January 12–14, 2014
Princeton, New Jersey, USA

Association for Computing Machinery

Advancing Computing as a Science & Profession

ITCS'14

Proceedings of the 2014 Conference on Innovations in Theoretical Computer Science

Sponsored by:

ACM SIGACT

Supported by:

Princeton School of Engineering and Applied Science, and Center for Computational Intractability

Association for
Computing Machinery

Advancing Computing as a Science & Profession

The Association for Computing Machinery
2 Penn Plaza, Suite 701
New York, New York 10121-0701

ISBN: 978-1-4503-2698-8 (Digital)

ISBN: 978-1-4503-3094-7 (Print)

Additional copies may be ordered prepaid from:

ACM Order Department
PO Box 30777
New York, NY 10087-0777, USA

Phone: 1-800-342-6626 (USA and Canada)
+1-212-626-0500 (Global)
Fax: +1-212-944-1318
E-mail: acmhelp@acm.org
Hours of Operation: 8:30 am – 4:30 pm ET

Printed in the USA

Preface

The papers in this volume were presented at the 5th Innovations in Theoretical Computer Science (ITCS 2014) conference, sponsored by the ACM Special Interest Group on Algorithms and Computation Theory (SIGACT). The conference was held in Princeton, New Jersey, USA, January 11–14, 2014. ITCS (previously known as ICS) seeks to promote research that carries a strong conceptual message, for instance, introducing a new concept or model, opening a new line of inquiry within traditional or cross-interdisciplinary areas, or introducing new techniques or new applications of known techniques).

The call for papers welcomed all submissions, whether aligned with current theory of computation research directions or deviating from them. Altogether 116 submissions were received worldwide. Of these the program committee selected 48 papers. The accepted papers cover a wide range of topics in theoretical computer science, including algorithms, complexity, cryptography, learning, data privacy, quantum, physical and biological computing and relations between computing and social sciences. In addition to the selected papers the committee invited Professor Peter Winkler of Dartmouth to give an evening talk and we are grateful for his acceptance. Another evening was devoted to "Graduating Bits" – short talks by recent graduates.

The program committee consisted of 24 members (plus the chair): Deeparnab Chakrabarty (Microsoft Research India), Timothy Chan (University of Waterloo), Costis Daskalakis (MIT), Yuval Emek (ETH and Technion), Kousha Etessami (University of Edinburgh), Yuval Filmus (University of Toronto and Simons Institute, Berkeley), Arpita Ghosh (Cornell University), Monika Henzinger (University of Vienna), Sandy Irani (University of California Irvine), Michael Kearns (University of Pennsylvania), Lap Chi Lau (The Chinese University of Hong Kong), Nati Linial (Hebrew University of Jerusalem), Kobbi Nissim (Ben-Gurion University), Rasmus Pagh (IT University of Copenhagen), Shubhangi Saraf (Rutgers University), Ola Svensson (EPFL), Vinod Vaikuntanathan (University of Toronto and MIT), Jan Vondrak (IBM Almaden Research Center), Manfred Warmuth (University of California, Santa Cruz), Daniel Wichs (Northeastern University), Udi Wieder (Microsoft Research SVC), Ryan Williams (Stanford University), Ronald de Wolf (CWI and University of Amsterdam), David Xiao (CNRS and Université Paris 7). I wish to express my admiration for their hard work of reading, evaluating and debating the merits of the submissions. The many individuals who assisted the reviewing process as subreviewers and extended the expertise of the committee deserve acknowledgments as well.

The organizing committee consisted of Princeton professors Sanjeev Arora, Moses Charikar and Bernard Chazelle. They, as well as Princeton University, deserve big thanks. I wish to express my gratitude to Robert Kleinberg, Program Chair of ITCS 2013, and Shafi Goldwasser, Chair of the Steering Committee of ITCS, for their guidance and advice. Above all, I thank the authors for contributing their work to ITCS 2014. I trust you will find that their papers present a varied and stimulating perspective of the field.

Moni Naor
ITCS 2014 Program Chair
Weizmann Institute of Science Rehovot,
ISRAEL

Table of Contents

ITCS 2014 Conference Organization ix

ITCS 2014 Sponsors & Supporters xii

Session 1: 08:30—8:40
Session Chair: Kobbi Nissim *(Ben-Gurion University)*

- **Lattice-Based FHE as Secure as PKE** 1
  Zvika Brakerski *(Weizmann Institute of Science)*, Vinod Vaikuntanathan *(MIT and University of Toronto)*
- **Cryptogenography** 13
  Joshua Brody *(Swarthmore College)*, Sune K. Jakobsen *(Queen Mary, University of London)*, Dominik Scheder *(University of California, Berkeley)*, Peter Winkler *(Dartmouth College)*
- **Limits of Random Oracles in Secure Computation** 23
  Mohammad Mahmoody *(University of Virginia)*, Hemanta K. Maji *(University of California, Los Angeles)*, Manoj Prabhakaran *(University of Illinois)*
- **Robust Device Independent Quantum Key Distribution** 35
  Umesh Vazirani *(University of California, Berkeley)*, Thomas Vidick *(Newton Institute, Cambridge, UK & Centre for Quantum Technologies NUS, Singapore)*

Session 2: 10:30-10:40
Session Chair: Nati Linial *(Hebrew University)*

- **On the Structure of Boolean Functions with Small Spectral Norm** 37
  Amir Shpilka *(Technion - Israel Institute of Technology)*, Avishay Tal *(Weizmann Institute of Science)*, Ben lee Volk *(Technion - Israel Institute of Technology)*
- **Non-Commutative Arithmetic Circuits with Division** 49
  Pavel Hrubeš *(University of Washington)*, Avi Wigderson *(Institute for Advanced Study)*
- **Decision Trees, Protocols and the Entropy-Influence Conjecture** 67
  Andrew Wan *(University of California, Berkeley)*, John Wright *(Carnegie Mellon University)*, Chenggang Wu *(IIIS, Tsinghua University)*
- **Locally Testable Codes and Cayley Graphs** 81
  Parikshit Gopalan *(Microsoft Research Silicon Valley)*, Salil Vadhan *(Harvard University)*, Yuan Zhou *(Carnegie Mellon University)*

Session 3: 14:00-14:10
Session Chair: Michael Kearns *(University of Pennsylvania)*

- **Invitation Games and the Price of Stability** 93
  Uriel Feige *(Weizmann Institute)*, Moshe Tennenholtz *(Microsoft Research, Haifa)*
- **The Computational Hardness of Pricing Compound Options** 103
  Mark Braverman, Kanika Pasricha *(Princeton Unviersity)*
- **Welfare Maximization and Truthfulness in Mechanism Design with Ordinal Preferences** 105
  Deeparnab Chakrabarty *(Microsoft Research, India)*, Chaitanya Swamy *(University of Waterloo)*
- **Coordination Mechanisms from (almost) all Scheduling Policies** 121
  Sayan Bhattacharya *(Max Plank Institute for Informatics)*, Sungjin Im *(University of California)*, Janardhan Kulkarni, Kamesh Munagala *(Duke University)*

Session 4: 16:00-16:10

Session Chair: David Xiao *(CNRS and Université Paris 7)*

- **Private Interactive Communication Across an Adversarial Channel** ... 135
  Ran Gelles, Amit Sahai, Akshay Wadia *(University of California, Los Angeles)*
- **Tree Codes and a Conjecture on Exponential Sums** ... 145
  Cristopher Moore *(Santa Fe Institute)*, Leonard J. Schulman *(Caltech)*
- **Capacity of Non-Malleable Codes** ... 155
  Mahdi Cheraghchi *(Massachusetts Institute of Technology)*, Venkatesan Guruswami *(Carnegie Mellon University)*
- **Linear-Time Encodable Codes Meeting the Gilbert-Varshamov Bound and Their Cryptographic Applications** ... 169
  Erez Druk, Yuval Ishai *(Technion)*

Session 5: 08:30-08:40

Session Chair: Costis Daskalakis *(MIT)*

- **Adversarial Hypothesis Testing and a Quantum Stein's Lemma for Restricted Measurements** ... 183
  Fernando G. S. L. Brandão *(University College London)*, Aram W. Harrow *(Massachusetts Institute of Technology)*, James R. Lee *(University of Washington)*, Yuval Peres *(Microsoft Research)*
- **Sequential Decision Making with Vector Outcomes** ... 195
  Yossi Azar *(Tel Aviv University)*, Uriel Felge *(Weizmann Institute)*, Michal Feldman *(Tel Aviv University)*, Moshe Tennenholtz *(Microsoft Research & Technion)*
- **Learning Mixtures of Arbitrary Distributions Over Large Discrete Domains** ... 207
  Yuval Rabani *(The Hebrew University)*, Leonard J. Schulman *(Caltech)*, Chaitanya Swamy *(University of Waterloo)*
- **Why Do Simple Algorithms for Triangle Enumeration Work in the Real World?** ... 225
  Jonathan W. Berry *(Sandia National Laboratories)*, Luke K. Fostvedt, Daniel J. Nordman *(Iowa State University)*, Cynthia A. Phillips, C. Seshadhri *(Sandia National Laboratories)*, Alyson G. Wilson *(North Carolina State University)*

Session 6: 10:30-10:40

Session Chair: Vinod Vaikuntanathan *(University of Toronto and MIT)*

- **Black-Box Obfuscation for d-CNFs** ... 235
  Zvika Brakerski *(Weizmann Institute of Science)*, Guy N. Rothblum *(Microsoft Research)*
- **Candidate Weak Pseudorandom Functions in AC0 \Circ MOD2** ... 251
  Adi Akavia *(Tel Aviv Academic College)*, Andrej Bogdanov, Siyao Guo *(Chinese University of Hong Kong)*, Akshay Kamath *(Chennai Mathematics Institute)*, Alon Rosen *(IDC Herzliya)*
- **Iterated Group Products and Leakage Resilience Against NC1** ... 261
  Eric Miles *(Northeastern University)*
- **Building One-Time Memories from Isolated Qubits** ... 269
  Yi-Kai Liu *(National Institute of Standards and Technology)*

Session 7: 14:00-14:10

Session Chair: Sandy Irani *(University of California, Irvine)*

- **Attribute-Efficient Evolvability of Linear Functions** ... 287
  Elaine Angelino *(Harvard University)*, Varun Kanade *(University of California, Berkeley)*
- **An Efficient Algorithm for Finding the Ground State of 1D Gapped Local Hamiltonians** ... 301
  Zeph Landau, Umesh Vazirani *(University of California, Berkeley)*, Thomas Vidick *(Newton Institute, Cambridge, UK & Centre for Quantum Technologies NUS, Singapore)*
- **Energy-Efficient Circuit Design** ... 303
  Antonios Antoniadis, Neal Barcelo, Michael Nugent, Kirk Pruhs, Michele Scquizzato *(University of Pittsburgh)*

- **Rate-Independent Computation in Continuous Chemical Reaction Networks** 313
  Ho-Lin Chen *(National Taiwan University)*, David Doty *(California Institute of Technology)*,
  David Soloveichik *(University of California, San Francisco)*

Session 8: 16:00-16:10

Session Chair: Yuval Filmus *(University of Toronto and Simons Institute, Berkeley)*

- **Testers and Their Applications** 327
  Nader H. Bshouty *(Technion, Haifa)*
- **Expanders with Respect to Hadamard Spaces and Random Graphs** 353
  Manor Mendel *(The Open University of Israel)*, Assaf Naor *(New York University)*
- **On the Automorphism Groups of Strongly Regular Graphs I** 359
  László Babai *(University of Chicago)*
- **Limits of Local Algorithms Over Sparse Random Graphs** 369
  David Gamarnik *(Massachusetts Institute of Technology)*, Madhu Sudan *(Microsoft Research)*

Session 9: 08:30-08:40

Session Chair: Daniel Wichs *(Northeastern University)*

- **Deterministic Compression with Uncertain Priors** 377
  Elad Haramaty *(Technion, Haifa)*, Madhu Sudan *(Microsoft Research)*
- **Faster Private Release of Marginals on Small Databases** 387
  Karthekeyan Chandrasekaran, Justin Thaler, Jonathan Ullman *(Harvard University)*,
  Andrew Wan *(Simons Institute for the Theory of Computing, U.C. Berkeley)*
- **Mechanism Design in Large Games: Incentives and Privacy** 403
  Michael Kearns, Mallesh M. Pai, Aaron Roth *(University of Pennsylvania)*,
  Jonathan Ullman *(Harvard University)*
- **Redrawing the Boundaries on Purchasing Data from Privacy-Sensitive Individuals** 411
  Kobbi Nissim *(Ben-Gurion University & Harvard University)*, Salil Vadhan *(Harvard University)*,
  David Xiao *(CNRS and Université Paris 7)*

Session 10: 10:30-10:40

Session Chair: Deeparnab Chakrabarty *(Microsoft Research India)*

- **Approximation Schemes via Sherali-Adams Hierarchy for Dense Constraint Satisfaction Problems and Assignment Problems** 423
  Yuichi Yoshida *(National Institute of Informatics & Preferred Infrastructure, Inc.)*,
  Yuan Zhou *(Carnegie Mellon University)*
- **Complexity of Approximating CSP with Balance / Hard Constraints** 439
  Venkatesan Guruswami, Euiwoong Lee *(Carnegie Mellon University)*
- **Integer Feasibility of Random Polytopes** 449
  Karthekeyan Chandrasekaran *(Harvard University)*, Santosh S. Vempala *(Georgia Institute of Technology)*
- **Multireference Alignment Using Semidefinite Programming** 459
  Afonso S. Bandeira, Moses Charikar, Amit Singer, Andy Zhu *(Princeton University)*

Session 11: 14:00-14:10

Session Chair: Shubhangi Saraf *(Rutgers University)*

- **Decompositions of Triangle-Dense Graphs** 471
  Rishi Gupta, Tim Roughgarden *(Stanford University)*, C. Seshadhri *(Sandia National Laboratories)*
- **Partial Tests, Universal Tests and Decomposability** 483
  Eldar Fischer, Yonatan Goldhirsh *(Technion – Israel Institute of Technology)*,
  Oded Lachish *(Birkbeck, University of London)*
- **High Dimensional Expanders and Property Testing** 501
  Tali Kaufman *(Bar-Ilan University)*, Alexander Lubotzky *(Hebrew University)*

- **Parameterized Testability** 507
  Kazuo Iwama *(Kyoto University)*,
  Yuichi Yoshida *(National Institute of Informatics and Preferred Infrastructure, Inc.)*

Session 12: 16:00-16:10

Session Chair: Kousha Etessami *(University of Edinburgh)*

- **Direct Sum Fails for Zero Error Average Communication** 517
  Gillat Kol *(Institute for Advanced Study)*, Shay Moran, Amir Shpilka, Amir Yehudayoff *(Technion)*
- **Rational Arguments: Single Round Delegation with Sublinear Verification** 523
  Siyao Guo *(Chinese University of Hong Kong)*, Pavel Hubáček *(Aarhus University)*,
  Alon Rosen *(IDC Herzliya)*, Margarita Vald *(Tel Aviv University)*
- **Optimal Provision-After-Wait in Healthcare** 541
  Mark Braverman *(Princeton University)*, Jing Chen *(Stony Brook University)*,
  Sampath Kannan *(University of Pennsylvania)*
- **The Truth Behind the Myth of the Folk Theorem** 543
  Joseph Y. Halpern, Rafael Pass, Lior Seeman *(Cornell University)*

Author Index 553

ITCS 2014 Conference Organization

Program Chair: Moni Naor *(Weizmann Institute of Science)*

Organization Committee: Sanjeev Arora *(Princeton University)*
Moses Charikar *(Princeton University)*
Bernard Chazelle *(Princeton University)*

Steering Committee Chair: Shafi Goldwasser *(Massachusetts Institute of Technology and Weizmann Institute of Science)*

Steering Committee: Sanjeev Arora *(Princeton University)*
Manuel Blum *(Carnegie Mellon University)*
Bernard Chazelle *(Princeton University)*
Oded Goldreich *(Weizmann Institute of Science)*
Richard Karp *(University of California, Berkeley)*
Ueli Maurer *(ETH Zürich)*
Silvio Micali *(Massachusetts Institute of Technology)*
Peter Bro Miltersen *(Aarhus University)*
Christos Papadimitriou *(University of California, Berkeley)*
Michael Rabin *(Harvard University)*
Madhu Sudan *(Microsoft Research)*
Leslie Valiant *(Harvard University)*
Umesh Vazirani *(University of California, Berkeley)*
Avi Wigderson *(Institute of Advanced Study)*
Andy Yao *(Tsinghua University)*

Program Committee: Deeparnab Chakrabarty *(Microsoft Research)*
Timothy Chan *(University of Waterloo)*
Costis Daskalakis *(Massachusetts Institute of Technology)*
Yuval Emek *(ETH and Technion)*
Kousha Etessami *(University of Edinburgh)*
Yuval Filmus *(University of Toronto and Simons Institute, Berkeley)*
Arpita Ghosh *(Cornell University)*
Monika Henzinger *(University of Vienna)*
Sandy Irani *(University of California Irvine)*
Michael Kearns *(University of Pennsylvania)*
Lap Chi Lau *(The Chinese University of Hong Kong)*
Nati Linial *(Hebrew University of Jerusalem)*
Kobbi Nissim (*Ben-Gurion University*)
Rasmus Pagh *(IT University of Copenhagen)*
Shubhangi Saraf *(Rutgers University)*
Ola Svensson *(EPFL)*
Vinod Vaikuntanathan *(University of Toronto and MIT)*

Program Committee (continued):

Jan Vondrak *(IBM Almaden Research Center)*
Manfred Warmuth *(University of California, Santa Cruz)*
Daniel Wichs *(Northeastern University)*
Udi Wieder *(Microsoft Research SVC)*
Ryan Williams *(Stanford University)*
Ronald de Wolf *(CWI and University of Amsterdam)*
David Xiao *(CNRS and Université Paris 7)*

Additional reviewers:

Ittai Abraham
Bruno Abrahao
Gagan Aggarwal
Andris Ambainis
Benny Applebaum
Michael Bender
Oren Ben-zwi
Sayan Bhattacharya
Eric Blais
Zvika Brakerski
Philipp Brandes
Mark Braverman
Joshua Brody
Gabriel Carroll
Hubert Chan
Siu On Chan
Ning Chen
Xi Chen
Yiling Chen
Kai-Min Chung
Roger Colbeck
Richard Cole
Seshadhri Comandur
Anne Condon
Michel De Rougemont
Ilias Diakonikolas
Itai Dinur
Thomas Dueholm Hansen
Paul Duetting
Zeev Dvir
Wolfgang Dvorak
Stefan Dziembowski
David Eppstein
Sebastian Faust
Michal Feldman
Jeremy Fineman
Abraham Flaxman
Lila Fontes
Dimitris Fotakis
Ehud Friedgut
Rafael Frongillo
Hu Fu
Pu Gao
Naveen Garg
Rong Ge
Ran Gelles
Wesley George
Costis Georgiou
Kaveh Ghasemloo
Sergey Gorbunov
Nikolai Gravin
Alan Guo
Gus Gutoski
Mika Goos
Anupam Gupta
Shai Halevi
Thore Husfeldt
Nicole Immorlica
Abhishek Jain
Brendan Juba
Adam Kalai
Satyen Kale
Petteri Kaski
Sanjeev Khanna
Robert Kleinberg
Swastik Kopparty
Wojciech Kotlovski
Robert Krauthgamer
Sebastian Krinninger
Fabian Kuhn

Additional reviewers (continued):

Amit Kumar
Mrinal Kumar
James Lee
Virginie Lerays
Kevin Lewi
Ke Li
Katrina Ligett
Veronika Loitzenbauer
Alex Lubotsky
Brendan Lucier
Hamid Mahini
Konstantin Makarychev
Daniel Marx
Will Matthews
Or Meir
Raghu Meka
Daniele Micciancio
Mladen Miksa
Tobais Momke
Hart Montgomery
Viswanath Nagarajan
Danupon Nanongkai
Thanh Nguyen
Jiazhong Nie
Eran Omri
Krzysztof Onak
Renato Paes Leme
Omer Paneth
Luís Paquete
Sunoo Park
Ron Peled
Chris Peikert
Raluca Ada Popa
Ariel Procaccia
Kirk Pruhs
Youming Qiao
Satish Rao
Ilya Razenshteyn
Sebastien Roch
Liam Roditty
Dana Ron
Ben Rossman
Guy Rothblum
Ron Rothblum
Thomas Rothvoss
Alexander Russell
Alex Samorodnitsky
Mathias Schacht
Thomas Schmitz
Henning Schnoor
Norbert Schuch
Jochen Seidel
Rocco Servedio
Igor Shinkar
Ali Sinop
Adam Smith
Troels Sørensen
Martin Starnberger
Uri Stemmer
Mukund Sundararajan
Vasilis Syrgkanis
Kunal Talwar
Tami Tamir
Omer Tamuz
Ross Tate
Abhradeep Thakurta
Justin Thaler
Madhur Tulsiani
Paul Valiant
Tim van Erven
Santosh S. Vempala
Thomas Vidick
Vladimir Voroninsky
Jens Vygen
Stephanie Wehner
Matt Weinberg
Renato Werneck
David Woodruff
Yi Wu
Eylon Yogev
Yuichi Yoshida
Hila Zarosim
Shengyu Zhang
Martin Zinkevich
Uri Zwick

ITCS 2014 Sponsor & Supporters

Sponsor:

SIGACT

Supporters:

PRINCETON

School of Engineering and Applied Science

Center for Computational Intractability

Lattice-based FHE as Secure as PKE

Zvika Brakerski
Weizmann Institute of Science
zvika.brakerski@weizmann.ac.il

Vinod Vaikuntanathan*
MIT and University of Toronto
vinodv@csail.mit.edu

ABSTRACT

We show that (leveled) fully homomorphic encryption (FHE) can be based on the hardness of $O(n^{1.5+\epsilon})$-approximation for lattice problems (such as GapSVP) under quantum reductions for any $\epsilon > 0$ (or $O(n^{2+\epsilon})$-approximation under classical reductions). This matches the best known hardness for "regular" (non-homomorphic) lattice based public-key encryption up to the ϵ factor. A number of previous methods had hit a roadblock at quasipolynomial approximation. (As usual, a circular security assumption can be used to achieve a non-leveled FHE scheme.)

Our approach consists of three main ideas: Noise-bounded sequential evaluation of high fan-in operations; Circuit sequentialization using Barrington's Theorem; and finally, successive dimension-modulus reduction.

Categories and Subject Descriptors

E.3 [**Data Encryption**]: Miscellaneous

Keywords

Cryptography, Fully Homomorphic Encryption, Lattice Based Cryptography

1. INTRODUCTION

Fully homomorphic encryption (FHE) allows us to convert an encryption of a message $\mathsf{Enc}(m)$ into an encryption of a related message $\mathsf{Enc}(f(m))$ for *any* efficient f, using only public information and without revealing anything about m itself. FHE has numerous theoretical and practical applications, the canonical one being to the problem of *outsourcing* computation to a remote server without compromising one's privacy.

Until 2008, FHE was considered practically science fiction as no constructions or even viable approaches were known. A breakthrough by Gentry [9, 10, 8] presented the first plausible candidate construction. The security of Gentry's scheme relied on much stronger assumptions than standard (non homomorphic) public-key encryption (PKE), namely the hardness of problems on specially chosen ideal lattices as well as a new assumption called the sparse subset sum assumption. This state of affairs coincided with many researchers' intuition that FHE, being much more versatile, should naturally be harder to achieve and should require stronger assumptions than regular public-key encryption. Brakerski and Vaikuntanathan [7] subsequently constructed an FHE scheme[1] based on the worst-case hardness of approximating lattice problems such as GapSVP (a promise version of the shortest vector problem on lattices) which have been studied extensively and are by now considered standard cryptographic assumptions. However, they required that the problem is hard to approximate to within a subexponential factor (in the dimension of the underlying lattice). This is in contrast to standard lattice-based public-key encryption which can be based on the hardness of approximating the problem to within polynomial factors (explicitly $\widetilde{O}(n^{1.5})$ using quantum reductions [18] or $\widetilde{O}(n^2)$ using classical reductions [16]). Closing this gap has been a central goal in the study of FHE from both a theoretical and a practical perspective (since relying on a weaker assumption allows us to use shorter parameters resulting in better efficiency). Starting with [5], several works using different approaches [4, 12] have reduced the required factor of approximation to $n^{O(\log n)}$, which seemed to be a barrier for known methods.

In this work, we match the best known approximation factors up to any $\epsilon > 0$ and show that "science fiction" FHE can be as secure as any other lattice-based public-key encryption scheme. Furthermore, the keys and ciphertexts in our scheme (with the exception of the evaluation key which is only used for homomorphic evaluation) are identical to Regev's original lattice-based PKE [18], with parameters that are optimal up to a factor of $1 + \epsilon$.

Our results are summarized in the following theorem.

THEOREM 1.1. *For every $\epsilon > 0$, there exists a leveled fully homomorphic encryption scheme based on the* $\mathsf{DLWE}_{n,q,\alpha}$

*Supported by an NSERC Discovery Grant, DARPA Grant number FA8750-11-2-0225, Connaught New Researcher Award, a Qatar Computing Research Institute (QCRI) grant, and an Alfred P. Sloan Fellowship.

ITCS'14, January 12–14, 2014, Princeton, New Jersey, USA.
Copyright 2014 ACM 978-1-4503-2698-8/14/01 ...$15.00.
http://dx.doi.org/10.1145/2554797.2554799.

[1]Here, and in the rest of the introduction, when we say FHE, we mean a leveled FHE scheme that can evaluate circuits of any a-priori bounded polynomial depth. The only known way to achieve non-leveled FHE schemes is to make a circular security assumption, in addition.

assumption (n-dimensional decisional LWE modulo q, with discrete Gaussian noise with parameter α), where $\alpha = 1/O(n^{\epsilon} \cdot \sqrt{n\log(q)} \cdot q)$.

Thus, the scheme is secure based on either the quantum *worst-case hardness of* $\mathsf{GapSVP}_{\tilde{O}(n^{1.5+\epsilon})}$, *or the* classical *worst-case hardness of* $\mathsf{GapSVP}_{\tilde{O}(n^{2+\epsilon})}$.

As we further explain below, to achieve the best approximation factor, we reduce from the hardness of *several instances* of the LWE problem, each with a different, yet polynomially-related, dimension n (q and α remain the same as a function of n). The sizes of the ciphertexts and keys in our scheme, with the exception of the evaluation key, are derived from the *smallest* LWE instance, which is comparable to Regev's parameters as we mentioned above. The evaluation key, however, contains elements that relate to all instances, and therefore its size relates (roughly) to $n = k^{1/\epsilon}$, where k is the smallest modulus. This also implies that the efficiency of the reduction (in the worst case) decreases with power $1/\epsilon$, which remains to be improved.

High Level Overview.

Our starting point is a new LWE-based FHE scheme by Gentry, Sahai and Waters [12]. They present an encryption scheme where the public key is identical to Regev's scheme, but the ciphertexts are square matrices rather than vectors. It was then possible to add and multiply ciphertexts using (roughly) matrix addition and multiplication. As in previous LWE-based FHE schemes, the ciphertext contains a "noise" element that grows with homomorphic operations and must be kept under a certain threshold in order for the ciphertext to be decryptable. The scheme is instantiated by a dimension n and modulus q, which correspond to the parameters of the LWE problem. The initial noise level is $\mathrm{poly}(n)$ and the scheme is decryptable so long as the noise remains under (say) $q/8$. In order to base the scheme on the hardness of polynomial approximation to lattice problems, we would like to characterize the class of functions that can be homomorphically evaluated using $q = \mathrm{poly}(n)$. The analysis of Gentry, Sahai and Waters [12] shows that the evaluation of each Boolean gate increases the noise by a $\mathrm{poly}(n)$ factor, and thus the class of functions that can be evaluated setting $q = \mathrm{poly}(n)$ is NC^0.

Our first observation is that the asymmetric (namely, non-commutative) nature of matrix multiplication gives rise to an interesting phenomenon in the GSW scheme: when multiplying two ciphertexts with noise levels e_1 and e_2, the noise in the output turns out to be $e_1 + \mathrm{poly}(n) \cdot e_2$. That is, the noise grows in an asymmetric manner. This means that if we want to multiply ℓ ciphertexts, for example, which all start with the same noise level, we can consecutively multiply them one after the other, and the final noise will only grow by a $\ell \cdot \mathrm{poly}(n)$ factor. This is in contrast to the conventional wisdom that favors the use of a multiplication tree, which in this case would have resulted in a $\mathrm{poly}(n)^{\log \ell}$ noise blowup. This observation already allows us to evaluate AC^0 circuits in a setting where the modulus $q = \mathrm{poly}(n)$. (Using an additional trick, this can be extended to $\mathsf{AC}^0[\oplus]$, namely AC^0 circuits augmented with XOR gates).

Our second idea is to push this technique forward by "sequentializing" larger circuit classes. A particularly potent tool in this direction of thought is Barrington's Theorem [2] which allows us to transform any NC^1 circuit into a polynomial length, width-5 permutation branching program. Homomorphic evaluation of a length-ℓ branching program essentially requires homomorphically multiplying ℓ 5-by-5 encrypted permutation matrices, in contrast to the simple product operation on bits that we just accomplished. We show that this is in fact possible, namely a method of homomorphically multiplying ℓ permutation matrices that only increases the noise by an $\ell \cdot \mathrm{poly}(n)$ factor. This gives us a way to evaluate any NC^1 circuit in a setting where the modulus $q = \mathrm{poly}(n)$. In a high level, our technique here is reminiscent of Ishai and Paskin's method of evaluating branching programs on encrypted data [13].

Evaluating NC^1 circuits with low noise blowup is a highly sought-after goal in the study of FHE schemes. The reason is Gentry's bootstrapping theorem [9], which shows how to convert a scheme with some homomorphic properties into a fully homomorphic one, assuming that it can evaluate its own decryption circuit. Since the decryption circuit of the scheme in question lies in NC^1, we can apply the bootstrapping theorem and obtain and FHE scheme with $q = \mathrm{poly}(n)$, thus basing its security on the worst-case hardness of approximating lattice problems to within a (somewhat large) polynomial factor.

To obtain the optimal approximation factor (up to an arbitrarily small ϵ), we employ our third idea, namely a variant of the *dimension-modulus reduction* technique, originating in [7]. Our noise analysis of the NC^1 scheme shows that in order to obtain parameters that are optimal up to ϵ, the decryption circuit of our scheme must have depth at most $\epsilon \cdot \log(n)/2$, which seems unachievable. After all, an NC^1 circuit with n inputs and depth less than $\log n$ cannot even look at all the inputs! To solve this conundrum, we apply the *dimension-modulus reduction* technique, which allows us to "shrink" the ciphertext into a "smaller copy" of the same scheme. We show that by applying this method consecutively several times (as opposed to a single time as was done in [7]), we can reduce the ciphertext to a small enough size that decrypting it becomes possible in depth $\epsilon \log(n)/2$. This allows us to obtain an FHE scheme based on the worst-case hardness of approximating GapSVP within a factor of $\tilde{O}(n^{2+\epsilon})$ by classical algorithms, or a factor of $\tilde{O}(n^{1.5+\epsilon})$ by quantum algorithms.

Let us now explain at a high level how dimension-modulus reduction is employed in our scheme. We recall from [7] that dimension-modulus reduction allows to convert a ciphertext of dimension n and modulus q into another ciphertext of dimension k and modulus p, at the cost of increasing the noise in the resulting ciphertext by a factor of $\approx \sqrt{n \log q}$ (as an example, think about $q = n^3$ and $p = k^3$). In order to achieve optimal approximation factor for our reduction, the noise increase must be no more than $\approx k^{\epsilon} \cdot \sqrt{k \log p}$. It therefore follows that if we wish to keep our parameters close to optimal, we must take $n \approx k^{1+\epsilon}$. Since we want to end up with k which is much smaller than n, we must apply this procedure successively $\approx 1/\epsilon$ times in order to both maintain the approximation factor and reduce the modulus.

Organization of the Paper.

We start with some background and preliminaries: the reader should consult section 2.1 for background on Gaussian distributions, section 2.2 for the learning with error problem, and section 2.5 for homomorphic encryption. Our main result is described in Section 3 where we construct a (leveled) FHE scheme secure under the polynomial LWE assumption. We conclude in Section 4 by showing how to show how to reduce and optimize the assumption to match the best known LWE assumption for lattice-based PKE.

2. PRELIMINARIES

Matrices are denoted by bold-face capital letters, and vectors are denoted by bold-face small letters. All logarithms are taken to base 2, unless otherwise specified. For an integer q, we define the set $\mathbb{Z}_q \triangleq (-q/2, q/2] \cap \mathbb{Z}$. For any $x \in \mathbb{Q}$, we let $y = [x]_q$ denote the unique value $y \in (-q/2, q/2]$ such that $y = x \pmod q$ (i.e. y is congruent to x modulo q).

We let κ denote a security parameter. When we speak of a negligible function $\mathrm{negl}(\kappa)$, we mean a function that grows slower than $1/\kappa^c$ for any constant $c > 0$ and sufficiently large values of κ. When we say that an event happens with overwhelming probability, we mean that it happens with probability at least $1 - \mathrm{negl}(\kappa)$ for some negligible function $\mathrm{negl}(\kappa)$. We denote $y = \widetilde{O}_\kappa(x)$ if $y = O(x \cdot \mathrm{polylog}(\kappa))$, and $y = \widetilde{O}(x)$ if $y = \widetilde{O}_x(x)$. The notation $\widetilde{\Theta}_\kappa(\cdot)$, $\widetilde{\Omega}_\kappa(\cdot)$ is defined analogously.

The security parameter underlies all of our constructions. The parameters n, k etc. should all be considered to be a function of the security parameter κ, which is chosen according to the level of confidence desired by the user of the scheme. (The dimension of the LWE problem, defined below, should be considered to be polynomially related to the security parameter.)

2.1 Gaussians and Discrete Gaussians

In this work we will only consider one-dimensional Gaussians, and one-dimensional discrete Gaussians over the integers.

For $r > 0$, the (one-dimensional) Gaussian function $\rho_r : \mathbb{R} \to (0, 1]$ is defined as

$$\rho_r(x) \triangleq \exp(-\pi |x|^2 / r^2).$$

The (spherical) continuous Gaussian distribution D_r is the distribution with density function proportional to ρ_r. The (one-dimensional, integer-coset) discrete Gaussian $D_{\mathbb{Z}-c,r}$ is the discrete distribution supported on $\mathbb{Z} - c$ for $c \in \mathbb{R}$, whose probability mass function is proportional to ρ_r.

Gaussian Rounding..

To achieve the tightest results, we will need to use a simple Gaussian rounding procedure. The following is an immediate corollary of [6, Lemma 2.3].

COROLLARY 2.1. *There exists a randomized procedure $\lfloor \cdot \rceil_G$ such that given $x \in \mathbb{R}$, it holds that $y \leftarrow \lfloor x \rceil_G$ is such that $y - x \sim D_{\mathbb{Z}-x,1}$.*

In fact, a slightly smaller standard deviation is achievable, but we use 1 for the sake of simplicity.

Sum of Discrete Gaussians..

We wish to bound the absolute value of a sum of discrete Gaussians. The following are immediate corollaries from [19, Corollary 3.10] and [11, Lemma 3.1].

PROPOSITION 2.2. *Let $\kappa \in \mathbb{N}$ be a security parameter. Then with all but $\mathrm{negl}(\kappa)$ probability, if $x \sim D_r$, then $|x| \le r \cdot \omega(\sqrt{\log \kappa})$. Similarly, if $x \sim D_{\mathbb{Z}^n - c, r}$ then with all but negligible probability, $|x| \le \max\{r, \omega(\sqrt{\log \kappa})\} \cdot \omega(\sqrt{\log \kappa})$.*

PROPOSITION 2.3. *Let $\kappa \in \mathbb{N}$ be a security parameter. Let $n \in \mathbb{N}$, let $\mathbf{z} \in \{0,1\}^n$ and $\mathbf{c} \in \mathbb{R}^n$ be arbitrary, and let $\mathbf{e} \sim D_{\mathbb{Z}^n - \mathbf{c}, r}$. Then with all but negligible probability*

$$|\langle \mathbf{z}, \mathbf{e} \rangle| \le \sqrt{n} \cdot \max\{r, \omega(\sqrt{\log \kappa})\} \cdot \omega(\sqrt{\log \kappa}) = \widetilde{O}_\kappa(\sqrt{n}) \cdot r\ .$$

PROPOSITION 2.4. *Let $\kappa \in \mathbb{N}$ be a security parameter. Let $n \in \mathbb{N}$, let $\mathbf{c} \in \mathbb{R}^n$ be arbitrary, let $\mathbf{e} \sim D_{\mathbb{Z} - \mathbf{c}, r}$, and let $\mathbf{z} \in \{0,1\}^n$ be possibly dependent on $\mathbf{e}$. Then with all but negligible probability*

$$|\langle \mathbf{z}, \mathbf{e} \rangle| \le n \cdot \max\{r, \omega(\sqrt{\log \kappa})\} \cdot \omega(\sqrt{\log \kappa}) = \widetilde{O}_\kappa(n) \cdot r\ .$$

2.2 Learning With Errors (LWE)

The LWE problem was introduced by Regev [18] as a generalization of "learning parity with noise". For positive integers n and $q \ge 2$, a vector $\mathbf{s} \in \mathbb{Z}_q^n$, and a probability distribution χ on $\mathbb{Z}$, let $A_{\mathbf{s},\chi}$ be the distribution obtained by choosing a vector $\mathbf{a} \stackrel{\$}{\leftarrow} \mathbb{Z}_q^n$ uniformly at random and a noise term $e \stackrel{\$}{\leftarrow} \chi$, and outputting $(\mathbf{a}, [\langle \mathbf{a}, \mathbf{s} \rangle + e]_q) \in \mathbb{Z}_q^n \times \mathbb{Z}_q$. Decisional LWE (DLWE) is defined as follows.

DEFINITION 2.5 (DLWE). *For an integer $q = q(n)$ and an error distribution $\chi = \chi(n)$ over $\mathbb{Z}$, the (average-case) decision learning with errors problem, denoted $\mathsf{DLWE}_{n,m,q,\chi}$, is to distinguish (with non-negligible advantage) m samples chosen according to $A_{\mathbf{s},\chi}$ (for uniformly random $\mathbf{s} \stackrel{\$}{\leftarrow} \mathbb{Z}_q^n$), from m samples chosen according to the uniform distribution over $\mathbb{Z}_q^n \times \mathbb{Z}_q$. We denote by $\mathsf{DLWE}_{n,q,\chi}$ the variant where the adversary gets oracle access to $A_{\mathbf{s},\chi}$, and is not a-priori bounded in the number of samples.*

There are known quantum (Regev [18]) and classical (Peikert [16]) reductions between $\mathsf{DLWE}_{n,m,q,\chi}$ and approximating short vector problems in lattices. Specifically, these reductions take χ to be a discrete Gaussian distribution $D_{\mathbb{Z},\alpha q}$ for some $\alpha < 1$. We sometimes write $\mathsf{DLWE}_{n,m,q,\alpha}$ (resp. $\mathsf{DLWE}_{n,q,\alpha}$) to indicate this instantiation (it will be clear from the context when we use a distribution χ and when a Gaussian parameter α). We now state a corollary of the results of [18, 16] (in conjunction with the search to decision reduction of Micciancio and Mol [14] and Micciancio and Peikert [15]). These results also extend to additional forms of q (see [14, 15]).

COROLLARY 2.6 ([18, 16, 14, 15]). *Let $q = q(n) \in \mathbb{N}$ be either a prime power $q = p^r$, or a product of co-prime numbers $q = \prod q_i$ such that for all i, $q_i = \mathrm{poly}(n)$, and let $\alpha \ge \sqrt{n}/q$. If there is an efficient algorithm that solves the (average-case) $\mathsf{DLWE}_{n,q,\alpha}$ problem, then:*

- *There is an efficient quantum algorithm that solves $\mathsf{GapSVP}_{\widetilde{O}(n/\alpha)}$ (and $\mathsf{SIVP}_{\widetilde{O}(n/\alpha)}$) on any n-dimensional lattice.*
- *If in addition $q \ge \widetilde{O}(2^{n/2})$, there is an efficient classical algorithm for $\mathsf{GapSVP}_{\widetilde{O}(n/\alpha)}$ on any n-dimensional lattice.*

Recall that GapSVP_γ is the (promise) problem of distinguishing, given a basis for a lattice and a parameter d, between the case where the lattice has a vector shorter than

d, and the case where the lattice doesn't have any vector shorter than $\gamma \cdot d$. SIVP is the search problem of finding a set of "short" vectors. We refer the reader to [18, 16] for more information.

The best known algorithms for GapSVP_γ ([20]) require at least $2^{\tilde{\Omega}(n/\log\gamma)}$ time.

In this work, we will only consider the case where $q \leq 2^n$. Furthermore, the underlying security parameter κ is assumed to be polynomially related to the dimension n.

2.3 Vector Decomposition and Key Switching

We show how to decompose vectors in a way that makes their norm smaller, and yet preserves certain inner products. Our notation is generally adopted from [5].

Vector Decomposition.

We often break vectors into their bit representations as defined below:

- $\mathsf{BitDecomp}_q(\mathbf{x})$: For $\mathbf{x} \in \mathbb{Z}^n$, let $w_{i,j} \in \{0,1\}$ be such that $\mathbf{x}[i] = \sum_{j=0}^{\lceil \log q \rceil - 1} 2^j \cdot w_{i,j} \pmod q$. Output the vector

$$(w_{1,\lceil \log q \rceil-1}, \ldots, w_{1,0}, \ldots, w_{n,\lceil \log q \rceil -1}, \ldots, w_{n,0}) \in \{0,1\}^{n \cdot \lceil \log q \rceil} .$$

- $\mathsf{PowersOfTwo}_q(\mathbf{y})$: For $\mathbf{y} \in \mathbb{Z}^n$, output

$$\left[2^{\lceil \log q \rceil -1}\mathbf{y}[1], \ldots, 2\mathbf{y}[1], \mathbf{y}[1], \ldots, 2^{\lceil \log q \rceil -1} \cdot \mathbf{y}[n], \ldots, 2\mathbf{y}[n], \mathbf{y}[n])\right] \in \mathbb{Z}_q^{n \cdot \lceil \log q \rceil} .$$

We will usually omit the subscript q when it is clear from the context.

CLAIM 2.7. *For all $q \in \mathbb{N}$ and $\mathbf{x}, \mathbf{y} \in \mathbb{Z}^n$, it holds that*

$$\langle \mathbf{x}, \mathbf{y} \rangle = \langle \mathsf{BitDecomp}_q(\mathbf{x}), \mathsf{PowersOfTwo}_q(\mathbf{y}) \rangle \pmod q .$$

Additionally, we define the procedure Flatten following [12], along with the procedure Combine.

Let $\mathbf{g} = (2^{\lceil \log(q) \rceil -1}, 2^{\lceil \log(q) \rceil -2} \ldots, 4, 2, 1) \in \mathbb{Z}^{\lceil \log q \rceil}$ and let $\mathbf{G} := \mathbf{g} \otimes \mathbf{I}_n \in \mathbb{Z}^{n \times (n \cdot \lceil \log q \rceil)}$ denote the tensor product of $\mathbf{g}$ with the n-by-n identity matrix $\mathbf{I}_n$.

- $\mathsf{Combine}_q(\mathbf{z})$: For $\mathbf{z} \in \mathbb{Z}^{n \cdot \lceil \log q \rceil}$, output $[\mathbf{G} \cdot \mathbf{z}]_q \in \mathbb{Z}_q^n$.
- $\mathsf{Flatten}_q(\mathbf{z})$: For $\mathbf{z} \in \mathbb{Z}^{n \cdot \lceil \log q \rceil}$, output

$$\mathsf{BitDecomp}_q(\mathsf{Combine}(\mathbf{z})) \in \{0,1\}^{n \cdot \lceil \log q \rceil}$$

CLAIM 2.8. *For all $q \in \mathbb{N}$, and $\mathbf{x}, \mathbf{z} \in \mathbb{Z}^{n \cdot \lceil \log q \rceil}$, it holds that*

$$\langle \mathsf{PowersOfTwo}(\mathbf{x}), \mathbf{z} \rangle = \langle \mathsf{PowersOfTwo}(\mathbf{x}), \mathsf{Flatten}(\mathbf{z}) \rangle \pmod q .$$

2.4 Partial Randomization Using LWE

We describe a procedure that allows us to partially randomize vectors while preserving their inner product with an LWE secret $\mathbf{s}$. This procedure will be useful to us when trying to manipulate ciphertexts that are a result of a homomorphic operation (and thus may have arbitrary dependence on the public parameters).

Let n, q, α be parameters for the DLWE problem, let $\chi = D_{\mathbb{Z},\alpha q}$. Let $\mathbf{s} \in \mathbb{Z}_q^n$ be some (arbitrary) vector.

- $\mathsf{RandParam}(\mathbf{s})$: Let $m \triangleq (n+1) \cdot (\log q + O(1))$. Sample $\mathbf{A} \xleftarrow{\$} \mathbb{Z}_q^{m \times n}$ and $\mathbf{e} \xleftarrow{\$} \chi^m$. Compute $\mathbf{b} := [\mathbf{A} \cdot \mathbf{s} + \mathbf{e}]_q$, and define

  $$\mathbf{P}_{\mathsf{rand}} := [\mathbf{b} \| -\mathbf{A}] \in \mathbb{Z}_q^{m \times (n+1)} .$$

  Output $\mathbf{P}_{\mathsf{rand}}$.

  We note that this is identical to the public key generation process in Regev's encryption scheme.

- $\mathsf{Rand}(\mathbf{P}_{\mathsf{rand}}, \mathbf{c})$: For $\mathbf{c} \in \mathbb{Z}_q^{n+1}$, sample $\mathbf{r} \xleftarrow{\$} \{0,1\}^m$, and compute

  $$\mathbf{c}_{\mathsf{rand}} := \left[\mathbf{c} + \mathbf{r}^T \mathbf{P}_{\mathsf{rand}}\right]_q .$$

  Output $\mathbf{c}_{\mathsf{rand}}$.

The properties of this process are summarized below.

First, we state the security of our procedure, namely that $\mathbf{P}_{\mathsf{rand}}$ does not reveal information about $\mathbf{s}$. The proof is straightforward and omitted.

LEMMA 2.9. *If $\mathbf{s}$ is uniformly sampled and*

$$\mathbf{P}_{\mathsf{rand}} \leftarrow \mathsf{RandParam}(\mathbf{s})$$

then under the $\mathsf{DLWE}_{n,q,\alpha}$ assumption, $\mathbf{P}_{\mathsf{rand}}$ is computationally indistinguishable from uniform.

Next, we state that the inner product of the randomized vector with $(1, \mathbf{s})$ does not change by much.

LEMMA 2.10. *Let $\mathbf{s} \in \mathbb{Z}_q^n$ be arbitrary, and let*

$$\mathbf{P}_{\mathsf{rand}} \leftarrow \mathsf{RandParam}(\mathbf{s})$$

Let $\mathbf{c} \in \mathbb{Z}_q^{n+1}$ be arbitrary, and $\mathbf{c}_{\mathsf{rand}} \leftarrow \mathsf{Rand}(\mathbf{P}_{\mathsf{rand}}, \mathbf{c})$, then there exists δ such that

$$\langle \mathbf{c}, (1, \mathbf{s}) \rangle - \langle \mathbf{c}_{\mathsf{rand}}, (1, \mathbf{s}) \rangle = \delta \pmod q ,$$

and $|\delta| \leq \widetilde{O}_\kappa(\sqrt{n \log(q)}) \cdot \alpha q$ with all but $\mathrm{negl}(\kappa)$ probability.

PROOF. We start by noting that

$$\langle \mathbf{r}^T \mathbf{P}_{\mathsf{rand}}, (1, \mathbf{s}) \rangle = \langle \mathbf{r}, \mathbf{e} \rangle \pmod q ,$$

where $\mathbf{e}$ is the noise used to generate $\mathbf{P}_{\mathsf{rand}}$. Using Proposition 2.3, the result follows. □

Finally, we state the randomization property of our procedure.

LEMMA 2.11. *Let $q \leq 2^n$. Let $\mathbf{s} \in \mathbb{Z}_q^n$ be arbitrary, and let $\mathbf{P}_{\mathsf{rand}} \leftarrow \mathsf{RandParam}(\mathbf{s})$. Let $\mathbf{f} \xleftarrow{\$} D_{\mathbb{Z},t}^{(n+1) \cdot \lceil \log(q) \rceil}$ for some t, and let $\mathbf{c} \in \mathbb{Z}_q^{n+1}$ be arbitrary (possibly dependent on $\mathbf{f}$). Finally, let $\mathbf{c}_{\mathsf{rand}} \leftarrow \mathsf{Rand}(\mathbf{P}_{\mathsf{rand}}, \mathbf{c})$, then*

$$\left|\langle \mathsf{BitDecomp}_q(\mathbf{c}_{\mathsf{rand}}), \mathbf{f} \rangle\right| \leq \widetilde{O}_\kappa(\sqrt{n \log(q)}) \cdot t ,$$

with all but $\mathrm{negl}(\kappa)$ probability.

PROOF. By the leftover hash lemma, the last n coordinates of $\mathbf{c}_{\mathsf{rand}}$ are distributed uniformly, and independently of $\mathbf{f}, \mathbf{c}$. By Proposition 2.3, this part of $\mathbf{c}_{\mathsf{rand}}$ contributes $\widetilde{O}_\kappa(\sqrt{n \log(q)}) \cdot t$ to the inner product (with all but negligible probability).

The first coordinate of $\mathbf{c}_{\mathsf{rand}}$ may have dependence on $\mathbf{f}$, but it only decomposes to $O(\log q)$ bits, and therefore by Proposition 2.4, its contribution to the inner product is at most $\widetilde{O}_\kappa(\log(q)) \cdot t$ with all but negligible probability. Recalling that $q \leq 2^n$, this is at most $\widetilde{O}_\kappa(\sqrt{n}\log(q)) \cdot t$.

The union bound completes the proof. □

2.5 Homomorphic Encryption and Bootstrapping

We now define homomorphic encryption and introduce Gentry's bootstrapping theorem. Our definitions are mostly taken from [7, 5].

A homomorphic (public-key) encryption scheme $\mathsf{HE} = (\mathsf{HE.Keygen}, \mathsf{HE.Enc}, \mathsf{HE.Dec}, \mathsf{HE.Eval})$ is a quadruple of PPT algorithms as follows (κ is the security parameter):

- **Key generation** $(pk, evk, sk) \leftarrow \mathsf{HE.Keygen}(1^\kappa)$**:** Outputs a public encryption key pk, a public evaluation key evk and a secret decryption key sk.[2]
- **Encryption** $c \leftarrow \mathsf{HE.Enc}_{pk}(\mu)$**:** Using the public key pk, encrypts a single bit message $\mu \in \{0,1\}$ into a ciphertext c.
- **Decryption** $\mu \leftarrow \mathsf{HE.Dec}_{sk}(c)$**:** Using the secret key sk, decrypts a ciphertext c to recover the message $\mu \in \{0,1\}$.
- **Homomorphic evaluation** $c_f \leftarrow \mathsf{HE.Eval}_{evk}(f, c_1, \ldots, c_\ell)$**:** Using the evaluation key evk, applies a function $f : \{0,1\}^\ell \to \{0,1\}$ to $c_1, \ldots, c_\ell$, and outputs a ciphertext c_f.

A homomorphic encryption scheme is said to be secure if it is semantically secure (note that the adversary is given both pk and evk).

Homomorphism w.r.t depth-bounded circuits and full homomorphism are defined next:

DEFINITION 2.12 (COMPACTNESS AND HOMOMORPHISM). *A homomorphic encryption scheme is compact if its decryption circuit is independent of the evaluated function. A compact scheme is (pure) fully homomorphic if it can evaluate any efficiently computable function. The scheme is leveled fully homomorphic if it takes 1^L as additional input in key generation, and can only evaluate depth L Boolean circuits.*

Gentry's bootstrapping theorem shows how to go from limited amount of homomorphism to full homomorphism. This method has to do with the *augmented decryption circuit.*

DEFINITION 2.13. *Consider a homomorphic encryption scheme* HE. *Let* (sk, pk, evk) *be properly generated keys and let* $\mathcal{C}$ *be the set of properly decryptable ciphertexts. Then the set of augmented decryption functions,* $\{f_{c_1,c_2}\}_{c_1,c_2 \in \mathcal{C}}$ *is defined by* $f_{c_1,c_2}(x) = \overline{\mathsf{HE.Dec}_x(c_1) \wedge \mathsf{HE.Dec}_x(c_2)}$. *Namely, the function that uses its input as secret key, decrypts* c_1, c_2 *and returns the NAND of the results.*

The bootstrapping theorem is thus as follows.

[2]We adopt the terminology of [7] that treats the evaluation key as a separate entity from the public key.

THEOREM 2.14 (BOOTSTRAPPING [9, 8]). *A scheme that can homomorphically evaluate its family of augmented decryption circuits can be transformed into a leveled fully homomorphic encryption scheme with the same decryption circuit, ciphertext space and public key.*

Furthermore, if the aforementioned scheme is also weak circular secure (remains secure even against an adversary who gets encryptions of the bits of the secret key), then it can be made into a pure fully homomorphic encryption scheme.

3. OUR FHE SCHEME

In this section, we describe an FHE scheme secure under a polynomial LWE assumption which, using known reductions [18, 16], translates to the worst-case hardness of solving various lattice problems to within polynomial approximation factors. We start with the basic encryption scheme in Section 3.1, and describe "proto-homomorphic" addition and multiplication subroutines in Section 3.2. Departing from the "conventional wisdom" in FHE, our circuit evaluation procedure in Section 3.3 will *not* be a naive combination of these proto-homomorphic operations, but rather a carefully designed procedure that manages the noise growth effectively.

Finally, in Section 3.4, we put this all together to get our FHE scheme under the decisional LWE assumption $\mathsf{DLWE}_{n,q,\alpha}$ with $\alpha = n^{-c}$ for some constant $c > 0$. This polynomial factor is rather large: thus, in Section 4, we apply a carefully designed variant of the dimension-modulus reduction procedure of [7] to obtain our final FHE scheme that is secure under the hardness of $\mathsf{DLWE}_{n,q,\alpha}$ with $\alpha \leq 1/\widetilde{O}_\kappa(n^\epsilon \cdot \sqrt{n}\log(q))$ which is weakest LWE hardness assumption that underlies the (non-homomorphic) lattice-based public key encryption schemes [1, 17, 18, 16, 6].

3.1 The Basic Encryption Scheme

Our basic encryption scheme closely follows the Gentry-Sahai-Waters FHE scheme [12]. We refer the reader to Section 2.3 for the description of the vector decomposition routines $\mathsf{PowersOfTwo}$, $\mathsf{BitDecomp}$ and $\mathsf{Flatten}$ used in the scheme below.

System Parameters.

Let n be the LWE dimension and q be an LWE modulus. Define $N := (n+1) \cdot \lceil \log q \rceil$. Let d denote the maximal homomorphism depth that is allowed by the scheme. Let χ be an error distribution over $\mathbb{Z}$. Typically χ will be a discrete Gaussian $D_{\mathbb{Z},\alpha q}$ for $\alpha = 1/\widetilde{O}_\kappa(\sqrt{n}\log(q) \cdot 4^d)$. Recall that we identify $\mathbb{Z}_q$ with the set $(-q/2, q/2] \cap \mathbb{Z}$.

- $\mathsf{NCCrypt.Keygen}(1^n, q, 4^d)$: Sample a vector $\mathbf{s} \xleftarrow{\$} \mathbb{Z}_q^n$. Let $m \triangleq (n+1) \cdot (\log q + O(1))$. Sample $\mathbf{A} \xleftarrow{\$} \mathbb{Z}_q^{m \times n}$ and $\mathbf{e} \xleftarrow{\$} \chi^m$. Compute $\mathbf{b} := [\mathbf{A} \cdot \mathbf{s} + \mathbf{e}]_q$, and define
$$\mathbf{P} := [\mathbf{b} \| -\mathbf{A}] \in \mathbb{Z}_q^{m \times (n+1)} .$$
Output $sk = \mathbf{s}$ and $pk = evk = \mathbf{P}$.

We describe public-key as well as secret-key encryption algorithms. Looking ahead, we remark that a secret-key encryption of μ is somewhat less "noisy" than a public-key encryption of μ.

- $\mathsf{NCCrypt.PubEnc}(pk, \mu)$: To encrypt a bit $\mu \in \{0,1\}$, using the public key $pk = \mathbf{P}$, we let $\mathbf{R} \xleftarrow{\$} \{0,1\}^{N\times m}$, and output the ciphertext

$$\mathbf{C} = \mathsf{Flatten}\left(\mathsf{BitDecomp}(\mathbf{R}\cdot\mathbf{P}) + \mu\cdot\mathbf{I}\right) \in \{0,1\}^{N\times N}.$$

- $\mathsf{NCCrypt.SecEnc}(sk, \mu)$: A symmetric encryption of a bit $\mu \in \{0,1\}$, using the secret key $sk = \mathbf{s}$, is performed by sampling $\mathbf{A} \xleftarrow{\$} \mathbb{Z}_q^{N\times n}$ and $\mathbf{e} \xleftarrow{\$} \chi^N$, computing $\mathbf{b} := [\mathbf{A}\cdot\mathbf{s} + \mathbf{e}]_q$, and defining

$$\mathbf{C} = \mathsf{Flatten}\left(\mathsf{BitDecomp}\left([\mathbf{b}\| - \mathbf{A}]\right) + \mu\cdot\mathbf{I}\right) \in \{0,1\}^{N\times N}.$$

- $\mathsf{NCCrypt.Dec}(sk, \mathbf{C})$: Let $\mathbf{c}$ be the second row of $\mathbf{C}$. We use standard Regev decryption on $\mathbf{c}$. Namely, we output $\mu^* = 0$ if $\left|[\langle \mathbf{c}, \mathsf{PowersOfTwo}(1,\mathbf{s})\rangle]_q\right| < q/8$, and $\mu^* = 1$ otherwise.

Correctness..

In order to show correctness of this scheme, we analyze the noise magnitude of ciphertexts produced by both the public-key and secret-key encryption algorithms. As we will show shortly, for ciphertexts $\mathbf{C}$ produced by either encryption algorithm, we have

$$\mathbf{C}\cdot\mathsf{PowersOfTwo}(1,\mathbf{s}) = \mu\cdot\mathsf{PowersOfTwo}(1,\mathbf{s}) + \mathbf{e} \pmod q$$

for a noise vector $\mathbf{e}$ of "small magnitude". This motivates our definition of the noise in the ciphertext $\mathbf{C}$ with respect to a secret key vector $\mathbf{s}$ and a message μ as follows.

DEFINITION 3.1. *For every $\mathbf{C} \in \{0,1\}^{N\times N}$, $\mathbf{s} \in \mathbb{Z}_q^n$ and $\mu \in \mathbb{Z}$, we define*

$$\mathsf{noise}_{\mathbf{s},\mu}(\mathbf{C}) \triangleq \|(\mathbf{C} - \mu\mathbf{I})\cdot\mathsf{PowersOfTwo}(1,\mathbf{s}) \pmod q\|_\infty$$

The significance of this definition is captured by the following claims. The first claim shows that any ciphertext with small noise is decrypted correctly.

LEMMA 3.2. *For every $\mathbf{C} \in \{0,1\}^{N\times N}$, $\mathbf{s} \in \mathbb{Z}_q^n$ and $\mu \in \mathbb{Z}$ such that $\mathsf{noise}_{\mathbf{s},\mu}(\mathbf{C}) < q/8$,*

$$\mathsf{NCCrypt.Dec}(\mathbf{s}, \mathbf{C}) = \mu$$

PROOF. Since $\mathsf{noise}_{\mathbf{s},\mu}(\mathbf{C}) < q/8$, we have

$$\mathbf{C}\cdot\mathsf{PowersOfTwo}(1,\mathbf{s}) = \boldsymbol{\eta} + \mu\cdot\mathsf{PowersOfTwo}(1,\mathbf{s}) \pmod q$$

where $\|\boldsymbol{\eta}\|_\infty < q/8$. Thus, for the second row of $\mathbf{C}$ it holds that

$$\langle \mathbf{c}, \mathsf{PowersOfTwo}(1,\mathbf{s})\rangle = \eta + 2^{\lceil\log(q)\rceil-2}\cdot\mu \pmod q$$

where $|\eta| < q/8$. Thus, when $\mu = 0$,

$$\left|[\langle \mathbf{c}, \mathsf{PowersOfTwo}(1,\mathbf{s})\rangle]_q\right| = |\eta| < q/8$$

When $\mu = 1$,

$$\left|[\langle \mathbf{c}, \mathsf{PowersOfTwo}(1,\mathbf{s})\rangle]_q\right| \geq q/4 - |\eta| \geq q/8$$

since $q/4 \leq 2^{\lceil\log(q)\rceil-2} < q/2$. This shows correctness of decryption for ciphertexts with small noise. □

The next claim demonstrates parameter settings for which the (public key and secret key) encryption algorithms produce ciphertexts with small noise.

LEMMA 3.3. *Let n be the LWE dimension, q be the LWE modulus and $\chi = D_{\mathbb{Z},\alpha q}$ be the discrete Gaussian distribution. Then, for every $\mathbf{s} \in \mathbb{Z}_q^n$ and $\mu \in \{0,1\}$,*

- *for $\mathbf{C}_{\mathsf{pub}} \leftarrow \mathsf{NCCrypt.PubEnc}(pk, \mu)$, we have*

$$\mathsf{noise}_{\mathbf{s},\mu}(\mathbf{C}_{\mathsf{pub}}) = \widetilde{O}_\kappa(\alpha q\cdot\sqrt{m})$$

- *for $\mathbf{C}_{\mathsf{sec}} \leftarrow \mathsf{NCCrypt.SecEnc}(sk, \mu)$, we have*

$$\mathsf{noise}_{\mathbf{s},\mu}(\mathbf{C}_{\mathsf{sec}}) = \widetilde{O}_\kappa(\alpha q)$$

with all but negligible (in κ) probability over the coins of $\mathsf{NCCrypt.Keygen}$.

In particular, we have correctness of decryption for the public key encryption for $\alpha < 1/\widetilde{\Omega}_\kappa(\sqrt{m})$, and for the secret key encryption for $\alpha < 1/\widetilde{\Omega}_\kappa(1)$.

PROOF. We first show the analysis for the public-key encryption.

$$\begin{aligned}
&\mathbf{C}_{\mathsf{pub}}\cdot\mathsf{PowersOfTwo}(1,\mathbf{s})\\
&= \mathsf{Flatten}\Big(\mathsf{BitDecomp}(\mathbf{R}\cdot\mathbf{P}) + \mu\cdot\mathbf{I}\Big)\cdot\mathsf{PowersOfTwo}(1,\mathbf{s})\\
&= \Big(\mathsf{BitDecomp}(\mathbf{R}\cdot\mathbf{P}) + \mu\cdot\mathbf{I}\Big)\cdot\mathsf{PowersOfTwo}(1,\mathbf{s})\\
&= \mathbf{R}\cdot\mathbf{P}\cdot(1,\mathbf{s})^T + \mu\cdot\mathsf{PowersOfTwo}(1,\mathbf{s})\\
&= \mathbf{R}\cdot\mathbf{e} + \mu\cdot\mathsf{PowersOfTwo}(1,\mathbf{s})
\end{aligned}$$

Thus, by Proposition 2.3,

$$\mathsf{noise}(\mathbf{C}_{\mathsf{pub}}) = \|\mathbf{R}\cdot\mathbf{e}\|_\infty = \widetilde{O}_\kappa(\sqrt{m}\cdot\alpha q)$$

This is less than $q/8$ by the choice of $\alpha < 1/\widetilde{\Omega}_\kappa(\sqrt{m})$.

The analysis for the secret key encryption follows analogously, except that

$$\mathbf{C}_{\mathsf{sec}}\cdot\mathsf{PowersOfTwo}(1,\mathbf{s}) = \mathbf{e} + \mu\cdot\mathsf{PowersOfTwo}(1,\mathbf{s})$$

Thus,

$$\mathsf{noise}(\mathbf{C}_{\mathsf{sec}}) = \|\mathbf{e}\|_\infty = \widetilde{O}_\kappa(\alpha q)$$

which is less than $q/8$ by the choice of $\alpha < 1/\widetilde{\Omega}_\kappa(1)$. □

Security.

Semantic security of the scheme follows from the decisional LWE assumption $\mathsf{DLWE}_{n,q,\alpha}$, similarly to Regev's encryption scheme (see [18, 7, 12] for similar arguments).

Complexity of Decryption.

Our decryption algorithm is essentially the same as the decryption algorithm in Regev's encryption scheme, the complexity of which has been thoroughly studied in the context of FHE. The following is an immediate corollary from [7, Lemma 4.1].

PROPOSITION 3.4. *There exists a constant c_{dec} such that the decryption circuit of the scheme* $\mathsf{NCCrypt}$, *with parameters n, q, has depth at most $c_{\mathsf{dec}}\cdot\log(n\log q)$.*

3.2 Proto-Homomorphic Operations

We now describe proto-homomorphic addition and multiplication algorithms which will be used in Section 3.3 for homomorphic circuit evaluation. Departing from the "conventional wisdom" in FHE, our circuit evaluation procedure will *not* be a naive combination of homomorphic addition and multiplication, but a carefully designed procedure that manages the noise growth effectively. To further stress the fact that we do not intend for these procedures to be used independently, we call them proto-homomorphic operations.

Proto-Homomorphic Addition.

This is a simple addition of the ciphertext matrices.

- $\mathsf{NCCrypt.ProtoAdd}(\mathbf{C}_1, \mathbf{C}_2)$: Output

$$\mathbf{C}_+ := \mathsf{Flatten}(\mathbf{C}_1 + \mathbf{C}_2)$$

Jumping ahead, we note that in our use of NCCrypt.ProtoAdd in Section 3.3, both $\mathbf{C}_1$ and $\mathbf{C}_2$ will be encryptions of bits, and at most one of them will be an encryption of 1. The following claim analyzes the noise growth in homomorphic addition.

CLAIM 3.4.1 (NOISE GROWTH IN NCCrypt.ProtoAdd.). *For every* $\mathbf{s} \in \mathbb{Z}_q^n$, $\mu_1, \mu_2 \in \mathbb{Z}$ *and* $\mathbf{C}_1, \mathbf{C}_2 \in \{0,1\}^{N \times N}$, *we have*

$$\begin{aligned}&\mathsf{noise}_{\mathbf{s},\mu_1+\mu_2}(\mathsf{NCCrypt.ProtoAdd}(\mathbf{C}_1, \mathbf{C}_2))\\&\qquad \le \mathsf{noise}_{\mathbf{s},\mu_1}(\mathbf{C}_1) + \mathsf{noise}_{\mathbf{s},\mu_2}(\mathbf{C}_2)\end{aligned}$$

PROOF. Let $\mathbf{C}_+ \leftarrow \mathsf{NCCrypt.ProtoAdd}(\mathbf{C}_1, \mathbf{C}_2)$. We note that

$$\begin{aligned}&\mathbf{C}_+ \cdot \mathsf{PowersOfTwo}(1, \mathbf{s})\\&= \mathsf{Flatten}(\mathbf{C}_1 + \mathbf{C}_2) \cdot \mathsf{PowersOfTwo}(1, \mathbf{s})\\&= (\mathbf{C}_1 + \mathbf{C}_2) \cdot \mathsf{PowersOfTwo}(1, \mathbf{s})\\&= \mathbf{C}_1 \cdot \mathsf{PowersOfTwo}(1, \mathbf{s}) + \mathbf{C}_2 \cdot \mathsf{PowersOfTwo}(1, \mathbf{s})\\&= (\mathbf{e}_1 + \mathbf{e}_2) + (\mu_1 + \mu_2) \cdot \mathbf{I}\end{aligned}$$

Thus, by the definition of $\mathsf{noise}_{\mathbf{s},\mu_1+\mu_2}$, we have

$$\mathsf{noise}_{\mathbf{s},\mu_1+\mu_2}(\mathbf{C}_+) \le \mathsf{noise}_{\mathbf{s},\mu_1}(\mathbf{C}_1) + \mathsf{noise}_{\mathbf{s},\mu_2}(\mathbf{C}_2)$$

□

Homomorphic Multiplication.

This is essentially a multiplication of the ciphertext matrices, except that we randomize the first ciphertext.

- $\mathsf{NCCrypt.ProtoMult}(evk, \mathbf{C}_1, \mathbf{C}_2)$:
  - Randomize $\mathbf{C}_1 \in \{0,1\}^{N \times N}$ into a matrix $\widetilde{\mathbf{C}}_1 \in \{0,1\}^{N \times N}$ by replacing each row $\mathbf{c}$ in $\mathbf{C}_1$ by the row

    $$\widetilde{\mathbf{c}} \leftarrow \mathsf{BitDecomp}(\mathsf{Rand}(pk, \mathsf{Combine}(\mathbf{c})))$$

    where Rand is the LWE randomization procedure from Section 2.4.
  - Output $\mathbf{C}_\times \leftarrow \mathsf{Flatten}(\widetilde{\mathbf{C}}_1 \cdot \mathbf{C}_2)$.

Jumping ahead, we remark that when we use the proto multiplication algorithm NCCrypt.ProtoMult in our homomorphic circuit evaluation in Section 3.3, the first ciphertext will be an "evaluated ciphertext" (namely, a result of previous homomorphic evaluations), whereas the second ciphertext will be a "fresh ciphertext" (namely an output of the *secret key* encryption algorithm).

The first new idea in this work is that while the order of the arguments does not matter in homomorphic addition, the multiplication algorithm NCCrypt.ProtoMult is inherently asymmetric, since it is essentially the matrix multiplication operation which is non-commutative. This asymmetry turns out to be the key to achieving improved noise growth, as Claim 3.4.2 below will demonstrate.

CLAIM 3.4.2 (NOISE GROWTH IN NCCrypt.ProtoMult.). *For every* $\mathbf{s} \in \mathbb{Z}_q^n$, $\mu_1, \mu_2 \in \{0,1\}$ *and* $\mathbf{C}_1 \in \{0,1\}^{N \times N}$ *and* $\mathbf{C}_2 \leftarrow \mathsf{NCCrypt.SecEnc}(sk, \mu_2)$, *we have*

$$\begin{aligned}&\mathsf{noise}_{\mathbf{s},\mu_1\mu_2}(\mathsf{NCCrypt.ProtoMult}(\mathbf{C}_1, \mathbf{C}_2))\\&\qquad \le |\mu_2| \cdot \mathsf{noise}_{\mathbf{s},\mu_1}(\mathbf{C}_1) + \widetilde{O}_\kappa(\alpha q \cdot \sqrt{n \log q})\end{aligned}$$

with all but negligible probability over the randomness of NCCrypt.Keygen, NCCrypt.SecEnc *and* NCCrypt.ProtoMult.

Remark. In words, Claim 3.4.2 says that if $\mu_2 \in \{0,1\}$ (as will be the case in our homomorphic circuit evaluation in Section 3.3), the noise in $\mathbf{C}_\times$ is at most the noise in $\mathbf{C}_1$, plus a fixed additive term. What's more, if $\mu_2 = 0$, then the noise in $\mathbf{C}_\times$ is independent of that in $\mathbf{C}_1$! *These two facts are the key new ideas that enable our main result.*

PROOF. (of Claim 3.4.2.)
Let $\mathbf{C}_\times \leftarrow \mathsf{NCCrypt.ProtoMult}(evk, \mathbf{C}_1, \mathbf{C}_2)$. Note that

$$\begin{aligned}&\mathbf{C}_\times \cdot \mathsf{PowersOfTwo}(1, \mathbf{s})\\&= \mathsf{Flatten}(\widetilde{\mathbf{C}}_1 \cdot \mathbf{C}_2) \cdot \mathsf{PowersOfTwo}(1, \mathbf{s})\\&= \widetilde{\mathbf{C}}_1 \cdot (\mathbf{C}_2 \cdot \mathsf{PowersOfTwo}(1, \mathbf{s}))\\&= \widetilde{\mathbf{C}}_1 \cdot (\mathbf{e}_2 + \mu_2 \cdot \mathsf{PowersOfTwo}(1, \mathbf{s}))\\&= \widetilde{\mathbf{C}}_1 \cdot \mathbf{e}_2 + \mu_2 \cdot \widetilde{\mathbf{C}}_1 \cdot \mathsf{PowersOfTwo}(1, \mathbf{s})\\&= \widetilde{\mathbf{C}}_1 \cdot \mathbf{e}_2 + \mu_2 \cdot (\widetilde{\mathbf{e}}_1 + \mu_1 \cdot \mathsf{PowersOfTwo}(1, \mathbf{s}))\\&= (\widetilde{\mathbf{C}}_1 \cdot \mathbf{e}_2 + \mu_2 \cdot \widetilde{\mathbf{e}}_1) + \mu_1\mu_2 \cdot \mathsf{PowersOfTwo}(1, \mathbf{s}) \qquad (1)\end{aligned}$$

Since $\mathbf{e}_2 \leftarrow D_{\mathbb{Z},\alpha q}^N$ and each row of $\widetilde{\mathbf{C}}_1 \in \{0,1\}^{N \times N}$ is the result of Rand, by Lemma 2.11, we have

$$\left\| \widetilde{\mathbf{C}}_1 \cdot \mathbf{e}_2 \right\|_\infty \le \widetilde{O}_\kappa(\alpha q \cdot \sqrt{n \log q}) \qquad (2)$$

with all but negligible probability.
Also, by lemma 2.10, we have

$$\|\widetilde{\mathbf{e}}_1\|_\infty \le \|\mathbf{e}_1\|_\infty + \widetilde{O}_\kappa(\alpha q \cdot \sqrt{n \log q}) \qquad (3)$$

with all but negligible probability.

Putting together Eq. (1),(2) and (3), we have

$$\begin{aligned}\mathsf{noise}_{\mathbf{s},\mu_1\mu_2}(\mathbf{C}_\times) &\le \left\| \widetilde{\mathbf{C}}_1 \cdot \mathbf{e}_2 \right\|_\infty + |\mu_2| \cdot \|\widetilde{\mathbf{e}}_1\|_\infty\\&\le |\mu_2| \cdot \mathsf{noise}_{\mathbf{s},\mu_1}(\mathbf{C}_1) + \widetilde{O}_\kappa(\alpha q \cdot \sqrt{n \log q})\end{aligned}$$

which finishes the proof. □

3.3 Homomorphic Evaluation of Circuits

We will now describe how to homomorphically evaluate a Boolean circuit Ψ with two-input NAND gates that takes ℓ inputs, and has depth d. In particular, our scheme will be able to evaluate circuits of depth $c \cdot \log n$ (for any constant c) under a polynomial LWE assumption, namely $\mathsf{DLWE}_{n,q,\chi}$ where $\chi = D_{\mathbb{Z},\alpha}$ and $\alpha = 1/n^{\Theta(c)}$. Since the depth of the decryption circuit is $c_{\mathsf{dec}} \cdot \log(n \log(q)) \le 2c_{\mathsf{dec}} \cdot \log(n)$ (for some constant $c_{\mathsf{dec}} > 0$), the scheme is bootstrappable, and by the bootstrapping theorem (Theorem 2.14), we get a leveled FHE scheme under the same assumption.

To evaluate a circuit, our scheme first turns it into a width-5 permutation branching program [3, 2], a model of computation that we describe below.

Width-5 Permutation Branching Programs. A permutation branching program Π of length L with input space $\{0,1\}^\ell$ is a sequence of L tuples of the form $(\mathsf{var}(t), \sigma_{t,0}, \sigma_{t,1})$ where

- $\mathsf{var} : [L] \to [\ell]$ is a function that associates the t-th tuple with an input bit $x_{\mathsf{var}(t)}$.
- $\sigma_{j,0}$ and $\sigma_{j,1}$ are permutations on 5 elements. We will think of $\sigma_{j,0}$ and $\sigma_{j,1}$ as bijective functions from the set $\{1,2,3,4,5\}$ to itself.

The computation of Π on input $\mathbf{x} = (x_1, \ldots, x_\ell)$ proceeds as follows. The state of the computation at any point in time t is a number $\zeta_t \in \{1,2,3,4,5\}$. Computation starts with the initial state $\zeta_0 = 1$. The state ζ_t is computed recursively as

$$\zeta_t = \sigma_{t,\mathsf{var}(t)}(\zeta_{t-1})$$

Finally, after L steps, our state is ζ_L. The output of the computation is 1 if $\zeta_L = 1$, and 0 otherwise.

To manage the growth of noise in homomorphic evaluation, we need to work with bits rather than numbers. Thus, we prefer to represent the state $\zeta_t \in \{1,2,3,4,5\}$ by a 0-1 vector $\mathbf{v}_t$ which is the unit vector $\mathbf{u}_{\zeta_t}$ in 5 dimensions.

The computation then proceeds as follows. The idea is that $\mathbf{v}_t[i] = 1$ if and only if $\sigma_{t,\mathsf{var}(t)}(\zeta_{t-1}) = i$. Turning this around, $\mathbf{v}_t[i] = 1$ if and only if either:

- $\mathbf{v}_{t-1}[\sigma_{t,0}^{-1}(i)] = 1$ and $x_{\mathsf{var}(t)} = 0$; or
- $\mathbf{v}_{t-1}[\sigma_{t,1}^{-1}(i)] = 1$ and $x_{\mathsf{var}(t)} = 1$.

The following formula captures this condition. For $t = 1, \ldots, L$, and $i \in \{1,2,3,4,5\}$, we have:

$$\begin{aligned}\mathbf{v}_t[i] &:= \mathbf{v}_{t-1}[\sigma_{t,0}^{-1}(i)] \cdot (1 - x_{\mathsf{var}(t)}) + \mathbf{v}_{t-1}[\sigma_{t,1}^{-1}(i)] \cdot x_{\mathsf{var}(t)} \\ &= \mathbf{v}_{t-1}[\gamma_{t,i,0}] \cdot (1 - x_{\mathsf{var}(t)}) + \mathbf{v}_{t-1}[\gamma_{t,i,1}] \cdot x_{\mathsf{var}(t)} \qquad (4)\end{aligned}$$

where $\gamma_{t,i,0} \triangleq \sigma_{t,0}^{-1}(i)$ and $\gamma_{t,i,1} \triangleq \sigma_{t,1}^{-1}(i)$ are constants that are publicly computable given the description of the branching program. It is this form that we will work with in our homomorphic evaluation.

The important property that we will use is that circuits of depth d can be simulated by branching programs of depth $L = 4^d$.

THEOREM 3.5 (BARRINGTON'S THEOREM [2]). *Every Boolean NAND circuit Ψ that acts on ℓ inputs and has depth d can be computed by a width-5 permutation branching program Π of length 4^d. Given the description of the circuit Ψ, the description of the branching program Π can be computed in $\mathrm{poly}(\ell, 4^d)$ time.*

Homomorphic Evaluation $\mathsf{NCCrypt.Eval}(\Psi, \mathbf{C}_1, \ldots, \mathbf{C}_\ell)$. The homomorphic evaluation procedure will first convert the depth-d circuit Ψ into a width-5 permutation branching program Π of length $L = 4^d$.

- **[Initialization]** We maintain the encrypted state of the computation of the branching program for every step t. We denote this state by the vector $\mathbf{V}_t = (\mathbf{V}_{t,1}, \mathbf{V}_{t,2}, \mathbf{V}_{t,3}, \mathbf{V}_{t,4}, \mathbf{V}_{t,5})$, where each $\mathbf{V}_{t,i} \in \{0,1\}^{N\times N}$ will be an encryption of $\mathbf{v}_t[i]$.
  - We initialize the state as follows. Compute $\mathbf{V}_{0,i} := \mathbf{v}_0[i] \cdot \mathbf{I}$.
    Note that $\mathbf{V}_{0,i}$ is in fact a valid encryption of the bit $\mathbf{v}_0[i]$ with zero noise.
  - We also compute encryptions of the complements of the input bits, for convenience. That is, set $\bar{\mathbf{C}}_k := \mathbf{I} - \mathbf{C}_k$. Note that $\bar{\mathbf{C}}_k$ is an encryption of $\bar{x}_k = 1 - x_k$ with the same noise as $\mathbf{C}_k$.
- **[Evaluation]** The evaluation proceeds iteratively for $t = 1, \ldots, L$, where L is the length of the branching program Π. Assuming that we have
  $$\mathbf{V}_{t-1} := (\mathbf{V}_{t-1,1}, \mathbf{V}_{t-1,2}, \ldots, \mathbf{V}_{t-1,5})$$
  the encryption of the state of the branching program computation at time $t-1$, we compute
  $$\mathbf{V}_t := (\mathbf{V}_{t,1}, \mathbf{V}_{t,2}, \ldots, \mathbf{V}_{t,5})$$
  by homomorphically evaluating Eq. (4) above.
  That is, for $i \in \{1,2,3,4,5\}$, we compute
  $$\begin{aligned}\mathbf{V}_{t,i} := \mathsf{NCCrypt.ProtoAdd}\Big(& \mathsf{NCCrypt.ProtoMult}(\mathbf{V}_{t-1,\gamma_0}, \bar{\mathbf{C}}_{\mathsf{var}(t)}), \\ & \mathsf{NCCrypt.ProtoMult}(\mathbf{V}_{t-1,\gamma_1}, \mathbf{C}_{\mathsf{var}(t)})\Big) \qquad (5)\end{aligned}$$
- **[Output]** Upon finishing the evaluation stage, we have $\mathbf{V}_L := (\mathbf{V}_{L,1}, \mathbf{V}_{L,2}, \ldots, \mathbf{V}_{L,5})$. Output $\mathbf{V}_{L,1}$ as the result of the homomorphic evaluation.

We now show that the scheme correctly evaluates circuits.

LEMMA 3.6 (CORRECTNESS OF HOM. EVALUATION). *Let n be the LWE dimension, q the LWE modulus, Ψ be any Boolean circuit of depth d, and*

$$\alpha \le 1/\widetilde{\Theta}_\kappa(4^d \cdot \sqrt{n \log q})$$

For every $x_1, \ldots, x_\ell \in \{0,1\}$, every Boolean circuit Ψ of depth at most d, and every secret key sk, letting $\mathbf{C}_k \leftarrow$ $\mathsf{NCCrypt.SecEnc}(sk, x_k)$ be the secret key *encryptions of the inputs, and $\mathbf{C}_\Psi \leftarrow \mathsf{NCCrypt.Eval}(evk, \Psi, \mathbf{C}_1, \ldots, \mathbf{C}_k)$ be the evaluated ciphertext, we have:*

$$\mathsf{NCCrypt.Dec}(sk, \mathbf{C}_\Psi) = \Psi(x_1, \ldots, x_\ell)$$

with overwhelming probability over the coin tosses of all the algorithms. $\mathsf{NCCrypt.Eval}$ *runs in time* $\mathrm{poly}(4^d, \ell, n, \log q)$.

Note that we stated the correctness of homomorphic evaluation on ciphertexts produced by the secret-key encryption algorithm $\mathsf{NCCrypt.SecEnc}$. A similar lemma can be shown in the case of public-key encryption, if α is smaller by a factor of $\sqrt{n \log q}$. However, in our "optimal FHE" scheme in Section 4, we will only need to invoke this lemma with secret-key encryption.

PROOF. It is easy to see that each step of the homomorphic evaluation algorithm, given by Eq. (5), simulates the execution of the branching program, given by Eq. (4). It remains to bound the noise growth during NCCrypt.Eval. We show this by induction.

In the sequel, we will abbreviate the noise function $\mathsf{noise}_{\mathbf{s},\mu}(\mathbf{C})$ to $\mathsf{noise}(\mathbf{C})$ since the secret key is fixed throughout the evaluation, and the message μ is clear from the context.

Clearly, $\mathsf{noise}(\mathbf{V}_{0,i}) = 0$, since they $\mathbf{V}_{0,i}$ are just the messages, with no noise. Assume, as the inductive hypothesis, that for all $i \in \{1,2,3,4,5\}$,

$$\mathsf{noise}(\mathbf{V}_{t-1,i}) = (t-1) \cdot \widetilde{O}_\kappa(\alpha q \cdot \sqrt{n \log q})$$

We will now bound $\mathsf{noise}(\mathbf{V}_{t,i})$ for all $i \in \{1,2,3,4,5\}$. Note that

$$\begin{aligned}\mathsf{noise}(\mathbf{V}_{t,i}) &\le \mathsf{noise}\Big(\mathsf{NCCrypt.ProtoMult}(\mathbf{V}_{t-1,\gamma_0}, \bar{\mathbf{C}}_{\mathsf{var}(t)})\Big) + \\ &\quad \mathsf{noise}\Big(\mathsf{NCCrypt.ProtoMult}(\mathbf{V}_{t-1,\gamma_1}, \mathbf{C}_{\mathsf{var}(t)})\Big) \\ &\le |1 - x_{\mathsf{var}(t)}| \cdot \mathsf{noise}(\mathbf{V}_{t-1,\gamma_0}) + \\ &\quad |x_{\mathsf{var}(t)}| \cdot \mathsf{noise}(\mathbf{V}_{t-1,\gamma_1}) + \widetilde{O}_\kappa(\alpha q \cdot \sqrt{n \log q})\end{aligned}$$

where the second inequality holds by Claim 3.4.2 since all the ciphertexts encrypt bits, $\mathbf{C}_{\mathsf{var}(t)}$ is a fresh secret-key encryption, and $\bar{\mathbf{C}}_{\mathsf{var}(t)}$ contains exactly the same noise as $\mathbf{C}_{\mathsf{var}(t)}$.

Since exactly one of $x_{\mathsf{var}(t)}$ and $1 - x_{\mathsf{var}(t)}$ is non-zero, we have

$$\begin{aligned}\mathsf{noise}(\mathbf{V}_{t,i}) &\le \max(\mathsf{noise}(\mathbf{V}_{t-1,\gamma_0}), \mathsf{noise}(\mathbf{V}_{t-1,\gamma_1})) + \\ &\quad \widetilde{O}_\kappa(\alpha q \cdot \sqrt{n \log q}) \\ &\le t \cdot \widetilde{O}_\kappa(\alpha q \cdot \sqrt{n \log q})\end{aligned}$$

by the inductive hypothesis.

Thus, in particular,

$$\mathsf{noise}(\mathbf{V}_\Psi) = \mathsf{noise}(\mathbf{V}_{L,1}) \le 4^d \cdot \widetilde{O}_\kappa(\alpha q \cdot \sqrt{n \log q}) < q/8$$

by our setting of the parameter α. □

3.4 Achieving Fully Homomorphic Encryption

We know by Lemma 3.4 that the depth of the decryption circuit of NCCrypt is $c_{\mathsf{dec}} \cdot \log(n \log q) = c_{\mathsf{dec}} \log N$ for some constant $c_{\mathsf{dec}} > 0$. Setting the depth $d = c \log N$ for some constant $c > c_{\mathsf{dec}}$ in Lemma 3.6 and $\alpha \le 1/\widetilde{\Theta}_\kappa(4^d \cdot \sqrt{n \log q})$ gives us a bootstrappable encryption scheme. By the bootstrapping theorem (Theorem 2.14), this can be turned into a leveled FHE scheme, without additional assumptions. We state this theorem below:

THEOREM 3.7. *Let n be the LWE dimension, q be the LWE modulus, $N := (n+1) \cdot \lceil \log q \rceil$, and let $c > c_{\mathsf{dec}}$ be a large enough constant (where c_{dec} is the decryption depth constant from Proposition 3.4), and*

$$\alpha \le 1/\widetilde{\Theta}_\kappa((n \log q)^{2c+1/2})$$

Then, there is a leveled FHE scheme that is secure under the decisional LWE assumption $\mathsf{DLWE}_{n,q,\alpha}$.

In the next section, we will use a variant of the dimension-modulus reduction of [7], the effect of which will be to reduce the constant c above to a very small $\epsilon \to 0$, thus achieving a value of α that matches the best known lattice-based PKE schemes.

4. SUCCESSIVE DIMENSION-MODULUS REDUCTION

In this section we revisit the dimension-modulus reduction technique from [7] and show that by successive application of this technique, we can achieve comparable lattice approximation factor to the best known factor for public key encryption.

We start by revisiting [7]'s dimension-modulus reduction in Section 4.1, and then proceed in Section 4.2 to present a bootstrappable homomorphic encryption scheme that is based on $\widetilde{O}(n^{1+\epsilon} \cdot \sqrt{n \log(q)})$-approximate GapSVP.

4.1 Dimension-Modulus Reduction (Revisited)

In the functions below, q is an integer and χ is a distribution over $\mathbb{Z}$:

- $\mathsf{SwitchKeyGen}_{q:p,\chi}(\mathbf{s}, \mathbf{t})$: For a "source" key $\mathbf{s} \in \mathbb{Z}^{n_s}$ and "target" key $\mathbf{t} \in \mathbb{Z}^{n_t}$, we define a set of parameters that allow to switch ciphertexts under $\mathbf{s}$ into ciphertexts under $(1, \mathbf{t})$.

  Let $\hat{n}_s \triangleq n_s \cdot \lceil \log q \rceil$ be the dimension of $\mathsf{PowersOfTwo}_q(\mathbf{s})$. Sample a uniform matrix $\mathbf{A}_{\mathbf{s}:\mathbf{t}} \xleftarrow{\$} \mathbb{Z}_p^{\hat{n}_s \times n_t}$ and a noise vector $\mathbf{e}_{\mathbf{s}:\mathbf{t}} \xleftarrow{\$} \chi^{\hat{n}_s}$. The function's output is a matrix

  $$\mathbf{P}_{\mathbf{s}:\mathbf{t}} = [\mathbf{b}_{\mathbf{s}:\mathbf{t}} \| - \mathbf{A}_{\mathbf{s}:\mathbf{t}}] \in \mathbb{Z}_p^{\hat{n}_s \times (n_t+1)} ,$$

  where

  $$\mathbf{b}_{\mathbf{s}:\mathbf{t}} := \Big[\mathbf{A}_{\mathbf{s}:\mathbf{t}} \cdot \mathbf{t} + \mathbf{e}_{\mathbf{s}:\mathbf{t}} + \lfloor (p/q) \cdot \mathsf{PowersOfTwo}_q(\mathbf{s}) \rceil_G\Big]_p \in \mathbb{Z}_p^{\hat{n}_s} .$$

  Here, $\lfloor \cdot \rceil_G$ is the Gaussian rounding procedure from Corollary 2.1.

- $\mathsf{SwitchKey}_q(\mathbf{P}_{\mathbf{s}:\mathbf{t}}, \mathbf{c}_s)$: To switch a source ciphertext $\mathbf{c}_s \in \mathbb{Z}_q^{n_s}$ from a secret key $\mathbf{s}$ to $(1, \mathbf{t})$, output

  $$\mathbf{c}_t := \Big[\mathbf{P}_{\mathbf{s}:\mathbf{t}}^T \cdot \mathsf{BitDecomp}_q(\mathbf{c}_s)\Big]_p \in \mathbb{Z}_p^{n_t+1} .$$

LEMMA 4.1 (CORRECTNESS). *Let $\mathbf{s} \in \mathbb{Z}^n$, $\mathbf{t} \in \mathbb{Z}^k$ be some vectors. Let χ be the discrete Gaussian $D_{\mathbb{Z},\alpha p}$, and let $\mathbf{P}_{\mathbf{s}:\mathbf{t}} \leftarrow \mathsf{SwitchKeyGen}_{q:p,\chi}(\mathbf{s}, \mathbf{t})$ and $\mathbf{P}_{\mathsf{rand}} \leftarrow \mathsf{RandParam}_{D_{\mathbb{Z},\beta q}}(\mathbf{s})$. Let $\mathbf{c}_s \in \mathbb{Z}_q^n$ and let $\mathbf{c}'_s \leftarrow \mathsf{Rand}(\mathbf{P}_{\mathsf{rand}}, \mathbf{c}_s)$.*

Finally, set $\mathbf{c}_t \leftarrow \mathsf{SwitchKey}(\mathbf{P}_{\mathbf{s}:\mathbf{t}}, \mathbf{c}'_s)$. Then there exists δ such that

$$(p/q) \cdot \langle \mathbf{c}_s, \mathbf{s} \rangle - \delta = \langle \mathbf{c}_t, (1, \mathbf{t}) \rangle \pmod p ,$$

and $|\delta| < \widetilde{O}_\kappa(\sqrt{n \log(q)}) \cdot \alpha p$ with all but $\mathrm{negl}(\kappa)$ probability (over the coins in the experiment, and regardless of the generation of $\mathbf{s}, \mathbf{t}, \mathbf{c}_s$).

PROOF. We expand the expression for $\langle \mathbf{c}_t, (1, \mathbf{t}) \rangle$:

$$\begin{aligned}\langle \mathbf{c}_t, (1, \mathbf{t}) \rangle &= \langle \mathbf{P}_{\mathbf{s}:\mathbf{t}}^T \cdot \mathsf{BitDecomp}_q(\mathbf{c}'_s), (1, \mathbf{t}) \rangle \\ &= \langle \mathsf{BitDecomp}_q(\mathbf{c}'_s), \mathbf{P}_{\mathbf{s}:\mathbf{t}} \cdot (1, \mathbf{t}) \rangle \\ &= \langle \mathsf{BitDecomp}_q(\mathbf{c}'_s), \mathbf{e}_{\mathbf{s}:\mathbf{t}} + \lfloor (p/q) \cdot \mathsf{PowersOfTwo}_q(\mathbf{s}) \rceil_G \rangle .\end{aligned}$$

It follows that $\delta = \delta_1 + \delta_2$ where

$$\delta_1 = \langle \mathsf{BitDecomp}_q(\mathbf{c}'_s), \mathbf{e}_{\mathbf{s}:\mathbf{t}} \rangle ,$$

which, by Lemma 2.11, is bounded by $|\delta_1| \le \widetilde{O}_\kappa(\sqrt{n\log(q)})\alpha p$ with all but negl(κ) probability; and

$$\delta_2 = \left\langle \mathsf{BitDecomp}_q(\mathbf{c}'_s), \lfloor (p/q) \cdot \mathsf{PowersOfTwo}_q(\mathbf{s}) \rceil_G \right\rangle - (p/q) \cdot \langle \mathbf{c}'_s, \mathbf{s} \rangle$$
$$= \left\langle \mathsf{BitDecomp}_q(\mathbf{c}'_s), \lfloor (p/q) \cdot \mathsf{PowersOfTwo}_q(\mathbf{s}) \rceil_G - (p/q) \cdot \mathsf{PowersOfTwo}_q(\mathbf{s}) \right\rangle .$$

Applying Lemma 2.11, we get that $|\delta_2| \le \widetilde{O}_\kappa(\sqrt{n\log(q)})$ with all but negl(κ) probability. □

Security follows in a straightforward manner, the proof is omitted.

LEMMA 4.2 (SECURITY). *Let $\mathbf{s} \in \mathbb{Z}^{n_s}$ be any vector. If we generate $\mathbf{t} \xleftarrow{\$} \mathbb{Z}_p^k$ and $\mathbf{P} \leftarrow \mathsf{SwitchKeyGen}_{q:p,\chi}(\mathbf{s}, \mathbf{t})$, then $\mathbf{P}$ is computationally indistinguishable from uniform over $\mathbb{Z}_p^{\hat{n}_s \times (n_t+1)}$, assuming the decisional LWE assumption $\mathsf{DLWE}_{k,p,\chi}$.*

4.2 A Bootstrappable Scheme

Let $q : \mathbb{N} \to \mathbb{N}$ be a monotone function such that $q(n) \le 2^n$ for all n, and $\alpha : \mathbb{N} \to \mathbb{R}$. Let $\chi(n)$ denote the discrete Gaussian distribution $D_{\mathbb{Z},\alpha(n)q(n)}$. Finally, let $\epsilon > 0$.

The typical value of $\alpha(n)$ will be $1/\widetilde{O}_\kappa(\sqrt{n\log(q)} \cdot n^\epsilon)$, where κ is the security parameter. As to the function $q(n)$, we will be interested in two ranges of parameters: In the first we will set $q(n)$ such that $\alpha(n) \cdot q(n) \approx \sqrt{n}$ (i.e. we set q such that $q(n) = \widetilde{O}_\kappa(n^{1+\epsilon}\sqrt{\log(q)})$. This is the minimal q that allows to apply worst-case to average-case reductions for LWE. The second case is where $q(n) = 2^{n/2}$, which is the minimal q that allows to apply *classical* worst-case to average case reductions to the GapSVP problem.

The scheme DimReduced is defined as follows.

- $\mathsf{DimReduced.Keygen}(1^k)$: Define $n \triangleq (k\log(q(k)))^{2c_{\mathsf{dec}}/\epsilon}$ (namely, $n^\epsilon = 4^{c_{\mathsf{dec}} \cdot \log(k\log(q(k)))}$), where c_{dec} is as in Proposition 3.4. Assume for convenience that $n = k^{(1+\epsilon)^L}$ for some $L \in \mathbb{N}$ (otherwise round n to the next power up). Further define $k_i = k^{(1+\epsilon)^i}$, so $k_0 = k$ and $k_L = n$, and define $q_i = q(k_i)$. For convenience we denote $p \triangleq q_0$.
  Let
  $$(\mathsf{ncsk}, \mathsf{ncevk}, \mathsf{ncpk}) \leftarrow \mathsf{NCCrypt.Keygen}(1^n, q(n), 4^{c_{\mathsf{dec}} \cdot \log(k\log(q(k)))+1}) .$$
  Define $\mathbf{s}_L \triangleq \mathsf{ncsk} \in \mathbb{Z}_{q_L}^{n_L}$. For all $i = 0, \ldots, L-1$, sample $\mathbf{s}_i \xleftarrow{\$} \mathbb{Z}_{q_i}^{n_i}$.
  Next, we generate dimension-modulus switching parameters (see Section 4.1), and randomization parameters (see Section 2.4) for all $i \in [L]$:
  $$\mathbf{P}_{i:(i-1)} \leftarrow \mathsf{SwitchKeyGen}_{q_i:q_{i-1}}((1, \mathbf{s}_i), \mathbf{s}_{i-1}) ,$$
  and
  $$\mathbf{P}_{\mathsf{rand},i} \leftarrow \mathsf{RandParam}_{D_{\mathbb{Z},\alpha(k_i)q_i}}(\mathbf{s}_i) .$$
  Finally, output the keys $sk \triangleq (\mathbf{s}_0, \mathbf{s}_L)$, $pk \triangleq \mathsf{ncpk}$, $evk \triangleq (\mathsf{ncevk}, \{\mathbf{P}_{i:(i-1)}\}_{i\in[L]}, \{\mathbf{P}_{\mathsf{rand},i}\}_{i\in[L]})$.
  We note that as ϵ approaches 0, $n = k^{\Theta(1/\epsilon)}$ becomes larger. If k is proportional to the security parameter, then ϵ must be bounded by a constant to keep n polynomially bounded. We further note that $L = \Theta(\log(1/\epsilon)/\epsilon)$.
- $\mathsf{DimReduced.PubEnc}_{pk}(\mu)$ / $\mathsf{DimReduced.SecEnc}_{sk}(\mu)$: The asymmetric and symmetric encryption procedures are identical to NCCrypt. Since DimReduced's public key and secret key contain those of NCCrypt, this can be done in a straightforward manner.
- $\mathsf{DimReduced.Eval}_{evk}(f, \mathbf{C}_1, \ldots, \mathbf{C}_t)$: To perform homomorphic evaluation, we first compute
  $$\mathbf{C}_f \leftarrow \mathsf{NCCrypt.Eval}_{\mathsf{ncevk}}(f, \mathbf{C}_1, \ldots, \mathbf{C}_t) .$$
  We then consider $\mathbf{c}_f \in \{0,1\}^{n\lceil\log(q_L)\rceil}$, which is the second row of $\mathbf{C}_f$. We set $\mathbf{c}_L := \mathsf{Combine}_{q_L}(\mathbf{c}_f)$.
  We then compute, in order for $i = L-1, \ldots, 0$, the ciphertexts $\mathbf{c}_{\mathsf{rand},i+1} \leftarrow \mathsf{Rand}(\mathbf{P}_{\mathsf{rand},i+1}, \mathbf{c}_{i+1})$, and then $\mathbf{c}_i \leftarrow \mathsf{SwitchKey}(\mathbf{P}_{(i+1):i}, \mathbf{c}_{\mathsf{rand},i+1})$. Finally, $\mathbf{c}_0 \in \mathbb{Z}_p^k$ is output as the final ciphertext.
- $\mathsf{DimReduced.Dec}_{sk}(\mathbf{c})$: We recall that $\mathbf{c} \in \mathbb{Z}_p^k$. We output $\mu^* = 0$ if $\left|[\langle \mathbf{c}, (1, \mathbf{s}_0)\rangle]_p\right| < p/8$, and $\mu^* = 1$ otherwise.

Security is stated in the next lemma and follows immediately using a hybrid argument and using the security properties of the scheme NCCrypt, the ciphertext randomization procedure (Lemma 2.9) and the dimension-modulus reduction procedure (Lemma 4.2). The formal proof is omitted.

LEMMA 4.3. *The scheme DimReduced is secure under the $\mathsf{DLWE}_{k,q(k),\alpha(k)}$ assumption.*

Correctness poses a more challenging task. We want to prove that DimReduced can homomorphically evaluate an augmented decryption circuit. Proving this when $\alpha(n)$ is small (e.g. $\alpha(n) = 1/n^3$) is fairly easy. However, since we wish to achieve optimal parameters, the analysis is more involved and appears in the following lemma.

We define $\tau \triangleq 2^{\lceil\log(q_L)\rceil-2}/q_L$ and notice that $\tau \in (1/4, 1/2]$.

LEMMA 4.4. *Let $\alpha(n) = 1/\widetilde{O}_\kappa(\sqrt{n\log(q)} \cdot n^\epsilon)$, and let $q(n) \ge \widetilde{O}(\sqrt{n}/\alpha(n))$. Consider a set of keys generated by $(sk, pk, evk) \leftarrow \mathsf{DimReduced.Keygen}(1^k)$, and recall that $sk = (\mathbf{s}_0, \mathbf{s}_L)$. Let $\mathbf{K}_i \leftarrow \mathsf{DimReduced.SecEnc}_{sk}(\mathsf{BitDecomp}(\mathbf{s}_0)[i])$. Namely, $\mathbf{K}_i$ is the symmetric encryption of the ith bit of $\mathbf{s}_0$.*

Let f be an augmented decryption circuit as per Definition 2.13. Namely, let $\mathbf{c}, \mathbf{c}' \in \mathbb{Z}_p^k$ and $\mu, \mu' \in \{0,1\}$ be such that

$$[\langle \mathbf{c}, \mathbf{s}_0 \rangle]_p = \mu \cdot \tau p + e ,$$

where $|e| < p/8$, and similarly for $\mathbf{c}'$. The function f is the function that on input x, treats x as a secret key and decrypts $\mathbf{c}, \mathbf{c}'$, and outputs the NAND of their decryptions.

Let

$$\mathbf{c}_0 \leftarrow \mathsf{DimReduced.Eval}_{evk}(f, \mathbf{K}_1, \mathbf{K}_2, \ldots) ,$$

and note that this is syntactically well defined since f can be represented as a Boolean circuit of depth $c_{\mathsf{dec}} \cdot \log(k\log(q(k))) + 1$.

Then with all but negl(κ) probability,

$$[\langle \mathbf{c}_0, \mathbf{s}_0 \rangle]_p = \mu^* \cdot \tau p + e_f ,$$

where $\mu^* = \overline{(\mu \wedge \mu')}$, $|e_f| < p/8$ are as above.

PROOF. Consider the process of execution of $\mathsf{DimReduced.Eval}_{evk}(f, \mathbf{K}_1, \mathbf{K}_2, \ldots)$. It starts by generating

$\mathbf{c}_L$, where we are guaranteed by the correctness of NCCrypt that

$$[\langle \mathbf{c}_L, \mathbf{s}_L \rangle]_{q_L} = \mu^* \cdot \tau q_L + e_L \ ,$$

where

$$\begin{aligned} |e_L|/q_L &\leq \widetilde{O}_\kappa(\sqrt{n \log(q_L)} \cdot 4^{c_{\mathsf{dec}} \cdot \log(k \log(q(k)))+1}) \alpha(n) \\ &= \widetilde{O}_\kappa(n^\epsilon \cdot \sqrt{n \log(q_L)}) \cdot \alpha(n) \ , \end{aligned}$$

and we will set $\alpha(n) = 1/(\sqrt{n \log(q)} \cdot n^\epsilon \text{polylog}(\kappa))$ with sufficiently large polylogarithmic factor to offset the one coming from the noise so that

$$|e_L|/q_L \leq 1/\text{polylog}(\kappa) \ .$$

We then commence with $L = O(1)$ levels of randomization followed by modulus-dimension reduction. Let us consider the effect of these operations at level i.

Lemma 2.10 guarantees that in the randomization step, the relative noise grows by an additive factor of at most $\widetilde{O}_\kappa(\sqrt{k_i \log(q_i)}) \cdot \alpha(k_i) = k_i^{-\epsilon} \cdot \widetilde{O}_\kappa(1)/\text{polylog}(\kappa)$. Again, the idea is to define α with sufficiently large polylogarithmic factor to offset those coming from $\widetilde{O}_\kappa(\cdot)$.

Lemma 4.1 guarantees that in the key switching step, the relative noise grows by an additive factor of $\widetilde{O}_\kappa(\sqrt{k_i \log(q_i)}) \cdot \alpha(k_{i-1})$. We recall that $k_i = k_{i-1}^{1+\epsilon}$ and that $q(n) < 2^n$. Therefore

$$\sqrt{k_i \log(q_i)} \leq \sqrt{(k_{i-1} \log(q_{i-1}))^{1+\epsilon}} \leq \sqrt{(k_{i-1} \log(q_{i-1}))} \cdot k_{i-1}^{\epsilon} \ .$$

Therefore, setting the polylogarithmic factors right, we get an additive relative error of at most $1/\text{polylog}(\kappa)$.

Putting all of these together, we get that

$$|e_f| \leq L/\text{polylog}(\kappa) \ll p/8 \ ,$$

and the result follows. □

Finally, we derive the worst-case lattice approximation factor based on Corollary 2.6. We recall that a bootstrappable homomorphic encryption scheme implies a leveled FHE scheme under the same assumptions, and a pure FHE scheme with an additional circular security assumption.

COROLLARY 4.5. *For all $\epsilon > 0$, there exist:*

- *A bootstrappable homomorphic encryption scheme based on the worst-case* quantum *hardness of solving* $\mathsf{GapSVP}_{\widetilde{O}(n^{1.5+\epsilon})}$ *and* $\mathsf{SIVP}_{\widetilde{O}(n^{1.5+\epsilon})}$.
- *A bootstrappable homomorphic encryption scheme based on the worst-case* classical *hardness of solving* $\mathsf{GapSVP}_{\widetilde{O}(n^{2+\epsilon})}$.

The first (quantum) case is derived from Lemma 4.4 by setting $q(n) = \sqrt{n}/\alpha(n) = \text{poly}(n)$, and the second (classical) case is derived by setting $q(n) = 2^{n/2}$.

Improving Key and Ciphertext sizes..

The scheme DimReduced uses a ladder of LWE instances, ranging from short (k, p) to polynomially larger (n, q). In the description above, the public key of the scheme is derived from that of NCCrypt, and therefore depends on n and not on k. Likewise, the "input ciphertexts" (the ones before homomorphic evaluation) also depend on n.

We note here that this can be fixed in such a way that only the *evk* depends on n, and the rest of the parameters are exactly the same as Regev's scheme with parameters (k, p). This is done in a standard way (used e.g. in [7]) as follows.

We will generate the public key as a standard Regev public key with parameters (k, p), and in the evaluation key we will encrypt the bits of the respective secret key using NCCrypt. This will allow to perform homomorphic operations by evaluating the augmented decryption circuit. Namely, the ciphertexts visible to the user of the scheme will always be short, but in the process of homomorphic evaluation, larger ciphertexts are used to accommodate the homomorphic operation, and once it is done dimension-modulus reduction will be used to shrink the output ciphertext back to the original size. Since this is standard practice, we omit the technical description.

5. REFERENCES

[1] M. Ajtai and C. Dwork. A public-key cryptosystem with worst-case/average-case equivalence. In F. T. Leighton and P. W. Shor, editors, *STOC*, pages 284–293. ACM, 1997.

[2] D. A. M. Barrington. Bounded-width polynomial-size branching programs recognize exactly those languages in nc^1. *J. Comput. Syst. Sci.*, 38(1):150–164, 1989.

[3] A. Borodin, D. Dolev, F. E. Fich, and W. J. Paul. Bounds for width two branching programs. *SIAM J. Comput.*, 15(2):549–560, 1986.

[4] Z. Brakerski. Fully homomorphic encryption without modulus switching from classical GapSVP. In R. Safavi-Naini and R. Canetti, editors, *CRYPTO*, volume 7417 of *Lecture Notes in Computer Science*, pages 868–886. Springer, 2012.

[5] Z. Brakerski, C. Gentry, and V. Vaikuntanathan. (Leveled) fully homomorphic encryption without bootstrapping. In S. Goldwasser, editor, *ITCS*, pages 309–325. ACM, 2012. Invited to ACM Transactions on Computation Theory.

[6] Z. Brakerski, A. Langlois, C. Peikert, O. Regev, and D. Stehlé. Classical hardness of learning with errors. *CoRR*, abs/1306.0281, 2013. Preliminary version in STOC 2013.

[7] Z. Brakerski and V. Vaikuntanathan. Efficient fully homomorphic encryption from (standard) LWE. In R. Ostrovsky, editor, *FOCS*, pages 97–106. IEEE, 2011. Invited to SIAM Journal on Computing.

[8] C. Gentry. *A fully homomorphic encryption scheme.* PhD thesis, Stanford University, 2009.

[9] C. Gentry. Fully homomorphic encryption using ideal lattices. In *STOC*, pages 169–178, 2009.

[10] C. Gentry. Toward basing fully homomorphic encryption on worst-case hardness. In *CRYPTO*, pages 116–137, 2010.

[11] C. Gentry, C. Peikert, and V. Vaikuntanathan. Trapdoors for hard lattices and new cryptographic constructions. In C. Dwork, editor, *STOC*, pages 197–206. ACM, 2008.

[12] C. Gentry, A. Sahai, and B. Waters. Homomorphic encryption from learning with errors: Conceptually-simpler, asymptotically-faster, attribute-based. *IACR Cryptology ePrint Archive*, 2013:340, 2013. Preliminary version in CRYPTO 2013.

[13] Y. Ishai and A. Paskin. Evaluating branching programs on encrypted data. In S. P. Vadhan, editor,

TCC, volume 4392 of *Lecture Notes in Computer Science*, pages 575–594. Springer, 2007.

[14] D. Micciancio and P. Mol. Pseudorandom knapsacks and the sample complexity of lwe search-to-decision reductions. In P. Rogaway, editor, *CRYPTO*, volume 6841 of *Lecture Notes in Computer Science*, pages 465–484. Springer, 2011.

[15] D. Micciancio and C. Peikert. Trapdoors for lattices: Simpler, tighter, faster, smaller. *IACR Cryptology ePrint Archive*, 2011:501, 2011. Extended abstract in Eurocrypt 2012.

[16] C. Peikert. Public-key cryptosystems from the worst-case shortest vector problem: extended abstract. In M. Mitzenmacher, editor, *STOC*, pages 333–342. ACM, 2009.

[17] O. Regev. New lattice-based cryptographic constructions. *J. ACM*, 51(6):899–942, 2004.

[18] O. Regev. On lattices, learning with errors, random linear codes, and cryptography. In H. N. Gabow and R. Fagin, editors, *STOC*, pages 84–93. ACM, 2005. Full version in [19].

[19] O. Regev. On lattices, learning with errors, random linear codes, and cryptography. *J. ACM*, 56(6), 2009.

[20] C.-P. Schnorr. A hierarchy of polynomial time lattice basis reduction algorithms. *Theor. Comput. Sci.*, 53:201–224, 1987.

Cryptogenography

Joshua Brody
Swarthmore College
Swarthmore, PA
joshua.e.brody@gmail.com

Sune K. Jakobsen
Queen Mary, University of London
London, United Kingdom
s.k.jakobsen@qmul.ac.uk

Dominik Scheder
Simons Institute for the Theory of Computing, UC Berkeley
Berkeley, CA
dominik.scheder@gmail.com

Peter Winkler
Dartmouth College
Hanover, NH
peter.winkler@dartmouth.edu

ABSTRACT

We consider the following cryptographic secret leaking problem. A group of players communicate with the goal of learning (and perhaps revealing) a secret held initially by one of them. Their conversation is monitored by a computationally unlimited eavesdropper, who wants to learn the identity of the secret-holder. Despite the unavailability of key, some protection can be provided to the identity of the secret-holder. We call the study of such communication problems, either from the group's or the eavesdropper's point of view, *cryptogenography.*

We introduce a basic cryptogenography problem and show that two players can force the eavesdropper to missguess the origin of a secret bit with probability $1/3$; we complement this with a hardness result showing that they cannot do better than than $3/8$. We prove that larger numbers of players can do better than 0.5644, but no group of any size can achieve 0.75.

Categories and Subject Descriptors

E.4 [**Coding and Information Theory**]; F.m [**Theory of Computation**]: Miscellaneous

Keywords

cryptogenography, cryptography, information theory, communication complexity

1. INTRODUCTION

We consider a cryptographic secret leaking problem where the goal is hiding the identity of the person leaking a secret, rather than protecting the secret itself. Indeed, assuming the communicators share no prior key, the secret is unprotectable unless eavesdroppers are computationally limited *and* some complexity assumptions are made. What is perhaps surprising is that under these circumstances, it is nonetheless possible to protect the identity of the secret-owner.

In the simplest scenario the secret is a bit X held by one of a group of $k > 1$ cooperating players; initially, neither the secret bit nor (except in the $k = 2$ case) the identity of its holder is known to the rest of the group. Ultimately the secret bit is revealed, but the identity of the initial bit-holder must not be revealed to an eavesdropper, even though the eavesdropper hears everything and is not computationally limited.

A protocol's success is measured by the "success probability" p that the secret is correctly revealed and the eavesdropper misguesses the identity of the secret-owner. The group's goal of maximizing p, and the eavesdropper's goal of minimizing it, comprise the two sides of what we call *cryptogenography* ("hidden source writing"). We give a formal definition of a cryptogenography problem in Section 2.

Motivation.
The standard cryptographic setting, in which players want to share a secret but keep it hidden from an adversary, is a well-studied and well-motivated problem. However, there are several applications where hiding the identity of the secret-owner is as important as, or more important than, hiding the secret itself.

The most obvious such situation arises when someone wants to publicize some secret information but fears retribution for making the information public, e.g., when dissidents protest against a government that responds by cracking down on protesters. In this case, protesters might want to broadcast the time and place for anticipated crackdowns, but fear arrest for disseminating this information.

Alternatively, the secret-owner might be publishing information obtained (legally or otherwise) from an organization that wants to keep this information from being leaked, as in the recent mass surveillance disclosures of Edward Snowden [12] and the Wikileaks scandal [13].

Groups who are already in possession of private keys, or capable of setting up a public-key system (and willing to make the necessary assumptions about computational complexity and adversarial limitations), can protect the identity of a source using standard cryptologic methods. Protection against traffic analysis can be achieved by having all parties send messages of sufficient length to include the secret.

ITCS'14, January 12–14, 2014, Princeton, New Jersey, USA.
Copyright 2014 ACM 978-1-4503-2698-8/14/01 ...$15.00.
http://dx.doi.org/10.1145/2554797.2554800.

That cryptogenography can protect the source identity without key or computational assumptions is of potential interest, we think, as are upper bounds on the degree to which this protection can be achieved. The toy problem studied below (in which the secret is just one bit) may not be directly applicable to real-life situations, but will serve, we hope, to get the subject of cryptogenography started.

1.1 Our Results

We introduce the cryptogenography problem[1] and provide both upper and lower bounds on the best possible success probability achievable by the players. Our first results are protocols, both in the two-player and general k-player cases.

THEOREM 1.1. *In the two-player problem, players can achieve success probability* $1/3$.

THEOREM 1.2. *For all large* k*, there exists a cryptogenography protocol achieving success probablity* 0.5644.

The proofs of the above theorems are constructive. For Theorem 1.2, we provide a series of protocols. First, we give a "majority vote" protocol which achieves success probability $1/2 + \Theta(1/\sqrt{k})$. For large k, this is essentially $1/2$, but for smaller k, we get something better. The success of the majority-votes protocol is maximized at roughly 54% for $k = 23$ players. We then show how a larger number of players can emulate the majority-votes protocol by first communicating to decide on 23 players to participate in the majority-votes protocol. The success probability decreases as a result, but the decrease can be made arbitrarily small. Surprisingly, it turns out that *reversing these operations*—having all k players vote, then adaptively deciding which players' votes will count—can boost the success probability up to ≈ 0.5644. We formalize and analyze these protocols in Section 3.

On the other side, we provide hardness results in Section 4, both in the 2-player case and in the general k-player case.

THEOREM 1.3. *No two-player cryptogenography protocol can achieve success probability greater than* 0.375.

Given that with many players, one can achieve success greater than $1/2$, one might suspect that as $k \to \infty$, players' success probability approaches 1. We show this is actually not the case.

THEOREM 1.4. *No* k*-player cryptogenography protocol can achieve success probability greater than* 0.75.

To show these upper bounds we generalize the problem, so that instead of starting with secret and secret-holder being uniformly distributed and independent, they can have an arbitrary joint distribution. We show that if a function from the set of such distributions to $[0, 1]$ is an upper bound on the probability of winning if communication is not allowed, and the function satisfy some concavity requirements, then the function is an upper bound on the probability of winning. We further show that the function that sends a probability distribution over secret and secret-holder to the probability of winning starting from this distribution, will satisfy these requirements. Thus, our method can find tight upper bounds.

1.2 Previous Work

The problem of secret sharing in the presence of an adversarial eavesdropper is a classic and fundamental problem in cryptography [11, 4, 9, 10, 5, 1]. However, to our knowledge our work is the first to consider how to hide the *identity* of the secret-owner rather than the secret itself.

While we are not aware of other work considering other cryptogenography research, some of our techniques are similar to techniques used in recent works in information complexity and information theory. The most relevant is the recent paper of Braverman et al. [3], who give *exact* bounds for the information complexity of zero-error protocols computing the AND of two bits and further use this bound to achieve nearly exact bounds on the randomized communication complexity of computing DISJOINTNESS, perhaps the most studied problem in communication complexity. Specifically, their optimal "protocol" for AND is similar to our "continuous protocol" for cryptogenography (see Section 3.2). Furthermore, their characterization of zero-error information complexity in terms of local concavity constraints is very similar to our convexity arguments in Section 4. Similar arguments appeared first in work of Ma and Ishwar [8, 7].

Cryptography in the absence of private key or computational assumptions is the setting for [2], in which it is shown that information can be passed in secret over an open channel when the parties have shared knowledge, even though that knowledge may not include shared secrets. In our cryptogenography setting, the players do indeed have some shared knowledge: each knows whether he/she is or is not the original secret-owner. This amounts to a shared secret only in the $k = 2$ case, and is otherwise insufficient to protect even a one-bit secret. In our development below, we neutralize even this small scrap of shared information by asking that the secret be revealed—in other words, that a hypothetical extra party, who has zero shared knowledge, be able to deduce the secret from the conversation.

1.3 Paper Outline

We formalize the cryptogenography problem and provide some initial insights in Section 2. In Section 3, we develop our cryptogenography protocols. We give hardness results in Section 4. Finally, Section 5 concludes the paper and lists some open problems for followup work.

2. PRELIMINARIES

Let $[k]$ denote the set $\{1, \ldots, k\}$. We use calligraphic letters, lower case letters, and capital letters to refer respectively to sets, elements of a set, and random variables. Random variables are uniformly distributed unless specified otherwise. We use π to denote a communication protocol

[1]There are many cryptogenography questions that can be asked. The amount of information to be leaked can be varied, as well as the number of players who originally have the information; likewise, what is known about who knows the information (e.g., one player knows the information, another only knows which player was given the information). Conceivably some of the players may try to prevent the information from being leaked by sending misleading messages. The objective itelf can be altered; e.g., instead of measuring success by the probability that Eve guess wrong, it might only be required that Eve cannot be more than 95% sure of who the secret-holder is. Here we only consider one of these questions, calling it "the" cryptogenography problem.

and assume by default that each player has a source of private randomness they can use to decide what messages to send. We further assume that messages are broadcast[2] and abuse notation somewhat by also using π to denote the *protocol transcript*; i.e., the concatenation of all messages sent during a protocol.

The (k-player) cryptogenography problem is formally defined as follows. There are k players, denoted $\text{PLR}_1, \ldots, \text{PLR}_k$. Inputs consist of $(X, J) \sim \mu$, where μ is uniform over $\{0,1\} \times [k]$. We refer to X as the *secret* and say that PLR_J is the *secret-owner*, or that PLR_J owns the secret. Both X and J are given to PLR_J; other players receive no input. Players communicate using a protocol π, after which they compute a guess $\text{Out} : \{0,1\}^* \to \{0,1\}$ for the secret. Let $\text{Eve} : \{0,1\}^* \to [k]$ be the function that maximizes $\Pr[\text{Eve}(\pi) = J \mid \text{Out}(\pi) = X]$ for each possible value of the protocol transcript. This function represents the best possible guess of an adversary (whom we call Eve), who sees all communication between the players and wants to determine the identity of the secret-owner. Note that $\text{Out}(\pi)$ and $\text{Eve}(\pi)$ are functions of the messages sent in π. We define the success of a protocol as

$$\text{succ}(\pi) := \Pr[\text{Out}(\pi) = X \text{ and } \text{Eve}(\pi) \neq J] .$$

The *communication cost* of π, denoted $\text{CC}(\pi)$, is the maximum amount of communication sent during π, taken over all possible inputs (x, j) and all choices of randomness. In this work, we focus on understanding the maximum possible $\text{succ}(\pi)$ of a protocol, not the communication cost.

The following lemma shows that one can assume without loss of generality that players learn the secret with certainty.

LEMMA 2.1. *For all protocols π there exists a cryptogenography protocol π' with $\text{succ}(\pi') = \text{succ}(\pi)$, $\text{CC}(\pi') = \text{CC}(\pi) + k$, and such that $\Pr[\text{Out}(\pi') = X] = 1$.*

PROOF. Players first execute π, after which each player sends an additional bit, which equals 1 if (i) the player is the secret-owner and (ii) $\text{Out}(\pi) \neq X$, and is 0 otherwise. Define $\text{Out}(\pi')$ to equal $\text{Out}(\pi)$ if all players communicate a 0 in the extra round of communication; otherwise, set $\text{Out}(\pi') = 1 - \text{Out}(\pi)$.

It is easy to see that $\text{Out}(\pi') = X$ with certainty—either π correctly computes X already, or the secret-owner announces that $\text{Out}(\pi) \neq X$. It is also trivial to verify that $\text{CC}(\pi') = \text{CC}(\pi) + k$. Thus, it remains to show that $\text{succ}(\pi') = \text{succ}(\pi)$. This can be seen through the following chain of equalities.

$$\begin{aligned}
\text{succ}(\pi') &= \Pr[\text{Out}(\pi') = X \wedge \text{Eve}(\pi') \neq J] \\
&= \Pr[\text{Eve}(\pi') \neq J] \\
&= \Pr[\text{Eve}(\pi') \neq J \mid \text{Out}(\pi) = X] \cdot \Pr[\text{Out}(\pi) = X] \\
&\quad + \Pr[\text{Eve}(\pi') \neq J \mid \text{Out}(\pi) \neq X] \cdot \Pr[\text{Out}(\pi) \neq X] \\
&= \Pr[\text{Eve}(\pi') \neq J \mid \text{Out}(\pi) = X] \cdot \Pr[\text{Out}(\pi) = X] \\
&= \Pr[\text{Eve}(\pi) \neq J \mid \text{Out}(\pi) = X] \cdot \Pr[\text{Out}(\pi) = X] \\
&= \text{succ}(\pi) ,
\end{aligned}$$

where the second equality holds because players always learn X in π', the third equality holds by conditioning on $\text{Out}(\pi)$, and the penultimate equality holds because, conditioned on π correctly computing X, the eavesdropper in π' learns nothing new about J. □

[2]We make this assumption for concreteness only. Our focus in this work is on the success probability and not the communication complexity, and in this case, the type of communication (e.g., broadcast vs. point-to-point) is equivalent.

3. CRYPTOGENOGRAPHY PROTOCOLS

In this section, we present a series of protocols that demonstrate what is possible for the players to achieve.

3.1 Two Player Cryptogenography

When $k = 2$, we refer to players as Alice and Bob instead of PLR_1 and PLR_2.

THEOREM 3.1 (RESTATEMENT OF THEOREM 1.1). *There is a two-player cryptogenography protocol π with $\text{succ}(\pi) = 1/3$ and $\text{CC}(\pi) = 2$.*

PROOF. This protocol proceeds in two rounds. In the first round of communication, Alice decides whether to "pass" or "speak". If she passes, then Bob speaks in the second round; otherwise she speaks. In the second round of communication, whoever speaks will (i) send the secret if she owns it and (ii) send a random bit otherwise. Both players output the second bit of communication as their guess for the secret.

All that remains is to complete the protocol is to specify how Alice chooses to pass or speak in the first round. If Alice owns the secret, she passes with probabilty $2/3$ and speaks with probability $1/3$; otherwise, she passes with probability $1/3$ and speaks with probability $2/3$.

Note that Alice is more likely to speak in round 2 when she *doesn't* own the secret. This is perhaps counterintuitive—the players output the second bit of communication, so intuitively Alice should speak more often when she actually owns the bit. Is there an a priori reason why Alice shouldn't just announce the secret if she owns it and pass otherwise? Unfortunately in this case, Eve will learn with certainty who owns the bit. Alice's probablities of passing are chosen to give Eve no information about the secret-owner *conditioned on players successfully outputting the secret.*

CLAIM 3.2. $\Pr[\text{Out}(\pi) = X] = 2/3$.

PROOF. The secret-owner speaks in the second round with probablity $1/3$. In this case, players output correctly with certainty. Otherwise, players output a random bit and are correct with probability $1/2$. Overall, they output the correct bit with probability $1/3 + (2/3) \cdot (1/2) = 2/3$. □

CLAIM 3.3. $\Pr[\text{Eve}(\pi) = J \mid \text{Out}(\pi) = X] = 1/2$.

PROOF. Without loss of generality, assume Alice speaks in the second round. From Eve's point of view, there are three cases: (i) Alice is the secret-owner and therefore outputs the correct bit in round 2, (ii) Alice is not the secret-owner but outputs the correct bit anyway, and (iii) Alice is not the secret-owner and outputs incorrectly in round 2. Simple calculation shows that all three events are equally likely; however, in the third case, the players have already failed. Thus, *conditioned on players correctly outputting the secret,* Alice and Bob are equally likely to be the secret-owner, and Eve can only guess at random. □

In this protocol, players output the secret with probability $2/3$ and given this, Eve guesses the secret-owner with probablity $1/2$. Thus, the overall success probability is $1/3$.

3.2 General Cryptogenography Protocols

Next, we present a series of protocols for the general case.

The Majority-Votes Protocol.

In this protocol π_{MAJ}, there is a single round of communication, with each player sending a single bit. PLR_j sends X if she owns the secret; otherwise, PLR_j sends a random bit. At the end of the protocol, players output the MAJORITY of the bits communicated. Let b_j denote the bit communicated by PLR_j, and define $\text{Out}(\pi_{\text{MAJ}}) := \text{MAJ}(b_1, \ldots, b_k)$. When k is odd, the distribution of $\text{MAJ}(b_1, \ldots, b_k)$ is biased slightly towards X. This enables players to achieve success probablity somewhat larger than $1/2$.

LEMMA 3.4. *If k is odd, then π_{MAJ} succeeds with probability $1/2 + \Theta(1/\sqrt{k})$.*

PROOF. The communication $b_1, \ldots, b_k$ consists of $k-1$ random bits, along with the secret X. It will be helpful to be more explicit about the success probability. Let z_j be an indicator variable for the event $b_j = X$. Note that since $\{b_j\}$ are uniform and independent, so are $\{z_j\}$. In π_{MAJ}, players output $\text{MAJ}(b_1, \ldots, b_k)$; therefore, $\text{Out}(\pi_{\text{MAJ}}) = X$ iff $\sum_{j \neq j} z_j \geq \frac{k-1}{2}$. Thus, we have

$$\begin{aligned}\Pr[\text{Out}(\pi_{\text{MAJ}}) = X] &= \Pr\left[\sum_{j \neq J} z_j \geq \frac{k-1}{2}\right] \\ &= \frac{1}{2} + 2^{-k}\binom{k-1}{(k-1)/2} \\ &= \frac{1}{2} + \Theta\left(\frac{1}{\sqrt{k}}\right).\end{aligned}$$

It is easy to see that the best choice for Eve is to guess a random player j whose bit agrees with the majority. There are at least $k/2$ such bits; therefore, $\Pr[\text{Eve}(\pi_{\text{MAJ}}) = J \mid \text{Out}(\pi_{\text{MAJ}}) = X] = 1/2 + \Theta(1/\sqrt{k}) - O(1/k) = 1/2 + \Theta(1/\sqrt{k})$. □

We can achieve a more precise analysis by conditioning on $\sum_j z_j$. We have

$$\begin{aligned}&\text{succ}(\pi_{\text{MAJ}}) = \\ &\sum_{\ell=(k-1)/2}^{k-1} \Pr\left[\sum_j z_j = \ell\right] \Pr\left[\text{Eve}(\pi_{\text{MAJ}}) \neq J \mid \sum z_j = \ell\right] \\ &= \sum_{\ell=(k-1)/2}^{k-1} 2^{-(k-1)} \cdot \binom{k-1}{\ell} \cdot \left(1 - \frac{1}{\ell+1}\right).\end{aligned}$$

A straightforward calculation shows that the success probablity of π_{MAJ} is maximized at $\text{succ}(\pi_{\text{MAJ}}) \approx 0.5406$ when $k = 23$. However, for large k, the success probablity decreases and approaches $1/2$. Furthermore, when k is even, π_{MAJ} has success probability less than one half.[3] Our next protocol handles both cases by emulating a protocol for a smaller number of players.

A Continuous Protocol for large k.

Let $k > k'$ be given, and fix a k'-player protocol π'. We construct a protocol π for k players in the following manner.

[3]If k is even then $\Pr[\text{Out}(\pi_{\text{MAJ}}) = X] = 1/2$, and the overall success is only $1/2 - O(1/k)$.

This protocol assumes the existence of a real-valued "clock" that all players see; i.e., the protocol assumes that all players have access to some $\eta \in \mathbb{R}_{\geq 0}$. When the protocol begins, $\eta = 0$, and η increases as the protocol progresses.

Each player generates a real number $t_j \in [0, 1]$. The secret-owner PLR_J sets $t_J := 1$; for $j \neq J$, PLR_j sets t_j uniformly in $[0, 1]$. As η increases, each player announces when $\eta = t_j$. When all but k' players have spoken, the remaining players run π'. We call the communication before emulating π' the *continuous* phase of communication. It is easy to see that at the end of this continuous phase, J is uniformly distributed over the k' remaining players. Thus π has precisely the same success probability as π'.

LEMMA 3.5. *Given any k' player protocol π' and any $k > k'$, there exists a k-player continuous protocol achieving* $\text{succ}(\pi) = \text{succ}(\pi')$.

Together with Lemma 3.4, we get an efficient protocol for all large k.

COROLLARY 3.6. *For all $k \geq 23$, there is a continuous protocol π achieving* $\text{succ}(\pi) \geq 0.5406$.

The assumption that all players have shared access to a continuous clock is perhaps unnatural, and it is unclear how players can emulate such a protocol without access to this clock. Nevertheless, it is a useful abstraction, and while it is hard to see how such protocols can be emulated, it is easy to construct a protocol that *approximates* them. Our next protocol is just such a construction.

LEMMA 3.7. *Fix k, k' with $k > k'$, and let $\epsilon > 0$. For any k'-player protocol π', there exists a k-player protocol π with* $\text{succ}(\pi) \geq \text{succ}(\pi') - \epsilon$ *and* $\text{CC}(\pi) = \text{CC}(\pi') + O(k^3/\epsilon)$.

PROOF. Given ϵ, let $m = \Theta(k^2/\epsilon)$ be determined later. Similar to the continuous protocol, each PLR_j ($j \neq J$) generates $t_j \in [m]$ uniformly. The secret-owner then sets $t_J := m + 1$. In the first phase of communication, players proceed in rounds $i = 1, 2$, etc. In the ith round, each PLR_j announces whether $t_j < i$. Call PLR_j *alive* if $t_j > i$. Communication in the first phase continues until $i = m$ or until at most k' players remain alive. In the second phase, the remaining alive players execute π' if exactly k' players remain; otherwise, they output something arbitrary.

There are $O(k^2/\epsilon)$ rounds of communication in the first phase of π, and each player sends a single bit in each of these rounds. Thus, π uses $O(k^3/\epsilon)$ additional communication over π'.

It is easy to see that conditioned on the communication in the first phase of π, J is uniformly distributed over the remaining alive players. Simple balls-and-bins analysis shows that the set $\{t_j \leq m\}$ are distinct with probability at least $1-\epsilon$. Thus, the probability that players do *not* execute π' is at most ϵ. □

Taking the majority-votes protocol and fixing ϵ to be a suitably small constant yields the following corollary.

COROLLARY 3.8. *For all $k \geq 23$, there exists a protocol π with* $\text{succ}(\pi) > 0.5406$ *and* $\text{CC}(\pi) = O(k^3)$.

Beating Majority-Votes.

For our final protocol we show that, perhaps surprisingly, one can boost success by reversing the above operations. Specifically, we consider a k-player protocol with two phases of communication. In the first phase, each player votes, as in π_{MAJ}. In the second phase of communication, players communicate to decide one-by-one who will *not* participate in the vote. Call a player "dead" if he has been chosen to no longer participate. Eventually, players decide to end the second phase of communicate and compute the majority of the remaining votes. By voting first, and elminating players from the vote one-by-one, the protocol can *adaptively* decide when to stop the protocol. At a high level, the protocol ends when the votes of the remaining players form a *super-majority*. Say that $b_1, \dots b_k$ form a t-super-majority if t of the k bits agree.

Fix a function $\tau : \mathbb{N} \to \mathbb{N}$. For each τ, we define a protocol π_τ as follows. First, the k players vote. Then, while there is no $\tau(k')$-super-majority among the remaining k' live players, they communicate to decide on a player to bow out of the protocol. The protocol ends when a super-majority of the remaining votes is achieved. In general, determining the optimal τ appears to be nontrivial; however, for small k (we used $k = 1200$), we can compute τ and the resulting $\text{succ}(\pi_\tau)$ easily using Mathematica and dynamic programming. Along with Lemma 3.7, this gives a protocol with success probability greater than 0.5644, thus proving Theorem 1.2.

THEOREM 3.9 (RESTATEMENT OF THEOREM 1.2). *For all $k \geq 1200$, there exists a k-player cryptogenography protocol π with* $\text{succ}(\pi) > 0.5644$.

4. HARDNESS RESULTS

In this section, we show the limits of cryptogenography—in both the two-player and general case, we give upper bounds on the best possible success probability. The proofs in this section are more technical, so we start with a high-level description of our approach.

In Section 3 we gave several protocols achieving high success probability under the uniform distribution on inputs (X, J). In this section, it will be helpful to consider the space of all possible input distributions. Let $\Delta(\{0,1\} \times [k])$ denote the set of all possible distributions on (X, J). Given a (partial) communication transcript $t \in \{0,1\}^m$, define μ_t to be the input distribution μ, conditioned on the first m bits of communication equaling t. Our motivation here is two-fold: first, examining general distributions allows us to appeal to the geometry of $\Delta(\{0,1\} \times [k])$. In particular, we show that the success of a protocol satisfies certain concavity conditions when viewed as a function $s : \Delta(\{0,1\} \times [k]) \to [0,1]$ over the distribution space. Second, our arguments will examine how a protocol π affects μ_t. We show that μ is a convex combination of $\{\mu_t\}$. We are particularly interested in how μ "splits" into distributions μ_0 and μ_1; i.e., we look at convex combinations on conditional distributions one bit at a time. Importantly, we show that for each player PLR_p, the set of all possible distributions obtainable by splitting μ forms a plane in $\Delta(\{0,1\} \times [k])$; we call this the *$\text{PLR}_p$-allowed plane through μ*. Any plane, that is an allowed plane through μ' for some distribution μ' is called an *allowed plane.* Our first lemma characterizes the possible distribution splits made by a cryptogenography protocol.

LEMMA 4.1. *Let π be a protocol where only one message gets sent, this message is in $\{0,1\}$, and this message is sent by PLR_p. If π is used with prior distribution μ, let $\nu(i)$ denote the probability that PLR_p sends message i and let μ_i be the distribution given that PLR_p sent message i. Then*

1. $\mu = \nu(0)\mu_0 + \nu(1)\mu_1$.
2. *Each μ_i is proportional to μ on* $\{0,1\} \times ([k] \setminus \{p\})$.

PROOF. 1: Let M denote the message sent in π. Then we have

$$\begin{aligned}\mu(x,j) &= \Pr(X = x, J = j) \\ &= \sum_{i=0}^{1} \Pr(X = x, J = j, M = i) \\ &= \sum_{i=0}^{1} \nu(i)\mu_i(x,j)\end{aligned}$$

2: Let $x' \in \{0,1\}$ and $p' \in [k] \setminus \{p\}$. Then by Bayes' theorem

$$\begin{aligned}\mu_i(x',p') =& \Pr(X = x', J = p' | M = i) \\ =& \frac{\Pr(M = i | X = x', J = p') \Pr(X = x', J = p')}{\Pr(M = i)} \\ =& \frac{\Pr(M = i | X = x', J = p')}{\Pr(M = i)} \mu(x',p')\end{aligned}$$

The probability distribution PLR_p use to chose his message only depends on his information, and thus does not depend on x' and p' (as long as $p' \neq p$). So $\frac{\Pr(M=i|X=x',J=p')}{\Pr(M=i)}$ is a constant, and μ_i is indeed proportional to μ on $\{0,1\} \times ([k] \setminus \{p\})$ □

Our second lemma is the converse of Lemma 4.1. It says that every possible split conforming to the restrictions of Lemma 4.1 are possible in a communication protocol.

LEMMA 4.2. *Let PLR_p be a player, μ, μ_0, μ_1 be distributions over $\{0,1\} \times [k]$, let ν be a distribution with support $\{0,1\}$ such that*

1. $\mu = \nu(0)\mu_0 + \nu(1)\mu_1$.
2. *Each μ_i is proportional to μ on* $\{0,1\} \times ([k] \setminus \{p\})$.

Then there is a protocol π where only player PLR_p sends messages, he only sends one message, he sends message $i \in \{0,1\}$ with probability $\nu(i)$, and the posterior probability distribution given that he sends the message i is μ_i.

PROOF. If PLR_p has the information and it is 0, he should send the message $i \in \{0,1\}$ with probability $\frac{\nu(i)\mu_i(0,p)}{\mu(0,p)}$, if he has the information and it is 1 he should send the message $i \in \{0,1\}$ with probability $\frac{\nu(i)\mu_i(1,p)}{\mu(1,p)}$ and if he does not have the information, he should send message i with probability $\frac{\nu(i)\mu_i(\{0,1\}\times([k]\setminus\{k\}))}{\mu(\{0,1\}\times([k]\setminus\{k\}))}$. It is easy to check that this protocol satisfies the claim in the theorem. □

Instead of playing the cryptogenography game starting from the uniform distribution over $\{0,1\} \times [k]$, we could start from any other distribution μ (and let all the players know that we are starting from distribution μ). Let $\text{succ}(\mu, \pi)$ denote the probability of winning, when using protocol π starting from distribution μ. Let $\text{succ}(\mu) = \sup_\pi \text{succ}(\mu, \pi)$ where the supremum is over all protocols π, and let $\text{succ}_n(\mu) = \sup_{CC(\pi)\le n} \text{succ}(\mu,\pi)$.

For a distribution μ we now know that the PLR_p-allowed plane through μ, as define previously, is the set of all distributions μ' that are proportional to μ on $\{0,1\}\times([k]\setminus\{p\})$. We see that this is indeed a plane in the set $\Delta(\{0,1\}\times[k])$ of distributions over $\{0,1\}\times[k]$.

LEMMA 4.3. *The function* succ : $\Delta(\{0,1\}\times[k]) \to [0,1]$ *satisfies:*

1. $\text{succ}(\mu) \ge \text{succ}(\mu,\pi_0)$ *where* π_0 *is the protocol where they do not communicate at all.*
2. *For any allowed plane,* succ *restricted to that plane is concave.*

PROOF. 1: $\text{succ}(\mu) = \sup_\pi \text{succ}(\mu,\pi) \ge \text{succ}(\mu,\pi_0)$.

2: Whenever μ_0,μ_1 are distributions in the PLR_p-allowed plane, and $\nu(i)$ is a distribution with support $\{0,1\}$ such that $\mu = \sum_{i=0}^{1}\nu(i)\mu_i$, Lemma 4.2 says that we can find a protocol where PLR_p sends one message, sends message i with probability $\nu(i)$, and the distribution given that PLR_p sends i is μ_i. For every $\epsilon > 0$ we can now construct a protocol π_ϵ such that $\text{succ}(\mu,\pi_\epsilon) \ge \sum_{i=0}^{1}\nu(i)\,\text{succ}(\mu_i) - \epsilon$. The protocol π_ϵ starts with the one-message protocol we obtain from Lemma 4.2. If the message i is sent, they continue from there, using a protocol π_i with $\text{succ}(\mu_i,\pi_i) \ge \text{succ}(\mu_i) - \epsilon$. The existence of such a protocol follows from the definition of $\text{succ}(\mu_i)$. It is clear that the resulting π_ϵ satisfies the required inequality. As we can do this for all $\epsilon > 0$ we get $\text{succ}(\mu) \ge \sum_{i=0}^{1}\nu(i)\,\text{succ}(\mu_i)$. It follows from the converse of Jensens inequality that succ is concave in the PLR_p-allowed plane. ☐

We are now ready for a characterisation of succ.

THEOREM 4.4. *The function* succ : $\Delta(\{0,1\}\times[k]) \to [0,1]$ *is the point-wise smallest function* $s : \Delta(\{0,1\}\times[k])$ *that satisfies*

1. $s(\mu) \ge \text{succ}(\mu,\pi_0)$ *where* π_0 *is the protocol where they do not communicate at all.*
2. *For any allowed plane,* s *restricted to that plane is concave.*

PROOF. We know from Lemma 4.3 that succ satisfies the two requirements. It is clear that the point-wise infimum of a family of functions satisfying requirement 1 will itself satisfy requirement 1, and similar for requirement 2. Thus, there is a smallest function s^* satisfying both requirements.

Requirement 1 simply says that $s^*(\mu) \ge \text{succ}_0(\mu)$. Assume for induction that $s^*(\mu) \ge \text{succ}_n(\mu)$, and consider a protocol π with $CC(\pi) \le n+1$. We can view the protocol π as first sending one message $i \in \{0,1\}$ sent by PLR_p (if he can send more than two messages in the first round, we simply let him send one bit of the message at a time), and for each possible message i calling some subsequent protocol π_i with $CC(\pi_i) \le n$. If we let $\nu(i)$ denote the probability that PLR_p sends i and let μ_i denote probability distribution given the PLR_p sends i, we know from Lemma 4.1 that all the μ_is are in the p-allowed plane through μ and that $\mu = \sum_{i=0}^{1}\nu(i)\mu_i$. So

$$\text{succ}(\mu,\pi) \le \sum_{i=0}^{1}\nu(i)\,\text{succ}_n(\mu_i) \le \sum_{i=0}^{1}\nu(i)s^*(\mu_i) \le s^*(\mu)$$

Here the second inequality follows from induction hypothesis, and the third follows from the fact that s is concave in the p-allowed plane. As this holds for all π with $CC(\pi) \le n+1$ we get $\text{succ}_{n+1}(\mu) \le s^*(\mu)$, and by induction we have $\text{succ}_n \le s^*$ for all n.

Now $s^*(\mu) \ge \lim_{n\to\infty}\text{succ}_n(\mu) = \text{succ}(\mu)$ but succ satisfies the two requirement in the theorem, and s^* is the smallest function satisfying the two requirements. Thus $s^* = \text{succ}$. ☐

This theorem gives us a way to show upper bounds on $\text{succ}(\mu)$: Whenever we have a function s satisfying the two requirements, $s(\mu) \ge \text{succ}(\mu)$. In the rest of this section we will show upper bounds on succ by guessing such functions s. These are the best functions we have, but we do not think that they are optimal.

THEOREM 4.5 (RESTATEMENT OF THEOREM 1.3). *Let* μ_2 *denote the uniform distribution on* $\{0,1\}\times[2]$. *Then* $\text{succ}(\mu_2) \le \frac{3}{8}$.

PROOF. For brevity, write $x_j := \mu(0,j), y_j := \mu(1,j)$ for $j \in \{1,2\}$ being one of the players. Define

$$f(x_1,x_2,y_1,y_2) := x_1^2 + x_2^2 + y_1^2 + y_2^2 - 6(x_1x_2 + y_1y_2) \quad \text{and}$$

$$s(x_1,x_2,y_1,y_2) := \frac{1 - f(x_1,x_2,y_1,y_2)}{4} .$$

PROPOSITION 4.6. *Let* μ_2 *be the uniform distribution on* $\{0,1\}\times[2]$. *Then* $s(\mu_2) = \frac{3}{8}$.

The proof is a simple calculation.

LEMMA 4.7. *The function* s *is concave on all allowed planes.*

PROOF. We focus on PLR_1-allowed planes. Let μ be a distribution and let $(\mu_t)_{t\in\mathbb{R}}$ be a line in a PLR_1-allowed plane through μ (let us say we get μ at $t = 0$). We show that f is convex (and thus s is concave) along this line. Since $(\mu_t)_{t\in\mathbb{R}}$ is an allowed line, the values $(x_2(t), y_2(t))$ will be proportional to (x_2,y_2) throughout.

First we handle the case that $(x_2(t), y_2(t)) = (x_2,y_2)$. That is, PLR_1's message does not change the probabilities involving PLR_2. In words, she talks only about the value of her bit, not about whether she owns it or not. In this case we can assume that

$$\mu_t = (x_1 + t, x_2, y_1 - t, y_2) .$$

Now $f(\mu_t)$ is a quadratic polynomial in t with leading monomial $2t^2$, and thus is convex.

From now on, we assume that $(x_2(t), y_2(t)) \ne (x_2,y_2)$ unless $t = 0$. Let $b := x_2 + y_2$ be the probability that PLR_2 has the bit. Note that $b > 0$, because the case $b = 0$ would mean $(x_2(t) = y_2(t)) = (0,0)$ throughout, and we have handled this case already above. Now μ_t is of the form

	0	1
P_1	$x_1 + ctb$	$y_1 + \bar{c}tb$
P_2	$x_2(1-t)$	$y_2(1-t)$

where c is a parameter that describes, if you will, the "slope" of the line $(\mu_t)_{t\in\mathbb{R}}$, and $\bar{c} := 1 - c$. Again, $t = 0$ recovers the original distribution μ. Again, $f(\mu_t)$ is quadratic in t, and the leading monomial is

$$(c^2 + \bar{c}^2)b^2 + x_2^2 + y_2^2 + 6b(cx_2 + \bar{c}y_2) . \qquad (1)$$

We want to show that this is non-negative. It is quadratic in c^2 with leading monomial $2b^2c^2$ (note that $\bar{c}^2 = 1-2c+c^2$). Thus (1) is minimized when the derivative with respect to c is 0:

$$\frac{\partial(1)}{\partial c} = 2cb^2 - 2\bar{c}b^2 + 6b(x_2 - y_2) = 0 \Leftrightarrow$$
$$cb - (1-c)b + 3(x_2 - y_2) = 0 \Leftrightarrow$$
$$cb = 2y_2 - x_2 \; ,$$

and $\bar{c}b = 2x_2 - y_2$ (recall that $b = x_2 + y_2$ when micro-checking the above calculation). Plugging the values of cb and $\bar{c}b$ into (1), we obtain

$$\begin{aligned}(c^2 + \bar{c}^2)b^2 &+ x_2^2 + y_2^2 + 6b(cx_2 + \bar{c}y_2)\\ &= (2y_2 - x_2)^2 + (2x_2 - y_2)^2 + x_2^2 + y_2^2\\ &\quad + 6x_2(2y_2 - x_2) + 6y_2(2x_2 - y_2)\\ &= 16x_2y_2\\ &\geq 0 \; .\end{aligned}$$

This shows that f is convex on all allowed planes. □

LEMMA 4.8. *Let $\mu \in \Delta(\{0,1\} \times [2])$ be a distribution and let π_0 be the empty protocol, i.e., the one without any communication. Then $s(\mu) \geq \mathrm{succ}(\mu, \pi_0)$.*

PROOF. First, let us compute $\mathrm{succ}(\mu, \pi_0)$. Since there is no communication, Out only depends on μ. If Out $= 0$, then Eve guesses the player j that maxizes x_j. If Out $= 1$, she maximizes y_j. It therefore follows that $\mathrm{succ}(\mu, \pi_0) = \max(\min(x_1, x_2), \min(y_1, y_2))$. Next, we claim that $s(\mu) \geq \min(x_1, x_2)$. The proof that $s(\mu) \geq \min(y_1, y_2)$ will be symmetric. We introduce the shorthand $s_x := x_1 + x_2$ and $m_x := \max(x_1, x_2)$, and similarly for y. So $\min(x_1, x_2) = s_x - m_x$.

$$s \geq \min(x_1, x_2) \Leftrightarrow 1 - f - 4\min(x_1, x_2) \geq 0 \quad (2)$$
$$\Leftrightarrow 1 - 4s_x + 4m_x - f \geq 0 \; . \quad (3)$$

Let us bound f from above:

$$\begin{aligned}f(x_1, x_2, y_1, y_2) &= x_1^2 + x_2^2 + y_1^2 + y_2^2 - 6(x_1x_2 + y_1y_2)\\ &= 4(x_1^2 + x_2^2) + 4(y_1^2 + y_2^2)\\ &\quad - 3(x_1 + x_2)^2 - 3(y_1 + y_2)^2\\ &= 4(x_1^2 + x_2^2) + 4(y_1^2 + y_2^2) - 3s_x^2 - 3s_y^2\\ &\leq 4s_xm_x + 4s_ym_y - 3s_x^2 - 3s_y^2 \; .\end{aligned}$$

Let us combine this with (3):

$$\begin{aligned}1 - 4s_x &+ 4m_x - f\\ &\geq 1 - 4s_x + 4m_x - 4m_xs_x - 4s_ym_y + 3s_x^2 + 3s_y^2\\ &= (1 - s_x)(1 - 3s_x) + 4m_x(1 - s_x) - 4m_ys_y + 3s_y^2\\ &= s_y(1 - 3s_x + 4m_x - 4m_y + 3s_y)\\ &\qquad \text{(note that } 1 - s_x = s_y)\\ &\geq s_y(1 - 3s_x + 2s_x - 4s_y + 3s_y)\\ &\qquad \text{(since } m_x \geq \tfrac{s_x}{2} \text{ and } m_y \leq s_y)\\ &= s_y(1 - s_x - s_y) = 0 \; .\end{aligned}$$

This shows that $s(\mu) \geq \max(\min(x_1, x_2), \min(y_1, y_2)) = \mathrm{succ}(\mu, \pi_0)$ and proves the lemma. □

By Theorem 4.4 this implies that $\mathrm{succ}(\mu_2) \leq s(\mu_2) = \frac{3}{8}$.

A function similar to the above s was suggested by "fedja" on Mathoverflow [6] and this function was then improved by Wadim Zudilin to the above function also on Mathoverflow.

Our final theorem generalizes the above argument to k players.

THEOREM 4.9 (RESTATEMENT OF THEOREM 1.4). *Let μ_k denote the uniform distribution on $\{0,1\} \times [k]$. Then $\mathrm{succ}(\mu_k) \leq \frac{3}{4} - \frac{1}{2k}$.*

PROOF. For brevity, we denote by x_j the probability that player j has the bit, and it is 0, that is, $x_j := \mu(0, j)$. Similarly, $y_j := \mu(1, j)$. We define

$$f(\vec{x}, \vec{y}) := 2\|\vec{x}\|_2^2 + 2\|\vec{y}\|_2^2 - \|x\|_1^2 - \|y\|_1^2 \; .$$

where $\|\vec{x}\|_p := \left(\sum_{i=1}^k x_i^p\right)^{1/p}$ and define

$$s_k(\vec{x}, \vec{y}) := \frac{1 - f(\vec{x}, \vec{y})}{2} \; .$$

We will prove three things. First, $s_k(\mu_k) = \frac{3}{4} - \frac{1}{2k}$. Second, $s_k(\mu) \geq \mathrm{succ}(\mu, \pi_0)$, where π_0 is the "empty" protocol without any communication. Third, and most important, s_k is concave along allowed planes. This will conclude the proof.

PROPOSITION 4.10. *Let μ_k be the uniform distribution on $\{0,1\} \times [k]$. Then $s_k(\mu_k) = \frac{3}{4} - \frac{1}{2k}$.*

PROOF. Every (X, J) has probability $\frac{1}{2k}$. Therefore $\|\vec{x}\|_2^2 = \|\vec{y}\|_2^2 = k \cdot \left(\frac{1}{2k}\right)^2$ and $\|\vec{x}\|_1^2 = \|\vec{y}\|_1^2 = \left(\frac{1}{2}\right)^2 = \frac{1}{4}$. Thus, $f(\mu_k) = 4k \cdot \left(\frac{1}{2k}\right)^2 - 2 \cdot \left(\frac{1}{2}\right)^2 = \frac{1}{k} - \frac{1}{2}$, and $s_k(\mu_k) = \frac{3}{4} - \frac{1}{2k}$. □

PROPOSITION 4.11. *Let $\mu \in \Delta(\{0,1\} \times [k])$ be a distribution and let π_0 be the empty protocol, i.e., the one without any communication. Then $s_k(\mu) \geq \mathrm{succ}(\mu, \pi_0)$.*

PROOF. What is $\mathrm{succ}(\mu, \pi_0)$? The transcript of π_0 is empty, thus $\mathrm{Out}(\pi)$ only depends on μ. If Out $= 0$, then Eve optimally guesses the player j that maximizes x_j, and the success probability for the players is $\mu(0, [k]) - \max_j \mu(0, j)$. Similarly, if Out $= 1$, she chooses the j maximizing y_j, and the success probability is $\mu(1, [k]) - \max_j \mu(1, j)$. Thus, the success probability of π_0 is

$$\max\left(\mu(0, [k]) - \max_j \mu(0, j), \quad \mu(1, [k]) - \max_j \mu(1, j)\right) \; .$$

For brevity, we define $m_x := \max_j x_j = \max_j \mu(0, j)$, $m_y := \max_j y_j = \max_j \mu(1, j)$, $s_x := \sum_j x_j = \mu(0, [k])$, and $s_y := \sum_j y_j = \mu(1, [k])$. We want to show that $s_k(\mu) \geq \mathrm{succ}(\mu, \pi_0) = \max(s_x - m_x, s_y - m_y)$. We will show that $s_k(\mu) \geq s_x - m_x$. The inequality $s_m(\mu) \geq s_y - m_y$ will follow analogously.

$$s_k(\mu) \geq s_x - m_x \iff \frac{1 - f(\vec{x}, \vec{y})}{2} \geq s_x - m_x \quad (4)$$
$$\iff 1 - 2s_x + 2m_x - f(\vec{x}, \vec{y}) \geq 0 \; . \quad (5)$$

Let us bound $f(\vec{x}, \vec{y})$ from above:

$$\begin{aligned}f(\vec{x}, \vec{y}) &= 2\|\vec{x}\|_2^2 + 2\|\vec{y}\|_2^2 - \|x\|_1^2 - \|y\|_1^2\\ &\leq 2m_xs_x + 2m_ys_y - s_x^2 - s_y^2 \; .\end{aligned}$$

Thus, we evaluate (5):

$$\begin{aligned}1 - 2s_x + 2m_x - f(\vec{x}, \vec{y}) \\ &\geq 1 - 2s_x + 2m_x - 2m_x s_x - 2m_y s_y + s_x^2 + s_y^2 \\ &= 1 - 2s_x + s_x^2 + s_y^2 + 2m_x(1 - s_x) - 2m_y s_y \\ &= 2s_y^2 + 2m_x s_y - 2m_y s_y \\ &= 2s_y(s_y + m_x - m_y) \geq 0 \ .\end{aligned}$$

The last inequality follows from $s_y - m_y \geq 0$. Replacing the roles of x and y, a similar calculation shows that $s_k(\mu) \geq s_y - m_y$, and thus $s_k(\mu) \geq \operatorname{succ}(\mu, \pi_0)$. □

PROPOSITION 4.12. *For any allowed plane, s_k restricted to that plane is concave.*

PROOF. By symmetry, we can restrict ourselves to PLR$_1$-allowed planes. That is, all distributions μ' that are proportional to μ on $\{0,1\} \times ([k] \setminus \{1\})$. Let μ be any distribution and let $(\mu_t)_{t \in \mathbb{R}}$ be a line through μ that is contained in a PLR$_1$-allowed plane. It suffices to show that s_k is concave along all such lines.

First suppose that in our line, each μ_t is not only proportional to μ on $\{0,1\} \times ([k] \setminus \{1\})$, but actually identical to it. Then μ_t looks as follows:

	0	1
P_1	$x_1 + t$	$y_1 - t$
P_2	x_2	y_2
$\vdots$	$\vdots$	$\vdots$
P_n	x_n	y_n

(6)

and $f(\mu_t)$ is quadratic in t with leading monomial $2t^2$. Therefore, it is convex, and s_k is concave, along $(\mu_t)_{t \in \mathbb{R}}$.

Suppose from now on that μ_t is not identical to μ on $\{0,1\} \times ([k] \setminus \{1\})$. How does a line $(\mu_t)_{t \in \mathbb{R}}$ through μ in a PLR$_1$-allowed plane look? The probabilities $x_2, \ldots, x_n$ and $y_2, \ldots, y_n$ get multiplied by a factor $(1 - t)$. Let $b_0 := x_2 + \cdots + x_n$, $b_1 := y_2 + \cdots + y_n$, and $b = b_0 + b_1$. Note that $b > 0$, otherwise all μ_t are 0 on $\{0,1\} \times ([k] \setminus \{1\})$, and this belongs to the above case. The distribution μ_t on the PLR$_1$-allowed plane containing μ has the form

	0	1
P_1	$x_1 + ctb$	$y_1 + \bar{c}tb$
P_2	$x_2(1-t)$	$y_2(1-t)$
$\vdots$	$\vdots$	$\vdots$
P_n	$x_n(1-t)$	$y_n(1-t)$

(7)

where $c \in \mathbb{R}$ is some parameter specific to the line $(\mu_t)_{t \in \mathbb{R}}$, and $\bar{c} := 1 - c$. For fixed $\vec{x}, \vec{y}, c$, all μ_t lie on a line. It remains to show that f is convex along this line. We evaluate $f(\mu_t)$, which is a quadratic polynomial in t, and analyze the coefficient of the monomial t^2: In the terms $\|\vec{x}\|_2^2$, $\|\vec{y}\|_2^2$, $\|\vec{x}\|_1^2$, $\|\vec{y}\|_1^2$, evaluated at μ_t, the monomial t^2 has the following coefficients:

$$\begin{aligned}\|\vec{x}\|_2^2 &\longrightarrow c^2b^2 + x_2^2 + \cdots + x_k^2 \geq c^2b^2 \\ \|\vec{y}\|_2^2 &\longrightarrow \bar{c}^2b^2 + y_2^2 + \cdots + y_k^2 \geq \bar{c}^2b^2 \\ \|\vec{x}\|_1^2 &\longrightarrow (cb - x_2 - \cdots - x_k)^2 = (cb - b_0)^2 = c^2b^2 - 2cbb_0 + b_0^2 \\ \|\vec{y}\|_1^2 &\longrightarrow (\bar{c}b - y_2 - \cdots - y_k)^2 = (\bar{c}b - b_1)^2 = \bar{c}^2b^2 - 2\bar{c}bb_1 + b_1^2\end{aligned}$$

Thus, the coefficient of t^2 of $f(\vec{x}, \vec{y}) = 2\|\vec{x}\|_2^2 + 2\|\vec{y}\|_2^2 - \|x\|_1^2 - \|y\|_1^2$ is at least

$$b^2(c^2 + \bar{c}^2) - b_0^2 - b_1^2 + 2b(cb_0 + \bar{c}b_1) \ . \qquad (8)$$

It remains to show that this is non-negative. Recall that b is the probability that PLR$_1$ does not own the bit. Since we assume $b > 0$, the expression in (8) is quadratic in c with leading monomial $2b^2c^2$ (note that $\bar{c}^2 = (1-c)^2 = 1-2c+c^2$). Thus, (8) is minimized if its derivate with respect to c is 0:

$$\begin{aligned}\frac{\partial(8)}{\partial c} &= 2b^2(c - \bar{c}) + 2b(b_0 - b_1) \\ &= 2b^2(2c - 1) + 2b(b - 2b_1) \\ &= 4b^2c - 4bb_1 \ .\end{aligned}$$

This is 0 if and only if $c = \frac{b_1}{b}$. At that point, $\bar{c} = \frac{b_0}{b}$. In particular, $c, \bar{c} \geq 0$. This is not a priori clear, since c is a parameter of the line (μ_t), not a probability. Let us evaluate (8) at $c = \frac{b_1}{b}$:

$$\begin{aligned}(8) &= b^2(c^2 + \bar{c}^2) - b_0^2 - b_1^2 + 2b(cb_0 + \bar{c}b_1) \\ &\geq b^2(c^2 + \bar{c}^2) - b_0^2 - b_1^2 \\ &= b^2\left(\left(\frac{b_1}{b}\right)^2 + \left(\frac{b_0}{b}\right)^2\right) - b_0^2 - b_1^2 = 0 \ .\end{aligned}$$

This shows that f is convex along the line $(\mu_t)_{t \in \mathbb{R}}$, and thus on whole PLR$_1$-allowed plane containing μ. Thus, s_k is concave along those planes, which proves the proposition. □

5. CONCLUSIONS AND OPEN PROBLEMS

In this work we considered a game where a group of people is collaborating, to let one of them publish one bit of information, while minimising the probability that an observer will guess who leaked the bit. This problem is easy to analyse under standard cryptographic assumption, and assuming that the observer has bounded computational power, but we wanted to analyse the problem with the assumption that the observer has unbounded computational power. We gave a characterisation of the optimal probability that the secret-holder is not guessed as a function of the prior distribution of secret-value and secret-holder, and using this characterisation we showed that no matter how many people are in the group, they will always lose the game with probability at least $\frac{1}{4}$. We also gave a general protocol that ensures the group wins with probability > 0.5644. In the case with only two players, we gave a protocol that ensures that the group wins with probability $\frac{1}{3}$, and we showed that they cannot win with probability more than $\frac{3}{8}$.

There are several interesting open questions to look at next. First of all, it is still an open problem to determine $\operatorname{succ}(\mu_2)$ and $\lim_{k \to \infty} \operatorname{succ}(\mu_k)$. More interestingly, we could ask the same problem, but where more than one player knows the information and/or the information is more than one bit. How fast does the number of player who know the information have to grow as a function of the amount of information to make it possible to leak the information?

Finally we see that a version of Theorem 4.4 holds for any game where a group of collaborating players receive some utility depending on the posterior distribution at the end of a communication round. A special case is the result in information complexity in [3] and [8], where the utility received in the end is either internal privacy or external privacy. We believe that it would be interesting to study this class of problems in general.

6. ACKNOWLEDGEMENTS

We thank Søren Riis for several stimulating discussions during the development of this work. Joshua Brody and Dominik Scheder acknowledge support from the Danish National Research Foundation and The National Science Foundation of China (under the grant 61061130540) for the Sino-Danish Center for the Theory of Interactive Computation, within which this work was performed. Dominik Scheder acknowledges support from the Simons Institute for the Theory of Computing, UC Berkeley.

7. REFERENCES

[1] R. Ahlswede and I. Csiszar. Common randomness in information theory and cryptography. I. Secret sharing. *IEEE Trans. Inf. Theory*, 39(4):1121–1132, 1993.

[2] Donald Beaver, Stuart Haber, and Peter Winkler. On the isolation of a common secret. In R.L. Graham and J. Nešetřil, editors, *The Mathematics of Paul Erdős Vol. II*, pages 121–135, Berlin, 1996. Springer-Verlag. (Reprinted and updated 2013.).

[3] Mark Braverman, Ankit Garg, Denis Pankratov, and Omri Weinstein. From information to exact communication. In *Proc. 45th Annual ACM Symposium on the Theory of Computing*, 2013.

[4] W. Diffie and M.E. Hellman. New directions in cryptography. *IEEE Trans. Inf. Theory*, 22(6):644–654, 1976.

[5] Shafi Goldwasser and Silvio Micali. Probabilistic encryption. *J. Comput. Syst. Sci.*, 28(2):270 – 299, 1984.

[6] Sune Jakobsen. Greatest function satisfying some convexity requirements. mathoverflow.net/questions/81753. (2011).

[7] N. Ma and P. Ishwar. Interactive source coding for function computation in collocated networks. *IEEE Trans. Inf. Theory*, 58(7):4289–4305, 2012.

[8] N. Ma and P. Ishwar. The infinite-message limit of two-terminal interactive source coding. *IEEE Trans. Inf. Theory*, 59(7):4071–4094, 2013.

[9] Ralph C. Merkle. Secure communications over insecure channels. *Commun. ACM*, 21(4):294–299, 1978.

[10] R. L. Rivest, A. Shamir, and L. Adleman. A method for obtaining digital signatures and public-key cryptosystems. *Commun. ACM*, 21(2):120–126, 1978.

[11] Claude E Shannon. Communication theory of secrecy systems. *Bell system technical journal*, 28(4):656–715, 1949.

[12] Wikipedia. 2013 mass surveillance disclosures. http://en.wikipedia.org/wiki/2013_mass_surveillance_-disclosures. (2013).

[13] Wikipedia. United states diplomatic cables leak. http://en.wikipedia.org/wiki/united_states_-diplomatic_cables_leak. (2010).

Limits of Random Oracles in Secure Computation

[Extended Abstract][*]

Mohammad Mahmoody[†]
University of Virginia
Charlottesville, VA, USA
mohammad@cs.virginia.edu

Hemanta K. Maji[‡]
University of California
Los Angeles, CA, USA
hmaji@cs.ucla.edu

Manoj Prabhakaran[§]
University of Illinois
Urbana-Champaign, IL, USA
mmp@cs.uiuc.edu

ABSTRACT

The seminal result of Impagliazzo and Rudich (STOC 1989) gave a black-box separation between one-way functions and public-key encryption: a public-key encryption scheme cannot be constructed using one-way functions in a black-box way. In addition, their result implied black-box separations between one-way functions and protocols for certain Secure Function Evaluation (SFE) functionalities (in particular, Oblivious Transfer). Surprisingly, however, *since then there has been no further progress in separating one-way functions and SFE functionalities.* In this work, we present the complete picture for finite deterministic 2-party SFE functionalities, vis a vis one-way functions. We show that in case of semi-honest adversaries, one-way functions are black-box separated from *all such SFE functionalities,* except the ones which have unconditionally secure protocols (and hence do not rely on any computational hardness). In the case of active adversaries, a black-box one-way function is indeed useful for SFE, but we show that it is useful only as much as access to an ideal commitment functionality is useful.

Technically, our main result establishes the limitations of random oracles for secure computation. We show that a two-party deterministic functionality f has a secure protocol in the random oracle model that is (statistically) secure against semi-honest adversaries if and only if f has a protocol *in the plain model* that is (perfectly) secure against semi-honest adversaries. Further, in the case of active adversaries, a deterministic SFE functionality f has a (UC or standalone) statistically secure protocol in the random oracle model if and only if f has a (UC or standalone) statistically secure protocol in the commitment-hybrid model.

Our proof is based on a "frontier analysis" of two-party protocols, combining it with (extensions of) the "independence learners" of Impagliazzo-Rudich/Barak-Mahmoody. We make essential use of a combinatorial property, originally discovered by Kushilevitz (FOCS 1989), of functions that have semi-honest secure protocols in the plain model (and hence our analysis applies only to functions of polynomial-sized domains, for which such a characterization is known).

Our result could be seen as a first step towards proving a conjecture that we put forth in this work and call it the *Many-Worlds Conjecture.* For every 2-party SFE functionality f, one can consider a "world" where f can be *semi-honest securely* realized in the computational setting. Many-Worlds Conjecture states that there are infinitely many "distinct worlds" between *minicrypt* and *cryptomania* in the universe of Impagliazzo's Worlds.

Categories and Subject Descriptors

F.1.3 [**COMPUTATION BY ABSTRACT DEVICES**]: Complexity Measures and Classes—*Reducibility and completeness*

General Terms

Security; Theory

Keywords

Random Oracle Model; Secure Function Evaluation; Black-box Separation; One-Way Functions; Impagliazzo's Worlds

1. INTRODUCTION

How useful is a random oracle in two-party secure function evaluation (SFE)? One obvious use of a random oracle is for implementing commitment. We show that, remarkably, for finite 2-party SFE[1] *a random oracle by itself is only as useful as a commitment functionality.* This is remarkable since in many other contexts in cryptography (including many protocol settings, like the use of Fiat-Shamir heuristics for NIZK), the random oracle is vastly more useful than standard primitives.

[*]A full version of this paper is available at [36]

[†]Research done while at Cornell and supported in part by NSF Awards CNS-1217821 and CCF-0746990, AFOSR Award FA9550-10-1-0093, and DARPA and AFRL under contract FA8750-11-2- 0211.

[‡]Supported by NSF CI Postdoctoral Fellowship.

[§]Research supported in part by NSF grants 1228856 and 0747027.

ITCS'14, January 12–14, 2014, Princeton, New Jersey, USA.

http://dx.doi.org/10.1145/2554797.2554801.

[1]Our results hold not just for finite SFE functionalities, but also those that have polynomial-size domains. However, we do not consider SFE functionalities with super-polynomial-size domains, for which, even without random oracles, a characterization of realizable functionalities is not known.

This result has important implications in understanding the "complexity" of secure function evaluation functionalities vis a vis computational primitives like one-way functions. An important goal in cryptography is to understand the qualitative complexity of various cryptographic primitives. In the seminal work of Impagliazzo and Rudich [21] a formal framework was established to qualitatively separate cryptographic primitives like symmetric-key encryption and public-key encryption from each other. Understanding that such a separation exists has been hugely influential in theoretical and practical cryptographic research in the subsequent decades: to optimize on both security and efficiency dimensions, a cryptographic construction would be based on symmetric-key primitives when possible, and otherwise is shown to "require" public-key primitives.

Beyond encryption, the result in [21] already implies the separation of certain SFE functionalities (in particular, Oblivious Transfer) from one-way functions. Surprisingly, however, *since then there has been no further progress on separating SFE functionalities and one-way functions*, although several other black-box separation results have emerged [48, 12, 13, 7, 24, 43, 18]. In this work, we present the complete picture for finite deterministic 2-party SFE functionalities vis a vis one-way functions: we show that in the case of security against semi-honest adversaries, *all of them* are black-box separated from one-way functions, except the ones which are trivial (which have unconditionally perfectly secure protocols). In the case of active adversaries, a black-box one-way function is indeed useful for SFE, but we show that it is useful only as much as access to a commitment functionality is useful (and explicitly characterize the functions for evaluating which it is useful).

Our work could be viewed as a confluence of two largely disjoint lines of work — one on black-box one-way functions, and one on the structure of secure function evaluation functionalities. The former line essentially started with [21]. The latter can be traced back to concurrent work [8, 5, 33] which combinatorially characterized which finite functionalities have (perfectly) semi-honest secure protocols. This characterization of 2-party functionalities, in terms of a combinatorial property called decomposability [33], will be important for us. Several later works obtained such combinatorial characterizations of SFE functionalities in different contexts (e.g., [25, 6, 27, 41, 30, 31, 29]).

An important ingredient of our proof is the "**frontier analysis**" approach from [39, 38]. As we shall see, frontier analysis provides a powerful means to work with otherwise-subtle conditional probabilities, especially as arising in 2-party protocols. In essence, it is simply a means to explicitly keep track of the order in which various events occur in a protocol (or more generally, in a sequence of random variables). But as we shall see, having an explicit mental picture lets us define frontiers and reason about their properties that are *a priori* not obvious. The proof in [9] could in fact be viewed as an instance of frontier analysis (and is one of the earliest ones that the authors are aware of). Another example (in a non-cryptographic setting) is the work of Barak et al. [2] who consider frontiers in a protocol where significant amounts of "new and relevant" information is revealed, and use this to reduce the total amount of communication.

Blackbox Separations. *Black-box constructions* form a general framework of obtaining a (more complex) cryptographic primitive $\mathcal{Q}$ (e.g., pseudorandom generators) from another (perhaps simpler) cryptographic primitive $\mathcal{P}$ (e.g., one-way functions) while $\mathcal{P}$ is used in the implementation of $\mathcal{Q}$ only as a black-box and the security of $\mathcal{Q}$ is proved based on the security of $\mathcal{P}$ also through a black-box argument. Apart from being the most common kind of reductions used in cryptographic constructions (with "provable security"), black-box reductions provide us with a framework to understand "complexity" of cryptographic primitives. This line of research was initiated in the seminal work of Impagliazzo and Rudich [21] who showed that public-key cryptography is strictly more complex than symmetric-key cryptography (say, one-way functions) under this framework.

Our main technical results are proven in the computationally unbounded setting, and the (honest-but-curious) adversaries implicit in our proofs use super-polynomial computational power (even if the honest parties were polynomial time). However, similar to the results in [21], this can be translated to a statement about black-box separation of semi-honest SFE protocols (for functions without perfectly secure protocols) from one-way functions, in a probabilistic polynomial time (PPT) setting. Intuitively, this is so because a random oracle is a strong one-way function (but for the drawback that it does not have a small code to implement it); so, if one-way function is the sole computational primitive needed for a construction, and it is used in a black-box manner, then it should be possible to base the construction on a random oracle instead. Hence, ruling out secure protocols in the random oracle model in the computationally unbounded setting would rule out protocols in the PPT setting that base their security on one-way functions in a black-box manner.

The Many-Worlds Conjecture. An added significance of our black-box separation is that it is part of proving a larger conjecture regarding computational assumptions associated with cryptographic reductions. In [40], a cryptographic complexity theory was introduced, where the objects of study were secure reductions between 2-party (or more generally, multi-party) functionalities. The existence of each such reduction in the PPT setting could be considered as a *computational assumption.* There it was conjectured that there are only a few (in particular, finitely many) "distinct" assumptions, when the notion of secure reduction used is that of universally composable (UC) security. This was based on the fact that a large range of such assumptions were shown to be equivalent to either the existence of one-way functions or oblivious transfer protocols. In terms of "Impagliazzo's Worlds," [19], this conjecture states that *there are only a few worlds between minicrypt and cryptomania* that correspond to these reductions. We refer to this conjecture from [40] as the **Few Worlds Conjecture**.

In this work, we conjecture that *there are infinitely many worlds intermediate to minicrypt and cryptomania, that correspond to semi-honest secure reductions between 2-party functionalities.* In fact, we conjecture that the same holds, even restricted to making one of the functionalities trivial (i.e., each world corresponds to a finite function f having a semi-honest secure protocol in the plain model). Note that this new conjecture – which we term the **Many Worlds Conjecture** (or MWC, for short) – does not contradict the Few Worlds Conjecture, since it considers semi-honest security rather than UC security. (The technical difference between the two settings is that for UC secure reductions, the simulator is required to "extract" an adversary's input, and this often implies a secure oblivious transfer protocol.)

The black-box separation result we prove could be considered as a first step towards proving the MWC. It shows that the assumption that an undecomposable function has a semi-honest protocol (i.e., it can be semi-honest securely reduced to a trivial functionality) is distinct from the assumption that one-way functions exist. In subsequent work, we further strengthened this separation to show that it is distinct from the assumption that public-key encryption exists [37]. In ongoing work, we investigate an approach to proving the MWC by showing that, corresponding to any two 2-party functionalities such that one cannot be semi-honest-securely reduced to the other information-theoretically, there are two "distinct worlds."[2] This approach relies on the result in this work as a basic building block.

1.1 Our Results

Our main result is the following.

THEOREM 1.1. *A deterministic two-party function f, with a polynomially large domain, has a semi-honest secure protocol against computationally unbounded adversaries in the random oracle model if and only if f has a perfectly semi-honest secure protocol in the plain model.*

We remark that such f can be explicitly characterized as decomposable functions as defined in [33] (if f is symmetric), or more generally, as those for which the symmetric function f' obtained as the "common information" part of f[3] is decomposable and f and f' are "isomorphic."[4] We remark that decomposability was originally defined for finite functions that do not depend on the security parameter; in our treatment, where we allow the function to depend on the security parameter, a function is said to be decomposable if for all but finitely many values of the security parameter, it is decomposable in the original sense.

In this theorem, as is conventional in much of the work on the combinatorial structure of SFE functionalities, we restrict ourselves to functions whose domain size is polynomial in the security parameter. A full combinatorial characterization of semi-honest securely realizable functions (even in the plain model) is known only with this restriction. In particular, there are undecomposable functions, with super polynomial domain size, which are semi-honest securely realizable. Henceforth, unless mentioned otherwise, whenever we consider a function we shall assume that its domain size is polynomial in the security parameter.

The above result — that random oracles are useless for 2-party SFE — does *not* hold in the case of security against active adversaries. In particular, note that the commitment functionality $\mathcal{F}_{\text{COM}}$, can be constructed UC-securely in a black-box manner from random oracles, and so, all the functions which can be UC-securely computed in the $\mathcal{F}_{\text{COM}}$ hybrid can also be UC-securely computed in the random oracle model. But we shall show that this is all that a random oracle is useful for in 2-party SFE. This follows from Theorem 1.1 and a compiler from [39] that turns semi-honest secure protocols to UC-secure protocols in the $\mathcal{F}_{\text{COM}}$-hybrid model (refer to the full version of this paper [36] for proof).

THEOREM 1.2. *A deterministic two-party function f, with a polynomially large domain, has a statistically UC-secure (and equivalently, a statistically standalone-secure) protocol in the random oracle model if and only if f has a statistically UC-secure (and equivalently, a statistically standalone-secure) protocol in the $\mathcal{F}_{\text{COM}}$ hybrid.*

We remark that such f can be characterized as those for which, on removing all "redundant inputs"[5] one at a time, we obtain a function of the kind in Theorem 1.1.

As mentioned earlier, these results for random oracles in the computationally unbounded setting translate to black-box separation results from one-way functions, in the PPT setting. We follow the definitions in [47], with slight technical modifications, to state our results. A formal statement appears in the full version of this paper [36]. We summarize this result informally below.

THEOREM 1.3. *(Informal.) For a deterministic two-party function f, with a polynomially large domain, there is a fully black-box reduction of semi-honest secure function evaluation of f to one-way functions if and only if f has a perfectly semi-honest secure protocol in the plain model.*

As in the case of Theorem 1.1, the above statement can be extended to the case of security against active adversaries.

THEOREM 1.4. [Informal.] *For a deterministic two-party function f with a polynomially large domain, there is a black-box reduction of UC (or stand-alone) secure function evaluation of f to one-way functions if and only if f has a statistically UC (or stand-alone) secure protocol in the $\mathcal{F}_{\text{COM}}$-hybrid model.*

Note that, though commitment is already known to be black-box equivalent to one-way functions, *statistical* (standalone) security in the $\mathcal{F}_{\text{COM}}$-hybrid is, *a priori*, more restrictive than standalone security in the PPT setting using fully black-box commitments. Further, the theorem holds for not only one-way functions, but also the other computational primitives mentioned above.

[2]It is known that the existence of "simple" (e.g., constant round) protocols for a functionality could be used to realize a complete functionality; this was discussed in [12] and recently explicitly proven in [35]. However, this does not contradict the above approach to proving the MWC, since these results apply only for restricted classes of protocols.

[3]For a deterministic two-party function $f : \mathcal{X} \times \mathcal{Y} \to \mathcal{Z}_A \times \mathcal{Z}_B$, the common information function f' is defined as follows (see for e.g., [42]): consider the bipartite graph consisting of nodes of the form $(x, a) \in \mathcal{X} \times \mathcal{Z}_A$ and $(y, b) \in \mathcal{Y} \times \mathcal{Z}_B$, with an edge between (x, a) and (y, b) iff $f(x, y) = (a, b)$. Then f' maps (x, y) to the connected component containing (x, a) and (y, b) where $f(x, y) = (a, b)$. Intuitively, $f'(x, y)$ reveals only that part of the information about (x, y) that f reveals to "commonly" to both Alice and Bob (and so they know that it is known to the other party as well).

[4] As defined in [42], f_0 and f_1 are isomorphic if there is a UC and semi-honest secure protocol for evaluating either function which uses a single instance of the other function with no other communication. In particular, if either function has a semi-honest secure protocol in the random oracle model (resp. plain model), then the other one has such a protocol too.

[5]Alice's input x to f is said to be redundant (for security against active adversaries) if there is an input $x' \neq x$ that dominates x: i.e., Alice can substitute x' for x without Bob noticing while still being able to calculate her correct output.

Though we state the result for one-way functions, in fact, any collection of primitives that can be constructed from a random oracle (or ideal cipher) or a random permutation oracle[6] in a black-box manner – one-way functions, one-way permutations, collision resistant hash functions, block-ciphers (including exponentially hard versions of these primitives) – is useless for 2-party SFE, if the primitives are used in a fully black-box manner.

1.2 Related Work

Impagliazzo and Rudich [21] showed that random oracles are not useful against a computationally unbounded adversary for the task of secure key agreement. This analysis was recently simplified and sharpened in [4, 18]. These results and techniques are one starting point for our result. Indeed, a partial version of our result — when the protocols are restricted to have only $\kappa/\log\kappa$ rounds where κ is the length of the inputs to the random oracle (or one-way function) — could be derived using techniques in [10, 18]. In subsequent work [37], by combining the frontier analytic techniques in this work with a more general eavesdropper strategy, we show that public-key encryption (which is significantly more involved than random oracles) is only as useful as the $\mathcal{F}_{\text{COM}}$-hyrbid for two-party deterministic secure function evaluation.

Following [21] many other black-box separation results have appeared (e.g., [48, 13, 7, 24, 43]). In particular, Gertner et al. [12] insightfully asked the question of comparing oblivious-transfer (OT) and key agreement (KA) and showed that OT is strictly more complex (in the sense of [21]). Another trend of results has been to prove lower-bounds on the efficiency of the implementation reduction in black-box constructions (e.g., [28, 11, 34, 15, 3, 4, 15]). A complementary approach has been to find black-box reductions when they exist (e.g., [20, 44, 45, 14, 16]). Also, results in the black-box separation framework of [21, 47] have immediate consequences for computational complexity theory. Indeed, as mentioned above, separations in this framework can be interpreted as new worlds in Impagliazzo's universe [19].

Frontier analysis is implicit in previous works on proving impossibility or lower bounds for protocols. For instance, the analysis in [9] fits our notion of what frontier analysis is. The analysis of protocols in [8, 5, 33] also have some elements of a frontier analysis, but of a rudimentary form which was sufficient for analysis of perfect security. In [39] frontier analysis was explicitly introduced and used to prove several protocol impossibility results and characterizations. [32] also presented similar results and used somewhat similar techniques (but relied on analyzing the protocol by rounds, instead of frontiers, and incurred significant restrictions on the round complexity of the protocols for which the impossibility could be shown). We also rely on results from [38] to extend the result to general SFE functionalities as opposed to symmetric SFE functionalities.

[6]We point out that Theorem 1.1 extends to a random permutation oracle, as argued in [21]: otherwise, we can construct an efficient distinguisher between a length preserving random oracle and a length preserving random permutation oracle for "long" inputs, and this can be shown to be impossible (as it is improbable to find collisions in a random oracle with non-negligible probability using only a polynomial number of queries).

In a concurrent work with related, but incomparable results, Haitner, Omri, and Zarosim [17, 18] show that random oracles are essentially useless in any *inputless protocol.* While [18] provide a general compiler to remove random oracles from inputless protocols, which has wider applications, the implications of their result for SFE are already provided by the separation in [21] (combined with a result in [26] which shows that inputless functionalities are either trivial or complete). In contrast, our result holds only for secure evaluation of deterministic functions with polynomial sized domains, but yields *new* black-box separations between one-way functions and SFE functionalities.

2. TECHNICAL OVERVIEW

We rely on a careful combination of the techniques in the black-box separation literature (in particular [21, 4, 10]) and new frontier analysis techniques. In this section, we briefly explain the overall approach and point out some of the highlights.

A clear starting point of our investigation is the "independence learner" of [21, 4] which shows, in a protocol between Alice and Bob involving private queries to a random oracle, how to make several (but polynomially many) additional queries to the random oracle and make Alice's and Bob's views (conditioned on their inputs) independent of each other. However, from this independence property it is not immediate to conclude that random oracles are useless in SFE protocols. One conjecture (which we are not able to prove) would be that the effect of the random oracle can be "securely simulated" in the plain model, and then any protocol in the random oracle model can be compiled into a plain-model protocol that is as secure as the original one. This would avoid the need to rely on combinatorial characterizations of SFE functionalities, and indeed show that random oracles are useless for virtually any protocol (up to small, but non-negligible errors inherent in the independence learner). However, in this work we do not obtain such a compiler. In particular, *we do not rule out the possibility that in fact random oracles could have unsimulatable effects, and may aid in secure computation of randomized functionalities, or functionalities with super-polynomial input domains.*

This leads us to the techniques used in showing that a symmetric SFE functionality f is semi-honest securely realizable if and only if it is decomposable. The strongest version of this result was proven using frontier analysis in [39]. However, as we shall see, we need a significantly more sophisticated argument here.

2.1 Frontier Analysis Meets Random Oracles

First we describe why naïve attempts at generalizing the argument used to characterize functions with SFE protocols in the plain model [39] fail in the random oracle setting.

The plain model result crucially relies on the following "locality" property. When Alice sends the next message in a plain model protocol, she can reveal (i.e., add to the transcript) new information only about her own input but *not* about Bob's inputs. So, during the execution of the protocol, Alice and Bob would alternately reveal information about their inputs x and y respectively. We define two frontiers:

F_X, where (significant, additional) information about x is first revealed, and F_Y where (significant, additional) information about y is first revealed in the transcript.

By the locality property, the frontiers F_X and F_Y are disjoint: at nodes in F_X Alice has just sent out a message, and at nodes in F_Y Bob has just sent out a message. Firstly, for the sake of correctness, information about x and y need to be revealed by the end of the protocol, and hence, F_X and F_Y are almost "full" frontiers (i.e., there is only a small probability that an execution finishes without passing through both frontiers).[7] To draw a contradiction we rely on the property that, *for an undecomposable function*[8] *it will be insecure for either party to reveal information about their input first.* In terms of the frontiers, this says that it will be insecure if, a (significantly probable) portion of F_X appears above F_Y, or if a (significantly probable) portion of F_Y appears above F_X. Combined with the fact that both frontiers are almost full, this rules out secure protocols for undecomposable functions.

Handling the Random Oracle. In the presence of a random oracle, we lose the locality property (that Alice's message is independent of Bob's input, conditioned on the transcript). It becomes possible that a correlation is established between Alice's and Bob's views via the common random oracle, even conditioned on the transcript. Indeed, given a random oracle, a secure protocol for even OT is possible unless the curious parties query the oracle on points other than what is prescribed by the protocol. Hence, to be meaningful in the presence of an oracle, we must define the information revealed by a transcript as what a curious eavesdropper making additional (polynomially bounded) queries to the oracle, can learn. This is where the independence learner "Eve" of [21, 4] is relevant.

Intuitively, Eve attempts to learn as much as possible (staying within a budget of polynomially many oracle queries), by making all "important" queries to the oracle after each message in the protocol. By including the information obtained by Eve into the transcript itself, we can ensure that the frontiers do correspond to points where certain information is revealed, conditioned on the information obtained by Eve. Being a semi-honest setting, it is not relevant when these queries are performed; but for our frontier analysis, it will be important to consider the curious eavesdropper as running concurrently with the protocol, querying the oracle as many times as it wants, after each message in the protocol.

Main Challenge. Once the transcript is augmented with Eve's view, one could hope that the previous analysis from [39] can be applied. Indeed, in this augmented protocol, the locality property is restored. However, now we have introduced new messages in the transcript (namely Eve's interaction with the random oracle), and these messages could be correlated with *both* Alice's and Bob's inputs! This is the core issue that we need to tackle.

Our Solution. Now we give an intuitive (but imprecise) description of our proof. As above, we shall define the frontiers F_X and F_Y where information about x and (respectively) about y is first revealed in the (augmented) transcript. Now, information about x or y could be revealed when Alice sends out a message, Bob sends out a message, or Eve obtains its answers from the oracle. We will be able to rule out information about x being revealed by a message from Bob, or information about y being revealed by a message from Alice (see "Locality Guarantee" in Section 2.2), but this leaves open the possibility that *the oracle's response to a query by Eve reveals information about x and y simultaneously.* In other words, while we can still rule out the possibility that F_X occurs strictly above F_Y with significant probability and vice versa, we are left with the possibility that they can almost always coincide.

To address this, we pursue the following intuition: suppose it turns out that in an execution of the protocol, augmented with Eve's queries, the first time significant information about x is revealed is simultaneously (and hence, possibly, safely) with information about y; thus, for instance, if $f(\hat{x}_0, \hat{y}_0) = f(\hat{x}_1, \hat{y}_0)$, but $f(\hat{x}_0, \hat{y}_1) \neq f(\hat{x}_1, \hat{y}_1)$, then the distinction between $x = \hat{x}_0$ and $x = \hat{x}_1$ could be revealed in this execution only when Bob's input is $\hat{y}_1$ and not when his input is $\hat{y}_0$. Nevertheless, by using our strategy, Bob can learn this distinction even if his input is $\hat{y}_0$. This rules out the possibility that the frontiers F_X and F_Y can coincide with significant probability.

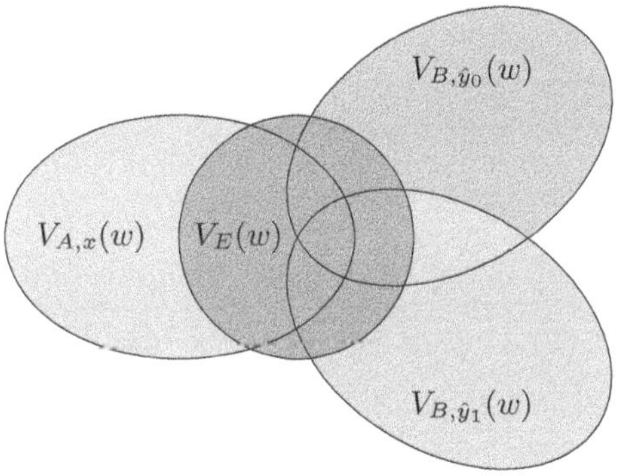

Figure 1: Simulating the oracle answers when mentally switching inputs.

We sketch the idea behind the curious-Bob strategy. Suppose an execution of the augmented protocol reaches a point w where Bob wants to mentally switch his input from his actual input $\hat{y}_0$ to a distinguishing input $\hat{y}_1$. Let Alice, Bob and Eve have views $V_{A,x}(w)$, $V_{B,\hat{y}_0}(w)$ and $V_E(w)$. Bob can sample for himself a view $V_{B,\hat{y}_1}(w)$ conditioned on his input being $\hat{y}_1$, consistent with $V_E(w)$. To simulate the next step (prior to the next message from Alice) in the execution with the new view, Bob needs to simulate the random oracle correctly. However, the actual random oracle he has access to is conditioned on the view $V_{B,\hat{y}_0}(w)$, and it will be pointless to use this oracle with the freshly sampled view $V_{B,\hat{y}_1}(w)$. Instead, Bob will simulate a random oracle as shown in Figure 1. The ovals represent the sets of

[7]As we shall see, *for undecomposable functions*, this must hold even if there are inputs for one party (say Bob) for which the function becomes constant. That is, F_Y needs to be crossed even for executions in which Bob's input is a value y for which the function $f(\cdot, y)$ is constant. This is because, by undecomposability, for certain values of Alice's input x, and another input y' for Bob, $f(x, y) = f(x, y')$ where $f(\cdot, y')$ is not constant, and then by security, the execution with input (x, y) has to be close to the execution with input (x, y'). In the latter, information about y needs to be revealed.

[8]Strictly speaking, this is true only for functions which are undecomposable at the "top-most" level. In our proof, it suffices to consider such functions.

queries in the views $V_{A,x}(w)$, $V_E(w)$, $V_{B,\hat{y}_0}(w)$ and $V_{B,\hat{y}_1}(w)$. Queries already answered in $V_E(w)$ (blue) or in the hypothetical Bob view $V_{B,\hat{y}_1}(w)$ (orange) are answered according to these views. Answers to the remaining queries in $V_{B,\hat{y}_0}(w)$ (green), are freshly sampled. All other queries are answered using the actual random oracle. Note that the queries in the orange and green regions are not answered according to the actual random oracle. Conditioned on none of those queries being present in Alice's view (which we refer to as a "safety" condition, below), the simulation with the switched input is perfect, and then, based on the outcome of this simulation (a single step in the execution) Bob can distinguish between $\hat{x}_0$ and $\hat{x}_1$. To complete the above argument, we show that at the points at which Bob carries out this simulation, the safety condition does indeed hold with high probability (see "Safety Guarantee" from Eve, in Section 2.2).

Technical Issues. Formalizing the above intuitive description presents several challenges. Recall that above we argued in terms of "the probability of reaching (a segment of) a frontier". One important issue is that this probability depends on the inputs. Whether these probabilities are similar or different for different inputs depends on whether the inputs have already been distinguished or not–that is, which frontiers occur above this frontier. Note that we use properties of the distribution over frontiers to reason about the ordering of the frontiers. But these distributions themselves depend on the ordering of the frontiers! Nevertheless, by employing appropriately defined frontiers we manage to implement the above outline while avoiding circularities.

2.2 Using the Independence Learner

As mentioned above, a crucial tool for analyzing protocols using a random oracle is to show that by making polynomially many queries to the oracle, an eavesdropper Eve can get sufficient information conditioned on which, Alice and Bob's views in the protocol are almost always close to being independent (up to an inverse polynomially small error). This is a delicate argument implicitly proved in [4] building on ideas from [21], and was first explicitly described in [10].

In our proof outlined above, we need to adapt this Eve and the guarantees provided by it.

Adapting the Independence Learner. A subtle issue to address when adapting the Eve strategy of [4] is that, in our case, Alice and Bob receive arbitrary inputs which Eve does not see. In particular, Alice and Bob could receive correlated inputs, and we cannot claim that their views, conditioned on Eve's view, are (almost always, close to being) independent. However, we can create an Eve which is oblivious to the actual inputs, but for *every* input pair (x, y) of inputs, when the protocol is executed with these inputs, Alice's and Bob's views conditioned on Eve's view are (almost always, close to being) independent. For this, we take Eve to be as defined in [4], but applied to an inputless protocol obtained by invoking the original protocols with *independent, random* inputs (x, y). Note that initially, from the point of view of this Eve, the actual inputs would have significant probability to be the randomly chosen inputs (since the inputs come from a polynomially large domain). In analyzing this Eve, we rely on an argument that with significant probability, at any round of the protocol, this Eve will continue to consider the actual input to be a likely input (refer to the full version [36] for a formal statement).

In our analysis sketched above, there are two guarantees from this Eve that we rely on:

Locality Guarantee: Alice's Message Independent of Bob's Input. Firstly, recall that the purpose of introducing Eve's view into the transcript was to restore the "locality property" – i.e., Alice's messages, conditioned on Eve's view, are independent of Bob's view. More precisely, for our setting with inputs, the guarantee from our Eve is that, at a point where Alice is about to send a message, if two inputs of Bob, y and y' are both somewhat likely, then Alice's message is almost independent of which of these two inputs Bob has. Note that we need this to hold (and this holds) only at points where both of Bob's inputs y and y' are somewhat likely. (In using this claim, the points considered will be above the frontier F_Y where all inputs for Bob are indeed significantly probable.)

Safety Guarantee: Collisions of Private Queries Unlikely. As mentioned in the outline above, the second place where we rely on Eve's properties is in arguing the "safety" of the *curious Bob strategy*: i.e., when curious Bob samples a view for himself after Alice sends a message, it is unlikely that there will be an oracle query that is not present in Eve's view, but exists both in Alice's actual view and in either Bob's actual view or the freshly sampled view. (Note that we need the safety condition to occur only when the "fake" input y' used for the sampled view is somewhat likely. Again, the claim will be applied to points above the frontier F_Y, and indeed all inputs are somewhat likely there.) We remark that, just for the actual views, similar statements were already explicitly proven in [21, 4], bounding the probability of an "intersection query" (query present in Alice's and Bob's views) that is not present in Eve's view. The additional twist in our case is that rather than Bob's actual view alone, we need to consider the view sampled for a "fake" input as well; further, Bob's views we consider are not at the point Eve finishes a round of oracle queries, but after he receives a subsequent message from Alice (before he makes his own oracle queries). Nevertheless, a careful analysis shows that our Eve does give this stronger guarantee (refer to the full version [36] for details).

3. PRELIMINARIES

Here we summarize some of the basic terminology; we refer the interested readers to the full version of the paper [36] for details.

2-Party Functions. A (deterministic) *2-party function* $f : \mathcal{X} \times \mathcal{Y} \mapsto \mathcal{Z}_A \times \mathcal{Z}_B$ maps a pairs of inputs (x, y) (associated with Alice and Bob respectively) to a pair of outputs (a, b) (for the two parties, respectively). For most part in our proofs, we shall be dealing with *symmetric* 2-party functions which produce two identical outputs (or equivalently, a single output given to both parties).

For symmetric functions, an *Alice-cut* is a partition $(X, \bar{X})$ of the input space $\mathcal{X}$ such that for any $x \in X$, $\bar{x} \in \bar{X}$ and $y \in \mathcal{Y}$ $f(x, y) \neq f(\bar{x}, y)$. The *functions associated with an Alice-cut* $(X, \bar{X})$ are the two restrictions of f, restricted to domain $X \times \mathcal{Y}$ and to domain $\bar{X} \times \mathcal{Y}$. A Bob-cut and functions associated with it are defined similarly.

Now, we define *decomposable* functions f in the following recursive manner [33, 5]:

- A constant function is decomposable.

• If f has an Alice-cut or a Bob-cut and the two functions associated with that cut are both decomposable then f is decomposable.

A function is *undecomposable* if it is *not* decomposable. Moreover, it is said to be *undecomposable at the top-most level*, if $f : \mathcal{X} \times \mathcal{Y} \mapsto \mathcal{Z}$ does not have an Alice-cut or Bob-cut (refer to the full version of the paper [36] for some examples).

Secure Function Evaluation and Security Definitions. We use standard definitions of Secure Function Evaluation (SFE) and simulation based security definitions for semi-honest, standalone and UC security. More detailed definitions can be found in the full version of the paper [36].

Random Oracles. Given a security parameter κ, a random oracle $\mathcal{O}$ randomly maps κ-bit strings to κ-bit strings. Security requirements for a protocol are over the random choice of this oracle. The parties do not learn the value of $\mathcal{O}(x)$ until they query the oracle on x. In a protocol, each party can query the random oracle privately; but the oracle is common, in that if the parties query it at at the same input, they receive the same output.

Frontiers. Consider a (possibly infinite) sequence of correlated random variables $(\mathbf{m}_1, \mathbf{m}_2, \ldots)$. We consider a natural representation of such a sequence as a rooted tree, with each level corresponding to a random variable $\mathbf{m}_i$ and each node v at depth t in the tree is uniquely identified with an assignment of values $(m_1, \ldots, m_t)$ to $(\mathbf{m}_1, \ldots, \mathbf{m}_t)$, such that $(m_1, \ldots, m_{t-1})$ is equal to the values identified with its parent node. Then we can identify the sequence of values of these random variables with a unique path in this tree, starting at the root.

We can identify a set of nodes S in this tree with the event that the path corresponding to the values taken by the random variables intersects S. A *frontier* on this tree corresponds to a set F of nodes which is "prefix-free" (i.e., no two nodes in F are on the same path starting at the root). We often define a frontier using a predicate, as the set of nodes which satisfy the predicate but do not have an ancestor which satisfies the predicate (i.e., the predicate is satisfied for the "first time"). Note that the frontier event is deterministic given a node in the tree (though the event could be in terms of the probability of other events at that node).

The tree naturally defines an "ancestor" partial order of the nodes in the tree: we say $u \preceq v$ if u occurs somewhere on the path from the root of the tree to v (u could be identical to v). If $u \preceq v$, but $u \neq v$, then we write $u \prec v$.

Invariably, we consider this tree only with sequence of random variables corresponding to the messages exchanged in a protocol (but possibly augmented by additional messages added for analysis). Though not necessary, it will be convenient to consider the underlying process as consisting of picking a uniformly random input and then executing the protocol. However, clearly, the tree and frontiers can be used to represent any sequence of random variables.

3.1 Transcript Tree

Augmented Protocol Execution. We shall consider two-party protocols Π where Alice and Bob interact to evaluate a (symmetric) function $f : \mathcal{X} \times \mathcal{Y} \to \mathcal{Z}$ on their respective local inputs $x \in \mathcal{X}$ and $y \in \mathcal{Y}$. We shall assume that $|\mathcal{X}|$ and $|\mathcal{Y}|$ are both polynomial in the security parameter. Alice and Bob have access to a random oracle $\mathcal{O}$. We "augment" the protocol Π with a "public query strategy" Eve, which can see the publicly generated transcript and can also query the random oracle. For simplicity, we consider Eve to be deterministic (as will be the case in our instantiation of Eve). We shall instantiate Eve as described in the full version of this paper [36] (applied to an input less protocol obtained by using uniformly randomly chosen inputs for Π).

When Alice is supposed to generate the next message, she queries the random oracle at some points. Based on her local view, she then generates the next message of the protocol using her next message generation algorithm. Similarly, Bob also generates the next message of the protocol during his turns. Eve, on the other hand, simply performs several queries to the random oracle and announces all her queries and their corresponding answers at the end of her turn. For concreteness we shall assume that the protocol starts with Alice sending a message. Alice and Bob take turns alternately, with Eve getting a turn after every Alice or Bob message (i.e., the messages will be sent by Alice, Eve, Bob, Eve, ...).

We shall refer to this protocol as the "augmented protocol" (Π, Eve). The total number of Alice and Bob messages is N. A *round* in this augmented protocol corresponds to a party sending a message followed by Eve adding a list of query-answer pairs.

Augmented Transcript Tree $\mathbb{T}^+$. Our analysis considers the transcript tree $\mathbb{T}^+$ of an execution of Π augmented with a public query strategy Eve. The $\mathbb{T}^+$ associated with an augmented protocol (Π, Eve), is the tree as defined in Section 3 with the sequence of random variables $(\mathbf{m}_1, \mathbf{m}_2, \ldots)$ being the messages added to the transcript of the augmented protocol by Alice, Eve and Bob during an execution. In other words, the nodes in the transcript tree are all the possible partial transcripts in the augmented protocol execution, with a directed edge from a node u to a node v, if the partial transcript associated with v is obtained by adding exactly one message (from Alice, Bob or Eve) to the partial transcript of u.

For convenience we add an initial "dummy" round, in which Alice sends a fixed message followed by Bob sending a fixed message. These correspond to two dummy nodes at the root of $\mathbb{T}^+$. We shall denote by Anodes and Bnodes the sets of Alice and Bob nodes, and by $\mathsf{Achildren}$ and $\mathsf{Bchildren}$ the sets of (Eve) nodes that are children of, respectively, Alice nodes and Bob nodes. The tree $\mathbb{T}^+$ naturally defines an "ancestor" partial order of the nodes in the tree: we say $u \preceq v$ if u occurs somewhere on the path from the root of the tree to v (u could be identical to v). If $u \preceq v$, but $u \neq v$, then we write $u \prec v$. We define $\mathsf{ancstrs}(v) = \{w | w \preceq v\}$.

Parent of u (represented by $\mathsf{parent}(u)$) is defined as w such that $w \prec u$ and $\forall v,\ v \prec u \Rightarrow v \preceq w$. A partial transcript u is said to intersect v if $v \preceq u$. We emphasize that although a round in the augmented protocol comprises of a party sending a message and Eve adding oracle queries-answer pairs to the transcript, we represent them separately in the tree, i.e., in a root to leaf path in $\mathbb{T}^+$ has Alice and Bob nodes followed by Eve nodes (except the two initial dummy nodes).

For any partial transcript w, we define the views of Alice, Bob and Eve consistent with the partial transcript w. The Eve view consistent with w is represented by $V_E(w)$. When considering distribution of Alice/Bob views consistent with a partial transcript, probability is over the choice of random tapes for Alice and Bob and the random oracle. We emphasize that the local views of parties contain only those query-answer pairs which were generated during next message generation of messages already present in w. So, if Alice sends the next message in a round and the resulting transcript was w, then Bob's views consistent with w will contain only query-answer pairs which were generated in previous rounds. Bob's view gets updated with new query-answer pairs when he sends the next message in the protocol.

Strictly Above a Set: $u \prec F$ and $F_1 \prec F_2$. We shall abuse the $\prec$ notation slightly, and use it in the following senses too: if u is a node and F is a set of nodes, we write $u \prec F$ (read as u is strictly above F) if u can be reached from the root without passing through any node in F (i.e., there is no $v \in F$ such that $v \preceq u$); note that for u to be strictly above F, it is not necessary to have any $v \in F$ such that $u \prec v$. For two sets of nodes F_1, F_2, we define the *event* $F_1 \prec F_2$ to occur if the transcript path of an execution passes through a node $v \in F_1$ strictly before passing through any node in F_2 (it may or may not pass through a node in F_2 afterwards).

4. PROOF OUTLINE

In this section we start presenting our formal proofs, including the definitions of the main frontiers used. The complete proof appears in the full version of the paper [36].

First we prove that there is no semi-honest secure protocol for a 2-party *symmetric* function f that is *undecomposable at the top-most level*, which forms the bulk of our proof. Then we extend this result to more general functions to complete the proof of Theorem 1.1. Finally, this impossibility result against semi-honest secure adversaries can be extended to malicious adversaries in the $\mathcal{F}_{\text{COM}}$-hybrid, to prove Theorem 1.2. In the rest of this section, we restrict ourselves to the proof for symmetric function that are undecomposable at the top-most level.

4.1 Frontiers

Recall that the main bottleneck of our proof is that curious eavesdropper's queries could simultaneously reveal information about both Alice and Bob's private inputs. We shall carefully deal with this issue by defining suitable frontiers, F_X^θ and F_Y^θ. F_X^θ is defined as the the following set:[9]

$$\{v : v \text{ is the first node on the path from root to } v \text{ s.t. } \exists y \in \mathcal{Y}, x, x' \in \mathcal{X}, \mathsf{P}[y|v] \geq \theta \text{ and } \mathsf{P}[v|\mathsf{parent}(v); x, y] > (1+\delta)\mathsf{P}[v|\mathsf{parent}(v); x', y]\}$$

Intuitively, F_X^θ is the first place where, for some input y of Bob, a significant distinction is made between some two inputs of Alice, x and x'. We require this distinction to be in terms of information revealed in a single message in the augmented protocol (hence the conditioning on $\mathsf{parent}(v)$). We also count this distinction as valid only if it occurs for an input of Bob that is somewhat likely (assuming a uniform prior over Bob's inputs).[10] Similarly, we define F_Y^θ.

Before proceeding further, it is useful to recall how the frontier analysis proceeds in [39] for proving the same result in the plain model setting (without random oracles). The frontiers there are (something similar to) F_X^0 and F_Y^0 defined above. Firstly, from the correctness of the protocol, both these frontiers are almost *full*, i.e., nearly all transcripts (except with probability $1/\text{poly}(\kappa)$) intersect both F_X^0 and F_Y^0. Further, in the plain model setting, F_X^0 has only Bob nodes (where Alice has just sent out a message) and similarly, F_Y^0 has only Alice nodes; so the two frontiers do not intersect. Since both the frontiers are almost full and do not intersect, at least one of them should occur above the other with at least about $\frac{1}{2}$ probability (when a transcript is randomly generated by an honest execution). But if F_X^0 occurs above (i.e., before) F_Y^0 with significant probability, then a semi-honest Bob would learn significant amount of information about Alice's input, irrespective of his own input, thereby breaking the security of the protocol. On the other hand, if F_Y^0 occurs above F_X^0 with significant probability, then a semi-honest Alice would break the security of the protocol. Thus, in either case the protocol is not secure.

In our case, similar to above, again we have that F_X^θ and F_Y^θ are almost full frontiers (when θ is small enough). But in trying to follow the above plan, the main bottleneck for us is that it is no more true that the two frontiers cannot intersect: indeed, on nodes where Eve has just added its message to the transcript, information about both Alice's and Bob's private inputs could be simultaneously revealed, and the two frontiers could coincide. The key element in the proof is to show that an honest-but-curious Bob could render the protocol insecure if nodes in F_X^θ occurs *at or above* F_Y^θ with significant probability (and symmetrically for Alice) — as opposed to giving an attack by Bob that works only when the nodes in F_X^θ occur strictly above F_Y^θ. Formally, we define the frontier

$$\check{F}_X = \left\{u : u \in F_X^\theta \text{ and } u \preceq F_Y^\theta\right\}.$$

Then, our goal is to show that if $\check{F}_X$ (resp. $\check{F}_Y$, defined symmetrically) has a significant probability, then an honest-but-curious Bob (resp. Alice) can violate the security of the protocol.

4.2 Steps of the Proof

Below, we present the proof ideas in a top down fashion, starting with the final contradiction. We provide an intuitive summary of each step.

Assuming that there is a secure protocol for an undecomposable 2-party function f, we derive a contradiction. This contradiction follows from the following (informally stated) claims below.

1. **Frontiers are full.** The frontiers F_X^θ and F_Y^θ are both almost always encountered by an honest protocol execution. This claim leverages the correctness of the protocol as well as the fact that the function f is not constant (i.e., each parties reveals information about their private input to the other.

[9] In all our equations, we use the convention that the probability of an event conditioned on a zero-probability event is zero. Alternately, we can avoid this by assuming, adding a negligible security error, that for any pair of inputs, any node in $\mathbb{T}^+$ is reached with positive probability.

[10] This technicality is relevant to applying the Safety Guarantee, discussed in Section 2.2, which holds only when the relevant inputs have significant probability.

2. **Frontier Ordering.** $\breve{F}_X$ and $\breve{F}_Y$ have low probability (i.e., , nodes in F_X^θ are unlikely to occur on or above F_Y^θ, and vice versa). This claim leverages that the function f is undecomposable at the top-most level, i.e., no party can reveal information about its private input before the other party.

The proof of the first claim above relies on the correctness of the protocol. The proof of the second claim, which relies on the security of the protocol, is more involved, and is broken up into parts, as described next. Note that to prove this claim, it suffices to bound the probability of $\breve{F}_X$; the claim for $\breve{F}_Y$ is symmetric.

Proving the Frontier Ordering. It turns out that instead of $\breve{F}_X$, it is easier to work with $\widetilde{F}_X$, which consists of nodes $u \in F_X^\theta$ such that u is on or above F_Y^0 (rather than on or above F_Y^θ). The proof relies on the following claims:

1. **Frontier F_Y^0 is full.** This follows from the claim that the frontier F_Y^θ is full, except that $\theta = 0$ in this case.
2. **Probability of encountering F_Y^0 before F_X^θ and F_Y^θ is small.**
3. **Probability of encountering $\widetilde{F}_X$ is small.**

Of these, the last claim has an involved proof. It comprises of the following steps:

1. **Part 1:** Identifying a Minor. First, we show that there are two inputs each, $\{\hat{x}_0, \hat{x}_1\}$ for Alice and $\{\hat{y}_0, \hat{y}_1\}$ for Bob (i.e., , a 2×2 minor in the function) that we can focus on, to show that the protocol cannot be secure if $\widetilde{F}_X$ has significant probability. We identify a segment $\widehat{F}_X \subseteq \widetilde{F}_X$ with a significant fraction of the probability mass on $\widetilde{F}_X$, which we then bound in the next two steps. This region $\widehat{F}_X$ is further partitioned into two parts: $\widehat{S}_X$ and $\widehat{R}_X$ based on whether the partial transcript is just after Alice has spoken or not. The final two steps of the proof deal with these two regions separately.
2. **Part 2:** Bounding the probability of $\widehat{S}_X$. This part is similar to the proof for the problem in the case of plain model protocols. It uses the Locality Property of the *augmented* protocol. Recall that $\widehat{S}_X$ is just after Alice has sent a message so any information revealed by Alice about her input is independent of the private input of Bob. Then, at any node in $\widehat{S}_X$ (where information about Alice input is divulged), Bob can break the security of the protocol.
3. **Part 3:** Bounding the probability of $\widehat{R}_X$. This is the most technical part of our proof. It essentially shows that even if the information about Alice input is revealed during Eve queries, Bob can violate the semi-honest security of the protocol by being curious. The strategy of Bob as introduced in Figure 1 is used.

Eavesdropper Strategy and Properties. We use the curious eavesdropper developed for input-less protocol by [4, 10] to ensure the Locality and Safety guarantees for protocols where parties also have private inputs.

- **Independence Learner.** We start from the Eve algorithm presented in [4, 10] for input-less protocols. This eavesdropper gathers enough information from the random oracle, so that conditioned on its view, Alice's and Bob's views are independent of each other (conditioned on the public transcript generated).
- **Locality Property.** Based on the input-less Eve presented above, we construct an Eve strategy where parties have private inputs. Intuitively, it assumes that parties sample their inputs uniformly at random and runs the "input-less Eve" in this hypothetical setting. This lemma can be strengthened to assert that when a party speaks, she can only divulge information about her own private inputs (conditioned on our eavesdropper's view).
- **Safety Property.** The previous result can be further strengthened to show that intersection queries of Bob's actual and hypothetical views with Alice queries are contained in our Eve's query list. This result is also proven based on the eavesdropper properties of the "input-less Eve."

5. CONCLUSION & OPEN PROBLEMS

We have shown a black-box separation between one-way functions and semi-honest SFE protocols for 2-party secure function evaluation for any finite deterministic function which does not already have a semi-honest SFE protocol in the plain model. Intuitively, this provides strong evidence that there could be numerous, if not infinitely many, natural, distinct "worlds" (a la *Impagliazzo's Worlds*) between *Minicrypt* and *Cryptomania*: the Many Worlds Conjecture (MWC, see Section 1).

We leave proving the MWC as the main open problem from this work. In particular, we have only established that the world with (semi-honest) SFE for various functions is "strictly stronger" than minicrypt, but not that it is "strictly weaker" than cryptomania (where oblivious transfer protocols exist). The first step in proving the MWC would be to show that there exist functions which yield worlds strictly intermediate to minicrypt and cryptomania.

Another open problem is to extend our current result to a larger class of functions. Our result relies on the combinatorial properties of undecomposable functions. In particular, we do not "compile out" the random oracle — i.e., we do not give a strategy to transform any protocol in the random oracle model to one in the plain model that is as secure as the original one. This leaves open the possibility that for certain classes of 2-party computation problems, like randomized functions (for which the characterization of non-triviality in terms of undecomposability is not applicable), the random oracle model could enable secure computation. We ask if random oracles can indeed be compiled out from all 2-party secure computation protocols.

6. REFERENCES

[1] *30th Annual Symposium on Foundations of Computer Science, 30 October-1 November 1989, Research Triangle Park, North Carolina, USA*. IEEE, 1989.

[2] B. Barak, M. Braverman, X. Chen, and A. Rao. How to compress interactive communication. In L. J. Schulman, editor, *STOC*, pages 67–76. ACM, 2010.

[3] B. Barak and M. Mahmoody. Lower bounds on signatures from symmetric primitives. In *FOCS: IEEE Symposium on Foundations of Computer Science (FOCS)*, 2007.

[4] B. Barak and M. Mahmoody. Merkle puzzles are optimal - an $O(n^2)$-query attack on any key exchange from a random oracle. In S. Halevi, editor, *CRYPTO*, volume 5677 of *Lecture Notes in Computer Science*, pages 374–390. Springer, 2009.

[5] D. Beaver. Perfect privacy for two-party protocols. In J. Feigenbaum and M. Merritt, editors, *Proceedings of DIMACS Workshop on Distributed Computing and Cryptography*, volume 2, pages 65–77. American Mathematical Society, 1989.

[6] A. Beimel, T. Malkin, and S. Micali. The all-or-nothing nature of two-party secure computation. In *CRYPTO*, pages 80–97, 1999.

[7] D. Boneh, P. A. Papakonstantinou, C. Rackoff, Y. Vahlis, and B. Waters. On the impossibility of basing identity based encryption on trapdoor permutations. In *FOCS*, pages 283–292. IEEE Computer Society, 2008.

[8] B. Chor and E. Kushilevitz. A zero-one law for boolean privacy (extended abstract). In Johnson [23], pages 62–72.

[9] R. Cleve and R. Impagliazzo. Martingales, collective coin flipping and discrete control processes (extended abstract), 1993.

[10] D. Dachman-Soled, Y. Lindell, M. Mahmoody, and T. Malkin. On black-box complexity of optimally-fair coin-tossing. In *Theory of Cryptography Conference - TCC 2011*, 2011.

[11] R. Gennaro, Y. Gertner, J. Katz, and L. Trevisan. Bounds on the efficiency of generic cryptographic constructions. *SIAM J. Comput.*, 35(1):217–246, 2005.

[12] Y. Gertner, S. Kannan, T. Malkin, O. Reingold, and M. Viswanathan. The relationship between public key encryption and oblivious transfer. In *FOCS*, pages 325–335. IEEE Computer Society, 2000.

[13] Y. Gertner, T. Malkin, and O. Reingold. On the impossibility of basing trapdoor functions on trapdoor predicates. In *FOCS*, pages 126–135, 2001.

[14] I. Haitner. Semi-honest to malicious oblivious transfer - the black-box way. In *TCC*, pages 412–426, 2008.

[15] I. Haitner, J. J. Hoch, O. Reingold, and G. Segev. Finding collisions in interactive protocols - a tight lower bound on the round complexity of statistically-hiding commitments. In *FOCS*, pages 669–679. IEEE Computer Society, 2007.

[16] I. Haitner, M.-H. Nguyen, S. J. Ong, O. Reingold, and S. P. Vadhan. Statistically hiding commitments and statistical zero-knowledge arguments from any one-way function. *SIAM J. Comput.*, 39(3):1153–1218, 2009.

[17] I. Haitner, E. Omri, and H. Zarosim. On the power of random oracles. *Electronic Colloquium on Computational Complexity (ECCC)*, 19:129, 2012.

[18] I. Haitner, E. Omri, and H. Zarosim. Limits on the usefulness of random oracles. *Theory of Cryptography Conference (TCC, to appear)*, 2013.

[19] R. Impagliazzo. A personal view of average-case complexity. In *Structure in Complexity Theory Conference*, pages 134–147, 1995.

[20] R. Impagliazzo and M. Luby. One-way functions are essential for complexity based cryptography (extended abstract). In *FOCS* [1], pages 230–235.

[21] R. Impagliazzo and S. Rudich. Limits on the provable consequences of one-way permutations. In Johnson [23], pages 44–61.

[22] Y. Ishai, editor. *Theory of Cryptography - 8th Theory of Cryptography Conference, TCC 2011, Providence, RI, USA, March 28-30, 2011. Proceedings*, volume 6597 of *Lecture Notes in Computer Science*. Springer, 2011.

[23] D. S. Johnson, editor. *Proceedings of the Twenty-First Annual ACM Symposium on Theory of Computing, 15-17 May 1989, Seattle, Washington, USA*. ACM, 1989.

[24] J. Katz, D. Schröder, and A. Yerukhimovich. Impossibility of blind signatures from one-way permutations. In Ishai [22], pages 615–629.

[25] J. Kilian. A general completeness theorem for two-party games. In *STOC*, pages 553–560. ACM, 1991.

[26] J. Kilian. More general completeness theorems for secure two-party computation. In *STOC*, pages 316–324, 2000.

[27] J. Kilian, E. Kushilevitz, S. Micali, and R. Ostrovsky. Reducibility and completeness in private computations. *SIAM J. Comput.*, 29(4):1189–1208, 2000.

[28] J. H. Kim, D. R. Simon, and P. Tetali. Limits on the efficiency of one-way permutation-based hash functions. In *FOCS*, pages 535–542, 1999.

[29] D. Kraschewski, H. K. Maji, M. Prabhakaran, and A. Sahai. A full characterization of completeness for two-party randomized function evaluation. Manuscript, 2013.

[30] D. Kraschewski and J. Müller-Quade. Completeness theorems with constructive proofs for finite deterministic 2-party functions. In *TCC*, 2011.

[31] G. Kreitz. A zero-one law for secure multi-party computation with ternary outputs. In Ishai [22], pages 382–399.

[32] R. Künzler, J. Müller-Quade, and D. Raub. Secure computability of functions in the it setting with dishonest majority and applications to long-term security. In Reingold [46], pages 238–255.

[33] E. Kushilevitz. Privacy and communication complexity. In *FOCS* [1], pages 416–421.

[34] H. C. Lin, L. Trevisan, and H. Wee. On hardness amplification of one-way functions. In J. Kilian, editor, *TCC*, volume 3378 of *Lecture Notes in Computer Science*, pages 34–49. Springer, 2005.

[35] Y. Lindell, E. Omri, and H. Zarosim. Completeness for symmetric two-party functionalities - revisited. In X. Wang and K. Sako, editors, *ASIACRYPT*, volume 7658 of *Lecture Notes in Computer Science*, pages 116–133. Springer, 2012.

[36] M. Mahmoody, H. K. Maji, and M. Prabhakaran. Limits of random oracles in secure computation.

Electronic Colloquium on Computational Complexity (ECCC), 19:65, 2012. http://eccc.hpi-web.de/report/2012/065/.

[37] M. Mahmoody, H. K. Maji, and M. Prabhakaran. On the power of public-key encryption in secure computation. In *TCC (To Appear)*, 2014. Full version available from IACR Eprint Archive: http://eccc.hpi-web.de/report/2013/137/.

[38] H. K. Maji, P. Ouppaphan, M. Prabhakaran, and M. Rosulek. Exploring the limits of common coins using frontier analysis of protocols. In *TCC*, 2011.

[39] H. K. Maji, M. Prabhakaran, and M. Rosulek. Complexity of multi-party computation problems: The case of 2-party symmetric secure function evaluation. In Reingold [46], pages 256–273. Full version available from IACR Eprint Archive: http://eprint.iacr.org.

[40] H. K. Maji, M. Prabhakaran, and M. Rosulek. Cryptographic complexity classes and computational intractability assumptions. In A. C.-C. Yao, editor, *ICS*, pages 266–289. Tsinghua University Press, 2010.

[41] H. K. Maji, M. Prabhakaran, and M. Rosulek. A zero-one law for cryptographic complexity with respect to computational uc security. In *CRYPTO*, pages 595–612, 2010.

[42] H. K. Maji, M. Prabhakaran, and M. Rosulek. A unified characterization of completeness and triviality for secure function evaluation. In *INDOCRYPT*, pages 40–59, 2012.

[43] T. Matsuda and K. Matsuura. On black-box separations among injective one-way functions. In Ishai [22], pages 597–614.

[44] R. Ostrovsky. One-way functions, hard on average problems, and statistical zero-knowledge proofs. In *Structure in Complexity Theory Conference*, pages 133–138, 1991.

[45] R. Ostrovsky and A. Wigderson. One-way functions are essential for non-trivial zero-knowledge. Technical Report TR-93-073, International Computer Science Institute, Berkeley, CA, Nov. 1993. Preliminary version in Proc. 2nd Israeli Symp. on Theory of Computing and Systems, 1993, pp. 3–17.

[46] O. Reingold, editor. *Theory of Cryptography, 6th Theory of Cryptography Conference, TCC 2009, San Francisco, CA, USA, March 15-17, 2009. Proceedings*, volume 5444 of *Lecture Notes in Computer Science*. Springer, 2009.

[47] O. Reingold, L. Trevisan, and S. P. Vadhan. Notions of reducibility between cryptographic primitives. In M. Naor, editor, *TCC*, volume 2951 of *Lecture Notes in Computer Science*, pages 1–20. Springer, 2004.

[48] D. R. Simon. Finding collisions on a one-way street: Can secure hash functions be based on general assumptions? In *EUROCRYPT*, pages 334–345, 1998.

Robust Device Independent Quantum Key Distribution

[Abstract]

Umesh Vazirani[*]
Computer Science Division
University of California, Berkeley

Thomas Vidick[†]
Newton Institute, Cambridge UK
and Centre for Quantum Technologies
NUS, Singapore

ABSTRACT

Quantum cryptography is based on the discovery that the laws of quantum mechanics allow levels of security that are impossible to replicate in a classical world [2, 8, 12]. Can such levels of security be guaranteed even when the quantum devices on which the protocol relies are untrusted? This fundamental question in quantum cryptography dates back to the early nineties when the challenge of achieving device independent quantum key distribution, or DIQKD, was first formulated [9]. We answer this challenge affirmatively by exhibiting a robust protocol for DIQKD and rigorously proving its security. The protocol achieves a linear key rate while tolerating a constant noise rate in the devices. The security proof assumes only that the devices can be modeled by the laws of quantum mechanics and are spatially isolated from each other and any adversary's laboratory. In particular, we emphasize that the devices may have quantum memory. All previous proofs of security relied either on the use of many independent pairs of devices [6, 4, 7], or on the absence of noise [10, 1].

To prove security for a DIQKD protocol it is necessary to establish at least that the generated key is truly random even in the presence of a quantum adversary. This is already a challenge, one that was recently resolved [14]. DIQKD is substantially harder, since now the protocol must also guarantee that the key is completely secret from the quantum adversary's point of view, and the entire protocol is robust against noise; this in spite of the substantial amounts of classical information leaked to the adversary throughout the protocol, as part of the error estimation and information reconciliation procedures.

Our proof of security builds upon a number of techniques, including randomness extractors that are secure against quantum storage [3] as well as ideas originating in the coding strategy used in the proof of the Holevo-Schumacher-Westmoreland theorem [5, 11] which we apply to bound correlations across multiple rounds in a way not unrelated to information-theoretic proofs of the parallel repetition property for multiplayer games. Our main result can be understood as a new bound on monogamy [13] of entanglement in the type of complex scenario that arises in a key distribution protocol.

Precise statements of our results and detailed proofs can be found at arXiv:1210.1810.

[*]Supported by ARO Grant W911NF-12-1-0541, NSF Grant CCF-0905626 and Templeton Foundation Grant 21674.

[†]Part of this work was completed while the author was visiting UC Berkeley. Supported by the National Science Foundation under Grant No. 0844626 and by the Ministry of Education, Singapore under the Tier 3 grant MOE2012-T3-1-009.

ITCS'14, January 12–14, 2014, Princeton, New Jersey, USA.
ACM 978-1-4503-2698-8/14/01.
http://dx.doi.org/10.1145/2554797.2554802.

Categories and Subject Descriptors

F.1 [**Computation by abstract devices**]: Miscellaneous

General Terms

Theory

Keywords

quantum key distribution; CHSH game; monogamy; certified randomness; device-independence

1. REFERENCES

[1] Jonathan Barrett, Roger Colbeck, and Adrian Kent. Unconditionally secure device-independent quantum key distribution with only two devices. Technical report arXiv:1209.0435, 2012.

[2] C. Bennett and G. Brassard. Quantum cryptography: Public key distribution and coin tossing. In *Proceedings of IEEE International Conference on Computers, Systems, and Signal Processing*, pages 175–179, 1984.

[3] A. De, C. Portmann, T. Vidick, and R. Renner. Trevisan's extractor in the presence of quantum side information. *SIAM Journal on Computing*, 41(4):915–940, 2012.

[4] Esther Hänggi, Renato Renner, and Stefan Wolf. Efficient device-independent quantum key distribution. In *Proceedings of the 29th Annual international conference on Theory and Applications of Cryptographic Techniques*, EUROCRYPT'10, pages 216–234, Berlin, Heidelberg, 2010. Springer-Verlag.

[5] A.S. Holevo. The capacity of the quantum channel with general signal states. *IEEE Transactions on Information Theory*, 44(1):269 –273, 1998.

[6] L. Masanes, R. Renner, M. Christandl, A. Winter, and J. Barrett. Unconditional security of key distribution from causality constraints. Technical report arXiv:quant-ph/0606049v4, 2009.

[7] Lluís Masanes, Stefano Pironio, and Antonio Acín. Secure device-independent quantum key distribution with causally

independent measurement devices. *Nature Communications*, 2(238):7, 2011.

[8] Dominic Mayers. Unconditional security in quantum cryptography. *J. ACM*, 48(3):351–406, May 2001.

[9] Dominic Mayers and Andrew Yao. Quantum cryptography with imperfect apparatus. In *Proceedings of the 39th Annual Symposium on Foundations of Computer Science*, FOCS '98, page 503, Washington, DC, USA, 1998. IEEE Computer Society.

[10] Ben Reichardt, Falk Unger, and Umesh Vazirani. A classical leash for a quantum system: Command of quantum systems via rigidity of CHSH games. Technical report arXiv:1209.0448, 2012.

[11] Benjamin Schumacher. Sending entanglement through noisy quantum channels. *Phys. Rev. A*, 54:2614–2628, Oct 1996.

[12] Peter W. Shor and John Preskill. Simple proof of security of the BB84 quantum key distribution protocol. *Phys. Rev. Lett.*, 85:441–444, Jul 2000.

[13] B. Terhal. Is entanglement monogamous? *IBM J. Res. Dev.*, 48:71–78, January 2004.

[14] Umesh Vazirani and Thomas Vidick. Certifiable quantum dice: or, true random number generation secure against quantum adversaries. In *Proceedings of the 44th symposium on Theory of Computing*, STOC '12, pages 61–76. ACM, 2011. Also available as arXiv:1111.6054.

On the Structure of Boolean Functions with Small Spectral Norm

Amir Shpilka*
Faculty of Computer Science, Technion — Israel Institute of Technology
Haifa, Israel
shpilka@cs.technion.ac.il

Avishay Tal†
Department of Computer Science and Applied Mathematics, Weizmann Institute of Science,
Rehovot, Israel
avishay.tal@weizmann.ac.il

Ben lee Volk*
Faculty of Computer Science, Technion — Israel Institute of Technology
Haifa, Israel
benlee@cs.technion.ac.il

ABSTRACT

In this paper we prove results regarding Boolean functions with small spectral norm (the spectral norm of f is $\|\hat{f}\|_1 = \sum_\alpha |\hat{f}(\alpha)|$). Specifically, we prove the following results for functions $f : \{0,1\}^n \to \{0,1\}$ with $\|\hat{f}\|_1 = A$.

1. There is a subspace V of co-dimension at most A^2 such that $f|_V$ is constant.
2. f can be computed by a parity decision tree of size $2^{A^2} n^{2A}$. (a parity decision tree is a decision tree whose nodes are labeled with arbitrary linear functions.)
3. f can be computed by a De Morgan formula of size $O(2^{A^2} n^{2A+2})$ and by a De Morgan formula of depth $O(A^2 + \log(n) \cdot A)$.
4. If in addition f has at most s nonzero Fourier coefficients, then f can be computed by a parity decision tree of depth $A^2 \log s$.
5. For every $\epsilon > 0$ there is a parity decision tree of depth $O(A^2 + \log(1/\epsilon))$ and size $2^{O(A^2)} \cdot \min\{1/\epsilon^2, O(\log(1/\epsilon))^{2A}\}$ that ϵ-approximates f. Furthermore, this tree can be learned, with probability $1-\delta$, using $\mathsf{poly}(n, \exp(A^2), 1/\epsilon, \log(1/\delta))$ membership queries.

All the results above (except 3) also hold (with a slight change in parameters) for functions $f : \mathbb{Z}_p^n \to \{0,1\}$.

Categories and Subject Descriptors

F.1.3 [**Complexity Measures and Classes**]: Relations among complexity measures

Keywords

Analysis of Boolean Functions; Decision Trees; Spectral Norm

1. INTRODUCTION

The Fourier transform is one of the most useful tools in the analysis of Boolean functions. It is a household name in many areas of theoretical computer science: Learning theory (cf. [15, 17, 18]); Hardness of approximation (cf. [12]); Property testing (cf. [4, 3, 8]); Social choice (cf. [13, 14]) and more. The reader interested in the Fourier transform and its applications is referred to the online book [20].

A common theme in the study of Fourier transform is the question of classifying all Boolean functions whose Fourier transforms share some natural property. For example, Friedgut proved that Boolean functions that have *small influence* are close to being juntas (i.e. functions that depend on a small number of coordinates) [6]. Friedgut, Kalai and Naor proved that Boolean functions whose Fourier spectrum is concentrated on the first two levels are close to dictator functions (i.e. functions of the form $f(x_1, \dots, x_n) = x_i$ or $1 - x_i$). In [24, 19] it was conjectured that a Boolean function that has a *sparse* Fourier spectrum (i.e. that has only s nonzero Fourier coefficients), can be computed by a parity decision tree (for short we denote parity decision tree by $\oplus$-DT) of depth $\mathsf{poly}(\log s)$. Recall that in a $\oplus$-DT nodes are labeled by linear functions (over $\mathbb{Z}_2$) rather than by variables. It is well known that a function that is computed by a depth d $\oplus$-DT has sparsity at most $\exp(d)$ (see Lemma 2.5), so this conjecture implies a (more or less) tight result. This conjecture was raised in the context of the log-rank conjecture in communication complexity and, if true, it would imply that the log-rank conjecture is true for functions of the form $F(x, y) = f(x \oplus y)$, for some Boolean function f.

In this paper we are interested in the structure of functions that have small spectral norm. Namely, in Boolean functions

*The research leading to these results has received funding from the European Community's Seventh Framework Programme (FP7/2007-2013) under grant agreement number 257575.

†Research supported by an Adams Fellowship of the Israel Academy of Sciences and Humanities, by an Israel Science Foundation grant and by the I-CORE Program of the Planning and Budgeting Committee and the Israel Science Foundation

ITCS'14, January 12–14, 2014, Princeton, New Jersey, USA.
Copyright 2014 ACM 978-1-4503-2698-8/14/01 ...$15.00.
http://dx.doi.org/10.1145/2554797.2554803.

$f : \{0,1\}^n \to \{0,1\}$ that for some number A satisfy

$$\|\hat{f}\|_1 \stackrel{\text{def}}{=} \sum_\alpha |\hat{f}(\alpha)| \leq A\,, \quad (1)$$

where A may depend on the number of variables n (for definitions see Section 2). Such functions were studied in the context of circuit complexity (cf. [11]) and, more notably, in learning theory, where it is one of the most general family of Boolean functions that can be learned efficiently [15, 18, 1]. In particular, Kushilevitz and Mansour proved that any Boolean function satisfying (1), can be well approximated by a sparse polynomial [15]. This already gives some rough structure for functions with small spectral norm, however one may ask for a more refined structure that captures the function exactly. Green and Sanders were the first to obtain such a result (and until this work this was the only such result). They proved that if f satisfies Equation (1) then it can be expressed as a sum of at most $2^{2^{O(A^4)}}$ characteristic functions of subspaces, that is,

$$f = \sum_{i=1}^{2^{2^{O(A^4)}}} \pm \mathbf{1}_{V_i}\,, \quad (2)$$

where each V_i is a subspace. Thus, when A is constant this gives a very strong result on the structure of such a function f. This result can be seen as an *inverse* theorem, as it is well known and easy to see that the spectral norm of the characteristic function of a subspace is constant. Thus, [9] show that in general, any function with a small spectral norm is a linear combination of a (relatively) small number of such characteristic functions. Of course, ideally one would like to show that the number of functions in the sum is at most $\mathsf{poly}(A)$ and not doubly exponential in A, however, Green and Sanders note that "it seems to us that it would be difficult to use our method to reduce the number of exponentials below two."

It is possible that another classification of Boolean functions with small spectral norm could be achieved using decision trees, or more generally, parity decision trees. It is not hard to show that if a Boolean function g is computed by a $\oplus$-DT with s leaves then the spectral norm of g is at most s (see Lemma 2.5). Interestingly, we are not aware of any Boolean function that has a small spectral norm and that cannot be computed by a small $\oplus$-DT. It is thus an interesting question whether this is indeed the general case, namely, that any function of small spectral norm can be computed by a small $\oplus$-DT. We note that the result of [9] does not yield such a structure. Indeed, if we were to represent the function given by Equation (2) as a $\oplus$-DT then, without knowing anything more about the function, then we do not see a more efficient representation than the brute-force one that yields a $\oplus$-DT of size $n^{2^{2^{O(A^4)}}}$.

Another interesting question concerning functions with small spectral norm comes from the learning theory perspective. As mentioned above, Kushilevitz and Mansour proved that for any Boolean function satisfying Equation (1) there is some sparse polynomial $g = \sum_{i=1}^{A^2/\epsilon} \hat{f}(\alpha_i)\chi_{\alpha_i}(x)$ (where the coefficients in the summation are the A^2/ϵ largest Fourier coefficient of f) such that $\Pr_x[f(x) \neq \mathrm{sgn}(g(x))] \leq \epsilon$. Thus, their learning algorithm always outputs as hypothesis the function $\mathrm{sgn}(g(x))$, also in the case where f is computed by a small decision tree or a small $\oplus$-DT. It would be desirable to output a hypothesis coming from the same complexity class as f, i.e. to output a decision tree or a $\oplus$-DT. However, a hardness result of [1] shows that under reasonable complexity assumptions, one cannot hope to output a small decision tree approximating f. So, a refinement of the question should be to try and output the smallest tree one can find for a function approximating f. For example, the function

$$\mathrm{sgn}(g) = \mathrm{sgn}\left(\sum_{i=1}^{A^2/\epsilon} \hat{f}(\alpha_i)\chi_{\alpha_i}(x)\right) \quad (3)$$

can be computed by a $\oplus$-DT of depth $O(A^2/\epsilon)$ in the natural way. Even when A is a constant and ϵ is polynomially small this does not give much information. Thus, a natural question is to try and find a better representation for such a range of parameters.

1.1 Our results

Our first result identifies a *local* structure shared by Boolean functions with small spectral norm.

THEOREM 1.1. *Let $f : \{0,1\}^n \to \{0,1\}$ be such that $\|\hat{f}\|_1 = A$, then, there is an affine subspace $V \subset \{0,1\}^n$ of co-dimension at most A^2 such that f is constant on V.*

We note that the proof of [9] does not imply the existence of such an affine subspace V of such a high dimension. Our next result gives a $\oplus$-DT computing f.

THEOREM 1.2. *Let $f : \{0,1\}^n \to \{0,1\}$ be such that $\|\hat{f}\|_1 = A$, then, f can be computed by a $\oplus$-DT of size $2^{A^2}n^{2A}$.*

In particular, the theorem implies that $f = \sum_{i=1}^{2^{A^2}n^{2A}} \pm \mathbf{1}_{V_i}$, where each V_i is a subspace.

The connections between parity decision trees and De Morgan formulas and between formula size and depth, along with Theorem 1.2, imply the following theorem. For completeness we give its proof, along with the formal definitions, in Appendix B.

THEOREM 1.3. *Let $f : \{0,1\}^n \to \{0,1\}$ be such that $\|\hat{f}\|_1 = A$, then, f can be computed by a De Morgan formula of size $O(2^{A^2} \cdot n^{2A} \cdot n^2)$ and by a De Morgan formula of depth $O(\log(n) \cdot A + A^2)$.*

Another result settles the conjecture of [24, 19] for the case of sparse Boolean functions with small spectral norm.

THEOREM 1.4. *Let $f : \{0,1\}^n \to \{0,1\}$ be such that $\|\hat{f}\|_1 = A$ and $|\{\alpha \mid \hat{f}(\alpha) \neq 0\}| = s$. Then f can be computed by a $\oplus$-DT of depth $A^2 \log s$.*

Thus, if the spectral norm of f is constant (or $\mathsf{poly}(\log s)$), Theorem 1.4 settles the conjecture affirmatively. The conjecture is still open for the case where the spectral norm of f is large.

Our last result (for functions over the Boolean cube) fits into the context of learning theory and provides a bound on the depth of a $\oplus$-DT *approximating* a function with a small spectral norm. Here, the distance between two Boolean functions is measured with respect to the uniform distribution, namely, $\mathrm{dist}(f, g) = \Pr_{x\in\{0,1\}^n}[f(x) \neq g(x)]$.

THEOREM 1.5. *Let* $f : \{0,1\}^n \to \{0,1\}$ *be such that* $\|\hat{f}\|_1 = A$. *Then for every* $\delta, \epsilon > 0$ *there is a randomized algorithm that, given a query oracle to* f, *outputs (with probability at least* $1 - \delta$*) a* $\oplus$*-DT of depth* $O(A^2 + \log(1/\epsilon))$ *and size* $2^{O(A^2)} \min\{1/\epsilon^2, O(\log(1/\epsilon))^{2A}\}$, *which computes a Boolean function* g_ϵ *such that* $dist(f, g_\epsilon) \leq \epsilon$. *The algorithm runs in time polynomial in* $n, \exp(A^2), 1/\epsilon$ *and* $\log(1/\delta)$.

Thus, when A is a constant and ϵ is polynomially small, the depth is $O(\log n)$ and the size is only poly-logarithmic in n. This greatly improves upon the representation guaranteed by Equation (3). If one insists on outputting a $\oplus$-DT, then, for all ranges of parameters, the tree that we obtain is much smaller than the tree guaranteed by Equation (3).

We also prove analogs of the theorems above for functions $f : \mathbb{Z}_p^n \to \{+1, -1\}$ having small spectral norm. Namely, in the theorems above one could instead talk of $f : \mathbb{Z}_p^n \to \{0,1\}$ and obtain essentially the same results.[1] Theorems 4.2, 4.3, 4.5 and 4.6 are the $\mathbb{Z}_p$ analogs to Theorems 1.1, 1.2, 1.4 and 1.5, respectively. We note that in [10] Green and Sanders extended their result to hold for functions mapping an abelian group G to $\{0,1\}$, obtaining the same bound as in [9], so our result for functions on $\mathbb{Z}_p^n$ could be seen as an analog to their result for such groups.

1.2 Comparison with [9]

Comparing Theorem 1.2 to Equation (2) (that was proved in [9]), we note that while Equation (2) does not involve the number of variables (i.e. the upper bound on the number of subspaces only depends on A), our result does depend on n. However, we give a more refined structure - that of a parity decision tree - which is not implied by Equation (2) (see also the discussion above). Moreover, when $A = \Omega((\log\log n)^{1/4})$, our bound is much better than the one given in Equation (2).

Our proof technique is also quite different than that of [9]. Their proof idea is to represent f as $f = f_1 + f_2$ where the Fourier supports of f_1 and f_2 are disjoint, and such that f_1 and f_2 are *close to being integer valued* and have a somewhat smaller spectral norm. Then, using recursion, they represent each f_i as a sum of a small number of characteristic functions of subspaces. In particular, Green and Sanders do not restrict their treatment to Boolean functions but rather study functions that at every point of the Boolean cube obtain a value that is almost an integer. Thus, they prove a more general result, namely, that $f_{\mathbb{Z}}$, the integer part of f, can be represented in the form of Equation (2). We on the other hand only work with Boolean functions, so their result is stronger from that respect. However, while their proof was a bit involved and required using results from additive combinatorics, our approach is more elementary and is based on exploiting the fact that f is Boolean. In particular, our starting point is an analysis of the simple equation $f^2 = 1$ (when we think of f as mapping $\{0,1\}^n$ to $\{\pm 1\}$). Furthermore, we are able to use the fact that f is Boolean in order to show that it can be computed by a small $\oplus$-DT, which does not seem to follow from [9].

[1] Of course, one would have to speak about the analog of a $\oplus$-DT for the case where the inputs come from $\mathbb{Z}_p^n$.

Green and Sanders later extended their technique and proved a similar result for functions over general abelian groups $f : G \to \{0,1\}$ [10]. Our technique do not extend to general groups, but we do obtain results for the case that $G = \mathbb{Z}_p^n$, which again has the same advantages and disadvantages compared to the result of [10] (although, the simplicity of our approach is even more evident here).

1.3 Proof idea

As mentioned above, our proof relies on the simple equation $f^2 = 1$ (when we think of $f : \{0,1\}^n \to \{\pm 1\}$). By expanding the Fourier representations (See Section 2 for definitions) of both sides we reach the identity

$$\sum_\gamma \hat{f}(\gamma)\hat{f}(\delta + \gamma) = 0,$$

that holds for all $\delta \neq 0$ (See Lemma 3.2). This identity could be interpreted as saying that the mass on pairs whose product is positive is the same as the mass on pairs whose product is negative. In particular, if we consider the two heaviest elements in the Fourier spectrum, say, $\hat{f}(\alpha)$ and $\hat{f}(\beta)$, and let $\delta = \alpha + \beta$, then by restricting f to one of the subspaces $\chi_\delta(x) = 1$ or $\chi_\delta(x) = -1$, we get a substantial saving in the spectral norm (see Lemma 3.1). This happens since there is a significant L_1 mass on pairs $\hat{f}(\gamma), \hat{f}(\delta + \gamma)$ that have different signs. By repeating this process we manage to prove the existence of small $\oplus$-DT for f.

The argument for functions over $\mathbb{Z}_p^n$ is similar, but requires more technical work. For that reason we decided to give a separate proof for the case of functions over the Boolean cube, and then, after the ideas were laid out in their simpler form, to prove the results in the more general case.

1.4 The work of Tsang et al. [23]

Independently and simultaneously to our work, Tsang et al. [23] obtained related results. The main objective of the work [23] was to study the communication complexity of sparse Boolean functions. These are functions f such that the *communication matrix* of the function $F(x, y) = f(x \oplus y)$ has low rank. Resolving the log-rank conjecture from communication complexity for such functions was the main motivation for the conjecture raised in [19] and [24].

Tsang et al. managed to prove a stronger version of our Theorem 1.1, namely, they proved that f is constant on a subspace of co-dimension at most $O(A)$. Their argument is identical to ours (namely, to the one given in Lemma 3.1) except that they observe that after $O(1/A)$ steps of increasing the largest Fourier coefficient of f, it grows to at least 1/2. At this point they observe that the proof of (their equivalent of) Lemma 3.1 actually guarantees that the restriction that saves the most in the spectral norm keeps increasing the largest coefficient. Thus, now at each step the spectral norm goes down by some constant factor and hence additional $O(1/A)$ many steps would make f constant.[2]

This immediately improves the results in Theorems 1.1 and 1.4; we can now change the factor A^2 to A in both.

The work [23] does not contain analogs for Theorems 1.2, 1.3 and 1.5. We also note that Tsang et al. did not study the case of functions from $\mathbb{Z}_p^n$ to $\{0,1\}$, and so they do not

[2] Our Lemma 3.1 only speaks about the spectral norm, but the effect on the largest Fourier coefficient is obvious from the proof.

have analogs of Theorems 4.2, 4.3, 4.5 and 4.6. Their work, however, contains structural results about Boolean functions with low $\mathbb{F}_2$ degree and with "light Fourier tail" (the exact definitions appear in their paper), which we do not consider.

1.5 Organization

Section 2 contains the basic background and definitions. In Section 3 we prove our results for functions $f : \mathbb{Z}_2^n \to \{+1, -1\}$. The results for functions on $\mathbb{Z}_p^n$ are given in Section 4. The proofs of those results are omitted from the conference proceedings version, and can be found in the full version ([21]). Finally, in Section 5 we discuss problems left open by this work.

2. NOTATION AND BASIC RESULTS

It will be more convenient for us to talk about functions $f : \{0,1\}^n \to \{\pm 1\}$. Note that if $f : \{0,1\}^n \to \{0,1\}$ then $1 - 2f : \{0,1\}^n \to \{\pm 1\}$ and $1 - 2f$ and f have roughly the same spectral norm (up to a multiplicative factor of 2) and the same Fourier sparsity (up to ± 1).

2.1 Decision trees and parity decision trees

In this section we define the basic computational models that we shall consider in the paper.

DEFINITION 2.1 (DECISION TREE). *A decision tree is a labeled binary tree T. Each internal node of T is labeled with a variable x_i, and each leaf by a bit $b \in \{+1, -1\}$. Given an input $x \in \mathbb{Z}_2^n$, a computation over the tree is executed as follows: Starting at the root, stop if it's a leaf, and output its label. Otherwise, query its label x_i. If $x_i = 0$, then recursively evaluate the left subtree, and if $x_i = 1$, evaluate the right subtree.*

A decision tree T computes a function f if for every $x \in \mathbb{Z}_2^n$, the computation of x over T outputs $f(x)$. The *depth* of a decision tree is the maximal length of a path from the root to a leaf. The decision tree complexity of f, denoted $D(f)$, is the depth of a minimal-depth tree computing f. Since one can always simply query all the variables of the input, it holds that for any Boolean function f, $D(f) \leq n$. A comprehensive survey of decision tree complexity, as well as other related complexity measures, can be found in [5].

In the context of Fourier analysis, even a function with simple Fourier spectrum, such as the parity function over n bits, which has only 1 nonzero Fourier coefficient, requires a full binary decision tree for its computation, and in particular its depth is n. This example suggests that a more suitable computational model for understanding the connection between the computational complexity and the Fourier expansion of a function is the *parity decision tree* model, first presented by Kushilevitz and Mansour ([15]).

DEFINITION 2.2 ($\oplus$-DT). *A parity decision tree is a labeled binary tree T, in which every internal node is labeled by a linear function $\alpha \in \mathbb{Z}_2^n$, and each leaf with a bit $b \in \{+1, -1\}$. Whenever a computation over an input x arrives at an internal node, it queries $\langle \alpha, x \rangle$ (where the inner product is carried modulo 2). If $\langle \alpha, x \rangle = 0$ it recursively evaluates the left subtree, and if $\langle \alpha, x \rangle = 1$, it evaluates the right subtree. When the computation reaches a leaf it outputs its label.*

Namely, a $\oplus$-DT can make an arbitrary linear query in every internal node (and in particular, compute the parity of n bits using a single query). Since a query of a single variable is linear, this model is an extension of the regular decision tree model.

The depth of the minimal-depth parity decision tree which computes f is denoted $D^{\oplus}(f)$, thus $D^{\oplus}(f) \leq D(f)$. As the example of the parity function shows, the parity decision tree model is strictly stronger than the model of decision trees. We also denote by $\text{size}_{\oplus}(f)$ the size (i.e. number of leaves) of a minimal-size $\oplus$-DT computing f.

2.2 Fourier Transform

We represent Boolean functions as functions $f : \mathbb{Z}_2^n \to \{+1, -1\} \subseteq \mathbb{R}$ where -1 represents the Boolean value "True" and 1 represents the Boolean value "False". For a vector of n bits α, α_i denotes its i-th coordinate. The set of 2^n group characters $\{\chi_\alpha : \mathbb{Z}_2^n \to \{+1, -1\} \mid \alpha \in \mathbb{Z}_2^n\}$, with $\chi_\alpha(x) = (-1)^{\sum_{i=1}^n \alpha_i x_i}$ for every $\alpha \in \mathbb{Z}_2^n$, forms a basis of the vector space of functions from $\mathbb{Z}_2^n$ into $\mathbb{R}$. Furthermore, the basis is orthonormal with respect to the inner product[3]

$$\langle f, g \rangle = \mathop{\mathbb{E}}_x [f(x)g(x)]$$

where the expectation is taken over the uniform distribution over $\mathbb{Z}_2^n$. The *Fourier expansion* of a function $f : \mathbb{Z}_2^n \to \{+1, -1\}$ is its unique representation as a linear combination of those group characters:

$$f(x) = \sum_{\alpha \in \mathbb{Z}_2^n} \hat{f}(\alpha)\chi_\alpha(x).$$

Two of the basic identities of Fourier analysis, which follow from the orthonormality of the basis, are:

1. $\hat{f}(\alpha) = \langle f, \chi_\alpha \rangle = \mathbb{E}_x [f(x)\chi_\alpha(x)]$
2. (Plancherel's Theorem) $\langle f, g \rangle = \mathbb{E}_x [f(x)g(x)] = \sum_{\alpha \in \mathbb{Z}_2^n} \hat{f}(\alpha)\hat{g}(\alpha)$.

The case $f = g$ in Plancherel's theorem is called *Parseval's Identity*. Furthermore, when f is Boolean, $f^2 = 1$, which implies

$$\sum_{\alpha \in \mathbb{Z}_2^n} \hat{f}(\alpha)^2 = 1. \qquad (4)$$

We define two basic complexity measures for Boolean functions:

DEFINITION 2.3. *Let $f : \mathbb{Z}_2^n \to \{+1, -1\}$ be a Boolean function. The* sparsity *of f, denoted* $\text{spar}(f)$*, is the number of non-zero Fourier coefficients, namely*

$$\text{spar}(f) = \#\left\{\alpha \in \mathbb{Z}_2^n \mid \hat{f}(\alpha) \neq 0\right\}.$$

A function f is said to be s-*sparse* if $\text{spar}(f) \leq s$.

DEFINITION 2.4. *Let $f : \mathbb{Z}_2^n \to \{+1, -1\}$ be a Boolean function. The L_1 norm (also dubbed the* spectral norm*) of f is defined as*

$$\|\hat{f}\|_1 = \sum_{\alpha \in \mathbb{Z}_2^n} |\hat{f}(\alpha)|.$$

[3]Later when we study of functions over $\mathbb{Z}_p^n$ we define the inner product to be $\mathbb{E}_x \left[f(x)\overline{g(x)}\right]$.

For every $f : \mathbb{Z}_2^n \to \{+1,-1\}$ it holds that $\|\hat{f}\|_1 \geq \|f\|_\infty = 1$ (where $\|f\|_\infty = \max_{x\in\mathbb{Z}_2^n} |f(x)|$). We later show (Lemma 3.5) that equality is obtained if and only if $f = \pm\chi_\alpha$ for some $\alpha \in \mathbb{Z}_2^n$.

These measures are related to parity decision trees using the following simple lemma, which is a special case of a more general result (see [2]). For completeness we give the proof of the lemma in Appendix A.

LEMMA 2.5. *Let $f : \mathbb{Z}_2^n \to \{+1,-1\}$ be a Boolean function computed by a $\oplus$-DT T of depth k and size m. Then:*

1. $\mathrm{spar}(f) \leq m2^k \leq 4^k$.
2. $\|\hat{f}\|_1 \leq m \leq 2^k$.

In the upcoming sections we consider restrictions of Boolean functions to (affine) subspaces of $\mathbb{Z}_2^n$. We denote by $f|_V$ the restriction of f to a subspace $V \subseteq \mathbb{Z}_2^n$. For any $\alpha \neq 0$, the set $\{x \mid \chi_\alpha(x) = 1\}$ is a subspace of $\mathbb{Z}_2^n$ of co-dimension 1. The restriction of f to this subspace is denoted $f|_{\chi_\alpha=1}$. Similarly, the set $\{x \mid \chi_\alpha(x) = -1\}$ is an affine subspace of co-dimension 1, and we denote with $f|_{\chi_\alpha=-1}$ the restriction of f to this affine subspace. It can be shown (cf. [20], Chapter 3, Section 3.3) that under such a restriction, the coefficients $\hat{f}(\beta)$ and $\hat{f}(\alpha+\beta)$ (for every $\beta \in \mathbb{Z}_2^n$) collapse to a single Fourier coefficient whose absolute value is $|\hat{f}(\beta) + \hat{f}(\alpha+\beta)|$. Similarly, in the Fourier transform of $f|_{\chi_\alpha=-1}$, they collapse to a single coefficient whose absolute value is $|\hat{f}(\beta) - \hat{f}(\alpha+\beta)|$. This in particular implies that $\|\hat{f}\|_1$ and $\mathrm{spar}(f)$ do not increase when f is restricted to such a subspace. Indeed, both facts follow easily from the representation

$$f(x) = \sum_{\beta\in\mathbb{Z}_2^n/\langle\alpha\rangle} \left(\hat{f}(\beta) + \hat{f}(\beta+\alpha)\chi_\alpha(x)\right)\chi_\beta(x)\,, \tag{5}$$

where $\mathbb{Z}_2^n/\langle\alpha\rangle$ denotes the cosets of the subgroup $\langle\alpha\rangle = \{0,\alpha\}$ in $\mathbb{Z}_2^n$. When studying a restricted function, say $f' = f|_{\chi_\alpha(x)=1}$, we shall abuse notation and denote with $\widehat{f'}(\beta)$ the term corresponding to the coset $\beta + \langle\alpha\rangle$. Namely, $\widehat{f'}(\beta) = \hat{f}(\beta) + \hat{f}(\beta+\alpha)$. (similarly, for $f'' = f|_{\chi_\alpha(x)=-1}$, we shall denote $\widehat{f''}(\beta) = \hat{f}(\beta) - \hat{f}(\beta+\alpha)$.) Thus, in f' both $\widehat{f'}(\beta)$ and $\widehat{f'}(\beta+\alpha)$ refer to the same Fourier coefficient as we only consider coefficients modulo $\langle\alpha\rangle$ (similarly for f'').

3. BOOLEAN FUNCTIONS WITH SMALL SPECTRAL NORM

In this section we prove our main results for functions over the Boolean cube. While many of the proofs and techniques used for general primes also apply to the case $p = 2$, we find the case $p = 2$ substantially simpler, so we present the proofs for this case separately.

3.1 Basic tools

In this section we prove the following lemma, which states that for every Boolean function $f : \mathbb{Z}_2^n \to \{+1,-1\}$, with small spectral norm, there exists a linear function χ_γ such that both restrictions $f|_{\chi_\gamma=1}$ and $f|_{\chi_\gamma=-1}$ have noticeable smaller spectral norms compared to f. In Section 4 we give a generalization of the lemma for functions $f : \mathbb{Z}_p^n \to \{+1,-1\}$ (Lemma 4.1).

LEMMA 3.1 (MAIN LEMMA FOR FUNCTIONS OVER $\mathbb{Z}_2^n$). *Let $f : \mathbb{Z}_2^n \to \{+1,-1\}$ be a Boolean function. Let $\hat{f}(\alpha)$ be f's maximal Fourier coefficient in absolute value, and $\hat{f}(\beta)$ be the second largest, and suppose $\hat{f}(\beta) \neq 0$. Let $f' = f|_{\chi_{\alpha+\beta}=1}$ and $f'' = f|_{\chi_{\alpha+\beta}=-1}$. Then, if $\hat{f}(\alpha)\hat{f}(\beta) > 0$ then it holds that*

$$\|\hat{f'}\|_1 \leq \|\hat{f}\|_1 - |\hat{f}(\alpha)| \quad \textit{and} \quad \|\hat{f''}\|_1 \leq \|\hat{f}\|_1 - |\hat{f}(\beta)|.$$

If $\hat{f}(\alpha)\hat{f}(\beta) < 0$ then

$$\|\hat{f'}\|_1 \leq \|\hat{f}\|_1 - |\hat{f}(\beta)| \quad \textit{and} \quad \|\hat{f''}\|_1 \leq \|\hat{f}\|_1 - |\hat{f}(\alpha)|.$$

The proof of the lemma follows from analyzing the simple equation $f^2 = 1$.

LEMMA 3.2. *Let $f : \mathbb{Z}_2^n \to \{+1,-1\}$ be a Boolean function. For all $\alpha \neq 0$, it holds that*

$$\sum_\gamma \hat{f}(\gamma)\hat{f}(\alpha+\gamma) = 0.$$

PROOF. Since f is Boolean we have that $f^2 = 1$. In the Fourier representation,

$$\left(\sum_\gamma \hat{f}(\gamma)\chi_\gamma(x)\right)\left(\sum_\beta \hat{f}(\beta)\chi_\beta(x)\right) = 1.$$

Then $\sum_\gamma \hat{f}(\gamma)\hat{f}(\alpha+\gamma)$ is the Fourier coefficient $\widehat{f^2}(\alpha)$ of the function f^2 at α. However, if $\alpha \neq 0$ then this coefficient equals 0 by the uniqueness of the Fourier expansion of the function $f^2 = 1$. ☐

PROOF OF LEMMA 3.1. Without loss of generality assume that $\hat{f}(\alpha)\hat{f}(\beta) > 0$, i.e. they have the same sign (the other case is completely analogous.) By Lemma 3.2,

$$\sum_{\gamma\in\mathbb{Z}_2^n} \hat{f}(\gamma)\hat{f}(\alpha+\beta+\gamma) = 0. \tag{6}$$

Let $N_{\alpha+\beta} \subseteq \mathbb{Z}_2^n$ be the set of vectors γ such that $\hat{f}(\gamma)\hat{f}(\alpha+\beta+\gamma) < 0$ (Note that by assumption, $\alpha, \beta \notin N_{\alpha+\beta}$). Switching sides in (6), we get:

$$2\left|\hat{f}(\alpha)\hat{f}(\beta)\right| = \sum_{\gamma\in N_{\alpha+\beta}} \left|\hat{f}(\gamma)\hat{f}(\alpha+\beta+\gamma)\right| - \sum_{\substack{\gamma\notin N_{\alpha+\beta}\\ \gamma\neq\alpha,\beta}} \left|\hat{f}(\gamma)\hat{f}(\alpha+\beta+\gamma)\right|.$$

In particular,

$$|\hat{f}(\alpha)||\hat{f}(\beta)| \leq \frac{1}{2}\sum_{\gamma\in N_{\alpha+\beta}} \left|\hat{f}(\gamma)\hat{f}(\alpha+\beta+\gamma)\right|. \tag{7}$$

We now use the fact that $\hat{f}(\beta)$ is the second largest in absolute value, and $\hat{f}(\alpha)$ does not appear in the sum, to bound the right hand side:

$$\sum_{\gamma\in N_{\alpha+\beta}} \left|\hat{f}(\gamma)\hat{f}(\alpha+\beta+\gamma)\right| \leq |\hat{f}(\beta)| \sum_{\gamma\in N_{\alpha+\beta}} \min\left\{|\hat{f}(\gamma)|, |\hat{f}(\alpha+\beta+\gamma)|\right\}. \tag{8}$$

Then (7) and (8) (as well as the assumption $|\hat{f}(\beta)| > 0$) together imply

$$|\hat{f}(\alpha)| \le \frac{1}{2} \sum_{\gamma \in N_{\alpha+\beta}} \min\left\{|\hat{f}(\gamma)|, |\hat{f}(\alpha+\beta+\gamma)|\right\}. \qquad (9)$$

Let $f' = f|_{\chi_{\alpha+\beta}=1}$. Then for every γ the coefficients $\hat{f}(\gamma)$ and $\hat{f}(\alpha+\beta+\gamma)$ collapse to a single coefficient whose absolute value is $|\hat{f}(\gamma) + \hat{f}(\alpha+\beta+\gamma)|$ (recall Equation (5)). For $\gamma \in N_{\alpha+\beta}$,

$$|\hat{f}(\gamma) + \hat{f}(\alpha+\beta+\gamma)| = \Big||\hat{f}(\gamma)| - |\hat{f}(\alpha+\beta+\gamma)|\Big|$$

which reduces the L_1 norm of f' compared to that of f by at least $\min(|\hat{f}(\gamma)|, |\hat{f}(\alpha+\beta+\gamma)|)$. In total, since both γ and $\alpha+\beta+\gamma$ belong to $N_{\alpha+\beta}$, we get:

$$\|\widehat{f'}\|_1 \le \|\hat{f}\|_1 - \frac{1}{2} \sum_{\gamma \in N_{\alpha+\beta}} \min\left\{|\hat{f}(\gamma)|, |\hat{f}(\alpha+\beta+\gamma)|\right\}.$$

Therefore by (9) we have

$$\|\widehat{f'}\|_1 \le \|\hat{f}\|_1 - |\hat{f}(\alpha)|.$$

When we consider $f'' = f|_{\chi_{\alpha+\beta}=-1}$ we clearly have that for $\gamma = \alpha$,

$$|\widehat{f''}(\gamma)| = |\hat{f}(\gamma) - \hat{f}(\alpha+\beta+\gamma)| = |\hat{f}(\alpha)| - |\hat{f}(\beta)|.$$

Hence,

$$\|\widehat{f''}\|_1 \le \|\hat{f}\|_1 - |\hat{f}(\beta)|.$$

□

Next, we show that any Boolean function with small spectral norm has a large Fourier coefficient.

LEMMA 3.3. *Let $f : \mathbb{Z}_2^n \to \{+1,-1\}$ be a Boolean function. Denote $A = \|\hat{f}\|_1$, and let $\hat{f}(\alpha)$ be f's maximal Fourier coefficient in absolute value. Then $|\hat{f}(\alpha)| \ge 1/A$. Furthermore, let $\hat{f}(\beta)$ be f's second largest Fourier coefficient in absolute value. Then $|\hat{f}(\beta)| > (1-\hat{f}(\alpha)^2)/\|\hat{f}\|_1 = (1-\hat{f}(\alpha)^2)/A$.*

PROOF. By Parseval's identity,

$$1 = \mathbb{E}[f^2] = \sum_\gamma \hat{f}(\gamma)^2.$$

Now note that

$$1 = \sum_\gamma \hat{f}(\gamma)^2 \le |\hat{f}(\alpha)| \sum_\gamma |\hat{f}(\gamma)| \le A|\hat{f}(\alpha)|,$$

which implies that indeed $|\hat{f}(\alpha)| \ge 1/A$. The second statement follows similarly, since

$$1 - \hat{f}(\alpha)^2 = \sum_{\gamma \ne \alpha} \hat{f}(\gamma)^2 \le |\hat{f}(\beta)| \sum_{\gamma \ne \alpha} |\hat{f}(\gamma)| < \|\hat{f}\|_1 \cdot |\hat{f}(\beta)| = A|\hat{f}(\beta)|.$$

□

COROLLARY 3.4. *Let $f : \mathbb{Z}_2^n \to \{+1,-1\}$ be a Boolean function such that $\|\hat{f}\|_1 = A > 1$. Then there exists $\gamma \in \mathbb{Z}_2^n$ and $b \in \{+1,-1\}$ such that $\|\widehat{f|_{\chi_\gamma=b}}\|_1 \le A - 1/A$.*

PROOF. The assumption $A > 1$ implies the second largest coefficient, $\hat{f}(\beta)$, is non-zero, and then the result is immediate from Lemma 3.1 and Lemma 3.3. □

3.2 Proofs of Theorems

We now show how Theorems 1.1,1.2,1.4 and 1.5 follow as simple consequences of Lemma 3.1.

LEMMA 3.5. *Let $f : \mathbb{Z}_2^n \to \{+1,-1\}$ be a Boolean function such that $\|\hat{f}\|_1 = 1$. Then $f = \pm\chi_\alpha$ for some $\alpha \in \mathbb{Z}_2^n$.*

PROOF. By Parseval's identity and the assumption, we get

$$\sum_\gamma \hat{f}(\gamma)^2 = 1 = \sum_\gamma |\hat{f}(\gamma)|.$$

For all γ we have that $|\hat{f}(\gamma)| \in [0,1]$, so $|\hat{f}(\gamma)| < \hat{f}(\gamma)^2$ unless $|\hat{f}(\gamma)| = 1$ or $\hat{f}(\gamma) = 0$, and the proposition follows. □

Corollary 3.4 and Lemma 3.5 imply Theorem 1.1:

THEOREM 3.6 (THEOREM 1.1, RESTATED). *Let $f : \mathbb{Z}_2^n \to \{+1,-1\}$ be such that $\|\hat{f}\|_1 = A$, then, there is an affine subspace $V \subseteq \mathbb{Z}_2^n$ of co-dimension at most A^2 such that f is constant on V.*

PROOF. Apply Corollary 3.4 iteratively on f. After less than A^2 steps, we are left with a function g which is a restriction of f on an affine subspace defined by the restrictions so far, such that $\|\hat{g}\|_1 = 1$. By Lemma 3.5, $g = \pm\chi_\alpha$ for some $\alpha \in \mathbb{Z}_2^n$. If $\alpha \ne 0$ we further restrict g on $\chi_\alpha = 1$ to get a restriction of f which is constant. □

We note that the proof of Theorem 1.1 actually implies that f is constant on a subspace of co-dimension at most $\binom{A+1}{2}$. As mentioned earlier, an extra observation improves the co-dimension to $O(A)$ [23].

THEOREM 3.7 (THEOREM 1.2, RESTATED). *Let $f : \mathbb{Z}_2^n \to \{+1,-1\}$ be such that $\|\hat{f}\|_1 = A$, then $\mathrm{size}_\oplus(f) \le 2^{A^2} n^{2A}$.*

PROOF. Let

$$L(n, A) \stackrel{\text{def}}{=} \max_{\substack{f:\mathbb{Z}_2^n \to \{+1,-1\} \\ \|\hat{f}\|_1 \le A}} \mathrm{size}_\oplus(f).$$

We show, by induction on n, that $L(n, A) \le 2^{A^2} \cdot n^{2A}$.

For $n = 1$ the result is trivial.

Let $n > 1$ and further assume that $A > 1$ (if $A = 1$ then the claim follows from Lemma 3.5). Let $\hat{f}(\alpha), \hat{f}(\beta)$ be the first and second largest Fourier coefficients in absolute value, respectively. By Lemma 3.3 we are in one of the following cases:

1. $|\hat{f}(\alpha)| \ge 1/2$
2. $1/2 > |\hat{f}(\alpha)| \ge 1/A$ and $|\hat{f}(\beta)| > \frac{1-\hat{f}(\alpha)^2}{A} \ge \frac{3}{4A}$.

Consider the tree whose first query is the linear function χ_γ where $\gamma = \alpha + \beta$ (i.e. we branch left or right according to the value of $\langle x, \gamma \rangle$). By the choice of γ we obtain the following recursion: In case 1,

$$L(n, A) \le L(n-1, A-1/2) + L(n-1, A);$$

While in case 2,

$$L(n, A) \le L(n-1, A-1/A) + L(n-1, A-3/(4A)).$$

Note also that in the second case $A \geq 2$, or else $|\hat{f}(\alpha)| \geq 1/2$ by Lemma 3.3. Induction follows in the first case as

$$\begin{aligned} L(n, A) &\leq L(n-1, A-1/2) + L(n-1, A) \\ &\leq 2^{(A-1/2)^2} \cdot (n-1)^{2(A-1/2)} + 2^{A^2} \cdot (n-1)^{2A} \\ &\leq 2^{A^2} \cdot (n-1)^{2(A-1/2)} (1 + (n-1)) \\ &< 2^{A^2} \cdot n^{2A} . \end{aligned}$$

In the second case we have

$$\begin{aligned} L(n, A) &\leq L(n-1, A-1/A) + L(n-1, A-3/(4A)) \\ &\leq 2^{(A-1/A)^2} \cdot (n-1)^{2(A-1/A)} + \\ &\quad 2^{(A-3/(4A))^2} \cdot (n-1)^{2(A-3/(4A))} \\ &\leq 2^{A^2} \cdot n^{2A} \left(2^{-2+1/A^2} + 2^{-3/2+(3/4)^2/A^2}\right) \\ &\leq 2^{A^2} \cdot n^{2A} , \end{aligned}$$

where in the last inequality we used the fact that $A \geq 2$. □

As the AND function demonstrates, this argument gives a result that is tight up to a polynomial factor in some cases.

THEOREM 3.8 (THEOREM 1.4, RESTATED). *Let $f : \mathbb{Z}_2^n \to \{+1, -1\}$ be such that $\|\hat{f}\|_1 = A$ and* spar$(f) = s$. *Then $D^{\oplus}(f) \leq A^2 \log s$.*

PROOF. By Theorem 1.1, there exist A^2 linear functions $\alpha_1, \ldots, \alpha_{A^2}$ that can be fixed to values $b_1, \ldots, b_{A^2}$, respectively, where $b_i \in \{+1, -1\}$ for $1 \leq i \leq A^2$, such that f restricted to the subspace $\{x \mid \chi_{\alpha_i}(x) = b_i \ , \ \forall 1 \leq i \leq A^2\}$ is constant. This implies that for any non-zero coefficient $\hat{f}(\beta)$ there exists at least one other non-zero coefficient $\hat{f}(\beta + \gamma)$ for $\gamma \in \text{span}\{\alpha_1, \ldots, \alpha_{A^2}\}$. Indeed, if no such coefficient exists then the restriction $f|_{\chi_{\alpha_1}(x)=b_1, \ldots, \chi_{\alpha_{A^2}}=b^2}$ will have the non-constant term $\hat{f}(\beta) \cdot \chi_\beta$ (for example, this can be easily obtained from Equation (5)). Therefore, for any other fixing of $\chi_{\alpha_1}, \ldots, \chi_{\alpha_{A^2}}$, both $\hat{f}(\beta)\chi_\beta$ and $\hat{f}(\beta+\gamma)\chi_{\beta+\gamma}$ collapse to the same (perhaps non-zero) linear function, which implies that spar$(f|_{\chi_{\alpha_1}=b'_1, \ldots, \chi_{\alpha_{A^2}}=b'_{A^2}}) \leq$ spar$(f)/2$ for any choice of $b'_1, \ldots, b'_{A^2}$. In other words, if we consider the tree of depth A^2 in which on level i all nodes branch according to $\langle \alpha_i, x \rangle$ then restricting f to any path yields a new function with half the sparsity. Thus, we can continue this process by induction for at most $\log s$ steps, until all the functions in the leaves are constant. The resulting tree has depth at most $A^2 \log s$ as claimed. □

Our next goal is proving Theorem 1.5. To this end, we use a lemma which shows that there exists a low depth $\oplus$-DT which computes a function g such that $\Pr_x[f(x) \neq g(x)] \leq \epsilon$, where x is drawn from the uniform distribution over $\mathbb{Z}_2^n$. Recall that the *bias* of a Boolean function f is defined to be

$$\text{bias}(f) \stackrel{\text{def}}{=} \left| \Pr_x[f(x) = 1] - \Pr_x[f(x) = -1] \right| .$$

Alternatively, bias$(f) = |\hat{f}(0)|$.

LEMMA 3.9. *Let $f : \mathbb{Z}_2^n \to \{+1, -1\}$ be a Boolean function with $\|\hat{f}\|_1 \leq A$. Then, there exists a $\oplus$-DT of depth at most $O(A^2 + \log(1/\epsilon))$ that computes a function g such that $\Pr_x[f(x) \neq g(x)] \leq 2\epsilon$. Furthermore, the size of the tree is at most $2^{O(A^2)} \min\{1/\epsilon^2, O(\log(1/\epsilon))^{2A}\}$.*

PROOF. Let $K = \max\{10A^2, 2\log(1/\epsilon)\}$ be a bound on the depth of the tree. In order to construct the $\oplus$-DT, we use a recursive argument that stops whenever we reach a highly biased leaf (with bias at least $1-2\epsilon$), or after K levels of recursion, and then show that for a uniformly random $x \in \mathbb{Z}_2^n$, x arrives at a highly biased leaf with probability $\geq 1 - \epsilon$, hence proving the statement of the lemma.

Let $\hat{f}(\alpha)$ be f's largest coefficient in absolute value, and $\hat{f}(\beta)$ the second largest. Note that if $|\hat{f}(0)| > 1 - 2\epsilon$ we are done. Hence, we consider two cases:

1. $|\hat{f}(\alpha)| > 1 - \epsilon$ for $\alpha \neq 0$:

   We first show that if $|\hat{f}(\alpha)| > 1-\epsilon$ then $|\hat{f}(0)| < \epsilon$. By considering $-f$ instead of f, if needed, we may assume without the loss of generality $\hat{f}(\alpha) > 1 - \epsilon$. Note that

   $$\begin{aligned} 1 - \epsilon < \hat{f}(\alpha) &= \Pr[f = \chi_\alpha] - \Pr[f \neq \chi_\alpha] \\ &= (1 - \Pr[f \neq \chi_\alpha]) - \Pr[f \neq \chi_\alpha], \end{aligned}$$

   so $\Pr[f \neq \chi_\alpha] < \epsilon/2$. Now, since $\mathbb{E}[\chi_\alpha] = 0$, we have

   $$\begin{aligned} |\hat{f}(0)| &= |\mathbb{E}[f]| = |\mathbb{E}[f] - \mathbb{E}[\chi_\alpha]| = |\mathbb{E}[f - \chi_\alpha]| \\ &\leq \mathbb{E}[|f - \chi_\alpha|] = 2\Pr[f \neq \chi_\alpha] < \epsilon. \end{aligned}$$

   In this case we query on χ_α. Note that no matter what value χ_α obtains, the restricted function has bias at least $|\hat{f}(\alpha)| - |\hat{f}(0)| > 1 - 2\epsilon$, and we terminate the recursion.

2. $|\hat{f}(\alpha)| \leq 1 - \epsilon$:

   In this case we query on $\chi_{\alpha+\beta}$. Let $f' = f|_{\chi_{\alpha+\beta}=1}$ and $f'' = f|_{\chi_{\alpha+\beta}=-1}$ By Lemma 3.1, for at least one of f' and f'', the spectral norm drops by at least $1/A$. We continue by induction the construction on f' and f'', terminating when all the leaves are highly biased (in particular this includes the case of a constant leaf), or after at most K levels of recursion.

Note that if we replace each highly biased leaf in the $\oplus$-DT with the constant it is biased towards (i.e. by the sign of its constant term), the total error of the $\oplus$-DT would increase by at most ϵ.

It remains to be shown that the fraction of inputs $x \in \mathbb{Z}_2^n$ that arrive at an unbiased leaf is at most ϵ. We say that an internal node labeled χ_γ is norm-reducing for x, if $\chi_\gamma(x) = b$ and the restriction on $\chi_\gamma = b$ reduces the spectral norm by at least $1/A$. Clearly, a computation over any input x which traverses A^2 norm reducing nodes for x arrives at a constant leaf. Furthermore, by construction, all the leaves which are not highly biased appear in the K-th level of the tree. Hence, an input which arrives at an unbiased node satisfies K independent linear equations, for which at most A^2 are norm reducing. Since for every fixed $0 \neq \gamma \in \mathbb{Z}_2^n$ and $b \in \{+1, -1\}$ the probability that $\chi_\gamma(x) = b$ is exactly $1/2$, the probability that x arrives at a non highly biased node is bounded by[4]

$$\sum_{i=0}^{A^2-1} \frac{\binom{K}{i}}{2^K} \leq 2^{-K} A^2 \binom{K}{A^2} \leq 2^{(-K/2)} \leq \epsilon$$

by the choice of K.

[4]We count how many words in $\{0,1\}^K$ with fewer than A^2 1's are there.

To prove the upper bound on the size of the tree we first note that 2^K is a trivial upper bound. Moreover, as in the proof of Theorem 1.2, the construction that we have satisfies the recursion formula

$$S(K-d,B) \leq$$
$$\max\{S(K-(d+1),B-1/2)+S(K-(d+1),B),$$
$$S(K-(d+1),B-1/B)+S(K-(d+1),B-3/(4B))\},$$

where $S(K-d,B)$ stands for the number of leaves in the tree rooted at a node v at depth d such that the function f_v computed at v satisfies $\|\hat{f}_v\|_1 \leq B$. As before, the solution to this recursion is $S(K,A) \leq 2^{A^2}K^{2A}$. Overall, we have that the size of the approximating parity decision tree is at most:

$$\begin{aligned}\min\left\{2^K, 2^{A^2}K^{2A}\right\} &= \min\left\{\max\left\{2^{10A^2}, \epsilon^{-2}\right\},\right.\\ &\left. 2^{A^2}\cdot\max\left\{(2\log(1/\epsilon))^{2A}, (10A^2)^{2A}\right\}\right\}\\ &\leq \min\left\{2^{10A^2}\cdot\epsilon^{-2},\right.\\ &\left. 2^{A^2}\cdot(10A^2)^{2A}\cdot(2\log(1/\epsilon))^{2A}\right\}\\ &\leq 2^{O(A^2)}\cdot\min\left\{\epsilon^{-2}, O(\log(1/\epsilon))^{2A}\right\}\end{aligned}$$

as claimed. □

In fact, in the proof of Lemma 3.9, we could have continued the recursion until reaching a constant leaf or depth K, but for the sake of understanding the proof of Theorem 1.5 it may be more clear to keep the current version in mind.

The proof of Theorem 1.5 follows by combining Lemma 3.9 with the well known result of Goldreich and Levin [7] and of Kushilevitz and Mansour [15], who showed that given a query oracle to a function f, with high probability, one can approximate its large Fourier coefficients in polynomial time.

Lemma 3.10 ([7, 15]). *There exists a randomized algorithm, such that given a query oracle to a function $f:\mathbb{Z}_2^n \to \{+1,-1\}$, and parameters δ,θ,η, outputs, with probability at least $1-\delta$, a list containing all of f's Fourier coefficients whose absolute value is at least θ. Furthermore, the algorithm outputs an additive approximation of at most η to each of these coefficients. The algorithm runs in polynomial time in n, $1/\theta$, $1/\eta$ and $\log(1/\delta)$.*

Proof of Theorem 1.5. We use the algorithm from Lemma 3.10 to find f's largest Fourier coefficient in absolute value, $\hat{f}(\alpha)$. Whenever $|\hat{f}(\alpha)| \leq 1-\epsilon$, Lemma 3.3 implies $|\hat{f}(\beta)| > \frac{1-\hat{f}(\alpha)^2}{\|\hat{f}\|_1} \geq \frac{1-\hat{f}(\alpha)^2}{A} > \epsilon/A$, so the same algorithm can be used to find the second largest coefficient, $\hat{f}(\beta)$, in time $\mathsf{poly}(n, A, 1/\epsilon, \log(1/\delta))$. We use Lemma 3.9 to construct a $\oplus$-DT. The bound on the running time follows from the size of the $\oplus$-DT and the running time of the algorithm from Lemma 3.10.

In fact, there is a slight inaccuracy in the argument above. Note that Lemma 3.10 only guarantees that we find a coefficient that is approximately the largest one. However, if it is the case that the second largest coefficient is very close to the largest one, then in Lemma 3.9 when we branch according to $\chi_{\alpha+\beta}$ both children have significantly smaller spectral norm.

If it is the case that we correctly identified the largest Fourier coefficient but failed to identify the second largest then we note that if our approximation is good enough, say better than $\epsilon/2A$, then even if we are mistaken and branch according to $\chi_{\alpha+\beta'}$ where $\left||\hat{f}(\beta)|-|\hat{f}(\beta')|\right| < \epsilon/2A$, the the argument in Lemma 3.9 still works, perhaps with a slightly worse constant in the big O. □

4. FUNCTIONS OVER $\mathbb{Z}_p^n$ WITH SMALL SPECTRAL NORM

In this section, we state our results to functions $f:\mathbb{Z}_p^n \to \{+1,-1\}$ where p is any fixed prime. Throughout this section we assume $p>2$. We start by giving some basic facts on the Fourier transform over $\mathbb{Z}_p^n$.

4.1 Preliminaries

Let $\omega = e^{\frac{2\pi i}{p}} \in \mathbb{C}$ be a primitive root of unity of order p. The set of p^n group characters

$$\{\chi_\alpha : \mathbb{Z}_p^n \to \mathbb{C} \mid \alpha \in \mathbb{Z}_p^n\}$$

where $\chi_\alpha(x) = \omega^{\langle\alpha,x\rangle}$, is a basis for the vector space of functions from $\mathbb{Z}_p^n$ into $\mathbb{C}$, and is orthonormal with respect to the inner product $\langle f,g\rangle = \mathbb{E}_x[f(x)\overline{g(x)}]$.[5] We now have that $\hat{f}(\alpha) = \mathbb{E}_x[f(x)\overline{\chi_\alpha(x)}]$ and $f = \sum_{\alpha\in\mathbb{Z}_p^n}\hat{f}(\alpha)\chi_\alpha$. Plancherel's theorem holds here as well and the sparsity and L_1 norm are defined in the same way as they were defined for functions $f:\mathbb{Z}_2^n \to \{+1,-1\}$. Lemma 3.3 also extends to functions $f:\mathbb{Z}_p^n \to \{+1,-1\}$, with virtually the same proof. When f is real-valued (and in particular, a Boolean function), then $\hat{f}(0) = \mathbb{E}[f]$ is real, and it can also be directly verified that $\hat{f}(\alpha) = \overline{\hat{f}(-\alpha)}$.

We have the analog to Equation (5):

$$f(x) = \sum_{\beta\in\mathbb{Z}_p^n/\langle\alpha\rangle}\left(\sum_{k=0}^{p-1}\hat{f}(\beta+k\cdot\alpha)(\chi_\alpha(x))^k\right)\chi_\beta(x)\,. \quad (10)$$

Hence, when f is restricted to an affine subspace on which $\chi_\alpha = \omega^\lambda$ (where $0\leq\lambda\leq p-1$), then for every[6] $\beta\in\mathbb{Z}_p^n/\langle\alpha\rangle$ we have

$$\hat{g}(\beta) = \sum_{k=0}^{p-1}\omega^{\lambda k}\hat{f}(\beta+k\alpha).$$

For every $\beta\in\mathbb{Z}_p^n$, we denote by $[\beta]_\alpha = \beta+\langle\alpha\rangle$ the coset of $\langle\alpha\rangle$ in which β resides.

Lemma 3.2 now becomes:

$$\sum_{\alpha\in\mathbb{Z}_p^n}\hat{f}(\alpha)\hat{f}(\beta-\alpha) = 0 \quad (11)$$

for all $0\neq\beta\in\mathbb{Z}_p^n$.

As a generalization of the $\oplus$-DT model, we define a p-ary linear decision tree, denoted $\oplus_p$-DT, to be a computation tree where every internal node v is labeled by a linear function $\gamma\in\mathbb{Z}_p^n$ and has p children. The edges between v and its children are labeled $0,1,\ldots,p-1$, and on an input x, it computes $\langle\gamma,x\rangle$ mod p and branches accordingly. We carry along from the binary case the notation $D^{\oplus_p}(f)$ and $\text{size}_{\oplus_p}(f)$, and define them to be the depth (respectively, size) of a minimal-depth (resp. size) $\oplus_p$-DT computing f.

[5] For a complex number z, we denote by $\overline{z}$ its complex conjugate.

[6] Recall that $\langle\alpha\rangle$ is the additive group generated by α and $\mathbb{Z}_p^n/\langle\alpha\rangle$ is the set of cosets of $\langle\alpha\rangle$.

4.2 Basic tools

In this section we state the basic tools required for generalizing the theorems for functions defined on $\mathbb{Z}_2^n$ to functions $f : \mathbb{Z}_p^n \to \{+1, -1\}$. As a generalization of Lemma 3.1, we show a slightly more complex and detailed argument:

LEMMA 4.1 (MAIN LEMMA FOR FUNCTIONS OVER $\mathbb{Z}_p^n$). *Let $f : \mathbb{Z}_p^n \to \{+1, -1\}$ be a non-constant Boolean function such that $\|\hat{f}\|_1 = A$. Let $\hat{f}(\alpha)$ be its largest coefficient in absolute value, and $\hat{f}(\beta)$ be the second largest. Then there exist a universal constant c_0 and a constant $c_1 = c_1(p) = O(1/p^2)$ such that*

1. *For all $\lambda \in \mathbb{Z}_p$, $\|\widehat{f|_{\chi_{\beta-\alpha}=\omega^\lambda}}\|_1 \leq A - c_0|\hat{f}(\beta)|$.*

2. *There exists at least $m := \lfloor p/3 \rfloor$ distinct elements $\lambda_1, \dots, \lambda_m \in \mathbb{Z}_p$ such that $\|\widehat{f|_{\chi_{\beta-\alpha}=\omega^{\lambda_k}}}\|_1 \leq A - c_0|\hat{f}(\alpha)| \leq A - c_0/A$ for $k = 1, \dots, m$.*

3. *There exists at least $p - 1$ distinct elements $\lambda_1, \dots, \lambda_{p-1} \in \mathbb{Z}_p$ such that $\|\widehat{f|_{\chi_{\beta-\alpha}=\omega^{\lambda_k}}}\|_1 \leq A - c_1 \cdot |\hat{f}(\alpha)| \leq A - c_1/A$ for $k = 1, \dots, p-1$.*

4.3 Analogs of Theorems 1.1, 1.2, 1.4 and 1.5

Theorems 4.2, 4.3, 4.5 and 4.6 now follow as consequences of Lemma 4.1. Their proofs use the same arguments we used to deduce their $\mathbb{Z}_2^n$ counterparts from Lemma 3.1. We use the notation $O_p(\cdot)$ when the underlying constant depends on p, whereas when we use $O(\cdot)$, the underlying constant is some absolute constant.

THEOREM 4.2. *Let $f : \mathbb{Z}_p^n \to \{+1, -1\}$ be a Boolean function with $\|\hat{f}\|_1 = A$. Then there exists an affine subspace $V \subseteq \mathbb{Z}_p^n$ of co-dimension at most $O(A^2)$ such that f is constant on V.*

THEOREM 4.3. *Let $f : \mathbb{Z}_p^n \to \{+1, -1\}$ be a Boolean function with $\|\hat{f}\|_1 = A$. Then $\mathrm{size}_{\oplus_p}(f) \leq p^{O_p(A^2)} n^{O_p(A)}$.*

As an immediate corollary, we get:

COROLLARY 4.4. *Let $f : \mathbb{Z}_p^n \to \{+1, -1\}$ be a Boolean function with $\|\hat{f}\|_1 = A$. Then $f = \sum_{i=1}^{p^{O_p(A^2)} n^{O_p(A)}} \pm \mathbf{1}_{V_i}$, where each V_i is an affine subspace of $\mathbb{Z}_p^n$.*

THEOREM 4.5. *Let $f : \mathbb{Z}_p^n \to \{+1, -1\}$ be such that $\|\hat{f}\|_1 = A$ and $|\{\alpha \mid \hat{f}(\alpha) \neq 0\}| = s$. Then f can be computed by a $\oplus_p$-DT of depth $O(A^2 \log s)$.*

THEOREM 4.6. *Let $f : \mathbb{Z}_p^n \to \{+1, -1\}$ be such that $\|\hat{f}\|_1 = A$. Then for every $\delta, \epsilon > 0$ there is a randomized algorithm that given a query oracle to f outputs (with probability at least $1 - \delta$) a $\oplus_p$-DT of depth $O(A^2 + \log(1/\epsilon))$ and size $\min\{p^{O(A^2+\log(1/\epsilon))}, p^{O_p(A^2)} \cdot O(A^2+\log(1/\epsilon))^{O_p(A)}\}$ that computes a Boolean function g_ϵ such that $dist(f, g_\epsilon) \leq \epsilon$. The algorithm runs in polynomial time in $n, \exp(A^2), 1/\epsilon$ and $\log(1/\delta)$.*

5. CONCLUSIONS AND OPEN PROBLEMS

In this work we obtained structural results for Boolean functions over $\mathbb{Z}_p^n$, for prime p. Our results provide a more refined structure than the one given in the works of Green and Sanders [9, 10]. For a certain range of parameters we also obtain improved results in the setting of the works [9, 10].

We were also able to achieve new results in the field of computational learning theory by showing that such functions can be learned with $\oplus$-DTs as the class of hypotheses.

There are still many intriguing open problems related to the structure of Boolean functions with small spectral norm. Most of these are related to the tightness of our results (as well as to the tightness of the results of Green and Sanders [9]).

We do not believe that the bound given in Equation (2) is tight. Perhaps it is even true that one could represent f as a sum of polynomially (in A) many characteristic functions of subspaces (note that this is not true for functions over general abelian groups. See [10]). Similarly, we do not believe that the bounds we obtain in Theorems 1.2 and 4.3 are tight. It seems more reasonable to believe that the true bound should be $\mathsf{poly}(n, A)$.

Recall that [24, 19] conjectured that Boolean functions with sparse Fourier spectrum can be computed by a $\oplus$-DT of depth $\mathsf{poly}(\log \mathrm{spar}\, f)$. Theorems 1.4 and 4.5 give an affirmative answer only for the case that f also has a small spectral norm. Thus, the general case is still open.

Finally, Theorems 1.5 and 4.6 give shallow $\oplus_p$-DTs approximating functions with small spectral norm. These results too do not seem tight. In particular, it is interesting to understand whether something better can be obtained if we assume in addition that f can be computed exactly by a small $\oplus_p$-DT. Namely, can one output a shallow $\oplus_p$-DT approximating f over the uniform distribution using polynomially many membership queries (i.e. oracle calls) to f, assuming that f can be exactly computed by such a $\oplus_p$-DT (and has a small spectral norm).

6. REFERENCES

[1] M. Alekhnovich, M. Braverman, V. Feldman, A. R. Klivans, and T. Pitassi. The complexity of properly learning simple concept classes. *J. Comput. Syst. Sci.*, 74(1):16–34, 2008.

[2] M. Bellare. A technique for upper bounding the spectral norm with applications to learning. In *Proceedings of the 5th annual COLT*, pages 62–70, 1992.

[3] M. Bellare, D. Coppersmith, J. Håstad, M. A. Kiwi, and M. Sudan. Linearity testing in characteristic two. *IEEE Trans. Inf. Theory.*, 42(6):1781–1795, 1996.

[4] M. Blum, M. Luby, and R. Rubinfeld. Self testing/correcting with applications to numerical problems. *J. Comput. Syst. Sci.*, 47(3):549–595, 1993.

[5] H. Buhrman and R. de Wolf. Complexity measures and decision tree complexity: a survey. *Theor. Comput. Sci.*, 288(1):21–43, 2002.

[6] E. Friedgut. Boolean functions with low average sensitivity depend on few coordinates. *Combinatorica*, 18(1):27–35, 1998.
[7] O. Goldreich and L. A. Levin. A hardcore predicate for all one-way functions. In *Proceedings of the 21st STOC*, pages 25–32, 1989.
[8] P. Gopalan, R. O'Donnell, R. Servedio, A. Shpilka, and K. Wimmer. Testing fourier dimensionality and sparsity. *SIAM J. Comput.*, 40(4):1075–1100, 2011.
[9] B. Green and T. Sanders. Boolean functions with small spectral norm. *GAFA*, 18:144–162, 2008.
[10] B. Green and T. Sanders. A quantitative version of the idempotent theorem in harmonic analysis. *Annals of Math.*, 168(3):1025–1054, 2008.
[11] V. Grolmusz. On the power of circuits with gates of low L_1 norms. *Theor. Comput. Sci.*, 188(1):117–128, 1997.
[12] J. Håstad. Some optimal inapproximability results. *J. ACM*, 48(4):798–859, 2001.
[13] J. Kahn, G. Kalai, and N. Linial. The influence of variables on Boolean functions. In *Proceedings of the 29th annual FOCS*, pages 68–80, 1988.
[14] G. Kalai. A Fourier-theoretic perspective on the Condorcet paradox and Arrow's theorem. *Adv. Appl. Math.*, 29(3):412–426, 2002.
[15] E. Kushilevitz and Y. Mansour. Learning Decision Trees Using the Fourier Spectrum. *SIAM J. Comput.*, 22(6):1331–1348, 1993.
[16] T. Lee. A new rank technique for formula size lower bounds. In *STACS*, pages 145–156, 2007.
[17] N. Linial, Y. Mansour, and N. Nisan. Constant depth circuits, Fourier transform and learnability. *J. ACM*, 40(3):607–620, 1993.
[18] Y. Mansour. Learning Boolean functions via the Fourier transform. In *Theoretical advances in neural computation and learning*, pages 391–424, 1994.
[19] A. Montanaro and T. Osborne. On the communication complexity of XOR functions. *CoRR*, abs/0909.3392, 2009.
[20] R. O'Donnell. Analysis of Boolean Functions. `http://www.analysisofbooleanfunctions.org/`, 2012.
[21] A. Shpilka, A. Tal, and B. L. Volk. On the structure of boolean functions with small spectral norm. *Electronic Colloquium on Computational Complexity (ECCC)*, 20:49, 2013.
[22] P. M. Spira. On time-hardware complexity tradeoffs for boolean functions. In *Proceedings of the 4th HICSS*, pages 525–527, 1971.
[23] H. Y. Tsang, C. H. Wong, N. Xie, and S. Zhang. Fourier sparsity, spectral norm, and the log-rank conjecture. In *Proceedings of the 54th Annual FOCS*, pages 658–667, 2013.
[24] Z. Zhang and Y. Shi. On the parity complexity measures of Boolean functions. *Theor. Comput. Sci.*, 411(26-28):2612 – 2618, 2010.

APPENDIX

A. PROOF OF LEMMA 2.5

The proof of Lemma 2.5 relies upon the following even simpler lemma.

LEMMA A.1. *Let $V \subseteq \mathbb{Z}_2^n$ be an affine subspace of co-dimension k, and let $\mathbf{1}_V : \mathbb{Z}_2^n \to \{0,1\}$ be its characteristic function. Then* $\mathrm{spar}(\mathbf{1}_V) = 2^k$ *and* $\|\widehat{\mathbf{1}_V}\|_1 = 1$.

PROOF. Denote $V = \alpha + U$ where U is a subspace of co-dimension k. There are k vectors $\gamma_1, \dots, \gamma_k \in \mathbb{Z}_2^n$ (a basis for $U^\perp$) and $b_1, \dots, b_k \in \{+1, -1\}$ such that $\mathbf{1}_V(x) = 1$ if and only if $\chi_{\gamma_i}(x) = b_i$ for all $1 \le i \le k$. Therefore

$$\mathbf{1}_V(x) = \prod_{i=1}^{k} \left(\frac{\chi_{\gamma_i}(x) + b_i}{2} \right).$$

Using the relation $\chi_\beta \chi_\gamma = \chi_{\beta+\gamma}$, and the fact that

$$\mathrm{span}\{\gamma_1, \dots, \gamma_k\} = U^\perp,$$

we get

$$\mathbf{1}_V(x) = \sum_{\gamma \in U^\perp} \pm 2^{-k} \chi_\gamma(x).$$

Since $|U^\perp| = 2^k$, both statements follow. □

PROOF OF LEMMA 2.5. Let L be the set of leaves of T, and for every $\ell \in L$ let b_ℓ be its label, and $\mathbf{1}_\ell : \mathbb{Z}_2^n \to \{0,1\}$ be the characteristic function of the set of inputs x such that computation upon x arrives at the leaf ℓ. Since T computes f, we may represent f as:

$$f = \sum_{\ell \in L} b_\ell \mathbf{1}_\ell(x).$$

Now note that if ℓ's depth is t, then $\mathbf{1}_\ell$ is a characteristic function of an affine subspace of co-dimension t. The maximal depth of T is k, hence for every $\ell \in L$ we have, by Lemma A.1, $\mathrm{spar}(\mathbf{1}_\ell) \le 2^k$ and $\|\widehat{\mathbf{1}_\ell}\|_1 = 1$. Finally, since $|L| = m$, we get

$$\mathrm{spar}(f) \le \sum_{\ell \in L} \mathrm{spar}(\mathbf{1}_\ell) \le m2^k,$$

and since $|b_\ell| = 1$, the triangle inequality implies

$$\|\hat{f}\|_1 \le \sum_{\ell \in L} \|\widehat{\mathbf{1}_\ell}\|_1 \le m.$$

□

B. FORMULA SIZE AND DEPTH OF BOOLEAN FUNCTIONS WITH SMALL SPECTRAL NORM

In this section, we give upper bounds on the formula size and depth of Boolean functions with small spectral norm.

A De Morgan formula is a Boolean formula over the basis $B_2 = \{\vee, \wedge, \neg\}$ with fan in at most 2. A De Morgan formula is represented by a tree such that every leaf is labeled by an input variable and every internal node is labeled by an operation from B_2. A formula is said to compute a function $f : \{0,1\}^n \to \{0,1\}$ if on all inputs $x \in \{0,1\}^n$ it outputs $f(x)$. The computation is done in the natural way from the leaves to the root. The size of a formula F, denoted by $L(F)$, is defined as the number of leaves it contains. The De Morgan formula size of a function $f : \{0,1\}^n \to \{0,1\}$, denoted by $L(f)$, is the size of the minimal De Morgan formula that computes f.

The next lemma states a natural connection between parity decision trees and De Morgan formulas:

LEMMA B.1. *Any Boolean function computed by a $\oplus$-DT of size s has a $O(n^2 \cdot s)$ size formula over the De Morgan basis.*

PROOF. We use the fact that any parity function (or its negation) on at most n variables can be computed by a De Morgan formula of size at most $9/8 \cdot n^2$ (see [16]).

For the rest of the proof, it will be convenient to use the number of nodes in the decision tree, s', instead of the number of leaves. As $s' = 2s - 1$, where s denotes the number of leaves in the $\oplus$-DT, it is enough to show that any $\oplus$-DT with s' nodes has an equivalent formula with $O(n^2 \cdot s')$ leaves.

We show, by induction on s', that any $\oplus$-DT on n input variables with s' nodes can be computed by a De Morgan formula of size $s' \cdot 9/4 \cdot n^2$.

For size $s' = 1$, the function must be constant and thus can be realized by a size 2 De Morgan formula: $x_1 \vee \neg x_1$ for the constant 1 and $x_1 \wedge \neg x_1$ for the constant 0.

For a $\oplus$-DT of size $s' > 1$, let $\ell(x_1, \ldots, x_n)$ be the linear function evaluated at the root of the $\oplus$-DT, and let f_L, f_R be the functions that the left subtree and right subtree compute, respectively. Also denote by s'_L, s'_R the number of nodes in the left subtree and right subtree, respectively.

We can write the function evaluated by the decision tree as

$$f(x_1,\ldots,x_n) = (\ell(x_1,\ldots,x_n) \wedge f_L(x_1,\ldots,x_n)) \vee \\ (\neg\ell(x_1,\ldots,x_n) \wedge f_R(x_1,\ldots,x_n)) \ .$$

The formula size of the above expression is at most $L(f_L) + L(f_R) + L(\ell) + L(\neg\ell)$. By the induction hypothesis $L(f_L) \le s'_L \cdot 9/4 \cdot n^2$ and $L(f_R) \le s'_R \cdot 9/4 \cdot n^2$. Overall, we get

$$L(f) \le L(f_R) + L(f_L) + L(\ell) + L(\neg\ell) \le \\ (s'_R + s'_L + 1) \cdot 9/4 \cdot n^2 = s' \cdot 9/4 \cdot n^2 \ ,$$

which completes the proof. □

A well known result of Spira ([22]) shows that every (De Morgan) formula of size S can be realized by a $O(\log(S))$ depth (De Morgan) formula. This result implies that every $\oplus$-DT of size s can be computed by a depth $O(\log(s) + \log(n))$ De Morgan formula. Theorem 1.3 is an immediate corollary of Lemma B.1 and Theorem 1.2. We restate it for convenience.

THEOREM B.2 (THEOREM 1.3, RESTATED). *Any $f : \mathbb{Z}_2^n \to \{+1,-1\}$ such that $\|\hat{f}\|_1 = A$ has a De Morgan formula of size $O(2^{A^2} \cdot n^{2A} \cdot n^2)$ and a De Morgan formula of depth $O(\log(n) \cdot A + A^2)$.*

Non-commutative Arithmetic Circuits with Division

Pavel Hrubeš [*]
Department of Computer Science and Engineering
University of Washington
pahrubes@gmail.com

Avi Wigderson [†]
School of Mathematics
Institute for Advanced Study
avi@ias.edu

ABSTRACT

We initiate the study of the complexity of arithmetic circuits with division gates over non-commuting variables. Such circuits and formulas compute *non-commutative* rational functions, which, despite their name, can no longer be expressed as ratios of polynomials. We prove some lower and upper bounds, completeness and simulation results, as follows.

If X is $n \times n$ matrix consisting of n^2 distinct mutually non-commuting variables, we show that:

(i). X^{-1} can be computed by a circuit of polynomial size,

(ii). every formula computing some entry of X^{-1} must have size at least $2^{\Omega(n)}$.

We also show that matrix inverse is complete in the following sense:

(i). Assume that a non-commutative rational function f can be computed by a formula of size s. Then there exists an invertible $2s \times 2s$-matrix A whose entries are variables or field elements such that f is an entry of A^{-1}.

(ii). If f is a non-commutative polynomial computed by a formula without inverse gates then A can be taken as an upper triangular matrix with field elements on the diagonal.

We show how divisions can be eliminated from non-commutative circuits and formulae which compute polynomials, and we address the non-commutative version of the "rational function identity testing" problem. As it happens, the complexity of both of these procedures depends on a single open problem in invariant theory.

Keywords

Arithmetic circuit complexity, Non-commutative rational function, Free skew field

[*]Supported by the NSF under agreement CCF-1016565

[†]Research partially supported by NSF grant CCF-0832797

ITCS'14, January 12–14, 2014, Princeton, New Jersey, USA.
Copyright 2014 ACM 978-1-4503-2698-8/14/01 ...$15.00.
http://dx.doi.org/10.1145/2554797.2554805 .

1. INTRODUCTION

Arithmetic circuit complexity studies the computation of polynomials and rational functions using the basic operations addition, multiplication, and division. It is chiefly interested in *commutative* polynomials or rational functions, defined over a set of multiplicatively commuting variables (see the survey [42], or the book [6]). The dominant computational models are the *arithmetic circuit* and its weakening, the *arithmetic formula*. The main open problem is to present an explicit polynomial which cannot be computed by a circuit – or a formula – of polynomial size.

The complexity of computing polynomials (not allowing division) in *non-commuting* variables has also been considered, for example, in [35, 25]. This was motivated partly by an apparent lack of progress in proving lower bounds in the commutative setting, partly by an interest in computations in matrix algebras[1]. And indeed, we do have nontrivial lower bounds in this setting. Most notably, Nisan [35] has proved thirty years ago that any arithmetic *formula* computing the non-commutative determinant or permanent must have an exponential size, and also gave an exponential separation between the power of circuits and formulae in this model. Despite much effort, a similar lower bound for non-commutative arithmetic *circuits* has not been achieved – indeed, the best known lower bounds for non-commutative circuits are as weak as the commutative ones.

In this paper, we take the study of non-commutative computation one step further and consider the complexity of non-commutative circuits which contain division (equivalently, inverse) gates. Such a circuit computes a "non-commutative rational function" – a far more complicated object than its commutative counterpart. Traditionally, arithmetic circuit complexity focuses on the computation of polynomials, with rational functions receiving minor attention. This is mainly because any commutative rational function can be expressed as a pair of polynomials fg^{-1}. Even on the computational level, commutative rational functions do not substantially differ from polynomials – apart from the omnipresent threat of dividing by zero. In contrast, the structure of non-commutative rational functions is far more complex, giving rise to host of new phenomena. It is not difficult to see that $x^{-1}+y^{-1}$ or $xy^{-1}x$ can no longer be expressed as fg^{-1} (or $g^{-1}f$), if x, y do not commute. More importantly, non-commutative rational functions may require *nested* inverses, as in $(u + xy^{-1}z)^{-1}$. Indeed, any

[1]Observe that Strassen's (and all subsequent) fast matrix multiplication algorithms *necessarily* work over non-commuting matrix entries

number of inverse operations, and nested inverse operations, may be needed to represent a rational function. Moreover, there is no "canonical" representation of non-commutative rational functions. Despite these facts, or rather thanks to them, non-commutative rational functions posses quite a lot of structure. They form a skew field[2] which is equipped with invariants not present in the standard commutative field of fractions. Our main hope is that this additional structure may be useful for proving lower bounds, even for polynomials. We make initial steps in this direction.

Non-commutative rational functions arise naturally in a variety of settings, beyond the abstract mathematical fields of non-commutative algebra and geometry[3]. One area is linear system theory and control theory, where the order of actions clearly matters, and the dynamics is often given by a rational function and its iterates. The paper [28] surveys some of this work, and also demonstrates situations where results in the commutative case were proven by "lifting" them to the non-commutative setting. Another area is formal language theory where regular expressions and formal series play analogous role. Indeed, these two areas are tightly connected, and the book [3] surveys some of the connections between the algebraic and linguistic settings (and more).

Note that non-commutative rational functions can often be more natural than non-commutative polynomials. For example, the determinant as a non-commutative *polynomial* has no longer any relevance to solving linear equations or a geometrical interpretation. In [20], it was argued that the correct analogy of the commutative determinant is the *quasideterminant*, which is a set of non-commutative rational functions sharing and extending many of the useful and beautiful properties of the commutative determinant. This development has important consequences in a variety of mathematics areas. The inverse of a matrix is probably the best example of a notion that makes perfect sense in the non-commutative setting, as a set of rational functions (and indeed the quasi-determinant of a matrix may be naturally defined from the entries of its inverse). Matrix inverse further plays a key role in one definition, due to Cohn [7], of the universal skew field of non-commutative rational functions.

Matrix inverse turns out to be central from a computational perspective. In this paper we will focus on the complexity of computing the inverse X^{-1} of an $n \times n$ matrix X consisting of n^2 non-commuting variables. We show that X^{-1} can be computed by a polynomial size circuit, but on the other hand, every formula computing an entry of X^{-1} must have an exponential size. This provides a non-trivial example[4] of an exponential gap between circuit and formula size – a counterpart of the above mentioned result of Nisan. We also prove the following completeness result: if a rational function f can be computed by a formula of size s then f can be expressed as an entry of A^{-1}, where A is a $2s \times 2s$-matrix whose entries are variables or field elements. This is an analog of Valiant's [45] theorem on completeness of determinant in the commutative, division-free, setting.

To see the origins of the lower bounds, let us return to examples of rational expressions. We noted that the expression $(x + xy^{-1}x)^{-1}$, which has *nested* inversions, can be simplified by Hua's identity to an equivalent expression without nesting: $(x + y)^{-1} - x^{-1}$. On the other hand, in the somewhat similar expression $(u + xy^{-1}z)^{-1}$, the nested inversion cannot be eliminated. This new phenomenon of nested inversion provides a new invariant not present in the commutative setting - the *height* of a rational function. The height is the minimum number of nested inversions in a formula computing this rational function. For a long time, it was not even clear that the height is unbounded, and it was a major result of C. Reutenauer [39] that it in fact is. Indeed, his result is much more precise and informative: any entry of the inverse of the generic $n \times n$ matrix X requires n nested inversions, namely has height n.

Our lower bound on formula size of matrix inverse is obtained by showing that a formula of size s can compute a function of height at most logarithmic in s. This is obtained via general balancing procedure of formulas, which is a bit more involved than the usual one due to the non-commutativity and presence of inversion gates. Combined with Reutenauer's theorem, this implies that the inverse of $n \times n$ matrix cannot be computed by a formula smaller than $2^{\Omega(n)}$. In circuit complexity, one keeps searching for properties that would imply that a function is hard to compute. For a polynomial f, there are not many such invariants at hand: for example, the degree or the number of variables, which both provide only very limited hardness results, and the more sophisticated rank of the partial derivative matrix used in Nisan's lower bound. In the context of non-commutative rational functions, we can now see that the inverse height is a new non-trivial invariant which can be successfully applied to obtain hardness results. Other non-trivial invariants are known in this setting, and it is quite possible that some of them can shed light on more classical problems of arithmetic circuit complexity.

We also prove a different characterization of the inverse height. We show that in a circuit, one never needs to use more inversion *gates* than the inversion height of the rational function computed, without significantly increasing the circuit size. Thus, e.g., the expression $x_1^{-1} + x_2^{-1} + \dots x_n^{-1}$ can be computed using only one inverse gate by an $O(n)$-sized circuit, and $n \times n$ matrix inverse can be computed by a polynomial size circuit with exactly n inverse gates.

We also consider the question of eliminating division from circuits or formulae whose output is a polynomial. Again, in the commutative setting this can be done with little overhead, as shown by Strassen [44]. His idea was to replace an inverse gate with an infinite power series expansion, and eventually truncate it according to the degree of the output polynomial. In the non-commutative setting, this approach faces a significant obstacle. In order to express f^{-1} as a power series, we need a point where f is non-zero, and so Strassen's argument hinges on the fact that a non-zero rational function does not vanish on some substitution from the underlying field (at least when the field is infinite). In contrast, assume that a non-commutative computation inverts the polynomial $xy - yx$. It is not identically zero, but vanishes on all inputs from any base field. A natural idea, which we indeed employ, is to evaluate the circuit on ma-

[2] A.k.a. "associative division algebra" – a field in which multiplication is not necessarily commutative.

[3] One of the best examples is the fact that the fundamental theorem of projective geometry follows rather simply from the fact that the following rational expression, $(x + xy^{-1}x)^{-1} + (x + y)^{-1} - x^{-1}$, is identically zero: this is called Hua's identity.

[4] The trivial example would be x^{2^n}.

trices instead of field elements. Extending relevant notions appropriately (namely, polynomials and power series with matrix coefficients), we can implement Strassen's idea and eliminate divisions, with the exception of one caveat – we don't know the size of matrices needed! As it turns out, it is a basic open problem, arising in non-commutative algebra as well as in commutative algebraic geometry, to determine any computable bound on the minimum size of matrices on which a nonzero rational expression does not vanish (resp. is invertible). Thus, our result is conditional: the simulation is polynomial in the size of the given circuit and in the size of the smallest dimension of matrices on which the given circuit can be correctly evaluated. Finally, we will see that this problem is also related to the question of deciding whether a rational expression computes the zero function. In the case of formulas, the "rational identity testing" problem can be decided by an efficient randomized algorithm, provided that the above matrix dimension is small.

Organization

In Section 2 we formally define our computational models, arithmetic circuits and formulae over non-commuting variables with division gates. We define rational functions, the skew field they live in and the notion of inverse height. Then we formally state our main results. In Section 3 we prove the circuit size upper bound on matrix inverse, and in Section 4 the formula size lower bound for it, via a general result about balancing formulae with division gates. In Section 5 we show that circuits require only as many inverse gates as the height, via an efficient simulation reducing the number of inverse gates to this bare minimum. In Section 6 we present several completeness results, most notably of matrix inverse for formulae. In Section 7 we define the identity testing problems for non-commutative polynomial and rational function and discuss their complexities. In Section 8 we explain how to eliminate divisions when computing polynomials. In Section 9 we discuss some future directions and open problems.

2. BACKGROUND AND MAIN RESULTS

Let $\mathbb{F}$ be a (commutative) field and $\bar{x} = x_1, \dots, x_n$ a set of variables. The ring of non-commutative polynomials in variables $\bar{x}$ will be denoted $\mathbb{F}\langle\bar{x}\rangle$, and $\mathbb{F}(\!\langle\bar{x}\rangle\!)$ denotes the free skew field of non-commutative rational functions. Two classical approaches to defining this field will be outlined below. For more detail see for example [8, 27]. The elements of $\mathbb{F}(\!\langle\bar{x}\rangle\!)$ are *non-commutative rational functions*, which we call simply *rational functions*.

Non-commutative arithmetic circuits with inverse gates

Non-commutative rational functions will be computed by means of *non-commutative arithmetic circuits with inverse gates*, which we call briefly *circuits*. This is a natural extension of both the notion of a commutative circuit with division gates, and the notion of a non-commutative circuit without divisions. We formally define the circuits, and then discuss how they lead to a definition of the free skew field.

A *circuit* Φ over a field $\mathbb{F}$ is a finite directed acyclic graph as follows. Nodes of in-degree zero are labelled by either a variable or a field element in $\mathbb{F}$. All the other nodes have in-degree one or two. The gates of in-degree one are labelled by $^{-1}$ and the gates of in-degree two by either $+$ or $\times$. The two edges going into a gate labelled by $\times$ are labelled by *left* and *right*, to determine the order of multiplication. The nodes are called input gates, inverse, sum and product gates. The nodes of out-degree zero are output gates. For nodes v, v_1, v_2, we write $v = v_1 \times v_2$ to indicate that v is a product gate with the two edges coming from v_1, v_2, and similarly for $v = v_1 + v_2$ or $v = v_1^{-1}$.

The *size* of a circuit Φ is the number of gates in Φ. Its *depth* is the length of the longest path in Φ. A *formula* is a circuit where every node has out-degree at most one.

For a node v in Φ, we denote Φ_v as the subcircuit of Φ rooted at v.

A node u in a circuit Φ in variables $x_1, \dots, x_n$ is intended to compute a non-commutative rational function $\widehat{u} \in \mathbb{F}(\!\langle x_1, \dots, x_n\rangle\!)$. However, the circuit may also contain division by zero, in which case we say that $\widehat{u}$ is *undefined*. The exact definition of $\widehat{u} \in \mathbb{F}(\!\langle x_1, \dots, x_n\rangle\!)$ is clear:

(*i*). If v is an input gate labelled by a (i.e., a is a variable or a field element), let $\widehat{v} := a$.

(*ii*). If $v = v_1 \times v_2$ resp. $v = v_1 + v_2$, let $\widehat{v} = \widehat{v}_1 \cdot \widehat{v}_2$ resp. $\widehat{v} = \widehat{v}_1 + \widehat{v}_2$, provided that both $\widehat{v}_1$ and $\widehat{v}_2$ are defined.

(*iii*). If $v = u^{-1}$, let $\widehat{v} := \widehat{u}^{-1}$, provided $\widehat{u}$ is defined and $\widehat{u} \neq 0$.

We say that a circuit Φ is a *correct circuit*, if $\widehat{u}$ is defined for every node in Φ. A correct circuit Φ *computes* a set of non-commutative rational functions $\widehat{\Phi} = \{\widehat{u}_1, \dots, \widehat{u}_m\}$, where $u_1, \dots, u_m$ are the output gates of Φ.

The free skew field - a computational definition

One classical definition of the field $\mathbb{F}(\!\langle\bar{x}\rangle\!)$ is through the computation of its elements as above, with equivalence of elements defined through evaluating their circuits on matrix algebras as we outline now.

Let R be a ring whose centre contains the field $\mathbb{F}$ (i.e., every element of $\mathbb{F}$ commutes with every element of R). Let Φ be a circuit in variables $x_1, \dots, x_n$ with a single output node. Then Φ can be viewed as computing a *partial* function $\widehat{\Phi}^R : R^n \to R$. That is, substitute $a_1, \dots, a_n$ for the variables $x_1, \dots . x_n$ and evaluate the circuit. $\widehat{\Phi}^R(a_1, \dots, a_n)$ is undefined if we come across an inverse gate whose input is not invertible in R. Note that

$$\widehat{\Phi}^R(x_1, \dots, x_n) = \widehat{\Phi}$$

if we interpret $x_1, \dots, x_n$ as elements of $R = \mathbb{F}(\!\langle x_1, \dots, x_n\rangle\!)$.

Looking at rings of $k \times k$ matrices $M_{k\times k}(\mathbb{F})$, we can obtain the following characterization of circuits and non-commutative rational functions (see [27] for proof):

(a) Φ is a correct circuit iff the domain of $\widehat{\Phi}^R$ is non-empty for some $R = M_{k\times k}(\mathbb{F})$.

(b) For correct circuits Φ_1, Φ_2, $\widehat{\Phi}_1 = \widehat{\Phi}_2$ iff $\widehat{\Phi}_1^R$ and $\widehat{\Phi}_2^R$ agree on the intersection of their domains, for every $R = M_{k\times k}(\mathbb{F})$.

In fact, those conditions could be used to define the skew field $\mathbb{F}(\!\langle x_1, \dots, x_n\rangle\!)$. It can be constructed as the set of all correct circuits modulo the equivalence class induced by (b).

Matrix inverse (and the quasi-determinant)

Let $A \in \mathrm{Mat}_{n\times n}(R)$ be an $n \times n$ matrix whose entries are elements of a unital ring R. Then $A^{-1} \in \mathrm{Mat}_{n\times n}(R)$ is the $n \times n$ matrix such that

$$A \cdot A^{-1} = A^{-1} \cdot A = I_n ,$$

where I_n is the identity matrix. The inverse A^{-1} does not always exists, but if it does, it is unique. We will be specifically interested in the inverse of the $n \times n$ *generic matrix* $X_n \in \mathrm{Mat}_{n\times n}(\mathbb{F}\langle\!\langle \bar{x} \rangle\!\rangle)$, which is the matrix $X_n = (x_{ij})_{i,j\in[n]}$ consisting of n^2 distinct variables.

Matrix inverse is a very close cousin of the *quasi-determinant*. In two influential papers, Gelfand and Retakh [21, 22] defined a non-commutative analog to the determinant, called *quasi-determinant*, which they argued to be the appropriate generalization of that fundamental polynomial. Its many beautiful properties and applications are surveyed in [19]. The quasi-determinant of a generic matrix is actually a *set* of n^2 rational functions, which can be simply defined from the entries of the matrix inverse. Indeed, the (i, j) quasi-determinant of X is simply the *inverse* of the (i, j) entry of X^{-1}. Thus, essentially everything we say about matrix inverse holds for the quasi-determinant as well.

That X_n^{-1} exists can be directly proved by induction on n, as in our construction in Section 3. However, one can also invoke an interesting theorem due to Cohn. Let R be a ring. A matrix $A \in \mathrm{Mat}_{n\times n}(R)$ is called *full in* R if it cannot be written as $A = B\cdot C$ with $B \in \mathrm{Mat}_{n\times k}(R)$, $C \in \mathrm{Mat}_{k\times n}(R)$ and $k < n$.

THEOREM 2.1 (COHN, [8]). *Let $A \in Mat_{n\times n}(\mathbb{F}\langle\bar{x}\rangle)$ be a matrix of non-commutative polynomials. Then A is invertible in the skew field $\mathbb{F}\langle\!\langle \bar{x} \rangle\!\rangle$ if and only if it is full in $\mathbb{F}\langle\bar{x}\rangle$. Moreover, if A is not full and its entries are polynomials of degree ≤ 1, then the entries of the factors B, C are without loss of generality degree ≤ 1 as well.*

This characterization of invertible matrices was then used by Cohn to give an alternative construction of the free field: we can identify an element of $\mathbb{F}\langle\!\langle \bar{x} \rangle\!\rangle$ with an element of A^{-1} for some full $A \in M_{n\times n}(\mathbb{F}\langle\bar{x}\rangle)$ This is another indication of the key role matrix inverse has in the study of non-commutative rational functions. Note that in the *commutative* polynomial ring, there exist matrices which are both full and singular.[5]

The height of a rational function

An important characteristic of a rational function is the number of nested inverse operations necessary to express it. For a circuit Φ, we define the *height* of Φ as the maximum number k such that there exists a path in Φ which contains k inverse gates. For example, the formula $xy^{-1}+zx^{-1}y^2$ has height 1 and $(1+xy^{-1}x)^{-1}$ has height 2. For a rational function f, the height of f is the smallest height of some circuit computing f (in this definition, one may equivalently consider formulas). Naturally, the depth of a circuit computing f must be at least the height of f.

In the commutative setting, every rational function can be written as fg^{-1} for some polynomials f, g and so has height at most 1. In the non-commutative setting, there exist rational functions of an arbitrary height. This is in itself a remarkable and non-trivial fact. However, we will use a stronger statement due to C. Reutenauer:

THEOREM 2.2 ([39]). *The height of any entry of the generic inverse matrix X_n^{-1} is n.*

In Section 5, we will give a different characterization of the inverse height of f: in Corollary 5.3, we point out that a rational function of height k can be computed by a circuit which *altogether* uses only k inverses. Hence the height of f can also be defined as the smallest *number* of inverse gates needed to compute f by means of a circuit.

Main results

We shall prove the following two theorems about the complexity of matrix inverse (recall that X_n is a matrix of n^2 distinct variables):

THEOREM 2.3. *X_n^{-1} can be computed by a circuit of size polynomial[6] in n.*

THEOREM 2.4. *Every formula computing some entry of X_n^{-1} has size $2^{\Omega(n)}$.*

Theorem 2.3 is an explicit construction. Theorem 2.4 is obtained by showing that a formula of size s can be balanced to obtain an equivalent formula of depth $O(\log s)$. This entails that if f can be computed by a formula of size s, then f has height at most logarithmic in s. This gives Theorem 2.4 by Theorem 2.2.

Theorems 2.3 and 2.4 can be strengthened as follows:

(*i*). X_n^{-1} can be computed by a polynomial size circuit which contains only n inverse gates (cf. Proposition 5.2).

(*ii*). Every formula computing some entry of X_n^{-1} has $2^{\Omega(n)}$ inverse gates. (cf. Corollary 4.4)

In his seminal paper [45], Valiant has shown that an arithmetic formula can be expressed as the determinant of a linear size matrix whose entries are variables or field elements. This result considers commutative formulas without inverse gates. That commutativity is not essential was later shown in [24]. Here, we show that a similar relationship holds between non-commutative arithmetic formulas and the matrix inverse:

THEOREM 2.5. *Assume that a rational function f can be computed by a formula Φ of size s. Then there exists $s' \leq 2s$ and an invertible $s' \times s'$-matrix A_Φ whose entries are variables or field elements such that f is an entry of A_Φ^{-1}.*

This is proved in Section 6. There, we also discuss some variants of the theorem. Namely, if f is computed without the use of inverse gates then A can be taken upper triangular, and we point out the connection with the non-commutative determinant.

We present several other results about the number of inverse gates in non-commutative circuits - how to minimize them when computing rational functions, and how to eliminate them when computing polynomials. More specifically:

[5]E.g., consider a generic skew-symmetric 3x3 matrix, or indeed one of every odd size.

[6]In fact, we show that X_n^{-1} can be computed by a circuit of size $O(n^\omega)$, where $2 \leq \omega < 3$ is the exponent of matrix multiplication.

- If f can be computed by a circuit of size s and height k, then f can be computed by a circuit of size $O(s(k+1))$ which contains k inverse gates.

In other words, f can be computed by a circuit which contains at most k inverses on any *directed path*, it can be computed by a circuit with k inverse gates *in total*, with only a small increase in circuit size. (Proposition 5.2 in Section 5).

- Let $f \in \mathbb{F}\langle \bar{x} \rangle$ be a polynomial of degree d which is computable by a circuit with divisions of size s. Assume that there exist matrices $a_1, \ldots, a_n \in R = \mathrm{Mat}_{m\times m}(\mathbb{F})$ such that $\widehat{\Phi}^R(a_1, \ldots, a_n)$ is defined. Then f can be computed by a division-free circuit of size $O(sd^3m^3)$.

This is an analogy of the elimination of division gates from commutative circuits. However, we do not know how large can the parameter $m = m(s, d)$ be for the worst such circuit, and hence we do not know whether our construction is polynomial in s and d. (See Section 8).

A version of this parameter appears again in Section 7 in connection with the *rational identity testing problem.*

- For a correct formula Φ of size s, one can decide whether $\widehat{\Phi} = 0$ by a randomized algorithm which runs in time polynomial in $s \cdot w(s)$.

Here, $w(s)$ is defined as the smallest k so that every correct formula of size s can be correctly evaluated on some $p \times p$ matrices with $p \leq k$. Via the completeness theorem above, an upper bound on $w(s)$ can be obtained by solving the following basic problem in invariant theory. This is also the most important open problem our work suggests, and we conclude this section by stating it. In a slightly different formulation, it is presented in Section 9 as Problem 4 (that the formulations are equivalent follows from Proposition 7.3), and is also discussed in Section 7.1. $\mathbb{F}$ can be any field, but it is especially interesting for algebraically closed fields, and specifically for the complex numbers.

- Find an upper bound on the smallest $k = k(s)$, such that for all $Q_1, \ldots, Q_s \in \mathrm{Mat}_{s\times s}(\mathbb{F})$ if[7] $\sum_{i=1}^{s} Q_i \otimes a_i$ is invertible for some $m \in \mathbb{N}$ and $a_1, \ldots, a_s \in \mathrm{Mat}_{m\times m}(\mathbb{F})$ then $\sum_{i=1}^{s} Q_i \otimes a_i$ is invertible for some $a_1, a_2, \cdots, a_s \in \mathrm{Mat}_{p\times p}(\mathbb{F})$ with $p \leq k$.

In other words, we want to find k such that $\det(\sum_{i=1}^{s} Q_i \otimes a_i)$ does not identically vanish on $(\leq k) \times (\leq k)$ matrices. Note that the vanishing of the determinant is invariant to acting on the sequence Q_i with left and right multiplication by any two invertible matrices - this provides the connection to invariant theory. This connection is further discussed in the Appendix.

3. A POLYNOMIAL-SIZE CIRCUIT FOR MATRIX INVERSE

In this section, we show that X_n^{-1} can be computed by a polynomial size circuit, thus proving Theorem 2.3. The algorithm is implicit in Strassen's paper [43].

[7] $\otimes$ is the Kronecker product.

The construction of X^{-1}

Let $X = X_n = (x_{ij})_{i,j\in[n]}$ be a matrix consisting of n^2 distinct variables. We define the matrix X^{-1} recursively. If $n = 1$, let $X^{-1} := (x_{11}^{-1})$. If $n > 1$, divide X into blocks as

$$X = \begin{pmatrix} a_1 & a_2 \\ a_3 & a_4 \end{pmatrix}, \tag{1}$$

where a_1, a_4 are square matrices of dimensions $p\times p$ and $(n-p)\times(n-p)$, respectively, and a_2, a_3 are in general rectangular matrices of dimension $p\times(n-p)$ and $(n-p)\times p$, respectively. (Later, we will choose p as roughly $n/2$.) Assume we have already constructed the matrix a_1^{-1}. Let

$$z := a_4 - a_3 a_1^{-1} a_2 ,$$

and

$$X^{-1} := \begin{pmatrix} a_1^{-1}(I + a_2 z^{-1} a_3 a_1^{-1}) & -a_1^{-1} a_2 z^{-1} \\ -z^{-1} a_3 a_1^{-1} & z^{-1} \end{pmatrix}. \tag{2}$$

Here, we should argue that z^{-1} exists, which is however apparent from the fact that $z = a_4$ if we set $a_3 = 0$.

Correctness

We must show that X^{-1}, as constructed above, indeed satisfies $X \cdot X^{-1} = I$ and $X^{-1} \cdot X = I$.

For $n = 1$, we have $x_{11} \cdot x_{11}^{-1} = x_{11}^{-1} \cdot x_{11} = 1$. Otherwise let $n > 1$ and let X be as in (1).

Using some rearrangements and the definition of z, we obtain

$$X \cdot X^{-1} =$$

$$\begin{pmatrix} a_1 & a_2 \\ a_3 & a_4 \end{pmatrix} \begin{pmatrix} a_1^{-1}(1 + a_2 z^{-1} a_3 a_1^{-1}) & -a_1^{-1} a_2 z^{-1} \\ -z^{-1} a_3 a_1^{-1} & z^{-1} \end{pmatrix} =$$

$$\begin{pmatrix} I + a_2 z^{-1} a_3 a_1^{-1} - a_2 z^{-1} a_3 a_1^{-1} & -a_2 z^{-1} + a_2 z^{-1} \\ a_3 a_1^{-1} + (a_3 a_1^{-1} a_2 - a_4) z^{-1} a_3 a_1^{-1} & (a_4 - a_3 a_1^{-1} a_2) z^{-1} \end{pmatrix}$$

$$= \begin{pmatrix} I & 0 \\ a_3 a_1^{-1} - z z^{-1} a_3 a_1^{-1} & z z^{-1} \end{pmatrix} = \begin{pmatrix} I & 0 \\ 0 & I \end{pmatrix}$$

The proof of $X^{-1} \cdot X = I$ is constructed in a similar fashion.

Complexity

Assume first that n is a power of two. Then X in (1) can be partitioned into four matrices of dimensions $n/2 \times n/2$. This shows that in order to compute the inverse of an $n \times n$ matrix, it is sufficient to compute the inverse of two $n/2 \times n/2$ matrices (a_1 and z), and add or multiply a constant number of $n/2 \times n/2$ matrices. Let $M(n)$ be the size of a smallest circuit which computes the product of two matrices and $C(n)$ the size of a smallest circuit computing X_n^{-1}. Then we obtain

$$C(n) \leq 2C(n/2) + c_1 M(n/2) + c_2 n^2 ,$$

for some constants c_1, c_2. If $M(n) = O(n^\omega)$, with $2 \leq \omega$, this implies that $C(n) = O(n^\omega)$.

If n is not a power of two, at each step partition X as evenly as possible, i.e., set $p := \lceil n/2 \rceil$. This gives that $C(n) \leq C(2^k)$, where k is the smallest integer such that $2^k \geq n$. Since $2^k \leq 2n$, this amounts to a loss of at most a constant factor.

Moreover, it is easy to see that the constructed circuit has height n.

4. MATRIX INVERSE HAS EXPONENTIAL FORMULA SIZE

In this section, we prove Theorem 2.4. For this purpose, we show that a formula of size s can be balanced to obtain an equivalent formula of depth $O(\log s)$. Both the statement and its proof are analogous to the commutative version given by Brent in [5]. On the other hand, the fact that this statement does hold for non-commutative rational functions is in itself slightly surprising.

PROPOSITION 4.1. *Assume that a non-commutative rational function f can be computed by a formula of size s. Then f can be computed by a formula of depth $O(\log s)$.*

This immediately implies:

COROLLARY 4.2. *If f can be computed by a formula of size s then f has height $O(\log s)$.*

This, together with Theorem 2.2, implies Theorem 2.4.

Let us first prove Proposition 4.1:

PROOF OF PROPOSITION 4.1. . The proof is almost identical to Brent's commutative version. Hence we just outline the argument and point out the peculiarities arising in the non-commutative setting.

The idea is to simultaneously prove the following two statements by induction on s. Let Φ be a correct formula of size s then, for sufficiently large s and suitable constant $c_1, c_2 > 0$, the following hold:

(i). $\widehat{\Phi}$ can be computed by a formula of depth $c_1 \log s$,

(ii). if z is a variable occurring at most once in Φ then

$$\widehat{\Phi} = (Az + B)(Cz + D)^{-1},$$

where A, B, C, D are non-commutative rational functions which do not depend on z and each is computable by a formula of depth $\leq c_2 \log s$. Moreover, $C\widehat{\Psi} + D \neq 0$ for any Ψ such that $\Phi(z/\Psi)$ is correct.

Here $\Phi(z/\Psi)$ means that Ψ is substituted for z in Φ. Furthermore, for a node v in Φ, Φ_v will stand for the subformula of Φ with the output v and $\Phi_{v:=z}$ is the formula obtained by replacing Φ_v in Φ by the variable z.

On the inductive step, (i) is obtained roughly as follows. Find a node v in Φ such that both Φ_v and $\Phi_{v:=z}$ are small (of size at most $2s/3$). Apply part (i) of the inductive assumption to bound the depth of $\widehat{\Phi}_v$. Apply (ii) to write $\widehat{\Phi}_{v:=z} = (Az+B)(Cz+D)^{-1}$, with A, B, C, D having small depth, which altogether gives a small depth formula for $\widehat{\Phi} = (A\widehat{\Phi}_v + B)(C\widehat{\Phi}_v + D)^{-1}$. To prove (ii), find an appropriate node v on the path between z and the output of Φ. (An "appropriate v" is a node v such that $\Phi_{v:=z_1}$ is small and Φ_{u_1} is small, where either $v = u_1^{-1}$, $v = u_1 + u_2$, $v = u_1 \times u_2$, or $v = u_2 \times u_1$, where u_2 does not depend on z.) Use the inductive assumptions to write

$$\begin{aligned} \widehat{\Phi}_{v:=z_1} &= (A_1 z_1 + B_1)(C_1 z_1 + D_1)^{-1}, \\ \widehat{\Phi}_v &= (A_2 z + B_2)(C_2 z + D_2)^{-1}, \end{aligned}$$

and compose these expressions to obtain (ii).

The main point that needs to be checked is that the representation

$$f = (Az + B)(Cz + D)^{-1} \qquad (3)$$

is well-behaved in the non-commutative setting. If A, B, C, D do not depend on z, we will say that f in (3) has *z-normal form*. It is not immediately clear that if Φ is as in (ii), then $\widehat{\Phi}$ has a z-normal form (even if we require nothing about the complexity of A, B, C, D). To see this, it is sufficient to show that if f has z-normal form and E does not depend on z, then $f+E, f\cdot E, E\cdot f$ and f^{-1} (if $f \neq 0$) have a z-normal form. This follows from the following identities, where we use that $(fg)^{-1} = g^{-1}f^{-1}$:

$$((Az+B)(Cz+D)^{-1})^{-1} = (Cz+D)(Az+B)^{-1},$$
$$(Az+B)(Cz+D)^{-1} + E = ((A+EC)z + (B+ED))(Cz+D)^{-1},$$
$$(Az+B)(Cz+D)^{-1} \cdot E = (Az+B)(E^{-1}Cz + E^{-1}D)^{-1}, \text{ if } E \neq 0,$$
$$E(Az+B)(Cz+D)^{-1} = (EAz + EB)(Cz+D)^{-1}.$$

However, it is more important that normal forms can be composed in the following sense. If

$$f = (A_1 z_1 + B_1)(C_1 z_1 + D_1)^{-1}, \; z_1 = (A_2 z + B_2)(C_2 z + D_2)^{-1},$$

then

$$f = (Az + B)(Cz + D)^{-1},$$

where $A = A_1A_2 + B_1C_2$, $B = A_1B_2 + B_1D_2$, $C = C_1A_2 + D_1C_2$ and $D = C_1B_2 + D_1D_2$. To see this, let $h_1 := A_2z + B_2$ and $h_2 := C_2z + D_2$ so that $z_1 = h_1h_2^{-1}$. Then

$$\begin{aligned} f &= (A_1h_1h_2^{-1} + B_1)(C_1h_1h_2^{-1} + D_1)^{-1} = \\ &= (A_1h_1 + B_1h_2)h_2^{-1}((C_1h_1 + D_1h_2)h_2^{-1})^{-1} = \\ &= (A_1h_1 + B_1h_2)h_2^{-1}h_2(C_1h_1 + D_1h_2)^{-1} = \\ &= (A_1h_1 + B_1h_2)(C_1h_1 + D_1h_2)^{-1}, \end{aligned}$$

and substitute for h_1, h_2.

The outlined properties of z-normal forms are quite sufficient to reconstruct Brent's proof. □

Let us note that the proof of Proposition 4.1 does not rely on the fact that the formula computes an element of a *free* skew field, and the proposition can be generalized as follows (recall the definition of $\widehat{\Phi}^R$ from Section 2):

PROPOSITION 4.3. *Let $\mathbb{F}$ be a field and R a skew field whose centre contains $\mathbb{F}$. Assume that $\Psi(x_1, \ldots, x_n)$ is a formula of size s and $\widehat{\Psi}^R(a_1, \ldots, a_n)$ is defined for given $a_1, \ldots, a_n \in R$. Then there exists a formula $\Phi(x_1, \ldots, x_n)$ of depth $O(\log s)$ such that*

$$\widehat{\Phi}^R(a_1, \ldots, a_n) = \widehat{\Psi}^R(a_1, \ldots, a_n).$$

This, together with Lemma 4.5 below, implies that Corollary 4.2 can be rephrased in terms of the number of inverse gates only:

COROLLARY 4.4. *Assume that f can be computed by a formula with k inverse gates. Then f has height $O(\log k)$.*

Consequently, any formula computing an entry of X_n^{-1} must have an exponential number of inverse gates. Corollary 4.4 follows from the following lemma, when we apply Proposition 4.3 to the formula $\Psi(z_1, \ldots, z_m)$.

LEMMA 4.5. *Assume that a rational function $f \in R = \mathbb{F}\langle\!\langle \bar{x} \rangle\!\rangle$ can be computed by a formula with k inverse gates. Then there exists a formula $\Psi(z_1, \ldots, z_m)$ such that*

(i). Ψ has size $O(k)$,

(ii). $f = \widehat{\Psi}^R(h_1, \ldots, h_m)$ for some polynomials $h_1, \ldots, h_m \in \mathbb{F}\langle \bar{x} \rangle$.

PROOF. Let us call a gate u in a formula Φ *trivial*, if Φ_u does not contain any inverse gate. Let us call u *maximal*, if it is trivial and for every trivial $v \neq u$, u is not a gate in Φ_v.

Assume that f can be computed by a formula with k inverse gates. It is sufficient to show that f can be computed by a formula Φ with $m = O(k)$ maximal gates. For let $u_1, \ldots, u_m$ be the maximal gates in Φ. Introduce new variables $z_1, \ldots, z_m$, and let Ψ be the formula obtained replacing every u_i by z_i in Φ. Clearly, $f = \widehat{\Psi}^R(h_1, \ldots, h_m)$, where h_i is the polynomial computed by Φ_{u_i}. Moreover, Ψ is a formula with m leaves. If we assume that Ψ does not contain redundant inverse gates $(u^{-1})^{-1}$, then Ψ has size $O(m)$.

To construct a formula with $O(k)$ maximal gates computing f, assume that $k > 0$. First, show that any formula with k inverses can be transformed to an equivalent formula Φ with k inverses such that every maximal gate u occurs in Φ in one of the following contexts:

(i). u^{-1},

(ii). $u \times v^{-1} \times u'$ or $u' \times v^{-1} \times u$, where u' is itself maximal,

(iii). $v_1 \times v_2 + u$, where $v_1 \times v_2$ is non-trivial.

This is easily proved by induction on k. If $k = 1$, we are supposed to compute f by a formula of the form $u_1 \times v^{-1} \times u_2 + u_3$, where v, u_1, u_2, u_3 do not contain inverse gates.

Finally, let us argue that Φ contains $O(k)$ maximal gates. For every inverse gate, there are at most 3 maximal gates corresponding to the conditions (i) and (ii). This also means that the number of non-trivial product gates $v_1 \times v_2$ in Ψ is $O(k)$ and so there are $O(k)$ maximal gates corresponding to the condition (iii). □

5. HEIGHT VERSUS THE NUMBER OF INVERSE GATES

Recall that the height of a circuit is the maximum number of inverse gates along *some directed path* in the circuit. Here we show that a circuit of height k can be transformed to an equivalent circuit which *altogether* uses only k inverse gates. This means that the height of f can be equivalently defined as the smallest number of inverse gates needed to compute f by a circuit.

This is based on the observation that $x_1^{-1}, \ldots, x_n^{-1}$ can be simultaneously computed using one inverse gate only:

LEMMA 5.1. *The rational functions $x_1^{-1}, \ldots, x_n^{-1}$ can be simultaneously computed by a circuit of size $O(n)$ which contains only one inverse gate.*

PROOF. Let $z := x_1 x_2 \ldots x_n$. As $z^{-1} = x_n^{-1} x_{n-1}^{-1} \ldots x_1^{-1}$, we have for every $j \in \{1, \ldots, n\}$

$$x_j^{-1} = (x_{j+1} x_{j+2} \ldots x_n) z^{-1} (x_1 x_2 \ldots x_{j-1}) .$$

Hence $x_1^{-1}, \ldots, x_n^{-1}$ can all be computed using just the inverse z^{-1}. To see that this gives a linear size circuit, it is sufficient to construct a linear size circuit simultaneously computing the polynomials $f_i = x_i x_{i+1} \ldots x_n$ and $g_i = x_1 x_2 \ldots x_i$, for $i \in \{1, \ldots, n\}$. This is clear because $f_{i+1} = x_{i+1} f_i$ and $g_{i+1} = g_i x_{i+1}$. □

PROPOSITION 5.2. *Assume that a rational function f can be computed by a circuit of size s and height k. Then f can be computed by a circuit of size $O(s(k+1))$ which contains k inverse gates.*

PROOF. Assume that Φ is a circuit of size s, inverse height k, which computes f. We construct the new circuit by induction on k. If $k = 0$, the statement is trivial, and so assume that $k > 0$. Let $u_1^{-1}, \ldots, u_n^{-1}$ be the inverse gates in Φ such that Φ_{u_i} does not contain any inverse gate. By the previous lemma, the rational functions computed by $u_1^{-1}, \ldots, u_n^{-1}$ can be computed by a circuit Ψ of size $c.s$ which contains only one inverse gate. Let Φ' be the circuit obtained from Φ by replacing the gate u_i^{-1} by a fresh variable z_i, for every $i \in \{1, \ldots, n\}$. The circuit Φ' has inverse height $k - 1$ and size $\leq s$, and so we can construct an equivalent circuit of size csk with only $k - 1$ division gates. Feeding the outputs of Ψ into the circuit Φ', we obtain a circuit computing f which has k inverse gates and size $csk + cs = cs(k + 1)$. □

COROLLARY 5.3. *The following are equivalent*

(i). f has inverse height $\leq k$,

(ii). f can be computed by a circuit with $\leq k$ inverse gates.

As follows from Corollary 4.4, the proposition or its corollary do not hold for formulas. Moreover, every formula computing $x_1^{-1} + \cdots + x_n^{-1}$ must contain a linear number of inverse gates (cf. Corollary 6.2 and Proposition 7.7.7 of [7]).

6. FORMULA COMPLETENESS OF MATRIX INVERSE

Here we prove Theorem 2.5. Our construction of matrices from formulae is similar to Malcolmson's approach for the construction of the skew field [31]. After this proof, we proceed in the following subsections to discuss the special case of formulae without inverse gates, in which the computation produces a non-commutative polynomial, and compare with the commutative case.

PROOF OF THEOREM 2.5. The matrix A is constructed by induction on s. We retain the property that f is the entry in the upper-right corner of A^{-1}. This entry will be denoted $\mathcal{R}A^{-1}$.

Let A, B be invertible matrices of dimension $p \times p$ and $q \times q$. For $k \in \{p, q\}$, let u_k resp. v_k be the $1 \times k$ vector whose first resp. last component is 1 and the others are zero. Furthermore, let a^t be the first column of A. The key observation are the following equalities (the unspecified entries are zero):

$$\mathcal{R}A^{-1} \cdot \mathcal{R}B^{-1} = \mathcal{R}\begin{pmatrix} A & -v_p^t \cdot u_q \\ & B \end{pmatrix}^{-1} \quad (4)$$

$$\mathcal{R}A^{-1} + \mathcal{R}B^{-1} = \mathcal{R}\begin{pmatrix} A & a^t \cdot u_q & -v_p^t \\ & B & v_q^t \\ & & 1 \end{pmatrix}^{-1} \quad (5)$$

$$(\mathcal{R}A^{-1})^{-1} = \mathcal{R}\begin{pmatrix} v_p^t & A \\ 0 & -u_p \end{pmatrix}^{-1}, \text{if } \mathcal{R}A^{-1} \neq 0 \quad (6)$$

To prove (4) and (5), note that

$$\begin{pmatrix} a_1 & a_2 \\ 0 & a_4 \end{pmatrix}^{-1} = \begin{pmatrix} a_1^{-1} & -a_1^{-1}a_2a_4^{-1} \\ 0 & a_4^{-1} \end{pmatrix},$$

whenever the right hand side makes sense. This follows from (2), noting that (2) holds whenever X is a matrix such that the right hand side makes sense. This gives

$$\mathcal{R}\begin{pmatrix} A & -v_p^t u_q \\ & B \end{pmatrix}^{-1} = \mathcal{R}\begin{pmatrix} A^{-1} & A^{-1}v_p^t u_q B^{-1} \\ & B^{-1} \end{pmatrix}$$
$$= \mathcal{R}(A^{-1}v_p^t u_q B^{-1}) = (\mathcal{R}A^{-1})(\mathcal{R}B^{-1}).$$

Similarly, one can verify that the entry in the upper-right corner of the matrix in (5) is the first entry of the $p\times 1$-vector

$$w = A^{-1}v_p^t + A^{-1}a^t u_q B^{-1} v_q^t = A^{-1}v_p^t + u_p^t u_q B^{-1} v_q^t =$$
$$= A^{-1}v_p^t + (\mathcal{R}B^{-1})u_p^t,$$

where we used that $A^{-1}a^t = u_p^t$. The first entry of w is therefore $\mathcal{R}A^{-1} + \mathcal{R}B^{-1}$.

To prove (6), apply (2), with $X_1 = A$ and $X_4 = 0$, to show that the entry in *lower*-right corner of

$$\begin{pmatrix} A & v_p^t \\ -u_p & 0 \end{pmatrix}^{-1}$$

is $(u_p A^{-1} v_p^t)^{-1} = -(\mathcal{R}A^{-1})^{-1}$. We have

$$\begin{pmatrix} v_p^t & A \\ 0 & -u_p \end{pmatrix}^{-1} = \left(\begin{pmatrix} A & v_p^t \\ -u_p & 0 \end{pmatrix}\begin{pmatrix} & I \\ 1 & \end{pmatrix}\right)^{-1} =$$
$$= \begin{pmatrix} & 1 \\ I & \end{pmatrix}\begin{pmatrix} A & v_p^t \\ -u_p & 0 \end{pmatrix}^{-1},$$

and so $\mathcal{R}\begin{pmatrix} v_p^t & A \\ 0 & -u_p \end{pmatrix} = (\mathcal{R}A^{-1})^{-1}$.

Equipped with (4)-(6), the statement of the theorem is directly proved by induction. If $s = 1$, f is either a variable or a field element and we have

$$f = \mathcal{R}\begin{pmatrix} 1 & f \\ 0 & -1 \end{pmatrix}.$$

If $s > 1$, consider the output node of the size-s formula computing f and apply (4)-(6) accordingly. □

The matrix A_Φ can be written as $Q_0 + x_1Q_1 + \cdots + x_nQ_n$, where Q_0 is a matrix in $\mathbb{F}$ and $Q_1, \ldots Q_n$ are 0,1-matrices. In general, if A is a matrix of the form

$$Q_0 + x_1Q_1 + \cdots + x_nQ_n\,, \text{ with } Q_0, \ldots, Q_n \in \mathrm{Mat}_{s'\times s'}(\mathbb{F})$$

R is a ring with $R \supseteq \mathbb{F}$, and $a_1, \ldots, a_n \in R$, we define

$$A(a_1, \ldots, a_n) := Q_0 + a_1Q_1 + \cdots + a_nQ_n\,;$$

it is a matrix in $\mathrm{Mat}_{s'\times s'}(R)$. Theorem 2.5 can be generalized in the following manner:

PROPOSITION 6.1. *Let $\mathbb{F}$ be a field and R a ring whose centre contains $\mathbb{F}$. Assume that $\Phi(x_1, \ldots, x_n)$ is a formula of size s and $a_1, \ldots, a_n \in R$ are such that $\widehat{\Phi}^R(a_1, \ldots, a_n)$ is defined. Then $A_\Phi(a_1, \ldots, a_n)$ is invertible in $M_{s'\times s'}(R)$, and $\widehat{\Phi}^R(a_1, \ldots, a_n)$ is an entry in A_Φ^{-1}.*

The proof is almost identical to that of Theorem 2.5. The only difference is that we do not assume that R is a skew field, and we must check that the constructed matrix A is indeed invertible. This follows from the assumption that $\widehat{\Phi}^R(a_1, \ldots, a_n)$ is defined.

By means of Lemma 4.5, Proposition 6.1 implies:

COROLLARY 6.2. *Assume that a rational function f can be computed by a formula with k inverses. Then there exists an $O(k) \times O(k)$ invertible matrix A whose entries are polynomials such that f is an entry of A^{-1}.*

The matrix inverse representation of rational functions will be directly used in the next section, on the *rational identity testing* problem. Before that we take a detour to discuss the special case of formulae without inverse gates.

6.1 Triangular matrices

As remarked in the "Main results" section, commutatively or not, the determinant is complete for formulas without inverse gates. That is, a polynomial f can be written as $f = \det(A)$, where A is a matrix of variables or field elements whose dimension is linear in the formula size of f. One difference between commutative and non-commutative setting is the following: the commutative determinant can be computed by a formula of size $n^{O(\log n)}$, but non-commutatively, it requires formula of exponential size (see [35]). However, let us remark here that this gulf is by no means necessary. Inspecting the construction presented in [24], one can see that it uses only matrices A of a specific form, and one can show the determinant of such matrices can be computed by a non-commutative formula of quasipolynomial size.

Let us first see what happens with our construction in Theorem 2.5, if we assume that f is a non-commutative polynomial computed by a formula without inverse gates. The constructed matrix A is then upper triangular with field elements on the diagonal. We summarize the properties of such matrices this in the following proposition:

PROPOSITION 6.3. *(i). Let A be an $n \times n$-upper triangular matrix whose entries are variables or field elements such that A has non-zero field elements on the diagonal. Then the entries of A^{-1} are polynomials. Moreover, every entry can be computed by a formula without inverse gates of size $n^{O(\log n)}$.*

(ii). Assume that a polynomial f can be computed by a formula without inverse gates of size s. Then there exists a $2s \times 2s$-upper triangular matrix A whose entries are variables or field elements, A has 1 or -1 on the diagonal, and f is the entry in the upper-right corner of A^{-1}.

PROOF. (*i*) Without loss of generality assume that A has the constant 1 on the diagonal, and write $A = I - J$, where J is an upper triangular matrix with zeros on the diagonal. This implies that $J^n = 0$ and therefore

$$A^{-1} = (I - J)^{-1} = I + J + J^2 + \ldots J^{n-1}.$$

In general, if B is $n \times n$ matrix then every entry of B^k can be computed by a formula of size $n^{O(\log k)}$. This means that A^{-1} has formula size $n^{O(\log n)}$.

(*ii*) Inspect the construction in the proof of Theorem 2.5. The equation (6) is never applied since f is computed without inverse gates. Equations (4) and (5) convert upper-triangular matrices A, B to an upper triangular matrix. □

One may wonder whether Proposition 6.3 can be improved to show that A^{-1} can be computed by a polynomial size formula, if A is upper triangular. However, this problem is – up to a polynomial – equivalent to the problem of computing the product $A_1A_2\dots A_k$ of $n\times n$ matrices $A_1,\dots,A_k$. We have seen one half of this statement in the proof of Proposition 6.3: in order to compute A^{-1}, it is sufficient to compute $J,J^2,\dots,J^{n-1}$. Conversely, suppose that we want to compute the product of $n\times n$ matrices $A_1A_2\dots A_k$. Let A be the $((k+1)n)\times((k+1)n)$- matrix

$$A:=\begin{pmatrix} I & -A_1 & & & \\ & I & -A_2 & & \\ & & \ddots & & \\ & & & I & -A_k \\ & & & & I\end{pmatrix}. \quad (7)$$

One can check that the $n\times n$-block in the upper right corner of A^{-1} equals $A_1A_2\dots A_k$. This means that the inverse of an upper triangular matrix has a polynomial size formula iff the power of a matrix can be computed by a polynomial size formula, which is believed to be unlikely.

This observation can be used to strengthen Proposition 6.3 to apply to algebraic branching programs instead of formulas. An *algebraic branching program*, ABP, is a directed acyclic graph without multiple edges and with exactly one source and one sink such that every edge is labelled by a (not necessarily homogeneous) linear function $\sum_i a_ix_i+b$. An ABP computes a polynomial which is the sum, over all paths from the source to the sink, of products of the linear functions on that path. We are considering non-commutative computation, and the order of multiplication is taken from the source to the sink. The size of an ABP is the number of vertices.

Algebraic branching programs can simulate formulas (without inverse gates), and are believed to be more powerful. This is because the product $A_1A_2\dots A_k$ of $n\times n$ matrices can be computed by an ABP of size $O(kn^2)$, but the best-known formula has size $n^{O(\log k)}$. In fact, algebraic branching programs can be characterized in terms of matrix product:

LEMMA 6.4. *Assume that a polynomial f in n variables can be computed by an ABP of size s. Then there exist $k\times k$ matrices $A_1,\dots,A_{2s}$ with $k=O(ns^2)$ such that their entries are variables or field elements and f is the entry in the upper-right corner of the product $A_1A_2\dots A_{2s}$.*

PROOF. Let f have n variables and let C be an ABP of size s computing f. First, show that f can be computed by an ABP B with the following properties:

(i). Every edge is labelled by a variable or a field element.

(ii). B has $2s+1$ levels: the vertices can be partitioned into disjoint sets $B_0,B_1,\dots B_{2s}$ with every edge going from B_i to B_{i+1} , and with B_0 and B_{2s} containing only the source and the sink, respectively.

(iii). For every $i\in\{1,\dots,2s-1\}$, B_i has size $k=O(ns^2)$.

(i) is obtained by taking every edge in C labelled by $a_1x_1+\dots a_nx_n+b$ and replacing it by n new vertices and $2n+1$ edges, labelled by $a_1,x_1,\dots,a_n,x_n$ and b respectively. Since C has at most $\binom{s}{2}$ edges, the new ABP has $k=O(ns^2)$ vertices. Moreover, since C had depth at most s, the new ABP has depth at most $2s$. The conditions (ii) and (iii) will be guaranteed by adding a copy of every vertex to every level $B_1,\dots,B_{2s-1}$, with appropriate labels of edges.

For $i\in 1,\dots,2s-1$, let v_i be the vector of the k polynomials computed by the nodes in B_i and let $v_0:=(1,0,\dots,0)$ and $v_{2s}:=(0,\dots,0,f)$. The condition (i) guarantees that we can find, for every $i\in\{1,\dots,2s\}$, a $k\times k$ matrix A_i of variables or field elements such that

$$v_i=v_{i-1}A_i\,.$$

Hence $v_{2s}=v_0A_1A_2\dots A_{2s}$, which implies that f is the entry in the upper-right corner of $A_1A_2\dots A_{2s}$. □

PROPOSITION 6.5. *(i). Let A be an $n\times n$-upper triangular matrix whose entries are variables or field elements such that A has non-zero field elements on the diagonal. Then every entry of A^{-1} can be computed by a polynomial size ABP.*

(ii). Assume that a polynomial f in n variables can be computed by an ABP of size s. Then there exists a $k\times k$-upper triangular matrix A with $k=O(ns^3)$ whose entries are variables or field elements, A has 1 on the diagonal, and f is the entry in the upper-right corner of A^{-1}.

PROOF. (i) is as in Proposition 6.3, where we note that J^k can be computed by a polynomial-size ABP.

(ii). Let $A_1,\dots,A_{2s}$ be the matrices from the previous lemma. Let

$$A:=\begin{pmatrix} I & A_1 & & & \\ & I & A_2 & & \\ & & \ddots & & \\ & & & I & A_{2s} \\ & & & & I\end{pmatrix}.$$

be as in (7). Then the upper-right block in A^{-1} is $A_1\cdots A_{2s}$ and hence f is the entry in the upper-right corner of A^{-1}. □

6.2 The determinant of nearly triangular matrices

We now discuss the connection between matrix inverse of triangular matrices and the determinant of *nearly* triangular matrices. If $X_n=(x_{i,j})_{i,j\in[n]}$, let

$$\det(X) = \sum_{\sigma\in S_n} sgn(\sigma)x_{1,\sigma(1)}\dots x_{n,\sigma(n)}$$

$$\mathrm{perm}(X) = \sum_{\sigma\in S_n} x_{1,\sigma(1)}\dots x_{n,\sigma(n)}.$$

A $n\times n$-matrix A will be called *nearly (upper) triangular*, if for every $i,j\in[n]$, $A_{i,j}\in\{1,-1\}$, if $j=i-1$, and $A_{i,j}=0$, if $j<i-1$. That is, A is upper triangular, except for a string of 1 and -1 below the main diagonal.

As an application of Propositions 6.3 and 6.5, we obtain:

PROPOSITION 6.6. *(i). Let A be a nearly triangular matrix consisting of variables or field elements. Then $\det(A)$ can be computed by a non-commutative formula of size $n^{O(\log n)}$ without inverse gates, and also by a polynomial size ABP.*

(ii). Let f be a polynomial in n variables which is computed by a) a formula of size s without inverse gates, or b) an

ABP of size s. Then $f = \det(A)$, where A is a $k \times k$-nearly triangular matrix whose entries are variables or field elements where a) $k = 2s$, or b) $k = O(ns^3)$.

PROOF. To prove (i), extend A to an upper triangular matrix

$$B = \begin{pmatrix} u^t & A \\ 0 & v \end{pmatrix} \text{ with } u = (1, 0, \ldots, 0), v = (0, \ldots, 0, 1).$$

Let g be the entry in the upper right corner of B^{-1}. By Propositions 6.3 and 6.5, g can be computed by a quasipolynomial size formula and a polynomial-size ABP. Commutatively, we would be done, since $\det(B)$ is either 1 or -1 and A is the minor of $B_{n+1,1}$. Hence g is equal – up to a sign – to $\det(A)$. Non-commutatively, one must check that the inverse of an upper triangular matrix can indeed be expressed in terms of determinants of minors. This we leave as an exercise. (Note that in the definition of the determinant, variables of X are multiplied row by row.)

Similarly, if A is the matrix from Proposition 6.3 or 6.5, such that f is the entry in the upper right corner of A^{-1}, we can argue that f is – up to a sign – equal to the determinant of the minor of $A_{2s,1}$, and this minor is a nearly upper triangular matrix. (The sign can be accounted for by adding an appropriate row and column.) □

A well-known, albeit not well-used, approach to lower-bounds on commutative formula size, is to try to bound the smallest s such that $f = \det(A)$, where A is an $s \times s$ matrix of variables or field elements. The previous Proposition shows that we can without loss of generality assume that A is nearly upper triangular. This restricted problem may perhaps be easier to solve. Also, one could hope to prove a lower bound even for the determinant itself: to ask what is the smallest s such that $\det(X) = \det(A)$, where A is a nearly triangular matrix of variables or field elements.

However, the following shows that the modified problem is different only in the non-commutative setting:

COROLLARY 6.7. *(i). Assume that $\det(X_n) = \det(A)$ or $\mathrm{perm}(X_n) = \det(A)$, where A is a nearly triangular matrix with entries variables or field elements, of dimension $s \times s$. Then $s \geq 2^{\Omega(n)}$.*

(ii). Assuming commutativity of variables, there exists a polynomial-size nearly triangular matrix A of variables or field elements such that $\det(X_n) = \det(A)$.

PROOF. (i) By [35], both $\det(X_n)$ and $\mathrm{perm}(X_n)$ require ABP of size $2^{\Omega(n)}$, but $\det(A)$ can be computed by a polynomial-size ABP.

(ii) Commutatively, $\det(X_n)$ can be computed by a branching program of a polynomial size, and use part (ii) of Proposition 6.6. □

7. THE RATIONAL IDENTITY TESTING PROBLEM

We will now address the following basic question: how can we decide whether two rational expressions define the same rational function? This is equivalent to testing whether a single rational expression defines the zero function. This problem can take several forms, and we will focus on deciding whether a *formula* computes the zero function, and refer to this question as the *rational identity testing* problem. As we shall see, the complexity of this problem will depend on a natural problem in (commutative) invariant theory of a simple linear-algebraic flavor, which will appear again in the next section on the elimination of divisions.

In the commutative setting, the rational identity testing problem can be reduced to the well-known *polynomial identity testing* problem, which can be solved quite efficiently by a polynomial time randomized algorithm, by means of Schwarz-Zippel Lemma. The reduction is possible due to the fact that a commutative rational function can be written as a ratio of two polynomials.

Given the complex structure of rational expressions, it is not even clear that the rational identity testing problem is decidable. This was shown in [9]. The algorithm eventually requires deciding whether a set of (commutative) polynomial equations has a solution, which puts this problem in $PSPACE$. We will outline a probabilistic algorithm whose efficiency depends on an extra parameter w arising from the above mentioned invariant-theory problem, and assuming the bound is polynomial in s will yield a BPP algorithm for the problem.

The parameter is defined as follows:

- $w(s)$ is the smallest k so that for every correct formula $\Phi(x_1, \ldots, x_n)$ of size s there exists $p \leq k$ and $a_1, \ldots, a_n \in R := \mathrm{Mat}_{p\times p}(\bar{\mathbb{F}})$ such that $\widehat{\Phi}^R(a_1, \ldots, a_n)$ is defined[8].

We will sketch a randomized algorithm for rational identity testing which runs in time polynomial in s and $w(s)$. We will also consider a different version of the parameter. Recall that a linear matrix is of the form

$$A = Q_0 + x_1 Q_1 + \cdots + x_n Q_n, \text{ with } Q_0, \ldots, Q_n \in \mathrm{Mat}_{s\times s}(\mathbb{F}). \quad (8)$$

The second parameter is defined as:

- $\tilde{w}(s)$ is the smallest k so that for every $s \times s$ matrix A of the form (8) with $Q_0 = 0$ and $n = s$, if A is invertible in $\mathbb{F}\langle x_1, \ldots, x_s \rangle$ then there exists $p \leq k$ and $a_1, \ldots, a_s \in \mathrm{Mat}_{p\times p}(\bar{\mathbb{F}})$ such that $Q_1 \otimes a_1 + \ldots Q_s \otimes a_s$ is invertible in $\mathrm{Mat}_{sp\times sp}(\bar{\mathbb{F}})$.

That both $w(s)$ and $\tilde{w}(s)$ are finite essentially follows from (a) in Section 2. We will prove this in Section 7.1 where the two parameters are further discussed. Note that the absence of the constant term Q_0 in $\tilde{w}$ is mostly cosmetic:

(a) $Q_0 + \sum_{i=1}^n x_i Q_i$ is invertible iff $x_0 Q_0 + \sum_{i=1}^n x_i Q_i$ is invertible,

(b) If $Q_0 \otimes a_0 + \sum_{i=1}^n Q_i \otimes a_i$ is invertible for some $a_0, \ldots, a_n \in \mathrm{Mat}_{p\times p}(\bar{\mathbb{F}})$ then a_0 can be assumed invertible ($\bar{\mathbb{F}}$ is infinite) and so $Q_0 \otimes I_p + \sum_{i=1}^n Q_i \otimes (a_0^{-1} a_i)$ is invertible.

Let us first observe that the rational identity problem is essentially equivalent to the following problem: decide whether a formula Φ is a correct formula. For, in order to see whether Φ is correct, we must only check that for every inverse gate u^{-1} in Φ, Φ_u doesn't compute the zero function. Conversely, a correct formula Φ computes the zero function if and only if Φ^{-1} is not a correct formula. Using the construction in Theorem 2.5, we can give the following criterion for the correctness of a formula:

[8] $\bar{\mathbb{F}}$ is the algebraic closure of $\mathbb{F}$

PROPOSITION 7.1. *Let $\mathbb{F}$ be a field and R a ring whose centre contains $\mathbb{F}$. For a formula Φ and $a_1, \dots, a_n \in R$, the following are equivalent:*

(i). $\widehat{\Phi}^R(a_1, \dots, a_n)$ is defined.

(ii). For every gate u in Φ, $A_{\Phi_u}(a_1, \dots, a_n)$ is invertible in $Mat(R)$.

PROOF. $(i)\rightarrow(ii)$ follows from Proposition 6.1. To prove the converse, assume that $\widehat{\Phi}^R(a_1, \dots, a_n)$ is not defined. Then there exists a gate u^{-1} in Φ such that $\widehat{\Phi}_u(a_1, \dots, a_n)$ is defined but $b := \widehat{\Phi}_u(a_1, \dots, a_n)$ is not invertible in R. Let $A := A_{\Phi_u}(a_1, \dots, a_n)$. From Proposition 6.1, we know that A is invertible and $b = \mathcal{R}A^{-1}$, where we invoke the notation from the proof Theorem 2.5. It is sufficient to show that $B := A_{\Phi_{u^{-1}}}(a_1, \dots, a_n)$ is not invertible.

From the construction of A_Φ, we have

$$B = \begin{pmatrix} v_p^t & A \\ 0 & -u_p \end{pmatrix}.$$

We can multiply this matrix by invertible matrices to show that B is invertible iff

$$\begin{pmatrix} A & 0 \\ 0 & u_p A^{-1} v_p^t \end{pmatrix} = \begin{pmatrix} A & 0 \\ 0 & \mathcal{R}A^{-1} \end{pmatrix} = \begin{pmatrix} A & 0 \\ 0 & b \end{pmatrix}$$

is invertible. A block-diagonal matrix is invertible iff each of the blocks is invertible. But b is not invertible and hence B is not invertible. $\square$

Specializing to the case $R = \mathbb{F}\langle\!\langle x_1, \dots, x_n \rangle\!\rangle$, we obtain:

COROLLARY 7.2. *Φ is a correct formula iff for every gate u in Φ, A_{Φ_u} is invertible.*

Hence, the problem of deciding whether Φ is a correct formula can be reduced to the problem of deciding whether a matrix A, whose entries are degree one polynomials, is invertible. The algorithm in [9] in fact solves this latter problem. The essence of the algorithm is Theorem 2.1. By the second part of the theorem, A of dimension $m \times m$ is invertible iff it cannot be written as $B \cdot C$ where B, C consist of degree-one polynomials and have dimensions $m \times k$ and $k \times m$, respectively, with $k < m$. Taking the coefficients of the polynomials in B, C as unknows, the problem is expressible in terms of solvability of a set of (commutative) polynomial equations over $\mathbb{F}$.

However, we will use a different invertibility test:

PROPOSITION 7.3. *Let A be as in (8). Then A is invertible in $Mat_{s\times s}(\mathbb{F}\langle\!\langle \bar{x} \rangle\!\rangle)$ iff there exists $k \in \mathbb{N}$ and $a_1, \dots, a_n \in Mat_{k\times k}(\mathbb{F})$ such that $Q_0 \otimes I_k + Q_1 \otimes a_1 + \dots Q_n \otimes a_n$ is invertible in $Mat_{sk\times sk}(\mathbb{F})$.*

PROOF. If A is invertible, there is $A^{-1} \in \mathrm{Mat}_{s\times s}(\mathbb{F}\langle\!\langle \bar{x} \rangle\!\rangle)$ with $A \cdot A^{-1} = A^{-1} \cdot A = I_s$. The entries of A^{-1} are rational functions. By (a) in Section 2, there exist $k \in \mathbb{N}$ and $a_1, \dots, a_n \in R := \mathrm{Mat}_{k\times k}(\bar{\mathbb{F}})$ such that every $A^{-1}_{i,j}$ is defined on $a_1, \dots, a_n$. (To obtain $a_1, \dots, a_n$ which work for every i, j, it is enough to consider a circuit in which every $A^{-1}_{i,j}$ is computed by some gate.) Evaluating A^{-1} at this point gives a matrix $B \in \mathrm{Mat}_{s\times s}(R)$ such that

$$A(a_1, \dots, a_n) \cdot B = B \cdot A(a_1, \dots, a_n) = I_s\,,$$

and so $A(a_1, \dots, a_n)$ is invertible in $\mathrm{Mat}_{s\times s}(R)$. It is a $s \times s$-matrix with $k \times k$-matrices as entries, and it can be identified with the $sk \times sk$-matrix $A(a_1, \dots, a_n)' = Q_0 \otimes I_k + Q_1 \otimes a_1 + \dots Q_n \otimes a_n$. Clearly, $A(a_1, \dots, a_n)$ is invertible iff $A(a_1, \dots, a_n)'$ is invertible. Hence $A(a_1, \dots, a_n)'$ is invertible.

If A is not invertible then it is not full by Theorem 2.1. Hence $A(a_1, \dots, a_n)$ is not full in R for every $R = \mathrm{Mat}_{k\times k}(\mathbb{F})$ and every $a_1, \dots, a_n$. Hence $A(a_1, \dots, a_n)$ and $A(a_1, \dots, a_n)'$ is never invertible. $\square$

The quantity $\tilde{w}$ is utilized as follows. Let A be an $s \times s$ matrix as in (8), and k a parameter. Introduce nk^2 distinct *commutative* variables $y^i_{p,q}, i \in \{1, \dots, n\}, p, q \in \{1, \dots, k\}$. For every variable x_i, consider the $k \times k$ matrix

$$x_i^\star := (y^i_{p,q})_{p,q\in\{1,\dots,k\}}\,,$$

and let

$$A^{(k)} := Q_0 \otimes I_s + Q_1 \otimes x_1^\star + \dots Q_n \otimes x_n^\star\,.$$

It is $sk \times sk$ matrix whose entries are commutative (linear) polynomials in the auxiliary variables Y.

Then we obtain the following invertibility test:

PROPOSITION 7.4. *Let A be as (8) with $n = s$ and $Q_0 = 0$. Then A is invertible iff there exists $k \le \tilde{w}(s)$ such that $\det(A^{(k)}) \neq 0$ (as a polynomial in $\mathbb{F}[Y]$).*

PROOF. By the definition of $\tilde{w}$, A is invertible (over the free skew field) iff there exists $k \le \tilde{w}(s)$ such that $A^{(k)}$ is invertible (over the field of fractions $\mathbb{F}(Y)$). The matrix $A^{(k)}$ has entries from the commutative ring $\mathbb{F}[Y] \subseteq \mathbb{F}(Y)$ and so it is invertible iff $\det(A^{(k)}) \neq 0$. $\square$

Setting $m := s\tilde{w}(s)$, each $A^{(k)}$ has dimension at most $m \times m$, and each entry is a linear polynomial in the commuting variables Y. Hence $\det(A^{(k)})$ is a polynomial of degree at most m, and it can be computed by a commutative arithmetic circuit of size polynomial in m. This allows to test invertibility of A by a randomized algorithm running in time polynomial in m.

By means of Proposition 7.1, this also gives an algorithm for rational identity testing whose complexity depends on $\tilde{w}$. However, such an algorithm can also be obtained using the parameter w instead. Proposition 7.1 gives:

PROPOSITION 7.5. *For a formula Φ of size s, the following are equivalent:*

(i). Φ is a correct formula.

(ii). There exists $k \le w(s)$ such that for every gate u in Φ, $\det(A^{(k)}_{\Phi_u}) \neq 0$.

By Theorem 2.5, each of the matrices $A^{(k)}_{\Phi_u}$ has size at most $2sw(s) \times 2sw(s)$ and each entry is again a linear polynomial in the commuting variables Y. This allows to reduce the non-commutative rational identity testing problem to s instances of the commutative polynomial identity testing problem.

Non-commutative polynomial *identity testing*

Let us add some comments about the special case of rational identity testing: decide whether a formula or a circuit *without* inverse gates computes the zero polynomial. In [37], Raz and Shpilka show that the problem can be decided by a polynomial time deterministic algorithm for a formula or even an arithmetic branching program. For a non-commutative circuit, no such deterministic algorithm is known. In [4], Bogdanov and Wee show it can be decided by a polynomial time randomized algorithm.

The main point is given by the celebrated Amitsur-Levitzki theorem ([2], discussed in a greater detail in Section 9): if a polynomial f vanishes on all $k \times k$ matrices over an infinite field then f must have degree at least $2k$. Hence, assume that we are given a division free circuit Φ computing a polynomial $f(x_1, \ldots, x_n)$ of degree $< 2k$. To check whether $f(x_1, \ldots, x_n) = 0$, it is now sufficient to check whether $f(a_1, \ldots, a_n) = 0$ for all $k \times k$ matrices $a_1, \ldots, a_n$, over an infinite field. As above, we can interpret $f(a_1, \ldots, a_n)$ as a matrix of k^2 polynomials in nk^2 commuting variables, each of degree $< 2k$, and hence reduce the non-commutative identity testing problem to k^2 instances of the commutative identity testing. This yields a polynomial time randomized algorithm, whenever we focus on a class of circuits computing polynomials of a polynomial degree.

7.1 The two parameters

Proposition 7.5 shows that in order to obtain an efficient rational identity testing algorithm, it is enough to show that $w(s)$ is small. The other parameter $\tilde{w}$ is designed to solve the more general problem of deciding whether a linear matrix is invertible. We now show a simple upper bound on w in terms of $\tilde{w}$ (and that the definitions of the parameters are indeed correct):

PROPOSITION 7.6. *Both w and $\tilde{w}$ are well-defined non-decreasing functions and $w(s) \leq \tilde{w}(s^2 + s)$.*

PROOF. We first show that $\tilde{w}(s)$ is well-defined (finite) for every s. Let T be the set of non-invertible linear matrices of the form $A = \sum_{i=1}^{s} x_i Q_i$ with $Q_1, \ldots, Q_s \in \mathrm{Mat}_{s\times s}(\mathbb{F})$. Proposition 7.3 asserts that $A \in T$ iff $\det(\sum_{i=1}^{s} Q_i \otimes a_i) = 0$ for every $k \in N$ and $a_1, \ldots, a_s \in \mathrm{Mat}_{k\times k}(\mathbb{F})$. We can view A as the s-tuple of the $s \times s$ matrices $Q_1, \ldots, Q_s$ and T as a subset of $\mathbb{F}^{s^3}$. Then we see that T is an algebraic set defined by the equations $\det(\sum_{i=1}^{s} Q_i \otimes a_i) = 0$, for all possible a_i's. By Hilbert's basis theorem, a finite subsets of the equations is enough to define T. Switching to the complement of T, this means that there exists $k \in \mathbb{N}$ such that A is invertible iff there exists $p \leq k$ and $a_1, \ldots, a_s \in \mathrm{Mat}_{k\times k}(\mathbb{F})$ such that $\sum_{i=1}^{s} Q_i \otimes a_i$ is invertible – and $\tilde{w}(s)$ is the smallest such k.

$\tilde{w}$ is non-decreasing because an invertible matrix A can be enlarged to a block-diagonal $(s+1) \times (s+1)$ invertible matrix A', the blocks being A and x_1.

We now prove the inequality $w(s) \leq \tilde{w}(s^2 + s)$. Let Φ be a correct formula of size s in variables $x_1, \ldots, x_n$. We can assume that $n < s$ for otherwise $n = s = 1$ and both $w(s) = \tilde{w}(s) = 1$. For a gate v in Φ, let s_v be the size of Φ_v and let A_{Φ_v} be of dimension $k_v \times k_v$. Let $k := \sum_v k_v$. It is easy to see that $\sum_v s_v \leq (s^2 + s)/2$. Since $k_v \leq 2s_v$ (Theorem 2.5), we have that $k \leq s^2 + s$. Let A be a $k \times k$-matrix which is block-diagonal with the blocks being the matrices A_{Φ_v}, for all gates v. Then A is invertible and of the form $Q_0 + \sum_{i=1}^{n} x_i Q_i$ with $Q_1, \ldots, Q_n \in \mathrm{Mat}_{k\times k}(\mathbb{F})$. Hence also $x_0 Q_0 + \sum_{i=1}^{n} x_i Q_i$ is invertible, where x_0 is a fresh variable. Since $n + 1 \leq k$, there exist $p \leq \tilde{w}(k)$ and $a_0, \ldots, a_n \in R := \mathrm{Mat}_{p\times p}(\mathbb{F})$ so that $Q_0 \otimes a_0 + \sum_{i=1}^{n} Q_i \otimes a_i$ is invertible. As in (b) above, we conclude that there exist $b_1, \ldots, b_n \in R$ so that $Q_0 \otimes I_p + \sum_{i=1}^{n} Q_i \otimes b_i$ is invertible. That is, $A(b_1, \ldots, b_n)$ is invertible in $\mathrm{Mat}_{k\times k}(R)$ – and hence all the blocks A_{Φ_v} are. This shows that $\Phi^R(b_1, \ldots, b_n)$ is defined by Proposition 7.1 and so $w(s) \leq \tilde{w}(k) = \tilde{w}(s^2 + s)$.

This entails that w is well-defined. It is non-decreasing because a correct formula Φ of size s can be modified to a correct formula of size $s + 1$ which contains all the inverse gates of Φ. (Hint: Φ^{-1} works whenever $\widehat{\Phi} \neq 0$.) □

We do not have a reason to believe that the inequality in Proposition 7.6 is even close to being tight. Hence, estimating w in terms of $\tilde{w}$ can turn out to be far too generous. However, the main appeal of $\tilde{w}$ is the simplicity of its definition. By means of Proposition 7.3, $\tilde{w}$ can be introduced without any reference to computations or even the skew field: in the definition of $\tilde{w}$, the assumption "A is invertible over $\mathbb{F}\langle\!\langle \bar{x} \rangle\!\rangle$" can be replaced by the assumption "$\sum_{i=1}^{s} Q_i \otimes a_i$ is invertible for some $m \in \mathbb{N}$ and $a_1, \ldots, a_s \in \mathrm{Mat}_{m\times m}(\mathbb{F})$". We also note that the suspected gap between w and $\tilde{w}$ disappears if in the definition of $\tilde{w}$, we consider only matrices A which come from a representation of some formula Φ as in Theorem 2.5 – i.e., $A = A_\Phi$ for some Φ.

8. HOW TO ELIMINATE DIVISIONS

A classical result of Strassen [44], see also [6] Chapter 7.1, asserts that division gates are not very helpful when computing commutative polynomials. If a commutative polynomial f of degree k can be computed by a circuit with divisions of size s then it can be computed by a circuit without divisions of size $O(sk^2)$. (The original argument assumes that the underlying field is infinite. It was noted in [26] that a similar statement holds over any field.) However, when dealing with non-commutative computations, the situation seems to be much more complicated. To outline the main issue, assume that we have computed a polynomial f using only one inverse g^{-1} for a polynomial g. Commutatively, if $g \neq 0$ and $\mathbb{F}$ is infinite, there must exist $a \in \mathbb{F}^n$ such that $g(a) \neq 0$. We can then rewrite g^{-1} as a power series around the point a. Supposing f has degree k, it is enough to truncate the series up to terms of degree k, obtaining a computation of f without divisions. Non-commutatively, no such substitution from $\mathbb{F}$ may exist. For example, $g = xy - yx$ is a non-zero polynomial which vanishes on every substitution from $\mathbb{F}$. An obvious remedy is to allow substitutions which are $m \times m$ matrices over $\mathbb{F}$, and then to work with power series in this matrix algebra. In the example $xy - yx$, it is easy to find 2×2 matrices a, b such that $ab - ba$ is invertible, and the power series argument yields a satisfactory answer. However, as g gets more complicated, we must substitute $m \times m$ matrices with a larger m. Computations with $m \times m$ matrices have cost roughly m^3 and in order to eliminate divisions efficiently, we want m to have polynomial size. The question now becomes: what is the dimension of matrices we need to make g invertible? We do not know how to answer this question and state it as Problem 3 in Section 9. As opposed to the running example, we cannot in general assume that g is a polynomial: it may itself contain inverses, and nested inverses. This makes the bound on m quite challenging; see Section 9 for further discussion. In Proposition 8.3, we will prove only a conditional result: if a polynomial f is computed by a circuit with divisions Φ such that $\widehat{\Phi}$ is defined for some matrices of small size, then f can be computed by a small circuit without division gates.

We now proceed towards proving Proposition 8.3. This requires introducing some definitions as well as extending definitions from Section 2. Let R be an arbitrary (unital) ring and let $\bar{x} = \{x_1, \ldots, x_n\}$ a set of variables. $R\langle\bar{x}\rangle$ will denote the set of polynomials in variables $\bar{x}$ with coefficients from R. The ring R is not in general commutative, and the variables do not multiplicatively commute, but we will assume that variables commute with elements of R. More exactly, a polynomial in $R\langle\bar{x}\rangle$ is a sum

$$\sum_\alpha c_\alpha \alpha ,$$

where α ranges over products of variables from $\bar{x}$ and $c_\alpha \in R$, with only finitely many c_α's being non-zero . Addition and multiplication are given by

$$\begin{aligned} \sum_\alpha c_\alpha\alpha + \sum_\alpha c'_\alpha\alpha &= \sum_\alpha (c_\alpha + c'_\alpha)\alpha , \\ \sum_\alpha c_\alpha\alpha \cdot \sum_\alpha c'_\alpha\alpha &= \sum_{\alpha,\beta} (c_\alpha c'_\beta)(\alpha\beta) . \end{aligned}$$

We will extend $R\langle\bar{x}\rangle$ to the ring of power-series[9] $R\{\bar{x}\}$. A power series $f \in R\{x\}$ is an infinite sum

$$f^{(0)} + f^{(1)} + f^{(2)} + \ldots ,$$

where every $f^{(k)} \in R\langle\bar{x}\rangle$ is a homogeneous polynomial of degree k. Addition and multiplication is defined in the obvious way:

$$(f+g)^{(k)} = f^{(k)} + g^{(k)} , \quad (f \cdot g)^{(k)} = \sum_{i+j=k} f^{(i)} \cdot g^{(j)} .$$

If $f^{(0)} = a \in R$ is invertible in R than f is invertible in $R\{\bar{x}\}$. Its inverse is given by

$$\begin{aligned} f^{-1} &= (a - (a - f))^{-1} = a^{-1}(1 - (1 - fa^{-1}))^{-1} = \\ &= a^{-1} \sum_{i=0}^{\infty} (1 - fa^{-1})^i . \end{aligned}$$

If we denote the partial sum $f^{(0)} + f^{(1)} + \cdots + f^{(k)}$ by $f^{(\leq k)}$ this can be written as

$$(f^{-1})^{(\leq k)} = a^{-1} \Big(\sum_{i=0}^{k} (1 - f^{(\leq k)} a^{-1})^i\Big)^{(\leq k)} , \qquad (9)$$

We also need to extend the definition of a circuit so that it can compute power series over R: this is achieved by taking circuits as introduced in Section 2, but allowing them to use elements of R in the computation (in the same way elements of the fields were). Such a circuit will be called an *R-circuit*. All other notions are generalized in an obvious manner. Mainly, an R-circuit computes an element of $R\{\bar{x}\}$: evaluate the circuit gate-by-gate over $R\{\bar{x}\}$. This either produces an element of $R\{\bar{x}\}$, or the evaluation fails due to attempting invasion of a non-invertible elements in $R\{\bar{x}\}$.

LEMMA 8.1. *Assume that $f \in R\{\bar{x}\}$ can be computed by an R-circuit of size s and depth d. Then for every $k \in \mathbb{N}$, $f^{(\leq k)} \in R\langle\bar{x}\rangle$ can be computed by an R-circuit without division gates of size $O(sk^3)$ and depth $O(d \log^2 k)$.*

PROOF. We divide the proof into two steps.

Step 1. Let Φ be the circuit computing f, and let us fix k. We will construct a division-free circuit Φ' of size $O(sk)$ and depth $O(d \log k)$ computing a polynomial $g \in R\langle\bar{x}\rangle$ such that $f^{(\leq k)} = g^{(\leq k)}$. Let $\lambda(z)$ be the univariate polynomial $\sum_{i=0}^{k} (1-z)^i$. Clearly, it can be computed by a division free circuit $\Lambda(z)$ of size $O(k)$ and depth $O(\log k)$ (actually, even of size $O(\log k)$). For any inverse gate u^{-1} in Φ, u computes an invertible element $\widehat{u} \in R\{\bar{x}\}$ and so $a := \widehat{u}^{(0)} \in R$ is invertible. Then Φ' is obtained by simultaneously replacing every inverse gate u^{-1} by the circuit $a^{-1}\Lambda(ua^{-1})$ and appropriately rewiring the inputs and outputs.

Since $a^{-1} \in R$, Φ' is an R-circuit without divisions, and it computes a polynomial $g \in R\langle\bar{x}\rangle$. That g satisfies $g^{(\leq k)} = f^{(\leq k)}$ is easily proved by induction on the size s. Note that for every f_1, f_2, $(f_1 \circ f_2)^{(\leq k)} = (f_1^{(\leq k)} \circ f_2^{(\leq k)})^{(\leq k)}$, where $\circ \in \{+, \cdot\}$, and (9) gives $(f_1^{-1})^{(\leq k)} = a^{-1}(\lambda(f_1^{(\leq k)} a^{-1}))^{(\leq k)}$, where $a = f_1^{(0)}$.

Step 2. Given a division-free Φ' of size s' and depth d' computing a polynomial g, $g^{(\leq k)}$ can be computed by a division-free circuit of size $O(s'k^2)$ and depth $O(d' \log k)$. This is a standard homogenization argument.

Altogether we have obtained a circuit of size $O(sk^3)$ and depth $O(d \log^2 k)$ computing $f^{(\leq k)}$. □

Next, we consider the ring of $m \times m$ matrices

$$R := \mathrm{Mat}_{m \times m}(\mathbb{F}) .$$

We want to interpret a polynomial $f \in R\langle\bar{x}\rangle$ as an $m \times m$ matrix $f^\star$ whose entries are polynomials in $\mathbb{F}\langle\bar{x}\rangle$. Let $f \in R\langle\bar{x}\rangle$ be written as $f = \sum_\alpha c_\alpha \alpha$, where $c_\alpha \in R$ and α ranges over products of the variables $\bar{x}$. Then $f^\star \in \mathrm{Mat}_{m \times m}(\mathbb{F}\langle\bar{x}\rangle)$ is the matrix with

$$f^\star_{i,j} = \sum_\alpha (c_\alpha)_{i,j}\alpha , \; i, j \in \{1, \ldots, m\} .$$

LEMMA 8.2. *Assume that $f \in R\langle\bar{x}\rangle$ can be computed by an R-circuit without divisions of size s and depth d. Then $f^\star$ can be computed by a circuit over $\mathbb{F}$ without divisions of size $O(sm^3)$ and depth $O(d \log m)$.*

PROOF. Note that $(f_1 + f_2)^\star = f_1^\star + f_2^\star$ and $(f_1 \cdot f_2)^\star = f_1^\star \cdot f_2^\star$, where on the right hand side we see a sum resp. product of $m \times m$ matrices. This means that a sum and a product gate in an R-circuit can be simulated by a sum resp. a product of $m \times m$ matrices over $\mathbb{F}$. This gives an increase in size of factor at most $O(m^3)$ and depth by a factor of $O(\log m)$. □

PROPOSITION 8.3. *Let $f \in \mathbb{F}\langle\bar{x}\rangle$ be a polynomial of degree k which is computable by a circuit Φ of size s and depth d. Assume that there exist matrices $a_1, \ldots, a_n \in R = Mat_{m \times m}(\mathbb{F})$ such that $\widehat{\Phi}^R(a_1, \ldots, a_n)$ is defined. Then f can be computed by a circuit without divisions of size $O(sk^3m^3)$ and depth $O(d \log^2 k \log m)$.*

PROOF. $\mathbb{F}$ can be embedded into R via the map $a \in \mathbb{F} \to aI_m \in R$. Similarly, each variable x_i is mapped to $x_i I_m$. So we can view f as en element of $R\langle\bar{x}\rangle$ and Φ as an R-circuit. Consider $g := f(x_1 + a_1, \ldots, x_n + a_n)$ and the R-circuit $\Phi' := \Phi(x_1 + a_1, \ldots, x_n + a_n)$. The assumption that $\widehat{\Phi}^R(a_1, \ldots, a_n)$ is defined guarantees that Φ' is a correct R-circuit computing $g \in R\langle\bar{x}\rangle \subseteq R\{\bar{x}\}$. By Lemma 8.1, $g^{(\leq k)}$ can be computed

[9]This ring is sometimes denoted $R\langle\langle\bar{x}\rangle\rangle$

by a division-free R-circuit Φ'' of size $O(sk^3)$ and depth $O(d\log^2 k)$. Since g has degree k, we have $g^{(\leq k)} = g$ and Ψ'' computes g. Moreover, $f = g(x_1 - a_1, \ldots, x_n - a_n)$ and so $\Phi''(x_1 - a_1, \ldots, x_n - a_n)$ computes f. Lemma 8.2 gives that $f^\star$ can be computed by a division-free circuit over $\mathbb{F}$ of size $O(sk^3m^3)$ and depth $O(d\log^2 k \log m)$. But $f^\star$ is simply the diagonal matrix with f on the diagonal and the statement of the proposition follows. □

Corollary 8.4. *Let $f \in \mathbb{F}\langle \bar{x} \rangle$ be a polynomial of degree k which is computable by a formula Φ of size s. Assume that there exist matrices $a_1, \ldots, a_n \in Mat_{m\times m}(\mathbb{F})$ such that $\widehat{\Phi}(a_1, \ldots, a_n)$ is defined. Then f can be computed by a formula without divisions of size $s^{O(\log^2 k \log m)}$.*

Recalling the definition of $w(s)$ from Section 7, the corollary implies that

- if $\mathbb{F}$ is algebraically closed then f can be computed by a formula without divisions of size $s^{O(\log^2 k \log w(s))}$.

The bounds presented in Proposition 8.3, and Corollary 8.4, are not intended to be optimal. A more careful calculation would show

- a size upper bound $O(sk^2 \log k{\cdot}m^\omega)$, where $\omega < 3$ is the (hitherto unknown) exponent of matrix multiplication
- depth upper bound $O(d\log k \log m)$ assuming that $\mathbb{F}$ is infinite (owing to savings in Step 2 in the proof of Lemma 8.1).

9. OPEN PROBLEMS

Problem 1. *Give an explicit polynomial $f \in \mathbb{F}\langle \bar{x} \rangle$ which cannot be computed by a polynomial size formula* with divisions.

Nisan's result [35] gives the solution for formulas without division gates. An obvious approach to Problem 1 is to show that division gates can be eliminated without increasing the formula size too much. This leads to the following question:

Problem 2. *Assume that a polynomial $f \in \mathbb{F}\langle \bar{x} \rangle$ of degree k can be computed by a circuit Φ with divisions of size s. Give a non-trivial upper bound on the size of a circuit without divisions computing f. Similarly for some other complexity measure of f, such as formula size.*

A conditional answer to Problem 2 was given in Proposition 8.3. There, we constructed a circuit without divisions computing f under the assumption that there exist matrices of small dimension for which the original circuit Φ is defined. (That is, matrices in $R = \mathrm{Mat}_{m\times m}(\mathbb{F})$ such that, when we evaluate Φ in R, we never come across an inverse gate computing a non-invertible matrix.) Hence:

Problem 3. *Assume that $\Phi(x_1, \ldots, x_n)$ is a correct circuit of size s. What is the smallest m so that there exist $a_1, \ldots, a_n \in R = Mat_{m\times m}(\mathbb{F})$ for which $\Phi^R(a_1, \ldots, a_n)$ is defined? Similarly, for some other complexity measure, such as formula size.*

As was explained in Section 7, the question is also relevant in the rational identity testing problem: to decide whether a formula computes the zero rational function. There, we also mentioned a related version of the question:

Problem 4. *Find an upper bound on the smallest $k = k(s)$, such that for all $Q_1, \ldots, Q_s \in Mat_{s\times s}(\mathbb{F})$ if $\sum_{i=1}^s x_i Q_i$ is invertible in $\mathbb{F}\langle\!\langle x_1, \ldots, x_s \rangle\!\rangle$ then $\sum_{i=1}^s Q_i \otimes a_i$ is invertible for some $a_1, a_2, \ldots, a_s \in Mat_{p\times p}(\mathbb{F})$ with $p \leq k$.*

Problems 3 and 4 are interesting from a purely algebraic perspective. The connection between them is explained in Section 7.1. Here, let us give few comments about Problem 3. First, such an m always exists, and can be bounded by a function of s. This is shown in Proposition 2.2 of [27] (cf. Proposition 7.1). Second, let us recall the celebrated Amitsur-Levitzki theorem [2]: for every p there exists a non-zero polynomial $f_p \in \mathbb{F}\langle x_1, \ldots, x_{2p} \rangle$ of degree $2p$ such that f_p vanishes on all $p\times p$ matrices. Conversely, every non-zero polynomial vanishing on all $p \times p$ matrices over an infinite field must have degree at least $2p$. The converse can be strengthened to show that if $0 \neq f \in \mathbb{F}\langle x_1, \ldots, x_n \rangle$ has degree $< 2p$, there exist $p \times p$ matrices $a_1, \ldots, a_n$ such that the matrix $f(a_1, \ldots, a_n)$ is invertible - indeed most tuples $(a_1, \ldots, a_n)$ will satisfy this property. This follows from another theorem of Amitsur (see [40] Theorem 3.2.6 and Exercise 2.4.2, as well as [30], Proposition 2.4). To apply this to Problem 3, suppose that the circuit Φ in Problem 3 contains a gate computing f_p^{-1}, where f_p is the Amitsur-Levitzki polynomial of degree $2p$. Then m must be at least $p + 1$, which shows that m grows with s. On the other hand, assume that Φ contains only one inverse gate computing g^{-1}, for some polynomial g of degree k. Then m can be taken $\leq k/2 + 1$. A similar bound can be obtained for any Φ of inverse height one. However, we do not know how to compose this argument, and what happens for circuits of general height – even the case of circuits of height two is far from clear.

Acknowledgement.

We thank Susan Durst, Peter Malcolmson and Aidan Schofield for useful references, Amir Yehudayoff and Klim Efremenko for comments on an earlier version of the paper.

10. REFERENCES

[1] B. Adsul, S. Nayak, and K. V. Subrahmanyam. A geometric approach to the Kronecker problem II: Invariants of matrices for simultaneous left-right actions. Manuscript, available in http://www.cmi.ac.in/ kv/ANS10.pdf, 2010.

[2] A. S. Amitsur and J. Levitzki. Minimal identities for algebras. *Proc. American Math Society*, 1:449–463, 1950.

[3] J. Berstel and C. Reutenauer. *Rational series and their applications*. Springer-Verlag, 1988.

[4] A. Bogdanov and H. Wee. More on noncommutative polynomial identity testing. In *IEEE Conference on Computational Complexity*, pages 92–99, 2005.

[5] R. P. Brent. The parallel evaluation of general arithmetic expressions. *J. ACM*, 21:201–206, 1974.

[6] P. Bürgisser, M. Clausen, and M. A. Shokrollahi. *Algebraic complexity theory*, volume 315 of *A series of comprehensive studies in mathematics*. Springer, 1997.

[7] P. M. Cohn. *Free rings and their relations*. Academic Press, 1985.

[8] P. M. Cohn. *Skew Fields*, volume 57 of *Encyclopedia of Mathematics*. Cambridge University Press, 1995.

[9] P. M. Cohn and C. Reutenauer. On the construction of the free field. *International Journal of Algebra and Computation*, 9(3-4):307–323, 1999.

[10] D. Cox, J. Little, and D. O'Shea. *Ideals, Varieties, and Algorithms*. Undergraduate Texts in Mathematics. Springer, New York, third edition, 2007.

[11] H. Derksen. Polynomial bounds for rings of invariants. *Proc. Amer. Math. Soc.*, 129:955–963, 2001.

[12] H. Derksen and G. Kemper. *Computational Invariant Theory*, volume 130 of *Encyclopaedia of Mathematical Sciences*. Springer-Verlag, Berlin, 2002.

[13] H. Derksen and J. Weyman. Semi-invariants of quivers and saturation for Littlewood-Richardson coefficients. *J. Amer. Math. Soc.*, 13:467–479, 2000.

[14] M. Domokos and A. N. Zubkov. Semi-invariants of quivers as determinants. *Transform. Groups*, 6(1):9–24, 2001.

[15] S. Donkin. Invariants of several matrices. *Invent. Math.*, 110(2):389–401, 1992.

[16] M. Forbes and A. Shpilka. Explicit Noether normalization for simultaneous conjugation via polynomial identity testing. *RANDOM*, 2013.

[17] E. Formanek. Invariants and the ring of generic matrices. *J. Algebra*, 89:178–223, 1984.

[18] P. Gabriel. Unzerlegbare darstellungen I. *Manuscripta Mathematica*, 6:72–103, 1972.

[19] I. Gelfand, S. Gelfand, V. Retakh, and R. Wilson. Quasideterminants. *Adv. Math.*, 193(1):56–141, 2005.

[20] I. Gelfand and V. Retakh. Determinants of matrices over noncommutative rings. *Funct. Anal. Appl.*, 25(2), 1991.

[21] I. Gelfand and V. Retakh. Determinants of matrices over noncommutative rings. *Funct. Anal. Appl.*, 25(2), 1991.

[22] I. Gelfand and V. Retakh. Theory of noncommutative determinants, and characteristic functions of graphs. *Funct. Anal. Appl.*, 26(4), 1992.

[23] D. Hilbert. Über die vollen invariantensysteme. *Math. Ann.*, 42:313–370, 1893.

[24] P. Hrubeš, A. Wigderson, and A. Yehudayoff. Relationless completeness and separations. In *IEEE Conference on Computational Complexity*, pages 280–290, 2010.

[25] P. Hrubeš, A. Wigderson, and A. Yehudayoff. Non-commutative circuits and the sum of squares problem. *J. Amer. Math. Soc.*, 24:871–898, 2011.

[26] P. Hrubeš and A. Yehudayoff. Arithmetic complexity in ring extensions. *Theory of Computing*, 7:119–129, 2011.

[27] D. Kaliuzhnyi-Verbovetskyi and V. Vinnikov. Noncommutative rational functions, their difference-differential calculus and realizations. *Multidimensional Systems and Signal Processing*, 2010.

[28] D. S. Kaliuzhnyi-Verbovetskyi and V. Vinnikov. Singularities of noncommutative rational functions and minimal factorizations. *Lin. Alg. Appl*, 430:869–889, 2009.

[29] H. Kraft and C. Procesi. *Classical Invariant Theory, a Primer*. 1996.

[30] T. Lee and Y. Zhou. Right ideals generated by an idempotent of finite rank. *Linear Algebra and its Applications*, 431:2118–2126, 2009.

[31] P. Malcolmson. A prime matrix ideal yields a skew field. *Journal of the London Mathematical Society*, 18:221–233, 1978.

[32] K. Mulmuley. On P vs. NP and geometric complexity theory. *J. ACM*, 58(2), 2011.

[33] K. Mulmuley. The GCT program toward the P vs. NP problem. *Communications of the ACM*, 55(6):98–107, 2012.

[34] K. Mulmuley. Geometric complexity theory V: Equivalence between blackbox derandomization of polynomial identity testing and derandomization of noether's normalization lemma. *CoRR*, abs/1209.5993, 2012.

[35] N. Nisan. Lower bounds for non-commutative computation. In *Proceeding of the 23th STOC*, pages 410–418, 1991.

[36] C. Procesi. The invariant theory of $n \times n$ matrices. *Adv. Math.*, 19:306–381, 1976.

[37] R. Raz and A. Shpilka. Deterministic polynomial identity testing in non commutative models. *Computational Complexity*, 14(1):1–19, 2005.

[38] Y. P. Razmyslov. Trace identities of full matrix algebras over a field of characteristic zero. *Izv. Akad. Nauk SSSR Ser. Mat.*, 38:723–760, 1974.

[39] C. Reutenauer. Inversion height in free fields. *Selecta Mathematica*, 2(1):93–109, 1996.

[40] L. H. Rowen. *Polynomial identities in ring theory*, volume 84. Academic Press, 1980.

[41] A. Schofield and M. V. den Bergh. Semi-invariants of quivers for arbitrary dimension vectors. *Indag. Math*, 12:125–138, 2001.

[42] A. Shpilka and A. Yehudayoff. Arithmetic circuits: A survey of recent results and open questions. *Foundations and Trends in Theoretical Computer Science*, 5(3):207–388, 2010.

[43] V. Strassen. Gaussian elimination is not optimal. *Numer. Math.*, 13:354–356, 1969.

[44] V. Strassen. Vermeidung von divisionen. *J. of Reine Angew. Math.*, 264:182–202, 1973.

[45] L. G. Valiant. Completeness classes in algebra. In *STOC*, pages 249–261, 1979.

Appendix: The Invariant Theory angle

In this section we give the necessary background from Invariant Theory to explain how our main open problem arises there (and mention a few other computational complexity questions which have recently been cast in this language). We will present only, in high level, the fragment of the theory which is relevant to us. Often, the stated results are known in greater generality. One can find much more in the books [10, 12, 29]. We stress that in this section all variables *commute*!

Fix a field $\mathbb{F}$ (while problems are interesting in every field, results mostly work for infinite fields only, and sometimes just for characteristic zero or algebraically closed ones). Let G be a group, and V a representation of G, namely a vector space on which G acts; for every $g, h \in G$ and $v \in V$ we have $gv \in V$ and $g(hv) = (gh)v$. When G acts on V, it also acts on $\mathbb{F}[V]$, the polynomial functions on V, also called the *coordinate ring* of V. We will denote gp the action of a group element g on a polynomial $p \in \mathbb{F}[X]$. In our setting V will have finite dimension (say m), and so $\mathbb{F}[V]$ is simply $\mathbb{F}[x_1, x_2, \cdots, x_m] = \mathbb{F}[X]$, the polynomial ring over $\mathbb{F}$ in m variables.

A polynomial $p(X) \in \mathbb{F}[X]$ is *invariant* if it is unchanged by this action, namely for every $g \in G$ we have $gp = p$. All invariant polynomials clearly form a subring of $\mathbb{F}[X]$, denoted $\mathbb{F}[X]^G$, called the ring of invariants of this action. Understanding the invariants of group actions is the main subject of Invariant Theory. In our setting, all these rings will be *finitely generated*, namely there will be a finite set of polynomials $\{q_1, q_2, \cdots q_t\}$ in $\mathbb{F}[X]^G$ so that for every polynomial $p \in \mathbb{F}[X]^G$ there is a t-variate polynomial r over $\mathbb{F}$ so that $p = r(q_1, q_2, \cdots, q_t)$. The following example must be familiar to the reader.

EXAMPLE 10.1. *Let $G = S_m$, the symmetric group on m letters, acting on the set of m formal variables X (and hence the vector space they generate) by simply permuting them. Then the set of invariant polynomials are simply all* symmetric polynomials. *As is well known, they are generated in the sense above by the m* elementary *symmetric polynomials (namely $q_1 = \sum_i x_i, q_2 = \sum_{i<j} x_i x_j, \cdots, q_m = \prod_i x_i$). Another generating set of the same size is provided by the* sums-of-powers *(namely $q_1' = \sum_i x_i, q_2' = \sum_i x_i^2, \cdots, q_m' = \sum_i x_i^m$).*

This example demonstrates a nearly perfect understanding of the ring of invariants. The first basic requirement is a finite set of generators of the ring of invariants. Establishing this for a group action is often called "First Fundamental Theorem", or FFT. The second requirement (naturally called the "Second Fundamental Theorem", or SFT, when established) is describing all algebraic relations between the given generating invariants. In the case of symmetric polynomials above, they are algebraically independent. Hence, we know FFT and SFT in this example.

Further requirements have to do with the explicitness and constructivity of the given invariants, their number, as a function of natural parameters like the dimension of the space V, size (when finite) or "dimension" of the group G. Finally, a more modern request is that the given invariants would be easy to compute. For the action of the symmetric group above, we are in an "optimal" situation. There are exactly m generating invariants (the dimension of V), explicitly given and very easy to compute. Some of these explicitness and computational notions are formally defined and discussed in [16], section 1.2.

This set of "computational" properties clearly directly related to the efficiency of solving perhaps the most basic *orbit* problem of this setting: given two points $u, v \in V$, are they in the same orbit under the group action? If they are, clearly their evaluation every invariant is identical (and the converse can be achieved with a somewhat more general notion of "separating invariants"). Many basic problems in many mathematical disciplines can be viewed in this way (e.g. Is a given knot unknotted? Can one turn a polygon into another via (straight) cutting and pasting?). More recently, basic problems of computational complexity were cast in these terms. Valiant [45] showed that to separate the arithmetic classes VP and VNP it suffices to show that the permanent polynomial is not a *linear projection* of a determinant of a not much larger matrix. While projection is not a group operation, the Geometric Complexity Theory (GCT) project of Mulmuley and Sohoni (see e.g. [33, 32] for surveys) describes it in similar terms, namely the intersection of the orbit *closure* of varieties defined respectively by permanent and determinant. In this last motivation the group acting are linear groups.

Most work and knowledge in Invariant Theory concerns linear groups[10]. The first seminal results came from Hilbert [23], who proved[11] the first and second fundamental theorems for the natural actions of the general and special linear groups, $GL(V)$ and $SL(V)$ on a vector space V. Again, a very familiar very special case, in which knowledge is complete, is the following.

EXAMPLE 10.2. *Consider the action of the group $SL_n(\mathbb{F})$ on the vector space of $n \times n$ matrices in $M_n(\mathbb{F})$, simply by matrix multiplication. Namely, $A \in SL_n$ acts on $M \in M_n$ by AM. The entries of such a generic matrix M may be viewed as $m = n^2$ variables $X = \{x_{ij}\}$. In this case all polynomial invariants are generated by the determinant $det(X)$.*

We shall be interested in invariants[12] of actions of SL_n on d-tuples of $n \times n$ matrices. So now the number of variables $m = dn^2$. The most well understood is the action of a single copy of SL_n by simultaneous conjugation of the d matrices, and the one we care about the action of two copies, $SL_n \times SL_n$, by simultaneous multiplication on the left and right. We define both next and discuss what is known, but first point out that these are very special cases of the general setting of *quivers* and their representation [18] and many of the results generalize to this setting.

Now a typical element of our vector space is a d-tuple of $n \times n$ matrices $(M_1, M_2, \cdots, M_d)$ and that the underlying variables X are now the $m = dn^2$ entries. Consider the action of a matrix $A \in SL_n$ on this tuple by simultaneous conjugation, namely transforming it to the tuple $(A^{-1}M_1A, A^{-1}M_2A, \cdots, A^{-1}M_dA)$. Which polynomials in X are invariant under this action? The first and second fundamental theorem were proved by Procesi, Formanek and Razmyslov and Donkin [36, 17, 38, 15]. More precisely, the invariants are generated by traces of products of length at most n^2 of the given matrices, namely by the set

$$\{Tr(M_{i_1}M_{i_2}\cdots M_{i_t}) : t \leq n^2\}.$$

These polynomials are explicit, have small degree and are easily computable. The one possible shortcoming, the exponential size of this set (a serious impediment to, e.g, solving the orbit problem above), was recently improved to quasi-polynomial by [16], who "derandomized" a probabilistic construction of Mulmuley [34]. That last paper further connected the problem of finding few invariants to solving the Polynomial Identity Testing problem (in the commutative setting).

[10] Here, we consider only actions on vector spaces, real interest of algebraic geometry is their actions on general affine varieties

[11] Among many other foundational results - this paper and its 1890 non-constructive predecessor contain in particular the Nullstellensatz theorem, the finite basis theorem and other cornerstones of commutative algebra and algebraic geometry.

[12] Often called semi-invariants, to distinguish them from invariants of GL_n

Finally, we get to the action we care about. Here a pair of matrices $(A, B) \in SL_n \times SL_n$ acts on $(M_1, M_2, \cdots, M_d)$ to give $(AM_1B, AM_2B, \cdots, AM_dB)$. Note that whether the symbolic matrix of linear forms $z_1M_1 + z_2M_2 + \cdots + z_dM_d$ is *full*[13] or not is unchanged by this action, which is the first relationship to the body of our paper. But in this case we only know an infinite set of generating invariants. They were determined (for arbitrary quivers) by [13, 41, 14] (and also for this specific left-right action in [1]). The invariants can be described in several ways. The papers [14, 13] describe them in terms of determinants of block matrices. Let $(X_1, X_2, \cdots, X_d)$ be the generic matrices of our variables X. For the left-right action the invariants are determinants of sums of the matrices $X_i \otimes T_i$ for some arbitrary d-tuple of $k \times k$ matrices $(T_1, T_2, \cdots, T_d)$. Namely, this is the set

$$\{\det(\sum_{i=1}^{d} X_i \otimes T_i) \, : \, k \in \mathbb{N}, \, T_i \in \mathrm{Mat}_{k\times k}(\mathbb{F})\}$$

These are precisely the polynomials we care about in the body of this paper, in both the non-commutative PIT problem, as well as in eliminating divisions from non-commutative circuits. By Hilbert's basis theorem, we know that a finite subset of this set generates all invariants, and hence in particular we can take them to be all invariants of degree below some finite bound (which puts an upper bound on the dimension k of the auxiliary matrices T_i). Attempts of giving an upper bound on the degree are surveyed in [11] who obtains the best estimate we know of, which unfortunately (despite the title of the paper) seems to be exponential in n. Note that a polynomial upper bound here implies one for Problem 4, and vice versa.

[13]As in the definition before Theorem 2.1

Decision Trees, Protocols, and the Fourier Entropy-Influence Conjecture

Andrew Wan *
Simons Institute, U.C. Berkeley
atw12@seas.harvard.edu

John Wright †
Carnegie Mellon University
jswright@cs.cmu.edu

Chenggang Wu ‡
IIIS, Tsinghua University
wcg06@mails.tsinghua.edu.cn

ABSTRACT

Given $f : \{-1,1\}^n \to \{-1,1\}$, define the *spectral distribution* of f to be the distribution on subsets of $[n]$ in which the set S is sampled with probability $\widehat{f}(S)^2$. Then the *Fourier Entropy-Influence (FEI) conjecture* of Friedgut and Kalai [2] states that there is some absolute constant C such that $\mathbf{H}[\widehat{f}^2] \leq C \cdot \mathbf{Inf}[f]$. Here, $\mathbf{H}[\widehat{f}^2]$ denotes the Shannon entropy of f's spectral distribution, and $\mathbf{Inf}[f]$ is the total influence of f. This conjecture is one of the major open problems in the analysis of Boolean functions, and settling it would have several interesting consequences.

Previous results on the FEI conjecture have been largely through direct calculation. In this paper we study a natural interpretation of the conjecture, which states that there exists a communication protocol which, given subset S of $[n]$ distributed as $\widehat{f}^2$, can communicate the value of S using at most $C \cdot \mathbf{Inf}[f]$ bits in expectation. Using this interpretation, we are able show the following results:

- First, if f is computable by a read-k decision tree, then $\mathbf{H}[\widehat{f}^2] \leq 9k \cdot \mathbf{Inf}[f]$.
- Next, if f has $\mathbf{Inf}[f] \geq 1$ and is computable by a decision tree with expected depth d, then $\mathbf{H}[\widehat{f}^2] \leq 12d \cdot \mathbf{Inf}[f]$.
- Finally, we give a new proof of the main theorem of O'Donnell and Tan [8], i.e. that their FEI$^+$ conjecture composes.

In addition, we show that natural improvements to our decision tree results would be sufficient to prove the FEI conjecture in its entirety. We believe that our methods give more illuminating proofs than previous results about the FEI conjecture.

*On leave from IIIS, Tsinghua University. Some of this work was completed at Harvard University and supported by NSF grant CCF-964401 and NSFC grant 61250110218.

†Supported by NSF grants CCF-0747250 and CCF-1116594 and a grant from the MSR–CMU Center for Computational Thinking. Some of this research done while visiting the Toyota Technological Institute at Chicago.

‡This work was supported in part by the National Basic Research Program of China Grant 2011CBA00300, 2011CBA00301, the National Natural Science Foundation of China Grant 61033001, 61061130540. Research done while visiting Carnegie Mellon University.

ITCS'14, January 12–14, 2014, Princeton, New Jersey, USA.

ACM 978-1-4503-2698-8/14/01 ...$15.00.
http://dx.doi.org/10.1145/2554797.2554806.

1. INTRODUCTION

Given a Boolean function $f : \{-1,1\}^n \to \{-1,1\}$, define the *spectral distribution* of f to be the distribution on subsets of $[n]$ in which the set S is sampled with probability $\widehat{f}(S)^2$. Overloading notation, we will denote this distribution by $\widehat{f}^2$. Write $\mathcal{X} \sim \widehat{f}^2$ for the random variable which is distributed according to $\widehat{f}^2$. The *Fourier Entropy-Influence (FEI) Conjecture* of Friedgut and Kalai [2] states that there is some absolute constant C such that $\mathbf{H}[\mathcal{X}] \leq C \cdot \mathbf{Inf}[f]$, where $\mathbf{Inf}[f]$ is the total influence of f, and $\mathbf{H}[\mathcal{X}]$ is the spectral entropy of f (equivalently, the Shannon entropy of $\mathcal{X}$), which equals

$$\mathbf{H}[\mathcal{X}] = \sum_{S \subseteq [n]} \widehat{f}(S)^2 \log\left(\frac{1}{\widehat{f}(S)^2}\right).$$

The FEI Conjecture has been shown to have several interesting consequences, including a learning algorithm for DNFs in the agnostic learning model [6, 3], and resolving it is a central question in the analysis of Boolean functions. See [9] for a comprehensive introduction to the subject.

Verifying the conjecture for individual functions—such as Majority, AND/OR, and Tribes—can be done via straightforward calculation. Verifying it for larger classes of functions requires more subtle argumentation. To date, it has been shown to hold for random DNFs [5], symmetric functions and read-once decision trees [9], and read-once formulas [8, 1]. Unfortunately, this conjecture lends itself to proofs which are at times opaque and conceptually unilluminating. Perhaps one of the reasons is that whereas the total influence $\mathbf{Inf}[f]$ is a central quantity in the analysis of Boolean functions, the spectral entropy $\mathbf{H}[\mathcal{X}]$ is rarely encountered and poorly understood.

In this paper we consider the natural interpretation of the FEI conjecture as stating the existence of a coding scheme for the random variable $\mathcal{X}$ with a certain performance. Roughly speaking, the coding scheme must use, on average, some fixed constant times the *size* of $\mathcal{X}$ (see Section 1.1 for a precise description). Using this interpretation, we give three results concerning the FEI conjecture; we believe that our proofs of these results are both straightforward and conceptually interesting.

For our first result, we verify the conjecture for read-k decision trees, where k is a constant. This is the class of decision trees in which each variable is queried at no more than k distinct locations in the entire tree. Previous results—those for read-once decision trees [9] and read-once formulas [8, 1]—failed to generalize even to the read-twice case, as allowing a decision tree to be read-twice introduces correlations between different parts of the tree, and this is difficult to analyze. In this paper, we surmount this barrier, proving:

THEOREM 1.1. *Suppose* $f : \{-1,1\}^n \to \{-1,1\}$ *can be computed by a read-k decision tree, and let* $\mathcal{X} \sim \widehat{f}^2$. *Then* $\mathbf{H}[\mathcal{X}] \leq 9k \cdot \mathbf{Inf}[f]$.

A natural question is whether this can be improved to show the FEI conjecture for read-$k(n)$ decision trees, where $k(n) = \omega(1)$ is a slowly growing function of n. However, a simple padding argument shows that this would be sufficient to prove the full FEI conjecture: given $f : \{-1,1\}^n \to \{-1,1\}$, one could add enough dummy variables to f so that $k(\cdot)$ is at least 2^n, and since any n-variable function is trivially computable by a read-2^n decision tree, f would satisfy the FEI conjecture.

Using much of the same proof as for Theorem 1.1, we then verify the conjecture for decision trees with expected depth d, where d is a constant. The FEI conjecture trivially holds for depth-d decision trees, which have a bounded number of variables, and so what makes this interesting is that we only require a bound on the *expected* depth of the tree. Our result is:

THEOREM 1.2. *Suppose* $f : \{-1,1\}^n \to \{-1,1\}$ *is computable by a decision tree whose expected depth is* d. *Further, suppose* $\mathbf{Inf}[f] \geq 1$. *Then* $\mathbf{H}[\widehat{f}^2] \leq 12d \cdot \mathbf{Inf}[f]$.

As before, if we could show the FEI conjecture for decision trees with expected depth $d(n)$, where $d(n) = \omega(1)$ is a slowly growing function of n, we would be able to show the full FEI conjecture. In addition, the requirement in Theorem 1.2 that $\mathbf{Inf}[f]$ be reasonably large is necessary, as we show in Appendix E. We note that this result (with a better constant) also follows from the bound $\mathbf{H}[\widehat{f}^2] \leq 2d$, which was proven independently by [1].

For our final result, we give a new proof of the main theorem from [8], which is a composition theorem for the FEI conjecture. Their main application is to verify the FEI conjecture for read-once formulas. For example, consider trying to prove the FEI conjecture for a read-once DNF formula (an OR of ANDs). It is easy to verify that both the AND and OR functions (of any input size) each individually satisfy the FEI conjecture, but it is not so obvious how to prove that their composition satisfies it.

More broadly, let f and $g_1, \ldots, g_k$ be Boolean functions, and consider the composition $h = f(g_1, \ldots, g_k)$, where each g_i is over its own set of variables. Their paper considers the following question: supposing that f and the g_i's satisfy the FEI conjecture with constant C, what can one conclude about h? Perhaps their main contribution is in noting that from f's perspective, it is not receiving perfectly unbiased bits as inputs, but $\mathbf{E}[g_i]$-biased bits. Thus it is natural that it shouldn't matter whether f satisfies the FEI conjecture, but rather whether it satisfies some $\mathbf{E}[g_i]$-biased version of the FEI conjecture. They formulate this biased version of the FEI conjecture, which they call the FEI$^+$ conjecture (which we will formally state later), and prove the following composition theorem:

THEOREM 1.3 (INFORMAL). *Suppose f and $g_1, \ldots, g_k$ satisfy the FEI$^+$ conjecture with constant C. Then $h = f(g_1, \ldots, g_k)$ also satisfies the FEI$^+$ conjecture with constant C.*

They proved this by expanding the expressions $\mathbf{H}[\mathcal{X}]$ and $\mathbf{Inf}[h]$ in terms of the Fourier coefficients of f and $g_1, \ldots, g_k$, and comparing the results. Using our coding theoretic interpretation of the FEI conjecture, we give a new proof of this theorem which shows that codes compose in a very clean way.

We now describe our interpretation of the FEI conjecture and discuss our main results in more detail.

1.1 The FEI Conjecture as a Coding Bound

Let $\mathcal{X} \sim \widehat{f}^2$. We view the Fourier Entropy-Influence Conjecture as stating the existence of highly efficient coding schemes for communicating the value of $\mathcal{X}$. To explain this, we begin with some standard information theory background. Given a domain $\mathcal{D}$ and an output alphabet Σ, a *code* on $\mathcal{D}$ is a function $c : \mathcal{D} \to \Sigma^*$. We say that c is *prefix-free* if $c(x)$ is never a prefix of $c(y)$ for distinct $x, y \in \mathcal{D}$. If $\boldsymbol{x}$ is a random variable which takes values in $\mathcal{D}$, then the average number of characters output by c, called the *length* of c, is $\mathbf{E}[|c(\boldsymbol{x})|]$, and we often care about finding a code c which minimizes this quantity. The source coding theorem of Shannon says that $\mathbf{H}[\boldsymbol{x}]$ is roughly the best possible length achievable by a prefix-free code:

THEOREM 1.4 (SHANNON [10]). *Let $\boldsymbol{x}$ be a random variable over a domain $\mathcal{D}$ and let Σ be a finite alphabet.*

1. *If $c : \mathcal{D} \to \Sigma^*$ is a prefix-free code for $\boldsymbol{x}$, then*

$$\mathbf{H}[\boldsymbol{x}]/\log_2|\Sigma| \leq \mathbf{E}[|c(\boldsymbol{x})|].$$

2. *Furthermore, there exists a prefix-free code $c : \mathcal{D} \to \Sigma^*$ such that $\mathbf{E}[|c(\boldsymbol{x})|] \leq \mathbf{H}[\boldsymbol{x}]/\log_2|\Sigma| + 1$.*

(In fact, this theorem applies to the more general class of *uniquely decodable* codes, but it is sufficient for our purposes that we only consider prefix-free codes.)

This suggests that if we want to upper bound the entropy of $\mathcal{X} \sim \widehat{f}^2$, we should try to design an efficient protocol for communicating the value of $\mathcal{X}$. The formula $\mathbf{Inf}[f] = \sum_S |S| \cdot \widehat{f}(S)^2$ shows that $\mathbf{Inf}[f]$ is actually the expected size of the set $\mathcal{X}$. Thus, showing a bound of the form $\mathbf{H}[\mathcal{X}] \leq C \cdot \mathbf{Inf}[f]$ for a function f requires showing a protocol for communicating the value of $\mathcal{X}$ which uses at most a constant number of bits on average for each element of $\mathcal{X}$. As an example, consider the following protocol for encoding the value of a set $S \subseteq [n]$:

$\mathcal{P}(S)$:

- For each $i \in S$, output the $\lceil \log n \rceil$-bit description of i.
- Output $\perp$.

Here $\perp$ is a termination character which prevents different codewords from being prefixes of each other. (Without it, the codeword for $\{1\}$ would be a prefix of the codeword for $\{1,2\}$, for example.)

Given the output of this protocol, one can uniquely determine the value of S. Furthermore, the protocol uses exactly $\lceil \log n \rceil \cdot |S| + 1$ characters to code S. As a result, we have

$$\mathbf{E}[|\mathcal{P}(\mathcal{X})|] = \lceil \log n \rceil \cdot \mathbf{E}[|\mathcal{X}|] + 1 = \lceil \log n \rceil \cdot \mathbf{Inf}[f] + 1, \quad (1)$$

giving an upper bound of $\mathbf{H}[\mathcal{X}] \le \log_2 3 \cdot (\lceil \log n \rceil \cdot \mathbf{Inf}[f] + 1)$. This is (ignoring the $\log_2 3$ factor) the well-known "weak" upper bound [9, 4], which is essentially the best-known upper bound for a general Boolean f (and is tight when f is real-valued).

With some extra work, we can remove the $(+1)$ from Equation (1) while adding only a small factor to the coefficient of $\mathbf{Inf}[f]$. This is important for the case when f is heavily biased and $\mathbf{Inf}[f]$ is small (for example, when f is the AND function). As a start, consider the modified protocol $\mathcal{P}'$ which has the same first line as $\mathcal{P}$ but the following second line instead:

- If $S \neq \emptyset$, output $\perp$.

This will only output $\perp$ when $S \neq \emptyset$. For $\mathcal{X} \sim \widehat{f}^2$, the probability that $\mathcal{X} \neq \emptyset$ is $\sum_{S \neq \emptyset} \widehat{f}^2(S) = \mathbf{Var}[f] \le \mathbf{Inf}[f]$. As a result, $\mathbf{E}[|\mathcal{P}'(\mathcal{X})|] \le (\lceil \log n \rceil + 1) \cdot \mathbf{Inf}[f]$. However, $\mathcal{P}'$ is no longer prefix-free: $\mathcal{P}'(\emptyset)$ is the empty string, and is therefore a prefix of $\mathcal{P}'(S)$ for *every* S. The following lemma, which is implicit in [9], shows that such a protocol still gives an entropy bound at a cost of $2 \cdot \mathbf{Inf}[f]$.

LEMMA 1.5. *Let $\mathcal{X} \sim \widehat{f}^2$, and let $\mathcal{P} : 2^{[n]} \to \Sigma^*$ be a prefix-free protocol, except it outputs an empty string on the input $\emptyset$. Then $\mathbf{H}[\mathcal{X}] \le \log_2 |\Sigma| \cdot \mathbf{E}[|\mathcal{P}(\mathcal{X})|] + 2 \cdot \mathbf{Inf}[f]$.*

For completeness, we include a proof of this lemma in Appendix B. Applying this lemma to the protocol $\mathcal{P}'$ in the previous example shows that $\mathbf{H}[\mathcal{X}] \le (\log_2 3 \cdot (\lceil \log n \rceil + 1) + 2) \cdot \mathbf{Inf}[f]$.

As the above example illustrates, it is natural for a protocol to output nothing when $\mathcal{X} = \emptyset$. For convenience, we will call such protocols *almost* prefix-free.[1]

1.2 Decision Tree Protocol

Let $f : \{-1,1\}^n \to \{-1,1\}$ be computed by a decision tree T, and let $\mathcal{X} \sim \widehat{f}^2$. To prove Theorems 1.1 and 1.2, we give an efficient protocol for communicating the value of $\mathcal{X}$. The protocol we use is simple: for a set $S \subseteq [n]$, $\widehat{f}(S)^2$ can be nonzero only if there is a root-to-leaf path in T which contains all the variables in S and, potentially, some extra variables. This means that any value which $\mathcal{X}$ takes with nonzero probability must correspond to at least one such path in the tree T. The protocol outputs the left/right description of such a path (stopping when the path has reached all the variables in $\mathcal{X}$), along with a sequence of bits indicating which indices along the path are contained in $\mathcal{X}$. Then, if $\mathcal{X} \neq \emptyset$, it terminates with a $\perp$.

For example, consider the tree in Figure 1. If the protocol were given the set $S = \{1,3\}$, then there are two paths it

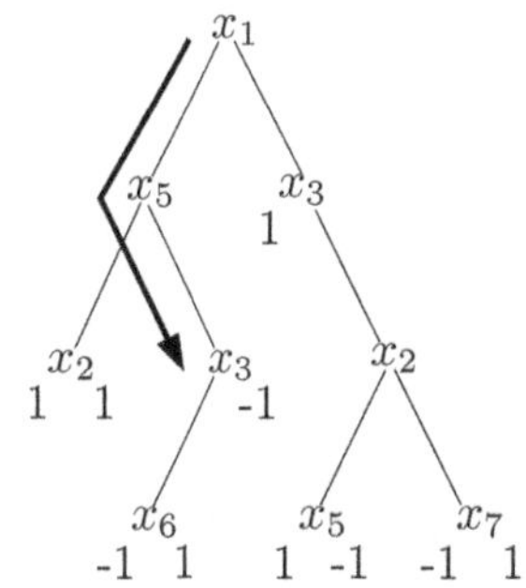

Figure 1: A path for the set $S = \{1,3\}$. The other possible path is $x_1 \to x_3$.

could use: $x_1 \to x_5 \to x_3$ and $x_1 \to x_3$. Supposing it chose the first path, it would output $0,1$ for the description of the path, then $1,0,1$ to indicate that x_1 and x_3 are in S but x_5 is not, and finally it would output $\perp$. So the total output string would be $0,1,1,0,1,\perp$. If it used the other path, the output string would be $1,1,1,\perp$. We defer the complete description of the protocol, including how it chooses between the possible paths, until Section 2.

Note that when $\mathcal{X} = \emptyset$, the protocol simply outputs an empty path. We show the following bound on the performance of this protocol which, when combined with Lemma 1.5 (and the fact that k and d are at least 1), yields Theorems 1.1 and 1.2:

THEOREM 1.6. *Suppose $f : \{-1,1\}^n \to \{-1,1\}$ is computable by a read-k decision tree whose expected depth is d, and let $\mathcal{X} \sim \widehat{f}^2$. Then there is an almost prefix-free protocol for $\mathcal{X}$ with length at most $\min\{(2k+2)\cdot\mathbf{Inf}[f], 4\cdot\mathbf{Inf}[f]+2d\}$ and alphabet size $|\Sigma| = 3$.*

This protocol relies heavily on the intuition that the structure of a decision tree should indicate which variables are significant. For example, the root variable should be very important, as should variables in the upper levels of the tree. Thus, even though the path outputted by the protocol always includes the root variable and almost always includes the variables in the upper levels of the tree, this should not be a problem given that these variables are highly influential.

It is possible, however, to construct trees which do not fit this intuition: for example, consider a decision tree T which contains one set of variables on levels 0 through $l-1$, and has rooted at every node on level l a copy of a decision tree T' over a different set of variables. An example of such a tree is given in Figure 2 for $l = 2$. As all paths lead to T', the variables in the first l levels clearly have influence zero. Unfortunately, the described protocol will always output a path containing a variable from each of these l levels, as each path from the root to an influential variable must go through these levels. Thus, for any arbitrary l, one can make this protocol output $2l$ extraneous characters for any nonempty input set, regardless of the influence of the function.

This is not so problematic for the case when T has small expected depth or is read-k, for k a small constant. In the above example, every level of dummy variables adds one to the depth of T, and so this construction is limited by the expected depth of T. Furthermore, since a copy of T' is rooted at every level-l node, T is itself at least a read-2^l decision tree, in which case the fact that the protocol

[1]An almost prefix-free protocol is implicit in the proof of the FEI conjecture for symmetric functions in [9], and ignoring the case when $\mathcal{X} = \emptyset$ is even explicitly built into the definition of the FEI$^+$ conjecture in [8].

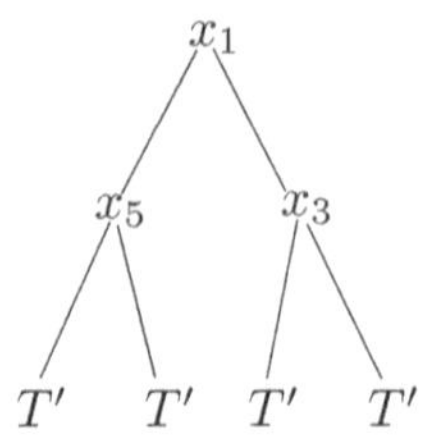

Figure 2: A bad tree. The T's are identical and do not contain x_1, x_3, or x_5.

outputs only $2l$ more bits than it should is perhaps not too concerning.

To analyze this example, we note that for each level i between 0 and $l-1$, every node at level i has a pair of highly covariant children. Here, by the covariance of two functions f and g we mean the quantity $\mathbf{Cov}[g, h] := \mathbf{E}_{\boldsymbol{x}}[(g(\boldsymbol{x}) - \mathbf{E}[g]) \cdot (h(\boldsymbol{x}) - \mathbf{E}[h])]$. In other words, for a node at level i, if g and h are the functions computed by that node's left and right subtrees, respectively, then as $g = h$, $\mathbf{Cov}[g, h] = \mathbf{Var}[f]$. Imagining that $\mathbf{Var}[f]$ is large, then it is exactly these nodes with highly covariant children which are troublesome. To keep track of these troublesome nodes, we define the quantity of *tree covariance* for T, written $\mathbf{Cov}[T]$. If T's left and right subtrees T_0 and T_1 compute the functions g and h, then $\mathbf{Cov}[T]$ can be defined recursively as $\mathbf{Cov}[T] = \mathbf{Cov}[g, h] + \frac{1}{2}(\mathbf{Cov}[T_0] + \mathbf{Cov}[T_1])$, with the base case that $\mathbf{Cov}[T] = 0$ if T computes a constant function. We show that the performance of this protocol on a general tree T depends on $\mathbf{Cov}[T]$:

LEMMA 1.7. *The length of the above protocol is* $4 \cdot \mathbf{Inf}[f] + 2 \cdot \mathbf{Cov}[T]$.

It is a simple fact (see Proposition 2.2) that $\mathbf{Cov}[T] \le d$ if T has expected depth d, and so Lemma 1.7 implies that the length of the protocol is at most $4 \cdot \mathbf{Inf}[f] + 2d$, which gives a part of Theorem 1.6.

Upper bounding $\mathbf{Cov}[T]$ for read-k decision trees is more complicated. For intuition, consider the case when $k = 2$. Again, suppose T's left and right subtrees T_0 and T_1 compute the functions g and h. At the extreme, if $\mathbf{Cov}[g, h]$ were to equal one, then this would mean that $g = h$, in which case every variable relevant to g is also relevant to h, and vice versa. In particular, every variable queried in T_0 to compute g must also be queried in T_1 to compute h, meaning that T_0 cannot have any variables which appear twice (as T is read-twice). And if T_0 is read-once, then the functions computed by its left and right subtrees must be entirely uncorrelated, as they depend on different variables. Thus, in this case $\mathbf{Cov}[T_0] = \mathbf{Cov}[T_1] = 0$, so $\mathbf{Cov}[T] = \mathbf{Cov}[g, h] = 1$. The result, intuitively, is that T has a finite amount of tree covariance to go around, and once it uses it up at a given level, the remaining levels must be uncorrelated. We extend this intuition into a bound on the tree covariance for read-k decision trees.

LEMMA 1.8. *Let* $f : \{-1,1\}^n \to \{-1,1\}$ *be computed by a read-k decision tree* T. *Then* $\mathbf{Cov}[T] \le (k-1) \cdot \mathbf{Var}[f]$.

Combining this lemma with Lemma 1.7 and the fact that $\mathbf{Var}[f] \le \mathbf{Inf}[f]$ shows that the length of the protocol is at most $(2k+2) \cdot \mathbf{Inf}[f]$, giving the remaining part of Theorem 1.6.

1.3 Read-Once Composition Protocol

Theorem 1.3 from [8] shows that composing functions which satisfy the FEI$^+$ conjecture will result in a function which also satisfies FEI$^+$. We give a new proof of this theorem by proving an analogous result (Theorem 1.12 below) for *protocols* instead of entropy; our proof shows how to construct an efficient protocol for the composed function using the efficient protocols of each of the functions in the composition. To complete the proof of Theorem 1.3, which is a statement about entropies, one might try to use the source coding theorem to translate our result about protocols to a result about entropies. This can't be done so simply, however, as Theorem 1.4 only gives an approximate correspondence between protocols and entropy. We are able to get this step to work by using a (mostly standard) parallelizing technique. We now describe each of these two steps in more detail.

The FEI$^+$ conjecture works with the spectral distribution conditioned on the sample being non-empty. We write this distribution as $\mathcal{Y} \sim \widehat{f}^2 \setminus \emptyset$, which is defined so that:

$$\mathbf{Pr}[\mathcal{Y} = \emptyset] = 0, \quad \text{and} \quad \mathbf{Pr}[\mathcal{Y} = S] = \frac{\widehat{f}(S)^2}{1 - \widehat{f}(\emptyset)^2},$$

for any $S \neq \emptyset$. We assume here that $\widehat{f}(\emptyset)^2 < 1$ (the FEI Conjecture is trivial when $\widehat{f}(\emptyset)^2 = 1$). For our purposes, a prefix-free protocol $\mathcal{P}$ for $\mathcal{Y}$ is the same as an almost prefix-free protocol for $\mathcal{X} \sim \widehat{f}^2$: the equality $\mathbf{E}[|\mathcal{P}(\mathcal{X})|] = \mathbf{Var}[f] \cdot \mathbf{E}[|\mathcal{P}(\mathcal{Y})|]$ holds, and Lemma 1.5 tells us that we may obtain a bound on the entropy of $\mathcal{X}$ using a prefix-free protocol for $\mathcal{Y}$.

The FEI$^+$ conjecture in [8] strengthens the FEI conjecture and generalizes it to product distributions, making it amenable to composition. We use $\widetilde{f}$ to denote the Fourier transform of f with respect to a product distribution μ (here each bit x_i is set so that $\mathbf{E}_\mu[x_i] = \mu_i$). We now state the main definition from [8]:

DEFINITION 1.9. *Let* $f : \{-1,1\}^n_\mu \to \{-1,1\}$ *be a Boolean function. The function f satisfies FEI$^+$ with constant C if*

$$\sum_{S \neq \emptyset} \widetilde{f}(S)^2 \log\left(\frac{\prod_{i \in S}(1 - \mu_i^2)}{\widetilde{f}(S)^2}\right) \le C \cdot \sum_{S \neq \emptyset} \widetilde{f}(S)^2 (|S| - 1).$$

In [8], it was conjectured that for some constant C, every Boolean function satisfies FEI$^+$ with constant C. They were in fact able to show that every Boolean function f satisfies FEI$^+$ with "constant" $2^{O(n)}$.[2]

Our first step is to reformulate what it means to "satisfy the FEI$^+$ conjecture with constant C" as a statement about the existence of an efficient protocol:

DEFINITION 1.10. *Let* $f : \{-1,1\}^n_\mu \to \{-1,1\}$ *be a function over the μ-biased variables* $x_1, \ldots, x_n$, *and let* $\mathcal{Y} \sim \widetilde{f}^2 \setminus \emptyset$. *Let P be a prefix-free protocol for communicating the value of $\mathcal{Y}$. Then P is a C-*good *protocol for f under bias μ if*

$$\mathbf{E}[|P(\mathcal{Y})|] \le C \cdot (\mathbf{E}[|\mathcal{Y}|] - 1) + \sum_i \mathbf{Pr}[i \in \mathcal{Y}] \cdot \log \frac{1}{1 - \mu_i^2} + \log \mathbf{Var}_p[f].$$

[2]It is known that one can improve this to $O(\log(n))$ in the unbiased case when all the μ_i's are zero.

This definition can be derived by rearranging the inequality in Definition 1.9 to place $\sum_{S\neq\emptyset} \widehat{f}(S)^2 \log \frac{1}{\widehat{f}(S)^2}$ on the left-hand side, and then replacing $\sum_{S\neq\emptyset} \widetilde{f}(S)^2 \log \frac{1}{\widetilde{f}(S)^2} = \mathbf{H}[\mathcal{Y}]$ with $\mathbf{E}[|P(\mathcal{Y})|]$. Because $\mathbf{H}[\mathcal{Y}] \leq \mathbf{E}[|P(\mathcal{Y})|]$, any function with a good protocol automatically satisfies FEI$^+$:

FACT 1.11. *Suppose there exists a C-good protocol for f under bias μ. Then f satisfies (the μ-biased) FEI$^+$ with constant C.*

We then prove the following composition theorem for protocols in Section 3:

THEOREM 1.12. *Let $h(x^1,\ldots,x^k) = f(g_1(x^1),\ldots,g_k(x^k))$, where the domain of h is endowed with a product distribution μ. Suppose there are C-good protocols for $g_1,\ldots,g_k$ under μ and a C-good protocol for f under bias $\eta = \langle \mathbf{E}_\mu[g_1],\ldots, \mathbf{E}_\mu[g_k]\rangle$. Then there exists a C-good protocol for h under bias μ.*

Given a good protocol P_f for f and good protocols $P_1,\ldots,P_k$ for $g_1,\ldots,g_k$, we construct a good protocol for h in the following way. Let $\mathcal{Y} = \mathcal{Y}_1 \circ \cdots \circ \mathcal{Y}_k$ be drawn from $\widetilde{h}^2 \setminus \emptyset$, where each $\mathcal{Y}_i$ denotes the restriction of $\mathcal{Y}$ to the relevant coordinates of g_i. Note that the $\mathcal{Y}_i$'s form a partition of $\mathcal{Y}$ because the g_i's have disjoint inputs. The protocol will use P_f to specify which $\mathcal{Y}_i$ are non-empty, and, for each such i, it will use $P_i(\mathcal{Y}_i)$ to specify which of the bits relevant to g_i are present in $\mathcal{Y}$. While outputting all of $P_1(\mathcal{Y}_1),\cdots,P_k(\mathcal{Y}_k)$ would be simpler and would suffice to completely specify $\mathcal{Y}$, this protocol will not be efficient when the g_i's have small variance (in this case the number of non-empty $\mathcal{Y}_i$ may be quite small).

In fact, the set $S \subseteq [k]$ of non-empty $\mathcal{Y}$ will be distributed according to $\widetilde{f}^2 \setminus \emptyset$, where $\widetilde{f}$ denotes the η-biased Fourier transformation of f, and furthermore, the sets $\mathcal{Y}_i$ are distributed according to $\widetilde{g_i}^2 \setminus \emptyset$. This fact is somewhat implicit in the analysis of [8], though we find it somewhat clearer and simpler to prove in isolation, without reference to entropy. The analysis of this protocol follows almost immediately from this fact, as the protocols P_f and $P_1,\ldots,P_k$ are designed for these distributions.

This yields a composition theorem for protocols. Our ultimate goal, however, is to prove the following composition theorem for FEI$^+$:

THEOREM 1.13. *Let $h(x^1,\ldots,x^k) = f(g_1(x^1),\ldots,g_k(x^k))$, where the domain of h is endowed with a product distribution μ. Suppose $g_1,\ldots,g_k$ satisfy μ-biased FEI$^+$ with constant C and f satisfies η-biased FEI$^+$ with constant C, where $\eta = \langle \mathbf{E}_\mu[g_1],\ldots,\mathbf{E}_\mu[g_k]\rangle$. Then h satisfies μ-biased FEI$^+$ with constant C.*

The naive strategy would be to apply Shannon's source coding theorem to derive C-good protocols for $f, g_1,\ldots,g_k$, apply Theorem 1.12 to give a C-good protocol for h, and then apply Fact 1.11 to show that h satisfies FEI$^+$. Unfortunately, this fails in the first step: the source coding theorem loses an additive factor of $(+1)$ when translating from entropy to protocols, and this $(+1)$ means that $f, g_1,\ldots,g_k$ don't necessarily have C-good protocols.

To fix this problem, we use the well-known observation that the length of a protocol can be made arbitrarily close to the entropy of a given random variable by encoding many independent copies of that random variable. Thus, by switching to protocols which encode multiple copies of $\mathcal{Y}$ instead of just one, we can ensure that the first step goes through properly, and the other steps (such as Theorem 1.12) go through nearly identically in this setting as well. As this part of the argument is essentially standard, we sketch it briefly in Appendix C.

1.4 Organization

The decision tree results can be found in Section 2 , and the FEI$^+$ results can be found in Section 3. The appendices mostly contain proofs of simple lemmas. Appendix E contains the argument for why the restriction on the total influence of f in Theorem 1.2 is necessary.

Proofs of the main theorems..
Theorem 1.1 and Theorem 1.2 follow from Lemma 1.5 and Theorem 1.6. Theorem 1.3 follows from Theorem 1.12 (proved in Section 3) and Theorem 1.13.

2. ENTROPY-INFLUENCE FOR READ-K DECISION TREES

In this section, we analyze our communication protocol for decision trees . We begin with some preliminary definitions in Section 2.1. Then, as a simple first step, we consider the case of read-once decision trees in Section 2.2. Finally, we prove Lemma 1.7 in Section 2.3 and Lemma 1.8 in Section 2.4. Together, these prove Theorem 1.6.

2.1 Definitions and Notation

Fourier analysis..
Unless stated otherwise, a random input $\boldsymbol{x} \in \{-1,1\}^n$ has the uniform distribution. Any function $f : \{-1,1\}^n \to \mathbb{R}$ can be written as

$$f(x) = \sum_{S\subseteq[n]} \widehat{f}(S)\chi_S(x).$$

The $\widehat{f}(S)$'s are the *Fourier coefficients* of f, and for each $S \subseteq [n]$, the parity function χ_S is defined as $\chi_S(x) = \prod_{i\in S} x_i$. *Parseval's equation* will be important for us, which states that $\mathbf{E}_{\boldsymbol{x}}[f(\boldsymbol{x})^2] = \sum_S \widehat{f}(S)^2$. In particular, if f is ±1-valued, then this sum equals one, and so the squared coefficients $\widehat{f}(S)^2$ form a probability distribution. We will also need the formula $\mathbf{Var}[f] = \sum_{S\neq\emptyset} \widehat{f}(S)^2$. We note that if $\mathcal{X} \sim \widehat{f}^2$, then $\mathbf{Pr}[\mathcal{X} \neq \emptyset] = \mathbf{Var}[f]$.

The *influence* of a variable x_i on f is $\mathbf{Inf}_i[f] := \mathbf{Pr}_{\boldsymbol{x}}[f(\boldsymbol{x}) \neq f(\boldsymbol{x}^{\oplus i})]$, where $\boldsymbol{x}^{\oplus i}$ is $\boldsymbol{x}$ with the i-th bit flipped. The *total influence* of f is $\mathbf{Inf}[f] := \sum_i \mathbf{Inf}_i[f]$, and it is simple to show that $\mathbf{Inf}[f]$ can also be written as $\mathbf{Inf}[f] = \sum_{S\neq\emptyset} |S|\widehat{f}(S)^2$. Comparing this to the formula for $\mathbf{Var}[f]$ shows that $\mathbf{Var}[f] \leq \mathbf{Inf}[f]$. This is all the Fourier analysis we will need; for a more comprehensive introduction to the subject, see [7].

Decision trees..
Decision trees are a standard model of computation, and we omit their definition (see, for example, [9] for a definition). Given a tree T, we will call the subtree corresponding

to the +1 edge the *left* subtree and the subtree corresponding to the −1 edge the *right* subtree. We will assume that if T is a decision tree, then no variable appears more than once in any root-to-leaf path of T. If this is not the case, then T can be simplified. We say that T is a *read-k* decision tree if no variable is queried in more than k locations of T.

Given a decision tree T, if v is a node of T, then $l(v)$ is the *label* of v, i.e. the coordinate in x which is queried at node v. Let $r(T)$ be the root node of T. Next, set $d(v)$ to be the depth of v in T. We start counting the depth at 0, so that $d(r(T)) = 0$. The *expected depth* of T is the average number of bits T queries on a uniformly random input $\boldsymbol{x}$. Since a given node v is reached with probability $2^{-d(v)}$, the expected depth of T may be written as

$$\sum_{v \in T} 2^{-d(v)}. \tag{2}$$

Given two functions $g, h : \{-1,1\}^n \to \mathbb{R}$, define $\mathbf{Cov}[g,h] := \mathbf{E}_{\boldsymbol{x}}[(g(\boldsymbol{x}) - \mathbf{E}[g]) \cdot (h(\boldsymbol{x}) - \mathbf{E}[h])]$. Now we may state our main definition:

DEFINITION 2.1. *Given a decision tree T and an internal node v, let g be the function computed by v's left subtree and h be the function computed by v's right subtree. Then define*

- $\mathbf{Cov}[v] := \mathbf{Cov}[g,h]$,
- $\mathbf{Cov}_i[T] := \sum_{v:l(v)=i} \mathbf{Cov}[v] \cdot 2^{-d(v)}$, *and*
- $\mathbf{Cov}[T] := \sum_{v \in T} \mathbf{Cov}[v] \cdot 2^{-d(v)}$.

Note that $\mathbf{Cov}[T]$ may also be written as

$$\mathbf{Cov}[T] = \sum_{i \in [n]} \mathbf{Cov}_i[T].$$

Furthermore, if T_0 is T's left subtree and T_1 is T's right subtree, then $\mathbf{Cov}[T]$ may also be written recursively as $\mathbf{Cov}[T] = \mathbf{Cov}[g,h] + \frac{1}{2}(\mathbf{Cov}[T_0] + \mathbf{Cov}[T_1])$, with the base case that $\mathbf{Cov}[T] = 0$ if T performs no queries. Intuitively, $\mathbf{Cov}[T]$ is a measure of the total correlation present in the structure of T. For example, $\mathbf{Cov}[T] = 0$ if T is a read-once decision tree. We note that when T computes a Boolean function, $\mathbf{Cov}[v] \le 1$ for each $v \in T$. Thus, in this case, it is immediate from Equation (2) that the expected depth of T is at least $\mathbf{Cov}[T]$. This gives the following proposition.

PROPOSITION 2.2. *Let $f : \{-1,1\}^n \to \{-1,1\}$ be computed by T, a decision tree with expected depth d. Then $\mathbf{Cov}[T] \le d$.*

We will also need the following two propositions, which are proven in Appendix A.

PROPOSITION 2.3. *Let f be computed by a decision tree T whose left and right subfunctions are g and h, respectively. If x_i is at the root of T and S is any subset of $[n] \setminus \{i\}$, then*

$$\widehat{f}(S)^2 + \widehat{f}(S \cup \{i\})^2 = \frac{1}{2}\left(\widehat{g}(S)^2 + \widehat{h}(S)^2\right).$$

PROPOSITION 2.4. *Assume the setup from Proposition 2.3. Then for all coordinates $j \ne i$,*

$$\mathbf{Inf}_j[f] = \frac{1}{2} \cdot (\mathbf{Inf}_j[g] + \mathbf{Inf}_j[h]).$$

2.2 Read-once decision trees

In this section, we will sketch the argument for read-once decision trees. Let $f : \{-1,1\}^n \to \{-1,1\}$ be computed by a read-once decision tree T. Given a decision tree T and a path $P = v_1 \to \cdots \to v_k$ in the tree (starting at the root v_1), the *description* of the path is the sequence of bits $b_1, \ldots, b_{k-1} \in \{0,1\}$ which, if read in that order, would result in traversing the given path (here we are using the standard $1 \leftrightarrow 0$ and $-1 \leftrightarrow 1$ correspondance). Given a set S for which $\widehat{f}(S) \ne 0$, our protocol will output the description of a path in which S is a subset of $\{l(v_1), \ldots, l(v_k)\}$. In fact, our protocol will choose a *minimal* such path containing S, in the sense that the path will stop once it has encountered all of the variables in S. In a general decision tree, there could be many minimal paths containing S and starting at the root, but because T is read-once, there can only be one such path. We may therefore state the protocol as:

Given $S \subseteq [n]$:

1. If $S = \emptyset$, output nothing.
2. There is a minimal path $P = p_1 \to \cdots \to p_k$ containing the indices in S which starts at T's root.
3. Output the description of that path.
4. Output a bit sequence $b_1, \ldots, b_k \in \{0,1\}$, where $b_i = 1$ iff $p_i \in \mathcal{X}$.
5. Terminate with a $\bot$.

We stress that the protocol is only required to work properly when S corresponds to a nonzero Fourier coefficient, i.e. $\widehat{f}(S) \ne 0$.

Suppose that the path P the protocol finds is of length l. Then because the description of a path of length l uses $l-1$ bits, the protocol outputs $2l$ characters in total. Furthermore, the protocol accurately communicates the value of S: given the output of the protocol, one could reconstruct S by following the path indicated by the first $l-1$ bits and including only those indices along the path which are tagged with a 1 in the second sequence. So long as $S \ne \emptyset$, the output is terminated with a $\bot$ character. Together, these mean that the protocol is an almost prefix-free protocol with alphabet size $|\Sigma| = 3$.

We are interested in the length of the protocol on input $\mathcal{X} \sim \widehat{f}^2$. As shown above, the number of characters this protocol outputs is exactly twice the length of the path P. Thus, we need to upper bound the average length of P.

Let us consider reasons why P might be on average too long. For example, because the protocol only considers paths starting at the root, the path output always contains the root variable (unless $\mathcal{X} = \emptyset$), even though this variable might have very low influence on f. However, a simple argument shows that this worry is unfounded. In particular, if x_i is T's root variable, then $\mathbf{Inf}_i[f] \ge \frac{1}{2}\mathbf{Var}[f]$ (we will show this later in Lemma 2.6). This inequality uses crucially the fact that T is read-once. The path P contains x_i whenever $\mathcal{X} \ne \emptyset$, which happens with probability $\mathbf{Var}[f]$. Thus, the probability that P contains x_i is at most $2 \cdot \mathbf{Inf}_i[f]$.

An inductive argument allows us to bring this inequality down to the rest of the variables in the tree, showing that the probability P contains a variable x_j is at most $2 \cdot \mathbf{Inf}_j[f]$ (we will show this later in Lemma 2.5). Summing this inequality over all j shows that the expected length of P is at most $2 \cdot \mathbf{Inf}[f]$. Thus, the protocol outputs at most $4 \cdot \mathbf{Inf}[f]$ characters in expectation, proving Theorem 1.7 in the $k = 1$ case.

2.3 General decision trees

Let $f : \{-1,1\}^n \to \{-1,1\}$ be computed by a decision tree T. Generalizing the above argument to work for T requires some modifications. The main change is that given $S \subseteq [n]$, there is no longer necessarily a unique minimal path starting from T's root which contains the indices in S. As Figure 1 shows, there could be two paths to select from when, for example, $S = \{1,3\}$. We want our protocol to use the fewest characters possible, so the obvious choice is for it to simply use the shortest path possible. This protocol is difficult to analyze, however, so we instead use a suboptimal protocol which constructs a path vertex-by-vertex probabilistically. If g is the function computed by T's left subtree and h is the function computed by T's right subtree, then the first step of the path will be chosen based on the relative weight that g and h place on the set S, i.e. $\widehat{g}(S)^2$ versus $\widehat{h}(S)^2$. As a result, the protocol is most easily stated recursively, as follows:

$\mathcal{P}(T, S)$:

1. If $S = \emptyset$, output nothing and terminate.
2. Let g be the function computed by T's left subtree T_0, and likewise let h be the function computed by T's right subtree T_1.
3. Let x_i be T's root variable. If $i \in S$, output a 1. Otherwise, output a 0.
4. Set $S' = S \setminus \{i\}$. If $S' = \emptyset$, output $\perp$ and terminate.
5. With probability proportional to $\widehat{g}(S')^2$, output 0 and run $\mathcal{P}(T_0, S')$.
6. With probability proportional to $\widehat{h}(S')^2$, output 1 and run $\mathcal{P}(T_1, S')$.

This protocol outputs the same information that the protocol in Section 2.2 does, only now the description of the path and the bit sequence are interleaved. If this protocol outputs $2k$ characters, then characters $2, 4, \ldots, 2k-2$ give a description of a path P, characters $1, 3, \ldots, 2k-1$ indicate which indices along the path P are included in S, and the $2k$-th character is a $\perp$. As a result, this protocol is an almost prefix-free protocol with alphabet size $|\Sigma| = 3$. We will refer to the path P as the path the protocol outputs, selects, etc.

Let us now consider the length of the protocol on input $\mathcal{X} \sim \widehat{f}^2$. The number of characters output is exactly twice the length of the path P the protocol outputs. Thus, we would like to upper bound the expected length of P. Our main lemma will show that for a given variable x_i, we can upper-bound the probability that it appears in P as follows:

LEMMA 2.5. *Let $f : \{-1,1\}^n \to \{-1,1\}$ be computed by a decision tree T, let $\mathcal{X} \sim \widehat{f}^2$, and let $p_i(T)$ be the probability that the path selected by $\mathcal{P}(T, \mathcal{X})$ contains index i. Then $p_i(T) \le 2 \cdot \mathbf{Inf}_i[f] + \mathbf{Cov}_i[T]$.*

By summing this lemma over $i \in [n]$, the expected length of P is at most $2 \cdot \mathbf{Inf}[f] + \mathbf{Cov}[T]$, and so the expected number of characters output by the protocol is at most $4 \cdot \mathbf{Inf}[f] + 2 \cdot \mathbf{Cov}[T]$, which proves Lemma 1.7.

In the special case when T has expected depth d, Proposition 2.2 tells us that $\mathbf{Cov}[T] \le d$, so the protocol uses at most $4 \cdot \mathbf{Inf}[f] + 2 \cdot d$ characters in expectation, the bound given in Theorem 1.6. If we further assume that $\mathbf{Inf}[f] \ge 1$, then this quantity is at most $6d \cdot \mathbf{Inf}[f]$. Combining this with Lemma 1.5 yields our FEI bound for decision trees of expected depth d, Theorem 1.2. In Appendix E, we argue that proving this theorem without the restriction that $\mathbf{Inf}[f] \ge 1$ is unlikely so long as the Fourier Entropy-Influence conjecture remains unproven. Next, as upper-bounding $\mathbf{Cov}[T]$ is more involved if T is read-k, we will defer the proof of the FEI conjecture for read-k decision trees to Section 2.4.

Now we prove Lemma 2.5. In Section 2.2, we stated that if x_i is T's root variable, then $\mathbf{Inf}_i[f] \ge \frac{1}{2}\mathbf{Var}[f]$, supposing that T is read-once. Unfortunately, this is not true for general (or even read-twice) decision trees. For example, the root variable could have two identical subtrees as its children, in which case it has influence zero. For this to happen, though, it must be the case that the two subfunctions have high covariance.

LEMMA 2.6. *Let $f : \{-1,1\}^n \to \{-1,1\}$ be computed by a decision tree T. If x_i is at the root of T, then $\mathbf{Inf}_i[f] \ge \frac{1}{2}\mathbf{Var}[f] - \frac{1}{2}\mathbf{Cov}[r(T)]$.*

PROOF. Let g be the function computed by T's left subtree and h be the function computed by T's right subtree, so that $f(x) = g(x)$ if $x_i = 1$, and $f(x) = h(x)$ if $x_i = -1$. Then $\hat{f}(\emptyset)^2 = \left(\frac{\hat{g}(\emptyset)+\hat{h}(\emptyset)}{2}\right)^2$. As a result,

$$\begin{aligned}
\mathbf{Inf}_i[f] &= \mathbf{Pr}[f(\boldsymbol{x}) \ne f(\boldsymbol{x}^{\oplus i})] \\
&= \mathbf{Pr}[g(\boldsymbol{x}) \ne h(\boldsymbol{x})] \\
&\qquad \text{(because } g \text{ and } h \text{ don't depend on } x_i\text{)} \\
&= \frac{1}{2} - \frac{1}{2}\mathbf{E}[g(\boldsymbol{x})h(\boldsymbol{x})] \\
&= \frac{1}{2} - \frac{1}{2}\hat{g}(\emptyset)\hat{h}(\emptyset) - \frac{1}{2}\mathbf{Cov}[g,h] \\
&\ge \frac{1}{2} - \frac{1}{2}\left(\frac{\hat{g}(\emptyset)+\hat{h}(\emptyset)}{2}\right)^2 - \frac{1}{2}\mathbf{Cov}[g,h] \\
&\qquad \text{(using } ab \le \left(\tfrac{a+b}{2}\right)^2\text{)} \\
&= \frac{1}{2}\left(1 - \hat{f}(\emptyset)^2\right) - \frac{1}{2}\mathbf{Cov}[g,h] \\
&= \frac{1}{2}\mathbf{Var}[f] - \frac{1}{2}\mathbf{Cov}[g,h].
\end{aligned}$$

Because $\mathbf{Cov}[r(T)] = \mathbf{Cov}[g,h]$, this proves the lemma. □

We now use this to prove Lemma 2.5:

PROOF PROOF OF LEMMA 2.5. We prove this by structural induction on the tree T, based on whether x_i is at the root of T. The lemma is clearly true if i doesn't appear in T, so we will assume that it does.

Base case:.

In this case, the root of T is x_i. By the protocol above, x_i will *always* be on the path P unless $\mathcal{X} = \emptyset$, i.e. the path is empty. Thus, the probability that x_i is outputted is $1-\hat{f}(\emptyset)^2 = \mathbf{Var}[f]$. By Lemma 2.6, we have that $2\cdot\mathbf{Inf}[f] \geq \mathbf{Var}[f] - \mathbf{Cov}[r(T)] = p_i(T) - \mathbf{Cov}[r(T)]$. Because x_i is at the root, it can appear nowhere else in T. This means that $\mathbf{Cov}_i[T] = \mathbf{Cov}[r(T)]$, which concludes the base case.

Inductive step:.

In this case, the root of T is not x_i, meaning that x_i is queried in one (or both) of T's subtrees. Let T_0 be the left subtree of T and T_1 its right subtree, and assume without loss of generality that the root of T is x_n. We will show the following pair of simple equalities:

1. $\mathbf{Inf}_i[f] = \frac{1}{2}\cdot(\mathbf{Inf}_i[g] + \mathbf{Inf}_i[h])$, and
2. $p_i(T) = \frac{1}{2}\cdot(p_i(T_0) + p_i(T_1))$.

Equality 1 follows directly from Proposition 2.4. Before proving Equality 2, let's see how they imply the lemma.

$$\begin{aligned} 2\cdot\mathbf{Inf}_i[f] &= \mathbf{Inf}_i[g] + \mathbf{Inf}_i[h] \\ &\geq \frac{1}{2}(p_i(T_0) + p_i(T_1) - \mathbf{Cov}_i[T_0] - \mathbf{Cov}_i[T_1]) \\ &= p_i(T) - \frac{1}{2}(\mathbf{Cov}_i[T_0] + \mathbf{Cov}_i[T_1]), \end{aligned} \tag{3}$$

where the second line follows from applying the inductive hypothesis to g and h. Since each vertex v in T_0 (or T_1) is one edge farther from the root in T than it is in T_0 (or T_1), we get that $\mathbf{Cov}_i[T] = \frac{1}{2}\mathbf{Cov}_i[T_0] + \frac{1}{2}\mathbf{Cov}_i[T_1]$. Note that $\mathbf{Cov}[r(T)]$ doesn't contribute anything to $\mathbf{Cov}_i[T]$ because x_i is not at the root of T. Plugging this equality into Equation (3) yields the lemma.

Now, we prove Equality 2. It will be convenient for us to define the modified protocol $\mathcal{P}'$:

> $\mathcal{P}'(T, S)$:
>
> 1. If $S \neq \emptyset$ and $S \neq \{j\}$, where x_j is T's root variable, then run $\mathcal{P}(T, S)$.
> 2. Otherwise:
>   (a) If $S = \{j\}$, output the characters $1, \bot$.
>   (b) With probability proportional to $\widehat{g}(\emptyset)^2$, run $\mathcal{P}(T_0, \emptyset)$.
>   (c) With probability proportional to $\widehat{h}(\emptyset)^2$, run $\mathcal{P}(T_1, \emptyset)$.

Note that $\mathcal{P}'$ always calls $\mathcal{P}$ as a subroutine. When $S \neq \emptyset, \{j\}$, then $\mathcal{P}'(T, S)$ is identical to $\mathcal{P}(T, S)$. On the other hand, when S equals $\emptyset$ or $\{j\}$, then $\mathcal{P}'(T, S)$ outputs exactly what $\mathcal{P}(T, S)$ would output, but then it calls either $\mathcal{P}(T_0, \emptyset)$ or $\mathcal{P}(T_1, \emptyset)$. These two will immediately terminate, so $\mathcal{P}'$ has the same output behavior as $\mathcal{P}$. Thus, to show that $p_i(T) = \frac{1}{2}\cdot(p_i(T_0) + p_i(T_1))$, it suffices to show that the probability that the path output by $\mathcal{P}'(T, \cdot)$ contains index i is $\frac{1}{2}\cdot(p_i(T_0) + p_i(T_1))$.

We will show that the probability $\mathcal{P}'(T, \cdot)$ makes a call to $\mathcal{P}(T_0, \cdot)$ versus $\mathcal{P}(T_1, \cdot)$ is exactly $\frac{1}{2}$. Next, we will show that the sets it calls $\mathcal{P}(T_0, \cdot)$ with are distributed as $\widehat{g}^2$, and similarly for $\mathcal{P}(T_1, \cdot)$, so that the recursion works.

Without loss of generality, assume that x_n is the root variable of T. Let $S \subseteq [n-1]$ be any set. The protocol $\mathcal{P}'(T, \mathcal{X})$ can only call $\mathcal{P}(T_0, S)$ when $\mathcal{X}$ is either S or $S \cup \{n\}$, which happens with probability $\widehat{f}(S)^2 + \widehat{f}(S \cup \{n\})^2$. By Proposition 2.3, $\widehat{f}(S)^2 + \widehat{f}(S \cup \{n\})^2 = \frac{1}{2}\left(\widehat{g}(S)^2 + \widehat{h}(S)^2\right)$. In either of these two cases, $\mathcal{P}(T_0, S)$ is called with probability proportional to $\widehat{g}(S)^2$, and $\mathcal{P}(T_1, S)$ is called with probability proportional to $\widehat{h}(S)^2$. Thus, the probability that $\mathcal{P}(T_0, S)$ is called is

$$\frac{1}{2}\left(\widehat{g}(S)^2 + \widehat{h}(S)^2\right) \cdot \frac{\widehat{g}(S)^2}{\widehat{g}(S)^2 + \widehat{h}(S)^2} = \frac{\widehat{g}(S)^2}{2}.$$

Summing over all sets S, the probability that $\mathcal{P}(T_0, \cdot)$ is called is exactly $1/2$, and conditioned on this occurring, the probability that $\mathcal{P}(T_0, S)$ is called is exactly $\widehat{g}(S)^2$. A similar argument holds with T_1 in place of T_0 and h in place of g.

Thus, when $\mathcal{P}'(T, \mathcal{X})$ calls $\mathcal{P}(T_0, \cdot)$, the input to the recursive call is distributed as $\widehat{g}^2$, meaning that the path constructed in the recursive call contains x_i with probability $p_i(T_0)$. Similarly, when $\mathcal{P}'(T, \mathcal{X})$ calls $\mathcal{P}(T_1, \cdot)$, the path constructed in the recursive call contains x_i with probability $p_i(T_1)$. Combining these, $p_i(T) = \frac{1}{2}(p_i(T_0) + p_i(T_1))$. □

2.4 A covariance bound for read-k decision trees

In this section, we prove Lemma 1.8.

LEMMA 2.7 (LEMMA 1.8 RESTATED.). *Let $f : \{-1,1\}^n \to \{-1,1\}$ be computed by a read-k decision tree T. Then* $\mathbf{Cov}[T] \leq (k-1)\cdot\mathbf{Var}[f]$.

Combining this with Lemma 1.7 and Lemma 1.5 yields our FEI bound for read-k decision trees:

THEOREM 2.8. *If $f : \{-1,1\}^n \to \{-1,1\}$ is computable by a read-k decision tree, then $\mathbf{H}[\widehat{f}^2] \leq (2+(2k+2)\cdot\log_2 3)\cdot \mathbf{Inf}[f]$.*

It is not at all clear whether our upper bound in Lemma 1.8 is tight. Potentially, this bound could be replaced with $\mathbf{Cov}[T] \leq \log_2 k \cdot \mathbf{Var}[f]$. The tight example of this was presented earlier: let T be the tree given in Figure 2, only with l layers of dummy variables rather than just two. Furthermore, suppose that T' is itself read-once. It is easy to see that T is read-2^l and has tree-covariance $\mathbf{Cov}[T] = l\cdot\mathbf{Var}[f]$. Thus, in this case, $\mathbf{Cov}[T] = \log 2^l \cdot \mathbf{Var}[f]$.

We will prove Lemma 1.8 by structural induction on T. As is often the case, we will need to strengthen the inductive hypothesis for the induction to go through. The reason for this is that the read-k decision tree definition only keeps track of the maximum number of times any variable appears in T, whereas we require a more fine-grained accounting of the number of times each variable appears. For a nonempty subset $S \subseteq [n]$, define $m_T(S)$ to be the maximum over $i \in S$ of the number of times x_i appears in the tree T. For example, if T is read-k then $m_T([n]) \leq k$. We will prove the following lemma:

LEMMA 2.9. *Let T be a decision tree which computes $f : \{-1,1\}^n \to \{-1,1\}$. Then*

$$\mathbf{Cov}[T] \leq \sum_{S\neq\emptyset}(m_T(S) - 1)\cdot \hat{f}(S)^2.$$

Note that if T is read-k, the right-hand side is at most $(k-1)\cdot\sum_{S\neq\emptyset}\hat{f}(S)^2 = (k-1)\cdot\mathbf{Var}[f]$, the bound we are looking for.

PROOF PROOF OF LEMMA 2.9. We prove this by structural induction on the tree T. The base case we consider is when T queries a single variable.

Base case:.

In this case, the left and right subtrees are constant functions, so their covariance is zero. For the sum on the right-hand side, any S for which $\widehat{f}(S)$ is nonzero must consist of variables queried by T, in which case $(m_T(S) - 1) \geq 0$. As a result, the right-hand side is always at least 0.

Inductive step:.

Suppose the root variable of T is x_n. Let T_0 and T_1 be the left and right subtrees of T, respectively. For convenience, we will upper-bound $2 \cdot \mathbf{Cov}[T]$, which can be written as

$$2 \cdot \mathbf{Cov}[T] = 2 \cdot \mathbf{Cov}[g, h] + \mathbf{Cov}[T_0] + \mathbf{Cov}[T_1].$$

We will begin with the first term on the right-hand side. Let J be the set of coordinates which appear in both T_0 and T_1. Because x_n is the root variable, it cannot appear in either T_0 or T_1, so J is a subset of $[n-1]$. Then

$$\begin{aligned} 2 \cdot \mathbf{Cov}[g, h] &= \sum_{S \neq \emptyset} 2 \cdot \widehat{g}(S)\widehat{h}(S) \\ &= \sum_{\emptyset \neq S \subseteq J} 2 \cdot \widehat{g}(S)\widehat{h}(S) \\ &\leq \sum_{\emptyset \neq S \subseteq J} \widehat{g}(S)^2 + \widehat{h}(S)^2, \end{aligned}$$

where the last line holds because $2ab \leq a^2 + b^2$.

Now we focus on the second term. Applying the inductive hypothesis to g and h yields

$$\mathbf{Cov}[T_0] + \mathbf{Cov}[T_1] \leq \sum_{\emptyset \neq S \subseteq [n-1]} (m_{T_0}(S) - 1) \cdot \widehat{g}(S)^2 + (m_{T_1}(S) - 1) \cdot \widehat{h}(S)^2. \quad (4)$$

For any S in the above sum, we have that $m_{T_0}(S) \leq m_T(S)$. This is because T_0 is a subtree of T. However, when $S \subseteq J$ we get the following improved bound: $m_{T_0}(S) \leq m_T(S) - 1$. This holds because every variable in S is queried at least once in T_1, and so it must be queried in T_0 at least one fewer time than in the whole of T. Similarly, all of these inequalities hold when T_0 is replaced with T_1. Rewriting Equation 4,

$$\begin{aligned} \mathbf{Cov}[T_0] + \mathbf{Cov}[T_1] \leq & \sum_{\emptyset \neq S \subseteq J} (m_T(S) - 2) \cdot \left(\widehat{g}(S)^2 + \widehat{h}(S)^2\right) \\ & + \sum_{\emptyset \neq S \not\subseteq J} (m_T(S) - 1) \cdot \left(\widehat{g}(S)^2 + \widehat{h}(S)^2\right) \end{aligned}$$

Now, if we add $2 \cdot \mathbf{Cov}[g, h]$ to this, we see that it will add 1 to the coefficient of $\widehat{g}(S)^2$ and $\widehat{h}(S)^2$ exactly when $\emptyset \neq S \subseteq J$. As a result,

$$2 \cdot \mathbf{Cov}[g, h] + \mathbf{Cov}[T_0] + \mathbf{Cov}[T_1] \leq \sum_{\emptyset \neq S \subseteq [n-1]} (m_T(S) - 1) \cdot \left(\widehat{g}(S)^2 + \widehat{h}(S)^2\right).$$

The left-hand side is $2 \cdot \mathbf{Cov}[T]$. As for the right-hand side, applying Proposition 2.3 shows that it is equal to

$$2 \cdot \sum_{\emptyset \neq S \subseteq [n-1]} (m_T(S) - 1) \cdot \left(\widehat{f}(S)^2 + \widehat{f}(S \cup \{n\})^2\right).$$

We would be done, except $\widehat{f}(S \cup \{n\})^2$ should have $m_T(S \cup \{n\})$ as its coefficient, not $m_T(S)$. However, $m_T(S) \leq m_T(S \cup \{n\})$ always, so we can perform this replacement. This yields the lemma. □

3. A COMPOSITION THEOREM FOR PROTOCOLS

In this section we prove Theorem 1.12. Theorem 1.12 concerns several different functions and their spectral distributions defined with respect to different product distributions. We assume here familiarity with Fourier analysis for product distributions over the Boolean cube (see [7] for an introduction) and briefly review some basic facts and notation used in the proof.

For a Boolean function $f : \{-1,1\}^n_\mu \to \{-1,1\}$, where $\mu = \langle \mu_1, \cdots, \mu_n \rangle$ is a sequence of biases, we think of $\{-1,1\}^n_\mu$ as endowed with the product distribution that sets each bit independently in $\{-1,1\}$ with expectation $\mathbf{E}_\mu[x_i] = \mu_i$ and $\mathbf{Var}_\mu[x_i] = 1 - \mu_i^2$. Then the μ-biased Fourier decomposition of f is

$$f = \sum_{S \subseteq [n]} \widetilde{f}(S)\phi^\mu_S$$

where

$$\phi^\mu_S(x) = \prod_{i \in S} \frac{x_i - \mu_i}{\mathbf{Var}_\mu[x_i]},$$

and $\widetilde{f}(S) = \mathbf{E}_\mu[f \cdot \prod_i i \in S]$. Thus, a spectral sample from $\widetilde{h}^2$ is distributed so that each $\mathcal{Y}$ appears with probability $\widetilde{h}(\mathcal{Y})^2$.

Now we proceed to prove Theorem 1.12. Let P_f be a C-good protocol for f under η and $P_1, \dots, P_k$ be C-good protocols for $g_1, \dots, g_k$ under μ. Recall that these protocols are prefix-free. Now, consider a spectral sample $\mathcal{Y} \sim \widetilde{h}^2$ and the following protocol $P_h(\mathcal{Y})$:

1. Let $S \subseteq [k]$ be the set containing those $i \in [k]$ such that $\mathcal{Y}_i \neq \emptyset$.
2. Output $P_f(S)$.
3. For each $i \in S$, output $P_i(\mathcal{Y}_i)$.

Because the subprotocols are prefix-free, $P_h(\mathcal{Y})$ is a prefix-free encoding of $\mathcal{Y}$. This is because if one scans the output of $P_h(\mathcal{Y})$ from left-to-right, the first prefix which could be output by $P_f(\cdot)$ must actually be the output of $P_f(S)$. This gives a description of the set S, from which one can recover $\mathcal{Y}_1, \dots, \mathcal{Y}_k$ by a similar process. We will show that if P_f and $P_1, \dots, P_k$ are efficient, then P_h is efficient as well. To begin, we will need the following pair of claims:

CLAIM 3.1. *Conditioned on $\mathcal{Y}_i \neq \emptyset$, $\mathcal{Y}_i$ is distributed as $\widetilde{g_i}^2 \setminus \emptyset$.*

CLAIM 3.2. *The set S is distributed as $\widetilde{f}^2 \setminus \emptyset$.*

The proofs of these claims, as well as the basic Fourier analytic facts used to prove them, may be found in the Appendix D. We now prove the composition theorem for C-good protocols.

LEMMA 3.3. *If P_i is a C-good protocol for each g_i and P_f is a C-good protocol for f, then P_h is a C-good protocol for h.*

PROOF. The expected output size of the protocol is

$$\mathbf{E}[|P_h(\mathcal{Y})|] = \mathbf{E}\left[|P_f(S)| + \sum_{i \in S} |P_i(\mathcal{Y}_i)|\right] = \mathbf{E}\left[|P_f(S)| + \sum_{i=1}^{k} \mathbf{1}[\mathcal{Y}_i \neq \emptyset] \cdot |P_i(\mathcal{Y}_i)|\right].$$

First, we upper bound the second term in the expectation. For a fixed i,

$$\mathbf{E}\left[\mathbf{1}[\mathcal{Y}_i \neq \emptyset] \cdot |P_i(\mathcal{Y}_i)|\right] = \mathbf{Pr}[\mathcal{Y}_i \neq \emptyset] \cdot \mathbf{E}\left[|P_i(\mathcal{Y}_i)| \big| \mathcal{Y}_i \neq \emptyset\right]. \tag{5}$$

From Claim 3.1, $\mathcal{Y}_i$ conditioned on $\mathcal{Y}_i \neq \emptyset$ is distributed as $\widetilde{g_i}^2 \setminus \emptyset$. Thus, as P_i is a C-good protocol for g_i, we may upper bound $\mathbf{E}\left[|P_i(\mathcal{Y}_i)| \big| \mathcal{Y}_i \neq \emptyset\right]$ with the expression in the definition of a C-good protocol, except where that definition uses an $\mathcal{Y}$, we have instead $\mathcal{Y}_i \big| (\mathcal{Y}_i \neq \emptyset)$. Note that $\mathbf{Pr}[\mathcal{Y}_i \neq \emptyset] \cdot \mathbf{E}\left[|\mathcal{Y}_i| \big| \mathcal{Y}_i \neq \emptyset\right] = \mathbf{E}[|\mathcal{Y}_i|]$ and that $\mathbf{Pr}[\mathcal{Y}_i \neq \emptyset] \cdot \mathbf{Pr}[j \in \mathcal{Y}_i | \mathcal{Y}_i \neq \emptyset] = \mathbf{Pr}[j \in \mathcal{Y}_i]$. As a result, the upper bound we get on Equation 5 is

$$C \cdot (\mathbf{E}[|\mathcal{Y}_i|] - \mathbf{Pr}[\mathcal{Y}_i \neq \emptyset]) + \sum_j \mathbf{Pr}[j \in \mathcal{Y}_i] \cdot \log \frac{1}{\mathbf{Var}_\mu[x_j]} + \mathbf{Pr}[\mathcal{Y}_i \neq \emptyset] \cdot \log \mathop{\mathbf{Var}}_{\mu}[g_i].$$

Note that $\mathcal{Y}_i \neq \emptyset$ exactly when $i \in S$. As a result, summing this over all $i \in [k]$ yields

$$\mathbf{E}\left[\sum_{i \in S} |P_i(\mathcal{Y}_i)|\right] \leq C \cdot (\mathbf{E}[|\mathcal{Y}|] - \mathbf{E}[|S|]) + \sum_{j \in [n]} \mathbf{Pr}[j \in \mathcal{Y}] \cdot \log \frac{1}{\mathbf{Var}_\mu[x_j]} + \sum_{i \in [k]} \mathbf{Pr}[i \in S] \cdot \log \mathop{\mathbf{Var}}_{\mu}[g_i]. \tag{6}$$

For the first term in the expectation, we know by Claim 3.2 that the random variable S defined in the protocol is distributed according to $\widetilde{f}^2 \setminus \emptyset$. Thus, because P_f is a C-good protocol,

$$\mathbf{E}[P_f(S)] \leq C \cdot (\mathbf{E}[|S|] - 1) + \sum_{i \in [k]} \mathbf{Pr}[i \in S] \cdot \log \frac{1}{\mathbf{Var}_\eta[y_i]} + \log \mathop{\mathbf{Var}}_{\eta}[f].$$

Note that $\mathbf{Var}_\eta[y_i] = \mathbf{Var}_\mu[g_i]$ and $\mathbf{Var}_\eta[f] = \mathbf{Var}_\mu[h]$. As a result, adding these together yields

$$\mathbf{E}[|P(\mathcal{Y})|] \leq C \cdot (\mathbf{E}[|\mathcal{Y}|] - 1) + \sum_{j \in [n]} \mathbf{Pr}[j \in \mathcal{Y}] \cdot \log \frac{1}{\mathbf{Var}_\mu[x_j]} + \log \mathop{\mathbf{Var}}_{\mu}[h],$$

which yields the theorem. ☐

4. REFERENCES

[1] S. Chakraborty, R. Kulkarni, S. Lokam, and N. Saurabh. Upper bounds on Fourier entropy. In *Electronic Colloquium on Computational Complexity TR13-052*, 2013. 1, 1

[2] E. Friedgut and G. Kalai. Every monotone graph property has a sharp threshold. *Proceedings of the American Mathematical Society*, 124(10):2993–3002, 1996. (document), 1

[3] P. Gopalan, A. Kalai, and A. Klivans. Agnostically learning decision trees. In *Proceedings of the 40th Annual ACM Symposium on Theory of Computing*, pages 527–536, 2008. 1

[4] N. Keller, E. Mossel, and T. Schlank. A note on the Entropy/Influence conjecture. *Discrete Mathematics*, 312(22):3364–3372, 2012. 1.1

[5] A. Klivans, H. Lee, and A. Wan. Mansour's Conjecture is true for random DNF formulas. In *Proceedings of the 23rd Annual Conference on Learning Theory*, 2010. 1

[6] Y. Mansour. Learning Boolean functions via the Fourier transform. In V. Roychowdhury, K.-Y. Siu, and A. Orlitsky, editors, *Theoretical Advances in Neural Computation and Learning*, chapter 11, pages 391–424. Kluwer Academic Publishers, 1994. 1

[7] R. O'Donnell. *Analysis of Boolean functions.* 2013. 2.1, 3

[8] R. O'Donnell and L.-Y. Tan. A composition theorem for the Fourier Entropy-Influence conjecture. In *Proceedings of the 40th International Colloquium on Automata, Languages and Programming*, pages 780–791, 2013. (document), 1, 1, 1, 1.3, 1.3, 1.3, C

[9] R. O'Donnell, J. Wright, and Y. Zhou. The Fourier Entropy–Influence Conjecture for certain classes of Boolean functions. In *Proceedings of the 38th International Colloquium on Automata, Languages and Programming*, pages 330–341, 2011. 1, 1.1, 1, 2.1, B, B

[10] C. Shannon. A mathematical theory of communication. *The Bell System Technical Journal*, 27:July 379–423, October 623–656, 1948. 1.4

APPENDIX

A. DECISION TREE PROOFS

We will repeatedly use the following proposition, which relates the Fourier coefficients of f to the Fourier coefficients of its subfunctions g and h.

PROPOSITION A.1. *Let f be computed by a decision tree T whose left and right subfunctions are g and h, respectively. If x_i is at the root of T and S is any subset of $[n] \setminus \{i\}$, then*

$$\widehat{f}(S)^2 + \widehat{f}(S \cup \{i\})^2 = \frac{1}{2}\left(\widehat{g}(S)^2 + \widehat{h}(S)^2\right).$$

PROOF. Write f as

$$f = \left(\frac{1+x_i}{2}\right) g + \left(\frac{1-x_i}{2}\right) h.$$

For any $S \subseteq [n] \setminus \{i\}$, $\widehat{f}(S) = \frac{1}{2}(\widehat{g}(S) + \widehat{h}(S))$ and $\widehat{f}(S \cup \{i\}) = \frac{1}{2}(\widehat{g}(S) - \widehat{h}(S))$. As a result,

$$\widehat{f}(S)^2 + \widehat{f}(S \cup \{i\})^2 = \frac{1}{2}\left(\widehat{g}(S)^2 + \widehat{h}(S)^2\right).$$

☐

We will also use the following proposition, which relates the influences of f to the influences of its subfunctions.

PROPOSITION A.2. *Assume the setup from Proposition 2.3. Then for a coordinate $j \neq i$,*

$$\mathbf{Inf}_j[f] = \frac{1}{2} \cdot (\mathbf{Inf}_j[g] + \mathbf{Inf}_j[h]).$$

PROOF.

$$\begin{aligned}\mathbf{Inf}_j[f] &= \mathbf{Pr}[f(\boldsymbol{x}) \neq f(\boldsymbol{x}^{\oplus j})] \\ &= \frac{1}{2}\mathbf{Pr}[g(\boldsymbol{x}) \neq g(\boldsymbol{x}^{\oplus j})] + \frac{1}{2}\mathbf{Pr}[h(\boldsymbol{x}) \neq h(\boldsymbol{x}^{\oplus j})] \\ &= \frac{1}{2}\left(\mathbf{Inf}_j[g] + \mathbf{Inf}_j[h]\right).\end{aligned}$$

□

B. PROOF OF LEMMA 1.5

In this section, we give a proof of Lemma 1.5, which was implicit in [9]; the proof we give here, included for completeness, is essentially the same. First, we have the following lemma:

LEMMA B.1. *Let $f : \{-1,1\}^n \to \{-1,1\}$ and write $\hat{f}(\emptyset)^2 = 1-\epsilon$. Then $2\cdot\mathbf{Inf}[f] \geq h(\epsilon)$, where $h(\cdot)$ is the binary entropy function.*

PROOF. First, we may assume $\epsilon \neq 0, 1$, otherwise the result is trivial. Now, $(1-\epsilon)\log\frac{1}{1-\epsilon} \leq \frac{1}{\ln 2}\epsilon \leq 2\epsilon$, so

$$h(\epsilon) = \epsilon\log\frac{1}{\epsilon} + (1-\epsilon)\log\frac{1}{1-\epsilon} \leq \epsilon\log\frac{1}{\epsilon} + 2\epsilon.$$

By Proposition 2 of [9], the right-hand side is at most $2 \cdot \mathbf{Inf}[f]$, and the lemma follows. □

LEMMA B.2 (RESTATEMENT OF LEMMA 1.5). *Suppose there is an almost prefix-free protocol for $\mathcal{X}$ with length B and alphabet Σ. Then $\mathbf{H}[\mathcal{X}] \leq \log_2|\Sigma| \cdot B + 2 \cdot \mathbf{Inf}[f]$.*

PROOF. Write $\hat{f}(\emptyset)^2 = 1-\epsilon$. If $\epsilon = 0$ then $\mathbf{H}[\mathcal{X}] = 0$, so the lemma follows. Otherwise, let $\mathcal{Y}$ be the indicator that $\mathcal{X} = \emptyset$. Then $\mathbf{H}[\mathcal{X}|\mathcal{Y} = 0] \leq \log_2|\Sigma|\ B/\epsilon$ by the source coding theorem, as the protocol outputs B/ϵ characters on average conditioned on $\mathcal{X}$ being nonempty.

$$\begin{aligned}\mathbf{H}[\mathcal{X}] &= \mathbf{H}[\mathcal{X},\mathcal{Y}] \\ &= \mathbf{H}[\mathcal{Y}] + \mathbf{H}[\mathcal{X}|\mathcal{Y}] && \text{(conditional entropy)} \\ &= \mathbf{H}[\mathcal{Y}] + (1-\epsilon)\cdot\mathbf{H}[\mathcal{X}|\mathcal{Y}=1] + \epsilon\cdot\mathbf{H}[\mathcal{X}|\mathcal{Y}=0] \\ &\leq \mathbf{H}[\mathcal{Y}] + \log_2|\Sigma|\cdot B && \text{(using } \mathbf{H}[\mathcal{X}|\mathcal{Y}=1]=0)\end{aligned}$$

Because $\mathcal{Y}$ is a $(1-\epsilon)$-biased random bit, $\mathbf{H}[\mathcal{Y}] = h(\epsilon)$, where $h(\cdot)$ is the binary entropy function. Thus, we may apply Lemma B.1 and get that $\mathbf{H}[\mathcal{X}] \leq 2\cdot\mathbf{Inf}[f] + \log_2|\Sigma|\cdot B$. □

C. PARALLELIZING THE PROTOCOL

The performance of Shannon's code gives the following guarantee:

FACT C.1. *Let $\mathcal{X}^1, \ldots, \mathcal{X}^t$ be t independent samples drawn from $\widetilde{f}^2 \setminus \emptyset$. Then there is a prefix-free protocol P_f^t for which*

$$\mathbf{E}\left[|P_f^t(\mathcal{X}^1, \ldots, \mathcal{X}^t)|\right] \leq t \cdot \boldsymbol{H}\left[\widetilde{f}^2 \setminus \emptyset\right] + 1.$$

In other words, the average number of bits used per copy of $\mathcal{X}$ is $1/t$ more than the theoretical best. In the limit as t tends to ∞, the excess number of bits tends to 0. Using this, we will show that the protocol from Section 3 may be analyzed as if the subprotocols are optimally efficient. We will do this by showing an efficient protocol to communicate sets $\mathcal{Y}^1, \ldots, \mathcal{Y}^t \sim \widetilde{h}^2 \setminus \emptyset$ which are chosen independently. As before, use $\mathcal{Y}_i^j$ to denote the restriction of $\mathcal{Y}^j$ to the coordinates relevant to g_i. We will assume that we have the efficient protocol P_f^t guaranteed by Fact C.1. In addition, for each $i \in [k]$ and $m \in [t]$ we will use the protocol P_i^m which Fact C.1 guarantees will efficiently communicate m samples from $\widetilde{g_i}^2 \setminus \emptyset$. Now, consider the following protocol $P_h^t(\mathcal{Y}^1, \ldots, \mathcal{Y}^t)$:

1. For each $j \in [t]$, let $S^j \subseteq [k]$ be the set containing those i such that $\mathcal{Y}_i^j \neq \emptyset$.
2. Output $P_f^t(S^1, \ldots, S^t)$.
3. For each $i \in [k]$:
   (a) Let $j_1, \ldots, j_m$ be the indices of the nonempty $\mathcal{Y}_i^j$ (in order).
   (b) If $m \neq 0$, output $P_i^m(\mathcal{Y}_i^{j_1}, \ldots, \mathcal{Y}_i^{j_m})$. Otherwise, output nothing.

The following lemma, which may be compared to Proposition 3.2 in [8], gives the performance of this protocol and suffices to recover their composition theorem for entropy.

LEMMA C.2. *Let S be distributed as in the protocol from Section 3. In the limit as $t \to \infty$,*

$$\frac{1}{t}\cdot\mathbf{E}\left[|P_h^t(\mathcal{Y}^1, \ldots, \mathcal{Y}^t)|\right] = \boldsymbol{H}\left[\widetilde{f}^2 \setminus \emptyset\right] + \sum_{i\in[k]}\mathbf{Pr}[i \in S]\cdot\boldsymbol{H}\left[\widetilde{g_i}^2 \setminus \emptyset\right].$$

PROOF PROOF SKETCH. Fix a coordinate $i \in [k]$ and consider the number m of nonempty $\mathcal{Y}_i^j$s. From Claim 3.1, we know that if $\mathcal{Y}_i^j$ is nonempty, then it is distributed as $\widetilde{g_i}^2 \setminus \emptyset$. As a result, for a fixed value of m, Fact C.1 tells us that the expected number of bits that P_i^m outputs per $\mathcal{Y}_i^j$ is at most $1/m$ in excess of $\mathbf{H}\left[\widetilde{g_i}^2 \setminus \emptyset\right]$. Now, m is distributed as $\mathrm{Bin}(t, r)$, where r is a probability independent of t. Thus, by taking $t \to \infty$ the expectation of $1/m$ (when m is nonzero) will tend towards 0. As a result, we may assume that $\mathbf{H}\left[\widetilde{g_i}^2 \setminus \emptyset\right]$ bits are used in expectation to communicate each nonzero $\mathcal{Y}_i^j$. A similar argument shows that we may assume that $\mathbf{H}[\widetilde{f}^2 \setminus \emptyset]$ bits are used in expectation to communicate each S^j.

Aside from packaging the different sets together when calling the subprotocols, the protocol acts as t independent copies of the protocol from Section 3. Let us focus on the case when $j = 1$. Then the expected number of bits spent outputting the sets for which $j = 1$ is

$$\mathbf{H}\left[\widetilde{f}^2 \setminus \emptyset\right] + \sum_{i\in[k]}\mathbf{Pr}[i \in S^1]\cdot\mathbf{H}\left[\widetilde{g_i}^2 \setminus \emptyset\right].$$

As S^1 is distributed identically to S in the protocol from Section 3, we may replace the event $i \in S^1$ with $i \in S$. Averaging this over all $j \in [t]$ yields the lemma. □

D. PROOFS OF CLAIMS

First, we recall several basic facts regarding μ-biased Fourier analysis. For $S \neq T$ and $S \neq \emptyset$, we have $\mathbf{E}_\mu[\phi_S^\mu] = 0$

and $\mathbf{E}_\mu[\phi^\mu_S \cdot \phi^\mu_T] = 0$. We also have Parseval's inequality, which states that for $f : \{-1,1\}^n \to \mathbb{R}$, the equality $\sum_{S\subseteq[n]} \widetilde{f}(S)^2 = \mathbf{E}_\mu[f^2]$ holds.

We now prove the following proposition, from which the claims follow immediately.

PROPOSITION D.1. *Given the setup of the first protocol,*

$$\widetilde{h}(\mathcal{Y}) = \widetilde{f}(S) \prod_{i\in S} \frac{\widetilde{g}(\mathcal{Y}_i)}{\sigma_i}.$$

PROOF. Let $\eta_i = \mathbf{E}_\mu[g_i]$ and $\sigma_i^2 = \mathbf{Var}_\mu[g_i]$. Let S be as defined in the protocol. Then

$$\begin{aligned}\widetilde{h}(\mathcal{Y}) &= \mathop{\mathbf{E}}_{\boldsymbol{x}\sim\mu}[h(\boldsymbol{x}) \cdot \phi^\mu_{\mathcal{Y}}(\boldsymbol{x})] \\ &= \mathop{\mathbf{E}}_{\boldsymbol{x}}\left[f(g_1(\boldsymbol{x}),\ldots,g_k(\boldsymbol{x})) \cdot \prod_{j\in S} \phi^\mu_{\mathcal{Y}_j}(\boldsymbol{x})\right] \\ &= \sum_{T\subseteq[k]} \widetilde{f}(T) \mathop{\mathbf{E}}_{\boldsymbol{x}}\left[\phi^\eta_T(g_1(\boldsymbol{x}),\ldots,g_k(\boldsymbol{x})) \cdot \prod_{j\in S} \phi^\mu_{\mathcal{Y}_j}(\boldsymbol{x})\right] \\ &= \sum_{T\subseteq[k]} \widetilde{f}(T) \mathop{\mathbf{E}}_{\boldsymbol{x}}\left[\prod_{i\in T}\left(\frac{g_i(\boldsymbol{x})-\eta_i}{\sigma_i}\right) \prod_{j\in S} \phi^\mu_{\mathcal{Y}_j}(\boldsymbol{x})\right].\end{aligned}$$

A standard calculation shows that the expectation is nonzero only if $S = T$. In this case, the expectation is equal to

$$\prod_{i\in S} \mathop{\mathbf{E}}_{\boldsymbol{x}}\left[\left(\frac{g_i(\boldsymbol{x})-\eta_i}{\sigma_i}\right) \cdot \phi^\mu_{\mathcal{Y}_i}(\boldsymbol{x})\right] = \prod_{i\in S} \frac{\widetilde{g}(\mathcal{Y}_i)}{\sigma_i},$$

where the equality holds because $\mathcal{Y}_i$ is nonempty, so the shift by η_i doesn't affect the calculation. The proposition now follows. □

Now we prove the claims:

PROOF PROOF OF CLAIM 3.1. Condition $\mathcal{Y}$ on $\mathcal{Y}_i \neq \emptyset$ and on any values for $\mathcal{Y}_1,\ldots,\mathcal{Y}_{i-1},\mathcal{Y}_{i+1},\ldots,\mathcal{Y}_k$. Then by Proposition D.1, $\mathcal{Y}_i$ is distributed as $\widetilde{g}_i{}^2 \setminus \emptyset$. As this holds conditioned on any values for the $\mathcal{Y}_j$'s, $j \neq i$, this also holds conditioned only on $\mathcal{Y}_i \neq \emptyset$. □

PROOF PROOF OF CLAIM 3.2. First, because f and h have the same mean, they also have the same variance, i.e.

$$\sum_{\mathcal{Y}\neq\emptyset} \widetilde{h}^2(\mathcal{Y}) = \sum_{S\neq\emptyset} \widetilde{f}^2(S).$$

Next, fix a particular value of $S \subseteq [k]$, $S \neq \emptyset$. The sets $\mathcal{Y}$ for which the protocol selects this particular S are those for which $\mathcal{Y}_i \neq \emptyset \iff i \in S$. Then the probability S is selected is just the sum over these sets:

$$\begin{aligned}\sum_{\mathcal{Y}:\mathcal{Y}_i\neq\emptyset \iff i\in S} \widetilde{h}(\mathcal{Y})^2 &= \sum_{\mathcal{Y}:\mathcal{Y}_i\neq\emptyset \iff i\in S} \widetilde{f}(S)^2 \prod_{i\in S} \frac{\widetilde{g}(\mathcal{Y}_i)^2}{\sigma_i^2} \\ &\qquad \text{(by Proposition D.1)} \\ &= \widetilde{f}(S)^2 \prod_{i\in S} \sum_{\mathcal{Y}_i\neq\emptyset} \frac{\widetilde{g}(\mathcal{Y}_i)^2}{\sigma_i^2} \\ &= \widetilde{f}(S)^2.\end{aligned}$$

Combining these two facts yields the claim. □

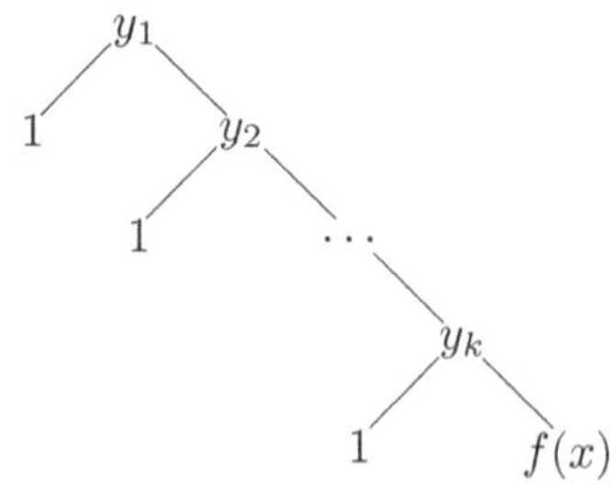

Figure 3: A decision tree computing $g(x,y)$.

E. SMALL INFLUENCE COUNTEREXAMPLE

Suppose we could prove Theorem 1.2 without the restriction on the function's total influence, i.e. the following statement:

CONJECTURE E.1. *Suppose $f : \{-1,1\}^n \to \{-1,1\}$ is computable by a decision tree with expected depth d, and let $\mathcal{X} \sim \widehat{f}^2$. Then $\mathbf{H}[\mathcal{X}] \leq C \cdot d \cdot \mathbf{Inf}[f]$, for some absolute constant C.*

This appears to be a weaker conjecture than the FEI conjecture. However, in this section we will show that this statement implies the FEI conjecture, at least for functions with sufficiently large influence.

PROPOSITION E.2. *Suppose Conjecture E.1 were true for some constant C. Let $f : \{-1,1\}^n \to \{-1,1\}$, and let $\mathcal{X} \sim \widehat{f}^2$. If $\mathbf{Inf}[f] \geq \log(n)$, then $\mathbf{H}[\mathcal{X}] \leq C' \cdot \mathbf{Inf}[f]$, where C' is some other absolute constant.*

Although this only shows that Conjecture E.1 implies a restricted form of the FEI conjecture, this restricted form does not appear to be especially easier than the full FEI conjecture. Thus, the restriction in Theorem 1.2 that f have large influence is a natural one.

Let $f : \{-1,1\}^n \to \{-1,1\}$ have $\mathbf{Inf}[f] \geq \log n$. We prove Proposition E.2 by "hiding" f in a low expected-depth decision tree. The resulting decision tree still has low expected-depth, and its spectral entropy and total influence terms are roughly proportional to f's. Thus, applying Conjecture E.1 to the decision tree shows that f itself satisfies the FEI conjecture.

PROOF. Let $f : \{-1,1\}^n \to \{-1,1\}$ have $\mathbf{Inf}[f] \geq \log n$, and let $\mathcal{X} \sim \widehat{f}^2$. We begin with the assumption that f is balanced, i.e. that $\mathbf{E}[f] = 0$, and we will later reduce the general case to this case. For simplicity, assume that n is a power of two. Consider the new function $g(x,y)$ defined as

$$g(x,y) = \begin{cases} f(x) & \text{if } AND(y_1,\ldots,y_k) = -1, \\ 1 & otherwise. \end{cases}$$

Pictorially, refer to Figure 3, where $f(x)$ is computed by some decision tree. Since f can be trivially computed by a decision tree of depth n, the decision tree pictured computes f with expected depth at most $2 + n/2^k$. By choosing $k = \log_2 n$, this decision tree has expected depth 3.

Each variable y_i is influential only when the rest of the y_j's are -1 and $f(x) = -1$ (which happens half of the time because f is balanced), so the influence of each y_i is exactly $1/2^k$. Each of the x_i variables is influential only when all of the $y_i's$ are -1, so the influence of variable x_i on g is exactly $\mathbf{Inf}_i[f]/2^k$. As a result,

$$\mathbf{Inf}[g] = \frac{k + \mathbf{Inf}[f]}{2^k} = \frac{\log n + \mathbf{Inf}[f]}{n}.$$

To compute the entropy, we can first write g as

$$g(x, y) = 1 - \frac{1}{2^k} \sum_S \chi_S(y) \left(\frac{1}{2} + \frac{f(x)}{2} \right).$$

From this, we can easily read off some of the Fourier coefficients of g: if $S \subseteq [k]$ and $T \subseteq [n]$ are both nonempty, then $\widehat{g}(S, T) = -\widehat{f}(T)/2^{k+1}$. As a result, if $\mathcal{X}' \sim \widehat{g}^2$, then we can lower bound $\mathbf{H}[\mathcal{X}']$ by summing over the terms in the entropy formula corresponding to these subsets:

$$\begin{aligned}
\mathbf{H}[\mathcal{X}'] &\geq \sum_{S,T \neq \emptyset} \frac{\widehat{f}(T)^2}{2^{2k+2}} \log\left(\frac{2^{2k+2}}{\widehat{f}(T)^2} \right) \\
&\geq \sum_T \frac{\widehat{f}(T)^2}{2^{k+3}} \log\left(\frac{2^{2k+2}}{\widehat{f}(T)^2} \right) \\
&\geq \sum_T \frac{(2k+2) \cdot \widehat{f}(T)^2}{2^{k+3}} + \sum_T \frac{\widehat{f}(T)^2}{2^{k+3}} \log\left(\frac{1}{\widehat{f}(T)^2} \right) \\
&= \frac{2k + 2 + \mathbf{H}[\mathcal{X}]}{2^{k+3}} = \frac{2\log n + 2 + \mathbf{H}[\mathcal{X}]}{8n}.
\end{aligned}$$

Here the second inequality follows because the sum is over $2^k - 1 \geq 2^{k-1}$ sets S and because $\widehat{f}(\emptyset) = 0$. The second-to-last equality follows because f is mean-zero, so $\sum_T \widehat{f}(T)^2 = 1$.

Now, applying Conjecture E.1 to g, we have that

$$\frac{3\log n + \mathbf{H}[\mathcal{X}]}{8n} \leq \mathbf{H}[\mathcal{X}'] \leq C\cdot 3\cdot \mathbf{Inf}[g] = C\cdot 3\cdot \frac{\log n + \mathbf{Inf}[f]}{n}.$$

This can be rearranged as

$$\mathbf{H}[\mathcal{X}] \leq (24C - 3) \cdot \log n + 24C \cdot \mathbf{Inf}[f].$$

Thus, if $\mathbf{Inf}[f] \geq \log n$, then $\mathbf{H}[\mathcal{X}] \leq C'\mathbf{Inf}[f]$, where $C' = 48C - 3$.

Now, if f is not balanced, consider the function $g(x_1, \ldots, x_n, x_{n+1}) = x_{n+1} \cdot f(x)$. Then g is balanced, has the same Fourier entropy as f, and $\mathbf{Inf}[g] = \mathbf{Inf}[f] + 1$. As we have just shown,

$$\begin{aligned}
\mathbf{H}[\mathcal{X}] &= \mathbf{H}[\widehat{g}^2] \\
&\leq C' \cdot \mathbf{Inf}[g] \\
&= C' \cdot (\mathbf{Inf}[f] + 1) \\
&\leq C' \cdot (\mathbf{Inf}[f] + \log n) \\
&\leq (C' + 1) \cdot \mathbf{Inf}[f].
\end{aligned}$$

Here, the last inequality uses the fact that $\log n \leq \mathbf{Inf}[f]$. Thus, f satisfies the FEI conjecture with constant $C'+1$. □

Locally Testable Codes and Cayley Graphs

Parikshit Gopalan
Microsoft Research
Silicon Valley
parik@microsoft.com

Salil Vadhan
School of Engineering
and Applied Sciences
Harvard University
salil@seas.harvard.edu

Yuan Zhou
Computer Science Department
Carnegie Mellon University
yuanzhou@cs.cmu.edu

ABSTRACT

We give two new characterizations of ($\mathbb{F}_2$-linear, smooth) locally testable error-correcting codes in terms of Cayley graphs over $\mathbb{F}_2^h$:

1. A locally testable code is equivalent to a Cayley graph over $\mathbb{F}_2^h$ whose set of generators is significantly larger than h and has no short linear dependencies, but yields a shortest-path metric that embeds into ℓ_1 with constant distortion. This extends and gives a converse to a result of Khot and Naor (2006), which showed that codes with large dual distance imply Cayley graphs that have no low-distortion embeddings into ℓ_1.

2. A locally testable code is equivalent to a Cayley graph over $\mathbb{F}_2^h$ that has significantly more than h eigenvalues near 1, which have no short linear dependencies among them and which "explain" all of the large eigenvalues. This extends and gives a converse to a recent construction of Barak et al. (2012), which showed that locally testable codes imply Cayley graphs that are small-set expanders but have many large eigenvalues.

Categories and Subject Descriptors

G.2.1 [**Mathematics of Computing**]: Discrete Mathematics—*Combinatorics*

Keywords

locally testable codes; Cayley graphs; metric embeddings; spectral graph theory; Fourier analysis

1. INTRODUCTION

In this work, we show that *locally testable codes* (with "smooth" testers) are equivalent to *Cayley graphs* with certain properties, thereby providing a new perspective from which to approach long-standing open problems about the achievable parameters of locally testable codes.

Before describing these results, we review the basics of both locally testable codes and Cayley graphs.

ITCS'14, January 12–14, 2014, Princeton, New Jersey, USA.

http://dx.doi.org/10.1145/2554797.2554807.

1.1 Locally Testable Codes

Informally, a *locally testable code (LTC)* is an error-correcting code in which one can distinguish received words that are in the code from those that are far from the code by a randomized test that probes only a few coordinates of the received word. Local testing algorithms for algebraic error-correcting codes (like the Hadamard code and the Reed–Muller code) were developed in the literature on program testing [BLR93, RS96], inspired the development of the field of property testing [GGR98], and played a key role in the constructions of multi-prover interactive proofs and the proof of the PCP Theorem [BFL91, FGL+96, BFLS91, AS98, ALM+98]. Indeed, they are considered to be the "combinatorial core" of PCPs (cf., [GS06, BGH+06]), and thus understanding what is possible and impossible with locally testable codes can point the way to a similarly improved understanding of PCPs. See the surveys [Tre04, Gol11, Ben10].

We focus on the commonly studied case of linear codes over $\mathbb{F}_2$. Thus a *code* is specified by a linear subspace $\mathcal{C} \subset \mathbb{F}_2^n$. n is called the *blocklength* of the code, and $k = \dim(\mathcal{C})$ is its *rate*. The *minimum distance* is $d = \min_{x \neq y \in \mathcal{C}} d(x,y) = \min_{x \in \mathcal{C}-\{0,\}} |x|$, where $d(\cdot,\cdot)$ denotes Hamming distance and $|\cdot|$ denotes Hamming weight. These parameters are typically summarized by referring to $\mathcal{C}$ as an $[n,k,d]_2$ *linear code*.

A *local tester* for $\mathcal{C}$ is a randomized algorithm T that, when given oracle access to a *received word* $r \in \mathbb{F}_2^n$, makes at most a small number q of queries to symbols of r and accepts or rejects. If $r \in \mathcal{C}$, then T^r should accept with high probability (completeness), and if r is "far" from $\mathcal{C}$ in Hamming distance, then T^r should reject with high probability (soundness). It was shown in [BHR05] that any tester for a linear code can be converted into one with the following structure: the tester T randomly samples a string $\alpha \leftarrow \mathcal{D}$ and accepts if $\alpha \cdot r = 0$, where $\mathcal{D} = \mathcal{D}_T$ is some distribution on the *dual code* $\mathcal{C}^\perp = \{\alpha \in \mathbb{F}_2^n : \alpha \cdot c = 0 \forall\, c \in \mathcal{C}\}$. In particular, such a tester has perfect completeness (accepts with probability 1 if $r \in \mathcal{C}$). We say the tester (which is now specified solely by $\mathcal{D}$) has *(strong) soundness* δ if for every $r \in \mathbb{F}_2^n$,

$$\Pr_{\alpha \leftarrow \mathcal{D}}[\alpha \cdot r = 1] \geq \delta \cdot d(r, \mathcal{C}),$$

where $d(r,\mathcal{C}) = \min_{c \in \mathcal{C}} d(r,c)$. This formulation of soundness is often referred to as *strong soundness* in the literature. Typically, we want $\delta = \Omega(1/d)$, where d is the minimum distance of the code, so that received words at distance $\Omega(d)$ from $\mathcal{C}$ are rejected with constant probability. If there are received words at distance $\omega(d)$ from $\mathcal{C}$, then it is common to cap the rejection probability at a constant (e.g. require $\Pr_{\alpha \leftarrow \mathcal{D}}[\alpha \cdot r = 1] \geq \min\{\delta \cdot d(r,\mathcal{C}), 1/3\}$), but we ignore this issue in the introduction for simplicity. An alternate formulation known as *weak soundness* only requires that the test reject with probability $\Omega(1)$ when r is at distance βd from the code, for some fixed constant $\beta < 1/2$.

We are interested in two parameter regimes for LTCs:

Asymptotically Good LTCs Here we seek rate $k = \Omega(n)$, minimum distance $d = \Omega(n)$, soundness $\delta = \Omega(1/d) = \Omega(1/n)$, and query complexity $q = O(1)$. Unfortunately, we do not know whether such codes exist — this is the major open problem about LTCs first posed by [GS06] , and it is closely related to the long-standing open question about whether SAT has constant-query PCPs of linear length (which would enable proving that various approximation problems require time $2^{\Omega(n)}$ under the exponential-time hypothesis). The closest we have is Dinur's construction [Din07], which has inverse-polylogarithmic (rather than constant) relative rate (i.e. $n = k \cdot \text{polylog}(k)$). A recent result by Viderman additionally achieves strong soundness [Vid13].

Constant-distance LTCs Here we are interested in codes where the minimum distance d is a fixed constant, and the traditional coding question is how large the rate k can be as $n \to \infty$. BCH codes have (optimal) rate $k = n - (d/2) \cdot \log n$, but do not have any local testability properties. Reed–Muller codes yield the best known locally testable codes in this regime, with rate $k = n - O((\log n)^{\log d})$ and query complexity $q = O(n/d)$ to achieve soundness $\delta = \Omega(1/d)$ [BKS+10].[1] (This query complexity is optimal, as $\Omega(n/d)$ queries is needed to detect $d/2$ random corruptions to a codeword with constant probability.) An open problem is whether rate $k = n - c_d \cdot \log n$ is possible, for some constant c_d depending only on d (but not on n).

In terms of limitations of LTCs, there are a number of results shedding light on the structure of an LTC with good parameters (see the survey [Ben10]), but there are essentially no nontrivial upper-bounds on rate known for arbitrary $\mathbb{F}_2$-linear LTCs.

Instead of bounding the query complexity of our LTCs, it is convenient for us to work with *smooth LTCs*, where we simply require that the tester does not query any one coordinate too often. Formally, a tester, specified by a distribution $\mathcal{D}$ on $\mathcal{C}^\perp$, is ε-*smooth* if for every $i \in [n]$, $\Pr_{\alpha \leftarrow \mathcal{D}}[\alpha_i = 1] \leq \varepsilon$. This is analogous to the notion of smooth locally *decodable* codes (LDCs) defined by Katz and Trevisan [KT00]. Like in the case of LDCs, bounding smoothness is closely related to bounding query complexity, where query complexity q corresponds to smoothness $\Theta(q/n)$ (as would be the case for testers that make q uniformly distributed queries). In particular, we want the smoothness to be $\varepsilon = O(1/n)$ in the asymptotically good regime, and $\varepsilon = O(1/d)$ in the constant-distance regime.

As we show in Appendix A, given a code with a q-query tester that gives weak soundness, we can convert it into a code with similar parameters and a tester with smoothness $O(q/d)$ that gives weak soundness. In the reverse direction, we can convert an ε-smooth tester for a code into a $O(\varepsilon n)$ query tester while preserving weak soundness. However, we are unaware of such reductions that preserve strong soundness, and there are examples of codes in the literature (such as those in [Vid13]) which have q-query testers that give strong soundness, but which are not known to have smooth testers with strong soundness. [2] Below we focus mainly on smooth testers with strong soundness, because our result statements are cleanest for such testers, but there are variants of our results for smooth testers with weak soundness.

1.2 Cayley Graphs

Cayley graphs are combinatorial structures associated with finite groups and are useful for applications ranging from pure group theory to reasoning about the mixing rates of Markov chains to explicit constructions of expander graphs [Big93, HLW06]. In this paper, we focus on the case that the group is a finite-dimensional vector space $\mathcal{V}$ over $\mathbb{F}_2$. (So $\mathcal{V} \cong \mathbb{F}_2^h$ for some $h \in \mathbb{N}$.) Given a multiset $S \subseteq \mathcal{V}$, the Cayley (multi)graph $\text{Cay}(\mathcal{V}, S)$ has vertex set $\mathcal{V}$ and edges $(x, x+s)$ for every $s \in S$ (with appropriate multiplicities if S is a multiset). Note that this is an $|S|$-regular undirected graph, since every element of $\mathcal{V}$ is its own additive inverse. If we take S to be a basis of $\mathcal{V}$, then $\text{Cay}(\mathcal{V}, S)$ is simply the h-dimensional hypercube, where $h = \dim \mathcal{V}$. We will be interested in the properties of such graphs when $|S|$ is larger than h.

1.3 LTCs and Metric Embeddings of Cayley Graphs

Our first result shows that locally testable codes are equivalent to Cayley graphs with low-distortion metric embeddings into ℓ_1. We refer the reader to [Mat02, Chapter 15] for background on metric embeddings. An *embedding* of a metric space (X_1, d_1) into metric space (X_2, d_2) with *distortion* $c \geq 1$ is a function $f : X_1 \to X_2$ such that for some $\alpha \in \mathbb{R}^+$ and every $x, y \in X_1$, we have

$$\alpha \cdot d_1(x,y) \leq d_2(f(x), f(y)) \leq c \cdot \alpha \cdot d_1(x,y).$$

A commonly studied case is when (X_1, d_1) is the shortest-path metric $d_{\mathcal{G}}$ on a graph $\mathcal{G}$, and (X_2, d_2) is an ℓ_p metric. Indeed, we will take (X_1, d_1) to be the shortest-path metric on a Cayley graph, and (X_2, d_2) to be an ℓ_1 metric. We will use the well-known characterization of ℓ_1 metrics as the cone of the "cut metrics": a finite metric space (X_2, d_2) is an ℓ_1 metric if and only if there is a constant $\alpha \in \mathbb{R}^+$ and a distribution F on boolean functions on X_2 such that for all $x, y \in X_2$, $d_2(x,y) = \alpha \cdot \Pr_{f \leftarrow F}[f(x) \neq f(y)]$.

Note that the shortest-path metric on the hypercube $\text{Cay}(\mathbb{F}_2^h, \{e_1, \ldots, e_h\})$ is an ℓ_1 metric. Indeed, this metric is simply the Hamming distance d, and $d(x,y) = n \cdot \Pr_{i \leftarrow [n]}[x_i \neq y_i]$. We show that the existence of locally testable codes is equivalent to being able to approximate this property (i.e. have low-distortion embeddings into ℓ_1) even when the number of generators is noticeably larger than h. To avoid trivial ways of increasing the number of generators (like duplicating generators, or taking small linear combinations), we will also require that the generators are d-wise linearly independent (i.e. have no linear dependency of length smaller than d).

THEOREM 1. *1. If there is an $\mathbb{F}_2$-linear code of blocklength n, rate k, and distance d with an ε-smooth local tester of strong soundness δ, then there is a Cayley graph $\mathcal{G} = \text{Cay}(\mathbb{F}_2^h, S)$ such that $|S| = n$, $h = n - k$, S is d-wise linearly independent, and the shortest path metric on $\mathcal{G}$ embeds into ℓ_1 with distortion at most ε/δ.*

2. If there is a Cayley graph $\mathcal{G} = \text{Cay}(\mathbb{F}_2^h, S)$ such that $|S| = n$, S is d-wise linearly independent, and the shortest path metric on $\mathcal{G}$ embeds into ℓ_1 with distortion at most c, then there is an $\mathbb{F}_2$-linear code of blocklength n, rate $k = n - h$, and distance d with an ε-smooth local tester of strong soundness δ, for some δ and ε such that $\varepsilon/\delta \leq c$.

Note that the theorem provides an exact equivalence between locally testable codes and ℓ_1 embeddings of Cayley graphs, except

[1]This is a case where the rejection probabilities need to be capped at a constant, since there may be received words at distance $\omega(d)$ from $\mathcal{C}$.

[2]We are thankful to Or Meir [Mei13] for clarifying this and pointing out an error in a previous version of this paper.

that the equivalence only preserves the ratio ε/δ rather than the two quantities separately. It turns out that this ratio is the appropriate parameter to measure when considering *strong* soundness. (See Section 3.1.) For weaker notions of soundness, we obtain equivalences with weaker notions of low-distortion embeddings, such as "single-scale embeddings" (where we replace the requirement that $d_2(f(x), f(y)) \geq \alpha d_1(x,y)$ with $d_1(x,y) \geq D \Rightarrow d_2(f(x), f(y)) \geq \alpha D$, see [Lee05] and references therein).

The theorem specializes as follows for the two main parameter regimes of interest:

COROLLARY 2. *There is an asymptotically good smooth LTC with strong soundness ($k = \Omega(n)$, $d = \Omega(n)$, $\varepsilon/\delta = O(1)$) iff there is a Cayley graph $\mathcal{G} = \mathrm{Cay}(\mathbb{F}_2^h, S)$ with $|S| = (1+\Omega(1))h$ such that S is $\Omega(h)$-wise linearly independent and the shortest path metric on $\mathcal{G}$ embeds into ℓ_1 with distortion $O(1)$.*

COROLLARY 3. *For a constant d, there is a distance d smooth LTC of blocklength n with rate $k = n - c_d \log n$ and $\varepsilon/\delta = O(1)$ iff there is a Cayley graph $\mathcal{G} = \mathrm{Cay}(\mathbb{F}_2^h, S)$ with $|S| = 2^{h/c_d}$ such that S is d-wise linearly independent and the shortest path metric on $\mathcal{G}$ embed into ℓ_1 with distortion $O(1)$.*

To interpret the theorem, let's consider what the conditions on the Cayley graph $\mathcal{G}$ mean. The condition that $|S| = n$ and the elements of S are d-wise independent means that locally, in balls of radius d, the graph $\mathcal{G}$ looks like the n-dimensional hypercube (which embeds into ℓ_1 with no distortion). However, it is squeezed into a hypercube of significantly lower dimension h (which may make even constant distortion impossible).

The canonical example of graphs that do not embed well into ℓ_1 are expanders. Specifically, an n-regular expander on $H = 2^h$ vertices with all nontrivial eigenvalues bounded away from 1 requires distortion $\Omega(h/\log n)$ to embed into ℓ_1. Roughly speaking, the reason is that by Cheeger's Inequality (or the Expander Mixing Lemma), cuts cannot distinguish random neighbors in the graph from random and independent pairs of vertices in the graph, and random pairs of vertices are typically at distance $\Omega(h/\log n)$.[3]

Thus, saying that a graph $\mathcal{G}$ embeds into ℓ_1 with constant distortion intuitively means that $\mathcal{G}$ is very far from being an expander. More precisely, to prove the nonexistence of an ℓ_1 embedding of distortion c amounts to exhibiting a distribution $\mathcal{D}_{\mathrm{close}}$ on edges of $\mathcal{G}$ and a distribution $\mathcal{D}_{\mathrm{far}}$ on pairs of vertices in $\mathcal{G}$ such that for every cut $f : \mathbb{F}_2^h \to \{0,1\}$,

$$\frac{\Pr_{(x,y)\leftarrow\mathcal{D}_{\mathrm{close}}}[f(x) \neq f(y)]}{c} > \frac{\Pr_{(x,y)\leftarrow\mathcal{D}_{\mathrm{far}}}[f(x) \neq f(y)]}{\mathbf{E}_{(x,y)\leftarrow\mathcal{D}_{\mathrm{far}}}[d_{\mathcal{G}}(x,y)]}.$$

As discussed above, if $\mathcal{G}$ were an expander, we could take $\mathcal{D}_{\mathrm{close}}$ to be the uniform distribution on edges and $\mathcal{D}_{\mathrm{far}}$ to be the uniform distribution on pairs of vertices, and deduce a superconstant lower bound on c. Showing an impossibility result for LTCs amounts to finding such expander-like distributions $\mathcal{D}_{\mathrm{close}}$ and $\mathcal{D}_{\mathrm{far}}$ in an arbitrary Cayley graph with a large (size n) set of d-wise linearly independent generators S.

Our construction of a Cayley graph from an LTC in Item 1 of Theorem 1 is a "quotient of hypercube" construction previously analyzed by Khot and Naor [KN06]. Specifically, they showed that if we start from a code $\mathcal{C}$ whose dual code $\mathcal{C}^\perp$ has large minimum distance, then the resulting Cayley graph $\mathcal{G}$ requires large distortion to embed into ℓ_1. Our contributions are to show that we can replace the hypothesis with the weaker condition that $\mathcal{C}$ is not locally testable, and to establish a tight converse by constructing LTCs from Cayley graphs with low-distortion embeddings.

[3]Actually, for Cayley graphs over $\mathbb{F}_2$ vector spaces, the bound can be improved to $\Omega(h/\log(n/h))$, using the fact that there are at most $\binom{n}{t}$ (rather than n^t) vertices at distance t from any given vertex.

1.4 LTCs and Spectral Properties of Cayley Graphs.

In our second result, we show that locally testable codes are equivalent to Cayley graphs with spectral properties similar to the "ε-noisy hypercube". We call such graphs derandomized hypercubes.

For Cayley graphs over $\mathbb{F}_2$ vector spaces (and more generally abelian groups), the spectrum can be described quite precisely using Fourier analysis. Let M be the transition matrix for the random walk on $\mathrm{Cay}(\mathcal{V}, S)$, i.e. the adjacency matrix divided by $|S|$. Then, regardless of the choice of S, the eigenvectors of M are exactly of the form $\chi_b(x) = (-1)^{b(x)}$ where $b : \mathcal{V} \to \mathbb{F}_2$ ranges over all $\mathbb{F}_2$-linear functions. (If we pick a basis so that $\mathcal{V} = \mathbb{F}_2^h$, then each such linear function is of the form $b(x) = \sum_i b_i x_i$.) The eigenvalue of M associated with χ_b is $(1/|S|) \cdot \sum_{s\in S} \chi_b(s)$. In particular, if S is a λ-biased space [NN93] for λ bounded away from 1, then all the nontrivial eigenvalues have magnitude at most λ, and hence the graph $\mathrm{Cay}(\mathcal{V}, S)$ is an expander. In contrast, for the case of the hypercube ($S = \{e_1, \ldots, e_h\}$ for a basis $e_1, \ldots, e_h$ of $\mathcal{V}$), the eigenvalue associated with $b = (b_1, \ldots, b_h)$ is $1 - 2|b|/h$ where $|b|$ is the Hamming weight of b, so there are $\binom{h}{i}$ eigenvalues of value $1 - 2i/h$.

In this section, it will be useful to generalize the notion of Cayley graph from multisets to distributions over $\mathcal{V}$. If S is a distribution over $\mathcal{V}$, then $\mathrm{Cay}(\mathcal{V}, S)$ is a weighted graph where we put weight $\Pr[S = s]$ on the edge $(x, x+s)$ for every $x, s \in \mathbb{F}_2^h$. $\Pr[S = s]$ is also the $(x, x+s)$ entry of the transition matrix of the random walk on $\mathrm{Cay}(\mathcal{V}, S)$. Now, the eigenvalues are $\lambda(b) = \mathbf{E}_{s\leftarrow S}[\chi_b(s)]$. Here a useful example is the ε-noisy hypercube, where $\mathcal{V} = \mathbb{F}_2^h$ and $S = (S_1, \ldots, S_h)$ has each coordinate independently set to 1 with probability ε, and hence the eigenvalues are $\lambda(b) = (1-2\varepsilon)^{|b|}$.

Neither the hypercube nor the ε-noisy hypercube are very good expanders, as they have eigenvalues of $1 - 2/h$ and $1 - 2\varepsilon$, respectively, corresponding to eigenvectors χ_b with $|b| = 1$ (which in turn correspond to the "coordinate cuts," partitioning $\mathbb{F}_2^h$ into the sets $\{x : x_i = 1\}$ and $\{x : x_i = 0\}$). However, their spectral properties do imply that small sets expand well. Indeed, Kahn, Kalai, and Linial [KKL88] showed that the indicator vectors of "small" sets in $\mathbb{F}_2^h$ are concentrated on the eigenvectors χ_b where $|b|$ is large, and hence small sets expand well in both the hypercube and ε-noisy hypercube (where "small" is $|\mathcal{V}|^{1-\Omega(1)}$ in the case of the hypercube, and $o(|\mathcal{V}|)$ in the case of the ε-noisy hypercube).

Our spectral characterization of locally testable codes is as follows.

THEOREM 4. *There is an $\mathbb{F}_2$-linear code of blocklength n, rate k, and distance d with an ε-smooth local tester of strong soundness δ if and only if there is a Cayley graph $\mathcal{G} = \mathrm{Cay}(\mathbb{F}_2^h, \mathcal{D})$ (for some distribution $\mathcal{D}$ on $\mathbb{F}_2^h$) and a set $S = \{b_1, \ldots, b_n\}$ of linear maps $b_i : \mathbb{F}_2^h \to \mathbb{F}_2$ satisfying:*

1. *$h = n - k$*
2. *S is d-wise linearly independent*
3. *$\lambda(b_i) \geq 1 - 2\varepsilon$ for $i = 1, \ldots, n$.*
4. *For every linear map $b : \mathbb{F}_2^h \to \mathbb{F}_2$, $\lambda(b) \leq 1 - 2\delta \cdot \mathrm{rank}_S(b)$, where $\mathrm{rank}_S(b) = \min\{|T| : T \subseteq S, b = \sum_{i\in T} b_i\}$.*

Let's compare these properties with those of the ε-noisy hypercube. Recall that, in the ε-noisy hypercube, the coordinate cuts $S = \{e_1, \ldots, e_h\}$ are linearly independent and all give eigenvalues of $1-2\varepsilon$. And for every b, $\lambda(b) = (1-2\varepsilon)^{|b|} = (1-2\varepsilon)^{\mathrm{rank}_S(b)} = 1 - \Omega(\varepsilon \cdot \mathrm{rank}_S(b))$ (provided $\mathrm{rank}_S(b) \leq O(1/\varepsilon)$).

Like in our metric embedding result, the main difference here is that we are asking for the set S to be of size larger than h (while retaining d-wise independence among the generators), so we need to squeeze many large eigenvalues into a low-dimensional space. One reason that these spectral properties are interesting is that they imply that the graph $\mathcal{G}$ is a small-set expander for sets of size $|\mathcal{V}|/\exp(d)$(see Lemma 18).

One direction of the above theorem (from LTCs to Cayley graphs) is extracted from the work of Barak et al. [BGH+12], who used locally testable codes (in the constant distance regime) to construct small-set expanders that have a large number of large eigenvalues (as a function of the number $H = 2^h$ of vertices). Such graphs provide barriers to improving the analysis of the Arora–Barak–Steurer algorithm for approximating small-set expansion and unique games [ABS10], and were also used by Barak et al. [BGH+12] to construct improved integrality gap instances for semidefinite programming relaxations of the unique games problem. Our contribution is showing that the connection can be reversed, when formulated appropriately (in terms of spectral properties rather than small-set expansion).

We can specialize Theorem 4 to the two parameter regimes of interest to us (see Corollaries 16 and 17 in Section 4.4 for precise statements). The existence of asymptotically good smooth LTCs with strong soundness is equivalent to the existence of Cayley graphs whose eigenvalue spectrum resembles the n-dimensional Boolean hypercube (for eigenevalues in the range $[0.5, 1]$) but where the number of vertices is $2^{(1-\Omega(1))n}$. In the constant d regime, the existence of $[n, n - c_d \log n, d]_2$ LTCs blocklength n with smoothness $\varepsilon = O(1/d)$, and soundness $\delta = \Omega(1/d)$ is equivalent to the existence of Cayley graphs whose eigenvalue spectrum resembles the n-dimensional Boolean hypercube (for eigenvalues in the range $[0.5, 1]$) but where the number of vertices is n^{c_d}.

Like our metric embedding result, Theorem 4 and its corollaries have analogues for weaker notions of soundness for the locally testable codes. Specifically, Item 4 changes in a way that is analogous to the soundness condition, for example only requiring that $\lambda(b)$ is small when $\mathrm{rank}_S(b)$ is large.

1.5 Perspective

For many of the problems about constructing codes or Cayley graphs studied in theoretical computer science, the main challenge is finding an *explicit* construction. Indeed, we know that a randomly chosen code has good rate and distance and that a randomly chosen set of generators yields a Cayley graph with high expansion, and much of the research on these topics is aimed at trying to match these parameters with efficient deterministic algorithms.

Locally testable codes (and the equivalent types of Cayley graphs that we formulate) are intriguing in that they combine properties of random objects (such as large distance) with very non-random properties (the existence of a local tester). Thus the major open questions (such as whether there are asymptotically good LTCs) are *existential* — do there even exist objects with the given parameters, regardless of the complexity of constructing them?

Our hope is that the alternative characterizations developed in this paper will be useful in approaching some of these existential questions, either positively (e.g. by using graph operations to construct Cayley graphs with the properties discussed above, analogously to Meir's construction of LTCs [Mei09]) or negatively (e.g. by reasoning about expander-like subgraphs of Cayley graphs, as discussed above in Section 1.3).

The connection between metric embeddings and local testability gives a new perspective on existing results in this area, for instance we use it to give a simple LTC-based proof of the non-embeddability result of Khot and Naor [KN06] (see Section 3.2). Similarly, the connection to derandomized hypercubes has been used by [BGH+12, KM13] to construct improved integrality gap instances for semidefinite programming relaxations of combinatorial optimization problems.

2. LOCALLY TESTABLE CODES REVISITED

In this section we reformulate the properties of Locally Testable Codes in terms of cosets, which makes our equivalences easier to show.

Recall that a local tester for an $[n, k, d]_2$ binary linear code $\mathcal{C}$ is specified by a a distribution $\mathcal{D}$ on $\mathcal{C}^{\perp}$. The tester $\mathcal{D}$ is ε-smooth if for every $i \in [n]$, $\Pr_{\alpha \leftarrow \mathcal{D}}[\alpha_i = 1] \leq \varepsilon$. For $v \in \mathbb{F}_2^n$ let $d(v, \mathcal{C}) = \min_{c \in \mathcal{C}} d(v, c)$ and $\mathrm{Rej}(v, \mathcal{D}) = \Pr_{\alpha \leftarrow \mathcal{D}}[\alpha \cdot v = 1]$. We say that $\mathcal{D}$ has soundness δ if $\mathrm{Rej}(v, \mathcal{D}) \geq \delta d(v, \mathcal{C})$ for all $v \in \mathbb{F}_2^n$. We say that an $[n, k, d]_2$ linear code is (ε, δ)-locally testable if it has a tester $\mathcal{D}$ which has smoothness ε and soundness δ. By considering received words at distance 1 from the code, we get $\delta \leq \mathrm{Rej}(e_i, \mathcal{D}) \leq \varepsilon$. The upper bound is an easy consequence of the smoothness. Ideally, we want $\delta = \Omega(\varepsilon)$.

Given $v \in \mathcal{V}$, let $\bar{v} \in \mathcal{V}/\mathcal{C}$ denote the coset of $\mathcal{C}$ containing it. Let $\bar{\mathcal{E}} = \{\bar{e}_1, \ldots, \bar{e}_n\}$ denote the coset representatives of the basis vectors $\{e_1, \ldots, e_n\}$. The $\bar{e}_i$s are not independent over $\mathbb{F}_2$, indeed we have

$$\sum_{i \in S} \bar{e}_i = 0 \iff \sum_{i \in S} e_i \in \mathcal{C}$$

Hence the shortest non-trivial linear dependence is of weight exactly d.

For $\bar{v} \in \mathcal{V}/\mathcal{C}$, there could be several ways to write it as a linear combination over $\bar{\mathcal{E}}$. We have

$$\bar{v} = \sum_{i \in S} \bar{e}_i \iff v + \sum_{i \in S} e_i \in \mathcal{C}$$

Hence if we define $d(\bar{v}, \mathcal{C}) = d(v, \mathcal{C})$ for any $v \in \bar{v}$ (the exact choice does not matter), it follows that $d(\bar{v}, \mathcal{C}) = \mathrm{rank}_{\bar{\mathcal{E}}}(v)$. Similarly, for every $c \in \mathcal{C}$, $v \in \mathcal{V}$ and $\alpha \in \mathcal{C}^{\perp}$, $\alpha(v) = \alpha(v + c)$. Hence

$$\mathrm{Rej}(v, \mathcal{D}) = \mathrm{Rej}(v + c, \mathcal{D}) \tag{1}$$

This lets us define $\mathrm{Rej}(\bar{v}, \mathcal{D}) = \mathrm{Rej}(v, \mathcal{D})$ for any $v \in \bar{v}$.

We can now rephrase smoothness and soundness in terms of coset representatives.

$$\Pr_{\alpha \leftarrow \mathcal{D}}[\alpha_i = 1] = \Pr_{\alpha \leftarrow \mathcal{D}}[\alpha(e_i) = 1] = \mathrm{Rej}(\bar{e}_i, \mathcal{D}) \tag{2}$$

Thus $\mathcal{D}$ is ε-smooth if every $\bar{e}_i$ is rejected with probability at most ε.

We say a set S of vectors in an $\mathbb{F}_2$-linear space is d-wise independent if every $T \subseteq S$ where $|T| < d$ is linearly independent over $\mathbb{F}_2$. For a set of vectors $S = \{s_1, \ldots, s_n\}$ which span a space $\mathcal{T}$, we use $\mathrm{rank}_S(t)$ for $t \in \mathcal{T}$ to denote the smallest k such that t can be expressed as the sum of k vectors from S. With this notation, $\mathcal{D}$ has soundness δ if for every $\bar{v} \in \mathcal{V}/\mathcal{C}$ such that $\mathrm{rank}_{\bar{\mathcal{E}}} \geq d'$, $\mathrm{Rej}(\bar{v}) \geq \delta d'$.

We summarize these observations in the following lemma:

LEMMA 5. *Let $\mathcal{C}$ be an $[n,k]_2$ code and let $\mathcal{D}$ be a tester for $\mathcal{C}$.*

- *$\mathcal{C}$ has distance d iff the set $\bar{\mathcal{E}}$ is d-wise independent.*
- *The tester $\mathcal{D}$ is ε-smooth iff $\mathrm{Rej}(\bar{e_i},\mathcal{D}) \le \varepsilon$ for all $i \in [n]$.*
- *For $\bar{v} \in \mathcal{V}/\mathcal{C}$, $d(\bar{v},\mathcal{C}) = \mathrm{rank}_{\bar{\mathcal{E}}}(\bar{v})$. Hence $\mathcal{D}$ has soundness δ iff for every $\bar{v} \in \mathcal{V}/\mathcal{C}$,*

$$\mathrm{Rej}(\bar{v},\mathcal{D}) \ge \delta \cdot \mathrm{rank}_{\bar{\mathcal{E}}}(\bar{v})$$

3. LOCALLY TESTABLE CODES AND METRIC EMBEDDINGS

Let $S = \{s_1,\ldots,s_n\} \subset \mathbb{F}_2^h$ be set of $n \ge h$ generators of $\mathbb{F}_2^h$ that are d-wise independent. Let $\mathcal{G} = \mathrm{Cay}(\mathbb{F}_2^h, S)$ be the Cayley graph whose edges correspond to the set S. The graph $\mathcal{G}$ can be naturally associated with a code $\mathcal{C}_\mathcal{G}$ which consists of all vectors $c = (c_1,\ldots,c_n)$ such that $\sum_i c_i s_i = 0$. It is easy to see that $\mathcal{C}_\mathcal{G}$ is an $[n, n-h, d]_2$ linear code.

Similarly, one can start from an $[n,k,d]_2$ linear code $\mathcal{C}$ and construct a Cayley graph $\mathcal{G}_\mathcal{C}$ on $\mathbb{F}_2^{n-k}$. We take the vertex set to be $\mathbb{F}_2^n/\mathcal{C}$. We add an edge $(\bar{x},\bar{y})$ if there exist $x \in \bar{x}$ and $y \in \bar{y}$ such that $d(x,y) = 1$. It is easy to see that is equivalent to taking $S = \{\bar{e_1},\ldots,\bar{e_n}\}$, and this set is d-wise independent by the distance property of $\mathcal{C}$.

It is easy to see that this construction inverts the previous construction. Henceforth we will fix a code $\mathcal{C}$ and a graph $\mathcal{G}$ that can be derived from one another. The vertex set of $\mathcal{G}$ is given by $V(\mathcal{G}) = \mathbb{F}_2^n/\mathcal{C}$ and the edge set $E(\mathcal{G})$ by $\{\bar{x}, \bar{x}+\bar{e_i}\}$ for $\bar{x} \in \mathbb{F}_2^n/\mathcal{C}$ and $i \in [n]$.

LEMMA 6. *Let $d_\mathcal{G}$ denote the shortest path metric on $\mathcal{G}$. We have*

$$d_\mathcal{G}(\bar{x},\bar{y}) = d_\mathcal{G}(\bar{x}+\bar{y},0) = d(x+y,\mathcal{C})$$

Proof: If $d_\mathcal{G}(\bar{x},\bar{y}) \le d$ then there exists $T \subset [n]$ of size d such that

$$\bar{y} = \bar{x} + \sum_{j\in T} \bar{e}_j \;\Rightarrow\; \bar{x}+\bar{y} = \sum_{j \in T} \bar{e}_j$$

hence $d(\bar{x}+\bar{y},\mathcal{C}) \le d$. Similarly, if $d(x+y,\mathcal{C}) \le d$, that gives an $\bar{x}$–$\bar{y}$ path of length d in $\mathcal{G}$. ∎

An ℓ_1-embedding of the shortest path metric $d_\mathcal{G}$ on the graph $\mathcal{G}$ is a distribution $\mathcal{D}$ over Boolean functions $f : V(\mathcal{G}) = \mathbb{F}_2^n/\mathcal{C} \to \{\pm 1\}$. The distance $\delta(\bar{x},\bar{y})$ between a pair of vertices $\bar{x}$ and $\bar{y}$ under this embedding is

$$\delta(\bar{x},\bar{y}) = \Pr_{f\in\mathcal{D}}[f(\bar{x}) \ne f(\bar{y})]$$

We define the stretch of an edge $(\bar{x},\bar{y})$ to be the ratio $\delta(\bar{x},\bar{y})/d(\bar{x},\bar{y})$. The distortion $c_\mathcal{D}$ of the embedding $\mathcal{D}$ is the ratio of the maximum to the minimum stretch of any pair of vertices. It is given by

$$c_\mathcal{D} = \frac{\max_{\bar{x},\bar{y}\in V(\mathcal{G})} \delta(\bar{x},\bar{y})/d_\mathcal{G}(\bar{x},\bar{y})}{\min_{\bar{x},\bar{y}} \delta(\bar{x},\bar{y})/d_\mathcal{G}(\bar{x},\bar{y})}$$

It follows by the triangle inequality that the stretch is maximized by some edge. Hence we get

$$c_\mathcal{D} = \frac{\max_{\bar{x}\in V(\mathcal{G}), i\in[n]} \delta(\bar{x},\bar{x}+\bar{e}_i)}{\min_{x,y} \delta(\bar{x},\bar{y})/d_\mathcal{G}(\bar{x},\bar{y})} \tag{3}$$

The minimum c achieved over all ℓ_1-embeddings of $\mathcal{G}$ is denoted $c_1(\mathcal{G})$.

DEFINITION 7. *An embedding $\mathcal{D}$ of $\mathcal{G} = \mathrm{Cay}(\mathbb{F}_2^h, S)$ into ℓ_1 is linear if $\mathcal{D}$ is supported on functions $\chi_\alpha(x) = (-1)^{\alpha(x)}$ where α is an $\mathbb{F}_2$-linear function on $V(\mathcal{G})$.*

The space of linear functions on $\mathbb{F}_2^n/\mathcal{C}$ is isomorphic to $\mathcal{C}^\perp$. In a linear embedding, we have

$$\begin{aligned}\delta(\bar{x},\bar{y}) &= \Pr_{\alpha\in\mathcal{D}}[\chi_\alpha(\bar{x}) \ne \chi_\alpha(\bar{y})]\\ &= \Pr_{\alpha\in\mathcal{D}}[\chi_\alpha(\bar{x}+\bar{y}) \ne 1]\\ &= \delta(\bar{x}+\bar{y},0)\end{aligned}$$

Thus, the distance δ is invariant under shifting in linear embeddings, just like the shortest path distance $d_\mathcal{G}$. Indeed, the next lemma shows that we can replace any embedding by a linear embedding without increasing the distortion.

LEMMA 8. *There is a linear embedding $\mathcal{D}$ of $\mathcal{G}$ into ℓ_1 achieving distortion $c_1(\mathcal{G})$.*

To prove this lemma, we set up some machinery. Let $f : \mathbb{F}_2^n/\mathcal{C} \to \{\pm 1\}$ be a Boolean function on $\mathbb{F}_2^n/\mathcal{C}$. We can extend f to a function on all of $\mathbb{F}_2^n$ by setting $f(x) = f(\bar{x})$. (We will henceforth switch freely between both notions). The resulting function is invariant under cosets of $\mathcal{C}$, which implies that its Fourier spectrum is supported on $\mathcal{C}^\perp$. Hence we have

$$f(x) = \sum_{\alpha\in\mathcal{C}^\perp} \hat{f}(\alpha)\chi_\alpha(x)$$

Further, we have $\sum_{\alpha\in\mathcal{C}^\perp} \hat{f}(\alpha)^2 = 1$.

We now proceed to the proof of Lemma 8.

Proof: Given an arbitrary distribution $\mathcal{D}$ on Boolean functions, we define a new distribution $\mathcal{D}'$ on functions where we sample $a \in \mathbb{F}_2^n$ uniformly at random, $f \in \mathcal{D}$, and return the function $f' : \mathbb{F}_2^n \to \{\pm 1\}$ defined by $f'(x) = f(x+a)$. We will show that $c'_\mathcal{D} \le c_\mathcal{D}$.

Let $\delta'(x,y) = \Pr_{f'\in\mathcal{D}'}[f'(x) \ne f'(y)]$. We have

$$\begin{aligned}\delta'(x,y) &= \Pr_{a\in\mathbb{F}_2^n, f\in\mathcal{D}}[f(x+a) \ne f(y+a)]\\ &= \mathbf{E}_{a\in\mathbb{F}_2^n}\left[\Pr_{f\in\mathcal{D}'}[f(x+a) \ne f(y+a)]\right]\\ &= \mathbf{E}_{a\in\mathbb{F}_2^n}[\delta(x+a,y+a)].\end{aligned}$$

Let a_1 and a_2 be the values of a that minimize and maximize $\delta(x+a,y+a)$ respectively. Then

$$\delta(x+a_1,y+a_1) \le \delta'(x,y) \le \delta(x+a_2,y+a_2)$$

Hence we have

$$\frac{\delta(x+a_1,y+a_1)}{d(x+a_1,y+a_1)} \le \frac{\delta'(x,y)}{d(x,y)} \le \frac{\delta(x+a_2,y+a_2)}{d(x+a_2,y+a_2)}$$

since all the denominators are equal. But this implies that

$$\min_{x,y}\frac{\delta'(x,y)}{d(x,y)} \ge \min_{x,y}\frac{\delta(x,y)}{d(x,y)},$$

$$\max_{x,y}\frac{\delta'(x,y)}{d(x,y)} \le \max_{x,y}\frac{\delta(x,y)}{d(x,y)}$$

and hence

$$c_{\mathcal{D}'} = \frac{\max_{x,y}\frac{\delta'(x,y)}{d(x,y)}}{\min_{x,y}\frac{\delta'(x,y)}{d(x,y)}} \le \frac{\max_{x,y}\frac{\delta(x,y)}{d(x,y)}}{\min_{x,y}\frac{\delta(x,y)}{d(x,y)}} = c_\mathcal{D}.$$

Next we show that there is a linear embedding $\mathcal{D}''$ with distortion $c_{\mathcal{D}''} = c_{\mathcal{D}'}$. The embedding is simple to describe: we first sample

$f \in \mathcal{D}$, we then sample $\chi_\alpha \in \mathcal{C}^\perp$ with probability $\hat{f}(\alpha)^2$. We denote this distribution on $\mathcal{C}^\perp$ by $\hat{f}^2$. Note that

$$\begin{aligned}
\delta'(x,y) &= \Pr_{a \in \mathbb{F}_2^n, f \in \mathcal{D}}[f(x+a) \neq f(y+a)] \\
&= \mathbf{E}_{f \in \mathcal{D}}\left[\frac{1}{2}\mathbf{E}_{a \in \mathbb{F}_2^n}[1 - f(x+a)f(y+a)]\right] \\
&= \mathbf{E}_{f \in \mathcal{D}}\Bigg[\frac{1}{2}\mathbf{E}_{a \in \mathbb{F}_2^n}\Bigg[1 - \\
&\quad \left(\sum_{\alpha \in \mathcal{C}^\perp} \hat{f}(\alpha)\chi_\alpha(x+a)\right)\left(\sum_{\beta \in \mathcal{C}^\perp} \hat{f}(\beta)\chi_\beta(y+a)\right)\Bigg]\Bigg] \\
&= \mathbf{E}_{f \in \mathcal{D}}\Bigg[\frac{1}{2}\Bigg(1 - \\
&\quad \sum_{\alpha,\beta \in \mathcal{C}^\perp} \hat{f}(\alpha)\hat{f}(\beta)\chi_\alpha(x)\chi_\beta(y)\mathbf{E}_{a \in \mathbb{F}_2^n}[\chi_\alpha(a)\chi_\beta(a)]\Bigg)\Bigg] \\
&= \mathbf{E}_{f \in \mathcal{D}}\left[\frac{1}{2}\left(1 - \sum_{\alpha \in \mathcal{C}^\perp} \hat{f}(\alpha)^2\chi_\alpha(x)\chi_\alpha(y)\right)\right] \\
&= \mathbf{E}_{f \in \mathcal{D}}\left[\sum_{\alpha \in \mathcal{C}^\perp} \hat{f}(\alpha)^2 \frac{(1 - \chi_\alpha(x)\chi_\alpha(y)}{2}\right] \\
&= \Pr_{f \in \mathcal{D}} \Pr_{\alpha \in \hat{f}^2}[\chi_\alpha(x) \neq \chi_\alpha(y)] \\
&= \delta''(x,y).
\end{aligned}$$

From this it follows that $c''_\mathcal{D} = c'_\mathcal{D} \leq c_\mathcal{D}$.

The lemma follows by taking $\mathcal{D}$ to be the ℓ_1 embedding of $\mathcal{G}$ that minimizes distortion. ∎

We now prove the main result of this section.

THEOREM 9. *We have $c_1(\mathcal{G}) \leq c$ iff there exists an (ε, δ)-tester for $\mathcal{C}$ where $\delta \geq \varepsilon/c$.*

Proof: For linear embeddings, we can use shift invariance to simplify the expression for distortion. Since $\mathcal{D}$ is a distribution on $C^\perp$, we can view it as a tester for $\mathcal{C}$. Note that $\mathrm{Rej}(\bar{x}, \mathcal{D}) = \delta(\bar{x}, 0)$. Recall by Equation (3)

$$c_\mathcal{D} = \frac{\max_{\bar{x} \in V(\mathcal{G}), i \in [n]} \delta(\bar{x}, \bar{x} + \bar{e}_i)}{\min_{x,y} \delta(\bar{x}, \bar{y})/d_\mathcal{G}(\bar{x}, \bar{y})}$$

We can use $\delta(\bar{x}, \bar{y}) = \delta(\bar{x} + \bar{y}, 0) = \mathrm{Rej}(\bar{x} + \bar{y}, \mathcal{D})$ to rewrite this as

$$c_\mathcal{D} = \frac{\max_{i \in [n]} \mathrm{Rej}(\bar{e}_i, \mathcal{D})}{\min_{\bar{x} \in V(\mathcal{G})} \mathrm{Rej}(\bar{x}, \mathcal{D})/d(\bar{x}, 0)} \tag{4}$$

Given a linear embedding specified by a distribution $\mathcal{D}$ that gives distortion $c_\mathcal{D}$, we view $\mathcal{D}$ as a tester. By definition, it has smoothness ε for

$$\varepsilon \geq \max_{i \in [n]} \mathrm{Rej}(\bar{e}_i, \mathcal{D}) \tag{5}$$

and has soundness δ for

$$\delta \leq \min_{\bar{x} \in V(\mathcal{G})} \mathrm{Rej}(\bar{x}, \mathcal{D})/d(\bar{x}, 0) \tag{6}$$

since any such δ satisfies the condition

$$\mathrm{Rej}(\bar{x}, \mathcal{D}) \geq \delta d(\bar{x}, 0).$$

By taking ε, δ to satisfy Equations 5 and 6 with equality, we get $\delta = \varepsilon / c_\mathcal{D}$.

In the other direction, assume we have a (ε, δ)-tester for $\mathcal{C}$ where $\delta \geq \varepsilon/c$. Note that ε, δ must satisfy Equations 5 and 6. Plugging these into Equation 4, we get

$$c_\mathcal{D} = \frac{\max_{i \in [n]} \mathrm{Rej}(\bar{e}_i, \mathcal{D})}{\min_{\bar{x} \in V(\mathcal{G})} \mathrm{Rej}(\bar{x}, \mathcal{D})/d(\bar{x}, 0)} \leq \frac{\varepsilon}{\delta} \leq c.$$

∎

3.1 Boosting the soundness

Theorem 9 implies the existance of an (ε, δ)-tester for $\mathcal{C}$, where

$$\frac{\varepsilon}{c_1(\mathcal{G})} \leq \delta \leq \varepsilon.$$

While this is the best ratio possible between ε and δ, Theorem 9 does not seem to guarantee the right absolute values for them. In this section, we show that one can achieve this by repeating the tests. First, we identify the right absolute values.

Let t denote the covering radius of $\mathcal{C}$, and let $\bar{x}$ be a codeword at distance t from $\mathcal{C}$. Since

$$1 \geq \mathrm{Rej}(\bar{x}, \mathcal{D}) \geq \delta t$$

we get $\delta \leq 1/t$. Given this upper bound, we would like ε to be $\Theta(1/t)$ and δ to be $\Theta(1/(c_1(\mathcal{G})t))$. We show that this is possible, with a small loss in constants (which we do not attempt to optimize).

THEOREM 10. *There is a $(1/(4t), 1/(16c_1(G)t))$-tester for $\mathcal{C}$.*

We defer the proof of this result to Appendix B.

Note that if $d = \Omega(n)$, then d and t differ by a constant factor. However, when $d = o(n)$, it could be that $t = \omega(d)$. In this case, we could relax the soundness requirement for words at distance $\omega(d)$ as follows:

$$\mathrm{Rej}(\bar{x}, \mathcal{D}) \geq \begin{cases} \delta d(\bar{x}, \mathcal{C}) & \text{if } d(\bar{x}, \mathcal{C}) \leq d \\ \delta d & \text{if } d(\bar{x}, \mathcal{C}) \geq d \end{cases}$$

It is possible to get such a tester where $\varepsilon = O(1/d), \delta = \Omega(1/(c_1(\mathcal{G})d))$ using the same argument as above, but replacing t with d. We omit the details.

3.2 Relation to previous work

This equivalence allows us to reformulate results about LTCs in the language of metric embeddings and vice versa. We present two examples where we feel such reformulations are particularly interesting.

Embedding lower bounds from dual distance: .

Khot and Naor show the following lower bound for $c_1(\mathcal{G})$ in terms of its dual distance.

THEOREM 11. *[KN06, Theorem 3.4] Let $\mathcal{C}$ be an $[n, n-h]_2$ code and let $\mathcal{G}$ be the associated Cayley graph. Let $d^\perp$ denote its dual distance. Then*

$$c_1(\mathcal{G}) \geq \Omega\left(d^\perp \frac{h}{n \log(n/h)}\right)$$

In the setting where $h/n = \Omega(1)$ (which is necessary to have constant relative distance), this gives a lower bound of $\Omega(d^\perp)$. Thus their result can be seen as the embedding analogue of the result of BenSasson et al. [BHR05], who showed that the existence of low-weight dual codewords is a necessary condition for local testability. Our results allow for a simple alternative proof of Theorem 11.

PROOF OF THEOREM 11. By Theorem 9, there exists a (ε, δ)-tester $\mathcal{D}$ so that $c_1(\mathcal{G}) = \epsilon/\delta$. We may assume without loss of generality that $\mathcal{D}$ is supported on non-zero code-words in $\mathcal{C}^\perp$, each of which is of weight at least $d^\perp$, so we have $\varepsilon \geq d^\perp/n$.

As in Section 3.1, we have $\delta \leq 1/t$ where t is the covering radius of $\mathcal{C}$. We lower bound t by a standard volume argument:

$$2^{n-h} \cdot \sum_{t'=0}^{t} \binom{n}{t'} \geq 2^n \Rightarrow t = \Omega\left(\frac{h}{\log(n/h)}\right).$$

So we have

$$c_1(\mathcal{G}) \geq \frac{\varepsilon}{\delta} \geq \frac{d^\perp}{n} t = \Omega\left(d^\perp \frac{h}{n \log(n/h)}\right).$$

□

Lower bounds for basis testers: .

A basis tester for a code $\mathcal{C}$ is a tester $\mathcal{D}$ which is supported on a basis for $\mathcal{C}$. Ben-Sasson et al. showed a strong lower bound for such testers [BSGK+10]. Their main result when restated in our notation says:

THEOREM 12. *[BSGK+10, Theorem 5] Let $\mathcal{C}$ be an $[n, k, d]_2$ code with an (ε, δ)-basis tester. Then*

$$\frac{\varepsilon}{\delta} \geq \frac{kd}{3n}.$$

If $\mathcal{C}$ is an $[n, k, d]_2$ code, a basis tester for $\mathcal{C}$ yields an embedding into $(n-k)$-dimensional space. Hence their result implies that any linear embedding of $\mathbb{F}_2^n/\mathcal{C}$ into $(n-k)$-dimensional space requires distortion $\Omega(kd/n)$ (even though $\mathbb{F}_2^n/\mathcal{C}$ has dimension $n-k$ as a vector space over $\mathbb{F}_2$), and hence low-distortion embeddings must have larger support. Note that since our reduction from arbitrary embeddings to linear embeddings could blow up the support, this does not imply a similar bound for arbitrary embeddings.

4. LOCALLY TESTABLE CODES AND DERANDOMIZED HYPERCUBES

4.1 Derandomized Hypercubes

We consider Cayley graphs over groups of characteristic 2. Let $\mathcal{A} = \mathbb{F}_2^h$ for some $h > 0$. A distribution $\mathcal{D}$ over $\mathcal{A}$ gives rise to a weighted graph $\mathrm{Cay}(\mathcal{A}, \mathcal{D})$ where the weight of edge (α, β) equals $\mathcal{D}(\alpha + \beta)$.

The symmetry of Cayley graphs makes it easy to compute their eigenvectors and eigenvalues explicitly. Let $\mathcal{A}^*$ denote the space of all linear functions $b : \mathcal{A} \to \mathbb{F}_2$. The characters of the group $\mathcal{A}$ are in 1-1 correspondence with linear functions: $b \in \mathcal{A}^*$ corresponds to a character $\chi_b : \mathcal{A} \to \{\pm 1\}$ given by $\chi_b(\alpha) = (-1)^{b(\alpha)}$. The eigenvectors of $\mathrm{Cay}(\mathcal{A}, \mathcal{D})$ are precisely the characters $\{\chi_b\}_{b \in \mathcal{A}^*}$. The corresponding eigenvalues are given by $\lambda(b) = \mathbf{E}_{\alpha \in \mathcal{D}}[\chi_b(\alpha)]$.

As mentioned earlier, the Cayley graphs we are interested in can be viewed as derandomizations of the ε-noisy hypercube, which retain many of the nice spectral properties of the Boolean hypercube. Before defining them formally, we list these properties that we would like preserved (at least approximately).

1. **Large Eigenvalues.** There are h "top" eigenvectors $\{\chi_{e_i}\}_{i=1}^h$ whose eigenvalues satisfy $\lambda(e_i) \geq 1 - \varepsilon$.
2. **Linear Independence.** The linear functions $\{e_1, \ldots, e_h\}$ corresponding to the top eigenvectors are linearly independent over $\mathbb{F}_2$.
3. **Spectral Decay.** For $a \in \mathcal{A}^*$, if $a = \sum_{i \in S} e_i$, then $\lambda(a) \leq (1-\varepsilon)^{|S|}$.

We are interested in Cayley graphs whose threshold rank n is possibly (much) larger than h. But this means that the corresponding dual vectors which lie in the space $\mathcal{A}^*$ of dimension $h < n$ can no longer be linearly independent. So we relax the Linear Independence condition, and only ask that there should be no *short* linear dependencies between these vectors. The Spectral Decay condition will stay the same, except that we need to modify the notion of rank to account for linear dependencies.

DEFINITION 13. *Let $\mathrm{Cay}(\mathcal{A}, \mathcal{D})$ be a Cayley graph on the group $\mathcal{A} = \mathbb{F}_2^h$. Let $\mu, \nu \in [0,1]$ and $d \in \{1, \ldots, n\}$. Let $\mathcal{B}^* = \{b_1, \ldots, b_n\}$ be a d-wise independent set of generators for $\mathcal{A}^*$ of cardinality n. We say that $\mathcal{B}^*$ is a (μ, ν)-spectrum generator for $\mathrm{Cay}(\mathcal{A}, \mathcal{D})$ if it satisfies the following properties:*

- **Large Eigenvalues.** $\lambda(b) \geq 1 - \mu$ *for every* $b \in \mathcal{B}^*$.
- **Spectral Decay.** *For* $a \in \mathcal{A}^*$, $\lambda(a) \leq 1 - \nu \cdot \mathrm{rank}_{\mathcal{B}^*}(a)$.

Note that any set of generators $\mathcal{B}^*$ for $\mathcal{A}^*$ gives us some values of n, d, μ and ν. We would like n, d to be large. Also, applying the Spectral decay condition to $b \in \mathcal{B}^*$, we see that

$$1 - \mu \leq \lambda(b) \leq 1 - \nu$$

hence $\mu \geq \nu$. Ideally, we would like them to be within a constant factor of each other.

We refer to such graphs as "derandomized hypercubes". The reason is that if there is a generating set of size n which is significantly larger than the dimension h, then the resulting graph has spectral properties that resemble the n dimensional hypercube, although it has only $2^h \ll 2^n$ vertices. Every Cayley graph $\mathrm{Cay}(\mathcal{A}, \mathcal{D})$ together with a generating set $\mathcal{B}^*$ gives us a derandomized hypercube, the parameters n, d, μ, ν tell us how good the derandomization is (just like any code $\mathcal{C}$ and dual distribution $\mathcal{D}$ gives us local tester, whose quality is governed by the parameters it achieves).

4.2 Derandomized hypercubes from Locally Testable Codes

Barak et al. proposed the following construction of Derandomized Hypercubes from any Locally Testable Code [BGH+12]. Given $\mathcal{C}$ which is an $[n, k, d]_2$ linear code with a local tester $\mathcal{D}$, they consider the Cayley graph $C(\mathcal{C}^\perp, \mathcal{D})$ on $\mathcal{C}^\perp \cong \mathbb{F}_2^{n-k}$ whose edge weights are distributed according to $\mathcal{D}$.

THEOREM 14. *Let $\mathcal{C}$ be an $[n, k, d]_2$ linear code for $d \geq 3$, and let $\mathcal{D}$ be an (ε, δ)-tester for $\mathcal{C}$. There exists a d-wise independent set $\bar{\mathcal{E}}$ of size n which is a $(2\varepsilon, 2\delta)$-spectrum generator for $\mathrm{Cay}(\mathcal{C}^\perp, \mathcal{D})$.*

PROOF. Observe that $(\mathcal{C}^\perp)^* \cong \mathcal{V}/\mathcal{C}$. This is because each $v \in \mathcal{V}$ defines a linear function on $\mathcal{C}^\perp$ given by $v(\alpha) = \alpha(v)$, and v, v' define the same function iff the lie in the same coset of $\mathcal{C}$.

We take $\bar{\mathcal{E}} = \{\bar{e}_1, \ldots, \bar{e}_n\}$ to be the cosets corresponding to the received words $e_1, \ldots, e_n$. By Lemma 5, since $\mathcal{C}$ has distance d, the set $\bar{\mathcal{E}}$ is d-wise independence. We will show that it is a $(2\varepsilon, 2\delta)$-spectrum generator for $\mathrm{Cay}(\mathcal{C}^\perp, \mathcal{D})$.

We bound the eigenvalues using the correspondence between the spectrum of $\text{Cay}(\mathcal{C}^{\perp}, \mathcal{D})$ and the soundness of the tester $\mathcal{D}$ established by Barak et al.. For $\bar{v} \in \mathcal{V}/\mathcal{C}$, let $\chi_{\bar{v}}$ and $\lambda(\bar{v})$ denote the corresponding eigenvalue. [BGH+12, Lemma 4.5] says that

$$\lambda(\bar{v}) = 1 - 2\text{Rej}(\bar{v}, \mathcal{D}). \tag{7}$$

- **Smoothness implies Large Eigenvalues.** By Lemma 5 the smoothness of $\mathcal{D}$ implies $\text{Rej}(\bar{e}_i, \mathcal{D}) \leq \varepsilon$. By Equation 7,

$$\lambda(\bar{e}_i) = 1 - 2\text{Rej}(e_i, \mathcal{D}) \geq 1 - 2\varepsilon.$$

- **Soundness implies Spectral decay.** Fix $\bar{v} \in \mathcal{V}/\mathcal{C}$ so that $\text{rank}_{\mathcal{B}^*}(\bar{v}) \geq d'$. By Lemma 5, the soundness of $\mathcal{D}$ implies $\text{Rej}(\bar{v}, \mathcal{D}) \geq \delta d'$. By Equation 7,

$$\lambda(\bar{v}) = 1 - 2\text{Rej}(\bar{v}, \mathcal{D}) \leq 1 - 2\delta d'.$$

□

4.3 Locally Testable Codes from Derandomized Hypercubes

We show how to start from a Cayley graph on $\mathcal{A} = \mathbb{F}_2^h$ and a set of generators for $\mathcal{A}^*$ and get a locally testable code from it. Our construction takes a Cayley graph $\text{Cay}(\mathcal{A}, \mathcal{D}')$ and a (d, μ, ν)-spectrum generator $\mathcal{B}^*$.

We define the locally testable code $\mathcal{C}$ by specifying the dual code $\mathcal{C}^{\perp}$ and the tester $\mathcal{D}$. We view elements $\alpha \in \mathcal{A}$ as messages, and embed them into $\mathbb{F}_2^n$ using the map

$$f(\alpha) = (b_1(\alpha), \ldots, b_n(\alpha)). \tag{8}$$

Since $\mathcal{B}^*$ generates $\mathcal{A}^*$, the mapping f is injective. Its image is a h-dimensional subspace of $\mathbb{F}_2^n$ which we denote by $\mathcal{C}^{\perp}$. The LTC will be $\mathcal{C}$, which is the dual of $\mathcal{C}^{\perp}$. The distribution $\mathcal{D}'$ on A induces a distribution $\mathcal{D} = f(\alpha)_{\alpha \in \mathcal{D}'}$ on $\mathcal{C}^{\perp}$, which is the tester for $\mathcal{C}$.

THEOREM 15. *Let $\text{Cay}(\mathcal{A} = F_2^h, \mathcal{D}')$ be a Cayley graph and let $\mathcal{B}^* = \{b_1, \ldots, b_n\}$ be a d-wise independent (μ, ν)-spectrum generator for it. Let $\mathcal{C}$ be the dual of the code specified by Equation 8. Then $\mathcal{C}$ is an $[n, n-h, d]_2$ linear code and $\mathcal{D}$ is a $(\mu/2, \nu/2)$-tester for $\mathcal{C}$.*

PROOF. It is clear that $\mathcal{C}^{\perp}$ is an $[n, h]_2$ code, and hence $\mathcal{C}$ is an $[n, n-h]_2$ code. Recall that $f : \mathcal{A} \to \mathcal{C}^{\perp}$ is an isomorphism. Since $\mathbb{F}_2^n/\mathcal{C} \cong (\mathcal{C}^{\perp})^*$, f induces an isomorphism $g : \mathcal{A}^* \to \mathbb{F}_2^n/\mathcal{C}$, with property that for $a \in \mathcal{A}^*$ and $\alpha \in \mathcal{A}$,

$$g(a)(f(\alpha)) = a(\alpha). \tag{9}$$

We observe that $g(b_i) = \bar{e}_i$, since

$$\bar{e}_i(f(\alpha)) = e_i \cdot f(\alpha) = b_i(\alpha).$$

Since $\mathcal{B}^*$ is d-wise independent, so is $\bar{\mathcal{E}}$, which by Lemma 5 implies that $\mathcal{C}$ has distance d. This also implies that for any $a \in \mathcal{A}^*$,

$$a = \sum_{i \in S} b_i \iff g(a) = \sum_{i \in S} \bar{e}_i$$

Hence by Lemma 5, we have $d(g(a), \mathcal{C}) = \text{rank}_{\mathcal{B}^*}(a)$. We can now deduce the local testability of $\mathcal{C}$ from the spectral properties of $\mathcal{B}^*$.

- **Large Eigenvalues Imply Smoothness.** In order to bound the smoothness of $\mathcal{D}$ we need to bound

$$\text{Rej}(\bar{e}_i, \mathcal{D}) = \Pr_{\alpha \in \mathcal{D}'}[\bar{e}_i \cdot f(\alpha) = 1] = \Pr_{\alpha \in \mathcal{D}'}[b_i(\alpha) = 1]$$

We have

$$\begin{aligned} 1 - \mu \leq \lambda(b_i) =& \mathbf{E}_{\alpha \in \mathcal{D}}[(-1)^{b_i(\alpha)}] \\ =& 1 - 2 \Pr_{\alpha \in \mathcal{D}}[b_i(\alpha) = 1] \end{aligned}$$

which implies that

$$\text{Rej}(\bar{e}_i, \mathcal{D}) \geq \frac{\mu}{2}.$$

- **Spectral decay implies soundness.** Consider $\bar{v} \in \mathbb{F}_2^n/\mathcal{C}$ such that $d(\bar{v}, \mathcal{C}) \geq d'$. Let $\bar{v} = g(a)$ for $a \in \mathcal{A}^*$, so that $\text{rank}_{\mathcal{B}^*}(g(a)) \geq d'$. From the spectral decay property of $\mathcal{B}^*$,

$$\begin{aligned} 1 - \nu d' \geq \lambda(a) =& \mathbf{E}_{\alpha \in \mathcal{D}'}[(-1)^{a(\alpha)}] \\ =& 1 - 2 \Pr_{\alpha \in \mathcal{D}'}[a(\alpha) = 1] \end{aligned}$$

hence

$$\Pr_{\alpha \in \mathcal{D}'}[a(\alpha) = 1] \geq \frac{\nu d'}{2}.$$

The soundness of the tester follows by noting that

$$\text{Rej}(\bar{v}, \mathcal{D}) = \Pr_{\alpha \in \mathcal{D}'}[g(a) \cdot f(\alpha) = 1] = \Pr_{\alpha \in \mathcal{D}'}[a(\alpha) = 1]$$

□

4.4 Some consequences of this equivalence

This equivalence lets us reformulate questions regarding LTCs as questions regarding the existence of certain families of derandomized hypercubes.

COROLLARY 16. *There exists an asymptotically good family of codes $\{\mathcal{C}_n\}$ where $\mathcal{C}_n$ has blocklength n and is $(O(1/n), \Omega(1/n))$-locally testable iff for infintitely many h there exists a Cayley graph $\mathcal{G}_h = \text{Cay}(\mathbb{F}_2^h, \mathcal{D})$ and a set $\mathcal{B}^*$ of generators for $(\mathbb{F}_2^h)^*$ such that*

- *the elements of $\mathcal{B}^*$ are $(\rho_0 h)$-wise independent for $\rho_0 > 0$,*
- *$|\mathcal{B}^*| \geq \rho_1 h$ for $\rho_1 > 1$,*
- *$\mathcal{B}^*$ is an $(O(1/h), \Omega(1/h))$-spectrum generator for $\mathcal{G}_h$.*

COROLLARY 17. *Let $d \geq 3$. There exists an asymptotic family of codes $\{\mathcal{C}_n\}$ where $\mathcal{C}_n$ has parameters $[n, n - c_d \log n, d]_2$ and is $(\varepsilon, \Omega(\varepsilon))$-locally testable iff for infinitely many h there exists a Cayley graph $\mathcal{G}_h = \text{Cay}(\mathbb{F}_2^h, \mathcal{D})$ and a set $\mathcal{B}^*$ of generators for $(\mathbb{F}_2^h)^*$ such that*

- *the elements of $\mathcal{B}^*$ are d-wise independent,*
- *$|\mathcal{B}^*| \geq 2^{h/c_d}$,*
- *$\mathcal{B}^*$ is an $(\varepsilon, \Omega(\varepsilon))$-spectrum generator for $\mathcal{G}_h$.*

Next we show that derandomized hypercubes are small-set expanders. We say that a regular graph G with n vertices is a (τ, ϕ)-expander if for every set S of at most τn vertices, at least a fraction ϕ of the edges incident to S leave S (i.e. are on the boundary between S and $\overline{S}$).

The following lemma says that if a graph has a (μ, ν) spectrum generator, then it is a (τ, ϕ)-expander for appropriately chosen τ and ϕ. The lemma is proved in [BGH+12]. Since our terminology and notation is different, we present a proof of the Lemma in Appendix C.

LEMMA 18. *[BGH+12] Let $G = \text{Cay}(\mathcal{A}, \mathcal{D})$ be a Cayley graph on the group $\mathcal{A} = \mathbb{F}_2^h$. Let $\mathcal{B}^*$ be a d-wise independent set which is a (μ, ν)-spectrum generator for G. Then G is a (τ, ϕ_τ) expander for $\phi_\tau = \nu d/4 - 3^{d/2}\tau^{1/4}$.*

To interpret the expansion bound, think of $\nu d/4 = \Omega(1)$ (we can assume that the graphs obtained from LTCs have this property, since this is analogous to saying that words at distance $d/4$ are rejected with constant probability). So if we take $\tau = \exp(-d)$, then $\phi_\tau = \Omega(1)$. A particularly interesting instantiation of this bound is obtained by combining Corollary 17 and Lemma 18:

COROLLARY 19. *For $d \geq 3$, suppose there exists an asymptotic family of codes $\{\mathcal{C}_n\}$ where $\mathcal{C}_n$ has parameters $[n, n - c_d \log n, d]_2$ and is $(O(1/d), \Omega(1/d))$-locally testable. There for infinitely many h there exists a Cayley graph $\mathcal{G}_h = \text{Cay}(\mathbb{F}_2^h, \mathcal{D})$ such that $\mathcal{G}_h$ is $(O(9^{-d}), \Omega(1))$-expander and has $2^{h/c_d}$ eigenvalues greater than $1 - O(1/d)$.*

In contrast, Arora et al. [ABS10] showed that if G is an $(\tau, \Omega(1))$-expander, then there are at most $n^{O(\epsilon)}/\tau$ eigenvalues greater than $1 - \epsilon$. Their bound implies that the graph $\mathcal{G}_h$ obtained in Corollary 19 can have at most $2^{O(h/d)}$ eigenvalues greater than $1 - O(1/d)$. If there exist LTCs where $c_d = O(d)$, the resulting graphs $\mathcal{G}_h$ would meet the ABS bound. The only lower bound we know of for c_d is $c_d \geq d/2$ by the Hamming bound.

5. ACKNOWLEDGEMENTS

This work was done in part when the second author was on leave as a Visiting Researcher at Microsoft Research Silicon Valley and a Visiting Scholar at Stanford University, and the third author was visiting Microsoft Research Silicon Valley.

The second author was supported in part by NSF grant CCF-1116616 and US-Israel BSF grant 2010196. The third author was supported in part by a grant from the Simons Foundation (Award Number 252545).

We thank Or Meir for pointing out an error in an earlier version of this paper, regarding the relationship between smoothness and bounded query complexity for locally testable codes. We thank Alex Andoni, Anupam Gupta and Kunal Talwar for useful discussions and pointers to the literature on metric embeddings. And we thank Raghu Meka, Prasad Raghavendra and Madhu Sudan for helpful discussions.

6. REFERENCES

[ABS10] Sanjeev Arora, Boaz Barak, and David Steurer. Subexponential algorithms for Unique Games and related problems. In *Proceedings of the 51st Annual IEEE Symposium on Foundations of Computer Science*, pages 563–572, 2010.

[ALM+98] Sanjeev Arora, Carsten Lund, Rajeev Motwani, Madhu Sudan, and Mario Szegedy. Proof verification and the hardness of approximation problems. *Journal of the ACM*, 45(3):501–555, May 1998.

[AS98] Sanjeev Arora and Shmuel Safra. Probabilistic checking of proofs: A new characterization of NP. *Journal of the ACM*, 45(1):70–122, January 1998.

[Ben10] Eli Ben-Sasson. Property testing. chapter Limitation on the rate of families of locally testable codes, pages 13–31. Springer-Verlag, Berlin, Heidelberg, 2010.

[BFL91] László Babai, Lance Fortnow, and Carsten Lund. Nondeterministic exponential time has two-prover interactive protocols. *Computational Complexity*, 1(1):3–40, 1991.

[BFLS91] László Babai, Lance Fortnow, Leonid A. Levin, and Mario Szegedy. Checking computations in polylogarithmic time. In Cris Koutsougeras and Jeffrey Scott Vitter, editors, *STOC*, pages 21–31. ACM, 1991.

[BGH+06] Eli Ben-Sasson, Oded Goldreich, Prahladh Harsha, Madhu Sudan, and Salil Vadhan. Robust PCPs of proximity, shorter PCPs and applications to coding. *SIAM Journal on Computing*, 36(4):889–974, 2006.

[BGH+12] Boaz Barak, Parikshit Gopalan, Johan Håstad, Raghu Meka, Prasad Raghavendra, and David Steurer. Making the long code shorter, with applications to the Unique Games Conjecture. In *Proceedings of the 53rd Annual IEEE Symposium on Foundations of Computer Science*, 2012.

[BHR05] Eli Ben-Sasson, Prahladh Harsha, and Sofya Raskhodnikova. Some 3CNF properties are hard to test. *SIAM J. Comput.*, 35(1):1–21 (electronic), 2005.

[Big93] Norman Biggs. *Algebraic graph theory*. Cambridge University Press, 1993.

[BKS+10] Arnab Bhattacharyya, Swastik Kopparty, Grant Schoenebeck, Madhu Sudan, and David Zuckerman. Optimal testing of reed-muller codes. In *FOCS*, pages 488–497, 2010.

[BLR93] Manuel Blum, Michael Luby, and Ronitt Rubinfeld. Self-testing/correcting with applications to numerical problems. *Journal of Computer and System Sciences*, 47(3):549–595, 1993.

[BSGK+10] Eli Ben-Sasson, Venkatesan Guruswami, Tali Kaufman, Madhu Sudan, and Michael Viderman. Locally testable codes require redundant testers. *SIAM J. Comput.*, 39(7):3230–3247, 2010.

[Din07] Irit Dinur. The PCP theorem by gap amplification. *Journal of the ACM*, 54(3):article 12, 44 pages (electronic), 2007.

[FGL+96] Uriel Feige, Shafi Goldwasser, Laszlo Lovász, Shmuel Safra, and Mario Szegedy. Interactive proofs and the hardness of approximating cliques. *Journal of the ACM*, 43(2):268–292, 1996.

[GGR98] Oded Goldreich, Shafi Goldwasser, and Dana Ron. Property testing and its connection to learning and approximation. *Journal of the ACM*, 45(4):653–750, 1998.

[Gol11] Oded Goldreich. Studies in complexity and cryptography. chapter Short locally testable codes and proofs, pages 333–372. Springer-Verlag, Berlin, Heidelberg, 2011.

[GS06] Oded Goldreich and Madhu Sudan. Locally testable codes and PCPs of almost-linear length. *Journal of the ACM*, 53(4):558–655 (electronic), 2006.

[HLW06] S. Hoory, N. Linial, and A. Wigderson. Expander graphs and their applications. *Bull. Amer. Math Soc.*, 43:439–561, 2006.

[KKL88] Jeff Kahn, Gil Kalai, and Nathan Linial. The influence of variables on Boolean functions (extended abstract). In *29th Annual Symposium on Foundations of Computer Science*, pages 68–80,

White Plains, New York, 24–26 October 1988. IEEE.

[KM13] Daniel M. Kane and Raghu Meka. A prg for lipschitz functions of polynomials with applications to sparsest cut. In *STOC*, pages 1–10, 2013.

[KN06] S. Khot and A. Naor. Nonembeddability theorems via Fourier analysis. *Mathematische Annalen*, 334(4):821–852, 2006.

[KT00] Jonathan Katz and Luca Trevisan. On the efficiency of local decoding procedures for error-correcting codes. In *Proceedings of the Thirty-Second Annual ACM Symposium on Theory of Computing*, pages 80–86 (electronic), New York, 2000. ACM.

[Lee05] James Lee. On distance scales, embeddings, and efficient relaxations of the cut cone. In *Proc. 16th ACM-SIAM Symposium on Discrete Algorithms*, pages 92–101, 2005.

[Mat02] Jiri Matousek. *Lectures on Discrete Geoemetry*. Springer, GTM, 2002.

[Mei09] Or Meir. Combinatorial construction of locally testable codes. *SIAM Journal on Computing*, 39(2):491–544, 2009.

[Mei13] Or Meir. Personal communication, 2013.

[NN93] Joseph Naor and Moni Naor. Small-bias probability spaces: Efficient constructions and applications. *SIAM Journal on Computing*, 22(4):838–856, August 1993.

[RS96] Ronitt Rubinfeld and Madhu Sudan. Robust characterizations of polynomials with applications to program testing. *SIAM Journal on Computing*, 25(2):252–271, 1996.

[Tre04] Luca Trevisan. Some applications of coding theory in computational complexity. *Quaderni di Matematica*, 13:347–424, 2004.

[Vid13] Michael Viderman. Strong LTCs with inverse poly-log rate and constant soundness. In *To appear in FOCS 2013*, 2013.

APPENDIX

A. SMOOTHNESS VERSUS BOUNDED QUERY COMPLEXITY

In this section, we describe an equivalence between constructing LTCs with smooth testers and constructing LTCs with bounded query complexity. The equivalence is only for *weak soundness*, so we define that more formally now.

DEFINITION 20. *Let $\mathcal{C} \subseteq \mathbb{F}_2^n$ be a linear code, and $\mathcal{D}$ a distribution on $\mathcal{C}^\perp$ (which we view as a tester for $\mathcal{C}$). For $\delta > 0$, we say that $\mathcal{D}$ has* weak soundness *at distance d', if for every received word $r \in \mathbb{F}_2^n$ such that $d(r, \mathcal{C}) \geq d'$, we have* $\Pr_{\alpha \leftarrow \mathcal{D}}[\alpha \cdot r = 1] \geq 1/2$.

Thus, a tester with strong soundness δ has weak soundness at distance $d' = 1/2\delta$, but the converse does not hold. If d is the minimimum distance of the code, we typically want strong soundness at distance $d' = \beta d$ for an arbitrarily small constant β. (If β is too large, e.g. $\beta \geq 1/2$, then there may be no received words at distance at least βd from the code, and weak soundness becomes vacuous.)

Now we note that it is easy to convert an ε-smooth tester into one with bounded query complexity. Since an ε-smooth tester for a code queries at most εn coordinates in expectation, we can get a tester with query complexity $q = O(\varepsilon n)$ by discarding tests that query more than q coordinates. However, this transformation costs an *additive* constant (namely $\varepsilon n/q$) in the soundness probability, and hence it only preserves weak soundness. (We can amplify the soundness probability back to $1/2$ by repeating the tester a constant number of times.)

The other direction is more involved and requires a modification to the underlying code.

THEOREM 21. *Let $\mathcal{C}$ be an $[n, k, d]_2$ code that has a q-query tester $\mathcal{D}$ giving weak soundness at distance d'. Then for every $d'' \in \mathbb{N}$ there exists an $[n', k, d]_2$ code $\mathcal{C}'$ that has a q/d''-smooth tester $\mathcal{D}'$ giving weak soundness at distance $d' + d''$, with blocklength $n' \leq n + d''$.*

Thus taking $d'' = \Theta(d')$, we only increase the distance at which we have soundness by a constant factor, and obtain smoothness $\varepsilon = O(q/d')$. In an asymptotically good LTC, we have $d' = \Omega(n)$, so smoothness $\varepsilon = O(q/n)$ is indeed equivalent to query complexity $O(q)$. When $d' = o(n)$, the relationship is not tight, and it would be nice to improve Theorem 21 to yield smoothness $O(q/n')$ in general.

Proof: Let $\mathcal{C}$ be an $[n, k, d]_2$ code that has a q-query tester $\mathcal{D}$ with weak soundness at distance d'. Our goal is to construct from it a smooth LTC with comparable parameters. Let ε_i denote the probability that $\mathcal{D}$ queries coordinate i. We define a new code $\mathcal{C}'$ by replicating coordinate i

$$m_i = \left\lceil \frac{\varepsilon_i d''}{q} \right\rceil$$

times. This operation cannot decrease the minimum distance of the code.

The tester $\mathcal{D}'$ for $\mathcal{C}'$ is obtained by first sampling a test α according to $\mathcal{D}$ and then for each i in the support of α, choosing one of the m_i copies at random. Now each copy of coordinate i is queried with probability $\varepsilon_i/m_i \leq q/d''$, so the resulting tester $\mathcal{D}'$ is q/d''-smooth.

We bound the blocklength of $\mathcal{C}'$ as follows:

$$\begin{aligned} n' &= \sum_{i=1}^{n} m_i \\ &\leq \sum_{i=1}^{n} \left(1 + \frac{\varepsilon_i d''}{q}\right) \\ &= n + \frac{d''}{q} \cdot \sum_{i=1}^{n} \varepsilon_i \\ &\leq n + d'', \end{aligned}$$

where the last inequality follows from the fact that $\mathcal{D}$ is a q-query tester. We now analyze the soundness. Running a test according to $\mathcal{D}'$ on a received word r' is the same as running a test from $\mathcal{D}$ on a distribution $\mathcal{R}(r')$ of recieved words in $\mathcal{C}$, where we sample $r \in \mathcal{R}(r')$ by setting the i-th coordinate in r randomly to one of the m_i coordinates of r' which are meant to be copies of coordinate i. Note that if r' is actually obtained by replicating coordinates of some received word r, then $\mathcal{R}(r')$ is supported entirely on r.

Now consider a received word r' where $d(r', \mathcal{C}') \geq d' + d''$. We claim that every r in the support of $\mathcal{R}(r')$ satisfies

$$d(r, \mathcal{C}) \geq d'.$$

Suppose there exists an $r \in \mathcal{R}(r')$ and $c \in \mathcal{C}$ so that $d(r, c) < d'$; equivalently r and c agree in more than $n - d'$ coordinates. Then consider the codeword $c' \in \mathcal{C}'$ that is obtained by replicating coordinates of c. Then r' and c' agree in at least as many coordinates as r and c, so

$$d(r', c') < n' - (n - d') \leq (n + d'') - (n - d') = d' + d'',$$

which contradicts our assumption that $d(d', \mathcal{C}') \geq d' + d''$.

Thus every every $r \in \mathcal{R}(r')$ is at distance at least d' from $\mathcal{C}$ and hence is rejected with probability at least $1/2$ by $\mathcal{D}$. Hence $\mathcal{D}'$ rejects words at distance $d' + d''$ from $\mathcal{C}'$ with probability at least $1/2$, and thus has weak soundness at distance $d' + d''$. ∎

B. PROOF OF THEOREM 10

Let $\mathcal{D}^{\oplus \ell}$ denote the distribution on $\mathcal{C}^{\perp}$ where we sample ℓ independent codewords according to $\mathcal{D}$ and add them. We claim that for suitable ℓ, both ε and δ scale by roughly a factor of ℓ.

LEMMA 22. *Let ℓ be such that*

$$\ell \leq \frac{1}{4\text{Rej}(\bar{x}, \mathcal{D})} \quad \textit{for all } \bar{x} \in \mathbb{F}_2^n/\mathcal{C}.$$

Then $\mathcal{D}^{\oplus \ell}$ is an $(\varepsilon\ell, \delta\ell/2)$-tester for $\mathcal{C}$.

Proof: The tester $\mathcal{D}^{\oplus \ell}$ is an $\ell\varepsilon$-smooth tester by the union bound. Its soundness can be analyzed by noting that

$$1 - 2\text{Rej}(\bar{x}, \mathcal{D}^{\oplus \ell}) = (1 - 2\text{Rej}(\bar{x}, \mathcal{D}))^{\ell}$$

Using the bound on ℓ to truncate the RHS, we get

$$\text{Rej}(\bar{x}, \mathcal{D}^{\oplus \ell}) \geq \frac{\ell}{2}\text{Rej}(\bar{x}, \mathcal{D}) \geq \frac{\ell\delta}{2} d(\bar{x}, 0). \tag{10}$$

∎

We use this to prove Theorem 10.

PROOF OF THEOREM 10. We start with an (ε, δ)-tester where $\delta \geq \varepsilon / c_1(\mathcal{G})$. If δ exceeds the claimed bound, we are already done. Assume this is not true, so

$$\delta \leq \frac{1}{16 c_1(\mathcal{G}) t}, \; \varepsilon \leq c_1(\mathcal{G})\delta \leq \frac{1}{16t}$$

Since the covering radius is t, we have that for every $\bar{x} \in \mathbb{F}_2^n$,

$$\text{Rej}(\bar{x}, \mathcal{D}) \leq t\varepsilon \leq 1/16$$

Let $\ell = \lfloor 1/(4t\varepsilon) \rfloor$ so that

$$\frac{1}{8t\varepsilon} \leq \ell \leq \frac{1}{4t\varepsilon}.$$

By Lemma 22, $\mathcal{D}^{\oplus \ell}$ has smoothness ε' where

$$\varepsilon' \leq \ell\varepsilon \leq \frac{1}{4t}$$

and soundness δ' where

$$\delta' \geq \frac{1}{2}\ell\delta \geq \frac{1}{2}\frac{1}{8t\varepsilon}\frac{\varepsilon}{c_1(G)} \geq \frac{1}{16 t c_1(G)}.$$

□

C. PROOF OF LEMMA 18

We first show the follow hypercontractive inequality:

CLAIM 23. *Let $B = \{b_1, \ldots, b_n\} \subseteq \mathbb{F}_2^h$ be $(4d+1)$-wise independent. For every function $f : \mathbb{F}_2^h \to \mathbb{R}$ defined as*

$$f(x) = \sum_{S \subseteq [n], |S| \leq d} \hat{f}(S) \prod_{i \in S} \chi_{b_i}(x),$$

we have $\mathbf{E}_x[f(x)^4] \leq 9^d \left(\mathbf{E}_x[f(x)^2]\right)^2$.

Proof: Let $g : \mathbb{F}_2^n \to \mathbb{R}$ be

$$g(y) = \sum_{S \subseteq [n], |S| \leq d} \hat{f}(S) \prod_{i \in S} y_i.$$

The statement is proved by the standard $(2,4)$-hypercontractive inequality (applied to g function) and the observation that

$$\mathbf{E}_x[f(x)^2] = \mathbf{E}_y[g(y)]^2 = \sum_{S \subseteq [n], |S| \leq d} \hat{f}(S)^2,$$

and

$$\begin{aligned}\mathbf{E}_x[f(x)^4] =& \mathbf{E}_y[g(y)^4] \\ =& \sum_{\substack{|S_1|,|S_2|,|S_3|,|S_4| \leq d \\ S_1 \Delta S_2 \Delta S_3 \Delta S_4 = \emptyset}} \hat{f}(S_1)\hat{f}(S_2)\hat{f}(S_3)\hat{f}(S_4).\end{aligned}$$

∎

We now proceed to prove Lemma 18.

PROOF OF LEMMA 18. For any two functions $f, g : \mathbb{F}_2^h \to \mathbb{R}$, define their inner-product as

$$\langle f, g \rangle = \mathbf{E}_{x \in \mathbb{F}_2^h}[f(x)g(x)]$$

and the p-norm of f to be

$$\|f\|_p = \left(\mathbf{E}_{x \in \mathbb{F}_2^h} f(x)^p\right)^{1/p}.$$

For every function $f : \mathbb{F}_2^h \to \mathbb{R}$ with Fourier expansion

$$f(x) = \sum_{a \in \mathbb{F}_2^h} \hat{f}_a \chi_a(x)$$

let

$$f^{<d/4}(x) = \sum_{a : \text{rank}_{\mathcal{B}^*}(a) < d/4} \hat{f}_a \chi_a(x),$$

$$f^{\geq d/4}(x) = \sum_{a : \text{rank}_{\mathcal{B}^*}(a) \geq d/4} \hat{f}_a \chi_a(x).$$

Fix a set $\mathcal{S} \subseteq \mathbb{F}_2^h$. Let $\tau = \mu(\mathcal{S})$ be the volume of $\mathcal{S}$. Let $\mathbf{1}_{\mathcal{S}}(x) = \mathbf{1}_{x \in \mathcal{S}}$ be the indicator function $\mathcal{S}$. Note that $\|\mathbf{1}_{\mathcal{S}}\|_p^p = \tau$ for every $p \geq 1$. We will lower bound the expansion $\Phi(\mathcal{S}) = 1 - \langle \mathbf{1}_{\mathcal{S}}, G\mathbf{1}_{\mathcal{S}} \rangle / \tau$, which is the fraction of the edges incident to $\mathcal{S}$ leaving $\mathcal{S}$. Observe that

$$\langle \mathbf{1}_{\mathcal{S}}, G\mathbf{1}_{\mathcal{S}} \rangle = \langle \mathbf{1}_{\mathcal{S}}, G\mathbf{1}_{\mathcal{S}}^{<d/4} \rangle + \langle \mathbf{1}_{\mathcal{S}}, G\mathbf{1}_{\mathcal{S}}^{\geq d/4} \rangle. \tag{11}$$

The first term in the RHS of (11) is upper bounded as

$$\begin{aligned}\langle \mathbf{1}_{\mathcal{S}}, G\mathbf{1}_{\mathcal{S}}^{<d/4} \rangle =& \|\mathbf{1}_{\mathcal{S}}\|_{4/3} \|G\mathbf{1}_{\mathcal{S}}^{<d/4}\|_4 \\ \leq& \|\mathbf{1}_{\mathcal{S}}\|_{4/3} \cdot \sqrt{3}^d \|\mathbf{1}_{\mathcal{S}}\|_2 = \sqrt{3}^d \tau^{5/4}\end{aligned}$$

by Hölder's inequality and Claim 23. The second term in the RHS of (11) is upper bounded as

$$\langle \mathbf{1}_{\mathcal{S}}, G\mathbf{1}_{\mathcal{S}}^{\geq d/4} \rangle \leq (1 - \nu d/4)\|\mathbf{1}_{\mathcal{S}}\|_2^2 = (1 - \nu d/4)\tau.$$

In all, we have

$$\begin{aligned}\Phi(\mathcal{S}) =& 1 - \frac{\langle \mathbf{1}_{\mathcal{S}}, G\mathbf{1}_{\mathcal{S}} \rangle}{\tau} \\ \geq& 1 - \sqrt{3}^d \tau^{1/4} - (1 - \nu d/4) = \nu d/4 - \sqrt{3}^d \tau^{1/4}.\end{aligned}$$

□

Invitation Games and the Price of Stability

Uriel Feige*
Department of Computer Science and Applied Mathematics
Weizmann Institute
Rehovot, Israel
uriel.feige@weizmann.ac.il

Moshe Tennenholtz
Microsoft Research, Herzliya
and Technion, Haifa
moshet@microsoft.com

ABSTRACT

Given an arbitrary 2-player game G that we refer to as the basic game, we propose a notion of a multiplayer *invitation game* that proceeds for a fixed number of rounds, where in each round some player (whose identity is determined by a scheduler) gets to invite a player of his choice to play a match of the basic game. The question that we study is how does the price of stability of the invitation game compare to that of the basic game. For a wide range of schedulers we prove a dichotomy result, showing that there are only two types of basic games, those that we call *invitation resistant* in which the price of stability of the invitation version is equal to that of the basic game, and those that we call *asymptotically efficient* in which the price of stability tends to 0 as the number of rounds grows. [1] In particular, when the basic game is the prisoners dilemma the game is asymptotically efficient if and only if the payoff when both players defect is nonzero.

Categories and Subject Descriptors

J.4 [**Computer Applications**]: Social and Behavioral Sciences; I.2.11 [**Artificial Intelligence**]: Distributed Artificial Intelligence—*Multiagent systems*

Keywords

Prisoners dilemma; multi-player games; sub-game perfect equilibrium

1. INVITATION GAMES

Theoretical games can be viewed as models of real life interaction among selfish agents. Some aspects of the real life situation are included in the abstract model, whereas others, judged not to have significant impact on the applicability of the abstract mathematical model to the real life motivation, are abstracted away. In some cases there appears to be a contradiction between the mathematical conclusions offered by game theory and real life experience, and this apparent contradiction can in general be attributed to some aspect of the real life situation that is not captured by the game theoretical model. The purpose of the current work is to consider one aspect that is typically abstracted away in game theoretic models. This aspect is the fact that often it is not the case that the players involved just happen to be playing the game, but rather the actual composition of players in the game is a result of strategic decisions on behalf of the players themselves. This aspect comes up naturally in diverse situations. Here are some examples.

1. Games of leisure, such as Bridge. A player may choose which friends to invite over to a game of Bridge depending on how much he enjoys playing with them.

2. Economic interactions that are modeled as games, such as bargaining games. A house owner may prefer inviting one plumber over another, depending not only on the quality of work of the plumber, but also on how stressful is the experience (game) of reaching agreement on a price.

3. Social interactions, e.g., in the sense of *games people play* [5]. People may choose their friends and spouses, and this affects who the other players will be in their subsequent social interactions that are modeled as games.

This aspect of having a choice with whom to play is captured explicitly in some economic models. For example, models of economic competition between firms involve the option for clients to choose which firm to do business with. However, it is our belief that this aspect has ramifications extending also to games in which this aspect is not traditionally modeled. To illustrate the effects of this aspect, we introduce an abstract model that we call *invitation games*, which is a variation on the previously studied model of repeated games. The main phenomenon that we consider is that of the effect of the invitation framework on the *price of stability* of games.

The price of stability of a given game measures the gap in welfare between the optimal social outcome of a game (the one that maximizes the sum of payoffs of the players) and the strategic outcome of the game (the one obtained in the most favorable Nash equilibrium). We prove that under quite mild conditions (for which we provide an exact charac-

*Work done in Microsoft Research, Herzliya.

[1] In our notation price of stability of 0 is best possible, and 1 is worse possible.

ITCS'14, January 12–14, 2014, Princeton, New Jersey, USA.

http://dx.doi.org/10.1145/2554797.2554808.

terization), this gap tends to 0 in invitation games. [2] Consequently, one may conclude that in the invitation framework socially optimal outcomes are natural results of selfish behavior.

1.1 The model

Consider an arbitrary game G with row player R and column player C. The payoff matrices for the players will also be denoted by R and C. Hence if R plays action i and C plays action j the payoff to R is $R_{i,j}$ and the payoff to C is $C_{i,j}$. Given G as above and a scheduler S, we define an *invitation* version of G, denoted by $G_{n,S}$, as follows. There are $n > 2$ players denoted by $P_1, \ldots, P_n$. The game $G_{n,S}$ proceeds sequentially in rounds, starting at round 1. In any given round t, the scheduler S may either choose to end the invitation game, or to output an index $s \in \{1, \ldots, n\}$, thus selecting a player P_s. (We shall shortly provide more details on how the scheduler makes its choices.) Then in round t, player P_s gets to invite a player of his choice (say, player P_q, where $q \neq s$) to a *match*, where a match is a game of G, with P_s playing the role of R and P_q playing the role of C. Hence the actions available to players in round t are as follows:

1. Player P_s (selected by the scheduler) has two actions to perform: to choose an index $q \neq s$, $1 \leq q \leq n$, thus inviting P_q to a match, and to choose an action i for player R in the game G.
2. Player P_q invited by P_s has one action to perform: to choose an action j for player C in game G.
3. Every other player $P_{q'}$ with $q' \notin \{s, q\}$ has no action to perform.

In a given round, let P_s be the player selected by the scheduler, let P_q be the player invited by P_s, let i be the action of player P_s in game G, and let j be the action of P_q in game G. The payoffs for the players are as follows

1. Player P_s gets payoff R_{ij}.
2. Player P_q gets payoff C_{ij}.
3. Every other player $P_{q'}$ gets payoff 0.

The total payoff of a player in $G_{n,S}$ is the sum of his payoffs over all rounds (when the scheduler ends the game).

In a given round, let P_s be the player selected by the scheduler, and let P_q be the player invited by P_s. Then the information revealed to the players at the end of the round is:

1. Player P_s learns the action played by P_q (and hence can infer the payoffs of all players in this round).
2. Player P_q learns that he was invited by P_s and the action of P_s (and hence can infer the payoffs of all players in this round).
3. In the *full information* version of the game, also every player $P_{q'}$ with $q' \notin \{s, q\}$ learns that the round took place, and also who P_s and P_q are and what they played. There are two *local information* (also referred to as *partial information*) versions of the game. In the *asynchronous* version $P_{q'}$ with $q' \notin \{s, q\}$ learns nothing (not even that the round took place). In the *synchronous version*, $P_{q'}$ with $q' \notin \{s, q\}$ learns that the round took place, that he himself was neither selected by the scheduler nor invited to a match, but nothing else.

Let us now present more details on the nature of the scheduler. Recall that in a given round t the scheduler needs to decide whether to end the game at that round, and if not, to decide which player P_s to select. In this work we shall restrict attention to *nonadaptive* schedulers, for which both decisions depend only on the round number t, but do not depend on the history of the game up to this round. (It makes sense to consider also adaptive scheduler, but this is beyond the scope of the current paper.) The nonadaptive scheduler may be either deterministic or randomized, where in the latter case its decision may also depend on random coin flips. For a nonadaptive deterministic scheduler, the total number of rounds in an invitation game is fixed in advance. In this paper, the total number of rounds of a randomized schedule will be fixed in advance, though we mention here that one may also consider the so called *unknown horizon* case in which the number of rounds is a random variable that depends on the randomness of the scheduler.

A special case of the nonadaptive deterministic scheduler is the *round robin* scheduler, for which the number of rounds T is divisible by n, and the rounds are partitioned into $B = T/n$ blocks of consecutive rounds. For any given block, in round s (for $1 \leq s \leq n$) within the block, the round robin scheduler selects player P_s (we say that it is P_s's *turn* to invite). The game $G_{n,S}$ with a round-robin scheduler and T rounds is denoted by $G_{n,T}$. For round robin schedulers with local information, there is no essential distinction between the synchronous version and the asynchronous versions of the game (because once a player gets to play a match, either by reaching his turn or by invitation, he gets synchronized again).

Throughout, given a 2-player game G, we refer to G as the *basic game* and to $G_{n,S}$ (or $G_{n,T}$ in the case of round robin scheduler) as the *invitation game*. Let us clarify that a nonadaptive scheduler is not a player in the invitation game, but rather part of the description of the rules of the game. Hence the scheduler is common knowledge to all players.

1.2 Strategies and solution concepts

Consider a 2-player game G, let A_R be the set of actions available to the row player R and let A_C be the set of actions available to the column player C. A *pure strategy* for player R (C, respectively) is a choice of a single action $i \in A_R$ ($j \in A_C$, respectively). A *mixed strategy* for player R (C, respectively) is a probability distribution over actions in A_R (in A_C, respectively). A *pure Nash equilibrium* (pure equilibrium, for short) is a pair of pure strategies, one for R and one for C, such that no player can increase his own payoff by deviating from his prescribed strategy, given that the other player has not deviated. A *mixed Nash equilibrium* (mixed equilibrium, for short) is a pair of mixed strategies, one for R and one for C, such that no player can increase his own expected payoff by deviating from his prescribed strategy, given that the other player has not deviated. A finite game has at least one equilibrium (possibly mixed).

[2]In our notation price of stability of 0 is best possible, and 1 is worse possible.

Given a basic game G, we consider its invitation version $G_{n,S}$. The notions of pure and mixed strategies extend naturally to $G_{n,S}$, but let us elaborate on this. A pure strategy for player P_i in the game $G_{n,S}$ is a function $H \longrightarrow ([n] \setminus \{i\}, A_R, A_C)$ mapping a history H of the game (the part observable by P_i in case of local information) to an action in the given round. The action in a round t has three components. The first component, a choice of an index from $[n]$ other than i, is the player that P_i would invite in round t given history H if the scheduler S dictates that it is P_i's turn to invite. This aspect of the action can be left empty if it is not P_i's turn to invite. The second component is P_i's choice of action in the basic game G, if P_i pays the role of R. Also this aspect of the action can be left empty if it is not P_i's turn to invite. The third component is P_i's choice of action in the basic game G, if P_i plays the role of C (that is, if P_i is invited and sees history H). This aspect of the action can be left empty if it is P_i's turn to invite. Mixed strategies are probability distributions over pure strategies.

For invitation games, we assume that every player P wishes to maximize the expected sum of payoffs that P receives from all rounds. As in the case of the basic 2-player game G, an *equilibrium* for $G_{n,S}$ is a profile of strategies, one for each player, such that no player can gain by unilaterally deviating from his strategy. However, due to the sequential aspect of $G_{n,S}$, the notion of equilibrium deserves further discussion. We envision a situation in which prior to the commencement of $G_{n,S}$ a profile of n (mixed) strategies is declared, with the ith strategy associated with player P_i. The profile of strategies is an equilibrium in the sense that if all players but one follow their declared strategies, the one deviating player does not gain by his deviation (compared to his expected payoff had he followed his declared strategy). Moreover, the declared profile needs to satisfy the additional property of *subgame perfect equilibrium* (see [15]). Namely, at any point of the game, regardless of the history of the game up to that point, the strategies when restricted to the remaining subgame form an equilibrium for that subgame. This requires strategies to be defined for every possible history H, including histories that lie outside the equilibrium path. [3]

Convention. The term *equilibrium* (whether pure or mixed) for an invitation game will always refer to a subgame perfect equilibrium.

1.3 Our results

Given a finite game G, let $W^+(G)$ denote the maximum welfare (sum of payoffs for all players) of an outcome of G, and let $W^-(G)$ denote the minimum welfare of an outcome of G. For example, if G is a basic two player game, then $W^+(G) = \max_{ij}[R_{ij} + C_{ij}]$ and $W^-(G) = \min_{ij}[R_{ij} + C_{ij}]$.

Definition 1. *The* price of anarchy *(PoA) of a finite game G is 0 if $W^+(G) = W^-(G)$, and otherwise*

$$PoA(G) = \max_N \frac{W^+(G) - W_N(G)}{W^+(G) - W^-(G)}$$

where N ranges over all (mixed) equilibria of G (recall also that if G is an invitation game, the equilibria need to be subgame perfect), and W_N denotes the expected welfare in equilibrium N. The price of stability *(PoS) of a game G is 0 if $W^+(G) = W^-(G)$ and otherwise*

$$PoS(G) = \min_N \frac{W^+(G) - W_N(G)}{W^+(G) - W^-(G)}.$$

Definition 1 is a natural variation on previous definitions of PoA and PoS [9, 14, 1], though we alert the reader that we took the liberty of rearranging some aspects of previous definitions. According to Definition 1, a price of anarchy (or stability) of 0 is best possible (no price needs to be paid), whereas a price of 1 is worst possible (all welfare is lost). In contrast, earlier work defines PoA and PoS (when payoffs are nonnegative) as $\max_N \frac{W^+(G)}{W_N(G)}$ and $\min_N \frac{W^+(G)}{W_N(G)}$, in which case a price of anarchy (or stability) of 1 is best possible, whereas a price of ∞ is worst possible.

Proposition 1. *For every finite 2-person game G, every $n \geq 3$ and every non-adaptive scheduler S, the following holds for the invitation games.*

1. *$PoA(G_{n,S}) \geq PoA(G)$.*
2. *$PoS(G_{n,s}) \leq PoS(G)$.*

For simplicity, the following definition, and consequently some of our results, are stated for a round robin schedule. Extensions of these results to other nonadaptive schedules (including randomized ones) appear in Section B.1.

Definition 2. *We say that a finite 2-player game G is* invitation-resilient *if for every $n \geq 3$, for every $T \geq 1$, in every subgame perfect equilibrium of the invitation game $G_{n,T}$ with a round robin schedule, in every match the corresponding two players play an equilibrium strategy for G.*

Definition 3. *We say that a finite 2-player game G is* asymptotically-efficient *if for every $n \geq 3$, the price of stability of the invitation game $G_{n,T}$ with a round robin schedule tends to 0 as T grows. Namely, $PoS(G_{n,T}) \to 0$ as $T \to \infty$.*

Our main theorem provides a dichotomy for invitation games.

Theorem 2. *Let G be an arbitrary finite 2-player game, and let $G_{n,T}$ be its corresponding full information invitation game with a round robin schedule and $n \geq 3$. Then either G is invitation resilient and then $Pos(G_{n,T}) = PoS(G)$ for every T, or G is asymptotically efficient ($PoS(G_{n,T})$ tends to 0 as T grows).*

The proof of Theorem 2 implies the following somewhat paradoxical corollary.

Corollary 3. *Given a basic game G, let G^- be the basic game obtained by reducing the payoff of every player in each outcome by a fixed universal constant (say, by 1). There is such a pair of basic games G and G^- for which the corresponding invitation games have the following property: $G^-_{n,T}$ has a subgame perfect equilibrium in which every player has higher payoff than the payoff of every player in every subgame perfect equilibrium of $G_{n,T}$.*

[3]One may think of deviations of players from their declared strategies as being accidental rather than deliberate. The declared strategy needs to include information on how players intend to act also in situations in which there were previous accidental deviations.

Given the payoff matrices of a two player game G that is asymptotically-efficient, the proof of Theorem 2 shows that there is an NP-witness (a proof polynomial in the size of the payoff matrices of G) certifying that G is asymptotically-efficient. However, finding such a witness need not be computationally easy.

Proposition 4. *Given the payoff matrices of the two players in a game G, the computational problem of determining that G is asymptotically-efficient is NP-complete.*

For games that are not invitation resilient, the price of anarchy offers a wide range of behaviors, unlike the price of stability (that necessarily tends to 0 as T grows).

Proposition 5. *Consider arbitrary $0 \leq \epsilon < \delta \leq 1$. Then there is a finite 2-player game G for which $PoA(G) = \epsilon$, and $PoA(G_{n,S})$ tends to δ as the number of rounds grows. ($G_{n,S}$ is the full information invitation game with an arbitrary nonadaptive schedule.)*

1.4 Related work

In our setting there is a basic game that is repeatedly played in the context of an invitation game, and as a result rational players might not play the equilibrium strategy in particular instances of the basic game. A similar phenomenon was previously illustrated in the context of repeated games, in which a basic game is repeated a fixed number of times, each time with the same set of players. We refer to this phenomenon as the repeated games principle, and it states that for certain classes of games, any feasible and individually rational payoff vector of the one-shot basic game can be approximated by the average payoff in a perfect equilibrium of a repeated game with a sufficiently long (but finite) horizon. Some special cases of the repeated game principle were presented in [7] using so called *trigger strategies*, and a characterization of the class of 2-player basic games for which the repeated game principle holds is presented in [4]. Our Proposition 12 in Section B.1 is implied by this characterization. We note however that the repeated games principle does not apply to all games, and in particular not to the game of prisoner's dilemma. The class of 2-player games for which the price of stability tends to 0 in the invitation version strictly contains the class of games for which the repeated games principle holds.

Despite the failure of the repeated games principle for the game of prisoners dilemma, various other explanations were suggested as to why players might choose to cooperate (hence play out of equilibrium) in repeated versions of this game. One aspect that may lead to cooperation is an unknown horizon – the players do not know how many times the game will be repeated. Technically, this allows to circumvent the issue of backward induction. See [12] for a complete treatment of this issue. An alternative explanation is offered (in a different context, but can easily be adapted to the prisoners dilemma) in [13]: players are willing to settle for a perfect ϵ-equilibrium (no player can gain more than ϵ by unilaterally deviating) instead of a perfect equilibrium. In repeated prisoners dilemma, cooperating in every game and defecting only if the other player previously deviated is an ϵ-equilibrium.

A different kind of explanation of how cooperation emerges in games of prisoners dilemma is demonstrated in [3, 2]: in a mixed population in which different players come up with their own strategies (not necessarily rational in the game theoretic sense), there is empirical evidence showing that some strategies that allow for cooperation perform better on average (when a player is matched for a sequence of games with a random player from the population) than the strategy of always defecting. If preference of either cooperation or defection is viewed as a hereditary property, then those strategies that do well on average have an evolutionary advantage, and hence become common.

The notion of price of anarchy was formally defined in [9, 14], and price of stability was formally defined in [1]. We note that we slightly change the standard definitions of these concepts so that the value ranges between 0 (no price) and 1 (as bad as it can get).

Our NP-hardness result (Proposition 4) has several predecessors with related results [10, 6], and implicitly follows from them. For completeness, we present a short proof of this proposition, using a characterization of Motzkin and Straus [11] of the size of the maximum independent set in a graph. This characterization has been previously used in NP-hardness proofs for so called *evolutionary stable strategies*, see [8].

2. SUBGAME PERFECT EQUILIBRIA OF INVITATION GAMES

Let G be an arbitrary finite 2-player game played between the row player R and the column player C. In a given match of G, we say that the players play an equilibrium strategy if their (mixed) strategies are in equilibrium. Proposition 1 is an immediate corollary of the following proposition, whose proof appears in Section A.

Proposition 6. *Let G be an arbitrary finite 2-player game, and let $G_{n,T}$ be its corresponding invitation game with full information and a non-adaptive scheduler. Consider an arbitrary equilibrium for G. Then there is a subgame perfect equilibrium for $G_{n,T}$ for which in every match both players (participating in the match) play the given equilibrium for the respective basic game G.*

Note that with an adaptive scheduler and $r \neq 0$, Proposition 6 need not hold. Suppose for example that R has a single dominating strategy in G that gives R payoff $r > 0$ and gives C payoff 0. Suppose that the adaptive scheduler makes P_1 the inviting player in round 1, and depending on P_1's action in round 1, decides whether P_1 will continue to be the inviting player in all future rounds (this happens if P_1 does not play his dominating strategy in round 1), or will never again be the inviting player (this happens if P_1 does play his dominating strategy in round 1). Then if the number of rounds is sufficiently large, P_1 will not play his dominating strategy in round 1.

Theorem 7. *Let G be an arbitrary finite 2-player game, and suppose that there is some value r such that in* every *equilibrium of G the expected payoff for R is r and the expected payoff for C is 0. Let $G_{n,T}$ be its corresponding invitation game with full information and a non-adaptive scheduler. Then in every subgame perfect equilibrium for $G_{n,T}$, in every match both players (participating in the match) play an equilibrium strategy for the respective basic game G.*

PROOF. Consider an arbitrary equilibrium for $G_{n,T}$. We use backwards induction to show that in every match both players play an equilibrium strategy for G. The base case is that of the last round. Let P the inviting player in round T. The first component of the action of P is a choice of player to invite. Let Q be this player. Regardless of the identity of P and Q, the subgame that one is left with is a match of G. By subgame perfection, in this match the players need to play an equilibrium strategy.

Consider now an arbitrary round t, and let P be the inviting player in that round. By our induction hypothesis, in every future round the respective matched players play equilibrium strategies. This implies that in future rounds the expected payoff for inviting players is always r, and the expected payoff for invited players is always 0. Hence players are indifferent to being invited in future rounds. Likewise, in future rounds inviting players are indifferent as to who they invite. Hence nothing that P does in round t effects his expected payoff in future rounds. This means that the match in round t is played without concern of the future, and subgame perfection implies that the match is played without concern of the past. Hence regardless of the identity of player Q invited by P in round T, the in a subgame perfect equilibrium of $G_{n,T}$ the players P and Q play an equilibrium strategy for G in round t. □

The maximum welfare of a game G is defined as $W^+(G) = \max_{ij}[R_{ij} + C_{ij}]$. In a given match of G, we say that the players play a maximum welfare strategy if R plays i and C plays j satisfying the equality above.

Theorem 8. *Let G be an arbitrary finite 2-player game, and let $G_{n,T}$ be its corresponding full information invitation game with a round robin schedule. Suppose that either one of the following holds:*

1. *There is some value $c \neq 0$ and an equilibrium of the basic game G in which the expected payoff for C is c.*
2. *There are two values $r \neq r'$ and two equilibria for the basic game G, in one of which the expected payoff for R is r and in the other it is r'. (It suffices to consider the case that in both equilibria for G the expected payoff for C is 0, as other cases are handled by 1 above.)*

Then there is some positive integer ℓ such that for every T there is a subgame perfect equilibrium for $G_{n,T}$ in which in all but ℓn matches the players play a maximum welfare strategy (and in other matches players play an equilibrium strategy).

A complete proof of Theorem 8 appears in Section B. Here we only sketch the main principles used in the proof. The set of all rounds is broken into the main set of rounds which includes the first $T - \ell n$ rounds, and the auxiliary set of rounds which includes the last ℓn rounds. The intention is that in the subgame perrfect equilibrium players will play a maximum welfare strategy in the main set of rounds. Players have no incentive to deviate because if they do they will get "punished" in the auxiliary set of rounds. The nature of the punishment depends on properties of equilibria of the basic games.

1. If there is an equilibrium of the basic game G in which the expected payoff for C is $c > 0$, then deviating players are punished by not being invited by other players in the auxiliary rounds, and hence not collecting a payoff of c.
2. If there is an equilibrium of the basic game G in which the expected payoff for C is $c < 0$, then deviating players are punished by being invited by other players in the auxiliary rounds, and consequently suffering a negative payoff of c.
3. If there is an "inferior" equilibrium for the basic game G in which the expected payoff for R is r and a "superior" equilibrium in which the expected payoff for R is $r' > r$, then a deviating player is punished by other players playing the inferior equilibrium whenever invited by the deviating player, rather than the superior equilibrium.

For more details regarding how the above principles can be implemented within a subgame perfect equilibrium, see the full proof in Section B.

It is convenient to think of a strategy for a player in an invitation game as composed of two components. One is the *invitation strategy*, specifying who a player invites when it is his turn to invite, and the other is the *G-strategy* specifying what to play in matches of G. We say that an invitation strategy in *nonadaptive* if it depends only on the round number but not of the history of the matches that the player played. In our proof of item 1 of Theorem 8 players use adaptive invitation strategies, whereas in the proof of item 2 players use nonadaptive invitation strategies.

We remark that even though Theorem 8 is stated for the full information setting, its proof applies without change also to the local information setting.

We now prove Theorem 2.

PROOF. Theorem 7 provides a sufficient condition for a finite 2-player game to be invitation resilient. This condition states that there is some value r such that in *every* equilibrium of G the expected payoff for R is r and the expected payoff for C is 0. Theorem 8 handles all those games for which this sufficient condition does not hold and claims that in all cases the game is asymptotically efficient. □

The price of anarchy does not provide the same sort of dichotomy provided by the price of stability. We now prove Proposition 5.

PROOF. Consider a basic game G with two pure strategies per player with payoff matrices $R = \begin{pmatrix} 0 & \frac{1-\delta}{2} \\ 0 & 0 \end{pmatrix}$ and $C = \begin{pmatrix} 1-\epsilon & \frac{1-\delta}{2} \\ 1-\epsilon & 1 \end{pmatrix}$. We have $W^+(G) = 1$ and $PoA(G) = \epsilon$ (in an equilibrium C must not play the second column as then R plays only the first row). For the invitation version of G, consider the equilibrium in which every player has a designated partner that he invites, as long as the designated partner agrees to play the $(\frac{1-\delta}{2}; \frac{1-\delta}{2})$ cell, and switches to an alternative partner once the designated partner deviates. As the number of rounds grows, all but a constant number of rounds (the constant depending on ϵ, δ) are played with $1 - \delta$ welfare. □

2.1 Prisoners dilemma as the basic game

Prisoners dilemma (PD) is a symmetric 2-player game. A player has two actions: *defect* (denoted here as 0) and *cooperate* (denoted here as 1). Defecting is a dominant action, but if both players cooperate they get a higher payoff than if they both defect. Hence we have $R_{10} < R_{00} < R_{11} < R_{01}$.

Corollary 9. *Let PD be the prisoners dilemma game and consider subgame perfect equilibria of the corresponding invitation game $PD_{n,T}$ with a round robin scheduler.*

1. *When the dominant payoff satisfies $R_{00} = 0$ then in every subgame perfect equilibria of the invitation game $PD_{n,T}$, in all matches both players defect.*

2. *When the dominant payoff satisfies $R_{00} \neq 0$ then there is a value of ℓ that depends only on PD such that for every T, the invitation game $PD_{n,T}$ has a subgame perfect equilibria for which in all but ℓn matches both players cooperate.*

PROOF. Item 1 is a special case of Theorem 7. If $2R_{00} \geq R_{01} + R_{10}$ then item 2 is a special case of (item 1 of) Theorem 8. If $2R_{00} < R_{01} + R_{10}$ then item 2 is technically not a special case of (item 1 of) Theorem 8, but it can be proved in exactly the same way in which item 1 of Theorem 8 is proved. □

2.2 A paradox for invitation games

One readily observes that Corollary 9 implies Corollary 3.

PROOF. Let G be the prisoners dilemma game with payoffs $R_{10} = -2$, $R_{00} = 0$, $R_{11} = 2$, $R_{01} = 4$ (where 0 signifies *defect* and 1 signifies *cooperate*). By item 1 of Corollary 9, in every subgame perfect equilibrium players always defect, and hence every player receives total payoff of 0. The game G^- is the prisoners dilemma with payoffs smaller by 1, namely $R_{10} = -3$, $R_{00} = -1$, $R_{11} = 1$, $R_{01} = 3$. Taking $\ell \geq 2$, the proof of item 2 of Corollary 9 shows (when n is even) a subgame perfect equilibrium in which every player P_i gets payoff of $2(T/n - \ell)R_{11} + 2\ell R_{00}$. Taking the number of blocks T/n to be at least five, the corollary is proved. (With extra work the proof can be extended also to the case that n is odd, but details are omitted.) □

Corollary 3 has a paradoxical flavor. The basic games G and G^- are the same game up to a fixed additive shift of payoffs. For the corresponding invitation games, if the number of matches that a player P_i participates in is fixed in advance to m_i (e.g., because players use nonadaptive invitation strategies) then the shift in payoffs for P_i between $G_{n,T}$ and $G^-_{n,T}$ is just the fixed constant m_i. The aspect that makes the proof of Corollary 3 possible is the use of adaptive invitation strategies, by which one player threatens to change the value of m_i if P_i deviates from the proposed equilibrium strategies.

2.3 Constant sum basic games

It is instructive to see what our results imply for the case that the basic game G is a constant sum game. By the minimax theorem, there are values r and c such that in all equilibria for G the expected payoff for R is r and the expected payoff for C is c (in a 0-sum game $r = -c$). In the special case that $c = 0$, Theorem 7 implies that in every subgame perfect equilibrium, in all matches both players play their minimax strategies. However, if $c \neq 0$, Theorem 7 no longer applies. Indeed, arguments similar to those appearing in the proof of Theorem 8 can be used in order to design a 0-sum game G and a subgame perfect equilibrium for the corresponding invitation games $G_{n,T}$ in which in all but the last few matches players do not play their minimax strategies.

2.4 Computational complexity

It is well known that for many natural restrictions on Nash equilibria, finding a Nash equilibrium satisfying these restrictions is NP-hard [10, 6]. In Lemma 10 we present yet another proof of such a result, that we shall use in order to prove Proposition 4.

Given a graph G, consider the following 2-player game that we refer to as the k-clique game. The payoff matrix A for the row player has $n + 1$ rows and n columns. The top n by n submatrix is the adjacency matrix of a graph G. All the entries of the bottom row are $\frac{k-1}{k}$. For the column player, the top n by n submatrix is the identity matrix, and the bottom row is all 0.

Lemma 10. *If G has a clique of size k, then there is a Nash equilibrium for the k-clique game in which the support for the row player has at least k rows, and the expected payoff for the column player is positive. If G does not have a clique of size k, then in all Nash equilibria the support for the row player is the last row, his payoff is $\frac{k-1}{k}$, and the payoff for the column player is 0.*

PROOF. If S is a maximal clique of size at least k, then both players playing uniformly over S gives a Nash equilibrium with payoff $1 - 1/|S|$ for the row player and $1/|S|$ for the column player. This proves the first part of the theorem.

We shall refer to a Nash equilibrium in which the row player plays row $n + 1$, the payoff for the row player is $\frac{k-1}{k}$ and the payoff for the column player is 0, as a *standard* equilibrium. If S is a maximal clique of size smaller than k, then the row player playing row $n+1$ and the column player playing uniformly over S gives a standard equilibrium. To prove the second part of the theorem it remains to show that if G has no clique of size k, there is no non-standard equilibrium. Suppose for the sake of contradiction that there is a non-standard equilibrium. Let x_i be the probability that the ith column is played in this equilibrium, and let S be the support for the mixed strategy for the column player (namely, $S = \{i|x_i > 0\}$). S must also be in the support for the row player (otherwise the payoff for one of the strategies of the column player is 0, implying that this is the payoff for all the column player's strategy, implying that only row $n+1$ is played, and hence this is a standard equilibrium). Being in the support of an equilibrium, all rows of S give the row player the same expected payoff, and it must be at least $\frac{k-1}{k}$ (otherwise the row player plays row $n + 1$ instead). Let y range over nonnegative vectors whose entries sum to 1, and let M be the adjacency matrix of G. We have thus established that $\max_y y^T My \geq \frac{k-1}{k}$, by taking $y = (x_1, \ldots x_n)$. The well known Motzkin-Straus theorem [11] implies that G contains a k-clique. □

We now prove Proposition 4.

PROOF. As implied by the proof of Theorem 2, a game is asymptotically efficient if and only if at list one of the two conditions listed in Theorem 8 holds. Each of these condition has a short witness (exhibiting the respective Nash equilibria) certifying that it holds (if it indeed holds). Hence the problem of determining that a game is asymptotically efficient is in NP. Lemma 10 implies that determining that a game is asymptotically efficient is NP-hard, because for the k-clique game is equivalent to determining whether the underlying graph has a k-clique. □

Acknowledgements

We thank Reshef Meir and an anonymous reviewer for directing us to related references.

3. REFERENCES

[1] Anshelevich, E., Dasgupta, A., Kleinberg, J., Tardos, E., Wexler, T., and Roughgarden, T. (2004). The Price of Stability for Network Design with Fair Cost Allocation. In Proceedings of the 45th IEEE Symposium on Foundations of Computer Science, (FOCS-04), pp. 59-73.

[2] Robert Axelrod. The Evolution of Cooperation, Basic Books, 1984.

[3] Robert Axelrod, William D. Hamilton. The Evolution of Cooperation. Science, New Series, Vol. 211, No. 4489. (March 27, 1981), pp. 1390-1396.

[4] Jean-Pierre Benoit and Vijay Krishna. Finitely Repeated Games. Econometrica, Vol. 53, No. 4 (July 1985), pp. 905-922.

[5] Eric Berne. Games People Play. New York: Ballantine Books. 1964.

[6] Vincent Conitzer, Tuomas Sandholm. Complexity Results about Nash Equilibria. IJCAI 2003: 765-771.

[7] James W. Friedman. Cooperative equilibria in finite horizon noncooperative supergames. Journal of Economic Theory, Volume 35, Issue 2, August 1985, Pages 390-398.

[8] Kousha Etessami, Andreas Lochbihler. The computational complexity of evolutionarily stable strategies. Int. J. Game Theory 37(1): 93-113 (2008).

[9] Koutsoupias, E., and Papadimitriou, C. (1999). Worst-Case Equilibria. In Proceedings of the 16th Annual Symposium on Theoretical Aspects of Computer Science, pp. 404-413.

[10] I. Gilboa and E. Zemel. Nash and Correlated Equilibria: Some Complexity Results. Games and Economic Behavior, 1 (1989), 80-93.

[11] T.S. Motzkin and E.G. Straus. Maxima for graphs and a new proof of a theorem of Turan. Can. J. Math. 17, 533-540 (1965).

[12] Abraham Neyman, Cooperation in Repeated Games when the Number of Stages is not Commonly Known. Econometrica, 67 (1999), pp. 45-64.

[13] Roy Radner. Collusive Behavior in Noncooperative Epsilon-Equilibria of Oligopolies with Long but Finite Lives. Journal of Economic theory 22, 136–154 (1980).

[14] Roughgarden, T., and Tardos, E. (2002). How Bad is Selfish Routing?. Journal of the ACM, 49(2), 236-259.

[15] R. Selten. Re-examination of the perfectness concept for equilibrium points in extensive games. Int. J. Game Theory 4 (1975), 25-55.

APPENDIX

A. PROOF OF PROPOSITION 6

In this section we prove Proposition 6.

Proof. Fix an arbitrary equilibrium for G. Let r (c, respectively) be the expected payoff of R (C, respectively) in this equilibrium. We say that a player plays his equilibrium strategy in G if he plays the strategy that corresponds to this given fixed equilibrium.

Consider the following profile of strategies for the players. For every i, when it is player's P_i turn to invite, he always invites player P_{i^+} (regardless of the history up to this round), where i^+ signifies addition in cyclic order, and its inverse i^- signifies subtraction in cyclic order. (This choice of using the function i^+ is arbitrary and was made for concreteness.) In every match (regardless of the history), both players play their equilibrium strategies.

Let m_i be the number of rounds in which P_i is the inviting player under the nonadaptive schedule. Then under the profile of strategies specified above, for each player P_i his expected payoff is $rm_i + cm_{i^-}$. Unilaterally deviating from the above strategy will not increase the expected payoff of P_i. Hence the profile of strategies is an equilibrium. It is subgame perfect, as can be shown by backward induction. □

B. PROOF OF THEOREM 8

For the proof of Theorem 8, we define various parameters of G:

The maximum welfare. $W^+(G) = \max_{ij}[R_{ij} + C_{ij}]$. For this optimal choice of ij that results in $W^+(G)$ (if there are several possible pairs of strategies i, j that lead to maximum welfare, fix one pair arbitrarily) we denote the respective payoffs by $r^* = R_{ij}$ and $c^* = C_{ij}$. In a given match of G, we say that the players play a maximum welfare strategy if R plays i and C plays j as above.

The maximum difference.
$D_R(G) = \max_{ii'j}[R_{ij} - R_{i'j}]$. $D_C(G) = \max_{ijj'}[C_{ij} - C_{ij'}]$. $D(G) = \max[D_R(G), D_C(G)]$. The parameter $D(G)$ provides an upper bound on how much a player can gain (in a single game of G) by replacing one strategy by another.

We now prove Theorem 8.

Proof. The proof involves a case analysis, but there is a common thread to all cases. Assume for simplicity that n is even. (After the proof we sketch how this assumption can be removed.) Arrange all players in disjoint pairs. Two players of the same pair will be called *partners*. We shall also have another arrangement of players in pairs, for which two players in the same pair are *fallback partners*. (For every player, his partner and fallback partners are different.)

Suppose that there is an equilibrium of G in which the expected payoff of C is $c > 0$, and let r denote the expected payoff of R in this equilibrium. Let ℓ be such that $c\ell \geq \max[D(G), r - r^*]$, and choose T such that $T/n > \ell$. We propose the following subgame perfect equilibrium for $G_{n,T}$. In equilibrium:

1. Every inviting player always invites his partner.
2. In every match in the first $T/n - \ell$ blocks the players play the maximum welfare strategy.
3. In every match in the last ℓ blocks the players play the equilibrium strategy.

We now describe how players respond to situations in which other players deviate from equilibrium:

1. If a player is invited by any player other than his partner, on that match he plays the equilibrium strategy.
2. If a player P observes a deviation by his partner Q in any of the matches that are (or should have been) held between them (either Q inviting a player other than P, or Q not playing the deterministic maximum welfare strategy in the first blocks, or Q not playing the

equilibrium strategy in the last blocks), then P never invites Q again. Instead P invites his fallback partner and plays the equilibrium strategy. Moreover, if Q invites P after Q has deviated, P plays the equilibrium strategy.

For subgame perfect equilibrium, we need to also describe how a player reacts to his own deviations from equilibrium. This represents what other players "believe" that this player will do, though of course once deviating, the player might deviate again. In our subgame perfect equilibrium strategy:

- If a player P previously deviated, then whenever it is P's turn to invite he invites his partner, and in every match P plays the equilibrium strategy for G.

If all players follow the above equilibrium strategy, every player receives expected payoff $(T/n - \ell)W^+(G) + \ell(c+r)$. A player has nothing to gain from unilaterally deviating. In the last ℓ blocks only equilibrium strategies for G are played. If a player deviates in any of the first $T/n-\ell$ blocks, he gains at most $D(G)$ (if the deviation was in a play of G against his partner) or at most expected $r-r^*$ (if the deviation was by inviting a player other than his partner), and loses an expected payoff of at least $c\ell$, by not being invited in the last ℓ blocks. The net gain is not positive. The equilibrium is subgame perfect because once a player deviates, all his games are played in an equilibrium for G, and backward induction applies.

Suppose now that there is no equilibrium of G in which the expected payoff of C is strictly positive, but there is an equilibrium of G in which the expected payoff of C is $c < 0$. Let r denote the expected payoff of R in this equilibrium. Let ℓ be such that $c\ell \geq \max[D(G), r - r^*]$, and choose T such that $T/n > \ell$. We propose the following equilibrium for $G_{n,T}$. In equilibrium:

1. In the first $T/n - \ell$ blocks every inviting player always invites his partner.
2. In the last ℓ blocks every inviting player always invites his fallback partner.
3. In every match in the first $T/n - \ell$ blocks the players play the maximum welfare strategy.
4. In every match in the last ℓ blocks the players play the equilibrium strategy.

We now describe how players respond to situations in which other players deviate from equilibrium:

1. If a player is invited by any player other than his partner, on that match he plays the equilibrium strategy for G.
2. If a player P observes a deviation by his partner Q in any of the matches that are (or should have been) held between them in the first $T/n - \ell$ blocks (either Q inviting a player other than P, or Q not playing the deterministic maximum welfare strategy), then P invites Q in all his remaining turns (including in the last ℓ blocks) and plays the equilibrium strategy for G. Moreover, if Q invites P after Q has deviated, P plays the equilibrium strategy for G.

We need to also describe how a player reacts to his own deviations from equilibrium. In our subgame perfect equilibrium strategy:

1. If a player P previously deviated then whenever it is P's turn to invite he invites his fallback partner, and in every match P plays the equilibrium strategy for G.

If all players follow the above equilibrium strategy, every player receives expected payoff $(T/n - \ell)W^+(G) + \ell(c+r)$. A player has nothing to gain from unilaterally deviating. In the last ℓ blocks only equilibrium strategies for G are played. If a player deviates in any of the first $T/n-\ell$ blocks, he gains at most $D(G)$ (if the deviation was in a play of G against his partner) or at most expected $r - r^*$ (if the deviation was by inviting a player other than his partner), and loses an expected payoff of at least $c\ell$, by being invited by his partner in the last ℓ blocks. The net gain is not positive. The above equilibrium is subgame perfect because once a player deviates, all his games are played in an equilibrium for G, and backward induction applies.

We now turn to prove item 2 of Theorem 8. Namely, the expected payoff of C is 0 in all equilibria for G, and there are two different equilibria, the *inferior* one in which the expected payoff of R is r, and the *superior* one in which the expected payoff of R is $r' > r$. Let ℓ be such that $(r'-r)\ell \geq \max[D(G), r - r^*]$, and choose T such that $T/n > \ell$. We propose the following subgame perfect equilibrium for $G_{n,T}$. In equilibrium:

1. Every inviting player always invites his partner.
2. In every match in the first $T/n - \ell$ blocks the players play the maximum welfare strategy.
3. In every match in the last ℓ blocks the players play the *superior* equilibrium strategy.

We now describe how players respond to situations in which other players deviate from equilibrium:

1. If a player is invited by any player other than his partner, on that match he plays the *inferior* equilibrium strategy.
2. If a player P observes a deviation by his partner Q in any of the matches that are (or should have been) held between them (either Q inviting a player other than P, or Q not playing the deterministic maximum welfare strategy in the first blocks, or Q not playing the superior equilibrium strategy when playing as C in the last blocks), then in future rounds P continues to invite Q. In matches with Q: if P is inviting he plays the superior equilibrium, and if Q is inviting P plays the inferior equilibrium.

We need to also describe how a player reacts to his own deviations from equilibrium. In our subgame perfect equilibrium strategy, a player P who previously deviated:

1. Always invites his partner and plays the inferior equilibrium.
2. When invited by his partner, P plays the superior equilibrium.
3. When invited by a player other than his partner, P plays the inferior equilibrium.

If all players follow the above strategy, every player receives expected payoff $(T/n - \ell)W^+(G) + \ell r'$. A player has nothing to gain from unilaterally deviating. In the last ℓ blocks invited players get 0 payoff, whereas and inviting player P gets payoff r, except for payoff of $r' > r$ when inviting their partner (conditioned on P not deviating earlier). If a player deviates in any of the first $T/n - \ell$ blocks, he gains at most $D(G)$ (if the deviation was in a play of G against his partner) or at most expected $r - r^*$ (if the deviation was by inviting a player other than his partner), and loses an expected payoff of at least $(r' - r)\ell$, by getting payoff r instead of r' in the last ℓ blocks. The net gain is not positive. The above equilibrium is subgame perfect because once a player deviates, all his games are played in an equilibrium for G, and backward induction applies. □

We presented the proof of Theorem 8 only for the case that n is even. We sketch how the proof of Theorem 8 can be extended to the case that n is odd. Because n is odd, we cannot partition all players into pairs, and instead we partition all but three of the players into pairs, and the remaining three players form a triple (P_1, P_2, P_3). In odd-numbered blocks, every player in the triple considers the player among the triple that follows him (in cyclic order) to be his partner, and the player that precedes him to be his auxiliary partner. In even-numbered blocks, every player in the triple considers the player that precedes him to be his partner, and the player that follows him to be his auxiliary partner. In two consecutive blocks (an odd block followed by an even block) we can identify three pairs of rounds, where in each such pair two players of the triple consider each other to be their partner, and the remaining player to be their auxiliary partner. Hence each player in the triple is in a situation equivalent to having one partner in one set of $T/2$ pairs of rounds (each player in the partnership invites in one round within a pair), and a different partner in a different set of $T/2$ pairs of round. The proof of Theorem 8 extends to this setting (with the modification that each player in the triplet is involved in 2ℓ blocks of an equilibrium strategy for G, instead of only ℓ blocks).

B.1 Extensions to other schedules

Theorem 8 shows how invitation games naturally lead to situations in which individual matches are not played in an equilibrium for the basic game. The statement of the theorem assumes a round robin schedule. However, variants of the theorem easily extend to other schedules. One natural schedule to consider is what we call the random schedule: in every round the inviting player is chosen uniformly at random, independently of all other events. Theorem 8 extends as is to this schedule.

Corollary 11. *Let G be an arbitrary finite 2-player game, and let $G_{n,T}$ be its corresponding full information invitation game with the random schedule. Suppose that either one of the following holds:*

1. *There is some value $c \neq 0$ and an equilibrium of the basic game G in which the expected payoff for C is c.*
2. *There are two values $r \neq r'$ and two equilibria for the basic game G, in one of which the expected payoff for R is r and in the other it is r'.*

Then there is some positive integer ℓ such that for every T there is a subgame perfect equilibrium for $G_{n,T}$ in which in all but ℓn matches the players play the maximum welfare strategy (and in other matches players play an equilibrium strategy).

Proof. The proof follows from that of Theorem 8 essentially with no change, because players are assumed to be expectation maximizers. Within every block of n matches, the round robin schedule lets every player invite exactly once, whereas the random schedule lets every player invite once in expectation. As expectation maximizers are concerned only with expectation, the arguments in the proof of Theorem 8 carry over to the case of a random scheduler. □

Recall that the proof of Theorem 8 applies not only in the full information setting, but also to the local information setting (both in the synchronous version and the asynchronous version). The proof of Corollary 11 as stated need not apply in the local information setting. Extending Corollary 11 so that it does apply in the local information setting is beyond the scope of this paper.

Returning to deterministic schedules, Theorem 8 need not hold as stated for arbitrary nonadaptive schedules, due to the fact that some players might invite less often than others. However, the main qualitative message of Theorem 8 still holds, namely, some matches may be governed by welfare considerations irrespective of consistency with equilibria for the basic game. We demonstrate this in two propositions for which we only sketch the proofs (as they follow principles similar to the proof of Theorem 8). Proposition 12 concerns the second class of basic games considered in Theorem 8. For that class, the proof applies even in the two player repeated game setting (without the need of an invitation setting), and is sketched mainly for completeness, as similar results already appeared in [7, 4]. This class of basic games does not include the prisoners dilemma.

Proposition 12. *Let G be an arbitrary finite 2-player game, and let G^T be its T-fold repeated setting. Let c denote the maximum possible payoff for C (the largest entry in C's payoff matrix). Suppose that among the equilibria for the basic game G, there is a* superior *equilibrium in which the expected payoffs for R and C are (r_1, c_1), and an* inferior *equilibrium in which the expected payoffs for R and C are (r_2, c_2), with $r_1 > r_2$ (there are no restrictions on the values of c_1 and c_2). Then there is some positive integer ℓ depending only on G such that if $T > \ell$, there is a subgame perfect equilibrium for G^T in which there is a match in which the payoff for C is c.*

Proof. The proposed equilibrium for G^T when no player deviates is as follows. In the first round, the players play the pure strategies that give C payoff c. In all future rounds the players play the superior equilibrium. If R deviates in the first round, then in all rounds the players play the inferior equilibrium. No other deviation affects future play of the players.

We sketch the proof of why this is a subgame perfect equilibrium. A unilateral deviation of C gains nothing for C, because in every round C is playing a best response. A unilateral deviation of R in round 1 may gain in round 1, but causes R to suffer the inferior equilibrium in all future rounds, instead of the superior equilibrium, hence losing $(r_1 - r_2)\ell$. In all other rounds R gains nothing by deviating, because he is playing a best response. □

Proposition 12 extends to the case when the roles of R and C are reversed. Namely, when r denotes the maximum possible payoff for R and $c_1 > c_2$, there is a subgame perfect equilibrium for G^T in which there is a match in which the payoff for R is r.

Proposition 13 corresponds to the first class of games considered in Theorem 8 (which does include the prisoners dilemma if the payoff for defect-defect is nonzero). This proposition does require the invitation setting and at least three players.

Proposition 13. *Let G be an arbitrary finite 2-player game, and let $G_{n,S}$ be its corresponding full information invitation game with schedule S. Let r denote the maximum possible payoff for R (the largest entry in R's payoff matrix). Suppose that there is some value $c \neq 0$ and a* distinguished *equilibrium of the basic game G in which the expected payoff for C is c. Then there is some positive integer ℓ depending only on G such that if the number of rounds in schedule S is larger than ℓn, there is a subgame perfect equilibrium for $G_{n,S}$ in which in some match the inviting player gets payoff r.*

PROOF. Given S, there is a player (say, P) that invites in more than ℓ rounds. Fix some arbitrary other player Q.

Suppose that $c > 0$. Then we propose the following subgame perfect equilibrium, All players always invite Q, and Q always invites P. In all matches the distinguished equilibrium is played, except for the first match among those in which it is P's turn to invite. In that match between P and Q they play the pure strategies that give R a payoff of r. If Q deviates from this strategy in this particular match, then P never invites Q again, and instead invites some other default player P' and they play the distinguished equilibrium. No other deviation results in a change of strategy of players.

We sketch the proof of why this is a subgame perfect equilibrium. A unilateral deviation of any player other than Q gains nothing for that player, because in every round the player is playing a best response. A unilateral deviation of Q in the first match in which Q is invited by P may result in Q gaining in that round, but causes Q to not be invited by P in future rounds, losing a payoff of $c\ell$. In all other rounds Q gains nothing by deviating, because he is playing a best response.

If $c < 0$ the same principles as above apply, except for exchanging Q for Q' (and Q' for Q) in the rounds in which P invites, except for P's first turn. $\square$

The Computational Hardness of Pricing Compound Options*

Mark Braverman
Department of Computer Science, Princeton University
mbraverm@cs.princeton.edu

Kanika Pasricha
Princeton University
pasricha@alumni.princeton.edu

ABSTRACT

It is generally assumed that you can make a financial asset out of any underlying event or combination thereof, and then sell a security. We show that while this is theoretically true from the financial engineering perspective, compound securities might be intractable to price. Even given no information asymmetries, or adversarial sellers, it might be computationally intractable to put a value on these, and the associated computational complexity might afford an advantage to the party with more compute power. We prove that the problem of pricing an option *on a single security* with unbounded compounding is PSPACE hard, even when the behavior of the underlying security is computationally tractable. We also show that in the oracle model, even when compounding is limited to at most k layers, the complexity of pricing securities grows exponentially in k.

Categories and Subject Descriptors

F.2.2 [**Theory of computation**]: Analysis of algorithms and problem complexity: Nonnumerical algorithms and problems

General Terms

Economics, Theory, Algorithms

Keywords

pricing, financial securities, computational finance, computational complexity

1. OVERVIEW

A financial security is an instrument representing financial value. Examples of securities include currencies, shares of companies, debt obligations, and commodity contracts. Simple securities generally directly correspond to actual future cash flows, or events. For example, a stock of a company can be viewed as a contract entitling one to the company's dividend payments. A simple oil futures contract entitles one for a given amount of oil to be delivered at a predetermined time. Simple securities therefore can be viewed as simple contracts that can be traded among agents.

Based on these simple securities one can construct more complicated ones, known as financial derivatives. The value of a derivative may depend on the value of one or multiple securities in a complicated fashion. For example, a *put option* may allow one to sell a stock at a later time at a predetermined price (e.g. the option to sell a share of GOOG for $1000 a year from now), thus realizing a piecewise linear function on the price of the stock. Collateralized debt obligations (CDOs), which were much publicized during the 2008 financial crisis, represent step functions on bundles of debt obligations. Financial derivatives are created for many different reasons, including risk-hedging and giving market participants greater flexibility in expressing their beliefs through their holdings.

Assigning values to financial securities and derivatives is one of the primary functions of financial markets and institutions. This function is at the heart of the stock market, and the operations of hedge funds who extract surplus by identifying (and helping correct) mispriced financial products. The subject of this paper is the *computational complexity* aspects of the hardness of pricing financial derivatives. The process of valuing securities can be abstracted as the process of (1) obtaining information about the present and the future that is relevant to the present and future value of the security; and (2) performing computations to obtain a price for the security based on the information. In this paper we focus on the computational complexity of performing the second step, and thus abstract away as much of the first step as possible. A common way of representing complex information about the future is through Monte-Carlo simulations. We will assume therefore that we have a model of the relevant future world-states and prices, either as a program or as a black-box oracle, and focus on the hardness of turning this model into the relevant price. Much of economic theory deals with information and uncertainty of the agents, which leads to various interesting phenomena. Here we assume no uncertainty in that the model available to the pricer is exhaustive and fully describes the system. Thus, a risk-neutral pricer *should* be able to produce the correct prices by herself. In the case of a simple security this is, more or less, the case: by running enough simula-

*The first author is supported by the Alfred P. Sloan Fellowship, an NSF CAREER award (CCF-1149888), NSF Award CCF-1215990, and a Turing Centenary Fellowship.

ITCS'14, January 12–14, 2014, Princeton, New Jersey, USA.

ACM 978-1-4503-2698-8/14/01 ...$15.00.
http://dx.doi.org/10.1145/2554797.2554809 .

tions of future returns and averaging them out, the pricer can estimate the security's value. What about compound securities? In this paper we restrict ourselves to the simplest case of a single security (with multiple securities, the combinatorial relations between them may induce computational hardness — an issue not present in the case of a single security). The simplest kind of a single compound security is obtained by compounding European options, which will be the main subject of study in this paper.

A *European call option* is the option to buy an asset at a given price that can only be exercised at a given point of time. An example of a European option O_1 is "The option to buy one GOOG share at \$900 on 07/01/2015". If the price of one GOOG share on that date is $\$X$, O_1 will be worth $\max(X - 900, 0)$ on that date. The closely related *European put option* is the option to *sell* an asset at a given price that can only be exercised at a given point of time. For example "The option to sell one GOOG share at \$900 on 07/01/2015". A compound option is an option on an option. An example of a compound option O_2 is "The option to buy two O_1 options at \$50 each on 07/01/2014". The focus of this paper is the *computational* hardness of pricing such options even in the presence of full information. To illustrate why compound options cannot be straightforwardly priced using Monte Carlo simulations, note that the price of O_2 today depends not only on our belief about the distribution of the eventual price of GOOG on 07/01/2015, but also on our belief on the distribution of our belief on 07/01/2014 about the price of GOOG a year from then. Intuitively, this roughly squares the amount of simulations that are needed to price O_2 as compared to O_1. In this paper, we make this intuition precise.

Main results

To the best of our knowledge, we give the first hardness results for pricing option contracts on a single security that rely only on computational complexity considerations. We obtain results both when the underlying security is modeled algorithmically, and when it can be queried through an oracle. The main results are as follows:

- With unbounded compounding, the problem of pricing of compound options (in the risk-neutral setting) is **PSPACE**-hard, even in the presence of full information, where the distribution of the future world-states is just uniform, and the function mapping future states to payoffs is a poly-time computable function. Specifically, options considered are compound European put options.
- We analyze the bounded compounding case in the oracle model, where the distribution of the future states is still uniform, and the pricing algorithm may access the ultimate value of the asset via an oracle that maps states to values. For options that are such that pricing $Option(\Phi)$ requires knowing the value of the security Φ with error δ, we show that the query complexity of pricing k-layered options scales as $(\Omega(\delta))^{-2k}$. Thus for small constant k's, such as $k = 3$ or $k = 4$ and $\delta = 10^{-3}$, the query complexity is on the order of $\sim 10^{18}$ or $\sim 10^{24}$, and differences in computing capacity may give the computationally stronger player a real advantage in pricing the security. This suggests one possible explanation for the vast computing resources utilized by financial firms.

Welfare Maximization and Truthfulness in Mechanism Design with Ordinal Preferences*

Deeparnab Chakrabarty
Microsoft Research
9 Lavelle Road, Bangalore 560001, India.
dechakr@microsoft.com

Chaitanya Swamy†
Dept. of Comb. and Opt., Univ. Waterloo
200 University Avenue, Waterloo, ON N2L 3G1
cswamy@math.uwaterloo.ca

ABSTRACT

In this paper, we study mechanism design problems in the *ordinal setting* wherein the preferences of agents are described by orderings over outcomes, as opposed to specific numerical values associated with them. This setting is relevant when agents can compare outcomes, but aren't able to evaluate precise utilities for them. Such a situation arises in diverse contexts including voting and matching markets.

Our paper addresses two issues that arise in ordinal mechanism design. To design social welfare maximizing mechanisms, one needs to be able to quantitatively measure the welfare of an outcome which is not clear in the ordinal setting. Second, since the impossibility results of Gibbard and Satterthwaite [14, 25] force one to move to randomized mechanisms, one needs a more nuanced notion of truthfulness.

We propose *rank approximation* as a metric for measuring the quality of an outcome, which allows us to evaluate mechanisms based on worst-case performance, and *lex-truthfulness* as a notion of truthfulness for randomized ordinal mechanisms. Lex-truthfulness is stronger than notions studied in the literature, and yet flexible enough to admit a rich class of mechanisms *circumventing classical impossibility results*. We demonstrate the usefulness of the above notions by devising lex-truthful mechanisms achieving good rank-approximation factors, both in the general ordinal setting, as well as structured settings such as *(one-sided) matching markets*, and its generalizations, *matroid* and *scheduling* markets.

Categories and Subject Descriptors

F.2.2 [**Analysis of Algorithms and Problem Complexity**]: Nonnumerical Algorithms and Problems; G.2 [**Discrete Mathematics**]; J.4 [**Computer Applications**]: Social and Behavioral Sciences—*Economics*

Keywords

Algorithmic game theory; Mechanism design; Ordinal preferences; Computational social choice theory; Social welfare and rank approximation; Truthfulness for randomized mechanisms; Linear programming; Matroids

1. INTRODUCTION

A central problem in social choice theory and mechanism design is that of choosing a "good" outcome by aggregating individuals' private preferences over outcomes, where individuals are rational agents. A *mechanism* implementing a *social choice function* (SCF) needs to elicit the preferences of agents in a truthful fashion, that is, in a way such that no agent may benefit by misreporting his preferences.

In this paper, we study mechanism-design problems in *ordinal* settings, wherein the preferences are described by orderings over the set of outcomes. This is in contrast with the *cardinal* setting, wherein an agent specifies a *value* to each outcome (which determines his preferences). Ordinal settings reduce the "informational burden" on an agent in the sense that he only needs to be able to compare outcomes rather than assign values to outcomes justifying his preferences. It is not hard to imagine settings where the former comparison task is easier, and more aptly describes the situation: examples span the spectrum between electoral settings and the setting of allocating dormitory rooms to students.

Two immediate issues arise in ordinal mechanism design. A typical mechanism-design goal is to maximize *social welfare*, but in order to approach this goal in ordinal settings, one needs to first be able to *quantitatively* measure the social-welfare value of an outcome. Second, since the Gibbard-Satterthwaite (GS) impossibility result [14, 25] precludes non-trivial deterministic truthful mechanisms, one is forced to move to *randomized mechanisms* for which one needs a more nuanced notion of truthfulness.

1.1 Our contributions

We propose a new framework for welfare-maximization and truthfulness for randomized ordinal mechanisms, and devise various near-optimal mechanisms in this framework. Our contributions are threefold.

1) We introduce a metric called *rank approximation* for measuring the quality of an outcome, which in turn allows us

*A single-column version is available from the CS arXiv [9].

†Supported in part by NSERC grant 327620-09, an NSERC Discovery Accelerator Supplement Award, and an Ontario Early Researcher Award.

ITCS'14, January 12–14, 2014, Princeton, New Jersey, USA.

ACM 978-1-4503-2698-8/14/01 ...$15.00.
http://dx.doi.org/10.1145/2554797.2554810.

to evaluate mechanisms in terms of their worst-case performance. We show that rank approximation is a robust notion that is appealing, and can be motivated, from various perspectives.

2) We propose a truthfulness notion called *lex-truthfulness* for randomized ordinal mechanisms. This is stronger than a notion studied in the literature, and yet flexible enough that it admits a rich class of mechanisms *bypassing classical impossibility results*. We provide a characterization result for lex-truthfulness, which we leverage to obtain lex-truthful mechanisms for various ordinal settings. We believe that this characterization will find application beyond the specific applications that we consider in this paper.

3) We demonstrate the usefulness of the above two notions by devising lex-truthful mechanisms achieving good rank-approximation factors both in the general ordinal setting, as well as structured settings such as *(one-sided) matching markets*, and its generalizations, *matroid* and *scheduling* markets.

We now elaborate on our contributions. Let n and m denote the number of agents and number of outcomes respectively, and $\succ_j$ denote agent j's ordering over outcomes, which we assume is strict and complete (i.e., for any two outcomes o, o', either $o \succ_j o'$ or vice versa).

Rank approximation (Section 3.1). We say that an outcome o has *rank approximation* α for preference profile $\succ$, if for *every* position r, the number of agents having o as one of their top-r outcomes is at least $\frac{1}{\alpha} \cdot \text{maxrank}_r(\succ)$, where $\text{maxrank}_r(\succ)$ denotes $\max_{\hat{o}}$(number of agents having $\hat{o}$ as one of their top-r outcomes). An *α-rank-approximation mechanism* is one that always returns an α-rank-approximate outcome. While the requirement of simultaneously approximating $\text{maxrank}_r(\succ)$ for all r seems too stringent, and even the *existence* of an α-rank-approximate outcome o, for non-trivial α seems doubtful, promisingly (as we elaborate later), we can achieve a 2-rank-approximation for matching and matroid markets, and a randomized $O(\log n)$-rank-approximation for general ordinal settings.

Rank approximation is a natural, purely ordinal notion with various desirable properties. Consider any cardinal-utility profile $\vec{U} = (U_1, \ldots, U_n)$, where each U_j is consistent with $\succ_j$, that is, $U_j(o) > U_j(o')$ i $o \succ_j o'$. Call such a utility profile *homogeneous*, if for all $r = 1, \ldots, m$, all U_js of every agent assign the same value to their r-th ranked outcome. An α-rank-approximation outcome o for $\succ$ is such that for *any* consistent homogeneous utility profile $\vec{U}$, its social welfare, $\sum_{j=1}^{n} U_j(o)$, for $\vec{U}$ is at least a $\frac{1}{\alpha}$-fraction of the optimum social welfare for $\vec{U}$. Thus, an α-rank-approximation mechanism *simultaneously yields an α-approximation to the optimum social-welfare for all consistent homogeneous utility profiles* (Theorem 3.1).

Consistent homogeneous utilities are also known as *scoring rules* [29]. A scoring rule assigns a score to each position and returns the outcome with highest total score; a prominent example is the *Borda rule*, which gives a score of $m - k$ to the k-th position. An outcome is α-approximate with respect to a scoring rule, if its score is at least a $\frac{1}{\alpha}$-fraction of the score of any other outcome. Translated to this setting, we obtain that an α-rank-approximation mechanism *simultaneously achieves an α-approximation to all scoring rules.* In other words, given an α-rank-approximation mechanism $\mathcal{M}$, one need not be overly concerned about which scoring rule is most suited to the problem, since $\mathcal{M}$ guarantees an α-approximation to all scoring rules!

To place these simultaneous-approximation bounds in perspective, it is useful to consider an even stronger notion: say that a mechanism has "strong welfare factor" α, if for every consistent (even non-homogeneous) cardinal-utility profile $\vec{U}$, the mechanism returns an α-approximation to the optimum social welfare for $\vec{U}$. Not surprisingly, this notion is too strong: it is easy to show that no mechanism (deterministic or randomized) can have any non-trivial strong welfare factor, even for matching markets.

Lex-truthfulness (Section 3.2). The classic impossibility results of [14, 25] show that the space of deterministic truthful mechanisms in general ordinal settings is extremely limited, forcing the move to randomized mechanisms. When seeking to define a notion of truthfulness for ordinal randomized mechanisms, one immediately encounters the following issue: *how should one extend an agent's preferences over outcomes to preferences over distributions of outcomes?* The usual approach in the economics literature is to use the *stochastic dominance* relation. Since this does not induce a total order over distributions, one obtains two notions of truthfulness: (i) *strong truthfulness* [15], where the truth-telling distribution stochastically dominates any distribution obtained via a misreport; and (ii) *weak truthfulness* [21, 7], where the truth-telling distribution is not stochastically dominated by any distribution obtained via a misreport. Gibbard [15] generalized [14, 25] to show that the space of strongly-truthful mechanisms in general ordinal settings is also limited, leaving weak-truthfulness as the only viable notion of truthfulness for randomized mechanisms.

We propose a new notion of truthfulness sandwiched (strictly) between the above two notions. A distribution **p** lex-dominates a distribution **q** with respect to ordering $\succ$, if, when considering outcomes in decreasing order of their ranking in $\succ$, at the first outcome o where **p** and **q** differ, **p** assigns a higher probability to o than **q**. Note that lex-dominance induces a *total order* on distributions. We say that a mechanism is *lex-truthful* (LT) if the truth-telling distribution lex-dominates any distribution obtained by a misreport.

We show that lex-truthfulness provides us with ample flexibility in mechanism design and allows us to *circumvent Gibbard's impossibility theorem.* Call a social choice function (SCF) f *fully lex-truthfully (LT) implementable* if for all $\varepsilon > 0$, there exists a lex-truthful mechanism that agrees with f with probability at least $(1-\varepsilon)$ on every preference profile. We isolate a property of an SCF, which we call *pseudomonotonicity*, that *completely characterizes* LT-implementability of the SCF (Theorem 3.3). Roughly speaking, an SCF is pseudomonotone if for any preference profile, if an agent j changes his ordering without altering his top k choices, then the new outcome cannot both be a better outcome for j and a top-$(k+1)$ outcome for j (see Definition 5).

This characterization turns out to be instrumental in making lex-truthfulness an amenable notion to work with, and opens up a host of SCFs to full LT-implementation. We show that various rank-approximation SCFs that we devise for matching, matroid, and scheduling markets—including the 2-rank-approximation mechanism for matching markets mentioned earlier—are pseudomonotone. For general ordinal settings, we identify a rich class of pseudomonotone SCFs which includes the *plurality scoring rule*. Thus, *all* of these SCFs are fully LT-implementable. We view the characterization of lex-truthfulness via pseudomonotonicity as one of our main contributions, which we believe will find further applications.

Matching, matroid, and scheduling markets (Sections 4 and 5). In addition to general ordinal mechanism-design settings, we also consider various structured settings, and obtain lex-truthful mechanisms with good rank-approximation factors.

Our most-compelling results are for *matching markets* (Section 4), which are one of the most well-studied ordinal settings (see, e.g., the surveys [28, 1]). Here, we have n agents and m items, and outcomes are matchings of agents to items. Each agent has a strict preference over items, which induces preferences over matchings based on the item the agent is assigned in a matching. Observe that agents are indifferent over matchings that give them the same item. The room allocation problem is an instance of this market.

We devise a simple deterministic 2-rank-approximation pseudomonotone algorithm MaxMatch (Theorem 4.1), which is therefore fully LT-implementable. In contrast, we show in Appendix B that various common algorithms proposed for matching markets, such as the top-trading-cycle algorithm, randomized serial dictatorship, probabilistic serial, *all have rank approximation at least* $\Omega(\sqrt{n})$. We prove a matching lower bound of 2 on the rank-approximation factor of deterministic SCFs (Theorem 4.2), and obtain super-constant lower bounds on the rank-approximation factor achievable by deterministic truthful mechanisms.

The 2-rank-approximation for matching markets extends to *matroid markets* (Theorem 4.6), which is the generalization where we have a matroid on the agent-set for every item, and the (possibly multiple) agents assigned to an item are required to form an independent set in that item's matroid. Besides the increased modeling power of matroids, this turns out to be a key component of our algorithms for scheduling markets.

In Section 5, we consider scheduling markets. Here the agents are jobs that need to be assigned to machines. Each job has a *private* ordering over the machines, and a public processing time on each machine, and there is makespan bound T that limits the amount of time available on each machine. An outcome is a partial assignment of some jobs to machines satisfying the makespan bound. This can be viewed as the matching problem with a *knapsack constraint*. For parallel machines, we obtain an LT-mechanism that always returns an $O(\log n)$-rank-approximation schedule with $O(T)$ makespan, and we show that this bound is tight (Theorems 5.2 and 5.3). We also obtain an $O(\log n)$-rank approximation for unrelated machines (Theorem 5.4), albeit not via an LT mechanism.

1.2 Other related work

The conundrum of social welfare in ordinal mechanisms which probably has its origins in the Condorcet paradox [11], which states that it may so happen that a majority of agents prefer outcome a to b, outcome b to c, and outcome c to a, was cemented by Arrow's impossibility theorem [4]. Subsequent to Arrow's result, most works in social choice theory has focused on Pareto optimality as the sole notion of efficiency for ordinal mechanisms.

Recent work, mostly in the CS literature, has led to a more nuanced notion of efficiency. Procaccia and Rosenchein [23] studied the strong welfare factor notion (that they call distortion), and noticed that deterministic mechanisms have unbounded distortion. Boutilier et al. [8] proposed randomized mechanisms and showed that the strong welfare factor is at most $O(\sqrt{m}\log^* m)$, if the consistent cardinal-utility profile is normalized. In contrast, our rank approximation results imply $O(\log n)$-approximate outcomes, but under a stronger restriction on the consistent cardinal utilities. The notion of approximations to scoring rules was studied by Procaccia [22] where he described strongly truthful mechanisms which 2-approximate Borda, but $O(\sqrt{m})$-approximate the plurality rule. In contrast, our (non-truthful) mechanism $O(\log n)$-rank approximates *any* scoring rule, and plurality can be arbitrarily well approximated by a lex-truthful mechanism.

Another notion of social welfare in ordinal mechanisms, called ordinal welfare factor (OWF), was recently proposed by Bhalgat et al [6]. A mechanism has OWF $\beta \in [0,1]$ if for any outcome o, at least βn agents prefer the outcome returned by the mechanism to o. This is in fact a *quantification* of the notion of *popular* outcomes; an outcome is popular if a majority prefer it to any other fixed outcome. Note that popular outcomes have OWF of at least 0.5. A popular outcome may not exist, but a popular distribution over outcomes always does. Popular outcomes were studied by economists in the matching setting [13], and as *strict maximal lotteries* in the general setting [12, 18]; subsequently, a large body of literature has been developed by computer scientists on popular matchings [2, 17, 16, 19]. The notions of rank approximation and OWF (and therefore the notion of popularity) are incomparable. That is, there are outcomes with "good" OWF and "bad" rank approximation, and vice-versa.

Subsequent to the Gibbard-Satterthwaite result, researchers focused on design of randomized mechanisms. As mentioned above, this led to differing notions of truthfulness. Strong truthfulness was proposed by Gibbard [15]. Postlewaite and Schmeidler [21] proposed weak truthfulness and proved that no weakly truthful mechanism on 4 or more outcomes, can be (ex ante) Pareto optimal if agents are allowed to have priors on their (own) preferences. Subsequently, Aziz et al [5] removed the prior condition, but prove impossibility of only certain *kinds* of mechanism. We remark that our lex-truthful mechanisms, which are also weakly truthful, do not contradict these results, since our mechanisms are not Pareto optimal. However, our mechanisms are ε-implementations of Pareto-optimal SCFs, so they satisfy Pareto optimality with probability at least $1-\varepsilon$. Thus, we bypass the above impossibility results while sacrificing a modicum of Pareto-optimality.

Matching markets are one of the most widely studied examples of the ordinal setting. There is a vast amount of literature, and we point to excellent surveys [24, 28, 1]. In Section B, we describe three well known mechanisms in this setting. These are the random serial dictatorship, Gale's top trading cycle algorithm [27], and the probabilistic serial (PS) mechanism [7]. The first two mechanisms are at least strongly truthful; PS is weakly truthful, and we show that it is lex-truthful as well. However, we show that all these three mechanisms have rank approximation as bad as $\Omega(\sqrt{n})$. In contrast, we obtain a fully LT-implementable 2-rank-approximation mechanism using our pseudomonotone 2-rank-approximation algorithm MaxMatch.

2. PRELIMINARIES

In the general *ordinal mechanism design* setting, we have a set N of n agents, and a set O of m outcomes (or alternatives). We use the terms agent and player interchangeably. Each agent $j \in N$ has a *private* complete preference list or ordering $\succeq_j$ over outcomes, that is, $o \succeq_j o'$ or $o' \succeq_j o$ for every $o, o' \in O$. This is typically referred to as *ordinal* utilities/preferences, to distinguish them from *cardinal* utilities wherein the utility function assigns a value to each outcome. Let Σ_j denote the publicly-known set of allowed preference lists for agent j, and $\Sigma := \prod_{j=1}^{n} \Sigma_j$. A preference profile is a combination $\succeq = (\succeq_1, \ldots, \succeq_n)$ of agents' preference lists. For $k \in \mathbb{Z}_+$, we use $[k]$ to denote the set $\{1, \ldots, k\}$. A preference list is called *strict*, and denoted $\succ$, if there are no indifferences: exactly one of $o \succ o'$ and $o' \succ o$ holds for every two distinct outcomes $o, o' \in O$. Given a strict preference $\succ$, we will sometimes say $o \succeq o'$ to denote that $o \succ o'$ or $o = o'$. Given a preference list $\succ$, let $\text{alt}(\succ, r) \in O$ denote the r-th ranked outcome in $\succ$, and $\text{pos}(\succ, o) \in [m]$ denote the rank of outcome o in $\succ$. For a tuple $x = (x_1, \ldots, x_n)$, we use x_{-j} to denote $(x_1, \ldots, x_{j-1}, x_{j+1}, \ldots, x_n)$. Similarly, let $\Sigma_{-j} := \prod_{k \neq j} \Sigma_k$.

In addition to the general setting mentioned above, we consider three specific mechanism-design settings in this paper: one-sided *matching markets*, which have been studied extensively in the literature (see, e.g., [28, 1]) and two generalizations of these, *matroid markets* and *scheduling markets*, that we introduce.

Matching markets (Section 4). We nave n agents and m items. Each agent j has a strict preference $\succ_j$ over the m items. The outcomes are matchings of agents to items. We say that an outcome M assigns an agent j the "null" item $\emptyset$ to denote that he is not assigned an item in M; we set $i \succ_j \emptyset$ for every item i. An agent is indifferent between matchings M and M' if they allot him the same item (counting $\emptyset$ as an item), and otherwise, prefers M to M' if he prefers the item allotted to him in M to the item allotted to him in M'.

Matroid markets (Section 4.1). We again have n agents who have a strict preference over m items. We also have a matroid $M_i = (N, \mathcal{I}_i)$ on the set N of agents, for each item $i \in [m]$. An outcome is an allocation that assigns at most one item to each agent j such that, for each item i, the set of agents allotted item i is an independent set of M_i. Note that multiple agents may be allocated the same item. An agent's ordering over outcomes is induced by his ordering of the items as in the setting of matching-markets. It is easy to see that a matching market is the special case where M_i encodes that at most one agent may be assigned to item i.

Scheduling markets (Section 5). The agents are n jobs that need to be scheduled on m machines, where the machines are in general *unrelated.* Each job j possesses a *private* strict complete preference order $\succ_j$ over the machines, and has a *publicly-known* processing time p_{ij} on machine i. Furthermore, there is a bound T on the maximum load allowed on any machine (i.e., makespan). An outcome is an (partial) assignment of some jobs to machines that respects the makespan bound. The ordering over outcomes is induced by the ordering over machines as in the above two cases. The parallel machines setting is the case where $p_{ij} = p_j$ for every machine i and job j.

Note that in the above three markets, agents' preferences over outcomes are *not* strict; however, for each agent j, the outcome-set may be partitioned into *indifference classes* such that j is indifferent between the outcomes in an indifference class, and has a strict ordering over the indifference classes. Our framework and results apply to such settings with cosmetic notational changes (see "Settings with indifferences" in Section 3), but we stick for the most part to the setting of strict preferences for notational ease.

A *social choice function* (SCF) is a function $f : \Sigma \mapsto O$. In settings with no monetary transfers, there is no formal distinction between an SCF and a *deterministic* algorithm or *direct-revelation* mechanism, which maps the preference profile given by the agents' reported preference lists to an outcome. An SCF f is said to be *implementable* or *truthful* if for every player j, every $\succ_j, \succ'_j \in \Sigma_j$, and every $\succ_{-j} \in \Sigma_{-j}$, we have $f(\succ_j, \succ_{-j}) \succeq_j f(\succ'_j, \succ_{-j})$; that is, no agent benefits by misreporting his preference list. A *randomized mechanism* is allowed to output a distribution (also called a *lottery*) over outcomes. Let $\mathcal{L}(O)$ denote the collection of distributions over the outcome-set O. A randomized mechanism is formally then a function mapping preference profiles to distributions in $\mathcal{L}(O)$. We sometimes refer to a mechanism that works with ordinal preferences as an ordinal mechanism.

Definition 1. A randomized mechanism $\mathcal{M}$ is said to *ε-implement* an SCF f (or that f is ε-implementable by $\mathcal{M}$), if $\mathbf{Pr}[\mathcal{M}(\succ) = f(\succ)] \geq 1 - \varepsilon$ for all $\succ \in \Sigma$, where the probability is over the random choices of $\mathcal{M}$. We say that a family $\{\mathcal{M}^{\varepsilon}\}$ of mechanisms *fully implements* f if for all $\varepsilon > 0$, $\mathcal{M}^{\varepsilon}$ ε-implements f. (This is in the same spirit as the notion of virtual implementation in Nash equilibrium [20, 3].)

Truthfulness for randomized mechanisms may be defined in various ways. The strongest notion is *universal truthfulness*, wherein a randomized truthful mechanism is a randomization (or mixture) over deterministic truthful mechanisms, where the mixture weights are input-independent. A somewhat weaker notion is obtained by considering the stochastic dominance relation. Given an ordering $\succ$ over O, and two lotteries $\mathbf{p}, \mathbf{q} \in \mathcal{L}(O)$, we say that $\mathbf{p}$ (first-order) *stochastically dominates* $\mathbf{q}$ with respect to $\succ$, if $\sum_{\ell \leq i} \mathbf{p}(\text{alt}(\succ, \ell)) \geq \sum_{\ell \leq i} \mathbf{q}(\text{alt}(\succ, \ell))$ for all $i = 1, \ldots, m$. Since stochastic dominance does not induce a total ordering on $\mathcal{L}(O)$, this yields two notions of truthfulness that have been studied in the literature.

Definition 2. A randomized mechanism $\mathcal{M}$ is said to be:

- *strongly truthful* [15]: if $\mathcal{M}(\succ_j, \succ_{-j})$ *stochastically dominates* $\mathcal{M}(\succ'_j, \succ_{-j})$ with respect to $\succ_j$, for all j, all $\succ_j, \succ'_j \in \Sigma_j$, and all $\succ_{-j} \in \Sigma_{-j}$.
- *weakly truthful* [21, 7]: if $\mathcal{M}(\succ_j, \succ_{-j})$ *is not stochastically dominated* by $\mathcal{M}(\succ'_j, \succ_{-j})$ with respect to $\succ_j$, for all j, all $\succ_j, \succ'_j \in \Sigma_j$, and all $\succ_{-j} \in \Sigma_{-j}$.

A universally truthful mechanism is also strongly truthful, and in fact, this inclusion is strict (Theorem 3.2). Gibbard [15] extended the impossibility result of [14, 25] to show that the space of strongly truthful mechanisms is also rather limited. A deterministic mechanism is: (i) *dictatorial* if there exists $j \in N$ such that the mechanism's output is always j's top choice; and (ii) *duple* if the mechanism's range $f(\Sigma)$ consists of at most two outcomes. A (deterministic or randomized) mechanism is *unilateral* if there exists some fixed $j \in N$ such that the mechanism's output depends only on j's (reported) preference list.

THEOREM 2.1. *(Gibbard-Satterthwaite and Gibbard impossibility results) (i) If $m \geq 3$ and $f(\Sigma) = O$, then f is truthful iff it is dictatorial. (ii) Any strongly truthful mechanism is a mixture of truthful unilateral and deterministic truthful duple mechanisms with input-independent mixture weights.*

Theorem 2.1 leaves weak truthfulness as the only notion that potentially allows for some sophisticated mechanisms. In Section 3.2, we propose a stronger notion of truthfulness and show that this is flexible enough that one can *bypass Gibbard's impossibility result* and obtain various interesting mechanisms including, in particular, mechanisms that yield "good" social welfare under the metric we introduce in Section 3.1.

3. RANK APPROXIMATION AND LEX-TRUTHFULNESS

3.1 Welfare in ordinal settings: rank approximation

We introduce a notion of social welfare that we call *rank approximation*. Given a preference profile $\succ = (\succ_1, \dots, \succ_n)$, the i-rank of an outcome $o \in O$ in $\succ$, denoted $\text{rank}_i(o; \succ)$, is the number of agents having o in their top i choices: $\text{rank}_i(o; \succ) = \big|\{j : \text{pos}(\succ_j, o) \leq i\}\big|$. Define $\text{maxrank}_i(\succ) := \max_{o \in O} \text{rank}_i(o; \succ)$.

Definition 3. A randomized mechanism $\mathcal{M}$ is an *α-rank-approximation* mechanism, if for every preference profile $\succ$, we have $\mathbf{E}\big[\text{rank}_i(\mathcal{M}(\succ); \succ)\big] \geq \text{maxrank}_i(\succ)/\alpha$ for *all* $i = 1, \dots, m$, where the expectation is taken over the random choices of $\mathcal{M}$. We say that α is the rank-approximation factor of $\mathcal{M}$.

As mentioned in the Introduction, rank approximation is an appealingly robust notion from various perspectives. A utility function U is consistent with a preference ordering $\succ$ if $U(o) > U(o')$ whenever $o \succ o'$. A collection of cardinal utility functions $(U_1, \dots, U_n)$ consistent with a preference profile $\succ$ is called *homogeneous* if for all $i \in [m]$, the value that an agent assigns to his i-th choice is the same across all agents, that is, $U_j(\text{alt}(\succ_j, i)) = U_{j'}(\text{alt}(\succ_{j'}, i))$ for all $i \in [m], j, j' \in N$.

An α-rank-approximation mechanism yields an α approximation to social welfare for *any* homogeneous cardinal-utility profile consistent with the agents' preferences.

THEOREM 3.1. *Let $\mathcal{M}$ be an α-rank-approximation randomized mechanism. Then, for every preference profile $\succ$, we have $\mathbf{E}\big[\sum_{j \in N} U_j\big(\mathcal{M}(\succ)\big)\big] \geq \frac{1}{\alpha} \cdot \max_{o \in O} \sum_{j \in N} U_j(o)$ for any homogeneous utility profile $(U_1, \dots, U_n)$ consistent with $\succ$.*

PROOF. Let $\mathbf{p} = \mathcal{M}(\succ)$. Let $U(i)$ be the common value of $U_j(\text{alt}(\succ_j, i))$. Define $\text{rank}_0(o; \succ) = 0$ for all $o \in O$, and $U(m+1) = 0$. Let $o^* = \text{argmax}_{o \in O} \sum_{j \in N} U_j(o)$. Then $\mathbf{E}\big[\sum_{j \in N} U_j\big(\mathcal{M}(\succ)\big)\big]$ is

$$
\begin{aligned}
&\sum_{o \in O} \mathbf{p}(o) \sum_{i=1}^{m} \big(\text{rank}_i(o; \succ) - \text{rank}_{i-1}(o; \succ)\big) U(i) \\
&= \sum_{o \in O} \mathbf{p}(o) \sum_{i=1}^{m} \text{rank}_i(o; \succ) \big(U(i) - U(i+1)\big) \\
&\geq \frac{1}{\alpha} \cdot \sum_{o \in O} \mathbf{p}(o) \sum_{i=1}^{m} \text{rank}_i(o^*; \succ) \big(U(i) - U(i+1)\big) \\
&= \frac{1}{\alpha} \cdot \sum_{j \in N} U_j(o^*).
\end{aligned}
$$

□

Consistent homogeneous utilities may be equivalently viewed as a *scoring rule*; Viewed from this perspective, Theorem 3.1 shows that an α-rank-approximation mechanism *simultaneously achieves an α-approximation to all scoring rules.*

In fact, rank approximation satisfies an even more general robustness property. Associate with each outcome o an m-vector called its *histogram*, given by $\text{hist}(o; \succ) = \{\text{rank}_i(o; \succ)\}_{i \in [m]}$. Define the g-value of an outcome o to be $g\big(\text{hist}(o; \succ); \succ\big)$, where $g(x; \succ) := \min_{i \in [m]} \frac{x_i}{\text{maxrank}_i(\succ)}$. It is not hard to see that g is a concave function of x and non-decreasing in each coordinate. A deterministic α-rank-approximation mechanism outputs an outcome with g-value at least $\frac{1}{\alpha}$.

Now suppose $h(x; \succ)$ is *any* concave non-decreasing function and we measure the value of an outcome o by $h\big(\text{hist}(o; \succ); \succ\big)$. This yields a natural SCF f^h, where $f^h(\succ)$ is $\text{argmax}_{o' \in O} h(o'; \succ)$. Note that scoring rules correspond to the special case where $h(\cdot)$ is linear with all coefficients non-negative. Analogous to α-rank-approximation, we can define an SCF f' to be an α-approximation for f^h if (h-value of $f'(\succ)$) $\geq \frac{1}{\alpha} \cdot$ (h-value of $f^h(\succ)$) for all $\succ$.

An α-rank-approximation mechanism *simultaneously* achieves an α-approximation mechanism for *all* such histogram-based concave SCFs: if o is the outcome returned, we get $g\big(\text{hist}(o; \succ); \succ\big) \geq \frac{1}{\alpha}$, and therefore $\text{hist}(o; \succ) \geq \frac{1}{\alpha} \cdot \text{hist}(o'; \succ)$ coordinate-wise for any $o' \in O$. Since h is non-decreasing and concave, this implies that $h\big(\text{hist}(o; \succ); \succ\big) \geq \frac{1}{\alpha} \cdot \max_{o' \in O} h\big(\text{hist}(o'; \succ); \succ\big) = \frac{1}{\alpha} \cdot f^h(\succ)$.

3.2 Truthfulness for randomized ordinal mechanisms: lex-truthfulness

We propose a new notion for truthfulness relying on lexicographic ordering. Given an ordering $\succ$ over O, and two lotteries $\mathbf{p} \neq \mathbf{q} \in \mathcal{L}(O)$, $\mathbf{p}$ *lexicographically dominates* $\mathbf{q}$ with respect to $\succ$, if there exists $i \in [m]$ such that $\mathbf{p}(\text{alt}(\succ, i)) > \mathbf{q}(\text{alt}(\succ, i))$ and $\mathbf{p}(\text{alt}(\succ, \ell)) = \mathbf{p}(\text{alt}(\succ, \ell))$ for all $\ell = 1, \dots, i-1$. Note that lex-dominance imposes a *total order* on $\mathcal{L}(O)$. This motivates the following definition of truthfulness.

Definition 4. A randomized mechanism $\mathcal{M}$ is called *lex-truthful* (LT) if for all $j \in N$, all $\succ_j \succ'_j \in \Sigma_j$, and all $\succ_{-j}$, we have that either $\mathcal{M}(\succ_j, \succ_{-j}) \equiv \mathcal{M}(\succ'_j, \succ_{-j})$, or $\mathcal{M}(\succ_j, \succ_{-j})$ *lexicographically dominates* $\mathcal{M}(\succ'_j, \succ_{-j})$ with respect to $\succ_j$.

Observe that if $\mathbf{p}$ stochastically dominates $\mathbf{q}$, then $\mathbf{p}$ lex-dominates $\mathbf{q}$ as well. Since lex-dominance is a total order, this implies that if $\mathbf{p}$ lex-dominates $\mathbf{q}$, then $\mathbf{q}$ cannot stochastically dominate $\mathbf{p}$. We obtain the following hierarchy between the various notions of truthfulness for randomized ordinal mechanisms.

THEOREM 3.2. *Let* UnivT, StrongT, WeakT, LexT *denote the classes of universally-, strongly-, weakly-, and lex-truthful mechanisms respectively. Then* UnivT $\subsetneq$ StrongT $\subsetneq$ LexT $\subsetneq$ WeakT.

We defer the proof of Theorem 3.2 to Appendix A. We shorten "implementable by a lex-truthful mechanism" to "lex-truthfully (LT) implementable" in the sequel. We show that lex-truthful implementability is equivalent to a property of the social-choice function that we call *pseudomonotonicity.* This characterization immediately opens up a host of SCFs that are fully LT-implementable. We heavily exploit this in Sections 4 and 5 to show that the rank-approximation SCFs that we devise for various problems are fully LT-implementable. In Section 6, we leverage this to show that an interesting class of SCFs in general ordinal settings are fully LT-implementable.

Definition 5. A social choice function f is *pseudomonotone* (or satisfies *pseudomonotonicity*) if the following holds. Consider any player j, $\succ_{-j}\in \Sigma_{-j}$, and $\succ_j,\succ'_j\in \Sigma_j$. Let $o = f(\succ)$ and $o' = f(\succ')$. Then, either (i) $o \succeq_j o'$, or (ii) there is an outcome o'' such that $o'' \succ_j o'$ and $\text{pos}(\succ_j, o'') < \text{pos}(\succ'_j, o'')$.

A useful way to view pseudomonotonicity is as follows: if a player's deviation leaves his first k preferences unaltered, then the deviation cannot both yield him a better outcome *and* a top-$(k+1)$ outcome.

THEOREM 3.3. *(i) Let f be a pseudomonotone SCF. Then f is ε-implementable by a lex-truthful mechanism for any $\varepsilon > 0$; that is, f is fully lex-truthfully implementable.*
(ii) Conversely, if f is ε-LT implementable for some $\varepsilon < \frac{1}{2}$, then f is pseudomonotone.

PROOF. First consider part (i). Given $\varepsilon > 0$, one can find $\varepsilon_1 > \varepsilon_2 > \cdots > \varepsilon_m > 0$ such that $\sum_i \varepsilon_i = \varepsilon$. Consider the randomized mechanism $\mathcal{M}$ that on input $\succ$, returns $f(\succ)$ with probability $(1-\varepsilon)$, and with probability ε it chooses a random agent a and returns his i-th preference with probability $\varepsilon_i/\varepsilon$.

It is clear by definition that $\mathcal{M}$ ε-implements f. To prove lex-truthfulness, fix an agent j and consider any $\succ' = (\succ'_j, \succ_{-j})$, where $\succ'_j \neq \succ_j$. Let $o = f(\succ)$ and let $o' = f(\succ')$. Also let $\mathbf{p} = \mathcal{M}(\succ)$, $\mathbf{q} = \mathcal{M}(\succ')$. Let $\mathbf{1}(A)$ be 1 if A is true, and 0 otherwise. For any outcome $\hat{o}$, we have

$$\mathbf{p}(\hat{o}) - \mathbf{q}(\hat{o}) = \frac{1}{n}\left(\varepsilon_{\text{pos}(\succ_j,\hat{o})} - \varepsilon_{\text{pos}(\succ'_j,\hat{o})}\right) + \mathbf{1}(\hat{o} = o)\cdot(1-\varepsilon) - \mathbf{1}(\hat{o} = o')\cdot(1-\varepsilon).$$

Considering outcomes in the preference order of $\succ_j$, let o'' be the first outcome such that $\text{pos}(\succ_j, o'') \neq \text{pos}(\succ'_j, o'')$. Then $\text{pos}(\succ_j, o'') < \text{pos}(\succ'_j, o'')$. By pseudomonotonicity of f, we know that $o \succeq_j o'$ or $o'' \succ_j o'$. In the latter case, we have $\mathbf{p}(\hat{o}) - \mathbf{q}(\hat{o}) \geq 0$ for all $\hat{o} \succeq_j o''$ and $\mathbf{p}(o'') - \mathbf{q}(o'') > 0$, so we are done. In the former case, if $o = o'$ or $o'' \succeq_j o$, then the same argument holds. So suppose $o \succ_j o''$ and $o \succ_j o'$. Then $\mathbf{p}(\hat{o}) - \mathbf{q}(\hat{o}) \geq 0$ for all $\hat{o} \succeq_j o$ and $\mathbf{p}(o) - \mathbf{q}(o) > 0$, so again we are done.

We now prove part (ii). Let $\mathcal{M}$ be an LT mechanism that ε-LT implements f, where $\varepsilon < \frac{1}{2}$. Suppose for a contradiction, there is some agent j, and $\succ = (\succ_j, \succ_{-j})$ and $\succ' = (\succ'_j, \succ_{-j})$ such that $o = f(\succ)$ and $o' = f(\succ')$ violate the conditions for pseudomonotonicity. That is, we have $o' \succ_j o$ and for every outcome $o'' \succ_j o'$, we have $\text{pos}(\succ_j, o'') \geq \text{pos}(\succ'_j, o'')$. This means that $\text{pos}(\succ_j, o'') = \text{pos}(\succ'_j, o'')$ for all $o'' \succ_j o'$. Let $\mathbf{p} = \mathcal{M}(\succ)$ and $\mathbf{q} = \mathcal{M}(\succ')$.

Since $\mathcal{M}$ ε-LT implements f, we have $\mathbf{p}(o') \leq \varepsilon$ and $\mathbf{q}(o') \geq 1-\varepsilon$, so $\mathbf{p}(o') < \mathbf{q}(o')$. Let $o_1, \ldots, o_r$ be the outcomes o'' such that $o'' \succ_j o'$ listed in decreasing preference order according to $\succ_j$. Since $\text{pos}(\succ_j, o'') = \text{pos}(\succ'_j, o'')$ for all $o'' \succ_j o'$, we have $o_\ell \succ'_j o'$ for all $\ell \in [r]$, and the ordering of the o_ℓs is the same in $\succ_j$ and $\succ'_j$. We claim that $\mathbf{p}(o_\ell) = \mathbf{q}(o_\ell)$ for all $\ell = 1, \ldots, r$, which contradicts the fact that $\mathcal{M}$ is lex-truthful.

We prove the claim by induction on ℓ. Considering $\succ_j$ to be j's true preference list, we must have $\mathbf{p}(o_1) \geq \mathbf{q}(o_1)$, and considering $\succ'_j$ to be j's true preference list, we must have $\mathbf{q}(o_1) \geq \mathbf{p}(o_1)$. Suppose that $\mathbf{p}(o_k) = \mathbf{q}(o_k)$ for $k = 1, \ldots, \ell-1$. Again considering $\succ_j$ and $\succ'_j$ be j's true preference lists in turn, we obtain that $\mathbf{p}(o_\ell) = \mathbf{q}(o_\ell)$. $\square$

Settings with indifferences.

As noted earlier, many of the settings we consider involve non-strict preferences. In these settings, the outcome set is partitioned into *indifference classes* $O^j_1, \ldots, O^j_{m_j}$ for each agent j. Agent j is indifferent between any two outcomes in the same indifference class, and has a strict complete ordering over his indifference classes that specifies his ordering between two outcomes in different classes. Formally, given $\succeq_j \in \Sigma_j$, we define $\text{pos}(\succeq_j, o) = r \in [m_j]$ if o lies in the indifference class of j ranked r under $\succeq_j$, and $\text{alt}(\succeq_j, r) \subseteq O$ is now the indifference class of j ranked r under $\succeq_j$ (that is, $\{o : \text{pos}(\succeq, o) = r\}$). The preferences induced over outcomes are then: $o \succeq_j o'$ iff $\text{pos}(\succeq_j, o) \leq \text{pos}(\succeq_j, o')$, and $o \succ_j o'$ iff $\text{pos}(\succeq_j, o) < \text{pos}(\succeq_j, o')$. Say that $o \sim_j o'$ if o and o' belong to the same indifference class of j.

One requires mostly notational changes to extend our framework and results to this more-general setting. With the above notation in place, the definitions of $\text{rank}_i(o; \succeq)$ (as $|\{j : \text{pos}(\succeq_j, o) \leq i\}|$, $\text{maxrank}_i(\succ)$, rank-approximation (Definition 3) and pseudomonotonicity (Definition 5) remain unchanged.

We extend lex-dominance and lex-truthfulness as follows. Since players have indifference classes it is not meaningful to consider probabilities assigned to individual outcomes; instead, we consider the total probability assigned to an indifference class. Given a lottery $\mathbf{p} \in \mathcal{L}(O)$ and $S \subseteq O$, define $\mathbf{p}(S) := \sum_{o\in S} \mathbf{p}(o)$. Given $\succeq_j \in \Sigma_j$, and lotteries $\mathbf{p} \neq \mathbf{q} \in \mathcal{L}(O)$, we say that $\mathbf{p}$ lex-dominates $\mathbf{q}$ with respect to $\succeq_j$ if there exists $r \in [m_j]$ such that $\mathbf{p}(\text{alt}(\succeq_j, r)) > \mathbf{q}(\text{alt}(\succeq_j, r))$ and $\mathbf{p}(\text{alt}(\succeq_j, \ell)) = \mathbf{q}(\text{alt}(\succeq_j, \ell))$ for all $\ell = 1, \ldots, r-1$. With this definition of lex-dominance, lex-truthfulness remains as defined in Definition 4.

We can now mimic the proof of Theorem 3.3 to prove the following analogue for the above setting, showing that pseudomonotonicity is necessary and sufficient for full LT-implementability. The proof appears in Appendix A.

THEOREM 3.4. *(i) Let f be a pseudomonotone SCF. Then f is fully lex-truthfully implementable.*

(ii) Conversely, if f is ε-lex-truthfully implementable for any $\varepsilon < \frac{1}{2}$, then f is pseudomonotone.

4. MATCHING MARKETS

Recall that in a matching market there are n agents and m items, and outcomes are matchings of agents to items. Each agent j has a strict total ordering over items, which induces his preferences over outcomes: j prefers outcome o to o' if he prefers his allotted item in o to the one in o'.

We show in Section B that various common mechanisms all have bad rank approximation. In contrast, we devise a simple deterministic algorithm, MaxMatch, that is a pseudomonotone, 2-rank-approximation algorithm (Theorem 4.1). We complement this by showing two lower bounds. Theorem 4.2 shows that 2 is the best rank approximation achievable by *any* deterministic algorithm, proving the tightness of our positive result. Next, Theorems 4.3 and 4.4 demonstrate limitations of *deterministic* truthful mechanisms for matching markets by showing that such mechanisms cannot achieve any constant rank approximation.

Algorithm MaxMatch .

Fix a tie-breaking rule over agents. On input $\succ$, MaxMatch allocates items to agents in m stages. In stage r, we consider the bipartite graph G_r with agents and items as vertices, and an edge from agent j to item i, if i is a top-r item of agent j. Note that $\text{maxrank}_r(\succ)$ is precisely the size of the maximum matching in G_r. Let M denote the current matching of agents to items (which is $\emptyset$ when $r = 1$), which is a matching in G_r. We maintain that at he beginning of stage r, M is a *maximal matching* in G_{r-1}; observe this is true when $r = 1$. Since M is a *maximal matching* in G_{r-1}, then any agent has an edge to at most one item in $G_r \setminus M$. For every unmatched item i that has non-zero degree in $G_r \setminus M$ (that is, i is a top-r item of some agent that is currently unmatched) we use our tie-breaking rule to pick an agent $j \in G_r \setminus M$; we assign item i to j and update M. Thus, M is updated to a maximal matching in G_r. We output the matching at the end of m stages.

THEOREM 4.1. MaxMatch *a pseudomonotone, 2-rank approximation algorithm for matching markets, and hence is fully LT-implementable.*

PROOF. The 2-rank-approximation guarantee of MaxMatch follows immediately from the fact that MaxMatch maintains a maximal matching in the "top-r" graph G_r for all r, and the size of any maximal matching is at least half the size of a maximum matching, and thus at least $\text{maxrank}_r(\succ)/2$.

Fix an agent j. Suppose that j deviates from $\succ_j$ to $\succ'_j$ without altering his top-r items and their ordering, that is, $\text{alt}(\succ_j, \ell) = \text{alt}(\succ'_j, \ell)$ for all $\ell = 1, \ldots, r$, and $\text{pos}(\succ'_j, i) > r + 1$ for $i = \text{alt}(\succ_j, r+1)$. Let $\succ = (\succ_j, \succ_{-j})$ and $\succ' = (\succ'_j, \succ_{-j})$. Since the other agents' inputs have not changed, MaxMatch$(\succ)$ and MaxMatch$(\succ')$ proceed identically up to the end of stage r. So if j has been assigned an item by this time (which happens in both runs) we are done. Otherwise, in MaxMatch$(\succ')$, all of j's top-r items are unavailable, and since j demotes i in $\succ'$, edge (j, i) does not belong to the graph G_{r+1} constructed in stage $r+1$; so j does not obtain i or a top-r item under input $\succ'$. This proves pseudomonotonicity. □

THEOREM 4.2. *No deterministic algorithm can have rank-approximation better than 2 for matching markets.*

PROOF. We create an instance with $n = 2K - 1$ players and items. We specify the first K preferences of the players; the remaining preferences may be set arbitrarily. Let $\succ$ denote the resulting input (with arbitrary remaining preferences). Since this is the only input we consider, we drop the $\succ$ in $\text{rank}_r(o; \succ)$ and $\text{maxrank}_r(\succ)$ in the sequel.

- For $r = 2, \ldots, K-1$, the r-th preference of a player j is item: $\begin{cases} r & ; \quad \text{if } j = r, \\ K + r - 1\ ; & \quad \text{if } j = r - 1, \\ r - 1 & ; \quad \text{otherwise.} \end{cases}$
- The first preference of a player j is: item 1 if $j = 1$, and item n otherwise.
- The K-th preference of a player j is: item K if $j = K-1$, and item $K - 1$ otherwise.

First, we claim that $\text{maxrank}_r \geq 2r$ for all $r \in [K-1]$. For $r = 1$, this is achieved by matching player 1 to item 1, and an arbitrary other player to item n. For $r = 2, \ldots, K-1$, this is achieved by matching player r to item r, each player $j \in [r-1]$ to item $K + j$, matching one player from $\{r + 1, \ldots, n\}$ to item n and $r - 1$ other arbitrary players from $\{r+1, \ldots, n\}$ arbitrarily to items in $[r-1]$. Note that each player is matched to a top-r item in this matching. Also, $\text{maxrank}_{K-1} = n$. This is achieved by matching player $K-1$ to item K, each player $j \in [K-2]$ to item $K + j$, matching one player from $\{K, \ldots, n\}$ to item $n-1$, and the remaining $K-1$ players from $\{K, \ldots, n\}$ arbitrarily to items in $[K-1]$.

Now fix a matching o. We show that if $\text{rank}_r(o) > \text{maxrank}_r/2$ for $r = 1, \ldots, K-1$, then we must have $\text{rank}_K(o) \leq K < \text{maxrank}_K/2$. Thus, we cannot have $\text{rank}_r(o) > \text{maxrank}_r/2$ for all $r \in [K]$.

We show by induction on r that if $\text{rank}_\ell(o) > \text{maxrank}_\ell/2$ for all $\ell \in [r]$, where $r < K$, then o must match player ℓ to item ℓ for all $\ell \in [r]$. For the base case, if $\text{rank}_1(o) > \text{maxrank}_1/2 \geq 1$, then o must match player 1 to item 1 since all other players have item n as their top item. For the induction step, suppose that $\text{rank}_\ell(o) > \text{maxrank}_\ell/2$ for all $\ell \in [r]$, where $1 < r < K$. Then, by the induction hypothesis, we know that o matches player ℓ to item ℓ for all $\ell \in [r-1]$. We require that $\text{rank}_r(o) \geq r+1$. Examining the preferences of the players in $\{r, \ldots, n\}$, we see that for player r, items r and n are the only unmatched items in his top-r list, and for a player $j \in \{r+1, \ldots, n\}$, item n is the only unmatched item in j's top-r list. Therefore, $\text{rank}_r(o) \geq r+1$ is only possible if o matches player r to item r.

Given the above claim, for players $j = K, \ldots, n$, item n is the only unmatched item in their top-K list, so $\text{rank}_K(o) \leq K$. □

We now show that randomization is necessary to achieve good rank approximation via truthful mechanisms. As a warm up, we first prove a lower bound of $n - 1$ on the rank-approximation factor achievable by truthful *no-bossy* mechanisms [25]. A *no-bossy mechanism* for matching markets is one where no agent can change his preference and modify the outcome without also modifying his own allocation.

Suppose there are n items. Let $\succ^* := (1, 2, \ldots, n)$ denote the ordering where item i is the i-th ranked item, for all $i \in [n]$. Let $\succ^* \circ (k-1, 1)$, denote the preference list that is identical to $\succ^*$ except that items $(k-1)$ and 1 are swapped. That is, $(k-1)$ is the top-item, 1 is the kth-choice, and item i is the i-th choice for all $i \neq 1, k-1$. Given n agents and any set $S \subseteq \{2, 3, \ldots, n\}$, let $\succ^S$ be the preference profile where each agent $k \in S$ has preference $\succ^* \circ (k-1, 1)$, while each $k \notin S$ has preference $\succ^*$. Thus, $\succ^\emptyset$ is the preference profile where every agent has the same preference order $\succ^*$ over items. For notational convenience, we think of a player who is not assigned an item as being assigned item $n+1$, which is lower ranked than any (true) item in $[n]$.

THEOREM 4.3. *No deterministic truthful no-bossy mechanism for matching markets can have rank-approximation smaller than* $(n-1)$.

PROOF. We consider a matching market with n (agents and) items. Let $\mathcal{M}$ be any deterministic truthful no-bossy mechanism. Suppose that $\mathcal{M}(\succ^\emptyset)$ assigns items to N players. By renaming players if necessary, we may assume that $\mathcal{M}(\succ^\emptyset)$ assigns item i to player i for all $i \in [N]$, and item $n+1$ to the remaining players.

Consider the input $\succ^{\{k\}}$. We claim that $\mathcal{M}(\succ^{\{k\}}) = \mathcal{M}(\succ^\emptyset)$. *Due to no-bossiness*, it suffices to show that agent k's allocation is the same in $\mathcal{M}(\succ^{\{k\}})$ and $\mathcal{M}(\succ^\emptyset)$. Suppose agent k obtains item i in $\mathcal{M}(\succ^{\{k\}})$. Invoking truthfulness when k's true preference list is $\succ^*$ (and the other players' preference lists are $\succ^*$), we obtain that $k \succeq^* i$, that is, $k \leq i$. Similarly, if k's true preference list were $\succ^* \circ (k-1,1)$, then truthfulness dictates that $i \leq k$. Hence, we have $i = k$.

The above argument can be generalized to show that for any $S \subseteq [n]$, we have $\mathcal{M}(\succ^S) = \mathcal{M}(\succ^{S \setminus k}) = \mathcal{M}(\succ^\emptyset)$ for all $k \in S$. In particular, $\mathcal{M}(\succ^{\{2,\dots,n\}})$ assigns item i to player i for all $i \in [n]$. Now, under the preference profile $\succ^{\{2,\dots,n\}}$, at most one agent, agent 1, gets his top choice; however, assigning every player $j > 1$ item $j-1$ yields an outcome where $n-1$ agents get their top choice. $\square$

While no-bossiness was crucial above, we show via a more sophisticated argument that no deterministic truthful mechanism can obtain constant rank approximation.

THEOREM 4.4. *Every deterministic truthful mechanism has rank approximation* $\Omega(\frac{\log\log n}{\log\log\log n})$.

PROOF. Let n be large enough so that $K := \left\lfloor \frac{\log\log n}{\log\log\log n} \right\rfloor - 2 \geq 1$. We show that on instances with n (agents and) items, no deterministic truthful mechanism can have rank approximation better than K.

As before, if $\mathcal{M}(\succ^\emptyset)$ assigns items to N players, we may assume that it matches agent i to item i for $i \in [N]$, and the remaining players are unassigned (i.e., assigned item $n+1$). Given agents $\{a_1,\dots,a_k\}$ and integers $r_1,\dots,r_k \geq 1$, we let $\succ^{(a_1,r_1),(a_2,r_2),\dots,(a_k,r_k)}$ denote the preference profile where all agents other than these a_ℓ's have preference order $\succ^*$, while each a_ℓ has preference order $\succ^* \circ (r_\ell, 1)$). That is, a_ℓ's top choice is item r_ℓ, his r_ℓ-th choice is item 1, and his i-th choice is item i for all $i \neq 1, r_\ell$. We show that there exist agents $a_1,\dots,a_K$ and *distinct* integers $r_1,\dots,r_K \in [K]$, such that, in $\mathcal{M}(\succ^{(a_1,r_1),\dots,(a_K,r_K)})$, every agent $a_1,\dots,a_K$ gets an item whose index is larger than K. Since all other agents have the same top item, the number of agents getting their top item is at most 1. This proves that the rank approximation is at least K, since assigning item r_ℓ to agent a_ℓ for all $\ell \in [K]$, yields an outcome where K agents obtain their top-choice item.

To find these K agents, we proceed in K stages. In stage ℓ, we will have a subset S_ℓ of agents with $|S_\ell| \geq \ell$ having the following property. For any $t < \ell$, any t agents $\{a_1,\dots,a_t\} \subseteq S_\ell$, and for any t distinct integers $r_1,\dots,r_t \in [K]$, $\mathcal{M}(\succ^{(a_1,r_1),\dots,(a_t,r_t)})$ allocates all agents in S_ℓ an item indexed larger than K.

Note that if we reach stage K, then we are done due to the following reason. Consider any K agents $a_1,\dots,a_K \in S_K$ and any K distinct integers $r_1,\dots,r_K \in [K]$. Consider any index $\ell \in [K]$. Let $\succ' = \succ^{(a_1,r_1),\dots,(a_{\ell-1},r_{\ell-1}),(a_{\ell+1},r_{\ell+1}),(a_{K-1},r_{K-1})}$ and $\succ = \succ^{(a_1,r_1),\dots,(a_K,r_K)}$. We know that $\mathcal{M}(\succ')$ allocates all agents in S_K an item indexed larger than K. This also implies that $o := \mathcal{M}(\succ)$ allocates a_ℓ an item indexed larger than K, otherwise given the preference profile $\succ'$, player ℓ has an incentive to deviate from his preference list $\succ^*$ and report $\succ^* \circ (r_\ell, 1)$. Since this holds for all ℓ, it follows that o allocates every agent $a_1,\dots,a_K$ an item indexed larger than K.

We now show how to obtain the S_ℓ sets. The base case is $S_1 = \{K+1,\dots,n\}$, which satisfies the stated property. Given a set S_ℓ at the end of stage $\ell < K$ we now show how to construct the set $S_{\ell+1} \subsetneq S_\ell$. We construct the following hypergraph H_ℓ. The vertices are the agents in S_ℓ. The hyperedges are subsets of vertices of size at most $(\ell+1)$ constructed as follows. For every ℓ-size subset $\{a_1,\dots,a_\ell\}$ of S_ℓ, and every $a \in S_\ell$ (which could be the same as one of the a_ts), we add the hyperedge $\{a_1,\dots,a_\ell,a\}$ if there exist ℓ distinct integers $r_1,\dots,r_\ell \in [K]$ such that $\mathcal{M}(\succ^{(a_1,r_1),\dots,(a_\ell,r_\ell)})$ allocates agent a an item with index at most K. Note that the number of hyperedges is at most $|S_\ell|^\ell \cdot K^{\ell+1}$ since there are $|S_\ell|$ choices for each a_t, and K choices for each r_t, and once these are fixed, there at most K choices for a.

Call a subset $U \subseteq S_\ell$ *independent* if no hyperedge is completely contained in it. Observe that U is a valid input to stage $(\ell+1)$ if $|U| \geq \ell+1$: consider any $t < \ell+1$ agents $a_1,\dots,a_t \in U$ and any distinct integers $r_1,\dots,r_t \in [K]$. Suppose that $\mathcal{M}(\succ^{(a_1,r_1),\dots,(a_t,r_t)})$ allocates some agent $a \in U$ an item with index at most K. Then we must have $t = \ell$, otherwise this would contradict the property assumed of S_ℓ, and then $\{a_1,\dots,a_t,a\}$ would be a hyperedge, contradicting independence of U.

Lemma 4.5 shows that there is an independent set $S_{\ell+1} \subseteq S_\ell$ such that $|S_{\ell+1}| \geq \frac{|S_\ell|^{\frac{1}{\ell+1}}}{K} - 1$. Therefore, if $|S_\ell|^{\frac{1}{\ell+1}} \geq 2K$ (and hence $|S_t|^{\frac{1}{t+1}} \geq 2K$ for all $t \leq \ell$), then

$$|S_{\ell+1}| \geq |S_\ell|^{\frac{1}{\ell+1}}/2K \geq |S_1|^{\frac{1}{(\ell+1)!}}/(2K)^\ell \geq \left(\frac{n}{2}\right)^{\frac{1}{(\ell+1)!}}/(2K)^\ell.$$

If $K \leq \frac{\log\log n}{\log\log\log n} - 2$, then this implies that $(\frac{n}{2})^{\frac{1}{K!}}/(2K)^{K-1} \geq 2K$. Hence, $|S_{\ell+1}| \geq 2K$, and moreover, if $\ell+1 < K$, then $|S_{\ell+1}|^{\frac{1}{\ell+2}}/2K \geq (\frac{n}{2})^{\frac{1}{(\ell+2)!}}/(2K)^{\ell+1} \geq 2K$. Thus, we obtain that $|S_K| \geq 2K$. $\square$

LEMMA 4.5. *There exists an independent set* $S_{\ell+1} \subseteq S_\ell$ *of size* $|S_{\ell+1}| \geq \frac{|S_\ell|^{\frac{1}{\ell+1}}}{K} - 1$.

PROOF. Let $\mathcal{N} = |S_\ell|$. Recall the number of hyperedges is at most $\mathcal{N}^\ell K^{\ell+1}$. We first argue that all hyperedges are of size $\ell+1$. Every hyperedge is of size at least ℓ. A size-ℓ hyperedge $\{a_1,\dots,a_\ell\}$ can only arise, if there are ℓ distinct integers $r_1,\dots,r_\ell \in [K]$ and some $a \in \{a_1,\dots,a_\ell\}$, say a_1 for notational convenience such that $\mathcal{M}(\succ^{(a_1,r_1),\dots,(a_\ell,r_\ell)})$ allots a an item indexed less than K. But the definition of S_ℓ implies that $\mathcal{M}(\succ^{(a_2,r_2),\dots,(a_\ell,r_\ell)})$ allots a_1 an item with index larger than K. This violates truthfulness, since agent

a_1 has an incentive to misreport $\succ^* o(r_1, 1)$ when his true preference is $\succ^*$ and obtain a better item.

Consider sampling each vertex of H_ℓ with probability $p = K^{-1} \cdot \mathcal{N}^{-\left(\frac{\ell}{\ell+1}\right)}$ to get a random subset X. If X contains a hyperedge, then we remove all its vertices from X. The probability that a hyperedge is present in X is at most $p^{\ell+1}$, since all hyperedges are of size $\ell + 1$. Therefore, in expectation, the size of X after removal is at least $p\mathcal{N} - p^{\ell+1}\mathcal{N}^\ell K^{\ell+1} = \frac{\mathcal{N}^{1/\ell+1}}{K} - 1$. □

4.1 A generalization: matroid markets

In this generalization of matching markets, there is a matroid $M_i = (N, \mathcal{I}_i)$ for each item i, and multiple agents may be assigned to item i provided they form an independent set of M_i. Here $\mathcal{I}_i$ is a collection of subsets of N with the following properties: (i) $\emptyset \in \mathcal{I}_i$; for all $A, B \subseteq N$ (ii) if $A \in \mathcal{I}_i$ and $B \subseteq A$, then $B \in \mathcal{I}_i$; (iii) if $A, B \in \mathcal{I}_i$ and $|A| > |B|$, then there exists some $j \in A \setminus B$ such that $B \cup \{j\} \in \mathcal{I}_i$. Clearly, the lower bounds obtained for matching markets also hold in this setting. Complementing this, we extend MaxMatch to obtain a pseudomonotone 2-rank-approximation algorithm for matroid markets.

THEOREM 4.6. *There is a pseudomonotone 2-rank approximation algorithm for matroid markets, and a mechanism that fully LT-implements it.*

PROOF. The algorithm is similar to MaxMatch. Again fix an agent-ordering and an item-ordering. Consider some input $\succ$.

We again proceed in m stages. In stage r, we consider the "top-r" graph $G_r = (N \cup O, E_r)$, where each agent j has edges to his top-r items. Note that every outcome induces a feasible solution to the *matroid-intersection* problem defined by the following two matroids on the universe E_r. One is M_A, which is the direct sum of the M_i matroids for all $i \in O$, i.e., a set $I \subseteq N \times O$ is independent if $\{j : (j, i) \in I\} \in \mathcal{I}_i$ for all $i \in O$. The second is the partition matroid $M_B(r)$ encoding that at most one edge of E_r is incident to each item j. Then every outcome induces a set that is independent in both M_A and $M_B(r)$, and $\text{maxrank}_r(\succ)$ is the size of the largest common independent set.

Let M consist of the edges denoting the current (i.e., at the start of stage r) assignment of items to agents. Our algorithm will maintain the invariant that at the end of stage r, M is a *maximal* set that is independent in both M_A and $M_B(r)$. The rank-approximation factor of 2 follows then from the well-known fact that every maximal common independent set of two matroids has size at least half the size of maximum-cardinality common independent set; Claim 4.7 gives a self-contained proof.

Let $\Gamma^r(u)$ denote the neighbors of node u in G_r, and $\Gamma^r_M(u) := \{v : (u, v) \in M\}$. Note that if M is a maximal common independent set in G_{r-1}, then for every agent j that is not assigned an item in M, among j's top-r items his r-th ranked item is the *only* item to which j can be possible assigned while preserving independence in the item's matroid.

We consider each item i and augment $\Gamma^r_M(i)$, the current set of agents assigned to item i, to a maximal subset $J_i \subseteq \Gamma^r(i)$ that is independent in M_i: we initialize J_i to $\Gamma^r_M(i)$. Next, we consider agents in $\Gamma^r(i) \setminus \Gamma^r_M(i)$ according to the fixed agent-ordering and add agent j to J_i if this maintains independence in M_i. Maximality of J_i follows from the matroid property. (In fact J_i is a maximum-size independent subset of $\Gamma^r(i)$.) Finally, we update M to reflect the new assignments in stage r.

The fact that M is a maximal common independent set of M_A and $M_B(r)$ is immediate: if some edge (j, i) can be added to M while preserving independence in M_A and $M_B(r)$, then j was unassigned at the start of stage r and when we considered item i, j could (and would) have been added to J_i in the iteration when j was considered.

We have already argued that the above algorithm is a 2-rank-approximation. Pseudomonotonicity of the above algorithm follows from exactly the same arguments as in Theorem 4.1. □

CLAIM 4.7. *Let $M_1(U, \mathcal{I}_1)$, $M_2 = (U, \mathcal{I}_2)$ be two matroids. Let $S \subseteq U$ be an inclusion-wise maximal set that is independent in both M_1 and M_2. Let A be a maximum-cardinality set that is independent in both M_1 and M_2. Then $|S| \geq |A|/2$*

PROOF. Suppose $|S| < |A|/2$. Let $T_1 = \{e \in A : S \cup \{e\} \in \mathcal{I}_1\}$. Since $A \in \mathcal{I}_1$, by the matroid exchange property, we have $|T_1| \geq |A| - |S| > |A|/2$. Similarly, if $T_2 = \{e \in A : S \cup \{e\} \in \mathcal{I}_2\}$, then we have $|T_2| > |A|/2$. But since $T_1, T_2 \subseteq A$, this means that $T_1 \cap T_2 \neq \emptyset$, and so if $e \in T_1 \cap T_2$, then e can be added to S while maintaining independence in both M_1 and M_2. This contradicts the maximality of S. □

5. SCHEDULING MARKETS

Recall that here the agents are n jobs that need to be assigned on m machines. Each job j has a private strict total ordering over the machines, and a publicly-known processing time p_{ij} on machine i. An outcome is a partial assignment of jobs to machines, also called a schedule, that has makespan at most a given value T. An agent prefers outcome o to outcome o' if he prefers his assigned machine in o to that in o'.

We obtain nearly tight results for scheduling markets. Say that an algorithm is an (α, β)-approximation if it always returns a schedule with rank-approximation factor α and makespan at most βT. For parallel machines ($p_{ij} = p_j$ for all i, j), we give an $\big(O(\log n), O(1)\big)$-approximation, fully lex-truthfully (LT) implementable algorithm (Theorem 5.2). We show that this bound is *tight* by proving an *algorithmic lower bound* showing that every (α, β)-approximation algorithm for parallel machines must have $\alpha = \Omega(\max\{\log m, \log n\}/\beta)$ (Theorem 5.3). For the setting of general unrelated machines, we devise an $\big(O(\log n), O(1)\big)$-approximation algorithm (Theorem 5.4), however we do not know how to achieve this via a fully LT-implementable algorithm. We leave this as an intriguing open question.

Let N denote the set of jobs. For $S \subseteq N$, let $\succ_S$ denote the restriction of $\succ$ to jobs in S, and $\text{maxrank}_r(\succ_S)$ denote the maximum number of jobs from S that can be assigned to one of their top-r machines with makespan at most T. Observe that $\text{maxrank}_r(\succ_{S \cup T}) \leq \text{maxrank}_r(\succ_S) + \text{maxrank}_r(\succ_T)$.

Parallel machines.

Our results rely on a bucketing argument coupled with Theorem 4.6 for matroid-markets and some insights from the matroid-intersection problem. We divide the set N of jobs into $k = O(\log n)$ disjoint classes $N_0, N_1, \ldots, N_k$ such that jobs in each class have roughly the same processing time. Set $N_0 := \{j : p_j \leq \frac{T}{n}\}$, and $N_\ell := \{j : 2^{\ell-1} \cdot \frac{T}{n} < p_j \leq 2^\ell \cdot \frac{T}{n}\}$

for $\ell = 1, \dots, k := \lceil \log_2 n \rceil$. Note that if $j \notin \bigcup_{\ell=0}^{k} N_\ell$, then $p_j > T$, so j cannot be assigned to any machine in any outcome and is not counted in $\text{maxrank}_r(\succ)$ for any position r. We assume for notational convenience that N does not contain any such job in the sequel. It will be convenient to ensure that $|N_0| \geq 1$. So we remove some fixed job a from the N_ℓ set containing it and add it to N_0.

Obtaining a good rank-approximation for a class N_ℓ, where $\ell \geq 1$, with makespan $O(T)$ amounts to a matroid-market problem (in fact, a *b-matching* problem) since the makespan bound can be encoded by the constraint that at most $\frac{n}{2^{\ell-1}}$ jobs are assigned to each machine. Any feasible schedule for N_ℓ yields a feasible allocation for the corresponding matroid-market problem. So Theorem 4.6 yields a pseudomonotone $(2,2)$-approximation algorithm f_ℓ for class N_ℓ, and a mechanism $\mathcal{M}_\ell^\varepsilon$ that ε-implements it, for all $\varepsilon > 0$.

THEOREM 5.1. *One can obtain a deterministic fully LT-implementable $\big(O(1), O(\log n)\big)$-approximation algorithm for parallel-machine markets.*

PROOF. On input $\succ$, we output the schedule obtained by concatenating the schedule where all jobs in N_0 are assigned to their top machine, and all the $f_\ell(\succ_{N_\ell})$ schedules. Note that the N_0-schedule has makespan at most $2T$. The resulting schedule, denoted $f(\succ)$, has makespan $O(T \log n)$ and rank-approximation factor 2 (since $\text{maxrank}_r(\succ_N) \leq \sum_{\ell=0}^{k} \text{maxrank}_r(\succ_{N_\ell})$). Fix $\varepsilon > 0$. The jobs in N_0 clearly have no incentive to lie. It is easy to see then that f is ε-LT implemented by the mechanism that outputs the N_0-schedule concatenated with the (random) schedules output by the $\mathcal{M}_\ell^\varepsilon$ mechanisms, where we couple the random choices of all the $\mathcal{M}_\ell^\varepsilon$ mechanisms (i.e., their decisions are based on the outcomes of the same random coins) so that $\mathbf{Pr}[\exists\ \ell : \mathcal{M}_\ell^\varepsilon(\succ_{N_\ell}) \neq f_\ell(\succ_{N_\ell})] \leq \varepsilon$. □

THEOREM 5.2. *There is a randomized fully LT-implementable $\big(O(\log n), O(1)\big)$-approximation algorithm for parallel-machine markets, where the rank-approximation and makespan bounds hold with probability 1.*

PROOF. Consider an input $\succ$. As before, we assign all jobs in N_0 to their top machine. Note that simply picking a class N_ℓ with probability $\frac{1}{k}$ and outputting the concatenation of the N_0-schedule and $f_\ell(\succ_{N_\ell})$ is not enough since this only yields $O(k)$ rank approximation in expectation. Instead, we build upon the above ideas and leverage some results about the matroid-intersection problem.

Consider the following bipartite graph representing the concatenation σ of all the $f_\ell(\succ_{N_\ell})$ schedules. We have a node for every machine, and every job not in N_0, and an edge (i,j) if j is assigned to machine i in schedule σ. Now set $x_{ij} = \frac{1}{k}$ for every edge (i,j). Define $A_{i,\ell} := \lceil \frac{n}{2^{\ell-1}k} \rceil$ for all i, ℓ and $B_r := \lfloor \text{rank}_r(\sigma; \succ_{N \setminus N_0})/k \rfloor$ for all r. Consider the following polytope:

$$\mathcal{P} := \Big\{ y \in \mathbb{R}^{[m] \times (N \setminus N_0)} : \sum_{j \in N_\ell} y_{ij} \leq A_{i,\ell} \quad \forall i \in [m], \ell \in [k],$$
$$\sum_{j:\text{pos}(\succ_j, \sigma(j)) \leq r} y_{ij} \geq B_r \quad \forall r \in [m],$$
$$0 \leq y_{ij} \leq 1 \quad \forall i \in [m],\ j \notin N_0 \Big\}.$$

We claim that $\mathcal{P}$ has integral extreme points. Any extreme point of $\mathcal{P}$ is defined by a linearly independent system of tight constraints comprising some $\sum_{j \in N_\ell} y_{ij} = A_{i,\ell}$ equalities whose supports are disjoint, and some $\sum_{j:\text{pos}(\succ_j,\sigma(j)) \leq r} y_{ij} = B_r$, $y_{ij} = 1$ equalities whose supports form a laminar family. The constraint matrix of such a system thus corresponds to equations coming from two laminar set systems; such a matrix is known to be totally unimodular (TU) (see, e.g., [26]), and hence a solution to this system is integral.

Note that $x \in \mathcal{P}$, so it can be expressed as a convex combination of some extreme points of $\mathcal{P}$. Equivalently, x yields a distribution over partial schedules for $N \setminus N_0$. Let Y be a random schedule, or equivalently vector in $\mathbb{R}^{[m] \times (N \setminus N_0)}$, sampled from this distribution. Note that $\mathbf{Pr}[j \text{ is assigned in } Y] = x_{ij} = \frac{1}{k}$ for $j \notin N_0$. The makespan of Y is at most $6T$ with probability 1. This is because $\sum_j p_j Y_{ij} \leq \sum_{\ell=1}^{k} (1 + \frac{n}{2^{\ell-1}k}) \cdot 2^\ell \cdot \frac{T}{n} \leq 2^{k+1} \cdot \frac{T}{n} + 2T \leq 6T$. Let Π be the (random) schedule obtained by concatenating the N_0-schedule with Y. Then Π has makespan at most $8T$ with probability 1. Also, $\text{rank}_r(\Pi; \succ) \geq |N_0| + B_r$ with probability 1. Now $B_r \geq \lfloor \text{maxrank}_r(\succ_{N \setminus N_0})/2k \rfloor$. Finally,

$$\begin{aligned} \text{maxrank}_r(\succ) &\leq |N_0| + \text{maxrank}_r(\succ_{N \setminus N_0}) \\ &\leq |N_0| + \max\{2k, 4k \lfloor \text{maxrank}_r(\succ_{N \setminus N_0}/2k) \rfloor\} \\ &\leq 4k(|N_0| + B_r), \end{aligned}$$

where the latter inequality follows since $|N_0| \geq 1$. Thus, the randomized algorithm f that outputs the random schedule Π is an $\big(O(\log n), O(1)\big)$-approximation with probability 1.

We now proceed as in the proof of Theorems 3.3 and 3.4 to devise a mechanism $\mathcal{M}$ that fully LT-implements f. Fix $\varepsilon > 0$, and $\varepsilon_1 > \ldots > \varepsilon_m$ such that $\sum_{r=1}^{m} \varepsilon_r = \varepsilon$. Consider input $\succ$. Let $Y^\succ$ be the random schedule for $N \setminus N_0$ for input $\succ_{N \setminus N_0}$ as obtained above. Mechanism $\mathcal{M}$ always assigns jobs in N_0 to their top machines. For jobs in $N \setminus N_0$, it returns schedule $Y^\succ$ with probability $1 - \varepsilon$. For each $j \notin N_0$ and $r \in [m]$, with probability $\frac{\varepsilon_r}{n}$, it returns the schedule where j is assigned to its r-th ranked machine $\text{alt}(\succ_j, r)$, and all other jobs are unassigned. Clearly, $\mathcal{M}(\succ) = f(\succ)$ with probability at least $1 - \varepsilon$.

Jobs in N_0 do not benefit by lying. Consider a job $j \in N_\ell$, where $\ell \geq 1$. Let $\succ' = (\succ_j, \succ_{-j})$, where $\succ'_j \neq \succ_j$. Let $x_{ij} = x_{ij}(\succ)$ and $x'_{ij} = x_{ij}(\succ')$ denote the probabilities that j is assigned to i under the random schedules $Y = Y^\succ$ and $Y' = Y^{\succ'}$ respectively. Then,

$$\begin{aligned} \Delta_{ij} &:= \mathbf{Pr}[j \text{ assigned to } i \text{ in } \mathcal{M}(\succ)] - \mathbf{Pr}[j \text{ assigned to } i \text{ in } \mathcal{M}(\succ')] \\ &= (1 - \varepsilon)(x_{ij} - x'_{ij}) + \frac{1}{n} \cdot \big(\varepsilon_{\text{pos}(\succ_j, i)} - \varepsilon_{\text{pos}(\succ'_j, i)}\big). \end{aligned}$$

Considering machines in the preference order of $\succ_j$, let $\hat{\imath}$ be the first machine such that $\text{pos}(\succ_j, \hat{\imath}) \neq \text{pos}(\succ'_j, \hat{\imath})$. Then $\text{pos}(\succ_j, \hat{\imath}) < \text{pos}(\succ'_j, \hat{\imath})$. If $x'_{ij} = 0$ for all $i \succeq_j \hat{\imath}$, then $\Delta_{ij} \geq 0$ for all $i \succeq_j \hat{\imath}$, and $\Delta_{\hat{\imath}j} > 0$, so we are done. Otherwise, j is assigned to some machine $i' \succeq_j \hat{\imath}$ in $f_\ell(\succ'_{N_\ell})$. Since all machines $i \succ_j i'$ have $\text{pos}(\succ_j, i) = \text{pos}(\succ'_j, i)$ and f_ℓ is pseudomonotone, it must be that j is assigned to $i'' \succeq_j i'$ in $f_\ell(\succ_{N_\ell})$. So $x_{ij} = x'_{ij}$, and hence, $\Delta_{ij} = 0$, for all $i \succ_j i''$. If $i'' \neq i'$, then $\Delta_{i''j} > 0$, otherwise $\Delta_{ij} = 0$ for all $i \succ_j \hat{\imath}$ and $\Delta_{\hat{\imath}j} > 0$. Thus, $\mathcal{M}$ is lex-truthful. □

THEOREM 5.3. *There exists an instance of a parallel-machine market where any schedule with βT makespan has rank-approximation factor $\Omega(\max\{\log m, \log n\}/\beta)$.*

PROOF. We create an instance with $n = O(m \ln m)$ jobs as follows. We create a set $A^{(1)}$ of m jobs of size (i.e., p_j) T partitioned into $A_1^{(1)}, \ldots, A_m^{(1)}$, where each $A_i^{(1)}$ consists of a single job whose first preference is machine i. We create a set $A^{(2)}$ of $2(m-1)$ jobs of size $\frac{T}{2}$ partitioned into $A_2^{(2)}, \ldots, A_m^{(2)}$, all of which have machine 1 as their first preference. Each set $A_i^{(2)}$ has two jobs, both having machine i as their 2nd preference. In general for $i < k$, we have a set $A^{(i)}$ of $2^{i-1}(m-i+1)$ jobs of size $\frac{T}{2^{i-1}}$ partitioned into $A_i^{(i)}, \ldots, A_m^{(i)}$, all of which have machine r as their r-th preference for $r = 1, \ldots, i-1$. Each set $A_\ell^{(i)}$ has 2^{i-1} jobs, all of which have machine ℓ as their i-th preference. Finally, we have a set $A^{(k)}$ of $2^k m$ jobs of size $\frac{T}{2^k}$ partitioned into $A_k^{(k)}, \ldots, A_m^{(k)}$, all having machine r as their r-th preference for $r = 1, \ldots, k-1$. Each set $A_\ell^{(k)}$ has at least 2^k jobs, all of which have machine ℓ as their k-th preference. The remaining preferences of the jobs play no role, and may be set arbitrarily. Let $\succ$ be the resulting preference profile.

For $r \in [k]$, we have $\text{maxrank}_r(\succ) \geq 2^{r-1}(m-r+1) + 2^k(r-1) \geq 2^{r-1}m$ obtained by assigning all jobs in $A_\ell^{(r)}$ to machine ℓ for $\ell = r, \ldots, m$, and any $2^k(r-1)$ jobs from $A^{(k)}$ to machines $1, \ldots, r-1$. Suppose we have a schedule σ with makespan βT that achieves α rank approximation. Then, $\text{rank}_r(\sigma; \succ) \geq \frac{2^{r-1}m}{\alpha}$ for all $r = 1, \ldots, k$. Let s_r be the number of jobs assigned to their r-th ranked machine in σ, and t_r be the number of jobs of size at least $\frac{T}{2^{r-1}}$ assigned to their r-th ranked machine in σ. Observe that $t_r \geq s_r - \beta 2^k$ since the jobs counted in s_r but not in t_r lie in $\bigcup_{\ell=r+1}^{k} A^{(\ell)}$, all of which have machine r as their r-th ranked machine; at most $\beta 2^k$ such jobs can be accommodated within makespan βT. Now $\beta m T$ is at least the total size of all jobs scheduled by σ, which is at least $\sum_{r=1}^k (s_r - \beta 2^k) \cdot \frac{T}{2^{r-1}} \geq \sum_{r=1}^k s_r \cdot \frac{T}{2^{r-1}} - \beta 2^{k+1} T$. So

$$\begin{aligned} \beta(mT + 2^{k+1}T) &\geq \frac{1}{2} \sum_{r=1}^{k} s_r \sum_{\ell=r}^{k} \frac{T}{2^{\ell-1}} \\ &= \frac{1}{2} \sum_{\ell=1}^{k} \frac{T}{2^{\ell-1}} \sum_{r=1}^{\ell} s_r = \frac{1}{2} \sum_{\ell=1}^{k} \frac{T}{2^{\ell-1}} \cdot \text{rank}_\ell(\sigma; \succ) \\ &\geq \frac{1}{2} \sum_{\ell=1}^{k} \frac{T}{2^{\ell-1}} \cdot \frac{2^{\ell-1}m}{\alpha}. \end{aligned}$$

Taking $k = \log_2 m$, this gives $3\beta m T \geq \frac{kmT}{2\alpha}$, so $\alpha \geq \frac{k}{6\beta} = \Omega(\log m/\beta)$. Also, the number of jobs is at most $k \cdot 2^k = O(m \log m)$, so α is also $\Omega(\log n/\beta)$. ☐

Unrelated machines.

We obtain an $\big(O(\log n), O(1)\big)$ approximation for the general setting of unrelated machines.

THEOREM 5.4. *There is a deterministic $\big(O(\log n), O(1)\big)$ approximation algorithm for scheduling markets.*

PROOF. We will need Lemma 5.5 stated below. Fix an input $\succ$. We use a different kind of bucketing argument where we group ranks that have roughly the same value of $\text{maxrank}_r(\succ)$. For $r \in [m]$, let σ^r be the schedule given by Lemma 5.5 that yields a 2-approximation to $\text{maxrank}_r(\succ)$, N_r be the set of jobs assigned by σ_r, and $n_r = |N_r|$. We may assume that $n_1 \leq n_2 \leq \ldots n_m$. Define $n_0 = 0$. If $n_m = 0$, then $\text{maxrank}_r(\succ) = 0$ for all $r \in [m]$, and we return the null assignment. So assume otherwise in the sequel.

Define $r_0 := 0 < r_1 < r_2 < \ldots < r_k < r_{k+1} = m+1$ as follows: r_ℓ is the smallest r such that $n_r > 4n_{r_{\ell-1}}$ for $\ell = 1, \ldots, k$, and $n_m \leq 4n_{r_k}$. Thus, $k \leq \lceil \log_4 n \rceil$ and $n_{r_\ell} \leq n_r \leq 4n_{r_\ell}$ for all $r \in [r_\ell, r_{\ell+1})$ and all $\ell = 0, \ldots, k$. For $\ell \in [k]$, define $S_{r_\ell} := N_{r_\ell} \setminus (\bigcup_{q=1}^{\ell-1} N_{r_q})$; note that $|S_{r_\ell}| \geq \frac{2n_{r_\ell}}{3}$.

If $n_{r_k} < 2k$ for all r, we simply return the assignment σ^{r_1}. Clearly, this yields a $2k$ rank approximation. Otherwise, let q be the smallest index ℓ such that $n_{r_\ell} \geq 2k$. Let $S = \bigcup_{\ell=q}^k S_{r_\ell}$. Let σ be the schedule for S, where each job $j \in S_{r_\ell}$ is assigned to the machine $\sigma^{r_\ell}(j)$, for $\ell = q, \ldots, k$. Let $L_i := |\{j : \sigma(j) = i\}|$. Consider the following bipartite graph, which is similar to the bipartite graph constructed in the GAP-rounding algorithm [10]. We have a node for every job in S, and a node (i,c) for every machine i and $c = 1, \ldots, \left\lceil \frac{L_i}{k-q+1} \right\rceil$. We sort the jobs assigned to i in σ in non-increasing p_{ij} order (breaking ties arbitrarily), and create an edge $\big((i,c),j\big)$ if $\sigma(j) = i$ and its position in this ordering lies in $\{(c-1)(k-q+1)+1, \ldots, c(k-q+1)\}$. Let E be the edge-set of this bipartite graph. Consider the following polytope:

$$\begin{aligned} \mathcal{Q} := \Big\{ y \in \mathbb{R}^E : \quad & \sum_{j:((i,c),j) \in E} y_{(i,c),j} \leq 1 \\ & \forall i \in [m], c = 1, \ldots, \left\lceil \tfrac{L_i}{k-q+1} \right\rceil, \\ & \sum_{((i,c),j) \in E : j \in S_{r_\ell}} y_{(i,c),j} \geq \left\lfloor \frac{|S_{r_\ell}|}{k-q+1} \right\rfloor \\ & \forall \ell = q, \ldots, k, \\ & 0 \leq y_{(i,c),j} \leq 1 \quad \forall \big((i,c),j\big) \in E \Big\}. \end{aligned}$$

As with the polytope $\mathcal{P}$ (see Theorem 5.2), the constraint-matrix defining an extreme point of $\mathcal{Q}$ corresponds to equations coming from two laminar systems, which is TU, so $\mathcal{Q}$ has integral extreme points. Setting $x_{(i,c),j} = \frac{1}{k-q+1}$ for every edge $\big((i,c),j\big)$, note that $x \in \mathcal{Q}$. So we can find an integral $y \in \mathcal{Q}$, which we interchangeably view as a partial assignment of S. We return the schedule π obtained by concatenating σ^{r_1} with this assignment y.

The schedule σ^{r_1} has makespan at most T. By the standard GAP-rounding proof in [10], the makespan of y is at most

$$T + \tfrac{1}{k-q+1} \cdot \sum_{j:\sigma(j)=i} p_{ij} = T + \tfrac{1}{k-q+1} \cdot \sum_{\ell=q}^{k} \sum_{j \in S_{r_\ell} : \sigma^{r_\ell}(j)=i} p_{ij} \leq 2T.$$

So π has makespan at most $3T$. Fix some rank r. If $r < r_1$, then $\text{maxrank}_r(\succ) = 0$. If $r_1 \leq r < r_q$, we have $\text{rank}_r(\pi; \succ) \geq n_{r_1} \geq 1 > n_r/2k \geq \text{maxrank}_r(\succ)/4k$. Otherwise, suppose $r \in [r_\ell, r_{\ell+1})$, where $\ell \geq q$. Then $\text{rank}_r(\pi; \succ) \geq \left\lfloor \frac{|S_{r_\ell}|}{k} \right\rfloor \geq \left\lfloor \frac{2n_{r_\ell}}{3k} \right\rfloor \geq \frac{n_{r_\ell}}{3k}$, where the last inequality follows since $n_{r_\ell} \geq n_{r_q} \geq 2k$, and $\frac{n_{r_\ell}}{3k} \geq \frac{n_r}{12k} \geq \frac{\text{maxrank}_r(\succ)}{24k}$. So π has $O(k)$ rank approximation. ☐

LEMMA 5.5. *For any preference-profile $\succ$, any set $S \subseteq N$, and any rank r, one can efficiently compute a 2-approximation to* $\text{maxrank}_r(\succ_S)$.

PROOF. Shmoys and Tardos [10] proved the following result about GAP. Let $\{c_{ij}\}$ be "assignment costs" for assigning jobs to machines, *which could also be negative.* Consider the following LP, where i indexes the machines and j indexes the jobs.

$$\min \sum_{i,j} c_{ij}x_{ij} \qquad \text{(P)}$$

$$\text{s.t.} \quad \sum_i x_{ij} = 1 \quad \forall j \qquad (1)$$

$$\sum_j t_{ij}x_{ij} \leq L_i \quad \forall i$$

$$x_{ij} \geq 0 \quad \forall i,j$$

$$x_{ij} = 0 \quad \forall i,j \text{ s.t. } t_{ij} > L_i.$$

[10] showed that a fractional solution x to (P) can be rounded to an integer solution $\tilde{x}$ of cost at most the cost of x such that the total load $\sum_j t_{ij}\tilde{x}_{ij}$ on each machine i is at most $2L_i$. Examining their rounding algorithm more closely, one can infer that the total load on each machine i under $\tilde{x}$ is at most L_i if $\sum_j x_{ij} \leq 1$, and at most $L_i + \max_{j:x_{ij}>0} t_{ij}$ otherwise.

We apply this result to our problem of approximating $\text{maxrank}_r(\succ_S)$ as follows. The set of jobs is S. Our problem is a prize-collecting problem, which we can reduce to GAP by creating a "machine" I_j for every job $j \in S$ and setting $t_{I_j k} = 0$ if $k = j$ and ∞ otherwise. There is no makespan bound for these I_j machines. For every (regular) machine i and job j, we set $t_{ij} = p_{ij}$ if $\text{pos}(\succ_j, i) \leq r$ and ∞ otherwise; the makespan bound for i is T. Finally, our objective is to maximize the number of jobs assigned to the regular machines (with $t_{ij} < \infty$). In terms of the LP (P), constraint (1) now reads $\sum_i x_{ij} + z_j = 1$ for every $j \in S$, where z_j indicates if j is assigned to I_j, and the objective function is to maximize $\sum_i \sum_{j \in S} x_{ij}$.

Applying the GAP-rounding algorithm, we obtain an assignment $\tilde{x}$ with makespan at most $2T$ such that $\text{rank}_r(\tilde{x}; \succ_S) = \text{maxrank}_r(\succ_S)$. To turn this into a feasible schedule with makespan T, we leverage the stronger property of the rounding algorithm mentioned above. If the load on machine i under $\tilde{x}$ is more than T, then we know that i has at least two jobs assigned to it, and there is a job assigned to i whose removal decreases the load on i to at most T. We simply remove this job from every overloaded machine i. This reduces the number of jobs assigned to an overloaded machine i by a factor of at most 2 (since $\sum_j \tilde{x}_{ij} \geq 2$), so now we obtain a schedule with makespan T where the number of jobs assigned (to one of their top-r machines) is at least $\text{maxrank}_r(\succ_S)/2$. $\square$

6. MECHANISMS FOR GENERAL ORDINAL SETTINGS

In this section, we evaluate the strength and flexibility provided by the notions of rank approximation and lex-truthfulness in general ordinal settings. We devise an $O(\log n)$-rank-approximation randomized mechanism, and show that this guarantee is tight for randomized mechanisms (Theorems 6.2 and 6.3). We also observe that deterministic mechanisms cannot in general achieve good rank approximation. Next, we consider lex-truthfulness and justify our earlier remark that lex-truthfulness allows one to circumvent Gibbard's impossibility result. We describe a rich class of pseudomonotone SCFs called *top-choice SCFs*, which thus lead to (non-unilateral, non-duple) LT mechanisms.

Rank approximation.

It is easy to see that any deterministic dictatorial SCF has rank approximation (at most) n. Also, the *plurality scoring rule* f^{Pl}, which returns the outcome that maximizes the number of agents who have it as their top choice, has $\text{rank}_1(f^{\mathsf{Pl}}(\succ); \succ) \geq \frac{n}{m}$, so its rank-approximation factor is at most m. It is not hard to prove a matching lower bound for deterministic mechanisms.

THEOREM 6.1. *No deterministic mechanism can have rank approximation better factor than* $\min\{n, m-1\}$ *in general ordinal settings.*

PROOF. Consider a preference profile with n agents and $n+1$ outcomes, where the top choices of all agents are the distinct outcomes $\{1, \ldots, n\}$, while the second choice of all agents is $n+1$. $\square$

Randomization leads to an exponential improvement (but no more), but we do not know how to achieve this in a lex-truthful manner.

THEOREM 6.2. *There is a randomized* $O(\log n)$*-rank approximation mechanism for general ordinal settings.*

PROOF. We first describe the mechanism, and then analyze its rank approximation. Fix a preference profile $\succ$. For brevity, let $n_r = \text{maxrank}_r(\succ)$. Let o_r^* be an outcome with $\text{rank}_r(o_r^*; \succ) = n_r$. We use a bucketing argument where we group ranks that have roughly the same n_r value. Define $r_1 := 1 < r_2 < \ldots < r_k < r_{k+1} := m+1$ be such that $n_{r_\ell} \leq n_r \leq 2n_{r_\ell} \quad \forall r \in [r_\ell, r_{\ell+1}) \cap \mathbb{Z}$, for all $\ell = 1, \ldots, k$ Observe that $k \leq \lceil \log_2 n \rceil$. The mechanism chooses an index $\ell \in [k]$ uniformly at random, and outputs $o_{r_\ell}^*$.

To argue about the rank approximation, consider any rank r. Suppose $r \in [r_\ell, r_{\ell+1})$. If we choose index ℓ, which happens with probability $1/k$, then at least $\text{rank}_r(o_{r_\ell}^*; \succ) \geq \text{rank}_{r_\ell}(o_{r_\ell}^*; \succ) = n_{r_\ell} \geq \frac{n_r}{2}$ agents are allotted a top-r item. So $\mathbf{E}[\text{rank}_r(\mathcal{M}(\succ); \succ)] \geq \frac{n_r}{2k}$. $\square$

THEOREM 6.3. *Every randomized mechanism has rank approximation factor* $\Omega(\log n)$.

PROOF. Fix a parameter k. We construct an instance with $n = 2^{k+1} - 2$ agents and $m = (k-1) \cdot (2^{k+1} - 2) + k$ outcomes. The agents are divided into k groups $A_1, \ldots, A_k$, where $|A_\ell| = 2^\ell$. There are k special outcomes $\{o_1, \ldots, o_k\}$. The remaining $m - k$ outcomes are partitioned into n groups $O_1, \ldots, O_n$, each having $k-1$ outcomes. We now describe the preference lists. For every agent j in group A_ℓ, outcome o_ℓ is their ℓ-th ranked outcome, and the outcomes in O_j occupy the other positions in $[k] \setminus \{\ell\}$; the exact positions of these outcomes are irrelevant. The outcomes in positions $r \geq k+1$ are also immaterial. Thus, the top-k outcome sets of agents j and j' are: disjoint if they are from different groups, and have exactly one outcome, o_ℓ, in common, at the ℓ-th position, if they both belong to group A_ℓ. Let $\succ$ denote this input.

Observe that $\text{maxrank}_r(\succ) = 2^r$ for all $r \in [k]$, and the outcome achieving this is o_r. Furthermore, $\text{rank}_r(o)$ is 2^ℓ if $o = o_\ell$ for $\ell \in [r]$, and is at most 1 otherwise.

Now consider a randomized mechanism that attains rank approximation α. Let p_ℓ be the probability with which it returns the outcome o_ℓ. Let q be the probability with which it returns an outcome in $\bigcup_{j=1}^n O_j$. Then, by the definition of rank approximation we have $q+\sum_{\ell>r} p_r+\sum_{\ell\leq r} p_\ell \cdot 2^\ell \geq \alpha \cdot 2^r$ for all $r \in [k]$. Dividing this inequality by 2^r and summing over all $r = 1,\ldots,k$, we obtain that $k\alpha \leq q \cdot \sum_{r=1}^k \left(\frac{1}{2^r}\right) + \sum_{\ell=1}^k p_\ell \cdot \left(\sum_{r<\ell} \frac{1}{2^r} + \sum_{r\geq\ell} \frac{2^\ell}{2^r}\right) \leq q \cdot 1 + \sum_{\ell=1}^k p_\ell \cdot 3 \leq 3$. Hence, $\alpha \leq \frac{3}{k}$. □

Lex-truthful mechanisms.
Consider any SCF of the form $f(\succ) = g(\{\text{alt}(\succ_j, 1)\}_{j=1}^n)$, where $g : O^n \mapsto O$ has the following property: for all $o_{-j} = (o_1, \ldots, o_{j-1}, o_{j+1}, \ldots, o_n) \in O^{n-1}$ and all $o \in O$, if $g(o, o_{-j}) = o'$ then $g(o', o_{-j}) = o'$. We call such an SCF a *top-choice SCF* since it only looks at the top choices of the players. It is not hard to see that the plurality scoring rule f^{Pl} mentioned earlier (with a fixed tie-breaking rule for outcomes) is an example of such an SCF. We show that *any* top-choice SCF is pseudomonotone, and so by Theorem 3.3 is fully LT-implementable.

THEOREM 6.4. *Every top-choice SCF is pseudomonotone, and hence is fully LT-implementable.*

PROOF. Let f be a top-choice SCF defined by $g : O^n \mapsto O$ having the required property. Consider an agent j, and $\succ = (\succ_j, \succ_{-j})$, $\succ' = (\succ'_j, \succ_{-j})$. Let $o = \text{alt}(\succ_j, 1)$. If $f(\succ) = o$ or $f(\succ) = f(\succ')$, then we are done. Otherwise, since $f(\succ) \neq o$, we also have $f(\succ') \neq o$ due to the property of g, and also $\text{pos}(\succ'_j, o) > 1$ (otherwise $f(\succ) = f(\succ')$), and so the pseudomonotonicity condition (Definition 5) is satisfied. □

7. REFERENCES

[1] A. Abdulkadiroglu and T. Sönmez. Matching markets: Theory and practice. *Prepared for the Econometric Society World Congress, China*, 2010. Available at the first author's website.

[2] D. Abraham, R. Irving, T. Kavitha, and K. Melhorn. Popular matchings. *SIAM Journ. of Computing*, 37:1030 –1045, 2007.

[3] D. Abreu and A. Sen. Virtual implementation in Nash equilibrium. *Econometrica*, 59:997 – 1021, 1991.

[4] Kenneth Arrow. *Social Choice and Individual Values.* Yale University Press, 1951, 2nd ed 1963.

[5] H. Aziz, F. Brandt, and M. Brill. On the tradeoff between economic efficiency and strategyproofness in randomized social choice. In *Proceedings of the 12th international conference on Autonomous agents and multiagent systems (AAMAS)*, 2013.

[6] A. Bhalgat, D. Chakrabarty, and S. Khanna. Social welfare in one sided matching markets without money. In *LNCS Proceedings of Workshop on Approximation Algorithms for Combinatorial Optimization Problems (APPROX)*, 2011.

[7] A. Bogomolnaia and H. Moulin. A new solution to the random assignment problem. *Journal of Economic Theory*, 100:295 – 328, 2001.

[8] C. Boutilier, I. Caragiannis, S. Haber, T. Lu, A. D. Procaccia, and O. Sheffet. Optimal social choice functions: A utilitarian view. In *Proceedings of the 13th ACM Conference on Electronic Commerce (EC)*, 2012.

[9] D. Chakrabarty and C. Swamy. Welfare maximization and truthfulness in mechanism design with ordinal preferences. *CS arXiv*, `http://arxiv.org/abs/1312.1831`, December 2013.

[10] David B. Shmoys and Eva Tardos. An approximation algorithm for the generalized assignment problem. *Mathematical Programming*, 62:461–474, 1993.

[11] Marie-Jean-Antoine-Nicolas de Caritat de Marquis de Condorcet. Essay on the application of analysis to the probability of majority decisions., 1785.

[12] P. C. Fishburn. Probabilistic social choice based on simple voting comparisons. *Review of Economic Studies*, 51(167):683 – 692, 1984.

[13] P. Gardenfors. Match making: assignments based on bilateral preferences. *Behavioral Sciences*, 20:166 – 173, 1975.

[14] A. Gibbard. Manipulation of voting schemes: a general result. *Econometrica*, 41:587 – 601, 1973.

[15] A. Gibbard. Manipulation of schemes that mix voting with chance. *Econometrica*, 45(3):665 – 681, 1977.

[16] Chien-Chung Huang, Telikepalli Kavitha, Dimitrios Michail, and Meghana Nasre. Bounded unpopularity matchings. In *Proceedings of the 11th Scandinavian Workshop on Algorithm Theory*, 2008.

[17] T. Kavitha, J. Mestre, and M. Nasre. Popular mixed matchings. *Theoretical Computer Science*, Article in Press, 2010.

[18] G. Kreweras. Aggregation of preference orderings. In *Mathematics and Social Sciences I: Proceedings of the seminar on Menthon-Saint-Bernard, France and of Gosing, Austria*, pages 73 – 79, 1965.

[19] Mohammad Mahdian. Random popular matchings. In *Proceedings of the 7th ACM Conference on Electronic commerce*, 2006.

[20] H. Matsushima. A new approach to the implementation problem. *Journal of Economic Theory*, 45:128 – 144, 1988.

[21] A. Postlewaite and D. Schmeidler. Strategic behavior and a notion of ex ante efficiency in a voting model. *Soc. Choice and Welfare*, 3:37 – 49, 1986.

[22] A. D. Procaccia. Can approximation circumvent Gibbard-Satterwaithe? In *Proceedings of 24th AAAI Conference on Artificial Intelligence*, 2010.

[23] A. D. Procaccia and J. S. Rosenschein. The distortion of cardinal preferences in voting. In *Proceedings of 10th CIA, LNCS Series*, volume 4149, pages 317-331. Springer, 2006.

[24] A. E. Roth and M. Sotomayor. *Two-Sided Matching: A Study on Game- Theoretic Modelling.* Cambridge University Press, 1990.

[25] M. Satterthwaite. Strategy-proofness and Arrow's conditions: Existence and correspondence theorems for voting procedures and social welfare functions. *J. Econ. Theory*, 10:187 – 217, 1975.

[26] A. Schrijver. *Combinatorial Optimization.* Springer, New York, 2003.

[27] L. Shapley and H. Scarf. On cores and indivisibility. *Journal of Mathematical Economics.*, 1:23 – 28, 1974.

[28] T. Sönmez and U. Ünver. Matching, allocation, and exchange of discrete resources. *Handbook of Social*

Economics, forthcoming, available at second author's website.

[29] H. P. Young. Social choice scoring functions. *SIAM J. Appl. Math.*, 28(4):824–838, 1975.

APPENDIX

A. PROOFS OMITTED FROM SECTION 3

Proof of Theorem 3.2. Clearly UnivT $\subseteq$ StrongT. If $\mathbf{p}$ stochastically dominates $\mathbf{q}$, then $\mathbf{p}$ lex-dominates $\mathbf{q}$, so StrongT $\subseteq$ LexT. If $\mathbf{p}$ lex-dominates $\mathbf{q}$, then $\mathbf{q}$ cannot stochastically dominate $\mathbf{p}$, so LexT $\subseteq$ WeakT. We now prove that the various inclusions are strict.

UnivT $\subsetneq$ StrongT. Fix a player j. Consider the unilateral mechanism $\mathcal{M}$ that returns one of the top 2 outcomes of j, each with probability $\frac{1}{2}$. $\mathcal{M}$ is clearly strongly truthful. But it is not universally truthful. Consider some input $\succ = (\succ_j, \succ_{-j})$. If $\mathcal{M}$ is a mixture of deterministic truthful mechanisms, then this mixture must assign a probability mass exactly $\frac{1}{2}$ to deterministic truthful mechanisms $\mathcal{M}_1$ satisfying $\mathcal{M}_1(\succ) = o = \text{alt}(\succ_j, 1)$; call these type-1 mechanisms. Similarly, it must assign probability mass exactly $\frac{1}{2}$ to deterministic truthful mechanisms $\mathcal{M}_2$ satisfying $\mathcal{M}_2(\succ) = o' = \text{alt}(\succ_j, 2)$; call these type-2 mechanisms.

For any preference list $\succ_j^*$, a type-2 mechanism cannot return o under the input $(\succ_j^*, \succ_{-j})$ due to truthfulness, otherwise on input $\succ$, j has an incentive to lie in the type-2 mechanism and report $\succ_j^*$. Hence, for any preference list $\succ_j^*$, where o is one of the top two outcomes, *every* type-1 mechanism must return o on input $(\succ_j^*, \succ_{-j})$. A symmetric argument shows that for any preference list $\succ_j^*$ where o' is one of the top two outcomes, every type-2 mechanism must return o' on input $(\succ_j^*, \succ_{-j})$.

Now consider some $\succ'_j$, where the top two outcomes are $o'', \hat{o} \notin \{o, o'\}$. Applying the arguments above we obtain that there are type-3 and type-4 deterministic truthful mechanisms, both of which are assigned probability mass $\frac{1}{2}$ (in the mixture yielding $\mathcal{M}$): the type-3 mechanisms which always return o'' whenever j's preference list has o'' as one of the top two outcomes, and the type-4 mechanisms always return $\hat{o}$ whenever j's preference list has $\hat{o}$ as one of the top two outcomes.

Now some mechanism $\mathcal{M}'$ in the mixture yielding $\mathcal{M}$, must be of multiple types, say type-1 and type-3 for illustration. Then, if $\succ''_j$ has o and o'' as the top two outcomes of j, $\mathcal{M}'$ must return both o and o'' on input $(\succ''_j, \succ_{-j})$, which cannot happen.

StrongT $\subsetneq$ LexT. Consider a setting with one player and three outcomes: a, b, c. Consider the top-choice SCF f defined by the following function: $g(a) = a$, $g(b) = g(c) = c$, which satisfies the property required for f to be a top-choice SCF. By Theorem 6.4, f is pseudomonotone. Let $\mathcal{M}$ be the LT mechanism that $\frac{1}{3}$-implements f. Let $\succ = (b, a, c)$ denoting that b is top-outcome, and $\succ' = (a, b, c)$. Let $\mathbf{p} = \mathcal{M}(\succ)$ and $\mathbf{q} = \mathcal{M}(\succ')$. Then $\mathbf{p}(b) + \mathbf{p}(a) \leq \frac{1}{3}$ since $f(\succ) = g(b) = c$, but $\mathbf{q}(b) + \mathbf{q}(a) \geq \frac{2}{3}$ since $f(\succ') = g(a) = a$. Thus, $\mathcal{M}$ is not strongly truthful.

LexT $\subsetneq$ WeakT. Consider a setting with one player and four outcomes: a, b, c, d. Let $\succ^* = (a, b, c, d)$, denoting that a is the top outcome. Define the following randomized mechanism $\mathcal{M}$: $\mathcal{M}(\succ^*)$ returns a with probability $\frac{1}{2}$ and b, c, d with probability $\frac{1}{6}$; on every other input $\succ$, $\mathcal{M}$ returns one of the top three outcomes of $\succ$ with probability $\frac{1}{3}$. $\mathcal{M}$ is weakly truthful, because if $\succ \neq \succ^*$ then $\mathcal{M}$ assigns total probability 1 to the top three outcomes of $\succ$. If $\succ = \succ^*$, then $\mathcal{M}$ assigns probability $\frac{1}{2}$ to the top outcome a under $\succ^*$, whereas for every other input $\mathcal{M}$ assigns probability at most $\frac{1}{3}$ to a.

But $\mathcal{M}$ is not lex-truthful: if $\succ = (a, b, d, c)$, then by reporting (a, b, c, d), the player can increase the probability of his top-outcome a from $\frac{1}{3}$ to $\frac{1}{2}$. □

Proof of Theorem 3.4. We mimic the proof of Theorem 3.3. For all j, and all $r \in [m_j]$, fix some outcome $o_r^j \in O_r^j$ form the indifference class O_r^j of agent j.

We prove part (i) first. Our randomized mechanism $\mathcal{M}$ does the following. On input $\succeq$, it returns $f(\succeq)$ with probability $(1 - \varepsilon)$; with probability ε, it picks a random agent a and returns outcome o_r^a with probability $\varepsilon_r^a / \varepsilon$, where $\varepsilon_1^a > \cdots > \varepsilon_{m_a}^a > 0$ are such that $\sum_{r=1}^{m_a} \varepsilon_r^a = \varepsilon$.

Clearly, $\mathcal{M}$ ε-implements f. To prove lex-truthfulness, fix an agent j and consider any $\succeq' = (\succeq'_j, \succeq_{-j})$, where $\succeq'_j \neq \succeq_j$. Let $o = f(\succeq)$ and let $o' = f(\succeq')$. Let $O_{t_1}^j$ and $O_{t_2}^j$ be the indifference classes of j containing outcomes o and o' respectively. Also, let $\mathbf{p} = \mathcal{M}(\succeq)$, $\mathbf{q} = \mathcal{M}(\succeq')$.

Considering indifference classes in the preference order of $\succeq_j$, let O_r^j be the first indifference class such that $\text{pos}(\succeq_j, o_r^j) < \text{pos}(\succeq'_j, o_r^j)$. Let $o'' = o_r^j$. By pseudomonotonicity of f, we know that $o \succeq_j o'$ or $o'' \succ_j o'$. In the latter case, we have $\mathbf{p}(O_t^j) - \mathbf{q}(O_t^j) \geq 0$ for all t such that $o_t^j \succeq_j o''$, and $\mathbf{p}(O_r^j) - \mathbf{q}(O_r^j) > 0$, so we are done.

If $o \succeq_j o'$, and $O_{t_1}^j = O_{t_2}^j$ or $o'' \succeq_j o$, then the above argument still holds. So suppose $o \succ_j o'$ and $o \succ_j o''$. Then $\mathbf{p}(O_t^j) - \mathbf{q}(O_t^j) \geq 0$ for all t such that $o_t^j \succeq_j o$ and $\mathbf{p}(O_{t_1}^j) - \mathbf{q}(O_{t_1}^j) > 0$, so again we are done.

Now consider part (ii). Let $\mathcal{M}$ be an LT mechanism that ε-LT implements f, where $\varepsilon < \frac{1}{2}$. Suppose for a contradiction, there is some agent j, and $\succeq = (\succeq_j, \succeq_{-j})$ and $\succeq' = (\succ'_j, \succeq_{-j})$ such that $o = f(\succ)$ and $o' = f(\succ')$ violate the conditions for pseudomonotonicity. Then we have $o' \succ_j o$ and for every outcome $o'' \succ_j o'$, we have $\text{pos}(\succ_j, o'') = \text{pos}(\succ'_j, o'')$. Let $O_{t_1}^j$ and $O_{t_2}^j$ be the indifference classes of j containing outcomes o and o' respectively. Let $\mathbf{p} = \mathcal{M}(\succeq)$ and $\mathbf{q} = \mathcal{M}(\succeq')$.

Since $\mathcal{M}$ ε-LT implements f, we have $\mathbf{p}(O_{t_2}^j) \leq \varepsilon$ and $\mathbf{q}(O_{t_2}^j) \geq \mathbf{q}(o') \geq 1 - \varepsilon$, so $\mathbf{p}(O_{t_2}^j) < \mathbf{q}(O_{t_2}^j)$. Let $O_{r_1}^j, \ldots, O_{r_\ell}^j$ be the indifference classes of j that are ranked higher than $O_{t_2}^j$ under $\succeq_j$, ordered so that $o_{r_1}^j \succ_j o_{r_2}^j \succ_j \cdots \succ_j o_{r_\ell}^j$. Since $\text{pos}(\succ_j, o'') = \text{pos}(\succ'_j, o'')$ for all $o'' \succ_j o'$, $O_{r_1}^j, \ldots, O_{r_\ell}^j$ are also the indifference class of j that are ranked higher than $O_{t_2}^j$ under $\succeq'_j$, and we have $o_{r_1}^j \succ'_j o_{r_2}^j \succ'_j \cdots \succ'_j o_{r_\ell}^j$. As in the proof of Theorem 3.3, this implies that $\mathbf{p}(O_{r_t}^j) = \mathbf{q}(O_{r_t}^j)$ for all $t = 1, \ldots, \ell$, which contradicts the fact that $\mathcal{M}$ is lex-truthful. □

B. QUALITY OF KNOWN MECHANISMS FOR MATCHING MARKETS

In this section, we investigate the rank approximation and lex-truthfulness of three extensively studied mechanisms for matching markets. These are *random serial dictatorship* mechanism (RSD), Gale's *top-trading-cycle algorithm* (TTCA), and the *probabilistic serial* mechanism (PS).

Random Serial Dictatorship.

Initially all items are marked unallocated. A random permutation of agents is sampled and the agents are considered according to this order. Each agent is allocated his best item among the unallocated items. This item henceforth is marked allocated.

Top Trading Cycle.

This appears in a paper by Shapley and Shubik [27] who attributed it to David Gale and is applicable when the number of items equals the number of agents.

The algorithm starts with an arbitrary assignment σ of agents to items. This assignment, which is called the initial endowment of agents, is independent of the preference orders of the agents. Subsequently, the agents will *trade* among themselves to return the final allocation.

The algorithm then proceeds in rounds. Initially all agents are marked active. In each round, one constructs a directed graph with the active agents as nodes. There is an arc from agent j to agent j', if the item $\sigma(j')$ is the top choice of agent j among the items owned by the active agents, that is, the set $\{\sigma(j) : j \text{ active }\}$. Note that each agent has out-degree exactly 1 (self loops are allowed and counted as both out and in degree). Therefore, there exists at least one directed cycle in the graph. A cycle (self loops are also cycles) is picked arbitrarily. For each arc (j, j') in the cycle, we allocate agents j the item $\sigma(j')$. We mark all agents in this cycle inactive and proceed to the next round. The algorithm stops when all agents are marked inactive.

Probabilistic Serial.

This algorithm is due to Bogomolnaia and Moulin [7]. We first describe the algorithm when the number of agents equals the number of items.

The algorithm first finds a *fractional matching*, that is, x_{ij}'s for items i and agents j such that each $x_{ij} \geq 0$ and $\sum_{i \in I} x_{ij} = 1$ for all agents j, and $\sum_{j \in A} x_{ij} = 1$ for all items i. By the Birkhoff-von Neumann theorem, we can find a distribution on matchings such that the probability agent j is allocated item i is exactly x_{ij}. This is the distribution returned by the algorithm.

The algorithm proceeds in rounds. Initially all x_{ij}'s are 0. For any item i, we denote its capacity as $\sum_{j \in A} x_{ij}$. Any item with capacity strictly < 1 is called unallocated. In each round, every agent points to the best item among the unallocated items. For each unallocated item i we simultaneously raise the x_{ij} for agents j which point to item i at the *same* rate. This continues till some unallocated item's capacity becomes 1. At this point we end the round and proceed to the next round. The algorithm terminates when all items are allocated. Since the procedure maintains that $\sum_{i \in I} x_{ij}$ is same for agents always, at the end we end up with a fractional matching.

A lot of literature exists on all three mechanisms; we point the reader to surveys [28, 1] for a detailed reference. Before stating the rank approximations and lex truthfulness, let us mention some relevant known facts. RSD is strongly truthful (in fact, it is universally truthful). TTCA is the only deterministic algorithm among the three. It is known that for *any* initial endowment, the algorithm is truthful [27]. PS is known to be weakly truthful and not strongly truthful [7]. Bhalgat et al [6] proved that the ordinal welfare factor (cf. Section 1.2) of RS and PSD are 1/2, which is the best possible. The OWF of TTCA is $1/n$ since it is deterministic.

Rank Approximations of RSD, TTCA, and PS.

We show that all three mechanisms have 'bad' rank approximation. Rank approximation of TTCA is at least $(n-1)$, while RSD and PS have rank approximation of $\Omega(\sqrt{n})$. Recall that MaxMatch has rank approximation 2.

We know that TTCA is deterministic and truthful. It is also non-bossy; if an agent changes his preference but still gets the same item, it implies that in the round when he gets allocated an item, the cycle is the same as before, since no other changes preferences. Therefore from Theorem 4.3, we get the rank apporximation is at least $(n-1)$.

Consider an instance $\succ$ with n agents and n items with preference lists as follows. Let $k = \lceil\sqrt{n}\rceil$. Agents $1 \leq i \leq k$ have item i as their top choice. Agents $k+1 \leq i \leq n$ have item n as their top choice. These agents are now grouped into k groups $G_1, \ldots, G_k$, each group containing $n/k - 1$ agents. Agents in group G_ℓ have item ℓ as their second choice. All the other choices of all agents is immaterial and can be assumed to be arbitrary. Observe that $\text{maxrank}_1(\succ) = k+1$.

Let's first take RSD and calculate the expected number of agents who get their top choice. With $1 - k/n$ probability, an agent $k+1 \leq j \leq n$ shows up as the first agent; he picks item n. No other agent $k+1 \leq j \leq n$ gets his top choice. Henceforth, for any $1 \leq \ell \leq k$, the probability that a guy in G_ℓ shows up before agent ℓ is at least $1 - \frac{2k}{n}$. If that occurs, then agent ℓ doesn't get his top choice. Therefore, the expected number of agents getting their top choice is at most $1 + 2k^2/n + o(n)$. Thus, setting $k = \Theta(\sqrt{n})$, the rank approximation is $\Omega(\sqrt{n})$.

In PS, the calculation is easier. For $1 \leq \ell \leq k$, we get $x_{\ell\ell} = \frac{1}{n-k} + \frac{k}{n}\left(1 - \frac{1}{n-k}\right) = \frac{k-1}{n}$. For agent $k+1 \leq \ell \leq n$, we get $x_{n\ell} = \frac{1}{n-k}$. Therefore, the expected number of agents getting their top choice in PS is precisely $1 + \frac{k(k-1)}{n}$. Setting $k = \Theta(\sqrt{n})$, we get that the rank approximation is $\Omega(\sqrt{n})$.

We do not know if the rank approximation for RSD and PS is $\Theta(\sqrt{n})$ or not.

Lex-Truthfulness of RSD, TTCA, and PS.

TTCA is truthful and RSD is universally truthful. Therefore, they are lex-truthful as well. PS was shown to be weakly truthful by [7]. We show that in fact PS is lex-truthful as well. The proof below is akin to the proof of weak truthfulness in [7] mentioned above; we include it for completeness.

THEOREM B.1. *PS is lex-truthful.*

PROOF. Consider any preference profile $\succ$. By renaming items we may assume $\succ_j = (1, 2, \ldots, n)$ for some agent j. Suppose agent j misreports his preference as $\succ'_j \neq \succ_j$, and let $\succ' := (\succ'_j, \succ_{-j})$. Let k be the first position at which $\succ_j$ and $\succ'_j$ differ. That is, for $r < k$, $\text{alt}(\succ'_j, r) = \text{alt}(\succ_j, r) = r$. Note that j has 'demoted' k in the misreported preference, that is, $\text{pos}(\succ'_j, k) > k$. Let $\mathbf{p}$ and $\mathbf{q}$ be the distributions over items that j obtains on reporting $\succ_j$ and $\succ'_j$ respectively. Let x and x' be the respective fractional matchings.

Observe that since PS has a notion of time (since x_{ij}'s are incremented at a certain rate), we can define $x(t)$ as the assignment at time t. So $x(0) \equiv 0$. Let $t_0 \geq 0$ be the time till which we have $x(t_0) \equiv x'(t_0)$. If t_0 is ill defined, then $x \equiv x'$ and so $\mathbf{p} \equiv \mathbf{q}$ and there's nothing to prove. We must have that till time t_0, agent j points to the same items in both runs, and right after that instant agent j points to different items in the two runs. Say at t_0, agent j pointed to item k in the original run, and k' in the new run. Observe that all items $r < k$ have been completely allocated in both runs since j is pointing to k in the original run. Thus, $\mathbf{p}(r) = \mathbf{q}(r)$ for $r < k$ since $x(t_0) \equiv x'(t_0)$.

We claim $\mathbf{p}(k) > \mathbf{q}(k)$. This will show $\mathbf{p}$ lexicographically dominates $\mathbf{q}$. To do so, we need to introduce some notation. Let t^* and t' be the times at which k is completely allocated in the original and new run respectively. Let t_1 be the time at which j points to k in the new run. Observe $t_0 < t_1 \leq t'$. Also observe that $x_{jk} = t^* - t_0$ and $x'_{jk} = t' - t_1$.

Now, if $t' \leq t^*$, we get $x_{jk} > x'_{jk}$, and we are done. So we may assume $t' > t^*$. For $t \geq t_0$, let $S(t,k)$ and $S'(t,k)$ be the set of agents pointing to item k at time t. Observe that PS satisfies the following monotonicity condition: if an agent points to an item at time t, then he continues to do so till the item is fully allocated. Using this, one can prove the following claim; we defer the proof to the end.

Claim B.2. *For all* $t_0 \leq t < t_1$, $|S'(t,k)| \geq |S(t,k)| - 1$, *for* $t_1 \leq t < t^*$, $|S'(t,k)| \geq |S(t,k)|$, *and for* $t^* \leq t < t'$, $|S'(t,k)| \geq |S(t^*,k)|$.

Using the claim, we now show $x_{jk} > x'_{jk}$. Let C denote the capacity of item k at time t_0. We know that $C < 1$. Now, from the run of PS we get

$$\int_{t_0}^{t^*} |S(t,k)|dt = (1 - C) = \int_{t_0}^{t'} |S'(t,k)|dt \quad (2)$$

Using the claim above and rearranging, we get

$$t_0 - t_1 \leq -\int_{t^*}^{t'} |S(t^*,k)|dt$$

Now suppose $|S(t^*,k)| = 1$, that is, in the original run only one guy points to item k. This must be agent j. This implies $|S(t,k)| = 0$ for $t < t_0$, the time at which j points to k. In particular, we get $C = 0$, and thus $x_{jk} = 1$. We know that $x'_{jk'} > 0$ since j points to $k' \neq k$ in the new run. Therefore, $x'_{jk} < 1$ since $\sum_{k \in I} x_{jk} = 1$. Thus, we may assume $|S(t^*,k)| > 1$, which implies that $t_0 - t_1 < -(t' - t^*)$. Thus,

$$x'_{jk} = t' - t_1 < t^* - t_0 = x_{jk}$$

Proof of Claim B.2. (Sketch) In fact, we claim that for every item $i \neq k$, the subset $S(t,i) \subseteq S'(t,i)$ for $t_0 \leq t < t'$. This can be proved by induction. Suppose the claim is true at some time; it is true at time t_0. The next interesting time t is when some item is i is completely allocated in one of the runs. By our assumption, this time t occurs in the new run since $S'(t,i) \geq S(t,i)$ for $i \neq k$. At this point the agents pointing to i point to different items increasing their corresponding $S'(t,\cdot)$s. The same occurs in the original run albeit at a later time say t''; however, by monotonicity property $S'(t'',i) \supseteq S'(t,i)$, and therefore $|S'(t'',i)| \geq |S(t'',i)|$. For the item k, note that the above argument implies $|S'(t,i) \setminus k| \geq |S(t,i) \setminus k|$, and then after t_1, j enters $S'(t,k)$ as well. □

Coordination Mechanisms from (almost) all Scheduling Policies*

Sayan Bhattacharya[†]
Max Plank Institute for Informatics
Saarbrucken, Germany
bsayan@mpi-inf.mpg.de

Sungjin Im[‡]
EECS
University of California
Merced, CA 95344
sim3@ucmerced.edu

Janardhan Kulkarni
Dept. of Computer Science
Durham, NC 27708
kulkarni@cs.duke.edu

Kamesh Munagala
Dept. of Computer Science
Durham, NC 27708
kamesh@cs.duke.edu

ABSTRACT

We study the *price of anarchy* of coordination mechanisms for a scheduling problem where each job j has a weight w_j, processing time p_{ij}, assignment cost h_{ij}, and communication delay (or release date) r_{ij} on machine i. Each machine is free to declare its own scheduling policy. Each job is a selfish agent and selects a machine that minimizes its own disutility, which is equal to its weighted completion time plus its assignment cost. The goal is to minimize the total disutility incurred by all the jobs. Our model is general enough to capture scheduling jobs in a distributed environment with heterogeneous machines (or data centers) that are situated across different locations.

Our main result is a *characterization* of scheduling policies that give a small (robust) Price of Anarchy. More precisely, we show that whenever each machine independently declares any scheduling policy that satisfies a certain *bounded stretch* condition introduced in this paper, the game induced between the jobs has a small Price of Anarchy. Our characterization is powerful enough to test almost all popular scheduling policies. On the technical side, to derive our results, we use a potential function whose derivative leads to an instantaneous smoothness condition, and linear programming and dual fitting. To the best of our knowledge, this is a novel application of these techniques in the context of coordination mechanisms, and we believe these tools will find more applications in analyzing PoA of games. We also extend our results to the ℓ_k-norms and ℓ_∞ norm (makespan) objectives.

*This work is supported by Munagala's Alfred P. Sloan Research Fellowship, an award from Cisco, and by NSF grants CCF-0745761, CCF-1008065, and IIS-0964560.

[†]Work done while the author was in Duke University.

[‡]Work done while the author was in Duke University.

ITCS'14, January 12–14, 2014, Princeton, New Jersey, USA.
Copyright 2014 ACM 978-1-4503-2698-8/14/01 ...$15.00.
http://dx.doi.org/10.1145/2554797.2554811 .

1. INTRODUCTION

Explosive growth of data has driven distributed computing to evolve at an unprecedented pace. In modern distributed systems, there are a large number of machines which are clustered and connected in a variety of topologies, and situated across different geographical locations. Hence routing jobs can incur considerable costs and communication delays. Machines are also inherently heterogeneous, having very different architectures and accesses to energy resources – some machines can process some jobs more efficiently and at cheaper costs. Due to the large scale of such systems, centralized algorithms for scheduling jobs is not very practical. Moreover, in many scenarios each job is a selfish agent that strategically selects a machine for getting processed. Can such a decentralized system perform well in spite of the strategic behaviors of the jobs? We explore this question under a mechanism design paradigm called *coordination mechanisms* [8].

1.1 Model

There is a set $\mathcal{J}$ of n jobs, and a set $\mathcal{M}$ of m unrelated machines. A job j has a weight w_j, and it needs p_{ij} units of *processing time* if scheduled on machine i – our analysis can be easily extended to unrelated weights w_{ij}. The job j has a *communication delay* (or *release date*) r_{ij} on machine i, i.e, the machine can start processing the job only after time r_{ij}. Further, the job j incurs an *assignment cost* h_{ij} if it is assigned to the machine i. This, for example, captures the energy costs.

In a sharp contrast with the centralized view of classical scheduling models, here each job is a self-interested and autonomous agent free to select its own machine. Every machine declares its scheduling policy in advance, and this induces a *simultaneous-move* game between the jobs. The strategy of a job consists of choosing the machine where it will get processed. Each job wants to minimize its own *disutility*, which is its weighted completion time plus its assignment cost. A Nash equilibrium of this game is a stable outcome where no job can reduce its disutility by switching to another machine. The strategic interactions among the jobs may lead to overall degradation in system performance. The standard benchmark to measure this deterioration is the Price of Anarchy (PoA), first introduced in [18]. This is the worst case (maximum possible) ratio of total disutility of the jobs in a Nash Equilibrium to that in an optimal solution (which assumes centralized assignment and no strategic behavior).

We let different machines declare different scheduling policies. Each of these policies, however, must be *strongly local*: each machine i only knows the w_j, p_{ij}, r_{ij}, and h_{ij} values of the jobs j that were assigned to it, but is not aware of the characteristics (processing lengths, release dates etc.) of the jobs on other machines. In the absence of a global view of the input, a reasonable option for a machine is to declare a scheduling policy that (approximately) minimizes its own share of the objective, namely, the total weighted completion time of all the jobs assigned to it. This raises a compelling question:

- *Do all scheduling policies that are $O(1)$-approximate on a single machine result in coordination mechanisms with $O(1)$ price of anarchy? If the answer is no, is there a characterization of single-machine scheduling policies that induce $O(1)$ price of anarchy?*

1.2 Our Results

In this paper, we present a general recipe for designing coordination mechanisms for minimizing the total weighted completion time of the jobs plus their assignment costs. The machines need not agree upon a specific scheduling policy. Nevertheless, the system will have small constant price of anarchy as long as every machine selects a scheduling policy that satisfies a certain *bounded stretch* condition introduced in this paper (see Sections 1.2.1,1.2.2). We further show that almost all scheduling policies used in practice satisfy this condition. We complement this positive result by showing that there exists a widely used $O(1)$-approximate single-machine scheduling policy that does not satisfy the bounded stretch condition, *and* induces a game with large price of anarchy. Finally, we extend our results to *all norms* of completion times of the jobs (see Section 1.2.3), and present a general black box reduction to *non-preemptive* scheduling policies (see Section 1.2.4).

All the previous works on coordination mechanisms for completion time scheduling [10, 9] focused on the case without communication delays (release dates) and assignment costs, i.e., $r_{ij} = h_{ij} = 0$. We note that release dates introduce a significant complexity in scheduling, and algorithms for problems without release dates typically do not generalize to those with release dates. For example, the underlying optimization problem on a single machine is polynomial time solvable via a greedy algorithm without release dates, but is NP-HARD with release dates [23]. Furthermore, the previous works [10, 9] analyze very specific scheduling policies, and restrict all machines to announce the same scheduling policy. In contrast, we give a new dimension to the problem by allowing different machines to declare different scheduling policies. This generalization models the real world applications more accurately, since the machines (or data centers) are typically owned and operated by different entities.

Our results rely upon two novel techniques. (a) A potential function that leads to an instantaneous *smoothness* condition; and (b) Linear programming and dual fitting.

1.2.1 *Characterization of Good Single-machine Scheduling Policies*

We introduce the notion of a scheduling policy with *bounded stretch* in the definition given below. We note that our notion of stretch is different from the standard definition of stretch used in scheduling literature.

DEFINITION 1. *Suppose that a machine is processing a given set of jobs. The scheduling policy followed by the machine has a stretch α iff the completion time C_j of each job j (with weight w_j, release date r_j, and processing time p_j) satisfies the inequality:*

$$C_j \leq r_j + p_j + \sum_{j' \neq j : C_{j'} \geq r_j} \alpha \cdot \min\left(p_{j'}, (w_{j'}/w_j) \cdot p_j\right)$$

To understand the above definition, assume for a while that all the jobs have unit weight, and note that the total *delay* encountered by a job j is equal to $C_j - (r_j + p_j)$. What should be a reasonable upper bound on the contribution (say $\eta_{j'}$) of some specific job $j' \neq j$ towards this delay $C_j - (r_j + p_j)$? Without any loss of generality, we can assume that the job j' completes after the release date of the job j, i.e. $C_{j'} \geq r_j$; otherwise $\eta_{j'}$ is zero. The α-stretch condition says that $\eta_{j'}$ can be at most α times $\min(p_j, p_{j'})$. Note that the job j' can delay the job j when it gets processed with a higher priority, and this can happen for an amount of time equal to the job j''s size, which is $p_{j'}$. Further, the α-stretch condition requires that the policy is fair to both the jobs and hence the bound $\alpha \cdot \min(p_j, p_{j'})$. Finally, the weights of the jobs are also factored in.

Our notion of 'bounded stretch' is closely related to the concepts of 'slowdown' and 'liability' considered in the work [19]. In [19], the slowdown of a job is defined as its 'flowtime' $(C_j - r_j)$ divided by its processing length p_j. Furthermore, the liability of a job is the worst possible slowdown it can experience. The goal is to design 'fair' scheduling policies where the liability of every job j is bounded by the size of the machine's queue, and in particular, is independent of the processing lengths of other jobs. For example, if all the jobs have unit weights and are released at time $t = 0$, then in any scheduling policy with stretch α the liability of every job is at most $(1 + \alpha n)$, where n is the number of jobs assigned to the machine.

This seemingly simple characterization turns out to be quite powerful. In Appendix A, we describe many scheduling policies that are used in practice, and most of these policies have bounded stretch.

THEOREM 1. *The scheduling policies – Highest Density First, Highest Residual Density First, Weighted Round Robin, and Weighted Shortest Elapsed Time First – all have stretch $\alpha = 1$.*

The reader may find it helpful to compare Definition 1 with the definition of the Weighted Round Robin (WRR) scheduling policy (see Appendix A). An important distinction between the two definitions is that the stretch condition does not specify a scheduling policy but is only concerned with the *final* completion times of the jobs. On the other hand, the scheduling policies with bounded stretch behave similar to WRR, in the sense that each job delays another job by at most α times it own processing length. This provides an intuitive explanation as to why such policies should lead to equilibria with small PoA.

1.2.2 Price of Anarchy Bounds for Coordination Mechanisms

With the above definition of bounded stretch, we prove the following general result.

THEOREM 2. *Suppose that each machine declares a (possibly different) scheduling policy with stretch α. Then the resulting game has a robust (smooth) price of anarchy of at most*

$$\frac{1+\alpha(\sqrt{\alpha^2+1}+\alpha)}{1-\alpha(\sqrt{\alpha^2+1}-\alpha)} \leq 4\alpha^2+2\alpha = O(\alpha^2)$$

Particularly when $\alpha = 1$, the bound is at most 5.8284, and this holds for many popular scheduling policies.

The interesting aspect of the above result is the analysis. We present two analysis techniques which yield somewhat different bounds - potential functions and dual fitting. Conceptually, our techniques are inspired by the elegant work on online scheduling [7, 1, 15] – the connection being that in both cases, we need to compare the decisions made by the optimal solution (that is non-strategic and omniscient) with the solution that arises due to the execution of the implemented policy. However, the similarity ends there - unlike online algorithms, in a coordination game, a job is selfish and cannot be forced to go to a specific machine and hence equilibrium state cannot be controlled by an algorithm. Moreover, a game can have multiple equilibria, and the analysis should hold for all them simultaneously.

Potential Functions. Our first technique uses a smoothness argument (see Section 2) via a carefully constructed *potential function* (see Section 3). The difficulty in a direct smoothness argument is that we have to compare the execution of two policies that make decisions over time, and these decisions could be very divergent. Note that unlike the case without release dates [10], we cannot write closed form expressions for the completion time induced by specific policies. Instead, we show that the *derivative* of the potential function (w.r.t. time) gives an *instantaneous* smoothness inequality that is easy to compute. We then integrate this inequality over time to derive the final smoothness bound. To our knowledge, this type of approach inspired by online algorithms has not been used before in the context of price of anarchy.

Dual Fitting. (See Section 4.) Consider the optimization problem underlying our game-theoretic framework, where the goal is to minimize the total weighted completion time of the jobs plus their assignment costs. We write a time-indexed LP-relaxation of the problem, similar to the one in [1]. Using the dual of this LP, we bound the price of anarchy of the game induced between the jobs, when every machine declares a scheduling policy satisfying certain natural conditions (see Section 4). The idea is to take any Nash equilibrium of the game, and appropriately charge the disutility of each job to the dual variables in a way such that (a) all the dual constraints are satisfied, and (b) the dual objective is at least η times the total disutility incurred by all the jobs in the Nash equilibrium, for some $\eta \in (0, 1]$. This shows that the price of anarchy is at most $1/\eta$ due to weak duality.

In contrast to a potential function based argument, one apparent drawback of the dual-fitting framework is that for technical reasons we need to impose two restrictions on the allowable class of scheduling policies in addition to the bounded stretch condition. These restrictions, however, are fairly intuitive. We are not aware of any simple, combinatorial scheduling policy with bounded stretch that violates the additional assumptions required in the dual-fitting proof. Further, unlike the potential function analysis, the dual-fitting proof only bounds the price of anarchy of pure, mixed Nash and correlated equilibria, and at present we do not see any way to extend the proof to get a robust (smooth) price of anarchy bound which, in addition to these three solution concepts, also applies to no regret sequences [20].

Nevertheless, we feel the dual-fitting framework is interesting in its own right, as it establishes a connection between the price of anarchy of a coordination mechanism and the LP relaxation of the underlying optimization problem. Further, it yields the following improved theorem:

THEOREM 3. *The price of anarchy (of pure, mixed, and correlated equilibria) of the Highest Density First scheduling policy (see Appendix A for definition) is at most 4.*

This matches the lower bound [10] known for non-preemptive scheduling policies when there are no release dates and assignment costs – note that Highest Density First is a non-preemptive policy in the absence of release dates. The dual-fitting approach also helps us compare against an optimal migratory solution where a job is processed over multiple machines. To our knowledge, this type of approach to bound the price of anarchy of games has not been considered previously in the literature.

Scheduling Policies with Large Stretch. As our α-stretch condition is fairly general and most of the popular scheduling policies have bounded stretch, the reader may be tempted to conjecture that all scheduling policies that are $O(1)$-approximation on a single machine lead to coordination mechanisms with $O(1)$ price of anarchy. However, we show in Appendix B that this is not the case. The scheduling policy Weighted Latest Arrival Processor Sharing (WLAPS) gives $O(1)$-approximation to the total weighted completion time on a single machine. But it does not induce a game with constant price of anarchy. The scheduling policy WLAPS generalizes Round Robin to favor more recent jobs, and has been extensively studied in scheduling theory – particularly in broadcast scheduling problems [12, 3]. Not surprisingly, WLAPS fails our bounded stretch condition (α is $\Omega(n)$). Thus, our characterization seems to separate scheduling policies which are good in non-strategic settings from those which lead to small Price of Anarchy.

1.2.3 Extension to ℓ_k-norms

Next, we extend our result to the more general objective of minimizing ℓ_k-norms of completion time where $1 \leq k < \infty$. Note that the total completion time is the ℓ_1-norm and the maximum completion time (makespan) is the ℓ_∞-norm. The ℓ_1-norm objective may starve some jobs for an unacceptably long time while focusing too much on average performance. In contrast, the ℓ_∞-norm tries to be as fair as possible at the expense of average performance. The ℓ_k-norms, $k \geq 2$ make a natural balance between average performance and fairness [4, 14, 1]. We prove the following theorem in Section 6.

THEOREM 4. *Suppose that each machine declares a (possibly different) scheduling policy with stretch α. Then the* *resulting game has a robust price of anarchy of $O(k\alpha^{k+1})$ for minimizing the ℓ_k-norm of completion time of jobs, for any $k \geq 1$.*

We present our result only for the unweighted jobs case, and will extend our result to the ℓ_k-norm of weighted completion time in the full version of the paper. We note that previous work [9] considered only SHORTEST JOB FIRST (SJF) and ROUND ROBIN (RR) policies without release dates, and showed that they have robust price of anarchy of $O(k)$ and $O(2^k)$, respectively. (In [9], the authors present the analysis for unweighted ℓ_k-norms of completion time, and claim that their analysis extends to weighted ℓ_k norms. We remind the reader that SJF is the unweighted version of HDF). Theorem 4 implies an exponential improvement for ROUND ROBIN (which has stretch $\alpha = 1$), and this holds even with release dates. As observed in [9], due to a well-known relationship between ℓ_k-norms and the ℓ_∞-norm we have the following theorem as a corollary.

THEOREM 5. *Suppose that each machine declares a (possibly different) strongly local scheduling policy with stretch $\alpha = 1$. Then the resulting game has a robust price of anarchy of $O(\log n)$ w.r.t. the objective of minimizing the makespan, where n is the number of jobs.*

The above theorem complments the lower bound of $\Omega(m)$ known for the price of anarchy of strongly local scheduling policies [2], where m is the number of machines (see Section 1.3).

1.2.4 Non-preemptive Scheduling Policies

In some applications, preempting a job can be costly, and non-preemptive scheduling policies are highly desirable. When the jobs arrive online, however, no natural non-preemptive scheduling policy gives $O(1)$ approximation to the weighted completion time, even on a single machine. This is particularly relevant since both our potential function and dual-fitting proofs are inspired by the frameworks developed for online scheduling problems [7, 1]. Nevertheless, in Section 5 we present a general black box reduction from preemptive scheduling policies to non-preemptive scheduling policies that preserve the stretch within a factor of two. This reduction is an adaptation of the idea used in [13].

THEOREM 6. *There exists a reduction that takes any preemptive scheduling policy with stretch α and outputs a non-preemptive scheduling policy with stretch at most 2α.*

The above theorem, along with Theorem 1 and Theorem 2, shows how to construct non-preemptive (offline) scheduling policies that lead to small constant price of anarchy.

1.2.5 Pure Nash Equilibrium

Although a correlated equilibrium (which can be computed in polynomial time) and a mixed Nash equilibrium is guaranteed to exist in every finite game, not all games have pure Nash equilibrium (PNE). For example, when there are no communication delays (release dates) and assignment costs, it is known that the game induced by the Highest Density First policy might not have a PNE [10]. In contrast, a PNE is guaranteed to exist in the game induced by the Weighted Round Robin (WRR) policy (see Appendix A for definitions). It is not clear if this property of WRR continues to hold in the presence of release dates and assignment costs. We address this concern by transforming the WRR policy. The idea is to run the WRR schedule but delay the completion time of a job, forcing it to satisfy the following condition.

$$w_j C_j = \sum_{j'} \min(w_j p_{j'}, w_{j'} p_j)$$

One way to achieve this is to process the last ϵ portion of job j at time $t = (1/w_j) \cdot \sum_{j'} \min(w_j p_{j'}, w_{j'} p_j)$. It is easy to verify that the stretch of the resulting schedule is at most 2. The proof for WRR in [10] can be easily extended to show that this induces a *potential game*. Hence, a PNE is guaranteed to exist, and the Nash dynamics converges toward a PNE in pseudo-polynomial time.

1.3 Related Work

There has been a lot of work on approximation algorithms for minimizing the weighted sum of completion times [13, 21, 22]. Our potential function and dual-fitting techniques are inspired by the elegant framework developed for online scheduling in [7, 1]. We note that their framework can be adapted to yield combinatorial scheduling policies for weighted completion time that are also $O(1)$-approximations. Here, each machine simply schedules the set of jobs assigned to it using, for example, the Highest Residual Density First policy (see Appendix A for definition). The algorithm considers the jobs in increasing order of their release dates and applies a *greedy dispatch* rule, assigning a job j to that machine i which increases the overall objective function (for the currently dispatched jobs) by the least amount. Although our potential function and dual-fitting proofs are inspired by this framework, as mentioned above, the settings are actually very different. For instance, there is a scheduling policy (see Section B) that gives $O(1)$-approximation to the online optimization problem when used in conjunction with the greedy dispatch rule, but induces a game with very large price of anarchy.

Coordination mechanisms were first introduced in [8]. See the survey [16] for various selfish scheduling models. The study of coordination mechanisms for the completion time objective was initiated in [10, 11]. In the absence of release dates and assignment costs, they show constant factor price of anarchy bounds for for three specific policies - WEIGHTED ROUND ROBIN (WRR), HIGHEST DENSITY FIRST (HDF), and RANDOM (RAND). In particular, their bounds are tight for the first two policies.

They also show that, both WRR and RAND induce pure Nash Equilibrium while HDF does not. The l_k-norms of the completion time were considered [9]. They prove a price of anarchy of $O(k)$ for SHORTEST JOB FIRST (when there are no weights, release dates, and assignment costs), and show that no strongly local deterministic policy can achieve a price of anarchy better than $O(k/\log\log k)$.

Azar et al [2] design coordination mechanisms for the makespan objective. They show a lower bound of $\Omega(m)$ for any strongly local scheduling policy (see Section 1.1 for definition), where m is the number of machines. In contrast, they present a weakly local scheduling policy (where a machine knows everything about the jobs assigned to it, including their processing lengths on other machines) that achieves a price of anarchy of $O(\log m)$, and a policy that induces a pure Nash Equilibrium with PoA of $O(\log^2 m)$. These results were later extended by Caragiannis [6]. Similar to our work, he showed a strong connection between coordination mechanisms and online algorithms [5]. It will be interesting to study whether this is purely coincidental, or if there is a deeper connection between price of anarchy and competitive ratios.

2. PRELIMINARIES

Recall the concepts and notations introduced in Section 1.1. We index a machine by $i \in \mathcal{M}$, and a job by $j \in \mathcal{J}$. Each machine $i \in \mathcal{M}$ declares a strongly local scheduling policy A_i. Let the symbol $A = (A_1, \ldots A_i, \ldots A_{|\mathcal{M}|})$ denote the profile of scheduling policies. Let $\text{GAME}(A)$ denote the resulting game induced between the jobs. An outcome of this game is a strategy-profile $\theta = (\theta_1, \ldots \theta_j, \ldots \theta_{|\mathcal{J}|})$, where $\theta_j \in \mathcal{M}$ is the machine selected by the job $j \in \mathcal{J}$. For notational convenience, we also define an *assignment-vector* Q that summarizes the outcome from the perspective of the machines. The vector $Q = (Q_1, \ldots Q_i, \ldots Q_{|\mathcal{M}|})$ has $|\mathcal{M}|$ components, and the ith component of this vector refers to the set of jobs assigned to machine $i \in \mathcal{M}$. Thus, we have $Q_i = \{j \in \mathcal{J} : \theta_j = i\}$. The completion time of a job j under this outcome is given by $C_j^A(\theta)$. The disutility of the job equals its assignment cost plus its weighted completion time, and this is denoted by $\texttt{COST}_j^A(\theta) = h_{\theta_j,j} + w_j \cdot C_j^A(\theta)$. The outcome is a pure Nash equilibrium iff no job can reduce its disutility by switching to another machine, i.e., $\texttt{COST}_j^A(\theta) \leq \texttt{COST}_j^A(i, \theta_{-j})$ for all $j \in \mathcal{J}, i \in \mathcal{M}$, where θ_{-j} is the strategy-profile of all the jobs except the job j.

We reserve the term *scenario* for a triple $S = (A, Q, \theta)$. This specifies the scheduling policy followed by every machine, and an outcome of the resulting game. The symbol $p_{ij}(t)$ denotes the remaining processing length of a job $j \in Q_i$ on machine i at time t. We say that the job is *unfinished* at time t iff $p_{ij}(t) > 0$. The symbol $W_i(t)$ denotes the total weight of the unfinished jobs on machine i at time t.

Fix any profile of scheduling policies A, and let $\text{NE}(A)$ be the set of all pure Nash equilibria of $\text{GAME}(A)$. The objective is to minimize the total disutility of the jobs. The price of anarchy of this game is:

$$\text{PoA}(A) = \frac{\max_{\theta \in \text{NE}(A)} \sum_j \texttt{COST}_j^A(\theta)}{\min_{A', \theta'} \sum_j \texttt{COST}_j^{A'}(\theta')}$$

Note that the above expression compares the worst Nash equilibrium of $\text{GAME}(A)$ with the optimal solution to the underlying optimization problem, which may use an entirely different profile of scheduling policies.

The notion of price of anarchy as defined above is not applicable in games that do not admit any pure Nash equilibrium. To address this issue, Roughgarden [20] introduced a *smoothness framework* which gives *robust* price of anarchy bounds for generalized solution concepts such as mixed Nash and correlated equilibria and no regret sequences. Adapting the smoothness framework to our context, we say that the $\text{GAME}(A)$ is (λ, μ)-smooth iff the following inequality holds for any two scenarios $S = (A, Q, \theta)$ and $S' = (A', Q', \theta')$.

$$\sum_{j \in \mathcal{J}} \texttt{COST}_j^A(\theta'_j, \theta_{-j}) \leq \lambda \cdot \sum_{j \in \mathcal{J}} \texttt{COST}_j^{A'}(\theta') + \mu \cdot \sum_{j \in \mathcal{J}} \texttt{COST}_j^A(\theta) \quad (1)$$

The reader may find it helpful to think of the scenario S as a pure Nash equilibrium of $\text{GAME}(A)$, and the scenario S' as an optimal solution to the underlying optimization problem. It can be shown that the price of anarchy of any (λ, μ)-smooth game is at most $\lambda/(1-\mu)$ for mixed Nash, correlated equilibria and no regret sequences [20]. Hence, it is also as termed *robust* PoA.

3. ROBUST PRICE OF ANARCHY BOUND VIA POTENTIAL FUNCTION

We devote this entire section to proving Theorem 2 by a potential function based argument. Throughout this section, we fix two scenarios $S = (A, Q, \theta)$ and $S' = (A', Q', \theta')$. Further, we assume that all the scheduling polices A_i (specified by A) under the scenario S have stretch α (see Definition 1). We will prove Equation 1. The quantities λ and μ depend on α and will be decided later.

Zero Assignment Costs. For ease of analysis, we ignore the jobs' assignment costs throughout this section, i.e. $h_{ij} = 0$. It is straightforward to extend our analysis to incorporate nonnegative assignment costs – the dual fitting proof in Section 4 is presented in its full generality, and does not require this simplifying assumption.

Note that the left hand side of Equation 1 results from mixing two completely different scenarios S and S'. Hence, it is not easy to relate this quantity with the right hand side, which consists of the weighted completion times under the two individual scenarios. This is the case particularly when the jobs are released over time, as it becomes extremely difficult to derive mathematical expressions for the terms in Equation 1.

To circumvent this difficulty, we upper bound the left hand side by a carefully chosen potential function, and consider its derivative with respect to time. The advantage of this approach is that we have a good understanding of how an algorithm makes instantaneous scheduling decision. For example, the instantaneous increase in the total weighted completion time is simply the total weight of the unfinished jobs. In other words, each unfinished job j incurs a penalty of w_j at each time step.

For a technical reason that will become clear as we proceed with the proof, we slow down the schedule under S' by a (suitably chosen) constant factor $\delta \in (0, 1)$. Let $A'(\delta)$ denote the new profile of scheduling policies, and let $S'(\delta) = (A'(\delta), Q', \theta')$ denote the new resulting scenario. More precisely, a job is processed on machine i at time t in S' iff it is processed on the same machine i at time t/δ in $S'(\delta)$. Note that the assignment vector and the strategy-profile remain the same across the two scenarios S' and $S'(\delta)$.

We emphasize that $S'(\delta)$ is *not* the schedule that results from the machines executing the policies A' with speed δ. Rather, $S'(\delta)$ is obtained by *stretching out* the schedule S by a factor of $1/\delta$ over the time horizon. It is easy to see that this transformation increases the completion time of a job by a factor of $1/\delta$.

FACT 1. *The completion time of every job j' under $S'(\delta)$ is exactly $1/\delta$ times its completion time under S'.*

Overview of our approach. Recall the notations introduced in Section 2. We will always index the jobs by j under the scenario S, and by j' under the scenario $S'(\delta)$. The remaining processing lengths will be denoted by $p_{ij}(t)$ under the scenario S, and by $p^*_{ij'}(t)$ under the scenario $S'(\delta)$. Similarly, the total weight of the unfinished jobs on a machine will be denoted by $W_i(t)$ under the scenario S, and by $W^*_i(t)$

under the scenario $S'(\delta)$. With these notations in place, we are now ready to define our potential function.

$$\Phi(t) = \sum_{i \in \mathcal{M}} \sum_{j' \in Q'_i} \sum_{j \in Q_i} \min\left(w_{j'} \cdot p_{ij}(t), w_j \cdot p^*_{ij'}(t)\right) \quad (2)$$

Let $\texttt{COST}^S = \sum_j \texttt{COST}_j^A(\theta)$ denote the total disutility of all the jobs under the scenario $S = (A, Q, \theta)$, which is the same as their total weighted completion time (assuming zero assignment costs). Hence, we can write this quantity as $\texttt{COST}^S = \int_0^\infty \frac{\mathrm{d}}{\mathrm{d}t}\texttt{COST}^S(t)$, where the derivative $\frac{\mathrm{d}}{\mathrm{d}t}\texttt{COST}^S(t)$ equals the total weight of the unfinished jobs at time t under the scenario S. Similarly, let $\texttt{COST}^{S'}$ (resp. $\texttt{COST}^{S'(\delta)}$) denote the total disutility of all the jobs under the scenario S' (resp. $S'(\delta)$). Fact 1 implies that $\texttt{COST}^{S'(\delta)} = (1/\delta) \cdot \texttt{COST}^{S'}$. We will show that $\Phi(t)$ is a good estimate of the left hand side of Equation 1. In particular, we will prove that $\Phi(t)$ satisfies the following conditions.

$$\Phi(\infty) = 0 \quad (3)$$

$$\sum_{i \in \mathcal{M}} \sum_{j' \in Q'_i} \texttt{COST}_{j'}^A(i, \theta_{-j'}) \leq \texttt{COST}^{S'} + \alpha \cdot \Phi(0) \quad (4)$$

$$-\frac{\mathrm{d}}{\mathrm{d}t}\Phi(t) \leq \frac{\mathrm{d}}{\mathrm{d}t}\texttt{COST}^{S'(\delta)}(t) + \delta \cdot \frac{\mathrm{d}}{\mathrm{d}t}\texttt{COST}^S(t) \quad \text{at every time } t \quad (5)$$

In Equation 4, the symbol α denotes the stretch of the scheduling policies declared by the machines (see Definition 1) under the scenario S.

THEOREM 7. *The potential function as defined in Equation 2 satisfies Equations 3, 4, 5.*

We now use Theorem 7 to derive:

$$\begin{aligned}
& \text{Left hand side of Equation 1} \\
= & \sum_{i \in \mathcal{M}} \sum_{j' \in Q'_i} \texttt{COST}_{j'}^A(i, \theta_{-j'}) \\
\leq & \texttt{COST}^{S'} + \alpha \cdot \Phi(0) \quad [\text{Due to 4}] \\
= & \texttt{COST}^{S'} - \alpha \cdot \int_{t=0}^{\infty} \frac{\mathrm{d}}{\mathrm{d}t}\Phi(t)\mathrm{d}t \quad [\text{Due to 3}] \\
\leq & \texttt{COST}^{S'} + \alpha \cdot \int_{t=0}^{\infty} \left[\frac{\mathrm{d}}{\mathrm{d}t}\texttt{COST}^{S'(\delta)}(t) + \delta \cdot \frac{\mathrm{d}}{\mathrm{d}t}\texttt{COST}^S(t)\right]\mathrm{d}t \\
\leq & \texttt{COST}^{S'} + \alpha \cdot \texttt{COST}^{S'(\delta)} + (\alpha\delta) \cdot \texttt{COST}^S \\
= & (1 + \alpha/\delta) \cdot \texttt{COST}^{S'} + (\alpha\delta) \cdot \texttt{COST}^S
\end{aligned}$$

The last equality follows from Fact 1.

Thus, setting $\lambda = (1 + \alpha/\delta)$ and $\mu = \alpha\delta$, we get a robust price of anarchy bound of $(1 + \alpha/\delta)/(1 - \alpha\delta)$. This leads to Theorem 2. More specifically, by setting $\delta = 1/(2\alpha)$, we obtain a robust PoA bound of $2(1 + 2\alpha^2)$. The best bound we can obtain here is $\frac{1+\alpha(\sqrt{\alpha^2+1}+\alpha)}{1-\alpha(\sqrt{\alpha^2+1}-\alpha)}$ when $\delta = \sqrt{\alpha^2+1} - \alpha$. This bound becomes $(\sqrt{2}+1)/(\sqrt{2}-1) \simeq 5.8284$ when $\alpha = 1$.

Remark. When all the release dates are zero, the robust price of anarchy bound improves to $4\alpha^2$. This improvement follows from a better bound for Equation 4, namely, we can show that its left hand side is at most $\alpha \cdot \Phi(0)$. Note that this bound is tight [10] when $\alpha = 1$ (see Theorem 1).

Full analysis. Let $\Phi_i(t)$ denote the contribution towards $\Phi(t)$ by machine $i \in \mathcal{M}$, and let $\Phi_{ij'}(t)$ denote the contribution towards $\Phi_i(t)$ by job $j' \in Q'_i$. Thus, we have:

$$\Phi_{ij'}(t) = \sum_{j \in Q_i} \min\left(w_{j'} \cdot p_{ij}(t), w_j \cdot p^*_{ij'}(t)\right) \quad (6)$$

$$\Phi_i(t) = \sum_{j' \in Q'_i} \Phi_{ij'}(t) \quad (7)$$

$$\Phi(t) = \sum_{i \in \mathcal{M}} \Phi_i(t) \quad (8)$$

The next two lemmas show that $\Phi(t)$ satisfies the boundary conditions at $t = 0$ and $t = \infty$.

LEMMA 1. *The potential function $\Phi(t)$ satisfies Equation 3.*

PROOF. Follows from the observation that each job has zero remaining processing length at time $t = \infty$. □

LEMMA 2. *The potential function $\Phi(t)$ satisfies Equation 4.*

PROOF. Fix any machine $i \in \mathcal{M}$. For every job $j' \in Q'_i$, As justified below, we have:

$$\begin{aligned}
& w_{j'} \cdot C_{j'}^A(i, \theta_{-j'}) \\
\leq & w_{j'} \cdot r_{ij'} + w_{j'} \cdot p_{ij'} + \alpha \cdot \sum_{j \in Q_i} \min\left(w_{j'} \cdot p_{ij}, w_j \cdot p_{ij'}\right) \\
= & w_{j'} \cdot (r_{ij'} + p_{ij'}) + \alpha \cdot \sum_{j \in Q_i} \min\left(w_{j'} \cdot p_{ij}(0), w_j \cdot p^*_{ij'}(0)\right) \\
= & w_{j'} \cdot (r_{ij'} + p_{ij'}) + \alpha \cdot \Phi_{ij'}(0) \\
\leq & w_{j'} \cdot C_{j'}^{A'}(\theta') + \alpha \cdot \Phi_{ij'}(0) \quad (9)
\end{aligned}$$

The first inequality holds since the scheduling policy A_i has stretch α (see Definition 1). The last inequality holds since the completion time of job j' under any feasible schedule is at least $r_{ij'} + p_{ij'}$. Finally, note that $w_{j'} \cdot C_{j'}^A(i, \theta_{-j'}) = \texttt{COST}_{j'}^A(i, \theta_{-j'})$ in the absence of assignment costs. So the lemma follows when we sum both sides of Equation 9 over all machines $i \in \mathcal{M}$ and jobs $j' \in Q'_i$. □

It remains to show that $\Phi(t)$ satisfies Equation 5. We will first make some simple observations.

FACT 2. *The functions $p_{ij}(t), p^*_{ij'}(t)$, and $\Phi_{ij'}(t)$ are all continuous and non-increasing in t.*

The following facts hold since the machines operate at speed δ (resp. 1) under scenario $S'(\delta)$ (resp. S).

FACT 3. *Fix any machine $i \in \mathcal{M}$, and any two jobs $j' \in Q'_i$ and $j \in Q_i$. At any time t, we have:*

$$0 \geq \frac{d}{dt}\left(p^*_{ij'}(t)\right) \geq -\delta, \quad \text{and} \quad 0 \geq \frac{d}{dt}\left(p_{ij}(t)\right) \geq -1.$$

FACT 4. *At any time t, on any machine $i \in \mathcal{M}$, we have:*

$$0 \geq \frac{d}{dt}\Big(\sum_{j' \in Q'_i} p^*_{ij'}(t)\Big) \geq -\delta, \quad \text{and} \quad 0 \geq \frac{d}{dt}\Big(\sum_{j \in Q_i} p_{ij}(t)\Big) \geq -1.$$

We now bound the rate of change in $\Phi_i(t)$ due to any unfinished job under the scenario $S'(\delta)$.

CLAIM 1. *For every job $j' \in Q'_i$ that completes after time t under the scenario $S'(\delta)$, we have:*

$$\frac{d}{dt}\left(\Phi_{ij'}(t)\right) \geq -w_{j'} + W_i(t) \cdot \frac{d}{dt}\left(p^*_{ij'}(t)\right).$$

PROOF. Recall that $\Phi_{ij'}(t)$ is a summation over a set of terms, each corresponding to a job $j \in Q_i$ assigned to the same machine i, but under a different scenario S (see Equation 6). Each such term is the minimum of two functions: $w_{j'} \cdot p_{ij}(t)$ and $w_j \cdot p^*_{ij'}(t)$. We partition all the jobs in Q_i into two subsets Y and Z, depending on which of the two functions attain the minimum value:

$$Y = \{j \in Q_i : w_{j'} \cdot p_{ij}(t) \leq w_j \cdot p^*_{ij'}(t)\}, \text{ and}$$

$$Z = \{j \in Q_i : w_{j'} \cdot p_{ij}(t) > w_j \cdot p^*_{ij'}(t)\}.$$

The functions $f^Y(t), f^Z(t)$ capture the respective contributions of the subsets Y and Z towards $\Phi_{ij'}(t)$.

$$f^Y(t) = w_{j'} \cdot \sum_{j \in Y} p_{ij}(t), \text{ and } f^Z(t) = \Big(\sum_{j \in Z} w_j\Big) \cdot p^*_{ij'}(t).$$

Note that $\Phi_{ij'}(t) = f^Y(t) + f^Z(t)$. Further, since the job j' completes after time t under the scenario $S'(\delta)$, we have $p^*_{ij'}(t) > 0$. It follows that every job $j \in Z$ has $p_{ij}(t) > 0$. In other words, every job in Z completes after time t under the scenario S, which implies that $\sum_{j \in Z} w_j \leq W_i(t)$. Hence, we conclude:

$$\begin{aligned}
\frac{d}{dt}(\Phi_{ij'}(t)) &= \frac{d}{dt} f^Y(t) + \frac{d}{dt} f^Z(t) \\
&= w_{j'} \cdot \frac{d}{dt} \sum_{j \in Y} p_{ij}(t) + \Big(\sum_{j \in Z} w_j\Big) \cdot \frac{d}{dt}(p^*_{ij'}(t)) \\
&\geq -w_{j'} + \Big(\sum_{j \in Z} w_j\Big) \cdot \frac{d}{dt}(p^*_{ij'}(t)) \qquad (10) \\
&\geq -w_{j'} + W_i(t) \cdot \frac{d}{dt}(p^*_{ij'}(t)) \qquad (11)
\end{aligned}$$

Equation 10 follows from Fact 4. Equation 11 holds since $\sum_{j \in Z} w_j \leq W_i(t)$ and $\frac{d}{dt}(p^*_{ij'}(t)) \leq 0$. □

The next claim shows that we can ignore the jobs that finishes before time t under the scenario $S'(\delta)$.

CLAIM 2. *For every job $j' \in Q'_i$ that completes before time t under the scenario $S'(\delta)$, we have:*

$$\frac{d}{dt}(\Phi_{ij'}(t)) = 0.$$

PROOF. Follows from the observation that such a job j' has $p^*_{ij'}(t') = 0$ for all $t' \geq t$. □

The next claim bounds the overall rate of change of $\Phi_i(t)$.

CLAIM 3. *For any machine $i \in \mathcal{M}$ and any time t, we have:*

$$\frac{d}{dt}(\Phi_i(t)) \geq -W^*_i(t) - \delta \cdot W_i(t).$$

PROOF. We infer that:

$$\begin{aligned}
\frac{d}{dt}\Phi_i(t) &= \sum_{j' \in Q'_i} \frac{d}{dt}\Phi_{ij'}(t) \\
&\geq -W^*_i(t) + W_i(t) \cdot \sum_{j' \in Q'_i} \frac{d}{dt}(p^*_{ij'}(t)) \qquad (12) \\
&\geq -W^*_i(t) - \delta \cdot W_i(t) \qquad (13)
\end{aligned}$$

Equation 12 follows from Claim 1 and Claim 2. Equation 13 follows from Fact 4. □

Now we are ready to bound the overall rate of change of $\Phi(t)$.

LEMMA 3. *The potential function $\Phi(t)$ satisfies Equation 5.*

PROOF. Follows from summing both sides of the inequality in Claim 3 over all machines $i \in \mathcal{M}$, and recalling that $\frac{d}{dt}\texttt{COST}^{S'(\delta)}(t) = \sum_i W^*_i(t)$, and $\frac{d}{dt}\texttt{COST}^S(t) = \sum_i W_i(t)$. □

4. PRICE OF ANARCHY USING DUAL FITTING

In this section, we improve the bound on the PoA of α-stretch scheduling policies to 4α using dual fitting. For simplicity of exposition, we only derive the PoA of pure Nash equilibria, and defer the extension to mixed Nash and correlated equilibria to Section 4.1. We require that the scheduling policies satisfy two properties in addition to the bounded stretch condition.

DEFINITION 2 (MYOPIC POLICY). *A scheduling policy is myopic iff its scheduling decision depends only on the status of the jobs available for processing at the present time instant. In particular, the decision is independent of the jobs that will be released in future.*

Assume for a while that all the jobs have unit weights, and consider a machine which follows the SRPT scheduling policy. At time t, this machine looks at the set of jobs available in its queue, and works on the job j with shortest remaining processing time $p_j(t)$. At time $t+1$, it repeats the same process. This policy is myopic, since its scheduling decision depends only on the jobs currently available in the machine's queue. The reader may find it helpful to keep this example in mind while going through the rest of this section.

DEFINITION 3 (MONOTONE POLICY). *A scheduling policy is monotone iff it satisfies three properties. (1) Everything else remaining the same, the completion time of a job can never increase if it is released at an earlier date. (2) Everything else remaining the same, the completion time of a job j can never decrease if the machine is asked to process an extra job j'. (3) For any two jobs j and j' with $w_j = w_{j'}$, $r_j \leq r_{j'}$, and $p_j \leq p_{j'}$, the completion time of job j is at most the completion time of job j', i.e, $C_j \leq C_{j'}$.*

All scheduling policies that give $O(1)$-approximations on a single machine (see Appendix A), with the exception of WLAPS, are myopic and monotone, and have stretch $\alpha = 1$. We prove the following theorem.

THEOREM 8. *Suppose that each machine declares a (possibly different) scheduling policy which is myopic, monotone and has stretch $\alpha \geq 1$. Then the price of anarchy of the induced game is at most 4α.*

First we derive a bound on the completion time of a job. The next lemma justifies our use of the term "bounded stretch", for traditionally the "stretch" of a job is defined as its completion time minus its release date divided by its processing length.

LEMMA 4. *If a machine runs a scheduling policy with stretch $\alpha \geq 1$, then a job j (with weight w_j, release date r_j, processing length p_j, and completion time C_j) on the machine satisfies the following condition.*

$$C_j \leq r_j + \alpha \cdot (W(r_j)/w_j) \cdot p_j.$$

Here, the symbol $W(t)$ denotes the total weight of the unfinished jobs at time t.

PROOF. Since the scheduling policy has stretch $\alpha \geq 1$, Definition 1 implies that:

$$\begin{aligned} C_j &\leq r_j + p_j + \sum_{j' \neq j : C_{j'} \geq r_j} \alpha \cdot \min(p_{j'}, (w_{j'}/w_j) \cdot p_j) \\ &\leq r_j + \sum_{j' : C_{j'} \geq r_j} \alpha \cdot (w_{j'}/w_j) \cdot p_j \\ &= r_j + \alpha \cdot (W(r_j)/w_j) \cdot p_j \end{aligned}$$

□

LP-relaxation..

Consider the LP PRIMAL described below [1]. It has a variable x_{ijt} for each machine $i \in \mathcal{M}$, each job $j \in \mathcal{J}$ and each unit time-slot $t \geq r_{ij}$. If the machine i processes the job j during the whole time-slot t, then this variable is set to 1. The first constraint says that every job has to be completely processed. The second constraint says that a machine cannot process more than one unit of the jobs during any time-slot. Note that the LP allows a job to be processed simultaneously across different machines.

In the objective function, the term $\sum_i \sum_{t \geq r_{ij}} h_{ij} \cdot (x_{ijt}/p_{ij})$ gives the assignment cost incurred by the job j. The term $\sum_i \sum_{t \geq r_{ij}} w_j \cdot x_{ijt} \cdot (t/p_{ij})$ is known as the *fractional weighted completion time* of the job j. In a feasible schedule this quantity is no more than its integral weighted completion time, minus half of its weighted processing time. Finally, the remaining term $\sum_i \sum_{t \geq r_{ij}} w_j \cdot x_{ijt} \cdot (1/2)$ equals half of the weighted processing time of the job. Thus, adding up these three terms, we see that the disutility of a job j is at least $\sum_i \sum_{t \geq r_{ij}} h_{ij} \cdot (x_{ijt}/p_{ij}) + \sum_i \sum_{t \geq r_{ij}} w_j \cdot x_{ijt} \cdot (t/p_{ij} + 1/2)$. Hence, the linear program PRIMAL is a valid relaxation of our problem.

$$\begin{aligned} \text{Min} \quad & \sum_j \sum_i \sum_{t \geq r_{ij}} h_{ij} \cdot (x_{ijt}/p_{ij}) \\ & + \sum_j \sum_i \sum_{t \geq r_{ij}} w_j \cdot x_{ijt} \cdot (t/p_{ij} + 1/2) \qquad (\text{PRIMAL}) \end{aligned}$$

$$\begin{aligned} \textstyle\sum_i \sum_{t \geq r_{ij}} x_{ijt}/p_{ij} &\geq 1 && \forall j \\ \textstyle\sum_{j : t \geq r_{ij}} x_{ijt} &\leq 1 && \forall i, t \\ x_{ijt} &\geq 0 && \forall i, j, t : t \geq r_{ij} \end{aligned}$$

Now, suppose that we constrain each machine to run at a reduced speed of $1/2\alpha$. In other words, each machine can process at most $1/2\alpha$ units of the jobs during one unit of time. It is easy to see that the modified LP described below is a valid relaxation under this new constraint. This transformation increases the objective by at most a factor of 2α.

$$\begin{aligned} \text{Min} \quad & \sum_j \sum_i \sum_{t \geq r_{ij}} h_{ij} \cdot (x_{ijt}/p_{ij}) \\ & + \sum_j \sum_i \sum_{t \geq r_{ij}} w_j \cdot x_{ijt} \cdot (t/p_{ij} + \alpha) \qquad \text{PRIMAL}(\alpha) \end{aligned}$$

$$\begin{aligned} \textstyle\sum_i \sum_{t \geq r_{ij}} x_{ijt}/p_{ij} &\geq 1 && \forall j \\ \textstyle\sum_{j : t \geq r_{ij}} x_{ijt} &\leq 1/(2\alpha) && \forall i, t \\ x_{ijt} &\geq 0 && \forall i, j, t : t \geq r_{ij} \end{aligned}$$

LEMMA 5. *The optimal objective of the linear program* PRIMAL(α) *is at most 2α times the total disutility of the jobs in any feasible integral schedule.*

Finally, we write down the dual of the above linear program.

$$\text{Max} \quad \sum_j y_j - \sum_i \sum_t z_{it} \qquad \text{DUAL}(\alpha)$$

$$\begin{aligned} y_j &\leq h_{ij} + w_j \cdot (t + \alpha \cdot p_{ij} + (2\alpha) \cdot (z_{it}/w_j) \cdot p_{ij}) \\ & \qquad\qquad\qquad\qquad \forall i, j, t : t \geq r_{ij} \\ y_j &\geq 0 \qquad\qquad \forall j \\ z_{it} &\geq 0 \qquad\qquad \forall i, t \end{aligned}$$

Analysis..

Fix a profile of scheduling policies $A = (A_1, \ldots, A_{|\mathcal{M}|})$, where A_i gives the scheduling policy declared by the machine i. For all $i \in \mathcal{M}$, the scheduling policy A_i is myopic, monotone and has a stretch α. Recall the notations introduced in Section 2. For the rest of this section, we focus on any scenario $S = (A, Q, \theta)$ where the strategy-profile θ is a pure Nash equilibrium of GAME(A).

We will set the variables of the linear program DUAL(α) so as to get a feasible dual solution, with an objective that is at least $1/2$ times the total disutility of the jobs under the scenario S. This, combined with Lemma 5 and weak duality, will imply that the price of anarchy of GAME(A) is at most 4α.

Setting the dual variables:.

The variable y_j is set to be the disutility of the job j under the scenario S. Further, the variable z_{it} is set to be half of the total weight of the unfinished jobs on machine i at time t, under the scenario S.

$$\begin{aligned} y_j = \texttt{COST}_j^A(\theta) &= h_{\theta_j, j} + w_j \cdot C_j^A(\theta) && (14) \\ z_{it} &= (1/2) \cdot W_i(t) && (15) \end{aligned}$$

LEMMA 6. *If the dual variables are set as in the equations 14, 15, then the objective of the linear program* DUAL(α) *is at least* $(1/2) \cdot \sum_j \texttt{COST}_j^A(\theta)$.

PROOF. We use the well-known fact that the total weighted completion time of all the jobs assigned to any specific machine i is equal to $\sum_t W_i(t)$. Thus, we infer that:

$$\sum_{i,t} z_{it} = (1/2) \cdot \sum_j w_j \cdot C_j^A(\theta) \leq (1/2) \cdot \sum_j \texttt{COST}_j^A(\theta).$$

The lemma follows from the above inequality and the fact that $\sum_j y_j = \sum_j \texttt{COST}_j^A(\theta)$. □

LEMMA 7. *If the dual variables are set as in the equations 14, 15, then all the constraints of the linear program* DUAL(α) *are satisfied.*

Theorem 8 will follow from Lemma 5, Lemma 6, and Lemma 7. We present the proof of Lemma 7 to complete the analysis. Clearly, the dual variables are set to nonnegative values. For the rest of the proof, we fix a job j, a machine i, and a time $t \geq r_{ij}$, and show that the corresponding dual constraint is satisfied.

A Thought Experiment..

We create a job j' with $p_{ij'} = p_{ij}$, $w_{j'} = w_j$, and $r_{ij'} = t$. The machine i is now asked to process the set of jobs $Q_i \cup \{j'\}$ using the scheduling policy A_i. Under this thought experiment, let $C^*_{j'}$ denote the completion time of the job j'. Recall that A_i is a myopic scheduling policy (Definition 2). Hence, under this thought experiment, the total weight of the unfinished jobs on machine i at time t is exactly $W_i(t) + w_{j'}$. Since the policy A_i also has stretch α, Lemma 4 gives:

$$C^*_{j'} \leq t + \alpha \cdot \left(\frac{W_i(t) + w_{j'}}{w_{j'}} \right) \cdot p_{ij'} = t + \alpha \cdot p_{ij'} + \alpha \cdot (W_i(t)/w_{j'}) \cdot p_{ij'}$$

Plugging in the equalities $W_i(t) = 2z_{it}$, $w_{j'} = w_j$, and $p_{ij'} = p_{ij}$, we get:

$$C^*_{j'} \leq t + \alpha \cdot p_{ij} + (2\alpha) \cdot (z_{it}/w_j) \cdot p_{ij} \qquad (16)$$

We now consider two possible cases.

Case 1:.

Job j selects machine i under the outcome S, so that $\theta_j = i$.

Let C^*_j denote the completion time of the job j under the thought experiment. Recall that the machine follows a monotone scheduling policy. Hence, part 3 of Definition 3 implies that $C^*_j \leq C^*_{j'}$. Further, part 2 of Definition 3 implies that $C^A_j(\theta) \leq C^*_j$. Accordingly, we have $C^A_j(\theta) \leq C^*_{j'}$. Since $y_j = h_{ij} + w_j \cdot C^A_j(\theta)$, we infer that:

$$y_j \leq h_{ij} + w_j \cdot C^*_{j'} \qquad (17)$$

Equation 16 and Equation 17 imply that the dual constraint is satisfied.

Case 2:.

Job j does not select machine i under the scenario S, so that $\theta_j \neq i$.

Consider the scenario S. We want to bound the completion time of the job j when it switches to the machine i, and everything else remains the same. This is denoted by $C^A_j(i, \theta_{-j})$. This also corresponds to a thought experiment, where the machine i is asked to schedule the jobs in $Q_i \cup \{j\}$ using the scheduling policy A_i. The only difference between this thought experiment and the previous one is that here the job being inserted has an earlier release date ($r_{ij} \leq r_{ij'} = t$, $w_j = w_{j'}$, $p_{ij} = p_{ij'}$). Accordingly, part 1 of Definition 3 implies that $C^A_j(i, \theta_{-j}) \leq C^*_{j'}$. Since $\texttt{COST}^A_j(i, \theta_{-j}) = h_{ij} + w_j \cdot C^A_j(i, \theta_{-j})$, we get:

$$\texttt{COST}^A_j(i, \theta_{-j}) \leq h_{ij} + w_j \cdot C^*_{j'} \qquad (18)$$

Finally, recall that the strategy-profile θ is a pure Nash equilibrium of GAME(A). Hence, we have:

$$y_j = \texttt{COST}^A_j(\theta) \leq \texttt{COST}^A_j(i, \theta_{-j}) \qquad (19)$$

Equation 16, Equation 18, and Equation 19 imply that the dual constraint is satisfied.

4.1 Extension to Mixed and Correlated PoA

In this section, we give the complete proof of PoA bound for mixed Nash equilibrium using dual fitting. Reader can verify that, the same proof extends to Correlated Equilibrium. As a first step, we derive a (slightly) different bound on the completion time of a job when a scheduling policy satisfies the α-stretch (Def 1),is myopic (Def 2) and monotone (Def 3). Recall that for a scheduling policy A and an input set Q of jobs, C_j denotes the completion time of job $j \in Q$; $Q(t)$ denotes the set of unsatisfied jobs at time r_j and $W(t)$ denotes the total weight of unsatisfied jobs at time t.

LEMMA 8. *If a scheduling policy A which is myopic,monotone and has a stretch α, then the following inequalities hold for all input sets of jobs Q.*

$$C_j \leq r_j + \alpha \cdot \left(\frac{W(r_j)}{w_j} \right) \cdot p_j \quad \textit{for all } j \in Q.$$

PROOF. Recall the definition of an α-stretch policy. We know from Definition 1,

$$\begin{aligned} C^A_j &\leq r_j + \alpha \cdot \left(\sum_{j' \in Q(r_j)} \min(p_{j'}, (w_{j'}/w_j) \cdot p_j) \right) \\ &\leq r_j + \alpha \cdot \left(\sum_{j' \in Q(r_j)} (w_{j'}/w_j) \cdot p_j \right) \\ &\leq r_j + \alpha \cdot W(r_j)/w_j \cdot p_j \end{aligned}$$

□

Consider the game induced by a profile of scheduling policies $A = (A_1, \ldots, A_{|\mathcal{M}|})$, where A_i is the scheduling policy followed by the machine i. Furthermore, for all $i \in \mathcal{M}$, the scheduling policy A_i is myopic, monotone and has a stretch α. Fix any (mixed) Nash equilibrium of this game and let the corresponding strategy-profile of jobs be denoted by $\theta = (\theta_1, \ldots, \theta_{|\mathcal{J}|})$, where $\theta_j = (\sigma_1, \ldots \sigma_i, \ldots \sigma_{|M|})$ and σ_i is the probability with which machine i selected by the job j. Let (A, θ) be denoted by scenario S.

We will use $E[\text{COST}^S_j]$ to denote the expected total cost incurred by job j under the scenario S which includes the expected assignment cost + weighted expected completion time. For rest of the section, $E[C^S_j]$ and $E[H^S_j]$ will stand for the expected completion time of job j under the scenario S and $E[W^S_i(t)]$ denote the expected total weight of unsatisfied jobs on the machine i at time t.

Setting the dual variables.

The variable y_j is set to be the total penalty incurred by the job j, under the scenario S. On the other hand, the variable z_{it} is set to be half of the expected total weight of the unfinished jobs on machine i at time t.

$$\begin{aligned} y_j = E[\text{COST}^S_j] &= E[H^S_j] + w_j \cdot E[C^S_j] \qquad (20) \\ z_{it} &= (1/2) \cdot E[W^S_i(t)] \qquad (21) \end{aligned}$$

LEMMA 9. *If the dual variables are set as in the equations 20, 21, then the objective of the linear program* DUAL(α) *is at least* $(1/2) \cdot E[\text{COST}^S]$.

PROOF. We invoke a standard characterization of completion time, which says that the total weighted completion time of all the jobs assigned to any specific machine i is equal to $\sum_t W^S_i(t)$. Thus, we infer that:

$$\sum_{i,t} z_{it} = (1/2) \cdot \sum_{j \in \mathcal{J}} w_j \cdot E[C^S_j] \leq (1/2) \cdot E[\text{COST}^S].$$

The lemma follows from the above inequality and the fact that $\sum_j y_j = E[\text{Cost}^S]$. $\square$

LEMMA 10. *If the dual variables are set as in the equations 20, 21, then all the constraints of the linear program* DUAL(α) *are feasible.*

PROOF. Clearly, the dual variables are set to nonnegative values. To complete the proof, we need to show that the dual constraint corresponding to any job j, any machine i, and any time $t \geq r_{ij}$, is satisfied. Let $E[\text{Cost}_j^S(i, \theta_{-j})]$ denote the expected cost incurred by job j if it unilaterally deviates to machine i, everything else remaining the same. Similarly, let $E[C_j^S(i, \theta_{-j})]$ denotes the expected completion time of job j if it deviates to machine i. Since, $S = (A, \theta)$ is in Nash equilibrium, we have

$$E[\text{Cost}_j^S] \leq h_{ij} + w_j \cdot E[C_j^S(i, \theta_{-j})] \tag{22}$$

To show that all the dual constraints are satisfied, fix a job j, machine i and some time instant $t \geq r_{ij}$.

Consider the following thought experiment. We create a job j^* with $p_{ij^*} = p_{ij}$, $w_{j^*} = w_j$, and $r_{ij^*} = t$. Machine i is asked to process this job $j*$. In otherwords, we take the scenario $S = (A, \theta)$ which is in Nash equilibrium and modify it into a new scenario $S' = (A, \theta')$ as follows. $\theta' = \theta \cup \theta_{j*}$ and $\theta_{j*} = (0, \ldots, \sigma_i = 1, \ldots 0)$. Let $E[C_{j^*}]$ denote the expected completion time of the job j^*. Since A_i is a myopic scheduling policy (Definition 2), under this thought experiment the expected total weight of the unfinished jobs on machine i at time t is exactly $E[W_i^S(t)] + w_{j^*}$.

Since the policy A_i also has stretch α, simple extension of Lemma 8 gives:

$$E[C_{j^*}] \leq t + \alpha \cdot \left(\frac{E[W_i^S(t)] + w_{j^*}}{w_{j^*}} \right) \cdot p_{ij^*}$$

Plugging in the equalities $E[W_i^S(t)] = 2z_{it}$, $w_{j^*} = w_j$, and $p_{ij^*} = p_{ij}$, we get:

$$E[C_{j^*}] \leq t + \alpha \cdot (1 + 2z_{it}/w_j) \cdot p_{ij} \tag{23}$$

To complete the proof, we note that since A_i is a myopic and monotone scheduling policy,

$$E[C_j^S(i, \theta_{-j})] \leq E[C_{j^*}] \tag{24}$$

Therefore from Equations 22, 23 and 24 we have,

$$\begin{aligned} E[\text{Cost}_j^S] &\leq h_{ij} + E[C_j^S(i, \theta_{-j})] \\ &\leq h_{ij} + w_j \left(t + \alpha \cdot (1 + 2z_{it}/w_j) \cdot p_{ij}\right) \end{aligned} \tag{25}$$

Since $y_j = E[\text{Cost}_j^S]$ we get,

$$y_j \leq h_{ij} + w_j \left(t + \alpha \cdot p_{ij} + (2\alpha) \cdot (z_{it}/w_j) \cdot p_{ij}\right)$$

Therefore, dual constraints are feasible. This completes the proof. $\square$

From Theorem 5 and Lemma 9, it follows that PoA of α-stretch scheduling policies which are monotone and myopic is at most 4α.

5. NON-PREEMPTIVE SCHEDULING POLICIES

We show how to transform any preemptive policy into a non-preemptive policy in which the completion time of a job increases at most by a factor 2. This ensures that if the preemptive policy had a stretch α to begin with, then the resulting non-preemptive policy has a stretch 2α. This implies Theorem 6. Our transformation is similar in spirit to the one used in [13].

Consider any α-stretch scheduling policy A_i declared by machine i. Recall that Q_i denotes the set of jobs assigned to machine i. Let C_j be completion time of job j in the schedule produced by policy A_i on the set Q_i. Renumber the jobs in Q_i such that $C_{j-1} < C_j$. We modify the preemptive schedule produced by A_i into a non-preemptive schedule in the following manner.

- Consider the jobs in $j \in Q_i$ in increasing order of their completion time values C_j. Schedule the jobs non-preemptively in this order.

Let $\overline{C_j}$ denote the completion time of job j in this new schedule. The following theorem shows that, the completion time every job in the new schedule increases at most by a factor of 2.

THEOREM 9. $\overline{C_j} \leq 2C_j$

PROOF. Fix a job j. The completion time of the job j in the non-preemptive schedule can be bounded by:

$$\overline{C_j} \leq \max_{k \in [j]} \{r_{ik}\} + \sum_{k \in [j]} p_{ik}$$

Recall that we renumbered the jobs in the set Q_i in the increasing order of C_j values. The above inequality holds since there is no idle period after the job with highest release date in the set $[1 \ldots j]$ is released.

The proof of the theorem follows from the observations that $C_j \geq \max_{k \in [j]} r_{ik}$ and $C_j \geq \sum_{k \in [j]} p_{ik}$. $\square$

6. ℓ_K-NORMS OF COMPLETION TIME

In this section, we extend our result for total completion time to the objective of ℓ_k-norms of complete time. The ℓ_k-norms of complete time of all jobs is defined as $(\sum_j (C_j - r_{\theta_j, j})^k)^{1/k}$ when job j is assigned to machine θ_j and is completed at time C_j. The kth power of completion time is defined as $\sum_j (C_j - r_{\theta_j, j})^k$. For the sake of analysis, we will first bound the smoothness of the game for the kth power of completion time, and will take the kth root at the end of analysis. The notation will remain the same unless specifically stated. We will use COST to refer to kth power of completion time. For example, COST^S denotes the total kth power of completion time of all jobs under the schedule (scenario) S. We let $\text{COST}_j^{S,S'}$ denote the kth power of completion time of job j when the job j is scheduled on machine θ_j' with jobs $Q_{\theta_j'}$ by the scheduling policy $A_{\theta_j'}$. More intuitively, $\text{COST}_j^{S,S'}$ is job j's kth power of completion time when it moves to the machine on which S' scheduled the job. This section is devoted to proving the following theorem. In this paper, we only give a high-level overview of the analysis. The details will appear in the full version of this paper.

THEOREM 10. *For any integer $k \geq 2$, consider the objective of minimizing kth power of completion time. Also consider any two scenarios $S = (A, Q, \theta)$ and $S' = (A', Q', \theta')$ where all scheduling policies A_i (specified by A) have stretch α. Then it follows that*

$$\sum_{j \in \mathcal{J}} \mathtt{COST}_j^{S,S'} \leq \lambda \cdot \mathtt{COST}^S + \mu \cdot \mathtt{COST}^{S'},$$

where $\lambda = O(\alpha^{k^2+k} \cdot (36k)^{k^2+k})$ *and* $\mu = 1/2$.

Hence we derive an upper bound of $O(\alpha^{k^2+k} \cdot (36k)^{k-1})$ on the robust PoA of the game for kth power of completion time. By taking the kth root on this bound, we obtain an upper bound of $O(\alpha^{k+1}k)$ for the ℓ_k-norms of completion time, thereby proving Theorem 4 and 5. We note that this can be done since each job behaves in the same way for both objectives. For mixed and correlated Nash equilibria, this is not the case, and it should be assumed that each job's goal is to minimize its expected kth power of completion time, not its expected completion time. We also note that there is almost a tight lower bound of $\Omega(k/\log k)$ on the price of anarchy [9].

6.1 Overview of the Analysis

In this section we give an overview of the analysis. We define the following potential function. Consider any two scenarios $S = (A, Q, \theta)$ and $S' = (A', Q', \theta')$.Suppose that in S, every machine is running at a reduced speed of $\delta \in [0, 1]$. This situation shall be denoted by $S(\delta)$. More precisely, a job j is processed in S at time t if and only if the same job j is processed in $S(\delta)$ at time t/δ; both Q and θ are the same in S and $S(\delta)$.

For all machines $i \in \mathcal{M}$, time t, and $j \in \mathbf{Q}^{S(\delta)}$, define :

$$\Phi_{ij}^{S(\delta),S'}(t) := \Big(\sum_{j' \in Q'} \min(p_{ij}^{S(\delta)}(t), p_{ij'}^{S'}(t) \Big)^k$$

For all machines $i \in \mathcal{M}$, define:

$$\Phi_i^{S(\delta),S'}(t) := \sum_{j \in Q_i} \Phi_{i,j}^{S(\delta),S'}(t).$$

Our final potential function will be:

$$\Phi^{S(\delta),S'}(t) := \sum_{i \in \mathcal{M}} \Phi_i^{S(\delta),S'}(t).$$

Assuming that all algorithms in A' have a stretch of at most α, we have,

$$\begin{aligned}
&\mathtt{COST}^{S,S'} \\
&\leq \sum_{i \in \mathcal{M}} \sum_{j \in Q_i} \Big(r_{ij} + p_{ij} + \alpha \cdot \sum_{j' \in Q_i'} \min(p_{ij}, p_{ij'}) \Big)^k \\
&\leq (k+1)^k \sum_{i \in \mathcal{M}} \sum_{j \in Q_i} \Big(r_{ij} + p_{ij} \Big)^k \\
&\quad + 3\alpha^k \sum_{i \in \mathcal{M}} \sum_{j \in Q_i} \Big(\sum_{j' \in Q_i'} \min(p_{ij}, p_{ij'}) \Big)^k \\
&\leq (k+1)^k \mathtt{COST}^S + 3\alpha^k \Phi^{S(\delta),S'}(0) \qquad (26)
\end{aligned}$$

The second inequality follows from a simple inequality that $\forall x, y \geq 0, \quad (x+y)^k \leq (k+1)^k x^k + (1+1/k)^k y^k \leq (k+1)^k x^k + 3y^k$. The last inequality follows from the fact that $(r_{ij} + p_{ij})$ is a lower bound on the completion time of job j in any schedule where job j is assigned to machine i (which is the case in the assignment Q).

Hence our analysis will be focused on bounding $\Phi^{S(\delta),S'}(0)$. We will study $\frac{\mathrm{d}}{\mathrm{d}t}\Phi^{S(\delta),S'}(t)$, and to upper bound it, we define a very useful quantity

$$\mathtt{COST}^S(t) := \sum_{j: t \leq C_j^S} (C_j^S - t)^k,$$

which will help keep track of how the cost of S changes. Likewise we define $\mathtt{COST}^{S(\delta)}(t) := \sum_{j:t \leq C_j^{S(\delta)}} (C_j^S - t)^k$.

Note that $\mathtt{COST}^S(0) = \mathtt{COST}^S$ and $\mathtt{COST}^S(\infty) = 0$. To this end, we show that for any $\delta \in (0, 1]$, and $\epsilon \in (0, 1)$, we will show that at all times t,

$$\begin{aligned}
\frac{\mathrm{d}}{\mathrm{d}t}\Phi^{S(\delta),S'}(t) \;&\leq\; -\Big(\frac{\delta^{k-1}}{\epsilon^{k-1}} \frac{1}{\epsilon^{k-1}}\Big) \frac{\mathrm{d}}{\mathrm{d}t}\mathtt{COST}^{S(\delta)}(t) \\
&\quad -\Big(2\epsilon^{k-1} + 3\delta k\Big) \frac{\mathrm{d}}{\mathrm{d}t}\mathtt{COST}^{S'}(t)
\end{aligned}$$

By integrating this inequality and combining it with (26), we will have

$$\begin{aligned}
\mathtt{COST}^{S,S'} \;&\leq\; (k+1)^k \mathtt{COST}^S + \Big(\frac{3\alpha^k \cdot \delta^{k-1}}{\epsilon^{k-1}} + \frac{3\alpha^k}{\epsilon^{k-1}}\Big)\mathtt{COST}^{S(\delta)} \\
&\quad + 3\alpha^k \cdot \Big(2\epsilon^{k-1} + \delta k 2^{k+1}\Big)\mathtt{COST}^{S'} \\
&\leq\; \Big((k+1)^k + \frac{3\alpha^k}{\epsilon^{k-1}} + \frac{3\alpha^k}{\epsilon^{k-1}\delta^{k-1}}\Big)\mathtt{COST}^S \\
&\quad + 3\alpha^k \cdot \Big(2\epsilon^{k-1} + \delta k 2^{k+1}\Big)\mathtt{COST}^{S'}
\end{aligned}$$

We set $\delta = \frac{1}{36k\alpha^k}$ and $\epsilon^{k-1} = \frac{1}{24\alpha^k}$, and derive:

$$\mathtt{COST}^{S,S'} \;\leq\; O\Big(\alpha^{k^2+k} \cdot (36k)^{k-1}\Big)\mathtt{COST}^S + \frac{1}{2}\mathtt{COST}^{S'}$$

This will complete the proof of Theorem 10.

As mentioned, our remaining task is to upper bound $\frac{\mathrm{d}}{\mathrm{d}t}\Phi^{S(\delta),S'}(t)$. We will first introduce several useful technical lemmas. Then we will proceed our analysis by considering the effect of the processing in $S(\delta)$ and S', separately. Throughout the analysis all ties are broken in an arbitrary but a consistent way. Particularly, the reader may read the analysis assuming that no two different jobs have the same size, nor the same remaining size.

7. REFERENCES

[1] S. Anand, N. Garg, and A. Kumar. Resource augmentation for weighted flow-time explained by dual fitting. In *Proceedings of the Twenty-Third Annual ACM-SIAM Symposium on Discrete Algorithms*, SODA '12, pages 1228–1241. SIAM, 2012.

[2] Y. Azar, K. Jain, and V. Mirrokni. (almost) optimal coordination mechanisms for unrelated machine scheduling. In *Proceedings of the nineteenth annual ACM-SIAM symposium on Discrete algorithms*, SODA '08, pages 323–332, Philadelphia, PA, USA, 2008. Society for Industrial and Applied Mathematics.

[3] N. Bansal, R. Krishnaswamy, and V. Nagarajan. Better scalable algorithms for broadcast scheduling. In *Proceedings of the 37th international colloquium conference on Automata, languages and programming,*

ICALP'10, pages 324–335, Berlin, Heidelberg, 2010. Springer-Verlag.
[4] N. Bansal and K. R. Pruhs. Server scheduling to balance priorities, fairness, and average quality of service. *SIAM J. Comput.*, 39(7):3311–3335, July 2010.
[5] I. Caragiannis. Better bounds for online load balancing on unrelated machines. In *SODA*, pages 972–981, 2008.
[6] I. Caragiannis. Efficient coordination mechanisms for unrelated machine scheduling. In *SODA*, pages 815–824, 2009.
[7] J. S. Chadha, N. Garg, A. Kumar, and V. N. Muralidhara. A competitive algorithm for minimizing weighted flow time on unrelatedmachines with speed augmentation. In *STOC*, 2009.
[8] G. Christodoulou, E. Koutsoupias, and A. Nanavati. Coordination mechanisms. *Theor. Comput. Sci.*, 410(36):3327–3336, Aug. 2009.
[9] J. Cohen, C. Dürr, and N. K. Thang. Smooth inequalities and equilibrium inefficiency in scheduling games. In *WINE*, pages 350–363, 2012.
[10] R. Cole, J. R. Correa, V. Gkatzelis, V. Mirrokni, and N. Olver. Inner product spaces for minsum coordination mechanisms. In *Proceedings of the 43rd annual ACM symposium on Theory of computing*, STOC '11, pages 539–548, New York, NY, USA, 2011. ACM.
[11] J. R. Correa and M. Queyranne. Efficiency of equilibria in restricted uniform machine scheduling with total weighted completion time as social cost. In *Naval Research Logistics*, pages 384–395, 2012.
[12] J. Edmonds and K. Pruhs. Scalably scheduling processes with arbitrary speedup curves. In *SODA*, pages 685–692, 2009.
[13] L. A. Hall, D. B. Shmoys, and J. Wein. Scheduling to minimize average completion time: Off-line and on-line algorithms. In *SODA*, 1996.
[14] S. Im and B. Moseley. Online scalable algorithm for minimizing ;k-norms of weighted flow time on unrelated machines. In *SODA*, pages 95–108, 2011.
[15] S. Im, B. Moseley, and K. Pruhs. A tutorial on amortized local competitiveness in online scheduling. *SIGACT News*, 42(2):83–97, 2011.
[16] N. Immorlica, L. E. Li, V. S. Mirrokni, and A. S. Schulz. Coordination mechanisms for selfish scheduling. *Theor. Comput. Sci.*, 410(17):1589–1598, Apr. 2009.
[17] B. Kalyanasundaram and K. Pruhs. Speed is as powerful as clairvoyance. *J. ACM*, 47(4):617–643, July 2000.
[18] E. Koutsoupias and C. H. Papadimitriou. Worst-case equilibria. In *STACS*, pages 404–413, 1999.
[19] H. Moulin. Minimizing the worst slowdown: off-line and on-line. *Operations Research*, 55(5):876–889, 2007.
[20] T. Roughgarden. Intrinsic robustness of the price of anarchy. In *STOC*, pages 513–522, 2009.
[21] A. S. Schulz and M. Skutella. Scheduling unrelated machines by randomized rounding. *SIAM J. Discret. Math.*, 15(4):450–469, Apr. 2002.
[22] M. Skutella. Convex quadratic and semidefinite programming relaxations in scheduling. *J. ACM*, 48(2):206–242, Mar. 2001.
[23] M. Skutella and G. J. Woeginger. A ptas for minimizing the total weighted completion time on identical parallel machines, 1999.

APPENDIX

A. POPULAR SCHEDULING POLICIES

Here, we describe some well known scheduling policies. Fix a machine i which has to process a set of jobs Q_i. The symbol $J_i(t)$ denotes the set of unfinished jobs that are available for processing at time t. All the policies described below are simple, in the sense that they can be implemented in an "online" environment. Thus, at any time t, the processing decision depends only on the jobs in $J_i(t)$, their weights, and remaining processing lengths. In particular, the decision is independent of the jobs that are going to arrive in future.

First we give a brief description of scheduling policies which has bounded stretch (see Definition 1).

Highest Density First (HDF). At any time t, the machine works on the job $j \in J_i(t)$ which has the highest density w_j/p_{ij}. When the jobs are unweighted, this policy is known as "Shortest Processing Time First" (SPT).

Highest Residual Density First (HRDF). At any time t, the machine works on the job $j \in J_i(t)$ which has the highest residual density $w_j/p_{ij}(t)$. When the jobs are unweighted, this policy is known as "Shortest Remaining Processing Time First" (SRPT).

Weighted Round Robin (WRR). At any time t, the machine works on the jobs in $J_i(t)$ in proportion to their weights. Specifically, for all jobs $j \in J_i(t)$, we have:

$$\frac{d}{dt}(p_{ij}(t)) = -\frac{w_j}{\sum_{j' \in J_i(t)} w_{j'}}.$$

We note that WRR is an example of a *non-clairvoyant* scheduling policy. This refers to the property that a scheduling policy like WRR can be used even when the machine does not known the processing lengths in advance, and a job's processing length is revealed only when the machine finishes the job.

Weighted Shortest Elapsed Time First (WSETF). At any time t, the machine works on the job $j \in J_i(t)$ which maximizes the ratio $w_j/(p_{ij} - p_{ij}(t))$. Unweighted version of this scheduling policy is known as "Shortest Elapsed Time First", and here the machine works on the job which has been least processed so far. WSETF is a non-clairvoyant scheduling policy which has been extensively studied in scheduling literature [17, 4].

It is easy to verify that all the scheduling policies mentioned above satisfy the stretch condition with $\alpha = 1$, and are myopic and monotone. We skip the proof.

Next, we look at scheduling policies which do not satisfy our bounded stretch conditon. First we consider WLAPS, which gives $O(1)$ approximation on a single machine and has been extensively studied in scheduling theory [12, 3]. We show in Section B that WLAPS has $\alpha = \Omega(n)$, and it also has PoA $= \Omega(n)$.

WEIGHTED LATEST ARRIVAL PROCESSOR SHARING (WLAPS(ϵ)). This scheduling policy takes a parameter $\epsilon \in [0, 1]$ as input. Let $J_i^\epsilon(t)$ denote $\epsilon|J(t)|$ jobs in $J(t)$ with the highest release dates. At any time t, the machine works on the jobs $j \in J_i^\epsilon(t)$ in proportion to their weights, so that for all $j \in J_i^\epsilon(t)$ we have:

$$\frac{d}{dt}(p_{ij}(t)) = -\frac{w_j}{\sum_{j' \in J_i^\epsilon(t)} w_{j'}}.$$

This scheduling policy gives preference to the recently released jobs, and is non-clairvoyant. Note that if $\epsilon = 1$, then this policy reduces to WEIGHTED ROUND ROBIN. When the jobs are unweighted, this policy is known as LATEST ARRIVAL PROCESSOR SHARING (LAPS).

The following scheduling policies also fail to satisfy our bounded stretch condition.

- First in First Out (FIFO) – this schedules the jobs in the increasing order of their release dates.
- Longest Job First (LJF) – this schedules the longest job available for processing.
- Biggest Weight First (BWF) – this schedules the job with the highest weight.
- The policy which schedules a job uniformly at random.

However, unlike WLAPS, these polices are not $O(1)$ approximation to the weighted completion objective and hence have bad PoA.

Remark:.

The scheduling policy RAND considered in [10] does indeed satisfy our condition with $\alpha = 1$ in expectation. However, we do not analyze RAND, since it is not clear how to extend RAND in the presence of release dates.

B. PRICE OF ANARCHY OF A SCHEDULING POLICY WITH LARGE STRETCH

In this section, we consider a policy called Weighted Latest Arrival Processor Sharing (WLAPS) which has been extensively studied in scheduling theory [12, 3]. Although this policy gives $O(1)$-approximation to weighted completion time on a single machine, we show that its induced game has large PoA (see Lemma 11). Further, we show that WLAPS fails our α-stretch condition (see Lemma 12), hence making a case for bounded stretch policies.

Fix a machine i which has to process a set of jobs, and let $J_i(t)$ denote the set of unfinished jobs that are available for processing at time t. The scheduling policy WLAPS takes a parameter $\epsilon \in [0, 1]$ as input. Let $J_i^\epsilon(t)$ denote the $\epsilon|J_i(t)|$ jobs in $J_i(t)$ with the highest release dates. At any time t, the machine works on the jobs $j \in J_i^\epsilon(t)$ in proportion to their weights, so that for all $j \in J_i^\epsilon(t)$ we have:

$$\frac{d}{dt}(p_{ij}(t)) = -\frac{w_j}{\sum_{j' \in J_i^\epsilon(t)} w_{j'}}.$$

WLAPS is an example of a *non-clairvoyant* scheduling policy, and reduces to Weighted Round Robin (see Appendix A) when $\epsilon = 1$. For simplicity, we fix $\epsilon = 1/2$ in the following proof; however, the proof can be easily extended to any value of ϵ.

LEMMA 11. *If every machine follows the scheduling policy WLAPS(ϵ) with $\epsilon = 1/2$, then the PoA of the resulting game is $\Omega(n)$, where n denotes the total number of jobs.*

PROOF. Consider the following instance. There are n jobs and n machines. Each job has unit weight. Among the n jobs, there is one *big* job j^* which has processing length $p_{ij^*} = n$ and release date $r_{ij^*} = \kappa$ on all the machines. Here, κ is an arbitrarily small positive value. The remaining $n - 1$ *small* jobs have processing lengths $p_{1j} = \kappa + \beta$ (which is an arbitrarily small positive value) on machine $i = 1$, and processing length $p_{ij} = n$ on the other machines $i \neq 1$. Further, these small jobs have release dates $r_{ij} = 0$ on all the machines.

In an optimal solution, all the small jobs are assigned to machine 1, and the big job is assigned to any other machine. Hence, the sum of the completion times of the jobs is at most $O(n)$. In contrast, there exists a bad equilibrium - the big job on machine 1, and each small job on a distinct machine. Here, the total completion time of all the jobs is at least $\Omega(n^2)$. It is easy to see that this is a Nash Equilibrium. In particular, no small job wants to deviate to machine 1, since that machine would make the small job wait till it finishes the big job. □

LEMMA 12. *The scheduling policy $WLAPS(\epsilon)$ has stretch $\alpha = \Omega(n)$ when $\epsilon = 1/2$. Here, the symbol n denotes the number of jobs processed by the machine.*

PROOF. Consider the following instance. A machine is processing a set of n jobs $X_1 \cup X_2$ using the scheduling policy WLAPS(1/2). Each job $j \in X_1 \cup X_2$ has weight $w_j = 1$. The subset X_1 consists of $n/2$ jobs. Each job $j \in X_1$ has a processing length $p_j = 1$ and release date $r_j = 0$. The subset X_2 also consists of $n/2$ jobs. Each job $j \in X_2$ has a processing length $p_j = n$ and release date $r_j = \kappa$, where κ is an arbitrarily small positive value.

It is easy to see that the machine starves the jobs in X_1 in favor of the jobs in X_2 from time $t = \kappa$ onwards. Hence, all the jobs in X_2 complete at time $t = n^2/2 + \kappa$, and the completion time of any job $j \in X_1$ is at least $\Omega(n^2)$. On the other hand, the bounded stretch condition (see Definition 1) requires the completion time of such a job to be at most αn. Thus, WLAPS(ϵ) has stretch $\alpha = \Omega(n)$ when $\epsilon = 1/2$. □

Private Interactive Communication Across an Adversarial Channel

Ran Gelles
Department of Computer Science, UCLA
gelles@cs.ucla.edu

Amit Sahai
Department of Computer Science, UCLA
sahai@cs.ucla.edu

Akshay Wadia
Department of Computer Science, UCLA
awadia@cs.ucla.edu

ABSTRACT

Consider two parties Alice and Bob, who hold private inputs x and y, and wish to compute a function $f(x, y)$ *privately* in the information theoretic sense; that is, each party should learn nothing beyond $f(x, y)$. However, the communication channel available to them is *noisy*. This means that the channel can introduce errors in the transmission between the two parties. Moreover, the channel is *adversarial* in the sense that it knows the protocol that Alice and Bob are running, and maliciously introduces errors to disrupt the communication, subject to some bound on the total number of errors. A fundamental question in this setting is to design a protocol that remains private in the presence of large number of errors.

If Alice and Bob are only interested in computing $f(x, y)$ correctly, and not privately, then quite robust protocols are known that can tolerate a *constant* fraction of errors. However, none of these solutions is applicable in the setting of privacy, as they inherently leak information about the parties' inputs. This leads to the question whether we can simultaneously achieve privacy and error-resilience against a constant fraction of errors.

We show that privacy and error-resilience are contradictory goals. In particular, we show that for every constant $c > 0$, there exists a function f which is privately computable in the error-less setting, but for which no private and correct protocol is resilient against a c-fraction of errors. The same impossibility holds also for sub-constant noise rate, e.g., when c is exponentially small (as a function of the input size).

Categories and Subject Descriptors

E.4 [**Data**]: Coding and Information Theory; F.1.2 [**Theory of Computation**]: Modes of Computation—*Interactive and reactive computation*

General Terms

Theory

ITCS'14, January 12–14, 2014, Princeton, New Jersey, USA.

ACM 978-1-4503-2698-8/14/01 ...$15.00.
http://dx.doi.org/10.1145/2554797.2554812.

Keywords

Interactive communication; coding; adversarial noise; private function evaluation; information-theoretic security

1. INTRODUCTION

Consider two parties, A and B that wish to compute some function $f(x, y)$ of their respective private inputs x, y. The channel connecting the parties might be prone to error, and in order to compute f the parties run some error-resilient interactive protocol that is guaranteed to output $f(x, y)$ as long as the amount of error is small (e.g., the fraction of corrupt messages is below some threshold $c > 0$).

If efficiency is not concerned, party A can simply encode its input using a standard (Shannon) error-correcting code that corrects a fraction $c < 1/2$ of errors [Sha48]; party B computes the output $f(x, y)$ and sends it back (encoded with the same parameters) to A. This allows a global error rate of up to $1/4$. However, x might be very large, and more efficient protocols (communication-wise) can be found. In 1993, Schulman [Sch93, Sch96] showed a way to compile any interactive protocol π that assumes no error, into an error-resilient protocol Π that withstands a fraction of errors of up to $1/240$, whose overhead is linear (i.e., the communication of Π, is linear in the communication of π). This was followed by a flow of other works [RS94, BR11, GMS11, BK12, BN13, FGOS13] trying to improve the efficiency or error-resilience in various settings. Notably, the work of Braverman and Rao [BR11] showed how to compile a (noiseless) π into an error-resilient Π that correctly computes f as long as the error fraction is less than $1/4$. Their construction, similar to the construction of Schulman, has a linear overhead (such constructions are also called *constant rate*). The recent elegant work of Brakerski and Kalai [BK12] shows how to achieve *efficient* computation in the presence of adversarial noise of rates less than $1/32$ (for binary alphabet).

All the above works consider only the correctness of the protocol in the presence of adversarial error. In this work we aim at achieving other properties as well, specifically, privacy. We ask the following question:

> *Can error-resilient protocols tolerating some constant fraction of errors be devised, if we also require the protocol to be* **private**, *that is, not to leak any information besides $f(x, y)$?*

Some functions cannot be privately computed even when the communication channel is noise-free, so the above question should only apply to functions that can be privately computed over a noiseless channel. The set of such functions was defined by Kushilevitz [Kus92] and independently by Beaver [Bea91]. Although this set is rather small, it still contains some very interesting functions such as the Vickrey function for 2nd-price auctions [Vic61] (see more details below).

Evidently, privacy is no longer guaranteed when compiling a private (error-free) protocol π for f using the methods of Schulman or Braverman and Rao. For instance, Schulman's scheme works by 'running' π until the users suspect their views are 'inconsistent' due to channel errors. Then, the users 'backtrack' to the last consistent point and continue from there. This "rewinding" is vital for the protocol's ability to recover from errors, yet it is fatal for its privacy.

We answer the above question in the negative, and show that privacy and error-resilience are in fact contradicting aspirations.

THEOREM 1.1 (SEPARATION THEOREM). *For any constant $c > 0$, there exists a function f such that a private protocol for f exists in the error-free setting, but no protocol is both private and correctly computes f over a noisy channel with at most a c-fraction of adversarial errors.*

In fact, our impossibility result is even stronger, as it rules out protocols even when the error-rate is below constant:

THEOREM 1.2 (MAIN, INFORMAL). *There is a function f taking two inputs of size n, such that there is a private protocol for f in the error-free setting, but no private protocol correctly computes f over a noisy channel with $O(2^{-n})$-fraction of adversarial errors.*

With our result, it is very interesting to compare private computations in the *error-free* model, the *random-noise* model, and the *adversarial-error* model. As first shown by Kushilevitz [Kus89, Kus92] and Beaver [Bea91], in the error-free model, some functions are privately-computable and others are not. The set of functions that can be privately computed is fully characterized in [Bea91, Kus92], wherein an optimal protocol for any function in this set is also provided. In the random-noise model, it is possible to obtain oblivious transfer over several types of channels, e.g., the binary symmetric channel [CK88] and the unfair noisy channel [DFMS04]. Since any function f can be privately computed assuming oblivious transfer [Kil88], *any* function can be privately computed assuming a (certain types of) random noise.

In the adversarial-error model, on the other hand, we show that depending on the error rate, there are functions that can be privately computed in the error-free setting but not in the adversarial-error model. Thus, there is no hope to achieve constant-rate schemes for any function f, or even for any f which can be computed privately in the error-free setting.

Techniques. Our key insight is that resilience to errors implies that the protocol must be able to "backtrack" its course from an incorrect track reached due to channel errors, while, at least intuitively, privacy should prevent the protocol from taking any course other than the correct one and prevent "rewinding" the protocol and changing its intermediates inputs. Hence, showing that privacy forces the protocol to advance in a specific order, say, through specific ordered steps, would imply that error-correction can be performed only *within* a single step, but not *between steps.*

The line of work initiated by Kushilevitz [Kus89, Kus92] and Beaver [Bea91] helps us with this problem. In particular, the result of Maji, Prabhakaran and Rosulek [MPR09], shows that private protocols in the error-free model must advance in very specific ways. The progress of such a protocol can be split into steps where at each step only a single quantum of information is revealed (namely, a single decomposition of the domain, see formal definitions in Section 2). Moreover, revealing the information of step i before the information of step $j < i$ is revealed leads to violating privacy. The amount of steps depends only on f, and for any $d \leq 2(2^n - 1)$ there exists a privately-computable function with exactly d steps [Kus92].

We revisit the works of [Bea91, Kus92, MPR09] and examine them in the adversarial error model. We show that a similar property exists in any private, error-resilient protocol. Next, we show that if a channel completely changes the messages of two consecutive steps, the privacy is compromised. This gives an upper bound of $O(1/d)$ on the proportion of allowed error, and proves our main theorem.

More specifically, We identify the point in the protocol where A reveals that his input is in some set P rather than in Q (where $P \cup Q$ is some subset of his domain). The adversarial channel changes the messages of this "step" to lead B to believe that A's input is actually in Q. Then, at the next "step" it's B's turn to reveal whether his input is in some partition V, W of (a subset of) his domain. The channel keeps changing A's messages until the end of this step. However, this violates the privacy of B since his partition is done assuming A's input is in Q. Conditioned on the fact it is in P, the next step of B should have been decomposing his sub-domain into $\tilde{V}, \tilde{W} \neq V, W$. Hence, some information was leaked, and the protocol is not private.

Independent Work. Concurrently and independently of our work, Chung, Pass and Telang [CPT13] also examine impossibility results for coding schemes for secure interactive communication. They prove that there is no compiler that takes a protocol and generates a noise-resilient protocol with good parameters (i.e., constant rate) such that the compiled version exactly imitates the information revelation of the original protocol. Their work extends also to the *computational setting* where they show an interesting tradeoff between the noise susceptibility and the rate of any possible scheme.

We note that their work considers a model where a *party* can be adversarial together with the (rate-limited) adversarial channel. In contrast, our impossibility result works in a model where parties are *semi-honest*, and only the channel can be adversarial (and rate-limited). Thus, the model of [CPT13] and ours are incomparable (but closely related).

Roadmap. We start with preliminaries and definitions in Section 2. Of special importance is Section 2.2, where we model the adversarial channel, and give definitions of privacy and correctness in the presence of such a channel. In Section 3 we study the structure of transcripts generated by a perfectly private and correct protocol in the presence of adversarial channel. The main result of this section is Theorem 3.7 which proves that a private protocol must advance in a very specific sequence of steps. This fact is used in Section 4 to construct a channel that introduces errors at well-chosen points in the protocol execution and violates privacy. Section 5 states our main theorem for the case of protocols which are not perfectly secure. Full details can be found in the long version of this manuscript [GSW13].

2. INTERACTIVE COMPUTATION WITH AND WITHOUT NOISE

2.1 Preliminaries: two-party computation in the noiseless model

We begin by recalling some definitions of two-party computation, assuming noiseless communication. Two parties, A and B hold inputs $x \in X$ and $y \in Y$ respectively. The parties wish to compute the value of $f : X \times Y \to Z$ for some finite set Z. The computation is done via an interactive probabilistic protocol $\pi = (\pi_A, \pi_B)$. The protocol works in rounds and defines for each party, at each round, the next message to be transmitted as a function of its input, randomness, and received messages.[1] The parties send massages $m \in \Sigma$ according to π in an alternating[2] way: for odd rounds, $m_i = \pi_A(x, R_A, m_2 m_4 \cdots m_{i-1})$ and for even rounds $m_i = \pi_B(y, R_B, m_1 m_3 \cdots m_{i-1})$. We denote the transcript of a specific instance $t = m_1 m_2 \cdots$ as the messages transmitted within that instance. We assume messages are delimited so it is possible to parse the transcript into specific messages.

At the end of an execution of π, the parties compute their outputs as a function of their respective inputs, randomness, and views. These functions will be denoted by $\mathsf{out}_A^\pi(\cdot,\cdot,\cdot)$ and $\mathsf{out}_B^\pi(\cdot,\cdot,\cdot)$ respectively. That is, for inputs $(x, y) \in X \times Y$, transcript t, and randomness R_A, R_B, party A's output will be $\mathsf{out}_A^\pi(x, R_A, t)$, and B's output is $\mathsf{out}_B^\pi(y, R_B, t)$. We will usually omit the randomness, and implicitly treat π (along with the output function) as a single randomized protocol.

Correctness and Privacy. We recall the standard definitions for correctness and privacy, assuming the computation is over an error-free channel.

DEFINITION 1. *A protocol is said to be perfectly correct if*

$$\forall x, y : \Pr_{t \leftarrow \pi(x,y)} [\mathsf{out}_A^\pi(x, t) = \mathsf{out}_B^\pi(y, t) = f(x, y)] = 1.$$

As for privacy, we follow the notions developed by Chor, Kushilevitz and Beaver [Kus89, CK91, Bea91, Kus92].

DEFINITION 2 (PRIVACY FOR NOISELESS PROTOCOLS). *A protocol is private (with respect to party A) if, for any $x, x' \in X$ and $y \in Y$ such that $f(x, y) = f(x', y)$, the protocol generates the same distribution of transcripts for inputs (x, y) and (x', y). Formally, for any $t \in \Sigma^*$, $\Pr[t \mid x, y] = \Pr[t \mid x', y]$. Similarly, privacy of party B is given if for any $x \in X$ and $y, y' \in Y$ such that $f(x, y) = f(x, y')$, for any $t \in \Sigma^*$, $\Pr[t \mid x, y] = \Pr[t \mid x, y']$.*

Kushilevtiz [Kus92] and Beaver [Bea91] gave a full characterization for functions that can be computed privately (in the noiseless model). We now recall this characterization.

We say that f is *column-partitionable* if there exists a non-trivial partition of Y into disjoint $P, Q \subset Y$ such that for any $x \in X$ and for any $y \in P, y' \in Q$, it holds that $f(x, y) \neq f(x, y')$. We refer to such P, Q as *valid column-partitions.* We let $f_{X \times P}$ and $f_{X \times Q}$ be f restricted to the domains $X \times P$ and $X \times Q$. Similarly, f is *row-partitionable* if we can partition X into Q and P such that for any $y \in Y$ and any $x \in P$, $x' \in Q$, it holds that $f(x, y) \neq f(x', y)$. Domains that were achieved by a sequence of valid partitionings are called *restricted domains.* We say that some subdomain $X' \times Y'$ is a restricted domain of depth d if it takes d recursive decompositions to obtain $X' \times Y'$. Furthermore, we can generalize the notion of f being row-partitionable, if X can be partitioned into $m > 1$ disjoint sets $X_1, X_2, \ldots, X_m$ and for any $u \in X_i$ and any $v \in X_j$ where $j \neq i$, it holds that for every $y \in Y$, $f(u, y) \neq f(v, y)$. A partition of X into m^* disjoint sets is called *maximal* if any other partition of X has $m \leq m^*$. We will mostly consider *binary decomposable* functions—functions which are maximally partitionable into at most $m = 2$ partitions.

We say that f is *partitionable* if: (1) f is constant; or, (2) f is either row-partitionable or column-partitionable, and each of the restricted functions is also partitionable.

The following lemma, which appears in [Bea91, Kus92], identifies the set of privately-computable functions exactly as the set of *partitionable* functions.

LEMMA 2.1 ([BEA91, KUS92]). *A function f has a perfectly correct protocol π (in the noiseless model) which is private with respect to both parties if and only if f is partitionable.*

2.2 The noisy model: two-party computation over a noisy channel

Let us now augment the above model into a noisy version. First, let us define the notion of a channel. We assume an arbitrary, *causal* channel (possibly with memory). The channel's instantiation at the ℓ-th round $\mathsf{Ch}_\ell(m_\ell \mid (m_1, m_1')(m_2, m_2') \cdots (m_{\ell-1} m_{\ell-1}'))$ is a distribution on Σ characterized by the (input, output) channel messages up to that round. Hence, the probability that the channel takes $\mathbf{m} = m_1 \cdots m_n$ and outputs $\mathbf{m}' = m_1' \cdots m_n'$ is given by

$$\begin{aligned}
&\Pr[\mathsf{Ch}(\mathbf{m}) = \mathbf{m}'] := \\
&\quad \Pr[\mathsf{Ch}_1(m_1 \mid \emptyset) = m_1'] \times \Pr[\mathsf{Ch}_2(m_2 \mid (m_1, m_1')) = m_2'] \cdots \\
&\quad \times \Pr[\mathsf{Ch}_n(m_n \mid (m_1, m_1')(m_2, m_2') \cdots (m_{n-1} m_{n-1}')) = m_n']
\end{aligned}$$

Again we assume that the parties alternately send messages. For a specific instance of the protocol, we denote the *transcript* $\mathbf{t} = (t^s, t^r) = (m_1 m_2 \cdots, m_1' m_2' \cdots)$ as the messages observed for that instance (where t^s denotes the messages the parties send, and t^r the massages they receive). We denote by $t_A^s = m_1 m_3 m_5 \cdots$ the messages sent by A and similarly $t_B^s = m_2 m_4 m_6 \cdots$ is the messages sent by B. The messages received by each party, t_A^r, t_B^r are defined in a similar way.

A protocol $\pi = (\pi_A, \pi_B)$ over a noisy channel Ch is defined in a similar way to the noiseless case: the protocol defines for each party, at each round the next message to send as a function of its inputs, randomness and all the messages *received* up to that round. Explicitly, A's messages on odd rounds are $m_{2i-1} = \pi_A(x, R_A, m_2' m_4' \cdots m_{2i-2}')$, and B's messages on even rounds are $m_{2i} = \pi_B(y, R_B, m_1' m_3' \cdots m_{2i-1}')$, with $\mathbf{m}' = \mathsf{Ch}(\mathbf{m})$.

For some protocol π over a channel Ch and some input (x, y) we can ask what is the set of possible transcripts generated by π for that input, and what is the probability to observe each such transcript. Formally, let $T^s(x, y, t^r)$ be the random variable describing $t^s = m_1 m_2 \cdots$ defined by π on inputs (x, y) given that $t^r = m_1' m_2' \cdots$ is received by the parties. Then, the probability that an instance of π sending messages

[1]Note that previously sent messages are function of the above and need not be given explicitly to the protocol.

[2]This assumption can be avoided with changing our results by a factor of at most 2.

over a channel Ch on inputs (x, y) produces $\mathbf{t} = (t^s, t^r)$ is given by

$$\Pr[\mathbf{t} \mid x, y, \mathsf{Ch}] := P_{T^s(x,y,t^r)}(t^s) \cdot \Pr[\mathsf{Ch}(t^s) = t^r]. \quad (1)$$

The probability can be generalized to any prefix of $\mathbf{t}$ in the standard way, quantifying the probability that π over Ch produces that prefix on (x, y). The probabilities to have a specific *sent-messages* transcript t^s, and a specific *received-messages* transcript t^r are given by the marginal probabilities,

$$\Pr[t^s \mid x, y, \mathsf{Ch}] = \sum_{t^r} P_{T^s(x,y,t^r)}(t^s) \cdot \Pr\left[\mathsf{Ch}(t^s) = t^r\right], \quad (2)$$

$$\Pr[t^r \mid x, y, \mathsf{Ch}] = \sum_{t^s} P_{T^s(x,y,t^r)}(t^s) \cdot \Pr\left[\mathsf{Ch}(t^s) = t^r\right]. \quad (3)$$

For a given input $(x, y) \in X \times Y$ the execution of π with inputs (x, y) over channel Ch induces a distribution over the set of all transcripts according to the above equations. Let $\mathbf{u}$ be a fixed partial transcript. For a given string $\mathbf{u}'$ such that the concatenation of $\mathbf{u}$ with $\mathbf{u}'$ is a complete transcript, we can compute the probability that the protocol π (with inputs (x, y) and channel Ch) will produce $\mathbf{u}'$ *when executed with the history* $\mathbf{u}$. We will use $\pi^{\mathsf{Ch}}(x, y; \mathbf{u})$ to refer to this distribution over completions $\mathbf{u}'$. We will use $\tau^{\mathsf{Ch}}(x, y) := \left\{\mathbf{t} \leftarrow \pi^{\mathsf{Ch}}(x, y)\right\}$ to denote the set of all possible (complete) transcripts generated by π on inputs (x, y) assuming messages are being sent over the channel Ch. The output function for A is defined as above, $\mathsf{out}_A^\pi(x, R_A, t_A^r)$ where t_A^r are the even indices of t^r, i.e., the messages received by A. Similarly, the output for B is $\mathsf{out}_B^\pi(y, R_B, t_B^r)$.

Error Rate. For $i = 1, 2, \ldots$, by $t^r[i]$ and $t^s[i]$ we denote the i-th message in t^r and t^s, respectively, and let $\mathbf{t}[i] = (t^s[i], t^r[i])$. We define $t^r[0]$ and $t^s[0]$ to be the empty string. By $|t^r|$ (resp. $|t^s|$), we denote the number of messages in transcript t^r (resp. t^s). We denote by $|\mathbf{t}|$ the number of pairs in $\mathbf{t}$ so that $|\mathbf{t}| = |t^r| = |t^s|$. If no noise is added by the channel, then for all $i = 1, 2, \ldots$, we have $t^r[i] = t^s[i]$. Define the *error weight* $\eta(\mathbf{t})$ of a transcript $\mathbf{t} = (t^r, t^s)$ as $\eta(\mathbf{t}) := |\{\, i \mid t^r[i] \neq t^s[i] \,\}|$.

Definition 3 (Error Rate of a Channel). *We say that a channel* Ch *has error rate* $\mu \in [0, 1]$, *if for any inputs* (x, y) *and any transcript* $\mathbf{t} \in \tau^{\mathsf{Ch}}(x, y)$, *it holds that* $\eta(\mathbf{t}) \leq \mu|\mathbf{t}|$.

Correctness and Privacy. We now augment the privacy and correctness definitions to the noisy case. The correctness definition is straightforward.

Definition 4 (Perfect Correctness). *A protocol* π *is* perfectly *correct with respect to some function* f *over* Ch *if for any inputs* x, y,

$$\Pr_{\substack{R_A, R_B, R_{\mathsf{Ch}} \\ (t^s, t^r) \leftarrow \pi^{\mathsf{Ch}}(x,y)}} [\mathsf{out}_A^\pi(x, t_A^r) = \mathsf{out}_B^\pi(y, t_B^r) = f(x, y)] = 1.$$

We further say a protocol π *is* perfectly correct with rate μ *if* π *is perfectly correct over every channel* Ch *with error rate* μ.

We define privacy in a similar way to the noiseless case, where the transcript doesn't leak more than what is trivially conveyed by the function's output.

Definition 5 (Perfect Privacy). *A protocol* π *for* f *is perfectly private over* Ch *with respect to* A *if for any inputs such that* $f(x, y) = f(x', y)$, *it holds that for any* $\mathbf{t}$

$$\Pr[\mathbf{t} \mid x, y, \mathsf{Ch}] = \Pr[\mathbf{t} \mid x', y, \mathsf{Ch}].$$

Similarly, perfect privacy with respect to B *requires that whenever* $f(x, y) = f(x, y')$ *it also holds that* $\Pr[\mathbf{t} \mid x, y, \mathsf{Ch}] = \Pr[\mathbf{t} \mid x, y', \mathsf{Ch}]$.
Furthermore, We say that a protocol π *is* perfectly private with rate μ *if it is perfectly private (for both players) over every channel* Ch *with rate* μ.

We mention the following difference between our setting and the one used in [Bea91, Kus92, MPR09]. One of the assumptions used by these works is that the last message of π is the output $f(x, y)$ (this doesn't restrict the generality of those results). However in our noisy model, this assumption doesn't make much sense as the channel can always "violate" the correctness of the protocol by changing this single message. To avoid this inconvenience we assume the output is given by the functions $\mathsf{out}_A, \mathsf{out}_B$ and is not part of the transcript. The next lemma shows that this change has no effect on the distribution of transcripts, namely, that different outputs imply different transcripts, regardless of the parties' randomness (which is trivially the case when the output is part of the transcript).

Lemma 2.2. *Let* π *be a perfectly correct and perfectly private protocol for a function* f, *and let* x, y, y' *be inputs such that* $f(x, y) \neq f(x, y')$. *Then, for any channel* Ch *and for any transcript* $\mathbf{t}$,

$$\textit{if } \Pr[\mathbf{t} \mid x, y, \mathsf{Ch}] > 0, \textit{ then } \Pr[\mathbf{t} \mid x, y', \mathsf{Ch}] = 0.$$

Proof. We say that A's random tape R_A *is consistent with* transcript $\mathbf{t}$ and input x if for $1 \leq i \leq |\mathbf{t}|$,

$$\pi_A(x, R_A, t^r[0 \ldots i-1]) = t^s[i].$$

Let $\mathbf{t}^*$ be a transcript such that both $\Pr[\mathbf{t}^* \mid x, y, \mathsf{Ch}] > 0$ and $\Pr[\mathbf{t}^* \mid x, y', \mathsf{Ch}] > 0$. Consider the set,

$$S_{\mathbf{t}^*} = \{\, R_A \mid R_A \textit{ is consistent with } \mathbf{t}^* \textit{ and } x \,\}$$

As $\Pr[\mathbf{t}^* \mid x, y, \mathsf{Ch}] > 0$, by perfect correctness, for all $R_A \in S_{\mathbf{t}^*}$, we have $\mathsf{out}_A(x, R_A, \mathbf{t}^*) = f(x, y)$. Similarly, as $\Pr[\mathbf{t}^* \mid x, y', \mathsf{Ch}] > 0$, for all $R_A \in S_{\mathbf{t}^*}$, we have that $\mathsf{out}_A(x, R_A, \mathbf{t}^*) = f(x, y')$. But these statements are mutually contradictory as $f(x, y) \neq f(x, y')$. Therefore, it must be that either $\Pr[\mathbf{t}^* \mid x, y, \mathsf{Ch}] = 0$ or $\Pr[\mathbf{t}^* \mid x, y', \mathsf{Ch}] = 0$. □

3. PRIVATE PROTOCOLS: THE PERFECT CASE

The goal of this section is to show that a private protocol reveals information about the parties' inputs in a particular well-defined order. This section extends the results in [MPR09] to the noisy channel setting. In particular, we analyze the transcripts of the protocol and show that they proceed through well-defined stages that depend upon the partitioning of the function. At each such stage, one of the parties necessarily reveals a particular partition of its input space in which its current input lies. This is formalized by the concept of "frontiers"(see Definition 7 for the formal definition). A frontier is a prefix-free set of partial transcripts which is maximal in the sense that every transcript has a prefix in the frontier. The main result of this section is

Theorem 3.7, where we construct a set of frontiers which correspond to the stages where the transcripts reveal the partitions.

We focus on functions that have a certain structure, which we call *binary-uniquely decomposable*: their domain is maximally row-partitionable into 2 partitions and is not column-partitionable. Each one of the two restricted domains is either constant or (maximally, binary) column-partitionable but not row-partitionable. This continues recursively in an alternating manner (i.e., one level row-partitionable and the next level is column-partitionable). Although the proofs could be extended to a more general case, this simpler class of functions is enough for our impossibility result, as we are only required to provide *one* function that has no perfectly-correct and private protocol over a noisy channel (of certain parameters). A simple example of such a function is the following Vickrey auction function [Vic61]

$$f(x,y) = \begin{cases} 2x & x \le y \\ 2y+1 & x > y \end{cases}$$

where the inputs x and y are integers less than a certain bound N. This function is very useful for performing private 2nd-price (Vickrey) auctions, as it practically outputs (to both parties and the auctioneer) the value of $\min(x,y)$ as well as the identity of the party that holds the minimal value, encoded via the parity of the output.

Our first step is to identify certain inputs that form a *minor*. These will be associated with each level of f's decomposition.

Definition 6 (Minor). *We say that x, x', y, y' form a $\boxminus$-minor (resp., a $\boxplus$-minor) if*

$$\begin{matrix} f(x,y) & = & f(x,y') \\ \neq & & \neq \\ f(x',y) & \neq & f(x',y') \end{matrix} \quad \textit{(resp., if} \quad \begin{matrix} f(x,y) & \neq & f(x,y') \\ = & & \neq \\ f(x',y) & \neq & f(x',y') \end{matrix} \textit{).}$$

Lemma 3.1. *Assume a binary-uniquely decomposable function f on $X \times Y$ which is row-partitionable into P, Q, but not column-partitionable. Then, exactly one of the following happens.*

1. *Both $f_{Q\times Y}$ and $f_{P\times Y}$ are constant.*
2. *Only one of $f_{Q\times Y}, f_{P\times Y}$ is constant, and there exists a $\boxminus$-minor (x,x',y,y') with x and x' in different sets of the partition (specifically x is in the constant partition). Furthermore, y, y' are in different sets of the column-partitioning of the non-constant restricted function.*
3. *Both $f_{Q\times Y}$ and $f_{P\times Y}$ are non constants, and there are at least two "overlapping" minors: if $f_{Q\times Y}$ is partitioned into Y_{Q_0}, Y_{Q_1} and $f_{P\times Y}$ is partitioned into Y_{P_0}, Y_{P_1}, there exist minors (x,x',y,y') and (x,x',w,w') where $x \in P$ and $x' \in Q$. And if both y, y' are in the same partition Y_{P_i} and both w, w' are in Y_{Q_j} then $Y_{P_i} \cap Y_{Q_j}$ contains one of w, w' and one of y, y'.*

Proof. We note that cases 1 and 2 are simple, and prove case 3. First, we mention that Y_{P_0}, Y_{P_1} is *not* a valid partition for $f_{Q\times Y}$, since if it was, then f would be column-partitionable in contradiction to its definition. The same applies to Y_{Q_0}, Y_{Q_1} and $f_{P\times Y}$.

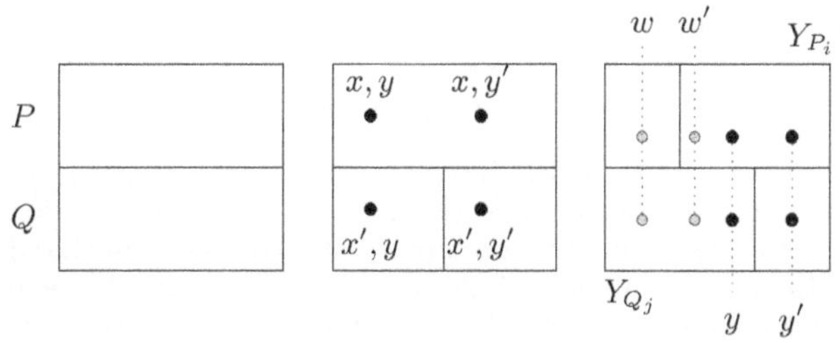

Figure 1: A simplified illustration of the three cases. A closed area means a constant value of f within this area.

Consider $f_{P\times Y}$. There must exist $x \in P$ and $y \in Y_{Q_0}, y' \in Y_{Q_1}$ such that $f(x,y) = f(x,y')$, or otherwise Y_{Q_0}, Y_{Q_1} is a valid column partition of $f_{P\times Y}$. It follows that y, y' must be in the same partition Y_{P_i}. Note that for any $x' \in Q$, (x,x',y,y') is a minor.

Let Y_{Q_j} be the partition that has non-empty intersection with both Y_{P_0}, Y_{P_1} (at least one of Y_{Q_0}, Y_{Q_1} must intersect both Y_{P_0}, Y_{P_1}, or otherwise f is column-partitionable). There must exist $u' \in Q$ and $w \in Y_{Q_j} \cap Y_{P_0}$, $w' \in Y_{Q_j} \cap Y_{P_1}$ such that $f(u',w) = f(u',w')$, or otherwise Y_{P_0}, Y_{P_1} is a valid partition for $f_{Q\times Y}$. Then, for any $u \in P$ (and specifically for x), (u',u,w,w') is a $\boxminus$-minor. Finally, note that we are allowed to choose any $x' \in Q, u \in P$; we choose $x' = u'$ and $u = x$ and complete the proof. $\square$

With this setting we can start exploring the sequential revelation of information in private protocols. Consider inputs (x,x',y,y') which form a $\boxminus$-minor. The following lemma shows that transcripts produced by inputs (x,y) and those produced by inputs (x',y) must differ at some point. Further, the earliest point where they differ must be a point where party A speaks.

Lemma 3.2. *For a perfectly correct π for f over Ch, the following holds. If $f(x,y) \neq f(x',y)$, then for any $\mathbf{t} \in \tau^{\mathsf{Ch}}(x,y) \cup \tau^{\mathsf{Ch}}(x',y)$ there exists an odd round ρ such that $\Pr[\mathbf{t}_{[1..\rho]} \mid x,y,\mathsf{Ch}] \neq \Pr[\mathbf{t}_{[1..\rho]} \mid x',y,\mathsf{Ch}]$, yet for any $\ell < \rho$ it holds that $\Pr[\mathbf{t}_{[1..\ell]} \mid x,y,\mathsf{Ch}] = \Pr[\mathbf{t}_{[1..\ell]} \mid x',y,\mathsf{Ch}]$.*

Proof. Let $\mathbf{t} = (t^s, t^r) \in \tau^{\mathsf{Ch}}(x,y) \cup \tau^{\mathsf{Ch}}(x',y)$. Since $f(x,y) \neq f(x',y)$ and the protocol is perfectly-correct, Lemma 2.2 suggests that there must exist some round k for which $\Pr[\mathbf{t}_{[1..k]} \mid x,y,\mathsf{Ch}] \neq \Pr[\mathbf{t}_{[1..k]} \mid x',y,\mathsf{Ch}]$. Let ρ be the minimal round that satisfies this condition.

Assume towards contradiction that ρ is even, i.e., B sends a message at round ρ. Then,

$$\begin{aligned} &\Pr\left[\mathbf{t}_{[1..\rho]} \mid x,y,\mathsf{Ch}\right] \\ &= \Pr\left[\pi(x,y,t^r{}_{[1..\rho]}) = t^s{}_{[1..\rho]}\right] \Pr\left[\mathsf{Ch}(t^s{}_{[1..\rho]}) = t^r{}_{[1..\rho]}\right] \\ &= \Pr\left[\pi_B(y,t^r{}_{[1..\rho-1]}) = t^s[\rho]\right] \\ &\quad \times \Pr\left[\pi(x,y,t^r{}_{[1..\rho-1]}) = t^s{}_{[1..\rho-1]}\right] \\ &\quad \times \Pr\left[\mathsf{Ch}(t^s[\rho] \mid \mathbf{t}_{[1..\rho-1]}) = t^r[\rho]\right] \\ &\quad \times \Pr\left[\mathsf{Ch}(t^s{}_{[1..\rho-1]}) = t^r{}_{[1..\rho-1]}\right] \\ &= \Pr\left[\pi_B(y,t^r{}_{[1..\rho-1]}) = t^s[\rho]\right] \\ &\quad \times \Pr\left[(\mathsf{Ch}(t^s[\rho] \mid \mathbf{t}_{[1..\rho-1]}) = t^r[\rho]\right] \Pr\left[\mathbf{t}_{[1..\rho-1]} \mid x',y,\mathsf{Ch}\right] \\ &= \Pr[\mathbf{t}_{[1..\rho]} \mid x',y,\mathsf{Ch}] \end{aligned}$$

which leads to a contradiction. The third transition is due the fact that for any round $k < \rho$, $\Pr[\mathbf{t}_{[1..k]} \mid x, y, \mathsf{Ch}] = \Pr[\mathbf{t}_{[1..k]} \mid x', y, \mathsf{Ch}]$, by the way we define ρ. □

The next two lemmas show that when considering two consecutive levels of the decomposition (say, row-decomposition followed by a column-decomposition; those are associated with some ⊞-minor (x, x', y, y')), if party B reveals some information about whether his input is y or y' (i.e. the column-decomposition), it must be the case, that party A has completely revealed whether his input is x or x', or more precisely, whether his input is in P or Q for the matching row-partition.

LEMMA 3.3. *For a perfectly correct π for f over Ch, the following holds. For any x, x', y, y' that form a ⊞-minor, let $\mathbf{t} \in \tau^{\mathsf{Ch}}(x', y) \cup \tau^{\mathsf{Ch}}(x', y')$, and let ρ be the first round where $\Pr[\mathbf{t}_{[1..\rho]} \mid x', y] \neq \Pr[\mathbf{t}_{[1..\rho]} \mid x', y']$. Then,*

$$\Pr\left[\mathbf{t}_{[1..\rho-1]} \mid x, y, \mathsf{Ch}\right] = \Pr\left[\mathbf{t}_{[1..\rho-1]} \mid x, y', \mathsf{Ch}\right] = 0.$$

PROOF. First, note that ρ must be even (this follows from Lemma 3.2). Assume towards contradiction that $\Pr[\mathbf{t}_{[1..\rho-1]} \mid x, y', \mathsf{Ch}] > 0$. Now,

$$\begin{aligned}
&\Pr[\mathbf{t}_{[1..\rho]} \mid x, y, \mathsf{Ch}] = \\
&\quad = \Pr\left[\pi_B\left(y, t^r_B{}_{[1..\rho-1]}\right) = t^s[\rho]\right] \\
&\quad\quad \times \Pr\left[\mathsf{Ch}\left(t^s[\rho] \mid \mathbf{t}_{[1..\rho-1]}\right) = t^r[\rho]\right] \Pr[\mathbf{t}_{[1..\rho-1]} \mid x, y, \mathsf{Ch}] \\
&\quad = \Pr\left[\mathbf{t}[\rho] \mid y, \mathbf{t}_{[1..\rho-1]}, \mathsf{Ch}\right] \Pr[\mathbf{t}_{[1..\rho-1]} \mid x, y', \mathsf{Ch}].
\end{aligned}$$

In addition, due to B's privacy and the fact that $f(x,y) = f(x,y')$, for any round ρ' and specifically for the above ρ we have, $\Pr[\mathbf{t}_{[1..\rho]} \mid x, y, \mathsf{Ch}] = \Pr[\mathbf{t}_{[1..\rho]} \mid x, y', \mathsf{Ch}]$ thus

$$\begin{aligned}
&\Pr[\mathbf{t}_{[1..\rho]} \mid x, y, \mathsf{Ch}] = \\
&\qquad \Pr\left[\mathbf{t}[\rho] \mid y', \mathbf{t}_{[1..\rho-1]}, \mathsf{Ch}\right] \Pr[\mathbf{t}_{[1..\rho-1]} \mid x, y', \mathsf{Ch}].
\end{aligned}$$

Since $\Pr[\mathbf{t}_{[1..\rho-1]} \mid x, y'] \neq 0$, it must be that

$$\Pr\left[\mathbf{t}[\rho] \mid y, \mathbf{t}_{[1..\rho-1]}, \mathsf{Ch}\right] = \Pr\left[\mathbf{t}[\rho] \mid y', \mathbf{t}_{[1..\rho-1]}, \mathsf{Ch}\right]. \quad (4)$$

On the other hand, we know that ρ is the first round such that $\Pr\left[\mathbf{t}_{[1..\rho]} \mid x', y\right] \neq \Pr\left[\mathbf{t}_{[1..\rho]} \mid x', y'\right]$, thus,

$$\begin{aligned}
&\Pr[\mathbf{t}_{[1..\rho]} \mid x', y, \mathsf{Ch}] \\
&\quad = \Pr\left[\mathbf{t}[\rho] \mid y, \mathbf{t}_{[1..\rho-1]}, \mathsf{Ch}\right] \Pr[\mathbf{t}_{[1..\rho-1]} \mid x', y, \mathsf{Ch}] \\
&\quad = \Pr\left[\mathbf{t}[\rho] \mid y, \mathbf{t}_{[1..\rho-1]}, \mathsf{Ch}\right] \Pr[\mathbf{t}_{[1..\rho-1]} \mid x', y', \mathsf{Ch}] \\
&\qquad\qquad \neq \\
&\quad \Pr\left[\mathbf{t}[\rho] \mid y', \mathbf{t}_{[1..\rho-1]}, \mathsf{Ch}\right] \Pr[\mathbf{t}_{[1..\rho-1]} \mid x', y', \mathsf{Ch}] \\
&\qquad\qquad = \Pr[\mathbf{t}_{[1..\rho]} \mid x', y', \mathsf{Ch}]
\end{aligned}$$

and since $\mathbf{t} \in \tau^{\mathsf{Ch}}(x', y) \cup \tau^{\mathsf{Ch}}(x', y')$ it holds that $\Pr[\mathbf{t}_{[1..\rho-1]} \mid x', y', \mathsf{Ch}] > 0$ and we conclude that

$$\Pr\left[\mathbf{t}[\rho] \mid y, \mathbf{t}_{[1..\rho-1]}, \mathsf{Ch}\right] \neq \Pr\left[\mathbf{t}[\rho] \mid y', \mathbf{t}_{[1..\rho-1]}, \mathsf{Ch}\right], \quad (5)$$

contradicting Eq. (4). A similar proof works for (x, y). □

LEMMA 3.4. *Let π be a perfectly-correct private protocol for f over Ch. For any x, x', y, y' that form a ⊞-minor, let $\mathbf{t} \in \tau^{\mathsf{Ch}}(x, y) \cup \tau^{\mathsf{Ch}}(x, y')$. Then, there exists a round ρ such that*

$$\Pr[\mathbf{t}_{[1..\rho-1]} \mid x', y, \mathsf{Ch}] = 0, \quad \Pr[\mathbf{t}_{[1..\rho-1]} \mid x', y', \mathsf{Ch}] = 0$$

Moreover, for any $\mathbf{t}^* \in \tau^{\mathsf{Ch}}(x', y) \cup \tau^{\mathsf{Ch}}(x', y')$ such that $\mathbf{t}_{[1..\rho']} = \mathbf{t}^*{}_{[1..\rho']}$ for some ρ', it holds that $\rho' < \rho$.

PROOF. The existence of ρ is trivially guaranteed by the perfect correctness. Clearly $\rho > \rho'$ since at least one of $\Pr[\mathbf{t}_{[1..\rho']} \mid x', y, \mathsf{Ch}]$, $\Pr[\mathbf{t}_{[1..\rho']} \mid x', y', \mathsf{Ch}]$ must be non zero, by the way we pick $\mathbf{t}^*$ and the fact that $\mathbf{t}_{[1..\rho']} = \mathbf{t}^*{}_{[1..\rho']}$. □

We conclude with the following Theorem, which is an immediate corollary of the above lemmas, and formalizes the fact that there is a round in which we fully know the row-partition but nothing about the next-level column-decomposition.

THEOREM 3.5. *Let π be perfectly-correct private protocol for f over Ch. Let x, x', y, y' form a ⊞-minor. Then, for any transcript $\mathbf{t}$, there is a round ρ such that at least one of the following is satisfied.*

1. $\Pr[\mathbf{t}_{[1..\rho]} \mid x, y, \mathsf{Ch}] = \Pr[\mathbf{t}_{[1..\rho]} \mid x, y', \mathsf{Ch}] = 0$, *and* $\Pr[\mathbf{t}_{[1..\rho]} \mid x', y, \mathsf{Ch}] = \Pr[\mathbf{t}_{[1..\rho]} \mid x', y', \mathsf{Ch}]$.
2. $\Pr[\mathbf{t}_{[1..\rho]} \mid x', y, \mathsf{Ch}] = \Pr[\mathbf{t}_{[1..\rho]} \mid x', y', \mathsf{Ch}] = 0$, *and* $\Pr[\mathbf{t}_{[1..\rho]} \mid x, y, \mathsf{Ch}] = \Pr[\mathbf{t}_{[1..\rho]} \mid x, y', \mathsf{Ch}]$.

It is important to note at this point that analogous claims for the above Lemma 3.1 through Theorem 3.5 can similarly be shown for a binary-uniquely decomposable f which is column-partitionable but not row-partitionable, and for (x, x', y, y') being a ⊞-minor instead of a ⊞-minor, etc.

3.1 Frontiers: dealing with more than a single transcript

While above we have analyzed one transcript at a time, we now extend the definitions to treat many transcripts (e.g., the entire $\tau^{\mathsf{Ch}}(x, y)$) at the same time. In the spirit of [MPR09] we define *frontiers* as a means to deal with several transcripts rather than a single transcript. We begin with a few definitions.

DEFINITION 7 (FRONTIERS). *A set F of partial transcripts is called a* frontier *if,*

1. *F is prefix-free[3].*
2. *F is* maximal, *i.e., $\Pr[F \mid x, y, \mathsf{Ch}] = 1$ for all inputs x, y, where*

$$\Pr[F \mid x, y, \mathsf{Ch}] \quad := \quad \sum_{\mathbf{u} \in F} \Pr[\mathbf{u} \mid x, y, \mathsf{Ch}].$$

Informally, we say that a partial transcript $\mathbf{u}$ has reached frontier F if $\mathbf{u} \in F$. For frontiers F and G, we will also be interested in the probability that F 'precedes' G; that is, the probability that the protocol reaches frontier F before it reaches frontier G.

DEFINITION 8. *For any frontiers F and G, define*

$$\Pr[F \leq G \mid x, y, \mathsf{Ch}] = \sum_{\{\mathbf{u} \in F \mid \mathbf{u} \text{ is a prefix of some } \mathbf{u}' \in G\}} \Pr[\mathbf{u} \mid x, y, \mathsf{Ch}]$$

the weighted probability of all the transcripts in F that are prefixes of transcripts in G. In the same manner define $\Pr[F < G \mid x, y, \mathsf{Ch}]$ for transcripts which are strict prefixes.

[3]That is, no string in F is a proper prefix of another string in F. Formally, for any $\mathbf{t}, \mathbf{t}' \in F$ where $|\mathbf{t}| \leq |\mathbf{t}'|$, it holds that $\mathbf{t} \neq \mathbf{t}'_{[1..|\mathbf{t}|]}$.

For notational conciseness, for fixed x, y, Ch, we will use the statement "$F \le G$" as a shorthand for the statement "$\Pr[F \le G \mid x, y, \mathsf{Ch}] = 1$". The same holds for the statement "$F < G$".

Given a minor (x, x', y, y') we define the set $F(x, x', y, y')$ as the collection of transcripts prefixes up to the point where the partitioning related with this minor "happens". Note that the length of each prefix can be different.

DEFINITION 9. *For a minor (x, x', y, y') define*

$$F(x,x',y,y') := \left\{ \mathbf{t}_{[1..\rho]} \;\middle|\; \begin{array}{l} \mathbf{t} \textit{ is a transcript and } \rho = \rho(\mathbf{t}) \\ \textit{is the minimal round satisfying} \\ \textit{Theorem 3.5.} \end{array} \right\}$$

LEMMA 3.6. *Given a minor (x, x', y, y'), the set $F(x, x', y, y')$ is a frontier.*

PROOF. First, we show that $F = F(x, x', y, y')$ is prefix free. Assume that $\mathbf{u}, \mathbf{v} \in F$ such that $\mathbf{u}$ is a strict prefix of $\mathbf{v}$. Let $\mathbf{t}$ be any transcript with prefix $\mathbf{v}$. The minimal ρ that satisfies Theorem 3.5 for $\mathbf{t}$ is $|\mathbf{u}|$, therefore it cannot be that $\mathbf{v} \in F$ because of $\mathbf{t}$. However, this claim holds for any $\mathbf{t}$ whose prefix is $\mathbf{v}$, thus $\mathbf{v} \notin F$. Second, observe that F is maximal since we consider all possible transcripts $\mathbf{t}$. □

We are now ready for the main theorem of this section. Let f be a binary-uniquely decomposable function on $X \times Y$ and let π be a perfectly correct and private protocol for f. We define a sequence of domains $X_1 \times Y_1 \subseteq \cdots \subseteq X_d \times Y_d$, according to the partitioning of f, where $X_d \times Y_d = X \times Y$. For any such sequence we define a sequence of frontiers $F_i = F(X_i \times Y_i)$ where F_i represents one decomposition step of the protocol (i.e., the decomposition of $X_i \times Y_i$ into $X_{i-1} \times Y_{i-1}$ and $(X_i \setminus X_{i-1}) \times Y_{i-1}$, assuming that the i-th decomposition level is a row-partition). Furthermore, it holds that $F_{i+1} \le F_i$, that is, the protocol reaches these frontiers exactly in their order (i.e., the information about f's decomposition is revealed exactly in this order).

THEOREM 3.7. *Suppose that f is binary-uniquely decomposable and assume that the maximal number of decomposition in f is $d \ge 1$. Let π be a perfectly-correct private protocol for f over Ch. Let $X_1 \times Y_1 \subseteq \cdots \subseteq X_d \times Y_d$ be a sequence of restricted domains such that $X_d \times Y_d = X \times Y$, and $X_i \times Y_i$ is one of the partitions of $X_{i+1} \times Y_{i+1}$. Then, for any $X_i \times Y_i$ there exists a frontier $F_i = F(X_i \times Y_i)$ such that (assuming $f_{X_i \times Y_i}$ is row-partitionable; a similar claim holds if $f_{X_i \times Y_i}$ is column-partitionable.), for any $x, x' \in X_i$ and $y, y' \in Y_i$, and any $\mathbf{u} \in F_i$,*

1. *if x, x' are in the same partition,* $\Pr[\mathbf{u} \mid x, y, \mathsf{Ch}] = \Pr[\mathbf{u} \mid x', y', \mathsf{Ch}]$.
2. *if x, x' belong to different partitions, at least one of* $\Pr[\mathbf{u} \mid x, y, \mathsf{Ch}]$, $\Pr[\mathbf{u} \mid x', y', \mathsf{Ch}]$ *is zero.*

Moreover, for any restricted domain $X_j \times Y_j$ such that $X_i \times Y_i \subset X_j \times Y_j$, it holds that $F_j \le F_i$.

PROOF. Assume $f_{X_i \times Y_i}$ is row-partitionable into $P, Q \subset X$. We prove the claim by induction on $i = 1 \ldots d$. We split the proof into cases according to Lemma 3.1.

Case I: $f_{P \times Y_i}, f_{Q \times Y_i}$ are constant. Let F_i be the set of complete transcripts $F_i = \{\mathbf{t} \in \tau^{\mathsf{Ch}}(x, y) \mid x, y \in X_i \times Y_i\}$, and the claim follows from privacy, and Lemma 2.2. Also note that this must be the case for the induction's base case $X_1 \times Y_1$.

Case II: $f_{P \times Y_i}$ is constant but $f_{Q \times Y_i}$ is not.

By Lemma 3.1 we know that there exists a minor $(x_\circ, x'_\circ, y_\circ, y'_\circ)$ where $x_\circ \in P$ and $x'_\circ \in Q$. Define $F_i = F(x_\circ, x'_\circ, y_\circ, y'_\circ)$ as given by Definition 9. We begin with proving the first property.

If $x, x' \in P$ the first property trivially holds from the privacy of (the constant) $f_{P \times Y_i}$.

If $x, x' \in Q$ then, assume $f_{Q \times Y_i}$ is column-partitionable into Y_i^0, Y_i^1, and recall that Lemma 3.1 suggests that $y_\circ$ and $y'_\circ$ are in different partitions, say $y_\circ \in Y_i^0$ and $y'_\circ \in Y_i^1$. Now, if y, y' are in the same partition, then the first property holds due to the induction hypothesis on $Q \times Y_i$. Namely, $Q \times Y_i \subset X_i \times Y_i$ and the induction implies that any string $\mathbf{u}'$ in $F_{i-1} = F(Q \times Y_i)$ satisfies property (1.); since $F_i \le F_{i-1}$, then any $\mathbf{u} \in F_i$ is a prefix of some $u' \in F_{i-1}$ and must satisfy the same property.

If $y \in Y_i^0$ and $y' \in Y_i^1$ then, again using the induction hypothesis we know that for any $\mathbf{u} \in F_i$ and for any $x, x' \in Q$, it holds that $\Pr[\mathbf{u} \mid x, y, \mathsf{Ch}] = \Pr[\mathbf{u} \mid x'_\circ, y_\circ, \mathsf{Ch}]$ and $\Pr[\mathbf{u} \mid x', y', \mathsf{Ch}] = \Pr[\mathbf{u} \mid x'_\circ, y'_\circ, \mathsf{Ch}]$. The claim follows since $\Pr[\mathbf{u} \mid x'_\circ, y_\circ, \mathsf{Ch}] = \Pr[\mathbf{u} \mid x'_\circ, y'_\circ, \mathsf{Ch}]$ as given by Theorem 3.5, and the way we have defined F_i.

We now prove the second property. Let $x \in P, x' \in Q$ and $y, y' \in Y_i$. Note that due to Theorem 3.5, for any $\mathbf{u} \in F_i$ it holds that at least one of $\Pr[\mathbf{u} \mid x'_\circ, y_\circ, \mathsf{Ch}]$ and $\Pr[\mathbf{u} \mid x_\circ, y'_\circ, \mathsf{Ch}]$ is zero. Also note that $\Pr[\mathbf{u} \mid x, y, \mathsf{Ch}] = \Pr[\mathbf{u} \mid x_\circ, y, \mathsf{Ch}]$ and $\Pr[\mathbf{u} \mid x', y', \mathsf{Ch}] = \Pr[\mathbf{u} \mid x'_\circ, y', \mathsf{Ch}]$, the former due to privacy (recall that $f_{P \times Y_i}$ is constant) and the latter due to the induction hypothesis on $Q \times Y_i$. This completes the proof of property (2.) for this case.

Case III: both $f_{P \times Y_i}$ and $f_{Q \times Y_i}$ are non constant.

Assume $f_{P \times Y_i}$ is column-partitionable to Y_p^0, Y_p^1 and that $f_{Q \times Y_i}$ to Y_q^0, Y_q^1. Let $(x_\circ, x'_\circ, y_\circ, y'_\circ)$ and $(x_\circ, x'_\circ, w_\circ, w'_\circ)$ be the minors guaranteed by Lemma 3.1. Define F_i to be $F(x_\circ, x'_\circ, y_\circ, y'_\circ)$, and note that $F(x_\circ, x'_\circ, y_\circ, y'_\circ) = F(x_\circ, x'_\circ, w_\circ, w'_\circ)$: by using the induction hypothesis on each of the domains $Q \times Y_{Q_0}$, $Q \times Y_{Q_1}$, $P \times Y_{P_0}$, $P \times Y_{P_1}$ we get that $\Pr[\mathbf{u} \mid x, y, \mathsf{Ch}] = \Pr[\mathbf{u} \mid x, y', \mathsf{Ch}] = \Pr[\mathbf{u} \mid x, w', \mathsf{Ch}]$ and $\Pr[\mathbf{u} \mid x', w, \mathsf{Ch}] = \Pr[\mathbf{u} \mid x', w', \mathsf{Ch}] = \Pr[\mathbf{u} \mid x', y, \mathsf{Ch}]$ (refer to Figure 1). By using the same reasoning as in Case II, the first term also equals $\Pr[\mathbf{u} \mid x, w, \mathsf{Ch}]$ and the second also equals $\Pr[\mathbf{u}' \mid x', y', \mathsf{Ch}]$ which implies these frontiers are in fact the same.

It is easy to verify that the induction holds for this case as well: the first property holds due to the same reason as the case where $x, x' \in Q$ in Case II; when $x, x' \in P$ we use the minor $(x_\circ, x'_\circ, w_\circ, w'_\circ)$ and when $x, x' \in Q$ we use the minor $(x_\circ, x'_\circ, y_\circ, y'_\circ)$.

The second property follows the same way as in Case II.

Finally, we complete the induction by showing that $F_i \le F_{i-1}$ (assuming the induction holds for all F_j with $j < i$). Suppose not, and let $\mathbf{u} \in F_i$ be a transcript that violates this condition, that is, there exists $\mathbf{u}' \in F_{i-1}$ such that $\mathbf{u}'$ is a strict prefix of $\mathbf{u}$. Due to the way we construct the frontiers, either F_i contains only complete transcripts (and then any frontier F_j satisfies $F_j \le F_i$) or otherwise F_{i-1} is defined via Definition 9 by some minor x, x', y, y' where $x, x' \in X_{i-1}$ and $y, y' \in Y_{i-1}$ (wlog, a $\boxplus$-minor); additionally, let v, v', w, w' be the ($\boxplus$-)minor that defines F_i, where $v, v' \in X_i$ and $w, w' \in Y_i$.

By Theorem 3.5 we know that for any $\mathbf{u}' \in F_{i-1}$, either $\Pr[\mathbf{u}' \mid x, y, \mathsf{Ch}] = 0$ or $\Pr[\mathbf{u}' \mid x, y', \mathsf{Ch}] = 0$. If both are 0 then $\mathbf{u}'$ (or prefix or it) is in F_i by its construction and it can't be that $\mathbf{u} \in F_i$ for any $\mathbf{u}$ that has a proper prefix $\mathbf{u}'$.

Otherwise, since $\mathbf{u}'$ is a prefix of $\mathbf{u}$, it follows that also either $\Pr[\mathbf{u} \mid x, y, \mathsf{Ch}] = 0$ or $\Pr[\mathbf{u} \mid x', y, \mathsf{Ch}] = 0$. However, X_{i-1} and $X_i \setminus X_{i-1}$ form a valid partitioning of X_i, thus x, x' are both in the same partition after the decomposition step of F_i. By the way we construct F_i, it holds that $\Pr[\mathbf{u} \mid v', w, \mathsf{Ch}] = \Pr[\mathbf{u} \mid v', w', \mathsf{Ch}]$. Furthermore, using the induction hypothesis on the two partitions of F_{i-1}, we get that $\Pr[\mathbf{u} \mid x, y, \mathsf{Ch}] = \Pr[\mathbf{u} \mid x', y, \mathsf{Ch}] = \Pr[\mathbf{u} \mid v', w, \mathsf{Ch}]$ as well as $\Pr[\mathbf{u} \mid x, y', \mathsf{Ch}] = \Pr[\mathbf{u} \mid x', y', \mathsf{Ch}] = \Pr[\mathbf{u} \mid v', w', \mathsf{Ch}]$. It follows that $\Pr[\mathbf{u} \mid x, y', \mathsf{Ch}] = \Pr[\mathbf{u} \mid x, y, \mathsf{Ch}] = 0$ and we reached a contradiction. □

4. IMPOSSIBILITY OF PRIVATE, NOISE-RESILIENT PROTOCOLS

Intuitively, Theorem 3.7 implies that information is leaked by order: first A speaks and tells where, in the first decomposition his input lies (and until then, B doesn't say anything meaningful); then it's B's turn to reveal where his input lies in the next decomposition, etc. It is not allowed to give information beyond the current point of decomposition (this will damage privacy), and moreover, if the other side does not acknowledge the correct partition of the decomposition, he might violate his privacy (or at least the protocol outputs a wrong output). This gives a strict bound on the error rate any such protocol can withstand.

Before we prove our impossibility result, we discuss a subtlety regarding the definition of error rate in protocols of varying length. Consider a (deterministic) protocol so that for any input x, y we can match a single transcript $t_{(x,y)}$. Assume that for any $(x, y) \neq (x', y')$ it holds that $|t_{(x,y)}| \neq |t_{(x',y')}|$. In this setting, Definition 3 has no practical meaning. Indeed, if the channel is allowed to corrupt a fraction $c \in (0, 1)$ of the transmission, and the protocol runs on the input whose transcript t is the longest, the protocol might terminate before round $|t|$, and the 'effective' fraction of errors in the observed transcript will be higher than c.

To overcome this issue, we restrict our discussion only to protocols whose output length is the same for every transcript. This doesn't restrict the power of the protocol: after executing $\mathsf{out}_A, \mathsf{out}_B$ the parties can send "0" as many times as needed, ignoring any received messages. On the other hand, the channel is potentially stronger, as it is allowed a higher proportion of errors for transcripts that prematurely terminate (if any exists). We also mention that protocols in which both parties always have consensus about whose turn it is to speak and whether or not the protocol has ended, *must* be of the same length for any input; see Claim 9 in [BR11].

THEOREM 4.1 (MAIN). *Let f be a binary-uniquely decomposable function with maximal decomposition depth d. Then, no private protocol for f is perfectly correct and perfectly private with error rate $1/d$. Namely, for every perfectly correct protocol π for f, there exists a channel Ch^* with error rate $1/d$, such that π^{Ch^*} is not private.*

We begin with an intuitive outline of the proof. For any protocol π, we will construct a channel Ch^* which violates party B's privacy. In particular, we will show there exist inputs $x \in X, y, y' \in Y$, and a transcript $\mathbf{t}$, such that $f(x, y) = f(x, y')$, but $\Pr[\mathbf{t} \mid x, y, \mathsf{Ch}^*] \neq \Pr[\mathbf{t} \mid x, y', \mathsf{Ch}^*]$.

We start with inputs $x_0, x_1 \in X, y_0, y_1 \in Y$ which form a ⊞-minor, and analyze protocol π with the noiseless channel Ch^0. Theorem 3.7 tells us precisely how information about the inputs (x_0, x_1, y_0, y_1) is revealed by π: *first* A reveals whether its input is in the partition corresponding to x_0 or x_1, *then,* if A's input is in the partition corresponding to x_1, B reveals whether its input is in the partition corresponding to y_0 or y_1. More precisely, there exists $1 \leq i \leq d$, such that,

- till frontier F_i, party A does not reveal any information that can distinguish the partitions corresponding to x_0 from x_1,
- at frontier F_{i+1}, party A reveals whether its input is in the partition corresponding to x_0 or x_1,
- if A's input was in partition corresponding to x_1, B reveals the partition of its own input at frontier F_{i+2}.

We use the above observations to design the adversarial channel Ch^*. Consider an execution of π with inputs x_0, y_0. The channel lets the messages go back and forth unmodified till the protocol reaches frontier F_i. At this stage, it samples a random tape R_A for A consistent with the transcript so far, *and input* x_1. Thereafter, the channel replaces A's messages with what it would have sent had its input been x_1 and random tape R_A. Note that as transcripts for x_0 and x_1 are identically distributed till frontier F_i, B's view is consistent with the execution of π with inputs x_1, y_0 with the *noiseless channel.* The channel Ch^* continues modifying A's messages this way until in B's view, the protocol reaches frontier F_{i+2}. At this point party B has revealed information about the partition of its input, which violates its privacy.

The crucial missing piece in the above is the rate of the channel Ch^*. Recall that our channel is allowed to introduce only a $1/d$ fraction of errors. If we pick an arbitrary minor (x_0, x_1, y_0, y_1) and launch the above attack, it is possible that the frontiers F_{i+2} and F_i are "far apart", and thus the channel has to introduce large number of errors. To avoid this, we start by picking inputs x_1, y_0 from a restricted subdomain of depth d, and a transcript $\mathbf{t}$ in $\tau^{\mathsf{Ch}}(x_1, y_0)$. As there are d frontiers, by an averaging argument, there exists an i such that the fraction of messages in $\mathbf{t}$ between F_i and F_{i+2} is $2/d$. Further, there must exist x_0, y_1 such that (x_0, x_1, y_0, y_1) forms a ⊞-minor which corresponds to the frontier F_i. The channel Ch^* uses this minor for the attack described above. The formal proof follows.

PROOF. (**Theorem 4.1**) Let Ch^0 be the 'noiseless channel', that is, for any $\ell \in \mathbb{N}$ and any sequence of messages $\mathbf{m} = m_1 \cdots m_\ell$,

$$\Pr[\mathsf{Ch}^0(\mathbf{m}) = \mathbf{m}] = 1.$$

Suppose $d > 2$ (the theorem trivially holds for $d \leq 2$) and let $X_\circ \times Y_\circ$ be a subdomain obtained by recursively performing d decomposition of f's domain (a restricted domain of depth d). Let $F_1, \ldots, F_d$ be the frontiers given by Theorem 3.7, and let F_0 be the empty set. We re-index the frontiers in a reverse order so that $F_d = F(X_\circ \times Y_\circ)$ and $F_1 \leq \cdots \leq F_d$. Let $x, y \in X_\circ \times Y_\circ$ and fix $\mathbf{t} \in \tau^{\mathsf{Ch}^0}(x, y)$. For $1 \leq j \leq d$, let $\lambda_j(\mathbf{t})$ be the length of the longest prefix of $\mathbf{t}$ in F_j. Then for $0 \leq j < k \leq d$, we can define the *number of messages in* $\mathbf{t}$ *between* F_j *and* F_k, $\lambda_{j,k}(\mathbf{t})$, as

$$\lambda_{j,k}(\mathbf{t}) := \lambda_k(\mathbf{t}) - \lambda_j(\mathbf{t}).$$

Since $\sum_{j=1}^{d} \lambda_{j-1,j}(\mathbf{t}) = |\mathbf{t}|$, there must exist i such that $\lambda := \lambda_{i,i+2}(\mathbf{t})$ satisfies $\lambda \leq 2|\mathbf{t}|/d$.

For any partial transcript $\mathbf{u}$, we define the *active domain at* $\mathbf{u}$ as the set of inputs that have a non-zero probability of producing a transcript with prefix $\mathbf{u}$. Let $X_i \times Y_i$ be the active domain at the longest prefix of $\mathbf{t}$ in F_i (clearly $(x,y) \in X_i \times Y_i$)). Let the next decomposition step be a row-decomposition, with row partitions $X_i^0, X_i^1 \subset X_i$. Let us rename the partitions so that $x \in X_i^1$. First, as the decomposition depth of (x,y) is $d \geq i+2$, it can not be the case that both $f_{X_i^0,Y_i}$ is constant, and $f_{X_i^1,Y_i}$ is constant. In particular, as $x \in X_i^1$, $f_{X_i^1,Y_i}$ is not constant. Let $Y_i^0, Y_i^1 \subset Y_i$ be the next column-partition of $X_i^1 \times Y_i$. Then, by Lemma 3.1, there exist $x_0 \in X_i^0, x_1 \in X_i^1, y_0 \in Y_i^0, y_1 \in Y_i^1$ such that (x_0, x_1, y_0, y_1) form a ⊞-minor. As $f(x,y_0) \neq f(x,y_1)$, inputs (x_0, x, y_0, y_1) also form a ⊞-minor.

Now we will construct a channel Ch^* that violates B's privacy. Let $\mathbf{u}$ be the longest prefix of $\mathbf{t}$ in F_i. Fix, $\mathbf{t}' \in \tau^{\mathsf{Ch}^0}(x_0, y_0)$ that also has $\mathbf{u}$ as a prefix. The existence of $\mathbf{t}'$ is guaranteed by Theorem 3.7. Define the channel Ch^* as follows:

- Ch^* does not introduce any errors till $|\mathbf{u}|$ rounds. If the partial transcript so far is not identical to $\mathbf{u}$, the channel acts as the noiseless channel Ch^0 for the entire protocol.

- If the partial transcript up to round $|\mathbf{u}|$ is identical to $\mathbf{u}$, then the channel modifies messages as follows: sample a random tape R_A for party A from the conditional distribution over random tapes given the transcript so far and the input $x \in X_i^1$. For the next $\lambda = \lambda_{i,i+2}$ rounds, send B's messages to A without change. Change A's sent messages to what A would have sent when using input x and the random tape sampled earlier. That is, for every message m, every odd round j such that $|\mathbf{u}| < j \leq |\mathbf{u}| + \lambda$,

$$\Pr\left[\mathsf{Ch}^*\left(t'^s[j] \mid \mathbf{t}'_{[1..(j-1)]}\right) = m\right] = \Pr\left[\pi_A\left(x, R_A, t^s{}_{[1..(j-1)]}\right) = m\right].$$

  The channel continues with the remaining protocol without modifying any messages.

First, note that Ch^* introduces only $1/d$ fraction of errors. This is because it only changes half of the messages between frontiers F_i and F_{i+2}, of which there are only a fraction $2/d$ of the length of transcript $\mathbf{t}$. As all transcripts are of the same length, the channel makes only $1/d$ fraction errors.

Next, we argue that channel Ch^* violates B's privacy. Fix a transcript $\mathbf{t}^* \in \tau^{\mathsf{Ch}^*}(x_0, y_0)$ which has $\mathbf{u}$ as a prefix. Again, the existence of $\mathbf{t}^*$ is guaranteed by Theorem 3.7. We will show that $\Pr[\mathbf{t}^* \mid x_0, y_1, \mathsf{Ch}^*] = 0$.

We have,

$$\Pr[(t^{*s}, t^{*r}) \mid x_0, y_1, \mathsf{Ch}^*] = \Pr[\pi_A(x_0, t^{*r}_A) = t^{*s}_A] \times \Pr[\mathsf{Ch}^*(t^{*s}) = t^{*r}] \Pr[\pi_B(y_1, t^{*r}_B) = t^{*s}_B]. \quad (6)$$

To maintain readability of the probability calculations below, we take two notational short-cuts: (1) all probabilities below are conditioned on observing the prefix $\mathbf{u}$, but we do not explicitly mention this conditioning, and (2) we analyze $\mathbf{t}^*$ only up to round $|\mathbf{u}| + \lambda$, so from now on we will take $\mathbf{t}^*$ to mean the prefix $\mathbf{t}^*{}_{[1..(|\mathbf{u}|+\lambda)]}$ (same for t^{*s}, t^{*r}).

By the channel's definition,

$$\Pr[\mathsf{Ch}^*(t^{*s}) = t^{*r}] = \left(\prod_{j=|\mathbf{u}|+1}^{(|\mathbf{u}|+\lambda)/2} \Pr\left[\mathsf{Ch}^*(t^{*s}[2j-1] \mid \mathbf{t}^*{}_{[|\mathbf{u}|..(2j-2)]}) = t^{*r}[2j-1]\right]\right) \times \left(\prod_{j=|\mathbf{u}|+1}^{(|\mathbf{u}|+\lambda)/2} \Pr\left[\mathsf{Ch}^*(t^{*s}[2j] \mid \mathbf{t}^*{}_{[|\mathbf{u}|..(2j-1)]}) = t^{*r}[2j]\right]\right).$$

Note that for every even round j, $t^{*s}[j] = t^{*r}[j]$, as Ch^* does not modify B's messages to A. Thus, the second product on the right hand side above is 1. By construction of Ch^*, for every odd $|\mathbf{u}| + 1 \leq j \leq (|\mathbf{u}| + \lambda)$,

$$\Pr\left[\mathsf{Ch}^*(t^{*s}[2j-1] \mid \mathbf{t}^*{}_{[|\mathbf{u}|..(2j-2)]}) = t^{*r}[2j-1]\right] = \Pr\left[\pi_A(x, t^{*s}{}_{[|\mathbf{u}|..(2j-2)]}) = t^{*r}[2j-1]\right].$$

Going back to Eq. (6), we have,

$$\begin{aligned}
&\Pr[(t^{*s}, t^{*r}) \mid x_0, y_1, \mathsf{Ch}^*] \\
&= \Pr[\pi_A(x_0, t^{*r}_A) = t^{*s}_A] \\
&\quad \times \Pr[\mathsf{Ch}^*(t^{*s}) = t^{*r}] \Pr[\pi_B(y_1, t^{*r}_B) = t^{*s}_B] \\
&= \Pr[\pi_A(x_0, t^{*r}_A) = t^{*s}_A] \\
&\quad \times \prod_{j=|\mathbf{u}|}^{(|\mathbf{u}|+\lambda)/2} \Big(\Pr\left[\pi_A(x, t^{*s}{}_{[|\mathbf{u}|..(2j-2)]}) = t^{*r}[2j-1]\right] \\
&\qquad \times \Pr\left[\pi_B(y_1, t^{*r}{}_{[|\mathbf{u}|..(2j-1)]}) = t^{*s}[2j]\right]\Big) \\
&= \Pr[\pi_A(x_0, t^{*r}_A) = t^{*s}_A] \Pr[\mathbf{t}^{**} \mid x, y_1, \mathsf{Ch}^0],
\end{aligned}$$

where $\mathbf{t}^{**} = (t^{**s}, t^{**r})$ is the following transcript: t^{**s} consists of all messages sent by the channel to B and all messages sent by B, and $t^{**r} = t^{**s}$. We now prove that $\Pr[\mathbf{t}^{**} \mid x, y_1, \mathsf{Ch}^0] = 0$.

Recall that y_0 and y_1 are in different (column) partitions of $X_i^1 \times Y_i$. Also, by construction of Ch^*, $\Pr[\mathbf{t}^{**} \mid x, y_0, \mathsf{Ch}^0] > 0$. Therefore, by Theorem 3.7, $\Pr[\mathbf{t}^{**} \mid x_0, y_1, \mathsf{Ch}^0] = 0$. Thus,

$$\Pr[\mathbf{t}^* \mid x_0, y_1, \mathsf{Ch}^*] = 0,$$

and although $f(x_0, y_0) = f(x_0, y_1)$ we learn that B holds y_0 rather than y_1, in violation of B's privacy according to Definition 4. □

5. PRIVATE PROTOCOLS: THE NON-PERFECT CASE

The above results assume the protocol to be perfectly-correct, which is interesting on its own. Indeed, possibility results for computing non-private functions over adversarial channels [Sch96, BR11] do achieve *perfect* correctness for error rate less than 1/4. However, from a practical point of view, the question of computing private functions over a noisy channel is interesting also for the non-perfect case, that is, where the protocol is only $(1-\varepsilon)$-correct and $(1-\delta)$-private, for some $\varepsilon, \delta > 0$.

Definition 10 (Correctness). *A protocol π is $(1-\varepsilon)$-correct with respect to some function f over* Ch *if for any inputs x, y,*

$$\Pr_{\substack{R_A, R_B, R_{\mathsf{Ch}} \\ (t^s, t^r) \leftarrow \pi^{\mathsf{Ch}}(x,y)}} [\mathsf{out}_A^{\pi}(x, t_A^r) = \mathsf{out}_B^{\pi}(y, t_B^r) = f(x,y)] \geq 1 - \varepsilon.$$

DEFINITION 11 (PRIVACY). *We say that a protocol π is $(1-\delta)$-private with respect to party A over a channel* Ch, *if for any $x, x' \in X$, $y \in Y$ such that $f(x,y) = f(x',y)$, and for any frontier F, it holds that* $\mathsf{SD}_F^{\mathsf{Ch}}((x,y),(x',y)) \le \delta$, *where*

$$\mathsf{SD}_F^{\mathsf{Ch}}((x,y),(u,v)) \triangleq \frac{1}{2}\sum_{\mathbf{t}\in F} |\Pr[\mathbf{t} \mid x,y,\mathsf{Ch}] - \Pr[\mathbf{t} \mid u,v,\mathsf{Ch}]| \,.$$

Finally, we say that π is an (ε,δ)-protocol for f if π is $(1-\varepsilon)$-correct and $(1-\delta)$-private.

Our main result for (ε,δ)-protocols is the following.

THEOREM 5.1 (MAIN, (ε,δ)-CASE). *Let f be a function that is binary-uniquely decomposable and has maximal decomposition depth d. Then, for every protocol π and for any small enough $\varepsilon,\delta > 0$, there exists a channel* Ch^* *with error rate $1/d$, such that* π^{Ch^*} *is not (ε,δ)-protocol for f.*

6. ACKNOWLEDGMENTS

We would like to thank Hemanta Maji and Sanjam Garg for useful discussions. Research supported in part from a DARPA/ONR PROCEED award, NSF grants 1228984, 1136174, 1118096, and 1065276, a Xerox Faculty Research Award, a Google Faculty Research Award, an equipment grant from Intel, and an Okawa Foundation Research Grant. This material is based upon work supported by the Defense Advanced Research Projects Agency through the U.S. Office of Naval Research under Contract N00014-11-1-0389. The views expressed are those of the author and do not reflect the official policy or position of the Department of Defense, the National Science Foundation, or the U.S. Government.

7. REFERENCES

[Bea91] D. Beaver. Perfect privacy for two-party protocols. *Proceedings of DIMACS Workshop on Distributed Computing and Cryptography*, vol. 2, pp. 65–77. 1991.

[BK12] Z. Brakerski and Y. T. Kalai. Efficient interactive coding against adversarial noise. FOCS '12, pp. 160–166. 2012.

[BN13] Z. Brakerski and M. Naor. Fast algorithms for interactive coding. SODA '13, pp. 443–456. 2013.

[BR11] M. Braverman and A. Rao. Towards coding for maximum errors in interactive communication. STOC '11, pp. 159–166. 2011.

[CK88] C. Crépeau and J. Kilian. Achieving oblivious transfer using weakened security assumptions. FOCS '88, pp. 42–52. 1988.

[CK91] B. Chor and E. Kushilevitz. A zero-one law for boolean privacy. *SIAM Journal on Discrete Mathematics*, 4(1):36–47, 1991.

[CPT13] K.-M. Chung, R. Pass, and S. Telang. Knowledge-preserving interactive coding. FOCS '13, pp. 449–458. 2013.

[DFMS04] I. Damgård, S. Fehr, K. Morozov, and L. Salvail. Unfair noisy channels and oblivious transfer. M. Naor, ed., *Theory of Cryptography, LNCS*, vol. 2951, pp. 355–373. Springer Berlin, 2004.

[FGOS13] M. Franklin, R. Gelles, R. Ostrovsky, and L. J. Schulman. Optimal coding for streaming authentication and interactive communication. R. Canetti and J. A. Garay, eds., *Advances in Cryptology – CRYPTO 2013, LNCS*, vol. 8043. Springer Berlin, 2013.

[GMS11] R. Gelles, A. Moitra, and A. Sahai. Efficient and explicit coding for interactive communication. FOCS '11, pp. 768–777. 2011.

[GSW13] R. Gelles, A. Sahai, and A. Wadia. Private interactive communication across an adversarial channel. Cryptology ePrint Archive, Report 2013/259, 2013.

[Kil88] J. Kilian. Founding crytpography on oblivious transfer. STOC '88, pp. 20–31. 1988.

[Kus89] E. Kushilevitz. Privacy and communication complexity. FOCS '89, pp. 416–421. IEEE Computer Society, 1989.

[Kus92] E. Kushilevitz. Privacy and communication complexity. *SIAM Journal on Discrete Mathematics*, 5(2):273–284, 1992.

[MPR09] H. K. Maji, M. Prabhakaran, and M. Rosulek. Complexity of multi-party computation problems: The case of 2-party symmetric secure function evaluation. O. Reingold, ed., *Theory of Cryptography, LNCS*, vol. 5444, pp. 256–273. Springer Berlin, 2009.

[RS94] S. Rajagopalan and L. Schulman. A coding theorem for distributed computation. STOC '94, pp. 790–799. 1994.

[Sch93] L. J. Schulman. Deterministic coding for interactive communication. STOC '93, pp. 747–756. 1993.

[Sch96] L. J. Schulman. Coding for interactive communication. *IEEE Transactions on Information Theory*, 42(6):1745–1756, 1996.

[Sha48] C. E. Shannon. A mathematical theory of communication. *ACM SIGMOBILE Mobile Computing and Communications Review*, 5(1):3–55, 2001. Originally appeared in *Bell System Tech. J.* 27:379–423, 623–656, 1948.

[Vic61] W. Vickrey. Counterspeculation, auctions, and competitive sealed tenders. *The Journal of Finance*, 16(1):8–37, 1961.

Tree Codes and a Conjecture on Exponential Sums

Cristopher Moore
Santa Fe Institute
1399 Hyde Park Rd., Santa Fe NM 87501, USA
moore@santafe.edu

Leonard J. Schulman
Caltech
MC305-16, Pasadena CA 91125, USA
schulman@caltech.edu

ABSTRACT

We propose a new conjecture on some exponential sums. These particular sums have not apparently been considered in the literature. Subject to the conjecture we obtain the first effective construction of asymptotically good tree codes. The available numerical evidence is consistent with the conjecture and is sufficient to certify codes for significant-length communications.

Categories and Subject Descriptors

E.4 [**Coding and Information Theory**]:

Keywords

Interactive communication; error-correcting codes; exponential sums

1. INTRODUCTION

Tree codes are a class of error-correcting codes that were introduced in [24, 25] as the main combinatorial tool underlying the interactive coding theorem. They play a role in general (two-way) communication protocols that is analogous to the role of block error correcting codes in Shannon's theory of (one-way) message transmission.

In spite of the existence proof provided in [24, 25], and in spite of efforts by researchers in the interim, to date no effective construction of tree codes is known. By "effective construction" we mean a deterministic algorithm that provides any requested code-word entry within time polynomial in the address-length of that entry (see detailed definitions below). In fact, even randomized constructions are unknown. The best known results have been, first, elementary ideas giving polynomial (rather than constant) size alphabet or else providing a weaker tree code property [23]; a modified existence proof with slightly better parameters by Peczarski [21]; and a construction of Braverman [5] giving a tree of depth n in time $2^{n^{\varepsilon}}$.

ITCS'14, January 12–14, 2014, Princeton, New Jersey, USA.

ACM 978-1-4503-2698-8/14/01 ...$15.00.
http://dx.doi.org/10.1145/2554797.2554813 .

Because of this gap, researchers have come up with several innovative ways to skirt the challenge of constructing tree codes yet still obtain noise robustness for communication protocols. Ostrovsky, Rabani, and Schulman [20] designed effective codes that can replace tree codes in a restricted class of communication protocols. Gelles, Moitra, and Sahai [12] introduced another class of codes, also weaker than tree codes, called "potent tree codes", which are again sufficient to recover the coding theorem; they showed that a random construction suffices to provide a potent tree code with high probability, but deterministic constructions remain unknown even for this weaker object.

In spite of these considerable advances in protocol design, the basic problem of effectively and deterministically constructing the underlying class of tree codes has remained open since 1993. This question will still remain open after the current paper, but we present here what is the first plausible candidate for an effective (i.e., deterministic, polynomial-time) construction of tree codes. The validity of the construction, namely whether the codes actually satisfy the required minimum-distance condition, depends on a conjecture about some particular exponential sums. Apparently, no bounds for these sums are known. However, analogous sums have drawn considerable attention, which we will discuss in Sec. 3.

Outline of the paper: In Sec. 2 we recall the definition of tree codes. In Sec. 3, as a warm-up, we show an elementary application of our method to the classic problem of constructing block codes. This will demonstrate that an extremely simple construction of asymptotically good block codes over bounded alphabets would be implied by an correspondingly bold conjecture about short exponential sums (of the type that has already been studied in analytic number theory). This section has no direct bearing on tree codes, however. In Sec. 4 we provide our candidate construction of tree codes and our associated conjecture. In Sec. 5 we disgress to discuss the relationship between our construction and the long-studied question of the distribution of the sequence $\xi\theta^n \bmod 1$, in particular for $\theta = 3/2$. In Sec. 6 we present numerical tests of our conjecture that rule out small counterexamples. In particular our own tests (which required only a few days of machine time) validate the use of our codes for communication protocols up to 90 rounds, well beyond the range at which the algorithms for other constructions can be validated with comparable computational effort, and similar calculations by students went even further and validate our codes up to 145 rounds.

1.1 Other literature

A few words on how tree codes are used. In [24, 25], tree codes were introduced as part of a particular protocol to simulate noiseless channels on noisy ones. This protocol is computationally efficient in the case of stochastic noise; the protocol also works for adversarial noise, up to fractional Hamming distance 1/240, but in this case is not computationally efficient. Braverman and Rao [6] improved the distance bound to 1/4 by modifying how the protocol uses the underlying tree codes. In [11] tree codes were used both for cryptographic ends, namely to authenticate data streams and interactive protocols, and in order to improve the above 1/4 to 1/2 under the additional assumption of shared randomness. Brakerski and Kalai [3] and Brakerski and Naor [4] showed how to handle even adversarial error with low computational overhead (first polynomial and then near-linear). In these recent two papers, tree codes of logarithmic depth (in the number of rounds of communication) are all that is needed, so (depending on the noise level and the constants in the protocols), our numerical results may be enough to enable some applications.

2. PRELIMINARIES

The infinite binary rooted tree T is the undirected graph whose vertices are the finite binary sequences $\{0,1\}^*$, and in which each vertex $x = (x_1, \ldots, x_n) \in \{0,1\}^n$ is connected to its parent $(x_1, \ldots, x_{n-1})$. We say x is at level n, and we let $L_n = \{0,1\}^n$ denote the set of vertices at level n. The root is the empty sequence ε, at level 0.

We are interested in T as a *leveled* metric space, that is to say, we define a distance function on each set L_n but use a common notation d_T. If $x, y \in L_n$ and $\ell + 1$ is the least integer i such that $x_i \neq y_i$, then we set $d_T(x,y) = n - \ell$. (This metric can be straightforwardly extended to a distance function on the full tree but we shall not need this.)

Let Σ be any alphabet. The set of finite sequences Σ^* is also a leveled metric space, using Hamming distance on strings of the same length: if $\sigma, \tau \in \Sigma^n$, then $d_\Sigma(\sigma, \tau) = |\{i : \sigma_i \neq \tau_i\}|$.

Let α be a mapping from $\bigcup_{n>0} L_n$ to Σ, assigning a label in Σ to every node in T other than the root. This induces a secondary mapping α^* from the vertices of T into Σ^*, where $\alpha^*(x)$ is the sequence of labels on the path from the root to x. That is, $\alpha^*(\varepsilon) = \varepsilon$, and for $n > 0$, $x \in L_n$,

$$\alpha^*(x_1, \ldots, x_n) = \alpha^*(x_1, \ldots, x_{n-1}) \circ \alpha(x_1, \ldots, x_n),$$

where $\circ$ denotes composition. In particular, α^* maps L_n into Σ^n.

We say that α satisfies the *tree code distance property* if α^* is bi-Lipschitz: that is, if there is a constant $c > 0$ such that for all $n \geq 0$ and all $x, y \in L_n$,

$$d_\Sigma(\alpha^*(x), \alpha^*(y)) \geq c\, d_T(x,y).$$

There is no particular need for the host metric d_Σ to be the Hamming distance, but for bounded alphabets the choice matters little. Below we will embed sequences Σ^* in the complex numbers $\mathbb{C}$, in which case we will replace d_Σ with the usual norm on $\mathbb{C}$.

We say that α is a *deterministic, effective, asymptotically good tree code* if $|\Sigma| < \infty$, the tree code distance property is satisfied, and α is computable in deterministic polynomial time. The question of whether such codes exist (even if we replace deterministic with randomized computation) is still open. Our goal in this paper is to present a construction α, and a number-theoretic conjecture regarding exponential sums, such that α is indeed asymptotically good if the conjecture is true.

3. AN ILLUSTRATION: BLOCK CODES

As a warm-up, in this section we show how the simple step of embedding the vertices of T in the complex numbers $\mathbb{C}$ can be applied toward a much simpler problem, namely the construction of asymptotically good block error codes—assuming that a certain conjecture regarding short exponential sums is true.

A probabilistic method argument due to Shannon in 1948 [26] shows the existence of asymptotically good block codes—namely, mappings from $\{0,1\}^n$ to Σ^n for Σ independent of n, such that for some $c > 0$ every two points in the image of the map have Hamming distance at least cn. It was not until 1966 that Forney [10] (improved by Justesen in 1972 [13]) gave a construction for effectively computable codes with bounded alphabet size, this by first making the construction in a finite field of unbounded size (roughly n), and then concatenating with a secondary code that maps each element of the finite field to a string over a bounded-size alphabet. (In [13], this code is location-dependent.)

The construction we describe now is simpler, although somewhat analogous: again we use as intermediary a code over a large field, in this case $\mathbb{C}$. The secondary mapping now carries each field element to a single character (rather than a sequence) in a bounded-size alphabet $\Sigma = \{0, \ldots, \kappa - 1\}$. Of course this secondary mapping can no longer be injective.

We treat sequences $\{0,1\}^n$ as elements of the cyclic group $\mathbb{Z}/2^n$. Then the construction is a composite mapping

$$\gamma^{n'} \circ (\beta_1, \ldots, \beta_{n'}) : \mathbb{Z}/2^n \to \Sigma^{n'},$$

for $n' = cn$ where c is a sufficiently large constant. Here each β_k maps $\mathbb{Z}/2^n$ into $\mathbb{C}$, γ maps the unit circle in $\mathbb{C}$ to Σ, and $\gamma^{n'}$ is the n'-fold direct product of γ with itself. Specifically, let

$$e(x) = \exp(2\pi i x).$$

Then β_k is defined by

$$\beta_k(m) = e\left(3^k \frac{m}{2^n}\right)$$

for each $0 \leq k < cn$. Observe that for any $m, m' \in \mathbb{Z}/2^n$,

$$\beta_k(m)\, \beta_k(m')^\dagger = \beta_k(m - m')$$

where $\dagger$ denotes complex conjugation. Finally, recalling that $\Sigma = \{0, \ldots, \kappa - 1\}$, γ rounds each component z_k according to which of the κ intervals of width $2\pi/\kappa$ it lies in:

$$\gamma(z_k) = \ell \quad \text{such that} \quad -\pi/\kappa \leq \arg \frac{z_k}{e(\ell/\kappa)} < \pi/\kappa.$$

Below we give a linear lower bound on the Hamming distance d_Σ between

$$(\gamma^{cn} \circ (\beta_1, \ldots, \beta_{cn}))(m)$$

and

$$(\gamma^{cn} \circ (\beta_1, \ldots, \beta_{cn}))(m')$$

for $m, m' \in \mathbb{Z}/2^n$ conditional on the following conjecture.

CONJECTURE 1. *There are constants $c < \infty$ and $\delta > 0$ such that for all n and all nonzero $m \in \mathbb{Z}/2^n$,*

$$\Re\left(\frac{1}{cn}\sum_{0\le k<cn} e\Big(3^k\frac{m}{2^n}\Big)\right) \le 1-\delta \tag{3.1}$$

(where $\Re$ denotes real part).

We emphasize that we are unaware of implications in either direction between this conjecture and Conjecture 3 (or 4), which are the main focus of this paper.

We make several remarks about the exponential sum appearing in this conjecture. First, note that it is the Fourier transform, at frequency $m \in \mathbb{Z}/2^n$, of the uniform distribution on the geometric series $\{1, 3, 3^2, \dots, 3^{cn-1}\}$. If we replace the modulus 2^n with a prime p so that $\mathbb{Z}/2^n$ becomes the finite field $\mathbb{F}_p$, and replace 3 with a primitive root g, then results of Korobov [16] give the following bound on the absolute value (which is obviously also a bound on the real part):

$$\left|\frac{1}{N}\sum_{0\le k<N} e(g^k m/p)\right| \le \frac{p^{1/2}\log p}{N}.$$

However, this bound becomes nontrivial only when $N > p^{1/2}\log p$. Improved bounds were given by Bourgain and Garaev [1] and Konyagin and Shparlinski [15]; see also Bourgain and Glibichuk [2] for complete sums over multiplicative subgroups, i.e., over all the powers of some element g that is not a primitive root, and Kerr [14] for incomplete sums of this type. However, all of these only become nontrivial when $N \ge p^\alpha$ for some $\alpha > 0$.

In contrast, we are interested in the average of the first $N = cn$ terms of the sum (for any sufficiently large constant c), which corresponds to $O(\log p)$ terms in the finite field case; in this regime, despite the results cited and related recent advances in additive combinatorics, nothing appears to be known.

Note that, at the least, Conjecture 1 requires that $c > \log_3 2$. Otherwise, taking $m = 1$, most terms of the summation are close to 1, as is the real part of their average. For the very modest value $n = 20$ and for $c = 2$ we have computed the LHS of Eqn. 3.1 for all m, and the evidence is consistent with Conjecture 1, and even makes plausible that the distribution of the LHS (with m uniformly random) tends to normal, with variance sufficiently small for the minimum distance guarantee. This is a phenomenon familiar in coding theory (see [19] p. 287 or [17] and references therein).

As another remark, note that the geometric series appearing in Eqn. 3.1 is generated by the fixed element 3, no matter the value of n. Arbitrary geometric series will not do. Consider replacing the generator 3 by 3^{2^r}. It is known that the order of 3 modulo 2^n is 2^{n-2} for $n \ge 3$. As a consequence, for $r \ge 1$, 3^{2^r} generates a multiplicative cyclic group $G \subset \mathbb{Z}/2^n$ which equals the additive coset $1 + 2^{r+2}\mathbb{Z}$. Now consider the additive subgroup $H = 2^{n-r-2}\mathbb{Z}$. If $m \notin H$, the sum in Eqn. 3.1 is zero; however, if $m \in H$, it is $e(m/2^n)$. As we vary m in the latter case, these values are spread evenly on the unit circle and in particular there are (many) nonzero m with real part arbitrarily close to 1.

Despite having little confidence in, and very limited evidence for, Conjecture 1, we plow ahead, showing that, if true, it implies that the above construction is an asymptotically good block error-correcting code. The following lemma (which we later employ again in the tree code section) provides the connection with Hamming distance.

LEMMA 2. *Let $z = (z_1, \dots, z_{n'})$ and $z' = (z'_1, \dots, z'_{n'})$ with $|z_k| = |z'_k| = 1$ for all $1 \le k \le n'$. Then*

$$d_\Sigma(\gamma^{n'}(z), \gamma^{n'}(z')) \ge \eta n'$$

where $$\eta = \frac{\cos 2\pi/\kappa - (1/n')\Re\sum_k z_k z_k'^{\dagger}}{1+\cos 2\pi/\kappa}.$$

(Note this bound is meaningful only for $\kappa > 4$.)

PROOF. Observe that if $\gamma(z_k) = \gamma(z'_k)$ then $\Re\left(z_k z_k'^{\dagger}\right) \ge 1 - \cos 2\pi/\kappa$. On the other hand for any z_k, z'_k we have $\Re\left(z_k z_k'^{\dagger}\right) \ge -1$. Therefore, with $h = d_\Sigma(\gamma^{n'}(z), \gamma^{n'}(z'))$,

$$\frac{1}{n'}\Re\sum_{k=1}^{n'}(1 - z_k z_k'^{\dagger}) = 1 - \frac{1}{n'}\sum_k \Re\left(z_k z_k'^{\dagger}\right)$$
$$\le 1 - \cos 2\pi/\kappa + \frac{h}{n'}(1 + \cos 2\pi/\kappa),$$

and rearranging completes the proof. □

Finally, if Conjecture 1 is true with a given c and δ, we choose κ such that $\cos 2\pi/\kappa > 1-\delta$. Then Lemma 2 tells us that $(\gamma^{n'} \circ (\beta_1, \dots, \beta_{n'}))(\mathbb{Z}/2^n)$ is an error-correcting code of length $n' = cn$ and distance $\eta n'$ where $\eta > 0$.

4. THE TREE CODE CONSTRUCTION AND THE MAIN CONJECTURE

Even if the rather strong conjecture in the preceding section can be proven, coding theory has of course long had other effective constructions of block codes. The main purpose of that section was to prepare for the following construction of tree codes.

Define a mapping β from $\{0,1\}^*$ to $\mathbb{C}$ as follows. Set $\beta(\varepsilon) = 1$. If $k > 0$, β has been defined on L_{k-1}, and $x = (x_1, \dots, x_k) \in L_k$, define $\beta(x)$ inductively using

$$\beta(x_1, \dots, x_k)^2 = \beta(x_1, \dots, x_{k-1})^3;$$

This equation has of course two roots, and we use one for each child of $(x_1, \dots, x_{k-1})$. Specifically, let $b \in [0, 1)$ such that

$$\beta(x_1, \dots, x_{k-1}) = e(b),$$

i.e., $b = (1/2\pi)\arg\beta(x_1, \dots, x_{k-1})$. Then make the assignment to each of the children following the arbitrary convention

$$\beta(x_1, \dots, x_k) = e\Big(\frac{3}{2}b + \frac{x_k}{2}\Big). \tag{4.1}$$

Now let $\alpha = \gamma \circ \beta$, with $\gamma : \mathbb{C} \to \Sigma$ the rounding function defined in the previous section, and define $\alpha^* : T \to \Sigma^*$ as in Sec. 2.

A key feature of this tree code design is that, in analogy with (one of the) original existence proofs in [24, 25], it has the property that its metric properties can be understood solely in terms of what happens to pairs of paths that diverge at the root. The convolutional construction in [24, 25], let us call it τ, had the following "translation invariant" property: Suppose that $x, x' \in L_n$ and that $d_T(x, x') = \ell$. Write

$$x = (x_1, \dots, x_{n-\ell}, 1, x_{n-\ell+2}, \dots, x_n) \tag{4.2}$$
$$x' = (x_1, \dots, x_{n-\ell}, 0, x'_{n-\ell+2}, \dots, x'_n).$$

Then

$$d_\Sigma(\tau^*(x), \tau^*(x')) \\ = d_\Sigma(\tau^*(1, x_{n-\ell+2}, \ldots, x_n), \tau^*(0, x'_{n-\ell+2}, \ldots, x'_n)).$$

That is to say, Hamming distances in τ are "translation invariant" as we shift pairs of paths about the tree: adding, removing, or changing their common initial subsequence. In particular, they are invariant if we remove their common initial subsequence completely so they diverge at the root.

This translation invariance *almost* holds in the present construction. Specifically, the inner product employed in Lemma 2 to lower bound the Hamming distance, does have this translation invariance. The invariance is lost only in the rounding by γ. Therefore it suffices to study inner products for pairs of paths which diverge at the root. The construction also has additional symmetry which we discuss below.

The lower bound method for our construction is as follows. Let $x, x' \in L_n$ be as in Eqn. (4.2). Then

$$d_\Sigma(\alpha^*(x), \alpha^*(x')) = \sum_{k=n-\ell+1}^{n} d_\Sigma(\gamma\beta(x_1, \ldots, x_k), \gamma\beta(x'_1, \ldots, x'_k)).$$

By Lemma 2 (with ℓ here corresponding to n' in the lemma), this is bounded below by

$$d_\Sigma(\alpha^*(x), \alpha^*(x')) \geq \tag{4.3}$$
$$\frac{\cos 2\pi/\kappa - (1/\ell)\Re \sum_{k=n-\ell+1}^{n} \beta(x_1, \ldots, x_k)\,\beta(x'_1, \ldots, x'_k)^\dagger}{1 + \cos 2\pi/\kappa}\,\ell.$$

We can now eliminate the common initial subsequence in $x_1, \ldots, x_{n-\ell}$ from this bound; this lets us reduce to the case where the paths diverge at the root. Let $b \in [0, 1)$ such that

$$\beta(x_1, \ldots, x_{n-\ell}) = e(b).$$

Then (4.1) gives

$$\begin{aligned}
&\sum_{k=n-\ell+1}^{n} \beta(x_1, \ldots, x_k)\,\beta(x'_1, \ldots, x'_k)^\dagger \\
&= e\left(\frac{3}{2}b + \frac{1}{2}\right) e\left(-\frac{3}{2}b\right) \\
&\quad + e\left(\frac{3}{2}\left(\frac{3}{2}b + \frac{1}{2}\right) + \frac{x_{n-\ell+2}}{2}\right) e\left(-\frac{3}{2}\left(\frac{3}{2}b\right) - \frac{x'_{n-\ell+2}}{2}\right) \\
&\quad + e\left(\frac{3}{2}\left(\frac{3}{2}\left(\frac{3}{2}b + \frac{1}{2}\right) + \frac{x_{n-\ell+2}}{2}\right) + \frac{x_{n-\ell+3}}{2}\right) \\
&\qquad \cdot e\left(-\frac{3}{2}\left(\frac{3}{2}\left(\frac{3}{2}b\right) + \frac{x'_{n-\ell+2}}{2}\right) - \frac{x'_{n-\ell+3}}{2}\right) + \cdots \\
&= e\left(\frac{1}{2}\right) + e\left(\frac{3}{2}\frac{1}{2} + \frac{x_{n-\ell+2} - x'_{n-\ell+2}}{2}\right) \\
&\quad + e\left(\left(\frac{3}{2}\right)^2 \frac{1}{2} + \left(\frac{3}{2}\right) \frac{x_{n-\ell+2} - x'_{n-\ell+2}}{2} + \frac{x_{n-\ell+3} - x'_{n-\ell+3}}{2}\right) \\
&\quad + \cdots \\
&\quad + e\left(\left(\frac{3}{2}\right)^{\ell-1} \frac{1}{2} + \left(\frac{3}{2}\right)^{\ell-2} \frac{x_{n-\ell+2} - x'_{n-\ell+2}}{2}\right. \\
&\qquad \left. + \left(\frac{3}{2}\right)^{\ell-3} \frac{x_{n-\ell+3} - x'_{n-\ell+3}}{2} + \cdots + \frac{x_n - x'_n}{2}\right) \\
&= \sum_{i=1}^{\ell} e\left(\frac{1}{2}\left(\left(\frac{3}{2}\right)^{i-1} + \sum_{j=2}^{i} \left(\frac{3}{2}\right)^{i-j} (x_{n-\ell+j} - x'_{n-\ell+j})\right)\right).
\end{aligned}$$

Now write $y_j = x_{n-\ell+j} - x'_{n-\ell+j}$. Then in order to show that α is a deterministic, effective, asymptotically good tree code, it is sufficient to show the following:

CONJECTURE 3. *There is a $\delta > 0$ such that for any $\ell \geq 1$ and any sequence $y_1, \ldots, y_\ell$ with $y_1 = 1$ and all $y_j \in \{-1, 0, 1\}$,*

$$\Re\left[\frac{1}{\ell}\sum_{i=1}^{\ell} e\left(\frac{1}{2}\sum_{j=1}^{i}\left(\frac{3}{2}\right)^{i-j} y_j\right)\right] \leq 1 - \delta. \tag{4.4}$$

Before proceeding further we point out a computational implication of the sufficiency of this conjecture. The fractional-distance bound for a tree code of depth n is the minimum of $\Theta(4^n)$ pairwise distances; in general, for a proposed tree code, verification to depth n may require this many calculations. But for the present construction, it is evidently sufficient to check $\Theta(3^n)$ distances. (Further improvement will be discussed below.)

It is easier to read Conjecture 3 as being about exponential sums if we define $e_N : \mathbb{Z}/N \to \mathbb{C}$ as $e_N(z) = e(z/N)$; note that all arithmetic in the argument of e_N is performed in $\mathbb{Z}/N$. Now if (for $y_1, \ldots, y_\ell$ with $y_1 = 1$) we write

$$z = \sum_{j=1}^{\ell} 2^{j-1} 3^{\ell-j} y_j \in \mathbb{Z}, \tag{4.5}$$

then we have

$$\begin{aligned}
e\left(\frac{1}{2}\sum_{j=1}^{i}\left(\frac{3}{2}\right)^{i-j} y_j\right) &= e_{2^i}\left(\sum_{j=1}^{i} 2^{j-1} 3^{i-j} y_j\right) \\
&= e_{2^\ell}\left(\left(\frac{2}{3}\right)^{\ell-i} z\right)
\end{aligned}$$

(where in the argument of e_{2^ℓ}, negative powers of 3 are of course positive powers of $3^{-1} \bmod 2^\ell$). Note that the terms $i < j \leq \ell$ in the last sum disappear, as they are divisible by 2^ℓ. Substituting $m = \ell - i$ transforms the left-hand side of (4.4) into

$$\Re\left[\frac{1}{\ell}\sum_{m=0}^{\ell-1} e_{2^\ell}\left(\left(\frac{2}{3}\right)^m z\right)\right].$$

Inspecting (4.5), we see that our condition that $y_1 = 1$ forces z to be odd; conversely, any odd $z \in \mathbb{Z}/2^\ell$ corresponds to a sequence $y_1 = 1, y_2, \ldots, y_\ell$ (and usually to many such sequences). This is easy to see by induction. Let $z' \in \mathbb{Z}/2^{\ell-1}$ satisfy $3z' = z \pmod{2^{\ell-1}}$ and let $y_1, y_2, \ldots, y_{\ell-1}$ be a sequence to which z' corresponds as in (4.5). Then an appropriate choice of y_ℓ extends the representation of z' to one of z. This gives us the following equivalent form of Conjecture 3:

CONJECTURE 4. *There is a $\delta > 0$ such that for any $\ell \geq 1$ and any odd integer z,*

$$\Re\left[\frac{1}{\ell}\sum_{m=0}^{\ell-1} e_{2^\ell}\left(\left(\frac{2}{3}\right)^m z\right)\right] \leq 1 - \delta. \tag{4.6}$$

Conjecture 4.6 has the following advantage over its equivalent sibling: verification of the conjecture for all $\ell \leq n$ (which is all that is required in order to certify a tree code of depth n) requires only $\Theta(2^n)$ calculations, i.e., one for each z between 1 and 2^ℓ, rather than $\Theta(3^n)$.

We end this section with some remarks on the sum in (4.6). We begin with an odd $z \in \mathbb{Z}/2^\ell$. We repeatedly multiply it by $2 \cdot 3^{-1}$, producing a sequence $z_0 = z, z_1 = (2/3)z, z_2 = (2/3)^2 z, \ldots$ Each such step maps z into a smaller subgroup: z_1 is even, z_2 is a multiple of 4, and so on until $z_{\ell-1} = 2^{\ell-1}$. The function e_{2^ℓ} maps these onto the unit circle with arguments $2\pi z/2^\ell$, and after $\ell - 1$ steps we arrive at $\beta = e_{2^\ell}(2^{\ell-1}) = -1$.

Alternatively, we can view this process in reverse. We start with $\beta = -1$, and then repeatedly map β to one of the square roots of β^3, mapping its argument $\theta = \arg \beta$ to $(3/2)\theta$ or $(3/2)\theta + \pi$. After k steps, θ is a multiple of $2\pi/2^k$. Taking $\ell - 1$ steps produces $2^{\ell-1}$ different sequences of points on the unit circle, which correspond to the $2^{\ell-1}$ odd elements of $\mathbb{Z}/2^\ell$.

Now imagine an adversary seeking to maximize the real part of the sum in (4.6). In order to do this effectively he must create long runs of terms close to 1 on the unit circle. He can do this if he can generate a small argument θ, so that successive arguments $(3/2)\theta, (3/2)^2\theta, \ldots$ will also be small. In particular, if on some step he generates $\theta = \Theta(2^{-k})$, then roughly the next $\log_{3/2}(1/\theta) = \Theta(k)$ terms will have arguments close to zero, contributing 1 to the average.

At the end of such a run, the arguments will again be $\Theta(1)$, with large successive angles between terms. However, if the adversary can generate an argument close to $2\pi/3$ or $4\pi/3$, i.e., a β close to a cube root of 1, he can generate another small argument on the next step, and start another run. If he can do this repeatedly, so that a $1 - o(1)$ fraction of the terms are close to 1, then Conjecture 4 is false. Thus our construction relies on the hope that he cannot design long sequences of runs with just a few terms between the end of each run and the start of the next. Equivalently, our conjecture holds if there are constants $c, \phi > 0$ such that, for all $2^{\ell-1}$ sequences, at least cn of the adjacent pairs of terms in (4.6) have an angle ϕ between them.

5. RELATED QUESTIONS, AND BASE-3/2 REPRESENTATIONS OF ONE

Since the early work of Pisot [22] and Vijayaraghavan [27] (see [9] for more recent work and other references) it has been of interest in number theory to study the distribution of the sequence $\xi\theta^n \bmod 1$, and in particular for $\theta = 3/2$. The extent of the relationship to our question is unclear, as we require an understanding of sequences generated by the operation $\times(3/2) + x/2$ for $x \in \{0, 1\}$, whereas these works are restricted to $x = 0$.

However, we can relate our main conjecture to a question of a similar flavor. Consider its statement in the form of Conjecture 4. Let us identify each element of $\mathbb{Z}/2^\ell$ with an integer in the range $-2^{\ell-1} < z \leq 2^{\ell-1}$. Then if

$$z' \equiv_{2^\ell} \frac{2}{3} z \,,$$

(where as before 3^{-1} refers to the inverse of 3 mod 2^ℓ) the corresponding integers obey

$$z' = \frac{2}{3}\left(z + a 2^{\ell-1}\right) \quad \text{for some} \quad a \in \{-2, -1, 0, 1, 2\} \,.$$

In other words, the function $(2/3)z$ has several "branches", where the relevant branch depends on z mod 3, and also on whether z is greater or smaller than $\pm 2^{\ell-2}$ due to wraparound effects; see Fig. 1.

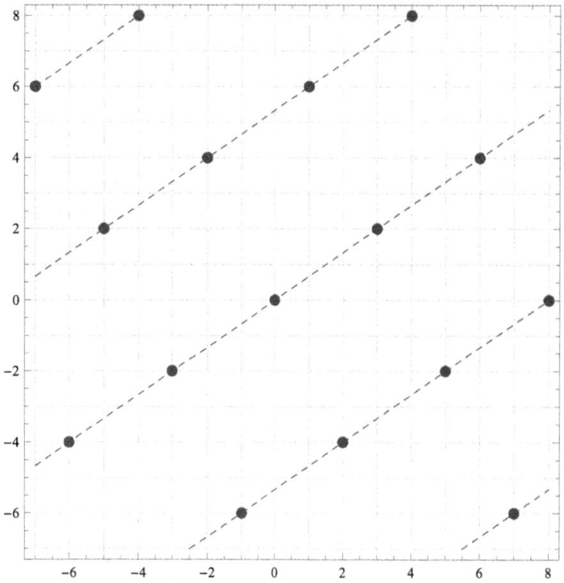

Figure 1: The five branches of the function $(2/3)z$ when we identify $z \in \mathbb{Z}/2^\ell$ with an integer in the range $-2^{\ell-1} < z \leq 2^{\ell-1}$. Here $\ell = 4$.

Now consider the sequence $z_0 = z, z_1 = (2/3)z, z_2 = (2/3)^2 z, \ldots$ discussed at the end of Section 4. We have

$$z_1 = \frac{2}{3}\left(z + a_1 2^{\ell-1}\right)$$

$$z_2 = \frac{2}{3}\left(\frac{2}{3}\left(z + a_1 2^{\ell-1}\right) + a_2 2^{\ell-1}\right)$$

$$\vdots$$

$$z_{\ell-1} = \left(\frac{2}{3}\right)^{\ell-1} z + 2^{\ell-1} \sum_{i=1}^{\ell-1} \left(\frac{2}{3}\right)^{\ell-i} a_i \,.$$

However, we also know that $z_{\ell-1} = 2^{\ell-1}$ since that is the only integer such that $-2^{\ell-1} < z \leq 2^{\ell-1}$ and $z_{\ell-1} \equiv_{2^\ell} 2^{\ell-1}$. Since $|z| \leq 2^{\ell-1}$, rearranging then gives

$$\left| 1 - \sum_{j=1}^{\ell-1} \left(\frac{2}{3}\right)^j a_{\ell-j} \right| \leq \left(\frac{2}{3}\right)^{\ell-1} . \tag{5.1}$$

Thus the coefficients a_i form a series that sums to 1, with an error term that decreases as $(2/3)^\ell$.

There are certainly many such series, i.e., many ways to "write 1 in base 3/2 with integer coefficients ranging from −2 to 2". However, we conjecture that, in any such series, a constant fraction of the coefficients a_i must be nonzero: in other words, that the sequence is forced to jump from branch to branch of the function $(2/3)z$ a constant fraction of the time. Since the branches with $a \neq 0$ are all a constant fraction of 2^ℓ away from z in the range $-2^{\ell-1} < z \leq 2^{\ell-1}$, this implies that a constant fraction of adjacent terms in (4.6) have a constant angle between them. Thus the following conjecture would imply Conjecture 4 (or equivalently Conjecture 3):

CONJECTURE 5. *There is a constant $c > 0$ such that, if $\ell \geq 1$ and (5.1) holds where $a_i \in \{-2, -1, 0, 1, 2\}$ for all* *i, then* $|\{i : a_i \neq 0\}| \geq c\ell$. *In particular, for any infinite sequence* $a_1, a_2, \ldots$ *with* $a_i \in \{-2, -1, 0, 1, 2\}$ *such that* $\sum_{i=1}^{\infty} (2/3)^i a_i = 1$, *any initial subsequence of length* ℓ *contains at least* $c\ell$ *nonzero terms.*

We offer no tools for proving Conjecture 5, but it seems of independent interest from a purely number-theoretic point of view. Perhaps it is too strong to be true; but if it fails while the main conjecture survives, that will be a fascinating distinction. A distantly-related conjecture of Erdős [8] states that there are only finitely many n such that the ternary expansion of 2^n avoids the digit 2. Lagarias [18] showed, among other things, that the set of real numbers $\lambda > 0$ such that the ternary expansion of $\lfloor 2^n \lambda \rfloor$ avoids 2 for infinitely many n has Hausdorff dimension bounded below 1. See also de Faria and Tresser [7], who conjecture that for any integer $b > 0$, in the base-b expansion of the product of any n primes that does not include all of b's prime factors, the digits $\{0, 1, \ldots, b-1\}$ become asymptotically equidistributed as $n \to \infty$.

Like our main conjecture, Conjecture 5 involves the length of "runs" that an adversary can arrange. Certainly he needs to use at least one of the first four coefficients before the terms become too small to sum to 1. However, if he can achieve a partial sum extremely close to 1 in an initial subsequence, making the error term much smaller than $(2/3)^k$ in the first k terms, then he can have a long string of zero coefficients before he needs to correct the sum further. We believe that he cannot do this repeatedly, creating arbitrarily long runs of zeros with only a few nonzero coefficients between each run, but we have no proof.

6. NUMERICAL RESULTS

As mentioned earlier, the design we have proposed has the attractive computational property that a fractional-distance bound to depth n can be verified by checking the minimum over just $\Theta(2^n)$, rather than $\Theta(4^n)$, distances between pairs of paths. Namely, if we write

$$1 - \delta_\ell = \max_{z \in \mathbb{Z}/2^\ell} \Re \left[\frac{1}{\ell} \sum_{m=0}^{\ell-1} e_{2^\ell} \left(\left(\frac{2}{3} \right)^m z \right) \right],$$

then our main conjecture is that $\sup_\ell (1 - \delta_\ell) < 1$, and verification of the distance property for a tree of depth n requires bounding the above "max" for all $\ell \leq n$. Applying Lemma 2, and specifically (4.3), we then obtain an asymptotically good tree code with alphabet size κ for

$$\kappa > \frac{2\pi}{\cos^{-1} \sup_\ell (1 - \delta_\ell)}.$$

We can speed up the computation even further by employing a branch-and-bound strategy as follows. Use a data structure which maintains at any time some of the nodes of the tree (initially just the root), and for each of these nodes, the real part of sum of β along the the path from the root. At all times, maintain the record-holding lower bound for $1 - \delta_\ell$ found so far (initially the record is -1). In each round, "pop" a node from the data structure; if it is possible for some descendant of the node to break the record, if the remainder of the path to that descendant turns out to consist solely of 1's, then "push" both children of the node onto the data structure. Empirically, this strategy runs in time $O(2^{c\ell})$ where $c \approx 0.27$.

We implemented this strategy in Mathematica (see Appendix A) and used it to compute $1 - \delta_\ell$ up to $\ell = 90$. In this range, the largest $1 - \delta_\ell$ is $1 - \delta_{88} = 0.7512$. Later, this problem was presented as a branch-and-bound exercise in a Caltech undergraduate algorithms course. Several teams of students, implementing various optimizations of the above basic strategy in C or C++, in some cases employing clusters of computers, were able to carry the computation even further. All of these calculations were conducted in double precision arithmetic, and the algorithm is numerically stable, so we have little concern about the accuracy aside from the possibility of programming errors. The latter risk is minimal due to the duplication of results by independently written programs; all results agreed to within 10^{-6} up to $\ell = 99$, 10^{-4} up to $\ell = 130$, and $2 \cdot 10^{-3}$ up to $\ell = 145$. The team of Shival Dasu, Albert Gural, Nicholas Schiefer and Kevin Yuh computed $1 - \delta_\ell$ up to $\ell = 149$, the largest in this range being $1 - \delta_{126} = 0.7861$. The team of Matt Mayers and Eric Wang computed $1 - \delta_\ell$ up to $\ell = 145$, and William Hoza's computation reached up to $\ell = 133$. See Appendix B for the numerical values, which are also depicted in Figure 2.

If Conjecture 3 (equivalently 4) should hold with $1 - \delta = 0.9$, then we would obtain an asymptotically good tree code with alphabet size $\kappa = 14$.

We note incidentally that a simple greedy algorithm, that always chooses the square root of β^3 with positive real part, appears to achieve an asymptotic lower bound on $1 - \delta_\ell$ of ≈ 0.335. A somewhat better greedy algorithm, that takes the root whose argument is between $-\pi/3$ and $2\pi/3$, appears to converge to $1 - \delta_\ell \approx 0.631$. However, these are both much inferior to the true values found by the branch and bound algorithm.

Acknowledgments

C.M. is supported by NSF grants CCF-1117426 and CCF-1219117, and ARO contract W911NF-04-R-0009. L.J.S. is supported by NSF grant CCF-1038578. Many students' branch and bound implementations were very successful (23 students crossed the $\ell = 100$ threshold); we thank all for their dedication and enthusiasm. Specific results are cited with permission. We also thank Alex Russell and Anup Rao for helpful discussions.

7. REFERENCES

[1] J. Bourgain and M. Z. Garaev. On a variant of sum-product estimates and explicit exponential sum bounds in prime fields. *Mathematical Proceedings of the Cambridge Philosophical Society*, 146:1–21, 1 2009.

[2] J. Bourgain and A. Glibichuk. Exponential sum estimates over a subgroup in an arbitrary finite field. *Journal d'Analyse Mathématique*, 115:51–70, 2011.

[3] Z. Brakerski and Y. T. Kalai. Efficient interactive coding against adversarial noise. In *FOCS*, pages 160–166, 2012.

[4] Z. Brakerski and M. Naor. Fast algorithms for interactive coding. *Electronic Colloquium on Computational Complexity (ECCC)*, 20:14, 2013.

[5] M. Braverman. Towards deterministic tree code constructions. In *Proceedings of the 3rd Innovations in Theoretical Computer Science Conference*, ITCS '12, pages 161–167, New York, NY, USA, 2012. ACM.

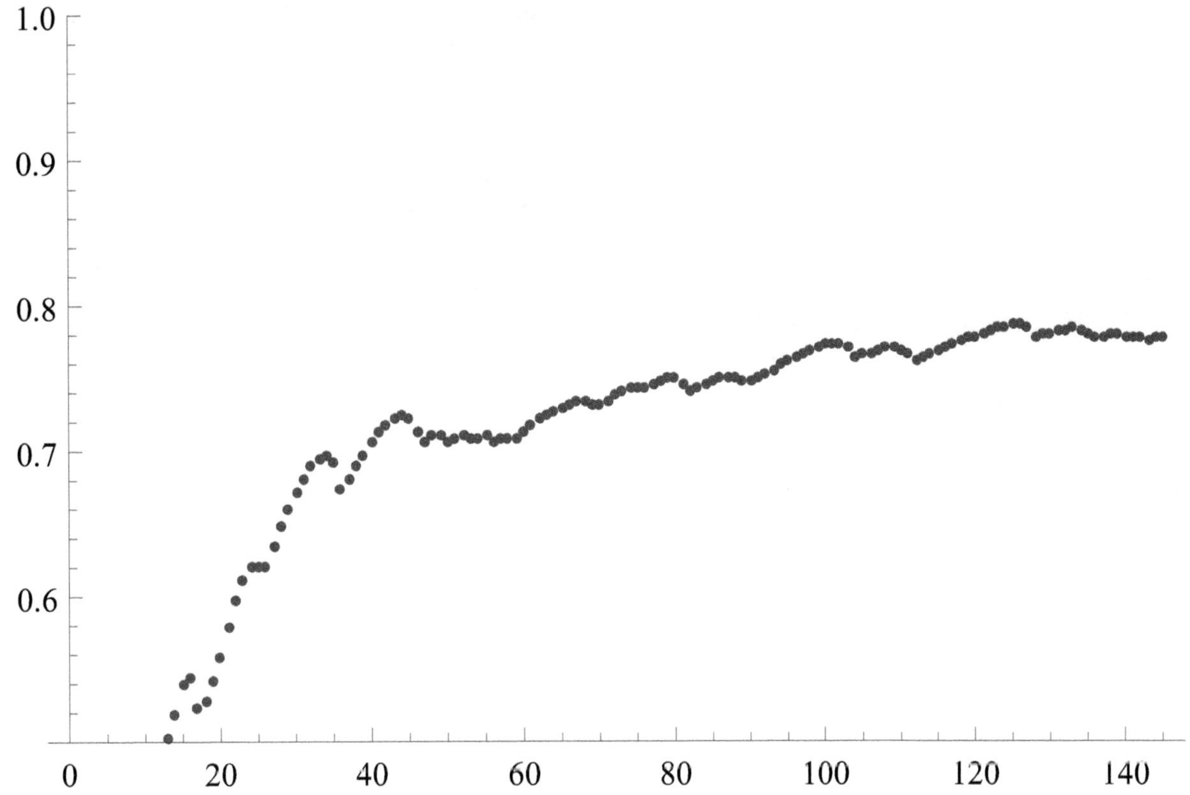

Figure 2: $1-\delta_\ell$ plotted up to $\ell = 145$; for the numerical values see Appendix B. ($1-\delta_\ell < 0.5$ for $\ell \leq 12$.)

[6] M. Braverman and A. Rao. Towards coding for maximum errors in interactive communication. In *Proceedings of the 43rd annual ACM symposium on Theory of computing*, STOC '11, pages 159–166, New York, NY, USA, 2011. ACM.

[7] E. de Faria and C. Tresser. On Sloane's persistence problem, 2013. http://arxiv.org/pdf/1307.1188v1.pdf.

[8] P. Erdős. Some unconventional problems in number theory. *Mathematics Magazine*, 52(2):67–70, 1979.

[9] L. Flatto, J. C. Lagarias, and A. D. Pollington. On the range of fractional parts $\{\xi(p/q)^n\}$. *Acta Arithmetica*, 70(2):125–147, 1995.

[10] G. D. Forney. *Concatenated Codes*. MIT Press, 1966.

[11] M. K. Franklin, R. Gelles, R. Ostrovsky, and L. J. Schulman. Optimal coding for streaming authentication and interactive communication. In *CRYPTO*, pages 258–276, 2013.

[12] R. Gelles, A. Moitra, and A. Sahai. Efficient and explicit coding for interactive communication. In *FOCS*, pages 768–777, 2011.

[13] J. Justesen. A class of constructive, asymptotically good algebraic codes. *IEEE Transactions on Information Theory*, IT-18:652–656, September 1972.

[14] B. Kerr. Incomplete exponential sums over exponential functions, 2013. http://arxiv.org/pdf/1302.4170v1.pdf.

[15] S. V. Konyagin and I. E. Shparlinski. On the consecutive powers of a primitive root: Gaps and exponential sums. *Mathematika*, 58:11–20, 1 2012.

[16] N. M. Korobov. On the distribution of digits in periodic fractions. *Mathematics of the USSR-Sbornik*, 18(4):659, 1972.

[17] I. Krasikov and S. Litsyn. Bounds on spectra of codes with known dual distance. *Designs, Codes and Cryptography*, 13:285–298, 1998.

[18] J. C. Lagarias. Ternary expansions of powers of 2. *Journal of the London Mathematical Society*, 79(3):562–588, 2009.

[19] F. J. MacWilliams and N. J. A. Sloane. *The Theory of Error-Correcting Codes*. North-Holland, 1977.

[20] R. Ostrovsky, Y. Rabani, and L.J. Schulman. Error-correcting codes for automatic control. *IEEE Transactions on Information Theory*, 55(7):2931–2941, July 2009.

[21] M. Peczarski. An improvement of the tree code construction. *Inf. Process. Lett.*, 99(3):92–95, 2006.

[22] C. Pisot. La répartition modulo 1 et nombres algébriques. *Ann. Scuola Norm. Sup. Pisa*, 2(7):205–248, 1938.

[23] L. J. Schulman. Postscript of 21 September 2003 to Coding for Interactive Communication. http://www.cs.caltech.edu/~schulman/Papers/intercodingpostscript.txt.

[24] L. J. Schulman. Deterministic Coding for Interactive Communication. In *Proceedings of the 25th Annual Symposium on Theory of Computing*, pages 747–756, 1993.

[25] L. J. Schulman. Coding for Interactive Communication. *Special Issue on Codes and*

Complexity of the IEEE Transactions on Information Theory, 42(6):1745–1756, November 1996.

[26] C. E. Shannon. A Mathematical Theory of Communication. *Bell System Tech. J.*, 27:379–423; 623–656, 1948.

[27] T. Vijayaraghavan. On the fractional parts of the powers of a number, I. *J. London Math. Soc.*, 15:159–160, 1940.

APPENDIX

A. BRANCH AND BOUND PROGRAM

This program implements a branch-and-bound strategy for computing the maximum $1 - \delta_\ell$ of the left-hand side of (4.6) over all odd $z \in \mathbb{Z}/2^\ell$, or equivalently over all sequences where we start with $\beta = -1$ and, for $\ell - 1$ steps, take one of the two square roots of β^3. We prune nodes from the search tree whenever their subtree cannot match the largest real part we have seen so far, even if we assume that all subsequent terms contribute 1. When we go from ℓ to $\ell + 1$, we simply assume that the next term has real part at least zero (since one of the square roots always does).

The main function `BandB[maxlen]` computes these bounds for all $2 \leq \ell =$ `maxlen`. It returns an array `Relist` containing entries of the form $\{\ell, N, z/2^\ell, 1 - \delta_\ell\}$ where N is the number of nodes explored, $z/2^\ell$ is the initial value of the worst sequence, and $1 - \delta_\ell$ is the maximum achieved.

```
(* branch-and-bound program for Conjecture 4 *)

(* t is an angle divided by 2pi *)
e[t_] := E^(2 Pi I t)
(* list of terms is stored in the form {sum, l, t} *)
score[terms_] := Re[terms[[1]]]

(* branch and bound: should we call off the search? *)
abandon[largrestResofar_, terms_] :=
  (score[terms] + len - terms[[2]] <= largrestResofar)

branch[terms_, lowerBound_] :=
 Module[{nextt1, nextt2, tmp, t, sum, re, l},
  nodes++;
  sum = terms[[1]];
  re = score[terms];
  l = terms[[2]];
  t = terms[[3]];

  If[l == len,
   If[re > largestRe,
    largestRe = re;
    worstseq = t,
    ];
   Return[re]
   ];

  If[abandon[Max[largestRe, lowerBound], terms],
    Return[0],];

  (* next points to try: two square roots *)
  nextt1 := Mod[3 t/2, 1];
  nextt2 := Mod[(3 t + 1)/2, 1];
  If[1/4 < next1 < 3/4,
   tmp = next1;
   nextt1 = next2;
   nextt2 = tmp,
   ];
  (* try root with positive real part first:*)
  (* saves some time *)

  branch[{sum + e[nextt1] // N, l + 1, nextt1},
    lowerBound];
  branch[{sum + e[nextt2] // N, l + 1, nextt2},
    lowerBound];
  Return[largestRe]
]

BandB[maxlen_] :=
 Module[{lowerBound, Relist, worstlen, largestoverall},
  lowerBound = -1.;
  Relist = {};
  worstlen = 0;
  largestAvgRe = 0; (* worst among all l *)

  For[len = 2, len <= maxlen, len++,
   largestRe = -1;
   worstseq = {};
   nodes = 0; (* number of nodes searched *)
   (* initial list consisting of -1, -I *)

   branch[{-1 - I, 2, 3/4}, lowerBound];
   Print["l=", len,
     " nodes explored=", nodes,
     " largest average Re=", largestRe/len
   ];

   If[largestRe/len > largestAvgRe,
    largestAvgRe = largestRe/len;
    worstlen = len,
    ];

   lowerBound = largestRe;
   AppendTo[Relist,
     {len, nodes, worstseq, largestRe/len}];
   ];

  Print["worst overall: l=", worstlen,
   ", worst average Re=", largestAvgRe];
  Return[Relist]
]

(* check up to length 90 *)
BandB[90];
```

B. NUMERICAL DATA FOR $\ell = 1, \ldots, 145$

Computed values of $1 - \delta_\ell$, in blocks of 5:

-1, -0.5, -0.09763107, 0.02244755, 0.06104173,
0.21035816, 0.30944832, 0.36931059, 0.38886774, 0.37897848,
0.43264236, 0.47419939, 0.50293127, 0.51902248, 0.53922673,
0.54395341, 0.52409779, 0.52756127, 0.54191323, 0.55916641,
0.57941523, 0.59694159, 0.61106656, 0.62006287, 0.62026151,
0.62094591, 0.63495312, 0.64792145, 0.65991213, 0.67092253,
0.68082984, 0.68926756, 0.6953662, 0.69724859, 0.69122805,
0.67276814, 0.68159584, 0.68993896, 0.69781049, 0.70519257,
0.71200453, 0.718033, 0.7227827, 0.72517324, 0.72299356,
0.71226017, 0.70661433, 0.70962287, 0.70963933, 0.70543927,
0.70942025, 0.71112421, 0.70837005, 0.70860827, 0.7097255,
0.7064789, 0.7078381, 0.70891003, 0.70956335, 0.71419406,
0.71841608, 0.72193815, 0.7241241, 0.72616951, 0.72938946,
0.7313194, 0.73375238, 0.73427986, 0.73113851, 0.7311115,

0.73415884, 0.73760456, 0.74065397, 0.74295896, 0.74377264,
0.74217703, 0.74522741, 0.74783505, 0.7495795, 0.74957126,
0.74606473, 0.74129791, 0.74394143, 0.745946, 0.74665782,
0.74908835, 0.75083691, 0.75119509, 0.74874461, 0.74762941,
0.7504024, 0.75311471, 0.75576782, 0.75836253, 0.7608983,
0.76337161, 0.76577249, 0.76807669, 0.77022843, 0.77210255,
0.77342368, 0.77360272, 0.77145276, 0.76491854, 0.76515789,
0.76717188, 0.76890072, 0.77005378, 0.77001304, 0.76844771,
0.76712548, 0.76278831, 0.76488747, 0.76694975, 0.76897601,
0.77096703, 0.77292332, 0.77484488, 0.77673065, 0.7785772,
0.78037586, 0.78210629, 0.78372238, 0.78512108, 0.78607595,
0.78610236, 0.78422349, 0.77874941, 0.77903028, 0.78064159,
0.78211905, 0.78333206, 0.78399579, 0.78351048, 0.78071408,
0.77733999, 0.77850478, 0.77909491, 0.779437, 0.77883906,
0.77796443, 0.77750376, 0.77602639, 0.7769396, 0.77717729

Capacity of Non-Malleable Codes*

Mahdi Cheraghchi†
CSAIL
Massachusetts Institute of Technology
Cambridge, MA 02139

Venkatesan Guruswami‡
Computer Science Department
Carnegie Mellon University
Pittsburgh, PA 15213

ABSTRACT

Non-malleable codes, introduced by Dziembowski, Pietrzak and Wichs (ICS 2010), encode messages s in a manner so that tampering the codeword causes the decoder to either output s or a message that is independent of s. While this is an impossible goal to achieve against unrestricted tampering functions, rather surprisingly non-malleable coding becomes possible against every fixed family $\mathcal{F}$ of tampering functions that is not too large (for instance, when $|\mathcal{F}| \leqslant 2^{2^{\alpha n}}$ for some $\alpha < 1$ where n is the number of bits in a codeword).

In this work, we study the "capacity of non-malleable coding," and establish optimal bounds on the achievable rate as a function of the family size, answering an open problem from Dziembowski et al. (ICS 2010). Specifically,

- We prove that for every family $\mathcal{F}$ with $|\mathcal{F}| \leqslant 2^{2^{\alpha n}}$, there exist non-malleable codes against $\mathcal{F}$ with rate arbitrarily close to $1 - \alpha$ (this is achieved w.h.p. by a randomized construction).
- We show the existence of families of size $\exp(n^{O(1)} 2^{\alpha n})$ against which there is no non-malleable code of rate $1 - \alpha$ (in fact this is the case w.h.p for a random family of this size).
- We also show that $1 - \alpha$ is the best achievable rate for the family of functions which are only allowed to tamper the first αn bits of the codeword, which is of special interest.

As a corollary, this implies that the capacity of non-malleable coding in the split-state model (where the tampering function acts independently but arbitrarily on the two halves of the codeword, a model which has received some attention recently) equals $1/2$.

We also give an efficient Monte Carlo construction of codes of rate close to 1 with polynomial time encoding and decoding that is non-malleable against any fixed $c > 0$ and family $\mathcal{F}$ of size 2^{n^c}, in particular tampering functions with say cubic size circuits.

*A draft of the full version of this paper appears in [2].

†Email: ⟨mahdi@csail.mit.edu⟩. Research supported in part by the Swiss National Science Foundation research grant PA00P2-141980, V. Guruswami's Packard Fellowship, and MSR-CMU Center for Computational Thinking.

‡Email: ⟨guruswami@cmu.edu⟩. Research supported in part by the National Science Foundation under Grant No. CCF-0963975. Any opinions, findings, and conclusions or recommendations expressed in this material are those of the author(s) and do not necessarily reflect the views of the National Science Foundation.

ITCS'14, January 12–14, 2014, Princeton, New Jersey, USA.

http://dx.doi.org/10.1145/2554797.2554814.

Categories and Subject Descriptors

E.3 [**Data**]: Data Encryption; E.4 [**Data**]: Coding and Information Theory; G.2.1 [**Discrete Mathematics**]: Combinatorics

General Terms

Theory

Keywords

coding theory; cryptography; error detection; information theory; probabilistic method; tamper-resilient storage

1. INTRODUCTION

Non-malleable codes are a fascinating new concept put forth in [7], following the program on non-malleable cryptography which was introduced by the seminal work of Dolev, Dwork and Naor [5]. Non-malleable codes are aimed at protecting the integrity of data in situations where it might be corrupted in ways that precludes error-correction or even error-detection. Informally, a code is non-malleable if the corrupted codeword either encodes the original message, or a completely unrelated value. This is akin to the notion of non-malleable encryption in cryptography which requires the intractability of, given a ciphertext, producing a different ciphertext so that the corresponding plaintexts are related to each other.

A non-malleable (binary) code against a family $\mathcal{F}$ of tampering functions each mapping $\{0,1\}^n$ to $\{0,1\}^n$, consists of a randomized encoding function $\mathsf{Enc} : \{0,1\}^k \to \{0,1\}^n$ and a deterministic decoding function $\mathsf{Dec} : \{0,1\}^n \to \{0,1\}^k \cup \{\perp\}$ (where $\perp$ denotes error-detection) which always satisfy $\mathsf{Dec}(\mathsf{Enc}(s)) = s$, and the following non-malleability property with error ϵ: For every message $s \in \{0,1\}^k$ and every function $f \in \mathcal{F}$, the distribution of $\mathsf{Dec}(f(\mathsf{Enc}(s)))$ is ϵ-close to a distribution $\mathcal{D}_f$ that depends only on f and is independent[1] of s. In other words, if some adversary (who has full knowledge of the code and the message s, but not the internal randomness of the encoder) tampers with the codeword $\mathsf{Enc}(s)$ corrupting it to $f(\mathsf{Enc}(s))$, he cannot control the relationship between s and the message the corrupted codeword $f(\mathsf{Enc}(s))$ encodes.

In general, it is impossible to achieve non-malleability against arbitrary tampering functions. Indeed, the tampering function can decode the codeword to compute the original message s, flip the last bit of s to obtain a related message $\tilde{s}$, and then reencode $\tilde{s}$. This clearly violates non-malleability as the tampered codeword encodes the message $\tilde{s}$ which is closely related to s. Therefore, in order to construct non-malleable codes, one focuses on a restricted class of tampering functions. For example, the body of work on error-correcting codes consists of functions which can flip an arbitrary subset of bits up to a prescribed limit on the total number of bit flips.

The notion of non-malleable coding becomes more interesting for families against which error-correction is not possible. A simple and natural such family is the set of functions causing arbitrary "additive errors," namely $\mathcal{F}_{\mathsf{add}} = \{f_\Delta \mid \Delta \in \{0,1\}^n\}$ where $f_\Delta(x) := x+\Delta$. Note that there is no restriction on the Hamming weight of Δ as in the case of channels causing bounded number of bit flips. While error-correction is impossible against $\mathcal{F}_{\mathsf{add}}$, *error-detection* is still possible — the work of Cramer et al. [4] constructed codes of rate approaching 1 (which they called "Algebraic Manipulation Detection" (AMD) codes) such that offset by an arbitrary $\Delta \neq 0$ will be detected with high probability. AMD codes give a construction of non-malleable codes against the family $\mathcal{F}_{\mathsf{add}}$.

Even error-detection becomes impossible against many other natural families of tampering functions. A particularly simple such class consists of all constant functions $f_c(x) := c$ for $c \in \{0,1\}^n$. This family includes some function that maps all inputs to a valid codeword c^*, and hence one cannot detect tampering. Note, however, that non-malleability is trivial to achieve against this family — the rate 1 code with identity encoding function is itself non-malleable as the output distribution of a constant function is trivially independent of the message. A natural function family for which non-malleability is non-trivial to achieve consists of *bit-tampering functions* f in which the different of bits of the codewords are tampered independently (i.e., either flipped, set to 0/1, or left unchanged); formally $f(x) = (f_1(x_1), f_2(x_2), \ldots, f_n(x_n))$ for arbitrary 1-bit functions $f_1, f_2, \ldots, f_n$ [7].

The family $\mathcal{F}_{\mathsf{all}}$ of all functions $f : \{0,1\}^n \to \{0,1\}^n$ has size given by $\log\log|\mathcal{F}_{\mathsf{all}}| = n + \log n$. The authors of [7] show the existence of a non-malleable code against *any* small enough family $\mathcal{F}$ (for which $\log\log|\mathcal{F}| < n$). The rate of the code is constant if $\log\log|\mathcal{F}| \leqslant \alpha n$ for some constant $\alpha \in (0,1)$. The question of figuring out the optimal rates of non-malleable codes for various families of tampering functions was left as an open problem in [7]. In this work we give a satisfactory answer to this question, pinning down the rate for many natural function families. We describe our results next.

1.1 Our results

Our results include improvements to the rate achievable as a function of the size of the family of tampering functions, as well as limitations of non-malleable codes demonstrating that the achieved rate cannot be improved for natural families of the stipulated size. Specifically, we establish the following results concerning the possible rates for non-malleable coding as a function of the size of the family of tampering functions:

1. (Rate lower bound) We prove in Section 3 that if $|\mathcal{F}| \leqslant 2^{2^{\alpha n}}$, then there exists a (strong) non-malleable code of rate arbitrarily close to $1-\alpha$ which is non-malleable w.r.t $\mathcal{F}$ with error $\exp(-\Omega(n))$. This significantly improves the probabilistic construction of [7], which achieves a rate close to $(1-\alpha)/3$ using a delicate Martingale argument. In particular, for arbitrary small families, of size $2^{2^{o(n)}}$, our result shows that the rate can be made arbitrarily close to 1. This was not known to be possible even for the family of bit-tampering functions (which has size 4^n), for which 1/3 was the best known rate[2] [7]. In fact, it can be shown that the proof strategy of [7] is limited to a rate of 1/2 even for a very simple tampering function such as the one that flips the first bit (we defer the proof to the full version of the paper). We note that our probabilistic construction is equipped with an encoder and decoder that can be efficiently and exactly implemented with access to a uniformly random permutation oracle and its inverse (corresponding to the ideal-cipher model in cryptography). This is a slight additional advantage over [7], where only an approximation of the encoder and decoder is shown to be efficiently computable.

2. (Upper bound/limitations on rate) The above coding theorem shows that the "capacity" of a function family $|\mathcal{F}|$ for non-malleable coding is at least $1 - (\log\log|\mathcal{F}|)/n$. We also address the natural "converse coding quesiton" of whether this rate bound is the best achievable (Section 5). This turns out to be false in general due to the existence of uninteresting large families for which non-malleable coding with rate close to 1 is easy. But we do prove that the $1-\alpha$ rate is best achievable in "virtually all" situations:

   (a) We prove that for *random* families of size $2^{2^{\alpha n}}$, with high probability it is not possible to exceed a rate of $1-\alpha$ for non-malleable coding with small error.

   (b) For the family of tampering functions which leave the last $(1-\alpha)n$ bits intact and act arbitrarily on the first αn bits, we prove that $1-\alpha$ is the best achievable rate for non-malleable coding. (Note that a rate of $1-\alpha$ is trivial to achieve for this family, by placing the message bits in the last

[1] The formal definition (see Definition2.3) has to accommodate the possibility that Dec error-corrects the tampered codeword to the original message s; and this is handled in a manner independent of s by including a special element $\underline{\mathsf{same}}$ in the support of $\mathcal{D}_f$.

[2] Assuming the existence of one-way functions, an explicit construction of non-malleable codes of rate close to 1 was proposed in [7]. This construction, however, only satisfies a weaker definition of non-malleability that considers computational indistinguishability rather than statistical security.

$(1-\alpha)n$ bits of the codeword, and setting the first αn bits of the codeword to all 0s.)

The result 2b, together with the existential result 1 above, pins down the optimal rate for non-malleable codes in the *split-state model* to 1/2. In the split-state model, which was the focus of a couple of recent works [6, 1], the tampering function operates independently (but in otherwise arbitary ways) on the two halves of the codeword, i.e., $f(x) = ((f_1(x_1), f_2(x_2))$ where x_1, x_2 are the two halves of x and f_1, f_2 are functions mapping $n/2$ bits to $n/2$ bits. The recent work [1] gave an explicit construction in this model with polynomially small rate. Our work shows that the capacity of the split-state model is 1/2, but we do not offer any explicit construction. For the more restrictive class of bit tampering functions (where each bit is tampered independently), in a follow-up work [3] we give an explicit construction with rate approaching 1 [3]. We also present in that work a reduction of non-malleable coding for the split-state model to a new notion of non-malleable two-source extraction.

Monte Carlo construction for small families. Our result 1 above is based on a random construction which takes exponential time (and space). Derandomizing this construction, in Section 4 we are able to obtain an efficient Monte Carlo construction of non-malleable codes of rate close to 1 (with polynomial time encoding and decoding, and inverse polynomially small error) for an *arbitrary* family of size $\exp(n^c)$ for any fixed $c > 0$. Note that in particular this includes tampering functions that can be implemented by circuits of any fixed polynomial size, or simpler families such as bit-tampering adversaries. The construction does not rely on any computational hardness assumptions, at the cost of using a small amount of randomness.

Subsequent work. Recently, Faust et al. [8] obtain a Monte-Carlo construction achieving a slightly worse rate (roughly, $1 - 3\alpha$ for families of size $2^{2^{\alpha n}}$ as opposed to $1 - \alpha$ achieved by our construction). However, the dependence of the time complexity of the encoder and decoder on the error parameter ϵ (as made precise in Definition 2.3) is $\log^{O(1)}(1/\epsilon)$ in [8] while our construction only achieves a polynomial dependence of $(1/\epsilon)^{O(1)}$.

1.2 Proof ideas

Rate lower bound. Our construction of codes of rate $\approx 1-(\log\log|\mathcal{F}|)/n$ is obtained by picking for each message, a random blob of t codewords, such that blobs corresponding to distinct messages are disjoint. For each tampering function f, our proof analyzes the distribution of $\mathsf{Dec}(f(\mathsf{Enc}(s))$ for each message s separately, and shows that w.h.p. they are essentially close to the same distribution $\mathcal{D}_f$. In order to achieve sufficiently small error probability allowing for a union bound, the proof uses a number of additional ideas, including a randomized process that gradually reveals information about the code while examining the t codewords in each blob in sequence. The analysis ensures that as little information is revealed in each step as possible, so that enough independence remains in the conditional joint distribution of the codewords throughout the analysis. Finally, strong concentration bounds are used to derive the desired bound on the failure probability. The proof for the special case of bijective tampering functions turns out to be quite straightforward, and as a warm-up we present this special case first in Section 3.1.

Monte Carlo construction. Since the analysis of the probabilistic code construction considers each message s separately, we observe that it only needs limited (t-wise) independence of the codewords. On the other hand, the code construction is designed to be sparse, namely taking $t = \mathrm{poly}(n, \log|\mathcal{F}|, 1/\epsilon)$ suffices for the analysis. This is the key idea behind our efficient Monte Carlo construction for small families with $\log|\mathcal{F}| \leqslant \mathrm{poly}(n)$.

The birthday paradox implies that picking the blob of codewords encoding each message independently of other messages, while maintaining disjointness of the various blobs, limits the rate to 1/2. Therefore, we construct the code by means of a t-wise independent *decoding* function implemented via a random low-degree polynomial. After overcoming some complications to ensure an efficient encoding function, we get our efficient randomized construction for small families of tampering functions.

Rate upper bounds. Our main impossibility result for the family of adversaries that only tamper the first αn bits of the codeword uses an information theoretic argument. We argue that if the rate of the code is sufficiently large, one can always find messages s_0 and s_1 and a set $X_\eta \subseteq \{0,1\}^{\alpha n}$ such that the following holds: The first αn bits of the encoding of s_0 has a noticeable chance of being in X_η, whereas this chance for s_1 is quite small. Using this property, we design an adversary that maps the first αn bits of the encoding to a dummy string if they belong to X_η and leaves the codeword intact otherwise. This suffices to violate non-malleability of the code.

2. PRELIMINARIES

2.1 Notation

We use $\mathcal{U}_n$ for the uniform distribution on $\{0,1\}^n$ and U_n for the random variable sampled from $\mathcal{U}_n$ and independently of any existing randomness. For a random variable X, we denote by $\mathscr{D}(X)$ the probability distribution that X is sampled from. Moreover, for an event $\mathcal{E}$, we use $\mathscr{D}(X|\mathcal{E})$ to denote the conditional distribution of the random variable X on the event $\mathcal{E}$. Generally, we will use calligraphic symbols (such as $\mathcal{X}$) for probability distributions and the corresponding capital letters (such as X) for related random variables. For a discrete distribution $\mathcal{X}$, we denote by $\mathcal{X}(x)$ the probability mass assigned to x by $\mathcal{X}$. Two distributions $\mathcal{X}$ and $\mathcal{Y}$ being ϵ-close in statistical distance is denoted by $\mathcal{X} \approx_\epsilon \mathcal{Y}$. We will use $(\mathcal{X}, \mathcal{Y})$ for the product distribution with the two coordinates independently sampled from $\mathcal{X}$ and $\mathcal{Y}$. All unsubscripted logarithms are taken to the base 2. Support of a discrete random variable (or distribution) X is denoted by $\mathsf{supp}(X)$. With a slight abuse of notation, for various bounds we condition probabilities and expectations on random variables rather than events (e.g., $\mathbb{E}[X|Y]$, or $\Pr[\mathcal{E}|Y]$). In such instances, the notation means that the statement holds for *every* possible realization of the random variables that we condition on.

2.2 Definitions

In this section, we review the formal definition of non-malleable codes as introduced in [7]. First, we recall the notion of *coding schemes*.

Definition 2.1 (Coding schemes). *A pair of functions* $\mathsf{Enc}\colon \{0,1\}^k \to \{0,1\}^n$ *and* $\mathsf{Dec}\colon \{0,1\}^n \to \{0,1\}^k \cup \{\perp\}$ *where* $k \leqslant n$ *is said to be a coding scheme with block length* n *and message length* k *if the following conditions hold.*

1. *The encoder* Enc *is a randomized function; i.e., at each call it receives a uniformly random sequence of coin flips that the output may depend on. This random input is usually omitted from the notation and taken to be implicit. Thus for any* $s \in \{0,1\}^k$, $\mathsf{Enc}(s)$ *is a random variable over* $\{0,1\}^n$. *The decoder* Dec *is; however, deterministic.*

2. *For every* $s \in \{0,1\}^k$, *we have* $\mathsf{Dec}(\mathsf{Enc}(s)) = s$ *with probability* 1.

The rate *of the coding scheme is the ratio* k/n. *A coding scheme is said to have relative distance* δ, *for some* $\delta \in [0,1)$, *if for every* $s \in \{0,1\}^k$ *the following holds. Let* $X := \mathsf{Enc}(s)$. *Then, for any* $\Delta \in \{0,1\}^n$ *of Hamming weight at most* δn, $\mathsf{Dec}(X + \Delta) = \perp$ *with probability* 1. □

Before defining non-malleable coding schemes, we find it convenient to define the following notation.

Definition 2.2. *For a finite set* Γ, *the function* $\mathsf{copy}\colon (\Gamma \cup \{\underline{\mathsf{same}}\}) \times \Gamma \to \Gamma$ *is defined as follows:*

$$\mathsf{copy}(x,y) := \begin{cases} x & x \neq \underline{\mathsf{same}}, \\ y & x = \underline{\mathsf{same}}. \end{cases} \qquad \square$$

The notion of non-malleable coding schemes from [7] can now be rephrased as follows.

Definition 2.3 (Non-malleability). *A coding scheme* (Enc, Dec) *with message length* k *and block length* n *is said to be non-malleable with error* ϵ *(also called* exact security*) with respect to a family* $\mathcal{F}$ *of tampering functions acting on* $\{0,1\}^n$ *(i.e., each* $f \in \mathcal{F}$ *maps* $\{0,1\}^n$ *to* $\{0,1\}^n$*) if for every* $f \in \mathcal{F}$ *there is a distribution* $\mathcal{D}_f$ *over* $\{0,1\}^k \cup \{\perp, \underline{\mathsf{same}}\}$ *such that the following holds for all* $s \in \{0,1\}^k$. *Define the random variable* $S := \mathsf{Dec}(f(\mathsf{Enc}(s)))$, *and let* S' *be independently sampled from* $\mathcal{D}_f$. *Then,* $\mathscr{D}(S) \approx_\epsilon \mathscr{D}(\mathsf{copy}(S', s))$. □

Remark 2.4. *The above definition allows the decoder to output a special symbol* $\perp$ *that corresponds to error detection. It is easy to note that any such code can be transformed to one where the decoder never outputs* $\perp$ *without affecting the parameters (e.g., the new decoder may simply output* 0^k *whenever the original decoder outputs* $\perp$*).*

Dziembowski et al. [7] also consider the following stronger variation of non-malleable codes.

Definition 2.5 (Strong non-malleability). *A pair of functions as in Definition 2.3 is said to be a* strong non-malleable coding scheme *with error* ϵ *with respect to a family* $\mathcal{F}$ *of tampering functions acting on* $\{0,1\}^n$ *if the following holds. For any message* $s \in \{0,1\}^k$, *let* $E_s := \mathsf{Enc}(s)$, *consider the random variable*

$$D_s := \begin{cases} \underline{\mathsf{same}} & \text{if } f(E_s) = E_s, \\ \mathsf{Dec}(f(E_s)) & \text{otherwise,} \end{cases}$$

and let $\mathcal{D}_{f,s} := \mathscr{D}(D_s)$. *It must be the case that for every pair of distinct messages* $s_1, s_2 \in \{0,1\}^k$, $\mathcal{D}_{f,s_1} \approx_\epsilon \mathcal{D}_{f,s_2}$. □

Remark 2.6 (Computational security). *Dziembowski et al. also consider the case where statistical distance is replaced with computational indistinguishability with respect to a bounded computational model. As our goal is to understand information-theoretic limitations of non-malleable codes, we do not consider this variation in this work. It is clear, however, that our negative results in Section 5 apply to this model as well. A related (but incomparable) model that we consider in Section 4 is when the distinguishability criterion is still statistical; however the adversary is computationally bounded (e.g., one may consider the family of polynomial sized Boolean circuits). For this case, we construct an efficient Monte Carlo coding scheme that achieves any rate arbitrarily close to* 1.

Remark 2.7 (Efficiency of sampling $\mathcal{D}_f$). *The original definition of non-malleable codes in [7] also requires the distribution* $\mathcal{D}_f$ *to be efficiently samplable given oracle access to the tampering function* f. *We find it more natural to remove this requirement from the definition since even combinatorial non-malleable codes that are not necessarily equipped with efficient components (such as the encoder, decoder, and sampler for* $\mathcal{D}_f$*) are interesting and highly nontrivial to construct. It should be noted; however, that for any non-malleable coding scheme equipped with an efficient encoder and decoder, it can be shown that the following is a valid and efficiently samplable choice for the distribution* $\mathcal{D}_f$ *(possibly incurring a constant factor increase in the error parameter):*

1. *Let* $S \sim \mathcal{U}_k$, *and* $X := f(\mathsf{Enc}(S))$.

2. *If* $\mathsf{Dec}(X) = S$, *output* $\underline{\mathsf{same}}$. *Otherwise, output* $\mathsf{Dec}(X)$.

Our Monte Carlo construction in Section 4 is equipped with a polynomial-time encoder and decoder. So is the case for our probabilistic construction in Section 3 in the random oracle model.

3. PROBABILISTIC CONSTRUCTION OF NON-MALLEABLE CODES

In this section, we introduce our probabilistic construction of non-malleable codes. Contrary to the original construction of Dziembowski et al. [7], where they pick a uniformly random truth table for the decoder and do not allow the $\perp$ symbol, our code is quite sparse. In fact, in our construction $\mathsf{Dec}(U_n) = \perp$ with high probability. In fact, this is the key to our improvement, since uniformly random decoders cannot achieve non-malleability even against extremely simple adversaries at rates better than 1/2 (we defer the proof to the full version of this paper). Moreover, our sparse construction offers the added feature of having a large minimum distance in the standard coding sense; any tampering scheme that perturbs the codeword in a fraction of the positions bounded by a prescribed limit will be detected by the decoder with probability 1. Another advantage of sparsity is allowing a compact representation for the code. We exploit this feature in our Monte Carlo construction of Section 4. Our probabilistic coding scheme is described in Construction 1.

We remark that Construction 1 can be efficiently implemented in the ideal-cipher model, which in turn implies an efficient approximate implementation in the random oracle model. In turn, this implies that the distribution $\mathcal{D}_f$ in Definition 2.3 for this construction can be efficiently sampled in both models (see Remark 2.7).

- *Given:* Integer parameters $0 < k \leqslant n$ and integer $t > 0$ such that $t2^k \leqslant 2^n$, and a relative distance parameter δ, $0 \leqslant \delta < 1/2$.
- *Output:* A pair of functions $\mathsf{Enc}\colon \{0,1\}^k \to \{0,1\}^n$ and $\mathsf{Dec}\colon \{0,1\}^n \to \{0,1\}^k$, where Enc may also use a uniformly random seed which is hidden from that notation, but Dec is deterministic.
- *Construction:*
  1. Let $\mathcal{N} := \{0,1\}^n$.
  2. For each $s \in \{0,1\}^k$, in an arbitrary order,
     - Let $E(s) := \emptyset$.
     - For $i \in \{1, \ldots, t\}$:
       (a) Pick a uniformly random vector $w \in \mathcal{N}$.
       (b) Add w to $E(s)$.
       (c) Let $\Gamma(w)$ be the Hamming ball of radius δn centered at w. Remove $\Gamma(w)$ from $\mathcal{N}$ (note that when $\delta = 0$, we have $\Gamma(w) = \{w\}$).
  3. Given $s \in \{0,1\}^k$, $\mathsf{Enc}(s)$ outputs an element of $E(s)$ uniformly at random.
  4. Given $w \in \{0,1\}^n$, $\mathsf{Dec}(s)$ outputs the unique s such that $w \in E(s)$, or $\perp$ if no such s exists.

Construction 1: Probabilistic construction of non-malleable codes.

The main theorem of this section is the result below that proves non-malleability of the coding scheme in Construction 1.

THEOREM 3.1. *Let $\mathcal{F}\colon \{0,1\}^n \to \{0,1\}^n$ be any family of tampering functions. For any $\epsilon, \eta > 0$, with probability at least $1-\eta$, the coding scheme* (Enc, Dec) *of Construction 1 is a strong non-malleable code with respect to $\mathcal{F}$ and with error ϵ and relative distance δ, provided that both of the following conditions are satisfied.*

1. $t \geqslant t_0$, for some

$$t_0 = O\left(\frac{1}{\epsilon^6}\left(\log \frac{|\mathcal{F}|N}{\eta}\right)\right). \tag{1}$$

2. $k \leqslant k_0$, for some

$$k_0 \geqslant n(1-h(\delta)) - \log t - 3\log(1/\epsilon) - O(1), \tag{2}$$

where $h(\cdot)$ denotes the binary entropy function.

Thus by choosing $t = t_0$ and $k = k_0$, the construction satisfies $k \geqslant n(1-h(\delta)) - \log\log(|\mathcal{F}|/\eta) - \log n - 9\log(1/\epsilon) - O(1)$. In particular, if $|\mathcal{F}| \leqslant 2^{2^{\alpha n}}$ for any constant $\alpha \in (0,1)$, the rate of the code can be made arbitrarily close to $1 - h(\delta) - \alpha$ while allowing $\epsilon = 2^{-\Omega(n)}$. □

REMARK 3.2. *(Error detection) An added feature of our sparse coding scheme is the error-detection capability. However, observe that any probabilistic coding scheme that is non-malleable against all families of adversaries of bounded size over $\{0,1\}^n$ (such as Construction 1, Construction 2, and the probabilistic construction of [7]) can be turned into one having relative distance δ (and satisfying the same non-malleability guarantees) by composing the construction with a fixed outer code $\mathcal{C}$ of block length n and relative distance δ. Indeed, any class $\mathcal{F}$ of tampering functions for the composed code corresponds to a class $\mathcal{F}'$ of the same size or less for the original construction. Namely, each function $f' \in \mathcal{F}'$ equals* $\mathsf{Dec}_\mathcal{C} \circ f$ *($\mathsf{Dec}_\mathcal{C}$ being the decoder of $\mathcal{C}$) for some $f \in \mathcal{F}$. The caveat with this approach (rather than directly addressing distance as in Construction 1) is that the composition may lose strong non-malleability even if the original code is strongly non-malleable. Indeed, it may be the case that f is a sophisticated tampering function whereas its projection f' becomes as simple as the identity function. If so, non-malleability may be satisfied by choosing $\mathcal{D}_f := \mathscr{D}(\underline{\mathsf{same}})$ whereas strong non-malleability does not hold.*

3.1 Proof of Theorem 3.1 for bijective adversaries

We first prove the theorem for adversaries that are bijective and have no fixed points. This case is still broad enough to contain interesting families of adversaries such as additive error adversaries $\mathcal{F}_{\mathsf{add}}$ mentioned in the introduction, for which case we reconstruct the existence proof of AMD codes (although optimal explicit constructions of AMD codes are already known [4]).

As it turns out, the analysis for this case is quite straightforward, and significantly simpler than the general case that we will address in Section 3.2.

Let $N := 2^n$, $K := 2^k$, and consider a fixed message $s \in \{0,1\}^k$ and a fixed bijective tampering function $f\colon \{0,1\}^n \to \{0,1\}^n$ such that for all $x \in \{0,1\}^n$, $f(x) \neq x$. We show that the non-malleability requirement of Definition 2.3 holds with respect to the distribution $\mathcal{D}_f$ that is entirely supported on $\{\perp\}$. That is, we wish to show that with high probability, the coding scheme (Enc, Dec) of Construction 1 is so that

$$\Pr[\mathsf{Dec}(f(\mathsf{Enc}(s))) \neq \perp] \leqslant \epsilon. \tag{3}$$

By taking a union bound over all choices of f and s, this would imply that with high probability, the code is non-malleable (in fact, strongly non-malleable) for the entire family $\mathcal{F}$.

Let $E(s) := \mathsf{supp}(\mathsf{Enc}(s))$ be the set of the t codewords that are mapped to s by the decoder. Let $E_1, \ldots, E_t$ be the codewords in this set in the order they are picked by the code construction. For any fixed $x \in \{0,1\}^n$, we know that $\Pr[\mathsf{Dec}(x) \neq \perp] \leqslant t(K-1)/(N-t) \leqslant \frac{\gamma}{1-\gamma}$, where $\gamma := tK/N$. This can be seen by observing that the code construction chooses the codewords uniformly at random and without replacement, combined with a union bound. Thus, in particular, $\Pr[\mathsf{Dec}(f(E_1)) \neq \perp] \leqslant \frac{\gamma}{1-\gamma}$ (since $f(E_1) \neq E_1$, the knowledge of $E_1 \in E(s)$ only decreases this probability). In fact, the same argument holds for $\mathsf{Dec}(f(E_2))$ conditioned on any realization of $f(E_1)$, and more generally, since $f(E_1), \ldots, f(E_t)$ are distinct, one can derive for each $i \in [t]$,

$$\Pr[\mathsf{Dec}(f(E_i)) \neq \perp | f(E_1), \ldots, f(E_{i-1})] \leqslant \frac{\gamma}{1-\gamma}. \tag{4}$$

Define indicator random variables $0 = X_0, X_1, \ldots, X_t \in \{0,1\}$, where $X_i = 1$ iff $\mathsf{Dec}(f(E_i)) \neq \perp$. From (4) and using Proposition B.1, we can deduce that for all $i \in [t]$, $\Pr[X_i = 1 | X_0, \ldots, X_{i-1}] \leqslant \frac{\gamma}{1-\gamma}$. Now, using Proposition B.5, letting $X := X_1 + \cdots + X_t$, it follows that $\Pr[X > \epsilon t] \leqslant \left(\frac{e\gamma}{\epsilon(1-\gamma)}\right)^{\epsilon t}$.

Assuming $\gamma \leqslant \epsilon/4$, the above upper bound simplifies to $\exp(-\Omega(\epsilon t))$. By taking a union bound over all possible choices of s and f (that we trivially upper bound by $N|\mathcal{F}|$), it can be seen that, as long as $t \geqslant t_0$ for some choice of $t_0 = O\Big(\frac{1}{\epsilon}\log(\frac{N|\mathcal{F}|}{\eta})\Big)$, the probability that (Enc, Dec) fails to satisfy (3) for some choice of s and f is at most η.

Finally, observe that the assumption $\gamma \leqslant \epsilon/4$ can be satisfied provided that $K \leqslant K_0$ for some choice of $K_0 = \Omega(\epsilon N/t)$, or equivalently, when $k \leqslant k_0$ for some choice of $k \geqslant n - \log t - \log(1/\epsilon)$. Note that for this case the proof obtains a better dependence on ϵ compared to (1) and (2).

3.2 Proof of Theorem 3.1 for general adversaries

Below we present a proof sketch describing the ideas an intuitions behind the general proof. The complete proof appears in Appendix A.

In the proof for bijective adversaries, we heavily used the fact that the tampering of each set $E(s)$ of codewords is a disjoint set of the same size. For general adversaries; however, this may not be true. Intuitively, since the codewords in $E(s)$ are chosen uniformly and almost independently at random (ignoring the distinctness dependencies), the tampered distribution $f(E(s))$ should look similar to $f(\mathcal{U}_n)$ for all s, if $|E(s)|$ is sufficiently large. Indeed, this is what is shown in the proof. The proof also adjusts the probability mass of same according to the fraction of the fixed points of f, but we ignore this technicality for the proof sketch.

Note that the distribution $f(\mathcal{U}_n)$ may be arbitrary, and may assign a large probability mass to a small set of the probability space. For example, f may assign half of the probability mass to a single point. We call the points in $\{0,1\}^n$ receiving a noticeable share of the probability mass in $f(\mathcal{U}_n)$ the *heavy elements* of $\{0,1\}^n$, and fix the randomness of the code construction so that the decoder's values at heavy elements are revealed before analyzing each individual message s. Doing so allows us to analyze each message s separately and take a union bound on various choices of s as in the case of bijective adversaries. Contrary to the bijective case; however, the distribution $\mathcal{D}_f$ is no longer entirely supported on $\perp$; but we show that it still can be made to have a fairly small support; roughly $\mathsf{poly}(n, \log|\mathcal{F}|)$. More precisely, the proof shows non-malleability with respect to the choice of $\mathcal{D}_f$ which is explicitly defined to be the distribution of the following random variable:

$$D := \begin{cases} \underline{\mathsf{same}} & \text{if } f(U_n) = U_n, \\ \mathsf{Dec}(f(U_n)) & \text{if } f(U_n) \neq U_n \text{ and } f(U_n) \in H, \\ \perp & \text{otherwise,} \end{cases}$$

where $H \subseteq \{0,1\}^n$ is the set of heavy elements formally defined as

$$H := \{x \in \{0,1\}^n \colon \Pr[f(U_n) = x] > 1/r\},$$

for an appropriately chosen $r = \Theta(\epsilon^2 t)$.

Although the above intuition is natural, turning it into a rigorous proof requires substantially more work than the bijective case, and the final proof turns out to be rather delicate even though it only uses elementary probability tools. The first subtlety is that revealing the decoder at the heavy elements creates dependencies between various random variables used in the analysis. In order to make the proof more intuitive, we introduce a random process, described as an algorithm Reveal, that gradually reveals information about the code as the proof considers the codewords $E_1, \ldots, E_t$ corresponding to the picked message s. The process outputs a list of elements in $\{0,1\}^k$, and we show that the empirical distribution of this list is close to the desired $\mathcal{D}_f$ for all messages s.

Roughly speaking, at each step $i \in [t]$ the analysis estimates the distribution of $\mathsf{Dec}(f(E_i))$ conditioned on the particular realizations of the previous codewords. There are three subtleties that we need to handle to make this work:

1. The randomness corresponding to some of the E_i is previously revealed by the analysis and thus such codewords cannot be assumed to be uniformly distributed any more. This issue may arise due to the revealing of the decoder's values at heavy elements in the beginning of analysis, or existence of cycles in the evaluation graph of the tampering function f. Fortunately, it is straightforward to show that the number of such codewords remain much smaller than t with high probability, and thus they may simply be ignored.

2. At each step of the analysis, the revealed information make the distribution of $\mathsf{Dec}(f(E_i))$ gradually farther from the desired $\mathcal{D}_f$. The proof ensures that the expected increase at each step is small, and using standard Martingale concentration bounds the total deviation from $\mathcal{D}_f$ remains sufficiently small with high probability at the end of the analysis.

3. Obtaining small upper bounds (e.g., $\exp(-cn)$ for some $c < 1$) on the probability of various bad events in the analysis (e.g., $\mathsf{Dec}(f(\mathsf{Enc}(s)))$ significantly deviating from $\mathcal{D}_f$) is not difficult to achieve. However, extra care is needed to ensure that the probabilities are much smaller than $1/(2^k|\mathcal{F}|)$ (to accommodate the final union bound), where the latter may easily be doubly-exponentially small in n. An exponential upper bound of $\exp(-cn)$ does not even suffice for moderately large families of adversaries such as bit-tampering adversaries, for which we have $|\mathcal{F}| = 4^n$.

4. A MONTE CARLO CONSTRUCTION FOR COMPUTATIONALLY BOUNDED ADVERSARIES

An important feature of Construction 1 is that the proof of non-malleability, Theorem 3.1, only uses limited independence (in fact $(3t)$-wise independence) of the permutation defining the codewords of the coding scheme. This is because the proof analyzes the distribution of $\mathsf{Dec}(f(\mathsf{Enc}(s)))$ for each individual message separately, and then takes a union bound on all choice of s.

In order to implement an efficient $(3t)$-wise independent coding scheme, we use the bounded independence property of polynomial evaluations over finite fields. More precisely, we consider the coding scheme given in Construction 2.

The advantage of using the derandomized Monte Carlo construction is that the number of random bits required to describe the code is dramatically reduced from $O(tnK)$ bits (which can be exponentially large if the rate of the code is $\Omega(1)$) to only $O(tn)$ bits, which is only polynomially large if $t = \mathsf{poly}(n)$. In order to efficiently implement the derandomized construction, we use bounded independence properties of polynomial evaluation. Using known algorithms for finite field operations and root finding, the implementation can be done in polynomial time.

- *Given:* Integer parameters $0 < k \leqslant n$ and integer $t > 1$ which is a power of two. Let $b := \log(2t)$ and $m := n - k - b$.
- *Output:* A coding scheme $(\mathsf{EncMC}, \mathsf{DecMC})$ of block length n and message length k.
- *Randomness of the construction:* A uniformly random polynomial $P \in \mathbb{F}_{2^n}[9t - 1]$.
- *Construction of* EncMC*:* Given $s \in \{0,1\}^k$,
  1. Initialize a set $E \subseteq \{0,1\}^n$ to the empty set.
  2. For every $z \in \{0,1\}^b$,
     (a) Construct a vector $y := (s, 0^m, z) \in \{0,1\}^n$ and regard it as an element of $\mathbb{F}_{2^n}$.
     (b) Solve $P(X) = y$, and add the set of solutions (which is of size at most $9t - 1$) to E.
  3. Output a uniformly random element of E.
- *Construction of* DecMC*:* Given $x \in \{0,1\}^n$, interpret x as an element of $\mathbb{F}_{2^n}$, and let $y := P(x)$, interpreted as a vector $(y_1, \ldots, y_n) \in \{0,1\}^n$. If $(y_{k+1}, y_{k+2}, \ldots, y_{k+m}) = 0^m$, output $(y_1, \ldots, y_k)$. Otherwise, output $\perp$.

Construction 2: The Monte Carlo Construction.

We state the following result on the performance and non-malleability of Construction 2. Proof of this result appears in the full version of the paper.

THEOREM 4.1. *Let $\mathcal{F}\colon \{0,1\}^n \to \{0,1\}^n$ be any family of tampering functions. For any $\epsilon, \eta > 0$, with probability at least $1 - \eta$, the pair* $(\mathsf{EncMC}, \mathsf{DecMC})$ *in Construction 2 can be set up to achieve a non-malleable coding scheme with respect to $\mathcal{F}$ and with error ϵ. Moreover, the scheme satisfies the following.*

1. *The code achieves $k \geqslant n - \log\log(|\mathcal{F}|/\eta) - \log n - 9\log(1/\epsilon) - O(1)$.*
2. *The number of random bits needed to specify the code is $O\Big((n + \log(|\mathcal{F}|/\eta))n/\epsilon^6\Big)$.*
3. *The encoder and the decoder run in worst case time* $\mathsf{poly}(\log(|\mathcal{F}|/\eta)n/\epsilon)$.

As a corollary, we observe that the rate of the Monte Carlo construction can be made arbitrarily close to 1 while keeping the bit-representation of the code as well as the running time of the encoder and decoder at $\mathsf{poly}(n)$ provided that $\epsilon = 1/\mathsf{poly}(n)$ and $|\mathcal{F}| = 2^{\mathsf{poly}(n)}$. In particular, we see that the Monte Carlo construction achieves strong non-malleability even with respect to such powerful classes of adversaries as polynomial-sized Boolean circuits (with n outputs bits) and virtually any interesting computationally bounded model.

REMARK 4.2. *Since in this construction the error ϵ is only polynomially small, for cryptographic applications such as tamper-resilient security it is important to set up the code so as to ensure that $1/\epsilon$ is significantly larger than the total number of tampering attempts made by the adversary.*

CAVEAT 4.3. *We point out that any explicit coding scheme for computationally bounded models (such as polynomial-sized Boolean circuits) necessarily implies an explicit lower bound for the respective computational model. This is because a function in the restricted model cannot be powerful enough to compute the decoder function, as otherwise, the following adversary would violate non-malleability:*

> *Consider fixed tuples $(s_1, x_1), (s_2, x_2) \in \{0,1\}^k \times \{0,1\}^n$, where $s_1 \neq s_2$, $\mathsf{Dec}(x_1) = s_1$ and $\mathsf{Dec}(x_2) = s_2$. Given a codeword $x \in \{0,1\}^n$, compute $s := \mathsf{Dec}(x)$. If $s = s_1$, output x_2. If $s = s_2$, output x_1. Otherwise, output x.*

5. IMPOSSIBILITY BOUNDS

In this section, we show that the bounds obtained by Theorem 3.1 are essentially optimal. In order to do so, we consider three families of adversaries. Throughout the section, we use k and n for the message length and block length of coding schemes and define $N := 2^n$ and $K := 2^k$.

The first hope is to demonstrate that Theorem 3.1 is the best possible for *every* family of the tampering functions of a prescribed size. We rule out this possibility and demonstrate a simple family $\mathcal{F}$ of tampering functions achieving $\log\log|\mathcal{F}| \approx n$ for which there is a non-malleable code achieving rate $1 - \gamma$ for arbitrarily small $\gamma > 0$. Details of this construction appear in the full version of the paper.

Despite the above negative result, we are able to show that for "virtually all" families of tampering functions of a certain size, Theorem 3.1 gives the best possible bound. More precisely, we consider a random family $\mathcal{F}$ of tampering functions with designed size M as follows: For each $i \in [M]$, sample a uniformly random function $f_i\colon \{0,1\}^n \to \{0,1\}^n$ and add f_i to the family. Since some of the f_i may turn out to be the same (albeit with negligible probability), $|\mathcal{F}|$ may in general be lower than M (which can only make a lower bound stronger).

We state the following result, which is proved in the full version of the paper.

THEOREM 5.1. *For any $\alpha > 0$, there is an M_0 satisfying $\log\log M_0 \leqslant \alpha n + O(\log n)$, such that with probability $1 - \exp(-n)$, a random family $\mathcal{F}$ with designed size $M \geqslant M_0$ satisfies the following: There is no coding scheme achieving rate at least $1 - \alpha$ and error $\epsilon < 1$ that is non-malleable with respect to the tampering family $\mathcal{F}$.* □

Finally, we consider an important family of adversaries which is only restricted by the subset of bits it acts upon. More precisely, let $T \subseteq [n]$ be a fixed set of size αn, for a parameter $\alpha \in (0,1)$. For $x \in \{0,1\}^n$, we use the notation $x_T \in \{0,1\}^{|T|}$ for the restriction of x to the positions in T. Without loss of generality, assume that T contains the first $|T|$ coordinate positions so that $x = (x_T, x_{\bar{T}})$, where $\bar{T} := [n] \setminus T$. We consider the family $\mathcal{F}_T$ of all functions $f\colon \{0,1\}^n \to \{0,1\}^n$ such that $f(x) = (g(x_T), x_{\bar{T}})$ for some $g\colon \{0,1\}^{|T|} \to \{0,1\}^{|T|}$. Observe that $|\mathcal{F}_T| \leqslant N^{(\alpha N^\alpha)}$ which implies $\log\log|\mathcal{F}_T| \leqslant \alpha n$.

Observe that construction of a non-malleable code of rate $1 - \alpha$ for the above family is trivial: Simply encode a given

$s \in \{0,1\}^{n(1-\alpha)}$ to $(0^{\alpha n}, s)$. Rather surprisingly, we prove that this coding scheme is optimal for the family $\mathcal{F}_T$.

This result can be seen as a variation of the classical Singleton bound for non-malleable codes. What makes this variation much more challenging to prove is the fact that 1) non-malleable codes allow a randomized encoder, and 2) non-malleability is a more relaxed requirement than error detection, and hence the proof must rule out the case where the decoder does not detect errors (i.e., outputs a wrong message) while still satisfies non-malleability.

THEOREM 5.2. *Let $T \subseteq [n]$ be of size αn and consider the family $\mathcal{F}_T$ of the tampering functions that only act on the coordinate positions in T (as defined above). Then, there is a $\delta_0 = O((\log n)/n)$ such that the following holds. Let $(\mathsf{Enc}, \mathsf{Dec})$ be any coding scheme which is non-malleable for the family $\mathcal{F}_T$ and achieves rate $1-\alpha+\delta$, for any $\delta \in [\delta_0, \alpha]$ and error ϵ. Then, $\epsilon \geqslant \delta/(16\alpha)$. In particular, when α and δ are absolute constants, $\epsilon = \Omega(1)$.* □

Before discussing the proof of the above theorem, we state the following immediate corollary.

COROLLARY 5.3. *Let $\mathcal{F}$ be the family of split-state adversaries acting on n bits. That is, each $f \in \mathcal{F}$ interprets the input as a pair (x_1, x_2) where $x_2 \in \{0,1\}^{\lfloor n/2 \rfloor}$ and $x_2 \in \{0,1\}^{\lceil n/2 \rceil}$, and outputs $(f_1(x_1), f_2(x_2))$ for arbitrary tampering functions f_1 and f_2 (acting on their respective input lengths).*

Moreover, for a fixed constant $\delta \in (0,1)$, let $\mathcal{F}_\delta$ be the class of tampering functions where $f \in \mathcal{F}_\delta$ iff every bit of $f(x)$ depends on at most $\lfloor \delta n \rfloor$ of ths bits of x.

Let $(\mathsf{Enc}_1, \mathsf{Dec}_1)$ (resp., $(\mathsf{Enc}_\delta, \mathsf{Dec}_\delta)$) be any coding scheme which is non-malleable for the class $\mathcal{F}$ (resp., $\mathcal{F}_\delta$) achieving error at most ϵ and rate R (resp., R_δ). Then, for every fixed constant $\gamma > 0$, there is a fixed constant $\epsilon_0 > 0$ such that if $\epsilon \leqslant \epsilon_0$, the following bounds hold.

(i) $R \leqslant 1/2 - \gamma$,

(ii) $R_\delta \leqslant 1 - \delta - \gamma$.

The proof of Theorem 5.2 (appearing in the full version) uses basic tools from information theory. However, the core ideas can be described as follows. Assume that the codeword is (X_1, X_2) where the adversary acts on X_1, which is of length αn. We show that for any coding scheme with rate slightly larger than $(1-\alpha)n$, there is a set $X_\eta \subseteq \{0,1\}^{\alpha n}$ such that

1. For some message s_0, X_1 lies in X_η with noticeable probability.
2. For a "typical" message s_1, X_1 is unlikely to land in X_η.
3. There is a vector $w \in \{0,1\}^{\alpha n}$ that cannot be extended to a codeword (w, w') that maps to either s_0 or s_1 by the decoder.

We then use the above properties to design the following strategy that violates non-malleability of the code: Given (X_1, X_2), if $X_1 \in X_\eta$, the adversary tampers the codeword to (w, X_2), which decodes to a message outside $\{s_0, s_1\}$. This ensures that $\mathsf{Dec}(f(\mathsf{Enc}(s_0)))$ has a noticeable chance of being tampered to an incorrect message. Otherwise, the adversary leaves the codeword unchanged, ensuring that $\mathsf{Dec}(f(\mathsf{Enc}(s_1)))$ has little chance of being tampered at all. Thus there is no choice for a distribution $\mathcal{D}_f$ that sufficiently matches both $\mathsf{Dec}(f(\mathsf{Enc}(s_0)))$ and $\mathsf{Dec}(f(\mathsf{Enc}(s_1)))$.

6. REFERENCES

[1] D. Aggarwal, Y. Dodis, and S. Lovett. Non-malleable codes from additive combinatorics. *ECCC* Technical Report TR13-081, 2013.

[2] M. Cheraghchi and V. Guruswami. Capacity of non-malleable codes. *ECCC* Technical Report TR13-118, 2013.

[3] M. Cheraghchi and V. Guruswami. Explicit optimal rate non-malleable codes for bit-tampering. In *Proceedings of Theory of Cryptography Conference (TCC)*, 2014.

[4] R. Cramer, Y. Dodis, S. Fehr, C. Padró, and D. Wichs. Detection of algebraic manipulation with applications to robust secret sharing and fuzzy extractors. In *Proceedings of EUROCRYPT 2008*, pages 471–488, 2008.

[5] D. Dolev, C. Dwork, and M. Naor. Nonmalleable cryptography. *SIAM Journal on Computing*, 30(2):391–437, 2000.

[6] S. Dziembowski, T. Kazana, and M. Obremski. Non-malleable codes from two-source extractors. In *Proceedings of CRYPTO*, 2013.

[7] S. Dziembowski, K. Pietrzak, and D. Wichs. Non-malleable codes. In *Proceedings of Innovations in Computer Science (ICS)*, 2010.

[8] S. Faust, P. Mukherjee, D. Venturi, and D. Wichs. Efficient non-malleable codes and key-derivation for poly-size tampering circuits. Cryptology ePrint Archive, Report 2013/702, 2013.

[9] R. Motwani and P. Raghavan. *Randomized Algorithms*. Cambridge University Press, 1995.

APPENDIX

A. COMPLETE PROOF OF THEOREM 3.1

In this section, we present a complete proof of Theorem 3.1, which is restated below.

THEOREM 3.1 (RESTATED). *Let $\mathcal{F}\colon \{0,1\}^n \to \{0,1\}^n$ be any family of tampering functions. For any $\epsilon, \eta > 0$, with probability at least $1-\eta$, the coding scheme $(\mathsf{Enc}, \mathsf{Dec})$ of Construction 1 is a strong non-malleable code with respect to $\mathcal{F}$ and with error ϵ and relative distance δ, provided that both of the following conditions are satisfied.*

1. $t \geqslant t_0$, *for some*

$$t_0 = O\left(\frac{1}{\epsilon^6}\left(\log \frac{|\mathcal{F}|N}{\eta}\right)\right). \tag{1}$$

2. $k \leqslant k_0$, *for some*

$$k_0 \geqslant n(1-h(\delta)) - \log t - 3\log(1/\epsilon) - O(1), \tag{2}$$

where $h(\cdot)$ denotes the binary entropy function.

Thus by choosing $t = t_0$ and $k = k_0$, the construction satisfies

$$k \geqslant n(1-h(\delta)) - \log\log(|\mathcal{F}|/\eta) - \log n - 9\log(1/\epsilon) - O(1).$$

In particular, if $|\mathcal{F}| \leqslant 2^{2^{\alpha n}}$ for any constant $\alpha \in (0,1)$, the rate of the code can be made arbitrarily close to $1-h(\delta)-\alpha$ while allowing $\epsilon = 2^{-\Omega(n)}$.

PROOF. First, observe that by construction, the minimum distance of the final code is always greater than δn; that is, whenever $\mathsf{Dec}(w_1) \neq \perp$ and $\mathsf{Dec}(w_2) \neq \perp$ for any pair of vectors $w_1 \neq w_2$, we have

$$\mathsf{dist}_h(w_1, w_2) > \delta n,$$

where $\mathsf{dist}_h(\cdot)$ denotes the Hamming distance. This is because whenever a codeword is picked, its δn neighborhood is removed from the sample space for the future codewords. Let V denote the volume of a Hamming ball of radius δn. It is well known that $V \leqslant 2^{nh(\delta)}$, where $h(\cdot)$ is the binary entropy function.

Fix an adversary $f \in \mathcal{F}$. We wish to show that the coding scheme $(\mathsf{Enc}, \mathsf{Dec})$ defined by Construction 1 is non-malleable with high probability for the chosen f.

Define $p_0 := \Pr[f(U_n) = U_n]$. In the sequel, assume that $p_0 < 1$ (otherwise, there is nothing to prove). For every $x \in \{0,1\}^n$, define $p(x) := \Pr[f(U_n) = x \wedge x \neq U_n]$. Observe that

$$\sum_x p(x) = 1 - p_0.$$

We say that a string $x \in \{0,1\}^n$ is *heavy* if

$$p(x) > 1/r,$$

for a parameter $r \leqslant t$ to be determined later. Note that the number of heavy strings must be less than r. Define

$$H := \{x \in \{0,1\}^n : p(x) > 1/r\},$$
$$\gamma := t/N,$$
$$\gamma' := tK/N.$$

Fix the randomness of the code construction so that $\mathsf{Dec}(x)$ is revealed for every heavy x. We will argue that no matter how the decoder's outcome on heavy elements is decided by the randomness of the code construction, the construction is non-malleable for every message s and the chosen function f with overwhelming probability. We will then finish the proof with a union bound over all choices of s and f.

Consider a random variable D defined over $\{0,1\}^k \cup \{\perp, \underline{\mathsf{same}}\}$ in the following way:

$$D := \begin{cases} \underline{\mathsf{same}} & \text{if } f(U_n) = U_n, \\ \mathsf{Dec}(f(U_n)) & \text{if } f(U_n) \neq U_n \text{ and } f(U_n) \in H, \\ \perp & \text{otherwise.} \end{cases} \quad (7)$$

For the chosen f, we explicitly define the distribution $\mathcal{D}_f$ as $\mathcal{D}_f := \mathscr{D}(D)$.

Now, consider a fixed message $s \in \{0,1\}^k$, and define the random variable $E_s := \mathsf{Enc}(s)$. That is, E_s is uniformly supported on the set $E(s)$ (this holds by the way that the encoder is defined). Observe that the marginal distribution of each individual set $E(s)$ (with respect to the randomness of the code construction) is the same for all choices of s, regardless of the ordering assumed by Construction 1 on the message space $\{0,1\}^k$.

Furthermore, define the random variable D_s as follows.

$$D_s := \begin{cases} \underline{\mathsf{same}} & \text{if } f(E_s) = E_s, \\ \mathsf{Dec}(f(E_s)) & \text{otherwise.} \end{cases} \quad (8)$$

Our goal is to show that the distribution of D_s (for the final realization of the code) is ϵ-close to $\mathcal{D}_f$ with high probability over the randomness of the code construction. Such assertion is quite intuitive by comparing the way the two distributions D_s and $\mathcal{D}_f$ are defined. In fact, it is not hard to show that the assertion holds with probability $1 - \exp(-\Omega(n))$. However, such a bound would be insufficient to accommodate a union bound of even moderate sizes such as 2^n, which is needed for relatively simple classes such as bit-tampering adversaries. More work needs to be done to ensure that it is possible to achieve a high probability statement with failure probability much smaller than $1/|\mathcal{F}|$, which may in general be doubly exponentially small in n.

The claim below shows that closeness of $\mathscr{D}(D_s)$ to $\mathcal{D}_f$ would imply non-malleability of the code.

CLAIM A.2. *Suppose that for every $s \in \{0,1\}^k$, we have $\mathscr{D}(D_s) \approx_\epsilon \mathcal{D}_f$ for the choice of $\mathcal{D}_f$ defined in (7). Then, $(\mathsf{Enc}, \mathsf{Dec})$ is a non-malleable coding scheme with error ϵ and a strong non-malleable coding scheme with error 2ϵ.*

PROOF. In order to verify Definition 2.5, we need to verify that for every distinct pair of messages $s_1, s_2 \in \{0,1\}^k$, $\mathscr{D}(D_{s_1}) \approx_{2\epsilon} \mathscr{D}(D_{s_2})$. But from the assumption, we know that $\mathscr{D}(D_{s_1})$ and $\mathscr{D}(D_{s_2})$ are both ϵ-close to $\mathcal{D}_f$. Thus the result follows by the triangle inequality.

It is of course possible now to use [7, Theorem 3.1] to deduce that Definition 2.3 is also satisfied. However, for the clarity of presentation, here we give a direct argument that shows that non-malleability is satisfied with the precise choice of $\mathcal{D}_f$ defined in (7) and error ϵ. Let $s \in \{0,1\}^k$, and let $E_s := \mathsf{Enc}(s)$ and $S := \mathsf{Dec}(f(E_s))$. Let $S' \sim \mathcal{D}_f$ and $S'' \sim \mathscr{D}(D_s)$ be sampled independently. We need to show that

$$\mathscr{D}(S) \approx_\epsilon \mathscr{D}(\mathsf{copy}(S', s)). \quad (9)$$

From the definition of D_s in (8), since $\mathsf{Dec}(f(E_s)) = s$ when $f(E_s) = E_s$, we see that $\mathscr{D}(\mathsf{copy}(S'', s)) = \mathscr{D}(\mathsf{Dec}(f(E_s))) = \mathscr{D}(S)$. Now, since by assumption $\mathscr{D}(S') \approx_\epsilon \mathscr{D}(S'')$, it follows that $\mathscr{D}(\mathsf{copy}(S', s)) \approx_\epsilon \mathscr{D}(\mathsf{copy}(S'', s))$ which proves (9). □

Let the random variables $E_1, \ldots, E_t$ be the elements of $E(s)$, in the order they are sampled by Construction 1.

Define, for $i \in [t]$,

$$S_i := \begin{cases} \underline{\mathsf{same}} & \text{if } f(E_i) = E_i, \\ \mathsf{Dec}(f(E_i)) & \text{otherwise.} \end{cases}$$

We note that, no matter how the final code is realized by the randomness of the construction, the distribution D_s is precisely the empirical distribution of $S_1, \ldots, S_t$ as determined by the code construction.

In the sequel, for each $i \in [t]$, we analyze the distribution of the variable S_i conditioned on the values of $S_1, \ldots S_{i-1}$ and use this analysis to prove that the empirical distribution of the sequence $(S_1, \ldots, S_t)$ is close to $\mathcal{D}_f$.

In order to understand the empirical distribution of the S_i, we consider the following process Reveal that considers the picked codewords $E_1, \ldots, E_t$ in order, gradually reveals information about the code construction, and outputs a subset of the S_i. We will ensure that

1. The process outputs a large subset of $\{S_1, \ldots, S_t\}$, and,
2. The empirical distribution of the sequence output by the process is close to $\mathcal{D}_f$ with high probability.

The above guarantees would in turn imply that the empirical distribution of the entire sequence S_i is also close to $\mathcal{D}_f$ with high probability. We define the process as follows.

Process Reveal*:*

1. Initialize the set $\mathsf{Skip} \subseteq [t]$ with the empty set. Recall that the values of $\mathsf{Dec}(w)$ for all $w \in H$ are already revealed in the analysis, as well as $\mathsf{Dec}(\Gamma(w))$ for those for which $\mathsf{Dec}(w) \neq \perp$.
2. For each heavy element $w \in H$, if $\mathsf{Dec}(w) = s$, consider the unique $j \in [t]$ such that $E_j = w$. Reveal[3] j and E_j, and add j to Skip.
3. For i from 1 to t, define *the ith stage* as follows:
   - **3.1.** If $i \in \mathsf{Skip}$, declare a *skip* and continue the loop with the next i. Otherwise, follow the remaining steps.
   - **3.2.** Reveal $\Gamma(E_i)$. Note that revealing E_i implies that $\mathsf{Dec}(E_i)$ is revealed as well, since $\mathsf{Dec}(E_i) = s$. Moreover, recall that for any $x \in \Gamma(E_i) \setminus E_i$, we have $\mathsf{Dec}(x) = \perp$ by the code construction.
   - **3.3.** If $\mathsf{Dec}(f(E_i))$ is not already revealed:
     - **3.3.1.** Reveal $\mathsf{Dec}(f(E_i))$.
     - **3.2.2.** If $\mathsf{Dec}(f(E_i)) = s$, consider the unique $j \in [t]$ such that $E_j = f(E_i)$. It must be that $j > i$, since $\mathsf{Dec}(E_j)$ has not been revealed before. Reveal j and add it to Skip.
     - **3.3.3.** Declare that an *unveil* has happened if $\mathsf{Dec}(f(E_i)) \neq \perp$. If so, reveal $\mathsf{Dec}(f(x))$ for all $x \in \Gamma(f(E_i)) \setminus E_i$ to equal $\perp$.
   - **3.4.** Reveal and output S_i.

For $i \in [t]$, we use the notation Reveal_i to refer to all the information revealed from the beginning of the process up to the time the ith stage begins. We also denote by $\mathsf{Next}(i)$ the least $j > i$ such that a skip does not occur at stage j; define $\mathsf{Next}(i) := t + 1$ if no such j exists, and define $\mathsf{Next}(0)$ to be the index of the first stage that is not skipped. Moreover, for $w \in \{0,1\}^n$, we use the notation $w \in \mathsf{Reveal}_i$ as a shorthand to denote the event that the process Reveal has revealed the value of $\mathsf{Dec}(w)$ at the time the ith stage begins.

By the way the code is constructed, the decoder's value at each given point is most likely $\perp$. We make this intuition more rigorous and show that the same holds even conditioned on the information reveal by the process Reveal.

Claim A.3. *For all $i \in [t]$ and any $a \in \mathsf{supp}(\mathsf{Reveal}_i)$,*

$$\Pr[\mathsf{Dec}(x) \neq \perp | (\mathsf{Reveal}_i = a) \wedge (x \notin \mathsf{Reveal}_i)] \leqslant \gamma'/(1-3\gamma V).$$

Proof. Suppose $x \notin \mathsf{Reveal}_i$, and observe that Reveal_i at each step reveals at most the values of the decoder at $2V$ points; namely, $\Gamma(E_i)$ and $\Gamma(f(E_i))$. Moreover, before the first stage, decoder's value is revealed at up to r heavy points and its Hamming neighborhood at radius δn. In total, the total number of points at which decoder's value is revealed by the information in Reveal_i is at most

$$(|H| + 2(i-1))|V| \leqslant (2t + r)V \leqslant 3\gamma V N.$$

Let

$$\mathcal{C} := \bigcup_s E(s)$$

be the set of all codewords of the coding scheme. Some of the elements of $\mathcal{C}$ are already included in Reveal_i, and by assumption we know that none of these is equal to x.

The distribution of each unrevealed codeword, seen in isolation, is uniform over the $N(1 - 3\gamma V)$ remaining vectors in $\{0,1\}^n$. Thus by taking a union bound on the probability of each such codeword hitting the point x (which is the only way to make $\mathsf{Dec}(x) \neq \perp$, we deduce that

$$\Pr[\mathsf{Dec}(x) \neq \perp | \mathsf{Reveal}_i = a] \leqslant \frac{tK}{N(1-3\gamma V)} = \gamma'/(1-3\gamma V).$$

□

Ideally, for each $i \in [t]$ we desire to have E_i almost uniformly distributed, conditioned on the revealed information, so that the distribution of $\mathsf{Dec}(f(E_i))$ (which is described by S_i when E_i does not hit a fixed point of f) becomes close to $\mathsf{Dec}(f(U_n))$. However, this is not necessarily true; for example, when the process Reveal determines the decoder's value on the heavy elements, the value of, say, E_1 may be revealed, at which point there is no hope to ensure that E_1 is nearly uniform. This is exactly what the set Skip is designed for, to isolate the instances when the value of E_i is already determined by the prior information. More precisely, we have the following.

Claim A.4. *Suppose that $i \notin \mathsf{Skip}$ when the ith stage of* Reveal *begins. Then, for any $a \in \mathsf{supp}(\mathsf{Reveal}_i)$,*

$$\mathscr{D}(E_i | \mathsf{Reveal}_i = a) \approx_\nu \mathcal{U}_n,$$

where $\nu := (3\gamma V)/(1 - 3\gamma V)$.

Proof. Note that, without any conditioning, the distribution of E_i is exactly uniform on $\{0,1\}^n$. If at any point prior to reaching the ith stage it is revealed that $\mathsf{Dec}(E_i) = s$, either line 2 or line 3.2.2 of process Reveal ensures that i is added to the set Skip.

If, on the other hand, the fact that $\mathsf{Dec}(E_i) = s$ has not been revealed when the ith stage begins, the distribution of E_i becomes uniform on the points in $\{0,1\}^n$ that have not been revealed yet. As in Claim A.3, the number of revealed points is at most $(2t + r)V \leqslant 3\gamma V N$. Thus, the conditional distribution E_i remains $((3\gamma V)/(1 - 3\gamma V))$-close to uniform by Proposition B.2. □

For each $i \in [t]$, define a random variable $S'_i \in \{0,1\}^k \cup \{\underline{\mathsf{same}}, \perp\}$ as follows (where U_n is independently sampled from $\mathcal{U}_n$):

$$S'_i := \begin{cases} \underline{\mathsf{same}} & \text{if } f(U_n) = U_n, \\ \mathsf{Dec}(f(U_n)) & \text{if } f(U_n) \neq U_n \wedge f(U_n) \in \mathsf{Reveal}_i, \\ \perp & \text{otherwise.} \end{cases} \tag{10}$$

Note that $\mathscr{D}(S'_1) = \mathcal{D}_f$.

[3]In a rigorous sense, by revealing a random variable we mean that we condition the probability space on the event that a particular value is assumed by the variable. For example, revealing E_i means that the analysis branches to a conditional world where the value of E_i is fixed to the revealed value. In an intuitive way, one may think of a reveal as writing constraints on the realization of the code construction on a blackboard, which is subsequently consulted by the analysis (in form of the random variable Reveal_i that the analysis defines to denote the information revealed by the process before stage i).

Intuitively, S'_i is the "cleaned up" version of the random variable S_i that we are interested in. As defined, S'_i is an independent random variable, and as such we are more interested in its *distribution* than value. Observe that the distribution of S'_i is randomly determined according to the randomness of the code construction (in particular, the knowledge of Reveal_i completely determines $\mathscr{D}(S'_i)$). The variable S'_i is defined so that its distribution approximates the distribution of the actual S_i conditioned on the revealed information before stage i. Formally, we can show that conditional distributions of these two variables are (typically) similar. Namely,

CLAIM A.5. *Suppose that $i \notin \mathsf{Skip}$ when the ith stage of Reveal begins. Then, for any $a \in \mathsf{supp}(\mathsf{Reveal}_i)$,*

$$\mathscr{D}(S_i|\mathsf{Reveal}_i = a) \approx_\nu \mathscr{D}(S'_i|\mathsf{Reveal}_i = a),$$

where $\nu := (3\gamma V + \gamma')/(1 - 3\gamma V)$.

PROOF. First, we apply Claim A.4 to ensure that

$$\mathscr{D}(E_i|\mathsf{Reveal}_i = a) \approx_{\nu'} \mathcal{U}_n,$$

where $\nu' = (3\gamma V)/(1 - 3\gamma V)$. Thus we can assume that the conditional distribution of E_i is exactly uniform at cost of a ν' increase in the final estimate.

Now, observe that, conditioned on the revealed information, the way S_i is sampled at stage i of Reveal can be rewritten as follows:

1. Sample $E_i \sim \mathcal{U}_n$.
2. If $f(E_i) = E_i$, set $S_i \leftarrow$ <u>same</u>.
3. Otherwise, if $f(E_i) \in \mathsf{Reveal}_i$, set S_i to $\mathsf{Dec}(f(E_i))$ as determined by the revealed information.
4. Otherwise, reveal $\mathsf{Dec}(f(E_i))$ (according to its conditional distribution on the knowledge of Reveal_i) and set S accordingly.

This procedure is exactly the same as how S'_i is sampled by (10); with the difference that at the third step, S'_i is set to $\perp$ whereas S_i is sampled according to the conditional distribution of $\mathsf{Dec}(f(E_i))$. However, we know by Claim A.3 that in this case,

$$\Pr[\mathsf{Dec}(f(E_i)) \neq \perp |\mathsf{Reveal}_i = a] \leqslant \gamma'/(1 - 3\gamma V).$$

Thus we see that S_i changes the probability mass of $\perp$ in $\mathscr{D}(S'_i)$ by at most $\gamma'/(1 - 3\gamma V)$. The claim follows. □

Recall that the distribution of S'_1 is the same as $\mathcal{D}_f$. However, for subsequent stages this distribution may deviate from $\mathcal{D}_f$. We wish to ensure that by the end of process Reveal, the deviation remains sufficiently small.

For $i \in [t-1]$, define Δ_i as

$$\Delta_i := \mathsf{dist}(\mathscr{D}(S'_{i+1}), \mathscr{D}(S'_i)).$$

where $\mathsf{dist}(\cdot)$ denotes statistical distance. Note that Δ_i is a random variable that is determined by the knowledge of Reveal_{i+1} (recall that Reveal_i determines the exact distribution of S'_i). We show that the conditional values attained by this random variable are small in expectation.

CLAIM A.6. *For each $i \in [t-1]$, and all $a \in \mathsf{supp}(\mathsf{Reveal}_i)$,*

$$\mathbb{E}[\Delta_i|\mathsf{Reveal}_i = a] \leqslant \frac{2\gamma'}{r(1 - 3\gamma V)}. \quad (11)$$

Moreover, $\Pr[\Delta_i \leqslant 2/r \mid \mathsf{Reveal}_i = a] = 1$.

PROOF. Recall that the distribution of S'_{i+1} is different from S'_i depending on the points at which the decoder's value is revealed during stage i of Reveal. If a skip is declared at stage i, we have $\mathsf{Reveal}_{i+1} = \mathsf{Reveal}_i$ and thus, $\Delta_i = 0$. Thus in the following we may assume that this is not the case.

However, observe that whenever for some $x \in \{0,1\}^n$, the decoder's value $\mathsf{Dec}(x)$ is revealed at stage i, the new information affects the probability distribution of S'_i only if $\mathsf{Dec}(x) \neq \perp$. This is because when $\mathsf{Dec}(x) = \perp$, some of the probability mass assigned by S_i to $\perp$ in (10) is removed and reassigned by S'_{i+1} to $\mathsf{Dec}(x)$, which is still equal to $\perp$. Thus, changes of this type can have no effect on the distribution of S'_i. We conclude that only revealing the value of E_i and an unveil (as defined in line 3.3.3 of process Reveal) can contribute to the statistical distance between S'_i and S'_{i+1}.

Whenever an unveil occurs at stage i, say at point $x \in \{0,1\}^n$, some of the probability mass assigned to $\perp$ by S'_i is moved to $\mathsf{Dec}(x)$ in the distribution of S'_{i+1}. Since we know that $x \notin H$, the resulting change in the distance between the two distributions is bounded by $1/r$, *no matter* what the realization of x and $\mathsf{Dec}(x)$ are. Overall, using Claim A.3, the expected change between the two distributions contributed by the occurrence of an unveil is upper bounded by the probability of an unveil occurring times $1/r$, which is at most

$$\frac{\gamma'/r}{1 - 3\gamma V}. \quad (12)$$

The only remaining factor that may contribute to an increase in the distance between distribution of S'_i and S'_{i+1} is the revealing of E_i at stage i. The effect of this reveal in the statistical distance between the two distributions is $p(E_i)$, since according to (10) the value of S'_{i+1} is determined by the outcome of $f(\mathcal{U}_n)$, and thus the probability mass assigned to $\mathsf{Dec}(E_i)$ by S'_{i+1} is indeed $\Pr[f(\mathcal{U}_n) = E_i]$. Let $\mathcal{D}_E$ be the distribution of E_i conditioned on the knowledge of Reveal_i. Observe that, since the values $\{p(x) \colon x \in \{0,1\}^n\}$ defines a probability distribution on N points, we clearly have

$$\sum_{x \in \mathsf{supp}(\mathcal{D}_E)} p(x) \leqslant 1. \quad (13)$$

On the other hand, by the assumption that a skip has not occurred at stage i, we can deduce using the argument in Claim A.4 that $\mathcal{D}_E$ is uniformly supported on a support of size at least $N(1-3\gamma V)$. Therefore, using (13), the expected contribution to Δ_i by the revealing of E_i is (which is the expected value of $p(E_i)$) is at most

$$\frac{1}{N(1 - 3\gamma V)} \leqslant \frac{\gamma'/r}{(1 - 3\gamma V)}, \quad (14)$$

where the inequality uses $r \leqslant \gamma' N = tK$. The desired bound follows by adding up the two perturbations (12) and (14) considered.

Finally, observe that each of the perturbations considered above cannot be more than $1/r$, since stage i never reveals the decoder's value on a heavy element (recall that all heavy elements are revealed before the first stage begins and the choices of E_i that correspond to heavy elements are added to Skip when Reveal begins). Thus, the conditional value of Δ_i is never more than $2/r$. □

Using the above result, we can deduce a concentration bound on the summation of the differences Δ_i.

CLAIM A.7. *Let $\Delta := \Delta_1 + \cdots + \Delta_{t-1}$, and suppose*

$$\frac{\gamma'}{1-3\gamma V} \leqslant \frac{\epsilon r}{32t}. \quad (15)$$

Then,

$$\Pr[\Delta \geqslant \epsilon/8] \leqslant \exp(-\epsilon^2 r^2/(2048t)) =: \eta_0. \quad (16)$$

PROOF. For $i \in [t-1]$, define $\Delta'_i := \Delta_i r/2$, $\Delta'_0 := 0$, and $\Delta' := \Delta'_1 + \cdots + \Delta'_{t-1}$. Since Reveal_i determines Δ'_{i-1}, by Claim A.6 we know that

$$\mathbb{E}[\Delta'_i | \Delta'_0, \ldots, \Delta'_{i-1}] \leqslant \nu,$$

where $\nu := \frac{\gamma'}{1-3\gamma V} \leqslant \epsilon r/(32t)$ In the above, conditioning on $\Delta'_0, \ldots, \Delta'_{i-1}$ instead of Reveal_i (for which Claim A.6 applies), is valid in light of Proposition B.1, since the knowledge of Reveal_i determines $\Delta'_0, \ldots, \Delta'_{i-1}$.

Moreover, again by the Claim A.6, we know that the Δ'_i are between 0 and 1. Using Proposition B.3, it follows that

$$\Pr[\Delta \geqslant \epsilon/8] = \Pr[\Delta' \geqslant \frac{\epsilon r}{16t} \cdot t] \leqslant \eta_0.$$

□

Next, we prove a concentration bound for the total number of unveils that can occur in line 3.3.3 of process Reveal.

CLAIM A.8. *Let u be the total number of unveils that occur in process Reveal. Assuming $\gamma'/(1-3\gamma V) \leqslant \epsilon/8$ (which is implied by (15)), we have*

$$\Pr[u \geqslant \epsilon t/4] \leqslant \exp(-\epsilon^2 t/128) \leqslant \eta_0.$$

PROOF. Let $X_1, \ldots, X_t$ be indicator random variable such that $X_i = 1$ iff an unveil occurs at stage i, and let $X_0 := 0$. Recall that an unveil can only occur at a stage that is not skipped. Thus, if $i \in [t]$ when the ith stage begins, we can deduce that $X_i = 0$.

Consider $i \in [t]$ such that $i \notin \mathsf{Skip}$ when the ith stage begins. An unveil occurs when $\mathsf{Dec}(f(E_i)) \notin \mathsf{Reveal}_i$. In this case, by Claim A.3, we get that

$$\Pr[\mathsf{Dec}(f(E_i)) \neq \perp | \mathsf{Reveal}_i] \leqslant \gamma'/(1-3\gamma V).$$

Since Reveal_i determines all the revealed information in each prior stage, and in particular the values of $X_0, \ldots, X_{i-1}$, we can use Proposition B.1 to deduce that

$$\Pr[X_i = 1 | X_0, \ldots, X_{i-1}] \leqslant \gamma'/(1-3\gamma V).$$

Finally, Proposition B.3 derives the desired concentration bound on the number of unveils, which is $X_1 + \cdots + X_t$. □

We are now ready to wrap up the proof and show that with overwhelming probability, the empirical distribution of $S_1, \ldots, S_t$ is ϵ-close to $\mathcal{D}_f$.

Suppose that process Reveal outputs a subset of the S_i. Let $T \subseteq [t]$ be the set of indices i such Reveal outputs S_i in the end of the ith stage. Note that $T = [t] \setminus \mathsf{Skip}$, where Skip denotes the skip set when Reveal terminates. Observe that $|\mathsf{Skip}|$ is at most the total number of unveils occurring at line 3.3.3 of Reveal plus r (which upper bounds the number of heavy elements in H). Thus, using Claim A.8 we see that, assuming (15),

$$\Pr[t - |T| \geqslant r + \epsilon t/4] \leqslant \eta_0. \quad (17)$$

Let δ_i for $i \in [t]$ denote the statistical distance between S'_i and $\mathcal{D}_f$. We know that δ_i is a random variable depending on Reveal_i. Thus, the value of δ_i becomes known to a particular fixed value conditioned on the outcome of every Reveal_j, $j \geqslant i$. Define $\delta_0 := \max_i \delta_i$, which is a random variable that becomes revealed by the knowledge of Reveal_t in the end of the process.

Using Claim A.5, we thus know that for any choice of $a \in \mathsf{supp}(\mathsf{Reveal}_i)$ and $i \in T$,

$$\mathscr{D}(S_i | \mathsf{Reveal}_i = a) \approx_{\nu_0 + \delta_0} \mathcal{D}_f,$$

where

$$\nu_0 := (3\gamma V + \gamma')/(1 - 3\gamma V).$$

Let $\mathcal{S}$ denote the empirical distribution of $\{S_i : i \in T\}$, and define $S_0 := \perp$. From the above conclusion, using Proposition B.1 we can now write, for $i \in T$,

$$\mathscr{D}(S_i | (S_j : j \in T \cap \{1, \ldots, i-1\}) \approx_{\nu_0 + \delta_0} \mathcal{D}_f.$$

Recall that $|\mathsf{supp}(\mathcal{D}_f)| \leqslant r + 2$. Assuming that

$$\nu_0 + \delta_0 \leqslant \epsilon/4, \quad (18)$$

Proposition B.6 implies (after simple manipulations) that with probability $1 - \eta_1$, where

$$\eta_1 \leqslant 2^{r+4-\Omega(\epsilon^2 |T|)}, \quad (19)$$

$\mathcal{S}$ is $(\epsilon/2)$-close to $\mathcal{D}_f$.

Recall that $\mathscr{D}(S'_1) = \mathcal{D}_f$. Using the triangle inequality for statistical distance, for every $i \in [t]$ we can write

$$\mathsf{dist}(S'_i, \mathcal{D}_f) = \mathsf{dist}(S'_i, S'_1) \leqslant \Delta_1 + \cdots + \Delta_{i-1} \leqslant \Delta,$$

and thus deduce that $\delta_0 \leqslant \Delta$. Recall that by Claim A.7, we can ensure that, assuming (15), $\Delta \leqslant \epsilon/8$ (and thus, $\delta_0 \leqslant \epsilon/8$) with probability at least $1 - \eta_0$. Thus under the assumption that

$$\nu_0 \leqslant \epsilon/8, \quad (20)$$

and (15), which we recall below

$$\frac{\gamma'}{1-3\gamma V} \leqslant \frac{\epsilon r}{32t},$$

we can ensure that $\nu_0 + \delta_0 \leqslant \epsilon/4$ with probability at least $1 - \eta_0$. Moreover, conditioned on the event $\nu_0 + \delta_0 \leqslant \epsilon/4$ (recall that δ_0 is a random variable), we have already demonstrated that with probability at least $1 - \eta_1$, $\mathcal{S}$ is $(\epsilon/2)$-close to $\mathcal{D}_f$. After removing conditioning on the bound on δ_0, we may deduce that overall (under the assumed inequalities (15) and (20)), with probability at least $1 - O(\eta_0 + \eta_1)$,

$$\mathcal{S} \approx_{\epsilon/2} \mathcal{D}_f,$$

which in turn, implies that the empirical distribution of $S_1, \ldots, S_t$ becomes ϵ'-close to uniform, where

$$\epsilon' := \epsilon/2 + (1 - |T|/t).$$

Finally, we can use (17) to ensure that (assuming (15)), $\epsilon' \leqslant \epsilon$ and $|T|/t \geqslant 1 - \epsilon/2$ with probability at least $1 - O(\eta_0 + \eta_1)$ as long as

$$r \leqslant \epsilon t/4. \quad (21)$$

By comparing (19) with (16), we also deduce that $\eta_1 = O(\eta_0)$ (and also that (21) holds) as long as $r \leqslant r_0$ for some

$$r_0 = \Omega(\epsilon^2 t). \quad (22)$$

Altogether, we arrive at the conclusion that under assumptions (15), (20), and by taking $r := r_0$, with probability at least $1 - O(\eta_0)$,

$$\text{(empirical distribution of } (S_1, \ldots, S_t)) \approx_\epsilon \mathcal{D}_f,$$

which ensures the required non-malleability condition for message s and tampering function f. By taking a union bound over all possible choices of s and f, the probability of failure becomes bounded by

$$O(\eta_0 K|\mathcal{F}|) =: \eta_2.$$

We can now ensure that $\eta_2 \leqslant \eta$ for the chosen value for r by taking $t \geqslant t_0$ for some

$$t_0 = O\left(\frac{1}{\epsilon^6}\left(\log \frac{|\mathcal{F}|N}{\eta}\right)\right). \tag{23}$$

Furthermore, in order to satisfy assumptions (15), (20), and the requirement $tKV \leqslant 1$ which is needed to make the construction possible, it suffices to have $K \leqslant K_0$ for some

$$K_0 = \Omega(\epsilon^3 N/(tV)).$$

Using the bound $V \leqslant 2^{nh(\delta)}$, where $h(\cdot)$ is the binary entropy function, and taking the logarithm of both sides, we see that it suffices to have $k \leqslant k_0$ for some

$$k_0 \geqslant n(1 - h(\delta)) - \log t - 3\log(1/\epsilon) - O(1).$$

This concludes the proof of Theorem 3.1.

B. USEFUL TOOLS

In many occasions in the paper, we deal with a chain of correlated random variables $0 = X_0, X_1, \ldots, X_n$ where we wish to understand an event depending on X_i conditioned on the knowledge of the previous variables. That is, we wish to understand

$$\mathbb{E}[f(X_i)|X_0, \ldots, X_{i-1}].$$

The following proposition shows that in order to understand the above quantity, it suffices to have an estimate with respect to a more restricted event than the knowledge of $X_0, \ldots, X_{i-1}$. Formally, we can state the following, where X stands for X_i in the above example and Y stands for $(X_0, \ldots, X_{i-1})$.

Proposition B.1. *Let X and Y be possibly correlated random variables and let Z be a random variable such that the knowledge of Z determines Y; that is, $Y = f(Z)$ for some function f. Suppose that for every possible outcome of the random variable Z, namely, for every $z \in \mathsf{supp}(Z)$, and for some real-valued function g, we have*

$$\mathbb{E}[g(X)|Z = z] \in I. \tag{24}$$

for a particular interval I. Then, for every $y \in \mathsf{supp}(Y)$,

$$\mathbb{E}[g(X)|Y = y] \in I.$$

Similarly, suppose for some distribution $\mathcal{D}$, and all $z \in \mathsf{supp}(Z)$,

$$\mathscr{D}(X|Z = z) \approx_\epsilon \mathcal{D}.$$

Then, for all $y \in \mathsf{supp}(Y)$,

$$\mathscr{D}(X|Y = y) \approx_\epsilon \mathcal{D}.$$

Proof. Let $T = \{z \in \mathsf{supp}(Z) \colon f(z) = y\}$, and let $p(z) := \Pr[Z = z|Y = y]$. Then,

$$\mathbb{E}[g(X)|Y = y] = \sum_{z \in T} p(z)\mathbb{E}[g(X)|Z = z].$$

Since by (24), each $\mathbb{E}[g(X)|Z = z]$ lies in I and $\sum_{z\in T} p(z) = 1$, we deduce that

$$\mathbb{E}[g(X)|Y = y] \in I.$$

Proof of the second part is similar, by observing that if a collection of distributions is statistically close to a particular distribution $\mathcal{D}$, any convex combination of them is equally close to $\mathcal{D}$ as well. □

Proposition B.2. *Let the random variable $X \in \{0,1\}^n$ be uniform on a set of size at least $(1-\epsilon)2^n$. Then, $\mathcal{D}(X)$ is $(\epsilon/(1-\epsilon))$-close to $\mathcal{U}_n$.*

We will use the following tail bounds on summation of possibly dependent random variables, which are direct consequences of Azuma's inequality.

Proposition B.3. *Let $0 = X_0, X_1, \ldots, X_n$ be possibly correlated random variables in $[0,1]$ such that for every $i \in [n]$ and for some $\gamma \geqslant 0$,*

$$\mathbb{E}[X_i|X_0, \ldots, X_{i-1}] \leqslant \gamma.$$

Then, for every $c \geqslant 1$,

$$\Pr[\sum_{i=1}^n X_i \geqslant cn\gamma] \leqslant \exp(-n\gamma^2(c-1)^2/2),$$

or equivalently, for every $\delta > \gamma$,

$$\Pr[\sum_{i=1}^n X_i \geqslant n\delta] \leqslant \exp(-n(\delta-\gamma)^2/2).$$

Proof. The proof is a standard Martingale argument. For $i \in [n]$, define

$$X_i' := X_i - \gamma,$$

and

$$S_i := \sum_{j=1}^i X_i' = \sum_{j-1}^i X_i - i\gamma.$$

By assumption, S_i is a super-martingale, that is, assuming $S_0 := 0$,

$$\mathbb{E}[S_{i+1}|S_0, \ldots, S_i] \leqslant S_i.$$

Thus, by Azuma's inequality, for all $t \geqslant 0$,

$$\Pr[S_n \geqslant t] \leqslant \exp(-t^2/(2n)).$$

Substituting $t := (c-1)n\gamma$ proves the claim. □

In a similar fashion (using Azuma's inequality for sub-martingales rather than super-martingales in the proof), we may obtain a tail bound when we have a lower bound on conditional expectations.

Proposition B.4. *Let $0 = X_0, X_1, \ldots, X_n$ be possibly correlated random variables in $[0,1]$ such that for every $i \in [n]$ and for some $\gamma \geqslant 0$,*

$$\mathbb{E}[X_i|X_0, \ldots, X_{i-1}] \geqslant \gamma.$$

Then, for every $\delta < \gamma$,

$$\Pr[\sum_{i=1}^{n} X_i \leqslant n\delta] \leqslant \exp(-n(\delta-\gamma)^2/2).$$

The following tail bound is similar in flavor to the one given by Proposition B.3, but only applies to indicator random variables. However, it can be better when the individual expectations are low and the target deviation from mean is very large.

PROPOSITION B.5. *Let $0 = X_0, X_1, \ldots, X_n \in \{0,1\}$ be indicator, possibly dependent, random variables such that for every $i \in [n]$,*

$$\mathbb{E}[X_i|X_1,\ldots,X_{i-1}] \leqslant p,$$

for some $p \in [0,1]$. Let $X := X_1 + \cdots + X_n$. Then, for every $c \geqslant 1$,

$$\Pr[X > cnp] \leqslant (e/c)^{cnp}.$$

PROOF. We closely follow the standard proof of Chernoff bounds for independent indicator random variables (see, e.g., [9]). Using Markov's bound on the exponential moment of X, we can write, for a parameter $t > 0$ to be determined later,

$$\Pr[X > cnp] \leqslant \frac{\mathbb{E}[\exp(tX)]}{\exp(tcnp)} = \frac{\mathbb{E}[\exp(tX_1)\cdots\exp(tX_n)]}{\exp(tcnp)}. \quad (25)$$

However, we can write down the expectation of product as the following chain of conditional expectations

$$\mathbb{E}_{(X_1,\ldots,X_n)}[\exp(tX)] = \mathbb{E}_{X_1}\Big[e^{tX_1}\mathbb{E}_{(X_2|X_1)}\big[e^{tX_2}\ldots\mathbb{E}_{(X_n|X_1,\ldots,X_{n-1})}e^{tX_n}]\ldots\big]\Big] \leqslant (p\exp(t)+1)^n.$$

where the inequality uses the fact that the X_i are Bernoulli random variables and thus

$$\mathbb{E}[\exp(tX_i)|X_1,\ldots,X_{i-1}] \leqslant p\exp(t) + (1-p)\exp(0) \leqslant p\exp(t)+1.$$

Using the inequality $(1+x)^n \leqslant \exp(nx)$ the above simplifies to

$$\mathbb{E}[\exp(tX)] \leqslant \exp(np\exp(t)),$$

and thus, plugging the above result into (25),

$$\Pr[X > cnp] \leqslant \frac{\exp(np\exp(t))}{\exp(tcnp)}.$$

Choosing $t := \ln c$ yields the desired conclusion. □

Approximating distributions by fuzzy correlated sampling

In this section, we show that it is possible to sharply approximate a distribution $\mathcal{D}$ with finite support by sampling possibly correlated random variables $X_1, \ldots, X_n$ where the distribution of each X_i is close to $\mathcal{D}$ conditioned on the previous outcomes, and computing the empirical distribution of the drawn samples.

LEMMA B.6. *Let $\mathcal{D}$ be a distribution over a finite set Σ such that $|\mathsf{supp}(\mathcal{D})| \leqslant r$. For any $\eta, \epsilon, \gamma > 0$ such that $\gamma < \epsilon$, there is a choice of*

$$n = O((r+2+\log(1/\eta))/(\epsilon-\gamma)^2)$$

such that the following holds. Suppose $0 = X_0, X_1, \ldots, X_n \in \Sigma$ are possibly correlated random variables such that for all $i \in [n]$ and all values $0 = x_0, x_1 \ldots, x_n \in \mathsf{supp}(\mathcal{D})$,

$$\mathscr{D}(X_i|X_0 = x_0, \ldots, X_{i-1} = x_{i-1}) \approx_\gamma \mathcal{D}.$$

Then, with probability at least $1-\eta$, the empirical distribution of the outcomes $X_1, \ldots, X_n$ is ϵ-close to $\mathcal{D}$.

PROOF. First, we argue that without loss of generality, we can assume that $|\Sigma| \leqslant r+1$. This is because if not, we can define a function $f\colon \Sigma \to \mathsf{supp}(\mathcal{D}) \cup \{\star\}$ as follows:

$$f(x) := \begin{cases} x & \text{if } x \in \mathsf{supp}(\mathcal{D}) \\ \star & \text{otherwise.} \end{cases}$$

Observe that for any distribution $\mathcal{D}'$ over Σ, $\mathsf{dist}(\mathcal{D}', \mathcal{D}) = \mathsf{dist}(f(\mathcal{D}'), \mathcal{D})$, since the elements outside $\mathsf{supp}(\mathcal{D})$ always contribute to the statistical distance and we aggregate all such mass on a single extra point $\star$, and by doing so do not affect the statistical distance. Thus the empirical distribution of $(X_1, \ldots, X_n)$ is ϵ-close to $\mathcal{D}$ iff the empirical distribution of $(f(X_1), \ldots, f(X_n))$ is.

Now suppose $|\Sigma| \leqslant r+1$. Let $A \subseteq \Sigma$ be any non-empty event, and denote by $\mathcal{D}'$ the empirical distribution of the outcomes $X_1, \ldots, X_n$. Let $p := \mathcal{D}(A)$, and define indicator random variables

$$Y_i := \begin{cases} 0 & X_i \notin A, \\ 1 & X_i \in A. \end{cases}$$

for $i \in [n]$ and $Y_0 := 0$. Observe that

$$\mathcal{D}'(A) = \frac{\sum_{i=1}^{n} Y_i}{n},$$

and, by the assumption on the closeness of conditional distributions of the X_i to $\mathcal{D}$,

$$\mathbb{E}[Y_i|Y_0, \ldots, Y_{i-1}] \in [p-\gamma, p+\gamma].$$

By Propositions B.3 and B.4, we can thus obtain a concentration bound

$$\Pr[|\mathcal{D}'(A) - p| > \epsilon] \leqslant 2\exp(-(\epsilon-\gamma)^2 n/2).$$

Now we can apply a union bound on all possible choices of A and conclude that

$$\Pr[\neg(\mathcal{D}' \approx_\epsilon \mathcal{D})] \leqslant 2^{r+2}\exp(-(\epsilon-\gamma)^2 n/2),$$

which can be ensured to be at most η for some choice of

$$n = O((r+2+\log(1/\eta))/(\epsilon-\gamma)^2).$$

□

Linear-Time Encodable Codes Meeting the Gilbert-Varshamov Bound and Their Cryptographic Applications*

Erez Druk
Computer Science, Technion
Haifa, Israel
druk@cs.technion.ac.il

Yuval Ishai
Computer Science, Technion
Haifa, Israel
yuvali@cs.technion.ac.il

ABSTRACT

A random linear code has good minimal distance with high probability. The conjectured intractability of decoding random linear codes has recently found many applications in cryptography. One disadvantage of random linear codes is that their encoding complexity grows quadratically with the message length. Motivated by this disadvantage, we present a randomized construction of linear error-correcting codes which can be encoded in linear time and yet enjoy several useful features of random linear codes. Our construction is based on a linear-time computable hash function due to Ishai, Kushilevitz, Ostrovsky and Sahai [25].

We demonstrate the usefulness of these new codes by presenting several applications in coding theory and cryptography. These include the first family of linear-time encodable codes meeting the Gilbert-Varshamov bound, the first non-trivial linear-time secret sharing schemes, and plausible candidates for symmetric encryption and identification schemes which can be conjectured to achieve better asymptotic efficiency/security tradeoffs than all current candidates.

Categories and Subject Descriptors

F.2 [**Theory of Computation**]: Analysis of Algorithms and Problem Complexity

General Terms

Security, Reliability, Theory

Keywords

Error-correcting codes, Gilbert-Varshamov bound, linear-time encodable codes, cryptography

*This research has received funding from the European Union's Tenth Framework Programme under grant agreement no. 259426 ERC-CaC, ISF grant 1361/10, and BSF grant 2008411.

ITCS'14, January 12–14, 2014, Princeton, New Jersey, USA.
Copyright 2014 ACM 978-1-4503-2698-8/14/01 ...$15.00.
http://dx.doi.org/10.1145/2554797.2554815.

1. INTRODUCTION

This work is concerned with error correcting codes and their applications in cryptography. We start by explaining some of the standard coding theory terminology we will use.

A *linear code* over a finite field $\mathbb{F}$ with message length k and block length n is a k-dimensional linear subspace $C \subseteq \mathbb{F}^n$. The *rate* of C is the normalized dimension $R(C) = k/n$. The *minimal distance* of C, denoted by d, is the minimal Hamming distance between any two distinct codewords $c, c' \in C$, namely the number of entries in which c and c' differ. The *relative distance* of C is the normalized minimal distance $\delta(C) = d/n$. Using an injective function $E : \mathbb{F}^k \to C$, called an *encoder*, any message $x \in \mathbb{F}^k$ can be encoded into a codeword $c = E(x)$ such that even if up to $d-1$ entries of c are erased or up to $(d-1)/2$ entries are modified, there is still sufficient information to recover x. An algorithm which recovers x from a corrupted version of $E(x)$ is called a *decoder*. All of the above notions can be naturally generalized to an arbitrary (rather than linear) code $C \subseteq \Sigma^n$ over the alphabet Σ.

The minimal distance and rate of C are the two main parameters by which the quality of C as an error correcting code is measured. Increasing any of these values increases the quality of the code in hand either by improving its error handling capabilities or by increasing the amount of information carried by the codewords. These code parameters are contradictory in nature and the possible tradeoffs between them are yet to be fully understood. One of the early goals of coding theory was to construct *asymptotically good codes,* namely infinite families of codes in which both the rate and relative distance are bounded away from zero.

As is often the case with combinatorial objects, a *random* family of codes, whether linear or not, is asymptotically good with high probability. In fact, random codes achieve the best known rate/distance tradeoff in the binary case and are only slightly inferior to the best known constructions over larger fields (achieved by codes based on algebraic geometry [43]). The rate/distance tradeoff achieved by random codes is captured by the *Gilbert-Varshamov (GV) bound* [17, 44]. The GV bound tells us that for any prime power q and $\delta \in (0, 1-1/q)$ there is an infinite family C_k of linear codes over $\mathbb{F}_q$ with relative distance of at least δ and rate $R(C_k)$ which tends to $1 - \mathrm{H}_q(\delta)$ when k tends to infinity, where $\mathrm{H}_q(x) = x\log_q(q-1) - x\log_q x - (1-x)\log_q(1-x)$ is the q-ary entropy function. In particular, the GV bound shows the existence of asymptotically good codes.

In addition to maximizing the rate and minimal distance of codes, another important optimization goal is to minimize the *computational complexity* of encoding and decoding. By default, we will measure computational complexity by the size of an arithmetic circuit performing the computation (whose gates may perform addition, subtraction or multiplication of two field elements). We will also refer to this measure of complexity as the encoding and decoding *time*. See Section 2.2 for more details on the computational model.

The main focus of this work is on minimizing the encoding complexity of codes. Random codes perform poorly by this measure, having exponential encoding complexity in the general case and quadratic in the linear case. Since the best asymptotic encoding complexity one could hope for is linear in n, it is natural to ask whether there are asymptotically good families of linear-time encodable codes. The first proof that such codes exist is due to Gelfand, Dobrushin and Pinsker [16], who presented a randomized construction of linear-time encodable linear codes over the binary field which have positive rate and relative minimal distance. An explicit construction of such codes, which also admits a linear-time[1] decoding algorithm, was given in a celebrated work of Spielman [42].

The concrete rate/distance tradeoff achieved by Spielman's codes is far from the GV bound. Guruswami and Indyk [23] construct linear-time encodable codes whose rate and distance parameters can get arbitrarily close to the GV bound. Unfortunately, the closer one wishes to get to the bound the larger the size of the underlying field becomes. A randomized construction of linear binary codes known as Wozencraft's ensemble [33, 26] meets the GV bound with high probability and uses only $O(n)$ random bits, but requires $n\cdot$polylog(n) time to encode. These results leave open the existence of linear-time encodable *binary*codes that meet the GV bound, or even get close to this bound. This question serves as a primary motivating question for our work.

1.1 Our Contribution

We present a randomized construction of linear-time encodable codes which enjoy several useful features of random linear codes. In particular, our construction answers the above question in the affirmative over every finite field, giving the first families of linear-time encodable codes that meet the GV bound.

Our construction relies on a pseudorandom object called a *linear uniform output family.* A linear uniform output family over a finite field $\mathbb{F}$ is a family of linear functions $A : \mathbb{F}^k \to \mathbb{F}^n$ such that for any fixed nonzero $x \in \mathbb{F}^k$, a random choice of A from the family makes $A(x)$ uniformly distributed over $\mathbb{F}^n$. We apply a variant of a construction of linear-time computable pairwise independent hash functions due to Ishai, Kushilevitz, Ostrovsky and Sahai [25] to obtain a linear uniform output family in which each A is computable in linear time. Furthermore, $A(x)$ can be computed in time $O(n)$ given x and a succinct description of A of length $O(n)$. This construction applies over any finite field $\mathbb{F}$ and for any choice of message length k and block length $n(k) > k$.

A linear uniform output family over the binary field was recently used by Baron, Ishai, and Ostrovsky [5] for obtaining linear-time computable hardcore functions and pseudorandom generators. Our construction applies over general fields (this generalization is needed for the results of Section 4) and its presentation is more self-contained. In contrast to our work, the applications in [5] rely on families which shrink (rather than expand) the input, and require the family to satisfy an additional "bilinearity" property.

The construction of linear uniform output families that can be computed in linear time is presented in Section 3, which also presents applications in coding theory. In particular, Section 3 presents the application to linear-time encodable codes meeting the GV bound, and establishes other properties of these codes which are used in Sections 4 and 5.

In contrast to the linear-time encodable codes from [42, 23], our codes are not fully explicit.[2] However, even without the linear-time encoding requirement, the question of explicitly constructing codes which meet the GV bound is wide open (cf. [22, 13]).

Another difference between our codes and the linear-time encodable codes from [42, 23] is that we do not know whether our codes support efficient decoding. This is not necessarily a problem for two reasons. First, there are natural applications of codes that only require decoding in the presence of *erasures* rather than errors, which can be done in polynomial time for any linear code. Second, and perhaps more interestingly, if the decoding problem for our codes indeed turns out to be intractable (as we conjecture), this can potentially make them useful for cryptographic applications. Indeed, there are quite a few cryptographic constructions that rely on the conjectured intractability of decoding random linear codes. Our new family serves as a plausible candidate for a smaller family of linear codes that has linear description and encoding complexity and yet enjoys the minimal distance and intractability features of random linear codes.

In Sections 4 and 5 we discuss applications of our codes in the field of cryptography. We make a distinction between applications to "information-theoretic cryptography," which require security against computationally unbounded adversaries but whose security can be proved unconditionally, and applications to "complexity-based cryptography," which settle for security against bounded adversaries but need to rely on unproven intractability assumptions. These two types of applications differ not only in the security guarantees they provide and the type of assumptions they rely on, but also in the required properties of the underlying codes.

We begin in Section 4 with an information-theoretic application, obtaining the first linear-time implementation of nontrivial secret sharing schemes. More concretely, we show that for any constants $0 < c_s < c_r < 1$ there is a "near-threshold" scheme for sharing a secret bit among n players, such that any set of at most $c_s n$ players learn nothing about the secret, any set of at least $c_r n$ players can jointly reconstruct the secret, and the share generation can be implemented in time $O(n)$ given the secret and uniformly random bits. This should be compared to the well known secret sharing scheme due to Shamir [40], which achieves a sharp threshold between the secrecy and reconstruction require-

[1]Linear-time decoding can be carried out in a more liberal computation model, namely a RAM model. In our default circuit model the codes of [42] and similar "linear-time decodable" codes can be decoded in quasi-linear time.

[2]The codes are semi-explicit in the sense that a linear-size encoding circuit meeting the required bound on the minimal distance can be generated in probabilistic polynomial time with negligible failure probability.

ments, but its implementation requires $n \cdot \text{polylog}(n)$ time. This application relies on known connections between linear codes and secret sharing, and exploits the fact that codes from our family (like random linear codes) do not only have a good minimal distance but also a good *dual distance*.

For the complexity-based cryptographic applications, discussed in Section 5, we naturally adapt previous applications of the "learning parity with noise" (LPN) problem in cryptography to use our new family of codes. In the LPN problem one is asked to recover a random k-bit vector x from samples of the form $(A, Ax + e)$, where A is a random $n \times k$ binary matrix and e is a random n-bit noise vector of low Hamming weight. An appealing feature of the LPN problem is that the related intractability question is of a "win-win" flavor: If the problem is indeed intractable, this implies the security of a variety of LPN-based cryptographic constructions (see [37] for a recent survey). On the other hand, if the problem turns out to be tractable (even in a weak sense), this will be considered a major breakthrough in coding theory, showing that random linear codes support efficient decoding.

Most applications of LPN in cryptography rely on the fact that the LPN problem admits a search to decision reduction. Roughly speaking, this means that recovering x from $(A, Ax + e)$ is reduces to distinguishing between $(A, Ax + e)$ and (A, U_n), where U_n is a uniformly random n-bit vector. We obtain a similar search to decision reduction for our new family of codes. More accurately, the intractability of the decision problem for our code family can be based on the intractability of a search problem for a related code family which has similar properties. We then observe that LPN-based constructions from the literature can be applied with arbitrary distributions of the matrix A as long as the corresponding decision assumption holds.

As applications, we get plausible candidates for stateless symmetric encryption and identification schemes which may achieve better asymptotic efficiency/security tradeoffs than all current candidates. Concretely, if the time complexity of the honest parties is n, then the best known attacks [30, 28] require $2^{O(n/\log\log n)}$ time. This should be compared with the original LPN-based constructions, which require the honest parties to spend $O(n^2)$ time for achieving a similar security guarantee, and an optimized variant suggested in [18] (based on Toeplitz matrices) which requires $n \cdot \text{polylog}(n)$ time. Similarly to LPN-based constructions, our constructions have a win-win flavor in that disproving their conjectured security would lead to an interesting progress in coding theory.

2. PRELIMINARIES

2.1 Basic Notation

For a prime power q, we denote by $\mathbb{F}_q$ the field $\text{GF}(q)$, i.e., the finite field with q elements. We let $\mathbb{N}$ denote the set of natural numbers. For any $n \in \mathbb{N}$, we denote by $[n]$ the set $\{1, 2, \ldots, n\}$. We use lower case letters i, j, k to denote indices, x, y, z to denote column vectors in $\mathbb{F}_q^n$, and upper case letters A, B, C to denote matrices in $\mathbb{F}_q^{n \times k}$. The transpose of a column vector x or a matrix A are denoted by x^T and A^T respectively. We let x_i denote the i-th entry of x and a_{ij} denote the entry in the i-th row and j-th column of A.

2.2 Models of Computation

The main model of computation by which we measure the efficiency of algorithms in this work is the model of arithmetic circuits over a finite field $\mathbb{F}$. Each wire in one of these circuits carries a field element. Each gate in the circuit has two input wires, and outputs the addition, subtraction, or multiplication of its two inputs. We allow gates to have an arbitrary fan-out and a fan-in of either 2 or 0, where a gate with fan-in 0 is labeled by either an input variable or a constant. We also consider *probabilistic circuits* which contain randomness gates with fan-in 0. The values of such gates are picked uniformly and independently from $\mathbb{F}$. The *size* and *depth* of a circuit are the number of wires and the length of the longest path in the graph of the circuit, respectively. See [9] and [39] for more precise definitions of this circuit model. We will consider polynomial-time uniform families of circuits, namely an infinite family of circuits C_k over $\mathbb{F}$, where C_k has k inputs and there is a polynomial-time algorithm which on input 1^k outputs a description of C_k.

Previous works on linear-time encodable and decodable codes (e.g., [41, 42]) also consider the model of a RAM machine [1]. A RAM has a central processor that can access data from a memory. This processor should have a few basic operations: addition, subtraction, read from memory, store to memory, and branch if zero. Each of these operations costs one unit of time. While the circuit model is generally considered more restrictive, the two models are technically incomparable. However, allowing a polynomial-time computable advice that depends only on the input length, any uniform family of circuits of size $s(k)$ can be simulated by such a RAM machine running in time $O(s(k))$.

We will often argue that some object X can be computed in linear-time or by linear-size circuits. By this we mean that the functions associated with X can be computed by a polynomial-time uniform family of linear-size circuits, implying that they can also be computed by a linear-time RAM machine with polynomial-time computable advice. For the sake of concreteness, our default model will be that of uniform arithmetic circuits.

2.3 Coding Theory

A *code* over an *alphabet* Σ with *block length* n is a subset $C \subseteq \Sigma^n$. For two vectors $u, v \in \Sigma^n$, we denote by $\Delta(u, v)$ the *Hamming distance* between u and v, that is, the number of coordinates in which u and v differ. The *Hamming weight* of y is $\Delta(y) = \Delta(y, \vec{0})$. The code's *minimal distance* is defined to be $\min_{c,c' \in C, c \neq c'} \Delta(c, c')$ and is denoted by d while the code's *relative distance* is the value $\delta(C) = \frac{d}{n}$.

The code's *message length* and *rate* are defined as $k = \log_q |C|$ and $R = \frac{k}{n}$, respectively, where $q = |\Sigma|$. We often view the code as the image of an injective *encoding function* (or *encoder*) $E_C : \Sigma^k \to \Sigma^n$. A code C as above is referred to as an $(n, k, d)_q$ code. In our case, Σ will usually be a finite field $\mathbb{F} = \mathbb{F}_q$ and C a k-dimensional linear subspace of $\mathbb{F}^n$. In such a case we say that C is a *linear code* or an $[n, k, d]_q$ code and refer to the orthogonal space of C as the *dual code* whose minimal distance $d^\perp$ is referred to as the *dual distance* of C. An $[n, k, d]_q$ code C admits an encoding function of the form $E_C(x) = Ax$, where A is a $n \times k$ matrix of rank k over $\mathbb{F}$ referred to as a *generator matrix* for C.

We define analogues of the quantities above for infinite families of codes. An infinite family of codes is a family $\mathcal{C} = \{C_i | i \in \mathbb{N}\}$ where C_i is a code of block length n_i with

$n_i > n_{i-1}$ and message length k_i. The rate of $\mathcal{C}$ is defined to be $R(\mathcal{C}) = \liminf_i R(C_i)$ and the relative distance is $\delta(\mathcal{C}) = \liminf_i \delta(C_i)$. We say that $\mathcal{C}$ is *asymptotically good* if $R(\mathcal{C}), \delta(\mathcal{C}) > 0$. We say that $\mathcal{C}$ is encodable in time $t(n)$ if each C_i is the image of an injective encoding function $E_i : \mathbb{F}_q^{k_i} \to \mathbb{F}_q^{n_i}$ where E_i is computable in time $t(n_i)$. When $\mathcal{C}$ is a family of linear codes we require each E_i to be a linear function.

The following definitions and claims are taken almost verbatim from [20].

DEFINITION 1. *For integers q, n, l denote by $\text{VOL}_q(n,l)$ the number of elements in a Hamming ball of radius l in $\mathbb{F}_q^n$. This value is independent of the center of the ball and equals*

$$\text{VOL}_q(n,l) = \sum_{i=0}^{l} \binom{n}{i} (q-1)^i$$

DEFINITION 2. *For a positive integer $q \geq 2$,* the q-ary entropy function $\text{H}_q : [0,1] \to \mathbb{R}$ *is defined as follows:*

$$\text{H}_q(x) = x \log_q(q-1) - x \log_q x - (1-x) \log_q(1-x)$$

For every $y \in [0,1]$ there exists a unique value $x \in [0, 1 - 1/q]$ such that $H_q(x) = y$. This allows us to define a inverse entropy function in following manner.

DEFINITION 3. *For a positive integer $q \geq 2$, the* inverse q-ary entropy function $\text{H}_q^{-1} : [0,1] \to [0,1]$ *is defined as $\text{H}_q^{-1}(y) = x$ where $x \in [0, 1 - 1/q]$ is the unique value satisfying $H_q(x) = y$.*

LEMMA 1. *For an integer $q \geq 2$ and $p \in [0, 1 - \frac{1}{q}]$,*

$$\text{VOL}_q(n, pn) \leq q^{\text{H}_q(p)n}$$

THEOREM 1. **(Asymptotic Gilbert-Varshamov bound)** *For every prime power q and $\delta \in (0, 1 - \frac{1}{q})$, there exists an infinite family $\mathcal{C}$ of linear codes over $\mathbb{F}_q$ with relative distance $\delta(\mathcal{C}) \geq \delta$ and rate $R(\mathcal{C}) \geq 1 - \text{H}_q(\delta)$.*

2.4 Probability

We use calligraphic letters $\mathcal{A}, \mathcal{B}, \mathcal{C}$ to denote discrete probability distributions. We use the notation $a \in_R \mathcal{A}$ to denote a random choice of a from the distribution $\mathcal{A}$. For $n \in \mathbb{N}$ and $\mu \in [0,1]$, we denote by BER_μ^n the distribution over n-bit vectors where each entry is chosen to be 1 with probability μ (independently of the other entries). The uniform distribution over n bit vectors, $\text{BER}_{1/2}^n$, is also denoted by U_n. For a sequence of (possibly randomized) operations $O_1, \ldots, O_m$ and an event A, we let $\Pr[O_1; \ldots; O_m : A]$ denote the probability of the occurrence of A after the sequential execution of $O_1, \ldots, O_m$.

LEMMA 2. **(XOR-lemma [14])** *Let $X = (X_1, \ldots, X_n)$ be a random variable distributed over $\mathbb{F}_q^n$. Then X is uniformly distributed if and only if for every nonzero $y \in \mathbb{F}_q^n$, the random variable $y^T X$ is uniformly distributed over $\mathbb{F}_q$.*

DEFINITION 4. **(Extractor for Bit-Fixing Sources)** *An (l, m, n)* extractor for bit-fixing sources *over $\mathbb{F}$ is a function $g : \mathbb{F}^m \to \mathbb{F}^n$ such that for every distribution X over $\mathbb{F}^m$ that fixes at most l entries and distributes the rest uniformly, the output $g(X)$ is uniformly distributed over $\mathbb{F}^n$.*

DEFINITION 5. **(Pairwise independence)** *A distribution $\mathcal{H}$ over functions $h : X \to Y$ is* pairwise independent *if for every $x, x' \in X$ such that $x \neq x'$ and every $y, y' \in Y$ it holds that*

$$\Pr_{h \in_R \mathcal{H}}[h(x) = y \wedge h(x') = y'] = |Y|^{-2}.$$

When $\mathcal{H}$ is a set or multiset of functions, the corresponding distribution is understood to be uniform over $\mathcal{H}$.

2.5 Asymptotics

A function $\epsilon(k)$ is said to be *negligible* if for every polynomial p and all sufficiently large k we have $\epsilon(k) < 1/p(k)$. When we say that an infinite sequence of events E_k occurs with negligible probability, we mean that the probability $\epsilon(k)$ of E_k is negligible. We will make a standard use of big-O and big-Ω notation.

In asymptotic expressions that involve multiple variables, the variables not explicitly included inside the $O(\cdot)$ or $\Omega(\cdot)$ are treated as constants. For instance, the expression $\epsilon(q,n) = q^{-\Omega(n)}$ means that for every q there exists $\theta > 0$ such that for all sufficiently large n, $\epsilon(q,n) \leq q^{-\theta n}$.

3. LINEAR-TIME ENCODABLE CODES MEETING THE GV BOUND

In this section we present a probabilistic construction of linear-time encodable codes that meet the GV bound. Our main tool is a new pseudorandom object which we call a *linear uniform output family.* Section 3.1 presents a linear-time computable linear uniform output family. In Section 3.2 we discuss applications to coding theory, including linear-time encodable codes that meet the GV bound.

3.1 Linear Uniform Output Families

DEFINITION 6. **(Linear Uniform Output Family)** *A (q,k,n)* linear uniform output family *is a distribution $\mathcal{A}$ over linear functions $A : \mathbb{F}_q^k \to \mathbb{F}_q^n$, such that for every nonzero $x \in \mathbb{F}_q^k$ and $y \in \mathbb{F}_q^n$ it holds that $\Pr_{A \in_R \mathcal{A}}[A(x) = y] = q^{-n}$. Equivalently, for every fixed nonzero $x \in \mathbb{F}_q^k$ the distribution of $A(x)$ induced by a choice of A according to $\mathcal{A}$ is uniform over $\mathbb{F}_q^n$.*

For notational convenience, we will identify a function A in the support of $\mathcal{A}$ with the $n \times k$ matrix representing it.

A well known linear uniform output family is the family of $n \times k$ Toeplitz matrices over $\mathbb{F}_q$. Similarly to our construction, each Toeplitz matrix A has a linear size description. However, the function corresponding to A is only known to be computable in quasi-linear time (see [32, 29]).

We now present a linear-time computable linear uniform output family. Our construction is a variant of the pairwise independent hash function family from Theorem 3.3 of [25]. It generalizes this construction to work over arbitrary finite fields and slightly modifies it to directly yield a linear uniform output family (as oppose to a pairwise independent family). We start with a high level overview of the previous construction.

Overview of the construction from [25]:.
The key idea of the construction is to use a linear number of constant-size pairwise independent hash functions to implement a large pairwise independent hash function. This

is done in three phases. First, a linear-time encodable code C is being used to encode the input x, resulting in an encoding y. For the construction as a whole to work, the alphabet size may be increased in this phase to allow the fractional distance to be bigger than $1/2$. Next, an independent constant-size pairwise independent hash function h_i is applied to each i'th symbol of y, resulting in a randomized encoding y'. Finally, a linear-time computable extractor for bit-fixing sources, g, is applied to y' obtaining the final output. Such an extractor can be obtained by transposing a linear-time encoding function of a linear code with good minimal distance, where the transpose mapping can be shown to also be implementable in linear time. Each function in the family is hence of the form $g \circ \vec{h} \circ E_C$ and is specified by the choice of $\vec{h} = (h_i)$. Since all three phases may be implemented in linear time, so does the entire construction.

An informal argument as to why the above function is pairwise independent is as follows. For every distinct inputs x_1, x_2 we have that the corresponding encodings y_1 and y_2 differ in many of the coordinates and hence y'_1 and y'_2 are distributed uniformly and independently in all these coordinates. The final application of an extractor for bit-fixing sources turns this partial pairwise independence into full pairwise independence.

To construct a linear uniform output family, we instantiate the above construction so that all building blocks are implemented by linear functions, where the functions h_i are now taken from a (constant-size) linear uniform output family rather than an arbitrary pairwise independent family. Since we will need a generalized form of the construction that applies over arbitrary fields, we present here a similar generalization for each of the underlying building blocks.

The first building block is an asymptotically good family of linear-time encodable linear codes. Spielman [42] obtains an explicit construction of such codes over the binary field. Here we generalize this construction and its analysis to apply over any finite field. We rely on the explicit lossless expanders of Capalbo et al. [11] (Theorem 7.1).

LEMMA 3. *There exists a constant $c_0 > 0$ such that for every positive integers n, t such that $t \leq n$ and every $\epsilon > 0$ there exists a bipartite graph $G = (L, R, E)$ with $|L| = n, |R| = m = \lfloor n/t \rfloor$ and the following properties:*

- **Degree.** *The degree of every $a \in L$ is $\Delta = \mathrm{poly}(\log t, 1/\epsilon)$.*
- **Expansion.** *For every set $X \subset L$ with $|X| \leq \frac{c_0 \epsilon m}{\Delta}$, if $Y = \Gamma(X)$ is the set of neighbors of X in G, then $|Y| \geq (1-\epsilon)\Delta|X|$.*
- **Explicitness.** *G can be constructed in $\mathrm{poly}(n, 2^{\mathrm{poly}(t,1/\epsilon)})$ time.*

LEMMA 4. *There exist constants $d_1 > 1$ and $d_2 > 0$ such that for every field $\mathbb{F}$ there exists a family of $[\lfloor d_1 k \rfloor, k, \lceil d_2 k \rceil]$ linear codes over $\mathbb{F}$ which can be encoded by a uniform family of linear-size arithmetic circuits consisting of addition and fan-out gates only.*

PROOF. The construction is a simplified version of Spielman's code [42] generalized to any finite field. The differences are that we replace XOR with general addition gates over $\mathbb{F}$ and adapt the base code of the recursive construction to the underlying field. Moreover, since we only care about the minimal distance of the code the construction involves lossless expanders instead of error reducing codes which are required for the decoding process of the original code.

We will now describe a recursive construction of a family of encoding functions $E_h : \mathbb{F}^{n_0 2^{h-2}} \to \mathbb{F}^{n_0 2^h}$ for some constant n_0 divisible by 4 such that a circuit of size $O(2^h)$ which computes E_h using addition gates can be generated in time $\mathrm{poly}(2^h)$ and the code defined by E_h has constant relative distance. The general case follows by padding an input of length k with zeros such that the obtained input length is the closest value of the form $n_0 2^h$. Doing so affects the rate by a constant factor and preserves the relative distance of the code encoded by E_h.

The base encoding function E_0 would be the encoding function of a linear code C_0 of block length n_0, rate $1/4$ and relative distance $\delta' > 0$. We set $\epsilon < 0.1$ and for $h \geq -1$ we denote by $G_h = (L_h, R_h, E'_h)$ the expander graph from Lemma 3 with $|L_h| = n_0 2^h, |R_h| = n_0 2^{h-1}, c_0 > 0$ and $\Delta = \mathrm{poly}(1/\epsilon)$. We assume that Δ is not too small (say $\Delta > 10$; Since Δ is a function of $1/\epsilon$ we do not lose generality).

For every $h > 0$ we define E_h to encode a message m of length $n_0 2^{h-2}$ in the following manner. First, G_{h-2} is used to compute a message m_1 of length $n_0 2^{h-3}$. More concretely, $(m_1)_j = \Sigma_{i \in \Gamma(\{j\})} m_i$ is the sum of the entries of m indexed by the neighbors of $j \in R_{h-2}$. We next compute $c_1 = E_{h-1}(m_1)$ whose length is $n_0 2^{h-1}$. We use G_{h-1} and c_1 as done above to compute c_2 whose length is $n_0 2^{h-2}$. The final output is $c = m \circ c_1 \circ c_2$ whose length is $n_0 2^h$.

We will now show by induction that for $\delta = \min\{\frac{c_0 \epsilon}{8\Delta}, \delta'\}$ every encoding function E_h defines a code C_h with relative distance least δ. The other assertions on E_h are easy to validate. Let m be a nonzero message of length $n_0 2^{h-2}$ and consider the following two possible cases. First, when the relative Hamming weight of m is at least 4δ we have that the relative weight of $c = m \circ c_1 \circ c_2$ is at least δ. Otherwise, let X denote the index set of the nonzero entries of m. Since the relative weight of m is at most $4\delta \leq \frac{c_0 \epsilon}{2\Delta}$ we have that $|X| \leq \frac{c_0 \epsilon |B_{h-2}|}{\Delta}$ and hence $\Gamma(X) \geq (1-\epsilon)\Delta|X|$. A simple counting argument shows that at least $(1-2\epsilon)\Delta|X| > 8|X| > 0$ of the vertices in B_{h-2} have a unique neighbor in X. All these vertices correspond to a nonzero entry in m_1. Since m_1 is nonzero, the relative weight of c_1 is at least $\delta' \geq \delta$. We have two possible sub-cases to consider. If the relative weight of c_1 is at least 2δ then we are done. Otherwise, the relative weight of c_1 is at least δ and at most 2δ. An argument as above with X' denoting the index set of the nonzero entries of c_1 shows the the weight of c_2 is at least $(1-2\epsilon)\Delta|X'| \geq 8\delta n_0 2^{h-1} > \delta n_0 2^h$ as promised. □

The first component of the construction, namely the code C in the overview, is obtained by permuting and grouping symbols of a code as above into constant-size blocks so that its relative minimal distance becomes a sufficiently large constant. The construction of C is similar in spirit to the expander based construction of Guruswami and Indyk [21] which applies the distance boosting technique of ABNNR [3] to an asymptotically good linear-time encodable code. We will need the following object which is a simplified version of the expander graph used in Theorem 11.4 of [19].

LEMMA 5. *There exists a constant $c_1 > 0$ such that for every $\epsilon > 0$ and positive integer n there exists a bipartite graph $G = (L, R, E)$ with $|L| = |R| = n$ and the following properties:*

- **Degree.** *The degree of every vertex in* G *is* $\Delta = \lceil c_1/\epsilon^3 \rceil$.
- **Expansion.** *For every set* $X \subset L$ *with* $|X| \geq \epsilon n$, *if* Y *is the set of neighbors of* X *in* G, *then* $|Y| \geq (1-\epsilon)|R|$.
- **Explicitness.** G *can be constructed in* $\text{poly}(n, 1/\epsilon)$ *time.*

The following theorem combines Lemma 4 and Lemma 5 to get the first component in our construction.

THEOREM 2. *For every prime power* q *and* $0 < \delta < 1$ *there exist* $0 < \rho < 1$, *a positive integer* β *and a family of linear encoding functions* $E_{C_k} : \mathbb{F}_q^k \to \mathbb{F}_q^{n(k)}$ *satisfying the following requirements for all* k:

- **Rate.** $k < n(k) \leq k/\rho$ *and* β *divides* $n(k)$.
- **Relative** β**-distance.** *Parsing the output of* C_k *as* $n(k)/\beta$ *blocks of length* β, *the resulting code has relative distance* $\geq \delta$.

Furthermore, C_k *can be computed by a uniform family of linear-size arithmetic circuits over* F_q.

PROOF. The construction combines a linear-time encoding function E_k of the $[\lfloor d_1 k \rfloor, k, \lceil d_2 k \rceil]_q$ code C'_k from Lemma 4 and the bipartite graph G with parameters $\epsilon = \min\{\frac{d_2}{d_1}, 1-\delta\}$ and $n = \lfloor d_1 k \rfloor$ from Lemma 5. To encode a message $x \in \mathbb{F}_q^k$ we compute $y = E_k(x) \in \mathbb{F}_q^n$ and redistribute the symbols according to G. More concretely, For every $i \in [n]$ and $j \in [\Delta]$ let $\gamma(i,j)$ be the index of the j'th neighbor of the i'th vertex in R. The $(i-1) \cdot \Delta + j$ entry of $E_{C_k}(x)$ is defined to be the $y_{\gamma(i,j)}$.

Since $\Delta = \lceil c_1/\epsilon^3 \rceil$ we have that $\frac{1}{d_1 \Delta}$, the rate of C_k, is bounded away from zero. The linearity and linear encoding complexity of C_k are inherited from C'_k. For the relative block distance, let $\beta = \Delta$ and $x, x' \in \mathbb{F}_q^k$ such that $x \neq x'$. Since the relative distance of C'_k is at least $\frac{d_2}{d_1}$, there exists a set $X \subset A$ of size at least $\frac{d_2}{d_1} n$ such that for every $i \in X$ we have $E_k(x)_i \neq E_k(x')_i$. Since $\epsilon \leq \frac{d_2}{d_1}$ the expansion property of G guarantees that at least $1 - \epsilon \geq \delta$ fraction of the blocks (of size $\beta = \Delta$) of $E_{C_k}(x_1)$ and $E_{C_k}(x_2)$ are different. □

The linear-time computable extractor for bit-fixing sources we use generalizes the one from Theorem 3.2 of [25] to arbitrary fields and is proved similarly. We rely on the following generalized transposition principle [10].

LEMMA 6. **(Implicit in [10],[25])** *There exists a constant* $c_4 > 0$ *such that for every finite field* $\mathbb{F}$ *the following holds. Let* C *be an arithmetic circuit over* $\mathbb{F}$ *of size* t *which consists of only addition gates and computes the function* $f(x) = Ax$. *Then there exists an arithmetic circuit* C' *of size at most* $c_4 t$ *that computes the function* $f'(x) = A^T x$.

Applying Lemma 6 to the codes from Lemma 4 and using the known relation between extractors for bit-fixing sources and linear codes [15], we get the following.

THEOREM 3. *There exist constants* $c_2, c_3 > 0$ *such that for every field* $\mathbb{F}$ *there exists a family of linear* $(\lceil c_2 k \rceil, k, \lfloor c_3 k \rfloor)$ *extractors for bit fixing sources over* $\mathbb{F}$ *that are computable by a uniform family of linear-size arithmetic circuits.*

We now show how to use the above components for the construction of linear uniform output families. The following construction takes an input length k and outputs a linear-size arithmetic circuit D_k representing a linear uniform output family from $\mathbb{F}^k$ to $\mathbb{F}^n$ where $n = \Theta(k)$.

CONSTRUCTION 1. *Parameter: prime power* q. *Input: positive integer* k.

Fix c_2 *and* c_3 *as in Theorem 3 and* δ *such that* $1 - c_2 < \delta < 1$. *Let* C *be a code over* $\mathbb{F}_q$ *with message length* k, *block length* $n(k)$, *rate parameter* ρ *and relative* β*-distance* $\geq \delta$ *as promised by Theorem 2.*

Let H *be a random block diagonal matrix over* $\mathbb{F}_q$ *with* $\frac{n(k)}{\beta}$ *blocks each of size* $\beta \times \beta$. H *can be naturally identified with a vector* $r \in \mathbb{F}_q^{\beta n(k)}$. *We denote by* H_r *the matrix* H *corresponding to* r.

Finally, let $k' = n(k)$ *and let* g *be a linear* $(\lceil c_2 k' \rceil, k', \lfloor c_3 k' \rfloor)$ *extractor for bit fixing sources over* $\mathbb{F}_q$ *due to Theorem 3.*

The output of the construction is the circuit $D_k : \mathbb{F}_q^k \times \mathbb{F}_q^{\beta n(k)} \to \mathbb{F}_q^{c_3 n(k)}$ *computing* $D_k(x, r) = g \circ H_r \circ E_C(x)$.

LEMMA 7. *Construction 1 outputs a circuit* $D_k : \mathbb{F}_q^k \times \mathbb{F}_q^{m(k)} \to \mathbb{F}_q^{n'(k)}$ *such that* $m(k) = O(k)$,$n'(k) = \Omega(k)$, D_k *is of size* $O(k)$, *and* $A_r(x) = D_k(x, r)$ *defines a linear uniform output family when* r *is chosen uniformly from* $\mathbb{F}_q^{m(k)}$.

PROOF. The length parameters, linearity, and linear circuit size of A_r are directly inherited from the building blocks. For the purpose of showing that the family is indeed uniform, let us view C as a code over $\Sigma = \mathbb{F}_q^\beta$ with relative distance $\geq \delta$. For any nonzero $x \in \mathbb{F}^k$ we consider $A_r x$, where r is chosen uniformly from $\mathbb{F}_q^{m(k)}$. Let L denote the places where $E_C(x)_i \neq 0$ and observe that the L-entries of $H_r(E_C(x))$ are distributed uniformly and independently whereas the rest of the entries are always zero. By the choice of C, the L-entries contain at least $\delta > 1 - c_2$ fraction of the symbols and by the choice of g having at least $1 - c_2$ fraction of the input being random is enough to ensure that the output is completely random. Together we have that $A_r x = D_k(x, r)$ is uniformly distributed. Finally, note that the size of the output is $c_3 n(k) > c_3 k$ as promised. □

Note that padding the input with zeros and truncating the output allow us to respectively decrease and increase the ratio between k and n. The main theorem of this subsection thus follows.

THEOREM 4. **(Linear Uniform Output Families)** *Let* $\mathbb{F}$ *be a finite field. For every positive integer* c *there is a polynomial-time constructible circuit family* $D_k : \mathbb{F}^k \times \mathbb{F}^{m(k)} \to \mathbb{F}^{ck}$ *such that* $m(k) = O(k)$, D_k *is of size* $O(k)$ *and* $A_r(x) = D_k(x, r)$ *defines a linear uniform output family when* r *is chosen uniformly from* $\mathbb{F}^{m(k)}$.

3.2 Applications in Coding Theory

We are interested in linear uniform output families because of their pseudorandom nature. It is well known that a purely random (linear) function defines a good code with overwhelming probability. We show that the relaxed requirement of linear uniform output families is enough for them to match the rate/distance tradeoff achieved by purely random codes. We will also establish other useful properties to be used in Sections 4 and 5.

We start by showing that a random member of a linear uniform output family meets the GV bound with high probability. This means that the best rate/distance tradeoff known for random linear codes is achieved by any linear uniform output family. Our proof is essentially the same as the one for random linear codes which can be found, e.g., in [20] (see Notes 2, Theorem 8), and is given here for self-containment.

THEOREM 5. **(GV Bound for Linear Uniform Output Families)** *For every prime power q, $\delta \in [0, 1-1/q)$ and $\epsilon > 0$, the following holds for all positive integers n. Let $k = \lceil (1 - H_q(\delta) - \epsilon)n \rceil$. If $\mathcal{A}$ is a (q,k,n) linear uniform output family over $\mathbb{F}_q$, then the image of $A \in_R \mathcal{A}$ is a linear code with rate $R = k/n$ and relative distance at least δ, except with at most $q^{-\Omega(n)}$ probability (over the choice of A from $\mathcal{A}$).*

PROOF. By the linearity of A both assertions are implied by showing that for any nonzero $x \in \mathbb{F}_q^k$ we have $\Delta(Ax) > \delta n$ except with exponentially small probability. Since $\mathcal{A}$ is a linear uniform output family, one has

$$\Pr[\Delta(Ax) \leq \delta n] \leq \frac{\mathrm{VOL}_q(n, \delta n)}{q^n}.$$

Recalling that

$$\mathrm{VOL}_q(n, \delta n) \leq q^{H_q(\delta)n},$$

a union bound over all $x \in \mathbb{F}_q^k$ yields

$$\Pr[\exists x \in \mathbb{F}_q^k \setminus \{0\} : \Delta(Ax) \leq \delta n)] \leq$$

$$q^k \frac{q^{H_q(\delta)n}}{q^n} \leq q^{(1-H_q(\delta)-\epsilon)n+1} q^{(H_q(\delta)-1)n} =$$

$$q \cdot q^{-\epsilon n}.$$

□

We will also need the following equivalent formulation.

COROLLARY 6. *Let $R \in (0,1)$ and let $\mathcal{A}$ be a (q, Rn, n) linear uniform output family. For every $\epsilon > 0$ a random $A \in_R \mathcal{A}$ defines a code with rate R and relative distance at least $H_q^{-1}(1-R) - \epsilon$ with probability $1 - q^{-\Omega(n)}$.*

We next show that the uniform output property is symmetric in the sense that a uniform output family has uniform output when multiplied from the left by any nonzero vector. This will allow us to deduce that the dual codes of codes obtained by uniform output families are good on their own right. This property of the dual codes will be useful for the application to secret sharing discussed in the next section.

LEMMA 8. *If $\mathcal{A}$ is a linear uniform output family then for any nonzero $y \in \mathbb{F}_q^n$ and $z \in \mathbb{F}_q^k$ it holds that*

$$\Pr_{A \in_R \mathcal{A}}[y^T A = z] = q^{-k}.$$

PROOF. Let x, y be nonzero vectors in $\mathbb{F}_q^k$ and $\mathbb{F}_q^n$ respectively. The uniform output of $\mathcal{A}$ ensures us that Ax is uniformly distributed whenever A is chosen according to $\mathcal{A}$. The fact that y is nonzero thus implies that $(y^T A)x = y^T(Ax)$ is uniform as well. Recalling that this holds for every nonzero x allows us to apply the XOR-lemma (Lemma 2) on $y^T A$ which completes the proof. □

LEMMA 9. *Let $R \in (0,1)$ and let $\mathcal{A}$ be a (q, Rn, n) linear uniform output family. For every $\epsilon > 0$ a random $A \in_R \mathcal{A}$ defines a code D whose dual code $D^\perp$ has rate $R^\perp = 1 - R$ and relative distance at least $H_q^{-1}(1-R^\perp) - \epsilon$ with probability $1 - q^{-\Omega(n)}$.*

PROOF. By the above lemma and the fact that $D^\perp = \{y : y^T A = 0\}$ one has $\Pr[y \in D^\perp] \leq q^{-k}$ where $k = Rn$. Following the exact proof outline of Theorem 5 we get that for every $\epsilon > 0$, $D^\perp$ has relative distance $H_q^{-1}(1 - (n-k)/n) - \epsilon$ with probability $1 - q^{-\Omega(n)}$. Observing that the dimension $k^\perp$ of $D^\perp$ is $n - k$ with probability $1 - q^{-\Omega(n)}$ completes the proof. □

The following theorem follows directly from the previous lemmas and will be used as the main tool in Section 4.

THEOREM 7. **(Simultaneous GV Bound)** *Let $R \in (0,1)$ and $A \in_R \mathcal{A}$ be a random member of a (q, Rn, n) linear uniform output family. Let $D = Im(A)$ be the code associated with the generator matrix A and $k = Rn$. Then for every $\epsilon > 0$ the following holds with probability $1 - q^{-\Omega(n)}$:*

- *D has relative distance $\geq H_q^{-1}(1 - k/n) - \epsilon$ and dimension k.*
- *$D^\perp$ has relative distance $\geq H_q^{-1}(1-(n-k)/n) - \epsilon$ and dimension $k^\perp = n - k$.*

4. APPLICATIONS IN INFORMATION THEORETIC CRYPTOGRAPHY

In this section we apply our new code family towards a linear-time implementation of secret sharing, a central tool in information-theoretic cryptography.

A secret sharing scheme [40, 6] allows a dealer to share a secret among n players so that only certain subsets of players can reconstruct the secret and others learn nothing about it. The typical case of interest is that of threshold secret sharing, where every set of at most t players learn nothing about the secret and every larger set of players can jointly reconstruct it. We consider the natural relaxation of *near-threshold* secret sharing, where there may be a small gap between the secrecy and reconstruction thresholds. More concretely, an (n, t, r) secret sharing scheme is an algorithm which given a secret s (a single bit by default) and a sequence of random bits produces an n-tuple of strings, called shares, such that any t shares reveal nothing about s and any r shares can be used to reconstruct s. The scheme is called an *ϵ-threshold* scheme if $t \geq (1-\epsilon)(r-1)$ and simply a *threshold* scheme when $t = r - 1$.

We start by reviewing some known connections between linear codes and secret sharing schemes. We give a self-contained general transformation from codes to secret sharing and tie the underlying code's parameters with the parameters of the resulting secret sharing scheme. We then prove that by plugging our codes into that transformation one obtains an ϵ-threshold scheme for every arbitrarily small $\epsilon > 0$ such that the secret sharing phase and reconstruction can be performed by linear-size circuits.

4.1 From Codes to Secret Sharing

The general relation between codes and secret sharing was put forward in [36] and relies on the following observation.

Given a code C, a codeword $c \in C$ and access to enough entries of c, one may reconstruct all the entries of c correctly. On the other hand, for some choices of C, access to a small amount of entries of c gives us no information about the other entries. Thus, to share a secret s one may choose a codeword c whose last entry is s and distribute the rest of the entries of c among the different players. This idea is the basis for the construction of Massey [34, 35] which was further generalized by Chen et al. [12]. We now describe a variant of these transformations which respects the time complexity of the encoding.

4.1.1 The Transformation

Given a $[n+1, k, d]_q$ code C over $\mathbb{F}_q$, we define the following secret sharing scheme for n players.

Algorithm 1 Share ($s \in \mathbb{F}_q$)

Choose a random $c \in C$ such that $c_{n+1} = s$
Let $s_i \leftarrow c_i$ for $i = 1, 2, \ldots, n$.

Choosing such a c can be done in the following manner. Fix a global $c^* \in C$ with $c^*_{n+1} \neq 0$ and choose a random $c' \in C$. Set $c = c' + \alpha \cdot c^*$ where $\alpha \in \mathbb{F}_q$ is chosen such that $c_{n+1} = s$, i.e. $\alpha = \frac{s - c'_{n+1}}{c^*_{n+1}}$. To do this in linear-time when C is a code from our family with an encoding matrix $A \in \mathcal{A}$ one need only choose a random $x \in \mathbb{F}_q^k$ and compute $c' = Ax$ using the corresponding linear size circuit.

Algorithm 2 Reconstruct $R = (s_i)_{i \in I}$

Find $c' \in C$ such that $s_i = c'_i$ for all $i \in I$.
Return c'_{n+1}

Note that finding such a c can be done by solving the corresponding linear system.

Lemma 10. *If $|I| \geq n - d + 2$ then Reconstruct(R)=s.*

Proof. Since R is missing at most $d-1$ pieces of c there is a unique c' which agrees with c on the indices of I, namely c itself. □

The following lemma shows that a set of at most $d^\perp - 2$ players learn nothing about the secret.

Lemma 11. *If $|I| \leq d^\perp - 2$ then the distribution over the possible values of $R = (s_i)_{i \in I}$ induced by Share(s) is independent of s.*

Proof. We first show that any possible sequence R does not determine the value of s. Indeed, if the opposite is correct then one has the relation $x_{n+1} = \sum_{i \in I} \alpha_i x_i$ for some field elements $(\alpha_i)_{i \in I}$ and hence $\sum_{i \in I} \alpha_i x_i - x_{n+1} = 0$ is one of the constraints that defines C as a linear subspace. Recalling that $C^\perp$ is exactly the set of all such constraints and that $|I| \leq d^\perp - 2$ shows that the minimal distance of $C^\perp$ is at most $d^\perp - 1$, a contradiction.

Let $K = \{c_i = s_i | i \in I\}$ be the set of constraints associated with a feasible sequence R. The above shows that these constraints, put together with those that define C, do not determine the value of c_{n+1} and since R is feasible they must have a freedom degree $l > 0$. Thus, setting c_{n+1} to be an arbitrary value $s' \in \mathbb{F}_q$ leaves us with exactly q^{l-1} codewords which agree with both R and $c_{n+1} = s'$, as promised. □

Corollary 8. *The general transformation applied to an $[n+1, k, d]_q$ code C yields a $(n, t, n-d+2)$ secret sharing scheme where $t \geq d^\perp - 2$.*

4.2 Linear-Time Near-Threshold Secret Sharing

Theorem 9. **(Linear-time secret sharing)** *Let c_s (relative secrecy threshold) and c_r (relative reconstruction threshold) be constants such that $0 < c_s < c_r < 1$. Then for any n there is a circuit D_n of size $O(n)$, which on input $s \in \{0,1\}$ and a random $r \in_R \{0,1\}^{O(n)}$ outputs an n-tuple of shares $(s_1, \ldots, s_n)$ where $s_i \in \{0,1\}^{O(1)}$ such that:*

- c_s**-secrecy.** *The joint distribution of every set of at most $c_s n$ shares is independent of s (and in particular, reveals nothing about s).*
- c_r**-reconstruction.** *The secret s can be recovered from any set of at least $c_r n$ shares.*

Furthermore, there exists a PPT algorithm Gen *which on input 1^n outputs a circuit D_n as above along with a corresponding reconstruction circuit except with $2^{-\Omega(n)}$ failure probability.*

Proof. Let $\epsilon > 0$ be a small constant to be fixed later and let q be large enough power of 2 such that for every $x \in [0,1]$ it holds that $H_q^{-1}(x) \geq x - \epsilon/2$. In this case, Theorem 7 insures that except for a $2^{-\Omega(n)}$ failure probability, a code C defined by a random generator matrix $A \in_R \mathcal{A}$ where $\mathcal{A}$ is a $(q, k = Rn, n+1)$ linear uniform output family due to Theorem 4 has relative distance $\delta \geq H_q^{-1}(1-R) - \epsilon/2 \geq 1 - R - \epsilon$ and dual relative distance $\delta^\perp \geq H_q^{-1}(1-R^\perp) - \epsilon/2 = H_q^{-1}(R) \geq R - \epsilon$. By using the general transformation we get a $(n, \lceil k - \epsilon n \rceil, \lfloor k + \epsilon n + 2 \rfloor)$ scheme over $\mathbb{F}_q$. Choosing $k = \lfloor (c_s + c_r)n/2 \rfloor$ and a small enough value for ϵ we get

$$\lfloor k + \epsilon n + 2 \rfloor \leq ((c_s + c_r)/2 + \epsilon)n + 2 < c_r n$$

reconstruction and

$$\lceil k - \epsilon n \rceil \geq ((c_s + c_r)/2 - \epsilon)n - 1 > c_s n$$

secrecy. The other assertions follow from the construction of our codes. □

Remark 1. **(On the efficiency of reconstruction)** *The circuit D_n computes a linear function of the secret and randomness. Hence, for every fixed reconstructing set I reconstruction can be performed by a linear size circuit.*

5. APPLICATIONS IN COMPLEXITY-BASED CRYPTOGRAPHY

This section demonstrates the potential usefulness of our codes for linear-time implementations of cryptographic primitives that rely on computational intractability. As usual, the security of such primitives must be based on plausible (but unproven) intractability assumptions. The intractability assumptions we employ are variants of the well studied intractability assumptions related to the learning parity with noise (LPN) problem. Roughly speaking, the LPN problem says that for a random generator matrix A, a random message x, and a low-weight random noise vector e, it is hard to decode x from $(A, Ax + e)$ except with negligible probability. We observe that LPN-based cryptographic constructions can be extended to other distributions over matrices A, provided that the corresponding intractability assumption still holds and the distribution satisfies a mild additional structural requirement. Combined with our new families of codes, this can yield improved computation time (linear instead of quadratic) with similar security. An advantage of our approach is its win-win flavor: refuting the underlying assumption would imply interesting progress in coding theory.

We introduce the relevant definitions in Section 5.1. A search to decision reduction for our variant of LPN is presented in Section 5.2. This reduction is essential to Section 5.3 in which we state and discuss our intractability assumption in further detail. Section 5.4 and Appendix A will show how to use our codes to construct symmetric encryption and identification schemes whose security is based on our new intractability assumption.

5.1 Preliminaries

DEFINITION 7. *For a distribution $\mathcal{A}$ over $n \times k$ binary matrices, a noise parameter μ and $x \in \{0,1\}^k$ we define the distribution $\mathcal{A}_{x,\mu}$ over $\mathbb{F}^{n\times k} \times \mathbb{F}^n$ where $(A, Ax+e)$ has the same probability as choosing A according to $\mathcal{A}$ and e according to BER_μ^n. The distribution $\mathcal{A} \times U_n$ is denoted by $\mathcal{A}_u$.*

DEFINITION 8. **(Intractability)** *For a family of distribution $\mathcal{L} = (\mathcal{A}^n)_{n=1}^\infty$ over $n \times k(n)$ binary matrices and a noise parameter μ the problem $\text{CODE}(\mathcal{L}, \mu)$ is defined as follows.*

- *Input: 1^n, oracle access to $\mathcal{A}_{x,\mu}^n$ where $x \in_R \{0,1\}^{k(n)}$ is a fixed random vector.*
- *Output: x.*

We say that $\text{CODE}(\mathcal{L}, \mu)$ is $(s(n), t(n), \epsilon(n))$ search secure *if every nonuniform adversary D of size $O(t(n))$ that makes $O(s(n))$ oracle queries solves the problem with probability at most $\epsilon(n)$. It is* search intractable *if every nonuniform polynomial size adversary D solves the problem with probability negligible in n.*

We say that $\text{CODE}(\mathcal{L}, \mu)$ is $(s(n), t(n), \epsilon(n))$ decision secure *if for every nonuniform adversary D of size $t(n)$ that makes $s(n)$ oracle queries it holds that*

$$|\Pr[x \in_R \{0,1\}^k : D^{\mathcal{A}_{x,\mu}^n}(1^n) = 1] - \Pr[D^{\mathcal{A}_u^n} = 1]| \le \epsilon(n)$$

for all sufficiently large n. We say that $\text{CODE}(\mathcal{L}, \mu)$ is just decision secure if it is $(p(n), p(n), 1/p(n))$ decision secure for every polynomial $p(n)$.

We will often omit the superscript n when it is clear from context. When referring to security with respect to function classes, it is assumed that security holds with respect to every choice of functions in these classes.

5.2 Search to Decision

In this section we show a two-step search to decision reduction for general distributions over linear codes $\mathcal{L} = (\mathcal{A}^n)_{n=1}^\infty$. The first step reduces $\text{CODE}(\tilde{\mathcal{L}}, \mu)$, where $\tilde{\mathcal{L}}$ is obtained by a simple transformation applied to $\mathcal{L}$, to the worst-case decision LPN problem for $\mathcal{L}$ with noise parameter μ. The second step is a worst-case to average-case reduction for the latter decision problem.

Using our notation, the LPN problem with parameters $R \in (0,1)$ and $\mu \in (0, 1/2)$ can be expressed as $\text{CODE}(\mathcal{L}, \mu)$ where $\mathcal{L} = (U_{n\times Rn})_{n=1}^\infty$. Put in words, it is the problem of recovering a random Rn-bit vector x given access to samples of the form $(A, Ax+e)$ where A is a random $n \times k$ binary matrix and e is sampled from BER_μ^n. (In each oracle call, A and e are picked independently whereas x if fixed.) One of the useful features of this problem is that it admits a search to decision reduction: an efficient distinguisher between samples from $(A, Ax + e)$ and samples from (A, U_n) implies an efficient algorithm to recover x from $(A, Ax + e)$ [7]. This allows one to conjecture the hardness of decoding a random linear code, whose refutation would imply a breakthrough in coding theory, and then rely on the pseudorandomness of $(A, Ax + e)$ for the construction of cryptographic primitives (see [4, 18, 24, 37, 31] for some examples).

Unfortunately, it seems that known search to decision reduction techniques do not apply to our family of codes. However, by applying a simple transformation to this family we show that in some useful sense these codes do admit to a search to decision reduction.

More concretely, we show a general transformation from a distribution over $n \times k$ matrices $\mathcal{A}$ to a distribution over $n \times (k+1)$ matrices $\tilde{\mathcal{A}}$ such that the search problem over $\tilde{\mathcal{A}}$ can be reduced to the decision problem over $\mathcal{A}$. Furthermore, if $\mathcal{A}$ is linear-time computable uniform output family then so is $\tilde{\mathcal{A}}$. The cryptographic results in the following sections rely on the intractability of solving the decision problem for our new family of codes. The search to decision reduction we prove next puts us in a win-win situation where either our cryptographic applications are secure or alternatively there are linear-time encodable codes meeting the GV bound that can be efficiently decoded. Concretely, the latter family of codes is the one obtained by concatenating polynomially many independent copies of $\tilde{\mathcal{A}}$.

For a $n \times k$ matrix $A = (a_1, \ldots, a_k)$, $i \in [k+1]$ and $r \in \{0,1\}^n$ we denote by $A_{i,r} = (a_1, \ldots a_{i-1}, r, a_i, \ldots, a_k)$ the matrix A with the vector r replacing the i'th column. For a distribution $\mathcal{A}$ over $n \times k$ matrices we define a new distribution $\tilde{\mathcal{A}}$ over matrices of the form $A_{i,r}$ where A is chosen according to $\mathcal{A}$ and i, r are chosen uniformly at random.

We will need the following technical lemmas. The first is a simple worst-case to average-case reduction for the problem of distinguishing $\mathcal{A}_{x,\mu}$ from $\mathcal{A}_u$. The second is a search to (worst-case) decision reduction which is similar in spirit to the ones from [38], Lemma 4.2, and [27], Lemma 1.

LEMMA 12. **(Decisional Worst-Case to Average-Case)** *Let $\mathcal{A}$ be a $n \times k$ matrix distribution such that the function $f : \mathcal{A} \times \{0,1\}^k \to \{0,1\}^n$ defined by $f(A, x) = Ax$ can be computed by a circuit of size t'. Assume that there exists a circuit D of size t making s oracle queries such that*

$$|\Pr[x \in_R \{0,1\}^k : D^{\mathcal{A}_{x,\mu}}(1^n) = 1] - \Pr[D^{\mathcal{A}_u} = 1]| \ge \delta.$$

Then there exists a circuit $\hat{D}$ of size $\hat{t} = O(t + st')$ making s oracle queries such that for every $x \in \{0,1\}^k$ it holds that

$$|\Pr[\hat{D}^{\mathcal{A}_{x,\mu}}(1^n) = 1] - \Pr[\hat{D}^{\mathcal{A}_u} = 1]| \ge \delta.$$

PROOF. To see that Algorithm 3 is as promised we need to observe that it transforms $(A, Ax+e)$ samples into $(A, Ax + e + Ar) = (A, A(x+r)+e)$ samples, that is, $\mathcal{A}_{x,\mu}$ into $\mathcal{A}_{x+r,\mu}$. On the other hand, $\hat{D}$ transforms $\mathcal{A}_u$ into itself. Hence for any $x \in \{0,1\}^k$ we have

$$\Pr[\hat{D}^{\mathcal{A}_{x,\mu}}(1^n) = 1] = \Pr[r \in_R \{0,1\}^k : D^{\mathcal{A}_{x+r,\mu}}(1^n) = 1] =$$

$$\Pr[r \in_R \{0,1\}^k : D^{\mathcal{A}_{r,\mu}}(1^n) = 1]$$

and

$$\Pr[\hat{D}^{\mathcal{A}_u} = 1] = \Pr[D^{\mathcal{A}_u} = 1]$$

which completes the proof. □

Algorithm 3 $\hat{D}(1^n)$

$r \leftarrow_R \{0,1\}^k$
Collect s oracle samples (A, y).
Simulate D. Answer each oracle query by transforming a sample (A, y) into $(A, y + Ar)$.

REMARK 2. *The size of* $\hat{D}$ *is* $\hat{t} = O(t + sn)$ *when* $\mathcal{A}$ *is a linear uniform output family obtained by our construction.*

LEMMA 13. *Let* $\mathcal{A}$ *be a* $n \times k$ *matrix distribution and assume that there exists a circuit* D *of size* t *making* s *oracle queries such that for every* $x \in \{0,1\}^k$ *it holds that*

$$|\Pr[D^{\mathcal{A}_{x,\mu}}(1^n) = 1] - \Pr[D^{\mathcal{A}_u} = 1]| \geq \delta.$$

Then for $m = \delta^{-2} sk \log k$ *there exists a circuit* $\tilde{D}$ *making* $\tilde{s} = O(km \log m)$ *oracle queries of size* $\tilde{t} = O(t\tilde{s})$ *such that for every* $x \in \{0,1\}^{k+1}$ *it holds that*

$$|\Pr[\tilde{D}^{\tilde{\mathcal{A}}_{x,\mu}}(1^n) = x] \geq 1/2.$$

PROOF. We let x^i denote the vector x after the removal of its i'th coordinate. The main idea is to extract the i'th bit of x by transforming the distribution $\tilde{\mathcal{A}}$ into either $\mathcal{A}_u$ or $\mathcal{A}_{x^i,\mu}$ depending on the value of x_i. Distinguishing between the two cases is then done by simulating D.

We start off by showing that choosing $l = O(\delta^{-2} \log k)$ for Algorithm 4 implies that $\tilde{D}_i(1^n) = x_i$ except with failure probability at most $1/10k$. Let p_u and p_{x^i} denote the values $\Pr[D^{\mathcal{A}_u} = 1]$ and $\Pr[D^{\mathcal{A}_{x^i,\mu}}(1^n) = 1]$ respectively. When $x_i = 0$ we have $y = A_{i,r}x = Ax^i + x_i \cdot r = Ax^i$ and hence $(A, y + r)$ is distributed according to $\mathcal{A}_u$ meaning that p and p' are both estimates of $\Pr[D^{\mathcal{A}_u} = 1]$. By the Chernoff bound taking l as above gives $|p - p'| \geq \delta/2$ (a wrong answer) with probability $O(1/k)$. On the other hand, when $x_i = 1$ we have $y = A_{i,r}x = Ax^i + x_i \cdot r = Ax^i + r$ and hence $(A, y + r)$ is distributed according to $\mathcal{A}_{x^i,\mu}$ meaning that p and p' are estimations of $\Pr[D^{\mathcal{A}_{x^i,\mu}}(1^n) = 1]$ and $\Pr[D^{\mathcal{A}_u} = 1]$ respectively. Another invocation of the Chernoff bound together with the fact that $|\Pr[D^{\mathcal{A}_{x^i,\mu}}(1^n) = 1] - \Pr[D^{\mathcal{A}_u} = 1] \geq \delta$ shows that $|p - p'| < \delta/2$ with probability at most $1/10k$.

A union bound over all $i \in [k+1]$ shows that we can recover x correctly with constant probability. The additional overhead is due to the fact that we need to collect $sl = O(s\delta^{-2} \log k)$ samples for each i. Greedily waiting for the needed sample by collecting at most $\log m$ samples (and outputting a random answer if the needed sample did not appear) adds at most $1/10k$ error probability for each i. □

The following search to decision theorem is a direct consequence of the above lemmas.

Algorithm 4 $\tilde{D}_i(1^n)$

$real, rand \leftarrow 0$
for all $j \in [l]$ **do**
  Collect s samples of the form $(A_{i,r}, y)$.
  Simulate D. Answer each oracle query by transforming a sample $(A_{i,r}, y)$ into $(A, y + r)$
  If D outputs 1 then $real \leftarrow real + 1$
  Simulate D answering oracle queries according to $\mathcal{A}_u$
  If D outputs 1 then $rand \leftarrow rand + 1$
end for
Let $p = \frac{real}{l}, p' = \frac{rand}{l}$ be the estimations of the accept probability of D in the above simulations
Output 1 if $|p - p'| \geq \delta/2$, otherwise output 0

THEOREM 10. *A matrix distribution* $\mathcal{A}$ *is decision secure iff the corresponding distribution* $\tilde{\mathcal{A}}$ *is search secure.*

Theorem 10 will allow us to base our cryptographic applications on an intractability assumption that has a win-win flavor. The exact statement we use is the next corollary.

COROLLARY 11. *Let* $\mathcal{A}$ *be a linear uniform output family for which the function* $f(A, x) = Ax$ *has linear circuit complexity. Then* $\mathcal{A}$ *is decision secure iff* $\tilde{\mathcal{A}}$ *is search secure. Moreover,* $\tilde{\mathcal{A}}$ *is a linear uniform output family and has linear circuit complexity as well.*

5.3 Intractability

In Section 5.4 and Appendix A we give some examples of how LPN based cryptographic constructions can be generalized to any (not necessarily uniform) matrix distribution and consider their instantiation with our new codes as the underlying distribution. The security of these constructions will follow directly from the decision intractability of the underlying codes. The advantage of using our new codes is in that their encoding complexity is linear, resulting in a linear-time implementation of the cryptographic primitive. Since cryptographic constructions can be made more efficient by reducing their level of security, it is important to consider the tradeoff between security and efficiency when comparing different constructions.

For the standard LPN problem, the best known algorithm, due to Blum et al. [8], has time and query complexity $2^{O(n/\log n)}$. When insisting on polynomial query complexity, which is most relevant to cryptographic applications, the best known running time is $2^{O(n/\log\log n)}$ [28, 30]. For constant query complexity, the problem is only known to be solved in exponential time. It seems plausible to conjecture that decoding random codes from our family and from the related family obtained by the security reduction has the same asymptotic hardness as decoding random linear codes. If this conjecture is refuted, this would imply the existence of linear-time encodable *and efficiently decodable* codes that meet the GV bound, which would be quite interesting.

5.4 Symmetric Encryption

DEFINITION 9. **(Symmetric Encryption)** *Let* $l = l(n)$ *be a message length parameter. We say that* $\Pi =$ (GEN, ENC, DEC) *is an* $(s(n), t(n), \epsilon(n))$ *secure stateless symmetric encryption scheme if the following holds:*

- *Correctness. For every n and $m \in \{0,1\}^{l(n)}$ we have*

$$\Pr[k \leftarrow \textsc{Gen}(1^n); c \leftarrow \textsc{Enc}(k,m); m' \leftarrow \textsc{Dec}(k,c) : m = m'] = 1$$

- *Security. For every nonuniform polynomial time adversary D of size at most $t(n)$,*

$$\Pr[\mathsf{E}_\mathsf{D}(1^n) = 1] \le 1/2 + \epsilon(n)$$

where the experiment $\mathsf{E}_\mathsf{D}(1^n)$ is defined as follows:

  - *$D(1^n)$ outputs a pair of messages vectors $\vec{M}_0 = (m_0^1, \ldots, m_0^{s(n)})$ and $\vec{M}_1 = (m_1^1, \ldots, m_1^{s(n)})$ where $m_b^i \in \{0,1\}^{l(n)}$*
  - *$k \leftarrow_R \textsc{Gen}(1^n)$; $b \leftarrow_R \{0,1\}$*
  - *For $i \in [s(n)]$, $c^i \leftarrow_R \textsc{Enc}(k, m_b^i)$*
  - *$b' \leftarrow_R D(c^1, \ldots, c^{s(n)})$*
  - *The output of the experiment E_D is defined to be 1 if $b' = b$, and 0 otherwise*

We construct a symmetric encryption scheme based on the conjectured intractability of decoding our codes. The construction enjoys linear (in the message length) size secret key as well as linear size encryption and decryption circuits and hence may achieve the best efficiecy/security tradeoff currently known for LPN-based symmetric encryption schemes. Our construction is a straightforward generalization from [4] (Construction 7) and [18] (Figure 1) for general matrix distributions.

Construction 2. *Let $\mathcal{L} = (\mathcal{A}^n)_{n=1}^\infty$ be a distribution over $n \times k(n)$ matrices, $l = l(n)$ a message length parameter, $\mu \in (0, 1/2)$ a noise parameter and $\mathcal{G} = (G_n)_{n=1}^\infty$ a family of rate $R_n = l(n)/n$ error correcting codes generator matrices. The private key x is a random k bit vector.*

- *Encryption. To encrypt a message $m \in \{0,1\}^{l(n)}$, choose a matrix $A \in_R \mathcal{A}^n$ and a random noise vector $e \in \mathrm{Ber}_\mu^n$. Output to ciphertext*

$$(A, Ax + e + G_n m).$$

- *Decoding. Given a ciphertext (A, y), apply the decoding algorithm of the code G_n to the vector $y - Ax$.*

We denote this scheme by $\mathrm{SE}(\mathcal{L}, \mu, \mathcal{G})$.

The next lemma ties the security of $\mathrm{SE}(\mathcal{L}, \mu, \mathcal{G})$ with the decision intractability of $\mathcal{L}$. Note that the lemma does not take the scheme's correctness into consideration.

Lemma 14. *Let $\mathcal{L} = (\mathcal{A}^n)_{n=1}^\infty$ be a family of $n \times Rn$ distributions, $\mu \in (0, 1/2)$ be a noise parameter and $\Pi = \mathrm{SE}(\mathcal{L}, \mu, \mathcal{G})$ such that $\mathcal{G}$ is encodable in time $t'(n)$. Let D be an adversary of size $t(n)$ making $s(n)$ oracle queries such that for infinitely many n*

$$\Pr[\mathsf{E}_\mathsf{D}(1^n) = 1] > 1/2 + \epsilon(n).$$

Then there exists an adversary D' of size $O(t(n) + s(n) \cdot t'(n))$ making $s(n)$ oracle queries such that for infinitely many n

$$\Pr[x \in_R \{0,1\}^k : D'^{\mathcal{A}_{x,\mu}}(1^n) = 1] - \Pr[D'^{\mathcal{A}_u} = 1] > \epsilon(n).$$

Proof. We define an adversary D' having oracle access to samples of the form (A, y) to simulate D with $\vec{c} = ((A_1, y_1 + G_n m_b^1), \ldots, (A_t, y_t + G_n m_b^{s(n)}))$ where b is a random bit and all the (A_i, y_i) are fresh oracle samples.

One can check that

$$\Pr[x \in_R \{0,1\}^k : D'^{\mathcal{A}_{x,\mu}}(1^n) = 1] = \Pr[\mathsf{E}_\mathsf{D}(1^n) = 1] > 1/2 + \epsilon(n),$$

whereas

$$\Pr[D'^{\mathcal{A}_u} = 1] = 1/2.$$

Putting the two together we get that for infinitely many n

$$\Pr[x \in_R \{0,1\}^k : D'^{\mathcal{A}_{x,\mu}}(1^n) = 1] - \Pr[D'^{\mathcal{A}_u} = 1] > \epsilon(n).$$

□

By plugging in our new family of codes we obtain a new symmetric encryption scheme candidate enjoying the best known efficiency/security tradeoff.

Theorem 12. **(Symmetric Encryption)** *For $R, \mu \in (0,1)$, let $\mathcal{A}^n$ be the linear uniform output family over $n \times Rn$ matrices obtained via Construction 1 and let $\mathcal{L} = (\mathcal{A}^n)_{n=1}^\infty$. Let $l(n) = n/\log n$. Suppose that $\mathrm{CODE}(\mathcal{L}, \mu)$ is $(s(n), t(n), \epsilon(n))$ decision secure. Then there exists a symmetric encryption scheme $\Pi = (\textsc{Gen}, \textsc{Enc}, \textsc{Dec})$ with message length $l(n)$ and the following properties:*

- *$\textsc{Gen}$, $\textsc{Enc}$ and $\textsc{Dec}$ can all be implemented by a polynomial time uniform family of linear-size circuits.*
- *Π is $(s(n), t(n) - ns(n), \epsilon(n))$ secure.*

Proof. We only need to put all the pieces together. Let $\mathcal{C}$ be Spielman's code CODES96, which can be used to encode and decode messages of length $l(n)$ using circuits of size $O(n)$. Let $\Pi = \mathrm{SE}(\mathcal{L}, \mu, \mathcal{G})$ be the symmetric encryption scheme obtained by applying construction 2 to $\mathcal{L}$ and $\mathcal{G}$. The security of the scheme follows directly from Lemma 14 and the assertions on $\textsc{Gen}, \textsc{Enc}, \textsc{Dec}$ follow from the properties of our linear uniform output family and the properties of $\mathcal{C}$. □

The following corollary states the best asymptotic security/efficiency tradeoffs one could hope for given the best known LPN attacks [8, 28, 30]. We are not aware of any candidate constructions of symmetric encryption schemes from the literature (including heuristic ones) that may achieve similar tradeoffs.

Corollary 13. *For $R, \mu \in (0,1)$ let $\mathcal{A}^n$ be the linear uniform output family over $n \times Rn$ matrices obtained via Construction 1, and let $\mathcal{L} = (\mathcal{A}^n)_{n=1}^\infty$. Let $l(n) = n/\log n$. Define the function classes $T_1 = 2^{o(n/\log\log n)}$, $T_2 = 2^{o(n/\log n)}$, and $T_3 = 2^{o(n)}$. Suppose that $\mathrm{CODE}(\mathcal{L}, \mu)$ is $(\mathrm{poly}(n), T_1, T_1^{-1})$ [resp. (T_2, T_2, T_2^{-1}), $(O(1), T_3, T_3^{-1})$] decision secure. Then there exists a $(\mathrm{poly}(n), T_1, T_1^{-1})$ [resp., (T_2, T_2, T_2^{-1}), $(O(1), T_3, T_3^{-1})$] secure symmetric encryption scheme $\Pi = (\textsc{Gen}, \textsc{Enc}, \textsc{Dec})$ with message length $l(n)$ such that $\textsc{Gen}$, $\textsc{Enc}$ and $\textsc{Dec}$ can all be implemented by polynomial-time uniform families of linear-size circuits.*

Similar results for the problem of *identification* are described in Appendix A.

6. CONCLUSION AND OPEN QUESTIONS

In this work we put forward a new family of linear codes which shares several useful properties of random linear codes while supporting linear-time encoding. This family yields the first randomized constructions of linear-time encodable codes that meet the Gilbert-Varshamov bound. It also gives rise to several cryptographic applications, including the first nontrivial linear-time secret sharing schemes and new candidate constructions of symmetric encryption and identification schemes which may be conjectured to exhibit better asymptotic efficiency/security tradeoffs than existing candidates.

We leave open several natural questions. A first is to try and gain better understanding of the decoding complexity of codes from our family. Do such codes admit significantly better decoding algorithms than those known for random linear codes? Is there a different (randomized) construction of linear-time encodable binary codes which meet the GV bound and yet support efficient decoding, even only in the presence of a small constant fraction of random errors?

A second question is to get an explicit family of codes which match the parameters of our randomized construction. This question appears to be very difficult even without the linear time encoding requirement. Indeed, obtaining an explicit family of binary codes which meet the GV bound is a longstanding problem, and in fact even the relaxed goal of meeting the GV bound using only $o(n)$ random bits seems challenging. The latter is only known to be achievable under strong derandomization assumptions [13].

The applications of our new codes to complexity-based cryptography mainly rely on the conjectured intractability of decoding and are less sensitive to the exact rate/distance tradeoff. Are there simpler randomized constructions of linear-time encodable codes which may suffice for these applications?

Finally, it may be interesting to extend the application domain of our technique to include linear-time implementations of other pseudorandom objects. In particular, there are several applications of dimension reduction via linear functions (such as the Johnson-Lindenstrauss transform and related problems, cf. [2]) for which no linear-time implementation is known.

Acknowledgements. We thank Venkatesan Guruswami, Elad Haramaty, Swastik Kopparty, Ronny Roth, Shubhangi Saraf, Amir Yehudayoff, and Gilles Zémor for helpful discussions, comments and pointers.

7. REFERENCES

[1] A. V. Aho, J. E. Hopcroft, and J. D. Ullman. *The Design and Analysis of Computer Algorithms.* Addison-Wesley, 1974.

[2] N. Ailon and B. Chazelle. Approximate nearest neighbors and the fast Johnson-Lindenstrauss transform. In *STOC*, pages 557–563, 2006.

[3] N. Alon, J. Bruck, J. Naor, M. Naor, and R. M. Roth. Construction of asymptotically good low-rate error-correcting codes through pseudo-random graphs. *IEEE Transactions on Information Theory*, 38(2):509–516, 1992.

[4] B. Applebaum, D. Cash, C. Peikert, and A. Sahai. Fast cryptographic primitives and circular-secure encryption based on hard learning problems. In *CRYPTO*, pages 595–618, 2009.

[5] J. Baron, Y. Ishai, and R. Ostrovsky. On linear-size pseudorandom generators and hardcore functions. In *COCOON*, pages 169–181, 2013.

[6] G. R. Blakley. Safeguarding cryptographic keys. In *Proceedings of the 1979 AFIPS National Computer Conference*, pages 313–317, Monval, NJ, USA, 1979. AFIPS Press.

[7] A. Blum, M. L. Furst, M. J. Kearns, and R. J. Lipton. Cryptographic primitives based on hard learning problems. In *CRYPTO*, pages 278–291, 1993.

[8] A. Blum, A. Kalai, and H. Wasserman. Noise-tolerant learning, the parity problem, and the statistical query model. *J. ACM*, 50(4):506–519, 2003.

[9] R. B. Boppana and M. Sipser. The complexity of finite functions. In *Handbook of Theoretical Computer Science, Volume A: Algorithms and Complexity (A)*, pages 757–804. 1990.

[10] J. L. Bordewijk. Inter-reciprocity applied to electrical networks. *Applied Scientific Research B: Electrophysics, Acoustics, Optics, Mathematical Methods*, 6:1–74, 1956.

[11] M. R. Capalbo, O. Reingold, S. P. Vadhan, and A. Wigderson. Randomness conductors and constant-degree lossless expanders. In *IEEE Conference on Computational Complexity*, page 15, 2002.

[12] H. Chen, R. Cramer, S. Goldwasser, R. de Haan, and V. Vaikuntanathan. Secure computation from random error correcting codes. In *EUROCRYPT*, pages 291–310, 2007.

[13] M. Cheraghchi, A. Shokrollahi, and A. Wigderson. Computational hardness and explicit constructions of error correcting codes. In *Fourty-Fourth Annual Allerton Conference on Communication, Control and Computing*, 2006.

[14] B. Chor, O. Goldreich, J. Håstad, J. Friedman, S. Rudich, and R. Smolensky. The bit extraction problem of t-resilient functions (preliminary version). In *FOCS*, pages 396–407, 1985.

[15] B. Chor, O. Goldreich, J. Håstad, J. Friedman, S. Rudich, and R. Smolensky. The bit extraction problem of t-resilient functions (preliminary version). In *FOCS*, pages 396–407, 1985.

[16] R. L. Dobrushin, S. I. Gelfand, and M. S. Pinsker. On the complexity of coding. *Proc. 2nd Internat. Symp. on Information Theory*, pages 174–184, 1973.

[17] E. N. Gilbert. A comparison of signalling alphabets. *Bell System Technical Journal*, 31:504–522, 1952.

[18] H. Gilbert, M. J. Robshaw, and Y. Seurin. How to encrypt with the LPN problem. In *Proceedings of the 35th international colloquium on Automata, Languages and Programming, Part II*, ICALP '08, pages 679–690, Berlin, Heidelberg, 2008. Springer-Verlag.

[19] V. Guruswami. *List Decoding of Error-Correcting Codes (Winning Thesis of the 2002 ACM Doctoral Dissertation Competition)*, volume 3282 of *Lecture Notes in Computer Science*. Springer, 2004.

[20] V. Guruswami. Introduction to coding theory - lecture notes, 2010.

[21] V. Guruswami and P. Indyk. Expander-based constructions of efficiently decodable codes. In *FOCS*, pages 658–667, 2001.
[22] V. Guruswami and P. Indyk. Efficiently decodable codes meeting Gilbert-Varshamov bound for low rates. In *SODA*, pages 756–757, 2004.
[23] V. Guruswami and P. Indyk. Linear-time encodable/decodable codes with near-optimal rate. *IEEE Transactions on Information Theory*, 51(10):3393–3400, 2005.
[24] N. J. Hopper and M. Blum. Secure human identification protocols. In *ASIACRYPT*, pages 52–66, 2001.
[25] Y. Ishai, E. Kushilevitz, R. Ostrovsky, and A. Sahai. Cryptography with constant computational overhead. In *STOC*, pages 433–442, 2008.
[26] J. Justesen. A class of constructive asymptotically good algebraic codes. *IEEE Trans. Info. Theory*, 18:652–656, 1972.
[27] J. Katz and J. S. Shin. Parallel and concurrent security of the HB and HB+ protocols. In *Proceedings of the 24th annual international conference on The Theory and Applications of Cryptographic Techniques*, EUROCRYPT'06, pages 73–87, Berlin, Heidelberg, 2006. Springer-Verlag.
[28] S. Kopparty and S. Saraf. Local list-decoding and testing of random linear codes from high error. *SIAM J. Comput.*, 42(3):1302–1326, 2013.
[29] H. Krawczyk. LFSR-based hashing and authentication. In *CRYPTO*, pages 129–139, 1994.
[30] V. Lyubashevsky. The parity problem in the presence of noise, decoding random linear codes, and the subset sum problem. In *APPROX-RANDOM*, pages 378–389, 2005.
[31] V. Lyubashevsky and D. Masny. Man-in-the-middle secure authentication schemes from LPN and weak PRFs. In *CRYPTO (2)*, pages 308–325, 2013.
[32] Y. Mansour, N. Nisan, and P. Tiwari. The computational complexity of universal hashing. *Theor. Comput. Sci.*, 107(1):121–133, 1993.
[33] J. L. Massey. *Threshold decoding*. MIT Press, Cambridge, Massachusetts, USA, 1963.
[34] J. L. Massey. Minimal codewords and secret sharing. In *Proceedings of the 6th Joint Swedish-Russian International Workshop on Information Theory*, pages 276–279, 1993.
[35] J. L. Massey. Some applications of coding theory in cryptography. In *Codes and Ciphers: Cryptography and Coding IV*, pages 33–47, 1995.
[36] R. J. McEliece and D. V. Sarwate. On sharing secrets and reed-solomon codes. *Commun. ACM*, 24(9):583–584, 1981.
[37] K. Pietrzak. Cryptography from learning parity with noise. In *SOFSEM*, pages 99–114, 2012.
[38] O. Regev. On lattices, learning with errors, random linear codes, and cryptography. *J. ACM*, 56(6), 2009.
[39] J. E. Savage. *The Complexity of Computing*. Krieger Publishing Co., Inc., Melbourne, FL, USA, 1987.
[40] A. Shamir. How to share a secret. *Commun. ACM*, 22(11):612–613, 1979.
[41] M. Sipser and D. A. Spielman. Expander codes. *IEEE Transactions on Information Theory*, 42(6):1710–1722, 1996.
[42] D. A. Spielman. Linear-time encodable and decodable error-correcting codes. *IEEE Transactions on Information Theory*, 42(6):1723–1731, 1996.
[43] M. A. Tsfasman. Goppa codes that are better than the Varshamov–Gilbert bound. *Probl. Peredachi Inf.*, 18:3–6, 1982.
[44] R. R. Varshamov. Estimate of the number of signals in error correcting codes. *Doklady Akadamii Nauk*, 117:739–741, 1957.

APPENDIX

A. LINEAR-TIME IDENTIFICATION

DEFINITION 10. **(Identification)** *An $(s(n), t(n), \epsilon(n))$ secure identification protocol is a tuple $\Pi = (\text{GEN}, \text{CHA}, \text{RES}, \text{VER})$ where GEN, CHA, RES are PPT algorithms and VER is a polynomial-time algorithm for which the following correctness and security conditions hold:*

- *Correctness. For any secret key and challenge, a response generated with the same secret key is always accepted. Formally:*

$$\Pr[k \leftarrow \text{GEN}(1^n); c \leftarrow \text{CHA}(k); a \leftarrow \text{RES}(c, k) :$$

$$\text{VER}(a, c, k)] = 1.$$

- *Security against passive adversaries. Let O_k denote the distribution over challenge/response pairs (c, a) where $c \leftarrow \text{CHA}(k)$ and $a \leftarrow \text{RES}(c, k)$. For every nonuniform adversary D of size $O(t(n))$ making $O(s(n))$ oracle queries it holds that*

$$\Pr[\mathsf{E}_D(1^n) = 1] \leq \epsilon(n)$$

where the experiment $\mathsf{E}_D(1^n)$ is defined as follows:

  - $k \leftarrow \text{GEN}(1^n)$
  - $c^* \leftarrow \text{CHA}(k)$
  - $a^* \leftarrow D^{O_k}(c^*)$
  - *The output of the experiment is defined to be 1 if $\text{VER}(a^*, c^*, k) = 1$*

Our Identification scheme is in essence a generalization of the well known HB protocol [24] (Protocol 1) for general code families. With resemblance to our symmetric encryption construction, the scheme enjoys linear (in the security parameter) circuit and communication complexities and hence achieves the best efficiency/security tradeoff currently known for LPN-based constructions.

CONSTRUCTION 3. *Let $\mathcal{L} = (\mathcal{A}^n)_{n=1}^{\infty}$ be a distribution over $n \times k(n)$ matrices and $\mu \in (0, 1/2)$ a noise parameter. We define the scheme $\text{HB}(\mathcal{L}, \mu)$ as follows.*

- $\text{GEN}(1^n)$ *outputs a random* $x \in_R \{0,1\}^{k(n)}$
- $\text{CHA}(x)$ *outputs a random* $A \in_R \mathcal{A}^n$
- $\text{RES}(x, A)$ *outputs* $y = Ax + e$ *where* $e \in \text{BER}_\mu^n$
- $\text{VER}(y, x, A)$ *accepts if* $\Delta(y - Ax) \leq (1 + \epsilon')\mu n$ *where* ϵ' *is a small constant (which exact value is discussed shortly)*

We denote this scheme by $\mathrm{HB}(\mathcal{L},\mu)$. The next lemma ties the security of $\mathrm{HB}(\mathcal{L},\mu)$ with the decision intractability of $\mathcal{L}$.

LEMMA 15. *Let $\mathcal{L} = (\mathcal{A}^n)_{n=1}^{\infty}$ be a sequence of linear uniform output families over $n \times Rn$ matrices and $\mu < H(1-R)/2$ be a noise parameter such that $\mathrm{CODE}(\mathcal{L},\mu)$ is $(s(n), t(n), \epsilon(n))$ decision inractable. Then there exists an $(s(n), t(n), \epsilon(n))$ secure identification scheme $\Pi = (\text{GEN}, \text{CHA}, \text{RES}, \text{VER})$.*

PROOF. Assume towards a contradiction that an adversary D of size $O(t(n))$ making $O(s(n))$ oracle queries exists such that for infinitely many n we have

$$\Pr[\mathsf{E}_\mathsf{D}(1^n) = 1] > \epsilon(n).$$

We define an adversary D' having oracle access to samples of the form (A, y) to simulate D by answering oracle queries with its own oracle samples (A, y).

One can check that

$$\Pr[x \in_R \{0,1\}^k : D'^{\mathcal{A}_{x,\mu}}(1^n) = 1] = \Pr[\mathsf{E}_\mathsf{D}(1^n) = 1] > \epsilon(n).$$

On the other hand, with access to $\mathcal{A}_u$ we provide D with samples (A, r) where r is random and independent of x and hence D has no information about x. Furthermore, from Corollary 6 the challenge A^* defines a code with relative distance greater then $H(1-R) > 2(1+\epsilon')\mu$ except for exponentially small in n failure probability. This means that from D's perspective, the correct response $A^*x + e$ can belong to any of the 2^{Rn} disjoint Hamming balls around codewords A^*x' and thus

$$\Pr[D'^{\mathcal{A}_u} = 1] = 2^{-\Omega(n)}.$$

Putting the two together we get that

$$\Pr[x \in_R \{0,1\}^k : D'^{\mathcal{A}_{x,\mu}}(1^n) = 1] - \Pr[D'^{\mathcal{A}_u} = 1] > \epsilon(n) - 2^{-\Omega(n)}$$

for infinitely many n in contradiction to the assumption that $\mathcal{L}$ is is $(s(n), t(n), \epsilon(n))$ decision intractable. Note that the only constraints on ϵ' are that $\epsilon' > 0$ and $H(1-R) > 2(1+\epsilon')\mu$. □

We now present the main theorem of this subsection

THEOREM 14. **(Identification)** *For $R \in (0,1)$ and $\mu < H(1-R)/2$ let $\mathcal{A}^n$ be the linear uniform output family over $n \times Rn$ matrices obtained via Construction 1 and let $\mathcal{L} = (\mathcal{A}^n)_{n=1}^{\infty}$. Then there exists an identification scheme $\Pi = (\text{GEN}, \text{CHA}, \text{RES}, \text{VER})$ with the following properties:*

- *GEN, CHA, RES and VER can be implemented by a polynomial time uniform family of linear-size circuits.*
- *if $\mathrm{CODE}(\mathcal{L},\mu)$ is $(s(n), t(n), \epsilon(n))$ decision secure then Π is $(s(n), t(n), \epsilon(n))$ secure.*

PROOF. Let $\Pi = \mathrm{HB}(\mathcal{L},\mu)$ be the identification scheme obtained by applying construction 3 to $\mathcal{L}$. The security of the scheme follows directly from lemma 15 and the assertions on GEN, CHA, RES, VER follow from the properties of our linear uniform output family. Finally, an honest identifier responds correctly whenever the weight of the noise e is less than $(1+\epsilon')\mu n$, this does not happen only with exponentially negligible in n probability. For perfect correctness one may choose $e \in \mathrm{BER}_\mu^n$ conditioned on $\Delta(e) < (1+\epsilon')\mu n$. Such a noise distribution is exponentially close to the original one and hence the scheme's security is only negligibly affected. □

COROLLARY 15. *For $R \in (0,1)$ and $\mu \in (0,1)$ such that $\mu < H(1-R)/2$ let $\mathcal{A}^n$ be the linear uniform output family over $n \times Rn$ matrices via Construction 1 and let $\mathcal{L} = (\mathcal{A}^n)_{n=1}^{\infty}$. Define the function classes $T_1 = 2^{o(n/\log\log n)}$, $T_2 = 2^{o(n/\log n)}$, and $T_3 = 2^{o(n)}$. Suppose that $\mathrm{CODE}(\mathcal{L},\mu)$ is $(\mathrm{poly}(n), T_1, T_1^{-1})$ [resp. (T_2, T_2, T_2^{-1}), $(O(1), T_3, T_3^{-1})$] decision secure. Then there exists a $(\mathrm{poly}(n), T_1, T_1^{-1})$ [resp., (T_2, T_2, T_2^{-1}), $(O(1), T_3, T_3^{-1})$] secure identification scheme $\Pi = (\text{GEN}, \text{CHA}, \text{RES}, \text{VER})$ such that GEN, CHA, RES and VER can all be implemented by a polynomial-time uniform family of linear-size circuits.*

Adversarial Hypothesis Testing and a Quantum Stein's Lemma for Restricted Measurements

[Extended abstract]*

Fernando G. S. L. Brandão
University College London
fgslbrandao@gmail.com

Aram W. Harrow
MIT
aram@mit.edu

James R. Lee
University of Washington
jrl@cs.washington.edu

Yuval Peres
Microsoft Research, Redmond
peres@microsoft.com

ABSTRACT

Recall the classical hypothesis testing setting with two sets of probability distributions P and Q. One receives either n i.i.d. samples from a distribution $p \in P$ or from a distribution $q \in Q$ and wants to decide from which set the points were sampled. It is known that the optimal exponential rate at which errors decrease can be achieved by a simple maximum-likelihood ratio test which does not depend on p or q, but only on the sets P and Q.

We consider an adaptive generalization of this model where the choice of $p \in P$ and $q \in Q$ can change in each sample in some way that depends arbitrarily on the previous samples. In other words, in the kth round, an adversary, having observed all the previous samples in rounds $1, \ldots, k-1$, chooses $p_k \in P$ and $q_k \in Q$, with the goal of confusing the hypothesis test. We prove that even in this case, the optimal exponential error rate can be achieved by a simple maximum-likelihood test that depends only on P and Q.

We then show that the adversarial model has applications in hypothesis testing for *quantum states* using restricted measurements. For example, it can be used to study the problem of distinguishing entangled states from the set of all separable states using only measurements that can be implemented with local operations and classical communication (LOCC). The basic idea is that in our setup, the deleterious effects of entanglement can be simulated by an adaptive classical adversary.

We prove a quantum Stein's Lemma in this setting: In many circumstances, the optimal hypothesis testing rate is equal to an appropriate notion of quantum relative entropy between two states. In particular, our arguments yield an alternate proof of Li and Winter's recent strengthening of strong subadditivity for von Neumann entropy.

*A full version of this paper is available at http://arxiv.org/abs/1308.6702.

ITCS'14, January 12–14, 2014, Princeton, New Jersey, USA.

ACM 978-1-4503-2698-8/14/01 ...$15.00.
http://dx.doi.org/10.1145/2554797.2554816.

Categories and Subject Descriptors

G.3 [**Mathematics of computing**]: Probability and statistics; H.1.1 [**Information systems**]: Models and principles—*Systems and information theory*

General Terms

Theory

Keywords

quantum information theory, entanglement testing, composite hypothesis testing

1. INTRODUCTION

Asymmetric hypothesis testing is the problem of distinguishing between two sources where one wants to minimize the rate of false positives (type-1 error) subject to a constraint on the rate of false negatives (type-2 error). In the case of n i.i.d. samples from a classical or quantum source, a central result is the Chernoff-Stein Lemma [11, 13, 1] which states that for any constant bound on the type-2 error, the optimal type-1 error decreases at an exponential rate whose exponent is given by the classical (respectively, quantum) relative entropy. Similar results hold even when we generalize the problem so that the sources are described by an unknown parameter and one needs to design a test that works for any choice of the parameter.

Adversarial hypothesis testing. In the first part of this paper (Section 2), we generalize this problem further to allow the parameter to vary adaptively from sample to sample. Since we will allow the parameter to depend arbitrarily on previous samples, this can be thought of as *adversarial* hypothesis testing. That is, we wish to devise a test that can distinguish between samples from two different sets even against an adversary that can choose the distribution in each round based on which samples have previously been observed.

There are some simple cases where it is not hard to see that this additional power cannot help the adversary. For example, suppose we are given a coin with heads probability p

and wish to distinguish between the cases where $p \in [0, 1/3]$ and where $p \in [2/3, 1]$. It is straightforward to show that this general problem is no harder than simply distinguishing a 1/3-biased coin from a 2/3-biased coin; equivalently, the adversary gains no advantage from the ability to be adaptive. On the other hand, distinguishing between the two settings $p \in \{1/3, 2/3\}$ and $p = 1/2$ is clearly impossible, as the adversary can simply choose with probability 1/2 to flip the 1/3-biased coin, and with probability 1/2 to flip the 2/3-biased coin. The resulting distribution of samples is indistinguishable from the one arising from $p = 1/2$. This stresses the role of *convexity* since even a non-adaptive adversary can simulate a convex combination of distributions by choosing randomly among them.

We will prove in Theorem 2 that this property is sufficient to characterize the optimal error rate for asymmetric hypothesis testing against an adaptive adversary. Specifically, if the two sources vary over convex sets of probability distributions, then the problem is no harder than in the i.i.d. case. Our Theorem 6 also establishes a version of this claim for symmetric hypothesis testing. These two results can be thought of as adversarial versions of the classic Chernoff-Stein Lemma and Chernoff Theorem, respectively.

Quantum hypothesis testing, entanglement, and additivity. One of our main applications for our adversarial Chernoff-Stein Lemma is in quantum hypothesis testing, when the states to be distinguished need not be i.i.d. Indeed, a recurrent challenge in quantum information theory is that even apparently i.i.d. problems can involve complicated entangled states (meaning that they cannot be written as a convex combination of independent states). For example, the quantum capacity of an i.i.d channel requires maximizing over all n-component inputs, and in general it is known that achieving the capacity requires using states that are entangled across channel uses [14, 17]. This phenomenon in quantum information theory—where information-theoretic quantities for n copies of a system are not simply n times the one-copy quantity—is known generally as the "additivity" problem.

A similar additivity problem arises in quantum hypothesis testing when we wish to distinguish many copies of a fixed state against a family of states that include non-i.i.d. states. One important example is the *relative entropy of entanglement* E_R, which is a method of quantifying the entanglement in a state ρ as the minimum of its relative entropy with respect to any separable (i.e. non-entangled) state. Here, ρ is a multipartite state (e.g., shared between systems A, B, C) and separability refers to this partition. However, to establish the asymptotic hypothesis testing rate of ρ against separable states, we need to compare n copies of ρ against states that are separable with respect to our original partition, but not necessarily across the different copies. In our example, $\rho^{\otimes n}$ lives on systems $A_1, B_1, C_1, \ldots, A_n, B_n, C_n$ and we need to compare against states that are separable across the $A_1 \ldots A_n : B_1 \ldots, B_n : C_1 \ldots C_n$ partition, but possibly entangled within the $A_1, \ldots, A_n$ systems (and the $B_1, \ldots, B_n$ and $C_1, \ldots, C_n$ systems). Indeed, such entanglement across copies is known to be necessary to compute the relative entropy of entanglement, since examples exist [39] where $E_R(\rho \otimes \rho) < 2E_R(\rho)$.

Restricted measurements. A further difficulty arises in the quantum setting when we consider restricted families of measurements, such as those arising from locality restrictions. Here, too, the optimal measurement can be entangled across copies. Moreover, since the hypothesis testing problem involves maximizing distinguishability over allowable measurements and minimizing over states, it is possible for entanglement to either increase or decrease the rate.

One particularly relevant example for our work involves distinguishing many copies of a state ρ against a general separable state, using measurements from a class (such as 1-LOCC, defined below) which preserves the set of separable states. This distinguishability scenario was studied extensively in [33, 9, 25, 8]. Though it may initially seem to be an obscure question, it has found applications to understanding the quantum conditional mutual information [9], to channel coding [28], and to classical algorithms for separability testing [10] and the small-set expansion problem [2].

The main result of Section 3 provides quantum versions of the Chernoff-Stein Lemma and Chernoff's theorem for restricted measurements. The main idea is that the deleterious effects of entanglement in this setting are no worse than what could be achieved by an adaptive adversary. Thus quantum analogues follow as a corollary of our classical results. One application of these results is an alternate proof of the improved strong subadditivity inequality of Li and Winter [25].

2. HYPOTHESIS TESTING AGAINST AN ADAPTIVE ADVERSARY

2.1 Asymmetric hypothesis testing

Fix two distributions p and q over a finite domain Ω. Given i.i.d. samples $X_1, X_2, \ldots, X_n$ from a distribution $r \in \{p, q\}$, the goal is to design a test which distinguishes the two possibilities based on the sample. The classical *Chernoff-Stein Lemma* characterizes the optimal exponential rate of error decay achievable in the one-sided error setting.

Consider any acceptance region $A_n \subseteq \Omega^n$ and the corresponding error probabilities $\alpha_n = p^n(A_n^c)$ and $\beta_n = q^n(A_n)$, where we use S^c to denote the complement of a set S. Then for $0 < \varepsilon < 1$, define

$$\beta_n^\varepsilon := \min_{\substack{A_n \subseteq \Omega^n \\ \alpha_n < \varepsilon}} \beta_n .$$

We define the optimal error exponent by

$$\mathcal{E}(p, q) := \lim_{\varepsilon \to 0} \lim_{n \to \infty} \frac{-\log \beta_n^\varepsilon}{n} .$$

The following well-known lemma characterizes $\mathcal{E}$ in terms of the relative entropy (see, e.g., Theorem 11.8.3 of [13]).

LEMMA 1 (CHERNOFF-STEIN LEMMA). *Consider any two distributions p and q over a finite domain Ω with $D(p \,\|\, q) < \infty$. Then $\mathcal{E}(p, q) = D(p \,\|\, q)$.*

Here, $D(p \,\|\, q)$ is the *relative entropy*, given by

$$D(p \,\|\, q) := \sum_{x \in \Omega} p(x) \log \frac{p(x)}{q(x)} ,$$

and we take $D(p \,\|\, q) := \infty$ when there is an $x \in \Omega$ such that $p(x) \neq 0$ but $q(x) = 0$.

The adaptive setting. Suppose now that $P, Q \subseteq \mathbb{R}^\Omega$ are closed, convex sets of probability distributions. An *adaptive*

P-*strategy* $\hat{p}$ is a collection of functions $\{\hat{p}_k : \Omega^{k-1} \to P : k = 1, 2, \ldots\}$. Let $\mathcal{A}(P)$ denote the set of all adaptive P-strategies. For $x \in \Omega^n$, we denote

$$\hat{p}(x) := \prod_{k=1}^{n} \hat{p}_k(x_1, \ldots, x_{k-1})(x_k).$$

As before, let $A_n \subseteq \Omega^n$ be an acceptance region, but now we define

$$\alpha_n := \sup_{\hat{p} \in \mathcal{A}(P)} \hat{p}(A_n^c),$$

and

$$\beta_n^\varepsilon := \min_{\substack{A_n \subseteq \Omega^n \\ \alpha_n < \varepsilon}} \sup_{\hat{q} \in \mathcal{A}(Q)} \hat{q}(A_n).$$

We denote the *adversarial one-sided error exponent* by

$$\mathcal{E}_{\mathrm{adv}}(P, Q) := \lim_{\varepsilon \to 0} \lim_{n \to \infty} \frac{-\log \beta_n^\varepsilon}{n}.$$

Observe that for single distributions $p, q \in \mathbb{R}^\Omega$, we have $\mathcal{E}_{\mathrm{adv}}(\{p\}, \{q\}) = \mathcal{E}(p, q)$.

THEOREM 2 (ADVERSARIAL CHERNOFF-STEIN). *Let Ω be a finite domain. For any closed, convex sets of probability distributions $P, Q \subseteq \mathbb{R}^\Omega$, we have*

$$\mathcal{E}_{\mathrm{adv}}(P, Q) = \min_{p \in P, q \in Q} D(p \,\|\, q) \tag{1}$$

whenever the right-hand side is finite.

Thus in the asymptotic regime, adversarial adaptive hypothesis testing is no harder than the i.i.d. setting. Indeed, the hypothesis test used is a simple Neyman-Pearson test for p, q minimizing the RHS of (1). This result was previously known in the non-adaptive case, where it is sometimes referred to as *composite hypothesis testing* [23].

PROOF. Let $p^* \in P$ and $q^* \in Q$ be the minimizers of $D(p \,\|\, q)$ as p and q vary over P and Q, respectively. We assume they exist and that $0 < D(p^* \,\|\, q^*) < \infty$, else the theorem is vacuously true. By considering non-adaptive strategies that simply play p^* and q^* in each coordinate, one sees that

$$\mathcal{E}_{\mathrm{adv}}(P, Q) \le \mathcal{E}_{\mathrm{adv}}(\{p^*\}, \{q^*\}) = \mathcal{E}(p^*, q^*) = D(p^* \,\|\, q^*),$$

where the last equality is Lemma 1. Thus we need only prove that $\mathcal{E}_{\mathrm{adv}}(P, Q) \ge D(p^* \,\|\, q^*)$.

To this end, for $n \in \mathbb{N}$ and $0 < \varepsilon$, we define an acceptance region

$$A_{n,\varepsilon} = \left\{ x \in \Omega^n : \log \frac{p^*(x_1)p^*(x_2)\cdots p^*(x_n)}{q^*(x_1)q^*(x_2)\cdots q^*(x_n)} \ge n(D(p^* \,\|\, q^*) - \varepsilon) \right\}.$$

Our first goal is to argue that, for every adaptive P-strategy $\hat{p}$, and every $\varepsilon > 0$, we have

$$\lim_{n \to \infty} \hat{p}(A_{n,\varepsilon}) = 1. \tag{2}$$

We will then show that for any adaptive Q-strategy $\hat{q}$, we have

$$\hat{q}(A_{n,\varepsilon}) \le e^{-n(D(p^* \,\|\, q^*) - \varepsilon)}. \tag{3}$$

Once these are proved, letting $\varepsilon \to 0$ yields the desired claim.

Toward proving (2), observe that, for every $\varepsilon > 0$, $\lim_{n \to \infty} (p^*)^n(A_{n,\varepsilon}) = 1$ by the law of large numbers. The following lemma will imply that the same is true for $\hat{p}$.

LEMMA 3. *For any $p \in P$, we have*

$$\sum_{x \in \Omega} p(x) \log \frac{p^*(x)}{q^*(x)} \ge \sum_{x \in \Omega} p^*(x) \log \frac{p^*(x)}{q^*(x)}.$$

PROOF. By Theorem 11.6.1 in [13], we have

$$D(p \,\|\, q^*) \ge D(p \,\|\, p^*) + D(p^* \,\|\, q^*).$$

Observing that $D(p \,\|\, q^*) - D(p \,\|\, p^*) = \sum_{x \in \Omega} p(x) \log \frac{p^*(x)}{q^*(x)}$, we see that this is precisely the desired inequality. □

Now, for $x \in \Omega$, let $L(x) = \log \frac{p^*(x)}{q^*(x)}$. The preceding lemma states that for any $p \in P$, we have

$$\mathbb{E}_p[L(x)] \ge \mathbb{E}_{p^*}[L(x)] = D(p^* \,\|\, q^*). \tag{4}$$

Consider a sequence of random variables $\{X_k\}$ distributed according to $\hat{p}$ (in other words, X_k is sampled according to the measure $\hat{p}_k(X_1, X_2, \ldots, X_{k-1})$), and the corresponding martingale difference sequence

$$D_k := L(X_k) - \mathbb{E}[L(X_k) \mid X_1, \ldots, X_{k-1}].$$

Since the differences are uniformly bounded, Chebyshev's inequality implies that for any $\varepsilon > 0$,

$$\lim_{n \to \infty} \mathbb{P}\left(\sum_{k=1}^{n} D_k \ge -\varepsilon n \right) = 1. \tag{5}$$

On the other hand, (4) implies that for each k, one has $\mathbb{E}[L(X_k) \mid X_1, \ldots, X_{k-1}] \ge D(p^* \,\|\, q^*)$. Combining this with (5) yields

$$\lim_{n \to \infty} \hat{p}(A_{n,\varepsilon}) = \lim_{n \to \infty} \mathbb{P}\left(\sum_{k=1}^{n} L(X_k) \ge n(D(p^* \,\|\, q^*) - \varepsilon) \right)$$
$$\ge \lim_{n \to \infty} \mathbb{P}\left(\sum_{k=1}^{n} D_k \ge -\varepsilon n \right) = 1,$$

confirming (2).

We now turn to verifying (3).

LEMMA 4. *For any $q \in Q$, we have*

$$\sum_{x \in \Omega} q(x) \frac{p^*(x)}{q^*(x)} \le 1.$$

PROOF. For $\lambda \in [0, 1]$, write $q_\lambda = \lambda q + (1 - \lambda) q^*$. Since q^* is the minimizer of $D(p^* \,\|\, q)$ for q in the convex set Q, we know that the derivative of $D(p^* \,\|\, q_\lambda)$ at $\lambda = 0$ is non-negative.

Calculate

$$\begin{aligned} \frac{d}{d\lambda} D(p^* \,\|\, q_\lambda) &= \sum_{x \in \Omega} p^*(x) \frac{d}{d\lambda} \log \frac{p^*(x)}{q_\lambda(x)} \\ &= -\sum_{x \in \Omega} p^*(x) \frac{d}{d\lambda} \log \left(\frac{\lambda q(x) + (1 - \lambda) q^*(x)}{p^*(x)} \right) \\ &= -\sum_{x \in \Omega} p^*(x) \frac{q(x) - q^*(x)}{\lambda q(x) + (1 - \lambda) q^*(x)}. \end{aligned}$$

Using the fact that the derivative is non-negative at $\lambda = 0$ yields

$$\sum_{x \in \Omega} \frac{p^*(x) q^*(x)}{q^*(x)} \ge \sum_{i=1}^{k} \frac{p^*(x) q(x)}{q^*(x)},$$

but the left-hand side is equal to 1, yielding the desired result. □

With the preceding lemma in hand, we finish the proof of (3). Fix some adaptive Q-strategy $\hat{q}$. By Markov's inequality,

$$\hat{q}(A_{n,\varepsilon}) \leq e^{-n(D(p^* \| q^*)-\varepsilon)} \mathbb{E}_{\hat{q}} \left[\frac{p^*(x_1)\cdots p^*(x_n)}{q^*(x_1)\cdots q^*(x_n)} \right]. \quad (6)$$

We now use the fact that, by Lemma 4, the sequence of likelihood ratios $\prod_{i=1}^n \frac{p^*(x_i)}{q^*(x_i)}$ is a supermartingale with respect to $\hat{q}$. In particular,

$$\begin{aligned}
&\mathbb{E}_{\hat{q}} \left[\frac{p^*(x_1)\cdots p^*(x_n)}{q^*(x_1)\cdots q^*(x_n)} \right] \\
&= \mathbb{E}_{\hat{q}} \left[\frac{p^*(x_1)\cdots p^*(x_{n-1})}{q^*(x_1)\cdots q^*(x_{n-1})} \mathbb{E}_{\hat{q}_n(x_1,x_2,\ldots,x_{n-1})} \frac{p^*(x)}{q^*(x)} \right] \\
&\leq \mathbb{E}_{\hat{q}} \left[\frac{p^*(x_1)\cdots p^*(x_{n-1})}{q^*(x_1)\cdots q^*(x_{n-1})} \right] \\
&\leq \cdots \\
&\leq 1,
\end{aligned}$$

where in the third line we have applied Lemma 4 to the distribution $\hat{q}_n(x_1, x_2, \ldots, x_{n-1}) \in Q$, and then we have continued by induction. Combining this with (6) completes our verification of (3) and hence our proof of the theorem.

2.2 Chernoff information and symmetric hypothesis testing

Suppose again that we have two distributions p and q over a finite domain Ω. We also have n i.i.d. samples $X_1, X_2, \ldots, X_n$ from a distribution $r \in \{p, q\}$, and a Bayesian hypothesis: The samples come from p with probability π_p and from q with probability π_q. Consider a test $T_n \subseteq \Omega^n$. If $(X_1, X_2, \ldots, X_n) \in T_n$, we declare that the sample came from p.

Our goal is to minimize the expected error

$$\delta_n(T_n) := \pi_p \, p^n(T_n^c) + \pi_q \, q^n(T_n) .$$

In this case, the best achievable error exponent is

$$\gamma(p,q) := \lim_{n\to\infty} -\frac{1}{n} \min_{T_n \subseteq \Omega^n} \log \delta_n(T_n) .$$

Observe that the constants π_p and π_q do not affect $\gamma(p,q)$.

For $\lambda \in [0,1]$, let us define

$$\Gamma^\lambda(p,q) := -\log \sum_{x\in\Omega} p(x)^\lambda q(x)^{1-\lambda} ,$$

and for p and q distinct, let $\lambda(p,q)$ be the value of $\lambda \in [0,1]$ that maximizes $\Gamma^\lambda(p,q)$. Finally, put $\Gamma^*(p,q) := \Gamma^{\lambda(p,q)}(p,q)$. We have the following characterization due to Chernoff (see, e.g., Theorem 11.9.1 of [13]).

THEOREM 5. *For any distributions p and q, one has*

$$\gamma(p,q) = \Gamma^*(p,q) = D(r \,\|\, q) = D(p \,\|\, r) ,$$

where r is the distribution given by

$$r(x) := \frac{p(x)^{\lambda(p,q)} q(x)^{1-\lambda(p,q)}}{\sum_{y\in\Omega} p(y)^{\lambda(p,q)} q(y)^{1-\lambda(p,q)}}$$

We will prove a corresponding theorem in the adaptive setting. To this end consider again two closed, convex sets of distributions $P, Q \subseteq \mathbb{R}^\Omega$. Define the *adversarial two-sided error exponent*

$$\gamma_{\text{adv}}(P,Q) := \lim_{n\to\infty} -\frac{1}{n} \min_{T_n \subseteq \Omega^n} \max_{\hat{p},\hat{q}} \log\left(\hat{p}(T_n^c) + \hat{q}(T_n)\right)$$

where the maximum is over all adaptive P-strategies $\hat{p}$ and adaptive Q-strategies $\hat{q}$.

THEOREM 6 (ADVERSARIAL CHERNOFF THEOREM). *For any finite domain Ω and closed, convex sets of distributions $P, Q \subseteq \mathbb{R}^\Omega$, we have*

$$\gamma_{\text{adv}}(P,Q) = \min_{p\in P, q\in Q} \Gamma^*(p,q) .$$

PROOF. Assume P and Q are disjoint, since otherwise both $\gamma_{\text{adv}}(P,Q)$ and $\Gamma^*(P,Q)$ are trivially equal to zero. Let $p^* \in P$ and $q^* \in Q$ denote the minimizers of $\Gamma^*(p,q)$ and put $\lambda^* = \lambda(p,q)$. First, we have

$$\gamma_{\text{adv}}(P,Q) \leq \gamma_{\text{adv}}(\{p^*\},\{q^*\}) = \gamma(p^*,q^*) = \Gamma^*(p^*,q^*) ,$$

where the latter equality is given by Theorem 6. Thus we are left to prove $\gamma_{\text{adv}}(P,Q) \geq \Gamma^*(p^*,q^*)$.

To this end, for $n \in \mathbb{N}$, define

$$T_n := \left\{ x \in \Omega_n : \prod_{i=1}^n p^*(x_i) \geq \prod_{i=1}^n q^*(x_i) \right\} .$$

Fix also an adaptive P-strategy $\hat{p}$ and an adaptive Q-strategy $\hat{q}$. We will show that

$$\lim_{n\to\infty} \frac{-\log(\hat{p}(T_n^c) + \hat{q}(T_n))}{n} \leq \Gamma^*(p^*,q^*) . \quad (7)$$

We will need to employ the following easy variant of the "envelope theorem."

LEMMA 7. *Consider a differentiable function $f : [0,1]^2 \to \mathbb{R}$. Define $V(t) = \inf_{\lambda\in[0,1]} f(\lambda,t)$ and suppose that for every $t \in [0,1]$, there is a unique $\lambda^*(t) \in (0,1)$ such that $V(t) = f(\lambda^*(t),t)$. If λ^* is differentiable at $t \in [0,1]$, then $V'(t) = f_2(\lambda^*(t),t)$ where f_2 is the partial derivative of f with respect to its second argument.*

PROOF. Let f_1 denote the partial derivative of f with respect to its first argument. Writing $V(t) = f(\lambda^*(t),t)$ and applying the chain rule yields

$$V'(t) = f_2(\lambda^*(t),t) + f_1(\lambda^*(t),t)\frac{d}{dt}\lambda^*(t).$$

The second term is zero because $f_1(\lambda^*(t),t) = 0$ by optimality of $\lambda^*(t)$. □

REMARK 8. *Observe that if $f(\lambda,t)$ has $\frac{\partial^2}{\partial\lambda^2} f(\lambda,t) > 0$ for some $t \in [0,1]$, then $\lambda^*(t)$ is the unique solution of $\frac{\partial}{\partial\lambda} f(\lambda,t) = 0$ and is differentiable by the implicit function theorem. Note that the assumptions of Lemma 7 can be relaxed considerably; see, e.g., [29, Ch. 3].*

This allows us to prove the following.

LEMMA 9. *For any distribution $q \in Q$, one has*

$$\sum_{x\in\Omega} q(x) \frac{p^*(x)^{\lambda^*}}{q^*(x)^{\lambda^*}} \leq \sum_{x\in\Omega} q^*(x) \frac{p^*(x)^{\lambda^*}}{q^*(x)^{\lambda^*}} .$$

PROOF. For $t \in [0,1]$, define a distribution $q_t := tq + (1-t)q^* \in Q$. Moreover, define a function $f : [0,1]^2 \to \mathbb{R}$ by

$$f(\lambda, t) = \sum_{x \in \Omega} q_t(x)^{1-\lambda} p^*(x)^\lambda .$$

Observe that since $q_t \neq p^*$ for any t, we have

$$\frac{\partial^2}{\partial \lambda^2} f(\lambda, t) = \sum_x q_t(x)^{1-\lambda} p^*(x)^\lambda \left(\ln \left(\frac{p^*(x)}{q_t(x)} \right) \right)^2 > 0$$

for all $t \in [0,1]$ and $\lambda \in (0,1)$. Moreover, for fixed t, the minimum of $f(\lambda, t)$ is achieved for some $\lambda \in (0,1)$.

Let f_2 be the partial derivative of f in its second argument; then one computes:

$$f_2(\lambda, t) = \sum_{x \in \Omega} (q(x) - q^*(x))(1-\lambda) q_t(x)^{-\lambda} p^*(x)^\lambda .$$

If we let $V(t) = \min_{\lambda \in (0,1)} f(\lambda, t)$, then optimality of q^* implies $V'(0) \leq 0$. But now Lemma 7 (in conjunction with Remark 8) yields

$$\begin{aligned} 0 \geq V'(0) &= f_2(\lambda^*, 0) \\ &= \sum_{x \in \Omega} (q(x) - q^*(x))(1-\lambda^*) q^*(x)^{-\lambda^*} p^*(x)^{\lambda^*} . \end{aligned}$$

Rearranging yields the desired claim. □

The preceding lemma shows that the sequence $\prod_{i=1}^n \frac{p^*(x_i)^{\lambda^*}}{q^*(x_i)^{\lambda^*}}$ is a supermartingale with respect to $\hat{q}$. Thus we can write

$$\begin{aligned} &\mathbb{E}_{\hat{q}} \left[\prod_{i=1}^{n} \frac{p^*(x_i)^{\lambda^*}}{q^*(x_i)^{\lambda^*}} \right] \\ &= \mathbb{E}_{\hat{q}} \left[\prod_{i=1}^{n-1} \frac{p^*(x_i)^{\lambda^*}}{q^*(x_i)^{\lambda^*}} \mathbb{E}_{\hat{q}_n(x_1,\ldots,x_{n-1})} \frac{p^*(x_n)^{\lambda^*}}{q^*(x_n)^{\lambda^*}} \right] \\ &\leq e^{-\Gamma^*(p^*,q^*)} \mathbb{E}_{\hat{q}} \left[\prod_{i=1}^{n-1} \frac{p^*(x_i)^{\lambda^*}}{q^*(x_i)^{\lambda^*}} \right] \\ &\leq \cdots \\ &\leq e^{-n\Gamma^*(p^*,q^*)} , \end{aligned}$$

where in the third line we have used Lemma 9 along with the fact that $q = \hat{q}_n(x_1, \ldots, x_{n-1}) \in Q$, and then we have continued by induction.

By Markov's inequality, this implies $\hat{q}(T_n) \leq e^{-n\Gamma^*(p^*,q^*)}$. By the symmetry of the preceding argument with respect to P and Q, the same bound of $\hat{p}(T_n^c) \leq e^{-n\Gamma^*(p^*,q^*)}$ holds for $\hat{p}$. Combining these yields $\gamma_{\text{adv}}(P,Q) \geq \Gamma^*(p^*,q^*)$, completing the proof.

3. DISTINGUISHING QUANTUM STATES WITH RESTRICTED MEASUREMENTS

A central problem in quantum information is to distinguish between a pair of quantum states ρ and σ. Necessary background and definitions for the reader unfamiliar with quantum information theory can be found in Appendix A. As usual, there is a tradeoff between errors of type 1 and 2, i.e., mistaking ρ for σ and vice versa. The quantum Neyman-Pearson lemma states that the optimal tradeoff curve between errors of type 1 and 2 is achieved by choosing

$$\mathcal{M} = \{\theta\rho - \sigma \geq 0\},$$

for some $\theta \geq 0$, where $\{X \geq 0\}$ denotes the projector onto the eigenvectors of X with nonnegative eigenvalue. The estimation strategy is then to perform the measurement $\{\mathcal{M}, I - \mathcal{M}\}$ and guess ρ upon obtaining outcome $\mathcal{M}$ or σ upon obtaining outcome $I - \mathcal{M}$.

One well-known case is when ρ and σ have prior probabilities p and $1-p$, respectively, and we wish to minimize the total probability of error. In this case the optimal $\mathcal{M}$ is given by $\mathcal{M} = \{p\rho - (1-p)\sigma \geq 0\}$, and the probability of error is $\frac{1 - \|p\rho - (1-p)\sigma\|_1}{2}$, where $\|\cdot\|_1$ denotes the Schatten 1-norm. The familiar *trace distance* $\frac{1}{2}\|\rho - \sigma\|_1$ corresponds to the case $p = 1/2$.

We modify this basic problem of state distinguishability in three (simultaneous) ways:

1. We consider only measurements $\mathcal{M}$ from some restricted class M.
2. We allow ρ, σ to be drawn adversarially from some sets R, S, respectively.
3. We consider the asymptotic limit in which M, R, S are replaced by families $\mathbf{M} = (M_1, M_2, \ldots), \mathbf{R} = (R_1, R_2, \ldots), \mathbf{S} = (S_1, S_2, \ldots)$ with M_n, R_n, S_n describing measurements and states on $V^{\otimes n}$. Our goal is then, for each n, to find a measurement $\mathcal{M} \in M_n$ that will effectively distinguish any state $\rho \in R_n$ from any state $\sigma \in S_n$.

These changes render the problem a good deal more abstract, and introduce a large number of new parameters. Thus, it may be helpful to keep in mind a prototypical example that was one of the motivations for this work. For some fixed bipartite state ρ over $A \otimes B$, let R_n be the singleton set $\{\rho^{\otimes n}\}$, and let $S_n := \text{Sep}(A^{\otimes n} : B^{\otimes n})$. This corresponds to studying the asymptotic distinguishability of many copies of ρ from a separable state on the same number of systems. For this special case, we introduce the notation $\boldsymbol{\rho} := (\{\rho\}, \{\rho^{\otimes 2}\}, \ldots)$ and $\mathbf{Sep}(A : B) := (\text{Sep}(A : B), \text{Sep}(A^{\otimes 2} : B^{\otimes 2}), \ldots)$. Where the context is understood, we will often omit the reference to A, B and simply write Sep or $\mathbf{Sep}$. Finally, we will consider a restricted class of measurements $\mathbf{M}$, such as the class of 1-LOCC measurements (as discussed in [33, 9, 25, 8]).

3.1 Background on restricted quantum measurements

We begin by introducing notation, describing known results on restricted-measurement distinguishability, and presenting a few small new results to help clean up the landscape. In Section 3.2, we describe our restricted-measurement version of the quantum Stein's Lemma, and in Section 3.3 we give an application to quantum conditional mutual information.

3.1.1 *Quantum Stein's Lemma*

Let us first introduce some definitions analogous to the classical setup discussed in Section 2. We replace our finite domain Ω with a finite-dimensional vector space V, and denote the set of density matrices over V by $\mathcal{D}(V)$. Often we will be interested in the case where V is a composite system, e.g., a bipartite space $A \otimes B$. If ρ, σ are density matrices on V, then the *relative entropy of ρ with respect to σ* is

$$D(\rho \,\|\, \sigma) := \text{tr}\,(\rho(\log\rho - \log\sigma)) . \qquad (8)$$

If $\ker(\sigma) \not\subseteq \ker(\rho)$, we take $D(\rho \| \sigma) := \infty$.

Following the classical case, we define an *acceptance operator* $\mathcal{M}_n$ (analogous to the acceptance region T_n) to be an operator on $V^{\otimes n}$ satisfying $0 \le \mathcal{M}_n \le I$ (i.e., a POVM element), with corresponding error probabilities $\alpha_n = \operatorname{tr}\left((I - \mathcal{M}_n)\rho^{\otimes n}\right)$ and $\beta_n := \operatorname{tr}\left(\mathcal{M}_n\sigma^{\otimes n}\right)$. Again we can define $\beta_n^\varepsilon := \min\{\beta_n : \alpha_n < \varepsilon\}$ and

$$E(\rho, \sigma) := \lim_{\varepsilon \to 0} \lim_{n \to \infty} \frac{-\log \beta_n^\varepsilon}{n} \tag{9}$$

Hiai and Petz [19] proved the following quantum analogue of Lemma 1:

$$D(\rho \| \sigma) = E(\rho, \sigma). \tag{10}$$

See also [5, 24] for elegant and elementary proofs. The "strong converse" of (10) was proved by Ogawa and Nagaoka [31], and can be thought of as showing that (10) holds when the limit of $\varepsilon \to 0$ in (9) is replaced by any fixed $\varepsilon \in (0, 1)$.

3.1.2 Asymptotic composite hypothesis testing

An important generalization of hypothesis testing is when ρ and σ are chosen from sets $R, S \subseteq \mathcal{D}(V)$, respectively, and we need to design our test with knowledge only of R and S. This problem is known as *composite hypothesis testing* and is closely related to the classical Sanov's theorem. In [4, 18], it is proved that the best error exponent when R is general and S is the singleton set $S = \{\sigma\}$ is given by

$$D(R \| \sigma) := \min_{\rho \in R} D(\rho \| \sigma)\,. \tag{11}$$

One case of particular interest to quantum information is when $\rho \in \mathcal{D}(A \otimes B)$ and S is the set of separable states on $A \otimes B$, i.e., $S = \operatorname{Sep}(A : B)$. The quantity $D(\rho \| \operatorname{Sep}) := D(\rho \| \operatorname{Sep}(A : B))$ is known as the *relative entropy of entanglement* [38] and has been widely studied as an entanglement measure (see, e.g., Table I in [9]); note that it is usually written as $E_R(\rho)$.

One challenge in working with the relative entropy of entanglement is that $D(\rho^{\otimes n} \| \operatorname{Sep})$ will not in general be equal to $n \cdot D(\rho \| \operatorname{Sep})$, reflecting the fact that $\operatorname{Sep}(A^{\otimes n} : B^{\otimes n})$ is larger than the convex hull of $\{\sigma_1 \otimes \cdots \otimes \sigma_n : \sigma_1, \ldots, \sigma_n \in \operatorname{Sep}(A : B)\}$. Intuitively, $\operatorname{Sep}(A^{\otimes n} : B^{\otimes n})$ can be thought of as the set of states on the $2n$ systems $A_1 \ldots A_n B_1 \ldots B_n$ which are separable across the $A_1 \ldots A_n : B_1 \ldots B_n$ cut, but may be entangled arbitrarily among the A systems and among the B systems. This is an example of the quantum-information phenomenon known as the *additivity* problem (see, e.g., [41, 36]).

DEFINITION 1. *Let* $\mathbf{R} = (R_1, R_2, \ldots)$, $\mathbf{S} = (S_1, S_2, \ldots)$, *with* $R_n, S_n \subseteq \mathcal{D}(V^{\otimes n})$. *Then the* asymptotic relative entropy *of* $\mathbf{R}$ *with respect to* $\mathbf{S}$ *is*

$$D(\mathbf{R} \| \mathbf{S}) := \lim_{n \to \infty} \inf_{\substack{\rho \in R_n \\ \sigma \in S_n}} \frac{D(\rho \| \sigma)}{n}. \tag{12}$$

We further define

$$\alpha_n(\mathcal{M}) := \sup_{\rho \in R_n} \operatorname{tr}\left((I - \mathcal{M})\rho\right) \tag{13}$$

$$\beta_n(\mathcal{M}) := \sup_{\sigma \in S_n} \operatorname{tr}\left(\mathcal{M}\sigma\right) \tag{14}$$

$$\beta_n^\varepsilon := \inf\{\beta_n(\mathcal{M}) : \alpha_n(\mathcal{M}) < \varepsilon\} \tag{15}$$

$$E(\mathbf{R}, \mathbf{S}) := \lim_{\varepsilon \to 0} \lim_{n \to \infty} \frac{-\log \beta_n^\varepsilon}{n} \tag{16}$$

Note that the limits of Eq. (12) (resp. Eq. (16)) may not exist, in which case we leave $D(\mathbf{R} \| \mathbf{S})$ (resp. $E(\mathbf{R}, \mathbf{S})$) undefined. See [6] for a discussion of replacing the lim with lim inf or lim sup.

An important special case of Eq. (12) is the *regularized relative entropy of entanglement* [37], which is defined to be $\lim_{n\to\infty} \frac{1}{n} D(\rho^{\otimes n} \| \operatorname{Sep})$, and is normally denoted $E_R^\infty(\rho)$. In our notation this quantity is given by

$$D(\boldsymbol{\rho} \| \mathbf{Sep}), \tag{17}$$

In terms of Definition 1, the result of [4, 18] can be expressed as

$$D(\mathbf{R} \| \mathbf{S}) = E(\mathbf{R}, \mathbf{S}), \tag{18}$$

whenever $\mathbf{R}, \mathbf{S}$ are of the form $R_n = \{\rho^{\otimes n} : \rho \in R_1\}$ and $S_n = \{\sigma^{\otimes n}\}$, for some set R_1 and some state σ. We call results of the form (18) "quantum Stein's Lemmas," because, like the classical Chernoff-Stein Lemma, they give an equality between a relative entropy and an error exponent for hypothesis testing.

A quantum Stein's Lemma has also been proven in the case when $\mathbf{R} = \boldsymbol{\rho}$ for a fixed state ρ and $\mathbf{S}$ is a family of sets. In this case, (18) is proved in [7] in the case where $\mathbf{S}$ is a *self-consistent* family of states, meaning that:

1. Each S_n is convex and closed.
2. There exists a full-rank state σ such that each S_n contains $\sigma^{\otimes n}$.
3. For each $\sigma \in S_n$, $\operatorname{tr}_n \sigma \in S_{n-1}$.
4. If $\sigma_n \in S_n, \sigma_m \in S_m$ then $\sigma_n \otimes \sigma_m \in S_{n+m}$.
5. S_n is closed under permutation.

Some important cases of self-consistent families of states are **Sep** (defined in Section 3.1.1), PPT (defined in Appendix A, although it will not be used in this paper) and $\boldsymbol{\sigma}$ for any full-rank state σ.

3.1.3 Hypothesis testing with restricted measurements

We now introduce the problem of quantum hypothesis testing with restricted measurements. In general, two-outcome measurements on $V^{\otimes n}$ have the form $\{\mathcal{M}, I - \mathcal{M}\}$ where $0 \le \mathcal{M} \le I$. However, it is often useful to consider smaller classes of measurements, such as those that two parties can perform with local operations and classical communication (LOCC).

DEFINITION 2. *Let* $\mathbf{R} = (R_1, R_2, \ldots)$, $\mathbf{S} = (S_1, S_2, \ldots)$, *with* $R_n, S_n \subseteq \mathcal{D}(V^{\otimes n})$, *and* $\mathbf{M} = (M_1, M_2, \ldots)$, *with* M_n *a set of measurements on* $\mathcal{D}(V^{\otimes n})$. *Then the* asymptotic relative entropy *of* $\mathbf{R}$ *with respect to* $\mathbf{S}$ *under measurements* $\mathbf{M}$ *is*

$$D_{\mathbf{M}}(\mathbf{R} \| \mathbf{S}) := \lim_{n \to \infty} \sup_{\mathcal{M} \in M_n} \inf_{\substack{\rho \in R_n \\ \sigma \in S_n}} \frac{D(\mathcal{M}(\rho) \| \mathcal{M}(\sigma))}{n}. \tag{19}$$

We further define

$$\alpha_n(\mathcal{M}) := \sup_{\rho\in R_n} \mathrm{tr}\,((I-\mathcal{M})\rho) \tag{20}$$

$$\beta_n(\mathcal{M}) := \sup_{\sigma\in S_n} \mathrm{tr}\,(\mathcal{M}\sigma) \tag{21}$$

$$\beta_n^\varepsilon(\mathbf{M}) := \inf_{\mathcal{M}\in\mathbf{M}} \{\beta_n(\mathcal{M}) : \alpha(\mathcal{M}) < \varepsilon\} \tag{22}$$

$$E_{\mathbf{M}}(\mathbf{R},\mathbf{S}) := \lim_{\varepsilon\to 0}\lim_{n\to\infty} \frac{-\log\beta_n^\varepsilon}{n} \tag{23}$$

As before, the quantities (19) *and* (23) *are left undefined when the corresponding limit does not exist.*

Following our notation for families of states, we use boldface (e.g. $\mathbf{M}$) to denote families of measurements. In particular, we define $\mathrm{SEP}(A:B)$ to denote separable measurements on $A:B$ (i.e. M of the form $\sum_i X_i\otimes Y_i$ with $X_i, Y_i \geq 0$) and denote the corresponding family by

$$\mathbf{SEP}(A:B) = (\mathrm{SEP}(A:B), \mathrm{SEP}(A^{\otimes 2}:B^{\otimes 2}),\ldots).$$

Again we will often write SEP or **SEP** where the systems A, B are clear from context. Note that $\mathrm{Sep}(A:B)$ and $\mathrm{SEP}(A:B)$ both refer to sets of matrices that can be written as $\sum_i X_i\otimes Y_i$ with $X_i, Y_i \geq 0$; the difference is that Sep refers to density matrices (i.e. matrices with trace one) and SEP to measurement outcomes (i.e. matrices with operator norm ≤ 1).

Another important class of measurements is ALL, which is simply the set of all valid quantum measurements: i.e. $\mathsf{ALL} = \{0 \leq M \leq I\}$. The corresponding family is denoted $\mathbf{ALL}$.

One further definition we will need (following [33], but with different notation) is the idea of a *compatible pair.*

Definition 3. *For* $\mathbf{M}$ *is a collection of measurements and* $\mathbf{S}$ *is a collection of states, we say that* $(\mathbf{M},\mathbf{S})$ *are a compatible pair if applying a measurement in* $\mathbf{M}$ *to a state in* $\mathbf{S}$ *and conditioning on any outcome leaves a residual state that is still in* $\mathbf{S}$*. In other words, for any positive integers* n,k*, applying a measurement in* M_k *to* S_{n+k} *and conditioning on any outcome leaves a state that is still in* S_n*.*

For example $(\mathbf{SEP},\mathbf{Sep})$ is a compatible pair. Our main results (in Sections 3.2 and 3.4) involve compatible pairs, and we also discuss previously known results about compatible pairs in Section 3.1.5.

3.1.4 Relations between distinguishability measures

Finally, we state some known and new results that relate the different versions of $D, E, D_{\mathbf{M}}, E_{\mathbf{M}}$. The following statement is a consequence of the minimax theorem.

Lemma 10. *Let* R*,* S *and* M *be closed convex sets. Then*

$$\max_{\mathcal{M}\in M}\min_{\substack{\rho\in R\\ \sigma\in S}} D(\mathcal{M}(\rho)\,\|\,\mathcal{M}(\sigma)) = \min_{\substack{\rho\in R\\ \sigma\in S}}\max_{\mathcal{M}\in M} D(\mathcal{M}(\rho)\,\|\,\mathcal{M}(\sigma)) \tag{24}$$

The notation $\mathcal{M}(rho)$ refers to the probability distribution of measurement outcomes resulting from applying $\mathcal{M}$ to ρ.

Proof. The proof is an application of Sion's minimax theorem [35]. The function $f(\mathcal{M},(\rho,\sigma)) := D(\mathcal{M}(\rho)\,\|\,\mathcal{M}(\sigma))$ is jointly convex in ρ and σ [27]. However, to apply minimax we also need that it is quasi-concave in the measurement $\mathcal{M}$. In order to do so, we linearize the function in the measurement by maximizing over the set of probability measures on M instead. Let $\mathcal{P}(M)$ be the set of probability measures over M. We have,

$$\begin{aligned}
&\max_{\mathcal{M}\in M}\min_{\substack{\rho\in R\\ \sigma\in S}} D(\mathcal{M}(\rho)\,\|\,\mathcal{M}(\sigma))\\
&\quad= \max_{\mu\in\mathcal{P}(M)}\min_{\substack{\rho\in R\\ \sigma\in S}} \mathbb{E}_{\mathcal{M}\sim\mu} D(\mathcal{M}(\rho)\,\|\,\mathcal{M}(\sigma))\\
&\quad= \min_{\substack{\rho\in R\\ \sigma\in S}}\max_{\mu\in\mathcal{P}(M)} \mathbb{E}_{\mathcal{M}\sim\mu} D(\mathcal{M}(\rho)\,\|\,\mathcal{M}(\sigma))\\
&\quad= \min_{\substack{\rho\in R\\ \sigma\in S}}\max_{\mathcal{M}\in M} D(\mathcal{M}(\rho)\,\|\,\mathcal{M}(\sigma)),
\end{aligned} \tag{25}$$

where the second equality follows from Sion's minimax theorem applied to the function $g(\mu,(\rho,\sigma)) := \mathbb{E}_{\mathcal{M}\sim\mu} D(\mathcal{M}(\rho)\,\|\,\mathcal{M}(\sigma))$, which is linear in μ and convex in (ρ,σ). □

Known facts: The following relations between the quantities have been derived previously.

$$E(\boldsymbol{\rho},\boldsymbol{\sigma}) = D(\rho\,\|\,\sigma) \tag{26}$$

quantum Stein's Lemma [19]

$$D(\{\rho\}\,\|\,S_1) \geq D(\boldsymbol{\rho}\,\|\,\mathbf{S}\}) \tag{27}$$

for $\mathbf{S}$ satisfying self-consistency property (4)

$$D(\mathbf{R}\,\|\,\mathbf{S}) \geq D_{\mathbf{M}}(\mathbf{R}\,\|\,\mathbf{S}) \tag{28}$$

from monotonicity of relative entropy

$$E(\boldsymbol{\rho},\mathbf{S}) = D(\boldsymbol{\rho}\,\|\,\mathbf{S}) \tag{29}$$

for S a self-consistent class [7]

We can, in fact, relate D_{ALL}, D, E using

$$D_{\mathsf{ALL}}(\cdot\,\|\,\mathbf{S}) \overset{(41)}{\geq} E(\cdot,S) \overset{(29)}{=} D(\cdot\,\|\,\mathbf{S}) \overset{(28)}{\geq} D_{\mathsf{ALL}}(\cdot\,\|\,\mathbf{S}) \tag{30}$$

3.1.5 Superadditivity

When we consider families of states and measurements, it is not *a priori* clear whether the distinguishability per system should increase or decrease with the number of systems. We say that a quantity $f(\rho)$ is *subadditive* if $f(\rho_{XY}) \leq f(\rho_X) + f(\rho_Y)$ (e.g., entropy) and *superadditive* if $f(\rho_{XY}) \geq f(\rho_X) + f(\rho_Y)$ (e.g., most entanglement measures). A function f is weakly subadditive (resp. superadditive) if $f(\rho^{\otimes n})$ is $\leq nf(\rho)$ (resp., $\geq nf(\rho)$). If a function is both (weakly) subadditive and superadditive then we say it is (weakly) *additive*.

One of the main results known so far about relative entropy with restricted measurements is due to Piani [33], who used these measures to prove a superadditivity inequality:

$$D(\rho_{XY}\,\|\,S_2) \geq D_{\mathbf{M}}(\rho_X\,\|\,S_1) + D(\rho_Y\,\|\,S_1) \tag{31}$$

for compatible $(\mathbf{M},S)$ [33]

$$D(\boldsymbol{\rho}\,\|\,\mathbf{S}) \geq D_{\mathbf{M}}(\rho\,\|\,S_1) \tag{32}$$

as a corollary of (31) [33]

In fact, Piani's result can easily be improved to show that $D_{\mathbf{M}}(\mathbf{R}\,\|\,\mathbf{S})$ is superadditive whenever $(\mathbf{M},\mathbf{R})$ and $(\mathbf{M},\mathbf{S})$ are compatible pairs.

Lemma 11. *Let* $(\mathbf{M},\mathbf{R})$ *and* $(\mathbf{M},\mathbf{S})$ *be compatible pairs. Then for all* ρ_{XY}

$$D_{M_2}(\rho_{XY}\,\|\,S_2) \geq D_{M_1}(\rho_X\,\|\,S_1) + D_{M_1}(\rho_Y\,\|\,S_1). \tag{33}$$

Moreover,

$$D_{\mathbf{M}}(\mathbf{R} \,\|\, \mathbf{S}) \geq D_{M_1}(R_1 \,\|\, S_1), \tag{34}$$

PROOF. The argument is a direct adaptation of the proof of Theorem 1 in [33].

Let $\rho_{XY}, \sigma_{XY} \in S_2$ be states and $\mathcal{M}_X, \mathcal{M}_Y \in M_1$ optimal measurements for $D_{M_1}(\rho_X \,\|\, S_1)$ and $D_{M_1}(\rho_Y \,\|\, S_1)$, respectively. Let k be the number of outcomes of $\mathcal{M}_X$, and let $e_1, \ldots, e_k$ be an orthonormal basis of $\mathbb{C}^k$. Then:

$$\begin{aligned}
&D\left((\mathcal{M}_X \otimes \mathcal{M}_Y)(\rho_{XY}) \,\|\, (\mathcal{M}_X \otimes \mathcal{M}_Y)(\sigma_{XY})\right)\\
&= D\left(\sum_{i=1}^{k} p_i(\rho_X) e_i e_i^* \otimes \mathcal{M}_Y(\rho_Y^i) \,\|\, \sum_{i=1}^{k} p_i(\sigma_X) e_i e_i^* \otimes \mathcal{M}_Y(\sigma_Y^i)\right)\\
&= D\left(p_i(\rho_X) \,\|\, p_i(\sigma_X)\right) + \sum_{i=1}^{k} p_i(\rho_X) D\left(\mathcal{M}_Y(\rho_Y^i) \,\|\, \mathcal{M}_Y(\sigma_Y^i)\right)\\
&\geq D\left(\mathcal{M}_X(\rho_X) \,\|\, \mathcal{M}_X(\sigma_X)\right)\\
&\quad + D\left(\sum_{i=1}^{k} p_i(\rho_X) \mathcal{M}_Y(\rho_Y^i) \,\|\, \sum_{i=1}^{k} p_i(\rho_X) \mathcal{M}_Y(\sigma_Y^i)\right)\\
&= D\left(\mathcal{M}_X(\rho_X) \,\|\, \mathcal{M}_X(\sigma_X)\right)\\
&\quad + D\left(\mathcal{M}_Y(\rho_Y) \,\|\, \mathcal{M}_Y\left(\sum_{i=1}^{k} p_i(\sigma_X)\sigma_Y^i\right)\right),
\end{aligned} \tag{35}$$

where the first inequality follows from Proposition 1 of [33], the second by definition with $p_i(\rho_X) = \operatorname{tr}(M_X^i \rho_X)$ and $\rho_Y^i = \operatorname{tr}_X(M_X^i \otimes I_Y \rho_{XY})/p_i(\rho_X)$, the third from Lemma 1 of [33], and the fourth from property 2 of Proposition 1 of [33].

Since $(\mathbf{M}, \mathbf{R})$ and $(\mathbf{M}, \mathbf{S})$ are compatible, we can lower bound the last term of (35) by $D_{M_1}(\rho_X \,\|\, S_1) + D_{M_1}(\rho_Y \,\|\, S_1)$, from which (33) follows. (34), in turn, is a direct consequence of (33). □

The preceding lemma says that $D_{\mathbf{M}}(\cdot \,\|\, \mathbf{S})$ is superadditive for compatible pairs $(\mathbf{M}, \mathbf{S})$. The compatibility requirement here is essential. The pair $(\mathsf{ALL}, \mathbf{Sep})$ is not compatible, and here $D(\cdot \,\|\, \mathbf{S})$ is known to be strictly subadditive (i.e. not superadditive) in some cases [39].

On the other hand, $D_{\mathbf{M}}(\cdot \,\|\, \mathbf{S})$ can be strictly superadditive (i.e., not subadditive). Let us consider the simple situation in which $R_n = \{\rho^{\otimes n}\}$ and $S_n = \{\sigma^{\otimes n}\}$. It is a consequence of the quantum Stein's Lemma (10) that

$$D(\rho \,\|\, \sigma) = \lim_{n \to \infty} \frac{1}{n} D_{\mathsf{ALL}}(\rho^{\otimes n} \,\|\, \sigma^{\otimes n}).$$

Thus, any example in which

$$\max_{M \in \mathsf{ALL}} D(M(\rho) \,\|\, M(\sigma)) < D(\rho \,\|\, \sigma) \tag{36}$$

will yield an example in which $D_{\mathbf{M}}(\cdot \,\|\, \mathbf{S})$ is strictly superadditive. In fact, Lemma 1 of [32] states that (36) holds whenever $D(\rho \,\|\, \sigma)$ is finite and $\rho\sigma \neq \sigma\rho$. Thus superadditivity is a generic property of $D_{\mathbf{M}}(\cdot \,\|\, \cdot)$.

3.2 A quantum Stein's Lemma for restricted measurements

The following theorem can be thought of as a Quantum Stein's Lemma for restricted measurements.

THEOREM 12. *For any compatible pairs* $(\mathbf{M}, \mathbf{R})$ *and* $(\mathbf{M}, \mathbf{S})$,

$$D_{\mathbf{M}}(\mathbf{R} \,\|\, \mathbf{S}) = E_{\mathbf{M}}(\mathbf{R}, \mathbf{S}). \tag{37}$$

PROOF. For any positive integer k, let $E_k := D_{M_k}(R_k \,\|\, S_k)$, and choose some $\mathcal{M}_k \in M_k$ achieving the maximum in $D_{M_k}(R_k \,\|\, S_k)$. Let $P := \mathcal{M}_k(R_k)$ and $Q := \mathcal{M}_k(S_k)$. By our choice of $\mathcal{M}$, we have

$$D(p \,\|\, q) \geq E_k \qquad \forall p \in P, q \in Q. \tag{38}$$

Given a state $\rho \in \mathcal{D}(V^{\otimes nk})$, we apply $\mathcal{M}_k$ to each block of k systems, obtaining outcomes $x_1, \ldots, x_n$. Then since $(\mathbf{M}, \mathbf{R})$ and $(\mathbf{M}, \mathbf{S})$ are compatible pairs, the distribution of each x_i, conditioned on any possible value of $x_1, \ldots, x_{i-1}$, is an element of P (if $\rho \in R_{nk}$) or Q (if $\rho \in S_{nk}$). Thus, according to Theorem 2, there is an acceptance region that achieves the rate E_k. Thus

$$E_{\mathbf{M}}(\mathbf{R}, \mathbf{S}) \geq E_k. \tag{39}$$

Since (39) holds for any k, we obtain

$$E_{\mathbf{M}}(\mathbf{R}, \mathbf{S}) \geq D_{\mathbf{M}}(\mathbf{R} \| \mathbf{S}). \tag{40}$$

The reverse inequality can be obtained by the following standard argument: Let $\mathcal{M}_n \in M_n$ be an optimal sequence of measurements in $D_{\mathbf{M}}(\mathbf{R} \,\|\, \mathbf{S})$ and $\rho_n \in R_n$, and $\sigma_n \in S_n$ optimal sequences of states in $E_{\mathbf{M}}(\mathbf{R}, \mathbf{S})$. (Here "optimal" is in the sense of Lemma 10; i.e. $\mathcal{M}_n$ achieves the maximum on the LHS of (24) and ρ_n, σ_n achieve the minimum on the RHS of (24).) Then by monotonicity of relative entropy (see, e.g., [31]),

$$\begin{aligned}
D_{\mathbf{M}}(\mathbf{R} \,\|\, \mathbf{S}) &\geq \lim_{n \to \infty} \frac{D(\mathcal{M}_n(\rho_n) \,\|\, \mathcal{M}_n(\sigma_n))}{n}\\
&\geq -\lim_{n \to \infty} \frac{(1 - \alpha_n(\mathcal{M})) \log \beta_n(\mathcal{M})}{n}\\
&\geq E_{\mathbf{M}}(\mathbf{R}, \mathbf{S}).
\end{aligned} \tag{41}$$

□

This is analogous to the result in [7], which established $E(\boldsymbol{\rho}, \mathbf{S}) = D_{\mathsf{ALL}}(\boldsymbol{\rho} \,\|\, \mathbf{S})$ for self-consistent sets of states $\mathbf{S}$, but incomparable because in general $(\mathsf{ALL}, \mathbf{S})$ will not be a compatible pair.

3.3 Stronger Subadditivity of Quantum Entropy

We now present an application of Theorem 12 to a strengthening of the celebrated strong subadditivity inequality of Lieb and Ruskai for the quantum entropy [26], which can be written as

$$I(A : B \mid C)_\rho \geq 0 \tag{42}$$

where

$$\begin{aligned}
I(A : B \mid C)_\rho &:= H(AC)_\rho + H(BC)_\rho - H(ABC)_\rho - H(C)_\rho\\
&:= H(\rho_{AC}) + H(\rho_{BC}) - H(\rho_{ABC}) - H(\rho_C)
\end{aligned}$$

denotes the conditional mutual information of a state ρ_{ABC}. In what follows we will often omit the subscript ρ when the state is understood. See Appendix A for additional discussion.

In [9], the following lower bound was shown for any state ρ_{ABC}:

$$\begin{aligned}
&I(A : B \mid C) \geq\\
&D_{\mathsf{ALL}}(\boldsymbol{\rho}_{ABC} \,\|\, \mathbf{Sep}(A : BC)) - D_{\mathsf{ALL}}(\boldsymbol{\rho}_{AC} \,\|\, \mathbf{Sep}(A : C))
\end{aligned}$$

Moreover the following inequality was shown

$$D_{\mathsf{ALL}}(\boldsymbol{\rho}_{ABC} \,\|\, \mathbf{Sep}(A:BC)) - D_{\mathsf{ALL}}(\boldsymbol{\rho}_{AC} \,\|\, \mathbf{Sep}(A:C)) \geq E_{\text{1-LOCC}}(\boldsymbol{\rho}, \mathbf{Sep}(A:B)), \quad (43)$$

with 1-LOCC the class of all measurements that can be implemented by quantum local operations and classical communication from Bob to Alice (see Appendix A for the precise definition). This implies that the conditional mutual information is lower bounded by $E_{\text{1-LOCC}}(\boldsymbol{\rho}, \mathbf{Sep}(A:B))$.

In [25] the following strengthening of (43) was obtained:

$$D_{\mathsf{ALL}}(\boldsymbol{\rho}_{ABC} \,\|\, \mathbf{Sep}(A:BC)) \geq D_{\mathsf{ALL}}(\boldsymbol{\rho}_{AC} \,\|\, \mathbf{Sep}(A:C)) + D_{\text{1-LOCC}}(\boldsymbol{\rho}_{AB} \,\|\, \mathbf{Sep}(A:B)), \quad (44)$$

which implies

$$I(A:B \mid C) \geq D_{\text{1-LOCC}}(\boldsymbol{\rho}_{AB} \,\|\, \mathbf{Sep}(A:B)). \quad (45)$$

Theorem 12 shows that (44) is equivalent to (43) and so it can be used in conjunction with [9] to give an alternative proof of (45).

3.4 Symmetric hypothesis testing with restricted measurements

Our main result on symmetric hypothesis testing against an adaptive adversary (Theorem 6) implies a corresponding result for symmetric quantum hypothesis testing. For quantum states ρ, σ, define

$$\Gamma^*(\rho,\sigma) := \max_{0\leq\lambda\leq 1} \Gamma^\lambda(\rho,\sigma) := \max_{0\leq\lambda\leq 1} -\log\operatorname{tr}(\rho^\lambda\sigma^{1-\lambda})$$

$$\Gamma^*_{\mathbf{M}}(\mathbf{R},\mathbf{S}) := \lim_{n\to\infty} \sup_{\mathcal{M}\in M_n} \inf_{\substack{\rho\in R_n\\ \sigma\in S_n}} \frac{\Gamma^*(\mathcal{M}(\rho) \,\|\, \mathcal{M}(\sigma))}{n}$$

$$\gamma_{\mathbf{M}}(\mathbf{R},\mathbf{S}) := \lim_{n\to\infty} \sup_{\mathcal{M}\in M_n} \inf_{\substack{\rho\in R_n\\ \sigma\in S_n}} -\frac{1}{n}\log\operatorname{tr}(\mathcal{M}\sigma + (I-\mathcal{M})\rho)$$

A quantum analogue of the Chernoff Theorem was proven in [1] and in our notation can be expressed as

$$\gamma_{\mathsf{ALL}}(\boldsymbol{\rho},\boldsymbol{\sigma}) = \Gamma^*(\rho,\sigma).$$

Using the same idea behind the proof of Theorem 12, one can prove a restricted-measurement quantum Chernoff Theorem.

THEOREM 13. *If* $(\mathbf{M},\mathbf{R})$ *and* $(\mathbf{M},\mathbf{S})$ *are compatible pairs, then*

$$\gamma_{\mathbf{M}}(\mathbf{R},\mathbf{S}) = \Gamma^*_{\mathbf{M}}(\mathbf{R},\mathbf{S}).$$

The proof is essentially the same as that of Theorem 12 with the adversarial Chernoff-Stein's Lemma replaced by the adversarial Chernoff Theorem (Theorem 6). We omit the details.

3.5 Open questions

Having established a quantum Stein's Lemma for restricted measurements, we would like to know if a strong converse can also be proven, or more generally if we can calculate the error exponent for type-2 error when type-1 error is required to be $< \varepsilon$ for some fixed $\varepsilon \in (0,1)$. The difficulty is that $D_{\mathbf{M}}(\cdot \,\|\, \mathbf{S}) > D_{M_1}(\cdot \,\|\, S_1)$ in general, and we would need to control the rate of convergence as a function of n in the lim used to define $D_{\mathbf{M}}(\cdot \,\|\, \mathbf{S})$.

Like many information-theoretic quantities, $D(\boldsymbol{\rho} \,\|\, \mathbf{Sep})$ and $D_{\mathbf{M}}(\boldsymbol{\rho} \,\|\, \mathbf{Sep})$ (for various natural choices of $\mathbf{M}$) are operationally interesting, but are hard in practice to compute. We would like to know the complexity of estimating them (which is a variant of the usual question about the hardness of testing separability, cf. [16, 10]) and whether good relaxations exist (cf. [3]).

Finally, a major application of restricted-measurement distinguishability is to the related questions of k-extendable states[1], tripartite states with low conditional mutual information (i.e. "approximate Markov states", cf. [20]), and the quality of approximations achieved by the sum-of-squares hierarchy (cf. [2]). A few of the more prominent open questions here are:

- If $I(A:B \mid E)_\rho \leq \varepsilon$ then does there exist an "approximate recovery" map $T: E \to E \otimes B$ such that $(\mathrm{id} \otimes T)\rho_{AE} \approx_\delta \rho_{ABE}$, with $\delta \to 0$ as $\varepsilon \to 0$? (Here we use A, B, E both to denote quantum subsystems and the corresponding vector spaces.) This conjecture is due to Andreas Winter, and would imply an approximate equivalence between k-extendability and low conditional mutual information.

- How large can $D_{\mathbf{M}}(\rho \,\|\, \mathrm{Sep})$ be when ρ is k-extendable and $\mathbf{M}$ is the class of separable measurements? Sharp bounds are known [10] when $\mathbf{M}$ = 1-LOCC, and if they could be extended to separable measurements it would have implications for quantum Merlin-Arthur games with multiple Merlins [16] as well as for classical optimization algorithms.

- The ability of semidefinite programming hierarchies to estimate small-set expansion can be understood in terms of a restricted-measurement distinguishability problem [2]. A major open question is whether small-set expansion on graphs of size n can be well-approximated by $O(\log n)$ levels of these hierarchies, which would imply a quasipolynomial-time algorithm for the problem. Can tools from quantum information shed further light here?

APPENDIX

A. APPENDIX: BACKGROUND ON QUANTUM INFORMATION

This appendix contains a very brief review of the quantum formalism and notation used in this paper. For a much more detailed introduction to quantum information theory, see [40], or for an overview of the field of quantum computing and quantum information more generally see [30, 22].

Density matrices. The quantum analogue of a probability distribution over $[d] = \{1,\ldots,d\}$ is called a *density matrix*, or simply a *state*. Density matrices must be positive semi-definite and have trace one. These conditions are analogous to the requirement that probabilities must be

[1]A bipartite state ρ_{AB} is said to be k-extendable if there exists a state $\tilde{\rho}_{AB_1\ldots B_k}$ such that $\tilde{\rho}_{AB_i} = \rho_{AB}$ for each i. The idea of k-extendability was introduced in [34, 15], where it was proved that for any fixed dimension of A and/or B, the set of k-extendable states approaches the set of separable states. However, the rate of convergence is an open question.

nonnegative and normalized; indeed diagonal density matrices correspond exactly to probability distributions. If A is a complex vector space, then define $\mathcal{D}(A)$ to be the set of density matrices on A, meaning the set of operators on A that are positive semi-definite and have trace one. Let $\mathcal{L}(A, B)$ denote the set of linear operators from A to B, and let $\mathcal{L}(A) := \mathcal{L}(A, A)$.

Tensor product. To describe composite quantum systems, we use the tensor product. The tensor product of a vector $x \in \mathbb{C}^{d_1}$ and a vector $y \in \mathbb{C}^{d_2}$ is denoted $x \otimes y$ and has entries that run over all $x_{i_1} y_{i_2}$ for $i_1 \in [d_1], i_2 \in [d_2]$. Similarly, if X and Y are matrices, then their tensor product $X \otimes Y$ has matrix elements $(X \otimes Y)_{(i_1,i_2),(j_1,j_2)} = X_{i_1,j_1} Y_{i_2,j_2}$. For vector spaces A, B, we let $A \otimes B$ denote the span of $\{a \otimes b : a \in A, b \in B\}$. Note that $\mathbb{C}^{d_1} \otimes \mathbb{C}^{d_2} \cong \mathbb{C}^{d_1 d_2}$. Finally, in each case we use the tensor power notation $X^{\otimes n}$ to stand for

$$\overbrace{X \otimes X \otimes \cdots \otimes X}^{n \text{ times}}.$$

Product and separable states. The tensor product is used to combine quantum states in the same way that independent classical probability distributions are combined to form a joint distribution. Indeed, if p, q are probability distributions of independent random variables, then $p \otimes q$ denotes the joint distribution. Similarly, if ρ and σ are density matrices, then $\rho \otimes \sigma$ denotes the state of a system that is in a so-called *product state*. The convex hull of the set of product states is called the set of *separable states*. We write $\mathrm{Sep}(A : B)$ to indicate the split along which we demand that the states be separable, e.g.

$$\mathrm{Sep}(A : B) = \mathrm{conv}\{\alpha \otimes \beta : \alpha \in \mathcal{D}(A), \beta \in \mathcal{D}(\beta)\}. \quad (46)$$

Although the set $\mathrm{Sep}(A : B)$ is convex, it is not easy to work with. For example, computational hardness results are known for the weak membership problem. Instead, it is sometimes more convenient to consider the relaxation PPT, which denotes the set of states with Positive Partial Transpose. The partial transpose operator Γ (meant to resemble the right half of the T that usually denotes transpose) acts linearly on $\mathcal{L}(A \otimes B)$ by mapping $X \otimes Y$ to $X \otimes Y^T$; equivalently we can write it as $\mathrm{id}_A \otimes T_B$, where id_A is the identity operator on $\mathcal{L}(A)$ and T_B is the transpose operator on $\mathcal{L}(B)$. We define $\mathrm{PPT}(A : B) = \{\rho \in \mathcal{D}(A \otimes B) : \rho^\Gamma \in \mathcal{D}(A : B)\}$. This set is easier to work with because it has a semidefinite-programming characterization. Moreover, it is straightforward to show that $\mathrm{Sep}(A : B) \subset \mathrm{PPT}(A : B)$. However, in general this inclusion is strict, and as the dimensions of A, B grow large, PPT can be an arbitrarily bad approximation for Sep [3].

Partial trace. Another concept from probability theory that we will need to generalize is the idea of a marginal distribution. Say we have a density matrix $\rho_{AB} \in \mathcal{D}(A \otimes B)$. The subscript emphasizes the systems which ρ describes, which are analogous to the random variables corresponding to a probability distribution. To obtain the state on only the A system, we apply the *partial trace* operator $\mathrm{tr}_B := \mathrm{id}_A \otimes \mathrm{tr}_B$ to ρ_{AB}. The action of the partial trace is often denoted by writing only the subscripts, as in

$$\rho_A := \mathrm{tr}_B \, \rho_{AB} \quad \text{and} \quad \rho_B := \mathrm{tr}_A \, \rho_{AB}. \quad (47)$$

(This notation generalizes; e.g. if $\rho \in \mathcal{D}(A \otimes B \otimes C)$, then $\rho_B = \mathrm{tr}_{AC} \, \rho_{ABC} = \mathrm{tr}_A \, \mathrm{tr}_C \, \rho_{ABC}$, etc.) Concretely, $(\rho_A)_{i,i'} = \sum_j (\rho_{AB})_{(i,j),(i',j)}$ and $(\rho_B)_{j,j'} = \sum_i (\rho_{AB})_{(i,j),(i,j')}$. We see that if ρ is diagonal then this coincides with the idea of a marginal distribution from classical probability theory.

Measurements. Although technically all of physics is described by quantum mechanics, it is often convenient to make a distinction between quantum information, which is often carried in very small systems such as single atoms or single photons, and classical information, which is carried in macroscopic systems, such as a bit in a classical RAM. The bridge from quantum state to probability distribution is given by a *measurement* (also sometimes called a POVM), which formally is a collection of matrices $\mathcal{M} = (\mathcal{M}_1, \ldots, \mathcal{M}_k)$ satisfying $\mathcal{M}_i \geq 0$ for each i (meaning each $\mathcal{M}_i$ is positive semi-definite) and $\mathcal{M}_1 + \cdots + \mathcal{M}_k = I$. Performing the measurement $\mathcal{M}$ on state ρ yields outcome i with probability $\mathrm{tr}[\rho \mathcal{M}_i]$. Thus we can interpret $\mathcal{M}$ as a linear map from $\mathcal{L}(V)$ to $\mathbb{R}^k$, with the psd and normalization conditions serving to guarantee that $\mathcal{M}$ maps $\mathcal{D}(V)$ to valid probability distributions.

Measurements on multipartite states. For our purposes, we will consider a quantum state to be destroyed after it is measured. However, if we have a quantum state on multiple systems, such as $A \otimes B$, and we measure only system A, then we will still have a quantum state on system B. In this case, the probability of obtaining outcome i is $\mathbb{P}[i] = \mathrm{tr}[\mathcal{M}_i \rho_A]$ and the residual state in this case is

$$\frac{\mathrm{tr}_A[(\mathcal{M}_i \otimes I)\rho_{AB}]}{\mathbb{P}[i]}. \quad (48)$$

Since $\sum_i \mathcal{M}_i = I$, we can verify that if we average over all measurement outcomes, then system B is left in the state ρ_B, independent of the choice of measurement. This is an important feature of quantum mechanics; despite the possibility of entanglement, there is no way for Alice (who controls system A) to signal to Bob (who controls system B) through her choice of measurement.

Restricted classes of measurements. Consider a bipartite system $A \otimes B$, with systems A, B held by Alice and Bob respectively. Performing a general measurement on $A \otimes B$ may require that Alice and Bob exchange quantum messages, so it is often more practical for them to consider only measurements that they can perform using Local Operations and Classical Communication (LOCC). Although such restricted measurements were initially introduced to model these practical restrictions, they have since arisen in settings such as [9, 25] for completely different reasons. The class LOCC is difficult to work with and is cumbersome to even properly define—see [12] for a discussion—so we will often work with various restrictions or relaxations of it. A restriction which is interesting in its own right is the class 1-LOCC, which corresponds to Alice performing a measurement locally and sending the outcome to Bob. We say that $\mathcal{M} \in$ 1-LOCC if $\mathcal{M} = \{\mathcal{M}_{i,j}\}$ with $\mathcal{M}_{i,j} = X_i \otimes Y_{i,j}$, each $X_i, Y_{i,j} \geq 0$, $\sum_i X_i = I$ and for each i, $\sum_j Y_{i,j} = I$. On the other hand, a useful relaxation is the set SEP, for which each $\mathcal{M}_i$ should have the form $\mathcal{M}_i = \sum_j X_{i,j} \otimes Y_{i,j}$ with each $X_{i,j}, Y_{i,j} \geq 0$. An even further relaxation is PPT for which we demand only that each $\mathcal{M}_i^\Gamma \geq 0$ (apart from the usual conditions that $\sum_i \mathcal{M}_i = I$ and each $\mathcal{M}_i \geq 0$). Finally we use ALL to denote the set of all measurements. Summarizing, we have

$$\text{1-LOCC} \subset \text{LOCC} \subset \text{SEP} \subset \text{PPT} \subset \text{ALL}.$$

In each case, we consider measurements with any finite number of outcomes, so these classes are technically not compact.

Entanglement swapping. An important concept in our work (building on [33]) is that of compatible pairs of families of measurements and states. We say that a measurement outcome $\mathcal{M}_i$ is compatible with a family of states $\mathbf{S}$ if for each n and each $\rho \in S_n$, applying $\mathcal{M}_i$ to the first system leaves a residual state (defined by (48)) that is in S_{n-1}. A family of measurements $\mathbf{M}$ is compatible with $\mathbf{S}$ if each outcome of each measurement in $\mathbf{M}$ is compatible with $\mathbf{S}$. If $\mathbf{S} = \text{Sep}$, then 1-LOCC, LOCC, SEP are all compatible with $\mathbf{S}$. If $\mathbf{S} = \text{PPT}$ then the set of compatible measurements includes PPT. However, it is easy to construct examples of incompatible pairs. Let $e_1, \ldots, e_d$ be an orthonormal basis for $\mathbb{C}^d$ and define $\Psi = \frac{1}{d}\sum_{i,j\in[d]} e_i \otimes e_j \otimes e_i \otimes e_j$. Observe that Ψ has entanglement between systems 1:3 and systems 2:4, but is product across the 13:24 cut. Now consider a measurement acting on systems 12. One can calculate that

$$\operatorname{tr}_{12}[(\mathcal{M}_i \otimes I)\Psi\Psi^*] = \frac{\mathcal{M}_i^T}{d}. \tag{49}$$

Thus, if $\mathcal{M}_i^T$ is proportional to an entangled state, then the measurement can create entanglement on the previous unentangled states 3,4 that were not measured. This phenomenon—in which we start with $A_1 : A_2$ and $B_1 : B_2$ entanglement, measure A_1B_1 and end with $A_2 : B_2$ entanglement—is called entanglement swapping [21] and is one of the main new difficulties encountered in attempting to perform hypothesis testing with respect to classes such as Sep.

Entropy. The classical (Shannon) entropy of a distribution p is given by $H(p) = -\sum_i p_i \log(p_i)$. The quantum analogue is called the von Neumann entropy, and is given by $H(\rho) = -\operatorname{tr}[\rho \log \rho]$. Observe that $H(\rho)$ is the Shannon entropy of the eigenvalues of ρ, and coincides with the Shannon entropy when we consider probability distributions to be diagonal density matrices. If ρ_{ABC} is a multipartite state, then we let $H(A)_\rho := H(\rho_A), H(AB)_\rho = H(\rho_{AB})$, etc. When ρ is understood, we may write simply $H(A), H(AB), \ldots$. Analogous to the classical mutual information, conditional entropy, etc. we can define

$$H(A \mid B) := H(AB) - H(B) \tag{50}$$

$$I(A : B) := H(A) + H(B) - H(AB) \tag{51}$$

$$I(A : B \mid C) := H(AC) + H(BC) - H(ABC) - H(C), \tag{52}$$

in each case with an implicit dependence on some state ρ. Finally, the quantum relative entropy is $D(\rho \,\|\, \sigma) := \operatorname{tr}[\rho(\log \rho - \log \sigma)]$. Many of these quantities behave similarly to their classical analogues, but a number of new subtleties emerge; see Chapter 11 of [10] or Chapter 11 of [30] for more information.

Acknowledgments

We are grateful to Keiji Matsumoto for helpful conversations about hypothesis testing, and AWH and FGSLB also thank the Mittag-Leffler Institute for their hospitality while some of this work was done. FB was funded by EPSRC. AWH was funded by NSF grant CCF-1111382 and ARO contract W911NF-12-1-0486. JRL was supported by NSF grants CCF-1217256 and CCF-0905626.

B. REFERENCES

[1] K. Audenaert, J. Calsamiglia, L. Masanes, R. Munoz-Tapia, A. Acin, E. Bagan, and F. Verstraete. Discriminating states: The quantum Chernoff bound. *Phys. Rev. Lett.*, 98, 2007, arXiv:quant-ph/0610027.

[2] B. Barak, F. G. Brandão, A. W. Harrow, J. Kelner, D. Steurer, and Y. Zhou. Hypercontractivity, sum-of-squares proofs, and their applications. In *Proceedings of the 44th symposium on Theory of Computing*, STOC '12, pages 307–326, 2012, arXiv:1205.4484.

[3] S. Beigi and P. W. Shor. Approximating the set of separable states using the positive partial transpose test. *J. Math. Phys.*, 51(4):042202, 2010, arXiv:0902.1806.

[4] I. Bjelaković, J.-D. Deuschel, T. Krüger, R. Seiler, R. Siegmund-Schultze, and A. Szkoła. A quantum version of Sanov's theorem. *Commun. Math. Phys.*, 260(3):659–671, 2005, arXiv:quant-ph/0412157.

[5] I. Bjelaković and R. Siegmund-Schultze. Quantum Stein's lemma revisited, inequalities for quantum entropies, and a concavity theorem of Lieb, 2012, arXiv:quant-ph/0307170.

[6] G. Bowen and N. Datta. Beyond i.i.d. in quantum information theory, 2006, arXiv:quant-ph/0604013.

[7] F. G. Brandão and M. B. Plenio. A generalization of quantum Stein's lemma. *Commun. Math. Phys.*, 295:791, 2010, arXiv:0904.0281.

[8] F. G. S. L. Brandão and A. W. Harrow. Quantum de Finetti theorems under local measurements with applications, 2012, arXiv:1210.6367.

[9] F. G. S. L. Brandão, M. Christandl, and J. Yard. Faithful squashed entanglement. *Commun. Math. Phys.*, 306(3):805–830, 2011, arXiv:1010.1750.

[10] F. G. S. L. Brandão, M. Christandl, and J. Yard. A quasipolynomial-time algorithm for the quantum separability problem. pages 343–351, NY, USA, 2011. ACM New York, arXiv:1011.2751.

[11] H. Chernoff. A measure of asymptotic efficiency for tests of a hypothesis based on the sum of observations. *The Annals of Mathematical Statistics*, 23(4):493–507, 1952.

[12] E. Chitambar, D. Leung, L. Mancinska, M. Ozols, and A. Winter. Everything you always wanted to know about LOCC (but were afraid to ask), 2012, arXiv:1210.4583.

[13] T. M. Cover and J. A. Thomas. *Elements of Information Theory*. Series in Telecommunication. John Wiley and Sons, New York, 1991.

[14] D. P. DiVincenzo, P. W. Shor, and J. A. Smolin. Quantum channel capacity of very noisy channels. *Phys. Rev. A*, 57:830, 1998, arXiv:quant-ph/9706061.

[15] A. C. Doherty, P. A. Parrilo, and F. M. Spedalieri. Complete family of separability criteria. *Phys. Rev. A*, 69:022308, Feb 2004, arXiv:quant-ph/0308032.

[16] A. W. Harrow and A. Montanaro. An efficient test for product states, with applications to quantum Merlin-Arthur games. In *Proc. 51st Symp. on FOCS*, pages 633–642, 2010, arXiv:1001.0017.

[17] M. B. Hastings. A counterexample to additivity of minimum output entropy. *Nature Physics*, 5, 2009, arXiv:0809.3972.

[18] M. Hayashi. Optimal sequence of quantum measurements in the sense of Stein's lemma in quantum hypothesis testing. *J. Phys. A*, 35(50):10759–10773, 2002, arXiv:quant-ph/0208020.

[19] F. Hiai and D. Petz. The proper formula for relative entropy and its asymptotics in quantum probability. *Commun. Math. Phys.*, 143(1):99–114, 1991.

[20] B. Ibinson, N. Linden, and A. Winter. Robustness of quantum markov chains. *Commun. Math. Phys.*, 277(2):289–304, 2008, arXiv:quant-ph/0611057.

[21] M. Żukowski, A. Zeilinger, M. A. Horne, and A. K. Ekert. "Event-ready-detectors" Bell experiment via entanglement swapping. *Phys. Rev. Lett.*, 71:4287–4290, Dec 1993.

[22] A. Y. Kitaev, A. H. Shen, and M. N. Vyalyi. *Classical and Quantum Computation*, volume 47 of *Graduate Studies in Mathematics*. AMS, 2002.

[23] E. Levitan and N. Merhav. A competitive Neyman-Pearson approach to universal hypothesis testing with applications. *Information Theory, IEEE Transactions on*, 48(8):2215–2229, 2002.

[24] K. Li. Second order asymptotics for quantum hypothesis testing, 2012, arXiv:1208.1400.

[25] K. Li and A. Winter. Relative entropy and squashed entanglement, 2012, arXiv:1210.3181.

[26] E. Lieb and M. Ruskai. Proof of the strong subadditivity of quantum-mechanical entropy. *J. Math. Phys.*, 14(12):1938, 1973.

[27] G. Lindblad. Expectations and entropy inequalities for finite quantum systems. *Comm. Math. Phys.*, 39:111–119, 1974.

[28] W. Matthews and S. Wehner. Finite blocklength converse bounds for quantum channels, 2012, arXiv:1210.4722.

[29] P. Milgrom. *Putting Auction Theory to Work.* Cambridge University Press, 2004.

[30] M. A. Nielsen and I. L. Chuang. *Quantum Computation and Quantum Information.* Cambridge University Press, New York, 2000.

[31] T. Ogawa and H. Nagaoka. Strong converse and Stein's lemma in quantum hypothesis testing. *Information Theory, IEEE Transactions on*, 46(7):2428–2433, 2000, arXiv:quant-ph/9906090.

[32] D. Petz. Monotonicity of quantum relative entropy revisited. *Rev. Math. Phys.*, 15(01):79–91, 2003, arXiv:quant-ph/0209053.

[33] M. Piani. Relative entropy of entanglement and restricted measurements. *Phys. Rev. Lett.*, 103:160504, Oct 2009, arXiv:0904.2705.

[34] G. A. Raggio and R. F. Werner. Quantum statistical mechanics of general mean field systems. *Helv. Phys. Acta*, 62:980–1003, 1989.

[35] M. Sion. On general minimax theorems. *Pacific J. Math.*, 8:171–176, 1958.

[36] G. Smith. Quantum channel capacities. In *Information Theory Workshop (ITW), 2010 IEEE*, pages 1–5, 2010, arXiv:1007.2855.

[37] V. Vedral and M. B. Plenio. Entanglement measures and purification procedures. *Phys. Rev. A*, 57:1619–1633, Mar 1998, arXiv:quant-ph/9707035.

[38] V. Vedral, M. B. Plenio, M. A. Rippin, and P. L. Knight. Quantifying entanglement. *Phys. Rev. Lett.*, 78:2275–2279, Mar 1997, arXiv:quant-ph/9702027.

[39] K. G. H. Vollbrecht and R. F. Werner. Entanglement measures under symmetry. *Phys. Rev. A*, 64:062307, Nov 2001, arXiv:quant-ph/0010095.

[40] M. M. Wilde. *Quantum Information Theory.* Cambridge University Press, 2013, arXiv:1106.1445.

[41] M. M. Wolf, T. S. Cubitt, and D. Perez-Garcia. Are problems in quantum information theory (un)decidable?, 2011, arXiv:1111.5425.

Sequential Decision Making with Vector Outcomes

Yossi Azar
Tel Aviv University
azar@post.tau.ac.il

Uriel Feige*
Weizmann Institute
uriel.feige@weizmann.ac.il

Michal Feldman
Tel Aviv University
mfeldman@tau.ac.il

Moshe Tennenholtz
Microsoft Research, Israel, and Technion
moshet@ie.technion.ac.il

ABSTRACT

We study a multi-round optimization setting in which in each round a player may select one of several actions, and each action produces an outcome *vector*, not observable to the player until the round ends. The final payoff for the player is computed by applying some known function f to the sum of all outcome vectors (e.g., the minimum of all coordinates of the sum). We show that standard notions of performance measure (such as comparison to the best single action) used in related expert and bandit settings (in which the payoff in each round is scalar) are not useful in our vector setting. Instead, we propose a different performance measure, and design algorithms that have vanishing regret with respect to our new measure.

Categories and Subject Descriptors

I.2.6 [**Artificial Intelligence**]: Learning; I.2.1 [**Artificial Intelligence**]: Applications and Expert Systems—*games*; F.2 [**Analysis of Algorithms and Problem Complexity**]: Miscellaneous

Keywords

expert; bandit; vector outcome

1. INTRODUCTION

We consider the following multiround optimization setting. There is one player, m *actions* A_i for $1 \leq i \leq m$ and T *rounds* t for $1 \leq t \leq T$. With every action A_i and round t there is some associated *outcome* of the action for that round, denoted by $O_{i,t}$. The outcome is represented by a vector of dimension d. The values $O_{i,t}$ are a-priori unknown to the player. However, for every t, the outcomes $O_{i,t}$ for all A_i are revealed to the player at the end of round t. The multiround optimization proceeds as follows. In every round t, the player who already observed $O_{i,t'}$ for all $t' < t$ chooses one action, say A_j. Thereafter, the outcomes $O_{i,t}$ of all actions for round t are revealed to the player, and the player accumulates $O_{j,t}$ for the action A_j that was selected in round t. This proceeds for T rounds. After round T, the vector of accumulated outcomes is divided by T (thus averaging over all rounds). Let V denote the resulting vector. The goal of the player is to achieve a most favorable vector V. The quality of vectors is measured using a value function f. Namely, the *value* that the player gets is $f(V)$. Our goal is to characterize the maximum value achievable by the player in such settings, and to design strategies for the player that achieve this value.

To make the setting less abstract, consider the following motivating example. The player is an advertiser (or more accurately, its bidding agent) who wishes to run an advertising campaign on an ad exchange over a month. Ad opportunities from various publishers arrive repeatedly, and the bidding agent needs to decide how to use advertising budget (e.g., on which keywords to bid, and how much), say every hour. This situation can be modeled using our framework, where the bidding agent needs to make real-time decisions over $T = 720$ instances (i.e., the number of hours in a month), and every instance there are m actions available to the agent, where actions here correspond to different bidding strategies. On any given instance t, the agent, using information available to it from previous instances, may choose an action for that instance. The outcome of the action is represented by a vector, where each component of the vector specifies some aspect of the campaign. For example, one component can be the number of impressions (denote it $N(t)$), another component can be the number of clicks (denote it $C(t)$), and yet another component can be the amount of budget spent (denote it $B(t)$). After every instance, the agent can estimate the outcome of each action for that instance. (For example, using statistics released by the ad exchange.) The same set of actions are available on every instance, but the outcomes of the same action on different instances may differ from each other, and are largely unpredictable. The overall value of the campaign is determined only at the end of T time periods (in our example, a month). The outcome vectors are added up (or equivalently, averaged), and then some value function f is applied to the resulting monthly vector so as to measure its quality. A concrete function may be, for example, $f = \min(N/10, C) - |B - 1000|$, where N, C and B denote the sum of $N(t), C(t)$ and $B(t)$, respectively, over the T time periods. This function has two aspects of

*Work carried out at MSR Herzlyia.

ITCS'14, January 12–14, 2014, Princeton, New Jersey, USA.

ACM 978-1-4503-2698-8/14/01 ...$15.00.
http://dx.doi.org/10.1145/2554797.2554817.

non-linearity: The first term is a non-linear aggregation of two linear components, and the second term is a non-linear operation applied to a single component. The goal of the player is to run a campaign (that is, choose actions on each instance) that maximizes the value of f at the end of the month.

It should be noted that while this work has been motivated by challenges in advertising and pricing, our goal here is to present and study a stylized model, extending upon previous theoretical work, and not to provide concrete implementation that can be used "as is" to solving these highly practical problems. Nonetheless, in many cases, our results extend beyond these that are stated in the formal results, and thus are more applicable than might be first perceived. Some of these issues are elucidated in Section 4, which perhaps allows the reader to better understand the scope of applicability of our results.

Finally, while the guarantees given by our algorithms are appropriate for multiround optimization settings, but not necessarily so for multiround *games*, our framework is appropriate for 0-sum game settings with vector outcomes. A particular application of interest is a situation in which a *master* player who plays on behalf of several players in a repeated game, wishes to guarantee good performance to all the players under his control (independent of the actions of the other players). A related setting, motivated by [10], has been studied in [3], which considered a player who observes the actions taken by the opponent but not the obtained payoff. We study the complementary problem, where the obtained payoff is observed, but not the action. See Section 5 for a discussion of these issues.

1.1 A scalar setting and restrictions on the value function

To gain intuition to our problem and put it in context of earlier work, it is instructive to first consider the simpler case in which the outcome is one dimensional, namely, $d = 1$. If in addition we impose the condition that f is the identity function, we recover exactly a well known setting often referred to as *expert algorithms*. In the corresponding literature, what we refer to as actions is referred to as *experts*. Informally, the main result associated with expert algorithms is that the player has a strategy that obtains a value essentially as good as the value of the best single expert. This well known result suggests that we should be seeking a similar result in our setting. However, as we shall see, there are substantial differences between our setting and the classical expert setting.

Let us comment first that the aspect that specialized our model to the known expert setting was not really the issue of a one dimensional outcome, but rather a choice of f that is linear. Even if the outcome is multidimensional, if f is linear, then applying f commutes with averaging (applying f to the average of outcome vectors is the same as first applying f to each outcome vector and then averaging), and hence in every round it suffices to consider only a one dimensional value (rather than a multidimensional outcome) and average all values at the end.

Given the above comment, we return to the special case that $d = 1$, but now f is not linear. The first question that we address is whether any function f is reasonable in our context, or whether we must place some restrictions on f. The answer of course depends on what we want to achieve. Let us put forward one goal that seems to be a minimum requirement in our setting.

Conservative goal. If among all actions there is one action (say, action A_1) that on every round gives the same outcome V, then the algorithm should be able to obtain a value of at least $f(V) - o(1)$, where the $o(1)$ term is a term that tends to 0 as T grows.

To achieve an $o(1)$ term as in the conservative goal, we need to have f continuous. Otherwise, choosing the desirable action A_1 on all rounds but one might still not give a value of $f(V) - o(1)$. Continuity is a qualitative property, whereas we will wish to achieve quantitative guarantees (give an explicit bound on the $o(1)$ term). A quantitative version of continuity is a Lipschitz condition. Namely, for some $c > 0$ and every two vectors u and v, we have that $|f(u) - f(v)| \leq c|u - v|$ (where distance between vectors is computed in the ℓ_2 norm). The Lipschitz condition ensures that if the player manages to attain a vector close (in ℓ_2 distance) to a vector of high value, then the player also attains high value. To make the Lipschitz constant c meaningful, we use the convention (that can be attained by some simple scaling) that outcome vectors have ℓ_2 norm at most 1, and that f when applied to such vectors has value in the range $[-1, 1]$.

A Lipschitz condition by itself will not suffice in order to attain the conservative goal.

Example 1. Consider the function $f(x) = |x|$, attaining its maximum at $x = \pm 1$. Let A_1 be an action that on the first $T/2$ rounds gives outcome $+1$, and let A_2 be an action that on the first $T/2$ rounds gives outcome -1. In the last $T/2$ rounds, either both actions give the outcome $+1$, or both give -1, but before completing round $T/2+1$ the player does not know which case holds. Note that in either case, the conservative goal requires that the player achieves a value of $1 - o(1)$, but regardless of what the player does in the first $T/2$ rounds, his average value over these two cases is at most $1/2$.

To overcome such negative examples, we shall require that f is *quasiconcave*. Recall that a function f is *convex* if for every $0 \leq \lambda \leq 1$ and vectors u and v, we have $f(\lambda u + (1 - \lambda)v) \leq \lambda f(u) + (1 - \lambda) f(v)$, and *concave* if for every $0 \leq \lambda \leq 1$ and vectors u and v, we have $f(\lambda u + (1 - \lambda)v) \geq \lambda f(u) + (1 - \lambda) f(v)$. A function is *quasiconcave* if for every $0 \leq \lambda \leq 1$ and vectors u and v, we have the weaker condition $f(\lambda u + (1 - \lambda)v) \geq \min[f(u), f(v)]$ (and for *quasiconvex* we have $f(\lambda u + (1 - \lambda)v) \leq \max[f(u), f(v)]$). Equivalently, for every c, for quasiconvex functions the region of vectors for which $f(v) \leq c$ is convex, and for quasiconcave functions the region of vectors for which $f(v) \geq c$ is convex. An example of a quasiconcave function that is not concave (in fact, it is strictly convex) is the scalar function $f(x) = x^2$ over the domain $x \geq 0$. For the motivating example that we started with, quasiconcavity of f is a natural assumption. It is also natural that a property such as quasiconcavity will be necessary in our setting. It is inherent in our model that the player averages the outcome vectors from different rounds, and quasiconcavity ensures that averaging vectors cannot reduce the value below that of the least valuable vector contributing to the average.

Summarizing the discussion above, we say that f is *admissible* if the following requirements and conventions hold.

1. Outcome vectors have ℓ_2 norm at most 1

2. The value function f when applied to such vectors has value in the range $[-1, 1]$.

3. The value function f is continuous with a Lipschitz constant $c > 0$.

4. The value function f is quasiconcave. Namely, for every $0 \leq \lambda \leq 1$ and vectors u and v, one has $f(\lambda u + (1-\lambda)v) \geq \min[f(u), f(v)]$.

If f is admissible, can we achieve the same goals as those achieved in the standard expert setting? That is, can the player attain a value at least as high as the value of the best action (up to low order terms)? Interestingly, the answer is negative.

Example 2. Consider the concave function $f(x) = -|x|$, attaining its maximum at $x = 0$. As in example 1, let A_1 be an action that on the first $T/2$ rounds gives outcome $+1$, and let A_2 be an action that on the first $T/2$ rounds gives outcome -1. In the last $T/2$ rounds, either both actions give the outcome $+1$, or both give -1, but before completing round $T/2 + 1$ the player does not know which case holds. Note that in either case, there is one action whose average outcome is 0. However, regardless of what the player does in the first $T/2$ rounds, his average value over these two cases is at most $-1/2$.

Example 2 illustrates that to be able to nearly match the performance of the best action, one may need to place additional restrictions on the value function f. Indeed, earlier work of [9] (when adapted to our setting, see more detailed discussion in Section 1.4) can be viewed as implementing such an approach, in combination with placing restrictions on the outcome vectors $O_{i,t}$. However, in this work we do not wish to place such restrictions, as then the results will not be applicable for our intended applications. Instead we shall consider a different performance measure for our algorithms.

1.2 Maxmin comparison classes

When quantifying the performance of an algorithm for the player, one often specifies a class of algorithms against which to compare the performance of the player's algorithm (or using standard jargon, against which to measure the *regret* of the algorithm). Much of previous work on expert algorithms uses as a comparison class those algorithms that in every round perform the same action, and wishes to nearly match the performance of the best algorithm in this class. As Example 2 shows, in our setting it is impossible to do so. Instead, in this work we follow a different approach. We define a collection $\mathcal{B}$, where each $B \in \mathcal{B}$ is a block of rounds that may serve as an *excuse block*. In addition, we define a comparison class $\mathcal{A}$ of algorithms. Let $f_A(B)$ be the value achieved by algorithm A on block B of rounds. Then the value that we attempt to attain is $\min_{B\in\mathcal{B}}[\max_{A\in\mathcal{A}} f_A(B)]$. One interpretation for this expression is that any block from $\mathcal{B}$ can serve as an excuse of why our algorithm did not attain a high value – no algorithm from the comparison class can do well on the block B, and hence we are excused from doing well on the whole sequence of T rounds. A special case of this maxmin comparison class is when $\mathcal{B}$ contains only a single block, that of all rounds (we call this the *standard excuse block*), and $\mathcal{A}$ contains those algorithms that in every round perform the same action. This special case is the same as the comparison class conventionally used for expert algorithms.

Before presenting our results, we introduce the following terminology.

Definition 1. We say that a strategy *asymptotically matches* a target value g, if the expected difference between g and the value obtained by the strategy is $O(\nu(T))$, where T is the number of rounds and $\nu(T)$ is a nonnegative function that tends to 0 as T grows.

An interesting choice for $\mathcal{B}$ is to take as excuse blocks all suffixes. Namely, for $1 \leq t \leq T$, block B_t contains rounds t up to T. We call this the *suffix blocks.* As above, $\mathcal{A}$ contains those algorithms that in every round perform the same action. We call this, the *pure strategies.* The proof of the next proposition appears in Appendix A.

PROPOSITION 1. *If f is admissible and the outcome is one dimensional, then there is a strategy that asymptotically matches* $\min_{B\in\mathcal{B}}[\max_{A\in\mathcal{A}} f_A(B)]$, *where $\mathcal{B}$ is the suffix blocks and $\mathcal{A}$ are the pure strategies.*

The requirement that the outcome is one dimensional is essential in Proposition 1. For multidimensional outcomes, suffix blocks do not suffice, and neither does a natural larger class of blocks. This is established in the following theorem, whose proof appears in Appendix A.

THEOREM 1. *Even for admissible f and when $\mathcal{A}$ are the pure strategies, no strategy asymptotically matches* $\min_{B\in\mathcal{B}}[\max_{A\in\mathcal{A}} f_A(B)]$ *for $\mathcal{B}$ that contains all single rounds, all prefixes and all suffixes.*

Remark. Our proof of Theorem 1 has interesting consequences beyond those stated in the theorem. Consider the following *transparent version* of the multiple round optimization problem: in every round the player is first told what are the outcome vectors associated with each action on that particular round, and only then needs to choose an action. Then if any round can serve as an excuse block, the player now has a strategy that achieves at least $\min_{B\in\mathcal{B}}[\max_{A\in\mathcal{A}} f_A(B)]$. Namely, in each round the player chooses the action that gives the outcome vector of highest value, and by quasiconcavity of the value function f, this gives the desired global guarantee. However, if the excuse blocks are only all prefixes and all suffixes, then the proof of Theorem 1 actually shows that no strategy asymptotically matches $\min_{B\in\mathcal{B}}[\max_{A\in\mathcal{A}} f_A(B)]$, not even in the transparent version.

Given the negative results of Theorem 1, in our Theorem 2 we identify a collection of excuse blocks with respect to which the player does have a good strategy.

1.3 Main theorem

For our positive results, the comparison class $\mathcal{A}$ need not be restricted to that of pure strategies. It can be generalized to be that of *fixed mixed strategies.* A fixed mixed strategy is a probability vector α over actions, and the value resulting from it within a block B is that of the α weighted average of the pure strategies, namely, $f(\frac{1}{|B|}\sum_i \alpha_i \sum_{t\in B} O_{i,t})$. The collection of excuse blocks that we use are described next.

Medium size blocks. Blocks of $\sqrt{T}$ consecutive rounds that end at a round that is a multiple of $\sqrt{T}$. For concreteness, let $\mathcal{B}$ contain $\sqrt{T}$ blocks, where block j contains rounds $(j-1)\sqrt{T}+1$ up to $j\sqrt{T}$.

THEOREM 2. *Let f be admissible with Lipschitz constant c, let $\mathcal{B}$ be the medium size collection of blocks, and let $\mathcal{A}$ be the class of fixed mixed strategies. Then there is a randomized strategy that asymptotically matches* $\min_{B\in\mathcal{B}}[\max_{A\in\mathcal{A}} f_A(B)]$.

The proof of Theorem 2 (which appears in Section 2) combines expert algorithms with Blackwell's approachability theorem [6]. The ability to have fixed mixed strategies rather than only pure strategies as the comparison class is a natural consequence of the use of Blackwell's approachability theorem, and a similar extension of the comparison class appears also in [9].

An important aspect of Theorem 2 is that it uses the medium size collection of blocks rather than the standard one (that only contains all rounds as a single block). As implied by Theorem 1, this is unavoidable in our setting. (Of course, some variations on the medium size collection of blocks would also work for us, but Theorem 1 places limitations on what these variations might be.)

From a motivational point of view, the two versions of excuse blocks are incomparable. In a *stock market* example, actions correspond to buying stocks in the stock market. There it is natural to assume that in the long run (say, in a 15 years period) the stock market goes up, but this assumption is not made for periods of medium length (say, three months). Hence it is desirable to use the standard excuse block, comparing our outcome with that of the best stock that we could have bought and held on to, rather than with the collection of medium size excuse blocks, which might contain excuse blocks in which the value attainable is very poor, and this will reflect badly on our guarantees. In the *tennis player* example, actions correspond to supporting a tennis player, and making profit in times in which the tennis player is ranked among the top players in the world. There is no single tennis player that maintains high rank over a long period of 30 years, but within every medium length period (say one year), there always is some player who is consistently ranked high. In this setting it is desirable to use the medium size excuse blocks rather than the standard excuse block.

From a technical point of view, achieving results with respect to the standard excuse block (when possible) are preferable over results with respect to the collection of medium size excuse blocks, since the former can be used to obtain results also for the latter (apply the former algorithm to each medium size block treating it as a standard block, and concatenate the outcomes – the proof that this works uses quasiconcavity of f), but not vice versa.

The proof of Theorem 2 establishes a regret of $\tilde{O}(T^{3/4})$ (or an average of $\tilde{O}(T^{-1/4})$ per round with respect to medium size excuse blocks, where the $\tilde{O}$ notation hides factors that are either logarithmic or independent of T (such as number of actions, or Lipschitz constant c). We next show that this result is tight; i.e., a regret of $\Omega(T^{3/4})$ is unavoidable.

THEOREM 3. *Even with only two actions and scalar outcome, no algorithm has expected regret smaller than $\Omega(T^{3/4})$ with respect to medium size excuse blocks.*

In Section 3, we establish the robustness of this lower bound. Specifically, we show that a regret of $\Omega(T^{3/4})$ is unavoidable not only with respect to medium size excuse blocks, but also with respect to other natural excuse blocks.

There are some natural directions in which one may want to extend Theorem 2. One of them is to raise the bar and rather than compare the value attained by the player to that attainable by an algorithm from the comparison class in the worst block, compare it to the kth-worst block for some suitably small value k. That is, a single bad block no longer serves as an excuse for bad performance – only multiple bad blocks do. Another is to consider a *bandit* setting in which the player can only observe the outcomes of those actions that he performed (rather than of all actions). With these extensions one can still design strategies for which the expected regret term tends to 0 as T grows, though the rate at which the regret term tends to 0 is slower than that of Theorem 2. These extensions are discussed in Section 4.

1.4 Related work

In the classical *expert* setting (see, e.g., [13]), there are m experts and T rounds. In every round t, every expert j provides some scalar payoff $p_{j,t}$ in the range $[-1,1]$. There is a player that does not know these payoffs a-priori. In every round t the player may select one expert (say, j), receive the payoff from that expert ($p_{j,t}$ in our example), and in addition the values $p_{i,t}$ for all i are revealed. The *bandit* setting (see, e.g., [2]) is the same except that only $p_{j,t}$ for the selected expert j is revealed in round t, but not $p_{i,t}$ for $i \neq j$. The goal of the player in either setting is to maximize the some of payoffs received in al rounds. As the selection of a player may be randomized, one considers the expected total payoff. The basic theorems in these settings relate the expected payoff achievable by the player with that given by the best expert – namely, with payoffs achievable by the best fixed strategy that selects the same expert in every round, with hindsight of knowing which is the expert with highest total payoff. Many bounds have been established over the years for different variants of the problem. Here, we present the best existing bounds (to the best of our knowledge) to the expert and bandit settings described above.

THEOREM 4. *[8] In the above expert setting, there is a randomized strategy for the player that achieves payoff at least* $\max_j \sum_t p_{j,t} - O\left(\sqrt{T\ln(m/\delta)}\right)$ *with probability at least* $1-\delta$ *for every* $\delta \in (0,1)$.

THEOREM 5. *[8] In the above bandit setting, there is a randomized strategy for the player that achieves expected payoff*[1] *at least* $\max_j \sum_t p_{j,t} - O\left(\sqrt{mT\ln(m)}\ln(1/\delta)\right)$ *with probability at least* $1-\delta$ *for every* $\delta \in (0,1)$.

[6] considered vector-valued games (where the payoff of an agent is given by a vector of unexchangeable values), and defined the notion of "approachability" of a convex set in such games. Specifically, a convex set is said to be approachable if the player has a strategy, in the repeated game, that guarantees an average payoff vector (over all rounds) that is approaching the convex set; i.e., whose distance from the convex set goes to zero as the number of rounds goes to infinity. The convex regions that are feasible in this setting were exactly characterized by Blackwell's approachability theorem [6]. Blackwell's approachability theorem applies in a

[1]Note that the $\ln(m)$ factor in the regret expression can be discarded if one is interested in a regret bound that holds in expectation rather than with high probability [1].

special case of the vector setting, when the experts represent pure strategies for the approaching player, the payoff vectors represent payoffs obtained from mixed strategies of the other player, and the payoff matrix of the game is known.

The work closest to ours that we are aware of is that of [9]. A motivating example presented in [9] is as follows. There are m machines and T rounds. In every round t, a load balancing scheduler needs to place a job J_t on a machine. The marginal load $l_{i,t}$ that will be suffered by machine i if job J_t is placed on it is not a-priori known, but is revealed after round t (for all machines, not only for the machine on which J_t was actually placed). After T rounds one has the m-dimensional vector whose jth entry is the total load (over all rounds) placed on machine j. The goal is to achieve a vector that minimizes some function f (e.g., the load of the most loaded machine, or the sum of squares of loads). The problem studied in [9] can readily be seen to be a special case of the problem that we study. It too is concerned with optimizing a function of the sum of outcomes, and the outcome in each round is a vector. As such, much of what we do in our current paper was already done in [9]. This includes placing restrictions on f (it is required to be convex in [9] and quasiconcave in our setting, where the switch between convexity and concavity is explained by a switch between minimization and maximization), using Blackwell's approachability theorem in the proofs, and using a comparison class that allows for fixed mixed strategies. However, there is a major aspect in which our setting is more general than that of [9], which significantly changes the nature of results. In our setting, the outcome of an action can be an arbitrary vector (of norm at most 1). In [9], for every i the outcome of action i is a vector for which all coordinates except for i are 0. This restriction in [9] corresponds to a model in which all load on the machines is a consequence of the jobs that the load balancing scheduler places on them (e.g., nobody else is using the machines except for the scheduler), and hence each round adds load only to the machine on which the corresponding job is placed. This restriction allows [9] to use the standard excuse block (whereas in our more general setting this is impossible, as Example 2 above shows). A major technical ingredient in their proof is to show that in their setting, when f is an ℓ_p norm with $p > 1$, the value of the outcome of the best fixed mixed strategy enjoys a concavity property. The proof uses heavily the fact that the outcome vectors are of special form, and the concavity property is simply incorrect in our more general setting. (To see where the concavity property fails in Example 2 above, consider only the last $T/2$ rounds. Each of the two options given for outcome vectors has poor value, but averaging the two outcome vectors gives good value. This holds regardless of the action chosen, and hence also with respect to the best fixed mixed strategy. Translating this example to the terminology of [9], this contradicts the concavity property.)

Our vector setting can be also seen as a generalization of some nonlinear bandit or expert settings that have previously appeared in the literature. An example of such a setting is that of dynamic pricing with unknown demand [4, 5]. In this setting, a seller has a set of identical items, and is facing n potential buyers, who arrive sequentially. The seller's goal is to maximize profit; to do so, the seller can make a "take it or leave it" offer to each arriving buyer. If supply were unlimited, then this situation corresponds to a standard bandit setting [7, 12]. If, however, the number of items is smaller than n (as is the case in [4, 5]), then the payoff becomes nonlinear and hence a blackbox application of bandit algorithms is inappropriate[2].

To avoid possible confusion, let us emphasize that our framework is different from that of Online Convex Optimization in the sense of [14]. We average the outcome vectors over all rounds, and then compute the payoff of the average. Zinkevich allows a choice of an action vector (which is different from having an outcome vector), and the loss function in a round is convex function of this vector (and revealed only at the end of the round). The main difference is that the loss is computed per round, and then averaged. Our setting should also not be confused with that of [11], where the *strategy* taken by the decision maker can be represented as a vector, while the obtained payoff is a scalar.

2. MEDIUM SIZE EXCUSE BLOCKS

We restate and prove Theorem 2 and Theorem 3.

Theorem 2 *Let f be admissible with Lipschitz constant c, let $\mathcal{B}$ be the medium size collection of blocks, and let $\mathcal{A}$ be the class of fixed mixed strategies. Then there is a randomized strategy that asymptotically matches* $\min_{B\in\mathcal{B}}[\max_{A\in\mathcal{A}} f_A(B)]$.

We break the proof of the theorem into two parts. In the first part, we assume that the algorithm knows which value it needs to approach. The result of this part is summarized in the following theorem.

THEOREM 6. *Let f be admissible with Lipschitz constant c, let $\mathcal{B}$ be the medium size collection of blocks, and let $\mathcal{A}$ be the class of fixed mixed strategies. Let $g = \min_{B\in\mathcal{B}}[\max_{A\in\mathcal{A}} f_A(B)]$ be the minimum over all blocks of the value achievable by the fixed mixed strategy of highest value in that block. Then there is a randomized strategy that given g achieves value $g - O(c\sqrt{\log(mT/\delta)}/T^{1/4})$ with probability at least $1-\delta$.*

PROOF. Let K denote the set of vectors u in R^d that satisfy $f(u) \geq g$. By quasiconcavity of f we have that K is a convex set. We are required to design a strategy that over the T rounds obtains an average outcome vector that is either in K or very close to K. This requirement is similar to the requirement in Blackwell's approachability theorem. However, the premises of Blackwell's theorem do not hold, and hence we cannot apply Blackwell's theorem directly. Instead, we shall use algorithms from the (scalar) expert setting on each block separately and use this in order to obtain an approximate version of Blackwell's setting with T/B rounds, where $B = \sqrt{T}$ is the number of rounds in a block. In our proof of Theorem 6 we shall use Theorem 4 (regarding the expert setting) as a blackbox, in combination with the proof technique that is used in the proof of Blackwell's approachability theorem.

We now describe the randomized algorithm. Recall that the outcome of each action is a d-dimensional vector. Partition the T rounds into T/B blocks $B_1, B_2, \ldots$. We describe what our algorithm does in block B_j given the outcomes in previous blocks. Let u^j denote the average of outcome vectors achieved by our algorithm in all rounds up to the beginning of block B^j, with $u^1 = 0$. Observe that u^j is a

[2]A major difference between their setting and ours is that their setting is stochastic while we employ a worst-case approach.

random variable (because our algorithm is randomized), but the algorithm knows its value when block B^j is about to begin. If $u^j \in K$ we refer to the block as a *dormant block*, and in all rounds of block B^j our algorithm performs arbitrary actions. (For out theoretical bounds, it does not matter which actions are performed in dormant blocks, though in practice it may matter. See Section 4.) If $u^j \notin K$ we refer to the block as an *active block*, and then let K^j denote the point in K closest to u^j (in Euclidean distance). At an intuitive level, our algorithm attempts to move towards K^j. Formally, let d^j be a unit vector pointing in the desirable direction of movement (namely, $d^j = K^j - u^j$ normalized to be a unit vector). Within the block B^j our algorithm would like to obtain an outcome vector O^j that maximizes the movement in direction d^j. This is the vector that maximizes the inner product $\langle (O^j - u^j), d^j \rangle$. Observe that this inner product is a scalar and not a vector. Hence within block B^j our algorithm shall employ the expert algorithm from Theorem 4, where in each round the value of each outcome O is considered to be $\langle (O - u_j), d^j \rangle$. This completes the description of the strategy of our algorithm in block B^j, and by induction, on the whole sequence of T rounds.

We now analyze the performance of our algorithm. Let B^j be an active block. Let O_i^j denote the average outcome vector of action A_i on the rounds of block B^j. Within block B^j the premises of Theorem 6 imply that there is a convex combination $\sum_i \lambda_i O_i^j$ (where $\lambda_i \geq 0$ and $\sum_i \lambda_i = 1$) that lies within K. For this particular convex combination it must hold $\langle (\sum_i \lambda_i O_i^j - u^j), d^j \rangle \geq \langle (K^j - u^j), d^j \rangle$. In particular, there must be some action (say A_i) for which $\langle (O_i^j - u^j), d^j \rangle \geq \langle (K^j - u^j), d^j \rangle$. As a consequence of Theorem 4, there is probability at least $1 - \delta$ that the outcome vector O^j of our algorithm in block B^j satisfies

$$\langle (O_i^j - u^j), d^j \rangle \geq \langle (K^j - u^j), d^j \rangle - O(\frac{1}{\sqrt{B}} \sqrt{\log(m/\delta)}) \quad (1)$$

For a vector u, let $|u - K|$ denote the ℓ_2 distance between u and the point closest to u in the convex body K. We consider the sequence of average vectors $u^1, u^2, \ldots$ obtained by our algorithm at the beginning of blocks and upper bound the distance of these vectors from K. It will be more convenient for us to scale the distance by the number of rounds that passed up to that point, e.g., replace $|u^j - K|$ by $D^j = (j-1)B|u^j - K|$. In our analysis we will assume that inequality (1) always holds. This can be enforced on all blocks simultaneously with probability $(1 - \delta)$ by taking $\delta < 1/T^2$ and applying the union bound.

We now show that if inequality (1) always holds then for all $1 \leq j \leq T/B$ we have $D^j \leq O(B^{3/2}\sqrt{\log(m/\delta)})$. The proof is by induction on j. Let j_0 be the largest index satisfying $D^{j_0} < B^{3/2}$. Then $D^{j_0+1} \leq D^{j_0} + 2B$ (because in each round the worst that can happen is that the outcome and K are two antipodal points on the unit sphere). Thereafter, for every $j > j_0$ we claim that $D^{j+1} \leq D^j + O(\sqrt{B \log(m/\delta)})$. This follows from the fact that in block $j+1$ the total backward movement along the direction d^{j+1} is no worse than $O(\sqrt{B\log(m/\delta)})$ (by inequality (1)), and in the perpendicular direction it is no worse than B (because this is the number rounds in a block). Hence $(D^{j+1})^2 \leq (D^j + O(\sqrt{B\log(m/\delta)}))^2 + B^2 \leq (D^j + O(\sqrt{B\log(m/\delta)}))^2$, where the last inequality uses the fact that $D^j > B^{3/2}$ and assumes a change of constant in the O notation. As there are B blocks we have that the final value of D is at most $B^{3/2} + B + O(B^{3/2}\sqrt{\log(m/\delta)}) = O(B^{3/2}\sqrt{\log(m/\delta)})$.

It follows that the final average outcome vector u of the algorithm satisfies $|u - K| \leq O(B^{3/2}\sqrt{\log(m/\delta)}/T) = O(\sqrt{\log(m/\delta)}/T^{1/4})$. By the Lipschitz condition on f the final value is no worse than $g - O(c\sqrt{\log(m/\delta)}/T^{1/4})$. Finally, the requirement that $\delta \leq 1/T^2$ gives the bound claimed in the theorem.

□

Remark. If excuse blocks are of size $\sqrt{T\log(mT/\delta)}$ rather than $\sqrt{T}$, the proof in Theorem 6 gives an improved bound of $g - O(c(\log(mT/\delta)/T)^{1/4})$. However, for simplicity, in this manuscript we fix the size of excuse blocks to be $\sqrt{T}$ and do not attempt to optimize the logarithmic terms.

With Theorem 6 at hand, we are now able to prove Theorem 2.

PROOF. Consider a nested sequence of convex bodies $K_1 \subset K_2 \subset K_3 \ldots$, where for every $1 \leq i < T^{1/4}$ we have that K_i is the set of vectors whose value under f is above $1 - 2i/T^{1/4}$ (recall that f takes on values in the range $[-1, 1]$). Our strategy is similar to that of Theorem 6 with the difference that there is no one fixed convex body K that we attempt to approach, but rather the convex body may change from block to block. Namely, suppose that in block B_j the algorithm K_i played the role of K. Then before block B_{j+1} begins, the algorithm determines whether there was a fixed mixed strategy whose average outcome vector for block B_j lies within K_i. If there was such a strategy, then also in block B_{j+1} the algorithm attempts to approach K_i. If there was no such strategy, then in block B_{j+1} the algorithm attempts to approach K_{i+1}. (In a different version of our algorithm, rather than approaching K_{i+1} the algorithm may attempt to approach $K_{i'}$ for the largest i' that is consistent with all previous blocks. However, doing the conservative change to $i+1$ rather than an aggressive change to i' has certain advantages that will become apparent in Section 4.)

We now analyze the strategy. Let $g = \min_{B \in \mathcal{B}}[\max_{A \in \mathcal{A}} f_A(B)]$ and let K be the convex body containing all vectors whose value according to f is at least g. Our goal is to approach K, though K is not known to the algorithm. Let i be the least index for which $K \subset K_i$. In every block there is a fixed mixed strategy whose average outcome vector lies within K_i. Hence in every block B_j it must be the case that our algorithm attempts to approach some convex body $K_{i'}$ with $i' \leq i$, where i' may depend on j. In some blocks it may happen to be the case that there is no fixed mixed strategy whose average outcome vector lies within the respective $K_{i'}$ (since $K_{i'} \subset K_i$ rather than $K_{i'} = K_i$). On these blocks the expert algorithm that is employed on the block offers no guarantees. Luckily, there can be at most $T^{1/4}$ such blocks, because each such block causes the value of i' to increase. Hence altogether they can contribute at most $2BT^{1/4} = O(T^{3/4})$ to the loss in D (where D is as in the proof of Theorem 6), which translates to a loss of $O(1/T^{1/4})$ in the final value. Another source of loss compared to the proof of Theorem 6 is due to the quantization in specifying the convex body, namely, due to the difference between K_i and K. This incurs an additional loss of at most $2/T^{1/4}$ in the final value. Other than the above two issues, the bounds are precisely like in the proof of Theorem 6, and hence with probability $1-\delta$ the strategy achieves a value of $g - O(c\sqrt{\log(mT/\delta)}/T^{1/4})$. This completes the proof of Theorem 2.

□

Finally, we show that an average regret of $\Omega(T^{-1/4})$ per round with respect to medium size excuse blocks is unavoidable. The following result, as well as the results in the next section, refer to the total regret. An average regret of $\Omega(T^{-1/4})$ is equivalent to a total regret of $\Omega(T^{3/4})$ as the total regret is simply T times the average regret.

Theorem 3 *Even with only two actions and scalar outcome, no algorithm has expected regret smaller than $\Omega(T^{3/4})$ with respect to medium size excuse blocks.*

PROOF. In each block, for each of the two actions, the outcome of the first $\sqrt{T} - T^{1/4}\log T$ rounds is set independently at random to be either $+1$ or -1. In each block B_j, for each of the two actions, the outcome of each of the last $T^{1/4}\log T$ rounds is set to be a_j, where a_j is chosen such that the better of the two actions in the block averages to 0 in that block. Hence the value for every excuse block is 0.

Observe that the expectation of $a_j T^{1/4}\log T$ is in the order of $-\theta(T^{1/4})$, because the maximum of two random ± 1 walks of length roughly $\sqrt{T}$ is in the order of $T^{1/4}$. Hence any algorithm is expected to average 0 on the first $\sqrt{T} - T^{1/4}\log T$ rounds and then lose $\Omega(T^{1/4})$ on the last rounds of the block. Hence altogether the algorithm has regret $\Omega(T^{3/4})$, or average regret $\Omega(T^{-1/4})$ per round. □

3. LOWER BOUNDS

In Section 2 we showed an algorithm that obtains a regret of $\tilde{O}(T^{3/4})$ with respect to medium size excuse blocks. We also showed that a regret of $\Omega(T^{3/4})$ is unavoidable. In this section we extend this lower bound and show that a regret of $\Omega(T^{3/4})$ is unavoidable not only with respect to medium size excuse blocks, but also with respect to many other natural excuse blocks.

We begin with the introduction of several classes of excuse blocks.

- *Small interval blocks.* Blocks of up to $\sqrt{T}$ consecutive rounds, starting at an arbitrary round.
- *Binary tree blocks.* T is assumed to be a power of 2. The rounds are placed on the leaves of a full binary tree of depth $\log T$, and every node of the tree represents a block that contains the rounds in its subtree.
- *Sliding window blocks.* Some arbitrary but fixed value ℓ serves as the size of the window. Every interval of ℓ consecutive rounds is a block.
- *Interval excuse blocks.* Every consecutive set of rounds of arbitrary length serves as an excuse block.

Recall that by Theorem 3, even with only two actions, a regret smaller than $\Omega(T^{3/4})$ is unavoidable with respect to medium size excuse blocks. In the proof of the following theorem the number of actions grows with T.

THEOREM 7. *Even with $O(\log T)$ actions and scalar outcome, no algorithm has expected regret smaller than $\Omega(T^{3/4})$ with respect to small interval blocks.*

PROOF. Each of the $m = \Theta(\log T)$ actions is a random string of ± 1. Each $+1$ counts as payoff of $1 - 1/T^{1/4}$, whereas each -1 counts as payoff of -1.

For a small interval of length ℓ, every action has expected average payoff of $-\ell/2T^{1/4}$ and standard deviation of $\Omega(\sqrt{\ell})$. Hence when $\ell \le \sqrt{T}$ an action has constant probability of giving positive average payoff on the interval. The probability that no action gives positive payoff is $2^{-\Omega(m)}$. Taking a union bound over all $O(T^{3/2})$ intervals, there is high probability that for every small interval there is an action with positive average payoff.

On the other hand, the player gets an average payoff of $-1/2T^{1/4}$ per round, giving total expected regret $\Omega(T^{3/4})$.

□

In the proof of the following theorem, also the number of dimensions grows with T.

THEOREM 8. *No algorithm has expected regret smaller than $\Omega(T^{3/4})$ with respect to binary tree blocks.*

PROOF. Blocks of size at most $\sqrt{T}$ are already handled by Theorem 7. Hence it remains to deal with those blocks of size larger than $\sqrt{T}$. There are $O(\sqrt{T})$ such blocks in the binary tree. Each such block will be associated with two fresh dimensions and two fresh actions. Consider one such block of length $\ell > \sqrt{T}$. In the first half of the block one action offers an outcome of $(1, -1)$ in the dimensions associated with the block (and 0 in other dimensions). The other action offers an outcome of $(-1, 1)$. In the second half of the block, with probability 1/2 both actions give $(1, -1)$, and with probability 1/2 they both give $(-1, 1)$. If an action associated with an interval is played outside the interval, it gives an outcome of $(-1, -1)$. The function f computing the payoff of an average outcome vector is the negative of the ℓ_2 norm of the vector.

If on at least half the rounds the player takes actions that are associated with small intervals, the theorem follows from Theorem 7. Hence on at least half the rounds the player takes actions associated with large intervals. For every such action, the expected regret is linear in the number of rounds on which it was played. Hence to minimize regret (when measured as an ℓ_2 norm), the player needs to spread the regret (which is linear in ℓ_1 norm) on as many coordinates as possible, namely, on $O(T^{1/2})$ coordinates. This reduces the regret from $O(T)$ (had it been measured in ℓ_1 norm) to $O(T^{3/4})$. □

We note that unlike the proofs of Theorems 3 and 7, the proof of Theorem 8 only establishes a bound on the expected regret, but does not show that this bound holds with high probability.

THEOREM 9. *For every even ℓ, no algorithm has expected regret smaller than $\Omega(T^{3/4})$ with respect to sliding window blocks of size ℓ. When $\ell > \sqrt{T}$, this holds even if the number of actions is a constant independent of ℓ and T.*

PROOF. The case of $\ell \le \sqrt{T}$ is handled by Theorem 7. Hence we may assume that $\ell > \sqrt{T}$. We first prove the theorem under the assumptions that $\ell \le T/2$ and T is divisible by ℓ.

Recall that ℓ is assumed to be divisible by 2. Partition T into $2T/\ell$ intervals of $\ell/2$ consecutive rounds. A *quadruple* is four consecutive intervals. A quadruple is of type Q_i if it starts at an interval whose index is i modulo 4. Note that the rounds covered by two quadruples of the same type do not overlap. We shall consider only quadruples of type Q_1 and Q_3. We shall have four actions associated with type Q_1 quadruples, and four actions associated with type Q_3 quadruples. With each quadruple we associate four patterns, $(+1, +1, +1, +1)$, $(+1, -1, -1, -1)$, $(+1, -1, +1, +1)$ and $(+1, -1, +1, -1)$. Given a quadruple (say of type Q_1), with each pattern we associate at random one of the four actions associated with the type of the quadruple, and one fresh dimension (without the player knowing which action is associated with each pattern). The pattern associated with an action shows which outcome to give (in the corresponding dimension) in each of the four intervals that make up the quadruple. Observe that only the last of the four patterns ensures that in every block of ℓ consecutive rounds that lies within the quadruple, the average outcome is 0. The payoff function is the ℓ_2 norm of the average vector.

Observe that for every block of size ℓ there is some action with average payoff 0. However, the player does not know which action is associated with each pattern. Because of that, within a block of length ℓ the player has expected regret $\Omega(\ell)$. As the number of dimensions is $O(T/\ell)$, the total regret is $\Omega(\sqrt{T\ell}) \geq \Omega(T^{3/4})$ (because $\ell > \sqrt{T}$).

To remove the assumption that T is divisible by ℓ, let $T' < T$ be the largest integer smaller than T and divisible by ℓ. Make two copies of the construction above, one with eight actions on the first T' rounds (and giving -1 payoffs on the $T - T'$ last rounds), the other with eight actions on the last T' rounds (and giving -1 payoffs on the first $T - T'$ rounds).

Finally, it remains to deal with the case that $\ell > T/2$. In this case, one cannot fit even a single quadruple in T rounds. However, this does not matter. Let $T' = 2\ell > T$, which is the number of rounds that suffices in order to support a quadruple. Make two independent constructions of a single quadruple and four patterns and four actions on T' rounds, align one of them to start at the beginning of the T rounds, and the other to end at the end of the T rounds. It does not matter that the quadruples spill beyond the borders of the T rounds. □

THEOREM 10. *No algorithm has expected regret smaller than $\Omega(T^{3/4})$ with respect to the set of interval excuse blocks.*

PROOF. One can use the proof of Theorem 7 on blocks of size at most $\sqrt{T}$. To handle blocks of size $\ell > \sqrt{T}$ one would like to use the proof of Theorem 9. However, to do so for every possible value of $\sqrt{T} < \ell \leq T/2$ would be too costly, because than the total number of dimensions would no longer be $O(\sqrt{T})$, and even if the ℓ_1 regret is $\Omega(T)$, the ℓ_2 regret need not be $\Omega(T^{3/4})$. To keep the number of dimensions at most $O(\sqrt{T})$ we use the proof of Theorem 9 only with values of ℓ that are multiples of $1 + \epsilon$. To handle other values of $\ell > \sqrt{T}$ we introduce some slackness in the proof of Theorem 9. Namely, rather than give a coordinate ± 1 values, the coordinate is split into two coordinates, where $+1$ corresponds to $(1, -1 + \epsilon)$ and -1 corresponds to $(-1 + \epsilon, 1)$. The function f is now the ℓ_2 norms of the average outcome vector, but computed only of those coordinates that have negative value (coordinates with positive value cost nothing). □

4. EXTENSIONS

In Theorem 2 we assumed a so called *expert* setting in which after each round the outcomes of all actions for that round are revealed. Theorem 2 (with somewhat different quantitative parameters) extends also to the bandit setting in which only the outcomes of actions chosen by the player are revealed.

THEOREM 11. *Let f be admissible with Lipschitz constant c, let $\mathcal{B}$ be the medium size collection of blocks, and let $\mathcal{A}$ be the class of fixed mixed strategies. Then in the bandit setting there is a randomized strategy that asymptotically matches* $\min_{B \in \mathcal{B}}[\max_{A \in \mathcal{A}} f_A(B)]$.

PROOF. We first adapt the statement and proof of Theorem 6 to the bandit setting. The only change in the proof is a blackbox replacement of the algorithm from Theorem 4 by the algorithm of Theorem 5. This changes the value achieved to $g - O(c\sqrt{m}\log(T/\delta)/T^{1/4})$. [3]

Now we adapt the proof of Theorem 2 to the bandit setting. The difficulty is that in the bandit setting the algorithm does not know after block B_j whether there was a fixed mixed strategy whose average outcome vector lies within K_i. Hence instead we employ a different strategy. If in block B_j the movement away from the respective K_i along the direction d^j turned out to be significantly larger than expected (namely, D^j increased by more than $O(c\sqrt{mB}\log(T/\delta))$), then the algorithm infers (and this inference is correct with probability at least $1 - \delta/T$) that block B^j can serve an excuse block for failing to approach K_i, and raises i by 1. The analysis then proceeds exactly as in the proof of Theorem 2. □

How robust are our algorithms? In what follows we emphasize some of the issues that are not stated in the formal results, which can perhaps allow the reader to better understand the robustness of our algorithms.

First, notice that the division into blocks of size $\sqrt{T}$ can be replaced by division into other block sizes, and in fact, not all block sizes need to be the same. This will only change the quantitative guarantees on the regret term, but the qualitative guarantee (of being a term that tends to 0 as the number of rounds grow) will remain. For example, our bounds apply in a realistic setting of a campaign on an ad exchange, which runs for a year, when a block corresponds to a day, in which bidding is done approximately every minute.

Also, our guarantee for being no worse than the best expert on the worst block, can be replaced by referring to the k worst blocks; this is important from a pragmatic perspective as one may claim that some blocks (e.g. days) may be really bad as far as payoffs or budget spent are concerned due to the nature of supply arrival (in the ads example) or demand arrival (in the pricing example). Suppose that for some value g it happens that k of the excuse blocks are such that no fixed mixed strategy can attain g on these blocks. Then our algorithms with no change are still useful, provided that k is not too large. The bounds in Theorem 6 suffer an additive loss of at most $2kB/T$ (because in k blocks the algorithm

[3]The $\sqrt{m}$ term is an exploration cost associated with the bandit algorithm. For simplicity of notation, we equated the space of actions with the space of bandits. We note that in cases where the number of bandits exceeds number of actions (for example, if bandits represent complicated strategies over a small set of actions) the exploration term can be decreased.

might behave erratically), which for $k \leq T^{1/4}$ is smaller than the loss that they already allow. The bounds in Theorems 2 and 11 suffer a larger additive loss of $O(k/T^{1/4})$ (because the algorithm may end up trying to approach K_{i+k} instead of K_i), which is still tolerable when $k = o(T^{1/4})$. The possibility of such sources of error suggest that in practice, in dormant blocks (see proof of Theorem 6), rather than taking arbitrary actions, it may be advisable to try to pick a direction in which f increases and use the expert algorithm (of Theorem 4) in an attempt to move in that direction.

One might also think that our definitions imply that our algorithms would necessarily divide resources such as budget equally among blocks. However, this is not the case: our algorithms may well spend budget at higher rate in some blocks, and compensate for this by spending budget at slower rates at other blocks.

Finally, our algorithm is well defined, and moreover, may potentially work great, even if there is no block in which our experts do well; this is due to the fact that the derivatives of the multi-dimensional changes in different blocks may cancel each other, so that the overall average output may have high value even if the average output of each individual block has low value.

5. A GAME-THEORETIC SETTING

The low regret guarantees given by our algorithms are appropriate for multiround optimization settings, but not necessarily so for multiround games. The distinction is that in multiround optimization settings we think of the sequence of outcomes of every action as being fixed in advance (though unknown to the player), whereas in multiround games the outcomes depend on actions of other players, and the choice of actions that the other players make may depend on the actions of the optimizing player. This point is well illustrated by considering repeated play of the well known prisoner's dilemma game. For our notion of regret, defecting in every round is an optimal policy. But if this game is played against another player whose strategy is to play at each round whatever the other player played in the previous round, the optimal strategy would be to always cooperate (except for the last round). Hence despite being optimal with respect to our notion of regret, always defecting is a strategy that might carry high regret in the multiround game setting (when the player learns after the game that had he chosen to cooperate his payoff would have been much larger). This aspect is not captured by our modeling (and neither by the standard experts and bandits models). On the other hand, for multiround 0-sum games, the multiround optimization framework is appropriate.

A particular multiround 0-sum game setting with vector outcomes was studied in [3]. In that setting there is a *master* player who plays on behalf of several players in a repeated game, and wishes to guarantee good performance to all the players under his control, independent of the actions of the other players. While in [3] the player observes the actions taken by the opponent but not the obtained payoff, we consider here the complementary problem, where the obtained payoff is observed, but not the action. This situation can be modeled as a two player game between players P_1 (the *master* player) and P_2. The master player, P_1, plays on behalf of n players, and therefore the outcome of a round can be viewed as an n-dimensional vector of payoffs, with one coordinate for each player he represents. Payoff matrices are unknown and cannot be inferred (since the actions of P_2 are not observable). The master player can only observe the realized payoff vector (the outcome) after each round of play. As the payoffs for P_2 are never observed by P_1, we wish to obtain guarantees for P_1 that hold regardless of the payoff matrix for P_2, and the worst case from this respect is the 0-sum setting. For symmetric games, a natural goal for P_1 is to maximize the sum of payoffs of his n players, and this task can be cast as a bandit problem. For nonsymmetric games, the situation becomes more complicated. The master player wishes to achieve some goal over the obtained payoff vector, which corresponds to some master payoff function f (that returns a real value v given a payoff vector V). Our work establishes sufficient conditions for a value v to be approachable in the repeated game. In particular, by Theorem 2 (or rather Theorem 11, we shall not distinguish between them here), v is approachable if the master payoff function is quasiconcave, and every medium sized block has an action that achieves v. A natural goal for P_1 is to guarantee good performance to every player he represents. In this case, f is the *minimum* function, given by $f(V) = \min(V_1, \ldots, V_n)$, where V_i is the payoff for player i, averaged over all rounds. Theorem 2 establishes that P_1 has a strategy that guarantees good performance to every player if every medium sized block of rounds has an action that exhibits good performance with respect to every player.

Two remarks are in order here. One is that it is natural and desirable to make use of the extra power offered by Theorem 2 to compare with fixed mixed strategies rather than fixed actions. This is because in any given block, it could be that each action is bad for some player, but a mixed strategy offers a vector of payoffs that is not bad for any player.

The other remark is that in the game setting there will be a natural class of vectors $\mathcal{V}$ such that for every vector $V \in \mathcal{V}$, in each medium size block there is a fixed mixed strategy that achieves V. Moreover, in every block of rounds (regardless of the number of rounds in the block and regardless of whether they are consecutive or not) there is a fixed mixed strategy achieving this vector. This class contains those vectors that in each coordinate have the *product-minimax value* [3] for the corresponding player. The product-minimax value of a player in a game is defined as the value that a player can guarantee herself if the other players announce their most harmful product mixed strategy first, and in response she chooses her best strategy. This value is at least as high as the minimax value and is often higher. In particular, if we let v be the minimum product-minimax value across all players the master represents, then our results imply that v is approachable for the master for the function $f(V) = \min(V_1, \ldots, V_n)$.

6. OPEN QUESTIONS

We do not know if the lower bounds of Section 3 hold when the dimension and/or the number of actions is a constant independent of T (except for those theorems that state so explicitly). When block size can be large (e.g., as large as T) this relates also to the question of whether the bound of $\Omega(T^{3/4})$ is only on the expected regret or also a high probability bound. If the number of actions is k and the complete block can serve as an excuse block then the probability of having no regret is at least $1/k$.

Another situation in which the $\Omega(T^{3/4})$ lower bound need not hold is when every set of rounds is an excuse block (and not only intervals). This case may come up in situations like those discussed in Section 5. The number of possible excuse blocks is then exponential in T rather than polynomial in T which makes the construction of negative examples difficult.

7. REFERENCES

[1] J. Y. Audibert, U. P. Est, and S. Bubeck. Minimax policies for adversarial and stochastic bandits, in. In *Proceedings of the 22nd Annual Conference on Learning Theory, Omnipress*, pages 773–818, 2004.

[2] P. Auer, N. Cesa-Bianchi, Y. Freund, and R. E. Schapire. The nonstochastic multiarmed bandit problem. *SIAM J. Comput.*, 32(1):48–77, Jan. 2003.

[3] Y. Azar, U. Feige, M. Tennenholtz, and M. Feldman. Mastering multi-player games. In *Proceedings of the 11th International Conference on Autonomous Agents and Multiagent Systems - Volume 2*, AAMAS '12, pages 897–904, Richland, SC, 2012. International Foundation for Autonomous Agents and Multiagent Systems.

[4] M. Babaioff, S. Dughmi, R. Kleinberg, and A. Slivkins. Dynamic pricing with limited supply. In *Proceedings of the 13th ACM Conference on Electronic Commerce*, EC '12, pages 74–91, New York, NY, USA, 2012. ACM.

[5] O. Besbes and A. Zeevi. On the minimax complexity of pricing in a changing environment. *Oper. Res.*, 59(1):66–79, Jan. 2011.

[6] D. Blackwell. An analog of the minimax theorem for vector payoffs. *Pacific Journal of Mathematics*, 6:1–8, 1956.

[7] A. Blum, V. Kumar, A. Rudra, and F. Wu. Online learning in online auctions. In *SODA*, pages 202–204, 2003.

[8] V. Dani and T. P. Hayes. How to beat the adaptive multi-armed bandit. *CoRR*, abs/cs/0602053, 2006.

[9] E. Even-Dar, R. Kleinberg, S. Mannor, and Y. Mansour. Online learning with global cost functions. In *22nd Annual Conference on Learning Theory, COLT*, 2009.

[10] M. Feldman, A. Kalai, and M. Tennenholtz. Playing games without observing payoffs. In *ICS*, pages 106–110, 2010.

[11] A. Kalai and S. Vempala. Efficient algorithms for online decision problems. In *COLT*, pages 26–40, 2003.

[12] R. Kleinberg and T. Leighton. The value of knowing a demand curve: Bounds on regret for online posted-price auctions. In *Proceedings of the 44th Annual IEEE Symposium on Foundations of Computer Science*, FOCS '03, pages 594–, Washington, DC, USA, 2003. IEEE Computer Society.

[13] N. Littlestone and M. Warmuth. The weighted majority algorithm. *Informat. Comput.*, 108:212–261, 1994.

[14] M. Zinkevich. Online convex programming and generalized infinitesimal gradient ascent. In *ICML*, pages 928–936, 2003.

APPENDIX

A. THE SUFFIX EXCUSE BLOCKS

We restate and prove Proposition 1 and Theorem 1.

Proposition 1 *If f is admissible and the outcome is one dimensional, then there is a strategy that asymptotically matches $\min_{B\in\mathcal{B}}[\max_{A\in\mathcal{A}} f_A(B)]$, where $\mathcal{B}$ is the suffix blocks and $\mathcal{A}$ are the pure strategies.*

Theorem 4 does not directly prove Proposition 1 because in Proposition 1 the player does not need to maximize the outcome, but rather some function f of the average outcome. This function need not be nondecreasing. However, Theorem 4 can be used as a blackbox in order to prove Proposition 1, which we now prove.

PROOF. As f is admissible it is quasiconcave. When the outcome is scalar, this implies that f is unimodular. That is, there is some value $p \in [-1, 1]$ such that $f(x)$ is nondecreasing in the range $x \in [-1, p]$ and nonincreasing in the range $x \in [p, 1]$. Furthermore, f is continuous with Lipschitz constant $c > 0$, and hence for every $x \in [-1, 1]$, $f(p) - f(x) \le c|x - p|$.

For the sake of devising a strategy for the player, ignore the function f and treat the outcome of a round as a payoff. Consider two strategies for the player. Strategy *max* attempts to maximize the sum of payoffs over all rounds, and is the strategy from the proof of Theorem 4. Strategy *min* attempts to minimize the sum of payoffs over all rounds, and is the strategy one obtains from the proof of Theorem 4 by negating all payoffs. Let p_t denote the payoff obtained by the player in round t, and let $P_t = \frac{\sum_{i\le t} p_i}{t}$ (with $P_0 = 0$). Then the *zooming in* strategy is as follows: for every $t \ge 0$, in round $t+1$ use strategy *max* if $P_t \le p$, and use strategy *min* if $P_t > p$.

Let v be the minimum over all suffixes of the value of f obtained by averaging the outcomes of the expert who maximizes this value over the respective suffix. We now prove that for every $\delta > 0$, there is probability at least $1-\delta$ that the expected value obtained by the zooming in strategy is at least $v - O(c\sqrt{\frac{\log(mT/\delta)}{T}})$.

We first make some preliminary calculations that will later be used in our analysis. For $0 \le t \le T-1$, let u_t denote the maximum over all actions of the average outcome on rounds $[t+1, T]$, and let ℓ_t denote the minimum over all actions of the average outcome on these rounds. Suppose that a player uses strategy *max* from round $t+1$ until round T (regardless of whether the *zooming in* strategy actually dictates using *max* on these rounds). Then we denote by U_t the event that in these rounds the sum of outcomes obtained by the *max* strategy is below $u_t(T-t) - O(\sqrt{T\log(mT/\delta)})$. Theorem 4 implies that $Pr[U_t] \le \frac{\delta}{2T}$. Likewise, denote by L_t the event that in rounds $[t+1, T]$ the sum of outcomes obtained by the *min* strategy is above $l_t(T-t) + O(\sqrt{T\log(mT/\delta)})$. Theorem 4 implies that $Pr[L_t] \le \frac{\delta}{2T}$. The union bound implies that with probability at least $1-\delta$ there is no value of t for which either U_t or L_t happens.

We now return to the analysis of the *zooming in* strategy. Let $-1 \le q_1 \le p \le q_2 \le 1$ be such that $[q_1, q_2]$ is the maximal range of values for which $f(x) \ge v$ (by quasiconcavity of f there must be such an interval). Partition values into three ranges: *under* ($< q_1$), *good* ($\in [q_1, q_2]$) and *over* ($> q_2$). Consider what happens when the zooming in strategy is played.

As t increases, the corresponding average value P_t may drift. For some values of t, it changes range (say from *good* to *under*). Let t_0 be the latest round for which the range in which P_{t_0} lies is different from that in which P_{t_0-1} lies. Consider the range in which P_{t_0} lies. If this range is *good* then we are done, because then $f(P_T) \geq v$. Hence we may assume that this range is either *under* or *over*, and without loss of generality let it be *under*. This implies that also P_T is *under*, and it is left to estimate by how much. In round t_0 the player got a payoff p_{t_0} that caused P_{t_0} to drift into under. Hence $-1 \leq p_{t_0} < q_1$. In the suffix starting from round t_0+1, there is an expert whose average outcome lies in $[q_1, q_2]$. As was shown above, even if the value t_0 is chosen in an adversarial manner, there is probability at least $1-\delta$ that the strategy *max* of the player on these rounds gives a sum of outcomes of at least $(T-t_0)q_1 - O(\sqrt{T\log(mT/\delta)})$. In the first $t_0 - 1$ rounds the sum of outcomes was at least $(t_0 - 1)q_1$. Hence the average outcome is at least $q_1 - O(\sqrt{\frac{\log(mT/\delta)}{T}})$ (and at most q_1), and hence the value obtained by the player is at least $v - O(c\sqrt{\frac{\log(mT/\delta)}{T}})$. □

Remark. Our proof of Proposition 1 shows that with probability at least $1-\delta$ the regret is at most $O(c\sqrt{\frac{\log(mT/\delta)}{T}})$. The T factor within the log was a consequence of using Theorem 4 as a blackbox and applying a union bound on $2T$ events. A smaller regret of $O(c\sqrt{\frac{\log(m/\delta)}{T}})$ can be obtained by a more sophisticated argument that we sketch here. A common approach of devising algorithms in the expert setting is via the multiplicative weight update approach. Within that framework, one can consider fractional expert algorithms (rather than randomized ones), and for them the regret is $O(\sqrt{\frac{\log m}{T}})$ (this is a deterministic statement). The dependence on δ only enters once one uses randomized rounding to transform the fractional algorithms into randomized ones. For the randomized rounding process, with probability $1-\delta$ the error introduced in T rounds is at most $\sqrt{1/T \log \delta}$. But in fact, this is be true for every prefix of rounds simultaneously. (Suppose otherwise. Then after the first time an exceptionally high value is reached, there is probability 1/2 of maintaining this value until the end.) By symmetry, a similar property holds for all suffixes. Hence there is no need of suffering a union bound over $O(T)$ events. (A formal proof based on this remark becomes simpler if one modifies the *zooming in* strategy to switch between *max* and *min* only at points when the fractional expert algorithm would have switched. However, then it does not apply to the bandit setting.)

We now restate and prove Theorem 1.

Theorem 1 *Even for admissible f and when $\mathcal{A}$ are the pure strategies, no strategy asymptotically matches* $\min_{B\in\mathcal{B}}[\max_{A\in\mathcal{A}} f_A(B)]$ *for $\mathcal{B}$ that contains all single rounds, all prefixes and all suffixes.*

PROOF. In our proof there will be four actions, that we call P_1, P_2, S_1 and S_2 (P for *prefix*, S for *suffix*). The outcome vectors will be 4-dimensional. For convenience of the presentation, their ℓ_2 norm will be bounded by 3 rather than by 1. Likewise, the total number of rounds will be denoted by $4T$ rather than T. For a vector $x = (x_1, x_2, x_3, x_4)$, the value function will be $f(x) = \min[x_1, x_2, x_3, x_4, 0]$, which is nonpositive. Observe that f is continuous with Lipschitz constant 1, and quasiconcave, as required from value functions. We first prove the theorem when the excuse blocks are all prefixes and all suffixes, and later extend the proof to capture also all single rounds.

We shall consider four possible input sequences, that we shall denote by $I_{11}, I_{12}, I_{21}, I_{22}$. The first subscript determines which of the prefix actions attains a value of 0 on all prefix blocks, whereas the second subscript determines which of the suffix actions attains a value of 0 on all suffix blocks.

Action P_1 gives an outcome of $(3,0,0,0)$ on each of the first T rounds. Action P_2 gives an outcome of $(0,3,0,0)$ on each of the first T rounds. On the last $3T$ rounds, both P_1 and P_2 give an outcome of $(-1,0,0,0)$ for inputs sequences I_{11} and I_{12}, and an outcome of $(0,-1,0,0)$ for inputs sequences I_{21} and I_{22}.

Action S_1 gives an outcome of $(0,0,-1,0)$ on each of the first $3T$ rounds. Action S_2 gives an outcome of $(0,0,0,-1)$ on each of the first $3T$ rounds. On the last T rounds, both S_1 and S_2 gives an outcome of $(0,0,3,0)$ for inputs sequences I_{11} and I_{21}, and an outcome of $(0,0,0,3)$ for inputs sequences I_{12} and I_{22}.

One can readily verify that for input sequence I_{ij} (with $1 \leq i,j \leq 2$), for every prefix the average outcome of action P_i has value 0, and for every suffix the average outcome of action S_j has value 0.

Consider now a player faced with an input sequence chosen at random from the four possible input sequences I_{ij} (the player does not know which one). In the first T rounds, at least one of the actions P_1 or P_2 is played at most $T/2$ times. Without loss of generality, let P_1 be this action. Then after T rounds the accumulated outcome vector has value at most $3T/2$ on its first coordinate. Then, with probability half, it turns out that the input sequence is one of I_{11} or I_{12}. As a consequence, in the middle $2T$ rounds, the player may choose an action from P_1 or P_2 at most $5T/3$ times, as otherwise the first coordinate of the accumulated output vector becomes $-T/6$, and can never recover from being negative. Hence at least one of the actions S_1 or S_2 is played at least $T/6$ times. Without loss of generality, let S_1 be this action. Then in the input sequence turns out to be I_{12} the third coordinate of the aggregate outcome vector ends up being at most $-T/6$, and the overall value of the outcome vector is at most $-\frac{T}{6}\frac{1}{4T} = -1/24$. As this happens with probability at least $1/4$, the expected value obtained by the player is negative and bounded away from 0, proving the theorem when the excuse blocks are all prefixes and all suffixes.

Extending the proof to allow also for single round excuse blocks is fairly straightforward. One option is to add two auxiliary actions A_1 and A_2, where in each round one of them (chosen at random independently in each round) gives an outcome vector of $(0,0,0,0)$ and the other an outcome vector of $(-2,-2,0,0)$. The player gains nothing by playing these actions because their expected outcome vector is $(-1,-1,0,0)$ which is worse than playing P_1. However now in each round some outcome vector has value 0. Another option is not to add auxiliary actions, but instead, in every round to replace the outcome of one of the $P_1/P_2/S_1/S_2$ actions (chosen at random) by $(0,0,0,0)$. □

Learning Mixtures of Arbitrary Distributions over Large Discrete Domains

Yuval Rabani
The Hebrew University
Jerusalem 91904, Israel.
yrabani@cs.huji.ac.il

Leonard J. Schulman*
Caltech
Pasadena, CA 91125, USA.
schulman@caltech.edu

Chaitanya Swamy†
Univ. Waterloo
Waterloo, ON N2L 3G1, Canada.
cswamy@math.uwaterloo.ca

ABSTRACT

We give an algorithm for learning a mixture of *unstructured* distributions. This problem arises in various unsupervised learning scenarios, for example in learning *topic models* from a corpus of documents spanning several topics. We show how to learn the constituents of a mixture of k arbitrary distributions over a large discrete domain $[n] = \{1, 2, \ldots, n\}$ and the mixture weights, using $O(n \operatorname{polylog} n)$ samples. (In the topic-model learning setting, the mixture constituents correspond to the topic distributions.)

This task is information-theoretically impossible for $k > 1$ under the usual sampling process from a mixture distribution. However, there are situations (such as the above-mentioned topic model case) in which each sample point consists of several observations from the same mixture constituent. This number of observations, which we call the *"sampling aperture"*, is a crucial parameter of the problem.

We obtain the *first* bounds for this mixture-learning problem *without imposing any assumptions on the mixture constituents.* We show that efficient learning is possible exactly at the information-theoretically least-possible aperture of $2k - 1$. Thus, we achieve near-optimal dependence on n and optimal aperture. While the sample-size required by our algorithm depends exponentially on k, we prove that such a dependence is *unavoidable* when one considers general mixtures.

A sequence of tools contribute to the algorithm, such as concentration results for random matrices, dimension reduction, moment estimations, and sensitivity analysis.

*Supported in part by NSF CCF-1038578, NSF CCF-0515342, NSA H98230-06-1-0074, and NSF ITR CCR-0326554.

†Supported in part by NSERC grant 32760-06, an NSERC Discovery Accelerator Supplement Award, and an Ontario Early Researcher Award.

ITCS'14, January 12–14, 2014, Princeton, New Jersey, USA.

ACM 978-1-4503-2698-8/14/01 ...$15.00.
http://dx.doi.org/10.1145/2554797.2554818.

Categories and Subject Descriptors

F.2.2 [**Analysis of Algorithms and Problem Complexity**]: Nonnumerical Algorithms and Problems; G.2 [**Discrete Mathematics**]; G.3 [**Probability and Statistics**]

Keywords

Randomized algorithms; mixture learning; topic models; spectral techniques; moment methods; linear programming; convex geometry

1. INTRODUCTION

We give an algorithm for learning a mixture of *unstructured* distributions. More specifically, we consider the problem of learning a mixture of k arbitrary distributions over a large finite domain $[n] = \{1, 2, \ldots, n\}$. This finds applications in various unsupervised learning scenarios including *collaborative filtering* [29], and learning *topic models* from a corpus of documents spanning several topics [39, 11], which is often used as the prototypical motivating example for this problem. Our goal is to learn the probabilistic model that is hypothesized to generate the observed data. In particular, we learn the constituents of the mixture and their weights in the mixture. (In the topic models application, the mixture constituents are the topic distributions.)

It is information-theoretically impossible to reconstruct the mixture model from single-snapshot samples. Thus, our work relies on multi-snapshot samples. To illustrate, in the (pure documents) topic model introduced in [39], each document consists of a *bag of words* generated by selecting a topic with probability proportional to its mixture weight and then taking independent samples from this topic's distribution (over words); so n is the size of the vocabulary and k is the number of topics. Notice that typically n will be quite large, and substantially larger than k. Also, clearly, if very long documents are available, the problem becomes easy, as each document already provides a very good sample for the distribution of its topic. Thus, it is desirable to keep the dependence of the sample size on n as low as possible, while at the same time minimize what we call the *aperture*, which is the number of snapshots per sample point (i.e., words per document). These parameters govern both the applicability of an algorithm and its computational complexity.

Our results. We provide the *first* bounds for the mixture-learning problem *without making any limiting assumptions* on the mixture constituents. Let probability distributions $p^1, \ldots, p^k \in \Delta^{n-1}$ denote the k-mixture constituents, where Δ^{n-1} is the $(n-1)$-simplex, and $w_1, \ldots, w_k$ denote the mixture weights. Our algorithm uses

$$O\left(\frac{k^3 n \ln n}{\epsilon^6}\right) + O\left(\frac{k^2 n \ln^6 n \ln(\frac{k}{\epsilon})}{\epsilon^4}\right) + O\left(\frac{k}{\epsilon}\right)^{O(k^2)} \quad (1)$$

documents (i.e., samples) and reconstructs with high probability (see Theorem 4.1) each mixture constituent up to ℓ_1-error ϵ, and each mixture weight up to additive error ϵ. We make no assumptions on the constituents. The asymptotic notation hides factors that are polynomial in $w_{\min} := \min_t w_t$ and the *"width"* of the mixture (which intuitively measures the minimum variation distance between any two constituents). The three terms in (1) correspond to the requirements for the number of 1-, 2-, and $(2k-1)$-snapshots respectively. So we need aperture $2k-1$ only for a small part of the sample (and this is necessary).

Notably, we achieve *near-optimal dependence on n and optimal aperture.* To see this, and put our bounds in perspective, notice importantly that we recover the mixture constituents within *ℓ_1-distance* ϵ. One needs $\Omega(n/\epsilon^2)$ samples to learn even a single arbitrary distribution over $[n]$ (i.e., $k=1$) within ℓ_1-error ϵ; for larger k but fixed aperture (independent of n), a sample size of $\Omega(n)$ is *necessary* to recover even the expectation of the mixture distribution with constant ℓ_1-error. On the other hand, aperture $\Omega((n+k^2)\log nk)$ is sufficient for algorithmically trivial recovery of the model with constant ℓ_∞ error using few samples. Restricting the aperture to $2k-2$ makes recovery *impossible* to arbitrary accuracy (without additional assumptions): we show that there are two far-apart k-mixtures that generate exactly the same aperture-$(2k-2)$ sample distribution; moreover, we prove that with $O(k)$ aperture, an exponential in k sample size is *necessary* for arbitrary-accuracy reconstruction. These lower bounds hold even for $n=2$, and hence apply to arbitrary mixtures even if we allow $O(k\log n)$ aperture. Also, they apply even if we only want to construct a k-mixture source that is close in transportation distance to the true k-mixture source (as opposed to recovering the parameters of the true mixture). Section 6 presents these lower bounds. (Interestingly, an exponential in k sample-size lower bound is also known for the problem of learning a mixture of k Gaussians [36], but this lower bound applies for the parameter-recovery problem and not for reconstructing a mixture that is close to the true Gaussian mixture.)

Our work yields new insights into the mixture-learning problem that nicely complements the recent interesting work of [4, 3, 2]. These papers posit certain assumptions on the mixture constituents, use constant aperture, and obtain incomparable sample-size bounds: they recover the constituents up to ℓ_2 or ℓ_∞ error using sample size that is poly(k) and sublinear in (or independent of) n. An important new insight revealed by our work is that such bounds of constant aperture and poly(k) sample size are *impossible* to achieve for arbitrary mixtures. Moreover, if we seek to achieve ℓ_1-error ϵ, there are inputs for which their sample size is $\Omega(n^3)$ (or worse, again ignoring dependence on $w_{\min}$ and "width"; see Appendix B). This is a significantly poorer dependence on n compared to our near-linear dependence (so our bounds are better when n is large but k is small). To appreciate a key distinction between our work and [4, 3, 2], observe that with $\Omega(n^3)$ samples, the entire distribution on 3-snapshots can be estimated fairly accurately; the challenge in [4, 3, 2] is therefore to recover the model from this relatively noiseless data. In contrast, a major challenge for achieving ℓ_1-reconstruction with $O(n \operatorname{polylog} n)$ samples is to ensure that the error remains bounded despite the presence of very noisy data due to the small sample size, and we develop suitable machinery to achieve this.

We now give a rough sketch of our algorithm (see Section 3) and the ideas behind its analysis (Section 4). Let $P = (p^1, \dots, p^k)$, $r = \sum_t w_t p^t$ be the expectation of the mixture, and $k' = \operatorname{rank}(p^1 - r, \dots, p^k - r)$. We first argue that it suffices to focus on isotropic mixtures (Lemma 3.3). Our algorithm reduces the problem to the problem of learning *one-dimensional mixtures.* Note that this is a special case of the general learning problem that we need to be able to solve (since we do not make any assumptions about the rank of P). We choose k' random lines that are close to the affine hull, aff(P), of P and "project" the mixture on to these k' lines. We learn each projected mixture, which is a one-dimensional mixture-learning problem, and combine the inferred projections on these k' lines to obtain k points that are close to aff(P). Finally, we project these k' points on to Δ^{n-1} to obtain k distributions over $[n]$, which we argue are close (in ℓ_1-distance) to $p^1, \dots, p^k$.

Various difficulties arise in implementing this plan. We first learn a good approximation to aff(P) using spectral techniques and 2-snapshots. We use ideas similar to [35, 6, 34], but our challenge is to show that the covariance matrix $A = \sum_t w_t (p^t - r)(p^t - r)^\dagger$ can be well-approximated by the empirical covariance matrix with only $O(n \ln^6 n)$ 2-snapshots. A random orthonormal basis of the learned affine space supplies the k' lines on which we project our mixture. Of course, we do not know P, so "projecting" on to a basis vector b actually means that we project snapshots from P on to b by mapping item i to b_i. For this to be meaningful, we need to ensure that if the mixture constituents are far apart in variation distance then their projections $(b^\dagger p^t)_{t\in[k]}$ are also well separated relative to the spread of the support $\{b_1, \dots b_n\}$ of the one-dimensional distribution. In general, we can only claim a relative separation of $\Theta(\frac{1}{\sqrt{n}})$ (since $\min_{t\neq t'} \|p^t - p^{t'}\|_2$ may be $\Theta(\frac{1}{\sqrt{n}})$). We avoid this via a careful balancing act: we prove (Lemma 4.3) that the ℓ_∞ norm of unit vectors in aff(P) is $O(\frac{1}{\sqrt{n}})$, and argue that this isotropy property suffices since b is close to aff(P).

Finally, a key ingredient of our algorithm (see Section 5) is to show how to solve the one-dimensional mixture-learning problem and learn the real projections $(b^\dagger p^t)_{t\in[k]}$ from the projected snapshots. This is technically the most difficult step and the one that requires aperture $2k-1$ (the smallest aperture at which this is possible). We show that the projected snapshots on b yield empirical moments of a related distribution and use this to learn the projections and the mixture weights via a method of moments (see, e.g., [25, 24, 31, 10, 36, 3]). One technical difficulty is that variation distance in Δ^{n-1} translates to transportation distance [42] in the one-dimensional projection. We use a combination of convex programming and numerical-analysis techniques to learn the projections from the empirical "directional" moments. In the process, we establish some novel properties about the *moment curve*—an object that plays a central role in convex and polyhedral geometry [8]—that may be of independent interest.

Related work. The past decade has witnessed tremendous progress in the theory of learning statistical mixture models. The most striking example is that of learning mixtures of high dimensional Gaussians. Starting with Dasgupta's groundbreaking paper [20], a long sequence of improvements [21, 5, 41, 32, 1, 24, 13] culminated in the recent results [31, 10, 36] that essentially resolve the problem in its general form. In this vein, other highly structured mixture models, such as mixtures of discrete product distributions [33, 26, 18, 25, 14, 16] and similar models [18, 9, 37, 32, 19, 15, 22], have been studied intensively. One important difference between this line of work and ours is that the structure of those mixtures enables learning using single-snapshot samples, whereas this is impossible in our case. Another interesting difference between our setting and the work on structured models (and this is typical of most results on PAC-style learning) is that the amount of information in each sample point is roughly in the same ballpark as the information needed to describe the model. In our setting, the amount of information in each sample point is exponentially sparser than the information needed to describe the model to good accuracy. Thus, the topic-model learning problem motivates the natural question of inference from sparse samples. This issue is also encountered in collaborative filtering; see [34] for some related theoretical problems.

Recently and independently, [4, 3, 2] have considered much the same question as ours.[1] They make certain assumptions about the mixture constituents which makes it possible to learn the mixture with constant aperture and poly(n, k) sample size (for ℓ_1-error). In comparison with our work, their sample bounds are attractive in terms of k but come at the expense of added assumptions (which are necessary), and have a worse dependence on n.

The assumptions in [4, 3, 2] impose some limitations on the applicability of their algorithms. To understand this, it is illuminating to consider the case where all the p^ts lie on a line-segment in Δ^{n-1} as an illustration. This poses no problems for our algorithm: we recover the p^ts along with their mixture weights. However, as we show below, the algorithms in [4, 3, 2] all fail to reconstruct this mixture. Anandkumar et al. [3] solve the same problem that we consider, under the assumption that P (viewed as an $n \times k$ matrix) has rank k. This is clearly violated here, rendering their algorithm inapplicable. The other two papers [4, 2] consider the setting where each multi-snapshot is generated from a combination of mixture constituents [39, 28]: first a convex combination $\lambda \in \Delta^{k-1}$ is sampled from a mixture distribution $\mathcal{T}$ on Δ^{k-1}, then the snapshot is generated by sampling from the distribution $\sum_{t=1}^{k} \lambda_t p^t$. The goal is to learn the mixture constituents and the mixture distribution. (The problem we consider is the special case where $\mathcal{T}$ places weight w^t on the t-th vertex of Δ^{k-1}.) [4] posits a *ρ-separability* assumption on the mixture constituents, wherein each p^t has a unique "anchor word" i such that $p_i^t \geq \rho$ and $p_i^{t'} = 0$ for every $t' \neq t$, whereas [2] weakens this to the requirement that P has rank k. Both papers handle the case where $\mathcal{T}$ is the Dirichlet distribution (which gives the latent Dirichlet model [12]); [4] obtains results for other mixture distributions as well.

In order to apply these algorithms, we can view the input as being specified by two constituents, x and y, which are the end points of the line segment; $\mathcal{T}$ then places weight w_t on the convex combination $(\lambda_t, 1-\lambda_t)^\dagger$, where $p^t = \lambda_t x + (1-\lambda_t)y$. This $\mathcal{T}$ is far from the Dirichlet distribution, so [3] does not apply here. Suppose that x and y satisfy the ρ-separability condition. (Note that ρ may only be $O(\frac{1}{n})$, even if x and y have *disjoint* supports.) We can then apply the algorithm of Arora et al. [4]. But this *does not* recover $\mathcal{T}$; it returns the "topic correlation" matrix $\mathrm{E}_{\mathcal{T}}[\lambda\lambda^\dagger]$, which does not reconstruct the mixture (w, P).

This limitation should not be surprising since [4] uses constant aperture. Indeed, [4] notes that it is impossible to reconstruct $\mathcal{T}$ with arbitrary accuracy (with any constant aperture) even if one knows the constituents x and y. In this context, we remark that our earlier work [40] uses the approach presented in this paper and solves the problem for *arbitrary* mixtures of two distributions, yielding a crisp statement about the tradeoff between the sampling aperture and the accuracy with which $\mathcal{T}$ can be learnt.

Our methods bear some resemblance with the recent independent work of Gravin et al. [27] who consider the problem of recovering the vertices of a polytope from its directional moments. [27] solves this problem for a polynomial density function assuming that exact directional moments are available; they do not perform any sensitivity analysis for measuring the error in their output if one has noisy information. In contrast, we solve this problem given only noisy empirical moment statistics and using much smaller aperture, albeit when the polytope is a subset of the $(n-1)$-simplex and the distribution is concentrated on its vertices.

Finally, it is also pertinent to compare our mixture-learning problem with the problem of learning a mixture of product distributions (e.g., [25]). Multi-snapshot samples can be thought of as single-snapshot samples from the power distribution on $[n]^K$, where K is the aperture. The product distribution literature typically deals with samples spaces that are the product of many small cardinality components, whereas our problem deals with samples spaces that are the product of few large cardinality components.

2. PRELIMINARIES

2.1 Mixture sources, snapshots, and projections

Let $[n]$ denote $\{1, 2, \ldots, n\}$, and Δ^{n-1} denote the $(n-1)$-simplex $\{x \in \mathbb{R}^n_{\geq 0} : \sum_i x_i = 1\}$. A *$k$-mixture source (w, P) on $[n]$* consists of k mixture constituents $P = (p^1, \ldots, p^k)$, where p^t has support $[n]$ for all $t \in [k]$, along with the corresponding mixture weights $w = (w_1, \ldots, w_k) \in \Delta^{k-1}$. An m-snapshot from (w, P) is obtained by choosing $t \in [k]$ according to the distribution w, and then choosing $i \in [n]$ m times independently according to the distribution p^t. The probability distribution on m-snapshots is thus a mixture of k power distributions on the product space $[n]^m$. We also consider mixture sources whose constituents are distributions on $\mathbb{R}$. A *k-mixture source (w, P) on $\mathbb{R}$* consists of k mixture constituents $P = (p^1, p^2, \ldots, p^k)$, where each p^t is a probability distribution on $\mathbb{R}$, along with corresponding mixture weights $w = (w_1, \ldots, w_k) \in \Delta^{k-1}$.

Given a distribution p on $[n]$ and a vector $x \in \mathbb{R}^n$, we define the projection of p on x, denoted $\pi_x(p)$, to be the discrete distribution on $\mathbb{R}$ that assigns probability mass $\sum_{i:x_i=\beta} p_i$ to $\beta \in \mathbb{R}$. (Thus, $\pi_x(p)$ has support $\{x_1, \ldots, x_n\}$ and $\mathrm{E}[\pi_x(p)] = x^\dagger p$.) Given a k-mixture source (w, P) on $[n]$, we define the

[1] An earlier stage of this work, including the case $k = 2$ as well as some other results that are not subsumed by this paper, dates to 2007. The last version of that phase has been posted since May 2008 at [40]. The extension to arbitrary k is from 2012.

projected k-mixture source $(w, \pi_x(P))$ on $\mathbb{R}$ to be the k-mixture source on $\mathbb{R}$ given by $(w, (\pi_x(p^1), \ldots, \pi_x(p^k)))$.

We also denote by $(w, \mathrm{E}[\pi_x(P)])$ the distribution that assigns probability mass w_t to $\mathrm{E}[\pi_x(p^t)] = x^\dagger p^t$ for all $t \in [k]$. This is an example of what we call a *k-spike distribution*, which is a distribution on $\mathbb{R}$ that assigns positive probability mass to k points in $\mathbb{R}$.

2.2 Transportation distance for mixtures

Let $(w, (p^1, \ldots, p^k))$ and $(\tilde{w}, (\tilde{p}^1, \ldots, \tilde{p}^\ell))$ be k- and ℓ-mixture sources on $[n]$ respectively. The *transportation distance* (with respect to the total variation distance $\frac{1}{2}\|x-y\|_1$ on measures on Δ^{n-1}) between these two sources, denoted by $\mathrm{Tran}(w, P; \tilde{w}, \tilde{P})$, is the optimum value of the following linear program (LP).

$$\text{minimize} \quad \sum_{i=1}^{k}\sum_{j=1}^{\ell} x_{ij} \cdot \frac{1}{2}\|p^i - \tilde{p}^j\|_1 \qquad \text{subject to}$$

$$\sum_{j=1}^{\ell} x_{ij} = w_i \quad \forall i \in [k], \qquad \sum_{i=1}^{k} x_{ij} = \tilde{w}_j \quad \forall j \in [\ell], \qquad x \geq 0.$$

The transportation distance $\mathrm{Tran}(w, \alpha; \tilde{w}, \tilde{\alpha})$ between a k-spike distribution $(w, \alpha = (\alpha_1, \ldots, \alpha_k))$ and an ℓ-spike distribution $(\tilde{w}, \tilde{\alpha} = (\tilde{\alpha}_1, \ldots, \tilde{\alpha}_\ell))$ is defined as the optimum value of the above LP with the objective function replaced by $\sum_{i\in[k], j\in[\ell]} x_{ij}|\alpha_i - \tilde{\alpha}_j|$.

2.3 Perturbation results and operator norm of random matrices

Definition 1. The *operator norm* of A (induced by the ℓ_2 norm) is defined by $\|A\|_{\mathrm{op}} = \max_{x\neq 0} \frac{\|Ax\|_2}{\|x\|_2}$. The *Frobenius norm* of $A = (A_{i,j})$ is defined by $\|A\|_F = \sqrt{\sum_{i,j} A_{i,j}^2}$.

LEMMA 2.1 (Weyl; see Theorem 4.3.1 in [30]). *Let A and B be $n \times n$ matrices such that $\|A - B\|_{\mathrm{op}} \leq \rho$. Let $\lambda_1(A) \geq \ldots \geq \lambda_n(A)$, and $\lambda_1(B) \geq \ldots \geq \lambda_n(B)$ be the sorted list of eigenvalues of A and B respectively. Then $|\lambda_i(A) - \lambda_i(B)| \leq \rho$ for all $i = 1, \ldots, n$.*

LEMMA 2.2. *Let A, B be $n\times n$ positive semi-definite (PSD) matrices whose nonzero eigenvalues are at least $\varepsilon > 0$. Let Π_A and Π_B be the projection operators onto the column spaces of A and B respectively. Let $\|A - B\|_{\mathrm{op}} \leq \rho$. Then $\|\Pi_A - \Pi_B\|_{\mathrm{op}} \leq \sqrt{4\rho/\varepsilon}$.*

PROOF. Note that $A\Pi_A = A$, $\Pi_A^2 = \Pi_A$, $B\Pi_B = B$, and $\Pi_B^2 = \Pi_B$. Let x be a unit vector. Since $\|(A-B)\|_{\mathrm{op}} \leq \rho$ and Π_B is a contraction, $\|(A - B)\Pi_B x\| \leq \rho\|\Pi_B x\| \leq \rho$. Now note that $(A - B)\Pi_B x = A\Pi_B x - Bx$ so by the triangle inequality, we have $\|A\Pi_B x - Ax\| \leq 2\rho$. Now we can also write $A\Pi_B x - Ax = A(\Pi_B - I)x = A(\Pi_A\Pi_B - \Pi_A)x$. Since A here is acting on a vector that has already been projected down by Π_A, we can conclude

$$2\rho \geq \|A\Pi_B x - Ax\| = \|A(\Pi_A\Pi_B - \Pi_A)x\| \geq \varepsilon\|(\Pi_A\Pi_B - \Pi_A)x\|.$$

Thus, $2\rho/\varepsilon \geq \|(\Pi_A - \Pi_A\Pi_B)x\|$. By the symmetric argument we also can write $2\rho/\varepsilon \geq \|(\Pi_B - \Pi_B\Pi_A)x\|$. Adding these and applying the triangle inequality we have

$$\begin{aligned} 4\rho/\varepsilon &\geq \|(\Pi_A - \Pi_A\Pi_B + \Pi_B - \Pi_B\Pi_A)x\| \\ &= \|(\Pi_A^2 - \Pi_A\Pi_B - \Pi_B\Pi_A + \Pi_B^2)x\| \\ &= \|(\Pi_A - \Pi_B)^2 x\| \qquad \square \end{aligned}$$

THEOREM 2.3 ([43]). *For every $\mu > 0$, there is a constant $\kappa = \kappa(\mu) = O(\mu) > 0$ such that the following holds. Let $X_{i,j}, 1 \leq i \leq j \leq n$ be independent random variables with $|X_{ij}| \leq K$, $\mathrm{E}[X_{i,j}] = 0$, and $\mathrm{Var}(X_{i,j}) \leq \sigma^2$ for all $i, j \in [n]$, where $\sigma \geq \kappa^2 n^{-1/2} K \ln^2 n$. Let A be the symmetric matrix with entries $A_{i,j} = X_{\min(i,j),\max(i,j)}$ for all $i, j \in [n]$. Then, $\Pr\left[\|A\|_{\mathrm{op}} \leq 2\sigma\sqrt{n} + \kappa(K\sigma)^{1/2} n^{1/4} \ln n\right] \geq 1 - n^{-\mu}$.*

3. OUR ALGORITHM

We now describe our algorithm that uses 1-, 2-, and $(2k-1)$-snapshots from the mixture source (w, P). Given a matrix Z, we use $\mathrm{Span}(Z)$ to denote the column space of Z. Let $r = \sum_{t=1}^k w_t p^t$ denote the 1-snapshot distribution of (w, P). Let M be the $n \times n$ symmetric matrix representing the 2-snapshot distribution of (w, P); so $M_{i,j}$ is the probability of obtaining the 2-snapshot $(i, j) \in [n]^2$. Let $R = rr^\dagger$.

PROPOSITION 3.1. *$M = \sum_{t=1}^k w_t p^t p^{t\dagger} = R + A$, where $A = \sum_{t=1}^k w_t(p^t - r)(p^t - r)^\dagger$.*

Note that M and A are both PSD. We say that (w, P) is *ζ-wide* if (i) $\|p - q\|_2 \geq \frac{\zeta}{\sqrt{n}}$ for any two distinct $p, q \in P$; and (ii) the smallest non-zero eigenvalue of A is at least $\zeta^2\|r\|_\infty \geq \frac{\zeta^2}{n}$. We assume that $w_{\min} := \min_t w_t > 0$. Let $k' = \mathrm{rank}(A) \leq k-1$. It is easy to estimate r using Chernoff bounds (Lemma A.1).

LEMMA 3.2. *For every $\mu \in \mathbb{N}$ and every $\sigma > 0$, if we use $N \geq \frac{8(\mu+2)}{\sigma^3} \cdot n \ln n$ independent 1-snapshots and set $\tilde{r}_i$ to be the frequency of i in these 1-snapshots for all $i \in [n]$, then with probability at least $1 - n^{-\mu}$ the following hold.*

$$\begin{aligned} (1-\sigma)r_i \leq \tilde{r}_i &\leq (1+\sigma)r_i & \forall i \text{ with } r_i \geq \frac{\sigma}{2n} \\ \tilde{r}_i &\leq (1+\sigma)\sigma/2n & \forall i \text{ with } r_i < \frac{\sigma}{2n}. \end{aligned} \tag{2}$$

It will be convenient in the sequel to assume that our mixture source (w, P) is *isotropic*, by which we mean that $\frac{1}{2n} \leq r_i \leq \frac{2}{n}$ for all $i \in [n]$; notice that this implies that $p_i^t \leq \frac{2}{w_{\min} n}$ for all $i \in [n]$. We show below that this can be assumed at the expense of a small additive error.

LEMMA 3.3. *Suppose that we can learn, with probability $1 - \frac{1}{\omega}$, the constituents of an isotropic ζ-wide k-mixture source on $[n]$ to within transportation distance ϵ using $N_1(n; \zeta, \omega, \epsilon)$, $N_2(n; \zeta, \omega, \epsilon)$, and $N_{2k-1}(n; \zeta, \omega, \epsilon)$ 1-, 2-, and $(2k-1)$-snapshots respectively. Then, we can learn, with probability $1 - O(\frac{1}{\omega})$, the constituents of an arbitrary ζ-wide k-mixture source (w, P) on $[n]$ to within transportation distance 2ϵ using $O\big(\frac{\ln\omega}{\sigma^3} \cdot n \ln n\big) + 6\omega N_1\big(\frac{n}{\sigma}, \frac{\zeta}{2}, \omega, \epsilon\big)$, $6\omega N_2\big(\frac{n}{\sigma}, \frac{\zeta}{2}, \omega, \epsilon\big)$, and $6\omega N_{2k-1}\big(\frac{n}{\sigma}, \frac{\zeta}{2}, \omega, \epsilon\big)$ 1-, 2-, and $(2k-1)$-snapshots respectively, where $\sigma = \frac{\epsilon\zeta^2}{32kw_{\min}}$.*

PROOF. Given (w, P), we first compute an estimate $\tilde{r}$ satisfying (2), where $\mu = 2 + \ln\omega$, using $O\big(\frac{\ln\omega}{\sigma^3} \cdot n \ln n\big)$ 1-snapshots. We assume in the sequel that (2) holds. Consider the following modification of the mixture constituents. We eliminate items i such that $\tilde{r}_i < \frac{2\sigma}{n}$. Each remaining item i is "split" into $n_i = \lfloor n\tilde{r}_i/\sigma \rfloor$ items, and the probability of i is split equally among its copies. The mixture weights are unchanged. From (2), we have that $r_i < \frac{4\sigma}{n}$ if i is eliminated. So the total weight of eliminated items is at most 4σ. Let $n' = \sum_{i:\tilde{r}_i \geq 2\sigma/n} n_i \leq \frac{n}{\sigma}$ be the number of new items. Let $\hat{P} = (\hat{p}^1, \ldots, \hat{p}^k)$ denote the modified mixture constituents, and $\hat{r}$ denote the distribution of the modified 1-snapshots. We prove below that the modified mixture $(w, \hat{P})$ is isotropic and $\zeta/2$-wide.

We use the algorithm for isotropic mixture sources to learn $(w, \hat{P})$ within transportation distance ϵ, using the following procedure to sample m-snapshots from $(w, \hat{P})$. We obtain an m-snapshot from (w, P). We eliminate this snapshot if it includes an eliminated item; otherwise, each item i in the snapshot is replaced by one of its n_i copies, chosen uniformly at random (and independently of previous such choices). From the inferred modified mixture source, we can obtain an estimate of the original mixture source by aggregating, for each inferred mixture constituent, the probabilities of the items that we split, and setting the probability of each eliminated item to 0. This degrades the quality of the solution by the weight of the eliminated items, which is at most an additive $4\sigma \leq \epsilon$ term in the transportation distance.

The probability that an m-snapshot from (w, P) survives is at least $(1-4\sigma)^m \geq \frac{1}{2}$ for $m \leq 2k-1$. Therefore, with probability at least $1 - \frac{1}{3\omega}$, we need at most $6\omega N$ m-snapshots from (w, P) to obtain N m-snapshots from $(w, \hat{P})$. (If we violate this bound, we declare failure.) Thus, we use at most the stated number of 1-, 2-, and $(2k-1)$-snapshots from (w, P) and succeed with probability $1 - O(\frac{1}{\omega})$.

We conclude by showing that $(w, \hat{P})$ is isotropic and $\zeta/2$-wide. Let $S = \{i \in [n] : \tilde{r}_i < 2\sigma/n\}$ denote the set of eliminated items. Recall that $\tilde{r}$ satisfies (2). So we have $\frac{31}{32} \leq \frac{\tilde{r}_i}{r_i} \leq \frac{33}{32}$ for every non-eliminated item. We use i_ℓ, where $\ell = 1, \ldots, n_i$, to denote a new item obtained by splitting item i. Define $n_i = 0$ if i is eliminated.

The number n' of new items is at most $\frac{n}{\sigma}$ and at least $\sum_{i \notin S} \frac{2}{3} \cdot \frac{n\tilde{r}_i}{\sigma} \geq \frac{2}{3} \cdot \frac{n}{\sigma} \cdot (1-2\sigma) \geq \frac{5n}{8\sigma}$. Let $K = \sum_{i \notin S} r_i \geq 1 - 4\sigma \geq 7/8$. For every new item i_ℓ, we have $\hat{r}_{i_\ell} \geq \frac{r_i}{n\tilde{r}_i/\sigma} \geq \frac{32\sigma}{33n} \geq \frac{1}{2n'}$ and $\hat{r}_{i_\ell} \leq \frac{1}{K} \cdot \frac{3}{2} \cdot \frac{r_i}{n\tilde{r}_i/\sigma} \leq \frac{384\sigma}{217n} \leq \frac{2}{n'}$. Thus, $(w, \hat{P})$ is isotropic.

Now consider the width of $(w, \hat{P})$. For $t = 1, \ldots, k$, define $p'^t \in \mathbb{R}^n$ to be the vector where $p'^t_i = 0$ if $i \in S$, and $p'^t_i = p^t_i$ otherwise. For any distinct $t, t' \in [k]$, we have $\|\hat{p}^t - \hat{p}^{t'}\|_2 \geq \frac{\|\hat{p}^t - \hat{p}^{t'}\|_1}{\sqrt{n'}}$ and

$$\|\hat{p}^t - \hat{p}^{t'}\|_1 = \frac{\|p'^t - p'^{t'}\|_1}{K} \geq \|p^t - p^{t'}\|_1 - \sum_{i \in S} \max\{p^t_i, p^{t'}_i\}$$
$$\geq \zeta - n \cdot \frac{4\sigma}{w_{\min} n} \geq \zeta/2.$$

Let $\hat{A} = \sum_{t=1}^k w_t (\hat{p}^t - \hat{r})(\hat{p}^t - \hat{r})^\dagger$, which is an $n' \times n'$ matrix. We need to prove that the smallest non-zero eigenvalue of $\hat{A}$ is at least $\frac{\zeta^2}{4} \cdot \|\hat{r}\|_\infty$. It will be convenient to define the following matrices. Let $B \in \mathbb{R}^{([n]\setminus S)\times([n]\setminus S)}$ be the matrix defined by setting $B_{i,j} = A_{i,j}$ for all $i, j \notin S$. Define A' to be the $n \times n$ matrix obtained by padding B with 0s: set $A'_{i,j} = A_{i,j} = B_{i,j}$ if $i, j \notin S$, and equal to 0 otherwise. It is easy to see that the non-zero eigenvalues of A' coincide with the non-zero eigenvalues of B. Define $X \in \mathbb{R}^{n' \times ([n]\setminus S)}$ as follows. Letting $\{i_\ell\}_{i \notin S, \ell=1,\ldots,n_i}$ index the rows of X, we set $X_{i_\ell, j} = \frac{1}{Kn_i}$ if $j = i$, and 0 otherwise. Notice that $\hat{A} = XBX^\dagger$. To see this, it is convenient to define a padded version $Y \in \mathbb{R}^{n' \times [n]}$ of X by setting $Y_{i_\ell, j} = X_{i_\ell, j}$ if $j \notin S$ and 0 otherwise. Then, we have $\hat{p}^t = Yp^t$ for all $t \in [k]$, and hence, $\hat{A} = YAY^\dagger = XBX^\dagger$.

Note that $\mathrm{rank}(A') \leq \mathrm{rank}(A) = k'$. Consider $A - A'$. Suppose $i \in S$, so $p^t_i \leq \frac{4\sigma}{w_{\min} n}$ for all $t \in [k]$. Then,

$$|(A - A')_{i,j}| = |A_{i,j}| = |M_{i,j} - R_{i,j}| \leq \max\Big\{\sum_{t=1}^k w_t p^t_i p^t_j, r_i r_j\Big\}$$
$$\leq \frac{4\sigma}{w_{\min} n} \cdot r_j \leq \frac{4\sigma}{w_{\min} n} \cdot \|r\|_\infty.$$

Hence, $\|A - A'\|_{\mathrm{op}} \leq \|A - A'\|_F \leq \frac{8\sigma}{w_{\min}} \cdot \|r\|_\infty$. By Lemma 2.1, this implies that

$$\lambda_{k'}(B) = \lambda_{k'}(A') \geq \lambda_{k'}(A) - \|A - A'\|_{\mathrm{op}}$$
$$\geq \Big(\zeta^2 - \frac{8\sigma}{w_{\min}}\Big)\|r\|_\infty \geq \frac{\zeta^2}{2} \cdot \|r\|_\infty.$$

We now argue that $\lambda_{k'}(XBX^\dagger) \geq \lambda_{k'}(B)/(\max_i n_i)$. By the Courant-Fischer theorem (see, e.g., Theorem 4.2.11 in [30]), this is equivalent to showing that there exist vectors $y^1, \ldots, y^{k'} \in \mathbb{R}^{n'}$, such that for every unit vector $v \in \mathrm{Span}(y^1, \ldots, y^{k'})$, we have $v^\dagger(XBX^\dagger)v \geq \frac{\lambda_{k'}(B)}{\max_i n_i}$. We know that there are vectors $u^1, \ldots, u^{k'} \in \mathbb{R}^{[n]\setminus S}$ such that $zBz^\dagger \geq \lambda_{k'}(B)\|z\|_2$ for every $z \in \mathrm{Span}(u^1, \ldots, u^{k'})$. Set $y^t_{i_\ell} = u^t_i$ for every copy i_ℓ of item $i \in [n] \setminus S$, and every $t \in [k']$. Consider any $v \in \mathrm{Span}(y^1, \ldots, y^{k'})$. We have that $z = X^\dagger v \in \mathrm{Span}(u^1, \ldots, u^{k'})$, and since $v_{i_\ell} = z_i$ for every copy i_ℓ of item $i \in [n] \setminus S$ we have that $\|v\|_2^2 \leq (\max_i n_i)\|z\|_2^2$. Therefore, if v is a unit vector, we have $v^\dagger XBX^\dagger v = z^\dagger Bz \geq \lambda_{k'}(B)\|z\|_2^2 \geq \frac{\lambda_{k'}(B)}{\max_i n_i}$.

Putting everything together, we have that $\lambda_{k'}(\hat{A}) \geq \frac{\zeta^2 \|r\|_\infty}{2 \max_i n_i}$. Note that $\|r\|_\infty \geq \frac{32}{33}\|\tilde{r}\|_\infty$ and $\frac{\|\tilde{r}\|_\infty}{\max_i n_i} \geq \frac{\sigma}{n} \geq \frac{217}{384}\|\hat{r}\|_\infty$. So the smallest non-zero eigenvalue of $\hat{A}$ is $\lambda_{k'}(\hat{A}) \geq \frac{\zeta^2}{4}\|\hat{r}\|_\infty$. □

Algorithm overview. Our algorithm for learning an isotropic k-mixture source on $[n]$ takes three parameters: $\zeta \leq 1$ such that (w, P) is ζ-wide, $\omega \in \mathbb{N}$, which controls the success probability of the algorithm, and $\delta \in (0,1)$, which controls the statistical distance between the constituents of the learnt model and the constituents of the correct model. For convenience, we assume that δ is sufficiently small. The output of the algorithm is a k-mixture source $(\tilde{w}, \tilde{P})$ such that with probability $1 - O(\frac{1}{\omega})$, $\|w - \tilde{w}\|_\infty$ and $\|p^t - \tilde{p}^t\|_1$ for all $t \in [k]$ tend to 0 as $\delta \to 0$ (see Theorem 4.1).

The algorithm (see Algorithm 1) consists of three stages. First, we reduce the dimensionality of the problem from n to k' using only 1- and 2-snapshots. By Lemma 3.2, we have an estimate $\tilde{r}$ that is component-wise close to r. Thus, $\tilde{R} = \tilde{r}\tilde{r}^\dagger$ is close in operator norm to R. So we focus on learning the column space of A for which we employ spectral techniques. Leveraging Theorem 2.3, we argue (Lemma 4.2) that by using $O(n \ln^6 n)$ 2-snapshots, one can compute (with high probability) a good enough estimate $\tilde{M}$ of M, and hence obtain a PSD matrix $\tilde{A}$ such that $\|A - \tilde{A}\|_{\mathrm{op}}$ is small.

The remaining task is to learn the projection of P on the affine space $\tilde{r} + \text{Span}(\tilde{A})$, and the mixture weights, which then yields the desired k-mixture source $(\tilde{w}, \tilde{P})$. We divide this into two steps. We choose a random orthonormal basis $\{b_1, \ldots, b_{k'}\}$ of $\text{Span}(\tilde{A})$. For each b_j, we consider the projected k-mixture source $(w, \pi_{b_j}(P))$ on $\mathbb{R}$. In Section 5, we devise a procedure to learn the corresponding k-spike distribution $(w, \text{E}[\pi_{b_j}(P)])$ using $(2k-1)$-snapshots from $(w, \pi_{b_j}(P))$ (which we can obtain using $(2k-1)$-snapshots from (w, P)). Applying this procedure (see Lemma 4.7), we obtain weights $\tilde{w}_1^j, \ldots, \tilde{w}_k^j$ and k (distinct) values $\alpha_1^j, \ldots, \alpha_k^j$ such that each true spike $(w_t, b_j^\dagger p^t)$ maps to a distinct inferred spike $(\tilde{w}_{\sigma^j(t)}^j, \alpha_{\sigma^j(t)}^j)$.

Finally, we match up σ_j and $\sigma_{k'}$ for all $j \in [k'-1]$ to obtain k points in $\tilde{r} + \text{Span}(\tilde{A})$ that are close to the projection of P on $\tilde{r} + \text{Span}(\tilde{A})$. For every $j \in [k'-1]$, we generate a random unit "test vector" z_j in $\text{Span}(b_j, b_{k'})$ and learn the projections $\{z_j^\dagger p^t\}_{t \in [k]}$. Since (w, P) is ζ-wide, results about random projections and the guarantees obtained from our k-spike learning procedure imply that $z_j^\dagger(\alpha_{t_1}^j b_j + \alpha_{t_2}^{k'} b_{k'})$ is close to some value in $\{z_j^\dagger p^t\}_{t \in [k]}$ iff there is some t such that $\alpha_{t_1}^j$ and $\alpha_{t_2}^{k'}$ are close respectively to $b_j^\dagger p_t$ and $b_{k'}^\dagger p^t$ (Lemma 4.8). Thus, we can use the learned projections of $\{z_j^\dagger p^t\}_{t \in [k]}$ to match up $\{\alpha_t^j\}_{t \in [k]}$ and $\{\alpha_t^{k'}\}_{t \in [k]}$.

ALGORITHM 1. *Input: an isotropic ζ-wide k-mixture source (w, P) on $[n]$, and parameters $\omega > 1$ and $\delta > 0$.*
Output: a k-mixture source $(\tilde{w}, \tilde{P})$ on $[n]$ that is "close" to (w, P). Define $T = 3\omega k^4$, $H = \frac{4}{w_{\min}^2 \zeta \sqrt{n}}$ and $L = \frac{\zeta}{64\omega^{1.5} k^4 \sqrt{n}}$. We assume that $\delta \le \frac{w_{\min}^3 \zeta^4}{2^{29}\omega^5 k^{16}}$. Let $\kappa = \kappa(2 + \ln \omega)$ be given by Theorem 2.3; we assume $\kappa \ge 1$ for convenience. Define $c = \frac{6400\kappa^2}{w_{\min}^2 \delta^2} \cdot \ln\left(\frac{1}{\delta}\right)$. We assume that $w_{\min}^2 \ge \frac{240\kappa \ln^{2.5} n}{\sqrt{n}}$.

A1. **Dimension reduction.**
   - A1.1 Use Lemma 3.2 with $\mu = 2 + \ln \omega$ and $\sigma = \frac{\delta}{48}$ to compute an estimate $\tilde{r}$ of r. Set $\tilde{R} = \tilde{r}\tilde{r}^\dagger$.
   - A1.2 Independent of all other random variables, choose a Poisson random variable N_2 with expectation $\text{E}[N_2] = cn \ln^6 n$. Choose N_2 independent 2-snapshots and construct a symmetric $n \times n$ matrix $\tilde{M}$ as follows: set $\tilde{M}_{i,i}$ = frequency of the 2-snapshot (i, i) in the sample for all $i \in [n]$, and $\tilde{M}_{i,j} = \tilde{M}_{j,i}$ = half the combined frequency of 2-snapshots (i, j) and (j, i) in the sample, for all $i, j \in [n], i \ne j$.
   - A1.3 Compute the spectral decomposition $\tilde{M} - \tilde{R} = \sum_{i=1}^n \lambda_i v_i v_i^\dagger$, where $\lambda_1 \ge \ldots \ge \lambda_n$.
   - A1.4 Set $\tilde{A} = \sum_{i:\lambda_i \ge \zeta^2/2n} \lambda_i v_i v_i^\dagger$. Note that $\tilde{A}$ is PSD.

A2. **Learning projections of (w, P) on random vectors in $\text{Span}(\tilde{A})$.**
   - A2.1 Pick an orthonormal basis $B = \{b_1, \ldots, b_{k'}\}$ for $\text{Span}(\tilde{A})$ uniformly at random.
   - A2.2 Set $(\tilde{w}^j, \alpha^j) \leftarrow \text{Learn}\left(b_j, \delta, \frac{1}{6\omega k}\right)$ for all $j = 1, \ldots, k'$.

A3. **Combining the projections to obtain $(\tilde{w}, \tilde{P})$.**
   - A3.1 Pick $\theta \in [0, 2\pi]$ uniformly at random.
   - A3.2 For each $j = 1, \ldots, k' - 1$, we do the following.
     - Let $z_j = b_j \cos\theta + b_{k'} \sin\theta$.
     - Set $(\hat{w}^j, \hat{\alpha}^j) \leftarrow \text{Learn}\left(z_j, \delta, \frac{1}{6\omega k}\right)$.
     - For each $t_1, t_2 \in [k]$, if there exists $t \in [k]$ such that $\left|(\alpha_{t_1}^j b_j + \alpha_{t_2}^{k'} b_{k'})^\dagger z_j - \hat{\alpha}_t^j\right| \le (\sqrt{2} + 1)L/(2 + 5T)$ then set $\varrho^j(t_2) = t_1$.
   - A3.3 Define $\varrho^{k'}(t) = t$ for all $t \in [k]$.
   - A3.4 For every $t \in [k]$: set $\tilde{w}_t = \left(\sum_{j=1}^{k'} \tilde{w}_{\varrho^j(t)}^j\right)/k'$, $\hat{p}^t = \tilde{r} + \sum_{j=1}^{k'} (\alpha_{\varrho^j(t)}^j - b_j^\dagger \tilde{r}) b_j$, and $\tilde{p}^t = \arg\min_{x \in \Delta^{n-1}} \|x - \hat{p}^t\|_1$, which can be computed by solving an LP. Return $(\tilde{w}, \tilde{P} = (\tilde{p}^1, \ldots, \tilde{p}^k))$.

ALGORITHM $\text{Learn}(v, \varsigma, \varepsilon)$
Input: a unit vector $v \in \text{Span}(\tilde{A})$, and parameters $\varsigma > 0$, $\varepsilon > 0$. We assume that (a) $|v^\dagger(p - q)| \ge L$ for all distinct $p, q \in P$; and (b) $1024k\varsigma < \frac{w_{\min} L}{16H}$.
Output: a k-spike distribution $(\bar{w}, (\gamma_1, \ldots, \gamma_k))$ close to $(w, \text{E}[\pi_v(P)])$.

L1. Solve the following convex program:

$$\min \quad \|x\|_\infty \quad \text{s.t.} \quad v^\dagger x \ge 1 - \frac{4\delta}{\zeta^2}, \quad \|x\|_2^2 \le 1 \qquad (Q_v)$$

to obtain x^*; set $a = \frac{x^*}{\|x^*\|_2}$. We prove in Lemma 4.4 that $\|a\|_\infty \le H$ and $|a^\dagger(p - q)| \ge \frac{L}{2}$ for all $p, q \in P$, $p \ne q$.

L2. Let $s = \varsigma^{4k}$. Apply the procedure in Section 5 leading to Theorem 5.1 for $(w, \pi_{a/2H}(P))$ to infer a k-spike distribution $(\bar{w}, \beta)$ that, with probability at least $1 - \varepsilon$, is within transportation distance $O(s^{\Omega(1/k)})$ from $(w, \text{E}[\pi_{a/2H}(P)])$. This uses a sample of $(2k-1)$-snapshots of size $3k2^{4k}s^{-4k}\ln(4k/\varepsilon)$.

L3. For every $t \in [k]$, set $\gamma_t = (2H\beta_t)(a^\dagger v)$. Return $(\bar{w}, \gamma)$.

Remark 1. We cannot compute the spectral decomposition in step A1.3 exactly, or solve (Q_v) exactly in step L1, since the output may be irrational. However, one can obtain a decomposition such that $\|\tilde{M} - \tilde{R} - \sum_{i=1}^n \lambda_i v_i v_i^\dagger\|_{\text{op}} = O\left(\frac{\delta}{n}\right)$ and compute a 2-approximate solution to (Q_v) in polytime, and this suffices: slightly modifying the constants H and c makes the entire analysis go through. We have chosen the presentation above to keep exposition simple.

---

4. ANALYSIS

THEOREM 4.1. *Algorithm 1 uses $O\left(\frac{\ln \omega}{\delta^3} \cdot n \ln n\right)$ 1-snapshots, $O\left(\frac{\ln^2 \omega \ln(1/\delta)}{\delta^2 w_{\min}^2} \cdot n \ln^6 n\right)$ 2-snapshots, and $O\left(\frac{k2^{4k}}{\delta^{16k^2}} \cdot \ln(24\omega k^2)\right)$ $(2k-1)$-snapshots, and computes a k-mixture source $(\tilde{w}, \tilde{P})$ on $[n]$ such that with probability $1 - O\left(\frac{1}{\omega}\right)$, there is a permutation $\sigma : [k] \mapsto [k]$ such that for all $t = 1, \ldots, k$,*

$$|w_t - \tilde{w}_{\sigma(t)}| = O\left(\frac{\delta \omega^{1.5} k^5}{w_{\min}^2 \zeta^2}\right) \quad \text{and} \quad \|p^t - \tilde{p}^{\sigma(t)}\|_1 = O\left(\frac{\sqrt{k\delta}}{w_{\min}^{1.5}\zeta}\right).$$

Hence, $\text{Tran}(w, P; \tilde{w}, \tilde{P}) = O\left(\frac{\sqrt{k\delta}}{w_{\min}^{1.5}\zeta}\right)$. The running time is polynomial in the sample size.

The roadmap of the proof is as follows. By Lemma 3.2, with probability at least $1 - \frac{1}{\omega n^2}$, $\left(1 - \frac{\delta}{48}\right) r_i \le \tilde{r}_i \le \left(1 + \frac{\delta}{48}\right) r_i$ for all $i \in [n]$. We assume that this holds in the sequel. In Lemma 4.2, we prove that the matrix $\tilde{A}$ computed after step A1 is a good estimate of A. In Lemma 4.3, we derive some properties of the column space of A. Lemma 4.4 then uses these properties to show that algorithm Learn returns a good approximation to $(w, \text{E}[\pi_v(P)])$. Claim 4.5 and Lemma 4.6 prove that the projections of the mixture constituents on the b_js and the z_js are well-separated. Combining this with Lemma 4.4, we prove in Lemma 4.7 that with suitably large probability, every true spike $(w_t, b_j^\dagger p^t)$ maps to a distinct nearby inferred spike on every b_j, $j \in [k']$, and similarly every true spike $(w_t, z_j^\dagger p^t)$ maps to a distinct nearby inferred spike on every z_j, $j \in [k'-1]$. Lemma 4.8 shows that one can then match up the spikes on the different b_js. This yields k points in $\mathrm{Span}(\tilde{A})$ that are close to the projection of P on $\mathrm{Span}(\tilde{A})$. Finally, we argue that this can be mapped to a k-mixture source $(\tilde{w}, \tilde{P})$ that is close to (w, P).

LEMMA 4.2. *With probability at least $1 - \frac{1}{n\omega}$, the matrix $\tilde{A}$ computed after step A1 satisfies* $\mathrm{rank}(\tilde{A}) = k' = \mathrm{rank}(A)$ *and* $\|A - \tilde{A}\|_{\mathrm{op}} \le \frac{\delta}{n}$.

PROOF. Recall that $k' = \mathrm{rank}(A)$. Let $B = \tilde{M} - \tilde{R} = \sum_{i=1}^n \lambda_i v_i v_i^\dagger$, where $\lambda_1 \ge \ldots \ge \lambda_n$. We prove below that with probability at least $1 - \frac{1}{n\omega}$, we have $\|M - \tilde{M}\|_{\mathrm{op}} \le \frac{\delta}{4n}$ and $\|R - \tilde{R}\|_{\mathrm{op}} \le \frac{\delta}{4n}$. This implies that $\|A - B\|_{\mathrm{op}} \le \|M - \tilde{M}\|_{\mathrm{op}} + \|R - \tilde{R}\|_{\mathrm{op}} \le \frac{\delta}{2n}$. Hence, by Lemma 2.1, it follows that by the ζ-wide assumption, $\lambda_{k'} \ge \frac{\zeta^2}{n} - \frac{\delta}{2n} \ge \frac{3\zeta^2}{4n}$, and $|\lambda_i| \le \frac{\delta}{2n} \le \frac{\zeta^2}{4n}$ for all $i > k'$. Thus, we include exactly k' eigenvectors when defining $\tilde{A}$, so $\mathrm{rank}(\tilde{A}) = k'$. Since $\tilde{A}$ is the closest rank-k' approximation in operator norm to B, we have $\|A - \tilde{A}\|_{\mathrm{op}} \le \|A - B\|_{\mathrm{op}} + \|B - \tilde{A}\|_{\mathrm{op}} \le 2\|A - B\|_{\mathrm{op}} \le \frac{\delta}{n}$.

It is easy to see that $|\tilde{R}_{i,j} - R_{i,j}| \le 3\sigma r_{i,j}$, where $\sigma = \delta/48$, and so $\|R - \tilde{R}\|_{\mathrm{op}} \le \|R - \tilde{R}\|_F \le \frac{\delta}{4n}$. Bounding $\|M - \tilde{M}\|_{\mathrm{op}}$ is more challenging. We carefully define a matrix whose entries are independent random variables with bounded variance, and then apply Theorem 2.3.

Note that $M_{i,j} \le \min\{\frac{2}{n}, \frac{4}{w_{\min} n^2}\}$ due to isotropy. Let $K = \frac{4\ln(1/\delta)}{\delta}$ and $K' = \frac{5\ln(1/\delta)}{\delta}$. Let $D = N_2 \cdot (\tilde{M} - M)$. Let $X_{i,i}^\ell = 1$ if the ℓ-th snapshot is (i,i), for $i \in [n]$, and for $i, j \in [n], i \ne j$, let $X_{i,j}^\ell = X_{j,i}^\ell = \frac{1}{2}$ if the ℓ-th 2-snapshot is (i,j) or (j,i), and 0 otherwise. Let $Y_{i,j}^\ell = X_{i,j}^\ell - M_{i,j} = X_{i,j}^\ell - \mathrm{E}[X_{i,j}^\ell]$; so $D_{i,j} = \sum_{\ell=1}^{N_2} Y_{i,j}^\ell$ for all $i, j \in [n]$. We have $\sigma^2(n_2) := \mathrm{Var}[D_{i,j} | N_2 = n_2] = n_2 \mathrm{Var}[X_{i,j}^1] \le n_2 \mathrm{E}[(X_{i,j}^1)^2] \le n_2 M_{i,j}$. For $n_2 \le 2cn\ln^6 n$, we have $\sigma^2(n_2) \le \frac{8c\ln^6 n}{w_{\min}^2 n} \le \frac{\ln n \ln(1/\delta)}{\delta^2}$ (since $w_{\min}^4 \ge \frac{57600\kappa^2 \ln^5 n}{n}$). So by Bernstein's inequality (Lemma A.2),

$$\Pr[|D_{i,j}| > K\ln n | N_2 = n_2] \le 2\exp\Big(-\frac{K^2\ln^2 n}{2(\sigma^2(n_2) + K\ln n/3)}\Big)$$
$$\le 2\max\Big\{\exp(-\tfrac{K^2\ln^2 n}{4\sigma^2(n_2)}), \exp(-\tfrac{3K\ln n}{4})\Big\} \le \frac{2\delta}{n^3}.$$

Since $\Pr[N_2 > 2c\ln^6 n] \le n^{-3}$, we can say that with probability at least $1 - 2n^{-2}$, we have $|D_{i,j}| \le K\ln n$ for every $i, j \in [n]$ and $N_2 \le 2c\ln^6 n$.

Define a matrix D' by putting, for every $i, j \in [n]$, $D'_{i,j} = \mathrm{sign}(D_{i,j}) \cdot \min\{|D_{i,j}|, K\ln n\}$. Put $D'' = D' - \mathrm{E}[D']$. Clearly, $\mathrm{E}[D''_{i,j}] = 0$ for every $i, j \in [n]$. We prove below that $|\mathrm{E}[D'_{i,j}]| \le \frac{3\delta c\ln^6 n}{n^2} \le \frac{\ln n \ln(1/\delta)}{\delta}$; therefore, $|D''_{i,j}| \le K'\ln n$. The entries of D are independent random variables as N_2 is a Poisson random variable; hence, the entries of D'' are also independent random variables. Also $\mathrm{Var}[D''_{i,j}] \le \mathrm{Var}[D_{i,j}]$ since censoring a random variable to an interval can only reduce the variance. Note that $D_{i,j} = \sum_{\ell=1}^{N_2} Y_{i,j}^\ell$ follows the compound Poisson distribution. So we have

$$\mathrm{Var}[D_{i,j}] = \mathrm{E}[N_2] \cdot \mathrm{E}[(Y_{i,j}^1)^2] = \mathrm{E}[N_2] \cdot \mathrm{Var}[X_{i,j}^1]$$
$$\le \mathrm{E}[N_2] M_{i,j} \le \frac{4c\ln^6 n}{w_{\min}^2 \cdot n} \le \frac{\hat{c}^2 K'^2 \ln^6 n}{n}$$

where $\hat{c} = \max\{\frac{2\sqrt{c}}{w_{\min} K'}, \kappa^2\}$. Thus, by Theorem 2.3, the constant $\kappa = \kappa(2 + \ln\omega) > 0$ is such that with probability at least $1 - \frac{1}{n^2\omega}$

$$\|D''\|_{\mathrm{op}} \le 2 \cdot \frac{\hat{c}K'\ln^3 n}{\sqrt{n}} \cdot \sqrt{n} + \kappa\sqrt{K'\ln n \cdot \frac{\hat{c}K'\ln^3 n}{\sqrt{n}}} \cdot \sqrt[4]{n} \cdot \ln n$$
$$\le (2K'\hat{c} + \kappa K'\sqrt{\hat{c}}) \ln^3 n. \qquad (3)$$

We have $\Pr[N_2 \ge \frac{1}{2}\mathrm{E}[N_2]] \ge 1 - n^{-2}$, Thus, with probability at least $1 - \frac{1}{n\omega}$, we have that $N_2 \ge \frac{1}{2}\mathrm{E}[N_2]$, $D' = D$, and $\|D''\|_{\mathrm{op}}$ is bounded by (3). We show below that $2\|\mathrm{E}[D']\|_{\mathrm{op}} / \mathrm{E}[N_2] \le 6\delta n^{-2} \le \delta/20n$. One can verify that $4K'\hat{c}/c \le \delta/10$ and $2\kappa K'\sqrt{\hat{c}}/c \le \delta/10$. Therefore, with probability at least $1 - \frac{1}{n\omega}$, we have that $\|M - \tilde{M}\|_{\mathrm{op}} = \frac{1}{N_2} \cdot \|D\|_{\mathrm{op}} \le \frac{2}{\mathrm{E}[N_2]} \cdot (\|D''\|_{\mathrm{op}} + \|\mathrm{E}[D']\|_{\mathrm{op}}) \le \frac{\delta}{4n}$.

Finally, we bound $\|\mathrm{E}[D']\|_{\mathrm{op}}$. We have $\|\mathrm{E}[D']\|_{\mathrm{op}} \le \|\mathrm{E}[D']\|_F \le n \cdot \max_{i,j} |\mathrm{E}[D'_{i,j}]|$. Let $\mu = cn\ln^6 n = \mathrm{E}[N_2]$. Fix any i, j. We have $|\mathrm{E}[D'_{i,j}]| = |\mathrm{E}[D'_{i,j} - D_{i,j}]| \le \mathrm{E}[|D'_{i,j} - D_{i,j}|]$. For any $n_2 \le 2\ln(1/\delta)\mu$, we have $\mathrm{Var}[D_{i,j} | N_2 = n_2] \le n_2 M_{i,j} \le \frac{8c\ln(1/\delta)\ln^6 n}{w_{\min}^2 n}$. So by Bernstein's inequality, we have that $\Pr[|D_{i,j}| > K\ln n | N_2 \le 2\ln(1/\delta)\mu] < 2\delta n^{-3}$. Also, $|D'_{i,j} - D_{i,j}| \le N_2$ always. Therefore,

$$\mathrm{E}\big[|D'_{i,j} - D_{i,j}| | N_2 = n_2\big] \le \begin{cases} 2\delta n^{-3} n_2 & \text{if } n_2 \le 2\ln(\frac{1}{\delta})\mu; \\ n_2 & \text{otherwise} \end{cases}$$

and $\mathrm{E}\big[|D'_{i,j} - D_{i,j}|\big] \le \mu - \Pr[N_2 \le 2\ln(1/\delta)\mu]\, \mathrm{E}[N_2 | N_2 \le 2\ln(1/\delta)\mu](1 - 2\delta n^{-3})$. Since N_2 is Poisson distributed, we have

$$\Pr[N_2 \le 2\ln(1/\delta)\mu]\, \mathrm{E}[N_2 | N_2 \le 2\ln(1/\delta)\mu]$$
$$= \sum_{\ell=0}^{\lfloor 2\ln(1/\delta)\mu \rfloor} \ell \cdot \frac{\mu^\ell e^{-\mu}}{\ell!}$$
$$= \mu \sum_{\ell=0}^{\lfloor 2\ln(1/\delta)\mu \rfloor - 1} \frac{\mu^\ell e^{-\mu}}{\ell!}$$
$$\ge \mu \Pr[N_2 \le \ln(1/\delta)\mu] \ge \mu(1 - \delta n^{-3}).$$

Thus, $\mathrm{E}\big[|D'_{i,j} - D_{i,j}|\big] \le \mu - \mu(1 - \delta n^{-3})(1 - 2\delta n^{-3}) \le 3\delta n^{-3}\mu$, and $2\|\mathrm{E}[D']\|_{\mathrm{op}} / \mathrm{E}[N_2] \le 6\delta n^{-2}$. ☐

We assume in the sequel that the high-probability event stated in Lemma 4.2 happens. Thus, Lemma 2.2 implies that $\|\Pi_A - \Pi_{\tilde{A}}\|_{\mathrm{op}} \le \frac{2\sqrt{\delta}}{\zeta}$.

LEMMA 4.3. *For every unit vector $b \in \mathrm{Span}(A)$, $\|b\|_\infty \le \frac{2}{w_{\min}^2 \zeta\sqrt{n}}$.*

PROOF. Recall that $A = \sum_{t=1}^k w_t (p^t - r)(p^t - r)^\dagger$, and the smallest non-zero eigenvalue of A is at least ζ^2/n. Note that $\mathrm{Span}(A) = \mathrm{Span}\{p^1 - r, \ldots, p^k - r\}$. Let $Z = \mathrm{conv}(P)$. If $r + b \in Z$, then $\|r + b\|_\infty \le \frac{2}{w_{\min} n}$, $r + b \ge 0$, and $\|r\|_\infty \le \frac{2}{n}$ imply that $\|b\|_\infty \le \frac{2}{w_{\min} n}$. Otherwise, let the line segment $[r, r+b]$ intersect the boundary of Z at some point b'. We show that $\|r - b'\|_2^2 \ge \frac{\zeta^2 w_{\min}^2}{n}$. The lemma then follows since $b = (b' - r)/\|b' - r\|_2$ and so $\|b\|_\infty = \frac{\|b' - r\|_\infty}{\|b' - r\|_2} \le \frac{2}{w_{\min}^2 \zeta\sqrt{n}}$.

Let S be a facet of Z such that $b' \in S$, $r \notin S$ (note that r is in the strict interior of P). Since $Z \subseteq \mathrm{Span}(A)$, one can find a unit vector $v \in \text{Span}(A)$ such that S is exactly the set of points that minimize $v^\dagger x$ over $x \in Z$. Let $d_L = v^\dagger r - \min_{x \in Z} v^\dagger x = v^\dagger(r - b')$. We lower bound $\|r - b'\|_2$ by d_L. Note that $d_L > 0$. Clearly, $v^\dagger(p^t - r) \geq -d_L$ for all $t \in [k]$. Projecting P onto v, we have that (a) $\sum_{t=1}^k w_t v^\dagger(p^t - r) = 0$; and (b) $v^T A v = \sum_{t=1}^k w_t \left(v^\dagger(p^t - r)\right)^2 \geq \frac{\varsigma^2}{n}$ since $v \in \text{Span}(A)$ and (w, P) is ς-wide. Let $W_L = \sum_{t: v^\dagger(p^t - r) \leq 0} w_t$, let $W_R = 1 - W_L \geq w_{\min}$, and let $d_R = \max_t\{v^\dagger(p^t - r)\}$. Then, $0 = \sum_{t=1}^k w_t v^\dagger(p^t - r) \geq W_L(-d_L) + w_{\min} d_R$, so $d_R \leq d_L \cdot \frac{W_L}{w_{\min}}$, Also $\frac{\varsigma^2}{n} \leq \sum_{t=1}^k w_t \left(v^\dagger(p^t - r)\right)^2 \leq W_L \cdot d_L^2 + W_R \cdot d_R^2 \leq W_L \cdot d_L^2 + W_R \cdot d_L^2 \cdot \frac{W_L^2}{w_{\min}^2} \leq \frac{d_L^2}{w_{\min}^2}$. So, $d_L^2 \geq \frac{\varsigma^2 w_{\min}^2}{n}$. $\square$

LEMMA 4.4. *If the assumptions stated in Algorithm* Learn *are satisfied, then: (i) the vector a computed in* Learn *satisfies $\|a\|_\infty \leq H$, and $|a^\dagger(p-q)| \geq L/2$ for every two mixture constituents $p, q \in P$;*
(ii) with probability at least $1 - \varepsilon$, the output $(\bar{w}, \gamma)$ of Learn *satisfies the following: there is a permutation $\sigma : [k] \mapsto [k]$ such that for all $t = 1, \ldots, k$,*

$$|w_t - \bar{w}_{\sigma(t)}| = O\Big(\frac{\varsigma \omega^{1.5} k^5}{w_{\min}^2 \varsigma^2}\Big), \qquad \textit{and}$$

$$|v^\dagger p^t - \gamma_{\sigma(t)}| \leq \frac{2048 k H \varsigma}{w_{\min}} + \frac{8\sqrt{2\delta}}{w_{\min}\varsigma\sqrt{n}} \leq \frac{2048 k H \varsigma}{w_{\min}} + \frac{L}{8T}.$$

PROOF. We have $v^\dagger \Pi_A(v) = 1 - \|v - \Pi_A(v)\|_2^2 = 1 - \|(\Pi_{\tilde{A}} - \Pi_A)v\|_2^2 \geq 1 - \frac{4\delta}{\varsigma^2}$. Thus, $\Pi_A(v)$ is feasible to (Q_v), and since $\|\Pi_A(v)\|_2 \leq 1$, by Lemma 4.3, the optimal solution x^* to (Q_v) satisfies $\|x^*\|_\infty \leq 2\|\Pi_A(v)\|_\infty \leq H/2$. Also $\|x^*\|_2^2 \geq v^\dagger x^* \geq 1 - \frac{4\delta}{\varsigma^2} \geq \frac{1}{4}$, so $\|a\|_\infty \leq H$. Note that $\|v - a\|_2^2 = 2(1 - v^\dagger a) \leq 2(1 - v^\dagger x^*) \leq \frac{8\delta}{\varsigma^2}$. It follows that for any two mixture constituents p, q, we have

$$\begin{aligned}
|a^\dagger(p-q)| &\geq |v^\dagger(p-q)| - |(v-a)^\dagger(p-q)| \\
&\geq |v^\dagger(p-q)| - \frac{2\sqrt{2\delta}}{\varsigma}\|p-q\|_2 \\
&\geq |v^\dagger(p-q)| - \frac{8\sqrt{2\delta}}{w_{\min}\varsigma\sqrt{n}} \geq |v^\dagger(p-q)| - \frac{L}{2} \geq \frac{L}{2}.
\end{aligned}$$

This proves part (i). For part (ii), we note that any two spikes in the k-spike mixture $(w, \text{E}[\pi_{a/2H}(P)])$ are separated by a distance of at least $L/4H$. Since $s < L/4H$, Theorem 5.1 guarantees that with a sample of $(2k-1)$-snapshots of size $3k2^{4k}s^{-4k}\log(4k/\varepsilon)$, with probability at least $1 - \varepsilon$, the learned k-spike distribution $(\bar{w}, \beta)$ satisfies $\text{Tran}(w, \text{E}[\pi_{a/2H}(P)]; \bar{w}, \beta) \leq 1024 k s^{1/(4k)} = 1024 k \varsigma < \frac{L w_{\min}}{8H}$. Notice that this implies that there is a permutation $\sigma : [k] \mapsto [k]$ such that $\forall t = 1, \ldots, k$:

$$|(a/2H)^\dagger p^t - \beta_{\sigma(t)}| \leq \frac{1024 k \varsigma}{w_{\min}} < \frac{L}{8H}, \tag{4}$$

$$|w_t - \bar{w}_{\sigma(t)}| = O\Big(\frac{k\varsigma}{L/8H}\Big) = O\Big(\frac{\varsigma \omega^{1.5} k^5}{w_{\min}^2 \varsigma^2}\Big).$$

Fix some $t \in [k]$. Let $t' = \sigma(t)$. From (4), we know that $|a^\dagger p^t - 2H \cdot \beta_{t'}| = \frac{2048 k H \varsigma}{w_{\min}}$. We bound $|v^\dagger p^t - a^\dagger p^t|$ and $|2H\beta_{t'} - \gamma_{t'}|$, which together with the above will complete the proof of the lemma. We have $|(v-a)^\dagger p^t| \leq \|v - a\|_2 \|p^t\|_2 \leq \frac{4\sqrt{2\delta}}{w_{\min}\varsigma\sqrt{n}}$. Since $\gamma_{t'} = (2H\beta_{t'})a^\dagger v$ and $|\beta_{t'}| \leq \frac{1}{2}$, we have $|2H\beta_{t'} - \gamma_{t'}| \leq \frac{H \cdot 4\delta}{\varsigma^2} \leq \frac{16\delta}{w_{\min}^2 \varsigma^3 \sqrt{n}}$. It follows that $|v^\dagger p^t - \gamma_{t'}| \leq \frac{2048 k H \varsigma}{w_{\min}} + \frac{8\sqrt{2\delta}}{w_{\min}\varsigma\sqrt{n}} \leq \frac{2048 k H \varsigma}{w_{\min}} + \frac{L}{8T}$. $\square$

CLAIM 4.5. *Let Z be a random unit vector in $\text{Span}(\tilde{A})$ and $v \in \text{Span}(\tilde{A})$. $\Pr\big[|Z^\dagger v| < \frac{\|v\|_2}{32\omega^{1.5}k^4}\big] < \frac{1}{3\omega k' k^2}$.*

PROOF. One way of choosing the random unit vector Z is as follows. Fix an orthonormal basis $\{u_1, \ldots, u_{k'}\}$ for $\text{Span}(\tilde{A})$. We choose independent $N(0,1)$ random variables X_i for $i \in [k']$. Define $C = \sum_{i=1}^{k'} X_i u_i$ and set $Z = C/\|C\|_2$. Set $a_1 = \frac{\pi}{32\omega^2 k'^2 k^4}$ and $a_2 = 2 + \frac{4\ln(12\omega k' k^2)}{k'} \leq 96\omega k$.

Note that $C^\dagger v/\|v\|_2$ is distributed as $N(0,1)$. Therefore, $\Pr\big[|C^\dagger v| \leq \|v\|_2\sqrt{a_1}\big] \leq \sqrt{\frac{2a_1}{\pi}} \leq \frac{1}{4\omega k' k^2}$. Also, $\|C\|_2^2 = \sum_{i=1}^{k'} X_i^2$ follows the $\chi_{k'}^2$ distribution. So

$$\begin{aligned}
\Pr[\|C\|_2^2 > a_2 k'] &< \left(a_2 e^{1-a_2}\right)^{k'/2} \\
&< \exp\!\Big((1 - a_2/2)k'/2\Big) < \frac{1}{12\omega k' k^2}.
\end{aligned}$$

Observe that $\sqrt{\frac{a_1}{a_2 k'}} \geq \frac{1}{32\omega^{1.5}k^4}$. So if the "bad" event stated in the lemma happens, then $|C^\dagger v| \leq \|v\|_2\sqrt{a_1}$ or $\|C\|_2^2 \geq a_2 k'$ happens; the probability of this is at most $\frac{1}{3\omega k' k^2}$. $\square$

LEMMA 4.6. *With probability at least $1 - \frac{1}{3\omega}$, for every pair $p, q \in P$, we have (i) $|b_j^\dagger(p-q)| \geq L$ for every $j \in [k']$ and (ii) $|z_j^\dagger(p-q)| \geq L$ for every $j \in [k'-1]$.*

PROOF. Define $\tilde{p} = \Pi_{\tilde{A}}(p)$ for a mixture constituent p. Clearly, for any $v \in \text{Span}(\tilde{A})$, $v^\dagger \tilde{p} = v^\dagger p$. Recall that $\|\Pi_A - \Pi_{\tilde{A}}| \leq \frac{2\sqrt{\delta}}{\varsigma}$. So for every $p, q \in P$, $\|\tilde{p} - \tilde{q}\|_2^2 \geq \|p - q\|_2^2 - \|(\Pi_A - \Pi_{\tilde{A}})(p-q)\|_2^2 \geq \|p-q\|^2/4$; hence, $\|\tilde{p} - \tilde{q}\|_2 \geq \frac{\varsigma}{2\sqrt{n}}$. Notice that the z_j vectors are also random unit vectors in $\text{Span}(\tilde{A})$. Applying Claim 4.5 to each event involving one of the $\{b_j\}_{j \in [k']}, \{z_j\}_{j \in [k'-1]}$ random unit vectors, and one of the $\binom{k}{2}$ vectors $\|\tilde{p} - \tilde{q}\|$ for $\tilde{p}, \tilde{q} \in \Pi_{\tilde{A}}(P)$, and taking the union bound over the at most $k'k^2$ such events completes the proof. $\square$

LEMMA 4.7. *With probability at least $1 - \frac{2}{3\omega}$, the k-spike distributions obtained in steps A2 and A3 satisfy:*
(i) For every $j \in [k']$, there is a permutation $\sigma^j : [k] \mapsto [k]$ such that for all $t \in [k]$,

$$|w_t - \tilde{w}^j_{\sigma^j(t)}| = O\Big(\frac{\delta\omega^{1.5}k^5}{w_{\min}^2\varsigma^2}\Big),$$

$$|b_j^\dagger p^t - \alpha^j_{\sigma^j(t)}| = O\Big(\frac{\sqrt{\delta}}{w_{\min}^{1.5}\varsigma\sqrt{n}}\Big) \quad \textit{and is at most } \frac{L}{2+5T}.$$

Hence, $|\alpha^j_{t_1} - \alpha^j_{t_2}| \geq L - \frac{2L}{2+5T} = \frac{L}{1+0.4/T}$ for all distinct $t_1, t_2 \in [k]$.
(ii) For every $j \in [k'-1]$, for every $t \in [k]$, there is a distinct t' such that

$$|w_t - \hat{w}^j_{t'}| = O\Big(\frac{\delta\omega^{1.5}k^5}{w_{\min}^2\varsigma^2}\Big),$$

$$|z_j^\dagger p^t - \hat{\alpha}^j_{t'}| = O\Big(\frac{\sqrt{\delta}}{w_{\min}^{1.5}\varsigma\sqrt{n}}\Big) \quad \textit{and is at most } \frac{L}{2+5T}.$$

PROOF. Assume that the event stated in Lemma 4.6 happens. Then the inputs to Learn in steps A2 and A3 are "valid", i.e., satisfy the assumptions stated in Algorithm Learn. Plug in $\varsigma = \delta$ and $\varepsilon = \frac{1}{6\omega k}$ in Lemma 4.4. Taking the union bound over all the b_js and the z_js, we obtain that the probability that Learn fails on some input, when all the b_js and z_js are valid is at most $\frac{1}{3\omega}$. The lemma follows from Lemma 4.4 by noting that $\frac{2048kH\delta}{w_{\min}} = O\left(\frac{\sqrt{\delta}}{w_{min}^{1.5}\zeta\sqrt{n}}\right)$ and is at most $\frac{L}{24T}$, and $L/24T + L/8T \leq L/(2+5T)$. □

LEMMA 4.8. *With probability at least $1-\frac{1}{\omega}$, for every $j = 1,\ldots,k'-1$ ϱ^j is a well-defined function and $\varrho^j(\sigma^{k'}(t)) = \sigma^j(t)$ for every $t \in [k]$.*

PROOF. Assume that the events in Lemmas 4.6 and 4.7 occur. Fix $j \in [k'-1]$. We call a point $\alpha^j_{t_1} b_j + \alpha^{k'}_{t_2} b_{k'}$ a grid-j point. Call this grid point "genuine" if there exists $t \in [k]$ such that $\sigma^j(t) = t_1$ and $\sigma^{k'}(t) = t_2$, and "fake" otherwise. The distance between any two grid-j points is at least $L/(1+0.4/T)$ (by Lemma 4.7). So the probability there is a pair of genuine and fake grid-j points whose projections on z_j are less than $L/(T+0.4)$ away is at most $k^3 \cdot \frac{2}{\pi}\arcsin\left(\frac{1}{T}\right) \leq k^3 \cdot \frac{2}{\pi} \cdot \frac{6}{5T} \leq \frac{1}{3\omega k}$. Therefore, with probability at least $1-\omega$, the events in Lemma 4.6 and Lemma 4.7 happen, and for all $j \in [k'-1]$, every pair of genuine and fake grid-j points project to points on z_j that are at least $L/(T+0.4)$ apart. We condition on this in the sequel.

Now fix $j \in [k'-1]$ and consider any pair $t_1, t_2 \in [k]^2$. Let g be the grid-j point $b_j\alpha^j_{t_1} + b_{k'}\alpha^{k'}_{t_2}$ We show that $\varrho^j(t_2) = t_1$ iff g is a genuine grid-j point. If g is genuine, let t be such that $\sigma^j(t) = t_1$, $\sigma^{k'}(t) = t_2$. Let p' be the projection of p^t on $\mathrm{Span}(b_j, b_{k'})$. By Lemma 4.7, we have that $\|p'-g\|_2 \leq \frac{\sqrt{2}L}{2+5T}$. Also, there exists $t' \in [k]$ such that $|\hat{\alpha}^j_{t'} - z_j^\dagger p^t| \leq \frac{L}{2+5T}$. Since $z_j^\dagger p' = z_j^\dagger p^t$, this implies that $|z_j^\dagger g - \hat{\alpha}^j_{t'}| \leq |\hat{\alpha}^j_{t'} - z_j^\dagger p^t| + |z_j^\dagger(p'-g)| \leq \frac{(\sqrt{2}+1)L}{2+5T}$ and so $\varrho^j(t_2) = t_1$.

Now suppose g is fake but $|z_j^\dagger g - \hat{\alpha}^j_{t'}| \leq (\sqrt{2}+1)L/(2+5T)$ for some $t' \in [k]$. Let $t \in [k]$ be such that $|\hat{\alpha}^j_{t'} - z_j^\dagger p^t| \leq \frac{L}{2+5T}$. Let g' be the genuine grid point $b_j\alpha^j_{\sigma^j(t)} + b_{k'}\alpha^{k'}_{\sigma^{k'}(t)}$. So $|z_j^\dagger g' - \hat{\alpha}^j_{t'}| \leq (\sqrt{2}+1)L/(2+5T)$, and hence $|z_j^\dagger(g-g')| \leq \frac{2(\sqrt{2}+1)L}{2+5T} < \frac{L}{0.4+T}$ which is a contradiction. □

PROOF OF THEOREM 4.1. We condition on the fact that all the "good" events stated in Lemmas 3.2, 4.2, 4.6, 4.7, and 4.8 happen. The probability of success is thus $1 - O\left(\frac{1}{\omega}\right)$. The sample-size bounds follow from the description of the algorithm. For notational simplicity, let $\sigma^{k'}$ be the identity permutation, i.e., $\sigma^{k'}(t) = t$ for all $t \in [k]$. So by Lemma 4.8, we have $\varrho^j(t) = \sigma^j(t)$ for every $j \in [k'-1]$ and $t \in k$.

For $t = 1, 2, \ldots, k$, define $\bar{p}^t = \tilde{r} + \sum_{j=1}^{k'} b_j^\dagger(p^t - \tilde{r})b_j = \tilde{r} + \Pi_{\tilde{A}}(p^t - \tilde{r})$. Fix $t \in [k]$. Then

$$
\begin{aligned}
\|p^t - \tilde{p}^t\|_1 &\leq \|p^t - \hat{p}^t\|_1 + \|\hat{p}^t - \tilde{p}^t\|_1 \\
&\leq 2\|p^t - \hat{p}^t\|_1 \leq 2\left(\|p^t - \bar{p}^t\|_1 + \|\bar{p}^t - \hat{p}^t\|_1\right).
\end{aligned}
$$

We have

$$
\begin{aligned}
\|p^t - \bar{p}^t\|_2 &= \Big\|r - \tilde{r} + (p^t - r) - \sum_{j=1}^{k'} b_j^\dagger(p^t - \tilde{r})b_j\Big\|_2 \\
&= \left\|r - \tilde{r} + \Pi_{\tilde{A}}(\tilde{r} - r) + (p^t - r) - \Pi_{\tilde{A}}(p^t - r)\right\|_2 \\
&\leq 2 \cdot \|r - \tilde{r}\|_2 + \cdot\|\Pi_A - \Pi_{\tilde{A}}\|_{\mathrm{op}} \cdot \|p^t - r\|_2 \\
&\leq \frac{\delta}{12\sqrt{n}} + \frac{8\sqrt{2\delta}}{w_{\min}\zeta\sqrt{n}}.
\end{aligned}
$$

Also $\|\bar{p}^t - \hat{p}^t\|_2 \leq \Big\|\sum_{j=1}^{k'}(b_j^\dagger p^t - \alpha^j_{\sigma^j(t)})b_j\Big\|_2 = O\left(\frac{\sqrt{k\delta}}{w_{\min}^{1.5}\zeta\sqrt{n}}\right)$ where the last equality follows from Lemma 4.7. Thus, $\|p^t - \tilde{p}^t\|_1 = O\left(\frac{\sqrt{k\delta}}{w_{\min}^{1.5}\zeta}\right)$. Also, we have $|w_t - \tilde{w}_t| = O\left(\frac{\delta\omega^{1.5}k^5}{w_{\min}^2\zeta^2}\right)$ by Lemma 4.7. Finally, note that $\mathrm{Tran}(w, P; \tilde{w}, \tilde{P})$ is at most

$$
\begin{aligned}
&\frac{1}{2}\Big(\sum_{t=1}^{k}\min\{w_t, \tilde{w}_t\}\max_t\|p^t - \tilde{p}^t\|_1 + \|w - \tilde{w}\|_1\max_{t\neq t'}\|p^t - \tilde{p}^{t'}\|_1\Big) \\
&\leq \frac{1}{2}\Big(\sum_{t=1}^{k}\min\{w_t, \tilde{w}_t\}\max_t\|p^t - \tilde{p}^t\|_1 \\
&\qquad + \|w - \tilde{w}\|_1\big(\max_{t\neq t'}\|p^t - p^{t'}\|_1 + \max_t\|p^t - \tilde{p}^t\|_1\big)\Big) \\
&\leq \max_t\|p^t - \tilde{p}^t\|_1 + \|w - \tilde{w}\|_1 \cdot \frac{2}{w_{\min}} = O\left(\frac{\sqrt{k\delta}}{w_{\min}^{1.5}\zeta}\right).
\end{aligned}
$$

The running time is dominated by the time required to compute the spectral decomposition in step A1.3, the calls to Learn in steps A2.2 and A3.2, and the time to compute $\tilde{p}^t$ in step A3.4. The other steps are clearly polytime. As noted in Remark 1, it suffices to compute a decomposition such that $\|\tilde{M} - \tilde{R} - \sum_{i=1}^n \lambda_i v_i v_i^\dagger\| = O\left(\frac{\delta}{n}\right)$; this takes time $\mathrm{poly}\big(n, \ln(n/\delta)\big)$. The LP used in step A3.4 is of polynomial size, and hence can be solved in polytime. Procedure Learn requires solving (Q_v); again, an approximate solution suffices and can be computed in polytime. Theorem 5.1 proves that the one-dimensional learning problem can be solved in polytime; hence, Learn takes polytime. □

5. THE ONE-DIMENSIONAL PROBLEM: LEARNING MIXTURE SOURCES ON [0,1]

In this section, we supply the key subroutine called upon in step L2 of Algorithm Learn, which will complete the description of Algorithm 1. We are given a k-mixture source $\big(w, \pi_x(P)\big)$ on $\left[-\frac{1}{2}, \frac{1}{2}\right]$. (Recall that Learn invokes the procedure for the mixture $\big(w, \pi_{a/2H}(P)\big)$ where $\|a\|_\infty \leq H$.) It is clear that we *cannot* in general reconstruct this mixture source with an aperture size that is independent of n, let alone aperture $2k-1$. However, our goal is somewhat different and more modest. We seek to reconstruct the k-spike distribution $\big(w, \mathrm{E}[\pi_x(P)]\big)$, and we show that this *can* be achieved with aperture $2k-1$ (which is the smallest aperture at which this is information-theoretically possible).

It is easy to obtain a $(2k-1)$-snapshot from $(w, \pi_x(P))$ given a $(2k-1)$-snapshot from (w, P) by simply replacing each item $i \in [n]$ that appears in the snapshot by x_i. We will assume in the sequel that every constituent $\pi_x(p^t)$ is supported on $[0,1]$, which is simply a translation by $\frac{1}{2}$.

To simplify notation, we use $\boldsymbol{\theta} = (\vartheta, (q^1, \ldots, q^k))$ to denote the k-mixture source on $[0,1]$, and $(\vartheta, \alpha = (\alpha_1, \ldots, \alpha_k))$ to denote the corresponding k-spike distribution, where $\alpha_i \in [0,1]$ is the expectation of q^i for all $i \in [k]$. We equivalently view (ϑ, α) as a k-mixture source $(\vartheta, (f^1, \ldots, f^k))$ on $\{0,1\}$: each f^i is a "coin" whose bias is $f_1^i = \alpha_i$. In Section 5.1, we describe how to learn such a *binary* mixture source from its $(2k-1)$-snapshots (see Algorithm 2 and Theorem 5.3). Thus, if we can obtain $(2k-1)$-snapshots from the binary source $(\vartheta, (f^1, \ldots, f^k))$ (although our input is $\boldsymbol{\theta}$) then Theorem 5.3 would yield the the desired result. We show that this is indeed possible, and hence, obtain the following result (whose proof appears at the end of Section 5.1).

THEOREM 5.1. *Let $\boldsymbol{\theta} = (\vartheta, (q^1, \ldots, q^k))$ be a k-mixture source on $[0,1]$, and (ϑ, α) be the corresponding k-spike distribution. Let $\tau = \min_{j \neq j'} |\alpha_j - \alpha_{j'}|$. For any $s < \tau$ and $\psi > 0$, using $3k2^{4k}s^{-4k}\ln(4k/\psi)$ $(2k-1)$-snapshots from source $\boldsymbol{\theta}$, one can compute in polytime a k-spike distribution $(\tilde{\vartheta}, \tilde{\alpha})$ on $[0,1]$ such that $\text{Tran}(\vartheta, \alpha; \tilde{\vartheta}, \tilde{\alpha}) \leq 1024ks^{1/(4k)}$ with probability at least $1-\psi$.*

5.1 Learning a binary k-mixture source

Recall that $(\vartheta, (f^1, \ldots, f^k))$ denotes the binary k-mixture source, and $\alpha_i = f_1^i$ is the bias of the i-th "coin". We can collect from each $(2k-1)$-snapshot a random variable $0 \leq X \leq 2k-1$ denoting the number of times the outcome "1" occurs in the snapshot. Thus,

$$\Pr[X = i] = \binom{2k-1}{i} \sum_{j=1}^{k} \vartheta_j \alpha_j^i (1-\alpha_j)^{2k-1-i}.$$

Our objective is to use these statistics to reconstruct, in transportation distance (see Section 2.2), the binary source (i.e., the mixture weights and the k biases). Now consider the equivalent k-spike distribution (ϑ, α). The i-th moment, and (what we call) the i-th *normalized binomial moment* (NBM) of this distribution are respectively

$$g_i(\vartheta, \alpha) = \sum_{j=1}^{k} \vartheta_j \alpha_j^i, \qquad \nu_i(\vartheta, \alpha) = \sum_{j=1}^{k} \vartheta_j \alpha_j^i (1-\alpha_j)^{2k-1-i}$$

Up to the factors $\binom{2k-1}{i}$ the NBMs are precisely the statistics of the random variable X and so our objective in this section can be restated as: use the empirical NBMs to reconstruct the k-spike distribution (ϑ, α).

Let $g(\vartheta, \alpha) = \big(g_i(\vartheta, \alpha)\big)_{i=0}^{2k-1}$ and $\nu(\vartheta, \alpha) = \big(\nu_i(\vartheta, \alpha)\big)_{i=0}^{2k-1}$ denote the row-vectors of the first $2k-1$ moments and NBMs respectively of (ϑ, α). For an integer $b > 0$ and a vector $\beta = (\beta_1, \ldots, \beta_\ell)$, let $A_b(\beta)$ be the $\ell \times b$ matrix $(A_b(\beta))_{ij} = (1-\beta_i)^{b-1-j}\beta_i^j$ (with $1 \leq i \leq \ell$ and $0 \leq j \leq b-1$). Analogously, let $V_b(\beta)$ be the $\ell \times b$ "Vandermonde" matrix $(V_b(\beta))_{ij} = \beta_i^j$ (with $1 \leq i \leq \ell$ and $0 \leq j \leq b-1$). Let Pas be the $2k \times 2k$ lower-triangular "Pascal triangle" matrix with non-zero entries $\text{Pas}_{ij} = \binom{2k-1-j}{i-j}$ for $0 \leq j \leq 2k-1$ and $j \leq i \leq 2k-1$. Then $V_{2k}(\alpha) = A_{2k}(\alpha)\text{Pas}$, $\nu(\vartheta, \alpha) = \vartheta A_{2k}(\alpha)$, and $g(\vartheta, \alpha) = \vartheta V_{2k}(\alpha) = \nu(\vartheta, \alpha)\text{Pas}$.

In our algorithm it is convenient to use the empirical ordinary moments, but what we obtain are actually the empirical NBMs, so we need the following lemma.

LEMMA 5.2. $\|\text{Pas}\|_{\text{op}} \leq 4^k/\sqrt{3}$.

PROOF. The non-zero entries in column j of Pas are $\binom{m}{\ell}$ for $\ell = 0, \ldots, m = 2k-1-j$. Therefore, $\|\text{Pas}\|_{\text{op}} \leq \|\text{Pas}\|_F = \sqrt{\sum_{m=0}^{2k-1}\sum_{\ell=0}^{m}\binom{m}{\ell}^2}$. Since $\sum_{i=0}^{m}\binom{m}{i}^2 = \binom{2m}{m} \leq 2^{2m}$, we have $\|\text{Pas}\|_F \leq \sqrt{\sum_{m=0}^{2k-1} 2^{2m}}$. $\square$

Our algorithm uses two input parameters τ and ξ as input, and the empirical NBM vector $\tilde{\nu}$, which we convert to an empirical moment vector $\tilde{g}$ by multiplying by Pas. Since we infer (in the sampling limit) the locations of the k spikes exactly, there is a singularity in the process when spikes coincide. So we assume a minimum separation between spikes: $\tau = \min_{j \neq j'} |\alpha_j - \alpha_{j'}|$. (It is of course possible to simply run a doubling search for sufficiently small τ, but the required accuracy in the moments, and hence sample size, does increase as τ decreases.) We also assume a bound ξ on the accuracy of our empirical statistics. (When we utilize Theorem 5.3 to obtain Theorem 5.1, ξ is a consequence, and not an input parameter). We require that

$$\|\tilde{\nu} - \nu(\vartheta, \alpha)\|_2 \leq \xi 4^{-k}\sqrt{3}, \qquad \xi \leq \tau^{2k} \tag{5}$$

THEOREM 5.3. *There is a polytime algorithm that receives as input τ, ξ, an empirical NBM vector $\tilde{\nu} \in \mathbb{R}^{2k}$ satisfying (5), and outputs a k-spike distribution $(\tilde{\vartheta}, \tilde{\alpha})$ on $[0,1]$ such that $\text{Tran}(\vartheta, \alpha; \tilde{\vartheta}, \tilde{\alpha}) \leq O(\xi^{\Omega(1/k^2)})$.*

We first show the information-theoretic feasibility of Theorem 5.3: the transportation distance between two probability measures on $[0,1]$ is upper bounded by (a moderately-growing function of) the Euclidean distance between their moment maps. (To use Lemma 5.4 to prove Theorem 5.3, we have to also show how to compute $\tilde{\vartheta}$ and $\tilde{\alpha}$ from $\tilde{g}$ such that $\|\tilde{g} - g(\tilde{\vartheta}, \tilde{\alpha})\|_2$, and hence, $\|g(\vartheta, \alpha) - g(\tilde{\vartheta}, \tilde{\alpha})\|_2$ is small.)

LEMMA 5.4. *For any two (at most) k-spike distributions (ϑ, α) $(\tilde{\vartheta}, \tilde{\alpha})$ on $[0,1]$,*

$$\|g(\vartheta, \alpha) - g(\tilde{\vartheta}, \tilde{\alpha})\|_2 \geq \frac{1}{(2k-1)^{4k}2^{8k-5}} \cdot \left(\text{Tran}(\vartheta, \alpha; \tilde{\vartheta}, \tilde{\alpha})\right)^{4k-2}.$$

Lemma 5.4 can be geometrically interpreted as follows. The point $g(\vartheta, \alpha)$ is in the convex hull of the moment curve and is therefore, by Caratheodory's theorem, expressible as a convex combination of $2k$ points on the curve. However, this point is special in that it belongs to the collection of points expressible as a convex combination of merely k points of the curve. Lemma 5.4 shows that $g(\vartheta, \alpha)$ is in fact *uniquely* expressible in this way, and that moreover this combination is stable: any nearby point in this collection can only be expressed as a very similar convex combination. We utilize the following lemma, which can be understood as a global curvature property of the moment curve; we defer its proof to the end of this section. We prove a partial converse of Lemma 5.4 in Section 6, and hence obtain a sample-size lower bound that is exponential in k. The moment curve plays a central role in convex and polyhedral geometry [8], but as far as we know Lemmas 5.4 and 5.5 are new, and may be of independent interest.

LEMMA 5.5. *Let $0 \leq \beta_1 < \ldots < \beta_{\kappa+1} \leq 1$, $\ell \in [\kappa]$, and $s = \beta_{\ell+1} - \beta_\ell$. Let $\gamma(x) = \sum_{i=0}^{\kappa} \gamma_i x^i$ be a real polynomial of degree κ evaluating to 1 at the points $\beta_1, \ldots, \beta_\ell$ and evaluating to 0 at the points $\beta_{\ell+1}, \ldots, \beta_{\kappa+1}$. Then $\sum_{i=0}^{\kappa} \gamma_i^2 \leq \kappa^2 2^{4\kappa-1} s^{-2\kappa}$.*

PROOF OF LEMMA 5.4. Denote $\{\alpha_1,\ldots,\alpha_k\}\cup\{\tilde\alpha_1,\ldots,\tilde\alpha_k\}$ by $\overline{\alpha}=\{\overline{\alpha}_1,\ldots,\overline{\alpha}_K\}$ where $\overline{\alpha}_1<\ldots<\overline{\alpha}_K$. Define $\overline{\vartheta}_i=\sum_{j:\alpha_j=\overline{\alpha}_i}\vartheta_j-\sum_{j:\tilde\alpha_j=\overline{\alpha}_i}\tilde\vartheta_j$ for $i\in[K]$. Let $\overline{\vartheta}\in\mathbb{R}^K$ be the row vector $(\overline{\vartheta}_1,\ldots,\overline{\vartheta}_K)$. Let $\eta=\mathrm{Tran}(\vartheta,\alpha;\tilde\vartheta,\tilde\alpha)$. So we need to show that $\|\overline{\vartheta}V_{2k}(\overline{\alpha})\|_2\geq\frac{1}{(2k-1)^{4k}2^{8k-5}}\cdot\eta^{4k-2}$. It suffices to show that $\|\overline{\vartheta}V_K(\overline{\alpha})\|_2\geq\frac{1}{(K-1)^{2K}2^{4K-5}}\cdot\eta^{2K-2}$. There is an $1\leq\ell<K$ such that $\left|\sum_{i=1}^{\ell}\overline{\vartheta}_i\right|\cdot(\overline{\alpha}_{\ell+1}-\overline{\alpha}_\ell)\geq\eta/(K-1)$. Let $\delta=\sum_{i=1}^{\ell}\overline{\vartheta}_i$; without loss of generality $\delta\geq0$, and note that $\delta\leq1$. Let $s=\overline{\alpha}_{\ell+1}-\overline{\alpha}_\ell$, so $(K-1)\delta s\geq\eta$. Denote row i of a matrix Z by Z_{i*} and column j by Z_{*j}. We lower bound $\|\overline{\vartheta}V_K(\overline{\alpha})\|_2$, by considering its minimum value under the constraints $\sum_{i=1}^{\ell}\overline{\vartheta}_i=\delta$ and $\sum_{i=1}^{K}\overline{\vartheta}_i=0$.

A vector $y^\dagger=\overline{\vartheta}V_K(\overline{\alpha})$ minimizing $\|y\|_2$ must be orthogonal to $V_K(\overline{\alpha})_{i*}-V_K(\overline{\alpha})_{i'*}$ if $1\leq i<i'\leq\ell$ or if $\ell+1\leq i<i'\leq K$. This means that there are scalars c and d such that $V_K(\overline{\alpha})y=c(\sum_{j=1}^{\ell}e_j)+d(\sum_{j=\ell+1}^{K}e_j)$, where vector $e_j\in\mathbb{R}^K$ has a 1 in the j-th position and 0 everywhere else. Therefore, $y=c\gamma+d\gamma'$, where $\gamma=\sum_{j=1}^{\ell}(V_K(\overline{\alpha})^{-1})_{*j}$ and $\gamma'=\sum_{j=\ell+1}^{K}(V_K(\overline{\alpha})^{-1})_{*j}$. At the same time

$$\delta=\sum_{i=1}^{\ell}\overline{\vartheta}_i=\overline{\vartheta}V_K(\overline{\alpha})\gamma=y^\dagger\gamma=c\|\gamma\|_2^2+d\gamma'^\dagger\gamma$$

$$-\delta=\sum_{i=\ell+1}^{K}\overline{\vartheta}_i=\overline{\vartheta}V_K(\overline{\alpha})\gamma'=y^\dagger\gamma'=c\gamma^\dagger\gamma'+d\|\gamma'\|_2^2$$

and hence, $\|y\|_2^2=y\cdot(c\gamma+d\gamma')=(c-d)\delta$. Solving for c,d gives

$$c-d=\frac{\delta\|\gamma+\gamma'\|_2^2}{\|\gamma\|_2^2\cdot\|\gamma'\|_2^2-(\gamma^\dagger\cdot\gamma')^2}.$$

First we examine the numerator of $c-d$. Like any combination of the columns of $V_K(\overline{\alpha})^{-1}$, $\gamma+\gamma'$ is the list of coefficients of a polynomial of degree $K-1$, in the basis $1,x,\ldots,x^{K-1}$. By definition, $\gamma+\gamma'=\sum_j(V_K(\overline{\alpha})^{-1})_{*j}$, which is to say that for every i, $V_K(\overline{\alpha})_{i*}\cdot(\gamma+\gamma')=1$. So the polynomial $\gamma+\gamma'$ evaluates to 1 at every $\overline{\alpha}_i$. It can therefore only be the constant polynomial 1; this means that $(\gamma+\gamma')_i=1$ if $i=0$, and $(\gamma+\gamma')_i=0$ otherwise. Thus $\|\gamma+\gamma'\|_2^2=1$.

Next we examine the denominator, which we upper bound by $\|\gamma\|_2^2\cdot\|\gamma'\|_2^2$. When interpreted as a polynomial, γ takes the value 1 on a nonempty set of points $\overline{\alpha}_1,\ldots,\overline{\alpha}_\ell$ separated by the positive distance $s=\overline{\alpha}_{\ell+1}-\overline{\alpha}_\ell$ from another nonempty set of points $\overline{\alpha}_{\ell+1},\ldots,\overline{\alpha}_K$ upon which it takes the value 0. Observe that if the polynomial was required to change value by a large amount within a short interval, it would have to have large coefficients. A converse to this is the inequality stated in Lemma 5.5. Using this to bound $\|\gamma\|_2^2$ and $\|\gamma'\|_2^2$, and since $\delta s\geq\eta/(K-1)$, we obtain that

$$\|y\|_2^2=(c-d)\delta\geq\frac{\delta^2}{\|\gamma\|_2^2\cdot\|\gamma'\|_2^2}\geq\frac{\delta^2}{((K-1)^2 2^{4K-5}s^{-2K+2})^2}$$
$$\geq\frac{\eta^{4K-4}}{(K-1)^{4K}2^{8K-10}}.\quad\square$$

We now define the algorithm promised by Theorem 5.3. To give some intuition, suppose first that we are given the true moment vector $g(\vartheta,\alpha)=\vartheta V_{2k}(\alpha)$. Observe that there is a common vector $\lambda=(\lambda_0,\ldots,\lambda_k)^\dagger$ of length $k+1$ that is a dependency among every $k+1$ adjacent columns of $V_{2k}(\alpha)$. In other words, letting $\Lambda=\Lambda(\lambda)$ denote the $2k\times k$ matrix with $\Lambda_{ij}=\lambda_{i-j}$ (for $0\leq i<2k$, $0\leq j<k$ and with the understanding $\lambda_\ell=0$ for $\ell\notin\{0,\ldots,k\}$), $V_{2k}(\alpha)\Lambda=0$. Thus $g(\vartheta,\alpha)\Lambda=\vartheta V_{2k}(\alpha)\Lambda=0$. Overtly this is a system of $2k$ equations to determine λ. But we eliminate the redundancy in Λ by forming the $k\times(k+1)$ matrix $G=G(g(\vartheta,\alpha))$ defined by $G_{ij}=g(\vartheta,\alpha)_{i+j}$ for $i=0,\ldots,k-1$ and $j=0,\ldots,k$, and then solve the system of linear equations $G\lambda=0$ to obtain λ. This system does not have a unique solution, so in the sequel λ will denote a solution with $\lambda_k=1$. For each $i=1,\ldots,k$, we have $\left(V_{2k}(\alpha)\Lambda\right)_{i,1}=\sum_{\ell=0}^{k}\lambda_\ell{\alpha_i}^\ell=0$. This implies that we can obtain the α_i values by computing the roots of the polynomial $P_\lambda(x):=\sum_{\ell=0}^{k}\lambda_\ell x^\ell$. Once we have the α_i's, we can compute ϑ by solving the linear system $yV_{2k}(\alpha)=g(\vartheta,\alpha)$ for y.

Of course, we are actually given $\tilde g$ rather than the true vector $g(\vartheta,\alpha)$. So we need to control the error in estimating first α and then ϑ. The learning algorithm is as follows.

ALGORITHM 2. *Input: parameters ξ,τ and empirical moments $\tilde g$ such that $\|\tilde g-g(\vartheta,\alpha)\|_2\leq\xi$.*
Output: a k-spike distribution $(\tilde\vartheta,\tilde\alpha)$

B1. Solve the minimization problem:
$$\text{minimize}\quad\|x\|_1\quad\text{s.t.}\quad\|G(\tilde g)x\|_1\leq2^k k\xi,\quad x_k=1\qquad(\mathrm{P})$$
which can be encoded as a linear program and hence solved in polytime, to obtain a solution $\tilde\lambda$. Observe that since $G(\tilde g)$ has $k+1$ columns and k rows, there is always a feasible solution.

B2. Let $\bar\alpha_1,\ldots,\bar\alpha_k$ be the (possibly complex) roots of the polynomial $P_{\tilde\lambda}$. Thus, we have $V_{2k}(\bar\alpha)\Lambda(\tilde\lambda)=0$. We map the roots to values in $[0,1]$ as follows. Let $\epsilon=\frac{4}{\tau}(2k\xi)^{1/k}$. First we compute $\hat\alpha_1,\ldots,\hat\alpha_k$ such that $|\hat\alpha_i-\bar\alpha_i|\leq\epsilon$ for all i, in time $\mathrm{poly}(\log(\frac{1}{\epsilon}))$, using Pan's algorithm [38, Theorem 1.1][2]. We now set $\tilde\alpha_i=\max\{0,\min\{\mathrm{Re}(\hat\alpha_i),1\}\}$.

B3. Finally, we set $\tilde\vartheta$ to be the row-vector y that minimizes $\|yV_{2k}(\tilde\alpha)-\tilde g\|_2^2$ subject to $\|y\|_1=1$, $y\geq0$. Note that this is a convex quadratic program that can be solved exactly in polytime [17].

We now analyze Algorithm 2 and justify Theorem 5.3. Recall that $\tau=\min_{j\neq j'}|\alpha_j-\alpha_{j'}|$. We need the following lemma, whose proof appears at the end of this section.

LEMMA 5.6. *The weights $\tilde\vartheta$ satisfy $\|\tilde\vartheta V_{2k}(\tilde\alpha)-\tilde g\|_2\leq\|g(\vartheta,\alpha)-\tilde g\|_2+\frac{(8k)^{5/2}}{\tau}\cdot(2k\xi)^{1/k}$.*

PROOF OF THEOREM 5.3. We call Algorithm 2 with $\tilde g=\tilde\nu\mathrm{Pas}$. By Lemma 5.2, we obtain that $\|\tilde g-g(\vartheta,\alpha)\|_2\leq\xi$, and by Lemma 5.6, we have that $\|g(\vartheta,\alpha)-\tilde\vartheta V_{2k}(\tilde\alpha)\|_2\leq2\|g(\vartheta,\alpha)-\tilde g\|_2+\frac{8}{\tau}\cdot(8k)^{3/2}\left(2k\xi\right)^{1/k}$. Coupled with Lemma 5.4 and since $\xi\leq\tau^{2k}$, we obtain that $\mathrm{Tran}(\vartheta,\alpha;\tilde\vartheta,\tilde\alpha)$ is at most

$$\left[(2k-1)^{4k}2^{8k-5}\|g(\vartheta,\alpha)-g(\tilde\vartheta,\tilde\alpha)\|_2\right]^{\frac{1}{4k-2}}$$
$$\leq\left[(2k-1)^{4k}2^{8k-5}\left(2\xi+\frac{(8k)^{\frac{5}{2}}}{\tau}(2k\xi)^{\frac{1}{k}}\right)\right]^{\frac{1}{4k-2}}$$
$$\leq\left[(2k-1)^{4k}2^{8k-5}\left(2\xi+(8k)^{5/2}(2k\sqrt{\xi})^{1/2k}\right)\right]^{\frac{1}{4k-2}}$$
$$\leq1024\cdot k\xi^{\frac{1}{8k^2}}.\quad\square$$

[2]The theorem requires that the complex roots lie within the unit circle and that the coefficient of the highest-degree term is 1; but the discussion following it in [38] shows that this is essentially without loss of generality.

PROOF OF THEOREM 5.1. We convert $\boldsymbol{\theta}$ to the corresponding binary source $(\vartheta, (f^1, \ldots, f^k))$ by randomized rounding. Given a $(2k-1)$-snapshot $z = (z_1, \ldots, z_{2k-1}) \in [0,1]^{2k-1}$ from $\boldsymbol{\theta}$, we obtain a $(2k-1)$-snapshot from the binary source as follows. We choose $2k-1$ independent values $a_1, \ldots, a_{2k-1}$ uniformly at random from $[0,1]$ and set $X_i = 1$ if $z_i \geq a_i$ and 0 otherwise for all $i \in [2k-1]$. Note that if q^j is the constituent generating the $(2k-1)$-snapshot z, then $\Pr[X_i = 1 | q^j] = \mathrm{E}[X_i | q^j] = \alpha_j$, and so $X_1, \ldots, X_{2k-1}$ is a random $(2k-1)$-snapshot from the above binary source.

Now we apply Theorem 5.3, setting $\xi = s^{2k}$. Let $\tilde{\nu}$ be the empirical NBM-vector obtained from the $(2k-1)$-snapshots of the above binary source (i.e., $\tilde{\nu}_i = \binom{2k-1}{i}^{-1}$. (frequency with which the $(2k-1)$-snapshot has exactly i 1s)). The stated sample size ensures, via a Chernoff bound, that $\Pr\left[|\tilde{\nu}_i - \nu(\vartheta,\alpha)_i| \geq \frac{\xi 4^{-k}}{\sqrt{6k}}\right] < \frac{\psi}{2k}$ for all $i = 0, \ldots, 2k-1$. Hence, with probability at least $1-\psi$, we have $\|\tilde{\nu} - \nu(\vartheta,\alpha)\|_2 \leq \sqrt{2k} \cdot \|\tilde{\nu} - \nu(\vartheta,\alpha)\|_\infty \leq \xi 4^{-k}/\sqrt{3}$. □

PROOF OF LEMMA 5.5. There are two easy cases to dismiss before we reach the more subtle part of this lemma. The first easy case is $\ell = 1$. In this case γ is a single Lagrange interpolant: $\gamma(x) = \prod_{j=2}^{\kappa+1} \frac{x-\beta_j}{\beta_1-\beta_j}$. For $0 \leq i \leq \kappa$ let $e_i^\kappa(\beta_2, \ldots, \beta_{\kappa+1})$ be the i'th *elementary symmetric mean*,

$$e_i^\kappa(\beta_2, \ldots, \beta_{\kappa+1}) = \frac{1}{\binom{\kappa}{i}} \sum_{S \subseteq \{2,\ldots,\kappa+1\}:|S|=i} \prod_{j \in S} \beta_j$$

and observe that for all i, $0 \leq e_i^\kappa(\beta_2, \ldots, \beta_{\kappa+1}) \leq 1$. Now

$$\gamma(x) = \Big(\prod_{j=2}^{\kappa+1} \frac{1}{\beta_1 - \beta_j}\Big) \sum_{i=0}^{\kappa} (-1)^{\kappa-i} \binom{\kappa}{i} e_{\kappa-i}^\kappa(\beta_2, \ldots, \beta_{\kappa+1}) x^i$$

So $\sum_{i=0}^\kappa \gamma_i^2 = \Big(\prod_{j=2}^{\kappa+1} \frac{1}{\beta_1-\beta_j}\Big)^2 \sum_{i=0}^\kappa \left(\binom{\kappa}{i} e_i^\kappa(\beta_2, \ldots, \beta_{\kappa+1})\right)^2 \leq s^{-2\kappa} \sum_{i=0}^\kappa \binom{\kappa}{i}^2 = \binom{2\kappa}{\kappa} s^{-2\kappa}$.

The second easy case is $\ell = \kappa$; this is almost as simple. Merely note that the above argument applies to the polynomial $1-\gamma$, so that we have only to allow for the possible increase of $|\gamma_0|$ by 1. Hence $\sum_{i=0}^\kappa \gamma_i^2 \leq 4\binom{2\kappa}{\kappa} s^{-2\kappa}$.

We now consider the less trivial case of $1 < \ell < \kappa$. The difficulty here is that the Lagrange interpolants of γ may have very large coefficients, particularly if among $\beta_1, \ldots, \beta_\ell$ or among $\beta_{\ell+1}, \ldots, \beta_{\kappa+1}$ there are closely spaced roots, as well there may be. We must show that these large coefficients cancel out in γ.

The trick is to examine not γ but $\partial\gamma/\partial x$. The roots of the derivative interlace the two sets on which γ is constant, which is to say, with $\beta'_1 \leq \ldots \leq \beta'_{\kappa-1}$ denoting the roots of $\partial\gamma/\partial x$, that for $j < \ell$, $\beta_j \leq \beta'_j \leq \beta_{j+1}$, and for $j \geq \ell$, $\beta_{j+1} \leq \beta'_j \leq \beta_{j+2}$. In particular, none of the roots fall in the interval $(\beta_\ell, \beta_{\ell+1})$. For some constant C we can write $\partial\gamma/\partial x = C \prod_{j=0}^{\kappa-1} (x - \beta'_j)$ (with $\mathrm{sign}(C) = (-1)^{1+\kappa-\ell}$). Observe that $\int_{\beta_\ell}^{\beta_{\ell+1}} \frac{\partial\gamma}{\partial x}(x)\, dx = -1$. So $(-1)^{1+\kappa-\ell}/C = \int_{\beta_\ell}^{\beta_{\ell+1}} (-1)^{\kappa-\ell} \prod_{j=0}^{\kappa-1}(x-\beta'_j)\, dx$. Observe that if for any $j < \ell$, β'_j is increased, or if for any $j \geq \ell$, β'_j is decreased, then the integral decreases. So $(-1)^{1+\kappa-\ell}/C \geq \int_{\beta_\ell}^{\beta_{\ell+1}} (-1)^{\kappa-\ell}(x-\beta_\ell)^{\ell-1}(x-\beta_{\ell+1})^{\kappa-\ell}\, dx$. This is a definite integral that can be evaluated in closed form:

$$\int_{\beta_\ell}^{\beta_{\ell+1}} (-1)^{\kappa-\ell}(x-\beta_\ell)^{\ell-1}(x-\beta_{\ell+1})^{\kappa-\ell}\, dx = (\beta_{\ell+1}-\beta_\ell)^\kappa (\ell-1)!(\kappa-\ell)!/\kappa!\,.$$

Hence, $(-1)^{1+\kappa-\ell} C \leq \frac{\kappa!}{s^\kappa(\ell-1)!(\kappa-\ell)!}$. The sum of squares of coefficients of $\frac{\partial\gamma}{\partial x}$ is $C^2 \sum_{i=0}^{\kappa-1} \binom{\kappa-1}{i}^2 (e_i^{\kappa-1}(\beta'_1, \ldots, \beta'_{\kappa-1}))^2 \leq C^2 \binom{2\kappa-2}{\kappa-1}$. Integration only decreases the magnitude of the coefficients, so the same bound applies to γ, with the exception of the constant coefficient. The constant coefficient can be bounded by the fact that γ has a root in $(0,1)$, and that in that interval the derivative is bounded in magnitude by $C \sum_{i=0}^{\kappa-1} \binom{\kappa-1}{i} = C \cdot 2^\kappa$. So $|\gamma_0| \leq C \cdot 2^\kappa$. Consequently, $\sum_{i=0}^\kappa \gamma_i^2$ is at most

$$C^2 \left[\binom{2\kappa-2}{\kappa-1} + 2^{2\kappa}\right] \leq \frac{\binom{2\kappa-2}{\kappa-1} + 2^{2\kappa}}{s^{2\kappa}} \cdot \left(\frac{\kappa!}{(\ell-1)!(\kappa-\ell)!}\right)^2$$
$$\leq \frac{5\kappa^2 2^{2\kappa-2}}{s^{2\kappa}} \cdot \binom{\kappa-1}{\ell-1}^2 \leq \frac{5\kappa^2 2^{4\kappa-4}}{s^{2\kappa}},$$

which completes the proof of the lemma. □

Proof of Lemma 5.6.

Recall that $G = G(g(\vartheta,\alpha))$ is the $k \times (k+1)$ matrix defined by $G_{ij} = g(\vartheta,\alpha)_{i+j}$ for $i = 0, \ldots, k-1$ and $j = 0, \ldots, k$; λ is such that $G\lambda = 0$ and $\lambda_k = 1$; $\Lambda = \Lambda(\lambda)$ is the $2k \times k$ matrix with $\Lambda_{ij} = \lambda_{i-j}$ (for $0 \leq i < 2k$, $0 \leq j < k$ with the understanding $\lambda_\ell = 0$ for $\ell \notin \{0, \ldots, k\}$; and $P_\lambda(x)$ is the polynomial $\sum_{\ell=0}^k \lambda_\ell x^\ell$. We use V_k, V_{2k}, to denote $V_k(\alpha), V_{2k}(\alpha)$ respectively, and $\tilde{V}_k, \tilde{V}_{2k}, \tilde{G}, \tilde{\Lambda}$ to denote $V_k(\tilde{\alpha}), V_{2k}(\tilde{\alpha}), G(\tilde{g}), \Lambda(\tilde{\lambda})$ respectively. We abbreviate $g(\vartheta,\alpha)$ to g.

LEMMA 5.7. *If $\|\tilde{g} - g\|_2 \leq \xi$, then $\|G\tilde{\lambda}\|_1 \leq 2^{k+1}k\xi$.*

PROOF. First, observe that $\tilde{G}\lambda = G\lambda + (\tilde{G}-G)\lambda = (\tilde{G}-G)\lambda$. Also $\|\lambda\|_2 \leq \|\lambda\|_1 = \prod_{i=1}^k (1+\alpha_i) \leq 2^k$. The last two inequalities follows since $P_\lambda(x) = \prod_{i=1}^k (x - \alpha_i)$, and $P_\lambda(-1) = (-1)^k \|\lambda\|_1$. So for any $i = 1, \ldots, k$, $|(G-\tilde{G})_i \cdot \lambda| \leq \|\lambda\|_2 \|G_i - \tilde{G}_i\|_2 \leq 2^k \xi$. Thus, λ is a feasible solution to (P), which implies that $\|\tilde{\lambda}\|_1 \leq 2^k$. We have $\|G\tilde{\lambda}\|_1 \leq \|\tilde{G}\tilde{\lambda}\|_1 + \|(G-\tilde{G})\tilde{\lambda}\|_1 \leq 2^k k\xi + \|(G-\tilde{G})\tilde{\lambda}\|_1$. For any $i = 1, \ldots, k$, $|(G-\tilde{G})_i \cdot \tilde{\lambda}| \leq \|G_i - \tilde{G}_i\|_2 \|\tilde{\lambda}\|_2 \leq 2^k \xi$, so $\|G\tilde{\lambda}\|_1 \leq 2^{k+1}k\xi$. □

LEMMA 5.8. *For every α_i, $i = 1, \ldots, k$, there exists a $\sigma(i) \in \{1, \ldots, k\}$ such that $\vartheta_i |\alpha_i - \tilde{\alpha}_{\sigma(i)}| \leq \frac{8}{\tau}(2k\xi)^{1/k}$.*

PROOF. Since $\|G\tilde{\lambda}\|_2 \leq 2^{k+1}k\xi$ (by Lemma 5.7), we have equivalently that the $\|.\|_2$ norm of $g\tilde{\Lambda} = \vartheta V_{2k}\tilde{\Lambda}$ is at most $2^{k+1}k\xi$. We may write $\vartheta V_{2k}\tilde{\Lambda}$ as

$$\vartheta V_{2k}\tilde{\Lambda} = \vartheta \begin{pmatrix} P_{\tilde{\lambda}}(\alpha_1) & \alpha_1 P_{\tilde{\lambda}}(\alpha_1) & \cdots & \alpha_1^{k-1} P_{\tilde{\lambda}}(\alpha_1) \\ P_{\tilde{\lambda}}(\alpha_2) & \alpha_2 P_{\tilde{\lambda}}(\alpha_2) & \cdots & \alpha_2^{k-1} P_{\tilde{\lambda}}(\alpha_2) \\ \vdots & \vdots & \ddots & \vdots \\ P_{\tilde{\lambda}}(\alpha_k) & \alpha_k P_{\tilde{\lambda}}(\alpha_k) & \cdots & \alpha_k^{k-1} P_{\tilde{\lambda}}(\alpha_k) \end{pmatrix}$$

which is equal to $\vartheta' V_k(\alpha)$ where $\vartheta' = (\vartheta_1 P_{\tilde{\lambda}}(\alpha_1), \cdots, \vartheta_k P_{\tilde{\lambda}}(\alpha_k))$. Thus, we are given that $\|\vartheta' V_k\|_2 \leq 2^{k+1}k\xi$.

Let $(\gamma^i)^\dagger = (\arg\min_{y\in\mathbb{R}^k: y_i=1} \|yV_k\|_2)V_k$. Then, we also have $\|\vartheta' V_k\|_2 \geq \max_i |\vartheta'_i| \|\gamma^i\|_2$. Note that γ^i must be orthogonal to $(V_k)_{j*}$ for all $j \neq i$, and $(V_k)_{i*}\gamma^i = \|\gamma^i\|_2^2$. (Recall that Z_{i*} denotes row i of a matrix Z.) Let $Q_i(x) = \sum_{\ell=0}^{k-1} \gamma^i_\ell x^\ell$. Then, $Q_i(x) = \|\gamma^i\|_2^2 \prod_{j\neq i} \frac{x-\alpha_j}{\alpha_i - \alpha_j}$. Also, since the coefficients of $Q_i(x)$ have alternating signs, we have

$$|Q_i(-1)| = \|\gamma^i\|_1 = \|\gamma^i\|_2^2 \prod_{j\neq i} \frac{1+\alpha_j}{|\alpha_i - \alpha_j|}.$$

Hence, $\|\gamma^i\|_2 \geq \prod_{j\neq i} \frac{|\alpha_i - \alpha_j|}{1+\alpha_j}$. So we obtain the lower bound

$$\begin{aligned}\|\vartheta' V_k\|_2 &\geq \max_i \Big(|\vartheta'_i| \cdot \prod_{j\neq i} \frac{|\alpha_i - \alpha_j|}{1+\alpha_j} \Big) \\ &\geq \max_i \Big(\vartheta_i \Big(\frac{\tau}{2}\Big)^{k-1} \prod_{j=1}^{k} |\alpha_i - \bar{\alpha}_j| \Big) \\ &\geq \max_i \Big(\vartheta_i \Big(\frac{\tau}{2}\Big)^{k-1} \prod_{j=1}^{k} |\alpha_i - \mathrm{Re}(\bar{\alpha}_j)| \Big).\end{aligned}$$

The last inequality follows since complex roots occur in conjugate pairs, so if $\bar{\alpha}_\ell = a + bi$ is complex, then there must be some ℓ' such that $\bar{\alpha}_{\ell'} = a - bi$ and therefore,

$$\begin{aligned}\prod_j |\alpha_i - \bar{\alpha}_j| &= \big((\alpha_i - a)^2 + b^2\big) \cdot \prod_{j\neq \ell,\ell'} |\alpha_i - \bar{\alpha}_j| \\ &\geq (\alpha_i - a)^2 \cdot \prod_{j\neq \ell,\ell'} |\alpha_i - \bar{\alpha}_j|.\end{aligned}$$

Now, we claim that $|\alpha_i - \mathrm{Re}(\bar{\alpha}_j)| \geq \big||\alpha_i - \tilde{\alpha}_j| - \epsilon\big|$ for every j. If both $\mathrm{Re}(\bar{\alpha}_j)$ and $\mathrm{Re}(\hat{\alpha}_j)$ lie in $[0,1]$, or both of them are less than 0, or both are greater than 1, then this follows since $|\bar{\alpha}_j - \hat{\alpha}_j| \leq \epsilon$ and $\alpha_i \in [0,1]$. If $\mathrm{Re}(\bar{\alpha}_j) \notin [0,1]$ but $\mathrm{Re}(\hat{\alpha}_j) \in [0,1]$, or if $\mathrm{Re}(\bar{\alpha}_j) \in [0,1]$ but $\mathrm{Re}(\hat{\alpha}_j) \notin [0,1]$, then this again follows since $|\bar{\alpha}_j - \hat{\alpha}_j| \leq \epsilon$. Combining everything, we get that

$$2^k(2k\xi) \;\geq\; \|\vartheta' V_k\|_2 \;\geq\; \max_i \Big(\vartheta_i \Big(\frac{\tau}{2}\Big)^{k-1} \prod_{j=1}^{k} \big||\alpha_i - \tilde{\alpha}_j| - \epsilon\big| \Big).$$

This implies that for every $i = 1, \ldots, k$, there exists $\sigma(i) \in \{1, \ldots, k\}$ such that $\vartheta_i |\alpha_i - \tilde{\alpha}_{\sigma(i)}| \leq \frac{4}{\tau} \cdot (2k\xi)^{1/k} + \epsilon$. ☐

We can now wrap up the proof of Lemma 5.6. Let $\eta = \frac{8}{\tau} \cdot (2k\xi)^{1/k}$. We will bound $\|\tilde{\vartheta}\tilde{V}_{2k} - \tilde{g}\|_2$ by exhibiting a solution $y \in [0,1]^k$, $\|y\|_1 = 1$ such that $\|y\tilde{V}_{2k} - \tilde{g}\|_2 \leq \|g - \tilde{g}\| + k(8k)^{3/2}\eta$. Let σ be the function whose existence is proved in Lemma 5.8. For $j = 1, \ldots, k$, set $y_j = \sum_{i:\sigma(i)=j} \vartheta_i$ (if $\sigma^{-1}(j) = \emptyset$, then $y_j = 0$). We have $\|y\tilde{V}_{2k} - \tilde{g}\|_2 \leq \|g - \tilde{g}\|_2 + \|g - y\tilde{V}_{2k}\|_2$. We expand $g - y\tilde{V}_{2k} = \vartheta V_{2k} - y\tilde{V}_{2k} = \sum_{i=1}^k \vartheta_i \big((V_{2k})_{i*} - (\tilde{V}_{2k})_{\sigma(i)*}\big)$ For every i,

$$\vartheta_i^2 \|(V_{2k})_{i*} - (\tilde{V}_{2k})_{\sigma(i)*}\|_2^2 = \vartheta_i^2 \sum_{\ell=0}^{2k-1} (\alpha_i^\ell - \tilde{\alpha}_{\sigma(i)}^\ell)^2 \leq \vartheta_i^2 \cdot 8k^3 \cdot \eta^2.$$

Therefore, $\|g - y\tilde{V}_{2k}\|_2 \leq k(8k)^{3/2}\eta$. ☐

6. LOWER BOUNDS

In this section, we prove sample-size and aperture lower bounds that apply even to the setting where we have k-mixture sources on $\{0,1\}$ (so $n = 2$). Recall that a k-mixture source on $\{0,1\}$ may be equivalently viewed as a k-spike distribution supported on $[0,1]$; in the sequel, we therefore focus on k-spike distributions. The separation of a k-spike distribution (or the equivalent k-mixture source) is the minimum separation between its spikes. Theorem 6.2 proves that $2k-1$ is the smallest aperture at which it becomes possible to reconstruct a k-spike distribution. We emphasize that this is an *information-theoretic* lower bound. We show (Theorem 6.2) that there are two k-spike distributions supported on $[0,1]$ having separation $\Omega(\frac{1}{k})$ and transportation distance $\Omega(\frac{1}{k})$ that yield exactly the same first $2k-2$ moments. Moreover, for any $b \geq 2k-1$, by adjusting the constant in the $\Omega(.)$s, one can ensure that the $(2k-1)$-th, $\ldots$, b-th moments of these two k-spike distributions are exponentially close.

It follows immediately that even with infinite sample size it is impossible to reconstruct a k-mixture source (with arbitrarily small error) if we limit the aperture to $2k-2$. Furthermore, we leverage the exponential closeness of the moments to show that for any aperture $b \geq 2k-1$, there exists $\tau = \Omega(\frac{1}{k})$ such that reconstructing a k-mixture source on $\{0,1\}$ having separation τ to within transportation distance $\frac{\tau}{4}$ requires *exponential in* k sample size (Theorem 6.1). In fact, since $n = 2$, this means that with arbitrary mixtures, the exponential dependence of the sample size on k remains *even with aperture* $O(k \log n)$, and more generally, even with aperture $O(k \cdot \kappa(n))$ for any function $\kappa(.)$. (To place this in perspective, observe that with separation $\tau = \Omega(\frac{1}{k})$, if we have $\Omega(k^2 \log k)$ aperture, then $O(k^3)$ samples suffice to reconstruct the given mixture source to within transportation distance $\frac{\tau}{4}$. This is because with, with high probability, we will see every $\{0,1\}$ source or "coin" with weight $\vartheta_i \geq \frac{1}{\tau^2}$, and we can estimate its bias within additive error, say $\frac{\tau}{8}$, with probability $1 - \frac{1}{\mathrm{poly}(k)}$ since we have $\Omega(\frac{\log k}{\tau^2})$ coin tosses available. The unseen coins contribute $O(\tau)$ to the transportation distance, so we infer k-mixture source within transportation distance $\frac{\tau}{4}$.)

THEOREM 6.1. *(i) With aperture $2k-2$, it is impossible to reconstruct a k-mixture source having separation at least $\frac{1}{2k}$ to within transportation distance $\frac{1}{8k}$ even with infinite sample size.*
(ii) For any $\psi \in (0,1)$, and any constants $c_A \geq 1$, $c_E \geq 0$, there exists $\tau = \Omega(\frac{1}{k})$ such that reconstructing a k-mixture source having separation τ to within transportation distance $\frac{\tau}{4}$ with probability at least $1 - \psi$ using aperture $c_A(2k-1)$ requires $\Omega(3^{c_E k} \ln(\frac{1}{\psi}))$ samples.

Our approach for proving Theorem 6.1 is as follows. To prove the existence of two suitable k-spike distributions (Theorem 6.2), we fix some spike locations ensuring the required separation and transportation-distance bounds, and search for suitable probability weights to place on these locations so as to obtain the desired closeness of moments for the two k-spike distributions. Since moments are linear functions of the weights (and the spike locations are fixed), this search problem can be encoded as a minimization LP (P1). To upper bound the optimum, we move to the dual LP (D1), which can be interpreted as finding a polynomial satisfying certain conditions on its coefficients and roots, to maximize the variation between its values at certain spike locations. We upper bound the variation possible by such a polynomial using elementary properties of polynomials. Finally, the closeness of moments of the two k-spike distributions obtained this way implies that the distributions of b-snapshots of these two distributions have exponentially small variation distance (Lemma 6.3), and this yields the sample-size lower bound in Theorem 6.1.

THEOREM 6.2. *Let $b \geq 2k-1$, and $\rho \geq 2$. There are two k-spike distributions (y, α) and (z, β) on $[0, 1]$ with separation $\frac{2}{(2k-1)\rho}$ and $\mathrm{Tran}(y, \alpha; z, \beta) \geq \frac{1}{(2k-1)\rho}$ such that $g_\ell(y, \alpha) = g_\ell(z, \beta)$ for all $\ell = 0, \ldots, 2k-2$, and $\sum_{\ell=2k-1}^{b} \binom{b}{\ell} 2^\ell |g_\ell(y, \alpha) - g_\ell(z, \beta)| \leq 4 \cdot \frac{3^b}{\rho^{2k-1}}$.*

PROOF. Let $\epsilon = \frac{1}{\rho}$. We set $\alpha_i = \epsilon \cdot \frac{2(i-1)}{2k-1}$, and $\beta_i = \epsilon \cdot \frac{2i-1}{2k-1} = \alpha_i + \frac{\epsilon}{2k-1}$ for all $i = 1, \ldots, k$. Note that for any mixture weights $y_1, \ldots, y_k$, and $z_1, \ldots, z_k$, the separation of (y, α) and (z, β) is $\frac{2}{(2k-1)\rho}$ and $\mathrm{Tran}(y, \alpha; z, \beta) \geq \frac{1}{(2k-1)\rho}$. We obtain y and z by solving the following linear program (P1), whose optimal value we show is at most $4 \cdot \frac{3^b}{\rho^{2k-1}}$.

$$\min \quad \sum_{\ell=2k-1}^{b} \binom{b}{\ell} 2^\ell \lambda_\ell \tag{P1}$$

$$\text{s.t.} \quad \sum_{i=1}^{k} (z_i \beta_i^\ell - y_i \alpha_i^\ell) = 0 \qquad \forall \ell = 0, \ldots, 2k-2 \tag{6}$$

$$\sum_{i=1}^{k} (z_i \beta_i^\ell - y_i \alpha_i^\ell) \leq \lambda_\ell \qquad \forall \ell = 2k-1, \ldots, b \tag{7}$$

$$\sum_{i=1}^{k} (y_i \alpha_i^\ell - z_i \beta_i^\ell) \leq \lambda_\ell \qquad \forall \ell = 2k-1, \ldots, b \tag{8}$$

$$\sum_{i=1}^{k} y_i = 1, \quad y_i, z_i \geq 0 \qquad \forall i = 1, \ldots, k.$$

The dual of (P1) is the following linear program.

$$\max \quad c \tag{D1}$$

$$\text{s.t.} \quad c - \sum_{\ell=0}^{2k-2} \gamma_\ell \alpha_i^\ell - \sum_{\ell=2k-1}^{b} (\gamma_\ell - \theta_\ell) \alpha_i^\ell \leq 0 \qquad \forall i = 1, \ldots, k$$

$$\sum_{\ell=0}^{2k-2} \gamma_\ell \beta_i^\ell + \sum_{\ell=2k-1}^{b} (\gamma_\ell - \theta_\ell) \beta_i^\ell \leq 0 \qquad \forall i = 1, \ldots, k$$

$$\gamma_\ell + \theta_\ell \leq \binom{b}{\ell} 2^\ell \qquad \forall \ell = 2k-1, \ldots, b$$

$$\gamma_\ell, \theta_\ell \geq 0 \qquad \forall \ell.$$

The dual variable c corresponds to $\sum_i y_i = 1$, variables γ_ℓ for $\ell = 0, \ldots, b$ correspond to (6) and (8), and variables θ_ℓ for $\ell = 2k-1, \ldots, b$ correspond to (7). Given a feasible solution to (D1), if we set $\gamma'_\ell = \gamma_\ell - \min\{\gamma_\ell, \theta_\ell\}$, $\theta'_\ell = \theta_\ell - \min\{\gamma_\ell, \theta_\ell\}$ for all $\ell = 2k-1, \ldots, b$, then we obtain another feasible solution to (D1), where $\gamma'_\ell + \theta'_\ell = |\gamma'_\ell - \theta'_\ell| = |\gamma_\ell - \theta_\ell|$. Thus, an optimal solution to (D1) can be interpreted as a polynomial $f(x) = \sum_{\ell=0}^{b} f_\ell x^\ell$ satisfying $|f_\ell| \leq \binom{b}{\ell} 2^\ell$ for all $\ell = 2k-1, \ldots, b$, and $f(\alpha_i) \geq c > 0 \geq f(\beta_i)$ for all $i = 1, \ldots, k$ (where $c > 0$ follows from Lemma 5.4).

Let $c' = 3^b \cdot \frac{\rho/(\rho-1)}{\rho^{2k-1}} \leq 2 \cdot \frac{3^b}{\rho^{2k-1}}$. Suppose that $c > 2c'$. Observe that for any $x \in [0, \epsilon]$, by the Cauchy-Schwarz inequality and since the ℓ_2-norm is at most the ℓ_1 norm, we have

$$\begin{aligned} \Big| \sum_{\ell=2k-1}^{b} f_\ell x^\ell \Big| &\leq \Big(\sum_{\ell=2k-1}^{b} |f_\ell| \Big) \Big(\sum_{\ell=2k-1}^{b} x^\ell \Big) \\ &\leq \sum_{\ell=2k-1}^{b} \binom{b}{\ell} 2^\ell \cdot \frac{\rho/(\rho-1)}{\rho^{2k-1}} \leq c'. \end{aligned} \tag{9}$$

Let $h(x) = \sum_{\ell=0}^{2k-2} f_\ell x^\ell - c/2$. Then, due to (9), we have $f(x) - c/2 - c' \leq h(x) \leq f(x) - c/2 + c'$ for all $x \in [0, \epsilon]$, so $h(\alpha_i) > 0 > h(\beta_i)$ for all $i = 1, \ldots, k$. But then $h(x)$ has $2k-1$ roots—one in every (α_i, β_i) and (β_i, α_{i+1}) interval—which is impossible since $h(x)$ is a polynomial of degree $2k-2$. ☐

Given a k-spike distribution $(\vartheta, \alpha = (\alpha_1, \ldots, \alpha_k))$ on $[0, 1]$, we abuse notation and denote the equivalent k-mixture source on $\{0, 1\}$ also by (ϑ, α); that is, $\boldsymbol{\theta} = (\vartheta, \alpha)$ represents a mixture of k "coins", where coin i has bias α_i and is chosen with weight ϑ_i. Let $g(\vartheta, \alpha) = \big(g_i(\vartheta, \alpha)\big)_{i=0}^{2k-1}$. We use $D^{\boldsymbol{\theta}}$ (viewed as a vector in $\mathbb{R}_{\geq 0}^{\{0,1\}^{2k-1}}$) to denote the distribution of $(2k-1)$-snapshots induced by $\boldsymbol{\theta}$ on $\{0, 1\}^{2k-1}$. The total variation distance $d_{\mathrm{TV}}(D^{\boldsymbol{y}}, D^{\boldsymbol{z}})$ between two such distributions is defined to be $\frac{1}{2}\|D^{\boldsymbol{y}} - D^{\boldsymbol{z}}\|_1$.

LEMMA 6.3. *Let $b \geq 2k-1$. Given two k-mixture sources $\boldsymbol{y} = (y, \alpha)$ and $\boldsymbol{z} = (z, \beta)$ on $\{0, 1\}$ with identical first $2k-2$ moments, we have $d_{TV}(D^{\boldsymbol{y},b}, D^{\boldsymbol{z},b}) = \frac{1}{2} \sum_{\ell=2k-1}^{b} \binom{b}{\ell} 2^\ell |g_\ell(y, \alpha) - g_\ell(z, \beta)|$.*

PROOF. For any $s \in \{0, 1\}^b$ with i 1s, we have $D_s^{\boldsymbol{y},b} = \nu_i(y, \alpha)$ and $D_s^{\boldsymbol{z},b} = \nu_i(z, \beta)$. Therefore, $d_{\mathrm{TV}}(D^{\boldsymbol{y},b}, D^{\boldsymbol{z},b}) = \frac{1}{2} \sum_{i=0}^{b} \binom{b}{i} |\nu_i(y, \alpha) - \nu_i(z, \beta)|$. Let B be the $(b+1) \times (b+1)$ diagonal matrix with $B_{ii} = \binom{b}{i}$ for $0 \leq i \leq b$. Then, $\binom{b}{i} \nu_i(y, \alpha) = \big(g^b(y, \alpha) \mathrm{Pas}_{b+1}^{-1} B\big)_i$. Let $\Delta g^b := g^b(y, \alpha) - g^b(z, \beta)$. So $d_{\mathrm{TV}}(D^{\boldsymbol{y},b}, D^{\boldsymbol{z},b}) = \frac{1}{2}\|(\Delta g^b)(\mathrm{Pas}_{b+1}^{-1} B)\|_1$. We prove below that Pas_{b+1}^{-1} is the lower triangular matrix with entries $(\mathrm{Pas}_{b+1}^{-1})_{ij} = (-1)^{i-j} \binom{b-j}{i-j}$ for $0 \leq j \leq i \leq b$ (and 0 otherwise). Let Z_{i*} denote row i of matrix Z. Since $(\Delta g^b)_i = 0$ for $i = 0, \ldots, 2k-2$, we have that $d_{\mathrm{TV}}(D^{\boldsymbol{y},b}, D^{\boldsymbol{z},v})$ is at most

$$\begin{aligned} &\frac{1}{2} \sum_{\ell=2k-1}^{b} |(\Delta g^b)_\ell| \cdot \|(\mathrm{Pas}_{b+1}^{-1} B)_{\ell,*}\|_1 \\ &= \frac{1}{2} \sum_{\ell=2k-1}^{b} |(\Delta g^b)_\ell| \sum_{j=0}^{\ell} \binom{b-j}{\ell-j} \binom{b}{j} \\ &= \frac{1}{2} \sum_{\ell=2k-1}^{b} |(\Delta g^b)_\ell| \binom{b}{\ell} \sum_{j=0}^{\ell} \binom{\ell}{j} \\ &= \frac{1}{2} \sum_{\ell=2k-1}^{b} |(\Delta g^b)_\ell| \binom{b}{\ell} 2^\ell. \end{aligned}$$

To see the claim about Pas_{b+1}^{-1}, let Q be the claimed inverse matrix; so $Q_{ij} = (-1)^{i-j} \binom{b-j}{i-j}$ for $0 \leq j \leq i \leq b$. Then $(\mathrm{Pas}_{b+1} Q)_{ij} = 0$ for $j > i$, and is equal to $\sum_{\ell=j}^{i} \binom{b-\ell}{i-\ell} (-1)^{\ell-j} \binom{b-j}{\ell-j}$ otherwise. The latter expression evaluates to $\binom{b-j}{i-j} \sum_{\ell=j}^{i} (-1)^{\ell-j} \binom{i-j}{\ell-j} = \binom{b-j}{i-j} (1-1)^{i-j}$, which is 0 if $i > j$, and 1 if $i = j$. ☐

PROOF OF THEOREM 6.1. For part (i), take $\rho = 2$ and $b = 2k-1$. Consider the two k-mixture sources $\boldsymbol{y} = (y, \alpha)$

and $\boldsymbol{z} = (z, \beta)$ given by Theorem 6.2, which have separation $\frac{1}{2k-1}$ and transportation distance $\frac{1}{2(2k-1)}$. For any $b' \leq 2k-2$, the distributions $D^{\boldsymbol{y},b'}$ and $D^{\boldsymbol{z},b'}$ are *identical* and hence indistinguishable even with infinitely many samples, but the stated reconstruction task would allow us to do precisely this.

For part (ii), set $\rho = 3^{c_E+c_A}$, $b = c_A(2k-1)$, and $\tau = \frac{2}{(2k-1)\rho}$. Let $\boldsymbol{y} = (y, \alpha)$ and $\boldsymbol{z} = (z, \beta)$ be as given by Theorem 6.2 (for this b, ρ), which satisfy the required separation property. Suppose that we can perform the stated reconstruction task using N b-snapshots. Then, we can distinguish between $\boldsymbol{y}$ and $\boldsymbol{z}$ with probability at least $1-\psi$. But this probability is also upper bounded by $\left[1 + d_{\mathrm{TV}}\left((D^{\boldsymbol{y},b})^N, (D^{\boldsymbol{z},b})^N\right)\right]/2$, where $(D^{\boldsymbol{y},b})^N$ and $(D^{\boldsymbol{z},b})^N$ are the N-fold products of $D^{\boldsymbol{y},b}$ and $D^{\boldsymbol{z},b}$ respectively. Thus, $d_{\mathrm{TV}}\left((D^{\boldsymbol{y},b})^N, (D^{\boldsymbol{z},b})^N\right) \geq 1 - 2\psi$. By Proposition 11 and Lemma 12 in [7]

$$N \geq \frac{1}{4 d_{\mathrm{TV}}(D^{\boldsymbol{y},b}, D^{\boldsymbol{z},b})} \ln\left(\frac{1}{1-(1-2\psi)^2}\right)$$
$$\geq \frac{\rho^{2k-1}}{8 \cdot 3^b} \ln\left(\frac{1}{4\psi}\right) = \Omega\left(3^{c_E(2k-1)} \ln\left(\frac{1}{\psi}\right)\right)$$

where the second inequality follows from Theorem 6.2 and Lemma 6.3. □

7. REFERENCES

[1] D. Achlioptas and F. McSherry. On spectral learning of mixtures of distributions. In *Proc. 18th COLT*, pages 458–469, 2005.

[2] A. Anandkumar, D.P. Foster, D. Hsu, S.M. Kakade, and Y.-K. Liu. Two SVDs suffice: Spectral decompositions for probabilistic topic modeling and latent Dirichlet allocation. *CoRR*, abs/1204.6703, 2012. `http://arxiv.org/abs/1204.6703`.

[3] A. Anandkumar, D. Hsu, and S.M. Kakade. A method of moments for mixture models and hidden Markov models. In *Proc. 25th COLT*, pages 33.1–33.34, 2012. `http://arxiv.org/abs/1203.0683`.

[4] S. Arora, R. Ge, and A. Moitra. Learning topic models — going beyond SVD. In *Proc. 53rd FOCS*, pages 1–10, 2012.

[5] S. Arora and R. Kannan. Learning mixtures of separated nonspherical Gaussians. *Ann. Appl. Prob.*, 15:69–92, 2005.

[6] Y. Azar, A. Fiat, A. R. Karlin, F. McSherry, and J. Saia. Spectral analysis of data. In *Proc. 33rd STOC*, pages 619–626, 2001.

[7] Z. Bar-Yossef, R. Kumar, and D. Sivakumar. Sampling algorithms: lower bounds and applications. In *Proc. 33rd STOC*, pages 266–275, 2001.

[8] A. Barvinok. *A Course in Convexity*, volume 54 of *Graduate Studies in Mathematics*. AMS, 2002.

[9] T. Batu, S. Guha, and S. Kannan. Inferring mixtures of Markov chains. In *Proc. 17th COLT*, pages 186–199, 2004.

[10] M. Belkin and K. Sinha. Polynomial learning of distribution families. In *Proc. 51st FOCS*, pages 103–112, 2010.

[11] D.M. Blei. Probabilistic topic models. *Commun. ACM*, 55(4):77–84, 2012.

[12] D.M. Blei, A.Y. Ng, and M.I. Jordan. Latent Dirichlet allocation. *J. Machine Learning Res.*, 3:993–1022, 2003.

[13] S.C. Brubaker and S. Vempala. Isotropic PCA and affine-invariant clustering. In *Proc. 49th FOCS*, pages 551–560, 2008.

[14] K. Chaudhuri, E. Halperin, S. Rao, and S. Zhou. A rigorous analysis of population stratification with limited data. In *Proc. 18th SODA*, pages 1046–1055, 2007.

[15] K. Chaudhuri and S. Rao. Beyond Gaussians: Spectral methods for learning mixtures of heavy-tailed distributions. In *Proc. 21st COLT*, pages 21–32, 2008.

[16] K. Chaudhuri and S. Rao. Learning mixtures of product distributions using correlations and independence. In *Proc. 21st COLT*, pages 9–20, 2008.

[17] S. Chung and K. Murty. Polynomially bounded ellipsoid algorithms for convex quadratic programming. In O. Mangasarian, R. Meyer, and S. Robinson, editors, *Nonlinear Programming*, volume 4, pages 439–485. Academic Press, Orlando, Florida, 1981.

[18] M. Cryan, L. Goldberg, and P. Goldberg. Evolutionary trees can be learned in polynomial time in the two state general Markov model. *SICOMP*, 31(2):375–397, 2002.

[19] A. Dasgupta, J. Hopcroft, J. Kleinberg, and M. Sandler. On learning mixtures of heavy-tailed distributions. In *Proc. 46th FOCS*, pages 491–500, 2005.

[20] S. Dasgupta. Learning mixtures of Gaussians. In *Proc. 40th FOCS*, pages 634–644, 1999.

[21] S. Dasgupta and L.J. Schulman. A probabilistic analysis of EM for mixtures of separated, spherical Gaussians. *Journal of Machine Learning Research*, 8:203–226, 2007.

[22] C. Daskalakis, I. Diakonikolas, and R.A. Servedio. Learning k-modal distributions via testing. In *Proc. 23rd SODA*, pages 1371–1385, 2012.

[23] D. Dubhashi and A. Panconesi. *Concentration of measure for the analysis of randomized algorithms*. Cambridge University Press, 2009.

[24] J. Feldman, R. O'Donnell, and R.A. Servedio. PAC learning mixtures of axis-aligned Gaussians with no separation assumption. In *Proc. 19th COLT*, pages 20–34, 2006.

[25] J. Feldman, R. O'Donnell, and R.A. Servedio. Learning mixtures of product distributions over discrete domains. *SIAM J. Comput.*, 37(5):1536–1564, 2008.

[26] Y. Freund and Y. Mansour. Estimating a mixture of two product distributions. In *Proc. 12th COLT*, pages 183–192, 1999.

[27] N. Gravin, J. Lasserre, D. Pasechnik, and S. Robins. The inverse moment problem for convex polytopes. *J. Discrete and Computational Geometry*, 48(3):596–621, 2012.

[28] T. Hofmann. Probabilistic latent semantic analysis. In *Proc. 15th UAI*, pages 289–296, 1999.

[29] T. Hofmann and J. Puzicha. Latent class models for collaborative filtering. In *Proc. IJCAI*, pages 688–693, 1999.
[30] R. Horn and C. R. Johnson. *Matrix Analysis*. Cambridge University Press, 1985.
[31] A.T. Kalai, A. Moitra, and G. Valiant. Efficiently learning mixtures of two Gaussians. In *Proc. 42nd STOC*, pages 553–562, June 2010.
[32] R. Kannan, H. Salmasian, and S. Vempala. The spectral method for general mixture models. *SIAM J. Computing*, 38(3):1141–1156, 2008.
[33] M. Kearns, Y. Mansour, D. Ron, R. Rubinfeld, R. Schapire, and L. Sellie. On the learnability of discrete distributions. In *Proc. 26th STOC*, pages 273–282, 1994.
[34] J. Kleinberg and M. Sandler. Using mixture models for collaborative filtering. *J. Comput. Syst. Sci.*, 74:49–69, 2008.
[35] F. McSherry. Spectral partitioning of random graphs. In *Proc. 42nd FOCS*, pages 529–537, October 2001.
[36] A. Moitra and G. Valiant. Settling the polynomial learnability of mixtures of Gaussians. In *Proc. 51st FOCS*, pages 93–102, 2010.
[37] E. Mossel and S. Roch. Learning nonsingular phylogenies and hidden Markov models. In *Prof. 46th STOC*, pages 366–375, 2005.
[38] V. Y. Pan. Optimal and nearly optimal algorithms for approximating polynomial zeros. *Computers & Mathematics with Applications*, 31(12):97–138, 1996.
[39] C. Papadimitriou, P. Raghavan, H. Tamaki, and S. Vempala. Latent semantic indexing: A probabilistic analysis. *J. Comput. Syst. Sci.*, 61(2):217–235, 2000.
[40] Y. Rabani, L.J. Schulman, and C. Swamy. Inference from sparse sampling. `http://www.cs.technion.ac.il/~rabani/Papers/RabaniSS-manuscript.pdf`, 2008.
[41] S. Vempala and G. Wang. A spectral algorithm for learning mixtures of distributions. *J. Comput. Syst. Sci.*, 68(4):841–860, 2004.
[42] C. Villani. *Topics in optimal transportation*, volume 58 of *Graduate Studies in Mathematics*. AMS, 2003.
[43] V. H. Vu. Spectral norm of random matrices. In *Proc. 37th STOC*, pages 423–430, 2005.

APPENDIX

A. PROBABILITY BACKGROUND

We use the following large-deviation bounds in our analysis.

LEMMA A.1 (Chernoff bound; Theorem 1.1 in [23]). *Let $X_1, \ldots, X_N$ be independent random variables with $X_i \in [0,1]$ for all i, and $\mu = (\sum_i \mathrm{E}\, X_i)/N$. Then,* $\Pr\left[\left|\frac{1}{N}\sum_i X_i - \mu\right| > \epsilon\right] \le 2e^{-2\epsilon^2 N}$.

LEMMA A.2 (Bernstein's inequality; Theorem 1.2 in [23]). *Let $X_1, \ldots, X_N$ be independent random variables with $|X_i| \le b$, $\mathrm{E}[X_i] = 0$ for all i, and let $\sigma^2 = \sum_i \mathrm{Var}[X_i]$. Then,* $\Pr[|\ sum_i X_i| > t] \le 2\exp\left(-\frac{t^2}{2(\sigma^2 + bt/3)}\right)$.

B. SAMPLE-SIZE DEPENDENCE OF [2, 3, 4] ON n FOR ℓ_1-RECONSTRUCTION

We view $P = (p^1, \ldots, p^k)$ as an $n \times k$ matrix. Recall that $r = \sum_{t=1}^k w_t p_t p_t^\dagger$, $A = \sum_{t=1}^k w_t (p^t - r)(p^t - r)^\dagger$, and $M = rr^\dagger + A$. Let $w_{\max} := \max_t w_t$. We consider isotropic k-mixture sources, which is justified by Lemma 3.3. So $\frac{1}{2n} \le r_i \le \frac{2}{n}$ for all $i \in [n]$. Note that $\|r\|_1$, $\|r\|_2^2$, and $\|r\|_\infty$ are all $\Theta(\frac{1}{n})$. It will be convenient to split the width parameter ζ into two parameters. Let (i) $\frac{\zeta_1}{\sqrt{n}} = \min_{p,q \in P, p \ne q} \|p - q\|_2$; and (ii) $\zeta_2^2 \|r\|_\infty$ be the smallest non-zero eigenvalue of A. Then, the width of (w, P) is $\zeta = \min\{\zeta_1, \zeta_2\}$. We use $\sigma_i(Z)$ to denote the i-th largest singular value of a matrix Z. If Z has rank ℓ, its condition number is given by $\kappa(Z) := \sigma_1(Z)/\sigma_\ell(Z)$. For a square matrix Z with real eigenvalues, we use $\lambda_i(Z)$ to denote the i-th largest eigenvalue of Z. Note that if Z is an $n \times k$ matrix, then $\sigma_i(Z)^2 = \lambda_i(ZZ^\dagger) = \lambda_i(Z^\dagger Z)$ for all $i = 1, \ldots, k$. Also the singular values of $ZZ^\dagger$ coincide with its eigenvalues, and the same holds for $Z^\dagger Z$.

We now proceed to evaluate the sample-size dependence of [2, 3, 4] on n for reconstructing the mixture constituents within ℓ_1-distance ϵ. Since these papers use different parameters than we do, in order to obtain a meaningful comparison, we relate their bounds to our parameters ζ_1, ζ_2; we keep track of the resulting dependence on n but ignore the (polynomial) dependence on other quantities. We show that the sample size needed is at least $\Omega(\frac{n^4}{\epsilon^2})$, with the exception of Algorithm B in [3], which needs $\Omega(\frac{n^3}{\epsilon^2})$ samples. As required by [2, 3, 4], we assume that P has full column rank. It follows that M has rank k and A has rank $k-1$. The following inequality will be useful.

PROPOSITION B.1. *Let $D = \mathrm{diag}(d_1, \ldots, d_k)$ where $d_1 \ge d_2 \ge \ldots \ge d_k > 0$. Then $\lambda_k(PDP^\dagger) \ge d_k \lambda_k(PP^\dagger) = d_k \sigma_k(P)^2$.*

Comparison with [4]. The algorithm in [4] requires also that P be ρ-separable. This means that for every $t \in [k]$, there is some $i \in [n]$ such that $p_i^t \ge \rho$ and $p_i^{t'} = 0$ for all $t' \ne t$. This has the following implications. For any $t, t' \in [k]$, $t \ne t'$, we have $\|p^t - p^{t'}\|_2 \ge \sqrt{2}\rho$, so $\frac{\zeta_1}{\sqrt{n}} \ge \sqrt{2}\rho$. We can write $P^\dagger P = Y + Z$, where Y is a PSD matrix, and Z is a diagonal matrix whose diagonal entries are at least ρ^2. So $\lambda_k(P^\dagger P) = \lambda_k(PP^\dagger) \ge \rho^2$. Therefore,

$$\zeta_2^2 \|r\|_\infty + \|r\|_2^2 = \lambda_k(A) + \|r\|_2^2 \ge \lambda_k(M) \ge w_{\min} \cdot \rho^2$$

where the first inequality follows from Lemma 2.1, and the second from Proposition B.1. It follows that $\rho = O(\frac{1}{\sqrt{n}})$. The bound in [4] to obtain ℓ_∞ error ε is (ignoring dependence on other quantities) $\Omega(\frac{1}{\varepsilon^2 \rho^6})$. So setting $\varepsilon = \frac{\epsilon}{n}$ to guarantee ℓ_1-error at most ϵ and plugging in the above upper bounds on ρ, we obtain that the sample size is $\Omega(\frac{n^5}{\epsilon^2})$.

Comparison with [2]. The sample size required by [2] for the latent Dirichlet model for obtaining ℓ_2 error ε is $\Omega(\frac{1}{\varepsilon^2 \sigma_k(P)^6})$. Proposition B.1 yields $\lambda_k(M) \ge w_{\min} \cdot \sigma_k(P)^2$ and as argued above, $\lambda_k(M) \le \lambda_k(A) + \|r\|_2^2 = O(\frac{1}{n})$. So $\sigma_k(P)^6 = O(\frac{1}{n^3})$. Setting $\varepsilon = \frac{\epsilon}{\sqrt{n}}$ for ℓ_1 error ϵ, this yields a bound of $\Omega(\frac{n^4}{\epsilon^2})$.

Comparison with [3]. Algorithm A in [3] requires sample size $\Omega(\frac{1}{\sigma_k(P)^8 \sigma_k(M)^4 \varepsilon^2})$ to recover each p^t to within ℓ_2-distance $\varepsilon \max_{p \in P} \|p\|_2$. Since $\max_{p \in P} \|p\|_2 \leq \frac{2}{w_{\min}\sqrt{n}}$ due to isotropy, we can set $\varepsilon = \frac{\epsilon w_{\min}}{2}$ to obtain ℓ_1-error ϵ. Since $\sigma_k(P)^2$ and $\sigma_k(M) = \lambda_k(M)$ are both $O(\frac{1}{n})$, we obtain a bound of $\Omega(\frac{n^8}{\epsilon^2})$.

Algorithm B in [3] uses sample size $\Omega\Big(\kappa(P)^8/(\frac{\zeta_1^2}{n} \cdot \sigma_k(M)^2 \varepsilon^2)\Big)$ to recover each p^t to within ℓ_2-distance $\varepsilon \max_{p \in P} \|p\|_2$. Clearly $\kappa(P) \geq 1$. Again, setting $\varepsilon = \frac{\epsilon w_{\min}}{2}$, this yields a sample size of $\Omega(\frac{n^3}{\epsilon^2})$ for ℓ_1 error ϵ.

Why Do Simple Algorithms for Triangle Enumeration Work in the Real World?

Jonathan W. Berry
Sandia National Laboratories *
jberry@sandia.gov

Luke K. Fostvedt
Iowa State University
fostvedt@iastate.edu

Daniel J. Nordman
Iowa State University
dnordman@iastate.edu

Cynthia A. Phillips
Sandia National Laboratories
caphill@sandia.gov

C. Seshadhri
Sandia National Laboratories
csesha@sandia.gov

Alyson G. Wilson
North Carolina State University
alyson_wilson@ncsu.edu

Abstract

Triangle enumeration is a fundamental graph operation. Despite the lack of provably efficient (linear, or slightly superlinear) worst-case algorithms for this problem, practitioners run simple, efficient heuristics to find all triangles in graphs with millions of vertices. How are these heuristics exploiting the structure of these special graphs to provide major speedups in running time?

We study one of the most prevalent algorithms used by practitioners. A trivial algorithm enumerates all paths of length 2, and checks if each such path is incident to a triangle. A good heuristic is to enumerate only those paths of length 2 where the middle vertex has the lowest degree. It is easily implemented and is empirically known to give remarkable speedups over the trivial algorithm.

We study the behavior of this algorithm over graphs with heavy-tailed degree distributions, a defining feature of real-world graphs. The erased configuration model (ECM) efficiently generates a graph with asymptotically (almost) any desired degree sequence. We show that the expected running time of this algorithm over the distribution of graphs created by the ECM is controlled by the $\ell_{4/3}$-norm of the degree sequence. As a corollary of our main theorem, we prove expected linear-time performance for degree sequences following a power law with exponent $\alpha \geq 7/3$, and non-trivial speedup whenever $\alpha \in (2, 3)$.

*This manuscript has been authored by Sandia Corporation under Contract No. DE-AC04-94AL85000 with the U.S. Department of Energy. The United States Government retains and the publisher, by accepting the article for publication, acknowledges that the United States Government retains a non-exclusive, paid-up, irrevocable, world-wide license to publish or reproduce the published form of this manuscript, or allow others to do so, for United States Government purposes.

ITCS '14, January 12-14, 2014, Princeton, NJ, USA
Copyright 2013 ACM 978-1-4503-2698-8/14/01 ...$15.00.
http://dx.doi.org/10.1145/2554797.2554819

Categories and Subject Descriptors

F.2 [**Analysis of algorithms and problem complexity**]: Miscellaneous

Keywords

graph algorithms; heavy-tailed degree distribution; triangle enumeration; expected analysis

1. INTRODUCTION

Finding triangles in graphs is a classic theoretical problem with numerous practical applications. The recent explosion of work on social networks has led to a great interest in fast algorithms to find triangles in graphs. The social sciences and physics communities often study triangles in real networks and use them to reason about underlying social processes [Col88,Por98,WS98,Bur04,Bur07,FWVDC10]. Much of the information about triangles in the last four papers is determined by a complete enumeration of all triangles in a (small) graph. Triangle enumeration is also a fundamental subroutine for other more complex algorithmic tasks [BHLP11,FH97].

From a theoretical perspective, Itai and Rodeh [IR78] gave algorithms for triangle finding in $O(n^\omega)$ time (where n is the number of vertices and ω is the matrix multiplication constant) using fast matrix multiplication. Vassilevska Williams and Williams [WW10] show deep connections between matrix multiplication and (edge-weighted) triangle enumeration. But much of this work is focused on dense graphs. Practitioners usually deal with massive sparse graphs with large variance in degrees, where sub-quadratic time algorithms can be trivially obtained, but are still too slow to run.

Practioners enumerate triangles on massive graphs (with millions of vertices) using fairly simple heuristics, which are often easily parallelizable. This work is motivated by the following question: *can we theoretically explain why simple algorithms for triangle enumeration work in the real world?*

Consider a trivial algorithm. Take an undirected graph with n vertices, m edges, and degree sequence $d_1, d_2, \ldots, d_n$ (so the degree of vertex v is d_v). We refer to paths of length 2 as *wedges*. Call a wedge *closed* if it participates in a triangle and *open* otherwise. Simply enumerate all wedges and output the closed ones. The total running time is $\Theta(\sum_v d_v^2)$

(assume that checking if a wedge is closed can be done in constant time), since every wedge involves a pair of neighbors for the middle vertex. We will henceforth refer to this as *the* trivial algorithm. A simple heuristic is to only enumerate paths where the middle vertex has the lowest degree among the 3 vertices in the path. We call this algorithm MinBucket.

1. Create n empty buckets $B_1, B_2, \ldots, B_n$.
2. For each edge (u, v): if $d_u \leq d_v$, place it in B_u, otherwise place it in B_v. Break ties consistently.
3. For each bucket B_v: iterate over all wedges formed by edges in B_v and output closed ones.

MinBucket is quite common in practice (sometimes taking the somewhat strange name *nodeIterator++*) and has clean parallel implementations with no load balancing issues [SW05a, Coh09, SV11]. For such simple algorithms, the total work pretty much determines the parallel runtime. For example, it would take n processors with perfect speed up running a $\Theta(n^2)$-work algorithm to compete with a single processor running a $\Theta(n)$-work algorithm.

MinBucket is often the algorithm of choice for triangle enumeration because of its simplicity and because it beats the trivial algorithm by orders of magnitude, as shown in the previous citations. (A quick check shows at least 60 citations to [Coh09], mostly involving papers that deal with massive scale graph algorithms.) The algorithm itself has been discovered and rediscovered in various forms over the past decades. The earliest reference the authors could find was from the mid-80s where Chiba and Nishizeki [CN85] devised a sequential version of the above algorithm. We provide a more detailed history later.

Nonetheless, MinBucket has a poor worst-case behavior. It would perform terribly on a high degree regular bipartite graph. If the input sparse graph (with high variance in degree) simply consisted of many such bipartite graphs of varying sizes, MinBucket would perform no better than its trivial cousin. Then why is it good in practice?

1.1 Results

Since the seminal results of Barabási and Albert [BA99], Faloutsos et al [FFF99], Broder et al [BKM+00], researchers have assumed that massive graphs obtained from the real world have *heavy-tailed degree distributions* (often approximated as a power law). The average degree is thought to be a constant (or very slowly growing), but the variance is quite large. The usual approximation is to think of the number of vertices of degree d as decaying roughly as $1/d^\alpha$ for some small constant α.

This seems to have connections with MinBucket. If edges tend to connect vertices of fairly disparate degrees (quite likely in a graph with large variance in degrees), MinBucket might provably give good running times. This is exactly what we set out to prove, for a natural distribution on heavy-tailed graphs.

Consider any list of positive integers $\mathbf{d} = (d_1, d_2, \ldots, d_n)$, which we think of as a "desired" degree sequence. In other words, we wish to construct a graph on n vertices where vertex $v \in [n]$ has degree d_v. The *configuration model* (CM) [BC78, Bol80, MR98, New03] creates a random graph that almost achieves this. Imagine vertex v being incident to d_v "stubs", which can be thought of as half-edges. We take a random perfect matching between the stubs, so pairs of stubs are matched to each other. Each such pair creates an edge, and we end up with a multigraph with the desired degree sequence. Usually, this is converted to a simple graph by removing parallel edges and self-loops [BDML06]. We refer to this graph distribution as the erased configuration model, $ECM(\mathbf{d})$, for input degree sequence $\mathbf{d}$. This model has a fairly long history (which we relegate to a later section) and is a standard method to construct a graph with a desired degree sequence. It is closely connected to models given by Chung and Lu [CL02, CLV03] and Mihail and Papadimitriou [MP02], in the context of eigenvalues of graphs with a given degree sequence. These models simply connect vertices u and v independently with probability $d_u d_v/2m$, similarly to the Erdős-Rényi construction.

Our main theorem gives a bound on the expected running time of MinBucket for $ECM(\mathbf{d})$. We set $m = (\sum_v d_v)/2$. We will henceforth assume that $0 < d_1 \leq d_2 \ldots \leq d_n$ and that $d_n < \sqrt{m}/2$. This "truncation" is a standard assumption for analysis of the configuration model [MR98, CL02, MP02, CLV03, New03, BDML06]. We use $\sum_v$ as a shorthand for $\sum_{i=1}^{n}$, since it is a sum over all vertices. The run time bottleneck for MinBucket is in wedge enumeration, and checking whether a wedge is closed is often assumed to be a constant time operation. Henceforth, when we say "running time," we mean the number of wedges enumerated.

Theorem 1.1. *Consider a degree sequence* $\mathbf{d} = (d_1, d_2, \ldots, d_n)$, *where* $m = (\sum_v d_v)/2$ *and* $d_n < \sqrt{m}/2$. *The expected (over* $ECM(\mathbf{d})$*) number of wedges enumerated by* MinBucket *is* $O(n + m^{-2}(\sum_v d_v^{4/3})^3)$.

(Our main theorem applies to Chung-Lu graphs as well. Details are given in §6.) Before we actually make sense of this theorem, let us look at a corollary of this theorem. It has been repeatedly observed that degree sequences in real graphs have heavy tails, often approximated as a *power law* [BA99]. Power laws say something about the moments of the degree distribution (equivalently, norms of the degree sequence). Since it does not affect our main theorem or corollary, we choose a fairly loose definition of power law. This is a binned version of the usual definition, which states the number of vertices of degree d is proportional to n/d^α. (Even up to constants, this is never precisely true because there are many gaps in real degree sequences.)

Definition 1.2. *A degree sequence* $\mathbf{d}$ *satisfies a power law of exponent* $\alpha > 1$ *if the following holds for all* $k \leq \log_2 d_n - 1$*: for* $d = 2^k$, *the number of sequence terms in* $[d, 2d]$ *is* $\Theta(n/d^{\alpha-1})$.

The following shows an application of our theorem for common values of α. This bound is tight as we show in Section 5. (When $\alpha \geq 3$, the trivial algorithm runs in linear time because $\sum_v d_v^2 = O(n)$.)

Corollary 1.3. *Suppose a degree sequence* $\mathbf{d}$ *(with largest term* $< \sqrt{m}/2$*) satisfies a power law with exponent* $\alpha \in (2, 3)$. *Then the expected running time of* MinBucket *of* $ECM(\mathbf{d})$ *is asymptotically better than the trivial algorithm, and is* linear *when* $\alpha > 7/3$.

1.2 Making sense of Thm. 1.1

First, as a sanity check, let us actually show that Thm. 1.1 beats the trivial bound, $\sum_v d_v^2$. This is a direct application of Hölder's inequality for conjugates $p = 3$ and $q = 3/2$.

$$\begin{aligned}(\sum_v d_v^{4/3})^3 &= (\sum_v d_v^{2/3} \cdot d_v^{2/3})^3 \\ &\leq \Big(\sum_v d_v^{\frac{2}{3}\cdot 3}\Big)^{3\cdot\frac{1}{3}} \Big(\sum_v d_v^{\frac{2}{3}\cdot\frac{3}{2}}\Big)^{3\cdot\frac{2}{3}} \\ &= (2m)^2 (\sum_v d_v^2)\end{aligned}$$

Rearranging, we get $m^{-2}(\sum_v d_v^{4/3})^3 = O(\sum_v d_v^2)$, showing that our bound at least holds the promise of being non-trivial.

Consider the uniform distribution on the vertices. Assuming $m > n$, we can write our running time bound as $n(\mathbf{E}[d_v^{4/3}])^3$, as opposed to the trivial bound of $\sum_v d_v^2 = n\mathbf{E}[d_v^2]$. If the degree "distribution" (think of the random variable given by the degree of a uniform random vertex) has a small 4/3-moment, the running time is small. This can happen even though the second moment is large, and this is where MinBucketbeats the trivial algorithm. In other words, if the tail of the degree sequence is heavy but not too heavy, MinBucket will perform well.

And this is exactly what happens when $\alpha > 2$ for power law degree sequences. When $\alpha > 7/3$, the 4/3-moment becomes constant and the running time is linear. (It is known that for ECM graphs over power law degree sequences with $\alpha > 7/3$, the clustering coefficient (ratio of triangles to wedges) converges to zero [New03].) We show in §5 that the running time bound achieved in the following corollary for power laws with $\alpha > 2$ is tight. When $\alpha \leq 2$, MinBucket gets no asymptotic improvement over the trivial algorithm. For convenience, we will drop the big-Oh notation, and replace it by $\lessdot$. So $A \lessdot B$ means $A = O(B)$.

Proof. (of Cor. 1.3) First, let us understand the trivial bound. Remember than d_n is the maximum degree.

$$\begin{aligned}\sum_v d_v^2 \lessdot \sum_{k=1}^{\log_2 d_n - 1} (n/2^{k(\alpha-1)})2^{2k} &= n \sum_{k=1}^{\log_2 d_n - 1} 2^{k(3-\alpha)} \\ &\lessdot n + n d_n^{3-\alpha}\end{aligned}$$

We can argue that the expected number of wedges enumerated by the trivial algorithm is $\Omega(\sum_v d_v^2)$ (Claim 3.3). Now for the bound of Thm. 1.1.

$$\begin{aligned}m^{-2}(\sum_v d_v^{4/3})^3 &\lessdot n^{-2}\Big(\sum_{k=1}^{\log_2 d_n - 1} (n/2^{k(\alpha-1)})2^{4k/3}\Big)^3 \\ &= n\Big(\sum_{k=1}^{\log_2 d_n - 1} 2^{k(7/3-\alpha)}\Big)^3 \lessdot n + n d_n^{7-3\alpha}\end{aligned}$$

Regardless of d_n, if $\alpha > 7/3$, then the running time of MinBucket is linear. Whenever $\alpha \in (2,3)$, $7 - 3\alpha < 3 - \alpha$, and MinBucket is asymptotically faster than a trivial enumeration. □

1.3 Significance of Thm. 1.1

Thm. 1.1 connects the running time of a commonly used algorithm to the norms of the degree sequences, a well-studied property of real graphs. So this important property of heavy-tails in real graphs allows for the algorithmic benefit of MinBucket. We have discovered that for a fairly standard graph model inspired by real degree distributions, MinBucket is very efficient.

We think of this theorem as a proof of concept: theoretically showing that a common property of real world inputs allows for the efficient performance of a simple heuristic. Because of our distributional assumptions as well as bounds on α, we agree with the (skeptical) reader that this does not fully explain why MinBucket works in the real world[1]. Nonetheless, we feel that this makes progress towards that, especially for a question that is quite hard to formalize. After all, there is hardly any consensus in the social networks community on what real graphs look like.

But the notion that distinctive properties of real world graphs can be used to prove efficiency of simple algorithms is a useful way of thinking. This is one direction to follow for going beyond worst-case analysis. Our aim here is not to design better algorithms for triangle enumeration, but to give a theoretical argument for why current algorithms do well.

The proof is obtained (as expected) through various probabilistic arguments bounding the sizes of the different buckets. The erased configuration model, while easy to implement and clean to define, creates some niggling problems for analysis of algorithms. The edges are not truly independent of each other, and we have to take care of these weak dependencies.

Why the 4/3-norm? Indeed, that is one of the most surprising features of this result (especially since the bound is tight for power laws of $\alpha > 2$). As we bound the bucket sizes and make sense of the various expressions, the total running time is expressed as a sum of various degree terms. Using appropriate approximations, it tends to rearrange into norms of the degree sequence. Our proof goes over two sections. We give some probabilistic calculations for the degree behavior in §3, which sets the stage for the run-time accounting. In §4, we start bounding bucket sizes and finally get to the 4/3-moment. In §5, we show that bounds achieved in the proof of Cor. 1.3 are tight. This is mostly a matter of using the tools of the previous sections. In §7, we give a tighter theorem (proof in full version) that gives an explicit expression for strong upper bounds on running time and experimentally show these more careful bounds closely approximate the expected runtime of ECM graphs.

2. RELATED WORK

The idea of using some sort of degree binning, orienting edges, or thresholding for finding and enumerating triangles has been used in many results. Chiba and Nishizeki [CN85] give bounds for a sequential version of MinBucket using the degeneracy of a graph. This does not give bounds for MinBucket, although their algorithm is similar in spirit. Alon, Yuster, and Zwick [AYZ97] find triangles in $O(m^{1.41})$ using degree thresholding and matrix multiplication ideas from Itai and Rodeh [IR78]. Chrobak and Eppstien [CE91] use acyclic orientations for linear time triangle enumeration in planar graphs. Vassilevska Williams and Williams [WW10] show that fast algorithms for weighted triangle enumeration leads to remarkable consequences, like faster all-pairs shortest paths. In the work most closely to ours, Latapy [Lat08] discusses various triangle finding algorithms, and also fo-

[1] As the astute reader would have noticed, our title is a question, not a statement.

cuses on power-law graphs. He shows the trivial bound of $O(mn^{1/\alpha})$ when the power law exponent is α. Essentially, the maximum degree is $n^{1/\alpha}$ and that directly gives a bound on the number of wedges.

MINBUCKET has received attention from various experimental studies. Schank and Wagner [SW05b] perform an experimental study of many algorithms, including a sequential version of MINBUCKET which they show to be quite efficient. Cohen [Coh09] specifically describes MINBUCKET in the context of Map-Reduce. Suri and Vassilvitskii [SV11] do many experiments on real graphs in Map-Reduce and show major speedups (a few orders of magnitude) for MINBUCKET over the trivial enumeration. Tsourakakis [Tso08] gives a good survey of various methods used in practice for triangle counting and estimation.

Explicit triangle enumerations have been used for various applications on large graphs. Fudos and Hoffman [FH97] use triangle enumeration for a graph-based approach for solving systems of geometric constraints. Berry et al [BHLP11] touch every triangle as part of their community detection algorithm for large graphs.

Configuration models for generating random graphs with given degree sequences have a long history. Bender and Canfield [BC78] study this model for counting graphs with a given degree sequence. Wormald [Wor81] looks at the connectivity of these graphs. Molloy and Reed [MR95a, MR98] study various properties like the largest connected component of this graph distribution. Physicists studying complex networks have also paid attention to this model [NSW01]. Britton, Deijfen, and Martin-Löf [BDML06] show that the simple graph generated by the ECM asymptotically matches the desired degree sequence. Aiello, Chung, and Lu [ACL01] give a model for power-law graphs, where edges (u, v) are independently inserted with probability $d_u d_v/2m$. This was studied for more general degree sequences in subsequent work by Chung, Lu, and Vu [CL02, CLV03]. Mihail and Papadimitriou [MP02] independently discuss this model. Most of this work focused on eigenvalues and average distances in these graphs. Newman [New03] gives an excellent survey of these models, their similarities, and applications.

3. DEGREE BEHAVIOR OF $ECM(\mathbf{d})$

We fix a degree sequence $\mathbf{d}$ and focus on the distribution $ECM(\mathbf{d})$. All expectations and probabilities are over this distribution. Because of dependencies in the erased configuration model, we will need to formalize our arguments carefully. We first state a general lemma giving a one-sided tail bound for dependent random variables with special conditional properties. The proof is in the appendix.

LEMMA 3.1. *Let $Y_1, Y_2, \ldots, Y_k$ be independent random variables, and $X_i = f_i(Y_1, Y_2, \ldots, Y_i)$ be 0-1 random variables. Let $\alpha \in [0, 1]$. Suppose $\Pr[X_1] \geq \alpha$ and $\Pr[X_i = 1 | Y_1, Y_2, \ldots, Y_{i-1}] \geq \alpha$ for all i. Then, $\Pr[\sum_{i=1}^{k} X_i < \alpha k\delta] < \exp(-\alpha k(1-\delta)^2/2)$ for any $\delta \in (0, 1)$.*

We now prove a tail bound on degrees of vertices; the probability the degree of vertex v deviates by a constant factor of d_v is $\exp(-\Omega(d_v))$. Let $\beta, \beta', \delta, \delta'$ denote sufficiently small constants.

Before we proceed with our tail bounds, we describe a process to construct the random matching of stubs. We are interested in a particular vertex v. Order the stubs such that the d_v v-stubs are in the beginning; the remaining stubs are ordered arbitrarily. We start with the first stub, and match to a uniform random stub (other than itself). We then take the next unmatched stub, according to the order, and match to a uniform random unmatched stub. And so on and so forth. The final connections are clearly dependent, though the choice among unmatched stubs is done independently. This is formalized as follows. Let Y_i be an independent uniform random integer in $[1, 2m-2(i-1)-1]$. This represents the choice at the ith step, since in the ith step, we have exactly $2m-2(i-1)-1$ choices. Imagine that we first draw these independent Y_i's. Then we deterministically construct the matching on the basis of these numbers. (So the first stub is connected to the Y_1st stub, the second unmatched stub is connected to the Y_2nd unmatched stub, etc.)

LEMMA 3.2. *Assume $d_n < \sqrt{m}/2$. Let D_v be the random variable denoting the degree of v in the resulting graph. There exist sufficiently small constants $\beta, \beta' \in (0, 1)$, such that $\Pr[D_v < \beta' d_v] < \exp(-\beta d_v)$.*

PROOF. Suppose $d_v > 1$. We again order the stubs so that the d_v v-stubs are in the beginning. Let X_j be the indicator random variable for the jth matching forming a new edge with v. Note that $\sum_{j=1}^{\lfloor d_v/2 \rfloor} X_j \leq D_v$. Observe that X_j is a function of $Y_1, Y_2, \ldots, Y_j$. Consider any $Y_1, Y_2, \ldots, Y_{j-1}$ and suppose the matchings created by these variables link to vertices $v_0 = v, v_1, v_2, \ldots, v_{j-1}$ (distinct) such that there are n_j links to vertex v_j such that $\sum_{i=0}^{j-1} n_i = (j-1)$. Then, for $j = 1, \ldots, \lfloor d_v/2 \rfloor$,

$$\begin{aligned} & \mathbf{E}[X_j | Y_1, Y_2, \ldots, Y_{j-1}] \\ \geq \; & 1 - \frac{(d_v - j - n_0) + \sum_{1 \leq i \leq j-1; n_i \neq 0}(d_{v_i} - n_i)}{2m - 2(j-1) - 1} \\ \geq \; & 1 - \frac{-2(j-1) - 1 + \sum_{i=0}^{j-1} d_{v_i}}{2m - 2(j-1) - 1} \\ \geq \; & 1 - \frac{\sum_{i=0}^{j-1} d_{v_i}}{2m - 2d_v}. \end{aligned}$$

Note that $\sum_{i=0}^{j-1} d_{v_i} \leq (\sqrt{m}/2)^2 = m/4$, by the bound on the maximum degree. We also get $2m - 2d_v > m$, so we bound $\mathbf{E}[X_j | Y_1, Y_2, \ldots, Y_{j-1}] \geq 3/4$. By Lem. 3.1 (setting $\delta = 2/3$ and bounding $\alpha k > d_v/4$),

$$\begin{aligned} \Pr[D_v < d_v/8] & \leq \Pr\left[\sum_{j=1}^{\lfloor d_v/2 \rfloor} X_j < d_v/8\right] \\ & \leq \Pr\left[\sum_{j=1}^{\lfloor d_v/2 \rfloor} X_j < \lfloor d_v/2 \rfloor/2\right] \\ & < \exp(-d_v(1/3)^2/8) \end{aligned}$$

□

This suffices to prove the trivial bound for the trivial algorithm.

CLAIM 3.3. *The expected number of wedges enumerated by the trivial algorithm is $\Omega(\sum_v d_v^2)$.*

PROOF. The expected number of wedges enumerated is $\Omega(\sum_v D_v^2)$, where D_v is the actual degree of v. Using Lem. 3.2, $\mathbf{E}[D_v^2] = \Omega(d_v^2)$. □

We will need the following basic claim about the joint probability of two edges.

CLAIM 3.4. *Let v, w, w' be three distinct vertices. The probability that edges (v,w) and (v,w') are present in the final graph is at most $d_v^2 d_w d_{w'}/m^2$.*

PROOF. Assume $d_v > 1$. Let $C_{v,w}$ be the indicator random variable for edge (v,w) being present (likewise define $C_{v,w'}$). Label the stubs of each vertex as $s_1^v, \ldots, s_{d_v}^v$; $s_1^w, \ldots, s_{d_w}^w$; and $s_1^{w'}, \ldots, s_{d_{w'}}^{w'}$. Let $C_{s_i^v, s_j^w}$ be the indicator random variable for edge being present between stubs s_i^v and s_j^w (likewise define $C_{s_i^v, s_j^{w'}}$). Then the event $\{C_{v,w}C_{v,w'} = 1\}$ that edges (v,w) and (v,w') are present is a subset of the event $\cup_{1 \le i \ne j \le d_v} \cup_{k=1}^{d_w} \cup_{\ell=1}^{d_{w'}} \{C_{s_i^v, s_k^w} C_{s_j^v, s_\ell^{w'}} = 1\}$. Hence,

$$\Pr[C_{v,w}C_{v,w'} = 1] \le \sum_{1 \le i \ne j \le d_v} \sum_{k=1}^{d_w} \sum_{\ell=1}^{d_{w'}} \Pr[C_{s_i^v, s_k^w} C_{s_j^v, s_\ell^{w'}} = 1].$$

Fix $1 \le i \ne j \le d_v$, $1 \le k \le d_w$ and $1 \le \ell \le d_{w'}$ and order stubs s_i^v, s_j^v first in the ECM wiring. Then, we have $\Pr[C_{s_i^v, s_k^w} C_{s_j^v, s_\ell^{w'}} = 1] = \Pr[C_{s_i^v, s_k^w} = 1] \Pr[C_{s_j^v, s_\ell^{w'}} = 1 | C_{s_i^v, s_k^w} = 1]$ where $\Pr[C_{s_i^v, s_k^w} = 1] = [2m-1]^{-1}$ and $\Pr[C_{s_j^v, s_\ell^{w'}} = 1 | C_{s_i^v, s_k^w} = 1] = [2m-3]^{-1}$. Hence,

$$\Pr[C_{v,w}C_{v,w'} = 1] \le d_v(d_v - 1) d_w d_{w'}/m^2$$

using $(2m-1)(2m-3) \ge m^2$ when $m \ge 3$. □

4. GETTING THE 4/3 MOMENT

We will use a series of claims to express the running time of MINBUCKET in a convenient form. For vertex v, let X_v be the random variable denoting the number of edges in v's bin. The expected running time is at most $\mathbf{E}[\sum_v X_v(X_v - 1)]$. This is because number of wedges in each bin is $\binom{X_v}{2} \le X_v^2 - X_v$.

We further break X_v into the sum $\sum_w Y_{v,w}$, where $Y_{v,w}$ is the indicator for edge (v,w) being in v's bin. As mentioned earlier, $C_{v,w}$ is the indicator for edge (v,w) being present. Note that $Y_{v,w} \le C_{v,w}$, since (v,w) can only be in v's bin if it actually appears as an edge.

We list out some bounds on expectations. Only the second one really uses the binning of MINBUCKET.

CLAIM 4.1. *Consider vertices v, w, w' $(w \ne w')$.*

- $\mathbf{E}[Y_{v,w}Y_{v,w'}] \le d_v^2 d_w d_{w'}/m^2$.
- *There exist sufficient small constants $\delta, \delta' \in (0,1)$ such that: if $d_w < \delta d_v$ then* $\mathbf{E}[Y_{v,w}Y_{v,w'}] \le 2\exp(-\delta' d_v) d_v^2 d_w d_{w'}/m^2$.

PROOF. We use the trivial bound of $Y_{v,w}Y_{v,w'} \le C_{v,w}C_{v,w'}$. By Claim 3.4, $\mathbf{E}[Y_{v,w}Y_{v,w'}] \le \mathbf{E}[C_{v,w}C_{v,w'}] \le d_v^2 d_w d_{w'}/m^2$.

Now for the interesting bound. The quantity $\mathbf{E}[Y_{v,w}Y_{v,w'}]$ is the probability that both $Y_{v,w}$ and $Y_{v,w'}$ are 1. For this to happen, we definitely require both (v,w) and (v,w') to be present as edges. Call this event $\mathcal{E}$. We also require (at the very least) the degree of v to be at most the degree of w (otherwise the edge (v,w) will not be put in v's bin.) Call this event $\mathcal{F}$. If D_v, D_w denote the degrees of v and w, note that $D_w \le d_w < \delta d_v$, implying event $\mathcal{F}$ is contained in the event $\{D_v < \delta d_v\}$ when $d_w < \delta d_v$. Hence, the event $Y_{v,w}Y_{v,w'} = 1$ is contained in $\mathcal{E} \cap \{D_v < \delta d_v\}$. Assume $d_v > 2, d_w > 0, d_{w'} > 0$ or else $\mathbf{E}[Y_{v,w}Y_{v,w'}] = 0$ trivially when $\delta < 1/2$.

As in the proof of Claim 3.4, let $C_{s_i^v, s_j^w}$ be the indicator random variable for edge being present between stubs s_i^v and s_j^w of vertices v, w (and analogously define $C_{s_i^v, s_j^{w'}}$). Then $\mathcal{E}$ is contained in $\cup_{1 \le i \ne j \le d_v} \cup_{k=1}^{d_w} \cup_{\ell=1}^{d_{w'}} \{C_{s_i^v, s_k^w} C_{s_j^v, s_\ell^{w'}} = 1\}$ so that

$$\begin{aligned}
&\Pr[Y_{v,w}Y_{v,w'} = 1] \\
\le\ &\Pr[\mathcal{E}, D_v < \delta d_v] \\
\le\ &\sum_{1 \le i \ne j \le d_v} \sum_{k=1}^{d_w} \sum_{\ell=1}^{d_{w'}} \Pr[C_{s_i^v, s_k^w} C_{s_j^v, s_\ell^{w'}} = 1, D_v < \delta d_v] \\
=\ &\sum_{1 \le i \ne j \le d_v} \sum_{k=1}^{d_w} \sum_{\ell=1}^{d_{w'}} \Pr[C_{s_i^v, s_k^w} C_{s_j^v, s_\ell^{w'}} = 1] \times \\
&\qquad \Pr[D_v < \delta d_v | C_{s_i^v, s_k^w} C_{s_j^v, s_\ell^{w'}} = 1].
\end{aligned}$$

Given fixed values of i, j, k, ℓ and order stubs s_i^v, s_j^v first in the ECM wiring. Then, $\Pr[C_{s_i^v, s_k^w} C_{s_j^v, s_\ell^{w'}} = 1] \le m^{-2}$ as in the proof of Claim 3.4. Additionally, conditioned on $C_{s_i^v, s_k^w} C_{s_j^v, s_\ell^{w'}} = 1$, the remaining stubs form an ECM with respect to a new degree sequence formed by replacing $2m$, d_v, d_w, and $d_{w'}$ in the original degree sequence by $2\tilde{m} = 2m - 4$, $d_v - 2$, $d_w - 1$, and $d_{w'} - 1$. Let $\tilde{D}_v$ denote the degree of v in the final graph from the new degree sequence. Then, conditioned on $C_{s_i^v, s_k^w} C_{s_j^v, s_\ell^{w'}} = 1$, we have $D_v = 2 + \tilde{D}_v$ so that conditional probability is bounded by

$$\begin{aligned}
&\Pr[D_v < \delta d_v | C_{s_i^v, s_k^w} C_{s_j^v, s_\ell^{w'}} = 1] \\
=\ &\Pr[\tilde{D}_v < \delta d_v - 2 | C_{s_i^v, s_k^w} C_{s_j^v, s_\ell^{w'}} = 1] \\
\le\ &\Pr[\tilde{D}_v < \delta(d_v - 2) | C_{s_i^v, s_k^w} C_{s_j^v, s_\ell^{w'}} = 1] \\
\le\ &2\exp(-\delta' d_v)
\end{aligned}$$

since $\delta < 1$. That is, Lem. 3.2 applies to $\tilde{D}_v$ with respect to the new degree sequence where v has degree $d_v - 2$ and each degree in this new sequence is less than $\sqrt{\tilde{m}}/2$ by assumption. The bound $\Pr[Y_{v,w}Y_{v,w'} = 1] \le 2\exp(-\delta' d_v) d_v^2 d_w d_{w'}/m^2$ then follows. □

Armed with these facts, we can bound the expected number of wedges contained in a single bucket.

LEMMA 4.2.

$$\mathbf{E}[X_v(X_v - 1)] = O\left(1 + \left(\frac{d_v}{m} \times \sum_{w: d_w \ge \delta d_v} d_w\right)^2\right)$$

.

PROOF. We will write out

$$X_v^2 = \left(\sum_w Y_{v,w}\right)^2 = \sum_w Y_{v,w}^2 + \sum_w \sum_{w' \ne w} Y_{v,w}Y_{v,w'}$$

where $\sum_w Y_{v,w}^2 = \sum_w Y_{v,w} = X_v$ as each $Y_{v,w}$ is a 0-1 variable. Hence,

$$
\begin{aligned}
&\mathbf{E}[X_v(X_v-1)] \\
=\ & \sum_{w}\sum_{w'\neq w} \mathbf{E}[Y_{v,w}Y_{v,w'}] \\
\leq\ & \sum_{\substack{w:\\ d_w \geq \delta d_v}} \sum_{\substack{w\neq w':\\ d_{w'}\geq \delta d_v}} \mathbf{E}[Y_{v,w}Y_{v,w'}] + \sum_{\substack{w:\\ d_w<\delta d_v}} \sum_{w'\neq w} \mathbf{E}[Y_{v,w}Y_{v,w'}] \\
&+ \sum_{\substack{w':\\ d_{w'}<\delta d_v}} \sum_{w\neq w'} \mathbf{E}[Y_{v,w}Y_{v,w'}] \\
=\ & \sum_{\substack{w:\\ d_w \geq \delta d_v}} \sum_{\substack{w\neq w':\\ d_{w'}\geq \delta d_v}} \mathbf{E}[Y_{v,w}Y_{v,w'}] + 2\sum_{\substack{w:\\ d_w<\delta d_v}} \sum_{w'\neq w} \mathbf{E}[Y_{v,w}Y_{v,w'}] \\
\leq\ & \frac{d_v^2}{m^2}\Big(\sum_{w:d_w\geq \delta d_v} d_w\Big)^2 + 2\sum_{\substack{w:\\ d_w<\delta d_v}} \sum_{w'\neq w} \mathbf{E}[Y_{v,w}Y_{v,w'}]
\end{aligned}
$$

by splitting the sums into cases, $d_w \geq \delta d_v$ and $d_w < \delta d_v$, and using the trivial bound of Claim 4.1 for the first quantity. We satisfy the conditions to use the second part of Claim 4.1.

$$
\begin{aligned}
&\sum_{\substack{w:\\ d_w<\delta d_v}} \sum_{w'\neq w} \mathbf{E}[Y_{v,w}Y_{v,w'}] \leq \\
&2\sum_{\substack{w:\\ d_w<\delta d_v}} \sum_{w'\neq w} \exp(-\delta d_v) d_v^2 d_w d_{w'}/m^2 \leq \\
&8m^{-1}\exp(-\delta d_v) d_v^2,
\end{aligned}
$$

where $\sum_{i=1}^{n} d_i = 2m$, The latter is a decreasing function of d_v (for sufficiently large d_v) and is $O(1)$, completing the proof. □

With this bound for $\mathbf{E}[X_v(X_v-1)]$, we are ready to prove Thm. 1.1.

THEOREM 4.3. $\mathbf{E}[\sum_v X_v(X_v-1)] = O(n + m^{-2}(\sum_{i=1}^{n} d_i^{4/3})^3)$.

PROOF. We use linearity of expectation and sum the bound in Lem. 4.2 as

$$
\begin{aligned}
&\mathbf{E}[\sum_v X_v(X_v-1)] \\
\lessdot\ & n + m^{-2}\sum_v d_v^2\Big(\sum_{w:d_w\geq \delta d_v} d_w\Big)^2 \\
=\ & n + m^{-2}\sum_v \sum_{w:d_w\geq\delta d_v} \sum_{w':d_{w'}\geq \delta d_v} d_v^2 d_w d_{w'}
\end{aligned}
$$

This is the moment where the 4/3 moment will appear. Since $d_w \geq \delta d_v$ and $d_{w'} \geq \delta d_v$, $d_v^{2/3} \leq \delta^{-2/3} d_w^{1/3} d_{w'}^{1/3}$. Therefore, $d_v^2 d_w d_{w'} = d_v^{4/3} d_v^{2/3} d_w d_{w'} \leq \delta^{-2/3}(d_v d_w d_{w'})^{4/3}$. Wrapping it up,

$$
\begin{aligned}
& m^{-2}\sum_v \sum_{w:d_w\geq\delta d_v} \sum_{w':d_{w'}\geq \delta d_v} d_v^2 d_w d_{w'} \\
\lessdot\ & m^{-2}\sum_v \sum_{w:d_w\geq\delta d_v} \sum_{w':d_{w'}\geq \delta d_v} (d_v d_w d_{w'})^{4/3} \\
\lessdot\ & m^{-2}\Big(\sum_v d_v^{4/3}\Big)^3.
\end{aligned}
$$

□

5. PROVING TIGHTNESS

We show that the bound achieved by Thm. 1.1 is tight for power laws with $\alpha > 2$. This shows that the bounds given in the proof of Cor. 1.3 are tight. The proof, as expected, goes by reversing most of the inequalities given earlier. For convenience, we will assume for the lower bound that $d_n < \sqrt{m}/4$, instead of the $\sqrt{m}/2$ used for the upper bound. This makes for cleaner technical arguments (we could just as well prove it for $\sqrt{m}/2$, at the cost of more pain).

CLAIM 5.1. *Let* $\mathbf{d}$ *be a power law degree sequence with* $\alpha \in (2, 7/3)$ *with* $d_n < \sqrt{m}/4$. *Then the expected number of wedges enumerated by* MINBUCKET *over* $ECM(\mathbf{d})$ *is* $\Omega(n d_n^{7-3\alpha})$.

We need a technical claim give a lower bound for probabilities of edges falling in a bucket.

CLAIM 5.2. *Let* $d_v > 3$. *Consider vertices* v, w, w' $(w \neq w')$ *and let c be a sufficiently large constant. If* $\min(d_w, d_{w'}) > c d_v$, *then* $\mathbf{E}[Y_{v,w}Y_{v,w'}] = \Omega(d_v^2 d_w d_{w'}/m^2)$.

PROOF. The random variable $Y_{v,w}Y_{v,w'}$ is 1 if (v, w), (v, w') are edges and the degrees of w and w' are less than that of v. As before, we will start the matching process by matching stubs of v. We partition the stubs into two groups denoted by B_w and $B_{w'}$, and start by matching stubs in B_w. We set $|B_w| = \lfloor d_v/3 \rfloor$. What is the probability that a stub in B_w connects with a w-stub? This is at least $1-(1-d_w/2m)^{\lfloor d_v/3\rfloor} = \Omega(d_v d_w/m)$.

Condition on any matching of the stubs in B_w. What is the probability that a stub in $B_{w'}$ matches with a w'-stub? Since $\min(|B_{w'}|, d_{w'}) \geq 2|B_w|$, this probability is at least $1-(1-d_{w'}/4m)^{\lfloor d_v/3\rfloor} = \Omega(d_v d_{w'}/m)$.

Now condition on any matching of the v-stubs. The number of unmatched stubs connected to w is at least $d_w/2$ (similarly for w'). The remaining stubs connect according to a standard configuration model. For the remaining degree sequence, the total number of stubs is $2\tilde{m} = 2m - 2d_v$. For sufficiently large m, $d_n \leq \sqrt{m}/4 \leq \sqrt{\tilde{m}}/2$. Hence, we can use Lem. 3.2 (and a union bound) to argue that the probability that the final degrees of w and w' are at least d_v is $\Omega(1)$. Multiplying all the bounds together, the probability $Y_{v,w}Y_{v,w'} = 1$ is $\Omega(d_v^2 d_w d_{w'}/m^2)$. □

We prove Claim 5.1.

PROOF. Note that when $\alpha > 2$, then $m = O(n)$. We start with the arguments in the proof of Lem. 4.2. Applying Claim 5.2 for vertex v such that $d_v > 3$,

$$
\begin{aligned}
\mathbf{E}[X_v(X_v-1)] &= \sum_w \sum_{w'\neq w} \mathbf{E}[Y_{v,w}Y_{v,w'}] \\
&\geq \sum_{\substack{w:\\ d_w\geq c d_v}} \sum_{\substack{w\neq w':\\ d_{w'}\geq c d_v}} \mathbf{E}[Y_{v,w}Y_{v,w'}] \\
&\gg m^{-2} d_v^2 \sum_{\substack{w:\\ d_w\geq c d_v}} \sum_{\substack{w\neq w':\\ d_{w'}\geq c d_v}} d_w d_{w'} \\
&\geq m^{-2} d_v^2 \Big(\sum_{\substack{w:\\ d_w\geq c d_v}} d_w\Big)^2 - m^{-2} d_v^2 \sum_w d_w^2
\end{aligned}
$$

The latter part, summed over all v is at most

$$
m^{-2}\Big(\sum_v d_v^2\Big)^2 \leq m^{-2}\big(\max_v d_v \sum_v d_v\big)^2 \lessdot m
$$

Now we focus on the former part. Choose v so that $cd_v \leq d_n/2$, and let 2^r be the largest power of 2 greater than cd_v. (Note that $r \leq \log_2 d_n - 1$.) We bound $\sum_{w:d_w \geq cd_v} d_w \geq \sum_{w:d_w \geq 2^r} d_w \gg \sum_{k=r}^{\log_2 d_n - 1} 2^k n/2^{k(\alpha-1)}$. This is $\sum_{k=r}^{\log_2 d_n - 1} n/2^{k(\alpha-2)}$, which is convergent when $\alpha > 2$. Hence, it is at least $\Omega(n2^{-r(\alpha-2)}) = \Omega(nd_v^{-(\alpha-2)})$.

We sum over all (appropriate v).

$$\begin{aligned}
&\sum_{v:3<d_v\leq d_n/2c} m^{-2}d_v^2(\sum_{\substack{w:\\ d_w\geq cd_v}} d_w)^2 \\
\gg\ & (n/m)^2 \sum_{v:3<d_v\leq d_n/2c} d_v^2 d_v^{-(2\alpha-4)} \\
=\ & (n/m)^2 \sum_{v:3<d_v\leq d_n/2c} d_v^{6-2\alpha} \\
\gg\ & (n/m)^2 \sum_{k=2}^{\lfloor \log_2 n - \log_2(2c)\rfloor} n2^{k(7-3\alpha)}
\end{aligned}$$

When $\alpha < 7/3$, the sum is divergent. Noting that $m = \Theta(n)$, we bound by $\Omega(nd_n^{7-3\alpha})$. Overall, we lower bound the running time MinBucket by $\sum_{v:3<d_v\leq d_n/2c} \mathbf{E}[X_v(X_v-1)]$, which is $\Omega(nd_n^{7-3\alpha} - m)$. For $\alpha < 7/3$, this is $\Omega(nd_n^{7-3\alpha})$, matching the upper bound in Cor. 1.3. □

6. THE RUNNING TIME OF MinBucket FOR CHUNG-LU GRAPHS

Theorem 6.1. *Consider a Chung-Lu graph distribution with n vertices over a degree distribution $f_1, f_2, \ldots, f_n$. The expected running time of MinBucket is given by $O(m + n(\sum_v d_v{}^{4/3})^3)$.*

We remind the reader that the Chung-Lu (CL) model involves inserting edge (i,j) with probability $d_i d_j/2m$ for all unordered pairs (i,j). We need to prove Claim 4.1 for the Chung-Lu model. Thm. 6.1 will then follow directly using the arguments in §4.

We first state Bernstein's inequality.

Theorem 6.2. *[Bernstein's inequality] Let $X_1, X_2, \ldots, X_k$ be zero-mean independent random variables. Suppose $|X_i| \leq M$ almost surely. Then for all positive t,*

$$\Pr[\sum_{i=1}^k X_i > t] \leq \exp\Big(-\frac{t^2/2}{\sum_i \mathbf{E}[X_i^2] + Mt/3}\Big)$$

We now prove some tail bounds about degrees of vertices. The basic form of these statements is the probability that degree of vertex v deviates by a constant factor of d_v is $\exp(-\Omega(d_v))$. We state in terms of conditional events for easier application later. We use β to denote a sufficiently small constant.

Claim 6.3. *Let $d \geq 2$. Suppose v is a vertex such that $d_v \leq d$ and e, e' be two pairs. Let $\mathcal{E}$ be the event that e, e' are present, and D_v be the random variable denoting the degree of v. For sufficiently small constant β,*

$$\Pr[D_v > 3d|\mathcal{E}] < \exp(-\beta d)$$

Proof. All edges are inserted independently. So the occurrence of edge $e'' \neq e, e'$ is completely independent of $\mathcal{E}$. Let $\delta(v)$ be the set of all pairs involving v and $\hat{\delta}(v) = \delta(v) \setminus \{e, e'\}$. We express $D_v = \sum_{h\in\delta(v)} C_h$, where C_h is the indicator random variable for edge h being present. Let $\hat{D}_v = \sum_{h\in\hat{\delta}_v} C_h$. Note that $\mathbf{E}[\hat{D}_v] \leq \mathbf{E}[D_v] = d_v \leq d$. Set $C'_h = C_h - \mathbf{E}[C_h]$, so

$$\begin{aligned}
\Pr[\hat{D}_v - \mathbf{E}[\hat{D}_v] > d] &= \Pr[\sum_{h\in\hat{\delta}(v)} (C_h - \mathbf{E}[C_h]) > d] \\
&= \Pr[\sum_{h\in\hat{\delta}(v)} C'_h > d]
\end{aligned}$$

We wish to apply Bernstein's inequality to the C'_h random variables. Observe that $\mathbf{E}[C'_h] = 0$, and $|C'_h| \leq 1$. Setting $\mathbf{E}[C_h] = \mu$, note that

$$\mathbf{E}[(C'_h)^2] = \mathbf{E}[(C_h - \mu)^2] = \mathbf{E}[C_h^2] - \mu\mathbf{E}[C_h] + \mu^2 = \mathbf{E}[C_h].$$

So $\sum_{h\in\hat{\delta}(v)} \mathbf{E}[(C'_h)^2] = \sum_{h\in\hat{\delta}(v)} \mathbf{E}[C_h] = \mathbf{E}[\hat{D}_v] \leq d$. By Bernstein's inequality (Thm. 6.2),

$$\begin{aligned}
\Pr[\hat{D}_v - \mathbf{E}[\hat{D}_v] > d] &= \Pr[\sum_{h\in\hat{\delta}(v)} C'_h > d] \\
&\leq \exp\Big(-\frac{d^2/2}{\sum_{h\in\hat{\delta}(v)} \mathbf{E}[(C'_h)^2] + d/3}\Big) \\
&\leq \exp\Big(-\frac{d^2/2}{d + d/3}\Big) = \exp(-3d/8)
\end{aligned}$$

None of these random variables depend on the event $\mathcal{E}$, so we get that $\Pr[\hat{D}_v - \mathbf{E}[\hat{D}_v] > d \mid \mathcal{E}] \leq \exp(-3d/8)$. Suppose $\hat{D}_v \leq \mathbf{E}[\hat{D}_v] + d \leq 2d$. We always have $D_v \leq \hat{D}_v + 2$ and hence $D_v \leq 3d$ (using the bound that $d \geq 2$). Hence, $\Pr[D_v > 3d|\mathcal{E}] < \exp(-3d/8)$. We only require $\beta < 3/8$. □

Claim 6.4. *Suppose v is a vertex such that $d_v \geq 4$ and e, e' be two pairs. Let $\mathcal{E}$ be the event that e, e' are present, and D_v be the random variable denoting the degree of v. For sufficiently small constant β,*

$$\Pr[D_v < d_v/3|\mathcal{E}] < \exp(-\beta d_v)$$

Proof. This proof is almost identical to the previous one. Again, we express $D_v = \sum_{h\in\delta(v)} C_h$, where C_h is the indicator random variable for edge h being present. Let $\hat{D}_v = \sum_{h\in\hat{\delta}_v} C_h$. We have $\hat{D}_v \geq D_v - 2$, so $\mathbf{E}[\hat{D}_v] \geq \mathbf{E}[D_v] - d_v/2 = d_v/2$ (using the bound $d_v \geq 4$). Applying a multiplicative Chernoff bound to $\hat{D}_v$,

$$\Pr[\hat{D}_v < 2\mathbf{E}[\hat{D}_v]/3] < \exp(-d_v/36)$$

Since $\hat{D}_v$ is completely independent of $\mathcal{E}$, we can condition on $\mathcal{E}$ to get the same bound. Suppose $D_v < d_v/3$. Since $D_v \geq \hat{D}_v$ and $d_v \leq 2\mathbf{E}[\hat{D}_v]$, we get $\hat{D}_v < 2\mathbf{E}[\hat{D}_v]/3$. So the even $D_v < d_v/3|\mathcal{E}$ is contained in $\hat{D}_v < 2\mathbf{E}[\hat{D}_v]/3|\mathcal{E}$, completing the proof. We require $\beta < 1/36$. □

Finally, we need a simple claim about the second moment of sums of independent random variables.

Claim 6.5. *Let $X = \sum_i X_i$ be a sum of independent positive random variables with $X_i = O(1)$ for all i and $\mathbf{E}[X] = O(1)$. Then $\mathbf{E}[X^2] = O(1)$.*

PROOF. By linearity of expectation,

$$\mathbf{E}\left[X^2\right] = \mathbf{E}\Big[\big(\sum_i X_i\big)^2\Big] = \sum_i \mathbf{E}\left[X_i^2\right] + 2\sum_{i<j} \mathbf{E}[X_i]\mathbf{E}[X_j]$$
$$\leq \sum_i O\left(\mathbf{E}[X_i]\right) + \Big(\sum_i \mathbf{E}[X_i]\Big)^2 = O(1).$$

□

We prove the analogue of Claim 4.1.

CLAIM 6.6. *Consider vertices v, w, w' ($w \neq w'$).*

- *If $d_v \leq 4$, then $\mathbf{E}[X_v^2] = O(1)$.*
- *$\mathbf{E}[Y_{v,w}Y_{v,w'}] \leq d_v^2 d_w d_{w'}/4m^2$.*
- *If $d_w \leq d_v/10$ and $d_v \geq 4$, then $\mathbf{E}[Y_{v,w}Y_{v,w'}] \leq 2\exp(-\beta d_v) d_v^2 d_w d_{w'}/4m^2$.*

PROOF. Defining $\hat{X}_v = \sum_w C_{v,w}$, we have $X_v \leq \hat{X}_v$. Since these are all positive random variables, $X_v^2 \leq \hat{X}_v^2$. Applying Claim 6.5, $\mathbf{E}[\hat{X}_v^2] = O(1)$. That completes the first part.

For the second part, we use the trivial bound of $Y_{v,w}Y_{v,w'} \leq C_{v,w}C_{v,w'}$. Taking expectations and using independence, $\mathbf{E}[Y_{v,w}Y_{v,w'}] \leq C_{v,w}C_{v,w'} = d_v^2 d_w d_{w'}/4m^2$.

The third case is really the interesting one. The quantity $\mathbf{E}[Y_{v,w}Y_{v,w'}]$ is the probability that both $Y_{v,w}$ and $Y_{v,w'}$ are 1. For this to happen, we definitely required both (v, w) and (v, w') to be present as edges. Call this event $\mathcal{E}$. We also require (at the very least) the degree of v to be at most the degree of w (otherwise the edge (v, w) will not be put in v's bin.) Call this event $\mathcal{F}$. The event $Y_{v,w}Y_{v,w'} = 1$ is contained in $\mathcal{E} \cap \mathcal{F}$. Using conditional probabilities, $\Pr(\mathcal{E} \cap \mathcal{F}) = \Pr(\mathcal{F}|\mathcal{E})\Pr(\mathcal{E})$. Note that $\Pr(\mathcal{E}) = d_v^2 d_w d_{w'}/4m^2$.

Let D_v, D_w denote the degrees of v and w. Let $\mathcal{F}_v$ denote the event $D_v < d_v/3$ and $\mathcal{F}_w$ denote event $D_w > 3d_v/10$. If neither of these events happens, then $D_w \leq 3d_v/10 < d_v/3 \leq D_v$. So $\mathcal{F}$ cannot happen. Hence, $(\mathcal{F}|\mathcal{E})$ is contained in $(\mathcal{F}_v \cup \mathcal{F}_w|\mathcal{E})$. By the union bound, $\Pr(\mathcal{F}_v \cup \mathcal{F}_w|\mathcal{E}) \leq \Pr(\mathcal{F}_v|\mathcal{E}) + \Pr(\mathcal{F}_w|\mathcal{E})$. Applying Claim 6.4 to the latter and Claim 6.3 to the former, we bound $\Pr(\mathcal{F}|\mathcal{E}) \leq 2\exp(-\beta d_v)$. □

As mentioned earlier, we can now execute the arguments in §4 to prove Thm. 6.1.

7. A MORE CAREFUL ANALYSIS

Because we are interested in practical performance, we performed a more careful analysis to find stronger bounds on the performance of MINBUCKET, trying to understand the size of the constants in the big-Oh notation. We consider a slightly different ECM distribution. Rather than starting with a given degree sequence, we draw the degree for each vertex independently at random from a reference degree distribution f. Specifically, $f(d)$ is the probability that a node draws degree value d, for d an integer in $[0, \infty)$. After nodes draw degree values, the rest of the ECM construction proceeds as described in §1.1.

Our analysis assumes that when an edge joins two vertices of the same degree, the edge is placed in the bucket for both edges. Thus we slightly overcount the work for MINBUCKET. Let $X_{v=i,n}$ be the size of the bucket for an arbitrary node i in a graph generated by ECM with n nodes. We wish to bound the expected triangle-searching work $\mathbf{E}[\sum_{i=1}^n \binom{X_{i,n}}{2}]$ in an ECM graph, as the number of nodes $n \to \infty$. We denote the rth moment, $r > 0$, of the reference degree distribution f as $\mathbf{E}[D^r] = \sum_{d=0}^{\infty} d^r \cdot f(d)$.

The following theorem gives explicit expressions for the size of each bucket and the total work for MINBUCKET. The proof is quite involved and uses many measure-theoretic arguments. We provide it in the full version. Given a probability distribution $f(d)$, and a value n, the expression in this theorem computes a strong upper bound on the ratio between the work and n. We focus on linear regimes, where this is the constant in the running time.

THEOREM 7.1. *Under the ECM for generating random graphs (cf.§1.1), suppose the reference degree distribution f has a finite mean $\mathbf{E}[D] = \sum_{d=0}^{\infty} d \cdot f(d) \in (0, \infty)$ and $\mathbf{E}[D^{4/3}] \in (0, \infty)$. As $n \to \infty$, $\frac{1}{n}\mathbf{E}\left[\sum_{i=1}^n \binom{X_{i,n}}{2}\right]$ (the expected triangle-searching work per bucket) tends to*

$$\frac{1}{2(\mathbf{E}[D])^2} \sum_{d_1=0}^{\infty} d_1 f(d_1) \Big[\sum_{d_2=d_1}^{\infty} d_2 f(d_2) \Big]^2 \in (0, \infty).$$

7.1 Experimental Analysis

We experimentally show the bound of Thm. 7.1 does captures the expected performance of MINBUCKET on ECM graphs. We generated ECM graphs of various sizes based on a power-law degree distribution with power exponent $\alpha = 2.4 > 7/3$ (which guarantees a finite $\frac{4}{3}$ moment for the degree distribution). Figure 1(a) shows the average value of $\sum_{i=1}^n \binom{X_{i,n}}{2}$, total work over all buckets, computed over 10 Monte Carlo trials (i.e., taken as an approximation of $\mathbf{E}[\sum_{i=1}^n \binom{X_{i,n}}{2}]$) for ECM graphs of various sizes up to $n = 80$ million. Degrees are truncated at $\sqrt{n}$. The ECM uses power law reference degree distributions for $\alpha = 2.3$, where MINBUCKET runs in superlinear time, and for $\alpha = 2.4$, where it runs in linear time. Figure 1(a) also shows the theoretical linear bound on the overall expected work $\mathbf{E}[\sum_{i=1}^n \binom{X_{i,n}}{2}]$ for a power-law degree distribution with $\alpha = 2.4$. The constant we get from Thm. 7.1 is approximately $C = 0.687935$. As $n \to \infty$, we would anticipate from Thm. 7.1 that the value of $\mathbf{E}[\sum_{i=1}^n \binom{X_{i,n}}{2}]$ approximated by Monte Carlo trials should approach nC, also shown in the left part of Fig. 1. The right part of Fig. 1 shows the ratio of work to number of nodes n. For power law distributions with $\alpha = 2$, this ratio is not a constant. But by $\alpha = 2.4$, the factor is leveling off below 1.

Acknowledgments

This work was funded under the Sandia National Laboratories Laboratory Directed Research and Development (LDRD) program. We thank Ali Pinar for suggestions on improving the presentation.

8. REFERENCES

[ACL01] W. Aiello, F. Chung, and L. Lu. A random graph model for power law graphs. *Experimental Mathematics*, 10:53–66, 2001.

[AYZ97] N. Alon, R. Yuster, and U. Zwick. Finding and counting given length cycles. *Algorithmica*, 17:354–364, 1997.

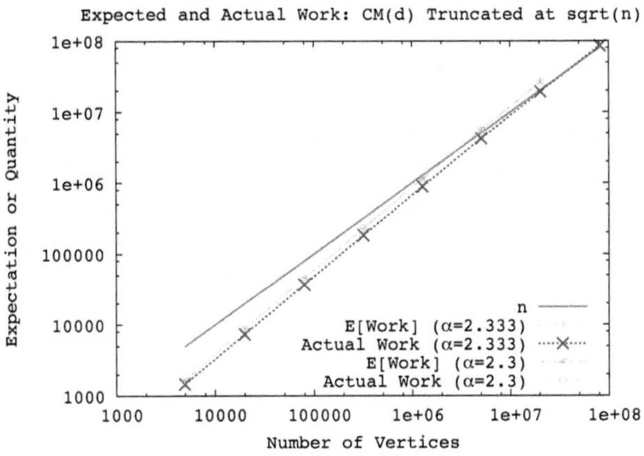

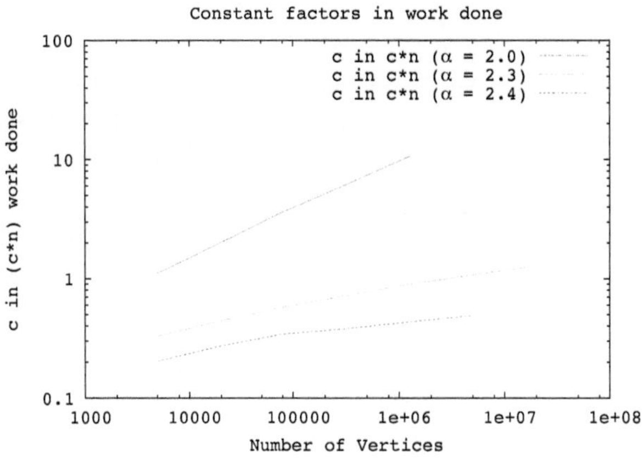

Figure 1: Experimental results with n-node ECM graphs with degrees $\leq n^{1/2}$ drawn from a power-law distribution with exponent $\alpha = 2.3$ or 2.4. The red solid line shows n. The green dashed line shows a theoretical bound $0.687935n$ on the expected number of pairs in buckets for an ECM graph with n vertices and exponent 2.4. The blue crosses shows the average value of pairs observed in 10 generations of ECM graphs. The magenta line and blue boxes show the same for exponent 2.3. (b) Experimental values of the ratio of work to n for power law exponents 2, 2.3, and 2.4.

[BA99] Albert-László Barabási and Réka Albert. Emergence of scaling in random networks. *Science*, 286:509–512, October 1999.

[BC78] E. A. Bender and E.R. Canfield. The asymptotic number of labeled graphs with given degree sequences. *Journal of Combinatorial Theory A*, 24:296–307, 1978.

[BDML06] T. Britton, M. Deijfen, and A. Martin-Löf. Generating simple random graphs with prescribed degree distribution. *Journal of Statistical Physics*, 124(6), September 2006.

[BHLP11] J. W. Berry, B. Hendrickson, R. A. LaViolette, and C. A. Phillips. Tolerating the Community Detection Resolution Limit with Edge Weighting. *Physical Review E*, 83(5), May 2011.

[BKM$^+$00] A. Broder, R. Kumar, F. Maghoul, P. Raghavan, S. Rajagopalan, R. Stata, A. Tomkins, and J. Wiener. Graph structure in the web. *Computer Networks*, 33:309–320, 2000.

[Bol80] B. Bollobás. A probabilistic proof of an asymptotic formula for the number of labelled regular graphs. *European Journal on Combinatorics*, 1:311–316, 1980.

[Bur04] R. S. Burt. Structural holes and good ideas. *American Journal of Sociology*, 110(2):349–399, 2004.

[Bur07] R. S. Burt. Secondhand brokerage: Evidence on the importance of local structure for managers, bankers, and analysts. *Academy of Management Journal*, 50, 2007.

[CE91] M. Chrobak and D. Eppstein. Planar orientations with low out-degree and compaction of adjacency matrices. *Theoretical Computer Science*, 86:243–266, 1991.

[CL02] F. Chung and L. Lu. The average distances in random graphs with given expected degrees. *PNAS*, 99:15879–15882, 2002.

[CLV03] F. Chung, L. Lu, and V. Vu. Eigenvalues of random power law graphs. *Annals of Combinatorics*, 7:21–33, 2003.

[CN85] N. Chiba and T.Takao Nishizeki. Arboricity and subgraph listing algorithms. *SIAM J. Comput.*, 14:210–223, February 1985.

[Coh09] J. Cohen. Graph twiddling in a MapReduce world. *Computing in Science & Engineering*, 11:29–41, 2009.

[Col88] J. S. Coleman. Social capital in the creation of human capital. *American Journal of Sociology*, 94:S95–S120, 1988.

[FFF99] M. Faloutsos, P. Faloutsos, and C. Faloutsos. On power-law relationships of the internet topology. In *Proceedings of SIGCOMM*, pages 251–262, 1999.

[FH97] I. Fudos and C. M. Hoffmann. A graph-constructive approach to solving systems of geometric constraints. *ACM Transactions on Graphics*, 16(2):179–216, 1997.

[FWVDC10] B. Foucault Welles, A. Van Devender, and N.Noshir Contractor. Is a friend a friend?: Investigating the structure of friendship networks in virtual worlds. In *CHI-EA'10*, pages 4027–4032, 2010.

[IR78] A. Ital and M. Rodeh. Finding a minimum circuit in a graph. *SIAM Journal on Computing*, 7:413–423, 1978.

[Lat08] M. Latapy. Main-memory triangle computations for very large (sparse (power-law)) graphs. *Theoretical Computer Science*, 407:458–473, 2008.

[MP02] M. Mihail and C. Papadimitriou. On the eigenvalue power law. In *RANDOM*, pages 254–262, 2002.

[MR95a] M. Molloy and B. Reed. A critical point for random graphs with a given degree sequence. *Random Structures and Algorithms*, 6:161–179, 1995.

[MR95b] R. Motwani and P. Raghavan. *Randomized Algorithms.* Cambridge University Press, 1995.

[MR98] M. Molloy and B. Reed. The size of the giant component of a random graph with a given degree sequence. *Combinatorics, Probability and Computing*, 7:295–305, 1998.

[New03] M.E.J. Newman. The structure and function of complex networks. *SIAM Review*, 45:167–256, 2003.

[NSW01] M. E. J. Newman, S. Strogatz, and D. Watts. Random graphs with arbitrary degree distributions and their applications. *Physical Review E*, 64:026118, 2001.

[Por98] A. Portes. Social capital: Its origins and applications in modern sociology. *Annual Review of Sociology*, 24(1):1–24, 1998.

[SV11] S. Suri and S. Vassilvitskii. Counting triangles and the curse of the last reducer. In *WWW'11*, pages 607–614, 2011.

[SW05a] T. Schank and D. Wagner. Finding, counting and listing all triangles in large graphs, an experimental study. In *Experimental and Efficient Algorithms*, pages 606–609. Springer Berlin / Heidelberg, 2005.

[SW05b] T. Schank and D. Wagner. Finding, counting, and listing all triangles in large graphs: an experimental study. *Workshop on Experimental and Efficient Algorithms (WEA)*, 2005.

[Tso08] C. E. Tsourakakis. Fast counting of triangles in large real networks without counting: Algorithms and laws. In *ICDM*, pages 608–617, 2008.

[Wor81] N. C. Wormald. The asymptotic connectivity of labelled regular graphs. *Journal of Combinatorial Theory B*, 31:156–167, 1981.

[WS98] D. Watts and S. Strogatz. Collective dynamics of 'small-world' networks. *Nature*, 393:440–442, 1998.

[WW10] V. Vassilevska Williams and R. Williams. Subcubic equivalences between path, matrix and triangle problems. In *Foundations of Computer Science (FOCS)*, pages 645–654, 2010.

APPENDIX

A. PROOF OF TECHNICAL LEMMA

PROOF. (of Lem. 3.1) Consider the sequence $X'_1, X'_2, \ldots, X'_k$ of i.i.d. Bernoulli random variables with $\mathbf{E}[X'_i] = \alpha$. We will shortly prove that for any $t > 0$, $\Pr[\sum_{i=1}^k X_i < t] \leq \Pr[\sum_{i=1}^k X'_i < t]$. Given this, we just apply a multiplicative Chernoff bound (Theorem 4.2 of [MR95b]) for $\sum_{i=1}^k X'_i$ with $\mu = \alpha k$. Hence, $\Pr[\sum_{i=1}^k X_i < \alpha k \delta] < \exp(-\alpha(1-\delta)^2/2)$.

For convenience, we show the contrapositive $\Pr[\sum_{i=1}^k X_i \geq t] \geq \Pr[\sum_{i=1}^k X'_i \geq t]$. This is proven by induction on k. First, the base case. Since X_1 and X'_1 are Bernoulli random variables, it suffices to show that $\Pr[X_1 = 1] \geq \Pr[X'_1 = 1] = \alpha$, which holds by assumption.

Now for the induction step. Assume for all $t > 0$ and some index j, $\Pr[\sum_{i=1}^j X_i \geq t] \geq \Pr[\sum_{i=1}^j X'_i \geq t]$. We prove this for $j+1$. Let $\mathcal{E}$ denote the event $\sum_{i=1}^j X_i \geq t$, and $\mathcal{E}'$ be the (disjoint) event $\sum_{i=1}^j X_i \in [t-1, t)$. Let $\mathbb{I}(A)$ denote the indicator function of event A. Because X_i is a 0-1 random variable, we get

$$\begin{aligned}
\Pr\left[\sum_{i=1}^{j+1} X_i \geq t\right] &= \Pr[\mathcal{E}] + \Pr[\mathcal{E}' \wedge (X_{j+1} = 1)] \\
&= \Pr[\mathcal{E}] + \mathbf{E}[\mathbb{I}(\mathcal{E}')\mathbb{I}(X_{j+1} = 1)] \\
& \Pr[\mathcal{E}] + \mathbf{E}\{\mathbf{E}[\mathbb{I}(\mathcal{E}')\mathbb{I}(X_{j+1} = 1) | Y_1, \ldots, Y_j]\}
\end{aligned}$$

Observe that $\sum_{i=1}^j X_i$ only depends on $Y_1, \ldots, Y_j$ so that $\mathbb{I}(\mathcal{E}')$ is a constant in the conditional expectation

$$\begin{aligned}
\mathbf{E}[\mathbb{I}(\mathcal{E}')\mathbb{I}(X_{j+1} = 1) | Y_1, \ldots, Y_j] &= \mathbb{I}(\mathcal{E}')\mathbf{E}[\mathbb{I}(X_{j+1} = 1) | Y_1, \ldots, Y_j] \\
&= \mathbb{I}(\mathcal{E}') \Pr[X_{j+1} = 1 | Y_1, \ldots, Y_j] \\
&\geq \mathbb{I}(\mathcal{E}')\alpha,
\end{aligned}$$

where $\Pr[X_{j+1} = 1 | Y_1, \ldots, Y_j] \geq \alpha$ by the lemma assumption.

Let us denote (for any $s > 0$) $\Pr[\sum_{i=1}^j X_i \geq s]$ by p_s and $\Pr[\sum_{i=1}^j X'_i \geq s]$ by p'_s. The above gives

$$\begin{aligned}
&\Pr\left[\sum_{i=1}^{j+1} X_i \geq t\right] \\
\geq\ & p_t + \alpha \mathbf{E}[\mathbb{I}(\mathcal{E}')] \\
=\ & p_t + (p_{t-1} - p_t)\alpha = p_{t-1}\alpha + p_t(1-\alpha) \\
\geq\ & p'_{t-1}\alpha + p'_t(1-\alpha) \quad \text{(using induction hypothesis and } \alpha \in [0,1]\text{)} \\
=\ & p'_t + (p'_{t-1} - p'_t)\alpha \\
=\ & \Pr\left[\sum_{i=1}^{j} X'_i \geq t\right] + \Pr\left[\left(\sum_{i=1}^{j} X'_i \in [t-1, t)\right) \wedge (X'_{j+1} = 1)\right] \\
=\ & \Pr\left[\sum_{i=1}^{j+1} X'_i \geq t\right]
\end{aligned}$$

□

Black-Box Obfuscation for d-CNFs

Zvika Brakerski
Weizmann Institute of Science
zvika.brakerski@weizmann.ac.il

Guy N. Rothblum
Microsoft Research
rothblum@alum.mit.edu

ABSTRACT

We show how to securely obfuscate a new class of functions: *conjunctions of $\mathcal{NC}_d^0$ circuits*. These are functions of the form $C(\vec{x}) = \bigwedge_{i=1}^{m} C_i(\vec{x})$, where each C_i is a boolean $\mathcal{NC}_d^0$ circuit, whose output bit is only a function of $d = O(1)$ bits of the input $\vec{x}$. For example, d-CNFs, where each clause is a disjunction of at most d variables, are in this class. Given such a function, we produce an obfuscated program that preserves the input-output functionality of the given function, but reveals nothing else. Our construction is based on multilinear maps, and can be instantiated using the recent candidates proposed by Garg, Gentry and Halevi (EUROCRYPT 2013) and by Coron, Lepoint and Tibouchi (CRYPTO 2013).

We prove that the construction is a secure obfuscation in a generic multilinear group model, under the black-box definition of Barak et al. (CRYPTO 2001). Security is based on a new *worst-case* hardness assumption about exponential hardness of the NP-complete problem 3-SAT, the *Bounded Speedup Hypothesis*.

One of the new techniques we introduce is a method for enforcing input consistency, which we call *randomizing sub-assignments*. We hope that this technique can find further application in constructing secure obfuscators.

The family of functions we obfuscate is considerably richer than previous works that consider black-box obfuscation.[1] As one application, we show how to achieve *obfuscated functional point testing*: namely, to construct a circuit that checks whether $f(\vec{x}) = \vec{y}$, where f is an arbitrary "public" polynomial-time computable function, but $\vec{y}$ is a "secret" point that is hidden in the obfuscation.

Categories and Subject Descriptors

E.3 [**Data Encryption**]: Miscellaneous

[1]A concurrent and independent work of Garg et al. [16] considers the weaker security notion of "indistinguishability obfuscation", and proposes a candidate obfuscator for any function computed by a polynomial size circuit.

ITCS'14, January 12–14, 2014, Princeton, New Jersey, USA.

http://dx.doi.org/10.1145/2554797.2554820.

Keywords

Cryptography, Program Obfuscation

1. INTRODUCTION

A code obfuscator is a compiler that makes computer programs impossible to reverse engineer, while preserving their input-output functionality. Code obfuscation is a central question in the theory and practice of cryptography. Despite the problem's importance, very few techniques or heuristics were known. Recently, however, several works have leveraged new constructions of cryptographically secure multilinear maps [15, 12] to construct obfuscators for complex functionalities [6, 16].

In this work, we present a candidate obfuscator for a rich new circuit class: conjunctions of $\mathcal{NC}^0$ circuits. In particular, this includes the family of d-CNF formulas (for constant d). Our construction relies on *(asymmetric) multilinear maps*, and can be instantiated using the new candidate constructions of Garg, Gentry and Halevi [15], or of Coron, Lepoint and Tibouchi [12].

We prove the construction's security in a generic multilinear map model, under a worst-case complexity assumption (see below). An important ingredient in this construction, which we hope will find further applications, is a new technique for enforcing input consistency using *randomizing sub-assignments*.

Obfuscation: Definitions. Intuitively, an obfuscator should generate a new program that preserves the the original program's functionality, but is impossible to reverse engineer. The theoretical study of this problem was initiated by Barak et al. [3]. They formalized a strong simulation-based security requirement of *black box obfuscation*: namely, the obfuscated program should expose nothing more than what can be learned via oracle access to its input-output behavior. We refer to this notion as "black-box" obfuscation, and we use this strong formalization throughout this work (except where we note otherwise).

A weaker notion of obfuscation, known as *indistinguishability* or *best-possible* obfuscation was studied in [3, 18]. An indistinguishability obfuscator guarantees that the obfuscations of any two programs (boolean circuits) with identical functionalities are indistinguishable. We note that, unlike the black-box definition of security, indistinguishability obfuscation does not quantify or qualify what information the obfuscation might expose. In particular, the obfuscation might reveal non-black-box information about the functionality.

Prior Work: Negative Results. In their work, [3] proved the impossibility of general-purpose black-box obfuscators (i.e. ones that work for any polynomial-time functionality) in the virtual black box model. This impossibility result was extended in [17]. While these negative results show serious limitations on the possibility of general-purpose obfuscation, they focus on specific (often cryptographic or contrived) functionalities. Thus, they do not rule out that obfuscation may be possible for many programs of interest. Goldwasser and Rothblum [18] showed obstacles to the possibility of achieving indistinguishability obfuscation with information-theoretic security, and to achieving it in the random oracle model.

Prior Work: Positive Results. Positive results on obfuscation focused on specific, simple programs. One program family, which has received extensive attention, is that of "point functions": password checking programs that only accept a single input string, and reject all others. Starting with the work of Canetti [8], several works have shown obfuscators for this family under various assumptions [10, 22, 27], as well as extensions [9, 4]. Canetti, Rothblum and Varia [11] showed how to obfuscate a function that checks membership in a hyperplane of constant dimension (over a large finite field). Other works showed how to obfuscate cryptographic function classes under different definitions and formalizations. These function classes include checking proximity to a hidden point [13], vote mixing [1], and re-encryption [20]. Several works [8, 10, 19, 20] relaxed the security requirement so that obfuscation only holds for a random choice of a program from the family.

More recently, Brakerski and Rothblum [6] showed that multilinear maps could be used to obfuscate richer function families. They constructed an obfuscator for *conjunctions*, the family of functions that test whether a subset of the input bits take on specified values. The construction was shown to be secure in the generic multilinear map model. It was also shown to be secure under (falsifiable [24]) multilinear DDH-like assumptions, so long as the conjunction is drawn from a family with sufficient entropy.

Related Concurrent Work [16]. In a concurrent and independent work, Garg et al. [16] use cryptographic multilinear maps to give a candidate indistinguishability obfuscator (see above) for all polynomial-size circuits. The main differences with our work are: (*i*) we construct an obfuscator with the stronger security notion of black-box obfuscation (albeit for a smaller class of functions). And (*ii*) we prove the security of our construction in the generic multilinear group model. See more on the generic multilinear group model below. Our proof uses a worst-case complexity-theoretic assumption. Garg et al. [16] pose the security of their construction in the generic multilinear group model as a major open question. We note that [16] do prove security in a new "generic colored matrix model", which restricts an adversary to a subset of the multilinear group operations.

Our Work: Black-Box Obfuscation for Conjunctions of $\mathcal{NC}^0$. An $\mathcal{NC}^0_d$ circuit is a boolean circuit on n-bit inputs, whose output depends only on d input bits. If a circuit (or rather a circuit ensemble) is in $\mathcal{NC}^0_d$ for some fixed $d \geq 0$, then we say that it is in $\mathcal{NC}^0$ (and we drop the d). A *conjunction of* $\mathcal{NC}^0$ *circuits* is a circuit $C = \bigwedge_{i=1}^{m} C_i$, where each C_i is an $\mathcal{NC}^0$ circuit. We use $\mathcal{CNC}^0$ to refer to the class of circuits that are conjunctions of $\mathcal{NC}^0$ circuits. For example, any d-CNF (a CNF formula, where each clause has at most d literals) is a $\mathcal{CNC}^0$ circuit. Another example is simple conjunction circuits: there each C_i only depends on (at most) a single input bit.

In this work we build a black-box obfuscator for $\mathcal{CNC}^0$ circuits. In more detail, the obfuscator takes as input a $\mathcal{CNC}^0_d$ circuit C, runs in time $O(n^d)$, and outputs and obfuscation that exposes nothing beyond the input-output functionality of C (the obfuscation also exposes d). We note that the class $\mathcal{CNC}^0$ is limited in computational power. In particular, it is contained in $\mathcal{AC}^0$, and so there are simple and natural functions (such as XOR) that cannot be computed in $\mathcal{CNC}^0$. Still, it is significantly richer than previous classes for which obfuscators were known. For example, the Cook-Levin Theorem shows that NP-complete statements can be verified in $\mathcal{CNC}^0$, and there are secure digital signature schemes where verification is in $\mathcal{CNC}^0$. Moreover, impossibility results [3, 17] rule out general-purpose black-box obfuscation even for $\mathcal{AC}^0$. Obfuscating $\mathcal{CNC}^0$ brings us close to the dovetailing with these impossibility results.

One important ingredient in this construction is a new technique for enforcing input consistency by *randomizing sub-assignments*. We are hopeful that this technique may find further applications.

We prove that the construction is a secure black-box obfuscator in the generic multilinear group model. In the generic multilinear group model, an adversary must operate independently of group elements' representations. Rather, the adversary is given arbitrary strings representing these elements, and can only manipulate them using oracles for addition, subtraction, multilinear maps and more (see below). In our proof, we make use of a new *worst-case* assumption about exponential hardness of the NP-complete problem 3-SAT. We call this new assumption the *bounded speedup hypothesis*, a strengthening of the long-standing exponential time hypothesis (ETH) for solving SAT [21].[2] See further details below.

We find this proof of security intriguing for several reasons. First, as stated above, it tells us that (under the bounded-speedup hypothesis) the construction is completely impervious to generic attacks—a rich class that of attacks, which in particular includes all known attacks against the candidate cryptographic multilinear groups. While we distrust the generic model (especially in light of impossibility results [3, 17]), results in this model can still be used to obfuscate provided we have simple secure hardware implementing the generic group. Finally, to the best of our knowledge, no impossibility results for black-box obfuscation are known in generic models (or in the random oracle model). This raises the possibility that our techniques could be used to construct a secure *black-box* obfuscator for richer classes, and even for any polynomial-size circuit, in the generic multilinear group model.

An Application: Obfuscated Functional Point Tests. Consider the following setting: there is an arbitrary polynomial-size "public" circuit computing a function f, and a "secret" target value $\vec{y}$. We want to release an obfuscation that can test, for any input $\vec{x}$, whether $f(\vec{x}) = \vec{y}$, but *without revealing anything about the secret* $\vec{y}$. For example, perhaps C checks that its input contains a message m, and a digital

[2] We note that is both the adversary and the simulator are allowed to run in quasi-polynomial tim, security can be based on the (standard) Exponential-Time Hypothesis.

signature on m from a trusted authority (otherwise C rejects). If this test passes, C runs a sophisticated analysis to determine m's topic, and flags whether m's topic equals y. An adversary that receives the obfuscation (and knows the topic analysis algorithm) should not be able to determine what the "target topic" y is—it can only test messages that have been signed by the trusted authority, and see whether their topic is y.

A obfuscator for $\mathcal{CNC}^0$ can be used for this application as follows. By the Cook-Levin theorem, for any polynomial-size C, there exists a $\mathcal{CNC}^0_3$ circuit C' that takes as input $(\vec{x}, C(\vec{x}), w)$, where w is "advice" computed as a function of C and of $\vec{x}$ only, and accept if and only if $C(\vec{x}) = y$. By obfuscating C' gives the desired application. We note that this type of application, involving general computations, is well beyond what was known to be possible for black-box obfuscation.

Followup Work. Brakerski and Rothblum [7] showed how to combine the techniques in this paper with those of [16] to introduce an obfuscator for $\mathcal{P}$ which is provably VBB secure in the generic model under the bounded speedup hypothesis. They also show that the construction is an indistinguishability obfuscator in the generic model without requiring further assumptions. Further building on their work, Barak et al. [2], give a construction and prove its VBB security in the generic model (without a complexity assumption).

We proceed with further details and discussions.

1.1 Our Construction and its Security

Background on Multilinear Maps and Graded Encoding Schemes. We begin by recalling the notion of multilinear maps, due to Boneh and Silverberg [5]. Rothblum [25] considered the asymmetric case, where the groups may be different (this is crucial for our construction, as we explain below).

DEFINITION 1.1 (ASYMMETRIC MULTILINEAR MAP [5, 25]). *For $\tau+1$ cyclic groups $G_1, \ldots, G_\tau$, G_T of the same order p, a τ-multilinear map $e : G_1 \times \ldots \times G_\tau \to G$ has the following properties:*

1. *For elements $\{g_i \in G_i\}_{i=1,\ldots,\tau}$, index $i \in [\tau]$ and integer $\alpha \in \mathbb{Z}_p$, it holds that:*

$$e(g_1, \ldots, \alpha \cdot g_i, \ldots, g_\tau) = \alpha \cdot e(g_1, \ldots, g_\tau)$$

2. *The map e is non-degenerate: when its inputs are all generators of their respective groups $\{G_i\}$, then its output is a generator of the group G.*

Recently, [15] suggested a candidate for graded encoding, a generalization of (symmetric or asymmetric) multilinear maps. See Section 2.1 for a more complete overview on these. For this introduction, we treat them as a generalization of asymmetric multilinear maps in the following way. For the i-th group G_i, of prime order p, we consider the ring $\mathbb{Z}_p$. For an element $\sigma \in \mathbb{Z}_p$, we can think of $\sigma \cdot g_i$ as an "encoding" of σ in G_i.[3] We denote this by $\mathsf{enc}_i(\sigma)$. We note that this encoding is easy to compute, but (presumably) hard to invert. The multilinear map e lets us take τ encodings $\{\mathsf{enc}_i(\sigma_i)\}_{i\in[\tau],\sigma_i\in\mathbb{Z}_p}$, and compute an encoding $\mathsf{enc}_T(\prod_i \sigma_i)$ in the "final group" G. Graded encoding schemes provide a similar functionality, albeit with randomized and noisy encodings, and with a procedure for testing equality of encoded elements in the final group G.

Obfuscating Conjunctions of Bit-Predicates [6]. Recently, [6] show how to obfuscate conjunction functions: conjunctions of single-bit predicates. A conjunction $C(\vec{x}) = \bigwedge_{i\in[n]} C_i(\vec{x}[i])$ is made up of a single circuit C_i for each input bit $\vec{x}[i]$. The circuit C_i can equal $\vec{x}[i]$, its negation, or be a constant 1 (meaning it has no effect) or 0 (meaning that $C \equiv 0$). For each $i \in [n]$, the [6] obfuscator chooses an "accepting" ring element $\alpha_{i,0}$ and a "rejecting" ring element $\alpha_{i,1}$. It then encodes the circuit C_i using a two-entry table, where each entry $v \in \{0,1\}$ contains *the encodings* of a pair of ring elements:

$$(\rho_{i,v}, (\rho_{i,v}) \cdot \alpha_{i,C_i(v)}))$$

(the $\rho_{i,v}$ value is uniformly random). We emphasize that the obfuscation only produces the *encodings* of these ring elements. Note that e.g. if $C_i \equiv 1$, then both of these table entries use the same α variable, and are thus not independent. Nonetheless, since the encodings are hard to invert, an adversary will not be able to tell that this is the case (which is essential for security).

To complete the obfuscation, the obfuscator also produces encodings of an "unlocking" or "checking" pair:

$$(\rho_{\mathsf{chk}}, (\rho_{\mathsf{chk}} \cdot (\prod_{i\in[n]} \alpha_{i,1})))$$

(where again ρ is uniformly random, and chk is just a notation for the last group, $n+1$ in this case).

To evaluate the obfuscated program on an input $\vec{x} \in \{0,1\}^n$, they use the multilinear map to test the equality:[4]

$$\left(\rho_{\mathsf{chk}} \cdot (\prod_{i\in[n]} (\rho_{i,\vec{x}[i]}) \cdot \alpha_{i,C_i(\vec{x}[i])})\right) \stackrel{?}{=} \left((\rho_{\mathsf{chk}} \cdot (\prod_{i\in[n]} \alpha_{i,1})) \cdot (\prod_{i\in[n]} \rho_{i,\vec{x}[i]})\right)$$

Correctness follows by construction: the equality holds if and only if $\forall i \in [n] : C_i(\vec{x}[i]) = 1$ (except for a negligible error probability).

Security is not as straightforward. Intuitively, security holds because for each $i \in [n]$, the entries of the i-th table do not reveal anything about C_i (the complication is that the "checking" pair creates correlations between the different table entries. See [6]).

The importance of using *asymmetric* multilinear maps (as opposed to symmetric) is apparent in this construction. We must not allow to multiply elements of the same group index, as that would trivially allow to identify for all i whether $C_i \equiv 1$, by cross-multiplying the 0 and 1 elements and checking for equality. This logic carries over to our construction below, although its manifestation is less apparent.

Our Contribution: Obfuscating Conjunctions of Multi-Bit Predicates. Our goal is obfuscating a $\mathcal{CNC}^0$ circuit C,

[3]Note that we are using additive group notation. In multiplicative notation this would be written as g_i^σ.

[4]For the candidate of [15], the encodings are randomized, but there is a procedure for testing equality between encoded elements in the final group.

where C is a conjunction of $\mathcal{NC}^0$ predicates $C_1, \ldots, C_m$. A natural initial approach is starting with the construction of [6], which obfuscates conjunctions of single-bit predicates, and trying to extend that construction to conjunctions of predicates on many (d) bits as follows. We can "group" every d-tuple of inputs bits into a "super-symbol". This stretches the n-bit input into a vector of $\binom{n}{d}$ "super-symbols" in $\{0,1\}^d$. Now, any predicate on d bits becomes a predicate on a single "super-symbol", and we might hope to directly apply the conjunction obfuscator.

There are two issues with this approach:

1. **Each input "super-symbol" is now in $\{0,1\}^d$ (rather than $\{0,1\}$)**

   Examine one such super-symbol I, corresponding to a d-tuple of input bits (i.e. I is a set of d elements out of $[n]$, which we denote $I \in \binom{[n]}{d}$). Let C_I be the circuit in C that takes the d bits in I as its input bits.[5] Of the 2^d assignments to the bits in I, there is a subset $S_1 \subseteq \{0,1\}^d$ that makes C_I accept. The remaining assignments $S_0 \subseteq \{0,1\}^d$, make C_I reject.

   Building on the conjunction obfuscator, we can now have a table of size 2^d for the circuit C_I, where each table entry corresponds to an assignment for the variables in I. We choose an "accepting ring element" $\alpha_{I,1}$ and a "rejecting group element" $\alpha_{I,0}$. In each entry $\vec{s} \in \{0,1\}^d$ we encode either an "accepting pair" $(\rho_{I,\vec{s}}, (\rho_{I,\vec{s}} \cdot \alpha_{I,1}))$, or a "rejecting pair" $(\rho_{I,\vec{s}}, (\rho_{I,\vec{s}} \cdot \alpha_{I,0}))$. Intuitively, hardness of discreet log problems guarantees that an adversary cannot use these table to distinguish whether or not any given assignment satisfies the I-th sub-circuit.

   Finally, to complete the obfuscation, we also include a "checking pair" that encodes a product of all the accepting group elements $(\rho_{\mathsf{chk}}, (\rho_{\mathsf{chk}} \cdot \prod_{I \in \binom{[n]}{d}} \alpha_{I,1}))$.

   To evaluate the obfuscated program on an input $\vec{x} \in \{0,1\}^n$, use the multilinear map, as in the conjunction obfuscator, to test the equality:

$$\left(\rho_{\mathsf{chk}} \cdot \Big(\prod_{I \in \binom{[n]}{d}} (\rho_{I,\vec{x}_{|I}} \cdot \alpha_{I,\vec{x}_{|I}})\Big)\right) \stackrel{?}{=} \left(\rho_{\mathsf{chk}} \cdot \Big(\prod_{I \in \binom{[n]}{d}} \alpha_{I,1}\Big) \cdot \Big(\prod_{I \in \binom{[n]}{d}} \rho_{I,\vec{x}_{|I}}\Big)\right)$$

   By construction, equality will hold if and only if $\vec{x}$ is an accepting input (except for a negligible error probability). The size of the resulting obfuscation is $O(n^d \cdot 2^d)$.

2. **Enforcing Consistency**

   A more serious issue with the idea above, is *enforcing consistency*. Namely, there is nothing to stop an adversary from picking $\binom{n}{d}$ arbitrary assignments $\{\vec{s}_I \in \{0,1\}^d\}_{I \in \binom{[n]}{d}}$, and evaluating the "checking equality":

$$\left(\rho_{\mathsf{chk}} \cdot \Big(\prod_{I \in \binom{[n]}{d}} (\rho_{I,\vec{s}_I} \cdot \alpha_{I,\vec{s}_I})\Big)\right) \stackrel{?}{=} \left(\rho_{\mathsf{chk}} \cdot \Big(\prod_{I \in \binom{[n]}{d}} \alpha_{I,1}\Big) \cdot \Big(\prod_{I \in \binom{[n]}{d}} \rho_{I,\vec{s}_I}\Big)\right)$$

   We emphasize that *the assignments $\vec{s}_I$ might not be consistent*: they need not correspond to any input $\vec{x} \in \{0,1\}^n$. For example, the first bit of $\vec{x}$ might be set to 0 in one set I, and to 1 in another set I'! Allowing an adversary to test such equalities would immediately leak non black-box information about the circuit C and would break security.

   The main technical challenge in our construction is disallowing such attacks, and enforcing consistency in the adversary's choices. We view this as one of our main contributions, and we hope that it can find further applications as a building-block for constructing secure obfuscators.

[5]We assume w.l.o.g. that there is a single such circuit C_I in C: if there is none, then C_I is the constant-1 circuits. If there are multiple such circuits, they can be merged into their conjunction, which is itself an $\mathcal{NC}^0_d$ circuit. Both transformations maintain the functionality of C and also maintain $|C| \le O(n)^d$.

Randomizing Sub-Assignments and Enforcing Consistency. We want to avoid letting an adversary choose inconsistent sub-assignments for the circuits $\{C_I\}_{I \in \binom{[n]}{d}}$. In particular, if $i \in I, I'$, then we want to ensure that the adversary can only pick sub-assignments $\vec{s}_I, \vec{s}_{I'}$ where $\vec{s}_I[i] = \vec{s}_{I'}[i] \in \{0,1\}$. Towards this end, we randomize each sub-assignment's table entry as follows.

For each $i \in [n]$ and $I \ni i$ (we use $I \ni i$ to denote $\{I \in \binom{[n]}{d} : i \in I\}$), and for each bit value $b \in \{0,1\}$, choose a uniformly random randomizer $\beta_{I,i,b}$, and multiply it into each entry $\vec{s} \in \{0,1\}^d$ of the table for I, so that entry now has encodings of:

$$(\rho_{I,\vec{s}}, (\rho_{I,\vec{s}} \cdot \alpha_{I,C_I(\vec{s})} \cdot (\prod_{i \in I} \beta_{I,i,\vec{s}[i]})))$$

Now in evaluating the "checking equality", on the left-hand side we have a product of all these β-randomizers, i.e. we get an additional multiplicative term:

$$\prod_{I \in \binom{[n]}{d}, i \in I} \beta_{I,i,\vec{s}_I[i]} = \prod_{i \in [n]} (\prod_{I \ni i} \beta_{I,i,\vec{s}_I[i]})$$

We pick the β-randomizers under the additional restriction that $\forall i \in [n]$:

$$(\prod_{I \ni i} \beta_{I,i,0}) = (\prod_{I \ni i} \beta_{I,i,1}) = \gamma_i$$

Otherwise the β variables are uniformly random. This has the effect that as long as the adversary picks the sub-assignments involving variable i *consistently*, the new multiplicative term is exactly γ_i, regardless of whether the bit value assigned to the i-th input bit is 0 or 1. However, if assignments involving input bit i get *inconsistent* values, then the added multiplicative term will be different from γ_i (indeed, it will be close to uniformly random and independent of γ_i).

We use the above randomization to enforce consistency. To allow functionality, we multiply the new terms into the "checking pair", which now has encodings of:

$$(\rho_{\mathsf{chk}}, (\rho_{\mathsf{chk}} \cdot \prod_{I \in \binom{[n]}{d}} \alpha_{I,1} \cdot \prod_{i \in [n]} \gamma_i))$$

The obfuscated program can now be evaluated using the target equation similarly to the above (with the added β terms enforcing consistency). Functionality follows by construction. Security is not so straightforward: while the randomized sub-assignments do intuitively seem to aid in avoiding inconsistent assignments to the sub-circuits, proving that the construction is secure seems to be considerably more difficult.

Security in the Generic Model and the Bounded-Speedup Hypothesis We prove that our construction is a secure black-box obfuscator in the generic multilinear group model. In this proof, we make use of a new *worst-case* assumption about exponential hardness of the NP-complete problem 3-SAT. We call this new assumption the *bounded speedup hypothesis*, a strengthening of the long-standing exponential time hypothesis for solving SAT [21]. The exponential-time hypothesis states that no sub-exponential time algorithm can resolve satisfiability of 3-CNF formulas. Intuitively, the bounded-speedup hypothesis states that no polynomial-time algorithm for resolving satisfiability of 3-CNFs can have "super-polynomial speedup" over a brute-force algorithm that tests assignments one-by-one. More formally, there does not exist an ensemble of polynomial-size circuits $\{\mathcal{A}_n\}$, and an ensemble of super-polynomial-size sets of assignments $\{\mathcal{X}_n\}$, such that on input a 3-CNF Φ on n-bit inputs, w.h.p. $\mathcal{A}_n$ finds a satisfying assignment for Φ in $\mathcal{X}_n$ if such an assignment exists. We emphasize that this is a worst-case hypothesis, i.e. it only says that for every ensemble $\mathcal{A}$, there *exists* some 3-CNF on which $\mathcal{A}$ fails. See Definition 5.3, and further discussion in Appendix A below.

In the proof of security, we consider a random generic graded encoding model, where each element is represented by a long random bit string. This allows the simulator to produce a fake obfuscated program simply by producing a sequence of random representations. The main problem is that in a real simulated program, there is a correlation between the underlying elements represented by the bit strings. For example, when properly evaluating the circuit on a legal input, we expect to get the right answer (which is very unlikely to be produced by a fake obfuscated program). We show that this challenge translates to the task of deciding whether a certain type of multilinear arithmetic circuits evaluate to zero under a certain distribution (which depends on C). We then show that this zero testing can be performed using only oracle access to C.

At an intuitive (and somewhat inaccurate) level, the security proof uses the randomizing sub-assignments to argue that the only "interesting" computations that an adversary can run in the generic model are: (i) evaluate the "checking equation" on a consistently chosen input $\vec{x}$, or (ii) evaluate a linear combination of the checking equations for a set $\mathcal{X}$ of inputs. For any other computations that the adversary runs, the answer is essentially independent of the obfuscated circuit C, and can be simulated.

For computations that evaluate a linear combination of the checking equation for inputs in a set $\mathcal{X}$, the answer can be simulated using only black-box access to C on those inputs. The remaining challenge is to argue that the adversary can only evaluate a linear combination of *polynomially* many inputs, i.e. that the set $\mathcal{X}$ must be of polynomial size. To show this, we prove that an adversary that computes a linear combination of the checking equation for a set of inputs $\mathcal{X}$, can also resolve 3-SAT on this same set $\mathcal{X}$: given any 3-CNF Φ, it can find a satisfying assignment for Φ in $\mathcal{X}$ (if one exists). Thus, under the Bounded Speedup Hypothesis, the set $\mathcal{X}$ must be of polynomial size, and the adversary can be simulated. We note that one detail (among many) omitted above, is how the simulator can "extract" the set $\mathcal{X}$ to complete the simulation. See details in Section 5.

2. PRELIMINARIES

For all $n, d \in \mathbb{N}$ we define $\binom{[n]}{d}$ to be the set of lexicographically ordered sets of cardinality d in $[n]$. More formally:

$$\binom{[n]}{d} = \left\{\langle i_1, \ldots, i_d\rangle \in [n]^d : i_1 < \cdots < i_d\right\} .$$

Note that $\left|\binom{[n]}{d}\right| = \binom{n}{d}$.

For $\vec{x} \in \{0,1\}^n$ and $I = \langle i_1, \ldots, i_d\rangle \in \binom{[n]}{d}$, we let $\vec{x}_{|I} \in \{0,1\}^d$ denote the vector $\langle \vec{x}[i_1], \ldots, \vec{x}[i_d]\rangle$. We often slightly abuse notation when working with $\vec{s} = \vec{x}_{|I}$, and let $\vec{s}[i_j]$ denote the element $x[i_j]$ (rather than the i_jth element in $\vec{s}$). We sometimes overload notation and use $I \in \binom{[n]}{d}$ to denote the lexicographic ordinal of I in $\binom{[n]}{d}$ (which is an integer in $\left[\binom{n}{d}\right]$). We use $I \ni i$ to denote the set of sets $\{I \in \binom{[n]}{d} : i \in I\}$. Namely, all the sets in $\binom{[n]}{d}$ which contain the element i.

2.1 Graded Encoding Schemes

We begin with the definition of a graded encoding scheme, due to Garg, Gentry and Halevi [15]. While their construction is very general, for our purposes a more restricted setting is sufficient as defined below.

Definition 2.1 (τ-Graded Encoding Scheme [15]). *A τ-encoding scheme for an integer $\tau \in \mathbb{N}$ and ring R, is a collection of sets $\mathcal{S} = \{S_{\vec{v}}^{(\alpha)} \subset \{0,1\}^* : \vec{v} \in \{0,1\}^\tau, \alpha \in R\}$ with the following properties:*

1. *For every index $\vec{v} \in \{0,1\}^\tau$, the sets $\{S_{\vec{v}}^{(\alpha)} : \alpha \in R\}$ are disjoint, and so they are a partition of the indexed set $S_{\vec{v}} = \bigcup_{\alpha \in R} S_{\vec{v}}^{(\alpha)}$.*

2. *There are binary operations "+" and "−" such that for all $\vec{v} \in \{0,1\}^\tau$, $\alpha_1, \alpha_2 \in R$ and for all $u_1 \in S_{\vec{v}}^{(\alpha_1)}$, $u_2 \in S_{\vec{v}}^{(\alpha_2)}$:*

   $$u_1 + u_2 \in S_{\vec{v}}^{(\alpha_1+\alpha_2)} \quad \text{and} \quad u_1 - u_2 \in S_{\vec{v}}^{(\alpha_1-\alpha_2)} ,$$

   where $\alpha_1+\alpha_2$ and $\alpha_1-\alpha_2$ are addition and subtraction in R.

3. *There is an associative binary operation "×" such that for all $\vec{v}_1, \vec{v}_2 \in \{0,1\}^\tau$ such that $\vec{v}_1 + \vec{v}_2 \in \{0,1\}^\tau$, for all $\alpha_1, \alpha_2 \in R$ and for all $u_1 \in S_{\vec{v}_1}^{(\alpha_1)}$, $u_2 \in S_{\vec{v}_2}^{(\alpha_2)}$, it holds that*

   $$u_1 \times u_2 \in S_{\vec{v}_1+\vec{v}_2}^{(\alpha_1\cdot\alpha_2)} ,$$

   where $\alpha_1 \cdot \alpha_2$ is multiplication in R.

In this work, the ring R will always be $\mathbb{Z}_p$ for a prime p.

For the reader who is familiar with [15], we note that the above is the special case of their construction, in which we consider only binary index vectors (in the [15] notation, this corresponds to setting $\kappa = 1$), and we construct our encoding schemes to be *asymmetric* (as will become apparent below when we define our zero-text index $\mathbf{vzt} = \vec{1}$).

We now define efficient procedures for a τ-graded encoding scheme [15].

DEFINITION 2.2. *We consider τ-graded encoding schemes (see above) where the following procedures are efficiently computable.*

- *Instance Generation:* $\mathsf{InstGen}(1^\lambda, 1^\tau)$ *outputs the set of parameters params, a description of a τ-Graded Encoding Scheme. (Recall that we only consider Graded Encoding Schemes over the set indices $\{0,1\}^\tau$, with zero testing in the set $S_{\vec{1}}$). In addition, the procedure outputs a subset evparams $\subset$ params that is sufficient for computing addition, multiplication and zero testing*[6] *(but possibly insufficient for encoding or for randomization).*
- *Ring Sampler:* $\mathsf{samp}(params)$ *outputs a "level zero encoding" $a \in S_0^{(\alpha)}$ for a nearly uniform $\alpha \in_R R$.*
- *Encode and Re-Randomize:*[7] $\mathsf{encRand}(params, i, a)$ *takes as input an index $i \in \tau$ and $a \in S_0^{(\alpha)}$, and outputs an encoding $u \in S_{\vec{e}_i}^{(\alpha)}$, where the distribution of u is (statistically close to being) only dependent on α and not otherwise dependent of a.*
- *Addition and Negation:* $\mathsf{add}(evparams, u_1, u_2)$ *takes $u_1 \in S_{\vec{v}}^{(\alpha_1)}$, $u_2 \in S_{\vec{v}}^{(\alpha_2)}$, and outputs $w \in S_{\vec{v}}^{(\alpha_1+\alpha_2)}$. (If the two operands are not in the same indexed set, then* add *returns $\perp$). We often use the notation $u_1 + u_2$ to denote this operation when evparams is clear from the context. Similarly,* $\mathsf{negate}(evparams, u_1) \in S_{\vec{v}}^{(-\alpha_1)}$.
- *Multiplication:* $\mathsf{mult}(evparams, u_1, u_2)$ *takes $u_1 \in S_{\vec{v}_1}^{(\alpha_1)}$, $u_2 \in S_{\vec{v}_2}^{(\alpha_2)}$. If $\vec{v}_1 + \vec{v}_2 \in \{0,1\}^\tau$ (i.e. every coordinate in $\vec{v}_1 + \vec{v}_2$ is at most 1), then* mult *outputs $w \in S_{\vec{v}_1+\vec{v}_2}^{(\alpha_1 \cdot \alpha_2)}$. Otherwise,* mult *outputs $\perp$. We often use the notation $u_1 \times u_2$ to denote this operation when evparams is clear from the context.*
- *Zero Test:* $\mathsf{isZero}(evparams, u)$ *outputs 1 if $u \in S_{\vec{1}}^{(0)}$, and 0 otherwise.*

In the [15, 12] constructions, encodings are noisy *and the noise level increases with addition and multiplication operations, so one has to be careful not to go over a specified noise bound. However, the parameters can be set so as to support $O(\tau)$ operations, which are sufficient for our purposes. We therefore ignore noise management throughout this manuscript. An additional subtle issue is that with negligible probability the initial noise may be too big. However this can be avoided by adding rejection sampling to* samp *and therefore ignored throughout the manuscript as well.*

[6]The "zero testing" parameter **pzt** defined in [15] is a part of *evparams*.

[7]This functionality is not explicitly provided by [15], however it can be obtained by combining their encoding and re-randomization procedures.

As was done in [6], our definition deviates from that of [15]. We define two sets of parameters *params* and *evparams*. While the former will be used by the obfuscator in our construction (and therefore will not be revealed to an external adversary), the latter will be used when evaluating an obfuscated program (and thus will be known to an adversary). When instantiating our definition, the guideline is to make *evparams* minimal so as to give the least amount of information to the adversary. In particular, in the known candidates [15, 12], *evparams* only needs to contain the zero-test parameter **pzt** (as well as the global modulus).

2.2 Obfuscation

DEFINITION 2.3 (VIRTUAL BLACK-BOX OBFUSCATOR [3]). *Let $\mathcal{C} = \{\mathcal{C}_n\}_{n \in \mathbb{N}}$ be a family of polynomial-size circuits, where $\mathcal{C}_n$ is a set of boolean circuits operating on inputs of length n. And let $\mathcal{O}$ be a PPTM algorithm, which takes as input an input length $n \in \mathbb{N}$, a circuit $C \in \mathcal{C}_n$, a security parameter $\lambda \in \mathbb{N}$, and outputs a boolean circuit $\mathcal{O}(C)$ (not necessarily in $\mathcal{C}$).*

$\mathcal{O}$ is an obfuscator *for the circuit family $\mathcal{C}$ if it satisfies:*

1. Preserving Functionality: *For every $n \in \mathbb{N}$, and every $C \in \mathcal{C}_n$, and every $\vec{x} \in \{0,1\}^n$, with all but negl(λ) probability over the coins of $\mathcal{O}$:*
$$(\mathcal{O}(C, 1^n, \lambda))(\vec{x}) = C(\vec{x})$$
2. Polynomial Slowdown: *For every $n, \lambda \in \mathbb{N}$ and $C \in \mathcal{C}$, the circuit $\mathcal{O}(C, 1^n, 1^\lambda)$ is of size at most poly($|C|, n, \lambda$).*
3. Virtual Black-Box: *For every (non-uniform) polynomial size adversary $\mathcal{A}$, there exists a (non-uniform) polynomial size simulator $\mathcal{S}$, such that for every $n \in \mathbb{N}$* and for every *$C \in \mathcal{C}_n$:*
$$\left|\Pr_{\mathcal{O},\mathcal{A}}[\mathcal{A}(\mathcal{O}(C, 1^n, 1^\lambda)) = 1] - \Pr_{\mathcal{S}}[\mathcal{S}^C(1^{|C|}, 1^n, 1^\lambda) = 1]\right| = negl(\lambda)$$

REMARK 2.4. *A stronger notion of functionality, which also appears in the literature, requires that with overwhelming probability the obfuscated circuit is correct on* every input simultaneously*. We use the relaxed requirement that for every input (individually) the obfuscated circuit is correct with overwhelming probability (in both cases the probability is only over the obfuscator's coins). We note that our construction can be modified to achieve the stronger functionality property (by using a ring of sufficiently large size and the union bound).*

3. THE GENERIC GRADED ENCODING SCHEME MODEL

We would like to prove the security of our construction against *generic adversaries*. To this end, we will use the *generic graded encoding scheme* model, which was previously used in [6], and is analogous to the *generic group model* (see Shoup [26] and Maurer [23]). In this model, an algorithm/adversary $\mathcal{A}$ can only interact with the graded encoding scheme via oracle calls to the add, mult, and isZero operations from Definition 2.2. Note that, in particular, we only allow access to the operations that can be run using *evparams*. To the best of our knowledge, non-generic attacks on known schemes, e.g. [15], require use of *params* and cannot be mounted when only *evparams* is given.

We use $\mathcal{G}$ to denote an oracle that answers adversary calls. The oracle operates as follows: for each index $\vec{v} \in \{0,1\}^\tau$, the elements of the indexed set $S_{\vec{v}} = \bigcup_{\alpha \in R} S_{\vec{v}}^{(\alpha)}$ are arbitrary binary strings. The adversary $\mathcal{A}$ can manipulate these strings using oracle calls (via $\mathcal{G}$) to the graded encoding scheme's functionalities. For example, the adversary can use $\mathcal{G}$ to perform an add call: taking strings $s_1 \in S_{\vec{v}}^{(\alpha_1)}$, $s_2 \in S_{\vec{v}}^{(\alpha_2)}$, encoding indexed ring elements $(\vec{v}, \alpha_1), (\vec{v}, \alpha_2)$ (respectively), and obtaining a string $s \in S_{\vec{v}}^{(\alpha_1+\alpha_2)}$, encoding the indexed ring element $(\vec{v}, (\alpha_1 + \alpha_2))$.

We say that $\mathcal{A}$ is a generic algorithm (or adversary) for a problem on graded encoding schemes (e.g. for computing a moral equivalent of discreet log), if it can accomplish this task with respect to *any* oracle representing a graded encoding scheme, see below.

In the add example above, there may be many strings/encodings in the set $S_{\vec{v}}^{(\alpha_1+\alpha_2)}$. One immediate question is *which* of these elements should be returned by the call to add. In our abstraction, for each $\vec{v} \in \{0,1\}^\tau$ and $\alpha \in R$, $\mathcal{G}$ always uses a *single unique encoding* of the indexed ring element $(\vec{v}, \alpha)$. I.e. the set $S_{\vec{v}}^{\alpha}$ is a singleton. Thus, the representation of items in the graded encoding scheme is given by a map $\sigma(\vec{v}, \alpha)$ from $\vec{v} \in \{0,1\}^\tau$ and $\alpha \in R$, to $\{0,1\}^*$. We restrict our attention to the case where this mapping has polynomial blowup.

REMARK 3.1. *We note that the known candidates of secure graded encoding schemes [15, 12]* do not provide unique encodings*: their encodings are probabilistic. Nonetheless, in the generic graded encoding scheme abstraction we find it helpful to restrict our attention to schemes with unique encodings. For the purposes of proving security against generic adversaries, this makes sense: a generic adversary should work for* any *implementation of the oracle $\mathcal{G}$, and in particular also for an implementation that uses unique encodings.*

Moreover, our perspective is that unique encodings are more "helpful" to an adversary than randomized encodings: a unique encoding gives the adversary the additional power to "automatically" check whether two encodings are of the same indexed ring element (without consulting the oracle). Thus, we prefer to prove security against generic adversaries even for unique representations.

It is important to note that the set of legal encodings may be very sparse within the set of images of σ, and indeed this is the main setting we will consider when we study the generic model. In this case, the only way for $\mathcal{A}$ to obtain a valid representation of any element in any graded set is via calls to the oracle (except with negligible probability). Finally, we note that if oracle calls contain invalid operators (e.g. the input is not an encoding of an element in any graded set, the inputs to add are not in the same graded set, etc.), then the oracle returns $\perp$.

Random Graded Encoding Scheme Oracle. We focus on a particular randomized oracle: the random generic encoding scheme (GES) oracle $\mathcal{RG}$. $\mathcal{RG}$ operates as follows: for each indexed ring element (with index $\vec{v} \in \{0,1\}^\tau$ and ring element $\sigma \in R$), its encoding is of length $\ell = (|\tau| \cdot \log|R| \cdot poly(\lambda))$ (where $|\tau|$ is the bit representation length of τ). The encoding of each indexed ring element is a uniformly random string of length ℓ. In particular, this implies that the only way that $\mathcal{A}$ can obtain valid encodings is by calls to the oracle $\mathcal{RG}$ (except with negligible probability).

The definition of secure obfuscation in the random GES model is as follows.

DEFINITION 3.2. *Let $\mathcal{C} = \{\mathcal{C}_n\}_{n\in\mathbb{N}}$ be a family of circuits and $\mathcal{O}$ a PPTM as in Definition 2.3.*

A generic algorithm $\mathcal{O}^{\mathcal{RG}}$ is an obfuscator in the random generic encoding scheme model, *if it satisfies the functionality and polynomial slowdown properties of Definition 2.3 with respect to $\mathcal{C}$ and to* any *GES oracle $\mathcal{RG}$, but the virtual black-box property is replaced with:*

3. Virtual Black-Box in the Random GES Model: *For every (non-uniform) polynomial size* generic *adversary $\mathcal{A}$, there exists a (non-uniform) generic polynomial size simulator $\mathcal{S}$, such that for every $n \in \mathbb{N}$ and every $C \in \mathcal{C}_n$:*

$$\Big|\big(\Pr_{\mathcal{RG},\mathcal{O},\mathcal{A}}[\mathcal{A}^{\mathcal{RG}}(\mathcal{O}^{\mathcal{RG}}(C, 1^n, 1^\lambda))] = 1\big) - \big(\Pr_{\mathcal{RG},\mathcal{S}}[\mathcal{S}^C(1^{|C|}, 1^n, 1^\lambda)] = 1\big)\Big| = negl(\lambda)$$

We remark that while it makes sense to allow $\mathcal{S}$ to access the oracle $\mathcal{RG}$, this is in fact not necessary. This is since $\mathcal{RG}$ can be implemented in polynomial time (as described below), and therefore $\mathcal{S}$ can just implement it by itself.

Online Random GES Oracle. In our proof, we will use the property that the oracle $\mathcal{RG}$ can be approximated to within negligible statistical distance by an *online polynomial time process*, which samples the representations on-the-fly. Specifically, the oracle will maintain a table of entries of the form $(\vec{v}, \alpha, \mathsf{label}_{\vec{v},\alpha})$, where $\mathsf{label}_{\vec{v},\alpha} \in \{0,1\}^\ell$ is the representation of $S_{\vec{v}}^{(\alpha)}$ in $\mathcal{RG}$ (the table is initially empty). Every time $\mathcal{RG}$ is called for some functionality, it checks that its operands indeed correspond to an entry in the table, in which case it can retrieve the appropriate $(\vec{v}, \alpha)$ to perform the operation (if the operands are not in the table, $\mathcal{RG}$ returns $\perp$). Whenever $\mathcal{RG}$ needs to return a value $S_{\vec{v}}^{(\alpha)}$, it checks whether $(\vec{v}, \alpha)$ is already in the table, and if so returns the appropriate $\mathsf{label}_{\vec{v},\alpha}$. Otherwise it samples a new uniform label, and inserts a new entry into the table.

When interacting with an adversary that only makes a polynomial number of calls, the online version of $\mathcal{RG}$ is within negligible statistical distance of the offline version (in fact, the statistical distance is exponentially small in λ) . This is because the only case when the online oracle implementation differs from the offline one is when when the adversary guesses a valid label that it has not seen (in the offline setting). This can only occur with exponentially small probability due to the sparsity of the labels. The running time of the online oracle is polynomial in the number of oracle calls.

4. OBFUSCATING $\mathcal{CNC}^0$

We formally define $\mathcal{CNC}^0$ circuits (conjunctions of $\mathcal{NC}_d^0$ circuits).

DEFINITION 4.1 ($\mathcal{CNC}_d^0$). *For an integer d and input length n, a $\mathcal{CNC}_d^0$ circuit C is a predicate on n-bit inputs. It* *is defined by a set of $\mathcal{NC}_d^0$ subcircuits $(C_1, \ldots, C_m)$, where $m \le \binom{n}{d}$.*

We associate each subcircuit C_I with a set $I \in [d]^n$ of input bits on which C_I operates. Without loss of generality, we always consider the case $m = \binom{n}{d}$, where for every d-tuple $I \in \binom{[n]}{d}$ of distinct input indices, there is a unique subcircuit C_I in C over the variables $\{x_i\}_{i \in I}$.

For every input $\vec{x} \in \{0,1\}^n$:

$$C(\vec{x}) \equiv \bigwedge_{I \in \binom{[n]}{d}} C_I(\vec{x})$$

Observe that any d-CNF is (by definition) a $\mathcal{CNC}_d^0$-circuit (where each sub-circuit computes a d-variable disjunction). We note that the above definition is without loss of generality, because we can always add dummy sub-circuits that output the constant 1 function so that C has a sub-circuit C_I for each $I \in \binom{[n]}{d}$. We can also eliminate multiple sub-circuits on the same I (or son subsets of I), by merging them into a single sub-circuit computing their conjunction (which is still in $\mathcal{CNC}_d^0$).

REMARK 4.2. *Unlike many classes of functionalities that were previously studied in the context of obfuscation, even given an accepting input to a $\mathcal{CNC}^0$ circuit C, it might still be hard to recover C using black-box access. This is in contract to, say, point functions [8], or even conjunctions [6], and it makes obfuscation more challenging.*

An ensemble of conjunctions of $\mathcal{CNC}^0$ circuits is defined in the natural way.

DEFINITION 4.3 (ENSEMBLE OF $\mathcal{CNC}_d^0$ CIRCUITS). *An ensemble $\mathcal{C} = \{C^{(n)}\}_{n \in \mathbb{N}}$ is a collection of $\mathcal{CNC}_d^0$ circuits, one for each input length.*

REMARK 4.4. *When we obfuscate a $\mathcal{CNC}_d^0$ circuit C, we allow the obfuscation to expose d (but nothing more). We also allow the obfuscator to run in time $poly(\lambda, n^d)$.*

Our obfuscator for the class of conjunctions is presented in Figure 1. Correctness follows in a straightforward manner as described in the following lemma (the proof is omitted). We note that the error is one sided, it is always the case that if $C(\vec{x}) = 1$ then for the obfuscated program $\mathcal{O}_C(\vec{x}) = 1$ as well.

LEMMA 4.5 (OBFUSCATOR FUNCTIONALITY). *Let C be an n-variable $\mathcal{CNC}_d^0$ circuit and let $\mathcal{O}_C = \mathsf{CNCZObf}(1^\lambda, 1^n, 1^d, C)$. Then for every $\vec{x} \in \{0,1\}^n$,*

$$\Pr[\mathcal{O}_C(\vec{x}) \ne \mathcal{C}(\vec{x})] \le poly(n)/p\ ,$$

where $p = 2^{\Omega(\lambda)}$ is the order of the group in the graded encoding scheme, and the probability is taken over the randomness of CNCZObf.

5. SECURITY AGAINST GENERIC ADVERSARIES

In this section, we prove virtual black-box security for the obfuscator CNCZObf in the random GES model, as per Definition 3.2. The security relies on a new *worst case* complexity theoretic assumption, which we call the *bounded speedup hypothesis* (BSH). This assumption is a "scaled-down" version of the exponential time hypothesis (ETH) [21]: whereas the latter asserts that SAT solvers cannot do much better than a brute force search over the space of 2^n solutions, BSH asserts that even solving SAT over smaller solution spaces cannot improve much over brute force search. See Assumption 5.3 below for a formal statement. In Appendix A we discuss the relation between BSH and ETH, and show that the latter implies the former for some parameter range. We find the occurrence of a complexity-theoretic worst-case assumption in a cryptographic proof fairly unusual and intriguing. Whether a proof can be derived without this assumption is left as open problem.

Formally, to conclude that CNCZObf is secure against generic adversaries the following theorem will be proven.

THEOREM 5.1. *Under the bounded speedup hypothesis,* CNCZObf *is a virtual black-box obfuscator in the random GES model for the class $\mathcal{CNC}^0$.*

The bounded speedup hypothesis is formally defined as follows.

DEFINITION 5.2. *Consider a family of sets $\mathcal{X} = \{X_n\}_{n \in \mathbb{N}}$ such that $X_n \subseteq \{0,1\}^n$. We say that an algorithm $\mathcal{A}$ is a $\mathcal{X}$-3-SAT solver if it solves the 3-SAT problem, restricted to inputs in $\mathcal{X}$. Namely, given a 3-CNF formula $\Phi : \{0,1\}^n \to \{0,1\}$, $\mathcal{A}$ finds whether there exists $x \in X_n$ such that $\Phi(x) = 1$.*

Note that a standard self reduction argument shows that if $\mathcal{A}$ is efficient, then the alleged x can also be found efficiently. This is done by restricting each variable in turn to either 0 or 1, and checking if the formula is still satisfiable by an assignment in X_n.

ASSUMPTION 5.3 (BSH). *There exists a polynomial $p(\cdot)$, such that for any $\mathcal{X}$-3-SAT solver that runs in time $t(\cdot)$, the family of sets $\mathcal{X}$ is of size at most $p(t(\cdot))$.*

In Appendix A we show that a quasi-polynomial version of BSH is in fact implied by ETH. We note that this implies that allowing quasi-polynomial time adversaries and quasi-polynomial time simulators, our proof can be based on ETH.

ASSUMPTION 5.4. *(quasi-Bounded Speedup Hypothesis (qBSH)) For any $\mathcal{X}$-3-SAT solver that runs in time $t(n)$, the family of sets $\mathcal{X}$ is of size at most $(t(n))^{O(\log(n))}$.*

The remainder of this section is dedicated to proving Theorem 5.1. We follow the methodology of [6] and share some of their notation. Our simulator will attempt to execute the adversary $\mathcal{A}$ while simulating the online $\mathcal{RG}$ oracle (see Section 3). In some cases, however, the simulator needs to output labels for unknown ring elements (most notably, the simulated obfuscated program itself). In those cases, $\mathcal{S}$ returns a completely random label, and marks the variable as an unknown in its table. Throughout the execution, $\mathcal{S}$ keeps track of the relations between the unknown variables. This is important because if two variables, whose underlying encoded ring elements are both unknown to the simulator, are supposed to be equal (when the real $\mathcal{RG}$ is used), then they should also be given the same label in the simulation. To

Obfuscator CNCZObf, on input $(1^\lambda, 1^n, 1^d, C = (C_1, \ldots, C_m))$ where $m = \binom{n}{d}$

1. generate $(params, evparams) \leftarrow \mathsf{InstGen}(1^\lambda, 1^{m+1})$
2. for each $I \in \binom{[n]}{d}$ and $z \in \{0,1\}$: $a_{I,z} \leftarrow \mathsf{samp}(params) \in S_0^{(\alpha_{I,z})}$:
3. for each $i \in [n]$, let I^* be the first set in $\binom{[n]}{d}$ s.t. $i \in I^*$:
   (a) for each $I \in (\binom{[n]}{d} \setminus I^*)$ s.t. $i \in I$, and each $v \in \{0,1\}$: $b_{I,i,v} \leftarrow \mathsf{samp}(params) \in S_0^{(\beta_{I,i,v})}$
   (b) $b'_i \leftarrow samp(params) \in S_0^{(\beta'_i)}$
   $b_{I^*,i,0} \leftarrow b'_i \times \left(\prod_{I \in (\binom{[n]}{d}) \setminus I^*): i \in I} b_{I,i,1}\right) \in S_0^{(\beta_{I^*,i,0})}$
   $b_{I^*,i,1} \leftarrow b'_i \times \left(\prod_{I \in (\binom{[n]}{d}) \setminus I^*): i \in I} b_{I,i,0}\right) \in S_0^{(\beta_{I^*,i,1})}$
   (c) $c_i \leftarrow \prod_{I \in \binom{[n]}{d}: i \in I} b_{I,i,0} \in S_0^{(\gamma_i)}$, where $\gamma_i = \prod_{I \in \binom{[n]}{d}: i \in I} \beta_{I,i,0}$,
   and note that $\gamma_i = \beta'_i \cdot \prod_{I \in (\binom{[n]}{d}) \setminus I^*): i \in I} (\beta_{I,i,0} \cdot \beta_{I,i,1}) = \prod_{I \in \binom{[n]}{d}: i \in I} \beta_{I,i,1}$
4. for each $I \in \binom{[n]}{d}$ and $\vec{s} \in \{0,1\}^d$:
   (a) $d_{I,\vec{s}} \leftarrow (a_{I,C_I(\vec{s})} \cdot \prod_{i \in I} b_{I,i,\vec{s}[i]}) \in S_0^{(\alpha_{I,C_I(\vec{s})} \cdot \prod_{i \in I} \beta_{I,i,\vec{s}[i]})}$
   and denote $\delta_{I,\vec{s}} = (\alpha_{I,C_I(\vec{s})} \cdot \prod_{i \in I} \beta_{I,i,\vec{s}[i]})$
   (b) $r_{I,\vec{s}} \leftarrow \mathsf{samp}(params) \in S_0^{(\rho_{I,\vec{s}})}$
   (c) $s_{I,\vec{s}} \leftarrow (r_{I,\vec{s}} \times d_{I,\vec{s}}) \in S_0^{(\rho_{I,\vec{s}} \cdot \delta_{I,\vec{s}})}$
   (d) $\mathbf{w}_{I,\vec{s}} \leftarrow \mathsf{encRand}(params, I, r_{I,\vec{s}}) \in S_{\vec{e}_I}^{(\rho_{I,\vec{s}})}$
   (e) $\mathbf{u}_{I,\vec{s}} \leftarrow \mathsf{encRand}(params, I, s_{I,\vec{s}}) \in S_{\vec{e}_I}^{(\rho_{I,\vec{s}} \cdot \delta_{I,\vec{s}})}$
5. Letting chk denote the $(m+1)$ group:
   $d_{\mathsf{chk}} \leftarrow (\prod_{I \in \binom{[n]}{d}} a_{I,1} \times \prod_{i \in I} c_i) \in S_0^{(\delta_{\mathsf{chk}})}$, where $\delta_{\mathsf{chk}} = (\prod_{I \in \binom{[n]}{d}} \alpha_{I,1} \cdot \prod_{i \in [n]} \gamma_i)$
   $r_{\mathsf{chk}} \leftarrow \mathsf{samp}(params) \in S_0^{(\rho_{\mathsf{chk}})}$
   $s_{\mathsf{chk}} \leftarrow r_{\mathsf{chk}} \times d_{\mathsf{chk}} \in S_0^{(\rho_{\mathsf{chk}} \cdot \delta_{\mathsf{chk}})}$
   $\mathbf{w}_{\mathsf{chk}} \leftarrow \mathsf{encRand}(params, \mathsf{chk}, r_{\mathsf{chk}}) \in S_{\vec{e}_{\mathsf{chk}}}^{(\rho_{\mathsf{chk}})}$
   $\mathbf{u}_{\mathsf{chk}} \leftarrow \mathsf{encRand}(params, \mathsf{chk}, s_{\mathsf{chk}}) \in S_{\vec{e}_{\mathsf{chk}}}^{(\rho_{\mathsf{chk}} \cdot \delta_{\mathsf{chk}})}$
6. output the obfuscation: $(evparams, (\mathbf{w}_{\mathsf{chk}}, \mathbf{u}_{\mathsf{chk}}), \{(\mathbf{w}_{I,\vec{s}}, \mathbf{u}_{I\vec{s}})\}_{I \in \binom{[n]}{d}, \vec{s} \in \{0,1\}^d})$

Evaluation, on input $\vec{x} \in \{0,1\}^n$

1. $\mathbf{t} \leftarrow (\mathbf{w}_{\mathsf{chk}} \times \prod_{I \in \binom{[n]}{d}} \mathbf{u}_{I,\vec{x}_{|I}}) \in S_{(1,1,\ldots,1)}^{(\rho_{\mathsf{chk}} \cdot (\prod_{I \in \binom{[n]}{d}} \rho_{I,\vec{x}_{|I}}) \cdot (\prod_{I \in \binom{[n]}{d}} \delta_{I,\vec{x}_{|I}}))}$
2. $\mathbf{t}' \leftarrow (\mathbf{u}_{\mathsf{chk}} \times \prod_{I \in \binom{[n]}{d}} \mathbf{w}_{I,\vec{x}_{|I}}) \in S_{(1,1,\ldots,1)}^{(\rho_{\mathsf{chk}} \cdot (\prod_{I \in \binom{[n]}{d}} \rho_{I,\vec{x}_{|I}}) \cdot \delta_{\mathsf{chk}})}$
3. output the bit: $\mathsf{isZero}(evparams, (\mathbf{t} - \mathbf{t}'))$.

Figure 1: Obfuscator for Conjunctions.

this end, we will show that $\mathcal{S}$ can always check for equality of two unknown variables in the obfuscation (or rather, test if their difference is equal to zero) given only oracle access to C. In our construction, the relations between the unknowns are much more complicated than in [6] and therefore we need to develop new tools in order to perform the simulation.

For a security parameter $\lambda \in \mathbb{N}$, consider the obfuscation of a $\mathcal{CNC}^0$ circuit C. The obfuscation is generated by choosing parameters for a graded encoding scheme, and then picking ring elements for the various labelings. The output labelings are defined by the underlying ring elements $\{\rho_{I,\vec{s}}, \delta_{I,\vec{s}}\}_{I \in \binom{[n]}{d} \cup \mathsf{chk}}$. *Note that these ring elements are not independently distributed* (though each of them, on its own, is close to uniformly random in R). In the security proof, we treat these ring elements as variables, since they are unknown to the simulator (all that $\mathcal{S}$ knows is that these variables were sampled in the process of obfuscating a circuit). We use $\vec{\rho}$ to denote the vector containing $\{\rho_{I,\vec{s}}\}_{I \in \binom{[n]}{d} \cup \mathsf{chk}}$, and we call these the ρ random variables. We use $\vec{\delta}$ to denote the vector containing $\{\delta_{I,\vec{s}}\}_{I \in \binom{[n]}{d} \cup \mathsf{chk}}$, and we call these the δ random variables. For a circuit C, we consider the joint distribution of these variables:

DEFINITION 5.5 (DISTRIBUTION D_C). *For a $\mathcal{CNC}^0$ circuit C, we define the distribution D_C over $(\vec{\rho}, \vec{\delta})$ to be the distribution of the ρ and δ variables in an obfuscation of C using the obfuscator* $\mathsf{CNCZObf}$ *in Figure 1.*

The Simulator $\mathcal{S}$. For a polynomial-size generic adversary $\mathcal{A}$ (w.l.o.g. we assume that $\mathcal{A}$ is deterministic), the simulator $\mathcal{S}$ simulates $\mathcal{A}$'s operation with an *online* random graded encoding scheme (GES) oracle $\mathcal{RG}$ (see Section 3), i.e. $\mathcal{S}$ answers $\mathcal{A}$'s oracle queries to $\mathcal{RG}$. For a circuit C, we consider the "real" view $\mathcal{A}^{\mathcal{RG}}(\mathsf{CNCZObf}(C))$, where the randomness is over the choice of random GES oracle and the obfuscator's random coins. We also consider a "simulated" view where $\mathcal{S}$ executes $\mathcal{A}$ on a "dummy obfuscation" and answers its oracle queries to $\mathcal{RG}$ (using a strategy specified below). In the simulated view the randomness is over $\mathcal{S}$'s coins.

As outlined above, $\mathcal{S}$ will maintain a table T, where each entry is of the form $(\vec{v}, \sigma, \mathsf{label}_{\vec{v},\sigma})$, similarly to the online version of $\mathcal{RG}$ (see Section 3). However, in some cases, instead of setting σ to be an explicit element in the ring R, it sets σ to be an unknown variable, or an arithmetic circuit over R on unknown variables (note that the indexed set $\vec{v}$ is always known).

Initially, the simulator $\mathcal{S}$ creates a "dummy obfuscation". This requires sampling values for $\vec{\rho}, \vec{\delta}$. However, $\mathcal{S}$ will mark these values as unknowns, and sample random labels for them, and insert them into the table.[8] By Claim 5.6, the view of the adversary in the simulated setting is statistically indistinguishable from the real setting. This is the only place in the simulation where new unknowns are introduced.

From this point and on, $\mathcal{S}$ needs to answer $\mathcal{A}$'s oracle queries to $\mathcal{RG}$. This is done exactly in the same way as the online implementation of $\mathcal{RG}$. For arithmetic operations, $\mathcal{S}$ can pull the operands from the table T and perform the required operation, either explicitly, if the σ values of the operands are known, or implicitly by creating an arithmetic circuit that combines the arithmetic circuits of the operands. The problem arises in determining the label to be returned as the output of the operation. Recall that if the $(\vec{v}, \sigma)$ of the output already appears in T, the same label is to be returned. This means that in order for the simulation to be successful, we must have a way to compare two implicit representations (in the form of arithmetic circuits over unknowns) and determine whether they represent the same value under the distribution D_C. $\mathcal{S}$ needs to do this using only black-box access to C (and the same technique can be used to simulate the isZero operation).

We show how $\mathcal{S}$ can use its *black-box* access to C to compare implicit representations. We use the *functional representation* of the elements encoded in the table entries, as functions of the $(\vec{\rho}, \vec{\delta})$ random variables (this method was introduced in [6]).

As outlined above, for each entry $t \in T$, by tracking $\mathcal{A}$'s oracle calls, the simulator $\mathcal{S}$ can compute a polynomial-size arithmetic circuit that computes entry t's functional representation f_t. The adversary is limited to multi-linear operations over the inputs, so the functional representations have very specific *cross-linear* structure (see below). We use this structure to show that whenever $\mathcal{S}$ needs to check equality of an entry t to 0, $\mathcal{S}$ can determine (given the arithmetic circuit that computes f_t and black-box access to C) whether w.h.p. over $(\vec{\rho}, \vec{\delta}) \sim D_C$, it is the case that $f_t(\vec{\rho}, \vec{\delta}) = 0$. Similarly, $\mathcal{S}$ can use this zero-testing procedure to identify whether two table entries are equal, by comparing their difference function to 0. This is used to determine whether the output of a new oracle call to $\mathcal{RG}$ is already in the table (and if so, to return its label rather than create a new one). Thus, $\mathcal{S}$ can answer all of the adversary's oracle queries, and generate a statistically close view to the real execution.

The remainder of the proof is organized as follows: first, we formalize the above notions of functional representations and their structural properties. We then show that for any table entry t, the simulator can determine with high accuracy and in polynomial time whether or not the functional representation $f_t(\vec{\rho}, \vec{\delta})$ equals 0 w.h.p. when $(\vec{\rho}, \vec{\delta})$ are drawn from D_C. This will allow to complete the simulation as described above. The latter is proven under the bounded speedup hypothesis (Assumption 5.3), which we view as a flavor of the exponential time hypothesis.

5.1 Functional Representations and Structural Properties

We start by exploring the probability space underlying the distribution D_C. As explained above, and can be seen from the description of $\mathsf{CNCZObf}$, the $\vec{\rho}$ variables are uniform and independent. The $\vec{\delta}$ variables, in contrast, are products of more basic variables. We recall that these variables include:

1. the variables $\{\alpha_{I,v}\}_{I \in \binom{[n]}{d}, v \in \{0,1\}}$, which are all uniform and independent in R.
2. The variables $\{\beta_{I,i,v}\}$, for all $i \in [n]$, $I \ni i$, except the lexicographically first I^* for each i, and $v \in \{0,1\}$. These are also uniform and independent (and also independent of the previous variables). We note that the variables $\beta_{I^*,i,v}$ are also defined, but are not independent of the other variables, see below.
3. The variables $\{\beta'_i\}_{i \in [n]}$ that are also uniform and in-

[8]We note that $\mathcal{S}$ could actually explicitly sample the $\vec{\rho}$ values since they are independent of the circuit C, however it is more convenient for our analysis to leave them undetermined.

dependent in R (and also independent of the previous variables).

Based on these variables, we define $\beta_{I^*,i,v}$, for all i, as follows:

$$\beta_{I^*,i,v} = \beta'_i \cdot \prod_{\substack{I \ni i, \\ I \neq I^*}} \beta_{I,i,1-v} \ .$$

Note that this implies that $\beta_{I^*,i,v}$ are uniform subject to the constraint that for all i,

$$\prod_{I \ni i} \beta_{I,i,0} = \prod_{I \ni i} \beta_{I,i,1} \quad (= \gamma_i) \ .$$

We note the important property that all $\beta_{I,i,v}, \beta'_i, \gamma_i$ variables are completely independent between different i's.

Finally, $\delta_{I,\vec{s}}$ is defined as

$$\delta_{I,\vec{s}} = \alpha_{I,C_I(\vec{s})} \cdot \prod_{i \in I} \beta_{I,i,\vec{s}[i]} \ ,$$

and

$$\delta_{\mathsf{chk}} = \prod_{I \in \binom{[n]}{d}} \alpha_{I,1} \cdot \prod_{i \in [n]} \gamma_i \ .$$

Note that the only variables that depend on the circuit C are $\delta_{I,\vec{s}}$, and in particular this dependence is only on whether the clause C_I is satisfied by $\vec{s}$. We observe that the ring elements encoded in the obfuscation are (w.h.p.) all distinct:

Claim 5.6. *Let $C \in \mathcal{CNC}^0$. With all but negl(λ) probability over $(\vec{\rho}, \vec{\delta}) \sim D_C$, the encoded ring elements in the obfuscation are all distinct.*

Proof. The encoded ring elements in the obfuscator's output are $\{\rho_{I,\vec{s}}, \rho_{I,\vec{s}} \cdot \delta_{I,\vec{s}}\}_{I \in \binom{[n]}{d} \cup \mathsf{chk}, \vec{s} \in \{0,1\}^d}$. By the properties of the probability space underlying D_C, we observe that with all but *negl*(λ) probability it is the case that $\delta_{I,\vec{s}} \notin \{0,1\}$. Moreover, the $\vec{\rho}$ variables are all uniform and independently random ring elements, and so the probability that the encoded ring elements in the obfuscation are not all distinct is *negl*(λ). □

Building on [6], we consider $\mathcal{A}$'s oracle calls, their functional representations, and the structure enforced by the random generic encoding scheme model. We examine $\mathcal{A}$'s oracle calls in sequence. For the add, negate, mult procedures, the indexed ring element in their output is always a multilinear function of the $(\vec{\rho}, \vec{\delta})$ random variables. Thus the table T will only contain multilinear functions of the unknowns $\vec{\rho}, \vec{\delta}$. In fact, these are multilinear functions of $(\vec{\rho}, \vec{\delta})$ with a very specific structure: we call these *cross-linear* functions, see Definition 5.11 and Claim 5.12 below. The difficulty in generating a simulated view is zero testing of a multilinear function under the distribution D_C of its unknowns (namely, the zero-test outcome may depend on the circuit C).

We proceed as follows. Recall that the oracle $\mathcal{RG}$ maintains a table T of all indexed ring elements whose labelings have already been specified (see Section 3). For each element in the table T, we consider its representation as a (cross-linear) function of the $(\vec{\rho}, \vec{\delta})$ random variables. After the obfuscated circuit is specified, the entries in T contain the indexed elements $\{\vec{\rho}_{I,\vec{s}}\}_{I \in \binom{[n]}{d} \cup \mathsf{chk}, \vec{s} \in \{0,1\}^d}$ and $\{\rho_{I,\vec{s}} \cdot \delta_{I,\vec{s}}\}_{I \in \binom{[n]}{d} \cup \mathsf{chk}, \vec{s} \in \{0,1\}^d}$. As $\mathcal{A}$ makes additional oracle calls, new entries are added to the table T. For these new entries, we consider the representations of their indexed ring elements as cross-linear functions of $(\vec{\rho}, \vec{\delta})$. We focus here on calls to the add, negate, mult, encRand procedures (calls to samp are handled by sampling an element and a labeling, and adding them as an entry to the table with $\tau = 0$).[9] For each such call, the inputs should be labelings that are in the table T: for any other string, the probability that it is a valid labeling is negligible, and the oracle $\mathcal{RG}$ just answers $\perp$ (in both the real execution with a random GES oracle, and in the simulated execution). Otherwise, the inputs are in the table T, and the output may form a new entry in T. The *functional representation* of a table entry is defined as follows.

Definition 5.7 (Functional Representation [6]). *For each entry in $\mathcal{RG}$'s table T, with indexed ring element $(\vec{v}, \sigma) \in \{0,1\}^\tau \times R$ and labeling $s \in \{0,1\}^*$, its* functional representation *$f(\vec{\rho}, \vec{\delta})$ is defined recursively:*

1. *Initially, the only table entries are labelings that appear in the obfuscation. I.e., the entries for the ring elements $\{(\rho_{I,\vec{s}}, (\rho_{I,\vec{s}} \cdot \delta_{I,\vec{s}}))\}_{I \in \binom{[n]}{d}, \vec{s} \in \{0,1\}^d}$, where the variables associated with the index set I are indexed by $\vec{e}_I$. These table entries are all distinct (except with negligible probability), and for each table entry its functional representation is simply $f(\vec{\rho}, \vec{\delta}) = \rho_{I,\vec{s}}$ or $f(\vec{\rho}, \vec{\delta}) = (\rho_{I,\vec{s}} \cdot \delta_{I,\vec{s}})$ (respectively).*
2. *For subsequent entries that are created on $\mathcal{A}$'s calls to $\mathcal{RG}$, their functional representation is defined recursively. E.g. for an* add *call, with input labelings s_1 and s_2, if s_1 or s_2 is not in $\mathcal{RG}$'s table T, then that input does not represent a valid labeling, the output is $\perp$ and no new table entry is created. If the inputs are in the table T, let $(\vec{v}_1, \sigma_1)$ and $(\vec{v}_2, \sigma_2)$ be the indexed ring elements that they encode. If $\vec{v}_1 \neq \vec{v}_2$ then again the output is $\perp$ and no new table entry is created. The remaining case is $\vec{v}_1 = \vec{v}_2 = \vec{v}$. In this case, let f_1 and f_2 be the functional representations of the input labeling. If a new table entry is created for the output, then its representation is $(f_1 + f_2)$.*

   The cases of samp, encRand, negate, mult *calls are handled similarly.*

We remark that for a table entry t, its functional representation is completely independent of the circuit being obfuscated. By definition, the functional representation indeed computes the ring element in a table entry (for any setting of $(\vec{\rho}, \vec{\delta})$). Moreover, for any table entry, $\mathcal{S}$ can compute a polynomial-size arithmetic circuit computing that table entry's functional representation (see [6] for the proofs):

Claim 5.8. *For any setting of the initial random variables $(\vec{\rho}, \vec{\delta})$, and for an entry t in the table T containing the indexed ring element $(\vec{v}_t, \sigma_t)$ and with functional functional representation f_t, it is the case that $\sigma_t = f_t(\vec{\rho}, \vec{\delta})$.*

[9] We note that in some implementations of Graded Encoding Schemes, e.g. in that of [15], the adversary is only given access to add, negate, mult, and so we could consider an even more restricted GES model. All of our results would hold in this restricted model (and no non-generic attacks are known for those schemes).

Claim 5.9. *For each entry t in $\mathcal{RG}$'s table T, the simulator $\mathcal{S}$ can compute a polynomial-size arithmetic circuit computing its functional representation $f_t(\vec{\rho}, \vec{\alpha})$.*

As noted above, the functional representations of all table entries are multilinear functions in $(\vec{\rho}, \vec{\delta})$. Moreover, they are multilinear functions with a specific structure, defined as *cross-linear* functions in [6]. We proceed to define structural properties of these functions, and then use these to prove security.

Definition 5.10 (cross-linear monomial). *A function $h(\vec{\rho})$ is a* cross-linear monomial *of $\vec{\rho}$, or a ρ-monomial, if it is of the form:*

$$h(\vec{\delta}) = \eta \cdot (\prod_{I \in S} \rho_{I,y(I)})$$

where $S \subseteq \left(\binom{[n]}{d} \cup \{\mathsf{chk}\}\right)$, $y : \binom{n}{d} \to \{0,1\}^d$ is a partial function defined over S (by notation $y(\mathsf{chk})$ is the empty string), and $\eta \in R$. We also say that h is a cross-linear monomial in the variables $\{\rho_{I,y(I)}\}_{I \in S}$.

Similarly, a function $h(\vec{\delta})$ is a cross-linear monomial *of $\vec{\delta}$, or a δ-monomial, if it is of the form:*

$$h(\vec{\delta}) = \eta \cdot (\prod_{I \in S} \delta_{I,y(I)})$$

where S, y, and η are as above. Similarly to the above, here we say that h is cross-linear in the variables $\{\delta_{I,y(I)}\}_{I \in S}$.

A cross-linear function *in the variables $\{\delta_{I,y(I)}\}_{I \in S}$ is a sum of cross-linear monomials in the same variables.*

Definition 5.11 (cross-linear polynomial [6]). *A function $g(\vec{\rho}, \vec{\delta})$ is a* cross-linear term *of $(\vec{\rho}, \vec{\delta})$ if it is of the form:*

$$g(\vec{\rho}, \vec{\delta}) = h_\rho(\vec{\rho}) \cdot \left(\sum_{h \in H} h(\vec{\delta})\right)$$

where h_ρ is a ρ-monomial (as per Definition 5.10) w.r.t a set S and assignment y, and for each $h \in H$, h is a δ-monomial over a subset of variables $S' \subseteq S$ and the assignment y.

A function f is a cross-linear polynomial *of $(\vec{\rho}, \vec{\delta})$ if it can be expressed as a sum of cross-linear terms. I.e., it is of the form:*

$$f(\vec{\rho}, \vec{\delta}) = \sum_{g \in G} g(\vec{\rho}, \vec{\delta})$$

where each $g \in G$ is a cross-linear term of $(\vec{\rho}, \vec{\delta})$ as above. We assume that the expansion is compact in the sense that the for each term g, the set S (of its ρ-monomial) is distinct. We call this particular expansion the cross-linear expansion *of f.*

It was shown in [6] that in the GES model, the functional representations of all table entries are cross-linear polynomials:

Claim 5.12. *For any entry in the table T, its functional representation is a cross-linear polynomial of $(\vec{\rho}, \vec{\delta})$.*

5.2 Testing Equality to Zero

For a given table entry t (or difference between table entries), $\mathcal{S}$ needs to test whether its functional representation equals 0. More formally: $\mathcal{S}$ wants to test whether it is the case that when $(\vec{\rho}, \vec{\delta}) \sim D_C$, with all but negligible probability the output of f_t is zero (we show below that it is always the case that either f_t is always 0, or it is only 0 with negligible probability). We assume that the functional representation $f_t(\vec{\rho}, \vec{\delta})$ contains at least one cross-linear term as per Definition 5.11 (otherwise f_t is trivially identically 0 under the distribution D_C).

At this point we deviate from [6], and present a new set of tools. To analyze the possible structure of f_t, we introduce the notion of consistent assignments, and consistent monomials:

Definition 5.13 (consistent and full assignments). *Let $y : \binom{[n]}{d} \to \{0,1\}^d$ be a partial function (i.e. one that is not necessarily defined on its entire domain). We say that y is* consistent with *$\vec{x} \in \{0,1\}^n$, if for all $I \in \binom{[n]}{d}$ for which $y(I)$ is defined, it holds that $\vec{x}_{|I} = y(I)$. We say that y is* consistent *if it is consistent with some $\vec{x}$. If y is a total function, we say that it is also* full.

Definition 5.14 (full and consistent ρ-monomials). *We say that h is a* full *ρ-monomial if it is a ρ-monomial of total degree $\binom{n}{d} + 1$, i.e. of maximal total degree. In this case, for some total function $y : \binom{[n]}{d} \to \{0,1\}^d$, we have $h = \eta \cdot \left((\prod_{I \in \binom{n}{d}} \rho_{I,y(I)}) \cdot \rho_{\mathsf{chk}}\right)$. We say that h is the* full ρ-monomial for *y. Further, if y is a* consistent *assignment for some $\vec{x} \in \{0,1\}^n$, as per Definition 5.13, then h is a* full and consistent ρ-monomial *(for the input $\vec{x}$).*

Lemma 5.15 below shows that if f_t is *not* a sum of full and consistent ρ-monomials corresponding to accepting inputs for C (each multiplied by a polynomial in δ), then f_t is only 0 with negligible probability over D_C.

The Zero Testing Procedure. The simulator $\mathcal{S}$ begins by identifying ρ-monomials of f_t. This can be done efficiently by Lemma 5.21. If $\mathcal{S}$ finds a non-full or non-consistent monomial, or a full and consistent monomial for $\vec{x}$ s.t. $C(\vec{x}) = 0$, then by Lemma 5.15 it knows that f_t is non-zero (under the distribution D_C). If f *is* a sum of full and consistent ρ-monomials that all correspond to accepting inputs for C (each multiplied by a polynomial in δ), then by Lemma 5.22, $\mathcal{S}$ can test whether f_t gets a 0 or non-zero value when $(\vec{\rho}, \vec{\delta})$ are drawn by D_C.

The only remaining issue is determining whether or not f is a sum of full and consistent ρ-monomials. Lemma 5.21 shows that $\mathcal{S}$ can identify any k ρ-monomials of f in time *poly*(k). This is not sufficient, however, because f might be a sum of *super polynomially* many full and consistent ρ-monomials. To rule this out, we show that for an efficient adversary $\mathcal{A}$, with all but negligible probability over its coins, all the differences between the functional representations of table entries that it creates can only be sums of a *polynomial* number of full and consistent ρ-monomials. This is where we use the bounded-speedup hypothesis.

We show in Lemma 5.18 that any function which is a sum of super-polynomially many full and consistent ρ-monomials can be used to solve 3-SAT on a super-polynomial set of inputs, which is in contradiction to the BSH (Assumption 5.3). We note that this only requires black-box access to the functional description.

This finalizes the proof of Theorem 5.1. The formal statements and proof of the aforementioned lemmas follows.

LEMMA 5.15. *Let C be any $\mathcal{CNC}^0$ circuit. Let f be any cross-linear polynomial of $(\vec{\rho}, \vec{\delta})$ s.t. $f \not\equiv 0$, where $f = \sum_{g \in G} g(\vec{\rho}, \vec{\delta})$, and each function $g \in G$ is a cross-linear term (as in Definition 5.11).*

If there exists $g^* \in G$ s.t. $g^*(\vec{\rho}, \vec{\delta}) = h_\rho(\vec{\rho}) \cdot \left(\sum_{h \in H} h(\vec{\delta})\right)$, where h_ρ is **not** *a full and consistent ρ-monomial for some input $x \in \{0,1\}^n$ s.t. $C(x) = 1$, then:*

$$\Pr_{(\vec{\rho},\vec{\delta}) \sim D_C} [f(\vec{\rho}, \vec{\delta}) = 0] = negl(\lambda)$$

PROOF. Consider the monomial g^* in the lemma statement. Since g^* is either not full and consistent, or is full and consistent with x such that $C(x) = 0$, we can apply either Claim 5.16 or Claim 5.17 below. We get that the variables $\vec{\delta}$ in g^*, when sampled from the distribution D_C, are statistically close to being uniform and independent. We can thus apply the Schwatz-Zippel lemma to argue that with all but $negl(\lambda)$ probability over $\vec{\delta}$, it holds that $\sum_{h \in H} h(\vec{\delta}) \neq 0$. This is because the total degree of $\sum_{h \in H} h(\vec{\delta}) \neq 0$ is at most $\binom{n}{d} + 1$.

Now, let us consider the function f, restricted to an assignment of *all* δ variables according to D_C. This is now a polynomial in the $\vec{\rho}$ variables, with total degree $\binom{n}{d} + 1$. Furthermore, this polynomial is non-zero with all but negligible probability, since the monomial that corresponds to g^* will not zero out. This implies that by Schwartz-Zippel again, that sampling all $\vec{\rho}$ values according to D_C (namely, independently and almost uniformly), $f(\vec{\rho}, \vec{\delta}) \neq 0$ and the lemma follows.

CLAIM 5.16. *Let $y : \binom{[n]}{d} \to \{0,1\}^d$ be an assignment that is not consistent or not full. Then the variables $\{\delta_{I,y(I)}\}$ in D_C for all $I \in \binom{[n]}{d} \cup \{\mathsf{chk}\}$ are $negl(\lambda)$-statistically close to uniform and independent.*

PROOF. We prove that if $\mathsf{samp}(params)$ samples labelings of uniform elements in $\mathbb{Z}_p^*$ (rather than in $\mathbb{Z}_p$), then the variables stated in the claim are uniform in $\mathbb{Z}_p^*$ and independent. Since the statistical distance from the real setting is $(poly(n)/p)$, the claim follows.

We show two properties:

1. For any assignment y, and for all $i \in [n]$, it holds that $\{\beta_{I,i,y(I)[i]}\}_{I \ni i}$ are uniform and independent. This immediately implies that $\{\beta_{I,i,y(I)[i]}\}_{i \in [n], I \in \binom{[n]}{d}}$ are uniform and independent (since the β values for each i are sampled independently).

2. Consider an assignment y and $j \in [n]$ such that y is either inconsistent or not full on j. Namely, either there exists $J \ni j$ such that J is not in the domain of y or there exist $J_1, J_2 \ni j$ such that $y(J_1)[j] \neq y(J_2)[j]$. Then $\{\beta_{J,j,y(J)[j]}\}_{J \ni j} \cup \{\gamma_j\}$ are all uniform and independent.

Given properties 1 and 2, the claim will follow: Given y as in the claim statement, there must exist j as in property 2. We first consider the set $\{\delta_{I,y(I)}\}_{I \not\ni j}$. This set is uniform and independent based on property 1, since each such $\delta_{I,y(I)}$ can be written a product of variables, where exactly one of these variables is $\beta_{I,i,y(I)[i]}$ (and further, $\beta_{I,i,y(I)[i]}$ does not appear in the product of any of the other $\delta_{I,y(I)}$).

To complete the argument, one needs to show that $\{\delta_{J,y(J)}\}_{J \ni j} \cup \{\delta_{\mathsf{chk}}\}$ are uniform and independent of the former variables. To see this, fix a value for all α, β variables, except for those of the form β'_j or $\beta_{I,j,b}$ (note that γ_j only depends on these variables). Now, each variable in $\{\delta_{J,y(J)}\}_{J \ni j} \cup \{\delta_{\mathsf{chk}}\}$ can be written as a scalar times exactly one variable of the set $\{\beta_{J,j,y(J)[j]})\}_{J \ni j} \cup \{\gamma_j\}$. Specifically $\delta_{J,y(J)}$ is a product of $\beta_{J,j,y(J)[j]}$ with a scalar, and δ_{chk} is a product of γ_j with a scalar. Applying property 2, the independence follows.

Proof of Property 1. Consider some $i \in [n]$ and let I^* be the lexicographically first element in $\{I \in \binom{[n]}{d} : I \ni i\}$. The set $\{\beta_{I,i,y(I)[i]}\}_{I \ni i, I \neq I^*}$ will be uniform and independent since each $\beta_{I,i,b}$ is chosen independently. Further, all of those variables are independent of $\beta_{I^*,i,y(I^*)[i]}$ since the latter contains β'_i which is independent of any of the former β values.

Proof of property 2. From the previous property we have that $\{\beta_{J,j,y(J)[j]}\}_{J \ni j}$ are uniform and independent. It is left to show that γ_j is independent of all of them - assume towards contradiction that this is false. Recall that $\gamma_j = \beta'_j \cdot \prod_{J \neq J^*} (\beta_{J,j,0} \cdot \beta_{J,j,1})$, where J^* is the lexicographically first set that contains j. Further recall that all variables $\beta_{J,j,b}$ for $J \neq J^*$ are sampled uniformly and independently, but for J^* the definition is $\beta_{J^*,j,b} = \beta'_j \cdot \prod_{J \neq J^*} \beta_{J,j,1-b}$, so β'_j only appears as a factor in $\beta_{J^*,j,b}$ (and in γ_j).

If indeed γ_j is not independent of all $\{\beta_{J,j,y(J)[j]}\}_{J \ni j}$, then it must be the case that $y(J^*)$ is defined, since otherwise β'_j will randomize γ_j and make it independent of all other values. Note that γ_j can be written as $\beta_{J^*,j,y(J^*)[j]} \cdot \prod_{J \neq J^*} \beta_{J,j,y(J^*)[j]}$. Since we assume that this product is not independent of $\{\beta_{J,j,y(J)[j]}\}_{J \ni j}$, then all of the factors in the product must appear in the aforementioned set. For counting reasons, and since we know that $\beta_{J^*,j,y(J^*)[j]}$ is indeed in the set, it must also be the case that $\beta_{J,j,y(J^*)[j]}$ is in the set for all J. This in turn implies that $y(J)$ is defined for all J and furthermore that $y(J)[j] = y(J^*)[j]$ for all J.We get a contradiction since we showed that y is consistent and full on j. ☐

CLAIM 5.17. *Let $y : \binom{[n]}{d} \to \{0,1\}^d$ be an assignment that is full and consistent with $x \in \{0,1\}^n$ for which $C(x) = 0$. Then the variables $\{\delta_{I,y(I)}\}_{I \in \binom{[n]}{d} \cup \{\delta_{\mathsf{chk}}\}}$ in D_C are $negl(\lambda)$-statistically close to uniform and independent.*

PROOF. As in Claim 5.16, we prove that if $\mathsf{samp}(params)$ samples labelings of uniform elements in $\mathbb{Z}_p^*$ (rather than in $\mathbb{Z}_p$), then the variables stated in the claim are uniform in $\mathbb{Z}_p^*$ and independent. Since the statistical distance from the real setting is $poly(n)/p$, the claim follows.

We show that:

- Letting y, x be as in the claim statement, the variables $\{\alpha_{I,C_I(x)}\} \cup \{\prod_I \alpha_{I,1}\}$ are all uniform and independent.

The claim immediately follows since even conditioned on all the β values, each $\delta_{I,y(I)}$ a product that contains $\alpha_{I,C_I(x)}$, and δ_{chk} is a product that contains $\prod_I \alpha_{I,1}$.

The proof of the above property is also fairly straightforward. Since $C(x) = 0$, there exists J such that $\alpha_{J,C_J(x)} = \alpha_{J,0}$. Now, all $\{\alpha_{I,C_I(x)}\}$ are independent by definition (since they are sampled independently), and $\prod_I \alpha_{I,1}$ is independent of all of them since it is a product that contains $\alpha_{J,1}$. ☐

LEMMA 5.18. *For $n, \lambda \in \mathbb{N}$, and $X \subseteq \{0,1\}^n$, let f be any cross-linear function of $(\vec{\rho}, \vec{\delta})$ s.t.*

$$f = \sum_{x \in X} h_x(\vec{\rho}) \cdot g_x(\vec{\delta})$$

where $\forall x \in X$, h_x is a full ρ-monomial which is consistent with x, *and $g_x \not\equiv 0$.*

Then there exists a polynomial-size circuit $\mathcal{A}^f$ s.t. for any circuit $B \in \mathcal{CNC}^0$ on n-bit inputs, the circuit $\mathcal{A}^f$ on input B decides whether there exist $x \in X$ that satisfies B. I.e.:

$$\forall B \in \mathcal{CNC}^0 : \Pr_{\mathcal{A}}[\mathcal{A}(B) = \mathbf{1}_{\exists x \in X : B(x)=1}] \geq 1 - negl(\lambda)$$

PROOF. Each $h_x(\vec{\rho})$ is a full ρ-monomial consistent with x, and so:

$$\forall x \in X : h_x(\vec{\rho}) = \prod_{I \in \left(\binom{[n]}{d} \cup \{\mathsf{chk}\}\right)} \vec{\rho}_{I, x_{|I}}$$

The algorithm $\mathcal{A}^f$ picks $(\vec{\rho}, \vec{\delta})$ from a distribution F_B, which depends on the circuit B (but is *not* the distribution D_B that these variables take in the obfuscation). $\mathcal{A}^f$ outputs 1 iff $f(\vec{\rho}, \vec{\delta}) \neq 0$. The distribution F_B is obtained as follows: each variable in $\vec{\delta}$ is chosen uniformly and random from the ring. For each variable $\rho_{I,\vec{s}}$, if $B_I(\vec{s}) = 1$ then it is chosen uniformly at random, but if $B_I(\vec{s}) = 0$ then it is always fixed to 0. The variable $\vec{\rho}_{\mathsf{chk}}$ is uniformly random and independent. The lemma follows from Claims 5.19 and 5.20 below.

CLAIM 5.19. *If $\forall x \in X, B(x) = 0$, then $\Pr_{\vec{\rho},\vec{\delta}}[f(\vec{\rho}, \vec{\delta}) = 0] = 1$*

PROOF. Since $\forall x \in X, B(x) = 0$, we conclude that $\forall x \in X, \exists I \in \binom{[n]}{d} : B_I(x_{|I}) = 0$. By the construction of F_B, we conclude that $\forall x \in X, \exists I \in \binom{[n]}{d} : \rho_{I,x_{|I}} = 0$. Thus $\forall x \in X$, the function $h_x(\vec{\rho})$, which is a product of all of the $\rho_{I,x_{|I}}$ variables, outputs 0. We conclude that $f(\vec{\rho}, \vec{\delta}) = \sum_{x \in X} h_x(\vec{\rho}) \cdot g_x(\vec{\delta})$ is a sum of 0's, and so when f's input is drawn from D_F, f's output is always 0. □

CLAIM 5.20. *If $\exists x^* \in X : B(x^*) = 1$, then $\Pr_{\vec{\rho},\vec{\delta}}[f(\vec{\rho}, \vec{\delta}) = 0] = negl(\lambda)$.*

PROOF. Set all variables in $\vec{\rho}$ that take value 0 in D_F to 0. This gives restricted functions: f' derived from f, and h'_x derived from h_x (for each $x \in X$). Choosing the input $(\vec{\rho}, \vec{\delta}) \sim D_F$ for f is equivalent to choosing a uniformly random input for f'.

For the promised $x^* \in X : B(x^*) = 1$, we get that h'_x is a non-zero polynomial of total degree at most $(\binom{n}{d} + 1)$. Thus f' is a non-zero polynomial of total degree $O(\binom{n}{d}+1)$, and we are choosing a uniformly random input for it. By Schwartz-Zippel, the probability that f' outputs 0 is $negl(\lambda)$. □

LEMMA 5.21. *There exists an algorithm that takes an arithmetic circuit computing a cross-linear polynomial*

$$f(\vec{\rho}, \vec{\delta}) = \sum_{k \in [K]} h_k(\vec{\rho}) \cdot \Big(\sum_{h \in H_k} h(\vec{\delta})\Big) ,$$

finds, with all but negligible probability, an arithmetic circuit for $h_{k^*}(\vec{\rho}) \cdot (\sum_{h \in H_{k^*}} h(\vec{\delta}))$ for some $k^* \in [K]$, and furthermore finds the assignment $y_{k^*} : (\binom{[n]}{d} \cup \mathsf{chk}) \to \{0,1\}^d$ that is associated with the monomial h_{k^*}.

PROOF. First, observe that it is easy to perform zero-testing for functions like f using Schwartz-Zippel (because f is a low-degree function of the underlying ρ, α, β variables, which are drawn uniformly at random). Our algorithm will start by finding a minimal set of ρ variables such that if all other ρ variables are set to 0, the function f remains non-zero. This is easy to do by setting one variable at a time to zero. Note that we need a *minimal* set, i.e. one that cannot be decreased further, and *not a minimum* set. From the structure of f, such a set must correspond to the set of variables in some monomial h_{k^*}. Furthermore, given this set of variables, the assignment y_{k^*} is immediately derived. More explicitly, for all $\rho_{I,\vec{s}}$ in the set, we define $y_{k^*}(I) = \vec{s}$. Since f is cross-linear, there can be no collisions in this definition.

Now, consider the arithmetic circuit obtained from f by fixing the value of all ρ variables, except the aforementioned set, to 0. This circuit computes the function $h_{k^*}(\vec{\rho}) \cdot (\sum_{h \in H_{k^*}} h(\vec{\delta}))$ as required. □

LEMMA 5.22. *Let C be any $\mathcal{CNC}^0$ circuit and let let $O \in \mathcal{CNC}^0$ be the circuit for the constant function* 1 *(the function that accepts any input). Let f be a cross-linear polynomial of the form:*

$$f(\vec{\rho}, \vec{\delta}) = \sum_{x \in X} h_x(\vec{\rho}) \cdot g_x(\vec{\delta}) ,$$

where h_x, g_x are consistent with x, and $\forall x \in X, C(x) = 1$. Then:

$$\Pr_{(\vec{\rho},\vec{\delta}) \sim D_C}[f(\vec{\rho}, \vec{\delta}) = 0] = \Pr_{(\vec{\rho},\vec{\delta}) \sim D_O}[f(\vec{\rho}, \vec{\delta}) = 0]$$

Moreover, when $(\vec{\rho}, \vec{\delta}) \sim D_C, D_O$, either it is always *the case that $f(\vec{\rho}, \vec{\delta})$ equals 0, or it only equals 0 with $negl(\lambda)$ probability (and these cases can be distinguished efficienctly).*

PROOF. Recall that for any circuit C, in the distribution D_C the variables $\vec{\rho}$ are uniform and independent, whereas the variables $\vec{\delta}$ are determined by the underlying random variables $\{\beta_{I,i,v}, \alpha_{I,v}\}$, which are sampled independently of the circuit C. Recall further that $\delta_{\mathsf{chk}} = \prod_I \alpha_{I,1} \cdot \prod_{i,I} \beta_{I,i,1}$, namely δ_{chk} is also independent of the circuit C.

In contrast, for all $I, \vec{s}$, $\delta_{I,\vec{s}} = \alpha_{I,C_I(\vec{s})} \cdot \prod_{i \in I} \beta_{I,i,\vec{s}[i]}$. I.e. these variables do depend on the circuit C and differ between D_C and D_O. However, since f is a sum of (products of) monomials that are consistent with accepting inputs of C, it follows that all of the δ variables in f are consistent with an accepting input x: i.e. they are of the form $\delta_{I,\vec{s}}$, where there exists an input $x \in X$ s.t. $C(x) = 1$ and $x_{|I} = \vec{s}$, so it must be the case that $C_I(\vec{s}) = 1$. In other words, for all δ values in f, it holds that

$$\delta_{I,\vec{s}} = \alpha_{I,C_I(\vec{s})} \cdot \prod_{i \in I} \beta_{I,i,\vec{s}[i]} = \alpha_{I,1} \cdot \prod_{i \in I} \beta_{I,i,\vec{s}[i]} = \alpha_{I,O_I(\vec{s})} \cdot \prod_{i \in I} \beta_{I,i,\vec{s}[i]} ,$$

Thus, the joint distributions of the δ variables in D_C and D_O are identical. The Lemma follows because, viewing $f(\vec{\rho}, \vec{\delta})$ as a function of the ρ, α, β variables (the same function when $(\vec{\rho}, \vec{\delta})$ are drawn from D_C or from D_O), either f is always

0, or it is only 0 with negligible probability (by Schwartz-Zippel, since f is a low-degree function of the uniformly random ρ, α, β). □

Acknowledgments. We thank Shafi Goldwasser for helpful and insightful comments, and Moni Naor for bring to our attention the connections between the Bounded Speedup Hypothesis and parameterized complexity theory. We are grateful to Ryan Williams for illuminating conversations about the Bounded Speedup Hypothesis, and in particular for pointing out the proof that qBSH is implied by ETH [28]. We also thank Amir Yehudayoff for helpful discussions on arithmetic circuit complexity.

6. REFERENCES

[1] B. Adida and D. Wikström. How to shuffle in public. In S. P. Vadhan, editor, *TCC*, volume 4392 of *Lecture Notes in Computer Science*, pages 555–574. Springer, 2007.

[2] B. Barak, S. Garg, Y. T. Kalai, O. Paneth, and A. Sahai. Protecting obfuscation against algebraic attacks. Cryptology ePrint Archive, Report 2013/631, 2013. `http://eprint.iacr.org/`.

[3] B. Barak, O. Goldreich, R. Impagliazzo, S. Rudich, A. Sahai, S. P. Vadhan, and K. Yang. On the (im)possibility of obfuscating programs. *J. ACM*, 59(2):6, 2012. Preliminary version in CRYPTO 2001.

[4] N. Bitansky and R. Canetti. On strong simulation and composable point obfuscation. In *CRYPTO*, pages 520–537, 2010.

[5] D. Boneh and A. Silverberg. Applications of multilinear forms to cryptography. *IACR Cryptology ePrint Archive*, 2002:80, 2002.

[6] Z. Brakerski and G. Rothblum. Obfuscating conjunctions, 2013. CRYPTO 2013.

[7] Z. Brakerski and G. N. Rothblum. Virtual black-box obfuscation for all circuits via generic graded encoding. Cryptology ePrint Archive, Report 2013/563, 2013. To appear in TCC 2014.

[8] R. Canetti. Towards realizing random oracles: Hash functions that hide all partial information. In *CRYPTO*, pages 455–469, 1997.

[9] R. Canetti and R. R. Dakdouk. Obfuscating point functions with multibit output. In *EUROCRYPT*, pages 489–508, 2008.

[10] R. Canetti, D. Micciancio, and O. Reingold. Perfectly one-way probabilistic hash functions (preliminary version). In *STOC*, pages 131–140, 1998.

[11] R. Canetti, G. N. Rothblum, and M. Varia. Obfuscation of hyperplane membership. In *TCC*, pages 72–89, 2010.

[12] J.-S. Coron, T. Lepoint, and M. Tibouchi. Practical multilinear maps over the integers. Cryptology ePrint Archive, Report 2013/183, 2013. CRYPTO 2013.

[13] Y. Dodis and A. Smith. Correcting errors without leaking partial information. In H. N. Gabow and R. Fagin, editors, *STOC*, pages 654–663. ACM, 2005.

[14] J. Flum and M. Grohe. *Parameterized Complexity Theory*. Springer, 2006.

[15] S. Garg, C. Gentry, and S. Halevi. Candidate multilinear maps from ideal lattices and applications. *IACR Cryptology ePrint Archive*, 2012:610, 2012. Extended abstract in EUROCRYPT 2013.

[16] S. Garg, C. Gentry, S. Halevi, M. Raykova, A. Sahai, and B. Waters. Candidate indistinguishability obfuscation and functional encryption for all circuits. Cryptology ePrint Archive, Report 2013/451, 2013. Extended abstract in FOCS 2013.

[17] S. Goldwasser and Y. T. Kalai. On the impossibility of obfuscation with auxiliary input. In *FOCS*, pages 553–562, 2005.

[18] S. Goldwasser and G. N. Rothblum. On best-possible obfuscation. In S. P. Vadhan, editor, *TCC*, volume 4392 of *Lecture Notes in Computer Science*, pages 194–213. Springer, 2007.

[19] D. Hofheinz, J. Malone-Lee, and M. Stam. Obfuscation for cryptographic purposes. *J. Cryptology*, 23(1):121–168, 2010.

[20] S. Hohenberger, G. N. Rothblum, A. Shelat, and V. Vaikuntanathan. Securely obfuscating re-encryption. *J. Cryptology*, 24(4):694–719, 2011.

[21] R. Impagliazzo and R. Paturi. Complexity of k-sat. In *IEEE Conference on Computational Complexity*, pages 237–240. IEEE Computer Society, 1999.

[22] B. Lynn, M. Prabhakaran, and A. Sahai. Positive results and techniques for obfuscation. In *EUROCRYPT*, pages 20–39, 2004.

[23] U. . Maurer. Abstract models of computation in cryptography. In *IMA Int. Conf.*, pages 1–12, 2005.

[24] M. Naor. On cryptographic assumptions and challenges. In D. Boneh, editor, *CRYPTO*, volume 2729 of *Lecture Notes in Computer Science*, pages 96–109. Springer, 2003.

[25] R. Rothblum. On the circular security of bit-encryption. In *TCC*, pages 579–598, 2013.

[26] V. Shoup. Lower bounds for discrete logarithms and related problems. In *EUROCRYPT*, pages 256–266, 1997.

[27] H. Wee. On obfuscating point functions. In H. N. Gabow and R. Fagin, editors, *STOC*, pages 523–532. ACM, 2005.

[28] R. Williams. Personal communication, 2013.

APPENDIX

A. THE BOUNDED SPEEDUP HYPOTHESIS

In this section we investigate the relation between BSH and ETH. We use an insight of Williams [28] to show that qBSH (quasi-polynomial BSH) is in fact implied by ETH. We also discuss a connection with parameterized complexity. We start by restating BSH, qBSH, ETH using similar terminology.

DEFINITION 5.2 ($\mathcal{X}$-3-SAT SOLVER, RESTATED). *Consider a family of sets $\mathcal{X} = \{X_n\}_{n \in \mathbb{N}}$ such that $X_n \subseteq \{0,1\}^n$. We say that an algorithm $\mathcal{A}$ is a $\mathcal{X}$-3-SAT solver if it solves the 3-SAT problem, restricted to inputs in $\mathcal{X}$. Namely, given a 3-CNF formula $\Phi : \{0,1\}^n \to \{0,1\}$, $\mathcal{A}$ finds whether there exists $x \in X_n$ such that $\Phi(x) = 1$.*

ASSUMPTION 5.3 (BSH, RESTATED). *There exists a polynomial $p(\cdot)$, such that for any $\mathcal{X}$-3-SAT solver that runs in time $t(\cdot)$, the family of sets $\mathcal{X}$ is of size at most $p(t(\cdot))$.*

The quasi-BSH (qBSH), is a variant where the polynomial $p(\cdot)$ is allowed to have degree $\log(n)$.

Assumption 5.4 (qBSH restated). *For any $\mathcal{X}$-3-SAT solver that runs in time $t(n)$, the family of sets $\mathcal{X}$ is of size at most $(t(n))^{O(\log(n))}$.*

We proceed with the exponential time hypothesis, presented by Impagliazzo and Paturi [21]. For our purposes, we use the weaker notion of ETH (the strong version makes claims about kCNF-SAT for all k).

Assumption A.1 (The Exponential Time Hypothesis). *There is no $2^{o(n)}$-time $\{0,1\}^n$-3-SAT solver.*

We further consider the following scaled down version of the ETH, which is not stronger than the original.

Assumption A.2 (Scaled-Down ETH). *There is no $t(n)$-time solver for $\omega(\log(t(n)))$-variable 3-SAT.*

Assumption A.1 implies Assumption A.2 by a scaling argument. The Scalded-Down ETH, in turn, is more similar to the BSH: we can view a solver for $\omega(\log(n))$-variable 3SAT as an $\mathcal{X}$ solver where $\mathcal{X}$ covers all possible assignments of the first $\omega(\log(n))$ variables (or rather, any subset of $\omega(\log(n))$ variables). The only difference from BSH thus is that the family $\mathcal{X}$ is "structured" in the sense of being concentrated on a small set of coordinates.

In fact, when we consider non-uniform solvers, the ETH implies qBSH (note that the scaling down above also applies to non-uniform solvers):

Lemma A.3 ([28]). *For non-uniform solvers, qBSH is implied by Scaled-Down ETH for (and therefore, qBSH is implied by ETH for non-uniform circuits).*

Proof. We start by recalling a learning theoretic argument. Given a family $\mathcal{X}$, we can consider the strings in X_n as functions in $\{0,1\}^k \rightarrow \{0,1\}$, where $k = \lceil\log(n)\rceil$ (the $(2^k - n)$ last bits can be set to zero). Recall that by Sauer's Lemma, the VC dimension of X_n (as a set of boolean functions) is at least $\mathsf{dim} = \Omega(\log(|X_n|)/k)$. This means that there exists a set of dim coordinates that is shuttered by X_n. Namely, such that there exists 2^{dim} functions in X_n that cover all possible assignments to this set of coordinates.

It follows, therefore, that if there exists a $\mathcal{X}$-3-SAT solver $\mathcal{A}$ that runs in time $t(n)$ with $|X_n| = (t(n))^{\omega(log(n))}$, then there is a set of

$$\Omega(\log(|X_n|)/\lceil\log(n)\rceil) = \omega(\log(t(n)))$$

coordinates that is shuttered by X_n (namely, they take all possible assignments when ranging over X_n). Mapping those to the variables of a scaled-down formula, yields a (non-uniform) solver for the Scaled-Down ETH (the coordinates to map to are specified by non-uniform advice). □

Connections with Parameterized Complexity. The bounded-speedup hypothesis implies that 3-SAT is hard even when restricted to super-polynomial-size subsets of inputs. One natural set to consider is the inputs of weight k, where k is super-constant or logarithmic (and weight is the L_1 norm, or the number of 1's in the assignment). This is a super-polynomial set, with a very short implicit description.

The problems of resolving SAT and 3-SAT on inputs of weight k, in time that is $f(k) \cdot poly(n)$ (for any function f, even super-exponential in k), has been studied in the context of parameterized complexity. "Weighted" 3-SAT is known to be complete for the class $W[1]$, and is not generally believed to be tractable. See e.g. [14].

This study shows an obstacle to finding a 3-SAT algorithm with significant speedup for *every* set $\mathcal{X}$ of inputs: in particular, doing so for the set of low-weight inputs seems hard. Still, we emphasize the Bounded Speedup Hypothesis asks for more: it says that there *exists no set* with super-polynomial speedup. Reducing this hypothesis to a more well studied worst-case problem is an intriguing direction for future work.

Candidate Weak Pseudorandom Functions in AC0 ∘ MOD2

Adi Akavia
Tel Aviv Academic College
akavia@mta.ac.il

Andrej Bogdanov
Chinese Univ. of Hong Kong
andrejb@cse.cuhk.edu.hk

Siyao Guo
Chinese Univ. of Hong Kong
syguo@cse.cuhk.edu.hk

Akshay Kamath
Chennai Math. Institute
adkamath@cmi.ac.in

Alon Rosen
IDC Herzliya
alon.rosen@idc.ac.il

ABSTRACT

Pseudorandom functions (PRFs) play a fundamental role in symmetric-key cryptography. However, they are inherently complex and cannot be implemented in the class $AC^0(MOD_2)$. Weak pseudorandom functions (weak PRFs) do not suffer from this complexity limitation, yet they suffice for many cryptographic applications.

We study the minimal complexity requirements for constructing weak PRFs. To this end

- We conjecture that the function family $F_A(x) = g(Ax)$, where A is a random square $GF(2)$ matrix and g is a carefully chosen function of constant depth, is a weak PRF. In support of our conjecture, we show that functions in this family are inapproximable by $GF(2)$ polynomials of low degree and do not correlate with any fixed Boolean function family of subexponential size.
- We study the class $AC^0 \circ MOD_2$ that captures the complexity of our construction. We conjecture that all functions in this class have a Fourier coefficient of magnitude $\exp(-\text{poly}\log n)$ and prove this conjecture in the case when the MOD_2 function is typical.
- We investigate the relation between the hardness of learning noisy parities and the existence of weak PRFs in $AC^0 \circ MOD_2$.

We argue that such a complexity-driven approach can play a role in bridging the gap between the theory and practice of cryptography.

Categories and Subject Descriptors

F.2.0 [**Theory of Computation**]: Analysis of Algorithms and Problem Complexity—*General*

Keywords

Weak Pseudorandom Functions; $AC^0 \circ MOD_2$; Parallel Cryptography; Inapproximability of AC^0; Learning Parity with Noise

ITCS'14, January 12–14, 2014, Princeton, New Jersey, USA.
Copyright 2014 ACM 978-1-4503-2698-8/14/01 ...$15.00.
http://dx.doi.org/10.1145/2554797.2554821.

1. INTRODUCTION

The design of symmetric-key cryptographic primitives can be roughly classified into two main categories: (1) the "theory-oriented" approach, in which claims on the security of one's design are supported by a reduction from a well-established hardness assumption, and (2) the "practice-oriented" approach, in which the construction is heuristically guided by practical experience and common sense. In both cases, confidence in the security of the design is gained through lack of cryptanalysis over time. In this respect, the theory-oriented approach is preferable over its practical counterpart, as it typically relies on simpler and mathematically more natural hardness assumptions. At the same time, the practice-oriented approach, not being constrained by burdensome proofs of security, results in significantly more efficient constructions.

Even though practical constructions that withstand the test of time are widely considered to be secure enough for applications, it is not clear whether the lack of cryptanalysis should be attributed to their secure design or to the fact that the design's complexity hinders analysis and theoretical understanding. This leaves us in an unsatisfactory state of affairs, in which the most widely used cryptographic primitives lack justification for their security. But is complex design really necessary for actual security, or is it only introduced to hinder cryptanalytic efforts in practice? Is simple design, one that is easy to understand from a theoretical perspective (and moreover lends itself to efficient implementation), incompatible with security?

The tension between the theoretical and practical approaches is perhaps most apparent in the design of *pseudorandom functions* (PRFs) [11], a fundamental cryptographic primitive that yields direct solutions to most central goals of symmetric cryptography (encryption, authentication, identification). While simple theory-oriented constructions of PRFs do exist, these constructions are inefficient and as a result the most widely deployed PRF in practice is AES [6]. It is true that, comparatively speaking, the design of AES can be considered simple. Yet, we are still quite far from understanding the role that many of its design choices play in its security as a PRF.

Our focus is on so called *weak pseudorandom functions*. An adversary for a weak PRF aims to distinguish a random member of the family from a truly random function after observing a polynomially-bounded number of samples $(x_1, f(x_1)), \ldots, (x_m, f(x_m))$, where $x_1, \ldots, x_m$ are independent uniformly random strings from $\{0,1\}^n$ and $f\colon \{0,1\}^n \to \{0,1\}$ is the function in question. Although strong PRFs (in which the x_i's can be adaptively chosen by the adversary) have traditionally played a more important role in cryptography, in many applications of interest they can be replaced by weak PRFs. Cryptographic applications of weak PRFs have been studied in several works [7, 17, 20, 8, 16].

In this paper we set out to better understand what makes a weak PRF secure from a complexity theoretic perspective, and in particular whether the efficiency of such functions is inherently tied to that of strong PRFs. We propose constructions of weak pseudorandom functions whose complexity of evaluation is minimal. To this end, we study the class $AC^0 \circ MOD_2$ of polynomial-size, constant-depth circuit families with a layer of MOD_2 gates at the bottom level followed by layers of AND/OR gates.

Unlike the typical theory-oriented construction, our design will not be accompanied by a reduction from an established problem. Instead, we let the choices in our design be guided by insights on the complexity of low-depth circuits. A useful byproduct of this process is that it identifies certain complexity theoretic properties of the class $AC^0 \circ MOD_2$ and gives rise to interesting conjectures that are of independent interest.

In addition to minimizing the computational complexity of our candidate weak pseudorandom functions, we also make deliberate effort to keep their design as simple as possible. This is done in order to make its cryptanalysis more appealing, and to examine to what extent the functions can withstand actual attacks (this approach was also explicitly advocated by Goldreich [10] and Miles and Viola [18]). The longer they do, the more confidence we will gain in their security.

1.1 Low-depth pseudorandom functions

Are parallel implementations of PRFs at all achievable? For the case of strong PRFs, a complexity-theoretic viewpoint provides a fairly satisfactory answer to this question. Razborov and Rudich [22], based on works of Razborov and Smolensky [21, 26], showed that the class $AC^0(MOD_2)$ of polynomial-size, constant-depth circuit families with unbounded fan-in AND, OR, and MOD_2 gates cannot contain strong PRFs of hardness[1] beyond $\exp \text{poly} \log n$.

Several works proposed candidate, theory-guided, constructions of strong PRFs that can be implemented in the class TC^0 of polynomial-size, constant-depth circuit families with unbounded fan-in threshold gates [19, 2]. The class TC^0 strictly contains $AC^0(MOD_2)$ and is believed to be of strictly lower complexity than the original construction of Goldreich et al. [11].

In the context of weak PRFs, Linial, Mansour, and Nisan [15] show that weak (and hence also strong) PRF implementations in the class AC^0 of polynomial-size, constant-depth circuit families with unbounded fan-in AND/OR gates can have hardness at most $\exp \text{poly} \log n$, which is considered inadequate for cryptographic practice. With this in mind, the class $AC^0 \circ MOD_2$, being a slight extension of AC^0, does indeed seem to be "minimal". Moreover, as mentioned above, this class (being contained in $AC^0(MOD_2)$) does not admit strong PRFs of adequate hardness.

Linial et al. prove that AC^0 function families have most of their Fourier mass concentrated on the first $t = \text{poly} \log n$ levels of the spectrum; thus such functions can be distinguished from random by detecting a noticeable correlation with one of the linear functions that depends on at most t variables. More generally, one could consider attacks that exploits the large correlation between the function being attacked and some other function h that belongs to some fixed family $\mathcal{H}$ of relatively small size.

These "LMN-type" attacks can be performed given access to the function at random (and in particular not adaptively chosen) inputs. Thus, at the very least a candidate weak pseudorandom function should exhibit low correlation with members of fixed families of small size.

[1] A pseudorandom function has hardness h if no adversary of size h can distinguish it from a random one with advantage better than $1/h$.

1.2 A Candidate weak pseudorandom function in $AC^0 \circ MOD_2$

For parameters $n, k \in \mathbb{N}$, such that $n/k = \Theta(2^k)$, and uniformly chosen $A \in \{0,1\}^{(n+1)\times(n+1)}$ our candidate weak PRF is:

$$F_A(x) = g(Ax) \quad \text{where} \quad g(y,z) = \text{TRIBES}_{n/k,k}(y) \oplus z.$$

Here, $\text{TRIBES}_{n/k,k}$ is the function defined as the OR of n/k ANDs over independent blocks with k bits in each block. In particular, for every A, F_A can be computed by $AC^0 \circ MOD_2$ circuits. The rationale behind the design of our candidate function takes the following considerations into account:

- Any function of the form $g(Ax)$ for $g \in AC^0$ and random A has known heavy Fourier coefficients, and hence can be learned from random samples by the algorithm of Linial et al. The matrix A randomly shuffles (and aggregates) the heavy Fourier coefficients of the TRIBES function. In fact, this transformation reduces the correlation of the function with any fixed Boolean function family of subexponential size. Keeping A secret is necessary for avoiding these types of attacks.

- The choice of the TRIBES function is driven by the need to prevent approximation of the function F_A by $GF(2)$ polynomials of low degree, which are learnable from random examples.

- We XOR the output of TRIBES with an independent bit in order to make the output of F_A unbiased.

Needless to say, it would have been preferable if we could also provide a reduction from a well-established hard problem. However, we currently do not know of such a reduction to any candidate weak pseudorandom function in $AC^0 \circ MOD_2$. As will become clear later, our results on the complexity class $AC^0 \circ MOD_2$ (combined with results of Feldman et al. [9]) imply that the computational hardness of the *Learning Parity With Noise* (LPN) problem [4] is necessary for the existence of weak PRFs in $AC^0 \circ MOD_2$.

We now turn to give a more detailed exposition of the rationale behind the choices made in the design of our candidate weak PRF, as well as connections to the complexity class $AC^0 \circ MOD_2$ and to the LPN problem.

1.3 The power of $AC^0 \circ MOD_2$ circuits

To better understand the security of our candidate weak PRFs, we study the class $AC^0 \circ MOD_2$ of polynomial-size, constant-depth circuit families consisting of a layer of MOD_2 gates at the bottom level followed by layers of AND/OR gates. Functions computed by such circuits can be represented in the form $f(x) = g(Ax)$, where A is an $m(n) \times n$ $GF(2)$ matrix and g is a constant-depth circuit of size polynomial in n.

We begin by conjecturing a structural property of all functions in this class.

CONJECTURE 1. *Let $\{f_n\colon \{0,1\}^n \to \{-1,1\}\}$ be a function family in $\mathrm{AC}^0 \circ \mathrm{MOD}_2$. There is a polynomial p such that for every n there exists an $a \in \{0,1\}^n$ satisfying $|\hat{f}_n(a)| \geq 2^{-p(\log n)}$.*

Here we identify the outputs "true" and "false" of the circuit with the values -1 and 1, respectively, and we use the notation $\hat{f}(a)$ for the a-th Fourier coefficient of f over $\mathbb{Z}_2^n$. In Section 2 we prove Conjecture 1 in the cases when

1. A is a random matrix (of arbitrary dimension) and g is an arbitrary AC^0 function, and
2. A is an arbitrary matrix and g is a polynomial-size depth-2 function (a CNF or a DNF).[2]

Our conjecture implies that functions in $\mathrm{AC}^0 \circ \mathrm{MOD}_2$ can be distinguished from random ones by the Goldreich-Levin and Kushilevitz-Mansour algorithms for learning Fourier coefficients. However, these algorithms require the examples $(x, f(x))$ to be chosen by the adversary. Similarly, the distinguisher of Razborov and Rudich that separates functions in $\mathrm{AC}^0(\mathrm{MOD}_2)$ from random ones requires chosen examples. Therefore these arguments do not rule out the possibility of weak PRFs in $\mathrm{AC}^0 \circ \mathrm{MOD}_2$.

Servedio and Viola [25] conjecture that the inner product function modulo 2 cannot be computed by polynomial-size $\mathrm{AC}^0 \circ \mathrm{MOD}_2$ circuits. This would follow from positive answer to Conjecture 1.

1.4 Some natural attacks on weak pseudorandom functions

The hardness of learning parity with noise (LPN) assumption for noise rate η postulates that the function family $F_{a,N}(x) = \langle a, x\rangle + N(x)$ (all operations are over $GF(2)$), where a is uniformly random in $\{0,1\}^n$ and the values $N(x)$ are independent Bernoulli(η) random bits is a weak PRF. Although this construction is of very low complexity, it is not efficient since describing the function N requires $\eta 2^n$ bits of entropy.

Some intuition about the hardness of LPN comes from the observation that known algorithms for learning $GF(2)$ linear functions from random examples are not robust to random noise. However, it is precisely the random nature of this noise that makes the implementation of $F_{a,N}$ inefficient. Is it possible to achieve the same effect with "deterministic" noise?

In this work we consider function families $F_A(x) = g(Ax)$, where A is a random $n \times n$ $GF(2)$ matrix and g is an almost unbiased "rounding" function of low complexity. For which choices of g is F_A a weak PRF? Clearly if g is a linear function then F_A is not weakly pseudorandom, as the algorithm for learning linear functions from random examples can be used to distinguish F_A from a random function. More generally, if g is a degree-d GF(2) polynomial, then the degree-d polynomial learning algorithm distinguishes F_A from a random function in time poly$\binom{n}{d}$. Even more generally, if g is ε-close to a degree-d polynomial p for $\varepsilon \ll 1/\binom{n}{d}$ we would expect F_A to appear indistinguishable from $p(Ax)$ from the perspective of the learning algorithm, and so F_A can again be distinguished from a random function.

Taking into account these bad choices of the function g, we propose the following conjecture regarding the pseudorandomness of F_A. We say g is *unbiased* if $\mathrm{E}_{x\sim\{0,1\}^n}[g(x)] = 0$.

CONJECTURE 2. *Let $\alpha < 1$ be a constant, n be sufficiently large and $g\colon \{0,1\}^n \to \{-1,1\}$ be an unbiased function. If g is $1/\binom{n}{d}^\alpha$-far from all $GF(2)$ polynomials of degree d then $F_A(x) = g(Ax)$ is a weak PRF of hardness $\binom{n}{d^{\Omega(1)}}$.*

Linial et al. showed that AC^0 function families have most of their Fourier mass concentrated on the first $t = \mathrm{poly}\log n$ levels of the spectrum; thus such functions can be distinguished from random by detecting a noticeable correlation among the function in question and one of the linear functions that depends on at most t variables.

In Section 4 we show that a more general form of this attack cannot work against our family F_A: For any fixed function family $\mathcal{H}$ of size at most $2^{n/4}$, the correlation between F_A and any function in $\mathcal{H}$ is exponentially small with overwhelming probability over the choice of the key A.

Razborov and Smolensky showed that the majority and MOD_q predicates on n input bits, where q is a power of a prime other than 2, are $\Omega(1)$-far from all $GF(2)$ polynomials of degree $\sqrt{n}$. Conjecture 2 predicts that the resulting weak pseudorandom functions have exponential hardness.

1.5 Inapproximability of $\mathrm{AC}^0 \circ \mathrm{MOD}_2$ by low-degree polynomials

Can we instantiate Conjecture 2 with a function g in the class $\mathrm{AC}^0 \circ \mathrm{MOD}_2$? Razborov shows that every AC^0 function g can be approximated by a polynomial of degree d with error $\varepsilon = \exp O(-d^{\alpha'}/\log n)$, where $\alpha' \leq 1$ is a constant that is inverse proportional to the circuit depth. In contrast, Conjecture 2 requires that g be $1/\binom{n}{d}^\alpha = \exp(-O(\alpha d \log n))$-far from all such polynomials (assuming $d \leq \sqrt{n}$). Thus we would like to find functions in $\mathrm{AC}^0 \circ \mathrm{MOD}_2$ whose Razborov approximating polynomials have essentially optimal degree-error tradeoff.

As an example of interest we consider the $\mathrm{TRIBES}_{n/k,k}$ function. This function is defined as the OR of n/k ANDs over independent blocks with k bits in each block. We will assume that the bias of $\mathrm{TRIBES}_{n/k,k}$ is constant, which is only possible if $n/k = \Theta(2^k)$). The Razborov approximation method gives approximating polynomials for $\mathrm{TRIBES}_{n/k,k}$ of degree d and error $\exp(-O(d/\log n))$ for every d. In particular, when $d = o(\log n)$, the Razborov approximating polynomials have very large error. We show that this is inevitable. Let $\mathrm{Corr}_d(f)$ denote the maximum correlation between $f\colon \{0,1\}^n \to \{-1,1\}$ and $GF(2)$ degree-d polynomials: $\mathrm{Corr}_d(f) = \max_{p\in S} \mathrm{E}_{x\sim\{0,1\}^n}[f(x)\cdot(-1)^{p(x)}]$ where $S = \{GF(2)$ degree-d polynomial$\}$.

THEOREM 3. *Let $\alpha > 0$ be a constant and K be a constant depending on α. Assume that $\alpha k 2^k \leq n \leq (1-\alpha)k2^k$. For every $d \leq \log n - \log(K \log n)$, $\mathrm{Corr}_d(\mathrm{TRIBES}_{n/k,k}) = 1 - \Omega(2^{-d})$.*

[2]This argument also appears in independent work of Servedio and Viola [25].

We conjecture that the bound in fact holds for all $d < n^{\Omega(1)}$. We leave this extension of Theorem 3 to higher degrees as an interesting open problem.

Despite this, the $\text{TRIBES}_{n/k,k}$ function may not be a suitable choice for g as we are not aware of any sequence of values $(n, k(n))$ that makes g unbiased (or of negligible bias). We therefore work with the function $g(y,z) = \text{TRIBES}_{n/k,k}(y) \oplus z$, which we show is unbiased yet cannot be approximated by polynomials of degree d any better than TRIBES.

COROLLARY 4. *The function $g(y,z) = \text{TRIBES}_{n/k,k}(y) \oplus z$ is unbiased and satisfies the conclusion of Theorem 3.*

In Section 3.3 we give another example of an unbiased AC^0 function family that has correlation at most $1 - \Omega(2^{-d})$ with all polynomials of degree $o(\log n)$. We conjecture that the bound also holds for larger degrees.

1.6 Learning noisy parities vs. weak pseudorandom functions in $\text{AC}^0 \circ \text{MOD}_2$

The Goldreich-Levin and Kushilevitz-Mansour algorithms efficiently learn all large Fourier coefficients of a boolean function f, but require that the examples $(x, f(x))$ be chosen by the algorithm. Feldman et al. [9] show that if noisy parities can be learned efficiently, then random examples can be used instead of chosen ones. Thus assuming Conjecture 1, the LPN assumption is necessary for the existence of weak PRFs in $\text{AC}^0 \circ \text{MOD}_2$. Is it also sufficient?

Banerjee et al. [2] observe that under the Learning with Errors (LWE) [23] assumption over a sufficiently large modulus q one can construct relatively simple weak PRFs. Their argument is based on the existence of an efficient *rounding function* g for which the distributions $g(Ax+e)$ and $g(Ax)$ are of negligible statistical distance. Here, A is a random $GF(q)$ matrix and e follows the noise model of the LWE assumption. Can this argument be modified to handle smaller values of q, specifically $q = 2$?

In Section 5 we show that no such reduction exists from LPN to breaking a weak PRF of the form $g(Ax)$ for any choice of the rounding function g: If samples of the form $g(Ax+e)$ and $g(Ax)$ are statistically indistinguishable, then g must be significantly biased.

In a recent work, Alwen et al. [1] use a different type of reduction to show hardness of "learning with rounding" for a bounded number of samples assuming the hardness of LWE over moduli q of magnitude polynomial in the hardness parameter.

2. THE FOURIER SPECTRUM OF $\text{AC}^0 \circ \text{MOD}_2$

In this section we prove two special cases of Conjecture 1. This conjecture postulates the existence of a large Fourier coefficient in functions of the form $f(x) = g(Ax)$, where A is an m by n matrix and g can be represented by a small AC^0 circuit.

Linial et al. showed that the Fourier spectrum of a function that can be computed by AC^0 circuits of size s and depth d is concentrated on the first $O(\log s)^d$ levels. It follows that at least one of these Fourier coefficients of low weight must have large value. If the rows of A are linearly independent (i.e. the map A^T is injective), then all the Fourier coefficients of g appear as coefficients of f and the conjecture follows easily.

The scenario where the rows of A are dependent is more interesting. In particular this always happens when $m > n$. In this case, every Fourier coefficient of f is a scaled sum of Fourier coefficients of g over some affine subspace. The concentration property of g proved by Linial et al. is no longer sufficient to obtain the conclusion of Conjecture 1.

We make the following partial progress towards the conjecture:

1. In Proposition 5 we prove that if g has small DNF size, then $g(Ax)$ has a large Fourier coefficient. This proof is inspired by the analysis of Jackson's algorithm for weakly learning DNF formulas.
2. In Proposition 7 we show that if no set of $\text{poly} \log s$ rows of A is linearly dependent, then $g(Ax)$ has a large Fourier coefficient. Curiously, in addition to Linial et al.'s characterization of the Fourier spectrum of AC^0 circuit, our proof relies on Braverman's theorem stating that polylogarithmically independent distributions are pseudo-random for AC^0 circuits.

   In particular, Proposition 7 applies to the cases when the map A^T is injective and when A is a random matrix of essentially arbitrary dimension.

2.1 g is a DNF and A is arbitrary

PROPOSITION 5. *Let $g\colon \{0,1\}^m \to \{-1,1\}$ be a DNF with s terms, A be an $m \times n$ $GF(2)$ matrix and $f(x) = g(Ax)$. There exists $a \in \{0,1\}^n$ such that $|\hat{f}(a)| \geq 1/(2s+1)$.*

The proof of Prop 5 uses the following Lemma of Jackson, which he used in the analysis of his weak learner for DNF formulas.

LEMMA 6 (JACKSON [14]). *For any DNF $g\colon \{0,1\}^m \to \{-1,1\}$ with s terms and any distribution D over $\{0,1\}^m$, there exists a vector $b \in \{0,1\}^m$ so that $\text{E}_{z\sim D}[g(z)\chi_b(z)] \geq 1/(2s+1)$.*

PROOF OF PROPOSITION 5. By Lemma 6, for distribution Ax where $x \sim \{0,1\}^n$, there exists $b \in \{0,1\}^m$ so that $\text{E}_{x\sim\{0,1\}^n}[g(Ax)\chi_b(Ax)] \geq 1/(2s+1)$. Notice that

$$\begin{aligned}
&\text{E}_{x\sim\{0,1\}^n}[g(Ax)\chi_b(Ax)] \\
&= \text{E}_{x\sim\{0,1\}^n}[f(x)\chi_{A^Tb}(x)] \\
&= \hat{f}(A^Tb).
\end{aligned}$$

Therefore there exists $a = A^Tb$, $|\hat{f}(a)| \geq 1/(2s+1)$. □

2.2 A is "typical" and g is arbitrary

In this section we consider the case where A is a random matrix and g is an arbitrary AC^0 function. We first prove, in Proposition 7, that Conjecture 1 holds for an arbitrary AC^0 function g and A with a certain property (specifically, the property that no $\text{poly} \log s$ rows of A are linearly dependent). Then in Corollary 10, we show that a random matrix A has this property with very high probability. Therefore Conjecture 1 holds for an arbitrary AC^0 function g and a random matrix A.

PROPOSITION 7. *Let $g\colon \{0,1\}^m \to \{-1,1\}$ be an AND/OR circuit of size $s \geq n$ and depth d, A be an $m \times n$ $GF(2)$ matrix so that every set of $r = (\log s)^{O(d^3)}$ rows of A is linearly independent, and $f(x) = g(Ax)$. Then there exists an $a \in \{0,1\}^n$ for which $|\hat{f}(a)| \geq m^{-O((\log s)^d)}$.*

Our proof relies on the following fundamental lemmas about AC^0 circuits of Linial et al. and Braverman.

LEMMA 8 (LINIAL ET AL. [15]). *Let $g\colon \{0,1\}^m \to \{-1, 1\}$ be an AND/OR circuit of size $s \geq n$ and depth d. For any t,*

$$\sum_{|b|>t} \hat{g}(b)^2 \leq 2s2^{-t^{1/d}/20}$$

LEMMA 9 (BRAVERMAN [5]). *Let $g\colon \{0,1\}^m \to \{-1,1\}$ be an AND/OR circuit of size $s \geq n$ and depth d, and $\mathcal{D}$ be an r-wise independent distribution over $\{0,1\}^n$, where $r \geq r(s,d,\varepsilon) = (\log(s/\varepsilon))^{O(d^2)}$. Then*

$$|\mathrm{E}_{z\sim\mathcal{D}}[g(z)] - \mathrm{E}_{z\sim\{0,1\}^n}[g(z)]| \leq \varepsilon.$$

PROOF OF PROPOSITION 7. We apply Lemma 8 with $t = (20\log 4s)^d$. In particular, there must exist at least one $b \in \{0,1\}^m$ with Hamming weight at most t for which

$$\hat{g}(b)^2 \geq 1/\Big(2\sum_{i=0}^{t}\tbinom{m}{i}\Big) = m^{-O(\log s)^d}.$$

Now we show for $a = A^T b$, $|\hat{f}(a)| \geq |\hat{g}(b)|/2 = m^{-O(\log s)^d}$.

Consider the function $h(z) = g(z)\chi_b(z)$, where $\chi_b(z) = (-1)^{\sum z_i}$. Håstad [13] observes that χ_b can be computed by a circuit of depth d and size $2^{t^{1/(d-1)}}$. Therefore h is computable by a circuit of size $s + 2^{O(t^{1/(d-1)})} = 2^{O(\log s)^{d/(d-1)}}$ and depth $d+1$. Instantiating Lemma 9 with the appropriate parameters, we get that

$$|\mathrm{E}_{z\sim\mathcal{D}}[h(z)] - \mathrm{E}_{z\sim\{0,1\}^m}[h(z)]| \leq |\hat{g}(b)|/2, \qquad (1)$$

as long as $\mathcal{D}$ is r-wise independent, where

$$r = r(2^{O(\log s)^{d/(d-1)}}, d+1, |\hat{g}(b)|/2)$$
$$\geq r(2^{O(\log s)^{d/(d-1)}}, d+1, m^{-O(\log s)^d}) = (\log s)^{O(d^3)}.$$

By our assumption on the matrix A, the distribution Ax, where $x \sim \{0,1\}^n$ is r-wise independent. Substituting into (1) we get

$$|\mathrm{E}_{x\sim\{0,1\}^n}[g(Ax)\chi_b(Ax)] - \mathrm{E}_{z\sim\{0,1\}^m}[g(z)\chi_b(z)]|$$
$$\leq |\hat{g}(b)|/2.$$

This inequality can be rewritten as

$$|\hat{f}(A^T b) - \hat{g}(b)| \leq |\hat{g}(b)|/2$$

so by the triangle inequality, $|\hat{f}(A^T b)| \geq |\hat{g}(b)|/2$. □

COROLLARY 10. *Let A be a random $m \times n$ $GF(2)$ matrix. With probability $1 - 2^{-\Omega(n)}$ over the choice of A, for every AND/OR circuit $g\colon \{0,1\}^m \to \{-1,1\}$ of size $n \leq s \leq \exp\big((n/\log m)^{1/O(d^3)}\big)$ and depth d, and $f(x) = g(Ax)$, there exists an $a \in \{0,1\}^n$ for which $|\hat{f}(a)| \geq m^{-O((\log s)^d)}$.*

PROOF. It is sufficient to show that with probability $1 - 2^{-\Omega(n)}$ over the choice of A, every $r = (\log s)^{\mathrm{poly} d}$ rows of A are linearly independent. By a union bound, the probability that there exists a linear dependence between r or fewer rows is at most

$$\frac{1}{2^n}\sum_{i=0}^{r}\tbinom{m}{i} \leq \frac{(r+1)m^r}{2^n} \leq 2^{-\Omega(n)},$$

where the last inequality follows from our assumption that $s \leq \exp\big((n/\log m)^{1/O(d^3)}\big)$. □

3. AC^0 FUNCTIONS INAPPROXIMABLE BY LOW-DEGREE POLYNOMIALS

In order to apply Conjecture 2 towards obtaining a weak PRF in the class $AC^0 \circ MOD_2$, we need a function g in the class $AC^0 \circ MOD_2$ that (1) is unbiased and (2) is inapproximable by $GF(2)$ polynomials of low degree.

We believe that a good candidate for condition (2) is the $\mathrm{TRIBES}_{n/k,k}$ function with $n = \Theta(k2^k)$. To this end we prove Theorem 3, which states that $\mathrm{TRIBES}_{n/k,k}$ is $\Omega(2^{-d})$-far from all polynomials of degree at most $C\log n$. We remark that we further believe that for every degree $d \leq \sqrt{n}$, $\mathrm{TRIBES}_{n/k,k}$ cannot be approximated within $2^{-O(d)}$ by a polynomial of degree d; we leave this extension of Theorem 3 to larger d as an interesting open question.

To prove Theorem 3, we rely on a result of Samorodnitsky and Trevisan [24] (Lemma 13 below) stating that functions of low maximum influence and small bias have small Gowers norm, which in turn implies inapproximability by low degree polynomials. Samorodnitsky and Trevisan used Lemma 13 in the design of a "dictator test" that emulates the computation of the Gowers norm of the function being queried. They use Lemma 13 to show that if the function passes the test, then it must have an influential variable, which can then be used to implement the "decoding step" in the corresponding PCP. Here we use Lemma 13 in the opposite direction: Because the TRIBES function has low maximum influence, it must have low Gowers norm.

To meet condition (1) (which the TRIBES function family does not appear to satisfy), we give a simple general transformation that preserves correlation with degree d polynomials for every d but turns any function into an unbiased one.

CLAIM 11. *Let $f\colon \{0,1\}^n \to \{-1,1\}$ be a boolean function and $g\colon \{0,1\}^{n+1} \to \{-1,1\}$ be given by $g(y,z) = f(y)\cdot(-1)^z$. Then for every $d \geq 1$, $\mathrm{Corr}_d(g) = \mathrm{Corr}_d(f)$.*

Combining Theorem 3 and Claim 11 yields Corollary 4.

3.1 Influence, bias, and inapproximability by low degree polynomials

The *bias* of a boolean function $f\colon \{0,1\}^n \to \{-1,1\}$ is the value $\mathrm{Bias}[f] = \mathrm{E}_{x\sim\{0,1\}^n}[f(x)]$. The *influence* $\mathrm{Inf}_i[f]$ of the i-th input on f where $1 \leq i \leq n$, is the probability of the event $f(x) \neq f(x^i)$ where x is random in $\{0,1\}^n$ and x^i is obtained by flipping the i-th bit of x.

PROPOSITION 12. *For any boolean function $f\colon \{0,1\}^n \to \{-1,1\}$ and $GF(2)$ polynomial p of degree at most d,*

$$\mathrm{E}_{x\sim\{0,1\}^n}[f(x)(-1)^{p(x)}]$$
$$\leq \big(\mathrm{Bias}[f]^2 + (2^{d-1}-1)\max_i \mathrm{Inf}_i[f]\big)^{1/2^d}.$$

Proposition 12 follows immediately from the lemmas of Gowers [12] and Samorodnitsky and Trevisan [24]. These lemmas refer to a sequence of measures on Boolean functions called the *Gowers uniformity norms* and denoted by $U_d[f]$. In this work we merely need one property of $U_d[f]$ so we will not define this norm, but refer the interested reader to the works of Gowers [12] and Viola and Wigderson [27]. We note here that for a given polynomial, if its correlation, $\mathrm{E}_{x\sim\{0,1\}^n}[f(x)(-1)^{p(x)}] < \epsilon$ then $f(x)$ is $\frac{1-\epsilon}{2}$-far from $p(x)$.

Lemma 13 (Samorodnitsky and Trevisan [24]). *For any boolean function $f\colon \{0,1\}^n \to \{-1,1\}$ and any $d \geq 1$,*

$$U_d[f] \leq \left(\mathrm{Bias}[f]^2 + (2^{d-1}-1)\max_i \mathrm{Inf}_i[f]\right)^{1/2^d}.$$

Lemma 14 (Gowers [12]). *For every $f\colon \{0,1\} \to \mathbb{R}$ and every polynomial p of degree at most d,*

$$\mathrm{E}_{x\sim\{0,1\}^n}[f(x)(-1)^{p(x)}] \leq U_d[f].$$

3.2 Proof of Theorem 3 and Claim 11

To prove Theorem 3, we use the well-known facts [3] that for $n = \Theta(k2^k)$, $\mathrm{TRIBES}_{n/k,k}$ has bias at most $1-\Omega(1)$ and maximum influence $O(\log n/n)$. When $d \leq \log n - \log(K\log n)$ for a sufficiently large constant K, we have that

$$\mathrm{Bias}[f]^2 + (2^{d-1}-1)\max_i \mathrm{Inf}_i[f] \leq 1-\Omega(1)$$

and by Proposition 12, $\mathrm{E}_{x\sim\{0,1\}^n}[f(x)(-1)^{p(x)}] \leq 1-\Omega(2^{-d})$.

To prove Claim 11, notice that the correlation of $f(y)$ with a polynomial $p(y)$ equals the correlation of $g(y,z)$ with the polynomial $p(y)\oplus z$. In the other direction, suppose $g(y,z)$ and $p(y,z)$ have correlation γ. By averaging z can be fixed to a constant $c\in\{0,1\}$ so that $g(y,c)$ and $p(y,c)$ have correlation at least γ. Then $f(y)$ has correlation at least γ with the polynomial $p(y,c)\oplus c$.

Corollary 4 follows from Theorem 3 and Claim 11.

3.3 Another example

We now give another example of an unbiased AC^0 function family g that has correlation at most $1-\Omega(2^{-d})$ with degree d polynomials for $d = o(\log n)$. We conjecture that this correlation bound holds as long as $d = n^{\Omega(1)}$.

The *addressing function* $a\colon \{0,1\}^{n+\log n} \to \{0,1\}$ takes an n-bit input x and a $\log n$-bit input y and outputs the y-th bit of x. We define the function $g\colon \{0,1\}^{n+n\log n} \to \{0,1\}$

$$\begin{aligned} &g(x, z_1, \ldots, z_{\log n}) \\ &= a(x, \mathrm{TRIBES}_{n/k,k}(z_1), \ldots, \mathrm{TRIBES}_{n/k,k}(z_{\log n})). \end{aligned}$$

where $z_1,\ldots,z_{\log n} \in \{0,1\}^n$ and $n = \Theta(k2^k)$.

Claim 15. *The function g is unbiased and all variables of g have influence at most $n^{-\Omega(1)}$.*

Proof. For every fixing of the inputs $z_1,\ldots,z_{\log n}$, the output of g is a specific bit of x, which is unbiased. We now bound the influence. The influence of every input z_{ij} is at the maximum influence of an input in the $\mathrm{TRIBES}_{n/k,k}$ function, which is $O(\log n/n)$. On the other hand, an input x_a is influential only if $a_i = \mathrm{TRIBES}_{n/k,k}(z_i)$ for all $\log n$ values of i. This event happens with probability at most $n^{-\Omega(1)}$. □

By Proposition 12, we obtain the desired conclusion.

4. LACK OF CORRELATION WITH FIXED FUNCTION FAMILIES

One way to distinguish a pseudorandom function from a random one is to seek correlations of the function in question with a fixed collection of functions $\mathcal{H} = \{h\colon \{0,1\}^n \to \{-1,1\}\}$. This is the approach used by Linial et al. to learn functions in AC^0. In their case, the collection in question consists of all linear functions on sufficiently few inputs.

In Corollary 17 below we show that for functions of the type $f(x) = g(Ax)$, with overwhelming probability over the choice of A, f fails to correlate with any sufficiently small collection of functions $\mathcal{H}$, as long as g has negligible bias. Our proof is essentially a second moment calculation which relies on the pairwise independence of the values Ax.

Proposition 16. *For any function $h\colon \{0,1\}^n \to \{-1,1\}$,*

$$\Pr_A\left[|\mathrm{E}_x[g(Ax)h(x)] - \mathrm{E}_x[g(x)]\,\mathrm{E}_x[h(x)]| > \varepsilon + 2^{-n+1}\right] = O(2^{-n}/\varepsilon^2)$$

where A is a random $n\times n$ $GF(2)$ matrix.

Proof. Let us consider the random variable $Z(A) = \mathrm{E}_x[g(Ax)h(x)]$. We will estimate the first and second moments of this random variable.

Conditioned on $x \neq 0$, Ax is uniformly distributed in $\{0,1\}^m$ and independent of x. Therefore $\mathrm{E}_A[Z(A)]$ is

$$\begin{aligned} &\frac{1}{2^n}\sum_{x\neq 0}\mathrm{E}_A[g(Ax)h(x)] + \frac{1}{2^n}g(0)h(0) \\ &= \frac{1}{2^n}\sum_{x\neq 0} h(x)\,\mathrm{E}_y[g(y)] + \frac{1}{2^n}g(0)h(0) \\ &= \mathrm{E}_x[h(x)]\,\mathrm{E}_y[g(y)] - \frac{1}{2^n}h(0)\,\mathrm{E}_y[g(y)] + \frac{1}{2^n}g(0)h(0). \end{aligned}$$

Since $|h(0)\,\mathrm{E}_y[g(y)]| \leq 1$ and $|g(0)h(0)| \leq 1$, we can obtain

$$\begin{aligned} &|\mathrm{E}_A[Z(A)] - \mathrm{E}_y[g(y)]\,\mathrm{E}_x[h(x)]| \\ &\leq |\frac{1}{2^n}h(0)\,\mathrm{E}_y[g(y)]| + |\frac{1}{2^n}g(0)h(0)| \leq 2^{-n+1}. \end{aligned}$$

All probabilities are over the uniform distribution. For the second moment, we have

$$\begin{aligned} \mathrm{E}_A[Z(A)^2] &= \mathrm{E}_A[\mathrm{E}_x[g(Ax)h(x)]^2] \\ &= \mathrm{E}_A\left[\mathrm{E}_x[g(Ax)h(x)]\,\mathrm{E}_{x'}[g(Ax')h(x')]\right] \\ &= \mathrm{E}_{x,x'}\left[h(x)h(x')\,\mathrm{E}_A[g(Ax)g(Ax')]\right]. \end{aligned}$$

Fix x and x' satisfying $x \neq x'$ and $x, x' \neq 0$. Then Ax and Ax' are independent and uniformly distributed in $\{0,1\}^n$ over the choice of A, so $\mathrm{E}_A[g(Ax)g(Ax')] = \mathrm{E}_y[g(y)]^2$. Since the event "$x = x'$ or $x' = 0$ or $x = 0$ happens with probability at most $3\cdot 2^{-n}$, it follows that

$$\mathrm{E}_A[Z(A)^2] \leq \mathrm{E}_x[h(x)]^2\,\mathrm{E}_x[g(x)]^2 + 3\cdot 2^{-n}$$

and

$$\mathrm{Var}_A[Z(A)] = \mathrm{E}_A[Z(A)^2] - \mathrm{E}_A[Z(A)]^2 \leq 7\cdot 2^{-n}.$$

The proposition follows by applying Chebyshev's inequality to $Z(A)$. □

By applying a union bound and setting parameters appropriately, we obtain the following corollary:

Corollary 17. *Let $\mathcal{H} = \{h\colon \{0,1\}^n \to \{-1,1\}\}$ be a collection of functions of size at most $2^{n/4}$. With probability $2^{-\Omega(n)}$ over the choice of A, for every $h\in\mathcal{H}$, $\mathrm{E}_x[g(Ax)h(x)] \leq \beta + 2^{-\Omega(n)}$, where $\beta = \mathrm{E}_x[g(x)]$.*

The β term is necessary; if g is biased then $g(Ax)$ correlates with the zero function.

5. NOISY PARITIES, ROUNDING, AND WEAK PSEUDORANDOM FUNCTIONS

As observed in the introduction, assuming Conjecture 1, the hardness of learning noisy parities (LPN) is a necessary assumption for the existence of weak PRFs in $AC^0 \circ MOD_2$. In this section we investigate whether this assumption is also sufficient.

For this purpose we view our function $f_A(x) = g(Ax)$ as applying a "rounding" function g that adds a "deterministic noise" to the samples Ax. This viewpoint has proved instrumental in the context of learning with errors (LWE), which is a generalization of LPN to larger modulus q. Specifically, Banerjee et al. [2] construct a weak PRF $f'_A(x) = g'(Ax)$ where A, x and all operations are over $GF(q)$ for a sufficiently large modulus q; they then prove that for a suitably chosen rounding function g', their "deterministic noise" is statistically close to an LWE noise, implying that their function f' is as hard as LWE; finally, as g' has negligible bias, they conclude that $f'_A(x) = g'(Ax)$ is computationally indistinguishable from uniform; namely, f' is a weak PRF. Can their proof techniques [2] be transferred to the field $GF(2)$ for basing the hardness of our candidate function on LPN? In Theorem 18 we give a negative answer to this question by showing that for every function g, if the "deterministic noise" incurred by g is statistically close to an LPN noise, then g is highly biased (ie, g is close to a constant function and thus $f(x) = g(Ax)$ cannot be a weak PRF).

Elaborating on the above, Banerjee et al. [2] observe that under the LWE assumption (and for a suitable g'), samples of the form $(x, g'(\langle a, x\rangle))$ are computationally indistinguishable from samples $(x, g'(u))$, where $x \sim GF(q)^n$ and $u \sim GF(q)$ is independent of x. This follows by looking at the auxiliary distribution $(x, g'(\langle a, x\rangle + e))$, where e follows the LWE noise distribution. On the one hand, for a suitable choice of g', $(x, g'(\langle a, x\rangle))$ and $(x, g'(\langle a, x\rangle + e))$ are statistically close. On the other hand, by the LWE assumption, $(x, g'(\langle a, x\rangle + e))$ and $(x, g'(u))$ are computationally close. Thus, as g' has negligible bias, they conclude that the samples $(x, g'(\langle a, x\rangle))$ are computationally indistinguishable from uniform samples (x, u); namely, f' is a weak PRF.

Transferring the proof technique of [2] to the case $q = 2$ would look as follows. Suppose the adversary sees t samples

$$(x_1, g(Ax_1)), \ldots, (x_t, g(Ax_t)), \qquad (2)$$

and consider the auxiliary distribution

$$(x_1, g(Ax_1 + e_1)), \ldots, (x_t, g(Ax_t + e_t)) \qquad (3)$$

where $e_1, \ldots, e_t \in \{0,1\}^m$ follow the LPN noise distribution with rate η (ie, their coordinates are i.i.d. random variables accepting 1 with probability η); denote this distribution $\{0,1\}^m_\eta$. On the one hand, argue for some choice of g that distributions (2) and (3) are statistically close. On the other hand, by the LPN assumption[3] distribution (3) is computationally close to

$$(x_1, g(u_1)), \ldots, (x_t, g(u_t))$$

where $u_1, \ldots, u_t \sim \{0,1\}^m$ are independent of $x_1, \ldots, x_t$. Finally, using the assumption that g has negligible bias, it would follow that $g(Ax)$ is pseudo-random.

The following theorem shows that this proof method cannot work: essentially if distributions (2) and (3) are statistically close, then g must be biased. Specifically, if the statistical distance is $\varepsilon \le \frac{\eta^2}{m^2} \cdot \frac{1}{n^{2c}}$ for $c > 0$ a constant and sufficiently many samples say $t = \frac{m^2}{\eta^2} \cdot mn \cdot n^{2c}$ (note that $t = \text{poly}(n)$ for $m = \text{poly}(n)$ and LPN noise rate η which is noticeable), then we obtain that $\text{Bias}[g]^2 = 1 - O(n^{-c})$.

THEOREM 18. *For n, m, t, η as above, function $g\colon \{0,1\}^m \to \{-1,1\}$, if distributions (2) and (3) are within statistical distance ε, then* $\text{Bias}[g]^2 \ge 1 - \frac{m}{\eta} \cdot (5\sqrt{\delta} + \sqrt{\varepsilon} + 1/2^n)$ *for* $\delta = \frac{1}{t} \cdot (nm \ln 2 + \ln(1 - \sqrt{\varepsilon}))$.

5.1 Proof of Theorem 18

In this section we prove Theorem 18 by showing that the following holds for a random matrix A (with high probability over the choice of the input x and the noise e): First we give a statistical test and show that if this test cannot distinguish distributions (2) and (3) then we can eliminate the noise e by replacing A with a related matrix A'; namely, $g(Ax + e) = g(A'x)$ (see Claim 19). Then we show that even with a slightly higher noise rate the above still holds, ie, $g(Ax + e + e') = g(A'x)$; implying that $g(Ax + e + e') = g(Ax + e)$ (see Claim 21). Next, we employ the above to upper bound the noise-sensitivity of g. Specifically, we observe that $Ax+e$ is uniform (because A is uniform), thus replacing $Ax + e$ by u in the above we conclude that $g(u + e') = g(u)$ with high probability; namely, g has low noise-sensitivity (see Claim 22). Finally we employ a simple relation between the noise-sensitivity and the bias to conclude that g has high bias (see Proposition 23). The proof details follow.

First we show that for most matrices A there is a matrix A' s.t. $g(Ax + e) = g(A'x)$ with high probability over the choice of x, e.

CLAIM 19. *With probability at least $1 - \sqrt{\varepsilon}$ over the choice of $A \sim \{0,1\}^{m\times n}$, there exists $A' \in \{0,1\}^{m\times n}$ such that*

$$\Pr_{x,e}[g(Ax + e) = g(A'x)] \ge 1 - \delta$$

where $x \sim \{0,1\}^n, e \sim \{0,1\}^m_\eta$.

PROOF. Let us consider following statistical test T: on input $(x_1, b_1, \ldots, x_t, b_t)$, output 1 if and only if there exists $A' \in \{0,1\}^{m\times n}$ such that $g(A'x_i) = b_i$ for all $1 \le i \le t$. Notice that T accepts distribution (2) with probability 1. Because distributions (2) and (3) are ε statistically close, T accepts distribution (3) with probability at least $1 - \varepsilon$. Moreover, by Markov's inequality, with probability at least $1 - \sqrt{\varepsilon}$ over the choice of A, T accepts distribution (3) with probability at least $1 - \sqrt{\varepsilon}$ over choice x_i, e_i, i.e.

$$\Pr_A[\Pr_{x_i,e_i}[\exists A' \forall i, g(Ax_i + e_i) = g(A'x_i)] \ge 1 - \sqrt{\varepsilon}] \ge 1 - \sqrt{\varepsilon}.$$

Then, we complete the proof by showing for any fixed choice of A, $\Pr_{x_i,e_i}[\exists A' \forall i, g(Ax_i + e_i) = g(A'x_i)] \ge 1 - \sqrt{\varepsilon}$ implies $\max_{A' \in \{0,1\}^{m\times n}} \Pr_{x,e}[g(Ax + e) = g(A'x)] \ge 1 - \delta$. We

[3]The values $(x_1, Ax_1 + e_1), \ldots, (x_t, Ax_t + e_t)$ can be viewed as noisy samples for multiple random secrets. Specifically, the random secrets are the rows a_j of the matrix A, and the corresponding noisy samples are $(x_1, \langle a_j, x_1\rangle + e_1), \ldots, (x_t, \langle a_j, x_t\rangle + e_t)$. Such samples are computational indistinguishable from uniform samples under LPN assumption (this is straightforward to prove, due to the self-reducibility of LPN).

show by assuming that $\max_{A' \in \{0,1\}^{m\times n}} \Pr_{x,e}[g(Ax+e) = g(A'x)] < 1-\delta$ and derive

$$\begin{aligned}
&\Pr_{x_i,e_i}[\exists A' \forall i, g(Ax_i + e_i) = g(A'x_i)] \\
&\leq \sum_{A' \in \{0,1\}^{m\times n}} \Pr_{x_i,e_i}[\forall i, g(Ax_i+e_i) = g(A'x_i)] \\
&\leq \sum_{A' \in \{0,1\}^{m\times n}} (\Pr_{x,e}[g(Ax+e) = g(A'x)])^t \\
&\leq 2^{mn} \max_{A' \in \{0,1\}^{m\times n}} (\Pr_{x,e}[g(Ax+e) = g(A'x)])^t \\
&< 2^{mn}(1-\delta)^t \leq 2^{mn}e^{-t\delta} = 1-\sqrt{\varepsilon}.
\end{aligned}$$

□

Next we show that $g(Ax+e+e') = g(Ax+e)$ (for most matrices A, and with high probability over x, e, e') in Claim 21. To prove this, we show how to eliminate noise of a slightly higher rate than considered in Claim 19, ie, $g(Ax+e+e') = g(A'x)$ which relies on following lemma.

LEMMA 20. *For any $0 < \eta < 1/2$ and $h\colon \{0,1\}^m \to \{0,1\}$, $\Pr_{e,e'}[h(e+e') \neq 0] \leq 3\Pr_e[h(e) \neq 0]$ where $e \sim \{0,1\}^m_\eta, e' \sim \{0,1\}^m_{\eta/m}$.*

PROOF. For any $z \in \{0,1\}^m$, $\Pr_{e,e'}[e+e' = z] \leq (1-\eta)^{m-|z|}(1+1/m)^m\eta^{|z|} \leq (1+1/m)^m \Pr_e[e=z] < 3\Pr_e[e=z]$ so that

$$\begin{aligned}
\Pr_{e,e'}[h(e+e') = 0] &= \sum_{z:h(z)=0} \Pr_{e,e'}[e+e' = z] \\
&\leq 3 \sum_{z:h(z)=0} \Pr_e[e=z] = 3\Pr_e[h(e) = 0].
\end{aligned}$$

□

CLAIM 21. *With probability at least $1-\sqrt{\varepsilon}$ over the choice of $A \sim \{0,1\}^{m\times n}$, there exists $A' \in \{0,1\}^{m\times n}$ such that*

$$\Pr_{x,e}[g(Ax+e) = g(Ax+e+e')] \geq 1 - 5\sqrt{\delta}$$

where $x \sim \{0,1\}^n, e \sim \{0,1\}^m_\eta, e' \sim \{0,1\}^m_{\eta/m}$.

PROOF. For A, A', x, let $h_{A,A',x}(z) = 0$ if and only if $g(Ax+z) \neq g(A'x)$. By union bound,

$$\begin{aligned}
&\Pr_{e,e'}[g(Ax+e) \neq g(Ax+e+e')] \\
&\leq \Pr_{e,e'}[g(Ax+e+e') \neq g(A'x)] + \Pr_e[g(Ax+e) \neq g(A'x)] \\
&= \Pr_{e,e'}[h_{A,A',x}(e+e') = 0] + \Pr_e[h_{A,A',x}(e) = 0] \\
&\leq 4\Pr_e[h_{A,A',x}(e) = 0]
\end{aligned}$$

where the last inequality is due to Lemma 20. By Claim 19 and Markov's inequality, for at least $1-\sqrt{\varepsilon}$ choice of A such that at least $1-\sqrt{\delta}$ choice of x,

$$\Pr_e[g(Ax+e) \neq g(A'x)] = \Pr_e[h_{A,A',x}(e) = 0] \leq \sqrt{\delta}.$$

Therefore for at least $1-\sqrt{\varepsilon}$ choice of A such that at least $1-\sqrt{\delta}$ choice of x, $\Pr_{e,e'}[g(Ax+e) \neq g(Ax+e+e')]$ is bounded by $4\Pr_e[h_{A,A',x}(e) = 0] \leq 4\sqrt{\delta}$. By averaging over x, we obtain for at least $1-\sqrt{\varepsilon}$ choice of A, $\Pr_{x,e,e'}[g(Ax+e) \neq g(Ax+e+e')] \leq 5\sqrt{\delta}$. □

Next we bound the noise-sensitivity of g, where recall that the noise sensitivity of a Boolean function g is defined to be

$$\mathsf{NS}_{e'}(g) = \Pr_{u,e'}[g(u+e') \neq g(u)],$$

where $u \sim \{0,1\}^m$ and $e' \in \{0,1\}^m_{\eta/m}$.

CLAIM 22. $\mathsf{NS}_{e'}(g) \leq 5\sqrt{\delta} + \sqrt{\varepsilon} + 1/2^n$.

PROOF. Claim 21 implies $\Pr_{A,x,e,e'}[g(Ax+e) = g(Ax+e+e')] \geq 1-5\sqrt{\delta}-\sqrt{\varepsilon}$. Since for any fixed e, e' and non-zero x, Ax is uniformly distributed, we can derive

$$\begin{aligned}
&\Pr_{u,e'}[g(u) = g(u+e')] \\
&\geq \Pr_{A,x,e,e'}[g(Ax+e) = g(Ax+e+e')] - 1/2^n \\
&= 1 - 5\sqrt{\delta} - \sqrt{\varepsilon} - 1/2^n.
\end{aligned}$$

Hence $\mathsf{NS}_{e'}(g) \leq 5\sqrt{\delta} + \sqrt{\varepsilon} + 1/2^n$. □

To conclude the proof we employ the above bound on the noise-sensitivity to bound the bias.

PROPOSITION 23. *For any $g\colon \{0,1\}^m \to \{-1,1\}$ and $0 < \eta' < 1/2$, $\mathrm{Bias}[g]^2 \geq 1 - \mathsf{NS}_{e'}(g)/\eta'$.*

PROOF. By $\sum_{a\in\{0,1\}^m} \hat{g}^2(a) = 1$ and $0 < \eta' < 1/2$,

$$\begin{aligned}
&\sum_{a\in\{0,1\}^m} \hat{g}^2(a)(1-2\eta')^{|a|} \\
&\leq \hat{g}^2(0^m) + \sum_{a\neq 0^m} \hat{g}^2(a)(1-2\eta') \\
&= 1 - 2\eta'(1-\hat{g}^2(0^m)).
\end{aligned}$$

Recall the fact $\mathsf{NS}_{e'}(g) = \frac{1}{2} - \frac{1}{2}\sum_{a\in\{0,1\}^m} \hat{g}^2(a)(1-2\eta')^{|a|}$. Therefore $\mathsf{NS}_{e'}(g) \geq \eta'(1-\hat{g}^2(0^m))$ which implies $\mathrm{Bias}[g]^2 = \hat{g}^2(0^m) \geq 1 - \mathsf{NS}_{e'}(g)/\eta'$. □

6. ACKNOWLEDGMENTS

Adi Akavia's research was conducted while visiting IDC Herzliya, supported by the ERC under the EU's Seventh Framework Programme (FP/2007-2013) ERC Grant Agreement n. 307952.

Part of Andrej Bogdanov's research was conducted while visiting IDC Herzliya, supported by the ERC under the EU's Seventh Framework Programme (FP/2007-2013) ERC Grant Agreement n. 307952 and supported by RGC GRF grants CUHK410111 and 410112.

Part of Siyao Guo's research was conducted while visiting IDC Herzliya, supported by the ERC under the EU's Seventh Framework Programme (FP/2007-2013) ERC Grant Agreement n. 307952. Siyao Guo acknowledges support from Computer Science and Engineering department of Chinese University of Hong Kong and CUHK Research Postgraduate Student Grants for Overseas Academic Activities.

Part of Akshay Kamath's research was conducted while visiting IDC Herzliya supported by the ERC under the EU's Seventh Framework Programme (FP/2007-2013) ERC Grant Agreement n. 307952.

Alon Rosen is supported by the ERC under the EU's Seventh Framework Programme (FP/2007-2013) ERC Grant Agreement n. 307952.

7. REFERENCES

[1] J. Alwen, S. Krenn, K. Pietrzak, and D. Wichs. Learning with rounding, revisited: New reduction, properties and applications. In *Advances in Cryptology - CRYPTO 2013 - 33rd Annual Cryptology Conference*, pages 57–74, 2013.

[2] A. Banerjee, C. Peikert, and A. Rosen. Pseudorandom functions and lattices. In *EUROCRYPT*, pages 719–737, 2012.

[3] M. Ben-Or and N. Linial. Collective coin flipping, robust voting schemes and minima of banzhaf values. In *FOCS*, pages 408–416, 1985.

[4] A. Blum, M. Furst, M. Kearns, and R. J. Lipton. Cryptographic primitives based on hard learning problems. In *Advances In Cryptology(CRYPTO 93)*, pages 278–291. Springer, 1994.

[5] M. Braverman. Poly-logarithmic independence fools bounded-depth boolean circuits. *Communications of the ACM*, 54(4):108–115, 2011.

[6] J. Daemen and V. Rijmen. *The Design of Rijndael: AES - The Advanced Encryption Standard.* Information Security and Cryptography. Springer, 2002.

[7] I. Damgård and J. B. Nielsen. Expanding pseudorandom functions; or: From known-plaintext security to chosen-plaintext security. In *CRYPTO*, pages 449–464, 2002.

[8] Y. Dodis, E. Kiltz, K. Pietrzak, and D. Wichs. Message authentication, revisited. In *EUROCRYPT*, pages 355–374, 2012.

[9] V. Feldman, P. Gopalan, S. Khot, and A. K. Ponnuswami. On agnostic learning of parities, monomials, and halfspaces. *SIAM J. Comput.*, 39(2):606–645, 2009.

[10] O. Goldreich. Candidate one-way functions based on expander graphs. *Electronic Colloquium on Computational Complexity (ECCC)*, 7(90), 2000.

[11] O. Goldreich, S. Goldwasser, and S. Micali. How to construct random functions (extended abstract). In *FOCS*, pages 464–479, 1984.

[12] W. T. Gowers. A new proof of Szemerédi's theorem. *Geom. Funct. Anal.*, 11(3):465–588, 2001.

[13] J. Håstad. *Computational limitations of small-depth circuits.* MIT press, 1987.

[14] J. C. Jackson. An efficient membership-query algorithm for learning dnf with respect to the uniform distribution. *Journal of Computer and System Sciences*, 55(3):414–440, 1997.

[15] N. Linial, Y. Mansour, and N. Nisan. Constant depth circuits, fourier transform, and learnability. *Journal of the ACM (JACM)*, 40(3):607–620, 1993.

[16] V. Lyubashevsky and D. Masny. Man-in-the-middle secure authentication schemes from lpn and weak prfs. *IACR Cryptology ePrint Archive*, 2013:92, 2013.

[17] U. M. Maurer and J. Sjödin. A fast and key-efficient reduction of chosen-ciphertext to known-plaintext security. In *EUROCRYPT*, pages 498–516, 2007.

[18] E. Miles and E. Viola. Substitution-permutation networks, pseudorandom functions, and natural proofs. In *CRYPTO*, pages 68–85, 2012.

[19] M. Naor and O. Reingold. Number-theoretic constructions of efficient pseudo-random functions. In *FOCS*, pages 458–467, 1997.

[20] K. Pietrzak. A leakage-resilient mode of operation. In *EUROCRYPT*, pages 462–482, 2009.

[21] A. A. Razborov. Lower bounds on the size of bounded depth circuits over a complete basis with logical addition. *Matematicheskie Zametki*, 41(4):598–607, 1987.

[22] A. A. Razborov and S. Rudich. Natural proofs. In *STOC*, pages 204–213, 1994.

[23] O. Regev. The learning with errors problem (invited survey). In *IEEE Conference on Computational Complexity*, pages 191–204, 2010.

[24] A. Samorodnitsky and L. Trevisan. Gowers uniformity, influence of variables, and pcps. *SIAM J. Comput.*, 39(1):323–360, 2009.

[25] R. Servedio and E. Viola. On a special case of rigidity. Technical Report TR12-144, Electronic Colloquium on Computational Complexity (ECCC), 2012.

[26] R. Smolensky. Algebraic methods in the theory of lower bounds for boolean circuit complexity. In *STOC*, pages 77–82, 1987.

[27] E. Viola and A. Wigderson. Norms, xor lemmas, and lower bounds for polynomials and protocols. *Theory of Computing*, 4(1):137–168, 2008.

Iterated Group Products and Leakage Resilience Against NC1*

Eric Miles
Northeastern University
enmiles@ccs.neu.edu

ABSTRACT

We show that if $\mathrm{NC}^1 \neq \mathrm{L}$, then for every element α of the alternating group A_t, circuits of depth $O(\log t)$ cannot distinguish between a uniform vector over $(A_t)^t$ with product $= \alpha$ and one with product $=$ identity. Combined with a recent construction by the author and Viola in the setting of leakage-resilient cryptography [STOC '13], this gives a compiler that produces circuits withstanding leakage from NC^1 (assuming $\mathrm{NC}^1 \neq \mathrm{L}$). For context, leakage from NC^1 breaks nearly all previous constructions, and security against leakage from P is impossible.

We build on work by Cook and McKenzie [J. Algorithms '87] establishing the relationship between L = logarithmic space and the symmetric group S_t. Our techniques include a novel algorithmic use of commutators to manipulate the cycle structure of permutations in A_t.

Categories and Subject Descriptors

F.1.1 [**Computation by Abstract Devices**]: Models of Computation; F.1.3 [**Computation by Abstract Devices**]: Complexity Measures and Classes

Keywords

leakage-resilient cryptography; iterated group products

1. INTRODUCTION

The interplay between *group theory* and *computational complexity* has been the source of a number of elegant constructions and computational insights. A line of work [Bar89, CM87, BT88, BC92, CL94, Cle91, IL95] in the late 1980s gave characterizations of various complexity classes in terms of products over finite groups. A primary motivation of some of this work was to obtain an efficient simulation of circuits by branching programs, such as in the celebrated theorem of Barrington [Bar89]. Beyond this however, the underlying encoding of computation by group products has proven to be a useful tool in other areas.

A typical encoding has the following form. Let G be a group with identity element id, let f be a Boolean function, and let x be an input to f. Then the encoding $E(f, x)$ is a vector $(g_1, \ldots, g_t) \in G^t$ such that $\prod_i g_i = \mathsf{id} \Leftrightarrow f(x) = 0$. For such encodings a number of efficiency aspects are of interest, including the size of the group, the length of the encoding, and the complexity of computing it. In some cases a short encoding can be computed with much fewer resources than are needed to compute f, yielding the result that the decoding problem, i.e. computing iterated products over G, is as hard as computing f.

Recently, the author and Viola [MV13] gave an application of these group encodings to *leakage-resilient cryptography.* This area studies cryptographic models in which the adversary obtains more information from an algorithm than just its input/output behavior. The extra information is commonly modeled by providing the adversary with the output of a computationally restricted "leakage function" of its choosing, applied to (the bits carried on) the wires of a circuit implementing the algorithm. A general goal in this area is to compile any circuit C into a functionally equivalent circuit $\widehat{C}$ such that any attack on $\widehat{C}$ exploiting this extra information can in fact be carried out just using input/output access, and hence does not succeed under standard hardness assumptions.

The [MV13] construction provides a rather generic way to construct such a compiler, given any group G satisfying the following property with respect to a set of leakage functions $\mathcal{L}$. This property says that for an element $\alpha \in G$, functions in $\mathcal{L}$ cannot distinguish between vectors with product $= \alpha$ and those with product $=$ id.

Definition 1.1. *Let G be a group. For $\alpha \in G$ and $t \in \mathbb{N}$, the* α-product problem over G^t *is to decide, given a tuple $(x_1, \ldots, x_t) \in G^t$ such that $\prod_i x_i \in \{\alpha, \mathit{id}\}$, which product it has.*

Let D_α denote the uniform distribution over $\{(x_1, \ldots, x_t) \in G^t \mid \prod_i x_i = \alpha\}$. A set of functions $\mathcal{L}$ is (ϵ, α)-fooled by G^t *if $\Delta(\ell(D_\alpha), \ell(D_{\mathit{id}})) \leq \epsilon$ for every $\ell \in \mathcal{L}$.*

The [MV13] construction obtains security against leakage classes that are (ϵ, α)-fooled by G^t for *every* $\alpha \in G$. A key technical contribution there is to show that a number of well-studied classes of functions have this property when $G = A_5$, where A_u denotes the group of even permutations on u points. In particular they show that for every $\alpha \in A_5$, functions including parity, majority, inner

*Supported by NSF grants CCF-0845003 and CCF-1319206.

ITCS'14, January 12–14, 2014, Princeton, NJ, USA.
Copyright 2014 ACM 978-1-4503-2698-8/14/01 ...$15.00
http://dx.doi.org/10.1145/2554797.2554822.

product, and communication protocols are $(t^{-\omega(1)}, \alpha)$-fooled by $(A_5)^t$, yielding a compiler that provides security against leakage from these functions.

They also make the following conjecture, whose proof would yield a compiler that provides security against leakage from the class NC^1 of log-depth, fan-in-2 circuits.

CONJECTURE 1 ([MV13]). *If* $\mathrm{NC}^1 \neq \mathrm{L}$ *then for every* $\alpha \in A_t$, NC^1 *is* $(t^{-\omega(1)}, \alpha)$*-fooled by* $(A_t)^t$.

Some support for this conjecture comes from the work of Cook and McKenzie [CM87] on the relationship between L = log-space and iterated group products. Their results can be used to show that the following problem is L-complete: given $x = (x_1, \ldots, x_t) \in (A_t)^t$, determine if $\prod_i x_i = \mathsf{id}$. (The difference from Definition 1.1 is that x's product is not guaranteed to be in $\{\alpha, \mathsf{id}\}$.) If one could instead show that the α-product problem is L-complete for every $\alpha \in A_t$, the conjecture follows from the random self-reducibility of iterated group products [Kil88]. However, it was not clear how to show this for even a single α.

1.1 Our results

We show that indeed the α-product problem is L-complete for every $\alpha \in A_t$, and as a result we prove the above conjecture.

THEOREM 1.2. *Assume that there is a circuit family* C *of depth* $O(\log t)$ *such that for sufficiently large* t*, there exists* $\alpha \in A_t$ *such that* C *decides the* α*-product problem over* $(A_t)^t$*. Then* $\mathrm{NC}^1 = \mathrm{L}$.

COROLLARY 1.3. *If* $\mathrm{NC}^1 \neq \mathrm{L}$*, then* NC^1 *is* $(t^{-\omega(1)}, \alpha)$*-fooled by* $(A_t)^t$ *for infinitely many* t *and all* $\alpha \in A_t$.

More precisely, if $\mathrm{NC}^1 \neq \mathrm{L}$ *then for all* k*, infinitely many* t*, and all* $\alpha \in A_t$*, the class of* NC^1 *circuits with depth* $k \log t$ *and output length* $k \log t$ *is* (t^{-k}, α)*-fooled by* $(A_t)^t$.

In combination with [MV13], Corollary 1.3 yields a compiler that is secure against NC^1 leakage. As noted in [MV13], even 1 bit of leakage from NC^1 breaks nearly all previous constructions [ISW03, FRR$^+$10, JV10, DF12, GR12, Rot12] (in fact leakage from $\mathrm{TC}^0 \subseteq \mathrm{NC}^1$ is already enough to break these). Furthermore, securing circuits against arbitrary polynomial-time leakage is known to be *impossible*, due to the impossibility of obfuscation [BGI$^+$01]. We note that, like some other compilers [FRR$^+$10, GR10, JV10, DF12], in the multi-query setting the [MV13] construction uses a so-called "secure hardware component". Specifically, the compiled circuits have a gate that produces a uniform sample from $(A_t)^t$ with product = id, and whose internal computation is not visible to the leakage function.

On the amount of leakage.

The amount of NC^1 leakage tolerated using Corollary 1.3 is logarithmic in the security parameter, which is smaller than one might wish (and smaller than can be achieved against other leakage classes). This limitation seems to be inherent when starting from an assumption such as $\mathrm{NC}^1 \neq \mathrm{L}$. One approach to circumventing this is by instead starting from a *compression bound*, i.e. a bound on the correlation between NC^1 circuits with > 1 output bit and functions in L. Indeed, the compression bound of Dubrov and Ishai [DI06] against AC^0 was used by [FRR$^+$10, MV13] to achieve security against a linear amount of AC^0 leakage.

In this setting however, there is an issue which is that the proof of Theorem 1.2 gives a Turing reduction to the α-product problem, as opposed to a many-one reduction. With such a reduction it is not clear how to translate a (hypothetical) NC^1 circuit compressing the α-product problem into a circuit compressing an arbitrary language in L, and therefore a generic assumption on the inability of NC^1 to compress L does not immediately yield improved leakage bounds. In light of this, it would be interesting to show that the α-product problem is L-complete under many-one reductions. Jumping ahead, showing this for any fixed $\alpha \in A_t$ would suffice to show it for all α via Theorem 2.1.

We refer the reader to [MV13] for further details on leakage-resilience, and now give an overview of the proof of Theorem 1.2. The proof of Corollary 1.3 given Theorem 1.2 uses straightforward techniques and appears in §4.

1.2 Techniques

The Cook-McKenzie construction.

Our starting point is the work by Cook and McKenzie [CM87] who show that a number of problems related to S_t, the group of all permutations on t points, are complete for L. A key tool in their work is the following construction of a permutation that encodes acceptance of a given branching program on a given input. (We equate L with the set of polynomial-size branching programs.)

THEOREM 1.4 ([CM87]). *There exists* $t = O(s)$ *and a circuit* C *of depth* $O(\log s)$ *such that, on input* (B, x) *where* B *is a branching program of size* $s \geq |x|$*,* C *outputs a permutation* $\sigma \in S_t$ *such that* B *accepts* x *iff* 1 *and* t *are in the same cycle in* σ*'s disjoint cycle representation.*

Recall that any permutation can be uniquely written as a product of disjoint cycles. Throughout, when a permutation $\sigma \in S_t$ is the input or output of an algorithm, it is given in $(t \log t)$-bit pointwise representation as $(\sigma(1), \ldots, \sigma(t))$. Inversion and pairwise multiplication in S_t can then be implemented in NC^1, because each essentially amounts to indexing an element from an array of length t.

Theorem 1.4 is proved by constructing a permutation σ that performs one step of a depth-first search in B when projecting to the edges consistent with the input x. The nodes are labeled by $[t]$, and the labels of the start and accept nodes (1 and t wlog) are in the same cycle of σ iff the accept node is reachable from the start node.

As observed to us by Eric Allender and V. Arvind (personal communication), Theorem 1.4 can be used to show that the following very natural problem is L-complete: given $(x_1, \ldots, x_t) \in (S_t)^t$, decide if $\prod_i x_i = \mathsf{id}$. A simple embedding trick shows that this problem remains L-complete even over the group A_t (see §3.1).

However it was not clear whether Theorem 1.4 could be used to show that the α-product problem is L-complete, for every or even for a single $\alpha \in A_t$. The issue is that the permutation σ constructed in Theorem 1.4 depends on the structure of the branching program B when projecting to the edges whose labels match the input x. So while the reduction to the "product $\stackrel{?}{=}$ id" problem always produces a vector with product = id when $B(x) = 0$, when $B(x) = 1$

the product can change depending on x, rather than being fixed to some α.

Before explaining how we overcome this, we briefly review some facts and terminology about permutations that will be used; a more detailed discussion appears in e.g. [Wil09, §2].

Permutation groups.

S_t is the group of all permutations on $[t] = \{1, \ldots, t\}$. Any permutation can be written as a product of transpositions, and the permutation is called *even* or *odd* depending on whether the number of transpositions in this product is even or odd. Thus the product of two permutations is even iff both are even or both are odd. $A_t \subset S_t$ is the group of all even permutations on $[t]$.

A *k-cycle* $(a_1 \ \cdots \ a_k)$ is a permutation that maps $a_i \mapsto a_{i+1}$ for $i < k$ and $a_k \mapsto a_1$. A k-cycle is an even permutation iff k is odd, because any k-cycle can be written as a product of $k-1$ transpositions $(a_1 \ a_2)(a_1 \ a_3) \cdots (a_1 \ a_k)$. Every permutation can be uniquely written as a product of disjoint cycles, and the list of these cycles' lengths is the *cycle type* of the permutation.

$\alpha, \beta \in G$ are *conjugate* if there exists $\gamma \in G$ such that $\gamma^{-1}\alpha\gamma = \beta$. Conjugacy is an equivalence relation and partitions G into its conjugacy classes. In S_t, two permutations are conjugate iff they have the same cycle type. In A_t this continues to hold if that cycle type contains either an even-length cycle or two cycles of the same length, but for cycle types consisting of distinct odd lengths (including length 1) there are two distinct conjugacy classes. For example, the two 5-cycles (1 2 3 4 5) and (1 2 3 5 4) are conjugate in S_5 and S_6 but not in A_5 nor A_6.

The *commutator* of two elements $\alpha, \beta \in G$ is denoted $[\alpha, \beta]$ and defined by $[\alpha, \beta] := \alpha\beta\alpha^{-1}\beta^{-1}$. We will use the fact that for every α, $[\alpha, \mathsf{id}] = [\mathsf{id}, \alpha] = \mathsf{id}$.

We now explain the proof of Theorem 1.2, which has two steps. We first show that if NC^1 can decide the α-product problem for any fixed $\alpha \in A_t$, then it can do so for every $\alpha \in A_t$. Next we show that the α-product problem is L-complete for the specific choice of $\alpha = (1\ 2)(3\ 4)$. The combination of these implies that if NC^1 can decide the α-product problem for any α, then $\mathrm{NC}^1 = \mathrm{L}$. In light of the above discussion on the amount of leakage, we remark that only the latter step uses a Turing reduction.

Mapping group products.

We reduce the α-product problem to the β-product problem, for any $\mathsf{id} \neq \alpha, \beta \in A_t$, by constructing an NC^1 map

$$f_{\alpha\to\beta} : (A_t)^m \to (A_t)^{O(tm)}$$

that maps α-products to β-products while preserving id-products. Namely, this map satisfies

$$\prod_i x_i = \alpha \Rightarrow \prod_i f_{\alpha\to\beta}(x)_i = \beta$$

$$\text{and} \qquad (1)$$

$$\prod_i x_i = \mathsf{id} \Rightarrow \prod_i f_{\alpha\to\beta}(x)_i = \mathsf{id}$$

for every $x = (x_1, \ldots, x_m) \in (A_t)^m$. (To prove Theorem 1.3 we choose $m = t$, but here we keep them separate to make the blowup in output length clear.) Moreover $f_{\alpha\to\beta}$ has the nice property that each output element depends on only 1 input element, i.e. it is *1-local.*

If α and β are in the same conjugacy class, then there is a simple 1-local NC^1 map with no blowup in length that satisfies (1). This map is

$$(x_1, \ldots, x_m) \mapsto (\gamma^{-1}x_1, \ldots, x_m\gamma)$$

where $\gamma \in A_t$ satisfies $\gamma^{-1}\alpha\gamma = \beta$. But because α and β are in the same conjugacy class only if they have the same cycle type, to map between permutations of different cycle types a different technique is needed.

Our idea is to use *commutation* to map between permutations of different cycle types, and combined with conjugation as above this allows us to construct a map from any α to any β. As noted previously commutation is identity-preserving, i.e. $[\gamma, \mathsf{id}] = [\mathsf{id}, \gamma] = \mathsf{id}$ for every γ, which makes it a good candidate for maps satisfying (1). One limitation is that commutation doubles the length of the vector, i.e. we compute

$$(x_1, \ldots, x_m) \mapsto (x_1, \ldots, x_m\gamma, x_m^{-1}, \ldots, x_1^{-1}\gamma^{-1})$$

to map α-products to $[\alpha, \gamma]$-products while preserving id-products. But by using $\leq \log t + O(1)$ commutations, here the total length increase is limited to a factor of $O(t)$.

We note that our use of commutation is different than in Barrington's construction [Bar89]. There it is used to simulate AND, and each commutator is formed from two vectors whose products are both unknown. Here we use it to manipulate cycle structure, and each commutator is formed from a vector whose product is unknown and a fixed group element.

Our framework for using commutation to map between different cycle types has three steps.

1. *Reduce to two disjoint transpositions.* (Lemma 2.3)

   We first convert any $\alpha \neq \mathsf{id}$ into a product of two disjoint transpositions. For example if α's disjoint cycle representation contains a 4-cycle $(a\ b\ c\ d)$, then commutating with $\gamma := (a\ b)(c\ d)$ yields $[\alpha, \gamma] = (a\ c)(b\ d)$.

2. *Grow the number of transpositions.* (Lemma 2.4)

   From a product of disjoint transpositions, we use one commutation to double the number of transpositions, and $\log k$ commutations to convert from 2 to $2k$ disjoint transpositions. For example if $\alpha = (a\ b)(c\ d)$, then commutating with $\gamma := (a\ e)(b\ f)(c\ g)(d\ h)$ yields $[\alpha, \gamma] = (a\ b)(c\ d)(e\ f)(g\ h)$.

3. *Combine transpositions into cycles.* (Lemmas 2.5-2.6)

   We finally convert products of disjoint transpositions into longer cycles. For example if $\alpha = (a_1\ b_1) \cdots (a_k\ b_k)$, then commutating with $\gamma := (a_1\ b_1\ a_2\ b_2\ \cdots\ a_k\ b_k\ c)$ yields the $(2k+1)$-cycle $[\alpha, \gamma] = (a_1\ \cdots\ a_k\ b_k\ \cdots\ b_1\ c)$.

In total we use $\leq \log t + O(1)$ commutations. This turns out to be tight for certain starting and target permutations as shown in the following theorem, and thus for these permutations a map satisfying (1) with smaller output length requires different techniques. (The theorem also holds if both commutations and conjugations are allowed.)

THEOREM 1.5. *There exist $\alpha, \beta \in A_t$ such that α cannot be converted to β with fewer than $\log(t) - 1$ commutations. That is, for every $\ell < \log(t) - 1$ and every sequence $\gamma_1, \ldots, \gamma_\ell \in A_t$, $\beta \neq [[\cdots[[\alpha, \gamma_1], \gamma_2], \cdots], \gamma_\ell]$.*

PROOF. For $\alpha \in A_t$, let $M(\alpha) := |\{i \in [t] \mid \alpha(i) \neq i\}|$ denote the number of points moved (i.e. not fixed) by α. We show that $M([\alpha,\gamma]) \leq 2 \cdot M(\alpha)$ for every α and γ, i.e. the number of points moved by $[\alpha,\gamma]$ is at most twice the number of points moved by α. This implies the theorem by choosing $\alpha = (1\ 2\ 3)$ and $\beta = (1\ 2\ \cdots\ t)$, because $M(\alpha) = 3$ and $M(\beta) = t$.

Pick $\gamma \in A_t$. Observe that $\gamma\alpha^{-1}\gamma^{-1}$ has the same cycle type as α because it is conjugate to α in S_t. This implies $M(\gamma\alpha^{-1}\gamma^{-1}) = M(\alpha)$, and therefore $[\alpha,\gamma] = \alpha\gamma\alpha^{-1}\gamma^{-1}$ moves at most $2 \cdot M(\alpha)$ points because any such point must be moved by either α or $\gamma\alpha^{-1}\gamma^{-1}$. □

Hardness for a single element.

To prove that the (1 2)(3 4)-product problem is L-complete, we reduce from the problem of deciding if $x \in (A_t)^t$ has product $=$ id. That is, from any $x \in (A_t)^t$ we compute a vector $y \in (A_t)^t$ such that y has product $=$ id if x does, and otherwise y has product $= (1\ 2)(3\ 4)$.

As in step 1 above, we first show that if $\prod_i x_i = \alpha \neq \mathsf{id}$ then there is some $\gamma_1 \in A_t$ (which depends on α) such that $[\alpha,\gamma_1]$ is a double-transposition, i.e. a product of two disjoint transpositions. Then because all double-transpositions are conjugate in A_t there is some $\gamma_2 \in A_t$ such that $\gamma_2^{-1} \cdot [\alpha,\gamma_1] \cdot \gamma_2 = (1\ 2)(3\ 4)$, and a vector with this product can be computed from x in NC^1 if we know γ_1, γ_2.

The problem of course is that we do not know γ_1, γ_2 without knowing $\alpha = \prod_i x_i$ which we cannot compute. We resolve this by showing that for any $\alpha \neq \mathsf{id}$, γ_1 and γ_2 as above can be taken from the set of permutations that are fixed on all but ≤ 8 points in $[t]$. Since there are $< \binom{t}{8} \cdot |A_8| = t^{O(1)}$ such permutations, we can thus construct a set of $t^{O(1)}$ vectors such that if x has product $=$ id then they all do, and otherwise some vector has product $= (1\ 2)(3\ 4)$. Then the proof is completed by applying an NC^1 circuit deciding the (1 2)(3 4)-product problem to each vector and a depth-$O(\log t)$ OR tree to the results.

Organization.

The rest of the paper is organized as follows. In §2 we describe our mapping between group products and construct the function $f_{\alpha\to\beta}$ defined above for any α and β. In §3 we show that the (1 2)(3 4)-product problem is L-complete. Together these prove Theorem 1.2, and in §4 we prove Corollary 1.3.

2. MAPPING GROUP PRODUCTS

In this section we prove the following theorem.

THEOREM 2.1. *Let $t \equiv 2 \pmod 4$ and let $\mathsf{id} \neq \alpha, \beta \in A_t$. Then for all m there is a 1-local function $f : (A_t)^m \to (A_t)^{O(tm)}$ computable in depth $O(\log t)$ that maps α-products to β-products while preserving the identity, i.e. that satisfies $\forall x = (x_1, \ldots, x_m) \in (A_t)^m$:*

$$\prod_i x_i = \alpha \Rightarrow \prod_i f(x)_i = \beta$$

and

$$\prod_i x_i = \mathsf{id} \Rightarrow \prod_i f(x)_i = \mathsf{id}.$$

The function f is constructed by concatenating compositions of functions from the following two families, where the compositions are given by Lemma 2.2.

$$\mathsf{Conj} = \{\mathsf{Conj}_\gamma(\alpha) := \gamma^{-1}\alpha\gamma \mid \gamma \in A_t\}$$

$$\mathsf{Comm} = \{\mathsf{Comm}_\gamma(\alpha) := \alpha\gamma\alpha^{-1}\gamma^{-1} \mid \gamma \in A_t\}$$

LEMMA 2.2. *Let $t \equiv 2 \pmod 4$ and let $\alpha, \beta \in A_t$ such that $\alpha \neq \mathsf{id}$ and β is either a cycle of odd length k or is the product of two disjoint even-length cycles of total length k. Then, there is a sequence $f_1, \ldots, f_\ell \in (\mathsf{Conj} \cup \mathsf{Comm})$ such that $f(\alpha) = \beta$, where $f := f_\ell \circ \cdots \circ f_1$ and $\ell = \log k + O(1)$.*

Any function given by this lemma yields a 1-local function $f : (A_t)^m \to (A_t)^{m \cdot 2^\ell}$ computable in depth $O(\log t)$ that maps α-products to β-products while preserving the identity.

PROOF OF THEOREM 2.1. We prove the case $m = 1$, but the argument extends immediately to any m. Fix $\alpha, \beta \in A_t$, and consider the unique representation of β as a set of disjoint cycles $C = \{\sigma_1, \ldots, \sigma_s\} \subset S_t$. (Here C contains only those cycles with length > 1.) The idea is to apply Lemma 2.2 to each cycle $\sigma \in C$, obtaining $f' : A_t \to (A_t)^{O(|\sigma|)}$ such that $\prod_i f'(\alpha)_i = \sigma$. Then letting f output the concatenation of these f', the resulting function maps α-products to β-products while preserving the identity. Further, its output length is $\sum_{\sigma \in C} O(|\sigma|) = O(t)$.

The only technical complication has to do with cycles of even length: if σ is a cycle of even length then it is an odd permutation, and so there can be no composition of functions from Conj and Comm that maps $\alpha \mapsto \sigma$. We handle this by pairing the cycles of even length, which we can do because C must contain an even number of cycles of even length as each is an odd permutation and β is an even permutation. So, for each such pair of even-length cycles $\sigma, \sigma' \in C$, we instead apply Lemma 2.2 to get a function f' such that $\prod_i f'(\alpha)_i = \sigma \cdot \sigma'$. □

2.1 Proof of Lemma 2.2

To prove Lemma 2.2, we implement the procedure described in §1.2. Namely, we first use ≤ 2 commutations to convert a given $\alpha \in A_t$ to a double-transposition, then $\log k$ commutations to convert to a product of roughly $k/2$ disjoint transpositions, and finally ≤ 2 commutations and 1 conjugation to convert to either a cycle of odd length k or to the product of two disjoint even-length cycles with total length k.

LEMMA 2.3. *Let $t \geq 4$. For every $\mathsf{id} \neq \alpha \in A_t$, there exist $\gamma_1, \gamma_2 \in A_t$ such that $[[\alpha,\gamma_1],\gamma_2]$ is a double-transposition. Further, each γ_i is either a double-transposition or a 3-cycle.*

PROOF. We consider five cases based on α's cycle structure. In all cases except the last, in fact only one commutation is needed to obtain a double-transposition, but we can use two by noting that $[(a\ b)(c\ d),(a\ b\ c)] = (a\ d)(b\ c)$.

1. If α contains a double-transposition $(a\ b)(c\ d)$, then $[\alpha,(a\ b\ c)] = (a\ d)(b\ c)$.
2. If α is a 3-cycle $(a\ b\ c)$, then $[\alpha,(a\ b)(c\ d)] = (a\ d)(b\ c)$.
3. If α contains two 3-cycles $(a\ b\ c)(d\ e\ f)$, then we have $[\alpha,(a\ d)(c\ f)] = (a\ d)(b\ e)$.

4. If α contains a 4-cycle $(a\ b\ c\ d)$, then $[\alpha, (a\ b)(c\ d)] = (a\ c)(b\ d)$.

5. If α contains a $(k \geq 5)$-cycle $(a_1\ \cdots\ a_k)$, then we have $[\alpha, (a_2\ a_3\ a_4)] = (a_1\ a_4\ a_3)$ and can apply case 2.

□

LEMMA 2.4. *$\forall$ double-transpositions $\alpha \in A_t$ and even $k \leq t/2$, $\exists \gamma_1, \ldots, \gamma_{\log k} \in A_t$ s.t. $[[\cdots[[\alpha, \gamma_1], \gamma_2], \cdots], \gamma_{\log k}]$ is a product of k disjoint transpositions.*

PROOF. Given $\alpha = (a\ b)(c\ d)$, we can double the number of transpositions by commutating with $\gamma = (a\ e)(b\ f)(c\ g)(d\ h)$ to get $[\alpha, \gamma] = (a\ b)(c\ d)(e\ f)(g\ h)$. Repeating this $\log(k)-1$ times (with appropriate modifications to γ) grows the number of transpositions from 2 to k. To handle k that is not a power of 2, note that any $(a\ b)(c\ d)$ can be "maintained" rather than doubled by instead commutating with $(a\ b\ c)$ as in the proof of Lemma 2.3. □

We now show how to commutate a product of disjoint transpositions to obtain either an odd-length cycle (Lemma 2.5) or the product of two even-length cycles (Lemma 2.6).

LEMMA 2.5. *Let t be even and $\beta \in A_t$ be any cycle of odd length $5 \leq k \leq t-1$. For any $\alpha \in A_t$ that is the product of either $(k-1)/2$ or $(k-3)/2$ disjoint transpositions (depending on which is even), there are $\gamma_1, \gamma_2, \gamma_3 \in A_t$ such that either $[\gamma_1^{-1}\alpha\gamma_1, \gamma_2] = \beta$ or $[[\gamma_1^{-1}\alpha\gamma_1, \gamma_2], \gamma_3] = \beta$.*

PROOF. We first show that α can be converted to a k-cycle with ≤ 2 commutations. Afterwards we observe that by first using 1 conjugation, these commutations can be made to produce the specific k-cycle β.

If $(k-1)/2$ is even, then let $\alpha := (a_1\ b_1)\cdots(a_{k'}\ b_{k'})$ be any product of $k' := (k-1)/2$ disjoint transpositions. Choosing $\gamma := (a_1\ b_1\ a_2\ b_2\ \cdots\ a_{k'}\ b_{k'}\ c) \in A_t$, where c is distinct from all $k-1$ points permuted by α, we get that

$$[\alpha, \gamma] = (a_1\ \cdots\ a_{k'}\ b_{k'}\ \cdots\ b_1\ c)$$

is a k-cycle. (We only need one commutation in this case.)

If instead $(k-3)/2$ is even (so $k \geq 7$), then let α be any product of $(k-3)/2$ disjoint transpositions. First, commutate once as above to get a $(k-2)$-cycle

$$\mu := (a_1\ \cdots\ a_{k-2}).$$

We now show that there is another $(k-2)$-cycle $\pi \in A_t$ such that $\mu\pi$ is a k-cycle. This implies that we can convert μ to a k-cycle with one more commutation, namely by commutating with $\gamma \in A_t$ such that $\gamma\mu^{-1}\gamma^{-1} = \pi$. (Such γ must exist because the set of $(k-2)$-cycles forms a conjugacy class in A_t when $t \geq k+1$.) Take the $(k-2)$-cycle

$$\pi := (a_1\ c_1\ c_2\ c_3\ a_3\ a_4\ \cdots\ a_{k-5}\ a_2)$$

where c_1, c_2, c_3 are distinct from the $k-2 \leq t-3$ points permuted by μ. Then letting $a_i \overset{\text{by } 2}{\cdots} a_j$ denote the sequence $a_i\ a_{i+2}\ a_{i+4}\ \cdots\ a_j$, we have that

$$\mu\pi = (a_2 \overset{\text{by } 2}{\cdots} a_{k-5}\ a_{k-4}\ a_{k-3}\ a_{k-2}\ c_1\ c_2\ c_3\ a_3 \overset{\text{by } 2}{\cdots} a_{k-6})$$

is a k-cycle (permuting points $a_2, \ldots, a_{k-2}, c_1, c_2, c_3$).

Having converted α to a k-cycle with ≤ 2 commutations, one might hope to then use 1 conjugation to convert to the specific k-cycle β. However when $k = t-1$, the k-cycles form two distinct conjugacy classes in A_t so we cannot do this. We instead note that the points permuted by the k-cycle depend directly on the points permuted by α (and the extra points c_i), and that products of an equal number of disjoint transpositions are conjugate in A_t. So by *first* using 1 conjugation to modify α appropriately, the above commutations yield β. □

LEMMA 2.6. *Let $t \equiv 2 \pmod 4$ and $\beta \in A_t$ be any product of two disjoint cycles of even lengths k_1, k_2. Denote $k = k_1 + k_2$. For any $\alpha \in A_t$ that is the product of either $k/2$ or $k/2-1$ disjoint transpositions (depending on which is even), there exist $\gamma_1, \gamma_2 \in A_t$ such that $\gamma_2^{-1} \cdot [\alpha, \gamma_1] \cdot \gamma_2 = \beta$.*

PROOF. We first use one commutation to convert α to the product of a k_1-cycle and a k_2-cycle, and then one conjugation to convert it to β (which here we can do without the complication mentioned at the end of Lemma 2.5). We assume that $k_1, k_2 \geq 4$, and at the end mention how to handle the two cases $k_1 = k_2 = 2$ and $k_1 = 2, k_2 = 4$.

If $k/2$ is even, let

$$\alpha := (a_1\ b_1)\cdots(a_{k'_1}\ b_{k'_1})(c_1\ d_1)\cdots(c_{k'_2}\ d_{k'_2})$$

be any product of $k/2 = k'_1 + k'_2$ disjoint transpositions, where $k'_1 := k_1/2$ and $k'_2 := k_2/2$. We will show that there exists $\pi \in A_t$ that is the product of $k/2$ disjoint transpositions such that $\alpha\pi$ is the product of a k_1-cycle and a k_2-cycle. As in Lemma 2.5, this implies that we can convert α to the desired form by commutating with $\gamma \in A_t$ such that $\gamma\alpha^{-1}\gamma^{-1} = \pi$. Define

$$\pi := \prod_{i=1}^{k'_1-1}(a_{i+1}\ b_i) \cdot \prod_{i=1}^{k'_2-2}(c_{i+1}\ d_i) \cdot (d_{k'_2-1}\ e_1)(c_{k'_2}\ d_{k'_2})(c_1\ e_2)$$

where $e_1, e_2 \in [t]$ are distinct from each point permuted by α. (Such e_1, e_2 must exist because $4|k$ and $t \equiv 2 \pmod 4$, and thus $k \leq t-2$.) Then we have that

$$\alpha\pi = (a_1\ \cdots\ a_{k'_1}\ b_{k'_1}\ \cdots\ b_1)(c_1\ \cdots\ c_{k'_2-1}\ e_1\ d_{k'_2-1}\ \cdots\ d_1\ e_2)$$

is the product of two disjoint cycles of lengths $2k'_1 = k_1$ and $2k'_2 = k_2$.

If instead $k/2-1$ is even, let

$$\alpha := (a_1\ b_1)\cdots(a_{k'_1}\ b_{k'_1})(c_1\ d_1)\cdots(c_{k'_2-1}\ d_{k'_2-1})$$

be any product of $k/2-1 = k'_1+k'_2-1$ disjoint transpositions. This time we define

$$\pi := \prod_{i=1}^{k'_1-1}(a_{i+1}\ b_i) \cdot \prod_{i=1}^{k'_2-3}(c_{i+1}\ d_i) \cdot (c_1\ c_{k'_2-1})(d_{k'_2-2}\ e_1)(d_{k'_2-1}\ e_2)$$

where again e_1, e_2 are distinct from each of the $2(k/2-1) \leq t-2$ points permuted by α (here we use $k'_1 \geq 2$, $k'_2 \geq 3$). Then we have that

$$\begin{aligned}\alpha\pi \;=\; & (a_1\ \cdots\ a_{k'_1}\ b_{k'_1}\ \cdots\ b_1) \\ & \cdot (c_1\ \cdots\ c_{k'_2-2}\ e_1\ d_{k'_2-2}\ \cdots\ d_1\ c_{k'_2-1}\ e_2\ d_{k'_2-1})\end{aligned}$$

is the product of two disjoint cycles of lengths $2k'_1 = k_1$ and $2k'_2 = k_2$.

Finally we handle the two cases $k_1 = k_2 = 2$ and $k_1 = 2, k_2 = 4$. If $k_1 = k_2 = 2$ then α and β are both double-transpositions and can be made equal with a single conjugation. Otherwise denote $\alpha = (a\ b)(c\ d)$, and note that there is another double-transposition $\pi = (c\ e)(d\ f)$ such that $\alpha\pi = (a\ b)(c\ f\ d\ e)$. Thus α can be commutated to the product of a 2-cycle and a 4-cycle, and a conjugation can make it equal to β. □

Lemma 2.2 follows immediately from Lemmas 2.3-2.6. The only cases not explicitly covered by these are when $t = 2$ in which case Lemma 2.2 is vacuous, and when β is a 3-cycle (because Lemma 2.5 only handles $(k \geq 5)$-cycles). For the latter, note that by assumption we must have $t \geq 6$. We first convert α to a 5-cycle $(a_1 \ \cdots \ a_5)$ using Lemmas 2.3-2.5, then use one commutation with $(a_2\ a_3\ a_4)$ to convert to $(a_1\ a_4\ a_3)$, and finally use one conjugation to convert to β.

3. HARDNESS FOR A SINGLE ELEMENT

In this section we show that the (1 2)(3 4)-product problem is L-complete.

THEOREM 3.1. *If for sufficiently large t there is a circuit of depth $O(\log t)$ that decides the* (1 2)(3 4)*-product problem over $(A_t)^t$, then* $\mathrm{NC}^1 = \mathrm{L}$.

We use the following theorem which is proved afterwards and says that deciding if an input vector has product = id is L-complete.

THEOREM 3.2. *If for sufficiently large t there is a circuit of depth $O(\log t)$ that decides if its input in $(A_t)^t$ has product = id, then* $\mathrm{NC}^1 = \mathrm{L}$.

To prove Theorem 3.1 from Theorem 3.2, we show how to construct a set of $t^{O(1)}$ vectors from an input vector $x \in (A_t)^t$ such that, if x has product = id then they all do, and otherwise some vector has product = (1 2)(3 4). Then we apply the circuit deciding the (1 2)(3 4)-product problem to each vector, and a depth-$O(\log t)$ OR tree to the outputs. The vectors are constructed using commutation and conjugation via Lemma 2.3.

PROOF OF THEOREM 3.1. Assume that there is a circuit C of depth $O(\log t)$ that decides the (1 2)(3 4)-product problem. We construct a circuit C' of depth $O(\log t)$ that decides if its input has product = id, which in combination with Theorem 3.2 proves the theorem.

Lemma 2.3 shows that for every id $\neq \alpha \in A_t$, there exist $\gamma_1, \gamma_2 \in A_t$ such that $\alpha' := [[\alpha, \gamma_1], \gamma_2]$ is a double-transposition and each γ_i is either a double-transposition or a 3-cycle. We observe in the claim following this proof that for every double-transposition α', there exists $\gamma_3 \in A_t$ such that $\gamma_3^{-1} \cdot \alpha' \cdot \gamma_3 = (1\ 2)(3\ 4)$ and γ_3 permutes ≤ 8 points.

For any such choice of $\gamma := (\gamma_1, \gamma_2, \gamma_3)$, let $C_\gamma : (A_t)^t \to (A_t)^t$ denote a circuit of depth $O(\log t)$ that satisfies

$$\prod_i x_i = \alpha \quad \Longrightarrow \quad \prod_i C_\gamma(x)_i = \gamma_3^{-1} \cdot [[\alpha, \gamma_1], \gamma_2] \cdot \gamma_3$$

for every $\alpha \in A_t$ and $x \in (A_t)^t$. The crucial point is that if $\prod_i x_i \neq \mathsf{id}$ then there exists γ such that $\prod_i C_\gamma(x)_i = (1\ 2)(3\ 4)$, and otherwise $\prod_i C_\gamma(x)_i = \mathsf{id}$ for every γ.

Observe that the number of double-transpositions in A_t is $\binom{t}{4} \cdot 3$, the number of 3-cycles is $\binom{t}{3} \cdot 2$, and the number of permutations that permute ≤ 8 points is $< \binom{t}{8} \cdot |A_8|$, all of which are $t^{O(1)}$. Thus on input x, C' checks in depth $O(\log t)$ if any of these $t^{O(1)}$ choices of $\gamma = (\gamma_1, \gamma_2, \gamma_3)$ satisfies $C(C_\gamma(x)) = 1$. □

CLAIM 1. *Let $t \geq 8$. For every double-transposition $\alpha \in A_t$, there exists $\gamma \in A_t$ such that $\gamma^{-1}\alpha\gamma = (1\ 2)(3\ 4)$ and γ permutes ≤ 8 points.*

PROOF. Denote $\alpha = (a\ b)(c\ d)$. Any injective function $\phi : \{1, 2, 3, 4\} \cup \{a, b, c, d\} \to [8]$ maps α and (1 2)(3 4) to two double-transpositions in A_8. Since the latter are conjugate, and since the $\gamma \in A_8$ that "witnesses" this conjugacy necessarily permutes ≤ 8 points, applying ϕ^{-1} (suitably defined) to γ yields an element in A_t that permutes ≤ 8 points and witnesses the conjugacy of α and (1 2)(3 4). □

3.1 Proof of Theorem 3.2

Recall from §1 the following encoding of branching programs by permutations. The proof of this theorem is implicit in [CM87, Prop. 1].

THEOREM 1.4 ([CM87]). *There exists $t = O(s)$ and a circuit C of depth $O(\log s)$ such that, on input (B, x) where B is a branching program of size $s \geq |x|$, C outputs a permutation $\sigma \in S_t$ such that B accepts x iff 1 and t are in the same cycle in σ's disjoint cycle representation.*

Next we use this to show that the problem of deciding if a vector over S_t has product = id is L-complete. This proof is due to Eric Allender and V. Arvind (personal communication), and we include it with their permission.

THEOREM 3.3. *If for sufficiently large t there is a circuit of depth $O(\log t)$ that decides if its input in $(S_t)^t$ has product = id, then* $\mathrm{NC}^1 = \mathrm{L}$.

PROOF. Let a string x and a branching program B of size $s = \mathrm{poly}(|x|)$ be given. Let $t = O(s)$ be as in Theorem 1.4.

We first construct t vectors in $(S_t)^t$ such that B accepts x iff the product of some vector is a permutation that maps $1 \mapsto t$. Let $\sigma \in S_t$ be given by Theorem 1.4. Notice that 1 and t are in the same cycle in σ's disjoint cycle representation iff $\exists k \leq t$ such that σ^k maps $1 \mapsto t$. Thus for $k = 1, \ldots, t$ we construct the kth vector to have product σ^k, by concatenating k copies of σ and $t - k$ copies of id. (Up to now this construction appears in [CM87].)

Next we transform $z \in (S_t)^t$ to $z' \in (S_{t+1})^{2t+2}$ satisfying

$$\prod_i z_i \text{ maps } 1 \mapsto t \quad \Longleftrightarrow \quad \prod_i z'_i = \mathsf{id}. \tag{2}$$

This is done via the map

$$z' := (z,\ (t\ \ t+1),\ z^{-1},\ (1\ \ t+1))$$

where $z^{-1} := (z_t^{-1}, \ldots, z_1^{-1}) \in (S_t)^t$ and we embed S_t into S_{t+1} in the canonical way. This is computable in depth $O(\log t)$.

To see that (2) holds, denote $\pi := \prod_i z_i$ and $\pi' := \prod_i z'_i$. If $\pi(1) \neq t$, then $\pi'(1) = t + 1$ and so $\pi' \neq \mathsf{id}$. On the other hand if $\pi(1) = t$, then it can be checked that $\pi'(1) = 1$ and $\pi'(t+1) = t+1$, and it is clear that $\pi'(j) = j$ for $1 < j < t+1$ since $\pi(j)$ is not touched by $(t\ \ t+1)$ and j is not touched by $(1\ \ t+1)$.

Thus we have constructed t vectors in $(S_{t+1})^{2t+2}$ such that B accepts x iff some vector has product = id. We can reduce the vectors' length to $t + 1$ in depth $O(\log t)$ by multiplying adjacent permutations. Finally, applying the circuit in the assumption of the theorem and an OR-tree yields a circuit of depth $O(\log t)$ that decides if B accepts x. □

To conclude the proof of Theorem 3.2, we observe that there is an embedding $M : S_t \to A_{t+2}$ computable in NC^1 that preserves the identity product. M is defined by $M(\alpha) := \alpha$ if α is even and $M(\alpha) := \alpha \cdot (t+1 \ \ t+2)$ if α is odd. It can be checked that this is a homomorphism, and thus $\prod_i x_i = \mathsf{id} \Leftrightarrow \prod_i M(x_i) = \mathsf{id}$. Computing M requires deciding if $\alpha \in S_t$ is odd or even, which can be done in depth $O(\log t)$ by checking if there are an odd or even number of pairs $i < j \leq t$ such that $\alpha(i) > j$.

4. PROOF OF COROLLARY 1.3

Theorem 1.2 is immediate from Theorems 2.1 and 3.1. We now prove Corollary 1.3 from Theorem 1.2 using the random self-reducibility of group products (cf. [MV13, Thm. 3.9]).

THEOREM 1.2. *Assume that there is a circuit family C of depth $O(\log t)$ such that for sufficiently large t, there exists $\alpha \in A_t$ such that C decides the α-product problem over $(A_t)^t$. Then $\mathrm{NC}^1 = \mathrm{L}$.*

COROLLARY 1.3. *If $\mathrm{NC}^1 \neq \mathrm{L}$, then NC^1 is $(t^{-\omega(1)}, \alpha)$-fooled by $(A_t)^t$ for infinitely many t and all $\alpha \in A_t$.*

More precisely, if $\mathrm{NC}^1 \neq \mathrm{L}$ then for all k, infinitely many t, and all $\alpha \in A_t$, the class of NC^1 circuits with depth $k \log t$ and output length $k \log t$ is (t^{-k}, α)-fooled by $(A_t)^t$.

PROOF OF COROLLARY 1.3. Assume that there exists k such that for sufficiently large t, there exists $\alpha \in A_t$ and a circuit C of depth $k \log t$ such that $\Delta(C(D_\alpha), C(D_{\mathsf{id}})) \geq t^{-k}$, where recall that D_g is the uniform distribution over $\{x \in (A_t)^t \mid \prod_i x_i = g\}$.

Let $S \subseteq \{0,1\}^{k \log t}$ be the set that maximizes $\Pr[C(D_\alpha) \in S] - \Pr[C(D_{\mathsf{id}}) \in S]$, and note that checking $x \in S$ can be done in depth $O(\log t)$. Thus, there exists $C' : (A_t)^t \to \{0,1\}$ of depth $O(\log t)$ such that

$$\Pr[C'(D_\alpha) = 1] - \Pr[C'(D_{\mathsf{id}}) = 1] \geq t^{-k}. \quad (3)$$

Define $\epsilon_\alpha := \Pr[C'(D_\alpha) = 1]$ and $\epsilon_{\mathsf{id}} := \Pr[C'(D_{\mathsf{id}}) = 1]$, and note that $\epsilon_\alpha \geq t^{-k}$.

Let C'' be the randomized circuit of depth $O(\log t)$ that computes as follows on input $x \in (A_t)^t$. First for $m := t^{3k+3}/\epsilon_\alpha = t^{O(k)}$, C'' samples $z_1, \ldots, z_m \in (A_t)^t$ independently from D_g where $g := \prod_i x_i \in \{\alpha, \mathsf{id}\}$. This is done by choosing uniform $r_1, \ldots, r_{t-1} \in A_t$ for each $i \leq m$ and computing $z_i := (x_1 r_1, \ r_1^{-1} x_2 r_2, \ \ldots, \ r_{t-1}^{-1} x_t)$. Then C'' outputs α if

$$(1 - 1/(2t^k)) \cdot m\epsilon_\alpha \ \leq \ \sum_{i=1}^{m} C'(z_i) \ \leq \ (1 + 1/(2t^k)) \cdot m\epsilon_\alpha$$

and otherwise outputs id.

We prove the following claim afterwards.

CLAIM 2. *For all $x \in (A_t)^t$ such that $\prod_i x_i \in \{\alpha, id\}$, we have $\Pr[C''(x) = \prod_i x_i] > 1 - |A_t|^{-t}$ over the random coins of C''.*

This implies the theorem, as follows. By a union bound there is a way to fix the random coins of C'' such that $C''(x) = \prod_i x_i$ for every x satsifying $\prod_i x_i \in \{\alpha, \mathsf{id}\}$. This solves the α-product problem in NC^1, and thus by Theorem 1.2 we have $\mathrm{NC}^1 = \mathrm{L}$. □

PROOF OF CLAIM 2. Denote $X := \sum_{i=1}^m C'(z_i)$, and $\mu := \mathbb{E}[X]$. Note that $|A_t|^t = (t!/2)^t < 2^{t^3}$.

Fix x, and first assume $\prod_i x_i = \alpha$ which means $\mu = m\epsilon_\alpha = t^{3k+3}$. Then

$$\begin{aligned} \Pr[C''(x) = \alpha] &= \Pr\left[|X - \mu| \leq \mu/(2t^k)\right] \\ &\geq 1 - 2e^{-\mu \cdot t^{-3k}} \\ &\geq 1 - 2^{-t^3} \end{aligned}$$

by a Chernoff bound.

Now assume $\prod_i x_i = \mathsf{id}$. Then $\mu = m\epsilon_{\mathsf{id}}$, and since $\epsilon_\alpha/\epsilon_{\mathsf{id}} \geq 1 + 1/t^k$ by (3), we have $(1 - 1/(2t^k)) \cdot m\epsilon_\alpha \geq \mu(1 + 1/(3t^k))$. Then using another Chernoff bound, we have

$$\begin{aligned} \Pr[C''(x) = \mathsf{id}] &\geq \Pr[X \geq \mu(1 + 1/(3t^k))] \\ &\geq 1 - e^{-\mu \cdot t^{-3k}} \\ &\geq 1 - 2^{-t^3}. \end{aligned}$$

□

Acknowledgements.

We are grateful to Eric Allender and V. Arvind for sharing the proof of Theorem 3.3 and allowing us to include it here, and to Emanuele Viola for helpful discussions and comments on a previous draft of this paper.

5. REFERENCES

[Bar89] David A. Mix Barrington. Bounded-width polynomial-size branching programs recognize exactly those languages in NC^1. *J. of Computer and System Sciences*, 38(1):150–164, 1989.

[BC92] Michael Ben-Or and Richard Cleve. Computing algebraic formulas using a constant number of registers. *SIAM J. Comput.*, 21(1):54–58, 1992.

[BGI+01] Boaz Barak, Oded Goldreich, Russell Impagliazzo, Steven Rudich, Amit Sahai, Salil P. Vadhan, and Ke Yang. On the (im)possibility of obfuscating programs. In *Int. Cryptology Conf. (CRYPTO)*, pages 1–18, 2001.

[BT88] David A. Mix Barrington and Denis Thèrien. Finite monoids and the fine structure of NC^1. *J. ACM*, 35(4):941–952, 1988.

[CL94] Jin-yi Cai and Richard J. Lipton. Subquadratic simulations of balanced formulae by branching programs. *SIAM J. on Computing*, 23(3):563–572, 1994.

[Cle91] Richard Cleve. Towards optimal simulations of formulas by bounded-width programs. *Computational Complexity*, 1:91–105, 1991.

[CM87] Stephen A. Cook and Pierre McKenzie. Problems complete for deterministic logarithmic space. *J. Algorithms*, 8(3):385–394, 1987.

[DF12] Stefan Dziembowski and Sebastian Faust. Leakage-resilient circuits without computational assumptions. In *Theory of Cryptography Conf. (TCC)*, pages 230–247, 2012.

[DI06] Bella Dubrov and Yuval Ishai. On the randomness complexity of efficient sampling. In *38th ACM Symposium on Theory of Computing (STOC)*, pages 711–720, 2006.

[FRR+10] Sebastian Faust, Tal Rabin, Leonid Reyzin, Eran Tromer, and Vinod Vaikuntanathan. Protecting circuits from leakage: the computationally-bounded and noisy cases. In *Int. Conf. on the Theory and Applications of Cryptographic Techniques (EUROCRYPT)*, pages 135–156, 2010.

[GR10] Shafi Goldwasser and Guy N. Rothblum. Securing computation against continuous leakage. In *Int. Cryptology Conf. (CRYPTO)*, pages 59–79, 2010.

[GR12] Shafi Goldwasser and Guy N. Rothblum. How to compute in the presence of leakage. In *IEEE Symp. on Foundations of Computer Science (FOCS)*, 2012.

[IL95] Neil Immerman and Susan Landau. The complexity of iterated multiplication. *Inf. Comput.*, 116(1):103–116, 1995.

[ISW03] Yuval Ishai, Amit Sahai, and David Wagner. Private circuits: Securing hardware against probing attacks. In *Int. Cryptology Conf. (CRYPTO)*, pages 463–481, 2003.

[JV10] Ali Juma and Yevgeniy Vahlis. Protecting cryptographic keys against continual leakage. In *Int. Cryptology Conf. (CRYPTO)*, pages 41–58, 2010.

[Kil88] Joe Kilian. Founding cryptography on oblivious transfer. In *ACM Symp. on the Theory of Computing (STOC)*, pages 20–31, 1988.

[MV13] Eric Miles and Emanuele Viola. Shielding circuits with groups. In *ACM Symp. on the Theory of Computing (STOC)*, 2013.

[Rot12] Guy N. Rothblum. How to compute under AC^0 leakage without secure hardware. In *Int. Cryptology Conf. (CRYPTO)*, pages 552–569, 2012.

[Wil09] Robert A. Wilson. *The Finite Simple Groups*. Springer, 2009.

Building One-Time Memories from Isolated Qubits

(Extended Abstract)

Yi-Kai Liu
Applied and Computational Mathematics Division
National Institute of Standards and Technology
Gaithersburg, MD, USA
yi-kai.liu@nist.gov

ABSTRACT

One-time memories (OTM's) are simple tamper-resistant cryptographic devices, which can be used to implement *one-time programs*, a very general form of software protection and program obfuscation. Here we investigate the possibility of building OTM's using quantum mechanical devices. It is known that OTM's cannot exist in a fully-quantum world or in a fully-classical world. Instead, we propose a new model based on *isolated qubits* — qubits that can only be accessed using *local operations and classical communication* (LOCC). This model combines a quantum resource (single-qubit measurements) with a classical restriction (on communication between qubits), and can be implemented using current technologies, such as nitrogen vacancy centers in diamond. In this model, we construct OTM's that are information-theoretically secure against one-pass LOCC adversaries that use 2-outcome measurements.

Our construction resembles Wiesner's old idea of quantum conjugate coding, implemented using random error-correcting codes; our proof of security uses entropy chaining to bound the supremum of a suitable empirical process. In addition, we conjecture that our random codes can be replaced by some class of efficiently-decodable codes, to get computationally-efficient OTM's that are secure against computationally-bounded LOCC adversaries.

In addition, we construct data-hiding states, which allow an LOCC sender to encode an $(n - O(1))$-bit messsage into n qubits, such that at most half of the message can be extracted by a one-pass LOCC receiver, but the whole message can be extracted by a general quantum receiver.

Categories and Subject Descriptors

F.1.1 [**Computation by Abstract Devices**]: Models of Computation; E.3 [**Data Encryption**]; E.4 [**Coding and Information Theory**]

ITCS'14, January 12–14, 2014, Princeton, New Jersey, USA.

ACM 978-1-4503-2698-8/14/01
http://dx.doi.org/10.1145/2554797.2554823.

Keywords

Quantum computation; cryptography; one-time programs; oblivious transfer; local operations and classical communication; data-hiding states; conjugate coding.

1. INTRODUCTION

One-time memories (OTM's) are a simple type of tamper-resistant cryptographic hardware [1]. An OTM device behaves as follows: one party (Alice) can write two messages $s, t \in \{0,1\}^k$ into the device, and then give the device to another party (Bob); after receiving the device, Bob can then choose to read either s or t, but not both. An OTM is far simpler than a general-purpose processor, but it can be used to implement sophisticated forms of secure computation, such as one-time programs[1] [1, 2, 3] (and, more recently, quantum one-time programs [4]). The remarkable fact about these constructions is that the OTM is the *only* piece of hardware that has to be tamper-resistant; everything else consists of cryptographic software running on untrusted general-purpose processors.

Intuitively, it seems much easier to build an OTM, rather than a general-purpose tamper-proof processor. Indeed, there are many practical approaches to building such devices. However, from a theoretical perspective, it would be nice if one could build *provably-secure* OTM's based on some clear *physical principle*, in the same way that one can build provably-secure encryption and signature schemes based on assumptions that certain problems are computationally intractable. But this line of investigation runs into a number of obstacles. OTM's cannot exist in a fully classical world, because information can always be copied without destroying it. One might hope to build OTM's in a quantum world, where the no-cloning principle limits an adversary's ability to copy an unknown quantum state. However, this is also impossible, because an OTM can be used to perform oblivious transfer with information-theoretic security, and there are strong no-go theorems for quantum oblivious transfer, quantum bit commitment, and many other kinds of two-party secure computation in a quantum world [5, 6, 7, 8].

[1] A one-time program is a package of hardware and software that is prepared by Alice and given to Bob. It can compute a function f (chosen by Alice when she prepares the package) on a single input x provided by Bob (when he runs the package). During its execution, the one-time program behaves like a black box, i.e., Bob learns nothing about its internal functioning. After running once, the one-time program "self-destructs," i.e., it stops functioning, and no more information can be extracted from it.

One way around these no-go theorems is to try to construct protocols that are secure against a restricted class of quantum adversaries. The adversaries in the no-go theorems (that break quantum bit commitment, oblivious transfer, etc.) seem to require the full power of a quantum computer, i.e., the ability to perform arbitrary quantum circuits with entangling gates. However, a number of authors have shown protocols for bit commitment and other functionalities that are secure against adversaries who can only perform k-local measurements [9], or adversaries who only have bounded or noisy quantum storage [10, 11, 12, 13].

In this paper, we propose a new model of this type, called the *isolated qubits* model. This model allows the adversary to perform *local operations and classical communication* (LOCC); intuitively, this is the class of operations that can generate classical correlations between the qubits, but not entanglement. We then aim to construct OTM's that are secure in this model.

The main challenge in this paper arises from the fact that OTM's are non-interactive: after Alice gives the OTM to Bob, there is no further communication between them. Thus, they cannot use standard cryptographic tools, such as privacy amplification, to give Bob an advantage over the adversary. This makes OTM's very different from most other protocols for bit-commitment and oblivious transfer. [2]

For our OTM's, we instead use an old idea called *conjugate coding*, which is due to Wiesner [16], and which works in this non-interactive setting. Conjugate coding uses quantum states that are not entangled, hence they can be prepared by honest parties in our model. Wiesner argued that conjugate coding *is* secure against non-adaptive adversaries who can only perform single-qubit destructive measurements, but that it is *not* secure against adversaries who can perform many-qubit entangled measurements. However, apart from those two extreme cases, little seems to be known about the security of conjugate coding. It is a natural question, then, whether conjugate coding *is* secure against the more general class of LOCC adversaries (which may be adaptive, and may perform repeated weak measurements on the same qubit). If the answer turned out to be yes, this would be a fairly realistic scenario in which conjugate coding provides useful security.

Unfortunately, proving good upper bounds on the power of LOCC adversaries is a long-standing open problem. Previous results in this area include demonstrations of "nonlocality without entanglement" (NLWE) [17] (see [18] for a recent survey), and constructions of data-hiding states [19, 20, 21, 22]. However, these results do not seem to apply to our OTM's. We are only able to prove partial results on the security of our OTM's, but given that strong bounds of this type are quite rare, we believe this is significant progress.

On a conceptual level, we show that information can be hidden from an LOCC adversary in a stronger and more sophisticated way, such that the adversary can retrieve one of the messages contained in the OTM, but not both. This contrasts with previous work on NLWE and data-hiding states. On a technical level, we prove security of our OTM's against "1-pass" LOCC adversaries (which may be adaptive, but are still restricted to destructive single-qubit measurements). This extends Wiesner's original claim, though not all the way to general LOCC adversaries. The techniques used to prove this result are quite nontrivial: we construct our OTM's using random codes, and we prove security using entropy chaining (also called Dudley's inequality for suprema of empirical processes [23], or "using correlations to beat the union bound").

1.1 Isolated qubits

In this paper we consider a model with *isolated qubits*, where all parties are only allowed to perform local quantum operations (on each qubit) and classical communication (between qubits). This class of operations is known as *n-partite LOCC*, where n is the number of qubits. (See Section 2 for details.) We will construct an OTM that consists of n isolated qubits. When Alice prepares the device, she can perform n-partite LOCC operations on the qubits, and likewise, when Bob reads the device, he can perform n-partite LOCC operations on the qubits. However, there is no communication or interaction between Alice and Bob, apart from the step where Alice gives the device (containing the n qubits) to Bob.

Note that this is a different scenario from most previous work on the power of LOCC operations [17, 19], where Alice and Bob share some *bipartite* quantum system, and a "local operation" refers to an arbitrary operation on either Alice's subsystem or Bob's subsystem, and "classical communication" refers to communication between Alice and Bob.

Our model of isolated qubits is motivated by recent experimental work on nitrogen vacancy centers in diamond [24]. Nitrogen vacancy (NV) centers can be used to implement single qubits that have relatively long coherence times (on the order of seconds or minutes), at room temperature in a solid-state material. Individual NV centers can be read out and manipulated optically, but it is difficult to perform entangling operations on pairs of NV centers, due to variations in their emission spectra. (Recent experiments have demonstrated entanglement between distant NV centers [25], but for our purposes there are natural ways of designing a device to prevent such entangling operations.) NV centers have been studied in connection with quantum money [26], and they are a plausible candidate to implement our model of isolated qubits.

Isolated qubits are similar (but not directly comparable) to Salvail's k-local measurement model [9]. In Salvail's model, the adversary can perform entangled measurements on up to k qubits, where k is proportional to n; however, the adversary is only allowed to perform projective measurements, not repeated weak measurements (which are allowed in LOCC).

We also argue that isolated qubits can exist in a world with quantum computers. Isolated qubits are simply designed to satisfy different requirements than the qubits in a quantum computer. More specifically, recall that in any quantum device, there is a tradeoff between two conflicting requirements: first, protecting the device from unwanted interactions with the environment, such as noise and decoherence; and second, providing strong coherent interactions

[2]More precisely, the difference is that OTM's are asynchronous, in the sense that there is only one message from Alice to Bob. In contrast, most other protocols (even those that only require one-way communication rather than two-way interaction [14]) still use a sequence of two messages from Alice to Bob, in such a way that any dishonest action occurs before the second message, so that the second message can be used to perform privacy amplification. A notable exception is the recent work [15], which considers a situation that is fully asynchronous, with a non-adaptive adversary.

between the device and an external probe, in order to perform some useful task. Isolated qubits represent one possible compromise between these requirements, namely strong protection from noise and decoherence, and only classical (not entangling) gates and measurements. (Note that one cannot teleport information to or from an isolated qubit.) In contrast, quantum computers and quantum memories must satisfy both of the above requirements, which is a different, possibly more difficult task. (Indeed, the bounded / noisy storage model [10, 13] assumes that it is hard to build large, high-fidelity quantum memories.)

In some sense, our isolated qubits model is complementary to the bounded / noisy storage model. In the bounded / noisy storage model, the honest parties Alice and Bob use qubits that may allow entangled measurements, but cannot be stored for a long time. In our model, Alice and Bob use qubits that can be stored for a long time, but do not allow entangled measurements.

1.2 Data-hiding states

Our first main result is a construction for data hiding states (see Section 3). These states are simpler to analyze than our one-time memories, and they demonstrate the basic point that a sender can use LOCC operations to "hide" information from a LOCC receiver. We consider a system of n isolated qubits, and we construct a set of $2^{\tilde{n}}$ states, where $\tilde{n} := n - \Theta(1)$, by sampling independently at random from the set $\{|0\rangle, |1\rangle, |+\rangle, |-\rangle\}^{\otimes n}$. (Here, $|+\rangle := (|0\rangle + |1\rangle)/\sqrt{2}$ and $|-\rangle := (|0\rangle - |1\rangle)/\sqrt{2}$ are the Hadamard basis states.) These states are all tensor products of single-qubit pure states, hence they can be prepared using only LOCC operations.

First, we show that these states can be distinguished almost perfectly using an entangled quantum measurement (the "pretty good measurement," see Section 3.1). Then we consider "one-pass" LOCC measurement strategies, i.e., measurement strategies that measure each qubit at most once. (For comparison, a general LOCC measurement strategy may perform many weak measurements on the same qubit. Note that bounding the power of general LOCC measurement strategies is a difficult open problem.) We show that a one-pass LOCC measurement strategy using 2-outcome measurements can extract at most $\approx n/2$ bits of information about which state was prepared[3] (see Section 3.2). Note that there exists a trivial LOCC measurement strategy that can extract $n/2$ bits of information, by measuring each qubit in the $\{|0\rangle, |1\rangle\}$ basis, for instance; hence the above bound is tight. In addition, we show that a one-pass LOCC measurement strategy using q-outcome measurements (for any constant q) can extract at most $\approx (0.7067)n$ bits of information (see Section 3.3).

The main point of this data-hiding result is to develop the proof techniques for our one-time memories, which will use a similar idea of sampling random states from the set $\{|0\rangle, |1\rangle, |+\rangle, |-\rangle\}^{\otimes n}$, but will restrict access to the data in a more subtle way. We use two proof techniques: *entropy chaining*, and a bound on the *collision entropy*. We will describe these techniques below.

In addition, our data-hiding states may also be of independent interest, as they differ from previous work in some significant ways. On one hand, most previous constructions of data-hiding states [19, 20, 21, 22] are secure against a much stronger class of LOCC adversaries (with infinite LOCC rather than one-pass LOCC). On the other hand, almost all of those constructions use entangled states, which cannot be realized in our isolated qubits model. (An exception is [20], which uses separable Werner states. This approach too is quite different from ours.)

We remark that another line of work has focused on "nonlocality without entanglement" [17], where one considers a bipartite system, and one constructs sets of separable states that are orthogonal but cannot be perfectly distinguished using LOCC; see [18] for a recent survey. Finally, there are a number of elegant results about unambiguous state discrimination using multipartite LOCC, which are applicable when the number of states to be distinguished is relatively small [27, 28, 29].

1.3 Entropy chaining

One of our proof techniques is "entropy chaining," aka Dudley's inequality for empirical processes [23]. This is similar to a union bound over the set of all one-pass adaptive LOCC measurement strategies, but it takes advantage of the positive correlations between the performance of strategies that are similar. This approach gives a tight bound for adversaries that use 2-outcome measurements, but it performs poorly when applied to adversaries that use q-outcome measurements for large q (see Section 3.2).

The basic idea is as follows. Let E denote the random choices made in the construction of our data-hiding states. Let the resulting collection of data-hiding states be denoted by $|E(u)\rangle$ (for all $u \in \{0,1\}^{\tilde{n}}$); note that the description of these states is public information. We imagine a game, where first an adversary chooses some measurement strategy M; then a referee chooses $u \in \{0,1\}^{\tilde{n}}$ uniformly at random, and prepares the state $|E(u)\rangle$; and finally the adversary performs the measurement strategy M on $|E(u)\rangle$, and outputs a string of measurement outcomes z. The adversary's goal is to maximize the mutual information $I(Z;U)$ (where Z and U are random variables containing the strings z and u). Note that $I(Z;U)$ is computed by averaging over the referee's choice of u and the adversary's measurement outcomes z; however, we do not average over the random choices E used to construct the data-hiding states, or the adversary's measurement strategy M. Thus $I(Z;U)$ is a random variable that depends on both E and M.

As a first step, note that if we fix a particular adversary strategy, then with high probability over E, $I(Z;U) \approx n/2$. To see this, write $I(Z;U) = H(Z) - H(Z|U)$; note that for 1-pass LOCC strategies using 2-outcome measurements, $H(Z) \leq n$; and note that $H(Z|U) = 2^{-\tilde{n}} \sum_u H(Z|U = u)$ is a sum of independent random variables with respect to E; hence by Hoeffding's inequality, with high probability over E, $H(Z|U)$ will be close to its expected value, which is roughly $n/2$.

We want to prove a much stronger statement, however. We want to estimate the probability (over the random choice of E) that the *best* LOCC strategy (chosen with knowledge of the states $|E(u)\rangle$) can extract more than $n/2$ bits of information about U. To achieve this, we can try to use the union bound over all possible LOCC strategies. However, note that adaptive LOCC strategies can be described by *decision trees*, and in the case of 1-pass LOCC strategies using 2-outcome measurements, there are $2^{\Theta(2^n)}$ such decision

[3]Formally, we upper-bound the Shannon mutual information.

trees. Meanwhile, the quantity $H(Z|U)$ is a sum of only $2^{\tilde{n}}$ independent random variables, so the failure probability in Hoeffding's inequality is only exponentially small in n, not doubly-exponentially small in n. Thus the union bound fails to give a useful result.

Entropy chaining fixes this problem by exploiting correlations among the different strategies — the fact that two strategies that make similar measurements will produce similar results, and hence their failure probabilities do not add up in the worst-case fashion described by the union bound. The term "entropy chaining" refers to the fact that one must use a sequence of these arguments, to capture both strong correlations between very similar strategies and weak correlations between less-similar strategies. Each such argument involves covering the set of strategies with an ε-net at a different resolution, which can be interpreted as bounding the entropy of the set.

1.4 Bounding the collision entropy

Our second proof technique involves calculating the collision entropy of the unknown message U, conditioned on every possible sequence of measurement outcomes. This approach does not give a tight bound, but it works fairly well for all values of q (see Section 3.3).

Here we take a different perspective: instead of considering LOCC measurement strategies (which correspond to decision trees), we consider measurement outcomes (which correspond to tensor products of single-qubit POVM elements). That is, a measurement outcome is described by a POVM element of the form $M_A = \bigotimes_{i\in A} M_i$, where $A \subset [n]$ is the set of qubits that were measured, and M_i is a POVM element acting on qubit i. (Measurement outcomes have this form when the adversary performs separable measurements, which include LOCC measurements as a special case; but this does not hold when the adversary performs entangled measurements.)

The basic idea is to fix some measurement outcome M_A, then lower-bound the collision entropy $H_2(U|M_A)$ (with high probability over E), and then use the union bound over all measurement outcomes M_A. To lower-bound $H_2(U|M_A)$, we proceed as follows. Essentially we want to upper-bound the collision probability

$$\begin{aligned}\Pr[\mathrm{col}|M_A] &= \sum_u \Pr[U=u|M_A]^2 \\ &= 4^{-\tilde{n}} \Pr[M_A]^{-2} \sum_u \Pr[M_A|U=u]^2.\end{aligned} \tag{1}$$

To do this, we note that both $\Pr[M_A] = 2^{-\tilde{n}} \sum_u \Pr[M_A|U = u]$ and $\sum_u \Pr[M_A|U=u]^2$ are sums of independent random variables (with respect to E), and we use large deviation bounds. Finally, to take the union bound over all M_A, we note that we only have to include those M_A that are of tensor product form, hence the number of M_A is exponential in $|A|$, rather than doubly exponential in $|A|$.

1.5 One-time memories

We now describe our construction for one-time memories (see Section 4.2). We consider a system of n isolated qubits, and we pick two random error-correcting codes, $C : \{0,1\}^k \to \{0,1\}^n$ and $D : \{0,1\}^k \to \{0,1\}^n$. (That is, each codeword is chosen independently and uniformly at random in $\{0,1\}^n$.) Given two messages s and t in $\{0,1\}^k$, we prepare each qubit i (for $i = 1, 2, \ldots, n$) as follows. Let $C(s)_i$ and $D(t)_i$ denote the i'th bit in the strings $C(s)$ and $D(t)$, respectively. We prepare the i'th qubit in a pure state that has the following properties: first, if the qubit is measured in the $\{|0\rangle, |1\rangle\}$ basis, the outcome is more likely to be $|0\rangle$ if $C(s)_i = 0$, and $|1\rangle$ if $C(s)_i = 1$; and second, if the qubit is measured in the $\{|+\rangle, |-\rangle\}$ basis, the outcome is more likely to be $|+\rangle$ if $D(t)_i = 0$, and $|-\rangle$ if $D(t)_i = 1$. This is similar to Wiesner's idea of quantum conjugate coding [16]. We refer to these states as one-time memory (OTM) states.

It is straightforward to check that these OTM states can be prepared using only LOCC operations, and that an honest party can recover either s or t using only LOCC operations (see Section 4.3).

However, the security of these OTM states is somewhat problematic. For instance, an LOCC adversary can always obtain partial information about both s and t, by measuring some of the qubits in the $\{|0\rangle, |1\rangle\}$ basis and some of the qubits in the $\{|+\rangle, |-\rangle\}$ basis. Also, these OTM states can "leak" extra information: there is a one-pass LOCC strategy that can extract $n/2 \approx (1.2528)k$ bits of information about s and t. [4] To address this issue, we define a notion of a "leaky OTM," which we believe is a useful first step towards constructing one-time programs from realistic physical devices (see Section 4.1).

We then present some evidence that our OTM states satisfy this notion of "leaky security". Essentially, we prove that our OTM states satisfy a weaker notion of security, in which the smoothed min-entropy H_∞^ε is replaced by the Shannon entropy H (see Section 4.2). We believe it should be possible to strengthen this result to show "leaky security." In particular, we note that certain parts of the proof already use the collision entropy H_2, which is stronger than H, and implies bounds on H_∞^ε.

Our technical result is that no 1-pass LOCC adversary using 2-outcome measurements can extract more than $\approx (1.9189)k < 2k$ bits of information about (s,t) (see Section 4.4). (We believe that this constant factor can be improved.) The proof uses a two-stage argument that applies both the collision entropy bound and entropy chaining; we will describe this below.

We remark that there is a subtle point involving the difference between 1-pass LOCC measurements and general LOCC measurements, when applied to our OTM's based on conjugate coding. For our OTM's, there is a 1-pass LOCC measurement that can reconstruct s (and there is a similar measurement for t). Also, Winter's "gentle measurement lemma" [39] implies that, if there is a *nondestructive* measurement that reconstructs s, and there is a similar measurement for t, then there is a measurement that reconstructs both s and t simultaneously. However, this does *not* imply the existence of a 2-pass LOCC measurement that can reconstruct both s and t simultaneously.

The reason is that, in order to reconstruct s (or t) using 1-pass LOCC operations, the measurement must be destructive (i.e., one must perform a projective measurement on each qubit, obtain a string of classical measurement outcomes, and then run the classical decoding algorithm). If

[4] Let $|\alpha_{C(s)_i D(t)_i}\rangle$ be the state used to encode $C(s)_i$ and $D(t)_i$ into qubit i (see Section 3 for the precise definition). It turns out that $|\alpha_{00}\rangle$ and $|\alpha_{11}\rangle$ are orthogonal, and likewise, $|\alpha_{01}\rangle$ and $|\alpha_{10}\rangle$ are orthogonal. So, a one-pass LOCC strategy that measures each qubit in the basis $\{|\alpha_{00}\rangle, |\alpha_{11}\rangle\}$ can extract $n/2 \approx (1.2528)k$ bits of information.

one wants to reconstruct s (or t) using a nondestructive measurement, one must use entangling operations (i.e., one must run the classical decoding algorithm on a superposition of many different inputs). Thus the gentle measurement lemma cannot be applied to these particular 1-pass LOCC measurements, and it does not rule out the possibility that our OTM's are secure against 2-pass or general LOCC adversaries.

1.6 Two-stage argument

Let us denote our OTM states by $|E(s,t)\rangle$ (for $s,t \in \{0,1\}^k$). These states resemble the data-hiding states studied previously, but there are some important differences. First, there are fewer OTM states (there are 4^k states in dimension 2^n, where $k \approx (0.3991)n$), hence the states are easier to distinguish. Also, the OTM states are not constructed independently at random: there are 4^k states $|E(s,t)\rangle$, but only $2 \cdot 2^k$ independent random variables (consisting of the codewords $C(s)$ and $D(t)$). As a result, there are positive correlations between states $|E(s,t)\rangle$ that have the same s but different t.

To deal with the correlations among the states $|E(s,t)\rangle$, we use large-deviation bounds for sums of locally dependent random variables [41, 38]. However, these large-deviation bounds are not as strong as the ones we had for data-hiding states, and so neither of our proof techniques (i.e., entropy chaining and collision entropy) gives a useful result by itself.

To get around this difficulty, we combine the two techniques in sequence. Let S and T be random variables containing the messages s and t. We use the collision entropy technique to analyze the first few steps taken by the adversary; this yields a lower-bound on $H_2(S,T|M_A)$, for any measurement outcome M_A observed by the adversary thus far. Then we use entropy chaining to prove bounds on the adversary's subsequent steps; this yields an upper-bound on $I(\tilde{Z};S,T|M_A)$, where $\tilde{Z}$ is the adversary's output from subsequent measurements. It is necessary to apply the two techniques in this order, because the collision entropy technique yields an upper-bound on $\sum_{st} \Pr[S=s,T=t|M_A]^2$; this helps us to get stronger large-deviation bounds for the quantity

$$H(\tilde{Z}|S,T,M_A) = \sum_{st} H(\tilde{Z}|S=s,T=t,M_A)\Pr[S=s,T=t|M_A], \quad (2)$$

which is crucial for entropy chaining.

1.7 Outlook

We think it is an interesting challenge to develop our OTM construction into a useful primitive for secure computation. In this paper we have taken a first step, by constructing OTM's based on isolated qubits, and analyzing their security in a simple information-theoretic framework (e.g., using random codes in the OTM's, and describing the adversary's knowledge in terms of mutual information). The next step is to make our OTM's efficient, and prove a stronger security guarantee that allows composition of OTM's to implement one-time programs.

First, we conjecture that the random codes C and D can be replaced by some class of efficiently-decodable codes, to construct computationally-efficient one-time memories that are secure against computationally-bounded LOCC adversaries. For comparison, note that the present construction, while not computationally efficient, also makes no assumptions about the adversary's computational power, i.e., it is secure against one-pass LOCC adversaries that have unbounded computational power.

Second, we conjecture that our OTM's satisfy a particular notion of "leaky security," which we believe will be useful for constructing one-time programs. This notion of "leaky security" uses the smoothed min-entropy to quantify the adversary's uncertainty about the messages s and t. Here we presented bounds that support this conjecture, using the Shannon entropy and the collision entropy.

Finally, it is an open problem to better understand the security of Wiesner's conjugate coding technique against general LOCC strategies (rather than the one-pass LOCC strategies considered here).

1.8 Notation

For any integer $n \geq 1$, we define the set $[n] := \{1,2,\dots,n\}$. For any vector $v \in \mathbb{C}^n$, we define the ℓ_2 norm $\|v\|_2 = (\sum_i |v_i|^2)^{1/2}$.

For any matrix $M \in \mathbb{C}^{m\times n}$, with singular values $\lambda_1(M) \geq \lambda_2(M) \geq \cdots$, we define the operator norm $\|M\| := \lambda_1(M)$ and the Frobenius norm $\|M\|_F := (\sum_i \lambda_i(M)^2)^{1/2}$. The notation $M \succeq 0$ means M is positive semidefinite.

An ε-net E (for a set S, with respect to some metric d) is a subset $E \subseteq S$ such that, for all $x \in S$, there exists some $x' \in E$, such that $d(x,x') \leq \varepsilon$. The covering number $N(S,d,\varepsilon)$ is the minimum cardinality of any such ε-net E.

Logarithms are denoted as follows: $\ln(\cdot)$ is the natural logarithm, $\lg(\cdot)$ is the base-2 logarithm, and $\log(\cdot)$ is the logarithm when the base does not matter (because the log appears inside a big-O expression).

The Hamming distance between two binary strings $s,t \in \{0,1\}^n$ is denoted $d_H(s,t)$.

The L_1 or total variation distance between two random variables X and X' is denoted by $\Delta(X,X') = \sum_x |\Pr[X=x] - \Pr[X'=x]|$.

The Shannon entropy of a random variable X is denoted by $H(X) = -\sum_x \Pr[X=x]\lg\Pr[X=x]$, and the mutual information between random variables X and Y is denoted by $I(X;Y) = H(X) - H(X|Y)$. (Note that I without parentheses denotes the identity operator. It will be clear from the context which one is meant.)

The Renyi collision entropy of X is denoted $H_2(X) = -\lg(\sum_x \Pr[X=x]^2)$. The min-entropy of X is given by $H_\infty(X) = -\lg(\max_x \Pr[X=x])$, and the smoothed min-entropy of X is given by $H_\infty^\varepsilon(X) = \max_{X' : \Delta(X,X')\leq\varepsilon} H_\infty(X')$.

2. ISOLATED QUBITS, AND LOCC MEASUREMENT STRATEGIES

In this section we introduce the model of isolated qubits, and the class of LOCC measurement strategies. Essentially, in a system of n isolated qubits, the allowed operations are local (single-qubit) quantum operations, and classical communication between qubits. These are n-party LOCC operations, where each party holds a single qubit.

Any n-party LOCC measurement strategy can be described as a sequence of steps, which outputs a sequence of measurement outcomes, as follows:

Begin at step 1.

At step a, conditioned on the output of the previous steps $1, 2, \ldots, a-1$:
Choose one of the parties, specified by $i \in \{1, 2, \ldots, n\}$.
Choose some measurement M. [5]
Perform the measurement M on the i'th party's qubits; this yields some outcome j.
Output j, and proceed to step $a+1$.

LOCC measurement strategies can use an unbounded number of steps, and can measure each qubit many times, for instance by using a sequence of weak measurements (which may be chosen adaptively). Strategies using unbounded LOCC are difficult to analyze; in particular, it is a long-standing open problem to prove strong quantitative bounds on the amount of information returned by strategies using unbounded LOCC.

Here we consider a restricted class of LOCC strategies: those that measure each qubit *at most once*. We will refer to these as *1-pass* LOCC strategies.

Let us introduce some notation. A 1-pass LOCC strategy consists of n steps, labeled by $a \in [n]$ (where we define $[n] := \{1, 2, \ldots, n\}$). Suppose the strategy uses single-qubit measurements that have at most q outcomes. At step a, let $z_{<a} := (z_1, z_2, \ldots, z_{a-1}) \in [q]^{a-1}$ be the output of the previous steps; let $Q_a(z_{<a}) \in [n]$ be the choice of which qubit to measure next; let $M_a(z_{<a}, \zeta) \in \mathbb{C}^{2\times 2}$ (for all $\zeta \in [q]$) be the POVM elements corresponding to the choice of measurement in this step; and let z_a be the actual measurement outcome that is obtained, so that $M_a(z_{\leq a})$ is the corresponding POVM element. We can write the complete strategy as a POVM measurement on n qubits, whose elements are given by

$$M(z) := \bigotimes_{a=1}^{n} M_a(z_{\leq a}), \quad \forall z \in [q]^n, \tag{3}$$

where $M_a(z_{\leq a})$ acts on the qubit indicated by $Q_a(z_{<a})$.

2.1 A state discrimination game

Consider a collection of n-qubit quantum states $|E(u)\rangle$, indexed by $u \in \mathcal{U}$. How well can an LOCC adversary distinguish among these states? To make this question precise, one can define the following *state discrimination game*: first the referee chooses $u \in \mathcal{U}$ uniformly at random, then prepares the corresponding state $|E(u)\rangle$, and gives it to the adversary; then the adversary carries out some LOCC measurement strategy, and outputs some string $z \in [q]^n$. We can measure the adversary's success in terms of the *mutual information* $I(Z;U)$, where U and Z are the random variables describing the referee's choice and the adversary's output.

Note that, in the isolated qubits model, each party holds a single qubit (rather than a higher-dimensional quantum system). We can make use of this fact, to further simplify the set of possible LOCC strategies.

[5] Any measurement can be described by a set of measurement operators $K_1, K_2, \ldots$ which satisfy $\sum_j K_j^\dagger K_j = I$. For a given state ρ, the measurement returns outcome j with probability $\mathrm{tr}(K_j \rho K_j^\dagger)$, and the post-measurement state (conditioned on observing j) is $K_j \rho K_j^\dagger / \mathrm{tr}(K_j \rho K_j^\dagger)$. Note that the measurement can also be described by a set of POVM elements $M_j = K_j^\dagger K_j$; the probability of observing outcome j can then be written as $\mathrm{tr}(M_j \rho)$.

LEMMA 2.1. *Let $\mathcal{M}$ be any 1-pass LOCC strategy in the isolated qubits model, which uses q-outcome measurements and returns output Z. Then there exists $\mathcal{M}'$, a 1-pass LOCC strategy in the isolated qubits model, which uses q-outcome measurements and returns output Z', and has the following additional properties:*

1. *$I(Z';U) \geq I(Z;U)$ (when playing the state discrimination game shown above).*
2. *In every measurement performed by $\mathcal{M}'$, the POVM elements all have rank 1.*

Proof: See Appendix A in the full version of this paper [42].

2.2 Discretization of LOCC strategies

Let $\mathcal{S}$ be the set of all single-qubit measurements with q outcomes, where every POVM element has rank 1:

$$\begin{aligned}\mathcal{S} = \{(M_1, \ldots, M_q) \mid M_i \in \mathbb{C}^{2\times 2},\ M_i \succeq 0, \\ \sum_{i=1}^{q} M_i = I,\ \mathrm{rank}(M_i) = 1\}.\end{aligned} \tag{4}$$

This is a continuous set. In our proofs, we would like to approximate it by a finite ε-net L, with respect to some appropriate metric t. It will be convenient to define t as follows:

$$t(M, \tilde{M}) := \max_{i \in [q]} \|M_i - \tilde{M}_i\|. \tag{5}$$

(Here $\|\cdot\|$ denotes the operator norm.) The following two lemmas bound the size of the ε-net L, first in the special case where $q = 2$ (for which we have a better bound), and then in the general case where $q \geq 2$.

LEMMA 2.2. *Let $q = 2$. For any $0 < \varepsilon \leq 1$, there exists an ε-net L for $\mathcal{S}$, with respect to the metric t, that has cardinality $|L| \leq C/\varepsilon^2$ (where C is some numerical constant). Equivalently, we have $N(\mathcal{S}, t, \varepsilon) \leq C/\varepsilon^2$.*

Proof: See Appendix A in the full version of this paper [42].

LEMMA 2.3. *Let $q \geq 2$. For any $0 < \varepsilon \leq 1$, there exists an ε-net L for $\mathcal{S}$, with respect to the metric t, that has cardinality $|L| \leq (C/\varepsilon)^{3q}$ (where C is some numerical constant). Equivalently, we have $N(\mathcal{S}, t, \varepsilon) \leq (C/\varepsilon)^{3q}$.*

Proof: See Appendix A in the full version of this paper [42].

We now bound the effect of this discretization when applied to a complete LOCC strategy. Essentially, if we choose $\varepsilon \leq O(1/qn)$, then the discretization has a negligible effect on the amount of information returned by the strategy.

LEMMA 2.4. *Let $\mathcal{M}$ be any 1-pass LOCC strategy in the isolated qubits model, which uses q-outcome measurements, where all POVM elements have rank 1, and which has output Z. Fix some $0 < \varepsilon \leq 1/(qne)$, and let L be the ε-net for $\mathcal{S}$ defined above. Let $\mathcal{M}'$ be the strategy that is obtained by duplicating the strategy $\mathcal{M}$, and replacing each measurement $M \in \mathcal{S}$ with the best approximating measurement $\tilde{M} \in L$. Let Z' be the output of the strategy $\mathcal{M}'$. Then*

$$|I(Z';U) - I(Z;U)| \leq 2qn^2\varepsilon + 2\eta(qn\varepsilon), \tag{6}$$

where $\eta(x) := -x \lg x$.

Proof: See Appendix A in the full version of this paper [42].

3. DATA-HIDING STATES

Consider a system of n qubits. We will construct a set B of $2^{\tilde{n}}$ quantum states, with $\tilde{n} \geq n - O(1)$, that has the following properties:

1. The states are pure and unentangled (i.e., they are tensor products of pure single-qubit states).
2. There exists an entangled quantum measurement that distinguishes these states almost perfectly. In particular, given a state chosen uniformly at random from B, this measurement recovers nearly $\tilde{n}$ bits of information about the identity of the state.
3. No n-party LOCC measurement strategy can distinguish these states very well. In particular, given a state chosen uniformly at random from B, no n-party LOCC measurement strategy using 2-outcome measurements can recover more than about $n/2$ bits of information about the identity of the state. Similar bounds hold for n-party LOCC measurement strategies using q-outcome measurements, for constant q.

We construct the set of states B as follows. Set $\tilde{n} = n - \Theta(1)$. Briefly, B is a set of $2^{\tilde{n}}$ states chosen independently and uniformly at random from the set $\{|0\rangle, |1\rangle, |+\rangle, |-\rangle\}^{\otimes n}$. To state this more explicitly, we define the following single-qubit states:

$$\begin{aligned} &|\alpha_{00}\rangle := |0\rangle, \quad |\alpha_{11}\rangle := |1\rangle, \\ &|\alpha_{01}\rangle := |+\rangle = \tfrac{1}{\sqrt{2}}(|0\rangle + |1\rangle), \\ &|\alpha_{10}\rangle := |-\rangle = \tfrac{1}{\sqrt{2}}(|0\rangle - |1\rangle). \end{aligned} \tag{7}$$

Choose a random mapping $E : \{0,1\}^{\tilde{n}} \rightarrow \{00,01,10,11\}^n$, i.e., for each $u \in \{0,1\}^{\tilde{n}}$, assign $E(u)$ a value chosen independently and uniformly at random in $\{00,01,10,11\}^n$. Also, for $a = 1,2,\dots,n$, let $E(u)_a \in \{00,01,10,11\}$ denote the a'th entry in the string $E(u)$. Then let B be the set of states $|E(u)\rangle$ defined as follows:

$$|E(u)\rangle := \bigotimes_{a=1}^{n} |\alpha_{E(u)_a}\rangle, \quad \forall u \in \{0,1\}^{\tilde{n}}. \tag{8}$$

We will consider the following state discrimination problem, which we describe as a game between a referee and a distinguisher. First, the referee chooses a random string u in $\{0,1\}^{\tilde{n}}$, and prepares the state $|E(u)\rangle$. Given this state, the distinguisher performs some measurement, and outputs a string z (over some alphabet). The goal of the distinguisher is to maximize the *mutual information* $I(Z;U)$, where U and Z are the random variables representing the referee's choice of the state and the distinguisher's output.

3.1 The pretty good measurement

In this section we show that the states $|E(u)\rangle$ can be distinguished almost perfectly by a measurement that uses entanglement among the n qubits. In particular, we will consider the "pretty good measurement" [32], which is defined as follows. Let ρ be the mixed state $\rho := 2^{-\tilde{n}} \sum_{u\in\{0,1\}^{\tilde{n}}} |E(u)\rangle\langle E(u)|$. Then the "pretty good measurement" is given by the following set of POVM elements:

$$\begin{aligned} M_{\mathrm{PGM}} &:= \{|M(z)\rangle\langle M(z)|,\ z \in \{0,1\}^{\tilde{n}}\}, \\ &\text{where } |M(z)\rangle := 2^{-\tilde{n}/2}\rho^{-1/2}|E(z)\rangle. \end{aligned} \tag{9}$$

(If ρ is not full-rank, then $\rho^{-1/2}$ is defined on the support of ρ.)

We will show that, with high probability over the choice of the states $|E(u)\rangle$, the pretty good measurement works well. In particular, let Z be the output of the pretty good measurement; we will show that $Z = U$ with probability close to 1, and the mutual information $I(Z;U)$ is close to $\tilde{n}$.

LEMMA 3.1. *Let $C \geq 1$. With probability $\geq 1 - \frac{1}{C}$ (over the choice of E), we have*

$$\Pr[Z = U] \geq 1 - 2\sqrt{C} \cdot 2^{(\tilde{n}-n)/2}. \tag{10}$$

In particular, for any $\varepsilon > 0$, suppose that $\tilde{n}$ satisfies $\tilde{n} \leq n - \lg(C/\varepsilon^2) - 2$. Then equation (10) implies that

$$\Pr[Z = U] \geq 1 - \varepsilon. \tag{11}$$

Proof: First, we will give a lower-bound for $\Pr[Z = U]$ in terms of the eigenvalues of the Gram matrix of the states $|E(u)\rangle$, using an argument due to Montanaro [33]. We write

$$\begin{aligned} \Pr[Z = U] &= 2^{-\tilde{n}} \sum_{u\in\{0,1\}^{\tilde{n}}} |\langle M(u)|E(u)\rangle|^2 \\ &= 4^{-\tilde{n}} \sum_{u\in\{0,1\}^{\tilde{n}}} \left|\langle E(u)|\rho^{-1/2}|E(u)\rangle\right|^2. \end{aligned} \tag{12}$$

We define the matrix $P \in \mathbb{C}^{2^{\tilde{n}}\times 2^{\tilde{n}}}$, whose entries are $P_{uv} = \langle E(u)|\rho^{-1/2}|E(v)\rangle$. In addition, we define the Gram matrix $G \in \mathbb{C}^{2^{\tilde{n}}\times 2^{\tilde{n}}}$, whose entries are $G_{uv} = \langle E(u)|E(v)\rangle$. It is easy to see that both P and G are positive semidefinite, and that $P^2 = 2^{\tilde{n}}G$; hence we can write $P = 2^{\tilde{n}/2}\sqrt{G}$. So we have

$$\Pr[Z = U] = 4^{-\tilde{n}} \sum_u |P_{uu}|^2 = 2^{-\tilde{n}} \sum_u ((\sqrt{G})_{uu})^2. \tag{13}$$

We can lower-bound this as follows, using the convexity of the square function, and letting $\lambda_u(G)$ denote the eigenvalues of G:

$$\begin{aligned} \Pr[Z = U] &\geq \Big(2^{-\tilde{n}} \sum_u (\sqrt{G})_{uu}\Big)^2 \\ &= \Big(2^{-\tilde{n}} \operatorname{tr}\sqrt{G}\Big)^2 = \Big(2^{-\tilde{n}} \sum_u \sqrt{\lambda_u(G)}\Big)^2. \end{aligned} \tag{14}$$

Next, define

$$\nu_u(G) := \begin{cases} \lambda_u(G) & \text{if } 0 \leq \lambda_u(G) \leq 1 \\ 1 & \text{if } \lambda_u(G) \geq 1 \end{cases} \tag{15}$$

and observe that $\sqrt{\lambda_u(G)} \geq \nu_u(G)$. So we have

$$\begin{aligned} \Pr[Z = U] &\geq \Big(2^{-\tilde{n}} \sum_u \nu_u(G)\Big)^2 = \Big(1 - 2^{-\tilde{n}} \sum_u (1 - \nu_u(G))\Big)^2 \\ &\geq 1 - 2 \cdot 2^{-\tilde{n}} \sum_u (1 - \nu_u(G)) \\ &\geq 1 - 2 \cdot 2^{-\tilde{n}} 2^{\tilde{n}/2} \|\vec{1} - \vec{\nu}(G)\|_2. \end{aligned} \tag{16}$$

Also note that $|1 - \nu_u(G)| \leq |1 - \lambda_u(G)|$, hence $\|\vec{1} - \vec{\nu}(G)\|_2 \leq \|\vec{1} - \vec{\lambda}(G)\|_2 = \|G - I\|_F$. So we have

$$\Pr[Z = U] \geq 1 - 2 \cdot 2^{-\tilde{n}/2} \|G - I\|_F. \tag{17}$$

Finally, we will use Markov's inequality to show that, with high probability (over the choice of E), $\|G-I\|_F$ is not too large. We write:

$$\mathbb{E}_E[\|G-I\|_F^2] = \mathbb{E}_E\Big[\sum_{u\neq v\in\{0,1\}^{\tilde{n}}} |G_{uv}|^2\Big], \tag{18}$$

$$\begin{aligned}\mathbb{E}_E[|G_{uv}|^2] &= \mathbb{E}_E\Big[\prod_{a=1}^{n} |\langle \alpha_{E(u)_a}|\alpha_{E(v)_a}\rangle|^2\Big] \\ &= \prod_{a=1}^{n} (\tfrac{1}{4}(1+0+\tfrac{1}{2}+\tfrac{1}{2})) \\ &= 2^{-n} \quad (\forall u\neq v),\end{aligned} \tag{19}$$

$$\mathbb{E}_E[\|G-I\|_F^2] = 2^{\tilde{n}}(2^{\tilde{n}}-1)2^{-n} < 4^{\tilde{n}}2^{-n}. \tag{20}$$

Hence, by Markov's inequality, for any $C\geq 1$,

$$\Pr_E[\|G-I\|_F^2 \geq C\cdot 4^{\tilde{n}}2^{-n}] \leq \tfrac{1}{C}. \tag{21}$$

That is, with probability $\geq 1-\frac{1}{C}$ (over the choice of E), we have $\|G-I\|_F \leq \sqrt{C}\cdot 2^{\tilde{n}}2^{-n/2}$. Combining this with equation (17) completes the proof. □

We have just shown a lower-bound on the success probability $\Pr[Z=U]$; this now implies a lower-bound on the mutual information $I(Z;U)$.

LEMMA 3.2. *Suppose that* $\Pr[Z=U]\geq 1-\varepsilon$, *and* ε *is sufficiently small that* $2\sqrt{\varepsilon}+2^{-\tilde{n}}\leq 1/e$. *Then* $I(Z;U)\geq (1-5\sqrt{\varepsilon})\tilde{n}-\eta(2\sqrt{\varepsilon})$, *where* $\eta(x) := -x\lg x$.

Proof: See Appendix B in the full version of this paper [42].

3.2 1-pass LOCC strategies with 2-outcome measurements

In this section, we prove that the states $|E(u)\rangle$ ($u\in\{0,1\}^{\tilde{n}}$) cannot be fully distinguished by any 1-pass LOCC strategy that uses 2-outcome measurements. In particular, we show that any such strategy cannot extract more than about $n/2$ bits of information about U. This claim holds with high probability over the randomized construction of the states $|E(u)\rangle$; more precisely, the claim holds with high probability over the choice of the map $E:\{0,1\}^{\tilde{n}}\to\{00,01,10,11\}^n$, which we view as a random variable.

The proof uses an entropy chaining argument, which is stated in Lemma A.1. This is essentially Dudley's inequality for bounding the supremum of an empirical process with Gaussian decaying correlations [23], with some minor technical modifications (in particular, the result is stated as a tail bound for the supremum, rather than a bound on the expected supremum).

THEOREM 3.3. *Let* $\mathbb{M}$ *be the set of all 1-pass LOCC strategies in the isolated qubits model using 2-outcome measurements. Let* $t_0>0$ *and* $u\geq 1$. *Then, with probability* $\geq 1-\exp(-2t_0^2)-2\cdot 2^{-u^2}$ *(over the choice of* E*), the following statement holds:*

$$\forall \mathcal{M}\in\mathbb{M},\ I(Z;U)\leq (0.54)n+O(1)+t_0\tilde{n}2^{-\tilde{n}/2}+u\cdot O(\sqrt{\log n}), \tag{22}$$

where Z *denotes the output of the strategy* $\mathcal{M}$.

Proof: First, let L be an ε-net for the set of single-qubit measurements with 2 outcomes where all POVM elements have rank 1, as described in Lemma 2.2; and set $\varepsilon = 1/(100n)$. Let $\mathbb{M}'$ be the set of all strategies that use measurements chosen from the set L. By Lemmas 2.1 and 2.4, any strategy in $\mathbb{M}$ can be approximated by one in $\mathbb{M}'$.

For any strategy $\mathcal{M}$, let Z denote its output. Note that Z takes values in $\{0,1\}^n$, and we can split its output into two pieces, $Z=(Z_{1,\dots,\tilde{n}}, Z_{\tilde{n}+1,\dots,n})$. So we can write

$$I(Z;U) = H(Z)-H(Z|U) \leq n - H(Z_{1,\dots,\tilde{n}}|U). \tag{23}$$

We want to show that $H(Z_{1,\dots,\tilde{n}}|U)$ is not too small.

Let $\mathbb{M}''$ be the set of all strategies with $\tilde{n}$ steps, whose behavior matches the first $\tilde{n}$ steps of some strategy in $\mathbb{M}'$. For any $\mathcal{M}\in\mathbb{M}''$, we now define

$$Q_{\mathcal{M}} := H(Z_{1,\dots,\tilde{n}}|U), \tag{24}$$

which is a random variable depending on E. Let $\mu_{\mathcal{M}} := \mathbb{E}_E\, Q_{\mathcal{M}}$; we will prove a lower bound for $\mu_{\mathcal{M}}$ below. We will then use entropy chaining (Lemma A.1) to lower-bound the quantity

$$\inf_{\mathcal{M}\in\mathbb{M}''} (Q_{\mathcal{M}}-\mu_{\mathcal{M}}). \tag{25}$$

First, we evaluate $\mu_{\mathcal{M}}$:

$$\begin{aligned}\mu_{\mathcal{M}} &= \mathbb{E}_E\big[H(Z_{1,\dots,\tilde{n}}|U)\big] \\ &= 2^{-\tilde{n}}\sum_{u\in\{0,1\}^{\tilde{n}}}\sum_{z\in\{0,1\}^{\tilde{n}}} \mathbb{E}_E\big[-\Pr(z|u)\lg\Pr(z|u)\big],\end{aligned} \tag{26}$$

where for convenience we wrote $\Pr(z|u)$ in place of $\Pr[Z_{1,\dots,\tilde{n}} = z|U=u]$. Consider any fixed $u,z\in\{0,1\}^{\tilde{n}}$. Recall that $|E(u)\rangle$ is chosen uniformly at random in $A^{\otimes n}$, where $A := \{|\alpha_{00}\rangle, |\alpha_{01}\rangle, |\alpha_{10}\rangle, |\alpha_{11}\rangle\}$. So we have

$$\begin{aligned}&\mathbb{E}_E\big[-\Pr(z|u)\lg\Pr(z|u)\big] \\ &\quad= 4^{-\tilde{n}}\sum_{|\psi\rangle\in A^{\otimes\tilde{n}}} -\langle\psi|M(z)|\psi\rangle \lg\langle\psi|M(z)|\psi\rangle.\end{aligned} \tag{27}$$

Furthermore, we know that $\langle\psi|M(z)|\psi\rangle = \prod_{a=1}^{\tilde{n}} \langle\psi_{Q_a(z_{<a})}|M_a(z_{\leq a})|\psi_{Q_a(z_{<a})}\rangle$, where we used the notation introduced in Section 2. Hence we can write

$$\begin{aligned}&\mathbb{E}_E\big[-\Pr(z|u)\lg\Pr(z|u)\big] \\ &= \sum_{a=1}^{\tilde{n}} 4^{-\tilde{n}} \sum_{|\psi\rangle\in A^{\otimes\tilde{n}}} -\langle\psi|M(z)|\psi\rangle\cdot \\ &\qquad\qquad \lg\langle\psi_{Q_a(z_{<a})}|M_a(z_{\leq a})|\psi_{Q_a(z_{<a})}\rangle \\ &= \sum_{a=1}^{\tilde{n}} 4^{-\tilde{n}}\Big[\sum_{\psi_a\in A} -\langle\psi_a|M_a(z_{\leq a})|\psi_a\rangle\lg\langle\psi_a|M_a(z_{\leq a})|\psi_a\rangle\Big]\cdot \\ &\qquad\qquad \prod_{b\neq a}\Big[\sum_{\psi_b\in A}\langle\psi_b|M_b(z_{\leq b})|\psi_b\rangle\Big]\end{aligned} \tag{28}$$

Recall that we are considering single-qubit measurements with 2 outcomes, where each outcome corresponds to a rank-1 POVM element. Hence each $M_b(z_{\leq b})$ is a rank-1 projector, i.e., it can be viewed as a density matrix of a quantum state. Hence we can write

$$\sum_{\psi_b\in A}\langle\psi_b|M_b(z_{\leq b})|\psi_b\rangle = 2\operatorname{tr} M_b(z_{\leq b}) = 2. \tag{29}$$

Also, suppose we let R_0 be the result of measuring the state $M_a(z_{\leq a})$ in the orthonormal basis $\{|\alpha_{00}\rangle, |\alpha_{11}\rangle\}$, and we let R_1 be the result of measuring the same state in the orthonormal basis $\{|\alpha_{01}\rangle, |\alpha_{10}\rangle\}$. Then we can write

$$\sum_{\psi_a \in A} -\langle\psi_a|M_a(z_{\leq a})|\psi_a\rangle \lg \langle\psi_a|M_a(z_{\leq a})|\psi_a\rangle = H(R_0) + H(R_1) \geq 1, \tag{30}$$

using an entropic uncertainty relation of Maassen and Uffink [35, 36]. Substituting into the previous equations, we get

$$\mathbb{E}_E\big[-\Pr(z|u)\lg \Pr(z|u)\big] \geq 2^{-\tilde{n}-1}\cdot \tilde{n}, \tag{31}$$

$$\mu_{\mathcal{M}} \geq \tilde{n}/2. \tag{32}$$

We now show several technical facts which are needed in order to apply the entropy chaining argument (Lemma A.1). First, fix some particular strategy $\mathcal{M}_0 \in \mathbb{M}''$. We will show that $Q_{\mathcal{M}_0}$ is tightly concentrated around its mean. Observe that $Q_{\mathcal{M}_0} = 2^{-\tilde{n}} \sum_{u\in\{0,1\}^{\tilde{n}}} H(Z_{1,\dots,\tilde{n}}|U = u)$ is a sum of $2^{\tilde{n}}$ independent random variables, since the strings $E(u)$ for different u are chosen independently at random. Using Hoeffding's inequality, we get that

$$\Pr_E[Q_{\mathcal{M}_0} < \mu_{\mathcal{M}_0} - t] \leq \exp\Big(-\frac{2t^2}{2^{\tilde{n}}(n/2^{\tilde{n}})^2}\Big) = \exp\Big(-\frac{2t^2\cdot 2^{\tilde{n}}}{\tilde{n}^2}\Big) \quad (\forall t > 0), \tag{33}$$

or equivalently

$$\Pr_E\Big[Q_{\mathcal{M}_0} < \mu_{\mathcal{M}_0} - \frac{t_0\tilde{n}}{2^{\tilde{n}/2}}\Big] \leq \exp(-2t_0^2), \quad (\forall t_0 > 0). \tag{34}$$

Next, we show that when two strategies $\mathcal{M}$ and $\mathcal{M}'$ are "similar," the random variables $Q_{\mathcal{M}}$ and $Q_{\mathcal{M}'}$ are positively correlated. In particular, suppose that $\mathcal{M}$ and $\mathcal{M}'$ behave identically for the first ℓ steps. Let $Z_{1,\dots,\tilde{n}}$ and $Z'_{1,\dots,\tilde{n}}$ be the output of these two strategies; then $(Z_{1,\dots,\ell}, U)$ and $(Z'_{1,\dots,\ell}, U)$ have the same distribution. So we can write

$$\begin{aligned} Q_{\mathcal{M}} - Q_{\mathcal{M}'} &= H(Z_{\ell+1,\dots,\tilde{n}}|Z_{1,\dots,\ell}, U) - H(Z'_{\ell+1,\dots,\tilde{n}}|Z'_{1,\dots,\ell}, U) \\ &= 2^{-\tilde{n}} \sum_{u\in\{0,1\}^{\tilde{n}}} H(Z_{\ell+1,\dots,\tilde{n}}|Z_{1,\dots,\ell}, U = u) - \\ &\qquad H(Z'_{\ell+1,\dots,\tilde{n}}|Z'_{1,\dots,\ell}, U = u), \end{aligned} \tag{35}$$

which again is a sum of $2^{\tilde{n}}$ independent random variables. By Hoeffding's inequality,

$$\Pr_E[Q_{\mathcal{M}} - Q_{\mathcal{M}'} - \mu_{\mathcal{M}} + \mu_{\mathcal{M}'} \geq t] \leq \exp\Big(-\frac{2t^2}{2^{\tilde{n}}(2(\tilde{n}-\ell)/2^{\tilde{n}})^2}\Big) = \exp\Big(-\frac{t^2\cdot 2^{\tilde{n}}}{2(\tilde{n}-\ell)^2}\Big). \tag{36}$$

We can rewrite this bound in terms of a metric d that measures the "distance" between strategies. We define d as follows: [6]

$$d(\mathcal{M},\mathcal{M}') := \sqrt{2}\cdot 2^{-\tilde{n}/2}(\tilde{n} - \ell(\mathcal{M},\mathcal{M}')), \text{ where} \tag{37}$$

$$\ell(\mathcal{M},\mathcal{M}') := \max\{\ell \mid 0 \leq \ell \leq \tilde{n}, \text{ and } \mathcal{M} \text{ and } \mathcal{M}' \text{ behave identically on steps } 1,2,\dots,\ell\}. \tag{38}$$

We then have

$$\Pr_E[Q_{\mathcal{M}} - Q_{\mathcal{M}'} - \mu_{\mathcal{M}} + \mu_{\mathcal{M}'} \geq t] \leq \exp\Big(-\frac{t^2}{d(\mathcal{M},\mathcal{M}')^2}\Big). \tag{39}$$

Next, we bound the covering numbers of $\mathbb{M}''$ with respect to the metric d. We use a simple bound:

$$N(\mathbb{M}'', d, \sqrt{2}\cdot 2^{-\tilde{n}/2}\varepsilon) \leq \begin{cases} (n|L|)^{2^{\lceil \tilde{n}-\varepsilon\rceil}} & \text{if } \varepsilon \leq \tilde{n} \\ 1 & \text{if } \varepsilon > \tilde{n}. \end{cases} \tag{40}$$

(This bound simply counts the number of possible strategies with $\lceil \tilde{n} - \varepsilon\rceil$ steps. Each such strategy is described by a binary tree of depth $\lceil \tilde{n} - \varepsilon\rceil$, and at every node there is a choice of which of the n qubits to measure next, and which of the measurements in the set L to perform.) We now bound the integral appearing in Lemma A.1 ("Dudley's entropy integral"): (here C_0 is a numerical constant)

$$\begin{aligned} S &\leq C_0 \int_0^\infty \sqrt{\log N(\mathbb{M}'', d, \varepsilon)}\, d\varepsilon \\ &= C_0 \int_0^\infty \sqrt{\log N(\mathbb{M}'', d, \sqrt{2}\cdot 2^{-\tilde{n}/2}\varepsilon)}\cdot \sqrt{2}\cdot 2^{-\tilde{n}/2} d\varepsilon \\ &\leq C_0 \int_0^{\tilde{n}} \sqrt{2^{\tilde{n}-\varepsilon+1}\log(n|L|)}\cdot\sqrt{2}\cdot 2^{-\tilde{n}/2} d\varepsilon \\ &= C_0 \int_0^{\tilde{n}} 2^{-\varepsilon/2} d\varepsilon \cdot 2\sqrt{\log(n|L|)} \\ &= C_0(\tfrac{2}{\ln 2})(1 - 2^{-\tilde{n}/2})\cdot 2\sqrt{\log(n|L|)} \\ &< C_0(\tfrac{2}{\ln 2})\cdot 2\sqrt{\log(n|L|)}. \end{aligned} \tag{41}$$

Recall that $|L| \leq O(1/\varepsilon^2) = O(n^2)$. Hence we have:

$$S \leq O(\sqrt{\log n}). \tag{42}$$

Finally, using Lemma A.1, we have that: for all $t_0 > 0$ and $u \geq 1$, with probability $\geq 1 - \exp(-2t_0^2) - 2\cdot 2^{-u^2}$, the following holds:

$$\forall \mathcal{M} \in \mathbb{M}'',\ Q_{\mathcal{M}} - \mu_{\mathcal{M}} > -\frac{t_0\tilde{n}}{2^{\tilde{n}/2}} - uS. \tag{43}$$

This implies that

$$\forall \mathcal{M} \in \mathbb{M}'',\ Q_{\mathcal{M}} > \frac{\tilde{n}}{2} - \frac{t_0\tilde{n}}{2^{\tilde{n}/2}} - u\cdot O(\sqrt{\log n}). \tag{44}$$

Plugging into equation (23), we get that

$$\forall \mathcal{M} \in \mathbb{M}',\ I(Z;U) < n - \frac{\tilde{n}}{2} + \frac{t_0\tilde{n}}{2^{\tilde{n}/2}} + u\cdot O(\sqrt{\log n}). \tag{45}$$

Finally, using Lemmas 2.1 and 2.4, we get that

$$\forall \mathcal{M} \in \mathbb{M},\ I(Z;U) < n - \frac{\tilde{n}}{2} + \frac{n}{25} + O(1) + \frac{t_0\tilde{n}}{2^{\tilde{n}/2}} + u\cdot O(\sqrt{\log n}). \tag{46}$$

This proves the claim. □

[6] Note that d is indeed a metric: It is easy to see that $d(\mathcal{M},\mathcal{M}') \geq 0$, with equality iff $\mathcal{M} = \mathcal{M}'$. Also, clearly $d(\mathcal{M},\mathcal{M}') = d(\mathcal{M}',\mathcal{M})$. It remains to show that $d(\mathcal{M},\mathcal{M}'') \leq d(\mathcal{M},\mathcal{M}') + d(\mathcal{M}',\mathcal{M}'')$. We consider two cases. On one hand, if $\mathcal{M}'$ satisfies $\ell(\mathcal{M},\mathcal{M}') \leq \ell(\mathcal{M},\mathcal{M}'')$ or $\ell(\mathcal{M}',\mathcal{M}'') \leq \ell(\mathcal{M},\mathcal{M}'')$, then the claim follows immediately. On the other hand, if $\mathcal{M}'$ satisfies $\ell(\mathcal{M},\mathcal{M}') > \ell(\mathcal{M},\mathcal{M}'')$ and $\ell(\mathcal{M}',\mathcal{M}'') > \ell(\mathcal{M},\mathcal{M}'')$, then this is impossible, since $\mathcal{M}$ and $\mathcal{M}''$ do not agree at step $\ell(\mathcal{M},\mathcal{M}'') + 1$; hence this case cannot occur.

3.3 1-pass LOCC strategies with q-outcome measurements

In this section, we consider a more general class of 1-pass LOCC strategies, that use q-outcome measurements (for any constant q). Again we show that the states $|E(u)\rangle$ ($u \in \{0,1\}^{\tilde{n}}$) cannot be perfectly distinguished by such an adversary. Quantitatively, we show that such an adversary can extract at most $\approx (0.71)\tilde{n}$ bits of information about U; we do not believe this bound is optimal, but it does nonetheless show that a constant fraction of the information in U is hidden from the adversary.

We use a different proof technique from the previous section: here we show an explicit lower bound on the Renyi collision entropy of U conditioned on the output $Z_{\leq m}$ of the first m steps of the adversary. This "collision entropy" proof is a useful alternative to the "entropy chaining" proof of the previous section. The collision entropy proof works quite well when q is large, whereas the entropy chaining proof has some difficulty because the number of possible measurement strategies grows rapidly with q. However, the collision entropy proof does not give a tight bound for any value of q, while the entropy chaining approach does give a tight bound when $q = 2$.

THEOREM 3.4. *Let $\mathbb{M}$ be the set of all 1-pass LOCC strategies in the isolated qubits model, using q-outcome measurements. Then, with probability $\geq 1 - e^{-\Omega(n)}$ (over the choice of E), the following statement holds:*

$$\forall \mathcal{M} \in \mathbb{M},\ I(Z;U) \leq (0.7067)n + O(1) + O(\lg(qn)), \tag{47}$$

where Z denotes the output of the strategy $\mathcal{M}$.

Proof: First, let L be an ε-net for the set of single-qubit measurements with q outcomes where all POVM elements have rank 1, as described in Lemma 2.3; and set $\varepsilon = 1/(200qn)$. Let $\mathbb{M}'$ be the set of all strategies that use measurements chosen from the set L. By Lemmas 2.1 and 2.4, any strategy in $\mathbb{M}$ can be approximated by one in $\mathbb{M}'$.

We will analyze the first m steps of any strategy in $\mathbb{M}'$, where $m = \lfloor \tilde{n}/\lg(8/3) \rfloor \approx (0.7067)\tilde{n}$. We will show the following bound:

LEMMA 3.5. *With probability $\geq 1 - e^{-\Omega(n)}$ (over the choice of E),*

$$\forall \mathcal{M} \in \mathbb{M}',\ \forall z_{1,\dots,m} \in [q]^m,$$
$$H_2(U|Z_{1,\dots,m} = z_{1,\dots,m}) \geq \tilde{n} - m\lg(\tfrac{3}{2}) - \lg(O(qn\lg(qn))), \tag{48}$$

where $Z_{1,\dots,m}$ denotes the output of the first m steps of the strategy $\mathcal{M}$, H_2 denotes the Renyi collision entropy, and $\lg(\frac{3}{2}) \approx 0.5850$.

Proof (of Lemma 3.5): Note that the lemma is equivalent to the following statement: with high probability (over the choice of E),

> for all subsets of qubits $A \subset [n]$, of size $|A| = m$,
> for all possible measurement outcomes M_A that correspond to measuring the qubits in the set A using any measurements in the set L,
> $H_2(U|M_A)$ (where we condition on observing the measurement outcome M_A) is large.

Note that a measurement outcome M_A is uniquely represented by a rank-1 POVM element of the form $M_A = \bigotimes_{i\in A} M_i$, where each M_i is a POVM element acting on qubit i, that corresponds to one possible outcome of some measurement in the set L.

We will now proceed as follows. First, we will show that, for every A and M_A, $\Pr[M_A]$ is approximately $\mathrm{tr}(M_A)/2^m$. Secondly, we will show that, for every A and M_A, $\sum_u \Pr[M_A|U = u]^2$ is small. (To show these claims, we will use large-deviation bounds for every fixed choice of A and M_A, followed by the union bound over all A and M_A.) Finally, we will combine these two claims to get a lower-bound on $H_2(U|M_A)$.

First, fix some subset of qubits $A \subset [n]$, of size $|A| = m$. Let ρ be the mixed state presented to the adversary, $\rho := 2^{-\tilde{n}} \sum_{u\in\{0,1\}^{\tilde{n}}} |E(u)\rangle\langle E(u)|$, and let ρ_A be the reduced state on the subset A,

$$\begin{aligned}\rho_A &:= \mathrm{tr}_{[n]\setminus A}(\rho) = 2^{-\tilde{n}} \sum_{u\in\{0,1\}^{\tilde{n}}} |E(u)_A\rangle\langle E(u)_A|,\\ &\text{where } |E(u)_A\rangle := \bigotimes_{a\in A} |\alpha_{E(u)_a}\rangle.\end{aligned} \tag{49}$$

Note that $\mathbb{E}_E\, \rho_A = I/2^m$. We claim that, with high probability (over the choice of E), ρ_A is close to the maximally mixed state $I/2^m$, and hence any measurement outcome M_A on the subset A will be observed with probability approximately $\mathrm{tr}(M_A)/2^m$. To show this, we will use the matrix Bernstein inequality [37].

For convenience, define $H := \sum_{u\in\{0,1\}^{\tilde{n}}} H_u$, where $H_u := |E(u)\rangle_A\langle E(u)|_A$. Note that $\mathbb{E}_E\, H = 2^{\tilde{n}-m} I$ and $\mathbb{E}_E\, H_u = 2^{-m} I$. Note that the H_u are bounded:

$$\|H_u - \mathbb{E}_E\, H_u\| = \max\{1 - 2^{-m}, 2^{-m}\} < 1 =: R. \tag{50}$$

The variance of H is described by

$$\begin{aligned}\mathbb{E}_E[(H - \mathbb{E}_E\, H)^2] &= \mathbb{E}_E[H^2] - (\mathbb{E}_E\, H)^2\\ &= \mathbb{E}_E[\sum_u H_u^2 + \sum_{u\neq v} H_u H_v] - 4^{\tilde{n}-m} I\\ &= \sum_u \mathbb{E}_E[H_u^2] + \sum_{u\neq v} \mathbb{E}_E[H_u]\,\mathbb{E}_E[H_v] - 4^{\tilde{n}-m} I\\ &= 2^{\tilde{n}-m} I + (4^{\tilde{n}} - 2^{\tilde{n}})4^{-m} I - 4^{\tilde{n}-m} I\\ &= 2^{\tilde{n}-m}(1 - 2^{-m}) I.\end{aligned} \tag{51}$$

In particular, note that

$$\sigma^2 := \|\mathbb{E}_E[(H - \mathbb{E}_E\, H)^2]\| < 2^{\tilde{n}-m}. \tag{52}$$

Then the matrix Bernstein inequality [37] implies that, for any $t > 0$,

$$\begin{aligned}\Pr_E[\|H - \mathbb{E}_E\, H\| \geq t] &\leq 2\cdot 2^m \exp\Big(-\frac{t^2}{2(\sigma^2 + \frac{1}{3}Rt)}\Big)\\ &= 2\cdot 2^m \exp\Big(-\frac{t^2}{2(2^{\tilde{n}-m} + \frac{1}{3}t)}\Big).\end{aligned} \tag{53}$$

Now set

$$t := t_0\sqrt{m}2^{(\tilde{n}-m)/2}, \text{ for any } t_0 \geq 1. \tag{54}$$

Recall that $0 \leq m \leq \tilde{n} - \lg\tilde{n}$. This implies that $\lg\tilde{n} \leq \tilde{n} - m$, hence $t < t_0\sqrt{\tilde{n}}2^{(\tilde{n}-m)/2} \leq t_0 2^{\tilde{n}-m}$, and hence $2^{\tilde{n}-m} + \frac{1}{3}t \leq$

$\frac{4}{3}t_0 2^{\tilde{n}-m}$. Substituting into the above equation, we get that

$$\Pr_E[\|H - \mathbb{E}_E H\| \geq t_0\sqrt{m}2^{(\tilde{n}-m)/2}] \leq 2 \cdot 2^m \exp(-\tfrac{3}{8}t_0 m). \quad (55)$$

Recall that $\rho_A = 2^{-\tilde{n}}H$, hence this implies a large-deviation bound for ρ_A:

$$\Pr_E[\|\rho_A - 2^{-m}I\| \geq 2^{-\tilde{n}}t_0\sqrt{m}2^{(\tilde{n}-m)/2}] \leq 2{\cdot}2^m \exp(-\tfrac{3}{8}t_0 m). \quad (56)$$

Now use the union bound over all subsets $A \subset [n]$ of size $|A| = m$. (There are $\binom{n}{m} < 2^n$ such sets.) So with probability $\geq 1 - 2^{n+m+1}\exp(-\frac{3}{8}t_0 m)$ (over the choice of E), we have that

for all subsets A of size m,

$$\|\rho_A - 2^{-m}I\| \leq 2^{-\tilde{n}}t_0\sqrt{m}2^{(\tilde{n}-m)/2} = 2^{-m}2^{-(\tilde{n}-m)/2}t_0\sqrt{m}. \quad (57)$$

By setting t_0 to be a sufficiently large constant, we can make the failure probability exponentially small in n. Finally, equation (57) implies that, for any subset A of size m, and any measurement outcome M_A, the probability of observing M_A (which is given by $\Pr[M_A] = \operatorname{tr}(M_A\rho_A)$) satisfies the bound

$$|\Pr[M_A] - 2^{-m}\operatorname{tr}(M_A)| \leq 2^{-m}\operatorname{tr}(M_A)2^{-(\tilde{n}-m)/2}t_0\sqrt{m}. \quad (58)$$

Next, fix some subset of qubits $A \subset [n]$, $|A| = m$, and some measurement outcome M_A. We will use Bernstein's inequality to upper-bound the quantity

$$F := \sum_{u\in\{0,1\}^{\tilde{n}}} F_u, \quad \text{where } F_u := (\operatorname{tr}(M_A))^{-2}\Pr[M_A|U = u]^2. \quad (59)$$

Recall that M_A is a tensor product of rank-1 operators acting on single qubits, and so $M_A/\operatorname{tr}(M_A)$ can be written in the form

$$\frac{M_A}{\operatorname{tr}(M_A)} = |\psi_A\rangle\langle\psi_A|, \quad \text{where } |\psi_A\rangle = \bigotimes_{a\in A}|\psi_a\rangle,\ |\psi_a\rangle \in \mathbb{C}^2,\ \langle\psi_a|\psi_a\rangle = 1. \quad (60)$$

So we can write

$$F_u = \Big(\langle E(u)_A|\tfrac{M_A}{\operatorname{tr}(M_A)}|E(u)_A\rangle\Big)^2 = |\langle\psi_A|E(u)_A\rangle|^4. \quad (61)$$

First, we will calculate $\mathbb{E}_E F = \sum_u \mathbb{E}_E F_u$. Note that $\mathbb{E}_E F_u = \prod_{a\in A}|\langle\psi_a|E(u)_a\rangle|^4$. We can upper-bound this as follows:

$$\begin{aligned}&\mathbb{E}_E\big[|\langle\psi_a|E(u)_a\rangle|^4\big]\\ &= \tfrac{1}{4}\big[|\langle\psi_a|\alpha_{00}\rangle|^4 + |\langle\psi_a|\alpha_{01}\rangle|^4 + |\langle\psi_a|\alpha_{10}\rangle|^4 + |\langle\psi_a|\alpha_{11}\rangle|^4\big]\\ &= \tfrac{1}{4}\langle\psi_a|^{\otimes 2}T|\psi_a\rangle^{\otimes 2},\end{aligned} \quad (62)$$

where we define the matrix $T \in \mathbb{C}^{4\times 4}$ to be

$$T := \Big(|0\rangle\langle 0|\Big)^{\otimes 2} + \Big(|1\rangle\langle 1|\Big)^{\otimes 2} + \Big(|+\rangle\langle +|\Big)^{\otimes 2} + \Big(|-\rangle\langle -|\Big)^{\otimes 2}. \quad (63)$$

Now write the spectral decomposition of T:

$$T = |\Psi^+\rangle\langle\Psi^+| + 2|\Phi^+\rangle\langle\Phi^+| + |\Phi^-\rangle\langle\Phi^-|, \quad (64)$$

where $|\Psi^\pm\rangle = \frac{1}{\sqrt{2}}(|01\rangle \pm |10\rangle)$ and $|\Phi^\pm\rangle = \frac{1}{\sqrt{2}}(|00\rangle \pm |11\rangle)$ are the Bell states. Now write $|\psi_a\rangle$ in the form $|\psi_a\rangle = \alpha|0\rangle + \beta|1\rangle$. This implies

$$|\psi_a\rangle^{\otimes 2} = \sqrt{2}\alpha\beta|\Psi^+\rangle + \tfrac{1}{\sqrt{2}}(\alpha^2+\beta^2)|\Phi^+\rangle + \tfrac{1}{\sqrt{2}}(\alpha^2-\beta^2)|\Phi^-\rangle. \quad (65)$$

Now we calculate

$$\begin{aligned}&\langle\psi_a|^{\otimes 2}(2T)|\psi_a\rangle^{\otimes 2}\\ &= 4|\alpha|^2|\beta|^2 + 2(\alpha^2+\beta^2)^*(\alpha^2+\beta^2) + (\alpha^2-\beta^2)^*(\alpha^2-\beta^2)\\ &= 4|\alpha|^2|\beta|^2 + 3|\alpha|^4 + (\alpha^2)^*\beta^2 + (\beta^2)^*\alpha^2 + 3|\beta|^4\\ &= 2(|\alpha|^2+|\beta|^2)^2 + |\alpha^2+\beta^2|^2\\ &\leq 3(|\alpha|^2+|\beta|^2)^2 = 3.\end{aligned} \quad (66)$$

This implies that $\mathbb{E}_E\big[|\langle\psi_a|E(u)_a\rangle|^4\big] \leq \frac{3}{8}$, and hence $\mathbb{E}_E F_u \leq (\frac{3}{8})^m$ and $\mathbb{E}_E F \leq 2^{\tilde{n}}(\frac{3}{8})^m$.

In addition, we bound the variance of F_u as follows (using the fact that $0 \leq F_u \leq 1$): $\operatorname{Var}_E F_u \leq \mathbb{E}_E(F_u^2) \leq \mathbb{E}_E F_u \leq (\frac{3}{8})^m$.

Now Bernstein's inequality [38] implies that, for all $t > 0$,

$$\Pr_E[F > \mathbb{E}_E F + t] \leq \exp\bigg(-\frac{t^2}{2\cdot 2^{\tilde{n}}(\frac{3}{8})^m + \frac{2}{3}t}\bigg). \quad (67)$$

Recall that $m \leq \tilde{n}/\lg(\frac{8}{3})$, and note that this implies $2^{\tilde{n}}(\frac{3}{8})^m \geq 1$. Now set

$$t = t_1[2^{\tilde{n}}(\tfrac{3}{8})^m]^{1/2}, \text{ for any } t_1 \geq 1. \quad (68)$$

This implies $2{\cdot}2^{\tilde{n}}(\frac{3}{8})^m + \frac{2}{3}t \leq (2+\frac{2}{3})t_1 2^{\tilde{n}}(\frac{3}{8})^m$. Substituting into the above equation, we get

$$\Pr_E[F > 2^{\tilde{n}}(\tfrac{3}{8})^m + t_1[2^{\tilde{n}}(\tfrac{3}{8})^m]^{1/2}] \leq \exp(-\tfrac{3}{8}t_1). \quad (69)$$

Now take the union bound over all subsets $A \subset [n]$ of size $|A| = m$, and all measurement outcomes M_A that correspond to measurements chosen from the set L and performed on the qubits in the set A. (There are $\binom{n}{m} < 2^n$ such sets, and $(q|L|)^m \leq (qO(1/\varepsilon)^{3q})^m \leq (qO(qn)^{3q})^m \leq 2^{O(qn\lg(qn))}$ such measurement outcomes.) Then, with probability $\geq 1 - 2^{O(qn\lg(qn))}\exp(-\frac{3}{8}t_1)$, we have that

for all subsets A of size m, and all measurement outcomes M_A,

$$F \leq 2^{\tilde{n}}(\tfrac{3}{8})^m + t_1[2^{\tilde{n}}(\tfrac{3}{8})^m]^{1/2}. \quad (70)$$

By setting $t_1 := \Theta(qn\lg(qn))$, we can make the failure probability exponentially small in n.

Finally, we will combine equations (58) and (70) to get a lower bound on $H_2(U|M_A)$. For any A and M_A, we write

$$\begin{aligned}
2^{-H_2(U|M_A)} &= \sum_{u\in\{0,1\}^{\tilde{n}}} \Pr[U=u|M_A]^2 \\
&= \Pr[M_A]^{-2} 4^{-\tilde{n}} \sum_{u\in\{0,1\}^{\tilde{n}}} \Pr[M_A|U=u]^2 \\
&= \Pr[M_A]^{-2} 4^{-\tilde{n}} (\mathrm{tr}(M_A))^2 F \\
&\le [2^{-m}\,\mathrm{tr}(M_A)(1-2^{-(\tilde{n}-m)/2} t_0\sqrt{m})]^{-2} 4^{-\tilde{n}} (\mathrm{tr}(M_A))^2 \cdot \\
&\quad [2^{\tilde{n}}(\tfrac{3}{8})^m + t_1[2^{\tilde{n}}(\tfrac{3}{8})^m]^{1/2}] \\
&\le 4^m (1-2^{-(\tilde{n}-m)/2} t_0\sqrt{m})^{-2} 4^{-\tilde{n}} 2^{\tilde{n}} (\tfrac{3}{8})^m (1+t_1) \\
&\le 2^{-\tilde{n}} (\tfrac{3}{2})^m O(qn\lg(qn)).
\end{aligned} \tag{71}$$

This implies

$$\begin{aligned}
H_2(U|M_A) &\ge \tilde{n} - m\lg(\tfrac{3}{2}) - \lg(O(qn\lg(qn))) \\
&\approx \tilde{n} - (0.5850)m - \lg(O(qn\lg(qn))).
\end{aligned} \tag{72}$$

This completes the proof of Lemma 3.5. □

We now return to the proof of Theorem 3.4. Consider any strategy $\mathcal{M} \in \mathbb{M}'$. We want to bound the mutual information

$$I(U;Z) = I(U;Z_{1,\dots,m}) + I(U;Z_{m+1,\dots,n}|Z_{1,\dots,m}). \tag{73}$$

We bound the first term using Lemma 3.5. First we write

$$\begin{aligned}
I(U;Z_{1,\dots,m}) &= H(U) - H(U|Z_{1,\dots,m}) \\
&\le \tilde{n} - \sum_{z_{1,\dots,m}\in[q]^m} \Pr[Z_{1,\dots,m} = z_{1,\dots,m}]\cdot \\
&\qquad H(U|Z_{1,\dots,m} = z_{1,\dots,m}).
\end{aligned} \tag{74}$$

For any particular string of measurement outcomes $z_{1,\dots,m} \in [q]^m$, let $A \subset [n]$ be the set of qubits that were measured, and let M_A be the corresponding POVM element. Then, by Lemma 3.5, we have

$$\begin{aligned}
H(U|Z_{1,\dots,m} = z_{1,\dots,m}) &\ge H_2(U|Z_{1,\dots,m} = z_{1,\dots,m}) \\
&\ge \tilde{n} - \tilde{n}\tfrac{\lg(3/2)}{\lg(8/3)} - O(\lg(qn)).
\end{aligned} \tag{75}$$

We bound the second term using Holevo's inequality [34]. First we write

$$\begin{aligned}
&I(U;Z_{m+1,\dots,n}|Z_{1,\dots,m}) \\
&= \sum_{z_{1,\dots,m}\in[q]^m} \Pr[Z_{1,\dots,m} = z_{1,\dots,m}]\cdot \\
&\qquad I(U;Z_{m+1,\dots,n}|Z_{1,\dots,m} = z_{1,\dots,m}).
\end{aligned} \tag{76}$$

For any particular string of measurement outcomes $z_{1,\dots,m} \in [q]^m$, let $A \subset [n]$ be the set of qubits that were measured, and let $p(u) = \Pr[U=u|Z_{1,\dots,m} = z_{1,\dots,m}]$. (Also, for any quantum state ρ, let $S(\rho)$ denote the von Neumann entropy of ρ.) Then we have

$$\begin{aligned}
&I(U;Z_{m+1,\dots,n}|Z_{1,\dots,m} = z_{1,\dots,m}) \\
&\le S\Big(\sum_{u\in\{0,1\}^{\tilde{n}}} p(u)|E(u)\rangle\langle E(u)|_{[n]\setminus A}\Big) \\
&\quad - \sum_{u\in\{0,1\}^{\tilde{n}}} p(u) S\Big(|E(u)\rangle\langle E(u)|_{[n]\setminus A}\Big) \\
&\le n - m \le n - \tfrac{\tilde{n}}{\lg(8/3)} + 1.
\end{aligned} \tag{77}$$

Combining these bounds, we get

$$\begin{aligned}
I(U;Z) &\le \tilde{n} - \tilde{n} + \tilde{n}\tfrac{\lg(3/2)}{\lg(8/3)} + O(\lg(qn)) + n - \tfrac{\tilde{n}}{\lg(8/3)} + 1 \\
&\le n - \tilde{n}\tfrac{\lg(4/3)}{\lg(8/3)} + O(\lg(qn)) \\
&\approx n - (0.2933)\tilde{n} + O(\lg(qn)).
\end{aligned} \tag{78}$$

□

4. ONE-TIME MEMORIES FROM ISOLATED QUBITS

A one-time memory (OTM) is a device that implements the following functionality [1]: one party (Alice) can write two messages $s, t \in \{0,1\}^k$ into the device, and then give the device to another party (Bob); after receiving the device, Bob can then choose to read either s or t, but not both. The main application of OTM's is to construct one-time programs [1, 2, 3].

In this section, we will construct devices which are similar to OTM's, in the isolated qubits model. Our devices will not implement the ideal OTM functionality described above, but we conjecture that they do provide a weaker "leaky OTM" functionality that is still sufficient to construct one-time programs. We will first define this "leaky OTM" functionality, and then describe our construction based on isolated qubits.

4.1 Leaky OTM's

DEFINITION 4.1. *Fix some class of adversary strategies $\mathbb{M}$, some leakage parameter $\delta \in [0,1]$, and some failure probability $\varepsilon \in [0,1]$. A* leaky one-time memory (leaky OTM) *with parameters $(\mathbb{M}, \delta, \varepsilon)$ is a device that has the following behavior. Suppose that the device is programmed with two messages s and t chosen uniformly at random in $\{0,1\}^k$; and let S and T be the random variables containing these messages. Then:*

1. *Correctness: There exists an honest strategy $\mathcal{M}^{(1)} \in \mathbb{M}$ that interacts with the device and recovers the message s with probability $\ge 1-\varepsilon$. Likewise, there exists an honest strategy $\mathcal{M}^{(2)} \in \mathbb{M}$ that recovers the message t with probability $\ge 1-\varepsilon$.*

2. *Leaky security: For every strategy $\mathcal{M} \in \mathbb{M}$, if Z is the random variable containing the classical information output by $\mathcal{M}$, then with probability $\ge 1-\varepsilon$, Z takes on a value z such that $H_\infty^\varepsilon(S,T|Z=z) \ge (1-\delta)k$. (Here H_∞^ε is the smoothed min-entropy.)*

This leaky OTM is weaker than the ideal OTM in two important respects: it assumes that the messages s and t are chosen uniformly at random, independent of all other variables; and it allows the adversary to obtain partial information about both s and t, so long as the adversary still has $(1-\delta)k$ bits of uncertainty (as measured by the smoothed min-entropy).

Also, note that when we choose $\mathbb{M}$ to be the class of LOCC adversaries, the above definition yields information-theoretic (rather than computational) notions of correctness and security. In particular, the honest strategies are not required to be computationally efficient, but at the same time, security holds against LOCC adversaries with unbounded computational power.

We remark that this definition is mostly classical, rather than quantum. In particular, this definition assumes that the party who programs the OTM is classical, so that the messages s and t are classical bit strings. This definition also assumes that the party who reads the OTM may make (quantum) LOCC measurements, but immediately outputs a classical string z. These assumptions are reasonable, since the isolated qubits model is mostly classical, as LOCC operations can never generate quantum entanglement.

We conjecture that one can build a (non-leaky) OTM by combining a leaky OTM with an encryption scheme. The (non-leaky) OTM is prepared as follows: given two messages s and t, choose two keys k_1 and k_2 uniformly at random; then prepare a leaky OTM containing k_1 and k_2, as well as ciphertexts $x = \text{Enc}_{k_1}(s)$ and $y = \text{Enc}_{k_2}(t)$. To recover the message s, one can extract the key k_1 from the leaky OTM, and then decrypt the ciphertext x; likewise, to recover the message t, one can extract the key k_2, and decrypt the ciphertext y.

For this (non-leaky) OTM to be secure, the encryption scheme must be able to tolerate partial leakage of the keys k_1 and k_2. This bears some resemblance to previous work on leakage-resilient encryption [30, 31], but with a different notion of leakage — in this case, the adversary's leakage function is constrained to use only LOCC operations, but may depend on side information (namely, the ciphertexts x and y). We think it should be possible to construct encryption schemes secure against this kind of leakage; intuitively, this is because the leakage function cannot make use of the ciphertexts x and y, because the decryption functions $\text{Dec}_{k_1}(x)$ and $\text{Dec}_{k_2}(y)$ are too complicated to evaluate using LOCC operations. However, we leave this as an open problem.

Finally, we conjecture that one can use similar ideas to construct garbled circuits, and thus one-time programs [1].

4.2 Construction using isolated qubits

We consider a system of n isolated qubits, and we construct a set of states $|E(s,t)\rangle$ (for $s,t \in \{0,1\}^k$), where $k \approx (0.3991)n$. First, choose a random function $C : \{0,1\}^k \to \{0,1\}^n$, i.e., for each $s \in \{0,1\}^k$, choose $C(s) \in \{0,1\}^n$ independently and uniformly at random. Similarly, choose a random function $D : \{0,1\}^k \to \{0,1\}^n$. Now define

$$|E(s,t)\rangle := \bigotimes_{a=1}^{n} |\alpha_{C(s)_a D(t)_a}\rangle, \tag{79}$$

where the single-qubit states $|\alpha_{00}\rangle$, $|\alpha_{01}\rangle$, $|\alpha_{10}\rangle$, $|\alpha_{11}\rangle$ are defined in the same way as in the previous section (see equation (7)). Note that these states can be prepared using single-qubit operations in the isolated qubits model.

We now describe the "honest" measurement strategies, that can be used to learn either s or t. The states $|E(s,t)\rangle$ are reminiscent of Wiesner's conjugate coding [16], in that measuring in one basis reveals information about s, while measuring in another basis reveals information about t. Let us define the states

$$|\beta_\phi\rangle := \cos(\phi)|0\rangle + \sin(\phi)|1\rangle, \quad \phi \in \mathbb{R}. \tag{80}$$

Then measuring each qubit in the basis $\{|\beta_{\pi/8}\rangle, |\beta_{5\pi/8}\rangle\}$ returns a "noisy" copy of the string $C(s)$, which can be decoded to recover s (since, with high probability, C is a good error-correcting code). Likewise, measuring each qubit in the basis $\{|\beta_{-\pi/8}\rangle, |\beta_{3\pi/8}\rangle\}$ returns a "noisy" copy of the string $D(t)$, which can be decoded to recover t.

Is there some measurement strategy that will reveal both s and t? Wiesner pointed out that there does exist a joint measurement on the n qubits that can recover both s and t; this also follows from the "gentle measurement lemma" of Winter [39]. However, when the codes C and D are "unstructured," one may expect this measurement to be highly entangled, hence impossible to perform using only LOCC operations. We will give rigorous evidence that this is indeed the case.

We will show that these states partially satisfy the definition of a leaky OTM. In particular, with high probability over the random choice of C and D, the following statements hold:

1. Suppose s and t are chosen uniformly at random. There exists a sequence of single-qubit projective measurements that can reconstruct s with probability $\geq 1 - e^{-\Omega(n)}$. Likewise, there exists a sequence of single-qubit projective measurements that can reconstruct t with probability $\geq 1 - e^{-\Omega(n)}$.

2. Suppose s and t are chosen uniformly at random. No 1-pass LOCC measurement strategy using 2-outcome measurements can recover more than $\approx (1.9190)k$ bits of information about s and t. That is, if S and T are the random variables containing the strings s and t, and Z is the output of the measurement strategy, then

$$I(Z; S, T) \leq (1.9190)k + O(\sqrt{n}\log n). \tag{81}$$

Note that we can write $I(Z; S, T) = H(S,T) - H(S,T|Z)$, hence this implies

$$H(S,T|Z) \geq (0.081)k - O(\sqrt{n}\log n). \tag{82}$$

These statements are similar to the definition of a leaky OTM, where $\mathbb{M}$ is the set of 1-pass LOCC measurement strategies using 2-outcome measurements, the leakage parameter is $\delta \approx 0.9190$, the failure probability is $\varepsilon = e^{-\Omega(n)}$, and the security condition is relaxed by replacing the smoothed min-entropy H_∞^ε with the Shannon entropy H. (Also, we set aside the requirement that the honest strategies must be computationally efficient.)

We believe it should be possible to prove much stronger results of this type. In particular, it should be possible to improve our bound on the leakage parameter δ, as our current proof technique is somewhat ad hoc. Also, we remark that some parts of our proof already imply bounds on the smoothed min-entropy H_∞^ε. Specifically, in Lemma 4.4, we actually lower-bound the collision entropy $H_2(S,T|Z_{1,\dots,m} = z_{1,\dots,m})$, where $Z_{1,\dots,m}$ represents the measurement outcomes of the first m qubits measured by the adversary, where $m \approx (0.7067)k$. This directly implies a lower-bound on the smoothed min-entropy $H^{\varepsilon}_{\infty}(S,T|Z_{1,\dots,m} = z_{1,\dots,m})$, using a standard argument.[7]

4.3 Correctness for honest parties

First, we show that the honest strategies for recovering either s or t (as described above) do succeed with high probability. Without loss of generality, suppose we want to recover s. Let S and T be random variables, distributed independently and uniformly on $\{0,1\}^k$. We are given the state $|E(S,T)\rangle$, and we measure each qubit in the basis $\{|\beta_{\pi/8}\rangle, |\beta_{5\pi/8}\rangle\}$. Let Z be the random variable containing the string of measurement outcomes, i.e., Z takes values in $\{0,1\}^n$.

We decode Z as follows: we output any string $t \in \{0,1\}^k$ such that $d_H(C(t), Z) \leq r$, where d_H denotes the Hamming distance, and r is a parameter that we will set below. If there are multiple candidate strings t, we pick one of them in some arbitrary fashion. Let $\hat{S}$ be the random variable containing the output of this procedure.

Observe that Z is the output of a binary symmetric channel $BSC(p_e)$ applied to the string $C(S)$, where the error probability p_e is given by

$$p_e := \sin^2(\pi/8) \approx 0.1464. \tag{83}$$

Recall that the channel $BSC(p_e)$ has capacity $1 - h(p_e) \approx 0.3991$, where $h(p)$ is the binary entropy function,

$$h(p) := -p\lg(p) - (1-p)\lg(1-p). \tag{84}$$

Also, note that the expected number of errors introduced by the channel is np_e.

This suggests that we should set the parameters k and r as follows:

$$k := n(1 - h(p_e) - \theta), \tag{85}$$

$$r := n(p_e + \tau), \tag{86}$$

where $0 < \theta \ll 1$ and $0 < \tau \ll 1$ are small constants.

We prove the following statement, which is essentially Shannon's noisy coding theorem for the binary symmetric channel, using an argument from [40]. This shows that, when we choose θ and τ appropriately, then with high probability over the choice of the random code C, $\Pr[\hat{S} = S]$ is close to 1.

PROPOSITION 4.2. *Fix any constants $\lambda \geq 1$, $0 < \tau \leq \frac{1}{2} - p_e \approx 0.3536$, and $\theta > \tau h'(p_e) \approx (2.5431)\tau$. Then for all sufficiently large n, the following statement holds: with probability $\geq 1 - \frac{1}{\lambda}$ (over the choice of C), we have*

$$\Pr[\hat{S} = S] \geq 1 - \lambda\big[e^{-2\tau^2 n} + 2^{-n(\theta - \tau h'(p_e))}\big] \geq 1 - \lambda e^{-\Omega(n)}. \tag{87}$$

Proof: See Appendix D in the full version of this paper [42].

4.4 Security against 1-pass LOCC adversaries using 2-outcome measurements

In this section we will upper-bound the amount of information that can be extracted from our OTM devices by any 1-pass LOCC adversary using 2-outcome measurements. We use the collision entropy technique to analyze the first few steps taken by the adversary; then we use the entropy chaining technique to prove bounds on the adversary's subsequent steps. To deal with the correlations among the states $|E(s,t)\rangle$, we will use large deviation bounds for sums of locally dependent random variables [41, 38].

THEOREM 4.3. *Let $\mathbb{M}$ be the set of all 1-pass LOCC strategies that use 2-outcome measurements. Then, with probability $\geq 1 - e^{-\Omega(n)}$ (over the choice of C and D), the following statement holds:*

$$\forall \mathcal{M} \in \mathbb{M},\ I(Z;S,T) \leq (1.9190)k + O(\sqrt{n}\log n), \tag{88}$$

where Z denotes the output of the strategy $\mathcal{M}$. Equivalently, we can write:

$$\forall \mathcal{M} \in \mathbb{M},\ H(S,T|Z) \geq (0.081)k - O(\sqrt{n}\log n). \tag{89}$$

Proof: First, let L be an ε-net for the set of single-qubit measurements with 2 outcomes where all POVM elements have rank 1, as described in Lemma 2.2; and set $\varepsilon = 1/(200n)$. Let $\mathbb{M}'$ be the set of all strategies that use measurements chosen from the set L. By Lemmas 2.1 and 2.4, any strategy in $\mathbb{M}$ can be approximated by one in $\mathbb{M}'$.

We will analyze the first m steps of any strategy in $\mathbb{M}'$, where

$$m := \lfloor k/\lg(8/3) \rfloor \approx (0.7067)k. \tag{90}$$

We will show the following bound:

LEMMA 4.4. *With probability $\geq 1 - e^{-\Omega(n)}$ (over the choice of C and D),*

$$\forall \mathcal{M} \in \mathbb{M}',\ \forall z_{1,\dots,m} \in \{0,1\}^m,$$
$$H_2(S,T|Z_{1,\dots,m} = z_{1,\dots,m}) \geq 2k - m\lg(\tfrac{3}{2}) - \lg(O(n\lg n)), \tag{91}$$

where $Z_{1,\dots,m}$ denotes the output of the first m steps of the strategy $\mathcal{M}$, H_2 denotes the Renyi collision entropy, and $\lg(\frac{3}{2}) \approx 0.5850$.

Note that equation (91) is equivalent to the following statement:

> for all subsets of qubits $A \subset [n]$, of size $|A| = m$,
> for all possible measurement outcomes M_A, that can be obtained by measuring the qubits in A (using measurements chosen from the set L),
> $H_2(S,T|M_A) \geq 2k - m\lg(\frac{3}{2}) - \lg(O(n\lg n))$.

Also, recall that a measurement outcome M_A is uniquely represented by a rank-1 POVM element of the form $M_A = \bigotimes_{i\in A} M_i$, where each M_i is a POVM element acting on qubit i, that corresponds to one possible outcome of some measurement in the set L.

The proof of Lemma 4.4 is similar to that of Lemma 3.5, except that here we use large-deviation bounds for sums of locally dependent random variables [41, 38]. See Section 4.4 in the full version of this paper [42] for details.

We now return to the proof of Theorem 4.3. Consider any measurement strategy $\mathcal{M} \in \mathbb{M}'$, and let Z be its output.

[7] In particular, for any $\theta \geq 0$, if we set $\varepsilon = 2^{-\theta}$, then $H^{\varepsilon}_{\infty}(X) \geq H_2(X) - \theta$; this follows from Markov's inequality.

We will upper-bound the amount of information extracted during the first m steps, using Lemma 4.4:

$$\begin{aligned} I(S,T;Z_{1,\ldots,m}) &\\ &= H(S,T) - H(S,T|Z_{1,\ldots,m}) \\ &\le H(S,T) - \sum_{z_{1,\ldots,m}} \Pr[Z_{1,\ldots,m} = z_{1,\ldots,m}]\cdot \\ &\qquad\qquad H_2(S,T|Z_{1,\ldots,m} = z_{1,\ldots,m}) \\ &\le 2k - [2k - m\lg(\tfrac{3}{2}) - \lg(O(n\lg n))] \\ &= m\lg(\tfrac{3}{2}) + \lg(O(n\lg n)) \\ &= k\tfrac{\lg(3/2)}{\lg(8/3)} + \lg(O(n\lg n)). \end{aligned} \tag{92}$$

Next, we will analyze the subsequent steps of the adversary. First, let us fix some subset of qubits $A \subset [n]$, of size $|A| = m$, and some measurement outcome M_A; these represent past actions of the adversary during its first m steps. We will then upper-bound the amount of information gained by the adversary in the next $\tilde{m}$ steps, conditioned on M_A. Finally, we will use the union bound to show that this result holds simultaneously for all choices of A and M_A.

To simplify the notation, let us define $h := H_2(S,T|M_A)$, and $p_{st} := \Pr[S=s, T=t|M_A]$; so we have

$$\sum_{s,t\in\{0,1\}^k} p_{st}^2 \le 2^{-h}. \tag{93}$$

Note that h and p_{st} depend only on the qubits in the set A; so they only depend on those random variables $C(s)_a$ and $D(t)_a$ with $a \in A$. As shown above, with probability $\ge 1 - e^{-\Omega(n)}$ (over this subset of the random variables C and D),

$$h \ge 2k - m\lg(\tfrac{3}{2}) - \lg(O(n\lg n)). \tag{94}$$

We will look at the next $\tilde{m}$ steps of the adversary, and we set

$$\tilde{m} := \lfloor h - k \rfloor \ge k - m\lg(\tfrac{3}{2}) - \lg(O(n\lg n)). \tag{95}$$

More precisely, we let $\tilde{\mathbb{M}}$ be the set of all possible measurement strategies that an adversary in $\mathbb{M}'$ may follow for the next $\tilde{m}$ steps, after having received measurement outcome M_A on the first m steps. We let $\tilde{Z} := (Z_{m+1}, \ldots, Z_{m+\tilde{m}})$ be the output of the adversary on the next $\tilde{m}$ steps. Note that this depends only on the qubits outside the set A; so it only depends on those random variables $C(s)_a$ and $D(t)_a$ with $a \notin A$. We refer to this subset of random variables as $\tilde{C}$ and $\tilde{D}$. We show the following lemma:

LEMMA 4.5. *Fix a particular subset of qubits A and a particular measurement outcome M_A, as described above. Let $t_0 > 0$ and $u \ge 1$. With probability $\ge 1 - \exp(-2t_0^2) - 2\cdot 2^{-u^2}$ (over the choice of $\tilde{C}$ and $\tilde{D}$), the following statement holds:*

$$\forall \mathcal{M} \in \tilde{\mathbb{M}},\; I(\tilde{Z}; S,T|M_A) < \frac{\tilde{m}}{2} + \frac{t_0\tilde{m}}{2^{\tilde{m}/2}} + u\cdot O(\sqrt{\log n}). \tag{96}$$

The proof of Lemma 4.5 is similar to that of Theorem 3.3, with appropriate modifications to the large deviation bounds to allow for locally dependent random variables. See Section 4.4 in the full version of this paper [42] for details.

We now return to the proof of Theorem 4.3. We take the union bound over all subsets $A \subset [n]$ of size $|A| = m$, and all measurement outcomes M_A that correspond to measurements chosen from the set L and performed on the qubits in the set A. Then, with probability $\ge 1 - 2^{O(n\lg n)}\cdot \exp(-2t_0^2) - 2^{O(n\lg n)}\cdot 2\cdot 2^{-u^2}$, we have that:

$$\begin{gathered} \text{for all subsets } A \text{ of size } m, \\ \text{and for all measurement outcomes } M_A, \\ I(\tilde{Z}; S,T|M_A) < \frac{\tilde{m}}{2} + \frac{t_0\tilde{m}}{2^{\tilde{m}/2}} + u\cdot O(\sqrt{\log n}). \end{gathered} \tag{97}$$

By setting $t_0 := \Theta(\sqrt{n\log n})$ and $u := \Theta(\sqrt{n\log n})$, we can make the failure probability exponentially small in n.

Hence, for any measurement strategy $\mathcal{M} \in \mathbb{M}'$, with output Z, and any sequence of measurement outcomes $z_{1,\ldots,m}$, we have

$$I(Z_{m+1,\ldots,m+\tilde{m}}; S,T|Z_{1,\ldots,m} = z_{1,\ldots,m}) < \frac{\tilde{m}}{2} + O(\sqrt{n}\log n), \tag{98}$$

and hence

$$I(Z_{m+1,\ldots,m+\tilde{m}}; S,T|Z_{1,\ldots,m}) < \frac{\tilde{m}}{2} + O(\sqrt{n}\log n). \tag{99}$$

Finally, we consider the remaining steps of the adversary. Using Holevo's inequality [34] (see the proof of Theorem 3.4), we get that

$$I(Z_{m+\tilde{m}+1,\ldots,n}; S,T|Z_{1,\ldots,m+\tilde{m}}) \le n - m - \tilde{m}. \tag{100}$$

Combining equations (92), (99) and (100), we get that

$$\begin{aligned} I(Z;S,T) &\le m\lg(\tfrac{3}{2}) + \lg(O(n\lg n)) + \tfrac{1}{2}\tilde{m} + O(\sqrt{n}\log n) \\ &\quad + n - m - \tilde{m} \\ &= n - m\lg(\tfrac{4}{3}) - \tfrac{1}{2}\tilde{m} + O(\sqrt{n}\log n). \end{aligned} \tag{101}$$

From equations (85), (90) and (95), we have that

$$n \le \tfrac{k}{1-h(p_e)} + O(\sqrt{n}) \approx (2.5056)k + O(\sqrt{n}), \tag{102}$$

$$m = \lfloor \tfrac{k}{\lg(8/3)} \rfloor \approx \lfloor (0.7067)k \rfloor, \tag{103}$$

$$\begin{aligned} \tilde{m} &\ge k - m\lg(\tfrac{3}{2}) - \lg(O(n\lg n)) \\ &\ge k - \tfrac{k\lg(3/2)}{\lg(8/3)} - \lg(O(n\lg n)) \\ &\approx (0.5866)k - \lg(O(n\lg n)). \end{aligned} \tag{104}$$

Combining these bounds, we get that

$$I(Z;S,T) \le (1.9190)k + O(\sqrt{n}\log n), \tag{105}$$

as desired. □

Acknowledgements

It is a pleasure to thank Anne Broadbent, Daniel Gottesman, Jonathan Katz, Dianne O'Leary, Rene Peralta, Christian Schaffner, Jake Taylor, Stephanie Wehner, and several anonymous referees, for helpful suggestions regarding this work. In particular, I am grateful for suggestions about improving the presentation of the results, and corrections about the security properties needed to construct one-time programs, though unfortunately some of these issues could not be fully addressed in this paper. This work is a contribution of NIST, an agency of the US government, and is not subject to US copyright laws.

5. REFERENCES

[1] S. Goldwasser, Y.T. Kalai and G.N. Rothblum, "One-Time Programs," *CRYPTO 2008*, pp.39-56.

[2] V. Goyal, Y. Ishai, A. Sahai, R. Venkatesan and A. Wadia, "Founding Cryptography on Tamper-Proof Hardware Tokens," *TCC 2010*, pp.308-326.

[3] M. Bellare, V. T. Hoang and P. Rogaway, "Adaptively Secure Garbling with Applications to One-Time Programs and Secure Outsourcing," *ASIACRYPT 2012*, pp.134-153.

[4] A. Broadbent, G. Gutoski and D. Stebila, "Quantum one-time programs," arXiv:1211.1080.

[5] H.-K. Lo and H.F. Chau, "Is quantum bit commitment really possible?" *Phys. Rev. Lett.* 78, 3410 (1997).

[6] H.-K. Lo, "Insecurity of quantum secure computations," *Phys. Rev. A*, 56(2): 1154-1162 (1997).

[7] D. Mayers, "Unconditionally secure quantum bit commitment is impossible," *Phys. Rev. Lett.*, 78:3414-3417 (1997).

[8] H. Buhrman, M. Christandl and C. Schaffner, "Complete Insecurity of Quantum Protocols for Classical Two-Party Computation," *Phys. Rev. Lett.* 109, 160501 (2012).

[9] L. Salvail, "Quantum Bit Commitment from a Physical Assumption," *CRYPTO 1998*, pp.338-353.

[10] I. Damgaard, S. Fehr, L. Salvail and C. Schaffner, "Cryptography In the Bounded Quantum-Storage Model," *FOCS 2005*, pp.449-458.

[11] R. Koenig and B.M. Terhal, "The Bounded Storage Model in the Presence of a Quantum Adversary," *IEEE Trans. Inf. Th.*, vol. 54, no. 2 (2008).

[12] I. Damgaard, S. Fehr, L. Salvail and C. Schaffner, "Secure Identification and QKD in the Bounded-Quantum-Storage Model," *CRYPTO 2007*, pp.342-359.

[13] S. Wehner, C. Schaffner and B. Terhal, "Cryptography from Noisy Storage," *Phys. Rev. Lett.* 100, 220502 (2008).

[14] I. Damgard, S. Fehr, R. Renner, L. Salvail and C. Schaffner, "A Tight High-Order Entropic Quantum Uncertainty Relation with Applications," *CRYPTO 2007*, pp.360-378.

[15] N. J. Bouman, S. Fehr, C. Gonzalez-Guillen and C. Schaffner, "An All-But-One Entropic Uncertainty Relation, and Application to Password-Based Identification," *TQC 2012*, pp.29-44.

[16] S. Wiesner, "Conjugate coding," *ACM SIGACT News*, Volume 15, Issue 1, 1983, pp.78-88.

[17] C.H. Bennett, D.P. DiVincenzo, C.A. Fuchs, T. Mor, E. Rains, P.W. Shor, J.A. Smolin and W.K. Wootters, "Quantum nonlocality without entanglement," *Phys. Rev. A* 59, pp.1070âĂ§1091 (1999).

[18] A.M. Childs, D. Leung, L. Mancinska and M. Ozols, "A framework for bounding nonlocality of state discrimination," arXiv:1206.5822.

[19] D.P. DiVincenzo, D.W. Leung and B.M. Terhal, "Quantum Data Hiding," *IEEE Trans. Inf. Theory*, Vol. 48, No. 3, pp.580-599 (2002).

[20] T. Eggeling and R. F. Werner, "Hiding Classical Data in Multipartite Quantum States," *Phys. Rev. Lett.* 89, 097905 (2002).

[21] D.P. DiVincenzo, P. Hayden and B.M. Terhal, "Hiding Quantum Data," *Found. Phys.* 33(11), pp.1629-1647, 2003.

[22] P. Hayden, D. Leung and G. Smith, "Multiparty data hiding of quantum information," *Phys. Rev. A* 71, 062339 (2005).

[23] M. Talagrand, "Majorizing measures: the generic chaining," *Ann. Probab.*, Vol. 24, No. 3 (1996), pp.1049-1103.

[24] F. Jelezko and J. Wrachtrup, "Single defect centres in diamond: A review," *Physica Status Solidi (A)*, Volume 203, Issue 13, pp. 3207-3225, Oct. 2006.

[25] H. Bernien, B. Hensen, W. Pfaff, G. Koolstra, M. S. Blok, L. Robledo, T. H. Taminiau, M. Markham, D. J. Twitchen, L. Childress and R. Hanson, "Heralded entanglement between solid-state qubits separated by 3 meters," *Nature* 497, pp.86-90 (2013).

[26] F. Pastawski, N. Y. Yao, L. Jiang, M. D. Lukin and J. I. Cirac, "Unforgeable Noise-Tolerant Quantum Tokens," *Proc. Nat. Acad. Sci.* 109, 16079-16082 (2012).

[27] J. Walgate, A.J. Short, L. Hardy and V. Vedral, "Local Distinguishability of Multipartite Orthogonal Quantum States," *Phys. Rev. Lett.* 85, 4972 (2000).

[28] P.-X. Chen and C.-Z. Li, "Orthogonality and distinguishability: Criterion for local distinguishability of arbitrary orthogonal states," *Phys. Rev. A* 68, 062107 (2003).

[29] J. Walgate and A.J. Scott, "Generic local distinguishability and completely entangled subspaces," *J. Phys. A* 41, 375305 (2008).

[30] A. Akavia, S. Goldwasser and V. Vaikuntanathan, "Simultaneous Hardcore Bits and Cryptography against Memory Attacks," *TCC 2009*, pp.474-495.

[31] M. Naor and G. Segev, "Public-Key Cryptosystems Resilient to Key Leakage," *CRYPTO 2009*, pp.18-35.

[32] P. Hausladen and W. Wootters, "A 'pretty good' measurement for distinguishing quantum states," *J. Mod. Opt.* 41, pp.2385 (1994).

[33] A. Montanaro, "On the distinguishability of random quantum states," *Comm. Math. Phys.* 273(3), pp. 619-636, 2007.

[34] M.A. Nielsen and I.L. Chuang, *Quantum Computation and Quantum Information*, Cambridge University Press, 2000.

[35] H. Maassen and J. Uffink, *Phys. Rev. Lett.*, Vol. 60, pp.1103 (1988).

[36] S. Wehner and A. Winter, "Entropic uncertainty relations - A survey," *New J. Phys.*, Vol. 12, 025009 (2010).

[37] J.A. Tropp, "User-Friendly Tools for Random Matrices: An Introduction," manuscript, 2012, http://users.cms.caltech.edu/~jtropp/notes/Tro12-User-Friendly-Tools-NIPS.pdf.

[38] D.P. Dubhashi and A. Panconesi, *Concentration of Measure for the Analysis of Randomized Algorithms*, Cambridge University Press, 2009.

[39] A. Winter, "Coding theorem and strong converse for quantum channels," *IEEE Trans. Inform. Theory* 45(7), pp.2481-2485 (1999).

[40] D. Welsh, *Codes and Cryptography*, Oxford University Press, 1988.
[41] S. Janson, "Large Deviations for Sums of Partly Dependent Random Variables," *Random Struct. Alg.*, Vol. 24, pp.234-248, 2004.
[42] Y.-K. Liu, "Building One-Time Memories from Isolated Qubits," Arxiv:1304.5007.

APPENDIX

A. ENTROPY CHAINING

We prove a variant of Dudley's inequality, for bounding the expected supremum of a family of correlated random variables, $\mathbb{E}\sup_t X_t$, using entropy chaining. Our claim is a slight generalization of the usual statement of Dudley's inequality, in that it allows the random variables X_t to have different means; also, we state our result as a tail bound on $\sup_t X_t$, which is stronger than the usual form of Dudley's inequality. Nonetheless, the proof is more or less the same as the usual one; see, e.g., [23].

LEMMA A.1 (DUDLEY'S INEQUALITY TAIL BOUND). *Let $\{X_t \mid t \in T\}$ be a family of random variables taking values in $\mathbb{R}$. Define $\mu_t := \mathbb{E}\,X_t$.*

Let $d(\cdot,\cdot)$ be a metric on the set T, such that the following "increment condition" holds:

$$\Pr[X_s - X_t - \mu_s + \mu_t > u] \leq \exp(-u^2/d(s,t)^2), \quad \forall s,t \in T,\ \forall u > 0. \tag{106}$$

(Note that, by exchanging s and t, this also implies a similar bound on the lower tail of $X_s - X_t$.) Also, suppose that, for any sequence $s_1, s_2, s_3, \ldots \in T$, and any $t \in T$, if $\lim_{j\to\infty} d(s_j,t) = 0$, then $\lim_{j\to\infty} \mu_{s_j} = \mu_t$.

Suppose there exist $t_0 \in T$ and $\delta, \varepsilon > 0$, such that $Pr[X_{t_0} - \mu_{t_0} > \delta] \leq \varepsilon$. Then we have the following bound:

$$\Pr[\sup_t (X_t - \mu_t) > \delta + uS] \leq \varepsilon + 2 \cdot 2^{-u^2}, \quad \forall u \geq 1, \tag{107}$$

where

$$S \leq C_0 \int_0^\infty \sqrt{\log N(T,d,\varepsilon)}\, d\varepsilon, \tag{108}$$

C_0 is a numerical constant, and $N(T,d,\varepsilon)$ is the covering number, i.e., the minimum cardinality of an ε-net for the set T with respect to the metric $d(\cdot,\cdot)$.

By applying the same argument to the random variables $\{-X_t \mid t \in T\}$, we also have a lower bound. Suppose there exist $t_0 \in T$ and $\delta, \varepsilon > 0$, such that $Pr[X_{t_0} - \mu_{t_0} < -\delta] \leq \varepsilon$. Then:

$$\Pr[\inf_t (X_t - \mu_t) < -\delta - uS] \leq \varepsilon + 2 \cdot 2^{-u^2}, \quad \forall u \geq 1. \tag{109}$$

Proof: See Appendix C in the full version of this paper [42].

Attribute-Efficient Evolvability of Linear Functions

Elaine Angelino [*]
Harvard University
elaine@eecs.harvard.edu

Varun Kanade [†]
University of California, Berkeley
vkanade@eecs.berkeley.edu

ABSTRACT

In a seminal paper, Valiant (2006) introduced a computational model for evolution to address the question of complexity that can arise through Darwinian mechanisms. Valiant views evolution as a restricted form of computational learning, where the goal is to *evolve* a hypothesis that is close to the *ideal function*. Feldman (2008) showed that (correlational) statistical query learning algorithms could be framed as evolutionary mechanisms in Valiant's model. P. Valiant (2012) considered evolvability of real-valued functions and also showed that weak-optimization algorithms that use weak-evaluation oracles could be converted to evolutionary mechanisms.

In this work, we focus on the *complexity* of representations of evolutionary mechanisms. In general, the reductions of Feldman and P. Valiant may result in intermediate representations that are arbitrarily complex (polynomial-sized circuits). We argue that biological constraints often dictate that the representations have low complexity, such as constant depth and fan-in circuits. We give mechanisms for evolving sparse linear functions under a large class of smooth distributions. These evolutionary algorithms are attribute-efficient in the sense that the size of the representations and the number of generations required depend only on the sparsity of the target function and the accuracy parameter, but have no dependence on the total number of attributes.

Categories and Subject Descriptors

F.2 [**Analysis of Algorithms and Problem Complexity**]: General

[*]This author is supported in part by a grant from the National Library of Medicine (4R01LM010213-04) and NSF grant CCF-09-64401.

[†]This author is supported by a Simons Postdoctoral Fellowship.

ITCS'14, January 12–14, 2014, Princeton, New Jersey, USA.

http://dx.doi.org/10.1145/2554797.2554824.

Keywords

Evolvability, Computational Learning Theory, Regression

1. INTRODUCTION

Darwin's theory of evolution through natural selection has been a cornerstone of biology for over a century and a half. Yet, a quantitative theory of complexity that could arise through Darwinian mechanisms has remained virtually unexplored. To address this question, Valiant introduced a computational model of evolution [28]. In his model, an organism is an entity that computes a function of its environment. There is a (possibly hypothetical) *ideal function* indicating the best behavior in every possible environment. The performance of the organism is measured by how close the function it computes is to the ideal. An organism produces a set of offspring, that may have mutations that alter the function computed. The performance (fitness) measure acting on a population of mutants forms the basis of natural selection. The resources allowed are the most generous while remaining feasible; the mutation mechanism may be any efficient randomized Turing machine, and the function represented by the organism may be arbitrary as long as it is computable by an efficient Turing machine.

Formulated this way, the question of evolvability can be asked in the language of computational learning theory. For what classes of ideal functions, C, can one expect to find an evolutionary mechanism that gets arbitrarily close to the ideal, within feasible computational resources? Darwinian selection is restrictive in the sense that the only feedback received is *aggregate* over life experiences. Valiant observed that any feasible evolutionary mechanism could be simulated in the statistical query framework of Kearns [19]. In a remarkable result, Feldman showed that in fact, evolvable concept classes are exactly captured by a restriction of Kearns' model, where the learning algorithm is only allowed to make *performance queries*, *i.e.*, it produces a hypothesis and then makes a query to an oracle that returns the (approximate) performance of that hypothesis under the distribution [9].[1] P. Valiant studied the evolvability of real-valued functions and showed that whenever the corresponding weak optimization problem, *i.e.*, approximately minimizing the expected loss, can be solved by using a weak evaluation oracle, such an algorithm can be converted into an evolutionary mechanism [29]. This implies that a large class of functions –

[1]Feldman calls these correlational statistical queries, because when working with boolean functions with range $\{-1, 1\}$, the performance of any hypothesis is its correlation with the ideal function.

fixed-degree real polynomials – can be evolved with respect to any convex loss function.

Direct evolutionary mechanisms, not invoking the general reductions of Feldman and P. Valiant, have been proposed for certain classes in restricted settings. Valiant showed that the class of disjunctions is evolvable using a simple set of mutations under the uniform distribution [28]. Kanade, Valiant and Vaughan proposed a simple mechanism for evolving homogeneous linear separators under radially symmetric distributions [17]. Feldman considered a model where the ideal function is boolean but the representation can be real-valued, allowing for more detailed feedback. He presents an algorithm for evolving large margin linear separators for a large class of convex loss functions [11]. P. Valiant also showed that with very simple mutations, the class of fixed-degree polynomials can be evolved with respect to the squared loss [29].

Current understanding of biology (or lack thereof) makes it difficult to formalize a notion of *naturalness* for mutations in these frameworks; in particular, it is not well understood how mutations to DNA relate to functional changes in an organism. That said, the more direct algorithms are appealing due to the simplicity of their mutations. Also, the "chemical computers" of organisms may be slow, and hence, representations that have low complexity are attractive. In general, Feldman's generic reduction from statistical query algorithms may use arbitrarily complex representations (polynomial-sized circuits), depending on the specific algorithm used. In the remainder of the introduction, we first describe a particular class of biological circuits, *transcription networks*, that motivate our study. We then frame the evolutionary question in the language of computational learning theory, summarize our contributions and discuss related work.

1.1 Representation in Biology

Biological systems appear to function successfully with greatly restricted representation classes. The nature of circuits found in biological systems may vary, but some aspects – such as *sparsity* – are common. Specifically, the interacting components in many biological circuits are sparsely connected. Biological circuits are often represented as networks or graphs, where the vertices correspond to entities such as neurons or molecules and the edges to connections or interactions between pairs of entities. For example, both neural networks [31] and networks of metabolic reactions in the cell [30, 14] have been described by "small-world" models, where a few "hub" nodes have many edges but most nodes have few edges (and consequently, the corresponding graphs have small diameter). An associated property observed in biological networks is *modularity*: a larger network of interacting entities is composed of smaller modules of (functionally related) entities [12]. Both the "small-world" description and modularity of biological networks are consistent with the more general theme of sparsity.

We focus on transcription networks, which are a specific class of networks of interacting genes and proteins that are involved in the production of new protein. Alon provides an accessible and mathematical introduction to transcription networks and other biological circuits [1]; below and in Figure 1(a), we present a simplified account that motivates this work. Genes are *transcribed* to produce mRNA, which is then *translated* into sequences of amino acids that ultimately

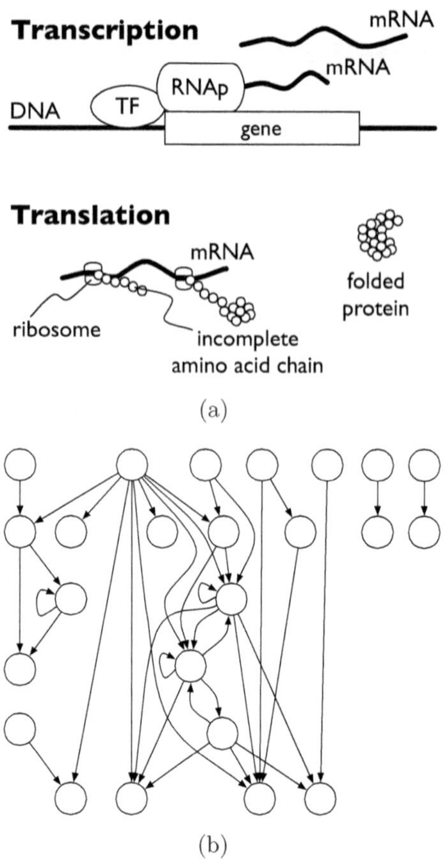

Figure 1: (a) Schematic of transcription (top) and translation (bottom). Here, a transcription factor (TF) binds to DNA close to a gene in a way that increases gene expression by encouraging RNA polymerase (RNAp) to transcribe the gene and so produce mRNA. The mRNA is then translated by ribosomes to produce sequences of amino acids that ultimately fold into proteins. Only a small number of transcription factors directly regulate any gene. Note that a transcription factor's action can also decrease gene expression. For a more complete picture, see *e.g.*, [1]. (b) Topology of the transcription network of respiration and redox reactions in yeast. $X \to Y$ represents that transcription factor X regulates the expression of Y. Note that this real network has cycles. Adapted from [23].

fold into proteins.[2] In a transcription network, a gene's transcription may be regulated by a set of proteins called *transcription factors*. These transcription factors may increase or decrease a gene's transcription by physically binding to regions of DNA that are typically close to the gene. In nat-

[2]In reality, this is a dynamical system where the rates of production are important. Note that this process need not be linear: a gene (mRNA transcript) can be transcribed (translated) multiple times, not only in series but also in parallel fashion. We also ignore other *epigenetic* effects, *i.e.*, molecular modifications to DNA that do not change its sequence but alter gene expression, *e.g.*, the addition of methyl groups to nucleotides in a way that physically blocks transcription.

ural systems, only a small number of transcription factors regulate any single gene, and so transcription networks are sparsely connected. For example, Balaji *et al.* studied a yeast transcription network of 157 transcription factors regulating 4,410 genes. They observed this network to have 12,873 interactions (edges) where each gene was regulated on average by about 2.9 transcription factors, the distribution of in-degrees was well-described by an exponential fit, and only about 45 genes had an in-degree of 15 or greater [3].

The number of transcription factors varies from hundreds in a bacterium to thousands in a human cell. Some transcription factors are always present in the cell and can be thought of as representing a *snapshot* of the environment [1]. For example, the presence of sugar molecules in the environment may cause specific transcription factors to be *activated*, enabling them to regulate the production of other proteins. One of these proteins could be an *end-product*, such as an enzyme that catalyzes a metabolic reaction involving the sugar. Alternatively, the transcription factor could regulate another transcription factor that itself regulates other genes – we view this as intermediate computation – and may participate in further "computation" to produce the desired end-result.

While transcription networks may include cycles (loops), here for simplicity we focus on systems that are directed acyclic graphs, and the resulting computation can be viewed as a circuit. We illustrate a small, real transcription network in Figure 1(b). These circuits are by necessity shallow due to a temporal constraint, that the time required for sufficient quantities of protein to be produced is of the same order of magnitude as cell-division time.[3] For example, Luscombe *et al.* measured the shortest path length (in number of intermediate nodes) between transcription factors and regulated genes corresponding to terminal nodes (leaves) in a yeast transcription network. In the static network, the mean such path length was 4.7 and the longest path involved 12 intermediate transcription factors [21].

1.2 Our Contributions

First, our contribution is conceptual. We believe that the study of evolvability from a computational standpoint will benefit by understanding the representation complexity required to evolve a certain concept class. Motivated by the previous discussion, in the case of transcription networks, it appears essential that the representation used be a constant depth and fan-in (boolean or arithmetic) circuit. Of course, any function that can be represented by such a circuit can depend only on a constant number of input variables. We ask the question, when we restrict attention to functions in a given class that depend only on a constant number of variables, when can evolution succeed?

Second, we show that the class of sparse linear functions, those that depend only on a constant number of variables, under a large class of smooth distributions, can be evolved using sparse linear functions as representations, when the performance is measured using squared error. The number of variables used by the representations is larger than the number of variables in the *ideal function* and depends on the *smoothness* parameter of the distribution. According to our notion of Δ-smooth G-nice distributions (Defn. 2), the density function of a smooth distribution is obtained by convolution of an arbitrary density with a product measure on $[-\sqrt{3}\Delta, \sqrt{3}\Delta]^n$ (alternatively, drawing a point from the smooth distribution is equivalent to drawing a point from an arbitrary distribution and adding a (noise) vector from a product distribution).

A linear function is represented by a weighted arithmetic circuit with only one addition gate (alternatively, by a depth-two circuit with a layer of multiplication gates and some constant inputs).[4] Also, the number of generations required for evolution to succeed depends polynomially on the sparsity k of the target linear function, the smoothness parameter Δ of the distribution and the inverse of the target accuracy ϵ, and has no dependence on the dimension n of the input space. The number of mutations explored at each generation depends polynomially in n and $1/\epsilon$. Thus, our result shows *attribute-efficient* evolvability of sparse linear functions, in the sense of Littlestone [20]. For the precise statement, see Theorem 1 in Section 3.1.

Valiant also proposed a stronger selection mechanism – when natural selection aggressively selects the (almost) best mutation, rather than merely a beneficial one – called evolution by optimization. Our second result requires a much stronger distributional assumption – that the correlation $\mathrm{corr}(x_i, x_j) \leq 1/(2k)$ – where k is the sparsity of the target linear function (see Defn. 3). Under such distributions, we show that under evolution by optimization, sparse linear functions can be evolved by representations with the same sparsity. The mechanism we propose and its analysis is inspired by the greedy orthogonal matching pursuit algorithms in signal processing [7, 27]. Unlike the previous evolutionary algorithm, this one requires initialization, *i.e.*, the evolutionary process begins with the 0 function. As in the previous case, the number of generations required depends polynomially on the sparsity k of the target linear function, the inverse of the accuracy parameter ϵ, but has no dependence on the total number of attributes n. The precise statement appears as Theorem 2 in Section 3.2.

1.3 Related Work

The question of proper vs. improper learning has been studied in computational learning theory. A separation between the two kinds is known, unless NP = RP. However, most interesting PAC-learnable classes can be learned using thresholds of low-degree polynomials, and do not seem to require the full generality of polynomial-sized circuits.[5] In this context, Valiant's disjunction algorithm under the uniform distribution [28], Kanade *et al.*'s algorithm for homogeneous half-spaces under radially symmetric distributions [17], and P. Valiant's algorithm for linear (polynomial) functions using squared loss [29], are *proper* evolutionary mechanisms, *i.e.*, the representation used is from the same class as the

[3]Other kinds of networks, such as signaling networks, operate by changing the shapes of proteins. The fact that these transformations are rapid may allow for much larger depth. Note that fast conformational changes govern how transcription factors directly process information from the environment in order to regulate gene expression. In our example, a sugar molecule binds to a transcription factor and changes its shape in a way that alters its ability to bind to DNA.

[4]There is a natural tradeoff between fan-in and depth, that may be useful, depending on which is the more severe constraint.

[5]For example, the classes of k-CNF, k-term DNF, decision lists and low-rank decision trees, can all be represented as PTFs.

ideal function. In the first two cases, it is straightforward to show that if the target depends only on a constant number of variables, the evolutionary mechanism also succeeds using representations that depend only on a constant number of variables. Thus, attribute-efficient evolution can be achieved.

The problem of learning sparse linear functions has been studied under various names in several fields for many applications, *e.g.*, recovering sparse solutions to (underdetermined) linear systems of equations [4], or recovering sparse representations with a redundant dictionary [22, 8]; compressive sampling or compressed sensing for sparse signal reconstruction [5]; optimization with regularization or sparsity-inducing penalties in machine learning [2]; sparse coding for learning an overcomplete basis [25], or for denoising in image and video processing [8]. This area is too vast to review here; Bruckstein *et al.* have an excellent survey [4]. Learning the sparsest linear function is equivalent to finding the sparsest solution to a system of linear equations (assuming there is no noise in the data). In general, this problem is NP-hard and the currently best-known approximation factor depends on the norm of the pseudo-inverse of the matrix [24]. Thus, some assumption on the distribution seems necessary. Our evolution based on optimization algorithm (Section 3.2) is essentially the greedy orthogonal matching pursuit algorithm of Tropp [27] and Donoho *et al.* [7], cast in the language of evolvability; these algorithms are also known in statistical modeling as forward stepwise regression [6, 13].

Finally, the question of *attribute-efficient* regression in the PAC (or SQ) model is a natural one. Here, the goal would be to design a polynomial time algorithm for producing an ϵ-accurate linear function, with sample complexity that is polynomial in the sparsity k of the target function and the inverse of the target accuracy ϵ, and only polylogarithmic in n, the total number of attributes. Under mild boundedness assumptions on the distribution, this can be achieved by setting up an L_1-regularized optimization problem; the output classifier may not be sparse in light of the NP-hardness result mentioned above. We note that under the distributional assumption made in this paper, finding the *sparsest* linear function that fits the data is also easy in the PAC/SQ setting, since the solution to the optimization problem in this case is unique. The focus in our work is different, namely showing that simple evolutionary mechanisms can succeed, while using representations that are themselves sparse linear functions at all times.

Organization

In Section 2, we give an overview of Valiant's evolution model and describe the concept classes and class of distributions considered in this paper. Section 3 contains the mechanisms for evolving sparse linear functions. We conclude in Section 4 with some discussion and directions for future work.

2. MODEL AND PRELIMINARIES

We first provide an overview of the evolvability framework of Valiant [28]. The description here differs slightly from Valiant's original formulation and includes some subsequent extensions (for more details the reader is referred to [28, 9, 10, 29, 16]).

2.1 Valiant's Evolvability Framework

Let X denote a set of instances, *e.g.*, $X = \mathbb{R}^n$ or $X = \{0,1\}^n$. We assume that the representation length of each $x \in X$ is captured by the parameter n. To avoid excessive notation, we will keep this size parameter implicit in our description of the model. Let D be a distribution over X. Each $x \in X$ can be thought of as the description of an environmental setting, the inputs to any circuit of an organism. D denotes the distribution over the possible environmental settings an organism may experience in a lifetime. Let $f : X \to Y$ (typically $Y = \mathbb{R}$ or $Y = \{0,1\}$) denote the *ideal function*, the best behavior in each possible environmental setting.

Representations

A creature is a string representation that encodes an efficiently computable function $r : X \to Y$, *i.e.*, there is an efficient Turing Machine that, given the description string $\langle r \rangle$ and $x \in X$, outputs $r(x)$.

In this work, our focus is characterizing different evolutionary mechanisms based on the complexity of representations used. The complexity of a representation is measured by the function it computes. Let $H : X \to Y$ be a class of functions. For $R \subseteq \{0,1\}^*$, we say that R *represents* H, if there is a map, $\sigma : R \to H$, and if there exists an *efficient* Turing machine that, given input $r \in R$ and $x \in X$, outputs $(\sigma(r))(x)$. Henceforth, by abuse of notation we will use r to denote both the representation and the function it computes, $\sigma(r)$.

Evolutionary Algorithms

The performance of a representation r is measured using a loss function $\ell : Y \times Y \to \mathbb{R}^+$, such that $\ell(y, y) = 0$. For a function $g : X \to Y$, define the expected loss with respect to the ideal function $f : X \to Y$, under distribution D, as $\mathrm{L}_{f,D}(g) = \mathbb{E}_{x\sim D}[\ell(g(x), f(x))]$.[6] The goal of evolution is to reach some representation r^* such that $\mathrm{L}_{f,D}(r^*) < \epsilon$. In the following discussion, we use the notation: f the ideal function, ϵ the target accuracy, D the target distribution over X and $\mathrm{L}_{f,D}(g)$ the expected loss function.

Mutator: A mutator $\mathsf{Mut}(r, \epsilon)$, for a set of representations R, is a polynomial-time randomized Turing machine that takes as input a representation $r \in R$ and accuracy parameter ϵ and outputs a multiset $\mathsf{Neigh}(r, \epsilon) \subseteq R$. The running time requirement on Mut also ensures that $|\mathsf{Neigh}(r, \epsilon)|$ is polynomially bounded.

Selection: (Natural) Selection is based on the empirical performance of each representation. Let $s : R \times [0,1] \to \mathbb{N}$ be a sample size function. First, the mutation algorithm, $\mathsf{Mut}(r, \epsilon)$, is run to produce multiset $\mathsf{Neigh}(r, \epsilon)$. Then, an i.i.d. sample $\langle x^i \rangle_{i=1}^s$ is drawn from the distribution D over X, where $s = s(r, \epsilon)$. Denote the empirical performance of each $r' \in \mathsf{Neigh}(r, \epsilon) \cup \{r\}$ as

$$\hat{\mathrm{L}}_{f,D}(r') = \frac{1}{s} \sum_{i=1}^{s} \ell(r'(x^i), f(x^i))$$

Finally, let $t : R \times [0,1] \to \mathbb{R}$ be a tolerance function. Two possible selection mechanisms are considered.

[6]This definition does not require the expected loss to be bounded, but we will mainly be interested in situations when that is the case.

1. **Selection based on beneficial and neutral mutations** (BN-Sel): Let

$$\mathsf{Bene} = \{r' \in \mathsf{Neigh}(r,\epsilon) \mid \hat{\mathrm{L}}_{f,D}(r') \leq \hat{\mathrm{L}}_{f,D}(r) - t(r,\epsilon)\}$$

denote the set of beneficial mutations and let

$$\mathsf{Neut} = \{r' \in \mathsf{Neigh}(r,\epsilon) \mid |\hat{\mathrm{L}}_{f,D}(r') - \hat{\mathrm{L}}_{f,D}(r)| < t(r,\epsilon)\}$$

denote the neutral mutations, with respect to tolerance function t. Both Bene and Neut are treated as multisets (the multiplicity of any representation is the same as that in $\mathsf{Neigh}(r,\epsilon)$). Selection operates as follows: if $\mathsf{Bene} \neq \emptyset$, r' is randomly selected from Bene as the surviving creature at the next generation. If $\mathsf{Bene} = \emptyset$ and $\mathsf{Neut} \neq \emptyset$, then r' is selected randomly from Neut as the surviving creature at the next generation. Otherwise, $\perp$ is produced signifying failure of evolution.

2. **Selection based on optimization** (Opt-Sel): Let $\widehat{\mathsf{opt}} = \min_{r' \in \mathsf{Neigh}(r,\epsilon)} \hat{\mathrm{L}}_{f,D}(r')$. If $\widehat{\mathsf{opt}} > \hat{\mathrm{L}}_{f,D}(r) + t(r,\epsilon)$, then $\perp$ is produced signifying failure of evolution. Otherwise, consider the multiset,

$$\mathsf{Best} = \{r' \in \mathsf{Neigh}(r,\epsilon) \mid \hat{\mathrm{L}}_{f,D}(r') \leq \widehat{\mathsf{opt}} + t(r,\epsilon)\},$$

and then r' is chosen from Best randomly as the surviving creature at the next generation.

Thus, while the selection rule BN-Sel only chooses some beneficial (or at least neutral) mutation, Opt-Sel aggressively picks the (almost) best mutation from the available pool.

We denote by $r' \leftarrow \mathsf{Sel}[R, \mathsf{Mut}, s, t](r,\epsilon)$ the fact that r' is the surviving creature in the next generation after one mutation and selection operation on the representation r and accuracy parameter ϵ. Here, Sel may be one of the two selection rules described above. For Sel to be feasible we require that the size function s is polynomially bounded (in n and $1/\epsilon$) and that the inverse of the tolerance function t is polynomially sandwiched, *i.e.*, there exists polynomials $p_1(n, 1/\epsilon)$ and $p_2(n, 1/\epsilon)$ such that $1/p_1(n,1/\epsilon) \leq t(r,\epsilon) \leq 1/p_2(n,1/\epsilon)$ for every $r \in R$ and $\epsilon > 0$.

Evolutionary Algorithm: An evolutionary algorithm $\mathcal{E}A$ is a tuple $(R, \mathsf{Mut}, s, t, \mathsf{Sel})$. When $\mathcal{E}A$ is run starting from $r_0 \in R$ with respect to distribution D over X, ideal function $f: X \to Y$, loss function ℓ and parameter ϵ, a sequence $r_0, r_1, r_2, \ldots$ is produced, where $r_i \leftarrow \mathsf{Sel}[R, \mathsf{Mut}, s, t](r_{i-1}, \epsilon)$. If $r_i = \perp$ for some i, we consider evolution as halted and $r_j = \perp$ for $j > i$. We say that $\mathcal{E}A$ succeeds at generation g, if g is the smallest index for which the expected loss $\mathrm{L}_{f,D}(r_g) \leq \epsilon$.

Definition 1 (Evolvability [28]). *We say that a concept class C is evolvable with respect to loss function ℓ and selection rule* Sel, *under a class of distributions $\mathcal{D}$ using a representation class H, if there exists a representation scheme $R \subseteq \{0,1\}^*$, such that R represents H, and there exists an evolutionary algorithm $\mathcal{E}A = (R, \mathsf{Mut}, s, t, \mathsf{Sel})$, such that for every $D \in \mathcal{D}$, every $f \in C$, every $\epsilon > 0$, and every $r_0 \in R$, with probability at least $1-\epsilon$, $\mathcal{E}A$ run starting from r_0 with respect to f, D, ℓ, ϵ, produces r_g for which $\mathrm{L}_{f,D}(r_g) < \epsilon$. Furthermore, the number of generations g required for evolution to succeed should be bounded by a polynomial in n and $1/\epsilon$.*

Remark 1. *If the evolutionary algorithm succeeds only for a specific starting representation r_0, we say C is evolvable with* initialization.

Remark 2. *If the functions in concept class C depend only on k variables, we say the evolutionary algorithm is attribute-efficient, if the size function, s, is polylogarithmic in n, and polynomial in k and $1/\epsilon$, and the number of generations, g, is polynomial in k and $1/\epsilon$, but does not depend on n.*

The definition presented above varies slightly from the definition of Valiant, in the sense that we explicitly focus on the complexity of representations used by the evolutionary algorithm. As discussed in the introduction, we focus on concept classes where each function depends on *few* (constant) input variables.[7]

2.2 Sparse Linear Functions

Our main result in this paper concerns the class of sparse linear functions. We represent a linear function from $\mathbb{R}^n \to \mathbb{R}$ by a vector $w \in \mathbb{R}^n$, where $x \mapsto w \cdot x$. For a vector $w \in \mathbb{R}^n$, sparsity(w) is the number of non-zero elements of w.

For any $0 \leq l < u$ and integer k, define the class of linear functions:

$$\mathsf{Lin}^k_{l,u} = \{x \mapsto w \cdot x \mid \mathrm{sparsity}(w) \leq k, \forall i, w_i = 0 \text{ or } l \leq |w_i| \leq u\}$$

Thus, $\mathsf{Lin}^k_{l,u}$ is the class of k-sparse linear functions, where the "influence" of each variable is upper and lower bounded.[8]

Let D be a distribution over $\mathbb{R}^n$. For $w, w' \in \mathbb{R}^n$, define the inner product $\langle w, w' \rangle = \mathbb{E}_{x \sim D}[(w \cdot x)(w' \cdot x)]$, where $w \cdot x = \sum_{i=1}^n w_i x_i$ denotes the standard dot product in $\mathbb{R}^n$. In this paper, we use $\|w\|$ to denote $\sqrt{\langle w, w \rangle}$ (and not $\sqrt{\sum_i w_i^2}$). To avoid confusion, whenever necessary, we will refer to the quantity $\sqrt{\sum_i w_i^2}$ explicitly if we mean the standard Euclidean norm.

Distribution Classes

We use two classes of distributions for our results in this paper. We define them formally here.

Smooth Bounded Distributions: We consider the class of smooth bounded distributions over $\mathbb{R}^n$. The concept of smoothed analysis of algorithms was introduced by Spielman and Teng [26] and recently the idea has been used in learning theory [15, 18]. We consider distributions that are bounded and have 0 mean. Formally, distributions we consider are defined as:

Definition 2 (Δ-Smooth G-Nice Distribution). *A distribution D is a Δ-smooth G-nice distribution if it is obtained as follows. Let $\tilde{D}$ be some distribution over $\mathbb{R}^n$, and let U^n_a denote the uniform distribution over $[-a,a]^n$. Then $D = \tilde{D} * U^n_{\sqrt{3}\Delta}$ is obtained by the convolution of $\tilde{D}$ with $U^n_{\sqrt{3}\Delta}$.*[9] *Furthermore, D satisfies the following:*

[7]These functions have been referred to as juntas in the theory literature. We avoid using this nomenclature as we restrict our attention to specific functional forms, such as linear functions, with k relevant variables.

[8]We do not use the word "influence" in the precise technical sense here.

[9]We could perform convolution with a spherical Gaussian distribution, however, this would make the resulting dis-

1. $\mathbb{E}_D[x] = 0$

2. For all i, $\mathbb{E}_D[x_i^2] \le 1$

3. For every x in the support of D, $\sum_{i=1}^n x_i^2 \le G^2$

Incoherent Distributions: We also consider *incoherent* distributions.[10] For a distribution D over $\mathbb{R}^n$, the coherence is defined as $\max_{i,j} \operatorname{corr}(x_i, x_j)$, where $\operatorname{corr}(x_i, x_j)$ is the correlation between x_i and x_j. Again, we consider bounded distributions with zero mean. We also require the variance to be upper and lower bounded in each dimension. Formally, the distributions we consider are defined as:

DEFINITION 3 (μ-INCOHERENT (Δ, G)-NICE DISTRIBUTION). *A distribution D is a μ-incoherent (Δ, G)-nice distribution if the following hold:*

1. $\mathbb{E}_D[x] = 0$

2. For all i, $\Delta^2 \le \mathbb{E}_D[x_i^2] \le 1$

3. For all i, j, $\max_{i,j} \operatorname{corr}(x_i, x_j) \le \mu$

4. For all x in the support of D, $\sum_{i=1}^n x_i^2 \le G^2$

We say a linear function represented by $w \in \mathbb{R}^n$ is W-bounded if $\sum_{i=1}^n w_i^2 \le W^2$. We use the notation $w(x) = w \cdot x$. Suppose f, w are W-bounded linear functions, and distribution D is such that for every x in the support of D, $\sum_{i=1}^n x_i^2 \le G^2$. We consider the squared loss function, which for $y, y' \in \mathbb{R}$ is $\ell(y', y) = (y' - y)^2$. Then, for any x in the support of D, $\ell(f(x), w(x)) \le 4W^2G^2$. Thus, standard Hoeffding bounds imply that if $\langle x^i \rangle_{i=1}^s$ is an i.i.d. sample drawn from D, then

$$\Pr\left[\left|\frac{1}{s}\sum_{i=1}^{s} \ell(w(x^i), f(x^i)) - \mathrm{L}_{f,D}(w)\right| \ge \tau\right] \le 2\exp\left(-\frac{s\tau^2}{8W^2G^2}\right) \quad (1)$$

Finally, for linear functions w ($x \mapsto w \cdot x$), let $\mathsf{NZ}(w) = \{i \mid w_i \neq 0\}$ denote the non-zero variables in w, so $\operatorname{sparsity}(w) = |\mathsf{NZ}(w)|$. Then, we have the following Lemma. The proof appears in Appendix A.1.

LEMMA 1. *Let D be a Δ-smooth G-nice distribution (Defn. 2), let $w \in \mathbb{R}^n$ be a vector and consider the corresponding linear function, $x \mapsto w \cdot x$. Then the following are true:*

1. For any $1 \le i \le n$, $w_i^2 \le \frac{\langle w, w \rangle}{\Delta^2}$.

2. There exists an i such that $w_i^2 \le \frac{\langle w, w \rangle}{|\mathsf{NZ}(w)|\Delta^2}$.

tribution unbounded. All results in this paper hold if we work with sub-Gaussian distributions and consider convolution with a spherical Gaussian distribution with variance Δ^2. In this case, we would be required to use Chebychev's inequality rather than Hoeffding's bound to show that the empirical estimate is close to the expected loss with high probability.

[10]This terminology is adapted from incoherence of matrices, *e.g.*, see [4].

3. EVOLVING SPARSE LINEAR FUNCTIONS

In this section, we describe two evolutionary algorithms for evolving sparse linear functions. The first evolves the class $\mathsf{Lin}_{l,u}^k$ under the class of Δ-smooth G-nice distributions (Defn. 2), using the selection rule $\mathsf{BN\text{-}Sel}$. The second evolves the class $\mathsf{Lin}_{0,u}^k$ under the more restricted class of $(1/2k)$-incoherent (Δ, G)-nice distributions (Defn. 3), using the selection rule $\mathsf{Opt\text{-}Sel}$. We first define the notation used in the rest of this section.

Notation: D denotes the target distribution over $X = \mathbb{R}^n$, f denotes the ideal (target) function. The inner product $\langle \cdot, \cdot \rangle$ and 2-norm $\|\cdot\|$ of functions are with respect to the distribution D. $[n]$ denotes the set $\{1, \ldots, n\}$. For $S \subseteq [n]$, f^S denotes the best linear approximation of f using the variables in the set S; formally,

$$f^S = \underset{w \in \mathbb{R}^n \,:\, w_i = 0 \;\vee\; i \in S}{\operatorname{argmin}} \|f - w\|^2$$

Finally, recall that for $w \in \mathbb{R}^n$, $\mathsf{NZ}(w) = \{i \mid w_i \neq 0\}$ and $\operatorname{sparsity}(w) = |\mathsf{NZ}(w)|$. A vector w represents a linear function, $x \mapsto w \cdot x$. The vector e^i has 1 in coordinate i and 0 elsewhere and corresponds to the linear function $x \mapsto x_i$. Thus, in this notation, $\operatorname{corr}(x_i, x_j) = \langle e^i, e^j \rangle / (\|e^i\|\|e^j\|)$. The accuracy parameter is denoted by ϵ.

3.1 Evolving Sparse Linear Functions Using BN-Sel

We present a simple mechanism that evolves the class of sparse linear functions $\mathsf{Lin}_{l,u}^k$ with respect to Δ-smooth G-nice distributions (see Defn. 2). The representation class also consists of sparse linear functions, but with a greater number of non-zero entries than the *ideal function*. We also assume that a linear function is represented by $w \in \mathbb{R}^n$, where each w_i is a real number. (Handling the issues of finite precision is standard and is avoided in favor of simplicity.) Define the parameters $K = 5184(k/\Delta)^4(u/l)^2$ and $B = 10uk/\Delta$. Formally, the representation class is:

$$R = \{w \mid \operatorname{sparsity}(w) \le K, w_i \in [-B, B]\}$$

The important point to note is that the parameters K and B do not depend on n, the total number of variables.

Next, we define the mutator. Recall that the mutator is a randomized algorithm that takes as input an element $r \in R$ and accuracy parameter ϵ, and outputs a multiset $\mathsf{Neigh}(r, \epsilon) \subseteq R$. Here, $\mathsf{Neigh}(r, \epsilon)$ is populated by m independent draws from the following procedure, where m will be specified later (see the proof of Theorem 1). Starting from $w \in R$, define the mutated representation w', output by the mutator, as:

1. *Scaling*: With probability 1/3, choose $\gamma \in [-1, 1]$ uniformly at random and let $w' = \gamma w$.

2. *Adjusting*: With probability 1/3, do the following. Pick $i \in \mathsf{NZ}(w) = \{i \mid w_i \neq 0\}$ uniformly at random. Let w' denote the mutated representation, where $w'_j = w_j$ for $j \neq i$, and choose $w'_i \in [-B, B]$ uniformly at random.

3. With the remaining 1/3 probability, do the following:

   (a) *Swapping*: If $|\mathsf{NZ}(w)| = K$, choose $i_1 \in \mathsf{NZ}(w)$ uniformly at random. Then, choose $i_2 \in [n] \setminus \mathsf{NZ}(w)$ uniformly at random. Let w' be the mutated representation, where $w'_j = w_j$ for $j \neq$

i_1, i_2. Set $w'_{i_1} = 0$ and choose $w'_{i_2} \in [-B, B]$ uniformly at random. In this case, $\text{sparsity}(w') = \text{sparsity}(w) = K$ with probability 1, and hence $w' \in R$.

(b) *Adding*: If $|\mathsf{NZ}(w)| < K$, choose $i \in [n] \setminus \mathsf{NZ}(w)$ uniformly at random. Let w' be the mutated representation, where $w'_j = w_j$ for $j \neq i$, and choose $w'_i \in [-B, B]$ uniformly at random.

Recall that $f \in \mathsf{Lin}^k_{l,u}$ denotes the ideal (target) function and D is the underlying distribution that is Δ-smooth G-nice (see Defn. 2). Since we are working with the squared loss metric, $\ell(y', y) = (y' - y)^2$, the expected loss for any $w \in R$ is given by $\mathrm{L}_{f,D}(w) = \|f - w\|^2 = \langle f - w, f - w\rangle$. We will show that for any $w \in R$, if $\|f - w\|^2 > \epsilon$, with non-negligible (inverse polynomial) probability, the above procedure produces a mutation w' that decreases the expected loss by at least some inverse polynomial amount. Thus, by setting the size of the neighborhood m large enough, we can guarantee that with high probability there will always exist a beneficial mutation.

To simplify notation, let $S = \mathsf{NZ}(w)$. Recall that f^S denotes the best approximation to f using variables in the set S; thus, $\|f - w\|^2 = \|f - f^S\|^2 + \|f^S - w\|^2$. At a high level, the argument for proving the success of our evolutionary mechanism is as follows: If $\|f^S - w\|^2$ is large, then a mutation of the type "scaling" or "adjusting" will get w closer to f^S, reducing the expected loss. (The role of "scaling" mutations is primarily to ensure that the representations remain bounded.) If $\|f^S - w\|^2$ is small and $S \neq \mathsf{NZ}(f)$, there must be a variable in $\mathsf{NZ}(f) \setminus S$, that when added to w (possibly by swapping), reduces the expected loss. Thus, as long as the representation is far from the evolutionary target, a *beneficial* mutation is produced with high probability.

More formally, let w' denote a random mutation produced as a result of the procedure described above. We will establish the desired result by proving the following claims.

CLAIM 1. *If $\|w\| \geq 2\|f^S\|$, then with probability at least $1/12$, $\mathrm{L}_{f,D}(w') \leq \mathrm{L}_{f,D}(w) - \|f^S - w\|^2/12$. In particular, a "scaling" type mutation achieves this.*

CLAIM 2. *When $\|w\| \leq 2\|f^S\|$, then with probability at least $\Delta\|f^S - w\|/(6K^2B)$, $\mathrm{L}_{f,D}(w') \leq \mathrm{L}_{f,D}(w) - 3\Delta^2\|f^S - w\|^2/(4|S|^2)$. In particular, an "adjusting" type mutation achieves this.*

CLAIM 3. *When $\|f^S - w\| \leq l^2\Delta^2/(4KB)$, but $\mathsf{NZ}(f) \not\subseteq S$, then with probability at least $\Delta\|f-w\|/(6KBnk)$, $\mathrm{L}_{f,D}(w') \leq \mathrm{L}_{f,D}(w) - \Delta^2\|f - w\|^2/(16k^2)$. In particular, a mutation of type "swapping" or "adding" achieves this.*

Note that when $\mathsf{NZ}(f) \subseteq S$, then $f^S = f$. Thus, in this case when $\mathrm{L}_{f,D}(w) = \|f^S - w\|^2 \leq \epsilon$, the evolutionary algorithm has succeeded.

The proofs of the above Claims are provided in Appendix A.2. We now prove our main result using the above claims.

THEOREM 1. *Let $\mathcal{D}$ be the class of Δ-smooth G-nice distributions over $\mathbb{R}^n$ (Defn. 2). Then the class $\mathsf{Lin}^k_{l,u}$ is evolvable with respect to $\mathcal{D}$, using the representation class $\mathsf{Lin}^K_{0,B}$, where $K = O((k/\Delta)^4(u/l)^2)$ and $B = O(uk/\Delta)$, using the mutation algorithm described in this section, and the selection rule* $\mathsf{BN\text{-}Sel}$. *Furthermore, the following are true:*

1. *The number of generations required is polynomial in (u/l), $1/\epsilon$, $1/\Delta$, and is independent of n, the total number of attributes.*

2. *The size function s, the number of points used to calculate empirical losses, depends polylogarithmically on n, and polynomially on the remaining parameters.*

PROOF. The mutator is as described in this section. Let

$$p = \min\left\{\frac{1}{12}, \frac{l^2\Delta^3}{24K^3B^2}, \frac{\Delta\sqrt{\epsilon}}{6KBnk}\right\},$$

and let

$$\alpha = \min\left\{\frac{l^4\Delta^4}{192K^2B^2}, \frac{3l^4\Delta^6}{64K^4B^2}, \frac{\epsilon\Delta^2}{16k^2}\right\}.$$

Now, by Claims 1, 2 and 3, if $\|f - w\|^2 \geq \epsilon$, then the mutator outputs a mutation that decreases the squared loss by α with probability at least p.

Recall that $K = 5184(k/\Delta)^4(u/l)^2$ and $B = 10uk/\Delta$. Now, let $g = 20KG^2B^2/\alpha$ (recall that G^2 is the bound on $\sum_i x_i^2$ for x in the support of the distribution). We will show that evolution succeeds in at most g generations. Note that g has no dependence on n, the number of attributes, and polynomial dependence on the remaining parameters. Define $m = p^{-1}\ln(2g/\epsilon)$, and at each time step we have that $|\mathsf{Neigh}(w, \epsilon)| = m$. Note that together with the observation above, this implies that except with probability $\epsilon/2$, for $1 \leq i \leq g$, if w^i is the representation at time step i, $\mathsf{Neigh}(w^i, \epsilon)$ contains a mutation that decreases the loss by at least α, if $\mathrm{L}_{f,D}(w^i) \geq \epsilon$.

Now, let $t = 3\alpha/5$ be the *tolerance function*, set $\tau = \alpha/5$ and let $s = (200gKG^2B^2/\alpha^2)\ln(4m/\epsilon)$ be the *size function*. Note that $\sum_i w_i^2 \leq KB^2$ for $w \in R$ (this also holds for f, since $k < K$ and $u < B$). If $\langle x^i\rangle_{i=1}^s$ is an i.i.d. sample drawn from D, for each $\bar{w}$ of the mg representations that may be considered in the neighborhoods for the first g time steps, using (1), it holds that $|\hat{\mathrm{L}}_{f,D}(\bar{w}) - \mathrm{L}_{f,D}(\bar{w})| \leq \tau$ simultaneously except with probability $\epsilon/2$ (by a union bound). Thus, allowing for failure probability ϵ, we assume that we are in the case when the neighborhood always has a mutation that decreases the expected loss by α (whenever the expected loss of the current representation is at least ϵ) and that all empirical expected losses are τ-close to the true expected losses.

Now let w be the representation at some generation such that $\mathrm{L}_{f,D}(w) \geq \epsilon$, let $w' \in \mathsf{Neigh}(w, \epsilon)$ such that $\mathrm{L}_{f,D}(w') \leq \mathrm{L}_{f,D}(w) - \alpha$. Then, it is the case that $\hat{\mathrm{L}}_{f,D}(w') \leq \hat{\mathrm{L}}_{f,D}(w) - 3\alpha/5$ (when $\tau = \alpha/5$). Hence, for tolerance function $t = 3\alpha/5$, for the selection rule using $\mathsf{BN\text{-}Sel}$, $w' \in \mathsf{Bene}$. Consequently $\mathsf{Bene} \neq \emptyset$. Hence, the representation at the next generation is chosen from Bene. Let $\tilde{w}$ be the chosen representation. It must be the case that $\hat{\mathrm{L}}_{f,D}(\tilde{w}) \leq \hat{\mathrm{L}}_{f,D}(w) - t$. Thus, we have $\mathrm{L}_{f,D}(\tilde{w}) \leq \mathrm{L}_{f,D}(w) - \alpha/5$. Hence, the expected loss decreases at least by $\alpha/5$.

Note that at no point can the expected loss be greater than $4KG^2B^2$ for any representation in R. Hence, in at most $20KG^2B^2/\alpha$ generations, evolution reaches a representation with expected loss at most ϵ. Note the only parameter introduced which has an inverse polynomial dependence on n is p. This implies that s only has polylogarithmic dependence on n. This concludes the proof of the theorem. □

REMARK 3. *We note that the same evolutionary mechanism works when evolving the class* $\mathsf{Lin}^k_{0,u}$, *as long as the sparsity* K *of the representation class is allowed polynomial dependence on* $1/\epsilon$, *the inverse of the accuracy parameter. This is consistent with the notion of attribute-efficiency, where the goal is that the information complexity should be polylogarithmic in the number of attributes, but may depend polynomially on* $1/\epsilon$.

3.2 Evolving Sparse Linear Functions Using Opt-Sel

In this section, we present a different evolutionary mechanism for evolving sparse linear functions. This algorithm essentially is an adaptation of a greedy algorithm commonly known as orthogonal matching pursuit (OMP) in the signal processing literature (see [7, 27]). Our analysis requires stronger properties on the distribution: we show that k-sparse linear functions can be evolved with respect to $1/(2k)$-incoherent (Δ, G)-nice distributions (Defn. 3). Here, the selection rule used is selection using *optimization* (Opt-Sel).[11] Also, the algorithm is guaranteed to succeed only with *initialization* from the 0 function. Nevertheless, this evolutionary algorithm is appealing due to its simplicity and because it never uses a representation that is not a k-sparse linear function.

Recall that $f \in \mathsf{Lin}^k_{0,u}$ is the ideal (target) function.[12] Let

$$R = \{w \mid \text{sparsity}(w) \le k, w_i \in [-B, B]\},$$

where $B = 10uk/\Delta$. Now, starting from $w \in R$, define the action of the mutator as follows (we will define the parameters λ and m later in the proof of Theorem 2):

1. *Adding*: With probability λ, do the following. Recall that $\mathsf{NZ}(w)$ denotes the non-zero entries of w. If $|\mathsf{NZ}(w)| < k$, choose $i \in [n] \setminus \mathsf{NZ}(w)$ uniformly at random. Let w' be such that $w'_j = w_i$ for $j \neq i$, and choose $w'_i \in [-B, B]$ uniformly at random. If $\mathsf{NZ}(w) = k$, let $w' = w$. Then, the multiset $\mathsf{Neigh}(w, \epsilon)$ is populated by m independent draws from the procedure just described.

2. With probability $1 - \lambda$, do the following:

   (a) *Identical*: With probability 1/2, output $w' = w$.

   (b) *Scaling*: With probability 1/4, choose $\gamma \in [-1, 1]$ uniformly at random and let $w' = \gamma w$.

   (c) *Adjusting*: With probability 1/4, do the following. Pick $i \in \mathsf{NZ}(w)$ uniformly at random. Let w' be such that $w'_j = w_j$ for $j \neq i$, and choose $w'_i \in [-B, B]$ uniformly at random.

   Then, the multiset $\mathsf{Neigh}(w, \epsilon)$ is populated by m independent draws from the procedure just described.

One thing to note in the above definition is that the mutations produced by the mutator at any given time are correlated, *i.e.*, they are all either of the kind that add a new variable, or all of the kind that just manipulate existing variables. At a high level, we prove the success of this mechanism as follows:

1. Using mutations of type "scaling" or "adjusting," a representation that is close to the *best* in the space, *i.e.*, f^S, is evolved.

2. When the representation is (close to) the best possible using current variables, adding one of the variables that is present in the *ideal function*, but not in the current representation, results in the greatest reduction of expected loss. Thus, selection based on optimization would always add a variable in $\mathsf{NZ}(f)$. By tuning λ appropriately, it is ensured that with high probability, candidate mutations that add new variables are not chosen until evolution has had time to approach the *best* representation using existing variables.

To complete the proof we establish the following claims.

CLAIM 4. *If* $\|f^S - w\| \le \sqrt{\epsilon}/2k$, *then if* $S \subsetneq \mathsf{NZ}(f)$, *there exists* $i \in \mathsf{NZ}(f) \setminus S$ *and* $-B < a < b < B$, *such that for any* $\gamma \in [a, b]$, $\mathrm{L}_{f,D}(w + \gamma e^i) \le \mathrm{L}_{f,D}(w) - \epsilon/(4k^2)$ *and for any* $j \notin \mathsf{NZ}(f)$, $\beta \in [-B, B]$, $\mathrm{L}_{f,D}(w + \beta e^j) \ge \mathrm{L}_{f,D}(w + \gamma e^i) + \epsilon/(4k^3)$. *Furthermore,* $b - a \ge \sqrt{(k+1)\epsilon}/k^2$.

CLAIM 5. *Conditioned on the mutator not outputting mutations that add a new variable, with probability at least* $\min\{1/16, \|f^S - w\|/(16k^2 B)\}$, *there exists a mutation that reduces the squared loss by at least* $\|f^S - w\|^2/(12k^2)$.

The proofs of Claims 4 and 5 are not difficult and are provided in Appendix A.3. Based on the above claims we can prove the following theorem:

THEOREM 2. *Let* $\mathcal{D}$ *be the class of* $1/(2k)$*-incoherent* (Δ, G)*-nice distributions over* $\mathbb{R}^n$ *(Defn. 3). Then, the class* $\mathsf{Lin}^k_{0,u}$ *is evolvable with respect to* $\mathcal{D}$ *by an evolutionary algorithm, using the mutation algorithm described in this section, selection rule* Opt-Sel, *and the representation class* $R = \mathsf{Lin}^k_{0,B}$, *where* $B = 10uk/\Delta$. *Furthermore, the following are true:*

1. *The number of generations* g *is polynomial in* $1/\epsilon$, k, $1/\Delta$, *but independent of the dimension* n.

2. *The size function* s, *the number of points used to calculate the empirical losses, depends polylogarithmically on* n *and polynomially on the remaining parameters.*

PROOF. The proof is straightforward, although a bit heavy on notation; we provide a sketch here. The mutator is as described in this section. Let

$$p = \min\left\{\frac{1}{16}, \frac{\sqrt{\epsilon}}{64k^3 B}, \frac{\sqrt{(k+1)\epsilon}}{k^2}\right\},$$

and let

$$\alpha = \min\left\{\frac{\epsilon}{4k^3}, \frac{\epsilon}{192k^4}\right\} = \frac{\epsilon}{192k^4}.$$

Also, let $\tau = \alpha/5$ and let $t = 3\alpha/5$ be the *tolerance function*.

First, we show that between the "rare" time steps when the mutator outputs mutations that add a new variable, evolution has enough time to *stabilize* (reach close to local optimal) using existing variables. To see this, consider a sequence of coin tosses, where the probability of heads is λ

[11] Valiant showed that selection using optimization was equivalent to selection using beneficial and neutral mutations [28]. However, this reduction uses representation classes that may be somewhat complex. For restricted representation classes, it is not clear that such a reduction holds. In particular, the necessary ingredient seems to be *polynomial-size* memory.

[12] Here, we no longer need the fact that each coefficient in the target linear function has magnitude at least l.

and the probability of tails is $1 - \lambda$. Let Y_i be the number of tails between the $(i-1)^{th}$ and i^{th} heads. Except with probability $\epsilon/(4(k+1))$, $Y_i > \epsilon/(4(k+1)\lambda)$ by a simple union bound. Also, by Markov's inequality, except with probability $\epsilon/(4(k+1))$, $Y_i < 4(k+1)/(\epsilon\lambda)$. Thus, except with probability $\epsilon/2$, we have $\epsilon/(4(k+1)\lambda) \leq Y_i \leq 4(k+1)/(\epsilon\lambda)$ for $i = 1, 2, \ldots, k+1$. Let $g = 4(k+1)^2/(\epsilon\lambda)+(k+1)$. This ensures that, except with probability $\epsilon/2$, after g time steps, at least $(k+1)$ time steps where the mutator outputs mutations of type "adding" have occurred, and the first k of these occurrences are all separated by at least $\epsilon/(4(k+1)\lambda)$ time steps of other types of mutations.

Also, let $m = p^{-1}\ln(4g/\epsilon)$ and let the *size function* be $s = (200gkG^2B^2/\alpha^2)\ln(4m/\epsilon)$. These values ensure that for g generations, except with probability $\epsilon/2$, the mutator always produces a mutation that had probability at least p of being produced (conditioned on the type of mutations output by the mutator at that time step), and that for all the representations concerned, $|\hat{\mathrm{L}}_{f,D}(w) - \mathrm{L}_{f,D}(w)| \leq \tau$, where $\tau = \alpha/5$. Thus, allowing the process to fail with probability ϵ, we assume that none of the undesirable events have occurred.

We will show that the steps with mutations other than "adding" are sufficient to ensure that evolution reaches the (almost) best possible target with the variables available to it. In particular, if the set of available variables is S, the representation w reached by evolution will satisfy $\|f^S - w\|^2 \leq \epsilon/(2k^2)$. For now, suppose that this is the case.

We claim by induction that evolution never adds a "wrong" variable, *i.e.*, one that is not present in the target function f. The base case is trivially true, since the starting representation is 0. Now suppose, just before a "heads" step, the representation is w, such that $S = \mathsf{NZ}(w)$ and $\|f^S - w\| \leq \epsilon/(2k^2)$. The current step is assumed to be a "heads" step, thus the mutator has produced mutations by adding a new variable. Then, using Claim 4, we know that there is a mutation w' in $\mathsf{Neigh}(w, \epsilon)$ such that $\mathrm{L}_{f,D}(w') < \mathrm{L}_{f,D}(w) - \epsilon/(4k^2)$ (obtained by adding a correct variable). Since $\alpha < \epsilon/(4k^2)$ and $\tau = \alpha/5$, it must be the case that $\hat{\mathrm{L}}_{f,D}(w') \leq \hat{\mathrm{L}}_{f,D}(w) - 3\alpha/5$. This ensures that the set Best, for selection rule $\mathsf{Opt\text{-}Sel}$ is not empty. Furthermore, we claim that no mutation that adds an *irrelevant* variable can be in Best. Suppose w'' is a mutation that adds an *irrelevant* variable; according to Claim 5, $\mathrm{L}_{f,D}(w'') > \mathrm{L}_{f,D}(w') + \alpha$, and hence $\hat{\mathrm{L}}_{f,D}(w'') > \hat{\mathrm{L}}_{f,D}(w') + t$. This ensures that every representation in Best corresponds to a mutation that adds some *relevant* variable. Thus, the evolutionary algorithm never adds any *irrelevant* variable.

Finally, note that during a "tails" step (when the mutator produces mutations of types other than "adding"), as long as $\|f^S - w\|^2 \geq \epsilon/(4k^2)$, there exists a mutation that reduces the expected loss by at least $\epsilon^2/(192k^4) = \alpha$. This implies that the set Best is non-empty and for the values of tolerance $t = 3\alpha/5$ and $\tau = \alpha/5$, any mutation from the set Best reduces the expected loss by at least $\alpha/5$. (This argument is identical to the one in Theorem 1.) Since the maximum loss is at most $4kB^2G^2$ for the class of distributions and a representation w from the set R; in at most $20kB^2G^2/\alpha$ steps, a representation satisfying $\mathrm{L}_{f,D}(w) \leq \epsilon/(4k^2)$ must be reached. Note that once such a representation is reached, it is ensured that the loss does not increase substantially, since with probability at least 1/2, the mutator outputs the same representation. Hence, it is guaranteed that there is always a neutral mutation. Thus, before the next "heads" step, it must be the case that $\|f^S - w\|^2 \leq \epsilon/2k^2$. If λ is set to $\epsilon\alpha/(80k(k+1)B^2G^2)$, the evolutionary algorithm using the selection rule $\mathsf{Opt\text{-}Sel}$ succeeds.

It is readily verified that the values of g and s satisfy the claims in the statement of the theorem. □

4. CONCLUSION AND FUTURE WORK

In this work, we provided simple evolutionary mechanisms for evolving sparse linear functions, under a large class of distributions. These evolutionary algorithms have the desirable properties that the representations used are themselves sparse linear functions, and that they are attribute-efficient in the sense that the number of generations required for evolution to succeed is independent of the total number of attributes.

Strong negative results are known for distribution-independent evolvability of boolean functions, *e.g.*, even the class of conjunctions is not evolvable [11]. However, along the lines of this work, it is interesting to study whether under restricted classes of distributions, evolution is possible for simple concept classes, using representations of low complexity. Currently, even under (biased) product distributions, no evolutionary mechanism is known for the class of disjunctions, except via Feldman's general reduction from CSQ algorithms. Even if the queries made by the CSQ algorithm are simple, Feldman's reduction uses intermediate representations that randomly combine queries made by the algorithm, making the representations quite complex.

A natural extension of our current results would be to study fixed-degree sparse polynomials. Another interesting direction is to study circuits with sigmoidal or other non-linear filters on the gates, which arise naturally in molecular systems. The suitable class of boolean functions to study is low-weight threshold functions, which includes disjunctions and conjunctions. The class of smooth bounded distributions may be an appropriate starting place for studying evolvability of these classes. For example, is the class of low-weight threshold functions evolvable under smooth distributions, or at least log-concave distributions?

Acknowledgments

We would like to thank Leslie Valiant for helpful discussions and comments on an earlier version of this paper. We are grateful to Frank Solomon for discussing biological aspects related to this work.

5. REFERENCES

[1] Uri Alon. *An Introduction to Systems Biology: Design Principles of Biological Circuits.* Chapman and Hall/CRC, Boca Raton, FL, 2006.

[2] Francis R. Bach, Rodolphe Jenatton, Julien Mairal, and Guillaume Obozinski. Optimization with sparsity-inducing penalties. *Foundations and Trends in Machine Learning*, 4(1):1–106, 2012.

[3] S. Balaji, Madan M. Babu, Lakshminarayan M. Iyer, Nicholas M. Luscombe, and L. Aravind. Comprehensive analysis of combinatorial regulation using the transcriptional regulatory network of yeast. *Journal of Molecular Biology*, 360(1):213–227, 2006.

[4] Alfred M. Bruckstein, David L. Donoho, and Michael Elad. From sparse solutions of systems of equations to

sparse modeling of signals and images. *SIAM Review*, 51(1):34–81, 2009.

[5] E. J. Candes and M. B. Wakin. An introduction to compressive sampling. *IEEE Signal Processing Magazine*, 25(2):21–30, 2008.

[6] Cuthbert Daniel and Fred S. Wood. *Fitting Equations to Data: Computer Analysis of Multifactor Data.* John Wiley & Sons, Inc., New York, NY, USA, 2nd edition, 1999.

[7] David L. Donoho, Michael Elad, and Vladimir N. Temlyakov. Stable recovery of sparse overcomplete representations in the presence of noise. *IEEE Transactions on Information Theory*, 52(1):6–18, 2006.

[8] M. Elad. *Sparse and Redundant Representations: From Theory to Applications in Signal and Image Processing.* Springer, 2010.

[9] Vitaly Feldman. Evolution from learning algorithms. In *Proceedings of the Symposium on the Theory of Computation (STOC)*, 2008.

[10] Vitaly Feldman. Robustness of evolvability. In *Proceedings of the Conference on Learning Theory (COLT)*, 2009.

[11] Vitaly Feldman. Distribution-independent evolution of linear threshold functions. In *Proceedings of the Conference on Learning Theory (COLT)*, 2011.

[12] L. H. Hartwell, J. J. Hopfield, S. Leibler, and A. W. Murray. From molecular to modular cell biology. *Nature*, 402(6761 Suppl):C47–C52, 1999.

[13] Trevor Hastie, Robert Tibshirani, and Jerome Friedman. *The Elements of Statistical Learning.* Springer New York Inc., New York, NY, USA, 2001.

[14] H. Jeong, B. Tombor, R. Albert, Z. N. Oltvai, and A. L. Barabasi. The large-scale organization of metabolic networks. *Nature*, 407(6804):651–654, 2000.

[15] Adam Tauman Kalai, Alex Samorodnitsky, and Shang-Hua Teng. Learning and smoothed analysis. In *Proceedings of IEEE Conference on the Foundations of Computer Science (FOCS)*, 2009.

[16] Varun Kanade. *Computational Questions in Evolution.* PhD thesis, Harvard University, 2012.

[17] Varun Kanade, Jennifer Wortman Vaughan, and Leslie G. Valiant. Evolution with drifting targets. In *Proceedings of the Conference on Learning Theory (COLT)*, 2010.

[18] Daniel M. Kane, Adam Klivans, and Raghu Meka. Learning halfspaces under log-concave densities: Polynomial approximations and moment matching. In *Proceedings of the Conference on Learning Theory (COLT)*, 2013.

[19] Michael Kearns. Efficient noise-tolerant learning from statistical queries. *J. ACM*, 45(6):983–1006, 1998.

[20] Nick Littlestone. Learning quickly when irrelevant attributes abound: A new linear-threshold algorithm. *Mach. Learn.*, 2(4):285–318, 1988.

[21] Nicholas M. Luscombe, M. Madan Babu, Haiyuan Yu, Michael Snyder, Sarah A. Teichmann, and Mark Gerstein. Genomic analysis of regulatory network dynamics reveals large topological changes. *Nature*, (7006):308–312.

[22] Stephane Mallat. *A Wavelet Tour of Signal Processing, Third Edition: The Sparse Way.* Academic Press, 3rd edition, 2008.

[23] Douglas B. Murray, Ken Haynes, and Masaru Tomita. Redox regulation in respiring *Saccharomyces cerevisiae. Biochimica et Biophysica Acta*, 1810(10):945–958, 2011.

[24] B. K. Natarajan. Sparse approximate solutions to linear systems. *SIAM J. Comput.*, 24(2):227–234, 1995.

[25] Bruno A. Olshausen and David J. Fieldt. Sparse coding with an overcomplete basis set: A strategy employed by V1? *Vision Research*, 37:3311–3325, 1997.

[26] Daniel A. Spielman and Shang-Hua Teng. Smoothed analysis of algorithms: Why the simplex algorithm usually takes polynomial time. *Journal of the ACM*, 51(3), 2004.

[27] Joel A. Tropp. Greed is good: Algorithmic results for sparse approximation. *IEEE Transactions on Information Theory*, 50(10):2231–2242, 2004.

[28] Leslie G. Valiant. Evolvability. *Journal of the ACM*, 56(1):3:1–3:21, 2009.

[29] Paul Valiant. Evolvability of real-valued functions. In *Proceedings of Innovations in Theoretical Computer Science (ITCS)*, 2012.

[30] Andreas Wagner and David A. Fell. The small world inside large metabolic networks. *Proceedings of the Royal Society of London. Series B: Biological Sciences*, 268(1478):1803–1810, 2001.

[31] Duncan J. Watts and Steven H. Strogatz. Collective dynamics of 'small-world' networks. *Nature*, 393(6684):440–442, 1998.

APPENDIX

A. OMITTED PROOFS

A.1 Proofs from Section 2.2

PROOF OF LEMMA 1. Note that for any $x \sim D$, we can write $x = \tilde{x}+\eta$, where $\tilde{x}$ is drawn from some smooth bounded distribution, and η is drawn from the uniform distribution over $[-\sqrt{3}\Delta, \sqrt{3}\Delta]^n$. Note that η and $\tilde{x}$ are independent, and all components of η are independent. First, we observe that $\mathbb{E}[x_i^2] = \mathbb{E}[(\tilde{x}_i + \eta_i)^2] \geq \mathbb{E}[\eta_i^2] = \Delta^2$. Now, consider the following:

$$
\begin{aligned}
\langle w, w\rangle &= \mathbb{E}\left[\left(\sum_{i=1}^{n} w_i x_i\right)^2\right] \\
&= \mathbb{E}\left[\left(\sum_{i=1}^{n} w_i(\tilde{x}_i + \eta_i)\right)^2\right] \\
&= \mathbb{E}\left[\left(\sum_{i=1}^{n} w_i\tilde{x}_i\right)^2\right] + 2\mathbb{E}\left[\left(\sum_{i=1}^{n} w_i\tilde{x}_i\right)\left(\sum_{i=1}^{n} w_i\eta_i\right)\right] \\
&\quad + \mathbb{E}\left[\left(\sum_{i=1}^{n} w_i\eta_i\right)^2\right] \\
&\geq \sum_{i=1}^{n} w_i^2\mathbb{E}[\eta_i^2] && \text{Since } \eta_i \text{ are all independent} \\
&\geq \sum_{i=1}^{n} w_i^2\Delta^2 && \text{Since } \mathbb{E}[\eta_i^2] = \Delta^2 \text{ by definition} \\
&= \sum_{i\in \mathsf{NZ}(w)} w_i^2\Delta^2
\end{aligned}
$$

The conclusions of the Lemma follow easily by looking at the above expression. □

A.2 Proofs from Section 3.1

PROOF OF CLAIM 1. We show that in this case, a "scaling" mutation achieves the desired result. Restricted to the direction w, the best approximation to f^S is $\frac{\langle f^S, w\rangle}{\|w\|^2}w$. We have that

$$\left\|\frac{\langle f^S, w\rangle}{\|w\|^2}w\right\| \leq \|f^S\| \leq \frac{\|w\|}{2}$$

Hence, if $\langle f^S, w\rangle > 0$, for $\gamma \in [1/4, 3/4]$ (and similarly if $\langle f^S, w\rangle < 0$ for $\gamma \in [-3/4, -1/4]$), we have that

$$
\begin{aligned}
\|f^S - \gamma w\|^2 &= \|f^S - w\|^2 + 2(1-\gamma)\langle f^S - w, w\rangle + (1-\gamma)^2\|w\|^2 \\
&\leq \|w - f^S\|^2 - (1-\gamma)\|w\|^2 + (1-\gamma)^2\|w\|^2 \\
&= \|w - f^S\|^2 - (\gamma - \gamma^2)\|w\|^2
\end{aligned}
$$

Finally, by observing that for $\gamma \in [1/4, 3/4]$, $\gamma - \gamma^2 \geq 3/16$ and that by the triangle inequality, $\|w\| \geq (2/3)\|f^S - w\|$ when $\|w\| \geq 2\|f^S\|$, we obtain

$$\|f^S - \gamma w\|^2 \leq \|f^S - w\|^2 - \frac{1}{12}\|f^S - w\|^2$$

We note that $\mathrm{L}_{f,D}(w') = \|f - f^S\|^2 + \|f^S - \gamma w\|^2$ and $\mathrm{L}_{f,D}(w) = \|f - f^S\|^2 + \|f^S - w\|^2$. An appropriate value of γ is chosen with probability at least 1/4, and combined with the probability of choosing a scaling mutation we get the desired result. □

PROOF OF CLAIM 2. Here, we appeal to a mutation that adjusts the relative weights of the variables within the set $S = \mathsf{NZ}(w)$. Consider the vector $f^S - w$, and note that $\mathsf{NZ}(f^S - w) \subseteq S$. Let $r^S = f^S - w$ denote the residual, which lies in the space spanned by S. Now consider

$$\|r_S\|^2 = \langle r^S, r^S\rangle = \sum_{i\in S} r_i^S\langle e^i, r^S\rangle$$

Here, e^i is the unit vector representing the linear function $x \mapsto e^i \cdot x = x_i$. Therefore, there must exist an i for which the following is true:

$$r_i^S\langle e^i, r^S\rangle \geq \frac{\|r^S\|^2}{|S|}$$

We appeal to Lemma 1 (part 1), which implies that $|r_i^S| \leq \sqrt{\langle r^S, r^S\rangle/\Delta^2} = \|r^S\|/\Delta$, to conclude that

$$|\langle e^i, r^S\rangle| \geq \frac{\|r^S\|\Delta}{|S|}$$

Let $\beta = \frac{\langle e^i, r^S\rangle}{\|e^i\|^2}$ and suppose $w' = w + \gamma e^i$ for $\gamma \in [\beta - |\beta|/2, \beta + |\beta|/2]$. We then have

$$\|f^S - (w + \gamma e^i)\|^2 = \|f^S - w\|^2 - 2\gamma\langle f^S - w, e^i\rangle + \gamma^2\|e^i\|^2$$

Recall that $f^S - w = r^S$ and note that $\langle e^i, r^S\rangle$ and γ have the same sign. This, combined with the above equation, gives

$$\|f^S - (w + \gamma e^i)\|^2 = \|f^S - w\|^2 - (2|\gamma||\beta| - \gamma^2)\|e^i\|^2$$

Finally, note that for $|\gamma| \in [|\beta|/2, 3|\beta|/2]$, $-2|\gamma||\beta| + \gamma^2 \leq -3|\beta|^2/4$, hence, the above equation and the fact that $\|e^i\| \leq 1$ together yield

$$
\begin{aligned}
\|f^S - (w + \gamma e^i)\|^2 &\leq \|f^S - w\|^2 - \frac{3}{4}\beta^2\|e^i\|^2 \\
&\leq \|f^S - w\|^2 - \frac{3}{4}\frac{\|f^S - w\|^2\Delta^2}{|S|^2}
\end{aligned}
$$

Note that a suitable mutation $w' = w + \gamma e^i$ is obtained with probability at least $|\beta|/(6KB)$ (1/3 for choosing the right type of mutation, $1/K$ for the correct choice of variable, and $|\beta|/(2B)$ for the choosing the correct value of w_i). Also note that $|\beta| \geq \Delta\|f^S - w\|/|S| \geq \Delta\|f^S - w\|/K$. For this to be a valid mutation, we also need to verify the fact that $w_i + \gamma \in [-B, B]$, which is ensured by our choice of B. To see this, note that $\|w\| \leq 2\|f^S\| \leq 2\|f\|$ (the last part is because f^S is a projection of f onto a lower dimensional space). Thus, by Lemma 1 (part 1), $w_i \leq 2\|f\|/\Delta$. Also, $|\beta| = |\langle e^i, r^S\rangle|/\|e^i\|^2 \leq \|r^S\|/\|e^i\| = \|f^S - w\|/\mathbb{E}[x_i^2] \leq 3\|f\|/\Delta$. Thus, if $B > 13\|f\|/(2\Delta)$, then $|w_i + \gamma| < B$ and the mutation will be a valid one. Note that the maximum value of $\|f\|$ for $f \in \mathsf{Lin}_{l,u}^k$ is uk. Thus, our choice of $B = 10uk/\Delta$ is sufficient. This completes the proof of Claim 2. □

PROOF OF CLAIM 3. Finally, we show that if $\|f^S - w\|$ is very small, but $\mathsf{NZ}(f) \not\subseteq S$, then it must be the case that a "swapping" or "adding" mutation is beneficial. We focus on the swapping case, *i.e.*, when $|S| = K$; the adding step is a special case of this. First, we observe that if there exists $i \in \mathsf{NZ}(f)$ such that $i \notin S$, then by using Lemma 1 (part 1), it must be the case that $\|f-w\|^2 \geq (f_i - w_i)^2\Delta^2 = f_i^2\Delta^2 \geq l^2\Delta^2$. Let $r = f - w$ denote the residual. Then, consider the following:

$$\langle r, r\rangle = \sum_{i \in \mathsf{NZ}(f)\setminus S} r_i \langle e^i, r\rangle + \sum_{i\in S} r_i \langle e^i, r\rangle$$

Note that for all $i \in S$, $\langle e^i, f - f^S\rangle = 0$, since f^S is the projection of f onto the space spanned by the variables in S. Hence, if $r^S = f^S - w$, the residual within the space spanned by S, then $r = f - f^S + r^S$. Thus, we have $\langle e^i, r\rangle = \langle e^i, r^S\rangle \leq \|r^S\|$. Using this we get,

$$\langle r, r\rangle \leq \sum_{i \in \mathsf{NZ}(f)\setminus S} r_i \langle e^i, r\rangle + \|r^S\| \sum_{i\in S} |r_i|$$

Now, even by a very crude estimate, $|r_i| = |f_i - w_i| \leq 2B$, and hence by the condition in the statement of Claim 3, that $\|r^S\| = \|f^S - w\| \leq l^2\Delta^2/(4KB)$, together with the previous observation that $\langle r, r\rangle = \|r\|^2 = \|f-w\|^2 \geq l^2\Delta^2$, we have that

$$\frac{1}{2}\langle r, r\rangle \leq \sum_{i \in \mathsf{NZ}(f)\setminus S} r_i \langle e^i, r\rangle$$

We now appeal to Lemma 1 (part 1), which shows that $|r_i| \leq \|r\|/\Delta$, and conclude that there exists an i for which

$$|\langle e^i, r\rangle| \geq \frac{\|r\|\Delta}{2k}$$

The crucial observation is that $|\mathsf{NZ}(f)| \leq k < K$. Let $\beta = \frac{\langle r, e^i\rangle}{\|e^i\|^2}$. Finally, Lemma 1 (part 2) implies that there exists an i' for which $w_{i'}^2 \leq \|w\|^2/K$. We consider the mutation, $w' = w + \gamma e^i - w_{i'} e^{i'}$ for $\gamma \in [\beta - |\beta|/2, \beta + |\beta|/2]$. Then, we have

$$\begin{aligned}&\|f - (w + \gamma e^i - w_{i'} e^{i'})\|^2 \\ &= \|f - (w+\gamma e^i)\|^2 - 2w_{i'}\langle f - (w + \gamma e^i), e^{i'}\rangle + w_{i'}^2\|e^{i'}\|^2\end{aligned} \quad (2)$$

We bound the first term on the right hand side of the above expression and then the latter two.

$$\begin{aligned}\|f - (w+\gamma e^i)\|^2 &= \|r\|^2 - 2\gamma\langle r, e^i\rangle + \gamma^2\|e^i\|^2 \\ &= \|r\|^2 - (2\gamma\beta - \gamma^2)\|e^i\|^2\end{aligned}$$

As in the proof of Claim 2, for $|\gamma| \in [|\beta|/2, 3|\beta|/2]$, we have that $-2\gamma\beta + \gamma^2 \leq -3\beta^2/4$. Hence,

$$\|f - (w + \gamma e^i)\|^2 \leq \|r\|^2 - \frac{3}{4}\beta^2 \quad (3)$$

To bound the remaining two terms in (2), recall that $f - w = f - f^S + r^S$ and that $\langle f - f^S, e^{i'}\rangle = 0$ (since $i' \in S$). Thus, we get that

$$\begin{aligned}&-2w_{i'}\langle f - (w+\gamma e^i), e^{i'}\rangle + w_{i'}^2\|e^{i'}\|^2 \\ &\leq 2|w_{i'}||\langle r^S + \gamma e^i, e^{i'}\rangle| + w_{i'}^2\|e^{i'}\|^2\end{aligned}$$

Using the fact that $\|r^S\| \leq \gamma$, $|w_{i'}| < \gamma$ (which can be verified by the setting of K below), $|\langle e^i, e^{i'}\rangle| \leq 1$ and $\|e^{i'}\| \leq 1$, we obtain

$$-2w_{i'}\langle f - (w+\gamma e^i), e^{i'}\rangle + w_{i'}^2\|e^{i'}\|^2 \leq 6|w_{i'}||\gamma| \quad (4)$$

Recall that $|w_{i'}| \leq \|w\|/\sqrt{K}$. Also $\|w\| \leq \|f^S\| + \|r^S\| \leq 2\|f^S\| \leq 2\|f\| \leq 2uk$, where we have used the fact that $\|r^S\|$ is small. Combining (2), (3), (4), the fact that $|w_i| \leq 2uk/\sqrt{K}$ and $|\gamma| \leq 3|\beta|/2$, we get

$$\|f - (w + \gamma e^i - w_{i'}e^{i'})\|^2 \leq \|r\|^2 - \frac{3}{4}\beta^2 + 18|\beta|uk/\sqrt{K}$$

Finally, we note that when $K > 5184(k/\Delta)^4(u/l)^2$, the above equation ensures that the expected loss drops by at least $\beta^2/4$. The probability of choosing a swapping operations is 1/3, of subsequently choosing the correct pair is at least $1/(nK)$, and subsequently choosing the correct value of w_i is at least $|\beta|/(2B)$. A simple calculation proves the statement of the claim. □

A.3 Proofs from Section 3.2

PROOF OF CLAIM 4. Since $S \subseteq \mathsf{NZ}(f)$, the residual $r = f - w$ is such that $\mathsf{NZ}(r) \subseteq \mathsf{NZ}(f)$. Consider $i \in \mathsf{NZ}(r)$ that maximizes $|r_i| \cdot \|e^i\|$. Then, we have:

$$\begin{aligned}\left|\frac{\langle e^i, r\rangle}{\|e^i\|}\right| &\geq \frac{|r_i|\langle e^i, e^i\rangle}{\|e^i\|} - \sum_{j\in\mathsf{NZ}(r), j\neq i} \frac{|r_j|\langle e^i, e^j\rangle}{\|e^i\|} \\ &\geq |r_i|\cdot\|e^i\| - \frac{1}{2k}\sum_{j\in\mathsf{NZ}(r), j\neq i} |r_j|\cdot\|e^j\| \quad (5) \\ &\geq |r_i|\cdot\|e^i\|\cdot\frac{k+1}{2k},\end{aligned}$$

where in the last two steps we used the fact that $\mathrm{corr}(x_i, x_j) = \langle e^i, e^j\rangle/(\|e^i\|\|e^j\|) \leq 1/(2k)$ and that $|\mathsf{NZ}(r) \setminus \{i\}| \leq k - 1$. On the other hand, for any $i' \notin \mathsf{NZ}(r)$, we have

$$\begin{aligned}\left|\frac{\langle e^{i'}, r\rangle}{\|e^{i'}\|}\right| &\leq \sum_{j\in\mathsf{NZ}(r)} \frac{|r_j\langle e^{i'}, e^j\rangle|}{\|e^{i'}\|} \\ &\leq \frac{1}{2k}\sum_{j\in\mathsf{NZ}(r)} |r_j|\cdot\|e^j\| \leq \frac{1}{2}|r_i|\cdot\|e^i\| \quad (6)\end{aligned}$$

Here, again in the last two steps, we have used the fact that $\mathrm{corr}(x_{i'}, x_j) \leq 1/(2k)$ and that $|r_i| \cdot \|e^i\|$ is the largest such term.

First, we claim that if $\|r\|^2 \geq \epsilon$, then the i that maximized $|r_i| \cdot \|e^i\|$ must be from the set $\mathsf{NZ}(f) \setminus S$. (Note that $\|r\|^2 = \|f - w\|^2 = \mathrm{L}_{f,D}(w)$, so if $\|r\|^2 \leq \epsilon$, evolution has reached its goal.) By the triangle inequality, $\sum_{i\in\mathsf{NZ}(r)} |r_i| \cdot \|e^i\| \geq \|r\| \geq \sqrt{\epsilon}$. Hence, it must be the case that $|r_i| \cdot \|e^i\| \geq \sqrt{\epsilon}/k$. For contradiction, assume that $i \in S$. Then, since f^S is the projection of f in the space spanned by S, we have $\langle e^i, r\rangle = \langle e^i, f^S - w\rangle$, since $r = f - f^S + f^S - w$ and $\langle e^i, f - f^S\rangle = 0$. But, by the assumption of the claim, $|\langle e^i, r\rangle| \leq \|e^i\| \cdot \|f^S - w\| \leq \|e^i\| \cdot \sqrt{\epsilon}/(2k)$, and by (5), we know that $|\langle e^i, r\rangle| \geq \|e^i\| \cdot (|r_i| \cdot \|e^i\|) \cdot (k+1)/(2k) > \|e^i\| \cdot \|r\|/(2k) \geq \|e^i\| \cdot \sqrt{\epsilon}/(2k)$. Thus, it cannot be the case that $i \in S$.

Let $w' = w + \gamma e^i$. Then,

$$\|f - (w + \gamma e^i)\|^2 - \|f - w\|^2 = -2\gamma\langle f - w, e^i\rangle + \gamma^2\|e^i\|^2$$
$$\leq -\|e^i\|^2 \left(|\gamma| \cdot |r_i| \cdot \frac{k+1}{k} - |\gamma|^2\right)$$

Now suppose γ satisfies $1 - \delta \leq (2|\gamma|k)/(|r_i|(k+1)) \leq 1+\delta$, then using the fact that the quadratic function on the RHS is maximized at $|\gamma| = (k+1)|r_i|/(2k)$, we have

$$\|f - (w + \gamma e^i)\|^2 - \|f - w\|^2 \leq -\|e^i\|^2 \cdot \frac{r_i^2}{4} \cdot \frac{(k+1)^2}{k^2} \cdot (1 - \delta^2)$$

Note that for any $i' \notin S$, the "best" representation of the form $w+\beta e^{i'}$ is when $\beta = \langle e^{i'}, r\rangle/\|e^{i'}\|^2$, and the corresponding reduction in squared loss is $(\langle e^{i'}, r\rangle)^2/\|e^{i'}\|^2$. Thus, for any $i' \neq i$, we have

$$\|f - (w + \beta e^{i'})\|^2 - \|f - w\|^2 \leq -\frac{\langle e^{i'}, r\rangle^2}{\|e^{i'}\|^2}$$
$$\leq -\frac{r_i^2}{4}\|e^i\|^2 \quad \text{Using (6)}$$

Setting $\delta = \sqrt{1/(k+1)}$ completes the proof of the claim. To see that $b - a \geq \sqrt{(k+1)\epsilon/k^2}$, notice that any γ, such that $|\gamma| \in [(1-\delta)((k+1)/(2k))|r_i|, (1-\delta)((k+1)/(2k))|r_i|]$, achieves the claimed reduction in squared loss. Since $|r_i| \cdot \|e^i\| \geq \sqrt{\epsilon}/k$, we have that $|r_i| \geq \sqrt{\epsilon}/k$. Hence, $b - a \geq 2\delta((k+1)/2k)(\sqrt{\epsilon}/k) \geq \sqrt{(k+1)\epsilon/k^2}$, for $\delta = \sqrt{1/(k+1)}$. □

Proof of Claim 5. The proof follows along the lines of the proofs of Claims 1 and 2. First, suppose that $\|w\| \geq 2\|f^S\|$. In this case, we claim that for $\gamma \in [1/2, 3/4]$, the mutation γw reduces the squared loss by at least $\|f^S - w\|^2/12$. This analysis is completely identical to that in Claim 1 and hence is omitted. The only difference is that the probability that such a mutation is selected is 1/16, conditioned on the event that the mutator chooses mutations that don't add an extra variable.

Next, we assume that $\|w\| \leq 2\|f^S\|$. Let $r^S = f^S - w$. Now, as in the proof of Claim 4, consider $i \in \mathsf{NZ}(r^S)$ (recall that $\mathsf{NZ}(r^S) = S$) that maximizes $|r_i^S| \cdot \|e^i\|$. Then, the following is true:

$$\left|\frac{\langle e^i, r^S\rangle}{\|e^i\|}\right| \geq |r_i^S|\frac{\langle e^i, e^i\rangle}{\|e^i\|} - \sum_{j\in S, j\neq i} |r_j^S|\frac{\langle e^i, e^j\rangle}{\|e^i\|}$$
$$\geq |r_i^S| \cdot \|e^i\| - \frac{1}{2k}\sum_{j\in S, j\neq i} |r_j^S| \cdot \|e^j\|$$
$$\geq |r_i^S| \cdot \|e^i\| \cdot \frac{k+1}{2k} \quad (7)$$

where in the last two steps we used the fact that $\mathrm{corr}(x_i, x_j) \leq 1/(2k)$ and that $|r_j^S| \cdot \|e^j\|$ is maximized for $j = i$, and the fact that $|S| \leq k$. Also, by the triangle inequality, we know that $\sum_{j\in S} |r_j^S| \cdot \|e^j\| \geq \|r^S\|$; hence, by definition of i, we have that $|r_i^S| \cdot \|e^i\| \geq \|r^S\|/k$. Now, let $\beta = \langle e^i, r^S\rangle/\|e^i\|^2$, and for $\gamma \in [\beta - |\beta|/2, \beta + |\beta|/2]$, consider the mutation $w + \gamma e^i$. We have,

$$\|f^S - (w + \gamma e^i)\|^2 - \|f^S - w\|^2 = -2\gamma\langle e^i, r^S\rangle + \gamma^2\|e^i\|^2$$
$$= -\|e^i\|^2(2|\gamma||\beta| - |\gamma|^2)$$
$$\leq -\frac{3}{4}\|e^i\|^2\beta^2$$
$$\leq -\frac{3}{16}\frac{\|r^S\|^2}{k^2}$$

Above $\gamma \in [\beta - |\beta|/2, \beta + |\beta|/2]$. The last step follows from (7) and the definition of β. In order for $w + \gamma e^i$ to be a valid mutation, we need to check that $|w_i| + 3|\beta|/2 < B$. To see this, observe the following:

$$\|w\|^2 \geq \sum_{j\in\mathsf{NZ}(w)} w_j^2\|e^j\|^2 - \sum_{j_1<j_2; j_1,j_2\in\mathsf{NZ}(w)} 2|w_{j_1}w_{j_2}||\langle e^{j_1}, e^{j_2}\rangle|$$
$$\geq \sum_{j\in\mathsf{NZ}(w)} w_j^2\|e^j\|^2 - \frac{1}{k}\sum_{j_1<j_2} |w_{j_1}w_{j_2}|\|e^{j_1}\|\|e^{j_2}\|$$
$$\geq \frac{1}{2}\sum_{j\in\mathsf{NZ}(w)} w_j^2\|e^j\|^2 + \frac{1}{2k}\sum_{j_1<j_2}(|w_{j_1}|\|e^{j_1}\| - |w_{j_2}|\|e^{j_2}\|)^2$$
$$\geq \frac{1}{2}\sum_{j\in\mathsf{NZ}(w)} w_j^2\|e^j\|^2$$

Hence, by a fairly loose analysis, $|w_i| \leq 2\|w\|/\Delta \leq 4\|f\|/\Delta \leq 4uk/\Delta$ (since $\|e^i\| \geq \Delta$ for the class of distributions defined in Defn. 3). Also $|\beta| = |\langle e^i, r^S\rangle|/\|e^i\|^2 \leq \|r^S\|/\|e^i\| \leq 3\|f\|/\Delta$ (since $\|r^S\| \leq \|f^S\| + \|w\| \leq 3\|f^S\| \leq 3\|f\|$). It's easy to see that $|w_i| + (3/2)|\beta| \leq B$, for $B = 10uk/\Delta$.

Finally, note that conditioned on the mutator choosing a mutation that doesn't add new variables, the probability of choosing such a mutation is at least $|\beta|/(8Bk)$ (1/4 for choosing a mutation of type "adjusting", $1/k$ for choosing the appropriate variable to adjust and $|\beta|/(2B)$ for choosing the correct value). Combining the claims for mutations of the "scaling" and "adjusting" types and taking the appropriate minimum values proves the statement of the claim. □

An Eff cient Algorithm for Finding the Ground State of 1D Gapped Local Hamiltonians

[Abstract]

Zeph Landau*
Computer Science Division
University of California, Berkeley

Umesh Vazirani†
Computer Science Division
University of California, Berkeley

Thomas Vidick‡
Newton Institute
Cambridge UK
and Centre for Quantum Technologies
NUS, Singapore

ABSTRACT

Computing ground states of local Hamiltonians is a fundamental problem in condensed matter physics. The problem is known to be QMA-complete, even for one-dimensional Hamiltonians [1]. This means that we do not even expect that there is a sub-exponential size description of the ground state that allows eff cient computation of local observables such as the energy. In sharp contrast, the heuristic density matrix renormalization group (DMRG) algorithm invented two decades ago [5] has been remarkably successful in practice on one-dimensional problems. The situation is reminiscent of the unexplained success of the simplex algorithm before the advent of ellipsoid and interior-point methods. Is there a principled explanation for this, in the form of a large class of one-dimensional Hamiltonians whose ground states can be provably eff ciently approximated? Here we give such an algorithm for gapped one-dimensional Hamiltonians: our algorithm outputs an (inverse-polynomial) approximation to the ground state, expressed as a matrix product state (MPS) of polynomial bond dimension. The running time of the algorithm is polynomial in the number of qudits n and the approximation quality δ, for a f xed local dimension d and gap $\Delta > 0$.

A key ingredient of our algorithm is a new construction of an operator called an approximate ground state projector (AGSP), a concept f rst introduced in [2] to derive an improved area law for gapped one-dimensional systems[3]. For this purpose the AGSP has to be eff ciently constructed; the particular AGSP we construct relies on matrix-valued Chernoff bounds [4]. Other ingredients of the algorithm include the use of convex programming, recently discovered structural features of gapped 1D quantum systems [2], and new techniques for manipulating and bounding the complexity of matrix product states.

Precise statements of our results and detailed proofs can be found at arXiv:1307.5143.

*Supported by ARO Grant W911NF-12-1-0541, NSF Grant CCF-0905626 and Templeton Foundation Grant 21674.

†Supported by ARO Grant W911NF-12-1-0541, NSF Grant CCF-0905626 and Templeton Foundation Grant 21674.

‡Part of this work was completed while the author was visiting UC Berkeley. Supported by the National Science Foundation under Grant No. 0844626 and by the Ministry of Education, Singapore under the Tier 3 grant MOE2012-T3-1-009.

ITCS'14, January 12–14, 2014, Princeton, New Jersey, USA.
ACM 978-1-4503-2698-8/14/01.
http://dx.doi.org/10.1145/2554797.2554825 .

Categories and Subject Descriptors

F.1 [**Computation by abstract devices**]: Miscellaneous

General Terms

Theory

Keywords

Local Hamiltonian; ground state; matrix product state; gapped Hamiltonian; 1d algorithm

1. REFERENCES

[1] Dorit Aharonov, Daniel Gottesman, Sandy Irani, and Julia Kempe. The power of quantum systems on a line. *Communications in Mathematical Physics*, 287(1):41–65, 2009.

[2] Itai Arad, Alexei Kitaev, Zeph Landau, and Umesh Vazirani. An area law and sub-exponential algorithm for 1D systems. In *Proceedings of the 4th Innovations in Theoretical Computer Science (ITCS)*, 2013.

[3] M B Hastings. An area law for one-dimensional quantum systems. *Journal of Statistical Mechanics: Theory and Experiment*, 2007(08):P08024, 2007.

[4] Joel A. Tropp. User-friendly tail bounds for sums of random matrices. *Foundations of Computational Mathematics*, 12:389–434, 2012.

[5] Steven R. White. Density matrix formulation for quantum renormalization groups. *Phys. Rev. Lett.*, 69:2863–2866, 1992.

Energy-Efficient Circuit Design

Antonios Antoniadis* Neal Barcelo† Michael Nugent‡ Kirk Pruhs§
Michele Scquizzato¶

Department of Computer Science
University of Pittsburgh
Pittsburgh, PA 15260, USA

ABSTRACT

We initiate the theoretical investigation of energy-efficient circuit design. We assume that the circuit design specifies the circuit layout as well as the supply voltages for the gates. To obtain maximum energy efficiency, the circuit design must balance the conflicting demands of minimizing the energy used per gate, and minimizing the number of gates in the circuit; If the energy supplied to the gates is small, then functional failures are likely, necessitating a circuit layout that is more fault-tolerant, and thus that has more gates. By leveraging previous work on fault-tolerant circuit design, we show general upper and lower bounds on the amount of energy required by a circuit to compute a given relation. We show that some circuits would be asymptotically more energy-efficient if heterogeneous supply voltages were allowed, and show that for some circuits the most energy-efficient supply voltages are homogeneous over all gates.

Categories and Subject Descriptors

F.0 [**Theory of Computation**]: General

General Terms

Theory

*Supported by a fellowship within the Postdoc-Programme of the German Academic Exchange Service (DAAD). E-mail: antonios@pitt.edu.

†This material is based upon work supported by the National Science Foundation Graduate Research Fellowship. E-mail: ncb30@cs.pitt.edu.

‡E-mail: mnugent@cs.pitt.edu.

§Supported in part by NSF grants CCF-1115575, CNS-1253218, and an IBM Faculty Award. E-mail: kirk@cs.pitt.edu.

¶Work supported, in part, by a fellowship of "Fondazione Ing. Aldo Gini", University of Padova, Italy. E-mail: scquizza@pitt.edu.

ITCS'14, January 12–14, 2014, Princeton, New Jersey, USA.

ACM 978-1-4503-2698-8/14/01 ...$15.00.
http://dx.doi.org/10.1145/2554797.2554826.

Keywords

Energy Efficiency; Circuit Design; Near-Threshold Computing

1. INTRODUCTION

The number of transistors per unit volume on a chip continues to double about every two years. However, about a decade ago chip makers hit a thermal wall as the cost of cooling chips with these transistor densities became prohibitive. This has resulted in Moore's gap, namely that increased transistor density no longer directly translates into a similar increase in performance, and in energy becoming the first order design constraint in CMOS-based technologies.

One promising technique to attain more energy-efficient circuits is *Near-Threshold Computing* (NTC). The threshold voltage of a transistor is the minimum voltage at which the transistor starts to conduct current, around 0.2-0.3V for modern processors. Of course, even for identically-designed transistors, there can be variations in the actual threshold voltage due to manufacturing variations; And even for the same transistor, the actual threshold voltage will vary with environmental conditions. Further, actual supply voltages may differ from the designed voltage due to manufacturing and environmental variance. Thus if the designed supply voltage was exactly the ideal threshold voltage, some transistors would likely fail to conduct current as designed. For example, for a typical 65 nm SRAM circuit, halving the supply voltage from the nominal level to 0.5V typically increases the failure rate by about 5 orders of magnitude [6]. The traditional design approach to achieving fault tolerance is to set the supply voltage to be sufficiently high so that with sufficiently high probability no transistor fails. Near-Threshold Computing simply means that the supply voltages are designed to be closer to the threshold voltage. As the power used by a transistor is roughly proportional to the square of the supply voltage [2], Near-Threshold Computing can potentially offer orders of magnitude improvements in energy efficiency, provided another, more energy-efficient, solution for the fault-tolerance issue can be found.

One strategy to achieve fault-tolerance is to design fault-tolerant circuits, namely circuits that correctly compute the desired output if the number of failures is not significantly higher than the expected number of failures. The study of fault-tolerant circuits is not new. Starting with the seminal paper by von Neumann [14], several papers [4, 5, 10, 11, 12, 8, 7] have considered the question of how many faulty gates, each (independently) having a (small) fixed probability of failure, are required to mimic the computation of

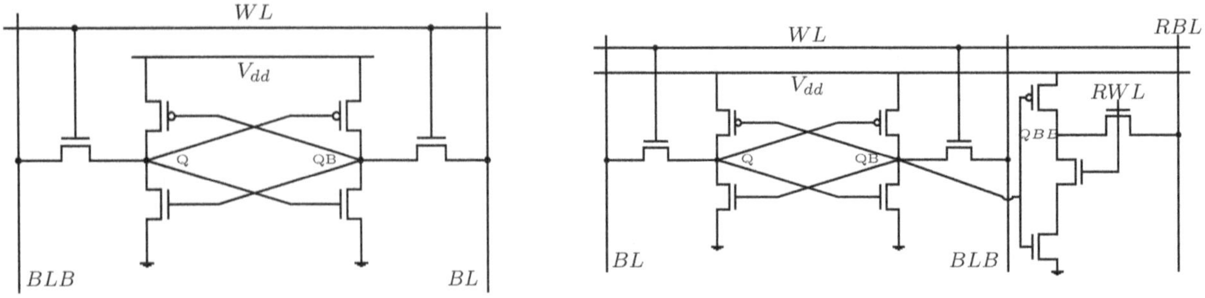

(a) Standard 6-transistor design.

(b) A more fault-tolerant 10-transistor design from [3].

Figure 1: Two SRAM circuits with the same functionality.

an ideal circuit with some desired probability of correctness. In general, as the probability of gate failure increases one would expect that more gates will be required to achieve a fixed probability of failure for the circuit. As an example from [6], the circuit shown in Figure 1a is the traditional 6-transistor design for an SRAM cell, while the circuit shown in Figure 1b is a more fault-tolerant, and thus more suited for Near-Threshold Computing, 10-transistor design for an SRAM cell.

Our goal here is to initiate the study of the design of energy-efficient circuits. We assume that the design of the circuit specifies both the circuit layout as well as the supply voltages for the gates. To obtain maximum energy efficiency, the circuit design must balance the conflicting demands of minimizing the energy used per gate, and minimizing the number of gates in the circuit; If the energy supplied to the gates is small, then functional failures are likely, necessitating a circuit layout that is more fault-tolerant, and thus that has more gates. Thus the design should find a "sweet spot" for the supply voltages that balances the competing demands of small circuit size and low per-gate energy. In Section 2 we formalize this in the natural way.

The paper [6] gives an excellent survey on Near-Threshold Computing. As an example of a technology that has at least the spirit of Near-Threshold Computing, IBM's production POWER7 servers use a technique called *Guardband* to save energy by dynamically lowering operating voltage [1].

1.1 Our Contribution

We give four main results, which we discuss in the following four paragraphs.

We show in Section 3 that the classic lower bound on circuit size from the fault-tolerant circuit literature can be extended to give a lower bound for energy. Gács and Gál [8], and independently Reischuk and Schmeltz [12], show that any Boolean function f with sensitivity s (roughly the number of input bits which affect the output) requires a circuit of size $\Omega(s \log s)$ to be reliably computed when the gates of the circuit fail independently with a fixed positive probability. We modify the techniques in [8] to prove an $\Omega\left(s \log\left(s(1-2\sqrt{\delta})/\delta\right)\right)$ lower bound on the energy required by any circuit that computes a relation with sensitivity s correctly with probability at least $(1-\delta)$.

We show in Section 4 that the classic upper bound on circuit size from the fault-tolerant circuit literature can be extended to give an upper bound on circuit energy consumption. Von Neumann [14] showed that given a Boolean function f and a circuit of size c which computes f, a circuit of size $O(c \log c)$ is sufficient for computing f correctly with high probability. Using techniques from [14] and from [10, 7], we show that a relation h that is computable by a circuit of size c can, with probability at least $(1-\delta)$, be computed by a circuit of faulty gates using $O(c \log(c/\delta))$ energy. In our construction, the supply voltages are homogeneous (that is, the same for all gates).

While it may not currently be practical, in principle the supply voltages need not be homogeneous over all gates, that is, different gates could be supplied with different voltages. This naturally leads to the question of whether allowing heterogeneous supply voltages might yield lower-energy circuits than is possible if the supply voltages are required to be homogeneous. In Section 5 we observe that there are relations, namely the parity function, for which allowing heterogeneous supply voltages will not allow one to achieve a circuit design that uses asymptotically less energy than is achievable with a circuit design with homogeneous supply voltages. Intuitively, the parity function has such high sensitivity that every gate in any reasonable circuit will be of equal importance, so nothing can be gained by heterogeneous supply voltages. Formally, the proof is essentially a corollary of our lower bounds from Section 3.

In contrast, in Section 6 we give a natural example where allowing heterogeneous supply voltages allows one to use asymptotically less energy than would be achievable using homogeneous supply voltages. In particular, we consider a natural super-majority relation, which outputs the majority of the input bits if this majority is sufficiently large, and the most natural circuit that computes this relation, a balanced tree of majority gates. We show that for homogeneous supply voltages the energy required by this circuit to compute this relation is $\Omega(nP(\delta))$, where n is the number of input bits, δ is the maximum probability of failure for the circuit that one is willing to tolerate, and $P(x)$ is the power required in order for one majority gate to fail with probability at most x. We then show that if supply voltages can be heterogeneous then this circuit can compute this relation using energy $O(n + 3^{1/\delta}P(\delta/10))$, which is asymptotically less than $nP(\delta)$ for functions P observed in current circuits. Intuitively, the gates closer to the output are more important, and one can obtain a greater increase in probability of correctness by investing more energy in these gates. In some sense this is our main result as the proof is not based on proofs in the fault-tolerant circuit literature.

2. PROBLEM DESCRIPTION AND NOTATION

We now formally define the problem. A *Boolean relation* h is a map from $\{0,1\}^n$ to $\{0,1\}$, where each input is mapped to 0, 1, or both 0 and 1. If x is mapped to both 0 and 1, this can be thought of as "don't care" (for example because the input x should not occur in a correctly functioning system). Note that a *Boolean function* is a Boolean relation where each input is uniquely mapped to either 0 or 1. For any input $x \in \{0,1\}^n$, denote by x^ℓ the input that has the same bits as x, except for the ℓ-th bit, which is flipped. A Boolean relation h is *sensitive* on the ℓ-th bit of x if neither $h(x)$ nor $h(x^\ell)$ is mapped to both 0 and 1, and $h(x) \neq h(x^\ell)$. The *sensitivity of* h *on* x is the number of bits of x that h is sensitive on. The *sensitivity of* h is the maximum over all x of the sensitivity of h on x.

A *gate* is a function $g : \{0,1\}^{n_g} \rightarrow \{0,1\}$, where n_g is the number of inputs (i.e., the *fan-in*) of the gate. We say that a gate *fails* when it produces an incorrect output, that is, when given an input x it produces an output other than $g(x)$. Every gate has some independent probability of failure ϵ. A gate that never fails is said to be *reliable.* A *Boolean circuit* C with n inputs is a directed acyclic graph in which every node is a gate. Among them there are n gates with fan-in zero, each of which outputs one of the n inputs of the circuit, i.e., the input gates are assumed to be reliable. One gate is designated as the output gate, which has out-degree zero. The *size* of a circuit is the number of gates it contains. Any Boolean relation can be represented by a Boolean circuit. Given a value $\delta \in (0,1/2)$ (δ may not be constant), a circuit that computes a Boolean relation h is said to be $(1-\delta)$-*reliable* if for every input x on which $h(x)$ is not both 0 and 1 it outputs $h(x)$ with probability at least $1-\delta$. We say that a circuit is *reliable* if it is 1-reliable (for example, because all its gates are reliable).

Every gate g is supplied with a voltage v_g. We say that the supply voltages are *homogeneous* when every gate of the circuit is supplied with the same voltage, and *heterogeneous* otherwise. A voltage-to-failure function $\epsilon(v) : \mathbb{R}^+ \rightarrow (0,1/2)$ maps a supply voltage to a probability of functional failure, that is, the probability that the gate fails when supplied with voltage v. For convenience, we refer to the probability of failure with ϵ when the supply voltage is implied by the context. Hence, every gate has a probability of failure of $\epsilon(v_g)$ which, to lighten notation, we denote as ϵ_g. There is also a voltage-to-energy function $E(v)$ mapping the supply voltage to the energy used by a gate with that supply voltage. The energy required by a circuit C is simply the aggregate energy used by the gates, $\sum_{g\in C} E(v_g)$ in our notation. For convenience, we define a failure-to-energy function $P(q) := E(\epsilon^{-1}(q))$, where ϵ^{-1} denotes the inverse of the function ϵ. Thus the energy of a circuit C can be rewritten as $\sum_{g\in C} P(\epsilon_g)$.

By observing a semi-log plot of voltage-to-failure for a current 65nm SRAM cell from [6] we can see that the relationship between voltage and the log of the failure is approximately linear. Hence, the error as a function of voltage is of the form of $\epsilon(v) = c^{-v}$, for some positive constant c. Thus using the fact that the energy is proportional to the square of the supply voltage, we conclude that the failure-to-energy function for a 65nm SRAM cell is approximately $P(\epsilon) = \Theta(\log^2(1/\epsilon))$.

3. A GENERAL ENERGY LOWER BOUND

Our main goal in this section is to prove Theorem 1, which roughly states that $\Omega(s \log s)$ energy is necessary to compute a relation with sensitivity s.

THEOREM 1. *Let $\delta < 1/4$, and let C be a circuit that $(1-\delta)$-reliably computes a relation h of sensitivity s. If each gate g of C fails independently with probability ϵ_g, and incurs an energy consumption of $P(\epsilon_g)$, with P being a proper failure-to-energy function, then C requires*

$$\Omega\left(s \log\left(s \frac{1-2\sqrt{\delta}}{\delta}\right)\right)$$

energy in order to $(1-\delta)$-reliably compute h.

The outline of this section is as follows. First, we define proper failure-to-energy functions (Definition 2), and discuss why proper functions are natural. Then, similarly to [8], we show how to translate our problem to an equivalent problem where the failures occur not only on gates, but on wires as well. This is formalized in Statement 3, which is implied by the proof of Lemma 3.1 in [4], and is also used in [8]. Lemma 6 then gives a lower bound on the energy necessary for $(1-\delta)$-reliable circuits within this new model with wire failures. The proof is based on the proof of Theorem 3.1 in [8], and uses a series of inequalities that relate the probability of an input being incorrectly transmitted to the probability of the circuit being incorrect. Using this, we can write the problem as a single-variable optimization problem and use standard techniques to give the desired lower bound. Finally, to prove Theorem 1 we show that given a $(1-\delta)$-reliable circuit C in our original model without wire failures, we can create a $(1-\delta)$-reliable circuit C' in the new model with wire failures, where the energy consumptions of C and C' differ only by a constant.

DEFINITION 2. *A failure-to-energy function P is called* proper *when it satisfies the four following properties:*

1. *P is nonincreasing,*
2. $\lim_{\epsilon\rightarrow 0^+} P(\epsilon)/(\log 1/\epsilon) > 0$,
3. $\lim_{\epsilon\rightarrow 1/2^-} P(\epsilon) > 0$,
4. $P(\epsilon_1) + P(\epsilon_2) \geq 2P(\sqrt{\epsilon_1\epsilon_2})$ *for all* $\epsilon_1, \epsilon_2 \in (0,1/2)$.

The first and third restrictions are natural, since they just require that the energy used decreases, but never becomes zero, as the probability of failure of a gate increases. The second property states that the energy must increase "quickly enough" as the probability of a gate's failure tends to 0, which is necessary in order to have any energy saving over gates that never (or almost never) fail. The last property provides a convexity constraint on the function P. We point out that failure-to-energy functions typically observed in real gates fall within this class of proper failure-to-energy functions [9, 6].

STATEMENT 3 ([4]). *Let g be a gate with fan-in n_g, in a circuit C where both gates and wires may fail. Furthermore, let $\epsilon \in (0,1/2), \zeta_g \in [0, \epsilon/n_g]$ and let $g(t)$ be the output of gate g assuming that its input-wires receive input t, and both g and g's input-wires are reliable. Then there exists a unique value $\eta_g(y, \zeta_g) \in [0,1]$ such that if*

- *the input wires of g fail independently with probability ζ_g, and*
- *gate g fails with probability $\eta_g(y, \zeta_g)$ when the gate receives input y,*

then the probability that g does not output $g(t)$ is equal to ϵ.

Note that in Statement 3, since we can now have failures on wires, the input y received by a gate g may be different than the input t received by the corresponding wires.

We need the following definition and technical lemma.

DEFINITION 4. *Given $x_{1,1}, x_{1,2}, \ldots, x_{1,n} \in \mathbb{R}$, we recursively define a sequence of numbers as follows. Let $m_j^u = \arg\max_i x_{j,i}$ and $m_j^l = \arg\min_i x_{j,i}$. Then, for all $i \neq \{m_j^u, m_j^l\}$, let $x_{(j+1),i} = x_{j,i}$, and let $x_{(j+1),m_j^u} = x_{(j+1),m_j^l} = \sqrt{x_{j,m_j^u} x_{j,m_j^l}}$.*

LEMMA 5. *Let $a_1, a_2, \ldots$ be a sequence of numbers such that $a_j = x_{j,m_j^u} - x_{j,m_j^l}$, with the terms x_{j,m_j^u} and x_{j,m_j^l} as defined above. Then,*

$$\lim_{j\to\infty} a_j = 0.$$

LEMMA 6. *Let f be a proper failure-to-energy function, and let C be a circuit that $(1-\delta)$-reliably computes a relation h of sensitivity s. If (i) each gate g of C fails independently with probability $\eta_g(y, \zeta_g)$ when receiving input y, (ii) g incurs an energy consumption of zero, and (iii) each wire i entering g fails independently with probability $\zeta_g \in (0, 1/4)$ and incurs an energy usage of $f(\zeta_g)$, then C requires*

$$\Omega\left(s \log\left(s \frac{1-2\sqrt{\delta}}{\delta}\right)\right)$$

energy in order to $(1-\delta)$-reliably compute h.

PROOF. We start by rephrasing our problem after borrowing a constraint on the number of wires and some notation from [8]. Specifically, let z be an input such that h has maximum sensitivity on z. Let $S \subset \{1, 2, \ldots, n\}$ be the set of indexes so that $\ell \in S$ if and only if h is sensitive to the ℓ-th bit on input z. Then $|S| = s$, where s is the sensitivity of h. For each $\ell \in S$ denote by B_ℓ the set of all wires originating from the ℓ-th input of the circuit. Let $m_\ell = |B_\ell|$. For any set $\beta \subset B_\ell$, let $H(\beta)$ be the event that the wires belonging to β fail and the other wires of B_ℓ are correct. Denote by β_ℓ the subset of B_ℓ where

$$\max_{\beta \subset B_\ell} \Pr[C(z^\ell) = h(z^\ell) \text{ s.t. } H(\beta)]$$

is obtained, where $C(z^\ell)$ is a random variable for the output of the circuit given input z^ℓ. Finally, let $H_\ell = H(B_\ell \setminus \beta_\ell)$. Note that since wires can now fail with different probabilities, we have that,

$$\Pr[H_\ell] = \prod_{i\in\beta_\ell} (1-\zeta_i) \prod_{i\notin\beta_\ell} \zeta_i \geq \prod_{i\in B_\ell} \zeta_i.$$

It follows from Inequalities (5) and (6) of [8] that

$$\frac{\delta}{1-2\sqrt{\delta}} \geq \sum_{\ell\in S} \prod_{i\in B_\ell} \zeta_i$$

and as in [8], using the inequality of arithmetic and geometric means, we have

$$\frac{\delta}{1-2\sqrt{\delta}} \geq s\left(\prod_{\ell\in S, i\in B_\ell} \zeta_i\right)^{1/s}.$$

Rewriting this to isolate the product term, we have

$$\prod_{\ell\in S, i\in B_\ell} \zeta_i \leq \left(\frac{\delta}{s(1-2\sqrt{\delta})}\right)^s.$$

Therefore, minimizing the energy consumption, is equivalent to the following optimization problem,

$$\text{minimize} \quad \sum_{\ell\in S, i\in B_\ell} f(\zeta_i)$$

$$\text{subject to} \quad \prod_{\ell\in S, i\in B_\ell} \zeta_i \leq \left(\frac{\delta}{s(1-2\sqrt{\delta})}\right)^s.$$

Now, take some feasible solution ζ^* to the above optimization problem. Let ζ_1^* and ζ_2^* denote the minimum and maximum ζ_i^* respectively, and M denote the total number of wires, i.e., $M = \sum_{\ell\in S} m_\ell$. Note that since we assume that $f(p_1) + f(p_2) \geq 2f(\sqrt{p_1 p_2})$ for all $p_1, p_2 \in (0, 1/2)$, we can set $\zeta_1^* = \zeta_2^* = \sqrt{\zeta_1^* \zeta_2^*}$, without increasing the value of the objective, and further the constraint remains feasible. By Lemma 5 this process, if repeated, will converge to a solution where all ζ_i are equal. Therefore, we can rewrite the optimization problem as

$$\text{minimize} \quad Mf(x)$$

$$\text{subject to} \quad x^M \leq \left(\frac{\delta}{s(1-2\sqrt{\delta})}\right)^s.$$

Isolating M in the constraint above, the problem is equivalent to that of minimizing

$$\left(\frac{s}{\log 1/x} \log\left(s\frac{1-2\sqrt{\delta}}{\delta}\right)\right) f(x).$$

Since the function satisfies properties 1, 2, and 3 of Definition 2, the above expression will be minimized either at some constant $x \in (0, 1/4)$, in which case $f(x)/\log(1/x) > 0$, or in the limit as x approaches 0, in which case

$$\lim_{x\to 0^+} f(x)/\log(1/x) > 0,$$

or in the limit as x approaches $1/4$, in which case

$$f(x)/\log(1/x) > 0.$$

The lemma follows. □

We are now ready to prove Theorem 1.

PROOF OF THEOREM 1. We start by constructing a new circuit C' for computing h, which is identical to C except that both wires and gates may fail, wires of C' incur some non-zero energy consumption (as a function of their probability of failure), and the gates in C' do not consume energy. First we argue that this can be done such that C' is $(1-\delta)$-reliable. Observe that if for each wire i entering gate g we set its probability of failure to $\zeta_g = \epsilon_g/n_g$, we can apply

Statement 3 and set the failure probability on gate g when receiving input y to $\eta_g(y, \zeta_g)$. The result is that when the input wires of gate g in C' receive input t, the probability that g does not output $g(t)$ is ϵ_g (the same as the probability of failure of g in the original circuit C). Thus by setting these failure probabilities for each gate and wire in C' we have that, for any input x, C and C' output $h(x)$ with the same probability, and so C' is $(1-\delta)$-reliable.

Now we set the energy consumption of the wires such that the energy of C' is at most the energy of C. First observe that if for each gate g we set the failure-to-energy function of the wires that are inputs to g to be $\tilde{P}_g(\zeta) = P(n_g \cdot \zeta)/n_g$, then since $\zeta_g = \epsilon_g/n_g$, the total energy of the wires entering g would be $n_g\tilde{P}_g(\zeta_g) = P(\epsilon_g)$ and the energy of C and C' would be equal. However, to apply Lemma 6, all wires must have the same failure-to-energy function. Therefore, let n_g^* be the maximum fan-in of any gate of C, i.e., $n_g^* = \max_{g\in C} n_g$. We set the failure-to-energy function of all wires in C' to be

$$\tilde{P}(\zeta) = \begin{cases} P(n_g^* \cdot \zeta)/n_g^* & \text{if } \zeta < \frac{1}{2n_g^*}, \\ \lim_{\epsilon\to 1/2^-} P(\epsilon)/n_g^* & \text{if } \zeta \geq \frac{1}{2n_g^*}. \end{cases}$$

First observe that $\tilde{P}_g(\zeta) \geq \tilde{P}(\zeta)$ for all $\zeta \in (0, 1/2)$ since P is nonincreasing so $P(n_g\zeta) \geq P(n_g^*\zeta)$. This implies that the energy of C' is at most the energy of C.

In order to apply Lemma 6, we need to verify that $\tilde{P}$ is a proper failure-to-energy function. The first property follows directly from the definition of $\tilde{P}$. For the second property, observe that

$$\lim_{\zeta\to 0^+} \frac{\tilde{P}(\zeta)}{\log\left(\frac{1}{\zeta}\right)} = \frac{1}{n_g^*} \lim_{\zeta\to 0^+} \frac{P(n_g^*\zeta)}{\log\left(\frac{1}{n_g^*\zeta}\right)} \cdot \lim_{\zeta\to 0^+} \frac{\log\left(\frac{1}{n_g^*\zeta}\right)}{\log\left(\frac{1}{\zeta}\right)}$$
$$= \lim_{\zeta\to 0^+} \frac{P(n_g^*\zeta)}{\log\left(\frac{1}{n_g^*\zeta}\right)} > 0.$$

The third property follows from the fact that

$$\lim_{\zeta\to 1/2^-} \tilde{P}(\zeta) = \lim_{\epsilon\to 1/2^-} P(\epsilon)/n_g^* > 0,$$

where we exploited the definition of $\tilde{P}$ and the fact that, by hypothesis, P is a proper failure-to-energy function. For the fourth property, let $\zeta_1, \zeta_2 \in (0, 1/2)$, and, w.l.o.g., $\zeta_1 < \zeta_2$. There are four cases, depending on the relationship between ζ_1, ζ_2, and n_g^*. When $\zeta_1 < \zeta_2 < 1/2n_g^*$, by applying the definition of $\tilde{P}$ and since P by hypothesis is a proper failure-to-energy function, we have

$$\tilde{P}(\zeta_1) + \tilde{P}(\zeta_2) = \frac{P(n_g^*\zeta_1)}{n_g^*} + \frac{P(n_g^*\zeta_2)}{n_g^*}$$
$$\geq 2\frac{P\left(\sqrt{n_g^*\zeta_1 n_g^*\zeta_2}\right)}{n_g^*}$$
$$= 2\tilde{P}\left(\sqrt{\zeta_1\zeta_2}\right).$$

When $\zeta_1 < \zeta_2 = 1/2n_g^*$, by the previous case we have that

$$\lim_{\zeta_2\to(1/(2n_g^*))^-} \left(\tilde{P}(\zeta_1) + \tilde{P}(\zeta_2) - 2\tilde{P}\left(\sqrt{\zeta_1\zeta_2}\right)\right) \geq 0,$$

and so in this case the property holds. When $\zeta_1 < 1/2n_g^* < \zeta_2$, we have that

$$\tilde{P}(\zeta_1) + \tilde{P}(\zeta_2) = \tilde{P}(\zeta_1) + \tilde{P}\left(\frac{1}{2n_g^*}\right)$$
$$\geq 2\tilde{P}\left(\sqrt{\frac{\zeta_1}{2n_g^*}}\right)$$
$$\geq 2\tilde{P}\left(\sqrt{\zeta_1\zeta_2}\right),$$

where the first equality holds by definition of $\tilde{P}$, the first inequality follows by the preceding case, and the second inequality holds since $\tilde{P}$ is nonincreasing ans since, in this case, $\sqrt{\zeta_1/2n_g^*} \leq \sqrt{\zeta_1\zeta_2}$. Finally, when $1/2n_g^* \leq \zeta_1 < \zeta_2$, $\sqrt{\zeta_1\zeta_2} > \zeta_1$ and thus, by definition, $\tilde{P}(\zeta_1) = \tilde{P}(\zeta_2) = \tilde{P}\left(\sqrt{\zeta_1\zeta_2}\right)$. We conclude that $\tilde{P}$ is a proper failure-to-energy function. The theorem then directly follows by applying Lemma 6 to C' and $\tilde{P}$. ☐

4. A GENERAL ENERGY UPPER BOUND

Our main goal in this section is to prove Theorem 7, which roughly states that $O(N \log N)$ energy is sufficient to simulate a circuit of size N.

THEOREM 7. *Given a reliable circuit C of size N and a non-trivial failure-to-energy function, it is possible to construct a circuit C' with homogeneous voltage supply that uses $O(N\log(N/\delta))$ units of energy and that $(1-\delta)$-reliably computes the same function computed by C.*

To prove Theorem 7 we use an upper bound on the number of gates for fault-tolerant circuits originally stated by Pippenger [10] and later proved in full generality by Gács [7]. This upper bound is stated in Theorem 8. The energy upper bound follows by choosing the voltage supply that minimizes the product of the total number of gates in the circuit constructed in Theorem 8, and the energy used by each gate. More specifically, we want to set the gate failure probability ϵ so as to minimize $P(\epsilon)/(\log(1/\epsilon) - r_0)$ for some constant r_0. As long as P is *non-trivial*, i.e., if for any $p^* \in (0, 1/2)$ it holds that $P(p^*) < +\infty$, one can find an ϵ such that $P(\epsilon) = O(1)$. This setting of ϵ then implies the upper bound of $O(N\log(N/\delta))$ on the energy used by this construction using homogeneous supply voltages.

THEOREM 8 ([7]). *There are constants $R_0, \epsilon_0, r_0 > 0$ such that for all $\epsilon < \epsilon_0$ and $\delta \geq 3\epsilon$, for every reliable circuit C of size N there is a circuit of size $R_0\frac{N\log(N/\delta)}{\log(1/\epsilon^*)-r_0}$ that computes the same result as C with probability at least $1-\delta$ if gates fail independently with probability at most ϵ, where $\epsilon^* = \max\{\epsilon, \delta/N\}$.*

PROOF. The main idea of this construction is to replace each gate of the reliable circuit with a gadget in the fault-tolerant circuit. A constant k is chosen as the level of redundancy for the circuit, meaning that each gadget has k outputs and each input to a gate in the reliable circuit is replaced by k inputs to a gadget. Another constant $\theta \in (0, 1)$ is chosen such that, with high probability, θk wires exiting each gadget carry the same value as the corresponding gate in the reliable circuit. Each gadget contains k copies of the corresponding gate from the reliable circuit, as well as an additional circuit that ensures that at least a θ fraction of the wires exiting the gadget are correct. ☐

5. SUPPLY VOLTAGE HETEROGENEITY MAY NOT HELP

In this section we observe in Theorem 9 that there are relations, namely the parity function, where heterogeneous supply voltages do not allow for an asymptotic reduction in energy.

THEOREM 9. *Let $\delta < 1/4$. The energy used by any circuit to $(1-\delta)$-reliably compute the parity function is $\Omega(n\log(n/\delta))$, and this is achievable by a circuit with homogeneous supply voltages.*

PROOF. The parity function can be reliably computed by a perfect binary tree of $2n-1$ XOR reliable gates. Thus, by Theorem 7 there exists a $(1-\delta)$-reliable circuit for the parity function that uses homogeneous voltage supplies and that incurs $O(n\log(n/\delta))$ energy consumption. Since the sensitivity of the parity function is n, by Theorem 1 this is the best possible to within a constant factor. □

6. SUPPLY VOLTAGE HETEROGENEITY CAN HELP

The goal of this section is to prove Theorem 13, which roughly states that heterogeneous supply voltages allow the natural majority circuit to compute a super-majority with asymptotically less energy than is possible with homogeneous supply voltages.

We start by defining the circuit and the logarithmic super-majority relation (LSR). Lemma 17 shows that $\Omega(n\cdot P(\delta))$ energy is required to $(1-\delta)$-reliably compute the LSR with homogeneous voltage supplies. The intuition behind the proof is that the output gate of any $(1-\delta)$-reliable circuit cannot have a probability of failure greater than δ and, since the voltage supplies are homogeneous, neither can any other gate. Then in Lemma 18 we show that there is a heterogeneous setting of the supply voltages so that this circuit $(1-\delta)$-reliably computes LSR with energy $O\left(n+3^{1/\delta}P(\delta/10)\right)$. Intuitively, we split the circuit into an "upper" part consisting of gates close to the output gate, and a "lower" part consisting of gates close to the input gates: Each gate in the lower part has a constant probability of failure and thus a small energy consumption which results in non-constant savings compared to the optimal homogeneous setting. With the help of technical Lemmas 14 and 15, we are able to show that although there exist gates in the lower part of the circuit that fail with a probability higher than δ, no such gate fails with a probability $o(1)$. This preserves enough information for the upper part of the circuit to still $(1-\delta)$-reliably compute LSR. In other words, in the upper part of the circuit we use a much smaller probability of failure for each gate in order to ensure that the circuit will "autocorrect" itself and output the correct result (see Lemma 16).

DEFINITION 10. *The* Logarithmic Supermajority Relation (LSR) *is the following Boolean relation:*

$$LSR(x)=\begin{cases}0 & \text{if the number of } 0\text{'s in } x \text{ is at least } n-\frac{1}{2}\log_3 n,\\ 1 & \text{if the number of } 1\text{'s in } x \text{ is at least } n-\frac{1}{2}\log_3 n, \text{ and}\\ 0 \text{ and } 1 & \text{otherwise,}\end{cases}$$

where x is the input and $|x|=n$.

This relation outputs 1 when the input contains at least $n-(1/2)\log_3 n$ ones, 0 when the input contains at least $n-(1/2)\log_3 n$ zeros, and otherwise we "don't care".

DEFINITION 11. *A* majority tree *is a Boolean circuit where the gates form a perfect ternary tree in which the leaves represent the inputs, and each internal gate, called* majority gate, *outputs the majority of its three children.*

DEFINITION 12. *A failure-to-energy function P is called* easy-going *when the following hold:*

- $\lim_{x\to 0}P(x)=+\infty$
- *There exists a constant $c>0$ such that $\frac{P(x/10)}{P(x)}\le c$ for all $x\in(0,1/2)$.*

Note that this class of failure-to-energy functions contains many natural functions. For example $P(x)=1/x^\alpha$ and $P(x)=(\log 1/x)^\alpha$ are both easy-going.

THEOREM 13. *Let P be an easy-going failure-to-energy function, and let $c\in(0,1)$ be a constant. Furthermore, let $E_1(\delta)$ be the optimal energy consumption of the $(1-\delta)$-reliable majority tree on n leaves where all the gates must have the same failure probability, and $E_2(\delta)$ be the optimal energy consumption of the same $(1-\delta)$-reliable majority tree when each gate can have an arbitrary failure probability. Then, for $\delta'=\frac{1}{(1-c)\log_3 n}$, there holds*

$$\frac{E_1(\delta')}{E_2(\delta')}=\omega(1).$$

Let p_i be the probability that a gate of height i in a majority tree outputs 1. Notice that

$$p_{i+1}=p_i^3(1-\epsilon)+3p_i^2(1-p_i)(1-\epsilon)+3p_i(1-p_i)^2\epsilon + (1-p_i)^3\epsilon=(3p_i^2-2p_i^3)(1-2\epsilon)+\epsilon.$$

Also, let $R(p_i):=p_{i+1}$, and let $\ell^*(\epsilon)$ be the largest real number such that $R(\ell^*(\epsilon))=\ell^*(\epsilon)$. Note that $\ell^*(\epsilon)$ only exists when $\epsilon<1/6$. Therefore for the following we assume that $\epsilon<1/6$.

LEMMA 14. *It holds that $\ell^*(\epsilon)=\frac{1}{2}+\frac{1}{2}\sqrt{\frac{1-6\epsilon}{1-2\epsilon}}$. Furthermore, if $1/2\le p_i\le\ell^*(\epsilon)$ then $p_i\le p_{i+1}\le\ell^*(\epsilon)$, and if $p_i\ge\ell^*(\epsilon)$ then $p_i\ge p_{i+1}\ge\ell^*(\epsilon)$, for all $i\in\{1,2,\ldots,\log_3 n\}$.*

Note that the above technical lemma implies that $\ell^*(\epsilon)$ is a *stable* fixed point. The next two lemmas will be useful for setting the failure probabilities and analyzing the upper part of the tree.

LEMMA 15. *Let G be a majority gate with input gates g_1,g_2 and g_3 which output 1 with probability $q_1>1/2, q_2>1/2$, and $q_3>1/2$, respectively. Furthermore let q_G be the probability that G outputs 1 (for the given probabilities of the inputs to output 1). If we alter g_1,g_2, and g_3 to have probabilities $q_1'>q_1, q_2'>q_2$, and $q_3'>q_3$ of outputting 1, then for the new probability q_G' of G outputting 1 it holds that $q_G'\ge q_G$.*

LEMMA 16. *Consider a majority tree T of height $\lfloor 1/\delta\rfloor$ (for δ small enough) where each input of T is 1 with probability at least 0.79, and suppose that each gate of T has a failure probability of $\delta/10$. Then T outputs 1 with probability at least $1-\delta$.*

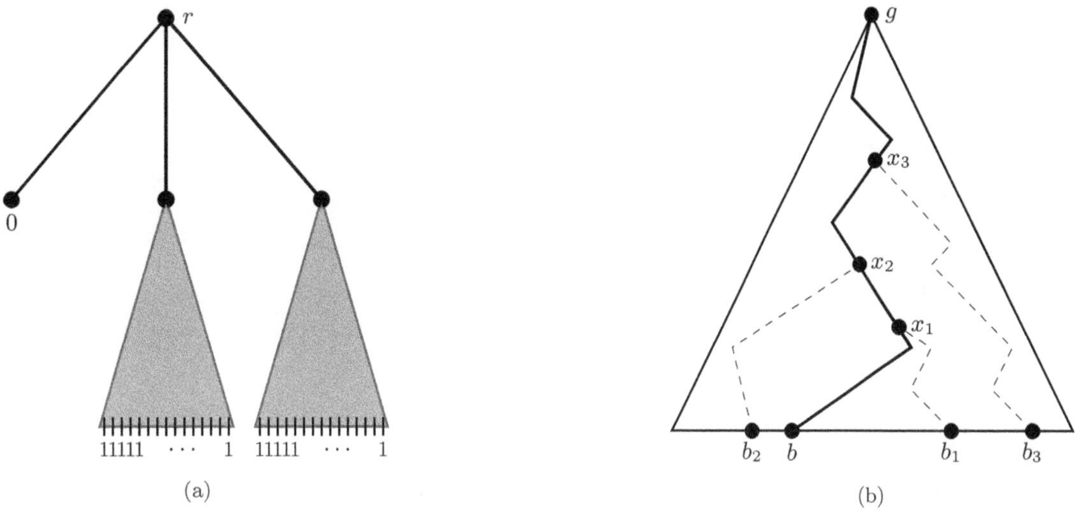

Figure 2: (a) Pr[r outputs 1] $\geq 1-p$. (b) The path from b to g. The input gates b_i receive input 0.

With the help of the above lemmas, we are now ready to bound E_1 and E_2.

LEMMA 17. *It holds that* $E_1(\delta) = \Omega(n \cdot P(\delta))$.

PROOF. In order to lower bound E_1, we will consider the case where each input bit is 1. Note that the root cannot have a probability of failure greater than δ, since then even with all its inputs being correct it would not give the right output with the desired probability, and by Lemma 15 this probability can only decrease as the probability that the input gates are correct decreases. Because all gates must have the same probability, we have that each of the $O(n)$ gates has an energy consumption of at least $P(\delta)$, and the lemma follows. □

LEMMA 18. *It holds that* $E_2(\delta) = O\left(n + 3^{1/\delta}P(\delta/10)\right)$.

PROOF. Assume without loss of generality that the input contains at least $n - (1/2)\log_3 n$ 1's, so that the desired output is 1. We assign a failure probability of $\delta/10$ to each gate located at a height of at least $\log_3 n - 1/\delta$, and a failure probability of 0.12 to each gate at a height strictly less than $\log_3 n - 1/\delta$. By Lemma 16, it suffices to show that each gate at height $\lfloor \log_3 n - 1/\delta \rfloor$ outputs 1 independently with probability at least 0.79.

Let $p = 0.36$. Consider a majority tree where each gate has a failure probability of 0.12. Then, by Lemma 14, and since for this tree $p_0 = 0.88 > \ell^*(0.12)$, we have that the root of the tree outputs 1 with probability at least $\ell^*(0.12) > 0.8$. Thus, a reliable majority gate whose inputs are one 0 and the outputs of two arbitrarily sized majority trees whose inputs are all 1's outputs 0 with probability at most $1 - 0.8^2 = p$. See Figure 2a.

Consider a majority tree of height h rooted at gate g, and fix an input to this tree that contains exactly d zeros as input, with $0 < d < h$. Let b be any of the input gates of the tree that was assigned a zero for this input. We first show that the probability that the path from b to gate g contains only 0's after each gate has computed is at most p^{h-d}. Let b_i for $i = 1, 2, \ldots, d-1$ be the other input gates that were assigned 0's. We may assume that the path from each b_i to g intersects the path from b to g, at a distinct gate x_i. Furthermore we may assume that each such x_i outputs a 0. See Figure 2b for an example. The probability of such a path from b to g to contain only 0's is equal to the probability that the $h - d - 1$ non-x_i gates on the path from b to g output a 0. Note that these non-x_i gates either receive a 0 and two inputs from majority subtrees whose inputs are all 1, or three inputs from majority subtrees whose inputs are all 1. Therefore, by the above observation about p and Lemma 15, the probability of such a path of all 0's is at most p^{h-d}.

Let T be any full (but not necessarily complete) majority tree of some height h_T. For any $h_A \geq h_T$, we can "complete" a copy of tree T by adding extra gates in order to obtain a perfect majority tree A of height h_A. We associate each gate in T with the corresponding gate in A. We claim that if the input at the leaves of both T and A consists of only 1's, then each gate of T is at least as likely to output 1 as the corresponding gate in A. We prove this claim by induction over the heights of gates in T. The base case, i.e., if a gate in T is a leaf, is straightforward. Assume now that each gate of T up to some height h', has a higher probability of outputting 1 than its corresponding gate in A, and consider a non-leaf gate g' of T at height $h' + 1$. Since T is a full tree, and g' is not a leaf, g' must have three children. The inductive step now directly follows from Lemma 15.

Next, consider any subtree B of our original majority tree that is rooted at a gate g of height $\lfloor \log_3 n - 1/\delta \rfloor$. Since we assumed that the input to the original tree contains at most $(1/2)\log_3 n$ 0's, clearly this holds for B as well. See Figure 3 for an example of a tree B.

Now we want to lower bound the probability that g outputs a 1 when there is no path of all 0's from a leaf to g. We note that if there is no path of all 0's from a leaf to g then there exists a full subtree T' of B that is also rooted at g and whose inputs can be assumed to be all 1's. The subtree T' can be constructed by truncating each leaf-to-root path in B at the first node that outputs 1. The existence of T' follows from the fact that there is no path of all 0's from a leaf in B to g, but the structure T' depends on the random events occurring at each gate in $B \setminus T'$ and the leaves of T'.

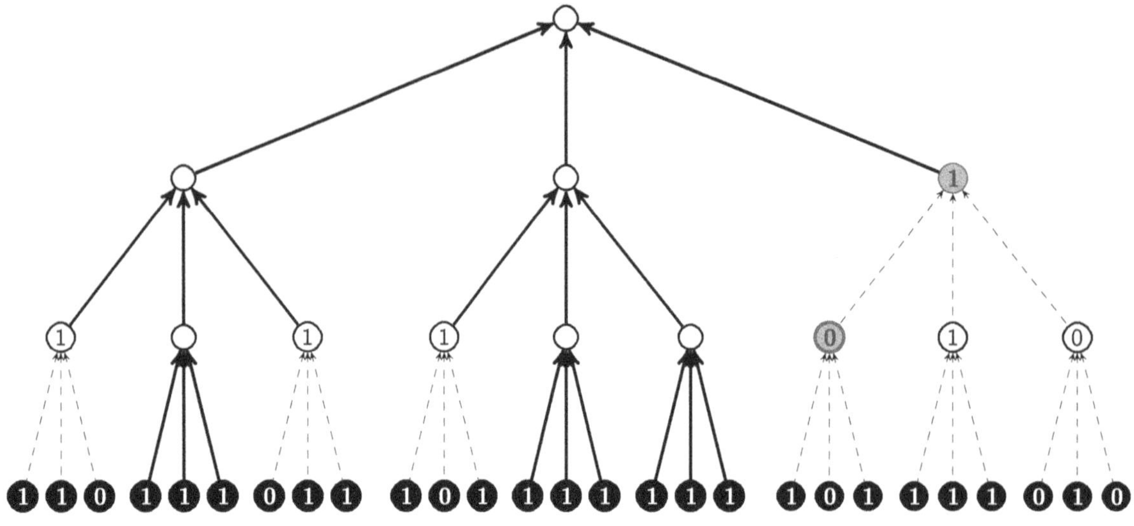

Figure 3: A subtree B. The solid edges denote the full ternary subtree $T \in \Gamma$. Note that T has 1's as inputs on its leafs. The dashed edges denote the edges in $B \setminus T$. The gray nodes denote gates that failed.

Conditioning on those random events, we have that B and T' output a 1 with the same probability.

Let Γ be the set of all full ternary trees of height at most $\lfloor \log_3 n - 1/\delta \rfloor$, and for $T \in \Gamma$ let X_T be the event that the truncated tree described above is T. We have that:

$$\Pr[B \text{ outputs } 1] \geq$$
$$\Pr[B \text{ outputs } 1 | \nexists \text{ path of all 0's}] \Pr[\nexists \text{ path of all 0's}] \geq$$
$$\Pr[\nexists \text{ path of all 0's}] \Pr[A \text{ outputs } 1].$$

The second inequality follows because

$$\Pr[B \text{ outputs } 1 | \nexists \text{ path of all 0's}] =$$
$$\sum_{T \in \Gamma} \Pr[X_T] \Pr[T \text{ outputs 1 when given only 1's as input}] \geq$$
$$\sum_{T \in \Gamma} \Pr[X_T] \Pr[A \text{ outputs } 1] =$$
$$\Pr[A \text{ outputs } 1].$$

It follows by the union bound over all possible leaf-to-root paths of all 0's that g, and therefore every gate of height $\lfloor \log_3 n - 1/\delta \rfloor$, outputs 1 independently with probability at least $\ell^*(\epsilon) \cdot (1 - \frac{1}{2}(\log_3 n) p^{\frac{1}{2} \log_3 n - \frac{1}{\delta}})$. For n large enough this is at least 0.79. By Lemma 16, the upper part of the majority tree outputs 1 with probability at least $1 - \delta$. The total energy of the circuit is at most $P(0.12)n + 3^{1/\delta} P(\delta/10)$. □

Proof of Theorem 13. By Lemmas 17 and 18, we have that for $\delta' = \frac{1}{(n-c)\log_3 n}$,

$$\frac{E_1(\delta')}{E_2(\delta')} = \Omega\left(\frac{n \cdot P(\delta')}{n + 3^{1/\delta'} P(\delta'/10)}\right)$$
$$= \Omega\left(\frac{n \cdot P\left(\frac{1}{(1-c)\log n}\right)}{n + n^{1-c} P\left(\frac{1}{(1-c)\log n}\right)}\right)$$
$$= \omega(1),$$

where the second equality follows by the second property of easy-going functions, and the third equality by the first property of easy-going functions when taking n large enough. □

We note that there are more trivial examples where heterogeneous supply voltages help. For example, consider a circuit that is a balanced binary tree of gates that each output the first bit, and the relation that outputs the first input bit. As most gates in this circuit are irrelevant to computing the desired relation, one can get an asymptotic energy saving by setting the supply voltages of the irrelevant gates to zero. Our example is more natural as one cannot simply power-off most of the gates. Although one might argue that our example is still not fully satisfactory as a more energy-efficient way to compute the super-majority relation is to use the majority circuit from [13] to compute the majority of the first $\log n$ bits with the supply voltages on each gate set so that the probability that any gate fails is at most δ. So a natural question is, "For every relation, is there is an asymptotically energy-optimal circuit for computing this relation that uses homogeneous supply voltages?"

7. CONCLUSIONS

This paper initiated the theoretical study of energy-efficient circuits. At this point, it seems that there are many interesting research lines in this area. Perhaps the most natural direction is to look at circuit design, namely determining the most energy-efficient circuit to compute a particular relation. But this design question is probably too difficult as a special case of this problem is the problem of designing a circuit with the least number of gates to compute a particular relation, which is a known hard problem. Perhaps questions related to circuit analysis are more amenable. A natural circuit analysis question would be: given a (perhaps special type of) relation, and (perhaps a special type of) circuit, how does one set the supply voltage, or voltages, so that the circuit $(1-\delta)$-reliably computes the relation using approximately minimal energy. Another natural direction is to try to better understand which relations and circuits can benefit from heterogeneous supply voltages. An additional natural direction is to study the effect of switching delays of gates, which increase as the supply voltage decreases.

8. ACKNOWLEDGEMENT

We thank Rami Melhem for insightful discussions about Near-Threshold Computing.

9. REFERENCES

[1] G. Anthes. Inexact design: beyond fault-tolerance. *Communications of the ACM*, 56(4):18–20, 2013.

[2] J. Butts and G. Sohi. A static power model for architects. In *Proceedings of the 33rd annual ACM/IEEE International Symposium on Microarchitecture (MICRO)*, pages 191–201, 2000.

[3] B. Calhoun and A. Chandrakasan. A 256-kb 65-nm sub-threshold SRAM design for ultra-low-voltage operation. *IEEE Journal of Solid-State Circuits*, 42(3):680–688, 2007.

[4] R. L. Dobrushin and S. I. Ortyukov. Lower bound for the redundancy of self-correcting arrangements of unreliable functional elements. *Problems of Information Transmission*, 13:59–65, 1977.

[5] R. L. Dobrushin and S. I. Ortyukov. Upper bound for the redundancy of self-correcting arrangements of unreliable functional elements. *Problems of Information Transmission*, 13:203–218, 1977.

[6] R. G. Dreslinski, M. Wieckowski, D. Blaauw, D. Sylvester, and T. N. Mudge. Near-threshold computing: Reclaiming Moore's law through energy efficient integrated circuits. *Proceedings of the IEEE*, 98(2):253–266, 2010.

[7] P. Gács. *Algorithms in Informatics*, volume 2, chapter Reliable Computation. ELTE Eötvös Kiadó, Budapest, 2005. Electronic version also in English: `http://www.cs.bu.edu/faculty/gacs/papers/iv-eng.pdf`.

[8] P. Gács and A. Gál. Lower bounds for the complexity of reliable boolean circuits with noisy gates. *IEEE Transactions on Information Theory*, 40(2):579–583, 1994.

[9] W. Ibrahim and V. Beiu. Reliability of NAND-2 CMOS gates from threshold voltage variations. In *Proceedings of the International Conference on Innovations in Information Technology (IIT)*, pages 310–314, 2009.

[10] N. Pippenger. On networks of noisy gates. In *Proceedings of the 26th Annual Symposium on Foundations of Computer Science (FOCS)*, pages 30–38, 1985.

[11] N. Pippenger, G. D. Stamoulis, and J. N. Tsitsiklis. On a lower bound for the redundancy of reliable networks with noisy gates. *IEEE Transactions on Information Theory*, 37(3):639–643, 1991.

[12] R. Reischuk and B. Schmeltz. Reliable computation with noisy circuits and decision trees–A general $n \log n$ lower bound. In *Proceedings of the 32nd Annual Symposium on Foundations of Computer Science (FOCS)*, pages 602–611, 1991.

[13] L. G. Valiant. Short monotone formulae for the majority function. *Journal of Algorithms*, 5(3):363–366, 1984.

[14] J. von Neumann. Probabilistic logics and the synthesis of reliable organisms from unreliable components. In C. E. Shannon and J. McCarthy, editors, *Automata Studies*, pages 329–378. Princeton University Press, 1956.

Rate-Independent Computation in Continuous Chemical Reaction Networks

Ho-Lin Chen
National Taiwan University
MD-718
Taipei 106, Taiwan
holinc@gmail.com

David Doty
California Institute of Technology
1200 E. California Blvd
MC 305-16
Pasadena, CA 91125
ddoty@caltech.edu

David Soloveichik
UCSF Center for Systems and Synthetic Biology
1700 4th Street
Byers Hall 401, Box 2540
San Francisco, CA 94158
david.soloveichik@ucsf.edu

ABSTRACT

Understanding the algorithmic behaviors that are *in principle* realizable in a chemical system is necessary for a rigorous understanding of the design principles of biological regulatory networks. Further, advances in synthetic biology herald the time when we'll be able to rationally engineer complex chemical systems, and when idealized formal models will become blueprints for engineering.

Coupled chemical interactions in a well-mixed solution are commonly formalized as chemical reaction networks (CRNs). However, despite the widespread use of CRNs in the natural sciences, the range of computational behaviors exhibited by CRNs is not well understood. Here we study the following problem: what functions $f : \mathbb{R}^k \to \mathbb{R}$ can be computed by a chemical reaction network, in which the CRN eventually produces the correct amount of the "output" molecule, no matter the rate at which reactions proceed? This captures a previously unexplored, but very natural class of computations: for example, the reaction $X_1+X_2 \to Y$ can be thought to compute the function $y = \min(x_1, x_2)$. Such a CRN is robust in the sense that it is correct whether its evolution is governed by the standard model of mass-action kinetics, alternatives such as Hill-function or Michaelis-Menten kinetics, or other arbitrary models of chemistry that respect the (fundamentally digital) stoichiometric constraints (what are the reactants and products?). We develop a formal definition of such computation using a novel notion of reachability, and prove that a function is computable in this manner if and only if it is *continuous piecewise linear*.

Categories and Subject Descriptors

F.1 [**Theory of Computation**]: Computation by Abstract Devices; C.1.3 [**Computer systems organization**]: Other Architecture Styles—*Analog computers*

ITCS'14, January 12–14, 2014, Princeton, New Jersey, USA.

ACM 978-1-4503-2698-8/14/01 ...$15.00.
http://dx.doi.org/10.1145/2554797.2554827.

Keywords

Chemical Reaction Networks, Mass-Action, Analog Computation, Piecewise-Linear

1. INTRODUCTION

Both the engineering of complex artificial molecular systems, as well as the understanding of the constraints imposed upon biology, require the understanding of what is, in principle, achievable in chemistry. The natural language for describing the interactions of molecular species in a well-mixed solution is that of chemical reaction networks (CRNs), i.e., finite sets of chemical reactions such as $A+B \to A+C$. The intuitive meaning of this expression is that a unit of chemical species A reacts with a unit of chemical species B, producing a unit of a new chemical species C and regenerating a unit of A back. Typically (in mass-action kinetics) the rate with which this occurs is proportional to the product of the amounts of the reactants A and B.

Traditionally CRNs have been used as a descriptive language to analyze naturally occurring chemical reactions, as well as various other systems with a large number of interacting components such as gene regulatory networks and animal populations. However, CRNs also constitute a natural choice of programming language for engineering artificial systems. For example, nucleic-acid networks can be rationally designed to implement arbitrary chemical reaction networks [7, 10, 20]. Thus, since in principle any CRN can be physically built, hypothetical CRNs with interesting behaviors are becoming of more than theoretical interest. One day artificial CRNs may underlie embedded controllers for biochemical, nanotechnological, or medical applications, where environments are inherently incompatible with traditional electronic controllers. However, to effectively program chemistry, we must understand the computational power at our disposal. In turn, the computer science approach to CRNs is also beginning to generate novel insights regarding natural cellular regulatory networks [8].

Informally speaking we can identify two sources of computational power in CRNs. First, the reaction *stoichiometry* transforms some specific ratios of reactants to products. For example, $X \to 2Y$ makes two units of Y for every unit of X. Second, in mass-action kinetics the reaction *rate laws* effectively perform multiplication of the reactant concentrations. In this work, we seek to disentangle the contributions of these two computational ingredients by focusing on the computational power of stoichiometry alone.

One reason to focus on *stoichiometric computation* is that algorithms that rely on stoichiometry make easier design targets. The rates of reactions are real-valued quantities that can fluctuate with reaction conditions and temperature, while the stoichiometries are immutable whole numbers set by the nature of the reaction. Methods for physically implementing CRNs naturally yield systems with digital stoichiometry that can be set exactly [7,20]. Further, relying on specific rate laws can be problematic: many systems do not follow mass-action rate laws[1] and chemists have developed an array of alternative rate laws such as Michaelis-Menten and Hill-function kinetics. Indeed, robustness of rate laws is a recurring motif in systems biology due to much evidence that biological regulatory networks tend to be robust to the form of the rate laws and the rate parameters [5]. Thus we are interested in what computations can be understood or engineered without regard for the reaction rate laws.

There are two well-studied models of chemical kinetics: *continuous* and *discrete*. In the discrete model, the amount of a species is a nonnegative *integer* representing the total count of molecules of that species in a given reaction vessel. In the continuous model, the amount of a species is a nonnegative *real number* representing its average count per unit volume or concentration. The discrete model is *stochastic* and reactions are modeled by a Markov jump process [11], while the continuous model is *deterministic*, governed by a system of ordinary differential equations with a unique solution. When the volume and counts are large, the discrete model converges to the continuous model [14]. While many cellular chemical processes operate at single-molecule precision, a significant amount of regulation is well-understood by continuous models [1]. Further, because of the difficulty of working at molecular resolution most experimental implementations of rationally designed chemical computation have been in bulk solution (e.g. [10,16,18]).

Here we study the continuous setting, and characterize the class of real-valued functions computable by CRNs when reaction rates are permitted to vary arbitrarily (and possibly adversarially) over time. Any computation in this setting must rely on stoichiometry alone. Our work is related to the study of *deterministic*[2] *computation* in stochastic CRNs: making reaction rates unreliable is the natural analog to error in the stochastic setting (where error corresponds to reactions occurring in an undesired order). (See Section 1.1.)

How can rate laws "preserve stoichiometry" while varying "arbitrarily over time"? Formally, preserving stoichiometry means that if we reach state $\mathbf{d}$ from state $\mathbf{c}$, then $\mathbf{d} = \mathbf{c} + \mathbf{M}\mathbf{u}$ for stoichiometry matrix $\mathbf{M}$, and some non-negative vector $\mathbf{u}$ of reaction fluxes. Subject to this constraint, the widest class of trajectories that still satisfies the intuitive meaning of the reaction semantics can be described informally as follows: (1) concentrations can't become negative, (2) all reactants must be non-zero for a reaction to occur (e.g. if a reaction uses a catalyst[3], it must be present).

[1]Although it is generally taken for granted that they would if properly decomposed into truly elementary reactions.

[2]Deterministic computation in the discrete/stochastic model should not be confused with the determinism of the continuous model, where any stochasticity is absent.

[3]A species acts catalytically in a reaction if it is both a reactant and product: e.g. C in reaction $A + C \to B + C$. Note that executing this reaction without C does not by itself violate condition (1).

a)

$$X_1 \to Z_1 + Y$$
$$X_2 \to Z_2 + Y$$
$$Z_1 + Z_2 \to K$$
$$Y + K \to \emptyset$$

b)

$$X_1^+ \to X_2^- + Y^+$$
$$X_2^+ \to X_1^- + Y^+$$
$$X_1^- + X_2^- \to Y^-$$

Figure 1: Examples of (a) *direct* and (b) *dual-rail* rate-independent computation of $f(x_1, x_2) = \max(x_1, x_2)$.

The example shown in Fig 1(a) illustrates the style of computation studied here. Let $f : \mathbb{R}^2_{\geq 0} \to \mathbb{R}_{\geq 0}$ be the max function $f(x_1, x_2) = \max(x_1, x_2)$ restricted to nonnegative x_1 and x_2. The CRN shown computes this function in the following sense. Inputs x_1 and x_2 are given as initial concentrations of input species X_1 and X_2. Then the CRN converges to the output value of species Y, under a very wide interpretation of rate laws. Intuitively, the first two reactions must eventually produce $x_1 + x_2$ of Y, and x_1, x_2 of Z_1 and Z_2, respectively. This is enforced by the stoichiometric constraint that the amount of Z_1 and Y produced is equal to the amount of X_1 consumed (and analogously for the second reaction). Stoichiometric constraints require the third reaction to produce the amount of K that is the minimum of the amount of Z_1 and Z_2 eventually produced in the first two reactions. Thus $\min(x_1, x_2)$ of K is eventually produced. Therefore, the fourth reaction eventually consumes $\min(x_1, x_2)$ molecules of Y leaving $x_1 + x_2 - \min(x_1, x_2) = \max(x_1, x_2)$ of Y behind. We can imagine an adversary pushing flux through these four reactions in any devious stratagem, but as long as he cannot take any concentration negative, the CRN can only converge to the correct output.

In this paper we further consider the natural extension of such computation to handle negative real values. The example shown in Fig. 1(b) computes $f(x_1, x_2) = \max(x_1, x_2)$ ($f : \mathbb{R}^2 \to \mathbb{R}$). In order to handle negative input and output values, we represent the value of each input and output by a pair of species (so-called "dual-rail" representation). For example, in state $\mathbf{c}$, $x_1 = \mathbf{c}(X_1^+) - \mathbf{c}(X_1^-)$ — i.e. the difference between the concentrations of species X_1^+ and X_1^-. Note that when X_1^- and X_2^- are initially absent, the CRN becomes equivalent to the first three reactions of Fig. 1(a) under relabeling of species. We do not need the last reaction of (a) because the output is represented as the difference of Y^+ and Y^- by our convention. For the argument that the computation is correct even if X_1^- and X_2^- are initially present, we refer the reader to Section 3.1.

In addition to handling negative values, the dual-rail representation has the benefit of allowing composition. Specifically, the dual-rail representation allows CRNs to never consume their output species (e.g. rather than consuming Y^+, it can produce Y^-). This monotonicity in the production of output allows directly composing CRN computations simply by mixing CRNs and relabeling species (e.g. to make the output of one be input to the other). Since the upstream CRN never consumes its output species, the downstream CRN is free to consume them without interfering with the upstream computation.

In order to formally delineate the class of functions (direct and dual-rail) computable in a rate-independent manner, we take the following approach. We first define a reachability relation that captures motion along trajectories satisfying the two intuitive properties above. Then we define rate-independent computation using this reachability relation. Roughly, to say that a function is correctly computed, it must be the case that from every reachable state, the correct output can be reached, and once reached the output cannot change. Our main results are that exactly functions that are positive-continuous, piecewise linear (direct) or continuous, piecewise linear (dual-rail) can be computed. (Positive-continuous means that the only discontinuities occur on a "face" of $\mathbb{R}^k_{\geq 0}$ — i.e., the function may discontinuously jump only at a point where some input goes from 0 to positive.)

In the constructive portion of our results, we supply rate-independent CRNs for computing any function in the above classes. Further, our constructions have the following property: If the same CRNs were simulated under mass-action kinetics from any reachable state, as the time $t \to \infty$ the concentration of the output species would approach its intended value. In other words, no matter how an adversary might have pushed us initially, letting the system evolve by mass-action will yield the correct answer. Although we prove that the correct output is reachable, and mass-action trajectories converge there, it remains an open problem to delineate the entire class of rate laws that force our constructions to converge.

1.1 Relation to Previous Work

The computational abilities of discrete CRNs have been investigated more thoroughly than of continuous CRNs, and have been shown to have a surprisingly rich computational structure. Of most relevance here is the work in the discrete setting showing that the class of functions that can be computed depends strongly on whether the computation must be deterministic (guaranteed to be correct), or just likely to be correct. While Turing universal computation is possible with an arbitrarily small, non-zero probability of error over all time [19], forbidding error altogether limits the computational power severely: Error-free computation by stochastic CRNs is limited to semilinear predicates and functions [4,9]. (Intuitively, semilinear functions are expressible as a finite union of affine functions, with "simple, periodic" domains of each affine function [9].)

Our paper was motivated by trying to extend the results on error-free computation to the continuous CRN model. As mentioned above, our notion of rate-independent computation is the natural extension of deterministic computation in the discrete model. However, there are many differences in the two settings. As broached in ref. [9], many of the CRNs that work in the discrete setting appear not to work in the continuous setting. For example, the CRNs computing discontinuous functions such as "$f(x_1, x_2) = x_2$ if $x_1 > x_2$ and 0 otherwise" provably fail to work in the continuous setting. Indeed, discrete CRNs can, for example, distinguish between even and odd inputs, whereas it does not even make sense to talk about the "parity" of a real-valued input. Further, the proof techniques appear to require very different machinery.

The relationship between the discrete and continuous CRN models is a complex and much studied one in the natural sciences [17]. While computational differences in the models are less understood, the distributed computing community is beginning to investigate the subject as well [6].

Our notion of reachability captures a wide diversity of possible rate laws. A related idea in the literature, albeit restricted to mass-action, is differential inclusion [12]. Generalized rate laws (extending mass-action, Michaelis-Menten, etc) have been previously studied, although not in a computational setting. For example, certain conditions were identified on global convergence to equilibrium based on properties intuitively similar to ours [2].

2. PRELIMINARIES

Let $\mathbb{N}$ and $\mathbb{R}$ denote the set of nonnegative integers and the set of real numbers, respectively. If $x \in \mathbb{R}$, let $\mathbb{R}_{\geq x} = \{ x' \in \mathbb{R} \mid x' \geq x \}$, and similarly for $\mathbb{R}_{>x}$. Given a vector $\mathbf{x} \in \mathbb{R}^k$, let $\|\mathbf{x}\| = \|\mathbf{x}\|_1 = \sum_{i=1}^k \mathbf{x}(i)$, where $\mathbf{x}(i)$ denotes the ith coordinate of $\mathbf{x}$. We abuse notation and consider the sets $\mathbb{R}^k \times \mathbb{R}^l$ and $\mathbb{R}^{k+l}$ to be the same, because it is sometimes convenient to treat an ordered pair of vectors as being concatenated into a single longer vector. If Λ is a finite set (in this paper, of chemical species), and A is any set, we write A^Λ to denote the set of functions $f : \Lambda \to A$. Equivalently, we view an element $\mathbf{c} \in A^\Lambda$ as a vector of $|\Lambda|$ elements of A, each coordinate "labeled" by an element of Λ. Write $\mathbf{c} \upharpoonright \Delta$ to denote the vector $\mathbf{d} \in \mathbb{N}^\Delta$ such that $\mathbf{c}(S) = \mathbf{d}(S)$ for all $S \in \Delta$.

2.1 Chemical reaction networks

Given $S \in \Lambda$ and $\mathbf{c} \in \mathbb{R}^\Lambda_{\geq 0}$, we refer to $\mathbf{c}(S)$ as the *concentration of S in* $\mathbf{c}$. For any $\mathbf{c} \in \mathbb{R}^\Lambda_{\geq 0}$, let $[\mathbf{c}] = \{S \in \Lambda \mid \mathbf{c}(S) > 0\}$, the set of species *present* in $\mathbf{c}$. We write $\mathbf{c} \leq \mathbf{c}'$ to denote that $\mathbf{c}(S) \leq \mathbf{c}'(S)$ for all $S \in \Lambda$. Given $\mathbf{c}, \mathbf{c}' \in \mathbb{R}^\Lambda_{\geq 0}$, we define the vector component-wise operations of addition $\mathbf{c} + \mathbf{c}'$, subtraction $\mathbf{c} - \mathbf{c}'$, and scalar multiplication $x\mathbf{c}$ for $x \in \mathbb{R}$. If $\Delta \subset \Lambda$, we view a vector $\mathbf{c} \in \mathbb{R}^\Delta_{\geq 0}$ equivalently as a vector $\mathbf{c} \in \mathbb{R}^\Lambda_{\geq 0}$ by assuming $\mathbf{c}(S) = 0$ for all $S \in \Lambda \setminus \Delta$. For $\Delta \subset \Lambda$, we write $\mathbf{c} \upharpoonright \Delta$ to denote $\mathbf{c}$ *restricted to* Δ; in particular, $\mathbf{c} \upharpoonright \Delta = \mathbf{0} \iff (\forall S \in \Delta)\ \mathbf{c}(S) = 0$.

Given a finite set of chemical species Λ, a *reaction* over Λ is a pair $\alpha = \langle \mathbf{r}, \mathbf{p} \rangle \in \mathbb{N}^\Lambda \times \mathbb{N}^\Lambda$, specifying the stoichiometry of the reactants and products, respectively.[4] In this paper, we assume that $\mathbf{r} \neq \mathbf{0}$, i.e., we have no reactions of the form $\varnothing \to \ldots$.[5] For instance, given $\Lambda = \{A, B, C\}$, the reaction $A + 2B \to A + 3C$ is the pair $\langle (1,2,0), (1,0,3) \rangle$. Note that we represent reversible reactions such as $A \rightleftharpoons B$ as two irreversible reactions $A \to B$ and $B \to A$. A *(finite) chemical reaction network (CRN)* is a pair $\mathcal{C} = (\Lambda, R)$, where Λ is a finite set of chemical *species*, and R is a finite set of reactions over Λ. A *state* of a CRN $\mathcal{C} = (\Lambda, R)$ is a vector $\mathbf{c} \in \mathbb{R}^\Lambda_{\geq 0}$. Given a state $\mathbf{c}$ and reaction $\alpha = \langle \mathbf{r}, \mathbf{p} \rangle$, we say that α is *applicable* in $\mathbf{c}$ if $[\mathbf{r}] \subseteq [\mathbf{c}]$ (i.e., $\mathbf{c}$ contains positive concentration of all of the reactants).

2.2 Reachability

[4]It is customary to define, for each reaction, a *rate constant* $k \in \mathbb{R}_{>0}$ specifying a constant multiplier on the mass-action rate (i.e., the product of the reactant concentrations), but as we are studying CRNs whose output is independent of the reaction rates, we leave the rate constants out of the definition.

[5]We allow high order reactions; i.e., those that consume more than two reactants. It is not difficult to show that such a reaction $S_1 + S_2 + \ldots + S_n \to P_1 + \ldots + P_m$ can be replaced by bimolecular reactions $S_1 + S_2 \rightleftharpoons S_{12}, S_{12} + S_3 \rightleftharpoons S_{123}, S_{123} + S_4 \rightleftharpoons S_{1234}, \ldots, S_n + S_{12\ldots n-1} \to P_1 + \ldots + P_m$ without affecting the correctness of the CRN.

In the previous section we defined the syntax of CRNs. We wish to define a semantic interpretation of them suitable for defining how they compute functions. In particular, we want to consider CRNs guaranteed to correctly compute a function of their inputs, regardless of the rate at which reactions proceed, calling this *stable computation*, defined in Section 2.4. This definition rests on another, which we must take care in defining, namely what it means for one state to be *reachable* from another, which is the focus of this section. Intuitively, $\mathbf{d}$ is reachable from $\mathbf{c}$ if applying some amount of reactions to $\mathbf{c}$ results in $\mathbf{d}$, such that no reaction is ever applied when any of its reactants are concentration 0. Formalizing this concept is a bit tricky and constitutes one of the contributions of this paper. Intuitively, we'll think of reachability via straight line segments. This may appear overly limiting; after all mass-action and other rate laws trace out smooth curves. However we show a number of properties of our definition that support its reasonableness.

Throughout this section, fix a CRN $\mathcal{C} = (\Lambda, R)$. All states $\mathbf{c}$, etc., are assumed to be states of $\mathcal{C}$. Let $m = |R|$ be the number of reactions in CRN $\mathcal{C}$, and let $n = |\Lambda|$ be the number of species in $\mathcal{C}$. We define the the $n \times m$ *reaction stoichiometry matrix* $\mathbf{M}$ such that $\mathbf{M}(i, j)$ is the net amount of the i'th species that is produced by the j'th reaction (negative if the species is consumed).[6] For example, if we have the reactions $X \to Y$ and $X + A \to 2X + 3Y$, and if the three rows correspond to X, A, and Y, in that order, then

$$\mathbf{M} = \begin{pmatrix} -1 & 1 \\ 0 & -1 \\ 1 & 3 \end{pmatrix}$$

DEFINITION 2.1. *State* $\mathbf{d}$ *is* straight-line reachable (aka 1-segment reachable) *from* $\mathbf{c}$, *written* $\mathbf{c} \to^1 \mathbf{d}$, *if* $(\exists \mathbf{u} \in \mathbb{R}^m_{\geq 0})$ $\mathbf{c} + \mathbf{M}\mathbf{u} = \mathbf{d}$ *and* $\mathbf{u}(j) > 0$ *only if reaction* j *is applicable at* $\mathbf{c}$. *In this case write* $\mathbf{c} \to^1_{\mathbf{u}} \mathbf{d}$.

Intuitively, by a single segment we mean running the reactions applicable at $\mathbf{c}$ at a constant (possibly 0) rate to get from $\mathbf{c}$ to $\mathbf{d}$. In the definition, $\mathbf{u}(j)$ represents the flux of reaction j.

DEFINITION 2.2. *State* $\mathbf{d}$ *is* l-segment reachable, *written* $\mathbf{c} \rightsquigarrow^l \mathbf{d}$ *from* $\mathbf{c}$ *if* $(\exists \mathbf{b}_1, \ldots, \mathbf{b}_{l+1})$ $\mathbf{c} = \mathbf{b}_1 \to^1 \mathbf{b}_2 \to^1 \mathbf{b}_3 \to^1 \ldots \to^1 \mathbf{b}_{l+1} = \mathbf{d}$.

DEFINITION 2.3. *State* $\mathbf{d}$ *is* segment-reachable *from* $\mathbf{c}$, *written* $\mathbf{c} \rightsquigarrow \mathbf{d}$, *if* $(\exists l \in \mathbb{N})$ $\mathbf{c} \rightsquigarrow^l \mathbf{d}$.

Suppose the reactions are $X \to C$ and $C + Y \to C + Z$, and we are in state $\{0C, 1X, 1Y, 0Z\}$. With straight-line segments, any state with a positive amount of Z must be reached in at least two segments: first to produce C, which allows the second reaction to occur, and then any combination of the first and second reactions. For example, $\{0C, 1X, 1Y, 0Z\} \to^1 \{0.1C, 0.9X, 1Y, 0Z\} \to^1 \{1C, 0X, 0Y, 1Z\}$. This is a simple example showing that more states are reachable with $\rightsquigarrow$ then $\to^1$. Often Definition 2.3 is used implicitly, when we make statements such as, "Run reaction 1 until its first reactant is 0, then run reaction 2", which implicitly defines two straight lines in concentration space.

[6] Note that $\mathbf{M}$ does not fully specify $\mathcal{C}$, since catalysts are not modeled: reactions $Z + X \to Z + Y$ and $X \to Y$ both correspond to the column vector $(-1, 1, 0)^\top$.

Given a curve, we can think about approximating it to an arbitrary accuracy using straight-line segments. But it may seem that we can never achieve the "full diversity" of states reachable with curves if we use only a finite number of line segments. However, the following lemma shows that increasing the number of straight-line segments beyond a certain point does not make any additional states reachable. Thus using a few line segments captures all the states reachable in the limit of infinitely many line segments.

LEMMA 2.4. *If* $\mathbf{c} \rightsquigarrow \mathbf{d}$, *then* $\mathbf{c} \rightsquigarrow^{m+1} \mathbf{d}$, *where* $m = |R|$ *is the number of reactions.*

PROOF. The intuitive idea of the proof is as follows. If $\mathbf{c} \rightsquigarrow \mathbf{d}$, then the path could use a huge number of segments, much greater than $m + 1$. We don't care precisely what these segments are, only that they give us an *ordering* $\prec$ *on species that need to become positive to reach* $\mathbf{d}$, such that, calling the species $S_1 \prec S_2 \prec \ldots \prec S_p$, for each i, there is a reaction to produce S_i that has only reactants in $[\mathbf{c}] \cup \{S_1, \ldots, S_{i-1}\}$. Therefore we can produce a small amount of each species $S_1, \ldots, S_n$, starting only from species in $[\mathbf{c}]$, by running these reactions in order, and running each reaction a smaller amount than the previous to ensure that nothing positive goes to 0. Once all these species are produced, a single straight line can take the CRN to state $\mathbf{d}$. The trick is that we should not produce *every* producible species, but only those needed to run the reactions corresponding to the final straight line. Otherwise, for example, we could create a species $X \notin [\mathbf{c}] \cup [\mathbf{d}]$, and if no reaction consumes X, $\mathbf{d}$ would become unreachable.

If $\mathbf{d}$ is reachable from $\mathbf{c}$ via fewer than $m+1$ straight line segments, then this can be re-expressed with precisely $m+1$ line segments by using length-0 line segments. It remains to show that at most $m+1$ straight line segments are necessary.

Suppose that $\mathbf{c} \rightsquigarrow \mathbf{d}$ via $l > m + 1$ straight line segments $\mathbf{c} = \mathbf{b}_0 \to^1 \mathbf{b}_1 \to^1 \ldots \to^1 \mathbf{b}_l = \mathbf{d}$. Let the reactions R be ordered as $\alpha_0, \alpha_1, \ldots$. For each $\mathbf{b}_i$, there exists $\mathbf{u}_i$ such that $\mathbf{b}_i + \mathbf{M}\mathbf{u}_i = \mathbf{b}_{i+1}$. Let $F_j = \sum_{i=0}^{l-1} \mathbf{u}_i(j)$ be the total flux through reaction α_j to get from $\mathbf{c}$ to $\mathbf{d}$ along the l straight line segments defined by the $\mathbf{b}_i$'s. Let $P = \{\ j \mid F_j > 0\ \}$ be the indices of reactions that occurred with strictly positive flux. If $\alpha_j = (\mathbf{r}_j, \mathbf{p}_j)$, let $\mathbf{v}_j = \mathbf{p}_j - \mathbf{r}_j$ be the vector representing the net change in concentrations if reaction α_j experiences unit flux. Then $\mathbf{d} = \mathbf{c} + \sum_{j \in P} F_j \mathbf{v}_j$. We use this fact to show that $\mathbf{c} \rightsquigarrow^{m+1} \mathbf{d}$.

Let $R(P) = \{\ \alpha_j \in R \mid j \in P\ \}$ be the reactions with indices in P. We first argue that there is an ordering $\prec$ of reactions in $R(P)$, such that for any reaction $\alpha = (\mathbf{r}, \mathbf{p})$, $[\mathbf{r}] \subseteq [\mathbf{c}] \cup \bigcup_{\alpha' = (\mathbf{r}', \mathbf{p}') \prec \alpha} [\mathbf{p}']$. In other words, if all products of reactions preceding α have positive concentration, as well as all species present in $\mathbf{c}$, this guarantees α is applicable. This in turn allows the reactions to proceed in the given order, so long as we are careful that no positive concentration species is allowed to be consumed back to 0. At the end, all products of all reactions in $R(P)$ are positive. To see that this ordering exists, it suffices to observe that the straight line segments given by the hypothesis $\mathbf{c} \rightsquigarrow \mathbf{d}$ give a *partial* order that respects the constraints, since any reactions with positive flux in the k'th straight line segment, which were not positive flux in any previous straight line segments, must consume only species that were either positive in $\mathbf{c}$, or that were produced by a reaction with positive flux in the l'th straight line segment, where $l < k$. Given all reactions having positive flux for the first time in the k'th straight line segment, they can be ordered arbitrarily relative to each other while obeying the constraint $\prec$. For the sake of brevity, assume without loss of generality that $P = \{0, 1, \ldots, |P| - 1\}$, and that $\alpha_0 \prec \alpha_1 \prec \ldots \prec \alpha_{|P|-1}$.

Let $K = \max_{S \in \Lambda} \max_{\alpha=(\mathbf{r},\mathbf{p}) \in R(P)} \mathbf{r}(S)$ be the maximum stoichiometry coefficient of any possible reactant. In the worst case, running a reaction by δ flux will decrease the concentration of any species by at most δK. Let

$$\epsilon = \min \left\{ \min_{S \in [\mathbf{c}]} \mathbf{c}(S), \min_{j \in P} F_j \right\}.$$

The significance of ϵ is that if we allow all reactions in $R(P)$ to go forward from $\mathbf{c}$ by strictly less than ϵ of flux, this will be less than the total flux experienced by each reaction, and also each species present in $\mathbf{c}$ will remain in positive concentration. Formally, define the following basis vectors (representing individual reaction vectors) $\mathbf{w}_j \in \mathbb{R}^m_{\geq 0}$ for $0 \leq j < |P|$. Let $\mathbf{w}_j(j) = \frac{\epsilon}{(2K)^{j+1}}$ and $\mathbf{w}_i(j) = 0$ if $i \neq j$. Then $\mathbf{M}\mathbf{w}_j$ is the j'th line segment to define. Let $\mathbf{a} = \mathbf{c} + \sum_{j=0}^{|P|-1} \mathbf{M}\mathbf{w}_j$ be the point reached after following these line segments. For each j, let $\mathbf{a}_j = \mathbf{c} + \sum_{i=0}^{j-1} \mathbf{M}\mathbf{w}_i$ be the state reached after following the first j straight line segments, letting $\mathbf{a}_0 = \mathbf{c}$.

We prove by induction on j that each $\mathbf{M}\mathbf{w}_j$ satisfies Definition 2.1 by showing that for all j, $S \in [\mathbf{a}_j] \implies \mathbf{a}_j(S) \geq \frac{\epsilon}{(2K)^{j+1}}$. I.e., all species are nonnegative at the start and end of the line (hence along the entire line), and the reactions experiencing positive flux along the line are applicable at the starting state.

We first establish the base case, where $\mathbf{w}_0(0) = \frac{\epsilon}{2K}$. By the definition of $\prec$, which ensures that for $\alpha_0 = (\mathbf{r}_0, \mathbf{p}_0)$, $[\mathbf{r}_0] \subseteq [\mathbf{c}]$, α_0 is applicable at $\mathbf{c}$. Note that $\epsilon \leq \mathbf{c}(S)$ for all $S \in [\mathbf{c}]$, i.e., running α_0 with flux $\frac{\epsilon}{2K}$ can cut the concentration of any species $S \in [\mathbf{c}]$ at most in half, so that in state $\mathbf{a}_1 = \mathbf{c} + \mathbf{M}\mathbf{w}_0$, $\mathbf{a}_1(S) \geq \frac{\epsilon}{2} \geq \frac{\epsilon}{2K}$, satisfying the base case for species in $[\mathbf{c}]$. Because α_0 experiences $\frac{\epsilon}{2K}$ of flux, each species produced $S \in [\mathbf{p}_0] \setminus [\mathbf{c}]$ initially absent in $\mathbf{c}$ but produced in $\mathbf{a}_1$ has increased in concentration by at least $\frac{\epsilon}{2K}$. Therefore all species in $[\mathbf{a}_1] \setminus [\mathbf{c}]$ have concentration at least $\frac{\epsilon}{2K}$, satisfying the base case for these species.

For the inductive case, inductively assume each species $S \in [\mathbf{a}_j]$ satisfies $\mathbf{a}_j(S) \geq \frac{\epsilon}{(2K)^{j+1}}$. Then by the definition of α_j and $\prec$, α_j is applicable in $\mathbf{a}_j$. Similarly to the base case, by running α_j by flux $\frac{\epsilon}{(2K)^{j+2}}$, the most any such species is consumed is $\frac{\epsilon}{(2K)^{j+2}}$, and since all such species S started with concentration $\mathbf{a}_j(S) \geq \frac{\epsilon}{(2K)^{j+1}}$, their concentrations are at most cut in half, i.e. $\mathbf{a}_{j+1}(S) \geq \frac{\epsilon}{(2K)^{j+2}}$. Therefore the inductive hypothesis for case $j+1$ is satisfied for species in $\mathbf{a}_j$. To show that the inductive hypothsis is satisfied for the rest of the species (i.e., those in $[\mathbf{a}_{j+1}] \setminus [\mathbf{a}_j]$), observe that all products $S \in [\mathbf{a}_{j+1}] \setminus [\mathbf{a}_j]$ have increased in concentration by at least $\frac{\epsilon}{(2K)^{j+2}}$.

The final line segment is a straight line from $\mathbf{a}$ to $\mathbf{d}$. By our choice of P, all reactions in $R(P)$ are applicable at $\mathbf{a}$. By our choice of $\mathbf{w}_j$'s, the total flux experienced by reaction α_j to get from $\mathbf{c}$ to $\mathbf{a}$ is strictly less than F_j, the total flux α_j experienced in the original straight line segments defining $\mathbf{c} \rightsquigarrow \mathbf{d}$. Therefore the final straight line from $\mathbf{a}$ can be defined by the vector $\mathbf{w}(j) = F_j - \mathbf{w}_j(j)$, so that $\mathbf{a} + \mathbf{M}\mathbf{w} = \mathbf{d}$. This shows that $\mathbf{c} \rightsquigarrow^{m+1} \mathbf{d}$. □

2.3 Relation to mass-action

For understanding the results of this paper, it is not necessary to be familiar with mass-action kinetics. However, as mass-action is the most commonly used model of chemical kinetics, we want to be satisfied that our notion of reachability at least considers states that can be reached by mass-action trajectories. Indeed, Lemma 2.8 shows that our notion of reachability is more general than mass-action.[7]

While a thorough discussion of mass-action kinetics is beyond the scope of this paper, we remind the reader that a CRN with rate constants assigned to each reaction defines a mass-action ODE system with a variable for each species. Each reaction contributes a term to the ODEs for all the species participating in it (except catalysts that are unchanged in the reaction). The term from reaction α appearing in the ODE for x is the product of: the rate constant, the reactant concentrations, and the net stoichiometry of x in α. For example, the CRN

$$X + X \to C$$
$$C + X \to C + Y$$

corresponds to ODEs:

$$\dot{x} = -2k_1x^2 - k_2cx$$
$$\dot{c} = k_1x^2$$
$$\dot{y} = k_2cx$$

where k_1, k_2 are the rate constants of the two reactions. We restrict our attention to CRNs whose mass-action trajectories are well-defined at all times $t \geq 0$, and where concentrations remain finite for all finite t.[8]

Definition 2.5. *A state* $\mathbf{d}$ *is* mass-action reachable *from* $\mathbf{c}$ *if there are non-zero rate constants such that the corresponding mass-action trajectory starting in* $\mathbf{c}$ *passes through* $\mathbf{d}$, *or approaches* $\mathbf{d}$ *as* $t \to \infty$.

In order to prove Lemma 2.8 we need to introduce the notion of a *siphon* from the Petri net literature. This notion will be used, as well, to prove negative results in later sections. Let $\mathcal{C} = (\Lambda, R)$ be a CRN. A *siphon* is a set of species $\Omega \subseteq \Lambda$ such that, for all reactions $\alpha = (\mathbf{r}, \mathbf{p}) \in R$, $[\mathbf{p}] \cap \Omega \neq \varnothing \implies [\mathbf{r}] \cap \Omega \neq \varnothing$, i.e., every reaction that produces an element of Ω requires a positive concentration of an element of Ω to be applicable. The following lemma, due to Angeli, De Leenheer, and Sontag [3], shows that this is equivalent to the notion that "the absence of Ω is forward-invariant" under mass-action: if all species in Ω are absent, then they can never again be produced (under mass-action).[9]

[7] It is much more general, in fact. For example, the reaction $X \to \varnothing$ can take X from a positive concentration to 0, whereas in mass-action kinetics the concentration of X would only approach 0 asymptotically as time $t \to \infty$.

[8] Although mass-action systems are free of many pathologies of more general dynamical systems, there are mass-action CRNs that reach infinite concentration in finite time: e.g. $2X \to 3X$

[9] It may appear obvious that if the rates of all reactions producing a particular species are zero, the species cannot be produced. However, this is a rather deep fact about mass-action ODEs. Consider the CRN $2X \to 3X$. The corresponding mass-action ODE is $\dot{x} = x^2$, and has the property that if you start with $x(0) = 0$, it cannot become positive.

LEMMA 2.6 ([3]). *Let $\Omega \subseteq \Lambda$ be a set of species. Then Ω is a siphon if and only if, for any state* $\mathbf{c}$ *such that* $\Omega \cap [\mathbf{c}] = \varnothing$ *and any state* $\mathbf{d}$ *that is mass-action reachable from* $\mathbf{c}$, $\Omega \cap [\mathbf{d}] = \varnothing$.

We show that the same holds true for segment-reachability.

LEMMA 2.7. *Let $\Omega \subseteq \Lambda$ be a set of species. Then Ω is a siphon if and only if, for any state* $\mathbf{c}$ *such that* $\Omega \cap [\mathbf{c}] = \varnothing$ *and any state* $\mathbf{d}$ *such that* $\mathbf{c} \rightsquigarrow \mathbf{d}$, $\Omega \cap [\mathbf{d}] = \varnothing$.

PROOF. Suppose Ω is a siphon, let $\mathbf{c}$ be a state such that $[\mathbf{c}] \cap \Omega = \varnothing$, and let $\mathbf{d}$ be such that $\mathbf{c} \rightsquigarrow \mathbf{d}$. Every straight line with end points $\mathbf{b}_i$ and $\mathbf{b}_{i+1}$ in the path from $\mathbf{c}$ to $\mathbf{d}$ is expressible as a sum of reaction vectors for reactions applicable in $\mathbf{b}_i$. Assuming inductively that $[\mathbf{b}_i] \cap \Omega = \varnothing$, the definition of siphon gives that $[\mathbf{b}_{i+1}] \cap \Omega = \varnothing$ as well. Therefore $\mathbf{d} \cap \Omega = \varnothing$.

To show the reverse direction, suppose that Ω is not a siphon. Then there is a reaction $\alpha = (\mathbf{r}, \mathbf{p})$ such that $[\mathbf{p}]$ contains an element $S \in \Omega$, but $[\mathbf{r}] \cap \Omega = \varnothing$. Then from any state $\mathbf{c}$ such that $[\mathbf{c}] = \Lambda \setminus \Omega$ (i.e., all species not in Ω are present), α is applicable. Running α produces S, hence results in a state $\mathbf{d}$ such that $\mathbf{c} \rightsquigarrow \mathbf{d}$ with $\Omega \cap [\mathbf{d}] \neq \varnothing$, since $S \in \Omega$. □

LEMMA 2.8. *If* $\mathbf{d}$ *is mass-action reachable from* $\mathbf{c}$, *then* $\mathbf{c} \rightsquigarrow \mathbf{d}$.

PROOF. This proof is similar to the proof of Lemma 2.4; the main difference is that we need to define the "reaction fluxes" each reaction experiences on the mass-action trajectory from $\mathbf{c}$ to $\mathbf{d}$, and that we need to find an ordering on those reactions with positive flux that allows us to apply them one-by-one in order to show $\mathbf{c} \rightsquigarrow^{m+1} \mathbf{d}$.

First, suppose $\mathbf{d}$ is reached in finite time t_f. The trajectory followed by mass-action kinetics to get from $\mathbf{c}$ to $\mathbf{d}$ defines a differentiable curve $\rho : [0, t_f] \to \mathbb{R}^n_{\geq 0}$. Let $\rho' = \frac{d\rho}{dt}$ be the corresponding mass-action differential equations. Let the reactions R be $\alpha_0, \alpha_1, \ldots$. Let $f_j : [0, t_f] \to \mathbb{R}_{\geq 0}$ be the "instantaneous flux" through the j'th reaction at time t. In other words, $\rho'(t) = \sum_j f_j(t)\mathbf{v}_j$, where index j ranges over all reactions, $\mathbf{v}_j$ represents the j'th reaction vector ($\mathbf{p} - \mathbf{r}$ if $\alpha_j = (\mathbf{r}, \mathbf{p})$, i.e., the j'th column of $\mathbf{M}$).

By the fundamental theorem of calculus,

$$\begin{aligned} \mathbf{d} - \mathbf{c} &= \rho(t_f) - \rho(0) = \int_0^{t_f} \rho'(t)dt \\ &= \int_0^{t_f} \sum_j f_j(t)\mathbf{v}_j dt = \sum_j \mathbf{v}_j \int_0^{t_f} f_j(t)dt, \end{aligned}$$

Let $F_j = \int_0^{t_f} f_j(t)dt$ be the total flux through the j'th reaction. Then $\mathbf{d} = \mathbf{c} + \sum_{j \in P} F_j \mathbf{v}_j$.

If $\mathbf{d}$ is not reached in finite time, then by the definition of mass-action reachability, $\mathbf{d} = \lim_{t_f \to \infty} \rho(t_f)$. Now, if we define $F_j = \int_0^{\infty} f_j(t)dt$ as above, the flux F_j could be infinite (consider $X \rightleftharpoons Y$, which approaches the point with equal concentrations of X and Y but has infinite flux through each reaction in the limit). Instead, we observe that for each species S being produced by one reaction whose flux is going to infinity, there must be a corresponding reaction consuming S whose flux is also going to infinity, for $\mathbf{d}(S)$ to be finite. Therefore we can find finite, positive values for each F_j such that $\mathbf{d} = \mathbf{c} + \sum_{j \in P} F_j \mathbf{v}_j$ as above.

Let $R_\rho = \{ \alpha_j \in R \mid F_j > 0 \}$ be the reactions that occurred with strictly positive flux along the curve ρ. We claim that there is an ordering $\prec$ of reactions in R_ρ, such that for any reaction $\alpha = (\mathbf{r}, \mathbf{p})$, $[\mathbf{r}] \subseteq [\mathbf{c}] \cup \bigcup_{\alpha' = (\mathbf{r}', \mathbf{p}') \prec \alpha} [\mathbf{p}']$.

Let $\mathcal{S}_0, \ldots, \mathcal{S}_l \subseteq \Lambda$ be a finite sequence of sets of species, and $\beta_1, \ldots, \beta_l \in R_\rho$ be a finite sequence of reactions which are generated as follows. Let $\mathcal{S}_0 = [\mathbf{c}]$. Given $\mathcal{S}_0, \ldots, \mathcal{S}_{i-1}$ and $\beta_1, \ldots, \beta_{i-1}$, let β_i be a new reaction in R_ρ whose reactants are in $\mathcal{S}_{i-1}$, and then form $\mathcal{S}_i$ by adding the products of β_i to $\mathcal{S}_{i-1}$. Let $\mathcal{S}$ be the final $\mathcal{S}_l$ such that we can no longer extend the sequence. Call the reactions appearing in the list of β's *processed.* If all of the reactions in R_ρ are processed, then the order in which they are processed can define the ordering $\prec$. We now claim that indeed all reactions in R_ρ will be processed.

We proceed by contradiction: we argue that the existence of an unprocessed reaction in R_ρ contradicts Lemma 2.6. Let $\overline{\mathcal{S}} = \Lambda \setminus \mathcal{S}$. For all unprocessed reactions in R_ρ, at least one reactant is in $\overline{\mathcal{S}}$. We also know that for all processed reactions in R_ρ, their products are not in $\overline{\mathcal{S}}$. Thus $\overline{\mathcal{S}}$ is a siphon for the CRN consisting of reactions in R_ρ. Let S^* be a reactant of the unprocessed reaction in R_ρ, and let F^* be its total flux. We know that $F^* > 0$, and thus there must be a point in the mass-action trajectory where S^* has positive concentration. However, $\mathbf{c}$ is zero on the siphon $\overline{\mathcal{S}}$, and $S^* \in \overline{\mathcal{S}}$. This violates Lemma 2.6.

The sequence $\beta_1, \ldots, \beta_l$ gives an ordering $\prec$ on reactions in R_ρ. Using this ordering, the remainder of the proof is identical to the proof of Lemma 2.4. □

Lemma 2.8 shows that our definition of reachability is at least as general as mass-action kinetics. In the other direction, ultimately we must appeal to intuition to justify that our definition does not reach too far. Our intuition says that the following properties are required of any reasonable notion of reachability: (1) concentrations must be nonnegative in all reachable states, (2) a reaction cannot execute in any state in which some reactant is 0,[10] (3) the relation should be reflexive, transitive, and "respect addition" (if $\mathbf{x} \to \mathbf{y}$, then for all $\mathbf{c}$, $\mathbf{x}+\mathbf{c} \to \mathbf{y}+\mathbf{c}$, since the presence of additional chemicals should not *prevent* reactions from being possible). Our definition was the most general one we could conceive that satisfied these properties.

Segment-reachability will serve as our main notion of reachability. Hence, throughout the rest of the paper, we say $\mathbf{d}$ is *reachable* from $\mathbf{c}$, written $\mathbf{c} \to \mathbf{d}$, if $\mathbf{c} \rightsquigarrow \mathbf{d}$.

2.4 Stable computation

In this section, we use our notion of reachability introduced above to formally define our notion of rate-independent computation. Intuitively, devious rate laws might take the system along trajectories anywhere in the reachable space. For the computation to be correct despite the rate laws, it must be able to reach a state with the final correct output from any reachable state. Further, in this setting an output

However, the very similar non-mass-action ODEs $\dot{x} = x^{1/2}$ has a perfectly valid solution $x(t) = t^2/4$ which starts at 0 but becomes positive, despite the fact that at $t = 0$, $\dot{x} = 0$.

[10] In particular, we want siphons to behave reasonably in that their absence is forward-invariant; i.e., that Lemmas 2.6 and 2.7 should apply to any reasonable notion of reachability.

can reasonably be called final only if no rate law can falsify it.

First, to formally define what it means for such a CRN to compute a function, we must first single out some aspects of the CRN as semantically meaningful. Formally, a *chemical reaction computer (CRC)* is a tuple $\mathcal{C} = (\Lambda, R, \Sigma, Y)$, where (Λ, R) is a CRN, $\Sigma \subset \Lambda$, written as $\Sigma = \{X_1, \ldots, X_k\}$,[11] is the *set of input species*, and $Y \in \Lambda \setminus \Sigma$ is the *output species*.

Definition 2.9. *A state* $\mathbf{o} \in \mathbb{R}^{\Lambda}_{\geq 0}$ *is* output stable *if, for all* $\mathbf{o}'$ *such that* $\mathbf{o} \to \mathbf{o}'$, $\mathbf{o}(Y) = \mathbf{o}'(Y)$, *i.e., once* $\mathbf{o}$ *is reached, no reactions can change the concentration of the output species* Y.

Definition 2.10. *Let* $f : \mathbb{R}^k_{\geq 0} \to \mathbb{R}_{\geq 0}$ *be a function*[12] *and let* $\mathcal{C}$ *be a CRC. We say that* $\mathcal{C}$ stably computes f *if, for all* $\mathbf{x} \in \mathbb{R}^k_{\geq 0}$, *for all* $\mathbf{c}$ *such that* $\mathbf{x} \to \mathbf{c}$, *there exists an output stable state* $\mathbf{o}$ *such that* $\mathbf{c} \to \mathbf{o}$ *and* $\mathbf{o}(Y) = f(\mathbf{x})$.

2.5 Dual-rail representations

In general, the output species of an upstream CRN may be used as the inputs to a downstream CRN if the upstream CRN only produces but never consumes the output species. We say that such a CRN computes its output *monotonically*. This is impossible for general stable CRNs. For example, any CRN computing the function $f(x_1, x_2) = x_1 - x_2$ must necessarily be able to consume its output species in order to account for some amount of species X_2 that has not yet reacted. Therefore, some of our CRNs represent their output Y in a "dual-rail" fashion as the difference of two species Y^+ and Y^-, both of which are only produced but never consumed by the CRN. Since these outputs are given as input to a downstream subroutine CRN, the downstream CRN must also be designed to accept inputs in this same dual-rail representation. Furthermore, representing values in this way allows us to take negative inputs and produce negative outputs, using only nonnegative concentrations, representing for example a negative output by a higher concentration of Y^- than Y^+.

Formally, let $f : \mathbb{R}^k \to \mathbb{R}$ be a function. A function $\hat{f} : \mathbb{R}^{2k} \to \mathbb{R}^2$ is a *dual-rail representation* of f if, for all $x^+, x^- \in \mathbb{R}^k$, if $(y^+, y^-) = \hat{f}(x^+, x^-)$, then $f(x^+ - x^-) = y^+ - y^-$. In other words, $\hat{f}$ represents f as the difference of its two outputs y^+ and y^-, and it works for any input pair (x^+, x^-) whose difference is the input value to f. We can define a CRC to stably compute such a function in the same manner as in Section 3.2, but having input species $X_1^+, X_1^-, X_2^+, X_2^-, \ldots, X_k^+, X_k^-, \ldots$, and two output species Y^+ and Y^-.

Definition 2.11. *We say that a CRC* stably dual-computes $f : \mathbb{R}^k \to \mathbb{R}$ *if it stably computes a dual-rail representation* $\hat{f} : \mathbb{R}^k \times \mathbb{R}^k \to \mathbb{R} \times \mathbb{R}$ *of* f.

Note that if a CRC monotonically outputs Y^+ and Y^- according to the dual-rail convention, and the output value is never negative, then it can be trivially modified to produce its output according to the direct computation convention (Def. 2.10) by adding the reaction $Y^+ + Y^- \to \varnothing$. Note that a single function has an infinite number of dual-rail representations. We require only that a CRN exists to compute one of them to say that the function is stably dual-computable by a CRN.

[11] We assume a canonical ordering of $\Sigma = \{X_1, \ldots, X_k\}$ so that a vector $\mathbf{x} \in \mathbb{R}^k_{\geq 0}$ (i.e., an input to f) can be viewed equivalently as a state $\mathbf{x} \in \mathbb{R}^{\Sigma}_{\geq 0}$ of $\mathcal{C}$ (i.e., an input to $\mathcal{C}$). Also, we have defined valid initial states to contain only the input species Σ; other species must have initial concentration 0. Our results would change slightly if we relaxed this assumption; however, considering any species $S \notin \Sigma$ as an "auxiliary input", the result would remain that what is computed is a (piecewise) linear function of those species present initially. Since the initial value of non-input species would be constant across all valid initial states, rather than linear functions $f(\mathbf{x}) = \sum_{i=1}^k a_i \mathbf{x}(i)$, we would instead deal with *affine* functions $f(\mathbf{x}) = c + \sum_{i=1}^k a_i \mathbf{x}(i)$, where the constant c would depend only on the initial concentrations of non-input species.

[12] Our results extend easily to functions $f : \mathbb{R}^k \to \mathbb{R}^l$, i.e., whose output is a vector of l real numbers. This is because such a function is equivalently l separate functions $f_i : \mathbb{R}^k \to \mathbb{R}$.

3. FUNCTIONS OVER REALS USING DUAL-RAIL REPRESENTATION

A function $f : \mathbb{R}^k \to \mathbb{R}$ is *rational linear* if there exist $a_1, \ldots, a_k \in \mathbb{Q}$ such that $f(\mathbf{x}) = \sum_{i=1}^k a_i \mathbf{x}(i)$. A function $f : \mathbb{R}^k \to \mathbb{R}$ is *piecewise rational linear* if there is a finite set of partial rational linear functions $f_1, \ldots, f_p : \mathbb{R}^k \dashrightarrow \mathbb{R}$, with $\bigcup_{j=1}^p \mathrm{dom}\ f_j = \mathbb{R}^k$, such that, for all $j \in \{1, \ldots, p\}$ and all $\mathbf{x} \in \mathrm{dom}\ f_j$, $f(\mathbf{x}) = f_j(\mathbf{x})$. In this case, we say that $f_1, \ldots, f_p$ are the *components* of f.

The following is the main theorem of this paper.

Theorem 3.1. *A function* $f : \mathbb{R}^k \to \mathbb{R}$ *is stably dual-computed by a CRN if and only if it is continuous and piecewise rational linear.*

We prove each direction of Theorem 3.1 separately via Lemmas 3.3 and 3.13.

3.1 Continuous piecewise rational linear functions are computable

We require the following theorem, due to Ovchinnikov [15], which characterizes continuous piecewise linear functions in a way that is conducive to computation by CRNs.

Theorem 3.2 ([15]). *Let* $D \subseteq \mathbb{R}^k$ *be convex. For every continuous piecewise linear function* $f : D \to \mathbb{R}$ *with components* $f_1, \ldots, f_p$, *there exists a family* $S_1, \ldots, S_q \subseteq \{1, \ldots, p\}$ *with* $S_i \not\subseteq S_j$ *if* $i \neq j$, *such that, for all* $\mathbf{x} \in D$, $f(\mathbf{x}) = \max_{i \in \{1,\ldots,q\}} \min_{j \in S_i} f_j(\mathbf{x})$.

The following lemma shows that any continuous piecewise rational linear function is stably computable by a CRN (in fact, with monotonic production of outputs in a dual-rail representation).

Lemma 3.3. *Let* $D \subseteq \mathbb{R}^k$ *be convex, and let* $f : D \to \mathbb{R}$ *be a continuous piecewise rational linear function. Then* f *is monotonically stably dual-computed by a CRN.*

Proof. By Theorem 3.2, it suffices to show how to compute a dual-rail representation of any rational linear function, a dual-rail representation of the minimum function with two inputs, and a dual-rail representation of the maximum function with two inputs. The latter two can be composed in a tree of depth $\log l$ to compute the minimum or maximum functions with input arity l.

Let $g : \mathbb{R}^k \to \mathbb{R}$ be a rational linear function $g(\mathbf{x}) = \sum_{i=1}^{k} a_i \mathbf{x}(i)$. By appropriate integer arithmetic, there exist $n_1, \ldots, n_k \in \mathbb{Z}$ and $d \in \mathbb{Z}^+$ such that $g(\mathbf{x}) = \frac{1}{d}\sum_{i=1}^{k} n_i \mathbf{x}(i)$. The following reactions compute a dual-rail representation of g with input species $X_1^+, \ldots, X_k^+, X_1^-, \ldots, X_k^-$ and output species Y^+, Y^-. For each i such that $n_i > 0$, add the reactions

$$\begin{aligned} X_i^+ &\to n_i W^+ \\ X_i^- &\to n_i W^- \end{aligned}$$

For each i such that $n_i < 0$, add the reactions

$$\begin{aligned} X_i^+ &\to |n_i| W^- \\ X_i^- &\to |n_i| W^+ \end{aligned}$$

To divide the values of W^- and W^+ by d, add the reactions

$$\begin{aligned} dW^+ &\to Y^+ \\ dW^- &\to Y^- \end{aligned}$$

To see that this works, for all states $\mathbf{c}$, define $x_i(\mathbf{c}) = \mathbf{c}(X_i^+) - \mathbf{c}(X_i^-)$, $w(\mathbf{c}) = \mathbf{c}(W^+) - \mathbf{c}(W^-)$, and $y(\mathbf{c}) = \mathbf{c}(Y^+) - \mathbf{c}(Y^-)$. Let $\mathbf{i}$ be the initial state. It is routine to check that the reactions enforce that for any state $\mathbf{c}$ reachable from $\mathbf{i}$,

$$y(\mathbf{c}) + \frac{1}{d} w(\mathbf{c}) + \frac{1}{d}\sum_{i=1}^{k} n_i x_i(\mathbf{c}) = \frac{1}{d}\sum_{i=1}^{k} n_i x_i(\mathbf{i}). \qquad (3.1)$$

(The right side is a constant depending only on the initial state, and each reaction increases one term on the left side by the same amount it decreases another term.)

If $\mathbf{c}$ is output stable, then $\mathbf{c}(X_i^+) = \mathbf{c}(X_i^-) = \mathbf{c}(W^+) = \mathbf{c}(W^-) = 0$, whence by (3.1) $y(\mathbf{c}) = \frac{1}{d}\sum_{i=1}^{k} n_i x_i(\mathbf{i})$, i.e, the output value of the CRN is the desired rational linear function of the inputs. Furthermore, observe that from any reachable state, it is always possible to reach an output stable state by executing the reactions above to completion in the order in which they are listed. This shows that a dual-rail representation of any rational linear function can be monotonically stably dual-computed by a CRN.

The following reactions monotonically stably compute a dual-rail representation of min with input species X_1^+, X_2^+, X_1^-, X_2^- and output species Y^+, Y^-. Add the reactions

$$\begin{aligned} X_1^+ + X_2^+ &\to Y^+ && (3.2) \\ X_1^- &\to X_2^+ + Y^- && (3.3) \\ X_2^- &\to X_1^+ + Y^- && (3.4) \end{aligned}$$

To see that this works, for all states $\mathbf{c}$, define $x_1(\mathbf{c}) = \mathbf{c}(X_1^+) - \mathbf{c}(X_1^-)$, $x_2(\mathbf{c}) = \mathbf{c}(X_2^+) - \mathbf{c}(X_2^-)$, and $y(\mathbf{c}) = \mathbf{c}(Y^+) - \mathbf{c}(Y^-)$. Let $\mathbf{i}$ be the initial state, and let $\mathbf{c}$ be a state reachable from $\mathbf{i}$. Let c_1, c_2, and c_3 be the amount of reactions (3.2), (3.3) and (3.4), respectively, that have executed to get from state $\mathbf{i}$ to state $\mathbf{c}$. Then we have $x_1(\mathbf{i}) - c_1 + c_2 + c_3 = x_1(\mathbf{c}), x_2(\mathbf{i}) - c_1 + c_2 + c_3 = x_2(\mathbf{c}), c_1 - c_2 - c_3 = y(\mathbf{c})$, which implies that $x_1(\mathbf{i}) = x_1(\mathbf{c}) + y(\mathbf{c}), x_2(\mathbf{i}) = x_2(\mathbf{c}) + y(\mathbf{c})$. In a stable state, either $\mathbf{c}(X_1^+) = 0$ or $\mathbf{c}(X_2^+) = 0$, otherwise reaction (3.2) is applicable. Further, in a stable state $\mathbf{c}$, $x_1(\mathbf{c}) = \mathbf{c}(X_1^+)$ and $x_2(\mathbf{c}) = \mathbf{c}(X_2^+)$, because $\mathbf{c}(X_1^-) = \mathbf{c}(X_2^-) = 0$ for reactions (3.3) and (3.4) not to be applicable. Thus, $x_1(\mathbf{c}) = 0$ or $x_2(\mathbf{c}) = 0$.

Thus, $x_1(\mathbf{i}) = y(\mathbf{c})$ and $x_2(\mathbf{i}) = x_2(\mathbf{c}) + y(\mathbf{c})$, or $x_2(\mathbf{i}) = y(\mathbf{c})$ and $x_1(\mathbf{i}) = x_1(\mathbf{c}) + y(\mathbf{c})$. So if $x_1(\mathbf{i}) < x_2(\mathbf{i})$, then it must be the first case (since $x_2(\mathbf{c}) > 0$). Otherwise, the second case holds. This shows that if stable state is reached, then computation is correct. Finally, observe that from any reachable state, by executing to completion the last applicable reaction among (3.3) and (3.4), followed by executing to completion (3.2), we obtain concentration zero of X_1^-, X_2^-, and one of X_1^+ or X_2^+, which implies that no reaction is applicable and the state is output stable.

To monotonically stably compute a dual-rail representation of max, observe that it is equivalent to computing the min function with the roles of the "plus" and "minus" species reversed (which negates the value represented in dual-rail), since $\max(x_1, x_2) = -\min(-x_1, -x_2)$. In other words, add the reactions

$$\begin{aligned} X_1^- + X_2^- &\to Y^- \\ X_1^+ &\to X_2^- + Y^+ \\ X_2^+ &\to X_1^- + Y^+ \end{aligned}$$

By appropriate renaming of input and output species of the three types of CRNs described above, they can be composed to compute $f(\mathbf{x}) = \max_{i \in \{1,\ldots,q\}} \min_{j \in S_i} f_j(\mathbf{x})$ as in Theorem 3.2. □

Although not essential to understanding the results of this paper, we now discuss the behavior of our construction with regards to mass-action kinetics. The following lemma shows that our construction actually converges to the correct output value under mass-action no matter how an adversary might have pushed us initially:

LEMMA 3.4. *For any input state $\mathbf{x}$, for any state $\mathbf{z}$ reachable from $\mathbf{x}$, the mass-action trajectory of the CRN of Lemma 3.3 with any non-zero rate constants starting at $\mathbf{z}$ converges to the output stable state in the limit $t \to \infty$.*

PROOF SKETCH. Our proof strategy is as follows. Using a Lyapunov function, we show that starting in any state $\mathbf{z}$ (not necessarily even reachable from $\mathbf{x}$), the CRN following mass-action kinetics converges to a steady-state as $t \to \infty$. Further, the CRN has the property that for every input state $\mathbf{x}$, there is exactly one mass-action steady-state that is segment-reachable from $\mathbf{x}$, and this state happens to be the output stable state. Since mass-action reachability (even in the limit) implies segment-reachability by Lemma 2.8, the convergence to steady-state implies convergence to the correct output.

We now show how to construct the appropriate Lyapunov function. The trajectory followed by mass-action kinetics starting from any state $\mathbf{z}$ defines a differentiable curve $\rho_\mathbf{z} : [0, \infty) \to \mathbb{R}^n_{\geq 0}$. Let $\rho'_\mathbf{z} = \frac{d\rho_\mathbf{z}}{dt}$ be the corresponding mass-action differential equations. Let $f_j^\mathbf{z} : [0, \infty) \to \mathbb{R}_{\geq 0}$ be the "instantaneous flux" through the j'th reaction at time t. (In other words, $\rho'_\mathbf{z}(t) = \sum_j f_j^\mathbf{z}(t)\mathbf{v}_j$, where index j ranges over all reactions, and $\mathbf{v}_j$ is the j'th column of stoichiometry matrix $\mathbf{M}$.) Our construction has the property that $F_j^\mathbf{z} = \int_0^\infty f_j^\mathbf{z}(t)dt$ (i.e. the total flux through the j'th reaction) is finite for any starting state $\mathbf{z}$. This follows because the CRN conserves mass up to multiplicative constants (due to stoichiometry) and our CRN is "feedforward" in the sense that there is an ordering on reactions according to which mass can flow, but it cannot flow back. Thus we can construct the Lyapunov function $\mathcal{L}(\mathbf{z}) : \mathbb{R}^n_{\geq 0} \to \mathbb{R}_{\geq 0}$ as $\mathcal{L}(\mathbf{z}) = \sum_j F_j^\mathbf{z}$.

To apply the standard Lyapunov machinery [13], we need to show three properties of the Lyapunov function: (1) $\mathcal{L} > 0$

everywhere except at a steady-state where $\mathcal{L} = 0$, (2) $\mathcal{L}$ gets arbitrarily large with increasing $\mathbf{z}$, (3) $\frac{d}{dt}\mathcal{L}(\rho_{\mathbf{z}}(t)) \leq 0$, and strictly negative everywhere except when $\rho_{\mathbf{z}}(t)$ is a steady state. This would guarantee that no matter where we start, the CRN converges to a steady-state under mass-action. The first two properties of the Lyapunov function are easily checked. To show the last property, we observe that $\frac{d}{dt}\mathcal{L}(\rho_{\mathbf{z}}(t)) = \sum_j \frac{d}{dt}\int_0^\infty f_j^{\rho_{\mathbf{z}}(t)}(t')dt' = \sum_j \frac{d}{dt}\int_t^\infty f_j^{\mathbf{z}}(t')dt' = \sum_j \frac{d}{dt}\left(\int_0^\infty f_j^{\mathbf{z}}(t')dt' - \int_0^t f_j^{\mathbf{z}}(t')dt'\right) = -\sum_j f_j^{\mathbf{z}}(t) \leq 0$ and equal to zero at exactly a steady state. □

3.2 Computable functions are continuous piecewise rational linear

Let $\mathcal{C} = (\Lambda, R, \Sigma, Y)$ be a CRC. We call any siphon Ω such that $(\mathbf{c} \upharpoonright \Omega = \mathbf{0}) \implies (\mathbf{c}$ is output stable) an *output stable siphon*. Lemma 3.5 shows the underlying relationship between output stability and siphons.

Lemma 3.5. *Either every state is output stable, or every state is output unstable, or there is a set of output stable siphons $\mathcal{S}$ such that a state $\mathbf{c}$ is output stable if and only if $\exists \Omega \in \mathcal{S}$ such that $\mathbf{c} \upharpoonright \Omega = \mathbf{0}$.*

We prove some facts about siphons first that will help us characterize output stability in terms of them.

Lemma 3.6. *Let $\mathbf{c}, \mathbf{d}_1, \ldots, \mathbf{d}_l$ be states such that $\mathbf{c} \to \mathbf{d}_1, \ldots, \mathbf{c} \to \mathbf{d}_l$. Then there exists $\mathbf{d}$ such that $\mathbf{c} \to \mathbf{d}$ and $[\mathbf{d}] = \bigcup_{i=1}^l [\mathbf{d}_i]$.*

Proof. Since $\mathbf{c} \to \mathbf{d}_1, \ldots, \mathbf{c} \to \mathbf{d}_l$, we have that for all $i \in \{1, \ldots, l\}$, $\frac{1}{l}\mathbf{c} \to \frac{1}{l}\mathbf{d}_i$. Hence $\mathbf{c} \to \frac{1}{l}\sum_{i=1}^l \mathbf{d}_i$. Letting $\mathbf{d} = \frac{1}{l}\sum_{i=1}^l \mathbf{d}_i$ completes the proof. □

The next lemma shows that if a set of species has even a single state from which none of the species can be produced, then it is a siphon.

Lemma 3.7. *If $\mathbf{c}$ is a state and Ω' is a set of species such that for all $\mathbf{d}$ reachable from $\mathbf{c}$, $\mathbf{d} \upharpoonright \Omega' = \mathbf{0}$, then there exists a siphon $\Omega \supseteq \Omega'$ such that $\mathbf{c} \upharpoonright \Omega = \mathbf{0}$.*

Proof. There is a unique largest set of species $\overline{\Omega}$ such that $\forall S \in \overline{\Omega}$, $\exists \mathbf{d}$ reachable from $\mathbf{c}$ and $\mathbf{d}(S) > 0$, i.e., $\overline{\Omega}$ is the set of species producible from $\mathbf{c}$. Let $\mathbf{d}$ be a state reachable from $\mathbf{c}$ such that, for all $S \in \overline{\Omega}$, $\mathbf{d}(S) > 0$; such a state exists by Lemma 3.6. Let $\Omega = \Lambda \setminus \overline{\Omega}$; we must show Ω is a siphon.

Suppose for the sake of contradiction that Ω is not a siphon. Then there exists some state $\mathbf{c}'$ with $\mathbf{c}' \upharpoonright \Omega = 0$ (implying $[\mathbf{c}'] \subseteq [\mathbf{d}]$), some state $\mathbf{d}'$ reachable from $\mathbf{c}'$, and $S \in \Omega$, such that $\mathbf{d}'(S) > 0$. Let $\epsilon > 0$ be sufficiently small that $\epsilon \cdot \mathbf{c}' \leq \mathbf{d}$; such an ϵ exists because $[\mathbf{c}'] \subseteq [\mathbf{d}]$. Then $\epsilon \cdot \mathbf{d}'$ is reachable from $\epsilon \cdot \mathbf{c}'$, and $\epsilon \cdot \mathbf{d}'(S) > 0$. Since $\epsilon \cdot \mathbf{c}' \leq \mathbf{d}$ and reachability respects addition, this implies that S is producible from $\mathbf{d}$ (hence from $\mathbf{c}$) as well, implying $S \in \overline{\Omega}$, a contradiction since we chose $S \in \Omega$ and $\Omega \cap \overline{\Omega} = \varnothing$. □

We are now ready to prove Lemma 3.5.

Proof. (of Lemma 3.5) We create the set of siphons as follows. Let $\{r_j = (\mathbf{r}_j, \mathbf{p}_j)\}_j$ be the set of all reactions that change Y (consume or produce; i.e., $\mathbf{r}_j(Y) \neq \mathbf{p}_j(Y)$). We construct sets of species $\{\Omega'_k\}_k$ by taking one reactant from each reaction in every possible way (i.e., the set of subsets of species $\{\ \Omega'_k \subseteq \Lambda \mid (\forall j)\ \Omega'_k \cap \mathbf{r}_j \neq \varnothing\ \}$). For each possible siphon Ω such that $\Omega \supseteq \Omega'_k$, add Ω to $\mathcal{S}$. It is easy to see that if $\mathbf{c}$ is zero on some siphon $\Omega \in \mathcal{S}$ then it is output stable.

For the other direction: Let $O(\mathbf{c}) = \{\ \Omega'_k \mid \mathbf{c} \upharpoonright \Omega'_k = \mathbf{0}\ \}$. If in some state $\mathbf{c}$, we have $O(\mathbf{c}) = \varnothing$, then there is a reaction r_j that changes Y and is applicable in $\mathbf{c}$. Then Y can change by this reaction and $\mathbf{c}$ cannot be output stable. So for output stable $\mathbf{c}$, $O(\mathbf{c})$ is non-empty. Now let $\mathbf{d}_1, \ldots, \mathbf{d}_l$ be some states reachable from $\mathbf{c}$ such that if $\mathbf{c} \to \mathbf{d}$ then $\exists i, O(\mathbf{d}_i) = O(\mathbf{d})$ (i.e. these states cover the whole variety of $O(\mathbf{d}_i)$'s). Lemma 3.6 implies that if $\cap_{i=1}^l O(\mathbf{d}_i) = \varnothing$ then $\mathbf{c} \to \mathbf{d}$ such that $O(\mathbf{d}) = \varnothing$. Thus, for an output stable $\mathbf{c}$, at least one of the original sets $\Omega'_k \in O(\mathbf{c})$ stays zero on all states reachable from $\mathbf{c}$. This implies that there is some siphon $\Omega \in \mathcal{S}$ that includes Ω'_k and $\mathbf{c} \upharpoonright \Omega = \mathbf{0}$ (by Lemma 3.7). □

Recall that we write the set of reactions as $R = \{\alpha_1, \alpha_2, \ldots, \alpha_m\}$.

Definition 3.8. *Let $\mathbf{s} = (R_1, \ldots, R_l) \in \mathcal{P}(R)^l$ denote a sequence of subsets of reactions. Say that $\mathbf{c} \to_{\mathbf{s}} \mathbf{d}$ if $\mathbf{c} = \mathbf{b}_0 \to^1_{\mathbf{u}_1} \mathbf{b}_1 \to^1_{\mathbf{u}_2} \mathbf{b}_2 \to^1_{\mathbf{u}_3} \cdots \to^1_{\mathbf{u}_l} \mathbf{b}_l = \mathbf{d}$, where, for each $i \in \{1, \ldots, l\}$ and $j \in \{1, \ldots, m\}$, $\mathbf{u}_i(j) > 0 \iff \alpha_j \in R_i$.*

In other words, $\mathbf{d}$ is reachable from $\mathbf{c}$ via l straight lines, in which the i'th straight line is defined by a strictly positive weighted sum of reactions in R_i.

Let $X_{\mathbf{s}}(\Omega) = \{\mathbf{x} \in \mathbb{R}^\Lambda_{\geq 0} \mid (\exists \mathbf{o})\ \mathbf{x} \to_{\mathbf{s}} \mathbf{o} \text{ and } \mathbf{o} \upharpoonright \Omega = \mathbf{0}\}$ denote those states from which Ω is drainable (thus the reached state is output stable since Ω is an output siphon) via straight lines respecting $\mathbf{s}$.

Note that the following lemma concerns *direct* stable computability.

Lemma 3.9. *Let $f : \mathbb{R}^k_{\geq 0} \to \mathbb{R}_{\geq 0}$ be stably computed by a CRC $\mathcal{C} = (\Lambda, R, \Sigma, Y)$. Let Ω be an output stable siphon and let $\mathbf{s} = (R_1, \ldots, R_l) \in \mathcal{P}(R)^l$ for some $l \in \mathbb{N}$. Then f restricted to inputs in $X_{\mathbf{s}}(\Omega)$ is rational linear.*

Proof. By the definition of output stable siphon, every state $\mathbf{o}$ such that $\mathbf{o} \upharpoonright \Omega = \mathbf{0}$ is output-stable. By the stability of $\mathcal{C}$, every such state $\mathbf{o}$ reachable from a particular initial state $\mathbf{x}$ must have the same value of $y = \mathbf{o}(Y) = f(\mathbf{x})$.

By the definition of $X_{\mathbf{s}}(\Omega)$, an output stable state $\mathbf{o}$ is reachable from $\mathbf{x}$, with $\mathbf{o} \upharpoonright \Omega = \mathbf{0}$, via straight-line segments respecting $\mathbf{s}$. Then by Definition 3.8, there are states $\mathbf{b}_0, \mathbf{b}_1, \ldots, \mathbf{b}_l \in \mathbb{R}^n_{\geq 0}$ such that $\mathbf{x} = \mathbf{b}_0 \to^1_{\mathbf{u}_1} \mathbf{b}_1 \to^1_{\mathbf{u}_2} \mathbf{b}_2 \to^1_{\mathbf{u}_3} \cdots \to^1_{\mathbf{u}_l} \mathbf{b}_l = \mathbf{o}$, where, for each $i \in \{1, \ldots, l\}$ and $j \in R_i$, $\mathbf{u}_i(j) > 0 \iff \alpha_j \in R_i$.

We claim that the condition "$\mathbf{x} \in X_{\mathbf{s}}(\Omega)$" is equivalent to a conjunction of linear inequalities (some strict and some non-strict). The fact that each $\mathbf{b}_i \to^1_{\mathbf{u}_{i+1}} \mathbf{b}_{i+1}$ is captured by the inequalities $\mathbf{b}_i(S) > 0$ for each species S that appears as a reactant of some reaction in R_i, and to the linear equations $\mathbf{b}_i = \mathbf{b}_{i-1} + \mathbf{M}\mathbf{u}_i$ (where $\mathbf{M}$ is the reaction stoichiometry matrix from Definition 2.1). The fact that all concentrations must be nonnegative corresponds to the linear inequalities $\mathbf{b}_i \geq \mathbf{0}$. The fact that all reactions must happen in the forward direction (recall we represent reversible reactions such as $A \rightleftharpoons B$ as two irreversible reactions $A \to B$ and $B \to A$) corresponds to the linear inequalities $\mathbf{u}_i \geq \mathbf{0}$. The fact that the siphon Ω is drained corresponds to the linear inequality $\mathbf{o}(S) \leq 0$ for each $S \in \Omega$, together with the existing constraint $\mathbf{o} \geq \mathbf{0}$.

These equations and inequalities can be expressed as a single system of linear inequalities $\mathbf{Az} \geq / > \mathbf{0}$, (i.e., some strict and some non-strict inequalities) where $\mathbf{A}$ is a constant rational matrix depending only on the constants $\mathbf{M}$ and Ω, and $\mathbf{z}$ is a single vector of unknowns corresponding to all the unknowns above, namely $\mathbf{x}$ (the initial species concentrations subject to the constraint that all non-input species start at 0), $\mathbf{o}$ (the final species concentrations subject to the constraint that all siphon species end up at 0), and the various $\mathbf{u}_i$'s (the fluxes through each reaction to get from $\mathbf{b}_i$ to $\mathbf{b}_{i+1}$), and the $\mathbf{b}_i$'s.

These inequalities define a convex subset S of $\mathbb{R}^d$ for some constant d. Let $G \subseteq \mathbb{R}^{k+1}$ be the projection of S to the $(k+1)$-dimensional subspace corresponding to $\mathbf{x}$ and $y = \mathbf{o}(Y)$. G is the graph of the function $y = f(\mathbf{x})$ restricted to inputs $\mathbf{x} \in X_{\mathbf{s}}(\Omega)$. Since S is convex, G is also convex. We claim that G must be a subset of a k-dimensional rational hyperplane. For the sake of contradiction, suppose not. The matrix defining the set S was rational, so G cannot be a subset of a k-dimensional *irrational* hyperplane. Then there are $k+1$ non-coplanar points in G. Since G is convex, it contains the entire $(k+1)$-dimensional convex hull H of these points. Since H is a $(k+1)$-dimensional convex polytope, it contains two different values of y corresponding to the same value of $\mathbf{x}$, contradicting the fact that only a single y value exists in all output-stable states reachable from $\mathbf{x}$. This establishes the claim that G must be a subset of a k-dimensional rational hyperplane.

Since the graph of f is a subset of a k-dimensional rational hyperplane, it is a rational affine function. Since there are no reactions of the form $\varnothing \to \ldots$, Y cannot be produced from the initial state $\mathbf{x} = \mathbf{0}$ (nor can any other species), so $f(\mathbf{0}) = 0$. Therefore this hyperplane passes through the origin, so it defines a rational linear function. □

In Lemma 3.9, the reason that we restrict attention to a single output siphon Ω *and* a single sequence $\mathbf{s}$ of subsets of reactions is as follows. If different output siphons are drained, then different linear functions may be computed by the CRC. For example, $X_1 + X_2 \to Y$ computes $f(x_1, x_2) = x_1$ if siphon $\{X_2\}$ is drained and $f(x_1, x_2) = x_2$ if siphon $\{X_1\}$ is drained. Further our proof technique relies on fixing $\mathbf{s}$ to obtain convexity. If we do not force a particular set of reactions to occur with positive flux on each line segment, then to logically express the condition that Ω is drainable from state $\mathbf{x}$ would require that we specify, for each each line segment and each species S, that either S has positive concentration at the start, *or* S is not a reactant used in that line segment. This would imply that the condition of Ω being drainable from $\mathbf{x}$ is expressible as a conjunction of disjunctions of linear inequalities, which is not necessarily a convex set as required in the proof.

LEMMA 3.10. *Let $f : \mathbb{R}^k \to \mathbb{R}$ be stably dual computed by a CRC. Let Ω be an output stable siphon and let $\mathbf{s} = (R_1, \ldots, R_l) \in \mathcal{P}(R)^l$ for some $l \in \mathbb{N}$. Then f restricted to inputs that have a dual rail representation in $X_{\mathbf{s}}(\Omega)$ is rational linear.*

PROOF. A dual-rail computing CRC can be thought to *directly* compute two separate functions $\hat{f}^+, \hat{f}^- : \mathbb{R}^{2k}_{\geq 0} \to \mathbb{R}_{\geq 0}$ such that $\hat{f} = \hat{f}^+ - \hat{f}^-$ where $\hat{f}$ is a dual rail representation of f. By Lemma 3.9 we know that $\hat{f}^+$ and $\hat{f}^-$ are rational linear when restricted to $X_{\mathbf{s}}(\Omega)$. The lemma then follows because rational linearity is closed under subtraction. □

LEMMA 3.11. *Let Ω be an output siphon and $R' \subseteq R$ be a subset of reactions. Let $\mathbf{a}_1, \mathbf{a}_2, \ldots, \in X_{(R')}(\Omega)$ be a convergent sequence of states, where $\mathbf{a} = \lim_{i\to\infty} \mathbf{a}_i$, i.e., Ω is drainable from every $\mathbf{a}_i$, via a single straight line segment that uses precisely reactions from R'. Suppose $[\mathbf{a}] = \Lambda$. Then $\mathbf{a} \in X_{(R')}(\Omega)$.*

PROOF. As in the proof of Lemma 3.9, the condition $\mathbf{a}_i \in X_{(R')}(\Omega)$ is equivalent to the condition that $\mathbf{a}_i$ satisfies a set of linear inequalities. Some inequalities may be strict; out goal is to show we can remove the strict inequalities so that the remainder define a closed set.

Unlike Lemma 3.9, because $[\mathbf{a}] = \Lambda$, every reaction in R (including those in R') is applicable to $\mathbf{a}$. Thus all states reachable from $\mathbf{a}$ are reachable via a single straight line. For all $\epsilon > 0$, let $\mathcal{B}_\epsilon(\mathbf{a}) = \{\mathbf{x} \in \mathbb{R}^n_{\geq 0} \mid (\forall S \in \Lambda)\, |\mathbf{x}(S) - \mathbf{a}(S)| \leq \epsilon\}$ be the ball of (L_∞) radius ϵ around $\mathbf{a}$. For any $0 < \epsilon < \min_{S\in\Lambda} \mathbf{a}(S)$, $\mathbf{x} \in \mathcal{B}_\epsilon(\mathbf{a}) \implies [\mathbf{x}] = \Lambda$, since being within ϵ of $\mathbf{a}$ implies that all species are present. Furthermore, note that this condition is expressible using non-strict inequalities.

Thus the condition that $\mathbf{x} \in X_{(R')}(\Omega) \cap \mathcal{B}_\epsilon(\mathbf{a})$ is expressible as a conjunction of linear inequalities, *without* using the strict inequality $\mathbf{b}_i(k) > 0$ enforcing that reactants of reactions in R' are present. Hence we are left with only nonstrict inequalities, which define a closed set. Thus $X_{(R')}(\Omega) \cap \mathcal{B}_\epsilon(\mathbf{a})$ is a closed set. Since $\mathbf{a} = \lim_{i\to\infty} \mathbf{a}_i$, for all but finitely many i, $\mathbf{a}_i \in X_{(R')}(\Omega) \cap \mathcal{B}_\epsilon(\mathbf{a})$. Since this set is closed, it contains all its limit points, whence $\mathbf{a} \in X_{(R')}(\Omega)$. □

Note that the hypothesis $[\mathbf{a}] = \Lambda$ is necessary. Otherwise, consider the reactions $A \to C$, $A + B \to \varnothing$, and $F + C \to C$, with $\mathbf{a}_i(C) = 0$, $\mathbf{a}_i(F) = 1$, $\mathbf{a}_i(B) = 1$, and $\mathbf{a}_i(A)$ approaching 1 from above as $i \to \infty$ (whence $C \notin [\mathbf{a}]$). Then the siphon $\Omega = \{A, B, F\}$ is drainable from each $\mathbf{a}_i$ by running $A \to C$ until A and B have the same concentration, then running the other two reactions to completion. However, $\mathbf{a}(A) = \mathbf{a}(B)$, so running any amount of reaction $A \to C$ prevents reaction $A + B \to \varnothing$ from draining B. Therefore $\mathbf{a} \notin X_{(R')}(\Omega)$ but $\mathbf{a}_i \in X_{(R')}(\Omega)$ for all i.

The following lemma concerns *direct* computability and will be useful for both direct and dual computation by CRCs. A function $f : \mathbb{R}^k_{\geq 0} \to \mathbb{R}_{\geq 0}$ is *positive-continuous* if, for all $U \subseteq \{1, \ldots, k\}$, f is continuous on the domain $D_U = \{\ \mathbf{x} \in \mathbb{R}^k_{\geq 0} \mid (\forall i \in \{1, \ldots, k\})\, \mathbf{x}(i) > 0 \iff i \in U\ \}$. In other words, f is continuous on any subset $D \subset \mathbb{R}^k_{\geq 0}$ that does not have any coordinate $i \in \{1, \ldots, k\}$ that takes both zero and positive values in D.

LEMMA 3.12. *Let $f : \mathbb{R}^k_{\geq 0} \to \mathbb{R}_{\geq 0}$ be stably computed by a CRC. Then f is positive-continuous.*

PROOF. Let $U \subseteq \{1, \ldots, k\}$, let $\mathbf{x} \in D_U$, and let $\mathbf{x}_1, \mathbf{x}_2, \ldots \in D_U$ be an infinite sequence of points such that $\lim_{i\to\infty} \mathbf{x}_i = \mathbf{x}$. It suffices to show that $\lim_{i\to\infty} f(\mathbf{x}_i) = f(\mathbf{x})$ — i.e. that f is continuous on D_U. We take $\mathbf{x}_i$ and $\mathbf{x}$ equivalently to be the initial state of the CRC giving the concentrations of species in $\Sigma = \{X_1, \ldots, X_k\}$.

In analyzing the behavior of the CRC on states in D_U, it will help us to consider the functionally equivalent CRC in which we remove species that are not producible from states in D_U. For the purposes of this proof we consider this reduced CRC, and let Λ be the corresponding reduced set of species.

Let $\delta = \min_{i \in U} \mathbf{x}(i)$ be the smallest concentration of an initially positive species. Let $\mathbf{d} \in \mathbb{R}^k_{\geq 0}$ be the state $\mathbf{d}(X_i) = \delta$ for all $i \in U$ and $\mathbf{d}(S) = 0$ for all other species S. By an argument similar to the proof of Lemma 2.4, we can reach from $\mathbf{d}$ by at most m straight line segments to a state $\mathbf{e}$ such that $[\mathbf{e}] = \Lambda$. Because of the way we defined $\mathbf{d}$, $\mathbf{x}_i \geq \mathbf{d}$ and $\mathbf{x} \geq \mathbf{d}$. Thus, letting $\mathbf{a}_i = \mathbf{x}_i + \mathbf{e} - \mathbf{d}$, we have that $\mathbf{x}_i \to_{\mathbf{s}} \mathbf{a}_i$ for some fixed $\mathbf{s}$, and $[\mathbf{a}_i] = \Lambda$. Further, $\mathbf{a} = \lim_{i\to\infty} \mathbf{a}_i = (\lim_{i\to\infty} \mathbf{x}_i) + \mathbf{e} - \mathbf{d} = \mathbf{x} + \mathbf{e} - \mathbf{d}$. Thus, $\mathbf{x} \to_{\mathbf{s}} \mathbf{a}$ and $[\mathbf{a}] = \Lambda$.

Since there are a finite number of output siphons, by the pigeonhole principle, one such output siphon Ω must be drainable from infinitely many such states $\mathbf{a}_i$ (via a straight line as observed previously since $[\mathbf{a}_i] = \Lambda$). Let $\mathbf{o}_i$ be an output-stable state such that $\mathbf{a}_i \to^1 \mathbf{o}_i$.

There is a finite number of subsets of reactions that may occur in the final straight line segment from $\mathbf{a}_i$ to $\mathbf{o}_i$ with strictly positive flux, so one (call it R') must repeat infinitely often. We used an identical prefix of straight line segments $\mathbf{s}$ for all i to reach from $\mathbf{x}_i$ to $\mathbf{a}_i$. Letting $\mathbf{s}'$ be $\mathbf{s}$ concatenated with R', we have that $\mathbf{s}'$ is infinitely often the sequence of subsets of reactions with strictly positive flux, i.e., for infinitely many i, $\mathbf{x}_i \to_{\mathbf{s}} \mathbf{a}_i \to^1_{(R')} \mathbf{o}_i$ and the same siphon Ω is drained in all these $\mathbf{o}_i$.

Let this infinite subsequence of $\mathbf{a}_i$ states agreeing on Ω and R' (and thus $\mathbf{s}'$) be denoted $\mathbf{a}'_1, \mathbf{a}'_2, \ldots \in \mathbb{R}^n_{\geq 0}$. Let $\mathbf{x}'_1, \mathbf{x}'_2, \ldots \in \mathbb{R}^k$ be the initial states corresponding to the subsequence $(\mathbf{a}'_i)$ (i.e., $\mathbf{x}'_i \to_{\mathbf{s}} \mathbf{a}'_i$ as described before).

Clearly, $\mathbf{x}'_i \in X_{\mathbf{s}'}(\Omega)$. Further, observe that the limit $\lim_{i\to\infty} \mathbf{a}'_i = \lim_{i\to\infty} \mathbf{a}_i = \mathbf{a}$, and recall $[\mathbf{a}] = \Lambda$. Since $\mathbf{a}'_i \in X_{(R')}(\Omega)$ and $[\mathbf{a}] = \Lambda$, this implies by Lemma 3.11, $\mathbf{a} \in X_{(R')}(\Omega)$. Since $(\mathbf{x}'_i)$ is a infinite subsequence of a sequence converging to $\mathbf{x}$, $\mathbf{x} = \lim_{i\to\infty} \mathbf{x}'_i$. Since $\mathbf{x} \to_{\mathbf{s}} \mathbf{a}$ and $\mathbf{a} \in X_{(R')}(\Omega)$, it follows that $\mathbf{x} \in X_{\mathbf{s}'}(\Omega)$.

By Lemma 3.9, f is rational linear – hence continuous – on inputs in $X_{\mathbf{s}'}(\Omega)$. Because $\mathbf{x}, \mathbf{x}'_1, \mathbf{x}'_2, \ldots \in X_{\mathbf{s}'}(\Omega)$, the continuity on inputs in $X_{\mathbf{s}'}(\Omega)$ implies that $f(\mathbf{x}) = \lim_{i\to\infty} f(\mathbf{x}'_i)$, which equals $\lim_{i\to\infty} f(\mathbf{x}_i)$ since $\mathbf{x}'_i$ is a subsequence of $\mathbf{x}_i$. Since $\mathbf{x}$ was arbitrary and $\mathbf{x}_1, \mathbf{x}_2, \ldots$ was an arbitrary sequence converging to $\mathbf{x}$, it follows that f is continuous. □

LEMMA 3.13. *Let $f : \mathbb{R}^k \to \mathbb{R}$ be stably dual-computable by a CRC. Then f is continuous and piecewise rational linear.*

PROOF. Let $\mathcal{C}$ be the CRC stably computing a dual-rail representation $\hat{f}$ of f, with input species $X_1^+, \ldots, X_k^+, X_1^-, \ldots, X_k^-$ and output species Y^+, Y^-.

Similarly to the proof of Lemma 3.10, a dual-rail computing CRC can be thought to *directly* compute two separate functions $\hat{f}^+, \hat{f}^- : \mathbb{R}^{2k}_{\geq 0} \to \mathbb{R}_{\geq 0}$ such that $\hat{f} = \hat{f}^+ - \hat{f}^-$ where $\hat{f}$ is a dual rail representation of f. Let $\delta > 0$. Then for *any* input $\mathbf{x}' \in \mathbb{R}^k$ to f, there is an initial state $\mathbf{x} \in \mathbb{R}^\Sigma_{\geq \delta}$ representing $\mathbf{x}'$. Any sequences inputs $\mathbf{x}'_1, \mathbf{x}'_2, \ldots \in \mathbb{R}^k$ to f such that $\lim_{i\to\infty} \mathbf{x}'_i = \mathbf{x}'$ are similarly represented by a sequence $\mathbf{x}_1, \mathbf{x}_2, \ldots \in \mathbb{R}^\Sigma_{\geq 0}$ of initial states of the CRC such that $\lim_{i\to\infty} \mathbf{x}_i = \mathbf{x}$ has the property that all but finitely many $\mathbf{x}_i$ obey $[\mathbf{x}_i] = \Sigma$. By Lemma 3.12, f is continuous on the domain in which all input species are positive, which includes the input represented by $\mathbf{x}$ and the inputs represented by all but finitely many of $\mathbf{x}_i$. Therefore, $f(\mathbf{x}') = \lim_{i\to\infty} f(\mathbf{x}'_i)$, so f is continuous.

It remains to show that f is piecewise rational linear. If $\mathbf{x}$ is an initial state and $\mathbf{x} \to \mathbf{o}$ where $\mathbf{o}$ is output stable, then by Lemma 2.4, $\mathbf{x} \rightsquigarrow^{m+1} \mathbf{o}$. Let Ω be an output siphon such that $\mathbf{o} \upharpoonright \Omega = \mathbf{0}$, which exists by Lemma 3.5. Let $\mathbf{s} = (R_1, \ldots, R_l) \in \mathcal{P}(R)^l$, where $\mathbf{x} \to_{\mathbf{s}} \mathbf{o}$, where by Lemma 2.4 we may assume $l \leq m+1$. By Lemma 3.10, this value of y is a rational linear function of $\mathbf{x}$. Since there are a finite number of output siphons and sequences in $\mathcal{P}(R)^{\leq m+1}$, this establishes the piecewise rational linearity of f. □

4. FUNCTIONS OVER NONNEGATIVE REALS USING DIRECT REPRESENTATION

In this section, we show an analogous result to Theorem 3.1 for CRNs that compute functions *directly*, instead of computing a dual-rail representation. As a result, since concentrations are nonnegative, we may only compute functions $f : \mathbb{R}^k_{\geq 0} \to \mathbb{R}_{\geq 0}$. Interestingly, the class of computable functions expands slightly to include some discontinuous functions, specifically the *positive-continuous* functions defined in Section 3.

THEOREM 4.1. *A function $f : \mathbb{R}^k_{\geq 0} \to \mathbb{R}_{\geq 0}$ is stably computable by a CRN if and only if f is positive-continuous and piecewise rational linear.*

We prove each direction of Theorem 4.1 separately via Lemmas 4.2 and 4.4.

4.1 Positive-continuous piecewise rational linear functions are computable

LEMMA 4.2. *Every positive-continuous piecewise linear function $f : \mathbb{R}^k_{\geq 0} \to \mathbb{R}_{\geq 0}$ is stably computable by a CRN.*

PROOF. The CRN will have input species $X_1, \ldots, X_k$ and output species Y^+. (While it will be helpful to think of a Y^+ and Y^- species, and during the computation the output will be encoded in their difference, the output of the CRC is only the Y^+ species as per direct computability.)

Let $f : \mathbb{R}^k_{\geq 0} \to \mathbb{R}_{\geq 0}$ be a positive-continuous piecewise linear function. Since it is positive-continuous, there exist 2^k domains

$$D_U = \{\mathbf{x} \in \mathbb{R}^k_{\geq 0} \mid (\forall i \in \{1, \ldots, k\})\ \mathbf{x}(i) > 0 \iff i \in U\},$$

one for each subset $U \subseteq \{1, \ldots, k\}$, such that $f \upharpoonright D_U$ is continuous on D_U. Define $f_U = f \upharpoonright D_U$.

Since each D_U is convex, by Lemma 3.3, there is a CRN $\mathcal{C}_U$ monotonically computing a dual-rail representation $\hat{f}_U : \mathbb{R}^k_{\geq 0} \times \mathbb{R}^k_{\geq 0} \to \mathbb{R} \times \mathbb{R}$ of f_U. By letting the initial concentration of the "minus" version of the i'th input species X_i^- be 0, we convert $\mathcal{C}_U$ into a CRN that directly computes an output dual-rail representation of f_U.

The intuition of the proof is as follows. The case $U = \varnothing$ is trivial, as we will have no reactions of the form $\varnothing \to A$ for any species A, so if no species are initially present, no species (including Y^+) will ever be produced. For each nonempty U, we compute f_U independently in parallel by CRN $\mathcal{C}_U$, modifying each reaction producing Y^+ to produce an equivalent amount of species Y_U, which is specific to U. For each such U there are inactive and active "indicator" species J_U and I_U. In parallel, there are reactions that will activate indicator species I_U (i.e. convert J_U to I_U) if and only if all species X_i are present initially for each $i \in U$. These I_U species will then counteract the effect of any CRN computing $f_{U'}$ for $U' \subset U$ by catalytically converting all $Y_{U'}$ to Y^-. If

U is the complete set of indices of non-zero inputs, then only CRNs computing $f_{U'}$ for subsets $U' \subset U$ have produced any amount of Y^+, so eventually all of these will be counteracted by I_U.

Formally, construct the CRN as follows. For each $i \in \{1,\ldots,k\}$, add the reaction $X_i \to I_{\{i\}} + J_{\{i\}} + J_{U_1} + X_i^{U_1} + J_{U_2} + X_i^{U_2} + \ldots + J_{U_l} + X_i^{U_l}$, where $U_1, U_2, \ldots, U_l$ are all subsets of $\{1,\ldots,k\}$ that are strict supersets of $\{i\}$. The extra versions of X_i are used as inputs to the parallel computation of each f_U. We generate the inactive indicator species from the input species in this manner, because the CRN is not allowed to start with anything other than the input.

The indicator species are activated as follows. For each nonempty $U, U' \subseteq \{1,\ldots,k\}$ such that $U \neq U'$, add the reaction $I_U + I_{U'} + J_{U \cup U'} \to I_U + I_{U'} + I_{U \cup U'}$.

For each nonempty $U \subseteq \{1,\ldots,k\}$, let $\mathcal{C}_U$ be the CRN computing an output dual-rail representation of f_U (i.e. dual rail on the output). Modify $\mathcal{C}_U$ as follows. Rename the output species of $\mathcal{C}_U$ to Y^+ and Y^-, i.e., all parallel CRNs share the same output species. For each reaction producing the output species Y^+, add the product Y_U^+ (which is a species specific to $\mathcal{C}_U$) with the same net stoichimetry. Similarly, for each reaction producing the output species Y^-, add the product Y_U^- with the same net stoichimetry. For instance, replace the reaction $A + B \to Y^+$ by the reaction $A + B \to Y^+ + Y_U^+$, and replace the reaction $A + Y^+ \to B + 4Y^+$ by the reaction $A + Y^+ \to B + 4Y^+ + 3Y_U^+$. Therefore the eventual amount of Y_U^+ is equal to the total amount of Y^+ produced by $\mathcal{C}_U$, and similarly for Y_U^- and Y^-. For each $U' \subset U$, add the reactions $I_U + Y_{U'}^+ \to I_U + Y^-$, $I_U + Y_{U'}^- \to I_U + Y^+$. Also, for each reaction in $\mathcal{C}_U$, add I_U as a catalyst. This ensures that $\mathcal{C}_U$ cannot execute any reactions (and therefore cannot produce any amount of Y^+ or Y^-) unless all species X_i for $i \in U$ are present. Finally, add the reaction $Y^+ + Y^- \to \varnothing$. □

The following lemma shows that our construction actually converges to the correct output value under mass-action kinetics; it follows similarly to Lemma 3.4.

LEMMA 4.3. *For any input state* $\mathbf{x}$, *for any state* $\mathbf{z}$ *reachable from* $\mathbf{x}$, *the mass-action trajectory of the CRN of Lemma 4.2 with any non-zero rate constants starting at* $\mathbf{z}$ *converges to the output stable state in the limit* $t \to \infty$.

4.2 Computable functions are positive-continuous piecewise rational linear

In this section we prove that stable CRNs can compute only the positive-continuous piecewise linear functions.

LEMMA 4.4. *Let* $f : \mathbb{R}^k_{\geq 0} \to \mathbb{R}_{\geq 0}$ *be stably computable by a CRC. Then* f *is positive-continuous and piecewise rational linear.*

PROOF. Let $\mathcal{C}$ be the CRC stably computing f, with input species $X_1, \ldots, X_k$ and output species Y. By Lemma 3.12, f is positive-continuous.

It remains to show that f is piecewise rational linear. If $\mathbf{x}$ is an initial state and $\mathbf{x} \to \mathbf{o}$ where $\mathbf{o}$ is output stable, then by Lemma 2.4, $\mathbf{x} \rightsquigarrow^{m+1} \mathbf{o}$. Let Ω be an output siphon such that $\mathbf{o} \upharpoonright \Omega = \mathbf{0}$, which exists by Lemma 3.5. Let $\mathbf{s} = (R_1, \ldots, R_l) \in \mathcal{P}(R)^l$, where $\mathbf{x} \to_{\mathbf{s}} \mathbf{o}$, where by Lemma 2.4 we may assume $l \leq m+1$. By Lemma 3.9, this value of y is a rational linear function of $\mathbf{x}$. Since there are a finite number of output siphons and sequences in $\mathcal{P}(R)^{\leq m+1}$, this establishes the piecewise rational linearity of f. □

5. ACKNOWLEDGEMENTS

We thank Manoj Gopalkrishnan, Elisa Franco, Damien Woods, and the organizers and participants of the American Mathematical Institute workshop on Mathematical Problems Arising from Biochemical Reaction Networks for insightful discussions. We are grateful to anonymous reviewers for insightful comments and suggestions that have improved this paper. DD was supported by the Molecular Programming Project under NSF grants 0832824 and 1317694 and by NSF grants CCF-1219274 and CCF-1162589. DS was supported by NIGMS Systems Biology Center grant P50 GM081879.

6. REFERENCES

[1] U. Alon. *Introduction to Systems Biology: Design Principles of Biological Circuits.* CRC press, 2006.

[2] D. Angeli, P. De Leenheer, and E. D. Sontag. On the structural monotonicity of chemical reaction networks. In *45th IEEE Conference on Decision and Control*, pages 7–12. IEEE, 2006.

[3] D. Angeli, P. De Leenheer, and E. D. Sontag. A Petri net approach to the study of persistence in chemical reaction networks. *Mathematical Biosciences*, 210(2):598–618, 2007.

[4] D. Angluin, J. Aspnes, and D. Eisenstat. Stably computable predicates are semilinear. In *PODC 2006: Proceedings of the twenty-fifth annual ACM symposium on Principles of distributed computing*, pages 292–299, New York, NY, USA, 2006. ACM Press.

[5] N. Barkai and S. Leibler. Robustness in simple biochemical networks. *Nature*, 387(6636):913–917, 1997.

[6] O. Bournez, P. Chassaing, J. Cohen, L. Gerin, and X. Koegler. On the convergence of population protocols when population goes to infinity. *Applied Mathematics and Computation*, 215(4):1340–1350, 2009.

[7] L. Cardelli. Strand algebras for DNA computing. *Natural Computing*, 10(1):407–428, 2011.

[8] L. Cardelli and A. Csikász-Nagy. The cell cycle switch computes approximate majority. *Scientific Reports*, 2, 2012.

[9] H.-L. Chen, D. Doty, and D. Soloveichik. Deterministic function computation with chemical reaction networks. *Natural Computing*, 2013. to appear. Preliminary version appeared in DNA 2012.

[10] Y.-J. Chen, N. Dalchau, N. Srinivas, A. Phillips, L. Cardelli, D. Soloveichik, and G. Seelig. Programmable chemical controllers made from DNA. *Nature Nanotechnology*, 8(10):755–762, 2013.

[11] D. T. Gillespie. Exact stochastic simulation of coupled chemical reactions. *Journal of Physical Chemistry*, 81(25):2340–2361, 1977.

[12] M. Gopalkrishnan, E. Miller, and A. Shiu. A projection argument for differential inclusions, with applications to persistence of mass-action kinetics. *Symmetry, Integrability and Geometry: Methods and Applications*, 9(0):25–25, 2013.

[13] H. K. Khalil. *Nonlinear systems.* Prentice Hall, 2002.

[14] T. G. Kurtz. The relationship between stochastic and deterministic models for chemical reactions. *The Journal of Chemical Physics*, 57(7):2976–2978, 1972.

[15] S. Ovchinnikov. Max-min representation of piecewise linear functions. *Contributions to Algebra and Geometry*, 43(1):297–302, 2002.

[16] L. Qian and E. Winfree. Scaling up digital circuit computation with DNA strand displacement cascades. *Science*, 332(6034):1196, 2011.

[17] M. S. Samoilov and A. P. Arkin. Deviant effects in molecular reaction pathways. *Nature biotechnology*, 24(10):1235–1240, 2006.

[18] G. Seelig, D. Soloveichik, D. Y. Zhang, and E. Winfree. Enzyme-free nucleic acid logic circuits. *Science*, 314(5805):1585–1588, 2006.

[19] D. Soloveichik, M. Cook, E. Winfree, and J. Bruck. Computation with finite stochastic chemical reaction networks. *Natural Computing*, 7(4):615–633, 2008.

[20] D. Soloveichik, G. Seelig, and E. Winfree. DNA as a universal substrate for chemical kinetics. *Proceedings of the National Academy of Sciences*, 107(12):5393, 2010. Preliminary version appeared in DNA 2008.

Testers and their Applications

[Extended Abstract] *

Nader H. Bshouty
Dept. of Computer Science
Technion, Haifa
bshouty@cs.technion.ac.il

ABSTRACT

We develop a new notion called *tester of a class $\mathcal{M}$ of functions $f : \mathcal{A} \to \mathcal{C}$* that maps the elements $\boldsymbol{a} \in \mathcal{A}$ in the domain $\mathcal{A}$ of the function to a finite number (the size of the tester) of elements $\boldsymbol{b}_1, \ldots, \boldsymbol{b}_t$ in a smaller sub-domain $\mathcal{B} \subset \mathcal{A}$ where the property $f(\boldsymbol{a}) \neq 0$ is preserved for all $f \in \mathcal{M}$. I.e., for all $f \in \mathcal{M}$ and $\boldsymbol{a} \in \mathcal{A}$ if $f(\boldsymbol{a}) \neq 0$ then $f(\boldsymbol{b}_i) \neq 0$ for some i.
We use tools from elementary algebra and algebraic function fields to construct testers of almost optimal size in deterministic polynomial time in the size of the tester. We then apply testers to deterministically construct new set of objects with some combinatorial and algebraic properties that can be used to derandomize some algorithms.
We show that those new constructions are almost optimal and for many of them meet the union bound of the problem. Constructions include, d-restriction problems, perfect hash, universal sets, cover-free families, separating hash functions, polynomial restriction problems, black box polynomial identity testing for polynomials and circuits over small fields and hitting sets.

Keywords

Combinatorial objects, Derandomization, d-Restriction problems, Perfect hash, Universal sets, Cover-Free families, Separating hash functions, Hitting sets, Polynomial restriction problems, Polynomial identity testing (PIT).

1. INTRODUCTION

1.1 Testers

A *tester* of a class of multivariate polynomials $\mathcal{M}$ over n variables is a set L of maps from a complex (algebraic) structure $\mathcal{A}^n$ to a simple one $\mathcal{B}^n$ that preserve the property $f(\boldsymbol{a}) \neq 0$ for every $f \in \mathcal{M}$, i.e., for all $f \in \mathcal{M}$ and $\boldsymbol{a} \in \mathcal{A}^n$ if $f(\boldsymbol{a}) \neq 0$ then $f(\ell(\boldsymbol{a})) \neq 0$ for some $\ell \in L$. In this paper we study testers when $\mathcal{A}$, the domain of the functions in $\mathcal{M}$, is a field or a subspace of a field and $\mathcal{B} \subset \mathcal{A}$ is a small subfield. We use tools from elementary algebra and algebraic function fields to construct testers of almost optimal size $|L|$ in deterministic polynomial time.
One application of testers is the following: Suppose we need to construct a small set of vectors $S \subset \Sigma^n$ for some alphabet Σ that satisfies some property P. We map Σ into a field $\mathbb{F}$ and find a set of functions $\mathcal{M}_P$ where $S \subset \mathbb{F}^n$ satisfies property P if and only if S is a hitting set for $\mathcal{M}_P$, i.e., for every $f \in \mathcal{M}_P$ there is $\boldsymbol{a} \in S$ such that $f(\boldsymbol{a}) \neq 0$. We then extend $\mathbb{F}$ to a larger field $\mathbb{K}$ (or $\mathbb{F}$-algebra $\mathcal{A}$). Find $S' \subset \mathbb{K}^n$ that is a hitting set for $\mathcal{M}_P$ (which supposed to be easier). Then use tester to change the hitting set $S' \subset \mathbb{K}^n$ over $\mathbb{K}$ to a hitting set $S \subset \mathbb{F}^n$ over $\mathbb{F}$.
In this paper we consider two main classes of multivariate polynomials over finite fields $\mathbb{F}_q$ with q elements. The first class is $\mathcal{P}(\mathbb{F}_q, n, d)$, the class of all multivariate polynomials with n variables and total degree d. The second class is $\mathcal{HLF}(\mathbb{F}_q, n, d)$, the class of all multivariate polynomials f with dn variables $x_{i,j}$, $i = 1, \ldots, d$, $j = 1, \ldots, n$ where each monomial in f is of the form $x_{1,i_1} x_{2,i_2} \cdots x_{d,i_d}$. Also called multilinear form.
For the class $\mathcal{P}(\mathbb{F}_q, n, d)$ we give the following testers that map elements from $\mathcal{A} = \mathbb{F}_{q^t}$ to $\mathcal{B} = \mathbb{F}_q$ (see the following two tables. The first is for deterministic poly time and 2^t time construction and the second is for explicit construction and lower bound)
In the table I.S. stands for "infinite sequence of integers t" and P.S. stands for "perfect square". The second column in the first table gives bounds on q, the size of the field. The parameter c is any constant greater than 1. Notice that when $q < d + 1$ no tester exists for $\mathcal{P}(\mathbb{F}_q, n, d)$. The third column gives the size of testers that can be constructed in polynomial time.

t	q	Poly time size=$O()$	2^t time size=$O()$
All	$q \geq d(t-1)+1$	dt	dt
I.S.	$q \geq c(d+1)^2$, q P.S.	d^3t	d^2t
All	$q \geq c(d+1)^2$, q P.S.	d^3t	d^2t
I.S.	$q \geq c(d+1)$	d^4t	d^3t
All	$q \geq c(d+1)$	d^4t	d^3t
I.S.	$q \geq d+1$	d^5t	d^4t
All	$q \geq d+1$	d^5t	d^4t
All	$q < d+1$		

*A full version of this paper is available in Electronic Colloquium on Computational Complexity, (ECCC), Report No. 11 (2012) at `http://eccc.hpi-web.de/`

ITCS'14, January 12–14, 2014, Princeton, New Jersey, USA.
Copyright 2014 ACM 978-1-4503-2698-8/14/01 ...$15.00.
http://dx.doi.org/10.1145/2554797.2554828 .

t	q	Explicit size=$O()$	Lower Bound size=$\Omega()$
All	$q \geq d(t-1)+1$	dt	dt
I.S.	$q \geq c(d+1)^2$, q P.S.	dt	dt
All	$q \geq c(d+1)^2$, q P.S.	d^2t	dt
I.S.	$q \geq c(d+1)$	d^2t	dt
All	$q \geq c(d+1)$	d^3t	dt
I.S.	$q \geq d+1$	d^3t	dt
All	$q \geq d+1$	d^4t	dt
All	$q < d+1$		∞

Table 1

The fourth column gives the size of the testers that can be constructed in time 2^t. This will be used for fields $\mathbb{F}_{q^r}$ where $r = O(\log t)$. The fifth column (the third column in the second table) gives the size of the testers that can be explicitly constructed[1] but are not known to be polynomial time constructed. The last column gives lower bounds. For example, the second row and third column in the table says that, for any constant $c > 1$, perfect square $q \geq c(d+1)^2$ there is a tester L for $\mathcal{P}(\mathbb{F}_q, n, d)$ of size $O(d^3t)$ for infinite sequence of integers t.
We then study testers for $\mathcal{P}(\mathbb{F}_q, n, d)$ that map subspaces $S \subseteq \mathbb{F}_{q^T}$ of size q^t to $\mathbb{F}_q$ for some $T > t$. We were able to give better bounds for the size of such testers that can be constructed in deterministic polynomial time. For small t those bounds match the size of the explicit constructions in the above table.
For the class $\mathcal{HLF}(\mathbb{F}_q, n, d)$ when $q \geq d+1$ the testers for $\mathcal{P}(\mathbb{F}_q, n, d)$ are also testers for $\mathcal{HLF}(\mathbb{F}_q, n, d)$. For $q = d$ we have a tester of size $O(d^6t)$. For $q < d$ we give the following testers that map elements from $\mathcal{A} = \mathbb{F}_{q^t}$ to $\mathcal{B} = \mathbb{F}_q$

q	Upper Bound size =	Lower Bound size =
2	$2^{1.66d} \cdot t$	$2^d \cdot t$
3	$2^{1.12d} \cdot t$	$2^{0.58d} \cdot t$
4	$2^{0.87d} \cdot t$	$2^{0.41d} \cdot t$
5	$2^{0.72d} \cdot t$	$2^{0.32d} \cdot t$
7	$2^{0.55d} \cdot t$	$2^{0.22d} \cdot t$
q	$2^{O(\log q/q)d} \cdot t$	$2^{\Omega(1/q)d} \cdot t$

Table 2

The upper bound and lower bounds are bounds on the size of the testers. The time complexity of constructing the above testers is within $poly(t)$ of their upper bound size.

1.2 d-Restriction Problems

We apply testers to the following problems.
d-Restriction Problems: A *d-restriction problem* [43, 4] is a problem of the following form: Given an alphabet Σ of size $|\Sigma| = q$, a length n and a class $\mathcal{M}$ of nonzero functions $f_i : \Sigma^d \to \{0,1\}$, $i = 1, 2, \ldots, t$. Find a set $A \subseteq \Sigma^n$ of small size such that: For any $1 \leq i_1 < i_2 < \cdots < i_d \leq n$ and $f \in \mathcal{M}$ there is $\boldsymbol{a} \in A$ such that $f(a_{i_1}, \ldots, a_{i_d}) \neq 0$.
The d-restriction problems considered in this paper are perfect hash, universal sets, cover-free families and separating hash functions. Using tester we achieve an asymptotically optimal construction for those problems.

Perfect Hash: For $d \leq q$ we say that the set H of functions $h : [n] \to \mathbb{F}_q$ is a (n, q, d)-*perfect hashing* [4] (or (n, d, q)-*splitter* [43]) if for all subsets $S \subseteq [n]$ of size $|S| = d$ there is a *hash function* $h \in H$ such that $h|_S$ is injective (one-to-one) on S, i.e., $|h|_S(S)| = d$. Obviously, perfect hash is a d-restriction problem with the alphabet $\Sigma = \mathbb{F}_q$. In [43, 4] it was shown that there is an (n, d^2, d)-perfect hashing of size $O(d^4 \log d \log n)$ that can be constructed in $poly(n, d)$ time. Wang and Xing [64] used algebraic function fields and gave an explicit (n, d^4, d)-perfect hashing of size $O((d^2/\log d)\log n)$ for infinite sequence of integers n. The only known polynomial time construction is of size $O(d^4 \log d \log n)$ when $q = O(d^2)$, [43, 4]. Blackburn and Wild [18] gave an explicit optimal construction when q is very large compared to d and $\log n$. In this paper we use testers to give a polynomial time construction that is almost optimal for any q and n as described in the following

n	$q \geq$	poly time Size =	Union Bound	Lower Bound
I.S.	$\frac{c}{4}d^4$	$d^2 \frac{\log n}{\log q}$	$d \frac{\log n}{\log q}$	$\frac{\log n}{\log q}$
all	$\frac{c}{4}d^4$	$d^4 \frac{\log n}{\log q}$	$d \frac{\log n}{\log q}$	$\frac{\log n}{\log q}$
I.S.	$\frac{c}{2}d^2$	$d^4 \frac{\log n}{\log d}$	$\frac{d \log n}{\log(2q/(d(d-1)))}$	$\frac{\log n}{\log q}$
all	$\frac{c}{2}d^2$	$d^6 \frac{\log n}{\log d}$	$\frac{d \log n}{\log(2q/(d(d-1)))}$	$\frac{\log n}{\log q}$
I.S.	$\frac{d^2+d+2}{2}$	$d^6 \frac{\log n}{\log d}$	$d \log n$	$\frac{\log n}{\log q}$
all	$\frac{d^2+d+2}{2}$	$d^8 \frac{\log n}{\log d}$	$d \log n$	$\frac{\log n}{\log q}$

Table 3

In the table, I.S. means "for infinite sequence of integers n" and $c > 1$ is any constant. The union bound is a non-constructive bound that can be achieved using probabilistic method by randomly uniformly choosing hash functions [6].
Our results improve all the results in the literature and give the first polynomial time $O(\log n/\log q)$ size construction for a fixed d and any n and q.

Universal sets: Another d-restriction problem is the problem of (n, d)-universal set over an alphabet of size q. This problem is d-restriction problem where $\mathcal{M}$ contains all the nonzero functions $f : \Sigma^d \to \{0,1\}$. That is, $A \subseteq \mathbb{F}_q^n$ is (n, k)-universal set if for every $1 \leq i_1 < i_2 < \cdots < i_d \leq n$ and $\alpha_1, \ldots, \alpha_d \in \mathbb{F}_q$ there is $\boldsymbol{a} \in A$ such that $a_{i_1} = \alpha_1, a_{i_2} = \alpha_2, \ldots, a_{i_d} = \alpha_d$.
The lower bound $\Omega(q^{d-1} \log n/\log q)$ for the size of (n, d)-universal set over $\mathbb{F}_q$ can be derived from [36]. The union bound gives the upper bound $O(dq^d \log n)$. The best known polynomial time[2] construction for this problem gives a universal set of size $d^{O(\log d/\log q)} q^d \log n$ for $q < d$ and $O(d^5 (\log d)^2 \, q^d \log n)$, for $q > d$ [43, 2]. For $q < d$ the size of the construction in [43], $d^{O(\log d/\log q)} q^d \log n$, is better than the size we get here. For $q \geq d$ we give a polynomial time construction of (n, d)-universal set of size $O(d^4 (q^d/\log q) \log n)$. When $q = \Omega(d^2)$ and perfect square, for infinite number of integers n, we give a polynomial time construction of size $O(d^2 (q^d/\log q) \log n)$ and an explicit construction of size $O(d(q^d/\log q) \log n)$. Although

[1] In this paper, when we say "explicit construction" we mean a construction that uses elementary algebra and algebraic function fields in which each step of the construction is indicated. But it is not clear if the construction is polynomial time construction.

[2] In this paper, when we say polynomial time we mean $poly(n) \cdot s$ where s is the size of the construction.

those results slightly improve the existing results from the literature, the latter bound is a surprising result since it exceeds the union bound $O(dq^d \log n)$ achieved by probabilistic method. This shows that our new technique may lead to new combinatorial bounds that exceed the union bounds.
The following two tables summarize the results

n	q	Poly Time Size=
I.S.	$q \ge c(d+1)^2$, q P.S.	$d^2 q^d \frac{\log n}{\log q}$
all	$q \ge c(d+1)^2$, q P.S.	$d^2 q^d \frac{\log n}{\log q}$
I.S.	$q \ge c(d+1)$	$d^3 q^d \frac{\log n}{\log d}$
all	$q \ge c(d+1)$	$d^3 q^d \frac{\log n}{\log d}$
I.S.	$q \ge d+1$	$d^4 q^d \frac{\log n}{\log d}$
all	$q \ge d+1$	$d^4 q^d \frac{\log n}{\log d}$
all	$q \le d+1$	$d^7 q^{(1+c_q/\log q)d} \log n$
all	$q = 2$	$d^7 2^{2.66d} \log n$

n	q	Explicit Size=
I.S.	$q \ge c(d+1)^2$, q P.S.	$dq^d \frac{\log n}{\log q}$
all	$q \ge c(d+1)^2$, q P.S.	$d^2 q^d \frac{\log n}{\log q}$
I.S.	$q \ge c(d+1)$	$d^2 q^d \frac{\log n}{\log d}$
all	$q \ge c(d+1)$	$d^3 q^d \frac{\log n}{\log d}$
I.S.	$q \ge d+1$	$d^3 q^d \frac{\log n}{\log d}$
all	$q \ge d+1$	$d^4 q^d \frac{\log n}{\log d}$
all	$q \le d+1$	$d^5 q^{(1+c_q/\log q)d} \log n$
all	$q = 2$	$d^5 2^{2.66d} \log n$

Table 4

In the table $c \ge 1$ is any constant, I.S. means "for infinite sequence of integers n", P.S. means "perfect square" and c_q is the constant from Theorem 21.

Cover-Free Families (CFF): Let X be a set with N elements and $\mathcal{B}$ be a set of subsets (blocks) of X. We say that $(X, \mathcal{B})$ is *(w,r)-cover-free family* ((w,r)-CFF), [35], if for any w blocks $B_1, \ldots, B_w \in \mathcal{B}$ and any other r blocks $A_1, \ldots, A_r \in \mathcal{B}$, we have $\bigcap_{i=1}^{w} B_i \not\subseteq \bigcup_{j=1}^{r} A_j$. The goal is to find (w,r)-CFF with small N. Let $N((w,r),n)$ denotes the minimum number of points in any (w,r)-CFF having n blocks. When $w=1$, the problem is called *group testing.* It is easy to see that CFF is d-restriction problem.
The problem (w,r)-cover-free family is equivalent to the following problem: A (w,r)-cover-free family is a set $\mathcal{F} \subseteq \{0,1\}^n$ such that for every $1 \le i_1 < i_2 < \cdots < i_d \le n$ where $d = w + r$ and every $J \subset [d]$ of size $|J| = w$ there is $\boldsymbol{a} \in \mathcal{F}$ such that $a_{i_k} = 0$ for all $k \notin J$ and $a_{i_j} = 1$ for all $j \in J$. Then $N((w,r),n)$ is the minimum size of such $\mathcal{F}$. There are several lower bounds for $N((w,r),n)$. We give the one in [61]

$$N((w,r),n) \ge \Omega\left(\frac{d\binom{d}{w}}{\log\binom{d}{w}} \log n\right).$$

It follows from [62], that for infinite sequence of integers n, a (w,r)-cover free family of size $M = O\left((wr)^{\log^* n} \log n\right)$ can be constructed in polynomial time. In [39], Liu and Shen show that for fixed d (and therefore fixed w,r) there is an explicit construction of size $O(\log n)$ for infinite sequence of integers n. This also follows, for all n and fixed d, from the (n,d)-universal set constructed in [42].

In this paper we show: for any constant $c > 1$, the following (w,r)-CFF can be constructed in polynomial time

n	w	Poly time Size=	Union Bound
I.S	$O(1)$	$\frac{r^{w+2}}{\log r} \log n$	$r^{w+1} \log n$
all	$O(1)$	$\frac{r^{w+3}}{\log r} \log n$	$r^{w+1} \log n$
I.S.	$o(r)$	$\frac{w^2 (ce)^w r^{w+2}}{\log r} \log n$	$\frac{r^{w+1}}{(w/e)^{w-1/2}} \log n$
all	$o(r)$	$\frac{w^3 (ce)^w r^{w+3}}{\log r} \log n$	$\frac{r^{w+1}}{(w/e)^{w-1/2}} \log n$

n	w	Lower Bound
I.S	$O(1)$	$\frac{r^{w+1}}{\log r} \log n$
all	$O(1)$	$\frac{r^{w+1}}{\log r} \log n$
I.S.	$o(r)$	$\frac{r^{w+1}}{(w/e)^{w+1} \log r} \log n$
all	$o(r)$	$\frac{r^{w+1}}{(w/e)^{w+1} \log r} \log n$

Table 5

To the best of our knowledge, this is the first asymptotically optimal (within $poly(r)$) construction for any d, $w = O(1)$ and n. For $w = o(r)$ our construction is within $r^{o(w)}$ of the lower bound.

Separating Hash Family: Let X and Σ be sets of size n and q, respectively. We call a set $\mathcal{F}$ of functions $f : X \to \Sigma$ an $(M; n, q, \{d_1, d_2, \ldots, d_r\})$ *separating hash family* (SHF), [58, 59], if $|\mathcal{F}| = M$ and for all pairwise disjoint subsets $C_1, C_2, \ldots, C_r \subseteq X$ with $|C_i| = d_i$ for $i = 1, 2, \ldots, r$, there is at least one function $f \in \mathcal{F}$ such that $f(C_1), f(C_2), \ldots, f(C_r)$ are pairwise disjoint subsets. The minimal M is denoted by $M(n, q, \{d_1, d_2, \ldots, d_r\})$. It is easy to see that this problem is d-restriction problem.
In [17], Bazrafshan and Trund proved that for $D_1 = d_1 + d_2 + \cdots + d_r$,

$$M(n, q, \{d_1, d_2, \ldots, d_r\}) = \Omega\left(D_1 \frac{\log n}{\log q}\right).$$

In [62], Stinson et. al. proved that an $(M; n, q, \{d_1, d_2\})$ separating hash families of size $M = O((d_1 d_2)^{\log^* n} \log n)$ can be constructed in polynomial time for infinite sequence of integers n and $q > d_1 d_2$. The same proof gives a polynomial time construction for any separating hash family of size $M = O(D_2^{\log^* n} \log n)$ where $D_2 = \sum_{1 \le i_1 < i_2 \le r} d_{i_1} d_{i_2}$ when $q > D_2$.
In [39], Liu and Shen provide an explicit construction of $(M; n, q, \{d_1, d_2\})$ separating hash family using algebraic curves over finite fields. They show that for infinite sequence of integers n there is an explicit $(M; n, q, \{d_1, d_2\})$ separating hash families of size $O(\log n)$ for fixed d_1 and d_2. This also follows from [42], an $(n, d_1 + d_2)$-universal set over $\{0,1\}$ is a separating hash family of size $O(\log n)$ for fixed d_1 and d_2. In this paper we give a polynomial time construction of an $(M; n, q, \{d_1, d_2\})$ separating hash family of size $M = ((d_1 d_2)^4 \log n / \log q)$ for any $q \ge d_1 d_2 (1 + o(1))$ and any n.
We show, for constant $c > 1$ and $q > D_2$, the following $(M; n, q, \{d_1, d_2, \ldots, d_r\})$ separating hash families can be constructed in polynomial time

n	q	poly time Size =	Union Bound	Lower Bound [15]
I.S.	$q \ge cD_2^2$	$D_2 \frac{\log n}{\log q}$	$D_1 \frac{\log n}{\log q}$	$D_1 \frac{\log n}{\log q}$
all	$q \ge cD_2^2$	$D_2^2 \frac{\log n}{\log q}$	$D_1 \frac{\log n}{\log q}$	$D_1 \frac{\log n}{\log q}$
I.S.	$q \ge cD_2$	$D_2^2 \frac{\log n}{\log d}$	$D_1 \frac{\log n}{\log(q/D_2))}$	$D_1 \frac{\log n}{\log q}$
all	$q \ge cD_2$	$D_2^3 \frac{\log n}{\log d}$	$D_1 \frac{\log n}{\log(q/D_2)}$	$D_1 \frac{\log n}{\log q}$
I.S.	$q > D_2$	$D_2^3 \frac{\log n}{\log q}$	$D_1 \log n$	$D_1 \frac{\log n}{\log q}$
all	$q > D_2$	$D_2^4 \frac{\log n}{\log q}$	$D_1 \log n$	$D_1 \frac{\log n}{\log q}$

Table 6

We now turn to another application of tester.

1.3 Black Box PIT

The second application of tester is getting asymptotically optimal black box PIT sets for classes of multivariate polynomials over finite fields with substitutions from an extension field of optimal dimension.

The black box Polynomial Identity Testing (PIT) problem is the following: Given an arithmetic circuit C that either identical to the zero function or from a class of circuits $\mathcal{C}$ over a field $\mathbb{F}$, with input variables $x_1, x_2, \ldots, x_n$ and given a *substitution oracle* that for an input $\boldsymbol{a} \in \mathbb{F}^n$ returns $f(\boldsymbol{a})$. Determine whether C computes the identically zero polynomial. We say that $S \subset \mathbb{F}^n$ is a *black box PIT set* for $\mathcal{C}$ if for every $f \in \mathcal{C}$ there is $\boldsymbol{a} \in S$ such that $f(\boldsymbol{a}) \neq 0$.

When the field is finite $\mathbb{F}_q$ many simple classes of circuits, such as circuits that compute monomials, require black box PIT sets of exponential size. Therefore, many papers in the literature allow the substitution oracle to receive assignment $\boldsymbol{a}$ from some extension field $\mathbb{F}_{q^t}$ of $\mathbb{F}_q$. We say that $S \subset \mathbb{F}_{q^t}^n$ is a *black box PIT set over* $\mathbb{F}_{q^t}$ for $\mathcal{C}$ if for every $f \in \mathcal{C}$ there is $\boldsymbol{a} \in S$ such that $f(\boldsymbol{a}) \neq 0$. Our goal will be to minimize the size of the black box PIT set $|S|$ and minimize the dimension of the extension field t.

For this problem we use testers in the following way. First we construct an optimal black box PIT set S for the class over a large field $\mathbb{F}_{q^T}$. We then use a tester to map the assignments in S to assignments in a smaller field $\mathbb{F}_{q^t}$.

Asymptotically Optimal Black Box PIT Sets for Polynomials: We study the following classes of multivariate polynomials: $\mathcal{P}(\mathbb{F}_q, n)$ is the class of all multivariate polynomials in $\mathbb{F}_q[x_1, \ldots, x_n]$ of variable degree (maximal degree of the variables) at most $q-1$, $\mathcal{P}(\mathbb{F}_q, n, (d, r))$ is the class of all multivariate polynomials in $\mathcal{P}(\mathbb{F}_q, n)$ of degree at most d and variable degree at most $r \le q-1$, $\mathcal{P}(\mathbb{F}_q, n, d) = \mathcal{P}(\mathbb{F}_q, n, (d, q-1))$, $\mathcal{P}(\mathbb{F}_q, n, s)$ is the class of all multivariate polynomials in $\mathcal{P}(\mathbb{F}_q, n)$ with at most s monomials. Polynomials in the latter class are called in the literature "sparse multivariate polynomials". $\mathcal{P}(\mathbb{F}_q, n, (d, r)$ $, s)$ is the class of all multivariate polynomials in $\mathcal{P}(\mathbb{F}_q, n)$ of degree at most d, variable degree at most r and with at most s monomials.

To the best of our knowledge all the algorithms in the literature that construct black box PIT sets for the above classes are either randomized, deterministic for some fixed extension field $\mathbb{F}_{q^t}$ or obtain non-optimal results in both the extension field dimension and the size of the black box PIT set [27, 19, 63, 31, 37, 8]. In this paper we give polynomial time constructions of black box PIT sets of size that are within *poly*(n) of the optimal size, Also, the dimensions of the extension fields are optimal.

The following table summarizes some of our main results. See other results in the full paper [11].

Class	Field $\mathbb{F}_{q^t}$	Lower Bound
$\mathcal{P}(\mathbb{F}_q, n)$	$t \ge \log_q n + 2$	$\frac{q^n}{t}$
$\mathcal{P}(\mathbb{F}_q, n, r)$	$t \ge \log_q n + 2$	$\frac{(r+1)^n}{t}$
$\mathcal{P}(\mathbb{F}_q, n, (d, r))$	$t \ge \log_q (d+1)$	$\frac{R(n,d,r)}{t}$
$\mathcal{P}(\mathbb{F}_q, n, s)$	$t \ge \log_q n + 2$	$\frac{n \cdot s}{t}$
$\mathcal{P}(\mathbb{F}_q, n, r, s)$	$t \ge \log_q n + 2$	$\frac{n \log(r+1)}{\log q} \cdot \frac{s}{t}$
$\mathcal{P}(\mathbb{F}_q, n, (d, r), s)$	$t \ge \log_q (d+1)$	$\frac{d \log n}{\log q} \cdot \frac{s}{t}$

Class	Upper Bound	Explicit Construction
$\mathcal{P}(\mathbb{F}_q, n)$	$\frac{(\log(qn)) \cdot q^n}{t}$	$\frac{n \cdot q^n}{t}$
$\mathcal{P}(\mathbb{F}_q, n, r)$	$\frac{(\log(rn)) \cdot (r+1)^n}{t}$	$\frac{n \cdot (r+1)^n}{t}$
$\mathcal{P}(\mathbb{F}_q, n, (d, r))$	$\frac{(\log d) \cdot R(n,d,r)}{t}$	$\frac{dn^{d+1}}{t}$
$\mathcal{P}(\mathbb{F}_q, n, s)$	$\frac{(\log n) n \cdot s}{t}$	$\frac{q^5 n^6 \cdot s}{t}$
$\mathcal{P}(\mathbb{F}_q, n, r, s)$	$\frac{n (\log n) \log(r+1)}{\log q} \cdot \frac{s}{t}$	$\frac{n^6 r^5 \log(r+1)}{\log q} \cdot \frac{s}{t}$
$\mathcal{P}(\mathbb{F}_q, n, (d, r), s)$	$\frac{d (\log d) \log n}{\log q} \cdot \frac{s}{t}$	$\frac{d^6 \log n}{\log q} \cdot \frac{s}{t}$

Class	Poly Time Construction
$\mathcal{P}(\mathbb{F}_q, n)$	$\frac{n \cdot q^n}{t}$
$\mathcal{P}(\mathbb{F}_q, n, r)$	$\frac{n \cdot (r+1)^n}{t}$
$\mathcal{P}(\mathbb{F}_q, n, (d, r))$	$\frac{dn^{d+1}}{t}$
$\mathcal{P}(\mathbb{F}_q, n, s)$	$\frac{n^7 q^{29} (\log^2 q) \cdot s}{t}$
$\mathcal{P}(\mathbb{F}_q, n, r, s)$	$\frac{n^7 r^5 q^{24} (\log^2 r) \cdot s}{t}$
$\mathcal{P}(\mathbb{F}_q, n, (d, r), s)$	$\frac{q^{24} d^7 (\log^2 n) \cdot s}{t}$

Table 7

Notice that our polynomial time constructions (column 2 in the third table) are optimal in the largest parameters (q^n, $(r+1)^n$, n^d and s in the last three rows of the table). For sparse polynomials $\mathcal{P}(\mathbb{F}_q, n, s)$, $\mathcal{P}(\mathbb{F}_q, n, r, s)$ and $\mathcal{P}(\mathbb{F}_q, n, (d, r), s)$, all the results in the literature give black box PIT sets of size that are at least quadratic in the size s. Also, the tight tradeoff with the field dimension $(\cdot/t)$ in each row of the table was not known before. The bound on the dimension of the field extension in the second column is $\log_q(degree) + 1$ and is known to be the best possible dimension (even for randomized algorithms) if one uses DeMillo-Lipton-Schwartz-Zippel Lemma. Therefore, our constructions are tight in the dimension of the field extension. For the class $\mathcal{P}(\mathbb{F}_q, n, (d, r), s)$ (the last row of the table), the best known result in the literature [37, 8] used field extension of dimension that depends on the number of the variables n. Our result uses field extension of dimension $\log_q(d+1)$ that is independent of the number of variables. Also notice, that when $q \ge d+1$ no extension field is needed. This will be further studied in [13] to give new Pseudorandom generators over small fields.

In this full paper we also develop a new bound that improves the upper bound of DeMillo-Lipton-Schwartz-Zippel Lemma. This new bound gives a randomized algorithm for polynomial size black box PIT set even over field extension of dimension 2. Our new bound also significantly improves the upper bounds when the size of the sparse multivariate polynomial is small. See the full paper [11].

Reduction of Black Box PIT Sets over Large Field to Sets over Small Field: We give several polynomial time reductions of black box PIT sets over large fields to black box PIT sets over small fields. For example, consider a subclass $\mathcal{C} \subseteq \mathcal{P}(\mathbb{F}_q, n, d)$ and t such that $q^t \ge d+1$. We give a polynomial time algorithm that takes a black box PIT set S of size w for $\mathcal{C}$ over an extended field $\mathbb{F}_{q^T}$ and constructs a black box PIT set for $\mathcal{C}$ over $\mathbb{F}_{q^t}$ of size $O(d^5 \cdot wT/t)$.

In particular, we apply this result to the results in [54, 56, 57, 5] and get black box PIT sets over smaller fields as indicated in the following table

Circuit Class	Field size $\ge$	Size of of PIT set	Ref.
$\Sigma\Pi\Sigma(k,d,n)$	dnk^2	$poly(n)\cdot d^k$	[54]
$\Sigma_r P_k$ROF	kn^3	$(kn)^{O(r+\log n)}$	[56]
ML $\Sigma\Pi\Sigma\Pi(k)$	n^2	$n^{O(k^3)}$	[57]
R_k ML	n^2	$n^{k^{O(k)}+O(k\log n)}$	[5]

Circuit Class	New Field size $\ge$	New Size of PIT set
$\Sigma\Pi\Sigma(k,d,n)$	$d+1$	$poly(n)\cdot d^{k+5}$
$\Sigma_r P_k$ROF	$kn+1$	$(kn)^{O(r+\log n)}$
ML $\Sigma\Pi\Sigma\Pi(k)$	$n+1$	$n^{O(k^3)}$
R_k ML	n^2	$n^{k^{O(k)}+O(k\log n)}$

Table 8

The classes in the table are: $\Sigma\Pi\Sigma(k,d,n)$ is the class of depth-3 circuits with n variables, degree d and top fanin k. P_kROF is the class of read once formulas (ROF, each variable appears at most once in the formula) with n variables in which we are allowed to replace each variable x_i with a univariate polynomial $T_i(x_i)$ of degree at most k. $\Sigma_r P_k$ROF is the sum of r P_kROF formulas. Multilinear (ML) $\Sigma\Pi\Sigma\Pi(k)$ is the class of depth 4 circuits with n variables in which the fan-in of the top Σ gate is a constant k and each multiplication gate computes a multilinear polynomial. R_k ML is the class of multilinear formulas with n variables where each variable appears at most k times in the formula.

The table shows the reduction to a smaller field. For example, in the first row in the table, in [54], Saxena and Seshadhri gave a black box PIT set for $\Sigma\Pi\Sigma(k,d,n)$ over fields of size at least dnk^2. We apply our reduction to give a black box PIT set for $\Sigma\Pi\Sigma(k,d,n)$ over fields of size at least $d+1$. Notice that our field size is independent of n and when the field $\mathbb{F}_q$ satisfies $q \ge d+1$, no extension field is needed.

1.4 Polynomial Restriction Problems

We now give another application of tester. Our new problem is called *polynomial restriction problem* and is a generalization of the d-restriction problem. In the d-restriction problems all the functions that determine the restrictions on the combinatorial structure depend on the same d variables. In the polynomial restriction problem the functions that determine the restrictions may depend on all the variables but are multivariate polynomials with some bounded parameters (such as degree, variable degree and size). Obviously, d-restriction problems are also polynomial restriction problems with polynomials of degree d. We show that also for those problems several polynomial time constructions are almost optimal. We now give a formal definition

Restriction Problem: A restriction problem is a problem of the following form: Given an alphabet Σ of size $|\Sigma| = q$, an integer n and a class $\mathcal{M}$ of nonzero functions $f : \Sigma^n \to \{0,1\}$. Find a small set $A \subseteq \Sigma^n$ such that: For every $f \in \mathcal{M}$ there is $\boldsymbol{a} \in A$ such that $f(\boldsymbol{a}) \ne 0$.

We will study restriction problems when $\mathcal{M}$ is a class of multivariate polynomials over $\mathbb{F}_q$.

(s,d)-Sparse (d,r)-Degree Polynomial Restriction Problem: Let $\mathcal{P}(\mathbb{F}_q, n, ((d,r),s))$ be the class of all multivariate polynomials in $\mathbb{F}_q[x_1,\ldots,x_n]$ of degree d and variable degree at most r with at most s monomials of degree d and any number of monomials of degree less than d. We denote $\mathcal{P}(\mathbb{F}_q, n, ((d,q-1),s))$ by $\mathcal{P}(\mathbb{F}_q, n, (d,s))$.

The *(s,d)-sparse (d,r)-degree polynomial problem* over $\mathbb{F}_q$ problem is the following: Given the class $\mathcal{P}(\mathbb{F}_q, n, ((d,r),s))$. Find a small set $S \subset \mathbb{F}_q^n$ such that for every $f \in \mathcal{P}(\mathbb{F}_q, n, ((d,r),s))$ there is $\boldsymbol{a} \in S$ such that $f(\boldsymbol{a}) \ne 0$. This problem can be regarded as black box PIT over $\mathbb{F}_q$, hitting set problem or polynomial restriction problem. We will call S a *hitting set* for $\mathcal{P}(\mathbb{F}_q, n, ((d,r),s))$. We note that this class is not studied in the literature. Also notice that if $f(\boldsymbol{x}) \in \mathcal{P}(\mathbb{F}_q, n, (d,r),s)$ then for any vector of constants $\boldsymbol{\alpha} \in \mathbb{F}_q^n$ we have $f(\boldsymbol{x}+\boldsymbol{\alpha}) \in \mathcal{P}(\mathbb{F}_q, n, ((d,r),s))$. The class $\mathcal{P}(\mathbb{F}_q, n, ((d,r),s))$ is much larger than $\mathcal{P}(\mathbb{F}_q, n, (d,r),s)$ since we allow any number of monomials of degree less than d in f and therefore the union bound does not give good bounds for this class. We develop new techniques that find lower and upper bounds for the size of a hitting set for this class and apply tester to construct almost optimal size hitting set.

The following table summarizes the results for the size of the hitting sets for $\mathcal{M} = \mathcal{P}(\mathbb{F}_q, n, ((d,r),s))$ when $r \le p-1$ where p is the characteristic of the field.

$\mathbb{F}_q, d$	Lower Bound	Upper Bound
$q=2$	$2^d s\log n$	$2^{2d} s\log n$
$q=2^\ell \le d$	$\pi_{q,r}^d s\frac{\log n}{\log q}$	$d(2\pi_{q,1})^d s\log n$
$q \le d$	$\pi_{q,r}^d s\frac{\log n}{\log q}$	$d(2\pi_{q,1})^d s\log n$
$q \le d = O(1)$	$s\log n$	$s\log n$
$q \ge d+1$	$ds\frac{\log n}{\log q}$	$d^2 s\frac{\log n}{\log(q/d)}$
$q \ge d+1 = O(1)$	$s\frac{\log n}{\log q}$	$s\frac{\log n}{\log(q/d)}$

$\mathbb{F}_q, d$	Explicit Construction	Poly Time Construction
$q=2$	$2^{2.66d} s\log n$	$2^{2.66d} s\log^2 n$
$q=2^\ell \le d$	$2^{(1+c_q)d} s\log n$	$2^{(1+c_q)d} s\log^2 n$
$q \le d$	$2^{(1+c_q)d} d! s\log n$	$2^{(1+c_q)d} d! s\log^2 n$
$q \le d = O(1)$	$s\log n$	$s\log n$
$q \ge d+1$	$d^6 s\frac{\log n}{\log q}$	$q^{24} d^7 s\cdot\log^2 n$
$q \ge d+1 = O(1)$	$s\frac{\log n}{\log q}$	$s\frac{\log n}{\log q}$

Table 9

In the table, the constant $\pi_{q,r}$ satisfies

$$1+\frac{1}{q-1} \le \pi_{q,r} := \left(\frac{q}{q-r}\right)^{1/r} \le q^{1/(q-1)} = 1+\frac{\ln q}{q-1}+O\left(\frac{\log^2 q}{q^2}\right) \le 2.$$

and the constant c_q satisfies

$$c_q = \sum_{i=0}^{\infty} \frac{\log(q^{2^i}+1)}{q^{2^i}} = \frac{\log(q+1)}{q} + O\left(\frac{\log q}{q^2}\right) < 1.66.$$

In the table all the bounds are tight in the parameter s, the number of monomials of degree d. The explicit constructions (see footnote in page) are also tight in $\log n$ where in the polynomial time constructions we get $(\log n)^2$. This is because our algorithm requires an element of the field of multiplicative order $n^{O(d)}$. When $d = O(1)$ (rows 4 and 6 in the table) n^d is polynomial and finding such element can be done in polynomial time.

2. TESTER

DEFINITION 1. *Let $\mathbb{F}$ be a field and $\mathcal{A}$ and $\mathcal{B}$ be two commutative $\mathbb{F}$-algebras. Let $\mathcal{M} \subseteq \mathbb{F}[x_1, x_2, \ldots, x_n]$ be a class of multivariate polynomials. Let $S \subseteq \mathcal{A}$ and $R \subseteq \mathcal{B}$ be linear sub-spaces over $\mathbb{F}$ and $L = \{\boldsymbol{\ell}_1, \ldots, \boldsymbol{\ell}_\nu\}$ be a set of maps $S^n \to R^n$. We denote by fL the map $S^n \to \mathcal{B}^\nu$ where for $\boldsymbol{a} \in S^n$, $(fL)(\boldsymbol{a}) = (f(\boldsymbol{\ell}_1(\boldsymbol{a})), \ldots, f(\boldsymbol{\ell}_\nu(\boldsymbol{a})))$. We say that L is an $(\mathcal{M}, S, R)$-tester if for every $\boldsymbol{a} \in S^n$ and $f \in \mathcal{M}$ we have (Here $\mathbf{0} = 0^\nu$ is the zero vector of length ν)*

$$(fL)(\boldsymbol{a}) = \mathbf{0} \implies f(\boldsymbol{a}) = 0.$$

The integer $\nu = |L|$ is called the *size of the tester.* The minimum size of an $(\mathcal{M}, S, R)$-tester is denoted by $\nu_R^\circ(\mathcal{M}, S)$. If no L exists then we write $\nu_R^\circ(\mathcal{M}, S) = \infty$. When S and R are known from the context we then just say *tester for* $\mathcal{M}$.

We will also allow $L = \{\ell_1, \ldots, \ell_\nu\}$ to be a set of maps $S \to R$. In that case $\boldsymbol{\ell}_i : S^n \to R^n$ is defined as $\boldsymbol{\ell}_i(\boldsymbol{a}) = (\ell_i(a_1), \ldots, \ell_i(a_n))$ where $\boldsymbol{a} = (a_1, \ldots, a_n) \in S^n$. In such case we call the tester *symmetric tester.*

We say that the tester is *componentwise tester* if $\boldsymbol{\ell}_i(\boldsymbol{a}) = (\ell_{i,1}(a_1), \ldots, \ell_{i,n}(a_n))$ for some $\ell_{i,j} : S \to R$. All the testers that will be considered in this paper are componentwise testers. A componentwise tester is called *reducible* if $\ell_{i,j}(1_\mathcal{A}) = 1_\mathcal{B}$ where $1_\mathcal{A}$ and $1_\mathcal{B}$ are the identities of the algebras $\mathcal{A}$ and $\mathcal{B}$ respectively.

Let $\boldsymbol{y} = (\boldsymbol{y}_1, \ldots, \boldsymbol{y}_d)$ and $\boldsymbol{y}_i = (y_{i,1}, \ldots, y_{i,n})$ be indeterminates over $\mathbb{F}$ for $i = 1, \ldots, d$. A multilinear polynomial in $\mathbb{F}[\boldsymbol{y}]$ is called *(n, d)-multilinear polynomial* if each monomial of f contains exactly one variable from each $\boldsymbol{y}_i$, $i = 1, \ldots, d$. Let $\mathcal{HLF}(\mathbb{F}, n, d)$ be the class of all (n, d)-multilinear polynomials in $\mathbb{F}[\boldsymbol{y}]$. Notice that $\mathcal{HLF}(\mathbb{F}, n, 2)$ is the class of all bilinear forms $\boldsymbol{y}_1^T A \boldsymbol{y}_2$ where $A \in \mathbb{F}^{n \times n}$. We denote $\nu_R(d, S) = \nu_R^\circ(\mathcal{HLF}(\mathbb{F}, n, d), S)$. Let $\mathcal{P}(\mathbb{F}, n, d)$ be the class of all multivariate polynomials in $\mathbb{F}[x_1, \cdots, x_n]$ of degree d and $\mathcal{HP}(\mathbb{F}, n, d)$ be the class of all homogeneous polynomials of degree d. We denote $\nu_R^\mathcal{P}(d, S) = \nu_R^\circ(\mathcal{P}(\mathbb{F}, n, d), S)$ and $\nu_R^{\mathcal{HP}}(d, S) = \nu_R^\circ(\mathcal{HP}(\mathbb{F}, n, d), S)$. Then

$$\nu_R(d, S) \le \nu_R^{\mathcal{HP}}(d, S) \le \nu_R^{\mathcal{P}}(d, S). \quad (1)$$

When $\mathbb{F}$ is not clear from the context then we write: $\nu_R((d, \mathbb{F}), S)$, $\nu_R^\mathcal{P}((d, \mathbb{F}), S)$ and $\nu_R^{\mathcal{HP}}((d, \mathbb{F}), S)$. In the following subsections we will study bounds for $\nu_{\mathbb{F}_q}$, $\nu_{\mathbb{F}_q}^\mathcal{P}$ and $\nu_{\mathbb{F}_q}^{\mathcal{HP}}$ where $\mathbb{F}_q$ is the finite field with q elements.

2.1 Preliminary Results for Testers

In this subsection we prove some elementary results on testers. The following three Lemmas immediately follows from the definition of tester

LEMMA 2. *Let $\mathcal{A}$ and $\mathcal{B}$ be commutative $\mathbb{F}$-algebras and $C \subseteq S \subseteq \mathcal{A}$ and $R \subset \mathcal{B}$ be subspaces over $\mathbb{F}$. Let $\mathcal{M} \subseteq \mathbb{F}[x_1, \ldots, x_n]$. If L is a $(\mathcal{M}, S, R)$-tester then L is a $(\mathcal{M}, C, R)$-tester. In particular, $\nu_R^\circ(\mathcal{M}, C) \le \nu_R^\circ(\mathcal{M}, S)$.*

LEMMA 3. *Let $\mathcal{A}$ and $\mathcal{B}$ be commutative $\mathbb{F}$-algebras and $S \subseteq \mathcal{A}$ and $R \subseteq \mathcal{B}$ be subspaces over $\mathbb{F}$. Let $\mathcal{M} \subset \mathcal{N} \subseteq \mathbb{F}[x_1, \ldots, x_n]$. If L is a $(\mathcal{N}, S, R)$-tester then L is a $(\mathcal{M}, S, R)$-tester. In particular, $\nu_R^\circ(\mathcal{M}, S) \le \nu_R^\circ(\mathcal{N}, S)$.*

LEMMA 4. *Let $\mathcal{A}, \mathcal{B}$ and $\mathcal{C}$ be commutative $\mathbb{F}$-algebras and $\mathcal{M} \subseteq \mathbb{F}[x_1, \ldots, x_n]$. Let $S_1 \subseteq \mathcal{A}$, $S_2 \subseteq \mathcal{B}$ and $S_3 \subseteq \mathcal{C}$ be subspaces over $\mathbb{F}$. If L_1 is a $(\mathcal{M}, S_1, S_2)$-tester and L_2 is a $(\mathcal{M}, S_2, S_3)$-tester then $L_2 \circ L_1 = \{\boldsymbol{\ell}_2(\boldsymbol{\ell}_1) \mid \boldsymbol{\ell}_1 \in L_1, \boldsymbol{\ell}_2 \in L_2\}$ is $(\mathcal{M}, S_1, S_3)$-tester. In particular, $\nu_{S_3}^\circ(\mathcal{M}, S_1) \le \nu_{S_3}^\circ(\mathcal{M}, S_2) \cdot \nu_{S_2}^\circ(\mathcal{M}, S_1)$.*

In particular we have

COROLLARY 5. *Let $\mathbb{K}$ be an extension field of $\mathbb{F}$, $\mathcal{A}$ be a $\mathbb{K}$-algebra and $S \subseteq \mathcal{A}$ be a linear subspace. Let $\mathcal{M} \subseteq \mathbb{F}[x_1, \ldots, x_n]$. Then $\nu_\mathbb{F}^\circ(\mathcal{M}, S) \le \nu_\mathbb{F}^\circ(\mathcal{M}, \mathbb{K}) \cdot \nu_\mathbb{K}^\circ(\mathcal{M}, S)$. In particular, for any integers t and m we have*

$$\nu_{\mathbb{F}_q}^\circ(\mathcal{M}, \mathbb{F}_{q^{tm}}) \le \nu_{\mathbb{F}_q}^\circ(\mathcal{M}, \mathbb{F}_{q^t}) \cdot \nu_{\mathbb{F}_{q^t}}^\circ(\mathcal{M}, \mathbb{F}_{q^{tm}})$$

and $\nu_{\mathbb{F}_q}^\mathcal{P}(d, \mathbb{F}_{q^{tm}}) \le \nu_{\mathbb{F}_q}^\mathcal{P}(d, \mathbb{F}_{q^t}) \cdot \nu_{\mathbb{F}_{q^t}}^\mathcal{P}(d, \mathbb{F}_{q^{tm}})$.

We must note here that $\nu_{\mathbb{F}_{q^t}}^\mathcal{P}(d, \mathbb{F}_{q^{tm}})$ may be understood as $\nu_{\mathbb{F}_{q^t}}^\circ(\mathcal{P}(\mathbb{F}_q, n, d), \mathbb{F}_{q^{tm}}) = \nu_{\mathbb{F}_{q^t}}^\mathcal{P}((d, \mathbb{F}_q), \mathbb{F}_{q^{tm}})$, which is what we meant in Corollary 5, or as $\nu_{\mathbb{F}_{q^t}}^\circ(\mathcal{P}(\mathbb{F}_{q^t}, n, d), \mathbb{F}_{q^{tm}}) = \nu_{\mathbb{F}_{q^t}}^\mathcal{P}((d, \mathbb{F}_{q^t}), \mathbb{F}_{q^{tm}})$. The inequality is true for both since, by Lemma 3

$$\nu_{\mathbb{F}_{q^t}}^\circ(\mathcal{P}(\mathbb{F}_q, n, d), \mathbb{F}_{q^{tm}}) \le \nu_{\mathbb{F}_{q^t}}^\circ(\mathcal{P}(\mathbb{F}_{q^t}, n, d), \mathbb{F}_{q^{tm}}).$$

In the full paper we prove

LEMMA 6. *Let $\mathcal{M} \subseteq$*

$$\mathbb{F}[\boldsymbol{x}]\mathbb{F}[\boldsymbol{y}] := \left\{ \sum_{i=1}^{s} h_i(\boldsymbol{x}) g_i(\boldsymbol{y}) \;\middle|\; h_i \in \mathbb{F}[\boldsymbol{x}], g_i \in \mathbb{F}[\boldsymbol{y}], s \in \mathbb{N} \right\}$$

be a class of multivariate polynomials where $\boldsymbol{x} = (x_1, \ldots, x_n)$ and $\boldsymbol{y} = (y_1, \ldots, y_m)$ are indeterminates. Let $\mathcal{A}$ be a commutative $\mathbb{F}$-algebra, $S \subseteq \mathcal{A}$ linear subspace, $\mathcal{M}_x =$

$$\left\{ \sum_{i=1}^{s} \lambda_i h_i(\boldsymbol{x}) \;\middle|\; \sum_{i=1}^{s} h_i(\boldsymbol{x}) g_i(\boldsymbol{y}) \in \mathcal{M}, \boldsymbol{\lambda} \in \mathbb{F}^s, s \in \mathbb{N} \right\}.$$

If L_x is an $(\mathcal{M}_x, S, \mathbb{F})$-tester and L_y is an $(\mathcal{M}_y, S, \mathbb{F})$-tester then $L_x \times L_y$ is a $(\mathcal{M}, S, \mathbb{F})$-tester. That is,

$$\nu_\mathbb{F}^\circ(\mathcal{M}, S) \le \nu_\mathbb{F}^\circ(\mathcal{M}_x, S) \cdot \nu_\mathbb{F}^\circ(\mathcal{M}_y, S).$$

In particular, for any d_1 and d_2

$$\nu_\mathbb{F}(d_1 + d_2, S) \le \nu_\mathbb{F}(d_1, S) \cdot \nu_\mathbb{F}(d_2, S).$$

We now prove two lemmas for $\nu_{\mathbb{F}_q}^\mathcal{P}$ and $\nu_{\mathbb{F}_q}^{\mathcal{HP}}$. Let $\mathbb{F}_q[X]_w$ be the linear space of polynomials in $\mathbb{F}_q[X]$ of degree at most w.

LEMMA 7. *We have*

1. *If $q \ge d(t-1)$ then*

$$\nu_{\mathbb{F}_q}^{\mathcal{HP}}(d, \mathbb{F}_{q^t}) \le \nu_{\mathbb{F}_q}^{\mathcal{HP}}(d, \mathbb{F}_q[X]_{t-1}) \le d(t-1) + 1.$$

2. *If* $q \ge d(t-1)+1$ *then*

$$\nu^{\mathcal{P}}_{\mathbb{F}_q}(d,\mathbb{F}_{q^t}) \le \nu^{\mathcal{P}}_{\mathbb{F}_q}(d,\mathbb{F}_q[X]_{t-1}) \le d(t-1)+1.$$

PROOF. Let $\mathbb{F}_{q^t} = \mathbb{F}_q[\alpha]/(g(\alpha))$ for some irreducible polynomial $g(\alpha) \in \mathbb{F}_q[\alpha]$ of degree t. Every element in $\mathbb{F}_{q^t}$ can be represented as $\omega_0+\omega_1\alpha+\cdots+\omega_{t-1}\alpha^{t-1}$ where $\omega_i \in \mathbb{F}_q$ for $i=0,1,\ldots,t-1$. We first define the map $\ell(\omega_0+\omega_1\alpha+\cdots+\omega_{t-1}\alpha^{t-1}) = \omega_0+\omega_1X+\cdots+\omega_{t-1}X^{t-1}$ where X is indeterminates over $\mathbb{F}_q$. Obviously, for any $f \in \mathbb{F}_q[x_1,\cdots,x_n]$ and $\boldsymbol{\beta}=(\beta_1,\ldots,\beta_n) \in \mathbb{F}^n_{q^t}$, if $f(\ell(\beta_1),\ldots,\ell(\beta_n))=0$ then $f(\beta_1,\ldots,\beta_n)=0$. This gives a $(\mathbb{F}_q[x_1,\cdots,x_n],\mathbb{F}_{q^t},\mathbb{F}_q[X]_{t-1})$-tester of size 1.
For every $f \in \mathcal{P}(\mathbb{F}_q,n,d)$ and $z_1,\ldots,z_n \in \mathbb{F}_q[X]_{t-1}$ we have $f(z_1,\ldots,z_n) \in \mathbb{F}_q[X]_{d(t-1)}$. Therefore, if $q \ge d(t-1)+1$, we can choose $F \subseteq \mathbb{F}_q$ of size $d(t-1)+1$ and if $f(z_1,\ldots,z_n)|_{X=\beta}=0$ for all $\beta \in F$ then $f(z_1,\ldots,z_n)=0$. Therefore, $L=\{\ell_\beta \mid \beta \in F\}$ where $\ell_\beta : \mathbb{F}_q[X]_{t-1} \to \mathbb{F}_q$ is defined as $\ell_\beta(z(X))=z(\beta)$ is a $(\mathcal{P}(\mathbb{F}_q,n,d),\mathbb{F}_q[X]_{t-1},\mathbb{F}_q)$-tester of size $d(t-1)+1$.
Combining both testers, by Lemma 3 and 4, we get a $(\mathcal{P}(\mathbb{F}_q,n,d),\mathbb{F}_{q^t},\mathbb{F}_q)$-tester of size $d(t-1)+1$. Therefore, for $q \ge d(t-1)+1$,

$$\nu^{\mathcal{HP}}_{\mathbb{F}_q}(d,\mathbb{F}_{q^t}) \le \nu^{\mathcal{P}}_{\mathbb{F}_q}(d,\mathbb{F}_{q^t}) \le \nu^{\mathcal{P}}_{\mathbb{F}_q}(d,\mathbb{F}_q[X]_{t-1}) \le d(t-1)+1.$$

This proves *1* and *2* for $q \ge d(t-1)+1$.
For *1*, when $q=d(t-1)$, consider $f \in \mathcal{HP}(\mathbb{F}_q,n,d)$ and $z_1,\ldots,z_n \in \mathbb{F}_q[X]_{t-1}$. Let $F=\mathbb{F}_q \cup \{\infty\}$ and define for $z \in \mathbb{F}_q[X]_{t-1}$, $\ell_\beta(z)=z(\beta)$ if $\beta \in \mathbb{F}_q$ and $\ell_\infty(z)$ to be the coefficient of X^{t-1} in z. Let $L=\{\ell_\beta \mid \beta \in \mathbb{F}_q \cup \{\infty\}\}$. It is easy to see that the coefficient of $X^{d(t-1)}$ in $f(z_1,\ldots,z_n)$ is $f(\ell_\infty(z_1),\ldots,\ell_\infty(z_n))$. Now if $f(\ell_\infty(z_1),\ldots,\ell_\infty(z_n))=0$ then $f(z_1,\ldots,z_n)$ is of degree $d(t-1)-1$ and then if we also have $f(\ell_\beta(z_1),\ldots,\ell_\beta(z_n)) = f(z_1,\ldots,z_n)|_{X=\beta}=0$ for all $\beta \in \mathbb{F}_q$ then $f(z_1,\ldots,z_n)\equiv 0$. Therefore $L=\{\ell_\beta \mid \beta \in F\}$ is a $(\mathcal{HP}(\mathbb{F}_q,n,d),\mathbb{F}_q[X]_{t-1},\mathbb{F}_q)$-tester of size $d(t-1)+1$. □

The next result shows how to reduce testers for degree d polynomials in $\mathbb{F}_{q^t}$ to testers in $\mathbb{F}_{q^{\log(dt)/\log q}}$. This will be used to construct testers that are almost (within *poly*(d)) optimal in polynomial time.
For any positive integer k, let $N_q(k)$ denotes the number of monic irreducible polynomial of degree k over $\mathbb{F}_q$ [38].

LEMMA 8. *For any finite field* $\mathbb{F}_q$ *and any integers* r *and* t *such that* $q^{r-1} \ge dt-d+1$, *we have*

$$\nu^{\mathcal{P}}_{\mathbb{F}_q}(d,\mathbb{F}_{q^t}) \le \left(\frac{dt-d+1}{r}+1\right)\cdot \nu^{\mathcal{P}}_{\mathbb{F}_q}(d,\mathbb{F}_{q^r}).$$

PROOF. By Lemma 7 and Lemma 4 we have

$$\begin{aligned}\nu^{\mathcal{P}}_{\mathbb{F}_q}(d,\mathbb{F}_{q^t}) &\le \nu^{\mathcal{P}}_{\mathbb{F}_q}(d,\mathbb{F}_q[X]_{t-1})\\ &\le \nu^{\mathcal{P}}_{\mathbb{F}_{q^r}}((d,\mathbb{F}_q),\mathbb{F}_q[X]_{t-1})\cdot \nu^{\mathcal{P}}_{\mathbb{F}_q}(d,\mathbb{F}_{q^r}).\quad(2)\end{aligned}$$

Now it is enough to prove the following lemma. □

LEMMA 9. *For any finite field* $\mathbb{F}_q$ *and any integers* r *and* t *such that* $q^{r-1} \ge dt-d+1$, *we have*

$$\nu^{\mathcal{P}}_{\mathbb{F}_{q^r}}((d,\mathbb{F}_q),\mathbb{F}_q[X]_{t-1}) \le \frac{dt-d+1}{r}+1. \qquad (3)$$

PROOF. It is known that $q^{r-1} < rN_q(r) \le q^r$, [38]. Let $\mathcal{R}'$ be the set of all monic irreducible polynomials of degree r. Since $deg(\prod_{p\in\mathcal{R}'} p) = rN_q(r) > q^{r-1} \ge dt-d+1$, we can choose $\mathcal{R} \subseteq \mathcal{R}'$ such that

$$dt-d+1 \le deg\left(\prod_{p\in\mathcal{R}} p\right) < dt-d+1+r.$$

Let $f \in \mathcal{P}(\mathbb{F}_q,n,d)$, $z_1,\ldots,z_n \in \mathbb{F}_q[X]_{t-1}$ and $g(X) = f(z_1,\ldots,z_n) \in \mathbb{F}_q[X]_{dt-d}$. Now $g\equiv 0$ if and only if $g \bmod (\prod_{p\in\mathcal{R}} p) \equiv 0$ if and only if $g \bmod p \equiv 0$ for all $p \in \mathcal{R}$. Now since $g \in \mathbb{F}_q[X]$ then $g \bmod p \equiv 0$ if and only if $g(\beta) = f(z_1(\beta),\ldots,z_n(\beta)) = 0$ for one root $\beta \in \mathbb{F}_{q^r}$ of p. See Theorem 3.33 (ii) in [38].
Therefore,

$$\nu^{\mathcal{P}}_{\mathbb{F}_{q^r}}((d,\mathbb{F}_q),\mathbb{F}_q[X]_{t-1}) \le |\mathcal{R}| \le \frac{dt-d+1+r}{r}.$$

□

Now notice that when $t_1=t$ and $t_{i+1}=\lceil\log(dt_i)/\log q\rceil+1$ then $q^{t_{i+1}-1} \ge dt_i-d+1$, and by Lemma 8 we have

$$\begin{aligned}\nu^{\mathcal{P}}_{\mathbb{F}_q}(d,\mathbb{F}_{q^{t_i}}) &\le \left(\frac{dt_i-d+1}{t_{i+1}}+1\right)\cdot \nu^{\mathcal{P}}_{\mathbb{F}_q}\left(d,\mathbb{F}_{q^{t_{i+1}}}\right)\\ &\le (d+1)\frac{t_i}{t_{i+1}}\cdot \nu^{\mathcal{P}}_{\mathbb{F}_q}\left(d,\mathbb{F}_{q^{t_{i+1}}}\right).\end{aligned}$$

Therefore, if $q \ge d+1$ and using Lemma 7 for the last step of the above recurrence, we get $\nu^{\mathcal{P}}_{\mathbb{F}_q}(d,\mathbb{F}_{q^t}) \le d^{\log^* t+O(1)}\cdot t$ where $\log^* t$ is the minimum integer i in which $t_i \le 4$ (or any other constant). In the next subsection we prove that for $q \ge d+1$ $\nu^{\mathcal{P}}_{\mathbb{F}_q}(d,\mathbb{F}_{q^t}) \le d^{O(1)}\cdot t$.
When r divides t then a better bound is proved in the following

LEMMA 10. *For any finite field* $\mathbb{F}_q$, *any integers* r *and* t *such that* $r|t$ *and* $q^r \ge d(t/r-1)+1$, *we have*

$$\nu^{\mathcal{P}}_{\mathbb{F}_q}(d,\mathbb{F}_{q^t}) \le \left(\frac{dt}{r}-d+1\right)\cdot \nu^{\mathcal{P}}_{\mathbb{F}_q}(d,\mathbb{F}_{q^r}).$$

PROOF. By Corollary 5 we have

$$\nu^{\mathcal{P}}_{\mathbb{F}_q}(d,\mathbb{F}_{q^t}) \le \nu^{\mathcal{P}}_{\mathbb{F}_q}(d,\mathbb{F}_{q^r})\cdot \nu^{\mathcal{P}}_{\mathbb{F}_{q^r}}((d,\mathbb{F}_q),\mathbb{F}_{(q^r)^{t/r}}).$$

Now by Lemma 7 and 3, if $q^r \ge d(t/r-1)+1$ we have

$$\nu^{\mathcal{P}}_{\mathbb{F}_{q^r}}((d,\mathbb{F}_q),\mathbb{F}_{(q^r)^{t/r}}) \le \nu^{\mathcal{P}}_{\mathbb{F}_{q^r}}(d,\mathbb{F}_{(q^r)^{t/r}}) \le \frac{dt}{r}-d+1.$$

□

2.2 Testers for Large Fields

In this subsection we use algebraic function fields to construct explicit testers for large fields. We prove

THEOREM 11. *For any* $q \ge d+1$ *and any* t *we have*

$$\nu^{\mathcal{P}}_{\mathbb{F}_q}(d,\mathbb{F}_{q^t}) \le poly(d)\cdot t.$$

In particular, the bound is also true for $\nu_{\mathbb{F}_q}(d,\mathbb{F}_{q^t})$ *and* $\nu^{\mathcal{HP}}_{\mathbb{F}_q}(d,\mathbb{F}_{q^t})$.

We will in fact prove the bound $\nu^{\mathcal{P}}_{\mathbb{F}_q}(d,\mathbb{F}_{q^t}) = O(d^4)\cdot t$. For better bounds when q is large see Corollary 17.
For notations used in this subsection we refer the reader to Appendix A in [11]. See also Subsections 1.1 – 1.4 in [52].
In this subsection we prove Theorem 11 and then in Subsection 3.4 we show how to construct such tester in polynomial time.

We first prove few lemmas using the technique used in [7], Lemma 2.2. (Here we use ℓ for linear maps and l for the dimension of divisors.)

LEMMA 12. *Let $F/\mathbb{F}_q$ be a function field, $P_1,\ldots,P_s$ be distinct places of $F/\mathbb{F}_q$ of degree 1 and $D = P_1 + P_2 + \cdots + P_s$. Let G be a divisor of $F/\mathbb{F}_q$ such that* $(\text{supp } D) \cap (\text{supp } G) = $. *Let $L = \{\ell_{P_1},\ldots,\ell_{P_s}\}$ where $\ell_{P_i} : \mathscr{L}(G) \to \mathbb{F}_q \cup \{\infty\}$ is defined as $\ell_{P_i}(x) = x(P_i)$. Then*

1. *If $s > d\deg(G)$ then any $L' \subseteq L$ where $|L'| = d\deg(G)+1$ is a symmetric and reducible $(\mathcal{P}(\mathbb{F}_q,n,d),\mathscr{L}(G),\mathbb{F}_q)$-tester.*
2. *If $s > d\deg(G)$ then there is $\bar{L} \subseteq L$ of size $l(dG) \le d\deg(G)+1$ such that $\bar{L}$ is a symmetric and reducible $(\mathcal{P}(\mathbb{F}_q,n,d),\mathscr{L}(G),\mathbb{F}_q)$-tester.*
3. *If $s > d\deg(G) \ge 2g-1$ then there is $\bar{L} \subseteq L$ of size $l(dG) = d\deg(G) - g + 1$ such that $\bar{L}$ is a symmetric and reducible $(\mathcal{P}(\mathbb{F}_q,n,d),\mathscr{L}(G),\mathbb{F}_q)$-tester. In particular, $\nu^{\mathcal{P}}_{\mathbb{F}_q}(d,\mathscr{L}(G)) \le l(dG) = d\deg(G) - g + 1$.*

PROOF. Let $\mathcal{M} = \mathcal{P}(\mathbb{F}_q,n,d)$ and $\mathcal{M}(\mathscr{L}(G)^n) = \{f(\boldsymbol{x}) \mid f \in \mathcal{M}, \boldsymbol{x} \in \mathscr{L}(G)^n\}$. We first show that ℓ_{P_i} is well defined, i.e., $\ell_{P_i} : \mathscr{L}(G) \to \mathbb{F}_q$. Let $z \in \mathscr{L}(G)$. Then for every i, $v_{P_i}(z) \ge -v_{P_i}(G) = 0$ and therefore $\ell_{P_i}(z) = z(P_i) \ne \infty$. Also, since P_i is of degree 1 we have $\ell_{P_i}(z) = z(P_i) \in \mathbb{F}_q$.
In the same way the linear function $\ell_{P_i} : \mathscr{L}(dG) \to \mathbb{F}_q$ is well defined. For $\boldsymbol{x} = (x_1,\ldots,x_n) \in \mathscr{L}(G)^n$ we have $f(\ell_{P_i}(x_1),\ldots,\ell_{P_i}(x_n)) = \ell_{P_i}(f(\boldsymbol{x}))$ and $f(\boldsymbol{x}) \in \mathcal{M}(\mathscr{L}(G)^n) \subseteq \mathscr{L}(dG)$. Now if $f(\ell_{P_i}(x_1),\ldots,\ell_{P_i}(x_n)) = 0$ for every $P_i \in L'$ then $\ell_{P_i}(f(\boldsymbol{x})) = 0$ for every $P_i \in L'$ and therefore $f(\boldsymbol{x}) \in \text{Ker}(\ell_{P_i})$ for every $P_i \in L'$. Therefore, it is enough to show that

$$\mathscr{L}(dG) \bigcap \left(\bigcap_{P_i \in L'} \text{Ker}(\ell_{P_i}) \right) = \{0\}.$$

If $z \in \mathscr{L}(dG) \cap \text{Ker}(\ell_{P_i})$ for all $P_i \in L'$ then $\ell_{P_i}(z) = z(P_i) = 0$ and therefore $v_{P_i}(z) \ge 1$. Then, since $(\text{supp } D) \cap (\text{supp } G) = $ we have $z \in \mathscr{L}(dG - D')$ where $D' = \sum_{P_i \in L'} P_i$. This implies that

$$\mathscr{L}(dG) \cap \bigcap_{P_i \in L'} \text{Ker}(\ell_{P_i}) \subseteq \mathscr{L}(dG - D').$$

Now since $\deg(dG - D') = d\deg G - |L'| = -1 < 0$, $\mathscr{L}(dG - D') = \{0\}$. Therefore L' is a symmetric and reducible $(\mathcal{P}(\mathbb{F}_q,n,d),\mathscr{L}(G),\mathbb{F}_q)$-tester.
Obviously, the tester L is symmetric. Since $\ell_{P_i}(1) = 1(P_i) = 1$, the tester is also reducible. This completes the proof of *1*.
Now consider the linear map

$$\begin{aligned} T : \mathscr{L}(dG) &\to \mathbb{F}_q^s \\ f &\mapsto (f(P_1), f(P_2),\ldots,f(P_s)). \end{aligned}$$

In *1* we actually have proved that $\ker T = \{0\}$. Therefore, there are $w = \dim \mathscr{L}(dG)$ places $P_{i_1},\ldots,P_{i_w}$ such that the map

$$\begin{aligned} T' : \mathscr{L}(dG) &\to \mathbb{F}_q^w \\ f &\mapsto (f(P_{i_1}), f(P_{i_2}),\ldots,f(P_{i_w})) \end{aligned}$$

is an isomorphism. This completes the proof of *2*.
Now we have $w = \dim \mathscr{L}(dG) = l(dG) = \deg(dG) - g + 1 = d\deg(G) - g + 1$. This proves *3*. □

LEMMA 13. *Let $F/\mathbb{F}_q$ be a function field. Let G be a divisor of $F/\mathbb{F}_q$ and Q be a prime divisor of degree $\deg Q = t = l(G)$ such that $v_Q(G) = 0$. If $l(G - Q) = 0$ then the map*

$$\begin{aligned} E : \mathscr{L}(G) &\to F_Q = \mathbb{F}_{q^t} \\ f &\mapsto f(Q) \end{aligned}$$

is isomorphism of vector spaces over $\mathbb{F}_q$ and $L = \{E^{-1}\}$ is a symmetric and reducible $(\mathbb{F}_q[\boldsymbol{x}],\mathbb{F}_{q^t},\mathscr{L}(G))$-tester where $\boldsymbol{x} = (x_1,\ldots,x_m)$. In particular, $\nu^{\circ}_{\mathscr{L}(G)}(\mathbb{F}_q[\boldsymbol{x}],\mathbb{F}_{q^t}) = 1$.

PROOF. We first show that the map E is an isomorphism of linear spaces. Let $f \in \mathscr{L}(G)$. Then $v_Q(f) \ge -v_Q(G) = 0$ and therefore $f(Q) \ne \infty$ and the map is well defined. Since Q is prime divisor of degree t we have $\dim \mathscr{L}(G) = l(G) = t = [F_Q : \mathbb{F}_q] = \dim F_Q$. Therefore, $F_Q = \mathbb{F}_{q^t}$.
Now we show that $\text{Ker}E = \{0\}$. Let $f \in \mathscr{L}(G)$. If $f \in \text{Ker}E$ then $f(Q) = 0$ and therefore $v_Q(f) > 0$. Since $v_Q(G) = 0$ and $l(G-Q) = 0$ we have $f \in \mathscr{L}(G-Q) = \{0\}$. Therefore E is an isomorphism of vector spaces.
Now suppose $h \in \mathbb{F}_q[\boldsymbol{x}]$ and let $\boldsymbol{E} = (E,E,\ldots,E)$ and $\boldsymbol{E}^{-1} = (E^{-1},E^{-1},\ldots,E^{-1})$. Let $\boldsymbol{a} \in \mathbb{F}_{q^t}^m$. If $(hL)(\boldsymbol{a}) = 0$ then $0 = ((hL)(\boldsymbol{a}))(Q) = h(\boldsymbol{E}^{-1}(\boldsymbol{a}))(Q) = h(\boldsymbol{E}(\boldsymbol{E}^{-1}(\boldsymbol{a}))) = h(\boldsymbol{a})$.
Since $E(1) = 1(Q) = 1$ we have $E^{-1}(1) = 1$ and the tester is reducible. □

Ballet in [7] shows that there is a divisor G and a prime divisor Q that satisfy the conditions in Lemma 13. We state the result in the following

LEMMA 14. *Let $F/\mathbb{F}_q$ be algebraic function field of genus g that contains at least $g+1$ places of degree 1. Let Q be a prime divisor of degree t. There is a divisor G that satisfies the following: (1) $v_Q(G) = 0$ (2) $v_P(G) = 0$ for any prime divisor P of degree 1 (3)$l(G) = \deg Q = t$. (4) $\deg(G) = t + g - 1$ (5) $l(G - Q) = 0$.*

PROOF. The proof follows immediately from Lemma 2.1 and 2.2 in [7]. □

We now use the above three lemmas to prove

LEMMA 15. *Let $F/\mathbb{F}_q$ be a function field of genus g and $t \ge 3 + 2\log_q(2g+1)$. If F has $d(t+g-1)+1$ places of degree 1 then $\nu^{\mathcal{P}}_{\mathbb{F}_q}(d,\mathbb{F}_{q^t}) \le dt + (d-1)(g-1)$.*

PROOF. First, by Corollary 5.2.10 (c) in [52], if $2g+1 \le q^{(t-1)/2}(q^{1/2}-1)$ then there is a prime divisor of degree t. Since $t \ge 3 + 2\log_q(2g+1)$ the inequality holds and there is at least one prime divisor of degree t. Let Q be such divisor. Let $P_1,\ldots,P_s$, $s = d(t+g-1)+1$, be distinct places of $F/\mathbb{F}_q$ of degree 1 and $D = P_1 + P_2 + \cdots + P_s$. In Lemma 14 we proved that there is a divisor G of $F/\mathbb{F}_q$ such that $(\text{supp } D) \cap (\text{supp } G) = $, $\deg Q = t = l(G)$, $v_Q(G) = 0$, $\deg G = t + g - 1$ and $l(G - Q) = 0$.
By Lemmas 13, 12 and Lemma 4 we have $\nu^{\mathcal{P}}_{\mathbb{F}_q}(d,\mathbb{F}_{q^t}) \le \nu^{\mathcal{P}}_{\mathbb{F}_q}(d,\mathscr{L}(G)) \cdot \nu^{\mathcal{P}}_{\mathscr{L}(G)}(d,\mathbb{F}_{q^t}) \le d\deg G - g + 1 = dt + (d-1)(g-1)$. □

We are now ready to give the explicit construction. A *tower* of function fields over $\mathbb{F}_q$ is a sequence $\mathcal{F} = (F^{(0)}, F^{(1)}, F^{(2)}, \cdots)$ of function fields $F^{(i)}/\mathbb{F}_q$ with $F^{(0)} \subseteq F^{(1)} \subseteq F^{(2)} \subseteq \cdots$ where each extension $F^{(k+1)}/F^{(k)}$ is finite and separable. There are many explicit towers known from the literature. We will use the following $\mathcal{W}_1$ tower defined in [29]. See also [30] Chapter 1.

LEMMA 16. *Let x_1 be indeterminate over $\mathbb{F}_{q^2}$ and $F^{(1)} = \mathbb{F}_{q^2}(x_1)$. For $k \geq 1$ let $F^{(k)} = F^{(k-1)}(x_k)$ where*

$$x_k^q + x_k = \frac{x_{k-1}^q}{x_{k-1}^{q-1}+1}.$$

Let g_k be the genus of $F^{(k)}/\mathbb{F}_{q^2}$ and N_k the number of places in $F^{(k)}/\mathbb{F}_{q^2}$ of degree 1. Then

$$g_k = \begin{cases} q^k - 2q^{k/2} + 1 & \text{if } k = 0 \mod 2 \\ q^k - q^{(k+1)/2} - q^{(k-1)/2} + 1 & \text{if } k = 1 \mod 2 \end{cases} \quad (4)$$

and

$$N_k = \begin{cases} (q^2 - q)q^{k-1} + 2q & \text{if } k \geq 3, q = 1 \mod 2 \\ (q^2 - q)q^{k-1} + 2q^2 & \text{if } k \geq 3, q = 0 \mod 2 \end{cases} \quad (5)$$

We are now ready to prove Theorem 11.

PROOF. We first prove the result for $q \geq 2(d+1)$. Let r be an integer such that $q^{r+1} < 2dt \leq q^{r+2}$. Consider the function field $F^{(r+1)}/\mathbb{F}_{q^2}$ defined in Lemma 16. By Lemma 16, $F^{(r+1)}$ is of genus $g \leq q^{r+1}$ and has $N \geq q^{r+2} - q^{r+1}$ places of degree 1. By Lemma 15, since

$$\begin{aligned} N &\geq q^{r+2} - q^{r+1} = \frac{q^{r+2}}{2} + \left(\frac{q^{r+2}}{2} - q^{r+1}\right) \\ &\geq dt + dq^{r+1} \geq d(t+g-1) + 1 \end{aligned}$$

we have

$$\nu^{\mathcal{P}}_{\mathbb{F}_{q^2}}(d, \mathbb{F}_{q^{2t}}) \leq dt + (d-1)(g-1) \leq d(2d+1)t. \quad (6)$$

Now by Lemma 2 and 7 and Corollary 5 we have

$$\begin{aligned} \nu^{\mathcal{P}}_{\mathbb{F}_q}(d, \mathbb{F}_{q^t}) &\leq \nu^{\mathcal{P}}_{\mathbb{F}_q}(d, \mathbb{F}_{q^{2t}}) \leq \nu^{\mathcal{P}}_{\mathbb{F}_q}(d, \mathbb{F}_{q^2}) \cdot \nu^{\mathcal{P}}_{\mathbb{F}_{q^2}}(d, \mathbb{F}_{q^{2t}}) \\ &= d(d+1)(2d+1)t. \end{aligned}$$

This proves the result for $q \geq 2(d+1)$.
Notice that thus far we have proved that: for any t and any $q \geq 2(d+1)$ we have $\nu^{\mathcal{P}}_{\mathbb{F}_q}(d, \mathbb{F}_{q^t}) \leq d(d+1)(2d+1)t$. In particular, for any t and any $q^2 \geq 2(d+1)$ we have

$$\nu^{\mathcal{P}}_{\mathbb{F}_{q^2}}(d, \mathbb{F}_{q^{2t}}) \leq d(d+1)(2d+1)t. \quad (7)$$

Now for $q \geq d+1$ we have $q^2 \geq 2(d+1)$ and with (7) we have $\nu^{\mathcal{P}}_{\mathbb{F}_q}(d, \mathbb{F}_{q^t}) \leq \nu^{\mathcal{P}}_{\mathbb{F}_q}(d, \mathbb{F}_{q^{2t}}) \leq \nu^{\mathcal{P}}_{\mathbb{F}_q}(d, \mathbb{F}_{q^2}) \cdot \nu^{\mathcal{P}}_{\mathbb{F}_{q^2}}(d, \mathbb{F}_{q^{2t}}) = d(d+1)^2(2d+1)t$. This proves the result. □

Recall that $\nu_{\mathbb{F}_q}(d, \mathbb{F}_{q^t}) \leq \nu^{\mathcal{HP}}_{\mathbb{F}_q}(d, \mathbb{F}_{q^t}) \leq \nu^{\mathcal{P}}_{\mathbb{F}_q}(d, \mathbb{F}_{q^t})$. Therefore all the above bounds and the bounds in the following Corollary are also true for $\nu^{\mathcal{HP}}_{\mathbb{F}_q}(d, \mathbb{F}_{q^t})$ and $\nu_{\mathbb{F}_q}(d, \mathbb{F}_{q^t})$. In the full paper we prove

COROLLARY 17. *Let $c > 1$ be any constant. We have*

1. *For perfect square q where $q \geq c(d+1)^2$ there is an infinite sequence of integers t such that $\nu^{\mathcal{P}}_{\mathbb{F}_q}(d, \mathbb{F}_{q^t}) = O(dt)$.*
2. *For perfect square q where $q \geq c(d+1)^2$ and any integer t we have $\nu^{\mathcal{P}}_{\mathbb{F}_q}(d, \mathbb{F}_{q^t}) = O(d^2t)$.*
3. *For any $q \geq c(d+1)$ there is an infinite sequence of integers t such that $\nu^{\mathcal{P}}_{\mathbb{F}_q}(d, \mathbb{F}_{q^t}) = O(d^2t)$.*
4. *For any $q \geq c(d+1)$ and any integers t we have $\nu^{\mathcal{P}}_{\mathbb{F}_q}(d, \mathbb{F}_{q^t}) = O(d^3t)$.*
5. *For any $q \geq d+1$ there is an infinite sequence of integers t such that $\nu^{\mathcal{P}}_{\mathbb{F}_q}(d, \mathbb{F}_{q^t}) = O(d^3t)$.*
6. *For any $q \geq d+1$ and any integers t we have $\nu^{\mathcal{P}}_{\mathbb{F}_q}(d, \mathbb{F}_{q^t}) = O(d^4t)$.*
7. *For any $q \geq d$ and any integers t we have $\nu^{\mathcal{HP}}_{\mathbb{F}_q}(d, \mathbb{F}_{q^t}) = O(d^4t)$.*
8. *For any $q < d+1$ and any integers $t > 1$ we have $\nu^{\mathcal{P}}_{\mathbb{F}_q}(d, \mathbb{F}_{q^t}) = \infty$.*
9. *For any $q < d$ and any integers $t > 1$ we have $\nu^{\mathcal{HP}}_{\mathbb{F}_q}(d, \mathbb{F}_{q^t}) = \infty$.*

In Subsection 3.4 we show that a tester with the bound in Theorem 11 can be constructed in polynomial time. In Subsection 2.6 we show that the size of the above tester is almost optimal.

2.3 Testers for Subspaces of Large Fields

In this subsection we study $(\mathcal{M}, S, \mathbb{F}_q)$-testers when $S \subset \mathbb{F}_{q^t}$ is a linear subspace over $\mathbb{F}_q$. In the next section we show that such testers can be easily constructed in polynomial time and, for many applications, are almost as good as the testers in the previous subsection.
We start with the following

LEMMA 18. *Let $F/\mathbb{F}_q$ be a function field of genus g. Let G be a divisor of $F/\mathbb{F}_q$ and Q be a prime divisor of degree $\deg Q = t = \deg G + 1$ such that $v_Q(G) = 0$. Then the map*

$$\begin{aligned} E : \mathscr{L}(G) &\to F_Q = \mathbb{F}_{q^t} \\ f &\mapsto f(Q) \end{aligned}$$

is one-to-one linear map and there is a symmetric and reducible $(\mathbb{F}_q[\boldsymbol{x}], S, \mathscr{L}(G))$-tester of size 1 where $S = E(\mathscr{L}(G))$ and $\boldsymbol{x} = (x_1, \ldots, x_m)$.
In particular, $S \subseteq \mathbb{F}_{q^t}$ is a linear subspace over $\mathbb{F}_q$, $|S| = q^{l(G)} \geq q^{t-g}$ and $\nu^{\circ}_{\mathscr{L}(G)}(\mathbb{F}_q[\boldsymbol{x}], S) = 1$.

PROOF. We first show that the map E is a one-to-one linear map. Let $f \in \mathscr{L}(G)$. Then $v_Q(f) \geq -v_Q(G) = 0$ and therefore $f(Q) \neq \infty$ and the map is well defined.
Now we show that $\mathrm{Ker}E = \{0\}$. Let $f \in \mathscr{L}(G)$. Then $(f) \geq -G$. If $f \in \mathrm{Ker}E$ then $f(Q) = 0$ and therefore $v_Q(f) > 0$. Since $v_Q(G) = 0$ we have $f \in \mathscr{L}(G - Q)$. Since $deg(G-Q) = -1$, $\mathscr{L}(G-Q) = \{0\}$ and therefore $f = 0$. Therefore E is a one-to-one linear map and the map $E_S : \mathscr{L}(G) \to S$ defined as $E_S(f) = E(f)$ is an isomorphism of linear spaces over $\mathbb{F}_q$.
Now suppose $h \in \mathbb{F}_q[\boldsymbol{x}]$ and let $\boldsymbol{E}_S = (E_S, E_S, \ldots, E_S)$ and $\boldsymbol{E}_S^{-1} = (E_S^{-1}, E_S^{-1}, \ldots, E_S^{-1})$. Consider the tester $L = \{\boldsymbol{E}_S^{-1}\}$. Let $\boldsymbol{a} \in S^m$. If $(hL)(\boldsymbol{a}) = 0$ then $0 = ((hL)(\boldsymbol{a}))(Q) = h(\boldsymbol{E}_S^{-1}(\boldsymbol{a}))(Q) = h(\boldsymbol{E}_S(\boldsymbol{E}_S^{-1}(\boldsymbol{a}))) = h(\boldsymbol{a})$. Since $E_S(1) = 1(Q) = 1$ we have $E_S^{-1}(1) = 1$ and the tester is reducible.

Since E_S is isomorphism we have $|S| = |\mathscr{L}(G)| = q^{(G)}$ and by the Riemann-Roch Theorem we have $(G) \geq \deg G + 1 - g = t - g$. □

We now prove

LEMMA 19. *Let $F/\mathbb{F}_q$ be a function field of genus g and let $t, g > 4$. If F has $d(t+g-1)+2$ places of degree 1 then there is a linear subspace $S \subseteq \mathbb{F}_{q^{t+g}}$ of size q^t such that $\nu^{\mathcal{P}}_{\mathbb{F}_q}(d,S) \leq d(t+g-1)+1$.*

PROOF. First, by Corollary 5.2.10 (c) in [52], if $2g + 1 \leq q^{(t+g-1)/2}(q^{1/2}-1)$ then there is a prime divisor of degree $t+g$. Since $t, g > 4$ the inequality holds and there is at least one prime divisor of degree $t+g$. Let Q be a prime divisor of degree $t+g$.
Let $P_1, \ldots, P_s, P_\infty$, $s = d(t+g-1)+1$, be distinct places of $F/\mathbb{F}_q$ of degree 1 and $D = P_1 + P_2 + \cdots + P_s$ and let $G = (t+g-1)P_\infty$. By Lemma 18 there is a subspace $S \subseteq \mathbb{F}_{q^{t+g}}$ of size $|S| = q^t$ such that $\nu^{\mathcal{P}}_{\mathscr{L}(G)}(d,S) = 1$.
By *1* in Lemma 12 and Lemma 4 we have $\nu^{\mathcal{P}}_{\mathbb{F}_q}(d,S) \leq \nu^{\mathcal{P}}_{\mathbb{F}_q}(d,\mathscr{L}(G)) \cdot \nu^{\mathcal{P}}_{\mathscr{L}(G)}(d,S) \leq d \deg G + 1 = d(t+g-1)+1$. □

Note that in the above lemma we could have used *2* in Lemma 12 and get $\nu^{\mathcal{P}}_{\mathbb{F}_q}(d,S) \leq dt + (d-1)(g-1)$. This will not effect the asymptotic bounds we get in this paper. Also, we will see in the next subsection that the construction of such tester is easier using this bound.
In the full paper we prove the following result that is similar to Corollary 17

COROLLARY 20. *Let $c > 1$ be any constant. For every t there is a linear subspace $S_t \subseteq \mathbb{F}_{q^T}$ over $\mathbb{F}_q$ for some $T = O(dt)$ of size $|S_t| = q^t$ such that:*

1. *For perfect square q where $q \geq c(d+1)^2$ and any integer t we have $\nu^{\mathcal{P}}_{\mathbb{F}_q}(d,S_t) = O(d^2t)$.*

2. *For any $q \geq c(d+1)$ and any integers t we have $\nu^{\mathcal{P}}_{\mathbb{F}_q}(d,S_t) = O(d^3t)$.*

3. *For any $q \geq d+1$ and any integers t we have $\nu^{\mathcal{P}}_{\mathbb{F}_q}(d,S_t) = O(d^4t)$.*

Let $c > 1$ be any constant. For every t there is a linear subspace $S_t \subseteq \mathbb{F}_{q^T}$ over $\mathbb{F}_q$ for some $T = O(t)$ of size $|S_t| = q^t$ such that:

4. *For perfect square q where $q \geq c(d+1)^2$ there is an infinite sequence of integers t such that $\nu^{\mathcal{P}}_{\mathbb{F}_q}(d,S_t) = O(dt)$.*

5. *For any $q \geq c(d+1)$ there is an infinite sequence of integers t such that $\nu^{\mathcal{P}}_{\mathbb{F}_q}(d,S_t) = O(d^2t)$.*

6. *For any $q \geq d+1$ there is an infinite sequence of integers t such that $\nu^{\mathcal{P}}_{\mathbb{F}_q}(d,S_t) = O(d^3t)$.*

We note here that Corollary 20 is subsumed by Corollary 17 but as we will show in the sequel, its construction requires less time complexity.

2.4 Testers for Small Fields

In this subsection we use some elementary algebra and Theorem 11 to construct testers for small fields. We prove

THEOREM 21. *For any $q < d+1$ and t we have*

$$\nu_{\mathbb{F}_q}(d, \mathbb{F}_{q^t}) \leq poly(d) \cdot 2^{c_q d} \cdot t$$

where

$$c_q = \sum_{i=0}^{\infty} \frac{\log(q^{2^i}+1)}{q^{2^i}} = O\left(\frac{\log q}{q}\right).$$

In particular $c_2 = 1.659945821$, $c_3 = 1.116191294$, $c_4 = 0.867464571$, $c_5 = 0.719921672$ and $c_7 = 0.548433289$.

PROOF. Let r be such that $q^{2^{r-1}} < d+1 \leq q^{2^r}$. By Lemma 2, Corollary 5, Lemma 6 and 7 and (1) and Theorem 11, $\nu_{\mathbb{F}_q}(d, \mathbb{F}_{q^t}) \leq \nu_{\mathbb{F}_q}(d, \mathbb{F}_{q^{t \cdot 2^r}})$

$$\begin{aligned}
&\leq \left(\prod_{i=0}^{r-1} \nu_{\mathbb{F}_{q^{2^i}}}(d, \mathbb{F}_{q^{2^{i+1}}})\right) \nu_{\mathbb{F}_{q^{2^r}}}(d, \mathbb{F}_{(q^{2^r})^t}) \\
&\leq \left(\prod_{i=0}^{r-1} \nu_{\mathbb{F}_{q^{2^i}}}(q^{2^i}, \mathbb{F}_{q^{2^{i+1}}})^{\lceil d/q^{2^i} \rceil}\right) \nu_{\mathbb{F}_{q^{2^r}}}(d, \mathbb{F}_{(q^{2^r})^t}) \\
&\leq \left(\prod_{i=0}^{r-1} \left(q^{2^i}+1\right)^{\lceil d/q^{2^i} \rceil}\right) \nu_{\mathbb{F}_{q^{2^r}}}(d, \mathbb{F}_{(q^{2^r})^t}) \\
&\leq \left(\left(\prod_{i=0}^{r-1} \left(q^{2^i}+1\right)\right) 2^{c_q d}\right) poly(d) \cdot t \\
&\leq poly(d) \cdot 2^{c_q d} \cdot t.
\end{aligned}$$

□

We note here that the $poly(d)$ part in the proof is at most $O(d^6)$. In the full paper we show how to reduce it to $O(d^5)$. In Subsection 3.6 we show that a tester with such size can be constructed in time $2^{c_q d} \cdot poly(t)$. In Subsection 2.6 we give the lower bound $\nu_{\mathbb{F}_q}(d, \mathbb{F}_{q^t}) = 2^{\Omega(d/q)}t$ for the above tester. This shows that the size of the above tester is almost optimal.

2.5 Symmetric and Reducible Testers

In this subsection we give a classification of symmetric and reducible tester. This classification will first help us understand the algebraic structure of symmetric and reducible tester. Then it will show that the problem of deciding, given a set of maps L, whether L is a symmetric and reducible $(\mathcal{P}(\mathbb{F}_q, n, d), \mathbb{F}_{q^t}, \mathbb{F}_q)$-tester is in NP. This will be used in the next subsection to construct a symmetric and reducible $(\mathcal{P}(\mathbb{F}_q, n, d), \mathbb{F}_{q^t}, \mathbb{F}_q)$-tester of almost (within d^2) optimal size in polynomial time. More general results are proved in [12].

2.5.1 Definition

We recall the definition of symmetric and reducible tester

DEFINITION 22. *Let $\mathbb{F}$ be a field and $\mathcal{A}$ and $\mathcal{B}$ be two commutative $\mathbb{F}$-algebras. Let $\mathcal{M} \subseteq \mathbb{F}[x_1, x_2, \ldots, x_n]$ be a class of multivariate polynomials. Let $S \subseteq \mathcal{A}$ and $R \subseteq \mathcal{B}$ be linear sub-spaces over $\mathbb{F}$ and $L = \{\ell_1, \ldots, \ell_\nu\}$ be a set of maps $S \to R$. Let $\boldsymbol{\ell}_i : S^n \to R^n$ where for $\boldsymbol{a} \in S^n$,*

$$\boldsymbol{\ell}_i(\boldsymbol{a}) = (\ell_i(a_1), \ell_i(a_2), \ldots, \ell_i(a_n)).$$

We denote by fL the map $S^n \to \mathcal{B}^\nu$ where for $\boldsymbol{a} \in S^n$, $(fL)(\boldsymbol{a}) = (f(\boldsymbol{\ell}_1(\boldsymbol{a})), \ldots, f(\boldsymbol{\ell}_\nu(\boldsymbol{a})))$. We say that L is an symmetric $(\mathcal{M}, S, R)$-tester if for every $\boldsymbol{a} \in S^n$ and $f \in \mathcal{M}$ we have

$$(fL)(\boldsymbol{a}) = 0^\nu \implies f(\boldsymbol{a}) = 0.$$

We say that L is reducible if for all i, $\ell_i(1_\mathcal{B}) = 1_\mathcal{A}$ where $1_\mathcal{A}$ and $1_\mathcal{B}$ are the identities of the algebras $\mathcal{A}$ and $\mathcal{B}$ respectively.

For $q \geq d+1$ we define $\tau(d,q,t)$ the constant for which a $(\mathcal{P}(\mathbb{F}_q,n,d), \mathbb{F}_{q^t}, \mathbb{F}_q)$-tester of size $O(d^{\tau(d,q,t)} \cdot t)$ exists. Define $\tau^*(d,q,t)$ the constant for which a symmetric and reducible $(\mathcal{P}(\mathbb{F}_q,n,d), \mathbb{F}_{q^t}, \mathbb{F}_q)$-tester of size $O(d^{\tau^*(d,q,t)} \cdot t)$ exists. Obviously $\tau(d,q,t) \leq \tau^*(d,q,t)$.
Since the testers in Lemma 12 and Lemma 13 are symmetric and reducible and Corollary 5 is also true for symmetric and reducible testers, the testers constructed in Theorem 11 and Corollary 17 are symmetric and reducible. Therefore

$$\tau^*(d,q,t) \leq 4 \tag{8}$$

for any $q \geq d+1$ and any t and

COROLLARY 23. *We have*

1. *For perfect square q where $q \geq c(d+1)^2$ there is infinite sequence of integers t such that $\tau^*(d,q,t) \leq 1$.*
2. *For perfect square q where $q \geq c(d+1)^2$ and any integer t we have $\tau^*(d,q,t) \leq 2$.*
3. *For any $q \geq c(d+1)$ there is an infinite sequence of integers t such that $\tau^*(d,q,t) \leq 2$.*
4. *For any $q \geq c(d+1)$ and any integers t we have $\tau^*(d,q,t) \leq 3$.*
5. *For any $q \geq d+1$ there is an infinite sequence of integers t such that $\tau^*(d,q,t) \leq 3$.*
6. *For any $q \geq d+1$ and any integers t we have $\tau^*(d,q,t) \leq 4$.*

2.5.2 Classification

In this subsection we give a classification of symmetric and reducible tester. In the full paper we prove the following

LEMMA 24. *We have: $L = \{\ell_1, \ldots, \ell_\nu\}$ is a symmetric $(\mathcal{HP}(\mathbb{F}_q,n,d), \mathbb{F}_{q^t}, \mathbb{F}_q)$-tester for all n if and only if there are $\beta_1, \ldots, \beta_\nu \in \mathbb{F}_{q^t}$ such that for every $a_1, a_2, \ldots, a_d \in \mathbb{F}_{q^t}$*

$$a_1 a_2 \cdots a_d = \sum_{i=1}^{\nu} \beta_i \ell_i(a_1) \ell_i(a_2) \cdots \ell_i(a_d).$$

LEMMA 25. *We have: $L = \{\ell_1, \ldots, \ell_\nu\}$ is a symmetric and reducible $(\mathcal{P}(\mathbb{F}_q,n,d), \mathbb{F}_{q^t}, \mathbb{F}_q)$-tester for all n if and only if there are $\beta_1, \ldots, \beta_\nu \in \mathbb{F}_{q^t}$ such that for every $a_1, a_2, \ldots, a_d \in \mathbb{F}_{q^t}$*

$$a_1 a_2 \cdots a_d = \sum_{i=1}^{\nu} \beta_i \ell_i(a_1) \ell_i(a_2) \cdots \ell_i(a_d) \tag{9}$$

and $\ell_i(1) = 1$ for all i.

In the following lemma we show that when the tester is symmetric then we may assume without loss of generality that all ℓ_i are linear functions from the dual vector space $\mathbb{F}_{q^t}^*$. The proof is in full paper

LEMMA 26. *If $L = \{\ell_1, \ldots, \ell_\nu\}$ is a symmetric (and reducible) $(\mathcal{P}(\mathbb{F}_q,n,d), \mathbb{F}_{q^t}, \mathbb{F}_q)$-tester for all n then there is a symmetric (and reducible) $(\mathcal{P}(\mathbb{F}_q,n,d), \mathbb{F}_{q^t}, \mathbb{F}_q)$-tester $\tilde{L} = \{\tilde{\ell}_1, \ldots, \tilde{\ell}_\nu\}$ with the same size where each $\tilde{\ell}_i$, $i = 1, \ldots, \nu$ is a linear function in $\mathbb{F}_{q^t}^*$.*

Testers of the form (9) are called symmetric linear simulator [12]. For $d = 2$, symmetric simulators and their connection to tensor rank are studied in [55]. We further study simulators in [12] and their connection to d-dimensional tensor rank and give other results.

2.6 Lower Bounds

In this subsection we give some lower bounds for the size of testers. In Theorem 21 we have proved that for any $q < d+1$ and t we have $\nu_{\mathbb{F}_q}(d, \mathbb{F}_{q^t}) \leq$

$$\left(1 + \frac{\ln(q+1)}{q} + O\left(\frac{\log q}{q^2}\right)\right)^d \cdot t = 2^{O\left(\frac{\log q}{q}\right)d} \cdot t.$$

In the full paper we give the following lower bound

THEOREM 27. *For any q, d and t we have*

$$\nu_{\mathbb{F}_q}(d, \mathbb{F}_{q^t}) \geq \left(1 + \frac{1}{q-1} - \frac{1}{(q-1)q^{t-1}}\right)^{d-1} \cdot t = 2^{\Omega\left(\frac{1}{q}\right)d} \cdot t.$$

For $\nu^\mathcal{P}$ and $\nu^{\mathcal{HP}}$, we first prove that there is no tester for $\mathcal{P}(\mathbb{F}_q,n,d)$ when $q \leq d$ and no tester for $\mathcal{HP}(\mathbb{F}_q,n,d)$ when $q \leq d-1$.

LEMMA 28. *For $q \leq d$ we have $\nu^\mathcal{P}_{\mathbb{F}_q}(d, \mathbb{F}_{q^t}) = \infty$ and for $q \leq d-1$ we have $\nu^{\mathcal{HP}}_{\mathbb{F}_q}(d, \mathbb{F}_{q^t}) = \infty$.*

PROOF. Let $\mathbb{F}_q = \{\alpha_1, \ldots, \alpha_q\}$ and consider the polynomial $f(x) = (x - \alpha_1)(x - \alpha_2) \cdots (x - \alpha_q)$. Let $\beta \in \mathbb{F}_{q^t}$ such that $f(\beta) \neq 0$. Since $f(\ell(\beta)) = 0$ for all $\ell : \mathbb{F}_{q^t} \to \mathbb{F}_q$ the first result follows.
For the second result we take $f(x_1, x_2) = x_2(x_1 - \alpha_1 x_2)(x_1 - \alpha_2 x_2) \cdots (x_1 - \alpha_q x_2)$. $\square$

In Corollary 17 we have shown that for $q \geq d+1$ we have $\nu^\mathcal{P}_{\mathbb{F}_q}(d, \mathbb{F}_{q^t}) = O(d^{\tau(d,q,t)} t)$ where for any constant $c > 1$

$$\tau(d,q,t) = \begin{cases} 1 & \text{if} \quad q \text{ perfect square}, q \geq c(d+1)^2, \text{ I.S. } t \\ 2 & \text{if} \quad q \text{ perfect square}, q \geq c(d+1)^2 \\ 2 & \text{if} \quad q \geq c(d+1), \text{ I.S. } t \\ 3 & \text{if} \quad q \geq c(d+1) \\ 3 & \text{if} \quad q \geq d+1, \text{ I.S. } t \\ 4 & \text{if} \quad q \geq d+1 \end{cases}$$

where I.S. stands for "infinite sequence of". In the following Theorem we give the lower bound $\tau(d,q,t) \geq 1$, which is tight for perfect square q, $q \geq c(d+1)^2$ and infinite sequence of t.

THEOREM 29. *For any $q \geq d+1$ and t we have*

$$\nu^\mathcal{P}_{\mathbb{F}_q}(d, \mathbb{F}_{q^t}) \geq \nu^{\mathcal{HP}}_{\mathbb{F}_q}(d, \mathbb{F}_{q^t}) \geq dt - d + 1.$$

In particular, $\tau(d,q,t) \geq 1$.

PROOF. Consider the set $\mathcal{M} = \{\prod_{k=1}^{d}(x_j - x_{i_k}) \mid 1 \le i_1 < i_2 < \cdots < i_d \le q^t, 1 \le j \le q^t, j \notin \{i_1, i_2, \ldots, i_d\}\}$. Obviously, $\mathcal{M} \subseteq \mathcal{HP}(\mathbb{F}_q, n, d)$. Let $L = \{\ell_1, \ldots, \ell_\nu\}$ be a $(\mathcal{HP}(\mathbb{F}_q, n, d), \mathbb{F}_{q^t}, \mathbb{F}_q)$-tester with minimal size $\nu = \nu_{\mathbb{F}_q}^{\mathcal{HP}}(d, \mathbb{F}_{q^t})$. By Lemma 3, L is a $(\mathcal{M}, \mathbb{F}_{q^t}, \mathbb{F}_q)$-tester. Let α be a primitive root in $\mathbb{F}_{q^t}$ and consider the assignment $\boldsymbol{z} = (0, \alpha^0, \alpha^1, \ldots, \alpha^{q^t-2}) \in \mathbb{F}_{q^t}^{q^t}$. Let $\boldsymbol{c}_i = \ell_i(\boldsymbol{z})$ for $i = 1, \ldots, \nu$ and $C = \{\boldsymbol{c}_i \mid i = 1, 2, \ldots, \nu\}$. Since $f(\boldsymbol{z}) \neq 0$ for all $f \in \mathcal{M}$ and L is a tester for $\mathcal{M}$, for every $f \in \mathcal{M}$ there is $\boldsymbol{c} \in C$ such that $f(\boldsymbol{c}) \neq 0$. That is, for every $1 \le j \le q^t$ and every $1 \le i_1 < i_2 < \cdots < i_d \le q^t$ such that $j \notin \{i_1, i_2, \ldots, i_d\}$ there is $\boldsymbol{c} \in C$ such that $c_j \notin \{c_{i_1}, \ldots, c_{i_d}\}$. Such set is called $(\nu; q^t, q, \{1, d\})$-separating hash family [58, 59]. See Subsection 4.4 in this paper. In [17], Bazrafshan and van Trang proved that

$$q^t \le dq^{\lceil \frac{\nu}{d} \rceil}.$$

See also [15]. Therefore

$$\left\lceil \frac{\nu}{d} \right\rceil \ge t - \frac{\log d}{\log q}.$$

If $q \ge d+1$ then $\lceil \nu/d \rceil \ge t$ and $\nu \ge dt - d + 1$. □

3. CONSTRUCTING TESTERS IN POLYNOMIAL TIME

In this subsection we show that testers of almost optimal size can be constructed in polynomial time.

3.1 Time Complexity of Constructing Irreducible Polynomials and $\mathbb{F}_{q^t}$

In some applications the construction of irreducible polynomials of degree n over $\mathbb{F}_q$ and the construction of the field $\mathbb{F}_{q^t}$ is also needed and their complexity must be included in the overall time complexity of the problem.
To construct the field $\mathbb{F}_{q^t}$ one should construct an irreducible polynomial $f(x)$ of degree t in $\mathbb{F}_q[x]$ and then use the representation $\mathbb{F}_{q^t} = \mathbb{F}_q[x]/(f(x))$. For a comprehensive survey on this problem see [50] Chapter 3. See also [3, 23, 47]. We give here the results that will be used in this paper.

LEMMA 30. *Let $\mathbb{F}_q$ be a field of characteristic p. There is a deterministic algorithm that constructs an irreducible polynomial of degree t with $T = O(p^{1/2+\epsilon}t^{3+\epsilon} + (\log q)^{2+\epsilon} t^{4+\epsilon}) = poly(p, t, \log q)$ arithmetic operations in the field $\mathbb{F}_q$. Assuming the Extended Riemann Hypothesis (ERH) there is a deterministic algorithm that constructs an irreducible polynomial of degree t with $T = O(\log^2 q + t^{4+\epsilon} \log q) = poly(t, \log q)$.*

In some of the applications it is enough to construct an extension field of dimension close to t. The following lemma is proved in [45]

LEMMA 31. *There is a deterministic algorithm that constructs an irreducible polynomial of degree d where $t \le d \le t \log q$ with $poly(t, \log q)$ arithmetic operations in the field $\mathbb{F}_q$.*

One constraint that follows from using finite fields as an alphabet is that the size of the alphabet must be a power of prime. Shparlinski showed in [49] that

LEMMA 32. *for any q large enough one can construct a finite field $\mathbb{F}_Q$ with $Q = q + o(q)$ elements in deterministic time $poly(\log q)$.*

In Lemma 8 one should construct many irreducible polynomials of certain degree. In the full paper we prove

LEMMA 33. *There is a deterministic algorithm that runs in time $m \cdot poly(t, p, \log q)$ (and $m \cdot poly(t, \log q)$ assuming ERH) and construct m distinct irreducible polynomials of degree t in $\mathbb{F}_q[x]$.*

Throughout this paper, when we say polynomial time or write $poly(t, p, \log q)$ we mean $poly(t, p, \log q)$ without any assumption and $poly(t, \log q)$ assuming ERH.

3.2 Preliminary Results

In this subsection we give some preliminary results
For $q \ge d+1$ we define $\tau_{poly}(d, q, t)$ the constant for which a $(\mathcal{P}(\mathbb{F}_q, n, d), \mathbb{F}_{q^t}, \mathbb{F}_q)$-tester of size $O(d^{\tau_{poly}(d,q,t)} \cdot t)$ can be constructed in deterministic polynomial time. Since some of the applications in this paper require testers for fields of logarithmic dimension we also define $\tau_{poly}(d, q, t, r)$ the constant for which a $(\mathcal{P}(\mathbb{F}_q, n, d), \mathbb{F}_{q^r}, \mathbb{F}_q)$-tester of size $O(d^{\tau_{poly}(d,q,t,r)} \cdot r)$ can be constructed in deterministic time $poly(t, p, \log q)$.
In Lemma 7 we have shown that when $q \ge d(t-1)+1$, then a $(\mathcal{P}(\mathbb{F}_q, n, d), \mathbb{F}_{q^t}, \mathbb{F}_q)$-tester can be constructed in time complexity that is equal to the time complexity of constructing the field $\mathbb{F}_{q^t}$. Therefore, such tester can be constructed in polynomial time $poly(t, p, \log q)$. Hence, we may assume that

$$d + 1 \le q \le d(t-1).$$

Notice that in this case, $poly(t, p, \log q) = poly(d, q, t) = poly(t)$.
The results in the following lemma follow immediately from Lemma 7, Corollary 5 and the proof of Corollary 17

LEMMA 34. *We have*

1. *For $q \ge d(t-1)+1$ we have $\tau_{poly}(d, q, t) = 1$.*
2. *For $q \ge d+1$ we have $\tau_{poly}(d, q, t) \le \tau_{poly}(d, q^2, t) + 1$.*
3. *For any $c > 1$, $q \ge c(d+1)^2$, q perfect square, any integer r and $t = \lfloor (\sqrt{c} - 1) q^{(r+2)/2} / \sqrt{c} d \rfloor$ we have $\tau^*(d, q, t) = 1$.*

We now prove the following lemma. The construction in this lemma is computationally expensive in its own right, but with the parameters we will be using it, it will take time polynomial in the parameters of the main problem.

LEMMA 35. *A $(\mathcal{P}(\mathbb{F}_q, n, d), \mathbb{F}_{q^t}, \mathbb{F}_q)$-tester of size $O(d^\tau t)$ can be constructed in $poly(q^{d^\tau t^2})$ time where $\tau = \tau^*(d, q, t)$.*

PROOF. By Corollary 23 there is a symmetric and reducible $(\mathcal{P}(\mathbb{F}_q, n, d), \mathbb{F}_{q^t}, \mathbb{F}_q)$-tester of size $O(d^\tau t)$. By Lemma 25 we have $L = \{\ell_1, \ldots, \ell_\nu\}$ is a symmetric and reducible $(\mathcal{P}(\mathbb{F}_q, n, d), \mathbb{F}_{q^t}, \mathbb{F}_q)$-tester if and only if $\ell_i(1) = 1$ for all i and there are $\beta_i \in \mathbb{F}_{q^t}$ such that for every $\boldsymbol{a} \in \mathbb{F}_{q^t}^d$ we have

$$a_1 a_2 \cdots a_d = \sum_{i=1}^{\nu} \beta_i \ell_i(a_1) \ell_i(a_2) \cdots \ell_i(a_d). \qquad (10)$$

Then by Lemma 26 we may assume without loss of generality that $\ell_i \in \mathbb{F}_{q^t}^*$ and $\ell_i(1) = 1$ for all $i = 1, 2, \ldots, \nu$.
Now to construct a symmetric and reducible tester we can exhaustively search for one. That is, we can try all possible $\beta_i \in \mathbb{F}_{q^t}$ and $\ell_i \in \mathbb{F}_{q^t}^*$ where $\ell_i(1) = 1$, $i = 1, 2, \ldots, \nu$ and check if (10) is true for all $\boldsymbol{a} \in \mathbb{F}_{q^t}^d$. The number of all possible testers of size ν is at most

$$\binom{|\mathbb{F}_{q^t}|}{\nu} \cdot \binom{|\mathbb{F}_{q^t}^*|}{\nu} = \binom{q^t}{\nu}^2 \le q^{2\nu t}.$$

Checking each tester takes $|\mathbb{F}_{q^t}^d| = q^{dt}$ substitutions in (10). Therefore, for $\tau = \tau^*(d, q, t)$, with at most $q^{O(d^\tau t^2)} q^{dt} = q^{O(d^\tau t^2)}$ arithmetic operations in the field $\mathbb{F}_{q^t}$ one can find a symmetric and reducible $(\mathcal{P}(\mathbb{F}_q, n, d), \mathbb{F}_{q^t}, \mathbb{F}_q)$-tester. This implies the result. □

In particular we have

LEMMA 36. *For every $q \ge d+1$ and $\tau = \tau^*(d, q, r)$ if*

$$r \le \sqrt{\frac{\log t}{d^\tau \log q}}$$

then $\tau_{poly}(d, q, t, r) \le \tau^*(d, q, r)$.

3.3 Reductions of the Problem

In this subsection we show that a $(\mathcal{P}(\mathbb{F}_q, n, d), \mathbb{F}_{q^t}, \mathbb{F}_q)$-tester can be reduced in deterministic polynomial time to a $(\mathcal{P}(\mathbb{F}_q, n, d), \mathbb{F}_{q^{t'}}, \mathbb{F}_q)$-tester where t' is logarithmic in t. This reduction blows up the size of the tester by at most a factor of d.
Our main technique for constructing testers in polynomial time is to reduce the dimension t of the field in the tester to a small dimension $r = o(t)$ (Lemma 8) and then construct the tester for dimension r in time polynomial in t. Formally,

LEMMA 37. *For any $t \le t'$ and any $r = O(\log_q t')$*

$$r \ge \left\lceil \frac{\log(dt)}{\log q} \right\rceil + 1$$

(or $q^{r-1} \ge dt - d + 1$) we have

$$\tau_{poly}(d, q, t', t) \le \tau_{poly}(d, q, t', r) + 1.$$

PROOF. We use Lemma 8. Since $r \ge \lceil \log(dt)/\log q \rceil + 1$ we have $q^{r-1} \ge dt - d + 1$. To use the construction in Lemma 8 we need to find $O(dt/r)$ polynomials of degree r. Since $r = O(\log_q t')$ we have $|\mathbb{F}_{q^r}| = poly(t')$. Therefore the field $\mathbb{F}_{q^r}$ can be constructed in $poly(t')$ time and a primitive root of the field and therefore $O(dt/r)$ irreducible polynomials of degree r over $\mathbb{F}_q$ can be constructed in $poly(t')$ time.
If there is a deterministic $poly(t', p, \log q)$ time construction algorithm for a $(\mathcal{P}(\mathbb{F}_q, n, d), \mathbb{F}_{q^r}, \mathbb{F}_q)$-tester of size $O(d^c r)$ then the construction in Lemma 8 is deterministic $poly(t', p, \log q)$ time construction for $(\mathcal{P}(\mathbb{F}_q, n, d), \mathbb{F}_{q^t}, \mathbb{F}_q)$-tester of size

$$\left(\frac{dt - d + 1}{r} + 1\right) \cdot O(d^c r) \le O(d^{c+1} t).$$

This implies the result. □

3.4 Testers for $q \ge d+1$ in Polynomial Time

In this subsection we prove that for every t, d and $q \ge d+1$ a $(\mathcal{P}(\mathbb{F}_q, n, d), \mathbb{F}_{q^t}, \mathbb{F}_q)$-tester of size $O(d^5 \cdot t)$ can be constructed in deterministic polynomial time.
We first prove

LEMMA 38. *For every t, constant $c > 1$, perfect square $q \ge c(d+1)^2$ and $d \ge 3$ a $(\mathcal{P}(\mathbb{F}_q, n, d), \mathbb{F}_{q^t}, \mathbb{F}_q)$-tester of size $O(d^3 t)$ can be constructed in deterministic polynomial time.*

PROOF. By *1* in Lemma 34, for $t \le d+2$ we have $q \ge d(t-1)+1$ and therefore $\tau_{poly}(d, q, t) = 1$. By Lemma 37, for $d + 3 \le t \le q^{d+1}/d$ we have

$$\tau_{poly}(d, q, t) \le \tau_{poly}(d, q, t, d+2) + 1 \le 2.$$

Then again by Lemma 37, for $q^{d+1}/d \le t \le q^{dq^d}$ and $r_0 = \lfloor q^{d+1}/d \rfloor - 1$ we have

$$\tau_{poly}(d, q, t) \le \tau_{poly}(d, q, t, r_0) + 1 \le 3.$$

Therefore, we may assume that

$$t \ge t_0 := q^{dq^d}.$$

Let

$$r_1 = \left\lceil \frac{\log dt}{\log q} \right\rceil + 1. \tag{11}$$

By Lemma 37, we have

$$\tau_{poly}(d, q, t) \le \tau_{poly}(d, q, t, r_1) + 1. \tag{12}$$

Let r be an integer such that

$$\frac{(\sqrt{c}-1)q^{(r+2)/2}}{\sqrt{c}d} \le \sqrt{\frac{\log t}{d \log q}} < \frac{(\sqrt{c}-1)q^{(r+3)/2}}{\sqrt{c}d} \tag{13}$$

and

$$r_2 := \left\lfloor \frac{(\sqrt{c}-1)q^{(r+2)/2}}{\sqrt{c}d} \right\rfloor. \tag{14}$$

By *3* in Lemma 34,

$$\tau^*(d, q, r_2) = 1. \tag{15}$$

In Claim 1 below we prove that $q^{r_2-1} \ge dr_1 - d + 1$. By Lemma 37, since $q^{r_2-1} \ge dr_1 - d + 1$ we have

$$\tau_{poly}(d, q, t, r_1) \le \tau_{poly}(d, q, t, r_2) + 1. \tag{16}$$

Finally, by Lemma 36, (13), (14) and (15) we have

$$\tau_{poly}(d, q, t, r_2) \le \tau^*(d, q, r_2) = 1.$$

This with (16) and (12) gives the result. □

It remains to prove

CLAIM 1. *We have $q^{r_2-1} \ge dr_1 - d + 1$.*

PROOF. Since $t \ge t_0 \ge q^{dq^d}$ we have $r_1 \ge \log_q t \ge dq^d$. By (11) we have $r_1 \le \log_q t + 3$ and therefore $t \ge q^{r_1-3}$. By (13) and (14) we have

$$\begin{aligned} r_2 \ &\ge \ \frac{(c-1)q^{(r+2)/2}}{cd} - 1 \ge \frac{1}{q^{1/2}} \frac{(c-1)q^{(r+3)/2}}{cd} - 1 \\ &\ge \ \sqrt{\frac{\log t}{qd \log q}} - 1 \ge \sqrt{\frac{r_1 - 3}{qd}} - 1. \end{aligned}$$

Therefore

$$q^{r_2-1} \geq q^{\sqrt{\frac{r_1-3}{qd}}-2}$$

and it is enough to prove that for $r_1 \geq dq^d$,

$$q^{\sqrt{\frac{r_1-3}{qd}}-2} \geq dr_1.$$

This is true since $d \geq 3$ and $q \geq (d+1)^2$.

□

We now prove

THEOREM 39. *For every n, t, d and $q \geq d+1$, a $(\mathcal{P}(\mathbb{F}_q, n, d), \mathbb{F}_{q^t}, \mathbb{F}_q)$-tester of size $O(d^5 t)$ can be constructed in polynomial time.*

PROOF. If $q \geq d+1$ then $q^4 \geq 2(d+1)^2$. Therefore by Lemma 38, $\tau_{poly}(d, q^4, t) \leq 3$. Now by *2* in Lemma 34 we have

$$\tau_{poly}(d,q,t) \leq \tau_{poly}(d,q^2,t)+1 \leq \tau_{poly}(d,q^4,t)+2 \leq 5.$$

□

By Corollary 23 and the proof of Theorem 39 we also get

COROLLARY 40. *Let $c > 1$ be a constant and $r = poly(d, \log t)$. We have the following upper bounds for $T_1 := \tau_{poly}(d, q, t, r)$ and $T_2 := \tau_{poly}(d, q, t)$*

q	t	τ^*	T_1	T_2
$q \geq c(d+1)^2$, q *P.S.*	*I.S.*	1	2	3
$q \geq c(d+1)^2$ q *P.S.*	*all*	2	2	3
$q \geq c(d+1)$	*I.S.*	2	3	4
$q \geq c(d+1)$	*all*	3	3	4
$q \geq d+1$	*I.S.*	3	4	5
$q \geq d+1$	*all*	4	4	5

where I.S. stands for "for infinite sequence of integers t" and P.S. for "perfect square".

3.5 Testers for Subspaces of Fields in Polynomial Time

In the full paper we discuss the explicit construction in Subsection 2.3 of testers for subspaces of fields and what is needed in order to get a polynomial time construction. We show that testers for subspaces of extension fields of logarithmic dimension can be constructed in polynomial time. Those testers will have better size than the testers in the previous subsection and will close the gaps in the table in Corollary 40 for $\tau_{poly}(d, q, t, r)$ when $r = O(\log t / \log q)$. In the full paper we prove

COROLLARY 41. *Let $c > 1$ be a constant and $r = O(\log t / \log q)$. There is a polynomial time algorithm that constructs a subspace $S \subseteq \mathbb{F}_{q^R}$ of size $|S| = q^r$ where $R \leq O(r)$ and a $(\mathcal{P}(\mathbb{F}_q, n, d), S, \mathbb{F}_q)$-tester of size $O(d^\tau r)$ where τ is as indicated in the following table (the fourth column in the table)*

q	t	*Upper B.* $\tau^*(d,q,t)$	*Upper B.* τ
$q \geq c(d+1)^2$, q *P.S.*	*I.S.*	1	1
$q \geq c(d+1)$	*I.S.*	2	2
$q \geq d+1$	*I.S.*	3	3

where I.S. stands for "for infinite sequence of integers t" and P.S. for "perfect square".

Notice that $\tau_{poly}(d, q, t, r)$ in Corollary 40 with τ in Corollary 41 give bounds that meet the bounds for $\tau^*(d, q, t)$ when the dimension is $O(\log t / \log q)$.

3.6 Testers for $q < d+1$ in Polynomial Time

In this subsection we study $(\mathcal{HLF}(\mathbb{F}_q, n, d), \mathbb{F}_{q^t}, \mathbb{F}_q)$-testers when $q < d+1$. The following result follows immediately from Lemma 30 and the testers constructed in Lemmas 2, 4, 6, 7, Theorem 21 and Theorem 39.

THEOREM 42. *For any $q < d+1$ and t a $(\mathcal{HLF}(\mathbb{F}_q, n, d), \mathbb{F}_{q^t}, \mathbb{F}_q)$-tester of size $O(d^7 \cdot 2^{c_q d} \cdot t)$ can be constructed in time $2^{c_q d} \cdot poly(t)$ where*

$$c_q = \sum_{i=0}^{\infty} \frac{\log(q^{2^i}+1)}{q^{2^i}} = O\left(\frac{\log q}{q}\right).$$

We denote by $\sigma(q)$ (respectively, $\sigma_{poly}(q)$) the constant for which a $(\mathcal{HLF}(\mathbb{F}_q, n, d), \mathbb{F}_{q^t}, \mathbb{F}_q)$-tester L of size $2^{\sigma(q)\cdot d + o(d)} \cdot t$ exists (respectively, and can be constructed in $2^{\sigma(q)\cdot d} \cdot poly(t)$ time). By Theorem 21 and Theorem 27 we have

$$O\left(\frac{\log q}{q}\right) = \sum_{i=0}^{\infty} \frac{\log(q^{2^i}+1)}{q^{2^i}} = c_q \geq \sigma_{poly}(q) \geq$$

$$\sigma(q) \geq \log\left(1+\frac{1}{q-1}\right) = \Omega\left(\frac{1}{q}\right).$$

3.7 Tester from any Field to any Field

In this subsection we study $(\mathcal{P}(\mathbb{F}_q, n, d), \mathbb{F}_{q^t}, \mathbb{F}_{q^{t'}})$-testers when $q^{t'} \geq d+1$. Those testers will be used to reduce the dimension of the extension field used in the black box interpolation and identity testing to a smaller dimension. Such tester can be constructed using the fact that $\mathbb{F}_{q^t}$ can be embedded into the field $\mathbb{F}_{(q^{t'})^t} \cong \mathbb{F}_{(q^t)^{t'}}$ and then the $(\mathcal{P}(\mathbb{F}_q, n, d), \mathbb{F}_{(q^{t'})^t}, \mathbb{F}_{q^{t'}})$-tester constructed in the previous subsections is also a $(\mathcal{P}(\mathbb{F}_q, n, d), \mathbb{F}_{q^t}, \mathbb{F}_{q^{t'}})$-tester. This tester is optimal within a factor of t'. Our goal in this subsection is to find such tester that is optimal within a factor of $poly(d)$.

One approach is to first construct a $(\mathcal{P}(\mathbb{F}_q, n, d), \mathbb{F}_{q^t}, \mathbb{F}_{q^T})$-tester such that $T > dt$ and $t'|T$. Then construct a $(\mathcal{P}(\mathbb{F}_q, n, d), \mathbb{F}_{q^T}, \mathbb{F}_{q^{t'}})$-tester and combine both testers. Another approach, that is used here, is to first construct a $(\mathcal{P}(\mathbb{F}_q, n, d), \mathbb{F}_{q^t}, \mathbb{F}_{q^T})$-tester where $t'|T$ and $T = O(\log(dt)/\log q)$. Then construct a $(\mathcal{P}(\mathbb{F}_q, n, d), \mathbb{F}_{q^T}, \mathbb{F}_{q^{t'}})$-tester and combine both testers.

In the full paper we prove

LEMMA 43. *Let $t' \geq 1$ be an integer such that $q^{t'} \geq d+1$. We have*

1. *If $t' \geq \lceil \log(dt)/\log q \rceil + 1$ then $\nu^{\mathcal{P}}_{\mathbb{F}_{q^{t'}}}((d, \mathbb{F}_q), \mathbb{F}_{q^t}) \leq (d+1)t/t'$ and a tester with such size can be constructed in polynomial time.*
2. *If $t' \geq \lceil \log(d \log(dt)/\log q)/\log q \rceil \geq 2$ then $\nu^{\mathcal{P}}_{\mathbb{F}_{q^{t'}}}((d, \mathbb{F}_q), \mathbb{F}_{q^t}) \leq d(d+1)t/t'$ and a tester with such size can be constructed in polynomial time.*

3. For any t' we have $\nu^{\mathcal{P}}_{\mathbb{F}_{q^{t'}}}((d,\mathbb{F}_q),\mathbb{F}_{q^t}) \le O(d^5t/t')$ and a tester with such size can be constructed in polynomial time.

4. D-RESTRICTION PROBLEMS

In this section we give some applications of testers for d-restriction problems. A *d-restriction problem* [43, 4] is a problem of the following form:

Given an alphabet Σ of size $|\Sigma| = q$, an integer n and a class $\mathcal{M}$ of nonzero functions $f_i : \Sigma^d \to \{0,1\}$, $i = 1,2,\ldots,t$.

Find a small set $A \subseteq \Sigma^n$ such that: For every $1 \le i_1 < i_2 < \cdots < i_d \le n$ and $f \in \mathcal{M}$ there is $\boldsymbol{a} \in A$ such that $f(a_{i_1},\ldots,a_{i_d}) \ne 0$.

We give applications of testers for the following four d-restriction problems: Perfect hash, universal set, cover-free family and separating hash family.

Note. For all the applications in this paper we will give deterministic polynomial time constructions, but in some cases some explicit constructions are also given. We remind the reader that when say an "explicit construction" we mean a construction using elementary algebra and algebraic function fields in which each step of the construction is indicated. But it is not clear whether the construction is polynomial time construction. For a construction that has exponential size, when we say that such construction can be constructed in "polynomial time" we mean in time $s \cdot poly(n)$ where s is the size of the construction.

4.1 Perfect Hash

In this subsection we show that testers can be used for constructing almost optimal perfect hashing in polynomial time.

Let H be a family of functions $h : [n] \to [q]$. We say that H is an *(n,q)-family of perfect hash functions* if for all subset $S \subseteq [n]$ of size $|S| = q$ there is an $h \in H$ such that the restriction of h to S, $h|_S$, is onto, i.e., $h|_S(S) = [q]$. In [43] Naor et. al. gave a deterministic construction of an (n,q)-family of perfect hash functions of size $s = e^q q^{O(\log q)} \log n$ that can be constructed in time $s \cdot poly(n)$.

For $d \le q$ we say that H is an *(n,q,d)-perfect hashing* [4] (or *(n,d,q)-splitter* [43]) if for all subsets $S \subseteq [n]$ of size $|S| = d$ there is a *hash function* $h \in H$ such that $h|_S$ is injective (one-to-one) on S, i.e., $|h|_S(S)| = d$. Thus (n,q)-family of perfect hash functions is (n,q,q)-perfect hashing. In [43, 4] it was shown that there are (n,d^2,d)-perfect hashing of size $O(d^4 \log d \log n)$ that can be constructed in *poly*(n,d) time. Wang and Xing [64] used algebraic function fields and gave an explicit (n,d^4,d)-perfect hashing of size $O((d^2/\log d)\log n)$ for infinite sequence of integers n. Their construction is similar to the construction of $(\mathcal{P}(\mathbb{F}_q,n,d),\mathscr{L}(G),\mathbb{F}_q)$-tester. The only known polynomial time construction is of size $O(d^4 \log d \log n)$ when $q = O(d^2)$, [43, 4]. Blackburn and Wild [18] gave an explicit optimal construction when q is very large compared to d and $\log n$.

Let $N(n,d,q)$ be the size of the smallest (n,q,d)-perfect hashing. Obviously, the problem of finding a small *(n,q,d)-perfect hashing* is a d-restriction problem where $\mathcal{M} = \{f\}$, $f : \Sigma^d \to \{0,1\}$ and $f(x_1,x_2,\ldots,x_d) = 1$ if and only if $|\{x_1,\ldots,x_d\}| = d$. We will be interested in the case where $d = o(n)$. We now use union bound to give a nonconstructive upper bound

LEMMA 44. *Let $q \ge d(d-1)/2+1$. Then*

$$N(n,q,d) \le \frac{\log\binom{n}{d}}{\log\left(\frac{1}{1-g(q,d)}\right)} \le \frac{d\log n}{\log\frac{2q}{d(d-1)}} \tag{17}$$

where $g(q,d) = (q-1)(q-2)\cdots(q-d+1)/q^d$.
In particular, when $q = \Theta(d^2)$ then $N(n,q,d) = O(d\log n)$ and when $q \ge d^{2+\epsilon}$ for some constant $\epsilon > 0$ then

$$N(n,q,d) \le \frac{d\log n}{\log q}.$$

PROOF. The bound (17) follows from union bound. □

By [40] (see also [26, 33, 34]) we have the following lower bound

LEMMA 45. *Let $q \ge d(d-1)/2+1$. Then*

$$N(n,q,d) \ge \frac{g(n,d-1)\log(n-d+2)}{g(q,d-1)\log(q-d+2)} = \Omega\left(\frac{\log n}{\log q}\right). \tag{18}$$

We now prove

LEMMA 46. *Let $q > d(d-1)/2$ be a power of prime. Let t be an integer such that $q^t \ge n$. Let $S \subseteq \mathbb{F}_{q^T}$ be a linear subspace for some $T \ge t$ where $|S| = q^t$. There is an explicit (n,q,d)-perfect hashing of size*

$$\nu^{\mathcal{HP}}_{\mathbb{F}_q}\left(\frac{d(d-1)}{2},S\right).$$

In particular, There is an explicit (n,q,d)-perfect hashing of size

$$\nu^{\mathcal{HP}}_{\mathbb{F}_q}\left(\frac{d(d-1)}{2},\mathbb{F}_{q^t}\right).$$

In particular, for a constant $c > 1$, the Table 3 (in the introduction) of the (n,q,d)-perfect hashing can be constructed in polynomial time

PROOF. Consider the set of functions

$$\mathcal{F} = \{\Delta_{\{i_1,\ldots,i_d\}}(x_1,\ldots,x_n) \mid 1 \le i_1 < \cdots < i_d \le n\}$$

in $\mathbb{F}_q[x_1,x_2,\ldots,x_n]$ where

$$\Delta_{\{i_1,\ldots,i_d\}}(x_1,\ldots,x_n) = \prod_{1\le k<j\le d}(x_{i_k}-x_{i_j}).$$

Consider n distinct elements $\alpha_1,\alpha_2,\ldots,\alpha_n \in S$ and let $\boldsymbol{\alpha} = (\alpha_1,\alpha_2,\ldots,\alpha_n)$. Since $g(\boldsymbol{\alpha}) \ne 0$ for every $g \in \mathcal{F}$, and since $\mathcal{F} \subset \mathcal{HP}(\mathbb{F}_q,n,d(d-1)/2)$, using testers, there is a set $B \subseteq \mathbb{F}_q^n$ of size $\nu^{\mathcal{HP}}_{\mathbb{F}_q}(d(d-1)/2,S)$ such that for every $g \in \mathcal{F}$ there is $\boldsymbol{b} \in B$ where $g(\boldsymbol{b}) \ne 0$. This gives an (n,q,d)-perfect hashing.

Now, the results in the table follows from Corollaries 40 and 41. □

When $q > d(d+1)/2$ is not a power of prime number then we can take the nearest prime $q' < q$ and construct an (n,q',d)-perfect hashing that is also (n,q,d)-perfect hashing. It is known that the nearest prime $q' \ge q - \Theta(q^{.525})$, [16], and therefore the result in the above table is also true for any integer $q \ge d(d+1)/2 + O(d^{1.05})$.

4.2 (n, d)-Universal Set

An (n, d)-universal set over an alphabet Σ is a set $\mathcal{F} \subseteq \Sigma^n$ such that for every $1 \le i_1 < i_2 < \cdots < i_d \le n$ and every $(\sigma_1, \ldots, \sigma_d) \in \Sigma^d$ there is $\boldsymbol{a} \in \mathcal{F}$ such that $a_{i_j} = \sigma_j$ for all $j = 1, \ldots, d$.

Let $|\Sigma| = q$. Let $U(n, d, q)$ be the size of the smallest (n, d)-universal set over the alphabet Σ. Obviously, finding a small (n, d)-universal set is a d-restriction problem.

The union bound shows that there is an (n, d)-universal set over an alphabet Σ of size

$$U(n, d, q) \le dq^d \left(\ln \frac{n}{d} + \ln q\right) = O\left(dq^d \log n\right).$$

In the full paper we give the following better bound when q is a power of prime

LEMMA 47. *Let $q > 2$ be a power of prime. We have*

$$U(n, d, q) = O\left(d \frac{q^d}{\log q} \log n\right).$$

For $q = 2$, a lower bound of $\Omega(2^d \log n)$ was proved in [36]. The following lower bound follows from [36] and [51]

LEMMA 48. *We have*

$$U(n, d, q) = \Omega\left(\frac{q^{d-1}}{\log q} \log n\right).$$

The best known construction for this problem gives a universal set of size $d^{O(\log d/\log q)} q^d \log n$ for $q < d$ and $O(d^5 (\log d)^2 q^d \log n)$, for $q > d$ [43, 2]. Those constructions are constructed in time $\omega(poly(d)) \cdot s$ where s is the size of the construction. Here we will show the following

LEMMA 49. *For any q, d and an integer r such that $q^r \ge n > q^{r-1}$ there is an explicit (n, d)-universal set over $\Sigma = \mathbb{F}_q$ of size*

$$q^d \cdot \nu_{\mathbb{F}_q}(d, \mathbb{F}_{q^r}).$$

In particular, for any constant $c > 1$, Table 4 (in the introduction) of (n, d)-universal sets over $\Sigma = \mathbb{F}_q$ can be constructed in deterministic polynomial time.

PROOF. Consider the Reed Solomon $[q^r, q^r - d, d + 1]$ code C over $\mathbb{F}_{q^r}$ where $q^r \ge n > q^{r-1}$. Consider the $d \times n$ matrix H_C that is the first n columns of the parity check matrix of C. Consider the set of (n, d)-multilinear polynomials $D_I(\boldsymbol{y}) = \det([y_{j,i_k}]_{j,k})$ where $j, k = 1, \ldots, d$, $I = \{i_1, \ldots, i_d\}$, $1 \le i_1 < i_2 < \cdots < i_d \le n$, $\boldsymbol{y} = (\boldsymbol{y}_1, \ldots, \boldsymbol{y}_d)^T$ and $\boldsymbol{y}_i = (y_{i,1}, \ldots, y_{i,n})$. Here for notational convenience we regard $\boldsymbol{y}$ as a $d \times n$ matrix of indeterminates. Since every d columns of H_C are linearly independent we have $D_I(H_C) \ne 0$ for all I.

Let $L = \{\boldsymbol{\ell}_1, \ldots, \boldsymbol{\ell}_\nu\}$, $\boldsymbol{\ell}_i : \mathbb{F}_{q^r}^{d \times n} \to \mathbb{F}_q^{d \times n}$, be a $(\mathcal{HLF}(\mathbb{F}, n, d), \mathbb{F}_{q^r}, \mathbb{F}_q)$-tester where $\nu = \nu_{\mathbb{F}_q}(d, \mathbb{F}_{q^r})$. Consider $G_i = \boldsymbol{\ell}_i(H_C) \in \mathbb{F}_q^{d \times n}$, $i = 1, 2, \ldots, \nu$. By the definition of tester, since for all I, $D_I(H_C) \ne 0$ we have: for every I there is j such that $D_I(G_j) \ne 0$. That is, for every d distinct indices $I = \{i_1, \ldots, i_d\}$ there is a matrix G_j such that the columns $i_1, \ldots, i_d$ in G_j are linearly independent.

Now consider the set $\mathcal{F} = \cup_i \mathrm{Span}_{\mathbb{F}_q} G_i$ where $\mathrm{Span}_{\mathbb{F}_q} G_i$ is the linear space spanned by the rows of G_i. It is obvious that $\mathcal{F}$ is (n, d)-universal set over $\mathbb{F}_q$ of size $q^d \cdot \nu_{\mathbb{F}_q}(d, \mathbb{F}_{q^r})$.

The results in the first 6 rows of the table follow from the fact that $\nu_{\mathbb{F}_q}(d, \mathbb{F}_{q^r}) \le \nu^{\mathcal{P}}_{\mathbb{F}_q}(d, \mathbb{F}_{q^r})$, Corollary 17 and Corollary 40. The results in the last two rows of the table follows from Theorem 21 and Theorem 42. $\square$

For $q \ge c(d+1)^2$, perfect square q and infinite sequence of integers n we get an explicit construction of size $O(dq^d \log n / \log q)$, and for all n, a polynomial time construction of size $O(d^2 q^d \log n / \log q)$. Notice that the bound in the explicit construction exceeds the union bound and meets the upper bound in Lemma 47. For constant d all the above bounds meet the bounds in Lemma 47. For $q = 2$ (and small q) the bound $2^{d+O(\log^2 d)} \log n$ in [43] exceeds our bound $d^5 2^{2.66d} \log n$. The advantage of our construction is in that each bit in the construction can be constructed in $poly(d, \log n)$ time where the construction in [43] needs $\omega(poly(d)) \cdot poly(\log n)$ time. This is studied in more details in [13].

4.3 Cover-Free Families

Let X be a set with N elements and let $\mathcal{B}$ be a set of subsets (blocks) of X. We say that $(X, \mathcal{B})$ is (w, r)-*cover-free family* ((w, r)-CFF), [35], if for any w blocks $B_1, \ldots, B_w \in \mathcal{B}$ and any other r blocks $A_1, \ldots, A_r \in \mathcal{B}$, we have

$$\bigcap_{i=1}^{w} B_i \not\subseteq \bigcup_{j=1}^{r} A_j.$$

Let $N((w, r), n)$ denotes the minimum number of points in any (w, r)-CFF having n blocks. When $w = 1$, the problem is called *group testing*. The problem of group testing which was first presented during World War II was presented as follows [20, 41]: Among n soldiers, at most r carry a fatal virus. We would like to blood test the soldiers to detect the infected ones. Testing each one separately will give n tests. To minimize the number of tests we can mix the blood of several soldiers and test the mixture. If the test comes negative then none of the tested soldiers are infected. If the test comes out positive, we know that at least one of them is infected. The problem is to come up with a small number of group test.

This problem is equivalent to $(1, r)$-CFF and is equivalent to finding a small set $\mathcal{F} \subseteq \{0, 1\}^n$ such that for every $1 \le i_1 < i_2 < \cdots < i_d \le n$ and every $1 \le j \le d$ there is $\boldsymbol{a} \in \mathcal{F}$ such that $a_{i_k} = 0$ for all $k \ne j$ and $a_{i_j} = 1$.

Group testing has the following lower bound [21, 22, 25]

$$N((1, r), n) \ge \Omega\left(\frac{r^2}{\log r} \log n\right). \tag{19}$$

It is known that a group testing of size $O(r^2 \log n)$ can be constructed in polynomial time [20, 44, 32].

The problem (w, r)-cover-free family is equivalent to the following problem: An (w, r)-cover-free family is a set $\mathcal{F} \subseteq \{0, 1\}^n$ such that for every $1 \le i_1 < i_2 < \cdots < i_d \le n$ where $d = w + r$ and every $J \subset [d]$ of size $|J| = w$ there is $\boldsymbol{a} \in \mathcal{F}$ such that $a_{i_k} = 0$ for all $k \notin J$ and $a_{i_j} = 1$ for all $j \in J$. Then $N((w, r), n)$ is the minimum size of such $\mathcal{F}$.

There are several lower bounds for $N((w, r), n)$. We give the one in [61]

$$N((w, r), n) \ge \Omega\left(\frac{d\binom{d}{w}}{\log \binom{d}{w}} \log n\right).$$

With union bound one can show

LEMMA 50. *For $d = w + r = o(n)$ we have*

$$N((w, r), n) \le O\left(\sqrt{wrd} \cdot \binom{d}{w} \log n\right).$$

It follows from [62], that for infinite sequence of integers n, a (w,r)-cover free family of size

$$M = O\left((wr)^{\log^* n}\log n\right)$$

can be constructed in polynomial time. For constant d, the (n,d)-universal set over $\Sigma = \{0,1\}$ constructed in [42] of size $M = O(2^{3d}\log n)$ (and in [43] of size $M = 2^{d+O(\log^2 d)}\log n$) is (w,r)-cover free family for any w and r of size $O(\log n)$. See also [39].
We now prove

LEMMA 51. *Let t be such that $q^t \ge n$ and $q \ge wr+1$. Let $S \subseteq \mathbb{F}_{q^T}$ be a linear subspace for some $T \ge t$ where $|S| = q^t$. Then*

$$N((w,r),n) \le N((w,r),q)\cdot \nu_{\mathbb{F}_q}^{\mathcal{HP}}(wr,S).$$

In particular, there is an explicit (w,r)-CFF of size

$$\binom{q}{w}\cdot \nu_{\mathbb{F}_q}^{\mathcal{HP}}(wr,S).$$

In particular, for any constant $c>1$, Table 5 (in the introduction) of (w,r)-CFF can be constructed in polynomial time in their sizes

PROOF. Consider the set of non-zero functions

$$\mathcal{M} = \{\Delta_{\boldsymbol{i}} \mid \boldsymbol{i}\in[n]^d,\ i_1,i_2,\ldots,i_d \text{ are distinct}\}$$

where

$$\Delta_{\boldsymbol{i}}(x_1,\ldots,x_n) = \prod_{1\le k\le w \text{ and } w<j\le d}(x_{i_k}-x_{i_j}).$$

Consider n distinct elements $\alpha_1,\alpha_2,\ldots,\alpha_n \in S$ and let $\boldsymbol{\alpha} = (\alpha_1,\alpha_2,\ldots,\alpha_n)$. Since $g(\boldsymbol{\alpha}) \ne 0$ for every $g\in\mathcal{M}$, and since $\mathcal{M}\subset \mathcal{HP}(\mathbb{F}_q,n,wr)$, using testers, there is a set $B\subseteq \mathbb{F}_q^n$ of size $\nu_{\mathbb{F}_q}^{\mathcal{HP}}(wr,S)$ such that for every $g\in\mathcal{M}$ there is $\boldsymbol{b}\in B$ where $g(\boldsymbol{b})\ne 0$.
Let $\mathcal{F}\subseteq\{0,1\}^q$ be a (w,r)-CFF with $|X| = q$ elements of size $N((w,r),q)$. Regard each $f\in\mathcal{F}$ as a function $f:\mathbb{F}_q\to\{0,1\}$. It is easy to see that

$$\{(f(b_1),f(b_2),\ldots,f(b_n)) \mid \boldsymbol{b}\in B, f\in\mathcal{F}\}\subseteq\{0,1\}^n$$

is (w,r)-CFF of size $|\mathcal{F}|\cdot|B| = N((w,r),q)\cdot\nu_{\mathbb{F}_q}^{\mathcal{HP}}(wr,S)$.
Now for every subset $R\subseteq\mathbb{F}_q$ define the function $\chi_R:\mathbb{F}_q\to\{0,1\}$ where for $\beta\in\mathbb{F}_q$ we have $\chi_R(\beta)=1$ if $\beta\in R$ and $\chi_R(\beta)=0$ otherwise. Then $\{\chi_R \mid R\subseteq\mathbb{F}_q, |R| = w\}\subseteq\{0,1\}^{\mathbb{F}_q}$ is a (w,r)-CFF with $|\mathbb{F}_q| = q$ elements of size $\binom{q}{w}$. Therefore $C = \{(\chi_R(b_1),\chi_R(b_2),\ldots,\chi_R(b_n)) \mid \boldsymbol{b}\in B, R\subseteq \mathbb{F}_q, |R| = w\}$ is (w,r)-CFF of size

$$|C| \le \binom{q}{w}\nu_{\mathbb{F}_q}^{\mathcal{HP}}(wr,S).$$

Now for the results in the table consider a constant $c>1$ and let q be a power of prime such that $q = cwr + o(wr)$. This is possible by [16]. Let $t = \lceil\log n/\log q\rceil$ and let $S\subseteq\mathbb{F}_{q^T}$ where $T = O(t)$ be the linear space defined in Corollary 20. By Corollaries 20, 41 and the above result, for infinite sequence of integers n, there is a (w,r)-CFF of size

$$\binom{q}{w}\cdot\nu_{\mathbb{F}_q}^{\mathcal{HP}}(wr,S) \le \left(\frac{qe}{w}\right)^w (wr)^2 t$$

$$= O\left((cer)^w (wr)^2\frac{\log n}{\log r}\right) = O\left(\frac{w^2(ce)^w r^{w+2}}{\log r}\log n\right)$$

that can be constructed in polynomial time. By Corollary 40 there is a (w,r)-CFF of size

$$\binom{q}{w}\cdot\nu_{\mathbb{F}_q}^{\mathcal{HP}}(wr,\mathbb{F}_{q^t}) \le \left(\frac{qe}{w}\right)^w (wr)^3 t =$$

$$O\left(\frac{w^3(ce)^w r^{w+3}}{\log r}\log n\right)$$

that can be constructed in polynomial time. □

In Corollary 17 we have showed that for any constant $c>1$ and $q\ge c(d+1)$, for infinite sequence of integers t we have $\nu_{\mathbb{F}_q}^{\mathcal{P}}(d,\mathbb{F}_{q^t}) = O(d^2t)$. One of the open problems in this paper is whether this bound can be improved to $O(dt)$. By the proof of Lemma 51, if for some constant $c>1$ and any $q = c(d+1)$ we have $\nu_{\mathbb{F}_q}^{\mathcal{P}}(d,\mathbb{F}_{q^t}) = O(dt)$ then for $w = O(1)$

$$N((w,r),n) = O\left(\frac{r^{w+1}}{\log r}\log n\right).$$

This bound matches the lower bound and therefore closes the gap between the union bound and the lower bound.
In particular, we will have

$$N((1,r),n) = \Theta\left(\frac{r^2}{\log r}\log n\right)$$

for the group testing problem. We state this in the following

LEMMA 52. *If for some constant $c>1$ and $q = c(d+1)$ we have $\nu_{\mathbb{F}_q}^{\mathcal{P}}(d,\mathbb{F}_{q^t}) = O(dt)$ then*

$$N((1,r),n) = \Theta\left(\frac{r^2}{\log r}\log n\right).$$

4.4 Separating Hash Family

See the results in the introduction. The proofs are similar to the above problems and appears in the full paper [11].

5. APPLICATION OF TESTER FOR BLACK BOX PIT SETS OVER SMALL FIELD

In this section we show how to reduce a black box PIT set over large field to a black box PIT set over small field. We then apply this to different subsets of multivariate polynomials.
The black box Polynomial Identity Testing (PIT) problem is the following: Given an arithmetic circuit C that either identical to the zero function or from a class of circuits $\mathcal{C}$ over a field $\mathbb{F}$, with input variables $x_1,x_2,\ldots,x_n$ and given a *substitution oracle* that for an input $\boldsymbol{a}\in\mathbb{F}^n$ returns $f(\boldsymbol{a})$. Determine whether C computes the identically zero polynomial. We say that $S\subset\mathbb{F}^n$ is a *black box PIT set* or a *hitting set* for $\mathcal{C}$ if for every $f\in\mathcal{C}$ there is $\boldsymbol{a}\in S$ such that $f(\boldsymbol{a})\ne 0$.
When the field is finite $\mathbb{F}_q$ many simple classes of circuits, such as circuits that computes monomials, requires black box PIT sets of exponential size. Therefore, many papers in the literature allow the substitution oracle to receive assignment $\boldsymbol{a}$ from some extension field $\mathbb{F}_{q^t}$ of $\mathbb{F}_q$. One

problem with that approach is that some functions, such as $x_1^q - x_1$, are identically zero over $\mathbb{F}_q$ but not over any extension field $\mathbb{F}_{q^t}$ of $\mathbb{F}_q$. Therefore, when using an extension field, they assume that each output node in the circuit computes a function of variable degree less than q. That is, the degree of each variable in the function is less than q. In that case, C is identically zero over $\mathbb{F}_q$ if and only if it is identically zero over $\mathbb{F}_{q^t}$ for any t. We say that $S \subset \mathbb{F}_{q^t}^n$ is a *black box PIT set over* $\mathbb{F}_{q^t}$ or a *hitting set over* $\mathbb{F}_{q^t}$ for $\mathcal{C}$ if for every $f \in \mathcal{C}$ there is $\boldsymbol{a} \in S$ such that $f(\boldsymbol{a}) \neq 0$. Our goal will be to minimize the size of the black box PIT set and the dimension of the extension field.

We first start with some definitions

5.1 Sets of Multivariate Polynomials

For a multivariate polynomial f the *total degree* (or just *degree*) of f is the maximum over the sums of the exponents of each multivariate monomial in f and the *variable degree* of f is the maximum over the degree of each variable in f. In this section we will study the following classes of multivariate polynomials

1. $\mathcal{P}(\mathbb{F}_q, n)$ is the class of all multivariate polynomials in $\mathbb{F}_q[x_1, \ldots, x_n]$ of variable degree at most $q-1$.
2. $\mathcal{P}(\mathbb{F}_q, n, (d, r))$ is the class of all multivariate polynomials in $\mathcal{P}(\mathbb{F}_q, n)$ of degree at most d and variable degree at most r.
3. $\mathcal{P}(\mathbb{F}_q, n, d) = \mathcal{P}(\mathbb{F}_q, n, (d, q-1))$ is the class of all multivariate polynomials in $\mathcal{P}(\mathbb{F}_q, n)$ of degree at most d.
4. $\mathcal{P}(\mathbb{F}_q, n, s)$ is the class of all multivariate polynomials in $\mathcal{P}(\mathbb{F}_q, n)$ with at most s monomials. This class is called in the literature "sparse multivariate polynomials".
5. $\mathcal{P}(\mathbb{F}_q, n, (d, r), s)$ is the class of all multivariate polynomials in $\mathcal{P}(\mathbb{F}_q, n)$ of degree at most d and variable degree at most r with at most s monomials.

In the same way we define the classes $\mathcal{P}(\mathbb{F}_q, n, r)$, $\mathcal{P}(\mathbb{F}_q, n, d, s)$ and $\mathcal{P}(\mathbb{F}_q, n, r, s)$. Notice that when we write $\mathcal{P}(\mathbb{F}_q, n, 1)$ it is not clear whether $r = 1$, $d = 1$ or $s = 1$. To avoid confusion we will use "=" in the definition of the class to indicate which parameter is meant. For example, $\mathcal{P}(\mathbb{F}_q, n, r = 1)$ is the class of multilinear polynomials where $\mathcal{P}(\mathbb{F}_q, n, s = 1)$ is the class of monomials and $\mathcal{P}(\mathbb{F}_q, n, d = 1)$ is the class of linear functions.

5.2 Main Results

We will study black box PIT sets for the above classes over $\mathbb{F}_{q^t}$. To the best of our knowledge all the algorithms in the literature that construct black box PIT sets for the above classes are either randomized, deterministic for some fixed extension field $\mathbb{F}_{q^t}$ or obtains non-optimal results in both the extension field dimension and the size of the black box PIT set [27, 19, 63, 31, 37, 8]. See more details in the next subsections. In this paper all the results we obtain are within *poly*(n) of the optimal black box PIT set size and the dimension of the extension field is optimal.

Table 7 in the introduction summarizes some of our main results. Notice that our polynomial time constructions (column 6 in the table) are optimal in the largest parameters (q^n, $(r+1)^n$, n^d and s in the last three rows of the table). For sparse polynomials $\mathcal{P}(\mathbb{F}_q, n, s)$, $\mathcal{P}(\mathbb{F}_q, n, r, s)$ and $\mathcal{P}(\mathbb{F}_q, n, (d, r), s)$, all the results in the literature give black box PIT sets of size that are at least quadratic in the size s. Also, the tight tradeoff with the field dimension $(\cdot/t)$ in each row of the table was not known before. The bound on the dimension of the field extension in the second column is $\log_q(\mathit{degree})+1$ and is known to be the best possible dimension (even for randomized algorithms) if one uses DeMillo-Lipton-Schwartz-Zippel Lemma. Therefore, our constructions are tight in the dimension of the field extension. For the class $\mathcal{P}(\mathbb{F}_q, n, (d, r), s)$ (the last row of the table), the best known result in the literature [37, 8] used field extension of dimension that depends on the number of the variables n. Our result uses field extension of dimension $\log_q(d+1)$ that is independent of the number of variables. Also notice, that when $q \geq d+1$ no extension field is needed. This will be further studied in [13] to give new Pseudorandom generators over small fields.

See other results in the following subsections.

5.3 Preliminary Results

Before we move to the constructions we give some preliminary results that will be needed in this section

5.3.1 A Primitive Root in the Field

In this subsection we give some results from the literature about deterministic algorithms for finding a primitive root (called also primitive element) and an element of large multiplicative order in the field. See more results in [50]. In [48] it is shown that

LEMMA 53. *In any field $\mathbb{F}_q$ a primitive root can be found in deterministic time $O(q^{1/4+\epsilon})$ for any constant $\epsilon > 0$.*

In some applications one can also use an element of large order in finite field instead of a primitive root. Von zur Gathen and Shparlinski in [28] showed

LEMMA 54. *There is a deterministic algorithm that for every integer n, gives $N = n + o(n)$ and finds an element in $\mathbb{F}_{q^N}$ of multiplicative order*

$$2^{(10n^{1/2}/q^{12})-25}$$

in time poly(n).

In [53], Shoup proved (see also [50], Theorem 2.6)

LEMMA 55. *There is a deterministic algorithm that for every integer n, gives $N = n + o(n)$ and finds a primitive root in $\mathbb{F}_{p^N}$ in time*

$$p^{O(n/\log\log n)}.$$

5.3.2 Sidon Sequences

In this subsection we define the Sidon Sequence and prove some results that will be used in the sequel

A sequence of non-negative integers $a_1, a_2, \cdots, a_n$ is called *Sidon B_d sequence* if the sums $a_{i_1} + \cdots + a_{i_d}$ for all $\boldsymbol{i} \in [n]^d$ are distinct up to rearrangements of the summands. The sequence is called *Sidon $B_{\leq d}$ sequence* if the sums $a_{i_1} + \cdots + a_{i_r}$ for all $\boldsymbol{i} \in [n]^d$ and $r \leq d$ are distinct up to rearrangements of the summands. We will study Sidon $B_{\leq d}$ sequences when $d = o(n)$. It is easy to see that $\max_j a_j \geq n^{d-o(d)}$. See more results in [10] and references within.

Several explicit constructions of Sidon B_d sequences were given in the literature [10]. Bose [9] constructed B_2 Sidon sequences by using finite affine geometry. His construction was extended in [14] to the following Sidon B_d sequences. Let q be a prime power and θ a primitive root of $\mathbb{F}_{q^d}$. Define

$$B_d(q,\theta) = \{a \in [q^d-1] \mid \theta^a - \theta \in \mathbb{F}_q\}.$$

Then $B_d(q,\theta)$ is a Sidon B_d sequence. The construction of this sequence requires discrete log and therefore it is not clear whether it can be done in polynomial time.
In the full paper we prove the following two results

LEMMA 56. *A Sidon $B_{\le d}$ sequence $a_1, a_2, \cdots, a_n$ with*

$$\max_j a_j \le (n + O(n^{0.525}))^{d+1}$$

can be constructed in deterministic $O(n^{d/2+1.5})$ time.

For $B_{\le d}$ Sidon sequence that can be constructed in polynomial time we prove

LEMMA 57. *A Sidon $B_{\le d}$ sequence $a_1, a_2, \cdots, a_n$ with*

$$\max_j a_j < (2dn)^{2d}$$

can be constructed in time poly(n).

5.3.3 The Operator ϕ_d

In this subsection we introduce a new notion that will be used in the sequel.
Let $\mathbb{F}$ be any field. Consider a multivariate polynomial $f \in \mathbb{F}[x_1,\ldots,x_n]$ of degree d. Let $\boldsymbol{y} = (\boldsymbol{y}_1,\ldots,\boldsymbol{y}_d)$ where $\boldsymbol{y}_i = (y_{i,1},\ldots,y_{i,n})$ are new indeterminates for $i = 1,\ldots,d$. Define the operator $\phi_d : \mathbb{F}[\boldsymbol{x}] \to \mathbb{F}[\boldsymbol{y}]$

$$\phi_d f = \sum_{J\subseteq[d]} (-1)^{d-|J|} f\left(\sum_{i\in J} \boldsymbol{y}_i\right), \tag{20}$$

where $\sum_{i\in\emptyset} \boldsymbol{y}_i = 0$. In the full paper we show

LEMMA 58. *We have*

1. *For a monomial M of degree less than d we have $\phi_d M = 0$*
2. *For a monomial $M_{\boldsymbol{i}} = x_{i_1}\cdots x_{i_d}$ of degree d we have $\phi_d M_{\boldsymbol{i}} = \mathrm{Perm} Y_{M_{\boldsymbol{i}}}$ where* Perm *is the permanent of matrices and*

$$Y_{M_{\boldsymbol{i}}}(\boldsymbol{y}) = \begin{pmatrix} y_{1,i_1} & y_{1,i_2} & \cdots & y_{1,i_d} \\ y_{2,i_1} & y_{2,i_2} & \cdots & y_{2,i_d} \\ \vdots & \vdots & \vdots & \vdots \\ y_{d,i_1} & y_{d,i_2} & \cdots & y_{d,i_d} \end{pmatrix}.$$

3. *For any monomial M of degree at most d we have $\phi_d M = 0$ if and only if M is of degree less than d or one of the variables in M has degree that is greater than or equal to the characteristic of the field p.*

Suppose

$$f(\boldsymbol{x}) = \sum_{\boldsymbol{i}\in I} \lambda_{\boldsymbol{i}} x_{i_1}\cdots x_{i_d} + g(\boldsymbol{x})$$

where $\boldsymbol{x} = (x_1,\ldots,x_n)$, $g(\boldsymbol{x})$ is a multivariate polynomial of degree less than d, $\boldsymbol{i} = (i_1, i_2, \ldots, i_d)$, $1 \le i_1 \le i_2 \le \cdots \le i_d \le n$, $\lambda_{\boldsymbol{i}} \ne 0$ and $I \subset [n]^d$. Since ϕ_d is linear we have

$$(\phi_d f)(\boldsymbol{y}_1,\ldots,\boldsymbol{y}_d) = \sum_{\boldsymbol{i}\in I} \lambda_{\boldsymbol{i}} \mathrm{Perm}\left(Y_{M_{\boldsymbol{i}}}(\boldsymbol{y}_1,\ldots,\boldsymbol{y}_d)\right). \tag{21}$$

5.4 The Reduction from Large Field to Small Field

In this subsection we show how to reduce a black box PIT set over an extension field $\mathbb{F}_{q^t}$ to a black box PIT set over $\mathbb{F}_{q^{t'}}$ where $t' < t$.
We prove

LEMMA 59. *If $\mathcal{M} \subseteq \mathbb{F}[x_1,\ldots,x_n]$ and there is a black box PIT set $T \subset S^n$ for $\mathcal{M}$ over a subspace $S \subseteq \mathcal{A}$ for an $\mathbb{F}$-algebra $\mathcal{A}$ then there is a black box PIT set $R \subset \mathbb{F}^n$ for $\mathcal{M}$ of size $|R| = |T| \cdot \nu^{\circ}_{\mathbb{F}}(\mathcal{M}, S)$.*
In particular,

1. *If $\mathcal{M} \subseteq \mathcal{HLF}(\mathbb{F}_q, n, d)$ and there is a black box PIT set over an extension field $\mathbb{F}_{q^t}$ for $\mathcal{M}$ of size w then there is a black box PIT set for $\mathcal{M}$ over $\mathbb{F}_q$ of size $w \cdot \nu_{\mathbb{F}_q}(d, \mathbb{F}_{q^t})$.*
2. *If $\mathcal{M} \subseteq \mathcal{P}(\mathbb{F}_q, n, d)$, $q \ge d+1$ and there is a black box PIT set for $\mathcal{M}$ over an extended field $\mathbb{F}_{q^t}$ of size w then there is a black box PIT set for $\mathcal{M}$ over $\mathbb{F}_q$ of size $w \cdot \nu^{\mathcal{P}}_{\mathbb{F}_q}(d, \mathbb{F}_{q^t})$.*
3. *If $\mathcal{M} \subseteq \mathcal{P}(\mathbb{F}_q, n, d)$, $q^{t'} \ge d+1$ and there is a black box PIT set for $\mathcal{M}$ over an extended field $\mathbb{F}_{q^t}$ of size w then there is a black box PIT set for $\mathcal{M}$ over $\mathbb{F}_{q^{t'}}$ of size $w \cdot \nu^{\mathcal{P}}_{\mathbb{F}_{q^{t'}}}((d, \mathbb{F}_q), \mathbb{F}_{q^t})$.*

PROOF. The results follow immediately from the definition of testers. □

By Corollary 40, Theorem 42 and Lemma 43 we have

LEMMA 60. *We have*

1. *Let $\mathcal{M} \subseteq \mathcal{HLF}(\mathbb{F}_q, n, d)$. Let S be a black box PIT set for $\mathcal{M}$ over an extended field $\mathbb{F}_{q^t}$ of size w. There is an algorithm that runs in time $w \cdot 2^{c_q d} \cdot poly(t)$ and constructs a black box PIT set for $\mathcal{M}$ over $\mathbb{F}_q$ of size $O(d^7 \cdot 2^{c_q d} \cdot tw)$.*
2. *Let $\mathcal{M} \subseteq \mathcal{P}(\mathbb{F}_q, n, d)$ and $q \ge d+1$. Let S be a black box PIT set for $\mathcal{M}$ over an extended field $\mathbb{F}_{q^t}$ of size w. There is an algorithm that runs in time $w \cdot poly(d,t)$ and constructs a black box PIT set for $\mathcal{M}$ over $\mathbb{F}_q$ of size $O(d^{\tau_{poly}(d,q,t)} \cdot tw) = O(d^5 \cdot tw)$.*
3. *Let $\mathcal{M} \subseteq \mathcal{P}(\mathbb{F}_q, n, d)$ and $q^{t'} \ge d+1$. Let S be a black box PIT set for $\mathcal{M}$ over an extended field $\mathbb{F}_{q^t}$ of size w. There is an algorithm that runs in time $w \cdot poly(d,t)$ and constructs a black box PIT set for $\mathcal{M}$ over $\mathbb{F}_{q^{t'}}$ of size $O(d^5 \cdot wt/t')$.*

We now prove

LEMMA 61. *If $\mathcal{M} \subseteq \mathcal{P}(\mathbb{F}_q, n, d, r = p-1) \backslash \mathcal{P}(\mathbb{F}_q, n, d-1, r = p-1)$ where p is the characteristic of the field, $q \le d$ and there is a black box PIT set for $\phi_d\mathcal{M} = \{\phi_d f \mid f \in \mathcal{M}\}$ over an extension field $\mathbb{F}_{q^t}$ of size w then there is a black box PIT set for $\mathcal{M}$ over $\mathbb{F}_q$ of size $2^d w \cdot \nu_{\mathbb{F}_q}(d, \mathbb{F}_{q^t})$.*

In particular, let S be a black box PIT set for $\phi_d\mathcal{M}$ over an extended field $\mathbb{F}_{q^t}$ of size w. There is an algorithm that runs in time $w\cdot 2^{(1+c_q)d}\cdot poly(t)$ and constructs a black box PIT set for $\mathcal{M}$ over $\mathbb{F}_q$ of size $O(d^7 2^{(1+c_q)d}\cdot tw)$.

PROOF. Let $S\subseteq(\mathbb{F}_{q^t}^n)^d$ be a black box PIT set for $\phi_d\mathcal{M}$ of size w. Let $f\in\mathcal{P}(\mathbb{F}_q,n,d,r=p-1)$ be of degree d and $f\not\equiv 0$. By Lemma 58, $\phi_d f\not\equiv 0$. Since $\phi_d\mathcal{M}\subset\mathcal{HLF}(\mathbb{F}_q,n,d)$ and S is a black box PIT set for $\phi_d\mathcal{M}$ over $\mathbb{F}_{q^t}$, by Lemma 59, there is a black box PIT set $R\subseteq(\mathbb{F}_q^n)^d$ for $\phi_d\mathcal{M}$ over $\mathbb{F}_q$ of size $|S|\cdot\nu_{\mathbb{F}_q}(d,\mathbb{F}_{q^t})$. Therefore, for every $f\in\mathcal{M}$ there is $\boldsymbol{a}=(\boldsymbol{a}_1,\ldots,\boldsymbol{a}_d)\in R$ such that $(\phi_d f)(\boldsymbol{a})\neq 0$. Now, by (20), there is $J\subseteq[d]$ such that $f(\sum_{j\in J}\boldsymbol{a}_j)\neq 0$. Therefore

$$\left\{\sum_{j\in J}\boldsymbol{a}_j\,\middle|\, J\subset[d],\boldsymbol{a}\in R\right\},$$

is a black box PIT set for $\mathcal{M}$ over $\mathbb{F}_q$ of size $2^d w\cdot\nu_{\mathbb{F}_q}(d,\mathbb{F}_{q^t})$. The other result follows from Theorem 42. □

5.5 Constructive Upper Bound for $\mathcal{P}(\mathbb{F}_q,n)$ and $\mathcal{P}(\mathbb{F}_q,n,r)$

In this subsection we give polynomial time constructions of a black box PIT sets for $\mathcal{P}(\mathbb{F}_q,n)$ and $\mathcal{P}(\mathbb{F}_q,n,r)$ of size that asymptotically match the lower bounds in Lemma 67 in [11]. We give two constructions. The first is a very simple construction that uses combinatorial Nullstellensatz [1] and is asymptotically tight for small fields and the other one uses testers and is asymptotically tight for large fields. Notice that since $\mathcal{P}(\mathbb{F}_q,n)=\mathcal{P}(\mathbb{F}_q,n,r=q-1)$, it is enough to study the class $\mathcal{P}(\mathbb{F}_q,n,r)$.
The first construction uses the following combinatorial Nullstellensatz

LEMMA 62. *([1]) Let $\mathbb{F}$ be a field and f be a multivariate polynomial in $\mathbb{F}[x_1,\ldots,x_n]$ of total degree d. Let $x_1^{r_1}x_2^{r_2}\cdots x_n^{r_n}$ be a monomial in f of degree d. If $S_1,\cdots,S_n$ are subsets of $\mathbb{F}$ with $|S_i|=r_i+1$, there is $s_1\in S_1, s_2\in S_2,\ldots,s_n\in S_n$ so that $f(s_1,\ldots,s_n)\neq 0$.*

This immediately gives the following construction

LEMMA 63. *Let $\mathbb{F}_q$ be any field. Let $S\subseteq\mathbb{F}_{q^t}$ be a set of size $r+1$. Then S^n is a black box PIT set for $\mathcal{P}(\mathbb{F}_q,n,r)$ of size $(r+1)^n$.*

We now use testers to prove the following

LEMMA 64. *For any q there is a black box PIT set for $\mathcal{P}(\mathbb{F}_q,n,r)$ over $\mathbb{F}_{q^t}$ of size at most*

$$2n\frac{(r+1)^n}{t}$$

that can be constructed in $(r+1)^n poly(t,n)$ time.
In particular, there is a black box PIT set for $\mathcal{P}(\mathbb{F}_q,n)$ over $\mathbb{F}_{q^t}$ of size at most

$$2n\frac{q^n}{t}$$

that can be constructed in $q^n poly(t,n)$ time.

PROOF. If $t\le 2n$ then the black box PIT set in Lemma 63 is of size $(r+1)^n\le 2n\cdot(r+1)^n/t$. Therefore we may assume that $t>2n$.

Consider the linear space $\mathbb{F}_q[x]_{T-1}$ where $T=(r+1)^{n-1}+1$. Since for two distinct monomials M_1 and M_2 with variable degree r we have $M_1(x^1,x^{(r+1)},x^{(r+1)^2},\ldots,x^{(r+1)^{n-1}})\not\equiv M_2(x^1,x^{(r+1)},x^{(r+1)^2},\ldots,x^{(r+1)^{n-1}})$ for $f\in\mathcal{P}(\mathbb{F}_q,n,r)$ we have $f\not\equiv 0$ if and only if $h(x):=f(x^1,x^{(r+1)},x^{(r+1)^2},\ldots,x^{(r+1)^{n-1}})\not\equiv 0$. This gives a black box PIT set for $\mathcal{P}(\mathbb{F}_q,n,r)$ over $\mathbb{F}_q[x]_{T-1}$ of size 1.
By Lemma 59, since $f\in\mathcal{P}(\mathbb{F}_q,n,d=rn)$ and $q^t\ge q^{2n+1}\ge rn+1$ there is a black box PIT set for $\mathcal{P}(\mathbb{F}_q,n,r)$ over $\mathbb{F}_{q^t}$ of size

$$\nu^{\mathcal{P}}_{\mathbb{F}_{q^t}}((rn,\mathbb{F}_q),\mathbb{F}_q[x]_{T-1}).$$

By Lemma 9, since

$$q^{t-1}\ge q^{2n}\ge rnT-rn+1$$

we have

$$\nu^{\mathcal{P}}_{\mathbb{F}_{q^t}}((rn,\mathbb{F}_q),\mathbb{F}_q[x]_T)\le(rn+1)\frac{T-1}{t}=2n\frac{(r+1)^n}{t}.$$

□

5.6 Constructive Upper Bound for $\mathcal{P}(\mathbb{F}_q,n,d)$ and $\mathcal{P}(\mathbb{F}_q,n,(d,r))$

In this subsection we give a black box PIT set for the class $\mathcal{P}(\mathbb{F}_q,n,(d,r))$ for every d,r and q. We give two constructions. The first is a very simple construction that uses combinatorial Nullstellensatz lemma and the second one uses testers. For small d, the size of the black box PIT set asymptotically matches the lower bound in Lemma 65 in [11].
By Lemma 67 and 72 in [11] we have that for $q^t\ge d+1$, a minimum size black box PIT set S over $\mathbb{F}_{q^t}$ for $\mathcal{P}(\mathbb{F}_q,n,(d,r))$ satisfies

$$\frac{R(n,d,r)}{t}\le|S|\le(\log d)\frac{R(n,d,r)}{t}$$

where $R(n,d,r)$ is the number of monomials in $\mathbb{F}_q[x_1,\ldots,x_n]$ of degree at most d and variable degree at most r. The function $R(n,d,r)$ satisfies the following bounds

$$\sum_{i=0}^{d}\binom{n}{i}=R(n,d,1)\le R(n,d,r)\le R(n,d,d)=\binom{n+d}{d}.$$

The combinatorial Nullstellensatz lemma gives the following construction

LEMMA 65. *Let $S'=\{\sigma_0,\sigma_1,\ldots,\sigma_r\}\subseteq\mathbb{F}$ where $|S'|=r+1$. The set $S=\{(\sigma_{i_1},\ldots,\sigma_{i_n})\mid 0\le i_0\le d,\ i_j\le r$ for $j=1,\ldots,n$, and $i_0+i_1+i_2+\cdots+i_n=d\}$ is a black box PIT set for $\mathcal{P}(\mathbb{F},n,(d,r))$ of size $|S|=R(n,d,r)$.*

Our second construction uses testers. We prove

LEMMA 66. *For any $q^t\ge d+1$ there is a black box PIT set for $\mathcal{P}(\mathbb{F}_q,n,d)$ over $\mathbb{F}_{q^t}$ of size*

$$\frac{d((1+o(1))n)^{d+1}}{t}$$

that can be constructed in time $n^{d+2}\cdot poly(t,d)$.

PROOF. If $t\le dn$ then by Lemma 66 we get the result. Therefore, we may assume that $t>dn$. Let $f\in\mathcal{P}(\mathbb{F}_q,n,d)$ where $q^t\ge d+1$. Then

$$f(\boldsymbol{x})=\sum_{\boldsymbol{i}\in I}\lambda_{\boldsymbol{i}}\cdot x_{i_1}\cdots x_{i_d}$$

where $\boldsymbol{x} = (x_0, x_1, \ldots, x_n)$, $x_0 = 1$, $I \subseteq \{(i_1, i_2, \ldots, i_d) \mid 0 \le i_1 \le i_2 \le \cdots \le i_d \le n\}$ and $\lambda_i \in \mathbb{F}_q$. Note here that we are using x_0 to create monomials of degree less than d. Consider the Sidon $B_{\le d}$ sequence $a_1, a_2, \cdots, a_n$ in Lemma 56 where $\max_j a_j \le N-1 = (n+o(n))^{d+1}$. In Lemma 56 we have shown that this sequence can be constructed in time $n^{d/2+1.5}$. Consider the assignment $\boldsymbol{x}' = (x^{a_0}, x^{a_1}, x^{a_2}, \ldots, x^{a_d})$ where $a_0 = 0$ and x is a new indeterminate. Then

$$f(\boldsymbol{x}') = \sum_{i \in I} \lambda_i \cdot x^{a_{i_1}+a_{i_2}+\cdots+a_{i_d}}.$$

Notice that $n_i := a_{i_1} + a_{i_2} + \cdots + a_{i_d}$, $\boldsymbol{i} \in I$ are distinct. Therefore, $f(\boldsymbol{x}') \ne 0$. That is, $S = \{\boldsymbol{x}'\}$ is a black box PIT set over $\mathbb{F}_q[x]_{N-1}$ of size 1. By Lemma 60 and 9 there is a black box PIT set over $\mathbb{F}_{q^t}$ of size $\nu^{\mathcal{P}}_{\mathbb{F}_{q^t}}((d, \mathbb{F}_q), \mathbb{F}_q[x]_{N-1})$

$$\le \frac{dN - d + 1}{t} + 1 \le \frac{d((1+o(1))n)^{d+1}}{t}.$$

□

5.7 Other Constructive Upper Bounds

Using similar techniques we give in the full paper polynomial time constructions for the classes $\mathcal{P}(\mathbb{F}_q, n, s)$ $\mathcal{P}(\mathbb{F}_q, n, r, s)$ $\mathcal{P}(\mathbb{F}_q, n, d, s)$ and $\mathcal{P}(\mathbb{F}_q, n, (d, r), s)$. Some of the results were improved in [13].

5.8 Field Reduction of Other Circuit Classes

In this subsection we apply the reduction in Lemma 59 for the black box PIT sets in [54, 56, 57, 5] and get a black box PIT sets over smaller fields. The results are in Table 8 in the introduction

The classes in the table are: $\Sigma\Pi\Sigma(k, d, n)$ is the class of depth-3 circuits with n variables, degree d and top fanin k. P_kROF is the class of read once formulas (ROF, each variable appears at most once in the formula) with n variables in which we are allowed to replace each variable x_i with a univariate polynomial $T_i(x_i)$ of degree at most k. $\Sigma_r\text{P}_k$ROF is the sum of r P_kROF formulas. Multilinear (ML) $\Sigma\Pi\Sigma\Pi(k)$ is the class of depth 4 circuits with n variables in which the fan-in of the top Σ gate is a constant k and each multiplication gate computes a multilinear polynomial. R_k ML is the class of multilinear formulas with n variables where each variable appears at most k times in the formula.

The table shows the reduction to a smaller field. For example, in the first row in the table, in [54], Saxena and Seshadhri gave a black box PIT set for $\Sigma\Pi\Sigma(k, d, n)$ over fields of size at least dnk^2. We apply our reduction to give a black box PIT set for $\Sigma\Pi\Sigma(k, d, n)$ over fields of size at least $d+1$. Notice that our field size is independent of n and when the field $\mathbb{F}_q$ satisfies $q \ge d+1$, no extension field is needed.

6. APPLICATION OF TESTER FOR POLYNOMIAL RESTRICTION PROBLEMS

A restriction problem is a problem of the following form: **Given** an alphabet Σ of size $|\Sigma| = q$, an integer n and a class $\mathcal{M}$ of nonzero functions $f : \Sigma^n \to \{0, 1\}$.

Find a small set $S \subseteq \Sigma^n$ such that: For any $f \in \mathcal{M}$ there is $\boldsymbol{a} \in S$ such that $f(\boldsymbol{a}) \ne 0$.

We will study restriction problems when $\mathcal{M}$ is a class of multivariate polynomials over $\mathbb{F}_q$.

We remind the reader that the *total degree* (or just *degree*) of a multivariate polynomial is the maximum over the sums of the exponents of each multivariate monomial and the *variable degree* is the maximum over the degree of each variable. We denote by $\mathcal{P}(\mathbb{F}_q, n, ((d, r), s))$ the class of all multivariate polynomial over $\mathbb{F}_q$ of degree exactly d and variable degree at most $r \le q-1$ that contains at most s monomials of degree d and any number of monomials of degree less than d. We denote $\mathcal{P}(\mathbb{F}_q, n, ((d, q-1), s))$ by $\mathcal{P}(\mathbb{F}_q, n, (d, s))$. Obviously, $\mathcal{P}(\mathbb{F}_q, n, d, s) \subseteq \mathcal{P}(\mathbb{F}_q, n, (d, s))$ and $\mathcal{P}(\mathbb{F}_q, n, (d, r), s) \subseteq \mathcal{P}(\mathbb{F}_q, n, ((d, r), s))$. Notice that, for example, $f = (x_1+1)(x_2+1)\cdots(x_d+1)$ is in $\mathcal{P}(\mathbb{F}_q, n, (d, 1), 2^d)$ and $\mathcal{P}(\mathbb{F}_q, n, ((d, 1), 1))$ but not in $\mathcal{P}(\mathbb{F}_q, n, (d, 1), s)$ for any $s < 2^d$.

In this section we consider the following **s-sparse (d, r)-degree polynomial problem** over $\mathbb{F}_q$: Given the class $\mathcal{P}(\mathbb{F}_q, n, ((d, r), s))$. Find a small set $S \subset \mathbb{F}_q^n$ such that for every $f \in \mathcal{P}(\mathbb{F}_q, n, ((d, r), s))$ there is $\boldsymbol{a} \in S$ such that $f(\boldsymbol{a}) \ne 0$.

This problem can be regarded as black box PIT set over $\mathbb{F}_q$ problem, hitting set problem or polynomial restriction problem. We will call S a *hitting set* for $\mathcal{P}(\mathbb{F}_q, n, ((d, r), s))$.

Note: Throughout this section we will assume

$$d, r, q = o(n). \tag{22}$$

Our technique can also handle other cases that will also be considered here. Although our results are true for any s, we will assume that $s \gg n$ and therefore we will concentrate on constructions that gives hitting sets of size that is linear in s. In [13] other constructions of hitting sets that have size quadratic in s are also studied.

6.1 Bounds for $\mathcal{P}(\mathbb{F}_q, n, ((d, r), s))$

In the full paper we give the following lower bound for the size of any hitting set for $\mathcal{P}(\mathbb{F}_q, n, ((d, r), s))$.

We prove

LEMMA 67. *For any n, d, r, s and ℓ, where $\ell \le n^{c_1}$ and $s \le n^{c_2(1-c_1)\ell}$ for some constants $c_1, c_2 < 1$, any hitting set S for $\mathcal{P}(\mathbb{F}_q, n, ((d, r), s))$ is of size*

$$|S| = \Omega\left(\left(\frac{q}{q-r}\right)^{\lfloor (d-\ell)/r \rfloor} \frac{\ell s \log n}{\log q}\right).$$

In particular, for $s = poly(n)$ there is infinite sequence of integers d such that

$$|S| = \Omega\left(\pi_{q,r}^d \cdot \frac{s \log n}{\log q}\right) \tag{23}$$

where

$$\pi_{q,r} = \left(\frac{q}{q-r}\right)^{1/r}$$

and for $s = poly(n)$ and $q = 2$

$$|S| = \Omega(2^d \cdot s \log n).$$

We then give the following nonconstructive upper bound for $\mathcal{P}(\mathbb{F}_q, n, (d, s))$

LEMMA 68. *For any non-zero function $f \in \mathcal{P}(\mathbb{F}_q, n, (d, r))$, $r \ge 1$ we have*

$$\mathbf{Pr}_{\boldsymbol{x} \in U(\mathbb{F}_q^n)}[f(\boldsymbol{x}) \ne 0] \ge \pi_{q,r}^{-d}$$

where

$$\pi_{q,r} = \left(\frac{q}{q-r}\right)^{1/r}$$

and $U(\mathbb{F}_q^n)$ is the uniform distribution over $\mathbb{F}_q^n$.

The union bound with Lemma 68 gives

LEMMA 69. *We have*

1. *There is a hitting set for $\mathcal{P}(\mathbb{F}_q, n, (d,r), s)$ of size*

$$\frac{\log|\mathcal{P}(\mathbb{F}_q, n, (d,r), s)|}{\log\left(\frac{1}{1-\pi_{q,r}^{-d}}\right)}$$

for $q \le d$ and of size

$$\frac{\log|\mathcal{P}(\mathbb{F}_q, n, (d,r), s)|}{\log(q/d)}$$

for $q \ge d+1$.

2. *In particular, for any $d \le n^{c_1}$ and $s \le n^{(1-c_1)c_2 d}$, for some constant $c_1, c_2 < 1$, there is a hitting set for $\mathcal{P}(\mathbb{F}_q, n, (d,r), s)$ of size*

$$O\left(d\pi_{q,r}^d s \log n\right)$$

for $q \le d$ and of size

$$O\left(\frac{ds\log n}{\log(q/d)}\right) = \begin{cases} O(d^2 s\log n) & q = d+c \\ O(ds\log n) & q = c(d+1) \\ O\left(\frac{d}{\log(q/d)} s\log n\right) & q = \omega(d) \\ O\left(\frac{d}{\log q} s\log n\right) & q \ge d^{1+c} \end{cases}$$

for $q \ge d+1$ and any constant $c > 0$.

3. *In particular, there is a hitting set for $\mathcal{P}(\mathbb{F}_2, n, d, s)$ of size $O(d2^d s\log n)$.*

Since $f \in \mathcal{P}(\mathbb{F}_q, n, ((d,r), s))$ can contain any number of monomials of degree less than d, the size of the class $\mathcal{P}(\mathbb{F}_q, n, ((d,r), s))$ is at least $q^{(n/d)^{d-1}}$ and therefore the union bound will not give a good bound. In the full paper we use a new technique that gives the following better bounds

LEMMA 70. *We have*

1. *Let $d \le n^{c_1}$ and $s \le n^{(1-c_1)c_2 d}$ for some constants $c_1, c_2 < 1$. If $r \le p-1$, where p is the characteristic of the field, and $q \le d$ then there is a hitting set for $\mathcal{P}(\mathbb{F}_q, n, ((d,r), s))$ of size $O(d(2\cdot\pi_{q,1})^d s\log n)$*

$$= O\left(d\left(2+\frac{2}{q-1}\right)^d s\log n\right).$$

2. *In particular, there is a hitting set for $\mathcal{P}(\mathbb{F}_2, n, (d,s))$ of size $O(d2^{2d}s\log n)$.*

3. *If $q \ge d+1$ then for any constant $c \ge 0$, there is a hitting set for $\mathcal{P}(\mathbb{F}_q, n, ((d,r), s))$ of size*

$$O\left(\frac{d^2 s\log n}{\log(q/d)}\right) = \begin{cases} O(d^3 s\log n) & q = d+c \\ O(d^2 s\log n) & q = c(d+1) \\ O\left(\frac{d^2}{\log(q/d)} s\log n\right) & q = \omega(d) \\ O\left(\frac{d^2}{\log q} s\log n\right) & q \ge d^{1+c}. \end{cases}$$

6.2 Constructive Upper Bound for $\mathcal{P}(\mathbb{F}_q, n, (d,s))$

In this subsection we give explicit and polynomial time constructions of hitting sets for $\mathcal{P}(\mathbb{F}_q, n, ((d,r), s))$.
Our first result is for $q \ge d+1$. We prove

LEMMA 71. *Let $q \ge d+1$ and $\mathcal{M} = \mathcal{P}(\mathbb{F}_q, n, (d,s))$.*

1. *There is an explicit hitting set for $\mathcal{M}$ of size*

$$O\left(d^{\tau+1} s\frac{\log n}{\log q}\right)$$

where $c > 1$ is any constant and $\tau \le 5$.

2. *For a constant d there is a hitting set for $\mathcal{M}$ of size*

$$O\left(s\frac{\log n}{\log q}\right)$$

that can be constructed in polynomial time poly(n).

3. *For $d = O(\log\log\log n)$ and a prime q there is a hitting set for $\mathcal{M}$ of size*

$$O\left(d^{\tau+1} s\frac{\log n}{\log q}\right)$$

that can be constructed in time $s\cdot$ poly(n).

4. *For any d there is a hitting set for $\mathcal{M}$ of size*

$$O\left(q^{24} d^7 s\cdot\log^2 n\right)$$

that can be constructed in time $s\cdot$ poly(n).

PROOF. Let $f \in \mathcal{P}(\mathbb{F}_q, n, (d,s))$. Consider the Sidon $B_{\ge d}$ sequence in Lemma 57, $a_1, a_2, \cdots, a_n$ where $\max a_j \le N := (2dn)^{2d}$ that can be constructed in polynomial time. Consider the assignment $\boldsymbol{x}' = (x^{a_1}y, \ldots, x^{a_n}y)$ where x and y are new indeterminates. Then $g(x,y) := f(\boldsymbol{x}') \in \mathbb{F}_q[x,y]$ can be represented as $g(x,y) = g_d(x)y^d + g_{d-1}(x)$ $y^{d-1} + \cdots + g_0(x)$. Since $f \in \mathcal{P}(\mathbb{F}_q, n, (d,s))$, $g_d(x)$ is a nonzero polynomial of degree at most dN with at most s monomials. Consider the field $\mathbb{F}_{q^t}$ such that $q^{t-1} < dN \le q^t$ and α a primitive root of $\mathbb{F}_{q^t}$. Since g_d contains at most s monomials of degree less than dN, one of the values $g_d(\alpha^0), \ldots, g_d(\alpha^{s-1})$ is not equal to 0. Since $g(x,y)$ is of degree d in y, we have $g(\alpha^i, \alpha^j) \ne 0$ for some $i = 0, \ldots, s-1$ and $j = 0, \ldots, d$. This gives a hitting set for $\mathcal{P}(\mathbb{F}_q, n, (d,s))$ over $\mathbb{F}_{q^t}$ of size $(d+1)s$. Now using a $(\mathcal{P}(\mathbb{F}_q, n, d), \mathbb{F}_{q^t}, \mathbb{F}_q)$-tester and by Corollary 17 we get a hitting set for $\mathcal{P}(\mathbb{F}_q, n, (d,s))$ of size

$$(d+1)s\cdot\nu_{\mathbb{F}_q}^{\mathcal{P}}(d, \mathbb{F}_{q^t}) = O\left(d^{\tau(d,q,t)+1} s\frac{\log n}{\log q}\right).$$

This proves *1.*
The bottleneck in the above algorithm is finding a primitive root in $\mathbb{F}_{q^t}$ where $q^t \ge dN$. By Lemma 53, this can be done in polynomial time when d is constant. This implies *2.*
For $d = O(\log\log\log n)$ we use Lemma 55. If q is prime then by Lemma 55 a primitive root in $\mathbb{F}_{q^T}$ where $T = t + o(t)$ can be found in time

$$q^{O(t/\log\log t)} = q^{O(d\log n/(\log q\log\log\log n))} = poly(n).$$

This with Corollaries 40 and 41 implies *3.*
One can also use, instead of a primitive root, an element in $\mathbb{F}_{q^t}$ of multiplicative order at least dN. By Lemma 54 for

$m = O(q^{24}d^2 \log^2 n)$ there is a polynomial time algorithm that constructs an element in $\mathbb{F}_{q^M}$ of order at least dN where $M \le m + o(m)$. This, with Corollary 40, gives a hitting set of size

$$(d+1)s \cdot \nu^{\mathcal{P}}_{\mathbb{F}_q}(d, \mathbb{F}_{q^m}) = O\left(q^{24}d^7 s \cdot \log^2 n\right).$$

This implies *4*. □

Notice that, for any constant $c > 1$ and perfect square $q \ge c(d+1)^2$, our explicit construction meets the non-constructive bound in Lemma 70.
We now study the problem for $q \le d$. We will first study the case where $q = 2$ and then consider other fields. We prove

LEMMA 72. *Let $\mathcal{M} = \mathcal{P}(\mathbb{F}_2, n, (d, s))$. Then*

1. *There is an explicit hitting set for $\mathcal{M}$ of size $O(2^{2.66d} s \log n)$.*
2. *For a constant d there is a hitting set for $\mathcal{M}$ of size $O(s \log n)$ that can be constructed in polynomial time $poly(n)$.*
3. *For $d = O(\log \log \log n)$, there is a hitting set for $\mathcal{M}$ of size $O(2^{2.66d} s \log n)$ that can be constructed in time $s \cdot poly(n)$.*
4. *There is a hitting set for $\mathcal{M}$ of size $O(2^{2.66d} s \log^2 n)$ that can be constructed in time $2^{2.66d} s \cdot poly(n)$.*

PROOF. The idea of the proof is the following: First we change the multivariate polynomials in $\mathcal{M}$ to (n, d)-multilinear polynomials in $\phi_d\mathcal{M}$. Then we use Sidon sequence to find a hitting set for $\phi_d\mathcal{M}$ over $\mathbb{F}_{2^r}$ where $r = O(d \log n)$. Then we use a tester to change the hitting set over $\mathbb{F}_{2^r}$ to a hitting set over $\mathbb{F}_2$. Then we use the hitting set for $\phi_d\mathcal{M}$ to get a hitting set for $\mathcal{M}$.
Let $\mathcal{M} = \mathcal{P}(\mathbb{F}_2, n, (d, s))$. Consider $f \in \mathcal{M}$ and suppose

$$f(\boldsymbol{x}) = \sum_{\boldsymbol{i} \in I} \lambda_{\boldsymbol{i}} x_{i_1} \cdots x_{i_d} + g(\boldsymbol{x})$$

where $\boldsymbol{x} = (x_1, \ldots, x_n)$, $g(\boldsymbol{x})$ is a multivariate polynomial of degree less than d, $\boldsymbol{i} = (i_1, i_2, \ldots, i_d)$, $1 \le i_1 < i_2 < \cdots < i_d \le n$, $\lambda_{\boldsymbol{i}} = 1$, $I \subset [n]^d$ and $|I| \le s$. Let $M_{\boldsymbol{i}} = x_{i_1} \cdots x_{i_d}$. Let $\boldsymbol{y} = (\boldsymbol{y}_1, \ldots, \boldsymbol{y}_d)$ where $\boldsymbol{y}_i = (y_{i,1}, \ldots, y_{i,n})$ are new indeterminates for $i = 1, \ldots, d$. Recall the operator $\phi_d : \mathbb{F}_2[\boldsymbol{x}] \to \mathbb{F}_2[\boldsymbol{y}]$ in (20). Since the field is of characteristic 2 and since ϕ_d is linear we have

$$\begin{aligned}(\phi_d f)(\boldsymbol{y}_1, \ldots, \boldsymbol{y}_d) &= \sum_{\boldsymbol{i} \in I} \lambda_{\boldsymbol{i}} \mathrm{Perm}\left(Y_{M_{\boldsymbol{i}}}(\boldsymbol{y}_1, \ldots, \boldsymbol{y}_d)\right) \\ &= \sum_{\boldsymbol{i} \in I} \lambda_{\boldsymbol{i}} \det\left(Y_{M_{\boldsymbol{i}}}(\boldsymbol{y}_1, \ldots, \boldsymbol{y}_d)\right) \quad (24)\end{aligned}$$

Notice that $\phi_d f$ is (n, d)-multilinear polynomial. Let $\boldsymbol{z} = (z_1, \ldots, z_n)$ be new indeterminates. Then $(\phi_d f)(\boldsymbol{z} \star \boldsymbol{y}_1, \ldots, \boldsymbol{z} \star \boldsymbol{y}_d) = \sum_{\boldsymbol{i} \in I} \lambda_{\boldsymbol{i}} z_{i_1} \cdots z_{i_d} \det(Y_{M_{\boldsymbol{i}}}(\boldsymbol{y}_1, \ldots, \boldsymbol{y}_d))$, where $\boldsymbol{z} \star \boldsymbol{y}_i = (z_1 y_{i,1}, \ldots, z_n y_{i,n})$.
Let $\mathbb{K} = \mathbb{F}_{2^r}$ where $r = \lceil 4d \log(2dn) \rceil$ and let α be a primitive root in $\mathbb{K}$. We substitute $\boldsymbol{y}' = (\boldsymbol{y}'_1, \ldots, \boldsymbol{y}'_d)$ in $\boldsymbol{y}$ where $y'_{i,j} = \alpha^{ij}$ and get $(\phi_d f)(\boldsymbol{z} \star \boldsymbol{y}'_1, \ldots, \boldsymbol{z} \star \boldsymbol{y}'_d) = \sum_{\boldsymbol{i} \in I} \lambda_{\boldsymbol{i}} z_{i_1} \cdots z_{i_d} \det\left([\alpha^{i_k j}]_{k,j}\right) = \sum_{\boldsymbol{i} \in I} \Lambda_{\boldsymbol{i}} z_{i_1} \cdots z_{i_d}$, where, by Vandermonde, $\Lambda_{\boldsymbol{i}} = \lambda_{\boldsymbol{i}} \det([\alpha^{i_k j}]_{k,j}) \ne 0$ for all $\boldsymbol{i} \in I$.
Let $a_1, a_2, \ldots, a_n$ be the Sidon $B_{\le d}$ sequence that is defined in Lemma 57 where $\max_j a_j \le (2dn)^{2d}$. We now substitute $\boldsymbol{z} = \boldsymbol{z}' := (w^{a_1}, \ldots, w^{a_n})$ for a new indeterminate w and get

$$t(w) := (\phi_d f)(\boldsymbol{z}' \star \boldsymbol{y}'_1, \ldots, \boldsymbol{z}' \star \boldsymbol{y}'_d) = \sum_{\boldsymbol{i} \in I} \Lambda_{\boldsymbol{i}} w^{a_{i_1} + \cdots + a_{i_d}}.$$

Since $t(w)$ is a polynomial in one variable w of size at most s and degree at most $d(2dn)^{2d} < |\mathbb{K}|$, one of the values $t(1), t(\alpha), \ldots, t(\alpha^{s-1})$ is not zero.
This gives a hitting set for $\phi_d\mathcal{M}$ over $\mathbb{K}$ of size s. By the definition of testers there is a hitting set for $\phi_d\mathcal{M}$ over $\mathbb{F}_2$ of size $s \cdot \nu_{\mathbb{F}_2}(d, \mathbb{F}_{2^r})$. Since each substitution in $\phi_d f$ can be simulated by 2^d substitutions in f and by Theorem 21, there is a hitting set for $\mathcal{M}$ over $\mathbb{F}_2$ of size $2^d s \cdot \nu_{\mathbb{F}_2}(d, \mathbb{F}_{2^r}) = 2^{d + c_2 d} d^5 s r \le d^6 2^{d + c_2 d} s \log n = O(2^{2.66d} s \log n)$. This proves *1*.
In Lemma 56 we show that a Sidon $B_{\le d}$ sequence $a_1, a_2, \cdots, a_d$ with $N := \max_j a_j \le (1 + o(1))^d n^d$ can be constructed in deterministic $O(n^{d/2+1})$ time. We can use this in the above proof. Then we can choose $\mathbb{K} = \mathbb{F}_{2^r}$ where $2^r \ge dN > 2^{r-1}$ and, by Lemma 53, a primitive root in $\mathbb{K}$ can be found in time $(dN)^{1/4} = O(n^{d/2+1})$. This gives a construction of size $O(2^{2.66d} s \log n)$ that can be constructed in time $n^{d/2+1}$. For constant d, we get *2*.
By Lemma 55, for some constant c, there is $M = 2d \log(2dn) + o(2d \log(2dn))$ such that a primitive root in $\mathbb{F}_{2^M}$ can be found in time

$$T = 2^{c \frac{2d \log(2dn)}{\log \log(2d \log(2dn))}}.$$

When $d = O(\log \log \log n)$ we have $T = poly(n)$. This implies *3*.
For the above construction one can also use an element of large multiplicative order in finite field instead of a primitive root. By Lemma 54, for $m = O(d^2 \log^2(dn)))$ one can find an element in $\mathbb{F}_{2^M}$ for some $m \le M \le m + o(m)$ of multiplicative order at least $(2dn)^{2d}$ in polynomial time. This gives a polynomial time construction of a hitting set of size $O(2^{2.66d} s \log^2 n)$. □

When applying the above to any other field we encounter two bottlenecks. The first is that in (24), $\mathrm{Perm}(Y_{M_{\boldsymbol{i}}}(\boldsymbol{y}_1, \ldots, \boldsymbol{y}_d) = \det(Y_{M_{\boldsymbol{i}}}(\boldsymbol{y}_1, \ldots, \boldsymbol{y}_d))$ is true only for multilinear polynomials over fields of characteristic 2. Using permanent instead of determinant for fields of characteristic not equal to 2 will add a factor of $d!$ to the size of the construction. The second bottleneck is that the operator in (20) gives a factor of 2^d to the size of the construction and this, for large field $\mathbb{F}_q$, gives a large gap from the lower bound $(q/(q-1))^d s \log n = 2^{\Omega(d/q)} s \log n$. We therefore get

LEMMA 73. *Let $q \le d$, $r \le p - 1$ and $\mathcal{M} = \mathcal{P}(\mathbb{F}_q, n, ((d, r), s))$. Then*

1. *There is an explicit hitting set for $\mathcal{M}$ of size $O(2^{(1+c_q)d} d! s \log n)$.*
2. *If $q = 2^\ell$ then there is an explicit hitting set for $\mathcal{M}$ of size $O(2^{(1+c_q)d} s \log n)$.*
3. *If d is constant then there is a hitting set for $\mathcal{M}$ of size $O(s \log n)$ that can be constructed in polynomial time $poly(n)$.*
4. *There is a hitting set for $\mathcal{M}$ of size $O(2^{(1+c_q)d} s d! \log^2 n)$ that can be constructed in time $2^{(1+c_q)d} d! s \cdot poly(n)$.*

5. *If $q = 2^\ell$ then there is a hitting set for $\mathcal{M}$ of size $O(2^{(1+c_q)d} s \log^2 n)$ that can be constructed in time $2^{(1+c_q)d} s \cdot poly(n)$.*

Table 9 in the introduction summarizes the results for $\mathcal{M} = \mathcal{P}(\mathbb{F}_q, n, ((d, r), s))$ where $r \le p - 1$.
We note here that the above results were substantially improved in [13].
Acknowledgement. I am grateful to Ronny Roth, Joachim von zur Gathen, Igor Shparlinski, Kenneth Shum and Ilya Volkovich for the number of interesting conversations.

7. REFERENCES

[1] N. Alon. Combinatorial Nullstellensatz. *Combinatorics, Probability and Computing*, 8(1-2), pp. 7–29. (1999).

[2] N. Alon, J. Bruck, J. Naor, M. Naor, R. M. Roth. Construction of asymptotically good low-rate error-correcting codes through pseudo-random graphs. *IEEE Transactions on Information Theory*, 38(2), pp. 509–516. (1992).

[3] L. M. Adleman, H. W. Lenstra. Finding irreducible polynomial over finite field. In Proc. 18th Annual ACM Symposium on Theory of Computing, (STOC 86), pp. 350–355. (1986).

[4] N. Alon, D. Moshkovitz, S. Safra. Algorithmic construction of sets for k-restrictions. *ACM Transactions on Algorithms*, 2(2), pp. 153–177. (2006).

[5] M. Anderson, D. van Melkebeek, I. Volkovich. Derandomizing polynomial identity testing for multilinear constant-read formulae. IEEE Conference on Computational Complexity 2011, pp. 273–282. (2011).

[6] N. Alon, J. H. Spencer. The probabilistic method, Wiley, Third Edition, (2008).

[7] S. Ballet. Curves with many points and multiplication complexity in any extension of $\mathbb{F}_q$. *Finite Fields and Their Applications*, 5(4) , pp. 364–377. (1999).

[8] A. Bogdanov. Pseudorandom generators for low degree polynomials. Proceedings of the 37th ACM Symposium on Theory of Computing, (STOC 2005), pp. 21–30. (2005).

[9] R. C. Bose. An affine analogue of Singer's theorem. *Journal of the Indian Mathematical Society,* 6, pp. 1–15. (1942).

[10] K. O'Bryant. A complete annotated bibliography of work related to Sidon sequences. *The Electric Journal of Combinatorics*, (2004).

[11] Nader H. Bshouty. Testers and their Applications. Electronic Colloquium on Computational Complexity (ECCC) 19: 11 (2012).

[12] Nader H. Bshouty. Multilinear Complexity is Equivalent to Optimal Tester Size. Electronic Colloquium on Computational Complexity (ECCC) 20: 11 (2013).

[13] N. H. Bshouty. Dense Testers and their Applications. In Preperation.

[14] R. C. Bose, S. Chowla. Theorems in additive theory of numbers. *Comment. Math. Helv.*, 37, pp. 141–147. (1962/1963).

[15] S. R. Blackburn, T. Etzion, D. R. Stinson, G. M. Zaverucha. A bound on the size of separating hash families. *Journal of Combinatorial Theory, Series A*, 115(7), pp. 1246–1256. (2008).

[16] R. C. Baker, G. Harman, J. Pintz. The difference between consecutive primes. II. Proceedings of the London Mathematical Society, 83(3), pp. 532–562. (2001).

[17] M. Bazrafshan, T. van Trung. Bounds for separating hash families. *Journal of Combinatorial Theory, Series A*, 118(3), pp. 1129–1135. (2011).

[18] S. R. Blackburn, P. R. Wild. Optimal linear perfect hash families. *Journal of Combinatorial Theory, Series A*, 83(2), pp. 233–250. (1998).

[19] M. Clausen, A. Dress, J. Grabmeier, M. Karpinski. On Zero-testing and interpolation of k-sparse multivariate polynomials over finite fields. *Theoretical Computer Science*, 84(2), pp. 151–164. (1991).

[20] D. Z. Du, F. K. Hwang. Combinatorial group testing and its applications. Volume 12 of Series on Applied Mathematics. World Scientific, New York, second edition, (2000).

[21] A. G. Dýachkov and V. V. Rykov. Bounds on the length of disjunctive codes. *Problemy Peredachi Inf*, 18(3), pp. 7–13. (1982).

[22] A. G. Dýachkov, V. V. Rykov, A. M. Rashad. Superimposed distance codes. Problems Control Inform. Theory/Problemy Upravlen. Teor. Inform., 18(4), pp. 237–250. (1989).

[23] S. A. Evdokimov. Factoring a solvable polynomial over finite fields and generalized Riemann hypothesis. *Zapiski Nauchn Semin. Leningr. Otdel Matem. Inst. Acad. Sci.*, USSR 176, pp. 104–117, (1989).

[24] W. Fulton. Algebraic curves: An introduction to algebraic geometry. W. A. Benjamin, Inc., New-York, Amesterdam. (1969).

[25] Z. Füredi. On r-cover-free families. *Journal of Combinatorial Theory, Series A*, 73(1), pp. 172–173. (1996).

[26] M. L. Fredman, J. Komlós. On the size of seperating systems and families of perfect hash function, *SIAM J. Algebraic and Discrete Methods*, 5(1), pp. 61–68. (1984).

[27] D. Y. Grigoriev, M. Karpinski, M. F. Singer. Fast parralel algorithms for sparse multivariate polynomial interpolation over finite fields. *SIAM J. Comput.*, 19(6), pp. 1059–1063. (1990).

[28] J. von zur Gathen and I. Shparlinski. Orders of Gauss periods in finite fields. *Applicable Algebra in Engineering, Communication and Computing*, 9(1), pp. 15–24. (1998).

[29] A. Garcia, H. Stichtenoth. On the asymptotic behaviour of some towers of function fields over finite fields. *Journal of Number Theory*, 61(2), pp. 248–273. (1996).

[30] A. Garcia, H. Stichtenoth. Topics in geometry, coding theory and cryptography. Algebra and applications. Springer. (2007).

[31] M. A. Huang, A. J. Rao. Interpolation of sparse multivariate polynomials over large finite fields with

applications. *J. of Algorithms*, 33(2), pp. 204–228. (1999).

[32] P. Indyk, H. Q. Ngo, A. Rudra. Efficiently decodable non-adaptive group testing. In the 21st Annual ACM-SIAM Symposium on Discrete Algorithms (SODA 10), pp. 1126–1142. (2010).

[33] J. Körner. Fredman-Komlós bounds and information theory, *SIAM J. Algebraic and Discrete Methods*, 7(4), pp. 560–570. (1986).

[34] J. Körner, K. Marton. New bounds for perfect hashing via information theory. *Europ. J. of Combinatorics*, 9(6), pp. 523–530. (1988).

[35] W. H. Kautz, R. C. Singleton, Nonrandom binary superimposed codes, *IEEE Trans. Inform. Theory*, 10(4), pp. 363–377. (1964).

[36] D. J. Kleitman, J. Spencer. Families of k-independent sets. *Discrete Mathematics*, 6(3), pp. 255–262. (1972).

[37] A. Klivans, D. A. Spielman. Randomness efficient identity testing of multivariate polynomials. In Proceedings on 33rd Annual ACM Symposium on Theory of Computing, (STOC 2001), pp. 216–223. (2001).

[38] R. Lidl, H. Niederreiter. Finite Fields. Encyclopedia of mathematics and its applications. Addison-Wesley Publishing Company. (1984).

[39] L. Liu, H. Shen. Explicit constructions of separating hash families from algebraic curves over finite fields. *Designs, Codes and Cryptography*, 41(2), pp. 221–233. (2006).

[40] A. Nilli. Perfect hashing and probability. *Combinatorics, Probability and Computing*, 3(3), pp. 407–409. (1994).

[41] H. Q. Ngo, D. Z. Du. A survey on combinatorial group testing algorithms with applications to DNA library screening. *Theoretical Computer Science*, 55, pp. 171–182. (2000).

[42] J. Naor, M. Naor. Small-bias probability spaces: efficient constructions and applications. *SIAM J. Comput.*, 22(4), pp. 838–856. (1993).

[43] M. Naor, L. J. Schulman, A. Srinivasan. Splitters and near-optimal derandomization, Proc. of the 36th IEEE Symp. on Foundations of Computer Science, (FOCS 95), pp. 182–191. (1995).

[44] E. Porat, A. Rothschild. Explicit non-adaptive combinatorial group testing schemes. *IEEE Transactions on Information Theory*, 57(12), pp. 7982–7989. (2011).

[45] C. Saha. A note on irreducible polynomials and identity testing. Manuscript. (2008).

[46] J. T. Schwartz. Fast probabilistic algorithms for verification of polynomial identities. *Journal of the ACM*, 27(4), pp. 701–717. (1980).

[47] V. Shoup. New algorithms for finding irreducible polynomial over finite field. *Mathematics of Computation*, 54(189), pp. 435–447. (1990).

[48] I. Shparlinski. On finding primitive roots in finite fields. *Theoretical Computer Science*, 157(2), pp. 273–275. (1996).

[49] I. Shparlinski. Finding irreducible and primitive polynomials. *Applicable Algebra in Engineering Communication and Computing*, 4(4), pp. 263–268. (1993).

[50] I. Shparlinski. Finite fields: theory and computation. Mathematics and Its Applications, Vol. 477. (1999).

[51] G. Seroussi, N. H. Bshouty. Vector sets for exhaustive testing of logic circuits. *IEEE transaction on information theory*, 34(3), pp. 513–522. (1988).

[52] H. Stichtenoth. Algebraic function fields and codes. Second Edition, Vol. 254, Springer. (2008).

[53] V. Shoup. Finding irreducible and primitive polynomials. *Appl. Algebra in Engin., Commun. and Computing*, 4, pp. 263–268. (1993).

[54] N. Saxena, C. Seshadhri. Blackbox identity testing for bounded top fanin depth-3 circuits: the field doesn't matter. Electronic Colloquium on Computational Complexity, Report No. 46. (2011).

[55] G. Seroussi, A. Lempel. On symmetric algorithms for bilinear forms over finite fields. *J. Algorithms*, 5(3), pp. 327–344. (1984).

[56] A. Shpilka, I. Volkovich. Improved polynomial identity testing for read-once formulas. Proceedings of the 12th International Workshop and 13th International Workshop on Approximation, Randomization, and Combinatorial Optimization, (APPROX-RANDOM 09), pp. 700–713. (2009).

[57] S. Saraf, I. Volkovich. Black-box identity testing of depth-4 multilinear circuits. Electronic Colloquium on Computational Complexity, Report No. 46. (2011).

[58] D.R. Stinson, T. van Trung, R. Wei. Secure frameproof codes, key distribution patterns, group testing algorithms and related structures, *J. Stat. Planning and Inference*, 86(2), pp. 595–617. (2000).

[59] D.R. Stinson, R. Wei, K. Chen. On generalised separating hash families. *Journal of Combinatorial Theory, Series A*, 115(1), pp. 105–120. (2008).

[60] D. R. Stinson, R. Wei, L. Zhu. New constructions for perfect hash families and related structures using combinatorial designs and codes. *Journal of Combinatorial Designs*, 8(3), pp. 189–200. (2000).

[61] D. R. Stinson, R. Wei, L. Zhu. Some new bounds for cover-free families, *Journal of Combinatorial Theory, Series A*, 90(1), pp. 224-Ű234. (2000).

[62] D. R. Stinson, R. Wei, L. Zhu. New constructions for perfect hash families and related structures using combintorial designs and codes, *J. Combin. Designs.*, 8(3), pp. 189–200. (2000).

[63] K. Werther. The complexity of sparse polynomial interpolation over finite fields. *Applicable Algebra in Engineering, Communication and Computing*, 5(2), pp. 91–103. (1994).

[64] H. Wang and C. P. Xing. Explicit Constructions of perfect hash families from algebraic curves over finite fields. *J. of Combinatorial Theory, Series A*, 93(1), pp. 112–124. (2001).

[65] R. Zippel. Probabilistic algorithms for sparse polynomials. In Proceedings of the International Symposiumon on Symbolic and Algebraic Computation, 72, pp. 216–226. (1979).

Expanders with Respect to Hadamard Spaces and Random Graphs

[Extended Abstract] *

Manor Mendel
Mathematics and Computer Science Department
The Open University of Israel
mendelma@gmail.com

Assaf Naor
Courant Institute
New York University
naor@cims.nyu.edu

ABSTRACT

It is shown that there exists a sequence of 3-regular graphs $\{G_n\}_{n=1}^\infty$ and a Hadamard space X such that $\{G_n\}_{n=1}^\infty$ forms an expander sequence with respect to X, yet random regular graphs are not expanders with respect to X. This answers a question of [31]. $\{G_n\}_{n=1}^\infty$ are also shown to be expanders with respect to random regular graphs, yielding a deterministic sublinear time constant factor approximation algorithm for computing the average squared distance in subsets of a random graph. The proof uses the Euclidean cone over a random graph, an auxiliary continuous geometric object that allows for the implementation of martingale methods.

This extended abstract does not contain proofs. The full version of this paper can be found at `arXiv:1306.5434`.

Categories and Subject Descriptors

[**Theory of computation**]: Randomness, geometry and discrete structures—*Pseudorandomness and derandomization, Random projections and metric embeddings*; [**Networks**]: Network types—*Overlay and other logical network structures*

Keywords

Expanders; random regular graphs; CAT(0); Hadamard spaces; Euclidean cone; metric embeddings

1. INTRODUCTION

Throughout this paper all graphs are unweighted, non-oriented, and finite, and they are allowed to have parallel edges and self-loops, unless stated otherwise. Given a graph G, we denote its vertices by V_G and its edges by E_G. If G is connected then we denote the shortest-path metric that it induces on V_G by d_G.

Fix $d \in \mathbb{N}$ and let $\{G_n\}_{n=1}^\infty$ be a sequence of d-regular graphs such that $\lim_{n\to\infty} |V_{G_n}| = \infty$. Then $\{G_n\}_{n=1}^\infty$ is an expander sequence (see e.g. [12]) if and only if for every sequence of Hilbert space valued functions $\{f_n : V_n \to \ell_2\}_{n=1}^\infty$ we have

$$\frac{1}{|V_{G_n}|^2} \sum_{(x,y)\in V_{G_n}\times V_{G_n}} \|f_n(x)-f_n(y)\|_2^2 \asymp \frac{1}{|E_{G_n}|} \sum_{\{u,v\}\in E_{G_n}} \|f_n(u)-f_n(v)\|_2^2. \quad (1)$$

Here and in what follows, when we write $A \asymp B$ we mean that there exist two universal constants $c, C \in (0,\infty)$ such that $cA \leqslant B \leqslant CB$. Also, in what follows the notations $A \lesssim B$ and $B \gtrsim A$ mean that $A \leqslant KB$ for some universal constant $K \in (0,\infty)$. If we need to allow K to depend on parameters, we indicate this by subscripts, thus e.g. $A \lesssim_{\alpha,\beta} B$ means that $A \leqslant K(\alpha,\beta)B$ for some $K(\alpha,\beta) \in (0,\infty)$ which is allowed to depend only on the parameters α and β.

The asymptotic identity (1) says that whenever one assigns a vector to each vertex of G_n, the average squared distance between these vectors can be estimated up to universal constant factors by averaging those squared distances that correspond to edges of G_n, an average of only $d|V_{G_n}|$ numbers rather than the full $|V_{G_n}|^2$ pairwise distances. This geometric characterization of expanders as "universal average Euclidean distance approximators" (following terminology of [2]) is easy to prove (its proof will also be explained in the ensuing discussion).

It is natural to investigate the possible validity of (1) when the Hilbertian metric is replaced with other metrics. (1) comprises of two asymptotic inequalities, one of which holds true in any metric space: if G is a d-regular graph and (X, d_X) is a metric space then for every $f : V_G \to X$ we have

$$\frac{1}{|E_G|} \sum_{\{u,v\}\in E_G} d_X\big(f(u), f(v)\big)^2 \leqslant \frac{4}{|V_G|^2} \sum_{(x,y)\in V_G\times V_G} d_X\big(f(x), f(y)\big)^2. \quad (2)$$

Indeed, by the triangle inequality and the convexity of the function $t \mapsto t^2$,

$$d_X(f(u), f(v))^2 \leqslant 2d_X(f(u), f(w))^2 + 2d_X(f(w), f(v))^2 \quad (3)$$

---

*A full version is available at `arXiv:1306.5434`.

ITCS'14, January 12–14, 2014, Princeton, New Jersey, USA.

ACM 978-1-4503-2698-8/14/01 ...$15.00.
http://dx.doi.org/10.1145/2554797.2554829.

for every $u, v, w \in V_G$. Since G is d-regular, the bound (2) follows by averaging (3) over the set $\{(u,v,w) \in V_G \times V_G \times V_G : \{u,v\} \in E_G\}$.

The nontrivial content of (1) is therefore the fact that the left hand side of (1) can be bounded by a multiple (independent of n and f) of the right hand side of (1). Thus, given a regular graph G and a metric space (X, d_X), let $\gamma(G, d_X^2)$ be the infimum over those $\gamma \in (0,\infty]$ such that for every $f : V_G \to X$,

$$\frac{1}{|V_G|^2} \sum_{(u,v)\in V_G\times V_G} d_X\big(f(u), f(v)\big)^2 \leqslant \frac{\gamma}{|E_G|} \sum_{\{u,v\}\in E_G} d_X\big(f(u), f(v)\big)^2. \quad (4)$$

If $X = \mathbb{R}$ with $d_{\mathbb{R}}(s,t) \stackrel{\mathrm{def}}{=} |s-t|$ then by expanding the squares in (4) one checks that

$$\gamma(G, d_{\mathbb{R}}^2) = \frac{1}{1-\lambda_2(G)},$$

where $\lambda_2(G)$ denotes the second largest eigenvalue of the normalized adjacency matrix of the graph G. Despite the fact that there is no actual spectrum present in this geometric context, we think of $\gamma(G, d_X^2)$ as the reciprocal of the spectral gap of G with respect to (X, d_X). The value of $\gamma(G, d_X^2)$ is sensitive to the choice of metric space (X, d_X) and it can be very different from the reciprocal of the spectral gap of G. We refer to [30] for more information on nonlinear spectral gaps.

Given $d \in \mathbb{N}$, a sequence of d-regular graphs $\{G_n\}_{n=1}^\infty$ is said to be an expander sequence with respect to a metric space (X, d_X) if $\lim_{n\to\infty} |V_{G_n}| = \infty$ and $\sup_{n\in\mathbb{N}} \gamma(G_n, d_X^2) < \infty$. Note that by Cheeger's inequality [7, 1] for every graph G we have

$$|X| \geqslant 2 \implies \gamma(G, d_X^2) \gtrsim \frac{1}{\sqrt{1-\lambda_2(G)}}.$$

Hence, unless X is a singleton, if $\{G_n\}_{n=1}^\infty$ is an expander sequence with respect to (X, d_X) then $\sup_{n\in\mathbb{N}} \lambda_2(G_n) < 1$. This means that for every nontrivial metric space (X, d_X), being an expander sequence with respect to (X, d_X) is a stronger requirement than being an expander sequence in the classical sense.

Nonlinear spectral gaps first arose in the context of bi-Lipschitz embeddings; notable examples include the works of Enflo [8], Gromov [9], Bourgain, Milman and Wolfson [5], Pisier [35], Linial, London and Rabinovich [23], and Matoušek [27] (examples of more recent applications of nonlinear spectral gaps to bi-Lipschitz embeddings appear in [3, 18]). Gromov [11] studied nonlinear spectral gaps in the context of coarse embeddings and the Novikov conjecture, a direction that has been pursued in the works of Ozawa [32], Kasparov and Yu [17], V. Lafforgue [20, 21, 22], Pisier [36], and ourselves [28, 30]. Nonlinear spectral gaps also arise in fixed point theory for group actions; see the works of Wang [39, 40], Gromov [11], Izeki and Nayatani [15], Pansu [33], Naor and Silberman [31], and Izeki, Kondo and Nayatani [14]. We refer to the works of Gromov [10] and Pichot [34] for additional geometric applications of nonlinear spectral gaps. In Section 2 we discuss the relevance of nonlinear spectral gaps to approximation algorithms, based on ideas of Indyk [13] and Barhum, Goldreich and Shraibman [2].

Answering a question of Kasparov and Yu [17], V. Lafforgue proved [20] that there exists a sequence of bounded degree graphs that are expanders with respect to *every* uniformly convex normed space; such graph sequences are called super-expanders. In [30] we found a different construction of super-expanders; here we show that our method can be applied to situations in which it seems difficult to use Lafforgue's (algebraic) approach.

It is a challenging question to characterize those metric spaces with respect to which there exist expander sequences. Random regular graphs are with high probability expanders in the classical sense (i.e., with respect to $\mathbb{R}$), but we are far from understanding those metric spaces with respect to which random regular graphs are expanders. One of the consequences of the results obtained here is that there exists a metric space (X, d_X) with respect to which there exists an expander sequence, yet almost surely random regular graphs are not expanders with respect to (X, d_X). No such example was previously known.

Let $\mathbb{G}_n$ be the set of all graphs on the vertex set $\{1, \ldots, n\}$. The subset of $\mathbb{G}_n$ consisting of all the connected graphs is denoted $\mathbb{G}_n^{\mathrm{con}}$. Given an integer $d \geqslant 3$, let $\mathcal{G}_{n,d}$ be the probability measure on $\mathbb{G}_n$ which is uniform over all those graphs in $\mathbb{G}_n$ that are d-regular and have no self-loops and no parallel edges. By [41], $\lim_{n\to\infty} \mathcal{G}_{n,d}(\mathbb{G}_n^{\mathrm{con}}) = 1$.

A Hadamard space (also known as a complete $CAT(0)$ space) is a complete metric space (X, d_X) with the property that for every $x, y \in X$ there exists a point $w \in X$ such that for every $z \in X$ we have

$$d_X(z,w)^2 + \frac{1}{4} d_X(x,y)^2 \leqslant \frac{1}{2} d_X(z,x)^2 + \frac{1}{2} d_X(z,y)^2. \quad (5)$$

See the books [16, 6] and the survey [38] for an extensive account of Hadamard spaces. One of the main questions left open in [31] (specifically, see page 1547 of [31]) is whether or not it is true that if (X, d_X) is a Hadamard space that admits at least one expander sequence then every classical expander sequence is also an expander sequence with respect to (X, d_X). Theorem 1.1 below, which is the first of our two main theorems, answers this question.

THEOREM 1.1. *There exist a Hadamard space (X, d_X) and a sequence of 3-regular graphs $\{G_n\}_{n=1}^\infty$ with $\lim_{n\to\infty} |V_{G_n}| = \infty$ such that*

$$\sup_{n\in\mathbb{N}} \gamma(G_n, d_X^2) < \infty, \quad (6)$$

yet there exists $c \in (0,\infty)$ such that for every $d \in \mathbb{N}$,

$$\lim_{n\to\infty} \mathcal{G}_{n,d}\left(\left\{H \in \mathbb{G}_n : \gamma(H, d_X^2) \geqslant c(\log_d n)^2\right\}\right) = 1. \quad (7)$$

Theorem 1.1 answers the above mentioned question from [31]. Indeed, by (6) the Hadamard space (X, d_X) admits some expander sequence. Random regular graphs are asymptotically almost surely classical expanders [4], i.e., there exists $C \in (0,\infty)$ such that for every integer $d \geqslant 3$,

$$\lim_{n\to\infty} \mathcal{G}_{n,d}\left(\left\{H \in \mathbb{G}_n : \gamma(H, d_{\mathbb{R}}^2) \leqslant C\right\}\right) = 1. \quad (8)$$

Consequently, it follows from (7) and (8) that not all classical expander sequences are expanders with respect to (X, d_X).

Theorem 1.1 yields the first known example of a metric space (X, d_X) with respect to which random regular graphs are asymptotically almost surely not expanders, yet there does exist a special graph sequence $\{G_n\}_{n=1}^\infty$ that is an expander sequence with respect to (X, d_X). Observe that $\{G_n\}_{n=1}^{\infty}$ is a fortiori a classical expander sequence.

The graphs $\{G_n\}_{n=1}^{\infty}$ of Theorem 1.1 have desirable properties which no other expander sequence is known to satisfy. Specifically, $\{G_n\}_{n=1}^{\infty}$ are expanders with respect to random regular graphs. This is made precise in the following theorem.

THEOREM 1.2. *There exists a universal constant $\Gamma \in (0, \infty)$ and a sequence of 3-regular graphs $\{G_n\}_{n=1}^{\infty}$ with*

$$\lim_{n\to\infty} |V_{G_n}| = \infty \qquad \text{and} \qquad \sup_{n\in\mathbb{N}} \frac{|V_{G_{n+1}}|}{|V_{G_n}|} < \infty, \tag{9}$$

such that for every integer $d \geqslant 3$ we have

$$\lim_{m\to\infty} \mathcal{G}_{m,d}\left(\left\{H \in \mathbb{G}_m^{\mathrm{con}} : \sup_{n\in\mathbb{N}} \gamma(G_n, d_H^2) < \Gamma\right\}\right) = 1. \tag{10}$$

In (10) we restrict to $H \in \mathbb{G}_m^{\mathrm{con}}$ because the metric d_H is defined only when H is connected. Explicit bounds on the rates of convergence in (7) and (10) are given in the full version.

Take $G \in \{G_n\}_{n=1}^{\infty}$ and write $V_G = \{1, \ldots, k\}$ for some $k \in \mathbb{N}$. Theorem 1.2 asserts that almost surely as $m \to \infty$, if H is a uniformly random m-vertex d-regular graph then for every $v_1, \ldots, v_k \in V_H$ the average of $d_H(v_i, v_j)^2$ over all $i, j \in \{1, \ldots, k\}$ is at most a constant multiple of the average of $d_H(v_i, v_j)^2$ over those $i, j \in \{1, \ldots, k\}$ that are joined by an edge of G. Note that the latter average is over $3k/2 \asymp k$ numbers while the former average is over $\binom{k}{2} \asymp k^2$ numbers.

Thus G is an especially constructed fixed graph that serves as a "sparse template" for computing the average squared distance between any k vertices in a random regular graph. This yields *sublinear (deterministic) time* approximate computation of average distances in random graphs: our input size is $\Omega(k^2)$, namely all the pairwise distances, while using G we estimate $\frac{1}{k^2}\sum_{i=1}^{k}\sum_{j=1}^{k} d_H(x_i, x_j)^2$ by making only $O(k)$ distance queries. See Section 2 for more on this topic.

Once the graph G is given to us, the above statement about the average squared shortest-path distance of any k vertices of the random graph H involves elementary combinatorics and probability. Nevertheless, our proof of this statement uses methods from analysis and geometry that are interesting in their own right.

Specifically, in [30] we introduced an iterative approach to the construction of super-expanders, building on the zigzag iteration of Reingold, Vadhan and Wigderson [37]. This approach uses estimates on martingales in uniformly convex Banach spaces. In [29] we extended the estimates that were needed for the construction of super-expanders (namely nonlinear spectral calculus inequalities) to Hadamard spaces using an appropriate notion of nonlinear martingale. In order to apply these methods in the present setting, we consider the one-dimensional simplicial complex obtained by including all the edges of H as unit intervals. We then work with the *Euclidean cone* over this one-dimensional simplicial complex, which is an auxiliary two-dimensional (random) continuous object on which martingale methods can be applied. The definition of the Euclidean cone over a metric space is recalled in the full version. We prove that if H is sampled from $\mathcal{G}_{n,d}$ then with high probability its Euclidean cone is a (non-disjoint) union of two sets A_1, A_2 such that A_1 admits a bi-Lipschitz embedding into L_1 and A_2 admits a bi-Lipschitz embedding into a Hadamard space. We then treat A_1 directly using Matoušek's extrapolation lemma for Poincaré inequalities [27], and we treat A_2 using the methods of [30, 29].

The implementation of the above strategy is not straightforward, relying on a variety of geometric and analytic tools; a more detailed overview of our proof of Theorem 1.2 appears in the full version. Here we only wish to stress that our proof of Theorem 1.2 introduces a way to reason about random graphs that is potentially useful in other contexts: we consider such a graph as being embedded in a larger auxiliary continuous geometric object that allows for the use of analytic methods, even though the statement being proved involves only the vertices of the original graph.

Previous work. Nonlinear spectral gaps have been studied in the literature from several points of view, leading to some notational inconsistencies. Here we use the notation that arises naturally from bi-Lipschitz embedding theory. Pichot [34] denotes the reciprocal of $\gamma(G, d_X^2)$ by $\lambda_1(G, X)$. In reference to Gromov's original definition [10, 11], Pansu [33] and Kondo [19] denote the same quantity by $\lambda^{\mathrm{Gro}}(G, X)$ and $\lambda_1^{\mathrm{Gro}}(G, X)$, respectively. When X is a Hadamard space, a closely related quantity, known today as Wang's invariant, was introduced by Wang [39, 40]; Wang's invariant is always within a factor of 2 of the reciprocal of $\gamma(G, d_X^2)$. For Hadamard spaces, Izeki and Nayatani [15] introduced an invariant that can be used to control the ratio between Wang's invariant for a graph G and the classical spectral gap of G.

We were motivated to revisit the question of [31] that Theorem 1.1 answers by the recent work of Kondo [19]. Kondo's goal in [19] was to construct a Hadamard space for which the Izeki-Nayatani invariant is trivial. He succeeded to do so by using the Euclidean cone over certain expander graphs. In particular he obtained a Hadamard space that contains bi-Lipschitzly copies of some (classical) expanders. Gromov considered the same construction in [10, 11] for a different but related purpose. The main point of Theorem 1.1 is to prove that the space X admits a sequence of expanders; we achieve this by modifying the Gromov-Kondo construction so that it will be compatible with the method to construct nonlinear expanders of [30]. The fact that our graphs are expanders with respect to random graphs requires additional work, relying on a structural result for Euclidean cones over random graphs.

2. SUBLINEAR AVERAGE DISTANCE APPROXIMATION ALGORITHMS

Suppose that (X, d_X) is a metric space and we have oracle access to pairwise distances in X. Given $x_1, \ldots, x_n \in X$ write

$$A \stackrel{\mathrm{def}}{=} \frac{1}{n^2}\sum_{i=1}^{n}\sum_{j=1}^{n} d_X(x_i, x_j)^2. \tag{11}$$

One can compute A exactly with k^2 distance queries. But, we wish to estimate A in *sublinear time*, i.e., with only $o(k^2)$ distance queries.

Indyk [13] proved that it is possible to approximate A up to a factor of $1 + \varepsilon$ by querying the distances between $O(n/\varepsilon^{7/2})$ pairs of points chosen uniformly at random. Barhum, Goldreich and Shraibman [2] improved the required number of uniformly random pairs of points to $O(n/\varepsilon^2)$, which is asymptotically tight [2].

The above simple randomized sampling algorithm shows that for every $x_1,\dots,x_n \in X$ one can find $O(n)$ pairs of points from $\{x_1,\dots,x_n\}$ whose average distance is within $O(1)$ of A, but these pairs depend on the initial point set $\{x_1,\dots,x_n\} \subseteq X$. Following [2], for $D \in [1,\infty)$ we say that a graph $G = (\{1,\dots,n\},E)$ is a *D-universal approximator* with respect to (X,d_X^2) if there exists (a scaling factor) $s \in (0,\infty)$ such that for every $x_1,\dots,x_n \in X$ we have

$$\frac{1}{n^2}\sum_{i=1}^{n}\sum_{j=1}^{n} d_X(x_i,x_j)^2 \leqslant \frac{s}{|E|}\sum_{\{i,j\}\in E} d_X(x_i,x_j)^2 \leqslant \frac{D}{n^2}\sum_{i=1}^{n}\sum_{j=1}^{n} d_X(x_i,x_j)^2.$$

In [2] it is shown that there exists $c \in (0,\infty)$ such that if $G = (\{1,\dots,n\},E)$ is a D-universal approximator with respect to (X,d_X^2) for *every* metric space (X,d_X) then

$$|E| \gtrsim \frac{n^{1+c/\sqrt{D}}}{\sqrt{D}}.$$

It was also shown in [2] that there exists $C \in (0,\infty)$ such that for every $D \in [1,\infty)$ and $n \in \mathbb{N}$ there exists a graph $G = (\{1,\dots,n\},E)$ that is a D-universal approximator with respect to (X,d_X^2) for *every* metric space (X,d_X), and such that

$$|E| \leqslant \sqrt{D}\cdot n^{1+C/\sqrt{D}}.$$

We note that [2] deals with the analogous question for universal approximators when the quantity A in (11) is defined with the distances raised to power 1 rather than being squared. However, the arguments of [2] easily extend mutatis mutandis to yield the above stated results (and, in fact, to analogous statements when A is defined in terms of distances raised to power p for any $p \geqslant 1$).

We thus have a satisfactory understanding of the size of universal approximators with respect to *all* metric spaces. But, for special metric spaces it is possible to obtain better tradeoffs. Indeed, in [2] it is observed that an expander graph is a linear size $O(1)$-universal approximator with respect to Hilbert space; this is nothing more than an interpretation of (1), though by being more careful, and using Ramanujan graphs [24, 26] of appropriate degree, it is shown in [2] how to obtain a $1+\varepsilon$ approximation for every $\varepsilon \in (0,1)$.

Due to (2) and (4), for every graph G and every metric space (X,d_X), if we set $D = 4\gamma(G,d_X^2)$ then G is D-universal approximator with respect to (X,d_X^2). Hence, the super-expanders of [21] and [30] are $O_X(1)$-universal approximators with respect to $(X,\|\cdot\|_X^2)$ for every uniformly convex Banach space $(X,\|\cdot\|_X)$ (by $O_X(1)$ we mean that the approximation factor depends only on X, in fact, it depends only on the modulus of uniform convexity of X).

Theorem 1.2 yields the only known construction of bounded degree $O(1)$-universal approximators with respect to random regular graphs; this is the content of Theorem 2.1 below. Graphs sampled from $\mathcal{G}_{n,d}$ occur in various application areas, e.g. in networking, where they serve as models for peer-to-peer networks [25]. Therefore, a data structure that can compute quickly the average squared distance of a given subset of a random regular graph is of theoretical interest. However, the potential practicality of our data structure is questionable because the approximation guarantee is a large universal constant; we made no attempt to improve this aspect of the construction.

THEOREM 2.1. *There exists $D \in [1,\infty)$ and for every $n \in \mathbb{N}$ there exists a graph $U_n = (\{1,\dots,n\},E_n)$ with $|E_n| = O(n)$ such that for every two integers $m,d \geqslant 3$, if H is sampled from the restriction of $\mathcal{G}_{m,d}$ to $\mathbb{G}_m^{\mathrm{con}}$ then with probability that tends to 1 as $m \to \infty$ the graphs $\{U_n\}_{n=1}^\infty$ are D-universal approximators with respect to (V_H,d_H^2).*

PROOF. Let $\{G_k\}_{k=1}^\infty$ be the graphs from Theorem 1.2. Fixing $n \in \mathbb{N}$, it follows from (9) that there exists $k \in \mathbb{N}$ such that $n \leqslant |V_{G_k}| \leqslant Mn$, where $M \in \mathbb{N}$ is a universal constant. Partition V_{G_k} into n disjoint sets $A_1,\dots,A_n \subseteq V_{G_k}$ satisfying

$$\forall i \in \{1,\dots,n\}, \qquad |A_i| \in \left\{\left\lfloor\frac{|V_{G_k}|}{n}\right\rfloor, \left\lfloor\frac{|V_{G_k}|}{n}\right\rfloor+1\right\}. \tag{12}$$

Define the edge multi-set E_n of U_n by letting the number of edges joining $i \in \{1,\dots,n\}$ and $j \in \{1,\dots,n\}$ be equal to the total number of edges joining A_i and A_j in G_k. Then $|E_n| \leqslant |E_{G_k}| = \frac{3}{2}|V_{G_k}| \leqslant \frac{3}{2}Mn$.

Suppose that $H \in \mathbb{G}_m$ is connected and

$$\sup_{k\in\mathbb{N}} \gamma\left(G_k, d_H^2\right) < \Gamma, \tag{13}$$

where Γ is the constant from Theorem 1.2. It follows from (10) that if $H \in \mathbb{G}_m$ is sampled from $\mathcal{G}_{m,d}$ then the above asumptions hold true with probability that tends to 1 as $m \to \infty$.

Fix $x_1,\dots,x_n \in V_H$ and define $f : V_{G_k} \to V_H$ by setting $f(u) = x_i$ for $u \in A_i$. By the definition of $\gamma(G_k,d_H^2)$ combined with (13) and (2),

$$\begin{aligned}\frac{1}{|V_{G_k}|^2}&\sum_{(u,v)\in V_{G_k}\times V_{G_k}} d_H(f(u),f(v))^2\\ &\leqslant \frac{\Gamma}{|E_{G_k}|}\sum_{\{u,v\}\in E_{G_k}} d_H(f(u),f(v))^2\\ &\leqslant \frac{4\Gamma}{|V_{G_k}|^2}\sum_{(u,v)\in V_{G_k}\times V_{G_k}} d_H(f(u),f(v))^2. \end{aligned}\tag{14}$$

Since

$$\sum_{(u,v)\in V_{G_k}\times V_{G_k}} d_H(f(u),f(v))^2 = \sum_{i=1}^{n}\sum_{j=1}^{n} |A_i|\cdot|A_j|\cdot d_H(x_i,x_j)^2,$$

it follows from (12) that

$$\begin{aligned}\frac{n^2\lfloor|V_{G_k}|/n\rfloor^2}{|V_G|^2} &\leqslant \frac{\frac{1}{|V_{G_k}|^2}\sum_{(u,v)\in V_{G_k}\times V_{G_k}} d_H(f(u),f(v))^2}{\frac{1}{n^2}\sum_{i=1}^{n}\sum_{j=1}^{n} d_H(x_i,x_j)^2}\\ &\leqslant \frac{n^2\left(\lfloor|V_{G_k}|/n\rfloor+1\right)^2}{|V_G|^2}.\end{aligned}\tag{15}$$

Also, by the definition of E_n and f we have

$$\sum_{(u,v)\in E_{G_k}} d_H(f(u),f(v))^2 = \sum_{(i,j)\in E_n} d_H(x_i,x_j)^2. \tag{16}$$

By substituting (15) and (16) into (14) we conclude that

$$\frac{1}{n^2}\sum_{i=1}^{n}\sum_{j=1}^{n} d_H(x_i,x_j)^2$$
$$\leqslant \frac{\Gamma|V_G|^2|E_n|}{n^2\lfloor|V_{G_k}|/n\rfloor^2|E_{G_k}|}\cdot\frac{1}{|E_n|}\sum_{\{i,j\}\in E_n} d_H(x_i,x_j)^2$$
$$\leqslant \frac{4\Gamma\left(1+\frac{1}{\lfloor|V_{G_k}|/n\rfloor}\right)^2}{n^2}\sum_{i=1}^{n}\sum_{j=1}^{n} d_H(x_i,x_j)^2$$
$$\leqslant \frac{16\Gamma}{n^2}\sum_{i=1}^{n}\sum_{j=1}^{n} d_H(x_i,x_j)^2.$$

This means that U_n is a D-universal approximator with respect to (V_H, d_H^2), where $D = 16\Gamma$. □

REMARK 2.2. *A straightforward inspection of our proof of Theorem 1.2 reveals that for every $n \in \mathbb{N}$ the universal approximator U_n of Theorem 2.1 can be constructed in deterministic $O(n)$ time.*

REMARK 2.3. *Let (X, d_X) be a metric space and $p \in [1,\infty)$. As noted above, one can study universal approximators with respect to (X, d_X^p), i.e., given $x_1,\dots,x_n \in X$ the goal is approximate computation of the quantity*

$$\frac{1}{n^2}\sum_{i=1}^{n}\sum_{j=1}^{n} d_X(x_i,x_j)^p$$

with $o(k^2)$ distance queries. The references [13, 2] deal with $p = 1$, but as we mentioned earlier, they extend painlessly to general $p \geqslant 1$. Here we have only dealt with the case $p = 2$, but we speculate that our argument can be modified to yield bounded degree universal approximators with respect to (H, d_H^p) for any $p \in (1,\infty)$, where H is a random d-regular graph. We did not, however, attempt to carry out our proof when $p \neq 2$. We also speculate that the case $p = 1$ requires more substantial new ideas, as the type of martingale arguments that we use typically fail at the endpoint $p = 1$.

2.1 A question of J. Kleinberg

In connection with Theorem 1.2 and the algorithmic context described in Section 2, Jon Kleinberg asked us whether or not two stochastically independent random 3-regular graphs are asymptotically almost surely expanders with respect to each other. Formally, we have the following open question.

QUESTION 2.4 (JON KLEINBERG). *Does there exist a universal constant $K \in (0,\infty)$ such that*

$$\lim_{\min\{m,n\}\to\infty} \mathcal{G}_{m,3}\times\mathcal{G}_{n,3}\left[\left\{(G,H)\in\mathbb{G}_m\times\mathbb{G}_n^{\mathrm{con}}:\ \gamma\left(G,d_H^2\right)\right\}\leqslant K\right]=1.$$

While a positive solution of Question 2.4 does not formally imply that there exist graphs $\{G_n\}_{n=1}^{\infty}$ as in Theorem 2, such a statement would be a step towards a probabilistic construction of such graphs. At present we do not have methods to argue about the nonlinear spectral gap of random graphs. In particular, it is a major open question whether or not random 3-regular graphs are super-expanders with positive probability. Thus, all the known constructions in the context of nonlinear spectral gaps are deterministic, with the only two methods that are currently available being Lafforgue's algebraic approach [20] and our iterative approach [30]. It seems, however, that the problem of obtaining a probabilistic proof of the existence of expanders with respect to random graphs is more tractable, and for this reason we believe that Question 2.4 is a promising research direction. The following proposition is a partial result towards a positive solution of Question 2.4 that we obtained through discussions with Uriel Feige; we thank him for allowing us to include his insights here.

PROPOSITION 2.5. *For $n \in \mathbb{N}$ even let G, H be two i.i.d. random graphs sampled from $\mathcal{G}_{n,3}$. Then with probability that tends to 1 as $n \to \infty$, for every permutation $\pi \in S_n$ we have*

$$\frac{1}{n^2}\sum_{i=1}^{n}\sum_{j=1}^{n} d_H(\pi(i),\pi(j))^2 \lesssim \frac{1}{n}\sum_{\{i,j\}\in E_G} d_H(\pi(i),\pi(j))^2. \tag{17}$$

A positive answer to Question 2.4 would require proving (17) when G, H are independent random 3-regular graphs of possibly different cardinalities, say G sampled from $\mathcal{G}_{n,3}$ and H sampled from $\mathcal{G}_{m,3}$, and with the permutation π of Proposition 2.5 replaced with a general mapping $f : \{1,\dots,n\} \to \{1,\dots,m\}$.

3. ACKNOWLEDGEMENTS

We are grateful to Uriel Feige, Konstantin Makarychev and Yuval Peres for helpful discussions, and to Jon Kleinberg for formulating Question 2.4. We also thank Takefumi Kondo for sending us a preliminary version of [19]. M. M. was supported by ISF grants 221/07 and 93/11, BSF grant 2010021, and NSF grants CCF-0832797 and DMS-0835373. Part of this work was completed while M. M. was visitor at Microsoft Research and a member of the Institute for Advanced Study at Princeton. A. N. was supported by NSF grant CCF-0832795, BSF grant 2010021, the Packard Foundation and the Simons Foundation. Part of this work was completed while A. N. was a Visiting Fellow at Princeton University.

4. REFERENCES

[1] N. Alon and V. D. Milman. λ_1, isoperimetric inequalities for graphs, and superconcentrators. *J. Combin. Theory Ser. B*, 38(1):73–88, 1985.

[2] K. Barhum, O. Goldreich, and A. Shraibman. On approximating the average distance between points. In *Approximation, Randomization, and Combinatorial Optimization. Algorithms and Techniques. Proccedings of 10th International Workshop APPROX 2007 and 11th International Workshop RANDOM 2007*, pages 296–310, 2007.

[3] Y. Bartal, N. Linial, M. Mendel, and A. Naor. On metric Ramsey-type phenomena. *Ann. of Math. (2)*, 162(2):643–709, 2005.

[4] B. Bollobás. The isoperimetric number of random regular graphs. *European J. Combin.*, 9(3):241–244, 1988.

[5] J. Bourgain, V. Milman, and H. Wolfson. On type of metric spaces. *Trans. Amer. Math. Soc.*, 294(1):295–317, 1986.

[6] M. R. Bridson and A. Haefliger. *Metric spaces of non-positive curvature*, volume 319 of *Grundlehren der Mathematischen Wissenschaften [Fundamental Principles of Mathematical Sciences]*. Springer-Verlag, Berlin, 1999.

[7] J. Cheeger. A lower bound for the smallest eigenvalue of the Laplacian. In *Problems in analysis (Papers dedicated to Salomon Bochner, 1969)*, pages 195–199. Princeton Univ. Press, Princeton, N. J., 1970.

[8] P. Enflo. Uniform homeomorphisms between Banach spaces. In *Séminaire Maurey-Schwartz (1975–1976), Espaces, L^p, applications radonifiantes et géométrie des espaces de Banach, Exp. No. 18*, page 7. Centre Math., École Polytech., Palaiseau, 1976.

[9] M. Gromov. Filling Riemannian manifolds. *J. Differential Geom.*, 18(1):1–147, 1983.

[10] M. Gromov. CAT(κ)-spaces: construction and concentration. *Zap. Nauchn. Sem. S.-Peterburg. Otdel. Mat. Inst. Steklov. (POMI)*, 280(Geom. i Topol. 7):100–140, 299–300, 2001.

[11] M. Gromov. Random walk in random groups. *Geom. Funct. Anal.*, 13(1):73–146, 2003.

[12] S. Hoory, N. Linial, and A. Wigderson. Expander graphs and their applications. *Bull. Amer. Math. Soc. (N.S.)*, 43(4):439–561 (electronic), 2006.

[13] P. Indyk. Sublinear time algorithms for metric space problems. In *Annual ACM Symposium on Theory of Computing (Atlanta, GA, 1999)*, pages 428–432 (electronic). ACM, New York, 1999.

[14] H. Izeki, T. Kondo, and S. Nayatani. N-step energy of maps and the fixed-point property of random groups. *Groups Geom. Dyn.*, 6(4):701–736, 2012.

[15] H. Izeki and S. Nayatani. Combinatorial harmonic maps and discrete-group actions on Hadamard spaces. *Geom. Dedicata*, 114:147–188, 2005.

[16] J. Jost. *Nonpositive curvature: geometric and analytic aspects.* Lectures in Mathematics ETH Zürich. Birkhäuser Verlag, Basel, 1997.

[17] G. Kasparov and G. Yu. The coarse geometric Novikov conjecture and uniform convexity. *Adv. Math.*, 206(1):1–56, 2006.

[18] S. Khot and A. Naor. Nonembeddability theorems via Fourier analysis. *Mathematische Annalen*, 334(4):821–852, 2006.

[19] T. Kondo. CAT(0) spaces and expanders. *Math. Z.*, 271(1-2):343–355, 2012.

[20] V. Lafforgue. Un renforcement de la propriété (T). *Duke Math. J.*, 143(3):559–602, 2008.

[21] V. Lafforgue. Propriété (T) renforcée Banachique et transformation de Fourier rapide. *J. Topol. Anal.*, 1(3):191–206, 2009.

[22] V. Lafforgue. Propriété (T) renforcée et conjecture de Baum-Connes. In *Quanta of maths*, volume 11 of *Clay Math. Proc.*, pages 323–345. Amer. Math. Soc., Providence, RI, 2010.

[23] N. Linial, E. London, and Y. Rabinovich. The geometry of graphs and some of its algorithmic applications. *Combinatorica*, 15(2):215–245, 1995.

[24] A. Lubotzky, R. Phillips, and P. Sarnak. Ramanujan graphs. *Combinatorica*, 8(3):261–277, 1988.

[25] P. Mahlmann and C. Schindelhauer. Peer-to-peer networks based on random transformations of connected regular undirected graphs. In *Proceedings of the seventeenth annual ACM symposium on Parallelism in algorithms and architectures*, SPAA'05, pages 155–164, New York, NY, USA, 2005. ACM.

[26] G. A. Margulis. Explicit group-theoretic constructions of combinatorial schemes and their applications in the construction of expanders and concentrators. *Problemy Peredachi Informatsii*, 24(1):51–60, 1988.

[27] J. Matoušek. On embedding expanders into ℓ_p spaces. *Israel J. Math.*, 102:189–ï£¡197, 1997.

[28] M. Mendel and A. Naor. Towards a calculus for non-linear spectral gaps. In *Proceedings of the Twenty-First Annual ACM-SIAM Symposium on Discrete Algorithms*, pages 236–255, 2010.

[29] M. Mendel and A. Naor. Spectral calculus and Lipschitz extension for barycentric metric spaces. *Anal. Geom. Metr. Spaces*, 1:163–199, 2012.

[30] M. Mendel and A. Naor. Nonlinear spectral calculus and super-expanders. *Publications mathématiques de l'IHÉS*, 2014. To appear.

[31] A. Naor and L. Silberman. Poincaré inequalities, embeddings, and wild groups. *Compos. Math.*, 147(5):1546–1572, 2011.

[32] N. Ozawa. A note on non-amenability of $\mathscr{B}(l_p)$ for $p = 1, 2$. *Internat. J. Math.*, 15(6):557–565, 2004.

[33] P. Pansu. Superrigidité géométique et applications harmoniques. In *Géométries à courbure négative ou nulle, groupes discrets et rigidités*, volume 18 of *Sémin. Congr.*, pages 373–420. Soc. Math. France, Paris, 2009.

[34] M. Pichot. Harmonic analysis from quasi-periodic domains. *Israel J. Math.*, 167:63–90, 2008.

[35] G. Pisier. Probabilistic methods in the geometry of Banach spaces. In *Probability and analysis (Varenna, 1985)*, volume 1206 of *Lecture Notes in Math.*, pages 167–241. Springer, Berlin, 1986.

[36] G. Pisier. Complex interpolation between Hilbert, Banach and operator spaces. *Mem. Amer. Math. Soc.*, 208(978), 2010.

[37] O. Reingold, S. Vadhan, and A. Wigderson. Entropy waves, the zig-zag graph product, and new constant-degree expanders. *Ann. of Math.*, 155(1):157–187, 2002.

[38] K.-T. Sturm. Probability measures on metric spaces of nonpositive curvature. In *Heat kernels and analysis on manifolds, graphs, and metric spaces (Paris, 2002)*, volume 338 of *Contemp. Math.*, pages 357–390. Amer. Math. Soc., Providence, RI, 2003.

[39] M.-T. Wang. A fixed point theorem of discrete group actions on Riemannian manifolds. *J. Differential Geom.*, 50(2):249–267, 1998.

[40] M.-T. Wang. Generalized harmonic maps and representations of discrete groups. *Comm. Anal. Geom.*, 8(3):545–563, 2000.

[41] N. C. Wormald. The asymptotic connectivity of labelled regular graphs. *J. Combin. Theory Ser. B*, 31(2):156–167, 1981.

On the Automorphism Groups of Strongly Regular Graphs I

László Babai
University of Chicago
1100 E 58th St
Chicago, IL 60637
laci@cs.uchicago.eduu

To the memory of Ákos Seress (1958–2013)

ABSTRACT

We derive structural constraints on the automorphism groups of strongly regular (s. r.) graphs, giving a surprisingly strong answer to a decades-old problem, with tantalizing implications to testing isomorphism of s. r. graphs, and raising new combinatorial challenges.

S. r. graphs, while not believed to be Graph Isomorphism (GI) complete, have long been recognized as hard cases for GI, and, in this author's view, present some of the core difficulties of the general GI problem. Progress on the complexity of testing their isomorphism has been intermittent (Babai 1980, Spielman 1996, BW & CST (STOC'13) and BCSTW (FOCS'13)), and the current best bound is $\exp(\widetilde{O}(n^{1/5}))$ (n is the number of vertices).

Our main result is that if X is a s. r. graph then, with straightforward exceptions, the degree of the largest alternating group involved in the automorphism group $\mathrm{Aut}(X)$ (as a quotient of a subgroup) is $O((\ln n)^2/\ln\ln n)$. (The exceptions admit trivial linear-time GI testing.)

The design of isomorphism tests for various classes of structures is intimately connected with the study of the automorphism groups of those structures. We include a brief survey of these connections, starting with an 1869 paper by Jordan on trees.

In particular, our result amplifies the *potential* of Luks's divide-and-conquer methods (1980) to be applicable to testing isomorphism of s. r. graphs in *quasipolynomial time.*

The challenge remains to find a hierarchy of combinatorial substructures through which this potential can be realized. We expect that the generality of our result will help in this regard; the result applies not only to s. r. graphs but to all graphs with strong spectral expansion and with a relatively small number of common neighbors for every pair of vertices. We state a purely mathematical conjecture that could bring us closer to finding the right kind of hierarchy. We also outline the broader GI context, and state conjectures in terms of "primitive coherent configurations." These are generalizations of s. r. graphs, relevant to the general GI problem.

Another consequence of the main result is the strongest argument to date against GI-completeness of s. r. graphs: we prove that no polynomial-time *categorical* reduction of GI to isomorphism of s. r. graphs is possible. All known reductions between isomorphism problems of various classes of structures fit into our notion of "categorical reduction."

The proof of the main result is elementary; it is based on known results in spectral graph theory and on a 1987 lemma on permutations by Ákos Seress and the author.

ITCS'14, January 12–14, 2014, Princeton, NJ, USA

http://dx.doi.org/10.1145/2554797.2554830 ...$15.00.

Categories and Subject Descriptors

Mathematics of computing [**Discrete mathematics**]: Graph theory; Theory of computation [**Design and analysis of algorithms**]: Graph algorithms analysis

Keywords

graphs, groups, automorphism groups, algorithms, isomorphism testing, strongly regular graphs

1. INTRODUCTION

In just a few lines and from mostly known igredients we derive a surprisingly strong and unanticipated answer to a decades-old mathematical question with implications to graph isomorphism testing, the combinatorics of highly regular configurations, and the theory of permutation groups.

Accordingly, this paper is short on proofs and long on motivation. The proofs, albeit simple, draw on diverse sources: two distinct areas of spectral graph theory (expansion, where the focus is on inequalities; and the spectral aspects of strong regularity, where identities play a central role), a lemma on permutations that initially arose in the context of parallel algorithms and the diameter of permutation groups; and a combinatorial lemma about strongly regular graphs, initially devised in the context of isomorphism testing.

We start with describing the main results, and discuss the motivation in a subsequent section. In a brief "Outlook" section (Sec. 8) we outline the broader graph isomorphism (GI) context and state relevant conjectures in terms of "primitive coherent configurations."

Nothing but the most basic group theory is required for the main results (the notion of the alternating group and of subgroups and quotient groups). Elements of the theory of permutation groups are required for the algorithmic motivation, specifically the notion of primitive permutation groups.

These concepts have been fundamental to the area of GI testing ever since Gene Luks's seminal 1980 paper [46]. We review basic permutation group concepts in the Appendix (Sec. A). The reader may understand much of the motivation by having just the vague notion that "primitive permutation groups" are those permutation groups where natural "divide and conquer" breaks down.

1.1 The main results

A graph X is *strongly regular* with parameters (n, k, λ, μ) if X has n vertices, every vertex has degree k, each pair of adjacent vertices has λ common neighbors, and each pair of non-adjacent vertices has μ common neighbors.

A group G is said to *involve* the group H if $H \cong L/N$ for some $N \triangleleft L \leq G$ (quotient of a subgroup).

Next we introduce a term motivated by the asymptotic theory of primitive permutation groups (see Theorem 6) that will be convenient to use in the statement of our main results.

Definition 1. The *thickness* $\theta(G)$ of a group G is the greatest t such that the alternating group A_t is involved in G.

We note that this is not standard terminology, but Peter Cameron, one of the architects of asymptotic group theory, agreed to use this term in the future[1].

We shall say that the strongly regular graph X is *trivial* if X or its complement is disconnected. In this case, X or its complement is the disjoint union of cliques of equal size. We shall say that X is *graphic* if X or its complement is the line graph of a graph. (The vertices of the line graph $L(Y)$ of the graph Y correspond to the edges of Y; two vertices of $L(Y)$ are adjacent in $L(Y)$ if the corresponding edges of Y share a vertex.) The line graph $L(Y)$ is s. r. exactly if Y is either a complete graph K_v ($n = \binom{v}{2}$) or a complete bipartite graph $K_{v,v}$ (with equal parts; $n = v^2$).

We note that it is straightforward to recognize trivial and graphic s. r. graphs and to test their isomorphism in linear time. We also note that the automorphism groups of these families of s. r. graphs have large thickness: at least $\sqrt{n}$ in each case.

THEOREM 2. *Let X be a non-trivial and non-graphic strongly regular graph with n vertices. Then the thickness of the automorphism group of X is*

$$\theta(\mathrm{Aut}(X)) = O((\ln n)^2 / \ln \ln n).$$

This will be proved in Section 5.2.

[1] Peter Cameron and this author together coined the term "asymptotic group theory" while organizing the first conference specifically dedicated to this area, the European Research Conference "Group Theory: Finite to Infinite," held at Il Ciocco, Lucca, Italy, July 1996. Weeks before the meeting, the sponsoring European Science Foundation informed me that the stellar list of speakers we invited was insufficiently European and therefore this "Russian–Israeli event," as they labeled it, referring to the nationalities of a significant fraction of the speakers, would be canceled. I also received the hint that I could avert this disaster by relabeling the nationalities of visiting scholars according to the countries they visited. Thus Rostislav Grigorchuk (Steklov Inst.) became Swiss (Geneva), Ehud Hrushovski (Hebrew U.) British (Cambridge), etc., and the Europeanness scores kept by the bean counters of Brussels worked out in the end. A happy outcome for asymptotic group theory.

The best previously known bound is $\theta(\mathrm{Aut}(X)) = \widetilde{O}(n^{1/5})$, inferable from [9] (see Section B in the Appendix); prior to 2013, the best known bound was $\widetilde{O}(n^{1/3})$, inferable from Spielman [59]. (The tilde hides polylogarithmic factors.)

One more piece of terminology will come in handy.

Definition 3. Let X be a regular graph of degree k. Let $k = \xi_1 \geq \xi_2 \geq \cdots \geq \xi_n$ denote the eigenvalues of the adjacency matrix of X. Set $\xi = \xi(X) = \max\{|\xi_i| \mid 2 \leq i \leq n\}$. We call this quantity the *zero-weight spectral radius* of X. (It is the spectral radius of the adjacency operator restricted to the subspace $\sum x_i = 0$.)

We shall actually prove the following more general result.

THEOREM 4. *Let X be a regular graph of degree k with zero-weight spectral radius of ξ. Suppose every pair of vertices in X has at most q common neighbors. Assume $q + \xi < k$. Then the thickness of* $\mathrm{Aut}(X)$ *is at most*

$$\frac{(\ln n)^2}{2 \ln \ln n} \cdot \frac{1 + o(1)}{\left(1 - \frac{q+\xi}{k}\right)^2}. \quad (1)$$

(Here the $o(1)$ term goes to zero as $n \to \infty$ uniformly regardless of the other parameters.)

This will be proved in Section 4.

To infer Theorem 2 from Theorem 4, we shall need to show that for non-trivial, non-graphic s. r. graphs, $q + \xi$ is bounded away from k. Since the complement of a s. r. graph is s. r., it suffices to prove this under the assumption that our s. r. graphs have degree $k \leq (n-1)/2$. In fact, we shall need to assume $k < n/4$. For the cases $k \geq n/4$ we shall take a more direct approach.

THEOREM 5. *Let X be a non-trivial, non-graphic strongly regular graph of degree k with $n \geq 29$ vertices and zero-weight spectral radius of ξ. Suppose every pair of vertices in X has at most q common neighbors. Assume $k \leq n/4$. Then $q + \xi < 7k/8$.*

This will be proved in Section 5.1.

Theorems 2 and 4 will immediately follow from bounds we establish on the order of automorphisms (Prop. 13 and Theorem 20, respectively). Specifically, we prove that the order of any automorphism of a non-trivial, non-graphic s. r. graph is at most n^8 (Theorem 20). We also indicate that in fact a stronger, $n^{1+o(1)}$ bound holds (Theorem 21).

2. MOTIVATION: THE GRAPH ISOMORPHISM PROBLEM

2.1 Complexity status

Graph Isomorphism (GI) continues to be one of the intriguing problems of usettled complexity status. It is unlikely to be NP-complete; an early indication of this was that for GI, existence and counting are polynomial-time equivalent [3, 49]. More compelling evidence was provided by the early theory of interactive proofs which demonstrated that if GI is NP-complete then the polynomial-time hierarchy collapses to $\Sigma_2^P = \Pi_2^P = \mathrm{AM}$ [33] (based on [7, 21, 34]). (For a self-contained proof, see [16].)

On the other hand, while GI $\in$ NP $\cap$ coAM, the GI problem is not known to belong to coNP. On the algorithmic front, the best complexity bound is $\exp(\widetilde{O}(\sqrt{n}))$ [14, 63, 12] which has not been improved in three decades.

2.2 Automorphism group vs. isomorphism testing

Algorithms for testing isomorphism of a class of objects are intimately related to the order and structure of the automorphism groups of those objects. There are examples in the history of the two subjects when structural information on the automorphism groups was the basis of the design of efficient isomorphism tests; and conversely, methods developed to test isomorphism of such structures had implications on the structure of the automorphism groups. Yet in other cases the two subjects evolved separately, pursued by separate communities with different context and terminology, yet with virtually identical underlying methods.

In an 1869 paper [41], Jordan counted the automorphisms of trees. His method easily yields a description of the structure of the automorphism groups of trees in terms of iterated direct products and wreath products of symmetric groups, and just as easily yields a canonical form (and therefore isomorphism test) of trees in linear time. Independent work in the early 1970s on the isomorphism problem for planar graphs [39, 40] by Hopcroft and Tarjan, and on the description of the structure of the automorphism groups of planar graphs [2] by this author is based on the same structural principles (canonical reduction to bi-connected and tri-connected components and the structure of three-connected planar graphs).

In 1938, Roberto Frucht [31] discovered that every finite group is isomorphic to the automorphism group of a finite graph. First he showed this to be the case for colored directed graphs, namely, the Cayley diagram of the group, and then applied gadgets to encode color and orientation by undirected, uncolored graphs. Decades later, Frucht's gadgets were reinvented in the context of the reduction of the isomorphism problem of directed (colored) graphs to undirected graphs [50].

Frucht's theme was further developed by the Prague category theory school in the 1960s and early 70s. In particular, Hedrlín and Pultr [35] showed in 1966 that every category of finite structures is "fully embeddable" in the category of finite graphs. (For a beautiful exposition, see [36].) A "full embedding" is a functor F that maps the set of $X \to Y$ morphisms bijectively *onto* the set of $F(X) \to F(Y)$ morphisms. In particular, F preserves the automorphism groups and the endomorphism monoids of objects, and $X \cong Y$ if and only if $F(X) \cong F(Y)$. The Hedrlín–Pultr construction is explicit and polynomial-time, thus an immediate (weak) corollary to their work is that the isomorphism problem for explicit structures reduces in polynomial time to the isomorphims problem for graphs. A decade later Miller [50] rediscovered this result and brought it to the attention of the theory community (STOC 1977).

In a 1963 paper, Erdős and Rényi [30] proved that almost all finite graphs have trivial automorphism group. An algorithmic version of this statement is that the naive vertex refinement method completely splits almost all graphs in linear time [11, 13].

The first result on testing isomorphism of strongly regular graphs [4] (1980) established the algorithmic time bound $\exp(\widetilde{O}(n^{1/2}))$; as a corollary, the same value is an upper bound on the number of automorphisms of non-trivial s. r. graphs. Generalizing the method of this proof, this author proved the same bounds for primitive coherent configurations [6] (certain highly regular colorings of the edges of the directed complete graph, cf. section 8), giving, as a corollary, a nearly tight upper bound on the orders of primitive but not doubly transitive groups, solving a then 150-year-old problem on permutation groups.

Motivated partly by a question of Peter Cameron on counting finite models, arising from his study of oligomorphic permutation groups (cf. [25]), Pyber and this author gave an $\exp(\widetilde{O}(n^{1/2}))$ bound on the number of automorphisms of Steiner 2-designs in a 1994 paper [17]. Independently, in 1996, Spielman [59] used the exact same method to test isomorphism of those structures. Spielman's time bound was reduced to $n^{O(\log n)}$ in 2013 [20, 27], yielding the same bound on the number of automorphisms of Steiner 2-designs.

Spielman's main result in [59] was an $\exp(\widetilde{O}(n^{1/3}))$ algorithm to test isomorphism of s. r. graphs; his proof also established this quantity as an upper bound on the number of automorphisms of non-trivial and non-graphic s. r. graphs. Both meanings of this bound (algorithmic and algebraic) were recently improved to $\exp(\widetilde{O}(n^{9/37}))$ by Chen, Sun, and Teng [27] (cf. [9]).

Godsil studied the automorphism groups of graphs with bounded eigenvalue multiplicity [32]; a closely related underlying structure was exploited in [10] to decide isomorphism of such graphs in polynomial time.

The advent of the group theory method (1979-80) brought about much closer ties between GI and automorphism group structure; we next review this connection.

2.3 The group theory method

The group theory method, first introduced into GI in [5] and developed into a profound theory by Luks [46] has been the most successful tool in GI, especially in combination with combinatorial individualization/refinement techniques (see Appendix, Sec. C for an explanation). This combination was also first explored in [5], giving a soon obsolete $\exp(\widetilde{O}(\sqrt{n}))$ isomorphism test for graphs of bounded degree, using very elementary group theory only. Luks's methods were first combined with the individualization/refinement heuristic in [14], yielding results that have not been improved upon to this day (e. g., testing isomorphism of block designs in quasipolynomial time assuming bounded-size blocks and bounded number of blocks passing through each pair of points, and testing isomorphism of tournaments in time $n^{\log n+O(1)}$). The combined method was used in [9] to test isomorphism of s. r. graphs of degrees $k \le n^{3/5}$.

For basic concepts on permutation groups needed for the rest of the discussion in this section, especially the notion of *primitive permutation groups*, see the Appendix (Sec. A). These concepts are only needed to motivate the results, not for the actual technical development.

Luks's method processes an intransitive permutation group orbit-by-orbit, and a transitive but imprimitive permutation group by the blocks of an invariant equivalence relation. We run out of such natural divide-and-conquer options when a primitive group is encountered; nothing much better than complete enumeration of G has been used in this case.

The efficiency of Luks's divide-and-conquer thus critically depends on bounds on the orders of primitive permutation groups the algorithm may encounter; these are typically permutation groups involved in the automorphism group of some subobject of the object in question.

Bounds on the order of a primitive permutation group in turn depend on the *thickness* of the group; by a result by Cameron, Pálfy, and this author [8] and its refinements ([56, 43, 44, 48], cf. [45, Sec. 3] for a survey) we have

THEOREM 6. *If G is a primitive permutation group of degree n and thickness t then $|G| = n^{O(t)}$.*

(This result heavily depends on the classification of finite simple groups [29]. We note that while the initial motivation for [8] came from the GI problem, this result found applications in group theory, including profinite groups (a class of infinite compact groups) [22].)

For example, it is easy to see that the automorphism group of a connected graph of degree $\le k$ with an individualized edge (an edge with a unique color) has thickness $\le k-1$; Luks's algorithm can then be analysed via Theorem 6 to imply that isomorphism of graphs of degree $\le k$ can be tested in time $n^{O(k)}$.

Our main result, Theorem 2, provides a polylogarithmic bound on the thickness of $\mathrm{Aut}(X)$ for all interesting strongly regular graphs, thereby raising *the possibility of a quasipolynomially efficient isomorphism test for s. r. graphs* via Luks's methods.

The question addressed by this result has been in plain view for over three decades; it is significant not only to the GI problem but also to the combinatorial study of highly regular objects such as s. r. graphs, and to the theory of primitive permutation groups. The result is surprising both for its strength and for the simplicity of its proof. It was unanticipated; just a few months earlier, an $n^{o(1)}$ bound was still only a vague hope, and the possibility of its failing seemed like a potential major obstacle to the ultimate goal of the BCSTW [9] project, namely, a subexponential isomorphism test for s. r. graphs.

In addition to the algorithmic perspectives this result opens, it also provides the strongest evidence yet against GI-completeness of s. r. graphs (see Theorem 22).

A caveat: this purely mathematical result does not in itself have immediate algorithmic consequences. While it removes a major obstacle to applying Luks's method to s. r. graphs with quasipolynomial efficiency, another major obstacle to applying Luks's method remains: the apparent lack of a recursive structure in s. r. graphs. In addition to a thickness bound on the automorphism groups, the known applications of Luks's method require a *hierarchy of substructures* that satisfy the same constraint on their automorphism groups. (E. g., a connected graph of degree $\le k$ with a uniquely colored edge can be built up layer by layer from graphs with the same defining properties.) S. r. graphs don't have such a hierarchical structure. Our result is more general, however, and applies to all graphs with strong spectral expansion and a relatively small number of common neighbors to every pair of vertices (Theorem 4).

This observation presents the **combinatorial challenge** to find such a hierarchical structure in s. r. graphs (after individualization of a moderate number of vertices), possibly capitalizing on the generality of our result as well as on the simplicity of its proof: the proof should be easy to adapt to a variety of circumstances.

There are encouraging initial results in the direction of building a hierarchy with a thickness bound; the paper [9] (FOCS'13) builds such a hierarchical structure after individualizing $O(\log n)$ vertices, where the automorphism group of every member of the hierarchy has thickness $\le \mu$, the number of common neighbors of a pair of non-adjacent vertices. Using Luks's method via [14] and a result of Miller [52], we then infer that isomorphism of s. r. graphs can be tested in time $n^{O(\mu+\log n)}$. This is one of the key results in [9]. In the cases of interest, we have $\mu \sim k^2/n$ [53, 54, 59], so this gives a strong bound when k is not much larger than its minimum possible value, $\sqrt{n-1}$.

Tournaments illustrate the difficulty of the combinatorial challenge. Their automorphism groups have odd order and therefore have thickness ≤ 2. It follows that the primitive permutation groups involved in them have polynomially bounded order. (This was first proved by Pálfy [55] and Wolf [62]. Pálfy's proof served as a model for [8].) Yet the best known bound on the complexity of testing isomorphism of tournaments is $n^{\log n+O(1)}$ [14] because the natural divide-and-conquer strategy for tournaments leads to a recursion of the form $T(n) = nT(n/2) + n^{O(1)}$, not as strong as would be hoped based on the group theory. Overcoming this combinatorial difficulty is a three-decades-old challenge.

We state a purely mathematical conjecture that could bring us closer to the possibility of a subexponential (or even quasipolynomial) application of Luks's method to s. r. graphs. Following Luks [46], we say that a group G belongs to the class Γ_d if every composition factor of G is a subgroup of the symmetric group S_d.

CONJECTURE 7. *Let X be a non-trivial and non-graphic strongly regular graph with n vertices. Then X has a set S of $O(\log n)$ vertices such that the stabilizer of S in $\mathrm{Aut}(X)$ belongs to the class $\Gamma_{m(n)}$ for some function $m(n) = n^{o(1)}$.*

The conclusion may hold even with a polylogarithmic bound on $m(n)$. If the goal is a subexponential isomorphism test, it may suffice to require that $|S| = n^{o(1)}$.

Most known applications of Luks's method are tied to Γ_d-groups for bounded or slowly growing d, resulting from a hierarchical structure called "color-d-bounded graphs" in [9, Sec. III]. One of the main results of [9] alluded to above establishes a "color-μ-bounded" structure for s. r. graphs after individualizing $O(\log n)$ vertices; this proves the Conjecture with $m(n) = O(\mu + \log n)$. – Tournaments are a notable exception; their automorphism groups do not fit in a Γ_d class with small d. Yet a quasi-polynomial-time isomorphism test for tournaments is based on the solvability of their automorphism groups [14].

2.4 Further motivation

We note that considerable added motivation for our results comes from outside the theory of computing: combinatorics and group theory. The relevant subarea of the former is the the study of the symmetries of highly regular objects; one of the relevant subareas of the latter is the study of primitive permutation groups. We mention a further result of interest to these fields which can be proved by our methods combined with group theory.

THEOREM 8. *Let X be a non-trivial and non-graphic strongly regular graph with n vertices. Assume $\mathrm{Aut}(X)$ is primitive. Then $|\mathrm{Aut}(X)| \le n^{(1+o(1))\log n}$.*

This answers, in a very strong sense, another question the author has considered for three decades, motivated by the seminal paper by Cameron [24].

It would be of great algorithmic interest if in Theorem 8 the assumption of primitivity could be dropped. In fact, motivated by [24] and [6], it has been this author's belief for more than three decades that non-trivial and non-graphic s. r. graphs have very small automorphism groups.

CONJECTURE 9. *Let X be a non-trivial and non-graphic strongly regular graph with n vertices. Then* $\mathrm{Aut}(X)$ *has subexponential order, i. e.,* $|\mathrm{Aut}(X)| < \exp(n^{o(1)})$.

The best result to date in this direction [28] (cf. [9]) is that

$$|\mathrm{Aut}(X)| < \exp(\widetilde{O}(n^{9/37})). \qquad (2)$$

The significance of the conjecture is that it would give purely combinatorial individualization/refinement techniques a chance to achieve a subexponential-time isomorphism test for s. r. graphs; it is no coincidence that the $\exp(\widetilde{O}(n^{9/37}))$ bound was obtained in this context (as were all previous bounds: $\exp(\widetilde{O}(n^{1/2}))$ [4] and $\exp(\widetilde{O}(n^{1/3}))$ [59]). On the other hand, if this conjecture is false, this would virtually rule out that individualization/refinement methods alone could succeed. The difficulties encountered in trying to reduce the $\exp(\widetilde{O}(n^{9/37}))$ bound may suggest that perhaps the conjecture is in fact false.

I note that a similar feeling of possible futility may arise from the considerable difficulties we had to overcome just to reduce Spielman's $\exp(\widetilde{O}(n^{1/3}))$ bound to $\exp(\widetilde{O}(n^{1/5}))$. The good news is that Theorem 2 removes the possibility of a similar obstacle to the group theory approach.

3. TWO LEMMAS

We shall need a variant of the "Expander Mixing Lemma" of Alon and Chung [1] which we state here.

LEMMA 10 (EXPANDER MIXING LEMMA). *Let $X = (V, E)$ be a regular graph of degree k with zero-weight spectral radius ξ. Let $d(S)$ denote the average degree of the subgraph induced by $S \subseteq V$. Then*

$$|d(S) - (|S|/n)k| \leq \xi. \qquad (3)$$

For the reader's convenience, we include the very short proof of this lemma in the Appendix, Sec. E.

The following lemma by Ákos Seress and the author is one of our main tools.

LEMMA 11 ([18]). *Let σ be a permutation of n elements. Assume σ has order n^α for some $\alpha > 0$. Then some non-identity power of σ has at least $(1 - 1/\alpha)n$ fixed points.*

The original statement of this lemma included an unnecessary condition, so for completeness, we include the short proof of this lemma as well in the Appendix, Sec. D.

This lemma played a key role in the proof that basic questions about permutation groups (membership, order, etc.) are in NC [15]. It was also central to the first non-trivial bound ($\exp(\sqrt{n \ln n}(1 + o(1)))$) on the (worst-case) diameter of the symmetric group [19]. In a recent breakthrough by Helfgott and Seress [37], this bound was reduced to quasi-polynomial, and this lemma was again one of the igredients.

Ákos Seress (1958–2013) was my #1 collaborator, with 15 joint papers over a period of 25 years, several of which I count among the highlights of my career. This collaboration began in summer 1986 at a conference in Szeged, Hungary, where, by a stroke of serendipity, both of us missed the sightseeing boat. This lemma was a fruit of the first hours of our collaboration, conceived at the banks of the river Tisza even before the return of the boat.

4. FIXED-POINTS OF AUTOMORPHISMS

PROPOSITION 12. *Let X be a regular graph of degree k with zero-weight spectral radius of ξ. Suppose every pair of vertices in X has at most q common neighbors. Then every nonidentity automorphism of X has at most $n(q+\xi)/k$ fixed points.*

PROOF. Let σ be a nonidentity automorphism. Let $S = \mathrm{supp}(\sigma) = \{x \in V \mid x^\sigma \neq x\}$ be the support of σ. Let $N(x)$ denote the set of neighbors of x outside S. Then, by the Expander Mixing Lemma (Lemma 10), there exists $x \in S$ such that $|N(x)| \geq (1 - |S|/n)k - \xi$. On the other hand, $N(x) = N(x^\sigma)$, therefore $|N(x)| \leq q$. We infer that $q \geq (1 - |S|/n)k - \xi$, and therefore the number of points fixed by x is $n - |S| \leq n(q+\xi)/k$. □

PROPOSITION 13. *Let X be a regular graph of degree k with zero-weight spectral radius of ξ. Suppose every pair of vertices in X has at most q common neighbors. Assume $q + \xi < k$. Then the order of any automorphism of X is at most $n^{k/(k-q-\xi)}$.*

PROOF. Combine Prop. 12 and the Lemma 11. □

PROOF OF THEOREM 4. Let $z(t)$ denote the largest among the orders of elements of A_t. It is known that $z(t) = \exp(\sqrt{t \ln t}(1 + o(1))$ [42]. In fact all we need is $z(t) \geq \exp(\sqrt{t \ln t}(1 + o(1))$ which easily follows from the Prime Number Theorem, taking the product of cycles of small odd prime lengths.

Suppose A_t is involved in $\mathrm{Aut}(X)$. Then $\mathrm{Aut}(X)$ has an element of order $\geq z(t)$. Therefore

$$n^{k/(k-q-\xi)} \geq z(t). \qquad (4)$$

Let us replace t by the greatest value t' for which inequality (4) holds. Then the statement follows with a $o(1)$ term that goes to zero as $t' \to \infty$. But $n \to \infty$ implies $t' \to \infty$ since $n^{k/(k-q-\xi)} \geq n$. □

5. STRONGLY REGULAR GRAPHS

Throughout this section, X will be a s. r. graph with parameters (n, k, λ, μ).

A *conference graph* is a strongly regular graph with parameters $k = (n-1)/2$, $\mu = (n-1)/4$, $\lambda = \mu - 1$.

5.1 Preparatory inequalities

The following well-known facts easily follow from the definition, cf. [23, Lemma 1.1.1 and Theorem 1.3.1].

PROPOSITION 14. *Let X be a nontrivial s. r. graph.*

(i) $\mu(n - k - 1) = k(k - \lambda - 1)$

(ii) X has three distinct eigenvalues, $k > r > -s$; here $r \geq 1$ and $s \geq 2$.

(iii) The eigenvalues of a conference graph are $r = (-1 + \sqrt{n})/2$ and $-s = (-1 - \sqrt{n})/2$.

(iv) Unless X is a conference graph, all eigenvalues are integers.

(v) $r - s = \lambda - \mu$ and $rs = k - \mu$.

The case $s = 2$ was characterized in the 1980s by Hoffman and Ray-Chaudhuri [38] and Seidel [57]. For a particularly elegant treatment, see [26].

THEOREM 15 (SEIDEL [57], CF. [26, THEOREM 4.13]). *If X is a nontrivial s. r. graph with $n \geq 29$ vertices and least eigenvalue $-s = -2$ then X is graphic (the line graph of K_v or $K_{v,v}$).*

Since the complement of a s. r. graph is s. r., we may assume $k \leq (n-1)/2$.

Notation. $\vartheta_1 = \max\{\lambda, \mu\}$ and $\vartheta_2 = \min\{\lambda, \mu\}$.

The following was proved by the author in a paper that appeared in 1980.

LEMMA 16 ([4]). *Let X be a non-trivial s. r. graph of degree $k \leq (n-1)/2$. Then*

(a) $k - \vartheta_2 \leq 2(k - \vartheta_1)$;

(b) $k^2 > n \cdot \vartheta_2$.

We derive further inequalities from Prop. 14 and Lemma 16.

LEMMA 17. *If X is non-trivial and $k \leq (n-1)/2$ then*

(A) $\vartheta_2 < k/2$ and $\vartheta_1 < 3k/4$.

(B) If in addition $s \geq 3$ and $k \leq n/4$ then $\vartheta_1 + r < 7k/8$.

PROOF. For part (A) we note that it follows from part (b) of Lemma 16 that $\vartheta_2 < k^2/n < k/2$; then from part (a) we infer that $\vartheta_1 < 3k/4$.

For part (B), assume first that $\lambda \geq \mu$. From part (v) of Proposition 14 we see that $rs - r + s = k - \lambda$ and therefore $(s-1)r + \lambda < k$. It follows that $(s-1)(\lambda+r) < (s-2)\lambda + k < (3(s-2)/4+1)k = (3s-2)k/4 < 7(s-1)k/8$, so $\lambda + r < 7k/8$.

Assume now that $\lambda < \mu$. From part (i) of Prop. 14 we see that $3\mu n/4 \leq \mu(n-k) \leq k^2$ and therefore $\mu \leq 4k^2/(3n) < k/3$. Moreover, by Part (v) of Prop. 14, we have $r < k/s \leq k/3$. Therefore $\mu + r < 2k/3$. ☐

We are essentially done proving one of our main auxiliary results, Theorem 5.

PROOF OF THEOREM 5. Modulo the change of notation ($q = \vartheta_1$ and $\xi = r$), the conclusion of Theorem 5 is the same as the conclusion of part (B) of Lemma 17. We only need to justify the assumption $s \geq 3$ made in Lemma 17, part (B). We have $s \geq 2$ by item (ii) of Prop. 14 since X is nontrivial. If X is a conference graph then $s \geq (1 + \sqrt{29})/2 > 3$ by item (iii) of Prop. 14 since $n \geq 29$. If X is not a conference graph then s is an integer by item (iv) of Prop. 14. So we only need to rule out the case $s = 2$; this is done by Seidel's theorem (Theorem 15). ☐

These preparations will suffice for the proof of our main result in the case $k < n/4$. For the cases when k is large, we use a different tool.

LEMMA 18. *Let X be a nontrivial s. r. graph of degree $k \leq (n-1)/2$. Then any nontrivial automorphism of X fixes fewer than $n - k/2$ vertices.*

For the proof of this lemma, we shall use the following result. Following [4], we say that vertex x *distinguishes* vertices y and z if x is adjacent to exactly one of y and z.

LEMMA 19 ([4]). *Let X be a nontrivial s. r. graph of degree $k \leq (n-1)/2$. Then every pair of distinct vertices is distinguished by at least $k - \vartheta_2$ vertices.*

PROOF OF LEMMA 18. According to part (A) of Lemma 17, we have $\vartheta_2 < k/2$ and therefore by Lemma 19, every pair of distinct vertices is distinguished by more than $k/2$ vertices.

Let now σ be a nontrivial automorphism that fixes the set F. Let $x \in V \setminus F$, so $x^\sigma \neq x$. Let D denote the set of vertices that distinguish x and x^σ. Clearly, $D \cap F = \emptyset$. Since $|D| > k/2$, it follows that $|F| < n - k/2$. ☐

5.2 Fixed points of automorphisms

Our main result will follow from the following inequalities.

THEOREM 20. *Let X be a non-trivial and non-graphic strongly regular graph with n vertices. Let σ be a non-identity automorphism of X. Then*

(i) σ has at most $7n/8$ fixed points; and

(ii) σ has order $\leq n^8$.

PROOF. Item (ii) follows from item (i) by Lemma 11. To prove item (i), we consider two cases.

I. If $k < n/4$ then by Theorem 5 we have $q + \xi < 7k/8$ and therefore, by Prop. 12, σ fixes fewer than $7n/8$ points.

II. Let us now assume $n/4 \leq k \leq (n-1)/2$. Then, by Lemma 18, σ fixes fewer than $n - k/2 \leq 7n/8$ points. ☐

Our main result, Theorem 2, follows from Theorem 20 by the same argument as the proof of Theorem 4 at the end of Section 4.

6. IMPROVED BOUNDS VIA NEUMAIER'S CLASSIFICATION OF S. R. GRAPHS

In this section we state a stronger version of Theorem 20.

THEOREM 21. *Let X be a non-trivial, non-graphic strongly regular graph with n vertices. Let σ be a non-identity automorphism of X. Then σ has order $\leq n^{1+o(1)}$.*

Moreover, either $|\operatorname{Aut}(X)| = n^{O(\log n)}$, or σ has $o(n)$ fixed points.

The proof of this result is based on a more substantial body of work. Neumaier [53, 54] classified s. r. graphs into several classes, one of which, following [9], we call *geometric.* These are the line graphs of certain "linear spaces" (transversal designs and Steiner 2-designs with lines of length at least 3 and at most $\approx v^{1/3}$ where v is the number of points in the geometry). These have been shown in [51, 20, 27] to satisfy the bound $|\operatorname{Aut}(X)| = n^{O(\log n)}$. Moreover, in these cases one can show that the order of σ is $O(n)$. Spielman [59] observed that in the remaining cases one can infer from Neumaier's results that both ξ and q are $o(k)$ and therefore Proposition 13 gives the bounds stated.

The details will be given elsewhere; [9] provides a good overview of the facts cited.

7. GI-COMPLETENESS

All known reductions between the isomorphism problems for various classes of structures are *functorial* in the following sense. Let $\mathrm{Iso}(X_1, X_2)$ denote the set of isomorphisms from object X_1 to object X_2.

Let $\mathcal{X}$ and $\mathcal{Y}$ be two classes of objects. A *functorial reduction* of the isomorphism problem for class $\mathcal{X}$ to the isomorphism problem of $\mathcal{Y}$ is a pair of maps (f, F) such that $f : \mathcal{X} \to \mathcal{Y}$, and F is a functor from the category of isomorphisms in $f(\mathcal{X})$ to the category of isomorphisms in $\mathcal{X}$ such that $F(\mathrm{Iso}(f(X_1), f(X_2)) = \mathrm{Iso}(X_1, X_2)$ (F is surjective).

We say that this reduction is *polynomial time* if f is computable in polynomial time.

This concept was introduced by the author in [3]. The main result of that paper regarding this concept was that there is no polynomial-time functorial reduction from degree-$(k+1)$ graphs to degree-k graphs when k is a prime number. This was motivated by Miller's result that for $k \neq 4$ no degree-$(k+1)$ to degree-k reduction can be constructed via a certain type of gadgets [50].

Our main result has the following consequence.

THEOREM 22. *There is no polynomial-time functorial reduction from GI to the isomorphism problem for s. r. graphs.*

For the proof, we need the following observation [3]. Let $\mathrm{maxord}(G)$ denote the maximum order of elements in the group G.

LEMMA 23. *Let (f, F) be a functorial reduction as above. Then for any object $X \in \mathcal{X}$, the group $\mathrm{Aut}(X)$ is a quotient of the group $\mathrm{Aut}(f(X))$. In particular, $\theta(\mathrm{Aut}(X)) \leq \theta(\mathrm{Aut}(f(X)))$ and $\mathrm{maxord}(\mathrm{Aut}(X)) \leq \mathrm{maxord}(\mathrm{Aut}(f(X)))$.*

PROOF. Indeed, $\mathrm{Aut}(X) = \mathrm{Iso}(X, X)$, so F gives a map from $\mathrm{Aut}(f(X))$ onto $\mathrm{Aut}(X)$. This map is a homomorphism, given that F is a functor. ☐

PROOF OF THEOREM 22. Suppose (f, F) is a functorial reduction from GI to the isomorphism problem for s. r. graphs. Let us consider 5 copies of the graph $K_{1,k}$ ($k+1$ vertices with one vertex of degree k (the "root") and k vertices of degree 1); and let us join the five roots in a 5-cycle to obtain the graph X. So X has $n = 5(k+1)$ vertices. Assume $k \geq 5$. Now $\mathrm{Aut}(X) = S_k \wr D_5$ (the wreath product of S_k by the dihedral group D_5). It is easy to see that the automorphism groups of the trivial and the graphic s. r. graphs do not map onto this group because they do not map onto D_5. Let now $f(X) = Y$; so Y is non-trivial and non-graphic. Let m be the number of vertices of Y. We claim that m is large. We could argue from Theorem 2, using the fact that $k = \theta(\mathrm{Aut}(X)) \leq \theta(\mathrm{Aut}(Y))$. Let us use Theorem 20 (ii) directly instead, using the inequality $\mathrm{maxord}(\mathrm{Aut}(X)) \leq \mathrm{maxord}(\mathrm{Aut}(f(X)))$. Now X has an automorphism of order $\exp(\sqrt{k \ln k}(1 + o(1)) = \exp(\sqrt{n \ln n}(1/\sqrt{5} + o(1))$, so $\mathrm{Aut}(f(X))$ must have an element of this order; so by item (ii) in Theorem 20 we have $\exp(\sqrt{n \ln n}(1/\sqrt{5} + o(1)) \leq m^8$ and therefore $m \geq \exp(\sqrt{n \ln n}(1/(8\sqrt{5} + o(1)))$, growing exponentially. ☐

8. OUTLOOK

We outline the broader context of this work. Consider the colored directed complete graph $\mathcal{X} = (V, c)$ where V is the set of vertices and the coloring $c : V \times V \to \{0, \ldots, r-1\}$ of the ordered pairs pairs satisfies the following conditions: (i) if $c(x,x) = c(y,z)$ then $y = z$; and (ii) $c(x,y)$ determines $c(y,x)$. We call $\mathcal{X}$ a "configuration." If c is onto, we say that $\mathrm{rank}(\mathcal{X}) = r$.

For $i, j < r$ and $x, y \in V$ let $p(x, y; i, j)$ denote the number of those $z \in V$ satisfying $c(x,z) = i$ and $c(z,y) = j$. The *Weisfeiler-Leman refinement* [61, 60] defines a refined coloring c' by making $c'(x,y) = c'(u,v)$ if and only if $c(x,y) = c(u,v)$ and for all $j, k < r$ we have $p(x, y; i, j) = p(u, v; i, j)$. The stable colorings (that do not get further refined) are called *coherent configurations*; these are characterized by the property that $p(x, y; i, j)$ is determined by i, j, and $c(x,y)$. (See [6] for more background on coherent configurations.)

It is clear that isomorphism of coherent configurations is GI-complete: given a graph $G = (V, E)$, view it as a rank-3 configuration by setting $c(x,y) = 0$ if $x = y$, $c(x,y) = 1$ if $\{x,y\} \in E$, and $c(x,y) = 2$ if $x \neq y$ and $\{x,y\} \notin E$; then refine this to stable coloring.

We say that the coherent configuration $\mathcal{X}$ is *homogeneous* if all diagonal pairs (x,x) have the same color; call this color 0. We say that the coherent configuration $\mathcal{X}$ is *primitive* if $\mathcal{X}$ is homogeneous and $(\forall i \geq 1)$ the digraph (V, R_i) is connected, where $R_i = \{(x,y) \mid c(x,y) = i\}$. We note that the rank-3 primitive coherent configurations are the s. r. graphs and the analogously defined s. r. tournaments.

The results of this paper represent progress in the context of the following problem, motivated by [24] and [6] and considered by the author for over three decades.

CONJECTURE 24. *Let $\mathcal{X}$ be a primitive coherent configuration with n vertices. For all $\epsilon > 0$ there exists $n_0(\epsilon)$ such that if $n \geq n_0(\epsilon)$ and $|\mathrm{Aut}(\mathcal{X})| \geq \exp(n^\epsilon)$ then $\mathrm{Aut}(\mathcal{X})$ is a primitive permutation group.*

This would be significant because of the detailed description of large primitive permutation groups by Cameron [24]. Since primitive coherent configurations are in a way the combinatorial building blocks of all coherent configurations, this problem would amplify the potential of combinatorial individualization/refinement methods to contribute to progress on the GI problem. We note that [6] confirms this conjecture for $\epsilon = 1/2 + o(1)$. In the rank-3 case, [27] (cf. [9]), combined with [6], confirms the conjecture for $\epsilon = 9/37 + o(1)$.

A weaker version of this conjecture in terms of the thickness of $\mathrm{Aut}(\mathcal{X})$, made plausible by the results of this paper, is the following.

CONJECTURE 25. *Let $\mathcal{X}$ be a primitive coherent configuration with n vertices. For all $\epsilon > 0$ there exists $n_0(\epsilon)$ such that if $n \geq n_0(\epsilon)$ and $\theta(\mathrm{Aut}(\mathcal{X})) \geq n^\epsilon$ then $\mathrm{Aut}(\mathcal{X})$ is a primitive permutation group.*

This version would amplify the potential of Luks's group theoretic divide-and-conquer methods, in conjunction with individualization/refinement, to achieve a subexponential upper bound on the complexity of the GI problem. Again, [6] confirms this conjecture for $\epsilon = 1/2 + o(1)$. In the rank-3 case, [9] confirms the conjecture for $\epsilon = 1/5 + o(1)$.

9. ACKNOWLEDGMENTS

I gratefully acknowledge the inspiration gained from two sources: the collaboration with my student John Wilmes and with Xi Chen, Xiaorui Sun, and Shang-Hua Teng on the isomorphism problem for strongly regular graphs [20,

27, 9]; and a conversation with Ian Wanless about the order of automorphisms of quasigroups, the subject of a paper by McKay, Wanless, and Zhang [47]. The latter discussion took place at the conference "Combinatorics, Algebra and More," celebrating Peter Cameron's 65th birthday at Queen Mary, University of London in July 2013. I thank the organizers, David Ellis and Leonard Soicher, for the opportunity to attend the meeting.

This research was supported in part by NSF Grant CCF-1017781.

10. REFERENCES

[1] Noga Alon, Fan R. K. Chung: Explicit construction of linear sized tolerant networks. *Discrete Math.* **72** (1988) 15–19

[2] László Babai: Automorphism groups of planar graphs II. In: *Infinite and Finite Sets* (Proc. Conf. Keszthely, Hungary, 1973, A. Hajnal et al eds.) Bolyai Society – North-Holland, 1975, pp. 29–84

[3] László Babai: On the isomorphism problem. Preprint, 1977 (10pp.) (cited in [49])

[4] László Babai: On the complexity of canonical labeling of strongly regular graphs. *SIAM J. Comput.* **9(1)** (1980), 212–216

[5] László Babai: Monte Carlo algorithms in graph isomorphism testing. Tech. Rep. 79–10, Dép. Math. et Stat., Univ. de Montréal, 1979.

[6] László Babai: On the order of uniprimitive permutation groups. *Annals of Math.* **113(3)** (1981) 553–568.

[7] László Babai: Trading group theory for randomness. *In: 17th STOC*, pp. 421–429, 1985.

[8] László Babai, Peter J. Cameron, Péter Pál Pálfy: On the orders of primitive groups with restricted nonabelian composition factors. *J. Algebra* **79** (1982), 161–168.

[9] László Babai, Xi Chen, Xiaorui Sun, Shang-Hua Teng, John Wilmes: Faster Canonical Forms For Strongly Regular Graphs. *In: 54th IEEE FOCS*, pp. 157–166, 2013.

[10] László Babai, Dmitry Yu. Grigor'ev, David M. Mount: Isomorphism of graphs with bounded eigenvalue multiplicity. In: *Proc. 14th ACM STOC*, 1982, pp. 310–324.

[11] László Babai, Paul Erdős, Stanley M. Selkow: Random graphs isomorphism, *SIAM J. on Computing* **9** (1980), 628-635.

[12] László Babai, William M. Kantor, Eugene M. Luks: Computational complexity and the classification of finite simple groups. *In: 24th IEEE FOCS*, pp. 162–171, 1983.

[13] László Babai, Luděk Kučera: Canonical labeling of graphs in linear average time. *In Proc. 20th FOCS.*, pp. 39–46, 1979.

[14] László Babai, Eugene M. Luks: Canonical labeling of graphs. *In: 15th ACM STOC*, pp. 171–183, 1983.

[15] László Babai, Eugene M. Luks, Ákos Seress: Permutation groups in NC. *In: Proc. 19th ACM STOC*, 1987, pp. 409–420

[16] László Babai, Shlomo Moran: Arthur-Merlin games: a randomized proof system, and a hierarchy of complexity classes. *J. Comput. Systems Science* **36** (1988), 254–276

[17] László Babai, László Pyber: Permutation groups without exponentially many orbits on the power set. *J. Combinat. Theory, Ser. A*, **66** (1994), 160–168.

[18] László Babai, Ákos Seress: On the degree of transitivity of permutation groups: a short proof. *J. Combinatorial Theory-A* **45** (1987), 310–315

[19] László Babai, Ákos Seress: On the diameter of Cayley graphs of the symmetric group. *J. Combinatorial Theory-A* **49** (1988), 175–179

[20] László Babai, John Wilmes: Quasipolynomial-time canonical form for Steiner designs. *In: 45th ACM STOC*, pp. 261-270, 2013.

[21] Ravi B. Boppana, Johan Håstad, Stathis Zachos: Does co-NP have short interactive proofs? *Information Processing Letters*, **25(2)** (1987), 127–132

[22] Alexandre V. Borovik, László Pyber, Aner Shalev: Maximal subgroups in finite and profinite groups. Trans. Amer. Math. Soc. **348(9)** (1996), 3745–3761.

[23] Andries E. Brouwer, Arjeh M. Cohen, Arnold Neumaier: *Distance-Regular Graphs.* Springer 1989.

[24] Peter J. Cameron: Finite permutation groups and finite simple groups. *Bull. London Math Soc.* **13** (1981) 1–22.

[25] Peter J. Cameron: *Oligomorphic Permutation Groups.* London Math. Soc. Lecture Notes 152. Cambridge Univ. Press, 1990.

[26] Peter J. Cameron, Jean-Marie Goethals, Johan Jacob Seidel, Ernest E. Shult: Line Graphs, Root Systems, and Elliptic Geometry. *J. Algebra* **43** (1976) 305-327

[27] Xi Chen, Xiaorui Sun, Shang-Hua Teng: Multi-stage design for quasipolynomial-time isomorphism testing of Steiner 2-systems. *In: 45th STOC*, pp. 271–280, 2013

[28] Xi Chen, Xiaorui Sun, Shang-Hua Teng: On the order of the automorphism groups of strongly regular graphs. In preparation.

[29] John H. Conway, Robert T. Curtis, Simon P. Norton, Richard A. Parker, Robert A. Wilson: *ATLAS of finite groups.* Oxford Univ. Press 1985, 2003.

[30] Paul Erdős, Alfréd Rényi: Asymmetric graphs. *Acta Math. Acad. Sci. Hung.* **14** (1963) 295–315

[31] Roberto Frucht: Herstellung von Graphen mit vorgegebener abstrakter Gruppe. *Composition Math.* **6** (1938) 239–250

[32] Chris D. Godsil: Graphs, groups, and polytopes. In: *Combinatorial Mathematics*, Springer LNM Vol. 686, 1978, pp. 157–164

[33] Oded Goldreich, Silvio Micali, Avi Wigderson: Proofs that yield nothing but their validity or all languages in NP have zero-knowledge proof system. *J. ACM*, **38(1)** (1991), 691–729

[34] Shafi Goldwasser, Michael Sipser: Private coins versus public coins in interactive proof systems. *In: 18th STOC*, pp. 59–68, 1986.

[35] Zdeněk Hedrlín, Aleš Pultr: On full embeddings of categories of algebras. *Ill. J. Math.* **10** (1966) 392–406

[36] Zdeněk Hedrlín, Joachim Lambek: How comprehensive is the category of semigroups? *J. Algebra* **11** (1969) 195–212

[37] Harald Helfgott, Ákos Seress: On the diameter of permutation groups. *Annals of Mathematics.* To appear

[38] Alan J. Hoffman, Dijen K. Ray-Chaudhury: On a spectral characterization of regular line graphs. Unpublished mansucript, cited by [26]

[39] John Hopcroft, Robert Endre Tarjan: Isomorphism of planar graphs. In: *Complexity of Computer Computations* R. M. Miller, J. W. Thatcher, eds., Plenum Press 1972, pp. 131–152.

[40] John Hopcroft, Robert Endre Tarjan: Dividing a graph into triconnected components. *SIAM J. Computing* **2** (1973) 135–158

[41] Camille Jordan: Sur les assemblages de lignes. *J. Reine Angew. Math.* **70** (1869), 185–190

[42] Edmund Landau: *Handbuch der Lehre von der Verteilung von Primzahlen., Bd I.* Teubner, Leipzig, 1909.

[43] Martin W. Liebeck: On minimal degrees and base sizes of primitive permutation groups. *Arch. Math.* **43** (1984) 11–15.

[44] Martin W. Liebeck, Aner Shalev: Simple groups, permutation groups, and probability. *J. AMS* **12** (1999) 497-520.

[45] Martin W. Liebeck, Aner Shalev: Bases of primitive permutation groups. *In: Groups, Combinatorics, and Geometry (Durham 2001)*, pp. 147–154. World Scientific 2003.

[46] Eugene M. Luks: Isomorphism of graphs of bounded valence can be tested in polynomial time. *J. Comput. Syst. Sci.* **25(1)** (1982) 42–65.

[47] Brendan D. McKay, Ian M. Wanless, Xiande Zhang: The order of automorphisms of quasigroups. Manuscript, submitted for publication. 2013.

[48] Attila Maróti: On the orders of primitive groups. *J. Algebra* **258(2)** (2002) 631–640.

[49] Rudi Mathon: A note on the graph isomorphism counting problem. *Inf. Proc. Letters* **8** (1979) 131–132.

[50] Gary L. Miller: Graph isomorphism, general remarks. *In: Proc. 9th STOC*, pp. 143-150, 1977

[51] Gary L. Miller: On the $n^{\log n}$ isomorphism technique: A preliminary report. *In: 10th ACM STOC*, pp. 51–58, 1978.

[52] Gary L. Miller: Isomorphism of graphs which are pairwise k-separable. *Information and Control* **56(1-2)** (1983) 21–33.

[53] Arnold Neumaier: Strongly regular graphs with smallest eigenvalue $-m$. *Arch. Math.* **33(4)** (1979) 392–400.

[54] Arnold Neumaier: Quasiresidual 2-designs, $1\frac{1}{2}$-designs, and strongly regular multigraphs. *Geom. Dedicata* **12(4)** (1982) 351–366.

[55] Péter P. Pálfy: A polynomial bound on the orders of primitive solvable groups. *J. Algebra* **77** (1982) 127–137

[56] László Pyber. Unpublished, cited by [45]

[57] Johan Jacob Seidel: Strongly regular graphs with $(-1, 1, 0)$-adjacency matrix having eigenvalue 3. *Linear Algebra Appl.* **1** (1968) 281-298

[58] Ákos Seress: *Permutation Group Algorithms.* Cambridge Univ. Press, 2003

[59] Daniel A. Spielman: Faster isomorphism testing of strongly regular graphs. *In: 28th STOC*, pages 576–584, 1996.

[60] Boris Weisfeiler (ed): *On Construction and Identification of Graphs.* Springer Lect. Notes in Math. Vol 558, 1976.

[61] Boris Weisfeiler, Andrei A. Leman: A reduction of a graph to a canonical form and an algebra arising during this reduction. *Nauchno-Technicheskaya Informatsiya* **9** (1968) 12–16.

[62] Thomas R. Wolf: Solvable and nilpotent subgroups of $GL(n, q^m)$. *Canad. J. Math.* **34** (1982) 1097–1111

[63] Viktor N. Zemlyachenko, N. M. Korneenko, Regina I. Tyshkevich: Graph isomorphism problem. *Zapiski Nauchnykh Seminarov LOMI* **118** (1982), 83–158, 215.

APPENDIX

A. PERMUTATION GROUP CONCEPTS

If G, H are groups, the notation $H \le G$ means H is a sugroup of G.

S_n denotes the symmetric group of degree n, i. e., the group of all permutations of a set Ω of n elements; Ω is the *permutation domain.*

G is a *permutation group of degree n* if $G \le S_n$.

The *order* of a group G is $|G|$, the number of elements of G. The order of an element $g \in G$ is the order of the subgroup generated by g. For $x \in \Omega$ and $g \in G$ we write x^g to denote the image of x under G. The *orbit* of x is the set $x^G = \{x^g \mid g \in G\}$. The orbits partition the permutation domain. G is *transitive* if $x^G = \Omega$ for some (and therefore, for any) $x \in \Omega$.

Definition 26. A transitive permutation group G is *primitive* if there is no nontrivial G-invariant equivalence relation on the permutation domain. Otherwise G is *imprimitive.*

The blocks of a G-invariant partition are called *blocks of imprimitivity.* Orbits and non-trivial blocks provide a natural setting for divide-and-conquer algorithms for permutation groups [46].

B. COMPARISON WITH PRIOR THICKNESS BOUNDS

In this section we explain the comment made immediately after Theorem 2 abut thickness bounds *inferable* from prior work.

Most prior results from which thickness bounds for $\mathrm{Aut}(X)$ are inferable were of the following form: "the pointwise stabilizer of ℓ points in $\mathrm{Aut}(X)$ is the identity." This was proved for all non-trivial s. r. graphs with $\ell = \widetilde{O}(n^{1/2})$ in [4]; for all non-trivial and non-graphic s. r. graphs with $\ell = \widetilde{O}(n^{1/3})$ in [59]; and with $\ell = \widetilde{O}(n^{1/5})$ for degree $k \gtrsim n^{3/5}$ in [9]. Now such a bound implies that $|\mathrm{Aut}(X)| \le n^{\ell}$ and therefore, if $\theta(\mathrm{Aut}(X)) = t$ then $t!/2 \le n^{\ell}$ which implies $t \lesssim \ell \ln n$, from which the bounds $\theta(\mathrm{Aut}(X)) = \widetilde{O}(n^s)$ follow with $s = 1/2, 1/3$, and $1/5$, respectively.

For $k \lesssim n^{3/5}$, [9] combined with [20] and [27] proved that by fixing $\ell = O(\log n)$ points, we obtain a group with thickness $\le \mu$ where $\mu \sim k^2/n$, so if $k \lesssim n^{3/5}$ then $\mu \lesssim n^{1/5}$. To understand the implication of this on the thickness of $\mathrm{Aut}(X)$, we need the following lemma.

LEMMA 27. *Let $G \le S_n$ be a permutation group. Suppose there is a subset Δ of the permutation domain such that $\theta(G_\Delta) = \tau$, where G_Δ denotes the pointwise stabilizer of Δ. Let $|\Delta| = \ell$ and $\theta(G) = t$. Then $t = O(\ell \log n + \tau)$, and if $\tau = n^{\Omega(1)}$ then $t = O(\ell + \tau)$.*

PROOF. Observe that $t!/\tau! \le n^\ell$. □

Taking $G = \mathrm{Aut}(X)$ and $\tau = \widetilde{O}(n^{1/5})$ we infer that $\theta(\mathrm{Aut}(X)) = \widetilde{O}(n^{1/5})$.

C. THE INDIVIDUALIZATION/REFINEMENT HEURISTIC

The most natural heuristic for isomorphism rejection colors the vertices in a canonical way (e. g., the color could indicate the degree of a vertex or the number of triangles containing the vertex) and then applies a canonical refinement procedure to the coloring (e. g., the new color of vertex v would encode the old color of v as well as the number of neighbors of v of any given old color). Iteration of the procedure leads to a stable coloring. In the case described, each color class of the stable refinement induces a regular graph and each pair of color-classes induces a biregular bipartite graph between the two color classes. Applying such a procedure simultaneously to two graphs leads to isomorphism rejection if in one of the graphs a color appears that does not exist in the other. (In connected graphs this automatically means that the sets of colors in the two graphs are disjoint.)

Canonicity of coloring and refinement means all isomorphisms are preserved. If the stable coloring *completely splits the graph*, i. e., it assigns a unique color to each vertex, then only one candidate isomorphism with any other (not rejected) graph remains, so this leads to a rapid isomorphism test. (This works for almost all graphs [11, 13].)

If the process does not lead to a satisfactory refinement (e. g., the process described does not even start if the graph is regular), *individualization* can be applied. This means the assignment of a unique color to each member of a set of say ℓ vertices. For valid isomorphism rejection, this process then needs to be repeated for every ordered ℓ-tuple. If for some ℓ-tuple the coloring leads to a complete split, this gives an isomorphism test (against any other graph) in time $n^{\ell+O(1)}$. This idea is the basis of the complexity bounds on testing isomorphism of s. r. graphs in [4, 59, 20, 27, 28] as well as in [9] for $k \gtrsim n^{2/3}$. For smaller degrees, [9] combines this idea with the group theoretic method.

D. THE B–SERESS LEMMA ON PERMUTATIONS: ORDER VS. FIXED POINTS

In this section we review the proof of Lemma 11. We repeat the statement.

LEMMA 28 ([18]). *Let σ be a permutation of n elements. Assume σ has order n^α for some $\alpha > 0$. Then some non-identity power of σ has at least $(1 - 1/\alpha)n$ fixed points.*

PROOF. Let σ act on the set Ω where $|\Omega| = n$. Let the order of σ be $N = n^\alpha = \prod_{i=1}^r q_i$ where $q_i = p_i^{\beta_i} > 1$ are powers of distinct primes p_i. For each $x \in \Omega$, let us consider the set $P(x)$ of those i for which q_i divides the length of the σ-cycle through x. Clearly, for each $x \in \Omega$,

$$\prod_{i \in P(x)} q_i \le n. \tag{5}$$

Let $n(i)$ denote the number of points $x \in \Omega$ such that $i \in P(x)$. Let us estimate the weighted average W of the $n(i)$ with weights $\log q_i$:

$$W = \frac{\sum n(i) \log q_i}{\sum \log q_i}. \tag{6}$$

Recall that the sum of weights is $\sum \log q_i = \log N = \alpha \log n$, therefore (using Eq. (5))

$$W = \sum_{x \in \Omega} \sum_{i \in P(x)} \frac{\log q_i}{\alpha \log n} \le \frac{n \log n}{\alpha \log n} = \frac{n}{\alpha}. \tag{7}$$

It follows that $n(i) \le n/\alpha$ for some $i \le r$. Let $m = N/p_i$ be the corresponding maximal divisor of N. Clearly σ^m is not the identity and it fixes all but $n(i)$ points. □

The original paper [18] made the unnecessary additional assumption that σ contains cycles of distinct *prime* lengths of which the product is $\ge n^\alpha$. While we drop this assumption here, the above proof is almost verbatim identical with the one in [18].

I ask those who may use the lemma in its present form to co-credit Seress.

E. THE EXPANDER MIXING LEMMA

While the simple proof of this result of Alon and Chung [1] has been reproduced in many places, we reproduce it here for the readers's convenience and because of its central role in our main result.

For a graph $X = (V, E)$ and subsets $S, T \subseteq V$ let $E(S, T)$ denote the set of ordered pairs (s, t) such that $s \in S$, $t \in T$, and s, t are adjacent. (Note that $|E(S, T)|$ doubly counts each edge in $S \cap T$.)

LEMMA 29. *Let $X = (V, E)$ be a k-regular graph with n vertices. Let $S, T \subseteq V$. Then*

$$\left| |E(S,T)| - \frac{|S||T|k}{n} \right| \le \xi \sqrt{|S||T|}. \tag{8}$$

where ξ is the zero-weight spectral radius of X (as defined before Thm. 4).

For completeness, we include the simple proof.

PROOF. Let $\mathbf{1}_W$ denote the incidence vector of the subset $W \subseteq V$ written as a column vector. Note that $||\mathbf{1}_W|| = \sqrt{|W|}$. Let J denote the $n \times n$ all-ones matrix (all entries 1). Then

$$|E(S,T)| = \mathbf{1}_S^* A \mathbf{1}_T \tag{9}$$

and

$$|S||T| = \mathbf{1}_S^* J \mathbf{1}_T. \tag{10}$$

(The asterisk indicates transpose.) It follows that the left-hand side in equation (8) is equal to

$$|\mathbf{1}_S^*(A - (k/n)J)\mathbf{1}_T| \tag{11}$$

which by Cauchy-Schwarz is not greater than $\sqrt{|S||T|}$ times the spectral norm of $A - (k/n)J$. If the eigenvalues of A are $k = \xi_1 \ge \xi_2 \ge \cdots \ge \xi_n$ then the eigenvalues of $A - (k/n)J$ are $0, \xi_2, \ldots, \xi_n$, so the spectral norm of $A - (k/n)J$ is ξ. □

Lemma 10 now follows, noting that $|E(S,S)| = |S|d(S)$ and applying Lemma 29 with $T = S$.

Limits of Local Algorithms over Sparse Random Graphs

[Extended Abstract] *

David Gamarnik†
MIT
gamarnik@mit.edu

Madhu Sudan
Microsoft Research
madhu@mit.edu

ABSTRACT

Local algorithms on graphs are algorithms that run in parallel on the nodes of a graph to compute some global structural feature of the graph. Such algorithms use only local information available at nodes to determine local aspects of the global structure, while also potentially using some randomness. Research over the years has shown that such algorithms can be surprisingly powerful in terms of computing structures like large independent sets in graphs locally. These algorithms have also been implicitly considered in the work on graph limits, where a conjecture due to Hatami, Lovász and Szegedy [17] implied that local algorithms may be able to compute near-maximum independent sets in (sparse) random d-regular graphs. In this paper we refute this conjecture and show that every independent set produced by local algorithms is smaller that the largest one by a multiplicative factor of at least $1/2 + 1/(2\sqrt{2}) \approx .853$, asymptotically as $d \to \infty$.

Our result is based on an important clustering phenomena predicted first in the literature on spin glasses, and recently proved rigorously for a variety of constraint satisfaction problems on random graphs. Such properties suggest that the geometry of the solution space can be quite intricate. The specific clustering property, that we prove and apply in this paper shows that typically every two large independent sets in a random graph either have a significant intersection, or have a nearly empty intersection. As a result, large independent sets are clustered according to the proximity to each other. While the clustering property was postulated earlier as an obstruction for the success of local algorithms, such as for example, the Belief Propagation algorithm, our result is the first one where the clustering property is used to formally prove limits on local algorithms.

*A full version of this paper is available as *Electronic Colloquium on Computational Complexity, Technical Report TR 13-055, February 20, 2013.*

†Research supported by the NSF grants CMMI-1031332.

ITCS'14, January 12–14, 2014, Princeton, New Jersey, USA.

http://dx.doi.org/10.1145/2554797.2554831.

Categories and Subject Descriptors

F.1.3 [**Complexity Measures and Classes**]: Lower Bounds

General Terms

Theory

Keywords

Local algorithms, lower bounds, random graphs

1. INTRODUCTION

Local algorithms are decentralized algorithms that run in parallel on nodes in a network using only information available from local neighborhoods to compute some global function of data that is spread over the network. Local algorithms have been studied in the past in various communities. They arise as natural solution concepts in parallel and distributed computing (see, e.g., [21, 19]). They also lead to efficient sub-linear algorithms — algorithms that run in time significantly less than the length of the input — and [26, 25, 16, 27] illustrate some of the progress in this direction. Finally local algorithms have also been proposed as natural heuristics for solving hard optimization problems with the popular Belief Propagation algorithm (see for instance [29, 23]) being one such example. In this work we study the performance of a natural class of local algorithms on *random regular graphs* and show limits on the performance of these algorithms.

1.1 Motivation

The motivation for our work comes from the a notion of local algorithms that has appeared in a completely different mathematical context, namely that of the theory of graph limits, developed in several papers, including [8], [7], [20], [6], [5], [12], [17]. In the realms of this theory it was conjectured that every "reasonable" combinatorial optimization problem on *random graphs* can be solved by means of some local algorithms. To the best of our knowledge this conjecture for the first time was formally stated in Hatami, Lovász and Szegedy in [17, Conjecture 7.13], and thus, from now on, we will refer to it as Hatami-Lovász-Szegedy (or HLS) conjecture, though informally it was posed by Szegedy earlier, and was referenced in several papers, including Lyons and Nazarov [22], and Csoka and Lippner [11]. In the concrete context of the problem of finding largest independent sets in sparse random regular graphs, the conjecture is stated as follows. Let $\mathbb{T}_{d,r}$ be a rooted d-regular tree with depth r.

Namely, every node including the root, has degree r, except for the leaves, and the distance from the root to every leaf is r. Consider a function $f_r : [0,1]^{\mathbb{T}_{d,r}} \to \{0,1\}$ which maps every such tree whose nodes are associated with real values from $[0,1]$ to a "decision" encoded by 0 and 1, where the decision is a function of the values associated with the nodes of the tree. In light of the fact that in a random d-regular graph $\mathbb{G}_d(r)$ the typical node has depth-r neighborhood isomorphic to $\mathbb{T}_{d,r}$, for any constant r, such a function f_r can be used to generate (random) subsets I of $\mathbb{G}_d(r)$ as follows: associate with every node of $\mathbb{G}_d(r)$ a uniform random values from $[0,1]$ (independently for each node) and apply function f_r to each node. The set of nodes for which f_r produces value 1 defines I, and is called "i.i.d. factor". It is clear that f_r essentially describes a local algorithm for producing sets I (sweeping issue of computability of f_r under the rug). The HLS conjecture postulates the existence of a sequence of $f_r, r = 1, 2, \ldots$, such that the set I thus produced is an independent subset of $\mathbb{G}_d(r)$ and asymptotically achieves the largest possible value as $r \to \infty$. Namely, largest independent subsets of random regular graphs are i.i.d. factors. The precise connection between this conjecture and the theory of graph limits is beyond the scope of this paper. Instead we refer the reader to the relevant papers [17],[12][1]. The concept of i.i.d. factors appears also in one of the open problem by David Aldous [2] in the context of coding invariant processes on infinite trees.

It turns out that an analogue for the HLS conjecture is indeed valid for another important combinatorial optimization problem - the matching problem. Lyons and Nazarov [22] established it for the case of bi-partite locally $\mathbb{T}_{d,r}$-tree-like graphs, and Csoka and Lippner established this result for general locally $\mathbb{T}_{d,r}$-tree-like graphs. Further, one can modify the framework of i.i.d. factors by encapsulating non-$\mathbb{T}_{d,r}$ type neighborhoods, for example by making f_r depend not only on the realization of random uniform in $[0,1]$ values, but also on the realization of the graph-theoretic neighborhoods around the nodes. Some probabilistic bound on a degree might be needed to make this definition rigorous (though we will not attempt this formalization in this paper). In this case one can consider, for example, i.i.d. factors when neighborhoods are distributed as r generations of a branching process with Poisson distribution, and then ask which combinatorial optimization problems defined now on sparse Erdös-Rényi graphs $\mathbb{G}(n, d/n)$ can be solved as i.i.d. factors. Here $\mathbb{G}(n, d/n)$ is a random graph on n nodes with each of the $\binom{n}{2}$ edges selected with probability d/n, independently for all edges, and $d > 0$ is a fixed constant. In this case it is possible to show that when $c \le e$, the maximum independent set problem on $\mathbb{G}(n, d/n)$ can be solved nearly optimally by the well known Belief Propagation (BP) algorithm with constantly many rounds. Since the BP is a local algorithm, then the maximum independent set on $\mathbb{G}(n, d/n)$ is an i.i.d. factor, in the extended framework defined above. (We should note that the original proof of Karp and Sipser [18] of the very similar result, relied on a different method.) Thus, the framework of local algorithms viewed as i.i.d. factors is rich enough to solve several interesting combinatorial optimization problems.

[1]We also remark that the language used in [17] is quite different from ours. Other works, e.g., [22] however do use langauge similar to ours in describing this conjecture.

Nevertheless, in this paper we refute the HLS conjecture in the context of maximum independent set problem on random regular graphs $\mathbb{G}_d(n)$. Specifically, we show that for large enough d, with high probability as $n \to \infty$, every independent set producible as an i.i.d. factor is a multiplicative factor $\gamma < 1$ smaller than the largest independent subset of $\mathbb{G}_d(n)$. We establish that γ is asymptotically at most $\frac{1}{2} + \frac{1}{2\sqrt{2}}$ (though we conjecture that the result holds simply for $\gamma = 1/2$, as we discuss in the body of the paper).

1.2 Techniques

Our result is proved in two steps. First we show that large independent sets in random regular graphs are somewhat clustered. Next we show that solutions of natural algorithms are not clustered. We elaborate on the two parts below.

Clustering is a powerful (though fairly simple to establish in our case) phenomenon associated with the solutions of some combinatorial optimization problems on random graphs. Roughly it states that such solutions are clustered in some natural topology associated with the solution space. (We will describe the precise version we care about shortly.) Such phenomena were first conjectured in the theory of spin glasses and later confirmed by rigorous means. Initially, this clustering property was discussed in terms of so-called overlap structure of the solutions of the Sherrington-Kirkpatrick model [28]. Later works highlighted this phenomenon in the context of random K-SAT problem. In particular, in independent works Achlioptas, Coja-Oghlan and Ricci-Tersenghi [1], and Mezard, Mora and Zecchina [24] proved this phenomenon rigorously. We do not define the random K-SAT problem here and instead refer the reader to the aforementioned papers. What these results state is that in certain regimes, the set of satisfying assignments, with high probability, can be clustered into groups such that two solutions within the same cluster agree on a certain minimum number of variables, while two solutions from different clusters have to disagree on a certain minimum number of variables. In particular, one can identify a certain non-empty interval $[z_1, z_2] \subset [0,1]$ such that *no* two solutions of the random K-SAT problem agree on precisely z fraction of variables for all $z \in [z_1, z_2]$. One can further show that the onset of clustering property occurs when the density of clauses to variables becomes at least $2^K/K$, while at the same time the formula remains satisfiable with high probability, when the density is below $2^K \log 2$. Interestingly, the known algorithms for finding solutions of random instances of K-SAT problem also stop working around the $2^K/K$ threshold. It was widely conjectured that the onset of the clustering phase is the main obstruction for finding such algorithms. In fact, Coja Oghlan [9] showed that the BP algorithm, which was earlier conjectured to be a good contender for solving the random instances of K-SAT problems, also fails when the density of clauses to variables is at least $2^K \log K/K$, though Coja-Oghlan's approach does not explicitly rely on the clustering property, and one could argue that the connection between the clustering property and the failure of the BP algorithm is coincidental.

Closer to the topic of this paper, the clustering property was also recently established for independent sets in Erdös-Rényi graphs by Coja-Oghlan and Efthymiou [10]. To describe their result, we first note a well-known fact that the largest independent subset of $\mathbb{G}(n, d/n)$ has size approximately $(2 \log d/d)n$, when d is large (see the next section for precise details). In [10] it is shown that the set of independent sets of size at least approximately $(\log d/d)n$ (namely those within factor $1/2$ of the optimal), are also clustered. Namely, one can split them into groups such that intersection of two independent sets within a group has a large cardinality, while intersection of two independent sets from different groups has a small cardinality. One should note that algorithms for producing large independent subsets of random graphs also stop short factor $1/2$ of the optimal, both in the case of sparse and in the dense random graph cases, as exhibited by the well-known Karp's open problem regarding independent subsets of $\mathbb{G}(n, 1/2)$ [3].

This is almost the result we need for our analysis with two exceptions. First, we need to establish this clustering property for random regular as opposed Erdös-Rényi graphs. Second, and more signficanlty, the result in [10] applies to *typical* independent sets and does not rule out the possibility that there exist two independent sets with some "intermediate" intersection cardinality, though the number of such pairs is insignificant compared to the total number of independent sets. For our result we need to show that, without exception, every pair of "large" independent sets has either large or small intersection. We indeed establish this, but at the cost of losing additional factor $1/(2\sqrt{2})$. In particular, we show (see Theorem 2.6) that for large enough d, with high probability as $n \to \infty$, every two independent subsets of $\mathbb{G}_d(n)$ with cardinality asymptotically $(1+\beta)(\log d/d)n$, where $1 \geq \beta > \frac{1}{2} + \frac{1}{2\sqrt{2}}$ either have intersection size at least $(1+z)(\log d/d)n$ or at most $(1-z)(\log d/d)n$, for some $z < \beta$. The result is established using a straightforward first moment argument: we compute the expected number of pairs of independent sets with intersection lying in the interval $[(1-z)(\log d/d)n, (1+z)(\log d/d)n]$, and show that this expectation converges to zero exponentially fast. We remark that even though our conclusion is somewhat stronger than that of previous clustering results, our proof of the clustering phenomenon is extremely simple.

With this result at hand, the refutation of the HLS conjecture is fairly simple to derive. We prove (see Theorem 2.7) that if local algorithms can construct independent sets of size asymptotically $(1+\beta)(\log d/d)n$, then, by means of a simple coupling construction, we can construct two independent sets with intersection size z for *all* z in the interval $[(1+\beta)^2(\log d/d)^2 n, (1+\beta)(\log d/d)n]$, clearly violating the clustering property. The additional factor $1/(2\sqrt{2})$ is an artifact of the analysis, and hence we believe that our result holds for all $\beta \in (0, 1]$. Namely, no local algorithm is capable of producing independent sets with size larger than factor $1/2$ of the optimal, asymptotically in d. We note again that this coincides with the barrier for known algorithms. It is noteworthy that our result is the first one where algorithmic hardness derivation relies directly on the the geometry of the solution space, viz a vi the clustering phenomena, and thus the connection between algorithmic hardness and clustering property is not coincidental.

The remainder of the paper is structured as follows. We introduce some basic material and the HLS conjecture in the next section. In the same section we state our main theorem — non-validity of the conjecture (Theorem 2.5). We also state two secondary theorems, the first describing the overlap structure of independent sets in random graphs (Theorem 2.6) - the main tool in the proof of our result, and the second describing overlaps that can be found if local algorithms work well (Theorem 2.7). We prove our main theorem easily from the two secondary theorems in Section 3. We prove Theorem 2.7 in Section 4. We omit the proof of Theorem 2.6 from this version.

2. PRELIMINARIES AND MAIN RESULT

For convenience, we repeat here some of the notions and definitions already introduced in the first section.

Basic graph terminology.

All graphs in this paper are understood to be simple undirected graphs. Given a graph $\mathbb{G}$ with node set $V(\mathbb{G})$ and edge set $E(\mathbb{G})$, a subset of nodes $I \subset V(\mathbb{G})$ is an independent set if $(u, v) \notin E(\mathbb{G})$ for all $u, v \in I$. A path between nodes u and v with length r is a sequence of nodes $u_1, \ldots, u_{r-1}$ such that $(u, u_1), (u_1, u_2), \ldots, (u_{r-1}, v) \in E(\mathbb{G})$. The distance between nodes u and v is the length of the shortest path between them. For every positive integer value r and every node $u \in V(\mathbb{G})$, $B_{\mathbb{G}}(u, r)$ denotes the depth-r neighborhood of u in $\mathbb{G}$. Namely, $B_{\mathbb{G}}(u, r)$ is the subgraph of $\mathbb{G}$ induced by nodes v with distance at most r from u. When $\mathbb{G}$ is clear from context we drop the subscript. The degree of a vertex $u \in V(\mathbb{G})$ is the number of vertices v such that $(u, v) \in E(\mathbb{G})$. The degree of a graph $\mathbb{G}$ is the maximum degree of a vertex of $\mathbb{G}$. A graph $\mathbb{G}$ is d-regular if the degree of every node is d.

Random graph preliminaries.

Given a positive real d, $\mathbb{G}(n, d/n)$ denotes the Erdös-Rényi graph on n nodes $[n] \triangleq \{1, 2, \ldots, n\}$, with edge probability d/n. Namely each of the $\binom{n}{2}$ edges of a complete graph on n nodes belongs to $E(\mathbb{G}(n, d/n))$ with probability d/n, independently for all edges. Given a positive integer d, $\mathbb{G}_d(n)$ denotes a graph chosen uniformly at random from the space of all d-regular graphs on n nodes. This definition is meaningful only when nd is an even number, which we assume from now on. Given a positive integer m, let $\mathcal{I}(n, d, m)$ denote the set of all independent sets in $\mathbb{G}(n, d/n)$ with cardinality m. $\mathcal{I}_d(n, m)$ stands for a similar set for the case of random regular graphs. Given integers $0 \leq k \leq m$, let $\mathcal{O}(n, d, m, k)$ denote the set of pairs $I, J \in \mathcal{I}(n, d, m)$ such that $|I \cap J| = k$. The definition of the set $\mathcal{O}_d(n, m, k)$ is similar. The sizes of the sets $\mathcal{O}(n, d, m, k)$ and $\mathcal{O}_d(n, m, k)$, and in particular whether these sets are empty or not, is one of our focuses.

Denote by $\alpha(n, d)$ the size of a largest in cardinality independent subset of $\mathbb{G}(n, d/n)$, normalized by n. Namely,

$$\alpha(n, d) = n^{-1} \max\{m : \mathcal{I}(n, d, m) \neq \emptyset\}.$$

$\alpha_d(n)$ stands for the similar quantity for random regular graphs. It is known that $\alpha(n, d)$ and $\alpha_d(n)$ have deterministic limits as $n \to \infty$.

THEOREM 2.1. *For every $d \in \mathbb{R}_+$ there exists $\alpha(d)$ such that w.h.p. as $n \to \infty$,*

$$\alpha(n, d) \to \alpha(d). \tag{1}$$

Similarly, for every positive integer d there exists α_d such that w.h.p. as $n \to \infty$

$$\alpha_d(n) \to \alpha_d. \tag{2}$$

Furthermore

$$\alpha(d) = \frac{2\log d}{d}(1 - o(1)), \quad (3)$$

$$\alpha_d = \frac{2\log d}{d}(1 - o(1)), \quad (4)$$

as $d \to \infty$.

The convergence (1) and (2) were established in Bayati, Gamarnik and Tetali [4]. The limits (3) and (4) follow from much older results by Frieze [13] for the case of Erdös-Rényi graphs and by Frieze and Łuczak [14] for the case of random regular graphs, which established these limits in the $\limsup_n$ and $\liminf_n$ sense. The fallout of these results is that graphs $\mathbb{G}(n, d/n)$ and $\mathbb{G}_d(n)$ have independent sets of size up to approximately $(2\log d/d)n$, when n and d are large, namely in the doubly asymptotic sense when we first take n to infinity and then d to infinity.

Local graph terminology.

A *decision function* is a measurable function $f = f(u, \mathbb{G}, \mathbf{x})$ where $\mathbb{G}$ is a graph on vertex set $[n]$ for some positive integer n, $u \in [n]$ is a vertex and $\mathbf{x} \in [0,1]^N$ is a sequence of real numbers for some $N \geq n$ and returns a Boolean value $\{0,1\}$. A decision function f is said to compute an independent set if for every graph $\mathbb{G}$ and every sequence $\mathbf{x}$ and for every pair $(u,v) \in E(\mathbb{G})$ it is the case that either $f(u, \mathbb{G}, \mathbf{x}) = 0$ or $f(v, \mathbb{G}, \mathbf{x}) = 0$, or both. We refer to such an f as an independence function. For an independence function f, graph $\mathbb{G}$ on vertex set $[n]$ and $\mathbf{x} \in [0,1]^N$ for $N \geq n$, we let $I_{\mathbb{G}}(f, \mathbf{x})$ denote the independent set of $\mathbb{G}$ returned by f, i.e., $I_{\mathbb{G}}(f, \mathbf{x}) = \{u \in [n] \mid f(u, \mathbb{G}, \mathbf{x}) = 1\}$. We will assume later that X is chosen randomly according to some probability distribution. In this case $I_{\mathbb{G}}(f, \mathbf{x})$ is a randomly chosen independent set in $\mathbb{G}$.

We now define the notion of a "local" decision function, i.e., one whose actions depend only on the local structure of a graph and the local randomness. The definition is a natural one, but we formalize it below for completeness. Let $\mathbb{G}_1$ and $\mathbb{G}_2$ be graphs on vertex sets $[n_1]$ and $[n_2]$ respectively. Let $u_1 \in [n_1]$ and $u_2 \in [n_2]$. We say that $\pi : [n_1] \to [n_2]$ is an r-local isomorphism mapping u_1 to u_2 if π is a graph isomorphism from $B_{\mathbb{G}_1}(u_1, r)$ to $B_{\mathbb{G}_2}(u_2, r)$ (so in particular it is a bijection from $B_{\mathbb{G}_1}(u_1, r)$ to $B_{\mathbb{G}_2}(u_2, r)$, and further it preserves adjacency within $B_{\mathbb{G}_1}(u_1, r)$ and $B_{\mathbb{G}_2}(u_2, r)$). For $\mathbb{G}_1, \mathbb{G}_2, u_1, u_2$ and an r-local isomorphism π, we say sequences $x^{(1)} \in [0,1]^{N_1}$ and $x^{(2)} \in [0,1]^{N_2}$ are r-locally equivalent if for every $v \in B_{\mathbb{G}_1}(u_1, r)$ we have $x^{(1)}_v = x^{(2)}_{\pi(v)}$. Finally we say $f(u, \mathbb{G}, x)$ is an r-local function if for every pair of graphs $\mathbb{G}_1, \mathbb{G}_2$, for every pair of vertices $u_1 \in V(\mathbb{G}_1)$ and $u_2 \in V(\mathbb{G}_2)$, for every r-local isomorphism π mapping u_1 to u_2 and r-locally equivalent sequences $x^{(1)}$ and $x^{(2)}$ we have $f(u_1, \mathbb{G}_1, x^{(1)}) = f(u_2, \mathbb{G}_2, x^{(2)})$. We often use the notation f_r to denote an r-local function.

Let $n_{d,r} \triangleq 1 + d \cdot ((d-1)^r - 1)/(d-2)$ denote the number of vertices in a rooted tree of degree d and depth r. We let $\mathbb{T}_{d,r}$ denote a canonical rooted tree on vertex set $[n_{d,r}]$ with root being 1. For $n \geq n_{d,r}, \mathbf{x} \in [0,1]^n$ and an r-local function f_r, we let $f_r(\mathbf{x})$ denote the quantity $f_r(1, \mathbb{T}_{d,r}, \mathbf{x})$. Let $\mathbf{X}$ be chosen according to a uniform distribution on $[0,1]^n$. The set subset of nodes $I_{\mathbb{G}_d(n)}(f_r, \mathbf{X})$ is called *i.i.d. factor* produced by the r-local function f_r. As we will see below the $\alpha(f_r) \triangleq \frac{1}{n} \cdot \mathbb{E}_{\mathbf{X}}[f_r(\mathbf{X})]$ accurately captures (to within an additive $o(1)$ factor) the density of an independent returned by an r-local independence function f_r on $\mathbb{G}_d(n)$.

First we recall the following folklore proposition which we will also use often in this paper.

PROPOSITION 2.2. *As $n \to \infty$, with probability tending to 1 almost all local neighborhoods in $\mathbb{G}_d(n)$ look like a tree. Formally, for every d, r and ϵ, for sufficiently large n,*

$$\mathbb{P}_{\mathbb{G}_d(n)}\left(|\{u \in [n] \mid B_{\mathbb{G}_d(n)}(u, r) \not\cong \mathbb{T}_{d,r}\}| \geq \epsilon n\right) \leq \epsilon.$$

This immediately implies that the expected value of the independent set $I_{\mathbb{G}_d(n)}(f_r, \mathbf{X})$ produced by f_r is $\alpha(f_r)n + o(n)$. In fact the following concentration result holds.

PROPOSITION 2.3. *As $n \to \infty$, with probability tending to 1 the independent set produced by a r-local function f on $\mathbb{G}_d(n)$ is of size $\alpha(f) \cdot n + o(n)$. Formally, for every d, r, ϵ and every r-local function f, for sufficiently large n,*

$$\mathbb{P}_{\mathbb{G}_d(n), \mathbf{X} \in [0,1]^N}\left(||I_{\mathbb{G}_d(n)}(f_r, \mathbf{X})| - \alpha(f_r)n| \geq \epsilon n\right) \leq \epsilon.$$

PROOF. The proof follows from by the fact that the variance of $|I_{\mathbb{G}_d(n), \mathbf{X}}|$ is $O(n)$ and its expectation is $\alpha(f_r)n + o(n)$, and so the concentration follows by Chebychev's inequality. The bound on the variance in turn follows from the fact that for every graph $\mathbb{G}$, there are at most $O(n)$ pairs of vertices u and v for which the events $f(u, \mathbb{G}, \mathbf{X})$ and $f(v, \mathbb{G}, \mathbf{X})$ are not independent for random $\mathbf{X}$. Details omitted. □

The Hatami-Lovász-Szegedy Conjecture and our result.

We now turn to describing the Hatami-Lovász-Szegedy (HLS) conjecture and our result. Recall α_d defined by (2). The HLS conjecture can be stated as follows.

CONJECTURE 2.4. *There exists a sequence of r-local independence functions $f_r, r \geq 1$ such that almost surely $I(f_r, n)$ is an independent set in $\mathbb{G}_d(n)$ and $\alpha(f_r) \to \alpha_d$ as $r \to \infty$.*

Namely, the conjecture asserts the existence of a local algorithm (r-local independence function f_r) which is capable of producing independent sets in $\mathbb{G}_d(r)$ of cardinality close to the largest that exist. For such an algorithm to be efficient the function $f_r(u, \mathbb{G}, \mathbf{x})$ should also be efficiently computable *uniformly*. Even setting this issue aside, we show that there is a limit on the power of local algorithms to find large independent sets in $\mathbb{G}_d(n)$ and in particular the HLS conjecture does not hold. Let $\hat{\alpha}_d = \sup_r \sup_{f_r} \alpha(f_r)$, where the second supremum is taken over all r-local independence functions f_r.

THEOREM 2.5. *[Main] For every $\epsilon > 0$ and all sufficiently large d,*

$$\frac{\hat{\alpha}_d}{\alpha_d} \leq \frac{1}{2} + \frac{1}{2\sqrt{2}} + \epsilon.$$

That is, for every $\epsilon > 0$ and for all sufficiently large d, a largest independent set obtainable by r-local functions is at most $\frac{1}{2} + \frac{1}{2\sqrt{2}} + \epsilon$ for all r.

Thus for all large enough d there is a multiplicative gap between $\hat{\alpha}_d$ and the independence ratio α_d. That being said, our result does not rule out that for small d, $\hat{\alpha}_d$ in fact equals α_d, thus leaving the HLS conjecture open in this regime.

The two main ingredients in our proof of Theorem 2.5 both deal with the *overlaps* between independent sets in random regular graphs. Informally, our first result on the size of the overlaps shows that in random graphs the overlaps are not of "intermediate" size — this is formalized in Theorem 2.6. We then show that we can apply any r-local function f_r twice, with coupled randomness, to produce two independent sets of intermediate overlap where the size of the overlap depends on the size of the independent sets found by f_r and the level of coupling. This is formalized in Theorem 2.7 Theorem 2.5 follows immediately by combinig the two theorems (and appropriate setting of parameters).

Overlaps in random graphs.

We now state our main theorem about the overlap of large independent sets. We interpret the statement after we make the formal statement.

THEOREM 2.6. *For $\beta \in (1/\sqrt{2}, 1)$ and $0 < z < \sqrt{2\beta^2 - 1} < \beta$ and d, let $s = (1+\beta)d^{-1}\log d$ and let $K(z)$ denote the set of integers between $\frac{(1-z)n\log d}{d}$ and $\frac{(1+z)n\log d}{d}$. Then, for all large enough d, we have*

$$\lim_{n\to\infty} \mathbb{P}\Big(\cup_{k\in K(z)} \mathcal{O}(n, d, \lfloor sn \rfloor, k) \neq \emptyset\Big) = 0, \qquad (5)$$

and

$$\lim_{n\to\infty} \mathbb{P}\Big(\cup_{k\in K(z)} \mathcal{O}_d(n, \lfloor sn \rfloor, k) \neq \emptyset\Big) = 0. \qquad (6)$$

In other words, both in the Erdös-Rényi and in the random regular graph models, when $\beta > 1/\sqrt{2}$, and d is large enough, with probability approaching unity as $n \to \infty$, one cannot find a pair of independent sets I and J with size $\lfloor ns \rfloor$, such that their overlap (intersection) has cardinality at least $\frac{n(1-z)\log d}{d}$ and at most $\frac{n(1+z)\log d}{d}$.

Note that for all $\beta > 1/\sqrt{2}$, there exists z satisfying $0 < z < \sqrt{2\beta^2 - 1}$ and so the theorem is not vacuous in this setting. Furthermore as $\beta \to 1$, z can be chosen arbitrarily close to 1 making the forbidden overlap region extremely broad. That is, as the size of the independent sets in consideration approaches the maximum possible (namely as $\beta \uparrow 1$), and as $d \to \infty$, we can take $z \to 1$. In other words, with probability approaching one, two nearly largest independent sets either overlap almost entirely or almost do not have an intersection. This is the key result for establishing our hardness bounds for existence of local algorithms.

A slightly different version of the first of these results can be found as Lemma 12 in [10]. The latter paper shows that if an independent set I is chosen uniformly at random from the set with size nearly $(1+\beta)n\log d/d$, then with high probability (with respect to the choice of I), there exists an empty overlap region in the sense described above. In fact, this empty overlap region exists for every $\beta \in (0,1)$, as opposed to just $1 > \beta > 1/2 + 1/(2\sqrt{2})$ as in our case. Unfortunately, this result cannot be used for our purposes, since this result does not rule out the existence of rare sets I for which no empty overlap exists.

Overlapping from local algorithms.

Next we turn to the formalizing the notion of using a local function f_r twice on coupled randomness to produce overlapping independent sets.

Fix an r-local independence function f_r. Given a vector $\mathbf{X} = (X_u, 1 \le u \le n)$ of variables $X_u \in [0,1]$, recall that $I_{\mathbb{G}}(f_r, \mathbf{X})$ denotes the independent set of $\mathbb{G}$ given by $u \in I_{\mathbb{G}}(f_r, \mathbf{X})$ if and only if $f_r(u, \mathbb{G}, \mathbf{X}) = 1$.

Recall that $\mathbf{X}$ is chosen according to the uniform distribution on $[0,1]^n$. Namely, X_u are independent and uniformly distributed over $[0,1]$. In what follows we consider some joint distributions on pairs of vectors $(\mathbf{X}, \mathbf{Y})$ such that marginal distributions on the vector $\mathbf{X}$ and $\mathbf{Y}$ are uniform on $[0,1]^n$, though $\mathbf{X}$ and $\mathbf{Y}$ are dependent on each other. The intuition behind the proof of Theorem 2.5 is as follows. Note that if $\mathbf{X} = \mathbf{Y}$ then $I_{\mathbb{G}}(f_r, \mathbf{X}) = I_{\mathbb{G}}(f_r, \mathbf{Y})$. As a result the overlap $I_{\mathbb{G}}(f_r, \mathbf{X}) \cap I_{\mathbb{G}}(f_r, \mathbf{Y})$ between $I_{\mathbb{G}}(f_r, \mathbf{X})$ and $I_{\mathbb{G}}(f_r, \mathbf{Y})$ is $\alpha(f_r)n + o(n)$ in expectation. On the other hand, if $\mathbf{X}$ and $\mathbf{Y}$ are independent, then the overlap between $I_{\mathbb{G}}(f_r, \mathbf{X})$ and $I_{\mathbb{G}}(f_r, \mathbf{Y})$ is $\alpha^2(f_r)n + o(n)$ in expectation, since the decision to pick a vertex u in I is independent for most vertices when $\mathbf{X}$ and $\mathbf{Y}$ are independent. (In particular, note that if the local neighborhood around u is a tree, which according to Proposition 2.2 happens with probability approaching unity, then the two decisions are independent, and $u \in I$ with probability $\alpha(f_r)$.) Our main theorem shows that by coupling the variables, the overlap can be arranged to be of any intermediate size, to within an additive $o(n)$ factor. In particular, if $\alpha(f_r)$ exceeds $\frac{1}{2} + \frac{1}{2\sqrt{2}}$ we will be able to show that the overlap can be arranged to be between the values $\frac{(1-z)n\log d}{d}$ and $\frac{(1+z)n\log d}{d}$, described in Theorem 2.6 which contradicts the statement of this theorem.

THEOREM 2.7. *Fix a positive integer d. For constant r, let $f_r(u, \mathbb{G}, \mathbf{x})$ be an r-local independence function and let $\alpha = \alpha(f_r)$. For every $\gamma \in [\alpha^2, \alpha]$ and $\epsilon > 0$, and for every sufficiently large n, there exists a distribution on variables $(\mathbf{X}, \mathbf{Y}) \in [0,1]^n \times [0,1]^n$ such that*

$$\mathbb{P}_{\mathbb{G}_d(n),(\mathbf{X},\mathbf{Y})}\left(|I_{\mathbb{G}_d(n)}(f_r, \mathbf{X}) \cap I_{\mathbb{G}_d(n)}(f_r, \mathbf{Y})| \notin (\gamma \pm \epsilon)n\right) \le \epsilon.$$

3. PROOF OF THEOREM 2.5

We now show how Theorems 2.6 and 2.7 immediately imply Theorem 2.5.

PROOF PROOF OF THEOREM 2.5. Fix an r-local function f_r and let $\alpha = \alpha(f_r)$. Fix $0 < \eta < 1$. We will prove below that for sufficiently large d we have $\alpha/\alpha_d \le 1/2 + 1/(2\sqrt{2}) + \eta$. The theorem will then follow.

Let $\epsilon = \frac{\eta \log d}{2d}$. By Proposition 2.3 we have that almost surely an independent set returned by f_r on $\mathbb{G}_d(n)$ is of size at least $(\alpha - \epsilon)n$. Furthermore for every $\gamma \in [\alpha^2, \alpha]$ we have, by Theorem 2.7, that $\mathbb{G}_d(n)$ almost surely has two independent sets I and J, with

$$|I|, |J| \ge (\alpha - \epsilon)n \text{ and } |I \cap J| \in [(\gamma - \epsilon)n, (\gamma + \epsilon)n]. \qquad (7)$$

Finally, by Theorem 2.1, we have that for sufficiently large d, $|I|, |J| \le (2d^{-1}\log d)(1+\eta)n \le 4d^{-1}\log dn$ and so $\alpha^2 \le d^{-1}\log d$, allowing us to set $\gamma = d^{-1}/\log d$.

Now we apply Theorem 2.6 with $z = \epsilon d/\log d$ and $\beta > \sqrt{\frac{1+z^2}{2}}$. (Note that for this choice we have $z < 1$ and $z < \sqrt{2\beta^2 - 1} < \beta < 1$. We will also use later the fact that for this choice we have $\beta \le 1/\sqrt{2} + z = 1/\sqrt{2} + \epsilon d^{-1}\log d$.) Theorem 2.6 asserts that almost surely $\mathbb{G}_d(n)$ has no independent sets of size at least $(1+\beta)d^{-1}\log dn$ with intersection size in $[(1-z)d^{-1}\log dn, (1+z)d^{-1}\log dn]$. Since $|I \cap J| \in [(\gamma - \epsilon)n, (\gamma + \epsilon)n] = [(1-z)d^{-1}\log dn, (1+z)d^{-1}\log dn]$, we conclude that $\min\{|I|, |J|\} \le (1+\beta)d^{-1}\log dn$. Combining with Equation (7) we get that $(\alpha - \epsilon)n \le \min\{|I|, |J|\} \le$

$(1+\beta)d^{-1}\log dn$ and so $\alpha \le (1+\beta)d^{-1}\log d + \epsilon$, which by the given bound on β yields $\alpha \le (1+1/\sqrt{2})d^{-1}\log d + 2\epsilon = (1+1/\sqrt{2}+\eta)d^{-1}\log d$. On the other hand we also have $\alpha_d \ge (2-\eta)d^{-1}\log d$. It follows that $\alpha/\alpha_d \le 1/2 + 1/2\sqrt{2}+\eta$ as desired.

□

4. PROOF OF THEOREM 2.7

For parameter $p \in [0,1]$, we define the p-correlated distribution on vectors of random variables $(\mathbf{X}, \mathbf{Y})$ to be the following: Let $\mathbf{X}, \mathbf{Z}$ be independent uniform vectors over $[0,1]^n$. Now let $Z_u = X_u$ with probability p and Y_u with probability $1-p$ independently for every $u \in V(G)$.

Let $f(u, \mathbb{G}, \mathbf{x})$ and α be as in the theorem statement. Recall that $f(\mathbf{x}) = f(1, \mathbb{T}_{d,r}, \mathbf{x})$ is the decision of f on the canonical tree of degree d and depth r rooted at the vertex 1. Let $\gamma(p)$ be the probability that $f(\mathbf{X}) = 1$ and $f(\mathbf{Y}) = 1$, for p-correlated variables $(\mathbf{X}, \mathbf{Y})$. As with Proposition 2.3 we have the following.

Lemma 4.1. *For every d, r, $\epsilon > 0$ and r-local function f, for sufficiently large n we have:*

$$\mathbb{P}\left(\left||I_{\mathbb{G}_d(n)}(f,\mathbf{X}) \cap I_{\mathbb{G}_d(n)}(f,\mathbf{Y})| - \gamma(p)\cdot n\right| \ge \epsilon n\right) \le \epsilon,$$

where $(\mathbf{X}, \mathbf{Y})$ are p-correlated distributions on $[0,1]^n$.

Proof. By Proposition 2.2 we have that almost surely almost all local neighborhoods are trees and so for most vertices u the probability that u is chosen to be in the independent sets $I(f,\mathbf{X})$ and $I(f,\mathbf{Y})$ is $\gamma(p)$. By linearity of expectations we get that $\mathbb{E}[|I(f,\mathbf{X}) \cap I(f,\mathbf{Y})|] = \gamma(p)\cdot n + o(n)$. Again observing that most local neighborhoods are disjoint we have that the variance of $|I(f,\mathbf{X}) \cap I(f,\mathbf{Y})|$ is $O(n)$. We conclude, by applying the Chebychev bound, that $|I(f,\mathbf{X}) \cap I(f,\mathbf{Y})|$ is concentrated around the expectation and the lemma follows. □

We also note that for $p=1$ and $p=0$ the quantity $\gamma(p)$ follow immediately from their definition.

Proposition 4.2. $\gamma(1) = \alpha$ *and* $\gamma(0) = \alpha^2$.

Now to prove Theorem 2.7 it suffices to prove that for every $\gamma \in [\alpha^2, \alpha]$ there exists a p such that $\gamma(p) = \gamma$. We show this next by showing that $\gamma(p)$ is continuous.

Lemma 4.3. *For every r, $\gamma(p)$ is a continuous function of p.*

Proof. Let $(W_u, u \in \mathbb{T}_{d,r})$ be random variables associated with nodes in $\mathbb{T}_{d,r}$, uniformly distributed over $[0,1]$, which are independent for different u and also independent from X_u and Z_u. We use W_u as generators for the events $Y_u = X_u$ vs $Y_u = Z_u$. In particular, given p, set $Y_u = X_u$ if $W_u \le p$ and $Y_u = Z_u$ otherwise. This process is exactly the process of setting variables Y_u to X_u and Z_u with probabilities p and $1-p$ respectively, independently for all nodes u. Now fix any $p_1 < p_2$, and let $\delta < (p_2 - p_1)/d^{r+1}$. We use the notation $f_r(X_u, Z_u, W_u, p)$ to denote the value of f_r when the seed variables realization is $(W_u, u \in \mathbb{T}_{d,r})$, and the threshold value p is used. Namely, $f_r(X_u, Z_u, W_u, p) = f_r\left(X_u \mathbf{1}\{W_u \le p\} + Z_u \mathbf{1}\{W_u > p\}, u \in \mathbb{T}_{d,r}\right)$. Here, for ease of notation, the reference to the tree $\mathbb{T}_{d,r}$ is dropped. Utilizing this notation we have

$$\gamma(p) = \mathbb{P}\left(f_r(X_u) = f_r(X_u, Z_u, W_u, p) = 1\right).$$

Manipulating the expressions somewhat we find

$$|\gamma(p_2) - \gamma(p_1)| \le d^{r+1}(p_2 - p_1).$$

Since r is fixed, the continuity of $\gamma(p)$ is established. □

We are now ready to prove Theorem 2.7.

Proof Proof of Theorem 2.7. Given $\gamma \in [\alpha^2, \alpha]$ by Lemma 4.3 we have that there exists a p such that $\gamma = \gamma(p)$. For this choice of p, let $(\mathbf{X}, \mathbf{Y})$ be a pair of p-correlated distributions. Applying Lemma 4.1 to this choice of p, we get that with probability at least $1-\epsilon$ we have $|I_{\mathbb{G}_d(n)}(f,\mathbf{X}) \cap I_{\mathbb{G}_d(n)}(f,\mathbf{Y})| \in [(\gamma-\epsilon)n, (\gamma+\epsilon)n]$ as desired. □

5. PROOF OF THEOREM 2.6

We omit the proof of this theorem from this version. Details can be found in the full version [15].

Acknowledgements

The first author wishes to thank Microsoft Research New England for providing exciting and hospitable environment during his visit in 2012 when this work was conducted. The same author also wishes acknowledge the general support of NSF grant CMMI-1031332.

6. REFERENCES

[1] D. Achlioptas, A. Coja-Oghlan, and F. Ricci-Tersenghi. On the solution space geometry of random formulas. *Random Structures and Algorithms*, 38:251–268, 2011.

[2] D. Aldous. Some open problems. *http://www.stat.berkeley.edu/~aldous/Research/OP/index.html.*

[3] N. Alon and J. Spencer. *Probabilistic Method.* Wiley, 1992.

[4] M. Bayati, D. Gamarnik, and P. Tetali. Combinatorial approach to the interpolation method and scaling limits in sparse random graphs. *Annals of Probability, to appear. Conference version in Proc. 42nd Ann. Symposium on the Theory of Computing (STOC)*, 2010.

[5] C. Borgs, J. Chayes, and D. Gamarnik. Convergent sequences of sparse graphs: A large deviations approach. arxiv:1302.4615 [math.PR], 2013.

[6] C. Borgs, J. Chayes, L. Lovász, and J. Kahn. Left and right convergence of graphs with bounded degree. *http://arxiv.org/abs/1002.0115*, 2010.

[7] C. Borgs, J. Chayes, L. Lovász, V. Sós, and K. Vesztergombi. Convergent graph sequences II: Multiway cuts and statistical physics. *Ann. of Math.*, 176:151–219, 2012.

[8] C. Borgs, J. Chayes, L. Lovász, V. Sós, and K. Vesztergombi. Convergent graph sequences I: Subgraph frequencies, metric properties, and testing. *Advances in Math.*, 219:1801–1851, 208.

[9] A. Coja-Oghlan. On belief propagation guided decimation for random k-sat. In *Proceedings of the Twenty-Second Annual ACM-SIAM Symposium on Discrete Algorithms*, pages 957–966. SIAM, 2011.

[10] A. Coja-Oghlan and C. Efthymiou. On independent sets in random graphs. In *Proceedings of the Twenty-Second Annual ACM-SIAM Symposium on Discrete Algorithms*, pages 136–144. SIAM, 2011.

[11] E. Csoka and G. Lippner. Invariant random matchings in cayley graphs. *arXiv preprint arXiv:1211.2374*, 2012.

[12] G. Elek and G. Lippner. Borel oracles. an analytical approach to constant-time algorithms. In *Proc. Amer. Math. Soc*, volume 138, pages 2939–2947, 2010.

[13] A. Frieze. On the independence number of random graphs. *Discrete Mathematics*, 81:171–175, 1990.

[14] A. Frieze and T. Łuczak. On the independence and chromatic numbers of random regular graphs. *Journal of Combinatorial Theory, Series B*, 54(1):123–132, 1992.

[15] D. Gamarnik and M. Sudan. Limits of local algorithms over sparse random graphs. *Electronic Colloquium on Computational Complexity (ECCC)*, 20:55, 2013.

[16] A. Hassidim, J. A. Kelner, H. N. Nguyen, and K. Onak. Local graph partitions for approximation and testing. In *FOCS*, pages 22–31. IEEE Computer Society, 2009.

[17] H. Hatami, L. Lovász, and B. Szegedy. Limits of local-global convergent graph sequences. *Preprint at http://arxiv.org/abs/1205.4356*, 2012.

[18] R. Karp and M. Sipser. Maximum matchings in sparse random graphs. In *22nd Annual Symposium on Foundations of Computer Science*, pages 364–375, 1981.

[19] N. Linial. Locality in distributed graph algorithms. *SIAM J. Comput.*, 21(1):193–201, 1992.

[20] L. Lovász and B. Szegedy. Limits of dense graph sequences. *Journal of Combinatorial Theory, Series B*, 96:933–957, 2006.

[21] M. Luby. A simple parallel algorithm for the maximal independent set problem. In R. Sedgewick, editor, *STOC*, pages 1–10. ACM, 1985.

[22] R. Lyons and F. Nazarov. Perfect matchings as iid factors on non-amenable groups. *European Journal of Combinatorics*, 32(7):1115–1125, 2011.

[23] M. Mezard and A. Montanari. *Information, Physics and Computation.* Oxford graduate texts, 2009.

[24] M. Mézard, T. Mora, and R. Zecchina. Clustering of solutions in the random satisfiability problem. *Physical Review Letters*, 94(19):197205, 2005.

[25] H. N. Nguyen and K. Onak. Constant-time approximation algorithms via local improvements. In *FOCS*, pages 327–336. IEEE Computer Society, 2008.

[26] M. Parnas and D. Ron. Approximating the minimum vertex cover in sublinear time and a connection to distributed algorithms. *Theor. Comput. Sci.*, 381(1-3):183–196, 2007.

[27] R. Rubinfeld, G. Tamir, S. Vardi, and N. Xie. Fast local computation algorithms. In B. Chazelle, editor, *ICS*, pages 223–238. Tsinghua University Press, 2011.

[28] M. Talagrand. *Mean Field Models for Spin Glasses: Volume I: Basic Examples.* Springer, 2010.

[29] M. J. Wainwright and M. I. Jordan. A variational principle for graphical models. In *New Directions in Statistical Signal Processing: From Systems to Brain. Cambridge, MA: MIT Press*, 2005.

Deterministic Compression with Uncertain Priors

[Extended Abstract] *

Elad Haramaty†
Department of Computer Science
Technion, Haifa.
eladh@cs.technion.ac.il.

Madhu Sudan
Microsoft Research
1 Memorial Drive, Cambridge, MA 02142.
madhu@mit.edu

ABSTRACT

Communication in "natural" settings, e.g., between humans, is distinctly different than that in classical designed settings, in that the former is characterized by the sender and receiver not being in perfect agreement with each other. Solutions to classical communication problems thus have to overcome an extra layer of uncertainty introduced by this lack of prior agreement. One of the classical goals of communication is compression of information, and in this context lack of agreement implies that sender and receiver may not agree on the "prior" from which information is being generated. Most classical mechanisms for compressing turn out to be non-robust when sender and receiver do not agree on the prior. Juba et al. (Proc. ITCS 2011) showed that there do exists compression schemes with *shared randomness* between sender and reciever that can compress information down roughly to its entropy.

In this work we explore the assumption of *shared* randomness between the sender and receiver and highlight why this assumption is problematic when dealing with natural communication. We initiate the study of deterministic compression schemes amid uncertain priors, and expose some the mathematical facets of this problem. We show some nontrivial determinstic compression schemes, and some lower bounds on natural classes of compression schemes. We show that a full understanding of deterministic communication turns into challenging (open) questions in graph theory and communication complexity.

Categories and Subject Descriptors

E.4 [**Coding And Information Theory**]: Data compaction and compression

*A full version of this paper is available as *ECCC* Technical Report TR 12-166, November 26, 2012.

†Work done in part when this author was visiting Microsoft Research New England.

ITCS'14, January 12–14, 2014, Princeton, New Jersey, USA.

http://dx.doi.org/10.1145/2554797.2554832 .

Keywords

Communication complexity, Graph coloring, Source coding

1. INTRODUCTION

In this work we consider the task of compressing information deterministically, in settings where the sender and receiver are not in agreement on the distribution from which the information is being generated. We start by first describing the general motivation for the study of this problem before formally describing the problem and our results.

1.1 Natural Communication: Context and Uncertainty

Natural communication, say between two humans, differs in significant ways from "designed communication", say between a cell phone and its nearby tower. The latter are carefully engineered to optimize use of the channel of communication, while introducing careful redundancy to overcome any unreliability of the channel. The resulting problems and solution concepts, such as compression schemes and error-correcting encoding schemes are well understood by now.

Natural communication, as characterized by the vagaries of natural language, is much less understood mathematically. Natural communication, often characterized by dictionaries and grammars, do not follow the rules they prescribe. They tend to be ambiguous locally, and seemingly needlessly redundant in other cases; without offering the same reliability as error-correcting codes do. At the same time, natural communication has remarkable capacity to overcome lack of "perfect engineering" of the sender or receiver of information, and in particular do not seem to require perfect agreement between then two (on the design of the protocol). Understanding this resilience mathematically would be a fruitful pursuit and forms the motivation for this and prior works in this stream.

The main goal here is to understand what does "language" look like and what parameters does it try to optimize. Roughly language takes an intended message in the sender's mind and attempts to describe how to convert this message to a sequence of, say, bits. This part is similar to the encoding map of a error-correcting scheme, However to model language more precisely, one should really take into account its context-sensitivity. A more precise description of a language would be as an *encoding* map from a pair *(context,message)* to a *word* which is a sequence of bits. For the time being, one may view context and message as elements of some abstract space (each being possibly a countable set). The language also gives rules on how a receiver should recover the message from the word: it does so by applying a *decoding* map that maps a pair *(context,word)* to a *message*. The goal hopefully is to make sure the receiver decodes to a message that is somehow *compatible* with the sender's intent. Defining compatibility is complex, and we will skirt this issue in this paper. (Such issues are considered, e.g., in [8, 4].) We will simply require receiver to decode to the *same* message as the sender wished to send (so in particular the message space for sender and receiver are identical). Even with this simplication, there remains a major hurdle to communication, namely that sender's context and receiver's context may not be identical! Remarkably, natural communication manages to function reasonably well even when these contexts are not identical, but reasonably close to each other, and it is this aspect that is the focus of this work.

In order to model contexts that are not identical, but are reasonably close, we need a more structured view of contexts (than merely as elements of an abstract set). Juba et al. [7] proposed a natural view: namely a context is simply a probability distribution on messages: The distribution that describes the message that the receiver is expecting to receive, or the distribution that the sender thinks the receiver is expecting to receive. In this framework, the encoding function becomes a map from a distribution P supported on some set U and message $m \in U$ to a word $w \in \{0,1\}^*$; and the decoding function becomes a map from a distribution Q also supported on U and word $w \in \{0,1\}^*$ to a message $\hat{m} \in U$ and the goal of the language is to ensure that $\hat{m} = m$ even if $P \neq Q$, provided they are reasonably close. At the same time the language would like to reduce the expected length of the communication, assuming say that the messages are generated from the distribution P. (More generally we could consider a setting where the messages are generated from some distribution R; our assumption that $R = P$ is mostly for simplicity.)

Classical communication dealt with the setting where $P = Q$. In the classical setting, it turns out that the entropy of the distribution P precisely describes the expected length of the transmission. Does entropy still give a good measure characterizing the expected length of the transmission in the natural setting, when $P \neq Q$? (We note that classical communication also considered the setting where $R \neq P = Q$ and this leads to notions such the KL-divergence, but the important aspect is that they did not consider settings where sender and receiver disagreed on the prior.)

Juba et al. consider the following notion of distance between distributions (a notion which is also used commonly in differential privacy): $\delta(P,Q) = max_{m \in U}\{|\log_2 P(m) - \log_2 Q(m)|\}$. (If $\delta(P,Q) \leq \Delta$ then for every $m \in U$ we have $2^{-\Delta}Q(m) \leq P(m) \leq 2^{\Delta}Q(m)$.) With this notion of distance in place, Juba et al. roughly show that entropy is a good measure of the compression length: Specifically they show that there exist encoding and decoding schemes that use shared randomness between sender and receiver and manage to compress information to a length of roughly $H(P)+2\delta(P,Q)$ where $H(\cdot)$ denotes the binary entropy function. (We note that works of Harsha et al. [6] and Braverman and Rao [1] also explore questions somewhat similar to the ones considered by Juba et al., though their motivations were quite different. Both works focus on the setting when sender and receiver have different priors and are trying to generate a random variable that is maximally correlated under their priors. In our case the sender gets a concrete message from its prior and wishes to communicate it. The focus in both works is on randomized solutions that get the communication complexity down to the minimum possible amount, whereas our thrust is to use less (or no) randomness at the expense of slightly larger communication complexity.)

The main goal of this paper is to explore the need for shared randomness in their work. The assumption of shared randomness takes the solution further away from the motivation of natural communication. Roughly their solution suggests that if the "dictionary", or any other codebook associated with language, is random, then information can be compressed. However in natural usage, the dictionary remains somewhat static whereas the contexts for communication vary vastly. Furthermore, it is even very plausible that the dictionary influences our communication and its context. We thus feel that a compression scheme based on shared randomness is not sufficient evidence to suggest that entropy is the natural complexity measure of capturing the complexity of communicating in natural settings. This leads us to study deterministic compression schemes in this paper, and as we stress below, this turns out to be surprisingly challenging to analyze. We illustrate the complexity by considering a rather simple problem in this space.

1.2 A toy problem

The following example illustrates the questions studied in this paper: Suppose Alice and Bob have a ranking of a set U of N elements, say, movies. Specifically Alice's rank function is $A : [N] \to U$ and Bob's rank function is $B : [N] \to U$ where $[N] = \{1, \ldots, N\}$ and A and B are bijections with $A(i)$ naming the ith ranked movie in Alice's ranking. Suppose further that Alice and Bob know that their rankings are "close", specifically for every $x \in U$, $|A^{-1}(x) - B^{-1}(x)| \leq 2$. How many bits does Alice have to send to Bob so that Bob knows her top-ranked movie, i.e., $A(1)$?

On the one hand Bob knows $A(1)$ is one of the three element set $S_1 = \{B(1), B(2), B(3)\}$ and so the information-content from his point of view is bounded by $\log_2 3$ bits. Indeed this leads to a randomized communication scheme, with Alice and Bob sharing common randomness with $O(1)$ bits of communication: Alice and Bob use their randomness to get a hash function hashing their universe to a constant number of bits. Alice sends the hash of $A(1)$, and Bob recovers the name of the movie provided the elements of S_1 hash to distinct values. However the deterministic communication complexity of the question is not as easily settled. Part of the reason is that Alice doesn't know S_1 and so has to "guess" it to communicate $A(1)$. Still she is not clueless: She knows it is contained in $T_2 = \{A(1), \ldots, A(5)\}$ and perhaps this can help her communicate $A(1)$ efficiently to Bob. The question of interest to us in this work is: Can Alice communicate $A(1)$ to Bob with a number of bits that is independent of N? (Unfortunately, we do not answer this question, though we do give a non-trivial upper bound. We will elaborate on this later.)

The question above is a prototypical example of "communication amid uncertainty", where the communicating players have fairly good information about each other (in the example above Alice and Bob know each others ranking of each movie to within ± 2), but are not sure of each other's information and do not have a common-ground to base communication on. As we elaborate on in this paper, solutions to this problem influence solutions to the general problems of communication amid uncertainty, while this problem is itself a special case (when Alice and Bob's distributions are geometric).

We describe our problems and solutions shortly, but to give a gist of the findings: We show in this work that there is a solution to the above toy problem communicating roughly $2^{O(\log^* N)}$ bits, which is a very slowly growing, but nevertheless growing, function of U. We are unable to resolve if a growing function of N bits is necessary for this problem; however we do show that any solution that looks at only a constant number of Alice's top movies (or a constant number of Bob's top movies) must communicate $\log^{(\Omega(1))} N$ bits (where $\log^{(i)}$ denotes the ith iterated logarithm function.

1.3 Formal definitions and main results

We start by defining the notion of an "uncertain compression scheme".

We let $\{0,1\}^*$ denote the set of all finite length binary strings. For $x \in \{0,1\}^*$, let $|x|$ denote its length. Throughout U, the set of all messages, will be a finite set of size N. Let $\mathcal{P}(U)$ denote the space of all probability distributions over U.

Definition 1.1. ((Basic) Uncertain Compression Scheme) *For positive real Δ an* Uncertain Compression Scheme (UCS) *for distance Δ over the universe U is given by a pair of $E : \mathcal{P}(U) \times U \to \{0,1\}^*$ and $D : \mathcal{P}(U) \times \{0,1\}^* \to U$ that satisfy the following correctness condition: For every pair of distributions $P, Q \in \mathcal{P}(U)$ that are Δ-close (i.e $\delta(P,Q) \leq \Delta$) and for every $m \in U$, we have $D(Q, E(P,m)) = m$. The* performance *of a UCS (E,D) is given by the function $L : \mathcal{P}(U) \to \Re^+$, where $L(P) = \mathbf{E}_{m \leftarrow_P U}[|E(P,m)|]$, i.e., the expected length of the encoding under the distribution P. We refer to such a scheme as a (Δ, L)-UCS.*

In English, the definition above explicitly provides the distribution as input to the encoding and decoding schemes, and expect the schemes to work correctly even if the distributions used by the encoder and decoder are not the same, as long as they are Δ-close to each other. While in general we would like compression schemes which work for all possible distributions P, Q that are within Δ of each other, and with no error (as expected in the definition above), some of our schemes are weaker and work with some error, or only for some class of distributions. We define such general UCS's below.

Definition 1.2. ((General) Uncertain Compression Scheme) *For positive real Δ (for distance), $\epsilon \in [0,1]$ (for error), a class of distributions $\mathcal{F} \subseteq \mathcal{P}$, and performance function $L : \mathcal{F} \to \Re^+$ a $(\Delta, \epsilon, \mathcal{F}, L)$-*Uncertain Compression Scheme (UCS) *over the universe U is given by a pair of $E : \mathcal{F} \times U \to \{0,1\}^* \cup \{\perp\}$ and $D : \mathcal{F} \times \{0,1\}^* \cup \{\perp\} \to U \cup \{\perp\}$ that satisfy the following conditions:*

1. *For every pair of distributions $P, Q \in \mathcal{F}$ that are Δ-close and for every $m \in U$, it is the case that if $E(P,m) \neq \perp$ then $D(Q, E(P,m)) = m$. Furthermore $D(\perp) = \perp$.*
2. $\Pr_{m \leftarrow_P U}[E(P,m) = \perp] \leq \epsilon$.
3. *For every $P \in \mathcal{F}$, we have $\mathbf{E}_{m \leftarrow_P U}[|E(P,m)|] \leq L(P)$.*

Note that we do not distinguish the two definitions above by name, but rather just by the number of parameters. So if the number of parameters is just two, then it is assumed that there is no error, and the performance holds for all distributions.

We note that the definitions above only cover deterministic compression schemes. A compression scheme with shared randomness can be defined analogously, but we don't do so here. We also stress that the choice of P and Q is "worst-case" within the family $\mathcal{F}$ (as formalized by the universal quantifier in the correctness condition). There are no assumptions that $\mathcal{F}$ is small (has only finitely many elements), which tends to be the setting for universal compression. Similarly, we do not consider a sequence of messages that need to be transmitted: Rather, we are considering one-shot communication with no assumptions on the distributions P and Q, other than that they are from $\mathcal{F}$ and Δ-close.

We recall that Juba et al. present a $(\Delta, H(P) + 2\Delta + c)$-UCS (with shared randomness) for some constant $c \leq 3$. We give two *deterministic* schemes in this paper, both having complexity depending on N, but both using substantially less than $\log N$ bits.

Theorem 1.3. *For every $\Delta \geq 0$, there exists a $(\Delta, O(H(P) + \Delta + \log\log N))$-UCS, i.e., a deterministic universal compression scheme that works for all pairs P, Q that are within distance Δ of each other, and where the expected length of encoding is at most $O(H(P) + \Delta + \log\log N)$.*

The dependence on N of this scheme is non-trivial and thus may even be reasonable in "natural circumstances". However it is not clear if such a dependency on N is necessary. Motivated by the quest to understand the dependence on N more closely, we explore schemes whose performance is not necessarily linear in $H(P)$. Simultaneously we relax our schemes to allow them to "drop" messages with ϵ probability. We note that if we don't do the latter, then the former is not really a relaxation: Any error-free scheme with superlinear dependence on $H(P)$ can be converted to one with linear dependence on $H(P)$ by a simple reduction (see Lemma 3.11).

Our next theorem gives a scheme that is weaker than the one from Theorem 1.3 in its dependence on the entropy $H(P)$ and in that it errs with non-zero probability. But it does achieve significantly better dependence on N.

Theorem 1.4. *For every $\epsilon > 0$ and $\Delta \geq 0$ there exists a $(\Delta, \epsilon, \mathcal{P}(U), \exp(H(P)/\epsilon + \Delta \log^* N))$-UCS, i.e., the scheme has error probability at most ϵ, it works for all pairs of distributions P, Q within distance Δ and the expected length of the encoding is at most $\exp(H(P)/\epsilon + \Delta \log^* N)$.*

In the above the notation $\exp(x)$ denotes a function of the form c^x for some universal constant c, and $\log^* N$ denotes the minimum integer i such $\log^{(i)} N \leq 1$ and $\log^{(i)}$ is the logarithm function iterated i times.

An alternate way to get around the barrier of Lemma 3.11, which insists that schemes must have linear dependence on $H(P)$ or make some error, is to have schemes that do not work for all possible pairs of distributions P and Q. As it turns out the scheme from Theorem 1.4 does have this behavior for many natural distributions. In Theorem 3.8 we show that our scheme from Theorem 1.4 works without error and with same performance as long as P (or Q) are close to a "flat distribution" (uniform over a subset), or a geometric distribution, or a binomial distribution. We stress that the scheme is not particularly carefully tailored to the class of distributions (though of course the encodings and decodings do depend on the distributions), but naturally adapts to being error-free for the above classes.

1.4 Techniques: Graph Coloring

While the most natural framework for studying our problem is as a question of communication complexity of a relational problem (as in [9]), this turns out not to be the most useful for studying the deterministic communication complexity. Indeed, as pointed out earlier, the modern stress in communication complexity is often on designing and understanding the limits of protocols that are interactive and use shared randomness, while in our case the thrust is in the opposite direction.

It turns out our questions are naturally also captured as graph-coloring questions. Furthermore such questions (or related ones) have been studied in the literature on distributed computing in the attempt to color graphs in a local distributed manner. In particular, the work of Linial [10] shows that a "local" algorithm for 3-coloring a cycle, due to Cole and Vishkin [2], implies that a large "high-degree graph" is 3-colorable. The ideas of Cole and Vishkin [2] and Linial [10] turn out to be quite useful in our context. Our work abstracts some of these techniques, and extends them to get combinatorial results, which we then convert to efficient compression schemes.

Uncertainty graphs and Chromatic number.

We start by defining a class of structured combinatorial graphs whose chromatic number turns out to be central to our problems. Let $[N] = \{1, \ldots, N\}$. Let S_N denote the set of all permutations on N elements, i.e., the set of all bijections from $[N]$ to itself. For $\pi, \sigma \in S_N$, let $\delta(\pi, \sigma) = \max_{i \in [N]} |\pi^{-1}(i) - \sigma^{-1}(i)|$.

DEFINITION 1.5 (UNCERTAINTY GRAPHS). *For integer N, ℓ the uncertainty graph $\mathcal{U}_{N,\ell}$ has as elements of S_N as its vertices, with $\pi \leftrightarrow \sigma$ if (1) $\pi(1) \neq \sigma(1)$ and $\delta(\pi, \sigma) \leq \ell$.*

It turns out that the chromatic number of the uncertainty graphs have a close connection to uncertain communication schemes. Roughly these graphs emerge from a very restricted version of the communication problem, where the distributions P and Q are geometric distributions (giving probability proportional to $\beta^{-\pi^{-1}(i)}$ and $\beta^{-\sigma^{-1}(i)}$ to the element $i \in [N]$). It follows that if $\delta(\pi, \sigma)$ is small, then P and Q are close to each other. Furthermore, for simplicity these graphs only consider the case that the message is the element with maximal probability under P. To understand how the chromatic number plays a role, fix a receiver with distribution Q and consider two possible senders P and P' that could communicate with this receiver. Consider coloring P and P' by $E(P, \text{argmax}_m\{P(m)\})$ and $E(P', \text{argmax}_m\{P'(m)\})$ respectively. This would lead to distinct colors on pairs P and P' that are too close to each other, provided their messages, i.e., $\text{argmax}_m\{P(m)\}$ and $\text{argmax}_m\{P'(m)\}$ are different. This exactly corresponds to adjacency in our graph: the underlying permutations π and σ are close, and the top ranked elements are different.

The results of Juba et al. imply that the "fractional chromatic number" of $\mathcal{U}_{N,\ell}$ is bounded by $O(\ell)$.[1] The (integral) chromatic number on the other hand does not immediately seem to be bounded as a function of ℓ alone. The implication of the low fractional chromatic number is that the chromatic number of $\mathcal{U}_{N,\ell}$ is at most $O(\ell N \log N)$, but this is worse that the naive upper bound of N, which can be obtained by setting the color of π to be $\pi^{-1}(1)$. (By definition of adjacency this is a valid coloring.) Our main technical contribution is in obtaining some non-trivial upper bounds on the chromatic number of this graph.

To derive our upper bounds, we look at "coarsened" versions of the graph $\mathcal{U}_{N,\ell}$. For positive integer k, we say that $\pi : [k] \to [N]$ is a *k-subpermutation* if π is injective. We let $S_{N,k}$ denoted the set of all k-subpermutations on $[N]$. For $k' \geq k$, we say subpermutation $\pi : [k] \to [N]$ *extends* the subpermutation $\sigma : [k'] \to [N]$ if $\sigma(i) = \pi(i)$ for all $i \in [k]$. For k-subpermutations π and σ, we let $\delta(\pi, \sigma) = \min_{\pi', \sigma' \in S_N \text{ extending } \pi, \sigma}\{\delta(\pi', \sigma')\}$.

DEFINITION 1.6 (RESTRICTED UNCERTAINTY GRAPHS). *For integers N, ℓ and k the k-restricted uncertainty graph $\mathcal{U}_{N,\ell,k}$ has elements of $S_{N,k}$ as its vertices, with $\pi \leftarrow \sigma$ if (1) $\pi(1) \neq \sigma(1)$ and $\delta(\pi, \sigma) \leq \ell$.*

Note that $\mathcal{U}_{N,\ell,N} = \mathcal{U}_{N,\ell}$. We derive our upper bounds on the chromatic number of $\mathcal{U}_{N,\ell}$ by giving non-trivial upper bounds on the chromatic number of $\mathcal{U}_{N,\ell,k}$.

LEMMA 1.7.

1. *For every $k \leq k'$, $\chi(\mathcal{U}_{N,\ell,k'}) \leq \chi(\mathcal{U}_{N,\ell,k})$.*
2. *For every N, ℓ, $\chi(\mathcal{U}_{N,\ell,2\ell}) \leq O(\ell^2 \log N)$.*
3. *For every N, ℓ and k that is an integral multiple of ℓ, we have $\chi(\mathcal{U}_{N,\ell,k}) \leq 2^{O(k \log \ell)} \log^{(k/\ell)} N$.*
4. *For every N, ℓ and k that is an integral multiple of ℓ, we have $\chi(\mathcal{U}_{N,\ell,k}) \geq \log^{(2k/\ell)}(N/\ell)$.*

As an immediate application we get the following theorem.

THEOREM 1.8. *For every N and ℓ, we have $\chi(\mathcal{U}_{N,\ell}) \leq O\left(\min\{\ell^2 \log N, 2^{O(\ell \log \ell \log^* N)}\}\right)$.*

Unfortunately, the lower bound from Part (4) of Lemma 1.7 goes to 0 as $k \to N$ and so we don't get a growing function of N as a lower bound. However, it does rule out most natural strategies for coloring $\mathcal{U}$, and shows limitations of the *intuition* that suggests $\mathcal{U}$ may be colorable with $f(\ell)$ colors independent of N. This is so since the intuition, as well most natural strategies, only use the top $O(\ell)$ ranking elements of a permutation π to determine its color; and such the lower bound shows that such strategies are inherently limited. In particular, it shows that there is no hope to extend the methods of Juba et al. (which was based on this intuition) in a simple way to get a deterministic UCS.

[1] The fractional chromatic number of a graph G is the smallest positive real w such that there exists a collection of independent sets $I_1, \ldots, I_t$ in G with weights $w_1, \ldots, w_t$ such that $\sum_{j=1}^{t} w_j = w$ and for every vertex $u \in V(G)$ it is the case that $\sum_{j: I_j \ni u} w_j \geq 1$.

1.5 Directions for further work

Given that most of the questions raised in this work haven't found tight answers, there is an obvious number of natural questions to resolve here — the most fundamental one being whether one can compress information down to its entropy (to within constant multiplicative factors) deterministically (or even just with private randomness) in the uncertain setting.

In addition to resolving open questions, a number of modelling challenges remain in trying to understand natural modes of communication. Language is an organically evolved concept with communicational, computational and societal pressures acting on it. The game that was played out with natural languages over the past millenia is now getting played out at a faster pace among computer networks: Protocols evolve, compete for survival, and develop a strange mix of tolerance for errors with intolerance for others. Most of the mechanics have not been studied mathematically and indeed little is known as to what the evolution process is trying to achieve, and what the steady state might look like, if at all one exists. Understanding aspects of language and its evolution definitely seem to be worthy causes.

One aspect in particular that we have not explored is the impact of "computational efficiency" of the encoding or decoding procedures. One of the reasons to set aside this concern for the time being is that ingredients like the dictionary suggest that natural language seems not to pay serious attention to the complexity of encoding/decoding relying instead on table look up for much of its performance; and tables don't appear to be particularly compact. Nevertheless, efficiency perhaps does play a significant role in the evolution of languages since some changes are more easy for humans to adapt to, as opposed to others. Understanding this aspect of efficiency is probably another challenge for the future.

Organization of this paper..

We start with the analysis of the chromatic number in Section 2. We then use the methods to build uncertain compression schemes in Section 3. Proofs omitted from this version may be found in the full version of the paper [5].

2. UNCERTAINTY GRAPHS

We start with some elementary material in Section 2.1 that already allows us to prove Parts (1) and (2) of Lemma 1.7. The lower bound mentioned in Part (4) of Lemma 1.7 follows also relatively easily from a result of Linial [10] and we show this in Section 2.2. Our main contribution, in Section 2.3, gives the upper bound from Part (3) of Lemma 1.7.

2.1 Preliminaries

We recall the concept of a homomorphism of graphs: For graph $G = (V, E)$ and $G' = (V', E')$, we say that $\phi : V \to V'$ is a homomorphism from G to G' if $(u, v) \in E \Rightarrow (\phi(u), \phi(v)) \in E'$. We say G is homomorphic to G' if there exists a homomorphism from G to G'.

PROPOSITION 2.1. *For every N, $\ell \geq 1$ and $k' \leq k \leq N$, the k-restricted uncertainty graph $\mathcal{U}_{N,\ell,k}$ is homomorphic to the k'-restricted uncertainty graph $\mathcal{U}_{N,\ell,k'}$.*

PROOF. We construct the homomorphism ϕ from $\mathcal{U}_{N,\ell,k}$ to $\mathcal{U}_{N,\ell,k'}$ as follows: For $\pi = \langle \pi(1), \ldots, \pi(k) \rangle \in S_{N,k}$ let $\phi(\pi) = \langle \pi(1), \ldots, \pi(k') \rangle \in S_{N,k'}$. >From the definitions it follows that this is a homomorphism. □

PROPOSITION 2.2. . *For every G and G' such that G is homomorphic to G', we have $\chi(G) \leq \chi(G')$.*

PROOF. Follows from the composability of homomorphisms and the fact that G is k-colorable if and only if it is homomorphic to K_k, the complete graph on k vertices. □

Part (1) of Lemma 1.7 follows immediately from Propositions 2.1 and 2.2.

PROPOSITION 2.3. *For every N, ℓ, and $k \geq \ell+1$ the fractional chromatic number of the restricted uncertainty graph $\mathcal{U}_{N,\ell,k}$ is at most 4ℓ.*

PROOF. For every function $f : [N] \to [2\ell]$ we associate the set $I_f = \{\pi \in S_{N,k} | f(\pi(1)) = 1 \text{ and } f(\pi(j)) \neq 1 \ \forall\, j \in \{2, \ldots, \ell+1\}\}$.

We claim that I_f is an independent set of $\mathcal{U}_{N,\ell,k}$ for every f. To see this consider an edge (π, σ) and suppose $\pi \in I_f$. Then $\sigma(1) \in \{\pi(2), \ldots, \pi(\ell+1)\}$ and so $f(\sigma(1)) \neq 1$ and so $\sigma \notin I_f$.

Next we note that for every π, the probability that $\pi \in I_f$ for f chosen uniformly at random is $1/(2\ell) \cdot (1 - 1/(2\ell))^\ell \geq 1/(4\ell)$.

Thus if we give each I_f a weight of $4\ell/(2\ell)^N$, then we have that the weight of independent sets containing any given vertex π is at least one, while the sum of all weights is 4ℓ, thus yielding the claimed bound on the fractional chromatic number. □

The following is a well-known connection between fractional chromatic number and chromatic number.

PROPOSITION 2.4. *For every graph G, $\chi(G) \leq \chi_f(G) \cdot \ln |V(G)|$.*

We are now ready to prove part (2) of Lemma 1.7.

LEMMA 2.5. $\chi(\mathcal{U}_{N,\ell}) \leq \chi(\mathcal{U}_{N,\ell,\ell+1})) \leq 4\ell(\ell+1) \ln N$

PROOF. The first inequality follows from Propositions 2.1 and 2.2. The second one follows from Proposition 2.4 and 2.3 and the fact that $\mathcal{U}_{N,\ell,\ell+1}$ has at most $N^{\ell+1}$ vertices. □

2.2 Lower Bound on Chromatic Number

We now prove Part (4) of Lemma 1.7 giving a lower bound on $\chi(\mathcal{U}_{N,\ell,k})$. We use a lower bound on a somewhat related family of graphs due to Linial [10].

DEFINITION 2.6 (SHIFT GRAPHS). *For integers N and $k < N$, we say that $\pi \in S_{N,k}$ is a* left shift *of $\sigma \in S_{N,k}$ if $\pi(i) = \sigma(i+1)$ for $i \in [k-1]$ and $\pi(k) \neq \sigma(1)$. We say π is a* right shift *of σ if σ is a left shift of π, and we say π is a shift of σ if π is a left shift or a right shift of σ. For integers N and k, the shift graph $\mathcal{S}_{N,k}$ is given by $V(\mathcal{S}_{N,k}) = S_{N,k}$ with $(\pi, \sigma) \in E(\mathcal{S}_{N,k})$ if π is a shift of σ.*

THEOREM 2.7 (LINIAL [10, PROOF OF THEOREM 2.1]). *For every odd k, $\chi(\mathcal{S}_{N,k}) \geq \log^{(k-1)} N$.*

(We note that the notation in [10] is somewhat different: The graph $\mathcal{S}_{N,k}$ is denoted $B_{N,t}$ for $t = (k-1)/2$ in [10].)

We show that the uncertainty graphs contain a subgraph isomorphic to the shift graph. This gives us our lower bound on the chromatic number of uncertainty graphs.

LEMMA 2.8. *For every N, ℓ and k that is an integral multiple of ℓ, we have $\chi(\mathcal{U}_{N,\ell,k}) \geq (\log^{(2k/\ell)}(N/\ell))$.*

PROOF. First without loss of generality we only consider the case of even ℓ. Then we reduce to the case $\ell = 2$, by considering only those permutations π which fix $\pi(i) = i$ if $\ell/2$ does not divide i. This still leaves us with $2N/\ell$ unfixed elements and subpermutations from $S_{2N/\ell,2k/\ell}$ that are within distance 2 of each other are within distance ℓ when mapped back to $S_{N,k}$.

So we assume $\ell = 2$ and show that $\mathcal{U}_{N,2,k}$ contains a subgraph isomorphic to the shift graph $\mathcal{S}_{N,k}$. Consider the map ϕ from $V(\mathcal{S}_{N,k})$ to $V(\mathcal{U}_{N,2,k})$ which sends $\pi = \langle\pi(1),\ldots,\pi(k)\rangle$ to $\phi(\pi) = \sigma = \langle\sigma(1),\ldots,\sigma(k)\rangle$ as follows: Let $t = \lfloor k/2 \rfloor$. Then $\sigma(2i) = \pi(t+i)$ and $\sigma(2i+1) = \pi(t-i)$ $\sigma(t+i) = \pi(2i)$ and $\sigma(t-i) = \pi(2i+1)$. It is easy to verify that the map is a bijection and if π and π' are shifts of each other, then $\phi(\pi)$ and $\phi(\pi')$ are within distance 2 of each other. It follows that $\mathcal{U}_{N,2,k}$ contains a copy of $\mathcal{S}_{N,k}$ and so $\chi(\mathcal{U}_{N,2,k}) \geq \chi(\mathcal{S}_{N,k}) \geq log^{(k-1)}N$. □

2.3 Upper Bound on Chromatic Number

In this section we give an upper bound on the chromatic number of the uncertainty graphs. We first describe our strategy. Fix N and ℓ. Now for every k, we know that there is a homomorphism from $\mathcal{U}_{N,\ell,k}$ to $\mathcal{U}_{N,\ell,k-1}$. However we note that if we jump from $\mathcal{U}_{N,\ell,k}$ to $\mathcal{U}_{N,\ell,k-\ell}$ then the homomorphism has an even nicer property. To describe this property, we introduce a new parameter associated with the homomorphism from $\mathcal{U}_{N,\ell,k}$ to $\mathcal{U}_{N,\ell,k-\ell}$. Let us denote this homomorphism ϕ_k. For $\pi \in S_{N,k}$ let $d_k(\pi) = |\{\phi_k(\sigma) \mid (\pi,\sigma) \in E(\mathcal{U}_{N,\ell,k})\}|$. Note that $d_k(\pi)$ is independent of π and so we just denote it d_k. We note first that d_k is small.

Recall that $\phi_k : S_{N,k} \to S_{N,k-\ell}$ and maps $\pi : [k] \to [N]$ to $\pi' : [k-\ell] \to [N]$ by setting $\pi'(i) = \pi(i)$.

CLAIM 2.9. *For every k, $d_k \leq (2\ell+1)^k$.*

PROOF. Let $(\sigma,\pi) \in E(\mathcal{U}_{N,\ell,k})$ then $\delta(\sigma,\pi) \leq \ell$. In particular for every $i \in [k-\ell]$, we have there exists $j(i) \in \{-\ell,\ldots,\ell\}$ such that $\sigma(i) = \pi(i+j(i))$. Thus the sequence $j(1),\ldots,j(k-\ell)$ completely specifies $\phi_k(\sigma)$. Since the number of such sequences is at most $(2\ell+1)^{k-\ell}$, we get our claim. □

The next lemma shows that a homomorphism with a small d-value yields especially good colorings.

LEMMA 2.10. *Let ϕ be a homomorphism from G to H and let $c = \chi(H)$ and $d = \max_{v \in V(G)} |\{\phi(w) \mid (v,w) \in E(G)\}|$. Then $\chi(G) \leq 2d(d+1)\log c = O(d^2 \log c)$.*

PROOF. For integers t and M, we start by building a small family of hash functions $\mathcal{H} = \{h_1,\ldots,h_M\} \subseteq \{h : [c] \to [t]\}$ with the property that for every subset $S \subseteq [c]$, with $|S| \leq d$, and for every $i \in [c] - S$, there exists $j \in [M]$ such that $h_j(i) \notin \{h_j(i') | i' \in S\}$.

Given such a hash family, we claim there is a coloring of G with $t \cdot M$ colors. To get such a coloring, let χ' be a coloring of H with colors $[c]$. Now, consider $v \in V(G)$ and let $S_v = \{\chi'(\phi(w)) \mid (w,v) \in E(H)\}$. By the definition of d, we have $|S_v| \leq d$. Also since χ' is a coloring of H and ϕ is a homomorphism, we have $\chi'(\phi(v)) \notin S_v$. Thus by the property of $\mathcal{H}$, we have that there exists a $j = j(v)$ such that $h_j(\chi'(\phi(v)) \notin \{h_j(i') | i' \in S_v\}$. We let the coloring χ of G be $\chi(v) = (j(v), h_{j(v)}(\chi'(\phi(v))\}$. Syntactically it is clear that this is a $t \cdot M$ coloring of G. To see it is valid, consider $(v,w) \in E(G)$. If $j(v) \neq j(w)$ then we are done. Else, suppose $j(v) = j(w) = j$. Then by definition of S_v we have $\chi'(\phi(w)) \in S_v$ and so $h_j(\chi'(v)) \neq h_j(\chi'(w)) \in \{h_j(i) | i \in S_v\}$, and thus $\chi(v) \neq \chi(w)$ as desired.

To conclude we need to give an upper bound on t and M.

CLAIM 2.11. *There exists such a hash family with $t \leq 2d$ and $M \leq \log(c^{d+1})$.*

PROOF. The proof is an elementary probabilistic method argument. Let $t = 2d$. We pick members of $\mathcal{H}$ at uniformly at random from $\{h : [c] \to [t]\}$. Fix a set S with $|S| \leq d$ and $i \in [c] - S$. Say that h separates i from S if $h(i) \notin \{h(i') | i' \in S\}$. The probability that a random h separates i from S is at least $1/2$ and the probability that there does not exist $h \in \mathcal{H}$ separating i from S is at most 2^{-M}. The probability that there exists S and $i \in [c] - S$ such that there does not exist $h \in \mathcal{H}$ separating i from S is strictly less than $c^{d+1} \cdot 2^{-M}$. It follows that if $M = \log c^{d+1}$ then such a family $\mathcal{H}$ exists. □

The lemma follows.

We are now ready to prove Part (3) of Lemma 1.7, restated below.

LEMMA 2.12. *There exists a constant c such that for every N, ℓ, k, we have $\chi(\mathcal{U}_{N,\ell,k}) \leq 2^{ck\log\ell} \log^{(\lfloor (k-1)/\ell \rfloor - 1)} N$.*

PROOF. We prove the lemma by induction on k. For notational simplicity assume $k-1$ is a multiple of ℓ. For $k \leq \ell$ the lemma is immediate from the fact that $\chi(\mathcal{U}_{N,\ell,1}) \leq N$. Assume the lemma is true for $k-\ell$. Then, by Lemma 2.10 we have that for $\chi(\mathcal{U}_{N,\ell,k}) \leq 2d_k(d_k+1) \cdot \log(\chi(\mathcal{U}_{N,\ell,k-\ell})) \leq 4d_k^2 \log \chi(\mathcal{U}_{N,\ell,k-\ell})$. By Claim 2.9, $d_k \leq (2\ell+1)^k \leq (4\ell)^k$ and so for $\chi(\mathcal{U}_{N,\ell,k}) \leq 4(4\ell)^{2k} \log(2^{c(k-\ell)\log\ell} \log^{(k-\ell-1)/ell} N \leq 2^{ck\log\ell} \log^{(k-1)/\ell)} N$ for a suitably large c. □

3. UNCERTAIN COMMUNICATION

We now convert some of the methods from the previous section into schemes for uncertain compression. In Section 3.1 we derive a simple compression scheme based on the relationship between fractional chromatic number and chromatic number from Section 2.1. We then use the "nested series of homomorphisms" from Section 2.3 to derive a second compression scheme in Section 3.2. The compression scheme of Section 3.2 can make errors with positive probability and has a non-linear dependence on entropy. In Section 3.3 we show that for some natural distributions, this scheme is error-free. In Section 3.4 we show how an error-free scheme working for all distributions would automatically have linear dependence on the entropy, suggesting some of the weaknesses in Section 3.2 are necessary.

3.1 A simple, zero-error compression scheme

Our first construction uses the notion of an isolating hash family as defined implicitly in Section 2.3, which we make explicit now. For positive integers ℓ, N and $m \in [N]$ and $S \subseteq [N] - \{m\}$, we say that a function $h : [N] \to \{0,1\}^\ell$ isolates m from S if $h(m) \notin \{h(m') | m' \in S\}$. We say that a hash family $\mathcal{H}_\ell = \{h_{1,\ell},\ldots,h_{M,\ell}\}$ is *(N,ℓ)-isolating* if for every $S \subseteq [N]$ with $|S| \leq 2^{\ell-1}$, and for every $m \in [N] - S$, there exists $j = j(m, S)$ such that $h_{j,\ell}(m) \notin h_{j,\ell}(S) \triangleq \{h_{j,\ell}(m') | m' \in S\}$.

We note first that small isolating families exist and then give a compression scheme based on small isolating families.

LEMMA 3.1. *For every ℓ and N, there exists an (N, ℓ)-isolating family of size at most $2^\ell \cdot \log N$.*

PROOF. The proof is straightforward application of the probabilistic method. We pick $\mathcal{H} = \{h_1, \ldots, h_M\}$ by picking h_i uniformly and independently from the set of all functions from $[N]$ to $\{0,1\}^\ell$. Fix $m \notin S \subseteq [N]$. The probability that a randomly chosen h isolates m from S is at least $1/2$. Thus the probability that some h_i in $\mathcal{H}$ does not isolate m from S is at most 2^{-M}. Taking the union bound over all m, S we find that the probability that $\mathcal{H}$ does not isolate some m from S is at most $N^{2^\ell}/2^M$. We conclude that $M \leq 2^\ell \cdot \log N$ suffices for the existence of such a $\mathcal{H}$. □

We are now ready to describe our encoding and decoding schemes.

Encoding: Given m, P let $S = \{m' \in [N] \setminus \{m\} \mid P(m') \geq P(m)/2^{2\Delta}\}$ and let $\ell = \log_2 1/P(m) + 2\Delta$. Let $\mathcal{H}$ be an (N, ℓ)-isolating family of size M and let $\mathcal{H} = \{h_{1,\ell}, \ldots, h_{M,\ell}\}$. Now let $j \in [M]$ be such that $h_{j,\ell}(m) \notin \{h_{j,\ell}(m') \mid m' \in S\}$. The encoding $E(P, m)$ is defined to be $(j, h_{j,\ell}(m))$.

Decoding: Given Q and $y = (j, z) \in \mathbb{Z}^+ \times \{0,1\}^*$, let $\ell = |z|$ and let $\hat{m} = \text{argmax}_{m \in [N]: h_{j,\ell}(m) = z}\{Q(m)\}$. The decoding of the pair (Q, y) is given by $D(Q, y) = \hat{m}$.

Our next proposition verifies the correctness of the compression scheme.

PROPOSITION 3.2. *For every pair of distributions P, Q such that $\delta(P, Q) \leq \Delta$, and for every message $m \in [N]$, it is the case that $D(Q, E(P, m)) = m$.*

PROOF. Fix P, Q and m such that $\delta(P, Q) \leq \Delta$. Let $E(m, P) = (j, z)$ with $\ell = |z|$ and let $D((j, z), Q) = \hat{m}$. We will show that $\hat{m} = m$. By definition of E, we have $h_{j,\ell}(m) = z$ and by definition of D we have $h_{j,\ell}(\hat{m}) = z$. Thus, by the condition that $\hat{m}$ maximizes probability under Q of messages satisfying $h_{j,\ell}(m') = z$, we have $Q(\hat{m}) \geq Q(m)$. Since the distance of P and Q is at most Δ, we have $P(m) \leq Q(m)2^\Delta$ and $P(\hat{m}) \geq Q(\hat{m})/2^\Delta$. Combining the inequalities we get $P(\hat{m}) \geq P(m)/2^{2\Delta}$. Now let $S = \{m' \in [N] - \{m\} \mid P(m') \geq P(m)/2^{2\Delta}\}$. We have $\hat{m} \in S \cup \{m\}$. But by definition of j, we have $h_{j,\ell}(m) \notin \{h_{j,\ell}(m') | m' \in S\}$ and since $h_{j,\ell}(m) = h_{j,\ell}(\hat{m})$, we must have $m = \hat{m}$. □

Finally we analyze the performance of our scheme.

LEMMA 3.3. *The expected length of the encoding E is $O(H(P) + \Delta + \log\log N)$.*

PROOF. Fix $m \in S$. Then we have $\ell \leq 1 + \log 1/P(m) + 2\Delta$ and $M \leq (2^\ell \log N)$. Thus, the length of $E(P, m)$ is at most $2\ell + \log\log N = O(\log 1/P(m) + \Delta + \log\log N)$. Taking expectation over m drawn from P, we have the expected length of the encoding is at most $O(H(P) + \Delta + \log\log N)$. □

Theorem 1.3 follows immediately from Proposition 3.2 and Lemma 3.3.

3.2 Compression with error in the low entropy setting

Our compression for the low entropy setting (with better dependence on N) relies on an extension of our coloring scheme for the uncertainty graphs. We describe this extension in the next section and then use that to present our compression scheme afterwards.

3.2.1 Compression for chains

We start with some terminology. We say that a finite sequence of sets $A_0, \ldots, A_k$ with $A_i \subseteq [N]$ is a *chain* in $[N]$ if $|A_0| = 1$ and $A_i \subseteq A_{i+1}$ for every i. We say that w is the *leader* of the chain if $A_0 = \{w\}$. We use Chain(N) to denote the set of all chains in $[N]$.

In this section we will show how to compress the leader of a chain so that it is unambiguous relative to "nearby" chains. This is in the spirit of the coloring of uncertainty graphs. Indeed vertices of the uncertainty graph $\mathcal{U}_{N,\ell,k}$ correspond to chains with the vertex $\langle\pi(1), \ldots, \pi(k)\rangle$ corresponding to the chain $\mathcal{A}$ with $A_0 = \{\pi(1)\}$ and $A_i = \{\pi(1), \ldots, \pi(\ell \cdot i)\}$ for $i \geq 1$. The compressing scheme will thus be similar to the coloring scheme, however there are two distinguishing factors: We will want to compress some chains more than others - a notion that would correspond to asking some vertices to use small colors while allowing others to use larger ones. Furthermore our chains will now grow arbitrarily fast (and not just in steps of 1 or more generally ℓ). We now describe the precise problem.

For a chain $\mathcal{A} = \langle A_0, \ldots, A_k\rangle$ we say the length of the chain, denoted lgt$(\mathcal{A})$, is the parameter k. We use sz$(\mathcal{A})$ denote the size of the final set $|A_k|$. For a chain $\mathcal{A}$ of length at least i, we let $\mathcal{A}_i$ denote its prefix of length i, i.e., $\mathcal{A}_i = \langle A_0, \ldots, A_i\rangle$.

For chain $\mathcal{A} = \langle A_0, \ldots, A_k\rangle$ and chain $\mathcal{B} = \langle B_0, \ldots, B_{k-d}\rangle$, we say $\mathcal{B}$ is within distance d from $\mathcal{A}$ if for all $i \in \{0, ..., k-d\}$, $A_{i-d} \subseteq B_i \subseteq A_{i+d}$ (where we consider sets with negative index to be the empty set). We denote the set of all chains that are within d distance from $\mathcal{A}$ by $S^d(\mathcal{A})$. Our goal next is to compress the leader of chains so that the length of the compression is small as a function of sz$(\mathcal{A})$, while it remains unambiguous to chains that are nearby.

LEMMA 3.4. *There exists a coloring scheme* Col : $\mathbb{Z}^+ \times$ Chain$(N) \to \mathbb{Z}^+$ *with the following properties:*

1. *If* lgt$(\mathcal{A}) \geq 2k$, *then for every $s \geq$* sz$(\mathcal{A}_{2k})$, Col$(s, \mathcal{A}_{2k}) \leq 2^{6(s+1)} \log^{(k)} N$.
2. *Let $\mathcal{A}$ and $\mathcal{A}'$ be chains of the same length, with* lgt$(\mathcal{A}) \geq 2k$ *and of size at most s. Then, if $S^1(\mathcal{A}) \cap S^1(\mathcal{A}') \neq \emptyset$ and $A_0 \neq A'_0$, then* Col$(s, \mathcal{A}_{2k}) \neq$ Col$(s, \mathcal{A}'_{2k})$.

Proof omitted from this version.

3.2.2 The Compression Scheme

We are now ready to define our final compression scheme.

Encoding: Given m, P define $r = \lfloor -\log P(m) \rfloor$ and $f = 2\lfloor \log^* N \rfloor - 1$. Further define the chain $\mathcal{A}$ of length f as follows. $A_0 = \{m\}$ and $A_k = \{m' \in [N] \mid |\log 1/P(m') - r| \leq \Delta(k+1) + 1\}$ (so that A_k is the set of messages of probability roughly $P(m)$ with the difference in logarithms being at most $(k+1)\Delta+1$). Let $s = \mathrm{sz}(\mathcal{A})$. The encoding $E_{\mathrm{low}}(P,m) = E(P,m)$ is

$$E(P,m) = \begin{cases} (s, r, \mathrm{Col}(s, \mathcal{A})) & \text{if } s \le 2^{\frac{H(P)}{\epsilon}+2\Delta\log^* N+1} \\ \perp & \text{otherwise.} \end{cases}$$

(We assume that s and r above are encoded in some prefix-free encoding, so that the receiver can separate the three parts.)

Decoding: The decoding function $D_{\mathrm{low}}(Q,y) = D(Q,y)$ works as follows: If $y = \perp$ then the decoder outputs $\perp$. Else let $y = (s,r,c)$ and let $f = 2\lfloor \log^* N \rfloor - 1$. Let $\mathcal{B} = \langle B_0, \ldots, B_{f-1}\rangle$ be as follows: $B_0 = \{w\}$ for some w such that $|\log 1/Q(w) - r| \le \Delta + 1$. For $k \ge 1$, $B_k = \{m' \mid |\log 1/Q(m') - r| \le (k+1)\Delta + 1\}$. Find a chain $\mathcal{A}'$ with the following properties: $\mathcal{B} \in S^1(\mathcal{A}')$, $\mathrm{lgt}(\mathcal{A}') = f$, $\mathrm{sz}(\mathcal{A}') \le s$ and $\mathrm{Col}(s, \mathcal{A}') = c$. Let $\hat{m}$ be the leader of $\mathcal{A}'$. The decoding $D(Q,y)$ is set to be $\hat{m}$.

We first analyze the correctness of the decoder.

LEMMA 3.5. *For every pair of distributions P, Q such that $\delta(P,Q) \le \Delta$ and for every message $m \in [N]$ such that $E_{\mathrm{low}}(P,m) \ne \perp$, it holds that $D_{\mathrm{low}}(Q, E_{\mathrm{low}}(P,m)) = m$.*

PROOF. Fix $P \in \mathcal{P}([N])$ and a message $m \in [N]$ such that $E_{\mathrm{low}}(P,m) \ne \perp$. The following claims will show that the decoding process is well defined (and then correctness will be essentially be immediate).

CLAIM 3.6. *There exists $w \in [N]$ such that $|\log 1/Q(w) - r| \le \Delta + 1$.*

PROOF. By our choice of r, we have $|\log 1/P(m) - r| \le 1$. Now using $\delta(P,Q) \le \Delta$, we have $|\log 1/P(m) - \log 1/Q(m)| \le \Delta$, and so $|\log 1/Q(m) - r| \le \Delta + 1$. So $w = m$ gives an element in $[N]$ with the desired property. □

Thus the chain $\mathcal{B}$ is now well-defined. It remains to show that there exists a chain $\mathcal{A}'$ satisfying the required properties. The next claim shows that $\mathcal{B} \in S^1(\mathcal{A})$, therefore $\mathcal{A}$ is a candidate for the role of $\mathcal{A}'$.

CLAIM 3.7. $\mathcal{B} \in S^1(\mathcal{A})$.

PROOF. The proof follows easily from our choice of $\mathcal{A}$, $\mathcal{B}$ and the fact that P and Q are Δ-close. Let $k \in \{0, ..., f-1\}$. We need to show that B_k is sandwiched between A_{k-1} and A_{k+1}.

First, We will show that $B_k \subseteq A_{k+1}$. When $k = 0$, we need to show that $w \in A_1$. Indeed,

$$\begin{aligned} & |\log 1/Q(w) - r| \le \Delta + 1 \\ \Rightarrow\ & |\log 1/P(w) - r| \le 2\Delta + 1 \\ \Rightarrow\ & w \in A_1 \ . \end{aligned}$$

Now consider $1 \le k \le f-1$. We have,

$$\begin{aligned} B_k &= \{m' \in [N] \mid |\log 1/Q(m') - r| \le (k+1)\Delta + 1\} \\ &\subseteq \{m' \in [N] \mid |\log 1/P(m') - r| \le (k+2)\Delta + 1\} \\ &= A_{k+1} \ . \end{aligned}$$

This shows that $B_k \subseteq A_{k+1}$. Next we show that $A_{k-1} \subseteq B_k$, for $2 \le k \le f-1$. We have

$$\begin{aligned} A_{k-1} &= \{m' \in [N] \mid |\log 1/P(m') - r| \le k\Delta + 1\} \\ &\subseteq \{m' \in [N] \mid |\log 1/Q(m') - r| \le (k+1)\Delta + 1\} \\ &= B_k \ . \end{aligned}$$

The case where $k = 1$ and $w \in B_1$ was proved in Claim 3.6. So we are done. □

To conclude, the decoder can find a chain $\mathcal{A}'$ such that $\mathrm{sz}(\mathcal{A}') \le s$, $\mathrm{lgt}(\mathcal{A}') = \mathrm{lgt}(\mathcal{A})$, $\mathrm{Col}(s, \mathcal{A}') = \mathrm{Col}(s, \mathcal{A})$ and there exists a chain $\mathcal{B} \in S^1(\mathcal{A}') \cap S^1(\mathcal{A})$. >From Lemma 3.4 the leader of A' is m as required.

We are now ready to prove Theorem 1.4.

PROOF. We now estimate the probability that the encoder will fail. Fix some probability P and a message m such that $E(P,m) = \perp$. We will first show that $P(m) \le 2^{-\frac{H(P)}{\epsilon}}$. Later, we will bound the probability that "m has such small probability" by ϵ.

Consider the chain $\mathcal{A} = \langle A_0, \ldots, A_f \rangle$ as defined by the encoder. In this case, the size of the largest set, $|A_f|$, is more then the threshold $T = 2^{\frac{H(P)}{\epsilon}+2\Delta\log^* N+1}$. So, there is some element $m' \in A_f$ such that $P(m') \le \frac{1}{T}$. By our choice of A_f, $P(m') \ge 2^{-\lfloor -\log P(m) \rfloor - (f+1)\Delta - 1} \ge P(m)2^{-2\Delta\log^* N - 1}$. Calculating,

$$\frac{1}{T} \ge P(m)2^{-2\Delta\log^* N-1} \Rightarrow P(m) \le \frac{2^{2\Delta\log^* N+1}}{T} = 2^{-\frac{H(P)}{\epsilon}}$$

Therefore, we can bound the failure probability by the probability that $P(m) \le 2^{-\frac{H(P)}{\epsilon}}$. Using the fact that $\mathbf{E}_{m \leftarrow P[N]}\left[\log \frac{1}{P(m)}\right] = H(P)$, we deduce the following by Markov's inequality,

$$\Pr_{m \leftarrow P[N]}\left[P(m) \le 2^{-\frac{H(P)}{\epsilon}}\right] = \Pr_{m \leftarrow P[N]}\left[\log \frac{1}{P(m)} \ge \frac{H(P)}{\epsilon}\right] \le \epsilon$$

We will finish the proof by bounding the performance of the scheme. To this end consider a distribution P and a message $m \in [N]$ such that $E(P,m) \ne \perp$ (i.e $\mathrm{sz}(\mathcal{A}) \le T$). The encoder sends $r = \lfloor -\log P(m) \rfloor$, $s = \mathrm{sz}(\mathcal{A})$ and $\mathrm{Col}(s, \mathcal{A})$. We first analyze the contribution of sending r to the performance. Because $\log|r| = O\left(\log(\frac{1}{P(m)})\right)$, the accepted length of sending r in a prefix-free encoding is at most $O\left(\mathbf{E}_{m \leftarrow P[N]} \log(\frac{1}{P(m)})\right) = O(H(P))$.

Now we analyze the length of $(s, \mathrm{Col}(s, \mathcal{A}))$. By Lemma 3.4:

$$C(s, \mathcal{A}) \le 2^{6(s+1)} \log^{(f)} N = 2^{O(s)}$$

Hence, the length of $(s, \mathrm{Col}(s, \mathcal{A}))$ is at most

$$O(\log s) + \log C(s, \mathcal{A}) = O(s) = 2^{\frac{H(P)}{\epsilon}+2\Delta\log^* n+O(1)} \ .$$

Thus, from the linearity of expectations, it follow that the total performance is at most $2^{\frac{H(P)}{\epsilon}+2\Delta\log^* n+O(1)}$. □

3.3 Error-free Compression for Natural Distributions

In this section we will show that for a large class of natural distributions, the above scheme is error free. We start by describing the natural distributions we can capture.

We say that a distribution $P \in \mathcal{P}([N])$ is *flat* it there exists a set $S \subseteq [N]$ such that P is uniform on S. The distribution is called *geometric* if there exists parameter $\alpha \in (0,1)$ and a permutation π on $[N]$ such that for all $k \in [N-1]$ it holds that $P(\pi(k+1)) = \alpha P(\pi(k))$. We call P *binomial* if there exists a parameter $p \in (0,1)$ and a permutation π on $[N]$

such that $\forall k \in [N]$, $P(\pi(k)) = \binom{N}{k} p^k (1-p)^{n-k}$. The sets of all flat, geometric and binomial distributions over $[N]$ are denoted by Flat_N, Geo_N and Bin_N respectively.

The following theorem shows that the scheme $(E_{\text{low}}, D_{\text{low}})$ performs well *without error* on all of the above natural distributions. Moreover, this theorem is stable in the sense that the guarantee on the performance holds even if a distribution is only close to one of the above-mentioned natural distributions.

THEOREM 3.8. *Let* $\mathcal{F} \triangleq \text{Flat}_N \cup \text{Geo}_N \cup \text{Bin}_N$ *and* $L(P) \triangleq 2^{H(P)} \lceil \Delta \log^* N \rceil$. *Then the scheme* $(E_{\text{low}}, D_{\text{low}})$ *(with* ϵ *set to* 0*) is a* $(\Delta, 0, \mathcal{F}, O(L(P)))$*-UCS. Moreover, if* $P \in \mathcal{P}([N])$ *is* $\Delta \log^* N$*-close to a distribution* $\tilde{P} \in \mathcal{F}$ *then the performance of the scheme on* P *is* $\mathbf{E}_{m \leftarrow_P U}[|E(P,m)|] = O\left(L(\tilde{P})\right)$.

We prove the theorem above by identifying a broad condition on distributions, which we call the *capacity*, and showing that the performance of our scheme is good if the capacity is small. We define this notion next, show that it is small for the distributions under consideration in Lemma 3.9 next, and finally bound the performance as a function of the capacity in Lemma 3.10 afterwards, thus leading to a proof of Theorem 3.8.

Let $P \in \mathcal{P}([N])$ be a distribution and let $S \subseteq [N]$ be its support. We say that $U \subseteq S$ is a *unit set* of P if for any two elements $m_1, m_2 \in U$ the distance $|\log P(m_1) - \log P(m_2)| \leq 1$. We define the *capacity* of P, denoted by $\mathscr{C}(P)$, to be the minimal $c \in \Re$ such that the size of every unit set of P is bounded by 2^c.

Later, we will prove the following lemma, showing that for the previously discussed distributions, the capacity is roughly the entropy.

LEMMA 3.9. *Let* $P \in \text{Flat}_N \cup \text{Geo}_N \cup \text{Bin}_N$. *Then* $\mathscr{C}(P) \leq H(P) + O(1)$.

Theorem 3.8 follows immediately from Lemma 3.9 combined with the following lemma.

LEMMA 3.10. *For every* P $(E_{\text{low}}, D_{\text{low}})$ *(with respect to* $\epsilon = 0$*) is a* $\left(\Delta, O\left(\log(H(P)) + 2^{\mathscr{C}(P)} \lceil \Delta \log^* N \rceil\right)\right)$ *scheme. Moreover, if* P *is* $\Delta \log^* N$ *close to a distribution* $\tilde{P}$*, then the performance of the scheme on* P *is* $O\left(\log(H(P)) + 2^{\mathscr{C}(\tilde{P})} \lceil \Delta \log^* N \rceil\right)$.

We omit the proofs of the lemmas above from this version.

3.4 Dependence of communication on entropy

In the previous sections we gave a scheme with performance that is exponential in the entropy. This scheme is error-free for some natural distributions and had positive error for general distributions. The next lemma shows that if we cannot find a scheme with performance that is linear in the entropy, then any scheme that we will find must have positive error for some distributions.

LEMMA 3.11. *For every non-decreasing function* $L : \Re^+ \to \Re^+$ *there exists a constant* $c = c_L$ *such that the following holds: If there exists* $(\Delta, L(H(P)))$*-UCS for some* $\Delta > 0$*, then there exists a* $(\Delta, c \cdot (1 + H(P)))$*-UCS.*

Proof omitted from this version.

4. REFERENCES

[1] M. Braverman and A. Rao. Information equals amortized communication. In R. Ostrovsky, editor, *FOCS*, pages 748–757. IEEE, 2011.

[2] R. Cole and U. Vishkin. Deterministic coin tossing with applications to optimal parallel list ranking. *Information and Control*, 70(1):32–53, 1986.

[3] T. M. Cover and J. A. Thomas. *Elements of Information Theory*. Wiley, 1991.

[4] O. Goldreich, B. Juba, and M. Sudan. A theory of goal-oriented communication. *J. ACM*, 59(2):8, 2012.

[5] E. Haramaty and M. Sudan. Deterministic compression with uncertain priors. *Electronic Colloquium on Computational Complexity (ECCC)*, 19:166, 2012.

[6] P. Harsha, R. Jain, D. A. McAllester, and J. Radhakrishnan. The communication complexity of correlation. *IEEE Transactions on Information Theory*, 56(1):438–449, 2010. Preliminary version in IEEE CCC 2007.

[7] B. Juba, A. T. Kalai, S. Khanna, and M. Sudan. Compression without a common prior: an information-theoretic justification for ambiguity in language. In B. Chazelle, editor, *ICS*, pages 79–86. Tsinghua University Press, 2011.

[8] B. Juba and M. Sudan. Universal semantic communication I. In *Proceedings of the 2008 ACM International Symposium on Theory of Computing, Victoria, British Columbia, Canada, May 17-20, 2008*, pages 123–132. ACM, 2008.

[9] E. Kushilevitz and N. Nisan. *Communication Complexity*. Cambridge University Press, 1997.

[10] N. Linial. Locality in distributed graph algorithms. *SIAM J. Comput.*, 21(1):193–201, 1992.

[11] C. E. Shannon. A mathematical theory of communication. *Bell System Technical Journal*, 27:379–423, 623–656, 1948.

[12] J. Ziv and A. Lempel. A universal algorithm for sequential data compression. *IEEE Transactions on Information Theory*, 23(3):337–342, 1977.

Faster Private Release of Marginals on Small Databases

Karthekeyan Chandrasekaran*
School of Engineering and Applied Sciences
Harvard University
karthe@seas.harvard.edu

Justin Thaler†
School of Engineering and Applied Sciences
Harvard University
jthaler@seas.harvard.edu

Jonathan Ullman‡
School of Engineering and Applied Sciences
Harvard University
jullman@seas.harvard.edu

Andrew Wan§
Simons institute for the Theory of Computing
U.C. Berkeley
atw12@seas.harvard.edu

ABSTRACT

We study the problem of answering k-*way marginal* queries on a database $D \in (\{0,1\}^d)^n$, while preserving differential privacy. The answer to a k-way marginal query is the fraction of the database's records $x \in \{0,1\}^d$ with a given value in each of a given set of up to k columns. Marginal queries enable a rich class of statistical analyses on a dataset, and designing efficient algorithms for privately answering marginal queries has been identified as an important open problem in private data analysis. For any k, we give a differentially private online algorithm that runs in time poly $\left(n, 2^{o(d)}\right)$ per query and answers any sequence of poly(n) many k-way marginal queries with error at most ± 0.01 on every query, provided $n \gtrsim d^{0.51}$. To the best of our knowledge, this is the first algorithm capable of privately answering marginal queries with a non-trivial worst-case accuracy guarantee for databases containing poly(d,k) records in time $\exp(o(d))$. Our algorithm runs the private multiplicative weights algorithm (Hardt and Rothblum, FOCS '10) on a new approximate polynomial representation of the database.

We derive our representation for the database by approximating the OR function restricted to low Hamming weight inputs using low-degree polynomials with coefficients of bounded L_1-norm. In doing so, we show new upper and lower bounds on the degree of such polynomials, which may be of independent approximation-theoretic interest.

*Supported by Simons Fellowship.

†Supported by an NSF Graduate Research Fellowship and NSF grants CNS-1011840 and CCF-0915922.

‡Supported by NSF grant CNS-1237235 and a Siebel Scholarship.

§On leave from IIIS, Tsinghua University. This work was completed while at Harvard University and supported by NSF grant CCF-0964401 and NSFC grant 61250110218.

ITCS'14, January 12–14, 2014, Princeton, New Jersey, USA.

http://dx.doi.org/10.1145/2554797.2554833.

1. INTRODUCTION

Consider a database $D \in (\{0,1\}^d)^n$ in which each of the $n(=|D|)$ rows corresponds to an individual's record, and each record consists of d binary attributes. The goal of privacy-preserving data analysis is to enable rich statistical analyses on the database while protecting the privacy of the individuals. In this work, we seek to achieve *differential privacy* [10], which guarantees that no individual's data has a significant influence on the information released about the database.

One of the most important classes of statistics on a dataset is its *marginals.* A marginal query is specified by a set $S \subseteq [d]$ and a pattern $t \in \{0,1\}^{|S|}$. The query asks, "What fraction of the individual records in D has each of the attributes $j \in S$ set to t_j?" A major open problem in privacy-preserving data analysis is to *efficiently* release a differentially private summary of the database that enables analysts to answer each of the 3^d marginal queries. A natural subclass of marginals are k-*way marginals*, the subset of marginals specified by sets $S \subseteq [d]$ such that $|S| \leq k$.

Privately answering marginal queries is a special case of the more general problem of privately answering *counting queries* on the database, which are queries of the form, "What fraction of individual records in D satisfy some property q?" Early work in differential privacy [2,9,10] showed how to privately answer any set of counting queries $\mathcal{Q}$ approximately by perturbing the answers with appropriately calibrated noise, ensuring good accuracy (say, within $\pm.01$ of the true answer) provided $|D| \gtrsim |\mathcal{Q}|^{1/2}$.

However, in many settings data is difficult or expensive to obtain, and the requirement that $|D| \gtrsim |\mathcal{Q}|^{1/2}$ is too restrictive. For instance, if the query set $\mathcal{Q}$ includes all k-way marginal queries then $|\mathcal{Q}| \geq d^{\Theta(k)}$, and it may be impractical to collect enough data to ensure $|D| \gtrsim |\mathcal{Q}|^{1/2}$, even for moderate values of k. Fortunately, a remarkable line of work initiated by Blum et al. [3] and continuing with [11, 14, 17–19, 21, 28], has shown how to privately release approximate answers to any set of counting queries, even when $|\mathcal{Q}|$ is *exponentially larger* than $|D|$. For example, the *online private multiplicative weights algorithm* of Hardt and Rothblum [19] gives accurate answers to any (possibly adaptively chosen) sequence of queries $\mathcal{Q}$ provided $|D| \gtrsim \sqrt{d} \log |\mathcal{Q}|$. Hence, if the sequence consists of all k-way marginal queries, then the algorithm will give accurate answers provided $|D| \gtrsim k\sqrt{d}$. Unfortunately, all of these algorithms have running time at least 2^d per query, even in the simplest setting where $\mathcal{Q}$ is the set of 2-way marginals.

Given this state of affairs, it is natural to seek *efficient* algorithms capable of privately releasing approximate answers to marginal queries even when $|D| \ll d^k$. The most efficient algorithm known for this problem, due to Thaler, Ullman, and Vadhan [34] (building on the work of Hardt, Rothblum, and Servedio [20]) runs in time $d^{O(\sqrt{k})}$ and releases a summary from which an analyst can compute the answer to any k-way marginal query in time $d^{O(\sqrt{k})}$.

Even though $|D|$ can be much smaller than $|\mathcal{Q}|^{1/2}$, a major drawback of this algorithm and other efficient algorithms for releasing marginals (e.g. [7,12,15,16,20]) is that the database still must be significantly larger than $\tilde{\Theta}(k\sqrt{d})$, which we know would suffice for inefficient algorithms. Recent experimental work of Hardt, Ligett, and McSherry [18] demonstrates that for some databases of interest, even the 2^d-time private multiplicative weights algorithm is practical, and also shows that more efficient algorithms based on adding independent noise do not provide good accuracy for these databases. Motivated by these findings, we believe that an important approach to designing practical algorithms is to achieve a minimum database size comparable to that of private multiplicative weights, and seek to optimize the running time of the algorithm as much as possible. In this paper we give the first algorithms for privately answering marginal queries for this parameter regime.

1.1 Our Results

In this paper we give faster algorithms for privately answering marginal queries on databases of size $\tilde{O}(d^{0.51}/\varepsilon)$, which is nearly the smallest a database can be while admitting any differentially private approximation to marginal queries [6].

THEOREM 1.1. *There exists a constant $C > 0$ such that for every $k, d, n \in \mathbb{N}$, $k \le d$, and every $\varepsilon, \delta > 0$, there is an (ε, δ)-differentially private online algorithm that, on input a database $D \in (\{0,1\}^d)^n$, runs in time*

$$\mathrm{poly}\left(n, \min\left\{\exp\left(d^{1-1/C\sqrt{k}}\right), \exp\left(d/\log^{0.99} d\right)\right\}\right)$$

per query and answers any sequence $\mathcal{Q}$ of (possibly adaptively chosen) k-way marginal queries on D up to an additive error of at most ± 0.01 on every query with probability at least 0.99, provided that $n \ge C d^{0.51} \log |\mathcal{Q}| \log(1/\delta)/\varepsilon$.

When k is much smaller than d, it may be useful to view our algorithm as an offline algorithm for releasing answers to all k-way marginal queries. This offline algorithm can be obtained simply by requesting answers to each of the $d^{\Theta(k)}$ distinct k-way marginal queries from the online mechanism. In this case we obtain the following corollary.

COROLLARY 1.2. *There exists a constant $C > 0$ such that for every $k, d, n \in \mathbb{N}$, $k = O(d/\log d)$, and every $\varepsilon, \delta > 0$, there is an (ε, δ)-differentially private offline algorithm that, on input a database $D \in (\{0,1\}^d)^n$, runs in time*

$$\mathrm{poly}\left(n, \min\left\{\exp\left(d^{1-1/C\sqrt{k}}\right), \exp\left(d/\log^{0.99} d\right)\right\}\right)$$

and, with probability at least 0.99, releases answers to every k-way marginal query on D up to an additive error of at most ± 0.01, provided that $n \ge Ckd^{0.51} \log(1/\delta)/\varepsilon$.

Here $\binom{d}{\le k} := \sum_{i=0}^{k} \binom{d}{i}$, and the number of k-way marginals on $\{0,1\}^d$ is bounded by a polynomial in this quantity. See Table 1 for a comparison of relevant results on privately answering marginal queries.

Remarks.

1. When $k = \Omega(\log^2 d)$, the minimum database size requirement can be improved to
$$n \ge Ckd^{0.5+o(1)} \log(1/\delta)/\varepsilon,$$
but we have stated the theorems with a weaker bound for simplicity. (Here $C > 0$ is a universal constant and the $o(1)$ is with respect to d.)

2. Our algorithm can be modified so that instead of releasing approximate answers to each k-way marginal explicitly, it releases a summary of the database of size $\tilde{O}(kd^{0.01})$ from which an analyst can compute an approximate answer to any k-way marginal in time $\tilde{O}(kd^{1.01})$.

A key ingredient in our algorithm is a new approximate representation of the database using polynomial approximations to the d-variate OR function restricted to inputs of Hamming weight at most k. For any such polynomial, the degree determines the runtime of our algorithm, while the L_1-weight of the coefficient vector determines the minimum required database size. Although low-degree low L_1-weight polynomial approximations to the OR function have been studied in the context of approximation theory and learning theory [29], our setting requires an approximation only over a restricted subset of the inputs. When the polynomial needs to approximate the OR function only on a subset of the inputs, is it possible to reduce the degree and $L1$-weight (in comparison to [29]) of the polynomial?

Our main technical contribution addresses this variant of the polynomial approximation problem. We believe that our construction of such polynomials (Theorem 1.3) as well as the lower bound (Theorem 1.4) could be of independent approximation-theoretic interest. The following theorem shows a construction of polynomials that achieve better degree and L_1-weight in comparison to [29] for small values of k. Let $\mathrm{OR}_d : \{-1,1\}^d \to \{-1,1\}$ denote the OR function on d variables with the convention that -1 is TRUE, and for any vector $x \in \{-1,1\}^d$, let $|x|$ denote the number of coordinates of x equal to -1.

THEOREM 1.3. *Let $k \in [d]$. For some constant $C > 0$, there exists a polynomial p such that*

(i) $|p(x) - OR_d(x)| \le 1/400$ for every $x \in \{-1,1\}^d : |x| \le k$,

Reference	Running Time per Query	Database Size
[2,9,10,13]	$O(1)$	$\widetilde{O}(d^{k/2})$
[17,19]	$2^{O(d)}$	$\widetilde{O}(k\sqrt{d})$
[20,34]	$d^{O(\sqrt{k})}$	$d^{O(\sqrt{k})}$
[12]	$d^{O(k)}$	$\widetilde{O}(d^{\lceil k/2\rceil/2})$
This paper	$2^{O(d/\log^{0.99} d)}$	$kd^{0.5+o(1)}$
This paper	$2^{d^{1-\Omega(1/\sqrt{k})}}$	$\widetilde{O}(kd^{.51})$

Table 1: Prior results on differentially private release of k-way marginals with error ± 0.01 on every marginal. (The running time ignores dependence on the database size, privacy parameters, and the time required to evaluate the query non-privately.)

(ii) the L_1-weight of the coefficient vector of p is at most $d^{0.01}$, and

(iii) the degree of p is at most

$$\min\left\{d^{1-\frac{1}{C\sqrt{k}}}, \frac{d}{\log^{0.995} d}\right\}.$$

The degree bound of $d/\log^{0.995} d$ in the above theorem follows directly from techniques developed in [29], while the degree bound of $d^{1-\frac{1}{C\sqrt{k}}}$ requires additional insight. We also show a lower bound to exhibit the tightness of our construction.

THEOREM 1.4. *Let $k = o(\log d)$, and let p be a real d-variate polynomial satisfying $|p(x) - OR_d(x)| \leq 1/6$ for all $x \in \{-1,1\}^d$ with $|x| \leq k$. If the L_1-weight of the coefficient vector of p is $d^{O(1)}$, then the degree of p is at least $d^{1-O(1/\sqrt{k})}$.*

We note that our algorithmic approach for designing efficient private data release algorithms would work equally well if we have any small set of functions whose low-L_1-weight linear combinations approximate disjunctions restricted to inputs of Hamming weight at most k. Our lower bound limits the applicability of our approach if we choose to use low-degree monomials as the set of functions. We observe that this also rules out several natural candidates that can themselves be computed exactly by a low-weight polynomial of low-degree (e.g., the set of small-width conjunctions). There is some additional evidence from prior work that low-degree monomials may be the optimal choice: if we only care about the *size* of the set of functions used to approximate disjunctions on inputs of Hamming weight at most k, then prior work shows that low-degree monomials are indeed optimal [31] (see also Section 5 in the full version of [34]). It remains an interesting open question to determine whether this optimality still holds when we restrict the L_1 weight of the linear combinations used in the approximations to be poly(d).

1.2 Techniques

For notational convenience, we focus on *monotone k-way disjunction queries.* However, our results extend straightforwardly to general non-monotone k-way marginal queries via simple transformations on the database and queries. A monotone k-way disjunction is specified by a set $S \subseteq [d]$ of size k and asks what fraction of records in D have at least one of the attributes in S set to 1.

Following the approach introduced by Gupta et al. [16] and developed into a general theory in [20], we view the problem of releasing answers to conjunction queries as a learning problem. That is, we view the database as specifying a function $f_D\colon \{-1,1\}^d \to [0,1]$, in which each input vector $s \in \{-1,1\}^d$ is interpreted as the indicator vector of a set $S \subseteq \{1,\ldots,d\}$, with $s_i = -1$ iff $i \in S$, and $f_D(s)$ equals the evaluation of the conjunction query specified by S on the database D. Then, our goal is to privately learn to approximate the function f_D; this is accomplished in [20] by approximating f_D succinctly with polynomials and learning the polynomial privately. Polynomial approximation is central to our approach as well, as we explain below.

We begin with a description of how the parameters of the online learning algorithm determine the parameters of the online differentially private learning algorithm. We consider the "IDC framework" [17]—which captures the private multiplicative weights algorithm [19] among others [17,21,28]—for deriving differentially private online algorithms from any *online learning algorithm* that may not necessarily be privacy preserving.

Informally, an online learning algorithm is one that takes a (possibly adaptively chosen) sequence of inputs $s_1, s_2, \ldots$ and returns answers $a_1, a_2, \ldots$ to each, representing "guesses" about the values $f_D(s_1), f_D(s_2), \ldots$ for the unknown function f_D. After making each guess a_i, the learner is given some information about the value of $f_D(s_i)$. The quantities of interest are the running time required by the online learner to produce each guess a_i and the number of "mistakes" made by the learner, which is the number of rounds i in which a_i is "far" from $f_D(s_i)$. Ultimately, for the differentially private algorithm derived in the IDC framework, the notion of far will correspond to the accuracy, the per query running time will essentially be equal to the running time of the online learning algorithm, and the minimum database size required by the private algorithm will be proportional to the square root of the number of mistakes.

We next describe the well-known technique of deriving faster online learning algorithms that commit fewer mistakes using *polynomial approximations* to the target function. Indeed, it is well-known that if f_D can be approximated to high accuracy by a d-variate polynomial $p_D\colon \{-1,1\}^d \to \mathbb{R}$ of degree t and L_1-weight at most W, where the weight is defined to be the sum of the absolute values of the coefficients, then there is an online learning algorithm that runs in time poly$(\binom{d}{\leq t})$ and makes $O(W^2 d)$ mistakes. Thus, if $t \ll d$, the running time of such an online learning algorithm will be significantly less than 2^d and the number of mistakes (and thus the minimum database size of the resulting private algorithm) will only blow up by a factor of W.

Consequently, our goal boils down to constructing the best possible polynomial representation p_D for any database D – one with low-degree, low-L_1-weight such that $|p_D(s) - f_D(s)|$ is small for all vectors $s \in \{-1,1\}^d$ corresponding to monotone k-way disjunction queries. To accomplish this goal, it is sufficient to construct a low-degree, low-L_1-weight polynomial that can approximate the d-variate OR function on inputs of Hamming weight at most k (i.e., those that have -1 in at most k indices). Such problems are well-studied in the approximation-theory literature, however our variant requires polynomials to be accurate only on a restricted subset of inputs. In fact, the existence of a polynomial with degree $d/\log^{0.99} d$ and L_1-weight $d^{o(1)}$ that approximates the d-variate OR function on all inputs follows from the work of Servedio et al. [29]. We improve these bounds for small values of k by constructing an approximating polynomial that has degree $d^{1-\Omega(1/\sqrt{k})}$ and L_1-weight $d^{0.01}$.

We also prove a new approximation-theoretic lower bound for polynomials that seek to approximate a target function for a restricted subset of inputs. Specifically, we show that for any $k = o(\log d)$, any polynomial p of weight poly(d) that satisfies $|p(s) - \mathrm{OR}(s)| \le 1/6$ for all inputs $s \in \{-1,1\}^d$ of Hamming weight at most k must have degree $d^{1-O(1/\sqrt{k})}$. We prove our lower bound by expressing the problem of constructing such a low-weight, low-degree polynomial p as a linear program, and exhibiting an explicit solution to the dual of this linear program. Our proof is inspired by recent work of Sherstov [30,31,33] and Bun-Thaler [5].

1.3 Related Work

Other Results on Privately Releasing Marginals. In work subsequent to our result, Dwork et al. [12] show how to privately release marginals in a very different parameter regime. Their algorithm is faster than ours, running in time poly$(\binom{d}{\le k})$, and has better dependence on the error parameter. However, their algorithm requires that the database size is $\tilde{\Omega}(d^{\lceil k/2 \rceil/2})$ for answering with error ± 0.01. This size is comparable to the optimal $\tilde{\Omega}(k\sqrt{d})$ only when $k \le 2$. In contrast, our algorithm has nearly-optimal minimum database size for every choice of k.

While we have focused on accurately answering *every* k-way marginal query, or more generally every query in a sequence of marginal queries, several other works have considered more relaxed notions of accuracy. These works show how to efficiently release a summary of the database from which an analyst can efficiently compute an approximate answer to marginal queries, with the guarantee that the *average* error of a marginal query is at most .01, when the query is chosen from a particular distribution. In particular, Feldman and Kothari [15] achieve small average error over the uniform distribution with running time and database size $\tilde{O}(d^2)$; Gupta et al. [16] achieve small average error over any product distribution with running time and minimum database size poly(d); finally Hardt et al. [20] show how to achieve small average error over arbitrary distributions with running time and minimum database size $2^{\tilde{O}(d^{1/3})}$. All of these results are based on the approach of learning the function f_D.

Several works have also considered information theoretic bounds on the minimum database size required to answer k-way marginals. Kasiviswanathan et al. [22] showed that $|D| \ge \min\{1/\alpha^2, d^{k/2}/\alpha\}$ is necessary to answer all k-way marginals with error $\pm\alpha$. De [8] extended this result to hold even when accuracy $\pm\alpha$ can be violated for a constant fraction of k-way marginals. In our regime, where $\alpha = \Omega(1)$, their results do not give a non-trivial lower bound. In forthcoming work, Bun, Ullman, and Vadhan [6] have proven a lower bound of $|D| \ge \tilde{\Omega}(k\sqrt{d})$, which is nearly optimal for $\alpha = \Omega(1)$.

Hardness of Differential Privacy. Ullman [35] (building on the results of Dwork et al. [11]), showed that any $2^{o(d)}$-time differentially private algorithm that answers *arbitrary* counting queries can only give accurate answers if $|D| \gtrsim |\mathcal{Q}|^{1/2}$, assuming the existence of exponentially hard one-way functions. Our algorithms have running time $2^{o(d)}$ and are accurate when $|D| \ll |\mathcal{Q}|^{1/2}$, and thus show a separation between answering marginal queries and answering arbitrary counting queries.

When viewed as an offline algorithm for answering all k-way marginals, our algorithm will return a list of values containing answers to each k-way marginal query. It would in some cases be more attractive if we could return a *synthetic database*, which is a new database $\widehat{D} \in (\{0,1\}^d)^{\widehat{n}}$ whose rows are "fake", but such that $\widehat{D}$ approximately preserves many of the statistical properties of the database D (e.g., all the marginals). Some of the previous work on counting query release has provided synthetic data [1,3,11,14,18].

Unfortunately, Ullman and Vadhan [36] (building on [11]) have shown that no differentially private sanitizer with running time poly(d) can take a database $D \in (\{0,1\}^d)^n$ and output a private synthetic database $\widehat{D}$, all of whose 2-way marginals are approximately equal to those of D, assuming the existence of one-way functions. They also showed that under certain strong cryptographic assumptions, there is no differentially private sanitizer with running time $2^{d^{1-\Omega(1)}}$ can output a private synthetic database, all of whose 2-way marginals are approximately equal to those of D. Our algorithms indeed achieve this running time and accuracy guarantee when releasing k-way marginals for constant k, and thus it may be inherent that our algorithms do not generate synthetic data.

Approximation Theory. Servedio et al. [29] focused on developing low-weight, low-degree polynomial threshold functions (PTFs) for decision lists, motivated by applications in computational learning theory. As an intermediate step in their PTF constructions, they constructed low-L_1-weight, low-degree polynomials that approximate the OR function on *all* Boolean inputs. Our construction of lower-weight, lower-degree polynomials that approximate the OR function on low Hamming weight inputs is inspired by and builds on Servedio et al.'s construction of approximations that are accurate on all Boolean inputs.

The proof of our lower bound is inspired by recent work that has established new approximate degree lower bounds via the construction of dual solutions to certain linear programs. In particular, Sherstov [30] showed that approximate degree and PTF degree behave roughly multiplicatively under function composition, while Bun and Thaler [5] gave a refinement of Sherstov's method in order to resolve the approximate degree of the two-level AND-OR tree, and also gave an explicit dual witness for the approximate degree of any symmetric Boolean function. We extend these lower bounds along two directions: (1) we show degree lower bounds that take into account the L_1-weight of the coefficient vector of the approximating polynomial, and (2) our lower bounds hold even when we only require the approximation to be accurate on inputs of low Hamming weight, while prior work only considered approximations that are accurate on all Boolean inputs.

Some prior work has studied the degree of polynomials that point-wise approximate *partial* Boolean functions [32, 33]. Here, a function $f : Y \to \mathbb{R}$ is said to be partial if its domain Y is a strict subset of $\{-1,1\}^d$, and a polynomial p is said to ϵ-approximate f if

1. $|f(x) - p(x)| \le \epsilon$ for all $x \in Y$, and
2. $|p(x)| \le 1 + \epsilon$ for all $x \in \{-1,1\}^d \setminus Y$.

In contrast, our lower bounds apply even in the absence of Condition 2, i.e., when $p(x)$ is allowed to take arbitrary values on inputs in $\{-1,1\}^d \setminus Y$.

Finally, while our motivation is private data release, our approximation theoretic results are similar in spirit to recent work of Long and Servedio [25], who are motivated by applications in computational learning theory. Long and Servedio consider halfspaces h defined on inputs of small Hamming weight, and (using different techniques very different from ours) give upper and lower bounds on the weight of these halfspaces when represented as linear threshold functions.

Organization. In Section 3, we describe our private online algorithm and show that it yields the claimed accuracy given the existence of sufficiently low-weight polynomials that approximate the d-variate OR function on inputs of low Hamming weight. The results of this section are a combination of known techniques in differential privacy [17, 19, 28] and learning theory (see e.g., [24]). Readers familiar with these literatures may prefer to skip Section 3 on first reading. In Section 4, we give our polynomial approximations to the OR function, both on low Hamming weight Boolean inputs and on all Boolean inputs. Finally, in Section 5, we state and prove our lower bounds for polynomial approximations to the OR function on restricted inputs.

2. PRELIMINARIES

2.1 Differentially Private Sanitizers

Let a *database* $D \in (\{0,1\}^d)^n$ be a collection of n rows $x^{(1)}, \dots, x^{(n)}$ from a *data universe* $\{0,1\}^d$. We say that two databases $D, D' \in (\{0,1\}^d)^n$ are *adjacent* if they differ only on a single row, and we denote this by $D \sim D'$.

Let $\mathcal{A} : (\{0,1\}^d)^n \to \mathcal{R}$ be an algorithm that takes a database as input and outputs some data structure in $\mathcal{R}$. We are interested in algorithms that satisfy *differential privacy.*

DEFINITION 2.1 (DIFFERENTIAL PRIVACY [10]). *An algorithm $\mathcal{A}$: $(\{0,1\}^d)^n \to \mathcal{R}$ is* (ε, δ)-differentially private *if for every two adjacent databases $D \sim D' \in (\{0,1\}^d)^n$ and every subset $S \subseteq \mathcal{R}$,*

$$\Pr[\mathcal{A}(D) \in S] \le e^{\varepsilon} \Pr[\mathcal{A}(D') \in S] + \delta.$$

Since a sanitizer that always outputs $\perp$ satisfies Definition 2.1, we focus on sanitizers that are accurate. In particular, we are interested in sanitizers that give accurate answers to *counting queries.* A counting query is defined by a boolean predicate q: $\{0,1\}^d \to \{0,1\}$. Abusing notation, we define the evaluation of the query q on a database $D \in (\{0,1\}^d)^n$ to be $q(D) = \frac{1}{n}\sum_{i=1}^n q(x^{(i)})$. Note that the value of a counting query is in $[0,1]$. We use $\mathcal{Q}$ to denote a set of counting queries.

For the purposes of this work, we assume that the range of $\mathcal{A}$ is simply $\mathbb{R}^{|\mathcal{Q}|}$. That is, $\mathcal{A}$ outputs a list of real numbers representing answers to each of the specified queries.

DEFINITION 2.2 (ACCURACY). *The output of $\mathcal{A}(D)$, $a = (a_q)_{q \in \mathcal{Q}}$, is* α-accurate *for the query set $\mathcal{Q}$ if*

$$\forall q \in \mathcal{Q},\ |a_q - q(D)| \le \alpha$$

A sanitizer is (α, β)-accurate *for the query set $\mathcal{Q}$ if for every database D, $\mathcal{A}(D)$ outputs a such that with probability at least $1 - \beta$, the output a is α-accurate for $\mathcal{Q}$, where the probability is taken over the coins of $\mathcal{A}$.*

We remark that the definition of both differential privacy and (α, β)-accuracy extend straightforwardly to the online setting. Here the algorithm receives a sequence of ℓ (possibly adaptively chosen) queries from $\mathcal{Q}$ and must give an answer to each before seeing the rest of the sequence. Here we require that with probability at least $1 - \beta$, *every* answer output by the algorithm is within $\pm\alpha$ of the true answer on D. See e.g., [19] for an elaborate treatment of the online setting.

2.2 Query Function Families

Given a set of queries of interest, $\mathcal{Q}$ (e.g., all marginal queries), we think of the database D as specifying a function f_D mapping queries q to their answers $q(D)$. We now describe this transformation more formally:

DEFINITION 2.3 ($\mathcal{Q}$-FUNCTION FAMILY). *Let*

$$\mathcal{Q} = \{q_y\}_{y \in Y_{\mathcal{Q}} \subseteq \{-1,1\}^m}$$

be a set of counting queries on a data universe $\{0,1\}^d$, where each query is indexed by an m-bit string. We define the index set of $\mathcal{Q}$ *to be the set $Y_{\mathcal{Q}} = \{y \in \{-1,1\}^m \mid q_y \in \mathcal{Q}\}$.*

We define the $\mathcal{Q}$-function family

$$\mathcal{F}_{\mathcal{Q}} = \{f_x : \{-1,1\}^m \to [0,1]\}_{x \in \{0,1\}^d}$$

as follows: For every possible database row $x \in \{0,1\}^d$, the function $f_x : \{-1,1\}^m \to [0,1]$ is defined as $f_x(y) = q_y(x)$. Given a database $D \in (\{0,1\}^d)^n$ we define the function $f_{\mathcal{Q},D} : \{-1,1\}^m \to [0,1]$ where $f_{\mathcal{Q},D}(y) = \frac{1}{n}\sum_{i=1}^n f_{x^{(i)}}(y)$. When $\mathcal{Q}$ is clear from context we will drop the subscript $\mathcal{Q}$ and simply write f_x, f_D, and $\mathcal{F}$.

When $\mathcal{Q}$ is the set of all monotone k-way disjunctions on a database $D \in (\{0,1\}^d)^n$, the queries are defined by sets $S \subseteq [d]$, $|S| \le k$. In this case, we represent each query by the d-bit $-1/1$ indicator vector y_S of the set S, where $y_S(i) = -1$ if and only if $i \in S$. Thus, y_S has at most k entries that are -1. Hence, we can take $m = d$ and $Y_{\mathcal{Q}} = \left\{y \in \{-1,1\}^d \mid \sum_{j=1}^d \mathbf{1}_{\{y_i=-1\}} \le k\right\}$.

2.3 Low-Weight Polynomial Approximations

Given an m-variate real polynomial p: $\{-1,1\}^m \to \mathbb{R}$,

$$p(y) = \sum_{S \subseteq [m]} c_S \cdot \prod_{i \in S} y_i,$$

we define the degree, weight $w(\cdot)$ and *non-constant weight* $w^*(\cdot)$ of the polynomial as follows:

$$\deg(p) := \max\{|S| : S \subseteq [m], c_S \neq 0\},$$
$$w(p) := \sum_{S \subseteq [m]} |c_S|, \text{and}$$
$$w^*(p) := \sum_{S \subseteq [m], S \neq \emptyset} |c_S|.$$

We use $\binom{[m]}{\leq t}$ to denote $\{S \subseteq [m] \mid |S| \leq t\}$ and $\binom{m}{\leq t} = \left|\binom{[m]}{\leq t}\right| = \sum_{j=0}^{t} \binom{m}{j}$.

We will attempt to approximate the functions

$$f_x : \{-1,1\}^m \to \{0,1\}$$

on all the indices in $Y_{\mathcal{Q}}$ by a family of polynomials with low degree and low weight. Formally and more generally:

Definition 2.4. *[RESTRICTED APPROXIMATION BY POLYNOMIALS] Given a function $f\colon Y \to \mathbb{R}$, where $Y \subseteq \mathbb{R}^m$, and a subset $Y' \subseteq Y$, we denote the restriction of f to Y' by $f|_{Y'}$. Given an m-variate real polynomial p, we say that p is a γ-*approximation *to the restriction $f|_{Y'}$, if $|f(y) - p(y)| \leq \gamma\ \forall y \in Y'$. Notice there is no restriction whatsoever placed on $p(y)$ for $y \in Y \setminus Y'$.*

Given a family of m-variate functions

$$\mathcal{F} = \{f_x\colon Y \to \mathbb{R}\}_{x \in \{0,1\}^d},$$

*where $Y \subseteq \mathbb{R}^m$, a set $Y' \subseteq Y$ we use $\mathcal{F}|_{Y'} = \{f_x|_{Y'}\}_{x\in\{0,1\}^d}$ to denote the family of restricted functions. Given a family $\mathcal{P}$ of m-variate real polynomials, we say that the family $\mathcal{P}$ is a γ-*approximation to the family $\mathcal{F}|_{Y'}$* if for every $x \in \{0,1\}^d$, there exists $p_x \in \mathcal{P}$ that is a γ-approximation to $f_x|_{Y'}$.*

Let $H_{m,k} = \{x \in \{-1,1\}^m : \sum_{i=1}^m (1-x_i)/2 \leq k\}$ denote the set of inputs of Hamming weight at most k. We view the d variate OR function, OR_d as mapping inputs from $\{-1,1\}^d$ to $\{-1,1\}$, with the convention that -1 is TRUE and 1 is FALSE. Let $\mathcal{P}_{t,W}(m)$ denote the family of all m-variate real polynomials of degree t and weight W. For the upper bound, we will show that for certain small values of t and W, the family $\mathcal{P}_{t,W}(d)$ is a γ-approximation to the family of all disjunctions restricted to $H_{d,k}$.

Fact 2.5. *If $\mathcal{Q}$ is the set of all monotone k-way disjunctions on a database $D \in (\{0,1\}^d)^n$, $\mathcal{F}$ is its function family, and $Y = H_{d,k}$ is its index set, then $\mathcal{P}_{t,W}(d)$ is a γ-approximation to the restriction $\mathcal{F}|_Y$ if and only if there is a degree t polynomial of weight $O(W)$ that γ-approximates $OR_d|_{H_{d,k}}$.*

The fact follows easily by observing that for any $x \in \{0,1\}^d$, $y \in \{-1,1\}^d$,

$$f_x(y) = \bigvee_{i \in x} \mathbf{1}_{\{y_i = -1\}} = \frac{1 - \mathrm{OR}_d(y_1^{x_1}, \ldots, y_d^{x_d})}{2}.$$

For the lower bound, we will show that any collection of polynomials with small weight that is a γ-approximation to the family of disjunctions restricted to $H_{m,k}$ should have large degree. We need the following definitions:

Definition 2.6 (Approximate Degree). *Given a function $f\colon Y \to \mathbb{R}$, where $Y \subseteq \mathbb{R}^m$, the γ-approximate degree of f is*

$$deg_\gamma(f) := min\{d : \exists \text{ real polynomial } p \text{ that is a } \gamma\text{-approximation to } f,\ deg(p) = d\}.$$

Analogously, the (γ, W)-approximate degree of f is

$$deg_{(\gamma,W)}(f) := min\{d : \exists \text{ real polynomial } p \text{ that is a } \gamma\text{-approximation to } f,\ deg(p) = d,\ w(p) \leq W\}.$$

It is clear that $deg_\gamma(f) = deg_{(\gamma,\infty)}(f)$.

We let $w^*(f,t)$ denote the degree-t non-constant margin weight *of f, defined to be:*

$$w^*(f,t) := \min\{w^*(p) : \exists \text{ real polynomial } p \text{ s.t. } deg(p) \leq t, f(y)p(y) \geq 1\ \forall\ y \in Y\}.$$

The above definitions extend naturally to the restricted function $f|_{Y'}$.

Our definition of non-constant margin weight is closely related to the well-studied notion of the degree-t polynomial threshold function (PTF) weight of f (see e.g., [31]), which is defined as $\min_p w(p)$, where the minimum is taken over all degree-t polynomials p with integer coefficients, such that $f(x) = \mathrm{sign}(p(x))$ for all $x \in \{-1,1\}^d$. Often, when studying PTF weight, the requirement that p have integer coefficients is used only to ensure that p has non-trivial margin, i.e. that $|p(x)| \geq 1$ for all $x \in \{-1,1\}^d$; this is precisely the requirement captured in our definition of non-constant margin weight. We choose to work with margin weight because it is a cleaner quantity to analyze using linear programming duality; PTF weight can also be studied using LP duality, but the integrality constraints on the coefficients of p introduces an integrality gap that causes some loss in the analysis (see e.g., Sherstov [31, Theorem 3.4] and Klauck [23, Section 4.3]).

3. PRIVATE DATA RELEASE USING LOW-WEIGHT APPROXIMATIONS

In this section we show that low-weight polynomial approximations imply data release algorithms that provide approximate answers even on small databases. The main goal of this section is to prove the following theorem.

Theorem 3.1. *Given $\alpha, \beta, \varepsilon, \delta > 0$, and a family of linear queries $\mathcal{Q}$ with index set $Y \subseteq \{-1,1\}^m$. Suppose for some $t \leq m$, $W > 0$, the family of polynomials $\mathcal{P}_{t,W}(m)$ $(\alpha/4)$-approximates the function family $\mathcal{F}_{\mathcal{Q}}|_Y$. Then there exists an (ϵ, δ)-differentially private online algorithm that is $(4\alpha, \beta)$-accurate for any sequence of ℓ (possibly adaptively chosen) queries from $\mathcal{Q}$ on a database $D \in (\{0,1\}^d)^n$, provided*

$$n \geq \frac{128W \log(\ell/\beta) \log(4/\delta)}{\alpha^2 \varepsilon} \sqrt{\log\left(2\binom{m}{\leq t} + 1\right)}.$$

The private algorithm has running time that is polynomial in $\left(n, \binom{m}{\leq t}, \log W, \log(1/\alpha), \log(1/\beta), \log(1/\varepsilon), \log(1/\delta)\right)$.

We note that the theorem can be assembled from known techniques in the design and analysis of differentially private algorithms and online learning algorithms. We include the proof of the theorem here for the sake of completeness, as to our knowledge they do not explicitly appear in the privacy literature.

We construct and analyze the algorithm in two steps. First, we use standard arguments to show that the non-private multiplicative weights algorithm can be used to construct a suitable online learning algorithm for $f_{\mathcal{Q},D}$ whenever $f_{\mathcal{Q},D}$ can be approximated by a low-weight, low-degree polynomial. Here, a suitable online learning algorithm is one that fits into the IDC framework of Gupta et al. [17]. We then apply the generic conversion from IDCs to differentially private online algorithms [17, 19, 28] to obtain our algorithm.

3.1 IDCs

We start by providing the relevant background on the *iterative database construction* framework. An IDC will maintain a sequence of functions $f_D^{(1)}, f_D^{(2)}, \ldots$ that give increasingly good approximations to the $f_{\mathcal{Q},D}$. In our case, these functions will be low-degree polynomials. Moreover, the mechanism produces the next approximation in the sequence by considering only one query $y^{(t)}$ that "distinguishes" the real database in the sense that $|f^{(t)}(y^{(t)}) - f_D(y^{(t)})|$ is large.

DEFINITION 3.2 (IDC [17, 19, 28]). *Let*

$$\mathcal{Q} = \{q_y\}_{y \in Y_\mathcal{Q} \subseteq \{-1,1\}^m}$$

be a family of counting queries indexed by m-bit strings. Let $\mathbf{U}$ *be an algorithm mapping a function* $f : Y_\mathcal{Q} \to \mathbb{R}$*, a query* $y \in Y_\mathcal{Q}$*, and a real number* a *to a new function* f'*. Let* $D \in (\{0,1\}^d)^n$ *be a database and* $\alpha > 0$ *be a parameter. Consider the following game with an adversary. Let* $f_D^{(1)}$ *be some function. In each round* $t = 1, 2, \ldots$*:*

1. *The adversary chooses a query* $y^{(t)} \in Y_\mathcal{Q}$ *(possibly depending on* $f_D^{(t)}$*).*
2. *If* $|f_D^{(t)}(y^{(t)}) - f_D(y^{(t)})| > \alpha$*, then we say that the algorithm has* made a mistake.
3. *If the algorithm made a mistake, then it receives a value* $a^{(t)} \in \mathbb{R}$ *such that* $|a^{(t)} - f_D(y^{(t)})| \le \alpha/2$ *and computes a new function* $f_D^{(t+1)} = \mathbf{U}(f_D^{(t)}, y^{(t)}, a^{(t)})$*. Otherwise let* $f_D^{(t+1)} = f_D^{(t)}$*.*

If the number of rounds t in which the algorithm makes a mistake is at most B for every adversary, then $\mathbf{U}$ *is a* iterative database construction *for* $\mathcal{Q}$ with mistake bound *B.*

THEOREM 3.3 (VARIANT OF [17]). *For any* $\alpha > 0$*, and any family of queries* $\mathcal{Q}$*, if there is an iterative database construction for* $\mathcal{Q}$ *with mistake bound B, then there is an* (ε, δ)*-differentially private online algorithm that is* $(4\alpha, \beta)$*-accurate for any sequence of* ℓ *(possibly adaptively chosen) queries from* $\mathcal{Q}$ *on a database* $D \in (\{0,1\}^d)^n$*, so long as*

$$n \ge \frac{32\sqrt{B}\log(\ell/\beta)\log(4/\delta)}{\alpha\varepsilon}.$$

Moreover, if the iterative database construction, $\mathbf{U}$*, runs in time* $T_\mathbf{U}$*, then the private algorithm has running time* $\mathrm{poly}(n, T_\mathbf{U}, \log(1/\alpha), \log(1/\beta), \log(1/\varepsilon), \log(1/\delta))$ *per query.*

The IDC we will use is specified in Algorithm 1. The IDC will use approximations $f_D^{(t)}$ in the form of low-degree polynomials of low-weight, and thus we need to specify how to represent such a function. Specifically, we will represent a polynomial p as a vector $\overline{p}$ of length $2\binom{m}{\le t}+1$ with only non-negative entries. For each coefficient $S \in \binom{[m]}{\le t}$, the vector will have two components $\overline{p}_S, \overline{p}_{\neg S}$. (Recall that $\binom{[m]}{\le t} := \{S \subseteq [m] \mid |S| \le t\}$.) Intuitively these two entries represent the positive part and negative part of the coefficient c_S of p. There will also be an additional entry $\overline{p}_0$ that is used to ensure that the L_1-norm of the vector is exactly 1. Given a polynomial $p \in \mathcal{P}_{t,W}$ with coefficients (c_S), we can construct this vector by setting

$$\overline{p}_S = \frac{\max\{0, c_S\}}{W} \qquad \overline{p}_{\neg S} = \frac{\max\{0, -c_S\}}{W}$$

and choosing $\overline{p}_0$ so that $\|\overline{p}\|_1 = 1$. Observe that $\overline{p}_0$ can always be set appropriately since the weight of p is at most W.

Similarly, we want to associate queries with vectors so that we can replace the evaluation of the polynomial p on a query y with the inner product $W\langle \overline{p}, \overline{y}\rangle$. We can do so by defining the vector $\overline{y}$ of length $2\binom{m}{\le t}+1$ such tha $\overline{y}_0 = 0$, $\overline{y}_S = \prod_{i \in S} y_i$ and $\overline{y}_{\neg S} = -\prod_{i\in S} y_i$.

FACT 3.4. *For every m-variate polynomial p of degree at most t and weight at most W, and every query* $y \in \{-1,1\}^m$*,* $W\langle \overline{p}, \overline{y}\rangle = p(y)$*.*

Algorithm 1 The Multiplicative Weights Algorithm for Low-Weight Polynomials.

$\mathbf{U}_\alpha^{MW}(\overline{p}^{(t)}, y^{(t)}, a^{(t)})$:
  Let $\eta \leftarrow \alpha/4W$.
  If: $p^{(t)} = \emptyset$ **then:** output

$$\overline{p}^{(t)} = \frac{1}{2\binom{m}{\le t}+1}(1, \ldots, 1)$$

  (representing the constant 0 polynomial).
  Else if: $a^{(t)} < W\langle \overline{p}^{(t)}, \overline{y}^{(t)}\rangle$
    Let $\overline{r}^{(t)} = \overline{y}^{(t)}$
  Else:
    Let $\overline{r}^{(t)} = -\overline{y}^{(t)}$
  Update: For all $I \in \left\{0, \binom{[m]}{\le t}, \neg\binom{[m]}{\le t}\right\}$ let

$$\overline{p}_I^{(t+1)} \leftarrow \exp(-\eta \overline{r}_I^{(t)}) \cdot \overline{p}_I^{(t)}$$

$$\overline{p}^{(t+1)} \leftarrow \frac{\overline{p}^{(t+1)}}{\|\overline{p}^{(t+1)}\|_1}$$

  Output $\overline{p}^{(t+1)}$.

We summarize the properties of the multiplicative weights algorithm in the following theorem:

THEOREM 3.5. *For any* $\alpha > 0$*, and any family of linear queries* $\mathcal{Q}$ *if* $\mathcal{P}_{t,W}$ $(\alpha/4)$*-approximates the restriction* $\mathcal{F}|_Y$ *then Algorithm 1 is an iterative database construction for* $\mathcal{Q}$ *with mistake bound B for*

$$B = B(W, m, t, \alpha) = \frac{16W^2 \log\left(2\binom{m}{\le t}+1\right)}{\alpha^2}.$$

Moreover, **U** *runs in time* $\text{poly}(\binom{m}{\le t}, \log W, \log(1/\alpha))$.

PROOF. Let $D \in (\{0,1\}^d)^n$ be any database. For every round t in which **U** makes a mistake, we consider the tuple $(\overline{p}^{(t)}, y^{(t)}, \widehat{a}^{(t)})$ representing the information used to update the approximation in round t. In order to bound the number of mistakes, it will be sufficient to show that after $B \le 16W^2 \log(2\binom{m}{\le t}+1)/\alpha^2$, the vector $\overline{p}^{(t)}$ is such that

$$\forall y \in Y_Q,\ |W\langle \overline{p}^{(t)}, \overline{y}\rangle - f_D(y)| \le \alpha.$$

That is, after making B mistakes $\overline{p}^{(t)}$ represents a polynomial that approximates f_D on every query, and thus there can be no more than B makes.

First, we note that there always exists a polynomial $p_D \in \mathcal{P}_{t,W}$ such that

$$\forall y \in Y_Q,\ |p_D(y) - f_D(y)| \le \frac{\alpha}{4}. \tag{1}$$

The assumption of our theorem is that for every $x^{(i)} \in D$, there exists $p_{x^{(i)}} \in \mathcal{P}_{t,W}$ such that

$$\forall y \in Y_Q,\ |p_{x^{(i)}}(y) - f_{x^{(i)}}(y)| \le \frac{\alpha}{4}.$$

Thus, since $f_D = \frac{1}{n}\sum_{i=1}^n f_{x^{(i)}}$, the polynomial

$$p_D = \frac{1}{n}\sum_{i=1}^n p_{x^{(i)}}$$

will satisfy (1). Note that $p_D \in \mathcal{P}_{t,W}$, thus if we represent p_D as a vector,

$$\forall y \in Y_Q,\ |W\langle \overline{p}_D, \overline{y}\rangle - f_D(y)| \le \frac{\alpha}{4}.$$

Given the existence of $\overline{p}_D$, we will define a potential function capturing how far $\overline{p}^{(t)}$ is from $\overline{p}_D$. Specifically, we define

$$\Psi_t := KL(\overline{p}_D \| \overline{p}^{(t)}) = \sum_{I \in \{0, \binom{[m]}{\le t}, \neg\binom{[m]}{\le t}\}} \overline{p}_{D,I} \log\left(\frac{\overline{p}_{D,I}}{\overline{p}_I^{(t)}}\right)$$

to be the KL divergence between $\overline{p}_D$ and the current approximation $\overline{p}^{(t)}$. Note that the sum iterates over all $2\binom{m}{\le t}+1$ indices in $\overline{p}$. We have the following fact about KL divergence.

FACT 3.6. *For all t: $\Psi_t \ge 0$, and $\Psi_0 \le \log\left(2\binom{m}{\le t}+1\right)$.*

We will argue that after each mistake the potential drops by at least $\alpha^2/16W^2$. Note that the potential only changes in rounds where a mistake was made. Because the potential begins at $\log\left(2\binom{m}{\le t}+1\right)$, and must always be non-negative, we know that there can be at most $B(\alpha) \le 16W^2 \log\left(2\binom{m}{\le t}+1\right)/\alpha^2$ mistakes before the algorithm outputs a (vector representation of) a polynomial that approximates f_D on Y_Q.

The following lemma is standard in the analysis of algorithms based on multiplicative-weights.

LEMMA 3.7.

$$\Psi_t - \Psi_{t+1} \ge \eta\left(\langle \overline{p}^{(t)}, r^{(t)}\rangle - \langle \overline{p}_D, r^{(t)}\rangle\right) - \eta^2$$

PROOF.

$$\begin{aligned}
\Psi_t - \Psi_{t+1} &= \sum_{I \in \{0, \binom{[m]}{\le t}, \neg\binom{[m]}{\le t}\}} \overline{p}_{D,I} \log\left(\frac{\overline{p}_I^{(t+1)}}{\overline{p}_I^{(t)}}\right) \\
&= -\eta\langle \overline{p}_D, r^{(t)}\rangle \\
&\quad - \log\left(\sum_{I \in \{0, \binom{[m]}{\le t}, \neg\binom{[m]}{\le t}\}} \exp(-\eta r_I^{(t)})\overline{p}_I^{(t)}\right) \\
&\ge -\eta\langle \overline{p}_D, r^{(t)}\rangle \\
&\quad - \log\left(\sum_{I \in \{0, \binom{[m]}{\le t}, \neg\binom{[m]}{\le t}\}} \overline{p}_I^{(t)}(1 + \eta^2 - \eta r_I^{(t)})\right) \\
&\ge \eta\left(\langle \overline{p}^{(t)}, r^{(t)}\rangle - \langle \overline{p}_D, r^{(t)}\rangle\right) - \eta^2
\end{aligned}$$

□

The rest of the proof now follows easily. By the conditions of an iterative database construction algorithm, $|\widehat{a}^{(t)} - f_D(y^{(t)})| \le \alpha/2$. Hence, for each t such that $|W\langle \overline{p}^{(t)}, y^{(t)}\rangle - f_D(y^{(t)})| \ge \alpha$, we also have that $W\langle \overline{p}^{(t)}, y^{(t)}\rangle > f_D(y^{(t)})$ if and only if $W\langle \overline{p}^{(t)}, y^{(t)}\rangle > \widehat{a}^{(t)}$.

In particular, if $r^{(t)} = y^{(t)}$, then

$$W\langle \overline{p}^{(t)}, y^{(t)}\rangle - W\langle \overline{p}_D, y^{(t)}\rangle \ge \alpha/2.$$

Similarly, if $r^{(t)} = -y^{(t)}$, then

$$W\langle \overline{p}_D, y^{(t)}\rangle - W\langle \overline{p}^{(t)}, y^{(t)}\rangle \ge \alpha.$$

Here we have utilized the fact that $|p_D(y) - f_D(y)| \le \alpha/4$. Therefore, by Lemma 3.7 and the fact that $\eta = \alpha/4W$:

$$\begin{aligned}
\Psi_t - \Psi_{t+1} &\ge \frac{\alpha}{4W}\left(\langle \overline{p}^{(t)}, r^{(t)}\rangle - \langle \overline{p}_D, r^{(t)}\rangle\right) - \frac{\alpha^2}{16W^2} \\
&\ge \frac{\alpha}{4W}\left(\frac{\alpha}{2W}\right) - \frac{\alpha^2}{16W^2} = \frac{\alpha^2}{16W^2}
\end{aligned}$$

Theorem 3.1 follows immediately from Theorems 3.3 and 3.5.

4. UPPER BOUNDS

Fact 2.5 and Theorem 3.1 show that in order to develop a differentially private mechanism that can release all k-way marginals of a database, it is sufficient to construct a low-weight polynomial that approximates the OR_d, on all Boolean inputs of Hamming weight at most k. This is the purpose to which we now turn.

The OR_d function is easily seen to have an exact polynomial representation of constant weight and degree d (see Fact 4.3 below); however, an approximation with smaller degree may be achieved at the expense of larger weight. The best known weight-degree tradeoff, implicit in the work of Servedio et al. [29], can be stated as follows: there exists a polynomial p of degree t and weight $(d \log(1/\gamma)/t)^{(d(\log 1/\gamma)^2/t)}$ that γ-approximates the function OR_d on all Boolean inputs, for every t larger than $\sqrt{d}\log(1/\gamma)$. Setting the degree t to be $O(d/\log^{0.99} d)$ yields a polynomial of weight at most $d^{0.01}$ that approximates the OR_d function on all Boolean inputs to any desired constant accuracy. On the other hand, Lemma 8 of [29] can be shown to imply that any polynomial of weight

W that 1/3-approximates the OR_d function requires degree $\Omega(d/\log W)$, essentially matching the $O(d/\log^{.99} d)$ upper bound of Servedio et al. when $W = d^{\Omega(1)}$.

However, in order to privately release k-way marginals, we have shown that it suffices to construct polynomials that are accurate *only* on inputs of low Hamming weight. In this section, we give a construction that achieves significantly improved weight degree trade-offs in this setting. In the next section, we demonstrate the tightness of our construction by proving matching lower bounds.

We construct our approximations by decomposing the d-variate OR function into an OR of OR's, which is the same approach taken by Servedio et al. [29]. Here, the outer OR has fan-in m and the inner OR has fan-in d/m, where the subsequent analysis will determine the appropriate choice of m. In order to obtain an approximation that is accurate on all Boolean inputs, Servedio et al. approximate the outer OR using a transformation of the Chebyshev polynomials of degree $\sqrt{m}$, and compute each of the inner OR's exactly.

For $k \ll \log^2 d$, we are able to substantially reduce the degree of the approximating polynomial, relative to the construction of Servedio et al., by leveraging the fact that we are interested in approximations that are accurate only on inputs of Hamming weight at most k. Specifically, we are able to approximate the outer OR function using a polynomial of degree only $\sqrt{k}$ rather than $\sqrt{m}$, and argue that the weight of the resulting polynomial is still bounded by a polynomial in d.

We now proceed to prove the main lemmas. For the sake of intuition, we begin with weight-degree tradeoffs in the simpler setting in which we are concerned with approximating the OR_d function over all Boolean inputs. The following lemma, proved below for completeness, is implicit in the work of [29].

LEMMA 4.1. *For every $\gamma > 0$ and $m \in [d]$, there is a polynomial of degree $t = O((d/\sqrt{m})\log(1/\gamma))$ and weight $W = m^{O(\sqrt{m}\log(1/\gamma))}$ that γ-approximates the OR_d function.*

Our main contribution in this section is the following lemma that gives an improved polynomial approximation to the OR_d function restricted to inputs of low Hamming weight.

LEMMA 4.2. *For every $\gamma > 0$, $k < d$ and $m \in [d] \setminus [k]$, there is a polynomial of degree $t = O(d\sqrt{k}\log(1/\gamma)/m)$ and weight $W = m^{O(\sqrt{k}\log(1/\gamma))}$ that γ-approximates the OR_d function restricted to inputs of Hamming weight at most k.*

For any constant γ, one may take $m = d^{O(1/\sqrt{k})}$ in the lemma (here the choice of constant depends on the constants in Fact 4.4) and obtain a polynomial of degree $d^{1-\Omega(1/\sqrt{k})}$ and weight $d^{0.01}$.

Our constructions use the following basic facts.

FACT 4.3. *The real polynomial $p_d : \{-1,1\}^d \to \mathbb{R}$*

$$p_d(x) = 2\left(\sum_{S\subseteq[d]} 2^{-d}\prod_{i\in S} x_i\right) - 1 = 2\prod_{i=1}^{d}\left(\frac{1+x_i}{2}\right) - 1$$

computes $OR_d(x)$ and has weight $w(p_d) \leq 3$.

FACT 4.4. *[see e.g., [34]] For every $k \in \mathbb{N}$ and $\gamma > 0$, there exists a univariate real polynomial $p = \sum_{i=0}^{t_k} c_i x^i$ of degree t_k such that*

1. *$t_k = O(\sqrt{k}\log(1/\gamma))$,*
2. *for every $i \in [t_k]$, $|c_i| \leq 2^{O(\sqrt{k}\log(1/\gamma))}$,*
3. *$p(0) = 0$, and*
4. *for every $x \in [2k]$, $|p(x) - 1| \leq \gamma/2$.*

PROOF OF LEMMA 4.1. We can compute $\mathrm{OR}_d(y)$ as a disjunction of disjunctions by partitioning the inputs $y_1, \dots, y_d$ into blocks of size d/m and computing:

$$\mathrm{OR}_m(\mathrm{OR}_{d/m}(y_1, \dots, y_{d/m}), \dots, \mathrm{OR}_{d/m}(y_{d-d/m+1}, \dots, y_d)).$$

In order to approximately compute $\mathrm{OR}_d(y)$, we compute the inner disjunctions exactly using the polynomial $p_{d/m}$ given in Fact 4.3 and approximate the outer disjunction using the polynomial from Fact 4.4. Let

$$Z(y) = p_{d/m}(y_1, \dots, y_{d/m}) + \dots + p_{d/m}(y_{d-d/m+1}, \dots, y_d).$$

Setting $k = m$ in Fact 4.4, let q_m be the resulting polynomial of degree $O(\sqrt{m}\log(1/\gamma))$ and weight $O(m^{\sqrt{m}\log(1/\gamma)})$. Our final polynomial is

$$1 - 2q_m(m - Z(y)).$$

Note that $m - Z(y)$ takes values in $\{0, \dots, m\}$ and is 0 exactly when all inputs $y_1, \dots, y_d$ are FALSE. It follows that our final polynomial indeed approximates OR_d to additive error γ on all Boolean inputs.

We bound the degree and weight of this polynomial in y. By Fact 4.3, the inner disjunctions are computed exactly using degree d/m and weight at most 3. Hence, the total degree is $O(\sqrt{m}\log(1/\gamma)\cdot d/m)$. To bound the weight, we observe that the outer polynomial $q_m(\cdot)$ has at most $T = m^{O(\sqrt{m}\log(1/\gamma))}$ terms where each one has degree at most $D_{\text{outer}} = O(\sqrt{m}\log(1/\gamma))$ and coefficients of absolute value at most $c_{\text{outer}} = 2^{O(\sqrt{m}\log(1/\gamma))}$. Expanding the polynomials for $Z(y)$, the weight of each term incurs a multiplicative factor of $c_{\text{inner}} \leq 3^{D_{\text{outer}}} = 3^{O(\sqrt{m}\log 1/\gamma)}$ so the total weight is at most $c_{\text{inner}} \cdot c_{\text{outer}} \cdot T = m^{O(\sqrt{m}\log 1/\gamma)}$.

□

PROOF OF LEMMA 4.2. Again we partition the inputs $y_1, \dots, y_d$ into blocks of size d/m and view the disjunction as:

$$\mathrm{OR}_m(\mathrm{OR}_{d/m}(y_1, \dots, y_{d/m}), \dots, \mathrm{OR}_{d/m}(y_{d-d/m+1}, \dots, y_d)).$$

Once again, we compute the inner disjunctions exactly using the polynomial from Fact 4.3. Let

$$Z(y) = p_{d/m}(y_1, \dots, y_{d/m}) + \dots + p_{d/m}(y_{d-d/m+1}, \dots, y_d).$$

If the input y has Hamming weight at most k, then $Z(y)$ also takes values in $\{m, \dots, m-2k\}$. Thus, we may approximate the outer disjunction using a polynomial of degree $O(\sqrt{k}\log(1/\gamma))$ from Fact 4.4. Our final polynomial is:

$$1 - 2q_k(m - Z).$$

The bound on degree and weight may be obtained as in the previous lemma. □

4.1 Proof of upper bound theorems

We first present the proof of Theorem 1.3.

PROOF OF THEOREM 1.3. Taking

$$m = O\big((\log d/\log\log d)^2\big)$$

in Lemma 4.1 and $m = d^{O(1/\sqrt{k})}$ in Lemma 4.2, it follows that for some constant $C > 0$, the d-variate disjunction restricted to $H_{d,k}$ is (1/400)-approximated by a d-variate real polynomial of degree t and weight W where

$$t = \min\left\{d^{1-\frac{1}{C\sqrt{k}}}, \frac{d}{\log^{0.995} d}\right\} \text{ and } W = d^{0.01}.$$

□

PROOF OF THEOREM 1.1. By Theorem 1.3, we have a polynomial p that (1/400)-approximates the function $OR_d|_{H_{d,k}}$. Moreover, p has weight $W <= d^{0.01}$ and degree

$$t \le \min\left\{d^{1-\frac{1}{C\sqrt{k}}}, \frac{d}{\log^{0.995} d}\right\}.$$

Thus, by Fact 2.5, we have a family of polynomials $\mathcal{P}_{t,W}(d)$ that (1/400)-approximates the function family $\mathcal{F}_{\mathcal{Q}}|_{H_{d,k}}$. We have the ingredients needed to apply Theorem 3.1. Taking $\alpha = 1/100$, $\beta = 1/100$ gives the conclusion. □

Remark 1 in the Introduction follows from using a slightly different choice of m in Lemma 4.1, namely

$$m = O(\log^2 d/\log^3 \log d).$$

To obtain the summary of the database promised in Remark 2, we request an answer to each of the k-way marginal queries $B(1/400)$ times. Doing so, will ensure that we obtain a maximal database update sequence, and it was argued in Section 2.1 that the polynomial resulting from any maximal database update sequence accurately answers every k-way marginal query. Finally, we obtain a compact summary by randomly choosing $\tilde{O}(kd^{0.01})$ samples from the normalized coefficient vector of this polynomial to obtain a new sparse polynomial that accurately answers every k-way marginal query (see e.g. [4]). Our compact summary is this final sparse polynomial.

5. LOWER BOUNDS

In this section, we address the general problem of approximating a block-composed function $G = F(\ldots, f(.), \ldots)$, where $F\colon \{-1,1\}^k \to \{-1,1\}$, $f\colon Y \to \{-1,1\}$, $Y \subseteq \mathbb{R}^{d/k}$ over inputs restricted to a set $\mathcal{Y} \subseteq Y^k$ using low-weight polynomials. We give a lower bound on the minimum degree of such polynomials. In our main application, G will be OR_d, and $\mathcal{Y}$ will be the set of all d-dimensional Boolean vectors of Hamming weight at most k.

Our proof technique is inspired by the composition theorem lower bounds of [30, Theorem 3.1], where it is shown that the γ-approximate degree of the composed function G is at least the product of the γ-approximate degree of the outer function and the PTF degree of the inner function. Our main contribution is a generalization of such a composition theorem along two directions: (1) we show degree lower bounds that take into account the L1-norm of the coefficient vector of the approximating polynomial, and (2) our lower bounds hold even when we require the approximation to be accurate only on inputs of low Hamming weight, while prior work only considered approximations that are accurate on all Boolean inputs.

Our main theorem is stated below. In parsing the statement of the theorem, it may be helpful to think of $G = \mathrm{OR}_d$, $\mathcal{Y} = H_{d,k}$, the set of all d-dimensional Boolean vectors of Hamming weight at most k, $f = \mathrm{OR}_{d/k}$, $F = \mathrm{OR}_k$, $Y = \{-1,1\}^{d/k}$, and $H = H_{d/k,1}$. This will be the setting of interest in our main application of the theorem.

THEOREM 5.1. *Let $Y \subset \mathbb{R}^{d/k}$ be a finite set and $\gamma > 0$. Given $f : Y \to \{-1,1\}$ and $F : \{-1,1\}^k \to \{-1,1\}$ such that $deg_{2\gamma}(F) = D$, let $G : Y^k \to \{-1,1\}$ denote the composed function defined by $G(Y_1, \ldots, Y_k) = F(f(Y_1), \ldots, f(Y_k))$. Let $\mathcal{Y} \subseteq Y^k$. Suppose there exists $H \subseteq Y$ such that for every $(Y_1, \ldots, Y_k) \in Y^k \setminus \mathcal{Y}$ there exists $i \in [k]$ such that $Y_i \in Y \setminus H$. Then, for every $t \in \mathbb{Z}_+$,*

$$deg_{(\gamma,W)}(G|_{\mathcal{Y}}) \ge \frac{1}{2}tD \text{ for every } W \le \gamma 2^{-k} w^*(f|_H, t)^{\frac{D}{2}}.$$

We will derive the following corollary from Theorem 5.1. Theorem 1.4 follows immediately from Corollary 5.2 by considering any $k = o(\log d)$.

COROLLARY 5.2. *Let $k \in [d]$. Then, there exists a universal constant $C > 0$ such that*

$$deg_{(1/6,W)}(OR_d|_{H_{d,k}}) = \Omega\left(\frac{d}{\sqrt{k}} \cdot \frac{W^{-\frac{1}{C\sqrt{k}}}}{2^{\sqrt{k}/C}}\right)$$

for every

$$W \le \frac{1}{6.2^k}\left(\frac{d}{k}\right)^{C\sqrt{k}}.$$

Intuition underlying our proof technique. Recall that our upper bound in Section 4 worked as follows. We viewed OR_d as an "OR of ORs", and we approximated the outer OR with a polynomial p of degree $\deg_{\text{outer}}$ chosen to be as small as possible, and composed p with a low-weight but high-degree polynomial computing each inner OR. We needed to make sure the weight W_{inner} of the inner polynomials was very low, because the composition step potentially blows the weight up to roughly $W_{\text{inner}}^{\deg_{\text{outer}}}$. As a result, the inner polynomials had to have very high degree, to keep their weight low.

Intuitively, we construct a dual solution to a certain linear program that captures the intuition that any low-weight, low-degree polynomial approximation to OR_d must look something like our primal solution, composing a low-degree approximation to an "outer" OR with low-weight approximations to inner ORs. Moreover, our dual solution formalizes the intuition that the composition step must result in a massive blowup in weight, from W_{inner} to roughly $W_{\text{inner}}^{\deg_{\text{outer}}}$.

In more detail, our dual construction works by writing OR_d as an OR of ORs, where the outer OR is over k variables, and each inner ORs is over d/k variables. We obtain our dual solution by carefully combining a dual witness Γ to the high approximate degree of the outer OR, with a dual witness ψ to the fact that any low-degree polynomial with margin at least 1 for each inner OR, must have "large" weight, even if the polynomial must satisfy the margin constraint only on inputs of Hamming weight 0 or 1. This latter condition, that ψ must witness high non-constant margin weight even if restricted to inputs of Hamming weight 0 or 1, is essential to ensuring that our combined dual witness does not place any "mass" on irrelevant inputs, i.e. those of Hamming weight larger than k.

5.1 Duality Theorems

In the rest of the section, we let $\chi_S(x) = \prod_{i \in S} x_i$ for any given set $S \subseteq [d]$. The question of existence of a weight W polynomial with small degree that γ-approximates a given function can be expressed as a feasibility problem for a linear program. Now, in order to show the non-existence of such a polynomial, it is sufficient to show infeasibility of the linear program. By duality, this is equivalent to demonstrating the existence of a solution to the corresponding dual program. We begin by summarizing the duality theorems that will be useful in exhibiting this witness.

THEOREM 5.3 ((γ, W)-APPROXIMATE DEGREE). *Fix $\gamma \geq 0$ and let $f : Y \to \{-1, 1\}$ be given for some finite set $Y \subset \mathbb{R}^d$. Then, $deg_{(\gamma,W)}(f) \geq t + 1$ if and only if there exists a function $\Psi : Y \to \mathbb{R}$ such that*

1. $\sum_{y \in Y} |\Psi(y)| = 1$,
2. $\sum_{y \in Y} \Psi(y) f(y) - W \cdot |\sum_{y \in Y} \Psi(y) \chi_S(y)| > \gamma$ *for every $S \subseteq [d], |S| \leq t$.*

PROOF. By definition, $\deg_{(\gamma,W)}(f) \leq t$ if and only if $\exists (\lambda_S)_{S \subseteq [d], |S| \leq t}$:

$$\sum_{S \subseteq [d], |S| \leq t} |\lambda_S| \leq W, \text{ and}$$

$$\left| f(y) - \sum_{S \subseteq [d], |S| \leq t} \lambda_S \chi_S(y) \right| \leq \gamma \ \forall\, y \in Y.$$

By Farkas' lemma, $\deg_{(\gamma,W)}(f) \leq t$ if and only if $\nexists\ \Psi : Y \to \mathbb{R}$ such that

$$\frac{1}{W} \sum_{y \in Y} (f(y)\Psi(y) - \gamma|\Psi(y)|) > \left| \sum_{y \in Y} \chi_S(y) \Psi(y) \right|$$

$\forall\, S \subseteq [d], |S| \leq t$. □

The dual witness that we construct to prove Theorem 5.1 is obtained by combining a dual witness for the large non-constant margin weight of the inner function with a dual witness for the large approximate degree for the outer function. The duality conditions for these are given below. The proof of the duality condition for the case of γ-approximate degree is well-known, so we omit the proof for brevity.

THEOREM 5.4 (γ-APPROXIMATE DEGREE). *[5, 31, 37] Fix $\gamma \geq 0$ and let $f : Y \to \{-1, 1\}$ be given, where $Y \subset \mathbb{R}^d$ is a finite set. Then, $deg_\gamma(f) \geq t + 1$ if and only if there exists a function $\Gamma : Y \to \mathbb{R}$ such that*

1. $\sum_{y \in Y} |\Gamma(y)| = 1$,
2. $\sum_{y \in Y} \Gamma(y) p(y) = 0$ *for every polynomial p of degree at most t, and*
3. $\sum_{y \in Y} \Gamma(y) f(y) > \gamma$.

THEOREM 5.5 (NON-CONSTANT MARGIN WEIGHT). *Let $Y \subset \mathbb{R}^d$ be a finite set, let $f : Y \to \{1, -1\}$ be a given function and $w > 0$. The non-constant margin weight $w^*(f, t) \geq w$ if and only if there exists a distribution $\mu : Y \to [0, 1]$ such that*

1. $\sum_{y \in Y} \mu(y) f(y) = 0$
2. $\left| \sum_{y \in Y} \mu(y) f(y) \chi_S(y) \right| \leq \frac{1}{w}$ *for every $S \subseteq [d]$, $|S| \leq t$.*

PROOF. Let $\mathcal{S} = \{S \subseteq [d] : |S| \leq t\}$, $\overline{\mathcal{S}} = \mathcal{S} \setminus \{\emptyset\}$. By definition, $w^*(f, t)$ is expressed by the following linear program:

$$\min \sum_{S \in \overline{\mathcal{S}}} |\lambda_S|$$

$$f(y) \sum_{S \in \mathcal{S}} \lambda_S \chi_S(y) \geq 1 \ \forall\, y \in Y.$$

The above linear program can be restated as follows:

$$\min \sum_{S \in \overline{\mathcal{S}}} \alpha_S$$

$$\alpha_S + \lambda_S \geq 0 \ \forall\, S \in \overline{\mathcal{S}},$$

$$\alpha_S - \lambda_S \geq 0 \ \forall\, S \in \overline{\mathcal{S}},$$

$$f(y) \sum_{S \in \mathcal{S}} \lambda_S \chi_S(y) \geq 1 \ \forall\, y \in Y, \text{ and}$$

$$\alpha_S \geq 0 \ \forall\, S \in \overline{\mathcal{S}}.$$

The dual program is expressed below:

$$\max \sum_y \mu(y)$$

$$u_1(S) + u_2(S) \leq 1 \ \forall\, S \in \overline{\mathcal{S}},$$

$$\sum_{y \in Y} \mu(y) f(y) \chi_S(y) + u_1(S) - u_2(S) = 0 \ \forall\, S \in \overline{\mathcal{S}},$$

$$\sum_{y \in Y} \mu(y) f(y) = 0,$$

$$\mu(y) \geq 0 \ \forall\, y \in Y,\ u_1(S), u_2(S) \geq 0 \ \forall\, S \in \overline{\mathcal{S}}.$$

By standard manipulations, the above dual program is equivalent to

$$\max \sum_y \mu(y)$$

$$|\sum_{y \in Y} \mu(y) \chi_S(y) f(y)| \leq 1 \ \forall\, S \in \overline{\mathcal{S}}$$

$$\sum_{y \in Y} \mu(y) f(y) = 0,$$

$$\mu(y) \geq 0 \ \forall\, y \in Y$$

Finally, given a distribution μ' satisfying the hypothesis of the theorem, one can obtain a dual solution μ to show that $w^*(f, t) \geq w$ by taking

$$w^{-1} = \max_{S \in \mathcal{S}} |\sum_{y \in Y} \mu'(y) \chi_S(y) f(y)|$$

and setting $\mu(y) = w\mu'(y) \ \forall\, y \in Y$. In the other direction, if $w^*(f, t) \geq w$, then we have a dual solution μ satisfying the above dual program such that $\sum_{y \in Y} \mu(y) = w^*(f, t)$. By setting $\mu'(y) = \mu(y)/w^*(f, t) \ \forall\, y \in Y$, we obtain the desired distribution. □

5.2 Proof of Theorem 5.1

Our approach to exhibiting a dual witness as per Theorem 5.3 is to build a dual witness by appropriately combining the dual witnesses for the "hardness" of the inner and outer functions. Our method of combining the dual witnesses is inspired by the technique of [30, Theorem 3.7].

PROOF OF THEOREM 5.1. Let $w = w^*(f|_H, t)$. We will exhibit a dual witness function $\Psi : \mathcal{Y} \to \mathbb{R}$ corresponding to Theorem 5.3 for the specified choice of degree and weight. For $y \in Y^k$, let $Y_i = (y_{(i-1)(d/k)+1}, \ldots, y_{id/k})$. By Theorem 5.5, we know that there exists a distribution $\mu : H \to \mathbb{R}$ such that

$$\sum_{y\in H} \mu(y)f(y) = 0, \tag{2}$$

$$\left|\sum_{y\in H} \mu(y)f(y)\chi_S(y)\right| \le \frac{1}{w} \; \forall\, S \subseteq \left[\frac{d}{k}\right], |S| \le t \tag{3}$$

We set $\mu(y) = 0$ for $y \in Y \setminus H$.

Since $\deg_{2\gamma}(F) = D$, by Theorem 5.4, we know that there exists a function $\Gamma : \{-1,1\}^k \to \mathbb{R}$ such that

$$\sum_{x\in\{-1,1\}^k} |\Gamma(x)| = 1, \tag{4}$$

$$\sum_{x\in\{-1,1\}^k} \Gamma(x)p(x) = 0$$

for every polynomial p of degree at most D, and (5)

$$\sum_{x\in\{-1,1\}^k} \Gamma(x)F(x) > 2\gamma. \tag{6}$$

Consider the function $\Psi : Y^k \to \mathbb{R}$ defined as $\Psi(y) = 2^k\Gamma(f(Y_1), \ldots, f(Y_k))\prod_{i=1}^k \mu(Y_i)$. By the hypothesis of the theorem, we know that if $(Y_1, \ldots, Y_k) \in Y^k \setminus \mathcal{Y}$, then there exists $i \in [k]$ such that $Y_i \in Y \setminus H$ and hence $\mu(Y_i) = 0$ and therefore $\Psi(Y_1, \ldots, Y_k) = 0$.

1.
$$\sum_{y\in\mathcal{Y}} |\Psi(y)| = \sum_{y\in\mathcal{Y}} 2^k|\Gamma(f(Y_1), \ldots, f(Y_k))| \prod_{i=1}^k \mu(Y_i)$$
$$= 2^k\mathbb{E}_{y\sim\Phi}(|\Gamma(f(Y_1), \ldots, f(Y_k))|)$$

where $y \sim \Phi$ denotes y chosen from the product distribution $\Phi : Y^k \to [0,1]$ defined by $\Phi(y) = \prod_{i\in[k]} \mu(Y_i)$. Since $\sum_{y\in Y} \mu(y)f(y) = 0$, it follows that if Y_i is chosen with probability $\mu(Y_i)$, then $f(Y_i)$ is uniformly distributed in $\{-1,1\}$. Consequently,

$$\sum_{y\in\mathcal{Y}} |\Psi(y)| = 2^k\mathbb{E}_{z\sim_U\{-1,1\}^k}(|\Gamma(z_1, \ldots, z_k)|) = 1.$$

The last equality is by using (4).

2. By the same reasoning as above, it follows from (6) that

$$\sum_{y\in\mathcal{Y}} \Psi(y)G(y) = \sum_{z\in\{-1,1\}^k} \Gamma(z)F(z) > 2\gamma.$$

3. Fix a subset $S \subseteq [d]$ of size at most $tD/2$. Let $S_i = S \cap \{(i-1)(d/k)+1, \ldots, id/k\}$ for each $i \in [k]$. Consequently, $\chi_S(y) = \prod_{i=1}^k \chi_{S_i}(Y_i)$.

Now using the Fourier coefficients $\hat{\Gamma}(T)$ of the function Γ, we can express

$$\Gamma(z_1, \ldots, z_k) = \sum_{T\subseteq[k]} \hat{\Gamma}(T)\prod_{i\in T} z_i = \sum_{\substack{T\subseteq[k],\\ |T|\ge D}} \hat{\Gamma}(T)\prod_{i\in T} z_i$$

since $\hat{\Gamma}(T) = 0$ if $|T| < D$ by (5). Hence,

$$\Psi(y) = 2^k \sum_{\substack{T\subseteq[k],\\ |T|\ge D}} \hat{\Gamma}(T)\prod_{i\in T} f(Y_i)\mu(Y_i) \cdot \prod_{i\in[k]\setminus T} \mu(Y_i)$$

Therefore, $\sum_{y\in\mathcal{Y}} \Psi(y)\chi_S(y)$

$$= \sum_{y\in\mathcal{Y}} \Psi(y) \prod_{i\in[k]} \chi_{S_i}(Y_i)$$

$$= 2^k \sum_{y\in\mathcal{Y}} \left(\sum_{\substack{T\subseteq[k],\\ |T|\ge D}} \hat{\Gamma}(T)\prod_{i\in T} f(Y_i)\mu(Y_i) \cdot \prod_{i\in[k]\setminus T} \mu(Y_i)\right) \prod_{i\in[k]} \chi_{S_i}(Y_i)$$

$$= 2^k \sum_{\substack{T\subseteq[k],\\ |T|\ge D}} \hat{\Gamma}(T) \sum_{y\in\mathcal{Y}} \left(\prod_{i\in T} f(Y_i)\mu(Y_i) \cdot \prod_{i\in[k]\setminus T} \mu(Y_i) \prod_{i\in[k]} \chi_{S_i}(Y_i)\right)$$

$$= 2^k \sum_{\substack{T\subseteq[k],\\ |T|\ge D}} \hat{\Gamma}(T) \sum_{Y_1,\ldots,Y_k\in H} \left(\prod_{i\in T} f(Y_i)\mu(Y_i)\chi_{S_i}(Y_i) \cdot \prod_{i\in[k]\setminus T} \mu(Y_i)\chi_{S_i}(Y_i)\right).$$

Rearranging, we have $\sum_{y\in\mathcal{Y}} \Psi(y)\chi_S(y) =$

$$2^k \sum_{\substack{T\subseteq[k],\\ |T|\ge D}} \hat{\Gamma}(T) \prod_{i\in T} \left(\sum_{Y_i\in H} f(Y_i)\mu(Y_i)\chi_{S_i}(Y_i)\right) \prod_{i\in[k]\setminus T} \left(\sum_{Y_i\in H} \mu(Y_i)\chi_{S_i}(Y_i)\right). \tag{7}$$

Now, we will bound each product term in the outer sum by $w^{-D/2}$. We first observe that for every $i \in [k]$,

$$\sum_{x\in H} \mu(x)\chi_{S_i}(x) \le \sum_{x\in H} \mu(x) = 1.$$

If $|S_i| \le t$, by (3)

$$\left|\sum_{x\in H} f(x)\mu(x)\chi_{S_i}(x)\right| \le \frac{1}{w}.$$

If $|S_i| > t$, then

$$\left|\sum_{x\in H} f(x)\mu(x)\chi_{S_i}(x)\right| \le \sum_{x\in H} \mu(x) = 1.$$

Since $\sum_{i=1}^k |S_i| \le tD/2$, it follows that $|S_i| \le t$ for more than $k - D/2$ indices $i \in [k]$. Thus, for each $T \subseteq [k]$ such that $|T| \ge D$, there are at least $D/2$

indices $i \in T$ such that $|S_i| \leq t$. Hence,

$$\left|\sum_{y \in \mathcal{Y}} \Psi(y)\chi_S(y)\right| \leq 2^k w^{-\frac{D}{2}} \sum_{\substack{T \subseteq [k] \\ |T| \geq D}} \left|\hat{\Gamma}(T)\right| \leq 2^k w^{-\frac{D}{2}}.$$

Here, the last inequality is because $|\hat{\Gamma}(T)| \leq 2^{-k}$ from (4).

From 1, 2 and 3, we have

$$\sum_{y \in \mathcal{Y}} \Psi(y)G(y) - W \max_{S \subseteq [d], |S| \leq \frac{tD}{2}} \left|\sum_{y \in \mathcal{Y}} \Psi(y)\chi_S(y)\right| > \gamma$$

if $W \leq \gamma 2^{-k} w^{D/2}$. □

We now derive Corollary 5.2. We need the following theorems on the approximate degree and the non-constant margin weight of the OR_d function.

THEOREM 5.6 (APPROXIMATE DEGREE OF OR_d [27]).

$$deg_{1/3}(OR_d) = \Theta(\sqrt{d}).$$

LEMMA 5.7 (MARGIN WEIGHT OF OR_d).

$$w^*(OR_d|_{H_{d,1}}, t) \geq d/t.$$

PROOF. The function

$$\mu(x) = \begin{cases} 1/2 & \text{if } x = (1, \ldots, 1), \\ 1/2d & \text{if } x \in H_{d,1} \setminus \{(1, \ldots, 1)\}. \end{cases}$$

acts as the dual witness in Theorem 5.5. □

PROOF OF COROLLARY 5.2. We use Theorem 5.1 in the following setting. Let $Y = \{-1,1\}^{d/k}$, the inner function $f : Y \to \{-1,1\}$ be $\mathrm{OR}_{d/k}$ and the outer function $F : \{-1,1\}^k \to \{-1,1\}$ be OR_k, $\mathcal{Y} = H_{d,k}$ and $H = H_{d/k,1}$. By a simple counting argument, if $(Y_1, \ldots, Y_k) \in \{-1,1\}^d \setminus H_{d,k}$, then there exists $i \in [k]$ such that $Y_i \in \{-1,1\}^{d/k} \setminus H_{d/k,1}$. Further, by Theorem 5.6, we know that $\deg_{1/3}(F) = \Theta(\sqrt{k})$ and by Claim 5.7, we know that $w^*(f|_H, t) \geq d/kt$. Therefore, by Theorem 5.1, we have that, for every $t \in \mathbb{Z}_+$,

$$\deg_{1/6,W}(OR_d|_{H_{d,k}}) = \Omega\left(t\sqrt{k}\right)$$

for every

$$W \leq \frac{1}{6} 2^{-k} \left(\frac{d}{kt}\right)^{C\sqrt{k}}.$$

We obtain the conclusion by taking

$$t = \lfloor (d/k)(6W2^k)^{-1/C\sqrt{k}} \rfloor.$$

Since $W \leq (1/6)2^{-k}(d/k)^{C\sqrt{k}}$, it follows that $t \geq 1$ and hence is a valid choice for t in applying Theorem 5.1. □

Comparison to [29]. As described in the beginning of Section 4, Lemma 8 of the work of Servedio et al. [29] can be shown to imply that any polynomial p of weight W that 1/3-approximates the OR_d function on all Boolean inputs requires degree $\Omega(d/\log W)$.[1] The proof in [29] relies on a Markov-type inequality that bounds the derivative of a univariate polynomial in terms of its degree and the size of its coefficients. The proof of this Markov-type inequality is non-constructive and relies on complex analysis.

Here, we observe that our dual witness construction used to prove Corollary 5.2 also yields a general lower bound on the tradeoffs achievable between the weight and degree of the approximating polynomial p, even when we require p to be accurate only on inputs of Hamming weight at most $O(\log W)$ (see Theorem 5.8). The methods of Servedio et al. do not yield any non-trivial lower bound on the degree in this setting. We also believe our proof technique is of interest in comparison to the methods of Servedio et al. as it is constructive (exhibiting an explicit dual witness for the lower bound) and avoids the use of complex analysis.

THEOREM 5.8. *Any polynomial p of weight W that 1/6-approximates the OR_d function on all Boolean inputs requires degree $d/2^{O(\sqrt{\log W})}$.*

PROOF. As p is accurate on the entire Boolen hypercube, it is accurate on inputs of Hamming weight at most $\log W$. The theorem follows by setting $k = \log W$ in the statement of Corollary 5.2. □

6. DISCUSSION

We gave a differentially private online algorithm for answering k-way marginal queries that runs in time $2^{o(d)}$ per query, and guarantees accurate answers for databases of size $\mathrm{poly}(d,k)$. More precisely, we showed that if there exists a polynomial of degree t and weight W approximating the d-variate OR function on Boolean inputs of Hamming weight at most k, then a variant of the private multiplicative weights algorithm can answer k-way marginal queries in time roughly $\binom{d}{t}$ per query and guarantee accurate answers on databases of size roughly $W\sqrt{d}$. To this end, we gave a new construction showing the existence of polynomial approximations to the OR function on inputs of low Hamming weight. Specifically, we showed that polynomials of weight $d^{0.01}$ and degree $d^{1-\Omega(1/\sqrt{k})}$ exist.

Practical Considerations. Our algorithm for answering k-way marginals is essentially the same as in [19] except for using a different set of base functions (specifically, the set of all low-degree parities), which leads to an efficiency gain. We note that our algorithm degrades smoothly to the private multiplicative weights algorithm as the degree of the promised polynomial approximation increases, and never gives a worse running time. This behavior suggests that our algorithm may lead to practical improvements even for relatively small values of d, for which the asymptotic analysis does not apply. In such cases one might use an alternative

[1]More precisely, [29, Lemma 8] as stated shows that if the coefficients of a univariate polynomial P each have absolute value at most W, and $1/2 \leq \max_{x\in[0,1]} |P(x)| \leq R$, then $\max_{x\in[0,1]} |P'(x)| = O(\deg(P) \cdot R \cdot (\log W + \log \deg(P)))$, where $P'(x)$ denotes the derivative of P at x, and $\deg(P)$ denotes the degree of P. By inspection of the proof, it is easily seen that if the L_1-norm of the coefficients of P is bounded by W, then the following slightly stronger conclusion holds: $\max_{x\in[0,1]} |P'(x)| = O(\deg(P) \cdot R \cdot \log W)$. When combined with the symmetrization argument of [29], this stronger conclusion implies: any polynomial p of weight W that 1/3-approximates the OR_d function on all Boolean inputs requires degree $\Omega(d/\log W)$.

but similar analysis that shows the existence of a polynomial of degree $kd^{1-c/k}$ and weight d^c (for any $0 < c < k$) that *exactly* computes the d-variate OR function on inputs of Hamming weight at most k. Such a polynomial may be obtained as in our construction, by breaking the d-variate OR function into an OR of ORs, and using a degree k polynomial defined via polynomial interpolation, instead of Chebyshev polynomials, to approximate the outer OR on inputs of Hamming weight at most k. This variant does achieve asymptotic properties not shared by the algorithm of Theorem 1.1, owing to the fact that it uses exact rather than approximate representations of the database: for any constant k, this variant also runs in time $\exp\left(d^{1-\Omega(1)}\right)$, and achieves worst-case additive error $o(1)$ for sufficiently large databases, i.e., for $n \gtrsim \tilde{O}(d^c)$.

Relationship with [12, 26]. As we mentioned in the introduction, in subsequent work, Dwork et al. [12] show how to privately release marginals in a very different parameter regime from what we consider here. Although their algorithm is quite different from ours, there are some important similarities. Their algorithm is based on a recent algorithm of Nikolov et. al. [26] for answering arbitrary counting queries. This algorithm proceeds as follows. First, it adds noise $O(|\mathcal{Q}|^{1/2}/|D|)$ to the answer to every query to obtain a vector of noisy answers. The noise is sufficient to ensure differential privacy. Second, it "projects" the vector of noisy answers onto the convex body K consisting of all vectors of answers that are consistent with some real database. Surprisingly, the projection step will improve the accuracy. In fact, Nikolov et al. [26] show that the projected answers will be accurate even for very small databases. However current best algorithms for projecting on the body K require time $2^{O(d)}$ for an arbitrary set of queries.

Dwork et al. [12] show that for the set of k-way marginals there is a convex body L such that the projection into L can be computed in time $\text{poly}(\binom{d}{\leq k})$ and L approximates K well enough to achieve accuracy on smaller databases than would be achievable with independent noise (however, these databases still have size $d^{\Omega(k)}$). Our approximation of f_D by low-weight polynomials of degree $t = o(d)$ can be shown to imply a polytope L' with $2^{o(d)}$ vertices—which is sufficient to imply that projection can be computed in time $2^{o(d)}$—that approximates K well enough to achieve accuracy on databases of nearly optimal size (i.e., size roughly $kd^{0.51}$). Thus our approximation-theoretic approach is relevant for understanding the capabilities and limitations of algorithms in the Nikolov et al. [26] framework.

Future Directions. Our lower bounds show that our polynomial approximation to the OR_d function on inputs of Hamming weight k is essentially the best possible; in particular, we cannot hope to substantially improve the running time on $\text{poly}(d, k)$ size databases by giving approximating polynomials with better weight and degree bounds. This also rules out several natural candidates that can themselves be computed exactly by a low-weight polynomial of low-degree (e.g., the set of small-width conjunctions).

However, we do not know if it is possible to do better by using different feature spaces (other than the set of all low-degree monomials) to approximate all disjunctions over d variables. There is some additional evidence from prior work that low-degree monomials may be the optimal choice: if the parameter of significance is the *size* of the set of functions used to approximate disjunctions on inputs of Hamming weight at most k, then low-degree monomials are indeed optimal [31] (see also Section 5 in the full version of [34]). It would be interesting to determine whether this optimality still holds when we restrict the L_1 weight of the linear combinations used in the approximations to be $\text{poly}(d)$.

Acknowledgments. We thank Salil Vadhan for helpful discussions about this work.

7. REFERENCES

[1] B. Barak, K. Chaudhuri, C. Dwork, S. Kale, F. McSherry, and K. Talwar. Privacy, accuracy, and consistency too: a holistic solution to contingency table release. In *PODS*, pages 273–282, 2007.

[2] A. Blum, C. Dwork, F. McSherry, and K. Nissim. Practical privacy: the sulq framework. In *PODS*, pages 128–138, 2005.

[3] A. Blum, K. Ligett, and A. Roth. A learning theory approach to non-interactive database privacy. In *STOC*, pages 609–618, 2008.

[4] J. Bruck and R. Smolensky. Polynomial Threshold Functions, AC^0 Functions, and Spectral Norms. *SIAM J. Comput.*, 21(1):33–42, 1992.

[5] M. Bun and J. Thaler. Dual lower bounds for approximate degree and markov-bernstein inequalities. In *Proceedings of 40th International Colloquium on Automata, Languages, and Programming*, pages 303–314, 2013.

[6] M. Bun, J. Ullman, and S. P. Vadhan. Fingerprinting codes and the price of approximate differential privacy. *CoRR*, abs/1311.3158, 2013.

[7] M. Cheraghchi, A. Klivans, P. Kothari, and H. K. Lee. Submodular functions are noise stable. In *Proceedings of the Twenty-Second Annual ACM-SIAM Symposium on Discrete Algorithms*, SODA, pages 1586–1592, 2012.

[8] A. De. Lower bounds in differential privacy. In *TCC*, pages 321–338, 2012.

[9] I. Dinur and K. Nissim. Revealing information while preserving privacy. In *PODS*, pages 202–210, 2003.

[10] C. Dwork, F. McSherry, K. Nissim, and A. Smith. Calibrating noise to sensitivity in private data analysis. In *TCC '06*, pages 265–284, 2006.

[11] C. Dwork, M. Naor, O. Reingold, G. N. Rothblum, and S. P. Vadhan. On the complexity of differentially private data release: efficient algorithms and hardness results. In *STOC '09*, pages 381–390, 2009.

[12] C. Dwork, A. Nikolov, and K. Talwar. Efficient algorithms for privately releasing marginals via convex relaxations. *CoRR*, abs/1308.1385, 2013.

[13] C. Dwork and K. Nissim. Privacy-preserving datamining on vertically partitioned databases. In *CRYPTO*, pages 528–544, 2004.

[14] C. Dwork, G. N. Rothblum, and S. P. Vadhan. Boosting and differential privacy. In *FOCS*, pages 51–60, 2010.

[15] V. Feldman and P. Kothari. Learning coverage functions. *Manuscript*, 2013.

[16] A. Gupta, M. Hardt, A. Roth, and J. Ullman. Privately releasing conjunctions and the statistical query barrier. In *STOC '11*, pages 803–812, 2011.

[17] A. Gupta, A. Roth, and J. Ullman. Iterative constructions and private data release. In *TCC*, pages 339–356, 2012.

[18] M. Hardt, K. Ligett, and F. McSherry. A simple and practical algorithm for differentially private data release. *NIPS '12*, 2012.

[19] M. Hardt and G. N. Rothblum. A multiplicative weights mechanism for privacy-preserving data analysis. In *FOCS*, pages 61–70, 2010.

[20] M. Hardt, G. N. Rothblum, and R. A. Servedio. Private data release via learning thresholds. In *SODA*, pages 168–187, 2012.

[21] P. Jain and A. Thakurta. Mirror descent based database privacy. In *APPROX-RANDOM*, pages 579–590, 2012.

[22] S. P. Kasiviswanathan, M. Rudelson, A. Smith, and J. Ullman. The price of privately releasing contingency tables and the spectra of random matrices with correlated rows. In *STOC*, pages 775–784, 2010.

[23] H. Klauck. On arthur merlin games in communication complexity. In *Proceedings of the 26th Annual Conference on Computational Complexity (CCC)*, CCC, pages 189–199, 2011.

[24] A. R. Klivans and R. A. Servedio. Toward attribute efficient learning of decision lists and parities. In J. Shawe-Taylor and Y. Singer, editors, *COLT*, volume 3120 of *Lecture Notes in Computer Science*, pages 224–238. Springer, 2004.

[25] P. M. Long and R. A. Servedio. Low-weight halfspaces for sparse boolean vectors. In *ITCS*, pages 21–36, 2013.

[26] A. Nikolov, K. Talwar, and L. Zhang. The geometry of differential privacy: the sparse and approximate cases. In *STOC*, pages 351–360, 2013.

[27] R. Paturi. On the degree of polynomials that approximate symmetric boolean functions. In *Proceedings of the twenty-fourth annual ACM Symposium on Theory of Computing*, pages 468–474, 1992.

[28] A. Roth and T. Roughgarden. Interactive privacy via the median mechanism. In *STOC '10*, pages 765–774, 2010.

[29] R. Servedio, L.-Y. Tan, and J. Thaler. Attribute-efficient learning and weight-degree tradeoffs for polynomial threshold functions. In *25th Annual Conference on Computational Learning Theory (COLT), JMLR Workshop and Conference Proceeding*, volume 23, pages 14.1–14.19, 2012.

[30] A. A. Sherstov. The intersection of two halfspaces has high threshold degree. In *Proceedings of the 2009 50th Annual IEEE Symposium on Foundations of Computer Science*, FOCS '09, pages 343–362, 2009.

[31] A. A. Sherstov. The pattern matrix method. *SIAM Journal on Computing*, 40(6):1969–2000, 2011.

[32] A. A. Sherstov. The multiparty communication complexity of set disjointness. In *STOC*, pages 525–548, 2012.

[33] A. A. Sherstov. Strong direct product theorems for quantum communication and query complexity. *SIAM J. Comput.*, 41(5):1122–1165, 2012.

[34] J. Thaler, J. Ullman, and S. P. Vadhan. Faster algorithms for privately releasing marginals. In *ICALP*, pages 810–821, 2012.

[35] J. Ullman. Answering $n^{2+o(1)}$ counting queries with differential privacy is hard. In *STOC*, pages 361–370, 2013.

[36] J. Ullman and S. P. Vadhan. PCPs and the hardness of generating private synthetic data. In *TCC '11*, pages 400–416, 2011.

[37] R. Špalek. A dual polynomial for OR. *CoRR*, abs/0803.4516, 2008.

Mechanism Design in Large Games: Incentives and Privacy *

[Extended Abstract]†

Michael Kearns
Department of Computer and Information Science
University of Pennsylvania
Philadelphia, PA
mkearns@cis.upenn.edu

Mallesh M. Pai
Department of Economics
University of Pennsylvania
Philadelphia, PA
mallesh@econ.upenn.edu

Aaron Roth
Department of Computer and Information Science
University of Pennsylvania
Philadelphia, PA
aaroth@cis.upenn.edu

Jonathan Ullman
School of Engineering and Applied Sciences
Harvard University
Cambridge, MA
jullman@seas.harvard.edu

ABSTRACT

We study the problem of implementing equilibria of complete information games in settings of incomplete information, and address this problem using "recommender mechanisms." A recommender mechanism is one that does not have the power to enforce outcomes or to force participation, rather it only has the power to suggestion outcomes on the basis of voluntary participation. We show that despite these restrictions, recommender mechanisms can implement equilibria of complete information games in settings of incomplete information under the condition that the game is *large*—i.e. that there are a large number of players, and any player's action affects any other's payoff by at most a small amount.

Our result follows from a novel application of *differential privacy.* We show that any algorithm that computes a correlated equilibrium of a complete information game while satisfying a variant of differential privacy—which we call *joint differential privacy*—can be used as a recommender mechanism while satisfying our desired incentive properties. Our main technical result is an algorithm for computing a correlated equilibrium of a large game while satisfying joint differential privacy.

Although our recommender mechanisms are designed to satisfy game-theoretic properties, our solution ends up satisfying a strong privacy property as well. No group of players can learn "much" about the type of any player outside the group from the recommendations of the mechanism, even if these players collude in an arbitrary way. As such, our algorithm is able to implement equilibria of complete information games, without revealing information about the realized types.

Categories and Subject Descriptors

Theory of Computation [**Algorithmic Game Theory and Mechanism Design**]: Algorithmic Mechanism Design

Keywords

Game Theory, Mechanism Design, Large Games, Differential Privacy

1. INTRODUCTION

A useful simplification common in game theory is the model of *games of complete (or full) information.* Informally, in a game of complete information, each player knows with certainty the utility function of every other player. In games of complete information, there are a number of solution concepts at our disposal, such as Nash equilibrium and correlated equilibrium. Common to these is the idea that each player is playing a best response against his opponents—because of randomness, players might be uncertain about what actions their opponents are taking, but they understand their opponents' incentives exactly.

In many situations, it is unreasonable to assume that players have exact knowledge of each other's utilities. For example, players may have few means of communication outside of the game, or may regard their type as valuable private information. These are *games of incomplete (or partial) in-*

*We gratefully acknowledge the support of NSF Grant CCF-1101389. We thank Nabil Al-Najjar, Eduardo Azevdeo, Eric Budish, Tymofiy Mylovanov, Andy Postlewaite, Al Roth and Tim Roughgarden for helpful comments and discussions.

†A full version of this working paper appears on the arXiv preprint site [KPRU13].

ITCS'14, January 12–14, 2014, Princeton, New Jersey, USA.
Copyright 2014 ACM 978-1-4503-2698-8/14/01 ...$15.00.
http://dx.doi.org/10.1145/2554797.2554834.

formation, which are commonly modeled as Bayesian games in which the players' utilities functions, or types, are drawn from a commonly known prior distribution. The most common solution concept in such games is Bayes-Nash Equilibrium. This stipulates that every player i, as a function of his type, plays an action that maximizes his expected payoff, in expectation *both* over the random draw of the types of his opponents from the prior distribution and over the possible randomization of the other players.

Unsurprisingly, equilibrium welfare can suffer in games of incomplete information, because coordination becomes more difficult amongst players who do not know each other's types. One way to measure the quality of equilibria is via the "price of anarchy"—how much worse the social welfare can be in an equilibrium outcome, as opposed to the welfare-maximizing outcome. The price of anarchy can depend significantly on the notion of equilibrium. For example, Roughgarden [Rou12] notes that even smooth games[1] that have a constant price of anarchy under full information solution concepts (e.g. Nash or correlated equilibrium) can have an unboundedly large price of anarchy under partial information solution concepts (e.g. Bayes-Nash Equilibrium). Therefore, given a game of partial information, where all that we can predict is that players will choose some Bayes-Nash Equilibrium (if even that), it may be preferable to implement an equilibrium of the complete information game defined by the actual realized types of the players. Doing so would guarantee welfare bounded by the price of anarchy of the full information game, rather than suffering from the large price of anarchy of the partial information setting. In a smooth game, we would be just as happy implementing a correlated equilibrium as a Nash equilibrium, since the price of anarchy is no worse over correlated equilibria.

In this paper we ask whether it is possible to help coordinate on an equilibrium of the realized full information game using a certain type of proxy that we call a "recommender mechanism." That is, we augment the game with an additional option for each player to use a proxy. If players opt in to using the proxy, and reveal their type to the proxy, then it will suggest some action for them to take. However, players may also simply opt out of using the proxy and play the original game using any strategy they choose. We make the assumption that if players use the proxy, then they must report their type truthfully (or, alternatively, that the proxy has the ability to verify a player's type and punish those who report dishonestly). However, the proxy has very limited power in other respects, because it does not have the ability to modify payoffs of the game (i.e. make payments) or to enforce that its recommendations be followed.

Our main result is that it is indeed possible to implement approximate correlated equilibria of the realized full information game using recommender mechanisms, assuming the original game is "large". Informally, a game is large if there are many players and that each player has individually only a small affect on the utility of any other player. We show that in such games there exists a recommender mechanism such that for any prior on agent types, it is an approximate Bayes-Nash equilibrium for every agent in the game to opt in to the proxy, and then follow its recommended action. Moreover, when players do so, the resulting play forms an approximate correlated equilibrium of the full information game. The approximation error we require tends to 0 as the number of players grows.

1.1 Overview of Techniques and Results

A tempting approach is to use the following form of proxy: The proxy accepts a report of each agent's type, which defines an instance of a full information game. It then computes a correlated equilibrium of the full information game, and suggests an action to each player which is a draw from this correlated equilibrium. By definition of a correlated equilibrium, if all players opt into the proxy, then they can do no better than subsequently following the recommended action. However, this proxy does not solve the problem, as it may not be in a player's best interest to opt in, even if the other $n-1$ players do opt in! Intuitively, by opting out, the player can cause the proxy to compute a correlated equilibrium of the wrong game, or to compute a different correlated equilibrium of the same game![2] The problem is an instance of the well known equilibrium-selection problem—even in a game of full information, different players may disagree on their preferred equilibrium, and may have trouble coordinating. The problem is only more difficult in settings of incomplete information. In our case, by opting out of the mechanism, a player can have a substantial affect on the computed equilibrium, even if each player has only small affect on the utilities of other players.

Our solution is to devise a means of computing correlated equilibria such that any single player's reported type to the algorithm only has a small effect on the distribution of suggested actions to all other players. The precise notion of "small effect" that we use is a variant of the well studied notion of *differential privacy*. It is not hard to see that computing an equilibrium of even a large game is not

[1]Of particular interest to us are *smooth games*, defined by Roughgarden [Rou09]. Almost all known price of anarchy bounds (including those for the well studied model of traffic routing games) are bounds on smooth games, and many are quite good. Although price of anarchy bounds are typically proven for exact Nash equilibria of the full information games, in smooth games, the price of anarchy bounds extend without loss to (and even beyond) approximate correlated equilibria, again of the full information game.

[2]As a simple example, consider a large number n of people who must each choose whether to go to the beach (B) or mountains (M). People privately know their types— each person's utility depends on his own type, his action, and the fraction of other people p who go to the beach. A Beach type gets a payoff of $10p$ if he visits the beach, and $5(1-p)$ if he visits the mountain. A mountain type gets a payoff $5p$ from visiting the beach, and $10(1-p)$ from visiting the mountain. Note that the game is 'insensitive' (an agent's visit decision has a small impact on others' payoffs). Further, note that "everyone visits beach" and "everyone visits mountain" are both equilibria of the game, regardless of the realization of types. Consider the mechanism that attempts to implement the following social choice rule—"if the number of beach types is less than half the population, send everyone to the beach, and vice versa." It should be clear that if mountain types are just in the majority, then each mountain type has an incentive to opt out of the mechanism, and vice versa. As a result, even though the game is "large" and agents' actions do not affect others' payoffs significantly, simply computing equilibria from reported type profiles does not in general lead to even approximately truthful mechanisms. This is a general phenomenon that is not specific to our example. Finding an exact correlated equilibrium subject to any objective is a linear programming problem, and in general small changes in the objective (or constraints) of an LP can lead to wild changes in its solution.

possible under the standard constraint of differential privacy, because although agent's actions have only a small affect on the utilities of other players in large games, they can have large affect on their own utility functions. Thus, it is not possible to privately announce a best response for player i while protecting the privacy of i's type. Instead, we introduce a variant which we call *joint differential privacy*, which requires that simultaneously for every player i, the joint distribution on the suggested actions to all players $j \neq i$ be differentially private in the type of agent i. We show that a proxy mechanism which calculates an α-approximate correlated equilibrium of the game induced by players reported types, under the constraint of ϵ-joint differential privacy makes it an $(\epsilon + \alpha)$-approximate Bayes-Nash equilibrium for players to opt into the proxy, and then follow their suggested action, as desired.

Our main technical result is an instantiation of this plan: a pair of algorithms for computing α-approximate correlated equilibria in large games, such that we can take the approximation parameter $\epsilon + \alpha$ tending to zero. The first algorithm is efficient, but has a suboptimal dependence on the number of actions k in the game. The other algorithm is inefficient, but has a nearly optimal dependence on k. Both have an optimal dependence on the number of players n in the game, which we show by exhibiting a matching lower bound.

We introduce joint differential privacy, large games, and our game theoretic solution concepts in Section 2. In Section 3, we formally introduce our notion of a proxy, and state our main results. Formal proofs are deferred to the full working paper version available at on the arXiv preprint site [KPRU13].

1.2 Related Work and Discussion

Market and Mechanism Design Our work is related to the large body of literature on mechanism/ market design in "large games," which uses the large number of agents to provide mechanisms which have good incentive properties, even when the small market versions do not. It stretches back to [RP76] who showed that market (Walrasian) equilibria are approximately strategy proof in large economies. More recently [IM05], [KP09], [KPR10] have shown that various two-sided matching mechanisms are approximately strategy proof in large markets. There are similar results in the literature for one-sided matching markets, market economies, and double auctions. The most general result is that of [AB11] who design incentive compatible mechanisms for large economies that satisfy a smoothness assumption. While we only allow agents to opt in/ opt out rather than mis-report, we do not assume any such smoothness condition. Further, the literature on mechanism design normally gives the mechanism the power to "enforce" actions, while here our mechanism can only "recommend" actions.

Our work is also related to mediators in games [MT03, MT09]. This line of work aims to modify the equilibrium structure of full information games by introducing a mediator, which can coordinate agent actions if they choose to opt in using the mediator. Mediators can be used to convert Nash equilibria into dominant strategy equilibria [MT03], or implement equilibrium that are robust to collusion [MT09]. Our notion of a recommender mechanism is related, but is even weaker than that of a mediator. For example, our mechanisms do not need the power to make payments [MT03], or the power to enforce suggested actions [MT09]. Our mediators are thus closer to the communication devices in the "communication equilibria" of Forges [For86]—that work investigates the set of achievable payoffs via such mediators rather than how to design one, which we do here. It also does not allow players to opt out of using the mediator.

Large Games Our results hold under a "largeness condition", i.e. a player's action affects the payoff of all others by a small amount. These are closely related to the literature on large games, see e.g. [ANS00] or [Kal04]. There has been recent work studying large games using tools from theoretical computer science (but in this case, studying robustness of equilibrium concepts)—see [GR08, GR10].

Differential Privacy Differential privacy was first defined by [DMNS06], and is now the standard privacy "solution concept" in the theoretical computer science literature. It quantifies the *worst-case harm* that can befall an individual from allowing his data to be used in a computation, as compared to if he did not provide his data. There is by now a very large literature on differential privacy, readers can consult [Dwo08] for a more thorough introduction to the field.

[MT07] were the first to observe that a differentially private algorithm is also approximately truthful. This line of work was extended by [NST12] to give mechanisms in several special cases which are exactly truthful by combining private mechanisms with non-private mechanisms which explicitly punish non-truthful reporting. [HK12] showed that the mechanism of [MT07] (the "exponential mechanism") is in fact maximal in distributional range, and so can be made exactly truthful with the addition of payments. This immediate connection between privacy and truthfulness does not carry over to the notion of joint-differential privacy that we study here, but as we show, it is regained if the object that we compute privately is an equilibrium of the underlying game.

Another interesting line of work considers the problem of designing truthful mechanisms for agents who explicitly experience a cost for privacy loss as part of their utility function [CCK+13, NOS12, Xia13]. The main challenge in this line of work is to formulate a reasonable model for how agents experience cost as a function of privacy. We remark that the approaches taken in the former two can also be adapted to work in our setting, for agents who explicitly value privacy. [Gra12] studies the problem of implementation for various assumptions about players' preference for privacy and permissible game forms. A related line of work which also takes into account agent values for privacy considers the problem of designing markets by which analysts can procure private data from agents who explicitly experience costs for privacy loss [FL12, GR11, LR12, RS12]. See [PR13] for a survey.

Finally, our results rely on several technical solutions in the differential privacy literature. The most well studied problem is that of accurately answering numeric-valued queries on a data set. A basic result of [DMNS06] is that any low sensitivity query (i.e. the addition or removal of a single entry can change the value of the query by at most 1) can be answered efficiently and (ϵ-differential) privately while introducing only $O(1/\epsilon)$ error. Another fundamental result of [DKM+06, DRV10] is that differential privacy composes gracefully. Any algorithm composed of T subroutines, each of which are $O(\epsilon)$-differentially private, is itself $\sqrt{T}\epsilon$-

differentially private. Combined, these give an efficient algorithm for privately answering any T low sensitivity queries with $O(\sqrt{T})$ effort, a result which we make use of.

Using computationally inefficient algorithms, it is possible to privately answer queries much more accurately [BLR08, DRV10, RR10, HR10, GHRU11, GRU12]. Combining the results of the latter two yields an algorithm which can privately answer arbitrary low sensitivity queries as they arrive, with error that scales only logarithmically in the number of queries. We use this when we consider games with large action spaces.

Our lower bounds for privately computing equilibria use recent information theoretic lower bounds on the accuracy queries can be answered while preserving differential privacy [DN03, DMT07, DY08, De12]. Namely, we construct games whose equilibria encode answers to large numbers of queries on a database.

Variants of differential privacy related to joint differential privacy have been considered in the setting of query release, specifically for analyst privacy [DNV12]. Specifically, the definition of one-analyst-to-many-analyst privacy used by [HRU13] can be seen as an instantiation of joint differential privacy.

2. MODEL & PRELIMINARIES

We consider games $\mathcal{G}$ of up to n players $\{1, 2, \dots, n\}$, indexed by i. Player i can take actions in a set A, $|A| = k$. To allow our games to be defined also for fewer than n players, we will imagine that the null action $\perp \in A$, which corresponds to "opting out" of the game. We index actions by j. A tuple of actions, one for each player, will be denoted $\mathbf{a} = (a_1, a_2, \dots a_n) \in A^n$.[3]

Let $\mathcal{U}$ be the set of player types.[4] There is a utility function $u : \mathcal{U} \times A^n \to \Re$ that determines the payoff for a player given his type t_i and a joint action profile $\mathbf{a}$ for all players. When it is clear from context, we will refer to the utility function of player i, writing $u_i : A^n \to \Re$ to denote $u(t_i, \cdot)$. We write a generic profile of utilities $\mathbf{u} = (u_1, u_2, \dots u_n) \in \mathcal{U}^n$. We will be interested in implementing equilibria of the *complete information game* in settings of *incomplete information.* In the complete information setting, the types t_i of each player is fixed and commonly known to all players. In such settings, we can ignore the abstraction of 'types' and consider each player i simply to have a fixed utility function u_i. In models of *incomplete* information, players know their own type, but do not know the types of others. In the Bayesian model of incomplete information, there is a commonly known prior distribution τ from which each agent's type is jointly drawn: $(t_1, \dots, t_n) \sim \tau$. We now define the solution concepts we will use, both in the full information setting and in the Bayesian setting.

Denote a distribution over A^n by π, the marginal distribution over the actions of player i by π_i, and the marginal distribution over the (joint tuple of) actions of every player but player i by π_{-i}. We now present two standard solution concepts— approximate correlated and coarse correlated equilibrium.

[3]In general, subscripts will refer indices i.e. players and periods, while superscripts will refer to components of vectors.
[4]It is trivial to extend our results when agents have different typesets, $\mathcal{U}_i$. $\mathcal{U}$ will then be $\bigcup_{i=1}^n \mathcal{U}_i$.

DEFINITION 1 (APPROXIMATE CE). *Let $(u_1, u_2, \dots u_n)$ be a tuple of utility functions, one for each player. Let π be a distribution over tuples of actions A^n. We say that π is an* α-approximate correlated equilibrium *of the (complete information) game defined by $(u_1, u_2, \dots u_n)$ if for every player $i \in [N]$, and any function $f\colon A \to A$,*

$$\mathop{\mathbb{E}}_{\pi}[u_i(\mathbf{a})] \geq \mathop{\mathbb{E}}_{\pi}[u_i(f(a_i), a_{-i})] - \alpha$$

We now define a solution concept in the Bayesian model. Let τ be a commonly known joint distribution over $\mathcal{U}^n$, and let $\tau_{|t_i}$ be the posterior distribution on types conditioned on the type of player i being t_i. A (pure) *strategy* for player i is a function $s_i : \mathcal{U} \to A$, and we write $\mathbf{s} = (s_1, \dots, s_n)$ to denote a vector of strategy profiles.

DEFINITION 2 (APPROXIMATE BNE). *Let τ be a distribution over $\mathcal{U}^n$, and let $\mathbf{s} = (s_1, \dots, s_n)$ be a vector of strategies. We say that* $\mathbf{s}$ *is an* α-approximate (pure strategy) Bayes Nash Equilibrium *under τ if for every player i, for every $t_i \in \mathcal{U}$, and for every alternative strategy s_i':*

$$\mathop{\mathbb{E}}_{\mathbf{t}_{-i} \sim \tau_{|t_i}}[u_i(t_i, s_i(t_i), s_{-i}(t_{-i}))] \geq$$

$$\mathop{\mathbb{E}}_{\mathbf{t}_{-i} \sim \tau_{|t_i}}[u_i(t_i, s_i'(t_i), s_{-i}(t_{-i}))] - \epsilon$$

We restrict attention to 'insensitive' games. Roughly speaking a game is γ-sensitive if a player's choice of action affects any other player's payoff by at most γ. Note that we do not constrain the effect of a player's *own* actions on his payoff— *a player's action can have a large impact on his own payoff.* Formally:

DEFINITION 3 (γ-SENSITIVE). *A game is said to be γ-sensitive if for any two distinct players $i \neq i'$, any two actions a_i, a_i' and type t_i for player i and any tuple of actions a_{-i} for everyone else:*

$$|u_{i'}(a_i, a_{-i}) - u_{i'}(a_i', a_{-i})| \leq \gamma. \qquad (1)$$

A key tool in our paper is the design of differentially private "proxy" algorithms for suggesting actions to play. Agents can able to opt out of participating in the proxy: so each agent can submit to the proxy either their type t_i, or else a null symbol $\perp$ which represents opting out. A proxy algorithm is then a function from a profile of utility functions (and $\perp$ symbols) to a probability distribution over $\mathcal{R}^n$, i.e. $\mathcal{M}\colon (\mathcal{U} \cup \{\perp\})^n \to \Delta\mathcal{R}^n$. Here $\mathcal{R}$ is an appropriately defined range space.

First we recall the definition of differential privacy, both to provide a basis for our modified definition, and since it will be a technical building block in our algorithms. Roughly speaking, a mechanism is differentially private if for every $\mathbf{u}$ and every i, knowledge of the output $\mathcal{M}(\mathbf{u})$ as well as u_{-i} does not reveal 'much' about u_i.

DEFINITION 4 ((STANDARD) DIFFERENTIAL PRIVACY). *A mechanism $\mathcal{M}$ satisfies (ε, δ)-differential privacy if for any player i, any two types for player i, t_i and $t_i' \in \mathcal{U} \cup \{\perp\}$, and any tuple of types for every else $t_{-i} \in (\mathcal{U} \cup \{\perp\})^{n-1}$ and any $S \subseteq \mathcal{R}^n$,*

$$\mathop{\mathbb{P}}_{\mathcal{M}}[(\mathcal{M}(t_i; t_{-i})) \in S] \leq e^{\varepsilon} \mathop{\mathbb{P}}_{\mathcal{M}}[(\mathcal{M}(t_i'; t_{-i})) \in S] + \delta.$$

We would like something slightly different for our setting. We propose a relaxation of the above definition, motivated by the fact that when computing a correlated equilibrium, the action recommended to a player is only observed by her. Roughly speaking, a mechanism is *jointly differentially private* if, for each player i, knowledge of the other $n-1$ recommendations (and submitted types) does not reveal 'much' about player i's report. Note that this relaxation is necessary in our setting if we are going to privately compute correlated equilibria, since knowledge of player i's recommended action can reveal a lot of information about his type. It is still very strong- the privacy guarantee remains *even if* everyone else colludes against a given player i, so long as i does not himself make the component reported to him public.

DEFINITION 5 (JOINT DIFFERENTIAL PRIVACY). *A mechanism $\mathcal{M}$ satisfies (ε, δ)-joint differential privacy if for any player i, any two possible types for player i, t_i and $t_i' \in \mathcal{U} \cup \{\perp\}$, any tuple of utilities for everyone else t_{-i} and $S \subseteq \mathcal{R}^{n-1}$,*

$$\mathop{\mathbb{P}}_{\mathcal{M}}\left[(\mathcal{M}(t_i;t_{-i}))_{-i} \in S\right] \leq e^{\varepsilon} \mathop{\mathbb{P}}_{\mathcal{M}}\left[(\mathcal{M}(t_i';t_{-i}))_{-i} \in S\right] + \delta.$$

3. JOINT DIFFERENTIAL PRIVACY AND TRUTHFULNESS

The main result of this paper is a reduction that takes an arbitrary large game $\mathcal{G}$ of incomplete information and modifies it to have equilibrium implementing equilibrium outcomes of the corresponding full information game defined by the *realized* agent types. Specifically, we modify the game by introducing the option for players to use a *proxy* that can recommend actions to the players. The modified game is called $\mathcal{G}'$. For any prior on agent types, it will be an approximate Bayes Nash equilibrium of $\mathcal{G}'$ for every player to opt in to using the proxy, and to subsequently follow its recommendation. Moreover, the resulting set of actions will correspond to an approximate correlated equilibrium of the complete information game $\mathcal{G}$ defined by the realized agent types. For concreteness, we consider Bayesian games, however our results are not specific to this model of incomplete information.

More precisely, the modified game $\mathcal{G}'$ will be identical to $\mathcal{G}$ with an added option. Each player i has the opportunity to submit their type to a proxy, which will then suggest to them an action $\hat{a}_i \in A$ to play. They can use this advice however they like: that is, they can choose any function $f : A \to A$ and choose to play the action $a_i = f(\hat{a}_i)$. Alternately, they can opt out of the proxy (and not submit their type), and choose an action to play $a_i \in A$ directly. In the end, each player experiences utility $u(t_i, (a_1, \ldots, a_n))$, just as in the original game $\mathcal{G}$. We assume that types are verifiable—agent i does not have the ability to opt in to the proxy but report a false type $t_i' \neq t_i$. However, he does have the ability to opt out (and submit $\perp$), and the proxy has no power to do anything other than suggest which action he should play. In the end, each player is free to play any action a_i, regardless of what the proxy suggests, even if he opts in.

Formally, given a game $\mathcal{G}$ defined by an action set A, a type space $\mathcal{U}$, and a utility function u, we define a *proxy game* $\mathcal{G}'_M$, parameterized by an algorithm $M : \{\mathcal{U} \cup \{\perp\}\}^n \to A^n$. In $\mathcal{G}'$, each agent has two types of actions: they can *opt in* to the proxy, which means they submit their type, receive an action recommendation $\hat{a}$, and choose a function $f : A \to A$ which determines how they use that recommendation. We denote this set of choices $A_1' = \{(\top, f) | f : A \to A\}$. Alternately, they can *opt out* of the proxy, which means that they do not submit their type, and directly choose an action to play. We denote this set of choices $A_2' = \{(\perp, a) | a \in A\}$. Together, the action set in $\mathcal{G}'_M$ is $A' = A_1' \cup A_2'$. Given a set of choices by the players, we define a vector $\mathbf{x}$ such that $\mathbf{x}_i = t_i$ for each player i who chose $(\top, f_i) \in A_1'$ (each player who opted in), and $\mathbf{x}_i = \perp$ for each player i who chose $(\perp, a_i) \in A_2'$ (each player who opted out). The proxy then computes $M(\mathbf{x}) = \hat{\mathbf{a}}$. Finally, this results in a vector of actions $\mathbf{a}$ from the game $\mathcal{G}$, one for each player. For each player who opted in, they play the action $\mathbf{a}_i = f_i(\hat{\mathbf{a}}_i)$. For each person who opted out, they play the action $\mathbf{a}_i = a_i$. Finally, each player receives utility $u(t_i, \mathbf{a})$ as in the original game $\mathcal{G}$.

We now show that if the algorithm M satisfies certain properties, then for any prior on agent types, it is always an approximate Bayes Nash equilibrium for every player to opt in and follow the recommendation of the proxy.

THEOREM 6. *Let M be an algorithm that satisfies (ϵ, δ)-joint differential privacy, and be such that for every vector of types $\mathbf{t} \in \mathcal{U}^n$, $M(\mathbf{t})$ induces a distribution over actions that is an α-approximate correlated equilibrium of the full information game $\mathcal{G}$ induced by the type vector $\mathbf{t}$. Then for every prior distribution on types τ, it is an η-approximate Bayes Nash equilibrium of $\mathcal{G}'_M$ for every player to play $(\top, f)$ for the identity function $f(a) = a$. (i.e. for every player to opt into the proxy, and then follow its suggested action), where $\eta = \epsilon + \delta + \alpha$.*

REMARK 7. *Observe that when agents play according to the approximate Bayes Nash equilibrium of $\mathcal{G}'_M$ guaranteed by Theorem 6, then the resulting distribution over actions played, and the resulting utilities of the players, correspond to an α-approximate correlated equilibrium of the full information game $\mathcal{G}'_M$, induced by the realized type vector $\mathbf{t}$.*

PROOF PROOF OF THEOREM 6. Fix any prior distribution on player types τ, and let $s_1, \ldots, s_n$ be the strategies corresponding to the action $(\top, f)$ for each player, where f is the identify function. (i.e. the strategy corresponding to opting into the proxy and following the suggested action). There are two types of deviations that a player i can consider: $(\top, f_i')$ for some function $f_i' : A \to A$ not the identity function, and $(\perp, a_i)$ for some action a_i. First, we consider deviations of the first kind. Let $s_i'(t_i)$ be the strategy corresponding to playing $(\top, f'_{\hat{s}(t_i)})$ for some function $\hat{s}(t_i)$. For every type t_i:

$$\begin{aligned}
\mathop{\mathbb{E}}_{\mathbf{t}_{-i} \sim \tau|_{t_i}}\left[u_i(t_i, s_i(t_i), s_{-i}(t_{-i}))\right] &= \sum_{\mathbf{t}_{-i}} \Pr_{\tau|_{t_i}}[\mathbf{t}_{-i}] \cdot \mathop{\mathbb{E}}_{\mathbf{a} \sim M(\mathbf{t})}\left[u_i(\mathbf{a})\right] \\
&\geq \sum_{\mathbf{t}_{-i}} \Pr_{\tau|_{t_i}}[\mathbf{t}_{-i}] \cdot \mathop{\mathbb{E}}_{\mathbf{a} \sim M(\mathbf{t})}\left[u_i(f'_{\hat{s}(t_i)}(\mathbf{a}_i), \mathbf{a}_{-i})\right] - \alpha \\
&= \mathop{\mathbb{E}}_{\mathbf{t}_{-i} \sim \tau|_{t_i}}\left[u_i(t_i, s_i'(t_i), s_{-i}(t_{-i}))\right] - \alpha
\end{aligned}$$

where the inequality follows from the fact that M computes an α-approximate correlated equilibrium. Now, consider a deviation of the second kind. Let $s_i'(t_i)$ be the strategy corresponding to playing $(\perp, a_{\hat{s}(t_i)})$ for some function $\hat{s}(t_i)$. For every type t_i:

$$\mathop{\mathbb{E}}_{\mathbf{t}_{-i}\sim\tau_{|t_i}}[u_i(t_i, s_i(t_i), s_{-i}(t_{-i}))]$$

$$= \sum_{\mathbf{t}_{-i}} \Pr_{\tau_{|t_i}}[\mathbf{t}_{-i}] \cdot \mathop{\mathbb{E}}_{\mathbf{a}\sim M(\mathbf{t})}[u_i(\mathbf{a})]$$

$$\geq \sum_{\mathbf{t}_{-i}} \Pr_{\tau_{|t_i}}[\mathbf{t}_{-i}] \cdot \mathop{\mathbb{E}}_{\mathbf{a}\sim M(\mathbf{t})}[u_i(a_{\hat{s}(t_i)}, \mathbf{a}_{-i})] - \alpha$$

$$\geq \sum_{\mathbf{t}_{-i}} \Pr_{\tau_{|t_i}}[\mathbf{t}_{-i}] \cdot \exp(-\epsilon) \cdot \mathop{\mathbb{E}}_{\mathbf{a}\sim M(\perp, \mathbf{t}_{-i})}[u_i(a_{\hat{s}(t_i)}, \mathbf{a}_{-i})] - \delta - \alpha$$

$$\geq \sum_{\mathbf{t}_{-i}} \Pr_{\tau_{|t_i}}[\mathbf{t}_{-i}] \cdot \mathop{\mathbb{E}}_{\mathbf{a}\sim M(\perp, \mathbf{t}_{-i})}[u_i(a_{\hat{s}(t_i)}, \mathbf{a}_{-i})] - \epsilon - \delta - \alpha$$

$$= \mathop{\mathbb{E}}_{\mathbf{t}_{-i}\sim\tau_{|t_i}}[u_i(t_i, s_i'(t_i), s_{-i}(t_{-i}))] - \varepsilon - \delta - \alpha$$

where the first inequality follows from the α-approximate correlated equilibrium condition, the second follows from the (ϵ, δ)-joint differential privacy condition, and the third follows from the fact that for $\epsilon \geq 0$, $\exp(-\epsilon) \geq 1 - \epsilon$ and that utilities are bounded in $[0, 1]$. □

The main technical contribution of the paper is an algorithm M which satisfies (ϵ, δ)-joint differential privacy, and computes an α-approximate correlated equilibrium of games which are γ-large. We in fact give two such algorithms: one that runs in time polynomial in n and $|A| = k$, and one that runs in time exponential in n and k. The efficient algorithm computes an α_1-approximate correlated equilibrium, and the inefficient algorithm computes an α_2-approximate correlated equilibrium, where:

$$\alpha_1 = \tilde{O}\left(\frac{\gamma k^{3/2}\sqrt{n}\log(1/\delta)}{\epsilon}\right)$$

$$\alpha_2 = \tilde{O}\left(\frac{\gamma \log k \log^{3/2}(\mathcal{U})\sqrt{n}\log(1/\delta)}{\epsilon}\right).$$

In combination with Theorem 6, the existence of these algorithms together with optimal choices of ϵ and δ give our main result:

THEOREM 8. *Let $\mathcal{G}$ be any γ-large game. Then there exists a proxy game $\mathcal{G}'$ such that for any prior distribution on types τ, it is an η-approximate Bayes-Nash equilibrium to opt into the proxy and follow its advice. Moreover, the resulting distribution on actions forms an η-approximate correlated equilibrium of the full information game induced by the realized types. If we insist that the proxy be implemented using a computationally efficient algorithm, then we can take:*

$$\eta = \tilde{O}\left(\sqrt{\gamma}n^{1/4}k^{3/4}\right)$$

If we can take the proxy to be computationally inefficient, then we can take:

$$\eta = \tilde{O}\left(\sqrt{\gamma}n^{1/4}\sqrt{\log k}\log^{3/4}|\mathcal{U}|\right)$$

REMARK 9. *In large games, the parameter γ tends to zero as n grows large. For $\gamma = 1/n$, our approximation error is $\eta = \tilde{O}(k^{3/4}/n^{1/4})$ and $\eta = \tilde{O}(\sqrt{\log k}\log^{3/4}|\mathcal{U}|/n^{1/4})$ respectively. Note that the approximation error η in the equilibrium concepts tends to zero in any γ-large game such that $\gamma = o(\frac{1}{\sqrt{n}k^{3/2}})$ or $\gamma = o(\frac{1}{\sqrt{n}\log k \log^{3/2}|\mathcal{U}|})$ respectively.*

4. DISCUSSION

In this work, we have introduced a new variant of differential privacy (joint differential privacy), and have shown how it can be used as a tool to construct extremely weak proxy mechanisms which can implement equilibria of full information games, even when the game is being played in a setting of only partial information. Moreover, our privacy solution concept maintains the property that no coalition of players can learn (much) more about any player's type outside of the coalition than they could have learned in the original Bayesian game, and thus players have almost no incentive not to participate even if they view their type as sensitive information. Although our proxies are weak in most respects (they cannot enforce actions, they cannot make payments or charge fees, they cannot compel participation), we do make the assumption that player types are verifiable in the event that they choose to opt into the proxy. This assumption is reasonable in many settings: for example, in financial markets, there may be legal penalties for a firm misrepresenting relevant facts about itself, and in traffic routing games, the proxy may be embodied as a physical device (e.g. a GPS device) that can itself verify player types (e.g. physical location). Nevertheless, we view relaxing this assumption as an important direction for future work.

In this extended abstract, we have merely summarized our results. Our full paper [KPRU13] includes a formal description of our algorithms, formal statements of our theorems, and proofs of all results.

5. REFERENCES

[AB11] E. Azevedo and E. Budish. Strategyproofness in the large as a desideratum for market design. Technical report, University of Chicago, 2011.

[ANS00] N.I. Al-Najjar and R. Smorodinsky. Pivotal players and the characterization of influence. *Journal of Economic Theory*, 92(2):318–342, 2000.

[BLR08] Avrim Blum, Katrina Ligett, and Aaron Roth. A learning theory approach to non-interactive database privacy. In Cynthia Dwork, editor, *STOC*, pages 609–618. ACM, 2008.

[CCK+13] Yiling Chen, Stephen Chong, Ian A Kash, Tal Moran, and Salil Vadhan. Truthful mechanisms for agents that value privacy. In *Proceedings of the fourteenth ACM conference on Electronic commerce*, pages 215–232. ACM, 2013.

[De12] Anindya De. Lower bounds in differential privacy. In *TCC*, pages 321–338, 2012.

[DKM+06] Cynthia Dwork, Krishnaram Kenthapadi, Frank McSherry, Ilya Mironov, and Moni Naor. Our data, ourselves: Privacy via distributed noise generation. In *EUROCRYPT*, pages 486–503, 2006.

[DMNS06] Cynthia Dwork, Frank McSherry, Kobbi Nissim, and Adam Smith. Calibrating noise to sensitivity in private data analysis. In *TCC '06*, pages 265–284, 2006.

[DMT07] Cynthia Dwork, Frank McSherry, and Kunal Talwar. The price of privacy and the limits of lp decoding. In *STOC*, pages 85–94, 2007.

[DN03] Irit Dinur and Kobbi Nissim. Revealing information while preserving privacy. In *PODS*, pages 202–210, 2003.

[DNV12] Cynthia Dwork, Moni Naor, and Salil Vadhan. The privacy of the analyst and the power of the state. In *Foundations of Computer Science (FOCS), 2012 IEEE 53rd Annual Symposium on*, pages 400–409. IEEE, 2012.

[DRV10] Cynthia Dwork, Guy N. Rothblum, and Salil P. Vadhan. Boosting and differential privacy. In *FOCS*, pages 51–60. IEEE Computer Society, 2010.

[Dwo08] C. Dwork. Differential privacy: A survey of results. *Theory and Applications of Models of Computation*, pages 1–19, 2008.

[DY08] Cynthia Dwork and Sergey Yekhanin. New efficient attacks on statistical disclosure control mechanisms. In *CRYPTO*, pages 469–480, 2008.

[FL12] Lisa Fleischer and Yu-Han Lyu. Approximately optimal auctions for selling privacy when costs are correlated with data. In *EC*, pages 568–585, 2012.

[For86] Françoise Forges. An approach to communication equilibria. *Econometrica: Journal of the Econometric Society*, pages 1375–1385, 1986.

[GHRU11] Anupam Gupta, Moritz Hardt, Aaron Roth, and Jonathan Ullman. Privately releasing conjunctions and the statistical query barrier. In *STOC '11*, pages 803–812, 2011.

[GR08] R. Gradwohl and O. Reingold. Fault tolerance in large games. In *EC*, pages 274–283. ACM, 2008.

[GR10] R. Gradwohl and O. Reingold. Partial exposure in large games. *Games and Economic Behavior*, 68(2):602–613, 2010.

[GR11] Arpita Ghosh and Aaron Roth. Selling privacy at auction. In *EC*, pages 199–208, 2011.

[Gra12] R. Gradwohl. Privacy in implementation. 2012.

[GRU12] Anupam Gupta, Aaron Roth, and Jonathan Ullman. Iterative constructions and private data release. In *TCC*, pages 339–356, 2012.

[HK12] Zhiyi Huang and Sampath Kannan. The exponential mechanism for social welfare: Private, truthful, and nearly optimal. In *FOCS*, 2012.

[HR10] Moritz Hardt and Guy N. Rothblum. A multiplicative weights mechanism for privacy-preserving data analysis. In *FOCS*, pages 61–70, 2010.

[HRU13] Justin Hsu, Aaron Roth, and Jonathan Ullman. Differential privacy for the analyst via private equilibrium computation. In *Proceedings of the 45th annual ACM symposium on Symposium on theory of computing*, pages 341–350. ACM, 2013.

[IM05] N. Immorlica and M. Mahdian. Marriage, honesty, and stability. In *SODA*, pages 53–62. Society for Industrial and Applied Mathematics, 2005.

[Kal04] E. Kalai. Large robust games. *Econometrica*, 72(6):1631–1665, 2004.

[KP09] F. Kojima and P.A. Pathak. Incentives and stability in large two-sided matching markets. *American Economic Review*, 99(3):608–627, 2009.

[KPR10] F. Kojima, P.A. Pathak, and A.E. Roth. Matching with couples: Stability and incentives in large markets. Technical report, National Bureau of Economic Research, 2010.

[KPRU13] Michael Kearns, Mallesh M Pai, Aaron Roth, and Jonathan Ullman. Mechanism design in large games: Incentives and privacy. *arXiv preprint arXiv:1207.4084*, 2013.

[LR12] Katrina Ligett and Aaron Roth. Take it or leave it: Running a survey when privacy comes at a cost. *CoRR*, abs/1202.4741, 2012.

[MT03] Dov Monderer and Moshe Tennenholtz. k-implementation. In *Proceedings of the 4th ACM conference on Electronic commerce*, pages 19–28. ACM, 2003.

[MT07] Frank McSherry and Kunal Talwar. Mechanism design via differential privacy. In *FOCS*, pages 94–103, 2007.

[MT09] Dov Monderer and Moshe Tennenholtz. Strong mediated equilibrium. *Artificial Intelligence*, 173(1):180–195, 2009.

[NOS12] Kobbi Nissim, Claudio Orlandi, and Rann Smorodinsky. Privacy-aware mechanism design. In *EC*, pages 774–789, 2012.

[NST12] Kobbi Nissim, Rann Smorodinsky, and Moshe Tennenholtz. Approximately optimal mechanism design via differential privacy. In *ITCS*, pages 203–213, 2012.

[PR13] Mallesh Pai and Aaron Roth. Privacy and mechanism design. *Sigecom Exchanges*, pages 8–29, 2013.

[Rou09] T. Roughgarden. Intrinsic robustness of the price of anarchy. In *STOC*, pages 513–522. ACM, 2009.

[Rou12] T. Roughgarden. The price of anarchy in games of incomplete information. In *Proceedings of the 13th ACM Conference on Electronic Commerce*, pages 862–879. ACM, 2012.

[RP76] D.J. Roberts and A. Postlewaite. The incentives for price-taking behavior in large exchange economies. *Econometrica*, pages 115–127, 1976.

[RR10] Aaron Roth and Tim Roughgarden. Interactive privacy via the median mechanism. In *STOC '10*, pages 765–774, 2010.

[RS12] Aaron Roth and Grant Schoenebeck. Conducting truthful surveys, cheaply. In *EC*, pages 826–843, 2012.

[Xia13] David Xiao. Is privacy compatible with truthfulness? In *Proceedings of the 4th conference on Innovations in Theoretical Computer Science*, pages 67–86. ACM, 2013.

Redrawing the Boundaries on Purchasing Data from Privacy-Sensitive Individuals

Kobbi Nissim
Ben-Gurion University and Harvard University.
Be'er Sheva, Israel and Cambridge, MA
kobbi@cs.bgu.ac.il

Salil Vadhan
Center for Research on Computation & Society and School of Engineering & Applied Sciences
Harvard University
Cambridge, MA
salil@seas.harvard.edu

David Xiao
CNRS
LIAFA and Université Paris 7
Paris, France
dxiao@liafa.univ-paris-diderot.fr

ABSTRACT

We prove new positive and negative results concerning the existence of truthful and individually rational mechanisms for purchasing private data from individuals with unbounded and sensitive privacy preferences. We strengthen the impossibility results of Ghosh and Roth (EC 2011) by extending it to a much wider class of privacy valuations. In particular, these include privacy valuations that are based on (ε, δ)-differentially private mechanisms for non-zero δ, ones where the privacy costs are measured in a per-database manner (rather than taking the worst case), and ones that do not depend on the payments made to players (which might not be observable to an adversary).

To bypass this impossibility result, we study a natural special setting where individuals have *monotonic privacy valuations*, which captures common contexts where certain values for private data are expected to lead to higher valuations for privacy (*e.g.* having a particular disease). We give new mechanisms that are individually rational for all players with monotonic privacy valuations, truthful for all players whose privacy valuations are not too large, and accurate if there are not too many players with too-large privacy valuations. We also prove matching lower bounds showing that in some respects our mechanism cannot be improved significantly.

Categories and Subject Descriptors

F.0 [**Theory of computation**]: General; K.4.1 [**Computers and society**]: Privacy

Keywords

differential privacy, mechanism design

ITCS'14, January 12–14, 2014, Princeton, New Jersey, USA.

ACM 978-1-4503-2698-8/14/01 ...$15.00.
http://dx.doi.org/10.1145/2554797.2554835.

1. INTRODUCTION

Computing over individuals' private data is extremely useful for various purposes, such as medical or demographic studies. Recent work on *differential privacy* first defined in [DMNS06, Dwo06] has focused on ensuring that analyses using private data can be carried out accurately while providing individuals a strong quantitative guarantee of privacy.

While differential privacy provides formal guarantees on how much information is leaked about an individual's data, it is silent about what incentivizes the individuals to share their data in the first place. A recent line of work [MT07, GR11, NST12, Xia13, NOS12, CCK$^+$13, FL12, LR12, RS12] has begun exploring this question, by relating differential privacy to questions of mechanism design.

One way to incentivize individuals to consent to the usage of their private data is simply to pay them for using it. For example, a medical study may compensate its participants for the use of their medical data. However, determining the correct price is challenging: low payments may not draw enough participants, causing insufficient data for an accurate study, while high payments may be impossible for budgetary reasons.

Ghosh and Roth [GR11] approached this problem by allowing the mechanism to elicit *privacy valuations* from individuals. A privacy valuation is a description of how much disutility an individual experiences from having information about their private data revealed. By eliciting valuations, the mechanism is hopefully able to tailor payments to incentivize enough participants to produce an accurate result, while not paying too much.

1.1 The setting and previous work

We continue the study of purchasing private data from individuals as first proposed by Ghosh and Roth [GR11] (see [Rot12, PR13] for a survey of this area). Since we work in a game-theoretic framework, we will also call individuals "players". As in [GR11], we study the simple case where the private information consists of a single data bit, which players can refuse to provide but cannot modify (e.g. because the data is already certified in a trusted database, such as a medical record database).

To determine the price to pay players for their data bits, the mechanism elicits *privacy valuations* from them. We study the simple case where each player i's privacy valuation is parameterized by a single real parameter v_i. For example, in Ghosh and Roth [GR11] they assume that player i loses $v_i\varepsilon$ utility when their data bit is used in an ε-differentially private mechanism. We will study a wider variety of privacy valuation functions in this paper. The valuations are known only to the players themselves, and therefore players may report false valuations if it increases their utility. Furthermore, because these valuations may be correlated with the data bits, the players may wish to keep their valuations private as well. It is instructive to keep in mind the application of paying for access to medical data (*e.g.* HIV status), where players cannot control the actual data bit, but their valuation might be strongly correlated to their data bit.

The goal of the mechanism is to approximate the sum of data bits while not paying too much. Based on the declared valuations, the mechanism computes payments to each of the players and obtains access to the purchased data bits from the players that accept the payments. The mechanism then computes and publishes an approximation to the sum of the data bits, which can cause the players some loss of privacy, which should be compensated for by the mechanism's payment.

The mechanism designer aims to achieve three goals, standard in the game theory literature: the mechanism should be individually rational, truthful, and accurate. A mechanism is *individually rational* if all players receive non-negative utility from participating in the game. In our context, this means that the mechanism is sufficiently compensating players for their loss in privacy, something that may be important for ethical reasons, beyond just incentivizing participation. Informally, a mechanism is *truthful* for player i on a tuple $x = (x_1, \ldots, x_n)$ of reports from the players if player i does not gain in utility by declaring some false type x'_i (while the other players' types remain unchanged). We aim to build mechanisms that are individually rational for all players, and truthful for as many players and inputs as possible (ideally for all players and inputs). A mechanism is *accurate* if the output of the mechanism is close to the true function it wishes to compute, in our case the sum of the data bits.

Ghosh and Roth [GR11] study the restricted setting (in their terminology the "insensitive value model") where players do not care about leaking their privacy valuations, as well as the general model (the "sensitive value model") where they may care and their valuations can be unbounded. They present two mechanisms in the insensitive value model, one that optimizes accuracy given a fixed budget and another that optimizes budget given a fixed accuracy constraint. They also prove that their mechanisms are individually rational and truthful under the assumption that each player i experiences a disutility of *exactly* $v_i\varepsilon$ when his data bit is used in an ε-differentially private mechanism.

In the general sensitive value model, they prove the following impossibility result: there is no individually rational mechanism with finite payments that can distinguish between the case where all players have data bit 0 and the case where all players have data bit 1.

This impossibility result spurred a line of work attempting to bypass it. Fleischer and Lyu [FL12] propose a Bayesian setting, where (for simplicity considering just Boolean inputs) there are publically known distributions D_0 and D_1 over privacy valuations, and each player who has data bit b_i receives a valuation v_i drawn from D_{b_i}. They show that in this model, it is possible to build a Bayes-Nash truthful, individually rational, and accurate mechanism.

In a related work, Roth and Schoenebeck [RS12] study a Bayesian setting where the agents' actual (dis)utilities are drawn from a known prior, and construct individually rational and ex-post truthful mechanism that are optimal for minimizing variance given a fixed budget and minimizing expected cost given a fixed variance goal. In comparison to [FL12], [RS12] studies a disutility value that does not quantitively relate to the privacy properties of the mechanism (but rather just a fixed, per-player disutility for participation), while it results in mechanisms satisfying a stronger notion of truthfulness.

Ligett and Roth [LR12] measure the privacy loss incurred from a player's decision to participate separately from the information leaked about the actual data (effectively ruling out arbitrary correlations between privacy valuations and data bits). They work in a worst-case (non-Bayesian) model and construct a mechanism that satisfies a relaxed "one-sided" notion of truthfulness and accuracy. However, their mechanism only satisfies individual rationality for players whose privacy valuation is not too high.

1.1.1 Improving the negative results

This line of work leaves several interesting questions open. The first is whether the impossibility result of [GR11] really closes the door on all meaningful mechanisms when players can have unbounded privacy valuations that can be arbitrarily correlated with their sensitive data.

There are two important loopholes that the result leaves open. First, their notion of privacy loss is pure ε-differential privacy, and they crucially use the fact that for pure ε-differentially private mechanisms the support of the output distribution must be identical for all inputs. This prevents their result from ruling out notions of privacy loss based on more relaxed notions of privacy, such as (ε, δ)-differential privacy for $\delta > 0$. As a number of examples in the differential privacy literature show, relaxing to (ε, δ)-differential privacy can be extremely powerful, even when δ is negligibly small but non-zero [DL09, HT10, DRV10, De12, BNS13]. Furthermore, even (ε, δ) differential privacy measures the worst-case privacy loss over all databases, and it may be the case that on most databases, the players' expected privacy loss is much less than the worst case bound.[1] Thus it is more realistic to use per-database measure of privacy loss (as done in [CCK$^+$13]).

Second, the [GR11] notion of privacy includes as observable and hence potentially disclosive output the (sum of the) payments made to *all* the players, not just the sum of the data bits. This leaves open the possibility of constructing mechanisms for the setting where an outside observer is not able to to see some of the player's payments. For example, it may be natural to assume that, when trying to learn about

[1]For example, consider a mechanism that computes an ε-differentially private noisy sum of the first $n-1$ rows (which we assume are bits), and if the result is 0, also outputs a ε-differentially private noisy version of the n'th row (e.g. via "randomized response"). The worst case privacy loss for player n is ε. On databases of the form $(0, 0, \ldots, 0, b)$ the first computation results with 0 with probability $\approx \varepsilon$ and player n suffers ε privacy loss with this probability. However, if it is known that the database is very unlikely to be almost entirely zero, then player n may experience any privacy loss with only exponentially small probability.

player i, an observer learns the payments to all players *except* player i. In the extreme case, we could even restrict the outside observer to not see any of the payments, but only the approximation to the sum of the data bits. The Ghosh-Rosh impossibility proof fails in these cases. Indeed in this case where player i's own payment is not visible to the observer, there *does exist* an individually rational and accurate mechanism with finite payments: simply ask each player for their valuation v_i and pay them $v_i\varepsilon$, then output the sum of all the bits with noise of magnitude $O(1/\varepsilon)$. (The reason that this mechanism is unsatisfactory is that it is completely untruthful — players always gain by reporting a higher valuations.)

We will close both these gaps: our results will hold even under very mild conditions on how the players experience privacy loss (in particular capturing a per-database analogue of (ε, δ)-differential privacy), and even when *only* the approximate count of data bits is observable and *none* of the payments are observable.

1.1.2 Improving the positive results

Another question left open by the previous work is if we can achieve individual rationality and some form of truthfulness under a worst-case setting. Recall that [FL12] and [RS12] work in a Bayesian model, while [LR12] does not guarantee individual rationality for all players. Furthermore, in both [FL12] and [RS12] the priors are heavily used in *designing the mechanism*, and therefore their results break if the mechanism designer does not accurately know the priors. We will replace the Bayesian assumption with a simple qualitative assumption on the monotonicity of the correlation between players' data bits and their privacy valuation. For accuracy (but not individual rationality), we will assume a rough bound on how many players exceed a given threshold in their privacy valuations (similarly to [NOS12]).

Another question is the interpretation of the privacy loss functions. We observe that the truthfulness of the mechanisms in [GR11] crucially relies on the assumption that $v_i\varepsilon$ is the *exact* privacy loss incurred. As was argued by [NOS12] and [CCK$^+$13], it seems hard to quantify the exact privacy loss a player experiences, as it may depend on the mechanism, all of the players' inputs, as well as an adversary's auxiliary information about the database. (See footnote 1 for an example.) It is much more reasonable to assume that the privacy valuations v_i declared by the players and the differential privacy parameter ε yield an *upper bound* on their privacy loss. When using this interpretation, the truthfulness of [GR11] no longer holds. The mechanisms we construct will remain truthful using the privacy loss function only as an upper bound on privacy loss (for players whose privacy valuations are not too large, similarly to the truthfulness guarantees of [NOS12, CCK$^+$13, LR12]).

1.2 Our results

In our model there are n players labelled $1, \ldots, n$ each with a data bit $b_i \in \{0, 1\}$ and a privacy valuation $v_i \in \mathbb{R}$, which we describe as a $2n$-tuple $(b, v) \in \{0,1\}^n \times \mathbb{R}^n$. The mechanism designer is interested in learning (an approximation of) $\sum b_i$. The players may lie about their valuation but they cannot lie about their data bit. A mechanism M is a pair of randomized functions $(M_{\mathsf{out}}, M_{\mathsf{pay}})$, where $M_{\mathsf{out}} : \{0,1\}^n \times \mathbb{R}^n \to \mathbb{Z}$ and $M_{\mathsf{pay}} : \{0,1\}^n \times \mathbb{R}^n \to \mathbb{R}^n$. Namely M_{out} produces an integer that should approximate $\sum b_i$ while M_{pay} produces payments to each of the n players.

Because the players are privacy-aware, the utility they derive from the game can be separated into two parts as follows:

$$\text{utility}_i = \text{payment}_i - \text{privacy loss}_i.$$

(Note that in this paper, we assume the players have no (dis)interest in the integer that M_{out} produces.) The privacy loss term will be quantified by a *privacy loss function* that depends on the identity of the player, his bit, his privacy valuation, and his declared valuation i, b, v, v'_i (where v'_i is not necessarily his true type v_i), the mechanism M, and the outcome (s, p) produced by $(M_{\mathsf{out}}, M_{\mathsf{pay}})$.

Strengthened impossibility result of non-trivial accuracy with privacy..

Our first result significantly strengthens the impossibility result of Ghosh-Roth [GR11].

THEOREM 1.1. *(Main impossibility result, informal. See Theorem 3.4.) Fix any mechanism M and any reasonable privacy loss functions. Then if M is truthful (even if only for players with privacy valuation 0) and individually rational and makes finite payments to the players (even if only when all players have privacy valuation 0), then M cannot distinguish between inputs $(b, v) = (0^n, 0^n)$ and $(b', v) = (1^n, 0^n)$.*

By "reasonable privacy loss functions," we mean that if from observing the output of the mechanism on an input (b, v), an adversary can distinguish the case that player i has data bit $b_i = 0$ from data bit $b_i = 1$ (while keeping all other inputs the same), then player i experiences a significant privacy loss (proportional to v_i) on database (b, v). In particular, we allow for a per-database notion of privacy loss. Moreover, we only need the adversary to be able to observe the mechanism's estimate of the count $\sum_j b_j$, and not any of the payments made to players. And our notion of indistinguishability captures not only pure ε-differential privacy but also (ε, δ)-differential privacy for $\delta > 0$. The conclusion of the result is as strong as conceivably possible, stating that M cannot distinguish between the two most different inputs (data bits all 0 vs. data bits all 1) even in the case where none of the players care about privacy.

We also remark that in our main impossibility result, in order to handle privacy loss functions that depend only on the distribution of the observable count and not the payment information, we crucially use the requirement that M be truthful for players with 0 privacy valuation. As we remarked earlier in Section 1.1.1 there exist M that are individually rational and accurate (but not truthful).

New notions of privacy and positive results..

One of the main conceptual contributions of this work is restricting our attention to a special class of privacy loss functions, which we use to bypass our main impossibility result. Essential to the definition of differential privacy (Definition 2.2) is the notion of *neighboring inputs*. Two inputs to the mechanism are considered neighboring if they differ only in the information of a single player, and in the usual notion of differential privacy, one player's information may differ arbitrarily. This view also characterized how previous work modeled privacy loss functions: in the sensitive value model of [GR11], the privacy loss function to a player i

on an input (b_i, v_i) was computed by considering how much changing to any possible neighbor (b'_i, v'_i) would affect the output of the mechanism. In contrast, we will restrict our attention to privacy loss functions that consider only how much changing to a specific subset of possible neighbors (b'_i, v'_i) would affect the output of the mechanism. By restricting to such privacy loss functions, we can bypass our impossibility results.

We now describe how we restrict (b'_i, v'_i). Recall that in our setting a single player's type information is a pair (b_i, v_i) where $b_i \in \{0, 1\}$ is a data bit and $v_i \in \mathbb{R}$ is a value for privacy. We observe that in many cases there is a natural sensitive value of the bit b_i, for example, if b_i represents HIV status, then we would expect that $b_i = 1$ is more sensitive than $b_i = 0$.

Therefore we consider only the following *monotonic valuations*: $(0, v_i)$ is a neighbor of $(1, v'_i)$ iff $v_i \leq v'_i$. Thus, if a player's true type is $(1, v'_i)$, then he is only concerned with how much the output of the mechanism differs from the case that her actual type were $(0, v_i)$ for $v_i \leq v'_i$.

Consider the pairs that we have excluded from consideration: any pairs $(b_i, v_i), (b_i, v'_i)$ (*i.e.* the data bit does not change) and any pairs $(0, v_i), (1, v'_i)$ where $v_i > v'_i$. By excluding these pairs we formally capture the idea that players are not concerned about revealing their privacy valuations *except* inasmuch as they may be correlated with their data bits b_i and therefore may reveal something about b_i. Since $b_i = 1$ is more sensitive than $b_i = 0$, the correlation says that privacy valuation when $b_i = 1$ should be larger than when $b_i = 0$. This can be seen as an intermediate notion between a model where players do not care at all about leaking their privacy valuation (the insensitive value model of [GR11]), and a model where players care about leaking any and all information about their privacy valuation (the sensitive value model of [GR11]).

Of course the assumption that players are not concerned about revealing their privacy valuation except inasmuch as it is correlated with their data is highly context-dependent. There may settings where the privacy valuation is intrinsically sensitive, independently of the players' data bits, and in these cases using our notion of monotonic valuations would be inappropriate. However, we believe that there are many settings where our relaxation is reasonable.

By using this relaxed notion of privacy, we are able to bypass our main impossibility result and prove the following:

THEOREM 1.2. *(Main positive result, informal. See Theorem 4.6.) For any fixed budget B and $\varepsilon > 0$, for privacy loss functions that only depend on how the output distribution changes between monotonic valuations, there exists a mechanism M that is individually rational for all players and truthful for players with low privacy valuation (specifically $v_i \leq B/2\varepsilon n$). Furthermore, as long as the players with low privacy valuation do indeed behave truthfully, then regardless of the behavior of the players with high privacy valuation, the mechanism's output estimates the sum $\sum_i b_i$ to within $\pm(h + O(1/\varepsilon))$ where h is the number of players with high privacy valuation.*

Note that even though we fix a budget B beforehand and thus cannot make arbitrarily high payments, we still achieve individual rationality for all players, even those with extremely high privacy valuations v_i. We do so by ensuring that such players experience perfect privacy ($\varepsilon_i = 0$), assuming they have monotonic valuations. We also remark that while we do not achieve truthfulness for all players, this is not a significant problem as long as the number h of players with high privacy valuation is not too large. This is because the accuracy guarantee holds even if the non-truthful players lie about their valuations. We also give a small improvement to our mechanism that ensures truthfulness for all players with data bit 0, but at some additional practical inconvenience; we defer the details to the body of the paper.

We remark that besides our specific restriction to monotonic valuations in this paper, the underlying principle of studying restricted notions of privacy loss functions by considering only subsets of neighbors (where the subset should be chosen appropriately based on the specific context) could turn out to be a more generally meaningful and powerful technique that is useful to bypass impossibility results elsewhere in the study of privacy.

Lower bounds on accuracy..

The above positive result raises the question: can we adaptively select the budget B in order to achieve accuracy for all inputs, even those where some players have arbitrarily high privacy valuations? Recall that Theorem 1.1 does not preclude this because we are now only looking at monotonic valuations, whereas Theorem 1.1 considers arbitrary valuations. We nevertheless show that it is impossible:

THEOREM 1.3. *(Impossibility of accuracy for all privacy valuations, informal, see Theorem 5.3) For reasonable privacy loss functions that are only sensitive to changes in output distribution of monotonic neighbors, any M with finite payments that is truthful (even if only on players with 0 privacy valuation) and individually rational, there exist player privacy valuations v, v' such that M cannot distinguish between $(0^n, v)$ and $(1^n, v')$.*

The exact formal condition on finite payments is somewhat stronger here than in Theorem 1.1, but it remains reasonable; we defer the formal statement to the body of the paper.

Finally, we also prove a trade-off showing that when there is a limit on the maximum payment the mechanism makes, then accuracy cannot be improved beyond a certain point, even when considering only monotonic valuations. We defer the statement of this result to Section 5.2.

1.3 Related work

The relationship between differential privacy and mechanism design was first explored by [MT07]. Besides the already mentioned works, this relationship was explored and extended in a series of works [NST12], [Xia13] (see also [Xia11]), [NOS12], [CCK+13] (see also [CCK+11]), [HK12], [KPRU13]. In [MT07, NST12, HK12, KPRU13], truthfulness refers only to the utility that players derive from the outcome of the game (as in standard mechanism design) and differential privacy is treated as a separate property. The papers [Xia13, NOS12, CCK+13] study whether and when such mechanisms, which are separately truthful and differentially private, remain truthful even if the players are privacy-aware and may incur some loss in utility from the leakage of the private information. Differential privacy has also been used as a technical tool to solve problems that are not necessarily immediately obvious as being privacy-related; the original work of [MT07] does this, by using differential privacy to construct approximately truthful and optimal mechanisms, while more recently, [KPRU13] use differential privacy as a tool to compute approximate equilibria. For more details, we refer the reader to the recent surveys of [Rot12, PR13].

Two ideas we draw on from this literature (particularly [NOS12, CCK+13]) are (1) the idea that privacy loss cannot be used as a threat because we do not know if a player will actually experience the maximal privacy loss possible, and therefore we should treat privacy loss functions only as upper bounds on the actual privacy loss, and (2) the idea that it is meaningful to construct mechanisms that are truthful for players with reasonable privacy valuations and accurate if most players satisfy this condition. Our mechanisms are truthful not for all players but only for players with low privacy valuation; it will be accurate if the mechanism designer knows enough about the population to set a budget such that most players have low privacy valuation (with respect to the budget).

2. DEFINITIONS

2.1 Notation

For two distributions X, Y we let $\Delta(X, Y)$ denote their total variation distance (i.e. statistical distance). For an integer i let $[i] = \{1, \ldots, i\}$. For any set S and any vector $v \in S^n$, we let $v_{-i} \in S^{n-1}$ denote the vector with entries $v_1, \ldots, v_{i-1}, v_{i+1}, \ldots, v_n$. We use the following convention: a vector of n entries consisting of $n-1$ variables or constants followed by an *indexed* variable denotes the vector of n entries with the last variable inserted at its index. For example *e.g.* $(0^{n-1}, v_i)$ denotes the vector with all zeros except at the i'th entry, which contains v_i. Some notation about the setting regarding mechanisms etc. was already introduced in Section 1.2.

2.2 Differential privacy

Definition 2.1. *Two inputs $(b, v), (b', v') \in \{0,1\}^n \times \mathbb{R}^n$ are* i-neighbors *if $b_j = b'_j$ and $v_j = v'_j$ for all $j \neq i$. They are* neighbors *if they are i-neighbors for some $i \in [n]$.*

Definition 2.2. *A randomized function f is said to be* (ε, δ)-differentially private *if for all neighbors $(b, v), (b', v')$, it holds that for all subsets S of the range of f:*

$$\Pr[f(b, v) \in S] \leq e^{\varepsilon} \Pr[f(b', v') \in S] + \delta. \quad (2.1)$$

We say f is ε-differentially private if it is $(\varepsilon, 0)$-differentially private.

The symmetric geometric random variable $\mathrm{Geom}(\varepsilon)$ takes integer values with the probability mass function given by $\Pr_{x \leftarrow_{\mathrm{R}} \mathrm{Geom}(\varepsilon)}[x = k] \propto e^{-\varepsilon|k|}$ for all $k \in \mathbb{Z}$. It is well-known and easy to verify that for $b \in \{0,1\}^n$, the output $\sum b_i + \mathrm{Geom}(\varepsilon)$ is ε-differentially private.

2.3 Privacy loss functions

A *privacy loss function* for player i is a real-valued function $\lambda_i^{(M)}(b, v, v'_i, s, p_{-i})$ taking as inputs the vectors of all player types b, v, player i's declaration v'_i (not necessarily equal to v_i), and a possible outcome $(s, p_{-i}) \in \mathbb{Z} \times \mathbb{R}^{n-1}$ of M. The function also depends on the mechanism $M = (M_{\mathsf{out}}, M_{\mathsf{pay}})$. Finally we define

$$\mathsf{Loss}_i^{(M)}(b, v, v'_i) = \mathbb{E}_{(s,p) \leftarrow_{\mathrm{R}} M(b,(v_{-i}, v'_i))}[\lambda_i^{(M)}(b, v, v'_i, s, p_{-i})]. \quad (2.2)$$

Observe that we have excluded player i's own payment from the output, as we will assume that an outside observer cannot see player i's payment. We let M_{-i} denote the randomized function $M_{-i}(b, v) = (M_{\mathsf{out}}(b, v), M_{\mathsf{pay}}(b, v)_{-i})$.

We comment that, in contrast to [CCK+13], we allow $\lambda_i^{(M)}$ to depend on the player's declaration v'_i to model the possibility that a player's privacy loss depends on his declaration. Allowing this dependence only strengthens our positive results, while our negative results hold even if we exclude this dependence on v'_i. We remark that even if $\lambda_i^{(M)}$ doesn't depend on v'_i, then $\mathsf{Loss}_i^{(M)}$ will still depend on v'_i, since it is an expectation over the output distribution of $M_{\mathsf{out}}(b, (v_{-i}, v'_i))$. (See Equation 2.2).)

Since the choice of a specific privacy loss function depends heavily on the context of the mechanism being studied, we avoid fixing a single privacy loss function and rather study several reasonable properties that privacy loss functions should have. Also, while we typically think of privacy valuation as being positive and privacy losses as positive, our definition does not exclude the possibility that players may *want* to lose their privacy, and therefore we allow privacy valuations (and losses) to be negative. Our impossibility results will only assume non-negative privacy loss, while our constructions handle possibly negative privacy loss functions as long as the *absolute value* of the privacy loss function is bounded appropriately.

2.4 Mechanism design criteria

Definition 2.3. *A mechanism $M = (M_{\mathsf{out}}, M_{\mathsf{pay}})$ is said to be* $([\alpha, \alpha'], \beta)$-accurate *on an input $(b, v) \in \{0,1\}^n \times \mathbb{R}^n$ if, setting $\bar{b} = \frac{1}{n}\sum_{i=1}^n b_i$, it holds that*

$$\Pr[M_{\mathsf{out}}(b, v) \notin ((\bar{b} - \alpha)n, (\bar{b} + \alpha')n)] < \beta.$$

We say that M is (α, β)-accurate *on (b, v) if it is $([\alpha, \alpha], \beta)$-accurate.*

We define $\mathsf{Pay}_i^{(M)}(b, v) = \mathbb{E}_{p \leftarrow_{\mathrm{R}} M_{\mathsf{pay}}(b,v)}[p_i]$.

Definition 2.4. *Fix n, a mechanism M on n players, and privacy loss functions $\lambda_1^{(M)}, \ldots, \lambda_n^{(M)}$. We say M is* individually rational *if for all inputs $(b, v) \in \{0,1\}^n \times \mathbb{R}^n$ and all $i \in [n]$:*

$$\mathsf{Pay}_i^{(M)}(b, v) \geq \mathsf{Loss}_i^{(M)}(b, v, v_i).$$

M is truthful for input (b, v) and player i *if for all v'_i it holds that*

$$\mathsf{Pay}_i^{(M)}(b, v) - \mathsf{Loss}_i^{(M)}(b, v, v_i) \geq \mathsf{Pay}^{(M)}(b, (v_{-i}, v'_i)) - \mathsf{Loss}_i^{(M)}(b, v, v'_i)$$

M is simply truthful *if it is truthful for all inputs and all players.*

3. IMPOSSIBILITY OF NON-TRIVIAL ACCURACY WITH PRIVACY

We will use a notion of distinguishability that captures when a function leaks information about an input pertaining to a particular player.

Definition 3.1. *An input $(b, v) \in \{0,1\}^n \times \mathbb{R}^n$ is said to be* δ-distinguishable *for player i with respect to a randomized function f if there is an i-neighbor (b', v') such that $\Delta(f(b, v), f(b', v')) \geq \delta$.*

We choose a notion based on statistical distance because it allows us to capture (ε, δ)-differential privacy even for $\delta > 0$. Namely, if there is an input $(b, v) \in \{0,1\}^n \times \mathbb{R}^n$ that is δ-distinguishable for player i with respect to f, then f cannot be (ε, δ')-differentially private for any ε, δ' satisfying $\delta > \delta' + e^{\varepsilon} - 1 \approx \delta' + \varepsilon$. However, note that, unlike differential privacy, δ-distinguishability is a *per-input* notion, measuring how much privacy loss a player can experience on a particular input (b, v), *not* taking the worst case over all inputs.

For our impossibility result we will require that any specified privacy loss should be attainable if the player's privacy valuation is large enough, as long as there is in fact a noticeable amount of information about the player's type being leaked (*i.e.* the player's input is somewhat distinguishable). Note that having unbounded privacy losses is necessary for having any kind of negative result. If the privacy losses were always upper-bounded by some value L, then a trivially truthful and individually rational mechanism would simply pay every player L and output the exact sum of data bits.

DEFINITION 3.2. *A privacy loss function $\lambda_i^{(M)}$ for a mechanism M and player i is* increasing for δ-distinguishability *if there exists a real-valued function T_i such that for all $\ell > 0$, $b \in \{0,1\}^n$ and $v_{-i} \in \mathbb{R}^{n-1}$, if $v_i \geq T_i(\ell, b, v_{-i})$ and if (b, v) is δ-distinguishable for player i with respect to M_{out}, then $\mathsf{Loss}_i^{(M)}(b, v, v_i) > \ell$.*

Notice that in our definition of increasing for δ-distinguishability we only consider distinguishability for M_{out} and not for $(M_{\mathsf{out}}, M_{\mathsf{pay}})$. Being able to handle this definition is what makes our impossibility rule out mechanisms even for privacy loss functions depending only on the distribution of M_{out}.

Definition 3.2 implies that the privacy loss functions are unbounded. We next define a natural property of loss functions, that for privacy-indifferent players privacy loss is not affected by the particular value reported for v_i.

DEFINITION 3.3. *A privacy loss function $\lambda_i^{(M)}$ for a mechanism M and player i* respects indifference *if whenever $v_i = 0$ it follows that $\mathsf{Loss}_i^{(M)}(b, v, v_i') = \mathsf{Loss}_i^{(M)}(b, v, v_i'')$ for all v_i', v_i''.*

THEOREM 3.4. *Fix a mechanism M, a number of players n, and non-negative privacy loss functions $\lambda_1^{(M)}, \ldots, \lambda_n^{(M)}$. Suppose that the $\lambda_i^{(M)}$ respect indifference, and are increasing for δ-distinguishability for some $\delta \leq \frac{1}{6n}$.*

Suppose that M that satisfies all of the following:

- *M is individually rational.*
- *M has finite payments when all players are privacy-indifferent, in the sense that for all $b \in \{0,1\}^n$ and all $i \in [n]$, it holds that $\mathsf{Pay}_i^{(M)}(b, 0^n)$ is finite.*
- *M is truthful for privacy-indifferent players, namely M is truthful for all inputs (b, v) and players i such that $v_i = 0$.*

Then it follows that M cannot have non-trivial accuracy in the sense that it cannot be $(1/2, 1/3)$-accurate on $(0^n, 0^n)$ and $(1^n, 0^n)$.

PROOF. Let $\mathsf{Pay}_i, \mathsf{Loss}_i, \lambda_i$ denote $\mathsf{Pay}_i^{(M)}, \mathsf{Loss}_i^{(M)}, \lambda_i^{(M)}$. By the assumption that M has finite payments when all players are privacy-indifferent, we can define

$$P = \max_{i \in [n], b \in \{0,1\}^n} \mathsf{Pay}_i(b, 0^n) < \infty.$$

By the assumption that all the λ_i are increasing for δ-indistinguishability, we may define a threshold

$$L = \max_{i \in [n], b \in \{0,1\}^n} T_i(P, b, 0^{n-1})$$

such that for all $i \in [n], b \in \{0,1\}^n, v_i \geq L$, if $(b, (0^{n-1}, v_i))$ is δ-distinguishable, then $\mathsf{Loss}_i(b, (0^{n-1}, v_i), v_i) > P$.

We construct a sequence of $2n + 1$ inputs $x^{(1,0)}, x^{(1,1)}, x^{(2,0)}, x^{(2,1)}, \ldots, x^{(n,0)}, x^{(n,1)}, x^{(n+1,0)}$. In $x^{(1,0)}$, all players have data bit 0 and privacy valuation 0. That is, $x^{(1,0)} = (0^n, 0^n)$. From $x^{(i,0)}$, we construct $x^{(i,1)}$ by changing player i's data bit b_i from 0 to 1 and valuation v_i from 0 to L. From $x^{(i,1)}$, we construct $x^{(i+1,0)}$ by changing player i's valuation v_i back from L to 0 (but b_i remains 1). Thus,

$$\begin{aligned} x^{(i,0)} &= ((1^{i-1}, 0, 0^{n-i}), (0^{i-1}, 0, 0^{n-i})), \quad \text{and} \\ x^{(i,1)} &= ((1^{i-1}, 1, 0^{n-i}), (0^{i-1}, L, 0^{n-i})) \end{aligned}$$

In particular, $x^{(n+1,0)} = (1^n, 0^n)$. Define the hybrid distributions $H^{(i,j)} = M_{\mathsf{out}}(x^{(i,j)})$.

CLAIM 3.5. *For all $i \in [n]$, $\mathsf{Pay}_i(x^{(i,1)}) \leq \mathsf{Pay}_i(x^{(i+1,0)}) \leq P$.*

To prove this claim, we first note that all players have privacy valuation 0 in $x^{(i+1,0)}$, so $\mathsf{Pay}_i(x^{(i+1,0)}) \leq P$ by the definition of P. Since player i has privacy valuation 0 in $x^{(i+1,0)}$, we also know that privacy loss of player i in input $x^{(i+1,0)}$ is independent of her declaration (since λ_i respects indifference). If player i declares L as her valuation instead of 0, she would get payment $\mathsf{Pay}_i(x^{(i,1)})$. By truthfulness for privacy-indifferent players, we must have $\mathsf{Pay}_i(x^{(i,1)}) \leq \mathsf{Pay}_i(x^{(i+1,0)})$.

By the definition of L it follows that $x^{(i,1)}$ cannot be δ-distinguishable for player i with respect to M_{out}. Otherwise, this would contradict individual rationality because on input $x^{(i,1)}$ player i would have privacy loss $> P$ while only getting payoff $\leq P$.

Since $x^{(i,1)}$ is not δ-distinguishable for player i with respect to M_{out}, and because $x^{(i,1)}$ is an i-neighbor of $x^{(i,0)}$ as well as $x^{(i+1,0)}$, it follows that

$$\Delta(H^{(i,0)}, H^{(i,1)}) < \delta \text{ and } \Delta(H^{(i,1)}, H^{(i+1,0)}) < \delta \quad (3.1)$$

Finally, since Equation 3.1 holds for all $i \in [n]$, and since $H^{(1,0)} = M_{\mathsf{out}}(0^n, 0^n)$ and $H^{(n+1,0)} = M_{\mathsf{out}}(1^n, 0^n)$, we have by the triangle inequality that

$$\Delta(M_{\mathsf{out}}(0^n, 0^n), M_{\mathsf{out}}(1^n, 0^n)) < 2n\delta$$

But since $\delta \leq 1/6n$, this contradicts the fact that M has non-trivial accuracy, since non-trivial accuracy implies that we can distinguish between the output of M_{out} on inputs $(0^n, 0^n)$ and $(1^n, 0^n)$ with advantage greater than 1/3, simply by checking whether the output is greater than $n/2$. □

3.1 Using sub-sampling for privacy loss functions with low distinguishability

We comment that the $\delta \leq 1/6n$ bound in Theorem 3.4 is tight up to a constant factor. Indeed, if players do not incur significant losses when their inputs are $O(1/n)$-distinguishable, then an extremely simple mechanisms based on subsampling can be used to achieve truthfulness, individual rationality, and accuracy with finite budget.

Namely, suppose that the privacy loss functions are such that if for all i, if player i's input is not C/n-distinguishable for some constant C, then regardless of v_i, the loss to player i is bounded by P. Then the following mechanism is truthful, individually rational, and accurate: pay all players P, select at random a subset A of size k for some $k < C$ from the population, and output $(n/|A|) \cdot \sum_{i \in A} b_i$. By a Chernoff Bound, this mechanism is $(\eta, 2e^{-\eta^2 k})$-accurate for all $\eta > 0$. By construction no player's input is C/n-distinguishable and therefore their privacy loss is at most P and the mechanism is individually rational. Finally mechanism is truthful since it behaves independently of the player declarations.

4. POSITIVE RESULTS

For our positive results, we will require the following natural property from our privacy loss functions. Recall that we allow the privacy loss functions $\lambda_i^{(M)}$ to depend on a player's report v_i', in addition the the player's true type. We require the dependence on v_i' to be well-behaved in that if changing declarations does not change the output distribution, then it also does not change the privacy loss.

DEFINITION 4.1. *A privacy loss function* $\lambda_i^{(M)}$ respects identical output distributions *if the following holds: for all* b, v, *if the distribution of* $M_{-i}(b, v)$ *is identical to the distribution of* $M_{-i}(b, (v_{-i}, v_i'))$, *then for all* s, p, *it holds that* $\lambda_i^{(M)}(b, v, v_i', s, p) = \lambda_i^{(M)}(b, v, v_i, s, p)$.

The above definition captures the idea that if what the privacy adversary can see (namely the output of M_{-i}) doesn't change, then player i's privacy loss should not change.

4.1 Monotonic valuations

We now define our main conceptual restriction of the privacy loss functions to consider only *monotonic valuations.*

DEFINITION 4.2. *Two player types* $(b_i, v_i), (b_i', v_i')$ *taking value in* $\{0,1\} \times \mathbb{R}$ *are said to be* monotonically related *iff* ($b_i = 0$, $b_i' = 1$, *and* $v_i \le v_i'$) *or* ($b_i = 1$, $b_i' = 0$, *and* $v_i \ge v_i'$). *Two inputs* $(b, v), (b', v') \in \{0,1\}^n \times \mathbb{R}^n$ *are* monotonic i-neighbors *if they are* i*-neighbors and furthermore* $(b_i, v_i), (b_i', v_i')$ *are monotonically related. They are* monotonic neighbors *if they are monotonic* i*-neighbors for some* $i \in [n]$.

Following [CCK+13], we also make the assumption that the privacy loss functions on a given output (s, p_{-i}) are bounded by the amount of influence that player i's report has on the probability of the output:

DEFINITION 4.3. *A privacy loss function* $\lambda_i^{(M)}$ *is* bounded by differential privacy *if the following holds:*

$$\left|\lambda_i^{(M)}(b, v, v_i', s, p_{-i})\right| \le v_i \cdot \left(\max_{(b_i'', v_i'')} \log \frac{\Pr[M_{-i}(b, v) = (s, p_{-i})]}{\Pr[M_{-i}((b_{-i}, b_i''), (v_{-i}, v_i'')) = (s, p_{-i})]} \right) \tag{4.1}$$

Input: $(b, v) \in \{0,1\}^n \times \mathbb{R}^n$. Auxiliary inputs: budget $B > 0$, privacy parameter $\varepsilon > 0$.

1. For all $i \in [n]$, set $b_i' = b_i$ if $2\varepsilon v_i \le B/n$, otherwise set $b_i' = 0$.
2. Output $\sum_{i=1}^n b_i' + \mathrm{Geom}(\varepsilon)$.
3. Pay B/n to player i if $2\varepsilon v_i \le B/n$, else pay player i nothing.

ALGORITHM 4.5. *Mechanism for monotonic valuations*

A privacy loss function $\lambda_i^{(M)}$ *is* bounded by differential privacy for monotonic valuations *if Equation 4.1 holds but the maximum is restricted to be only over* (b_i'', v_i'') *monotonically related to* (b_i, v_i).

As noted and used in [CCK+13], the RHS in the above definition can be upper-bounded by the level of (pure) differential privacy, and the same holds for monotonic valuations:

FACT 4.4. *If* M_{-i} *is* ε*-differentially private for* i*-neighbors (*i.e. *Equation 2.1 holds for all* i*-neighbors) and* $\lambda_i^{(M)}$ *is bounded by differential privacy (even if only for monotonic valuations), then player* i*'s privacy loss is bounded by* $v_i\varepsilon$ *regardless of other player types, player declarations, or outcomes.*

As hinted at in the definition of privacy loss functions bounded by differential privacy for monotonic valuations, one can define an analogue of differential privacy where we take the maximum over just monotonically related neighbors. However this notion is not that different from the original notion of differential privacy, since satisfying such a definition for some privacy parameter ε immediately implies satisfying (standard) differential privacy for privacy parameter 3ε, since every two pairs (b_i, v_i) and (b_i', v_i') are at distance at most 3 in the monotonic-neighbor graph. The monotonic neighbor notion becomes more interesting if we consider a further variant of differential privacy where the privacy guarantee ε_i afforded to an individual depends on her data (b_i, v_i) (e.g. $\varepsilon_i = 1/v_i$). We defer exploration of this notion to a future version of this paper.

4.2 Mechanism for monotonic valuations

The idea behind our mechanism for players with monotic valuations (Algorithm 4.5) is simply to treat the data bit as 0 (the insensitive value) for all players who value privacy too much.

THEOREM 4.6. *For privacy loss functions that are bounded by differential privacy for monotonic valuations and respect identical output distributions, the mechanism* M *in Algorithm 4.5 satisfies the following:*

1. *M is truthful for all players with* $2\varepsilon v_i \le B/n$.
2. *M is individually rational for all players*
3. *Assume only that the truthful players described in Point 1 do indeed declare their true types. Letting* η *denote*

the fraction of players where $b_i = 1$ and $2\varepsilon v_i > B/n$, it holds that M is $([\eta + \gamma, \gamma], 2e^{-\varepsilon\gamma n})$-accurate.

PROOF. **Truthfulness for players with $2\varepsilon v_i \le B/n$:** if $2\varepsilon v_i \le B/n$, then declaring any $v'_i \le B/(2\varepsilon n)$ has no effect on the output of the mechanism, and so there is no change in utility since the privacy loss functions respect identical output distributions. If player i declares some $v'_i > B/(2\varepsilon n)$, then he loses B/n in payment. Because M_{-i} is ε-differentially private if for i-neighbors (recall we assume an observer cannot see the change in p_i) and we assumed that the privacy loss functions are bounded by differential privacy for monotonic valuations, it follows that player i's privacy loss has absolute value at most $2\varepsilon v_i$ under a report of v_i and under a report of v'_i (Fact 4.4). Thus, there is at most a change of $2\varepsilon v_i$ in privacy, which is not sufficient to overcome the payment loss of B/n.

Individual rationality: consider any vector of types b, v and any player i. If $v_i \le B/2\varepsilon n$ then player i receives payment B/n. By the hypothesis that the privacy loss functions are bounded by differential privacy for monotonic valuations, and because the mechanism is ε-differentially private, the privacy loss to player i is bounded by $\varepsilon v_i < B/n$ (Fact 4.4), satisfying individual rationality.

Now suppose that player i has valuation $v_i > \frac{B}{2\varepsilon n}$. In this case the payment is 0. The mechanism sets $b'_i = 0$, and for every (b''_i, v''_i) monotonically related to (b_i, v_i) the mechanism also sets $b'_i = 0$. Since the report of player i does not affect b'_j or the payment to player j for $j \neq i$, monotonic neighbors will produce the *exact* same output distribution of M_{-i}.

Therefore the privacy loss of player i is 0. Indeed, since the privacy loss function is bounded by differential privacy for monotonic valuations, we have:

$$\left|\lambda_i^{(M)}(b, v, v'_i, s, p_{-i})\right|$$

$$\le v_i \cdot \left(\max_{(b''_i, v''_i)} \log \frac{\Pr[M_{-i}(b, v) = (s, p_{-i})]}{\Pr[M_{-i}((b_{-i}, b''_i), (v_{-i}, v''_i)) = (s, p_{-i})]} \right) \tag{4.2}$$

$$= 0$$

where in Equation 4.2 the maximum is taken over (b''_i, v''_i) monotonically related to (b_i, v_i).

Accuracy: the bits of the $(1 - \eta)$ fraction of truthful players and players with $b_i = 0$ are always counted correctly, while the bits of the η fraction of players with $b_i = 1$ and large privacy valuation $v_i \ge B/(2\varepsilon n)$ are either counted correctly (if they declare a value less than $B/(2\varepsilon n)$) or are counted as 0 (if they declare otherwise).

This means that $\overline{b'} = \sum_{i=1}^n b'_i$ and $\overline{b} = \sum_{i=1}^n b_i$ satisfy $\overline{b'} \in [\overline{b} - \eta n, \overline{b'}]$.

By the definition of symmetric geometric noise, it follows that (letting v' be the declared valuations of the players) it holds that

$$\Pr[|M_{\mathsf{out}}(b, v') - \overline{b'}| \ge \gamma n] < 2e^{-\varepsilon\gamma n}.$$

The theorem follows.

□

4.2.1 Achieving better truthfulness

We can improve the truthfulness of Theorem 4.6 to include all players with data bit 0.

THEOREM 4.7. *Let M' be the same as in Algorithm 4.5, except that* all *players with $b_i = 0$ are paid B/n, even those with large privacy valuations. Suppose that the $\lambda_i^{(M')}$ are bounded by differential privacy for monotonic valuations and also respect identical output distributions. Then the conclusions of Theorem 4.6 hold and in addition the mechanism is truthful for all players with data bit $b_i = 0$.*

Note that, unlike Algorithm 4.5, here the payment that the mechanism makes to players depends on their data bit, and not just on their reported valuation. This might make it impractical in some settings (e.g. if payment is needed before players give permission to view their data bits).

PROOF. Increasing the payments to the players with $b_i = 0$ and privacy valuation $v_i > \frac{B}{2\varepsilon n}$ does not hurt individual rationality or accuracy. We must however verify that we have not harmed truthfulness. Since players are not allowed to lie about their data bit, the same argument for truthfulness of players with $b_i = 1$ and $v_i \le B/(2\varepsilon n)$ remains valid. It is only necessary to verify that truthfulness holds for all players with $b_i = 0$.

Observe that for players with $b_i = 0$, the output distribution of the mechanism is identical regardless of their declaration for v_i. Therefore by the assumption that the $\lambda_i^{(M)}$ respect identical output distributions, changing their declaration does not change their privacy loss. Furthermore, by the definition of M' changing their declaration does not change their payment as all players with $b_i = 0$ are paid B/n. Therefore, there is no advantage to declaring a false valuation. □

We remark that the only setting where Theorem 4.7 is preferable to Theorem 4.6 is when knowing the true valuations is important beyond simply helping to achieve an accurate output; in particular, notice that M' as defined in Theorem 4.7 does not guarantee any better accuracy or any lower payments (indeed, it may make more payments than the original Algorithm 4.5).

5. LOWER BOUNDS

5.1 Impossibility of non-trivial accuracy for all privacy valuations with monotonic privacy

One natural question that Algorithm 4.5 raises is whether we can hope to adaptively set the budget B based on the valuations of the players and thereby achieve accuracy for all inputs, not just inputs where most players' privacy valuations are small relative to some predetermined budget. In this section we show that this is not possible, even when only considering players who care about privacy for monotonic neighbors.

DEFINITION 5.1. *An input $(b, v) \in \{0,1\}^n \times \mathbb{R}^n$ is δ-*monotonically distinguishable *for player i with respect to a randomized function f if there is a monotonic i-neighbor (b', v') such that $\Delta(f(b, v), f(b', v')) \ge \delta$.*

DEFINITION 5.2. *A privacy loss function $\lambda_i^{(M)}$ for a mechanism M and player i is* increasing for δ-monotonic distinguishability *if there exists a real-valued function T_i such that for all $\ell > 0$, $b \in \{0,1\}^n$ and $v_{-i} \in \mathbb{R}^{n-1}$, if $v_i \ge T_i(\ell, b, v_{-i})$ and if (b, v) is δ-monotonically distinguishable for player i with respect to M_{out}, then $\mathsf{Loss}_i^{(M)}(b, v, v_i) > \ell$.*

THEOREM 5.3. *Fix any mechanism M and any number of players n, and fix any non-negative privacy loss functions $\lambda_1^{(M)}, \ldots, \lambda_n^{(M)}$. Suppose that the $\lambda_i^{(M)}$ respect indifference and are increasing for δ-monotonic distinguishability for $\delta \leq \frac{1}{3n}$.*

Suppose M satisfies all the following:

- *M is individually rational.*
- *M always has finite payments, in the sense that for all $b \in \{0,1\}^n, v \in \mathbb{R}^n$ and all $i \in [n]$ it holds that $\mathsf{Pay}_i^{(M)}(b,v)$ is finite.*
- *M is truthful for privacy-indifferent players, as defined in Theorem 3.4*

Then M does not have non-trivial accuracy for all privacy valuations, i.e. *M cannot be $(1/2, 1/3)$-accurate on $(0^n, v)$ and $(1^n, v)$ for all $v \in \mathbb{R}^n$.*

PROOF. The argument follows the same outline as the proof of Theorem 3.4, *i.e.* by constructing a sequence of hybrid inputs and using truthfulness for privacy-indifferent players and individual rationality to argue that the neighboring hybrids must produce statistically close outputs. However, we have to take more care here because for the hybrids in this proof there is no uniform way to set the maximum payment P and threshold valuation L for achieving privacy loss $> P$ at the beginning of the argument, since here we allow the finite payment bound to depend on the valuations (whereas Theorem 3.4 only refers to the payment bound when all valuations are zero). Instead, we set P_i, L_i for the i'th hybrids in a way that depends on $L_{[i-1]} = (L_1, \ldots, L_{i-1})$.

As before, we define $2n+1$ hybrid inputs $x^{(1,0)}, x^{(1,1)}, x^{(2,0)}, x^{(2,1)}, \ldots, x^{(n,0)}, x^{(n,1)}, x^{(n+1,0)}$ inductively as follows. In $x^{(1,0)}$, all players have data bit 0 and privacy valuation 0. That is, $x^{(1,0)} = (0^n, 0^n)$. From $x^{(i,0)}$, we define $x^{(i,1)}$ by changing player i's data bit from 0 to 1. From $x^{(i,1)} = (b^{(i)}, v^{(i)})$, we define $P_i = \mathsf{Pay}_i(x^{(i,1)})$ to be the amount that player i is paid in $x^{(i,1)}$, and $L_i = T_i(P_i, b^{(i)}, v_{-i}^{(i)})$ to be a privacy valuation beyond which payment P_i does not compensate for δ-distinguishability (as promised by Definition 5.2). Then we define $x^{(i+1,0)}$ by increasing the valuation of player i from 0 to L_i. By induction, for $i = 1, \ldots, n+1$, we have

$$x^{(i,0)} = (1^{i-1}0^{n-i+1}, L_{[i-1]}0^{n-i+1}).$$

Define the distribution $H^{(i)} = M_{\mathsf{out}}(x^{(i,0)})$.

CLAIM 5.4. $\mathsf{Pay}_i(x^{(i+1,0)}) \leq \mathsf{Pay}_i(x^{(i,1)}) = P_i$

On input $x^{(i,1)}$, player i has privacy valuation 0, so his privacy loss is independent of his declaration (since λ_i respects indifference). Declaring L_i would change the input to $x^{(i+1,0)}$, so by truthfulness for privacy-indifferent players, we have $\mathsf{Pay}_i(x^{(i+1,0)}) \leq \mathsf{Pay}_i(x^{(i,1)})$.

By the definition of L_i, $x^{(i+1,0)}$ cannot be δ-monotonically distinguishable for player i with respect to M_{out}. Otherwise, this would contradict individual rationality because on input $x^{(i+1,0)}$ player i would have privacy loss greater than P_i while only getting a payoff of at most P_i (by Claim 5.4).

Since $x^{(i+1,0)}$ is not δ-monotonically distinguishable for player i with respect to M_{out}, and because $x^{(i,0)}$ is an i-monotonic neighbor of $x^{(i+1,0)}$, we therefore deduce that $\Delta(H^{(i-1)}, H^{(i)}) < \delta$. Finally, since this holds for all $i \in [n]$, the triangle inequality implies that $\Delta(H^{(0)}, H^{(n)}) < n\delta$. But since $\delta \leq 1/3n$, this implies that

$$\Delta(M_{\mathsf{out}}(0^n, 0^n), M_{\mathsf{out}}(1^n, L)) < 1/3$$

contradicting the fact that M has non-trivial accuracy for all privacy valuations. ☐

5.2 Tradeoff between payments and accuracy

One could also ask whether the accuracy of Theorem 4.6 can be improved, *i.e.* whether it is possible to beat $(\eta + \gamma, 2e^{-\varepsilon\gamma n})$-accuracy. We now present a result that, assuming the mechanism does not exceed a certain amount of payment, limits the best accuracy it can achieve. (We note however that this bound is loose and does not match our mechanism.)

In order to prove optimality we will require that the privacy loss functions be growing with statistical distance, a strictly stronger condition than being increasing for δ-distinguishability. However, a stronger requirement is unavoidable since one can invent contrived privacy loss functions that are increasing but for which one can achieve $(\eta, 0)$-accuracy by simply by outputting $\sum b_i'$ as constructed in Algorithm 4.5 without noise (while preserving the same truthfulness and individual rationality guarantees). Nevertheless, being growing with statistical distance for monotonic neighbors is compatible with being bounded by differential privacy for monotonic neighbors (*i.e.* there exist functions that satisfy both properties), and therefore the following result still implies limits to how much one can improve the accuracy of our positive result Theorem 4.6 for all privacy loss functions bounded by differential privacy for monotonic neighbors.

DEFINITION 5.5. *$\lambda_i^{(M)}(b, v, v_i', s, p_{-i})$ is* growing with statistical distance (for monotonic neighbors) *if:*

$$\mathsf{Loss}_i^{(M)}(b, v, v_i) \geq v_i \cdot \left(\max_{(b',v')} \Delta(M_{\mathsf{out}}(b,v), M_{\mathsf{out}}(b',v')) \right)$$

where the maximum is taken over (b', v') that are (monotonic) i-neighbors of (b, v).

THEOREM 5.6. *Fix a mechanism M, a number of players n, and privacy loss functions $\lambda_i^{(M)}$ for $i = 1, \ldots, n$. Suppose that the $\lambda_i^{(M)}$ respect indifference and are growing with statistical distance for monotonic neighbors.*

Suppose that M satisfies the following:

- *M is individually rational.*
- *There exists a maximum payment over all possible inputs that M makes to any player who declares 0 privacy valuation. Call this maximum value P.*
- *M is truthful for privacy-indifferent players as defined in Theorem 3.4.*

Then it holds that for any $\tau, \gamma, \eta > 0$ such that $\eta + 2\gamma \leq 1$, and any $\beta < \frac{1}{2} - \frac{P}{\tau}\gamma n$, the mechanism M cannot be $([\eta + \gamma, \gamma], \beta)$-accurate on all inputs where at most an η fraction of the players' valuations exceed τ.

PROOF. Fix any $\tau, \eta, \gamma > 0$ and any $\beta < \frac{1}{2} - \frac{P}{\tau}\gamma n$. We prove the theorem by showing that M cannot be $([\eta + \gamma, \gamma], \beta)$-accurate. Let $h = \eta n$ denote the number of players with high privacy valuation allowed.

Fix any $L \geq Ph/(1 - 2\frac{P}{\tau}\gamma n - 2\beta)$. Consider the following sequence of hybrid inputs. Let $x^{(1,0)} = (0^n, 0^n)$. From $x^{(i,0)}$, define $x^{(i,1)}$ by flipping player i's data bit from 0 to 1. From $x^{(i,1)}$, define $x^{(i+1,0)}$ by increasing the valuation of player i from 0 to L if $i \in [h+1]$, or from 0 to τ if $i \in (h+1, h+2\gamma n+1]$. By induction, we have:

$$\begin{aligned}\forall i \in & [h+1], \\ & x^{(i,0)} = (1^{i-1}0^{n-i+1}, L^{i-1}0^{n-i+1}) \\ \forall i \in & (h+1, h+2\gamma n+1], \\ & x^{(i,0)} = (1^{i-1}0^{n-i+1}, L^{h}\tau^{i-h-1}0^{n-i+1})\end{aligned}$$

These are well-defined since $h + 2\gamma = (\eta + 2\gamma)n \le n$. Define the hybrids $H^{(i,0)} = M_{\mathsf{out}}(x^{(i,0)})$. To analyze these hybrids, we use the following claims.

Claim 5.7. *For any input (b, v) where player i is paid at most P, it holds that (b, v) is not δ-distinguishable for monotonic neighbors for player i with respect to M_{out} for any $\delta \ge P/v_i$.*

Claim 5.7 holds because by individual rationality, it holds that the privacy loss does not exceed P. By the assumption that the privacy loss functions are growing with statistical distance for monotonic neighbors, it follows that $\Delta(M_{\mathsf{out}}(b, v), M_{\mathsf{out}}(b', v')) \le P/v_i$ for all (b', v') monotonic neighbors of (b, v).

Claim 5.8. $\mathsf{Pay}_i(x^{(i+1,0)}) \le \mathsf{Pay}_i(x^{(i,1)}) \le P$.

As in the proof of Theorem 5.3, this claim holds because on input $x^{(i,1)}$, player $i+1$ has 0 privacy valuation, and so $\mathsf{Pay}_i(x^{(i,1)}) \le P$ by our assumption that the mechanism pays at most P to players with 0 privacy valuation. The inequality $\mathsf{Pay}_i(x^{(i+1,0)}) \le \mathsf{Pay}_i(x^{(i,1)})$ follows as in the proof of Theorem 5.3 from the truthfulness of the mechanism for privacy-indifferent players and by the fact that the privacy loss functions respect indifference.

We may apply Claim 5.7 to conclude that for all $i \in [h]$, since player i has valuation L in $x^{(i+1,0)}$, it therefore holds that $x^{(i+1,0)}$ cannot be (P/L)-distinguishable for monotonic neighbors for player i. Since $x^{(i,0)}, x^{(i+1,0)}$ are monotonic i-neighbors, it follows that $\Delta(H^{(i,0)}, H^{(i+1,0)}) < P/L$.

Repeating the same argument for all $i \in [h+1, h+2\gamma n]$ and using the fact that player i has valuation τ in $x^{(i+1,0)}$ for these i, it follows that $\Delta(H^{(i,0)}, H^{(i+1,0)}) < P/\tau$.

Combining the above using the triangle inequality and applying the definition of L, we deduce that

$$\Delta(H^{(1,0)}, H^{(h+2\gamma n+1,0)}) < \frac{\eta n P}{L} + \frac{2\gamma n P}{\tau} \le 1 - 2\beta \quad (5.1)$$

For $i \in [n]$, define the open interval on the real line $A(i) = (i-1-(\eta+\gamma)n, i-1+\gamma n)$. Since the sum of the data bits in $x^{(i,0)}$ is exactly $i-1$, in order for M to be $([\eta+\gamma, \gamma], \beta)$-accurate, it is necessary that

$$\Pr[H^{(i)} \in A(i)] > 1 - \beta \text{ for all } i \in [h+2\gamma n+1] \quad (5.2)$$

Observe that $A(1)$ and $A(h+2\gamma n+1)$ are disjoint. Therefore, Equation 5.1 implies that

$$\Pr[H^{(1,0)} \in A(1)] < \Pr[H^{(h+2\gamma n+1,0)} \in A(1)] + 1 - 2\beta$$

By Equation 5.2 it follows that $\Pr[H^{(h+2\gamma n+1,0)} \in A(1)] < \beta$ and therefore from the previous inequality we deduce that $\Pr[H^{(1,0)} \in A(1)] < 1-\beta$. But this contradicts Equation 5.2, and therefore it must be the case that M is not $([\eta+\gamma, \gamma], \beta)$-accurate. □

Remark 5.9. *A different way to evaluate the accuracy guarantee of our mechanism, (the one taken in the work of Ghosh and Roth [GR11]) would be to compare it to the optimal accuracy achievable in the class of all envy-free mechanisms with budget B. However, in our context it is not clear how to define envy-freeness: while it is clear what it means for player i to receive player j's payment, it is not at all clear (without making further assumptions) how to define the privacy loss of player i as if he were treated like player j, since this loss may depend on the functional relationship between the player i's type and the output of the mechanism. Because of this, our mechanism may not envy-free (for reasonable privacy loss functions), and so we refrain from using envy-free mechanisms as a benchmark.*

6. ACKNOWLEDGEMENTS

K.N., S.V., and D.X., were supported in part by NSF grant CNS-1237235, a gift from Google, Inc., and a Simons Investigator grant to Salil Vadhan. K.N. was also supported by ISF grant (276/12). D.X. was also supported by the French ANR Blanc program under contract ANR-12-BS02-005 (RDAM project).

References

[BNS13] A. Beimel, K. Nissim, and U. Stemmer. Private Learning and Sanitization: Pure vs. Approximate Differential Privacy. In *Proceedings of the 17th International Workshop on Randomization and Computation (RANDOM '13)*, Lecture Notes in Computer Science, pages 363–378. Springer-Verlag, 21–23 August 2013.

[CCK+13] Y. Chen, S. Chong, I. A. Kash, T. Moran, and S. Vadhan. Truthful mechanisms for agents that value privacy. In *Proceedings of the fourteenth ACM conference on Electronic commerce*, EC '13, pages 215–232, New York, NY, USA, 2013. ACM.

[CCK+11] Y. Chen, S. Chong, I. A. Kash, T. Moran, and S. P. Vadhan. Truthful Mechanisms for Agents that Value Privacy. *CoRR*, abs/1111.5472, 2011.

[De12] A. De. Lower bounds in differential privacy. In *Theory of cryptography conference (TCC '12)*, volume 7194 of *Lecture Notes in Comput. Sci.*, pages 321–338. Springer, Heidelberg, 2012.

[Dwo06] C. Dwork. Differential privacy. In *In Proc. ICALP*, pages 1–12. Springer, 2006.

[DL09] C. Dwork and J. Lei. Differential privacy and robust statistics. In *STOC'09—Proceedings of the 2009 ACM International Symposium on Theory of Computing*, pages 371–380. ACM, New York, 2009.

[DMNS06] C. Dwork, F. Mcsherry, K. Nissim, and A. Smith. Calibrating noise to sensitivity in private data analysis. In *In Proc. of the 3rd TCC*, pages 265–284. Springer, 2006.

[DRV10] C. Dwork, G. Rothblum, and S. Vadhan. Boosting and Differential Privacy. In *Proceedings of the 51st Annual IEEE Symposium on Foundations of Computer Science (FOCS '10)*, pages 51–60. IEEE, 23–26 October 2010.

[FL12] L. K. Fleischer and Y.-H. Lyu. Approximately optimal auctions for selling privacy when costs are correlated with data. In *Proceedings of the 13th ACM Conference on Electronic Commerce*, EC '12, pages 568–585, New York, NY, USA, 2012. ACM.

[GR11] A. Ghosh and A. Roth. Selling privacy at auction. In *Proc. 12th EC*, EC '11, pages 199–208, New York, NY, USA, 2011. ACM.

[HT10] M. Hardt and K. Talwar. On the geometry of differential privacy. In *STOC'10—Proceedings of the 2010 ACM International Symposium on Theory of Computing*, pages 705–714. ACM, New York, 2010.

[HK12] Z. Huang and S. Kannan. The Exponential Mechanism for Social Welfare: Private, Truthful, and Nearly Optimal: In *Proc. FOCS '12*, pages 140–149, 2012.

[KPRU13] M. Kearns, M. M. Pai, A. Roth, and J. Ullman. Mechanism Design in Large Games: Incentives and Privacy. In *Proc. ITCS 2013*, 2013. Available at `http://arxiv.org/abs/1207.4084`.

[LR12] K. Ligett and A. Roth. Take it or Leave it: Running a Survey when Privacy Comes at a Cost. In *Proceedings of the 8th Workshop on Internet and Network Economics*, pages 378–391. Springer, 2012.

[MT07] F. McSherry and K. Talwar. Mechanism design via differential privacy. In *Proceedings of the 48th Annual Symposium on Foundations of Computer Science.* Citeseer, 2007.

[NOS12] K. Nissim, C. Orlandi, and R. Smorodinsky. Privacy-aware mechanism design. In *Proceedings of the 13th ACM Conference on Electronic Commerce*, EC '12, pages 774–789, New York, NY, USA, 2012. ACM.

[NST12] K. Nissim, R. Smorodinsky, and M. Tennenholtz. Approximately optimal mechanism design via differential privacy. In *Proceedings of the 3rd Innovations in Theoretical Computer Science Conference*, ITCS '12, pages 203–213, New York, NY, USA, 2012. ACM.

[PR13] M. M. Pai and A. Roth. Privacy and mechanism design. *SIGecom Exch.*, 12(1):8–29, June 2013.

[Rot12] A. Roth. Buying private data at auction: the sensitive surveyor's problem. *SIGecom Exch.*, 11(1):1–8, June 2012.

[RS12] A. Roth and G. Schoenebeck. Conducting truthful surveys, cheaply. In *Proceedings of the 13th ACM Conference on Electronic Commerce*, EC '12, pages 826–843, New York, NY, USA, 2012. ACM.

[Xia11] D. Xiao. Is privacy compatible with truthfulness? Technical Report 2011/005, Cryptology ePrint Archive, 2011.

[Xia13] D. Xiao. Is privacy compatible with truthfulness? In *In Proc. ITCS 2013*, pages 67–86, 2013.

Approximation Schemes via Sherali-Adams Hierarchy for Dense Constraint Satisfaction Problems and Assignment Problems

Yuichi Yoshida
National Institute of Informatics
and Preferred Infrastructure, Inc.
yyoshida@nii.ac.jp

Yuan Zhou
Computer Science Department
Carnegie Mellon University
yuanzhou@cs.cmu.edu

ABSTRACT

We consider approximation schemes for the maximum constraint satisfaction problems and the maximum assignment problems. Though they are NP-Hard in general, if the instance is "dense" or "locally dense", then they are known to have approximation schemes that run in polynomial time or quasi-polynomial time. In this paper, we give a unified method of showing these approximation schemes based on the Sherali-Adams linear programming relaxation hierarchy. We also use our linear programming-based framework to show new algorithmic results on the optimization version of the hypergraph isomorphism problem.

Categories and Subject Descriptors

G.1.6 [**Mathematics of Computing**]: Numerical Analysis—*Optimization*; F.2.0 [**Theory of Computation**]: Analysis of Algorithms and Problem Complexity—*General*

Keywords

Sherali-Adams hierarchy; approximation schemes; constraint satisfaction problems; assignment problems; dense instances; locally-dense instances

1. INTRODUCTION

In the maximum constraint satisfaction problem (Max-CSP), given a variable set V over the domain D and a set of constraints $\mathcal{C}$ over the variables in V, we want to find an assignment $\alpha : V \to D$ that maximizes the fraction of constraints satisfied by α. Max-CSP includes many fundamental problems such as Max-Cut and Max-SAT.

In general, Max-CSP is NP-Hard, and it is even NP-Hard to approximate within a constant factor [ALM$^+$98]. However, de la Vega [dlV96] showed that there is a polynomial-time approximation scheme for Max-Cut if the input graph is *dense*, i.e., it has $\Omega(n^2)$ edges. Here, a *polynomial-time approximation scheme* (PTAS) is an algorithm that, given $\epsilon > 0$ as a parameter, gives a $(1 - \epsilon)$-approximation to the optimal value, and runs in polynomial time for any constant ϵ. Max-k-CSP is a subproblem of Max-CSP, in which each constraint involves at most k variables, where k is a constant. Arora et al. [AKK99] and Frieze and Kannan [FK96] showed PTASs for dense Max-k-CSP, i.e., the input instance has $\Omega(n^k)$ constraints. Now it is known that we can compute $(1-\epsilon)$-approximation to the optimal value in time that depends only on k and ϵ [AdlVKK03].

There are two directions to generalize PTASs for dense Max-k-CSP. The first one is to generalize the notion of the density condition. We say that an instance of Max-2-CSP is *metric* if the weights of the constraints form a metric. Max-Cut [dlVK01] and Max-Bisection [FdlVKK04] admit PTASs if the instance is metric. The notion of *local density* is introduced to generalize the notion of metric to constraints over more than two variables. If the instance is locally dense, Max-k-CSP admits PTASs [dlVKKV05].

The second direction is to handle the maximum assignment problems (Max-AP). In this problem, given a variable set V and a set of constraints, we want to find a permutation π of V to maximize the fraction of satisfied constraints. Max-AP includes many fundamental problems such as Maximum Acyclic Subgraph, Betweenness, Maximum Graph Isomorphism, Densest k-Subgraph, and Quadratic Assignment Problem. Max-k-AP is a special case of Max-AP, in which each constraint involves at most k variables (see Section 2 for the precise definition). We say that an instance of Max-k-AP is dense if it has $\Omega(n^k)$ constraints. Arora et al. [AFK02] showed a quasi-polynomial-time approximation scheme for dense Max-k-AP and PTASs for many special cases.

As we have seen, Max-CSP and Max-k-AP admit PTASs (or quasi-PTASs) in the dense case and the locally dense case. However, the techniques to obtain them vary a lot. For example, [AKK99] is based on the idea of exhaustively trying all assignments for a small number of variables and then solving the rest using the partial assignment. On the other hand, [FK96] used a variant of Szemerédi's regularity lemma [Sze78]. To deal with the metric case, [dlVK01] used the method of copying important variables, and [dlVKKV05] considered a variant of singular value decomposition of tensors to deal with the locally dense case.

1.1 Linear Programming (LP) relaxation and LP relaxation hierarchies

LP relaxations are a standard tool to design approximation algorithms. In this well-known algorithmic framework,

ITCS'14, January 12–14, 2014, Princeton, New Jersey, USA.

http://dx.doi.org/10.1145/2554797.2554836 .

we typically model the given problem as an integer program, solve an LP relaxation, and use the optimal fractional solution to construct a feasible integral solution for the original problem (which is called a *rounding procedure*). We usually analyze the algorithm by comparing the value of the rounded solution to the value of the optimal fractional solution (which is an upper bound on the value of the optimal integral solution). In this way, the best approximation guarantee we can hope for, is the maximum gap (over all instance) between the values of optimal integral solution and the optimal fractional solution, which is usually referred to as the *integrality gap* of the relaxation.

In order to make the integrality gap smaller, we can strengthen the LP relaxation by additional constraints. People have proposed systematic ways to add additional constraints, such as Lovász-Schrijver LP relaxation hierarchy [LS91] and Sherali-Adams LP relaxation hierarchy [SA90]. These LP relaxation hierarchies contain a sequence of LP relaxations, where each LP relaxation is obtained by strengthening the previous one in the sequence. The ℓ-th LP relaxation in the sequence is usually called the *ℓ-round relaxation*, and typically can be solved in $n^{O(\ell)}$ time (where n is the number of variables in the original integer programming). The relaxation usually becomes as strong as the integer programming when ℓ becomes n; but it also takes exponential time to solve it.

It is known that $o(n)$-round Lovász-Schrijver LP relaxation and $n^{o(1)}$-round Sherali-Adams LP relaxation do not help to reduce the integrality gap for Max-Cut [STT07, CMM09]. For some other CSPs, the integrality gap remains even after strengthening the linear-round LP relaxation hierarchies with the power of semidefinite constraints (a.k.a. the Lasserre hierarchy) [Sch08]. On the other hand, it is known that LP hierarchies *do* help for some CSPs when the instance is dense. [dlVKM07] showed that the integrality gap of the $O_\epsilon(1)$-round Sherali-Adams LP relaxation drops to an arbitrarily small constant ϵ for dense Max-Cut instances.

LP relaxation and its hierarchies have found many connections to other known algorithmic frameworks, and to be a unified approach to solve several classes of problems. A few examples are listed as follows. Assuming the Unique Games Conjecture, a canonical LP relaxation (also referred to as the *Basic LP*) is shown to provide optimal approximation guarantee for CSPs with strict constraints [KMTV11]. It is known to the authors that constant-round Sherali-Adams LP relaxation decides the satisfiability of bounded-width CSPs; Atserias and Maneva [AM13] recently showed that the Sherali-Adams LP relaxation hierarchy for graph isomorphism interleaves with the levels of pebble-game equivalence with counting (i.e. higher-dimensional Weisfeiler-Lehman color refinement algorithm).

1.2 Our results

In this paper, we present the Sherali-Adams LP relaxation hierarchy as a unified approach to dense and locally dense problems – we show that a small number of rounds of the Sherali-Adams LP relaxation gives an approximation scheme to dense Max-k-CSP and all their variants studied in the previous works.

Our first main theorem deals with dense and locally dense Max-k-CSP.

Theorem 1.1 (Informal version of Theorem 5.1). *For any $\epsilon > 0$, $O(\frac{1}{\epsilon^2})$-round Sherali-Adams LP relaxation gives $(1-\epsilon)$-approximation to dense or locally dense Max-k-CSP.*

Then, we turn to dense and locally dense Max-k-CSP with global cardinality constraints. For explanatory purposes, we only consider *bisection* constraint, i.e., the domain is $\{0,1\}$ and the number of variables that are assigned to 0 should be equal to the number of variables that are assigned to 1. We show that

Theorem 1.2 (Informal version of Theorem C.2). *For any $\epsilon > 0$, $O(\frac{1}{\epsilon^2})$-round Sherali-Adams LP relaxation gives $(1-\epsilon)$-approximation to dense or locally dense bisection Max-k-CSP.*

Finally, we consider the dense Max-k-AP problems, and show that

Theorem 1.3 (Informal version of Theorem 5.2). *For any $\epsilon > 0$, $O(\frac{\log n}{\epsilon^2})$-round Sherali-Adams LP relaxation gives $(1-\epsilon)$-approximation to dense or locally dense Max-k-AP problems with n variables.*

In all the precise theorem statements, we actually show additive approximation guarantee (i.e. the value of the rounded solution being at least the fractional optimal value minus a constant error) instead of multiplicative approximation guarantee. However, since we define the problems in a way that the optimal solution is $\Omega(1)$ (see Section 2 for the precise definition of the problems), an additive approximation scheme implies a multiplicative approximation scheme.

1.2.1 New algorithmic guarantees

Let us define the problem Maximum k-Hypergraph Isomorphism as follows. Given two weighted k-uniform hypergraph $G = (V, \omega')$ and $H = (V, \omega'')$, where $\omega', \omega'' : V^k \to [0,1]$ are the weight functions over all possible hyperedges. The goal is to find a permutation π over V so that $\sum_{e \in V^k} \omega'(e)\omega''(\pi(e))$ is maximized (where $\pi(e)$ is the edge obtained by applying π on each incident vertex of e). It is easy to see Theorem 1.3 implies that $O(\frac{\log n}{\epsilon^2})$-round Sherali-Adams LP relaxation gives $(1-\epsilon)$-approximation to Maximum k-Hypergraph Isomorphism when both G and H are dense.

We are able to apply our analysis framework for the Sherali-Adams LP relaxation to another special case of Maximum k-Hypergraph Isomorphism, getting the following new algorithmic guarantee.

Theorem 1.4 (Informal version of Theorem 5.3). *For any $\epsilon > 0$, $O(\frac{\log n}{\epsilon^2})$-round Sherali-Adams LP relaxation gives $(1-\epsilon)$ approximation to the Maximum k-Hypergraph Isomorphism problem when one of the two graphs is locally dense and the other graph is dense, where n is the number of vertices in the hypergraphs. Therefore, this special case of the problem admits a $(1-\epsilon)$-approximation algorithm in time $n^{O(\frac{\log n}{\epsilon^2})}$.*

1.3 Proof overview

The first step of our algorithms is to condition on a set of random variables in a solution to the Sherali-Adams LP relaxation. In the *ℓ-round Sherali-Adams LP relaxation* (or the SA relaxation for short), for each set of variables S of size at most ℓ, we have a probability distribution $\boldsymbol{\mu}_S$ over assignments on S. First we solve $(k+\ell)$-round SA relaxation, where ℓ is a parameter depending on the error parameter ϵ. Then, we randomly sample a set of variables

$u_1, \ldots, u_\ell$ and assign values to them by sampling values from $\boldsymbol{\mu}_{\{u_1\}}, \ldots, \boldsymbol{\mu}_{\{u_\ell\}}$, respectively. By this conditioning, we obtain a solution to k-round Sherali-Adams relaxation $\boldsymbol{\mu}'$ with the same LP value in expectation. An important fact here is that variables become almost independent in the sense that, if we sample a k-tuple $(v_1, \ldots, v_k)$ according to a dense (or locally dense) distribution (this distribution corresponds to the weights of the constraints in k-CSP and k-AP instances), the distribution $\boldsymbol{\mu}_{\{v_1,\ldots,v_k\}}$ and the product distribution $\boldsymbol{\mu}_{\{v_1\}} \times \cdots \times \boldsymbol{\mu}_{\{v_k\}}$ are close in expectation.

The second step of our algorithms is to round the solution to the SA relaxation where the variables are almost independent. For dense (or locally dense) k-CSP and bisection k-CSP, the rounding algorithm just samples a value from $\boldsymbol{\mu}_{\{v\}}$ and assigning it to v for each variable v. It is relatively easy to show that the expected value of the sampled solution is close to the LP value, and therefore gives a $(1-\epsilon)$-approximation.

For k-AP problems, however, such independent sampling method does not work – there might be more than one variables assigned to the same value and we do not get a permutation when this happens. Instead, we view the marginal probability distributions on single variables, $\boldsymbol{\mu}_{\{u\}}(w)$, as a doubly stochastic matrix. We view this doubly stochastic matrix as a probability distribution of permutations. We iteratively choose two permutations in the support of the distribution and merge them into a new permutation, until there is only one permutation left in the support – which is the output of our rounding algorithm. The operation of merging two permutations is interestingly similar to the merging operation used in [AFK02], although the purposes are different. See Section 4.2 for more details.

1.4 Comparison to previous works

We first compare the running time of our SA relaxation-based algorithms with the previously known counterparts. For Max-k-CSP, the running time $n^{O(1/\epsilon^2)}$ of our method matches the one of the method by [AKK99]. For Max-k-AP the running time $n^{O(\log n/\epsilon^2)}$ of our method matches the one of the method by [AFK02]. [AFK02] improved the running time to $n^{O(1/\epsilon^2)}$ for various problems by reducing them to CSPs. We can use the same techniques to obtain the same running time for these problems.

The number of rounds ($O(\frac{1}{\epsilon^2})$) in Theorem 1.1 improves the corresponding theorem in [dlVKM07] which showed that $\tilde{O}(\frac{1}{\epsilon^4})$-round SA relaxation gives $(1-\epsilon)$-approximation to dense Max-Cut.

The idea of conditioning variables of a solution to LP/SDP hierarchies is used in [RT12, BRS11] to solve variants of Max-2-CSP. Let $G = (V, E)$ be the underlying graph of an instance of Max-2-CSP. Barak et al. [BRS11] showed that (i) the covariance between u and v over V^2 gets close to zero by conditioning, and (ii) the covariance between u and v over E gets close to the covariance between u and v over V^2 by conditioning if G is expander-like. Combining these two results, they show a PTAS for Max-2-CSP when G is expander-like. This method can be also applied to dense graphs, but it is not clear how to generalize it to metric graphs and k-CSP.

Raghavendra and Tan [RT12] used mutual information instead of covariance to measure correlation between two variables and simplified the proof. They noticed that conditioning is useful to deal with global constraints such as cardinality constraints since after conditioning we can sample variables independently and the resulting solution will not break global constraints much. With this idea, they gave a 0.85-approximation algorithm for Max-Bisection. Though our method and analysis are similar to theirs, we use the independence for obtaining PTASs for the dense and locally dense case as well as supporting global constraints. Also, to handle constraints of larger arities, we use total correlation instead of mutual information to measure correlation among variables.

Coja-Oghlan et al. [COCF09] showed that, even if the instance is sparse, if it satisfies a certain pseudo-random condition, then Max-k-CSP admits PTASs. If $k = 2$, this results can be seen as a special case of [RT12] because the pseudo-random condition would imply that the underlying graph is expander-like. Their result is incomparable to ours because it is not clear how the pseudo-random condition and the locally dense condition.

1.5 Organization

In Section 2, we introduce definitions and notions used in this paper. In Section 3, we show an algorithm that obtains an almost independent solution to the Sherali-Adams LP relaxation. Section 4 is devoted to show how to round the obtained solution to the Sherali-Adams LP relaxation. We combine the two steps together in Section 5. Appendix A and B are devoted to prove auxiliary lemmas. We consider CSPs with global cardinality constraints in Appendix C.

2. PRELIMINARIES

For an integer $a \geq 1$, $[a]$ denotes the set $\{1, \ldots, a\}$. For a set Y and $0 \leq k \leq |Y|$, $\binom{Y}{k}$ denotes the family of sets $X \subseteq Y$ with $|X| = k$. We usually use V to denote the set of variables in a problem, and use $n = |V|$ to denote the number of variables. For an event A, $\mathbf{1}[A]$ denotes the corresponding indicator function.

Probability theoretic notions.

We recall several notions from probability theory. For a probability distribution $\boldsymbol{\mu}$ on Ω, $\mathrm{supp}(\boldsymbol{\mu})$ denotes the *support* of $\boldsymbol{\mu}$, i.e., $\mathrm{supp}(\boldsymbol{\mu}) = \{i \in \Omega \mid \boldsymbol{\mu}(i) > 0\}$. For a set S, $i \sim S$ means that we sample i uniformly at random from S.

Let $\boldsymbol{\mu}_1$ and $\boldsymbol{\mu}_2$ be two probability distributions on a finite set Ω. Then, the L_1 distance between them is defined as $\|\boldsymbol{\mu}_1 - \boldsymbol{\mu}_2\|_1 = \sum_{i\in\Omega} \|\boldsymbol{\mu}_1(i) - \boldsymbol{\mu}_2(i)\|$. The Kullback-Leibler divergence between them is defined as

$$d_{KL}(\boldsymbol{\mu}_1 \| \boldsymbol{\mu}_2) = \sum_{i\in\Omega} \boldsymbol{\mu}_1(i) \log \frac{\boldsymbol{\mu}_1(i)}{\boldsymbol{\mu}_2(i)}.$$

We provide the following fact without proof.

LEMMA 2.1. *Let $\boldsymbol{\mu}_1$ and $\boldsymbol{\mu}_2$ be two probability distributions on a finite set Ω. Then, $\|\boldsymbol{\mu}_1 - \boldsymbol{\mu}_2\|_1 \leq \sqrt{2 d_{KL}(\boldsymbol{\mu}_1 \| \boldsymbol{\mu}_2)}$.*

Information theoretic notions.

We now recall some definitions from information theory. For a random variable $\boldsymbol{x}$, $\boldsymbol{\mu}_{\boldsymbol{x}}$ denotes the corresponding probability distribution. That is, for any i, we have $\boldsymbol{\mu}_{\boldsymbol{x}}(i) = \Pr[\boldsymbol{x} = i]$.

Let $\boldsymbol{x}$ be a random variable on a finite set Ω. The *entropy* of $\boldsymbol{x}$ is defined as $H(\boldsymbol{x}) = -\sum_{i\in\Omega} \Pr[\boldsymbol{x} = i] \log \Pr[\boldsymbol{x} = i]$.

Let $\boldsymbol{x}$ and $\boldsymbol{y}$ be jointly distributed variables on a finite set Ω. The *entropy* of $\boldsymbol{x}$ conditioned on $\boldsymbol{y}$ is defined as $H(\boldsymbol{x} \mid \boldsymbol{y}) = \mathop{\mathbf{E}}_{i \sim \boldsymbol{\mu}_{\boldsymbol{y}}} [H(\boldsymbol{x} \mid \boldsymbol{y} = i)]$. The *mutual information* of $\boldsymbol{x}$ and $\boldsymbol{y}$ is defined as $I(\boldsymbol{x}; \boldsymbol{y}) = d_{KL}(\boldsymbol{\mu}_{(\boldsymbol{x},\boldsymbol{y})} \| \boldsymbol{\mu}_{\boldsymbol{x}} \times \boldsymbol{\mu}_{\boldsymbol{y}})$.

Let $\boldsymbol{x}_1, \ldots, \boldsymbol{x}_k$ ($k \geq 2$) be jointly distributed variables on a finite set Ω. The *mutual information* of $\boldsymbol{x}_1, \ldots, \boldsymbol{x}_k$ is defined as $I(\boldsymbol{x}_1; \ldots; \boldsymbol{x}_k) = I(\boldsymbol{x}_1; \ldots; \boldsymbol{x}_{k-1}) - I(\boldsymbol{x}_1; \ldots; \boldsymbol{x}_{k-1} \mid \boldsymbol{x}_k)$, where $I(\boldsymbol{x}_1; \ldots; \boldsymbol{x}_{k-1} \mid \boldsymbol{x}_k) = \mathbf{E}_{i \sim \boldsymbol{\mu}_{\boldsymbol{x}_k}} [I(\boldsymbol{x}_1; \ldots; \boldsymbol{x}_{k-1} \mid \boldsymbol{x}_k = i)]$. The *total correlation* of $\boldsymbol{x}_1, \ldots, \boldsymbol{x}_k$ is defined as $C(\boldsymbol{x}_1, \ldots, \boldsymbol{x}_k) = d_{KL}(\boldsymbol{\mu}_{(\boldsymbol{x}_1,\ldots,\boldsymbol{x}_k)} \| \boldsymbol{\mu}_{\boldsymbol{x}_1} \times \cdots \times \boldsymbol{\mu}_{\boldsymbol{x}_k})$.

We give two well-known facts in information theory below.

LEMMA 2.2. *Let $\boldsymbol{x}$ and $\boldsymbol{y}$ be two jointly distributed variables on a finite set Ω. Then*

$$I(\boldsymbol{x}; \boldsymbol{y}) = H(\boldsymbol{x}) - H(\boldsymbol{x} \mid \boldsymbol{y}).$$

Let $\boldsymbol{x}_1, \ldots, \boldsymbol{x}_k$ be jointly distributed variables on a finite set Ω. Then

$$I(\boldsymbol{x}_1; \ldots; \boldsymbol{x}_k) = \sum_{(i_1,\ldots,i_t) \subseteq [k], t \geq 1} (-1)^{t-1} H(\boldsymbol{x}_{i_1}, \ldots, \boldsymbol{x}_{i_t}).$$

LEMMA 2.3. *Let $\boldsymbol{x}_1, \ldots, \boldsymbol{x}_k$ be jointly distributed variables on a finite set Ω. Then*

$$C(\boldsymbol{x}_1, \ldots, \boldsymbol{x}_k) = \sum_{(i_1,\ldots,i_t) \subseteq [k], t \geq 2} I(\boldsymbol{x}_{i_1}; \ldots; \boldsymbol{x}_{i_t}).$$

Constraint satisfaction problems.

Let D be a nonempty finite domain and $k \geq 2$ be an integer. An *instance* $\mathcal{I} = (V, \omega, P)$ of k-CSP consists of a set V of *variables*, a *scope distribution* ω over V^k, and a set of *payoff functions* $P = \{P_S : D^S \to [0,1] \mid S \in V^k\}$. An *assignment* for an instance $\mathcal{I} = (V, \omega, P)$ is a mapping $\alpha : V \to D$. The *value* of the assignment, denoted $\mathbf{val}(\mathcal{I}, \alpha) \in [0,1]$, is defined as $\mathbf{val}(\mathcal{I}, \alpha) = \Pr_{S \sim \omega}[P_S(\alpha|_S)]$, where $\alpha|_S$ is the projection of α to S. We define the *optimum value* of the instance $\mathcal{I}$ to be $\mathbf{opt}(\mathcal{I}) = \max_\alpha \{\mathbf{val}(\mathcal{I}, \alpha)\}$.

Let $\mathcal{I} = (V, \omega, P)$ be an instance of CSP. A *solution* to the ℓ-round Sherali-Adams relaxation consists of a probability distribution $\boldsymbol{\mu}_S$ over D^S for each set $S \subseteq V$ of size at most ℓ. The objective function is the probability that α is in P_S, where S is sampled from ω and α is sampled from $\boldsymbol{\mu}_S$. Strictly speaking, we sample a tuple $(v_1, \ldots, v_k)$ from ω, but we regard it as the set $\{v_1, \ldots, v_k\}$ when we use it as a subscript of $\boldsymbol{\mu}$. In other words, $\boldsymbol{\mu}_S$ and $\boldsymbol{\mu}_T$ are the same distribution for two tuples S and T if they are the same as sets. Also, for every pair of sets S and T with $|S \cup T| \leq \ell$, the corresponding probability distributions $\boldsymbol{\mu}_S$ and $\boldsymbol{\mu}_T$ must be consistent on $S \cap T$. Formally, the ℓ-round Sherali-Adams relaxation for a k-CSP instance $\mathcal{I} = (V, \omega, P)$ ($\ell \geq k$) is written as follows.

$$\begin{aligned}
\text{maximize} \quad & \mathop{\mathbf{E}}_{S \sim \omega} \mathop{\mathbf{E}}_{\alpha \sim \boldsymbol{\mu}_S} [P_S(\alpha)] \\
\text{subject to} \quad & \Pr_{\alpha \sim \boldsymbol{\mu}_S} [\alpha|_{S \cap T} = \beta] = \Pr_{\alpha \sim \boldsymbol{\mu}_T} [\alpha|_{S \cap T} = \beta] \\
& \forall S, T \subseteq V, |S \cup T| \leq \ell, \beta \in D^{S \cap T}.
\end{aligned}$$

It is not hard to see that the relaxation above can be written as a linear programming (see, e.g., [RS09] for details). We define $\boldsymbol{x}_v$ as the random variable sampled from the distribution $\boldsymbol{\mu}_{\{v\}}$. We use $\mathbf{val}_{\mathrm{LP}}(\mathcal{I}, \boldsymbol{\mu})$ to denote the objective value of the LP solution $\boldsymbol{\mu}$. The same definition applies to the following subsections.

Assignment problems.

The assignment problem differs from CSP in that we want to maximize the objective function over the set of permutations. Similarly to CSP, for an integer $k \geq 2$, an instance of the degree-k assignment problem is given as $\mathcal{I} = (V, \omega)$, where V is the set of variables, ω is a distribution over $V^k \times V^k$. The *scope distribution* of $\mathcal{I}$ is the marginal distribution of ω on the first k elements. An *assignment* for an instance $\mathcal{I} = (V, \omega)$ is a permutation π of V. The *value* of the assignment π, denoted $\mathbf{val}(\mathcal{I}, \pi)$, is defined as

$$\mathbf{val}(\mathcal{I}, \pi) = n^k \Pr_{(U,W) \sim \omega} [\forall i \in [k] : \pi(u_i) = w_i],$$

where $U = (u_1, u_2, \ldots, u_k)$ and $W = (w_1, w_2, \ldots, w_k)$. We define the optimum value of $\mathcal{I}$ to be $\mathbf{opt}(\mathcal{I}) = \max_\pi \{\mathbf{val}(\mathcal{I}, \pi)\}$.

Though the definition of $\mathbf{val}(\mathcal{I}, \pi)$ may look non-standard, it is just the objective function used in [AFK02] with a normalization factor that is multiplied to make the optimum $\Omega(1)$ when ω is dense.

The ℓ-round Sherali-Adams relaxation of an k-AP instance $\mathcal{I} = (V, \omega)$ ($\ell \geq k$) is as follows.

$$\begin{aligned}
\text{maximize} \quad & \mathop{\mathbf{E}}_{(U,W) \sim \omega} \Pr_{\alpha \sim \boldsymbol{\mu}_U} [\forall i \in [k] : \alpha(u_i) = w_i] \\
\text{subject to} \quad & \Pr_{\beta \sim \boldsymbol{\mu}_S} [\beta|_{S \cap T} = \alpha] = \Pr_{\beta \sim \boldsymbol{\mu}_T} [\beta|_{S \cap T} = \alpha] \\
& \forall S, T \subseteq V, |S \cup T| \leq \ell, \alpha \in V^{S \cap T} \\
& \sum_{\alpha \in V^S} \sum_{u \in V \setminus S} \boldsymbol{\mu}_{S \cup \{u\}}(\alpha \cup \{u \to w\}) \\
& = \textstyle\sum_{\alpha \in V^S} \boldsymbol{\mu}_S(\alpha) \quad \forall w \in V, S \subseteq V, |S| < \ell.
\end{aligned}$$

The difference from the Sherali-Adams relaxation for CSP is that we have extra constraints in the last line whose intended meaning is that each value i can be taken by at most one variable.

Density condition.

We now introduce the notion of dense and locally dense distributions.

Let ω be a probability distribution over a finite set Ω. For $\Delta \in (0,1]$, we say ω is Δ-*dense* if for every $a \in \Omega$, it holds that $\Delta \cdot \omega(a) \leq \frac{1}{|\Omega|}$.

Let ω be a probability distribution over V^k. Let $d_i(v) = \Pr_{S \sim \omega}[S_i = v_i]$ be the probability that the i-th coordinate is v under ω. For $\Delta \in (0,1]$, we say ω is Δ-*locally dense* if for every $(v_1, \ldots, v_k) \in V^k$, it holds that

$$\Delta \cdot \omega(v_1, \ldots, v_k) \leq \frac{1}{|V|^{k-1}} \sum_{1 \leq i \leq k} d_i(v_i).$$

Since $d_i(v) = \sum_{S \in V^k : S_i = v} \omega(S)$, the RHS of the locally dense condition is equal to $\sum_{1 \leq i \leq k} \mathop{\mathbf{E}}_{S \sim V^k} [\omega(S) \mid S_i = v_i]$. Thus the locally dense condition says that no tuple $(v_1, \ldots, v_k)$ is "wild" in that $\omega(v_1, \ldots, v_k)$ is at most constant times the sum over i of the average probability mass of S with $S_i = v_i$.

The notion of local density is introduced in [dlVKKV05] to generalize the metric condition. To see this, suppose $\omega : V^2 \to \mathbb{R}$ is a metric. Then, ω is 1-locally dense since, for any $u, v \in V$, we have $\frac{1}{n}(d_1(u) + d_2(v)) = \frac{1}{n} \sum_w (\omega(u, w) + \omega(w, v)) \geq \frac{1}{n} \sum_w \omega(u, v) \geq \omega(u, v)$.

It is immediate to verify the following lemma.

Lemma 2.4. *Let ω be a probability distribution over $\Omega_1 \times \Omega_2$. If ω is Δ-dense (resp., Δ-locally dense), then the marginal distribution ω_1 of ω on Ω_1 is also Δ-dense (resp., Δ-locally dense).*

3. CONDITIONING OPERATIONS FOR SHERALI-ADAMS LP HIERARCHY

Recall that, a solution to the ℓ-round SA relaxation consists of distributions over sets of ℓ variables. In this section, we show that, if the scope distribution is dense or locally dense, then by conditioning a small number of variables, we can make variables almost independent in these distributions. Once variables become almost independent, we can round variables independently without losing the objective value much (see Section 4).

Let $\mathcal{I}$ be an instance of k-CSP or k-AP with a variable set V. Fix ℓ and let $\boldsymbol{\mu}$ be a solution to the ℓ-round Sherali-Adams relaxation. For a variable set $S = (v_1, \ldots, v_k)$, $C_{\boldsymbol{\mu}}(\boldsymbol{x}_S)$ denotes the total correlation $C(\boldsymbol{x}_{v_1}, \ldots, \boldsymbol{x}_{v_k})$ under the probability distribution $\boldsymbol{\mu}_S$. We use the following notion to measure independence of variables.

Definition 3.1. *Let $\mathcal{I}$ be an instance of k-CSP or k-AP with a scope distribution ω. A solution $\boldsymbol{\mu}$ to the ℓ-round SA relaxation for $\mathcal{I}$ with $\ell \geq k$ is* κ-independent *with respect to distribution ω' if*

$$\mathop{\mathbf{E}}_{S \sim \omega'} [C_{\boldsymbol{\mu}}(\boldsymbol{x}_S)] \leq \kappa.$$

We say that $\boldsymbol{\mu}$ is κ-independent *if it is κ-independent with respect to ω.*

In Section 3.1, we explain how to condition variables. In Sections 3.2 and 3.3, we show that the conditioning operation outputs κ-independent LP solutions for the dense case and the locally dense case, respectively.

3.1 Conditioning operations

We first describe the operation of conditioning one variable. Given a solution $\boldsymbol{\mu}$ to the ℓ-round SA relaxation with $\ell \geq 2$, we sample a vertex u uniformly at random and then set $\boldsymbol{x}_u = i$, where i is a value sampled from $\boldsymbol{\mu}_{\{u\}}$. This operation gives a solution $\boldsymbol{\mu}'$ to the $(\ell-1)$-round SA relaxation: For each tuple $(v_1, \ldots, v_{\ell-1})$ of $\ell - 1$ variables, we define $\boldsymbol{\mu}'_{\{v_1,\ldots,v_{k-1}\}}(i_1, i_2, \ldots, i_{k-1}) = \boldsymbol{\mu}_{\{v_1,\ldots,v_{k-1},u\}}(i_1, i_2, \ldots, i_{k-1}, i)$. It is not hard to check that $\boldsymbol{\mu}'$ is indeed a solution to the $(\ell-1)$-round SA relaxation.

Our algorithm is given in Algorithm 1. Given an solution $\boldsymbol{\mu}$ to the $(\ell+\ell')$-round SA relaxation, it iteratively conditions variables. We will show in subsequent sections that, if ω is Δ-dense or Δ-locally dense, then Algorithm 1 outputs a κ-independent LP solution in ℓ' steps on average, where $\kappa = \frac{k4^k \log|D|}{\ell'}$. (If ω is Δ-dense, κ can be slightly smaller.)

We mention here the following simple fact.

Lemma 3.2. *Let $\boldsymbol{\mu}'$ be the solution output by Algorithm 1. Then,* $\mathbf{E}\,\mathbf{val}_{\mathrm{LP}}(\mathcal{I}, \boldsymbol{\mu}') = \mathbf{val}_{\mathrm{LP}}(\mathcal{I}, \boldsymbol{\mu})$.

Proof. Notice that the algorithm respects the marginal distributions provided by the SA relaxation during sampling the values to variables. Thus, the expected objective value is preserved. □

Algorithm 1

Input: A feasible solution $\boldsymbol{\mu}$ to the $(\ell+\ell')$-round SA relaxation for a CSP instance $\mathcal{I} = (V, \omega)$.
Output: An κ-independent solution to the ℓ-round SA relaxation, where $\kappa = \frac{k4^k \log|D|}{\ell'}$
Set $t = 1$.
while the current LP solution is not κ-independent **do**
  Sample a variable $u_t \in V$ uniformly at random.
  Sample a value a from its marginal distribution $\boldsymbol{\mu}_{\{u_t\}}$ after the first $t-1$ fixings, and condition the LP solution by setting $\boldsymbol{x}_{u_t} = a$.
  $t = t + 1$.

3.2 The dense case

We consider the dense case, that is, ω is a uniform distribution.

Lemma 3.3. *If ω is uniform distribution over V^k, there exists $t \leq \ell'$ such that*

$$\mathop{\mathbf{E}}_{U \sim V^t} \mathop{\mathbf{E}}_{S \sim V^k} [C_{\boldsymbol{\mu}}(\boldsymbol{x}_S \mid \boldsymbol{x}_U)] \leq \frac{3^k \log|D|}{\ell'}.$$

Proof. We consider the value

$$\sum_{1 \leq t \leq \ell'} \mathop{\mathbf{E}}_{U \sim V^t} \mathop{\mathbf{E}}_{S \sim V^k} [C_{\boldsymbol{\mu}}(\boldsymbol{x}_S \mid \boldsymbol{x}_U)].$$

From Lemma 2.3, this value can be decomposed as

$$\sum_{1 \leq t \leq \ell'} \mathop{\mathbf{E}}_{U \sim V^t} \mathop{\mathbf{E}}_{S \sim V^k} \left[\sum_{2 \leq r \leq k} \sum_{R \in \binom{S}{r}} I_{\boldsymbol{\mu}}(\boldsymbol{x}_R \mid \boldsymbol{x}_U) \right]$$
$$= \sum_{2 \leq r \leq k} \binom{k}{r} \sum_{1 \leq t \leq \ell'} \mathop{\mathbf{E}}_{U \sim V^t} \mathop{\mathbf{E}}_{R \sim V^r} [I_{\boldsymbol{\mu}}(\boldsymbol{x}_R \mid \boldsymbol{x}_U)],$$

where for a set $R = (v_1, \ldots, v_r)$, $I_{\boldsymbol{\mu}}(\boldsymbol{x}_R)$ denotes the mutual information $I_{\boldsymbol{\mu}_R}(v_1; \ldots; v_r)$.

To bound this value, we recall the definition of mutual information. For any $t \leq \ell'$,

$$\mathop{\mathbf{E}}_{\substack{U \sim V^t \\ R \sim V^r}} [I_{\boldsymbol{\mu}}(\boldsymbol{x}_R \mid \boldsymbol{x}_U)] =$$
$$\mathop{\mathbf{E}}_{\substack{U \sim V^t \\ R \sim V^{r-1}}} [I_{\boldsymbol{\mu}}(\boldsymbol{x}_R \mid \boldsymbol{x}_U)] - \mathop{\mathbf{E}}_{\substack{U \sim V^{t+1} \\ R \sim V^{r-1}}} [I_{\boldsymbol{\mu}}(\boldsymbol{x}_R \mid \boldsymbol{x}_U)].$$

Adding the equalities from $t = 0$ to ℓ', we get

$$\sum_{0 \leq t \leq \ell'} \mathop{\mathbf{E}}_{\substack{U \sim V^t \\ R \sim V^r}} [I_{\boldsymbol{\mu}}(\boldsymbol{x}_R \mid \boldsymbol{x}_U)] =$$
$$\mathop{\mathbf{E}}_{R \sim V^{r-1}} [I(\boldsymbol{x}_R)] - \mathop{\mathbf{E}}_{\substack{U \sim V^{\ell'+1} \\ R \sim V^{r-1}}} [I_{\boldsymbol{\mu}}(\boldsymbol{x}_R \mid \boldsymbol{x}_U)] \leq 2^r \log|D|,$$

where the last inequality holds from $I_{\boldsymbol{\mu}}(\boldsymbol{x}_R) \leq 2^{|R|} \log|D|$ by Lemma 2.2. Thus, we have

$$\sum_{0 \leq t \leq \ell'} \mathop{\mathbf{E}}_{U \sim V^t} \mathop{\mathbf{E}}_{S \sim V^k} [C(\boldsymbol{x}_S \mid \boldsymbol{x}_U)] \leq 3^k \log|D|,$$

and the lemma follows. □

The following corollary is immediate.

COROLLARY 3.4. *If ω is a Δ-dense distribution over V^k. Then there exists $t \le \ell'$ such that*

$$\mathop{\mathbf{E}}_{U\sim V^t}\mathop{\mathbf{E}}_{S\sim\omega}[C_{\boldsymbol{\mu}}(\boldsymbol{x}_S \mid \boldsymbol{x}_U)] \le \frac{3^k \log|D|}{\Delta\ell'}.$$

3.3 The locally dense case

We now consider the case that the scope distribution ω is 1-locally dense.

LEMMA 3.5. *If ω is a 1-locally dense distribution over V^k, then there exists $t \le \ell'$ such that*

$$\mathop{\mathbf{E}}_{U\sim V^t}\mathop{\mathbf{E}}_{S\sim\omega}[C_{\boldsymbol{\mu}}(\boldsymbol{x}_S \mid \boldsymbol{x}_U)] \le \frac{k4^k \log k|D|}{\ell'}.$$

PROOF. We consider the value

$$\sum_{1\le t\le \ell'}\mathop{\mathbf{E}}_{U\sim V^t}\mathop{\mathbf{E}}_{S\sim\omega}[C_{\boldsymbol{\mu}}(\boldsymbol{x}_S \mid \boldsymbol{x}_U)]. \qquad (1)$$

From Lemma 2.3, this value can be decomposed as

$$\sum_{1\le t\le\ell'}\mathop{\mathbf{E}}_{U\sim V^t}\mathop{\mathbf{E}}_{S\sim\omega}\left[\sum_{2\le r\le k}\sum_{R\in\binom{S}{r}} I_{\boldsymbol{\mu}}(\boldsymbol{x}_R \mid \boldsymbol{x}_U)\right]$$
$$= \sum_{J\subseteq[k]:2\le|J|\le k}\sum_{1\le t\le\ell'}\mathop{\mathbf{E}}_{U\sim V^t}\mathop{\mathbf{E}}_{R\sim\omega|_J}[I_{\boldsymbol{\mu}}(\boldsymbol{x}_R \mid \boldsymbol{x}_U)],$$

where $\omega|_J$ denotes the marginal distribution of ω on J.

Fix $J \subseteq [k]$ with $|J| = r \ge 2$. Let ω_i be the marginal distribution of ω on the i-th coordinate. Let $\Omega_i = \omega_i \times V^{r-1}$ and $\Omega'_i = \omega_i \times V^{r-2}$. We first analyze $I(\boldsymbol{x}_R)$ under Ω_i instead of $\omega|_J$.

From the definition, for any i and $t \le \ell'$,

$$\mathop{\mathbf{E}}_{\substack{U\sim V^t\\ R\sim\Omega_i}} I(\boldsymbol{x}_R \mid \boldsymbol{x}_U) = \mathop{\mathbf{E}}_{\substack{U\sim V^t\\ R\sim\Omega'_i}} I(\boldsymbol{x}_R \mid \boldsymbol{x}_U) - \mathop{\mathbf{E}}_{\substack{U\sim V^{t+1}\\ R\sim\Omega'_i}} I(\boldsymbol{x}_R \mid \boldsymbol{x}_U).$$

Adding the equalities from $t = 0$ to $t = \ell'$, we get

$$\sum_{0\le t\le\ell'}\mathop{\mathbf{E}}_{\substack{U\sim V^t\\ R\sim\Omega_i}} I(\boldsymbol{x}_R \mid \boldsymbol{x}_U) =$$
$$\mathop{\mathbf{E}}_{R\sim\Omega'_i} I(\boldsymbol{x}_R) - \mathop{\mathbf{E}}_{\substack{U\sim V^{\ell'+1}\\ R\sim\Omega'_i}} H(\boldsymbol{x}_R \mid \boldsymbol{x}_U) \le 2^r \log|D|. \qquad (2)$$

Now we turn to analyze $I(\boldsymbol{x}_{v_1};\cdots;\boldsymbol{x}_{v_r})$ under $\omega|_J$.

$$\mathop{\mathbf{E}}_{\substack{U\sim V^t\\ R\sim\omega|_J}} I(\boldsymbol{x}_R \mid \boldsymbol{x}_U) = \mathop{\mathbf{E}}_{U\sim V^t}\sum_{R\sim V^r}\omega|_J(R) I(\boldsymbol{x}_R \mid \boldsymbol{x}_U)$$
$$\le \mathop{\mathbf{E}}_{U\sim V^t}\sum_{(v_1,\dots,v_r)\sim V^r}\frac{1}{n^{r-1}}\sum_{1\le i\le r} d_i(v_i) I(\boldsymbol{x}_{v_1};\cdots;\boldsymbol{x}_{v_r} \mid \boldsymbol{x}_U)$$

(by local density and Lemma 2.4)

$$= \sum_{1\le i\le r}\mathop{\mathbf{E}}_{U\sim V^t}\sum_{(v_1,\dots,v_r)\sim V^r}$$
$$\frac{1}{n^{r-1}}\Pr_{S\sim\omega}[S_i = v_i] I(\boldsymbol{x}_{v_1};\cdots;\boldsymbol{x}_{v_r} \mid \boldsymbol{x}_U)$$
$$= \sum_{1\le i\le r}\mathop{\mathbf{E}}_{U\sim V^t}\sum_{R\sim V^r}\Omega_i(R) I(\boldsymbol{x}_{v_1};\cdots;\boldsymbol{x}_{v_r} \mid \boldsymbol{x}_U)$$
$$= \sum_{1\le i\le r}\mathop{\mathbf{E}}_{\substack{U\sim V^t\\ R\sim\Omega_i}} I(\boldsymbol{x}_R \mid \boldsymbol{x}_U).$$

Thus from (2),

$$\sum_{0\le t\le\ell'}\mathop{\mathbf{E}}_{\substack{U\sim V^t\\ R\sim\omega|_J}} I(\boldsymbol{x}_R \mid \boldsymbol{x}_U) \le \sum_{1\le i\le r} 2^r \log|D| = r2^r \log|D|.$$

It follows that (1) $\le k4^k \log|D|$ and the lemma holds. □

The following corollary is immediate.

COROLLARY 3.6. *If ω is a Δ-locally dense distribution over V^k, then there exists $t \le \ell'$ such that*

$$\mathop{\mathbf{E}}_{U\sim V^t}\mathop{\mathbf{E}}_{S\sim\omega}[C_{\boldsymbol{\mu}}(\boldsymbol{x}_S \mid \boldsymbol{x}_U)] \le \frac{k4^k \log|D|}{\Delta\ell'}.$$

4. ROUNDING κ-INDEPENDENT SOLUTIONS

4.1 Constraint satisfaction problems

LEMMA 4.1. *Let $\mathcal{I} = (V,\omega,P)$ be a k-CSP instance over finite domain D. Let $\boldsymbol{\mu}$ be a κ-independent solution to the k-round Sherali-Adams LP relaxation. There is a randomized polynomial time algorithm to find an assignment $\alpha : V \to D$ such that $\mathbf{val}(\mathcal{I},\alpha) \ge \mathbf{val}_{\mathrm{LP}}(\mathcal{I},\boldsymbol{\mu}) - 3\sqrt{\kappa}$.*

PROOF. For each $v \in V$, let $\alpha(v)$ be independently sampled from $\boldsymbol{\mu}_{\{v\}}$. For each $S \in V^k$, by the definition of total correlation, Lemma 2.1, and the fact that $P_S(\beta) \in [0,1]$ we have

$$\left|\mathop{\mathbf{E}}_{\beta\sim\boldsymbol{\mu}_S} P_S(\beta) - \mathop{\mathbf{E}}_{\alpha} P_S(\alpha|_S)\right| \le 2\sqrt{C(\boldsymbol{x}_S)}.$$

Therefore by κ-independence,

$$\left|\mathop{\mathbf{E}}_{S\sim\omega}\left(\mathop{\mathbf{E}}_{\beta\sim\boldsymbol{\mu}_S} P_S(\beta) - \mathop{\mathbf{E}}_{\alpha} P_S(\alpha|_S)\right)\right|$$
$$\le \mathop{\mathbf{E}}_{S\sim\omega} 2\sqrt{C(\boldsymbol{x}_S)} \le 2\sqrt{\mathop{\mathbf{E}}_{S\sim\omega} C(\boldsymbol{x}_S)} \le 2\sqrt{\kappa}\,.$$

We have proved that $\mathbf{E}_\alpha[\mathbf{val}(\mathcal{I},\alpha)] \ge \mathbf{val}_{\mathrm{LP}}(\mathcal{I},\boldsymbol{\mu}) - 2\sqrt{\kappa}$. Therefore we can sample an α in expected polynomial time such that $\mathbf{val}(\mathcal{I},\alpha) \ge \mathbf{val}_{\mathrm{LP}}(\mathcal{I},\boldsymbol{\mu}) - 3\sqrt{\kappa}$. □

4.2 Assignment problems

Let $\mathcal{I} = (V,\omega)$ be a Δ-dense k-AP instance. We introduce the following relaxation $\mathcal{H}$, and let $\mathbf{val}_{\mathcal{H}}(\mathcal{I})$ be its optimal value.

$$\begin{array}{lll}
\text{maximize} & n^k \mathop{\mathbf{E}}_{(U,W)\sim\omega}\prod_{i=1}^{k} \boldsymbol{x}_{u_i,w_i} & \\
\text{subject to} & \boldsymbol{x}_{u,w} \ge 0 & \forall u,w \in V^k \\
& \sum_{u\in V} \boldsymbol{x}_{u,w} = 1 & \forall w \in V \\
& \sum_{w\in V} \boldsymbol{x}_{u,w} = 1 & \forall u \in V.
\end{array}$$

4.2.1 From κ-independence to relaxation $\mathcal{H}$

We first see that we can find a good solution to $\mathcal{H}$ using a solution to the Sherali-Adams LP relaxation of a dense instance $\mathcal{I}$.

LEMMA 4.2. *Let $\mathcal{I} = (V,\omega)$ be a k-AP instance such that ω is Δ-dense. Let $\boldsymbol{\mu}$ be a κ-independent solution (with respect to the uniform distribution rather than ω) to the k-round Sherali-Adams LP relaxation of $\mathcal{I}$. There is a polynomial-time algorithm, on input $\boldsymbol{\mu}$, to find a solution to $\mathcal{H}$ that certifies that $\mathbf{val}_{\mathcal{H}}(\mathcal{I}) \ge \mathbf{val}_{\mathrm{LP}}(\mathcal{I},\boldsymbol{\mu}) - 2\sqrt{\kappa}/\Delta$.*

PROOF. Let $\boldsymbol{x}_{u,w} = \boldsymbol{\mu}_u(w)$ for all $u, w \in V$. For each $S = (u_1, u_2, \ldots, u_k) \in V^k$, by the definition of total correlation and Lemma 2.1 we have

$$\sum_{T=(w_1,\ldots,w_k)} \left| \boldsymbol{\mu}_S(T) - \prod_{i=1}^{k} x_{u_i,w_i} \right| \le 2\sqrt{C(\boldsymbol{x}_S)}. \tag{3}$$

Therefore,

$$\left| \mathop{\mathbf{E}}_{(S,T)=(u_1,\ldots u_k,v_1,\ldots,v_k)\sim\omega} \left(\boldsymbol{\mu}_S(T) - \prod_{i=1}^{k} x_{u_i,w_i} \right) \right|$$

$$\le \frac{1}{\Delta} \mathop{\mathbf{E}}_{(S,T)=(u_1,\ldots u_k,v_1,\ldots,v_k)\sim V^{2k}} \left| \boldsymbol{\mu}_S(T) - \prod_{i=1}^{k} x_{u_i,w_i} \right| \quad \text{(by density)}$$

$$\le \frac{1}{\Delta n^k} \mathop{\mathbf{E}}_{S\sim V^k} 2\sqrt{C(\boldsymbol{x}_S)} \quad \text{(by (3))}$$

$$\le \frac{2}{\Delta n^k} \sqrt{\mathop{\mathbf{E}}_{S\sim V^k} C(\boldsymbol{x}_S)} \le n^{-k} \cdot \frac{2\sqrt{\kappa}}{\Delta}. \quad \text{(by } \kappa\text{-independence)}$$

□

The following variant of Lemma 4.2 is used when dealing with the locally dense case later.

LEMMA 4.3. *Let $\mathcal{I} = (V, \omega)$ be a k-AP instance such that $\omega(u_1, \ldots, u_k, w_1, \ldots, w_k) = \omega'(u_1, \ldots, u_k) \cdot \omega''(w_1, \ldots, w_k)$ where ω'' is a Δ-dense distribution over V^k. Let $\boldsymbol{\mu}$ be a κ-independent solution to the k-round Sherali-Adams LP relaxation of $\mathcal{I}$. There is a polynomial-time algorithm, on input $\boldsymbol{\mu}$, to find a solution to $\mathcal{H}$ that certifies that $\mathbf{val}_{\mathcal{H}}(\mathcal{I}) \ge \mathbf{val}_{\mathrm{LP}}(\mathcal{I}, \boldsymbol{\mu}) - 2\sqrt{\kappa}/\Delta$.*

PROOF. Let $x_{u,w} = \boldsymbol{\mu}_u(w)$ for all $u, w \in V$. Similar to the proof of Lemma 4.2, we have

$$\left| \mathop{\mathbf{E}}_{(S,T)=(u_1,\ldots u_k,v_1,\ldots,v_k)\sim\omega} \left(\boldsymbol{\mu}_S(T) - \prod_{i=1}^{k} x_{u_i,w_i} \right) \right|$$

$$\le \frac{1}{\Delta} \mathop{\mathbf{E}}_{\substack{S=(u_1,\ldots u_k)\sim\omega' \\ T=(v_1,\ldots,v_k)\sim V^k}} \left| \boldsymbol{\mu}_S(T) - \prod_{i=1}^{k} x_{u_i,w_i} \right| \quad \text{(by density of } \omega''\text{)}$$

$$\le \frac{1}{\Delta n^k} \mathop{\mathbf{E}}_{S\sim\omega'} 2\sqrt{C(\boldsymbol{x}_S)} \quad \text{(by (3))}$$

$$\le \frac{2}{\Delta n^k} \sqrt{\mathop{\mathbf{E}}_{S\sim\omega'} C(\boldsymbol{x}_S)} \le n^{-k} \cdot \frac{2\sqrt{\kappa}}{\Delta}. \quad \text{(by } \kappa\text{-independence)}$$

□

4.2.2 *From relaxation $\mathcal{H}$ to an integral solution*

At a first look, $\mathcal{H}$ is very close to the k-AP problem itself. However, we cannot independently sample $\pi(v)$ from each $\boldsymbol{x}_v$ in $\mathcal{H}$ to get a solution to k-AP, since there is chance that $\pi(v) = \pi(v')$, rendering π not a permutation. Indeed, we show in Appendix D that for some k-AP instance $\mathcal{I}$, there is a gap between $\mathbf{val}_{\mathcal{H}}(\mathcal{I})$ and $\mathbf{val}(\mathcal{I})$. However, our following lemma shows that this gap cannot be very big for k-AP instances $\mathcal{I} = (V, \omega)$ when ω is Δ-dense. The proof is given later in Appendix A.

LEMMA 4.4. *Let $\mathcal{I} = (V, \omega)$ be a k-AP instance such that ω is Δ-dense. Given a solution $\boldsymbol{x}$ to relaxation $\mathcal{H}$, let $\mathbf{val}_{\mathcal{H}}(\mathcal{I}, \boldsymbol{x})$ be the value of the solution. There is a randomized polynomial-time algorithm to compute a permutation π such that $\mathbf{val}(\mathcal{I}, \pi) \ge \mathbf{val}_{\mathcal{H}}(\mathcal{I}, \boldsymbol{x}) - \frac{7k^2 \log n}{\Delta\sqrt{n}}$.*

In Appendix B, we prove the following variant of Lemma 4.4.

LEMMA 4.5. *Let $\mathcal{I} = (V, \omega)$ be a k-AP instance such that $\omega(u_1, \ldots, u_k, w_1, \ldots, w_k) = \omega'(u_1, \ldots, u_k) \cdot \omega''(w_1, \ldots, w_k)$, where ω' is Δ'-locally dense and ω'' is Δ-dense. Given a solution $\boldsymbol{x}$ to the relaxation $\mathcal{H}$, let $\mathbf{val}_{\mathcal{H}}(\mathcal{I}, \boldsymbol{x})$ be the value of the solution. There is a randomized polynomial-time algorithm to compute a permutation π such that $\mathbf{val}(\mathcal{I}, \pi) \ge \mathbf{val}_{\mathcal{H}}(\mathcal{I}, \boldsymbol{x}) - \frac{7k^2 \log n}{\Delta\Delta'\sqrt{n}}$.*

4.2.3 *The rounding lemmas*

Combining Lemma 4.2 and Lemma 4.4, and Lemma 4.3 and Lemma 4.5, we get the following main rounding lemmas for this subsection.

LEMMA 4.6. *Let $\mathcal{I} = (V, \omega)$ be a k-AP instance such that ω is Δ-dense. Let $\boldsymbol{\mu}$ be a κ-independent solution (with respect to the uniform distribution rather than ω) to the k-round Sherali-Adams LP relaxation for $\mathcal{I}$. There is a polynomial-time algorithm, on input $\boldsymbol{\mu}$, to find a permutation π such that $\mathbf{val}(\mathcal{I}, \pi) \ge \mathbf{val}_{\mathrm{LP}}(\mathcal{I}, \boldsymbol{\mu}) - \frac{2\sqrt{\kappa}}{\Delta} - \frac{7k^2 \log n}{\Delta\sqrt{n}}$.*

LEMMA 4.7. *Let $\mathcal{I} = (V, \omega)$ be a k-AP instance such that $\omega(u_1, \ldots, u_k, w_1, \ldots, w_k) = \omega'(u_1, \ldots, u_k) \cdot \omega''(w_1, \ldots, w_k)$ where ω' is Δ'-locally dense and ω'' is Δ-dense. Let $\boldsymbol{\mu}$ be a κ-independent solution to the k-round Sherali-Adams LP relaxation of $\mathcal{I}$. There is a randomized polynomial-time algorithm, on input $\boldsymbol{\mu}$, to find a permutation π such that $\mathbf{val}(\mathcal{I}, \pi) \ge \mathbf{val}_{\mathrm{LP}}(\mathcal{I}, \boldsymbol{\mu}) - \frac{2\sqrt{\kappa}}{\Delta} - \frac{7k^2 \log n}{\Delta\Delta'\sqrt{n}}$.*

5. PUTTING THINGS TOGETHER

The following theorem gives PTASs for dense and locally dense Max-CSP.

THEOREM 5.1. *Let $\mathcal{I} = (V, \omega, P)$ be a k-CSP instance over finite domain D such that ω is Δ-dense or Δ-locally dense. For any $\epsilon > 0$, let $\ell = \frac{9k^2 4^k \log |D|}{\epsilon^2 \Delta}$. The additive integrality gaps of the $(\ell+k)$-round Sherali-Adams LP relaxation is at most ϵ; and there is a randomized rounding algorithm producing a solution whose value is at least $\mathbf{opt}(\mathcal{I}) - \epsilon$, in expected $n^{O(\ell)}$ time.*

PROOF. Let $\boldsymbol{\mu}$ be a solution to the $(\ell + k)$-round Sherali Adams LP relaxation. Let the random variable $(\boldsymbol{\mu}|\boldsymbol{x}_U)$ be the solution after conditioning on the variables in U. By Corollary 3.4 and Corollary 3.6, we know that there exists $t \le \ell$ such that

$$\mathop{\mathbf{E}}_{U\sim V^t} \sqrt{\mathop{\mathbf{E}}_{S\sim\omega} C_{\mu}(\boldsymbol{x}_S|\boldsymbol{x}_U)} \le \sqrt{\mathop{\mathbf{E}}_{U\sim V^t} \mathop{\mathbf{E}}_{S\sim\omega} C_{\mu}(\boldsymbol{x}_S|\boldsymbol{x}_U)} \le \sqrt{\frac{k^2 4^k \log |D|}{\Delta \ell}} = \frac{\epsilon}{3}.$$

Together with Lemma 3.2, we have

$$\mathop{\mathbf{E}}_{U\sim V^t}\left(\mathbf{val}_{\mathrm{LP}}(\mathcal{I},\boldsymbol{\mu}|\boldsymbol{x}_U) - 3\sqrt{\mathop{\mathbf{E}}_{S\sim\omega} C_{\boldsymbol{\mu}}(\boldsymbol{x}_S|\boldsymbol{x}_U)}\right) \geq \mathbf{val}_{\mathrm{LP}}(\mathcal{I},\boldsymbol{\mu}) - \epsilon.$$

We enumerate all the possible ways of conditioning, and find out a solution $\boldsymbol{\mu}'$ to the $(k+\ell-t)$-round Sherali-Adams LP relaxation such that $\mathbf{val}_{\mathrm{LP}}(\mathcal{I},\boldsymbol{\mu}') - 3\sqrt{\mathbf{E}_{S\sim\omega} C_{\boldsymbol{\mu}'}(\boldsymbol{x}_S)} \geq \mathbf{val}_{\mathrm{LP}}(\mathcal{I},\boldsymbol{\mu})-\epsilon$. Since $\boldsymbol{\mu}'$ is always a $\mathbf{E}_{S\sim\omega} C_{\boldsymbol{\mu}'}(\boldsymbol{x}_S)$-independent solution, by Lemma 4.1, given $\boldsymbol{\mu}'$, we can find an assignment with value at least $\mathbf{val}_{\mathrm{LP}}(\mathcal{I},\boldsymbol{\mu})-\epsilon$ in randomized polynomial time. □

Now we prove that there is a quasi-polynomial-time approximation scheme for dense Max-AP.

THEOREM 5.2. *Let $\mathcal{I} = (V,\omega)$ be a k-AP instance such that ω is Δ-dense. For any $\epsilon > 0$, let $\ell = \frac{4k4^k \log|D|}{\epsilon^2\Delta^2}$. The additive integrality gaps of the $(\ell+k)$-round Sherali-Adams LP relaxation is at most $\epsilon + \frac{7k^2\log n}{\Delta\sqrt{n}}$; and there is a randomized rounding algorithm producing a solution whose value is at least $\mathbf{opt}(\mathcal{I}) - \epsilon - \frac{7k^2\log n}{\Delta\sqrt{n}}$, in expected $n^{O(\ell)}$ time.*

PROOF. Let $\boldsymbol{\mu}$ be a solution to the $(\ell+k)$-round Sherali Adams LP relaxation. By Lemma 3.3, we know that there exists $t \leq \ell$ such that

$$\mathop{\mathbf{E}}_{U\sim V^t}\sqrt{\mathop{\mathbf{E}}_{S\sim V^k} C_{\boldsymbol{\mu}}(\boldsymbol{x}_S|\boldsymbol{x}_U)} \leq \sqrt{\mathop{\mathbf{E}}_{U\sim V^t}\mathop{\mathbf{E}}_{S\sim V^k} C_{\boldsymbol{\mu}}(\boldsymbol{x}_S|\boldsymbol{x}_U)} \leq \sqrt{\frac{k4^k\log n}{\ell}} = \frac{\epsilon\Delta}{2}.$$

Together with Lemma 3.2, we have

$$\mathop{\mathbf{E}}_{U\sim V^t}\left(\mathbf{val}_{\mathrm{LP}}(\mathcal{I},\boldsymbol{\mu}|\boldsymbol{x}_U) - \frac{2}{\Delta}\sqrt{\mathop{\mathbf{E}}_{S\sim V^k} C_{\boldsymbol{\mu}}(\boldsymbol{x}_S|\boldsymbol{x}_U)}\right) \geq \mathbf{val}_{\mathrm{LP}}(\mathcal{I},\boldsymbol{\mu}) - \epsilon.$$

We enumerate all the possible ways of conditioning, and find out a solution $\boldsymbol{\mu}'$ to the $(k+\ell-t)$-round Sherali-Adams LP relaxation such that $\mathbf{val}_{\mathrm{LP}}(\mathcal{I},\boldsymbol{\mu}')-2\sqrt{E_{S\sim V^k}C_{\boldsymbol{\mu}'}(\boldsymbol{x}_S)} \geq \mathbf{val}_{\mathrm{LP}}(\mathcal{I},\boldsymbol{\mu}) - \epsilon$. By Lemma 4.6, given $\boldsymbol{\mu}'$, we can find a permutation with value at least $\mathbf{val}_{\mathrm{LP}}(\mathcal{I},\boldsymbol{\mu})-\epsilon-\frac{7k^2\log n}{\Delta\sqrt{n}}$. □

Using Corollary 3.6 and Lemma 4.7 instead of Lemma 3.3 and Lemma 4.6, the same argument shows that there is a quasi-polynomial-time approximation scheme for locally dense Max-AP.

THEOREM 5.3. *Let $\mathcal{I} = (V,\omega)$ be a k-AP instance such that $\omega(u_1,\ldots,u_k,w_1,\ldots,w_k) = \omega'(u_1,\ldots,u_k)\cdot\omega''(w_1,\ldots,w_k)$ where ω' is Δ'-locally dense and ω'' is Δ-dense. For any $\epsilon > 0$, let $\ell = \frac{4k^2 4^k \log|D|}{\epsilon^2\Delta'\Delta^2}$. The additive integrality gaps of the $(\ell+k)$-round Sherali-Adams LP relaxation is at most $\epsilon + \frac{7k^2\log n}{\Delta\Delta'\sqrt{n}}$; and there is a randomized rounding algorithm producing a solution whose value is at least $\mathbf{opt}(\mathcal{I}) - \epsilon - \frac{7k^2\log n}{\Delta\Delta'\sqrt{n}}$, in expected $n^{O(\ell)}$ time.*

6. ACKNOWLEDGEMENTS

Y.Y. is supported by JSPS Grant-in-Aid for Research Activity Start-up (24800082), MEXT Grant-in-Aid for Scientific Research on Innovative Areas (24106001), and JST, ERATO, Kawarabayashi Large Graph Project. Y. Z. is supported by a grant from the Simons Foundation (Award Number 252545). Part of the work has been done while visiting Toyota Technological Institute at Chicago.

We would like to thank Ryan O'Donnell for valuable discussions.

7. REFERENCES

[AdlVKK03] Noga Alon, W Fernandez de la Vega, Ravi Kannan, and Marek Karpinski. Random sampling and approximation of Max-CSPs. *Journal of computer and system sciences*, 67(2):212–243, 2003.

[AFK02] Sanjeev Arora, Alan Frieze, and Haim Kaplan. A new rounding procedure for the assignment problem with applications to dense graph arrangement problems. *Mathematical Programming*, 92(1):1–36, 2002.

[AKK99] Sanjeev Arora, David Karger, and Marek Karpinski. Polynomial time approximation schemes for dense instances of np-hard problems. *Journal of computer and system sciences*, 58(1):193–210, 1999.

[ALM+98] Sanjeev Arora, Carsten Lund, Rajeev Motwani, Madhu Sudan, and Mario Szegedy. Proof verification and the hardness of approximation problems. *Journal of the ACM*, 45(3):501–555, 1998.

[AM13] Albert Atserias and Elitza Maneva. Sherali–adams relaxations and indistinguishability in counting logics. *SIAM Journal on Computing*, 42(1):112–137, 2013.

[BRS11] Boaz Barak, Prasad Raghavendra, and David Steurer. Rounding semidefinite programming hierarchies via global correlation. In *Proc. 52nd Annual IEEE Symposium on Foundations of Computer Science (FOCS)*, pages 472–481, 2011.

[CMM09] Moses Charikar, Konstantin Makarychev, and Yury Makarychev. Integrality gaps for sherali-adams relaxations. In *Proceedings of the 41st annual ACM symposium on Theory of computing*, pages 283–292. ACM, 2009.

[COCF09] Amin Coja-Oghlan, Colin Cooper, and Alan Frieze. An efficient sparse regularity concept. *SIAM Journal on Discrete Mathematics*, 23(4):2000–2034, 2009.

[dlV96] W Fernandez de la Vega. Max-Cut has a randomized approximation scheme in dense graphs. *Random Structures & Algorithms*, 8(3), 1996.

[dlVK01] W Fernandez de la Vega and Claire Kenyon. A randomized approximation scheme for metric Max-Cut. *Journal of computer and system sciences*, 63(4):531–541, 2001.

[dlVKKV05] W Fernandez de la Vega, Marek Karpinski, Ravi Kannan, and Santosh Vempala. Tensor decomposition and approximation schemes for constraint satisfaction problems. In *Proc. 37th Annual ACM Symposium on Theory of Computing (STOC)*, pages 747–754, 2005.

[dlVKM07] Wenceslas Fernandez de la Vega and Claire Kenyon-Mathieu. Linear programming relaxations of maxcut. In *Proc. 18th Annual ACM-SIAM Symposium on Discrete Algorithms (SODA)*, pages 53–61, 2007.

[FdlVKK04] W Fernandez de la Vega, Marek Karpinski, and Claire Kenyon. Approximation schemes for metric bisection and partitioning. In *Proc. 15th Annual ACM-SIAM symposium on Discrete algorithms (SODA)*, pages 506–515, 2004.

[FK96] A Frieze and R Kannan. The regularity lemma and approximation schemes for dense problems. In *Proc. 37th Annual Symposium on Foundations of Computer Science (FOCS)*, pages 12–20, 1996.

[KMTV11] Amit Kumar, Rajsekar Manokaran, Madhur Tulsiani, and Nisheeth K Vishnoi. On lp-based approximability for strict csps. In *Proceedings of the Twenty-Second Annual ACM-SIAM Symposium on Discrete Algorithms*, pages 1560–1573. SIAM, 2011.

[LS91] L Lovász and A Schrijver. Cones of matrices and set-functions and 0-1 optimization. *SIAM Journal on Optimization*, 1(2):166–190, 1991.

[RS09] Prasad Raghavendra and David Steurer. How to round any CSP. In *Proc. 50th Annual IEEE Symposium on Foundations of Computer Science (FOCS)*, pages 586–594, 2009.

[RT12] Prasad Raghavendra and Ning Tan. Approximating CSPs with global cardinality constraints using sdp hierarchies. In *Proc. 23rd Annual ACM-SIAM Symposium on Discrete Algorithms (SODA)*, pages 373–387, 2012.

[SA90] Hanif D Sherali and Warren P Adams. A hierarchy of relaxations between the continuous and convex hull representations for zero-one programming problems. *SIAM Journal on Discrete Mathematics*, 3(3):411–430, 1990.

[Sch08] Grant Schoenebeck. Linear level lasserre lower bounds for certain k-CSPs. In *Proc. 49th Annual IEEE Symposium on Foundations of Computer Science (FOCS)*, pages 593–602, 2008.

[STT07] Grant Schoenebeck, Luca Trevisan, and Madhur Tulsiani. Tight integrality gaps for lovasz-schrijver lp relaxations of vertex cover and max cut. In *Proc. 39th Annual ACM Symposium on Theory of Computing (STOC)*, pages 302–310, 2007.

[Sze78] E. Szemerédi. Regular partitions of graphs. In *Proc. Colloque Inter. CNRS (J. C. Bermond, J. C. Fournier, M. Las Vergnas and D. Sotteau, eds.)*, pages 399–401, 1978.

APPENDIX

A. PROOF OF LEMMA 4.4

Observe that a solution $\boldsymbol{x}$ to the relaxation $\mathcal{H}$ corresponds to a doubly stochastic matrix. Now let us decompose $\boldsymbol{x}$ into a distribution of permutations $\mathcal{D} = \{\pi : V \to V\}$ such that for any $u, w \in V$, we have $\Pr_{\pi\sim\mathcal{D}}[\pi(u) = w] = \boldsymbol{x}_{u,w}$. Let $\mathbf{val}_{\mathcal{H}}(\mathcal{I}, \mathcal{D}) = \mathbf{val}_{\mathcal{H}}(\mathcal{I}, \boldsymbol{x})$ be the value of relaxation $\mathcal{H}$ on $\boldsymbol{x}$ for instance $\mathcal{I}$. Our goal is to "merge" the permutations in $\mathcal{D}$ into one permutation while not losing much in the objective value. The following lemma proves this for the special case when $\mathcal{D}$ is supported on only two permutations.

LEMMA A.1. *Let $\mathcal{D}$ be the distribution over π_1 and π_2 such that π_1 is chosen with probability p and π_2 is chosen with probability $(1-p)$. There exists a distribution $\mathcal{D}'$ over permutations such that for any $k \geq 2$ and any k-AP instance $\mathcal{I} = (V, \omega)$ such that ω is Δ-dense , we have*

$$\mathop{\mathbf{E}}_{\pi\sim\mathcal{D}'}[\mathbf{val}(\mathcal{I}, \pi)] \geq \mathbf{val}_{\mathcal{H}}(\mathcal{I}, \mathcal{D}) - \frac{2k^2}{\Delta\sqrt{n}}.$$

Moreover, $\mathcal{D}'$ can be sampled in polynomial time.

PROOF. Let us assume w.l.o.g. that $V = [n]$, $\pi_1 = \mathrm{id}$ (i.e. $\pi_1(i) = i$ for all $i \in [n]$). For any set $A = \{a_i : a_1 < a_2 < \cdots < a_{|A|} = n\} \subseteq [n]$, let us define π_A be the permutation over $[n]$ so that $\pi_A(i) = a_{t-1} + 1$ if $i = a_t$ for some $t \in [|A|]$ and $\pi_A(i) = i + 1$ otherwise (assuming $a_0 = 0$). We can also assume w.l.o.g. that there exists $A \subseteq [n]$ such that $\pi_2 = \pi_A$. See Figure 1. We can add at most $\sqrt{n}$ elements into A to get $A' \subseteq [n]$ such that there is no set of $\sqrt{n}$ consecutive integers that does not intersect A'. It is easy to show that π_A and $\pi_{A'}$ differ at most $2\sqrt{n}$ places. Let $\mathcal{D}_{A'}$ be the probability distribution that chooses π_1 with probability p and $\pi_{A'}$ with probability $(1-p)$. For any k and any k-AP instance $\mathcal{I} = (V, \omega)$ such that ω is Δ-dense, we have

$$\begin{aligned}
&\mathbf{val}_{\mathcal{H}}(\mathcal{I}, \mathcal{D}) - \mathbf{val}_{\mathcal{H}}(\mathcal{I}, \mathcal{D}_{A'}) \\
=& n^k \mathop{\mathbf{E}}_{(U,W)\sim\omega}\left(\prod_{i=1}^{k}\Pr_{\pi\sim\mathcal{D}}[\pi(u_i) = w_i] - \prod_{i=1}^{k}\Pr_{\pi\sim\mathcal{D}_{A'}}[\pi(u_i) = w_i]\right) \\
\leq& n^k \mathop{\mathbf{E}}_{(U,W)\sim\omega} \mathbf{1}[\exists i \in [k] : \pi_{A'}(u_i) \neq \pi_A(u_i)] \\
&\qquad\cdot \prod_{i=1}^{k}\Pr_{\pi\sim\mathcal{D}}[\pi(u_i) = w_i] \\
\leq& \frac{n^k}{\Delta} \cdot \mathop{\mathbf{E}}_{(U,W)\sim V^{2k}} \mathbf{1}[\exists i \in [k] : \pi_{A'}(u_i) \neq \pi_A(u_i)] \\
&\qquad\cdot \prod_{i=1}^{k}\Pr_{\pi\sim\mathcal{D}}[\pi(u_i) = w_i], \qquad (4)
\end{aligned}$$

where the last inequality is by the density of ω.

Since

$$n^k \mathop{\mathbf{E}}_{W\sim V^k} \prod_{i=1}^{k} \Pr_{\pi\sim\mathcal{D}}[\pi(u_i) = w_i] = \prod_{i=1}^{k}\sum_{w_i\sim V}\Pr_{\pi\sim\mathcal{D}}[\pi(u_i) = w_i] = 1, \quad (5)$$

we have

$$(4) \leq \frac{1}{\Delta} \cdot \Pr_{U\sim V^k}[\exists i \in [k] : \pi_{A'}(u_i) \neq \pi_A(u_i)] \leq \frac{2k}{\Delta\sqrt{n}}. \quad (6)$$

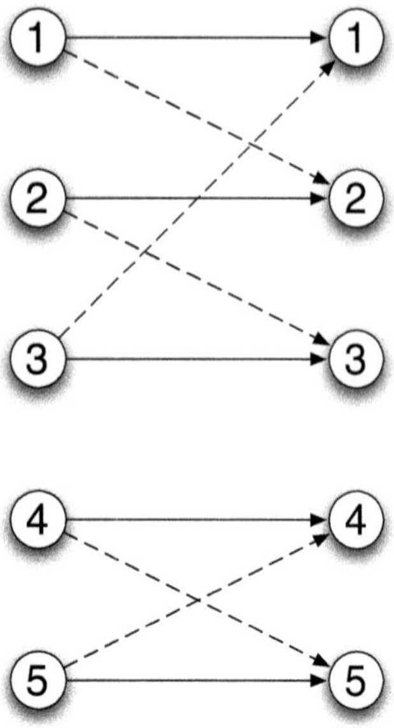

Figure 1: Permutations π_1 and π_2 over $[5]$ are shown as mappings from $[5]$ to $[5]$. Solid arrow represents π_1 and dashed arrows represent π_2. For any permutation π_1, we can move vertices in the right side (and relabeling them accordingly) so that the resulting π_1 is the identity permutation. Then for any permutation π_2, we can move pairs of vertices (and relabeling them accordingly) so that π_1 remains the identity permutation whereas the cycles formed by π_1 and π_2 are drawn disjointly. In such a case, π_2 satisfies the condition in the body text.

Now we define the distribution $\mathcal{D}'$. Let us assume that the elements in A' are $a'_1 < a'_2 < \ldots < a'_{|A'|} = n$; let $a'_0 = 0$ for convenience. To draw a permutation $\pi \sim \mathcal{D}'$, we sample $|A'|$ i.i.d. 0/1 bits $b_1, b_2, \ldots, b_{|A'|}$, each of which has mean p. For each i, we find out the unique $t \in [|A'|]$ so that $a'_{t-1} < i \le a'_t$; let $\pi(i) = \pi_1(i) = i$ if $b_t = 0$; let $\pi(i) = \pi_{A'}(i)$ otherwise.

For any k and any Δ-dense k-AP instance $\mathcal{I} = (V, \omega)$, we have

$$\begin{aligned}
&\mathbf{val}_{\mathcal{H}}(\mathcal{I}, \mathcal{D}_{A'}) - \mathop{\mathbf{E}}_{\pi\sim\mathcal{D}'} \mathbf{val}(\mathcal{I}, \pi) \\
=&n^k \mathop{\mathbf{E}}_{(U,W)\sim\omega} \left(\prod_{i=1}^{k} \Pr_{\pi\sim\mathcal{D}_{A'}} [\pi(u_i) = w_i] \right. \\
&\qquad \left. - \Pr_{\pi\sim\mathcal{D}'} [\forall i \in [k] : \pi(u_i) = w_i] \right) \\
=&n^k \mathop{\mathbf{E}}_{(U,W)\sim\omega} \left(\prod_{i=1}^{k} \Pr_{\pi\sim\mathcal{D}_{A'}} [\pi(u_i) = w_i] \right. \\
&\qquad \left. - \prod_{t=1}^{|A'|} \Pr_{\pi\sim\mathcal{D}'} [\forall i \in [k], a'_{t-1} < u_i \le a'_t : \pi(u_i) = w_i] \right) \\
\le&n^k \mathop{\mathbf{E}}_{(U,W)\sim\omega} \\
&\qquad \mathbf{1}\left[\exists t \in [|A'|] : \exists \text{ more than one } i \text{ s.t. } a'_{t-1} < u_i \le a'_t\right] \\
&\qquad \cdot \prod_{i=1}^{k} \Pr_{\pi\sim\mathcal{D}_{A'}} [\pi(u_i) = w_i] \\
\le&\frac{n^k}{\Delta} \mathop{\mathbf{E}}_{(U,W)\sim V^{2k}} \\
&\qquad \mathbf{1}\left[\exists t \in [|A'|] : \exists \text{ more than one } i \text{ s.t. } a'_{t-1} < u_i \le a'_t\right] \\
&\qquad \cdot \prod_{i=1}^{k} \Pr_{\pi\sim\mathcal{D}_{A'}} [\pi(u_i) = w_i] \qquad \text{(by density)} \\
=&\frac{1}{\Delta} \Pr_{U\sim V^k} \left[\exists t \in [|A'|] : \exists \text{ more than one } i \text{ s.t. } a'_{t-1} < u_i \le a'_t\right] \\
&\qquad \text{(by (5))} \\
\le&\frac{1}{\Delta} \cdot \binom{k}{2} \cdot \sum_{t\in[|A'|]} \left(\frac{a'_t - a'_{t-1}}{n}\right)^2 \\
\le&\frac{1}{\Delta} \cdot \binom{k}{2} \cdot \sum_{t\in[|A'|]} \left(\frac{a'_t - a'_{t-1}}{n}\right) \cdot \frac{1}{\sqrt{n}} \le \frac{k^2}{\sqrt{n}}. \qquad (7)
\end{aligned}$$

The lemma is proved by combining (6) and (7). □

Proof of Lemma 4.4. Let $\mathcal{D}$ be supported on $\pi_1, \pi_2, \ldots, \pi_m$, each π_i is chosen with probability p_i. We can assume that $m \le n^2$ by preserving only the n^2 permutations with the largest probabilities and proper normalization, which would cause a loss of at most n^{-1} in the objective value $\mathbf{val}_{\mathcal{H}}(\mathcal{I}, \mathcal{D})$. Now we show that for any such distribution, we can find a distribution $\mathcal{E}$ that is supported on $(m-1)$ permutations, such that

$$\mathbf{val}_{\mathcal{H}}(\mathcal{I}, \mathcal{E}) \ge \mathbf{val}_{\mathcal{H}}(\mathcal{I}, \mathcal{D}) - (p_1 + p_2)\frac{2k^2}{\Delta\sqrt{n}}. \qquad (8)$$

In other words, since π_1 and π_2 are arbitrary, we are able to "merge" any two permutations π_i and π_j in $\mathcal{D}$ by paying a loss of $(p_i + p_j)\frac{2k^2}{\Delta\sqrt{n}}$ in the objective value. We repeatedly merge the two permutations with the smallest probability mass in the distribution until there is only one permutation left, during this process we lose at most $\lceil \log m \rceil \frac{2k^2}{\Delta\sqrt{n}} \le \frac{6k^2 \log n}{\Delta\sqrt{n}}$ in objective value. Together with the n^{-1} loss at the beginning of the proof, we lose at most $\frac{7k^2 \log n}{\Delta\sqrt{n}}$ for sufficiently large n.

In order to show (8), let us define a distribution $\tilde{\mathcal{E}}$ of distributions of permutations as follows. Let $\mathcal{F}$ to be the distribution of permutations that chooses π_1 with probability $\frac{p_1}{p_1+p_2}$ and π_2 with the remaining probability. Apply Lemma A.1 on $\mathcal{F}$ to get $\mathcal{F}'$. A distribution $\mathcal{E}$ from $\tilde{\mathcal{E}}$ is sampled by first sampling a permutation π from $\mathcal{F}'$, and returning the distribution that puts probability mass $(p_1 + p_2)$ on π and p_i on π_i for all $i : 3 \le i \le m$. For every $u, w \in V$, let

$\gamma_{u,w} = \sum_{t=3}^m p_t \mathbf{1}[\pi_t(u) = w] \le 1$. We have

$$\mathop{\mathbf{E}}_{\mathcal{E}\sim\tilde{\mathcal{E}}} \mathbf{val}_{\mathcal{H}}(\mathcal{I},\mathcal{E}) = \mathop{\mathbf{E}}_{\mathcal{E}\sim\tilde{\mathcal{E}}} \mathop{\mathbf{E}}_{(U,W)\sim\omega} \prod_{i=1}^{k} \Pr_{\pi\sim\mathcal{E}}[\pi(u_i) = w_i]$$

$$= \mathop{\mathbf{E}}_{\pi\sim\mathcal{F}'} \mathop{\mathbf{E}}_{(U,W)\sim\omega} \prod_{i=1}^{k} ((p_1+p_2)\mathbf{1}[\pi(u_i) = w_i] + \gamma_{u_i,w_i})$$

$$= \sum_{Q\subseteq[k]} \mathop{\mathbf{E}}_{(U,W)\sim\omega} \left(\mathop{\mathbf{E}}_{\pi\sim\mathcal{F}'} \prod_{i\in Q} (p_1+p_2)\mathbf{1}[\pi(u_i) = w_i]\right)\left(\prod_{i\in\overline{Q}} \gamma_{u_i,w_i}\right)$$

$$= \sum_{Q\subseteq[k]} \mathop{\mathbf{E}}_{\substack{(U_{\overline{Q}},W_{\overline{Q}})\\ \sim\omega_{(\overline{Q},\overline{Q})}}} \left(\prod_{i\in\overline{Q}} \gamma_{u_i,w_i}\right)(p_1+p_2)^{|Q|}$$

$$\mathop{\mathbf{E}}_{\substack{(U_Q,W_Q)\\ \sim\omega|(U_{\overline{Q}},W_{\overline{Q}})}} \left(\mathop{\mathbf{E}}_{\pi\sim\mathcal{F}'} \prod_{i\in Q} \mathbf{1}[\pi(u_i) = w_i]\right), \qquad (9)$$

where U_A is the restriction of vector U over coordinates in A, $\omega_{(A,B)}$ is the marginal distribution of ω over A in the first k coordinates and B in the last k coordinates, and $\omega|(U_A, W_B)$ is the distribution ω conditioned on that coordinates in A are assigned U and coordinates in B are assigned W. Let $\mathcal{I}_{U_{\overline{Q}},W_{\overline{Q}}}$ be the $|Q|$-AP instance $(V, \omega|(U_{\overline{Q}}, W_{\overline{Q}}))$. We know that $\omega|(U_{\overline{Q}}, W_{\overline{Q}})$ is $\Delta\cdot n^{2|\overline{Q}|}\cdot\omega_{(\overline{Q},\overline{Q})}(U_{\overline{Q}}, W_{\overline{Q}})$-dense. Therefore for every $Q \ne \emptyset$, by Lemma A.1, we have

$$\mathop{\mathbf{E}}_{\substack{(U_Q,W_Q)\\ \sim\omega|(U_{\overline{Q}},W_{\overline{Q}})}} \left(\mathop{\mathbf{E}}_{\pi\sim\mathcal{F}'} \prod_{i\in Q} \mathbf{1}[\pi(u_i) = w_i]\right)$$

$$= \mathop{\mathbf{E}}_{\pi\sim\mathcal{F}'} \mathbf{val}(\mathcal{I}_{U_{\overline{Q}},W_{\overline{Q}}}, \pi)$$

$$\ge \mathbf{val}_{\mathcal{H}}(\mathcal{I}_{U_{\overline{Q}},W_{\overline{Q}}}, \mathcal{F}) - \frac{2k^2 n^{-2|\overline{Q}|}}{\Delta\omega_{(\overline{Q},\overline{Q})}(U_{\overline{Q}}, W_{\overline{Q}})\sqrt{n}}$$

$$= \mathop{\mathbf{E}}_{\substack{(U_Q,W_Q)\\ \sim\omega|(U_{\overline{Q}},W_{\overline{Q}})}} \prod_{i\in Q}\left(\frac{p_1\mathbf{1}[\pi_1(u_i) = w_i] + p_2\mathbf{1}[\pi_2(u_i) = w_i]}{p_1+p_2}\right)$$

$$- \frac{2k^2 n^{-2|\overline{Q}|}}{\Delta\omega_{(\overline{Q},\overline{Q})}(U_{\overline{Q}}, W_{\overline{Q}})\sqrt{n}}.$$

Therefore we have

(9)

$$\ge \sum_{Q\subseteq[k]} \mathop{\mathbf{E}}_{\substack{(U_{\overline{Q}},W_{\overline{Q}})\\ \sim\omega_{(\overline{Q},\overline{Q})}}} \left(\prod_{i\in\overline{Q}} \gamma_{u_i,w_i}\right)$$

$$\mathop{\mathbf{E}}_{\substack{(U_Q,W_Q)\\ \sim\omega|(U_{\overline{Q}},W_{\overline{Q}})}} \prod_{i\in Q} (p_1\mathbf{1}[\pi_1(u_i) = w_i] + p_2\mathbf{1}[\pi_2(u_i) = w_i])$$

$$- \sum_{\emptyset\ne Q\subseteq[k]} \mathop{\mathbf{E}}_{\substack{(U_{\overline{Q}},W_{\overline{Q}})\\ \sim\omega_{(\overline{Q},\overline{Q})}}} \left(\prod_{i\in\overline{Q}} \gamma_{u_i,w_i}\right)(p_1+p_2)^{|Q|}$$

$$\cdot \frac{2k^2 n^{-2|\overline{Q}|}}{\Delta\omega_{(\overline{Q},\overline{Q})}(U_{\overline{Q}}, W_{\overline{Q}})\sqrt{n}}$$

$$= \mathop{\mathbf{E}}_{(U,W)\sim\omega} \left(\sum_{t=1}^{m} p_t\mathbf{1}[\pi_t(u_i) = w_i]\right)$$

$$- \sum_{\emptyset\ne Q\subseteq[k]} \mathop{\mathbf{E}}_{\substack{(U_{\overline{Q}},W_{\overline{Q}})\\ \sim V^{\overline{Q}\times\overline{Q}}}} \left(\prod_{i\in\overline{Q}} \gamma_{u_i,w_i}\right)(p_1+p_2)^{|Q|} \cdot \frac{2k^2}{\Delta\sqrt{n}}$$

$$\ge \mathbf{val}_{\mathcal{H}}(\mathcal{I},\mathcal{D}) - (p_1+p_2)\frac{2k^2}{\Delta\sqrt{n}}.$$

In all, we have proved that $\mathbf{E}_{\mathcal{E}\sim\tilde{\mathcal{E}}}\,\mathbf{val}_{\mathcal{H}}(\mathcal{I},\mathcal{E}) \ge \mathbf{val}_{\mathcal{H}}(\mathcal{I},\mathcal{D}) - (p_1+p_2)\frac{2k^2}{\Delta\sqrt{n}}$. Since $\tilde{\mathcal{E}}$ can be sampled in polynomial time, there is a randomized polynomial-time algorithm to find out a $\mathcal{E}$ satisfying (8). □

B. PROOF OF LEMMA 4.5

We say a distribution ω' over V^k is Δ'-*well spread* if for every $i, j \in [k]$ such that $i \ne j$, and for every disjoint partition $V = V_1 \cup V_2 \cup \cdots \cup V_t$, we have

$$\Delta' \cdot \Pr_{(u_1,\ldots,u_k)\sim\omega'}[\exists t' \in [t] : u_i \in V_{t'} \text{ and } u_j \in V_{t'}] \le \frac{\max_{t'\in[t]} |V_{t'}|}{n}.$$

Claim B.1. *A Δ'-locally dense distribution ω' is (Δ'/k)-well spread.*

Proof. W.l.o.g. we assume that $i = 1$ and $j = 2$. For every $Z \subseteq V$, we have

$$\Pr_{(u_1,\ldots,u_k)\sim\omega'}[\exists t' \in [t] : u_i \in V_{t'} \text{ and } u_j \in V_{t'}]$$

$$= \sum_{t'\in[t]} \sum_{\substack{u_1,u_2\in V_{t'}\\ u_3,\ldots,u_k\in V}} \omega'(u_1,\ldots,u_k)$$

$$\le \sum_{t'\in[t]} \sum_{\substack{u_1,u_2\in V_{t'}\\ u_3,\ldots,u_k\in V}} \frac{\sum_{i=1}^k d_i(u_i)}{\Delta' n^{k-1}}$$

$$= \sum_{t'\in[t]} \left(\sum_{\substack{u_2\in V_{t'}\\ u_3,\ldots,u_k\in V}} \frac{\sum_{u_1\in V_{t'}} d_1(u_1)}{\Delta' n^{k-1}} + \sum_{\substack{u_1\in V_{t'}\\ u_3,\ldots,u_k\in V}} \frac{\sum_{u_2\in V_{t'}} d_2(u_2)}{\Delta' n^{k-1}} + \sum_{i=3}^{k} \sum_{\substack{u_1,u_2\in V_{t'}\\ u_3,\ldots,u_{i-1},u_{i+1},\ldots,u_k\in V}} \frac{\sum_{u_i\in V} d_i(u_i)}{\Delta' n^{k-1}} \right)$$

$$\le 2\cdot\frac{\max_{t'\in[t]}|V_{t'}|}{\Delta' n} + (k-2)\cdot\frac{\Delta'\max_{t'\in[t]}|V_{t'}|^2}{n^2}$$

$$\le \frac{k\max_{t'\in[t]}|V_{t'}|}{\Delta' n}.$$

□

We will prove a slightly stronger statement than that of Lemma 4.5, in the sense that we prove the lemma for every ω such that $\omega = \omega'\cdot\omega''$ where ω' is Δ'-well spread and ω'' is Δ-dense.

The proof goes along the lines of the proof of Lemma 4.4. We decompose x into a distribution of permutations $\mathcal{D} =$

$\{\pi : V \to V\}$ such that for any $u, w \in V$, we have

$$\Pr_{\pi \sim \mathcal{D}}[\pi(u) = w] = x_{u,w}.$$

We first prove following lemma, which is an analogy of Lemma A.1.

LEMMA B.2. *Let $\mathcal{D}$ be the distribution over π_1 and π_2 such that π_1 is chosen with probability p and π_2 is chosen with probability $(1-p)$. There exists a distribution $\mathcal{D}'$ over permutations and a distribution $\mathcal{V}$ over the disjoint partitions $\{(V_1 \cup \cdots \cup V_t)\}$ where each V_i has at most $2\sqrt{n}$ elements, such that for any $k \geq 2$ and any k-AP instance $\mathcal{I} = (V, \omega)$ such that $\omega = \omega' \cdot \omega''$ where ω'' is Δ-dense, we have*

$$\mathop{\mathbf{E}}_{\pi \sim \mathcal{D}'}[\mathbf{val}(\mathcal{I}, \pi)] \geq \mathbf{val}_{\mathcal{H}}(\mathcal{I}, \mathcal{D}) - \frac{2k}{\Delta\sqrt{n}} - \frac{1}{\Delta} \sum_{1 \leq i < j \leq k} \mathop{\mathbf{E}}_{(V_1 \cup \ldots \cup V_t) \sim \mathcal{V}} \sum_{t' \in [t]} \Pr_{(u_1, \ldots, u_k) \sim \omega'}[u_i \in V_{t'} \text{ and } u_j \in V_{t'}].$$

Moreover, $\mathcal{D}'$ can be sampled in polynomial time.

PROOF. Let us assume w.l.o.g. that $V = [n]$, $\pi_1 = \mathrm{id}$ (i.e. $\pi_1(i) = i$ for all $i \in [n]$). For any set $A = \{a_i : a_1 < a_2 < \cdots < a_{|A|} = n\} \subseteq [n]$, let us define π_A be the permutation over $[n]$ so that $\pi_A(i) = a_{t-1} + 1$ if $i = a_t$ for some $t \in [|A|]$ and $\pi_A(i) = i + 1$ otherwise (assuming $a_0 = 0$). We can also assume w.l.o.g. that there exists $A \subseteq [n]$ such that $\pi_2 = \pi_A$.

Now we define the random set variable $A' : A \subseteq A \subseteq V$ as follows. We start from $A' = A$, and for each $i \in [\sqrt{n}]$, we uniformly sample an element a from $((i-1)\sqrt{n}, i\sqrt{n}]$ and let $A' \leftarrow A' \cup \{a\}$. In this way, we know that there is no set of $2\sqrt{n}$ consecutive integers that does not intersect A'. It is easy to show that for every $v \in V$, $\Pr_{A'}[\pi_A(v) \neq \pi_{A'}(v)] \leq \frac{2}{\sqrt{n}}$.

Let $\mathcal{D}_{A'}$ be the probability distribution that chooses π_1 with probability p and $\pi_{A'}$ with probability $(1-p)$. For any k and any k-AP instance $\mathcal{I} = (V, \omega)$ such that ω is Δ-dense, we have

$$\begin{aligned}
&\mathbf{val}_{\mathcal{H}}(\mathcal{I}, \mathcal{D}) - \mathop{\mathbf{E}}_{A'} \mathbf{val}_{\mathcal{H}}(\mathcal{I}, \mathcal{D}_{A'}) \\
=& n^k \mathop{\mathbf{E}}_{(U,W) \sim \omega} \left(\prod_{i=1}^{k} \Pr_{\pi \sim \mathcal{D}}[\pi(u_i) = w_i] - \prod_{i=1}^{k} \Pr_{\pi \sim \mathcal{D}_{A'}}[\pi(u_i) = w_i] \right) \\
\leq& n^k \mathop{\mathbf{E}}_{U \sim \omega', W \sim \omega''} \mathop{\mathbf{E}}_{A'} \mathbf{1}[\exists i \in [k] : \pi_{A'}(u_i) \neq \pi_A(u_i)] \cdot \prod_{i=1}^{k} \Pr_{\pi \sim \mathcal{D}}[\pi(u_i) = w_i] \\
\leq& \frac{n^k}{\Delta} \cdot \mathop{\mathbf{E}}_{U \sim \omega'} \mathop{\mathbf{E}}_{A'} \mathbf{1}[\exists i \in [k] : \pi_{A'}(u_i) \neq \pi_A(u_i)] \cdot \mathop{\mathbf{E}}_{W \sim V^k} \prod_{i=1}^{k} \Pr_{\pi \sim \mathcal{D}}[\pi(u_i) = w_i], \qquad (10)
\end{aligned}$$

where the last inequality is by the density of ω''. By (5), we have

$$(10) \leq \frac{1}{\Delta} \cdot \mathop{\mathbf{E}}_{U \sim \omega'} \Pr_{A'}[\exists i \in [k] : \pi_{A'}(u_i) \neq \pi_A(u_i)] \leq \frac{2k}{\Delta\sqrt{n}}. \qquad (11)$$

For every $A' \subseteq [n]$, we define the distribution $\mathcal{D}'_{A'}$. Let us assume that the elements in A' are $a'_1 < a'_2 < \ldots < a'_{|A'|} = n$; let $a'_0 = 0$ for convenience. To draw a permutation $\pi \sim \mathcal{D}'_{A'}$, we sample $|A'|$ i.i.d. 0/1 bits $b_1, b_2, \ldots, b_{|A'|}$, each of which has mean p. For each i, we find out the unique $t \in [|A'|]$ so that $a'_{t-1} < i \leq a'_t$; let $\pi(i) = \pi_1(i) = i$ if $b_t = 0$; let $\pi(i) = \pi_{A'}(i)$ otherwise.

Now we define the distribution $\mathcal{D}'$. To draw a permutation $\pi \sim \mathcal{D}'$, we first sample a random set A', and then draw a permutation from $\mathcal{D}'_{A'}$.

For any k and any k-AP instance $\mathcal{I} = (V, \omega)$ such that $\omega = \omega' \cdot \omega''$ where ω'' is Δ-dense, we have

$$\begin{aligned}
&\mathop{\mathbf{E}}_{A'} \mathbf{val}_{\mathcal{H}}(\mathcal{I}, \mathcal{D}_{A'}) - \mathop{\mathbf{E}}_{\pi \sim \mathcal{D}'} \mathbf{val}(\mathcal{I}, \pi) \\
=& n^k \mathop{\mathbf{E}}_{(U,W) \sim \omega} \mathop{\mathbf{E}}_{A'} \left(\prod_{i=1}^{k} \Pr_{\pi \sim \mathcal{D}_{A'}}[\pi(u_i) = w_i] - \Pr_{\pi \sim \mathcal{D}'_{A'}}[\forall i \in [k] : \pi(u_i) = w_i] \right) \\
=& n^k \mathop{\mathbf{E}}_{(U,W) \sim \omega} \mathop{\mathbf{E}}_{A'} \left(\prod_{i=1}^{k} \Pr_{\pi \sim \mathcal{D}_{A'}}[\pi(u_i) = w_i] - \prod_{t=1}^{|A'|} \Pr_{\pi \sim \mathcal{D}'_{A'}}[\forall i \in [k], a'_{t-1} < u_i \leq a'_t : \pi(u_i) = w_i] \right) \\
\leq& n^k \mathop{\mathbf{E}}_{(U,W) \sim \omega} \mathop{\mathbf{E}}_{A'} \mathbf{1}[\exists t \in [|A'|] : \exists \text{ more than one } i \text{ s.t. } a'_{t-1} < u_i \leq a'_t] \cdot \prod_{i=1}^{k} \Pr_{\pi \sim \mathcal{D}_{A'}}[\pi(u_i) = w_i] \\
\leq& \frac{n^k}{\Delta} \mathop{\mathbf{E}}_{U \sim \omega'} \mathop{\mathbf{E}}_{A'} \mathbf{1}[\exists t \in [|A'|] : \exists \text{ more than one } i \text{ s.t. } a'_{t-1} < u_i \leq a'_t] \cdot \mathop{\mathbf{E}}_{W \sim V^k} \prod_{i=1}^{k} \Pr_{\pi \sim \mathcal{D}_{A'}}[\pi(u_i) = w_i] \quad \text{(by density)} \\
\leq& \frac{1}{\Delta} \mathop{\mathbf{E}}_{U \sim \omega'} \mathop{\mathbf{E}}_{A'} \mathbf{1}[\exists t \in [|A'|] : \exists \text{ more than one } i \text{ s.t. } a'_{t-1} < u_i \leq a'_t] \quad \text{(by (5))} \\
\leq& \frac{1}{\Delta} \sum_{1 \leq i < j \leq k} \mathop{\mathbf{E}}_{A'} \sum_{t \in [|A'|]} \Pr_{(u_1, \ldots, u_k) \sim \omega'}[a'_{t-1} < u_i, u_j \leq a'_t]. \qquad (12)
\end{aligned}$$

The lemma is proved by combining (11) and (12). □

Now we are ready to prove Lemma 4.5.

PROOF OF LEMMA 4.5. Let $\mathcal{D}$ be supported on $\pi_1, \pi_2, \ldots, \pi_m$, each π_i is chosen with probability p_i. We can assume that $m \leq n^2$ by preserving only the n^2 permutations with the largest probabilities and proper normalization, which would cause a loss of at most n^{-1} in the objective value $\mathbf{val}_{\mathcal{H}}(\mathcal{I}, \mathcal{D})$. Now we show that for any such distribution, we can find a distribution $\mathcal{E}$ that is supported on $(m-1)$ permutations, such that

$$\mathbf{val}_{\mathcal{H}}(\mathcal{I}, \mathcal{E}) \geq \mathbf{val}_{\mathcal{H}}(\mathcal{I}, \mathcal{D}) - (p_1 + p_2)\frac{2k^2}{\Delta\Delta'\sqrt{n}}. \qquad (13)$$

In other words, since π_1 and π_2 are arbitrary, we are able to "merge" any two permutations π_i and π_j in $\mathcal{D}$ by paying a loss of $(p_i + p_j)\frac{2k^2}{\Delta\Delta'\sqrt{n}}$ in the objective value. We repeatedly merge the two permutations with the smallest probability mass in the distribution until there is only one permutation left, during this process we lose at most $\lceil \log m \rceil \frac{2k^2}{\Delta\sqrt{n}} \leq \frac{6k^2 \log n}{\Delta\Delta'\sqrt{n}}$ in objective value. Together with the n^{-1} loss at the beginning of the proof, we lose at most $\frac{7k^2 \log n}{\Delta\Delta'\sqrt{n}}$ for sufficiently large n.

In order to show (13), let us define a distribution $\tilde{\mathcal{E}}$ of distributions of permutations as follows. Let $\mathcal{F}$ to be the distribution of permutations that chooses π_1 with probability $\frac{p_1}{p_1+p_2}$ and π_2 with the remaining probability. Apply Lemma B.2 on $\mathcal{F}$ to get $\mathcal{F}'$. A distribution $\mathcal{E}$ from $\tilde{\mathcal{E}}$ is sampled by first sampling a permutation π from $\mathcal{F}'$, and returning the distribution that puts probability mass $(p_1 + p_2)$ on π and p_i on π_i for all $i : 3 \leq i \leq m$. For every $u, w \in V$, let $\gamma_{u,w} = \sum_{t=3}^{m} p_t \mathbf{1}[\pi_t(u) = w] < 1$. We have

$$\mathop{\mathbf{E}}_{\mathcal{E}\sim\tilde{\mathcal{E}}} \mathbf{val}_{\mathcal{H}}(\mathcal{I}, \mathcal{E}) = \mathop{\mathbf{E}}_{\mathcal{E}\sim\tilde{\mathcal{E}}} \mathop{\mathbf{E}}_{(U,W)\sim\omega} \prod_{i=1}^{k} \Pr_{\pi\sim\mathcal{E}}[\pi(u_i) = w_i]$$

$$= \mathop{\mathbf{E}}_{\pi\sim\mathcal{F}'} \mathop{\mathbf{E}}_{(U,W)\sim\omega} \prod_{i=1}^{k} ((p_1 + p_2)\mathbf{1}[\pi(u_i) = w_i] + \gamma_{u_i,w_i})$$

$$= \sum_{Q\subseteq[k]} \mathop{\mathbf{E}}_{(U,W)\sim\omega}$$

$$\left(\mathop{\mathbf{E}}_{\pi\sim\mathcal{F}'} \prod_{i\in Q}(p_1 + p_2)\mathbf{1}[\pi(u_i) = w_i]\right)\left(\prod_{i\in\overline{Q}} \gamma_{u_i,w_i}\right)$$

$$= \sum_{Q\subseteq[k]} \mathop{\mathbf{E}}_{\substack{(U_{\overline{Q}},W_{\overline{Q}})\\ \sim\omega_{(\overline{Q},\overline{Q})}}} \left(\prod_{i\in\overline{Q}} \gamma_{u_i,w_i}\right) (p_1 + p_2)^{|Q|}$$

$$\mathop{\mathbf{E}}_{\substack{(U_Q,W_Q)\\ \sim\omega|(U_{\overline{Q}},W_{\overline{Q}})}} \left(\mathop{\mathbf{E}}_{\pi\sim\mathcal{F}'} \prod_{i\in Q} \mathbf{1}[\pi(u_i) = w_i]\right), \qquad (14)$$

where U_A is the restriction of vector U over coordinates in A, ω''_A is the marginal distribution of ω'' over the coordinates in A, and $\omega_{(A,B)}$ is the marginal distribution of ω over A in the first k coordinates and B in the last k coordinates. Let $\mathcal{I}_{U_{\overline{Q}},W_{\overline{Q}}}$ be the $|Q|$-AP instance $\big(V, \omega|(U_{\overline{Q}}, W_{\overline{Q}})\big)$. We know that $\omega|(U_{\overline{Q}}, W_{\overline{Q}}) = (\omega'|U_{\overline{Q}}) \cdot (\omega''|W_{\overline{Q}})$, and $\omega''|W_{\overline{Q}}$ is $\Delta \cdot n^{|\overline{Q}|} \cdot \omega''_{\overline{Q}}(W_{\overline{Q}})$-dense. Therefore for every $Q \neq \emptyset$, by Lemma B.2, we have

$$\mathop{\mathbf{E}}_{\substack{(U_Q,W_Q)\\ \sim\omega|(U_{\overline{Q}},W_{\overline{Q}})}} \left(\mathop{\mathbf{E}}_{\pi\sim\mathcal{F}'} \prod_{i\in Q} \mathbf{1}[\pi(u_i) = w_i]\right)$$

$$= \mathop{\mathbf{E}}_{\pi\sim\mathcal{F}'} \mathbf{val}(\mathcal{I}_{U_{\overline{Q}},W_{\overline{Q}}}, \pi)$$

$$\geq \mathbf{val}_{\mathcal{H}}(\mathcal{I}_{U_{\overline{Q}},W_{\overline{Q}}}, \mathcal{F}) - \frac{2kn^{-|\overline{Q}|}}{\Delta\omega''_{\overline{Q}}(W_{\overline{Q}})\sqrt{n}}$$

$$- \frac{n^{-|\overline{Q}|}}{\Delta\omega''_{\overline{Q}}(W_{\overline{Q}})} \sum_{\substack{i,j\in Q\\ i\neq j}} \mathop{\mathbf{E}}_{(V_1\cup\ldots\cup V_t)\sim\mathcal{V}}$$

$$\sum_{t'\in[t]} \Pr_{U_Q\sim\omega'|U_{\overline{Q}}}[u_i \in V_{t'} \text{ and } u_j \in V_{t'}]$$

$$= \mathop{\mathbf{E}}_{\substack{(U_Q,W_Q)\\ \sim\omega|(U_{\overline{Q}},W_{\overline{Q}})}} \prod_{i\in Q} \left(\frac{p_1\mathbf{1}[\pi_1(u_i) = w_i] + p_2\mathbf{1}[\pi_2(u_i) = w_i]}{p_1 + p_2}\right)$$

$$- \frac{2kn^{-|\overline{Q}|}}{\Delta\omega''_{\overline{Q}}(W_{\overline{Q}})\sqrt{n}}$$

$$- \frac{n^{-|\overline{Q}|}}{\Delta\omega''_{\overline{Q}}(W_{\overline{Q}})} \sum_{\substack{i,j\in Q\\ i\neq j}} \mathop{\mathbf{E}}_{(V_1\cup\ldots\cup V_t)\sim\mathcal{V}}$$

$$\sum_{t'\in[t]} \Pr_{U_Q\sim\omega'|U_{\overline{Q}}}[u_i \in V_{t'} \text{ and } u_j \in V_{t'}].$$

Therefore we have

(14)

$$\geq \sum_{Q\subseteq[k]} \mathop{\mathbf{E}}_{\substack{(U_{\overline{Q}},W_{\overline{Q}})\\ \sim\omega_{(\overline{Q},\overline{Q})}}} \left(\prod_{i\in\overline{Q}} \gamma_{u_i,w_i}\right)$$

$$\mathop{\mathbf{E}}_{\substack{(U_Q,W_Q)\\ \sim\omega|(U_{\overline{Q}},W_{\overline{Q}})}} \prod_{i\in Q} (p_1\mathbf{1}[\pi_1(u_i) = w_i] + p_2\mathbf{1}[\pi_2(u_i) = w_i])$$

$$- \sum_{\emptyset\neq Q\subseteq[k]} \mathop{\mathbf{E}}_{\substack{(U_{\overline{Q}},W_{\overline{Q}})\\ \sim\omega_{(\overline{Q},\overline{Q})}}} \left(\prod_{i\in\overline{Q}} \gamma_{u_i,w_i}\right) (p_1 + p_2)^{|Q|}$$

$$\cdot \frac{2kn^{-|\overline{Q}|}}{\Delta\omega''_{\overline{Q}}(W_{\overline{Q}})\sqrt{n}}$$

$$- \sum_{\emptyset\neq Q\subseteq[k]} \mathop{\mathbf{E}}_{\substack{(U_{\overline{Q}},W_{\overline{Q}})\\ \sim\omega_{(\overline{Q},\overline{Q})}}} \left(\prod_{i\in\overline{Q}} \gamma_{u_i,w_i}\right) (p_1 + p_2)^{|Q|}$$

$$\cdot \frac{n^{|\overline{Q}|}}{\Delta\omega''_{\overline{Q}}(W_{\overline{Q}})} \sum_{\substack{i,j\in Q\\ i\neq j}} \mathop{\mathbf{E}}_{\substack{(V_1\cup\ldots\cup V_t)\\ \sim\mathcal{V}}} \sum_{t'\in[t]} \Pr_{\substack{U_Q\sim\\ \omega'|U_{\overline{Q}}}} [u_i, u_j \in V_{t'}]$$

$$= \mathop{\mathbf{E}}_{(U,W)\sim\omega} \left(\sum_{t=1}^{m} p_t\mathbf{1}[\pi_t(u_i) = w_i]\right)$$

$$- \sum_{\emptyset\neq Q\subseteq[k]} \mathop{\mathbf{E}}_{\substack{U_{\overline{Q}}\sim\omega'_{\overline{Q}}\\ W_{\overline{Q}}\sim V^{\overline{Q}}}} \left(\prod_{i\in\overline{Q}} \gamma_{u_i,w_i}\right) (p_1 + p_2)^{|Q|} \cdot \frac{2k}{\Delta\sqrt{n}}$$

$$- \sum_{\emptyset\neq Q\subseteq[k]} \mathop{\mathbf{E}}_{\substack{U\sim\omega'\\ W_{\overline{Q}}\sim V^{\overline{Q}}}} \left(\prod_{i\in\overline{Q}} \gamma_{u_i,w_i}\right) (p_1 + p_2)^{|Q|}$$

$$\cdot \frac{1}{\Delta} \sum_{\substack{i,j\in Q\\ i\neq j}} \mathop{\mathbf{E}}_{(V_1\cup\ldots\cup V_t)\sim\mathcal{V}} \sum_{t'\in[t]} \mathbf{1}[u_i, u_j \in V_{t'}]$$

$$\geq \mathbf{val}_{\mathcal{H}}(\mathcal{I}, \mathcal{D}) - (p_1 + p_2)\frac{1}{\Delta}\left(\frac{2k}{\sqrt{n}} + \frac{k^2}{\Delta'\sqrt{n}}\right)$$

$$\geq \mathbf{val}_{\mathcal{H}}(\mathcal{I},\mathcal{D}) - (p_1+p_2)\frac{2k^2}{\Delta\Delta'\sqrt{n}},$$

where the last inequality is because of the well-spreadness of ω' and the maximum size of $|V_t|$ In all, we have proved that $\mathbf{E}_{\mathcal{E}\sim\tilde{\mathcal{E}}}\,\mathbf{val}_{\mathcal{H}}(\mathcal{I},\mathcal{E}) \geq \mathbf{val}_{\mathcal{H}}(\mathcal{I},\mathcal{D}) - (p_1+p_2)\frac{2k^2}{\Delta\Delta'\sqrt{n}}$. Since $\tilde{\mathcal{E}}$ can be sampled in polynomial time, there is a randomized polynomial-time algorithm to find out a $\mathcal{E}$ satisfying (13). □

C. BISECTION Max-k-CSP

In this section, we consider the bisection Max-CSP as a notable example of Max-CSP with globally cardinality constraints.

We start with definitions. Fix a finite domain D and a k-CSP instance $\mathcal{I}$ over D. A global cardinality constraint is a linear constraint on the numbers of variables that are assigned to the values in D. For simplicity and illustration purpose, here we only consider the bisection constraint – i.e., assuming $D = \{0,1\}$, the number of variables that take value 1 is exactly $n/2$ (for even integers n). For a bisection k-CSP instance $\mathcal{I} = (V,\omega,P)$, we define its *optimal value* to be

$$\mathbf{opt}(\mathcal{I}) = \max_{\alpha:|\{v\in V:\alpha(v)=1\}|=n/2}\{\mathbf{val}(\mathcal{I},\alpha)\},$$

where the definition of $\mathbf{val}(\mathcal{I},\alpha)$ remains the same as in the ordinary k-CSP case.

The ℓ-round Sherali-Adams relaxation for a bisection k-CSP instance $\mathcal{I} = (V,\omega,P)$ $(\ell \geq k)$ is written as follows.

$$\begin{aligned}
\text{maximize}\quad & \mathop{\mathbf{E}}_{S\sim\omega}\mathop{\mathbf{E}}_{\alpha\sim\boldsymbol{\mu}_S}[P_S(\alpha)]\\
\text{subject to}\quad & \Pr_{\alpha\sim\boldsymbol{\mu}_S}[\alpha|_{S\cap T}=\beta] = \Pr_{\alpha\sim\boldsymbol{\mu}_T}[\alpha|_{S\cap T}=\beta]\\
& \qquad \forall S,T\subseteq V, |S\cup T|\leq \ell, \beta\in D^{S\cap T}\\
& \sum_{v\in V}\Pr_{\alpha\sim\boldsymbol{\mu}_{S\cup\{v\}}}[\alpha|_S=\beta \text{ and } \alpha(v)=1] = \frac{n}{2}\cdot\boldsymbol{\mu}_S(\beta)\\
& \qquad \forall S\subseteq V, S<\ell, \beta\in\{0,1\}^S,
\end{aligned}$$

where the last constraint corresponds to the bisection constraint.

We now turn to how to round κ-independent solutions. The following lemma is similar to Lemma 4.1.

Lemma C.1. *Let $\mathcal{I} = (V,\omega,P)$ be a bisection k-CSP instance. Let $\boldsymbol{\mu}$ be an κ-independent solution (with respect to both uniform distribution and ω, $0\leq\kappa\leq 1$) to the k-round Sherali-Adams LP relaxation. There is a randomized polynomial time algorithm to find an assignment $\alpha: V\to\{0,1\}$ such that $\mathbf{val}(\mathcal{I},\alpha) \geq \mathbf{val}_{\mathrm{LP}}(\mathcal{I},\boldsymbol{\mu}) - 3k\kappa^{1/4}$ and $|\{v\in V: \alpha(v)=1\}| = n/2$.*

Proof. We sample α in the same way as we did in the proof of Lemma 4.1, and we see that $\mathbf{E}_\alpha[\mathbf{val}(\mathcal{I},\alpha)] \geq \mathbf{val}_{\mathrm{LP}}(\mathcal{I}) - 2\sqrt{\kappa}$. Also observe that

$$\begin{aligned}
&\mathop{\mathbf{E}}_{\alpha}\left|\sum_{v\in V}\alpha(v) - \frac{n}{2}\right| \leq \sqrt{\mathop{\mathbf{E}}_{\alpha}\left(\sum_{v\in V}\alpha(v)-\frac{n}{2}\right)^2}\\
=&\sqrt{\sum_{v_1,v_2\in V}\mathop{\mathbf{E}}_{\alpha}[\alpha(v_1)\alpha(v_2)] - n\sum_{v\in V}\mathop{\mathbf{E}}_{\alpha}[\alpha(v)] + \frac{n^2}{4}}\\
=&\sqrt{\sum_{v_1,v_2\in V}\mathop{\mathbf{E}}_{\alpha}[\alpha(v_1)\alpha(v_2)] - \frac{n^2}{4}}\\
\leq&\sqrt{\sum_{v_1,v_2\in V}\Pr_{\beta\sim\boldsymbol{\mu}_{\{v_1,v_2\}}}[\beta(v_1)=\beta(v_2)=1] + \sqrt{\kappa} - \frac{n^2}{4}}\\
=&\kappa^{1/4},
\end{aligned}$$

where the last inequality is because of κ-independence with respect to uniform distribution, the definition of total correlation, and Lemma 2.1; the last equality is because of Sherali-Adams constraints.

In all, we have

$$\begin{aligned}
\mathop{\mathbf{E}}_{\alpha}\left(\mathbf{val}(\mathcal{I},\alpha) - k\left|\sum_{v\in V}\alpha(v)-\frac{n}{2}\right|\right)
&\geq \mathbf{val}_{\mathrm{LP}}(\mathcal{I},\boldsymbol{\mu}) - 2\sqrt{\kappa} - k\kappa^{1/4}\\
&\geq \mathbf{val}_{\mathrm{LP}}(\mathcal{I},\boldsymbol{\mu}) - 2k\kappa^{1/4}.
\end{aligned}$$

We can sample an α in expected polynomial time so that

$$\mathop{\mathbf{E}}_{\alpha}\left[\mathbf{val}(\mathcal{I},\alpha) - \left|\sum_{v\in V}\alpha(v)-\frac{n}{2}\right|\right] \geq \mathbf{val}_{\mathrm{LP}}(\mathcal{I}) - 3k\kappa^{1/4}.$$

By greedily rearranging $\left|\mathbf{E}_{v\in V}[\alpha(v)] - \frac{1}{2}\right|$-fraction of the entries in α, we get a bisection assignment α' such that

$$\mathbf{val}(\mathcal{I},\alpha') \geq \mathbf{val}_{\mathrm{LP}}(\mathcal{I},\boldsymbol{\mu}) - 3k\kappa^{1/4}.$$

□

Finally as a counterpart to Theorem 5.1, we show the following.

Theorem C.2. *Let $\mathcal{I} = (V,\omega,P)$ be a bisection k-CSP instance over domain $\{0,1\}$ such that ω is Δ-dense or Δ-locally dense. For any $\epsilon > 0$, let $\ell = \frac{2\cdot 3^4k^6 4^k\log|D|}{\epsilon^4\Delta}$. The additive integrality gaps of the $(\ell+k)$-round Sherali-Adams LP relaxation is at most ϵ; and there is a randomized rounding algorithm producing a solution whose value is at least $\mathbf{opt}(\mathcal{I}) - \epsilon$, in expected $n^{O(\ell)}$ time.*

Proof. Let $\boldsymbol{\mu}$ be a solution to the $(\ell+k)$-round Sherali Adams LP relaxation. Similar as in the proof of Theorem 5.1, Corollary 3.4 and Corollary 3.6, we know that there exists $t\leq\ell$ such that

$$\begin{aligned}
&\mathop{\mathbf{E}}_{U\sim V^t}\sqrt[4]{\mathop{\mathbf{E}}_{S\sim V^k}C_{\boldsymbol{\mu}}(\boldsymbol{x}_S|\boldsymbol{x}_U) + \mathop{\mathbf{E}}_{S\sim\omega}C_{\boldsymbol{\mu}}(\boldsymbol{x}_S|\boldsymbol{x}_U)}\\
\leq&\sqrt[4]{\mathop{\mathbf{E}}_{U\sim V^t}\left(\mathop{\mathbf{E}}_{S\sim V^k}C_{\boldsymbol{\mu}}(\boldsymbol{x}_S|\boldsymbol{x}_U) + \mathop{\mathbf{E}}_{S\sim\omega}C_{\boldsymbol{\mu}}(\boldsymbol{x}_S|\boldsymbol{x}_U)\right)}\\
\leq&\sqrt[4]{2\cdot\frac{k^2 4^k\log|D|}{\Delta\ell}} \leq \frac{\epsilon}{3k^2}.
\end{aligned}$$

Therefore, together with Lemma 3.2, we have

$$\mathop{\mathbf{E}}_{U\sim V^t}\Bigg(\mathbf{val}_{\mathrm{LP}}(\mathcal{I},\boldsymbol{\mu}|\boldsymbol{x}_U) - 3k\left(\sqrt[4]{\mathop{\mathbf{E}}_{S\sim V^k} C_{\boldsymbol{\mu}}(\boldsymbol{x}_S|\boldsymbol{x}_U)} + \sqrt[4]{\mathop{\mathbf{E}}_{S\sim \omega} C_{\boldsymbol{\mu}}(\boldsymbol{x}_S|\boldsymbol{x}_U)}\right)\Bigg) \geq \mathbf{val}_{\mathrm{LP}}(\mathcal{I},\boldsymbol{\mu}) - \epsilon.$$

We enumerate all the possible ways of conditioning, and find out a solution $\boldsymbol{\mu}'$ to the $(k+\ell-t)$-round Sherali-Adams LP relaxation such that

$$\mathbf{val}_{\mathrm{LP}}(\mathcal{I},\boldsymbol{\mu}') - 3k\left(\sqrt[4]{\mathop{\mathbf{E}}_{S\sim V^k} C_{\boldsymbol{\mu}'}(\boldsymbol{x}_S)} + \sqrt[4]{\mathop{\mathbf{E}}_{S\sim \omega} C_{\boldsymbol{\mu}'}(\boldsymbol{x}_S)}\right) \geq \mathbf{val}_{\mathrm{LP}}(\mathcal{I},\boldsymbol{\mu}) - \epsilon.$$

Since $\boldsymbol{\mu}'$ is always κ-independent with respect to both uniform distribution and ω for $\kappa = \mathbf{E}_{S\sim V^k} C_{\boldsymbol{\mu}'}(\boldsymbol{x}_S)+\mathbf{E}_{S\sim\omega} C_{\boldsymbol{\mu}'}(\boldsymbol{x}_S)$, by Lemma C.1, given $\boldsymbol{\mu}'$, we can find an assigment with value at least $\mathbf{val}_{\mathrm{LP}}(\mathcal{I},\boldsymbol{\mu}) - \epsilon$ in randomized polynomial time. □

D. A GAP INSTANCE FOR RELAXATION $\mathcal{H}$

In this section, we show a gap instance for the relaxation $\mathcal{H}$. Consider the following 2-AP instance $\mathcal{I}([5],\omega)$. Let us define $\omega_{i,j,p,q} = \frac{1}{64}A_{i,j}B_{p,q}$, where

$$A = \begin{bmatrix} 0 & 1 & 1 & 0 & 0 \\ 1 & 0 & 0 & 0 & 1 \\ 1 & 0 & 0 & 0 & 1 \\ 0 & 0 & 0 & 0 & 0 \\ 0 & 1 & 1 & 0 & 0 \end{bmatrix}, \quad \text{and} \quad B = \begin{bmatrix} 0 & 1 & 1 & 0 & 0 \\ 1 & 0 & 1 & 0 & 0 \\ 1 & 1 & 0 & 0 & 0 \\ 0 & 0 & 0 & 0 & 1 \\ 0 & 0 & 0 & 1 & 0 \end{bmatrix}.$$

If we view A and B as the adjacency matrices of two 5-vertex graphs, $\mathbf{val}(\mathcal{I},\pi)$ is the number of edges in A that are mapped to an edge in B by π, multiplied by $\frac{25}{32}$. Since A is a 4-cycle with one isolated vertex, and B is a 3-cycle plus an edge, at most 2 edges in A can be mapped to B. Therefore, $\mathbf{opt}(\mathcal{I}) = \frac{25}{16}$.

On the other hand, let us consider the following distribution $\mathcal{D}$ of permutations, where $\mathcal{D}$ is supported on π_1 and π_2 with equal probability (1/2). π_1 is the identity permutation; $\pi_2(i) = (i \bmod 5) + 1$ for all $i \in [5]$. We have

$$\begin{aligned}&\mathbf{val}(\mathcal{I},\mathcal{D})\\ =&\frac{25}{64}\cdot\sum_{i,j}\sum_{p,q} A_{i,j}B_{p,q}\frac{1}{2}\left(\mathbf{1}[\pi_1(i)=p \text{ or } \pi_2(i)=p]\right)\\ &\cdot\frac{1}{2}\left(\mathbf{1}[\pi_1(j)=q \text{ or } \pi_2(j)=q]\right)\\ =&\frac{225}{128} > \mathbf{opt}(\mathcal{I}).\end{aligned}$$

Complexity of Approximating CSP with Balance / Hard Constraints *

Venkatesan Guruswami†
Computer Science Department
Carnegie Mellon University
Pittsburgh, PA 15213
guruswami@cmu.edu

Euiwoong Lee‡
Computer Science Department
Carnegie Mellon University
Pittsburgh, PA 15213
euiwoonl@cs.cmu.edu

ABSTRACT

We study two natural extensions of Constraint Satisfaction Problems (CSPs). *Balance*-Max-CSP requires that in any feasible assignment each element in the domain is used an equal number of times. An instance of *Hard*-Max-CSP consists of *soft constraints* and *hard constraints*, and the goal is to maximize the weight of satisfied soft constraints while satisfying *all* the hard constraints. These two extensions contain many fundamental problems not captured by CSPs, and challenge traditional theories about CSPs in a more general framework.

Max-2-SAT and Max-Horn-SAT are the only two nontrivial classes of Boolean CSPs that admit a *robust* satisfibiality algorithm, i.e., an algorithm that finds an assignment satisfying at least $(1-g(\varepsilon))$ fraction of constraints given a $(1-\varepsilon)$-satisfiable instance, where $g(\varepsilon) \to 0$ as $\varepsilon \to 0$, and $g(0) = 0$. We prove the inapproximability of these problems with balance or hard constraints, showing that each variant changes the nature of the problems significantly (in different ways). For instance, deciding whether an instance of 2-SAT admits a balanced assignment is NP-hard, and for Max-2-SAT with hard constraints, it is hard to find a constant-factor approximation even on $(1-\varepsilon)$-satisfiable instances (in particular, the version with hard constraints does not admit a robust satisfiability algorithm).

Categories and Subject Descriptors

F.2.2 [**Analysis of Algorithms and Problem Complexity**]: Nonnumerical Algorithms and Problems

*The full version of this paper is available on ECCC [15].

†Supported in part by a Packard Fellowship and NSF grant CCF-1115525.

‡Supported by a Samsung Fellowship, MSR-CMU Center for Computational Thinking, and NSF CCF-1115525.

ITCS'14, January 12–14, 2014, Princeton, New Jersey, USA.

ACM 978-1-4503-2698-8/14/01 ...$15.00.
http://dx.doi.org/10.1145/2554797.2554837 .

Keywords

complexity dichotomy; constraint satisfaction problem; dictatorship testing; inapproximability; robust satisfiability; unique games conjecture

1. INTRODUCTION

The study of the complexity of Constraint Satisfaction Problems (CSPs) has seen much progress, with beautiful well-developed theories explaining when they admit efficient satisfiability and approximation algorithms. A CSP is specified by a finite set Π of relations (relations can have different arities) over some finite domain Q. An instance of a Max-CSP(Π) consists of a set of variables $X = \{x_1, ..., x_n\}$ and a collection of constraints $C = \{C_1, ..., C_m\}$ each of which is a relation from Π applied to some tuple of variables from X. Constraints are weighted and we assume that $\sum_i \mathsf{wt}(C_i) = 1$. For any assignment $\sigma : X \to Q$, $\mathsf{val}(\sigma)$ is the total weight of satisfied constraints by σ, and our goal is to find σ that maximizes $\mathsf{val}(\sigma)$. We consider two natural extensions of Max-CSP(Π).

DEFINITION 1.1 (CSP WITH BALANCE CONSTRAINTS). *An instance of Balance-Max-CSP(Π) over domain Q, $\mathcal{I} = (X, C)$ consists of set of variables X and a collection of constraints C, as in Max-CSP(Π). An assignment $\sigma : X \to Q$ is called balanced if for each $q \in Q$, $|\sigma^{-1}(q)| = \frac{n}{|Q|}$. Define* $\mathsf{val}_B(\sigma) = \mathsf{val}(\sigma)$ *if σ is balanced, and* $\mathsf{val}_B(\sigma) = 0$ *otherwise. Let* $\mathsf{opt}_B(\mathcal{I}) = \max_\sigma \mathsf{val}_B(\sigma)$. *Our goal is to find σ that maximizes* $\mathsf{val}_B(\sigma)$.

The notion of Balance-Max-CSP is interesting both practically and theoretically. Partitioning a set of objects into equal-sized subsets with desired properties is a basic scheme used in Divide and Conquer algorithm. Balance-Max-Cut, also known as Max-Bisection, is one of the most well-known example of Balance-Max-CSP. Theoretically, the balance constraint is one of the most simple *non-local* constraints where the current algorithmic and hardness results on ordinary CSPs do not work.

DEFINITION 1.2 (CSP WITH HARD CONSTRAINTS). *An instance of Hard-Max-CSP(Π) $\mathcal{I} = (X, S, H)$ consists of set of variables X and a two collections of constraints $S = \{S_1, ..., S_{m_S}\}$ and $H = \{H_1, ..., H_{m_H}\}$ (S stands for* soft *constraints and H stands for* hard *constraints, and only soft constraints are weighted). An assignment $\sigma : X \to Q$ is* feasible *if it satisfies all constraints in H. Let* $\mathsf{val}_H(\sigma)$ *be the total weight of satisfied constraints in S if σ is feasible, and*

0 *otherwise. Let* $\mathsf{opt}_H(\mathcal{I}) = \max_\sigma \mathsf{val}_H(\sigma)$. *Our goal is to find* σ *that maximizes* $\mathsf{val}_H(\sigma)$.

Hard-Max-CSP contains every Max-CSP by definition, and also several additional fundamental combinatorial optimization problems, such as (Hypergraph) Independent Set, Multicut, Graph-k-Coloring, and many other covering/packing problems. While every assignment is *feasible* in ordinary Max-CSP, in Hard-Max-CSP only certain assignments which satisfy all the hard constraints are considered as feasible, giving a more general framework to study combinatorial optimization problems.

By the seminal work of Schaefer [28], there are only three nontrivial classes of Boolean CSPs for which satisfiability can be checked in polynomial time: 2-SAT, Horn-SAT, and LIN-mod-2.[1] Even among them, there is a stark difference in terms of approximability. Hastad [19] showed that for Max-LIN-mod-2, it is NP-hard to find an assignment that satisfies $(\frac{1}{2}+\varepsilon)$ fraction of constraints even when there is an assignment that satisfies $(1-\varepsilon)$ fraction of constraints, for any $\varepsilon > 0$. On the other hand, a series of works [13, 30, 7] showed that Max-2-SAT and Max-Horn-SAT admit a *robust* algorithm, which outputs an assignment satisfying at least $(1 - g(\varepsilon))$ fraction of constraints given a $(1-\varepsilon)$-satisfiable instance, where $g(\varepsilon) \to 0$ as $\varepsilon \to 0$, and $g(0) = 0$. The exact behavior of the function $g()$ for Max-2-SAT and Max-Horn-3SAT has been pinned down under the Unique Games conjecture [22, 17]. Generalizing this, all Boolean CSPs were classified with respect to how well they can be robustly approximated (i.e., the behavior of the function $g(\cdot)$) in [9]. From our perspective, it is natural to investigate the effects of balance and hard constraints applied to the *most tractable* classes of Boolean CSPs (Max-2-SAT, Max-Horn-SAT, Max-Cut) and study how hard each variant becomes. This is the task we undertake in this paper.

Between balance and hard constraints, which one makes the original problem harder? They are not directly comparable since each variant inherits different characteristics of the original problem. For Balance-Max-SAT which includes both Balance-Max-2SAT and Balance-Max-Horn-SAT, it is easy to find σ with $\mathsf{val}_B(\sigma) \geq 0.5$ – choose an arbitrary assignment with the same number of 0's and 1's, and try it and its complement. Therefore, Balance-Max-SAT admits a constant-factor approximation algorithm, but given an instance that admits a balanced satisfying assignment, even for 2-SAT and Horn-SAT, it is not clear how to find such an assignment.

The situation is exactly opposite in the case of Hard-Max-2-SAT or Hard-Max-Horn-SAT. Given an instance $\mathcal{I}$ that admits a satisfying (both hard and soft constraints) assignment (i.e., $\mathsf{opt}_H(\mathcal{I}) = 1$), well-known algorithms for 2-SAT or Horn-SAT will find such an assignment. However, for any $\varepsilon > 0$, when $\mathsf{opt}_H(\mathcal{I}) = 1-\varepsilon$, it is not clear how to find σ such that $\mathsf{val}_H(\sigma) \geq c$ for some absolute constant c, or even $\mathsf{val}_H(\sigma) \geq \varepsilon$. Therefore, adding hard constraints preserves the fact that satisfiability can be checked in polynomial time, but does not preserve a simple constant-factor approximation algorithm.

Though each of balance and hard constraints does not preserve one of the important characteristics of the original CSP in a simple way, there might be a hope that a more sophisticated algorithmic idea gives an efficient algorithm deciding satisfiability for Balance-Max-CSP, a constant-factor approximation algorithm for Hard-Max-CSP, or a robust algorithm for both of them.

1.1 Our Results

In this work, we prove strong hardness results for these problems, proving APX-hardness of deciding satisfiability of balanced versions and Unique Games-hardness of constant factor approximation algorithms on $(1-\varepsilon)$-satisfiable instances of hard versions, of both Max-2-SAT and Max-Horn-SAT. The results are formally stated below.

Balanced CSP. For Balance-Max-2-SAT and Balance-Max-Horn-SAT, the Schaefer-like dichotomy due to [8] for the (decision version of) Boolean Balance-CSP, implies that we cannot efficiently decide whether the given instance is satisfiable or not. (This dichotomy was extended to all domains in [6], which is somewhat surprising given the status of the dichotomy conjecture for CSPs without any balance/cardinality constraint.)

We show the following stronger statement that rules out even a robust satisfiability algorithm for the common special case Balance-Max-Horn-2-SAT.

THEOREM 1.3. *There exists an absolute constant* $\delta > 0$ *such that given an instance* $\mathcal{I}$ *of Balance-Max-Horn-2-SAT (special case of Balance-Max-2-SAT and Balance-Max-Horn-SAT), it is NP-hard to distinguish the following cases.*

- $\mathsf{opt}_B(\mathcal{I}) = 1$
- $\mathsf{opt}_B(\mathcal{I}) \leq 1-\delta$

This result should be contrasted with the fact that a special case of Balance-Max-2-SAT, namely Balance-Max-Cut (Max-Bisection), does admit a robust algorithm [16, 27, 2]. The work [2] also shows that the guaranteed approximation ratio for Balance-Max-2-SAT (which is the worst ratio $\frac{\mathsf{val}_B(\sigma)}{\mathsf{opt}_B(\mathcal{I})}$ over every instance $\mathcal{I}$ and σ found by the algorithm) is indeed equal to the best known approximation ratio for Max-2-SAT [24], i.e., $\alpha_{LLZ} \approx 0.9401$, so adding the balance constraint does not make the problem harder in this regard.

While several nontrivial approximation algorithms for Balance-Max-2-SAT have been studied, as far as we know, no algorithm for Balance-Max-Horn-SAT or even Balance-Max-SAT has been suggested in the literature. Other than the trivial 0.5-approximation algorithm given above, we also show that a slight modification to $\frac{3}{4}$-approximation algorithm due to Goemans and Williamson [13] gives the algorithm with the same ratio.

THEOREM 1.4. *For any* $\varepsilon > 0$, *there is a randomized algorithm such that given an instace* $\mathcal{I}$ *of Balance-Max-SAT, in time poly(size(*$\mathcal{I}$*),* $\frac{1}{\varepsilon}$*), outputs* σ *with* $\mathsf{val}_B(\sigma) \geq (\frac{3}{4} - \varepsilon)\mathsf{opt}_B(\mathcal{I})$ *with constant probability.*

Hard CSP. In Hard-Max-2SAT, robust algorithms are ruled out in a more radical way, assuming the Unique Games Conjecture. In the sequel, we use the phrase "UG-hard" for a decision problem to mean that it is NP-hard under the Unique Games Conjecture (Conjecture 2.3).

[1]An instance of Horn-SAT is a set of Horn clauses, each with at most one unnegated literal. An instance of LIN-mod-2 is linear equations mod 2. Dual-Horn-SAT in which clauses have at most one negated literal also admits an efficient satisfability algorithm, but as it obviously has the same properties as Horn-SAT, we focus on Horn-SAT in this paper.

THEOREM 1.5. *For any $\varepsilon > 0$, given an instance $\mathcal{I}$ of Hard-Max-2-SAT, it is UG-hard to distinguish the following cases.*

- $\mathsf{opt}_H(\mathcal{I}) \geq 1 - \varepsilon$
- $\mathsf{opt}_H(\mathcal{I}) \leq \varepsilon$

The above result again shows a stark difference between Max-2-SAT and Max-Cut since the famous algorithm of Goemans and Williamson [14] works well with hard constraints; if vertices u and v must be separated, we require the vectors corresponding to them to be placed in antipodal positions, and any hyperplane rounding separates them. It shows that Hard-Max-Cut admits *both* a constant-factor approximation algorithm and a robust algorithm while Hard-Max-2-SAT admits *neither* of them.

For Hard-Max-Horn-2-SAT, simple algorithmic and hardness tricks show that finding σ with $\mathsf{val}_H(\sigma) \geq 1 - 2\varepsilon$ given $\mathsf{opt}_H(\mathcal{I}) = 1 - \varepsilon$ is the best possible, assuming the Unique Games Conjecture.

OBSERVATION 1.6. *There is an algorithm that for any $\varepsilon > 0$, if the given instance $\mathcal{I}$ of Max-Horn-2-SAT satisfies $\mathsf{opt}_H(\mathcal{I}) = 1 - \varepsilon$, finds σ with $\mathsf{val}_H(\sigma) \geq 1 - 2\varepsilon$. Furthermore, for any $\varepsilon, \delta > 0$, it is UG-hard to distinguish the following cases.*

- $\mathsf{opt}_H(\mathcal{I}) \geq 1 - \varepsilon - \delta$.
- $\mathsf{opt}_H(\mathcal{I}) \leq 1 - 2\varepsilon + \delta$.

The above algorithmic trick does not work for other robust algorithms, and for Hard-Max-Horn-3-SAT (or higher arities), we have the following NP-hardness result.

THEOREM 1.7. *For any $\varepsilon > 0$, given an instance $\mathcal{I}$ of Hard-Max-Horn-3-SAT, it is NP-hard to distinguish the following cases.*

- $\mathsf{opt}_H(\mathcal{I}) \geq 1 - \varepsilon$
- $\mathsf{opt}_H(\mathcal{I}) \leq \varepsilon$

The complete algorithmic and hardness results are summarized in Table 1 and Table 2.

Ordering constraints over larger domain. If we go beyond the Boolean domain, the situation is not as clear; indeed even satisfiabilities of ordinary CSPs are not completely classified yet. We consider a simple and natural CSP of arity two over larger domains, namely Max-CSP(<) over domain $[q] = \{1, 2, ..., q\}$ – every constraint says that one variable must be less than another. This problem can also be understood as a graph-theoretic problem; given a directed graph $G = (V, E)$, delete the minimum number of edges so that the remaining graph has no *walk* of length q.If the domain is unbounded (indeed, $[n]$ is enough), this is exactly the well-known Max-Acyclic-Subgraph problem.

For all of these problems, a random assignment will give a constant-factor approximation algorithm. We observe that for fixed q, Max-CSP(<) over $[q]$ also admits a robust algorithm, and the same holds also for Hard-Max-CSP(<) over $[q]$. However, we show that adding hard constraints rules out the possibility of a constant-factor approximation algorithm, regardless of whether $[q]$ is fixed or unbounded.

THEOREM 1.8. *For any $k \geq 2$ and $\varepsilon > 0$, given an instance $\mathcal{I}$ of Hard-Max-CSP(<) over $[2k+1]$, it is UG-hard to distinguish the following cases.*

- $\mathsf{opt}_H(\mathcal{I}) \geq (1 - \varepsilon)\frac{k-1}{k}$
- $\mathsf{opt}_H(\mathcal{I}) \leq \varepsilon$

Over $\{1, 2, 3, 4\}$, it is also UG-hard to distinguish whether $\mathsf{opt}_H(\mathcal{I}) \geq \frac{1-\varepsilon}{2}$ or $\mathsf{opt}_H(\mathcal{I}) \leq \varepsilon$.

Also, for any $\varepsilon > 0$, given an instance $\mathcal{I}$ of Hard-Max-CSP(<) over the unbounded domain (an instance of Max-Acyclic-Subgraph with several edges that must be included), it is UG-hard to distinguish the following cases.

- $\mathsf{opt}_H(\mathcal{I}) \geq 1 - \varepsilon$
- $\mathsf{opt}_H(\mathcal{I}) \leq \varepsilon$

We also provide a constant-factor approximation algorithm for Hard-Max-CSP(<) over $\{1, 2, 3\}$ (albeit with a worse ratio than its ordinary counterpart), showing a difference between $\{1, 2, 3\}$ and $\{1, 2, 3, 4\}$, and complete the

		Ordinary
2-SAT	Ratio	0.9401 [24]
	Robust	$(1-\varepsilon, 1-O(\sqrt{\varepsilon}))$ [7]
	Hardness	UG: $(1-\varepsilon, 1-\Omega(\sqrt{\varepsilon}))$ [22]
Max-Cut	Ratio	0.8786 [13]
	Robust	$(1-\varepsilon, 1-O(\sqrt{\varepsilon}))$ [13]
	Hardness	UG: $(1-\varepsilon, 1-\Omega(\sqrt{\varepsilon}))$ [22]
Horn-2-SAT	Ratio	0.9401 [24]
	Robust	$(1-\varepsilon, 1-2\varepsilon)$ [17]
	Hardness	
Horn-SAT	Ratio	0.7968 [4]
	Robust	$(1-\varepsilon, 1-O(\frac{\log\log(1/\varepsilon)}{\log(1/\varepsilon)}))$ [17]
	Hardness	UG: $(1-\varepsilon, 1-\Omega(\frac{1}{\log(1/\varepsilon)}))$ [30]

Table 1: Summary of several Max-CSPs. $\varepsilon > 0$ indicates an arbitrary positive constant. Ratio indicates the best approximation ratio. $(1-\varepsilon, 1-f(\varepsilon))$ in a row labeled Robust indicates that there is a robust algorithm that find an assignment satisfying $(1-f(\varepsilon))$ fraction of constraints given an $(1-\varepsilon)$-satisfiable instance. $(1-\varepsilon, 1-f(\varepsilon))$ in a row labeled Hardness indicates that it is NP-hard to find an assignment satisfying $(1-f(\varepsilon))$ fraction of constraints given an $(1-\varepsilon)$-satisfiable instance. NP indicates that it is an NP-hardness result; UG indicates that it is based on the Unique Games Conjecture.

		Balance	Hard
2-SAT	Ratio	0.9401 [2]	**N/A**
	Robust	**N/A**	**N/A**
	Hardness	**NP:** $(1, 1-\delta)$	**UG:**$(1-\varepsilon, \varepsilon)$
Max-Cut	Ratio	0.8776 [2]	0.8786 [13]
	Robust	Same [27]	Same [13]
	Hardness	Same [22]	Same [22]
Horn-2-SAT	Ratio	0.9401 [2]	**N/A**
	Robust	**N/A**	$(1-\varepsilon, 1-2\varepsilon)$ [17]
	Hardness	**NP:** $(1, 1-\delta)$	**UG:**$(1-\varepsilon, 1-2\varepsilon)$
Horn-SAT	Ratio	**0.75**	**N/A**
	Robust	**N/A**	**N/A**
	Hardness	**NP:** $(1, 1-\delta)$	**NP:**$(1-\varepsilon, \varepsilon)$

Table 2: Summary of several Balance-Max-CSP and Hard-Max-CSP. $\varepsilon > 0$ indicates an arbitrary positive constant, while $\delta > 0$ is a fixed absolute constant. The results of this work are in boldface. N/A means that a robust or constant-factor approximation algorithm are ruled out by the hardness results.

picture of the approximability of these Ordering CSPs with hard constraints. The proofs and more detailed discussion can be found in the full version of this paper available on ECCC [15].

1.2 Discussion

Max-Cut is one of the simplest and well-studied CSPs. Its variants with balance or hard variants also inherit the desirable algorithmic properties of the original version — in particular both these variants admit robust satisfiability as well as constant-factor approximation algorithms. However, these algorithmic results do not extend even slightly more general CSPs; in Max-2-SAT, even one of balance and hard variants rule out the possibility of a robust algorithm. Furthermore, Hard-Max-2-SAT does not have a constant-factor approximation algorithm as well, and the hardness result for Balance-Max-2-SAT also holds for Balance-Max-Horn-2-SAT (which does not even capture Max-Cut).

These delicate differences even for CSPs of arity two over Boolean domain (where satisfiability is always in P) suggest that adding balance or hard constraints highlights previously unnoticed characteristics with respect to the approximability of each predicate. This work settles the approximability of almost all interesting arity two CSPs over Boolean domain, demonstrating the effect of hard and balance constraints on some classic problems.

While our techniques are relatively simple twists to known ones (with the one underlying the inapproximability of Hard-Max-2-SAT being the most significant), we think the body of results highlights subtle (and perhaps surprising) differences between CSPs in the presence of hard/balance constraints, and raises the challenge of extending our study to larger arity or domains. Attempts at such a generalization should be interesting by itself and also illuminate new aspects of CSPs.

In this regard, we record some simple observations on robust algorithms for Hard-Max-CSP(Π). In the weighted minimization version (Min-Uncut, Min-CNF-Deletion and Min-Feedback-Arc-Set are minimization versions of some problems we studied in this work), where the goal is to *minimize* the weight of *unsatisfied* constraints, hard constraints do not add to the difficulty of the original version as can be seen via the simple trick of converting all hard constraints to soft constraints and giving them large enough weight. Therefore, a constant-factor approximation algorithm for the minimization version will yield a robust satisfiability algorithm for Hard-Max-CSP(Π) as well. In general we do not have a reduction in the reverse direction as the robust algorithm might be allowed runtime exponential in ε (e.g. $n^{O(\frac{1}{\varepsilon})}$) on $(1-\varepsilon)$-satisfiable instances. Also, when the approximation factor for the minimization version depends on the instance size (e.g. $O(\sqrt{\log n})$ for Min-CNF-Deletion [1]), we do not automatically get a robust algorithm for the associated CSP with hard constraints.

We have an example, namely Hard-Max-2-SAT, where constant-factor and robust approximations are both hard in the presence of hard constraints, and an example (Hard-Max-Horn-2-SAT) where robust approximation is possible but a constant-factor approximation is hard. It is easy to see that Hard-Max-Lin-mod-2 admits an efficient constant factor approximation but not a robust algorithm; its ordinary version (without hard constraints), however, also has the same property. This raises the following interesting question: Is there a CSP which admits an efficient robust satisfiability algorithm, and whose hard version admits a constant-factor approximation algorithm but no robust algorithm? Or must a robust algorithm also exist for the hard version under these conditions?

1.3 Organization

Section 2 proves the results about Hard-CSP; Hard-Max-2-SAT in Section 2.2 and Hard-Max-Horn-SAT in Section 2.3. This section requires some understanding of the inner workings of the reduction from Unique Games to Min-Vertex-Cover [23, 5], so we present the relevant preliminaries in Section 2.1. Section 3 proves the results about Balance-CSP; hardness results in Section 3.1 and algorithmic results in Section 3.2.

2. CSP WITH HARD CONSTRAINTS

2.1 Preliminaries

Unique Games.

Our hardness result for Hard-Max-2-SAT relies on the Unique Games Conjecture [21], which is stated below.

DEFINITION 2.1. *An instance $\mathcal{L}(G(V,W,E),[R],\{\pi(v,w)\}_{(v,w)\in E})$ of Unique Games consists of a regular bipartite graph $G(V,W,E)$ and a set $[R]$ of labels. For each edge $(v,w)\in E$ there is a constraint specified by a permutation $\pi(v,w):[R]\to[R]$. The goal is to find a labeling $l: V\cup W\to[R]$ of the vertices such that as many edges as possible are satisfied, where an edge $e=(v,w)$ is said to be satisfied if $l(v)=\pi(v,w)(l(w))$.*

DEFINITION 2.2. *Given a Unique Games instance $\mathcal{L}$, let $\mathsf{opt}(\mathcal{L})$ denote the maximum fraction of simultaneously satisfied edges of $\mathcal{L}$ by any labeling, i.e.*

$$\mathsf{opt}(\mathcal{L}) := \frac{1}{|E|}\max_{l:V\cup W\to[R]} |\{e\in E : l \text{ satisfies } e\}|$$

CONJECTURE 2.3 ([21]). *For any constants $\varepsilon>0$, there is $R=R(\varepsilon)$ such that, for a Unique Games instance $\mathcal{L}$ with label set $[R]$, it is NP-hard to distinguish between*

- $\mathsf{opt}(\mathcal{L})\geq 1-\varepsilon$.
- $\mathsf{opt}(\mathcal{L})\leq \varepsilon$.

To show the optimal hardness result for Min-Vertex-Cover, Khot and Regev [23] introduced the following stronger conjecture, and proved that it is in fact equivalent to the original the Unique Games Conjecture.

CONJECTURE 2.4 ([23]). *For any constants $\varepsilon>0$, there is $R=R(\varepsilon)$ such that, for a Unique Games instance $\mathcal{L}$ with label set $[R]$, it is NP-hard to distinguish between*

- *There is a set $V'\subseteq V$ such that $|V'|\geq(1-\varepsilon)|V|$ and a labeling $l: V\cup W\to[R]$ that satisfies every edge (v,w) for $v\in V'$ and $w\in W$.*
- $\mathsf{opt}(\mathcal{L})\leq \varepsilon$.

Fourier Analysis on Biased Hypercubes.

Fix $p = 1/2 - \varepsilon$ for some $\varepsilon > 0$. We let $\{0,1\}^R_{(p)}$ be the R-dimensional boolean hypercube with p-biased distribution; each coordinate of $x \in \{0,1\}^R_{(p)}$ is independently set to 1 with probability p and 0 with probability $1-p$. Let $f : \{0,1\}^n_{(p)} \to \mathbb{R}$.

DEFINITION 2.5. *The* influence *of the ith coordinate on f is given by*

$$\mathsf{Inf}_i(f) = \mathbb{E}_{(x_j)_{j\neq i}}[\mathsf{Var}_{x_i}[f(x)|(x_j)_{j\neq i}]]$$

DEFINITION 2.6. *Let $\rho \in [-p/(1-p), 1]$. The* noisy operator *T_ρ acts on f by*

$$T_\rho f(x) = \mathbb{E}_y[f(y)] \ ,$$

where each bit y_i of y is independently sampled such that it is equal to x_i with probability ρ and sampled according to p-biased distribution with probability $(1-\rho)$. We call

$$\mathsf{Inf}_i(T_\rho f)$$

the noisy influence *of the ith coordinate.*

2.2 Hard-Max-2-SAT

At the heart of every hardness result based on the Unique Games Conjecture is an appropriate dictatorship test. The dictatorship test for Min-Vertex-Cover (and its maximization version Max-Independent-Set) is a graph $G = (V, E)$ where $V = \{0,1\}^R_{(p)}$ (vertices are weighted according to p-biased distribution). This graph must ensure that

- Completeness: For each $1 \leq i \leq R$, ith dictator function $f_i(x_1, ..., x_R) = x_i$ is the indicator function of a large independent set.
- Soundness: For every moderate-sized independent set D, its indicator function has a coordinate with large noisy influence.

The edges are constructed such that there is an edge between $(x_1, ..., x_R)$ and $(y_1, ..., y_R)$ if and only if there is no coordinate i such that $x_i = y_i = 1$. The first condition can be easily checked since $f_i(x) = f_i(y) = 1$ for some i means $x_i = y_i = 1$ and there is no edge between x and y. This construction was first used in Khot and Regev [23]. Later Austrin et al. [3] gave a different (and arguably simpler) analysis of the same test, relying on the invariance principle of Mossel et al. [25].

THEOREM 2.7 (IMPLICIT IN [3]). *Let $G = (V, E)$ be the graph constructed as above.*

- *Completeness: For each $1 \leq i \leq R$, ith dictator function $f_i(x_1, ..., x_R) = x_i$ is the indicator function of a large independent set of weight p.*
- *Soundness: For every $\varepsilon > 0$, there exist $\tau > 0$ and $\delta > 0$ such that the following holds. If D is an independent set of weight at least ε and $f : \{0,1\}^R_{(p)} \to \{0,1\}$ is the indicator function of D, then there exists i such that $\mathsf{Inf}_i(T_{1-\delta}f) \geq \tau$.*

Combined with the standard technique converting a dictatorship test to a hardness result based on the Unique Games Conjecture, it is shown that it is UG-hard to distinguish whether the maximum independent set has weight at least $1/2 - \varepsilon$ or at most ε.

There is a simple approximation-preserving reduction from Max-Independent-Set to Hard-Max-Horn-2-SAT. Given G constructed as above,

- $X = V$; each variable corresponds to one vertex.
- For each edge $(x, y) \in E$, add a hard constraint $(\neg x \vee \neg y)$.
- For each vertex $x \in V$, add a soft constraint x.

Hard constraints ensure that two variables corresponding to neighboring vertices cannot be set to True simultaneously, and maximizing the total weight of satisfied soft constraints is equivalent to maximizing the total weight of the vertices set to True. Therefore, the same hardness result also holds for Hard-Max-2-SAT. This hardness result rules out any constant-factor approximation algorithm, but does not apply to instances that are almost satisfiable. In fact, Hard-Max-Horn-2-SAT inherits the same hardness result (as the above reduction only uses Horn clauses), but it has a robust algorithm (See Section 2.3).

Our crucial observation to *amplify* this gap to $1-\varepsilon$ and ε is that dictatorship functions always give different values to a pair of antipodal points. Since our predicate is a disjunction of two variables (vertices), if we change soft constraints so that

$$S = \left\{(u \vee v) : \{u, v\} \text{ is an antipodal pair in } \{0,1\}^R_{(p)}\right\}$$

Then, every dictator function f_i will satisfy all the hard and soft constraints. To ensure the soundness, we have to *perturb* the distribution a little bit, but still almost all the weight will be concentrated around antipodal points. Given the dictatorship test $G = (V, E)$ for Min-Vertex-Cover, the dictatorship test for Hard-Max-2-SAT is $\mathcal{I} = (X, S, H)$ such that

- $X = V$; each variable corresponds to one vertex.
- For each edge $(x, y) \in E$, add a hard constraint $(\neg x \vee \neg y)$.
- Sample an ordered pair (x, y) such that for each i,

  $$\mathbb{P}[x_i = y_i = 0] = 2\varepsilon$$

  and

  $$\mathbb{P}[x_i = 1, y_i = 0] = \mathbb{P}[x_i = 0, y_i = 1] = 1/2 - \varepsilon \ .$$

  Add a soft constraint $(x \vee y)$ with the weight equal to the probability of (x, y).

With this trick, we can obtain a dictatorship test for Hard-Max-2-SAT with a much larger gap.

THEOREM 2.8. *Let $\mathcal{I} = (X, S, H)$ be the instance of Hard-Max-2-SAT constructed as above.*

- *Completeness: For each $1 \leq i \leq R$, ith dictator function $f_i(x_1, ..., x_R) = x_i$ satisfies $\mathsf{val}_H(f_i) = 1 - 2\varepsilon$.*
- *Soundness: For every $\varepsilon > 0$, there exist $\tau > 0$ and $\delta > 0$ such that the following holds. If $f : \{0,1\}^R_{(p)} \to \{0,1\}$ satisfies $\mathsf{val}_H(f) \geq 2\varepsilon$, then there exists i such that $\mathsf{Inf}_i(T_{1-\delta}f) \geq \tau$.*

PROOF. COMPLETENESS: It is already shown that ith dictator function f_i satisfies all the hard constraints. The only soft constraints that f_i fail to satisfy is $(x \vee y)$ where $x_i = y_i = 0$. Since the probability of picking $x_i = y_i = 0$ is 2ε, $\mathsf{val}_H(f_i) = 1 - 2\varepsilon$.

SOUNDNESS: If f is a function that satisfies all the hard constraints, it is also the indicator function of some independent set D. We claim that the weight of D in $\{0,1\}^R_{(p)}$ with $p = 1/2 - \varepsilon$ is at least $\mathsf{val}_H(f_i)/2$. For $z \in \{0,1\}^R_{(p)}$, let $\mathsf{deg}(z)$ be the sum of the weights of soft constraints $(z \vee x)$ or $(x \vee z)$ for some x ($(z \vee z)$ contributes twice). $(x, y) \sim S$ indicates that it is sampled according to its weight defined above. Note that its marginal distribution of x (and y) is exactly the p-biased distribution on $\{0,1\}^R_{(p)}$. Therefore,

$$\begin{aligned}\mathsf{deg}(z) &= \mathbb{P}_{(x,y)\sim S}[z = x] + \mathbb{P}_{(x,y)\sim S}[z = y] \\ &= 2\,\mathbb{P}_{(x,y)\sim S}[z = x] \\ &= 2\,\mathbb{P}_{x\sim\{0,1\}^R_{(p)}}[z = x] \\ &= 2\,\mathsf{wt}(z)\ .\end{aligned}$$

It means that for any z, switching $f(z)$ from 0 to 1 increases $\mathsf{val}_H(f)$ by at most $2\mathsf{wt}(z)$. Therefore, $\mathsf{val}_H(f)$ is at most two times the weight of D. Thus $\mathsf{val}_H(f) \geq 2\varepsilon$ indicates that the weight of D is at least ε. We can now use Theorem 2.7 to finish the argument. □

Combined with the standard technique converting a dictatorship test to a hardness result based on the Unique Games Conjecture, the main theorem of this section is proved.

THEOREM 2.9 (RESTATEMENT OF THEOREM 1.5). *For any $\varepsilon > 0$, given an instance $\mathcal{I}$ of Hard-Max-2-SAT, it is UG-hard to distinguish the following cases.*

- $\mathsf{opt}_H(\mathcal{I}) \geq 1 - \varepsilon$
- $\mathsf{opt}_H(\mathcal{I}) \leq \varepsilon$

PROOF. Given an instance of $\mathcal{L}(G(V, W, E), [R], \{\pi(v, w)\})$ of Unique Games, we construct an instance $\mathcal{I} = (X, S, H)$ of Hard-Max-2-SAT.

- $X = V \times \{0,1\}^R$. The weight of (v, x) is the weight of x in $\{0,1\}^R_{(1/2-\varepsilon)}$, divided by $|V|$ (weights are only used in the analysis).
- For every pair of edges $(w, v_1), (w, v_2)$ with the same endpoint $w \in W$, and every $x, y \in \{0,1\}^R$, such that there is no i such that $x_{\pi(v_1,w)(i)} = y_{\pi(v_2,w)(i)} = 1$, add a hard constraint $(\neg(v_1, x) \vee \neg(v_2, y))$.
- For each v, sample an ordered pair (x, y) such that for each i, $\mathbb{P}[x_i = y_i = 0] = 2\varepsilon$ and $\mathbb{P}[x_i = 1, y_i = 0] = \mathbb{P}[x_i = 0, y_i = 1] = 1/2 - \varepsilon$. Add a soft constraint $((v, x) \vee (v, y))$ with the weight equal to the probability of (x, y) divided by $|V|$.

Note that the variables and hard constraints of this construction are identical to that of Min-Vertex-Cover (Max-Independent-Set) of [3]. We use the variant of the Unique Games Conjecture (see Conjecture 2.4), and prove the following:

LEMMA 2.10. *Given an instance of Unique Games $\mathcal{L}$ and the instance $\mathcal{I}$ produced as above,*

- *If there is a set $V' \subseteq V$ such that $|V'| \geq (1 - \varepsilon)|V|$ and a labeling $l : V \cup W \to [R]$ that satisfies every edge (v, w) for $v \in V'$ and $w \in W$, then $\mathsf{opt}_H(\mathcal{I}) \geq 1 - 3\varepsilon$.*
- *There is a function $f : \mathbb{R}^+ \to \mathbb{R}^+$ such that if $\mathsf{opt}(\mathcal{L}) \leq f(\varepsilon)$, then $\mathsf{opt}_H(\mathcal{I}) \leq 2\varepsilon$.*

PROOF. We establish the completeness and soundness in turn.

COMPLETENESS: Let $V' \subseteq V$ and $l : V \cup W \to [R]$ be a subset and a labeling satisfying the above condition. For any $v \in V', x \in \{0,1\}$, set $(v, x) = x_{l(v)}$. If $v \notin V'$, $(v, x) = 0$ for all x. Note that this satisfies all the hard constraints; if there is a violated hard constraint $(\neg(v_1, x) \vee \neg(v_2, y))$, it means that $v_1, v_2 \in V'$, $x_{l(v_1)} = y_{l(v_2)} = 1$, but there exists $w \in W$ such that $\pi(v_1, w)(l(w)) = l(v_1), \pi(v_2, w)(l(w)) = l(v_2)$. It contradicts the above construction. For each v, the only soft constraints $((v, x) \vee (v, y))$ that are not satisfied by this assignment have $x_{l(v)} = y_{l(v)} = 0$, which happens with probability 2ε. Therefore, the total weight of soft constraints satisfied is at least $(1 - \varepsilon)(1 - 2\varepsilon) \geq 1 - 3\varepsilon$.

SOUNDNESS: Suppose there is an assignment $\sigma : V \times \{0,1\}^R \to \{0,1\}$ such that it satisfies all the hard constraints and $\mathsf{val}_H(\sigma) \geq 2\varepsilon$. Let $D \subseteq V \times \{0,1\}^R$ be the support of σ. Since σ satisfies all the hard constraints, D is an independent set of the graph whose vertex set is $V \times \{0,1\}^R$ and each pair of variables in a same hard constraint forms an edge. Note that this is the same graph used in the hardness of Min-Vertex-Cover in [3].

Since the soft constraints are defined within each hypercube $v \times \{0,1\}$ for each v, we can use the same analysis from Theorem 2.8 (which says that the sum of weights of the soft constraints containing a variable in the Hard-Max-2-SAT instance is exactly two times the weight of the corresponding vertex in the Max-Independent-Set instance) to conclude that the weight of D is at least ε. We can invoke Theorem 3.1 of [3] to argue that $\mathsf{opt}(\mathcal{L}) \geq f(\varepsilon)$ for some fixed function $f : \mathbb{R}^+ \to \mathbb{R}^+$. □

Therefore, if we can distinguish whether $\mathsf{opt}_H(\mathcal{L}) \geq 1 - 3\varepsilon$ or $\mathsf{opt}_H(\mathcal{L}) \leq 2\varepsilon$ for some $\varepsilon > 0$, then we can refute Conjecture 2.4, which is equivalent to the original Unique Games Conjecture. This proves Theorem 1.5.

2.3 Hard-Max-Horn-SAT

Suppose there is a very strong robust algorithm for Max-CSP(Π) in the sense that if the algorithm can find σ such that $\mathsf{val}_H(\sigma) \geq 1 - c\varepsilon$ whenever $\mathsf{opt}_H(\mathcal{I}) \geq 1 - \varepsilon$ for some absolute constant c (or in other words, we have a constant-factor approximation algorithm for the minimization version that seeks to minimize the weight of unsatisfied constraints). The performance of this algorithm is preserved for Hard-Max-CSP(Π) by the following trick: convert all hard constraints to soft constraints, but give them very large weight so that they will never be violated in the optimal solution. This will result in $\mathcal{I}'$ such that $\mathsf{opt}(\mathcal{I}') \geq 1 - \varepsilon'$ where $\varepsilon' \ll \varepsilon$, but the algorithm still finds σ such that $\mathsf{val}_H(\sigma) \geq 1 - c\varepsilon'$ as a solution to $\mathcal{I}'$, which also satisfies $\mathsf{val}_H(\sigma) \geq 1 - c\varepsilon$ as a solution to $\mathcal{I}$.

Now, Max-Horn-2-SAT is a problem that admits such a robust algorithm with $c = 2$ [17] ($c = 3$ was earlier shown in [20]), and therefore we can conclude that Hard-Horn-2-SAT admits a similar robust algorithm.

Furthermore, the reduction from Max-Independent-Set to Hard-Max-2-SAT introduced in Section 2.3 is an indeed a reduction to Hard-Max-Horn-2-SAT. Therefore, by previous results about Max-Independent-Set [23, 5], for any $\varepsilon > 0$, it is UG-hard to find σ with $\mathsf{val}_H(\sigma) \geq \varepsilon$ even when $\mathsf{opt}_H(\mathcal{I}) \geq 1/2 - \varepsilon$. By adding many dummy constraints that are always satisfiable, for any $\varepsilon, \delta > 0$, it is NP-hard to find σ with $\mathsf{val}_H(\sigma) \geq 1 - 2\varepsilon + \delta$ even when $\mathsf{opt}_H(\mathcal{I}) \geq 1 - \varepsilon - \delta$. These facts justfy the following observation made about Hard-Max-Horn-2-SAT.

OBSERVATION 2.11 (RESTATEMENT OF OBSERVATION 1.6). *There is an algorithm that for any $\varepsilon \geq 0$, if the given instance $\mathcal{I}$ of Max-Horn-2-SAT satisfies $\mathsf{opt}_H(\mathcal{I}) = 1-\varepsilon$, finds σ with $\mathsf{val}_H(\sigma) \geq 1 - 2\varepsilon$.*

Furthermore, for any $\varepsilon, \delta > 0$, it is UG-hard to distinguish the following cases.

- $\mathsf{opt}(\mathcal{I}) \geq 1 - \varepsilon - \delta$.
- $\mathsf{opt}(\mathcal{I}) \leq 1 - 2\varepsilon + \delta$.

The above algorithmic result for Max-Horn-2-SAT does not hold for Max-Horn-SAT in general since the robust algorithm is only guaranteed to find an assignment satisfying $1-O\left(\frac{\log\log(1/\varepsilon)}{\log(1/\varepsilon)}\right)$ fraction of clauses [30], and this exponential loss is inherent under the Unique Games conjecture [17]. In fact, even Horn-3-SAT is powerful enough to encode constraints of other hard problems with unbounded arity, which results in a very strong hardness result, stated below.[2]

THEOREM 2.12 (RESTATEMENT OF THEOREM 1.7). *For any $\varepsilon > 0$, given an instance $\mathcal{I}$ of Hard-Max-Horn-3-SAT, it is NP-hard to distinguish the following cases.*

- $\mathsf{opt}_H(\mathcal{I}) \geq 1 - \varepsilon$
- $\mathsf{opt}_H(\mathcal{I}) \leq \varepsilon$

PROOF. We reduce Max-Ek-Hypergraph-Independent-Set to Max-Horn-3-SAT. An instance of Max-Ek-Hypergraph-Independent-Set is a hypergraph $G = (V, E)$ where each hyperedge $e \in E$ contains exactly k vertices. Our goal is to find a set $D \subseteq V$ with the maximum weight such that no hyperedge e is a subset of D.

Given a graph $G = (V, E)$, we construct the instance $\mathcal{I} = (X, S, H)$ of Max-Horn-3-SAT as follows.

- $X = V \cup \{y_{e,j} : e \in E, 1 \leq j \leq k\}$; there is one variable for each vertex, and k variables for each hyperedge. Each variable corresponding to a vertex indicates that the vertex is picked or not.
- For each hyperedge $e = (v_1, ..., v_k) \in E$, add hard constraints
  - $(v_1 \to \neg y_{e,1}) \equiv (\neg v_1 \vee \neg y_{e,1})$
  - $2 \leq j \leq k$: $(\neg y_{e,i-1} \wedge v_i \to \neg y_{e,i}) \equiv (y_{e,i-1} \vee \neg v_i \vee \neg y_{e,i})$
  - $y_{e,k}$
- For each vertex $v \in V$, add a soft constraint v with the same weight as in G.

[2]We learned from Andrei Krokhin that this result, with essentially the same proof, was also shown by Siavosh Bennabas. But as we are not aware of a published reference, we include the simple proof.

The above construction ensures that there is at most one unnegated literal per each clause, so this is indeed an instance of Max-Horn-3-SAT. Once $v_1, ..., v_n$ are fixed, a quick check of the second set of constraints corresponding to hyperedge e ensures that there exists $y_{e,1}, ..., y_{e,k}$ that satisfy all the constraints if and only if at least one of $v_1, ..., v_k$ is set to False. Since the weight of satisfied soft constraints is equal to the weight of vertices picked, this is an approximation-preserving reduction from Max-Ek-Hypergraph-Independent-Set to Max-Horn-3-SAT. Dinur et al [10] showed that for the former, it is NP-hard to distinguish

- There is an independent set of weight $(1 - \frac{1}{k-1} - \varepsilon)$.
- Every independent set is of weight at most ε.

By taking k large and ε small, we get the desired result for Max-Horn-3-SAT. □

3. BALANCE CONSTRAINTS

3.1 Hardness Results

THEOREM 3.1 (RESTATEMENT OF THEOREM 1.3). *There exists an absolute constant $\delta > 0$ such that given an instance $\mathcal{I}$ of Balance-Max-Horn-2-SAT (special case of Balance-Max-2-SAT and Balance-Max-Horn-SAT), it is NP-hard to distinguish the following cases.*

- $\mathsf{opt}_B(\mathcal{I}) = 1$
- $\mathsf{opt}_B(\mathcal{I}) \leq 1 - \delta$

PROOF. We reduce from Max-3-SAT(B) to Max-Independent-Set to Balance-Max-Horn-2-SAT, where in Max-3-SAT(B) each variable occurs at most B times. The following description of the reduction from Max-3-SAT(B) to Max-Independent Set is from Papadimitriou and Yannakakis [26].

> *Construct a graph with one node for every occurrence of every literal. There is an edge connecting any two occurrences of complementary literals, and also, an edge connecting literal occurrences from the same clause (thus, there is a triangle for every clause with 3 literals, and an edge for a clause with 2 literals). The size of the maximum independent set in the graph is equal to the maximum number of clauses that can be satisfied. If every variable occurs at most B times in the clauses, then the degree is at most $B + 1$.*

Note that in the above reduction, there is an independent set of size l if and only if there is an assignment that satisfies l clauses. For some constants B and $\delta_0 > 0$, it is NP-hard to find an assignment satisfying $(1 - \delta_0)$ fraction of clauses in a satisfiable instance of Max-3-SAT(B). Let m be the number of clauses, and n be the number of variables of the given Max-3-SAT(B) instance, so we have $3m$ vertices, and at most $1.5(B+1)m \leq 2Bm$ edges in the graph. Our Balance-Max-Horn-2-SAT instance $\mathcal{I}$ consists of $4m$ variables; $3m$ of them correspond to the vertices of the graph, and m of them do not participate in any constraint. For each edge (u, v) we add the constraint $(\neg u \vee \neg v)$. Finally, we have the balance constraint that exactly $2m$ of them should be 1 (1 means True in 2-SAT, and that the vertex is picked in the Independent Set problem).

If the Max-3-SAT instance is satisfiable, we have an independent set of size $2m$ consisting of m vertices from the graph and m of the dummy vertices, so the Balance-Max-Horn-2-SAT instance is also satisfiable.

Now suppose that $\mathsf{opt}_B(\mathcal{I}) > 1-\delta$. This means that there is a balanced assignment (at least m 1's amongst the non-dummy variables) such that at most a fraction δ of the edges have both endpoints set to 1. By switching $2\delta Bm$ vertices from 1 to 0, all clauses of Balance-Max-Horn-2-SAT will be satisfied. This means that there is an independent set of size at least $(1-2\delta B)m$, and therefore also an assignment that satisfies $(1-2\delta B)m$ clauses of the Max-3-SAT(B) instance. It follows that we must have $\delta \geq \frac{\delta_0}{2B}$. □

Unlike the reduction from Max-Independent-Set to Hard-Max-Horn-2-SAT introduced in Section 2.2 (hard clauses for independence constraints, and soft clauses for the objective), we use clauses to enforce independence constraints, and the balance constraint to maximize the objective. For the soundness analysis, given a good assignment to Balance-Max-Horn-2-SAT, when viewed as a (slightly infeasible) solution to Max-Independent-Set, the balance constraint ensures that the objective is good, but there might be some adjacent vertices picked. The bounded degrees allow us to fix this solution to an independent set while still retaining many vertices.

3.2 Algorithmic Results

One of the most well-studied Balance-Max-CSP is Balance-Max-Cut (Max-Bisection). Over a long line of work [12, 18, 29, 11, 27, 2], the approximation ratio for Max-Bisection has become 0.8776 which is very close to the optimal (under the Unique Games Conjecture) approximation ratio for Max-Cut which is about 0.8786. Max-Bisection admits a robust algorithm as well [16, 27]. Note that Balance-Max-CSP(Π) is no easier to approximate than Max-CSP(Π), since any instance of Max-CSP(Π) can be reduced to an instance of Balance-Max-CSP(Π) by adding dummy variables that do not participate in any constraint.

For Balance-Max-2-SAT, the best known approximation ratio is 0.9401, matching the best known approximation ratio of Max-2-SAT [24]. This result indicates that in the approximation ratio perspective, adding the balance constraint does not make the problem harder. However, Theorem 3.1 rules out any robust algorithm for Balance-Max-2-SAT, which shows a stark difference between the balanced versions of Max-2-SAT and Max-Cut.

For Balance-Max-Horn-SAT, the same hardness result shows that we cannot hope for any robust algorithm. Therefore, the only remaining quetion is whether there is an algorithm whose approximation ratio nearly matches that of the best algorithm for ordinary Max-Horn-SAT. The best approximation ratio for Max-Horn-SAT is achieved by an algorithm for more general Max-SAT, which achieves 0.7968-approximation [4].[3]

The most recent results on Balance-Max-Cut and Balance-Max-2-SAT [27, 2] rely on Lasserre SDP hierarchies. The purpose of using a more sophisticated SDP rather than the basic SDP of Goemans and Williamson [14], is that during the rounding scheme, the vertices are not rounded independently; even if we add the balance constraint in the SDP relaxation, the final solution is not guaranteed to be approximately balanced when we do not have a guarantee about their correlations. The goal of Lasserre hierarchies is to produce an SDP solution with low global correlation so that each vertex can be rounded almost independently.

However, in the 3/4-approximation algorithm for Max-SAT by Goemans and Williamson [13], which is based on a LP-relaxation, each variable is rounded independently. Therefore, adding the balance constraint ensures that the final solution is almost balanced by a simple application of Chernoff bound. After a simple correction phase to get perfect balance (slightly more sophisticated than [27] since the arity is not bounded), we obtain an algorithm which is not far from the best algorithm for Max-SAT in terms of approximation ratio.

Theorem 3.2 (Restatement of Theorem 1.4). *For any $\varepsilon > 0$, there is a randomized algorithm such that given an instace $\mathcal{I}$ of Balance-Max-SAT, in time poly(size($\mathcal{I}$), $\frac{1}{\varepsilon}$), outputs σ with $\mathsf{val}_B(\sigma) \geq (\frac{3}{4}-\varepsilon)\mathsf{opt}_B(\mathcal{I})$ with constant probability.*

Proof. Let $\mathcal{I} = (X, C)$ be an instance Balance-Max-SAT, where $X = \{x_1, ..., x_n\}$ is the set of variables and $C = \{C_1, ..., C_m\}$ is the set of clauses. For each $1 \leq j \leq m$, let C_j^+ (resp. C_j^-) be the set of variables which appear in C_j *unnegated* (resp. *negated*). The following is a natural LP relaxation of Balance-Max-SAT.

$$\begin{aligned} \text{maximize} \quad & \sum_{j=1}^{m} \mathsf{wt}(C_j) z_j \\ \text{subject to} \quad & \forall 1 \leq j \leq m : \sum_{i \in C_j^+} y_i + \sum_{i \in C_j^-} (1-y_i) \geq z_j \\ & \forall 1 \leq j \leq m : 0 \leq z_j \leq 1 \\ & \forall 1 \leq i \leq n : 0 \leq y_i \leq 1 \\ & \sum_{i=1}^{n} y_i = \frac{n}{2} \end{aligned}$$

Given the solution (y_i, z_j) to the above LP, the rounding algorithm is simple:

1. Choose $a \in \{0,1\}$ uniformly at random.
2. If $a = 0$, set $\sigma(x_i) = 1$ with probability y_i independently; if $a = 1$, set $\sigma(x_i) = 1$ with probability 0.5 independently.
3. If the final solution is unbalanced (there exists $b \in \{0,1\}$ such that $|\sigma^{-1}(b)| = (0.5+\eta)n$ for some $\eta > 0$), pick exactly ηn variables from $\sigma^{-1}(b)$, set them to $1-b$.
4. Iterate it $O(1/\varepsilon)$ times.

Claim 3.3. *At the end of step 2, $\mathbb{E}[\mathsf{val}(\sigma)] \geq 3/4$ (note that it is $\mathsf{val}(\sigma)$, but not $\mathsf{val}_B(\sigma)$).*

Proof. For each C_j, let k be the number of variables in C_j and without loss of generality assume $C_j = x_1 \vee ... \vee x_k$ by renaming and negating variables. If $a = 0$, the probability that C_j is satisfied is

$$1-\Pi_{i=1}^{k}(1-y_i) \geq 1-(\frac{\sum_{i=1}^{k}(1-y_i)}{k})^k \geq 1-(1-\frac{z_i}{k})^k \geq \beta_k z_i$$

where $\beta_k = 1-(1-\frac{1}{k})^k$. If $a = 1$, the probability that C_j is satisfied is at least $\alpha_k = 1-2^{-k}$. Overall, the probability

[3]The same paper gives another algorithm whose approximation ratio is 0.8434 under some conjecture.

that C_j is satisfied is $\frac{\alpha_k+\beta_k}{2}$. For $k=1,2$, $\frac{\alpha_k+\beta_k}{2}=\frac{3}{4}$, and for $k\geq 3$, $\frac{\alpha_k+\beta_k}{2}\geq \frac{7/8+(1-1/e)}{2}\geq \frac{3}{4}$. □

By a simple averaging argument, with probability at least ε, $\mathsf{val}(\sigma)\geq 3/4-\varepsilon$. Since each variable is rounded independently once a is fixed, by Chernoff bound, $\mathbb{P}[|\sigma^{-1}(1)-\frac{n}{2}|>\varepsilon n]\leq 2exp(-\frac{2\varepsilon^2}{n})=o_n(1)$. Therefore, at the end of step 2, the probability that $\mathsf{val}(\sigma)\geq 3/4-\varepsilon$ and $|\sigma^{-1}(1)-\frac{n}{2}|\leq \varepsilon n$ is at least $\varepsilon/2$.

Let b be such that $|\sigma^{-1}(b)|=(1/2+\eta)n$ for some $0<\eta\leq\varepsilon$. In step 3, we randomly choose ηn variables from $\sigma^{-1}(b)$, and set them to $1-b$. Fix a constraint C_j that is satisfied by σ. Since C_j is a disjunction, there is only one assignment to the variables appearing C_j that makes C_j unsatisfied. Since C_j is already satisfied, to reach the only unsatisfying assignment, at least one variable must be switched. If there is a variable that must be switched from $1-b$ to b, then C_j is guaranteed to be satisfied even after step 3. Otherwise, there are k variables ($k\geq 1$) that must be swithced from b to $1-b$, and the probability of switching all of them is at most the probability of switching one of them, which is $\frac{\eta n}{(1/2+\eta)n}\leq 2\eta$. Therefore, in expectation, at most 2η fraction of already satisfied clauses can be unsatisfied, and with probability half, at most $4\eta\leq 4\varepsilon$ fraction of satisfied clauses can be unsatisfied. Combining step 2 and 3, in each iteration, we get a balanced σ with $\mathsf{val}_B(\sigma)\leq 3/4-5\varepsilon$ with probability $\varepsilon/4$. This probability can be made to a constant by repeating $O(1/\varepsilon)$ times.

Acknowledgments

We thank Andrei Krokhin for raising the question of whether Hard-2-SAT admits a robust satisfiability algorithm, which was the impetus for this work, and also for several useful comments on the write-up. We also thank Per Austrin for useful discussions.

4. REFERENCES

[1] A. Agarwal, M. Charikar, K. Makarychev, and Y. Makarychev. $O(\sqrt{\log n})$-approximation algorithms for Min UnCut, Min 2CNF deletion, and directed cut problems. In *Proceedings of the 37th annual ACM Symposium on Theory of Computing*, STOC '05, pages 573–581, 2005.

[2] P. Austrin, S. Benabbas, and K. Georgiou. Better balance by being biased: a 0.8776-approximation for Max Bisection. In *Proceedings of the 24th annual ACM-SIAM Symposium on Discrete Algorithms*, SODA '13, pages 373–387, 2013.

[3] P. Austrin, S. Khot, and M. Safra. Inapproximability of vertex cover and independent set in bounded degree graphs. In *Proceedings of the 24th annual IEEE Conference on Computational Complexity*, CCC '09, pages 74–80, 2009.

[4] A. Avidor, I. Berkovitch, and U. Zwick. Improved approximation algorithms for Max NAE-SAT and Max SAT. In T. Erlebach and G. Persinao, editors, *Approximation and Online Algorithms*, volume 3879 of *Lecture Notes in Computer Science*, pages 27–40. 2006.

[5] N. Bansal and S. Khot. Inapproximability of hypergraph vertex cover and applications to scheduling problems. In *Proceedings of the 37th International Colloquium on Automata, Languages and Programming*, ICALP '10, pages 250–261, 2010.

[6] A. A. Bulatov and D. Marx. Constraint satisfaction problems and global cardinality constraints. *Communications of the ACM*, 53(9):99–106, 2010.

[7] M. Charikar, K. Makarychev, and Y. Makarychev. Near-optimal algorithms for maximum constraint satisfaction problems. In *Proceedings of the 18th annual ACM-SIAM Symposium on Discrete Algorithms*, SODA '07, pages 62–68, 2007.

[8] N. Creignou, H. Schnoor, and I. Schnoor. Nonuniform boolean constraint satisfaction problems with cardinality constraint. *ACM Transactions on Computational Logic*, 11(4), 2010.

[9] V. Dalmau and A. Krokhin. Robust satisfiability for CSPs: hardness and algorithmic results. *ACM Transactions on Computation Theory*, 2013. To appear.

[10] I. Dinur, V. Guruswami, S. Khot, and O. Regev. A new multilayered PCP and the hardness of hypergraph vertex cover. *SIAM Journal on Computing*, 34(5):1129–1146, 2005.

[11] U. Feige and M. Langberg. The RPR2 rounding technique for semidefinite programs. In *Proceedings of the 28th International Colloquium on Automata, Languages and Programming*, ICALP '01, pages 213–224, 2001.

[12] A. M. Frieze and M. Jerrum. Improved approximation algorithms for Max k-Cut and Max Bisection. In *Proceedings of the 4th conference on Integer Programming and Combinatorial Optimization*, IPCO '95, pages 1–13, 1995.

[13] M. Goemans and D. Williamson. New $\frac{3}{4}$-approximation algorithms for the maximum satisfiability problem. *SIAM Journal on Discrete Mathematics*, 7(4):656–666, 1994.

[14] M. X. Goemans and D. P. Williamson. Improved approximation algorithms for maximum cut and satisfiability problems using semidefinite programming. *Journal of the ACM*, 42(6):1115–1145, Nov. 1995.

[15] V. Guruswami and E. Lee. Complexity of approximating CSP with balance / hard constraints. *Electronic Colloquium on Computational Complexity (ECCC)*, TR13-125, 2013.

[16] V. Guruswami, Y. Makarychev, P. Raghavendra, D. Steurer, and Y. Zhou. Finding almost-perfect graph bisections. In *Proceedings of the 2nd symposium on Innovations in Computer Science*, ICS '11, pages 321–337, 2011.

[17] V. Guruswami and Y. Zhou. Tight bounds on the approximability of almost-satisfiable horn SAT and exact hitting set. *Theory of Computing*, 8(1):239–267, 2012.

[18] E. Halperin and U. Zwick. A unified framework for obtaining improved approximation algorithms for maximum graph bisection problems. In *Proceedings of the 8th conference on Integer Programming and Combinatorial Optimization*, IPCO '01, pages 210–225, 2001.

[19] J. Håstad. Some optimal inapproximability results. *Journal of the ACM*, 48(4):798–859, July 2001.

[20] S. Khanna, M. Sudan, L. Trevisan, and D. P. Williamson. The approximability of constraint satisfaction problems. *SIAM Journal on Computing*, 30(6):1863–1920, 2000.

[21] S. Khot. On the power of unique 2-prover 1-round games. In *Proceedings of the 34th annual ACM Symposium on Theory of Computing*, STOC '02, pages 767–775, 2002.

[22] S. Khot, G. Kindler, E. Mossel, and R. O'Donnell. Optimal inapproximability results for max-cut and other 2-variable CSPs? *SIAM Journal on Computing*, 37(1):319–357, 2007.

[23] S. Khot and O. Regev. Vertex cover might be hard to approximate to within $2 - \varepsilon$. *Journal of Computer and System Sciences*, 74(3):335–349, 2008.

[24] M. Lewin, D. Livnat, and U. Zwick. Improved rounding techniques for the Max 2-SAT and Max Di-Cut problems. In *Proceedings of the 9th conference on Integer Programming and Combinatorial Optimization*, IPCO '02, pages 67–82, 2002.

[25] E. Mossel, R. O'Donnell, and K. Oleszkiewicz. Noise stability of functions with low influences: Invariance and optimality. *Annals of Mathematics*, 171:295–341, 2010.

[26] C. H. Papadimitriou and M. Yannakakis. Optimization, approximation, and complexity classes. *Journal of Computer and System Sciences*, 43(3):425 – 440, 1991.

[27] P. Raghavendra and N. Tan. Approximating CSPs with global cardinality constraints using SDP hierarchies. In *Proceedings of the 23rd Annual ACM-SIAM Symposium on Discrete Algorithms*, SODA '12, pages 373–387, 2012.

[28] T. J. Schaefer. The complexity of satisfiability problems. In *Proceedings of the 10th annual ACM Symposium on Theory of Computing*, STOC '78, pages 216–226, 1978.

[29] Y. Ye. A .699-approximation algorithm for Max-Bisection. *Mathematical Programming*, 90(1):101–111, 2001.

[30] U. Zwick. Finding almost-satisfying assignments. In *Proceedings of the 30th annual ACM Symposium on Theory of Computing*, STOC '98, pages 551–560, 1998.

Integer Feasibility of Random Polytopes

Karthekeyan Chandrasekaran*
School of Engineering and Applied Sciences
Harvard University
karthe@seas.harvard.edu

Santosh S. Vempala†
School of Computer Science
Georgia Institute of Technology
vempala@gatech.edu

ABSTRACT

We study the Chance-Constrained Integer Feasibility Problem, where the goal is to determine whether the random polytope

$$P(A,b) = \{x \in \mathbb{R}^n : A_i x \leq b_i, i \in [m]\}$$

obtained by choosing the constraint matrix A and vector b from a known distribution is integer feasible with probability at least $1-\epsilon$. We consider the case when the entries of the constraint matrix A are i.i.d. Gaussian (equivalently are i.i.d. from any spherically symmetric distribution). The radius of the largest inscribed ball is closely related to the existence of integer points in the polytope. We find that for m up to $2^{O(\sqrt{n})}$ constraints (rows of A), there exist constants $c_0 < c_1$ such that with high probability ($\epsilon = 1/\text{poly}(n)$), random polytopes are integer feasible if the radius of the largest ball contained in the polytope is at least $c_1\sqrt{\log(m/n)}$; and integer infeasible if the largest ball contained in the polytope is centered at $(1/2,\ldots,1/2)$ and has radius at most $c_0\sqrt{\log(m/n)}$. Thus, random polytopes transition from having no integer points to being integer feasible within a constant factor increase in the radius of the largest inscribed ball. Integer feasibility is based on a randomized polynomial-time algorithm for finding an integer point in the polytope.

Our main tool is a simple new connection between integer feasibility and linear discrepancy. We extend a recent algorithm for finding low-discrepancy solutions to give a constructive upper bound on the linear discrepancy of random Gaussian matrices. By our connection between discrepancy and integer feasibility, this upper bound on linear discrepancy translates to the radius bound that guarantees integer feasibility of random polytopes.

*This work was done while the author was a student at Georgia Institute of Technology supported in part by the Algorithms and Randomness Center (ARC) fellowship and the NSF.

†Supported in part by NSF Award CCF-1217793.

ITCS'14, January 12–14, 2014, Princeton, New Jersey, USA.

http://dx.doi.org/10.1145/2554797.2554838.

Categories and Subject Descriptors

G.1.6 [**Optimization**]: Integer Programming
; G.2.1 [**Discrete Mathematics**]: Combinatorics

General Terms

Theory, Algorithms

Keywords

Integer Programming, Probabilistic Instances, Discrepancy, Chance-Constrained Programs, Random Matrices

1. INTRODUCTION

Integer Linear Programming (IP) is a general and powerful formulation for combinatorial problems [29, 23]. One standard variant is the integer feasibility problem: given a polytope $P \in \mathbb{R}^n$ specified by linear constraints $Ax \leq b$, find an integer solution in P or report that none exists. The problem is NP-hard and appears in Karp's original list [15]. Dantzig [10] suggested the possibility of IP being a *complete* problem even before the Cook-Levin theory of NP-completeness. The best-known rigorous bound on the complexity of general IP is essentially $n^{O(n)}$ from 1987 [14] with only small improvements in the constant in the exponent since then [13, 9].

While IP in its general form is intractable, several special instances are very interesting and not yet well-understood. One such simple and natural family of instances is randomly generated IP instances, where the constraints describing random polytopes are drawn from a distribution. The class of optimization problems defined by such probabilistic constraints is known as Chance-Constrained Programming in Operations Research and their continuous optimization versions have been well-studied [7, 22, 26]. In its general form, a Chance-Constrained Linear Program (CCLP) with a joint probabilistic constraint is given by: $\max\{c^T x : A'x \leq b', \Pr(Ax \leq b) \geq 1-\epsilon\}$ for some chosen confidence parameter ϵ as required in the application. Here the probability is over the random choice of (A,b). CCLPs are powerful in modeling uncertainty in the availability of the resources and have found applications in supply chain management, circuit manufacturing, energy production, telecommunications, etc. [26, 27].

In this paper, we address the Chance-Constrained Integer Feasibility problem, where the goal is to determine whether the random polytope $\{x : Ax \leq b\}$ obtained by choosing A and b from a known distribution is integer feasible with probability at least $1-\epsilon$. We assume the constraint matrix

A is chosen randomly while the choice of b is deterministic, and ϵ is taken to be inverse polynomial in the dimension.

Random instances have been studied for several combinatorial problems e.g., random-SAT [4, 5, 8, 3, 11], random knapsack [1], and various other graph problems on random graphs [2]. Chance-constrained subset-sum IP was first studied by Furst and Kannan [12]. Their results were generalized to multi-row IP by Pataki et al. [25]. They showed that if each entry in the constraint matrix A is chosen independently and uniformly at random from the discrete set $\{1, 2, \ldots, M\}$, then with high probability, a certain reformulation of such random IP instances can be solved efficiently by the branch-and-bound algorithm provided that M is sufficiently large. These and other models for chance-constrained programs [28, 19, 18, 32] address the finite-case scenario in which the number of possible outcomes of (A, b) is finite. In contrast, here we address the continuous scenario.

Model for random IPs. A random IP instance in our model is described by a random constraint matrix $A \in \mathbb{R}^{m \times n}$ and an RHS vector b. Formally, we obtain random IP instances by generating random polytopes $P(n, m, x_0, R) = \{x \in \mathbb{R}^n : A_i x \leq b_i \ \forall \ i \in [m]\}$ as follows: pick a random $m \times n$ matrix A with i.i.d. entries from the Gaussian distribution $N(0, 1)$; and a vector b such that the hyperplane corresponding to each constraint is at distance at least R from x_0, i.e., denoting the i'th row of A as A_i,

$$\frac{b_i - A_i x_0}{\|A_i\|} \geq R$$

or

$$b_i \geq A_i x_0 + R\|A_i\|.$$

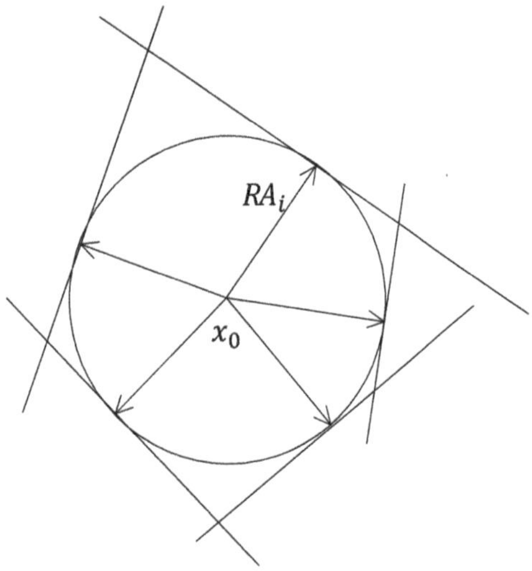

Figure 1: A Random IP instance $P(n, m, x_0, R)$ with facet normals being random unit vectors A_i and each facet at distance at least R from x_0.

An equivalent geometric interpretation for our model of random polytopes is the following (see Figure 1): we recall that if each row of the constraint matrix A is a unit vector, then they describe the normals to the facets of the polytope $P = \{x : Ax \leq b\}$. Thus, the random polytopes $P(n, m, x_0, R)$ in our model are obtained using m facets whose normal vectors are independent uniform random unit vectors in $\mathbb{R}^n$ and such that each facet is at distance R from the point x_0.

The condition that all facets are at distance at least R from x_0 is equivalent to the condition that $P(n, m, x_0, R)$ contains a ball of radius R centered at x_0. We study the integer feasibility of $P(n, m, x_0, R)$ for every x_0 as a function of the radius R. As R increases, intuitively it is more likely that the polytope contains an integer point.

Contributions. We show a phase-transition phenomenon regarding integer feasibility of random polytopes with respect to the radius used to generate these polytopes — we show an upper bound on R needed to guarantee integer feasibility with high probability for every $x_0 \in \mathbb{R}^n$; we show a lower bound that guarantees integer infeasibility with high probability for a fixed $x_0 = (1/2, \ldots, 1/2)$; our upper and lower bounds differ by a constant factor when m is at most $2^{O(\sqrt{n})}$. We show our upper bound via an efficient algorithm to find an integer feasible solution in the feasibility regime. This is an application of a recent constructive proof in discrepancy theory [17].

Alternatively, our results can be reinterpreted to bear resemblance to the well-known random SAT threshold: consider random polytopes in n-dimensions obtained by picking m random tangential hyperplanes to a ball of "constant" radius centered at x_0. If $m \leq c_0 n$, then random polytopes are integer feasible for every x_0 with high probability and if $m \geq c_1 n$, then random polytopes are integer infeasible for $x_0 = (1/2, \ldots, 1/2)$. Thus, integer feasibility of random polytopes exhibits a phase transition-like behavior when the number of hyperplanes increases beyond a constant times the number of variables, closely resembling the behavior of random k-SAT.

Our main conceptual (and simple) contribution is a new sufficient condition to guarantee integer feasibility of *arbitrary* polytopes. The idea is that a polytope is likely to contain an integer point if it contains a large ball. In fact, any polytope in n-dimensional space that contains a Euclidean ball of radius at least $\sqrt{n}/2$ is integer feasible. We refine this radius $r(A)$ of the largest inscribed ball that guarantees integer feasibility as a function of the constraint matrix A describing the polytope. This refined radius function is helpful in deriving bounds on the radius of the largest inscribed ball that guarantees integer feasibility of random polytopes.

For $R = \Omega(\sqrt{\log m})$ and $x_0 = (1/2, \ldots 1/2)$, there is a trivial algorithm: pick a random 0/1 vector. Most such vectors will be feasible in $P(n, m, x_0, R)$. But with smaller R, and arbitrary centers x_0, only an exponentially small fraction of nearby integer vectors might be feasible, so such direct sampling/enumeration would not give a feasible integer point. We use a more careful sampling technique for smaller R. As mentioned earlier, this is a straightforward extension of a recent algorithm for finding low discrepancy solutions [17].

1.1 Results

Our main theorem is stated as follows.

THEOREM 1. *Let* $1000n \leq m \leq 2^n$ *and*

$$R_0 = \sqrt{\frac{1}{6} \log \frac{m}{n}},$$

$$R_1 = 960 \left(\sqrt{\log \frac{m}{n}} + \sqrt{\frac{\log m \log (mn) \log (m/\log m)}{n}} \right).$$

Then,

1. *there exists a randomized polynomial time algorithm that with probability at least* $1 - (4/m^3) - 2me^{-n/96}$ *finds an integer point in the random polytope* $P(n, m, x_0, R)$ *for any* $x_0 \in \mathbb{R}^n$ *and* $R \geq R_1$,
2. *with probability at least* $1 - 2^{-n} - 2me^{-n/96}$, *the random polytope* $P(n, m, x_0 = (1/2, \ldots, 1/2), R)$ *does not contain an integer point if* $R \leq R_0$.

We remark that these results continue to hold in the equivalent random polytope model $P(n, m, x_0, R)$ obtained using random matrices A whose rows are chosen i.i.d. from any spherically symmetric distribution.

Remarks.

1. For $m = 2^{O(\sqrt{n})}$, the second term in R_1 is of the same order as the first and so R_0 and R_1 are within a constant factor of each other. Thus, in this case, the transition between infeasibility and feasibility happens within a constant factor increase in the radius.
2. When $m = cn$ for some sufficiently large constant c, our theorem shows that a constant radius ball inscribed in random polytopes is sufficient to guarantee integer feasibility with high probability (as opposed to the $\sqrt{n}/2$ radius ball needed in the case of arbitrary polytopes).

Underlying the above theorem is a simple yet powerful connection between the radius of the largest inscribed ball that guarantees integer feasibility and the linear discrepancy of the constraint matrix. If the radius is at least the linear discrepancy of the normalized constraint matrix (each row is normalized to a unit vector), then the polytope contains an integer point.

The linear discrepancy of a matrix $A \in \mathbb{R}^{m \times n}$ is defined as follows [20, 30, 31]:

$$\text{lin-disc}(A) := \max_{x_0 \in [0,1]^n} \min_{x \in \{0,1\}^n} \|A(x - x_0)\|_\infty .$$

Proposition 1. *Every polytope*

$$P_{x_0}(A) = \{x \in \mathbb{R}^n \mid |A_i(x - x_0)| \leq b_i \text{ for } i \in [m]\}$$

where $b_i \geq$ *lin-disc*(A) *contains an integer point for any* $x_0 \in \mathbb{R}^n$.

We elaborate on Proposition 1 in Section 1.2. To apply this connection to random IPs, we bound the linear discrepancy of Gaussian matrices.

Theorem 2. *Let* $A \in \mathbb{R}^{m \times n}$ *be a random matrix with i.i.d. entries from* $N(0, \sigma^2)$, *where* $2n \leq m \leq 2^n$. *There exists an algorithm that takes a point* $x_0 \in \mathbb{R}^n$ *as input and outputs a point* $x \in \mathbb{Z}^n$ *by rounding each coordinate of* x_0 *either up or down such that, for every* $i \in [m]$,

$$|A_i(x - x_0)| \leq 480\sigma \left(\sqrt{n \log \frac{m}{n}} + \sqrt{\log m \log (mn) \log \frac{m}{\log m}} \right).$$

with probability at least $1 - (4/m^3)$. *Moreover, the algorithm runs in expected time that is polynomial in* n *and* m.

In terms of classical discrepancy theory, Theorem 2 is equivalent to a bound of $O(\sigma R_1 \sqrt{n})$ on the linear discrepancy of random Gaussian matrices. The integer feasibility in Theorem 1 (part 1) follows from Theorem 2 by choosing $\sigma^2 = 1$ and observing that with probability at least $1 - 2me^{-n/96}$, all m random Gaussian vectors in n-dimension have length $O(\sqrt{n})$.

1.2 The Discrepancy Connection

To understand this connection, we begin with a simpler problem where $x_0 = 0$ and our goal is to find a point in the polytope with all coordinates in $\{-1, 1\}$ (as opposed to integer points). Given a matrix $A \in \mathbb{R}^{m \times n}$, and a real positive value r, consider the polytope $P(A, r) = \{x \in \mathbb{R}^n : |A_i x| \leq r \;\forall\, i \in [m]\}$. The discrepancy of a matrix A is defined to be the least r so that the polytope $P(A, r)$ contains a $-1/1$ point. This is equivalent to the classical definition of discrepancy [20, 30, 31]:

$$\text{disc}(A) := \min_{x \in \{-1,+1\}^n} \|Ax\|_\infty .$$

The following proposition is an immediate consequence of this definition.

Proposition 2. *The polytope* $P(A, disc(A)) = \{x \in \mathbb{R}^n : |A_i x| \leq disc(A) \;\forall\, i \in [m]\}$ *contains a point with all* $-1/1$ *coordinates.*

To see this, observe that the point $x \in \{-1, +1\}^n$ that minimizes discrepancy is in fact contained in the polytope $P(A, \text{disc}(A))$. Thus, if we can evaluate the discrepancy of the constraint matrix A, then by verifying whether the infinity norm of the RHS vector is at least disc(A), we have an easy heuristic to verify if the polytope contains a $-1/1$ point. Hence, if each row of A is a normalized unit vector, then the polytope $Ax \leq b$ contains a $-1/1$ point if it contains a ball of radius at least disc(A) centered at the origin.

The related notion of linear discrepancy helps in providing a sufficient condition for *integer feasibility* (as opposed to $-1/1$ feasibility) of arbitrary polytopes. Proposition 1, similar to Proposition 2, is an immediate consequence of the definition of linear discrepancy. This is because, by linear transformation, we may assume that x_0 is in the fundamental cube defined by the standard basis unit vectors. Thus, if each row of the matrix $A \in \mathbb{R}^{m \times n}$ is a unit vector, then the linear discrepancy of the constraint matrix gives a radius for the largest inscribed ball that guarantees integer feasibility of polytopes described by the constraint matrix A.

The approach suggested by Proposition 1 to verify integer feasibility of arbitrary polytopes requires the computation of linear discrepancy of arbitrary matrices. The related problem of computing the discrepancy of arbitrary matrices even to within an approximation factor of $\sqrt{n}$ is known to be NP-hard [6]. In recent work, Nikolov, Talwar and Zhang [24] have shown that *hereditary discrepancy*, which is an upper bound on linear discrepancy (see Theorem 4 below), can be efficiently computed to within an approximation factor of *poly*$(\log m, \log n)$; this could potentially be useful as a heuristic to verify integer feasibility (approximately).

In order to understand the integer feasibility of random polytopes using this approach, we seek a bound on the linear discrepancy of random matrices that holds with high probability. We obtain such a tight bound for random matrices algorithmically by extending a recent constructive algorithm that minimizes discrepancy [17] to an algorithm that minimizes *linear* discrepancy. Our infeasibility threshold is also based on discrepancy — we begin with a lower bound on the discrepancy of random matrices, which excludes any 0/1 point from being a feasible solution for $P(n, m, x_0 = (1/2, \dots, 1/2), R_0)$, and then extend this to exclude all integer points.

2. PRELIMINARIES

2.1 Related Work

The central quantity that leads to all known bounds on discrepancy and linear discrepancy in the literature is hereditary discrepancy defined as follows:

$$\text{herdisc}(A) := \max_{S \subseteq [n]} \text{disc}(A^S)$$

where A^S denotes the submatrix of A containing columns indexed by the set S. For a matrix $A \in \mathbb{R}^{m \times n}$ and any $S \subseteq [n]$, let $A_i{}^S$ denote the i'th row vector A_i restricted to the coordinates in S. The best known bound on discrepancy of arbitrary matrices is due to Spencer [30].

THEOREM 3. *[30] For any matrix $A \in \mathbb{R}^{m \times n}$, any subset $S \subseteq [n]$, there exists a point $z \in \{-1, +1\}^{|S|}$ such that for every $i \in [m]$,*

$$\left|A_i{}^S z\right| \le 11 \sqrt{|S| \log \frac{2m}{|S|}} \max_{k \in [m],\ j \in S} |A_{kj}|.$$

Lovász, Spencer and Vesztergombi [16] showed the following relation between hereditary discrepancy and linear discrepancy.

THEOREM 4. *[16] For any matrix A,*

$$\textit{lindisc}(A) \le \textit{herdisc}(A).$$

2.2 Concentration Inequalities

We will use the following well-known tail bounds.

LEMMA 3. *Let Y be a random variable drawn from the Gaussian distribution $N(0, \sigma^2)$. For any $\lambda > 0$,*

$$\Pr(Y \le \lambda\sigma) \le \min\left\{1 - \sqrt{\frac{1}{2\pi}}\left(\frac{\lambda}{\lambda^2 + 1}\right) e^{-\frac{\lambda^2}{2}}, \lambda\sqrt{\frac{1}{2\pi}}\right\}.$$

LEMMA 4. *Let Y be a random variable drawn from the Gaussian distribution $N(0, \sigma^2)$. For any $\lambda \ge 1$,*

$$\Pr(|X| \ge \lambda\sigma) \le 2e^{-\frac{\lambda^2}{4}}.$$

LEMMA 5. *Let $X_1, \dots, X_n$ be independent random variables each drawn from the Gaussian distribution $N(0, \sigma^2)$. For any $\lambda > 0$,*

$$\Pr\left(|\sum_{j \in [n]} X_j^2 - n\sigma^2| \ge \lambda\sqrt{n}\sigma^2\right) \le 2e^{-\frac{\lambda^2}{24}}.$$

LEMMA 6. *[21] Let $X_1, \dots, X_n$ be independent random variables each drawn uniformly from $\{-1, +1\}$. For a fixed set of vectors $a_1, \dots, a_m \in \mathbb{R}^n$, a fixed subset $S \subseteq [n]$, and any $\lambda \ge 0$,*

$$\Pr\left(|\sum_{j \in S} a_{ij} X_j| \ge \lambda\right) \le 2e^{-\frac{\lambda^2}{2\sum_{j \in S} a_{ij}^2}}.$$

3. LINEAR DISCREPANCY OF RANDOM MATRICES

Our first step towards an algorithm to identify an integer point in random polytopes is an algorithm to find small linear discrepancy solutions for random Gaussian matrices. The main goal of this section is to prove the bound on linear discrepancy of Gaussian matrices (Theorem 2).

Implications of known bounds. It is tempting to use known concentration inequalities in conjunction with Spencer's result (Theorem 3) to bound the hereditary discrepancy of Gaussian matrices; this would in turn lead to a bound on the linear discrepancy of Gaussian matrices by Theorem 4. In this setting, each entry A_{ij} is from $N(0, \sigma^2)$. Using standard concentration for $|A_{ij}|$ and a union bound to bound the maximum entry $|A_{ij}|$ leads to the following weak bound: with high probability, the polytope $P = \{x \in \mathbb{R}^n | |A_i(x - x_0)| \le b_i \text{ for } i \in [m]\}$ with $b_i = \Omega(\sigma\sqrt{n \log mn \log(2m/n)})$ contains an integer point for any $x_0 \in \mathbb{R}^n$. This is too weak for our purpose (recall that $\sqrt{n}$ radius ball in arbitrary polytopes already guarantees integer feasibility and our goal is to guarantee integer feasibility with smaller inscribed ball in *random* polytopes).

Our Strategy. Our overall strategy to bound discrepancy is similar to that of Spencer's: As a first step, show a partial coloring with low discrepancy – i.e., for any subset $U \subseteq [n]$, there exists a point $z \in \{0, -1, +1\}^{|U|}$ with at least $|U|/2$ non-zero coordinates such that $|A_i^U z|$ is small. Next for any $S \subseteq [n]$, repeatedly use the existence of this partial vector to derive a vector $x \in \{-1, 1\}^{|S|}$ with small discrepancy – start with $x = 0$, $U = S$ and use z to fix at least half of the coordinates of x to $+1$ or -1; then take U to be the set of coordinates that are set to zero in the current x and use z to fix at least half of the remaining coordinates of x to $+1$ or -1; repeat this until all coordinates of x are non-zero. Since at most $|U|/2$ coordinates are set to zero in each round of fixing coordinates, this might repeat at most $\log|S| \le \log n$ times. The total discrepancy is bounded by the sum of the discrepancies incurred in each round of fixing. Thus, the goal is to bound the discrepancy incurred in each partial coloring round.

The discrepancy incurred for the i'th constraint by the partial coloring can be bounded as follows[1]:

$$|A_i{}^U z| \le 4\,\|A_i{}^U\| \sqrt{\log \frac{2m}{|U|}} \quad \forall\, i \in [m],\ U \subseteq [n]. \quad (1)$$

Bounding discrepancy of partial vector. The discrepancy bound for the i'th constraint given in (1) depends on the length of the vector $A_i{}^U$. We describe a straightforward approach that does not lead to tight bounds.

[1]This is an improvement on the bound shown by Spencer: $|A_i{}^S z| = O\left(\max_{i \in [m], j \in S} |A_{ij}| \sqrt{|S| \log \frac{2m}{|S|}}\right)$ which can be recovered from (1). The proof of (1) is identical to the proof of Spencer's bound except for a stronger concentration inequality. We avoid the non-constructive proof for simplicity of presentation; we use an alternative algorithmic proof that follows from Lovett-Meka's partial coloring algorithm (see Lemma 9).

Approach 1. It is straightforward to obtain $\|A_i{}^U\| \leq 2\sigma\sqrt{|U|\log mn}$ with high probability for random Gaussian vectors A_i using well-known upper bound on the maximum coefficient of $A_i{}^U$. This leads to an upper bound of

$$8\sigma\sqrt{|S|\log(mn)\log\frac{2m}{|S|}}$$

on the discrepancy of A^S. Although this bound on the discrepancy of A^S is good enough when the cardinality of S is smaller than some threshold, it is too large for large sets S. E.g., when $S = [n]$, this gives a total discrepancy of at most $O(\sigma\sqrt{n\log(mn)\log(2m/n)})$.

New Approach. In order to obtain tighter bounds, we bound the length of partial vectors $A_i{}^U$ when each entry in the vector is from $N(0, \sigma^2)$ (as opposed to bounding the maximum coefficient). Using Lemma 5, we will show that

$$\|A_i{}^U\| = O\left(\sigma\sqrt{|U|}\left(\log\frac{en}{|U|}\right)^{\frac{1}{4}}\right)$$

for every $U \subseteq [n]$ of size larger than $\log m$ with probability at least $1-1/m^5$. Consequently, the total discrepancy incurred while the number of coordinates to be fixed is larger than $\log m$ is bounded by a geometric sum which is at most

$$O\left(\sigma\sqrt{n\log\frac{m}{n}}\right).$$

When the number of coordinates to be fixed is less than $\log m$, we use Approach 1 to bound the length of partial vectors, which in turn implies the required bound on the total discrepancy.

3.1 Bounding lengths of Gaussian subvectors

LEMMA 7. *Let $A \in \mathbb{R}^{m\times n}$ be a matrix whose entries are drawn i.i.d. from the Gaussian distribution $N(0, \sigma^2)$. Then, with probability at least $1 - 1/(mn)^3$,*

$$\|A_i{}^S\| \leq 2\sigma\sqrt{3|S|\log mn}\ \forall S \subseteq [n],\ \forall i \in [m].$$

PROOF. By Lemma 4 and union bound over the choices of $i \in [m], j \in [n]$, all entries $|A_{ij}| \leq 2\sigma\sqrt{3\log mn}$ with probability at least $1 - 1/(mn)^3$. Now, the squared length is at most the squared maximum entry multiplied by the number of coordinates. □

Next we obtain a bound on the length of $A_i{}^S$ when $|S|$ is large.

LEMMA 8. *Let $A \in \mathbb{R}^{m\times n}$ be a matrix whose entries are drawn i.i.d. from $N(0, \sigma^2)$ where $m \leq 2^n$. Then,*

$$Pr(\exists S \subseteq [n], |S| \geq \log m, \exists i \in [m] :$$

$$\|A_i{}^S\|^2 \geq 10\sigma^2|S|\sqrt{\log\left(\frac{en}{|S|}\right) + \frac{1}{|S|}\log m}\Bigg)$$

$$\leq \frac{1}{m^5}.$$

PROOF. Let

$$\lambda_s := 10s\sqrt{\log\left(\frac{en}{s}\right) + \frac{1}{s}\log m}.$$

Fix a subset $S \subseteq [n]$ of size $|S| = s$ and $i \in [m]$. Then, by Lemma 5, we have that

$$\Pr\left(\|A_i{}^S\|^2 \geq \lambda_s\sigma^2\right) \leq 2e^{-\frac{\lambda_s^2}{24s}}.$$

Hence,

$$\Pr\left(\exists S \subseteq [n], |S| = s, \exists i \in [m] : \|A_i{}^S\|^2 \geq \lambda_s\sigma^2\right)$$

$$\leq 2e^{-\frac{\lambda_s^2}{24s}} \cdot \binom{n}{s} \cdot m \leq 2e^{-\frac{\lambda_s^2}{24s}} \cdot \left(\frac{en}{s}\right)^s \cdot m$$

$$\leq 2e^{-\frac{\lambda_s^2}{24s} + s\log\frac{en}{s} + \log m} \leq 2e^{-3\left(s\log\frac{en}{s} + \log m\right)}.$$

Therefore,

$$\Pr\left(\exists S \subseteq [n], |S| \geq \log m, \exists i \in [m] : \|A_i{}^S\|^2 \geq \lambda_{|S|}\sigma^2\right)$$

$$= \Pr(\exists s \in \{\log m, \ldots, n\}, \exists S \subseteq [n], |S| = s, \exists i \in [m] :$$

$$\|A_i{}^S\|^2 \geq \lambda_{|S|}\sigma^2)$$

$$\leq \sum_{s=\log m}^{n} 2e^{-3\left(s\log\frac{en}{s} + \log m\right)} = \left(\frac{2}{m^3}\right)\sum_{s=\log m}^{n} e^{-3s\log\frac{en}{s}}$$

$$\leq \left(\frac{2n}{m^3}\right) e^{-3\log m\log\frac{en}{\log m}} \leq \frac{1}{m^5}.$$

The last but one inequality is because the largest term in the sum is $e^{-3\log m\log(en/\log m)}$. The last inequality is because $n \geq \log m$. □

3.2 Algorithmic Linear Discrepancy

Our algorithm is essentially a variation of Lovett-Meka's algorithm for constructive discrepancy minimization [17]. Lovett-Meka [17] provide a constructive partial coloring algorithm matching Spencer's bounds. The main difference in their approach from that of Spencer's is that, the partial coloring algorithm outputs a fractional point $z \in [-1, 1]^{|U|}$ such that at least $|U|/2$ coordinates are close to being 1 or -1. After at most $\log|S|$ rounds, all coordinates are close to being 1 or -1; a final randomized rounding step increases the total discrepancy incurred only by a small amount.

Their partial coloring algorithm can easily be extended to minimize linear discrepancy as opposed to discrepancy. In each partial coloring round, their algorithm starts with a point $x \in [-1, 1]^n$ and performs a random walk to arrive at a vector y such that the discrepancy overhead incurred by y (i.e., $|A_i(y - x)|$) is small. Further, at least half of the coordinates of x that are far from 1 or -1 are close to 1 or -1 in y. This can be extended to an algorithm which, in each phase, starts with a point $x \in [0, 1]^n$, and performs a random walk to arrive at a vector y such that the discrepancy overhead incurred by y (i.e., $|A_i(y - x)|$) is small. Further, at least half of the coordinates of x that are far from 0 or 1 are close to 0 or 1 in y. The functionality of such a partial coloring algorithm is summarized in the following lemma. In the rest of this section, given $x \in [0, 1]^n$, $\delta \in \mathbb{R}$, let $B(x) := \{j \in [n] : \delta < x(j) < 1 - \delta\}$.

LEMMA 9. *[17] Given $x \in [0, 1]^n$, $\delta \in (0, 0.5]$, $A_1, \ldots, A_m \in \mathbb{R}^n$, $c_1, \ldots, c_m \geq 0$ such that $\sum_{i=1}^{m} exp(-c_i^2/16) \leq |B(x)|/16$, there exists a randomized algorithm which with probability at least 0.1 finds a point $y \in [0, 1]^n$ such that*

1. $|A_i(y-x)| \le c_i ||A_i{}^{B(x)}||_2 \; \forall\, i \in [m]$,
2. $|B(y)| \le |B(x)|/2$
3. *If* $j \in [n] \setminus B(x)$, *then* $y(j) = x(j)$.

Moreover, the algorithm runs in time

$$O((m+n)^3 \delta^{-3} \log(nm/\delta)).$$

We denote the algorithm specified in Lemma 9 as Edge-Walk. To minimize the linear discrepancy of random Gaussian matrices, we repeatedly invoke the Edge-Walk algorithm. We repeat each invocation until it succeeds, so our algorithm is a Las Vegas algorithm. Each successful call reduces the number of coordinates that are far from being integer by at least a factor of 1/2. Thus, we terminate in at most $\log n$ successful calls to the algorithm. Further, the total discrepancy overhead incurred by x is at most the sum of the discrepancy overhead incurred in each successful call. The sum of the discrepancy overheads will be bounded using Lemmas 7 and 8. Finally, we do a randomized rounding to obtain integer coordinates from near-integer coordinates. By standard Chernoff bound, the discrepancy incurred due to randomized rounding will be shown to be small.

Algorithm 1 Algorithm Round-IP

Input: Point $x_0 \in \mathbb{R}^n$, matrix $A \in \mathbb{R}^{m\times n}$ where each $A_{ij} \sim N(0, \sigma^2)$.
Output: An integer point z.

1. **Initialize.** $x = x_0 - \lfloor x_0 \rfloor$, $\delta = 1/8 \log m$, $B(x) := \{j \in [n] : \delta < x(j) < 1-\delta\}$, $c_i = 8\sqrt{\log(m/|B(x)|)}$ for every $i \in [m]$.
2. While($|B(x)| > 0$)
   (i) Edge-Walk. $y \leftarrow$ Edge-Walk(x, δ, $A_1, \ldots, A_m$, $c_1, \ldots, c_m$).
   (ii) Verify and repeat. $B(y) := \{j \in [n] : \delta < y(j) < 1-\delta\}$. If $|B(y)| > |B(x)|/2$ or $|A_i(y-x)| > c_i ||A_i{}^{B(x)}||_2$ for some $i \in [m]$, then return to (i).
   (iii) Update. $x \leftarrow y$, $B(x) = \{j \in [n] : \delta < x(j) < 1-\delta\}$, $c_i = 8\sqrt{\log(m/|B(x)|)}\; \forall\, i \in [m]$.
3. **Randomized Rounding.** For each $j \in [n]$ set
$$z(j) = \begin{cases} \lceil x_0(j) \rceil & \text{with probability } x(j), \\ \lfloor x_0(j) \rfloor & \text{with probability } 1 - x(j). \end{cases}$$
4. Output z.

PROOF OF THEOREM 2. Without loss of generality, we may assume that $x_0 \in [0,1]^n$ and our objective is to find $x \in \{0,1\}^n$ with low discrepancy overhead. We use Algorithm Round-IP given in Figure 1. We will show that, with probability at least $1 - 4/m^3$, it outputs a point $z \in \{0,1\}^n$ such that

$$|A_i(z - x_0)| \le 192\sigma \left(\sqrt{n \log \frac{m}{n}} + \sqrt{\log m \log(mn) \log \frac{m}{\log m}} \right).$$

Let $\overline{x}$ denote the vector at the end of Step 2 in Algorithm Round-IP and let x_k denote the vector x in Algorithm Round-IP after k successful calls to the Edge-Walk algorithm. By a successful call, we mean that the call passes the verification procedure 2(ii) without having to return to 2(i). Let $S_k = B(x_k)$. We first observe that after $k-1$ successful calls to the Edge-Walk subroutine, we have $\sum_{i=1}^m exp(-c_i^2/16) \le |S_k|/16$ by the choice of c_is. By Lemma 9, the discrepancy overhead incurred in the k'th successful call to the Edge-Walk subroutine is

$$|A_i(x_k - x_{k-1})| \le 8 \left\| A_i{}^{S_k} \right\| \sqrt{\log \frac{m}{|S_k|}}.$$

Consequently, the total discrepancy is bounded by the sum of the discrepancy overhead incurred in each run. The discrepancy overhead incurred in the k'th successful run, where $k : |S_k| \ge \log m$, is at most

$$8\sigma \sqrt{10 |S_k| \log \frac{m}{|S_k|}} \left(\log \frac{en}{|S_k|} + \frac{1}{|S_k|} \log m \right)^{\frac{1}{4}}$$
$$\le 40\sigma \sqrt{|S_k| \log \frac{m}{|S_k|}} \left(\log \frac{en}{|S_k|} \right)^{\frac{1}{4}}$$

with probability at least $1 - (1/m^5)$. This is using the bound on the length of $A_i{}^{S_k}$ by Lemma 8.

Let k_1 be the largest integer such that $|S_{k_1}| > \log m$. Thus, with probability at least $1 - (1/m^5)$, the discrepancy overhead incurred after k_1 successful calls to the Edge-Walk subroutine is at most

$$D_1 := 40\sigma \sum_{k=0}^{\log \frac{n}{\log m}} \sqrt{n 2^{-k} \left(\log \frac{m}{n 2^{-k}} \right) \sqrt{\log \frac{e}{2^{-k}}}}$$
$$\le 240\sigma \sqrt{n \log \frac{m}{n}}.$$

The upper bound on D_1 follows from the following inequalities (by setting $A = m/n$),

$$\sqrt{\left(\log \frac{A}{2^{-k}} \right) \sqrt{\log \frac{e}{2^{-k}}}}$$
$$\le \left(\sqrt{\log A} + \sqrt{k \log 2} \right) (1 + k \log 2)^{\frac{1}{4}} \;\; \forall\, A \ge 1, \quad (2)$$

$$\sum_{k=0}^{\infty} \sqrt{2^{-k} (\log A)} (1 + k \log 2)^{\frac{1}{4}} \le 5 \sqrt{\log A}, \quad (3)$$

$$\sum_{k=0}^{\infty} \sqrt{2^{-k} \cdot k \log 2} (1 + k \log 2)^{\frac{1}{4}} \le 2 (\log 2)^{3/4} \sum_{k=0}^{\infty} \sqrt{2^{-k}} k^{3/4}$$
$$\le 10. \quad (4)$$

By Lemma 9, the discrepancy overhead incurred in the k'th successful call to the Edge-Walk subroutine, where $k : |S_k| \le \log m$, is

$$|A_i(x_k - x_{k-1})| \le 8 \left\| A_i{}^{S_k} \right\| \sqrt{\log \frac{m}{|S_k|}}$$
$$\le 32\sigma \sqrt{n 2^{-k} \log(mn) \log \frac{m}{n 2^{-k}}}$$

with probability at least $1 - 1/(mn)^3$. Here, the second inequality is by using Lemma 7 and $|S_k| \le n 2^{-k}$. Since each successful call to the Edge-Walk subroutine reduces $B(x)$ by at least half, the number of successful Edge-Walk subroutine calls is at most $\log n$.

Thus, with probability at least $1 - 1/(mn)^3$, the discrepancy overhead incurred by Step 2 in successful rounds $k : |S_k| \le \log m$ is at most

$$D_2 := \sum_{k=\log \frac{n}{\log m}}^{\log n} 32\sigma \sqrt{n2^{-k} \log (mn) \log \frac{m}{n2^{-k}}}$$

Now, using the inequalities (2), (3) and (4),

$$D_2 \le 64\sigma \sqrt{\log m \log (mn) \log \frac{m}{\log m}}.$$

Hence, with probability at least $(1 - 1/m^5)(1 - 1/(mn)^3)$, at the end of Step 2, we obtain a point $\overline{x}$ such that $\overline{x} \in [0, 1]^n$ and $\overline{x}(j) \ge 1 - \delta$ or $\overline{x}(j) \le \delta$ for every $j \in [n]$ and the total discrepancy overhead is bounded as follows:

$$\begin{aligned}\max_{i\in[m]} |A_i(\overline{x} - x_0)| &\le D_1 + D_2 \\ &\le 240\sigma \left(\sqrt{n \log \frac{m}{n}} \right. \\ &\quad \left. + \sqrt{\log m \log (mn) \log \frac{m}{\log m}} \right).\end{aligned}$$

Next we show that the randomized rounding performed in Step 3 incurs small discrepancy. Consider a coordinate $j \in [n]$ that is rounded. Then,

$$\mathbb{E}\left(z(j) - \overline{x}(j)\right) = 0,$$
$$\text{Var}\left(z(j) - \overline{x}(j)\right) \le \delta,$$

and thus,

$$\Delta_i^2 := \text{Var} \left(\sum_{j=1}^{n} A_{ij}(z(j) - \overline{x}(j)) \right) \le ||A_i||^2 \delta.$$

Therefore, for $i \in [m]$, by Chernoff bound,

$$\Pr \left(|\sum_{j=1}^{n} A_{ij}(z(j) - \overline{x}(j))| \ge 4\Delta_i \sqrt{\log m} \right) \le \frac{2}{m^8}.$$

Hence, by union bound, we get that

$$|A_i(z - \overline{x})| \le 4\Delta_i \sqrt{\log m} \le 4 \, ||A_i||$$

for every $i \in [m]$ with probability at least $1 - 1/m^7$. Now, applying Lemma 5, and using the condition that $\log m \le n$, we get that $|A_i(z - \overline{x})| \le 4\sigma\sqrt{n}$ with probability at least $(1 - 1/m^5)(1 - 1/m^7) \ge 1 - 2/m^5$. Thus,

$$\begin{aligned}|A_i(z - x_0)| &\le |A_i(z - \overline{x})| + |A_i(\overline{x} - x_0)| \\ &\le 480\sigma \left(\sqrt{n \log \frac{m}{n}} \right. \\ &\quad \left. + \sqrt{\log m \log (mn) \log \frac{m}{\log m}} \right) \quad \forall\, i \in [m]\end{aligned}$$

with probability at least $(1 - 1/m^5)(1 - 1/(mn)^3)(1 - 2/m^5) \ge 1 - 4/m^3$.

Finally, we compute the running time of the algorithm. Each call to the Edge-Walk subroutine succeeds with probability 0.1. Hence, the expected number of calls to the Edge-Walk subroutine is at most $10 \log n$. Since each call to the Edge-Walk subroutine takes

$$O((m + n)^3 \log^3 m \log (nm \log m))$$

time, the expected number of calls is $O(\log n)$ and the number of steps before each call is $O(m+n)$, the total number of steps is at most $O((m + n)^4 \log n \log^3 m \log (nm \log m))$. □

4. INFEASIBILITY RADIUS

The upper bound R_1 for the radius in Theorem 1 will follow from the linear discrepancy bound given in Theorem 2. For the lower bound, we show the following result for Gaussian matrices.

LEMMA 10. *For $m \ge 1000n$, let $A \in \mathbb{R}^{m\times n}$ be a matrix whose entries are chosen i.i.d. from the Gaussian distribution $N(0, \sigma^2)$. Let $x_0 := (1/2, \ldots, 1/2) \in \mathbb{R}^n$. Then,*

$$\Pr \left(\exists\, x \in \mathbb{Z}^n : A_i(x - x_0) \le \frac{\sigma}{2} \sqrt{n \log \frac{m}{n}} \; \forall i \in [m] \right) \le \frac{1}{2^n}.$$

We first show a lower bound on the radius necessary for the random polytope $P(n, m, 0, R)$ to contain an integer point with all nonzero coordinates. Lemma 10 will follow from the choice of x_0.

LEMMA 11. *For $m \ge 1000n$, let $A \in \mathbb{R}^{m\times n}$ be a matrix whose entries are chosen i.i.d. from the Gaussian distribution $N(0, \sigma^2)$. Then,*

$$\begin{aligned}Pr(\exists\, x \in \mathbb{Z}^n : |x_j| > 0 \;\forall\, j \in [n], \\ A_i x \le \sigma \sqrt{n \log \frac{m}{n}} \;\forall i \in [m]\Big) \\ \le \frac{1}{2^n}.\end{aligned}$$

PROOF. For each $r > 0$, we define the set

$$U_r := \mathbb{Z}^n \cap \{x : \|x\| = r, |x_j| > 0 \;\forall j \in [n]\}.$$

We will show that with probability at least $1 - 2^{-n}$ (over the choices of the matrix A), there does not exist $x \in \cup_{r \ge 0} U_r$ satisfying all the m inequalities. We first observe that U_r is non-empty only if $r \ge \sqrt{n}$. Fix $r \ge \sqrt{n}$ and a point $x \in U_r$. Now, for $i \in [m]$, since each A_{ij} is chosen from $N(0, \sigma^2)$, the dot product $A_i x$ is distributed according to the normal distribution $N(0, r^2\sigma^2)$. Let

$$P_x := \Pr \left(A_i x \le \sigma \sqrt{n \log \frac{m}{n}} \;\forall\, i \in [m] \right),$$

$$P_r := \Pr \left(\exists x \in U_r : A_i x \le \sigma \sqrt{n \log \frac{m}{n}} \;\forall\, i \in [m] \right).$$

By union bound,

$$P_r \le \sum_{x \in U_r} P_x \le |U_r| \max_{x \in U_r} P_x.$$

We will obtain an upper bound on P_x that depends only on r. To bound the size of the set U_r, we observe that every point in U_r is an integer point on the surface of a sphere of radius r centered around the origin and hence is contained in an euclidean ball of radius $r + 1$ centered around the origin. Thus, $|U_r|$ can be bounded by the volume of the sphere of radius $r + 1 \le 2r$ centered around the origin:

$$|U_r| \le \text{vol}\,(2r\mathbb{B}_0) \le \left(2r\sqrt{\frac{2\pi e}{n}} \right)^n \le \left(\frac{10r}{\sqrt{n}} \right)^n.$$

Next we bound P_r. We have two cases.

Case 1. Let $r \in \left[\sqrt{n}, \sqrt{n \log(m/n)}\right]$. Since $A_i x$ is distributed according to $N(0, r^2\sigma^2)$, by Lemma 3,

$$\Pr\left(A_i x \leq \sigma\sqrt{n \log \frac{m}{n}}\right) \leq 1 - \frac{1}{\sqrt{2\pi}}\left(\frac{r\sqrt{n\log\frac{m}{n}}}{r^2 + n\log\frac{m}{n}}\right)\cdot\left(\frac{n}{m}\right)^{\frac{n}{2r^2}}.$$

Since each A_{ij} is chosen independently, we have that

$$P_x = \prod_{i=1}^{m} \Pr\left(A_i x \leq \sigma\sqrt{n\log\frac{m}{n}}\right) < \left(1 - \frac{1}{\sqrt{2\pi}}\left(\frac{r\sqrt{n\log\frac{m}{n}}}{r^2 + n\log\frac{m}{n}}\right)\cdot\left(\frac{n}{m}\right)^{\frac{n}{2r^2}}\right)^m \leq e^{-\frac{1}{\sqrt{2\pi}}\left(\frac{r\sqrt{n\log\frac{m}{n}}}{r^2+n\log\frac{m}{n}}\right)\cdot\left(\frac{n}{m}\right)^{\frac{n}{2r^2}}\cdot m}.$$

Therefore, by union bound, it follows that

$$P_r \leq e^{-\frac{1}{\sqrt{2\pi}}\left(\frac{r\sqrt{n\log\frac{m}{n}}}{r^2+n\log\frac{m}{n}}\right)\cdot\left(\frac{n}{m}\right)^{\frac{n}{2r^2}}\cdot m + n\log\frac{10r}{\sqrt{n}}} \leq e^{-n\log\frac{10r}{\sqrt{n}}} \leq \left(\frac{\sqrt{n}}{10r}\right)^n.$$

Case 2. Let $r > \sqrt{n\log(m/n)}$. Since $A_i x$ is distributed according to $N(0, r^2\sigma^2)$, by Lemma 3, we have that

$$\Pr\left(A_i x \leq \sigma\sqrt{n\log\frac{m}{n}}\right) \leq \frac{1}{r}\sqrt{\frac{1}{2\pi}n\log\frac{m}{n}} \leq \frac{4}{5r}\sqrt{n\log\frac{m}{n}}.$$

The random variables $A_1 x, \ldots, A_m x$ are independent and identically distributed. Therefore,

$$P_x = \prod_{i=1}^{m}\Pr\left(|A_i x| \leq \sigma\sqrt{n\log\frac{m}{n}}\right) \leq \left(\frac{4}{5r}\sqrt{n\log\frac{m}{n}}\right)^m.$$

Hence, by union bound,

$$P_r \leq e^{-n\left(\frac{m}{n}\log\left(\frac{5r}{4\sqrt{n\log\frac{m}{n}}}\right) - \log\frac{10r}{\sqrt{n}}\right)} \leq e^{-n\left(\frac{m}{2n}\log\left(\frac{5r}{4\sqrt{n\log\frac{m}{n}}}\right)\right)} \leq \left(\frac{4\sqrt{n\log\frac{m}{n}}}{5r}\right)^{\frac{m}{2}}.$$

Finally,

$$\Pr\left(\exists x \in \cup_{r\geq\sqrt{n}} U_r : A_i x \leq \sigma\sqrt{n\log\frac{m}{n}}\ \forall i \in [m]\right)$$

$$= \sum_{r\geq\sqrt{n}} P_r = \sum_{r\in\left[\sqrt{n}, \sqrt{n\log\frac{m}{n}}\right]} P_r + \sum_{r>\sqrt{n\log\frac{m}{n}}} P_r$$

$$\leq \frac{1}{10^n}\int_{r=\sqrt{n}}^{\infty}\left(\frac{\sqrt{n}}{r}\right)^n dr + \left(\frac{4}{5}\right)^{\frac{m}{2}}\int_{r=\sqrt{n\log\frac{m}{n}}}^{\infty}\left(\frac{\sqrt{n\log\frac{m}{n}}}{r}\right)^{\frac{m}{2}} dr$$

$$\leq \frac{1}{10^n}\cdot\frac{\sqrt{n}}{n-1} + \left(\frac{4}{5}\right)^{\frac{m}{2}}\cdot\left(\frac{2\sqrt{n\log\frac{m}{n}}}{m-2}\right)$$

$$\leq \frac{1}{2^n} \qquad (\text{since } m \geq 1000n).$$

□

PROOF OF LEMMA 10. There exists $x \in \mathbb{Z}^n$ such that

$$A_i(x - x_0) \leq \frac{\sigma}{2}\sqrt{n\log\frac{m}{n}}\ \forall i \in [m]$$

if and only if there exists $x \in \mathbb{Z}^n \cap \{x \in \mathbb{R}^n : |x_j| \geq 1\ \forall\, j \in [n]\}$ such that

$$A_i x \leq \sigma\sqrt{n\log\frac{m}{n}}\ \forall i \in [m].$$

The result follows by Lemma 11. □

5. PROOF OF THRESHOLD RADIUS

We now have all the ingredients needed prove Theorem 1.

PROOF OF THEOREM 1. Let $P = \{x \in \mathbb{R}^n : a_i x \leq b_i\ \forall\, i \in [m]\}$, where each a_i is chosen from a spherically symmetric distribution. Then $\alpha_i = a_i / \|a_i\|$ for $i \in [m]$ is distributed randomly on the unit sphere. A random unit vector α_i can be obtained by drawing each coordinate from the Gaussian distribution $N(0, \sigma^2 = 1/n)$ and normalizing the resulting vector. Thus, we may assume $\alpha_i = A_i / \|A_i\|$ where each coordinate A_{ij} is drawn from the Gaussian distribution $N(0, 1/n)$. Here, we show that the probability that there exists a vector A_i that gets scaled by more than a constant is at most $2me^{-n/96}$.

Taking $\sigma^2 = 1/n$ in Lemma 5, we have

$$\Pr\left(\exists i \in [m] : |\,\|A_i\|^2 - 1| > \frac{1}{2}\right) \leq 2me^{-n/96}.$$

Hence, with probability at least $1 - 2me^{-n/96}$, we have that $\sqrt{1/2} \leq \|A_i\| \leq \sqrt{3/2}$ for every $i \in [m]$. We now show the upper and lower bounds.

1. Since P contains a ball of radius R_1, it follows that $P \supseteq Q$ where

$$Q = \{x \in \mathbb{R}^n |\ |\alpha_i(x - x_0)| \leq R_1 \text{ for } i \in [m]\}.$$

Using Theorem 2 and $\sigma^2 = 1/n$, we know that there exists a randomized algorithm that takes as input A and x_0 and outputs an integer point $x \in \mathbb{Z}^n$ such that for every $i \in [m]$

$$|A_i(x - x_0)| \le 480 \left(\sqrt{\log \frac{m}{n}} + \sqrt{\frac{\log m \log (mn)}{n} \log \frac{m}{\log m}}\right).$$

with probability at least $1-(4/m^3)$. Thus, with probability at least $1-(4/m^3)-2me^{-n/96}$, we obtain $x \in \mathbb{Z}^n$ satisfying

$$|\alpha_i(x - x_0)| = \frac{|A_i(x-x_0)|}{\|A_i\|} \le 960 \left(\sqrt{\log \frac{m}{n}} + \sqrt{\frac{\log m \log (mn)}{n} \log \frac{m}{\log m}}\right)$$

for every $i \in [m]$. Thus we have an integer point in the polytope Q and hence, an integer point in P.

2. For $x_0 = (1/2, \ldots, 1/2)$, let

$$P = \left\{x \in \mathbb{R}^n : A_i(x - x_0) \le \|A_i\| \sqrt{\frac{1}{6} \log \frac{m}{n}} \ \forall i \subset [m]\right\}.$$

Then, P contains a ball of radius R_0 centered around x_0 and hence is an instance of the random polytope $P(n, m, x_0, R_0)$. Further, with probability at least $1 - 2me^{-n/96}$, P is contained in

$$Q = \left\{x \in \mathbb{R}^n : A_i(x - x_0) \le \frac{1}{2}\sqrt{\log \frac{m}{n}} \ \forall i \in [m]\right\}.$$

By Lemma 10, with probability at least $1 - 2^{-n}$, we have that $Q \cap \mathbb{Z}^n = \emptyset$. Thus, with probability at least $1 - 2^{-n} - 2me^{-n/96}$, we have that $P \cap \mathbb{Z}^n = \emptyset$.

□

6. OPEN QUESTIONS

Propositions 1 and 2 hold for arbitrary constraint matrices describing the polytope. Are these observations useful for solving IP formulations of combinatorial optimization problems for families of instances? A concrete question is whether we can efficiently compute discrepancy or linear discrepancy for a reasonably general family of matrices.

Another open question is the complexity of integer linear optimization on random polytopes as given by our model, with an arbitrary, or even a random objective direction. Our work only addresses integer feasibility.

A natural question that arises there exists a sharp feasibility threshold R^* for the radius, i.e., with high probability, the random polytope $P(n, m, 0, R)$ is integer infeasible (for a nonzero integer point) if $R \le R^*$ and is integer feasible if $R > R^*$.

Finally, it would be interesting to explore similar phase transition phenomena when the rows of the matrix A are sparse, a setting that can be viewed as a geometric analog of random k-satisfiability.

7. REFERENCES

[1] R. Beier and B. Vöcking. Random knapsack in expected polynomial time. In *Proceedings of the 35th annual ACM symposium on theory of computing*, STOC '03, pages 232–241, 2003.

[2] B. Bollobás. *Random graphs*. Cambridge studies in advanced mathematics. Cambridge University Press, 2001.

[3] A. Broder, A. Frieze, and E. Upfal. On the satisfiability and maximum satisfiability of random 3-cnf formulas. In *Proceedings of the 4th annual ACM-SIAM symposium on discrete algorithms*, SODA '93, pages 322–330, 1993.

[4] M. T. Chao and J. Franco. Probabilistic analysis of two heuristics for the 3-satisfiability problem. *SIAM Journal on Computing*, 15:1106–1118, 1986.

[5] M. T. Chao and J. Franco. Probabilistic analysis of a generalization of the unit-clause literal selection heuristics for the k-satisfiability problem. *Information Sciences*, 51(3):289–314, Aug 1990.

[6] M. Charikar, A. Newman, and A. Nikolov. Tight hardness for minimizing discrepancy. In *Proceedings of the 22nd annual ACM-SIAM symposium on discrete algorithms*, SODA '11, pages 1607–1614, 2011.

[7] A. Charnes, W. W. Cooper, and G. H. Symonds. Cost horizons and certainty equivalents: An approach to stochastic programming of heating oil. *Management Science*, 4(3):pp. 235–263, 1958.

[8] V. Chvátal and B. Reed. Mick gets some (the odds are on his side). In *Proceedings of the 33rd annual symposium on foundations of computer science*, FOCS '92, pages 620–627, 1992.

[9] D. Dadush, C. Peikert, and S. Vempala. Enumerative lattice algorithms in any norm via m-ellipsoid coverings. In *FOCS*, pages 580–589, 2011.

[10] G. Dantzig. On the significance of solving some linear programs with some integer variables. *Econometrica*, 28:30–34, 1960.

[11] E. Friedgut. Sharp thresholds of graph properties and the k-sat problem. *Journal of the American Mathematical Society*, 12:1017–1054, 1998.

[12] M. Furst and R. Kannan. Succinct certificates for almost all subset sum problems. *SIAM J. Comput.*, 18:550–558, June 1989.

[13] R. Hildebrand and M. Köppe. A new lenstra-type algorithm for quasiconvex polynomial integer minimization with complexity $2^{O(n \log n)}$. *Discrete Optimization*, 10(1):69–84, 2013.

[14] R. Kannan. Minkowski's convex body theorem and integer programming. *Mathematics of Operations Research*, 12:415–440, 1987.

[15] R. Karp. Reducibility among combinatorial problems. *Complexity of Computer Computations*, pages 85–103, 1972.

[16] L. Lovász, J. Spencer, and K. Vesztergombi. Discrepancy of set-systems and matrices. *Eur. J. Comb.*, 7:151–160, April 1986.

[17] S. Lovett and R. Meka. Constructive discrepancy minimization by walking on the edges. In *Proceedings of the 53rd annual symposium on foundations of computer science*, FOCS '12, pages 61–67, 2012.

[18] J. Luedtke. An integer programming and decomposition approach to general chance-constrained mathematical programs. In *Integer Programming and Combinatorial Optimization*, pages 271–284. Springer, 2010.

[19] J. Luedtke, S. Ahmed, and G. L. Nemhauser. An integer programming approach for linear programs with probabilistic constraints. *Mathematical Programming*, 122(2):247–272, 2010.

[20] J. Matoušek. An Lp version of the Beck-Fiala conjecture. *Eur. J. Comb.*, 19:175–182, February 1998.

[21] J. Matoušek and J. Spencer. Discrepancy in arithmetic progressions. *American Mathematical Society*, 9(1):195–204, January 1996.

[22] B. L. Miller and H. M. Wagner. Chance constrained programming with joint constraints. *Operations Research*, 13(6):pp. 930–945, 1965.

[23] G. Nemhauser and L. Wolsey. *Integer and Combinatorial Optimization*. Wiley-Interscience, 1999.

[24] A. Nikolov, K. Talwar, and L. Zhang. The geometry of differential privacy: the sparse and approximate cases. In *Proceedings of the 45th annual ACM symposium on theory of computing*, STOC '13, pages 351–360, 2013.

[25] G. Pataki, M. Tural, and E. B. Wong. Basis reduction and the complexity of branch-and-bound. In *Proceedings of the 21st Annual ACM-SIAM symposium on Discrete Algorithms*, SODA '10, pages 1254–1261, 2010.

[26] A. Prékopa. On probabilistic constrained programming. In *Proceedings of the Princeton symposium on mathematical programming*, pages 113–138. Princeton University Press Princeton, NJ, 1970.

[27] A. Prékopa. Probabilistic programming. *Handbooks in operations research and management science*, 10:267–351, 2003.

[28] A. Ruszczyński. Probabilistic programming with discrete distributions and precedence constrained knapsack polyhedra. *Mathematical Programming*, 93(2):195–215, 2002.

[29] A. Schrijver. *Theory of Linear and Integer Programming*. John Wiley & sons, 1998.

[30] J. Spencer. Six standard deviations suffice. *Trans. Amer. Math. Soc.*, 289:679–706, 1985.

[31] J. Spencer. Ten lectures on the probabilistic method. *SBMS-NSF, SIAM*, 1987.

[32] H. Yanagisawa and T. Osogami. Improved integer programming approaches for chance-constrained stochastic programming. In *Proceedings of the 23rd international joint conference on Artificial Intelligence*, pages 2938–2944, 2013.

Multireference Alignment Using Semidefinite Programming

Afonso S. Bandeira
Program in Applied and Computational Math (PACM)
Princeton University
Princeton, New Jersey, USA
ajsb@math.princeton.edu

Moses Charikar
Department of Computer Science
Princeton University
Princeton, New Jersey, USA
moses@cs.princeton.edu

Amit Singer
Department of Mathematics and PACM
Princeton University
Princeton, New Jersey, USA
amits@math.princeton.edu

Andy Zhu
Department of Mathematics
Princeton University
Princeton, New Jersey, USA
azpujps@gmail.com

ABSTRACT

The multireference alignment problem consists of estimating a signal from multiple noisy shifted observations. Inspired by existing Unique-Games approximation algorithms, we provide a semidefinite program (SDP) based relaxation which approximates the maximum likelihood estimator (MLE) for the multireference alignment problem. Although we show this MLE problem is Unique-Games hard to approximate within any constant, we observe that our poly-time approximation algorithm for this problem appears to perform quite well in typical instances, outperforming existing methods. In an attempt to explain this behavior we provide stability guarantees for our SDP under a random noise model on the observations. This case is more challenging to analyze than traditional semi-random instances of Unique-Games: the noise model is on vertices of a graph and translates into dependent noise on the edges.

Interestingly, we show that if certain positivity constraints in the relaxation are dropped, its solution becomes equivalent to performing phase correlation, a popular method used for pairwise alignment in imaging applications. Finally, we describe how symmetry reduction techniques from matrix representation theory can greatly decrease the computational cost of the SDP considered.

Categories and Subject Descriptors

F.2.0 [**Theory of Computation**]: Analysis of Algorithms and Problem Complexity—*General*; G.0 [**Mathematics of Computing**]: General

ITCS'14, January 12–14, 2014, Princeton, New Jersey, USA.

ACM 978-1-4503-2698-8/14/01 ...$15.00.
http://dx.doi.org/10.1145/2554797.2554839.

Keywords

Multireference Alignment; Semidefinite Relaxation; Phase Correlation; Unique-Games

1. INTRODUCTION

The multireference alignment problem consists of estimating an unknown signal x from multiple noisy cyclically-shifted copies. More precisely, we are interested in the problem of estimating an unknown template vector $x \in \mathbb{R}^L$ from N measurements $y_1, \dots, y_N$ of the form:

$$y_i = R_{l_i}x + \xi_i \in \mathbb{R}^L, \tag{1}$$

where $\xi_i \sim \mathcal{N}(0, \sigma^2 I_L)$ is gaussian white noise with variance σ^2, and R_l denotes the index cyclic shift operator $(x_1, \dots, x_L) \mapsto (x_{1-l}, \dots, x_{L-l})$.

The difficulty of this problem resides in the fact that both the template x and the shifts $l_1, \dots, l_n$ are unknown (moreover, no model is presumed a-priori for their distribution). If the shifts were known, one could easily estimate x by unshifting the observations and averaging them. Motivated by this fact we will focus on the problem of estimating the shifts $l_1, \dots, l_n$ (up to a global shift).

This problem has a vast list of applications. Alignment is directly used in structural biology [8] [34]; radar [36] [29]; crystalline simulations [32]; and image registration in a number of important contexts, such as in geology, medicine, and paleontology [11] [12]. We will discuss below various methods to solve this problem, some of which are used in these communities (see also Appendix A).

Perhaps the most naïve approach to estimate the shifts in (1) would be to fix one of the observations, say y_i, as a reference template and align every other y_j with it by the shift δ_{ij} minimizing their distance

$$\delta_{ij} = \underset{l \in \mathbb{Z}_L}{\operatorname{argmin}} \|R_l y_j - y_i\|_2. \tag{2}$$

This solution works well at a high signal-to-noise ratio (SNR), but performs poorly at low SNR. A more democratic approach would be to calculate all of the pairwise relative shift estimates δ_{ij} before attempting to recover the shifts

$\{l_i\}$. The shifts could then be estimated by minimizing

$$\min_{l_1,\ldots,l_N \in \mathbb{Z}_L} \sum_{i,j=1}^{N} \left| e\left(\frac{l_i}{L}\right) - e\left(\frac{l_j+\delta_{ij}}{L}\right) \right|^2, \quad (3)$$

where $e(x) = e^{2\pi i x}$ denotes the classical Fourier basis function. This approach is known as angular synchronization [31, 3] and (3) can be approximated via a SDP-based relaxation or a spectral method.

The main shortcome of these methods is that the only information they use from the observations $\{y_i\}$ is the best relative shifts δ_{ij}. This means that the performance of a given choice of $\{l_i\}$ can only be evaluated by comparing $l_i - l_j$ with δ_{ij} (in shift space) across pairs (i, j). This does not take into account the cost associated with other possible relative shifts of y_i and y_j. On the other hand, for a candidate solution $\{l_i\}$, relating $R_{-l_i} y_i$ and $R_{-l_i} y_j$ (in signal space) would take into account information about all possible shifts instead of just the best one (2). The quasi maximum likelihood estimator (Section 2) attempts to do exactly that by solving the minimization problem:

$$\min_{l_1,\ldots,l_N \in \mathbb{Z}_L} \sum_{i,j=1}^{N} \left\| R_{-l_i} y_i - R_{-l_j} y_j \right\|^2. \quad (4)$$

Finding the MLE (4) is a non-trivial computational task because its parameter space is of exponential size, and the likelihood function is non-convex. While one can apply optimization methods such as gradient descent, simulated annealing, or expectation-maximization (EM), these are only guaranteed to find local minima of (4), but not the global minimum.

In this paper we take a different approach and propose a semidefinite relaxation for the quasi maximum likelihood problem (4). This particular SDP is inspired by an approximation algorithm designed to solve the Unique Games problem [7] (Section 3).

Convex relaxations of hard combinatorial problems have seen many successes in applied mathematics. They became particularly popular in the last decade with the introduction of Compressed Sensing, in the seminal work of Donoho, Candes, Tao, and others [5, 10]. This idea has since been applied to a vast list of problems. Semidefinite programming (SDP) has served as a convex surrogate for problems arising in applications such as low-rank matrix completion [4], phase retrieval [6], Robust PCA [23], multiple-input multiple-output (MIMO) channel detection [26], and many others. In many of these applications the same phenomenon is present: for typical instances, solving the convex problem is often equivalent to solving the original combinatorial problem [1].

Semidefinite relaxations also play a central role in the design of approximation algorithms in theoretical computer science. Almost two decades ago, Goemans and Williamson [13] proposed an SDP based approximation algorithm for the MAX-CUT problem with approximation ratio $\alpha^{\mathsf{GW}} \approx 0.878$. That is, for any instance of the problem, the computed solution is guaranteed to provide performance (in this case, a cut) at least α^{GW} of the optimum. Many semidefinite relaxations have since been proposed as approximation algorithms for a long list of NP-hard problems [35].

In order to better understand the theoretical limitations of approximation algorithms, substantial work has been done to establish limits on the approximation ratios achievable by poly-time algorithms for certain NP-hard problems (hardness of approximation). The Unique Games conjecture by Khot [16] is central to many recent developments: For $\delta, \varepsilon > 0$, it is impossible for a polynomial-time algorithm to distinguish between δ-satisfiable and $(1 - \varepsilon)$-satisfiable Unique-Games instances. A Unique-Games instance consists of a graph along with a permutations for each edge. The problem is to choose the best assignment of labels to each vertex such that as many of the edge permutations are satisfied. The validity of the UGC would imply the optimality of certain poly-time approximation ratios, in particular the Goemans-Williamson constant α^{GW} for the MAX-CUT problem [13, 17].

The best known polynomial time approximation to the unique games problem [7] is based on an SDP relaxation of a quadratic programming formulation that uses indicator variables. We note that this SDP is quite different from the relaxations normally used in applications (such as those described above). In particular, the variable matrix has size $NL \times NL$ and $\Omega\left(N^2L^2\right)$ constraints. The relaxation we propose consists of an adaptation of this SDP to approximate the quasi maximum likelihood problem (4).

As we show that it is Unique-Games hard to approximate (4) within any constant (assuming no noise model on $\{y_i\}$, see Section 2) it is hopeless to aim for good guarantees for general instances. However worst case analysis is often too pessimistic and not indicative of performance observed in practice. In fact, under the random noise model we assume for the observations, numerical simulations suggest that the SDP relaxation performs remarkably well, seeming to outperform existing methods. In an attempt to explain this phenomenon we show that, under our noise model, the SDP is stable at high SNR levels and even tight at extremely high SNR levels. By stability, we mean that with high probability the solution to the SDP does not deviate much from the true solution (see Section 4). The stability for this SDP is particularly interesting as it offers a new challenge in comparison with previously analyzed random instances of Unique-Games [2, 20]. This is because our noise model is on vertices, which translates into dependent noise on the edges. Still, these results fall short of properly explaining the remarkable performance that we see in simulations and more research is needed towards understanding the typical behavior of this relaxation.

In an attempt to simplify the SDP we also study a version with fewer constraints. Interestingly, this weaker SDP can be solved explicitly and is equivalent to the pairwise alignment method called phase correlation [14]. This method does not take into account information between all pairs of measurements, which suggests that the full complexity of the Unique-Games SDP [7] is needed to obtain a good approximation to (4).

The fact that a global shift does not affect the solution to (4) creates symmetries in our SDP relaxation. In fact, we leverage such structure, using symmetry reduction techniques to simplify the analysis of the SDP and greatly decrease its computational cost. This is particularly relevant given the high computational cost of state of the art semidefinite programming algorithms.

Contributions: Our main contribution is applying techniques from theoretical computer science to a problem from applied math. We introduce an Unique Games style SDP relaxation for the alignment problem, that is novel for the applied math community. From the theoretical computer science point of view, we introduce a new problem that has a similar flavor to the Unique Games problem, and show that a worst case version is at least as hard as Unique Games. We introduce a natural average case version of this alignment problem, aligning several shifted copies of a signal corrupted by independent Gaussian noise. Existing analyses of semi-random models of Unique Games do not seem to apply to this problem due to the structure of the noise. We show that for sufficiently high SNR, the SDP solution is close to an integer solution. This is a first step to establishing a signal recovery result which we leave as an open problem. We believe that future investigations into this problem will yield interesting insights into the Unique Games SDP and on dealing with correlated noise in average case analysis.

2. QUASI MAXIMUM LIKELIHOOD ESTIMATOR

The log likelihood function for model (1) is given by

$$\mathcal{L}(x, l_1, \ldots, l_N) = \frac{N\log(2\pi)}{2} - \frac{1}{2\sigma}\sum_{i\in[N]} \|R_{-l_i}y_i - x\|^2. \quad (5)$$

Maximizing $\mathcal{L}$ is equivalent to minimizing the sum of squared residuals $\sum \|R_{-l_i}y_i - x\|^2$. Fixing the l_i's, the minimal value of $\mathcal{L}$ occurs at the average $x = \frac{1}{N}\sum_{i=1}^N R_{-l_i}y_i$. Making the tame assumption that $\|x\|^2$ is estimable (indeed the norm is shift-invariant) and thus fixed in (5), maximizing (5) is equivalent to maximizing the sum of the inner products $\langle R_{-l_i}y_i, R_{-l_j}y_j\rangle$ across all pairs (i,j). Thus we consider the estimator

$$\operatorname*{argmax}_{l_1,\ldots,l_n\in\mathbb{Z}_L} \sum_{i,j\in[N]} \langle R_{-l_i}y_i, R_{-l_j}y_j\rangle \quad (6)$$

Unfortunately, the search space for this optimization problem has exponential size. Indeed, assuming no model for the vectors $\{y_i\}$, it is NP-hard to find the shifts which maximize (6), or even estimate it within a close constant factor.

THEOREM 2.1. *Assuming no model on the observatinos $\{y_i\}$, it is NP-hard (under randomized reductions) to find a set of labels approximating (6) within $16/17+\varepsilon$ of its optimum value. Furthermore, it is UG-hard (under randomized reductions) to approximate (6) within any constant factor.*

PROOF. (outline) We give a randomized reduction from the class of Γ-MAX-2LIN(q) instances consisting of a set of 2 variable linear equations of the form $x_i - x_j \equiv c_{ij} \pmod q$, with the goal of choosing an assignment for the variables which maximizes the number of satisfied equations. We construct a vector y_k for every variable x_k such that shifts of y_k correspond to an assignment to x_k. We pick a random vector z_{ij} corresponding to a constraint on variables x_i, x_j and place a copy of z_{ij} at specific locations in y_i and y_j. Shifts of y_i, y_j corresponding to satisfying assignments of the constraint results in a superposition of the copies of z_{ij}. We choose parameters so that the only non-trivial contributions to the objective function (6) come from such superposition. The value of the objective is (within small error) a scaled version of the number of constraints of the Γ-MAX-2LIN(q) instance satisfied by the assignment corresponding to the shifts. Thus hardness results for Γ-MAX-2LIN(q) directly translate to hardness results for the alignment problem. The details are given in Appendix C. ☐

The discrete optimization problem (6) may be formulated using indicator variables as an integer programming problem

$$\operatorname*{argmax}_{\{u_{ik}\}} \sum_{i,j=1}^{N}\sum_{k,l\in\mathbb{Z}_L} u_{ik}u_{jl}\langle R_{-k}y_i, R_{-l}y_j\rangle, \quad (7)$$

where $u_{ik}\in\{0,1\}$ and, for each i, $u_{ik}=1$ for exactly one index k, corresponding to indicator variables $u_{ik}=\delta\{l_i\equiv k\}$. These requirements can be described with quadratic constraints (up to global sign, which cannot be fixed by quadratic constraints)

$$\begin{aligned}\sum_{k,l\in\mathbb{Z}_L} u_{ik}u_{jl} &= 1, \quad i,j\in[N]\\ u_{ik}u_{il} &= 0, \quad i\in[N],\ k\neq l\in\mathbb{Z}_L \\ u_{ik}u_{jl} &\geq 0, \quad i,j\in[N],\ k,l\in\mathbb{Z}_L.\end{aligned} \quad (8)$$

Note that both the objective function (7) and the constraints (8) depend only on products of the form $u_{ik}u_{jl}$. This means that we can write the problem in terms of the Gram matrix $U\in\mathbb{R}^{NL\times NL}$ with entries $U_{ik;jl}=u_{ik}u_{jl}$. To ensure that $U\in\mathbb{R}^{NL\times NL}$ is indeed of the form $U=uu^T$ it suffices to require that $U\succeq 0$ and $\text{rank}(U)=1$. This means that (7) is equivalent to

$$\begin{aligned}\max_{U\in\mathbb{R}^{NL\times NL}} \quad & \text{tr}(CU) \\ \text{subject to} \quad & \sum_{k,l} U_{ik;jl} = 1 \text{ for } i,j\in[N] \\ & U_{ik;il} = 0 \text{ for } i\in[N],\ k\neq l\in\mathbb{Z}_L \\ & U\geq 0,\ U\succeq 0,\ \text{rank}(U)=1,\end{aligned} \quad (9)$$

where $C\in\mathbb{R}^{NL\times NL}$ is the data Gram matrix, with entries $C_{ik;jl}=\langle R_{-k}y_i, R_{-l}y_j\rangle$.

Due to the global shift redundancy of the multireference alignment problem, (9) will have L equivalent solutions (corresponding to the L shifts). We will deal with this redundancy by averaging the L solutions. This corresponds to a rank L matrix V satisfying $V_{ik;ik}=1/L$ for all $i\in[N]$ and $k\in\mathbb{Z}_L$. The L solutions u_{ik} lie in the L dimensional space spanned by the L non-zero eigenvectors of V. Hence the problem can be written as:

$$\begin{aligned}\max_{V\in\mathbb{R}^{NL\times NL}} \quad & \text{tr}(CV) \\ \text{subject to} \quad & \sum_{k,l} V_{ik;jl} = 1 \text{ for } i\neq j\in[N] \\ & V_{ik;ik} = 1/L \text{ for } i\in[N] \\ & V_{ik;il} = 0 \text{ for } i\in[N],\ k\neq l\in\mathbb{Z}_L \\ & V\geq 0,\ V\succeq 0,\ \text{rank}(V)\leq L.\end{aligned} \quad (10)$$

2.1 Data Gram matrix and a spectral method

The data Gram matrix C has special structural properties that may be leveraged. The following lemma describes this structure. Let $\mathcal{F}$ be the normalized Fourier transform $\mathcal{F}(y_i,k)=\frac{1}{\sqrt{L}}\sum_{l=0}^{L-1} e\left(\frac{-kl}{L}\right)(y_i)_l$.

LEMMA 2.2. *The data Gram matrix C with entries $C_{ik;jl} = \langle R_{-k}y_i, R_{-l}y_j\rangle$ satisfies:*

1. *$C\succeq 0$ and has rank L, with non-zero eigenvalues $\lambda_k = L\sum_{i=1}^N |\mathcal{F}(y_i,k)|^2$.*

2. *There is a unitary matrix $\mathcal{P}$ for which $\mathcal{P}C\mathcal{P}^* = \mathrm{diag}(\mathcal{C}_0, \ldots, \mathcal{C}_{L-1})$ is block diagonal, where each $\mathcal{C}_k \in \mathbb{C}^{N\times N}$ is a rank 1 matrix,*

where

PROOF. This follows from block circulance of (a permutation of) C. Refer to Lemma B.1. □

Ideally one would be able to read off the solution indicator vectors $\mathbf{1}\{ik : k \equiv l_i\} \in \mathbb{R}^{NL}$ from properties of C. In fact, it is not difficult to see that in the noiseless case ($\sigma = 0$), the span of the top L eigenvectors of C coincides with the span of the indicator vectors corresponding to the L globally shifted solutions.

Hence, one may try to recover a solution to (7) by examining the eigenvectors associated with the top eigenvalues in the spectrum of C. For random signals x, Lemma 2.2 indicates that the spectral gap between the top L eigenvalues and the remaining eigenvalues of C will be large, on the order $\min_k \sum_i |\mathcal{F}(y_i, k)|^2 = \Omega(LN)$. This suggests that a rounding procedure from the eigenvalues of C could be robust to noise, and motivate the application of a spectral method for the noisy case.

Unfortunately, this spectral gap will be rather small for a large class of signals. As long as a single power spectra $|\mathcal{F}(x, k)|^2$ of x is near zero, the corresponding eigenvalue λ_k will separate less from the small eigenvalues of C. Hence with additional noise, it would be less reliable to try and recover the solution indicator vector from the top L eigenvectors of C. This suggests that in this context, the SNR should be defined with respect to the spectral gap $\min_k |\mathcal{F}(x, k)|^2$. Furthermore, our simulations suggest that recovery from a spectral relaxation performs worse than the semidefinite relaxation we are about to propose.

3. SEMIDEFINITE RELAXATION

In (10), the only non-convex constraint imposed on V is that of rank deficiency, which obstructs the use of convex programming techniques. Removing this rank constraint yields a semidefinite program:

$$\begin{aligned}
\max_{V \in \mathbb{R}^{NL\times NL}} \quad & \mathrm{tr}(CV) && (11)\\
\text{subject to} \quad & \sum_{k,l} V_{ik;jl} = 1 \text{ for } i \neq j \in [N] \\
& V_{ik;ik} = 1/L,\ V_{ik;il} = 0 \text{ for } k \neq l, && (12)\\
& V \geq 0,\ V \succeq 0.
\end{aligned}$$

This SDP is extremely similar to and motivated by SDPs commonly used to approximate solutions to certain constraint satisfaction problems (CSPs), notably Unique-Games instances. An Unique-Games instance consists of a graph $G = ([N], E)$, a label set $\mathbb{Z}_L$, and a set of permutations $\pi_{ij} : \mathbb{Z}_L \to \mathbb{Z}_L$. The problem is to choose the best assignment of labels to each vertex such that as many of the permutations $(\pi_{ij})_{(i,j)\in E}$ as possible are satisfied. Γ-MAX-2LIN(L) is a special case where the permutations π_{ij} are cyclic. In our notation, the SDP studied for Unique-Games is usually of the form

$$\begin{aligned}
\max_{V} \quad & \frac{1}{2}\mathrm{tr}(\tilde{C}V) && (13)\\
\text{subject to} \quad & \tilde{C}, V \in \mathbb{R}^{NL\times NL},\ \tilde{C}_{ik;jl} = \delta\{l = \pi_{ij}(k)\}, \\
& \sum_k V_{ik;ik} = 1,\ V_{ik;il} = 0 \text{ for } k \neq l, && (14)\\
& V \geq 0,\ V \succeq 0.
\end{aligned}$$

This formulation attempts to count the number of satisfied edge constraints for an Unique-Games instance. In this context, the matrix $\tilde{C}$ is dubbed the label-extended adjacency matrix [18]. One can treat the SDP (11) as an instance of Γ-MAX-2LIN(L) on a weighted complete graph, with each cyclic permutation weighted by $C_{ik;jl} = \langle R_{-l_i} y_i, R_{-l_j} y_j \rangle$. Thus the significant body of literature conducted on Unique-Games may be useful in understanding (11). Another common feature of the aligment SDP with Γ-MAX-2LIN(L) instances is that the assigned labels may be chosen up to cyclic symmetry. This induces a block circulant symmetry in the semidefinite program. For example, it was this symmetry that allowed us to obtain the constraints $V_{ik;ik} = 1/L$ from the constraints $\sum_k V_{ik;ik} = 1$.

A major feature of (11) which distinguishes it from the general Unique-Games problem is the structure of the data coefficient matrix C (see Lemma 2.2). While Unique-Games specifies constraints on edges of a graph (there are N^2 pieces of information), the alignment problem only specifies information on its vertices (N pieces of information). While this does assist our understanding of the semidefinite program, since it enables us to apply more symmetry conditions, it also will complicate some of our analysis (see Section 4).

The number of constraints in our SDP (11) is dominated by the positivity constraints $V \geq 0$. One source of intuition behind it is that it enforces triangle inequality constraints $\|v_{ik} - \mathbf{0}\| + \|\mathbf{0} - v_{jl}\| \geq \|v_{ik} - v_{jl}\|$ [7]. From the next section, as well as from empirical results, we see that the constraint $V \geq 0$ seems to cause the SDP solution to be more stable around integral instances. As a trade-off, the computational cost of solving the SDP scales with the number of constraints, so we investigated the effect of removing the positivity constraints in (11). Interestingly, without this positivity constraint, the SDP (11) can be solved in closed form, and is effectively equivalent to applying phase correlation (see Appendix A) to each pair of the observations.

THEOREM 3.1. *There is a matrix $V \in \mathbb{R}^{NL\times NL}$ composed of circulant $L \times L$ blocks which solves the program (11), excluding the positivity constraint $V \geq 0$. V has rank L, corresponding to one eigenspace of eigenvalue N/L. This eigenspace contains the vector $v^{\mathsf{phase}} \in \mathbb{R}^{NL}$ satisfying*

$$v^{\mathsf{phase}}_{ik} = \frac{1}{\sqrt{L}} \sum_{l=0}^{L-1} e\left(\tfrac{-kl}{L}\right) \cdot \frac{\mathcal{F}(y_1, l)\mathcal{F}^*(y_i, l)}{|\mathcal{F}(y_1, l)\mathcal{F}^*(y_i, l)|}$$

which is the concatenation of phase correlation vectors between y_1 and y_i.

PROOF. (outline) The existence of a solution V composed of circulant blocks follows from symmetry. Hence, as in Lemma 2.2, V may block diagonalized as $\mathcal{P}V\mathcal{P}^* = \mathrm{diag}(\mathcal{V}_0, \ldots, \mathcal{V}_{L-1})$ for $\mathcal{V}_k \in \mathbb{C}^{N\times N}$. When the SDP constraints are written with respect to the entries of the $\mathcal{V}_k$'s, one resulting constraint is that the magnitude of each entry of $\mathcal{V}_k$ is bounded. As a consequence, the objective function (11) would be maximized when the entries of $\mathcal{V}_k$ have maximal magnitudes, and have the same complex phases as the corresponding entries in $\mathcal{C}_k$. This choice of V indeed lies in the SDP feasibility region (ignoring the positivity constraints). Analogous to phase correlation, the information used from the data matrix is entirely phase information. The details are given in the proof of Theorem B.3. □

From the SDP solution, one must round back to a solution in the original search space. There is a significant body of literature on the topic of rounding the solutions to various SDPs for Unique Games. The analysis and guarantees for these rounding schemes are usually expressed in terms of percentage of constraints satisfied by the SDP solution and do not immediately give a result about signal recovery in our setting. For example, in studying semi-random instances of Unique-Games, the authors of [19] give a rounding technique that uses both SDP and LP solutions when the SDP is known to be somewhat sparse. This is similar to a condition we obtain in the following stability section. Exploiting these ideas to establish an exact signal recovery guarantee is an interesting open problem.

4. STABILITY

For simplicity, we will assume, without loss of generality, that all the ground truth shifts correspond to the zero shift. Hence $y_i = x + \xi_i$, where $\xi_i \sim \mathcal{N}(0, \sigma^2 I_L)$ i.i.d.. The ground truth integral instance for the SDP will be (up to block cyclic symmetry) the indicator matrix $V^{int} \in \mathbb{R}^{NL\times NL}$, defined as $V^{int}_{ik;jl} = \delta_{k=l}/L$. It is not difficult to see that, if there is a set of labels $\{l_i\}$ which are pairwise optimal (in the sense that $\langle R_{-l_i} y_i, R_{-l_j} y_j\rangle = \max_k \langle y_i, R_{-k} y_j\rangle$ for all pairs (i,j)) the SDP (11) will return the integral instance. While this may be likely in a very high signal-to-noise setting, it is a rather stringent condition. We relax this condition and show that the SDP solution must still resemble the integral instance at a reasonably high SNR. The exact definition for the SNR will be deferred for later, but will be characterized in terms of the gap between the correct offset and incorrect shifts

$$\Delta = \|x\|^2 - \max_{l\neq 0}\langle x, R_l x\rangle, \tag{15}$$

and the noise level.

For any $V \in \mathbb{R}^{NL\times NL}$ lying in the SDP feasibility region, we can characterize the distance of V from the integral instance by the differences

$$D_{ij} = \sum_{k\neq l\in\mathbb{Z}_L} V_{ik;jl} = 1 - \sum_{k\in\mathbb{Z}_L} V_{ik;jk} \in [0,1].$$

D_{ij} is a measure of how much the SDP would weight shift preferences other than the ground truth. Note that D_{ij} is always non-negative and moreover, when all $D_{ij} = 0$ we obtain the integral instance.

For convenience, we make the definitions $\xi_0 = 2x$ and $\eta_{ij} = 2\max_l |\langle R_l \xi_i, \xi_j\rangle| \geq 0$ for $i,j = 0,1,\ldots,N$. The following Lemma provides a control on D_{ij} from the difference of the signal term Δ and the noise terms η_{ij}.

LEMMA 4.1. *If* $\operatorname{tr}(CV) \geq \operatorname{tr}(CV^{int})$, *then* $\sum_{i\neq j}(\Delta - \eta_{ij} - \eta_{j0})D_{ij} \leq 0$.

PROOF. We can find a block circulant matrix which attains the same SDP objective value as V, so without loss of generality presume V is block circulant. Hence $\sum_k V_{ik;j0} = 1/L$ and $D_{ij} = 1 - LV_{i0;j0}$. Expanding,

$$\begin{aligned}
0 &\geq \operatorname{tr}(CV^{int}) - \operatorname{tr}(CV) \\
&= \sum_{i,j}\sum_k \langle R_{-k} y_i, y_j\rangle\left(\delta_{k=0} - LV_{ik;j0}\right) \\
&\geq \sum_{i,j}\left(\langle y_i, y_j\rangle(1 - LV_{i0;j0}) - \max_{l\neq 0}\langle R_l y_i, y_j\rangle \sum_{k\neq 0} LV_{ik;j0}\right) \\
&= \sum_{i,j}\left(\langle y_i, y_j\rangle - \max_{l\neq 0}\langle R_l y_i, y_j\rangle\right) D_{ij}.
\end{aligned}$$

The second inequality requires the SDP constraint $V \geq 0$. Expanding the inner products and applying pessimistic bounds,

$$\langle y_i, y_j\rangle - \max_{l\neq 0}\langle R_l y_i, y_j\rangle \geq \Delta - (\eta_{i0}/2 + \eta_{j0}/2 + \eta_{ij}),$$

and rearrangement gives the desired inequality. □

THEOREM 4.2. *With probability* $1 - e^{-N+o(N)}$, *the solution to the SDP satisfies*

$$\sum_{i,j} D_{ij} \leq \frac{(\|x\| + \sigma^2\sqrt{L})\cdot 12\log eL}{\Delta}\cdot N^2.$$

PROOF. For sufficiently high SNR, we would expect that the inequality in Lemma 4.1 would fail to hold. Indeed, by Lemma D.2, the inequality

$$\sum_{i\neq j}(\eta_{ij} + \eta_{j0})D_{ij} \leq \mathcal{O}(\log L)\cdot\left(2\|x\| + \frac{1}{N}\sum_i \|\xi_i\|\right)N^2,$$

holds with probability at least $1 - e^{-N+\mathcal{O}(\log N)}$. It arises from tail bounds on the sum of slightly dependent random variables, and is independent of the structure of the SDP (as opposed to Lemma 4.1). Combined with Lemma 4.1, we can obtain a guarantee on the deviation between the SDP solution and the integral instance. The full proof may be found following Theorem D.3. □

Theorem 4.2 indicates that at a sufficiently high SNR, the UG-based SDP will produce a matrix V, of which each $L\times L$ block has most weight concentrated on its main diagonal. A rounding scheme would likely interpret this as the identity shift being the optimal shift. This motivates us to choose a definition for the SNR to be along the lines of $SNR = \Delta/[(\|x\| + \sigma^2\sqrt{L})\log L]$ (for reference, for random signals x, we would expect that $\Delta = L - \mathcal{O}(\sqrt{L})$). This characterization of SNR is significantly more lenient than that for spectral relaxation, in Section 2. For example, if the signal x was a sum of a few sinusoids, it would have several small power spectra, but as long as the least common multiple of their periods does not divide L, then Δ will still be large. Note further that we have more flexibility when defining Δ: for example, suppose there is a set of shifts $\boldsymbol{\ell}^*$ (including the identity element) of size $|\boldsymbol{\ell}^*| = \mathcal{O}(1)$ for which $\max_{l\in\boldsymbol{\ell}^*}\langle x, R_l x\rangle > \Delta + \min_{l\notin\boldsymbol{\ell}^*}\langle x, R_l x\rangle$. The above results may be modified to describe the concentration of the SDP solution on the entries of the shifts in $\boldsymbol{\ell}^*$ (not just along the identity shift) for each pair of observations y_i, y_j.

This result may be strengthened in other manners. For constants $0 < \delta, \varepsilon \ll 1$, we can attain a tighter concentration condition of the form

$$\sum D_{ij} \geq (1+\delta)^2 N \sqrt{\sum D_{ij}^2 / SNR} + 2\varepsilon N^2 \qquad (16)$$

instead of the current condition $\sum D_{ij} \geq N^2/SNR$. The argument is based on the analysis of the SDP for adversarial semi-random Unique-Games instances by [19]. However, the proof must be more nuanced in our case, due to correlations in the noise model of C, caused by the smaller source of randomness available to us. Hence we omit the full details, but provide a sketch below.

Any SDP feasible matrix V can alternatively be represented as $V_{ik;jl} = \langle v_{ik}, v_{jl} \rangle / L$ for a set of unit vectors $v_{ik} \in \mathbb{R}^{NL}$. With this notation, $2D_{ij} = 2(1 - LV_{i0;j0}) = \|v_{i0} - v_{j0}\|^2$. The space of these unit vectors can be approximately discretized by a random projection due to the Johnson-Lindenstrauss lemma. More precisely, Lemma D.4 provides a set of unit vectors $\mathfrak{N}$ of size $|\mathfrak{N}| = \exp\left(\mathcal{O}\left(\delta^{-2}\log^2(1/\varepsilon)\right)\right)$ such that the set of unit vectors $\{v_{i0}\}_{i=1}^N$ can be approximated under a random projection φ by an N-tuple in $\mathfrak{N}$. Specifically, if $D_{ij}^{\varphi} = \|\varphi(v_{i0}) - \varphi(v_{j0})\|^2/2$, then the D_{ij}'s lie within an α_{JL}-ball of D_{ij}^{φ}, this ball being defined as $\{D : \alpha_{JL}^{-1}(D^{\varphi}) \leq D \leq \alpha_{JL}(D^{\varphi})\}$ for $\alpha_{JL}(D) = (1+\delta)D + \varepsilon$.

Instead of finding a global tail bound in Lemma D.2, we can derive a local tail bound for each α_{JL}-ball of D_{ij}^{φ}'s, each tail bound holding with probability at least $1 - 2Ne^{-t^2 N}$. For $0 < \delta, \varepsilon = \varepsilon' \ll 1$ constants, the number of N-tuples of vectors in $\mathfrak{N}$ is of size $\exp(\mathcal{O}(N))$. With a sufficiently large constant t, the local tail bound may be union bounded across all balls of vectors in $\mathfrak{N}^N$, and thus will hold for all SDP-feasible V. With some care, this argument would yield a concentration condition of the form (16).

5. NUMERICAL RESULTS

We implemented several baseline methods for multireference alignment, and plotted their average error performance across 500 iterations in Figure 5. For each iteration, we chose a signal x randomly from the distribution $\mathcal{N}(0, I_L)$, as well as N i.i.d. noise vectors $\xi_i \sim \mathcal{N}(0, \sigma^2 I_L)$, and applied each of our methods. These simulations confirm our intuition that the UG-based SDP performs better than other benchmark techniques. In particular, they suggest that the UG-based SDP is highly stable around integral instances.

The implementation using bispectrum-like invariants is discussed in Appendix A. For each of the other procedures, we construct a $NL \times L$ matrix W which records alignment preferences of shifts of y_i with y_1. For cross- or phase-correlation, $W_{ik;l}$ is the $(k-l)$th entry of the cross- or phase-correlation vector between y_1 and y_i. For the spectral rounding off the Gram matrix C, and the solution of the UG-SDP, W is formed by the top L eigenvectors of the respective matrix. The shifts are read off this matrix, and the un-shifted y_i are averaged to produce an estimate for x. The first plot shows the difference between this estimate and x.

A second measurement of performance we looked at is how easy it would be to determine the best shifts from W. A natural method is to identify an indicator vector $\mathbf{1}\{ik : l_i \equiv k\}$ lying close to the column span of W, for some labelling $\{l_i\}$. The heuristic we implemented was to apply a linear transformation to W such that the top $L \times L$ block of W is the identity matrix I_L (although there is no reason to believe this rounding is robust, it is sufficient for the purpose of having an easy benchmark between multiple methods). Then, for each i, the maximal entry in the first column of W gives the choice of shift for y_i. The second plot shows the distance this indicator vector lies from the column span of W.

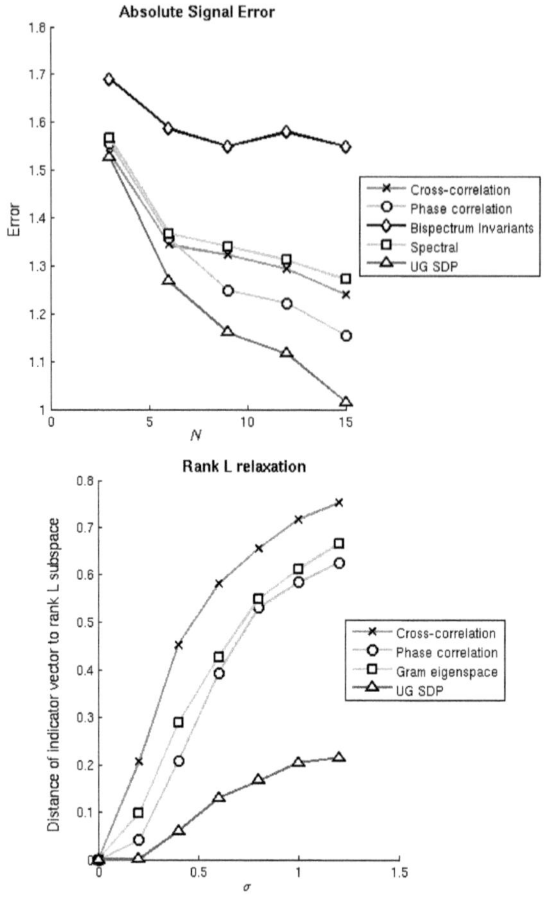

Figure 1: Averages of errors of several alignment methods across 500 iterations. The top plot has parameters $\sigma = 1$ and $L = 5$, and the bottom plot has parameters $N = 12$ and $L = 5$.

Another, perhaps more robust method, is to apply the theory of sparse recovery. The desired indicator vector $u \in \mathbb{R}^{NL}$ is a sparse vector lying near the column space of W. As suggested by Spielman, et al, in [33], such a sparse vector could be found by solving the ℓ_1-minimization problem $\min_{b \in \mathbb{R}^L} \|Wb\|_1$ and setting $u = Wb$. To prevent the solution from collapsing to zero, the search space can be limited by an affine constraint $b^T c = 1$ for an appropriate choice of $c \in \mathbb{R}^L$. In [33], this ℓ_1-minimization is done by choosing c from the rows of W.

6. GENERALIZATIONS AND FUTURE WORK

It is worth noting that the discrete multireference alignment problem naturally generalizes from shifts over $\mathbb{Z}_L$ to actions of finite groups G over finite spaces S. In this case, the analogue of phase correlation [25] is defined in terms of the generalized Fourier transform $\mathcal{F}_{G,S}(\cdot, \rho) : \mathbb{C}^S \to \mathbb{C}^{d_\rho \times d_\rho}$, where $\rho : G \to \mathbb{C}^{d_\rho \times d_\rho}$ are irreducible matrix representations. The Unique Games SDP may also be generalized in a natural manner, in rough analogy with SDP variants studied for Γ-MAX-2LIN instances. In the case of an abelian group $G = S$, the proof of Theorem 3.1 follows in the same fashion, and hence the alignment UG-based SDP without positivity constraints will remain equivalent to phase correlation.

The symmetry of the SDP in this case can be described naturally by the theory of $\mathbb{C}*$-matrix algebras. Symmetries in semidefinite programs can be written with respect to linear combinations of $\{0, 1\}$ matrices, which form a basis of a $*$-matrix algebra. Under sufficiently nice conditions, this basis can be block diagonalized, for example by Wedderburn's decomposition or by regular $*$-representations [28]. Hence, the $*$-matrix algebra can be represented by a lower-dimensional block diagonalized version. From a computational perspective, this can make highly symmetric SDPs much more amenable to sparse SDP solvers [9]. In our case, diagonalization by the block DFT allows the SDP to be rewritten as an optimization problem across L PSD matrices of size $N \times N$ instead of one PSD matrix of size $NL \times NL$.

It would be interesting to see how the performance of the SDP changes when we study the alignment problem across more difficult groups, especially non-abelian ones. For example, [32] applies angular synchronization to resolve an alignment problem over $SO(3)$.

The numerical simulations in Section 5 suggest that the UG-based SDP achieves exact recovery with high probability for sufficiently high SNR. That is, the resulting SDP matrix is integral, and by solving the SDP we obtain the solution to the quasi-ML estimator. Indeed, as the SNR decreases, there appears to be a phase transition during which the SDP almost always recovers an integral solution. Our analysis of the stability of the semidefinite program does not fully explain this phenomenon. The authors believe this to be an interesting direction for future work, especially since guarantees of exact recovery are attainable in high SNR settings for a few semidefinite relaxations, for example for the MIMO problem [26].

Another important question is to understand the sample complexity of our approach to the alignment problem. Since the objective is to recover the underlying signal x, a larger number of observations N should yield a better recovery. The question can be formalized as: for a given value of L and σ, how large does N need to be in order to allow for a reasonably accurate recovery? Methods like the bispectral invariants would be expected to require $N = \Omega(\sigma^2 L^2 \log L)$ observations. We would hypothesize, on the strength of our numerical results, that the UG-based SDP requires fewer observations for meaningful recovery.

Along with expanding the domain of the alignment problem, it would be interesting to attempt the style of analysis discussed in this paper for other maximum likelihood problems. Maximum likelihood estimators play an important role in many estimation problems, but often (as in our problem) computing or approximating the MLE is a challenging problem and semidefinite programming could perhaps provide a tractable alternative in an average case setting.

7. ACKNOWLEDGMENTS

The authors thank Yutong Chen for valuable assistance with the implementation of our algorithm. A. S. Bandeira was supported by AFOSR Grant No. FA9550-12-1-0317. M. Charikar was supported by NSF grants CCF 0832797, AF 0916218 and AF 1218687. A. Singer was partially supported by Award Number FA9550-12-1-0317 and FA9550-13-1-0076 from AFOSR, by Award Number R01GM090200 from the NIGMS, and by Award Number LTR DTD 06-05-2012 from the Simons Foundation. Parts of this work have appeared in A. Zhu's undergraduate thesis at Princeton University.

8. REFERENCES

[1] D. Amelunxen, M. Lotz, M. B. McCoy, and J. A. Tropp. Living on the edge: A geometric theory of phase transitions in convex optimization. *Available online at arXiv:1303.6672 [cs.IT]*, 2013.

[2] S. Arora, S. A. Khot, A. Kolla, D. Steurer, M. Tulsiani, and N. K. Vishnoi. Unique games on expanding constraint graphs are easy: extended abstract. In *Proceedings of the 40th annual ACM symposium on Theory of computing*, STOC '08, pages 21–28, New York, NY, USA, 2008. ACM.

[3] A. S. Bandeira, A. Singer, and D. A. Spielman. A Cheeger inequality for the graph connection Laplacian. *to appear in SIAM Journal on Matrix Analysis and Applications (SIMAX)*, 2013.

[4] E. J. Candès and B. Recht. Exact matrix completion via convex optimization. *Foundations of Computational Mathematics*, 9(6):717–772, 2009.

[5] E. J. Candès, J. Romberg, and T. Tao. Stable signal recovery from incomplete and inaccurate measurements. *Comm. Pure Appl. Math.*, 59:1207–1223, 2006.

[6] E. J. Candès, T. Strohmer, and V. Voroninski. Phaselift: Exact and stable signal recovery from magnitude measurements via convex programming. *Communications on Pure and Applied Mathematics*, 66(8):1241–1274, 2013.

[7] M. Charikar, K. Makarychev, and Y. Makarychev. Near-optimal algorithms for unique games. pages 205–214, 2006.

[8] R. Diamond. On the multiple simultaneous superposition of molecular structures by rigid body transformations. *Protein Science*, 1(10):1279–1287, October 1992.

[9] C. Dobre and E. de Klerk. Semidefinite programming approaches for structured combinatorial optimization problems, 2011.

[10] D. L. Donoho. Compressed sensing. *IEEE Trans. Inform. Theory*, 52:1289–1306, 2006.

[11] I. Dryden and K. Mardia. *Statistical shape analysis*. Wiley series in probability and statistics. Wiley, Chichester [u.a.], 1998.

[12] H. Foroosh, J. B. Zerubia, and M. Berthod. Extension of phase correlation to subpixel registration. *IEEE Transactions on Image Processing*, 11(3):188–200, 2002.

[13] M. X. Goemans and D. P. Williamson. Improved approximation algorithms for maximum cut and satisfiability problems using semidefine programming. *Journal of the Association for Computing Machinery*, 42:1115–1145, 1995.

[14] J. L. Horner and P. D. Gianino. Phase-only matched filtering. *Appl. Opt.*, 23(6):812–816, Mar 1984.

[15] R. Kakarala and G. J. Iverson. Uniqueness of results for multiple correlations of periodic functions. *J. Opt. Soc. Am. A*, 10(7):1517–1528, Jul 1993.

[16] S. Khot. On the power of unique 2-prover 1-round games. *Proceedings of the 34th Annual ACM Symposium on Theory of Computing*, pages 767–775, 2002.

[17] S. Khot, G. Kindler, E. Mossel, and R. O'Donnell. Optimal inapproximability results for max-cut and other 2-variable csps? *SIAM J. Comput.*, 37(1):319–357, 2007.

[18] A. Kolla. Spectral algorithms for unique games. *25th Annual IEEE Conference on Computational Complexity*, pages 122–130, 2010.

[19] A. Kolla, K. Makarychev, and Y. Makarychev. How to play unique games against a semi-random adversary: Study of semi-random models of unique games. *Foundations of Computer Science, IEEE Annual Symposium on*, pages 443–452, 2011.

[20] A. Kolla and M. Tulsiani. Playing random and expanding unique games. Unpublished, 2007.

[21] P. Kosir, R. DeWall, and R. Mitchell. A multiple measurement approach for feature alignment. In *Aerospace and Electronics Conference, 1995. NAECON 1995., Proceedings of the IEEE 1995 National*, volume 1, pages 94–101 vol.1, 1995.

[22] B. Laurent and P. Massart. Adaptive estimation of a quadratic functional by model selection. *The Annals of Statistics*, 28(5):pp. 1302–1338, 2000.

[23] G. Lerman, M. B. McCoy, J. A. Tropp, and T. Zhang. Robust computation of linear models, or how to find a needle in a haystack. *CoRR*, abs/1202.4044, 2012.

[24] W. Ligong, L. Xueliang, and H. C. Eigenvalues of a special kind of symmetric block circulant matrices. *Applied Math J. Chinese University Series B*, 19(1):17–26, 2004.

[25] A. Loneland. Non-commutative harmonic analysis: Generalization of phase correlation to the euclidean motion group. Master's thesis, University of Bergen, June 2010.

[26] A. Man-Cho So. Probabilistic analysis of the semidefinite relaxation detector in digital communications. In *Proceedings of the Twenty-First Annual ACM-SIAM Symposium on Discrete Algorithms*, SODA '10, pages 698–711, Philadelphia, PA, USA, 2010.

[27] A. Maurer. A bound on the deviation probability for sums of non-negative random variables. *J. Inequalities in Pure and Applied Mathematics*, 4(1):15, 2003.

[28] K. Murota. A numerical algorithm for block-diagonal decomposition of matrix *-algebras with application to semidefinite programming. *Japan Journal of Industrial and Applied Mathematics*, 27(1), 2007.

[29] R. G. Pita, M. R. Zurera, P. J. Amores, and F. L. Ferreras. Using multilayer perceptrons to align high range resolution radar signals. In W. Duch, J. Kacprzyk, E. Oja, and S. Zadrozny, editors, *Artificial Neural Networks: Formal Models and Their Applications - ICANN 2005*, volume 3697 of *Lecture Notes in Computer Science*, pages 911–916. Springer Berlin Heidelberg, 2005.

[30] B. M. Sadler and G. B. Giannakis. Shift- and rotation-invariant object reconstruction using the bispectrum. *J. Opt. Soc. Am. A*, 9(1):57–69, Jan 1992.

[31] A. Singer. Angular synchronization by eigenvectors and semidefinite programming. *Applied and Computational Harmonic Analysis*, 30(1):20 – 36, 2011.

[32] B. Sonday, A. Singer, and I. G. Kevrekidis. Noisy dynamic simulations in the presence of symmetry: Data alignment and model reduction. *Computers & Mathematics with Applications*, 65(10):1535 – 1557, 2013.

[33] D. A. Spielman, H. Wang, and J. Wright. Exact recovery of sparsely-used dictionaries. In *Proceedings of the Twenty-Third International Joint Conference on Artificial Intelligence*, IJCAI'13, pages 3087–3090. AAAI Press, 2013.

[34] D. L. Theobald and P. A. Steindel. Optimal simultaneous superpositioning of multiple structures with missing data. *Bioinformatics*, 28(15):1972–1979, 2012.

[35] D. P. Williamson and D. B. Shmoys. *The Design of Approximation Algorithms*. Cambridge University Press, New York, NY, USA, 1st edition, 2011.

[36] J. Zwart, R. van der Heiden, S. Gelsema, and F. Groen. Fast translation invariant classification of hrr range profiles in a zero phase representation. *Radar, Sonar and Navigation, IEE Proceedings*, 150(6):411–418, 2003.

APPENDIX

A. PHASE CORRELATION AND THE BISPECTRUM

Variations of the alignment problem crop up in many scientific fields, and thus many methods for alignment have been independently proposed. Such methods include iterative template aligning [21], zero phase representations [36], angular synchronization [32], and machine learning [29]. Unfortunately, to the authors' knowledge, no proposal exists for a multireference alignment method which fairly treats each input observation, makes use of all available information, and has rigorous performance discussion. We outline a couple of foundational techniques used in alignment literature in this section.

When aligning a pair of noisily shifted vectors ($N = 2$), a natural approach is to assign a score to each possible offset between the two vectors, and to estimate the best shift as the one with the highest score. A straightforward score is the inner product between the vectors, also known as cross-correlation. For two observations $y_i, y_j \in \mathbb{R}^L$, the selected shift is the maximal entry $\widehat{l} = \operatorname{argmax} v_l^{\mathsf{cross}}$ of the cross-correlation vector $v_l^{\mathsf{cross}} = \langle y_i, R_{-l} y_j \rangle$. More frequently used in practice is the phase correlation vector, whose components are

$$v_k^{\mathsf{phase}} = \frac{1}{\sqrt{L}} \sum_{l=0}^{L-1} e\left(\tfrac{-kl}{L}\right) \cdot \frac{\mathcal{F}(y_i, l)\mathcal{F}^*(y_j, l)}{|\mathcal{F}(y_i, l)\mathcal{F}^*(y_j, l)|}. \quad (17)$$

Essentially this measures the similarity of the observations in frequency space. For human-friendly images, phase correlation tends to be more appealing, since v^{phase} tends to have a sharper peak as compared to v^{cross} [14]. The relation between cross- and phase correlation can be seen from the convolution theorem:

LEMMA A.1. *Convolution theorem:* $(\mathcal{F}^* v^{\text{cross}})_k = \sqrt{L} \cdot \mathcal{F}(y_i, k)\mathcal{F}^*(y_j, k)$.

PROOF. Let M_l denote the modulation operator $(M_l x)_k = x_k e(kl/L)$, defined such that $\mathcal{F} R_l x = M_l \mathcal{F} x$. By Parseval's Theorem,

$$\langle y_i, R_{-l} y_j \rangle = \langle \mathcal{F} y_i, M_{-l} \mathcal{F} y_j \rangle = \sum_{l=0}^{L-1} e\left(\tfrac{-kl}{L}\right) \mathcal{F}(y_i, l)\mathcal{F}^*(y_j, l).$$

□

Cross- and phase correlation may be directly applied for the problem of multireference alignment, say by aligning all of the observations against the first one. However, this is not a robust method.

Another relevant notion for characterizing alignments are the moment spectra, which are shift-invariant properties of the observations. The kth power spectrum of a real signal $x \in \mathbb{R}^L$ is defined by $|\mathcal{F}(x,k)|^2 = \mathcal{F}(x,k)\mathcal{F}^*(x,k)$. This can be extended to the d-th order bispectrum (or moment spectra)

$$b(k_1, k_2, \ldots, k_d) = \mathcal{F}\left(x, \Sigma_{i=1}^d k_i\right) \prod_{i=1}^d \mathcal{F}^*(x, k_i); \tag{18}$$

its shift invariance can be seen since it is the Fourier transform of the d-th order autocorrelation function

$$a(k_1, k_2, \ldots, k_d) = \sum_{l=0}^{L-1} x_l \overline{x_{l-k_1} x_{l-k_2} \cdots x_{l-k_d}}, \tag{19}$$

by the Wiener-Khinchin theorem. How much information do these invariants capture about the signal x? Sadler and Giannakis give iterative and least squares algorithms in [30] for reconstructing the Fourier phases from full knowledge of the bispectrum, and Kakarala in [15] show the uniqueness of real function given all of its higher order moment spectra. These arguments generally tend to be of a more number-theoretic flavor and may be tedious to implement in practice.

A simple special case occurs when we take $k_1 = k_2 = \ldots = k_d = 1$ for $d = 1, \ldots, L$. This gives us the set of bispectral invariants $\mathcal{F}(x,d)\mathcal{F}^*(x,1)^d$, which can be consistently estimated from our observations y_i. With an estimate for the phase of the first Fourier coefficient $\mathcal{F}(x,1)$ (say, sample over a discretization of the unit circle), we can recover the remaining Fourier phases $\mathcal{F}(x,d)$ and thus the signal x. This approach is one of the baseline methods used in Section 5.

B. RELAXATIONS FOR MAXIMUM LIKELIHOOD

LEMMA B.1. *The data Gram matrix C with entries $C_{ik;jl} = \langle R_{-k} y_i, R_{-l} y_j \rangle$ satisfies the following properties:*

1. *$C \succeq 0$ and has rank L, with non-zero eigenvalues $\lambda_k = L \sum_{i=1}^N |\mathcal{F}(y_i,k)|^2$.*
2. *There is a unitary matrix $\mathcal{P}$ for which $\mathcal{P} C \mathcal{P}^* = \operatorname{diag}(\mathcal{C}_0, \ldots, \mathcal{C}_{L-1})$ is block diagonal, where each $\mathcal{C}_k \in \mathbb{C}^{N \times N}$.*

PROOF. C has Cholesky decomposition

$$C = (Ry)(Ry)^T \in \mathbb{R}^{LN \times LN} \quad \text{where } Ry = \begin{pmatrix} & \vdots & \\ - & R_{-k} y_i & - \\ & \vdots & \end{pmatrix}_{i,k},$$

so $C \succeq 0$ has rank L. Since the inner product of two observations is invariant under a global shift of all the observations, C is composed of $N \times N$ circulant blocks of size $L \times L$. After permuting the rows and columns of C, one may write C as a block circulant matrix

$$P^T C P = \begin{pmatrix} C_0 & C_1 & \cdots & C_{L-1} \\ C_{L-1} & C_0 & \cdots & C_{L-2} \\ \vdots & \vdots & \ddots & \vdots \\ C_1 & C_2 & \cdots & C_0 \end{pmatrix},$$

where $(C_k)_{ij} = \langle y_i, R_{-k} y_j \rangle$ encodes the pairwise information between y_i and y_j, and P is the appropriate permutation matrix. $P^T C P$ is block diagonalized by the block Discrete Fourier Transform matrix $DFT_L \otimes I_N$ [24], where $\otimes$ denotes the Kronecker product and DFT_L is the matrix representation of the normalized Discrete Fourier Transform on $\mathbb{C}^L$. $\mathcal{P} = (DFT_L \otimes I_N) P^T \in \mathbb{C}^{NL \times NL}$ is thus a unitary transformation such that

$$\mathcal{P} C \mathcal{P}^* = \operatorname{diag}(\mathcal{C}_0, \ldots, \mathcal{C}_{L-1}); \quad \mathcal{C}_k \in \mathbb{C}^{N \times N} \tag{20}$$

is block diagonal. These block diagonals are componentwise Discrete Fourier Transforms of the entries of $C_0, C_1, \ldots, C_{L-1}$:

$$\mathcal{C}_k = \sum_{l=0}^{L-1} e\left(\tfrac{kl}{L}\right) C_l = \{L \cdot \mathcal{F}(y_i,k)\mathcal{F}^*(y_j,k)\}_{ij}$$

by Lemma A.1. Note also that each $\mathcal{C}_k$ is Hermitian and rank 1 (C is of rank L, and each of the blocks $\mathcal{C}_k$ has positive rank). The unique nonzero eigenvalue λ_k of $\mathcal{C}_k$ is given by

$$\lambda_k = \operatorname{tr}(\mathcal{C}_k) = L \sum_{i=1}^N |\mathcal{F}(y_i,k)|^2. \tag{21}$$

□

For notation reference in the next lemma, consider a primal semidefinite problem of the form

$$\begin{aligned} &\text{minimize} \quad \operatorname{tr}(C_0 V) \\ &\text{subject to} \quad V \succeq 0 \quad \text{and} \quad \operatorname{tr}(C_i V) = b_i, \end{aligned} \tag{22}$$

where V is the semidefinite matrix to optimize over, and $C_i \in \mathbb{R}^{n \times n}$ are data matrix constraints and $b = (b_1, \ldots, b_m)$ are given, for $i \in \{1, 2, \ldots, m\}$. For a finite group G acting on a finite space S, let P_g denote the permutation matrix associated with the action of $g \in G$. A matrix $A \in \mathbb{C}^{|S| \times |S|}$ is G-invariant if $P_g^T A P_g = A$.

LEMMA B.2. *In the semidefinite program (22), suppose the constraint matrices $C_0, C_1, \ldots, C_m$ are G-invariant. Then there is a solution V to the SDP which is also G-invariant.*

PROOF. If V' is a solution of (22), then the matrix $V \in \mathbb{C}^{n \times n}$ given by

$$V = \mathcal{R}_G(V) := \frac{1}{|G|} \sum_{g \in G} P_g^T V' P_g$$

is G-invariant, feasible, and has the same objective value as V'. The averaging map $\mathcal{R}_G$ is known as the Reynolds operator.

This is a special case of a more general theorem about symmetry reductions in semidefinite programs from the theory of $*$-matrix algebras [9]. Informally speaking, if all of the constraint matrices $C_0, C_1, \ldots, C_m$ satisfy a class of symmetries, then there is a real solution V to (22) which also satisfies the same symmetries (for details refer to [9], Corollary 2.5.2). $\square$

THEOREM B.3. *There is a matrix $V \in \mathbb{R}^{NL\times NL}$ composed of circulant $L \times L$ blocks which solves the program (11), excluding the positivity constraint $V \geq 0$. V has rank L, corresponding to one eigenspace of eigenvalue N/L. This eigenspace contains the vector $v^{\mathsf{phase}} \in \mathbb{R}^{NL}$ satisfying*

$$v_{ik}^{\mathsf{phase}} = \frac{1}{\sqrt{L}} \sum_{l=0}^{L-1} e\left(\tfrac{-kl}{L}\right) \cdot \frac{\mathcal{F}(y_1,l)\mathcal{F}^*(y_i,l)}{|\mathcal{F}(y_1,l)\mathcal{F}^*(y_i,l)|}.$$

PROOF. The existence of a solution V composed of circulant blocks follows by a block-wise application of the Reynolds operator from Lemma B.2. Let $\mathcal{P}$ be the unitary matrix defined in Lemma 2.2. Then, $\mathcal{P}V\mathcal{P}^* = \operatorname{diag}(\mathcal{V}_0, \ldots, \mathcal{V}_{L-1})$ where $\mathcal{V}_k = \sum_{l=0}^{L-1} e\left(\frac{kl}{L}\right) V_l \in \mathbb{C}^{N\times N}$ is positive semidefinite. The SDP constraints

$$V \in \mathbb{R}_{NL\times NL}, \quad V \succeq 0, \quad V_{ik;il} = 0 \text{ for } k \neq l, \quad \sum_{k,l} V_{ik;jl} = 1$$

are respectively equivalent to the Fourier side constraints

$$\mathcal{V}_k = \overline{\mathcal{V}_{L-k}}, \quad \mathcal{V}_k \succeq 0, \quad (\mathcal{V}_k)_{ii} = 1/L, \quad (\mathcal{V}_0)_{ij} = 1/L. \quad (23)$$

Since $\mathcal{V}_k \succeq 0$, the magnitude of each entry of $\mathcal{V}_k$ is bounded by the maximum of its diagonal entries, which is $1/L$. Hence

$$\operatorname{tr}(CV) = \sum_{k\in\mathbb{Z}_L} \operatorname{tr}(\mathcal{C}_k\mathcal{V}_k) \leq \frac{1}{L} \sum_{k\in\mathbb{Z}_L} \sum_{i,j\in[N]} |(\mathcal{C}_k)_{ij}|, \quad (24)$$

with equality occuring when $\mathcal{V}_k$ has the entries of $\mathcal{C}_k$, normalized to magnitude $1/L$. Here, the $\mathcal{V}_k$'s are also rank-one matrices

$$(\mathcal{V}_k)_{ij} = \frac{\mathcal{F}(y_i,l)\mathcal{F}^*(y_j,l)}{|\mathcal{F}(y_i,l)\mathcal{F}^*(y_j,l)|}.$$

Define $w_i \in \mathbb{R}^L$ to be the vector with entries $(w_i)_k = (\mathcal{V}_k)_{i,1}$ (the choice of the index 1 is arbitrary). The concatenation of the w_i's is an eigenvector of the block diagonalization of V, and thus $v^{\mathsf{phase}} := \mathcal{P}^*w$ is an eigenvector of V. Its entries are given by

$$v_{ik}^{\mathsf{phase}} := \mathcal{F}^*(w_i,k) = \frac{1}{\sqrt{L}} \sum_{l=0}^{L-1} e\left(\tfrac{-kl}{L}\right) \cdot \frac{\mathcal{F}(y_1,l)\mathcal{F}^*(y_i,l)}{|\mathcal{F}(y_1,l)\mathcal{F}^*(y_i,l)|}.$$

Let $W^{\mathsf{phase}} \in \mathbb{R}^{NL\times L}$ be the matrix whose column vectors are generated by circulating the N blocks of L entries of v^{phase}. Its columns are linearly independent since the top $L \times L$ block of W^{phase} is the identity matrix I_L, and the column vectors span the eigenspace of V. $\square$

C. NP-HARDNESS OF QUASI MLE

A special case of the Unique-Games class of problems is that of MAX-2LIN(q). The labels $\{x_i\}$ can be thought of as equivalence classes modulo q, and each constraint is represented by a linear equation in two variables $a_{ij}x_i + b_{ij}x_j \equiv c_{ij} \pmod q$. The subclass Γ-MAX-2LIN(q) consists of the cases where each constraint has the form $x_i - x_j \equiv c_{ij} \pmod q$. It is known to be as hard as the general Unique-Games problem [17]. Associating each variable x_i as a vertex of a graph and each constraint as an edge, the instance is associated with a graph $G = (V(G), E(G))$, where $V(G) = [N]$ and $|E(G)| = M$.

THEOREM C.1. *Consider the problem* ALIGN$(y_1, \ldots, y_N)$*: for vectors $y_1, \ldots, y_N \in \mathbb{R}^L$, find the shifts $\boldsymbol{l} = (l_1, \ldots, l_N)$ which maximize*

$$\mathcal{A}(l_1, \ldots, l_N) = \sum_{i,j\in[N]} \langle R_{-l_i}y_i, R_{-l_i}y_j\rangle.$$

Let $\mathcal{A}^* = \max_{\boldsymbol{l}} \mathcal{A}(\boldsymbol{l})$. It is NP*-hard (under randomized reductions) to esimate $\mathcal{A}^*$ within $16/17 + \varepsilon$ of its true value. It is* UG*-hard (under randomized reductions) to estimate $\mathcal{A}^*$ within any constant factor.*

We demonstrate this by a poly-time approximation preserving reduction from (a connected instance of) Γ-MAX-2LIN(q). Suppose that at most ρ^* fraction of the M constraints $x_i - x_j \equiv c_{ij} \pmod q$ may be simultaneously satisfiable.

Let poly(M) be the space of integer functions which are bounded by polynomial order, i.e. $f \in$ poly(M) iff there are constants C, k such that $f(M) \leq CM^k$ for all $M \geq 1$. We say that an event occurs w.h.p if it occurs with probability $1 - \epsilon(q, G)$, where $\frac{1}{\epsilon(q,G)} \notin$ poly$(q \cdot |E(G)|)$. Notice under this definition that if poly(qM) events occur w.h.p, then by an union bound the event that all occur will also be w.h.p.

Construct a parameter $s = s(q, M) \in$ poly(qM). We take the vectors $y_1, \ldots, y_N$ to be of length $L = qMs$. The indices of the vector y_i can be expressed in mixed radix notation by elements of the tuple $(\mathbb{Z}_q, E(G), [s])$. For example, we would associate the tuple index (x, e_k, t) of y_i by the index $x \cdot qM + e_k \cdot M + t$, where e_k is the kth edge in some enumeration of $E(G)$. Note that a shift by $c \cdot qM$ takes this tuple index to $(x, e_k, t) + c \cdot qM \to (x + c, e_k, t)$.

For each edge constraint $x_i - x_j \equiv c_{ij}$, let z_{ij} be a vector uniformly at random chosen from $\{\pm 1\}^s$. Assign the entries $(0, \{i,j\}, \cdot)$ of y_i to z_{ij}, and the entries $(c_{ij}, \{i,j\}, \cdot)$ of y_j to z_{ij}. The remaining entries of the y_i's will be sampled from i.i.d Rademacher random variables ($\{\pm 1\}$ with probability $1/2$). Intuitively, a relative shift of $c_{ij} \cdot qM$ between y_i and y_j will produce a large inner product due to the overlapping of the z_{ij}'s, while any other shift between them would produce low inner products.

LEMMA C.2. *Suppose $\gamma \in$ poly(qM). Consider two random vectors y_1, y_2 of length γ whose entries are i.i.d sampled from the Rademacher distribution. W.h.p, for any $0 < \epsilon \ll 1$, the inner product of every possible shift $R_\ell y_1$ of y_1 with y_2 is bounded in absolute value by $\sqrt{\gamma} \cdot m^\epsilon$.*

PROOF. By independence, each inner product is the sum of γ independent Bernoulli random variables which take values ± 1 with probability $1/2$. Hoeffding's inequality indicates

$$\Pr(\langle R_\ell y_1, y_2\rangle \geq \sqrt{\gamma} \cdot (qM)^\epsilon) \leq 2\exp\left\{-(qM)^\epsilon/2\right\},$$

so $\frac{1}{\Pr(\langle R_\ell y_1, y_2\rangle \geq \sqrt{\gamma}(qM)^\epsilon)} \notin$ poly(qM). Union bounding over all $\gamma =$ poly(qM) such inner products, w.h.p all of the inner products are simultaneously bounded by $\sqrt{\gamma} \cdot (qM)^\epsilon$. $\square$

We say an edge $\{i,j\} \in E(G)$ is c_{ij}-satisfied under a labelling $\boldsymbol{\ell}$ if $l_i - l_j \equiv c_{ij}qM \pmod{L}$. From Lemma C.2, we observe that w.h.p, for any choices of shifts l_i, l_j,

$$|\langle R_{-l_i}y_i,\ R_{-l_j}y_j\rangle - s\cdot\delta(\{i,j\} \in E(G) \text{ is } c_{ij}\text{-satisfied})| < (qM)^{\epsilon}\sqrt{L}.$$

It follows that if the labelling $\boldsymbol{\ell}$ induces exactly k c_{ij}-satisfied edges, w.h.p

$$\begin{aligned}|\mathcal{A}(\boldsymbol{\ell}) - 2ks| &< k(qM)^{\epsilon}\sqrt{L} + (N^2 - k)(qM)^{\epsilon}\sqrt{L} \\ &\le q^{\epsilon}M^{2+\epsilon}\sqrt{L}. \end{aligned} \tag{25}$$

THEOREM C.3. *From a given labelling $\boldsymbol{\ell}$, w.h.p one may in polynomial time construct $(x_1,\ldots,x_N) \in \mathbb{Z}_q^N$ satisfying at least $\left(\mathcal{A}(\boldsymbol{\ell}) - q^{\epsilon}M^{2+\epsilon}\sqrt{L}\right)/(2s)$ edge-constraints $x_i - x_j \equiv c_{ij}$. Conversely, w.h.p there is a labelling $\boldsymbol{\ell}^{\max}$ w.h.p satisfying $\mathcal{A}(\boldsymbol{\ell}^{\max}) > 2s\cdot\rho^*M - q^{\epsilon}M^{2+\epsilon}\sqrt{L}$.*

PROOF. Consider the subgraph H of G with vertex set $V(G)$ and edge set comprising all edges c_{ij}-satisfied under $\boldsymbol{\ell}$. For each connected component of H, arbitrarily choose a vertex i of the component to have $x_i = 0$. Follow a spanning tree of each connected component and assign each neighbor j by $x_j \equiv x_i - c_{ij} \pmod{q}$. The first implication of the lemma follows immediately by applying (25). Conversely, construct the labelling $\boldsymbol{\ell}^{\max}$ by setting $l_i^{\max} = x_i \cdot qM$. This labelling induces at least ρ^*M c_{ij}-satisfied edges, and (25) completes the lemma. ☐

It is UG-hard (and thus NP-hard assuming the Unique Games conjecture) to approximate Γ-MAX-2LIN(q) within any constant factor [17]. As a corollary to Theorem C.3, any poly-time approximation ratio for ALIGN will also be a poly-time approximation ratio for Γ-MAX-2LIN(q). Thus the same hardness of approximation results for Γ-MAX-2LIN(q) hold for ALIGN (under randomized reductions). MAX-CUT is a special case of Γ-MAX-2LIN(q). Since it is NP-hard to approximate MAX-CUT within $16/17+\varepsilon$ (independent of the Unique Games conjecture), it is NP-hard (under randomized reductions) to approximate ALIGN within $16/17+\varepsilon$.

D. STABILITY

LEMMA D.1. *$\mathbb{E}[\eta_{ij}|\xi_i] \le \mu_\eta\|\xi_i\|$ and $\mathbb{E}[\eta_{ij}^2|\xi_i] \le \sigma_\eta\|\xi_i\|^2$, where $\mu_\eta = 2\sigma(\log L + 1)$ and $\sigma_\eta^2 = 4\sigma^2(\log^2 L + 1)$.*

PROOF. Take $\zeta \sim \mathcal{N}(0, I_L)$, and choose a unit vector $z \in \mathbb{R}^L$. Define $\eta(z) = \max_l \eta_l(z)$, where the distribution of $\eta_l(z) = |\langle R_l z, \zeta\rangle|$ is independent of the choice of z. Union bounding,

$$\begin{aligned}\Pr\left(\eta(z) \ge t\right) &\le \sum_{l\in\mathbb{Z}_L} \Pr\left(\eta_l(z) \ge \tfrac{t}{2}\right) \\ &= \sum_l \Pr\left(|\zeta_l| \ge \tfrac{t}{2}\right) \le \min\left\{1, \frac{2L}{t}\cdot\frac{e^{-t^2/2}}{\sqrt{2\pi}}\right\}.\end{aligned}$$

Thus, for $T > 1$,

$$\begin{aligned}\mu_\eta = \mathbb{E}\,\eta(z) &= \int_0^\infty \Pr\left(\eta(z) \ge t\right)dt \\ &\le T + \frac{2L}{\sqrt{2\pi}}\int_T^\infty te^{-t^2/2}\,dt \\ &\le T + Le^{-T}\end{aligned}$$

and

$$\begin{aligned}\sigma_\eta^2 = \mathbb{E}\,\eta(z)^2 &= \int_0^\infty 2t\Pr\left(\eta(z) \ge t\right)dt \\ &\le T^2 + \frac{L}{\sqrt{2\pi}}\int_T^\infty te^{-t^2/2}\,dt \\ &\le T^2 + Le^{-T}.\end{aligned}$$

The lemma follows by taking $T = \log L$, since $\eta_{ij} = 2\sigma\|\xi_i\|\cdot\eta(\xi_i/\|\xi_i\|)$ conditional on ξ_i. ☐

LEMMA D.2. *Let $t > 0$. With probability at least $1 - 2Ne^{-t^2N}$,*

$$\sum_{i\ne j}(\eta_{ij} + \eta_{j0})D_{ij} \le (\mu_\eta + \sigma_\eta t)\left(2\|x\| + \frac{1}{N}\sum_i \|\xi_i\|\right)N^2. \tag{26}$$

holds for all $D_{ij} \in [0,1]$.

PROOF. Define the random variables $Z_{ij} = (\eta_{ij}+\eta_{j0})D_{ij} \le \eta_{ij} + \eta_{j0}$. For fixed i, the η_{ij}'s are independent positive random variables. Applying the one-sided tail bound for independent positive random variables by Maurer [27], the probability the event

$$\sum_j(\eta_{ij} + \eta_{j0}) - \sum_j \mathbb{E}\left(\eta_{ij} + \eta_{j0}\right) \ge t_i\sqrt{\sum_j \mathbb{E}\left(\eta_{ij}^2 + \eta_{j0}^2\right)}$$

occurs is bounded under $2e^{-t_i^2}$. Choose $t_i = t\sqrt{N}$. By union bound, with probability at least $1 - 2Ne^{-t^2N}$,

$$\begin{aligned}\sum_{i,j} Z_{ij} &\le \sum_i \mu_\eta(2\|x\| + \|\xi_i\|)N + \sum_i t\sqrt{N^2\sigma_\eta^2(4\|x\|^2 + \|\xi_i\|^2)} \\ &\le (\mu_\eta + \sigma_\eta t)\left(2\|x\| + \frac{1}{N}\sum_i\|\xi_i\|\right)N^2.\end{aligned}$$

☐

THEOREM D.3. *With probability $1 - e^{-N+o(N)}$, the solution to SDP (11) satisfies*

$$\sum_{i,j} D_{ij} \le \frac{(\|x\| + \sigma^2\sqrt{L})\cdot 12\log eL}{\Delta}\cdot N^2.$$

PROOF. Let V be a solution matrix to the SDP, so that $\operatorname{tr}(CV) \ge \operatorname{tr}(CV^{int})$. It follows from Lemma 4.1 that

$$\Delta\sum_{ij} D_{ij} \le \sum_{ij}(\eta_{ij} + \eta_{j0})D_{ij}.$$

The χ^2-tail bound of Laurent-Massart [22] states

$$\Pr\left(\frac{1}{\sigma^2}\sum_i \|\xi_i\|^2 \le NL + 2\sqrt{NLt} + 2t\right) \ge 1 - \exp\{-t\}. \tag{27}$$

When $t = NL$ this gives

$$\sum_i \|\xi_i\| \le \sqrt{N\sum_i \|\xi_i\|^2} \le \sigma N\sqrt{5L}.$$

with probability at least $1 - e^{-NL}$. Union bounding with the tail bound of Lemma D.2, and applying Lemma D.1,

$$\begin{aligned}\Delta\sum_{ij} D_{ij} &\le (\mu_\eta + \sigma_\eta)\left(2\|x\| + \frac{1}{N}\sum_i \|\xi_i\|\right)N^2 \\ &\le 12\log eL(\|x\| + \sigma\sqrt{L})N^2\end{aligned}$$

with probability at least $1 - e^{-N+o(N)}$. □

LEMMA D.4. *Let $0 < \delta, \varepsilon, \varepsilon' \ll 1$ be small constants, and define $\alpha_{JL}(x) = (1+\delta)x + \varepsilon$. There is a set of unit vectors $\mathfrak{N}$ of size at most*

$$\exp\left(\mathcal{O}\left(\delta^{-2}\log(1/\varepsilon)\log(1/\varepsilon')\right)\right)$$

such that for any set of unit vectors $\{v_i\}$, there is a map $\varphi : \{v_i\} \to \mathfrak{N}$ satisfying the inequality

$$\alpha_{JL}^{-1}\left(\|v_i - v_j\|^2\right) \le \|\varphi(v_i) - \varphi(v_j)\|^2 \le \alpha_{JL}\left(\|v_i - v_j\|^2\right)$$

for at least $1 - \varepsilon'$ fraction of the pairs $(i, j) \in [N] \times [N]$.

PROOF. This lemma appears frequently in SDP literature, and in particular is used to analyze adversarial semi-random Unique-Games instances in [19]. Notice that the size of the set $\mathfrak{N}$ is independent of the number of vectors in the set $\{v_i\}$.

Construct a $\varepsilon/32$-net $\mathfrak{N}$ of the unit hypersphere in a $\mathcal{O}(\delta^2 \log(1/\varepsilon'))$-dimensional space $\mathfrak{L}$. By the (strong version of the) Johnson-Lindenstrauss lemma, there is a randomized mapping $\varphi' : \{v_i\} \to \mathfrak{L}$ satisfying

$$(1-\delta/2)\|v_i - v_j\|^2 \le \|\varphi'(v_i) - \varphi'(v_j)\|^2 \le (1+\delta/2)\|v_i - v_j\|^2$$

with probability at least $1 - \varepsilon'$. Define $\varphi(v_i)$ to be the closest point to $\varphi'(v_i)$ in $\mathfrak{N}$, and observe that

$$(1-\delta/2)x - \varepsilon \ge \frac{x - \varepsilon}{1+\delta} = \alpha_{JL}^{-1}(x), \quad (1+\delta/2)x + \varepsilon \le \alpha_{JL}(x)$$

for all $x > 0$, so φ satisfies the conditions of the lemma. □

Decompositions of Triangle-Dense Graphs

Rishi Gupta[*]
Stanford University
450 Serra Mall
Stanford, CA 94305
rishig@cs.stanford.edu

Tim Roughgarden[†]
Stanford University
450 Serra Mall
Stanford, CA 94305
tim@cs.stanford.edu

C. Seshadhri[‡]
Sandia National Labs
7011 East Ave
Livermore, CA 94550
scomand@sandia.gov

ABSTRACT

High triangle density — the graph property stating that a constant fraction of two-hop paths belong to a triangle — is a common signature of social networks. This paper studies triangle-dense graphs from a structural perspective. We prove constructively that significant portions of a triangle-dense graph are contained in a disjoint union of dense, radius 2 subgraphs. This result quantifies the extent to which triangle-dense graphs resemble unions of cliques. We also show that our algorithm recovers planted clusterings in approximation-stable k-median instances.

Categories and Subject Descriptors

F.2.0 [**Analysis of Algorithms and Problem Complexity**]: General; G.2.2 [**Discrete Mathematics**]: Graph theory

Keywords

Graph algorithms; Social and information networks; Clustering

1. INTRODUCTION

Can the special structure possessed by social networks be exploited algorithmically? Answering this question requires a formal definition of "social network structure." Extensive work on this topic has generated countless proposals but little consensus (see e.g. [CF06]). The most oft-mentioned (and arguably most validated) statistical properties of social networks include heavy-tailed degree distributions [BA99, BKM$^+$00, FFF99], a high density of triangles [WS98, SCW$^+$10, UKBM11] and other dense subgraphs or "communities" [For10, GN02, New03, New06, LLDM08], and low diameter and the small world property [Kle00a, Kle00b, Kle01, New01].

Much of the recent mathematical work on social networks has focused on the important goal of developing generative models that produce random networks with many of the above statistical properties. Well-known examples of such models include preferential attachment [BA99] and related copying models [KRR$^+$00], Kronecker graphs [CZF04, LCK$^+$10], and the Chung-Lu random graph model [CL02b, CL02a]. A generative model articulates a hypothesis about what "real-world" social networks look like, and is directly useful for generating synthetic data. Once a particular generative model of social networks is adopted, a natural goal is to design algorithms tailored to perform well on the instances generated by the model. It can also be used as a proxy to study the effect of random processes (like edge deletions) on a network. Examples of such results include [AJB00, LAS$^+$08, MS10].

This paper pursues a different approach. In lieu of adopting a particular generative model for social networks, we ask:

> *Is there a combinatorial assumption weak enough to hold in every "reasonable" model of social networks, yet strong enough to permit useful structural and algorithmic results?*

That is, we seek algorithms that offer non-trivial guarantees for *every* reasonable model of social networks, including those yet to be devised.

Triangle-Dense Graphs

We initiate the algorithmic study of *triangle-dense graphs.* Let a *wedge* be a two-hop path in an undirected graph.

Definition 1 (Triangle-Dense Graph). *The* triangle density *of an undirected graph $G = (V, E)$ is $\tau(G) := 3t(G)/w(G)$, where $t(G)$ is the number of triangles in G and $w(G)$ is the number of wedges in G (conventionally, $\tau(G) = 0$ if $w(G) = 0$). The class of* ϵ-triangle dense graphs *consists of the graphs G with $\tau(G) \geq \epsilon$.*

Since every triangle of a graph contains 3 wedges, and no two triangles share a wedge, the triangle density of a graph is between 0 and 1. We use the informal term "triangle

---

*Supported in part by the ONR PECASE Award of the second author.

†This research was supported in part by NSF Awards CCF-1016885 and CCF-1215965, an AFOSR MURI grant, and an ONR PECASE Award.

‡Sandia National Laboratories is a multi-program laboratory managed and operated by Sandia Corporation, a wholly owned subsidiary of Lockheed Martin Corporation, for the U.S. Department of Energy's National Nuclear Security Administration under contract DE-AC04-94AL85000.

ITCS'14, January 12–14, 2014, Princeton, New Jersey, USA.

ACM 978-1-4503-2698-8/14/01 ...$15.00.
http://dx.doi.org/10.1145/2554797.2554840.

dense graphs" to mean graphs with constant triangle density. In the social sciences, triangle density is usually called the *transitivity* of a graph [WF94]. We use the term triangle density because "transitivity" already has strong connotations in graph theory.

As an example, the triangle density of a graph is 1 if and only if it is the union of cliques. The triangle density of an Erdös-Renyi graph, drawn from $G(n,p)$, is concentrated around p. Thus, only very dense Erdös-Renyi graphs have constant triangle density. Social networks are generally sparse and yet have remarkably large triangle density; the Facebook graph, for instance, has triangle density 0.16 [UKBM11]. High triangle density is perhaps the least controversial signature of social networks (see related work below).

The class of ϵ-triangle dense graphs becomes quite diverse as soon as ϵ is bounded below 1. For example, the complete tripartite graph is triangle dense. Every graph obtained from a bounded-degree graph by replacing each vertex with a triangle is triangle dense. Adding a clique on $n^{1/3}$ vertices to an arbitrary n-vertex graph produces a triangle-dense graph. We give a litany of examples in §4. Can there be interesting structural or algorithmic results for this rich class of graphs?

Our Results: A Decomposition Theorem

Our main decomposition theorem quantifies the extent to which a triangle-dense graph resembles a union of cliques. The next definition gives our notion of an "approximate union of cliques." In it, we use $G|_S$ to denote the subgraph of a graph G induced by a subset S of vertices. Also, the *edge density* of a graph $G=(V,E)$ is $|E|/\binom{|V|}{2}$.

Definition 2 (Tightly Knit Family). *Let $\rho > 0$. A collection $V_1, V_2, \ldots, V_k$ of disjoint sets of vertices of a graph $G=(V,E)$ forms a* ρ-tightly-knit family *if:*

- *Each subgraph $G|_{V_i}$ has both edge density and triangle density at least ρ.*
- *Each subgraph $G|_{V_i}$ has radius at most 2.*

When ρ is a constant, we often refer simply to a tightly-knit family. Every "cluster" of a tightly-knit family is dense in edges and in triangles. In the context of social networks, an abundance of triangles is generally associated with meaningful social structure.

Our main decomposition theorem states that every triangle-dense graph contains a tightly-knit family that captures a constant fraction of the graph's triangles.

Theorem 3 (Main Decomposition Theorem). *For every triangle-dense graph G, there exists a tightly-knit family that contains a constant fraction of the triangles of G.*

We emphasize that Theorem 3 requires only that the input graph G is triangle dense — beyond this property, it could be sparse or dense, low- or high-diameter, and possess an arbitrary degree distribution. Graphs that are not triangle dense, such as sparse Erdös-Renyi random graphs, do not generally admit non-trivial tightly-knit families (even if the triangle density requirement for each cluster is dropped).

Our proof of Theorem 3 is constructive. Using suitable data structures, the resulting algorithm can be implemented to run in time proportional to the number of wedges of the graph; see Appendix A for more details. This running time is reasonable for many social networks. Our preliminary implementation of the algorithm requires only a few minutes to decompose networks with millions of edges.

Note that Theorem 3 is non-trivial only because we require that the tightly-knit family preserve the "interesting social information" of the original graph, in the form of the graph's triangles. Extracting a single low-diameter cluster rich in edges and triangles is easy — large triangle density implies that typical vertex neighborhoods have these properties. But extracting such a cluster carelessly can do more harm than good, destroying many triangles that only partially intersect the cluster. Our proof of Theorem 3 shows how to repeatedly extract low-diameter dense clusters while preserving at least a constant fraction of the triangles of the original graph.

A triangle-dense graph need not contain a tightly-knit family that contains a constant fraction of the graph's *edges*; see the examples in §4. The culprit is that triangle density is a "global" condition and does not guarantee good local triangle density everywhere, allowing room for a large number of edges that are intuitively spurious. Under the stronger condition of constant local triangle density, however, we can compute a tightly-knit family with a stronger guarantee.

Definition 4 (Jaccard Similarity). *The* Jaccard similarity *of an edge $e=(i,j)$ of a graph $G=(V,E)$ is the fraction of vertices in the neighborhood of e that participate in triangles:*

$$J_e = \frac{|N(i)\cap N(j)|}{|N(i)\cup N(j)\setminus\{i,j\}|}, \tag{1}$$

where $N(x)$ denotes the neighbors of a vertex x in G.

Definition 5 (Everywhere Triangle-Dense). *A graph is* everywhere ϵ-triangle dense *if $J_e \geq \epsilon$ for every edge e.*

Observe that an everywhere ϵ-triangle dense graph is ϵ-triangle dense. The following is proved as Theorem 15.

Theorem 6 (Stronger Decomposition Theorem). *Consider an everywhere triangle-dense graph $G=(V,E)$ with w wedges. There exists a tightly-knit family that contains a constant fraction of the* edges *and triangles of G.*

Applications to Planted Cluster Models.

We give an algorithmic application of our decomposition in §5, where the tightly knit family produced by our algorithm is meaningful in its own right. We consider the approximation-stable metric k-median instances introduced by Balcan, Blum, and Gupta [BBG09]. By definition, every solution of an approximation-stable instance that has near-optimal objective function value is structurally similar to the optimal solution. They reduce their problem to clustering a certain graph with "planted" clusters corresponding to the optimal solution. We prove that our algorithm recovers a close approximation to the the planted clusters, matching their guarantee.

1.1 Discussion

Structural Assumptions vs. Generative Models.

Pursuing structural results and algorithmic guarantees that assume only a combinatorial condition (namely, constant triangle density), rather than a particular model of social networks, has clear advantages and disadvantages. The class of graphs generated by a specific model will generally permit stronger structural and algorithmic guarantees than the class of graphs that share a single statistical property. On the other hand, algorithms and results tailored to a single model can lack robustness: they might not be meaningful if reality differs from the model, and are less likely to translate across different application domains that require different models. Our results for triangle-dense graphs are relevant for every model of social networks that generates such graphs with high probability, and we expect that all future social network models will have this property. And of course, our results can be used in any application domain that concerns triangle-dense graphs, whether motivated by social networks or not.

Beyond generality and robustness, a second reason to prefer a combinatorial assumption to a generative model is that the assumption can be easily verified for a given data set. Since computing the triangle density of a network is a well-studied problem, both theoretically and practically (see [SPK13] and the references therein), the extent to which a network meets the triangle density assumption can be quantified. By contrast, it is not clear how to argue that a network is a typical instance from a generative model, other than by verifying various statistical properties (such as triangle density). This difficulty of verification is amplified when there are multiple generative models vying for prominence, as is currently the case with social and information networks (e.g. [CF06]).

Why Triangle Density.

Social networks possess a number of statistical signatures, as discussed above. Why single out triangle density? First, there is tremendous empirical support for large triangle density in social networks. This property has been studied for decades in the social sciences [HL70, Col88, Bur04, Fau06, FWVDC10], and recently there have been numerous large-scale studies on online social networks [SCW$^+$10, UKBM11, SPK13]. Second, in light of this empirical evidence, generative models for social and information networks are explicitly designed to produce networks with high triangle density [WS98, CF06, SCW$^+$10, VB12]. Third, the assumption of constant triangle density seems to impose more exploitable structure than the other most widely accepted properties of social and information networks. For example, the property of having small diameter indicates little about the structure of a network — every network can be rendered small-diameter by adding one extra vertex connected to all other vertices. Similarly, merely assuming a power-law degree distribution does not seem to impose significant restrictions on a graph [FPP06]. For example, the Chung-Lu model [CL02b] generates power-law graphs with no natural decompositions. While constant triangle density is not a strong enough assumption to exclude all "obviously unrealistic graphs," it nevertheless enables non-trivial decomposition results. Finally, we freely admit that imposing one or more combinatorial conditions other than triangle density could lead to equally interesting results, and we welcome future work along such lines. For example, recent work by Ugander, Backstrom, and Kleinberg [UBK13] suggests that constraining the frequencies of additional small subgraphs could produce a refined model of social and information networks.

Why Tightly-Knit Families.

We have intentionally highlighted the existence and computation of tightly-knit families in triangle-dense graphs, rather than the (approximate) solution of any particular computational problem on such graphs. Our main structural result quantifies the extent to which we can "visualize" a triangle-dense graph as, approximately, a union of cliques. This is a familiar strategy for understanding restricted graph classes, analogous to using separator theorems to make precise how planar graphs resemble grids [LT79], tree decompositions to quantify how bounded-treewidth graphs resemble trees [RS86], and the regularity lemma to describe how dense graphs are approximately composed of "random-like" bipartite graphs [Sze78]. Such structural results provide a flexible foundation for future algorithmic applications. We offer a specific application to recovering planted clusterings and leave as future work the design of more applications.

2. AN INTUITIVE OVERVIEW

We give an intuitive description of our proof. Our approach to finding a tightly-knit family is an iterative extraction procedure. We find a single member of the family, remove this set from the graph (called the extraction), and repeat. Let us start with an everywhere triangle-dense graph G, and try to extract a single set S. It is easy to check that every vertex neighborhood is dense and has many triangles, and would qualify as a set in a tightly-knit family. But for vertex i, there may be many vertices outside $N(i)$ (the neighborhood of i) that form triangles with a single edge contained in $N(i)$. By extracting $N(i)$, we could destroy too many triangles. We give examples in §4 where such a naïve approach fails.

Here is a simple greedy fix to the procedure. We start by adding $N(i)$ and i to the set S. If any vertex outside $N(i)$ forms many triangles with the edges in $N(i)$, we just add it to S. It is not clear that we solve our problem by adding these vertices to S, since the extraction of S could still destroy many triangles. We prove that by adding at most d_i vertices (where d_i is the degree of i) with the highest number of triangles to $N(i)$, this "destruction" can be bounded. In other words, $G|_S$ will have a high density, obviously has radius 2 (from i), and will contain a constant fraction of the triangles incident to S.

Naturally, we can simply iterate this procedure and hope to get the entire tightly-knit family. But there is a catch. We crucially needed the graph to be *everywhere* triangle-dense for the previous argument. After extracting S, this need not hold. We therefore employ a *cleaning* procedure that iteratively removes edges of low Jaccard similarity and produces an everywhere triangle-dense graph for the next extraction. This procedure also destroys some triangles, but we can upper bound this number. As an aside, removing low Jaccard similarity edges has been used for sparsifying real-world graphs by Satuluri, Parthasarathy, and Ruan [SPR11].

When the algorithm starts with an arbitrary triangle-dense graph G, it first cleans the graph to get an everywhere triangle-dense graph. We may lose many edges during the initial cleaning, and this is inevitable, as examples in §4 show. In the end, this procedure constructs a tightly-knit family containing a constant fraction of the triangles of the original triangle-dense graph.

When G is everywhere triangle-dense, we can ensure that the tightly-knit family contains a constant fraction of the *edges* as well. Our proof is a non-trivial charging argument. By assigning an appropriate weight function to triangles and wedges, we can charge removed edges to removed triangles. This (constructively) proves the existence of a tightly-knit family with a constant fraction of edges and triangles.

3. EXTRACTING TIGHTLY-KNIT FAMILIES

In this section we walk through the proof outlined in §2 above. We first bound the losses from the cleaning procedure in §3.2. We then show how to extract a member of a tightly-knit family from a cleaned graph in §3.3. We combine these two procedures in Theorem 14 of §3.4 to obtain a full tightly-knit family from a triangle-dense graph. Finally, Theorem 15 of §3.5 shows that the procedure also preserves a constant fraction of the edges in an everywhere triangle-dense graph.

3.1 Preliminaries

We begin with some notation. Consider a graph $G = (V, E)$. We index vertices with $i, j, k, \ldots$. Vertex i has degree d_i. We use $w_i = \binom{d_i}{2}$ to denote the number of wedges where i is the middle vertex, and t_i to denote the number of triangles containing i. For edge $e = (i, j)$, we use $w_e = d_i + d_j - 2$ to denote the number of wedges including e, and t_e to denote the number of triangles including e. As mentioned earlier, the triangle density τ is $3t/w$. We define the local version (also called clustering coefficients [WS98]) by $\tau_i = t_i/w_i$. The Jaccard similarity J_e in (1) can be written as t_e/w_e (with the convention that if $w_e = 0$ then $J_e = 0$).

Let S be a set of vertices. The number of triangles including some vertex in S is denoted t_S. We use $G|_S$ for the induced subgraph on G, and $t_S^{(I)}$ for the number of triangles in $G|_S$ (the I is for "internal"). We will be repeatedly dealing with subgraphs H of G. We use the $\ldots(H)$ notation for the respective quantities in H. So, $t(H)$ would denote the number of triangles in H, $d_i(H)$ denotes the degree of i in H, etc.

3.2 Cleaning a graph

It will be convenient to have a "cleaning" procedure that constructs an everywhere triangle-dense graph.

DEFINITION 7. *Consider the following procedure $clean_\epsilon$ on a graph H that takes input $\epsilon \in (0, 1]$. Iteratively remove an arbitrary edge with Jaccard similarity less than ϵ, as long as such an edge exists. Finally remove all isolated vertices. This is called ϵ-cleaning. Abusing notation, the output is denoted by $clean_\epsilon(H)$.*

The output $clean_\epsilon(H)$ is dependent on the order in which edges are removed, but our results hold for an arbitrary removal order. Satuluri et al. [SPR11] use a more nuanced version of cleaning for graph sparsification of social networks. They provide much empirical evidence that removal of low Jaccard similarity edges does not affect graph structure. Our arguments below may provide some theoretical justification.

CLAIM 8. *The number of triangles in $clean_\epsilon(H)$ is at least $t(H) - \epsilon w(H)$.*

PROOF. The process $clean_\epsilon$ removes a sequence of edges $e_1, e_2, \ldots$. Let W_l and T_l be the set of wedges and triangles that are removed when e_l is removed. Since the Jaccard similarity of e_l *at this stage* is at most ϵ, $|T_l| \leq \epsilon(|W_l| - |T_l|) \leq \epsilon|W_l|$. All the W_l's (and T_l's) are disjoint. Hence, the total number of triangles removed is $\sum_l |T_l| \leq \epsilon \sum_l |W_l| \leq \epsilon w(H)$. □

We get an obvious corollary by noting that $t(H) = \tau(H) \cdot w(H)/3$.

COROLLARY 9. *The graph $clean_\epsilon(H)$ is everywhere ϵ-triangle dense and has at least $(\tau(H)/3 - \epsilon)w(H)$ triangles.*

We also state a simple lemma on the properties of everywhere triangle-dense graphs.

LEMMA 10. *If H is everywhere ϵ-triangle dense, then $d_i \geq \epsilon\, d_j$ for every edge (i, j). Furthermore, $N(i)$ is ϵ-edge dense for every vertex i.*

PROOF. If $d_i \geq d_j$ we are done. Otherwise

$$\epsilon \leq J_{(i,j)} = \frac{|N(i) \cap N(j)|}{|(N(i) \setminus \{j\}) \cup (N(j) \setminus \{i\})|} \leq \frac{d_i - 1}{d_j - 1} \leq \frac{d_i}{d_j}$$

as desired. To prove the second statement, let $S = N(i)$. The number of edges in S is at least

$$\frac{1}{2}\sum_{j \in S} |N(i) \cap N(j)| \geq \frac{1}{2}\sum_{j \in S} J_{(i,j)}(d_i - 1) \geq \frac{\epsilon d_i(d_i - 1)}{2} = \epsilon\binom{d_i}{2}.$$

□

3.3 Finding a single cluster

Suppose we have an everywhere ϵ-triangle dense graph H. We show how to remove a single cluster of a tightly-knit family. Since the entire focus of this subsection is on H, we drop the $\ldots(H)$ notation.

For a set S of vertices and $\rho \in (0, 1]$, we say that S is *ρ-extractable* if: $H|_S$ is ρ-edge dense, ρ-triangle dense, $H|_S$ has radius 2, and $t_S^{(I)} \geq \rho t_S$. We define a procedure that finds a single extractable cluster in graph H.

The extraction procedure: Let i be a vertex of maximum degree. For every vertex j, let θ_j be the number of triangles incident on j whose other two vertices are in $N(i)$. Let R be the set of d_i vertices with the largest θ_j values. Output $S = \{i\} \cup N(i) \cup R$.

It is not necessary to start with a vertex of maximum degree, but doing so provides a better dependence on ϵ.

Note: Strictly speaking, the $\{i\}$ above is redundant; a simple argument shows that $i \in R$.

We start with a simple technical lemma.

LEMMA 11. *Suppose $x_1 \geq x_2 \geq \cdots > 0$ with $\sum x_j \leq \alpha$ and $\sum x_j^2 \geq \beta$. For all $r \leq 2\alpha^2/\beta$, $\sum_{j \leq r} x_j^2 \geq \beta^2 r/4\alpha^2$.*

PROOF. If $x_{r+1} \geq \beta/2\alpha$, then $\sum_{j \leq r} x_j^2 \geq \beta^2 r/4\alpha^2$ as desired. Otherwise,

$$\sum_{j>r} x_j^2 \leq x_{r+1} \sum_j x_j \leq \beta/2.$$

Hence, $\sum_{j \leq r} x_j^2 = \sum x_j^2 - \sum_{j>r} x_j^2 \geq \beta/2 \geq \beta^2 r/4\alpha^2$, using the bound given for r. □

The main theorem of the section follows.

THEOREM 12. *Let H be an everywhere ϵ-triangle dense graph. The extraction procedure outputs an $\Omega(\epsilon^4)$-extractable set S of vertices. Furthermore, the number of edges in $H|_S$ is an $\Omega(\epsilon)$-fraction of the edges incident to S.*

PROOF. Let $\epsilon > 0$, i be a vertex of maximum degree, and $N = N(i)$.

We have $|S| \leq 2d_i$. By Lemma 10, $H|_N$ has at least $\epsilon\binom{d_i}{2}$ edges, so $H|_S$ is $\Omega(\epsilon)$-edge dense. By the size of S and maximality of d_i, the number of edges in $H|_S$ is an $\Omega(\epsilon)$-fraction of edges incident to S. It is also easy to see that $H|_S$ has radius 2. It remains to show that $H|_S$ is $\Omega(\epsilon^4)$-triangle dense, and that $t_S^{(I)} = \Omega(\epsilon^4)t_S$.

For any j, let η_j be the number of edges from j to N, and let θ_j be the number of triangles incident on j whose other two vertices are in N. Let $x_j = \sqrt{2\theta_j}$.

Lemma 11 tells us that if we can (appropriately) upper bound $\sum_j x_j$ and lower bound $\sum_j x_j^2$, then the sum of the largest few x_j^2's is significant. This implies that $H|_S$ has sufficiently many triangles. As we show below, using the appropriate setting of parameters, $H|_S$ contains $\Omega(\text{poly}(\epsilon) \cdot d_i^3)$ triangles, as opposed to trivial bounds that are quadratic in d_i.

CLAIM 13. *We have $\sum_j x_j \leq \sum_{k \in N} d_k$, and $\sum_j x_j^2 \geq \frac{\epsilon}{2}\sum_{k\in N} d_k(H|_N)\, d_k$, where $d_k(H|_N)$ is the degree of vertex k within $H|_N$.*

PROOF. We first upper bound $\sum_j x_j$:

$$\sum_j x_j \leq \sum_j \sqrt{2\binom{\eta_j}{2}} \leq \sum_j \eta_j = \sum_{k\in N} d_k.$$

The first inequality follows from $\theta_j \leq \binom{\eta_j}{2}$. The last equality is simply stating that the total number of edges to vertices in N is the same as the total number of edges from vertices in N.

Now, for any edge $e = (k_1, k_2)$, $t_e \geq J_e \cdot \max(d_{k_1} - 1, d_{k_2} - 1) \geq \epsilon \cdot \max(d_{k_1} - 1, d_{k_2} - 1)$. Since $\epsilon > 0$, each vertex is incident on at least 1 triangle. Hence all degrees are at least 2, and $d_k - 1 \geq d_k/2$ for all k. This means

$$t_e \geq \frac{\epsilon \cdot \max(d_{k_1}, d_{k_2})}{2} \geq \frac{\epsilon(d_{k_1} + d_{k_2})}{4} \qquad \text{for all } e = (k_1, k_2).$$

We can now lower bound $\sum_j x_j^2$. Abusing notation, $e \in H|_N$ refers to an edge in the induced subgraph. We have

$$\sum_j x_j^2 = \sum_j 2\theta_j = \sum_{e\in H|_N} 2t_e \geq \sum_{(k_1,k_2)\in H|_N} \frac{\epsilon}{2}(d_{k_1} + d_{k_2}) = \frac{\epsilon}{2}\sum_{k\in N} d_k(H|_N)\, d_k.$$

The two sides of the second equality are counting (twice) the number of triangles "to" and "from" the edges of N. □

We now use Lemma 11 with $\alpha = \sum_{k\in N} d_k$, $\beta = \frac{\epsilon}{2}\sum_{k\in N} d_k(H|_N)\, d_k$, and $r = d_i$. We first check that $r \leq 2\alpha^2/\beta$. Note that $d_i \geq d_k \geq \epsilon d_i$ for all $k \in N$, by Lemma 10 and by the maximality of d_i. Hence,

$$\frac{2\alpha^2}{\beta} = \frac{4}{\epsilon}\frac{\left(\sum_{k\in N} d_k\right)^2}{\sum_{k\in N} d_k(H|_N)\, d_k} \geq \frac{4}{\epsilon}\frac{\epsilon d_i |N| \sum_{k\in N} d_k}{d_i \sum_{k\in N} d_k} \geq 4d_i \geq r,$$

as desired. Let R be the set of $r = d_i$ vertices with the highest θ_j, or equivalently, with the highest x_j^2. By Lemma 11, $\sum_{j\in R} x_j^2 \geq \beta^2 r/4\alpha^2$, or $\sum_{j\in R}\theta_j \geq \beta^2 r/8\alpha^2$. We compute

$$\frac{\beta}{\alpha} = \frac{\epsilon}{2}\frac{\sum_{k\in N} d_k(H|_N)\, d_k}{\sum_{k\in N} d_k} \geq \frac{\epsilon}{2}\min_{k\in N} d_k(H|_N) \geq \frac{\epsilon^2 d_i}{4},$$

which gives $\sum_{j\in R}\theta_j \geq \epsilon^4 d_i^3/128$. For the first inequality above, think of the $d_k/\sum d_k$ as weights on the $d_k(H|_N)$. For the last inequality, $d_k(H|_N) = t_{(i,k)} \geq J_{(i,k)}(d_i - 1) \geq \epsilon d_i/2$ for all $k \in N$.

Recall $S = N \cup R$ and $|S| \leq 2d_i$. We have

$$t_S^{(I)} \geq \frac{\sum_{j\in R}\theta_j}{3} \geq \frac{\epsilon^4 d_i^3}{384},$$

since triangles contained in N get overcounted by a factor of 3. Since both t^S and the number of wedges in S are bounded above by $|S|\binom{d_i}{2} = \Theta(d_i^3)$, $H|_S$ is $\Omega(\epsilon^4)$-triangle dense, and $t_S^{(I)} = \Omega(\epsilon^4)t_S$ as desired.

3.4 Getting the entire family in a triangle-dense graph

We start with a triangle-dense graph G and explain how to get the desired entire tightly-knit family. Our procedure — called the decomposition procedure — takes as input a parameter ϵ.

The decomposition procedure: Clean the graph with *clean*$_\epsilon$, and run the extraction procedure to get a set S_1. Remove S_1 from the graph, run *clean*$_\epsilon$ again, and extract another set S_2. Repeat until the graph is empty. Output the sets $S_1, S_2, \ldots$.

We now prove our main theorem, Theorem 3, restated for convenience.

THEOREM 14. *Consider a τ-triangle dense graph G and $\epsilon \leq \tau/4$. The decomposition procedure outputs an $\Omega(\epsilon^4)$ tightly-knit family with an $\Omega(\epsilon^4)$-fraction of the triangles of G.*

PROOF. We are guaranteed by Theorem 12 that $G|_{S_i}$ is $\Omega(\epsilon^4)$-edge and $\Omega(\epsilon^4)$-triangle dense and has radius 2. It suffices to prove that an $\Omega(\epsilon^4)$-fraction of the triangles in G are contained in this family.

Consider the triangles that are *not* present in the tightly-knit family. We call these destroyed triangles. Such triangles fall in two categories: those destroyed in the cleaning phases, and those destroyed when an extractable set is removed. Let C be the triangles destroyed during cleaning, and let D_k be the triangles destroyed in the kth extraction. By the definition of extractable subsets and Theorem 12, $t(G|_{S_k}) = \Omega(\epsilon^4|D_k|)$. Note that C, D_k, and the triangles in $G|_{S_k}$ (over all k) partition the total set of triangles. Hence, we get that $\sum_k t(G|_{S_k}) = \Omega(\epsilon^4(t - |C|))$.

We now bound $|C|$. This follows the proof of Claim 8. Let $e_1, e_2, \ldots$ be all the edges removed during cleaning phases. Let W_l and T_l be the set of wedges and triangles that are destroyed when e_l is removed. Since the Jaccard similarity of e_l at the time of removal is at most ϵ, $|T_l| \leq \epsilon(|W_l| - |T_l|) \leq \epsilon|W_l|$. All the W_ls (and T_ls) are disjoint. Hence, $|C| = \sum_l |T_l| \leq \epsilon\sum_l |W_l| = \epsilon w = 3\epsilon t/\tau \leq 3t/4$, and $\sum_k t(G|_{S_k}) = \Omega(\epsilon^4 t)$ as desired. □

3.5 Preserving edges in an everywhere triangle-dense graph

For an everywhere triangle-dense graph, we can also preserve a constant fraction of the *edges*. This requires a more subtle argument. The aim of this subsection is to prove the following (cf. Theorem 6).

THEOREM 15. *Consider an everywhere γ-triangle dense graph G. The decomposition procedure, with $\epsilon \leq \gamma^2/4$, outputs an $\Omega(\epsilon^4)$ tightly-knit family with an $\Omega(\epsilon^4)$ fraction of the triangles of G and an $\Omega(\epsilon\gamma)$ fraction of the edges of G.*

The tightly-knit family and triangle conditions follow directly from Theorem 14, so we focus on the edge condition. By Theorem 12, the actual removal of the clusters preserves a large enough fraction of the edges. The difficulty is in bounding the edge removals during the cleaning phases. Even though G is everywhere triangle-dense, once a cluster is extracted, this condition may no longer hold. Indeed, the later cleaning phases may remove many edges, and we have to relate their behavior to the original graph.

We use E, W, and T to denote the sets of edges, wedges, and triangles in G. We use E^c, W^c, and T^c to be the respective sets destroyed during the cleaning phases. Let $T^s = T \setminus T^c$. Let E^s and V^s denote the edges and vertices, respectively, included in at least one triangle of T^s.

The main lemma shows that the cleaning phase does not destroy too many edges.

LEMMA 16. $|E^s| \geq \gamma|E|/6$.

Using this lemma, we complete the proof of Theorem 15.

PROOF. (of Theorem 15) As noted above, the tightly-knit family and triangle conditions follow directly from Theorem 14.

The proof of the edge condition follows a parallel argument to that of Theorem 14. Let D_k be the edges destroyed in the kth extraction, and let E_k be the edges in $G|_{S_k}$. By Theorem 12, $|E_k| = \Omega(\epsilon|D_k|)$. Since E^c, D_k, and E_k (over all k) partition E, we have $\sum_k |E_k| = \Omega(\epsilon(|E| - |E^c|))$. Since $|E^c| + |E^s| \leq |E|$, by Lemma 16 we have $\sum_k |E_k| = \Omega(\epsilon|E^s|) = \Omega(\epsilon\gamma|E|)$ as desired. □

To prove Lemma 16, we need additional definitions. For a triangle $t = (i_1, i_2, i_3)$, define the *weight* $r(t) = 1/d_{i_1} + 1/d_{i_2} + 1/d_{i_3}$. For a wedge w with central vertex i, define the weight $r(w) = 1/d_i$. Let $r(X) = \sum_{x \in X} r(x)$. Note that weights are always with respect to the degrees in the original graph G.

For an edge e, let W_e and T_e denote the sets of wedges and triangles incident to e. If e is removed by the cleaning phases, then let W_e^c and T_e^c denote the sets of wedges and triangles destroyed when e is removed. Note that W_e^c is not necessarily W_e, since some wedges in W_e may be removed prior to the removal of e.

We prove a series of bounds on various weights, crucially using the everywhere triangle-denseness of G. We finally chain them together to prove Lemma 16.

CLAIM 17. $r(T) \geq \gamma r(W)$.

PROOF. By Lemma 10 (every neighborhood is dense) and the everywhere γ-triangle denseness, $t_i \geq \gamma w_i$ for every i. Thus,

$$r(T) = \sum_i \frac{t_i}{d_i} \geq \sum_i \frac{\gamma w_i}{d_i} = \gamma\, r(W).$$

□

CLAIM 18. *For every edge e, $r(T_e) \geq 2\gamma$. If e is removed in a cleaning phase, $r(T_e^c) \leq (3\epsilon/\gamma)r(W_e^c)$.*

PROOF. Let $e = (i, j)$, where $d_i \geq d_j$. For any triangle δ incident to e, $r(\delta) \geq 2/d_i$. By the everywhere triangle density, $|T_e| \geq \gamma d_i$, so $r(T_e) = \sum_{\delta \in T_e} r(\delta) \geq 2\gamma$.

By Lemma 10 (edge balance), for any $\delta \in T_e^c$, $r(\delta) \leq 3/(\gamma d_i)$, and for any $w \in W_e^c$, $r(w) \geq 1/d_i$. Since $|T_e^c| < \epsilon(|W_e^c| - |T_e^c|) < \epsilon|W_e^c|$, $r(T_e^c) \leq (3\epsilon/\gamma)r(W_e^c)$. □

CLAIM 19. $|E^s| \geq r(T)/4$.

PROOF. We prove two bounds that imply the claim: $r(T^s) \geq r(T)/4$ and $|E^s| \geq r(T^s)$. For the first, we upper bound $r(T^c) = r(T) - r(T^s)$. We can express $r(T^c) = \sum_{e \in E^c} r(T_e^c)$. By Claim 18, $r(T_e^c) \leq (3\epsilon/\gamma)r(W_e^c)$. The second to last inequality in the chain below is Claim 17.

$$r(T^c) \leq \frac{3\epsilon}{\gamma} r(W^c) \leq \frac{3\epsilon}{\gamma} r(W) \leq \frac{3\epsilon}{\gamma^2} r(T) \leq \frac{3r(T)}{4}.$$

This implies $r(T^s) \geq r(T)/4$. Now to prove $|E^s| \geq r(T^s)$. For vertex $i \in V^s$, we use T_i^s for the set of triangles in T^s containing i. We have

$$r(T^s) = \sum_{(i_1,i_2,i_3) \in T^s} \left(\frac{1}{d_{i_1}} + \frac{1}{d_{i_2}} + \frac{1}{d_{i_3}}\right) = \sum_{i \in V^s} \frac{|T_i^s|}{d_i}.$$

Consider the subgraph G' obtained by only having the triangles of T^s. The non-isolated vertices of this subgraph are exactly V^s, and the edges are E^s. Denote the degree of $i \in V^s$ in G' as d_i'. Trivially, $|T_i^s| \leq d_i'(d_i' - 1)/2$. We can bound $d_i \geq d_i'$. Combining these, we get

$$r(T^s) \leq \sum_{i \in V^s} \frac{d_i'(d_i' - 1)}{2d_i} \leq \sum_{i \in V^s} \frac{d_i' - 1}{2} \leq |E^s| - \frac{|V^s|}{2} \leq |E^s|$$

as desired. □

We now have all the pieces needed to prove Lemma 16.

PROOF. (of Lemma 16) We observe that $r(T) = \sum_{e \in E} r(T_e)/3$, and use the bound $r(T_e) \geq 2\gamma$ (Claim 18). Starting with the bound of Claim 19,

$$|E^s| \geq \frac{r(T)}{4} \geq \sum_{e \in E} \frac{r(T_e)}{12} \geq \frac{2\gamma}{12}|E|.$$

□

3.6 Implementing the algorithm

We sketch an implementation of our decomposition procedure that runs in time proportional to the number of wedges of the graph; Appendix A gives further details. A preliminary implementation of the algorithm runs in a few minutes on a commodity laptop for networks with one million edges.

4. GALLERY OF "INCONVENIENT" GRAPHS

This section provides a number of examples of triangle-dense graphs. These examples show, in particular, that radius-1 clusters are not sufficient to capture a constant fraction of a triangle-dense graph's triangles, and that tightly knit families cannot always capture a constant fraction of a triangle-dense graph's edges.

- **Why radius 2?** Consider the complete tripartite graph. This is everywhere triangle-dense. If we removed the 1-hop neighborhood of any vertex, we would destroy a $1-\Theta(1/n)$-fraction of the triangles. The only tightly-knit family in this graph is the entire graph itself.

- **More on 1-hop neighborhoods.** All 1-hop neighborhoods in an everywhere triangle-dense graph are edge-dense, by Lemma 10. Maybe we could just take the 1-hop neighborhoods of an independent set, to get a tightly-knit family? Of course, the clusters would only be edge-disjoint (not vertex disjoint).

  We construct an everywhere triangle-dense graph where this does not work. There are $m+1$ disjoint sets of vertices, $A_1, \ldots, A_m, B$ each of size m. The graph induced on $\cup_k A_k$ is just a clique on m^2 vertices. Each vertex $b_k \in B$ is connected to all of A_k. Note that B is a maximal independent set, and the 1-hop neighborhoods of B contain $\Theta(m^4)$ triangles in total. However, the total number of triangles in the graph is $\Theta(m^6)$.

- **Why we can't preserve edges.** Theorem 3 only guarantees that the tightly-knit family contains a constant fraction of triangles, not edges. Consider a graph that has a clique on $n^{1/3}$ vertices and an arbitrary (or say, a random) constant-degree graph on the remaining $n-n^{1/3}$ vertices. No tightly-knit family can involve vertices outside the clique, so most of the edges must be removed. Of course, most edges in this case have low Jaccard similarity.

In general, the condition of constant triangle density is fairly weak, since it encompasses a seemingly wide variety of graphs. The following two examples provide some further intuition for this class of graphs.

- **A triangle-dense graph far from a disjoint union of cliques.** Define the graph Bracelet(m,d), for m nodes of degree d, when $m > 4d/3$, as follows: Let $B_1, \ldots, B_{3m/d}$ be sets of $d/3$ vertices each put in cyclic order. Note that $3m/d \geq 4$. Connect each vertex in B_k to each vertex in B_{k-1}, B_k and B_{k+1}. This is an everywhere triangle-dense d-regular graph on m vertices. Nonetheless, it is maximally far (i.e., $O(md)$ edges away) from a disjoint union of cliques. See Figure 1. A tightly-knit family is obtained by taking $B_1 \cup B_2 \cup B_3$, $B_4 \cup B_5 \cup B_6$, etc.

- **Hiding a tightly-knit family.** Start with $n/3$ disjoint triangles. Now, add an arbitrary bounded-degree graph (say, an expander) on these n vertices. The resulting graph has constant triangle density, but most of the structure is irrelevant for a tightly-knit family.

5. RECOVERING A PLANTED CLUSTERING

This section gives an algorithmic application of our decomposition procedure to recovering a "ground truth" clustering. We study the planted clustering model defined by Balcan, Blum, and Gupta [BBG09], and show that our algorithm gives guarantees similar to theirs. We do not subsume the results in [BBG09]. Rather, we observe that a graph problem that arises as a subroutine in their algorithm is essentially that of finding a tightly-knit family in a triangle-dense graph. Their assumptions ensure that there is (up to minor perturbations) a unique such family.

The main setting of [BBG09] is as follows. Given a set of points V is some metric space, we wish to k-cluster them according to some fixed objective function, such as the k-median objective. Denote the optimal k-clustering by $\mathcal{C}$ and the value by OPT. The instance satisfies (c,ϵ)-*approximation-stability* if for any k-clustering $\mathcal{C}'$ of V with objective function value at most $c \cdot OPT$, the "classification distance" between $\mathcal{C}$ and $\mathcal{C}'$ is at most ϵ. Thus, all solutions with near-optimal objective function value must be structurally close to $\mathcal{C}$.

In Lemma 5 of BaBlGu08, an approximation-stable k-median instance is converted into a *threshold graph*. This graph $G=(V,E)$ contains k disjoint cliques $\{X_a\}_{a=1}^{k}$, such that the cliques do not have any common neighbors. These cliques correspond to clusters in the ground-truth clustering, and their existence is a consequence of the approximation stability assumption. The aim is to get a k-clustering sufficiently close to $\{X_a\}$. Formally, a k-clustering $\{S_a\}$ of V is Δ-*incorrect* if there is a permutation σ such that $\sum |X_{\sigma(a)} \setminus S_a| \leq \Delta$.

Let $B = V \setminus \bigcup_a X_a$. It is shown in [BBG09] that when $|B|$ is small, good approximations to $\{X_a\}$ can be found efficiently. From our perspective, the interesting point is that when $|B|$ is much smaller than $\sum_a |X_a|$, the threshold graph has high triangle density. Furthermore, as we prove below, the clusters output by the extraction procedure of Theorem 12 are very close to the X_a's of the threshold graph.

Suppose we want a k-clustering of a threshold graph. We iteratively use the extraction procedure (from §3.3) k times to get clusters $S_1, S_2, \ldots, S_k$. In particular, recall that at each step we choose a vertex s_i with the current highest degree d_i. We set N_i to be the d_i neighbors of s_i at this time, and R to be the d_i vertices with the largest number of triangles to N_i. Then, $S_i = \{i\} \cup N_i \cup R$. The exact procedure of Theorem 14, which includes cleaning, also works fine. Foregoing the cleaning step does necessitate a small technical change to the extraction procedure: instead of adding all of R to S, we only add the elements of R which have a positive number of triangles to N_i.

We use the notation $N^*(U) = N(U) \cup U$. So $N^*(X_a) \cap N^*(X_b) = \emptyset$, when $a \neq b$. Unlike [BBG09], we assume that $|X_a| \geq 3$. The following parallels Theorem 3.3 of [BBG09], and the proof is similar to theirs.

THEOREM 20. *The output of the clustering algorithm above is $O(|B|)$-incorrect on G.*

PROOF. We first map the algorithm's clustering to the true clustering $\{X_a\}$. Our algorithm outputs k clusters, each with an associated "center" (the starting vertex). These are denoted $S_1, S_2, \ldots$, with centers $s_1, s_2, \ldots$, in order of extraction. We determine if there exists some true cluster X_a, such that $s_1 \in N^*(X_a)$. If so, we map S_1 to X_a. (Recall the $N^*(X_a)$'s are disjoint, so X_a is unique if it exists.) If no X_a exists, we simply do not map S_1. We then perform this for $S_2, S_3, \ldots$, except that we do not map S_k if we would be mapping it to an X_a that has previously been mapped to. We finally end up with a subset $P \subseteq [k]$, such that for each $a \in P$, S_a is mapped to some $X_{a'}$. By relabeling the true clustering, we can assume that for all $a \in P$, S_a is mapped

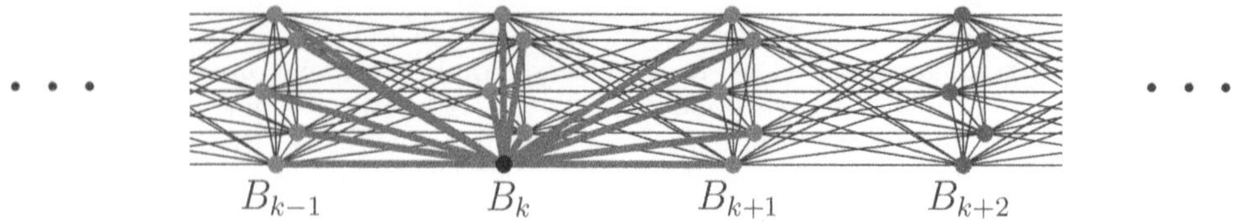

Figure 1: Bracelet graph with $d/3 = 5$.

to X_a. The remaining clusters (for $X_{a \notin P}$) can be labeled with an arbitrary permutation of $[k] \setminus P$.

Our aim is to bound $\sum_a |X_a \setminus S_a|$ by $O(|B|)$.

We perform some simple manipulations.

$$\begin{aligned}\bigcup_a (X_a \setminus S_a) &= \bigcup_{a \in P}(X_a \setminus S_a) \cup \bigcup_{a \notin P}(X_a \setminus S_a)\\ &= \bigcup_{a \in P}(X_a \cap \bigcup_{b<a} S_b) \cup \bigcup_{a \in P}(X_a \setminus \bigcup_{b \leq a} S_b) \cup \bigcup_{a \notin P}(X_a \setminus S_a)\\ &\subseteq \bigcup_{a}(X_a \cap \bigcup_{b<a} S_b) \cup \bigcup_{a \in P}(X_a \setminus \bigcup_{b \leq a} S_b) \cup \bigcup_{a \notin P} X_a.\end{aligned}$$

So we get the following sets of interest.

- $L_1 = \bigcup_a (X_a \cap \bigcup_{b<a} S_b) = \bigcup_b (S_b \cap \bigcup_{a>b} X_a)$ is the set of vertices that are "stolen" by clusters before S_a.
- $L_2 = \bigcup_{a \in P}(X_a \setminus \bigcup_{b \leq a} S_b)$ is the set of vertices that are left behind when S_a is created.
- $L_3 = \bigcup_{a \notin P} X_a$ is the set of vertices that are never clustered.

Note that $\sum_a |X_a \setminus S_a| = |\bigcup_a (X_a \setminus S_a)| \leq |L_1| + |L_2| + |L_3|$. The proof is completed by showing that $|L_1| + |L_2| + |L_3| = O(|B|)$. This will be done through a series of claims.

We first state a useful fact.

Claim 21. *Suppose for some $b \in \{1, 2, \ldots, k\}$, $s_b \in N(X_b)$. Then N_b is partitioned into $N_b \cap X_b$ and $N_b \cap B$.*

Proof. Any vertex in $N_b \setminus X_b$ must be in B. This is because N_b is contained in a two-hop neighborhood from X_b, which cannot intersect any other X_a. □

Claim 22. *For any b, $|S_b \cap \bigcup_{a>b} X_a| \leq 6|S_b \cap B|$.*

Proof. We split into three cases. For convenience, let U be the set of vertices $S_b \cap \bigcup_{a>b} X_a$. Recall that $|S_b| \leq 2d_b$.

- For some c, $s_b \in X_c$: Note that $c \leq b$ by the relabeling of clusters. Observe that S_b is contained in a two-hop neighborhood of s_b, and hence cannot intersect any cluster X_a for $a \neq c$. Hence, U is empty.
- For some (unique) c, $s_b \in N(X_c)$: Again, $c \leq b$. By Claim 21, $d_b = |N_b| = |N_b \cap X_c| + |N_b \cap B|$. Suppose $|N_b \cap B| \geq d_b/3$. Then $|S_b \cap B| \geq |N_b \cap B| \geq d_b/3$. We can easily bound $|S_b| \leq 2d_b \leq 6|S_b \cap B|$.

  Suppose instead $|N_b \cap B| < d_b/3$, and hence $|N_b \cap X_c| > 2d_b/3$. Note that $|N_b \cap X_c|$ is a clique. Each vertex in $N_b \cap X_c$ makes $\binom{|N_b \cap X_c|-1}{2} \geq \binom{\lfloor 2d_b/3 \rfloor}{2}$ triangles in N_b. On the other hand, the only vertices of N_b that any vertex in X_a for $a \neq c$ can connect to is in $N_b \cap B$. This forms fewer than $\binom{\lfloor d_b/3 \rfloor}{2}$ triangles in N_b. If $\binom{\lfloor d_b/3 \rfloor}{2} > 0$, then $\binom{\lfloor 2d_b/3 \rfloor}{2} > \binom{\lfloor d_b/3 \rfloor}{2}$.

  Consider the construction of S_b. We take the top d_b vertices with the most triangles to N_b, and say we insert them in decreasing order of this number. Note that in the modified version of the algorithm, we only insert them while this number is positive. Before any vertex of X_a ($a \neq b$) is added, all vertices of $N_b \cap X_c$ must be added. Hence, at most $d_b - |N_b \cap X_c| = |N_b \cap B| \leq |S_b \cap B|$ vertices of $\cup_{a \neq b} X_a$ can be added to S_b. Therefore, $|U| \leq |S_b \cap B|$.
- The vertex s_b is at least distance 2 from every X_c: Note that $N_b \subseteq S_b \cap B$. Hence, $|S_b| \leq 2d_b \leq 2|S_b \cap B|$.

□

Claim 23. *For any $a \in P$, $|X_a \setminus \bigcup_{b \leq a} S_b| \leq |S_a \cap B|$.*

Proof. Since $a \in P$, either $s_a \in X_a$ or $s_a \in N(X_a)$. Consider the situation of the algorithm after the first $a-1$ sets $S_1, S_2, \ldots, S_{a-1}$ are removed. There is some subset of X_a that remains; call it $X'_a = X_a \setminus \bigcup_{b<a} S_b$.

Suppose $s_a \in X_a$. Since X'_a is still a clique, $X'_a \subseteq N_a$, and $(X_a \setminus \bigcup_{b \leq a} S_b)$ is empty.

Suppose instead $s_a \in N(X_a)$. Because s_a has maximum degree and X'_a is a clique, $d_a \geq |X'_a| - 1$. Note that $|X'_a \setminus S_a|$ is what we wish to bound, and $|X'_a \setminus S_a| \leq |X'_a \setminus N_a|$. By Claim 21, N_a partitions into $N_a \cap X_a = N_a \cap X'_a$ and $N_a \cap B$. We have $|X'_a \setminus N_a| = |X'_a| - |N_a \cap X_a| \leq d_a + 1 - |N_a \cap X_a| = |N_a \cap B| + 1 \leq |S_a \cap B|$. □

Claim 24. $|L_3| \leq |B| + |L_1|$.

Proof. Consider some X_a for $a \notin P$. Look at the situation when $S_1, \ldots, S_{a-1}$ are removed. There is a subset X'_a (forming a clique) left in the graph. All the vertices in $X_a \setminus X'_a$ are contained in L_1. By maximality of degree, $d_a \geq |X'_a| - 1$. Furthermore, since $a \notin P$, $N_a \subseteq B$ implying $d_a \leq |S_a \cap B| - 1$. Therefore, $|X'_a| \leq |S_a \cap B|$. We can bound $\bigcup_{a \notin P}(X_a \setminus X'_a) \subseteq L_1$, and $\sum_{a \notin P} |X'_a| \leq |B|$, completing the proof. □

To put it all together, we sum the bound of Claim 22 and Claim 23 over $b \in [k]$ and $a \in P$ respectively to get $|L_1| \leq 6|B|$ and $|L_2| \leq |B|$. Claim 24 with the bound on $|L_1|$ yields $|L_3| \leq 7|B|$, completing the proof of Theorem 20.

6. REFERENCES

[AJB00] R. Albert, H. Jeong, and A.-L. Barab?si. Error and attack tolerance of complex networks. *Nature*, 406:378–382, 2000.

[BA99] A.-L. Barabasi and R. Albert. Emergence of scaling in random networks. *Science*, 286:509–512, October 1999.

[BBG09] M.-F. Balcan, A. Blum, and A. Gupta. Approximate clustering without the approximation. In *Proceedings of the Symposium on Discrete Algorithms (SODA)*, pages 1068–1077, 2009.

[BKM+00] A. Broder, R. Kumar, F. Maghoul, P. Raghavan, S. Rajagopalan, R. Stata, A. Tomkins, and J. Wiener. Graph structure in the web. *Computer Networks*, 33:309–320, 2000.

[Bur04] Ronald S Burt. Structural holes and good ideas. *American Journal of Sociology*, 110(2):349–399, 2004.

[CF06] Deepayan Chakrabarti and Christos Faloutsos. Graph mining: Laws, generators, and algorithms. *ACM Computing Surveys*, 38(1), 2006.

[CL02a] F. Chung and L. Lu. Connected components in random graphs with given degree sequences. *Annals of Combinatorics*, 6:125–145, 2002.

[CL02b] Fan Chung and Linyuan Lu. The average distances in random graphs with given expected degrees. *PNAS*, 99(25):15879–15882, 2002.

[Col88] James S. Coleman. Social capital in the creation of human capital. *American Journal of Sociology*, 94:S95–S120, 1988.

[CZF04] Deepayan Chakrabarti, Yiping Zhan, and Christos Faloutsos. R-MAT: A recursive model for graph mining. In *SDM '04*, pages 442–446, 2004.

[Fau06] Katherine Faust. Comparing social networks: Size, density, and local structure. *Metodoloski zvezki*, 3(2):185–216, 2006.

[FFF99] Michalis Faloutsos, Petros Faloutsos, and Christos Faloutsos. On power-law relationships of the internet topology. In *Proceedings of SIGCOMM*, pages 251–262, 1999.

[For10] S. Fortunato. Community detection in graphs. *Physics Reports*, 486:75–174, 2010.

[FPP06] Alessandro Ferrante, Gopal Pandurangan, and Kihong Park. On the hardness of optimization in power law graphs. In *Proceedings of Conference on Computing and Combinatorics*, 2006.

[FWVDC10] Brooke Foucault Welles, Anne Van Devender, and Noshir Contractor. Is a friend a friend?: Investigating the structure of friendship networks in virtual worlds. In *CHI-EA'10*, pages 4027–4032, 2010.

[GN02] M. Girvan and M. Newman. Community structure in social and biological networks. *Proceedings of the National Academy of Sciences*, 99(12):7821–7826, 2002.

[HL70] P. W. Holland and S. Leinhardt. A method for detecting structure in sociometric data. *American Journal of Sociology*, 76:492–513, 1970.

[Kle00a] Jon M. Kleinberg. Navigation in a small world. *Nature*, 406:845, 2000.

[Kle00b] Jon M. Kleinberg. The small-world phenomenon: An algorithmic perspective. In *Proceedings of ACM Symposium on Theory of Computing*, 2000.

[Kle01] Jon M. Kleinberg. Small-world phenomena and the dynamics of information. In *Advances in Neural Information Processing Systems (NIPS)*, volume 14, 2001.

[KRR+00] R. Kumar, P. Raghavan, S. Rajagopalan, D. Sivakumar, A. Tomkins, and E. Upfal. Stochastic models for the web graph. In *Proceedings of the 41st Annual Symposium on Foundations of Computer Science*, pages 57–65, 2000.

[LAS+08] H. Lin, C. Amanatidis, M. Sideri, R. M. Karp, and C. H. Papadimitriou. Linked decompositions of networks and the power of choice in polya urns. In *Proceedings of ACM-SIAM Symposium on Discrete Algorithms*, pages 993–1002, 2008.

[LCK+10] Jure Leskovec, Deepayan Chakrabarti, Jon Kleinberg, Christos Faloutsos, and Zoubin Ghahramani. Kronecker graphs: An approach to modeling networks. *J. Machine Learning Research*, 11:985–1042, February 2010.

[LLDM08] J. Leskovec, K. Lang, A. Dasgupta, and M. Mahoney. Community structure in large networks: Natural cluster sizes and the absence of large well-defined clusters. *Internet Mathematics*, 6(1):29–123, 2008.

[LT79] R. J. Lipton and R. E. Tarjan. A separator theorem for planar graphs. *SIAM Journal on Applied Mathematics*, 36(2):177–189, 1979.

[MS10] A. Montanari and A. Saberi. The spread of innovations in social networks. *Proceedings of the National Academy of Sciences*, 107(47):20196–20201, 2010.

[New01] M. E. J. Newman. The structure of scientific collaboration networks. *Proceedings of the National Academy of Sciences*, 98(2):404–409, 2001.

[New03] M. E. J. Newman. Properties of highly clustered networks. *Physical Review E*, 68(2):026121, August 2003.

[New06] M. E. J. Newman. Finding community structure in networks using the eigenvectors of matrices. *Physical Review E*, 74(3):036104, 2006.

[RS86] N. Robertson and P. D. Seymour. Graph minors III: Planar tree-width. *Journal of Combinatorial Theory, Series B*, 36(1):49–64, 1986.

[SCW+10] Alessandra Sala, Lili Cao, Christo Wilson, Robert Zablit, Haitao Zheng, and Ben Y. Zhao. Measurement-calibrated graph models for social network experiments. In *WWW '10*, pages 861–870. ACM, 2010.

[SPK13] C. Seshadhri, Ali Pinar, and Tamara G. Kolda. Fast triangle counting through wedge sampling. In *Proceedings of the SIAM Conference on Data Mining*, 2013.

[SPR11] V. Satuluri, S. Parthasarathy, and Y. Ruan. Local graph sparsification for scalable clustering. In *Proceedings of ACM SIGMOD*, pages 721–732, 2011.

[Sze78] E. Szemerédi. Regular partitions of graphs. *Problèmes combinatoires et th?orie des graphes*, 260:399–401, 1978.

[UBK13] J. Ugander, L. Backstrom, and J. Kleinberg. Subgraph frequencies: Mapping the empirical and extremal geography of large graph collections. In *Proceedings of World Wide Web Conference*, 2013.

[UKBM11] Johan Ugander, Brian Karrer, Lars Backstrom, and Cameron Marlow. The anatomy of the facebook social graph. Technical Report 1111.4503, Arxiv, 2011.

[VB12] J. Vivar and D. Banks. Models for networks: A cross-disciplinary science. *Wiley Interdisciplinary Reviews: Computational Statistics*, 4(1):13–27, 2012.

[WF94] S. Wasserman and K. Faust. *Social Network Analysis: Methods and Applications.* Cambridge University Press, 1994.

[WS98] D. Watts and S. Strogatz. Collective dynamics of 'small-world' networks. *Nature*, 393:440–442, 1998.

APPENDIX

A. IMPLEMENTATION DETAILS

A.1 High-Level Comments

This appendix describes how to implement the decomposition procedure in the proof of Theorem 14 in expected $O(|V| + |E| + w)$ time and $O(|E|)$ space, where w is the number of wedges of the graph.

The implementation includes a few improvements over a naive one. There are three operations that could potentially cause a slowdown: cleaning, finding the maximum degree vertex i, and finding vertices with many triangles incident on the neighborhoods M.

Naively computing all J_e's from scratch for every cleaning procedure could require $\Omega(|E|^2)$ time. To make cleaning fast, we note that $J_{(i,j)}$ only changes when edges incident on i or j get removed. Hence, we maintain a set of "dirtied" vertices after extraction and after each iteration of the cleaning procedure, and only recompute Jaccard similarities for the edges incident on those dirtied vertices. We also keep track of the number of triangles t_e incident on each edge and the degree d_i of each vertex so that computing J_e is an $O(1)$ operation.

To quickly find a maximum-degree vertex every extraction phase, we maintain a lookup from a degree d to the vertices of degree d, and also keep track of the maximum degree $d_{\max}$.

For finding vertices with many triangles incident on the neighborhoods M, we do $O(1)$ work for every triangle with an edge in M. The important point is to enumerate them by computing T_e for each $e \in M$, rather than directly computing the number of triangles from each vertex i, which would take $O(|V|w)$ time.

Sections §A.2 and §A.3 provide a more detailed description and analysis of the decomposition procedure.

A.2 Data Structures

We assume the following primitives:

- A *hash table*, or key-value store. With m keys, we assume $O(m)$ space, amortized or expected $O(1)$ time look-up, insertion, and deletion of any key, $O(m)$ enumeration of keys, expected $O(1)$ peek of a "random" key, and $O(1)$ look-up of number of keys. We denote hash tables by $\textsc{hash}(\mathcal{K}, k \to f(k))$, where $\mathcal{K}$ is the set of keys, and $k \to f(k)$ is the mapping from keys to values.
- A *set*, or key store. This is simply a degenerate hash table, where every value is 0. Note that the above properties imply $O(m_1 + m_2)$ time intersection of two sets with m_1 and m_2 keys respectively.
- A *multiset*, or key-count store. This is a hash table where the keys are the distinct elements, and the values are counts. We do not store keys with value zero.

Let V' be the set of non-isolated vertices, namely vertices i with $d_i > 0$. We maintain the following data structures throughout the course of the algorithm.

- A hash table $\mathcal{G} = \textsc{hash}(V', i \to \textsc{set}(N(i)))$ of vertex neighborhoods. This allows $O(N(i))$ lookup of $N(i)$.
- A hash table $\mathcal{D} = \textsc{hash}(V', i \to d_i)$ of vertex degrees.
- An array $\mathcal{A}$, where the d'th entry is a pointer to all the vertices of degree d, stored as a set. Note that we implicitly keep track of $|\mathcal{A}[d]|$ via our definition of set.
- An integer $d_{\max} = \max\{d : |\mathcal{A}[d]| > 0\}$.
- A hash table $\mathcal{T} = \textsc{hash}(E, e \to t_e)$ that keeps track of the number of triangles incident on e.

Note that we can iterate over all edges in $O(|E|)$ time, via $\mathcal{G}$. We can also iterate over all triangles in $O(w + |E|)$ time, by computing $N(i) \cap N(j)$ for each $(i, j) \in E$.

We define the following operations on the data structures above:

- $\textsc{DeleteEdge}(i, j)$ removes edge (i, j).
- $\textsc{Jaccard}(i, j)$ returns $J_{(i,j)} = \frac{\mathcal{T}(i,j)}{\mathcal{D}(i)+\mathcal{D}(j)-\mathcal{T}(i,j)}$, and takes $O(1)$ time.
- $\textsc{IsEmptyGraph}()$ returns True if $d_{\max}$ is 0, and takes $O(1)$ time.
- $\textsc{MaxDegreeVertex}()$ returns a vertex from $\mathcal{A}(d_{\max})$, and takes expected $O(1)$ time.

A.3 Procedure

We first define the two subroutines below.

$\textsc{Clean}$ starts with a dirty set of vertices $\mathcal{V}$. It iterates over edges incident on $\mathcal{V}$ until it finds one with $J_{(i,j)} < \epsilon$, after which it deletes (i, j), adds i and j to $\mathcal{V}$, and starts over. If it iterates over all the edges of some $i \in \mathcal{V}$ without finding one with low Jaccard similarity, it removes i from $\mathcal{V}$.

```
function CLEAN(𝒱, ε)
    while 𝒱 is non-empty do          ▷ 𝒱 is the set of dirty vertices
        for i ∈ 𝒱 do
            for j ∈ N(i) do
                if JACCARD(i, j) < ε then
```

6 DELETEEDGE(e)
7 Add j to $\mathcal{V}$ and go to line 2.
8 Remove i from $\mathcal{V}$.

Recall that θ_j is the number of triangles incident on j whose other two vertices are in $N(i)$. EXTRACT computes θ_j for each j where $\theta_j > 0$, by iterating over T_e for every edge $e \in N(i)$. It then takes the largest d_i such θ_js to form the extracted set S. It removes S from the graph, and dirties the vertices in the neighborhood of S for subsequent cleaning.

1 **function** EXTRACT
2 $i =$ MAXDEGREEVERTEX()
3 $\theta =$ a multiset over vertices ▷ $\theta(j)$ will count the number of triangles
4 in $N(i) \cup j$ incident on j.
5 **for** $j_1 \in N(i)$ **do**
6 **for** $j_2 \in N(j_1) \cap N(i)$ **do** ▷ (j_1, j_2) iterates over the edges of $N(i)$
7 **for** $j \in N(j_1) \cap N(j_2)$ **do**
8 Add j to θ.
9 $R =$ the $\mathcal{D}(i)$ keys of θ with the highest counts
10 $S = R \cup N(i)$
11 $\mathcal{V} = (\bigcup_{s \in S} N(s)) \setminus S$ ▷ dirtied vertices
12 **for** e incident on S **do**
13 DELETEEDGE(e)
14 **return** $S, \mathcal{V}$

Finally, we glue the two subroutines together to get the main function below. PARTITION alternatively CLEANs and EXTRACTs until the graph is gone.

1 **function** PARTITION(G, ϵ)
2 Construct the data structures $\mathcal{G}, \mathcal{D}, \mathcal{A}, d_{\max}, \mathcal{T}$ from G.
3 $\mathcal{P} =$ empty list ▷ stores the partition
4 CLEAN(V', ϵ)
5 **while** not ISEMPTYGRAPH() **do**
6 $S, \mathcal{V} =$ EXTRACT()
7 Append S to $\mathcal{P}$.
8 CLEAN($\mathcal{V}, \epsilon$)
9 **return** ($\mathcal{P}$)

We are now ready to prove the main theorem of this section.

THEOREM 25. *The procedure above runs in expected $O(|V| + |E| + w)$ time and $O(|E|)$ space.*

PROOF. The space bound is easy to check, so we focus on the time. We look at the total amount of time spent in DELETEEDGE, CLEAN, EXTRACT, and PARTITION in order; for each function, we ignore time spent in subroutines that have been previously accounted for. The *total cost* of a function or line of code refers to the time spent there over the course of the entire algorithm.

DELETEEDGE: Each edge gets deleted exactly once. It is easy to check that the total cost to $\mathcal{G}, \mathcal{D}$, and $\mathcal{A}$ is $O(|E|)$ each. The total cost to $d_{\max}$ is $O(|V|)$; every time $|\mathcal{A}(d_{\max})|$ drops to 0, we do a linear search downwards till we find a non-empty entry of $\mathcal{A}$. The total cost to $\mathcal{T}$ is at most $\sum_{(i,j)\in E} d_i + d_j = O(|E| + w)$; on deletion of (i, j), $\mathcal{T}(e)$ is decremented for $e = \{(i, k), (j, k) : k \in N(i) \cap N(j)\}$.

CLEAN: Say a vertex k gets "chosen" every time $i = k$ in lines 4–8. Each vertex $i \in V'$ gets chosen once from line 4 of PARTITION, and at most once each time d_i changes to a value > 0. Since d_i only decreases, each i is chosen at most d_i times. The cost of choosing a vertex i is at most d_i, so the total cost here is at most $\sum_{i \in V} d_i^2 = O(|E| + w)$.

EXTRACT: Over the course of the algorithm each edge ends up as a (j_1, i) pair at most once, so the total cost of lines 5–6 is at most $\sum_{(j_1,i)\in E} d_{j_1} + d_i = O(|E| + w)$. Similarly, each edge ends up as a (j_1, j_2) pair at most once, and so the total cost of lines 7–8 is also $O(|E| + w)$.

Line 9 can be computed in time proportional to the number of keys in θ. Each vertex i can be in θ at most d_i times, since once $i \in \theta$ it loses at least one edge to lines 12–13. Hence the total cost of line 9 is $O(|E|)$.

Finally, each vertex can be in S at most once, and so the total cost of line 11 is $O(|E|)$.

PARTITION: The only non-trivial step here is line 2. Initial construction of $\mathcal{G}, \mathcal{D}, \mathcal{A}$ and $d_{\max}$ takes $O(|V| + |E|)$ time, if the graph is originally presented as either as a list of edges or as an adjacency list. Initial construction of $\mathcal{T}$ takes $O(|E| + w)$ time, via iterating over all triangles. □

Partial Tests, Universal Tests and Decomposability

Eldar Fischer
Faculty of Computer Science
Technion – Israel Institute of Technology
Haifa 32000, Israel
eldar@cs.technion.ac.il

Yonatan Goldhirsh
Faculty of Computer Science
Technion – Israel Institute of Technology
Haifa 32000, Israel
jongold@cs.technion.ac.il

Oded Lachish
Department of Computer Science and Information Systems
Birkbeck, University of London
Malet St, London WC1E 7HX, United Kingdom
oded@dcs.bbk.ac.uk

ABSTRACT

For a property P and a sub-property P', we say that P is P'-*partially testable with* q *queries* if there exists an algorithm that distinguishes, with high probability, inputs in P' from inputs ϵ-far from P, using q queries. Some natural properties require many queries to test, but can be partitioned into a small number of subsets for which they are partially testable with very few queries, sometimes even a number independent of the input size.

For properties over 0, 1, the notion of being thus partitionable ties in closely with Merlin-Arthur proofs of Proximity (MAPs) as defined independently in [14]; a partition into r partially-testable properties is the same as a Merlin-Arthur system where the proof consists of the identity of one of the r partially-testable properties, giving a 2-way translation to an $O(\log r)$ size proof.

Our main result is that for some low complexity properties a partition as above cannot exist, and moreover that for each of our properties there does not exist even a single sub-property featuring both a large size and a query-efficient partial test, in particular improving the lower bound set in [14]. For this we use neither the traditional Yao-type arguments nor the more recent communication complexity method, but open up a new approach for proving lower bounds.

First, we use entropy analysis, which allows us to apply our arguments directly to 2-sided tests, thus avoiding the cost of the conversion in [14] from 2-sided to 1-sided tests. Broadly speaking we use "distinguishing instances" of a supposed test to show that a uniformly random choice of a member of the sub-property has "low entropy areas", ultimately leading to it having a low total entropy and hence having a small base set.

Additionally, to have our arguments apply to adaptive tests, we use a mechanism of "rearranging" the input bits (through a decision tree that adaptively reads the entire input) to expose the low entropy that would otherwise not be apparent.

We also explore the possibility of a connection in the other direction, namely whether the existence of a good partition (or MAP) can lead to a relatively query-efficient standard property test. We provide some preliminary results concerning this question, including a simple lower bound on the possible trade-off.

Our second major result is a positive trade-off result for the restricted framework of 1-sided proximity oblivious tests. This is achieved through the construction of a "universal tester" that works the same for all properties admitting the restricted test. Our tester is very related to the notion of sample-based testing (for a non-constant number of queries) as defined by Goldreich and Ron in [13]. In particular it partially resolves an open problem raised by [13].

ITCS'14, January 12–14, 2014, Princeton, New Jersey, USA.

ACM 978-1-4503-2698-8/14/01 ...$15.00.
http://dx.doi.org/10.1145/2554797.2554841 .

Categories and Subject Descriptors

F.1.2 [**Modes of Computation**]: Probabilistic computation; F.2.2 [**Nonnumerical Algorithms and Problems**]: Computations on discrete structures; G.3 [**Probability and Statistics**]: Probabilistic algorithms

General Terms

Theory, Algorithms

Keywords

property testing; universal testing; information theoretic lower bounds; sunflower theorems; partial testing

1. INTRODUCTION

Property Testing deals with randomized approximation algorithms that operate under low information situations. Formally, we deal with objects from some universe U which is parametrized by an integer n, usually Σ^n where Σ is some finite alphabet; with a notion of *distance* between two objects in U, usually the Hamming distance; and with a notion of a *query* to an object in U, usually corresponding to retrieving x_i for an index $i \in \{1, \ldots, n\}$.

Definition 1.1 (Testable property). *Suppose* $P \subseteq \{0,1\}^n$. *We say that* P *is* testable with q queries *if there exists an algorithm* A *that gets as input a parameter* $\epsilon > 0$ *and query access to an input string* $x \in \{0,1\}^n$ *and outputs* accept *or* reject *such that:*

- *If* $x \in P$*, then* A *accepts with probability at least* $2/3$.

- *If $d(x, P) > \epsilon$, then A rejects with probability at least* 2/3.

If furthermore all queries performed to the input can be decided before any of them are made, then the algorithm is non-adaptive, *and otherwise it is* adaptive. *If we require that whenever $x \in P$, then the algorithm accepts with probability* 1, *then the algorithm is* 1-sided, *and otherwise it is* 2-sided.

Property Testing was first addressed by Blum, Luby and Rubinfeld [6], and most of its general notions were first formulated by Rubinfeld and Sudan [24]. The first investigated properties were mostly of an algebraic nature, such as the property of a Boolean function being linear. The first investigation of combinatorial properties and the formal definition of testability was by Goldreich, Goldwasser and Ron [12]. Since then Property Testing has attracted significant attention. For surveys see [9, 21, 22].

When proving that testing a property requires many queries, one might ask "how strong is this requirement?", which can be illustrated with an example. Alon et. al. [3] studied the testability of formal languages, and proved that the language $L = \{uu^R vv^R | u, v \in \{0,1\}^*\}$ requires at least $\Omega(\sqrt{n})$ queries to test (formally, the property $L \cap \{0,1\}^n$ requires that many queries to test). Informally, one may say that the "reason" for this language being untestable is the difficulty in guessing the length of uu^R. This can be made formal by considering the languages $L_i = \{uu^R vv^R | u, v \in \{0,1\}^*, |u| = i\}$, which form a partition of L. A simple sampling algorithm can perform $O(\epsilon^{-1})$ queries to an input and distinguish between inputs in L_i and inputs ϵ-far from L. It is also important to note that $|L \cap \{0,1\}^n| = 2^{\Theta(n)}$, but its partition $L_0 \cap \{0,1\}^n, \ldots, L_n \cap \{0,1\}^n$ is only to a number of subsets linear in n.

This phenomenon is not unique to the language considered by Alon et. al. Another example is that of graph isomorphism, first considered in the property testing framework by Alon et. al. [2] (and later by Fischer and Matsliah [10]), and shown to require at least $\Omega(n)$ queries to test. In this setting we consider a pair of unknown graphs given by their adjacency matrices, and we are charged with distinguishing the case where they are isomorphic from the case where more than ϵn^2 of their edges must be changed to make them isomorphic. In this case, the size of the property is $2^{\Theta(n^2)}$, and we can partition the property into $n!$ properties $\{P_\pi | \pi \in S_n\}$, each defined by $P_\pi = \{(G_1, G_2) | \pi(G_1) = G_2\}$, such that a sampling algorithm can perform $O(\epsilon^{-1})$ queries to an input and distinguish between inputs in P_π and inputs ϵ-far from the original property.

Thus it is tempting to ask whether this is a general phenomenon. Can any property P be partitioned into $k = |P|^{o(1)}$ properties $P_1, \ldots, P_k$ such that the task of distinguishing inputs in P_i from inputs far from P can be performed with a number of queries that depends only on ϵ?

This question has a strong connection, in fact a near-equivalence, with the notion of a MAP as defined by an independent work of Gur and Rothblum [14]. They define a MAP (Merlin-Arthur proof of Proximity) as a testing algorithm that first read a "proof string" in whole, and uses it to test the given input. The requirement is that an input in P will have some corresponding proof that causes high probability acceptance, while for ϵ-far inputs for every proof there will be a high probability rejection. The connection to our framework is that the proof corresponds to the representation of the alleged i such that the input is in P_i, making the required proof length equal to $\lceil \log k \rceil$ for the optimal k.

The main result of the present paper is to prove that this is not always the case. In fact, there exist properties for which any such partition must be to a number of subsets exponential in n (and equivalently does not admit a MAP with an $o(n)$ proof size for testing with a number of queries independent of n).

To prove this result we in fact show the non-existence of a strictly weaker testing scenario, that would correspond to being able to test just for the biggest P_i in the alleged partition.

Definition 1.2 (Partially testable property). *If $P \subseteq \{0,1\}^n$ and $P' \subseteq P$. We say that P is P'*-partially testable with q queries *if there exists an algorithm A that gets as input a parameter $\epsilon > 0$ and query access to an input string $x \in \{0,1\}^n$ and outputs* accept *or* reject *such that:*

- *If $x \in P'$, then A accepts with probability at least 2/3.*
- *If $d(x, P) > \epsilon$, then A rejects with probability at least* 2/3.

If furthermore all queries performed to the input can be decided before any of them are made, then the algorithm is non-adaptive, *and else it is* adaptive.

Obviously, if P is testable with q queries, then for any subset $P' \subseteq P$ it is P'-partially testable with the same number of queries. On the other hand, for any property P and any element $x \in P$, we have that P is $\{x\}$-partially testable with $O(\epsilon^{-1})$ queries.

The partitions described above are in fact partitions of P into subsets $P_1, \ldots, P_k$ such that P is P_i-partially testable for every $1 \leq i \leq k$. If there exists such a partition into not too many sets, then there must be at least one set that is relatively large. Our main result shows that there exists a property P for which all subsets $P' \subseteq P$ such that P is P'-partially testable are small. In fact, all linear codes with large dual distance define such properties.

Theorem 1.3. *Let $C \subseteq \{0,1\}^n$ be a linear code of size $|C| \leq 2^{\frac{1}{64}n}$ and dual distance Γ. For every $C' \subseteq C$, if C is C'-partially testable with q adaptive queries, then $|C'| \leq |C| 2^{-\Theta(\Gamma/q)}$.*

We will first prove, as a warm-up, a weak version of Theorem 1.3 in Section 4 which will apply for q non-adaptive queries and imply the bound $|C'| \leq |C| 2^{-\Theta(\Gamma/q^3)}$. This proof will use some of the key ideas that will later manifest in the proof of the theorem in its full generality in Section 5.

Remark 1.4. *Theorem 1.3 holds for every property P which is Γ-wise independent. The only use of the linearity of C is in that dual distance Γ implies Γ-wise independence (see Theorem 3.9).*

An important question is the existence of codes with strong parameters. A random linear code C will have $\Gamma = \Theta(n)$ and $|C| = 2^{\Theta(n)}$ with high probability (this is implied by the Gilbert-Varshamov bound [11, 25]; MacWilliams et. al. [18] showed that this can also be obtained by codes which are self-dual and thus also have good distance), and thus by Theorem 1.3 we will have that for any $C' \subseteq C$ such that C is C'-partially testable with q queries, $|C'| \leq |C|2^{-\Theta(n/q)}$. For a constant q, this implies that partial testability will only be possible with exponentially small subsets. The best explicit (and low uniform decision complexity) construction known to us is that of [1], which gives $|C| = 2^{\Theta(n)}$ with $\Gamma = \Theta(n/\log n)$, and thus the bound deteriorates to $|C'| \leq n^{O(1)}|C|2^{-\Theta(n/q)}$, which is polynomially worse than the non-explicit bound, but is still a strong upper bound on the size of C'.

Theorem 1.3 implies that there exist properties P that require a lot of queries to test, and that every partition of P into subsets $P_1, \ldots, P_k$ such that P is P_i-partially testable for every $1 \leq i \leq k$ requires that k will be very big. One might ask if we can prove a converse. That is, if P can be tested with a few queries, can we find such a partition with a small k?

Open Problem 1.5. *Let P be a property testable with r queries. Is it true that we can partition P into subsets $P_1, \ldots, P_k$ such that P is P_i-partially testable using $O(1)$ queries for every $1 \leq i \leq k$ and k is bounded by some moderate function of r? What can be said about the converse direction?*

This problem can also be phrased as whether there exists a general trade-off between testing hardness and partitionability to easily partially testable properties. For the converse direction, of whether partitionability implies an efficient test for the whole property, we present preliminary results that revolve around the stricter notion of proximity oblivious testing:

Definition 1.6. *A* non-adaptive, 1-sided proximity-oblivious q-test *for a property P with* detection function $\rho(\epsilon)$ *is an algorithm that makes q non-adaptive queries to the input (i.e. the queries are all made before the answers to them are received), and based on those answers accepts or rejects the input in a way that satisfies the following:*

- *If the input satisfies P then the algorithm accepts with probability 1.*
- *If the input is ϵ-far from P, then the algorithm rejects with probability at least $\rho(\epsilon)$.*

Note that the algorithm is given the input length n in advance, but is not given ϵ. A partial proximity-oblivious q-test is defined in the analogous manner.

The simplest conceivable proximity-oblivious test would be a 2-test, making only 2 queries. Such tests exist for example in some monotonicity testing scenarios. We prove that partitionability into properties that are 2-testable implies a sublinear query test (that is not proximity-oblivious) for the entire property.

Theorem 1.7. *Let $P_1, P_2, \ldots, P_k \subseteq \{0,1\}^n$ be properties such that for every $i \in \{1, \ldots, k\}$, P_i has a 1-sided error proximity-oblivious 2-tester with detection function $\rho(\epsilon)$. If $\epsilon > 0$ is such that $\rho(\epsilon/2) > 0$, then for n large enough, as a polynomial function of $1/\rho(\epsilon/2)$, there is a one-sided error non-adaptive ϵ-tester for $P = \bigcup_{i=1}^{k} P_i$ with query complexity $\tilde{O}(n^{2/3}\epsilon^{-1}) \cdot \log(k)$ This is also true if for every P_i we only require a 1-sided error proximity-oblivious P_i-partial 2-test for P.*

The converse of the above immediately gives an observation interesting enough to state by itself.

Corollary 1.8. *If a property P requires $\Omega(n^\beta)$ many queries for some fixed $\beta > 2/3$, then there is no way to partition P into polynomially many properties (even not necessarily disjoint) admitting a 1-sided proximity-oblivious 2-tests (or even the corresponding partial tests).*

Theorem 1.7 is proved using a special test that we call a *universal test*, that works by selecting every index i for querying with probability $\tilde{O}(n^{-1/3}\epsilon^{-1}) \cdot \log(k)$, independently of other indexes. We prove in Theorem 6.8 below that such a kind of test will work for any property admitting a proximity oblivious 2-test, regardless of how that 2-test works. This universal test is very close to what is defined as a *sampling based test* in a new work [13] of Goldreich and Ron. In particular, our proof yields the following corollary, which partially addresses a question from [13] about whether proximity oblivious tests are translatable to sample-based ones:

Corollary 1.9. *Let P be a property that has a 1-sided error proximity-oblivious 2-tester with detection function $\rho(\epsilon)$. If $\epsilon > 0$ is such that $\rho(\epsilon/2) > 0$, then for n large enough, as a polynomial function of $1/\rho(\epsilon/2)$, there is a 1-sided error sample based test (see [13], Definition 2.3) with query complexity $\tilde{O}(n^{2/3}\epsilon^{-1}) \cdot \log(k)$.*

For proximity oblivious q-tests with $q > 2$ the situation is more complex, and we can only prove an analog of Theorem 6.8 (and by it Theorem 1.7) where the power of n in the query complexity depends (rather badly) on both q and $\rho(\epsilon/2)$.

To formulate the theorem achieving this, we say that a set R of indexes is a *witness against the input* for a property P, if the restriction of the input to R is such that it cannot be the restriction of any member of P (or alternatively, this restriction cannot be extended to an alternate input that satisfies P).

Definition 1.10. *For $\gamma \in (0,1)$, the* γ-universal sampler *selects a set $R \subseteq [n]$ where, for every $i \in [n]$, $\Pr[i \in R] = n^{-\gamma}$.*

We prove that the above sampling technique, essentially that of a sample-based tester as in [13], is indeed a core of a "universal test" for any property that has a (possibly "unknown") 1-sided proximity-oblivious q-test.

Theorem 1.11. *For every property P with a proximity oblivious q-test with detection function $\rho(\epsilon)$ there exists γ depending on q and $\rho(\epsilon/2)$ (for every ϵ), so that for n large enough and every ϵ-far input over $\{0,1\}^n$, the γ-universal sampler finds a witness against it with probability $1 - o(1)$.*

Its immediate corollary (through standard probability amplification and union bound) gives us a sub-linear query complexity test for any property decomposable into not too many (sub-exponential number of) properties where each of them has a proximity oblivious test, as long as they have the same detection function $\rho(\epsilon)$.

Corollary 1.12. *If $P = \bigcup_{i=1}^{\ell} P_i$ is a property such that every P_i has an oblivious 1-sided error (proximity oblivious)* *q-test, all with the same detection function $\rho(\epsilon)$ (but not necessarily the same test), then for n large enough the following is a test for P with $O(\log(\ell)n^{1-\gamma})$ query complexity, where we use the γ of Theorem 1.11:*

Select a set $R \subseteq [n]$ that is the union of $2\log(\ell)$ sets, each chosen according to the γ-universal sampler. If the set $|R| > 4\log(\ell)n^{1-\gamma}$ then accept immediately, and otherwise query the input on all indexes of R, reject if R is a P_i-witness against the input for every $i \in [\ell]$, and accept otherwise.

Finally, we prove a result in the other direction, hinting that maybe some role for proximity oblivious testing is essential. Using a very simple construction we prove the following:

THEOREM 1.13. *For every fixed k there is a property P, so that $1/5k$-testing P (even adaptively) requires $\Omega(n^{1-1/k})$ queries, while P is still decomposable to at most n^{k-1} many properties so that each of them is even ϵ-testable in itself with $O(1/\epsilon)$ many queries for every ϵ; in fact each of them will have a proximity-oblivious 1-sided k-test with the detection function $\rho(\epsilon) = O(k\epsilon)$.*

Until now we discussed the relation of Theorem 1.3 to the impossibility of decomposing a property to testable ones. However, there may be use in its stronger statement of not having even one large sub-property for which there exists an efficient test. The proof of Theorem 1.3 immediately gives the following corollary.

COROLLARY 1.14. *Suppose that P is a property for which $|P| \leq 2^{\frac{1}{64}n}$, and C is any linear code with dual distance Γ so that $|P \cap C| \geq |C|2^{-\Gamma/q}$. Then P requires at least $\Theta(q)$ many queries to test (or even $P \cap C$-partially test).*

We conclude this part of the introduction with an open question for which we cannot yet scratch the surface. Theorem 1.3 implies that for some properties, k might be as big as $2^{\Theta(n/q)}$. It is not clear whether this value of k can always be obtained. The trivial upper bound for every property is by partitioning into 2^{n-q} subsets of size 2^q. Are there properties for which this is required?

OPEN PROBLEM 1.15. *Does there exist a property P such that for every $P' \subseteq P$ where P is P'-partially testable with q queries we also have $|P'| \leq |P|2^{\Theta(q)-\Theta(n)}$?*

In [14] there is a non-constructive proof (by counting the number of possible algorithms) that there is a property that is not partitionable to less than $2^{\Theta(n)-\Theta(q)}$ properties admitting partial tests with q queries, which would result from a property as above.

1.1 Related work

The notion of partial testability, while not defined before, is implicit in previous works on PCPs (Probabilistically Checkable Proofs). The long code tester of Håstad [15] accepts inputs which are codewords in the long code, and rejects inputs which are far from being k-juntas for some k. Since codewords in the long code are dictatorships (1-juntas), this is an instance where the fact that being a dictatorship is k-junta-partially testable is used to construct PCPs.

Our notion of a partition is similar to existing notions in computational complexity. For a partition $P = P_1 \cup P_2 \cup \ldots \cup P_k$ where for every $1 \leq i \leq k$, P is P_i-partially testable, the designation of P_i can be seen as a "proof" that a certain x is in P. If $x \in P$, then there exists some P_i such that $x \in P_i$ and therefore a P_i-partial tester for P will accept it with high probability. If x is ϵ-far from P, then all P_i-partial testers for P will reject it with high probability.

This is similar to the notion of a *Probabilistically Checkable Proof of Proximity (PCPP)*, first introduced by Ben-Sasson et. al. [4]. PCPPs are to property testing as NP is to P. A q query PCPP for a property $P \subset U$ is an algorithm that gets as input $x \in U$ and a *proof of proximity* $\pi \in \{0,1\}^l$. The algorithm must perform at most q queries to x and π and fulfill the requirement that if $x \in P$ then there exists a proof π that causes the algorithm to accept with high probability, but when x is ϵ-far from P then for any proof π the algorithm rejects with high probability. In our setting, the algorithm is allowed free access to a proof of length $l = \log(k)$, but we expect l to be sublinear in the size of x. In particular, the property we analyze here cannot have a PCPP with a sublinear length proof. Note that a proof can always be seen as designating a specific subset of the property, the subset of inputs for which this proof is useful.

Rothblum et. al. [23] introduced the notion of an *Interactive Proof of Proximity (IPP)*. In an IPP for a property P, the tester can also communicate with a *prover* in addition to querying the input x. If $x \in P$ then the prover has a strategy that will cause the tester to accept with high probability. When x is ϵ-far from P, the prover cannot make the tester accept with high probability. Rothblum et. al. show that all languages in NC admit such a protocol with $\sqrt{n}$ query and communication complexity and polylog(n) communication rounds. Protocols of this kind are only interesting for the case where the communication complexity is sublinear, or else the prover may just give the input to the tester.

Independently of the present work, Gur and Rothblum [14] weakened the IPP model to create *Merlin-Arthur Proofs of Proximity (MAP)*. Gur and Rothblum define a MAP as a proof-system for a property P where for an input x and a proof π the verifier reads the entire proof π and queries q bits from the input x. If $x \in P$, then there exists a proof π such that the verifier accepts with high probability, and if x is far from P, then for every proof π the verifier rejects with high probability. Since we can trivially set $\pi = x$, the only interesting cases are where the length of π is sublinear.

The notion of a MAP with q queries and proofs of length ℓ for a property P is equivalent to the existence of $k = 2^\ell$ sets $P_1, \ldots, P_k$ such that $P = P_1 \cup P_2 \cup \ldots \cup P_k$ where for every $1 \leq i \leq k$, P is P_i-partially testable with q queries.

Gur and Rothblum give several constructions of properties where a MAP with a sublinear length proof greatly reduces query complexity. Gur and Rothblum also introduce the *Tensor Sum* family of properties, for which they prove that for every constant $\alpha > 0$ there exists an instantiation of Tensor Sum such that any MAP for it that performs q queries must require a proof of length $\Omega\left(\frac{n^{1-\alpha}}{q}\right)$. This bound is slightly weaker than the implication for decomposability of Theorem 1.3 proved in the present paper for our property (however, their property is not a high dual-distance code so our result would not apply directly). There is no known bound on the size of a sub-property of the Tensor Sum properties admitting a partial test, only on decomposability.

Their lower bound is proved by an extension of the communication complexity technique of Brody et. al. [5] to *Merlin-Arthur communication complexity*. First proving a lower bound for 1-sided testing this way, they then use a general conversion technique (at some cost to both proof length and query complexity, see below) to 2-sided testing. Their proof technique is fitting for the MAP setting, but does not apply to partial testing in general. Gur and Rothblum also prove that this trade-off is almost optimal for the Tensor Sum properties.

Additionally, Gur and Rothblum show separations between the power of MAPs and that of IPPs and PCPPs. For their proofs they also show that 2-sidedness may only give a MAP a polylog(n) factor improvement in proof length and query complexity over a 1-sided algorithm. Their result implies a connection also between 1-sided and 2-sided partial testability, though not one that would preserve O(1)-query partial testability.

Regarding the testing versus proof length trade-off question, they show it for the very simple case of "proof-oblivious" testers, i.e. algorithms that make their queries before reading the alleged proof. By contrast, the main difficulty in proving our preliminary trade-off result is exactly that the tests for different P_i could have differing query distributions (even that each of them in itself is proximity oblivious).

Another angle to our methods related to the above trade-off comes from the very recent work of Goldreich and Ron [13]. Their work is centered on what they call *sample-based algorithms*, which are testing algorithms that select all their queries uniformly and independently at random. For a number of queries that is a fixed power of n where n is large enough, this is virtually identical to the way our universal tests work, where every index is independently chosen to be queried with some fixed probability. Indeed they raised the question whether any property that is testable by a proximity-oblivious q-test can also be tested by a sublinear complexity sample-based test, and we give a partial positive answer, for 1-sided error tests ([13] also defines 2-sided error proximity oblivious q-tests, which we do not analyze here).

2. PLAN OF THE PAPER

The first major part of the paper is devoted to proving the partial testability lower bound, which is the most "mature" result. After the general preliminaries in Section 3, a warmup proof against non-adaptive testing is found in Section 4, and then additional ideas are incorporated to provide a proof against adaptive testing in Section 5.

The second major part deals with converting proximity-oblivious tests to universal ones that scale well when the property is only decomposable. The conversion from a partition into (proximity-oblivious) 2-testable properties to a test of the whole property is in Section 6, while Section 7 gives the (more expansive) conversion for q-testable properties.

Finally, Section 8 contains a property that requires relatively many queries to test for itself, while being partitionable into not too many highly testable properties. For the most part, the sections following the preliminaries can be read individually (Section 7 mildly uses some notions from Section 6).

The rest of this section is devoted to an informal description of the main ideas behind the proofs.

2.1 General themes for the partially untestable property

For the proofs of our main result we develop new techniques that are in some ways more flexible than the traditional use of Yao's method for proving property testing lower bounds. We believe that these techniques hold promise for other lower bound situations where using Yao's method seems to hit a wall.

As with Yao's method, we contrast the behavior of a supposed test when it is run over an input chosen according to some distribution over "yes" instances, with its behavior when it is run over an input chosen according to some distribution over "no" instances. However, while in the traditional method these two distributions are chosen based only on the property (and should work against all possible algorithms of a given class), here the distributions are in fact *tailor made* for the specific analyzed algorithm. Note that special care must be taken in the definition of such an input distribution. It may not depend on the "real-time" behavior of the algorithm (i.e. it may not adapt itself to the identity of the random queries that the algorithm has made), and is instead constructed based only on the *description* of the algorithm.

The second theme is the use of *Shannon entropy*. Our goal here is to prove that if C is C'-partially testable, then C' cannot be too large. For achieving this we assume that a testing algorithm exists, and then contrast a uniformly random choice of a word in C' with another word chosen from a "dangerous" distribution over words far from C. The assumption that the test in fact distinguishes the two distributions allows us to show that a uniformly random choice of a word in C' has low entropy, and hence C' must be small. Using entropy instead of direct counting is crucial to using our main method for obtaining a bound against 2-sided error tests, rather than only 1-sided error ones.

A third theme used in the proof against adaptive algorithms is that of first parsing the input through a specially constructed injective mapping, called a "reader", which is crucial to "exposing" low-entropy portions in this setting. We are in fact considering not just one input distribution, but several of them as the reader is constructed.

2.2 Proving a bound against non-adaptive algorithms

The bound against non-adaptive algorithms showcases many of the general themes. A supposed C'-partial test with q queries is in essence a distribution over query sets of size q, such that with high probability the chosen query set is one that highlights a difference between members of C' and inputs far from being in C. As a toy example, assume first that the test is additionally 1-sided, and "well-spread" with respect to the probabilities of querying any particular index. In this case, for every ϵ-far input, the high probability of finding a forbidden substructure (as this is the only way a 1-sided test can reject) translates to having many disjoint q-tuples of indexes where in each of them there is a value that a member of C' cannot take (as a hypothetical forbidden structure must exist). This would give a cross product bound on the size of C'.

As our tests are not necessarily "well-spread", we will construct a specialized distribution that depends on the specific testing algorithm (but is independent of any particular running instance). For handling 2-sided tests we use a feature of entropy that allows for bounds analogous to combinatorial cross product bounds, namely the subadditivity of the entropy measure.

To construct a "dangerous" distribution over words far from being in C, we first take note of the "heavy" indexes, which are those bits of the input that are with high probability part of the query subset of the investigated testing algorithm. There will be only few of those, and our distribution over far words would be that of starting with a restriction of a uniformly random word in C' to the set of heavy indexes, and augmenting it with independently and uniformly chosen values to all other input bits. When contrasted with the uniform distribution over all members of C', we obtain that there must be many query sets that show a distinction between the two distributions over the non-heavy indexes with respect to the heavy ones. This means that the values of the non-heavy indexes in each such query set do not behave like a uniformly independent choice, and thus have a corresponding entropy (conditioned on the heavy index bits) that is significantly less than the maximal possible entropy. Having many such query sets in essence means that we can find many such sets that are disjoint outside the heavy indexes, which in turn leads to an entropy bound by virtue of subadditivity (when coupled with general properties of linear codes).

2.3 Proving a bound against adaptive algorithms

An adaptive algorithm cannot be described as a distribution over query sets, but rather as a distribution over small decision trees of height q that determine the queries. Therefore low-entropy index sets cannot be readily found (and in fact do not always exist). To deal with this we employ a new technique, that allows us to "rearrange" the input in a way that preserves entropy, but now admits disjoint low-entropy sets.

This new construction is a *reader*, which in essence is an adaptive algorithm that reads the entire input bit by bit (without repetitions). As this adaptive algorithm always eventually reads the entire input, it defines a bijection between the input to be read and the "reading stream", i.e. the sequence of values in the order that the reader has read them.

The construction of this reader is fully based on the description of the q-query adaptive algorithm that C'-partially tests for C (again we assume that such an algorithm exists). In fact we contrast the uniform distribution over members of C' with not one but many possible distributions over inputs far from C. At every stage we obtain that, as long as our reader has not yet read a large portion of the input, the adaptive test can provide a decision tree over the yet-unread bits that shows a difference between a uniformly random member of C' (conditioned on the values of the bits already read) and an independently uniform random choice of values for the unread bits. Our reader will be the result of "concatenating" such decision trees as long as there are enough unread bits. Thus in the "reading stream" we have sets of q consecutive bits, each with low entropy (as it is distinguishable from independently uniform values). When there are not enough unread bits left, we read all remaining bits arbitrarily, and use general properties of codes to bound the entropy on that final chunk.

The method of constructing a reader not only allows us to do away with the exponential penalty usually associated with moving from non-adaptive to adaptive algorithms, but we additionally obtain better bounds for non-adaptive algorithms as well. This is because a reader can do away also with the penalty of moving from the situation of having many low-entropy query sets to having a family of sets disjoint outside the heavy indexes, in essence by constructing the reader for the uniform distribution over C' based on not one but many "dangerous" input distributions.

2.4 Testing decomposable properties through universal testing

Suppose that a property P defined over $\{0,1\}^n$ is decomposable to properties $P_1, \ldots, P_k$, so that each of them is in itself ϵ-testable with $q(\epsilon)$-queries for every $\epsilon > 0$ (the same arguments work also for partial testability, but we restrict the discussion here to proper testability for the sake of explanation). How can we test for all of P at once? The simplest way would be to juxtapose the individual tests for every P_i, which would give a test with $O(kq\log(k))$ many queries (accounting also for the necessary probability amplification). However, in our discussion here k rises too fast with n, so we would like the dependence on it to be at most polylogarithmic, even at the cost of replacing the "base complexity" k with a value that depends (sublinearly) on n.

If the tests for all P_i "behave the same", i.e. have the same query distribution, then instead of querying for every test individually we can do the querying once and feed it to all the tests, and then indeed get a test with $O(q\log(k))$ many queries. This is essentially what is done in the preliminary result from [14]. Our goal here is to replace the original test with a "universal" test that would work for *any* property for which an original test with the specified parameters exist, and then use it instead of the original individual tests.

In our first preliminary result we construct such a test whose number of queries is bounded by a fixed power of n, but only if every P_i was testable by the very restricted notion of a 1-sided non-adaptive proximity-oblivious test with 2 queries. Such tests allow for a combinatorial viewpoint through their underlying graphs (where an edge connects two indexes $i, j \in \{1, \ldots, n\}$ if with positive probability the test query set is $\{i, j\}$). This allows for some analysis of the probability of picking a "rejecting edge" when every index ("vertex") is picked and queried with probability $n^{-\beta}$ for an appropriate constant β. The hard part in the proof is when the test has some "heavy indexes", corresponding to high degree vertices.

Our second result handles proximity-oblivious q-tests for any fixed q, but unlike the first result, also the power of n in the resulting test depends on ϵ. We essentially make sure that the sampling is "forceful" enough so that any small "erroneous fragment" of the input cannot "propagate" much if it is altered (the test will detect all possible alterations with large propagations, so such alterations will be forbidden). This in turn allows us to analyze $1/\rho(\epsilon/2)$ many $\epsilon/2$-far inputs derived from the original input, showing that unless the universal test works, they cannot be all rejected by the original test. This is what causes a dependency on $\rho(\epsilon/2)$ of the power of n.

2.5 A non-testable property that is decomposable to testable ones

In the introduction, the property of being a concatenation of two palindromes was mentioned as one that requires

$\Omega(\sqrt{n})$ many queries to test, while being decomposable to $O(n)$ many testable properties (in fact properties admitting a proximity oblivious 2-test). The basic idea from this property is carried over to the properties constructed here. A parity condition ensures that instead of having to correlate two strings (an alleged palindrome and its reverse), we would have to correlate k strings, increasing the bound from $\Omega(\sqrt{n})$ to $\Omega(n^{1-1/k})$. As these k strings are allowed to "slide" relative to each other, the number of properties that we decompose to would be $O(n^{k-1})$, each one corresponding to a fixing of the locations of the strings.

3. PRELIMINARIES

Below we introduce the reader to some basic definitions and results regarding entropy and the dual distance of codes. We refer the reader who is interested in a more thorough introduction of entropy to [7, Chapter 2].

First, we introduce a standard notion of distance between distributions.

DEFINITION 3.1 (TOTAL VARIATION DISTANCE). *Let p and q be two distributions over the domain $\mathcal{D}$. The total variation distance between p and q is defined to be*

$$d_{TV}(p,q) = \frac{1}{2}\sum_{i\in\mathcal{D}} |p(i) - q(i)|.$$

We now introduce the notion of the entropy of a random variable, the entropy of a random variable conditioned on another one, and two well-known lemmas.

DEFINITION 3.2 (ENTROPY). *Let X be a random variable over the domain $\mathcal{D}$. The* entropy *of X is defined to be $H[X] = -\sum_{i\in\mathcal{D}} \Pr[X=i]\log(\Pr[X=i])$.*

DEFINITION 3.3 (CONDITIONAL ENTROPY). *Let X and Y be random variables over the domain $\mathcal{D}$. The* entropy of X conditioned on Y *is defined to be $H[X|Y] = \sum_{y\in\mathcal{D}} \Pr[Y = i]H[X|Y=y]$.*

LEMMA 3.4 (THE CHAIN RULE). *Assume that X and Y are random variables. The entropy of the combined state determined by both random variables is denoted $H[X,Y]$. This quantity obeys the chain rule $H[X,Y] = H[X|Y] + H[Y]$.*

LEMMA 3.5 (SUBADDITIVITY). *If X and Y are random variables, then $H[X,Y] \le H[X] + H[Y]$.*

The total variation distance is not a natural fit to the context of entropy. A more fitting notion of distance between distributions is divergence (also known as the Kullback-Liebler divergence [16]).

DEFINITION 3.6 (DIVERGENCE). *Let p and q be two distributions over $\mathcal{D}$. The* divergence of q from p *is defined to be $D(p\|q) = \sum_{i\in\mathcal{D}} p(i)\log\left(\frac{p(i)}{q(i)}\right)$.*

Fortunately, divergence and total variation distance are related via Pinsker's inequality. This was originally proved with worse bounds by Pinsker [19] and seen many subsequent improvements, the current definitive version being that of Reid and Williamson [20].

LEMMA 3.7 (PINSKER'S INEQUALITY). *Assume that p, q are two distributions over the domain $\mathcal{D}$. The total variation distance between p and q is related to the divergence of q from p by the inequality $\sqrt{\frac{1}{2}D(p\|q)} \ge d_{TV}(p,q)$.*

We will actually be using a simpler corollary of it.

LEMMA 3.8 (COROLLARY OF PINSKER'S INEQUALITY). *Assume that X is a random variable distributed according to p over $\mathcal{D}$, and denote the uniform distribution over $\mathcal{D}$ by p_u. The entropy of X is related to its total variation distance from the uniform distribution by $H[X] \le \log(|\mathcal{D}|) - 2(d_{TV}(p,p_u))^2$.*

PROOF.

$$H[X] = -\sum_{i\in\mathcal{D}} \Pr[X=i]\log(\Pr[X=i])$$

$$= -\sum_{i\in\mathcal{D}} \Pr[X=i]\log(\Pr[X=i]\cdot\frac{1}{|\mathcal{D}|}\cdot|\mathcal{D}|)$$

$$= -\sum_{i\in\mathcal{D}} \Pr[X=i]\log(\frac{1}{|\mathcal{D}|})$$

$$-\sum_{i\in\mathcal{D}} \Pr[X=i]\log(\Pr[X=i]\cdot|\mathcal{D}|)$$

$$= \log(|\mathcal{D}|) - D(p\|p_u) \le \log(|\mathcal{D}|) - 2(d_{TV}(p,p_u))^2$$

Where the last step follows from Pinsker's inequality. □

Let $x \in \{0,1\}^n$ and $J \subseteq [n]$. We use $x[J]$ to denote the restriction of x to the indices in J. That is, the vector $< x_j >_{j\in J}$. When $C \subseteq \{0,1\}^n$ we use $C[J] = \{x[J] | x \in C\}$.

Let $C \subseteq \{0,1\}^n$. We denote by $U(C)$ the uniform distribution over C. In accordance with the notation above, when $X \sim U(C)$, $X[J]$ denotes the random variable obtained by drawing uniformly from C and then restricting to the indices in J. As a shorthand we use $U(C)[J]$ for the distribution of $X[J]$. We use $U_J(C)$ to denote the result of first drawing a vector x according to $U(C)$, and then replacing $x\,[[n]\setminus J]$ with a uniformly random vector in $\{0,1\}^{n-|J|}$. In particular, in many cases we will take C to be a singleton, in which case we drop the curly braces and denote this probability distribution by $U_J(x)$.

We will make inherent use of the following result, which can be found e.g. in [17, Chapter 1, Theorem 10].

LEMMA 3.9. *Let C be a linear code with dual distance Γ. If $J \subseteq [n]$ is such that $|J| < \Gamma$ and $X \sim U(C)$, then $X[J]$ is distributed uniformly over $\{0,1\}^{|J|}$.*

We will also need the fact that a mostly random input is far from a code with high probability.

LEMMA 3.10. *Let $C \subseteq \{0,1\}^n$ such that $|C| \le 2^{\frac{1}{64}n}$, $\epsilon < 1/8$, and let $J \subseteq [n]$ be such that $|J| \le n/2$. $X \sim U_J(C)$ is ϵ-far from C with probability $1 - o(1)$. Furthermore, this is still true when conditioned on any value of $X[J]$.*

PROOF. By Chernoff bounds, the probability that a random element $X \sim U_J(C)$ will agree with $c \in C$ in more than $(1-\epsilon)n$ coordinates is at most $\exp\Big(-n(1/4-\epsilon)^2\Big)$.

Taking the union bound over all $c \in C$ gives us $|C| \cdot \exp\Big(-n(1/4-\epsilon)^2\Big) = o(1)$. Since this calculation assumes that $X[J]$ always agrees with $c[J]$, it holds when conditioned on any value of $X[J]$. □

Finally, we will also need to use Lemma 3.9 to help us calculate the entropy of uniform random variables in codes.

LEMMA 3.11. *Let C be a code with dual distance Γ, $J \subseteq [n]$ such that $|J| \leq \Gamma$, $C' \subseteq C$ and $X \sim U(C')$. Then $H[X|X[J]] \leq \log|C| - |J|$. Furthermore, this is true when conditioned on any particular value of $X[J]$.*

PROOF. We can partition C according to the values of the bits in J:

$$C = \bigcup_{z \in \{0,1\}^{|J|}} \{c \in C | c[J] = z\}$$

By Lemma 3.9, all sets on the right hand side are of size $2^{-|J|}|C|$. Obviously, for all $z \in \{0,1\}^{|J|}$, we have $\{c' \in C' | c'[J] = z\} \subseteq \{c \in C | c[J] = z\}$, simply because $C' \subseteq C$. Thus for every $x \in C'[J]$, we have that

$$H[X|X[J] = x] \leq \log|\{c' \in C' | c'[J] = z\}|$$

$$\leq \log|\{c \in C | c[J] = z\}|.$$

This completes the "furthermore" part of the lemma. To obtain the non-conditioned version, note that by the definition of conditional entropy,

$$H[X|X[J]] = \mathrm{E}_{x \sim U(C')[J]} H[X|X[J] = x] \leq \log\left(2^{-|J|}|C|\right)$$

$$= \log|C| - |J|.$$

□

We note (and use throughout) that trivially $H[X|X[J]] = H[X[\{1,\ldots,n\} \setminus J]|X[J]]$.

4. NONADAPTIVE LOWER BOUND

In this section we prove Theorem 1.3 for the case of a non-adaptive tester and with slightly worse quantitative bounds. For the rest of this section, set $C \subset \{0,1\}^n$ to be a code with dual distance Γ and $|C| \leq 2^{\frac{1}{64}n}$. Set $\epsilon < 1/8$ and assume that C is C'-partially testable for $C' \subseteq C$ with q non-adaptive queries.

Next we define a non-adaptive tester for a property. This definition is consistent with the standard one.

DEFINITION 4.1 (NON-ADAPTIVE PROPERTY TESTER). *A non-adaptive ϵ-tester for a code $C \subseteq \{0,1\}^n$ with query complexity $q(\epsilon, n)$ is defined by a collection of query sets $\{Q_i\}_{i \in I}$ of size q together with a predicate π_i for each query set and a distribution μ over I which satisfies:*

- *If $x \in C$, then with probability at least $2/3$ an $i \in I$ is picked such that $\pi_i(x[Q_i]) = 1$.*
- *If $d(x, C) > \epsilon$, then with probability at least $2/3$ an $i \in I$ is picked such that $\pi_i(x[Q_i]) = 0$.*

For a C'-partial tester the first item must hold only for $x \in C'$.

Set a non-adaptive tester for C', and let $\{Q_i\}_{i \in I}$ be its query sets.

We will be interested only in those query sets which are useful for telling a random element in C' from a mostly random element in $\{0,1\}^n$.

DEFINITION 4.2 (J-DISCERNING QUERY SET). *Let $J \subseteq [n]$ be such that $|J| \leq n/2$. A query set Q_i is a J-discerning set if $d_{TV}(U(C')[Q_i], U_J(C')[Q_i]) \geq 1/8$.*

Next we prove that a tester must have a lot of such good query sets.

LEMMA 4.3. *Set $J \subseteq [n]$ such that $|J| \leq n/2$. With probability at least $1/9$ the query set Q_i picked by the tester is a J-discerning set.*

PROOF. Assume the contrary, that is, that with probability greater than $8/9$ the query set Q_i picked by the tester is such that $d_{TV}(U(C')[Q_i], U_J(C')[Q_i]) < 1/8$.

Thus for every such Q_i,

$$|\Pr_{U(C')[Q_i]}[\text{tester accepts}] - \Pr_{U_J(C')[Q_i]}[\text{tester accepts}]| < 1/8.$$

For the case where the query set picked is not discerning, which occurs with probability smaller than $1/9$, we have no bound (better than 1) on the difference in probability.

Overall, over the randomness of the tester,

$$|\Pr_{U(C')}[\text{tester accepts}] - \Pr_{U_J(C')}[\text{tester accepts}]|$$

$$< 8/9 \cdot 1/8 + 1/9 = 2/9.$$

But by the correctness of the tester and Lemma 3.10, we arrive at $\Pr_{U(C')}[\text{tester accepts}] \geq 2/3$ while simultaneously $\Pr_{U_J(C')}[\text{tester accepts}] \leq 1/3$, a contradiction. □

We will later want to construct a collection of J-discerning sets disjoint outside of a small fixed portion of the input. Towards this end we prove that J-discerning sets show difference between an element in C' and a mostly random element in $\{0,1\}^n$ even when we only look outside of J.

LEMMA 4.4. *Assume that Q_i is a J-discerning set, draw $Z \sim U(C')[J]$ and then draw $X \sim U(C')[Q_i]$ conditioned on $X[J] = Z$. With probability at least $1/15$ (taken over the choice of Z), the distribution of $X[Q_i \setminus J]$ is $1/16$-far from $U(\{0,1\}^{|Q_i \setminus J|})$.*

PROOF. First note that the distance between $U(C')[Q_i]$ and $U_J(C')[Q_i]$ is the expectation over Z of the distance of $X[Q_i \setminus J]$ from $U(\{0,1\}^{|Q_i \setminus J|})$, conditioned on $X[J] = Z$. By definition, that is at least $1/8$. By simple probability bounds, with probability at least $1/15$, Z is such that the distance of $X[Q_i \setminus J]$ from $U(\{0,1\}^{|Q_i \setminus J|})$ conditioned on $X[J] = Z$ is at least $1/16$. □

However, total variation distance is not very handy for counting. We now use Lemma 3.8 to transform our total variation bounds into "entropy loss" bounds.

LEMMA 4.5. *If Q_i is a J-discerning set and pick $X \sim U(C')[Q_i]$, then $H[X[Q_i \setminus J]|X[J]] \leq |Q_i \setminus J| - 0.0005$.*

PROOF. Let $L \subseteq \{0,1\}^{|J|}$ be the set of values $z \in \{0,1\}^{|J|}$ such that when drawing $X \sim U(C')[Q_i]$ conditioned on having $X[J] = z$, the distribution of $X[Q_i \setminus J]$ is $1/16$-far from $U(\{0,1\}^{|Q_i \setminus J|})$.

Since the entropy is non-negative, we can upper bound

$$H[X[Q_i \setminus J]|X[J]]$$

$$\leq \sum_{z \in L} \Pr_{Z \sim U(C')[J]}[Z = z] H[[Q_i \setminus J]|X[J] = z]$$

$$+ \sum_{z \in \{0,1\}^J \setminus L} \Pr_{Z \sim U(C')[J]}[Z = z] |Q_i \setminus J|.$$

To treat the first summand on the right hand side, we invoke Lemma 3.8 to obtain

$$H[[Q_i \setminus J]|X[J] = z] \leq |Q_i \setminus J| - 0.007.$$

Overall we get

$$\sum_{z \in L} \Pr_{Z \sim U(C')[J]}[Z = z] H[[Q_i \setminus J]|X[J] = z]$$

$$+ \sum_{z \in \{0,1\}^J \setminus L} \Pr_{Z \sim U(C')[J]}[Z = z] |Q_i \setminus J|$$

$$\leq |Q_i \setminus J| - 0.0005.$$

□

Next, we would try to cover the indices in $[n]$ with as many discerning sets as possible. We will need these sets to be disjoint outside a not-too-big set, so that the "entropy loss" could be aggregated. This set of "bad" indices will be the set of bits read by the tester with the highest probability.

DEFINITION 4.6. *Define* $B = \{k \in [n] | \Pr_{Q \sim \mu}[k \in Q] \geq \frac{2q}{\Gamma}\}$.

OBSERVATION 4.7. $|B| \leq \Gamma/2 \leq n/2$. *Therefore Lemma 3.10 holds with* $J = B$.

Now we can prove that we can find many B-discerning sets which are disjoint outside of B.

LEMMA 4.8. *There exists a set* I_D *such that:*

- *For all* $i \in I_D$, Q_i *is a* B*-discerning set*
- *For all* $i, j \in I_D$, $Q_i \setminus B$ *and* $Q_j \setminus B$ *are disjoint*

$D = \cup_{i \in I_D}(Q_i \setminus B)$ *satisfies* $\Gamma/2 \geq |D| \geq \frac{\Gamma}{18q^2}$. *Additionally,* $|I_D| \geq \frac{\Gamma}{18q^3}$.

PROOF. We construct the set I_D greedily. Suppose that we have discerning sets covering k bits that are disjoint outside of B. Choose a set randomly using the tester's distribution conditioned on it being B-discerning. By Lemma 4.3, this increases the probability of every query set, and every bit to be in a query set, by at most 9. By the definition of B, if we choose a query set randomly using the tester's distribution, the probability that it intersects our already covered bits outside of B is at most $9\frac{2q^2}{\Gamma}k$. As long as this number is smaller than 1, such a set exists. Therefore, as long as $k < \frac{\Gamma}{18q^2}$ we have a set to add, leading to the bound. To get the upper bound on $|D|$ we can just stop the process before D gets too big.

The lower bound on the size of I_D follows from the lower bound on the size of D. □

Finally, we are ready to calculate the entropy of a uniformly random codeword from C'. We use the chain rule to split this into calculating the entropy of the bits in B, the entropy of the bits in D conditioned on the bits of B, and the entropy of everything else conditioned on the bits in $D \cup B$.

LEMMA 4.9. *If* $X \sim U(C')$, *then it's entropy is bounded away from maximal* $H[X] \leq \log|C| - 0.0005\frac{\Gamma}{18q^3}$

PROOF. First, by the chain rule for entropy and the fact that $D \setminus B = D$,

$$H[X] = H[X|X[D \cup B]] + H[X[D]|X[B]] + H[X[B]]$$

We proceed by bounding each element in the sum. First, trivially:

$$H[X[B]] \leq |B|$$

Next, invoke Lemma 3.11 for $D \cup B$, since $|D \cup B| \leq \Gamma$. This gives us:

$$H[X|X[D \cup B]] \leq \log|C| - |D \cup B|$$

Now, recall that $\cup_{i \in I_D}(Q_i \setminus B) = D$. Since these sets are disjoint outside of B, we employ subadditivity to get:

$$H[X[D \setminus B]|X[B]] \leq \sum_{i \in I_D} H[X[Q_i \setminus B]|X[B]]$$

Now, since these are all B-discerning sets, by Lemma 4.5 we know that for all $i \in I_D$ we have that $H[X[Q_i \setminus B]|X[B]] \leq |Q_i \setminus B| - 0.0005$. By Lemma 4.8 we know that $|I_D| \geq \frac{\Gamma}{18q^3}$. Summing up we get:

$$\sum_{i \in I_D} H[X[Q_i \setminus B]|X[B]] \leq |D| - 0.0005|I_D|$$

$$\leq |D| - 0.0005\frac{\Gamma}{18q^3}$$

That is,

$$H[X[D]|X[B]] \leq |D| - 0.0005\frac{\Gamma}{18q^3}$$

Summing up we get the statement of the lemma. □

From this it follows that:

THEOREM 4.10 (WEAK FORM OF THE MAIN THEOREM). *Let* $C' \subseteq C$, *if* C *is* C'*-partially testable with* q *non-adaptive queries, then*

$$|C'| = 2^{H[X]} \leq |C| 2^{-0.0005\frac{\Gamma}{18q^3}}.$$

5. ADAPTIVE LOWER BOUND

In this section we prove Theorem 1.3 in its full generality. We start by introducing the mechanism of a *reader*, which allows us to separate the adaptivity and randomness of the algorithm.

DEFINITION 5.1 (READER). *A* k*-reader* r *is a sequence* $r_0, r_1, \ldots, r_{k-1}$, *where* $r_i : \{0,1\}^i \to \{1, \ldots, n\}$ *satisfy for all* $i < j$ *and* $y \in \{0,1\}^j$ *that* $r_i(y[\{1, \ldots, i\}]) \neq r_j(y)$.

Given an input $x \in \{0,1\}^n$, the reader defines a sequence of its bits. This is the *reading* of x.

Definition 5.2 (Reading). *Given $x \in \{0,1\}^n$ and a k-reader r, the* reading $R_{r(x)}$ *of x according to r is a sequence $y_1, \dots, y_k$ defined inductively by $y_{i+1} = x_{r_i(y_1,\dots,y_i)}$. We define $r_i(x)$ to be $r_i(y_1, \dots, y_i)$. The set of* unread bits *$U_{r(x)}$ is the subset of $\{1, \dots, n\}$ that did not appear as values of $r_1, \dots, r_k$ in the reading.*

We can now define an adaptive tester as a distribution over readers and decision predicates.

Definition 5.3 (Adaptive tester). *An* adaptive ϵ-tester *for a code $C \subseteq \{0,1\}^n$ with query complexity $q = q(\epsilon, n)$ is defined by a collection of q-readers $\{r^i\}_{i \in I}$ together with predicates π_i for each reader, and a distribution μ over I which satisfies:*

- *For all $x \in C$, $\Pr_{i\sim\mu}\left[\pi_i(R_{r^i(x)}) = 1\right] \geq 2/3$.*
- *For all $x \in \{0,1\}^n$ such that $d(x, C) > \epsilon$, we have that $\Pr_{i\sim\mu}\left[\pi_i(R_{r^i(x)}) = 0\right] \geq 2/3$.*

Part of the usefulness of readers is that if we can construct a reader that reads the entire input, then reading the property C' through it preserves its size.

Observation 5.4. *If r is an n-reader, then the function mapping every $x \in \{0,1\}^n$ to its reading $R_{r(x)}$ is a bijection.*

Proof. Suppose that $x' \neq x$, and let $i \in \{1, \dots, n\}$ be the least index such that $x_{r_i(x)} \neq x'_{r_i(x)}$. Such an i must exist since r reads all bits, and $x' \neq x$. Note that $r_i(x) = r_i(x')$, since it is the first bit read to be different (and thus $y_1, \dots, y_i = y'_1, \dots, y'_i$). Thus $x_{r_i(x)} \neq x'_{r_i(x')}$ and therefore $R_{r(x)} \neq R_{r(x')}$. $\square$

In light of the above, we will construct an n-reader and bound the size of C' when permuted by its reading. However, while the end product of the construction is an n-reader, the intermediate steps might not be k-readers for any k. Thus we need to introduce a more general notion.

Definition 5.5 (Generalized reader). *A* generalized reader *r is a sequence $r_0, r_1, \dots, r_{n-1}$ where $r_i : \{0,1\}^i \to \{1, \dots, n\} \cup \{\star\}$ satisfy for all $i < j$ and $y \in \{0,1\}^j$ one of the following*

- *$r_i(y[\{1, \dots, i\}]) \in \{1, \dots, n\} \setminus r_j(y)$*
- *$r_i(y[\{1, \dots, i\}]) = r_j(y) = \star$*

Given a generalized reader r, a terminal sequence *in the reader is $y \in \{0,1\}^i$ such that $r_i(y_1, \dots, y_i) = \star$, while either $r_{i-1}(y_1, \dots, y_{i-1}) \neq \star$ or $i = 0$.*

If we fix a certain $x \in \{0,1\}^n$, a generalized reader defines a sequence of non-repeating indices that at some point may degenerate to a constant sequence of $\star$. Note that every k-reader naturally defines a generalized reader by setting all undefined functions to map everything to $\star$.

It is useful to think of a (possibly generalized) reader as a decision tree. With a generalized reader, we will often want to continue the branches of the tree with another reader. This operation is called *grafting*. We start with the notion of a 0-*branch* and a 1-*branch*.

Definition 5.6 (0-branch, 1-branch). *Let r be a reader, possibly generalized. The* 0-branch *of r is the reader r' defined by $r'_i(y_1, \dots, y_i) = r_{i+1}(0, y_1, \dots, y_i)$. Similarly, the* 1-branch *of r is the reader r'' defined by $r''_i(y_1, \dots, y_i) = r_{i+1}(1, y_1, \dots, y_i)$.*

We can now define grafting, and will do so recursively. Informally, grafting a reader t onto r at y means that at every $\star$ in the decision tree of r that can be reached after reading y, we continue the reading according to t. That is, this is the process of appending a decision tree t to another decision tree r given a certain history of reads y.

Definition 5.7 (Grafting). *Let r and t be generalized readers and $y \in \{0,1\}^i$ be a terminal sequence in r. The* grafting of t onto r on the branch y *is a new reader $r^{t,y}$ defined as follows.*

- *If $t_0 \in \{r_0(y_1, \dots, y_i), \dots, r_{i-1}(y_1, \dots, y_i)\}$, graft the y_{t_0}-branch of t onto r at $y_1, \dots, y_i$.*
- *If $t_0 \notin \{r_0(y_1, \dots, y_i), \dots, r_{i-1}(y_1, \dots, y_i)\}$, then set $r_i(y_1, \dots, y_i) = t_0$, call the new reader r', and graft the 0-branch of t onto r' at $y_0, \dots, y_i, 0$ and the 1-branch of t onto t at $y_0, \dots, y_i, 1$.*

Repeat the above recursively, with the base case being the grafting of an identically $\star$ reader onto r by not changing anything.

Note that the grafting of a generalized reader onto another results in a generalized reader. Note that it is also possible that $r^{t,y} = r$ when all bits that t may read were already read by r according as y.

To introduce the notion of a reader that discerns a random input from an input from C', we will first need to formulate a notion of executing a reader, which is inherently adaptive, on a partly random input.

Definition 5.8 (J-Simulation of a reader). *Let r be a q-reader, $J \subseteq [n]$ and $y \in \{0,1\}^{|J|}$. The* J-simulation *of r on y is the distribution $S(r, y, J)$ over $\{0,1\}^q$ defined to be $R_{r(x)}$ where $x[J] = y[J]$, and all bits of x outside of J are picked independently and uniformly at random from $\{0,1\}$.*

We now introduce the notion of a reader that discerns a random input from an input from C'.

Definition 5.9 (J-Discerning reader). *Let r be a (possibly generalized) reader, $J \subseteq [n]$ and $y \in \{0,1\}^{|J|}$. Let x be a uniform random variable in $\{c \in C' | c[J] = y\}$. We say that r is a* J-discerning reader *for y if it holds that $d_{TV}(R_{r(x)}, S(r, y, J)) \geq 1/8$.*

Next, we prove that many readers are indeed discerning.

Lemma 5.10. *Set $J \subseteq [n]$ such that $|J| \leq n/2$ and $y \in \{0,1\}^{|J|}$. With probability at least $1/9$ the q-reader r picked by the tester is J-discerning for y.*

Proof. Let r be a reader that is not J-discerning for y. Let $B \sim U_J(y)$ and $G \sim U(\{c \in C' | c[J] = y\})$. Denote by π_r the predicate associated with r. By our assumption,

$$|\Pr[\pi_r(R_{r(B)}) = 1] - \Pr[\pi_r(R_{r(G)}) = 1]| < 1/8.$$

Now assume that with probability greater than $8/9$, the q-reader picked is not J-discerning for y. Now consider the difference in acceptance probability when drawing a reader according to μ.

$$|\Pr_{r\sim\mu}[\pi_r(R_{r(B)})=1] - \Pr_{r\sim\mu}[\pi_r(R_{r(G)})=1]|$$

$$< 8/9 \cdot 1/8 + 1/9 = 2/9.$$

But by Lemma 3.10 and the correctness of the tester, we have that $\Pr_{r\sim\mu}[\pi_r(R_{r(B)})=1] \le 1/3$, and by the correctness of the tester $\Pr_{r\sim\mu}[\pi_r(R_{r(G)})=1] \ge 2/3$, a contradiction. □

A common operation will be to graft a discerning reader with additional arbitrary bits. This does not cause a discerning reader to stop being one.

DEFINITION 5.11. *Let r and s be generalized readers. We say that r* contains *s if for every $x \in \{0,1\}^n$, the sequence of non-$\star$ elements in $R_{s(x)}$ is a prefix of $R_{r(x)}$.*

Note that in particular, whenever we graft s onto r along some branch, we obtain a reader which contains r.

LEMMA 5.12. *Let r and s be generalized readers such that r contains s. Let $J \subseteq [n]$ and $y \in \{0,1\}^{|J|}$. If s is a J-discerning reader for y, then so is r.*

PROOF. Let $B \sim U_J(y)$ and $G \sim U(\{c \in C'|c[J]=y\})$. Consider $R_{r(B)}$. Its outcomes can be partitioned according to their $R_{s(B)}$ prefixes. Thus the probability of every event defined by values of $R_{r(B)}$ can be written as a weighted sum of the probabilities of events defined by values of $R_{s(B)}$. The same is true for $R_{r(G)}$ and $R_{s(G)}$. Therefore $d_{TV}(R_{r(x)}, S(r,y,J)) \ge d_{TV}(R_{s(x)}, S(s,y,J))$. □

To prove that a uniform choice in C' does not have high entropy we graft discerning readers one onto the other. We will want to make sure that all the branches of the decision tree are of the same height throughout the grafting, and thus we define the notion of a *padded grafting*.

DEFINITION 5.13 (q-PADDED GRAFTING). *Let r be a generalized reader, t be a q-reader and $y \in \{0,1\}^i$ be a terminal sequence in r. The* q-padded grafting *of t onto r on the branch y is defined by the following process. First, let r' be the grafting of t onto r at the branch y. Now perform the following repeatedly: Let $z_1,\dots,z_j$ with $j<q$ be such that $r'_{i+j-1}(y_1,\dots,y_i,z_1,\dots,z_{j-1}) \ne \star$ but also $r'_{i+j}(y_1,\dots,y_i,z_1,\dots,z_j)=\star$ (or $j=0$ and $r'_i(y_1,\dots,y_i)=\star$). Let k be an arbitrary index not in the set of indexes $\{r'_0,\dots,r'_{i+j-1}(y_1,\dots,y_i,z_1,\dots,z_{j-1})\}$, and redefine the reader $r'_{i+j}(y_1,\dots,y_i,z_1,\dots,z_j)=k$. Repeat this process as long as such $z_1,\dots,z_j$ with $j<q$ exist.*

The above is basically grafting additional arbitrary reads, so that the end-result will always read exactly q bits after reading the sequence $y_1,\dots,y_i$. The next observation together with Lemma 5.12 implies that q-padded grafting of a J-discerning reader is equivalent to a grafting of some other J-discerning reader.

OBSERVATION 5.14. *Let r be a generalized reader, t a q-reader and $y \in \{0,1\}^i$ a terminal sequence in r. There exists a reader s containing t such that the q-padded grafting of t onto r at y is equivalent to the grafting of s onto r at y.*

Now we can finally prove the main lemma, by performing repeated q-padded grafting of discerning readers one onto another.

LEMMA 5.15. *If $X \sim U(C')$, where C is C'-partially testable with q queries, then $H[X] \le \log|C| - \lfloor\frac{1}{32}\Gamma/q\rfloor$*

PROOF. Let us construct an n-reader and consider the entropy of C' when permuted by this reader.

Start with a 0-reader r^0. Let s be a $\emptyset$-discerning q-reader for the empty word, which must exist since the adaptive tester must pick one with positive probability. Set r^1 to be the grafting of s onto r^0 on the branch of the empty word.

Assume that we have constructed the jq-reader r^j. If $jq \ge \Gamma$, graft a reader that reads all remaining bits arbitrarily onto r^j on all branches. Else, perform the following for all branches $y \in \{0,1\}^{jq}$ to obtain r^{j+1} (noting that they are all terminal sequences in r^j):

- If there is no member of C' with the reading $R_{r^j(y)}$, perform a q-padded grafting of an arbitrary q-reader onto r^j at the branch y,
- If such a member exists, let s be a reader which is a $\{r_1^j(y), r_2^j(y),\dots,r_{jq}^j(y)\}$-discerning reader for y. Perform a q-padded grafting of s onto r^j at the branch y.

Now let r be the resulting n-reader, let $r_{R(C')}$ be the image of C' under the reading of r, and let $X \sim U(r_{R(C')})$. By Observation 5.4, the distribution of X is the same as starting with a uniformly random member of C' and then taking its reading according to r. By the chain rule $H[X] = H[X[\{1,\dots,\Gamma\}]] + H[X|X[\{1,\dots,\Gamma\}]]$.

Note that in the case of a word from C', the maximal j in the construction is equal to Γ/q. By the chain rule we may write

$$H[X[\{1,\dots,\Gamma\}]]$$

$$= \sum_{i=1}^{\Gamma/q} H[X[\{(i-1)q+1,\dots,iq-1\}]|X[\{1,\dots,(i-1)q-1\}]]$$

and since each sequence of q bits is from the grafting of a reader which is discerning with respect to all the previous ones, we may apply Lemma 3.8 to obtain

$$H[X[\{1,\dots,\Gamma\}]]$$

$$= \sum_{i=1}^{\Gamma/q} H[X[\{(i-1)q+1,\dots,iq-1\}]|X[\{1,\dots,(i-1)q-1\}]]$$

$$\le \sum_{i=1}^{\Gamma/q}\left(q-\frac{1}{32}\right) \le \Gamma - \Gamma/q \cdot \frac{1}{32}$$

.

By Lemma 3.11, $H[X|X[\{1,\dots,\Gamma\}]] \le \log|C| - \Gamma$, so by summing it all up we get $H[X] \le \log|C| - \Gamma/q \cdot \frac{1}{32}$.

□

This gives us Theorem 1.3 in its full generality, as it implies that $|C'| = 2^{H[X]} \le 2^{-\Gamma/32q} \cdot |C|$.

6. PROPERTIES WITH A PROXIMITY OBLIVIOUS 2-TESTABLE DECOMPOSITION

For simplicity of presentation all the proofs here are for a property P which is decomposable to properties $P_1, \ldots, P_\ell$ that in themselves admit a proximity oblivious 2-test rather than just a P_i-partial test for P. A sketch on how to extend this to the more general setting is found at the end of this section.

DEFINITION 6.1 (P-WITNESS). *Let $P \subseteq \{0,1\}^n$ be a property and $w \in \{0,1\}^n$. A P-witness against w is a set $Q \subseteq [n]$ such that for every $w' \in \{0,1\}^n$, if $w'_i = w_i$ for every $i \in Q$, then $w' \notin P$.*

The family of witness sets for a specific w is closed to supersets. Note that any 1-sided q-test essentially rejects only if their query set is a witness. A proximity oblivious 1-sided test is a non-adaptive one which is also independent of the proximity parameter ϵ, essentially just a probability distributions over query sets of a fixed size q. This means that the following definition of a proximity-oblivious test is in fact equivalent to Definition 1.6 from the introduction.

DEFINITION 6.2 (TEST DEFINED BY WITNESSES). *A proximity oblivious 1-sided q-test with the* detection function *$\rho(\epsilon)$ is a probability distributions over query sets of a fixed size q, so that for every ϵ-far input w (for every ϵ) the probability of obtaining a witness against w is at least $\rho(\epsilon)$.*

DEFINITION 6.3 (UNIVERSAL SAMPLER). *For parameters $\epsilon, \eta \in (0,1)$, the (ϵ, η)-*universal sampler *selects a set $R \subseteq [n]$ where, for every $i \in [n]$, $\Pr[i \in R] = \alpha n^{-1/3}$, with the parameter $\alpha = 2^{15}\epsilon^{-1}\log(\epsilon^{-1})\log \eta^{-1}$.*

Let $P_1, P_2, \ldots, P_\ell \subseteq \{0,1\}^n$ be properties, each having an oblivious one-sided error 2-tester with the same detection function $\rho(\epsilon)$. Given oracle access to input $w \in \{0,1\}^n$, the ϵ-universal algorithm *for $\bigcup_{i=1}^{\ell} P_i$, selects a set $R \subseteq [n]$ according to the $(\epsilon, 1/4\ell)$-universal sampler. If $|R| > 2\alpha n^{2/3}$ then it accepts immediately, and otherwise it queries the input on all indices of R, rejects if R is a P_i-witness against w for every $i \in [\ell]$, and accepts otherwise.*

LEMMA 6.4 (IMPLYING THEOREM 1.7). *Suppose that we have a sequence of properties $P_1, P_2, \ldots, P_\ell \subseteq \{0,1\}^n$ such that for every $i \in [\ell]$, P_i has a one-sided error oblivious 2-tester with detection function $\rho(\epsilon)$. If $\epsilon > 0$ is such that $\rho(\epsilon/2) > 0$, then for n large enough (as a polynomial function of $1/\rho(\epsilon/2)$) the ϵ-universal algorithm for $\bigcup_{i=1}^{\ell} P_i$ is a one-sided error non-adaptive ϵ-tester for $\bigcup_{i=1}^{\ell} P_i$ with query complexity bound $O(n^{2/3}(\log n)\epsilon^{-1}\log(\epsilon^{-1})\log \ell)$.*

To arrive at the theorem, we first need to "thin out" the possible test queries.

DEFINITION 6.5 (ϵ-TRAP). *A set $\mathcal{Q}$ of size-2 subsets of $[n]$ is called an* ϵ-trap *for a property P, if for every word $w \in \{0,1\}^n$ that is ϵ-far from P, there is some set $Q \in \mathcal{Q}$ which is a P-witness against w.*

LEMMA 6.6. *If P has a one-sided error oblivious 2-tester with the detection function $\rho(\epsilon)$, then for every ϵ it has an ϵ-trap $\mathcal{Q}$ with $|\mathcal{Q}| \le 9n/\rho(\epsilon)$.*

PROOF. This is immediate from running the 2-tester for $9n/\rho(\epsilon)$ many times (so with positive probability it will happen that every possible ϵ-far word is rejected by some iteration of it), and then setting $\mathcal{Q}$ to be the set of all query sets drawn in these iterations. □

We will also use as usual the following triviality.

OBSERVATION 6.7. *For n larger than some universal constant, the ϵ-universal test will do the "immediate accept" step (due to R being too large) with probability less than $1/12$.*

Lemma 6.4 and hence Theorem 1.7 now follows by first obtaining $\mathcal{Q}_1, \ldots, \mathcal{Q}_\ell$ as $\epsilon/2$-traps for $P_1, \ldots, P_\ell$ respectively, and then using the union bound for the respective applications of the following statement, which is in some ways the "true theorem" of this section.

THEOREM 6.8. *Let $\epsilon > 0$, $\eta > 0$, $\mathcal{Q}$ be an $\epsilon/2$-trap for a property P, and w be ϵ-far from P. For n larger than some polynomial function of $|\mathcal{Q}|/n$, the set R produced by the (ϵ, η)-universal sampler is a P-witness against w with probability exceeding $1 - \eta$.*

OBSERVATION 6.9.

1. $(1 - \alpha n^{-1/3})^{\epsilon n/4} < \eta 2^{-2\epsilon n^{2/3}}/3$,
2. $(1 - \alpha n^{-1/3})^{\epsilon n^{1/3}} < \eta/3n$,
3. $1 - e^{-\alpha\epsilon 2^{-4}/3\log n} > 1 - \eta/3$,
4. $1 - (1 - \alpha n^{-\frac{1}{3}})^{2^{-3}\epsilon\alpha n^{1/3}/\log n} > 1 - \eta/3$

From here on we fix P to be a property, $\mathcal{Q}$ to be its $\epsilon/2$-trap, and $w \in \{0,1\}^n$ to be ϵ-far from P.

DEFINITION 6.10 (DEGREE). *For every $i \in [n]$ and $\mathcal{Q}' \subseteq \mathcal{Q}$, we define $\deg_{\mathcal{Q}'}(i) = |\{Q \in \mathcal{Q}' \mid i \in Q\}|$.*

DEFINITION 6.11 ($\mathcal{W}_w$, $\mathcal{L}_w$ AND $\mathcal{M}_w$). *For every $w \in \{0,1\}^n$*

1. *$\mathcal{W}_w$ is the set of all members of $\mathcal{Q}$ that are witnesses against w, and for every $i \in [n]$, $\mathcal{W}_w^i$ is the set of all members of $\mathcal{W}_w$ that contain i.*
2. $\mathcal{L}_w = \left\{ Q \in \mathcal{W}_w \,\middle|\, \exists j \in Q \text{ s.t. } \deg_{\mathcal{W}_w}(j) > \epsilon n^{1/3} \right\}$
3. $\mathcal{M}_w = \mathcal{W}_w \setminus \mathcal{L}_w$.

DEFINITION 6.12 (THE $\Rightarrow$ NOTATION). *Let $(i,a), (j,b) \in [n] \times \{0,1\}$ be distinct. We write $(i,a) \Rightarrow (j,b)$ if $\mathcal{Q}$ has no witness against some $w' \in \{0,1\}^n$ such that $w'_j = \neg b$ while $\mathcal{Q}$ has a witness against every $w^* \in \{0,1\}^n$ such that $w^*_i = a$ and $w^*_j = \neg b$.*

DEFINITION 6.13 (VIABLE SUB-STRING). *Let $B \subset [n]$ be a set of indexes and $\sigma_B : B \to \{0,1\}$. σ_B is a* viable substring *if there exist no $h \in [n]$, $a \in \{0,1\}$ and $i, j \in B$, that are not necessarily distinct, such that $(i, \sigma_B(i)) \Rightarrow (h, a)$ and $(j, \sigma_B(j)) \Rightarrow (h, \neg a)$, or $(i, \sigma_B(i)) \Rightarrow (h, a)$ and $\mathcal{Q}$ has a witness against every $w^* \in \{0,1\}^n$ such that $w^*_h = a$.*

DEFINITION 6.14 (WITNESS AGAINST SUB-STRING). *Let $B \subset [n]$ and $\sigma_B : B \to \{0,1\}$ be a viable sub-string. $i \in [n]$ is a* witness against *σ_B in $w \in \{0,1\}^n$, if $i \in B$ and $w_i \ne \sigma_B(i)$, or if there exists $j \in B$ such that $(j, \sigma_B(j)) \Rightarrow (i, \neg w_i)$.*

Definition 6.15 (Inf_{σ_B}, σ_B^{Inf}). *Let $B \subset [n]$ and $\sigma_B : B \to \{0,1\}$ be a viable sub-string. We define Inf_{σ_B} to be the set containing all the possible witnesses against σ_B. We define $\sigma_B^{\mathrm{Inf}} : \mathrm{Inf}_{\sigma_B} \to \{0,1\}$ so that for every $i \in B$ and $j \in \mathrm{Inf}_{\sigma_B}$, if $(i, \sigma_B(i)) \Rightarrow (j, a)$, then $a = \sigma_B^{\mathrm{Inf}}(j)$.*

Lemma 6.16. *Let $B \subset [n]$, σ_B be a viable sub-string. For every $w^* \in \{0,1\}$ such that $w_i^* = \sigma_B^{\mathrm{Inf}}(i)$, for every $i \in \mathrm{Inf}_{\sigma_B}$, all of the members of $\mathcal{W}_{w^*}$ are disjoint from Inf_{σ_B}.*

Proof. Assume for the sake of contradiction that the lemma does not hold. If there exists a member of $\mathcal{W}_{w^*}$ that is contained in Inf_{σ_B}, then σ_B is not a viable sub-string and hence the contradiction. If $\mathcal{W}_{w^*}$ has a member $\{i,j\}$ such that $i \in \mathrm{Inf}_{\sigma_B}$ and $j \notin \mathrm{Inf}_{\sigma_B}$, then there exists $h \in B$ such that $(h, \sigma_B(h)) \Rightarrow (j, \neg w_j^*)$ (we take the h for which $(h, \sigma_B(h)) \Rightarrow (i, w_i^*)$). This is a contradiction to the definition of Inf_{σ_B} as containing all such j. □

Lemma 6.17. *If $\mathcal{W}_w \subseteq 2^B$, then Inf_{σ_B} contains at least $\epsilon n/2$ witnesses against σ_B for any viable sub-string $\sigma_B : B \to \{0,1\}$.*

Proof. Assume for the sake of contradiction that Inf_{σ_B} contains less than $\epsilon n/2$ witnesses against σ_B. Let $w^* \in \{0,1\}$ be such that $w_i^* = \sigma_B^{\mathrm{Inf}}(i)$ if $i \in \mathrm{Inf}_{\sigma_B}$ and otherwise $w_i^* = w_i$. Obviously, w^* is $\epsilon/2$-far from P.

By Lemma 6.16, $\mathcal{W}_{w^*}$ does not have any sets that intersect Inf_{σ_B}. Since $\mathcal{W}_w \subseteq 2^B$, $\mathcal{W}_{w^*} \cap 2^{[n]\setminus \mathrm{Inf}_{\sigma_B}} = \emptyset$. Thus, $\mathcal{W}_{w^*} = \emptyset$ and hence $\mathcal{Q}$ has no witness against w. This is a contradiction to $\mathcal{Q}$ being an $\epsilon/2$-trap for P. □

Lemma 6.18. *If $|\bigcup_{Q \in \mathcal{W}_w} Q| \leq 2\epsilon n^{2/3}$, then we have that $\Pr[R$ is a witness against $w] > 1 - \eta/3$, even if w is only $3\epsilon/4$-far from P.*

Proof. Let $W = \bigcup_{Q \in \mathcal{W}_w} Q$. By assumption, $|W| \leq 2\epsilon n^{2/3}$. Let σ_W be a viable sub-string. Since $\mathcal{W}_w \subseteq 2^W$, by Lemma 6.17, there are at least $\epsilon n/4$ witnesses against σ_W.

The probability that such a witness is not selected is at most $(1 - \alpha n^{-1/3})^{\epsilon n/4} < \eta 2^{-2\epsilon n^{2/3}}/3$, where the inequality is by Observation 6.9. The lemma follows by the union bound over all viable sub-strings for W. □

Lemma 6.19. *If $|\bigcup_{Q \in \mathcal{W}_w} Q| > 2\epsilon n^{2/3}$ and $|\bigcup_{Q \in \mathcal{M}_w} Q| < \epsilon n^{2/3}$, then the probability that R is a witness against w is at least $1 - \eta$, for n larger than some polynomial in $|\mathcal{Q}|/n$.*

Proof. Observe that $\mathcal{L}_w \neq \emptyset$ because by definition we have $\bigcup_{Q \in \mathcal{W}_w} Q = \bigcup_{Q \in \mathcal{M}_w \cup \mathcal{L}_w} Q$, and therefore $|\mathcal{L}_w| \geq \epsilon n^{1/3}$. Let $\mathrm{Piv} \subseteq [n]$ be the set of all i such that $\deg_{\mathcal{W}_w}(i) \geq \epsilon n^{1/3}$, and σ_{Piv} be such that $\sigma_{\mathrm{Piv}}(i) = \neg w_i$ for every $i \in \mathrm{Piv}$. Note that, for every $i \in \mathrm{Piv}$,

$$\Pr[R \text{ does not contain } j_i \text{ such that } \{i, j_i\} \in \mathcal{W}_w]$$

$$\leq (1 - \alpha n^{-1/3})^{\epsilon n^{1/3}} < \eta/3n,$$

where the last inequality is by Observation 6.9. Consequently, by the union bound

$$\Pr[\text{for every } i \in \mathrm{Piv},\ \exists j_i \in R \text{ s.t. } \{i, j_i\} \in \mathcal{W}_w] > 1 - \eta/3.$$

When the event above indeed occurs, it is only for $\sigma = \sigma_{\mathrm{Piv}}$ (out of any $\sigma : \mathrm{Piv} \to \{0,1\}$) that it may be the case that $\{j_i : i \in \mathrm{Piv}\}$ is not a witness against σ. In other words, with probability at least $1 - \eta/3$ we obtain the event that R contains witnesses against all possible assignments to Piv, apart from possibly σ_{Piv}. To conclude we partition to two cases that depend on the relationship of σ_{Piv} and w.

If w has at least $\epsilon n^{1/3}$ witnesses against σ_{Piv}, then the probability that such a witness is not selected is less than $(1 - \alpha n^{-1/3})^{\epsilon n^{1/3}} < \eta/3$, where the inequality is by Observation 6.9. Thus, by the union bound, with probability exceeding $1 - \eta$, R is a witness against w (as it contains witnesses against any possible assignment to Piv).

Assume now that there are less than $\epsilon n^{1/3}$ witnesses against σ_{Piv}. Let $w^* \in \{0,1\}^n$ be such that if $i \in \mathrm{Inf}_{\mathrm{Piv}}$, then $w_i^* = \sigma_{\mathrm{Piv}}^{\mathrm{Inf}}(i)$, and otherwise $w_i^* = w_i$. By the triangle inequality, w^* is $3\epsilon/4$-far from P (for n large enough so that $\epsilon n^{1/3} < \epsilon n/4$). By Lemma 6.16, none of the sets in $\mathcal{W}_{w^*}$ intersect $\mathrm{Inf}_{\mathrm{Piv}}$ and hence $\mathcal{W}_{w^*} \subseteq \mathcal{M}_w$ Consequently,

$$|\bigcup_{Q \in \mathcal{W}_{w^*}} Q| < |\bigcup_{Q \in \mathcal{M}_w} Q| \leq 2\epsilon n^{2/3}.$$

Thus, by Lemma 6.18, with probability exceeding $1 - \eta$, R is a witness against w^* and so against w (this case does not even require us to analyze witnesses against the possible assignments to Piv themselves). □

Lemma 6.20. *If $|\bigcup_{Q \in \mathcal{M}_w} Q| \geq \epsilon n^{2/3}$, then $\Pr[\mathcal{W}_w \cap 2^R = \emptyset] > 1 - \eta$.*

Proof. Let $H = \bigcup_{Q \in \mathcal{M}_w} Q$. Let H_1, H_2 be disjoint subsets of H, such that $|H_2| \geq |H|/2$ and every $i \in H_2$ is in a set $Q \in \mathcal{M}_w$ that intersects H_1 (this can be constructed iteratively, each time adding a new index i from H to H_2, and then possibly adding an index j to H_1 for some $\{i,j\} \in \mathcal{M}_w$ if i is not already "covered").

For every $k \in [0, \frac{\log n}{3} + \log \epsilon]$, let $H_1^k \subseteq H_1 \setminus \bigcup_{i=k+1}^{\frac{\log n}{3} + \log \epsilon} H_1^i$ be a maximal set such that for every $h \in H_1^k$,

$$\left| \bigcup_{Q \in \mathcal{M}_w | Q \cap H_1^k \neq \emptyset} Q \cap (H_2 \setminus \bigcup_{i=k+1}^{\frac{\log n}{3} + \log \epsilon} H_2^i) \right| - \left| \bigcup_{Q \in \mathcal{M}_w | Q \cap (H_1^k \setminus \{h\}) \neq \emptyset} Q \cap (H_2 \setminus \bigcup_{i=k+1}^{\frac{\log n}{3} + \log \epsilon} H_2^i) \right| \geq 2^k, \tag{1}$$

where for every $i \in [0, \frac{\log n}{3} + \log \epsilon]$, we have that $H_2^i = H_2 \cap \bigcup_{Q \in \mathcal{M}_w | Q \cap H_1^i \neq \emptyset} Q$. By the construction we have $H_2 = \bigcup_{i=0}^{\frac{\log n}{3} + \log \epsilon} H_2^i$. Let $k \in [0, \frac{\log n}{3} + \log \epsilon]$ be such that $|H_2^k| \geq \frac{|H_2|}{\log n}$. By the pigeon hole principle such a k indeed exists. Observe that

$$|H_1^k| \geq \frac{|H_2|}{2^{k+1} \log n} > \frac{\left|\bigcup_{Q \in \mathcal{M}_w} Q\right|}{2^{k+2} \log n} > \frac{\epsilon n^{1/3}}{2^2 \log n}, \tag{2}$$

where the last inequality is because $k \leq \frac{\log n}{3} + \log \epsilon$ and $|\bigcup_{Q \in \mathcal{M}_w} Q| \geq \epsilon n^{2/3}$. By the Chernoff inequality,

$$Pr\left[|H_1^k \cap R| \geq \frac{1}{2} \alpha n^{-1/3} |H_1^k|\right] > 1 - e^{-\alpha \epsilon 2^{-4}/3 \log n} > 1 - \eta/3, \tag{3}$$

where the last inequality is by Observation 6.9. Let

$$\mathcal{W}_w(H_1^k, R) = \left\{ i \in H_2^k \middle| \exists j \in H_1^k \cap R \text{ s.t. } \{i,j\} \in \mathcal{W}_w \right\}.$$

By (1),

$$\left|\mathcal{W}_w(H_1^k, R)\right| \geq 2^k |H_1^k \cap R| \tag{4}$$

Note that if $\mathcal{W}_w(H_1^k, R) \cap R \neq \emptyset$, then R is a witness against w. We will now bound the probability for this conditioned on the event of (3).

$$Pr\left[\mathcal{W}_w(H_1^k, R) \cap R \neq \emptyset \;\middle|\; |H_1^k \cap R| \geq \frac{1}{2}\alpha n^{-1/3} |H_1^k|\right]$$

$$\geq 1 - (1 - \alpha n^{-\frac{1}{3}})^{|\mathcal{W}_w(H_1^k, R)|}.$$

By (4) and (2),

$$1 - (1 - \alpha n^{-\frac{1}{3}})^{|\mathcal{W}_w(H_1^k, R)|} \geq 1 - (1 - \alpha n^{-\frac{1}{3}})^{2^{k-1}\alpha n^{-1/3}|H_1^k|}$$

$$\geq 1 - (1 - \alpha n^{-\frac{1}{3}})^{2^{k-1}\alpha n^{-1/3}\frac{|\bigcup_{Q \in \mathcal{M}_w} Q|}{2^{k+2}\log n}}$$

and hence

$$1 - (1 - \alpha n^{-\frac{1}{3}})^{|\mathcal{W}_w(H_1^k, R)|}$$

$$\geq 1 - (1 - \alpha n^{-\frac{1}{3}})^{2^{-3}\epsilon\alpha n^{1/3}/\log n} > 1 - \eta/3,$$

where the last inequality is by Observation 6.9. This conditional probability bound together with (3) concludes the proof by Bayes rule. □

PROOF PROOF OF THEOREM 6.8. An ϵ-far w must clearly fall under at least one of Lemma 6.18, Lemma 6.19 and Lemma 6.20. □

We conclude this section with a sketch of how to generalize the result for a decomposition admitting only partial sets. The key is in relaxing the definition of a trap. Under the new scheme, for every i, for a word $\epsilon/2$-far from P (rather than P_i), the "partial" trap $\mathcal{Q}_1$ would be required to contain a witness against P_i. The arguments translate almost verbatim to this setting, only one must be careful the definitions such as Definition 6.12) – the exact wording as the particular (partial) trap containing a witness against the words under consideration becomes even more important.

7. PROPERTIES WITH PROXIMITY OBLIVIOUS Q-TESTS

In the following we assume knowledge of the definitions and methods of Section 6. We also assume everywhere that n is large enough for the arguments to follow. To prove Theorem 1.11 we will make crucial use of sunflowers.

DEFINITION 7.1. *A* sunflower with center *A is a family of subsets $B_1, \ldots, B_t \subseteq \{1, \ldots, n\}$ so that every B_i contains A, and $B_1, \ldots, B_t$ are disjoint outside of A (a completely disjoint family is a sunflower with center $A = \emptyset$).*

LEMMA 7.2 (SUNFLOWER THEOREM). *(Erdös and Rado [8]) Any family of at least $s = q!t^{q+1}$ sets whose sizes are at most q contains a sub-family of size t which is a sunflower.*

In the following q would be the (constant) number of queries of the proximity-oblivious test, and t would be some power of n, so our required s would essentially be another power of n.

We next define fragments.

DEFINITION 7.3 (FRAGMENTS AND VIOLATIONS). *A fragment $\xi = (A, v)$ consists of a subset $A \subseteq \{1, \ldots, n\}$ and a function $v : A \to \{0, 1\}$. The special case where $A = \emptyset$ is called the* null fragment.

A fragment $\xi_1 = (A_1, v_1)$ contains *$\xi_2 = (A_2, v_2)$ if $A_2 \subseteq A_1$ and the restriction of v_1 to A_2 is v_2; in this case the* difference fragment *$\xi_3 = (A_3, v_3) = \xi_1 \setminus \xi_2$ is defined where $A_3 = A_1 \setminus A_2$ and v_3 is the restriction of v_1 to A_3.*

A fragment $\xi = (A, v)$ is said to be violated *by the input w if the restriction of w to A is v.*

It will be easier for us to redefine proximity oblivious tests as distributions over fragments.

DEFINITION 7.4 (FRAGMENT VERSION OF A q-TEST). *A* proximity oblivious q-test *for P is a distribution μ over a set Ξ of fragments of sizes bounded by q (some members of Ξ could be with probability 0) satisfying the following:*

- *If w satisfies P then no fragment is violated (not even probability 0 ones).*
- *If w is ϵ-far from P then the probability of picking a violated fragment is at least $\rho(\epsilon)$.*

When moving from a q-test as in the original definition of finding a witness against w, to a q-test as per the above definition, the original $\rho(\epsilon)$ might be divided by up to 2^q (every original query set is converted to all corresponding fragments that are possible witnesses against the input).

We next define how fragments can be "shortened" sometimes, through either queries or logic.

DEFINITION 7.5 (WITNESSES AND REFUTATIONS). *A* witness *for a fragment ξ is a containing fragment ξ', so that the difference $\xi' \setminus \xi$ is violated by the input w (ξ itself does not have to be violated by w).*

A refutation *for a fragment ξ is a set Ξ of fragments, one of which containing ξ, so that no possible input that satisfies the entire set Ξ may satisfy ξ.*

Note that in particular a set Ξ is a refutation of the null fragment if and only if it is unsatisfiable.

Our main tool of analyzing the universal sampler is the following:

DEFINITION 7.6 (R-REDUCTION OF A TEST). *Given a q-test for a property P, as a distribution μ over a set Ξ of fragments, and a set of queries $R \subseteq \{1, \ldots, n\}$, the* R-reduction *of the test is the result of the following process.*

1. *For every $i \in R$, we add the corresponding violated fragment $(i, \neg w(i))$, where w is the input, to Ξ, for the time being with probability 0 (this is essentially "adding the query i").*
2. *We add to Ξ (still with probability 0) every fragment for which there is a refutation in Ξ (note that, because of the previous item, this also includes fragments for which there is a witness whose corresponding difference was indeed verified to violate w through R).*

3. *For every fragment $\xi \in \Xi$ which contains another fragment in $\xi' \in \Xi$ (and is hence made "redundant" by it), we remove ξ from Ξ. If $\mu(\xi)$ was non-zero, we modify μ by adding this probability to the contained ξ' (we can pick any arbitrary ξ' which is not in itself contained in yet another member of Ξ).*

The R-reduction in itself is not necessarily a test for P. It may reject members of P, and it may even contain the null fragment (when that happens Ξ will contain only the null fragment and with probability 1; this in particular means that R is a witness for the property against the input, i.e., the input's restriction to R is not extensible to any possible string satisfying P).

On the other hand, the following is immediate.

OBSERVATION 7.7. *For every possible R, the R-reduction of the test is still a probability distribution over fragments. Moreover, for every possible input w, the probability of rejection (obtaining a violating fragment) by the R-reduction is at least the corresponding probability by the original test.*

Our main argument for Theorem 1.11 lies in the following: We prove that certain events concerning R and the resulting R-reduction of the test occur with probability $1-o(1)$. Given those events, we prove that if the null fragment is not in the resulting Ξ, then it may not be the case that all $\epsilon/2$-far inputs are rejected with probability $\rho(\epsilon/2)$ by the original test (we will construct too many "disjoint" inputs).

In the following, γ (of the universal sampler) will be chosen small enough as a function of all other parameters that will be defined. In the following we also view the universal sampler as consisting of q rounds, where in every round, every index is chosen with probability $n^{-2\gamma}$ (n is assumed large enough for this assumption to be viable).

First we define the following with respect to a β that will be chosen later (γ will depend on β).

DEFINITION 7.8 (SUNFLOWERS OF FRAGMENTS). *A family of fragments $\xi_1 = (A_1, v_1), \dots, \xi_t = (A_t, v_t)$ is called a* sunflower with center $\xi = (A, v)$ *if $A_1, \dots, A_t$ is a sunflower (of sets) with center A, and additionally the restriction of every v_i to A is v.*

Given a q-test with the set of fragments Ξ, all members of Ξ are said to be generation 0. *By induction, a fragment is said to be* generation i *if it is the center of a sunflower of n^β fragments whose generation is at most $i-1$ and which are all witnesses for it, or it has a refutation using fragments whose generation is at most i (and unless the fragment is already of a smaller generation).*

Fragments which do not have a designated generation by the above are said to be generation ∞.

We will only be interested in fragments of generation up to q due to this simple observation.

OBSERVATION 7.9. *A generation i fragment for $i < \infty$ has length at most $q-i$, so in particular all finite generations are at most q.*

A central claim is the following:

LEMMA 7.10. *Let $R = \bigcup_{j=1}^{q} R_j$ be the result of q rounds where in each round every index i is independently chosen to be in R_j with probability $n^{-2\gamma}$. With probability $1-o(1)$, after the j'th round, the $\bigcup_{k=1}^{j} R_k$-reduction of the test contains all generation j fragments or sub-fragments thereof. This is when γ is chosen to be $\beta/(4q)$.*

PROOF. This is proved by induction. The base is $j = 0$ (the $\emptyset$-reduction of the test will still have all the original fragments, or sub-fragments thereof if there were meaningful refutations).

Let us assume that the $\bigcup_{k=1}^{j-1} R_k$-reduction of the test includes all generation $j-1$ fragments or sub-fragments thereof. For a generation j fragment $\xi = (A, v)$ that is the center of a sunflower of witnesses, first let $\xi' = (A', v')$ be any member thereof. The probability that R_j contains $A' \setminus A$ is at least $n^{-2q\gamma}$. Note that when this happens, ξ or a sub-fragment thereof will be in the $\bigcup_{k=1}^{j} R_k$-reduction as required.

Now there are at least n^β members of the sunflower, and the events of each difference to be included in R_j are all independent (as this is a sunflower). Therefor the probability of none of the events happening is at most $(1-n^{-2q\gamma})^{n^\beta} < \exp(-n^{\beta-2q\gamma})$, which is $o(n^{-1-q})$ taking $\gamma = \beta/(4q)$. Noting that there are not more than n^{1+q} fragments in all, we are done for all such flower centers by a union bound.

The case where the generation j fragment has a refutation by other generation j fragments is immediate, once we know that all fragments that are generation j through being a center of a sunflower are included. □

This claim in turns motivates the following definition.

DEFINITION 7.11. *Given a test (as a distribution over a set of fragments Ξ) and an input w, the* generational reduction *thereof is the result of the following process:*

1. *We add to Ξ (with probability 0) every fragment which is of generation i for some $i < \infty$ (and hence $i \le q$).*

2. *For every fragment $\xi \in \Xi$ which contains another fragment in $\xi' \in \Xi$ (and is hence made "redundant" by it), we remove ξ from Ξ. If $\mu(\xi)$ was non-zero, we modify μ by adding this probability to the contained ξ' (we can pick any arbitrary ξ' which is not in itself contained in yet another member of Ξ).*

Again the following is straightforward.

OBSERVATION 7.12. *The generational reduction of the test is still a probability distribution over fragments. Moreover, for every possible input w, the probability of rejection (obtaining a violating fragment) by the generational reduction is at least the corresponding probability by the original test.*

It is important for us to note the following, as the generational reduction has a better structure than just any randomized R-reduction obtained through sampling.

LEMMA 7.13. *With probability $1-o(1)$, the R-reduction of the test is also a reduction of the generational reduction of the test.*

PROOF. This is equivalent to Lemma 7.10 for $j = q$, because it means that with probability $1-o(1)$ there will be witnesses in R to all finite generation fragments, recalling also Observation 7.9. □

In particular, if the generational reduction has the null fragment in its set of fragments, then with probability $1 - o(1)$ the γ-universal testing algorithm will reject the property. To complete the components required for the proof of Theorem 1.11, we will assume that the null fragment is not in this reduction (i.e. it is of generation ∞, which is equivalent to R not being a witness against the input) and reach a contradiction. At this point we use the sunflower theorem.

LEMMA 7.14. *Let Ξ_R denote the set of fragments of the generational reduction of the test, and assume that it does not contain the null fragment. For n large enough, there exists no fragment (regardless of whether it is violated itself) that is contained in more than $n^{(q+2)\beta}$ members of Ξ_R that are witnesses against it.*

PROOF. If $\xi = (A, v)$ was such a fragment, and $\xi_1 = (A_1, v_1), \ldots, \xi_t = (A_t, v_t)$ were (containing) members of Ξ_R for $t = n^{(q+2)\beta}$ that witness it, then (for n such that $n^\beta > q!$) by Lemma 7.2 there would have been a sunflower of sets $A_{j_1}, \ldots, A_{j_t}$ for $t = n^\beta$, whose center is some set A' that contains A. Now the restrictions of $v_{j_1}, \ldots, v_{j_t}$ to A' are all identical: Over A these are identical to v, and over $A' \setminus A$ these are identical to the restriction of w to this set. Let v' denote the common restriction of $v_{j_1}, \ldots, v_{j_t}$ to A'. $\xi_{j_1}, \ldots, \xi_{j_t}$ are now also a sunflower of fragments, all witnesses to their center $\xi' = (A', v')$. This would have meant that ξ' is a fragment of some finite generation, which is a contradiction to Ξ_R already corresponding to the generational reduction of the test. □

In particular (through the null fragment), the above means that there are no more than $n^{(q+2)\beta}$ members of Ξ_R that are violated by w. However, Ξ_R in itself could still be very large, for example it could contain many fragments that would be violated by the bit-wise negation of w.

In the following, we assume that w is an ϵ-far word for which the generational reduction does not contain the null fragment. We then do the following construction.

DEFINITION 7.15. *Assume that Ξ_R does not contain the null fragment (and is hence satisfiable). We define by induction the following sequences, where $w_0 = w$, $\Xi_0 = 0$ and $B_0 = \emptyset$. We let w^* be any word that violates no member of Ξ_R.*

- *Ξ_i is the set of the members of Ξ_R that are violated by w_{i-1}.*
- *$B_i = B_{i-1} \cup \bigcup\{A : \xi = (A, v) \in \Xi_i\}$.*
- *w_i is identical to w^* over B_i and identical to w outside of it.*

We are interested in taking $w_0, \ldots, w_r$, $\Xi_1, \ldots, \Xi_{r+1}$ and $B_1, \ldots, B_r$ for $r = 1/\rho(\epsilon/2)$. The following lemma gives us their required properties.

LEMMA 7.16. *Assume that R is not a witness, and equivalently Ξ_R does not contain the null fragment. All of the following hold for n large enough.*

- *The sets Ξ_i are all disjoint.*
- *$|\Xi_1| \le n^{(q+2)\beta}$ and $|B_1| \le qn^{(q+2)\beta}$.*
- *$|\Xi_i| \le n^{(q+2)\beta}|B_{i-1}|^q$ and additionally $|B_i| \le |B_{i-1}| + qn^{(q+2)\beta}|B_{i-1}|^q$ for $i > 1$.*
- *$|B_k| \le n^{(5q)^k\beta}$ for $k > 1$.*

PROOF. The first item is because Ξ_i cannot contain any fragment whose respective set is inside B_{i-1} (because w_{i-1} is identical to w^* there), or any fragment whose respective set is not contained in B_i (because of how B_i was defined), and we have successive containment $B_{i-1} \subseteq B_i$.

The second item is from the discussion after Lemma 7.14, noting also that all members of Ξ_R are of length bounded by q.

The third item is by Lemma 7.14 again. We note that violated fragments of Ξ_R here can only come from witnesses in Ξ_R for fragments inside B_{i-1}, and there are less than $|B_{i-1}|^q$ relevant fragments (all possible restrictions of w^* to subsets of size at most q of B_{i-1}).

The fourth item is by basic numeric induction. □

Now we finally have all the components for proving Theorem 1.11.

PROOF PROOF OF THEOREM 1.11. We take $\beta = \frac{1}{2}(5q)^{-r}$ (where $r = 1/\rho(\epsilon/2)$ and n to be large enough so that $n^{-1/2} \le \epsilon/2$). By Lemma 7.13, with probability $1 - o(1)$ the R-reduction of the test will include also its generational reduction. To conclude we prove that such an R is necessarily a witness against the input. Let us assume on the contrary that the R-reduction (and hence the generational reduction) does not contain the null fragment.

We refer to the construction of Definition 7.15. The choice of parameters above and Lemma 7.16 ensure that $|B_r| \le \epsilon n/2$, and so all the inputs $w_0, \ldots, w_r$ are $\epsilon/2$-close to w and hence are $\epsilon/2$-far from the property. Hence the original q-test and its generational reduction have to reject each of those inputs with probability at least $\rho(\epsilon/2)$. However, this means that in Ξ_R there are $r+1$ disjoint subsets $\Xi_1, \ldots, \Xi_{r+1}$ where each of which is assigned a probability of at least $\rho(\epsilon/2)$ by the generational reduction, which is the contradiction to the sum of all probabilities being 1. □

8. HIGHLY DECOMPOSABLE PROPERTIES

We prove here Theorem 1.13. The property that we will pick to show it will be the following one of being k-paritic.

DEFINITION 8.1. *A string $w = (w_1, \ldots, w_n) \in \{0,1\}^n$ is called* k-paritic *if there exist $i_1, \ldots, i_k$ for which $i_1 = 1$, $i_j + n/2k \le i_{j+1}$ for all $1 \le j < k$ and $i_k + n/2k \le n$, such that for every $0 \le r < n/2k$ we have $\bigoplus_{j=1}^k w_{i_j+r} = 0$.*

For fixed $i_1, \ldots, i_k$ as above, we let $P_{i_1,\ldots,i_k}$ denote the property of satisfying $\bigoplus_{j=1}^k w_{i_j+r} = 0$ for every $0 \le r < n/2k$ (for these particular $i_1, \ldots, i_k$).

Theorem 1.13 then immediately follows from Lemma 8.2 and Lemma 8.5 below.

LEMMA 8.2. *The property of being k-paritic is decomposable to at most n^{k-1} many properties, so that each of them has a proximity-oblivious 1-sided k-test with detection function $\rho(\epsilon) = O(k\epsilon)$.*

PROOF. We decompose the property of being k-paritic to the properties $P_{i_1,\dots,i_k}$ (as in Definition 8.1) where $i_1,\dots,i_k$ are any indexes such that $i_1 = 1$, $i_j + n/2k \le i_{j+1}$ for all $1 \le j < k$ and $i_k + n/2k \le n$ (note that these properties need not be disjoint). There are less than n^{k-1} such properties (i_1 has one value and every other i_j clearly can have less than n possible values), and clearly their union is the property of being k-paritic.

The proximity-oblivious k-test for every property $P_{i_1,\dots,i_k}$ is done by taking a uniformly drawn value from $\{0,\dots,n/2k\}$ for r, and checking that the requirement $\bigoplus_{j=1}^{k} w_{i_j+r} = 0$ is satisfied (which uses k queries). To get at the $O(k\epsilon)$ bound on the detection function, we note that for w to be ϵ-far from $P_{i_1,\dots,i_k}$, at least ϵn values of the possible $n/2k$ values for r must be such that $\bigoplus_{j=1}^{k} w_{i_j+r} = 1$, so the probability to get such a value for r is $\frac{\epsilon n}{n/2k} = O(k\epsilon)$. □

Before continuing we show that being k-paritic is not too dense.

LEMMA 8.3. *For every fixed k, a uniformly random member of $0,1^n$ (each bit being chosen uniformly and independently) is $1/10k$-far from being k-paritic with probability $1 - o(1)$.*

PROOF. First we consider a property $P_{i_1,\dots,i_k}$ for specific $i_1,\dots,i_k$ as in Definition 8.1. For every $0 \le r < n/2k$, the probability for $\bigoplus_{j=1}^{k} w_{i_j+r} = 1$ is exactly $\frac{1}{2}$, and these events are completely independent for different values of r. Hence by a straightforward large deviation inequality with probability at least $1 - 2^{n/10k}$ it holds that we have a set $R \subset \{0,\dots,\lceil n/2k\rceil - 1\}$ of size at least $n/10k$ so that for every $r \in R$ we have $\bigoplus_{j=1}^{k} w_{i_j+r} = 1$. When this occurs the word $w = (w_1,\dots,w_n)$ is clearly $1/10k$-far from $P_{i_1,\dots,i_k}$.

The lemma now follows from a union bound over all properties $P_{i_1,\dots,i_k}$ (whose number is less than n^{k-1}, see the proof of Lemma 8.2). □

We will also use a traditional Yao's argument. The following is similar to the form that appears in [9] (but was developed earlier).

LEMMA 8.4. *Suppose that $\mathcal{D}_P$ and $\mathcal{D}_N$ are two distributions over $\{0,1\}$. For an index set $Q \subset \{1,\dots,n\}$ of size q a word $v \in \{0,1\}^q$, let $\alpha(Q,v)$ be the probability that a word $w \in \{0.1\}$ drawn according to $\mathcal{D}_P$ agrees with v over Q (i.e., that setting $i_1,\dots,i_q$ to be the members of Q in sorted order, we have $w_{i_j} = v_j$ for all $1 \le j \le q$). Define $\beta(Q,v)$ similarly with $\mathcal{D}_N$ instead of $\mathcal{D}_P$.*

If for every Q of size q and every $v \in \{0,1\}^q$ we have that $\alpha(Q,v) \le (1-\eta)\beta(Q,v)$, then no algorithm making up to q queries can distinguish with probability more than η (even an adaptive one and in a 2-sided manner) between the case where w was drawn according to $\mathcal{D}_P$ and the case where it was drawn according to $\mathcal{D}_N$.

The following now concludes the proof of Theorem 1.13

LEMMA 8.5. *For any fixed k, The property of being k-paritic in itself cannot be $1/5k$-tested using $o(n^{1-1/k})$ many queries (even not by 2-sided adaptive algorithms).*

PROOF. Here we use Yao's method as per outlined in [9] (but developed earlier). We will assume that $n = 2kl$ for some integer l, as the move from this to general n involves simple padding. We define two distributions.

- The distribution $\mathcal{D}_P$ starts by first choosing uniformly and independently $2l(j-1)+1 \le i_j \le 2l(j-1)+l$ for every $1 \le j \le k$. Then we take $w \in \{0,1\}^n$ to be a uniformly random member of $P_{i_1,\dots,i_k}$, the corresponding property defined in the proof of Lemma 8.2 (out of the 2^{n-l} members thereof).

- The distribution $\mathcal{D}_N$ is just the uniform distribution over $\{0,1\}^n$.

It is clear that an input drawn according to $\mathcal{D}_P$ is always k-paritic. Also, by Lemma 8.3 we have that with probability $1 - o(1)$ an input drawn according to $\mathcal{D}_N$ is $1/5k$-far from being k-paritic.

Also note that for every $v \in \{0,1\}^q$ and an index set $Q \subseteq \{1,\dots,n\}$ of size q, the probability of a word w drawn according to $\mathcal{D}_N$ to agree with v over Q is exactly 2^{-q}. To complete the argument, by Lemma 8.4 it remains to show that for every $v \in \{0,1\}^q$ and every $Q \subseteq \{1,\dots,n\}$ of size q where $q = o(n^{1-1/k})$, the probability for such an agreement is at least $(1-o(1))2^{-q}$.

Let E be the event that there is no $0 \le r < l$ for which $\{j_1+r,\dots,j_k+r\} \subset Q$. Conditioned on E, the probability of w to agree with v over Q is exactly 2^{-q}, so it remains to show that E occurs with probability $1 - o(1)$. Let $s_1,\dots,s_k$ be members of Q. The only case where there can be a positive probability for the equalities $i_1+r = s_1,\dots,i_k+r = s_k$ is if $2l(j-1)+1 \le s_j \le 2lj$ for every $1 \le j \le k$, and also in this case the probability for all equalities to occur is bounded by $l^{1-k} = (2k/n)^{k-1}$ (by a union bound argument over the l possible values for r).

The number of possible eligible k-tuples $s_1,\dots,s_k$ in Q is at most $(q/k)^k$. By the union bound the probability for E not to occur is then bounded by $(2q/n)^{k-1}(q/k)$. For a fixed k, if $q = o(n^{1-1/k})$ then this probability bound evaluates to $o(1)$, concluding the proof. □

It would be interesting to find out whether there exists a property decomposable into a relatively small number of testable properties that in itself requires a linear number of queries to test. The following standard proposition shows that for being k-paritic our lower bounds are about as far they go.

PROPOSITION 8.6. *The property of being k-paritic is testable by a non-adaptive 1-sided test, with query complexity of $O(n^{1-1/k}(\log(n)/\epsilon)^{1/k})$ and detecting ϵ-far inputs with constant probability,*

PROOF. We will use the following algorithm:

- Choose a query set Q by choosing for every $1 \le j \le n$ independently whether $j \in Q$, where this occurs with probability $(10kn^{-1}\log(n)/\epsilon)^{1/k}$.

- If $|Q| > 2n(10kn^{-1}\log(n)/\epsilon)^{1/k}$ then accept the input without making any queries (by a large deviation inequality this occurs with probability $o(1)$).

- Otherwise, make all the queries in Q, and accept the input if and only if there exists a k-paritic word $u \in \{0,1\}^n$ whose restriction to Q agrees with all queries made to the input word w.

Clearly, if the input word w is k-paritic then it will always be accepted, either arbitrarily in the second step or by $u = w$ in the third step. It now remains to prove that ϵ-far words are rejected with high probability. The second step assures that the number of queries is always at most $2n(10kn^{-1}\log(n)/\epsilon)^{1/k} = O(n^{1-1/k}(\log(n)/\epsilon)^{1/k})$ (rather than being so only with probability $1 - o(1)$).

We may safely ignore the case where there is acceptance in the second step as it occurs with probability $o(1)$, and henceforth analyze the algorithm as if this step was removed from it. We start by analyzing the property $P_{i_1,\ldots,i_k}$ for specific $i_1, \ldots, i_k$ as in Definition 8.1. If w is ϵ-far from $P_{i_1,\ldots,i_k}$, then there is a set $R \subset \{0, \ldots, \lceil n/2k \rceil - 1\}$ of size at least ϵn so that for every $r \in R$ we have $\bigoplus_{j=1}^{k} w_{i_j+r} = 1$. For every fixed $r \in R$, the probability to query its corresponding witness of not being in $P_{i_1,\ldots,i_k}$, i.e. the probability for $\{i_1 + r, \ldots, i_k + r\} \in Q$, is $10kn^{-1}\log(n)/\epsilon$.

The above means that for the specific property $P_{i_1,\ldots,i_k}$, the probability of not detecting a witness for the input not being in the property is at most $(1 - 10kn^{-1}\log(n)/\epsilon)^{\epsilon n} < \exp(-10k\log(n)) = o(n^{k-1})$. All that remains to do is to perform a union bound over all properties $P_{i_1,\ldots,i_k}$, whose union is the property of being k-paritic (see Lemma 8.2 and its proof), to see that with probability $1-o(1)$ our query set is such that there is no k-paritic word u whose restriction to Q agrees with the queries made to w. □

9. ACKNOWLEDGMENTS

The research leading to these results has received funding from the European Union's - Seventh Framework Programme [FP7/2007-2013] under grant agreement no 202405 (PROPERTY TESTING).

10. REFERENCES

[1] Noga Alon, László Babai, and Alon Itai. A fast and simple randomized parallel algorithm for the maximal independent set problem. *Journal of Algorithms*, 7(4):567–583, December 1986.

[2] Noga Alon, Eldar Fischer, Michael Krivelevich, and Mario Szegedy. Efficient testing of large graphs. *Combinatorica*, 20(4):451–476, 2000.

[3] Noga Alon, Michael Krivelevich, Ilan Newman, and Mario Szegedy. Regular languages are testable with a constant number of queries. *SIAM J. Comput*, 30(6):1842–1862, 2000.

[4] Eli Ben-Sasson, Oded Goldreich, Prahladh Harsha, Madhu Sudan, and Salil P. Vadhan. Robust PCPs of proximity, shorter PCPs, and applications to coding. *SIAM J. Comput*, 36(4):889–974, 2006.

[5] Eric Blais, Joshua Brody, and Kevin Matulef. Property testing lower bounds via communication complexity. *Computational Complexity*, 21(2):311–358, 2012.

[6] Manuel Blum, Michael Luby, and Ronitt Rubinfeld. Self-testing/correcting with applications to numerical problems. *J. Comput. Syst. Sci.*, 47(3):549–595, 1993.

[7] Thomas M. Cover and Joy A. Thomas. *Elements of Information Theory.* Wiley-Interscience, New York, USA, 2000.

[8] Paul Erdős and Richard Rado. Intersection theorems for systems of sets. *J. London Math. Soc.*, 35:85–90, 1960.

[9] Eldar Fischer. The art of uninformed decisions: A primer to property testing. *Current Trends in Theoretical Computer Science: The Challenge of the New Century*, I:229–264, 2004.

[10] Eldar Fischer and Arie Matsliah. Testing graph isomorphism. *SIAM J. Comput*, 38(1):207–225, 2008.

[11] E. N. Gilbert. A comparison of signalling alphabets. *The Bell System Technical Journal*, 31(3):504–522, May 1952.

[12] Oded Goldreich, Shaffi Goldwasser, and Dana Ron. Property testing and its connection to learning and approximation. *J. ACM*, 45:653–750, July 1998.

[13] Oded Goldreich and Dana Ron. On sample-based testers. *Electronic Colloquium on Computational Complexity (ECCC)*, (109), 2013.

[14] Tom Gur and Ron Rothblum. Non-interactive proofs of proximity. *Electronic Colloquium on Computational Complexity (ECCC)*, (078), 2013.

[15] J. Håstad. Some optimal inapproximability results. *Journal of the ACM*, 48(4):798–859, 2001.

[16] Solomon Kullback and Richard A. Leibler. On information and sufficiency. *The Annals of Mathematical Statistics*, 22(1):79–86, March 1951.

[17] F. J. MacWilliams and N. J. A. Sloane. *The Theory of Error-Correcting Codes*, volume 16 of *North-Holland Mathematical Library.* North-Holland, 1977.

[18] F. J. MacWilliams, N. J. A. Sloane, and J. G. Thompson. Good self dual codes exist. *Discrete Math.*, 3:153–162, 1972.

[19] Mark S. Pinsker. *Information and information stability of random variables and processes.* Holden-Day Inc., San Francisco, Calif., 1964. Translated and edited by Amiel Feinstein.

[20] Mark D. Reid and Robert C. Williamson. Generalised pinsker inequalities. In *COLT*, 2009.

[21] Dana Ron. Property testing: A learning theory perspective. *Found. Trends Mach. Learn.*, 1:307–402, March 2008.

[22] Dana Ron. Algorithmic and analysis techniques in property testing. *Foundations and Trends in Theoretical Computer Science*, 5(2):73–205, 2010.

[23] Guy N. Rothblum, Salil Vadhan, and Avi Wigderson. Interactive proofs of proximity: delegating computation in sublinear time. In *Proceedings of the 45th annual ACM symposium on Symposium on theory of computing*, STOC '13, pages 793–802, New York, NY, USA, 2013. ACM.

[24] Ronitt Rubinfeld and Madhu Sudan. Robust characterizations of polynomials with applications to program testing. *SIAM J. Comput.*, 25(2):252–271, 1996.

[25] R. R. Varshamov. Estimate of the number of signals in error correcting codes. In *Dokl. Akad. Nauk SSSR*, volume 117, pages 739–741, 1957.

High Dimensional Expanders and Property Testing

Tali Kaufman
Bar-Ilan University
ISRAEL
kaufmant@mit.edu *

Alexander Lubotzky
Hebrew University
ISRAEL
alexlub@math.huji.ac.il †

ABSTRACT

We show that the high dimensional expansion property as defined by Gromov, Linial and Meshulam, for simplicial complexes is a form of testability. Namely, a simplicial complex is a high dimensional expander iff a suitable property is testable. Using this connection, we derive several testability results.

1. INTRODUCTION

1.1 High dimensional expanders

Expander graphs have been playing an important role in computer science in the last few decades (see [6]) and more recently also in pure mathematics (see [12]). In recent years a high dimensional theory of expanders is starting to emerge (see [13] and the references therein). It is not even clear what is the "right" definition of expanders for simplicial complexes of dimension greater equal 2. But, two essentially equivalent definitions were given in two seminal works: One by Linial and Meshulam [11] (see also [16]) whose motivation was to study the (homological) connectivity of random complexes, as a first step toward developing a higher dimensional version of the Erdos-Rèyni theory of random graphs. The second is by Gromov (see [5]) whose motivation was the study of fibers and overlapping properties of maps between complexes and manifolds. These two very different motivations led to a very similar definition, which we now give. We give a version that combines the two and which is most convenient for our needs. The homological/cohomological notions will be defined and explained in details in Section 2.

DEFINITION 1. *Let X be a finite simplicial complex of dimension d and let $i \in \{0, \cdots, d-1\}$. The i-th (coboundary) expansion constant ϵ_i of X is defined as follows:*

$$\epsilon_i = min \frac{||\delta f||}{||[f]||}$$

where the minimum is taken over all $f \in C^i(X, \mathbb{F}_2) \backslash B^i(X, \mathbb{F}_2)$, where $C^i(X, \mathbb{F}_2)$ is the $\mathbb{F}_2$-vector space of all i-cochains of X, $B^i(X, \mathbb{F}_2)$ is the subspace of the coboundaries and δf is the coboundary of f. The norm $||g||$ of $g \in C^i(X, \mathbb{F}_2)$ is the proportion of the i-cells on which g does not vanish. The symbol $[f]$ stands for the coset of f modulo $B^i(X, \mathbb{F}_2)$ and $||[f]|| = min\{||g|| | g \in [f]\}$.

While this definition looks mysterious in first sight, one can check that for $i = d-1 = 0$, i.e., for graphs, it gives the standard (normalized) edge expansion ("The Cheeger constant") of graphs. Namely, for a graph $X = (V, E)$:

$$\epsilon_0(X) = \frac{|V|}{|E|} \min_{A \neq \emptyset, V} \frac{|E(A, \bar{A})|}{\min\{|A|, |\bar{A}|\}}.$$

See Section 2 below for details.
A result proved independently by Meshulam and Wallach [16] and by Gromov [5] is the following.

THEOREM 2. *Let $X_n^{(d)}$ be the complete d-dimensional simplicial complex on n vertices, i.e., the complex of all subsets of $[n] = \{1, \cdots, n\}$ of size at most $d+1$. Then, for every $i = 0, \cdots, d-1$, $\epsilon_i \geq 1$.*

One of the difficult questions about simplicial complexes is to evaluate their expansion constants (see [4] for some results in this direction). Theorem 2 says informally that the complete d-dimensional simplicial complex is "an expander". It can be compared with the trivial result that this is the case for $d = 1$ i.e., the complete graph is an expander. It is less trivial to show that there are bounded degree expander graphs, though by now various methods are known: random, Kazhdan property T, Ramanujan conjecture, the zig-zag product etc. An outstanding open problem is to show that higher dimensional bounded degree expanders exist. For some results in this direction see [5, 8, 14].
The goal of this paper is to point out that this notion of high dimensional expansion is also of value and interest to theoretical computer science. We show below that the above expansion is intimately related to the area of "Property Testing".

1.2 Property Testing

Let us recall first what it means for a property to be testable.

*Research supported in part by the Alon Fellowship, and by an EU IRG grant.
†Research supported in part by the ERC and by the Israel Science Foundation.

ITCS'14, January 12–14, 2014, Princeton, New Jersey, USA.
Copyright 2014 ACM 978-1-4503-2698-8/14/01 ...$15.00.
http://dx.doi.org/10.1145/2554797.2554842 .

Definition 3. *((q,ϵ)-testability) Let A be a finite set, W_n a subset of A^n (the n-tuples of elements in A) and P_n a subset of W_n. We say that the membership of $\alpha \in P_n$ (given $\alpha \in W_n$) is* testable, *or that P_n is (q,ϵ)-testable, if there exist $0 < \epsilon \in \mathbb{R}$, $q \in \mathbb{N}$ and a randomized algorithm, called a tester, which queries only q (independent of n) coordinates of α and answers "yes" if $\alpha \in P_n$, while it answers "no" with probability at least $\epsilon \cdot \overline{dist}(\alpha, P_n)$ where $\overline{dist}(\alpha, P_n)$ is the normalized Hamming distance between α and the set P_n.*

One of the early works in the area of Property Testing is the work of Blum, Luby and Rubinfeld [2] which dealt with linearity testing (see [17] for low degree testing).
Linearity Testing: Let W be the space of all functions from $\{0,1\}^m$ to $\{0,1\}$. This space is of dimension $n = 2^m$ over $\mathbb{F}_2$, the field of two elements, and let W_0 be the subspace of all linear functions, so the dimension of W_0 is m.

Theorem 4. *[2]*

- *A function f in W is linear iff $f(x+y) = f(x) + f(y)$ for every $x, y \in \{0,1\}^m$.*
- *There exists a constant $\epsilon > 0$ such that for every $f \in W$*

$$Prob(f(x+y) \neq f(x)+f(y) | x, y \in \{0,1\}^m) \geq \frac{\epsilon \cdot dist(f, W_0)}{2^m}$$

where $dist(f, W_0)$ is the number of $x \in \{0,1\}^m$ on which f has to be changed to make it linear (i.e., the Hamming distance between f and W_0).

The first item in Theorem 4 is trivial (as this is the definition of a linear map!) and it also follows from the second item. The second part of Theorem 4 is not trivial. It implies, in particular, that if we want to ensure with probability at least $1 - \delta$ that a given $f \in W$ is linear (for some $\delta > 0$ e.g. $\delta = 0.001$), it suffices to check the equation $f(x+y) = f(x)+f(y)$ for a constant number k_0 of random inputs $x, y \in \{0,1\}^m$. The number k_0 depends on δ but is independent of n. One can take $k_0 = \min\{k | \epsilon^k < \delta\}$. In [2] it was proven that ϵ in Theorem 4 can be taken to be $\epsilon = \frac{2}{9}$, and better estimates have been given [7, 9].
So, Theorem 4 says (when $A = \{0,1\}$, $n = 2^m$, $W_n = A^n$ and P_n the m-dimensional linear functionals) that the property of linearity is testable.

1.3 Testability and Expansion

The main point of this paper is the observation that expansion and testability are intimately connected with each other. The formal way to express it is Theorem 8, whose proof is obtained by spelling out carefully the definitions, but it requires the notions to be defined in Section 2. Let us instead illustrate it here by a baby example.

The constant function property..
Let Γ be a connected graph on n vertices $[n] = \{1, \cdots, n\}$ and $f : [n] \to \{0,1\}$ a function on the vertices of Γ. Is f a constant function? Let us apply the following Γ-algorithm: choose a random edge of Γ and check whether f agrees on the two end points of the edge. Answer yes if it agrees and no otherwise.

Proposition 5. *The algorithm is a (2,ϵ)-tester for the "constant function" property iff Γ is an ϵ-expander graph.*

Before providing the proof of the proposition we recall that a graph $\Gamma = (V, E)$ is called an ϵ-expander if for every subset S of V

$$\frac{|E(S,\bar{S})|}{|E|} \geq \epsilon \cdot \frac{min(S,\bar{S})}{|V|}.$$

Where $E(S,\bar{S})$ is the set of edges from S to its complement $\bar{S}$. We are using this definition to take into account also graphs of unbounded degrees. For k-regular graphs (k fixed) this is equivalent to the usual definition (up to a change of ϵ).

Proof. Note that the constant function property P contains only two elements: the "all 0" function and the "all 1" function. Any function is a characteristic function of some subset S, $f = \chi_S$ and $\overline{dist}(f, P) = \frac{min(S,\bar{S})}{|V|}$. Now given such f (and hence S) the proportion of edges that cause the tester to reject is exactly $\frac{|E(S,\bar{S})|}{|E|}$. So, the result follows immediately from the definitions. □

Let us end this introduction by recalling that property testing is closely related to locally testable codes (LTCs). The fact that LTCs are related to expander graphs was shown in [3]. The results proven here show that if ϵ_i, the i-coboundary expansion of X, is positive then $B^i(X, \mathbb{F}_2)$ is a locally testable code inside $C^i(X, \mathbb{F}_2)$. Unfortunately, as a code, $B^i(X, \mathbb{F}_2)$ has a poor distance, as it contains the image of every $(i-1)$-cell $\triangle$, which are vectors whose support is equal to the $deg(\triangle) = \#\{i\text{-cells containing } \triangle\}$. In most cases of interest this is relatively small or even bounded.

2. HOMOLOGY AND COHOMOLOGY

2.1 Definitions and basic facts

In this section we will introduce the homological language needed in this paper. We will use only (co)homology with coefficients in the field $\mathbb{F}_2 = \{0,1\}$ of two elements, which makes life easier than the general case as we can ignore orientation.
Let X be a finite simplicial complex, i.e., X is a non-empty collection of subsets of a finite set V, called the set of vertices, satisfying $F \in X$ and $G \subseteq F$ implies $G \in X$. In particular, $\emptyset \in X$. For a subset $F \in X$, denote $\dim F = |F| - 1$. If $\dim F = i$ then F is called an *i-face* (or a face of dimension i or an i-cell).
The set of all i-faces is denoted $X(i)$, so $X(-1) = \{\emptyset\}$. We say that X is of dimension d if the face of largest size in X is of dimension d (i.e., of size $d+1$). A 1-cell is called an edge, a 2-cell a triangle etc.
Let us denote by $C_i = C_i(X, \mathbb{F}_2)$ the $\mathbb{F}_2$-vector space with basis $X(i)$ (or equivalently, the $\mathbb{F}_2$-vector space of subsets of $X(i)$), and $C^i = C^i(X, \mathbb{F}_2)$ the $\mathbb{F}_2$-vector space of functions from $X(i)$ to $\mathbb{F}_2$. It will be convenient sometimes to identify C_i with C^i in the obvious way. One can also think of C^i as the dual of C_i.
The boundary map $\partial_i : C_i(X, \mathbb{F}_2) \to C_{i-1}(X, \mathbb{F}_2)$ is:

$$\partial_i(F) = \sum_{G \subset F, |G| = |F|-1} G, \tag{1}$$

where $F \in X(i)$, and the coboundary map $\delta_i : C^i(X, \mathbb{F}_2) \to C^{i+1}(X, \mathbb{F}_2)$ is:

$$\delta_i(f)(G) = \sum_{F \subset G, |F| = |G|-1} f(F), \tag{2}$$

where $f \in C^i$ and $G \in X(i+1)$.
Using the identification between C^i and C_i and defining the bilinear form $C^i \times C^i \to \mathbb{F}_2$ by:

$$\langle f, g \rangle = \sum_{F \in X(i)} f(F)g(F).$$

(all in the $\mathbb{F}_2$ arithmetic) we have

$$\text{For } \alpha \in C^i = C_i \text{ and } \beta \in C_{i+1} = C^{i+1}: \langle \alpha, \partial\beta \rangle = \langle \delta\alpha, \beta \rangle. \quad (3)$$

Indeed to prove (3), it is sufficient to do it for $\alpha \in X(i)$ and $\beta \in X(i+1)$ and in such a case both sides of (3) are 1 if $\alpha \subseteq \beta$ and 0 otherwise.
Well known and easily calculated equations are:

$$\partial_i \circ \partial_{i+1} = 0 \text{ and } \delta_{i+1} \circ \delta_i = 0 \quad (4)$$

Or if we omit subscripts $\partial^2 = 0$ and $\delta^2 = 0$.
Thus, if we denote:
$B_i = B_i(X, \mathbb{F}_2) = \text{Image}(\partial_{i+1}) =$ the space of i-boundaries.
$Z_i = Z_i(X, \mathbb{F}_2) = \text{Ker}(\partial_i) =$ the space of i-cycles.
$B^i = B^i(X, \mathbb{F}_2) = \text{Image}(\delta_{i-1}) =$ the space of i-coboundaries.
$Z^i = Z^i(X, \mathbb{F}_2) = \text{Ker}(\delta_i) =$ the space of i-cocycles.
We get from (4)

$$B_i \subseteq Z_i \subseteq C_i \text{ and } B^i \subseteq Z^i \subseteq C^i. \quad (5)$$

Define the quotient spaces $H_i(X, \mathbb{F}_2) = Z_i/B_i$ and $H^i(X, \mathbb{F}_2) = Z^i/B^i$, the i-homology and the i-cohomology groups of X (with coefficients in $\mathbb{F}_2$).
A linear algebra exercise (as $\mathbb{F}_2$ is a field) shows that $\dim H_i(X, \mathbb{F}_2) = \dim H^i(X, \mathbb{F}_2)$. Another easy exercise gives that when $X = (V, E)$ is a graph with a set of vertices V and a set of edges E then $\delta_{-1} : C^{-1}(X, \mathbb{F}_2) \to C^0(X, \mathbb{F}_2)$ sends the one-dimensional space C^{-1} to $B^0 = \{0, \mathbf{1}\}$ where $\mathbf{1}$ is the "all" function giving 1 to every vertex. Furthermore, $\delta_0 : C^0 \to C^1$ sends every vertex to the "star" around it. It follows that a subset D of V is in $\text{Ker}\delta_0$ iff D is a union of connected components of the graph. Hence, $\dim H^0 = \dim Z^0 - \dim B^0 = -1 + \#$ connected components of X. Hence:

$$X \text{ is connected } \Leftrightarrow \dim H^0(X, \mathbb{F}_2) = 0 \quad (6)$$

Assuming X is connected, an easy computation shows that $\dim H^1(X, \mathbb{F}_2) = |E| - |V| - 1$. So, $H^1(X, \mathbb{F}_2) = 0$ iff X is a tree.
Going now back to general X we can deduce from (3) and (4) that

$$B_i^\perp = Z^i \text{ and } Z_i^\perp = B^i. \quad (7)$$

Indeed, if $\beta \in B_i$ and $\alpha \in Z^i$ then $\beta = \partial\gamma$ for some $\gamma \in C_{i+1}$ and so $\langle \beta, \alpha \rangle = \langle \partial\gamma, \alpha \rangle = \langle \gamma, \delta\alpha \rangle = \langle \gamma, 0 \rangle = 0$, hence $Z^i \subseteq B_i^\perp$. On the other hand, if $\alpha \in C^i$ and for every $\gamma \in C^{i+1}$, $\langle \partial\gamma, \alpha \rangle = 0$, then for every $\gamma \in C^{i+1}$, $\langle \gamma, \delta\alpha \rangle = 0$. The bilinear form is non-degenerate and hence $\delta\alpha = 0$ i.e., $\alpha \in Z^i$. In a similar way we deduce also the second equality.

2.2 $\mathbb{F}_2$-coboundary expansion

We are now ready to define following [11, 5] the expansion of a simplicial complex. Let X, as before, be a finite simplicial complex of dimension d and $\alpha \in C^i(X, \mathbb{F}_2)$ for some i, $0 \leq i \leq d$.
Denote: $|\alpha| = \#\{F \in X(i) | \alpha(F) \neq 0\}$ and $||\alpha|| = \frac{|\alpha|}{|X(i)|}$, i.e., the proportion of the number of i-cells on which α does not vanish. Of course, in our case, $\alpha(F) \neq 0$ means $\alpha(F) = 1$, but one may want to think also about this notion over other fields. In the case of $\mathbb{F}_2$, we can also think of α as simply a subset of $X(i)$, and $|\alpha|$ is its order.
For $\alpha \in C^i = C^i(X, \mathbb{F}_2)$ and W a subspace of C^i let:

$$\text{dist}(\alpha, W) = \min\{|\alpha_0| \; |\alpha_0 \in \alpha + W\}.$$

It is easy to see that if the minimum is obtained on $\bar{\alpha}$ in the coset $\alpha + W$ then $\alpha - \bar{\alpha}$ is the closest element to α in W in the Hamming distance and the distance is indeed $|\bar{\alpha}|$.
We should remark that this $\bar{\alpha}$ (and hence also $\alpha - \bar{\alpha}$) is not necessarily unique. This is a significant difference between "geometry over $\mathbb{F}_2$" versus "geometry over $\mathbb{R}$".
We also define the normalized distance:

$$\overline{dist}(\alpha, W) = ||\bar{\alpha}|| = \frac{\text{dist}(\alpha, W)}{|X(i)|}.$$

Let us give now Definition 1 in a slightly different form which will be more convenient for us.

Definition 6. *($\mathbb{F}_2$-coboundary expansion) For $i = 0, \cdots, d-1$ denote:*

$$\epsilon_i(X) = min \frac{||\delta_i f||}{\overline{dist}(f, B^i(X, \mathbb{F}_2))},$$

where the minimum is taken over all the functions $f \in C^i \setminus B^i$.

Definition 6 is equivalent to Definition 1 as $dist(\alpha, W)$ is equal to the minimum Hamming weight among the elements of the coset $\alpha + W$.

Remark 1. *The $\mathbb{F}_2$-coboundary expansion is defined essentially as in [11] and [5], but is slightly different from both. In [11], Linial and Meshulam studied the quotients $min \frac{|\delta_i f|}{||[f]||}$, without giving it a name, with a goal to prove that H^i vanishes. This is as our ϵ_i up to normalization factors. Gromov in [5] studied*

$$\mu_i = max_{0 \neq \beta \in B^{i+1}(X, \mathbb{F}_2)} \left(\frac{1}{||\beta||} \cdot min_{\alpha \in C^i(X, \mathbb{F}_2), \delta\alpha = \beta} ||\alpha|| \right).$$

It is easy to see that if $H^i = 0$ then $\mu_i = \frac{1}{\epsilon_i}$, but it is possible that $\mu_i < \infty$ even if $H^i \neq 0$ and $\epsilon_i = 0$. The name "coboundary expansion" was coined in [4].

An easy corollary of the definition is the following.

Corollary 1. *$\epsilon_i(X) \neq 0$ iff $H^i(X, \mathbb{F}_2) = 0$.*

Proof. If $H^i(X, \mathbb{F}_2) \neq 0$ then there exists $f \in C^i \setminus B^i$ with $\delta_i f = 0$, hence, $\epsilon_i(X) = 0$. On the other hand, if $H^i(X, \mathbb{F}_2) = 0$ then $\epsilon_i(X)$ is a minimum over a finite set of rational numbers each of which is non-zero. □

Let us spell out the definition for graphs. Here, $X = (V, E)$ and $d = 1$. A function $f \in C^0(X, \mathbb{F}_2)$ is a characteristic function 1_A of some subset A of V, $B^0(X, \mathbb{F}_2)$ is, as explained above, the 1-dimensional space of 0 and 1_V. Thus $\overline{dist}(1_A, B^0) = \frac{1}{|V|}\min(|A|, |V| \setminus |A|)$. On the other hand, one can easily check that $\delta_0(1_A) = E(A, \bar{A})$, i.e., the characteristic function of the set of all edges from A to its complement. Hence,

$$\epsilon_0(X) = \min_{\emptyset \neq A \subsetneq V} \frac{\frac{1}{|E|}|E(A, \bar{A})|}{\frac{1}{|V|}\min(|A|, |\bar{A}|)} = \frac{|V|}{|E|} \min_{A \neq \emptyset, V} \frac{|E(A, \bar{A})|}{\min\{|A|, |\bar{A}|\}}.$$

This gives us (up to the normalized factor $\frac{|V|}{|E|}$) the standard "edge expansion" (known also as the Cheeger constant) which defines expander graphs. Note also that when X is a k-regular graph, k fixed, $\frac{|V|}{|E|} = \frac{2}{k}$ is a constant.

2.3 The expansion of complete complexes

Theorem 2 of the introduction was proved independently by Linial and Meshulam [11] for $d = 2$, by Meshulam and Wallach [16] and Gromov [5], independently, for general d. It states:

Theorem 2 *Let $X_n^{(d)}$ be the complete d-dimensional simplicial complex on n vertices, i.e., the complex of all subsets of $[n] = \{1, \cdots, n\}$ of size at most $d+1$. Then, for every $i = 0, \cdots, d-1$, $\epsilon_i(X) \geq \frac{n}{n-i-1} \geq 1$.*

To get the flavor of this result, let us bring here the proof for $d = 2$. This is the case which we mostly use in Section 3, so it will make the proofs in the current paper self contained. Computing $\epsilon_0(X)$ in this case is easy as it depends only of the 1-skeleton of X and it is (as shown before) the normalized edge expansion, i.e.,

$$\epsilon_0(X) = \frac{|X(0)|}{|X(1)|}\min_{A\neq\emptyset, X(0)}\frac{|E(A,\bar{A})|}{\min\{|A|,|\bar{A}|\}}.$$

In our case the minimum is obtained for $|A| = \frac{n}{2}$, hence,

$$\epsilon_0(X) \geq \frac{n}{\binom{n}{2}}\frac{\frac{n}{2}\cdot\frac{n}{2}}{\frac{n}{2}} = \frac{n}{n-1} \geq 1.$$

Evaluating $\epsilon_1(X)$ is more involved. Let $\alpha \in C^1(X,\mathbb{F}_2)$, so α is a set of edges (or a function on the edges). For an edge $e \in X(1)$ and a vertex $u \in X(0)$ with $u \notin e$, denote by ue the triangle formed by u and e. Given α, define $\alpha_u \in C^0(X,\mathbb{F}_2)$, "the local view of α from u" by:

$$\alpha_u(v) = \alpha((u,v)) \text{ if } u \neq v, \text{ and } \alpha_u(v) = 0 \text{ otherwise .}$$

One can now checks that for every edge e:

$$(\alpha - \delta_0\alpha_u)(e) = (\delta_1\alpha)(ue) \text{ if } u \notin e, (\alpha - \delta_0\alpha_u)(e) = 0 \text{ if } u \in e \quad (8)$$

It now follows that:

$$\begin{aligned} 3|\delta_1\alpha| &= |\{(u,T) \in X(0)\times X(2) | u \in T, T \in \delta_1\alpha\}| && (9)\\ &= |\{(u,e) \in X(0)\times X(1) | e \in \alpha - \delta_0\alpha_u\}| && (10)\\ &= \sum_{u\in X(0)} |\alpha - \delta_0\alpha_u| \geq n \cdot \operatorname{dist}(\alpha, B^1). && (11)\end{aligned}$$

The first and the third equalities are just a careful spelling out of the notations, while the second follows from (8). The inequality follows from the fact that $\delta_0\alpha_u \in B^1$. We deduce that $\frac{|\delta_1\alpha|}{\operatorname{dist}(\alpha,B^1)} \geq \frac{n}{3}$. When we normalize by $|X(2)| = \binom{n}{3}$ and $|X(1)| = \binom{n}{2}$, we get:

$$\frac{||\delta_1\alpha||}{\overline{dist}(\alpha, B^1)} \geq \frac{n}{n-2} \geq 1.$$

3. EXPANSION AND TESTABILITY

We are ready now to give the main result, which shows that expansion is a form of testability.

DEFINITION 7. *(Cocycle Tester) Let X be a simplicial complex and $f \in C^i(X,\mathbb{F}_2)$. The* i-cocycle tester *for f is the test that picks a random $(i+1)$-cell F and evaluate $\delta(f)(F)$. The test accepts f iff $\delta(f)(F) = 0$.*
Note that, the number of queries performed by the i-cocycle tester is $i+2$ since every $(i+1)$-cell has exactly $i+2$ sub-cells of dim i (obtained by deleting one of its vertices).

Our main result is that high-dimensional (coboundary) expansion is equivalent to the local testability of the space of coboundaries. Namely:

THEOREM 8. *(Main) Let X be a d dimensional simplicial complex and let $i \in \{0, \cdots, d-1\}$. Then its i-th (coboundary) expansion is ϵ_i iff the subspace $B^i(X,\mathbb{F}_2) \subseteq C^i(X,\mathbb{F}_2)$ is $(i+2, \epsilon_i)$-testable via the "i-cocycle tester".*

REMARK 2. *Proposition 5 is a special case of Theorem 8 when $d = 1$ and $i = 0$.*

PROOF. Assume first that the i-cocycle tester is an $(i+2, \epsilon)$ tester for $B^i(X,\mathbb{F}_2)$ inside $C^i(X,\mathbb{F}_2)$. This means that the probability for a function $f \in C^i(X,\mathbb{F}_2)$ to fail the test is at least ϵ times its normalized Hamming distance from $B^i(X,\mathbb{F}_2)$. (In particular, it says that if f passes the test with probability 1, i.e., if $f \in Z^i(X,\mathbb{F}_2)$, then it is in $B^i(X,\mathbb{F}_2)$, hence $B^i(X,\mathbb{F}_2) = Z^i(X,\mathbb{F}_2)$, and so $H^i(X,\mathbb{F}_2) = 0$.)
This means that

$$\frac{\#\{F \in X(i+1) | \delta(f)(F) \neq 0\}}{|X(i+1)|} \geq \epsilon \cdot \overline{dist}(f, B^i(X,\mathbb{F}_2)).$$

which, by Definition 6, means exactly that the i-coboundary expansion of X is at least ϵ.
Conversely, assume that the i-coboundary expansion of X equals ϵ, then for every function $f \in C^i(X,\mathbb{F}_2) \setminus B^i(X,\mathbb{F}_2)$, $\frac{||\delta f||}{\overline{dist}(f,B^i(X,\mathbb{F}_2))} \geq \epsilon$, i.e.,

$$\frac{\#\{F \in X(i+1) | \delta(f)(F) \neq 0\}}{|X(i+1)|} \geq \epsilon \cdot \overline{dist}(f, B^i(X,\mathbb{F}_2)).$$

(see Definition 6). This exactly means that the probability of f to fail the i-cocycle test is at least ϵ times its (normalized) distance from $B^i(X,\mathbb{F}_2)$. Thus, the i-cocycle test is an $(i+2, \epsilon)$-test for $B^i(X,\mathbb{F}_2)$ inside $C^i(X,\mathbb{F}_2)$. □

Theorem 8 says that any expansion result for some simplicial complex gives automatically a testability result. Let us illustrate this by some applications of Theorem 2.

3.1 Sum functions on graphs

Let Γ be a finite graph on a set of vertices $[m] = \{1, \cdots, m\}$, and set of edges $E \subseteq \binom{[m]}{2}$ of size n. A function $f : E \to \{0,1\}$ will be called a *sum function* if there exists a function $g : [m] \to \{0,1\}$ such that for every edge $e = (i,j) \in E$, $f(e) = g(i) + g(j) \pmod 2$.

QUESTION 1. *Is the sum-function property testable?*

This depends on the structure of the graph. Let us start with a negative result.

PROPOSITION 9. *Let $\{X_i = (V_i, E_i)\}_{i\in I}$ be a family of finite graphs whose girth is going to infinity. Then, the sum function property on functions $f : E_i \to \{0,1\}$ is not testable.*

PROOF. In the notations above, the sum functions is exactly the space $B^1(X_i, \mathbb{F}_2)$. This is a linear space (or a code) and it is well known (see e.g. [1]) that such a code is locally testable only if it is an LDPC (Low Density Parity Check) code. I.e., its dual space is spanned by bounded weight constraints. However, in our case, $B^1(X_i, \mathbb{F}_2)^{\perp} = Z_1(X_i, \mathbb{F}_2)$ (see equation (7)). But, $Z_1(X_i, \mathbb{F}_2)$, the space of cycles, has no bounded weight vectors as the girth of X_i is unbounded. □

We now show that for the complete graphs the answer is positive.

PROPOSITION 10. *Let $\Gamma = K_m$ the complete graph on m vertices. Then the sum-function property on Γ is testable.*

PROOF. We embed $\Gamma = K_m$ as the 1-skeleton of $X = K_m^{(2)}$, the 2-dimensional complete complex on m vertices (i.e., the set of all subsets of $[m]$ of cardinality at most 3). Note that the space of sum functions is exactly $B^1(X, \mathbb{F}_2)$ - the space of coboundaries, as can be easily seen by spelling out the definitions. By Theorem 2, $\epsilon_1(K_m^{(2)}) \geq 1$. This means by Theorem 8, that the 1-cocycle tester is a $(3,1)$-tester for $B^1(X, \mathbb{F}_2)$ inside $C^1(X, \mathbb{F}_2)$. The meaning of the 1-cocycle tester is: choose a random tuple $\{r, j, k\} \in \binom{[m]}{3}$, accept a function f on the edges of $\Gamma = K_m$ (i.e. on $X(1)$) iff $f(rj) + f(jk) + f(kr) = 0$. Indeed, it performs 3 queries and the fact that it is a $(3,1)$-tester for $B^1(X, \mathbb{F}_2)$ exactly means that the probability of the test to reject f is at least its (normalized) distance from $B^1(X, \mathbb{F}_2)$, i.e., from the sum-functions. This proves the proposition.

□

REMARK 3. *Note that the proposition says in particular that a function on the edges of $\Gamma = K_m$ is a sum function iff it vanishes on triangles. This could be proved directly, but a conceptual way to see this is the following: $X = K_m^{(2)}$ is a triangulation of a bouquet of b two-dimensional spheres $Y = \bigvee_{i=1}^{b} S^2$, $S^2 = \{(x, y, z) \in \mathbb{R}^3 | x^2 + y^2 + z^2 = 1\}$. It has, therefore, the same cohomology/homology as S^2. Now, $H^1(S^2, \mathbb{F}) = 0$ for every field $\mathbb{F}$, and, in particular, $H^1(S^2, \mathbb{F}_2) = 0$. Hence also $H^1(Y, \mathbb{F}_2) = \bigoplus_{i=1}^{b} H^1(S^2, \mathbb{F}_2) = 0$, and so $H^1(X, \mathbb{F}_2) = 0$. This exactly means that every 1-cocycle of X is a coboundary. In particular, a function on the edges of $\Gamma = K_m$ is a sum function iff it vanishes on all triangles.*

The proof of Proposition 10 shows.

PROPOSITION 11. *Let X be a two dimensional simplicial complex and Γ its 1-skeleton. Then the "triangle checking algorithm" of X is a $(3, \epsilon)$-tester for the sum-function problem of Γ if and only if the first expansion constant of X is at least ϵ.*

3.2 Tensor power testing

Proposition 10 gives also a testability result of a different form (We are grateful to Irit Dinur for calling our attention to this fact).

Let $A = \{1, -1\}$ and $A^{\frac{m^2-m}{2}}$ is the set of all $m \times m$ symmetric matrices with 1 along the diagonal and $+1/-1$ outside the diagonal. Let P_m be the subset of all matrices M obtained as a tensor power, i.e., there exists a vector α of length m with $+1/-1$ entries, such that $M_{i,j} = \alpha_i \cdot \alpha_j$.

PROPOSITION 12. *P_m is testable within $A^{\frac{m^2-m}{2}}$ via the algorithm: choose three different indices $\{i, j, k\}$, answer "yes" if $M_{i,j} M_{j,k} M_{k,i} = 1$ and "no" otherwise.*

PROOF. This is just a reformulation of Proposition 10 when one switch notations from $\{0, 1\}$ to $\{1, -1\}$. With these notations the tensor powers are exactly the sum-functions and $A^{\frac{m^2-m}{2}}$ is the space of all symmetric functions on $[m] \times [m]$ with zeros along the diagonal. □

3.3 Seidel Switching

There is another interpretation for Proposition 10. Given a graph Γ with a set of vertices $[n] = \{1, \cdots, n\}$ and let v be a vertex of Γ. One defines the *Seidel switching* of Γ along v to be the graph obtained from Γ by deleting all the edges of Γ incident to v and connecting v to all vertices of $[n]$ which were not its neighbors in Γ. We say that the graph Γ' on $[n]$ is *Seidel equivalent* to Γ if it can be obtained from Γ by a sequence of such Seidel switchings. This is indeed an equivalence relation. The concept of Seidel switching appears in various areas of combinatorics and computer science. See for example [10] and the references therein.
We can now prove the following

PROPOSITION 13. *The property of Seidel equivalence of a pair of graphs is testable. I.e., given two graphs Γ,Γ' on $[n]$, there is a tester for the property that the pair of graphs are Seidel equivalent.*

PROOF. A graph Γ (resp Γ') on $[n]$ can be considered as a symmetric function from the set of 2-elements subsets of $[n]$ to $\{0, 1\}$, i.e., as a function on the edges of the complete graph K_n, so it is a 1-cochain of K_n. Now, one can see that if α is the cochain associated to Γ, then $\alpha + \delta_0(\chi_v)$ is the cochain associated with the Seidel switching of Γ along v (where χ_v is the characteristic function of $\{v\}$ and δ_0 the coboundary map).
As $B^1(K_n, \mathbb{F}_2)$ is generated by $\delta_0(\chi_v)$, $v \in [n]$, it follows that Γ' is Seidel equivalent to Γ iff α', the cochain associated with Γ', is in the same coset modulo $B^1(K_n, \mathbb{F}_2)$ as α, i.e., iff $\alpha - \alpha' \in B^1(K_n, \mathbb{F}_2)$. Theorem 2 implies, as explained in the proof of Theorem 8 and Proposition 10, that the question of whether a cochain of K_n is a coboundary, is testable. Applying this to $\alpha - \alpha'$ we deduce that "Seidel equivalence" is also testable. In fact the tester acts as follows. "Pick a random triangle and check whether $\delta_1(\alpha)$ and $\delta_1(\alpha')$ agree on it". □

Let us warn the reader that the last proposition says that the Seidel equivalence of graphs Γ and Γ' is testable when we consider them as labeled on the vertices $[n]$, and the Seidel switching preserves the label of the vertices. We do not expect the abstract Seidel switching to be testable since the decision version of that problem is equivalent to the problem of graph isomorphism [10].

4. REFERENCES

[1] E. Ben-Sasson, P. Harsha and S. Raskhodnikova, *Some 3CNF Properties are Hard to Test*, SIAM Journal on Computing, 35(1), 1–21, 2005.

[2] M. Blum, M. Luby, and R. Rubinfeld, *Self-Testing/Correcting with Applications to Numerical Problems*, In J. Comp. Sys. Sci. Vol. 47, No. 3, December 1993.

[3] I. Dinur and T. Kaufman, *Locally testable codes and expanders*, manuscript, 2012.

[4] D. Dotterrer and M. Kahle, *Coboundary expanders*, Journal of Topology and Analysis, 4(2012), 499-514.

[5] M. Gromov, *Singularities, expanders and topology of maps. part 2: From combinatorics to topology via algebraic isoperimetry*, Geometric And Functional Analysis, 20(2):416-Ű526, 2010.

[6] S. Hoory, N. Linial and A. Wigderson, *Expander graphs and their applications*, Bulletin of the American Mathematical Society, 43(4):439Ű-562, 2006.

[7] M. Bellare, D. Coppersmith, J. Håstad, Marcos, A. Kiwi and Madhu Sudan, *Linearity testing in characteristic two*, IEEE Transactions on Information Theory 42(6): 1781-1795 (1996).

[8] T. Kaufman, D. Kazhdan and A. Lubotzky, *Isoparametric inequlities for Ramanujan complexes and topological overlapping*, 2013, In preparations.

[9] T. Kaufman, S. Litsyn and N. Xie, *Breaking the Epsilon-Soundness Bound of the Linearity Test over GF(2)*, SIAM J. Comput. 39(5): 1988-2003 (2010).

[10] J. Kratochvíl, J. Nesetril and O. Zýka, *On the Computational Complexity of Seidel's Switching*, Annals of Discrete Mathematics, Volume 51, 161–166, 1992.

[11] N. Linial and R. Meshulam, *Homological connectivity of random 2-complexes*, Combinatorica, 26(4):475-Ű487, 2006.

[12] A. Lubotzky, *Discrete Groups, Expanding Graphs, and Invariant Measures*, Progress in Mathematics(125), Birkhausser Verlag, Basel 1994.

[13] A. Lubotzky, *Expander graphs in pure and applied mathematics*, Bull. Amer. Math. Soc, 49:113Ű-162, 2012.

[14] A. Lubotzky and R. Meshulam, *Random Latin squares and 2-dimensional expanders*, arXiv:1307.3582, 2013.

[15] A. Lubotzky, B. Samuels and U. Vishne, *Ramanujan complexes of type* $\tilde{A}_d$, Israel J. Math. Vol 149, 267–299, 2005.

[16] R. Meshulam and N. Wallach, *Homological connectivity of random k-dimensional complexes*, Random Struct. Algorithms, 34(2009) 408-417.

[17] R. Rubinfeld and M. Sudan, *Robust characterizations of polynomails with applications to program testing*, SIAM Journal of Computing, 25(2), 252–271, 1996.

[18] A. Gundert and U. Wagner, *On laplacians of random complexes*, Symposium on Computational Geometry 2012, 151-160.

Parameterized Testability

Kazuo Iwama*
School of Informatics
Kyoto University
iwama@kuis.kyoto-u.ac.jp

Yuichi Yoshida†
National Institute of Informatics, and
Preferred Infrastructure, Inc.
yyoshida@nii.ac.jp

ABSTRACT

This paper studies property testing for NP optimization problems with parameter k under the general graph model with an augmentation of random edge sampling capability. It is shown that a variety of such problems, including k-Vertex Cover, k-Feedback Vertex Set, k-Multicut, k-Path-Free and k-Dominating Set, are constant-time testable if k is constant. It should be noted that the first four problems are fixed parameter tractable (FPT) and it turns out that algorithmic techniques for their FPT algorithms (branch-and-bound search, color coding, etc.) are also useful for our testers. k-Dominating Set is $W[2]$-hard, but we can still test the property in constant time since the definition of ϵ-farness makes the problem trivial for non-sparse graphs that are the source of hardness for the original optimization problem. We also consider k-Odd Cycle Transversal, which is another well-known FPT problem, but we only give a sublinear-time tester when k is a constant.

Categories and Subject Descriptors

F.2 [**Theory of Computation**]: Analysis of Algorithms and Problem Complexity

General Terms

Theory

Keywords

Property testing, fixed parameter tractability

*Supported by JSPS Grant-in-Aid for Scientific Research (No. 25240002)

†Supported by JSPS Grant-in-Aid for Research Activity Start-up (No. 24800082), MEXT Grant-in-Aid for Scientific Research on Innovative Areas (No. 24106003), and JST, ERATO, Kawarabayashi Large Graph Project.

ITCS'14, January 12–14, 2014, Princeton, New Jersey, USA.

ACM 978-1-4503-2698-8/14/01 ...$15.00.
http://dx.doi.org/10.1145/2554797.2554843.

1. INTRODUCTION

In *graph property testing* [13], given a graph represented by an oracle, we want to test whether the graph satisfies some predetermined property or is ϵ-far from satisfying the property. Roughly speaking, a graph is called *ϵ-far* from a property if we need to modify an ϵ-fraction of the graph to make it satisfy the property. We also assume that we have a query access to the input graph. Then, many properties are known to be testable even with a constant number of queries, which is independent of the size of the input graph (see [12, 23, 24] for surveys of this area).

The most important question is finding general characterizations of constant-query testable properties, and there has been much progress in the last decade in this direction: For the dense graph model [13], any property $\mathcal{P}$ is constant-query testable if it is monotone [4] or hereditary [3], where a property is called *monotone* (resp., *hereditary*) if it is closed under edge deletions (resp., vertex deletions). The celebrated result by Alon et al. [1] finally obtains a purely combinatorial necessary and sufficient condition of constant-query testable properties that is closely related to Szemerédi's Regularity Lemma [25]. For the bounded-degree graph model [14], $\mathcal{P}$ is constant-query testable if it is minor-closed [7, 16] and any property is constant-query testable if the given graph is hyperfinite [18].

In this paper, we are still interested in a general framework of constant-query testable properties, but our approach is a bit different from the qualitative one as above. Rather, we are interested in "parameterized properties" that are quite common in NP optimization problems. A bit curiously, this direction has not been so popular in the context of property testing. The obvious reason is that the problem becomes less interesting in both the dense graph model and the bounded degree model. For instance, consider the problem k-Vertex Cover (whether a vertex cover of size at most k exists), where k is a constant. In the dense graph model, we want to decide whether a graph has a vertex cover of size at most k or we need to remove at least ϵn^2 edges to have the property, where n is the number of variables in the graph. This property is easily constant-query testable just by accepting only graphs with at most ϵn^2 edges. Indeed, if a graph has at most ϵn^2 edges, it is not ϵ-far from having a vertex cover of size 0 (and hence at most k). Also, if a graph has at least ϵn^2 edges, it cannot have a vertex cover of size at most k since at most $kn \ll \epsilon n^2$ edges can be covered by k vertices. We can use a similar argument for the bounded-degree model.

To avoid this triviality, we consider the general graph model. In the general graph model, a graph is called ϵ-

far from a property if we must remove or add at least ϵm edges, where m is the number of edges in the graph. By one query, we can ask for a random vertex, the degree of a vertex or a neighbor of a vertex. However, there is also an obstacle in this model. Let G_1 be an empty graph and let G_2 be a graph consisting of an $\sqrt{n}$-size clique and $n - \sqrt{n}$ isolated vertices. Note that G_1 has a vertex cover of size 0 and G_2 is clearly far from having a vertex cover of size 0. However, it is known that we cannot distinguish G_1 from G_2 with $o(\sqrt{n})$ queries, and it implies that even 0-Vertex Cover is not constant-query testable.

We can avoid this issue if we can find an edge in constant time. Thus in this paper, we consider the general graph model in which we can sample edges uniformly at random. We believe this model is natural and refer to Section 2 for details and comparison to other models. The goal of this paper is showing that, in the general graph model with random edge queries, many parameterized properties become constant-query testable. We hope our result will stimulate studies on testing under the general graph model and the relation between property testing and parameterized problems.

Our Contribution.

We say that a property $\mathcal{P}$ with parameter k is *sublinear-query fixed parameter testable* (*sublinear-time FPT* for short) if there is a tester that makes $f(\epsilon, \delta, k) \cdot g(n)$ queries for a sublinear function $g(n)$. Here n is the number of vertices in the input graph, and ϵ and δ are parameters corresponding to the ϵ-farness and the probability that the (randomized) algorithm fails to output the correct answer, respectively. Especially if $g(n)$ is constant, then we say that $\mathcal{P}$ is *constant-query FPT*. Our general graph model supports random vertex queries, random edge queries, degree queries and neighbor queries.

The first result is giving a general framework to construct testers for vertex and edge deletion problems. In a vertex (resp., edge) deletion problem, we want to decide whether a graph can be made satisfy some predetermined hereditary (resp., monotone) property $\mathcal{P}$ by removing at most k vertices (resp., edges). Vertex and edge deletion problems include k-Vertex Cover, k-Feedback Vertex Set (whether we can make a graph cycle-free by removing at most k vertices), k-Odd Cycle Transversal (whether we can make a graph bipartite by removing at most k vertices) and k-Multicut (whether we can disconnect specified terminal pairs by removing at most k edges). We show that k-Vertex Cover, k-Feedback Vertex Set and k-Multicut are constant-query FPT and k-Odd Cycle Transversal is testable with $O(\sqrt{n}\log^k n)$ queries.

Our framework is based on the simple brute-force search, but we need somewhat interesting idea to show that k-Feedback Vertex Set is constant-query FPT: Let $\mathcal{P}_{\text{forest}}$ be the property of being a forest (cycle-free). Then in each step of the brute-force search with an alleged feedback vertex set S, we want to test whether S is a feedback vertex set, in other words, $G \setminus S$ satisfies $\mathcal{P}_{\text{forest}}$. If it is the case, then we can accept. If it is not the case, then we want a cycle of constant length from $G \setminus S$ and to proceed to test whether $S \cup \{v\}$ is a feedback vertex set for each vertex v in the short cycle. An issue here is that we only have a two-sided error tester for $\mathcal{P}_{\text{forest}}$, and we cannot find short cycles in general even when G is ϵ-far from $\mathcal{P}_{\text{forest}}$. The first trick to overcome this issue is using a *tolerant tester* for $\mathcal{P}_{\text{forest}}$, which accepts if $G \setminus S$ is close to satisfying $\mathcal{P}_{\text{forest}}$ and rejects if $G \setminus S$ is far from satisfying $\mathcal{P}_{\text{forest}}$. Suppose that the tolerant tester accept. Then, since $G \setminus S$ is close to satisfying $\mathcal{P}_{\text{forest}}$, and in particular G is close to having a feedback vertex set of size at most k, we can safely accept. Suppose that the tolerant tester rejects. Then we know that $G \setminus S$ is far from satisfying $\mathcal{P}_{\text{forest}}$. Unfortunately, we cannot still find short cycles in general. However, we can design a constant-query algorithm that finds a short cycle if $G \setminus S$ is far from $\mathcal{P}_{\text{forest}}$, provided that $G \setminus S$ has a feedback vertex set of size at most k. Using the obtained short cycle, we can continue the brute-force search if G is a yes-instance. We do not really care what happens when G is a no-instance as it is sound to reject.

In summary, when we want to test whether a graph can be made satisfy $\mathcal{P}$ by removing k vertices or edges, what we need in our general framework is a tolerant tester for $\mathcal{P}$ and a one-sided error tester for $\mathcal{P}$ that is guaranteed to work when the input graph is a yes-instance.

Our second result is that k-Path-Free (whether *no* path of length k exists) is constant-query FPT. Note that the problem cannot be expressed as a vertex or edge deletion problem, and the main technique of its FPT algorithms is color coding [5]. Our tester for k-Path-Free is based on random walk and we analyze its behavior using color coding, indicating its usefulness in property testing.

Our third result is that k-Dominating Set (whether a dominating set of size k exists) is constant-query FPT. Recall that this problem is $W[2]$-hard [11], but its hardness seems to depend on the fact that underlying graphs are not sparse. In our context of property testing, the problem becomes trivial when the graph is not sparse because of the ϵ-farness. Therefore, it suffices to consider sparse graphs, for which we can design a tester in a way similar to the general framework for vertex and edge deletion problems. Although k-Dominating Set itself is $W[2]$-hard, what we test here is actually whether we can dominate at least $(1 - \epsilon)n$ vertices using k vertices, and the problem is known to be FPT.

k-Odd Cycle Transversal does not admit constant-query FPT as there is a lower bound of $\sqrt{n}$ for bipartiteness [14], but it still appears that FPT properties are easier to test rather than non-FPT properties in general. For instance, a polynomial lower bound on the query complexity for testing K_3-freeness (a special case of k-Clique, which is $W[1]$-hard), due to [2], does not seem to differ much even if we can use random edge sampling. We believe that revealing the relation between FPT and constant-query FPT is an interesting topic for future research.

We use random edge queries in testers for k-Vertex Cover, k-Feedback Vertex Set, k-Path-Free and k-Dominating Set to find edges or to approximate the number of edges. In the standard general graph model, without random edge queries, we can simulate these testers with $\widetilde{O}(\sqrt{n})$ queries using the technique in [15]. The only tester that runs in constant time even in the standard general graph model is the one for k-Multicut. But, it is basically because terminal pairs are given in advance and we do not have to find an edge.

Related Work.

Compared to the dense graph model and the bounded-degree model, the literature for the general graph model is rather limited. Usually we are allowed to use degree queries, neighbor queries, and sometimes pair queries, with which we can ask whether there is an edge between two vertices.

[17] showed that testing bipartiteness takes $\Theta(\min(\sqrt{n}, n/d))$ queries, where d is the average degree of the graph, and [2] studied mainly lower bounds of the query complexity for testing the K_3-freeness, obtaining polynomial lower bounds such as $\Omega(\sqrt{n})$ and $\Omega(n^{1/3})$ for d between $\omega(1)$ and $n^{1-o(n)}$. The reason we need such high query complexities is that we cannot quickly access a hidden dense subgraph of small size (say $\sqrt{n}$) using only vertex-based queries. Such high lower bounds would also hide the complexity of other (sometimes more inherent) parts of the testers, for instance, random walk becomes much easier and less interesting if we can use $\sqrt{n}$ queries. [6] introduced rather powerful query called a group query (allowing to ask if there are edges between a vertex and a set of vertices).

Testers provide just yes/no as their answer, but we can also consider their optimization version. Namely an algorithm $\mathcal{A}$ is said to be an (α, β)-approximation algorithm for a graph parameter x^* if $\mathcal{A}$ outputs a value x with $\alpha x^* - \beta \leq x \leq x^*$. A sequence of works [19, 21, 22, 27] obtained constant-query $(2, \epsilon n)$-approximation algorithms for the minimum size of a vertex cover for any $\epsilon > 0$. There is no direct relation to our result since, even if the correct value is constant, these algorithms may answer with a value of ϵn. Namely, such approximation algorithms are particularly useful when the target value is relatively large.

Organization.

In Section 2, we introduce definitions used throughout this paper. In Section 3, we first give a meta algorithm that is useful to design testers for vertex deletion problems. Then, we show that k-Feedback Vertex Set, k-Vertex Cover, k-Multicut are constant-query FPT and k-Odd Cycle Transversal is sublinear-query FPT. In Section 4 and Section 5, we show that k-Path-Free and k-Dominating Set are constant-query FPT, respectively.

2. PRELIMINARIES

For an integer n, let $[n]$ denote the set $\{1, \ldots, n\}$. Let $G = (V, E)$ be a graph. We always use n and m to denote the number of vertices and the number of edges in the input graph, respectively. In this paper, we only consider simple graphs. For a set of vertices $S \subseteq V$, let $G|_S$ be the subgraph induced by S, and let $G \setminus S$ be $G|_{V \setminus S}$. For a set of edges $F \subseteq E$, let $G \setminus F$ be the subgraph $(V, E \setminus F)$. For a vertex $v \in V$, let $d_G(v)$ be the degree of v and $N_G(v)$ be the set of neighbors of v (excluding v itself) in G. When the context is clear, we often omit the subscripts.

We often identify a graph property and the set of graphs satisfying the property. A property $\mathcal{P}$ is called *hereditary* if a graph G satisfies $\mathcal{P}$, then $G \setminus \{v\}$ also satisfies $\mathcal{P}$ for any vertex $v \in V$. For a hereditary property $\mathcal{P}$, $\mathcal{P} + kv$ (resp., $\mathcal{P} + ke$) denotes the set of graphs G such that we can make G satisfy $\mathcal{P}$ by removing at most k vertices (resp., edges).

Our algorithms run under the general graph model, defined as follows.

DEFINITION 2.1. *In the* general graph model with random edge queries, *an input graph $G = (V, E)$ is represented by an oracle supporting following four types of queries:*

- *Random vertex queries: The oracle returns a random vertex in V.*
- *Random edge queries: The oracle returns a random edge in E.*
- *Degree queries: Given a vertex v, the oracle returns the degree of v.*
- *Neighbor queries: Given a vertex v and $i \in [d(v)]$, the oracle returns the i-th neighbor of v.*

The number of vertices n and the number of edges m are given to algorithms in advance. The query complexity of an algorithm is the number of accesses to the oracle.

We mention other famous models used in graph property testing. In the *dense graph model* [13], a graph is represented by an oracle that supports random vertex queries and pair queries, for which the oracle returns whether there is an edge between two specified vertices. In the *bounded-degree graph model* [14] with degree bound d, we only consider graphs with maximum degree at most d, and a graph is represented by an oracle that supports random vertex queries and neighbor queries.

A value x is called an *(α, β)-approximation* to x^* if $\alpha x^* - \beta \leq x \leq x^*$. An *$(\alpha, 0)$-approximation* is simply called an *α-approximation*. An algorithm is called an *(α, β, δ)-approximation algorithm* for a parameter if it outputs (α, β)-approximation to the parameter with probability at least $1 - \delta$.

In the general graph model, a graph $G = (V, E)$ is called *ϵ-far* from a property $\mathcal{P}$ if we must add or remove at least ϵm edges to make G satisfy the property, and is called *ϵ-close* to $\mathcal{P}$ otherwise. An algorithm is called a *(two-sided error) (ϵ, δ)-tester* for a property $\mathcal{P}$ if it accepts with probability at least $1-\delta$ when G satisfies $\mathcal{P}$, and it rejects with probability at least $1-\delta$ when G is ϵ-far from $\mathcal{P}$. An algorithm is called a *one-sided error tester* for a property $\mathcal{P}$ if it is a tester and it always accepts graphs satisfying $\mathcal{P}$. For $\epsilon_1 \leq \epsilon_2$, an algorithm is called an $(\epsilon_1, \epsilon_2, \delta)$-tester if it accepts with probability at least $1 - \delta$ when G is ϵ_1-close to $\mathcal{P}$, and it rejects with probability at least $1-\delta$ when G is ϵ_2-far from $\mathcal{P}$. An $(\epsilon_1, \epsilon_2, \delta)$-tester is often referred to as a *tolerant tester*. We note that a $(0, \epsilon, \delta)$-tester is equivalent to an ϵ-tester.

A one-sided error tester, when it rejects, often outputs a "witness" that the input graph does not satisfy the property. In particular, when we are concerned with a hereditary property $\mathcal{P}$, an induced subgraph violating $\mathcal{P}$ will be a witness since any graph with it cannot satisfy $\mathcal{P}$. We formalize such a tester as a detector. We call an algorithm an *(ϵ, δ)-detector* for a hereditary property $\mathcal{P}$ if it is a one-sided error (ϵ, δ)-tester for $\mathcal{P}$ and it outputs an induced subgraph H with $H \notin \mathcal{P}$ when it rejects. The *witness size* of a detector is the number of vertices in the induced subgraph output by the detector.

For an (ϵ, δ)-tester and an (ϵ, δ)-detector, we refer ϵ to an *error parameter* and δ to a *confidence parameter*. When we say an algorithm is a tester (resp., a detector) *under a property $\mathcal{Q}$*, it means that it correctly works as a tester (resp., a detector) if the input graph satisfies $\mathcal{Q}$.

3. VERTEX DELETION PROBLEMS

In this section, we give a general method to construct a tester for $\mathcal{P} + kv$ where $\mathcal{P}$ is a hereditary property. First, we introduce several notions. We say that an algorithm is an *(ϵ, δ)-tester for $\mathcal{P}$ in subgraphs* if, given a query access to G and a set of vertices S, it accepts with probability at least $1-\delta$ if $G \setminus S$ satisfies $\mathcal{P}$ and rejects with probability at least $1-\delta$ if $G \setminus S$ is ϵ-far from $\mathcal{P}$, where ϵ-farness is defined with respect to the number of edges in G but not in $G \setminus S$. We similarly define tolerant testers and detectors for $\mathcal{P}$ in subgraphs.

In Subsection 3.1, we give a meta algorithm that constructs a tester for $\mathcal{P}+kv$ using a tolerant tester for $\mathcal{P}$ in $G \setminus S$ and a detector for $\mathcal{P}$ in $G \setminus S$ under $\mathcal{P}+kv$. As an illustrating application, we give a tester for k-Feedback Vertex Set in Subsection 3.2. Then, we show testers for k-Vertex Cover, k-Odd Cycle Transversal, and k-Multicut in subsequent sections.

3.1 A meta algorithm for vertex deletion problems

Let $\mathcal{P}$ be a hereditary property. Suppose that we have a tolerant tester $\mathsf{Test}_{\mathcal{P}}$ for $\mathcal{P}$ in subgraphs, and a detector $\mathsf{Detect}_{\mathcal{P}}$ for the property $\mathcal{P}$ in subgraphs under $\mathcal{P}+kv$. In this subsection, we give a meta algorithm that constructs a tester $\mathsf{Test}_{\mathcal{P}+kv}$ for $\mathcal{P}+kv$ using $\mathsf{Test}_{\mathcal{P}}$ and $\mathsf{Detect}_{\mathcal{P}}$.

Our algorithm is given in Algorithm 1. Here the procedure $\mathsf{Test}_{\mathcal{P}+kv}(G,\epsilon,\delta,S)$ is supposed to test whether $G \setminus S$ satisfies $\mathcal{P}+(k-|S|)v$, and the final output is $\mathsf{Test}_{\mathcal{P}+kv}(G,\epsilon,\delta,\emptyset)$. The idea behind $\mathsf{Test}_{\mathcal{P}+kv}(G,\epsilon,\delta,S)$ is as follows. We first run the tolerant tester for $\mathcal{P}$ in $G \setminus S$. If the tester accepts, we return **true** since G is sufficiently close to $\mathcal{P}+(k-|S|)v$. Suppose that the tester rejects. Then, we have two cases to consider: (1) $G \setminus S$ is far from $\mathcal{P}$ but satisfies $\mathcal{P}+(k-|S|)v$. (2) $G \setminus S$ is far from $\mathcal{P}+(k-|S|)v$. In the former case, the detector will output a small witness. Since we need to remove at least one vertex in the witness to make the input graph satisfy $\mathcal{P}$, for each vertex v in the witness, we recurse after adding v to S. In the latter case, we have no guarantee about the outcome of the detector. It may output a small witness or accept. If it outputs a small witness, then we recurse as in the former case. If it accepts, we simply return **false** (Line 7).

Now, we see how $\mathsf{Test}_{\mathcal{P}+kv}(G,\epsilon,\delta,\emptyset)$ works. Suppose that G satisfies $\mathcal{P}+kv$ and $G \setminus S^*$ satisfies $\mathcal{P}$ for some set S^* of at most k vertices. We will show that some vertex in S^* appears in the witness at each level. Then, $\mathsf{Test}_{\mathcal{P}+kv}(G,\epsilon,\delta,S^*)$ is called at level at most k and returns **true** at Line 2. It follows that $\mathsf{Test}_{\mathcal{P}+kv}(G,\epsilon,\delta,\emptyset)$ also returns **true**. Suppose that G is ϵ-far from $\mathcal{P}+kv$. Note that $G \setminus S$ is ϵ-far from $\mathcal{P}$ (with respect to the number of edges in G) for any $S \subseteq V$ with $|S| \le k$ since G is ϵ-far from $\mathcal{P}+kv$. Thus, the tolerant tester in $\mathsf{Test}_{\mathcal{P}+kv}(G,\epsilon,\delta,S)$ at level k will reject, and $\mathsf{Test}_{\mathcal{P}+kv}(G,\epsilon,\delta,S)$ returns **false** at Line 1. It follows that $\mathsf{Test}_{\mathcal{P}+kv}(G,\epsilon,\delta,\emptyset)$ also returns **false**. Now we give a formal statement.

THEOREM 3.1. *Let $\mathcal{P}$ be a hereditary property and $k \ge 0$ be an integer. Let $\mathsf{Test}_{\mathcal{P}}(G,\epsilon_1,\epsilon_2,\delta,S)$ be an $(\epsilon_1,\epsilon_2,\delta)$-tester for $\mathcal{P}$ in $G \setminus S$ with query complexity $q_T(n,\epsilon_1,\epsilon_2,\delta,|S|)$ and $\mathsf{Detect}_{\mathcal{P}}(G,\epsilon,\delta,S)$ be an (ϵ,δ)-detector for $\mathcal{P}$ in $G \setminus S$ under $\mathcal{P}+kv$ with query complexity $q_D(n,\epsilon,\delta,|S|)$ and the witness size at most $\ell(n,\epsilon,|S|)$. Then, there is an (ϵ,δ)-tester for $\mathcal{P}+kv$ with query complexity $(q_T(n,\frac{\epsilon}{2},\epsilon,\frac{\delta}{2\ell^k},k)+q_D(n,\frac{\epsilon}{2},\frac{\delta}{2\ell^k},k))\ell^{k+1}$, where $\ell=\ell(n,\frac{\epsilon}{2},k)$.*

PROOF. We can assume that $q_T(n,\epsilon_1,\epsilon_2,\delta,s)$, $q_D(n,\epsilon,\delta,s)$, and $\ell(n,\epsilon,s)$ are non-decreasing functions in s. Then, the query complexity is immediate since we recursively call $\mathsf{Test}_{\mathcal{P}+kv}$ at most ℓ^k times. We now show the correctness of $\mathsf{Test}_{\mathcal{P}+kv}$. We first note that, since we have chosen the confidence parameter as $\frac{\delta}{2\ell^k}$ for $\mathsf{Test}_{\mathcal{P}}$ and $\mathsf{Detect}_{\mathcal{P}}$, all executions of $\mathsf{Test}_{\mathcal{P}}$ and $\mathsf{Detect}_{\mathcal{P}}$ succeed with probability at least $1-\delta$. In what follows, we assume this happens. We have two cases to consider.

Algorithm 1 $\mathsf{Test}_{\mathcal{P}+kv}(G,\epsilon,\delta,S)$

Input: A graph $G=(V,E)$, $\epsilon \in (0,1), \delta \in (0,1)$ and a set of vertices $S \subseteq V$.
Output: Whether $G \setminus S$ satisfies $\mathcal{P}+(k-|S|)v$.
1: **if** $|S| \ge k+1$ **then return false**.
2: **if** $\mathsf{Test}_{\mathcal{P}}(G,\frac{\epsilon}{2},\epsilon,\frac{\delta}{2\ell^k},S)$ **then return true**.
3: **if** $\mathsf{Detect}_{\mathcal{P}}(G,\frac{\epsilon}{2},\frac{\delta}{2\ell^k},S)$ finds a witness $(G \setminus S)|_U$ that violates $\mathcal{P}$ **then**
4: **for** $v \in U$ **do**
5: **if** $\mathsf{Test}_{\mathcal{P}+kv}(G,\epsilon,\delta,S \cup \{v\})$ **then**
6: **return true**
7: **return false**

Case 1. Suppose G satisfies $\mathcal{P}+kv$. Since G satisfies $\mathcal{P}+kv$, there exists a set of vertices $S^* \subseteq V$ with $G \setminus S^* \in \mathcal{P}$. We shall show that, for each call of $\mathsf{Test}_{\mathcal{P}+kv}(G,\frac{\epsilon}{2},\epsilon,\delta,S)$, it returns **true** at Line 2, or it calls $\mathsf{Test}_{\mathcal{P}+kv}(G,\epsilon,\delta,S \cup \{v\})$ at Line 5 for some $v \in S^* \setminus S$. Then, after k recursive calls, $\mathsf{Test}_{\mathcal{P}+kv}(G,\epsilon,\delta,S^*)$ is called, and it returns **true** at Line 2. It follows that $\mathsf{Test}_{\mathcal{P}+kv}(G,\epsilon,\delta,\emptyset)$ also returns **true**.

Suppose $\mathsf{Test}_{\mathcal{P}}$ rejects G and we do not return **true** at Line 2. Then, since $G \setminus S \in \mathcal{P}+kv$ and $G \setminus S$ is $\frac{\epsilon}{2}$-far from $\mathcal{P}$ with respect to the number of edges in G, $\mathsf{Detect}_{\mathcal{P}}$ finds a witness $(G \setminus S)|_U \notin \mathcal{P}$ for some $U \subseteq V$ with $|U| \le \ell$. Since we must remove at least one vertex from $(G \setminus S)|_U$ to make G satisfy $\mathcal{P}$, there exists some $v \in U$ with $v \in S^* \setminus S$. It follows that $\mathsf{Test}_{\mathcal{P}+kv}(G,\epsilon,\delta,S \cup \{v\})$ is called at Line 5.

Case 2. Suppose G is ϵ-far from $\mathcal{P}+kv$. We consider the case that $\mathsf{Test}_{\mathcal{P}+kv}(G,\epsilon,\delta,S)$ is called with a set of vertices $|S|=k$ after k recursive calls. Note that $G \setminus S$ is still ϵ-far from $\mathcal{P}$ since G is ϵ-far from $\mathcal{P}+kv$. Thus, the tester at Line 2 does not accept, and we return **false** at Line 7 or Line 1 in the next recursion. It follows that $\mathsf{Test}_{\mathcal{P}+kv}(G,\epsilon,\delta,\emptyset)$ also returns **false**. □

Suppose that $\mathsf{Detect}_{\mathcal{P}}(G,\epsilon,\delta,S)$ is an (ϵ,δ)-detector for $\mathcal{P}$ in $G \setminus S$ that works in general. Then we do not need tolerant testers since we can simply run the detector to find witnesses. That is, we remove Line 2 and we return **true** if the detector at Line 3 does not find a witness.

COROLLARY 3.2. *Let $\mathcal{P}$ be a hereditary property and $k \ge 0$ be an integer. Let $\mathsf{Detect}_{\mathcal{P}}(G,\epsilon,\delta,S)$ be an (ϵ,δ)-detector for $\mathcal{P}$ in $G \setminus S$ with query complexity $q(n,\epsilon,\delta,|S|)$ and the witness size $\ell(n,\epsilon,|S|)$. Then, there is an (ϵ,δ)-tester for $\mathcal{P}+kv$ with query complexity $q(n,\epsilon,\frac{\delta}{\ell^k},k)\cdot\ell^{k+1}$, where $\ell=\ell(n,\epsilon,k)$.*

Simulating algorithms on induced subgraphs.

Given an oracle for a graph G and a set S of k vertices, we often want to run algorithms on the induced subgraph $G \setminus S$. For example, given a tester for a property $\mathcal{P}$, we want to transform it to a tester for $\mathcal{P}$ in $G \setminus S$. Some algorithms only use the oracle to sample neighbors of vertices uniformly at random, defined as follows. and we show that such algorithms can be easily transformed to algorithms for induced subgraphs. We define *random neighbor queries* as follows.

- Random neighbor queries: Given a vertex v, the oracle returns a random neighbor of v if it exists and returns $\perp$ otherwise.

Random neighbor queries can be simulated easily in $G \setminus S$.

LEMMA 3.3. *Given a set S of k vertices, we can simulate a random neighbor query in $G \setminus S$ with expected query complexity $O(k)$.*

PROOF. Let v be the vertex we are concerned with. We first obtain the degree $d_G(v)$ using a degree query. We have two cases depending on $d_G(v)$.

- Suppose $d_G(v) \leq k$. We first get all the neighbors $N_G(v)$ of v, and we return a random vertex from $U \setminus S$ if $|U \setminus S| > 0$ and return $\perp$ otherwise.
- Suppose $d_G(v) > k$. We repeat the following procedure until we return a vertex: Pick a random neighbor u of v in G, and return u if $u \notin S$.

It is clear that, when the algorithm above terminates, it returns a random neighbor of v in $G \setminus S$ if a neighbor exists, and it returns $\perp$ otherwise.

In the former case, the query complexity is $1 + k = O(k)$. In the latter case, since $d_G(v) > k$ and $|S| \leq k$, the probability that we find a vertex $u \notin S$ is at least $1/k$. Thus, the expected query complexity is also at most $1 + k = O(k)$. □

LEMMA 3.4. *Let $\mathcal{A}$ be an algorithm with query complexity q that only uses random vertex queries and random neighbor queries. Then, for any $\eta > 0$ and a set S of k vertices, with probability at least $1 - \eta$, we can finish running $\mathcal{A}$ on $G \setminus S$ with $O(\frac{kq}{\eta})$ queries.*

PROOF. We simply run $\mathcal{A}$ on $G \setminus S$. A random vertex query on $G \setminus S$ is exactly a random vertex query on G. Using Lemma 3.3, a random neighbor query on $G \setminus S$ can be simulated using random neighbor queries on G with expected query complexity $O(k)$. From Markov's inequality, we finish running $\mathcal{A}$ with query complexity $O(\frac{kq}{\eta})$ with probability at least $1 - \eta$. □

3.2 Feedback Vertex Set

A *feedback vertex set* of a graph $G = (V, E)$ is a set of vertices S such that $G \setminus S$ is a forest. In this subsection, we give a constant-query tester for k-Feedback Vertex Set, that is, the property of having a feedback vertex set of size at most k. Let $\mathcal{P}_{\text{forest}}$ be the property of being a forest. Then, a graph G has a feedback vertex set of size at most k if and only if $G \in \mathcal{P}_{\text{forest}} + kv$. We give a tolerant tester for $\mathcal{P}_{\text{forest}}$ in subgraphs and then a detector for $\mathcal{P}_{\text{forest}}$ in subgraphs under $\mathcal{P}_{\text{forest}} + kv$. Then, we obtain a tester for $\mathcal{P}_{\text{forest}} + kv$ from Theorem 3.1.

A tolerant tester for the property of being a forest.

For a graph $G = (V, E)$ with n vertices, m edges, and c connected components, we define $\rho(G) = m - n + c$. It is easy to observe that the distance to $\mathcal{P}_{\text{forest}}$ is precisely $\rho(G)/m$. Thus, we can obtain a tolerant tester for $\mathcal{P}_{\text{forest}}$ just by estimating $\rho(G)$. Since we want a tolerant tester for $\mathcal{P}_{\text{forest}}$ in subgraphs, we need to design algorithms that approximate the number of edges and the number of connected components in subgraphs.

LEMMA 3.5. *There is a $(1, \epsilon m, \delta)$-approximation algorithm for the number of edges in $G \setminus S$ with query complexity $O(\frac{1}{\epsilon^2} \log \frac{1}{\delta})$.*

PROOF. Let F be a multiset of $\Theta(\frac{1}{\epsilon^2} \log \frac{1}{\delta})$ edges obtained by using random edge queries. Then, we return $\frac{m}{|F|} \cdot |\{e \in F \mid e \text{ is not incident to } S\}| - \frac{\epsilon m}{2}$. From Hoeffding's inequality, the algorithm is indeed a $(1, \epsilon m, \delta)$-approximation algorithm with query complexity $O(\frac{1}{\epsilon^2} \log \frac{1}{\delta})$. □

We now turn to estimating the number of connected components. An approximation algorithm for the number of connected components already exists [9]. However, what we want here is an approximation algorithm in subgraphs. For a graph G and a vertex v in G, let $\gamma_G(v)$ be the size of the connected component v belongs to. Note that the number of connected components in G is $\sum_{v \in V} \frac{1}{\gamma_G(v)}$. Since we cannot compute $\gamma(v)$ in constant time, for an integer $\tau \geq 0$, we define an approximation $\gamma_G^\tau(v)$ to $\gamma_G(v)$ as $\gamma_G^\tau(v) = \gamma_G(v)$ if $\gamma_G(v) \leq \tau$ and $\gamma_G^\tau(v) = \infty$ otherwise.

LEMMA 3.6. *We can compute $\gamma_{G \setminus S}^\tau(v)$ with query complexity $O(\tau(\tau + |S|))$.*

PROOF. Using the oracle for G, we simulate a breadth first search in $G \setminus S$ from v until we reach more than τ vertices, and count the number of vertices in the connected component to compute $\gamma_{G \setminus S}^\tau(v)$. During the process, if we encounter a vertex with degree more than $\tau + |S|$, then we can conclude that $\gamma_{G \setminus S}^\tau(v) = \infty$ since the input graph is simple. Otherwise, we can obtain neighbors of v in $G \setminus S$ by using at most $\tau + |S|$ neighbor queries. The total query complexity is $O(\tau(\tau + |S|))$. □

LEMMA 3.7. *There is a $(1, \epsilon n, \delta)$-approximation algorithm to the number of connected components in $G \setminus S$ with query complexity $O(\frac{|S|}{\epsilon^4} \log \frac{1}{\delta})$.*

PROOF. We set $\tau = \frac{2}{\epsilon}$. Let T be a multiset of $t = \Theta(\frac{1}{\epsilon^2} \log \frac{1}{\delta})$ vertices chosen uniformly at random. For each vertex $v \in T$, we compute $\gamma_{G \setminus S}^\tau(v)$ using Lemma 3.6. Then, we return $\widetilde{c} = \frac{n}{t} \sum_{v \in T} \frac{1}{\gamma_{G \setminus S}^\tau(v)} - \frac{\epsilon n}{4}$. The query complexity is as stated.

Recall that the number of connected components in $G \setminus S$ is $c = \sum_{v \in V} \frac{1}{\gamma_{G \setminus S}(v)}$. Then, the value $\overline{c} = \sum_{v \in V} \frac{1}{\gamma_{G \setminus S}^\tau(v)}$ is a $(1, \frac{\epsilon n}{2})$-approximation to c since there are at most $\frac{\epsilon n}{2}$ connected components of size more than τ. Since the value $\frac{1}{\gamma_{G \setminus S}^\tau(v)}$ is between 0 and 1, from Hoeffding's inequality, the value $\widetilde{c}$ is a $(1, \frac{\epsilon n}{2})$-approximation to $\overline{c}$ with probability at least $1 - \delta$. It follows that $\widetilde{c}$ is a $(1, \epsilon n)$-approximation to c with probability at least $1 - \delta$. □

LEMMA 3.8. *There is an $(\epsilon_1, \epsilon_2, \delta)$-tester for $\mathcal{P}_{\text{forest}}$ in $G \setminus S$ with query complexity $O(\frac{|S|}{(\epsilon_2 - \epsilon_1)^4} \log \frac{1}{\delta})$.*

PROOF. Let m' and c' be the number of edges and connected components in $G \setminus S$, respectively. We set $\gamma = \epsilon_2 - \epsilon_1$. Let $\widetilde{m}$ and $\widetilde{c}$ be the output obtained by running the algorithm in Lemma 3.5 and the algorithm in Lemma 3.7, respectively, with an error parameter $\frac{\gamma}{4}$ and a confidence parameter $\frac{\delta}{2}$. Then, we accept if $\widetilde{m} - n + \widetilde{c} \leq \epsilon_1 m + \frac{\gamma m}{4}$ and reject otherwise. The query complexity is as stated.

From the union bound, with probability at least $1 - \delta$, it simultaneously holds that $\widetilde{m}$ is a $(1, \frac{\epsilon m}{4})$-approximation to

m' and $\widetilde{c}$ is a $(1, \frac{\epsilon n}{4})$-approximation to c'. If $G \setminus S$ is ϵ_1-close to $\mathcal{P}_{\text{forest}}$, then $\widetilde{m} - n + \widetilde{c} \leq m' - n + c' = \epsilon_1 m$ and we accept. If $G \setminus S$ is ϵ_2-far from being a forest, then $\widetilde{m} - n + \widetilde{c} \geq m' - \frac{\gamma m}{4} - n + c' - \frac{\gamma n}{4} \geq m' - n + c' - \frac{\gamma m}{2} \geq \epsilon_2 m - \frac{\gamma m}{2}$, and we reject. □

A detector for the property of being a forest.

Now, we give a constant-query detector for $\mathcal{P}_{\text{forest}}$ in subgraphs under $\mathcal{P}_{\text{forest}} + kv$ whose witness size is constant. Our detector will output a cycle (more precisely, an induced subgraph with a cycle if we follow the definition of detectors) as the witness that the input (sub)graph is not a forest. We note that no such detector exists in general since we can construct an expander that is ϵ-far from $\mathcal{P}_{\text{forest}}$ whereas its girth is $\Omega(\log n)$. However, we can overcome this issue by assuming that input graphs satisfy $\mathcal{P}_{\text{forest}} + kv$.

It is known that, for any minor-closed property $\mathcal{P}$, if a graph satisfies $\mathcal{P}$ and is ϵ-far from being bipartite, then we can find an odd-cycle in constant time with high probability [10]. Just by ignoring parities of cycles in the proof, we have the following. We note that its query complexity is not explicitly given in [10].

LEMMA 3.9 ([10]). *Let $\mathcal{P}$ be a minor-closed property. There is an (ϵ, δ)-detector for $\mathcal{P}_{\text{forest}}$ under $\mathcal{P}$ with query complexity $q_{3.9}(\epsilon, \delta, \mathcal{P})$ whose witness is a cycle of length at most $\ell_{3.9}(\epsilon, \mathcal{P})$. Furthermore, the detector only uses random vertex queries and random neighbor queries.* □

LEMMA 3.10. *There is an (ϵ, δ)-detector for the property $\mathcal{P}_{\text{forest}}$ in $G \setminus S$ under $\mathcal{P}_{\text{forest}} + kv$ with query complexity $q_{3.10}(\epsilon, \delta, k, |S|)$ and the witness size $\ell_{3.10}(\epsilon, k)$.*

PROOF. Note that $\mathcal{P}_{\text{forest}} + kv$ is a minor-closed property. From Lemma 3.9, we have an $(\epsilon, \frac{\delta}{2})$-detector for $\mathcal{P}_{\text{forest}}$ under $\mathcal{P}_{\text{forest}} + kv$ that only uses random vertex queries and random neighbor queries with query complexity $q_{3.9}(\epsilon, \delta, \mathcal{P}_{\text{forest}} + kv)$. From Lemma 3.4, we obtain an $(\epsilon, \frac{\delta}{2})$-detector for $\mathcal{P}_{\text{forest}}$ in $G \setminus S$ under $\mathcal{P}_{\text{forest}} + kv$ that, with probability at least $1 - \frac{\delta}{2}$, terminates within $q_{3.9}(\epsilon, \delta, \mathcal{P}_{\text{forest}} + kv)\frac{2|S|}{\delta}$ queries. It means that the detector is an (ϵ, δ)-detector for $\mathcal{P}_{\text{forest}}$ in $G \setminus S$ under $\mathcal{P}_{\text{forest}} + kv$ with query complexity $q_{3.9}(\epsilon, \delta, \mathcal{P}_{\text{forest}} + kv)\frac{2|S|}{\delta}$. (we can simply stop the algorithm if the number of queries becomes too large.) The witness size is $\ell_{3.9}(\epsilon, \mathcal{P}_{\text{forest}} + kv)$. □

THEOREM 3.11. *There is an (ϵ, δ)-tester for k-Feedback Vertex Set with query complexity $q_{3.11}(\epsilon, \delta, k)$.*

PROOF. The theorem follows by instantiating Theorem 3.1 with Lemma 3.8 and Lemma 3.10. □

3.3 Vertex Cover

Let $\mathcal{P}_{\text{empty}}$ be the property of having no edge. Then, a graph has a vertex cover of size at most k if and only if it satisfies $\mathcal{P}_{\text{empty}} + kv$. The following lemma gives a detector for $\mathcal{P}_{\text{empty}}$.

LEMMA 3.12. *There is a one-sided error (ϵ, δ)-detector for $\mathcal{P}_{\text{empty}}$ in subgraphs with query complexity $O(\frac{1}{\epsilon^2} \log \frac{1}{\delta})$ and the witness size 2.*

PROOF. We first describe our algorithm $\mathcal{A}$. Let $\widetilde{m}$ be the output by the algorithm given in Lemma 3.5 with an error parameter $\epsilon/2$ and a confidence parameter δ. Then, we accept the input graph G if $\widetilde{m} \leq 0$ and reject otherwise. The query complexity is clearly as stated.

Suppose $G \setminus S$ satisfies $\mathcal{P}_{\text{empty}}$. Seeing the algorithm in Lemma 3.5, we always have $\widetilde{m} \leq 0$ when $G \setminus S$ has no edge. Thus, $\mathcal{A}$ always accepts.

Suppose $G \setminus S$ is ϵ-far from $\mathcal{P}_{\text{empty}}$. Then, $|E(G \setminus S)| \geq \epsilon m$ holds. Thus, with probability at least $1 - \delta$, we have $\widetilde{m} \geq \epsilon m - \frac{\epsilon m}{2} \geq \frac{\epsilon m}{2}$ and $\mathcal{A}$ rejects. Since the algorithm in Lemma 3.5 always finds an edge when it outputs a positive value, $\mathcal{A}$ is indeed a detector. □

Since the detector above works for general graphs, we can use it also as a tester. Instantiating Corollary 3.2 with the detector in Lemma 3.12, we have the following.

THEOREM 3.13. *There is an (ϵ, δ)-tester for k-Vertex Cover with query complexity $O(\frac{2^k}{\epsilon^2} \log \frac{1}{\delta})$.* □

3.4 Odd cycle transversal

An *odd cycle transversal* of a graph $G = (V, E)$ is a set of vertices $S \subseteq V$ such that $G \setminus S$ is bipartite. Let $\mathcal{P}_{\text{bipartite}}$ be the property of being bipartite. Then, it is clear that a graph has an odd cycle transversal of size at most k if and only if G satisfies $\mathcal{P}_{\text{bipartite}} + kv$. We use the following detector for $\mathcal{P}_{\text{bipartite}}$.

LEMMA 3.14 ([17]). *There is an (ϵ, δ)-detector for bipartiteness with query complexity $O(\sqrt{n} \cdot \text{poly}(\frac{\log n}{\epsilon}) \log \frac{1}{\delta})$ that outputs an odd-cycle of length $\text{poly}(\frac{\log n}{\epsilon})$ as its witness. Furthermore, the detector only uses random vertex queries and random neighbor queries.* □

From Lemma 3.4, we obtain a detector for $\mathcal{P}_{\text{bipartite}}$ in subgraphs.

COROLLARY 3.15. *There is an (ϵ, δ)-detector for $\mathcal{P}_{\text{bipartite}}$ in $G \setminus S$ with query complexity $\widetilde{O}(\sqrt{n}\, \text{poly}(\frac{\log n}{\epsilon}) \cdot \frac{|S|}{\delta} \log \frac{1}{\delta})$ that outputs an odd-cycle of length $\text{poly}(\frac{\log n}{\epsilon})$ as its witness.* □

Since the detector above works for general graphs, we can use it also as a tester. Instantiating Corollary 3.2 with the detector in Corollary 3.15, we have the following.

THEOREM 3.16. *There is an (ϵ, δ)-tester for k-Odd Cycle Transversal with query complexity $O(\sqrt{n} \log^k n \cdot q_{3.16}(\epsilon, \delta, k))$.* □

3.5 Multicut

Let $G = (V, E)$ be a graph and $T = \{(s_1, t_1), \ldots, (s_\ell, t_\ell)\}$ be a set of terminal pairs in G. Then, the *multicut* with respect to T is a set of edges $F \subseteq E$ such that no terminal pair is connected in $G \setminus F$. We show that we can test whether the minimum size of a multicut is at most k in constant time assuming that the terminal pairs are given in advance.

The following lemma connects the minimum size of a multicut and the maximum number of edge disjoint paths between terminal pairs.

LEMMA 3.17 ([20]). *Let G be a graph with m edges and ℓ terminal pairs. If a minimum multicut has size at least ϵm, then there exists an $\frac{\epsilon^2 m}{\log \ell}$ edge-disjoint paths between terminal pairs.* □

When there are many edge-disjoint paths between two vertices, we can easily move from one to the other by random walk, as shown in the following lemma.

LEMMA 3.18 ([8]). *If a graph G with m edges contains p edge-disjoint (s,t)-paths of length at most ℓ, then the expected number of steps in a random walk that starts at s and ends upon first reaching t is at most $\frac{2ml}{p}$.* □

LEMMA 3.19. *Let G be a graph with ℓ terminal pairs (s_1, t_1), ..., (s_ℓ, t_ℓ) and the minimum size of a multicut at least ϵm. Then, with probability at least $1-\delta$, we can find a path of length at most $O(\frac{\ell^2 \log^2 \ell}{\epsilon^4 \delta})$ between some terminal pair with query complexity $O(\frac{\ell^3 \log^2 \ell}{\epsilon^4 \delta})$.*

PROOF. For each terminal s_i ($i \in [\ell]$), we perform a random walk of length $O(\frac{\ell^2 \log^2 \ell}{\epsilon^4 \delta})$ from s_i. If we have found a path from s_i to t_i, then we return the path. The length of returned paths and the query complexity is as stated.

We check the correctness of the algorithm. From Lemma 3.17, we have $\frac{\epsilon^2 m}{\log \ell}$ edge-disjoint paths between terminal pairs. It follows that there exists some $j \in [\ell]$ such that there are $\frac{\epsilon^2 m}{\ell \log \ell}$ edge-disjoint paths between s_j and t_j. Since the number of edges in G is m, we have at least $\frac{\epsilon^2 m}{2\ell \log \ell}$ edge-disjoint paths of length at most $\frac{2\ell \log \ell}{\epsilon^2}$ between s_j and t_j. From Lemma 3.18, the expected length of a random walk that starts at s_j and ends upon first reaching t_j is $\frac{8\ell^2 \log^2 \ell}{\epsilon^4}$. Thus, from Markov's inequality, we reach t_i in $\frac{8\ell^2 \log^2 \ell}{\epsilon^4 \delta}$ steps with probability at least $1-\delta$. □

We note that a similar argument already appeared in [26]. Since the detector above works for general graphs, we can use it also as a tester. Though Corollary 3.2 refers to testers for $\mathcal{P} + kv$, it can be easily modified to give a tester for $\mathcal{P} + ke$. Thus, combining this edge version of Corollary 3.2 and Lemma 3.19, we have the following.

THEOREM 3.20. *There is an (ϵ, δ)-tester for k-Multicut with query complexity $(\frac{\ell}{\epsilon\delta})^{O(k)}$ where ℓ is the number of terminal pairs.*

4. K-PATH-FREENESS

In this section, we give a tester for k-Path-Free. Recall that we want to test whether the input graph has *no* path of length k. The key component in our algorithm is a (k-step) *random walk* defined as follows. First, we pick an edge e using a random edge query and pick an end-point x_0 of e uniformly at random. Starting with the vertex x_0, we keep moving to an adjacent vertex k times using random neighbor queries. We stress again that we do not choose the starting vertex uniformly at random since it will take $\Omega(\sqrt{n})$ queries even to find a 1-path, that is, an edge.

In each step of the random walk, we have up to n possibilities for the next vertex. Color coding [5] lets us overcome this issue, which is also useful here. Note that we use this technique only for analysis. We call a graph *k-colored* if each vertex is assigned a value in $\{0, \ldots, k\}$ (Thus, we actually use $k+1$ colors). Let $\langle x_0, x_1, \ldots, x_k \rangle$ be a sequence of vertices that forms a k-path. Then, we call the path *colorful* if x_i has the i-th color for each $i \in \{0, \ldots, k\}$. We say that a colored graph G' is *obtained from* G when the graph G is exactly the graph G' if we ignore colors. The following claim is immediate since a colorful k-path in G' forms a k-path in G.

CLAIM 4.1. *Let G' be a k-colored graph obtained from G. The probability that a k-step random walk finds a k-path in G is as much as the probability that it finds a colorful k-path in G'.* □

Thus, our goal from now on is showing that there is a colored graph G' obtained from G such that a random walk finds a colorful k-path in G' with high probability.

LEMMA 4.2. *Let G be a graph ϵ-far from k-Path-Free. Then, there exists a k-colored graph G' obtained from G such that G' contains at least $\frac{2\epsilon m}{k(k+1)^{k+1}}$ edge-disjoint colorful k-paths.*

PROOF. Let P be a maximal set of edge-disjoint k-paths in G. Since we can remove all k-paths in G by removing $k|P|$ edges, we must have $|P| \geq \frac{\epsilon m}{k}$.

Consider a random coloring of vertices in G using $k+1$ colors. Since each k-path in P becomes colorful with probability $\frac{2}{(k+1)^{k+1}}$, the expected number of colorful k-paths in the resulting graph is $\frac{2\epsilon m}{k(k+1)^{k+1}}$. Thus, there exists a coloring that creates at least $\frac{2\epsilon m}{k(k+1)^{k+1}}$ many edge-disjoint colorful k-paths. □

Let G be a (colored) graph and $\mathcal{P}$ be a set of paths in G. we denote by $G|_{\mathcal{P}}$ the graph induced by $\mathcal{P}$. That is, $G|_{\mathcal{P}} = (V, E_{\mathcal{P}})$, where $E_{\mathcal{P}}$ is the set of edges from the paths in $\mathcal{P}$. The following lemma states that in order to show that a k-step random walk finds a colorful k-path in a colored graph G with a set $\mathcal{P}$ of edge-disjoint colorful k-paths, it suffices to show that the random walk finds a colorful k-path in $G|_{\mathcal{P}}$. A similar reasoning appeared in [10], but our proof is more delicate since we need to deal with random edge queries instead of random vertex queries as in [10].

LEMMA 4.3. *Let $G = (V, E)$ be a k-colored graph with a set $\mathcal{P}^*$ of at least αm ($\alpha < 1$) edge-disjoint colorful k-paths. Then, there is a function $\zeta(\alpha, k) = k\alpha^{O(k)}$ and a subset $\mathcal{P}$ of $\mathcal{P}^*$ of size at least $\frac{\alpha m}{2}$ such that, if the probability that a k-step random walk in $G|_{\mathcal{P}}$ finds a colorful k-path in $G|_{\mathcal{P}}$ is p, then the probability that a k-step random walk finds a colorful k-path in G is at least $\zeta \cdot p$.*

PROOF. To construct the subset $\mathcal{P}$, we first delete some k-paths from $\mathcal{P}^*$. The process of deleting the k-paths is based on the comparison of the original degree of the vertices with the current degree in $G|_{\mathcal{P}^*}$. To implement this scheme, we use the term *current degree* of a vertex v to denote its current degree in the graph $G|_{\mathcal{P}^*}$ induced by the current set of k-paths $\mathcal{P}^*$.

We repeat the following procedure as long as possible: if there is a vertex $v \in V$ with current degree in $G|_{\mathcal{P}^*}$ at most $\frac{1}{4}\alpha d_G(v)$, then we delete from $\mathcal{P}^*$ all k-paths going through v in $\mathcal{P}^*$. To estimate the number of deleted k-paths, we charge to v the number of deleted k-paths in each such operation.

Let $\mathcal{P}$ be the remaining set of k-paths from $\mathcal{P}^*$. Observe that each $v \in V$ can be processed above at most once. Indeed, once v has been used, it becomes isolated and hence it is not used again. Therefore, at most $\frac{1}{4}\alpha d_G(v)$ k-paths from $\mathcal{P}$ can be charged to any single vertex. This, together with the inequality $\sum_{v \in V} d_G(v) \leq 2m$, implies that the total number of k-paths removed from $\mathcal{P}^*$ is upper bounded by $\sum_{v \in V} \frac{1}{4}\alpha d_G(v) \leq \frac{1}{2}\alpha m$. Since $|\mathcal{P}^*| \geq \alpha m$, we conclude that $|\mathcal{P}| \geq |\mathcal{P}^*| - \frac{1}{2}\alpha m \geq \frac{1}{2}\alpha m$.

We have constructed a subset $\mathcal{P}$ of $\mathcal{P}^*$ with size at least $\frac{1}{2}\alpha m$ such that for every vertex $v \in V$, either v is isolated in $G|_{\mathcal{P}}$ or its degree is greater than $\frac{1}{4}\alpha d_G(v)$. We now use this property to show that if the probability that a k-step random walk in $G|_{\mathcal{P}}$ finds a colorful k-path is p, then a k-step random walk in G finds a colorful k-path with probability at least $\zeta \cdot p$, for appropriately chosen $\zeta = \zeta(\alpha, k)$. Then, we have the lemma.

Let us consider a fixed sequence of $k+1$ vertices $P = \langle x_0, x_1, ..., x_k \rangle$ in $G|_{\mathcal{P}}$ with $(x_i, x_{i+1}) \in E_{\mathcal{P}}, 0 \le i \le l - 1$, that forms a colorful k-path. Our claim is that, if the probability of this fixed sequence to be chosen as a k-step random walk in $G|_{\mathcal{P}}$ is p then it is at least $\zeta \cdot p$ in G.

The number of edges m' in $G|_{\mathcal{P}}$ satisfies that $m' \ge \frac{1}{2}\alpha k m$ since $|\mathcal{P}| \ge \frac{1}{2}\alpha m$ holds. Then, the probability that we choose x_0 as the starting vertex of a random walk in $G|_{\mathcal{P}}$ is $\frac{d_{G|_{\mathcal{P}}}(x_0)}{2m'} \le \frac{d_G(x_0)}{\alpha k m} = \frac{2}{\alpha k} \cdot \frac{d_G(x_0)}{2m}$. Therefore, when we choose x_0 as the starting vertex in G, we choose x_0 with probability at least $\frac{\alpha k}{2}$ times the probability that we choose x_0 in $G|_{\mathcal{P}}$.

Since x_0 cannot be isolated in $G|_{\mathcal{P}}$ (there is an edge (x_0, x_1)), we must have $d_{G|_{\mathcal{P}}}(x_0) \ge \frac{1}{4}\alpha d_G(x_0)$. Thus, when the random walk in G chooses a neighbor of x_0, it chooses x_1 with probability at least $\frac{\alpha}{4}$ times the probability that the random walk in $G|_{\mathcal{P}}$ chooses x_1. The same argument can be used to show that, if the random walk in G has chosen any vertex x_i, then it also chooses x_{i+1} with the probability at least $\frac{\alpha}{4}$ times the respective probability for the random walk in $G|_{\mathcal{P}}$. Therefore, if the random walk in $G_{\mathcal{P}}$ is chosen with probability p then the probability of choosing the same random walk in G is at least $\frac{\alpha k}{2}\left(\frac{\alpha}{4}\right)^k p$. Summing up over all sequences of $k+1$ vertices $\langle x_0, x_1, ..., x_k\rangle$ in $G|_{\mathcal{P}}$ with $(x_i, x_{i+1}) \in E_{\mathcal{P}}, 0 \le i \le k-1$ forming a colorful k-path, we obtain the claim with $\zeta = \frac{\alpha k}{2}\left(\frac{\alpha}{4}\right)^k = k\alpha^{O(k)}$. □

Now, we show that a k-step random walk finds a colorful k-path in a graph induced by colorful k-paths with high probability.

LEMMA 4.4. *Let G be a k-colored graph induced by a set $\mathcal{P}$ of edge-disjoint colorful k-paths. A k-step random walk on G finds a colorful k-path with probability at least $\frac{1}{k2^k}$.*

PROOF. Since G is a graph induced by $\mathcal{P}$, with probability $\frac{1}{k}$, we sample an edge with an end x_0 that is a starting vertex of some colorful k-path. Then, with probability $\frac{1}{2k}$, we choose x_0 as the starting vertex of a random walk.

Note that x_0 has color 0, the degree of x_0 is positive, and x_0 is adjacent to only vertices with color 1 since G is a graph induced by $\mathcal{P}$. Thus, after a single step of random walk, we move to a vertex x_1 with color 1 with probability one. Again, we note that the degree of x_1 is positive (since there is the edge (x_0, x_1)) and half of vertices adjacent to x_1 have color 0 and the other half of vertices adjacent to x_1 have color 2 since G is a graph induced by $\mathcal{P}$. Thus, after a single step of random walk, we move to a vertex x_2 with color 2 with probability half. Using the same argument, we conclude that we find a colorful k-path with probability at least $\frac{1}{2k} \cdot \frac{1}{2^{k-1}} = \frac{1}{k2^k}$. □

THEOREM 4.5. *There is a one-sided error (ϵ, δ)-tester for* k-Path-Free *with $(\frac{k}{\epsilon})^{O(k^2)} O(\log \frac{1}{\delta})$ queries.*

PROOF. We perform a k-step random walk $(\frac{k}{\epsilon})^{O(k^2)} \log \frac{1}{\delta}$ times, and we reject if we find a k-path and accept otherwise. It is indeed a one-sided error tester and the query complexity is as stated.

We show that the algorithm is indeed an (ϵ, δ)-tester. Let G be a graph ϵ-far from having no k-path. From Lemma 4.2, there exists a k-colored graph G' obtained from G with a set $\mathcal{P}$ of αm edge-disjoint colorful k-paths, where $\alpha = \frac{2\epsilon}{k(k+1)^{k+1}}$. From Lemma 4.3, there exists $\zeta = k\alpha^{O(k)}$ and a subset $\mathcal{P}'$ of $\mathcal{P}$ such that the probability that a random walk finds a colorful k-path in G' is at least ζ times the probability that a random walk finds a colorful k-path in $G'|_{\mathcal{P}'}$. However, the latter probability is at least $\frac{1}{k2^k}$ from Lemma 4.4. Thus, the former probability is at least $\zeta \cdot \frac{1}{k2^k} = \alpha^{O(k)}$. From Claim 4.1, the probability that a random walk finds a k-path in G is also at least $\alpha^{O(k)}$.

Thus, by performing random walks $(\frac{1}{\alpha})^{\Theta(k)} O(\log \frac{1}{\delta}) = (\frac{k}{\epsilon})^{O(k^2)} O(\log \frac{1}{\delta})$ times, we will find a k-path in G with probability at least $1 - \delta$. □

5. DOMINATING SET

A *dominating set* of a graph $G = (V, E)$ is a set of vertices S such that every vertex is adjacent to some vertex in S or is in S. In this section, we give a tester for k-Dominating Set, that is, the property of having a dominating set of size at most k. We assume $k \ge 1$ since the case $k = 0$ is trivial. We also assume $k \le \frac{n}{2}$ since otherwise we can exactly solve the problem with $O(k)$ queries.

For a set of vertices $S \subseteq V$, we call a vertex $v \in V$ *S-dominated* if v is adjacent to some vertex in S or v is in S, and we call v *non-S-dominated* otherwise. We call a graph G *S-dominated* if every vertex is S-dominated, that is, S is a dominating set.

The following lemma eliminates too sparse graphs and too dense graphs.

LEMMA 5.1. *Let $k \ge 1$. Any graph with less than $n - k$ edges cannot have a dominating set of size at most k. Also, any graph with more than $\frac{n}{\epsilon}$ edges is ϵ-close to having a dominating set of size at most k.*

PROOF. The first claim is trivial, and we show the second claim. Let v be some vertex in G. We add an edge to v from each vertex other than v, Then, the resulting graph has a dominating set $\{v\}$. Since we added $n-1$ edges and the graph has more than $\frac{n}{\epsilon}$ edges, the graph is ϵ-close to having a dominating set of size 1. □

LEMMA 5.2. *If a graph G is ϵ-far from being S-dominated for a set of vertices S with $|S| \ge 1$, then there are at least ϵm non-S-dominated vertices.*

PROOF. Suppose that we have at most ϵm non-S-dominated vertices. Then, by adding at most ϵm edges to some vertex in S, the resulting graph becomes S-dominated, which is contradiction. □

As we have used a detector for $\mathcal{P}$ in $G \setminus S$ to design a tester for $\mathcal{P} + kv$ in Section 3, in order to design a tester for k-Dominating Set, we use the following algorithm that tests whether a vertex set S is a dominating set.

LEMMA 5.3. *Let $k \ge 1$. Assume that the number of edges m satisfies $n - k \le m \le \frac{n}{\epsilon}$. Then, there is a one-sided error (ϵ, δ)-tester for the property of being S-dominated with query complexity $O(\frac{1}{\epsilon^3} \log \frac{1}{\delta})$. Furthermore, when the algorithm rejects, it outputs a non-S-dominated vertex with degree at most $O(\frac{1}{\epsilon^2})$.*

PROOF. Let T be a set of $t = \Theta(\frac{1}{\epsilon}\log\frac{1}{\delta})$ vertices chosen uniformly at random. For each vertex $v \in T$ with degree at most $\frac{8}{\epsilon^2}$, we check whether v is S-dominated. We reject if there is a non-S-dominated vertex and accept otherwise. The query complexity is immediate, and it is clear that the algorithm above can output a non-S-dominated vertex with degree $O(\frac{1}{\epsilon^2})$ when it rejects.

Now, we show that the algorithm is indeed an (ϵ, δ)-tester. Since the average degree is at most $\frac{2}{\epsilon}$, there are at most $\frac{\epsilon n}{4}$-fraction of vertices with degree more than $\frac{8}{\epsilon^2}$. Since G is ϵ-far from being S-dominated, from Lemma 5.2, there are at least $\epsilon m \geq \epsilon(n-k) \geq \frac{\epsilon n}{2}$ non-S-dominated vertices. Thus, the number of non-S-dominated vertices with degree at most $\frac{8}{\epsilon^2}$ is at least $\frac{\epsilon n}{2} - \frac{\epsilon n}{4} \geq \frac{\epsilon n}{4}$. Then, with probability at least $1-\delta$, such a vertex is contained in T, and we find a non-S-dominated vertex. □

THEOREM 5.4. *There is an (ϵ, δ)-tester for k-Dominating Set with query complexity $(\frac{1}{\epsilon})^{O(k)} O(\log\frac{1}{\delta})$.*

PROOF OF THEOREM 5.4. From Lemma 5.1, we can always reject if $m < n-k$, and we can always accept if $m > \frac{n}{\epsilon}$. Recall that n and m are given to algorithms in advance. Thus, we assume $n-k \leq m \leq \frac{n}{\epsilon}$ holds.

The outline of our algorithm is similar to Algorithm 1. We start with an empty set of vertices S. First, we run the tester given in Lemma 5.3 on $G \setminus S$ with an error parameter ϵ and a confidence parameter $\epsilon^k\delta$. If it accepts, then we accept the graph and terminate. Suppose that the tester rejects with a non-S-dominated vertex v with degree at most $O(\frac{1}{\epsilon^2})$. If $|S| = k$, then we reject the graph and terminate. Otherwise, we guess a vertex u (actually try every vertex) that is contained in the desired dominating set from the set of vertices $\{v\} \cup N_G(v)$. Then, we add the vertex u to S and recurse up to level k.

We omit the proof of correctness of the algorithm since it is almost same as the proof of Theorem 3.1. Since the number of neighbors of u is $O(\frac{1}{\epsilon^2})$, the total query complexity is $O(\frac{1}{\epsilon^3}\log\frac{1}{\epsilon^k\delta}) \cdot O(\frac{1}{\epsilon^2})^k = (\frac{1}{\epsilon})^{O(k)} O(\log\frac{1}{\delta})$. □

6. REFERENCES

[1] N. Alon, E. Fischer, I. Newman, and A. Shapira. A combinatorial characterization of the testable graph properties: It's all about regularity. *SIAM Journal on Computing*, 39:143–167, 2009.

[2] N. Alon, T. Kaufman, M. Krivelevich, and D. Ron. Testing triangle-freeness in general graphs. *SIAM Journal on Discrete Mathematics*, 22(2):786–819, 2008.

[3] N. Alon and A. Shapira. A characterization of the (natural) graph properties testable with one-sided error. *SIAM Journal on Computing*, 37(6):1703–1727, 2008.

[4] N. Alon and A. Shapira. Every monotone graph property is testable. *SIAM Journal on Computing*, 38(2):505–522, 2008.

[5] N. Alon, R. Yuster, and U. Zwick. Color-coding. *Journal of the ACM*, 42(4):844–856, 1995.

[6] I. Ben-Eliezer, T. Kaufman, M. Krivelevich, and D. Ron. Comparing the strength of query types in property testing: the case of testing k-colorability. In *Proc. 19th Annual ACM-SIAM Symposium on Discrete Algorithms (SODA)*, pages 1213–1222, 2008.

[7] I. Benjamini, O. Schramm, and A. Shapira. Every minor-closed property of sparse graphs is testable. *Advances in Mathematics*, 223(6):2200–2218, 2010.

[8] A. Chandra, P. Raghavan, W. Ruzzo, R. Smolensky, and P. Tiwari. The electrical resistance of a graph captures its commute and cover times. *Computational Complexity*, 6(4):312–340, 1996.

[9] B. Chazelle, R. Rubinfeld, and L. Trevisan. Approximating the minimum spanning tree weight in sublinear time. *SIAM Journal on Computing*, 34(6):1370–1379, 2005.

[10] A. Czumaj, M. Monemizadeh, K. Onak, and C. Sohler. Planar graphs: Random walks and bipartiteness testing. In *Proc. 52nd Annual IEEE Symposium on Foundations of Computer Science (FOCS)*, pages 423–432, 2011.

[11] R. Downey and M. Fellows. *Parameterized complexity*, volume 3. Springer, 1999.

[12] O. Goldreich, editor. *Property Testing: Current Research and Surveys*, volume 6390 of *LNCS*. Springer, 2010.

[13] O. Goldreich, S. Goldwasser, and D. Ron. Property testing and its connection to learning and approximation. *Journal of the ACM*, 45(4):653–750, 1998.

[14] O. Goldreich and D. Ron. Property testing in bounded degree graphs. *Algorithmica*, 32(2):302–343, 2002.

[15] O. Goldreich and D. Ron. Approximating average parameters of graphs. *Random Structures & Algorithms*, 32(4):473–493, 2008.

[16] A. Hassidim, J. A. Kelner, H. N. Nguyen, and K. Onak. Local graph partitions for approximation and testing. In *Proc. 50th Annual IEEE Symposium on Foundations of Computer Science (FOCS)*, pages 22–31, 2009.

[17] T. Kaufman, M. Krivelevich, and D. Ron. Tight bounds for testing bipartiteness in general graphs. *SIAM Journal on Computing*, 33(6):1441–1483, 2004.

[18] I. Newman and C. Sohler. Every property of hyperfinite graphs is testable. *SIAM Journal on Computing*, 42(3):1095–1112, 2013.

[19] H. Nguyen and K. Onak. Constant-time approximation algorithms via local improvements. In *Proc. 49th Annual IEEE Symposium on Foundations of Computer Science (FOCS)*, pages 327–336, 2008.

[20] K. Obata. Approximate max-integral-flow/min-multicut theorems. In *Proc. 36th Annual ACM Symposium on Theory of Computing (STOC)*, pages 539–545, 2004.

[21] K. Onak, D. Ron, M. Rosen, and R. Rubinfeld. A near-optimal sublinear-time algorithm for approximating the minimum vertex cover size. In *Proc. 23rd Annual ACM-SIAM Symposium on Discrete Algorithms (SODA)*, pages 1123–1131, 2012.

[22] M. Parnas and D. Ron. Approximating the minimum vertex cover in sublinear time and a connection to distributed algorithms. *Theoretical Computer Science*, 381(1-3):183–196, 2007.

[23] D. Ron. Algorithmic and analysis techniques in property testing. *Foundations and Trends in Theoretical Computer Science*, 5:73–205, 2010.

[24] R. Rubinfeld and A. Shapira. Sublinear time algorithms. *SIAM Journal on Discrete Mathematics*, 25(4):1562–1588, 2011.

[25] E. Szemerédi. Regular partitions of graphs. In *Proc. Colloque Inter. CNRS (J. C. Bermond, J. C. Fournier, M. Las Vergnas and D. Sotteau, eds.)*, pages 399–401, 1978.

[26] Y. Yoshida and Y. Kobayashi. Testing the (s,t)-disconnectivity of graphs and digraphs. *Theoretical Computer Science*, 435(25):98–113, 2012.

[27] Y. Yoshida, M. Yamamoto, and H. Ito. Improved constant-time approximation algorithms for maximum matchings and other optimization problems. *SIAM Journal on Computing*, 41(4):1074–1093, 2012.

Direct Sum Fails for Zero Error Average Communication

Gillat Kol *
School of Mathematics
Institute for Advanced Study
Princeton, USA
gillat.kol@gmail.com

Shay Moran
Department of Computer Science
Technion-IIT
Haifa, Israel
shaymoran1@gmail.com

Amir Shpilka †
Department of Computer Science
Technion-IIT
Haifa, Israel
shpilka@cs.technion.ac.il

Amir Yehudayoff ‡
Department of Mathematics
Technion-IIT
Haifa, Israel
amir.yehudayoff@gmail.com

ABSTRACT

We show that in the model of zero error communication complexity, direct sum fails for average communication complexity as well as for external information cost. Our example also refutes a version of a conjecture by Braverman et al. that in the zero error case amortized communication complexity equals external information cost.

In our examples the underlying distributions do not have full support. One interpretation of a distributions of non full support is as a promise given to the players (the players have a guarantee on their inputs). This brings up the issue of promise versus non-promise problems in this context.

1. INTRODUCTION

1.1 Direct Sum for Zero Error Communication

A *direct sum* problem asks whether solving n independent copies of a given task requires n times the amount of resources needed to solve a single copy. This fundamental question has been studied in many computational models. In the context of communication complexity, direct sum theorems in various settings have been the focus of many works [7, 6, 10, 8, 1, 11, 9]. We study the direct sum problem in the model of communication complexity with zero error.

1.1.1 Average Case Complexity Measures

Since we are interested in computations with zero error, we shall only consider here average case complexity measures. The reason is that worst case communication roughly corresponds to deterministic computation in the zero error case, since by fixing the randomness of a zero error protocol we get a deterministic zero error protocol with the same worst case complexity.

Let π be a communication protocol between two players, one holding an input x and the other y, where (x, y) are drawn from a mutual distribution μ. The protocol π has three average case complexity measures associated with it:

1. *Average communication complexity*, denoted $\mathsf{CC}_\mu^{\mathsf{avg}}(\pi)$: The expected number of bits exchanged by the players while executing π.
2. *External information cost*, denoted $\mathsf{IC}_\mu^{\mathsf{ext}}(\pi)$: The amount of information an observer who watches the execution of π learns about the players' inputs.
3. *Internal information cost*, denoted $\mathsf{IC}_\mu^{\mathsf{int}}(\pi)$: The amount of information the players learn about each other's input while executing π.

We focus on the first two measures, formally defined in Section 2. For a definition of internal information cost see [2]. The following inequality gives an order between the three measures (see Section 3.2 for the proof).

Claim 1. *For every protocol π,*

$$\mathsf{CC}_\mu^{\mathsf{avg}}(\pi) \geq \mathsf{IC}_\mu^{\mathsf{ext}}(\pi) \geq \mathsf{IC}_\mu^{\mathsf{int}}(\pi).$$

There are several possible definitions for the measures defined above. The options relate to randomized versus distributional complexities. A detailed discussion is given in Section 4. The definitions we use are given in Section 2.

For a given function f, a distribution μ and an error parameter $\epsilon \geq 0$, these three measures on protocols induce three measures on f over μ with error ϵ. For example, $\mathsf{CC}_\mu^{\mathsf{avg}}(f, \epsilon)$ is the minimum $\mathsf{CC}_\mu^{\mathsf{avg}}(\pi)$ for a protocol π that computes f with error ϵ over μ. We also discuss two options for the definition of "computes" in Section 4.

---

*This work was done while the author was at the Department of Computer Science, Technion, Haifa, Israel. The research leading to these results has received funding from the European Community's Seventh Framework Programme (FP7/2007-2013) under grant agreement number 257575

†The research leading to these results has received funding from the European Community's Seventh Framework Programme (FP7/2007-2013) under grant agreement number 257575.

‡Horev fellow – supported by the Taub foundation. Research is also supported by ISF and BSF

ITCS'14, January 12–14, 2014, Princeton, New Jersey, USA.

http://dx.doi.org/10.1145/2554797.2554844.

1.1.2 Direct Sum

We are interested in the complexity of computing n independent copies of a function f, that is, of the function $f^n((x_1,\dots,x_n),(y_1,\dots,y_n)) = (f(x_1,y_1),\dots,f(x_n,y_n))$ over the distribution μ^n.

It was shown in [1] that direct sum holds for internal information cost: For every f,μ and $\epsilon \geq 0$,

$$\mathsf{IC}^{\mathsf{int}}_{\mu^n}(f^n,\epsilon) = n\cdot \mathsf{IC}^{\mathsf{int}}_{\mu}(f,\epsilon).$$

Here we show (in a strong sense) that direct sum does *not* hold for average communication and for external information in the zero error case. For this part, we focus on average communication (external information is considered later on). A direct sum theorem for this model would say that if $\mathsf{CC}^{\mathsf{avg}}_{\mu}(f,0) \geq C$ then $\mathsf{CC}^{\mathsf{avg}}_{\mu^n}(f^n,0)$ is at least Cn or $Cn/100$ or even[1] $(C-1)n/100$. We show that this is far from true: For every $C > 0$ there exist a boolean function f and a distribution μ such that $\mathsf{CC}^{\mathsf{avg}}_{\mu}(f,0) \geq C$, but for every n it holds that $\mathsf{CC}^{\mathsf{avg}}_{\mu^n}(f^n,0)$ is at most roughly $C + C2^{-C}n \leq C+n$.

Observe that for "reasonable" computational models, if a function f requires an amount of C resources then f^n requires $\Omega(C+n)$ resources: The reason is that solving n copies is at least as hard as solving a single copy, and outputting the results of the n independent tasks requires at least $\Omega(n)$ resources.

1.2 Zero Error Amortized Cost Versus External Information

Another implication of our construction is the following. The amortized (average case) communication complexity of function f over μ with error $\epsilon \geq 0$ is the per-copy average communication cost, when we solve $n \to \infty$ copies of f simultaneously:

$$\mathsf{AC}^{\mathsf{avg}}_{\mu}(f,\epsilon) \triangleq \lim_{n\to\infty} \frac{\mathsf{CC}^{\mathsf{avg}}_{\mu^n}(f^n,\epsilon)}{n}.$$

Braveman et al. [2, 4] conjecture that in the zero error regime, the amortized communication complexity of a function is exactly captured by its external information complexity.

Conjecture 2 ([2, 4]). *For every function $f : \mathcal{X}\times\mathcal{Y}\to\mathcal{Z}$ and distribution μ over $\mathcal{X}\times\mathcal{Y}$, it holds that*

$$\mathsf{AC}^{\mathsf{avg}}_{\mu}(f,0) = \mathsf{IC}^{\mathsf{ext}}_{\mu}(f,0).$$

Conjecture 2 was proposed as a zero error analog of the fact that, for error $\epsilon > 0$, the internal information cost of a function is equal to its amortized (worst case) communication complexity: $\mathsf{AC}_{\mu}(f,\epsilon) = \mathsf{IC}^{\mathsf{int}}_{\mu}(f,\epsilon)$ [5]. This connection gives an "operational" meaning to the internal information of a function, but fails for $\epsilon = 0$.

The "$\leq$" direction of Conjecture 2 is known to hold [4, 8]. The conjecture is true for product distributions $\mu = \mu_x \times \mu_y$, since then the external and internal information costs coincide. Furthermore, the conjecture was shown to hold for well studied functions, such as the message transmission function $f(x,y) = x$, the bit equality function, and the AND function. Further discussion of the motivation for the conjecture can be found in [2, 4].

[1]This is because in any non trivial case the communication complexity is at least one.

The conjecture has several interpretations, depending on the meaning of "compute" and "average complexity" as discussed in detail in Section 4. With the definitions we use, our example refutes the conjecture.

1.3 Promise Versus Non-Promise

In our example, the measure μ does not have full support (i.e. $\mathrm{supp}(\mu) \neq \mathcal{X}\times\mathcal{Y}$). This seems to be a crucial property of μ in our proof. It, therefore, can still be the case that both direct sum and Conjecture 2 hold for measures of full support.

One way to think of a measure that does not have full support is as a "promise" that is given to the players about their inputs (the inputs are always from support). In this respect, our examples correspond to promise problems, whereas full support measures correspond to non-promise problems. This highlights a (possible) difference between promise and non-promise problems in this context that is worth a further investigation.

1.4 Results

Our main result is a construction of a function f and distribution μ on inputs with high external information and low amortized cost. The function f is the equality function on k-bit strings. The distribution μ puts almost all its weight on the diagonal (i.e., on input pairs with $x = y$). The remaining weight is on input pairs with $x < y$ (when we interpret both x and y as integers).

Theorem 3 (Main). *For every $k \in \mathbb{N}$, there exist a function $f : \{0,1\}^k \times \{0,1\}^k \to \{0,1\}$ and a distribution μ over $\{0,1\}^k \times \{0,1\}^k$ such that for every $n \in \mathbb{N}$,*

$$\mathsf{IC}^{\mathsf{ext}}_{\mu}(f,0) \geq 0.99k, \text{ while } \mathsf{CC}^{\mathsf{avg}}_{\mu^n}(f^n,0) \leq 5k + 10k2^{-k}n.$$

The following two corollaries show two cases where direct sum does not hold. Both corollaries follow from Theorem 3 using Claim 1.

Corollary 4. *For every $k \in \mathbb{N}$, there exist a function $f : \{0,1\}^k \times \{0,1\}^k \to \{0,1\}$ and a distribution μ over $\{0,1\}^k \times \{0,1\}^k$ such that for every $n \in \mathbb{N}$,*

$$\mathsf{CC}^{\mathsf{avg}}_{\mu}(f,0) \geq 0.99k, \text{ while } \mathsf{CC}^{\mathsf{avg}}_{\mu^n}(f^n,0) \leq 5k + 10k2^{-k}n.$$

Corollary 5. *For every $k \in \mathbb{N}$, there exist a function $f : \{0,1\}^k \times \{0,1\}^k \to \{0,1\}$ and a distribution μ over $\{0,1\}^k \times \{0,1\}^k$ such that for every $n \in \mathbb{N}$,*

$$\mathsf{IC}^{\mathsf{ext}}_{\mu}(f,0) \geq 0.99k, \text{ while } \mathsf{IC}^{\mathsf{ext}}_{\mu^n}(f^n,0) \leq 5k + 10k2^{-k}n.$$

Another corollary of Theorem 3 refutes a version of Conjecture 2.

Corollary 6. *For every $\alpha \in (0,1)$, there exist a function $f : \mathcal{X}\times\mathcal{Y}\to\{0,1\}$ and a distribution μ over $\mathcal{X}\times\mathcal{Y}$ such that*

$$\mathsf{AC}^{\mathsf{avg}}_{\mu}(f,0) < \alpha\cdot \mathsf{IC}^{\mathsf{ext}}_{\mu}(f,0).$$

We complement Theorem 3 and Corollaries 4 and 5 by the following Claim 7, which provides a matching lower bound.

Claim 7. *Let $f : \mathcal{X}\times\mathcal{Y}\to\mathcal{Z}$ be a function and μ a distribution over $\mathcal{X}\times\mathcal{Y}$. Assume that f is not constant on the support of μ, that is, there exist $(x,y) \neq (x',y')$ so that*

$\mu(x,y), \mu(x',y') > 0$ *and* $f(x,y) \neq f(x',y')$. *Then, there exists a constant* $\beta > 0$ *so that for every* $n \in \mathbb{N}$,

$$\mathsf{CC}^{\mathsf{avg}}_{\mu^n}(f^n, 0) \geq \tfrac{1}{2}\mathsf{CC}^{\mathsf{avg}}_{\mu}(f, 0) + \beta n$$

and

$$\mathsf{IC}^{\mathsf{ext}}_{\mu^n}(f^n, 0) \geq \tfrac{1}{2}\mathsf{IC}^{\mathsf{ext}}_{\mu}(f, 0) + \beta n.$$

The constant β in the claim above depends on f and μ. It is roughly the entropy of $f(x,y)$ for $(x,y) \sim \mu$. This lower bound almost matches the upper bound given in Theorem 3 where the $k2^{-k}$ term is roughly the entropy of the distribution given in the theorem.

2. PRELIMINARIES AND DEFINITIONS

2.1 Communication Complexity

We use the definitions of protocols from [3].

Private coin protocols.

Let $\mathcal{X}, \mathcal{Y}, \mathcal{Z}$ be finite sets. A *private coin protocol* π between two players, Alice and Bob, over inputs in $\mathcal{X} \times \mathcal{Y}$ and outputs in $\mathcal{Z}$, is a rooted tree with the following structure:

- Each non-leaf node is owned by either Alice or Bob.
- Each non-leaf node owned by a particular player has a set of children that are owned by the other player. Each of these children is labeled by a binary string. This labeling is prefix-free: No child has a label that is a prefix of a different child.
- Each non-leaf node owned by Alice is associated with a function mapping $\mathcal{X}$ to distributions on children of the node, and each non-leaf node owned by Bob is associated with a function mapping $\mathcal{Y}$ to distributions on children of the node.
- The leaves of the protocol are labeled by values from $\mathcal{Z}$.

On input $(x,y) \in \mathcal{X} \times \mathcal{Y}$, the protocol π is executed as in Algorithm 1.

Algorithm 1 (Generic Communication Protocol)

1. Alice gets x and Bob gets y.
2. Set v to be the root of the protocol tree.
3. If v is a leaf, the protocol ends and outputs[2] $\pi(x,y)$ which is the value labeling v. Otherwise, the player owning v samples a child of v according to the distribution associated with v and her input, and sends the child's label to the other player.
4. Set v to be the newly sampled node and return to the previous step.

Public coin protocols.

A *public coin protocol* is a distribution on private coin protocols. A public coin protocol is executed by first using the public randomness R to sample a private coin protocol π_R, and then running π_R. Every private coin protocol is thus also a public coin protocol.

[2]Observe that even for fixed x, y the value $\pi(x,y)$ may be random.

Notation.

In all that follows, we assume that f is a function $f : \mathcal{X} \times \mathcal{Y} \to \mathcal{Z}$, π is a public coin protocol over inputs in $\mathcal{X} \times \mathcal{Y}$, μ is a distribution over $\mathcal{X} \times \mathcal{Y}$, and $\epsilon \geq 0$ is an error parameter.

We denote by X, Y the (random) pair of inputs given to the players (i.e., they are distributed according to μ). We denote by T the random variable that is the *transcript* of the protocol π with respect to μ. That is, T is the concatenation of all the messages that are sent during the execution of π. Observe that $\mathrm{supp}(T)$ is a prefix-free code. Let $|T|$ denote the bit-length of T. We denote by R the public randomness of π.

Computing a function.

We say that π *computes* f with error ϵ with respect to μ if there exists a function d of the transcript T and public randomness R so that

$$\Pr[d(T,R) \neq f(x,y)] \leq \epsilon,$$

where the probability is over $(x,y) \sim \mu$ and the randomness of π. We denote by $\Pi_{\epsilon,\mu}(f)$ the set of all protocols that compute f with error ϵ with respect to μ.

DEFINITION 8 (**Average Communication**). *The* average communication complexity *of a protocol* π *with respect to a distribution* μ *is defined as*

$$\mathsf{CC}^{\mathsf{avg}}_{\mu}(\pi) = \mathbf{E}\left[|T|\right].$$

where the expectation is taken over μ*, as well as the player' private randomness and the public randomness. The* average communication complexity *of a function* f *with error* ϵ *with respect to a distribution* μ *is defined as*

$$\mathsf{CC}^{\mathsf{avg}}_{\mu}(f,\epsilon) = \inf\left\{\mathsf{CC}^{\mathsf{avg}}_{\mu}(\pi) : \pi \in \Pi_{\epsilon,\mu}(f)\right\}.$$

DEFINITION 9 (**Amortized Communication**). *The* (average case) amortized communication complexity *of a function* f *with error* ϵ *with respect to a distribution* μ *is defined as*

$$\mathsf{AC}^{\mathsf{avg}}_{\mu}(f,\epsilon) = \lim_{n\to\infty} \frac{\mathsf{CC}^{\mathsf{avg}}_{\mu^n}(f^n,\epsilon)}{n}.$$

We consider only average case amortized communication complexity since we focus on the zero error case where average case is more meaningful than worst case (worst case complexity depends only on the support of the distribution).

2.2 Information Cost

Information cost of protocols is defined using information theory notions (see e.g. [1]). Let A be a random variable taking values in a set $\mathcal{A}$. We denote by $\mathbf{H}(A)$ the *Shannon entropy* of the distribution over $\mathcal{A}$ induced by A. The logarithms in this work (including the log in the entropy function) are taken with base 2.

DEFINITION 10. *Let* A, B, C *be random variables. The* conditional entropy *of* A *given* B *is defined as*

$$\mathbf{H}(A|B) = \mathbf{H}(A,B) - \mathbf{H}(B).$$

The conditional mutual information *of* A *and* B *given* C *is*

$$\mathbf{I}(A;B|C) = \mathbf{H}(A|C) - \mathbf{H}(A|C).$$

DEFINITION 11 (**External Information**). *The* external information cost *of a public coin protocol π with respect to a distribution μ is defined as*

$$\mathsf{IC}^{\text{ext}}_{\mu}(\pi) = \mathbf{I}(X, Y; T|R),$$

where, as before, T is the transcript of π and R is the public randomness. The external information cost *of a function f with error ϵ with respect to a distribution μ is defined as*

$$\mathsf{IC}^{\text{ext}}_{\mu}(f, \epsilon) = \inf \left\{ \mathsf{IC}^{\text{ext}}_{\mu}(\pi) : \pi \in \Pi_{\epsilon,\mu}(f) \right\}.$$

3. PROOFS

3.1 An Example Violating Direct Sum

In this section we prove Theorem 3. The assertion of Theorem 3 follows directly from Lemma 12 (found in Section 3.1.2), Lemma 13 (found in Section 3.1.3), and Lemma 14 (found in Section 3.1.4). For the rest of the section we assume to be given $k, n \in \mathbb{N}$ as in the statement of Theorem 3.

3.1.1 The Example

The equality function.

Let $EQ : \{0,1\}^k \times \{0,1\}^k \to \{0,1\}$ be the equality function on k-bit strings. That is, $EQ(x, y) = 1$ if and only if $x = y$.

The input distribution.

We think of $x \in \{0,1\}^k$ both as a binary string and as an integer between 0 and $2^k - 1$. For $x, y \in \{0,1\}^k$, e.g., we write $x < y$ if x is smaller than y as integers. Let $\mu_{x=y}$ denote the uniform distribution on the set $\{(x, y) \mid x = y\} \subseteq \{0,1\}^k \times \{0,1\}^k$ and $\mu_{x<y}$ denote the uniform distribution on the set $\{(x, y) \mid x < y\} \subseteq \{0,1\}^k \times \{0,1\}^k$. Set

$$\delta = \frac{1}{25k2^{2k}}.$$

(This value of δ is taylored so that our protocols from subsection 3.1.3 and subsection 3.1.4 will give the average communication complexity as stated in Theorem 3) Define

$$\mu = (1 - \delta) \cdot \mu_{x=y} + \delta \cdot \mu_{x<y}.$$

3.1.2 The External Information of EQ

The following lemma gives a lower bound of $(1 - \delta)k$ on the zero error external information cost of EQ with respect to μ. Informally speaking, the reason is that in the case that $x = y = a$, the protocol must reveal a to make sure that x and y are equal.

LEMMA 12. $\mathsf{IC}^{\text{ext}}_{\mu}(EQ, 0) \geq (1 - \delta)k \geq 0.99k$.

Proof It suffices to prove the lemma for private coin protocols (as external information is defined as an average over the public randomness). Let π be a zero error private coin protocol for EQ.

Let t be a possible transcript of π. Denote by $A(t)$ the set of all input pairs (x, y) so that $\mu(x, y) > 0$ and[3] $\Pr[T(x, y) = t] > 0$. Since π has zero error, $A(t)$ is a *μ-monochromatic rectangle.* That is, there exist subsets $\mathcal{X}', \mathcal{Y}' \subseteq \{0,1\}^k$ such that $A(t) = (\mathcal{X}' \times \mathcal{Y}') \cap \text{supp}(\mu)$,[4] and for every $(x, y), (x', y') \in A(t)$ it holds that $EQ(x, y) = EQ(x', y')$.

Let $a \in \{0,1\}^k$. We claim that if $(a, a) \in A(t)$ then $A(t) = \{(a, a)\}$: By definition of μ, if $x > y$ then $(x, y) \notin A(t)$ (as it is not in supp(μ)). Since $A(t)$ is a μ-monochromatic rectangle, it cannot contain any (x, y) with $x < y$ as well. Finally, if $(a', a') \in A(t)$ for some $a' > a$, then since $A(t)$ is a μ-monochromatic rectangle it is also the case that $(a, a') \in A(t)$, which is impossible (a similar argument works for $a' < a$).

Let T denote the transcript of π and think of $A = A(T)$ as a random variable. Therefore,

$$\mathbf{H}(A \mid X = Y, X, Y) = 0.$$

Furthermore, conditioned on $X = Y$, the random variable $A(T)$ is uniform over $\{0,1\}^k$, and so

$$\mathbf{H}(A \mid X = Y) = k.$$

It follows that

$$\begin{aligned}\mathbf{I}(X, Y; A \mid X = Y) &= \mathbf{H}(A \mid X = Y) - \mathbf{H}(A \mid X = Y, X, Y)\\ &= k.\end{aligned}$$

Let E be indicator random variable of the event $X = Y$. Finally,

$$\begin{aligned}\mathsf{IC}^{\text{ext}}_{\mu}(\pi) &= \mathbf{I}(X, Y; T)\\ &\geq \mathbf{I}(X, Y; A) && (T \text{ determines } A)\\ &= \mathbf{I}(X, Y, E; A) && (XY \text{ determines } E)\\ &= \mathbf{I}(E; A) + \Pr[E = 1] \cdot \mathbf{I}(XY; A \mid E = 1)\\ &\quad + \Pr[E = 0] \cdot \mathbf{I}(XY; A \mid E = 0)\\ & && \text{(the chain rule)}\\ &\geq \Pr[X = Y] \cdot \mathbf{I}(XY; A \mid X = Y)\\ &= (1 - \delta)k.\end{aligned}$$

3.1.3 Efficiently Computing EQ^n for $n < 2^k$

Consider the zero error protocol π_n for EQ^n described in Algorithm 2:

Algorithm 2 (A zero error protocol π_n for EQ^n over μ^n, $n < 2^k$)

1. Alice computes $x = \sum_{i=1}^{n} x_i$ and Bob computes $y = \sum_{i=1}^{n} y_i$, where x_i, y_i are viewed as integers, and "+" is integer addition[5]. So, the bit-length of x, y is most $k + \log n + 1$.
2. Alice sends x to Bob, and Bob sends y to Alice. If $x = y$ the protocol terminates and outputs: "$\forall i \in [n] : EQ(x_i, y_i) = 1$".
3. Otherwise, Alice sends $x_1, \ldots, x_n$ to Bob, and Bob sends $y_1, \ldots, y_n$ to Alice. The protocol trivially outputs the true value of EQ^n.

[3]Even for fixed (x, y) the transcript $T(x, y)$ is a random variable that depends on the private coins.

[4]supp(μ) is the set of all $(x, y) \in \mathcal{X}' \times \mathcal{Y}'$ such that $\mu(x, y) > 0$.

[5]For example, $01 + 11 = 100$.

The protocol π_n works.

By choice of μ, for every $i \in [n]$, it holds that $x_i \leq y_i$. If strict inequality $x_i < y_i$ holds for some $i \in [n]$, then $x < y$. Therefore, $x = y$ if and only if $x_i = y_i$ for every $i \in [n]$.

LEMMA 13. *For $n < 2^k$ it holds that $\mathsf{CC}^{\mathsf{avg}}_{\mu^n}(\pi_n) \leq 5k$.*

Proof Denote by p the probability that there exists $i \in [n]$ such that $x_i \neq y_i$. It holds that

$$p = 1 - (1-\delta)^n \leq 1 - (1 - \delta n) = \delta n.$$

Step 2 of the protocol π_n exchanges at most $2(k + \log n + 1)$ bits. If $x = y$, the protocol ends after Step 2. Otherwise, if $x \neq y$, at most $2kn$ additional bits are sent in Step 3. We conclude that

$$\begin{aligned}\mathsf{CC}^{\mathsf{avg}}_{\mu^n}(\pi_n) &\leq (1-p) \cdot 2(k + \log n + 1) + p \cdot 2kn \\ &\leq 2(k + \log n + 1) + 2\delta k n^2 \\ &\leq 5k,\end{aligned}$$

where in the last inquality we used the fact that $\delta = \frac{1}{25k2^{2k}}$ and $n < 2^k$.

3.1.4 *Efficiently Computing EQ^n for $n \geq 2^k$*

Consider the zero error protocol π'_n for EQ^n described in Algorithm 3:

Algorithm 3 (A zero error protocol π'_n for EQ^n over μ^n, $n \geq 2^k$)

Express n as $n = d2^k + k'$ for $d \in \mathbb{N}$ and $k' \in \{0, \ldots, 2^k - 1\}$. Partition the input pairs into d disjoint sets of 2^k pairs each, and one set of k' pairs. Run the previous protocol (for small n) on each of these $d+1$ sets. That is, run

$$\pi_{2^k}\left((x_1, \ldots, x_{2^k}), (y_1, \ldots, y_{2^k})\right),$$
$$\pi_{2^k}\left((x_{2^k+1}, \ldots, x_{2 \cdot 2^k}), (y_{2^k+1}, \ldots, y_{2 \cdot 2^k})\right), \ldots,$$
$$\pi_{k'}\left((x_{d2^k+1}, \ldots, x_n), (y_{d2^k+1}, \ldots, y_n)\right).$$

LEMMA 14. *For $n \geq 2^k$ it holds that $\mathsf{CC}^{\mathsf{avg}}_{\mu^n}(\pi'_n) \leq 10k2^{-k}n$.*

Proof By Lemma 13,

$$\begin{aligned}\mathsf{CC}^{\mathsf{avg}}_{\mu^n}(\pi'_n) &\leq d \cdot \mathsf{CC}^{\mathsf{avg}}_{\mu^{2^k}}(\pi_{2^k}) + \mathsf{CC}^{\mathsf{avg}}_{\mu^{k'}}(\pi_{k'}) \\ &\leq (d+1)5k \\ &\leq 10k2^{-k}n.\end{aligned}$$

3.2 Order on Measures

Here we prove Claim 1. The inequality $\mathsf{IC}^{\mathsf{ext}}_{\mu}(\pi) \geq \mathsf{IC}^{\mathsf{int}}_{\mu}(\pi)$ is known to hold, see e.g. [1]. We show $\mathsf{CC}^{\mathsf{avg}}_{\mu}(\pi) \geq \mathsf{IC}^{\mathsf{ext}}_{\mu}(\pi)$. Intuitively, the proof uses the fact that each bit sent by the players can contain at most one bit of information about the inputs.

Formally, let π be a public coin protocol over an input space $\mathcal{X} \times \mathcal{Y}$, and let μ be a distribution over $\mathcal{X} \times \mathcal{Y}$. Denote by π_R the private coin protocol induced by public randomness R. Let T be the transcript of π and T_R be the transcript of π_R.

For every value r that R may attain, we know that T_r is a prefix-free code. So, since the expected length of a binary prefix-free code is at least its entropy, we know $\mathbf{E}[|T_r|] \geq \mathbf{H}(T_r)$. Therefore,

$$\begin{aligned}\mathsf{CC}^{\mathsf{avg}}_{\mu}(\pi) = \mathbf{E}[|T|] &= \mathbf{E}[\mathbf{E}[|T| \mid R]] \\ &\geq \mathbf{E}[\mathbf{H}(T)|R] = \mathbf{H}(T|R) \\ &\geq \mathbf{I}(X, Y; T|R) = \mathsf{IC}^{\mathsf{ext}}_{\mu}(\pi).\end{aligned}$$

□

3.3 Amortized Cost is Non Zero

Here we prove Claim 7. Informally speaking, the proof uses the fact that a protocol for f^n needs to encode the results of n independent evaluations of f, and each such result has constant entropy (since f is not constant on $\mathrm{supp}(\mu)$).

Denote by X, Y the (random) pair of inputs given to the players, distributed according to μ. Choose

$$\beta = \tfrac{1}{2}\min\{\mathbf{H}(f(X, Y)), 1\}.$$

Since f is not a constant function on the support of μ, it holds that $\beta > 0$.

Now, let π be a public coin protocol computing f^n with zero error. Denote by X^n, Y^n the n (random) pairs of inputs given to the players that are distributed according to μ^n. Let T denote the transcript of the protocol π. It holds that

$$\begin{aligned}\mathsf{IC}^{\mathsf{ext}}_{\mu^n}(\pi) &= \mathbf{I}(X^nY^n; T|R) \\ &\geq \mathbf{I}(X^nY^n; f^n(X^n, Y^n)|R) \\ &\quad (T \text{ determines } f^n \text{ as } \pi \text{ computes } f^n \text{ with zero error}) \\ &= \mathbf{H}(f^n(X^n, Y^n)|R) \\ &\quad (f^n \text{ is a deterministic function of } X^nY^n) \\ &= \mathbf{H}(f^n(X^n, Y^n)) \\ &\quad ((X^n, Y^n) \text{ is independent of } R) \\ &\geq 2\beta n. \\ &\quad (\text{the input pairs are independently selected})\end{aligned}$$

Claim 1, therefore, implies

$$\mathsf{CC}^{\mathsf{avg}}_{\mu^n}(f^n, 0) \geq \mathsf{IC}^{\mathsf{ext}}_{\mu^n}(f^n, 0) \geq 2\beta n.$$

Clearly,

$$\mathsf{CC}^{\mathsf{avg}}_{\mu^n}(f^n, 0) \geq \mathsf{CC}^{\mathsf{avg}}_{\mu}(f, 0) \text{ and } \mathsf{IC}^{\mathsf{ext}}_{\mu^n}(f^n, 0) \geq \mathsf{IC}^{\mathsf{ext}}_{\mu}(f, 0).$$

Hence,

$$\mathsf{CC}^{\mathsf{avg}}_{\mu^n}(f^n, 0) \geq \frac{1}{2} \cdot 2\beta n + \frac{1}{2}\mathsf{CC}^{\mathsf{avg}}_{\mu}(f, 0).$$

Similarly for $\mathsf{IC}^{\mathsf{ext}}_{\mu^n}(f^n, 0)$. □

4. DISCUSSION OF DEFINITIONS

We now discuss the definitions of "compute" and "average complexity" with a focus on zero error communication complexity and implications to Conjecture 2. The difference between the possible definitions relates to randomized computation versus distributional computation. We first explain two possible definitions for each notion and then discuss them in more detail.

We start by discussing the notion of "compute." Let f be a function defined over $\mathcal{X} \times \mathcal{Y}$ and let μ be a distribution over

$\mathcal{X}\times\mathcal{Y}$. We wish to define when does a protocol π computes f with error at most $\epsilon \geq 0$. Two possible definitions are:

(1) For every $(x,y) \in \mathcal{X}\times\mathcal{Y}$, we have[6] $\Pr_r[\pi(x,y,r) = f(x,y)] \geq 1-\epsilon$ where r is the randomness of the protocol.

(2) $\Pr_{(x,y)\sim\mu,r}[\pi(x,y,r) = f(x,y)] \geq 1-\epsilon$.

What does "average complexity" mean? Let π be a protocol with transcript T. We wish to define when does the average complexity of π is at most C. Two possible definitions are:

(a) For every $(x,y) \in \mathcal{X}\times\mathcal{Y}$, we have $\mathbf{E}_r[|T(x,y,r)|] \leq C$.

(b) $\mathbf{E}_{(x,y)\sim\mu,r}[|T(x,y,r)|] \leq C$.

Definitions (1) and (a) do not depend on μ at all, whereas Definitions (2) and (b) do. Definitions (1) and (a) are standard for randomized protocols when there is no distribution on inputs, see e.g. [12]. Definitions (2) and (b) are usually used in the distributional setting, for example, when studying information complexity, see e.g. [1].

There are therefore four options for defining $\mathsf{CC}^{\mathsf{avg}}_{\mu}(f,\epsilon)$: One that does not depend on μ at all (Definitions (1), (a) are used), and three options that depend on μ in different ways. Observe that the definition of "information complexity" of a protocol does not make sense in the randomized framework, and is defined in the distributional framework.

How many options to interpret Conjecture 2 are there? In any interpretation it seems reasonable to define "compute" in the same fashion for amortized cost and information cost. This leaves us with four interpretations:

The first two interpretations correspond to the definition of "average complexity" as per Definition (a). The two choices left are for the meaning of "compute." We claim that in these two interpretations the conjecture does not hold. The reason is that with these definitions, if μ has full support then $\mathsf{CC}^{\mathsf{avg}}_{\mu}(f,0)$ does not depend on μ at all, whereas $\mathsf{IC}^{\mathsf{ext}}_{\mu}(f,0)$ does. For example, if μ is $1-\delta$ times $\mu_{x=y}$ and δ times the uniform measure on $\mathcal{X}\times\mathcal{Y}$, then $\mathsf{IC}^{\mathsf{ext}}_{\mu}(EQ,0)$ depends on δ. (We use the fact that in the zero error case, for full support distributions, Definitions (1) and (2) have the same meaning.)

In the other two interpretations "average complexity" is given by Definition (b). Our example refutes the conjecture if "compute" is as in Definition (2). The case where "compute" is given by Definition (1) remains open. One drawback of this interpretation is that for $\epsilon > 0$ the standard way to define "compute" in the context of information complexity is as in Definition (2). So, this option leads to that $\mathsf{IC}^{\mathsf{ext}}_{\mu}(f,\epsilon)$ is not continuous at $\epsilon = 0$, for example, $\mathsf{IC}^{\mathsf{ext}}_{\mu_{x=y}}(EQ,\epsilon) = 0$ for $\epsilon > 0$ but $\mathsf{IC}^{\mathsf{ext}}_{\mu_{x=y}}(EQ,0) > 0$. We note that for measures μ of full support, external information cost is still continuous (which fits well with the possibility that Conjecture 2 is true for measures of full support).

[6] By $\pi(x,y,r) = f(x,y)$ we mean that knowledge of the transcript and the public randomness yields knowledge of f as in Section 2.1.

5. REFERENCES

[1] Boaz Barak, Mark Braverman, Xi Chen, and Anup Rao. How to compress interactive communication. In *STOC*, pages 67–76, 2010.

[2] Mark Braverman. Coding for interactive computation: Progress and challenges. In *Allerton*, 2012.

[3] Mark Braverman. Interactive information complexity. In *STOC*, pages 505–524, 2012.

[4] Mark Braverman, Ankit Garg, Denis Pankratov, and Omri Weinstein. From information to exact communication. In *STOC (to appear)*, 2013.

[5] Mark Braverman and Anup Rao. Information equals amortized communication. In *FOCS*, pages 748–757, 2011.

[6] Amit Chakrabarti, Yaoyun Shi, Anthony Wirth, and Andrew Yao. Informational complexity and the direct sum problem for simultaneous message complexity. In *In Proceedings of the 42nd Annual IEEE Symposium on Foundations of Computer Science*, pages 270–278, 2001.

[7] Tomás Feder, Eyal Kushilevitz, Moni Naor, and Noam Nisan. Amortized communication complexity. *SIAM J. Comput.*, 24(4):736–750, 1995.

[8] Prahladh Harsha, Rahul Jain, David A. McAllester, and Jaikumar Radhakrishnan. The communication complexity of correlation. In *IEEE Conference on Computational Complexity*, pages 10–23, 2007.

[9] Rahul Jain. New strong direct product results in communication complexity. *Electronic Colloquium on Computational Complexity (ECCC)*, 18:24, 2011.

[10] Rahul Jain, Jaikumar Radhakrishnan, and Pranab Sen. A direct sum theorem in communication complexity via message compression. In *ICALP*, pages 300–315, 2003.

[11] Hartmut Klauck. A strong direct product theorem for disjointness. In *STOC*, pages 77–86, 2010.

[12] Eyal Kushilevitz and Noam Nisan. Communication complexity. *Cambridge University Press*, 1997.

Rational Arguments: Single Round Delegation with Sublinear Verification

Siyao Guo*
Chinese Univ. of Hong Kong
syguo@cse.cuhk.edu.hk

Pavel Hubáček†
Aarhus University
hubacek@cs.au.dk

Alon Rosen‡
IDC Herzliya
alon.rosen@idc.ac.il

Margarita Vald§
Tel Aviv University
margarita.vald@cs.tau.ac.il

ABSTRACT

Rational proofs, recently introduced by Azar and Micali (STOC 2012), are a variant of interactive proofs in which the prover is neither honest nor malicious, but rather rational. The advantage of rational proofs over their classical counterparts is that they allow for extremely low communication and verification time. Azar and Micali demonstrated their potential by giving a one message rational proof for #SAT, in which the verifier runs in time $O(n)$, where n denotes the instance size. In a follow-up work (EC 2013), Azar and Micali proposed "super-efficient" and interactive versions of rational proofs and argued that they capture precisely the class TC0 of constant-depth, polynomial-size circuits with threshold gates.

In this paper, we show that by considering *rational arguments*, in which the prover is additionally restricted to be computationally bounded, the class NC1, of search problems computable by log-space uniform circuits of $O(\log n)$-depth, admits rational protocols that are *simultaneously* one-round and polylog(n) time verifiable. This demonstrates the potential of rational arguments as a way to extend the notion of "super-efficient" rational proofs beyond the class TC0.

The low interaction nature of our protocols, along with their sub-linear verification time, make them well suited for delegation of computation. While they provide a weaker (yet arguably meaningful) guarantee of soundness, they compare favorably with each of the known delegation schemes in at least one aspect. They are simple, rely on standard complexity hardness assumptions, provide a correctness guarantee for all instances, and do not require preprocessing.

*Work supported by the European Research Council under the European Union's Seventh Framework Programme (FP/2007-2013)/ERC Grant Agreement n. 307952.

†The author acknowledges support from the Danish National Research Foundation and The National Science Foundation of China (under the grant 61061130540) for the Sino-Danish Center for the Theory of Interactive Computation, within which part of this work was performed. The author did part of this work while visiting IDC Herzliya supported by ISF grant no. 334/08.

‡Work supported by ISF grant no. 334/08 and by the European Research Council under the European Union's Seventh Framework Programme (FP/2007-2013)/ ERC Grant Agreement n. 307952.

§Work supported by ISF grant no. 334/08.

ITCS'14, January 12–14, 2014, Princeton, New Jersey, USA.

http://dx.doi.org/10.1145/2554797.2554845 .

Categories and Subject Descriptors

F.2.0 [**Theory of Computation**]: Analysis of Algorithms and Problem Complexity—*General*

General Terms

Economics, Theory

Keywords

Delegation of Computation; Rational Cryptography; Succinct Arguments; Threshold Circuits

1. INTRODUCTION

With the advent of cloud computing there has been increased interest in schemes that allow devices with limited computing power to verify the correctness of computations done on their behalf. Such procedures are referred to as *delegation schemes*. In their most basic incarnation, the weak device (the *verifier*) delegates a computation to the cloud (the *prover*) by sending it an input $x \in \{0,1\}^n$ and expecting the cloud to return the value $f(x)$, where f is a function computable by a predetermined circuit C. To make the computation of $f(x)$ verifiable, the prover is expected to send along a "certificate of correct computation", which is then checked by the verifier, preferably investing less resources than it would have invested had he computed $f(x)$ on its own (for this notion to be meaningful the circuit C should be given in some succinct way, e.g. it can be efficiently generated by a small program).

1.1 Efficient Proofs/Arguments

The first approaches for delegating computation (which in fact pre-dated the cloud days by about two decades) proposed to use Computationally Sound proofs/efficient arguments (cf. Kilian [21], Micali [24]). These delegation schemes allow the verifier to run in time $O(\text{poly}(n, \log S))$, where S denotes f's circuit size. However, they require heavy machinery such as PCP for general circuits, and hence introduce significant overhead to both the prover and the verifier. Moreover, efficient arguments require four messages of interaction between the prover and the verifier, inflicting undesirable burden on the parties.

While the interaction can be removed by using Random Oracles [24], the question of whether there exist efficient non-interactive arguments under standard assumptions is still not well understood. One indication on the difficulty of resolving this problem is that no non-trivial language has a Succinct Non-interactive ARGument (SNARG) based on falsifiable assumptions (Gentry and Wichs [14]). Several works have been bypassing these limitations by relying on non-standard (and in particular not known to be falsifiable) assumptions (we survey these alternative proposals in Section 1.4), yet it is of interest to examine to what extent such assumptions are necessary for succinct delegation.

In any case, as observed by Goldwasser, Kalai and Rothblum [17], the impossibility results do not pose any limitation in the context of real-life delegation. This is simply because in delegation we are only interested in efficiently computable problems. This brought them to introduce a weaker notion of delegation, in which the prover is only required to work for languages computable in polynomial time, resulting in more efficient delegation schemes, both in the standard model (i.e., with no set-up), or in a model allowing an off-line preprocessing stage (used to amortize the cost of verification across multiple evaluations of f). One-round versions of such schemes are computationally sound, and in particular based on intractability assumptions (e.g. [8, 12, 1]), whereas interactive versions can be actually proved to be unconditionally sound [17].

It should be noted that, while many of these more recent schemes do not rely on full blown PCP machinery, they still induce significant computational overhead on the prover. Even leaving prover's complexity aside, in all the delegation schemes mentioned above the verifier's running time is $O(\text{poly}(n, \log S))$ (or at best $n + \text{polylog}(S)$), suggesting that the least the verifier should do is to read the input in its entirety. On the other hand, recent work by Rothblum, Vadhan and Wigderson [28], suggests that this apparent limitation can be actually bypassed by considering "Interactive Proofs of Proximity". For circuits of depth d, such proofs allow the verifier to work in time $(n/D+D)^{1+o(1)} \cdot \tilde{O}(d)$ (which is sub-linear for example when $D = \sqrt{n}$), but to reject only strings that are D-far from being the correct output of the computation.

1.2 Rational Proofs

Another recent line of work, initiated by Azar and Micali [2] proposes to relax the rigid soundness requirements of classical proofs. They do so by allowing the verifier to accept proofs of false statements, but make it *irrational* for the prover to provide them. While not good enough in case of a malicious prover (or say if one wants to detect faults), this still may fit very well a scenario in which a weak client delegates a complex computation to a more powerful server/cloud (think of delegation of some massive computation to Amazon, which would then be paid for its services). Thus, to the extent that such *Rational Proofs* are meaningful, one may consider them as an alternative to more traditional approaches to delegation.

Azar and Micali [2] give rational proofs for search problems in #P and more generally for the entire counting hierarchy. The main advantage of such proofs over their classical counterparts is that they are as simple as one could hope for. The basic idea is to let the prover simply give the verifier the result of the computation, and let the verifier randomly compute a "reward" based on the prover's answer. This reward reflects the quality of the prover's computation in that its expectation is maximized when the prover gives the correct answer. As a result there is almost no overhead both for the prover and for the verifier.

One natural question that comes to mind is whether rational proofs can be "scaled down" to lower complexity classes. This includes both classes such as NP, but also lower classes say within P (i.e., ones that are relevant to delegation). Towards this end, Azar and Micali [3] proposed "super-efficient" rational proofs, an extension of their notion, and showed that such super-efficient rational proofs capture precisely the class TC0 of *constant depth*, polynomial size circuits with threshold gates. The super-efficiency of their proofs, while introducing additional interaction, allows the reward to be computed by the verifier in sub-linear time (in the input size). This can be achieved in an extremely simple and natural manner, introducing hardly any overhead on the prover's work (beyond the computation of f).

Azar and Micali [3] also consider super-efficient one-round rational PCPs, in which the communication is $\text{poly}(n)$ and the verifier has random access to the message from prover. Rational PCPs can capture languages beyond TC0. However, given the differences in the communication model and constraints, they are not directly comparable to super-efficient proofs. Moreover rational PCPs seem unsuitable for delegation, since in this model the prover sends the whole proof to the verifier that queries only a limited number bits of it to check the correctness of computation.

1.3 Our Results

The main objective of this paper is to attain a simple (and in particular low-overhead), one-round delegation scheme that captures as large class of problems as possible, and in which the verifier works sub-linearly in the input size. To this end we introduce a new concept, called *Rational Arguments*, which beyond postulating a rational prover additionally assumes that he is computationally bounded. We show how to realize rational arguments based on standard (falsifiable) cryptographic hardness assumptions, resulting in an arguably meaningful alternative to known delegation schemes.

Our initial observation is that for the class of search problems computable by threshold circuits of depth $d = o(n)$, the efficiency of rational proofs can be strengthened beyond what was originally shown by Azar and Micali [2], in the sense that the verification time can be performed in as little as $\tilde{O}(d)$ time. This comes at the cost of making the proof interactive, and specifically requires d rounds of communication. The resulting rational proof is very simple and induces hardly any overhead. All that is required from the prover is to perform the computation as prescribed, storing intermediate values along the way. A small subset of these values is subsequently used to convince the verifier in the correctness of the actual computation. Moreover, the verification procedure requires the verifier to only access a *single* bit of the input, and to perform a computation with complexity proportional to d, the depth of the circuit.

Our rational proofs resemble by structure the super-efficient rational proofs of Azar and Micali [3], and traverse the circuit in a similar manner. However, the computation of reward by the verifier differs in that it requires the prover to send a single bit per gate (the corresponding intermediate value), unlike in the case of [3] where the prover needs to count and report the number of ones among the children of each gate queried by the verifier. This yields to substantial improvement in terms of communication complexity.

Next, we go on and convert the above interactive procedure into a one with a *single round*. This is done by applying a variant of a previously known transformation by Kalai and Raz [19]. This transformation makes use of a single server Private Information Retrieval Scheme (PIR) and assumes that the prover is computationally bounded. The "database" held by the prover in this transformation consists of precisely the intermediate computation values mentioned above, and as a result the overhead is kept minimal (the Kalai Raz transformation was previously used to convert significantly "heavier" protocols, resulting in increased work for the prover, beyond the mere computation of f). Jumping ahead, we note that our analysis departs from the original Kalai Raz analysis in several aspects.

Formalizing the above necessitates putting forward a completely new definition of *rational arguments*. This definition involves dealing with several subtleties and complications, arising from the combination of rational proofs with computational considerations and the presence of cost of computation. We view the formalization of this new concept as one of the main contributions of this paper. Our construction of rational arguments, along with the way it interacts with the definition, highlights the importance of the "gap" between the reward given in case of truthful behavior of the prover and the reward given in case of untruthful behavior. In our construction, the noticeable *reward gap* of our rational proofs for NC1 (in contrast to higher classes within NC) is exactly what allows us to successfully transform them into one-round rational arguments.

In addition to the above, we also establish strong limitations on the reward gap achievable by non-interactive public-coin rational proofs. Specifically, we show that non-trivial languages cannot have such rational proofs with both logarithmic communication complexity and noticeable reward gap. This suggests that the search for rational proofs with large reward gap should focus on private-coin and/or interactive protocols. Progress in this direction would be very interesting, as it might result in succinct non-interactive rational arguments, whose classical counterparts, as shown by Gentry and Wichs [14], cannot be achieved under falsifiable assumptions (at least not in a black box way).

To summarize, we view our main contributions to be the following:

- Downscaling rational proofs to efficiently handle a rich class of languages within P (specifically, the class of search problems computable by threshold circuits of depth $d = o(n)$). (Section 4.4)
- Defining a notion of rational arguments that bears meaningful semantics in the context of delegation of computation. (Section 3.1)
- Transforming any interactive rational proof with noticeable reward gap into highly efficient one-round rational arguments. (Section 3.2)
- Establishing limitations on the verification complexity (or more precisely on the complexity of computing the reward) in low communication rational proofs. (Section 4.5)
- Pointing out open questions related to the notions of rational proofs and arguments. (Section 5)

Our rational protocols, while providing a weaker (yet arguably meaningful) guarantee of soundness, compare favorably with each of the known delegation schemes in at least one aspect. They are simple, rely on standard complexity hardness assumptions, provide a correctness guarantee for all instances, and do not require preprocessing.

1.4 Previous Delegation Schemes

In classical model, the literature contains a variety of models for delegation. For problems within P the protocols can be roughly partitioned into *proofs* and *arguments*, where the latter has been considered both with and without *preprocessing*. For problems outside of P, the main notion considered is that of *succinct non-interactive arguments*. Arguments in preprocessing model and arguments for problems outside P are less relevant to this work. We survey some of them and note that the verification time is not sub-linear.

Before comparing with the classical setting, we present a comparison with other delegation schemes in the rational model. That is, we show a comparison between our rational arguments/rational proofs and rational proofs by Azar and Micali [3].

Rational proofs.

Independently of our work, Azar and Micali [3] show a rational proof for uniform constant depth threshold circuits (TC0) and prove that constant round, super-efficient rational proofs capture exactly this complexity class. Our rational arguments cover a potentially richer class of problems, while having only one round and only polylogarithmic overhead. We view it as an evidence that rational arguments have the potential to extend super-efficient rational proofs beyond class TC0.

The advantage of our rational proofs over rational proofs in [3] is minimality of communication, i.e., only one bit per round. For the restricted class of log-time constant depth threshold circuits, the verification time of our protocol as well as the one in Azar and Micali [3] is $O(\log n)$. A detailed comparison of parameters is in Table 1.

Proofs.

Goldwasser *et al.* [17] give a simple interactive proof for any log-space uniform circuit in NC. Their solution is to traverse the circuit from the top down, run a sum-check protocol and apply standard arithmetizing techniques which take only sub-linear time for each level. This approach yields very good efficiency for all levels except the last one (the input level), where the verifier performs a heavy computation (verifying the evaluation of a polynomial on the whole input) which takes quasi-linear time in the input size.

Rothblum *et al.* [28] study sub-linear verification in the model of interactive proofs of proximity, and gave a protocol based on parallel repetition of the Goldwasser *et al.* [17] pro-

Table 1: efficiency comparison of our rational proofs and arguments to [3]

	Complexity class	Rounds	Communication	Verification time
Azar and Micali [3]	TC0	constant	$O(\log n)$	polylog(n)
Our rational proofs	TC0	constant	constant	polylog(n)
Our rational proofs	NC1	$O(\log n)$	$O(\log n)$	polylog(n)
Our rational arguments	NC1	1	polylog(n)	polylog(n)

tocol. The main difference (and advantage) to Goldwasser *et al.* [17] is that the new model allows to avoid the costly verification procedure for the input level. Efficiency comes at the cost of correctness, which is no longer guaranteed to hold for instances that are only close to being in the language. In addition, communication and verification complexity are increased due to parallel repetition (used for the sake of distance amplification).

Our construction is even simpler than the protocol of Goldwasser *et al.* [17]. Not only our verifier runs in sublinear time, but also our rational prover runs in linear time in size of the circuit (in previous constructions the prover runs in polynomial time in the circuit size). As in previous constructions, the verifier in our protocol traverses the circuit from the top down, however he merely asks the rational prover for one bit at each level (value of a single gate).[1] Finally, in our protocols the verifier only needs to access one bit of the input (i.e., one query to the input) at the last level. See Table 2 for the full comparison. One other interesting approach is to consider a model with multiple provers. Based on Goldwasser *et al.* [17], Canetti, Riva and Rothblum [7] and Kol and Raz [22] show how to obtain more efficient proofs for NC in the competing prover model. Kalai, Raz and Rothblum [20] consider delegation for bounded space (which may also contain languages outside NC) in the model of multi-prover interactive proofs. The running time of verifiers in their constructions are at least quasi-linear.

Arguments.

Under cryptographic assumptions, it is in general possible to obtain more efficient protocols (though the soundness guarantee then only holds with respect to bounded cheating provers).

In order to minimize interaction, Kalai and Raz [19] give a transformation from specific type of interactive protocols into one-round arguments. Goldwasser *et al.* [17] noted that this transformation can be used to achieve non-interactivity also for their delegation scheme. Subsequently, Cormode *et al.* [9] optimized the efficiency of the prover into quasi-linear in circuit size, and Thaler [29] achieved even better efficiency for a natural class of structured circuits. Essentially the same transformation can make the work of Kalai *et al.* [20] one-round. Since the transformation preserves the complexity of the original interactive proof (with only a modest amount of overhead), the running time of the verifier in all the arguments obtained in this way is comparable to the original running time, but it still cannot get better than quasi-linear. In order to get a sub-linear one-round argument via this transformation, one would need to start with a sub-linear delegation scheme as in our case. The construction of Rothblum *et al.* [28] achieves sub-linear verification, however it is not obvious if the same transformation can turn it into a one-round argument. The problem of constructing arguments that are one-round with sub-linear verification time is still open in the classical setting. We show how to simultaneously achieve both in the rational setting.

Preprocessing model and SNARGs.

Gennaro, Gentry and Parno [12], Chung, Kalai and Vadhan [8] and Applebaum, Ishai and Kushilevitz [1] use a computationally demanding off-line phase to achieve efficiency during the run of the delegation scheme. The work of Parno, Raykova and Vaikuntanathan [26] further limits the amount of preprocessing needed to aim for *public-verifiability*. Other works consider delegation for NP languages based on non-falsifiable assumptions; the works of Bitansky *et al.* [4], Damgård, Faust and Hazay [10], Gennaro *et al.* [13], Groth [18] or Lipmaa [23] give succinct delegation schemes based on such assumptions.

2. PRELIMINARIES AND DEFINITIONS

Throughout the rest of the paper we use the following notation and definitions. For $n \in \mathbb{N}^+$, let $[n]$ denote the set of first n natural numbers, i.e., $[n] = \{1, \ldots, n\}$. A function $g : \mathbb{N} \to \mathbb{R}^+$ is *negligible* if it tends to 0 faster than any inverse polynomial, i.e., for all $c \in \mathbb{N}$ there exists $k_c \in \mathbb{N}$ such that for every $k > k_c$ it holds that $g(k) < k^{-c}$. We use negl$(\cdot)$ to talk about negligible function if we do not need to specify its name.

In a rational proof, Arthur pays Merlin a randomized reward according to the transcript of the communication, and the communication constitutes a rational Merlin Arthur game if the correct evaluation $y = f(x)$ can be derived from transcript that maximizes the expected reward.

For a pair of interactive Turing machines, P and V, we denote by $(P, V)(x)$ the random variable representing the transcript between P and V when interacting on common input x. Let $\mathsf{reward}(\cdot)$ denote a randomized function computed by V that given a transcript calculates a reward for P, and by $\mathsf{output}((P, V)(x))$ the output of V after interacting with P on common input x. In this setting, the goal of a *rational* P is to maximize the expected value of $\mathsf{reward}(\cdot)$, while the goal of V is to learn (and output) the true evaluation of the desired function f on x.

We extend the definition of rational Merlin Arthur [2] to multiple rounds. Our definition can be seen as a functional analogue of their decisional rational MA definition. Similar to classical proofs, where the statement is fixed ahead of time

[1] Unlike the previous works, we consider the class TC instead of NC. This is no limitation, since in general NC = TC. Moreover, we gain advantage in the case of constant depth, since $NC^0 \subset TC^0$. Note that TC^0 is a powerful model of bounded computation.

Table 2: efficiency comparison of our rational proofs to [17, 28]

	Queries	Rounds	Communication	Verification time	Remarks
Goldwasser *et al.* [17]	n	$\tilde{O}(d)$	$\tilde{O}(d)$	$\tilde{O}(n)$	NC of depth d
Rothblum *et al.* [28]	$\left(\frac{n}{D}\right)^{1+o(1)}$	$\tilde{O}(d)$	$D \cdot \left(\frac{n}{D}\right)^{o(1)} \cdot \tilde{O}(d)$	$\left(\frac{n}{D} + D\right)^{1+o(1)} \cdot \tilde{O}(d)$	D-proximity, NC of depth d
this work	1	d	d	$\tilde{O}(d)$	TC of depth d

(i.e., the statement is always proving x in the language), we consider the setting where a rational prover first declares his answer to $f(x)$, and only then tries to prove the correctness of the reported value.

Definition 1 (Functional Rational Merlin Arthur). *Let $C, T : \mathbb{N} \to \mathbb{R}$ be some functions. A function $f : \{0,1\}^* \to \{0,1\}^*$ is in* FRMA $[r, C, T]$ *if there exists an r-round public-coin protocol (P, V), referred as rational proof, and a randomized reward function* reward : $\{0,1\}^* \to \mathbb{R}_{\geq 0}$ *such that for all inputs $x \in \{0,1\}^*$:*

(a) $\Pr[\mathsf{output}((P,V)(x)) = f(x)] = 1$.

(b) Let $\mathcal{P}_i$ be the view of P up to his message at the ith-round. Then for every round i and for any prover $\tilde{P}$ that behaves as P up to round i and differs on round i it holds that:

$$\mathrm{E}[\mathsf{reward}((P,V)(x))] > \mathrm{E}[\mathsf{reward}((\tilde{P},V)(x))] ,$$

where the expectation is taken over the random coins of the verifier and the prover.

(c) The communication complexity of P is $C(|x|)$.

(d) The running time of V is $T(|x|)$.

We associate a language L with a function $f : \{0,1\}^* \to \{0,1\}$ where $f(x) = 1$ if and only if $x \in L$. That is, deciding membership in L is equivalent to computing f. The class *Decisional Rational Merlin Arthur*, or DRMA in short, is defined by restricting Definition 1 to binary functions.

3. RATIONAL ARGUMENTS

In this section we present the definition of rational arguments, and motivate the choices behind it. We then go on to construct a one-round rational argument, assuming a standard protocol for Private Information Retrieval. Our construction makes use of an interactive rational proof as a building block. The construction of the interactive rational proof is given in Section 4.4. The transformation we employ is similar to a transformation proposed by Kalai and Raz [19], with some significant differences in the analysis.

3.1 Definition

Rational arguments are designed to model what happens to the reward when restricting the prover to computationally bounded strategies. One difficulty in capturing the expected prover behavior lies in the fact that he always can attempt to solve the underlying hard problem, and in case of success can reap the highest payoff even while lying about the result. While these attempts will fail with overwhelming probability, one still has to account for those attempts that do succeed. Any definition of computationally bounded strategic behavior should thus take such strategies into consideration, and in particular accommodate negligible gains over the reward guaranteed by the prescribed behavior (but not more). This protects the verifier from giving out too high rewards on expectation, and at the same time ensures that the prover does not lose too much by honestly following the protocol (even though a purely rational prover might not follow the prescribed strategy, since it would try to solve the underlying hard problems).

However, such definition does not take into account the cost of computing $f(x)$. For example, it does not rule out a prover that always gives some default (possibly incorrect) output, without performing any computation, while getting just slightly less than the expectation of the prescribed behavior. Such strategy induces no cost to the prover and is certainly rational if the loss is smaller than the price of computing the function. To address this shortcoming we add another condition, whose objective is to "pin down" the profitability of deviating. Roughly speaking this condition requires that any strategy that lies about the value of $f(x)$ with noticeable probability does noticeably worse (in terms of expected reward) than the prescribed strategy (which always gives out the correct value of $f(x)$). This condition ensures that a rational prover will follow the prescribed strategy in order to increase his utility by a considerable amount.[2]

Definition 2 (Rational Argument). *A function $f : \{0,1\}^* \to \{0,1\}^*$ admits a* rational argument *with security parameter $\kappa : \mathbb{N} \to \mathbb{N}$ if there exists a protocol (P, V) and a randomized reward function* reward : $\{0,1\}^* \to \mathbb{R}_{\geq 0}$ *such that for any input $x \in \{0,1\}^*$ and any prover $\tilde{P}$ of size $\leq 2^{\kappa(|x|)}$ the following hold:*

(a) $\Pr[\mathsf{output}((P,V)(x)) = f(x)] = 1$.

(b) There exists a negligible function $\epsilon(\cdot)$ such that

$$\mathrm{E}[\mathsf{reward}((P,V)(x))] + \epsilon(|x|) \geq \mathrm{E}[\mathsf{reward}((\tilde{P},V)(x))] .$$

(c) If there exists a polynomial $p(\cdot)$ such that

$$\Pr[\mathsf{output}((\tilde{P},V)(x)) \neq f(x)] \geq p(|x|)^{-1}$$

then there exists a polynomial $q(\cdot)$ such that

$$\mathrm{E}[\mathsf{reward}((\tilde{P},V)(x))] + q(|x|)^{-1} \leq \mathrm{E}[\mathsf{reward}((P,V)(x))] .$$

The expectations and the probabilities are taken over the random coins of the respective prover and verifier. We say that the rational argument is efficient *if the running time of V is $o(|x|)$ for every $x \in \{0,1\}^*$.*

The three conditions ensure that the definition is both meaningful and nontrivial. Property (a) corresponds to the notion of *completeness* in classical protocols, and guarantees that a prover following the prescribed protocol will indeed

[2]Similarly to Azar and Micali [3], we consider strategies that induce a noticeable utility loss to be irrational.

report the correct value of $f(x)$ to the verifier. Property (b) guarantees that the gain attained by deviating from the prescribed strategy in a computationally bounded way is at most negligible. This by itself already guarantees that having both parties follow the protocol is a computational Nash equilibrium. Property (c) guarantees that not reporting $f(x)$ with noticeable probability results in a noticeable utility loss.

We note that Definition 1 of rational proofs (as well as the definition in [2]), does not rule out the above discussed "lazy" behavior of the prover once the computation has cost. Having this in mind, we propose to measure how big is the loss of a prover that always reports $f(x)$ incorrectly. A noticeable gap in expectation between such a prover and the prescribed behavior then assures that it is beneficial for the prover to perform the computation to significantly increase its utility. Namely, the verifier could in principle scale the reward by a polynomial factor to make it profitable for the prover to compute the function, while not blowing up too much the budget necessary for paying out the reward. This gives rise to a notion of *reward gap* that allows us to argue for rationality of our proofs in presence of computational cost; it is formalized as follows:

Definition 3 (Reward Gap). *Let $f \in \text{FRMA}[r, C, T]$ be some function and let (P, V) and $\mathsf{reward}(\cdot)$ be the guaranteed protocol and reward function. The* reward gap *of $\mathsf{reward}(\cdot)$ is a function $\Delta_{\mathsf{reward}} : \mathbb{N} \to \mathbb{R}$, such that for every $n \in \mathbb{N}$,*

$$\Delta_{\mathsf{reward}}(n) = \min_{x\in\{0,1\}^n} \min_{P^*\in S} \big(\mathrm{E}[\mathsf{reward}((P,V)(x))] - \mathrm{E}[\mathsf{reward}((P^*,V)(x))]\big) ,$$

where the expectation is taken over the random coins of the verifier and the prover, and S is the set of all P^* such that $\Pr[\mathsf{output}((P^*, V)(x)) \neq f(x)] = 1$.

By simple calculation it follows that the utility loss of an arbitrary prover $\tilde{P}$ is at least $\Delta \cdot \Pr[\mathsf{output}((\tilde{P}, V)(x)) \neq f(x)]$. Hence, rational proofs with noticeable reward gap provide similar guarantee to property (c) in Definition 2 of rational arguments, i.e., provers misreporting $f(x)$ with noticeable probability will face a noticeable utility loss. This hints on the importance of the reward gap measure when constructing rational arguments from rational proofs.

Azar and Micali [3] presented a stronger definition of rational proofs by introducing an additional requirement of constant utility gap between the prescribed and any other prover. However, such definition is extremely hard to satisfy. To illustrate the issue, consider a prover that is dishonest with only a negligible probability. The expected reward for such prover is only negligibly far from the reward of the prescribed behavior and hence has only negligible utility gap. Thus, no protocol can satisfy that any deviation results in a noticeable utility loss, and in particular the constructions in [3] seem to fail with respect to such strong utility gap requirement. Such cheating prover behavior renders the above alternative definition of reward gap meaningless (it would be negligible for any rational proof), and supports our choice of the reward gap definition that measures the gap with respect to provers that always report $f(x)$ incorrectly. Note that our definition of rational arguments does not suffer from this issue, since we only require the noticeable deviations to induce noticeable loss for the prover.

3.2 Building Blocks and Construction

In this section we provide a general transformation that is later applied to rational proofs that we construct in Section 4.4. The main theorem, Theorem 5, establishes that any suitable rational proof (with the required properties described below) can be made one-round, while preserving both its efficiency and the incentive for a rational prover to be truthful. Namely, it guarantees to the verifier that after eliminating interaction, he will be (almost always) provided with a correct answer, although he might need to pay negligibly more than in the interactive version.

We note that the increase in expected reward achieved by the rational prover and his truthfulness directly relate to the user privacy of the underlying PIR scheme.This hints that trying to violate the PIR user privacy is the best strategy to increase one's reward (though this reasoning heavily relies on the assumption that trying to break the PIR incurs no computational cost whatsoever). We use the following definition of PIR scheme.

Definition 4 (Poly-logarithmic PIR [19]). *Let κ be the security parameter and N be the database size. Let Q^{PIR} and D^{PIR} be probabilistic circuits, and let R^{PIR} be a deterministic circuit. We say that $(Q^{\mathrm{PIR}}, D^{\mathrm{PIR}}, R^{\mathrm{PIR}})$ is a* poly-logarithmic private information retrieval scheme *if the following conditions are satisfied:*

(a) (Size Restriction:) *Q^{PIR} and R^{PIR} are both of size $\leq \mathrm{poly}(\kappa, \log N)$, and D^{PIR} is of size $\leq \mathrm{poly}(\kappa, N)$. The output of Q^{PIR} and D^{PIR} is of size $\leq \mathrm{poly}(\kappa, \log N)$.*

(b) (Correctness:) *$\forall N, \forall \kappa, \forall$database $x = (x_1, \ldots, x_N) \in \{0,1\}^N$, and $\forall i \in [N]$,*

$$\Pr\left[R^{\mathrm{PIR}}(\kappa, N, i, (q,s), a) = x_i \,\middle|\, \begin{array}{c}(q,s) \leftarrow Q^{\mathrm{PIR}}(\kappa, N, i),\\ a \leftarrow D^{\mathrm{PIR}}(\kappa, x, q)\end{array}\right] \geq 1 - 2^{-\kappa^3} .$$

(c) (User Privacy:) *$\forall N, \forall \kappa, \forall i, j \in [N]$, and for every adversary $\mathcal{A}$ of size at most 2^{κ^3},*

$$|\Pr[\mathcal{A}(\kappa, N, q) = 1 | (q,s) \leftarrow Q^{\mathrm{PIR}}(\kappa, N, i)] - \Pr[\mathcal{A}(\kappa, N, q) = 1 | (q,s) \leftarrow Q^{\mathrm{PIR}}(\kappa, N, j)]| \leq 2^{-\kappa^3} .$$

Such PIR schemes exist under different computational assumptions, cf. Cachin, Micali and Stadler [6] who construct poly-logarithmic PIR for any $\kappa > \log N$ under the Φ-Hiding Assumption.

Admissible Protocols.

As in Kalai and Raz [19] we need the rational proof (P, V) to have the following properties: (1) history-ignorance: each message of the prover P can depend only on the message sent by the verifier at the same round. (2) each message of the verifier V can depend only on its random coins.[3] (3) the running time of the verifier V is sub-linear in the input size. We call such protocols *admissible rational proof.*

We can now present the main theorem that enables us to construct one-round rational arguments from interactive rational proofs (full proof is in Section 3.3). For simplicity

[3]The verifier's messages are independent of the function and the input; however, they can be correlated among themselves.

of exposition, we normalize the reward to be in $[0,1]$, and make the verifier output 1 with probability of the computed reward (in addition to the reported value of $f(x)$). Note that the probability of a verifier outputting 1 is then exactly the expected reward.

Theorem 5. *Let (P_I, V_I) be an r-round admissible rational proof for evaluating a polynomially bounded function $f : \{0,1\}^n \to \{0,1\}$ with communication complexity ℓ, and let $N = 2^\lambda$, where λ is the length of the longest message sent by V_I. Let $\mathsf{reward}(\cdot)$ and Δ be the reward function and the corresponding reward gap. Assume the existence of a poly-logarithmic PIR scheme with user-privacy $1-\delta$ (where $\delta = 2^{-\kappa^3}$), and let $\delta_0 = (r-1)\cdot\delta$.[4] Then for any security parameter $\kappa = \kappa(n) \geq \max\{\ell, \log n\}$, there exists a one-round protocol (P_A, V_A) with the following properties:*

(a) $\Pr[\mathsf{output}((P_A, V_A)(x)) = f(x)] = 1$.

(b) $\mathrm{E}[\mathsf{reward}((P_A, V_A)(x))] \geq \mathrm{E}[\mathsf{reward}((P_I, V_I)(x))]\cdot(1-\delta_0)$.

(c) The communication complexity is $\ell \cdot \mathrm{poly}(\kappa, \log N)$.

(d) The verifier V_A runs in time $\ell\cdot\mathrm{poly}(\kappa) + O(T_{V_I})$, where T_{V_I} is the running time of V_I.

(e) The prover P_A runs in time $\mathrm{poly}(\kappa, N, T_{P_I})$, where T_{P_I} is the running time of P_I.

(f) For any prover $\tilde{P}$ of size $\leq 2^{\kappa^2}$ that achieves

$$\mathrm{E}[\mathsf{reward}((\tilde{P}, V_A)(x))] = \mathrm{E}[\mathsf{reward}((P_A, V_A)(x))] + \delta^* ,$$

let $\mu = \Pr[\mathsf{output}((\tilde{P}, V_A)(x)) \neq f(x)]$. It holds that

(a) (Utility gain) $\delta^* \leq 2\delta_0$, *and*

(b) (Utility loss) $(-\delta^*) \geq \mu\Delta - (2+\Delta)\delta_0$.

As pointed out in Section 3.1, the utility loss of an arbitrary prover is at least $\mu\Delta$; hence Theorem 5 presents a construction that basically preserves (up to a negligible factor) the utility gain and loss of the underlying rational proof. Moreover, it guarantees that if the rational proof has noticeable utility loss (in particular, noticeable reward gap) then the constructed protocol will also have noticeable utility loss.

Theorem 6. *Let $f : \{0,1\}^n \to \{0,1\}$ be a function in* FRMA $[r, C, T]$. *Assume the existence of a PIR scheme with communication complexity* $\mathrm{poly}(\kappa)$ *and receiver work* $\mathrm{poly}(\kappa)$, *where $\kappa \geq \max\{C(n), \log n\}$ is the security parameter. If f has an admissible rational proof with noticeable reward gap Δ, then f admits rational argument which has the following properties:*

(a) The verifier runs in time $C(n)\cdot\mathrm{poly}(\kappa) + O(T(n))$.

(b) The communication complexity is $r\cdot\mathrm{poly}(\kappa, \log N)$ with N defined as above.

Proof. The running time of the verifier, the communication complexity, and property (a) of Definition 2 of rational argumetns are all explicitly provided by Theorem 5. It remains to show property (b) and property (c) of definition of rational arguments.

The utility gain is $\delta^* \leq 2\delta_0 \leq 2^{-\kappa^2+1} \leq 2^{-\log^2 n+1} = \mathrm{negl}(n)$. By the definition of δ^* we have,

$$\begin{aligned}&\mathrm{negl}(n) + \mathrm{E}[\mathsf{reward}((P_A, V_A)(x))]\\ &\geq \delta^* + \mathrm{E}[\mathsf{reward}((P_A, V_A)(x))]\\ &= \mathrm{E}[\mathsf{reward}((\tilde{P}, V_A)(x))] ,\end{aligned}$$

and hence property (b) of rational arguments follows.

To show property (c) of Definition 2, we assume that $\mu \geq p^{-1}(|x|)$ for some polynomial $p(\cdot)$. Due to the noticeable Δ, we know that $\mu\Delta \geq q_1^{-1}(|x|)$ for some polynomial $q_1(\cdot)$. From the utility loss bound we obtain that

$$\begin{aligned}(-\delta^*) &\geq \mu\Delta - (2+\Delta)\delta_0\\ &= \mu\Delta - \mathrm{negl}(n)\\ &\geq q_1^{-1}(|x|) - \mathrm{negl}(n)\\ &\geq q_1^{-1}(|x|)/2 .\end{aligned}$$

By defining polynomial $q(\cdot)$ to be $q(|x|) = 2q_1(|x|)$ we get

$$\begin{aligned}\mathrm{E}[\mathsf{reward}((P_A, V_A)(x))] &= \mathrm{E}[\mathsf{reward}((\tilde{P}, V_A)(x))] - \delta^*\\ &\geq \mathrm{E}[\mathsf{reward}((\tilde{P}, V_A)(x))] + q^{-1}(|x|)\end{aligned}$$

as desired. □

3.3 Proof of Theorem 5

First we present the transformation that allows to squash interaction to a single round, and then show that it achieves the claimed efficiency parameters. The transformation we apply to obtain rational arguments from rational proofs is essentially that of Kalai and Raz [19], and it is described for completeness below. Note that even though it uses PIR in order to hide verifier's queries from the prover, it does not introduce the issue of *spooky interactions* discussed in the work of Dwork *et al.* [11]. Indeed, Kalai and Raz [19] proved that the two-message argument obtained by their transformation from a suitable proof system is sound, which does not contradict the results of Dwork *et al.* [11] stating that in some cases such transformation need not to be secure when applied on an efficient PCP.

From interactive rational proofs to rational arguments.

Let (P_I, V_I) be an interactive rational proof for evaluating some function f, as in the statement of the Theorem 5. Recall that λ denotes length of the longest message sent by V_I in (P_I, V_I). For simplicity of exposition (and without loss of generality) we assume that this protocol consists of exactly ℓ rounds, where in the first round P_I sends $f(x)$, and in all other rounds V_I sends a message of size exactly λ, and P_I sends a single bit (i.e., $\ell = r$).

Fix any security parameter $\kappa \geq \max\{\ell, \log n\}$ and let $(Q^{\mathrm{PIR}}, D^{\mathrm{PIR}}, R^{\mathrm{PIR}})$ be a poly-logarithmic PIR scheme, with respect to security parameter κ and database size $N = 2^\lambda$. The one-round rational argument (P_A, V_A) is constructed as follows:

1. On common input $x \in \{0,1\}^n$, the verifier V_A proceeds as follows:

   (a) Emulate the verifier V_I to obtain the messages $m_2, \ldots, m_\ell \in \{0,1\}^\lambda$ to be sent by V_I.[5]

[4]We assume the existence of poly-logarithmic PIR for any κ and any database size.

[5]These messages can be computed in advance since in the protocol (P_I, V_I) all the messages sent by V_I depend only on V_I's random coin tosses (this follows from (P_I, V_I) being an admissible protocol).

(b) Compute $(q_i, s_i) \leftarrow Q^{\text{PIR}}(\kappa, N, m_i)$ for $2 \le i \le \ell$ and send $(q_2, \ldots, q_\ell)$ to P_A.

2. Upon receiving a message $(q_2, \ldots, q_\ell)$ from V_A, the prover P_A operates as follows:

   (a) Emulate P_I to obtain $f(x)$.

   (b) For each $2 \le i \le \ell$, compute a database DB_i (of size N), which is a collection of all emulated replies of P_I in the i'th round upon receiving any possible message $m \in \{0,1\}^\lambda$.[6]

   (c) For each $2 \le i \le \ell$, compute $a_i \leftarrow D^{\text{PIR}}(\kappa, DB_i, q_i)$ and send the message $(f(x), a_2, \ldots, a_\ell)$ to V_A.

3. Upon receiving the message $(f(x), a_2, \ldots, a_\ell)$ from P_A, the verifier V_A operates as follows:

   (a) For every $2 \le i \le \ell$, compute
   $$b_i' \leftarrow R^{\text{PIR}}(\kappa, N, m_i, (q_i, s_i), a_i) \ .$$

   (b) Emulate V_I on $(f(x), b_2', \ldots, b_\ell')$, as if each b_i' is P_I's response in the i'th round.

   (c) Output whatever V_I outputs (i.e., $f(x)$ and '1' with probability of the computed reward).

Correctness.

Let $x \in \{0,1\}^n$ be a common input. Let $m_2, \ldots, m_\ell \in \{0,1\}^\lambda$ be the messages generated by the underlying V_I. Let $b_2, \ldots, b_\ell$ be the responses to $m_2, \ldots, m_\ell$ of the underlying P_I. Let $b_2', \ldots, b_\ell'$ be the responses obtained by V_A after applying the algorithm R^{PIR}. According to the correctness property of the poly-logarithmic PIR scheme, for every $2 \le i \le \ell$ it holds that $\Pr[b_i' \ne b_i] < 2^{-\kappa^3}$ and by the union bound it follows that

$$\begin{aligned}\Pr[\text{no error in } R^{\text{PIR}}] &= \Pr[(b_2, \ldots, b_\ell) \\ &= (b_2', \ldots, b_\ell')] \\ &\ge 1 - (\ell - 1) \cdot 2^{-\kappa^3} = 1 - \delta_0 \ .\end{aligned}$$

Therefore,

$$\begin{aligned}&\mathrm{E}[\mathsf{reward}((P_A, V_A)(x))] \\ &\ge \mathrm{E}[\mathsf{reward}((P_A, V_A)(x)) | R^{\text{PIR}} \text{ correct}] \cdot \Pr[R^{\text{PIR}} \text{ correct}] \\ &\ge \mathrm{E}[\mathsf{reward}((P_I, V_I)(x))] \cdot (1 - \delta_0) \ .\end{aligned}$$

Item (a), which defines the output distribution of the constructed prover, simply follows from the definition of rational proofs and the transformation. More formally,

$$\begin{aligned}&\Pr[\mathsf{output}((P_A, V_A)(x)) = f(x)] \\ &= \Pr[\mathsf{output}((P_I, V_I)(x)) = f(x)] = 1 \ .\end{aligned}$$

Complexity.

The used PIR scheme is poly-logarithmic (see Definition 4), and hence the total communication complexity is

$$|f(x)| + \sum_{i=2}^{\ell} (|a_i| + |q_i|) \le \ell \cdot \text{poly}(\kappa, \log N) \ .$$

[6]These databases can be computed due to the history-ignorant property of (P_I, V_I).

The resulting verifier V_A emulates the verifier of the interactive rational proof V_I and additionally executes the algorithms Q^{PIR} and R^{PIR} $(\ell - 1)$-times. Therefore, its running time can be bounded by

$$\ell \cdot \text{poly}(\kappa, \log N) + O(T_{V_I}) \le \ell \cdot \text{poly}(\kappa) + O(T_{V_I}) \ .$$

Note that generating a single database requires $N \cdot T_{P_I}$, and each execution of the database algorithm D^{PIR} requires $\text{poly}(\kappa, N)$. Therefore, the running time of P_A can be bounded by

$$\text{poly}(\kappa, N, T_{P_I}) \ .$$

Before completing the proof of Theorem 5, we show how to convert any prover for the resulting (P_A, V_A) into a prover for the original (P_I, V_I). Our transformation preserves (up to a negligible amount) the expected reward and the probability of each answer.

Lemma 7. *Let (P_I, V_I) be an r-round interactive rational proof as in the statement of Theorem 5. Let (P_A, V_A) be the protocol after the transformation above, where we define κ, λ, ℓ, N also as above and assume the existence of poly-logarithmic PIR with user-privacy $1 - \delta$ (where $\delta = 2^{-\kappa^3}$), and let $\delta_0 = (r-1) \cdot \delta$. Given a prover $\tilde{P}_A$ of size at most 2^{κ^2} for (P_A, V_A), there exists a prover $\tilde{P}_I$ for (P_I, V_I) such that for all x*

(a) $|\Pr[\mathsf{output}((\tilde{P}_A, V_A)(x)) = f(x)] - \Pr[\mathsf{output}((\tilde{P}_I, V_I)(x)) = f(x)]| \le \delta_0$ *, and*

(b) $\mathrm{E}[\mathsf{reward}((\tilde{P}_A, V_A)(x))] - \mathrm{E}[\mathsf{reward}((\tilde{P}_I, V_I)(x))] \le \delta_0$.

Proof. Let $\tilde{P}_A$ of size $T_{\tilde{P}_A} \le 2^{\kappa^2}$ be some prover for (P_A, V_A), and let $x \in \{0,1\}^n$ be some input. Consider $\tilde{P}_I$, a prover for (P_I, V_I), that behaves as follows:

1. Pick $m_2', \ldots, m_r'$ independently at random from $\{0,1\}^\lambda$.
2. Compute $(q_j', s_j') \leftarrow Q^{\text{PIR}}(\kappa, N, m_j')$ for $2 \le j \le r$.
3. Internally run $\tilde{P}_A$ on $(q_2', \ldots, q_r')$, and obtain the message $(y, a_2, \ldots, a_r)$, where y is $\tilde{P}_A$'s answer to $f(x)$.
4. Send y to V_I.
5. Continue in the interaction with V_I. For every $2 \le j \le r$, reply to m_j by a message b_j' that maximizes the expected reward over the randomness V_I conditioned on m_j and the history up to this round.

Assume by a way of contradiction that the statement of lemma does not hold with respect to the $\tilde{P}_I$ above. That is, either item *(a)* does not hold:

$$\begin{aligned}&|\Pr[\mathsf{output}((\tilde{P}_A, V_A)(x)) = f(x)] \\ &- \Pr[\mathsf{output}((\tilde{P}_I, V_I)(x)) = f(x)]| > \delta_0 \ , \qquad (1)\end{aligned}$$

or item *(b)* does not hold:

$$\mathrm{E}[\mathsf{reward}((\tilde{P}_A, V_A)(x))] - \mathrm{E}[\mathsf{reward}((\tilde{P}_I, V_I)(x))] > \delta_0 \ . \quad (2)$$

Consider a sequence of hybrids $\{H_i = (\tilde{P}_A, V_i)\}_{i=1}^r$ (see Figure 1) defined by the following V_i:

1. Emulate V_I to obtain $m_2, \ldots, m_r$.
2. Choose independent and random $m_{i+1}', \ldots, m_r' \in \{0,1\}^\lambda$.

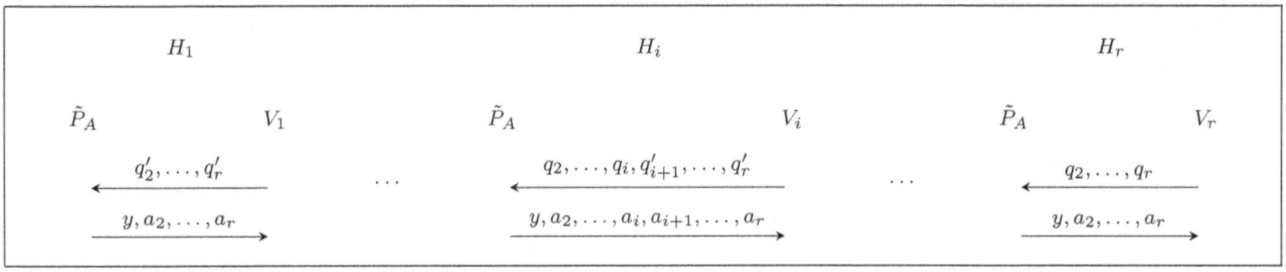

Figure 1: The sequence of hybrids H_i

3. Compute $(q_j, s_j) \leftarrow Q^{\text{PIR}}(\kappa, N, m_j)$ for $2 \leq j \leq i$, and $(q'_j, s'_j) \leftarrow Q^{\text{PIR}}(\kappa, N, m'_j)$ for $i+1 \leq j \leq r$.
4. Send $(q_2, \ldots, q_i, q'_{i+1} \ldots, q'_r)$ to $\tilde{P}_A$.
5. Upon receiving $(y, a_2, \ldots, a_r)$ compute
$$b_j \leftarrow R^{\text{PIR}}(\kappa, N, m_j, (q_j, s_j), a_j) \text{ for } 2 \leq j \leq i .$$
6. Emulate V_I as follows: first give y. Next, for $2 \leq j \leq i$ reply with b_j on m_j. For $i+1 \leq j \leq r$, on m_j reply with b'_j that maximizes the expected reward over the randomness of V_I conditioned on m_j and the history up to this round.
7. Output whatever V_I outputs.

By construction of the hybrids it holds that
$$\Pr[\mathsf{output}((\tilde{P}_I, V_I)(x)) = f(x)]$$
$$= \Pr[\mathsf{output}((\tilde{P}_A, V_1)(x)) = f(x)] ,$$
and
$$\text{E}[\mathsf{reward}((\tilde{P}_I, V_I)(x))] = \text{E}[\mathsf{reward}((\tilde{P}_A, V_1)(x))] .$$
Moreover,
$$\Pr[\mathsf{output}((\tilde{P}_A, V_A)(x)) = f(x)]$$
$$= \Pr[\mathsf{output}((\tilde{P}_A, V_r)(x)) = f(x)] ,$$
and
$$\text{E}[\mathsf{reward}((\tilde{P}_A, V_A)(x))] = \text{E}[\mathsf{reward}((\tilde{P}_A, V_r)(x))] .$$

If equation (1) does not hold, then by the hybrid argument, there exists $1 \leq k \leq r-1$ such that
$$|\Pr[\mathsf{output}((\tilde{P}_A, V_k)(x)) = f(x)]$$
$$- \Pr[\mathsf{output}((\tilde{P}_A, V_{k+1})(x)) = f(x)]| > \frac{\delta_0}{r-1} = \delta .$$
We show that this contradicts the user privacy of the underlying PIR scheme $(Q^{\text{PIR}}, D^{\text{PIR}}, R^{\text{PIR}})$. That is, we show that there exist an adversary $\mathcal{A}^k_x$ and two strings $m_{k+1}, m'_{k+1} \in \{0,1\}^\lambda$, such that $\mathcal{A}^k_x$ on input query q distinguishes whether q was created from m_{k+1} or m'_{k+1}. Let $\mathcal{A}^k_x$ be as follows:

1. Emulate V_I to obtain messages $m_2, \ldots, m_r$. In addition, choose $m'_{k+1}, \ldots, m'_r \in \{0,1\}^\lambda$ independently at random.
2. Compute $(q_j, s_j) \leftarrow Q^{\text{PIR}}(\kappa, N, m_j)$ for $2 \leq j \leq k$ and $(q'_j, s'_j) \leftarrow Q^{\text{PIR}}(\kappa, N, m'_j)$ for $k+2 \leq j \leq r$.
3. Upon receiving q, internally run $\tilde{P}_A$ on the queries $(q_2, \ldots, q_k, q, q'_{k+2}, \ldots, q'_r)$ to obtain $(y, a_2, \ldots, a_r)$.
4. Compute $f(x)$ and output 1 if $y = f(x)$, otherwise output 0.

Note that
$$\Pr[\mathsf{output}((\tilde{P}_A, V_{k+1})(x)) = f(x)]$$
$$= \Pr[\mathcal{A}^k_x(\kappa, N, q) = 1 | (q, s) \leftarrow Q^{\text{PIR}}(\kappa, N, m_{k+1})] \text{ , and}$$
$$\Pr[\mathsf{output}((\tilde{P}_A, V_k)(x)) = f(x)]$$
$$= \Pr[\mathcal{A}^k_x(\kappa, N, q) = 1 | (q, s) \leftarrow Q^{\text{PIR}}(\kappa, N, m'_{k+1})] .$$
Hence,
$$|\Pr[\mathcal{A}^k_x(\kappa, N, q) = 1 | (q, s) \leftarrow Q^{\text{PIR}}(\kappa, N, m_{k+1})]$$
$$- \Pr[\mathcal{A}^k_x(\kappa, N, q) = 1 | (q, s) \leftarrow Q^{\text{PIR}}(\kappa, N, m'_{k+1})]| > \delta .$$
Moreover, the size of $\mathcal{A}^k_x$ is at most $\text{poly}(2^\kappa) + T_{\tilde{P}_A} \leq 2^{\kappa^3}$ as desired.

Similarly, if equation (2) does not hold, then by the hybrid argument, there exists $1 \leq k \leq r-1$ such that
$$\text{E}[\mathsf{reward}((\tilde{P}_A, V_{k+1})(x))] - \text{E}[\mathsf{reward}((\tilde{P}_A, V_k)(x))] > \delta .$$
As before, we show that there exist an adversary $\mathcal{B}^k_x$ and two strings $m_{k+1}, m'_{k+1} \in \{0,1\}^\lambda$, such that $\mathcal{B}^k_x$ on input query q distinguishes whether q was created from m_{k+1} or m'_{k+1}. Let $\mathcal{B}^k_x$ be as follows:

1. Perform steps 1. - 3. as in the construction of $\mathcal{A}^k_x$.
2. Emulate V_I as follows: First give y. Next, for $2 \leq j \leq k$ reply with b_j on m_j. For $k+1 \leq j \leq r$, on m_j reply with b'_j that maximizes the expected reward over the randomness of V_I conditioned on m_j and the history up to this round. Note that each b'_j can be computed in time $\text{poly}(2^{\lambda \cdot \ell}) \leq \text{poly}(2^{\kappa^2})$.
3. Output whatever V_I outputs.

Note that
$$\text{E}[\mathsf{reward}((\tilde{P}_A, V_{k+1})(x))]$$
$$\geq \Pr[\mathcal{B}^k_x(\kappa, N, q) = 1 | (q, s) \leftarrow Q^{\text{PIR}}(\kappa, N, m_{k+1})] ,$$
and
$$\text{E}[\mathsf{reward}((\tilde{P}_A, V_k)(x))]$$
$$= \Pr[\mathcal{B}^k_x(\kappa, N, q) = 1 | (q, s) \leftarrow Q^{\text{PIR}}(\kappa, N, m'_{k+1})] .$$
Hence,
$$\Pr[\mathcal{B}^k_x(\kappa, N, q) = 1 | (q, s) \leftarrow Q^{\text{PIR}}(\kappa, N, m_{k+1})]$$
$$- \Pr[\mathcal{B}^k_x(\kappa, N, q) = 1 | (q, s) \leftarrow Q^{\text{PIR}}(\kappa, N, m'_{k+1})] > \delta .$$
To conclude the proof of the lemma, we note that the size of $\mathcal{B}^k_x$ is at most $\text{poly}(2^{\kappa^2}) + T_{\tilde{P}_A} \leq 2^{\kappa^3}$ as desired. □

Utility guarantee.

Let $\tilde{P}$ be some prover of size at most 2^{κ^2} for (P_A, V_A) that achieves $\mathrm{E}[\mathsf{reward}((\tilde{P}, V_A)(x))] = \mathrm{E}[\mathsf{reward}((P_A, V_A)(x))] + \delta^*$. By Lemma 7, there exists a prover $\tilde{P_I}$ such that:

$$|\Pr[\mathsf{output}((\tilde{P}, V_A)(x)) \neq f(x)] - \Pr[\mathsf{output}((\tilde{P_I}, V_I)(x)) \neq f(x)]| \leq \delta_0 , \quad (3)$$

and

$$\mathrm{E}[\mathsf{reward}((\tilde{P}, V_A)(x))] - \mathrm{E}[\mathsf{reward}((\tilde{P_I}, V_I)(x))] \leq \delta_0 . \quad (4)$$

Let $\mu_0 = \Pr[\mathsf{output}((\tilde{P_I}, V_I)(x)) \neq f(x)]$. By the definition of reward gap,

$$\begin{aligned} &\mathrm{E}[\mathsf{reward}((\tilde{P_I}, V_I)(x))] \\ &\leq \mu_0 \cdot (\mathrm{E}[\mathsf{reward}((P_I, V_I)(x))] - \Delta) \\ &\qquad +(1-\mu_0) \cdot \mathrm{E}[\mathsf{reward}((P_I, V_I)(x))] \\ &= \mathrm{E}[\mathsf{reward}((P_I, V_I)(x))] - \mu_0 \Delta . \end{aligned}$$

By combining (4) and the above, we obtain

$$\begin{aligned} &\mathrm{E}[\mathsf{reward}((\tilde{P}, V_A)(x))] \\ &\leq \mathrm{E}[\mathsf{reward}((\tilde{P_I}, V_I)(x))] + \delta_0 \\ &\leq \mathrm{E}[\mathsf{reward}((P_I, V_I)(x))] + \delta_0 - \mu_0 \Delta . \end{aligned}$$

On the other hand, from the already justified item (b) of Theorem 5 it follows that

$$\begin{aligned} &\mathrm{E}[\mathsf{reward}((\tilde{P}, V_A)(x))] \\ &= \mathrm{E}[\mathsf{reward}((P_A, V_A)(x))] + \delta^* \\ &\geq \mathrm{E}[\mathsf{reward}((P_I, V_I)(x))] \cdot (1-\delta_0) + \delta^* . \end{aligned}$$

Coupling the two above inequalities gives

$$\begin{aligned} &\mathrm{E}[\mathsf{reward}((P_I, V_I)(x))] \cdot (1-\delta_0) + \delta^* \\ &\leq \mathrm{E}[\mathsf{reward}((P_I, V_I)(x))] + \delta_0 - \mu_0 \Delta . \end{aligned}$$

Since the reward function assigns values from $[0,1]$ we get

$$\mu_0 \leq \frac{\delta_0(\mathrm{E}[\mathsf{reward}((P_I, V_I)(x))] + 1) - \delta^*}{\Delta} ,$$

$$\mu_0 \leq \frac{2\delta_0 - \delta^*}{\Delta} .$$

Since $\mu_0 \geq 0$, we get an upper bound $\delta^* \leq 2\delta_0$ on δ^*. Finally, combining the upper bound on μ_0 with equation (3) gives

$$\mu = \Pr[\mathsf{output}((\tilde{P}, V_A)(x)) \neq f(x)] \leq \mu_0 + \delta_0 \leq \frac{2\delta_0 - \delta^*}{\Delta} + \delta_0 ,$$

which implies $\delta^* \leq 2\delta_0 - (\mu - \delta_0)\Delta = (2+\Delta)\delta_0 - \mu\Delta$. Thus we obtain $(-\delta^*) \geq \mu\Delta - (2+\Delta)\delta_0$ which concludes the proof of Theorem 5.

3.4 Main result

We can now state our main result obtained by applying the transformation in Theorem 5 on an efficient interactive rational proofs with noticeable reward gap from Section 4.4. Thus, showing an explicit construction of efficient one-round rational arguments.

Corollary 8 (Main result). *Let $f : \{0,1\}^n \to \{0,1\}$ be a function computable by log-space uniform NC1 of size $S(n) =$ poly(n) and depth $d = O(\log n)$. Assume the existence of a PIR scheme with communication complexity* poly(κ) *and receiver work* poly(κ), *where $\kappa \geq \max\{d, \log n\}$ is the security parameter. Then f admits* efficient *rational argument which has the following properties:*

(a) The verifier runs in $d \cdot$ poly(κ) *and the prover runs in* poly(κ, n).

(b) The length of prover's message and the verifier's challenge is $d \cdot$ poly(κ). *The verifier's challenge depends only on his random coins and is independent of the input x.*

We note that for rational proofs with low complexity parameters, Corollary 8 is not that compelling due to the overhead introduced by the PIR. It is the case especially for constant round rational proofs with up to $O(\log n)$ communication and verification time, i.e., rational protocols for TC0 proposed both in this work or by [3].

We already mentioned that the reward gap of rational proofs limits the use of the transformation into rational arguments, however Corollary 8 could be in principle extended to all function in TC with respect to a slightly weaker notion of rational arguments. A rational prover in the corresponding *relaxed model* would need to be sensitive to negligible utility loss, and in a sense it would not be affected by the cost of computing the function. The only semantic difference between the original and relaxed variant of the definition is in the extra guarantee on the utility-loss with respect to deviating provers. That is, property (c) of Definition 2 would change as follows:

$$\begin{aligned} &\left(\mathrm{E}[\mathsf{reward}((\tilde{P}, V)(x))] \geq \mathrm{E}[\mathsf{reward}((P, V)(x))]\right) \\ &\Rightarrow \left(\Pr[\mathsf{output}((\tilde{P}, V)(x)) \neq f(x)] \leq \mathrm{negl}(\kappa)\right) . \end{aligned}$$

Which demands slightly less, i.e., restricting only the computationally bounded provers achieving more than the prescribed prover to lie with at most negligible probability.

4. DOWNSCALING RATIONAL PROOFS

In this section we first illustrate the power of rational proofs for #P (Section 4.1) and then explore the possibility of "scaling down" rational proofs for #P to NP and classes below. In Section 4.2, we give an extremely laconic rational proof where the prover only needs to send one bit for any language in NP, however the verification in this protocol is not sub-linear. In Section 4.3 we show evidence that existence of single round rational proofs with sub-linear verification time is unlikely. In Section 4.4 we consider multiple-round rational proofs, and we show a rational proof for any language computable by uniform threshold circuit of depth d, where the verification time is $\tilde{O}(d)$. In particular, we obtain sub-linear verification time when $d = o(n)$. In Section 4.5 we discuss the possibility to go beyond threshold circuits.

4.1 Rational Proofs for #P

The main tool used in the construction of rational Merlin Arthur games are *scoring rules* that allow to evaluate quality of a forecast about probability of an uncertain future event. Any scoring rule assigns a numerical value $S(\mathcal{Q}, x)$ to some predictive distribution $\mathcal{Q}$ and event x drawn from the actual distribution $\mathcal{P}$ that the prediction tries to forecast. The expectation of the score is maximized when the forecaster reports $\mathcal{Q} = \mathcal{P}$.

Definition 9 (Strictly Proper Scoring Rule). *Let $\mathcal{P}$ be a probability distribution over a probability space Ω, and S a scoring rule. We say that S is a* strictly proper scoring rule *with respect to $\mathcal{P}$ if for all $\mathcal{Q} \neq \mathcal{P}$*

$$\sum_{\omega \in \Omega} \mathcal{P}(\omega) S(\mathcal{P}, \omega) > \sum_{\omega \in \Omega} \mathcal{P}(\omega) S(\mathcal{Q}, \omega) ,$$

where $\mathcal{P}(\omega)$ is the probability that ω is drawn from $\mathcal{P}$.

The study of scoring rules was initiated by Brier [5], who introduced a first example of a strictly proper scoring rule in the context of meteorological forecasts. A variant of the *Brier's scoring rule* is given by the function

$$S(\mathcal{P}, \omega) = 2\mathcal{P}(\omega) - \sum_{\omega \in \Omega} \mathcal{P}(\omega)^2 - 1 .$$

Another example of strictly proper scoring rule is the *logarithmic scoring rule*:

$$S(\mathcal{P}, \omega) = \log(\mathcal{P}(\omega)) .$$

For an extensive survey of scoring rules see Gneiting and Raftery [15].

Rational Merlin Arthur games posses a surprising power when compared to classical Merlin Arthur protocols. Azar and Micali [2] showed that any problem in #P, the class of counting problems associated with the decision problems in NP, has a rational Merlin Arthur game with a single n bits message from Merlin and Arthur running in time poly(n). However in the classical setting, such extremely efficient protocol is unlikely to exist.

A notable example of a problem in #P is #SAT i.e., given a Boolean formula ϕ to find the number of satisfying assignments of ϕ. Azar and Micali gave Rational Merlin Arthur game for #SAT defined by the following randomized reward function Brier. for which Arthur wants to know the number of satisfying assignments. He selects a random assignment $z \in \{0,1\}^n$ and sets $b = \phi(z)$. The reward function is then

$$\mathsf{Brier}(\phi, y) = \begin{cases} 2(y/2^n) - (y/2^n)^2 - (1 - y/2^n)^2 + 1, & \text{if } b = 1, \\ 2(1 - y/2^n) - (y/2^n)^2 - (1 - y/2^n)^2 + 1, & \text{if } b = 0. \end{cases}$$

It is obviously a randomized function that can be computed in polynomial time in $|\phi|$ and $|y|$. Let y^* be the number of satisfying assignment of ϕ, by simple calculation,

$$\mathrm{E}[\mathsf{Brier}(\phi, y)] = -2(y/2^n - y^*/2^n)^2 + 2(y^*/2^n)^2 - 2(y^*/2^n) + 2 . \quad (5)$$

The fact that $\mathrm{E}[\mathsf{Brier}(\phi, y)]$ is maximized exactly when Merlin sends y^*, the number of satisfying assignments of ϕ, follows because $\mathsf{Brier}(\phi, y)$ is defined as the Brier's scoring rule. Note that any formula ϕ defines a probability distribution of a random variable that is one if a random assignment of ϕ is satisfying and zero otherwise. By sending some y to Arthur, Merlin gives out a prediction about this distribution. Since his reward is computed according to a strictly proper scoring rule, Merlin is incentivized to report the correct number of satisfying assignments.

On common input x and $L \in$ NP.

1. Merlin will send a bit y to Arthur denoting whether $x \in L$.
2. Arthur will sample a random candidate witness w for x, and compute the randomized reward $\mathsf{Brier}(x, y)$ for Merlin in the following way:

$$\begin{cases} 2\left(\frac{y}{|W_x|}\right) - \left(\frac{y}{|W_x|}\right)^2 - \left(1 - \frac{y}{|W_x|}\right)^2 + 1, & \text{if } (x, w) \in \mathcal{R}_L, \\ 2\left(1 - \frac{y}{|W_x|}\right) - \left(\frac{y}{|W_x|}\right)^2 - \left(1 - \frac{y}{|W_x|}\right)^2 + 1, & \text{if } (x, w) \notin \mathcal{R}_L. \end{cases}$$

Figure 2: Rational Merlin Arthur game for any NP language L

4.2 Extremely Laconic Rational Prover for any NP Language

In the rational Merlin Arthur game for #P of Azar and Micali, Merlin needs to send n bits to Arthur. We investigate on the possibility of existence of extremely succinct rational proofs. Towards this direction, let us restrict the communication to be only one bit. How can then Merlin convince Arthur about anything? Or else, what information can Arthur obtain in the #SAT protocol?

Recall the expected reward for announcing y for a formula ϕ which has y^* satisfying assignments given by (5). Our main observation is that the expected reward $\mathrm{E}[\mathsf{Brier}(\phi, y)]$ has the following favourable property; the smaller $|y - y^*|$ is, the larger is the expected reward $\mathrm{E}[\mathsf{Brier}(\phi, y)]$. If Merlin can only communicate one bit to Arthur (i.e., $y = 0$ or $y = 1$), he will choose the y which is closer to the true y^*. In particular, rational Merlin will tell Arthur $y = 0$ if $y^* = 0$, and he will announce $y = 1$ in the other case when $y^* \geq 1$. With one bit message from Merlin, Arthur does not expect to learn y^*. Nevertheless, he will obtain one bit information about y^* which is either that $y^* \geq 1$ or $y^* = 0$. And this is sufficient information for Arthur to decide whether $\phi \in$ SAT. It implies SAT has extremely succinct rational proof, and in fact any language in NP has such laconic rational proof where prover sends only one bit to the verifier. This gives the following theorem, that illuminates the power of rational proofs.

Theorem 10. NP $\subset$ DRMA$[1, 1, \mathrm{poly}(n)]$.

The general protocol for any NP language is given in Figure 2. Moreover, similar rational proof will work also for languages in coNP and PP. Thus, this two important classes are also contained in FRMA$[1, 1, \mathrm{poly}(n)]$, and unlike NP, both PP and coNP do not have classical one round interactive proof. For PP, our rational proof improves the efficiency of communication to only one bit message, compared to the rational proof of Azar and Micali with n bits of communication.

We formalize a general observation as following lemma which immediately implies Theorem 10.

Lemma 11 (Threshold Lemma). *For any polynomially bounded function $f : \{0,1\}^* \to \{0,1\}$. Let $C : \{0,1\}^* \times \{0,1\}^* \to \{0,1\}$ be a randomized procedure, and let β_0, β_1 :*

$\mathbb{N} \to [0,1]$ *be two functions such that* $\beta_0(n) < \beta_1(n)$ *for every* $n \in \mathbb{N}$. *If for any* $x \in \{0,1\}^*$ *it holds that*

(a) $\Pr_r[C(x;r) = 1 | f(x) = 1] \geq \beta_1(|x|)$, *and*

(b) $\Pr_r[C(x;r) = 1 | f(x) = 0] \leq \beta_0(|x|)$, *then*

$f \in \mathrm{FRMA}[1,1,t(\cdot)]$, *where* $t(\cdot)$ *is the running time of* C.

Proof. Let $x \in \{0,1\}^n$ be a common input on which Arthur wants to evaluate f. We show that the following protocol constitutes a rational Merlin Arthur game for f:

1. Merlin sends $y \in \{0,1\}$ to Arthur.

2. Arthur uniformly at random selects the random coins r for C and sets $b = C(x;r)$. He then pays Merlin $\mathsf{Brier}(x,y)$, where

$$\mathsf{Brier}(x,y) = \begin{cases} 2\beta_y(n) - (\beta_y(n))^2 - (1-\beta_y(n))^2 + 1, & \text{if } b = 1, \\ 2(1-\beta_y(n)) - (\beta_y(n))^2 - (1-\beta_y(n))^2 + 1, & \text{if } b = 0. \end{cases}$$

Clearly, the running time of Arthur is $t(n)$.

Let $\beta = \Pr_r[C(x;r) = 1]$ (note that β would differ for another input $x' \in \{0,1\}^*$). The expected reward for Merlin when sending y is $\mathrm{E}_r[\mathsf{Brier}(x,y)] = -2(\beta_y(n) - \beta)^2 + 2\beta^2 - 2\beta + 2$. Intuitively, β corresponds to the true distribution that Arthur wants to learn. However, Merlin is restricted to report either $\beta_0(n)$ or $\beta_1(n)$ by sending $y \in \{0,1\}$ to Arthur in the above protocol. In order to maximize his reward, Merlin must choose y such that $\beta_y(n)$ is the closer one to β.

Formally, if $f(x) = 1$ then $\beta \geq \beta_1(n) > \beta_0(n)$, thus $\mathrm{E}_r[\mathsf{Brier}(x,1)] - \mathrm{E}_r[\mathsf{Brier}(x,0)] = 2((\beta_0(n) - \beta)^2 - (\beta_1(n) - \beta)^2) > 0$. Moreover, if $f(x) = 0$ then $\beta \leq \beta_0(n) < \beta_1(n)$, thus $\mathrm{E}_r[\mathsf{Brier}(x,0)] - \mathrm{E}_r[\mathsf{Brier}(x,1)] = 2((\beta_1(n) - \beta)^2 - (\beta_0(n) - \beta)^2) > 0$. In both cases, rational Merlin has a clear incentive to truthfully send $y = f(x)$. □

Notice that the proof of Lemma 11 makes mainly use of the fact that the expected reward is a distance function; the closer y is to the true answer, the more reward Merlin can get. Hence, we can replace the Brier's scoring rule with other scoring rules which have this property. For distributions over 0 and 1, most strictly proper scoring rules have this property.

Proof of Theorem 10. For any $x \in L$, let W_x be the space of all possible witnesses for membership of x in the language L. We define the following randomized procedure C_L. Select a candidate witness w uniformly at random from W_x. Set $C_L(x;w) = 1$ if w is a witness for $x \in L$, and $C_L(x;w) = 0$ otherwise. Since L is an NP language, $C_L(x;w)$ can be computed in polynomial time in $|x|$. Moreover, $\Pr_{w \in W_x}[C_L(x;w) = 1] \geq \frac{1}{|W_x|}$ for every $x \in L$ and $\Pr_{w \in W_x}[C_L(x;w) = 1] = 0$ for any $x \notin L$. Thus, we can use Lemma 11 to conclude the proof. □

4.3 Impossibility for Parity

A natural question to ask is if one can improve the verification time in our extremely laconic rational proofs for NP to be sub-linear. Our first observation is that, even for such a simple function as parity, it is impossible to have an extremely laconic rational proof with sub-linear verification. However, the verifier can compute parity in linear time on his own. Consequently, any rational proof for parity with such extremely laconic Merlin is not interesting from the perspective of delegation of computation.

Theorem 12. $\bigoplus x = x_1 \oplus \cdots \oplus x_n \notin \mathrm{FRMA}[1,1,o(n)]$.

Proof. Suppose $\bigoplus x \in \mathrm{FRMA}[1,1,o(n)]$. Then there exists a randomized reward function $\mathsf{reward}(x,y;r)$ (here we explicitly use an argument r to denote the randomness of the reward function) of running time $o(n)$, such that for any $x \in \{0,1\}^n$, Merlin will get higher expected reward by sending $y = \bigoplus x$ than by sending $y' = \overline{\bigoplus x}$. Formally, for any $x \in \{0,1\}^n$

$$\mathrm{E}_r\left[\mathsf{reward}(x, \textstyle\bigoplus x; r)\right] > \mathrm{E}_r\left[\mathsf{reward}(x, \overline{\textstyle\bigoplus x}; r)\right] .$$

It implies that for all inputs, the average advantage of telling the truth to lying is greater than zero, i.e.,

$$\mathrm{E}_{x \sim \{0,1\}^n}\left[\mathrm{E}_r[\mathsf{reward}(x, \textstyle\bigoplus x; r)] - \mathrm{E}_r[\mathsf{reward}(x, \overline{\textstyle\bigoplus x}; r)]\right] > 0 .$$

By linearity of expectation and after changing the order of variables, we obtain the following inequality

$$\mathrm{E}_r\left[\mathrm{E}_{x \sim \{0,1\}^n}[\mathsf{reward}(x, \textstyle\bigoplus x; r) - \mathsf{reward}(x, \overline{\textstyle\bigoplus x}; r)]\right] > 0 .$$

To demonstrate the sought contradiction, it is sufficient to show that for any fixed r

$$\mathrm{E}_{x \sim \{0,1\}^n}\left[\mathsf{reward}(x, \textstyle\bigoplus x; r) - \mathsf{reward}(x, \overline{\textstyle\bigoplus x}; r)\right] = 0 . \quad (6)$$

Recall that for any fixed r, the reward function $\mathsf{reward}(\cdot,\cdot;r)$ runs in time $o(n)$. Thus, $\mathsf{reward}(\cdot,\cdot;r)$ depends on at most $n-1$ bits of the input. Without loss of generality, we assume that $\mathsf{reward}(\cdot,\cdot;r)$ does not depend on x_n. In such case, for any choice of $x_1, \ldots, x_{n-1}, y \in \{0,1\}$,

$$\mathsf{reward}(x_1, \ldots, x_{n-1}, 0, y; r) = \mathsf{reward}(x_1, \ldots, x_{n-1}, 1, y; r) .$$

For any choice of the bits $x_1, \ldots, x_{n-1}$ let $b = x_1 \oplus \cdots \oplus x_{n-1}$. We get that

$$\begin{aligned} &\mathrm{E}_{x_n \sim \{0,1\}}\left[\mathsf{reward}(x, \textstyle\bigoplus x; r) - \mathsf{reward}(x, \overline{\textstyle\bigoplus x}; r)\right] \\ &= \frac{1}{2}\Big((\mathsf{reward}(x, b \oplus 0; r) - \mathsf{reward}(x, b \oplus 1; r))|_{x_n=0} \\ &\qquad + (\mathsf{reward}(x, b \oplus 1; r) - \mathsf{reward}(x, b \oplus 0; r))|_{x_n=1}\Big) \\ &= \frac{1}{2}\Big((\mathsf{reward}(x, b \oplus 0; r) - \mathsf{reward}(x, b \oplus 1; r))|_{x_n=0} \\ &\qquad + (\mathsf{reward}(x, b \oplus 1; r) - \mathsf{reward}(x, b \oplus 0; r))|_{x_n=0}\Big) \\ &= \frac{1}{2}(\mathsf{reward}(x, b \oplus 0; r) - \mathsf{reward}(x, b \oplus 1; r) \\ &\qquad + \mathsf{reward}(x, b \oplus 1; r) - \mathsf{reward}(x, b \oplus 0; r))|_{x_n=0} \\ &= 0 . \end{aligned}$$

In fact, the above already shows that equation (6) holds, since for every fixed r,

$$\begin{aligned}&\mathrm{E}_{x\sim\{0,1\}^n}[\mathsf{reward}(x,\bigoplus x;r)-\mathsf{reward}(x,\overline{\bigoplus x};r)]\\&=\mathrm{E}_{x_1,\ldots,x_{n-1}\sim\{0,1\}}\big[\\&\qquad\mathrm{E}_{x_n\sim\{0,1\}}[\mathsf{reward}(x,\bigoplus x;r)-\mathsf{reward}(x,\overline{\bigoplus x};r)]\big]\\&=\mathrm{E}_{x_1,\ldots,x_{n-1}\sim\{0,1\}}[0]\\&=0\,.\end{aligned}$$

□

This result demonstrates the difficulty of getting sub-linear verification with extremely laconic rational proof (even for a very restricted problem in P). It hints that in order to circumvent this issue, we have to increase the communication or the number of rounds.

4.4 Efficient Rational Proofs for TC

By using multiple rounds, we show a general solution for functions computable by log-space uniform threshold circuits of depth d with d rounds, $d-1$ bit communication overhead and $d\cdot\mathrm{polylog}(n)$ verification time. In particular, for the case of $d=o(n)$, both communication and the verification time are sub-linear. Another implication of this result is that we can give a rational proof with constant rounds, constant communication bits and $\mathrm{polylog}(n)$ verification for parity since parity function is computable by constant depth threshold circuit.

Theorem 13. *If $f\colon\{0,1\}^*\to\{0,1\}$ is computable by a family of $O(\log(S(n)))$-space uniform threshold circuits of size $S(n)$ and depth $d(n)$, then $f\in\mathrm{FRMA}[d(n),d(n),O(d(n)\cdot\mathrm{polylog}(S(n))]$.*

We provide the efficiency comparison with known delegation schemes in Section 1.4. Additional discussion regarding threshold circuits, non-uniform model of computation and multi-output case are provided in Section 4.4.2. Description of the protocol is given below.

Protocol.

Let a circuit of depth d and $x\in\{0,1\}^n$ be the common input to Arthur and Merlin. The protocol begins with the following conversation,

1. Merlin: Evaluate the circuit on x and send y_1, the output value, to Arthur.
2. Arthur: Set $\gamma=1/(1+2m_0^2)$, where m_0 is the largest fan-in over all gates in the circuit.[7] Identify the 'root' gate g_1, and invoke $\mathrm{Round}(1,g_1,y_1)$,

where the procedure $\mathrm{Round}(i,g_i,y_i)$ for $1\le i\le d$ is

1. Arthur: Randomly chooses a "child" g_{i+1} of g_i.
   - If g_{i+1} is an input wire of value z then pay Merlin $\gamma^{d-i}/2\cdot\mathsf{Brier}(g_i,y_i)$ where $b=z$ and **STOP**.
   - Otherwise, ask M_{i+1} for the value of g_{i+1}.
2. Merlin: Send y_{i+1}, the value of g_{i+1}, to Arthur.
3. Arthur: Pay Merlin $\gamma^{d-i}/2\cdot\mathsf{Brier}(g_i,y_i)$ where $b=y_{i+1}$ and go to $\mathrm{Round}(i+1,g_{i+1},y_{i+1})$.

[7] In fact m_0 can be any number larger than the maximal fan-in (for example siz of the circuit). So that to settle m_0 we don't need exactly compute the maximal fan-in.

Notice that Brier is the reward function defined for single gate case (see (7)) and both Brier and the discounting factor γ are efficiently computable in $O(\mathrm{polylog}(m_0))=O(\mathrm{polylog}(S(n)))$ time.

Efficiency.

The protocol runs at most d rounds. In each round, Merlin sends one bit to Arthur, thus the communication complexity is at most d bits. The computation of Arthur is sampling a child and calculating the reward function in each round. By the uniformity of the circuit, any information about each gate (e.g. the type of the gate, identifying the children) can be computed in space $O(\log(S(n)))$ and time $O(\mathrm{polylog}(S(n)))$. In particular, sampling a child only takes $O(\mathrm{polylog}(S(n)))$ time. The reward function is computable in $\mathrm{polylog}(n)$ time. Hence, Arthur runs in $O(d\cdot\mathrm{polylog}(S(n)))$. Remark that the computation of Arthur can be done in space $O(\log(S(n)))$ since Arthur only needs to keep the information i,g_i,y_i for each $\mathrm{Round}(i,g_i,y_i)$ and compute the reward in space $O(\log(S(n)))$.

Reward Gap.

Recall the Definition 3 of reward gap. The above protocol achieves reward gap proportional to the depth of the circuit, in particular

$$\Delta(|x|)>\frac{\gamma^{d-1}}{2}\cdot\frac{1}{m_0^2}\ge\frac{1}{(2m_0^2+1)^{d-1}}\cdot\frac{1}{2m_0^2}\ge\frac{1}{(2m_0^2+1)^d},$$

where m_0 is the maximal fan-in over all gates in the circuit. This gives noticeable reward gap for TC0, where $m_0=O(\mathrm{poly}(|x|))$ and d is constant and similarly for NC1, where m_0 is constant and $d=O(\log|x|)$.

4.4.1 Proof of Theorem 13

First, we apply our Threshold lemma (Lemma 11) to obtain extremely laconic rational proof for any single threshold gate which is the main building block.

Lemma 14. *If $g(x)$ is a threshold gate with fan-in n and threshold a, i.e.,*

$$g(x)=\begin{cases}1, & \text{if } x_1+\cdots+x_n\ge a,\\ 0, & \text{if } x_1+\cdots+x_n\le a-1,\end{cases}$$

then $g(x)\in\mathrm{FRMA}[1,1,O(\log n)]$.

Proof. Let $C(x;r)$ be: on input $x=(x_1,\ldots,x_n)$, uniformly at random choose $r\in\{1,\ldots,n\}$, and output x_r. Notice that the running time of $C(x;r)$ is $O(\log n)$. Since g is a gate with threshold a, we get

1. $\Pr_r[C(x;r)=1|g(x)=1]\ge\beta_1(n)$, and
2. $\Pr_r[C(x;r)=1|g(x)=0]\le\beta_0(n)$,

where $\beta_1(n)=a/n,\beta_0(n)=(a-1)/n$. By Lemma 11, $C(x;r)$ allows us to construct a rational proof. In particular, if Merlin sends $y\in\{0,1\}$ to Arthur and the output of $C(x;r)$ is b, Arthur will pay Merlin $\mathsf{Brier}(g,y)$, where

$$\mathsf{Brier}(g, y) = \begin{cases} 2\beta_y(g) - (\beta_y(g))^2 - (1-\beta_y(g))^2 + 1, & \text{if } b = 1, \\ 2(1-\beta_y(g)) - (\beta_y(g))^2 - (1-\beta_y(g))^2 + 1, & \text{if } b = 0. \end{cases} \quad (7)$$

It follows that $g(x) \in \text{FRMA}[1, 1, O(\log n)]$. □

MAJORITY, AND, and OR are all threshold gates, hence this lemma implies that MAJORITY, AND, and OR are in FRMA$[1, 1, O(\log n)]$.[8] Let $d-$ FRMA denote the class of languages that admit rational proof with d independent Merlins. We show how to delegate threshold circuits using multiple independent Merlins, then replace independent Merlins by one Merlin.

Lemma 15. *If $f\colon \{0,1\}^* \to \{0,1\}$ is computable by a family of $O\big(\log(S(n))\big)$-space uniform threshold circuits of size $S(n)$ and depth $d(n)$, then*

$$f \in d(n) - \text{FRMA}[d(n), d(n), O\big(d(n) \cdot \text{polylog}(S(n))\big)] \ .$$

Proof. To give an idea of our proof, let us make the simplifying assumption that for x of length n, f is computable by a tree of depth $d = d(n)$. We denote M_i the ith Merlin and $y_i \in \{0,1\}$ the bit sent by M_i to Arthur in our rational proof.

The protocol constitutes of d rounds. In the first round, M_1 will tell Arthur the value y_1 of the root gate g_1. In Lemma 14, Arthur incetivizes Merlin to tell the truth for a single gate g by randomly picking an input bit b and paying $\mathsf{Brier}(g, y)$ defined as in equation (7) to Merlin. Similarly, Arthur will randomly pick a subtree and pay $\mathsf{Brier}(g_1, y_1)$ to M_1 where b is the value of the chosen subtree. Arthur can avoid computing b by paying another independent Merlin M_2 to get the bit b. Conditioned on M_2 telling the correct value of b, M_1 only maximizes his reward when telling the truth.

Thus, we reduce incentivizing M_1 to tell the truth for the root of a depth d tree to making M_2 tell the truth for any depth $d-1$ subtree. By repeating this idea, we reduce the whole problem to making M_d tell the truth for any tree of depth 1 which is just a threshold gate, and this case is guaranteed by Lemma 14. The complete protocol is as follows.

Protocol with d Merlins.

Let $x \in \{0,1\}^n$ and some depth d circuit be the common input to Arthur and $M_1, \ldots M_d$. The protocol begins with following conversation,

1. Merlin M_1: sends y_1 to Arthur.
2. Arthur: identifies the 'root' gate g_1 and invokes the procedure Round$(1, g_1, y_1)$,

where Round(i, g_i, y_i) for $1 \le i \le d$ is

1. Arthur: randomly chooses a 'child' g_{i+1} of g_i.
    - If g_{i+1} is an input wire of value z, then pay $\mathsf{reward}(g_i, y_i)$ to M_i where $b = z$ and **STOP**.
    - Otherwise, ask M_{i+1} for the value of g_{i+1}.
2. Merlin M_{i+1}: sends y_{i+1}.
3. Arthur: Pay $\mathsf{Brier}(g_i, y_i)$ to M_i where $b = y_{i+1}$ and go to Round$(i+1, g_{i+1}, y_{i+1})$.

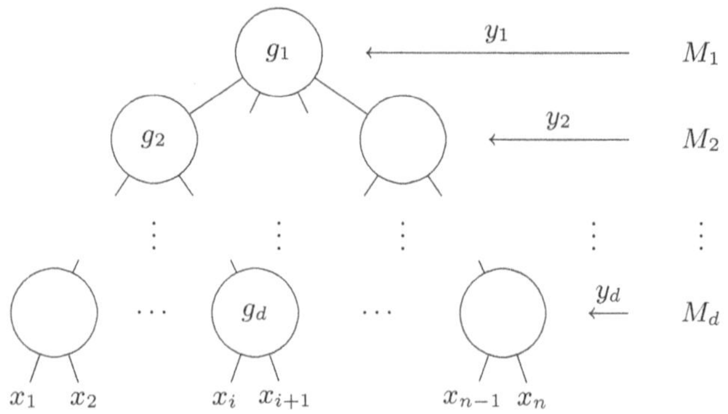

Figure 3: An independent Merlin M_i provides the intermediate value for each level i in the circuit according to Arthur's query g_i

Figure 3. depicts the process of selecting a random path in the circuit by Arthur from our protocol. Note that the achieved efficiency parameters are discussed in Section 4.4. Next, we prove the correctness.

Correctness.

We show by backward induction that for any $1 \le i \le d$, M_i prefers to answer Arthur with a correct value on the root for any depth $(d-i+1)$ threshold circuit. The base case is to show that M_d will tell the truth for any circuit of depth one, i.e., a threshold gate, which is guaranteed by Lemma 14. Assume that $M_d, \ldots, M_{i+1}$ are being truthful; we show that M_i will be consequently also truthful for any depth $d-i+1$ circuit X. Let the root gate g of X be connected to some depth (at most) $d-i$ sub-circuits $X_1, \ldots, X_m$. By the inductive hypothesis, $M_d, \ldots, M_{i+1}$ enable Arthur to learn the root value for each one of $X_1, \ldots, X_m$, and we can think of $X_1, \ldots, X_m$ as of fixed input bits each having depth zero, effectively reducing the depth of X to one. Hence, due to the help of $M_d, \ldots, M_{i+1}$, we only need to show that M_i will tell the truth for any threshold gate g. This case is the same as basic case ensured by Lemma 14. Hence, we can conclude that all of $M_1, \ldots, M_d$ prefer to truthfully report the value of the root for their respective sub-circuits. □

Arthur can in fact achieve the same when communicating with one Merlin. To merge the d independent Merlins into a protocol with a single Merlin, we discount the reward on the consecutive levels from the input gates to the root.[9]

Proof of Theorem 13. Besides the fact that Arthur is communicating with a single Merlin, the only difference between the protocol and the protocol described in Lemma 15 is that instead of paying $\mathsf{Brier}(g_i, y_i)$ in Round(i, g_i, y_i), Arthur now computes the reward as $\gamma^{d-i}/2 \cdot \mathsf{Brier}(g_i, y_i)$, where $\gamma = 1/(1+2m_0^2)$ and m_0 is the largest fan-in over all gates. After the protocol finishes, Arthur pays Merlin the total sum over all rounds.

[8]Remark that the NOT gate can be thought of as a threshold gate and has a similar rational proof, where one counts the number of zeros in the input instead of the number of ones. We therefore handle MAJORITY, AND, OR, and NOT gates.

[9]This idea resembles the proof of CH ⊂ DRMA presented in [2], however the discounting differs in our context.

The communication complexity and the number of rounds of the new protocol is exactly the same as of the protocol in Lemma 15. To check that it also constitutes a rational proof, we use backward induction to show that Merlin is truthful in each round when maximizing the expected reward. The base case is to prove that Merlin will tell the truth in $\text{Round}(d, g_d, y_d)$. If Merlin lies in this round his expected loss is

$$\begin{aligned}
&\gamma^{d-d}/2 \cdot |\,\mathrm{E}_r[\mathsf{Brier}(g_d, 0)] - \mathrm{E}_r[\mathsf{Brier}(g_d, 1)]| \\
&= \gamma^{d-d}/2 \cdot |(\beta - \beta_0(m))^2 - (\beta - \beta_1(m))^2| \\
&\geq \gamma^{d-d}/2 \cdot |(\beta_0(m) - \beta_1(m))(2\beta - \beta_0(m) - \beta_1(m))| \\
&\geq \gamma^{d-d}/2 \cdot (\beta_0(m) - \beta_1(m))^2 \\
&= \gamma^{d-d}/2 \cdot \frac{1}{m^2} \\
&\geq \frac{1}{2m_0^2},
\end{aligned}$$

where m is the fan-in of g_d. Since for every $1 \leq j \leq d$ we have $\mathsf{Brier}(g_j, y_j) \in [0, 2]$, the maximal total reward over the previous rounds $1, \ldots, d-1$ can be bound, i.e.,

$$\sum_{j=1}^{d-1} \gamma^{d-j}/2 \cdot \mathsf{Brier}(g_j, y_j) \leq \sum_{j=1}^{d-1} \gamma^{d-j} = \sum_{j=1}^{d-1} \left(\frac{1}{1+2m_0^2}\right)^{d-j} < \frac{1}{2m_0^2}.$$

Note that the total reward conditioned on lying in the last round is strictly smaller than the reward in the last round alone when telling the truth, hence a rational Merlin must be truthful in this round in order to maximize his total reward.

Assume that Merlin is truthful in rounds $d, \ldots, i+1$. Similarly to the base case, if he lies in $\text{Round}(i, g_i, y_i)$, then his expected loss is at least $\gamma^{d-i}/2 \cdot 1/m_0^2$ (conditioned on telling the truth in the next rounds). Moreover, the maximal total income over rounds $1, \ldots, i-1$ is also bounded, i.e.,

$$\sum_{j=1}^{i-1} \gamma^{d-j}/2 \cdot \mathsf{Brier}(g_j, y_j) \leq \sum_{j=1}^{i-1} \gamma^{d-j} < \gamma^{d-i} \cdot (1/2m_0^2).$$

By the same reasoning, Merlin is reporting the truth in Round (i, g_i, y_i) in order to maximize the total reward. Therefore, we can conclude that rational Merlin will report the truth in every round, and the protocol indeed constitutes a rational proof. □

4.4.2 *Discussion on Rational Proofs for* TC

Circuit Model.

Our rational proofs work for any circuit in TC, whereas interactive proofs of Goldwasser *et al.* [17] address circuits in NC. In general, the class TC and NC have the same computational power, indeed it is possible to simulate any threshold gate with AND and OR gates. However, once we take depth of the circuit into consideration, TC circuits may be much more powerful than NC circuits, and the advantage is remarkably evident in the case of constant depth.

Unlike TC0, the class NC0 can only compute functions which depend on constant number of input bits, since the fan-in of any gate is two. One can lift this restriction and allow the AND, and OR gates to have unbounded fan-in which corresponds to the class AC0. Nevertheless, we do know functions which are computable in TC0, but are outside AC0, e.g., parity, majority and some pseudorandom functions (under a computational assumption, see Naor and Reingold [25]). Note that TC0 is a class interesting also on its own (see Reif and Tate [27]). Many important practical problems are in TC0, such as sorting a list of n-bit numbers, multiplication of two n bit numbers, or integer division. Our result gives efficient delegation schemes for these problems in the rational setting with constant number of rounds, constant communication, and with a verifier running in polylog(n) time.

In the construction of both us and Goldwasser *et al.* [17], the number of rounds and the amount of communication is proportional to the depth of the circuit. However, for the same depth d, we need only d rounds but Goldwasser *et al.* [17] needs $\Omega(d \log n)$ rounds. Hence, for those function which are computable in TC0, our protocol only needs $O(1)$ rounds $O(1)$ bits communication that is in stark contrast to $\Omega(\log n)$ rounds and polylog(n) communication in [17].

Multi-Output Case.

Both our protocol and Goldwasser *et al.* [17] can be transformed to protocols that work for multi-output circuits of say m output bits. The general idea is to view these output bits as inputs to a virtual AND gate. This AND gate then outputs 1 if and only if all output bits are correct, and turns the circuit into a single-output circuit. The AND gate is however limited to fan-in two in NC, so the transformation adds $\log m$ factor to the depth of the circuit, and consequently to the number of rounds. Our transformation for multi-output circuits introduces only one additional round in which the verifier picks an output bit at random and runs the rational verification for the corresponding single-output circuit. More specifically, we show any $f\colon \{0,1\}^* \to \{0,1\}^\ell$ which can be computable by a family of $O(\log(S(n)))$-space uniform threshold circuits of size $S(n)$ and depth $d(n)$ is in $\text{FRMA}[d(n), d(n)+\ell-1, O(d(n) \cdot \text{polylog}(S(n)))]$. The protocol only differs from the protocol of Theorem 13 in the initial conversation where Merlin sends $z \in \{0,1\}^\ell$ then Arthur randomly chooses $r \in \{1, \ldots, \ell\}$, finds the corresponding "root" gate, denotes it as g_1, and starts $\text{Round}(1, g_1, z_r)$.

Suppose Merlin sends an incorrect $z \neq f(x)$, and a is the number of bits where z and $f(x)$ differ. With probability of a/ℓ, Arthur will start the first round with an incorrect z_r. As shown in Theorem 13, conditioned on z_r being incorrect, the expected loss of Merlin is at least $\Delta^d/2 \cdot 1/m_0^2$, where m_0 is the maximal fan-in over all gates. Thus, the expected loss of Merlin when lying on a bits of z will be at least $(a/\ell)(\Delta^d/2 \cdot 1/m_0^2)$. Merlin will again maximize the expected reward by sending $z = f(x)$.

Non-Uniform Circuits.

Uniformity of circuits describe how complex the circuits are. The statements of Goldwasser *et al.* [17] and our protocol demand $O(\log(S(n)))$ space uniform circuits where $S(n)$ is the size of circuit. It is because we want to get the information of circuit very efficiently without looking into the whole description of circuit. $O(\log S(n))$ space uniformity allows us to get the information of each gate in polylog$(S(n))$ time. As discussed in Goldwasser *et al.* [17], if preprocessing allowed, verifier can run poly$(S(n))$ time in off-line phase but keep poly$(d, \log(S))$ bits of information of the circuit. And in the online phase, verifier can get the information of each gate in time $\text{poly}(d, \log(S(n)))$ such that the total running time is $O(d \cdot \text{poly}(d, \log(S(n))))$. The running time of Goldwasser *et al.* [17] is $O(n \cdot \text{poly}(d, \log(S(n))))$.

4.5 Beyond TC

We show some limitation on extremely efficient rational proof for classes beyond TC. In the rational proof for any NP language described in Fig. 2, the assumption about rationality of Merlin allows him to convince Arthur while being extremely laconic. However, Goldreich *et al.* [16] showed that in the classical setting it is impossible to construct an interactive proof with a single, one bit message from the verifier for any NP-complete language.[10] We show that similar impossibility transfers also into the rational setting.

As mentioned earlier, Brier's score is not inherent to laconic rational proofs. However, for any bounded scoring rule computable in polynomial time, we show in following theorem that the reward gap is related to the randomized time needed for deciding the language, and we get as simple corollary that the reward gap cannot be noticeable in every extremely laconic rational Merlin Arthur game for any NP language, unless $\text{NP} \subset \text{BPP}$.

Theorem 16. *Let L be a language in $\text{DRMA}[1, 1, \text{poly}(|x|)]$, and $\mathsf{reward}(\cdot, \cdot)$ be any bounded reward function defining the corresponding rational Merlin-Arthur game with an extremely laconic Merlin. If $\Delta_{\mathsf{reward}}(\cdot)$ is a noticeable function, then L can be decided in randomized polynomial time with a constant error probability.*

Proof. Given $x \in \{0, 1\}^*$, consider the following procedure.

1. Evaluate t times both $\mathsf{reward}(x, 0)$ and $\mathsf{reward}(x, 1)$ to estimate $\mathrm{E}[\mathsf{reward}(x, 0)]$ respectively $\mathrm{E}[\mathsf{reward}(x, 1)]$.
2. If $\mathrm{E}[\mathsf{reward}(x, 0)] > \mathrm{E}[\mathsf{reward}(x, 1)]$ reject, and otherwise accept.

We use the Hoeffding's inequality to give an upper bound on the number t of evaluations of the reward function that suffices for the above procedure to decide L with a constant probability of error. The inequality states that if $X_1, \ldots, X_t$ are i.i.d. random variables such that $\mathrm{E}[X_i] = \mu$ and $0 \leq X_i \leq 1$ for all i, then for any $\epsilon > 0$,

$$\Pr\left[\left|\frac{1}{t}\sum_{i=1}^{t} X_i - \mu\right| \geq \epsilon\right] \leq 2\exp\left(-2t\epsilon^2\right) .$$

Assume without loss of generality that reward function assigns values form $[0, 1]$. Since $\Delta_{\mathsf{reward}}(\cdot)$ is noticeable function, there exists a polynomial p, such that $\Delta_{\mathsf{reward}}(|x|) > p(|x|)^{-1}$ for all large enough x.

If we approximate both $\mathrm{E}[\mathsf{reward}(x, 0)]$, and $\mathrm{E}[\mathsf{reward}(x, 1)]$ within $\epsilon = \Delta_{\mathsf{reward}}(|x|)/3$, the proposed procedure successfully determines if $x \in L$. The Hoeffding's inequality guarantees that after $t = \ln(12)/2\epsilon^2 = O(p(|x|)^2)$ evaluations of $\mathsf{reward}(x, b)$ we can approximate $\mathrm{E}[\mathsf{reward}(x, b)]$ within ϵ with probability greater than 5/6. Therefore, one can decide L in randomized polynomial time with probability greater than 2/3. □

Note that the proof can be easily extended for any $L \in \text{DRMA}[1, \log(|x|), \text{poly}(|x|)]$.

[10] Goldreich *et al.* [16] in fact showed that NP-complete languages cannot have interactive proofs in which the prover sends only poly-logarithmically many bits to the verifier.

5. CONCLUSION AND OPEN PROBLEMS

This work presents an alternative approach to constructing delegation schemes. Our approach, to the extent that it is meaningful, opens up the door for one-round protocols that demand minimal overhead for the prover and allow extremely fast verification. These dramatic efficiency improvements are a direct result of the relaxation in the soundness requirement. By penalizing the prover (on expectation) for even the slightest deviation from the correct computation, it is possible to focus the verification efforts on *local* parts of the computation (specifically paths along the computation), whose size is proportional to the depth of the circuit being computed. This stands in stark contrast to the more "rigid" approach to verification, whose soundness necessitates *global* dependence on the entire computation, and thus results in significantly more involved proof and verification procedures (inducing significant overhead beyond the actual computation).

Our work gives rise to several interesting open problems:

- While we give extremely laconic rational proofs for all NP languages (thus bypassing the impossibility result for interactive proofs), we also show that such succinct non-interactive public coin rational proofs NP cannot have non-negligible reward gap. An interesting research direction is to understand if this small gap is inherent. Specifically, can one construct succinct rational proofs for NP with large gap by increasing the number of rounds, or by having the verifier use private coins?
- In the context of the above question, it is natural to consider computationally bounded rational provers. Due to the impossibility result of Gentry and Wichs [14], constructions of succinct non-interactive arguments in the classical setting must be based on non-falsifiable assumptions. Can one overcome this limitation in the rational model and construct rational SNARGs?
- The main advantage of our rational delegation is the utmost simplicity. Still, the complexity of verification does depend on the depth of the underlying circuit. In particular, for P-complete problems the scheme is no longer succinct. Kalai, Raz and Rothblum [20] give a delegation scheme where the complexity of verification depends on the space of a Turing Machine instead of depth of circuit. Their scheme might potentially be simplified in the rational model, yielding a one-round succinct rational delegation for all problems in P.
- In this work, we propose to model rationality in presence of computational cost via noticeable reward gap. However, this modeling is not sensitive to different costs of computation while in reality a rational prover may behave differently on computations that have different complexity. It is an interesting open problem to refine our model, or even come up with a different approach, and capture rationality with respect to various measures of costs of computation.

6. ACKNOWLEDGMENTS

We would like to thank Andrej Bogdanov and the anonymous ITCS reviewers for valuable feedback that helped improve the paper.

7. REFERENCES

[1] B. Applebaum, Y. Ishai, and E. Kushilevitz. From secrecy to soundness: Efficient verification via secure computation. In S. Abramsky, C. Gavoille, C. Kirchner, F. Meyer auf der Heide, and P. G. Spirakis, editors, *ICALP (1)*, volume 6198 of *Lecture Notes in Computer Science*, pages 152–163. Springer, 2010.

[2] P. D. Azar and S. Micali. Rational proofs. In H. J. Karloff and T. Pitassi, editors, *STOC*, pages 1017–1028. ACM, 2012.

[3] P. D. Azar and S. Micali. Super-efficient rational proofs. In M. Kearns, R. P. McAfee, and É. Tardos, editors, *ACM Conference on Electronic Commerce*, pages 29–30. ACM, 2013.

[4] N. Bitansky, A. Chiesa, Y. Ishai, R. Ostrovsky, and O. Paneth. Succinct non-interactive arguments via linear interactive proofs. In *TCC*, pages 315–333, 2013.

[5] G. W. Brier. Verification of forecasts expressed in terms of probability. *Monthly Weather Review*, 78(1):1–3, 1950.

[6] C. Cachin, S. Micali, and M. Stadler. Computationally private information retrieval with polylogarithmic communication. In J. Stern, editor, *EUROCRYPT*, volume 1592 of *Lecture Notes in Computer Science*, pages 402–414. Springer, 1999.

[7] R. Canetti, B. Riva, and G. N. Rothblum. Refereed delegation of computation. *Inf. Comput.*, 226:16–36, 2013.

[8] K.-M. Chung, Y. T. Kalai, and S. P. Vadhan. Improved delegation of computation using fully homomorphic encryption. In T. Rabin, editor, *CRYPTO*, volume 6223 of *Lecture Notes in Computer Science*, pages 483–501. Springer, 2010.

[9] G. Cormode, M. Mitzenmacher, and J. Thaler. Practical verified computation with streaming interactive proofs. In S. Goldwasser, editor, *ITCS*, pages 90–112. ACM, 2012.

[10] I. Damgård, S. Faust, and C. Hazay. Secure two-party computation with low communication. In R. Cramer, editor, *TCC*, volume 7194 of *Lecture Notes in Computer Science*, pages 54–74. Springer, 2012.

[11] C. Dwork, M. Langberg, M. Naor, K. Nissim, and O. Reingold. Succinct NP proofs and spooky interactions. *Available at* www.openu.ac.il/home/mikel/papers/spooky.ps, 2004.

[12] R. Gennaro, C. Gentry, and B. Parno. Non-interactive verifiable computing: Outsourcing computation to untrusted workers. In T. Rabin, editor, *CRYPTO*, volume 6223 of *Lecture Notes in Computer Science*, pages 465–482. Springer, 2010.

[13] R. Gennaro, C. Gentry, B. Parno, and M. Raykova. Quadratic span programs and succinct NIZKs without PCPs. *IACR Cryptology ePrint Archive*, 2012:215, 2012.

[14] C. Gentry and D. Wichs. Separating succinct non-interactive arguments from all falsifiable assumptions. In L. Fortnow and S. P. Vadhan, editors, *STOC*, pages 99–108. ACM, 2011.

[15] T. Gneiting and A. E. Raftery. Strictly proper scoring rules, prediction, and estimation. *Journal of the American Statistical Association*, 102:359–378, 2007.

[16] O. Goldreich, S. P. Vadhan, and A. Wigderson. On interactive proofs with a laconic prover. *Computational Complexity*, 11(1-2):1–53, 2002.

[17] S. Goldwasser, Y. T. Kalai, and G. N. Rothblum. Delegating computation: interactive proofs for muggles. In C. Dwork, editor, *STOC*, pages 113–122. ACM, 2008.

[18] J. Groth. Short pairing-based non-interactive zero-knowledge arguments. In M. Abe, editor, *ASIACRYPT*, volume 6477 of *Lecture Notes in Computer Science*, pages 321–340. Springer, 2010.

[19] Y. T. Kalai and R. Raz. Probabilistically checkable arguments. In S. Halevi, editor, *CRYPTO*, volume 5677 of *Lecture Notes in Computer Science*, pages 143–159. Springer, 2009.

[20] Y. T. Kalai, R. Raz, and R. D. Rothblum. Delegation for bounded space. In D. Boneh, T. Roughgarden, and J. Feigenbaum, editors, *STOC*, pages 565–574. ACM, 2013.

[21] J. Kilian. A note on efficient zero-knowledge proofs and arguments (extended abstract). In S. R. Kosaraju, M. Fellows, A. Wigderson, and J. A. Ellis, editors, *STOC*, pages 723–732. ACM, 1992.

[22] G. Kol and R. Raz. Competing provers protocols for circuit evaluation. In R. D. Kleinberg, editor, *ITCS*, pages 473–484. ACM, 2013.

[23] H. Lipmaa. Progression-free sets and sublinear pairing-based non-interactive zero-knowledge arguments. In R. Cramer, editor, *TCC*, volume 7194 of *Lecture Notes in Computer Science*, pages 169–189. Springer, 2012.

[24] S. Micali. Computationally sound proofs. *SIAM J. Comput.*, 30(4):1253–1298, 2000.

[25] M. Naor and O. Reingold. Number-theoretic constructions of efficient pseudo-random functions. *J. ACM*, 51(2):231–262, 2004.

[26] B. Parno, M. Raykova, and V. Vaikuntanathan. How to delegate and verify in public: Verifiable computation from attribute-based encryption. In R. Cramer, editor, *TCC*, volume 7194 of *Lecture Notes in Computer Science*, pages 422–439. Springer, 2012.

[27] J. H. Reif and S. R. Tate. On threshold circuits and polynomial computation. *SIAM J. Comput.*, 21(5):896–908, 1992.

[28] G. N. Rothblum, S. P. Vadhan, and A. Wigderson. Interactive proofs of proximity: delegating computation in sublinear time. In D. Boneh, T. Roughgarden, and J. Feigenbaum, editors, *STOC*, pages 793–802. ACM, 2013.

[29] J. Thaler. Time-optimal interactive proofs for circuit evaluation. In R. Canetti and J. Garay, editors, *Advances in Cryptology - CRYPTO 2013*, volume 8043 of *Lecture Notes in Computer Science*, pages 71–89. Springer Berlin Heidelberg, 2013.

Optimal Provision-After-Wait in Healthcare*

Mark Braverman
Department of Computer Science, Princeton University
mbraverm@cs.princeton.edu

Jing Chen
Department of Computer Science, Stony Brook University
jingchen@cs.stonybrook.edu

Sampath Kannan
Department of Computer and Information Science, University of Pennsylvania
kannan@cis.upenn.edu

ABSTRACT

We investigate computational and mechanism design aspects of optimal scarce resource allocation, where the primary rationing mechanism is through waiting times. Specifically we consider the problem of allocating medical treatments to a population of patients. Each patient has demand for exactly one unit of treatment, and can choose to be treated in one of k hospitals, $H_1, \ldots, H_k$. Different hospitals have different costs per treatment, which are fully paid by a third party — the "payer"— and do not accrue to the patients. The payer has a fixed budget B and can only cover a limited number of treatments in the more expensive hospitals. Access to over-demanded hospitals is rationed through waiting times: each hospital H_i will have waiting time w_i. In equilibrium, each patient will choose his most preferred hospital given his intrinsic preferences and the waiting times. The payer thus computes the waiting times and the number of treatments authorized for each hospital, so that in equilibrium the budget constraint is satisfied and the social welfare is maximized.

We show that even if the patients' preferences are known to the payer, the task of optimizing social welfare in equilibrium subject to the budget constraint is NP-hard. We also show that, with constant number of hospitals, if the budget constraint can be relaxed from B to $(1+\epsilon)B$ for an arbitrarily small constant ϵ, then the original optimum under budget B can be approximated very efficiently.

Next, we study the endogenous emergence of waiting time from the dynamics between hospitals and patients, and show that there is no need for the payer to explicitly enforce the optimal equilibrium waiting times. When the patients arrive uniformly along time and when they have generic types, all that the payer needs to do is to enforce the total amount of money he would like to pay to each hospital. The waiting times will simply change according to the demand, and the dynamics will always converge to the desired waiting times in finite time.

We then go beyond equilibrium solutions and investigate the optimization problem over a much larger class of mechanisms containing the equilibrium ones as special cases. In the setting with two hospitals, we show that under a natural assumption on the patients' preference profiles, optimal welfare is in fact attained by the randomized assignment mechanism, which allocates patients to hospitals at random subject to the budget constraint, but avoids waiting times.

Finally, we discuss potential policy implications of our results, as well as follow-up directions and open problems.

Categories and Subject Descriptors

F.2 [**Theory of computation**]: Algorithmic game theory

General Terms

Economics, Complexity, Algorithms

Keywords

healthcare, mechanism design, budget constraint, waiting times

*The first author is supported by the Alfred P. Sloan Fellowship, an NSF CAREER award (CCF-1149888), NSF Award CCF-1215990, and a Turing Centenary Fellowship. The second author is supported in part by the Zurich Financial Services and NSF grant CCF-0832797. The third author is supported by NSF Award CCF-1137084. Part of this research was done when the second author was a postdoc at the Institute for Advanced Study and the third author was visiting Princeton University. The authors would like to thank Itai Ashlagi for pointing us to important references and three anonymous reviewers for their comments. A full version of this paper is available at http://arxiv.org/abs/1312.1955.

ITCS'14, January 12–14, 2014, Princeton, New Jersey, USA.

ACM 978-1-4503-2698-8/14/01 ...$15.00.
http://dx.doi.org/10.1145/2554797.2554846.

The Truth Behind the Myth of the Folk Theorem

Joseph Y. Halpern
Computer Science Dept.
Cornell University
Ithaca, NY
halpern@cs.cornell.edu

Rafael Pass
Computer Science Dept.
Cornell University
Ithaca, NY
rafael@cs.cornell.edu

Lior Seeman
Computer Science Dept.
Cornell University
Ithaca, NY
lseeman@cs.cornell.edu

ABSTRACT

We study the problem of computing an ϵ-Nash equilibrium in repeated games. Earlier work by Borgs et al. [2010] suggests that this problem is intractable. We show that if we make a slight change to their model—modeling the players as polynomial-time Turing machines that maintain state (rather than stateless polynomial-time Turing machines)—and make some standard cryptographic hardness assumptions (the existence of public-key encryption), the problem can actually be solved in polynomial time.

Categories and Subject Descriptors

F.2 [**Theory of Computation**]: Analysis of Algorithms and Problem Complexity; J.4 [**Computer Applications**]: Social and Behavioral Sciences-*Economics*

Keywords

Repeated games; folk theorem; computing Nash equilibrium

1. INTRODUCTION

The complexity of finding a Nash equilibrium (NE) is a fundamental question at the interface of game theory and computer science. A celebrated sequence of results showed that the complexity of finding a NE in a normal-form game is PPAD-complete [3, 5], even for 2-player games. Less restrictive concepts, such as ϵ-NE for an inverse-polynomial ϵ, are just as hard [4]. This suggests that these problems are computationally intractable.

There was some hope that the situation would be better in infinitely-repeated games. The *Folk Theorem* (see [19] for a review) informally states that in an infinitely-repeated game G, for any payoff profile that is *individually rational*, in that all players get more than[1] their minimax payoff (the highest payoff that a player can guarantee himself, no matter what the other players do) and is the outcome of some correlated strategy in G, there is a Nash equilibrium of G with this payoff profile. With such a large set of equilibria, the hope was that finding one would be less difficult. Indeed, Littman and Stone [17] showed that these ideas can be used to design an algorithm for finding a NE in a two-player repeated game.

Borgs et al. [2] (BC+ from now on) proved some results suggesting that, for more than two players, even in infinitely-repeated games it would be difficult to find a NE. Specifically, they showed that, under certain assumptions, the problem of finding a NE (or even an ϵ-NE for an inverse-polynomial ϵ) in an infinitely repeated game with three or more players where there is a discount factor bounded away from 1 by an inverse polynomial is also PPAD-hard. They prove this by showing that, given an arbitrary normal-form game G with $c \geq 2$ players, there is a game G' with $c+1$ players such that finding an $\epsilon/8c$-NE for the repeated game based on G' is equivalent to finding an ϵ-NE for G.

While their proof is indeed correct, in this paper, we challenge their conclusion. Not surprisingly, we do this by changing their assumptions in what we argue are natural ways. Like BC+, we assume that players are resource bounded.[2] Formally, we view players as probabilistic[3] polynomial-time Turing machines (PPT TMs). We differ from BC+ in two key respects. First, BC+ implicitly assume that players have no memory: they cannot remember computation from earlier rounds. By way of contrast, we allow players to have a bounded (polynomial) amount of memory. This allows players to remember the results of a few coin tosses from earlier rounds, and means that we can use some cryptography (making some standard cryptographic assumptions) to try to coordinate the players. We stress that this coordination happens in the process of the game play, not through communication. That is, there are no side channels; the only form of "communication" is by making moves in the game. We call such TMs *stateful*, and the BC+ TMs *stateless*. Second, since we restrict to (probabilistic) polynomial-time players, we restrict the deviations that can be made in

[1]For our results, since we consider ϵ-NE, we can replace "more than" by "at least".

[2]Although BC+ do not discuss modeling players in this way, the problem they show is NP-Hard is to find a polynomial-time TM profile that implements an equilibrium. There is an obvious exponential-time TM profile that implements an equilibrium: each TM in the profile just computes the single-shot NE and plays its part repeatedly.

[3]BC+ describe their TMs as deterministic, but allow them to output a mixed strategy. As they point out, there is no difference between this formulation and a probabilistic TM that outputs a specific action; their results hold for such probabilistic TMs as well.

ITCS'14, January 12–14, 2014, Princeton, New Jersey, USA.
Copyright 2014 ACM 978-1-4503-2698-8/14/01 ...$15.00.
http://dx.doi.org/10.1145/2554797.2554847.

equilibrium to those that can be computed by such players; BC+ allow arbitrary deviations. Without this extra restriction, there is no real difference between stateful TMs and stateless TMs in our setting (since a player with unbounded computational power can recreate the necessary state). With these assumptions (and the remaining assumptions of the BC+ model), we show that in fact an ϵ-NE in an infinitely-repeated game can be found in polynomial time.

Roughly speaking, the ϵ-NE can be described as proceeding in three stages. In the first stage, the players play a sequence of predefined actions repeatedly. If some player deviates from the sequence, the second stage begins, in which the other players use their actions to secretly exchange a random seed, through the use of public-key encryption. In the third stage, the players use a correlated minimax strategy to punish the deviator forever. To achieve this correlation, the players use the secret random seed as the seed of a pseudorandom function, and use the outputs of the pseudorandom function as the source of randomness for the correlated strategy. Since the existence of public-key encryption implies the existence of pseudorandom functions, the only cryptographic assumption needed is the existence of public-key encryptions—one of the most basic cryptographic hardness assumptions.

1.1 Related work

The idea of considering resource-bounded agents has a long history in game theory. It is known, for example, that cooperation is a NE of finitely-repeated prisoner's dilemma with resource-bounded players (see, e.g., [18, 22, 20]). The idea of using the structure of the game as a means of correlation is used by Lehrer [16] to show an equivalence between NE and correlated equilbrium in certain repeated games with nonstandard information structures. The use of cryptography in game theory goes back to Urbano and Vila [24, 23], who also used it to do coordination between players. More recently, it has been used by, for example, Dodis, Halevi, and Rabin [7].

The application of cryptography perhaps most closely related to ours is by Gossner [12], who uses cryptographic techniques to show how any payoff profile that is above the players' *correlated* minimax value can be achieved in a NE of a repeated game with public communication played by computationally bounded players. In [13], Gossner uses a strategy similar to the one that we use to prove that, even without communication, the same result holds. Gossner's results apply only to infinitely-repeated games with 3 players and no discounting; he claims that his results do not hold for games with discounting. Gossner does not discuss the complexity of finding a strategy of the type that he shows exists.

Recently, Andersen and Conitzer [1] described an algorithm for finding NE in repeated games with more than two players with high probability in *uniform games*. However, this algorithm is not guaranteed to work for all games, and uses the limit of means as its payoff criterion, and not discounting.

2. PRELIMINARIES

2.1 Infinitely repeated games

We define a game G as a triple $([c], A, \vec{u})$, where $[c] = \{1, \ldots, c\}$ is the set of players, A_i is the set of possible actions for player i, $A = A_1 \times \ldots \times A_c$ is the set of action profiles, and $\vec{u} : A \to \mathbb{R}^c$ is the utility function ($\vec{u}_i(\vec{a})$ is the utility of player i). A (mixed) *strategy* σ_i for player i is a probability distribution over A_i, that is, an element of $\Delta(A_i)$ (where, as usual, we denote by $\Delta(X)$ the set of probability distributions over the set X). We use the standard notation $\vec{x}_{-i}$ to denote vector $\vec{x}$ with its ith element removed, and $(x', \vec{x}_{-i})$ to denote $\vec{x}$ with its ith element replaced by x'.

DEFINITION 2.1. *(Nash Equilibrium)* $\sigma = (\sigma_1, ..., \sigma_c)$ *is an* ϵ*-NE of* G *if, for all players* $i \in [c]$ *and all actions* $a'_i \in A_i$,

$$E_{\sigma_{-i}}[u_i(a'_i, \vec{a}_{-i})] \leq E_{\sigma}[u_i(\vec{a})] + \epsilon.$$

A correlated strategy of a game G is an element $\sigma \in \Delta(A)$. It is a *correlated equilibrium* if, for all players i, they have no temptation to play a different action, given that the action profile was chosen according to σ. That is, for all players i for all $a_i \in A_i$ such that $\sigma_i(a_i) > 0$, $E_{\sigma|a_i} u_i(a_i, \vec{a}_{-i}) \geq E_{\sigma|a_i} u_i(a'_i, \vec{a}_{-i})$.

Player i's minimax value in a game G is the highest payoff i can guarantee himself if the other players are trying to push his payoff as low as possible. We call the strategy i plays in this case a minimax strategy for i; the strategy that the other players use is i's (correlated) punishment strategy. (Of course, there could be more than one minimax strategy or punishment strategy for player i.) Note that a correlated punishment strategy can be computed using linear programming.

DEFINITION 2.2. *Given a game* $G = ([c], A, \vec{u})$, *the strategies* $\vec{\sigma}_{-i} \in \Delta(A_{-i})$ *that minimize* $\max_{\sigma' \in \Delta(A_i)} E_{(\sigma', \vec{\sigma}_{-i})}[u_i(\vec{a})]$ *are the* punishment strategies *against player* i *in* G. *If* $\vec{\sigma}_{-i}$ *is a punishment strategy against player* i, *then* $mm_i(G) = \max_{a \in A_i} E_{\vec{\sigma}_{-i}}[u_i(a, a_{-i})]$ *is player* i*'s* minimax value *in* G

Simplifying assumption: We normalize all payoffs so that each player's minimax value is 0. Since, in an equilibrium, all players get at least their minimax value, this guarantees that all players get at least 0 in a NE. We also assume that each player has at least two actions in G. (This allows us to use the actions played in the infinitely-repeated game based on G to encode bit strings.) This assumption is without loss of generality—we can essentially ignore players for whom it does not hold.

Given a normal-form game G, we define the repeated game $G^t(\delta)$ as the game in which G is played repeatedly t times (in this context, G is called the *stage game*) and $1 - \delta$ is the discount factor (see below). Let $G^\infty(\delta)$ be the game where G is played infinitely many times. An infinite history h in this game is an infinite sequence $\langle \vec{a}^0, \vec{a}^1, \ldots \rangle$ of actions profiles. Intuitively, we can think of $\vec{a}^t$ as the action profile played in the tth stage game. We often omit the δ in $G^\infty(\delta)$ if it is not relevant to the discussion. Like BC+, we assume that G^∞ is *fully observable*, in the sense that, after each stage game, the players observe exactly what actions the other players played.

Since we consider computationally-bounded players, we take a player's strategy in G^∞ to be a (possibly probabilistic) Turing machine (TM), which outputs at each round an action to be played, based on its internal memory and the history of play so far. (The TMs considered in BC+ did not have internal memory.) We consider only TMs that at round

t use polynomial in nt many steps to compute the next action, where n is the maximum number of actions a player has in G. Thus, n is a measure of the size of G.[4] Denote by M_i the TM used by player i, and let $\vec{M} = (M_1, \dots, M_c)$.

Note that a profile $\vec{M}$ induces a distribution $\rho_{\vec{M}}$ on infinite histories of play. Let $\rho^t_{\vec{M}}$ denote the induced distribution on H^t, the set of histories of length t. (If $t = 0$, we take H^0 to consist of the unique history of length 0, namely $\langle\,\rangle$.) Player i's utility if $\vec{M}$ is played, denoted $p_i(\vec{M})$, is defined as follows:

$$p_i(\vec{M}) = \delta \sum_{t=0}^{\infty} (1-\delta)^t \sum_{h \in H^t, \vec{a} \in A} \rho^{t+1}_{\vec{M}}(h \cdot \vec{a})[u_i(\vec{a})].$$

Thus, the discount factor is $1 - \delta$. Note that the initial δ is a normalization factor. It guarantees that if $u_i(\vec{a}) \in [b_1, b_2]$ for all joint actions $\vec{a}$ in G, then i's utility is in $[b_1, b_2]$, no matter which TM profile $\vec{M}$ is played.

We are now ready to define the notion of equilibrium we use. Intuitively, as we model players as polynomial-time TMs, we consider a profile of TMs an equilibrium in a game if there is no player and no other polynomial-time TM that gives that player a higher expected payoff (or up to an ϵ for an ϵ-NE).

Since we consider (probabilistic) TMs that run in polynomial time in the size of the game, we cannot consider a single game. For any fixed game, running in polynomial time in the size of the game is meaningless. Instead, we need to consider a sequence of games. This leads to the following definition.

Definition 2.3. *An infinite sequence of strategy profiles $\vec{M}^1, \vec{M}^2, \ldots$, where $\vec{M}^k = (M^k_1, \ldots, M^k_c)$ is an ϵ-NE of an infinite sequence of games $G^\infty_1, G^\infty_2, \ldots$ where the size of G_k is k if, for all players $i \in [c]$ and all infinite sequences of polynomial-time TMs $M^1, M^2, \ldots$ (polynomial in n and t, as discussed above), there exist k_0 such that for all $k \geq k_0$*

$$p^k_i(M^k, \vec{M}^k_{-i}) \leq p^k_i(\vec{M}^k) + \epsilon(k).$$

where p^k_i is the payoff of player i in game G^∞_k.

We note that the equilibrium definition we use considers only deviations that can be implemented by polynomial-time TMs. This is different from both the usual definition of NE and from the definition used by BC+, who allow arbitrary deviations. The need to define polynomial-time deviation is the reason for considering sequences of games instead of a single game. There are other reasonable ways of capturing polynomial-time adversaries. As will be seen from our proof, our approach is quite robust, so our results should hold for any reasonable definition.

2.2 Cryptographic definitions

For a probabilistic algorithm A and an infinite bit string r, $A(x; r)$ denotes the output of A running on input x with randomness r; $A(x)$ denotes the distribution on outputs of A induced by considering $A(x; r)$, where r is chosen uniformly at random. A function $\epsilon : \mathbb{N} \to [0, 1]$ is *negligible* if, for every constant $c \in \mathbb{N}$, $\epsilon(k) < k^{-c}$ for sufficiently large k.

[4]When we talk about polynomial-time algorithms, we mean polynomial in n. We could use other measures of the size of G, such as the total number of actions. Since all reasonable choices of size are polynomially related, the choice does not affect our results.

In this section, when we mention a PPT algorithm, we mean a *non-uniform* PPT algorithm and, specifically, an algorithm that, in addition to its regular input, gets for every input length an additional input (of polynomial length) that is viewed as *advice* . It is common to assume that the cryptographic building blocks we define next and use in our constructions are secure against non-uniform PPT algorithms.

2.2.1 Computational Indistinguishability

Definition 2.4. *A probability ensemble is a sequence $X = \{X_n\}_{n \in \mathbb{N}}$ of random variables indexed by $\mathbb{N}$. (Typically, in an ensemble $X = \{X_n\}_{n \in \mathbb{N}}$, the domain of X_n consists of strings of length n.)*

We now recall the definition of computational indistinguishability [11].

Definition 2.5. *Two probability ensembles $\{X_n\}_{n \in \mathbb{N}}, \{Y_n\}_{n \in \mathbb{N}}$ are* computationally indistinguishable *if, for all PPT algorithms D, there exists a negligible function ϵ such that, for all $n \in \mathbb{N}$,*

$$|\Pr[D(1^n, X_n) = 1] - \Pr[D(1^n, Y_n) = 1]| \leq \epsilon(n).$$

To explain the Pr *in the last line, recall that X_n and Y_n are random variables. Although we write $D(1^n, X_n)$, D is a randomized algorithm, so what $D(1^n, X_n)$ returns depends on the outcome of random coin tosses. To be a little more formal, we should write $D(1^n, X_n, r)$, where r is an infinitely long random bit strong (of which D will only use a finite initial prefix). More formally, taking* Pr *to be the uniform distribution on bit-strings and over the value of X_n (or Y_n), we want*

$$|\Pr[\{r : D(1^n, X_n, r) = 1\}] - Pr[\{r : D(1^n, Y_n, r) = 1\}]| \leq \epsilon(n).$$

We similarly abuse notation elsewhere in writing Pr.

We often call a PPT algorithm that is supposed to distinguish between two probability ensembles a *distinguisher*.

2.2.2 Pseudorandom Functions

Definition 2.6. *A* function ensemble *is a sequence $F = \{F_n\}_{n \in \mathbb{N}}$ of random variables such that the range of F_n is the set of functions mapping n-bit strings to n-bit strings. The* uniform function ensemble, *denoted $H = \{H_n\}_{n \in \mathbb{N}}$, has H_n uniformly distributed over the set of all functions mapping n-bit strings to n-bit strings.*

We have the same notion of computational indistinguishablity for function ensembles as we had for probability ensembles, only that the distinguisher is now an oracle machine, meaning that it can query the value of the function at any point with one computation step, although it does not have the full description of the function. (See [9] for a detailed description.)

We now define *pseudorandom functions* (see [10]). Intuitively, this is a family of functions indexed by a seed, such that it is hard to distinguish a random member of the family from a truly randomly selected function.

Definition 2.7. *A* pseudorandom function ensemble (PRF) *is a set $\{f_s : \{0,1\}^{|s|} \to \{0,1\}^{|s|}\}_{s \in \{0,1\}^*}$ such that the following conditions hold:*

- *(easy to compute) $f_s(x)$ can be computed by a PPT algorithm that is given s and x;*
- *(pseudorandom) the function ensemble $F = \{F_n\}_{n\in\mathbb{N}}$, where F_n is uniformly distributed over the multiset $\{f_s\}_{s\in\{0,1\}^n}$, is computationally indistinguishable from H.*

We use the standard cryptographic assumption that a family of PRFs exists; this assumption is implied by the existence of one-way functions [14, 10]. We actually require the use of a seemingly stronger notion of a PRF, which requires that an attacker getting access to polynomially many instances of a PRF (i.e., f_s for polynomially many values of s) still cannot distinguish them from polynomially many truly random functions. Nevertheless, as we show in Appendix A, it follows using a standard "hybrid" argument that any PRF satisfies also this stronger "multi-instance" security notion.

2.2.3 Public-key Encryption Schemes

We now define public-key encryption schemes. Such a scheme has two keys. The first is public and used for encrypting messages (using a randomized algorithm). The second is secret and used for decrypting. The keys are generated in such a way that the probability that a decrypted message is equal to the encrypted message is equal to 1. The key generation algorithm takes as input a "security parameter" k that is used to determine the security of the protocols (inuitively, no polynomial-time attacker should be able to "break" the security of the protocol except possibly with a probability that is a negligible function of k).

We now recall the formal definitions of public-key encryption schemes [6, 21, 11].

DEFINITION 2.8. *Given a polynomial l, an l-*bit public-key encryption scheme *is a triple $\Pi = (Gen, Enc, Dec)$ of PPT algorithms where (a) Gen takes a security parameter 1^k as input and returns a (public key, private key) pair; (b) Enc takes a public key pk and a message m in a message space $\{0,1\}^{l(k)}$ as input and returns a ciphertext $Enc_{pk}(m)$; (c) Dec is a deterministic algorithm that takes a secret key sk and a ciphertext $\mathcal{C}$ as input and outputs $m' = Dec_{sk}(\mathcal{C})$, and (d)*

$$\Pr\left[\exists m \in \{0,1\}^{l(k)} \text{ s.t. } Dec_{sk}(Enc_{pk}(m)) \neq m\right] = 0.$$

We next define a security notion for public-key encryption. Such a security notion considers an adversary that is characterized by two PPT algorithms, A_1 and A_2. Intuitively, A_1 gets as input a public key that is part of a (public key, secret key) pair randomly generated by Gen, together with a security parameter k. A_1 then outputs two messages in $\{0,1\}^k$ (intuitively, messages it can distinguish), and some side information that it passes to A_2 (intuitively, this is information that A_2 needs, such as the messages chosen; An example of how this is used can be seen in Appendix B). A_2 gets as input the encryption of one of those messages and the side information passed on by A_1. A_2 must output which of the two messages m_0 and m_1 the encrypted message is the encryption of (where an output of $b \in \{0,1\}$ indicates that it is m_b). Since A_1 and A_2 are PPT algorithms, the output of A_2 can be viewed as a probability distribution over $\{0,1\}$. The scheme is secure if the two ensembles (i.e., the one generated by this process where the encryption of m_0 is always given to A_2, and the one where the encryption of m_1 is always given to A_2) are indistinguishable. More formally:

DEFINITION 2.9 (PUBLIC-KEY SECURITY). *An l-bit public-key encryption scheme $\Pi = (Gen, Enc, Dec)$ is* secure *if, for every probabilistic polynomial-time adversary $A = (A_1, A_2)$, the ensembles $\{IND_0^\Pi(A,k)\}_k$ and $\{IND_1^\Pi(A,k)\}_k$ are computationally indistinguishable, where $\{IND_b^\Pi(A,k)\}_k$ is the following PPT algorithm:*

$$\begin{aligned} IND_b^\Pi(A,k) := \quad & (pk, sk) \leftarrow Gen(1^k) \\ & (m_0, m_1, \tau) \leftarrow A_1(1^k, pk) \\ & \mathcal{C} \leftarrow Enc_{pk}(m_b) \\ & o \leftarrow A_2(\mathcal{C}, \tau) \\ & \text{Output } o. \end{aligned}$$

Intuitively, the $\leftarrow$ above functions as an assignment statement, but it is not quite that, since the various algorithms are actually PPT algorithms, so their output is randomized. Formally, $IND_b^\Pi(A,k)$ is a random variable on $(\{0,1\}^*)^4$. To compute $IND_b^\Pi(A,k,r_1,r_2,r_3,r_4)$, we view r_1, r_2, r_3, and r_4 as the random bitstrings that serve as the second arguments of Gen, A_1, Enc_{pk}, and A_2, respectively. Once we add these arguments (considering, e.g., $Gen(1^k, r_1)$ and $A_1(1^k, pk, r_2)$ rather than $Gen(1^k)$ and $A_1(1^k, pk)$) these algorithms become deterministic, and $\leftarrow$ can indeed be viewed as an assignment statement.

We assume a secure public-key encryption scheme exists. We actually require a seemingly stronger notion of "multi-instance" security, where an attacker gets to see encryptions of multiple messages, each of which is encrypted using multiple keys.

DEFINITION 2.10. *An l-bit public-key encryption scheme $\Pi = (Gen, Enc, Dec)$ is* multi-message multi-key secure *if, for all polynomials f and g, and for every probabilistic polynomial time adversary $A = (A_1, A_2)$, the ensembles $\{IND\text{-}MULT_0^\Pi(A,k,f,g)\}_k$ and $\{IND\text{-}MULT_1^\Pi(A,k,f,g)\}_k$ are computationally indistinguishable, where*

$$\begin{aligned} & IND\text{-}MULT_b^\Pi(A,k,f,g) := \\ & (pk_1, sk_1) \leftarrow Gen(1^k), \ldots (pk_{g(k)}, sk_{g(k)}) \leftarrow Gen(1^k), \\ & (m_0^1, \ldots, m_0^{f(k)}, m_1^1, \ldots, m_1^{f(k)}, \tau) \leftarrow \\ & \quad A_1(1^k, pk_1, \ldots, pk_{g(k)}) \ (m_0^i, m_1^i \in \{0,1\}^k) \\ & \mathcal{C} \leftarrow Enc_{pk_1}(m_b^1), \ldots, Enc_{pk_{g(k)}}(m_b^1), \\ & \quad \ldots, Enc_{pk_1}(m_b^{f(k)}), \ldots, Enc_{pk_{g(k)}}(m_b^{f(k)}) \\ & o \leftarrow A_2(\mathcal{C}, \tau) \\ & \text{Output } o \end{aligned}$$

In this definition, there are polynomially many messages being encrypted, and each message is encrypted a polynomial number of times, using a different key each time. Other than that, the process is similar to the standard definition of security. As we show in Appendix B, any secure encryption scheme is also multi-message multi-key secure.

3. THE COMPLEXITY OF FINDING ϵ-NE IN REPEATED GAMES PLAYED BY STATEFUL MACHINES

Our goal is to show that an ϵ-NE in infinitely-repeated games can be computed in polynomial time.

3.1 Preliminaries

DEFINITION 3.1. *Let $\mathcal{G}_{a,b,c,n}$ be the set of all games with c players, at most n actions per player, integral payoffs*[5]*, maximum payoff a, and minimum payoff b.*

Note that by our assumption that the minimax payoff is 0 for all players, we can assume $a \geq 0$, $b \leq 0$, and $a - b > 0$ (otherwise $a = b = 0$, which makes the game uninteresting). We start by showing that, given a correlated strategy σ in a game G, players can get an average payoff that is arbitrarily close to their payoff in σ by playing a fixed sequence of action profiles repeatedly.

LEMMA 3.2. *For all a, b, c, all polynomials q, all n, all games $G \in \mathcal{G}_{a,b,c,n}$, and all correlated strategies σ in G, if the expected payoff vector of playing σ is p then there exists a sequence sq of length $w(n)$, where $w(n) = ((a-b)q(n)+1)n^c$, such that player i's average payoff in sq is at least $p_i - 1/q(n)$.*

PROOF. Given σ, we create sq the obvious way: by playing each action in proportion to the probability $\sigma(\vec{a})$. More precisely, let $r = a - b$, and define $w(n) = (rq(n)+1)n^c$, as in the statement of the lemma. We create a sequence sq by playing each action profile $\vec{a}$ $\lfloor w(n)\sigma(\vec{a}) \rfloor$ times, in some fixed order. Notice that the length of this sequence is between $w(n) - n^c$ and $w(n)$. The average payoff player i gets in sq is

$$\begin{aligned}
v_i' &= \frac{1}{\sum_{\vec{a}\in A}\lfloor w(n)\sigma(\vec{a})\rfloor}\sum_{\vec{a}\in A}\lfloor w(n)\sigma(\vec{a})\rfloor u_i(\vec{a}) \\
&\geq \frac{1}{\sum_{\vec{a}\in A}\lfloor w(n)\sigma(\vec{a})\rfloor}\Big(\sum_{\vec{a}\in A, u_i(\vec{a})\geq 0}(w(n)\sigma(\vec{a})-1)u_i(\vec{a}) \\
&\quad + \sum_{\vec{a}\in A, u_i(\vec{a})<0} w(n)\sigma(\vec{a})u_i(\vec{a})\Big) \\
&= \frac{w(n)\sum_{\vec{a}\in A}\sigma(\vec{a})u_i(\vec{a})}{\sum_{\vec{a}\in A}\lfloor w(n)\sigma(\vec{a})\rfloor} - \frac{\sum_{\vec{a}\in A, u_i(\vec{a})\geq 0}u_i(\vec{a})}{\sum_{\vec{a}\in A}\lfloor w(n)\sigma(\vec{a})\rfloor} \\
&\geq \frac{w(n)p_i}{\sum_{\vec{a}\in A}\lfloor w(n)\sigma(\vec{a})\rfloor} - \frac{an^c}{w(n)-n^c}.
\end{aligned}$$

If $p_i < 0$,

$$\begin{aligned}
v_i' &\geq \frac{w(n)p_i}{\sum_{\vec{a}\in A}\lfloor w(n)\sigma(\vec{a})\rfloor} - \frac{an^c}{w(n)-n^c} \geq \frac{w(n)p_i - an^c}{w(n)-n^c} \\
&= \frac{(rq(n)+1)n^c p_i - an^c}{(rq(n)+1)n^c - n^c} = \frac{rq(n)n^c p_i - (a-p_i)n^c}{rq(n)n^c} \\
&\geq p_i - \frac{1}{q(n)}.
\end{aligned}$$

If $p_i \geq 0$,

$$\begin{aligned}
v_i' &\geq \frac{w(n)p_i}{\sum_{\vec{a}\in A}\lfloor w(n)\sigma(\vec{a})\rfloor} - \frac{an^c}{w(n)-n^c} \geq p_i - \frac{an^c}{w(n)-n^c} \\
&= p_i - \frac{an^c}{(rq(n)+1)n^c - n^c} = p_i - \frac{an^c}{rq(n)n^c} \geq p_i - \frac{1}{q(n)}.
\end{aligned}$$

□

[5]Our result also hold for rational payoffs except then the size of the game needs to take into account the bits needed to represent the payoffs

LEMMA 3.3. *For all a, b, c, all polynomials q and w, all $G \in \mathcal{G}_{a,b,c,n}$, and all sequences sq of length $w(n)$, if the average payoff vector of playing sq is p, then for all $\delta \leq 1/f(n)$, where $f(n) = (a-b)w(n)q(n)$, if sq is played infinitely often, player i's payoff in $G^\infty(\delta)$ is at least $p_i - 1/q(n)$.*

PROOF. Suppose that $sq = (a_0, \ldots, a_{w(n)-1})$, and let v_i be i's payoff from sq^∞ in $G^\infty(\delta)$. Then

$$\begin{aligned}
v_i &= \delta\sum_{t=0}^{\infty}(1-\delta)^{tw(n)}\sum_{k=0}^{w(n)-1}u(a_k)(1-\delta)^k \\
&= p_i + \delta\sum_{t=0}^{\infty}(1-\delta)^{tw(n)}\sum_{k=0}^{w(n)-1}(u(a_k)-p_i)(1-\delta)^k.
\end{aligned}$$

We want to bound the loss from the second part of the sum. Notice that this is a discounted sum of a sequence whose average payoff is 0. Call this sequence sq'. Observe that, because of the discounting, in the worst case, i gets all of his negative payoff in the first round of sq' and all his positive payoffs in the last round. Thus, we can bound the discounted average payoff by analyzing this case. Let the sum of i's negative payoffs in sq' be P_{neg}, which means that the sum of i's positive payoffs must be $-P_{neg}$. Let $r = a - b$, let $v_i' = \min_{\vec{a}\in A}(u_i(\vec{a}) - p_i) \geq -r$, and let $f(n) = rw(n)q(n)$, as in the statement of the lemma. So, if $\delta \leq 1/f(n)$, player i's average discounted payoff in the game is at least

$$\begin{aligned}
v_i &\geq p_i + \delta\sum_{t=0}^{\infty}P_{neg}(1-\delta)^{w(n)t} + (-P_{neg})(1-\delta)^{w(n)(t+1)-1} \\
&= p_i + \delta(P_{neg} + (-P_{neg})(1-\delta)^{w(n)-1})\sum_{t=0}^{\infty}(1-\delta)^{w(n)t} \\
&= p_i + \delta(P_{neg} + (-P_{neg})(1-\delta)^{w(n)-1})\frac{1}{1-(1-\delta)^{w(n)}} \\
&= p_i + P_{neg}\delta\frac{1-(1-\delta)^{w(n)-1}}{(1-(1-\delta)^{w(n)})} \geq p_i + \delta P_{neg} \\
&\geq p_i + \frac{P_{neg}}{f(n)} \geq p_i + \frac{v_i' w(n)}{f(n)} = p_i - 1/q(n).
\end{aligned}$$

□

The next lemma shows that, for every inverse polynomial, if we "cut off" the game after some appropriately large polynomial p number of rounds (and compute the discounted utility for the finitely repeated game considering only $p(n)$ repetitions), each player's utility in the finitely repeated game is negligibly close to his utility in the infinitely repeated game—that is, the finitely repeated game is a "good" approximation of the infinitely repeated game.

LEMMA 3.4. *For all a, b, c, all polynomials q, all n, all games $G \in \mathcal{G}_{a,b,c,n}$, all $0 < \delta < 1$, all strategy profiles $\vec{M}$, and all players i, i's expected utility $p_i[\vec{M}]$ in game $G^{\lceil n/\delta\rceil}(\delta)$ and $p_i[\vec{M}]$ in game $G^\infty(\delta)$ differ by at most a/e^n.*

PROOF. Let $p_i^t(\vec{M})$ denote player i's expected utility if the players are playing $\vec{M}$ and the game ends at round t.

Recall that $(1-\delta)^{1/\delta} \le 1/e$.

$$\begin{array}{rl} & p_i^{\infty}(\vec{M}) - p_i^{\lceil n/\delta \rceil}(\vec{M}) \\ = & \delta \sum_{t=0}^{\infty}(1-\delta)^t \sum_{h\in H^t, \vec{a}\in A} \rho_{\vec{M}}^{t+1}(h\cdot\vec{a})[u_i(\vec{a})] \\ & \quad -\delta \sum_{t=0}^{\lceil n/\delta \rceil}(1-\delta)^t \sum_{h\in H^t, \vec{a}\in A} \rho_{\vec{M}}^{t+1}(h\cdot\vec{a})[u_i(\vec{a})] \\ = & \delta \sum_{t=\lceil n/\delta \rceil+1}^{\infty}(1-\delta)^t \sum_{h\in H^t, \vec{a}\in A} \rho_{\vec{M}}^{t+1}(h\cdot\vec{a})[u_i(\vec{a})] \\ \le & \delta \sum_{t=\lceil n/\delta \rceil}^{\infty}(1-\delta)^t a \\ = & \delta(1-\delta)^{\lceil n/\delta \rceil} \sum_{t=0}^{\infty}(1-\delta)^t a = \delta(1-\delta)^{\lceil n/\delta \rceil} \frac{a}{\delta} \le \frac{a}{e^n}. \end{array}$$

□

3.2 An ϵ-NE

Let $sq = (s_1, s_2 \ldots, s_m)$ be a sequence of action profiles such that the average payoff (with no discounting) of player i from playing sq repeatedly is p_i. Let $a_i^0, a_i^1 \in A_i$ be two actions of player i. A player can broadcast an m-bit string by using these two actions for m rounds (treating a^0 as 0 and a^1 as 1). Let (Gen, Enc, Dec) be a multi-message multi-key secure l-bit public-key encryption scheme where, if the security parameter is k, the length of an encrypted message is $z(k)$ for some polynomial z. Fix a polynomial-time pseudorandom function ensemble $\{PS_s : s \in \{0,1\}^*\}$. For a game G such that $|G| = n$, consider the following strategy σ^{NE} for player i in $G^{\infty}(\delta)$:

1. Play according to sq (with wraparound) as long as sq was played in the previous round.
2. After detecting a deviation by player $j \neq i$ in round t_0 (note that here we are using the assumption that players can observe the action profile played in the previous stage):
   (a) Generate a pair (pk_i, sk_i) using Gen(1^n). Use the next $l(n)$ rounds to broadcast pk_i, as discussed above.
   (b) If $i = j+1$ (with wraparound), player i does the following:
      - i records $pk_{j'}$ for all players $j' \notin \{i, j\}$ (here we are using the fact that our TMs have memory);
      - i generates a random n-bit seed *seed*;
      - for each player $j' \notin \{i,j\}$, i computes $m = Enc_{pk_{j'}}(seed)$, and uses the next $(c-2)z(n)$ rounds to communicate these strings to the players other than i and j (in some predefined order).
   (c) If $i \neq j+1$, player i does the following:
      - i records the actions played by $j+1$ at time slots designated for i to retrieve $Enc_{Pk_i}(seed)$;
      - i decrypts to obtain *seed*, using Dec and sk_i.
3. At a round t after the communication phase ends, the players other than j compute $PS_{seed}(t)$ and use it to determine which action profile to play according to the distribution defined by a fixed (correlated) punishment strategy against j.

Note that if the players other than j had played a punishment strategy against j, then j would get his minimax payoff of 0. What the players other than j are actually doing is playing an approximation to a punishment strategy in two senses: first they are using a psuedorandom function to generate the randomness, which means that they are not quite playing according to the actual punishment strategy. Also, j might be able to guess which pure strategy profile they are actually playing at each round, and so do better than his minimax value. As we now show, j's expected gain during the punishment phase is negligible.

LEMMA 3.5. *For all a, b, c, all polynomials t and f, all n, and all games $G \in \mathcal{G}_{a,b,c,n}$, in $G^{\infty}(1/f(n))$, if the players other than j play σ_{-j}^{NE}, then if j deviates at round $t(n)$, j's expected payoff during the punishment phase is negligible.*

PROOF. Since we want to show j's expected payoff during the punishment phase (phase (3) only) is negligible, it suffices to consider only polynomially many rounds of playing phase (3) (more precisely, at most $nf(n)$ rounds); by Lemma 3.4, any payoff beyond then is guaranteed to be negligible due to the discounting.

We construct three variants of the strategy σ_{-j}^{NE}, that vary in phases (2) and (3). We can think of these variants as interpolating between the strategy above and the use of true randomness. (These variants assume an oracle that provides appropriate information; these variants are used only to make the claims precise.)

H1 In phase (2), the punishing players send their public keys to $j+1$. For each player j' not being punished, player $j+1$ then encrypts the seed 0 using (j')'s public key, and then sends the encrypted key to j'. In phase (3), the punishing players get the output of a truly random function (from an oracle), and use it to play the true punishment strategy. (In this case, phase (2) can be eliminated.)

H2 In phase (2), the punishing players send their public keys to $j+1$. For each player j' not being punished, player $j+1$ encrypts the seed 0 using (j')'s public key, and then sends the encrypted key to j'. In phase (3), the punishing players get a joint random seed *seed* (from an oracle) and use the outputs of PS_{seed} to decide which strategy profile to play in each round. (Again, in this case, phase (2) can be eliminated.)

H3 In phase (2), the punishing players send their public keys to $j+1$. Player $j+1$ chooses a random seed *seed* and, for each player j' not being punished, $j+1$ encrypts *seed* using (j')'s public key, and then sends the encrypted key to j'. In phase (3), the punishing players use the outputs of PS_{seed} to decide which strategy profile to play in each round.

It is obvious that in $H1$, j's expected payoff is negligible. (Actually, there is a slight subtlety here. As we observed above, using linear programming, we can compute a strategy that gives the correlated minimax, which gives j an expected payoff of 0. To actually implement this correlated minimax, the players need to sample according to the minimax distribution. They cannot necessarily do this exactly (for example, 1/3 can't be computed exactly using random bits). However, given n, the distribution can be discretized to the closest rational number of the form $m/2^n$ using at most n random bits. Using such a discretized distribution, the players other than j can ensure that j gets only a negligible payoff.)

We now claim that in $H2$, j's expected payoff during the punishment phase is negligible. Assume for contradiction that a player playing $H2$ has a non-negligible payoff $\mu(n)$ for all n (i.e., there exists some polynomial $g(\cdot)$ such that $\mu(n) \geq 1/g(n)$ for infinitely many n.). Let $h(n) = n(a-b)^2(1/\mu(n))^2$. We claim that if j's expected payoff is non-negligible, then we can distinguish $h(n)$ instances of the PRF $\{PS_s : s \in \{0,1\}^n\}$ with independently generated random seeds, from $h(n)$ independent truly random functions, contradicting the multi-instance security of the PRF PS.

More precisely, we construct a distinguisher D that, given 1^n and oracle access to a set of functions $f^1, f^2, \ldots, f^{h(n)}$, proceeds as follows. It simulates H_2 (it gets the description of the machines to play as its non-uniform advice) $h(n)$ times where in iteration i', it uses the function $f^{i'}$ as the randomization source of the correlated punishment strategy. D then computes the average payoff of player j in the $h(n)$ runs, and outputs 1 if this average exceeds $\mu(n)/2$. Note that if the functions $f^1, f^2, \ldots, f^{h(n)}$ are truly independent random functions, then D perfectly simulates H_1 and thus, in each iteration i', the expected payoff of player j (during the punishment phase) is negligible. On the other hand, if the functions $f^1, f^2, \ldots, f^{h(n)}$ are $h(n)$ independent randomly chosen instances of the PRF $\{PS_s : s \in \{0,1\}^n\}$, then D perfectly simulates H_2, and thus, in each iteration i', the expected payoff of player j (during the punishment phase) is at least $\mu(n)$.

By Hoeffding's inequality [15], given m random variables $X_1, \ldots, X_m$ all of which take on values in an interval of size c', $p(|\overline{X} - E(\overline{X})| \geq r) \leq 2\exp(-\frac{2mr^2}{c'^2})$. Since, in this setting, the range of the random variables is an interval of size $a - b$, the probability that D outputs 1 when the function are truly independent is at most $2/e^n$, while the probability that D outputs 1 when the functions are independent randomly chosen instances of the PRF $\{PS_s : s \in \{0,1\}^n\}$ is at least $1 - 2/e^n$. This, in turn, means that the difference between them is not negligible, which is a contradiction. Thus, j's expected payoff in $H2$ must be negligible.

We now claim that in $H3$, player j's expected payoff during the punishment phase is also negligible. Indeed, if j can get a non-negligible payoff, then we can break the multi-message multi-key secure encryption scheme.

Again, assume for contradiction that the punished player's expected payoff in the punishment phase is a non-negligible function $\mu(n)$ for all n. We can build a distinguisher $A = (A_1, A_2)$ (which also gets the description of the machines to play as its non-uniform advice) to distinguish $\{\text{IND-MULT}_0^\Pi(A, n, h, c)\}_n$ and $\{\text{IND-MULT}_1^\Pi(A, n, h, c)\}_n$ (where we abuse notation and identify c with the constant polynomial that always returns c). Given n, A_1 randomly selects $h(n)$ messages $r_1, \ldots, r_{h(n)}$ and outputs $(0, \ldots, 0, r_1, \ldots, r_{h(n)}, (pk_1, \ldots, pk_c))$. A_2 splits its input into pieces. The first piece contains the first c encryptions in $\mathcal{C}$ (i.e., the c encryptions of the first message chosen, according to the c different encryption functions), the second the next c encryptions and so on. Notice that each piece consists of c different encryptions of the same message in both cases. It can also simulate phase (1) by following the strategy for t rounds. It then uses each piece, along with the public keys, to simulate the communication in phase (2). For piece j it uses r_j as the seed of the PRF in phase (3). It repeats this experiment for all the different pieces of the input, for a total of $h(n)$ times, and outputs 1 if the punished player's average payoff over all experiments using its strategy is more than $\mu(n)/2$.

Note that if $b = 1$, player j faces $H3$ (i.e., the distributions over runs when $b = 1$ is identical to the distribution over runs with H3, since in both cases the seed is chosen at random and the corresponding messages are selected the same way), so player j's expected payoff in the punishment phase is $\mu(n)$. Thus, by Hoeffding's inequality the probability that player j's average payoff in the punishment phase is more then $\mu(n)/2$ is $1 - 2/e^n$, so A_2 outputs 1 with that probability in the case $b = 1$. On the other hand, if $b = 0$, then this is just H_2. We know player j's expected payoff in the punishment phase in each experiment is no more than negligible in H_2, so the probability that the average payoff is more than $\mu(n)/2$ after $h(n)$ rounds, is negligible. This means that there is a non-negligible difference between the probability A outputs 1 when $b = 1$ and when $b = 0$, which contradicts the assumption that the encryption scheme is multi-message multi-key secure public key secure. Thus, the gain in $H3$ must be negligible.

$H3$ is exactly the game that the punished player faces; thus, this shows he can't hope to gain more than a negligible payoff in expectation. □

We can now state and prove our main theorem, which says that σ^{NE} is an ϵ-NE for all inverse polynomials ϵ if δ is a small enough inverse polynomial.[6]

THEOREM 3.6. *For all a, b, c, and all polynomials q, there is a polynomial f and a polynomial-time algorithm that, for all sequences $G_1, G_2, \ldots$ of games with $G_j \in G_{a,b,c,j}$ and for all inverse polynomials $\delta \leq 1/f$, the sequence of outputs of the algorithm given the sequence $G_1, G_2, \ldots$ of inputs is a $(1/q)$-NE for $G_1^\infty(\delta(1)), G_2^\infty(\delta(2)), \ldots$.*

PROOF. Given a game $G^n \in \mathcal{G}(a, b, c, n)$, the first step of the algorithm is to find a correlated equilibrium σ of G^n. This can be done in polynomial time using linear programming. Since the minimax value of the game is 0 for all players, all players have an expected utility of at least 0 using σ. Let $r = a - b$. By Lemma 3.2, we can construct a sequence sq of length $w(n) = (3rnq(n) + 1)n^c$ that has an average payoff for each player that is at most $1/3q(n)$ less than his payoff using σ. By Lemma 3.3, it follows that by setting the discount factor $\delta < 1/f'(n)$, where $f'(n) = 3rw(n)q(n)$, the loss due to discounting is also at most $1/3q(n)$. We can also find a punishment strategy against each player in polynomial time, using linear programming.

We can now just take σ_n^* to be the strategy σ^{NE} described earlier that uses the sequence sq, the algorithm computed, and the punishment strategies. Let $m(n)$ be the length of phase (2). (Note that $m(n)$ is a polynomial that depends only on the choice of encryption scheme—that is, it depends on l, where an l-bit public-key encryption scheme is used, and on z, where $z(k)$ is the length of encrypted messages.) Let

$$f(n) = \max(3q(n)(m(n)a + 1), f'(n)).$$

[6]As pointed out by BC+, if the discount factor is exponentially close to 1 the problem becomes easy since the TMs can just spend the first rounds in computing the single-shot NE and then play it. Our range of δ is the range for which BC+ proved their hardness result.

Notice that f is independent of the actual game as required.

We now show that $\sigma_1^*, \ldots$ as defined above is a $(1/q)$-NE. If in game G^n a player follows σ_n^*, he gets at least $-2/3q(n)$. Suppose that player j defects at round t; that is, that he plays according to σ_n^* until round t, and then defects. By Lemma 3.4 if $t > \frac{n}{\delta(n)}$, then any gain from defection is negligible, so there exists some n_1 such that, for all $n > n_1$, a defection in round t cannot result in the player gaining more than $\frac{1}{q(n)}$. If player j defects at round $t \leq \frac{n}{\delta(n)}$, he gets at most a for the duration of phase (2), which is at most $m(n)$ rounds, and then, by Lemma 3.5, gains only a negligible amount, say $\epsilon_{neg}(n)$ (which may depend on the sequence of deviations), in phase (3). Let u_i^n be the payoff of player i in game G^n of the sequence. It suffices to show that

$$\delta(n)(\sum_{k=0}^{t} u_i^n(a_k)(1-\delta(n))^k + \sum_{k=0}^{m(n)} a(1-\delta(n))^{k+t} + (1-\delta(n))^{t+m(n)}\epsilon_{neg}(n)) - 1/q(n)$$
$$\leq \delta(n)(\sum_{k=0}^{t} u_i^n(a_k)(1-\delta(n))^k + \sum_{k=t}^{\infty} u_i^n(a_k)(1-\delta(n))^k).$$

By deleting the common terms from both side, rearranging, and noticing that $(1-\delta(n))^{m(n)}\epsilon_{neg(n)} \leq \epsilon_{neg(n)}$, it follows that it suffices to show

$$\delta(n)(1-\delta(n))^t(\sum_{k=0}^{m(n)} a(1-\delta(n))^k + \epsilon_{neg}(n)) - \frac{1}{q(n)}$$
$$\leq \delta(n)(1-\delta(n))^t(\sum_{k=0}^{\infty} u_i^n(a_{k+t})(1-\delta(n))^k).$$

We divide both sides of the equation by $(1-\delta(n))^t$. No matter at what step of the sequence the defection happens, the future expected discounted payoff from that point on is still at least $-2/3q(n)$, as our bound applies for the worst sequence for a player, and we assumed that in equilibrium all players get at least 0. It follows that we need to show

$$\delta(n)(\sum_{k=0}^{m(n)} a(1-\delta(n))^k + \epsilon_{neg}(n)) - \frac{1}{q(n)(1-\delta(n))^t} \leq -\frac{2}{3q(n)}.$$

Since ϵ_{neg} is negligible for all deviations, it follows that, for all sequences of deviations, there exists n_0 such that $\epsilon_{neg}(n) < 1$ for all $n \geq n_0$. For $n \geq n_0$,

$$\begin{aligned}\delta(n)(\sum_{k=0}^{m(n)} a(1-\delta(n))^k + \epsilon_{neg}(n)) - \frac{1}{q(n)(1-\delta(n))^t} &\leq \delta(n)(m(n)a + \epsilon_{neg}(n)) - \frac{1}{q(n)}\\ &\leq \frac{m(n)a + \epsilon_{neg}(n)}{f(n)} - \frac{1}{q(n)}\\ &\leq \frac{m(n)a + \epsilon_{neg}(n)}{3q(n)(m(n)a+1)} - \frac{1}{q(n)}\\ &\leq \frac{1}{3q(n)} - \frac{1}{q(n)} = -\frac{2}{3q(n)}.\end{aligned}$$

This shows that there is no deviating strategy that can result in the player gaining more than $\frac{1}{q(n)}$ in G^n for $n > \max\{n_0, n_1\}$. □

4. CONCLUSIONS

We have shown that computing an ϵ-NE for an infinitely-repeated game is indeed easier than computing one in a normal-form game. Our techniques use threats and punishment much in the same way that they are used to prove the Folk Theorem. However, there is a new twist to our results. We must assume that players are computationally bounded, and we use some cryptographic techniques that rely on standard cryptographic assumptions.

Our paper leaves many interesting open problems for future research:

- Our results are restricted to games with a fixed number of players. Can similar ideas be used when the number of players is part of the input?
- There are versions of the Folk Theorem that give *subgame-perfect* equilibria (see for example [8]). Can we find such an equilibrium in polynomial time?
- Our result is based on cryptographic hardness assumptions. Are these assumptions a necessary condition for an efficient computation of a repeated game equilibrium?

5. ACKNOWLEDGEMENTS

Joseph Halpern and Lior Seeman are supported in part by NSF grants IIS-0812045, IIS-0911036, and CCF-1214844, by AFOSR grant FA9550-08-1-0266, and by ARO grant W911NF-09-1-0281. Rafael Pass is supported in part by an Alfred P. Sloan Fellowship, a Microsoft Research Faculty Fellowship, NSF Awards CNS-1217821 and CCF-1214844, NSF CAREER Award CCF-0746990, AFOSR YIP Award FA9550-10-1-0093, and DARPA and AFRL under contract FA8750-11-2-0211. The views and conclusions contained in this document are those of the authors and should not be interpreted as representing the official policies, either expressed or implied, of the Defense Advanced Research Projects Agency or the US Government.

6. REFERENCES

[1] G. Andersen and V. Conitzer. Fast equilibrium computation for infinitely repeated games. In *Twenty-Seventh AAAI Conference on Artificial Intelligence*, 2013.

[2] C. Borgs, J. Chayes, N. Immorlica, A. Kalai, V. Mirrokni, and C. Papadimitriou. The myth of the folk theorem. *Games and Economic Behavior*, 70(1):34–43, 2010.

[3] X. Chen and X. Deng. Settling the complexity of two-player nash equilibrium. In *Proc. 47th IEEE Symposium on Foundations of Computer Science*, pages 261–272, 2006.

[4] X. Chen, X. Deng, and S. Teng. Computing Nash equilibria: Approximation and smoothed complexity. In *Proc. 47th IEEE Symposium on Foundations of Computer Science*, pages 603–612, 2006.

[5] C. Daskalakis, P. Goldberg, and C. Papadimitriou. The complexity of computing a nash equilibrium. In *Proc. 38th ACM Symposium on Theory of Computing*, pages 71–78, 2006.

[6] W. Diffie and M. Hellman. New directions in cryptography. *IEEE Transactions on Information Theory*, 22(6):644–654, 1976.

[7] Y. Dodis, S. Halevi, and T. Rabin. A cryptographic solution to a game theoretic problem. In *CRYPTO 2000: 20th International Cryptology Conference*, pages 112–130, 2000.

[8] D. Fudenberg and E. Maskin. The folk theorem in repeated games with discounting or with incomplete information. *Econometrica*, 54(3):533–554, 1986.

[9] O. Goldreich. *Foundation of Cryptography, Volume I Basic Tools*. 2001.

[10] O. Goldreich, S. Goldwasser, and S. Micali. How to construct random functions. *Journal of the ACM*, 33(4):792–807, 1986.

[11] S. Goldwasser and S. Micali. Probabilistic encryption. *Journal of Computer and System Sciences*, 28(2):270–299, 1984.

[12] O. Gossner. *Repeated games played by cryptographically sophisticated players*. Center for Operations Research & Econometrics. Université catholique de Louvain, 1998.

[13] O. Gossner. Sharing a long secret in a few public words. Technical report, THEMA (THéorie Economique, Modélisation et Applications), Université de Cergy-Pontoise, 2000.

[14] J. Håstad, R. Impagliazzo, L. A. Levin, and M. Luby. A pseudorandom generator from any one-way function. *SIAM Journal on Computing*, 28(4):1364–1396, 1999.

[15] W. Hoeffding. Probability inequalities for sums of bounded random variables. *Journal of the American Statistical Association*, 58(301):13–30, 1963.

[16] E. Lehrer. Internal correlation in repeated games. *International Journal of Game Theory*, 19(4):431–456, 1991.

[17] M. L. Littman and P. Stone. A polynomial-time nash equilibrium algorithm for repeated games. *Decision Support Systems*, 39(1):55–66, 2005.

[18] A. Neyman. Bounded complexity justifies cooperation in the finitely repeated prisoners' dilemma. *Economics Letters*, 19(3):227–229, 1985.

[19] M. J. Osborne and A. Rubinstein. *A Course in Game Theory*. MIT Press, Cambridge, Mass., 1994.

[20] C. H. Papadimitriou and M. Yannakakis. On complexity as bounded rationality. In *Proc. 26th ACM Symposium on Theory of Computing*, pages 726–733, 1994.

[21] R. L. Rivest, A. Shamir, and L. Adleman. A method for obtaining digital signatures and public-key cryptosystems. *Communications of the ACM*, 21(2):120–126, 1978.

[22] A. Rubinstein. Finite automata play the repeated prisoner's dilemma. *Journal of Economic Theory*, 39(1):83–96, 1986.

[23] A. Urbano and J. Vila. Unmediated communication in repeated games with imperfect monitoring. *Games and Economic Behavior*, 46(1):143–173, 2004.

[24] A. Urbano and J. E. Vila. Computational complexity and communication: Coordination in two-player games. *Econometrica*, 70(5):1893–1927, 2002.

APPENDIX

A. MULTI-INSTANCE PRFS

In this section, we show that for any family of PRF, even polynomially many random members of it are indistinguishable from polynomially many truly random functions.

LEMMA A.1. *For all polynomials q, if $\{f_s : \{0,1\}^{|s|} \to \{0,1\}^{|s|}\}_{s\in\{0,1\}^*}$ is a pseudorandom function ensemble, then the ensemble $F^q = \{F_n^1, \dots, F_n^{q(n)}\}_{n\in\mathbb{N}}$ where, for all i, F_n^i is uniformly distributed over the multi-set $\{f_s\}_{s\in\{0,1\}^n}$, is computationally indistinguishable from $H^q = \{H_n^1, \dots, H_n^{q(n)}\}_{n\in\mathbb{N}}$.*

PROOF. Assume for contradiction that the ensembles are distinguishable. This means there exist a polynomial q, a PPT D, and a polynomial p such that for infinitely many n's

$$|Pr[D(1^n, (H_n^1, \dots, H_n^{q(n)})) = 1] \\ -Pr[D(1^n, (F_n^1, \dots, F_n^{q(n)})) = 1]| > \frac{1}{p(n)}.$$

For each n, let $T_n^i = (1^n, (H_n^1, \dots, H_n^{i-1}, F_n^i, \dots, F_n^{q(n)}))$. We can now describe a PPT D' that distinguishes $\{F_n\}_{n\in\mathbb{N}}$ and $\{H_n\}_{n\in\mathbb{N}}$ for infinitely many n's. First notice that a PPT can easily simulate polynomially many oracle queries to both a truly random function and to a member of F_n. So D' on input $(1^n, X)$ randomly chooses $j \in \{1, \dots, q(n)\}$ and calls D with input $(1^n, (I^1, \dots, I^{j-1}, X, J^{j+1}, \dots, J^{q(n)}))$, where it simulates a query to I_k as a query to a random member of H_n, and a query to J_k as a query to a random member of F_n. (Notice that since D is a PPT, it can make only polynomially many oracle queries to any of the functions, which can be easily simulated). Whenever D makes an oracle query to X, D' makes an oracle query to X, and uses its answer as the answer to D. When D terminates, D' outputs the same value as D.

Now notice that if X is H_n, then the input to D is T_n^j, while if X is F_n, then the input to D is T_n^{j+1}. Thus, $Pr[D'(1^n, H_n) = 1] = \frac{1}{q(n)} \sum_{i=1}^{q(n)} Pr[D(T_n^{i+1}) = 1]$, and $Pr[D'(1^n, F_n) = 1] = \frac{1}{q(n)} \sum_{i=1}^{q(n)} Pr[D(T_n^i) = 1]$. It follows that

$$\begin{aligned} &|Pr[D'(1^n, H_n) = 1] - Pr[D'(1^n, F_n) = 1]| \\ &= \frac{1}{q(n)} |\sum_{i=1}^{q(n)} Pr[D(T_n^{i+1}) = 1] - Pr[D(T_n^i) = 1]| \\ &= \frac{1}{q(n)} |Pr[D(T_n^{q(n)+1}) = 1] - Pr[D(T_n^1) = 1]| \\ &> \frac{1}{q(n)p(n)}, \end{aligned}$$

where the last inequality is due to the fact that $T_n^{q(n)+1} = (1^n, (H_n^1, \dots, H_n^{q(n)}))$ and $T_n^1 = (1^n, (F_n^1, \dots, F_n^{q(n)}))$. But this means that for any such n, D' can distinguish $F = \{F_n\}_{n\in\mathbb{N}}$ and $H = \{H_n\}_{n\in\mathbb{N}}$ with non-negligible probability, and thus can do that for infinitely many n's. This is a contradiction to the assumption that $\{f_s : \{0,1\}^{|s|} \to \{0,1\}^{|s|}\}_{s\in\{0,1\}^*}$ is a pseudorandom function ensemble. □

B. MULTI-KEY MULTI-MESSAGE SECURITY

In this section, we show that any secure public-key encryption scheme is also multi-key multi-message secure.

LEMMA B.1. *If (Gen, Enc, Dec) is a secure public key encryption scheme, then it is also multi-message multi-key secure.*

PROOF. Assume for contradiction that (Gen, Enc, Dec) is a secure public key encryption scheme that is not multi-message multi-key secure. Then there exist polynomials f and g and an adversary $A = (A_1, A_2)$ such that $\{\text{IND-MULT}_0^{\Pi}(A,k,f,g)\}_k$ and $\{\text{IND-MULT}_1^{\Pi}(A,k,f,g)\}_k$ are distinguishable. That means there exist a PPT D and a polynomial p such that

$$|Pr[D(1^k, \{\text{IND-MULT}_0^{\Pi}(A,k,f,g)\}) = 1] \\ -Pr[D(1^k, \{\text{IND-MULT}_1^{\Pi}(A,k,f,g)\}) = 1]| > \frac{1}{p(n)}.$$

Let $T_{i,j}^{\pi}(A,k,f,g)$ be the following PPT algorithm:

$$\begin{aligned} T_{i,j}^{\pi}(A,k,f,g) := \quad & (pk_1, sk_1) \leftarrow \text{Gen}(1^k), \\ & \ldots, (pk_{g(k)}, sk_{g(k)}) \leftarrow \text{Gen}(1^k), \\ & (m_0^1, \ldots, m_0^{f(k)}, m_1^1, \ldots, m_1^{f(k)}, \tau) \\ & \quad \leftarrow A_1(1^k, pk_1, \ldots, pk_{g(k)}) \\ & \mathcal{C} \leftarrow \text{Enc}_{pk_1}(m_0^1), \ldots, \text{Enc}_{pk_{g(k)}}(m_0^1), \\ & \ldots, \text{Enc}_{pk_1}(m_0^j), \ldots, \text{Enc}_{pk_{i-1}}(m_0^j), \\ & \text{Enc}_{pk_i}(m_1^j), \ldots, \text{Enc}_{pk_{g(k)}}(m_1^j), \ldots, \\ & \text{Enc}_{pk_1}(m_1^{f(k)}), \ldots, \text{Enc}_{pk_{g(k)}}(m_1^{f(k)}) \\ & o \leftarrow A_2(\mathcal{C}, \tau) \\ & \text{Output } o. \end{aligned}$$

We now define an adversary $A' = (A'_1, A'_2)$, and show that $\{\text{IND}_0^{\Pi}(A',k,f,g)\}_k$ and $\{\text{IND}_1^{\Pi}(A',k,f,g)\}_k$ are not computationally indistinguishable. A'_1 on input $(1^k, pk)$ first chooses $i \in \{1, \ldots, g(k)\}$ uniformly at random. It then generates $g(k) - 1$ random key pairs $(pk_1, sk_1), \ldots, (pk_{i-1}, sk_{i-1}), (pk_{i+1}, sk_{i+1}), \ldots, (pk_{g(k)}, sk_{g(k)})$. It then calls A_1 with input $(1^k, pk_1, \ldots, pk_{i-1}, pk, pk_{i+1}, \ldots, pk_{g(k)})$. After getting A_1's output $M = (m_0^1, \ldots, m_0^{f(k)}, m_1^1, \ldots, m_1^{f(k)}, \tau)$, A'_1 chooses $j \in \{1, \ldots, f(n)\}$ uniformly at random, and returns as its output $(m_0^j, m_1^j, (i, j, pk, pk_1, sk_1, \ldots, pk_{g(k)}, sk_{g(k)}, M))$.

A'_2 on input $(\mathcal{C}, (i, j, pk, pk_1, sk_1, \ldots, pk_{g(k)}, sk_{g(k)}, M))$ constructs input $\mathcal{C}'$ for A_2 by first appending the encryptions of messages $m_0^1 \ldots, m_0^{j-1}$ with all the keys, then appending the encryption of m_0^j with keys $pk_1, \ldots, pk_i$ and then appends $\mathcal{C}$. It then appends the encryption of m_1^j with keys $pk_{i+2}, \ldots, pk_{g(k)}$ and also the encryption of the messages $m_1^{j+1}, \ldots, m_1^{f(k)}$ with each of the keys. It then outputs $A_2(\mathcal{C}', \tau)$. If $\mathcal{C}$ is the encryption of m_j^0 with key pk, then this algorithm is identical to $T_{i+1,j}^{\pi}(A,k,f,g)$ (if $i = g(k)$ then by $T_{i+1,j}^{\pi}$ we mean $T_{1,j+1}^{\pi}$; we use similar conventions elsewhere), while if it is the encryption of m_j^1 with key pk, then the algorithm is identical to $T_{i,j}^{\pi}(A,k,f,g)$.

We claim that D can distinguish $\{\text{IND}_0^{\Pi}(A',k,f,g)\}_k$ and $\{\text{IND}_1^{\Pi}(A',k,f,g)\}_k$. Note that

$$Pr[D(1^k, \{\text{IND}_0^{\Pi}(A',k,f,g)\}) = 1] \\ = \frac{1}{g(k)f(k)} \sum_{j=1}^{f(k)} \sum_{i=1}^{g(k)} Pr[D(1^k, T_{i+1,j}^{\pi}(A,k,f,g)) = 1]$$

and

$$Pr[D(1^k, \{\text{IND}_1^{\Pi}(A',k,f,g)\}) = 1] \\ = \frac{1}{g(k)f(k)} \sum_{j=1}^{f(k)} \sum_{i=1}^{g(k)} Pr[D(1^k, T_{i,j}^{\pi}(A,k,f,g)) = 1].$$

Thus,

$$\begin{aligned} & |Pr[D(1^k, \{\text{IND}_0^{\Pi}(A',k,f,g)\}) = 1] \\ & -Pr[D(1^k, \{\text{IND}_1^{\Pi}(A',k,f,g)\}) = 1]| \\ = \; & \tfrac{1}{g(k)f(k)} | \\ & \textstyle\sum_{j=1}^{f(k)} \sum_{i=1}^{g(k)} (Pr[D(1^k, T_{i+1,j}^{\pi}(A,k,f,g)) = 1] \\ & -Pr[D(1^k, T_{i,j}^{\pi}(A,k,f,g)) = 1])| \\ = \; & \tfrac{1}{g(k)f(k)} |Pr[D(1^k, \{\text{IND-MULT}_0^{\Pi}(A,k,f,g)\}) = 1] \\ & -Pr[D(1^k, \{\text{IND-MULT}_1^{\Pi}(A,k,f,g)\}) = 1]| \\ > \; & \tfrac{1}{g(k)f(k)p(k)}, \end{aligned}$$

where the next-to-last line follows because $T_{1,1}^{\pi}(A,k,f,g) = \text{IND-MULT}_1^{\Pi}(A,k,f,g)$ and $T_{g(k)+1,f(k)}^{\pi}(A,k,f,g) = \text{IND-MULT}_0^{\Pi}(A,k,f,g)$. Thus, we have a contradiction to the fact that the encryption scheme is secure. □

Author Index

Akavia, Adi 251
Angelino, Elaine 287
Antoniadis, Antonios 303
Azar, Yossi 195
Babai, László 359
Bandeira, Afonso S. 459
Barcelo, Neal 303
Berry, Jonathan W. 225
Bhattacharya, Sayan 121
Bogdanov, Andrej 251
Brakerski, Zvika 1, 235
Brandão, Fernando G. S. L. 183
Braverman, Mark 103, 541
Brody, Joshua 13
Bshouty, Nader H. 327
Chakrabarty, Deeparnab 105
Chandrasekaran, Karthekeyan 387, 449
Charikar, Moses 459
Chen, Ho-Lin 313
Chen, Jing 541
Cheraghchi, Mahdi 155
Doty, David 313
Druk, Erez 169
Feige, Uriel 93
Feldman, Michal 195
Felge, Uriel 195
Fischer, Eldar 483
Fostvedt, Luke K. 225
Gamarnik, David 369
Gelles, Ran 135
Goldhirsh, Yonatan 483
Gopalan, Parikshit 81
Guo, Siyao 251, 523
Gupta, Rishi 471
Guruswami, Venkatesan 155, 439
Halpern, Joseph Y. 543
Haramaty, Elad 377
Harrow, Aram W. 183
Hrubeš, Pavel 49
Hubáček, Pavel 523
Im, Sungjin 121
Ishai, Yuval 169
Iwama, Kazuo 507
Jakobsen, Sune K. 13
Kamath, Akshay 251
Kanade, Varun 287
Kannan, Sampath 541
Kaufman, Tali 501
Kearns, Michael 403
Kol, Gillat 517
Kulkarni, Janardhan 121
Lachish, Oded 483
Landau, Zeph 301
Lee, Euiwoong 439
Lee, James R. 183
Liu, Yi-Kai 269
Lubotzky, Alexander 501
Mahmoody, Mohammad 23
Maji, Hemanta K. 23
Mendel, Manor 353
Miles, Eric 261
Moore, Cristopher 145
Moran, Shay 517
Munagala, Kamesh 121
Naor, Assaf 353
Nissim, Kobbi 411
Nordman, Daniel J. 225
Nugent, Michael 303
Pai, Mallesh M. 403
Pasricha, Kanika 103
Pass, Rafael 543
Peres, Yuval 183
Phillips, Cynthia A. 225
Prabhakaran, Manoj 23
Pruhs, Kirk 303
Rabani, Yuval 207
Rosen, Alon 251, 523
Roth, Aaron 403
Rothblum, Guy N. 235
Roughgarden, Tim 471
Sahai, Amit 135
Scheder, Dominik 13
Schulman, Leonard J. 145, 207
Scquizzato, Michele 303
Seeman, Lior 543
Seshadhri, C. 225, 471
Shpilka, Amir 37, 517
Singer, Amit 459
Soloveichik, David 313
Sudan, Madhu 369, 377
Swamy, Chaitanya 105, 207
Tal, Avishay 37
Tennenholtz, Moshe 93, 195
Thaler, Justin 387
Ullman, Jonathan 387, 403
Vadhan, Salil 81, 411
Vaikuntanathan, Vinod 1
Vald, Margarita 523
Vazirani, Umesh 35, 301
Vempala, Santosh S. 449
Vidick, Thomas 35, 301
Volk, Ben lee 37
Wadia, Akshay 135
Wan, Andrew 67, 387
Wigderson, Avi 49
Wilson, Alyson G. 225
Winkler, Peter 13
Wright, John 67
Wu, Chenggang 67
Xiao, David 411
Yehudayoff, Amir 517
Yoshida, Yuichi 423, 507
Zhou, Yuan 81, 423
Zhu, Andy 459

www.ingramcontent.com/pod-product-compliance
Ingram Content Group UK Ltd.
Pitfield, Milton Keynes, MK11 3LW, UK
UKHW051416290926
15471UKWH00009B/1634

9 781450 330947